WITHDRAWN

EDITION 4

STRATEGIC MANAGEMENT

COMPETITIVENESS AND GLOBALIZATION

MICHAEL A. HITT

Arizona State University

R. DUANE IRELAND

University of Richmond

ROBERT E. HOSKISSON

The University of Oklahoma

Australia • Canada • Mexico • Singapore • Spain • United Kingdom • United States

HUNTINGTON CITY-TOWNSHIP
PUBLIC LIBRARY
200 W. Market Street
Huntington, IN 46750

Strategic Management: Competitiveness and Globalization (Concepts and Cases) 4e, by Michael A. Hitt, R. Duane Ireland & Robert E. Hoskisson

Vice President/Publisher: Jack W. Calhoun
Executive Editor: John Szilagyi
Marketing Manager: Rob Bloom
Project Manager: Katherine Pruitt-Schenck
Production Editor: Elizabeth A. Shipp
Media Production Editor: Kristen Meere
Manufacturing Coordinator: Sandee Milewski
Internal Design: Ann Small, A Small Design Studio
Cover Design: Ann Small, A Small Design Studio
Cover Image: DigitalVision
Photography Manager: Cary Benbow
Photo Researcher: Feldman & Associates, Inc.
Production House: WordCrafters Editorial Services, Inc.
Printer: QuebecorWorld—Versailles, KY

COPYRIGHT ©2001 by South-Western College Publishing, a division of Thomson Learning. The Thomson Learning logo is a registered trademark used herein under license.

All Rights Reserved. No part of this work covered by the copyright hereon may be reproduced or used in any form or by any means—graphic, electronic, or mechanical, including photocopying, recording, taping, or information storage and retrieval systems—without the written permission of the publisher.

Printed in the United States of America
1 2 3 4 5 03 02 01 00

For more information contact South-Western College Publishing, 5101 Madison Road, Cincinnati, Ohio, 45227 or find us on the Internet at http://www.swcollege.com

For permission to use material from this text or product, contact us by
- **telephone: 1-800-730-2214**
- **fax: 1-800-730-2215**
- **web: http://www.thomsonrights.com**

Library of Congress Cataloging-in-Publication Data
Hitt, Michael A.
Strategic management : competitiveness and globalization / Michael A. Hitt, R. Duane Ireland, Robert E. Hoskisson.—4th ed.
p. cm.
Includes bibliographical references and index.
ISBN 0-324-01731-6—ISBN 0-324-04892-0 (cases)—ISBN 0-324-04891-2 (concepts)
1. Strategic planning. 2. Industrial management. I. Ireland, R. Duane. II. Hoskisson, Robert E. III. Title.
HD30.28 .H586 2001
658.4'012—dc21

00-038775

ISBN: 0-324-01731-6 (Concepts and Cases Edition)
ISBN: 0-324-04891-2 (Concepts Edition)
ISBN: 0-324-04892-0 (Cases Edition)

This book is printed on acid-free paper.

R. Duane Ireland—
To my wife Mary Ann and our children, Rebecca and Scott. I love each of you deeply and look forward to the excitement and challenges of our new journeys. Truly, these are our Glory Days—the best of our lives.

Robert E. Hoskisson—
To my father, Claude W. Hoskisson, who taught me to be honest and dedicated in my work, and in memory of my mother, Carol B. Hoskisson, who provided my life with a foundation of love.

CONTENTS IN BRIEF

TABLE OF CONTENTS

PART 1
STRATEGIC MANAGEMENT INPUTS

CHAPTER ONE
STRATEGIC MANAGEMENT AND STRATEGIC COMPETITIVENESS 2

CHAPTER TWO
THE EXTERNAL ENVIRONMENT: OPPORTUNITIES, THREATS, INDUSTRY COMPETITION, AND COMPETITOR ANALYSIS 46

CHAPTER THREE
THE INTERNAL ENVIRONMENT: RESOURCES, CAPABILITIES, AND CORE COMPETENCIES 92

PART 2
STRATEGIC ACTIONS: STRATEGY FORMULATION

CHAPTER FOUR
BUSINESS-LEVEL STRATEGY 140

CHAPTER EIGHT
INTERNATIONAL STRATEGY 312

CHAPTER THIRTEEN
CORPORATE ENTREPRENEURSHIP AND INNOVATION 520

PART 4 CASES

Case Title	Manufacturing	Service	Consumer Goods	Industrial Goods
ABB in China: 1998	■			■
Adidas			■	
Alcoholes de Centroamerica, S.A. de C.V.	■		■	
Amazon.Com: Expanding Beyond Books		■	■	
Banking on the Internet: The Advance Bank in Germany		■		
Beano's Ice Cream Shop		■		
Ben & Jerrys Homemade Inc.: "Yo! I'm Your CEO!"	■		■	
Benecol: Raisio's Global Nutriceutical	■		■	
The Boeing Company: The Merger with McDonnell Douglas	■			■
BP-Mobil and the Restructuring of the Oil Refining Industry	■			■
British Airways: Latin America		■		
Circus Circus Enterprises, Inc., 1998		■		
Cisco Systems, Inc.	■			■
Cognex Corporation: "Work Hard, Play Hard"	■			■
Compaq in Crisis	■		■	
Enersis: Global Strategy in the Electric Power Sector		■	■	■
Internal Entrepreneurship at Ericsson: Finding Opportunities and Mobilizing Talent	■			■
E*Trade, Charles Schwab and Yahoo!: The Transformation of On-line Brokerage		■		
FEMSA Meets the 21st Century	■		■	
Fleming Companies, Inc.		■		
Gillette and the Men's Wet-Shaving Market	■		■	
Kiwi Travel International Airlines Ltd.		■		
KUVO Radio: Marketing an Oasis		■		
LEGO	■		■	
The Lincoln Electric Company, 1996	■		■	■
The Loewen Group		■		
Madd Snowboards—1999	■		■	
Mendocino Brewing Company, Inc.—1996	■		■	
Nucor Corp. and the U.S. Steel Industry	■			■
Odwalla, Inc., and the *E. Coli* Outbreak	■		■	
Outback Goes International		■		
Philip Morris	■		■	
Southwest Airlines, 1996		■		
Starbucks		■		
The Stone Group's Diversification Strategy: "Caught Between a Rock and a Hard Place"	■	■	■	
Sun Microsystems, Inc.	■		■	
The Merger of U.S. Bancorp and Piper Jaffray Companies		■		
The Wall Street Journal: Print versus Interactive		■		
Walt Disney Co.		■		
Western Pacific Airlines		■		

International Perspective	High Technology	Sports/ Entertainment	Food/Retail	Social/Ethical Issues	Entrepreneurial/Small-Medium Size	Industry Perspective	Chapters
■				■			2,3,8,11
■		■				■	2,3,4,5
■						■	4,5,8
■	■	■			■		4,5,6,9
■	■		■			■	2,4,5
			■		■	■	3,4,13
			■	■	■	■	3,12
■			■	■			5,8,13
■						■	2,4,5,7
■						■	5,6,7
■						■	8,9,11,12
		■				■	4,9,10
■	■						4,5,10,13
	■				■	■	4,5,13
	■						7,10,12
■							6,8,9
■	■				■		11,13
■	■				■	■	5,13
■			■				1,7,8,11
			■				2,3,7
■						■	7,8,10
■					■		5,8,12,13
		■			■		2,13
■							2,3,4,5
						■	3,7,8,12
■				■		■	5,6,7,12
		■			■	■	2,3,13
			■		■	■	2,3,13
						■	2,3,4
			■	■	■		1,5,12
■			■		■		4,8
■			■	■		■	2,6,11,12
						■	1,3,4,5
■			■		■		2,3,4,8
■			■				6,9,11
■	■				■		5,10,12,13
						■	2,3,7,10
■	■				■	■	1,4,13
		■				■	6,7,10
					■		4,5,7,13

ABOUT **THIS** BOOK

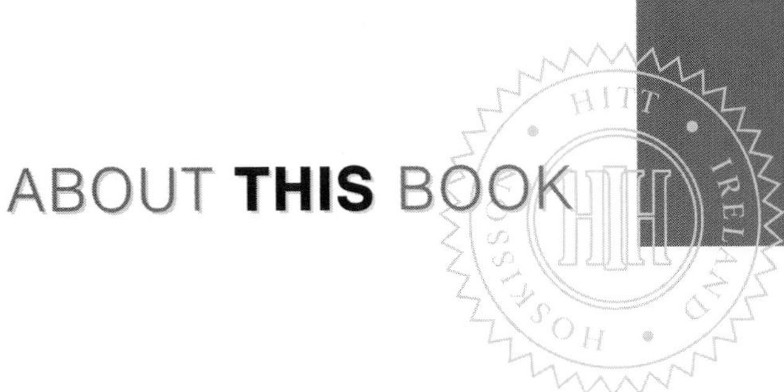

The fourth edition of *Strategic Management: Competitiveness and Globalization* continues the tradition from previous editions of integrating "cutting edge" research with an engaging writing style. In addition, we offer 35 all-new, full-length cases. Complementing the new cases are five Classic Cases that users selected from those appearing in the second and third editions. Thus, in this fourth edition, we present a combination of the "best" of previous cases and a new collection of excellent cases.

As we explain below, many new features to this edition enhance the value of our market-leading textbook. As with the first three editions, we have integrated the most current research with established research findings to prepare this fourth edition.

New Features

- All new chapter *Opening Cases* (13 in total).
- All new *Strategic Focus* segments (three per chapter for a total of 39).
- Many new company-specific examples that are integrated with each chapter's topic.
- Substantial emphasis on use of the Internet and e-commerce integrated throughout the book.
- Forty full-length cases representing highly current examples of strategy in action.
- Coverage of strategic issues in the 21st-century competitive landscape, including a strong emphasis on the competition created through *e-commerce ventures and start-ups.*
- Expanded *global coverage* with more emphasis on the international context and issues, both in the chapters and the cases.
- Updated Review Questions, Application Discussion Questions, and Ethics Questions at the end of each chapter that include issues suggested by the e-commerce phenomenon.
- *Internet exercises* and *e-projects* at the end of each chapter. These exercises and projects encourage readers to use the Internet as an information source and problem-solving tool.
- An updated and expanded case analysis guide.

These new features provide a unique competitive advantage for this book. With 13 new Opening Cases and 39 new Strategic Focus segments, we offer 52 major case examples in the chapters. In addition, *more than 75 percent of the shorter examples* used throughout each chapter are completely new. The 35 new full-length cases plus five user-selected Classic Cases comprehensively cover an interesting mix of industries and company sizes. In addition, many strategic issues such as mergers and acquisitions, Internet banking and services, competitive dynamics, and expansion into global markets are covered in the cases.

This edition remains focused on core topics that were the foundation for the first three editions. In addition, we also use a wide range of company-specific examples to discuss e-commerce applications of the strategic management process. E-commerce examples are presented in each chapter to show the pervasive effect of the Internet and e-commerce on competition in the global economy. Through these examples, our text is clearly differentiated from others regarding *e-commerce applications* of the strategic management process.

This new edition also emphasizes a *global advantage* with comprehensive coverage of international concepts and issues. In addition to comprehensive coverage of international strategies in Chapter 8, references to and discussions of the international context and issues are included in every chapter. The Opening Cases, Strategic Focus segments, and individual examples in each chapter cover numerous global issues. In addition, 60 percent of the 40 full-length cases focus on international contexts and markets (e.g., ABB in China: 1998; Alcoholes de Centroamerica, S.A. de C.V.; British Airways: Latin America).

Importantly, this new edition solidifies a research advantage for our book. For example, each chapter has more than 100 references. On average, 60 percent of these references are new to this edition. Drawn from the business literature and academic research, these materials are used to present current and accurate descriptions of how firms use the strategic management process. Additionally, we maintain our position as a market leader offering a full four-color format—a format that enhances the presentation of the materials as well as the book's overall design. Our goal while preparing this fourth edition has been to present you, our readers, with a complete, accurate, and up-to-date explanation of the strategic management process as it is used in the global economy.

The Book's Focus

The strategic management process is the focus of our textbook. Described in Chapter 1, organizations (both for-profit companies and not-for-profit agencies) use the strategic management process to understand competitive forces and to develop competitive advantages. The magnitude of this challenge is greater today than it has been historically. A new competitive landscape is developing in the 21st century as a result of the technological revolution (especially in e-commerce) and increasing globalization. The technological revolution has placed greater importance on product innovation and the ability to rapidly introduce new goods and services to the marketplace. The global economy, one in which goods and services flow relatively freely among nations, continuously pressures firms to become more competitive. By offering either valued goods or services to customers, competitive firms increase the probability of earning above-average returns. Thus, the strategic management process helps organizations identify *what* they intend to achieve and *how* they will do it.

This book is intended for use primarily in strategic management and business policy courses. The materials presented in the 13 chapters have been researched thoroughly. Both the academic, scholarly literature and the business, practitioner literatures were studied and then integrated to prepare this revision. The academic literature provides the foundation to develop an accurate, yet meaningful description of the strategic management process. The business practitioner literature yields a rich base of current domestic and global examples to show how the strategic management process's concepts, tools, and techniques are applied in different organizations.

The Strategic Management Process

Our discussion of the strategic management process is both traditional and contemporary. In maintaining tradition, we examine important materials that have historically been a part of understanding strategic management. For example, we thoroughly examine how to analyze a firm's external environment and internal environment.

Contemporary Treatment To explain the aforementioned important activities, we try to keep our treatments contemporary. In Chapter 3, for example, we emphasize the importance of identifying and determining the value-creating potential of a firm's resources, capabilities, and core competencies. The strategic actions taken as a result of understanding a firm's resources, capabilities, and core competencies have a direct link with the company's ability to establish a competitive advantage, achieve strategic competitiveness, and earn above-average returns.

Our contemporary treatment is also shown in the chapters on the dynamics of strategic change in the complex global economy. In Chapter 5, for example, we discuss how the dynamics of competition between firms, dynamics that are often "hypercompetitive," affect strategic outcomes. Chapter 5's discussion suggests that in most industries, a firm's strategic actions are influenced by its competitors' actions and reactions. Thus, competition in the global economy is fluid, dynamic, and fast-paced. Similarly, in Chapter 7, we explain the dynamics of strategic change at the corporate level, specifically addressing the motivation and consequences of mergers, acquisitions, and restructuring (e.g., divestitures) in the global economy.

We also emphasize that the set of strategic actions known as *strategy formulation* and *strategy implementation* (see Figure 1.1) must be integrated carefully if a firm is to achieve strategic competitiveness and earn above-average returns. Thus, this book shows that competitive success occurs when firms use implementation tools and actions that are consistent with the previously chosen business-level (Chapter 4), corporate-level (Chapter 6), acquisition (Chapter 7), international (Chapter 8), and cooperative (Chapter 9) strategies.

Contemporary Concepts Contemporary topics and concepts are the foundation for our in-depth analysis of strategic actions firms take to implement strategies. In Chapter 10, for example, we describe how different corporate governance mechanisms (e.g., boards of directors, institutional owners, executive compensation, etc.) affect strategy implementation. Chapter 11 explains how firms gain a competitive advantage by effectively using organizational structures that are matched properly to different strategies. The vital contributions of strategic leaders are examined in Chapter 12. Chapter 13 addresses the important topics of corporate entrepreneurship and innovation through internal corporate venturing, strategic alliances, and external acquisition or venture capital investments.

Key Features

To increase our book's value for you, several features are included.

Learning Objectives Each chapter begins with clearly stated learning objectives. Their purpose is to emphasize key points you will want to master while studying each chapter. To both facilitate and verify learning, you can revisit individual learning objectives while preparing answers to the review questions appearing at the end of each chapter.

Opening Cases An Opening Case follows the learning objectives in each chapter. The cases describe current strategic issues in modern companies such as Wal-Mart, Sony, General Motors, DaimlerChrysler, and Dell Computer Corporation, among others. The purpose of the Opening Cases is to demonstrate how specific firms apply individual chapter's strategic management concepts. Thus, the Opening Cases serve as a direct and often distinctive link between the theory and application of strategic management in different organizations and industries.

Key Terms Key terms that are critical to understanding the strategic management process are boldfaced throughout the chapters. Definitions of these key terms appear in chapter margins as well as in the text. Other terms and concepts throughout the text are italicized, signifying their importance.

Strategic Focus Segments Three all new Strategic Focus segments are presented in each chapter. As with the Opening Cases, the Strategic Focus segments highlight a variety of high-profile organizations, situations, and concepts. Each segment describes issues that can be addressed by applying a chapter's strategy-related concepts.

End-of-Chapter Summaries Closing each chapter is a summary that revisits the concepts outlined in the learning objectives. The summaries are presented in a bulleted format to highlight a chapter's concepts, tools, and techniques

Review Questions Review questions are pointedly tied to the learning objectives, prompting readers to reexamine the most important concepts in each chapter.

Application Discussion Questions These questions challenge readers to directly apply the part of the strategic management process highlighted in that chapter. The questions are designed to stimulate thoughtful classroom discussions and to help readers develop critical thinking skills.

Ethics Questions At the end of each chapter, readers are challenged by questions about ethical issues requiring careful thought and analysis. Preparing answers to these questions helps readers recognize and confront ongoing ethical issues facing management teams. Discussing these difficult issues in class heightens awareness of the ethical challenges encountered in today's global organizations and markets.

Internet Exercises The Internet is an invaluable source for exchanging information worldwide. In this edition, we present a totally new set of Internet exercises at the end of each chapter. Each exercise is designed to help readers develop an ability to recognize information sources that can aid in problem solution. Following each Internet exercise is a unique ****e-project*** module that can be used as a more comprehensive assignment—an assignment that challenges people to use the Internet for strategic purposes.

Examples In addition to the Opening Cases and Strategic Focus segments, each chapter is filled with real-world examples of companies in action. These examples illustrate key strategic management concepts and provide realistic applications of strategic management.

Indices Besides the traditional end of book Subject and Name indices, we offer a Company index as well. This index includes the names of all organizations discussed in the text for easier accessibility.

Full Four-Color Format Our presentation and discussion of the strategic management process is facilitated by the use of a full four-color format. This format provides the foundation for an interesting and visually appealing treatment of all parts of the strategic management process. Exhibits and photos further enhance the presentation by giving visual insight into the workings of companies competing in the global business environment.

The Strategic Advantage

The strategic management process is critical to organizational success. As described in Chapter 1, strategic competitiveness is achieved when a firm develops and exploits a sustained competitive advantage. Attaining such an advantage results in the earning of above-average returns; that is, returns that exceed those an investor could expect from other investments with similar amounts of risk. For example, Intel has developed and sustained a competitive advantage over time because of its significant emphasis on innovation even though it operates largely in highly competitive ever-changing high technology industries.

The Competitive Advantage

Success in the 21st-century competitive landscape requires specific capabilities, including the abilities to (1) use scarce resources wisely to maintain the lowest possible costs, (2) constantly anticipate frequent changes in customers' preferences, (3) adapt to rapid technological changes, (4) identify, emphasize, and effectively manage what a firm does better than its competitors, (5) continuously structure a firm's operations so objectives can be achieved more efficiently, and (6) successfully manage and gain commitments from a culturally diverse workforce.

The Global Advantage

Critical to the approach used in this text is the fact that all firms face increasing global competition. Firms no longer operate in relatively safe domestic markets as U.S. auto firms have discovered. In the past, many companies, including most in the United States, produced large quantities of standardized products. Today, firms typically compete in a global economy that is complex, highly uncertain, and unpredictable. To a greater degree than in a primarily domestic economy, the global economy rewards effective performers, whereas poor performers are forced to restructure significantly to enhance their strategic competitiveness. As noted earlier, increasing globalization and the technological revolution have produced a new competitive landscape in the 21st century. This landscape presents a challenging and complex environment for firms, but one that also has opportunities. The importance of developing and using these capabilities in the 21st century should not be underestimated.

Cases

Included in this fourth edition are 35 all-new case studies plus five Classic Cases. In total, the 40 cases speak to many different strategic issues. As shown by the cases, strategic issues surface for firms competing in e-commerce, manufacturing, service, consumer goods, and industrial goods industries. Importantly, given the 21st-century competitive landscape and the global economy, many of these cases represent international business concerns (e.g., ABB in China: 1998; Alcoholes de Centroamerica, S.A. de C.V.; British Airways: Latin America). Also, we offer cases dealing with the Internet (e.g., Banking on the Internet, The Advance Bank in Germany; E*Trade, Charles Schwab and Yahoo!; The Wall Street Journal: Print versus Interactive), entertainment (e.g., Circus Circus Enterprises, Inc.), and service firms (e.g., Amazon.com, Starbucks, and Outback Goes International). Some of the cases focus specifically on the wave of large merger and acquisition activity (The Boeing Company: The Merger with McDonnell Douglas, The Merger of U.S. Bancorp and Piper Jaffray Companies) while others emphasize strategic issues of entrepreneurial or small and medium-sized firms (e.g., Beano's Ice Cream Shop, Madd Snowboards—1999). Finally, a large number of the cases include detailed perspectives and information about the characteristics of the industry in which a particular focal firm or organization competes (e.g., Nucor Corp. and the U.S. Steel Industry).

Selected personally by the text authors, this unique case selection has been reviewed carefully. New to this edition are the Classic Cases. We polled the users of our text and selected their favorite cases from the last two editions. Our goal for the fourth edition has been to choose cases that are well written and deal with important strategic management issues. The comprehensive set of strategic management issues included in the cases yields a rich set of learning experiences for those performing case analyses.

Consistent with the nature of strategic issues, the cases included in this book are multidimensional in nature. Because of this, and for readers' convenience, a matrix listing all cases and the dimensions/characteristics of each one is provided following the table of contents. Furthermore, the matrix lists each text chapter that provides the best fit for teaching that particular case. While most of the cases are concerned with well-known national and international companies, several examine the strategic challenges experienced in smaller and entrepreneurial firms. Given the current challenge within the global economy, over 50 percent of the cases include an international perspective.

Support Material*

With this edition, we continue our commitment to present to you one of the most comprehensive and quality learning packages available for teaching strategic management. These supplements were prepared by talented and dedicated people—people who are recognized for their academic achievements and as excellent strategic management teachers. We worked jointly with each person to make certain that each part of the supplement package is integrated carefully and effectively with the text's materials.

For the Instructor

Instructor's Resource Manual with Video Guide and Transparency Masters (ISBN: 0-324-04276-0) Loren T. Gustafson, Seattle Pacific University, prepared a comprehensive Instructor's Manual. The manual provides teaching notes, suggestions for presentation, and chapter summaries. The teaching notes include discussion summaries or highlights of each Opening Case, Strategic Focus segment, table, and figure appearing in the text. The suggestions for presentation provide the instructor with a choice of strategies for integrating various text features into a lecture format.

The extensive Video Guide was prepared by Bruce Barringer of University of Central Florida. Now even more comprehensive in nature, the Guide provides information on length, alternative points of usage within the text, subjects to address, and discussion questions to stimulate classroom discussion. Suggested answers to these questions are also provided.

The transparency masters are printed from the PowerPoint Presentation Files and include figures from the text and innovative adaptations.

Test Bank (ISBN: 0-324-04273-6) The Test Bank, prepared by Les Palich, Baylor University, has been thoroughly revised for this new edition. It contains more than 1,200 multiple choice, true/false, and essay questions. Each question has been coded according to Bloom's taxonomy, a widely known testing and measurement device that is used to classify questions according to level (easy, medium, or hard) and type (application, recall, or comprehension).

ExamView™ Testing Software (ISBN: 0-324-04274-4) New to this edition, ExamView allows instructors to create, edit, store, and print exams more easily and efficiently.

*Adopters: Please contact your Thomson Learning sales representative to learn more about the book's supplements or visit http://hitt.swcollege.com.

Instructor's Case Notes (ISBN: 0-324-04277-9) Kendall W. Artz, Baylor University, prepared the Case Notes. Each note provides details about the case within the framework of case analysis. The structure of these case notes allows instructors to organize case discussions along common themes and concepts. For example, each case note details a firm's capabilities and resources, its industry and competitive environment, and key factors for success in the industry. In addition, the Case Notes feature aspects of the cases that make them unique. Thus, a common analytical framework—one that is tied to materials in the book's 13 chapters—yields multiple opportunities to apply the strategic management process in different organizational settings.

PowerPoint Presentation Files (ISBN: 0-324-04279-5) David Williams, University of Oklahoma, redefined and improved our comprehensive set of PowerPoint Presentation Files. Now with approximately 350 slides, the PowerPoint files feature figures from the text, lecture outlines, and innovative adaptations to enhance classroom presentation. Williams lends his academic media expertise in offering a unique and colorful set of presentations through which learning is guided and facilitated.

Transparency Acetates (ISBN: 0-324-04278-7) For those unable to access PowerPoint, a concise acetate package is available upon request.

Videos I & II (ISBNs: 0-324-01732-4 & 0-324-04275-2) A unique two-volume Video package is available that features video segments for each of the text's 13 chapters. Companies profiled include Mercedes-Benz, Ben & Jerry's, the World Gym, and Yahoo! Segments run 10-15 minutes each and focus on both small and large companies as they utilize the strategic management process. During the segments, questions are posed and viewers are asked to analyze different evolving strategic management situations. Segment cases focusing on topics found throughout the book's chapters are provided in the Instructor's Resource Manual.

For the Student

Insights: Readings in Strategic Management (ISBN: 0-538-88186-0) The comprehensive collection of readings from academic and popular business press offers an excellent and convenient literary supplement for your course. Three to four articles have been selected for each chapter. In combination, the articles deal with an individual chapter's core topics.

Web Tutor on WebCT (ISBN:0-324-06490-X) This interactive electronic study guide goes beyond the traditional print medium, providing students with vital interactive learning tools and tasks that will aid them in comprehending the conceptual material. Interested? Visit http://Webtutor.swcollege.com for more information and to demo a few sample chapters.

For the Student and Instructor

Web Site (http://hitt.swcollege.com) This continually updated site offers students and instructors access to case updates, strategy terms defined, an Internet index with important strategy URLs, and a section on how to write a case analysis. In addition, all Strategic Focus segments from the first three editions are offered for students and instructors to use as strategy examples. These are indexed by broad subject categories. All Internet exercises from editions 3 and 4 are available.

Acknowledgments

We want to thank those who helped us prepare the fourth edition. The professionalism, guidance, and support provided by the editorial team of John Szilagyi, Katherine Pruitt-Schenck, Libby Shipp, and Rob Bloom are gratefully acknowledged. We appreciate the excellent work of our supplement author team: Kendall Artz, Bruce Barringer, Loren Gustavson, Les Palich, and David Williams. In addition, we owe a debt of gratitude to our colleagues at Arizona State University, University of Richmond, and University of Oklahoma. Finally, we are sincerely grateful to those who took time to read and provide feedback on drafts of this fourth edition. Their insights and evaluations have enhanced this text, and we list them below with our thanks.

Catherine A. Maritan
State University of New York, Buffalo

Arieh A. Ullman
Binghamton University

Barbara R. Bartkus
Old Dominion University

Laszlo Tihanyi
Indiana University

Vincent P. Luchsinger
University of Baltimore

Anthony F. Chelte
Western New England College

R. Bruce Garrison
Houston Baptist University

Alfred L. Kahl
University of Ottawa

Final Comment

Organizations face exciting and dynamic competitive challenges in the 21st century. These challenges, and effective responses to them, are explored in this fourth edition of *Strategic Management: Competitiveness and Globalization*. The strategic management process conceptualized in this text offers valuable insights and knowledge to those committed to successfully meeting the challenge of dynamic competition. Thinking strategically, as this book challenges you to do, increases the likelihood that you will help your company achieve strategic success. In addition, continuous practice with strategic thinking and the use of the strategic management process gives you skills and knowledge that will contribute to career advancement and success. Finally, we want to wish you all the best and nothing other than complete success in all of your endeavors.

PART 1
STRATEGIC MANAGEMENT INPUTS

CHAPTER ONE
Strategic Management and Strategic Competitiveness

CHAPTER TWO
The External Environment: Opportunities, Threats, Industry Competition, and Competitor Analysis

CHAPTER THREE
The Internal Environment: Resources, Capabilities, and Core Competencies

STRATEGIC MANAGEMENT AND STRATEGIC COMPETITIVENESS

CHAPTER ONE OBJECTIVES

After reading this chapter, you should be able to:

1. Define strategic competitiveness, competitive advantage, and above-average returns.
2. Discuss the challenge of strategic management.
3. Describe the 21st-century competitive landscape and how global and technological changes shape it.
4. Use the industrial organization (I/O) model to explain how firms can earn above-average returns.
5. Use the resource-based model to explain how firms can earn above-average returns.
6. Describe strategic intent and strategic mission and discuss their value to the strategic management process.
7. Define stakeholders and describe the three primary stakeholder groups' ability to influence organizations.
8. Describe strategists' work.
9. Explain the strategic management process.

E-Commerce Strategy: Changing the Nature of Competition

Electronic commerce (e-commerce) is changing strategic management practices in many industries. The competition in the frenetic e-commerce environment often creates paranoia among CEOs. In his book, *Only the Paranoid Survive,* Intel's former CEO, Andrew Grove, suggests that continual change and quick strategic decisions are essential if a firm is to be successful in the new world of hypercompetition. Continuous change and rapid strategic decisions are particularly important for e-commerce firms such as Dell, Amazon.com, AOL, Yahoo, Cisco, and eBay.

The conditions facing e-commerce firms call for E-CEOs (CEOs of electronic-commerce firms) to evangelize, continuously making clear their vision as it changes. In addition, these CEOs must encourage employees consistently and meaningfully. Because the e-commerce world is so intangible, the E-CEO must spend a significant amount of time to position the company in the minds of customers, employees, the press, and numerous strategic alliance partners. A key reason for this is that a change of expectations in the minds of Wall Street analysts can diminish significantly an e-commerce firm's capital base in a short time.

E-CEOs must be much more than alert (and perhaps even paranoid) to survive the substantial competition and uncertainty of electronic commerce. For example, PointCast was a purveyor of "push technology" that continuously updated information on a screen throughout the day. A few years ago, this company and its technology were very "hot." However, large-business customers realized that push technology clogged up their corporate networks. Subsequently, many employees were ordered to discard PointCast from their PCs. The company was unable to adapt fast enough, and, as a result, it's a mere shadow of what it was several years ago.

The Internet is changing the patterns of competition among companies, thereby creating new opportunities and simultaneously affecting the way well-established firms traditionally conduct their business. Dell Computer Corporation is a prime example. Dell generates 80 percent of its revenue from business customers. The firm uses the Web to design a premier Web page that is individualized for each large customer. This personal page allows Dell to configure its PCs specifically for the particular job at each customer company. This capability reduces costs for both Dell and its customers. The customer receives a customized PC, while Dell is able to lower its paperwork flow, better coordinate its inventories, and schedule payments more efficiently.

Because the Internet makes it easier for new companies to enter markets, it also amplifies the market weaknesses of the existing companies. For example, Dell's approach has revealed weaknesses in a number of computer firms, such as Compaq,

Hewlett Packard, and IBM, that primarily use resellers. Dell's strategy requires fewer resources to implement and provides better customer satisfaction.

In addition, the Internet creates new strategic opportunities. For example, NextCard offers direct marketing services to sell financial products such as credit cards. NextCard has found that it attracted roughly $30 million in new revenues in one month; these revenues were acquired at 70 percent lower cost relative to traditional methods. Furthermore, those who have the sophistication to use the Web sites to apply for credit cards are the target customer group. These individuals tend to be professionals who pay their debts rapidly and maintain a good credit rating. The target customers represent an advantage for NextCard as it seeks to attract card users for its customers.

Amazon.com's Internet strategy also provides substantial customer service opportunities. For example, it makes recommendations for its customers based on their previous purchases and provides fast, quality service in regard to mailing its books and other items, such as CDs and videos. These services have created a loyal customer group for Amazon.com. More than 60 percent of the company's sales are from repeat business. Amazon.com treats its customers so well that they have little incentive to use competitors' services.

The Internet is also changing how firms manage strategy implementation through their traditional operations. Federal Express's (FedEx) business is moving from a phone-based to a Web-based package-tracking system. In fact, more customers now use the Internet to track their packages, rather than the telephone service. This system is much less costly for FedEx. It has to build fewer call centers, plus the existing call centers are able to focus on problem solving rather than on finding and providing information. Resulting from the use of a Web-based system are improved customer service and enhanced profitability.

Sun Microsystems uses the Internet to remain abreast of its hiring needs in the incredibly intense competition for knowledge workers in Silicon Valley. The firm examines Web sites and advertises on them to hire qualified people for critical engineering jobs. Also, Sun provides an incentive for current employees to refer high-potential candidates to it for possible employment.

Ford Motor Company is using its intranet (internal Web-based system) to allow better utilization of information among its group of approximately 100,000 employees. Top executives have supported and championed the intranet Web-only publication of divisional business plans, to engineer best practices and to prepare more precise product-development specifications. Their commitments and actions indicate clearly that Ford relies on its intranet. Approximately 80 percent of Ford's employees are connected to it on a daily basis. The average employee can check every car and truck model to examine and track design, production, quality control, and delivery processes. Through the company's information technology (IT) system, employees can examine whether a new dashboard will slow assembly or find out how many blue fenders are needed in tomorrow's shipment. A central information group tracks the intranet's performance and keeps its search engines operating effectively. The group also maintains over 700 Web page applications and servers. Employees can update their benefit plan details and examine new job postings, thereby creating a more effective internal labor market. Employees can even submit on-line evaluations of their bosses without fear of recrimination.

In summary, e-commerce has changed technology-based businesses and has

http://www.amazon.com

http://www.aol.com

http://cisco.com

http://compaq.com

http://dell.com

http://www.ebay.com

http://www.ford.com

http://www.fedex.com

http://www.hp.com

http://www.ibm.com

http://www.intel.com

http://www.nextcard.com

http://www.pointcast.com

http://sun.com

http://yahoo.com

greatly affected traditional businesses in the way they manage their suppliers, customers, and internal operations. Furthermore, and equally important, it has changed the way strategic leadership is practiced in all types of businesses.

SOURCES: T. Petzinger, Jr., 2000, There's a new economy out there—and it looks nothing like the old one, *Wall Street Journal,* January 1, R31; L. Armstrong, 1999, The rise and fall of an Internet star, *Business Week,* April 26, 88–94; E. Brown, 1999, Nine ways to win on the Web, *Fortune,* May 24, 112–125; G. Colvin, 1999, How to be a great E-CEO, *Fortune,* May 24, 104–110; H. Green, 1999, Throw out your old business model, *Business Week,* March 22, EB22–EB23; R. D. Hof, 1999, What every CEO needs to know about electronic business: A survival guide, *Business Week,* March 22, EB9–EB12; A. Reinherd, M. Moeller, & R. Siklos, 1999, As the web spins, *Business Week,* May 24, 31.

Electronic commerce (e-commerce) is changing strategic management practices. These changes are seen in e-commerce firms such as Amazon.com, Dell, and Yahoo and in what are thought of as more traditional firms, such as Ford and FedEx.

The expansion of on-line retailing efforts by major firms can affect the industry's competitive dynamics. This was the case when Wal-Mart formed an agreement with Fingerhut to handle many of its e-commerce orders. Observing this transaction, an analyst noted that "online retailers are awaiting news of Wal-Mart's e-commerce plans with some trepidation, concerned that the world's largest retailer could draw customers from less established Internet ventures."[1] Of course, all actions taken in these firms are intended to help companies achieve strategic competitiveness and earn above-average returns. *Strategic competitiveness* is achieved when a firm successfully formulates and implements a value-creating strategy. When a firm implements such a strategy that other companies are unable to duplicate or find too costly to imitate,[2] this firm has a **sustained, or sustainable, competitive advantage** (hereafter called simply competitive advantage). A firm is assured of a competitive advantage only after others' efforts to duplicate its strategy have ceased or failed. Even if a firm achieves a competitive advantage, it normally can sustain it only for a certain period.[3] The speed with which competitors are able to acquire the skills needed to duplicate the benefits of a firm's value-creating strategy determines how long a competitive advantage will last.[4] Understanding how to exploit its competitive advantage is necessary for a firm to earn above-average returns.[5]

A **sustained** or **sustainable competitive advantage** occurs when a firm implements a value-creating strategy of which other companies are unable to duplicate the benefits or find it too costly to imitate.

By achieving strategic competitiveness and successfully exploiting its competitive advantage, a firm is able to accomplish its primary objective: the earning of above-average returns. **Above-average returns** are returns in excess of what an investor expects to earn from other investments with a similar amount of risk. **Risk** is an investor's uncertainty about the economic gains or losses that will result from a particular investment.[6] Returns are often measured in terms of accounting figures, such as return on assets, return on equity, or return on sales. Alternatively, returns can be measured on the basis of stock market returns, such as daily, weekly, or monthly returns (the beginning stock price minus the end-of-the-period stock price, divided by the beginning stock price). Firms that are without a competitive advantage or that are not competing in an attractive industry earn, at best, only average returns. **Average returns** are returns equal to those an investor expects to earn from other investments with a similar amount of risk. In the long run, an inability to earn at least average returns results in failure. Failure occurs because investors will choose to invest in firms that earn at least average returns and will withdraw their investments from those earning less.[7]

Above-average returns are returns in excess of what an investor expects to earn from other investments with a similar amount of risk.

Risk is an investor's uncertainty about the economic gains or losses that will result from a particular investment.

Average returns are returns equal to those an investor expects to earn from other investments with a similar amount of risk.

The **strategic management process** is the full set of commitments, decisions, and actions required for a firm to achieve strategic competitiveness and earn above-average returns.

Dynamic in nature, the **strategic management process** (see Figure 1.1) is the full set of commitments, decisions, and actions required for a firm to achieve strategic competitiveness and earn above-average returns.[8] Relevant *strategic inputs,* from analyses of the internal and external environments, are necessary for effective strategy formulation and implementation. In turn, effective *strategic actions* are a prerequisite to achieving the desired outcomes of strategic competitiveness and above-average returns. Thus, the strategic management process is used to match the conditions of an ever-changing market and competitive structure with a firm's continuously evolving resources, capabilities, and competencies (the sources of strategic inputs). Effective

FIGURE 1.1 | The Strategic Management Process

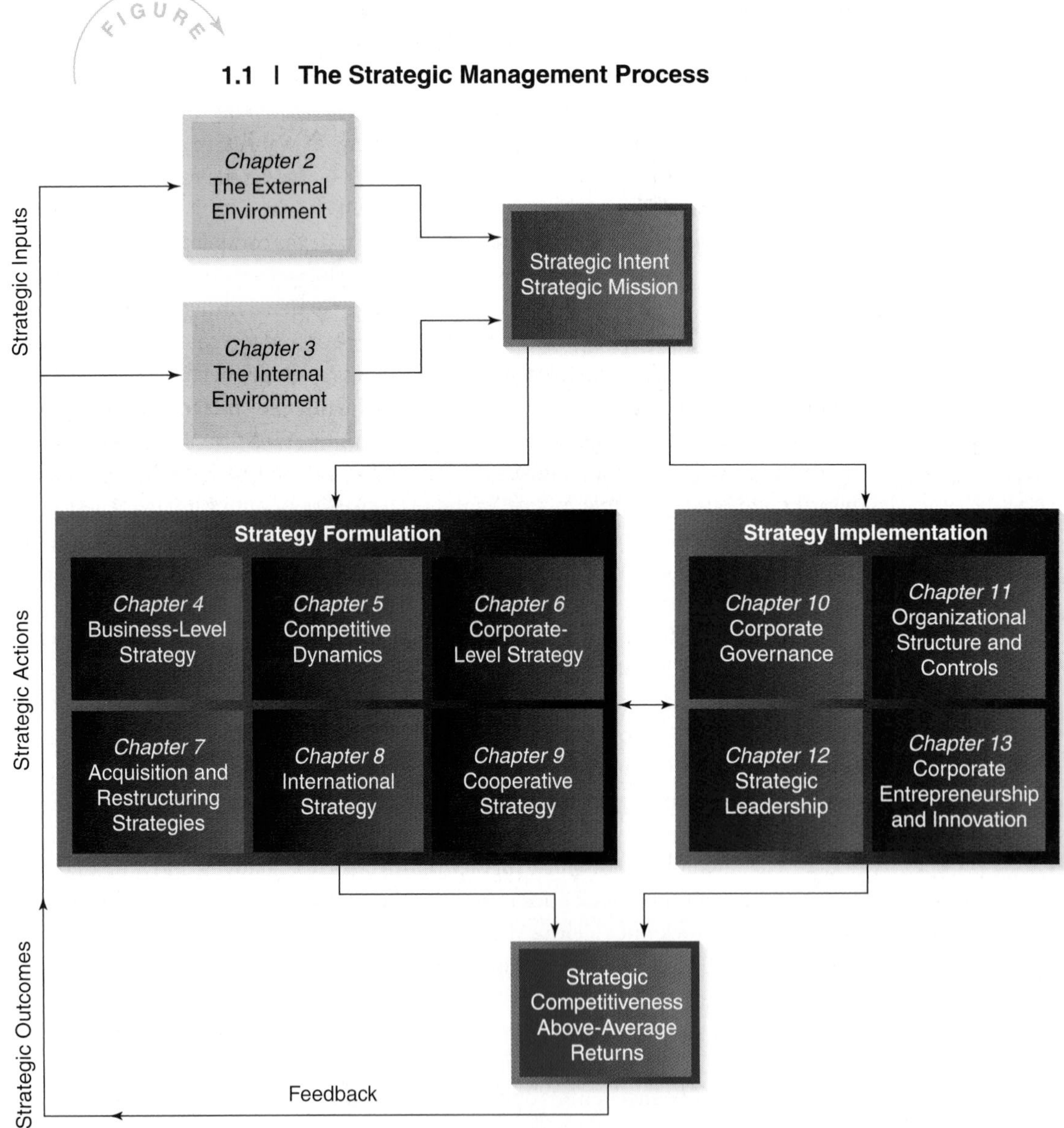

strategic actions that take place in the context of carefully integrated strategy formulation and implementation result in desired *strategic outcomes*.[9]

In the remaining chapters of this book, we use the strategic management process to explain what firms should do to achieve strategic competitiveness and earn above-average returns. Through these explanations, it becomes clear why some firms consistently achieve competitive success and others fail to do so.[10] As you will see, the reality of global competition is a critical part of the strategic management process.[11]

Several topics are discussed in this chapter. First, we examine the challenge of strategic management. This brief discussion highlights the fact that the strategic actions taken to achieve and then maintain strategic competitiveness demand the best of managers, employees, and their organizations on a continuous basis.[12] Second, we describe the 21st-century competitive landscape, created primarily by the emergence of a global economy and rapid technological changes. The 21st-century competitive landscape establishes the context of opportunities and threats within which the strategic management process is used by firms striving to meet the competitive challenge raised by demanding global standards.

We next examine two models that suggest conditions organizations should study to gain the strategic inputs needed to select strategic actions in the pursuit of strategic competitiveness and above-average returns. As we explain, the emphases of these two models differ. The first model (industrial organization) suggests that the *external environment* should be the primary determinant of a firm's strategic actions. The key to this model is identifying and competing successfully in an attractive (i.e., profitable) industry.[13] The second model (resource based) suggests that a firm's unique resources and capabilities are the critical link to strategic competitiveness.[14] Comprehensive explanations of these two models appear in this chapter, and the next two chapters show that through the combined use of these models, firms obtain the full set of strategic inputs needed to formulate and implement strategies successfully.

Analyses of its external and internal environments provide a firm with the information required to develop its strategic intent and strategic mission (intent and mission are defined later in this chapter).[15] As shown in Figure 1.1, strategic intent and strategic mission influence strategy formulation and implementation actions.

The chapter's discussion then turns to the stakeholders that organizations serve. The degree to which the stakeholders' needs can be met increases directly with enhancements in a firm's strategic competitiveness and its ability to earn above-average returns. Closing the chapter are introductions to organizational strategists and the elements of the strategic management process.

The Challenge of Strategic Management

The goals of achieving strategic competitiveness and earning above-average returns are challenging—not only for firms as large as IBM, but also for those as small as your local computer retail outlet or dry cleaners. The performance of some companies, of course, more than meets strategic management's challenge. At the end of the decade, a number of companies had shown extraordinary performance as illustrated in Table 1.1. For example, the stock prices for Cisco, AOL, Dell, EMC, CMGI, Solectron,

TABLE 1.1 | Best Performing Stocks of the 1990s

Best Stocks of the Decade	% Change 1990–99
Cisco	124,825
AOL	81,400
Dell	72,400
EMC	68,314
CMGI	57,191
Solectron	21,233
JDS Uniphase	18,755
Tellabs	16,921
Clear Channel Communications	13,700
Best Buy	9,376
Maxim Integrated	8,735
Veritas Software	8,536
Charles Schwab	7,985
Microsoft	7,483
Sun Microsystems	7,163
Safeguard Scientifics	6,816
Qlogic	6,764
Yahoo!	6,744
Qualcomm	6,388
Applied Materials	6,350

Source: www.zacks.com, January 31, 2000.

JDS Uniphase, Tellabs, and Clear Channel Communications all increased more than 10,000 percent during the decade.[16] Interestingly, in 1999, Microsoft became the first company to exceed $500 billion in market value. At the time, this value equaled that of the world's ninth-largest economy.[17]

However, the fact that only 16 of the 100 largest U.S. companies at the start of the 20th century are still identifiable today attests to the rigors of business competition and to strategic management's challenges.[18] Moreover, in a recent year, there were 44,367 business filings for bankruptcy, and there were many more actual U.S. business failures.[19] These statistics suggest that competitive success is transient.[20] Thomas J. Watson, Jr., formerly IBM's chairman, once cautioned people to remember that "corporations are expendable and that success—at best—is an impermanent achievement which can always slip out of hand."[21]

Successful performance may be transient and impermanent. The firms listed in Table 1.1 may not be listed there 10 years from now. This is also true for the firms in *Fortune* magazine's "Most Admired Corporation" list. In 1986, IBM held the number-one position on *Fortune*'s list for the fourth consecutive year. By 1995, IBM's position had slipped to number 281. Of course, IBM has come back, while the standing of another computer company, Compaq, has slipped[22] (this point is discussed later in the chapter).

It is interesting to note that, in a survey, CEOs did not place "strong and consistent profits" as their top priority; in fact, it was fifth. A "strong and well-thought-out strategy" was the top concern that will make a firm the most respected in the future. This was followed by maximizing customer satisfaction and loyalty, business leadership and quality products and services, and then concern for consistent profits.[23] This is consistent with the view that no matter how good a product or service is, the firm must select the "right" strategy and then implement it effectively.[24]

CEOs' concern for strategy is well founded. Some firms create their own problems by formulating the wrong strategy or implementing a strategy poorly. Such is the case with PointCast and Levi Strauss. Because of strategic errors, recent years have found each of these firms failing to earn the returns that shareholders expect. PointCast's strategic errors led to significant declines in the firm's market share and a decision to survive through retrenchment. At Levi Strauss, poor performance resulted in a decision to reduce costs substantially. It is interesting to note that Levi Strauss could not achieve its socially responsible ideals because it was not creating the customer value that had long resulted from implementation of its strategies. These firms' experiences are described in the Strategic Focus.

In recognition of strategic management's challenge, Andrew Grove, Intel's former CEO, observed that only paranoid companies survive and succeed. Intel is the number-one computer chip manufacturer in the world, with market capitalization greater than all the top U.S. automakers combined. Such firms know that current success does not guarantee future strategic competitiveness and above-average returns. In fact, in 1998, Intel lost ground to competitors. "It's fighting battles on many fronts, including the popular sub-$1,000 PC sector. Rather than cede this area to clonemakers such as AMD or National Semiconductor, Intel plans to win back the market share it lost last year."[25] By mid-1999, Intel had regained a great deal of the share it had lost. Much of the regained share was at AMD's expense. One business analysis suggested that AMD's CEO was "in denial" about recent losses and continually blamed Intel's "monopoly" position for his firm's performance difficulties.[26]

As this example indicates, Intel strives continuously to improve in order to remain competitive. For Intel and others that are competing in the 21st-century's competitive landscape, Andrew Grove believes that a key challenge is to try to do the impossible, namely, to anticipate the unexpected.[27]

The 21st-Century Competitive Landscape[28]

The fundamental nature of competition in many of the world's industries is changing.[29] The pace of this change is relentless and is increasing. Even determining the boundaries of an industry has become challenging. Consider, for example, how advances in interactive computer networks and telecommunications have blurred the definition of the television industry. The near future will find companies such as ABC, CBS, NBC, and HBO competing not only among themselves, but also with AT&T, Microsoft, and Sony.

An example of this new form of competition is occurring in the telephone and cable TV industries. In February 1996, U.S. West bought Continental Cablevision. In June 1998, AT&T agreed to buy TCI and made an offer in mid-1999 for MediaOne. AT&T is seeking cable assets to compete against the local bell monopolies. U.S. West

The Impermanence of Success

PointCast was a highly popular start-up that is now a small version of itself. The PointCast experience may not be unusual, given the frequent changes among Internet or e-commerce businesses. However, these experiences are less common among businesses with established brands, as is the case for Levi Strauss.

Internet businesses are often in an environment where revenues and profits seem to be afterthoughts. In 1996, before Yahoo!, Excite, Alta Vista, and other firms that began as search engines were on the Web, PointCast was recognized as a strong company in terms of delivering personalized information over the Web. Its software allowed customers to automatically transfer technology through the Internet to a select group of customers. PointCast generated its revenues from advertising charges. At one time, the PointCast network had 1.5 million users, $5 million in annual revenue, and a list of significant advertisers. Furthermore, it had attracted $48 million in funding from venture capitalists and corporations, such as Compaq Computer and General Electric Capital Services. PointCast's market valuation reached a high of $240 million.

Several strategic errors led to PointCast's downfall. First, the firm had built its entire business around proprietary software. In other words, PointCast had bet its future on this software; however, the market moved more toward Web-based services. Furthermore, the firm's board concluded that the company should be led by a CEO with broader and deeper experience than was the case with PointCast founder Christopher R. Hassett. However, six months passed before Pacific Bell's former CEO, David W. Dorman, was selected as a person with the leadership skills needed to chart PointCast's future. In the meantime, management was in turmoil and spending was out of control. Moreover, PointCast's corporate customers were turning increasingly to Web-based competitors such as Yahoo! and Excite. Additionally, corporations were concerned that PointCast's software would clog their intranet systems with too much useless information.

Ultimately, PointCast was unable to obtain capital through an IPO and had to reconfigure its business. It laid off nearly one-third of its 220 employees and is now pursuing a more focused strategy. Although PointCast had once filed for a $250 million stock offering, by April, 1999 the firm was seeking $15 million in order to remain solvent and to continue operating.

Beginning in 1997, Levi Strauss announced plans to close 29 factories in North America and Europe, thereby eliminating 16,310 jobs. Its 1998 sales dropped 13 percent from the year before, to just under $6 billion. In comparison, its crosstown (San Francisco) rival, Gap, Inc., grew much more rapidly during the same period. In 1996, Levi Strauss went through a leveraged buyout (LBO). Its stock had grown from $2.53 per share in 1985 to over $265 (adjusted for splits) per share in 1996. Robert Haas and other family shareholders decided to take the firm private to ensure that the company would be driven largely by social values and that it would not be hostage to profits alone.

Evidence suggests that Levi Strauss has not satisfied either its profit target or its social goals. In fact, many claim that it has mismanaged the Levi brand since 1990. Levi Strauss has always been a strong advocate of corporate philanthropy and social responsibility. In 1993,

Levi Strauss embarked on a project it called its customer-service supply-chain initiative. However, this supply-chain initiative changed over time to emphasize improving service to *all* retail customers. The initiative produced a reengineering team whose budget had swollen 70 percent by 1995, to over $850 million. While engaged in this restructuring, the company became overly focused on one brand for all customers.

During the period of Levi's restructuring efforts, other brands (e.g., Tommy Hilfiger) took some market share from Levi Strauss. Selling their clothing in new store concept outlets, such as Hot Tropic, Pacific Sunwear, and Gap, contributed to these other brands' success. In contrast to these new concept stores, Levi's clothing was being sold through channels (e.g., traditional department stores) that were less popular with the firm's target customers. Although Levi Strauss has now started a multibrand strategy—something its competitors have done for years—it's in a catch-up phase. Gap, for example, has its high-end Banana Republic stores, its midlevel brand Gap, and its low-priced Old Navy store concepts and associated brands. Although Gap has had some problems as well (see Strategic Focus in Chapter 4), they pale in comparison to Levi's mismanagement.

Another area where Levi Strauss fell behind was in its Web strategy. While Levi's market share shrank to 14 percent in 1998 from 16.9 percent in 1990, many direct-sale Internet sites were appearing. Levi's executives flirted with creating a site in 1994, but it wasn't until 1995 that the firm's first site was operational. Even then, the company was focused on giving customers a place to "hang, chat, and read about graffiti art and South African street styles." Feedback indicated that the site's capabilities frustrated customers, who expressed their desire to have an opportunity to buy jeans electronically. This interest troubled Levi personnel, who were concerned that such a site would offend its traditional retail outlet customers. These concerns may have surfaced because Levi did not launch its direct-sales strategy in collaboration with its retail outlets. Thus, while Lee jeans can be purchased at jcpenney.com and Calvin Klein jeans at macy.com, buying Levi's jeans from these retailers requires customers to visit "bricks and mortar" retail stores. Although Levi Strauss's Web approach is generating acceptable sales numbers, it's not clear how the firm's traditional customer–retailers will react. Affecting this reaction could be Levi's position that its e-commerce approach serves the *public* customer, not the retailer.

The PointCast and Levi Strauss examples suggest that an Internet venture (PointCast) and a firm competing on the basis of a strong brand (Levi Strauss) can both fail to achieve (PointCast) or maintain (Levi Strauss) strategic competitiveness. Such failure occurs when firms are unable to effectively use the strategic management process.

SOURCES: L. Himelstein & R. Siklos, 1999, The rise and fall of an Internet star, *Business Week*, April 26, 88–94; L. Kroll, 1998, Digital denim, *Forbes*, December 28, 102–103; N. Munk, 1999, How Levi's trashed a great American brand, *Fortune*, April 12, 83–90.

---

was seeking to pursue this potential substitute for local service. Also, both AT&T and U.S. West were attempting to establish competitive positions as deliverers of media services.[30] Later in 1999, U.S. West was acquired by a much smaller media company, Qwest Communications International[31] (see the Strategic Focus later in the chapter). As these examples illustrate, the pace of change among once-stable phone companies is as relentless as it is in the "traditional" grocery industry. Today, grocery stores (e.g.,

Albertson's) are selling gas, while oil firms (e.g., Chevron and Texaco) are building better food marts at their gas retail outlets. "And Wal-Mart? Wal-Mart wants to sell you everything—including gasoline and groceries."[32]

Still other characteristics of the 21st-century competitive landscape are noteworthy. Conventional sources of competitive advantage, such as economies of scale and huge advertising budgets, are not as effective in the 21st-century competitive landscape. Moreover, the traditional managerial mind-set cannot lead a firm to strategic competitiveness in the competitive landscape. In its place, managers must adopt a new mind-set—one that values flexibility, speed, innovation, integration, and the challenges that evolve from constantly changing conditions. The conditions of the competitive landscape result in a perilous business world, one where the investments required to compete on a global scale are enormous and the consequences of failure are severe.[33]

Hypercompetition is a term that is often used to capture the realities of the 21st-century competitive landscape (mentioned briefly here, hypercompetitive environments are discussed further in Chapter 5). According to Richard A. D'Aveni, hypercompetition results from the dynamics of strategic maneuvering among global and innovative combatants. It is a condition of rapidly escalating competition based on price–quality positioning, competition to create new know-how and establish first-mover advantage, competition to protect or invade established product or geographic markets, and competition based on deep pockets and the creation of even deeper pocketed alliances.[34]

Several factors have created hypercompetitive environments and the 21st-century competitive landscape. The two primary drivers are the emergence of a global economy and technology, specifically rapid technological changes.

The Global Economy

A **global economy** is one in which goods, services, people, skills, and ideas move freely across geographic borders.

A **global economy** is one in which goods, services, people, skills, and ideas move freely across geographic borders. Relatively unfettered by artificial constraints, such as tariffs, the global economy significantly expands and complicates a firm's competitive environment.[35]

Interesting opportunities and challenges are associated with the global economy's emergence. For example, Europe, instead of the United States, is now the world's largest single market. The European market, with 700 million potential customers, has a gross domestic product (GDP) of $8 trillion, which is comparable to that of the United States.[36] In addition, by 2015, China's total GDP will be greater than Japan's, although its per capita output will be much lower.[37] In recent years, as the competitiveness rankings in Table 1.2 indicate, the Japanese economy has lagged behind that of the United States and some European countries. However, other Asian countries—in particular Singapore and Hong Kong (now part of China)—have maintained their rankings. This is commendable, considering the severe Asian financial crisis of 1997.[38] Achieving improved competitiveness allows a country's citizens to have a higher standard of living. Some believe that entrepreneurial activity will continue to influence living standards during the 21st century. For example, a report describing European competitiveness concluded that "it is only through the creation of more new businesses and more fast-growing businesses that Europe will create more new jobs and achieve higher levels of economic well-being for all of its citizens" (we discuss the role of entrepreneurship further in Chapter 13).[39]

1.2 | Country Competitiveness Rankings

1999 Ranking	1998 Ranking	Country	Competitiveness Index 1999	Competitiveness Index 1998
1	1	Singapore	2.12	2.16
2	3	United States	1.58	1.41
3	2	Hong Kong	1.41	1.91
4	6	Taiwan	1.38	1.19
5	5	Canada	1.33	1.27
6	8	Switzerland	1.27	1.10
7	10	Luxembourg	1.25	1.05
8	4	United Kingdom	1.17	1.29
9	7	Netherlands	1.13	1.13
10	11	Ireland	1.11	1.05
11	15	Finland	1.11	0.70
12	14	Australia	1.04	0.79
13	13	New Zealand	1.01	0.84
14	12	Japan	1.00	0.97
15	9	Norway	0.92	1.09
16	17	Malaysia	0.86	0.59
17	16	Denmark	0.85	0.61
18	30	Iceland	0.59	–0.18
19	23	Sweden	0.58	0.25
20	20	Austria	0.57	0.37
21	18	Clile	0.57	0.57
22	19	Korea	0.46	0.39
23	22	France	0.44	0.25
24	27	Belgium	0.39	–0.03
25	24	Germany	0.37	0.15
26	25	Spain	0.16	0.02

Source: K. Schwab, M. E. Porter, J. D. Sachs, A. M Warner & M. Levinson, 1999, *The Global Competitiveness Report 1999*, New York: Oxford University Press, 11. Reprinted with permission.

A country's competitiveness is achieved through the accumulation of individual firms' strategic competitiveness in the global economy. Increasingly, to accomplish this, a firm must view the world as its marketplace. For example, Procter & Gamble believes that it still has tremendous potential to grow internationally because globally, the demand for household products is not as mature as it is in the United States.

Although a commitment to viewing the world as a company's marketplace creates a sense of direction, it is not without risks. For example, Whirlpool Corporation, the world's largest manufacturer of major home appliances, intends to maintain its global leadership position. With production facilities in 13 countries and through its marketing efforts in 140 nations, the company's sales volume outside the United States is now over 45 percent.[40] Recently, Whirlpool bought the white goods business of Gentrade of South Africa. The acquisition provides Whirlpool a sales and manufacturing base in that country. Whirlpool also has joint ventures with firms in various countries, including China, Taiwan, and India. However, with the global financial crisis initiated in Asia and spreading to Latin America, sales declined. For example, sales decreased by about 25 percent in Brazil in 1998. Furthermore, Whirlpool has been able to achieve only a 12 percent market share in Europe, compared with its goal of 20 percent, due to increased competition from firms such as Electrolux. Internet-ready products such as refrigerators and ovens may help the firm in efforts to reach its goals in various world markets. A Web-savvy oven, offered initially in Europe, was introduced in the U.S. market in 2000. Also introduced in the United States in 2000 was an Internet-ready refrigerator. Focusing on customer convenience, consumers can download a recipe from the Internet through a touch screen on the refrigerator and then automatically program the oven to cook the recipe.[41]

Large firms such as Whirlpool often commit to competition in the global economy more quickly than do midsize and small firms. Recently, however, U.S. midsize and small firms are demonstrating a strong commitment to competing in the global economy. For example, 60 percent of U.S. firms now exporting goods employ fewer than 100 people. And companies with fewer than 500 employees are selling over $200 billion a year to customers outside the United States.[42]

The March of Globalization

Globalization is the spread of economic innovations around the world and the political and cultural adjustments that accompany this diffusion. Globalization encourages international integration, which has increased substantially during the last generation. In globalized markets and industries, financial capital might be obtained in one national market and used to buy raw materials in another one. Manufacturing equipment bought from a third national market can be used to produce products that are sold in yet a fourth market. Thus, globalization increases the range of opportunities for firms competing in the 21st-century competitive landscape.

Many of Wal-Mart's initial international investments were in Canada and Mexico (a Mexican Wal-Mart shown here). Recently, it has expanded into Argentina, Brazil, Indonesia, and China. The company's goal is to offer lower priced goods to all customers, not just U.S. citizens.

For example, Wal-Mart is trying to achieve boundaryless retailing with global pricing, sourcing, and logistics. Most of Wal-Mart's international investments have been in Canada and Mexico, in close proximity to the United States. However, recently the company moved into Argentina, Brazil, Indonesia, and China. Supercenter stores in Buenos Aires sell as many as 15,000 items in a day, twice as many as in comparable U.S. superstores. Wal-Mart plans to export its North American dominance to other regions of the world as well. For instance, it recently made a large acquisition of stores in Germany and Europe.[43] One of Wal-Mart's objectives is to offer lower priced goods to the world's citizens—not just U.S. citizens.

The internationalization of markets and industries makes it increasingly difficult to think of some firms as domestic companies. For example, Daimler Benz, the parent company of Mercedes Benz, merged with Chrysler to create DaimlerChrysler. Moreover, even before these firms were integrated, Jurgen E. Schrempp, DaimlerChrysler CEO, tried to acquire cash-strapped Nissan Motor Co. The company needed better partnering arrangements in Asia. However, after the stock price declined, Daimler Chrysler's board decided that the deal was premature. DaimlerChrysler has now focused on getting the companies integrated around the world. In a similar move, Ford announced an acquisition of Volvo's car division. Ford now has six brands around the world: Ford, Lincoln, Mercury, Jaguar, Mazda, and Aston Martin. It can use these brands to spread its economies of scale in the purchase and sourcing of components that make up 60 percent of the value of a car.[44]

There are a number of other car companies that remain independent, such as Honda. However, Honda has become a target firm to be acquired.[45] Currently, Honda has a number of plants throughout the world. For instance, it produces in the United States over 70 percent of the cars it sells in the U.S. domestic market. Honda's decision to build a fourth U.S. plant in Alabama shows its commitment to trying to remain an independent global manufacturer. The Alabama facility is to build sport utility vehicles (SUVs) and will have a capacity of 120,000 vehicles annually by 2003.[46] Toyota Motor Corporation continues to reduce its total employment in Japan while expanding its global workforce. Toyota's Kentucky facility is the only place where the company builds its Avalon sedan and Camry Coupe and station wagon. In 1997, this plant became the sole producer of Toyota's new minivan, and, in 1998, the firm began to build its T100 pickup in the United States.[47] In August 1999, a red Tacoma pickup became the one-millionth truck to roll off the NUMMI assembly line (NUMMI is a GM-Toyota joint venture known as New United Motor Manufacturing, Inc.). Although seemingly foreign brands are quite domestic, U.S. carmakers have been accused of being asleep at the wheel: "For the 1999 model year, . . . four of the five top selling autos in the U.S. market (Camry, Accord, Civic, and Corolla) are made by Toyota and Honda. The only domestic car is the Ford Taurus, whose biggest customer is Hertz."[48] Unlike the 1980s, when imports increased their sales significantly, today foreign competitors have a 30 percent market share. Competition is even tougher for luxury brands, with BMW, Mercedes, and Lexus (Toyota) increasing their market share against Ford and GM brands. U.S. auto companies are also challenged to be more aware of other nations' cultures, including the languages. Ford, for example, launched a car that it had built in Europe in Japan. Called the Ka, this car's name translated into the word "mosquito" in the Japanese language.[49]

Given their operations, these automobile firms should not be thought of as European, Japanese, or American. Instead, they can be classified more accurately as global companies striving to achieve strategic competitiveness in the 21st-century competitive landscape. Some believe that because of its enormous economic benefits, globalization will not be stopped. It has been predicted, for example, that genuine free trade in manufactured goods among the United States, Europe, and Japan would add 5 to 10 percent to the triad's annual economic output; free trade in the triad's service sector would boost aggregate output by another 15 to 20 percent. Realizing these potential gains in economic output requires a commitment from the industrialized nations to cooperatively stimulate the higher levels of trade necessary for global growth. Eliminating national laws that impede free trade is an important stimulus to increased trading among nations.[50]

Global competition has increased performance standards in many dimensions, including those of quality, cost, productivity, product introduction time, and smooth, flowing operations. Moreover, these standards are not static; they are exacting, requiring continuous improvement from a firm and its employees. As they accept the challenges posed by these increasing standards, companies improve their capabilities and individual workers sharpen their skills. Thus, in the 21st-century competitive landscape, strategic competitiveness will be earned only by those capable of meeting, if not exceeding, global standards. This challenge exists for all companies that develop cooperative relationships (e.g., joint ventures) in order to capitalize on international growth opportunities.[51]

The development of emerging and transitional economies also is changing the global competitive landscape and significantly increasing competition in global markets. The economic development of Asian countries outside of Japan is increasing the significance of Asian markets. Firms in the emerging economies of Asia, such as South Korea, however, are becoming major competitors in global industries. For instance, Samsung has become a market leader in the semiconductor industry, taking market share away from Japanese and American firms. With increasing globalization and the spread of information technology, other countries are likely to develop their industrial bases as well. For instance, Taiwan's semiconductor industry has grown through firms such as United Microelectronics and Taiwan Semiconductor Manufacturing Co., which pursue a strategy of flexible contracting with other chip producers.[52] As this occurs, global markets will expand, but competition in those markets will also become more intense.

Firms such as Wal-Mart, Motorola, and Enron are moving more boldly into international markets. In particular, each of these firms is making important investments in Asia. Of course, there are also firms, such as Cemex (a large cement producer headquartered in Mexico), that have made investments in North America and Latin America. Thus, international investments come from many directions and are targeted for many different regions of the world. There are risks with these investments, however. We discuss a number of them in Chapter 8. Some people refer to these risks as the "liability of foreignness."[53] Recent research suggests that firms are challenged in their early ventures into international markets and can have difficulties if they enter too many different or challenging international markets. In other words, performance may suffer in early efforts to globalize until the skills required to manage it are developed.[54] Moreover, performance may suffer with substantial amounts of globalization. In this instance, firms may overdiversify internationally beyond their ability to manage the diversified operations that have been created.[55] The outcome can sometimes be quite painful to these firms.[56] Thus, entry into international markets, even for firms with substantial experience in such markets, requires careful planning and selection of the appropriate markets to enter and the most effective strategies to operate successfully in those markets.

Global markets are attractive strategic options for some companies, but they are not the only source of strategic competitiveness. In fact, for most companies—even for those capable of competing successfully in global markets—it is critical to remain committed to the domestic market.[57] In the 21st-century competitive landscape, firms are challenged to develop the optimal level of globalization, a level that results in appropriate concentrations on a company's domestic and global operations.

In many instances, strategically competitive companies are those that have learned how to apply competitive insights gained locally (or domestically) on a global scale.[58] These companies do not impose homogeneous solutions in a pluralistic world. Instead, they nourish local insights so they can modify and apply them appropriately in different regions around the world. Moreover, they are sensitive to globalization's potential effects. For example, a report issued by the World Health Organization and the International Labor Organization suggests that the "continuing shift of industrial production to low-cost sites in developing countries where worker protection is lower is likely to increase the global incidence of occupational disease and injury."[59] Firms with strong commitments to global success evaluate these possible outcomes in making their strategic choices.

Technology and Technological Changes

There are three categories of trends and conditions through which technology is significantly altering the nature of competition.

Increasing Rate of Technological Change and Diffusion

Both the rate of change of technology and the speed at which new technologies become available and are used have increased substantially over the last 15 to 20 years. *Perpetual innovation* is a term used to describe how rapidly and consistently new, information-intensive technologies replace older ones. The shorter product life cycles resulting from these rapid diffusions of new technologies place a competitive premium on being able to introduce new goods and services quickly into the marketplace. In fact, when products become somewhat indistinguishable because of the widespread and rapid diffusion of technologies, speed to market may be the only source of competitive advantage (see Chapter 5).[60]

There are other indicators of rapid technology diffusion. Some evidence suggests that after only 12 to 18 months, companies likely will have gathered information about their competitors' research and development and product decisions.[61] In the global economy, any idea that works can sometimes be imitated in a matter of a few days. Consider, for example, that approximately 75 percent of the product-life gross margins for a typical PC are earned within the first 90 days of sales.[62]

Once a source of competitive advantage, today's rate of technological diffusion stifles the protection firms possessed previously through their patents. Today, patents are thought by many to be an effective way of protecting proprietary technology only in the pharmaceutical and chemical industries. Indeed, many firms competing in the electronics industry often do not apply for patents to prevent competitors from gaining access to the technological knowledge included in the patent application!

The Information Age

Dramatic changes in information technology have occurred in recent years. Personal computers, cellular phones, artificial intelligence, virtual reality, and massive databases (e.g., Lexis/Nexis) are a few examples of how information is used differently as a result of technological developments. Intel's former CEO Andrew Grove believes that electronic mail (e-mail) systems are the first manifestation of a revolution in the flow and management of information in companies throughout the world. In Grove's view, "The informed use of e-mail has two simple but startling implications: It turns days into minutes, and allows each person to reach hundreds of co-workers with the same effort it takes to reach just one."[63] An important outcome of these changes is that the ability to access and use information effectively has become an important source of competitive advantage in virtually all industries.

Companies are now being wired to build electronic networks linking them to customers, employees, vendors, and suppliers. IBM has made this a major thrust in its drive to reorient and revive its business. These networks are often referred to as e-businesses by IBM and others.[64] E-business is big business. For example, Internet trade is predicted to reach $105 billion by 2000, up from only $7.8 billion in 1997. It is even predicted that e-business will eventually represent 75–80 percent of the U.S. gross domestic product. This means that most transactions will be accomplished electronically. It is interesting to note that e-commerce between businesses, about $43 billion in 1998, is five times larger than consumer e-business. By 2003, Forrester Research, Inc., estimates that it will balloon to $1.3 trillion.[65]

As the Opening Case suggests, e-businesses have a different form of competition and require a different leadership approach. Both the pace of change in information technology and its diffusion will continue to increase. It is predicted, for example, that the number of personal computers in use will grow from over 150 million today to 278 million in 2010. The declining costs of information technologies and the increased accessibility to them are also evident in the 21st-century competitive landscape. The global proliferation of relatively inexpensive computing power and its linkage on a global scale via computer networks combine to increase the speed and diffusion of information technologies. Thus, the competitive potential of information technologies is now available to companies throughout the world, rather than only to large firms in Europe, Japan, and North America.

Combined, the Internet and World Wide Web create an infrastructure that allows the delivery of information to computers in any location. Access to significant quantities of relatively inexpensive information yields strategic opportunities for a range of industries and companies. Retailers, for example, use the Internet to provide abundant shopping privileges to customers in multiple locations. To begin the competitive thrust into e-commerce, Nordstrom Inc., formed a partnership with venture capital firms.[66] Thus, as the Opening Case indicates, the power of this means of information

Compaq Is Flailing against Internet Technological Trends

In January 1998, Compaq Computer Corporation acquired Digital Equipment Corporation (DEC). This was ostensibly a defining moment for Compaq, showing that it was moving into a different league of competitors—ones offering larger machines and services as well as PCs. Eckhard Pfeiffer, then Compaq's CEO, was quoted as saying, "We want to do it all, and we want to do it now." However, a little over a year later, on April 18, 1999, Compaq chairman Benjamin M. Rosen, although praising Pfeiffer, announced through a press release that Pfeiffer was being asked to step down.

Pfeiffer had brought the company back from the precipice after Rod Canion, Compaq's founder, was deposed in 1991. Pfeiffer built the company from $3.3 billion to over $40 billion in sales since his 1991 ascent to the CEO position. In the process, Compaq became number one in overall PC sales in August of 1995. How did Pfeiffer's precipitous fall at Compaq happen? What went wrong?

In 1996, Compaq bought Tandem Computers, a minicomputer manufacturer focused on workstations. As already mentioned, in January 1998, it also purchased DEC, for $8.4 billion. The latter transaction was to help Compaq move into services, although DEC's business in workstations was declining. Thus, Compaq was moving into the territory of formidable competitors such as Sun Microsystems and IBM. IBM is excellent in services, but Compaq executives felt that acquiring DEC would help develop Compaq's services business in a growing high-tech world where services are the drivers that often foster sales in hardware and software. However, in so doing, Compaq executives lost focus on their main business, PCs, and were unable to execute Web-based direct selling as effectively as their main competitor, Dell Computer Corporation.

Compaq announced in February 1994 that by 1996 it would be implementing a build-to-order strategy that was similar to Dell's. At the time of the announcement, 55 percent of Compaq's PC sales were generated through direct and Web-based sales efforts. When Compaq announced a more significant move toward Internet sales, friction surfaced between the firm and its numerous resellers. This friction became especially pronounced when Compaq decided to sell its new Prosignia model exclusively on the Web. This decision was reversed in March 1999, following the initial announcement in November 1998. The reversal was due to an inventory buildup and an 8 percent drop in Compaq's stock price in 1998. Compaq subsequently announced that it would downsize the number of its resellers to 4 dominant distributors from approximately 20 major ones. This strategic decision was intended to provide Compaq more control over its resellers and allow the company to concentrate on its strategy of direct selling.

To add to Compaq's problems, the main strategist in charge of its service business, John Rando, resigned three weeks after Pfeiffer's forced departure. Compaq's service business ranked third behind IBM and EDS, just ahead of Hewlett-Packard (HP) and Andersen Consulting when Compaq acquired DEC in early 1998. Rando's departure created still additional uncertainty about the shape of Compaq's future.

Before Rando's replacement was chosen, many high-tech customers changed from DEC and Tandem technology-based workstations to systems from formidable competitors such as HP, IBM, and Sun Microsystems.

It is not unusual for an acquiring firm to encounter problems when it tries to integrate high-tech acquisitions into its operations. Silicon Graphics had trouble with its acquisition of Cray Research, while AT&T's acquisition of NCR and HP's acquisition of Apollo Computers never resulted in the positive outcomes executives expected when they decided to buy these other companies. Thus, as an acquirer, Compaq may be learning what some others in this industry (e.g., Silicon Graphics, AT&T, and HP) learned previously: It is difficult to compete successfully on several major fronts in an industry in which change is constant and dynamic.

SOURCES: P. Burrows, I. Sager, & M. Moeller, 1999, Can Compaq catch up? *Business Week,* May 3, 162–166; L. Kehoe, 1999, Compaq at the crossroads after Pfeiffer's departure, *Financial Times,* April 20, 17; G. McWilliams, 1999, Head of Compaq services unit resigns in third recent high-level departure, *Wall Street Journal Interactive Edition,* May 12, *www.interactive.wsj.com;* G. McWilliams & J. S. Lublin, 1999, Compaq Computer's board removes Chief Executive Officer Eckhard Pfeiffer, *Wall Street Journal Interactive Edition, April 19, www.interactive.wsj.com*; M. R. Zimmerman, 1999, Compaq and the road not taken, *PCWeek Online,* May 3, *www.zdnet.com*; J. G. Auerbach & W. M. Bulkeley, 1998, Compaq seeks Digital's prized asset: its world-famous service business, *Wall Street Journal Interactive Edition,* January 28, *www.interactive.wsj.com*; *Fortune,* 1998, Where Compaq went wrong, April 23, *http://www.fortune.com.*

access and application results in an almost astonishing array of strategic implications and possibilities.

Increasing Knowledge Intensity

Knowledge (information, intelligence, and expertise) is the basis of technology and its application. In the 21st-century competitive landscape, knowledge is a critical organizational resource and is increasingly a valuable source of competitive advantage. Because of this, many companies now strive to transmute the accumulated knowledge of individual employees into a corporate asset. Some argue that the value of intangible assets, including knowledge, is growing as a proportion of total shareholder value.[67] The probability of achieving strategic competitiveness in the 21st-century competitive landscape is enhanced for the firm that realizes that its survival depends on the ability to capture intelligence, transform it into usable knowledge, and diffuse it rapidly throughout the company.[68] Firms that accept this challenge shift their focus from merely obtaining the information to *exploiting* the information to gain a competitive advantage over rival firms.[69]

Strategic flexibility is a set of capabilities firms use to respond to various demands and opportunities that are a part of dynamic and uncertain competitive environments.

Our discussion of conditions in the 21st-century competitive landscape shows that firms must be able to adapt quickly to achieve strategic competitiveness and earn above-average returns. The term strategic flexibility describes a firm's ability to do this. **Strategic flexibility** is a set of capabilities firms use to respond to various demands and opportunities that are a part of dynamic and uncertain competitive environments.[70] Firms should develop strategic flexibility in all areas of their operations. Such capabilities in terms of manufacturing allow firms to "switch gears—from, for example, rapid product development to low cost—relatively quickly and with minimum resources."[71] As suggested in the Strategic Focus, one of Compaq Computer Corporation's problems in the late 1990s was a lack of strategic flexibility.[72]

To achieve strategic flexibility, many firms have to develop organizational slack. Slack resources allow the firm some flexibility to respond to environmental changes.[73] When the changes required are large, firms may have to undergo strategic reorientations. Such reorientations can drastically change a firm's competitive strategy.[74] Strategic reorientations are often the result of a firm's poor performance. For example, when a firm earns negative returns, its stakeholders (discussed later in this chapter) are likely to place pressure on the top executives to make major changes.[75] To be strategically flexible on a continuing basis, a firm has to develop the capacity to learn. The learning continuously provides the firm with new and current sets of skills. This allows the firm to adapt to its environment as it encounters changes.[76] As illustrated in the Strategic Focus, Compaq has had difficulties adjusting to the on-line selling approach pioneered by Dell. Although Compaq has maintained strategic flexibility in the past, its acquisition of Digital Equipment Corporation has created some difficult adjustment challenges. In addition, the firm has not adapted quickly in other strategic areas.

Next, we describe two models used by firms to generate the strategic inputs needed to successfully formulate and implement strategies and to maintain strategic flexibility in the process of doing so.

The I/O Model of Above-Average Returns

From the 1960s through the 1980s, the external environment was thought to be the *primary* determinant of strategies firms selected to be successful.[77] The industrial organization (I/O) model explains the dominant influence of the external environment on firms' strategic actions. The model specifies that the industry in which a firm chooses to compete has a stronger influence on the firm's performance than do the choices managers make inside their organizations.[78] The firm's performance is believed to be determined primarily by a range of an industry's properties, including economies of scale, barriers to market entry, diversification, product differentiation, and the degree of concentration of firms in the industry[79] (these industry characteristics are examined in Chapter 2).

Grounded in economics, the I/O model has four underlying assumptions. First, the external environment is assumed to impose pressures and constraints which determine the strategies that would result in above-average returns. Second, most firms competing within a particular industry or within a certain segment of an industry are assumed to control similar strategically relevant resources and to pursue similar strategies in light of those resources. The I/O model's third assumption is that resources used to implement strategies are highly mobile across firms. Because of resource mobility, any resource differences that might develop between firms will be short lived. Fourth, organizational decision makers are assumed to be rational and committed to acting in the firm's best interests, as shown by their profit-maximizing behaviors.[80]

The I/O model challenges firms to locate the most attractive industry in which to compete. Because most firms are assumed to have similar strategically relevant resources that are mobile across companies, competitiveness generally can be increased only when the firms find the industry with the highest profit potential and learn how to use their resources to implement the strategy required by the structural characteristics in that industry. The *five forces model of competition* is an analytical tool used to help firms with this task. The model (explained in detail in Chapter 2) encompasses many variables and tries to capture the complexity of competition.[81]

The five forces model suggests that an industry's profitability (i.e., its rate of return on invested capital relative to its cost of capital) is a function of interactions among five forces (suppliers, buyers, competitive rivalry among firms currently in the industry, product substitutes, and potential entrants to the industry).[82] Using this tool, a firm is challenged to understand an industry's profit potential and the strategy that should be implemented to establish a defensible competitive position, given the industry's structural characteristics. Typically, the model suggests that firms can earn above-average returns by manufacturing standardized products or producing standardized services at costs below those of competitors (a cost–leadership strategy) or differentiated products for which customers are willing to pay a price premium (a differentiation strategy). Cost–leadership and differentiation strategies are described fully in Chapter 4.

As shown in Figure 1.2, the I/O model suggests that above-average returns are earned when firms implement the strategy dictated by the characteristics of the general, industry, and competitor environments. Companies that develop or acquire the internal skills needed to implement strategies required by the external environment are likely to succeed, while those that do not are likely to fail. Hence, above-average returns are determined by external characteristics rather than the firm's unique internal resources and capabilities.

Recent research provides support for the I/O model. The research showed that approximately 20 percent of a firm's profitability was explained by the industry. In other words, 20 percent of a firm's profitability is determined by the industry(ies) in which it chooses to operate. This research also showed, however, that 36 percent of the variance in profitability could be attributed to the firm's characteristics and actions.[83] The results of the research suggest that both the environment and the firm's characteristics play a role in determining the firm's specific level of profitability. Thus, there is likely a reciprocal relationship between the environment and the firm's strategy, and this interrelationship affects the firm's performance.[84]

As the research results suggest, successful competition in the 21st-century competitive landscape mandates that a firm build a unique set of resources and capabilities. This should be done, however, within the framework of the dynamics of the industry (or industries) in which a firm competes. In that context, a firm is viewed as a bundle of market activities and a bundle of resources. Market activities are understood through the application of the I/O model. The development and effective use of a firm's resources, capabilities, and competencies is understood through the application of the resource-based model. Through an effective combination of results gained by using both the I/O and the resource-based model, firms dramatically increase the probability of achieving strategic competitiveness and earning above-average returns.

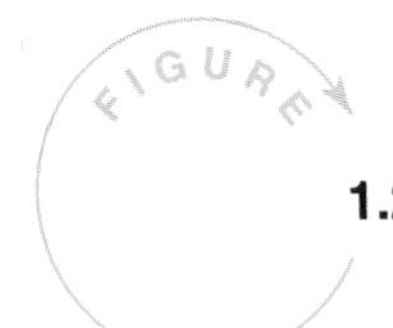

1.2 | The I/O Model of Superior Returns

1. Study the external environment, especially the industry environment.	**The External Environment** • The general environment • The industry environment • The competitor environment
2. Locate an industry with high potential for above-average returns.	**An Attractive Industry** • An industry whose structural characteristics suggest above-average returns
3. Identify the strategy called for by the attractive industry to earn above-average returns.	**Strategy Formulation** • Selection of a strategy linked with above-average returns in a particular industry
4. Develop or acquire assets and skills needed to implement the strategy.	**Assets and Skills** • Assets and skills required to implement a chosen strategy
5. Use the firm's strengths (its developed or acquired assets and skills) to implement the strategy.	**Strategy Implementation** • Selection of strategic actions linked with effective implementation of the chosen strategy
	Superior Returns • Earning of above-average returns

The Resource-Based Model of Above-Average Returns

The resource-based model assumes that each organization is a collection of unique resources and capabilities that provides the basis for its strategy and that is the primary source of its returns. In the 21st-century competitive landscape, this model argues that a firm is a collection of evolving capabilities that is managed dynamically in pursuit of above-average returns.[85] Thus, according to the model, differences in firms' performances across time are driven primarily by their unique resources and capabilities rather than by an industry's structural characteristics. This model also assumes that over time, a firm acquires different resources and develops unique capabilities. Therefore, not all firms competing within a particular industry possess the same strategically relevant resources and capabilities. Another assumption of the model is that resources may not be highly mobile across firms. The differences in resources form the basis of competitive advantage.

Resources are inputs into a firm's production process, such as capital equipment, the skills of individual employees, patents, finance, and talented managers.

Resources are inputs into a firm's production process, such as capital equipment, the skills of individual employees, patents, finances, and talented managers. In general, a firm's resources can be classified into three categories: physical, human, and organizational capital.[86] Described fully in Chapter 3, resources are either tangible or intangible in nature. With increasing effectiveness, the set of resources available to the firm tends to become larger.[87]

Individual resources alone may not yield a competitive advantage. For example, a sophisticated piece of manufacturing equipment may become a strategically relevant resource only when its use is integrated effectively with other aspects of a firm's operations (such as marketing and the work of employees). In general, it is through the combination and integration of sets of resources that competitive advantages are formed. A **capability** is the capacity for a set of resources to integratively perform a task or an activity. Through continued use, capabilities become stronger and more difficult for competitors to understand and imitate. As a source of competitive advantage, a capability "should be neither so simple that it is highly imitable, nor so complex that it defies internal steering and control."[88]

A **capability** is the capacity for a set of resources to integratively perform a task or an activity.

Amazon.com has taken the retail book market by storm. It was the first firm to sell books on the Internet. Because of this, Amazon.com has developed important capabilities for marketing and distributing books on-line. The firm has shown that a large inventory and beautiful facilities are not necessary to sell books. However, Amazon.com's capabilities may be imitable. In fact, the large and powerful Barnes & Noble sought to do just that when it opened its own on-line bookshop in 1997. Although developing Web pages and taking orders on-line are copied easily, Amazon.com had a 20-month lead, which, in Internet time, is significant. Barnes & Noble's strategic action could have had a significantly negative effect on Amazon.com, but the early evidence does not indicate this to be the case. In fact, the 1998 Christmas season was strong for Amazon.com: The firm realized one million new on-line customers, while Barnes & Noble achieved only 320,000. Accordingly, the firm's stock price skyrocketed, while Barnes & Noble's decreased. However, it remains to be seen whether the Internet resources of Amazon.com will continue to enjoy first-mover advantages against the brick and mortar of Barnes & Noble (see Chapter 5 for a full discussion of first-mover advantages). Although Amazon.com has won round one, the competitive battle will continue because Barnes & Noble has the resources to remain engaged in substantial competition.[89]

The resource-based model of superior returns is shown in Figure 1.3. In contrast to the I/O model, the resource-based view is grounded in the perspective that a firm's internal environment, in terms of its resources and capabilities, is more critical to the determination of strategic actions than is the external environment. Instead of focusing on the accumulation of resources necessary to implement the strategy dictated by conditions and constraints in the external environment (I/O model), the resource-based view suggests that a firm's unique resources and capabilities provide the basis

1.3 | **The Resource-Based Model of Superior Returns**

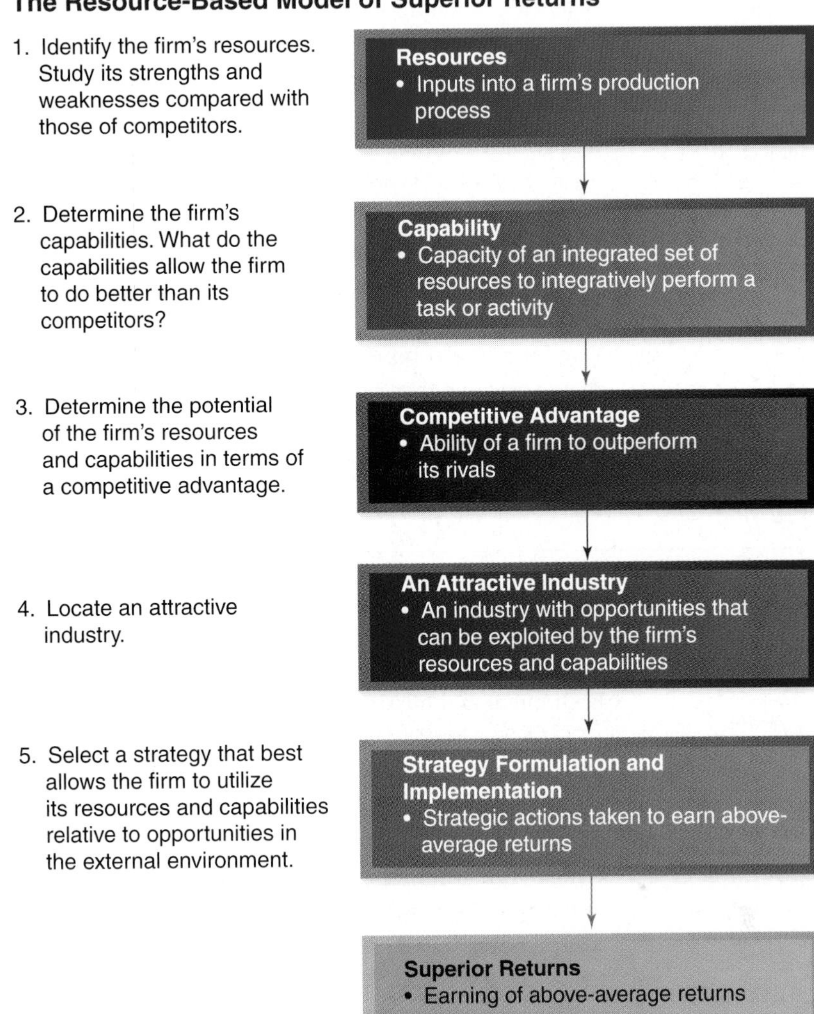

for a strategy. The strategy chosen should allow the firm to best exploit its core competencies relative to opportunities in the external environment.

Not all of a firm's resources and capabilities have the potential to be the basis for competitive advantage. This potential is realized when resources and capabilities are valuable, rare, costly to imitate, and nonsubstitutable.[90] Resources are *valuable* when they allow a firm to take advantage of opportunities or neutralize threats in its external environment; they are *rare* when possessed by few, if any, current and potential competitors; they are *costly to imitate* when other firms either cannot obtain them or are at a cost disadvantage in obtaining them compared with the firm that already possesses them; and they are *nonsubstitutable* when they have no structural equivalents.

When these four criteria are met, resources and capabilities become core compe-

Core competencies are resources and capabilities that serve as a source of competitive advantage for a firm over its rivals.

tencies. **Core competencies** are resources and capabilities that serve as a source of competitive advantage for a firm over its rivals. Often related to a firm's functional skills (e.g., the marketing function is a core competence at Philip Morris), core competencies, when developed, nurtured, and applied throughout a firm, may result in strategic competitiveness. Managerial competencies are important in most firms. For example, they have been shown to be critically important to successful entry into foreign markets.[91] Such competencies may include the capability to effectively organize and govern complex and diverse operations and the capability to create and communicate a strategic vision.[92] Another set of important competencies is product related. Included among these competencies are the capability to develop innovative new products and to reengineer existing products to satisfy changing consumer tastes.[93] Competencies must also be under continuous development to keep them up to date. This requires a systematic program for updating old skills and learning new ones.[94] Dynamic core competencies are especially important in rapidly changing environments, such as those that exist in high-technology industries.[95] Thus, the resource-based model argues that core competencies are the basis for a firm's competitive advantage, its strategic competitiveness, and its ability to earn above-average returns.

Strategic Intent and Strategic Mission

Resulting from analyses of a firm's internal and external environments is the information required to form a strategic intent and develop a strategic mission (see Figure 1.1). Both intent and mission are linked with strategic competitiveness.

Strategic Intent

Strategic intent is the leveraging of a firm's internal resources, capabilities, and core competencies to accomplish the firm's goals in the competitive environment.

Strategic intent is the leveraging of a firm's internal resources, capabilities, and core competencies to accomplish the firm's goals in the competitive environment.[96] Concerned with winning competitive battles and obtaining global leadership, strategic intent implies a significant stretch of an organization's resources, capabilities, and core competencies. When established effectively, a strategic intent can cause people to perform in ways they never imagined possible.[97] Strategic intent exists when all employees and levels of a firm are committed to the pursuit of a specific (and significant) performance criterion. Some argue that strategic intent provides employees with the only goal worthy of personal effort and commitment: to unseat the best or remain the best, worldwide.[98] Strategic intent has been formed effectively when people believe fervently in their product and industry and when they are focused totally on their firm's ability to outperform its competitors.[99]

The next few examples are expressions of strategic intent. Unocal Corporation intends "to become a high-performance multinational energy company—not the biggest, but the *best*." According to Eli Lilly and Company, "It's our strategic intent that customers worldwide view us as their most valued pharmaceutical partner." Phillips Petroleum Company seeks "to be the top performer in everything" the company does. Intel intends to become the premier building-block supplier to the computer industry. Microsoft believes that its "holy grail" is to be the Yellow Pages for an electronic marketplace of on-line information systems. Canon desires to "beat Xerox," and Honda strives to become a second Ford (a company it identified as a pioneer in the automobile industry). The CEO of Pep Boys does not believe in friendly competition; instead, he wants to dominate the competition and, by doing so, put them out of business. At Procter & Gamble (P&G), employees participate in a program the CEO calls "combat training." The program's intent is to focus on ways P&G can beat the competition.

But it is not enough for a firm only to know its own strategic intent: To perform well demands that the firm also identify its competitors' strategic intent. Only when the intentions of others are understood can a firm become aware of the resolve, stamina, and inventiveness (traits linked with effective strategic intents) of those competitors.[100] A company's success may be grounded in a keen and deep understanding of the strategic intent of customers, suppliers, partners, and competitors.[101] But more is needed: a mechanism that catalyzes intent into action.[102] Nucor Steel has implemented a pay plan in which hourly pay is 25 to 33 percent below the industry average, but an 80- to 200-percent bonus of base pay, based on team productivity, is paid weekly to all teams that meet or exceed productivity goals. If a person is late to work by 30 minutes, his or her bonus for the week is forfeited. If a product is returned for poor quality, bonus pay declines accordingly. If a machine breaks down, there is no compensating adjustment. The bonus for managers is even more pronounced: During the 1992 recession, CEO Ken Iverson's pay dropped 75 percent. The system also leaves no room for unproductive employees. In fact, those who are either unwilling or incapable of satisfying the team-based performance expectations often choose to resign from their jobs.

Strategic Mission

As the preceding discussion shows, strategic intent is internally focused. It is concerned with identifying the resources, capabilities, and core competencies on which a firm can base its strategic actions. Strategic intent reflects what a firm is capable of doing as a result of its core competencies and the unique ways they can be used to exploit a competitive advantage.

The **strategic mission** is a statement of a firm's unique purpose and the scope of its operations in product and market terms.

Strategic mission flows from strategic intent. Externally focused, the **strategic mission** is a statement of a firm's unique purpose and the scope of its operations in product and market terms.[103] A strategic mission provides general descriptions of the products a firm intends to produce and the markets it will serve using its internally based core competencies.

An effective strategic mission establishes a firm's individuality and is exciting, inspiring, and relevant to all stakeholders.[104] Together, strategic intent and strategic mission yield the insights required to formulate and implement the firm's strategies.

Basing their decisions partially on a firm's strategic intent and mission, top executives develop a *strategic orientation*—a predisposition to adopt a certain strategy or strategies over others.[105] Strategic orientation is also affected by the national culture in an executive's home country and the institutional environment where the firm's operations are located.[106]

When a firm is strategically competitive and earning above-average returns, it has the capacity to satisfy its stakeholders' interests. The stakeholder groups a firm serves are examined next.

Stakeholders

Stakeholders are the individuals and groups who can affect, and are affected by, the strategic outcomes achieved and who have enforceable claims on a firm's performance.

An organization is a system of primary stakeholder groups with whom it establishes and manages relationships.[107] **Stakeholders** are the individuals and groups who can affect, and are affected by, the strategic outcomes achieved and who have enforceable claims on a firm's performance.[108] Claims against an organization's performance are enforced through a stakeholder's ability to withhold participation essential to a firm's survival, competitiveness, and profitability.[109] Stakeholders continue to support an organization when its performance meets or exceeds their expectations.

Thus, organizations have dependency relationships with their stakeholders. Firms, however, are not equally dependent on all stakeholders at all times; as a consequence, not every stakeholder has the same level of influence. The more critical and valued a stakeholder's participation is, the greater a firm's dependency on it. Greater dependence, in turn, results in more potential influence for the stakeholder over a firm's commitments, decisions, and actions. In one sense, the challenge strategists face is to either accommodate or find ways to insulate the organization from the demands of stakeholders controlling critical resources.[110]

Classification of Stakeholders

The parties involved with a firm's operations can be separated into three groups.[111] As shown in Figure 1.4, these groups are the *capital market stakeholders* (shareholders and

1.4 | The Three Stakeholder Groups

Stakeholders → People who are affected by a firm's performance and who have claims on its performance

Capital Market Stakeholders
- Shareholders
- Major suppliers of capital (e.g., banks)

Product Market Stakeholders
- Primary customers
- Suppliers
- Host communities
- Unions

Organizational Stakeholders
- Employees
  - Managers
  - Nonmanagers

Shareholders, like those shown here at a General Electric shareholder meeting, have invested capital in the firm and expect at least an average return on their investments. However, short-term enhancement of shareholders' wealth can have a negative effect on a firm's future.

the major suppliers of a firm's capital), the *product market stakeholders* (the firm's primary customers, suppliers, host communities, and unions representing the workforce), and the *organizational stakeholders* (all of a firm's employees, including both nonmanagerial and managerial personnel).

Each stakeholder group expects those making strategic decisions in a firm to provide the leadership through which its valued objectives will be accomplished.[112] But these groups' objectives often differ from one another, sometimes placing managers in situations where trade-offs have to be made.

Grounded in laws governing private property and private enterprise, the most obvious stakeholders, at least in U.S. firms, are *shareholders*—those who have invested capital in a firm in the expectation of earning at least an average return on their investments. Shareholders want the return on their investment (and, hence, their wealth) to be maximized. This often can be accomplished at the expense of investing in a firm's future. Gains achieved by reducing investment in research and development, for example, could be returned to shareholders (thereby increasing the short-term return on their investments). However, a short-term enhancement of shareholders' wealth can negatively affect the firm's future competitive ability. Sophisticated shareholders, with diversified portfolios, may sell their interests if a firm fails to invest in its future. Those making strategic decisions are responsible for a firm's survival in both the short and the long term. Accordingly, it is in the interests of neither the organizational stakeholders nor the product market stakeholders for investments in the company to be unduly minimized.

In contrast to shareholders, customers prefer that investors receive a minimum return on their investments. In that way, customers could have their interests maximized when the quality and reliability of a firm's products are improved, but without a price increase. High returns to customers might come at the expense of lower returns negotiated with capital market shareholders.

Because of potential conflicts, each firm is challenged to manage its stakeholders. First, a firm must carefully identify all important stakeholders. Second, it must prioritize them in case it cannot satisfy all of them. In doing this, power is the most critical criterion. Other criteria might include the urgency of satisfying each particular stakeholder and the degree of importance to the firm.[113] When the firm earns above-average returns, this challenge is lessened substantially. With the capability and flexibility provided by above-average returns, a firm can more easily satisfy all stakeholders simultaneously.

When earning only average returns, however, a firm may find the management of stakeholders to be more difficult. In these situations, trade-offs must be made. With average returns, the firm is unable to maximize the interests of all stakeholders. The objective then becomes one of at least minimally satisfying each stakeholder. Trade-off decisions are made in light of how dependent the firm is on the support of the stakeholder groups. An example of how stakeholders can demand satisfaction of their claims on a firm's performance is provided in the next subsection. A firm earning below-average returns does not have the capacity to minimally satisfy all stakeholders. The managerial challenge in this case is to make trade-offs that minimize the amount of support lost from stakeholders.

Societal values influence the general weightings allocated among the three stakeholder groups. Although all three groups are served by firms in at least the major industrialized nations, the priorities in their service vary somewhat because of cultural differences. These differences are shown in the following commentary:

> In America . . . shareholders have a comparatively big say in the running of the enterprises they own; workers . . . have much less influence. In many European countries, shareholders have less say and workers more. . . . In Japan . . . managers have been left alone to run their companies as they see fit—namely for the benefit of employees and of allied companies, as much as for shareholders.[114]

A **global mind-set** is the capacity to appreciate the beliefs, values, behaviors, and business practices of individuals and organizations from a variety of regions and cultures.

Thus, it is important that those responsible for managing stakeholder relationships in a country outside their native land use a global mind-set. A **global mind-set** is the "capacity to appreciate the beliefs, values, behaviors, and business practices of individuals and organizations from a variety of regions and cultures."[115] The use of a global mind-set allows managers to better understand the realities and preferences that are a part of the world region and culture in which they are working. Thus, thinking globally means "taking the best [that] other cultures have to offer and blending that into a third culture."[116]

In the next three subsections, additional information is presented about the stakeholder groups that firms manage.

Capital Market Stakeholders

Both shareholders and lenders expect a firm to preserve and enhance the wealth they have entrusted to it. The returns expected are commensurate with the degree of risk accepted with those investments (that is, lower returns are expected with low-risk investments, and higher returns are expected with high-risk investments).

If lenders become dissatisfied, they can impose stricter covenants on subsequent borrowing of capital. Shareholders can reflect their dissatisfaction through several means, including selling their stock. When a firm is aware of potential or actual dissatisfactions among capital market stakeholders, it may respond to their concerns. The firm's response to dissatisfied stakeholders is affected by the nature of its dependency relationship with them (which, as noted earlier, is also influenced by a society's values). The greater and more significant the dependency relationship is, the more direct and significant the firm's response becomes.

As explained in the Strategic Focus, the power and influence of capital market stakeholders are exemplified in their effects on U.S. West in 1999. Capital market stakeholders, Global Crossing and Qwest Communication, put U.S. West in play during 1999. The interesting paradox is that as relatively recent start-up ventures, these two firms had shorter operating histories than did U.S. West, the firm that had become an acquisition target. The decision to attempt to acquire U.S. West illustrates the power that capital market stakeholders can wield when stock market evaluations skyrocket for start-up firms. Sometimes, at least in the short run, capital market stakeholders' interests may come at the expense of returns to other stakeholders. In this instance, though, product market stakeholders (customers) ultimately will determine the final outcome of an intense series of competitive actions and competitive reactions.

Product Market Stakeholders

Initial thoughts about customers, suppliers, host communities, and unions representing workers might suggest little commonality among these parties' interests. However, close inspection indicates that all four groups can benefit as firms engage in competitive battles. For example, depending on product and industry characteristics, marketplace competition may result in lower product prices being charged to a firm's customers and higher prices paid to its suppliers (the firm might be willing to pay higher supplier prices to ensure delivery of the types of goods and services that are linked with its competitive success).

As is noted in Chapter 4, customers, as stakeholders, demand reliable products at the lowest possible prices. Suppliers seek loyal customers who are willing to pay the highest sustainable prices for the goods and services they receive. Host communities want companies willing to be long-term employers and providers of tax revenues, without placing excessive demands on public support services. Union officials are interested in secure jobs, under highly desirable working conditions, for employees they represent. Thus, product market stakeholders are generally satisfied when a firm's profit margin yields the lowest acceptable return to capital market stakeholders (i.e., the lowest return lenders and shareholders will accept and still retain their interests in the firm).

All product market stakeholders are important in a competitive business environment. However, in many firms, customers are being emphasized. Jack Welch, former CEO of General Electric, is known for his position that satisfied customers are the only source of job security for the firm's organizational stakeholders. As the Strategic Focus suggests, although a firm's boundaries can be redrawn through the power of capital market stakeholders, the ultimate test of performance is customer satisfaction. The relationship between satisfaction of customers' needs and strategic competitiveness is examined in Chapter 4.

Organizational Stakeholders

Organizational employees expect the firm to provide a dynamic, stimulating, and rewarding working environment. As stakeholders, employees are usually satisfied

Both Qwest Communication and Global Crossing Make Offers for U.S. West

Because of high stock-market evaluations, which are an "Internet phenomenon," a small Bermuda-based company, such as Global Crossing, can offer to acquire a traditional large-monopoly phone company. Two years prior to the May 1999 announcement of the potential acquisition, Global Crossing was an idea instead of an operational company. By August 1998, the firm had posted revenues of $500 million. Since that time, Global Crossing's market value has soared to over $20 billion, seven times its initial public offering (IPO) price. Its market capitalization gave the firm the amount of financial resources required to pursue acquisitions of U.S. West and other telecommunications companies.

Global Crossing's lofty market evaluations of 40 times its cash flow occurred because Wall Street valued the firm's global strategy. Through its strategy, the firm intended to build state-of-the-art undersea fiber-optic phone lines to exploit the global explosion of the Internet and data traffic. In addition to its offer for U.S. West, Global Crossing made offers to acquire the wire-laying business of Cable & Wireless for $885 million and a local telephone service in Rochester, New York, Frontier Corporation, for $11.2 billion. If consummated, these transactions will create a firm with a pro forma stock market valuation of more than $30 billion.

While U.S. West's stock trades for roughly six times its cash flow, Global Crossing has been as high as 40 times its cash flow. Accordingly, the deal called for two issues of stock so that investors could track progress in the local phone business (U.S. West combined with Frontier) and the growth stock cabling 159 large cities around the world together in a large Internet pipeline.

Before these transactions could be completed, another player, Qwest Communication, launched bids for Frontier and U.S. West, seeking to forestall both agreements. Apparently, because of the steep stock price declines after announcing the U.S. West acquisition, Global Crossing's executives decided that the intended transaction might not serve the best interests of the firm's stockholders. Ultimately, however, Global Crossing agreed to proceed with the Frontier deal, which gives it "a nationwide U.S. network from which it can base its plans for global growth." Qwest and U.S. West agreed to merge with equal board representation "to balance the interests of both sets of shareholders."

These transactions are a sign of the times. The approach by Global Crossing is similar to WorldCom's acquisition of MCI. WorldCom had a hyperinflated stock price just like Global Crossing and pursued MCI, which had greater revenues, but a lower stock price, than WorldCom. Both Global Crossing and WorldCom are emphasizing the strategic action of selling telecommunications services to large businesses on a global basis. These firms' growth tracked the global growth in telecommunications and followed the globalization of businesses around the world.

The deal has also given Qwest and U.S. West an opportunity to expand their services into a full-service telecommunications company with local, long-distance, and Internet services. In addition, U.S. West has been building a cell-phone business. Although there may be some regulatory hurdles, because U.S. West is prohibited currently from offering long-distance service, the assets of the Qwest combination have little overlap with those of U.S. West.

The capital market stakeholders have given both Global Crossing and Qwest an opportunity to move into the "major leagues" of telecommunications. As globalization continues in telecommunication, nowhere is it written that the "global front-runners" (AT&T, Deutsche TeleKom, and British Telecommunications (BT)) will continue to be the leaders. In fact, start-up ventures such as Global Crossing and Qwest may have a technological lead because of the state-of-the-art data and voice networks they are developing. The state monopolies try to achieve connectivity through joint ventures. But one of these, Global One, is on the verge of breaking up because of the lack of a cohesive strategy, disagreements between partners, and system integration problems. Similarly, Concert (BT and MCI) stumbled when WorldCom bought MCI. Unisource partners have jumped in and out of the joint venture, causing instability. World Partners lost Australia's Telstra, and AT&T has signaled that it wants out. Although AT&T and BT have formed a joint venture, it took eight months to choose a CEO for the new operation. As the old monopolies, which were former competitors, try to work together, the start-ups are moving quickly to fill the services gaps. The new ventures such as Qwest and Global Crossing are more strategically flexible.

Whether they will be able to compete with the established brands of AT&T and MCI WorldCom, as well as other global competitors, will be determined by customer stakeholders. However, as it stands now, BellSouth is the only independent local telephone exchange left without some kind of joint venture, if the Qwest deal with U.S. West is approved. Thus, the stakeholders from both the capital and product markets will largely determine the outcome of these global combinations and partnerships.

SOURCES: R. Blumenstein, 1999, Qwest wins US West for $35 billion, *Wall Street Journal,* July 19, A3, A9; J. Creswell, 1999, A merger frenzy rich in fiber, *Fortune,* April 26, 44–46; *Financial Times,* 1999, Global Crossing: American dream, *Financial Times* FT.com, May 18, *http://www.ft.com.* S. Lipin & R. Blumenstein, 1999, Upstart's bid for US West is just a sign of the times, *Wall Street Journal,* interactive edition, May 17, *http://interactive.wsj.com.* S. Lipin, R. Blumenstein, & S. N. Mehta, 1999, Global Crossing is poised to merge with US West, *Wall Street Journal,* interactive edition, May 17, *http://interactive.wsj.com.* S. N. Mehta & J. S. Lublin, 1999, Global crossing, US West confirm plans to create firm to compete with AT&T, *Wall Street Journal,* May 18, A3, A8.

---

working for a company that is growing and is actively developing their skills, especially those required to be effective team members and to meet or exceed global work standards. Workers who learn how to productively use rapidly developing knowledge are thought to be critical to organizational success. In a collective sense, the education and skills of a nation's workforce may be its dominant competitive weapon in a global economy.[117]

In the next section, we describe the people responsible for the design and execution of strategic management processes. These individuals are variously named, including top-level managers, executives, strategists, the top management team, and general managers. Throughout this book, these names are used interchangeably. But, in each case, the name is used to describe the work of persons responsible for designing and implementing a successful strategic management process.

As is discussed in Chapter 12, top-level managers can be a source of competitive advantage. The decisions and actions these people make to combine resources to create capabilities often result in a competitive advantage. In fact, it may be that those ranked by *Business Week* as the world's top business leaders (see Table 1.3) are individually a source of competitive advantage to their firms.

Organizational Strategists

Small organizations may have a single strategist. In many cases, this person owns the firm and is involved deeply with its daily operations. At the other extreme, large, diversified firms have many top-level managers. In addition to the CEO and other top-level officials (e.g., the chief operating officer and chief financial officer), other managers of these companies are responsible for the performance of individual business units.

Top-level managers play critical roles in firms' efforts to achieve their desired strategic outcomes. In fact, some believe that every organizational failure is actually a failure of those who hold the final responsibility for the quality and effectiveness of a firm's decisions and actions. Failure can stem from the strategic assumptions changing, and the strategic mission may become a strategic blinder. The firm's method of operating may become routines that create strategic inertia. Established relationships may create shackles that prevent change. Finally, a shared set of beliefs could become dogmas that prevent a change in corporate culture.[118] Strategic managers need to stop and ask the right questions to overcome the inertia that is often created by success itself.

Decisions for which strategists are responsible include how resources will be developed or acquired, at what price they will be obtained, and how they will be used. Managerial decisions also influence how information flows in a company, the strategies a firm chooses to implement, and the scope of its operations. In making these decisions, managers must assess the risk involved in taking the actions being considered. This risk

Top-level managers play a critical role in firms' efforts to achieve their desired strategic outcomes. Organizational failure is often attributed to those who are responsible for the quality and effectiveness of a firm's decisions and actions.

1.3 | *Business Weeks*'s 25 Top Managers of the Year, 1999

Name	Company	Strategic Accomplishment
Minoru Arakawa	Nintendo America	Scored huge hit by bringing Pokémon to U.S. over objections of co-workers and negative market research
Bernard Arnault	LVMH	From just 23 in Oct. '98, LVMH's U.S. shares have vaulted 280 percent, to about 87
Arthur Blank	Home Depot	Profits should jump 46 percent, to $2.3 billion for fiscal year 1999. Sales are expected to grow 25 percent, to $38 billion
Peter Bijur	Texaco	After his company was labeled racist, attracted minorities to key jobs, including treasurer Ira Hall, a former IBM executive
Gordon Binder	Amgen	Boosted stock price by around 100 percent last year, to about $54
Steve Case	America Online	Deals to broaden AOL's availability and services will help boost income 102 percent this fiscal year, to $800 million
John Chambers	Cisco Systems	Broadened Cisco into strategic businesses such as software, consulting, and fiber-optic communications
Jim Curvey	Fidelity Investments	Reduced internal conflicts and spurred growth through management changes
Thierry Desmarest	Totalfina	Acquired rival French oil company ELF Aquitaine for $44 billion. Shares up about 35 percent in '99, as profits expected to grow 20 percent, to $3.1 billion
Bernie Ebbers	MCI WorldCom	Turned toward more profitable data, Internet, and international operations
Tom Engibous	Texas Instruments	Jump-started growth by focusing on key digital signal processing chip market
Chris Gent	Vodafone Airtouch	Shares have skyrocketed 243 percent, to around $48, in two years
Irwin Jacobs	Qualcomm	Developed digital technology that was adopted in 1999 as a global standard for next-generation wireless cell phones
Steve Jobs	Apple Computer, Pixar	Apple's stock increased roughly 140 percent in 1999, to about $99
Mel Karmazin	CBS/VIACOM	Arranged the $80 billion merger of CBS with Viacom
Jim Kelly	United Parcel Service	Made UPS the leader in e-commerce deliveries, with 55 percent market share
T. K. Koogle	Yahoo!	Yahoo should earn $131.6 million—a rare profitmaker in the Net world
Ken Lay	Enron	Shares rose about 50 percent last year, quadruple the S&P Natural Gas Index
Jenny Ming	Old Navy	Opened 135 locations in 1999, bringing the total to more than 500
Thomas Siebel	Siebel Systems	Landed key deal for IBM to push Siebel's customer-relationship software; increased stock price more than 400 percent last year, to about $88
Masayoshi Son	Softbank	Created a powerful Net empire by forging links between his 100-plus Net companies in the U.S. and Japan
Martha Stewart	Martha Stewart, Omnimedia	A splashy October IPO gave her empire a market cap of $1.1 billion
Keiji Tachikawa	NTT Docomo	Turned "i-mode" Net access service for wireless phones into smash hit in Japan
Jack Welch	General Electric	Profits should rise 15 percent, to $11 billion, on sales up 10 percent, to $110 billion
Yun Jong Yong	Samsung Electronics	Profits up tenfold in '99, to $2.4 billion, on sales up 24 percent, to $22 billion

Source: Special Report, 2000, The top 25 managers of the year, *Business Week,* January 10, 60–78.

HUNTINGTON CITY-TOWNSHIP
PUBLIC LIBRARY
200 W. Market Street
Huntington, IN 46750

is then factored into the decision.[119] The firm's strategic intent will affect the decisions managers make. Also, managers' strategic orientations, which include their personal values and beliefs, will affect their decisions.[120] Additionally, how strategists complete their work and their patterns of interactions with others significantly influence the way a firm does business and affect its ability to develop a competitive advantage.

Organizational culture refers to the complex set of ideologies, symbols, and core values shared throughout the firm and that influences the way it conducts business. It is the social energy that drives—or fails to drive—the organization.

How a firm does business is captured by the concept of organizational culture. Critical to strategic leadership practices and the implementation of strategies, **organizational culture** refers to the complex set of ideologies, symbols, and core values shared throughout the firm and that influences the way it conducts business. Thus, culture is the "social energy that drives—or fails to drive—the organization."[121] Andersen Consulting's core values include the requirement that employees attend company-sponsored training classes in professional attire, an expectation of hard work (up to 80 hours per week), and a willingness to work effectively with others to accomplish all tasks that are parts of the companywide demanding workload.[122] These core values at Andersen Consulting provide a particular type of social energy that drives the firm's efforts. As discussed in Chapters 3, 12, and 13, organizational culture is a potential source of competitive advantage.[123]

After evaluating available information and alternatives, top-level managers must frequently choose from among similarly attractive alternatives. The most effective strategists have the self-confidence necessary to select the best alternatives, allocate the required level of resources to them, and effectively explain to interested parties why certain alternatives were selected.[124]

When choosing among alternatives, strategists are accountable for treating employees, suppliers, customers, and others with fairness and respect. Evidence suggests that trust can be a source of competitive advantage, thereby supporting an organizational commitment to treat stakeholders fairly and with respect.[125] Nonetheless, firms cannot succeed without people who, following careful and sometimes difficult analyses, are willing to make tough decisions—the types of decisions that result in strategic competitiveness and above-average returns.[126]

The Work of Effective Strategists

Perhaps not surprisingly, hard work, thorough analyses, a willingness to be brutally honest, a penchant for always wanting the firm and its people to accomplish more, and common sense are prerequisites to an individual's success as a strategist.[127] In addition to possessing these characteristics, effective strategists must be able to think clearly and ask many questions. Their strategic effectiveness increases as they find ways for others also to think and inquire about what a firm is doing and why. But, in particular, top-level managers are challenged to "think seriously and deeply . . . about the purposes of the organizations they head or functions they perform, about the strategies, tactics, technologies, systems and people necessary to attain these purposes and about the important questions that always need to be asked."[128]

However, just as e-commerce is changing the nature of competition, it is also changing strategic decision making. Speed is becoming a much more prominent competitive factor, and it makes strategic thinking even more critical. Most high-tech firms operate in hypercompetitive industry environments. The intense competition in these industries has caused some product life cycles to decrease from a period of one to two years to a period of six to nine months, leaving precious little time for a company's products to generate revenue. For companies competing in these industries, speed and flexibility have become key sources of competitive advantage. For example, Sun Microsystems, a leading manufacturer of high-end workstations and networking systems, has made reducing product development times its key operational focus.[129] Thinking strategically, in concert with others, increases the probability of identifying bold, innovative ideas. When these ideas lead to the development of core competencies—that is, when the ideas result in exploiting resources and capabilities that are valuable, rare, costly to imitate, and nonsubstitutable—they become the foundation for taking advantage of environmental opportunities.

Our discussion highlights the nature of a strategist's work. The work is filled with ambiguous decision situations—situations for which the most effective solutions are not always easily determined. However, the opportunities suggested by this type of work are appealing. These jobs offer exciting chances to dream and to act. The following words, given as advice by his father to Steven J. Ross, the former chairman and co-CEO of Time-Warner, describe the opportunities in a strategist's work: "There are three categories of people—the person who goes into the office, puts his feet up on his desk, and dreams for 12 hours; the person who arrives at 5 A.M. and works for 16 hours, never once stopping to dream; and the person who puts his feet up, dreams for one hour, then does something about those dreams."[130] The organizational term used for a dream that challenges and energizes a company is strategic intent.[131]

Strategists have opportunities to dream and to act, and the most effective ones provide a vision (the strategic intent) to effectively elicit the help of others in creating a firm's competitive advantage.

The Strategic Management Process

The pursuit of competitiveness is at the heart of strategic management and the choices made in designing and using the strategic management process. Firms are in competition with one another—to gain access to the resources needed to earn above-average returns and to provide superior satisfaction of stakeholders' needs. Effective use of the interdependent parts of the strategic management process results in selecting the direction the firm will pursue and the means it utilizes to achieve the desired outcomes of strategic competitiveness and above-average returns.

As suggested by Figure 1.1, the strategic management process is intended to be a rational approach to help a firm respond effectively to the challenges of the 21st-century competitive landscape. This process calls for a firm to study its external (Chapter 2) and internal (Chapter 3) environments to identify its marketplace opportunities and threats and determine how to use its core competencies in the pursuit of desired strategic outcomes. With this knowledge, the firm forms its strategic intent so that it can leverage its resources, capabilities, and core competencies and win competitive battles in the global economy. Flowing from strategic intent, the strategic mission specifies, in writing, the products a firm intends to produce and the markets it will serve when leveraging its resources, capabilities, and competencies.

The firm's strategic inputs provide the foundation for its strategic actions to formulate and implement strategies. Both formulating strategies and implementing them are critical to achieving strategic competitiveness and earning above-average returns.

As suggested in Figure 1.1 by the horizontal arrow linking the two types of strategic actions, formulation and implementation must be integrated simultaneously. In formulating strategies, thought should be given to implementing them. During implementation, effective strategists seek feedback that allows them to improve the selected strategies. The separation of strategy formulation from strategy implementation in the figure is for discussion purposes only. In reality, these two sets of actions allow the firm to achieve its desired strategic outcomes only when they are integrated carefully. Some believe, for example, that Kodak's decline in performance in the late 1990s could be attributed partly to poor execution in terms of actions taken to implement the firm's strategies.[132]

Figure 1.1 shows the topics we examine to study the interdependent parts of the strategic management process. In Part 2 of this book, actions related to the formulation of strategies are explained. The first set of actions studied is the formulation of strategies at the business-unit level (Chapter 4). A diversified firm—one competing in multiple product markets and businesses—has a business-level strategy for each distinct product market area. A company competing in a single product market has but one business-level strategy. In all instances, a business-level strategy describes a firm's actions designed to exploit its competitive advantage over rivals. But, as is explained in Chapter 5, business-level strategies are not formulated and implemented in isolation. Competitors respond to, and try to anticipate, each other's actions. Thus, the dynamics of competition are an important input to the formulation and implementation of all strategies, but especially to business-level strategies.

For the diversified firm, corporate-level strategy (Chapter 6) is concerned with determining the businesses in which the company intends to compete, how resources are to be allocated among those businesses, and how the different units are to be managed. Other topics vital to strategy formulation, particularly in the diversified firm, include the acquisition of other companies and, as appropriate, the restructuring of the firm's portfolio of businesses (Chapter 7) and the selection of an international strategy that is consistent with the firm's resources, capabilities, core competencies, and external opportunities (Chapter 8). Chapter 9 examines cooperative strategies. Increasingly important in a global economy, these strategies are used by a firm to gain competitive advantage by forming advantageous relationships with other firms.

To examine more direct actions taken to implement strategies successfully, we consider several topics in Part 3 of the book. First, the different mechanisms used to govern firms are considered (Chapter 10). With demands for improved corporate governance voiced by various stakeholders, organizations are challenged to manage in ways that will result in the satisfaction of stakeholders' interests and the attainment of desired strategic outcomes. Finally, the matters of organizational structure and actions needed to control a firm's operations (Chapter 11), the patterns of strategic leadership appropriate for today's firms and competitive environments (Chapter 12), and the link among corporate entrepreneurship, innovation, and strategic competitiveness (Chapter 13) are addressed.

As noted earlier, competition requires firms to make choices to survive and succeed. Some of these choices are strategic in nature, including those of selecting a firm's strategic intent and strategic mission, determining which strategies to implement to offer a firm's products to customers, choosing an appropriate level of corporate scope, designing governance and organization structures that will properly coordinate a firm's work, and, through strategic leadership, encouraging and nurturing organizational innovation.[133] When made successfully, choices in terms of any one of these sets of actions have the potential to result in a competitive advantage for a firm over its rivals.

Primarily because they are related to how a firm interacts with its stakeholders, almost all strategic decisions have ethical dimensions.[134] Organizational ethics are revealed by an organization's culture; that is to say, a firm's strategic decisions are a product of the core values that are shared by most or all of a company's managers and employees. Especially in the turbulent and often ambiguous 21st-century competitive landscape, those making strategic decisions are challenged to recognize that their decisions do affect capital market, product market, and organizational stakeholders differently and to evaluate the ethical implications of their decisions. As the executives of Levi Strauss discovered, socially responsible actions are interwoven with their abilities to satisfy all stakeholders in the organization (see the first Strategic Focus).

As you will discover, the strategic management process examined in this text calls for disciplined approaches to the development of competitive advantage. These approaches provide the pathway through which firms will be able to achieve strategic competitiveness and earn above-average returns in the 21st century. Mastery of this strategic management process will effectively serve readers and the organizations for whom they choose to work.

Summary

- Through their actions, firms seek strategic competitiveness and above-average returns. Strategic competitiveness is achieved when a firm has developed and learned how to implement a value-creating strategy. Above-average returns—returns in excess of what investors expect to earn from other investments with similar levels of risk—allow a firm to simultaneously satisfy all of its stakeholders.
- A 21st-century competitive landscape—one in which the fundamental nature of competition is changing—has emerged. This landscape challenges those responsible for making effective strategic decisions to adopt a new mind-set, one that is global in nature. Through this mind-set, firms learn how to compete in what are highly turbulent and chaotic environments that produce disorder and a great deal of uncertainty. The globalization of industries and their markets and rapid and significant technological changes are the two primary realities that have created the 21st-century competitive landscape. Globalization—the spread of economic innovations around the world and the political and cultural adjustments that accompany this diffusion—is likely to continue. Globalization also increases the standards of performance companies must meet or exceed to be strategically competitive in the 21st-century. Developing the ability to satisfy these global performance standards also helps firms compete effectively in their critical domestic markets.
- There are two major models of what a firm should do to earn above-average returns. The I/O model argues that the external environment is the primary determinant of the firm's strategies. Above-average returns are earned when the firm locates an attractive industry and successfully implements the strategy dictated by the characteristics of that industry. The resource-based model assumes that each firm is a collection of unique resources and capabilities that determines a firm's strategy. In this model, above-average returns are earned when the firm uses its valuable, rare, costly-to-imitate, and nonsubstitutable resources and capabilities (i.e., core competencies) to establish a competitive advantage over its rivals.

- Strategic intent and strategic mission are formed in light of the information and insights gained from studying a firm's internal and external environments. Strategic intent suggests how resources, capabilities, and core competencies will be leveraged to achieve desired outcomes in the competitive environment. The strategic mission is an application of strategic intent. The mission is used to specify the product markets and customers a firm intends to serve through the leveraging of its resources, capabilities, and competencies.
- Stakeholders are those who can affect, and are affected by, a firm's strategic outcomes. Because a firm is dependent on the continuing support of stakeholders (shareholders, customers, suppliers, employees, host communities, etc.), they have enforceable claims on the company's performance. When earning above-average returns, a firm can adequately satisfy all stakeholders' interests. However, when earning only average returns, a firm's strategists must carefully manage all stakeholder groups in order to retain their support. A firm earning below-average returns must minimize the amount of support it loses from dissatisfied stakeholders.
- Organizational strategists are responsible for the design and execution of an effective strategic management process. Today, the most effective of these processes are grounded in ethical intentions and conduct. Strategists themselves—people with opportunities to dream and to act—can be a source of competitive advantage. The strategist's work demands decision trade-offs, often among attractive alternatives. Successful top-level managers work hard, conduct thorough analyses of situations, are brutally and consistently honest, and ask the right questions, of the right people, at the right time.

Review Questions

1. What are strategic competitiveness, competitive advantage, and above-average returns? Why are these terms important to those responsible for an organization's performance?
2. What is the challenge of strategic management?
3. What are the two factors that have created the 21st-century competitive landscape? What meaning does this landscape have for those interested in starting a business firm in the near future?
4. According to the I/O model, what should a firm do to earn above-average returns?
5. What does the resource-based model suggest a firm should do to achieve strategic competitiveness and earn above-average returns?
6. What are the differences between strategic intent and strategic mission? What is the value of the strategic intent and mission for a firm's strategic management process?
7. What are stakeholders? Why can they influence organizations? Do stakeholders always have the same amount of influence over an organization? Why or why not?
8. How would you describe the work of organizational strategists?
9. What are the parts of the strategic management process? How are these parts interrelated?

Application Discussion Questions

1. As suggested in the Opening Case, the outcomes in e-commerce are uncertain. Using the Internet, study Yahoo!'s current performance. Based on analysis, do you judge Yahoo! to be a success? Why or why not?
2. Choose several firms in your local community with which you are familiar. Describe the 21st-century competitive landscape to them, and ask for their feedback about how they anticipate that the landscape will affect their operations during the next five years.
3. Select an organization (e.g., school, club, or church) that is important to you. Who are the organization's stakeholders? What degree of influence do you believe each has over the organization, and why?
4. Are you a stakeholder at your university or college? If so, of what stakeholder group, or groups, are you a part?
5. Think of an industry in which you want to work. In your opinion, which of the three primary stakeholder groups is the most powerful in that industry today? Why? Which do you expect to be the most powerful group in five years? Why?
6. Do you agree or disagree with the following statement? "I think managers have little responsibility for the failure of business firms." Justify your view.
7. Do strategic intent and strategic mission have any meaning in your personal life? If so, describe it. Are your current actions being guided by an intent and mission? If not, why not?

Ethics Questions

1. Can a firm achieve a competitive advantage and, thereby, strategic competitiveness without acting ethically? Explain.
2. What are a firm's ethical responsibilities if it earns above-average returns?
3. What are some of the critical ethical challenges to firms competing in the global economy?
4. How should ethical considerations be included in analyses of a firm's internal and external environments?
5. Can ethical issues be integrated into a firm's strategic intent and mission? Explain.
6. What is the relationship between ethics and stakeholders?
7. What is the importance of ethics for organizational strategists?

Internet Exercise

Internet-based services depend heavily on continuous change and rapid strategic decision making. Companies such as Amazon.com that rely on Internet users for their customer base have demonstrated a distinct competitive advantage in serving their customers well. Barnes & Noble (**www.bn.com**) and Borders Books (**www.borders.com**) are some of Amazon.com's new competitors in the on-line book and music markets. How does this Web-based expansion affect the stakeholders of each? How does the entrance of these profitable retailers into the on-line market affect Amazon.com's competitive advantage?

***e-project:** Using other Web resources such as current business press and financial reports, discuss Amazon.com's continued growth despite recording no profits.

Notes

1. A. Edgecliff-Johnson, 1999, Fingerhut wins Wal-Mart deal, *Financial Times,* June 22, 26.
2. J. B. Barney, 1999, How firm's capabilities affect boundary decisions, *Sloan Management Review,* 40(3): 137–145; J. B. Barney, 1991, Firm resources and sustained competitive advantage, *Journal of Management,* 17: 99–120.
3. K. M. Eisenhardt & S. L. Brown, 1999, Patching: Restitching business portfolios in dynamic markets, *Harvard Business Review,* 77 (3): 72–84; D. J. Collis & C. A. Montgomery, 1995, Competing on resources: Strategy in the 1990s, *Harvard Business Review,* 73(4): 118–128.
4. D. Abell, 1999, Competing today while preparing for tomorrow, *Sloan Management Review,* 40(3): 73–81; D. J. Teece, G. Pisano, & A. Shuen, 1997, Dynamic capabilities and strategic management, *Strategic Management Journal,* 18: 509–533.
5. R. Coff, 1999, When competitive advantage doesn't lead to performance: The resource-based view and stakeholder bargaining power, *Organization Science,* 10: 119–133; R. A. D'Aveni, 1995, Coping with hypercompetition: Utilizing the new 7S's framework, *Academy of Management Executive,* IX (3): 54; D. Schendel, 1994, Introduction to the Summer 1994 special issue—Strategy: Search for new paradigms, *Strategic Management Journal,* 15 (Special Summer Issue): 3.
6. P. Shrivastava, 1995, Ecocentric management for a risk society, *Academy of Management Review,* 20: 119.
7. J. G. March & R. I. Sutton, 1998. Organizational performance as a dependent variable, *Organization Science,* 8: 698–706.
8. D. Lei, M. A. Hitt, & R. Bettis, 1996. Dynamic core competences through meta-learning and strategic context, *Journal of Management,* 22: 549–569; R. P. Rumelt, D. E. Schendel, & D. J. Teece (eds.), 1994, *Fundamental Issues in Strategy* (Boston: Harvard Business School Press), 527–530.
9. Schendel, Introduction to the Summer 1994 special issue, 1–3.
10. Rumelt, Schendel, & Teece, *Fundamental Issues in Strategy,* 543–547.
11. S. A. Zahra, R. D. Ireland, & M. A. Hitt, 2000, International expansion by new venture firms: International diversity, mode of market entry technological learning and performance, *Academy of Management* Journal, in press; M. E. Porter, 1994, Toward a dynamic theory of strategy, in R. P. Rumelt, D. E. Schendel, & D. J. Teece (eds.), *Fundamental Issues in Strategy* (Boston: Harvard Business School Press), 423–425.
12. J. Lee & D. Miller, 1999, People matter: Commitment to employees, strategy and performance in Korean firms, *Strategic Management Journal,* 20: 579–593.
13. A. M. McGahan & M. E. Porter, 1997, How much does industry matter, really? *Strategic Management Journal, 18* (Summer Special Issue): 15–30.
14. Barney, Firm resources and sustained competitive advantage.
15. Associated Press, 1999, Microsoft's now worth more than most countries, *Dallas Morning News,* July 17, F1.
16. A. Server, 2000, Street life, *Fortune,* January 10, 222.
17. Ibid.
18. M. S. Nevins & S. A. Stumpf, 1999, 21st century leadership: Redefining management education, *Strategy & Business,* 116: 41–51.
19. American Bankruptcy Institute, 1998, CY1998: Current bankruptcy statistics, *www.abiworld.org/stats/currentstats.html.*
20. Rumelt, Schendel, & Teece, *Fundamental Issues in Strategy,* 530.
21. C. J. Loomis, 1993, Dinosaurs, *Fortune,* May 3, 36–46.
22. E. Brown, 1999, America's most admired companies, *Fortune,* March 1, 68–73.
23. V. Marsh, 1998, Attributes: Strong strategy tops the list. *Financial Times,* November 30, www.ft.com.
24. J. Nocera, 1999, Five lessons from Iomega, *Fortune,* August 2, 251–254.

25. E. Schonfeld, 1999, The morphing of Intel, *Fortune,* February 15, 78.
26. P. Sellers, 1999, CEOs in denial, *Fortune,* June 21, 80–82.
27. A. Reinhardt, 1997, Paranoia, aggression, and other strengths, *Business Week,* October 13, 14; A. S. Grove, 1995, A high-tech CEO updates his views on managing and careers, *Fortune,* September 18, 229–230.
28. This section is based largely on information featured in two sources: M. A. Hitt, B. W. Keats, & S. M. DeMarie, 1998, Navigating in the new competitive landscape: Building competitive advantage and strategic flexibility in the 21st century, *Academy of Management Executive,* XII(4): 22–42; R. A. Bettis & M. A. Hitt, 1995, The new competitive landscape, *Strategic Management Journal,* 16 (Special Summer Issue): 7–19.
29. D. B. Yoffie & M. A. Cusumano, 1999, Judo strategy: The competitive dynamics of internet time, *Harvard Business Review,* 77(1): 70–81.
30. A. Kupfer, 1999, AT&T goes cable crazy, *Fortune,* May 24, 163–165.
31. R. Blumenstien, 1999, Qwest wins US West for $35 billion, *Wall Street Journal,* July 19, A3.
32. M. Halkias, 1999, Turf Wars, *Dallas Morning News,* February 20, F1, F3.
33. R. D. Ireland & M. A. Hitt, 1999, Achieving and maintaining strategic competitiveness in the 21st century: The role of strategic leadership, *Academy of Management Executive,* XIII (1): 22–42.
34. D'Aveni, Coping with hypercompetition, 46.
35. T. P. Murtha, S. A. Lenway, & R. Bagozzi, 1998, Global mind-sets and cognitive shifts in a complex multinational corporation, *Strategic Management Journal,* 19: 97–114.
36. S. Koudsi & L. A. Costa, 1998, America vs. the new Europe: By the numbers, *Fortune,* December 21, 149–156.
37. T. A. Stewart, 1993, The new face of American power, *Fortune,* July 26, 70–86.
38. K. Schwab, M. E. Porter, J. D. Sachs, A. W. Warner, & M. Levinson, 1999, *The Global Competitiveness Report 1999* (New York: Oxford University Press).
39. E. Tucker, 1999, More entrepreneurship urged, *Financial Times,* June 22, 2.
40. Whirlpool Home Page, 1999, Important company stuff, September 24, *www.whirlpoolcorp.com.*
41. S. Thurm & M. Tatge, 2000, Whirlpool to launch Internet-ready refrigerator, *Wall Street Journal,* January 7, B6; I. Katz, 1998, Whirlpool: In the wringer, *Business Week,* December 14, 83–87; G. Steinmetz & C. Quintanilla, 1998, Whirlpool expected easy going in Europe and it got a big shock. *Wall Street Journal,* April 10, A1, A6.
42. J. Landers, 1998, Small firms learning ways of global track, *Dallas Morning News,* August 17, D1, D4.
43. J. Kahn, 1999, Wal-Mart goes shopping in Europe, *Fortune,* July 7, 105–112.
44. Economist, 1999, Business: Ford swallows Volvo, *Economist,* January 30, 58.
45. E. Thornton, K. Kerwin, & K. Naughton, 1999, Can Honda go it alone? *Business Week,* July 5, 42–45.
46. B. Liu, 1999, Honda picks Alabama for next U.S. site, *Financial Times,* May 7, 7.
47. Toyota Home Page, 1999, *www.toyota.com,* September 24.
48. A. Taylor III, 1999, Asleep at the wheel, *Fortune,* March 15, 34–35.
49. R. McNast, 1999, Tora, tora, taurus, *Business Week,* April 12, 6.
50. R. Ruggiero, 1997, The high stakes of world trade, *Wall Street Journal,* April 28, A18.
51. S. A. Zahra, 1999, The changing rules of global competitiveness in the 21st century, *Academy of Management Executive,* 13(1): 36–42; R. M. Kanter, 1995, Thriving locally in the global economy, *Harvard Business Review* 73(5): 151–160.
52. D. P. Hamilton, 1999, As global chip industry reinvents itself again, Taiwan stands to gain, *Wall Street Journal,* February 17, A19.
53. S. Zaheer & E. Mosakowski, 1997, The dynamics of the liability of foreignness: A global study of survival in financial services, *Strategic Management Journal,* 18: 439–464.
54. J. S. Black & H. B. Gregersen, 1999, The right way to manage expats, *Harvard Business Review,* 77(2): 52–63; H. B. Gregersen, A. J. Morrison, & J. S. Black, 1998, Developing leaders for the global frontier, *Sloan Management Review,* 40(1): 21–32.
55. M. A. Hitt, R. E. Hoskisson, & H. Kim, 1997, International diversification: Effects on innovation and firm performance in product-diversified firms, *Academy of Management Journal,* 40: 767–798.
56. R. W. Moxon & C. Bourassa-Shaw, 1997, The global free-trade dilemma: Can you control the personal gale of creative destruction? *Business,* 18(Spring): 6–9.
57. T. Nakahara, 1997, Innovation in a borderless world economy, *Research-Technology Management,* May–June, 7–9.
58. N. Dawar & T. Frost, 1999, Competing with giants: Survival strategies for local companies in emerging markets, *Harvard Business Review,* 77 (2): 119–129.
59. F. Williams, 1999, Globalization bad for health, say UN agencies, *Financial Times,* June 10, 7.
60. K. M. Eisenhardt, 1999, Strategy as strategic decision making, *Sloan Management Review,* 40(3): 65–72.
61. C. W. L. Hill, 1997, Establishing a standard: Competitive strategy and technological standards in winner-take-all industries, *Academy of Management Executive,* XI(2): 7–25.
62. R. Karlgaard, 1999, Digital rules, *Forbes,* July 5, 43.
63. Grove, A high-tech CEO, 229.
64. B. Morris, 1997, IBM really wants your E-business, *Fortune,* November 10, 36–38.
65. R. D. Hof, 1999, What every CEO needs to know about electronic business: A survival guide, *Business Week,* March 22, EB9–EB12
66. W. Zellner, S. Anderson Forest, K. Morris, & L. Lee, 1999, The big guys go online, *Business Week,* September 6, 30–32.
67. B. L. Simonin, 1999, Ambiguity and the process of knowledge transfer in strategic alliances, *Strategic Management Journal,* 20: 595–624.
68. T. H. Davenport & L. Prusak, 1998, *Working knowledge: How organizations manage what they know* (Boston: Harvard Business School Press); C. A. Bartlett & S. Ghoshal, 1995, Changing the role of top management: Beyond systems to people, *Harvard Business Review,* 73(3): 141.
69. T. K. Kayworth & R. D. Ireland, 1998, The use of corporate IT standards as a means of implementing the cost leadership strategy, *Journal of Information Technology Management,* IX(4): 13–42.
70. R. Sanchez, 1995, Strategic flexibility in product competition, *Strategic Management Journal* (Special Summer Issue), 16: 135–159.
71. S. Kotha, 1995, Mass customization: Implementing the emerging paradigm for competitive advantage, *Strategic Management Journal,* 16: 21.
72. J. Browning & S. Reiss, 1999, *Wall Street Journal,* April 23, A14.
73. J. L. C. Cheng & I. F. Kesner, 1997, Organizational slack and response to environmental shifts: The impact of resource allocation patterns, *Journal of Management,* 23: 1–18.
74. C. Markides, 1998, Strategic innovation in established companies, *Sloan Management Review,* 39(3): 31–42; V. L. Barker III & I. M. Duhaime, 1997, Strategic change in the turnaround process: Theory and empirical evidence, *Strategic Management Journal,* 18: 13–38.
75. W. Boeker, 1997, Strategic change: The influence of managerial characteristics and organizational growth, *Academy of Management Journal,* 40: 152–170.
76. R. T. Pascale, 1999, Surving the edge of chaos, *Sloan Management Review,* 40(3): 83–94; E. D. Beinhocker, 1999, Robust adaptive strategies, *Sloan Management Review,* 40(3): 95–106; N. Rajagopalan & G. M. Spreitzer, 1997, Toward a theory of strategic

change: A multi-lens perspective and integrative framework, *Academy of Management Review*, 22: 48–79.

77. R. E. Hoskisson, M. A. Hitt, W. P. Wan, & D. Yiu, 1999, Swings of a pendulum: Theory and research in strategic management, *Journal of Management*, 25: 417–456.
78. D. Schendel, 1994, Introduction to competitive organizational behavior: Toward an organizationally-based theory of competitive advantage, *Strategic Management Journal*, 15 (Special Winter Issue): 2.
79. A. Seth & H. Thomas, 1994, Theories of the firm: Implications for strategy research, *Journal of Management Studies*, 31: 165–191.
80. Seth & Thomas, Theories of the firm, 169–173.
81. Porter, Toward a dynamic theory of strategy, 428.
82. M. E. Porter, 1985, *Competitive Advantage* (New York: Free Press); M. E. Porter, 1980, *Competitive Strategy* (New York: Free Press).
83. A. M. McGahan, 1999, Competition, strategy and business performance, *California Management Review*, 41(3): 74–101; A. M. McGahan & M. E. Porter, 1997, How much does industry matter, really? *Strategic Management Journal*, 18 (Special Summer Issue): 15–30.
84. R. Henderson & W. Mitchell, 1997, The interactions of organizational and competitive influences on strategy and performance, *Strategic Management Journal* (Special Summer Issue), 18: 5–14; C. Oliver, 1997, Sustainable competitive advantage: Combining institutional and resource-based views, *Strategic Management Journal*,18: 697–713; J. L. Stimpert & I. M. Duhaime, 1997, Seeing the big picture: The influence of industry, diversification, and business strategy on performance, *Academy of Management Journal*, 40: 560–583.
85. C. C. Markides, 1999, A dynamic view of strategy, *Sloan Management Review*, 40(3): 55–72; Abell, Competing today while preparing for tomorrow; J. R. Williams, 1994, Strategy and the search for rents: The evolution of diversity among firms, in R. P. Rumelt, D. E. Schendel, & D. J. Teece (eds.), *Fundamental Issues in Strategy* (Boston: Harvard Business School Press), 229–246.
86. Barney, Firm resources; Grant, Resource-based theory.
87. J. Kay, 1999, Total war and managers from Mars, *Financial Times*, August 4, 8.
88. P. J. H. Schoemaker & R. Amit, 1994, Investment in strategic assets: Industry and firm-level perspectives, in P. Shrivastava, A. Huff, & J. Dutton (eds.), *Advances in Strategic Management* (Greenwich, Conn.: JAI Press), 9.
89. N. Munk, 1999, Title fight, *Fortune*, June 21, 84–94.
90. J. B. Barney, 1995, Looking inside for competitive advantage, *Academy of Management Executive*, IX(4): 56.
91. A. Madhok, 1997, Cost, value and foreign market entry mode: The transaction and the firm, *Strategic Management Journal*, 18: 39–61.
92. A. A. Lado, N. G. Boyd, & S. C. Hanlon, 1997, Competition, cooperation, and the search for economic rents: A syncretic model, *Academy of Management Review*, 22: 110–141.
93. A. Arora & A. Gambardella, 1997, Domestic markets and international competitiveness: Generic and product specific competencies in the engineering sector, *Strategic Management Journal* 18 (Special Summer Issue): 53–74.
94. Teece, Pisano, & Shuen, Dynamic capabilities.
95. D. Lei, M. A. Hitt, & R. A. Bettis, 1996, Dynamic core competences through meta-learning and strategic context, *Journal of Management*, 22: 547–567.
96. G. Hamel & C. K. Prahalad, 1989, Strategic intent, *Harvard Business Review*, 67(3): 63–76.
97. S. Sherman, 1995, Stretch goals: The dark side of asking for miracles, *Fortune*, November 13, 231–232; G. Hamel & C. K. Prahalad, 1994, *Competing for the Future* (Boston: Harvard Business School Press), 129–136.
98. Hamel & Prahalad, Strategic intent, 66.
99. S. Sherman, 1993, The secret to Intel's success, 14.
100. Hamel & Prahalad, Strategic intent, 64.
101. M. A. Hitt, D. Park, C. Hardee, & B. B. Tyler, 1995, Understanding strategic intent in the global marketplace, *Academy of Management Executive*, IX(2): 12–19.
102. J. Collins, 1999, Turning goals into results: The power of catalytic mechanisms. *Harvard Business Review*, 77(4): 70–82.
103. R. D. Ireland & M. A. Hitt, 1992, Mission statements: Importance, challenge, and recommendations for development, *Business Horizons*, 35(3): 34–42.
104. W. J. Duncan, 1999, *Management: Ideas and Actions*. (New York: Oxford University Press), 122–125.
105. N. Rajagopalan, 1992, Strategic orientations, incentive plan adoptions, and firm performance: Evidence from electric utility firms, *Strategic Management Journal*, 18: 761–785.
106. M. A. Geletkanycz, 1997, The salience of culture's consequences: The effects of cultural values on top executive commitment to the status quo, *Strategic Management Journal*, 18: 615–634, M. A. Hitt, M. T. Dacin, B. B. Tyler, & D. Park, 1997, Understanding the differences in Korean and U.S. Executives' strategic orientation, *Strategic Management Journal*, 18: 159–167.
107. J. Frooman, 1999, Stakeholder influence strategies, *Academy of Management Review*, 24: 191–205.
108. T. M. Jones & A. C. Wicks, 1999, Convergent stakeholder theory, *Academy of Management Review*, 24: 206–221; R. E. Freeman, 1984, *Strategic Management: A Stakeholder Approach* (Boston: Pitman), 53–54.
109. G. Donaldson & J. W. Lorsch, 1983, *Decision Making at the Top: The Shaping of Strategic Direction* (New York: Basic Books), 37–40.
110. Rumelt, Schendel, & Teece, *Fundamental Issues in Strategy*, 33.
111. Donaldson & Lorsch, *Decision Making at the Top*, 37.
112. D. A. Gioia, 1999, Practicality, paradigms, and problems in stakeholder theorizing, *Academy of Management Review*, 24: 228–232.
113. R. K. Mitchell, B. R. Agle, & D. J. Wood, 1997, Toward a theory of stakeholder identification and salience: Defining the principle of who and what really count, *Academy of Management Review*, 22: 853–886.
114. Donaldson & Preston, The stakeholder theory of the corporation, citing a quote from *The Economist*, 1994, Corporate governance special section, September 11, 52–62.
115. Don't be an ugly-American manager, 1995, *Fortune*, October 16, 225.
116. G. Dutton, 1999, Building a global brain, *Management Review*, May: 23–30.
117. P. F. Drucker, 1999, *Management Challenges for the 21st Century* (New York: HarperCollins).
118. D. N. Sull, 1999, Why good companies go bad, *Harvard Business Review*, 77(4) 42–52.
119. G. McNamara & P. Bromiley, 1997, Decision making in an organizational setting: Cognitive and organizational influences on risk assessment in commercial lending, *Academy of Management Journal*, 40: 1063–1088.
120. L. Markoczy, 1997, Measuring beliefs: Accept no substitutes, *Academy of Management Journal*, 40: 1228–1242.
121. M. A. Hitt & R. E. Hoskisson, 1991, Strategic competitiveness, in L. W. Foster (ed.), *Advances in Applied Business Strategy* (Greenwich, Conn.: JAI Press), 1–36.
122. Bartlett & Ghoshal, Changing the role of top management, 139.
123. K. Weigelt & C. Camerer, 1988, Reputation and corporate strategy, *Strategic Management Journal*, 9: 443–454; J. B. Barney, 1986, Organizational culture: Can it be a source of sustained competitive advantage? *Academy of Management Review*, 11: 656–665.
124. R. D. Ireland, M. A. Hitt, & J. C. Williams, 1992, Self-confidence and decisiveness: Prerequisites for effective management in the 1990s, *Business Horizons*, 35(1): 36–43.

125. J. H. Davis, F. D. Schoorman, R. C. Mayer, & H. H. Tau, 2000, The trusted general manager and business unit performance: Empirical evidence of a competitive advantage, *Strategic Management Journal*, in press; R. C. Mayer, J. H. Davis, & F. D. Schoorman, 1995, An integrative model of organizational trust, *Academy of Management Review*, 20: 709–734,; J. B. Barney & M. H. Hansen, 1994, Trustworthiness as a source of competitive advantage, *Strategic Management Journal*, 15 (Winter Special Issue): 175–190.
126. E. Cohen & N. Tichy, 1999, Operation leadership, *Fast Company,* September, 278–286.
127. W. C. Taylor, 1999, Whatever happened to globalization, *Fast Company,* September, 288–294.
128. T. Leavitt, 1991, *Thinking About Management* (New York: Free Press), 9.
129. T. Minahan, 1997, Buyers tap suppliers to help them trim cycle times, *Purchasing,* November 27, 30–33.
130. M. Loeb, 1993, Steven J. Ross, 1927–1992, *Fortune,* January 25, 4.
131. Hamel & Prahalad, *Competing for the Future*, 129.
132. R. Waters, 1999, Fisher to step down as Kodak chief executive, *Financial Times,* June 10,17.
133. Rumelt, Schendel, & Teece, *Fundamental Issues in Strategy,* 9–10.
134. Our discussion of ethics and the strategic management process, both here and in other chapters, is informed by materials appearing in J. S. Harrison & C. H. St. John, 1994, *Strategic Management of Organizations and Stakeholders: Theory and Cases* (St. Paul, Minn.: West Publishing Company).

THE EXTERNAL ENVIRONMENT: OPPORTUNITIES, THREATS, INDUSTRY COMPETITION, AND COMPETITOR ANALYSIS

CHAPTER **TWO** OBJECTIVES

After reading this chapter, you should be able to:

1. Explain the importance of studying and understanding the firm's external environment.
2. Define and describe the general environment and the industry environment.
3. Discuss the four activities of the external environmental analysis process.
4. Name and describe the general environment's six segments.
5. Identify the five competitive forces and explain how they determine an industry's profit potential.
6. Define strategic groups and describe their influence on the firm's competitive actions.
7. Describe what firms need to know about their competitors and different methods used to collect intelligence on their competitors.

The Globalization of General Electric

Individual companies interpret and define globalization in ways that will have a positive influence on the actions they take to achieve strategic competitiveness and earn above-average returns. Critical to firms' efforts to interpret and define globalization is recognizing that effective worldwide competition requires meeting or exceeding global standards in terms of quality, service levels, safety, environmental concerns, and protection of intellectual property, among other performance dimensions. At General Electric (GE), globalization is one of three external shocks (the Internet and the move from manufacturing to services are the other two) that Jack Welch believed GE must confront with intensity and seriousness.

Inside GE, globalization means "globalizing every activity of the Company, including the sourcing of raw materials, components, and products to keep GE competitive in a price-sensitive deflationary world. Globalization *especially* means finding and attracting the unlimited pool of intellectual capital—the very best people—from all around the globe. The GE of the next century must provide high-value global products and services, designed and delivered by global talent, for global markets." To accomplish all that is associated with GE's brand of globalization, the firm's leaders are expected to have a global mind-set and to build and successfully use globally diverse work teams. Upper-level managers seem to be a globally diverse team, in that the head of the firm's Six Sigma Quality Initiative is Dutch (Six Sigma is a standard of excellence defined as having no more than 3.4 defects per million in any operation, whether it is manufacturing, billing, or loan processing), the head of the corporate audit staff is French, and non-Americans fill the firm's training classes for upper-level leaders in rough proportion to their numbers in GE's total employee base.

Toward the end of 1999 the ninth largest and second most profitable company in the world, GE is a company with multiple operations. Recently, the firm had 10 major product groups with approximately 250 business units spread among them. The firm's performance under Jack Welch's leadership has been stellar. Beginning in 1981 with his appointment as CEO, sales increased 3.7 times (from $27.2 billion to $100.5 billion), while profits grew 5.7 times (from $1.6 billion to $9.2 billion). In addition, GE's market capitalization grew from $14 billion to more than $400 billion during Welch's tenure. Contributing to these achievements were the significant restructurings that occurred. These actions resulted in layoffs of tens of thousands of employees, as well as the initialization of cost-cutting measures. However, the ability to make GE a truly global company may be Welch's most significant accomplishment and greatest legacy. Indicators of how globalized GE has become are the expectations that in the very near future, one-half of the firm's sales and most of its workforce will be outside the United States. In light of GE's globalization and Welch's other accomplishments, some suggest that he may be the world's most successful business leader/manager of the past quarter-century. (Welch's scheduled retirement from GE is April 2001.)

GE's transformation to a global powerhouse suggests processes that may be worthy of emulation. Until a little over a decade ago, the firm seemed to have an ethnocentric perspective, viewing the rest of the world as an export market while using mostly U.S. facilities to manufacture and distribute products. In 1987, 44 percent of GE's global sales were exports from the United States. In 1990, the situation had changed dramatically; Europe alone accounted for $24.4 billion of GE's 1998 revenue. Only 11 percent of this total sales volume came from exports from the United States.

Understanding different segments of the general environment, including the *economic, sociocultural,* and *political/legal* segments, is critical to GE's success as a global competitor. These segments, along with three others that together constitute a firm's general environment, are discussed in this chapter. Based in part on an understanding of the conditions in the general environment in different countries, GE has expertly acquired a number of companies to build its global presence. Several European acquisitions took place in 1994 and 1995 when a recession reduced the value of those companies' assets. In 1998 alone, GE spent $21 billion to acquire 108 companies. Promoting the success of its acquisitions in globalizing its operations is GE's commitment to carefully analyze a target firm before purchasing it. GE's analyses focus on both financial and human resource issues. Moving quickly once a company is bought, GE implements its own procedures and practices so that the acquisition can meet the firm's aggressive performance expectations. Work-Outs, a tool that allows a meeting to be called by any person to address any problem, has been applied successfully throughout GE. In use since 1989, this tool helps GE improve its procedures and practices. Essentially, the tool suggests that when presented with a solution to a problem during a Work-Out session, "the manager must say yes or no on the spot, no haggling, no waffling."

As the 21st century began, Welch believed that GE was prepared to derive full benefit from its globalization efforts through its commitment to globalize the company's intellect. According to Welch, globalizing intellect "means using Russian engineering and Indian software—not to arbitrage labor costs, but because these are the best people you can find." Although globalization is challenging, Welch was convinced that being able to learn through intellectual capital and transferring that learning quickly across the entire firm can provide the ultimate competitive advantage.

http://www.ge.com

SOURCES: GE Overview, 2000, General Electric Home Page, January 12, *www.ge.com*; G. Colvin, 1999, The ultimate manager, *Fortune,* November 22, 185–187; C. K. Prahalad, 1999, Changes in the competitive battlefield, Mastering Strategy (Part Two), *Financial Times,* October 4, 2–5; T. A. Stewart, 1999, See Jack. See Jack run, *Fortune,* September 27, 124–136; The house that Jack built, 1999, *The Economist,* September 18, 23–26.

Companies' experiences across time and research evidence suggest that the external environment affects firm growth and profitability.[1] Changes in political/legal realities, the strength of different nations' economies at different times, and the emergence of new technologies are a few examples of conditions in the external environment that are affecting GE and other firms throughout the world. Jack Welch believes, for example, that the capabilities of a major new technology, the Internet, will change everything, including relationships with employees, customers, and suppliers. Regarding suppliers, Welch decided that those supplying GE would be allowed no more than 18 months to gain the skills necessary to supply the firm on the Internet. Those failing to satisfy this expectation "won't do business with us," Welch declared.[2] One technique GE uses to impress the criticality of the Internet to each employee is to send materials about the need to change the way each unit conducts its business across the company under the heading "destroyyourbusiness.com."

The practice of using the Internet to work with suppliers is becoming common. Consistent with GE's actions, Ford Motor Company and Oracle Corp. formed a joint venture to put Ford's vast chain of suppliers on-line. The venture's new Internet company, called AutoXchange, put Ford's extended supply chain, with $300 billion in annual transactions, on the Web. Starting in the first quarter of 2000, the venture is expected to make each supplier more efficient, allowing Ford to reduce the time required to deliver vehicles to customers.[3]

This chapter focuses on what firms do to analyze and understand the external environment. As the discussion of GE shows, the external environment influences the firm's strategic options, as well as the decisions made in light of them. The firm's understanding of the external environment is matched with knowledge about its internal environment (the internal environment is discussed in the next chapter). Matching the conditions of the two environments is the foundation the firm needs to form its strategic intent, to develop its strategic mission, and to take strategic actions in the pursuit of strategic competitiveness and above-average returns (see Figure 1.1).

As noted in the first chapter, the environmental conditions facing firms in the global economy today differ from those firms faced previously. Technological changes and the explosion in information-gathering and processing capabilities demand more timely and effective competitive actions and responses.[4] The rapid sociological changes occurring in many countries affect labor practices and the nature of products demanded by increasingly diverse consumers. Governmental policies and laws affect where and how firms choose to compete.[5] Deregulation and local government changes, such as those being witnessed in the global electric utilities industry, affect the general competitive environment, as well as the strategic decisions that will be made by companies competing globally. Enron, for example, is among the hundreds of energy marketers, utilities, and banks seeking stakes in a $300 billion wholesale global gas and power business that is consolidating rapidly across the world's markets as a result of privatization activities. Through these actions, Enron has taken less than 10 years to transform itself into a global service powerhouse in energy, water, and other infrastructure industries.[6] Privatization, a form of deregulation, is a process in which ownership of an enterprise is transferred from the public sector to the private sector. To achieve strategic competitiveness, when dealing with all situations, including privatization activities, companies must be aware of and understand the implications of the realities of the external environment's different parts.

Firms attempt to understand the external environment by acquiring information about competitors, customers, and other stakeholders. In particular, firms seek to gain information to build their own base of knowledge and capabilities.[7] Firms may attempt to imitate the capabilities of able competitors or even successful firms in other industries, or they may build new knowledge and capabilities to develop a competitive advantage. On the basis of this new information, knowledge, and capabilities, firms may take actions to buffer environmental effects on them or to build relationships with stakeholders in their environment.[8] To build up their knowledge and capabilities and to take actions that buffer or build bridges to external stakeholders, organizations must effectively analyze the external environment.

The General, Industry, and Competitor Environments

Through an integrated understanding of the external and internal environments, firms gain the information they need to understand the present and predict the future.[9] As shown in Figure 2.1, a firm's external environment is divided into three major areas: the general, industry, and competitor environments.

The **general environment** is composed of elements in the broader society that influence an industry and the firms within it.

The **general environment** is composed of elements in the broader society that influence an industry and the firms within it.[10] We group these elements into six environmental *segments:* demographic, economic, political/legal, sociocultural, technological, and global. Examples of *elements* analyzed in each of these segments are shown in Table 2.1.

FIGURE 2.1 | The External Environment

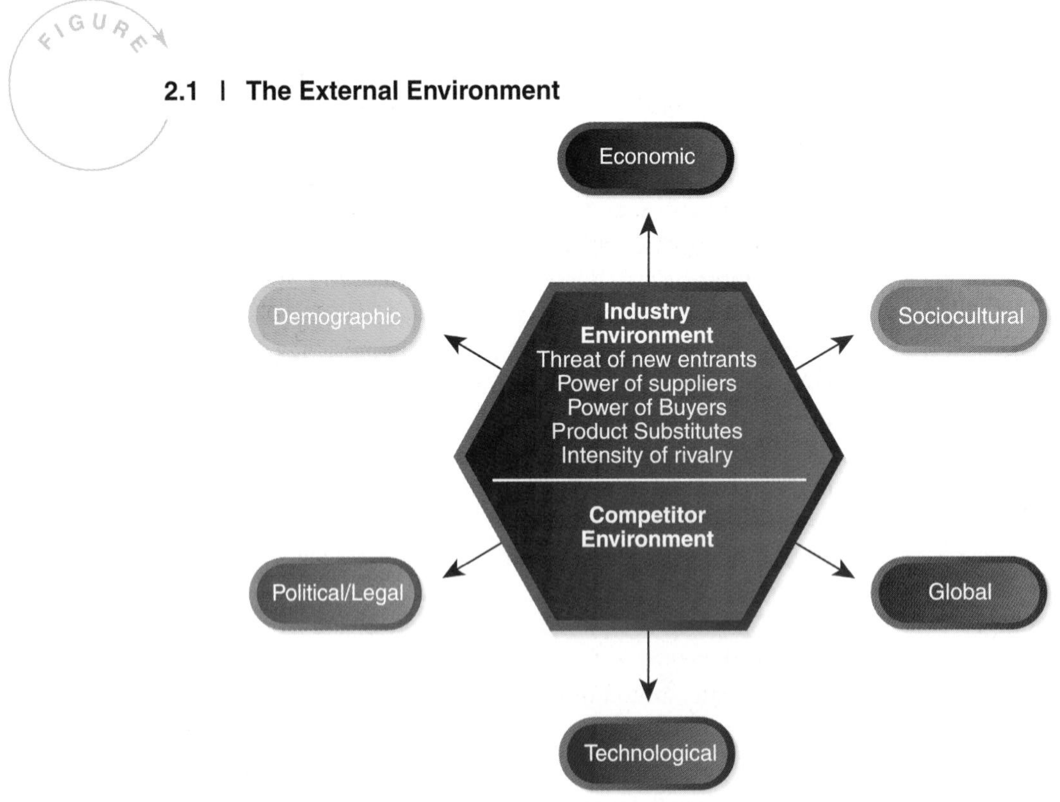

TABLE

2.1 | The General Environment: Segments and Elements

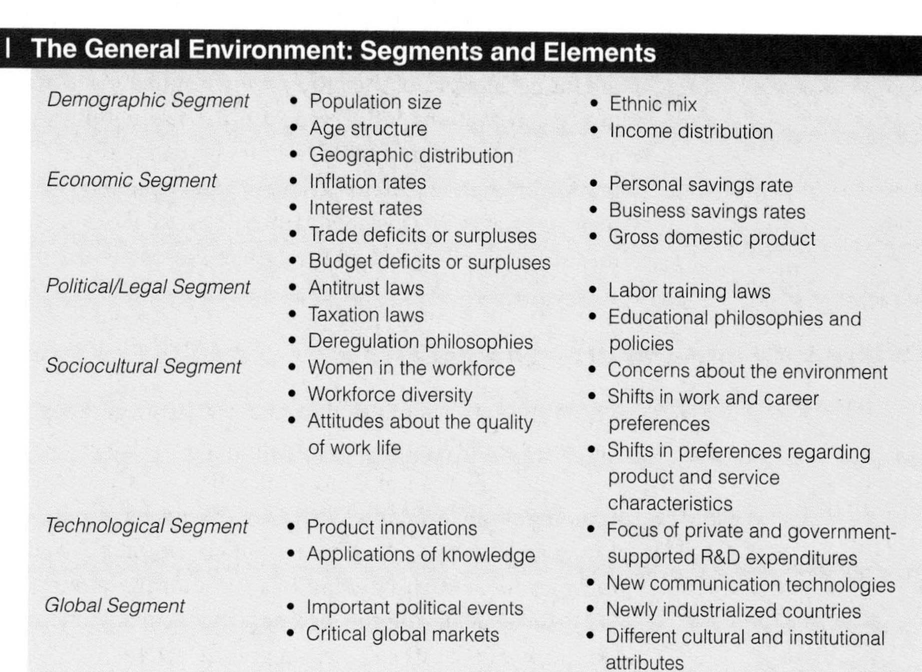

Segment	Elements	Elements
Demographic Segment	• Population size • Age structure • Geographic distribution	• Ethnic mix • Income distribution
Economic Segment	• Inflation rates • Interest rates • Trade deficits or surpluses • Budget deficits or surpluses	• Personal savings rate • Business savings rates • Gross domestic product
Political/Legal Segment	• Antitrust laws • Taxation laws • Deregulation philosophies	• Labor training laws • Educational philosophies and policies
Sociocultural Segment	• Women in the workforce • Workforce diversity • Attitudes about the quality of work life	• Concerns about the environment • Shifts in work and career preferences • Shifts in preferences regarding product and service characteristics
Technological Segment	• Product innovations • Applications of knowledge	• Focus of private and government-supported R&D expenditures • New communication technologies
Global Segment	• Important political events • Critical global markets	• Newly industrialized countries • Different cultural and institutional attributes

Firms cannot directly control the general environment's segments and elements. Accordingly, successful companies gather the types and amounts of data and information that are required to understand each segment and its implications so that appropriate strategies can be selected and used. For example, the "red-hot" United States economy during the latter part of the 1990s surprised countries throughout the world. During that time, the economy grew faster "than even the most optimistic forecasters thought possible, providing vital support to an ailing global economy in the process."[11] Although individual firms were affected differently, none could control the U.S. economy. Instead, companies around the globe were challenged to understand the effects of this economy's unexpectedly strong growth on their firm's current and future strategies.

The **industry environment** is the set of factors—the threat of new entrants, suppliers, buyers, product substitutes, and the intensity of rivalry among competitors—that directly influences a company and its competitive actions and responses.

The **industry environment** is the set of factors—the threat of new entrants, suppliers, buyers, product substitutes, and the intensity of rivalry among competitors—that directly influences a firm and its competitive actions and responses. In total, the interactions among these five factors determine an industry's profit potential. The challenge is to locate a position within an industry where a firm can favorably influence those factors or where it can successfully defend against their influence. The greater a firm's capacity to favorably influence its industry environment, the greater is the likelihood that the firm will earn above-average returns.

How companies gather and interpret information about their competitors is called *competitor analysis*. Understanding the firm's competitor environment complements the insights provided by studying the general and industry environments.

In combination, the results of the three analyses that are used to understand the external environment influence the development of the firm's strategic intent, strategic mission, and strategic actions. Analysis of the general environment is focused on the future; analysis of the industry environment is focused on understanding the factors and conditions influencing a firm's profitability; and analysis of competitors is focused on predicting the dynamics of competitors' actions, responses, and intentions. Although we discuss each analysis separately, performance improves when the firm integrates the insights gained from analyses of the general environment, the industry environment, and the competitor environment.

External Environmental Analysis

Most firms face external environments that are growing more turbulent, complex, and global—conditions that make interpretation increasingly difficult.[12] To cope with what are often ambiguous and incomplete environmental data and to increase their understanding of the general environment, firms engage in a process called external environmental analysis. The process, which should be conducted on a continuous basis. includes four activities: scanning, monitoring, forecasting, and assessing (see Table 2.2). Those analyzing the external environment should understand that completing this analysis is a difficult, yet significant, activity.[13]

An **opportunity** is a condition in the general environment that may help a company achieve strategic competitiveness.

An important objective of studying the general environment is identifying opportunities and threats. An **opportunity** is a condition in the general environment that may help a company achieve strategic competitiveness. General Motors believes that in the not-too-distant future, a person's car will be a mobile node on "the world-wide communications grid—plugged in by satellites and cellular links to digital audio, video, telecommunications and the Internet." GM executives see the possibility of selling billions of dollars of ancillary services to customers after they have purchased their automobiles as an "enormous opportunity."[14] An early action taken to exploit this perceived opportunity was the use of GM's OnStar satellite-based service to deliver e-mail, traffic reports, and other information to drivers of certain 2000-model luxury cars. Essentially, the OnStar system was being used as the portal for basic Internet services.[15] The fact that no more than one billion of the world's total population of 6 billion has anything close to cheap access to a telephone appears to be a huge opportunity for global telecommunications companies.[16] And General Electric believes that

2.2 | Components of the External Analysis

Scanning	• Identifying early signals of environmental changes and trends
Monitoring	• Detecting meaning through ongoing observations of environmental changes and trends
Forecasting	• Developing projections of anticipated outcomes based on monitored changes and trends
Assessing	• Determining the timing and importance of environmental changes and trends for firms' strategies and their management

"e-business represents a revolution that may be the greatest opportunity for growth that [the] Company has ever seen."[17]

A **threat** is a condition in the general environment that may hinder a company's efforts to achieve strategic competitiveness.

A **threat** is a condition in the general environment that may hinder a company's efforts to achieve strategic competitiveness.[18] In light of the Internet's growing use and promise, some graduate business schools are offering master's degrees focusing on electronic commerce. IBM is even offering such a degree in partnership with ESC Grenoble, a French business school.[19] For business schools lacking modern technology and a faculty that is fully conversant with the use of electronic commerce as a means of competitive survival and the development of a competitive advantage, the emergence of electronic commerce MBA degrees could appear threatening.[20] As our examples and discussion indicate, opportunities suggest competitive *possibilities,* while threats are potential *constraints*.

Several sources are used to analyze the general environment, including a wide variety of printed materials (e.g., trade publications, newspapers, business publications, and the results of academic research and public polls); attendance at and participation in trade shows; the content of conversations with suppliers, customers, and employees of public-sector organizations; and, business-related "rumors."[21] An additional source of data and information is people in "boundary-spanning" positions who interact with external constituents such as salespersons, purchasing managers, public relations directors, and human-resource managers. As discussed in sections to come, the Internet is increasingly a vital source of data and information for the purpose of understanding the general environment. In each case, though, the firm should verify the validity and reliability of the sources on which its environmental analyses are based.[22]

Scanning

Scanning entails the study of all segments in the general environment. Through scanning, firms identify early signals of potential changes in the general environment and detect changes that are already under way.[23] When scanning, the firm often deals with ambiguous, incomplete, or unconnected data and information. Environmental scanning is critically important for firms competing in highly volatile environments.[24] In addition, scanning activities must be aligned with the organizational context; a scanning system designed for a volatile environment is inappropriate for a firm in a stable environment.[25]

As the 1990s closed, a trend toward early retirement was emerging in western societies. One reason for this was the difficulty people age 50 and over were having locating work. Magnifying this difficulty was the virtual disappearance of some jobs. "The man from the Pru, the door-to-door collector of insurance premiums, is being outsourced, so it no longer matters where he comes from. Over-the-counter relationships are disappearing as customers are given electronic and Internet alternatives."[26]

Some analysts expect the pressure brought to bear by the early retirement trend on countries such as France, Germany, and Japan to be quite significant and challenging. Governments in these countries appear to be offering future elderly populations state-funded pensions that cannot be met with the present taxes and social-security contribution rates.[27] Those selling financial planning services and options should observe this trend to determine whether it represents an opportunity to help governments find ways to meet their previously agreed-upon responsibilities. In a similar vein, the fact that the number of students taking on-line courses is expected to grow from 1 million in 1999 to well over 2 million in 2002 is a trend for those delivering educational offerings via the Internet to study for opportunities. Early retirees might be an important customer segment for those providing education through electronic means.[28]

Monitoring

When *monitoring,* analysts observe environmental changes to see if an important trend is emerging from among those spotted by scanning.[29] Critical to successful monitoring is the ability to detect meaning in different environmental events. For example, a new law permitting shopping on Sunday for "touristic items" was introduced recently in eastern Germany. The limited Sunday store openings were a challenge to the nation's restrictive rules on shopping hours. Popular initially with consumers, the Sunday openings, said some analysts, might spread beyond the economically stricken east, even though the move toward longer hours was strongly opposed by the service sector union.[30] German retailers should monitor this change in their selling environment to determine if an important trend in shopping patterns might emerge. In the United States, the size of the middle class of African Americans continues to grow. With increasing wealth, this group of citizens is beginning to pursue investment options more aggressively.[31] Companies in the financial planning sector could monitor this change in the economic segment to determine the degree to which a competitively important trend and a business opportunity are emerging.

Forecasting

Scanning and monitoring are concerned with events in the general environment at a point in time. When *forecasting,* analysts develop feasible projections of what might happen, and how quickly, as a result of the changes and trends detected through scanning and monitoring.[32] For example, analysts might forecast the time that will be required for a new technology to reach the marketplace, the length of time before different corporate training procedures are required to deal with anticipated changes in the composition of the workforce, or how much time will elapse before changes in governmental taxation policies affect consumers' purchasing patterns.

The increasing use of the Internet by new companies called *infomediaries* is affecting business practices in the global economy. Infomediaries use technology to bring buyers and sellers together on-line. The company called E-Chemicals brokers 55-gallon drums of manufacturing chemicals between DuPont and thousands of heavy manufacturers located in the upper Midwest and east coast of the United States. PaperExchange.com maintains its Web site to enable paper suppliers and buyers from 40 countries to negotiate for products ranging from containerboard to writing paper. The firm's revenue source is the 3-percent commission it charges for each transaction completed by parties using its Web site.[33]

Assessing

The objective of *assessing* is to determine the timing and significance of the effects of environmental changes and trends on the strategic management of a firm.[34] Through scanning, monitoring, and forecasting, analysts are able to understand the general

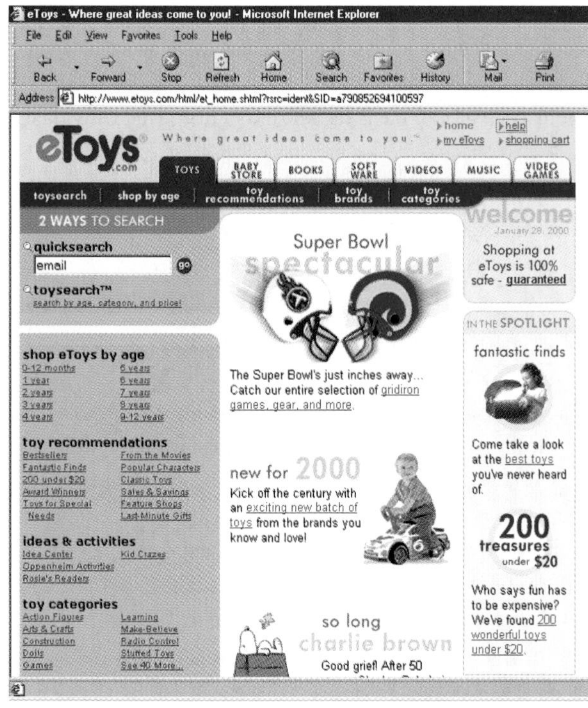

eToys, the Web's leading toy retailer, spent millions to promote its brand on the largest Internet portals. The firm is now facing competition from toymakers that are becoming more committed to selling their products on-line.

environment. Going a step further, the intent of assessment is to specify the implications of that understanding for the organization. Without assessment, the firm is left with data that are interesting, but of unknown competitive relevance.

In the U.S. automobile industry, Ford, General Motors, and DaimlerChrysler are selling increasing numbers of trucks, sport utility vehicles, and minivans. However, all three firms have lost market share in car sales to competitors such as Honda, Toyota, Volkswagen, Audi, and BMW. These three firms understand that if gasoline costs were to rise substantially or if consumer preferences shift from trucks to cars, they could be in trouble. However, shifting some production capacity to cars is a difficult decision for these companies, in that profits per unit on trucks, sport utility vehicles, and minivans vastly exceed those earned on cars.[35] Thus, the challenge for those firms is to continually assess the significance of possible decreases in demand for their most profitable products and to understand changes that would be necessary in their strategies to deal successfully with shifts in consumer preferences.

At the close of the 1990s, eToys was the Web's leading toy retailer. As with CDnow and Amazon.com, eToys' rapid success was a product of its decision to spend millions to promote its brand on the largest Internet portals. However, scanning, monitoring, and forecasting suggested interesting challenges from competitors for eToys to assess. Toymakers, especially Hasbro and Mattel, were becoming more committed to selling their products through electronic commerce, too. Similarly, Wal-Mart and Toys "R" Us decided to allocate significant resources to boost sales on their Web sites. Moreover, analysts suggested that these two giant firms might try to "turn the screws on the manufacturers to get first dibs on scarce items."[36] The implications of competitors' intentions should inform eToys' strategic decisions as it seeks to maintain its strategic competitiveness.

Segments of the General Environment

The general environment is composed of segments (and their individual elements) that are external to the firm (see Table 2.1). Although the degree of impact varies, these environmental segments affect each industry and the firms within it. The challenge is to scan, monitor, forecast, and assess those elements in each segment that are of the greatest importance. In addition, the results of an external environmental analysis should recognize environmental changes, trends, opportunities, and threats. Opportunities are then matched with a firm's core competencies (the matching process is discussed further in Chapter 3). Through proper matches, the firm achieves strategic competitiveness and earns above-average returns.

The Demographic Segment

The **demographic segment** is concerned with a population's size, age, structure, geographic distribution, ethnic mix, and income distribution.

The **demographic segment** is concerned with a population's size, age structure, geographic distribution, ethnic mix, and income distribution.[37] As previously noted, the firm analyzes demographic segments on a global basis rather than a domestic-only basis.

Population Size

In October 1999, the world's population reached 6 billion (growing from 5 billion in 1987). Combined, China and India accounted for one-third of the 6 billion. Experts speculate that the population might stabilize at 10 billion after 2200 if the deceleration in the rate of increase in the world's head count continues. By 2050, India (with over 1.5 billion people) and China (with just under 1.5 billion people) are expected to be the most populous countries.[38]

Observing demographic changes in populations highlights the importance of this environmental segment. For example, in some advanced nations, there is negative population growth (discounting the effects of immigration). In some countries, including the United States and several European nations, couples are averaging fewer than two children. Such a birthrate will produce a loss of population over time (even with the population living longer on average).[39] However, some analysts believe that a baby boom will occur in the United States during the first 12 years of the 21st century and that by 2012, the annual number of births could exceed 4.3 million. Such a birthrate in the United States would equal the all-time high that was set in 1957.[40]

In contrast to advanced nations, the rapid growth rate in the populations of some developing countries is depleting natural resources and reducing citizens' living standards. In the words of one writer, "If poor countries develop their economies in the same wasteful way industrial nations have, population growth will put an increasing burden on food and water supplies and the habitat of endangered species."[41] These projections suggest major 21st-century challenges and business opportunities.

Age Structure

In some countries, the population's average age is increasing. In the United States, for example, the percentage of the population aged 55 and older is expected to increase from roughly 6 percent in 1995 to approximately 37.5 percent in 2019.[42] Contributing to this change are declining birthrates and increasing life expectancies. Among others, these trends may suggest numerous opportunities for firms to develop goods and services to meet the needs of an increasingly older population.

It has been projected that up to one-half of the females and one-third of the males born at the end of the 1990s in developed countries could live to be 100 years old, with some of them possibly living to be 200 or more.[43] Also, the chance that a U.S. baby boomer (a person born between the years 1947 and 1964) will reach age 90 is now one in nine.[44] If such life spans become a reality, a host of interesting business opportunities and societal issues will emerge. For example, the effect on individuals' pension plans will be significant and will create potential opportunities for financial institutions, as well as possible threats to government-sponsored retirement and health plans.[45]

Geographic Distribution

For decades, the U.S. population has been shifting from the north and east to the west and south. Similarly, the trend of relocating from metropolitan to nonmetropolitan areas continues. These trends are changing local and state governments' tax bases. In turn, the locations of business firms are influenced by the degree of support different taxing agencies offer. Furthermore, the progress states are making to deal with the realities of the global economy differ (see Table 2.3). States in the top 10 of those that are trying to transform themselves to the realities and needs of a digital economy may experience an influx of high-tech companies and skilled workers, as well as increases in tax revenues.

The geographic distribution of populations throughout the world is being changed by the capabilities resulting from advances in communications technology. Through computer technologies, for example, people can remain in their homes, communicating with others in remote locations to complete their work. In the United States, self-employed travel agents find that it is more profitable to work from home rather than from a storefront office. Facing a decline in revenues from airlines and other sources, larger travel agencies "like to work with home-based agents because they cost less than an agent in the office and expand the agency's customer base."[46]

Ethnic Mix

The ethnic mix of countries' populations continues to change. Within the United States, the ethnicity of states and of cities within the states varies significantly. For business firms, the challenge is to be aware of and sensitive to these changes. Through careful study, firms can develop and market goods and services intended to satisfy the unique needs and interest of different ethnic groups.

Changes in the ethnic mix also affect a workforce's composition. In the United States, for example, the population and labor force will continue to diversify, as immigration accounts for a sizable part of growth. Projections are that the Hispanic and Asian population shares will increase from 14 percent in 1995 to 19 percent in 2020. By 2006, expectations are that (1) 72.7 percent of the U.S. labor force will be white non-Hispanic (down from 75.3 percent in 1996), (2) 11.7 percent will be Hispanic (compared with 9.5 percent in 1996), (3) 11.6 percent will be African-American (up from 11.3 percent in 1996), and (4) 5.4 percent will be Asian (up from 4.3 percent in

TABLE

2.3 | Top Ten U.S. States Moving Toward the Digital Economy

Rank	State
1	Massachusetts
2	California
3	Colorado
4	Washington
5	Connecticut
6	Utah
7	New Hampshire
8	New Jersey
9	Delaware
10	Arizona

Source: Adapted from *Across the Board*, 1999, October, 62.

1996). Moreover, "of the nearly 15 million worker increase in the 1996–2006 period, about 7 million will be Hispanic or Asian. Hispanic-Americans will raise their share of new workers slightly from 29 to 31 percent, as will Asian-Americans whose share will grow from 14.5 to 15.7 percent. By 2020, white non-Hispanic workers will make up only 68 percent of the work force."[47]

As with the U.S. labor force, other countries also are witnessing a trend toward an older workforce. By 2030, the proportion of OECD's total labor force of 45–59-year-olds is projected to increase from 25.6 to 31.8 percent; the share of workers age 60 and over is expected to increase from 4.7 to 7.8 percent. Because a labor force can be critical to competitive success, firms across the globe, including those competing in OECD countries, must learn to work effectively with labor forces that are becoming more diverse, as well as different (e.g., in terms of proportions along the dimensions of age and race), than they were previously.[48]

Workforce diversity is also a sociocultural issue. Effective management of a culturally diverse workforce can produce a competitive advantage. For example, heterogeneous work teams have been shown to produce more effective strategic analyses, more creativity and innovation, and higher quality decisions than homogeneous work teams.[49] However, evidence also suggests that work team diversity and team performance are complex.[50] Because of this complexity a number of companies promote cultural diversity in their workforces and facilitate effective management of such diversity through specialized management training.

Income Distribution

Understanding how income is distributed within and across populations informs firms of different groups' purchasing power and discretionary income. Studies of income distributions suggest that while living standards have improved over time, variations exist within and between nations.[51] Of interest to firms are the average incomes of households and individuals. For instance, a notable change is the increase in dual-career couples. Although, in general, real income has been declining, dual-career couples have increased their income. The actual figures yield strategically relevant information.

The Economic Segment

The health of a nation's economy affects the performance of individual firms and industries. Because of this, companies study the economic environment to identify changes, trends, and their strategic implications.

The **economic environment** refers to the nature and direction of the economy in which a firm competes or may compete.

The **economic environment** refers to the nature and direction of the economy in which a firm competes or may compete.[52] Because of the interconnectedness among nations that is resulting from the global economy, firms must scan, monitor, forecast, and assess the health of economies outside their host nation. Brazil's recent experiences highlight the need to do this.

In the middle to late 1990s, Brazil was one of Latin America's fastest growing economies and "was the darling of the international investment community." In particular, the country's middle class was experiencing significant work-related opportunities to improve its standard of living. However, the effects of late-1990 economic "meltdowns" in Russia and Asia were crippling for the Brazilian economy. For example, the global economic turmoil resulted in a decline in sales of 27.5 percent from 1997 to 1998 for Brazil's automobile industry alone. In response to the nation's crisis, the country's president instituted a major currency devaluation. In 1998, employers eliminated over 580,000 jobs. The fortunes of the middle class became bleak as job losses found them unable to cope with the demands of financial purchases they made during the "good times." In turn, Brazil's economic crisis affected companies throughout the world, including both large and small U.S. firms. Ford and General Motors decided to lay off workers in their facilities in Argentina because of the economic fallout from Brazil's devaluation.[53] A small Texas-based exporter of a home-repair franchising operation also suffered as a result of the devaluation of Brazil's currency.[54] Thus, any uncertainty in the world's interdependent economies affects firms of all types and sizes.

The cost of reversing the fortunes of an economy (such as Brazil's) once problems are encountered can be significant. For example, recent times found two-thirds of Indonesian and one-fourth of Thai companies to be virtually insolvent. According to a World Bank official, "cost estimates of financial-sector restructuring range[d] from a low of 18 percent of GDP in Indonesia to 30 percent in Thailand."[55] These estimated costs highlight the importance of a nation being able to govern itself and its business organizations in ways that facilitate continuous, uninterrupted economic success.

In light of the increasing interdependencies among the world's economies, some believe that it is in the best interests of all nations to create truly global markets. Doing this, it is argued, can create a future in which the common goals of creating wealth and fostering economic stability are achievable. Comments by members of the World Trade Organization speak to this matter: "A broad range of empirical studies conclude that open trade policies are conducive to growth. The conclusion appears to hold regardless of the level of development of the countries concerned, challenging the notion that a certain level of development is required before the benefits from trade can be fully realized."[56]

DaimlerChrysler's CEO, Jurgen E. Schrempp, who is a strong proponent of completing a transatlantic integration between Europe and North America, appears to support the position taken by the World Trade Organization regarding the benefits of unrestricted trade. Schrempp believes that an integration between Europe and North America is logical in that "Europe and the United States each account for close to 20 percent of the other's trade in goods while services account for more than 38 percent of bilateral trade." Principles developed by the Transatlantic Business Dialogue (a group of businesspersons and politicians) could support an integration effort. Among the principles are the removal of all trade barriers and differing regulatory controls and the acceptance of a product in all parts of the transatlantic marketplace once it has been approved.[57] The vice president of the European Commission believes that the Asian and Russian financial crises make it necessary to quickly integrate multiple economies, including those of Europe and the United States. In his view, "we must inject greater urgency into opening up world markets. And we must resist any moves to return to crippling pre-war protectionism."[58]

Creating truly "borderless commerce" that free trade among nations would permit is proving to be a significant challenge. Using the Internet to purchase books in Europe is an example of the barriers to borderless electronic commerce. A teacher of foreign languages living in Berlin purchases books from Amazon.com's Web site in the United Kingdom, rather than from the firm's German Web site. In his words, "If you buy from the U.K. site, it's much cheaper. Even if you include the shipping, it's a better deal in the U.K." The reason for the price differentials is that governments in Germany, France, and some other European nations allow publishing cartels to influence business practices. A group of book publishers, each cartel can legally dictate retail prices to booksellers—both in stores and on-line.[59] Thus, the selling of books in Europe via electronic commerce appears to be an example of a business transaction that could benefit a firm through the use of the principles designed by the members of the Transatlantic Business Dialogue group.

As our discussion of the economic segment suggests, economic issues are intertwined closely with the realities of the external environment's political/legal segment.

The Political/Legal Segment

The **political/legal segment** is the arena in which organizations and interest groups compete for attention, resources, and a voice of overseeing the body of laws and regulations guiding the interactions among nations.

The **political/legal segment** is the arena in which organizations and interest groups compete for attention, resources and a voice of overseeing the body of laws and regulations guiding the interactions among nations.[60] Essentially, this segment represents how organizations try to influence government and how governments influence them. Constantly changing, the segment influences the nature of competition (see Table 2.1). Because of this, firms must carefully analyze a new administration's business-related policies and philosophies. Antitrust laws, taxation laws, industries chosen for deregulation, labor training laws, and the degree of commitment to educational institutions are areas in which an administration's policies can affect the operations and profitability of industries and individual firms. Often, how the firm intends to interact with the political/legal segment is captured through the development and use of a political strategy. The effects of a host of global governmental policies on the firm's competitive position increases the importance of forming an effective political strategy.[61]

As the 21st century begins, business firms across the globe confront an interesting array of political/legal questions and issues. For example, the debate continues over trade policies. Some believe that a nation should erect trade barriers to protect products manufactured by its companies. Others argue that free trade across nations serves the best interests of individual countries and their citizens. The International Monetary Fund (IMF) classifies trade barriers as *restrictive* when tariffs total at least 25 percent of a product's price. At the other extreme, the IMF stipulates that a nation has *open trade* when its tariffs are between zero and 9 percent. To foster trade, New Zealand initially cut its tariffs from 16 to 8.5 percent and then to 3 percent in 2000. Columbia reduced its tariffs to less than 12 percent. The IMF classifies this percentage as "relatively open."[62] In a cooperative spirit, the European Union, Japan, Australia, Hong Kong, Singapore, Mexico, and Chile were among the countries that, beginning in January 2000, initiated a new round of global trade talks to try to develop multilateral negotiations that would reduce or eliminate trade barriers. Resulting from these actions, the countries hoped, would be a significant increase in the amount of free trade completed among their economies.[63]

An interesting debate occurring in the United States concerns the regulation of e-commerce. In part, laws regulating e-commerce are an attempt to prevent fraud, violations of privacy, and poor service. Beyond this, some think that governmental policies should be developed to influence the nature of Internet gambling.[64] Thus, as the 21st century started, U.S. government officials were trying to devise policies on a "host of knotty issues ranging from on-line pornography to Internet taxation." A concern of all parties is for government officials to develop policies that will not stifle the legitimate growth of e-commerce.[65]

Across the globe, governments are trying to develop policies that are in their countries' best economic interests. Japan's government is working actively to find policies that can stimulate economic growth. U.S. energy firms are investing heavily in Mexico as a result of recent favorable regulatory changes. Germany's government is seeking ways to support an entrepreneurial spirit that seems to have the potential to reduce the nation's unemployment rate. In the United Kingdom, regulators were working to end British Telecommunications PLC's dominance of local services as 1999 came to a close. Central America, once a proving ground for guerrilla-warfare tactics, is joining most of the rest of Latin America as a proving ground for free-market reform. Guatemala, for example, is implementing one of the most aggressive telecommunication reform laws in Latin America. It is essentially opening its market to full competition in all segments—local, long-distance, paging, and cellular services. Motorola and 14 other foreign telecommunications companies are negotiating to provide these services. Furthermore, Guatemala has already privatized railroad, radio, and electrical utility companies and has begun the process of privatizing its telecommunications company, Guatel. Other Central American countries are taking similar, if not identical, actions.[66]

The Sociocultural Segment

The **sociocultural segment** is concerned with a society's attitudes and cultural values.

The **sociocultural segment** is concerned with a society's attitudes and cultural values. Because attitudes and values form the cornerstone of a society, they often drive demographic, economic, political/legal, and technological conditions and changes.

Sociocultural segments differ across countries. For example, in the United States, 14 percent of the nation's GDP is spent on health care. This is the highest percentage of any OCED country. Germany allocates 10.4 percent of GDP to health care, while in Switzerland the percentage is 10.2.[67] Countries' citizens have different attitudes about retirement savings as well. In Italy, just 9 percent of the citizenry say that they are saving primarily for retirement, while the percentages are 18 percent in Germany and 48 percent in the United States.[68] Attitudes regarding one's savings for retirement affect a nation's economic and political/legal segments. Differences in attitudes about work seem to exist between France and some other nations, including the United States. In the United States, boundaries between work and home are becoming blurred, as employees' workweeks continue to be stretched, whereas working long hours has become a crime in France. Commenting about the situation in France, a business writer noted that "at a time when employees around the globe toil more and more, France is cutting the legal workweek to 35 hours from 39, even for white-collar staff. And after decades of ignoring the working habits of this workaholic group of employees known in France as *cadres,* labor inspectors are clamping down on companies where managers, engineers and researchers burn the midnight oil." Those supporting control of work hours suggest that doing so would reduce France's overall unemployment rate. From the strategic management perspective, the point is that a French company seeking to establish an operation in the United States and a U.S. firm attempting

The number of female workers is an important indicator of increased workforce diversity. In Japan, women now account for approximately 44 percent of the workforce.

to do the same in France should fully understand the effects of the sociocultural environment on expectations they can have of employees.[69]

Describing a culture's effect on a society, columnist George Will suggested that it is vital for people to understand that a nation's culture has a primary effect on its social character and health.[70] Thus, companies must understand the implications of a society's attitudes and its cultural values before they can expect to offer goods and services that will meet consumers' needs and interests.

As mentioned earlier, a significant trend in many countries is increased diversity of the workforce. The number of female workers is an important indicator of increasing workforce diversity, and women are a valuable source of highly productive employees. Some argue, for example, that "educated hardworking women double the talent pool in the U.S. and give the nation a big competitive advantage over countries that deny women full participation in their economies."[71] However, across multiple global workforces, women comprise an increasing percentage of employees. In the United States, women now account for approximately 47 percent of the workforce. In Sweden, they account for roughly 52 percent, in Japan 44 percent, in France 40 percent, in Germany 41 percent, and in Mexico 37 percent. In the United States, women hold 43 percent of the managerial jobs. In Sweden, women hold 17 percent of managerial positions, while in Japan, the figure is only 9.4 percent.[72]

In some instances, women hold high-profile executive positions. For example, three women now head one-half of General Motors' six vehicle divisions. Describing these executives' talent, the president for GM's North American operations suggested that they have the insights and skills required to make General Motors a successful company in the global economy.[73] Overall, though, women fill just 11.9 percent of senior executive positions in *Fortune* 500 companies.[74] Especially in terms of the CEO position, very limited progress is being made.[75] However, the number of women serving as members of the board of directors for *Fortune* 500 companies has increased substantially, as have their profiles.[76]

Pay differentials between men and women still exist, too, although because of equal pay and equal opportunity legislation in many countries, relative pay for women is increasing continuously. In Western European countries, the pay gap between men and women is greatest in the United Kingdom, where men earn 34 percent more than women do, and lowest in Sweden, where a 17-percent gap exists.[77]

The influx of women into the workforce and the increasing ethnic and cultural diversity yield exciting challenges and significant opportunities.[78] Included among these are the needs to combine the best of both men's and women's leadership styles for a firm's benefit and identify ways to facilitate all employees' contributions to their firms. An example of a firm attempting to meet these challenges and take advantage of such opportunities is Avon, where 4 of 11 board members and more than 40 percent of global managers are women and Andrea Jung was appointed CEO.[79] Some companies now provide training to nurture women's and ethnic minorities' leadership potential. Changes in organizational structure and management practices often are required to eliminate subtle barriers that may exist. Learning to manage diversity in the domestic workforce can increase a firm's effectiveness in managing a globally diverse workforce, as the firm acquires more international operations. These commitments to promote and manage diversity produce enhance the firm's performance.

Another manifestation of changing attitudes toward work is the continuing growth of contingency workers (part-time, temporary, and contract employees) throughout the global economy. Parts of the world in which this trend is significant include Canada, Japan, Latin America, Western Europe, and the United States. The fastest growing segment of contingency workers is in the technical and professional area. Because of tight labor markets for technical and professional workers, agencies providing contingency workers to companies are offering multiple inducements to those they hire. Snelling Personnel Services, for example, offers points to their employees for hours worked. The points can be used to purchase items from a gift catalog.[80] In Japan, analysts believe that the entire service sector, including the part dealing with contingency workers, is going to grow substantially. Creating this growth are corporate restructurings and a breakdown of lifetime employment practices. Pasona, Japan's largest temporary staffing agency, is moving quickly to take advantage of increasing demand for its services.[81]

Participating often in the workforce as contingency workers, cross-border electronic telecommuters are an interesting sociocultural trend. "Commuting" frequently from developing countries to work in developed countries, the number of electronic telecommuters is expected to increase rapidly in the 21st century. This work-style option is feasible because of changes in the technological segment, including the Internet's rapid growth and evolution.[82]

The Technological Segment

Pervasive and diversified in scope, technological changes affect many parts of societies. Their effects occur primarily through new products, processes, and materials. The **technological segment** includes the institutions and activities involved with creating new knowledge and translating that knowledge into new outputs, products, processes, and materials.

The **technological segment** includes the institutions and activities involved with creating new knowledge and translating that knowledge into new outputs, products, processes, and materials.

The knowledge and capabilities that are created by developing or using new technologies sometimes transform or revitalize an entire industry. This appears to be the case with the yo-yo. Stuck in an up-and-down cycle since being introduced in the United States in 1930, yo-yos have benefited from a technological innovation that created a demand which exceeds the industry's supply capacity. Recently, yo-yos were the second-largest-selling toy in the United States, behind only Beanie Babies. The transaxle, which is a sleeve around the yo-yo axle that reduces friction, is the technology contributing to the yo-yo's increase in popularity. This technology makes it possible for average users to easily perform more complicated tricks, such as the "long sleeper," in which the yo-yo spins at the bottom of the string for at least 15 seconds. The original technology allowed only "masters" to perform the trick.[83]

Given the rapid pace of technological change, it is vital for firms to study the technological segment quickly and thoroughly. The importance of such efforts is suggested by the finding that firms which are early adopters of new technology often achieve higher market shares and earn higher returns. Thus, executives must verify that their firm is continuously scanning the external environments to identify potential substitutes for technologies that are in current use, as well as to spot newly emerging technologies from which their firm could derive competitive benefits.[84]

As mentioned in Chapter 1 and highlighted in other chapters throughout the book, the Internet is a technology with important strategic implications for firms of all types and sizes. Sometimes referred to as "the information superhighway," the connectivity among different technologies and media that the Internet makes possible is thought by many to be at least as significant as were the changes brought about by the Industrial Revolution.[85]

Numerous surveys suggest that executives are aware of the Internet's potential. A survey completed by Booz Allen & Hamilton in partnership with *The Economist* revealed that (1) 92 percent of executives who participated in the survey believed that the Internet would continue to reshape their companies' markets, (2) 61 percent thought that effective use of the Internet would facilitate efforts to achieve their firms' strategic goals, and (3) 30 percent noted that their competitive strategies had already been altered because of the Internet's influence.[86] The growing number of college and university students pursuing degrees in electronic commerce suggests that tomorrow's businesspeople also recognize the Internet's importance and potential.[87] In contrast, the results of a survey of manufacturing executives suggests an opposite reaction: These respondents believe that on-line sales growth through 2003 will not be enough for the Internet to become a major force in the manufacturing industry. Commenting about the survey results, an industry analyst suggested that the manufacturing CEOs may be "missing the boat" in terms of the Internet's potential and influence.[88]

Among other valuable uses, the Internet is an excellent source of data and information for a firm to use in understanding its external environment. Using the Internet for this purpose supports the firm's efforts to complete an effective external environmental analysis. Access to experts on such topics as chemical engineering and semiconductor manufacturing, to the Library of Congress, and even to satellite photographs is available through the Internet. Other information available through this incredibly powerful and significant technology includes Security and Exchange Commission (SEC) filings, Commerce Department data, information from the Bureau of the Census, new patent filings, and stock market updates.

As a technology, the Internet is used to conduct business transactions between companies, as well as between a company and its customers. In late 1999, e-commerce between businesses accounted for the bulk (approximately 84 percent) of all Internet transactions. Projected to increase to 92 percent by 2003, the total value of business-to-business on-line commerce is expected to reach $1.3 trillion in the same year. This figure substantially dwarfs the estimated $108 billion in goods and services companies will sell on-line to consumers in 2003.[89] As an indication of the uncertainty associated with understanding how rapidly Internet business transactions with consumers will grow, another firm predicts that "the global consumer market for products and services ordered over the Internet may balloon to $380 billion by 2003."[90] The differences in these projections of Internet sales to consumers in 2003 ($108 billion versus $380 billion) could have important strategic implications (e.g., in terms of opportunities and threats) for firms competing in a variety of industries.

According to Dell Computer Corporation's CEO Michael Dell, the Internet also has great potential as a business-organization system. We discussed this point briefly in Chapter 1, where we noted that Dell reduces its paperwork flow, schedules its payments more efficiently, and is able to coordinate its inventories efficiently and effectively through the use of this technology. Dell Computer Corporation accomplishes all of this by linking personal computers with network servers, which the firm's CEO believes have the potential to revolutionize business processes "in a way that blurs traditional boundaries between supplier and manufacturer, and manufacturer and customer. This will eliminate paper-based functions, flatten organization hierarchies, and shrink time and distance to a degree not possible before."[91] Thus, a competitive premium may accrue to the company that is capable of deriving full value from the Internet in terms of both e-commerce activities and transactions taken to process the firm's workflow.

When coupled with Michael Dell's opinion, the sales volume data presented in the previous paragraph suggest that the Internet's power is recognized by today's successful firms, as well as by those seeking to enter an industry or to compete in ways that define a new market space.[92] Some companies are using the Internet to create new market space in the global music industry. It may be that digital distribution of music via the Internet will account for at least 8 percent ($4 billion in sales volume) of all recorded music sold worldwide in 2004 and up to 20 percent by 2010.[93] Some analysts believe that these expectations are stimulating the music industry to recognize the Internet as the key driver of its global future.[94] These examples suggest that companies which understand the Internet's potential and the business opportunities it creates embrace change and seek to use the Internet to increase their flexibility so that they can move rapidly when engaging in marketplace competition.[95]

The Global Segment

The **global segment** includes relevant new global markets, existing ones that are changing, important international political events, and critical cultural and institutional characteristics of global markets.

The **global segment** includes relevant new global markets, existing ones that are changing, important international political events, and critical cultural and institutional characteristics of global markets. Although the segments we have examined so far are analyzed in terms of their domestic and global implications, some additional specific global factors should be analyzed as well. For example, firms must attempt to identify critical new global markets, as well as those that are changing. Many global markets (e.g., those in some South American nations and in South Korea and Taiwan) are becoming borderless and integrated.[96] In addition to contemplating opportunities, firms should recognize potential threats in these countries and their marketplaces.

As explained in the Strategic Focus about Dell Computer Corporation, China is a nation with a business environment with both opportunities and threats. Creating additional opportunities is China's recent admission to the World Trade Organization (WTO). A Geneva-based organization, the WTO establishes rules for global trade.

China's membership in this organization suggests the possibility of increasing and less-restricted participation by the country in the global economy.[97] In return for gaining entry to the WTO, China agreed to cut duties on foreign goods from 22.1 percent to an average of 17 percent. Trade barriers were reduced in multiple industries, including telecommunications, banking, automobiles, movies, and professional services (e.g., the services of lawyers, physicians, and accountants).[98] The immediate reaction to the reduced barriers in China was positive among a host of countries. However, caution was also expressed, because most of the terms to which China agreed in order to gain entry to the WTO were to be phased in over roughly a five-year period. Also, an analyst noted that conducting business in China would challenge firms throughout the world, as China's environment and markets are "very unique" and really beyond easy comparison.[99]

Following an analysis of the conditions in the external environment and their implications, Dell decided to apply its direct business model in a market that skeptics suggested would not respond favorably to it. However, Dell thought that China was a market with potential that simply could not be overlooked, and therefore, deciding to compete in China was a strategic decision with acceptable risk.

The commitment to carefully evaluate its external environment before making strategic decisions is part of the pattern Dell follows when using its direct business model. The firm believes that its external environment is composed of a group of factors (e.g., general economic and industry conditions; competitors; international activities; product, customer, and geographic mixes; and seasonal trends) that are beyond its direct control. As a result, Dell examines these factors intensely to identify opportunities and threats.[100]

Firms must also have a reasonable understanding of the different sociocultural and institutional attributes of global markets in which they do compete or in which they hope to compete. Dell Computer Corporation, for example, continues to study China's political/legal and economic structures, as well as the attitudes and values that form and influence the nation's evolving culture.

Companies operating in South Korea must understand the value placed on hierarchical order, formality, and self-control, as well as on duty rather than rights. Furthermore, Korean ideology emphasizes communitarianism, a characteristic of many Asian countries. Korea's approach differs from those of Japan and China with its focus on *Inhwa*, or harmony. Inhwa is based on a respect of hierarchical relationships and an obedience to authority. Alternatively, the approach in China stresses *Guanxi*—personal relationships or good connections, while in Japan, the focus is on *Wa*, or group harmony and social cohesion.[101] The institutional context of Korea suggests a major emphasis on centralized planning by the government. Indeed, the emphasis placed on growth by many South Korean firms is the result of a government policy to promote economic growth.[102]

A key objective of analyzing the general environment is identifying anticipated significant changes and trends among external elements. With a focus on the future, the analysis of the general environment allows firms to identify opportunities and threats. Also critical to a firm's future operations is an understanding of its industry environment and its competitors; these issues are considered next.

Dell's Direct Business Model Leads to Strategic Success in China

According to a business writer, "One thing's for certain: The Dell model is working in China. And as long as China's PC market continues to grow, Dell is ready to grow with it—provided it sticks to that model and continues to execute it better than anyone else."

Dell's success in China is being achieved in spite of economic conditions that some believe are unfavorable. Examples of these conditions include the fact that only 40 percent of China's industrial output comes from private ventures and the reality that China suffers from a number of the symptoms that contributed to the trouble of neighboring Asian countries during the latter part of the 1990s. These symptoms include government interference with the economy and a host of traditional personal business arrangements that often require padding of egos and wallets. What is the Dell model, and why does it allow the firm to succeed when confronting conditions that do not necessarily predict success?

Commenting about Dell's origins, one writer noted that "Michael Dell began in 1984 with a simple business insight: he could bypass the dealership channel through which personal computers were then being sold. Instead, he would sell directly to customers and build products to order." Using this model, Dell has become the world's leading direct computer systems company, with recent annual revenues of over $22 billion. As the largest seller of personal computers in the United States, Dell does approximately two-thirds of its business with large corporations, government agencies, and educational institutions.

Manufacturing facilities are located in Round Rock, Texas; Nashville, Tennessee; Limerick, Ireland; Penang, Malaysia; and Xiamen, China. The company's direct business model allows it to sell personal computer systems directly to the consumer. Innovative when initially developed, the model allows Dell to better understand consumers' requirements and to reduce costs by eliminating the need for a group of wholesale and retail dealers between the firm and its customers. The model also allows Dell to maintain extremely low inventory levels of component parts, as it custom-manufactures products according to individual customers' specifications.

Dell's business transactions through the Internet continue to expand. The firm maintains country-specific sites in close to 50 countries. In the last quarter of 1999, Internet sales exceeded $14 million daily. Convinced that the Internet was turbocharging his firm's business, founder Michael Dell wants at least 50 percent of total revenue to be from Internet sales by the end of 2000.

An economy with huge potential, China was already the world's fifth largest PC market (behind the United States, Japan, Germany, and Britain) at the start of the 21st century. Along with competitors such as Compaq, IBM, and Hewlett-Packard, Dell concluded that the Chinese PC market was simply too large to ignore. Avoiding the consumer retail market (almost two years of a citizen's savings are required to buy a PC in China), Dell decided to sell directly to corporations instead. In contrast, its U.S.-based competitors relied largely on resellers. Avoiding the costs of middlemen, Dell believed that it could deliver products to customers at lower, more competitive prices. The fact that Dell's Chinese market share tripled in 1999 to 1.2 percent, while Compaq's declined from 3.5 to 2.7 percent, and the firm's ability to become the eighth largest PC seller in China in a mere eight months may be preliminary evidence supporting this belief.

To the surprise of competitors and analysts alike, Dell learned quickly how to sell to China's state-owned enterprises (SOEs). Contributing to this success was Dell's ability to gain support from these firms' chief information officers—company officials who were found to place high value on the speed, convenience, and service associated with Dell's products. In addition, Dell's salespeople learned that information managers in SOEs were far more "tech-savvy" than originally thought. Because of their increasing ability to solve many of their own technical problems, these managers and those working for them did not need the extensive (and more expensive) technical service support offered by Dell's competitors. In the words of Xiao Jian Yi, deputy general manager of China Pacific Insurance (a fast-growing state-owned insurance company), "We may still need some consulting services, but in our front offices we know how to choose our equipment." Speaking to Dell's advantages, Yi indicated that "Dell provides exactly what we need, and with Dell we can choose exactly what we want."

As noted by analysts, Dell intends to continue relying on the direct business model as it pursues strategic success: "By taking its direct business model and its associated customer experience to even higher levels, through the Internet and value-added services, Dell intends to continue to grow its business at a multiple of the high-growth rate anticipated for the computer-systems industry as a whole. Dell still has significant opportunity for expansion in all parts of the world, especially in markets outside of the U.S." Continuous scanning, monitoring, forecasting, and assessing of its external environment will help Dell identify opportunities for using the direct business model. In addition, these activities will help Dell identify conditions indicating that the model should be adapted to cope successfully with shifts in one or more of the external environment's segments.

SOURCES: N. Chowdhury, 1999, Dell cracks China, *Fortune,* June 21, 120–124; Dell Computer Corporation, 2000, January 17, *www.dell.com*; L. Kraar, 1999, Five Chinese myths, *Fortune,* May 10, 30; M. B. Regan, 1999, Industries adjust to e-commerce, *Waco Tribune-Herald,* April 11, B6, B7; J. Magretta, 1998, The power of virtual integration: An interview with Dell Computer's Michael Dell, *Harvard Business Review,* 76(2): 73–84.

Industry Environment Analysis

An **industry** is a group of firms producing products that are close substitutes.

An **industry** is a group of firms producing products that are close substitutes. In the course of competition, these firms influence one another. Typically, industries include a rich mix of competitive strategies that companies use in pursuing strategic competitiveness and above-average returns. In part, these strategies are chosen because of the influence of the effects of an industry's characteristics.[103] Some believe that technology-based industries in which e-commerce is a dominant means of competing differ from their more traditional predecessors. An important difference may be the virtually free exchange of information among e-commerce firms, partly to seek advice about how to improve their firms' operations. With a "communal bent," the belief is that sharing information allows each firm to learn how to improve its competitiveness.[104]

Compared to the general environment, the industry environment has a more direct effect on strategic competitiveness and above-average returns. The intensity of industry competition and an industry's profit potential (as measured by the long-run return on invested capital) are a function of five competitive forces: the threats posed by new entrants, suppliers, buyers, product substitutes, and the intensity of rivalry among competitors (see Figure 2.2).

The five forces model of competition expands the arena for competitive analysis. Historically, when studying the competitive environment, firms concentrated on companies with which they competed directly. However, today competition is viewed as a grouping of alternative ways for customers to obtain the value they desire, rather than as a battle among direct competitors. This is particularly important, because in recent years industry boundaries have become blurred. For example, in the electrical utilities industry, cogenerators, firms that also produce power, are competing with regional utility companies. Moreover, telecommunications companies now compete with broadcasters, software manufacturers also provide personal financial services, airlines sell mutual funds, and automakers sell insurance and provide financing.[105] In addition, to focus on customers rather than specific industry boundaries to define markets, geographic boundaries should be considered. The reason for this is that research evidence suggests that different geographic markets for the same product can have considerably different competitive conditions.[106]

The five forces model recognizes that suppliers could become a firm's competitor (by integrating forward), as could buyers (by integrating backward). The former strategy was illustrated graphically in the pharmaceuticals industry when Merck & Company acquired Medco Containment Services, a mail-order pharmacy and prescription benefits management company. In so doing, Merck integrated forward and became a competitor of other pharmacies and prescription benefits management companies.

2.2 | The Five Forces Model of Competition

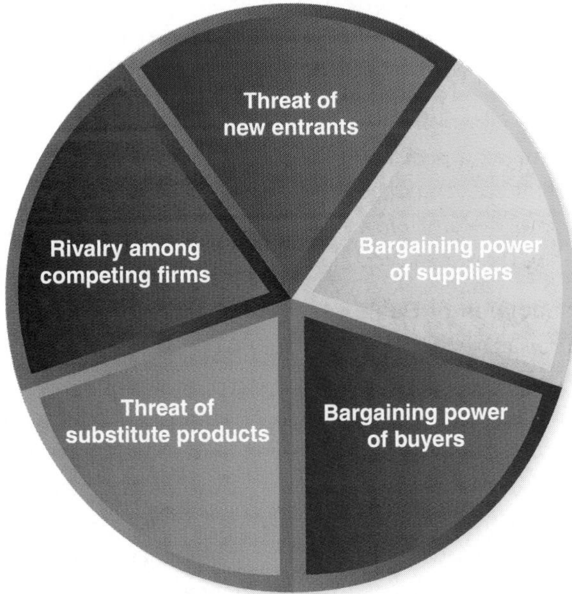

Perhaps most importantly, Merck guaranteed a major source of distribution for its products. Shortly after Merck's acquisition, SmithKline Beecham and Eli Lilly announced plans to acquire similar companies and integrate forward as well.[107] In addition, firms choosing to enter a new market and those producing products that are adequate substitutes for existing products could become competitors of a company.

Threat of New Entrants

Evidence suggests that companies have always found it difficult to identify new competitors.[108] This is unfortunate, in that new entrants often have the potential to be quite threatening to incumbents. One reason new entrants pose such a threat is that they bring additional production capacity. Unless the demand for a good or service is increasing, additional capacity holds consumers' costs down, resulting in less revenue and lower returns for an industry's firms. Often, new entrants have substantial resources and a keen interest in gaining a large market share. As a result, new competitors may force existing firms to be more effective and efficient and to learn how to compete on new dimensions (e.g., an Internet-based distribution channel).

The likelihood that firms will enter an industry is a function of two factors: barriers to entry and the retaliation expected from current industry participants. When firms find entry into a new industry difficult or when firms are at a competitive disadvantage entering a new industry, *entry barriers* exist.

Facing limited entry barriers and apparently convinced that it has the resources and capabilities required to cope successfully with potential retaliatory actions, Sylvan Learning Systems, Inc., known initially for its chain of tutorial centers, is entering other parts of the education industry. Largely through acquisitions, Sylvan seeks to "choose very attractive niches in education, where we bring a special advantage, and then to become the major leadership force in that niche." One of the firm's recent acquisitions is a for-profit university in Spain. Using this university as a foothold, Sylvan intends to form a network of universities in 10 European and Latin American countries. As a learning conglomerate, Sylvan now offers intensive instruction in troubled schools, English classes for overseas executives, and computerized testing ranging from Scholastic Aptitude Tests to professional licensure exams.[109]

Barriers to Entry

Existing competitors try to develop barriers to market entry. In contrast, potential entrants seek markets in which the entry barriers are relatively insignificant. The absence of entry barriers increases the probability that a new entrant can operate profitably. There are several kinds of potentially significant entry barriers.

Economies of Scale. An important characteristic of each production technology, *economies of scale* are "the marginal improvements in efficiency that a firm experiences as it incrementally increases its size."[110] From an operational perspective, economies of scale mean that as the quantity of a product produced during a given period increases, the costs of manufacturing each unit decline.

Also mentioned in Chapter 4, the Vanguard Group, Inc., sells multiple types of investment instruments to many institutions and individuals. Critical to the firm's strategy is its "at-cost" structure. By selling ever larger numbers of its products while keeping its expense ratios low, Vanguard believes that it is able to deliver the benefits

Gap achieves economies of scale through marketing, manufacturing, research and development, and purchasing. Small-scale entries into Gap's market are at a cost disadvantage, while large-scale entries risk strong competitive retaliation.

of the economies of scale it generates through its operations to shareholders in the form of low expense ratios—ratios the firm claims to be among the lowest of any major mutual fund group. In 1998, for example, the firm's average net assets increased by 33 percent, while its operating expenses as a percentage of U.S. fund assets held steady at 0.28 percent.[111] However, as might be anticipated, Vanguard's success is causing competitors to seek ways to gain scale economies to reduce their own cost structures.[112]

Economies of scale can be gained through most business functions (e.g., marketing, manufacturing, research and development, and purchasing). New entrants face a dilemma when confronting current competitors' scale economies. Small-scale entry places them at a cost disadvantage. However, large-scale entry, in which the new entrant manufactures large volumes of a product to gain economies of scale, risks strong competitive retaliation.

Also important (e.g., for automobile manufacturers) are instances of current competitive realities that reduce the ability of economies of scale to create an entry barrier. Many companies now customize their products for large numbers of small customer groups. Customized products are not manufactured in the volumes necessary to achieve economies of scale. Rather, customization is made possible by new flexible manufacturing systems. In fact, the new manufacturing technology facilitated by advanced computerization has allowed the development of mass customization in some industries. Mass customized products can be individualized to the customer in a very short time (e.g., within a day). Mass customization may become the norm in manufacturing products.[113] Companies manufacturing customized products learn how to respond quickly to customers' desires, rather than developing scale economies.

Product Differentiation. Over time, customers may come to believe that a firm's product is unique. This belief can result from service to the customer, effective advertising campaigns, or the firm being the first to market a good or service. Companies such as Coca-Cola, PepsiCo, and the world's automobile manufacturers spend a great deal of money on advertising to convince potential customers of their products' distinctiveness. Customers valuing a product's uniqueness tend to become loyal to both the product and the company producing it. Typically, new entrants must allocate many resources across time to overcome customer loyalties. To combat the perception of uniqueness, new entrants frequently offer products at lower prices. Doing this, however, may result in lower profits or even losses.

Capital Requirements. Competing in a new industry requires resources to invest. In addition to physical facilities, capital is needed for inventories, marketing activities, and other critical business functions. Even when competing in a new industry is attractive, the capital required for successful market entry may not be available to pursue an apparent market opportunity.

Switching Costs. *Switching costs* are the one-time costs customers incur when buying from a different supplier. The costs of buying new ancillary equipment and of retraining employees, and even the psychic costs of ending a relationship, may be incurred in switching to a new supplier. In some cases, switching costs are low, such as when the consumer switches to a different soft drink. Switching costs can vary as a function of time. For example, in terms of hours toward graduation, the cost to a student to transfer from one university to another as a freshman is much lower than it is when the student is entering the senior year. Occasionally, a decision made by manufacturers to produce a new, innovative product creates high switching costs for the final consumer. This was the case for the consumer who had to decide to switch from cassette tapes to CDs and for the customer contemplating switching from analog to digital cellular telephones. If switching costs are high, a new entrant must offer either a substantially lower price or a much better product to attract buyers. Usually, the more established the relationship between parties, the greater is the cost incurred to switch to an alternative offering.

Access to Distribution Channels. Over time, industry participants can develop effective means of distributing products. Once a relationship with distributors is developed, firms nurture it in order to create switching costs for them.

Access to distribution channels can be a strong entry barrier for new entrants, particularly in consumer nondurable goods industries (e.g., in grocery stores, shelf space is limited). Thus, new entrants have to persuade distributors to carry their products, either in addition to or in place of those already being stocked. Price breaks and cooperative advertising allowances may be used for this purpose; however, those practices reduce the new entrant's profit potential. As explained in the Strategic Focus, Dell uses its distribution channels to create value for customers in China, as well as throughout the world. To maintain the direct business model's advantage, Dell nurtures relationships with its customers by offering them services and responding to their needs.

Cost Disadvantages Independent of Scale. In some instance, established competitors have cost advantages that new entrants cannot duplicate. Proprietary product technology, favorable access to raw materials, favorable locations, and government subsidies are examples. Successful competition requires new entrants to find ways to reduce the strategic relevance of these factors. Delivering purchases directly to the buyer can counter the favorable location's advantage; new food establishments in an undesirable location follow this practice. Similarly, automobile dealerships located in unattractive areas (e.g., in a city's downtown area) can provide superior service (e.g., picking up and returning the car to be serviced to the customer) to overcome a competitor's location advantage.

Government Policy. Through licensing and permit requirements, governments can control entry into an industry. Liquor retailing, banking, and trucking are examples of industries in which government decisions and actions affect entry possibilities. Also, governments restrict entry into some utility industries because of the need to provide quality service to all and the capital requirements necessary to do so.

Expected Retaliation

Firms seeking to enter an industry also anticipate the reactions of firms in the industry. An expectation of swift and vigorous responses reduces the likelihood of entry. Vigorous retaliation can be expected when the firm has a major stake in the industry (e.g., having fixed assets with few, if any, alternative uses), when it has substantial resources, and when industry growth is slow or constrained.

Locating market niches not being served by incumbents allows the new entrant to avoid entry barriers. Small entrepreneurial firms are generally best suited for searching out and serving neglected market segments. When Honda first entered the U.S. market, it concentrated on small-engine motorcycles, a market that firms such as Harley-Davidson ignored. By targeting this neglected niche, Honda avoided competition. After consolidating its position, Honda used its strength to attack rivals by introducing larger motorcycles and competing in the broader market. Competitive actions and responses between firms such as Honda and Harley-Davidson are discussed fully in Chapter 5.

Bargaining Power of Suppliers

Increasing prices and reducing the quality of products sold are potential means through which suppliers can exert power over firms competing within an industry. If a firm is unable to recover cost increases through its pricing structure, its profitability is reduced by its suppliers' actions. A supplier group is powerful when

- it is dominated by a few large companies and is more concentrated than the industry to which it sells;
- satisfactory substitute products are not available to industry firms;
- industry firms are not a significant customer for the supplier group;
- suppliers' goods are critical to buyers' marketplace success;
- the effectiveness of suppliers' products has created high switching costs for industry firms; and
- suppliers are a credible threat to integrate forward into the buyers' industry (for example, a clothing manufacturer might choose to operate its own retail outlets). Credibility is enhanced when suppliers have substantial resources and provide the industry's firms with a highly differentiated product.

As a result of its success, initially in its domestic market and now globally as well, Wal-Mart is an example of a company over which few suppliers have power. The sheer size of its purchases and the relatively low switching costs it faces when choosing among suppliers often combine to yield significant power for the firm. Consider the relationship between Wal-Mart and the formerly independent Rubbermaid (recently acquired by Newell). At one point, approximately 15 percent of Rubbermaid's revenues were accounted for by sales to Wal-Mart. As Wal-Mart's largest customer, and in light of Wal-Mart's willingness to purchase products from Sterilite, an increasingly viable competitor of Rubbermaid, Rubbermaid found itself in a relatively powerless position with its major customer. To reduce Wal-Mart's influence, Rubbermaid decided to try to sell more of its products to specialty retailers and through its own Web site. A relationship with Amway to sell its products gives Rubbermaid another channel that differs from those of traditional retailers such as Wal-Mart.[114]

Bargaining Power of Buyers

Firms seek to maximize the return on their invested capital. Buyers (customers of an industry or firm) want to buy products at the lowest possible price, at which the industry earns the lowest acceptable rate of return on its invested capital. To reduce their costs, buyers bargain for higher quality, greater levels of service, and lower prices. These outcomes are achieved by encouraging competitive battles among the industry's firms. Customers (buyer groups) are powerful when

- they purchase a large portion of an industry's total output;
- the produce being purchased from an industry accounts for a significant portion of the buyers' costs;
- they could switch to another product at little, if any, cost; and
- the industry's products are undifferentiated or standardized, and the buyers pose a credible threat if they were to integrate backward into the sellers' industry.

Iceland is a niche frozen-food retailer operating in the United Kingdom. Recently, the firm announced that it was banning the use of genetically modified ingredients to manufacture its private-label products. This decision was in reaction to consumer demands for products to be prepared with unaltered food items. A recent poll taken in the United Kingdom showed that "40 percent of people had no trust in what scientists said on the safety of modified food" and that 56 percent thought modified foods were unsafe to eat, more than double the percentage thinking them safe." Initially, competitors' reaction to Iceland's decision was one of disdain. Separating modified from unmodified crops, they alleged, was virtually impossible. However, only 13 months after Iceland took its action, some giant manufacturers, including Unilever and Nestlé, began to phase out gene-altered ingredients from their food stocks. Actions taken by these companies were perhaps influenced by the size of the consumer group expressing concerns about the safety of items made with genetically altered crops.[115] An individual buyer lacks the degree of influence necessary to produce these responses; collectively, however, a large group of food consumers can account for a significant portion of the food-manufacturing and retailer industries' output.

Armed with greater amounts of information about the manufacturer's costs and the power of the Internet as a shopping and distribution alternative, the consumer appears to be stimulating a shift in power in the automobile industry. One reason for this shift is that individual buyers incur virtually zero switching costs when they decide to purchase from one manufacturer rather than another or from one dealer as opposed to a second or third one. These conditions are forcing companies in the automobile industry to become more focused on the needs and desires of the people actually buying cars, trucks, minivans, and sport utility vehicles. To retain a more direct relationship with their customers and possibly to reduce the power of their buyers, automobile companies are acting swiftly. General Motors, for example, has developed a new national on-line buying service. Called GM BuyPower, this service gives customers access to every vehicle available through participating dealers, as well as to independent data about competing models.[116]

Threat of Substitute Products

Substitute products are different goods or services from outside a given industry that perform similar or the same functions as a product that the industry produces. For example, as a sugar substitute, Nutrasweet places an upper limit on sugar manufacturers' prices (i.e., Nutrasweet and sugar perform the same function, but with different

Barnes & Noble has been an established bookseller for many years. When faced with strong competition from on-line bookseller Amazon.com, it retaliated by establishing its own Web business.

characteristics). Other product substitutes include fax machines instead of overnight deliveries, plastic containers rather than glass jars, paper bags in place of plastic bags, and tea substituted for coffee.[117]

In general, product substitutes are a strong threat to a firm when customers face few, if any, switching costs and when the substitute product's price is lower or its quality and performance capabilities are equal to or greater than those of the competing product. Differentiating a product along dimensions that customers value (e.g., price, quality, service after the sale, and location) reduces a substitute's attractiveness.

Intensity of Rivalry among Competitors

Because an industry's firms are mutually dependent, actions taken by one company usually invite competitive retaliation. Thus, in many industries, firms compete actively and vigorously as they pursue strategic competitiveness and above-average returns. Competitive rivalry intensifies when a firm is challenged by a competitor's actions or when an opportunity to improve a market position is recognized. Visible dimensions on which rivalry is based include price, quality, and innovation. Typically, firms seek to differentiate their products from competitors' offerings in terms of dimensions that customers value and in which the firms have a competitive advantage. As explained in the Strategic Focus, the rivalry between competitors Amazon.com and Barnesandnoble.com has been intense. However, given Amazon.com's recent strategic decisions, the nature of the rivalry may change.

Patterns of competitive actions and reactions also occur in the entertainment industry. Seeking first-mover advantages (discussed in Chapter 5) through a service innovation, NBC recently unveiled a three-way deal that made it the first major entertainment group to spin off its Internet activities into a separately traded company. NBC Internet (NBCi) was a product of combining NBC's Web activities with those of

Amazon.com and Barnesandnoble.com: A Continuing Rivalry

With a mission of using the Internet to transform book buying into the fastest, easiest, and most enjoyable shopping experience possible, Amazon.com opened its electronic doors in July 1995. The firm is credited widely for virtually creating the on-line retailing industry.

Businesspeople and business analysts alike consider Amazon.com's growth to be phenomenal. This perspective is highlighted by the following commentary from a business writer: "Amazon's four-year rise from upstart on-line bookseller to one of the largest retailers on the Web is now legendary. The company has defined e-commerce as we know it." Amazon's path-breaking success and its competitive aggressiveness is captured by the term "getting Amazoned," which is used to describe what happens when a conventional business is damaged severely by an on-line competitor.

In contrast to Amazon.com, Barnes and Noble's (B&N's) origins are in the "bricks-and-mortar" portion of book retailing. B&N was started in 1965 with a $5,000 investment in one bookstore. Len Riggio purchased the company six years later. At the time, B&N was a single 100-year-old bookstore on lower Fifth Avenue in New York City. In the mid-1980s, Riggio acquired the B. Dalton chain with a loan and junk bond financing. With these units as a foundation, Riggio developed his concept of a superstore for a retail bookseller. The concept was framed around the belief that independent bookstores were too small to be efficient. By stocking thousands of titles and placing sofas and coffee bars in large stores, Riggio was able to transform the book-retailing industry. The concept worked, analysts believe, because it "not only attracted traditional readers but tapped a whole new market—those who purchase the 53 percent of American books sold through supermarkets, mail-order clubs, or large wholesalers like Wal-Mart." Recently, Barnes & Noble, Inc., operated over 520 B&N units, as well as over 470 B. Dalton bookstores. Offering books from more than 50,000 publisher imprints, and with an emphasis on small, independent publishers and university presses, the company provides access to more than a million titles.

Amazon.com quickly became a serious, yet different, type of competitor for B&N. Because of the success of Amazon.com—a company that some believe B&N views as its "dreaded enemy"—Barnes and Noble, Inc., established barnesandnoble.com in 1997. Claiming that its Web site was built by booksellers for book lovers, B&N considers its on-line retailing operation to be one of the world's largest and most focused on-line booksellers. When the on-line aspect of the company started, Steve Riggio, founder Len Riggio's brother, predicted that barnesandnoble.com would use its national brand identity, its superstores, and its publisher network to make a "quantum leap beyond the current level of online bookselling." Roughly two and one-half years after this prediction, data showed that Amazon.com commanded 75 percent of the on-line bookselling market, while barnesandnoble.com controlled only 15 percent. During the first 30 months or so of head-to-head competition, Amazon.com and barnesandnoble.com established a new rivalry in the marketplace. However, recent strategic decisions may change the nature and intensity of the rivalry.

Following a study of the external environment and its internal environment, Amazon.com decided that its future would differ from the firm's origins. In late 1999, founder and CEO Jeff Bezos observed that "sixteen months ago Amazon.com was a place where you could find books. Tomorrow Amazon.com will be a place where you can find anything." With this announcement, Amazon.com indicated its intention of being at the center of the e-commerce world. In Bezos's vision, customers will be able to use Amazon.com as a portal to purchase virtually any item—pet food, pharmaceuticals, flowers, tennis shoes, and banjos, as well as books and thousands of other items. In total, Amazon.com offers over half a million items on its sites. Almost any item can be found in this assortment. However, a line of respectability does exist—no live animals, no pornography, and no contraband. To reflect its capabilities in terms of e-commerce, Amazon.com claims to have "the Earth's Biggest Selection of products, including free electronic greeting cards, online auctions, and millions of books, CDs, videos, DVDs, toys and games and electronics."

B&N is keenly aware of competitor Amazon.com's intention of becoming the center of the e-commerce world. Seeing its competitor's decision as an opportunity, B&N quickly suggested that "as Amazon becomes the place to sell anything on-line, it presents an opportunity for barnesandnoble.com to own books" by gaining a larger share of the retail book market. The perceived opportunity to "own books" is highly consistent with the firm's original mission of "bringing books and bookstores into the mainstream of American life." Thus, future competition between Amazon.com and barnesandnoble.com will differ from what it has been in the past. The difference is a product of Amazon.com's desire to be at the center of the e-commerce universe, while barnesandnoble.com views its future as one in which it becomes the dominant portal for the delivery of information. While remaining highly competitive, the competition between these two on-line retailers may not be as direct and intense as it previously was.

SOURCES: K. Brooker, 1999, Amazon vs. everybody, *Fortune,* November 8, 120–128; D. Carvajal, 1999, Amazon asks court to clear use of Times Best-Seller lists, *New York Times,* June 5, C3; K. Li, 1999, Big wheels & (maybe) big deals, *Daily News,* July 12, 23; J. Oleck, 1999, *Business Week,* May 24, 6; J. McHugh, 1999, The $29 billion flea market, *Forbes,* November 1, 66–68; J. Robins, 1999, Media: Sell first, print later, *The Independent,* October 19, 13; W. St. John, 1999, Barnes & Noble's epiphany, *Wired,* June, 132–144; B. Stavro, 1999, The cutting edge special report: E-commerce, *Los Angeles Times,* September 30, 6; D. Streitfeld, 1999, Barnes & Noble looses marketing virus, *The Washington Post,* July 15, E5.

Xoom.com and Snap.com. This competitive action was expected to "intensify the race among Internet media and entertainment companies to combine their fragmented audiences into larger blocks by merging several Web sites under a single umbrella." In the high-technology industry in which it operates, NBC expected quick and significant responses from competitors.[118] With this transaction completed, over one-half the value of NBC is now in new media operations, in its cable channels (especially CNBC), and in NBCi.[119]

The remainder of this section describes the various factors influencing the *intensity* of the rivalry between firms.

Numerous or Equally Balanced Competitors

Intense rivalries are common in industries with many companies. With multiple competitors, it is common for a few firms to believe that they can take actions without eliciting a response. However, evidence suggests that other firms generally are aware of competitors' actions, often choosing to respond to them. At the other extreme, industries with only a few firms of equivalent size and power also tend to have much rivalry. The large and often similar-sized resource bases of these firms permit vigorous actions and responses. The competitive battles between fast-food chains (e.g., McDonald's vs. Burger King) and footwear companies (e.g., Nike vs. Reebok) exemplify intense rivalries between relatively equivalent competitors.

Slow Industry Growth

When a market is growing, firms try to use resources effectively to serve an expanding customer base. Growing markets reduce pressures on firms to take customers from competitors. However, rivalry in nongrowth or slow-growth markets becomes more intense as firms battle to increase their market shares by attracting competitors' customers.

Typically, battles to protect market shares are fierce. Certainly, this has been the case with Amazon.com and barnesandnoble.com. The instability in the market that results from these competitive engagements reduces profitability for firms throughout the industry, as is demonstrated by the fast-food industry. Relative to past performance, the market for the industry's products in the United States is growing more slowly. To expand market share, fast-food companies (e.g., McDonald's, Burger King, and Wendy's) compete aggressively in terms of pricing strategies, the introduction of new products, and product and service differentiation. Promoting products through low-pricing options (e.g., 99-cent items) appeals to customers and may increase a firm's market share; however, these actions tend to reduce profits for individual firms, and they make it difficult for all competitors to stabilize their promotions around price categories that create profits.

High Fixed Costs or High Storage Costs

When fixed costs account for a large part of total costs, companies try to maximize the use of their productive capacity. Doing this allows the company to spread costs across a larger volume of output. However, when many firms attempt to maximize their productive capacity, excess capacity is created on an industrywide basis. To then reduce inventories, individual companies typically cut the price of their product and offer rebates and other special discounts to customers. These practices, however, often intensify competition. The pattern of excess capacity at the industry level followed by intense rivalry at the firm level is observed frequently in industries with high storage costs. Perishable products, for example, lose their value rapidly with the passage of time. As their inventories grow, producers of perishable goods often use pricing strategies to sell products quickly.

Lack of Differentiation or Low Switching Costs

When buyers find a differentiated product that satisfies their needs, they frequently purchase the product loyally over time. Industries with many companies that have successfully differentiated their products are less rivalrous, resulting in less competition for individual firms.[120] However, when buyers view products as commodities (i.e., as products with few differentiated features or capabilities), rivalry intensifies. In these instances, buyers' purchasing decisions are based primarily on price and, to a lesser degree, service.

The effect of switching costs is identical to that described for differentiated products. The lower the buyers' switching costs, the easier it is for competitors to attract buyers (through pricing and service offerings). High switching costs, however, at least partially insulate the firm from rivals' efforts to attract customers.

Capacity Augmented in Large Increments

In some industries (e.g., in the manufacture of vinyl chloride and chlorine), the competitive importance of economies of scale dictates that production capacity be added only on a large-scale basis. Substantial increases in capacity can be disruptive to a balance between industry supply and demand. Price cutting is often used to bring supply and demand back into balance. Achieving balance this way, though, has a negative effect on a firm's profitability.

Diverse Competitors

Not all companies seek to accomplish the same goals, nor do they operate with identical cultures. These differences make it difficult to identify an industry's competitive rules. Moreover, with greater diversity, it becomes increasingly difficult to be aware of the primary outcomes a competitor seeks through industry competition. Diversity among firms sometimes causes a company to take certain competitive actions just to see what competitors' responses will be. Doing this can improve the firm's ability to predict competitors' future actions.

High Strategic Stakes

Competitive rivalry is more intense when achieving success in a particular industry is important to many companies. For example, the success of a diversified firm in one industry may influence its effectiveness in other industries. This can be the case when the firm uses a related diversification corporate-level strategy (Chapter 6 presents a detailed discussion of this strategy).

High strategic stakes can also exist in terms of geographic locations. For example, Japanese automobile manufacturers are committed to a significant presence in the U.S. marketplace. A key reason for this is that the United States is the world's single largest market for auto manufacturers' products. Because of the stakes involved in this country for Japanese and U.S. manufacturers, rivalry among firms in the U.S. and global automobile industry is highly intense.

High Exit Barriers

Sometimes companies continue competing in an industry even though the returns on their invested capital are low or negative. Firms making this choice face high exit barriers, which include economic, strategic, and emotional factors causing companies to remain in an industry when the profitability of doing so is questionable. Common exit barriers are

- specialized assets (assets with values linked to a particular business or location);
- fixed costs of exit (e.g., labor agreements);
- strategic interrelationships (relationships of mutual dependence between one business and other parts of a company's operations, such as shared facilities and access to financial markets);
- emotional barriers (aversion to economically justified business decisions because of fear for one's own career, loyalty to employees, and so forth); and

- government and social restrictions. Common outside the United States, these restrictions often are based on government concerns for job losses and regional economic effects.

Interpreting Industry Analyses

Effective industry analyses are products of careful study and interpretation of data and information from multiple sources. A wealth of industry-specific data is available for analyzing an industry. Because of globalization, international markets and rivalries must be included in the firm's analyses. In fact, research shows that in some industries, international variables are more important than domestic ones as determinants of strategic competitiveness. Furthermore, because of the development of global markets, a country's borders no longer bound industry structures.[121]

Following study of the five industry forces, a firm has the insights required to determine an industry's attractiveness in terms of the potential to earn adequate or superior returns on its invested capital. In general, the stronger competitive forces are, the lower the profit potential for an industry's firms. An *unattractive industry* has low entry barriers, suppliers and buyers with strong bargaining positions, strong competitive threats from product substitutes, and intense rivalry among competitors. These industry characteristics make it very difficult for firms to achieve strategic competitiveness and earn above-average returns. Alternatively, an attractive industry has high entry barriers, suppliers and buyers with little bargaining power, few competitive threats from product substitutes, and relatively moderate rivalry.[122]

Strategic Groups

The term *strategic group* is used to capture competitive patterns that are visible across a set of firms competing against each other either on an industrywide basis or within a segment (e.g., a set of customers with unique needs) of an industry. The term originated when a researcher discovered that not all firms within the same industry were using the same strategy. This finding was a bit surprising, in that conventional wisdom at the time was that an industry's characteristics forced firms to compete in the same way (we talk about this view in greater detail in Chapter 3). Groups of firms following similar strategies were labeled strategic groups.[123] Formally, a **strategic group** is "a group of firms in an industry following the same or a similar strategy along the same strategic dimensions."[124] Examples of strategic dimensions that firms in a strategic group treat similarly or identically include the extent of technological leadership, the degree of product quality, pricing policies, the choice of distribution channels, and the degree and type of customer service the firms offer. Evidence suggests that "organizations in a strategic group occupy similar positions in the market, offer similar goods to similar customers, and may also make similar choices about production technology and other organizational features."[125] Thus, membership in a particular strategic group defines the essential characteristics of the firm's strategy.[126] The strategies of firms within a group are similar, but they differ from strategies being implemented by companies in the industry's other strategic groups.

A **strategic group** is a group of firms in an industry following the same or a similar strategy along the same strategic dimensions.

The notion of strategic groups is popular for analyzing an industry's competitive structure.[127] Contributing to its popularity is the assertion that strategic group analysis is a basic framework that should be used in diagnosing competition, positioning, and the profitability of firms within an industry.[128]

The use of strategic groups for analyzing industry structure requires that dimensions relevant to the firms' performances within an industry (e.g., price and image) be selected. Plotting companies along these dimensions helps to identify groups of firms competing in similar ways. For example, there are unique radio markets because consumers prefer different music formats, as well as different kinds of programming (news hours, talk radio, and so forth). It is estimated that approximately 30 different radio formats exist. These formats suggest 30 strategic groups. Typically, a format is created through choices made regarding music or nonmusic style, scheduling, and announcer style.[129] The strategies within each of the 30 formats are similar, while the strategies across the total set of formats are dissimilar.

Strategic groups have several implications. Because firms within a group are selling similar products to the same customers, the competitive rivalry among them can be intense. The more intense the rivalry, the greater is the threat to each firm's profitability. Second, the strengths of the five competitive forces (i.e., the threats posed by new entrants, suppliers, buyers, and product substitutes, and the intensity of rivalry among competitors) differ across strategic groups. Third, the closer the strategic groups are in terms of strategies followed and dimensions emphasized, the greater is the likelihood of rivalry between the groups. For example, two radio stations with a classical music format, but different announcer styles, are relatively close competitors, so the rivalry between them in a local market could be intense.

The Value of Strategic Group Analysis

Opinions vary about the value of strategic group analysis as a tool for understanding industry dynamics and structure. Some even argue that there is no convincing evidence that strategic groups exist or that a firm's financial performance is influenced by membership within a certain strategic group.[130] Another criticism is that studying the actions of companies within a strategic group may not yield any information that would not be captured by analyzing an entire industry and individual firms within it. However, recent research shows that there is "limited evidence that a rigorous search for strategic groups may prove fruitful."[131] This evidence suggests that caution should be taken in studying strategic groups, but that the analysis can help a firm in efforts to understand the industry in which it competes and to identify its most relevant competitors. Thus, as with all tools, the benefits and limitations of strategic group analysis should be recognized before the firm uses it to better understand an industry's structure.

Competitor Analysis

The *competitor environment* is the final part of the external environment requiring study. Competitor analysis focuses on each company against whom a firm competes directly. Important in all industries, competitor analyses are conducted energetically by companies competing in an industry with just a few companies possessing relatively equal capabilities. For example, Nike and Reebok are keenly interested in understanding each other's objectives, strategies, assumptions, and capabilities, as are Coca-Cola and PepsiCo. Furthermore, intense rivalry and desires to understand competitors characterize industries in which supply exceeds demand, such as retailing. A business writer suggested that U.S. "retailers are in the throes of a crisis. There are too many retail outlets and too few consumers—experts estimate 20% to 30% excess retail capacity—and the competition for eyes, ears, and dollars is downright savage." To better understand both competitors' customers and their own, some prominent retailers (e.g., Coca-Cola, General Mills, McDonald's, Burger King, and Starbucks) are using the services of Envirosell.[132] Viewing themselves as a group of "retail anthropologists," employees of Envirosell physically observe tens of thousands of shoppers across firms to determine why they buy what they buy. Thus, when engaged in a competitor analysis, the firm seeks to understand

- what drives the competitor, as shown by its *future objectives;*
- what the competitor is doing and can do, as is revealed by its *current strategy;*
- what the competitor believes about itself and the industry, as shown by its *assumptions;* and
- what the competitor's capabilities are, as shown by its *capabilities.*[133]

Information about these four issues helps the firm prepare an anticipated response profile for each competitor (see Figure 2.3). Thus, the results of an effective competitor analysis help a firm understand, interpret, and predict its competitors' actions and initiatives.[134]

Critical to effective competitor analysis is the gathering of data and information that can help the firm understand competitors' intentions and the strategic implications resulting from them.[135] Useful data and information combine to form **competitor intelligence:** the set of data and information the firm gathers to better understand and better anticipate competitors' objectives, strategies, assumptions, and capabilities.[136] In competitor analysis, the firm should gather intelligence not only about its competitors, but also regarding public policies in countries across the world. Intelligence about public policies "provides an early warning of threats and opportunities emerging from the global public policy environment, and analyzes how they will affect the achievement of the company's strategy."[137] Through effective competitive and public policy intelligence, the firm gains the insights it requires to help create a competitive advantage and to increase the quality of the strategic decisions it makes when choosing how to compete against its major rivals.[138]

Competitor intelligence is the ethical gathering of needed information and data about competitors' objectives, strategies, assumptions, and capabilities

Firms should follow generally accepted ethical practices in gathering competitor intelligence. Industry associations often develop lists of these practices that firms can adopt. Practices considered both legal and ethical include (1) obtaining publicly available information (e.g., court records, competitors' help-wanted advertisements, annual reports, financial reports of publicly held corporations, and Uniform Commercial Code filings), and (2) attending trade fairs and shows to obtain competitors' brochures, view their exhibits, and listen to discussions about their products. In contrast, certain practices (e.g., blackmail, trespassing, eavesdropping, and stealing drawings, samples, or documents) are viewed widely as unethical and often are illegal.

FIGURE 2.3 | Competitor Analysis Components

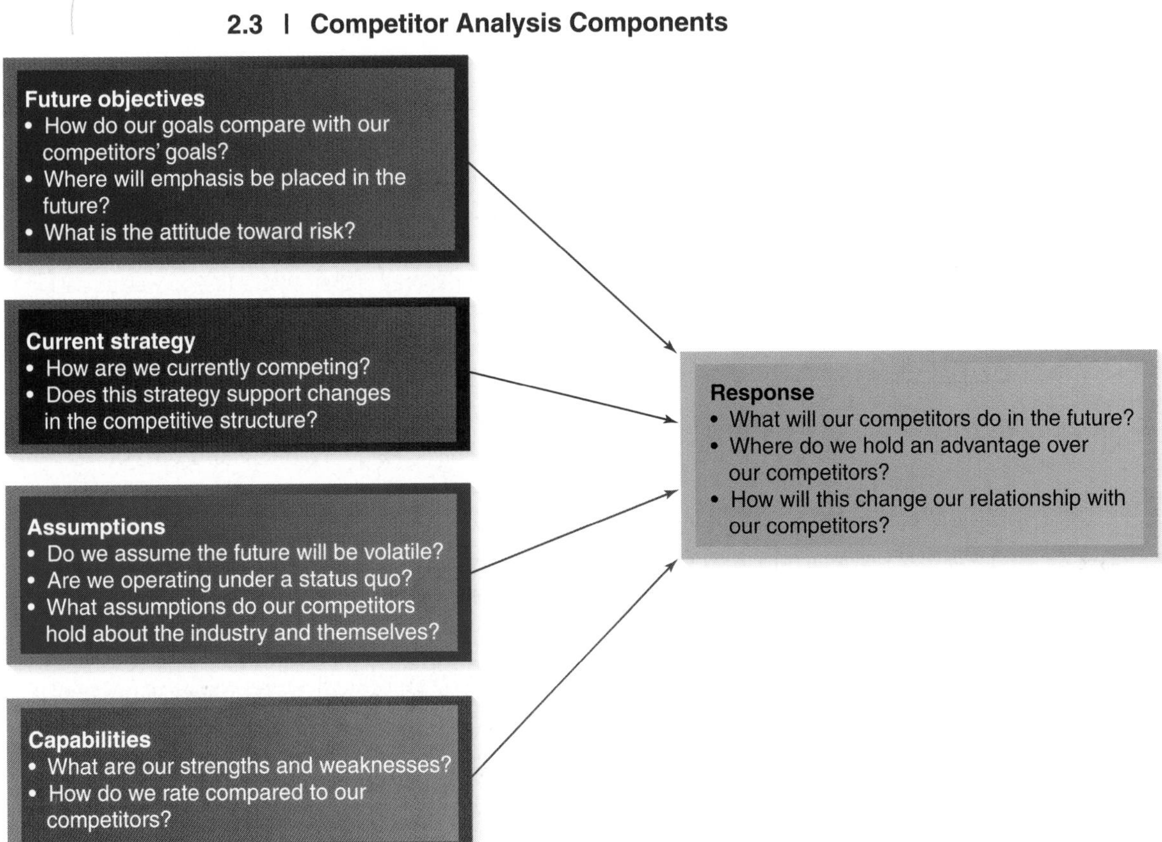

Breaking into PCs used by a competitor's personnel is an example of an illegal intelligence-gathering activity. In spite of this, the frequency with which such activity occurs seems to be increasing. A variant of this practice is trying to read the screen on a person's laptop computer during an airplane flight. Aware of the practice, a media consultant who travels frequently loads an interesting file if he finds that another person is trying to read his laptop's screen. The message reads, "If you can read this, you ought to be ashamed of yourself." Commenting about the message's effectiveness, the person said, "It works every time. It's a nice, polite two-by-four between the eyes."[139] To protect themselves from digital fraud or theft that occurs through breaking into employees' PCs, some companies are buying insurance to protect against PC hacking. Chubb's new ForeFront plan offers up to $10 million coverage against digital fraud, theft, and extortion. Cigna's information asset protection division sells antihacker policies that cover up to 10 percent of a firm's revenues. The number of clients making claims seems to suggest the value of having one of these policies.[140]

Some competitor intelligence practices are legal, but a firm must decide whether their use is ethical, given its culture and the image it desires as a corporate citizen. Especially with electronic transmissions, the line between legal and ethical practices

Competitive Intelligence and the Internet

The Internet is an excellent technology for distributing information to current and prospective customers. The tool appears to be effective, in that for many companies, customers are becoming increasingly comfortable with the practice of buying products through electronic commerce.

Interested in being recognized for the superiority of their Web sites, as well as selling to current customers and attracting new ones, a growing number of companies are offering a "digital cache of press releases and executive bios, job postings and research papers, price lists and details on strategic alliances," among other types of information, via their Web sites. For firms competing through e-commerce only, it is vital that they develop an effective Web site, because it is their single distribution channel. For example, started by Louis H. Borders, who also founded Borders Books & Music, Webvan sells groceries, meat and fish, and non-prescription drugs over the Internet. Strictly a Web-based business, Webvan has no operations from a "bricks and mortar" facility. The company is attractive to investors, and its stock price surged 66 percent on the day of its initial public offering. With a resulting market capitalization of $8 billion, Webvan immediately had one-half the capitalization of Safeway, Inc., and Kroger Co., the industry's traditional leaders. Webvan's competitors continue to increase, however, as the entry barriers to this type of business are low. In Dallas, Texas, GroceryWorks.com uses part of its Web site to emphasize, in an attractive manner, the superior freshness of its perishable items relative to those available through on-line competitors.

Providing competitive intelligence to competitors that historically was difficult for them to obtain is a downside to comprehensive Web sites. The seriousness of this problem is highlighted by the fact that the entry barriers to starting a Web-based business are very low. Commenting about the issue of providing intelligence to competitors through one's Web site, an analyst suggested that "Boeing's Web site is a gold mine for a competitor that would like to hire away staff who come with lots of sensitive information. And you know who[m] to talk to about each person. You can call their boss, work your way up the organizational chart and find out information about an executive, his background, how he is to work for." Other companies study the backgrounds of competitors' CEOs and top management teams. Knowing the functional backgrounds of a competitor's key decision makers yields valuable insights. For example, knowing that a CEO is from a marketing rather than, say, a finance background allows a firm to predict how the CEO "views the world" and the issues that likely have major effects on his or her strategic decisions. Corporations are well aware that others are studying their Web sites to develop competitor intelligence. One company official observed that "we know our competitors check out our Web site . . . And, of course, we do the same to them."

Another indicator of the value of competitor intelligence that is available from another firm's Web site is highlighted by the fact that new ventures have surfaced to provide what is called "Web-spying services." The need these companies satisfy is to help firms deal with "infoglut"—a term used to describe the vast amount of intelligence to which firms can gain access to study competitors. Called corporate intelligence firms, the charges for these firms' services can be over $1 million for a large project. One firm studied competitors' Web sites (and other publicly available information) to help Dow Chemical determine if there was a market for a promising new heat-resistant, superstrong composite of clay and plastic that it had developed (the answer was "yes") and if any of Dow's competitors were too far ahead in producing and distributing a competing product (the answer from the corporate intelligence firm was "maybe").

What should the firm do about Web spying? An obvious action is for the company to exercise caution about the type and level of information that is included on its Web site. The level of scrutiny devoted to assessing what is to be featured on a Web site should parallel the scrutiny an annual report undergoes before being published. The firm might also wish to verify, if it chooses to study competitors' sites, that any information included on a competing company's site about its own firm is accurate. According to a business writer, one firm has become "quite adept at spreading myths through its Web site" about the raw materials used to manufacture a competitor's product. Thus, if a firm chooses to study a competitor's Web site, it may also want to assess the accuracy of any information on that site that the competitor is providing about it.

SOURCES: G. Anders & R. Berner, 1999, Webvan's splashy stock debut may shake up staid grocery industry, *Wall Street Journal,* November 8, B1, B4; M. Fumento, 1999, Tampon terrorism, *Forbes,* May 17, 170–172; M. Halkias, 1999, New online grocer wants to grow with market, *Dallas Morning News,* November 9, D1, D6; K. Labich, 1999, Attention shoppers: This man is watching you. *Fortune,* July 19, 131–134; A. L. Penenberg, 1999, Is there a snoop on your site? *Forbes,* May 17, 323–326; Two new tech offerings are hits on Wall Street, *Dallas Morning News,* November 6, F11.

can be difficult to determine. For example, some firms develop Web-site addresses that are very similar to those of competitors. Occasionally, the firm then receives e-mail transmissions that were intended for its competitor. Is e-mail snagging legal? According to legal experts, the answer to this question remains unclear.[141] Nonetheless, the practice is an example of what companies face when determining how to gather intelligence and how to protect themselves from having too much of their own intelligence fall into competitors' hands.

Open discussions of intelligence-gathering techniques that a firm will use go a long way toward assuring that people understand the firm's convictions about what is ethical and acceptable for use and what is not when gathering competitor intelligence. An appropriate guideline about competitor intelligence practices that can frame these discussions is for the firm to respect the principles of common morality and the right of competitors not to reveal certain information about their products, operations, and strategic intentions.[142]

Despite the importance of studying competitors, evidence suggests that a relatively small percentage of firms use formal processes to do so. In fact, some believe that "only 10–15 percent of all businesses actually have a systematic process for collection and dissemination of competitive intelligence information."[143] Beyond this, some firms forget to analyze competitors' *future objectives* as they try to understand their current strategies' assumptions and capabilities. As previously stated, it is important to study the present *and* the future in examining competitors. Failure to do so yields incomplete insights about those competitors.[144]

Earlier in the chapter, we discussed the value of the Internet as a tool to help a firm scan, monitor, forecast, and assess the external environment. In the Strategic Focus, we discussed how the Internet's extensive capabilities may cause the firm to divulge too much about itself to competitors. Thus, through Web sites, the Internet creates interesting *opportunities* for the firm (e.g., to entice sales from current and future customers), as well as *threats* (e.g., giving too much competitive intelligence to competitors through its Web site) to the firm's survival.

As explained in Chapter 1, a firm's strategic actions are a product of its external and internal environments. Thus, to attain the outcomes of strategic competitiveness and above-average returns, the firm must integrate the insights gained by studying its external environment with those acquired by analyzing its internal environment. In this chapter, we discussed the insights the firm develops by studying the external environment. In the next, we describe what the firm seeks to understand about its internal environment and the tools that are used to develop those understandings.

Summary

- The firm's external environment is challenging and complex. Because of the effect the external environment has on performance, the firm must develop the skills required to identify opportunities and threats existing in that environment.
- The external environment has three major parts: (1) the general environment (elements in the broader society that affect industries and their firms), (2) the industry environment (factors that influence a firm, its competitive actions and responses, and the industry's profit potential—the threats of entry, suppliers, buyers, and product substitutes, and the intensity of rivalry among competitors), and (3) the competitor environment (in which the firm studies each major competitor's future objectives, current strategies, assumptions, and capabilities).
- Effective environmental analyses assume a nationless and borderless (i.e., global) business environment.
- The external environmental analysis process has four steps: scanning, monitoring, forecasting, and assessing. Through environmental analysis, the firm identifies opportunities and threats.
- The general environment has six segments: demographic, economic, political/legal, sociocultural, technological, and global. For each segment, the firm wants to determine the strategic relevance of environmental changes and trends.
- Compared to the general environment, the industry environment has a more direct effect on the firm's strategic actions.
- The five forces model of competition includes characteristics that determine the industry's profit potential. By studying these forces, the firm finds a position in an industry whereby it can influence the forces in its favor or whereby it can isolate itself from the power of the forces to reduce its ability to earn above-average returns.
- Industries are populated with different strategic groups. A strategic group is a collection of firms that follow similar strategies along similar dimensions. Competitive rivalry is greater within a strategic group than it is between strategic groups.
- Competitor analysis informs the firm about the future objectives, current strategies, assumptions, and capabilities of the companies with whom it competes directly.
- Different techniques are used to create competitor intelligence: the set of data, information, and knowledge that allows the firm to better understand those with whom it directly competes. At a minimum, the firm must use only legal practices to gather intelligence. Increasingly, the firm is being called on to determine those practices it will use because they are ethical as well as legal. The Internet's capabilities allow the firm to gather insights quickly about competitors and their intentions.

Review Questions

1. Why is it important for a firm to study and understand the external environment?
2. What are the differences between the general environment and the industry environment? Why are these differences important?
3. What is the external environmental analysis process? What does the firm want to learn as it scans, monitors, forecasts, and assesses its external environment?
4. What are the six segments of the general environment? Explain the differences among them.
5. Using information in the chapter, can you justify the following statement? "There are five competitive forces that determine an industry's profit potential." Explain.
6. What is a strategic group? Of what value is the strategic group concept in choosing a firm's strategy?
7. Why do firms want to understand how data and information about competitors are collected and interpreted? What practices should a firm use to gather competitor intelligence and why?

Application Discussion Questions

1. Given the importance of understanding the external environment, why do some firms fail to do so? Using the Internet, find an example of a firm that did not understand its external environment. What were the implications of the firm's failure to understand that environment?
2. Select a firm and describe its external environment. Suppose you are about to enter the business world. What actions do you believe the firm should take, given its external environment, and why?
3. How is it possible that one firm could see a condition in the external environment as an opportunity while a second firm sees it as a threat?
4. Select a firm in your local community. What materials would you read to understand the firm's external environment? How could the Internet help you to complete this activity?
5. Select an industry that is of interest to you. What actions could firms take to erect barriers of entry to this industry?
6. What conditions would cause a firm to retaliate aggressively against a new entrant to the industry?

Ethics Questions

1. How can a firm use its "code of ethics" to analyze the external environment?
2. What ethical issues, if any, may be relevant to a firm's monitoring of its external environment? Does use of the Internet to monitor the environment lead to additional ethical issues? If so, what are they?
3. Think of each segment in a firm's general environment. What is an ethical issue associated with each segment? Are firms across the globe doing enough to deal with the issue?
4. What is the importance of using ethical practices between a firm and its suppliers?
5. In an intense rivalry, especially one that involves competition in the global marketplace, how can the firm gather competitor intelligence ethically while maintaining its competitiveness?
6. What do you believe determines whether an intelligence-gathering practice is or is not ethical? Do you see this changing as the world's economies become more interdependent? If so, why? Do you see this changing because of the Internet? If so, how?

Internet Exercise

Firms rely on gathering and analyzing the general, industry, and competitor environments to assess their potential for global growth and profitability. Go to the Web site for the U.S. retail chain Wal-Mart at **http://www.wal-mart.com**. Wal-Mart's global expansion plans are extensive. List how each of the six segments of the general environment prompted Wal-Mart to expand into the markets that it has. Target is a major U.S. competitor of Wal-Mart. Check out the Target Web site at **http://www.target.com**. What are the firm's plans for global expansion? What types of opportunities and threats would prohibit Target from taking Wal-Mart's route? Would you consider Target a future key global rival of Wal-Mart?

***e-Project:** In addition to firms such as Amazon.com (with its own sites in the U.K. and Germany), what other U.S. firms offer global Web shopping in other countries' currencies and shipping specifications? How do these sites compare with the American ones?

Notes

1. D. J. Ketchen, Jr. & T. B. Palmer, 1999, Strategic responses to poor organizational performance: A test of competing perspectives, *Journal of Management,* 25: 683–706; V. P. Rindova & C. J. Fombrun, 1999, Constructing competitive advantage: The role of firm-constituent interactions, *Strategic Management Journal,* 20: 691–710; J. A. Wagner & R. Z. Gooding, 1997, Equivocal information and attribution: An investigation of patterns of managerial sensemaking, *Strategic Management Journal,* 16: 497–518.
2. N. Shirouzu & R. L. Simison, 2000, Toyota holds talks about joining GM in online market for suppliers' goods, *Wall Street Journal,* January 6, A4; T. A. Stewart, 1999, See Jack. See Jack run, *Fortune,* September 27, 124–136.
3. J. Ball & L. Gomes, 1999, Ford, Oracle announce joint venture to put automaker's suppliers online, *Wall Street Journal,* November 3, A4.
4. The great convergence: An introduction, 1999, *Forbes ASAP,* October 4, 15–16; C. M. Grimm & K. G. Smith, 1997, *Strategy As Action: Industry Rivalry and Coordination* (Cincinnati: South-Western); C. J. Fombrun, 1992, *Turning Point: Creating Strategic Change in Organizations* (New York: McGraw-Hill), 13.
5. T. E. Ricks & A. M. Squeo, 1999, Pentagon urges caution on big defense mergers, *Wall Street Journal,* October 22, A2.
6. H. Durgin, 1999, The plug is pulled on the fast buck crowd, *Financial Times,* March 25, 21; C. K. Prahalad, 1999, Changes in the competitive battlefield, Mastering Strategy (Part Two), *Financial Times,* October 4, 2–5.
7. S. A. Zahra, A. P. Nielsen, & W. C. Bogner, 1999, Corporate entrepreneurship, knowledge, and competence development, *Entrepreneurship: Theory and Practice,* 23(3), 169–189; M. Farjoun & L. Lei, 1997, Similarity judgments in strategy formulation: Role, process, and implications, *Strategic Management Journal,* 18: 255–273.
8. M. A. Hitt, J. E. Ricart I Costa, & R. D. Nixon, 1998, The new frontier, in M. A. Hitt, J. E. Ricart I Costa, & R. D. Nixon (eds.), *Managing Strategically in an Interconnected World* (Chichester: John Wiley & Sons), 1–12.
9. W. C. Bogner & P. Bansal, 1998, Controlling unique knowledge development as the basis of sustained high performance, in M. A. Hitt, J. E. Ricart I Costa, & R. D. Nixon (eds.), *Managing Strategically in an Interconnected World* (Chichester: John Wiley & Sons), 167–184; D. J. Teece, G. Pisano, & A. Shuen, 1997, Dynamic capabilities and strategic management, *Strategic Management Journal,* 18: 509–533.
10. L. Fahey, 1999, *Competitors* (New York: John Wiley & Sons); B. A. Walters & R. L. Priem, 1999, Business strategy and CEO intelligence acquisition, *Competitive Intelligence Review,* 10(2): 15–22; L. Fahey & V. K. Narayanan, 1986, *Macroenvironmental Analysis for Strategic Management* (St. Paul: West Publishing Company), 49–50.
11. G. Koretz, 1999, An unbalanced global economy, *Business Week,* March 15, 22.
12. R. D. Ireland & M. A. Hitt, 1999, Achieving and maintaining strategic competitiveness in the 21st century: The role of strategic leadership, *Academy of Management Executive,* 13(1): 43–57; M. A. Hitt, B. W. Keats, & S. M. DeMarie, 1998, Navigating in the new competitive landscape: Building strategic flexibility and competitive advantage in the 21st century, *Academy of Management Executive,* 12(4): 22–42.
13. J. Kay, 1999, Strategy and the delusion of grand designs, Mastering Strategy (Part One), *Financial Times,* September 27, 2.
14. G. L. White & J. B. White, 1999, At GM, Pearce returns to lead a push into high tech, *Wall Street Journal,* April 23, B1, B4.
15. J. Hyde, 1999, GM plans to offer car connected to Web, *Dallas Morning News,* November 3, D1, D12; G. L. White, 1999, GM will connect drivers to the World Wide Web, *Wall Street Journal,* November 3, B1, B4.
16. R. Karlgaard, 1999, Digital rules: Technology and the new economy, *Forbes,* May 17, 43.
17. GE Overview, 2000, General Electric Home Page, January 12, *www.ge.com.*
18. V. Prior, 1999, The language of competitive intelligence: Part four, *Competitive Intelligence Review,* 10(1): 84–87.
19. F. Beckett, 1999, IBM high technology meets European class, *Financial Times,* May 10, 12.
20. D. Kunde, 1999, Higher tech ed: Colleges focus on building e-commerce MBAs, *Dallas Morning News,* June 9, D1, D10.
21. G. Young, 1999, "Strategic value analysis" for competitive advantage, *Competitive Intelligence Review,* 10(2): 52–64.
22. D. N. Sull, 1999, Why good companies go bad, *Harvard Business Review,* 77(4): 42–52; H. Courtney, J. Kirkland, & P. Visuerie, 1997, Strategy under uncertainty, *Harvard Business Review,* 75(6): 66–79.
23. D. S. Elenkov, 1997, Strategic uncertainty and environmental scanning: The case for institutional influences on scanning behavior, *Strategic Management Journal,* 18: 287–302.
24. S. D. Hilmetz & R. S. Bridge, 1999, Gauging the returns on investments in competitive intelligence: A three-step analysis for executive decision makers, *Competitive Intelligence Review,* 10(1): 4–11; I. Goll & A. M. A. Rasheed, 1997, Rational decision-making and firm performance: The moderating role of environment, *Strategic Management Journal,* 18: 583–591.
25. R. Aggarwal, 1999, Technology and globalization as mutual reinforcers in business: Reorienting strategic thinking for the new millennium, *Management International Review,* 39(2): 83–104; M. Yasai-Ardekani & P. C. Nystrom, 1996, Designs for environmental scanning systems: Tests of contingency theory, *Management Science,* 42: 187–204.
26. R. Donkin, 1999, Too young to retire, *Financial Times,* July 2, 9.
27. Ibid., 9.
28. K. Morris, 1999, Wiring the ivory tower, *Business Week,* August 9, 90–92.
29. Fahey, *Competitors,* 71–73; Fahey & Narayanan, *Macroenvironmental Analysis,* 39.
30. H. Simonian, 1999, Germans buy new Sunday shopping laws, *Financial Times,* August 3, 2.
31. P. Yip, 1999, The road to wealth, *Dallas Morning News,* August 2, D1, D3.
32. Fahey, *Competitors*; Fahey & Narayanan, *Macroenvironmental Analysis,* 41.
33. Karlgaard, Digital rules, 43; M. B. Regan, 1999, Industries adjust to e-commerce, *Waco Tribunal Herald,* April 11, B6, B7.
34. Fahey, *Competitors,* 75–77; Fahey & Narayanan, *Macroenvironmental Analysis,* 42.
35. T. Box, 1999, Keep on truckin', *Dallas Morning News,* April 22, D1, D4.
36. P. Davidson, 1999, Net retailer eToys faces big risks as its star rises, *USA Today,* April 8, B1, B2.
37. Fahey & Narayanan, *Macroenvironmental Analysis,* 58.

38. D. Fishburn, 1999, The world in 1999, *The Economist Publications,* 9; Six billion . . . and counting, 1999, *Time,* October 4, 16.
39. J. F. Coates, J. B. Mahaffie, & A. Hines, 1997, *2025: Scenarios of US and Global Society Reshaped by Science and Technology* (Greensboro, NC: Oakhill Press).
40. R. Poe & C. L. Courter, 1999, The next baby boom, *Across the Board,* May, 1; Trends and forecasts for the next 25 years, 1999, *World Future Society,* 3.
41. Six billion, 16.
42. R. Stodghill, II, 1997, The coming job bottleneck, *Business Week,* March 24, 184–185.
43. D. Stipp, 1999, Hell no, we won't go!, *Fortune,* July 19, 102–108; G. Colvin, 1997, How to beat the boomer rush, *Fortune,* August 18, 59–63.
44. J. MacIntyre, 1999, Figuratively speaking, *Across the Board,* November/December, 15.
45. Colvin, How to beat the boomer rush, 60.
46. K. Hutt, 1999, On cruise control, *Dallas Morning News,* July 7, F1, F8.
47. U.S. Department of Labor, 1999, Demographic change and the future workforce, *Futurework,* November 8, *www.dol.gov.*
48. J. R. W. Joplin & C. S. Daus, 1997, Challenges of leading a diverse workforce, *Academy of Management Executive,* XI(3): 32–47; G. Robinson & K. Dechant, 1997, Building a business case for diversity, *Academy of Management Executive,* IX(3): 21–31.
49. G. Dessler, 1999, How to earn your employees' commitment, *Academy of Management Executive,* 13(2): 58–67; S. Finkelstein & D. C. Hambrick, 1996, *Strategic Leadership: Top Executives and Their Effect on Organizations* (Minneapolis: West).
50 L. H. Pelled, K. M. Eisenhardt, & K. R. Xin, 1999, Exploring the black box: An analysis of work group diversity, conflict, and performance, *Administrative Science Quarterly,* 44: 1–28.
51. E. S. Rubenstein, 1999, Inequality, *Forbes,* November 1, 158–160; J. Landers, 1997, Incomes rising around world, *Dallas Morning News,* September 15, D1, D4.
52. Fahey & Narayanan, *Macroenvironmental Analysis,* 105.
53. T. Robberson, 1999, Brazil's middle class scrambles to survive amid economic woes, *Dallas Morning News,* April 10, F1, F11.
54. E. Dufner, 1999, Export jolt, *Dallas Morning News,* February 2, D1, D14.
55. J. Wolfensohn, 1999, The world in 1999, A battle for corporate honesty, *The Economist Publications,* 38.
56. World Trade Organization, 1998, Annual Report, 5–6.
57. J. E. Schrempp, 1999, The world in 1999, Neighbours across the pond, *The Economist Publications,* 28.
58. L. Brittan, 1999, The world in 1999, The millennium round, *The Economist Publications,* 50.
59. M. E. Boudette, 1999, In Europe, surfing a Web of red tape, *Wall Street Journal,* October 29, B1, B4.
60. Fahey & Narayanan, *Macroenvironmental Analysis,* 139–157.
61. A. J. Hillman & M. A. Hitt, 1999, Corporate political strategy formulation: A model of approach, participation, and strategy decisions, *Academy of Management Review,* 24: 825–842.
62. M. Carson, 1998, *Global Competitiveness Quarterly,* March 9, 1.
63. Brittan, The millennium round, 50.
64. R. L. Riley, 1999, Will Uncle Sam trump Internet gamblers? *Wall Street Journal,* May 14, A14.
65. Cyberspace: Who will make the rules?, 1999, *Business Week,* March 22, 30D–30F.
66. S. Calian & S. Gruner, 1999, UK regulators move to open local phones to competition, *Wall Street Journal,* July 9, A14; J. Friedland & K. Kranhold, 1999, Mexico's energy reforms lure U.S. investors, *Wall Street Journal,* June 29, A8; P. Landers, 1999, Government involvement has boosted Japan's recovery, *Wall Street Journal,* June 15, A12; C. Murphy, 1999, Will the future belong to Germany?, *Fortune,* August 2, 129–136; T. Vogel, 1997, Central America goes from war zone to enterprise zone, *Wall Street Journal,* September 25, A18.
67. J. MacIntyre, 1999, Figuratively speaking, *Across the Board,* May, 11.
68. A. R. Varey & G. Lynn, 1999, Americans save for retirement, *USA Today,* November 16, B1.
69. D. Kunde, 1999, Survey finds technology blurring lines of work, home, *Dallas Morning News,* October 13, D1, D10; D. Woodruff, 1999, In France, working long hours becomes a crime, *Wall Street Journal,* June 25, A15.
70. G. F. Will, 1999, The primacy of culture, *Newsweek,* January 18, 64.
71. Woman power!, 1999, *Worth Magazine,* September, 100–101.
72. B. Beck, 1999, The world in 1999, Executive, thy name is woman, *The Economist Publications,* 89; P. Thomas, 1995, Success at a huge personal cost: Comparing women around the world, *Wall Street Journal,* July 26, B1.
73. T. Y. Jones, 1999, Gender motors, *Forbes,* May 17, 50–51.
74. D. Kunde, 1999, Women on slow track to top corporate jobs, survey finds, *Dallas Morning News,* November 12, D1, D11.
75. K. Jacobs, 1999, Women have scaled corporate ladder, but climb continues to be a slow one, *Wall Street Journal,* November 12, B4; P. Sellers, 1999, These women rule, *Fortune,* October 25, 94–132.
76. C. M. Daily, S. T. Certo, & D. R. Dalton, 1999, A decade of corporate women: Some progress in the boardroom, none in the executive suite, *Strategic Management Journal,* 20: 93–99.
77. R. Taylor, 1999, Pay gap between the sexes widest in W. Europe, *Financial Times,* June 29, 9.
78. Associated Press, 1999, Women-owned businesses making gains, *Dallas Morning News,* April 28, D2; N. Enbar, 1999, What do women want? Ask 'em, *Business Week,* March 29, 8.
79. S. Branch, 1999, Avon names Andrea Jung to CEO post, *Wall Street Journal,* November 5, A3; B. Morris, 1997, If women ran the world it would look a lot like Avon, *Fortune,* July 21, 74–79.
80. D. Kunde, 1999, Temporary shortage, *Dallas Morning News,* September 28, D1, D6.
81. N. Nakamae, 1999, Service sector shining in land of the rising sun, *Financial Times,* July 27, 4.
82. Trends and forecasts, 3.
83. P. Hochman, 1999, Yo-yos are back. This time they *mean* it, *Fortune,* May 24, 64.
84. X. M. Song, C. A. Di Benedetto, & Y. L. Zhao, 1999, Pioneering advantages in manufacturing and service industries, *Strategic Management Journal,* 20: 811–836.
85. C. Newman, 1999, Pearson to double Internet investment, *Financial Times,* August 3, 15.
86. Business ready for Internet revolution, 1999, *Financial Times,* May 21, 17.
87. K. S. Mangan, 1999, Business students flock to courses on electronic commerce, *The Chronicle of Higher Education,* April 30, A25.
88. K. Fairbank, 1999, CEOs downplay effect of Net sales, *Dallas Morning News,* November 12, D1, D10.
89. Regan, Industries adjust, B7.
90. A Goldstein, 1999, E-commerce may soar to $380 billion, *Dallas Morning News,* October 13, D1, D10.
91. M. Dell, 1999, The world in 1999, The virtual firm, *The Economist Publications,* 99.
92. W. C. Kim & R. Mauborgne, 1999, Creating new market space, *Harvard Business Review,* 77(1): 83–93; R. D. Nordstrom & R. L. Pinkerton, 1999, Taking advantage of Internet sources to build a competitive intelligence system, *Competitive Intelligence Review,* 10(1): 54–61.
93. A. Rawsthorn, 1999, Global Internet music sales to reach $4bn in five years, *Financial Times,* May 26, 8.
94. R. La Franco, 1999, Record companies, awake!, *Forbes,* November 15, 76–80.

95. D. B. Yoffie & M. A. Cusumano, 1999, Judo strategy: The competitive dynamics of Internet time, *Harvard Business Review,* 77(1): 71–81.
96. A. K. Gupta, V. Govindarajan, & A. Malhotra, 1999, Feedback-seeking behavior within multinational corporations, *Strategic Management Journal,* 20: 205–222.
97. China and the U.S. sign trade deal, clearing hurdle for WTO entry, 1999, *Wall Street Interactive Journal,* November 15, *www.interactive.wsj.com.*
98. J. Cox, 1999 USA could get billion Chinese customers, *USA Today,* November 16, B1; In historic pact, U.S. opens way for China to finally join WTO, 1999, *Wall Street Journal,* November 16, A1, A19.
99. U.S. companies eager for business in China, 1999, *Dallas Morning News,* November 16, D1, D9.
100. Dell Home Page, 2000, *www.dell.com*, January 12.
101. E. W. K. Tsang, 1998, Can *guanxi* be a source of sustained competitive advantage for doing business in China?, *Academy of Management Executive,* 12(2): 64–73; M. A. Hitt, M. T. Dacin, B. B. Tyler, & D. Park, 1997, Understanding the differences in Korean and U.S. executives' strategic orientations, *Strategic Management Journal,* 18: 159–167.
102. T. Khanna & K. Palepu, 1999, The right way to restructure conglomerates in emerging markets, *Harvard Business Review,* 77(4): 125–134;Hitt, Dacin, Tyler, & Park, 1997, Understanding the differences in Korean and U.S. executives' strategic orientations.
103. T. H. Brush, P. Bromiley, & M. Hendrickx, 1999, The relative influence of industry and corporation on business segment performance: An alternative estimate, *Strategic Management Journal,* 20: 519–547.
104. E. O. Welles, 1999, Not your father's industry, *Inc.,* January, 25–26.
105. Hitt, Ricart, Costa, & Nixon, The new frontier.
106. Y. Pan & P. S. K. Chi, 1999, Financial performance and survival of multinational corporations in China, *Strategic Management Journal,* 20: 359–374; G. R. Brooks, 1995, Defining market boundaries, *Strategic Management Journal,* 16: 535–549.
107. A. M. McGahan, 1994, Industry structure and competitive advantage, *Harvard Business Review,* 72(5): 115–124.
108. P. A. Geroski, 1999, Early warning of new rivals, *Sloan Management Review,* 40(3): 107–116.
109. D. W. Brin, 1999, Sylvan delves into higher education with purchase of university in Spain, *Wall Street Journal,* April 19, B7B.
110. R. Makadok, 1999, Interfirm differences in scale economies and the evolution of market shares, *Strategic Management Journal,* 20: 935–952.
111. In the Vanguard, 1999, The Vanguard cost advantage grows, Spring(2): 12.
112. J. Hechinger & P-W. Tam, 1999, Vanguard's index funds attract imitators, *Wall Street Journal,* November 12, C1, C23.
113. R. Wise & P. Baumgartner, 1999, Go downstream: The new profit imperative in manufacturing, *Harvard Business Review,* 77(5): 133–141; J. H. Gilmore & B. J. Pine, II, 1997, The four faces of mass customization, *Harvard Business Review,* 75(1): 91–101.
114. Rubbermaid Home Page, 2000, January 12, *www.rubbermaid.com;* T. Aeppel, 1997, Rubbermaid warns 3rd-quarter profits will come in far below expectations, *Wall Street Journal,* September 19, A4.
115. J. Willman, 1999, Consumer power forces food industry to modify approach, *Financial Times,* June 10, 11.
116. J. Muller, K. Naughton, & L. Armstrong, Old carmakers learn new tricks, 1999, *Business Week,* April 12, 116–118; O. Port, 1999, Customers move into the driver's seat, 1999, *Business Week,* October 4, 103–106.
117. S. Browder, 1997, Tea is bagging a bigger crowd, *Business Week,* August 25, 6.
118. R. Waters, 1999, NBC to spin off Web sites into new company, *Financial Times,* May 11, 15.
119. The house that Jack built, 1999, *The Economist,* September 18, 23–26.
120. D. L. Deephouse, 1999, To be different, or to be the same? It's a question (and theory) of strategic balance, *Strategic Management Journal,* 20: 147–166.
121. G. Lorenzoni & A. Lipparini, 1999, The leveraging of interfirm relationships as a distinctive organizational capability: A longitudinal study, *Strategic Management Journal,* 20: 317–338.
122. M. E. Porter, 1980, *Competitive Strategy* (New York: Free Press).
123. M. S. Hunt, 1972, Competition in the major home appliance industry, 1960–1970 (doctoral dissertation, Harvard University).
124. Porter, *Competitive Strategy,* 129.
125. H. R. Greve, 1999, Managerial cognition and the mimetic adoption of market positions: What you see is what you do, *Strategic Management Journal,* 19: 967–988.
126. R. K. Reger & A. S. Huff, 1993, Strategic groups: A cognitive perspective, *Strategic Management Journal,* 14: 103–123.
127. J. B. Barney & R. E. Hoskisson, 1990, Strategic groups: Untested assertions and research proposals, *Managerial and Decision Economics,* 11: 198–208.
128. M. Peteraf & M. Shanely, 1997, Getting to know you: A theory of strategic group identity, *Strategic Management Journal,* 18 (Special Issue): 165–186.
129. Greve, Managerial cognition, 972–973.
130. D. Nath & T. Gruca, 1997, Covergence across alternatives for forming strategic groups, *Strategic Management Journal,* 18: 745–760.
131. D. Dranove, M. Peteraf, & M. Shanley, 1998, Do strategic groups exist? An economic framework for analysis, *Strategic Management Journal,* 19: 1029–1044.
132. K. Labich, 1999, Attention shoppers: This man is watching you, *Fortune,* July 19, 131–134.
133. Porter, *Competitive Strategy,* 49.
134. Young, "Strategic value analysis," 52.
135. P. M. Norman, R. D. Ireland, K. W. Artz, & M. A. Hitt, 2000, Acquiring and using competitive intelligence in entrepreneurial teams. Working paper, Baylor University.
136. Nordstrom & Pinkerton, Taking advantage of Internet sources, 54.
137. C. S. Fleisher, 1999, Public policy competitive intelligence, *Competitive Intelligence Review,* 10(2): 24.
138. Young, "Strategic value analysis," 52.
139. E. de Lisser, 1999, Hearing and seeing business travel blab and laptop lapses, *Wall Street Journal,* November 8, A1, A20.
140. V. Drucker, 1999, Is your computer a sitting duck during a deal? *Mergers & Acquisitions,* July/August, 25–28; J. Hodges, 1999, Insuring your PC against hackers, *Fortune,* May 24, 280.
141. M. Moss, 1999, Inside the game of e-mail hijacking, *Wall Street Journal,* November 9, B1, B4.
142. J. H. Hallaq & K. Steinhorst, 1994, Business intelligence methods—How ethical?, *Journal of Business Ethics,* 13: 787–794.
143. Nordstrom & Pinkerton, Taking advantage of Internet sources, 55.
144. L. Fahey, 1999, Competitor scenarios: Projecting a rival's marketplace strategy, *Competitive Intelligence Review,* 10(2): 65–85.

THE INTERNAL ENVIRONMENT: RESOURCES, CAPABILITIES, AND CORE COMPETENCIES

CHAPTER THREE OBJECTIVES

After reading this chapter, you should be able to:

1. Explain the need for firms to study and understand their internal environment.
2. Define value and discuss its importance.
3. Describe the differences between tangible and intangible resources.
4. Define capabilities and discuss how they are developed.
5. Describe four criteria used to determine whether resources and capabilities are core competencies.
6. Explain how value chain analysis is used to identify and evaluate resources and capabilities.
7. Define outsourcing and discuss the reasons for its use.
8. Discuss the importance of preventing core competencies from becoming core rigidities.
9. Explain the relationship between strategic inputs and strategic actions.

Brands as a Source of Competitive Advantage

A set of differentiating features that link a good or service to its customers, a *brand* is recognized widely by businesspeople and academic researchers alike as one of the most sustainable and hence valuable of all competitive advantages. The world's leading marketer of juices and owner of many drinks, including Fruitopia, Barq's, Fanta, Fresca, Sprite, Surge, and Mello Yello, as well as its soft drinks, the Coca-Cola Company owns one of the world's most famous and, some think, most valuable brands. As an indicator of the brand's value, consider that in the early 1990s, some analysts suggested that if all of Coca-Cola's tangible assets were destroyed simultaneously, the company could borrow at least $100 billion with only its brand name as collateral. Because of concerns that surfaced in mid-1999 about the quality of some of its products in a few European countries, some estimated that the value of this brand had fallen to approximately $84 billion, an amount that still ranked Coca-Cola as the most valuable brand name in the world. At the same time, Microsoft was second with a brand value of almost $57 billion.

The top 60 global brands by value in 1999 are shown in Table 3.1. Absent from this list are financial sector organizations. In the words of an analyst, "The great failure of financial institutions has been their inability to create any relevant differentiation for themselves, other than at the edges." Of such institutions, Goldman Sachs is recognized as having one of the best brands in the global investment banking business. Citibank and American Express are thought to have strong brand identities in the general financial sector. Given that demand for savings and investment products is increasing on a worldwide basis, Fidelity is striving to become the global mutual fund brand.

Contributing to the sustainability of brand as a competitive advantage is the fact that a brand is an intangible resource. Discussed later in the chapter, intangible resources are less visible and more difficult for competitors to understand and imitate than are tangible resources. Increasingly, firms agree that, as an intangible resource or asset, a brand generates an identifiable stream of earnings over time. Once this perspective is adopted, brand value can then be defined and a net present value for future profits can be established for a brand.

Some of the world's most powerful brands result from the labor of inspired men and women who are leaders with visions of global expansion and dominance (see Table 3.2 for a listing of such "One-Person Brands"). These individuals' actions were founded on the belief that "while the day to day business might be about profits, brand building is about giving a single, often mundane product an identity that inspires loyalty and passion." For instance, when he became president of Coca-Cola in 1923, Robert Woodruff observed that his job was "to sell Coca-Cola, to see that as many people as possible are able to enjoy it." To inspire loyalty and to create a passion for his firm's products, Woodruff sent 64 portable bottling plants to follow American troops during their World War II travels. Following the war's end, these plants became part of the beachhead on which Coca-Cola began its global expansion—an expansion and operation that remains vital today to the firm's ability to earn above-average returns.

Other great "brand mechanics" include Sony Corporation's Akio Morita, McDonald's Ray Kroc, Nike's Phil Knight, and advertising executive Leo Burnett. Each of these leaders is credited with at least one key action that helped to create a powerful brand for his firm. Phil Knight, for example, pioneered celebrity sports marketing by signing athletes such as Michael Jordan and Tiger Woods to endorse his firm's products. Ray Kroc made fast food a global way of life by tirelessly building his company on the mantra of quality, service, cleanliness, and value. Kroc was famous for visiting McDonald's units

TABLE

3.1 | Banking on a Ranking: Top 60 Global Brands by Value

Brand Name	Country of Origin	Industry	Value ($m)	Brand Name	Country of Origin	Industry	brand Value ($m)
1 Coca-Cola	**US**	**Beverages**	**83,845**	31 Volkswagen	**Ger**	**Automobiles**	**6,603**
2 Microsoft	**US**	**Software**	**56,654**	32 Pepsi-Cola	**US**	**Beverages**	**5,932**
3 IBM	**US**	**Computers**	**43,781**	33 Kleenex	**US**	**Pers. care**	**4,602**
4 General Electric	**US**	**Diversified**	**33,502**	34 Wrigley's	**US**	**Food**	**4,404**
5 Ford	**US**	**Automobiles**	**33,197**	35 AOL	**US**	**Software**	**4,329**
6 Disney	**US**	**Entertainment**	**32,275**	36 Apple	**US**	**Computers**	**4,283**
7 Intel	**US**	**Computers**	**30,021**	37 Louis Vuitton	**Fra**	**Fashion**	**4,076**
8 McDonald's	**US**	**Food**	**26,231**	38 Barbie	**US**	**Toys**	**3,792**
9 AT&T	**US**	**Telecoms**	**24,181**	39 Motorola	**US**	**Telecoms**	**3,643**
10 Marlboro	**US**	**Tobacco**	**21,048**	40 Adidas	**Ger**	**Sports goods**	**3,596**
11 Nokia	**Fin**	**Telecoms**	**20,694**	41 Colgate	**US**	**Pers. care**	**3,568**
12 Mercedes	**Ger**	**Automobiles**	**17,781**	42 Hertz	**US**	**Car hire**	**3,527**
13 Nescafé	**Swit**	**Beverages**	**17,595**	43 Ikea	**Swe**	**Housewares**	**3,464**
14 Hewlett-Packard	**US**	**Computers**	**17,132**	44 Chanel	**Fra**	**Fashion**	**3,143**
15 Gillette	**US**	**Pers. care**	**15,894**	45 BP	**UK**	**Oil**	**2,985**
16 Kodak	**US**	**Imaging**	**14,830**	46 Bacardi	**Cuba**	**Alcohol**	**2,895**
17 Ericsson	**Swe**	**Telecoms**	**14,766**	47 Burger King	**US**	**Food**	**2,806**
18 Sony	**Jap**	**Electronics**	**14,231**	48 Moët & Chandon	**Fra**	**Alcohol**	**2,804**
19 Amex	**US**	**Fin. services**	**12,550**	49 Shell	**UK**	**Oil**	**2,681**
20 Toyota	**Jap**	**Automobiles**	**12,310**	50 Rolex	**Switz**	**Luxury**	**2,423**
21 Heinz	**US**	**Food**	**11,806**	51 Smirnoff	**Russ**	**Alcohol**	**2,313**
22 BMW	**Ger**	**Automobiles**	**11,281**	52 Heineken	**Neth**	**Alcohol**	**2,184**
23 Xerox	**US**	**Office equipmt**	**11,225**	53 Yahoo!	**US**	**Software**	**1,761**
24 Honda	**Jap**	**Automobiles**	**11,101**	54 Ralph Lauren	**US**	**Fashion**	**1,648**
25 Citibank	**US**	**Fin. services**	**9,147**	55 Johnnie Walker	**UK**	**Alcohol**	**1,634**
26 Dell	**US**	**Computers**	**9,043**	56 Pampers	**US**	**Pers. care**	**1,422**
27 Budweiser	**US**	**Alcohol**	**8,510**	57 Amazon.com	**US**	**Books**	**1,361**
28 Nike	**US**	**Sports goods**	**8,155**	58 Hilton	**US**	**Leisure**	**1,319**
29 Gap	**US**	**Apparel**	**7,909**	59 Guinness	**Ire**	**Alcohol**	**1,262**
30 Kellogg's	**US**	**Food**	**7,052**	60 Marriott	**US**	**Leisure**	**1,193**

Source: R. Tomkins, 1999, Assessing a name's worth, *Financial Times,* June 22, 12.

3.2 | One-Person Brands

SOME OF THE CENTURY'S GREAT BRANDS HAVE BEEN INSEPARABLE FROM THEIR BUILDERS.

Richard Branson	Virgin Atlantic	Flyboy, cola novice
Walt Disney	Disney	Cultural animator
Hugh Hefner	Playboy Enterprises	Dirty-mag mogul, pajama wearer
Mary Kay Ash	Mary Kay Cosmetics	Pancake peddler, direct seller
Frank Perdue	Perdue Farms	Poultry professional (raw material)
Colonel Sanders	KFC	Poultry professional (ready-to-eat)
Charles Schwab	Charles Schwab	Mutual funds populist
Martha Stewart	Martha Stewart	Lifestyle engineer
Dave Thomas	Wendy's	Regular guy
Donald Trump	Trump Organization	Transformer of old hotels, self

Source: S. Branch, 1999, The brand builders, *Fortune,* May 10, 134.

unannounced to verify that the actions demanded to fulfill his mantra were in place. Leo Burnett's stroke of genius, in terms of creating a powerful brand for his advertising agency, was creating characters, including the Marlboro Man and Tony the Tiger, to personify brands. Morita's decision to build a tiny portable stereo (a product that was to become known as the Walkman) over his engineers' objections caused Sony, which already had a formidable brand name, to become a global icon for innovation in consumer electronics products.

Individuals can also be a powerful brand. This is the case with Michael Jordan, the retired Chicago Bulls superstar and now president of the Washington Wizards NBA franchise. Chosen by the ESPN television network as the athlete of the 20th century, Jordan is thought to have transcended the sport of basketball. Viewed as a "powerbrand," Jordan is recognized as "a player whose popularity and reach is peerless in the history of sports business." The significance of Jordan as a powerbrand is evidenced by the fact that the National Basketball Association and the television networks broadcasting the league's games expressed serious concerns about how to retain fan interest when Jordan decided to retire after 13 "extraordinary years of skywalking across the NBA."

Only carefully managed brands are a source of competitive advantage. Coca-Cola, Sony Corporation, McDonald's, and Nike, for example, devote a significant amount of time and energy to managing their brand name to gain a competitive advantage. How a brand is managed varies from company to company. For instance, shelf space for cigarettes in convenience stores is critical to the management of the Philip Morris' cigarette brand. The firm has developed the Retail Leaders sales-incentive program to support its brand in the thousands of convenience stores that have displaced grocery stores, thus becoming the largest seller of cigarettes in the United States. The Retail Leaders program compensates retailers for favoring Philip Morris brands over competitors' offerings. To improve the recognition of its Knorr soups and sauces in the United States, Bestfoods is extending the product line and frequently advertising the full line on television. Convenience and innovation are the product attributes being emphasized to consumers through the advertising campaign. In a sense, the message is that, compared to competitors such as Campbell Soup, the Knorr brand provides the customer with greater convenience and superior innovations in food quality.

For large global branded firms, the challenge is to engage frequently in brand rationalization, a process that is "an opportunity to cut costs and improve purchasing efficiencies," as well as to improve products' positions in various global markets. Based in Switzerland, Nestlé SA offers more than 8,000 brands across the globe, including Nescafé instant coffee and Perrier mineral water. To manage the diversity of its brands, Nestlé relies on what it calls a "brand umbrella." Grouped as parts of the umbrella are World-Wide Corporate, World-Wide Strategic, Regional Strategic, and Local. Each umbrella part features multiple brands. Unit managers are responsible for managing and continuously rationalizing their brands in ways that contribute to strategic competitiveness and the earning of above-average returns.

Some preliminary evidence suggests that a brand name creates little, if any, value for young Internet users. In place of brand, perceived product utility is a key source of value. To date, Amazon.com has been quite successful in terms of demonstrating the utilities of its products to customers. Thus, companies with strong brand names may find it necessary to describe the actual utility of their products more precisely in terms of their functionality to at least young Internet users in order to earn their business. In the longer term, however, a group of analysts is very optimistic regarding the Internet's ability to generate value through brands. In the words of one commentator, "[T]he Internet is the greatest brand-building technique we've ever seen."

http://www.amazon.com

http://americanexpress.com

http://www.bestfoods.com

http://www.citibank.com

http://www.coca-cola.com

http://www.fidelity.com

http://www.goldmansachs.com

http://www.mcdonalds.com

http://www.microsoft.com

http://www.nba.com

http://www.nestle.com

http://www.nike.com

http://www.philipmorris.com

http://www.sony.com

SOURCES: G. Anders, 2000, Investing for the new millennium, *Wall Street Journal,* January 1, R20; E. Beck, 1999, Nestlé sticks to strategy of broad categories of brands, *Wall Street Journal,* September 14, B4; S. Branch, 1999, Bestfoods aims to spice up North American business, *Wall Street Journal,* November 10, B6; S. Branch, 1999, The brand builders, *Fortune,* May 10, 132–134; B. Copple, 1999, If you build it, will they sit down? *Forbes,* November 29, 132–134; T. Corrigan, 1999, Weighing up the value of one of banking's best brands, *Financial Times,* March 19, 28; R. O. Crockett, 1999, Yikes: Mike takes a hike, *Business Week,* January 25, 74–76; R. Heller, 1999, Gucci's $4 billion man, *Forbes,* February 8, 108–109; S. Lubove, 1999, Brand power, *Forbes,* August 9, 98–104; E. I. Schwartz, 1999, Brands aren't everything, *Industry Standard,* April 30, 27–30; R. Tomkins, 1999, Assessing a name's worth, *Financial Times,* June 22, 12; S. Reed, M. L. Clifford, B. Bremner, & G. Smith, 1998, Fidelity takes on the world, *Business Week,* May 18, *www.businessweek.com.*

The firms mentioned in the Opening Case have resources, capabilities, and core competencies (see Chapter 1) that have been used to create brand as a source of competitive advantage. Even cities can use resources, capabilities, and competencies to form a brand that is a source of competitive advantage. For example, New Orleans, Louisiana, historically has leaned "on its carnival reputation as a brand name" to attract tourists. Some believe, though, that the city's future growth depends on its ability to form a business brand identity. Officials and citizens hope to develop a business brand by emphasizing education and highlighting the quality of the city's scientific and technological business communities.[1]

Organizations that rely on brand as a competitive advantage want that advantage to be *sustainable*. However, as discussed in the first two chapters, several attributes of the global economy, including the rapid emergence of the Internet's capabilities, are making it increasingly difficult to develop a competitive advantage that can be sustained for any reasonable period of time. In these instances, firms try to create advantages that can be sustained longer than can others. Regardless of the period for which it can be sustained, a *sustainable competitive advantage* is achieved when firms implement a value-creating strategy that is grounded in their own unique resources, capabilities, and core competencies.

A key indicator of understanding the importance of the relationship between advantage and value-creating strategies is the fact that "competitive advantage continues to provide the central agenda in strategy research."[2] The reason for this is that "the basic notion behind strategy is that a successful, high performing business requires a distinctive (or core) competence or competitive advantage."[3] To identify and successfully use its competitive advantages across time, firms must think constantly about their strategic management process and how to continuously increase the value it creates as it is used throughout the company.[4] Thus, as the discussion in this chapter indicates, firms achieve strategic competitiveness and earn above-average returns when their unique core competencies are leveraged effectively to take advantage of opportunities in the external environment. Increasingly, employees or associates are an important source of competitive advantage for firms competing in the 21st century's global economy.[5] For example, GE executives believe that people and their ideas are an important competitive advantage for their widely globalized firm.[6]

Over time, the benefits of every firm's value-creating strategy can be duplicated. In other words, there are no absolutes or guarantees, in that all competitive advantages have a limited life.[7] The question of duplication is not *if* it will happen, but *when*. Speaking to the essence of this reality, Jack Welch argues that "to be vital, an organization has to repot itself, start again, get new ideas, renew itself."[8] Being brutally honest is a prelude to accepting the need for the firm to reinvent itself to develop new competitive advantages. In this context, failing to communicate fully and honestly with all people in the firm to make certain that the limited life of competitive advantages is fully understood can create problems. One such problem is that, without full understanding of an advantage's limited life, organizational change that is vital to continuously developing new advantages may be stifled.[9] For a time, this may have been the case at Nordstrom.

Nordstrom, Inc., the retailer that is legendary for its competitive advantage of *customer service,* has reported profit declines in recent quarters. As with other full-line department stores, Nordstrom has been affected by the success of focused retailers such as Gap, Inc. Competitors' success suggests that their value propositions are reducing the benefit that Nordstrom's service competitive advantage is providing to customers in a full-line department store setting. As explained in a Strategic Focus in Chapter 4, Gap creates value for customers through its limited offering of specialty apparel. Says William Nordstrom, one of the firm's six co-presidents, "We have always held that having the big box with a huge assortment was the way to go. Obviously, the Gap has proved that isn't so." To at least reenergize and partly reinvent itself, Nordstrom is seeking to create more value for customers through its recently established Internet venture, nordstrom.com. Approximately 62,000 items are available through the Web site. Nordstrom intends to use the competence it has in knowledge about its customers' needs to provide unparalleled Internet service. Thus, although through a different distribution channel—a different venue—the firm believes that service can again be a source of sustainable competitive advantage for it. Nordstrom is also evaluating the possibility of expanding its Façonnable boutiques, a three-store unit that sells mostly casual apparel. Driving the decision about Façonnable will be an assessment of whether Nordstrom has a competitive advantage in this business concept and, if so, how sustainable it is.[10]

Effective duplication by competitors may have contributed to Home Depot's mid-1990 performance difficulties. "Home Depot isn't such a nimble category killer anymore," says a business writer. Competitors such as Lowe's and Eagle Hardware have built hangar-size warehouses that offer an array of goods similar to that available from Home Depot. Moreover, these competitors' actions have reduced the service gap between them and Home Depot.[11] However, 1998 was a stellar year for Home Depot. Focusing on convenience and product selection as competitive advantages to restore profitability and regain the company's prominent industry position, Home Depot kept certain high-volume stores open 24 hours per day. In addition, truck rentals were introduced at some sites to reduce the inconvenience shoppers encountered when pondering the possibility of buying high-margin goods from Home Depot, such as flooring and carpet. Combined with cost-cutting efforts, these competitive actions (see Chapter 5) resulted in a 39 percent earnings increase for the year. With further changes throughout 1999, Home Depot's resurgence was even more pronounced in 2000.[12]

In general, the sustainability of a competitive advantage is a function of three factors: the rate of core competence obsolescence due to environmental changes, the availability of substitutes for the core competence, and the imitability of the core competence.[13] The challenge in all firms—a challenge that can be met through proper use of the strategic management process—is to manage current core competencies effectively while simultaneously developing new ones to use when the competitive advantage derived from the application of current ones has been eroded.[14] In the words of Michael Dell, CEO of Dell Computer Corporation, "No [competitive] advantage and no success is ever permanent. The winners are those who keep moving. The only constant in our business is that everything is changing. We have to be ahead of the game."[15] Thus, as with Dell Computer, only when firms are able to develop a continuous stream of competitive advantages (as explained further in Chapter 5) do they achieve strategic competitiveness, earn above-average returns, and remain ahead of competitors.

In Chapter 2, we examined the general, industry, and competitor environments. Armed with knowledge about the realities and conditions of their environments, firms have a better understanding of marketplace opportunities and the goods or services through which they can be pursued.

In this chapter, we focus on the firm. Through an analysis of the internal environment, a firm determines *what it can do*—that is, the actions permitted by its unique resources, capabilities, and core competencies. As discussed in Chapter 1, core competencies are a firm's source of competitive advantage. The magnitude of that competitive advantage is a function primarily of the uniqueness of those competencies compared to competitors' competencies.[16] The proper matching of what a firm *can do* with what it *might do* allows the development of strategic intent, the pursuit of strategic mission, and the formulation of strategies. When implemented effectively, a value-creating strategy leads to strategic competitiveness and above-average returns. Outcomes resulting from internal and external environmental analyses are shown in Figure 3.1.

3.1 | Outcomes from External and Internal Environmental Analyses

By studying the external environment, firms identify	By studying the internal environment, firms determine
• what they *might* choose to *do*	• what they *can do*

We examine several topics in this chapter. First, the importance and challenge of studying a firm's internal environment are addressed. We then discuss the roles of resources, capabilities, and core competencies in the development of sustainable competitive advantage. Included here are descriptions of the techniques used to identify and evaluate resources and capabilities and the criteria firms use to select core competencies from among them. While studying these materials, it is important to recall that resources, capabilities, and core competencies are not *inherently* valuable; they have value only because they allow the firm to perform certain activities that result in a competitive advantage. To create a *sustained* competitive advantage, these activities must be unique.[17]

As shown in Figure 1.1, strategic intent and strategic mission, coupled with insights gained through analyses of the internal and external environments, determine the strategies a firm will select and the actions it will take to implement those strategies successfully. In the final part of the chapter, we describe briefly the relationship between intent and mission and a firm's strategic actions in terms of formulation and implementation.

The Importance of Internal Analysis

In the 21st-century competitive landscape, traditional conditions and factors, such as labor costs, access to financial resources and raw materials, and protected or regulated markets, can still be a source of competitive advantage, but to a lesser degree than in the past.[18] One important reason for this decline is that the advantages created by these sources can be overcome through an international strategy (discussed in Chapter 8) and by the relatively free flow of resources throughout the global economy. In economist Lester Thurow's words, "Raw materials can be bought and moved to wherever they are needed. Financial capital is a commodity that can be borrowed in New York, Tokyo or London. Unique pieces of equipment that cannot be obtained or are too expensive for one's competitors to buy simply don't exist."[19] One of the outcomes of these conditions is a significant amount of excess capacity. In fact, it seems that overcapacity is the norm in a host of industries, increasing the difficulty of forming competitive advantages.[20] In this challenging competitive environment, few firms are able to consistently make the most effective strategic decisions. To improve the quality of decisions across events and time, 21st-century firms must develop the capability to change rapidly. A key challenge to developing this capability is fostering an

Michael Dell (shown here) firmly believes that the Internet can have a significant effect on the automobile industry in terms of procurement of materials, sales, and service. Dell Computer Corporation has used the Internet successfully to generate about a 160% annual return on investment.

organizational environment in which experimentation and learning are expected and promoted.[21]

The demands of the 21st-century competitive landscape make it necessary for top-level managers to rethink the concept of the corporation. Michael Dell, for example, believes that automobile executives should do this by learning how to use the Internet to streamline procurement and to reshape service and sales.[22] Dell is not the only person convinced about the Internet's significance to the automobile industry. In the words of Lee Sage, the global leader of Ernst & Young LLP's automotive-consulting practice, "The Internet is going to have as much of an impact on the automobile industry as Henry Ford's mass-merchandising and production methods did in the 1920s."[23] One reason car companies are intrigued by Dell's proposal and the Internet's potential is that, by following some of the principles that Michael Dell thinks could be used successfully by carmakers, Dell Computer Corporation has generated an annual return on its investment of approximately 160 percent.[24]

Although corporations are difficult to change, achieving strategic competitiveness in the 21st-century landscape requires development and the use of a different managerial mind-set.[25] This is true both for those leading some of the world's automobile manufacturers and for people leading a host of companies throughout the global economy.

Most top-level managers recognize the need to change their mind-sets, but many hesitate to do so. In the words of a European CEO of a major U.S. company, "It is more reassuring for all of us to stay as we are, even though we know the result will be certain failure . . . than to jump into a new way of working when we cannot be sure it will succeed."[26] However, Jacques Nasser, Ford Motor Company's CEO, is not hesitating to call for the adoption of a new mind-set throughout his firm. In fact, Nasser believes that all employees—but especially senior-level executives—must change their mind-set from one that concentrates on their own area of operation to one that encompasses a view of the company in its entirety. This is necessary, in Nasser's view, to generate the type of rapid decision making required for Ford to be successful in a "world driven by rapidly changing consumer needs and tastes."[27] Similarly, North American Bus Industries, a Hungarian-based company that was once part of a crumbling Soviet-era monolith, has transformed itself into a successful company that is selling its products in many countries, including the United States. According to the Hungarian-born venture capitalist who founded the firm in 1992, penetrating the U.S. bus market required the development of a "totally new mind-set" throughout the firm's 850-plus employees. In part, this new mind-set calls for the firm to listen carefully to customers so that it will be able to design products that fully satisfy their needs.[28]

Critical to the required mind-set is the view that a firm is a *bundle* of heterogeneous resources, capabilities, and core competencies that can be used to create an exclusive market position.[29] This view suggests that individual firms possess at least some resources and capabilities that other companies do not have—at least not in the same combination. Resources are the source of capabilities, some of which lead to the development of a firm's core competencies.[30] By using their core competencies, firms perform activities *better* than competitors or perform activities that competitors are unable to duplicate. Essentially, the mind-set needed in the 21st-century competitive landscape requires decision makers to define their firm's strategy in terms of a unique competitive position, rather than *strictly* in terms of operational effectiveness. For instance, Michael Porter argues that quests for productivity, quality, and speed from a number of management techniques (total quality management, benchmarking, time-based competition, and reengineering) have resulted in operational efficiency, but not strong sustainable strategies.[31] As we discussed in Chapter 1, strategic competitiveness results when the firm satisfies the operational efficiency demands of its external environment, while simultaneously using its own unique capabilities to establish a viable competitive position.

Increasingly, managers are being evaluated in terms of their ability to identify, nurture, and exploit their firm's core competencies.[32] A part of these evaluations is framed around the understanding that an effective internal environmental analysis includes the recognition of both what *are* and what *are not* the firm's core competencies.[33] By emphasizing the acquisition and development of competencies, organizations *learn how to learn*.[34] Being able to learn is a skill that is linked with the development of competitive advantage. This skill has been called *metalearning*.[35] Learning how to learn requires commitment, time, and the active support of top-level executives. At Deere & Co., a global firm operating in over 160 countries through commitments to product quality, customer service, and business integrity and a high regard for the contributions of individuals, managers have created an "in-house Yellow Pages" to help them find an expert inside or outside the firm.[36] The system is quite inexpensive—about the cost of one engineer to operate it—but it has paid for itself annually at least six times over, especially when there is a crisis, say, in production, and an expert is needed to solve it. In the final analysis, a corporatewide obsession with the development and use of knowledge, together with broader core competencies, may characterize companies that are able to compete effectively on a global basis.[37]

Value consists of the performance characteristics and attributes provided by companies in the form of goods or services for which customers are willing to pay.

By exploiting their core competencies and meeting the demanding standards of global competition, firms create value for customers. **Value** consists of the performance characteristics and attributes companies provide in the form of goods or services for which customers are willing to pay.[38] At JCPenney Co., the firm's newly appointed department store chief executive observes that the firm needs to focus its merchandise mix and take the confusion out of prices. Doing this, Vanessa Castagna believes, will create a situation in which Penney's prices will "shout unquestionable value for quality, fashionable merchandise."[39]

Ultimately, customer value is the source of a firm's potential to earn average or above-average returns. What the firm intends to do to create value affects its choice of business-level strategy (see Chapter 4) and its organizational structure (see Chapter 11).[40] In Chapter 4's discussion of business-level strategies, we note that value is created by a product's low cost or highly differentiated features, or by a combination of low cost and high differentiation, compared to competitors' offerings. For Herend Porcelain, the Hungarian company that designs and manufacturers hand-painted porcelain items, "the distinctive value of the Herend (product) is found in its unique design and fineness of detail."[41] Thus, this firm creates value through the differentiation business-level strategy (described in detail in the next chapter). At Herend, core competencies such as craftsmanship and material quality are actually a value-creating system through which the company seeks strategic competitiveness and above-average returns (the various relationships are shown in Figure 3.2). In the 21st-century competitive landscape, firms must continually evaluate the degree to which their core competencies create customer value.[42] Executives at Allen-Edmonds Shoe Corporation,

FIGURE 3.2 | Components of Internal Analysis Leading to Competitive Advantage and Strategic Competitiveness

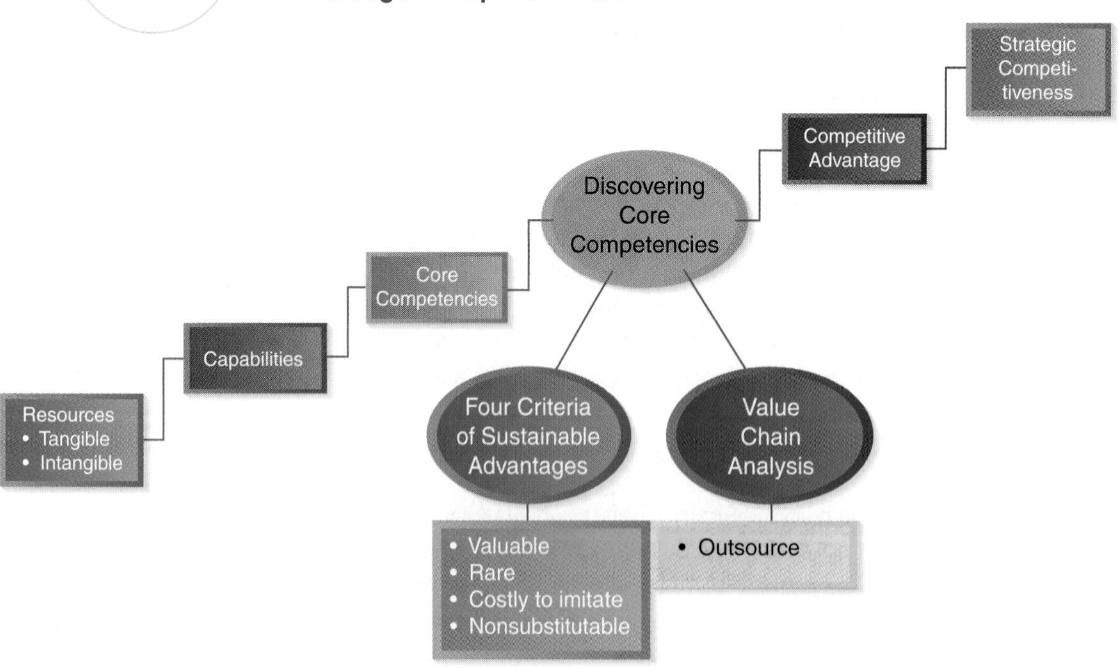

for example, believe that using the highest quality of leather available in the market and hiring the best craftspeople to work with that leather to design and manufacture shoes remain core competencies on which the firm's strategic competitiveness is based.[43]

During the last several decades, the strategic management process was concerned largely with understanding the characteristics of the industry in which a firm was competing and, in light of those characteristics, determining how the firm should position itself relative to competitors. The emphasis on industry characteristics and competitive strategy may have understated the role of organizational resources and capabilities in developing competitive advantage. A firm's core competencies, in addition to the results of an analysis of its general, industry, and competitor environments, should drive the selection of strategies. In this regard, core competencies, in combination with product-market positions or tactics, are the most important sources of competitive advantage in the 21st-century competitive landscape.[44] Emphasizing core competencies when formulating strategies is how companies learn to compete primarily on the basis of firm-specific differences, rather than seeking competitive advantage solely on the basis of an industry's structural characteristics.[45]

The Challenge of Internal Analysis

The decisions managers make in terms of resources, capabilities, and core competencies have a significant influence on a firm's ability to develop competitive advantages and earn above-average returns.[46] Making these decisions—that is, identifying, developing, deploying, and protecting resources, capabilities, and core competencies—may appear to be a relatively easy task. In fact, however, this work is as challenging and difficult as any other with which managers are involved; and it is becoming increasingly internationalized and linked with the firm's success.[47] The challenge and difficulty of making effective decisions is implied by preliminary evidence suggesting that one-half of organizational decisions fail.[48] Recognizing the firm's core competencies is required before the firm can make important strategic decisions, including those related to entering or exiting markets, investing in new technologies, building new or additional manufacturing capacity, and forming strategic partnerships.[49] Patterns of interactions between individuals and groups that occur as strategic decisions are made affect decision quality as well as how effectively and quickly they are implemented.[50]

Sometimes, mistakes are made when a firm conducts an internal analysis. Managers might, for example, select resources and capabilities as the firm's core competencies that do not, in fact, yield a competitive advantage (see Figure 3.5). When this occurs, decision makers must have the confidence to admit the mistake and take corrective actions. A firm can still grow through well-intended errors. Indeed, learning generated by making and correcting mistakes can be important to the creation of new competitive advantages.[51] Moreover, from the failure resulting from mistakes, firms learn what *not* to do when seeking competitive advantage.[52]

To facilitate the development and use of core competencies, managers must have courage, self-confidence, integrity, the capacity to deal with uncertainty and complexity, and a willingness to hold people accountable for their work *and* to be held accountable themselves. GE's CEO Jack Welch, scheduled to retire at the end of 2000, believes that upper-level executives should empower managers throughout the firm to take charge of their units to achieve stretch goals while expecting to be judged on the results accomplished by those units.[53] Thus, effective strategists try to create an organizational environment in which those working in operating units feel empowered to use core competencies to pursue marketplace opportunities.

Difficult managerial decisions concerning resources, capabilities, and core competencies are characterized by three conditions: uncertainty, complexity, and intraorganizational conflicts (see Figure 3.3).[54]

Managers face *uncertainty* in terms of the emergence of new proprietary technologies, rapidly changing economic and political trends, transformations in societal values, and shifts in customer demands.[55] Environmental uncertainty increases the *complexity* and the range of issues to examine when studying the internal environment. Biases about how to cope with uncertainty affect decisions about the resources and capabilities that will become the foundation of the firm's competitive advantage. Finally, *intraorganizational conflict* surfaces when decisions are made about core competencies that are to be nurtured and about how the nurturing is to take place.

In making decisions affected by these three conditions, judgment should be used. *Judgment* is the capability of making successful decisions when no obviously correct model or rule is available or when relevant data are unreliable or incomplete.[56] In this situation, one must be aware of possible cognitive biases. For instance, one must compare internal firm resources and make a judgment as to whether a resource is a strength or a weakness. When exercising judgment, decision makers demonstrate a willingness to take intelligent risks in a timely manner. In the 21st-century competitive landscape, executive judgment can be a particularly important source of competitive advantage. One reason for this is that, over time, effective judgment allows a firm to retain the loyalty of stakeholders whose support is linked to above-average returns.[57]

FIGURE

3.3 | Conditions Affecting Managerial Decisions About Resources, Capabilities, and Core Competencies

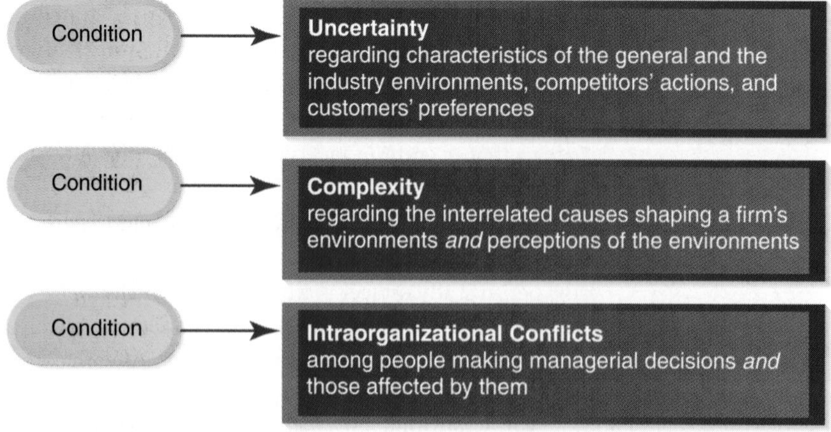

Source: Adapted from R. Amit & P. J. H. Schoemaker, 1993, Strategic assets and organizational rent, *Strategic Management Journal*, 14: 33.

Significant changes in the value-creating potential of a firm's resources and capabilities can occur in a rapidly changing global economy. Because these changes affect a company's power and social structure, inertia or resistance to change may surface. Even though that happens, decision makers should not deny the changes needed in their firm to assure its strategic competitiveness. *Denial* is an unconscious coping mechanism used to block out and not initiate painful changes.[58] Jack Welch, GE's former CEO, believes that top-level executives must demonstrate unflinching candor when making strategic decisions. Part of this candor demands that decision makers cause their firms and their people to face reality as it is—not as it once was or as they want it to be.[59] Successful firms learn that involving many people when making decisions about organizational change reduces denial as well as intraorganizational conflict.[60] Involving a *range* of individuals and groups is important, in that some people have a strong tendency to resist the types of changes that are needed to cope with the 21st century's intensely competitive environment.[61]

Resources, Capabilities, and Core Competencies

Our attention now turns to a description of resources, capabilities, and core competencies—characteristics that are the foundation of competitive advantage. As shown in Figure 3.2, combinations of resources and capabilities are managed to create core competencies. This subsection defines and provides examples of these internal aspects.

Resources

Defined in Chapter 1, *resources* are inputs into a firm's production process. Capital equipment, the skills of individual employees, patents, finances, and talented managers are all resources. Broad in scope, resources cover a spectrum of individual, social, and organizational phenomena.[62]

Typically, resources alone do not yield a competitive advantage.[63] A professional football team may benefit from employing the league's most talented running back, but it is only when the running back integrates his running style with the blocking schemes of the offensive linemen and the team's offensive strategy that a competitive advantage may develop. A competitive advantage is actually created through the *unique bundling of several resources*.[64] Dell Computer Corporation, for example, combines technological and human resources to use what analysts believe is a highly efficient business model (see the discussion about these actions in a Strategic Focus in Chapter 2). This model results in Dell selling PCs directly to customers, bypassing retailers and other middlemen. Thus, the model has created a unique distribution channel that is the company's main competitive advantage.[65] As with Dell, Frito-Lay's distribution system has long been cited "as the company's most important competitive advantage." Recently, though, the firm changed its distribution methods to better integrate its marketing capabilities with the physical delivery and support of products. A new emphasis is to have its army of 15,000-plus salespeople spend more time merchandising and selling chips in retail outlets, rather than loading and sorting products in their trucks.[66]

Tangible resources are assets that can be seen and quantified.

Some of a firm's resources are tangible, while others are intangible. **Tangible resources** are assets that can be seen and quantified. Production equipment, manu-

Intangible resources include assets that are rooted deeply in the firm's history and that have accumulated over time.

facturing plants, and formal reporting structures are examples of tangible resources. **Intangible resources** include assets that are rooted deeply in the firm's history and that have accumulated over time. Because they are embedded in unique patterns of routines, intangible resources are relatively difficult for competitors to understand and imitate. Knowledge, trust between managers and employees or associates, ideas, the capacity for innovation, managerial capabilities, organizational routines (the unique ways people work together), scientific capabilities, and the firm's reputation for its goods or services and the ways it interacts with people (e.g., employees, customers, and suppliers) are examples of intangible resources.[67]

The four types of tangible resources are financial, organizational, physical, and technological (see Table 3.3). The three types of intangible resources (human, innovation, and reputational) are shown in Table 3.4.

TABLE 3.3 | Tangible Resources

Financial Resources	• The firm's borrowing capacity • The firm's ability to generate internal funds
Organizational Resources	• The firm's formal reporting structure and its formal planning, controlling, and coordinating systems
Physical Resources	• Sophistication and location of a firm's plant and equipment • Access to raw materials
Technological Resources	• Stock of technology, such as patents, trademarks, copyrights, and trade secrets.

Source: Adapted from J. B. Barney, 1991, Firm resources and sustained competitive advantage, *Journal of Management,* 17: 101; R. M. Grant, 1991, *Contemporary Strategy Analysis* (Cambridge, U.K.: Blackwell Business), 100–102.

TABLE 3.4 | Intangible Resources

Human Resources	• Knowledge • Trust • Managerial capabilities • Organizational routines
Innovation Resources	• Ideas • Scientific capabilities • Capacity to innovate

Reputational Resources	• Reputation with customers
	  • Brand name
	  • Perceptions of product quality, durability, and reliability
	• Reputation with suppliers
	  • For efficient, effective, supportive, and mutually beneficial interactions and relationships

Source: Adapted from R. Hall, 1992, The strategic analysis of intangible resources, *Strategic Management Journal,* 13: 136–139; R. M. Grant, 1991, *Contemporary Strategy Analysis* (Cambridge, U.K.: Blackwell Business), 101–104.

Tangible Resources

As tangible resources, a firm's borrowing capacity and the status of its plant and equipment are visible to all. The value of many tangible resources can be established through financial statements, but these statements do not account for the value of all of a firm's assets, because they disregard some intangible resources.[68] As such, each of the firm's sources of competitive advantage may not be reflected fully on corporate financial statements. The value of tangible resources is also constrained because it is difficult to leverage them—that is, it is hard to derive additional business or value from a tangible resource. Consider the case of an airplane as a tangible resource or asset: "You can't use the same airplane on five different routes at the same time. You can't put the same crew on five different routes at the same time. And the same goes for the financial investment you've made in the airplane."[69]

Decision makers are challenged to understand fully the strategic value of their firm's tangible and intangible resources. The *strategic value of resources* is indicated by the degree to which they can contribute to the development of capabilities, core competencies, and, ultimately, a competitive advantage. For example, as a tangible resource, a distribution facility will be assigned a monetary value on the firm's balance sheet. The real value of the facility as a resource, however, is grounded in other factors, such as its proximity to raw materials and customers and the manner in which workers integrate their actions internally and with other stakeholders (e.g., suppliers and customers).[70]

Resources are the source of a firm's capabilities (see Figure 3.2). Capabilities in turn are the source of a firm's core competencies, which are the basis of competitive advantages. Compared to tangible resources, intangible resources are a superior and more potent source of core competencies.[71] In fact, in the global economy, "the success of a corporation lies more in its intellectual and systems capabilities than in its physical assets. [Moreover], the capacity to manage human intellect—and to convert it into useful products and services—is fast becoming the critical executive skill of the age."[72] There is some evidence that the value of intangible assets is growing relative to that of tangible assets. John Kendrick is a well-known economist studying the main drivers of economic growth. His findings indicate that there has been a general increase in the contribution of intangible assets to U.S. economic growth since the early 1900s: "In 1929, the ratio of intangible business capital to tangible business capital was 30 percent to 70 percent. In 1990, that ratio was 63 percent to 37 percent."[73]

Intangible Resources

Because they are less visible and more difficult for competitors to understand, purchase, imitate, or substitute for, firms prefer to rely on intangible resources as the foundation for their capabilities and core competencies. In fact, the more unobservable (that is, intangible) a resource is, the more sustainable will be the competitive advantage that is based on it.[74] Another benefit of intangible resources is that, unlike the case with most tangible resources, their use can be leveraged. For instance, sharing knowledge among employees does not diminish its value for any one person. To the contrary, two people sharing their individualized knowledge sets often can leverage them to create additional knowledge that is new to each of them and relevant to helping the firm pursue strategic competitiveness. With intangible resources, the larger the network of users, the greater is the benefit to each party.[75]

As illustrated in the Opening Case, brand names are an intangible resource that helps to create a firm's reputation and are recognized widely as an important source of competitive advantage for many companies, especially those manufacturing and selling consumer goods and services.[76] When effective, brand names inform customers of a product's performance characteristics, attributes, and value.[77] As part of an effort to revitalize Hewlett-Packard (HP), the newly appointed CEO, Carly Fiorina, is allocating $200 million to an advertising campaign. The campaign's primary purpose is to advance and support an overarching corporate image and brand name for the company itself. Historically, people managing the firm's 100-plus individual product lines (e.g., personal computers and LaserJet printers) have been responsible for developing advertising programs to support their products. Fiorina believes that HP would be served better if it were to use its advertising budget to develop a strong brand name as a company that is dedicated to producing a wide diversity of innovative products that are oriented toward providing solutions for customers.[78]

When a brand name yields a competitive advantage, some companies seek additional ways to exploit it in the marketplace. The Harley-Davidson brand name now has such cachet that it adorns a limited-edition Barbie doll, a popular restaurant in New York City, and a line of L'Oreal cologne. Moreover, Harley-Davidson Motorclothes annually generates over $100 million in revenue for the firm. The Harley brand adorns a broad range of clothing items, from black leather jackets to fashions for tots and French-cut women's undergarments.[79]

As a source of capabilities, tangible and intangible resources are a critical part of the pathway to the development of competitive advantage (see Figure 3.2). As discussed previously, the strategic value of resources is increased when they are integrated or combined. Unique combinations of the firm's tangible resources (see Table 3.3) and intangible resources (see Table 3.4), capabilities are what the firm is able to do as a result of teams of resources working together.

Capabilities

Capabilities are the firm's capacity to deploy resources that have been purposely *integrated* to achieve a desired end state.[80] As the glue that binds an organization together, capabilities emerge over time through complex interactions among tangible and intangible resources. Capabilities enable the firm "to create and exploit external opportunities and develop sustained advantages when used with insight and adroitness."[81] Critical to the pursuit of competitive advantage and strategic competitiveness, capabilities are often based on developing, carrying, and exchanging information and knowledge through the firm's human capital.[82] In the view of some representing one of the world's leading consultancies, greater numbers of executives "recognize that people's skills and commitment are [their firm's] best route to competitive advantage and stellar business results."[83] In competitively successful organizations, the firm's knowledge base is embedded in, and reflected by, its capabilities and is a key source of advantage in the 21st-century competitive landscape.[84] Because a knowledge base is grounded in organizational actions that may not be understood explicitly by all employees, the firm's capabilities become stronger and more valuable strategically through repetition and practice.

The foundation of many capabilities lies in the skills and knowledge of a firm's employees and, often, their functional expertise. Hence, the value of human capital in the development and use of capabilities and, ultimately, core competencies cannot be overstated. Specializing in front-end to back-end Web design that equips companies to conduct business on the Internet, Razorfish creates what it calls "unique user experiences" for its clients. Called "fish," the firm believes that its people are among the world's most accomplished in terms of creating value-enhancing user experiences. The knowledge possessed by Razorfish's employees is the pathway through which the company provides strategic, creative, and technology-based solutions for its clients' digital business operations.[85] Similarly, Microsoft believes that its best asset is the "intellectual horsepower" of its employees. To assure continued development of this capability and the core competence that flows from it, the firm strives continuously to hire people who are more talented than the current set of employees. Doing this facilitates satisfying Microsoft's desire to defend and extend the domain of its intellectual property.[86] Firms that are committed to continuously developing their people's capabilities seem to accept the adage that "the person who knows *how* will always have a job. The person who knows *why* will always be his boss."[87]

Thus, increasingly, global business leaders support the view that the knowledge possessed by the firm's human capital is among the most significant of an organization's capabilities and may ultimately be at the root of all competitive advantages. In the words of a business writer, "Today dominance rarely comes to the owner of a stockpile; in fact, it's not usually an issue of goods at all. Power is in the hands of people who hold valuable knowledge."[88] Similarly, researchers have suggested that "in the information age, things are ancillary, knowledge is central. A company's value derives not from things, but from knowledge, know-how, intellectual assets, competencies—all of it embedded in people."[89] Given this reality, the firm's challenge is to create an environment that allows people to fit their individual pieces of knowledge together so

A firm's human capital—the skills and knowledge of employees—is a key source of advantage in the 21st-century competitive landscape.

Knowledge Management and Sustainable Competitive Advantage

If compensation is used as an indicator, organizations appear to place high value on the expected contributions of individuals serving as their chief knowledge officer (CKO) or, somewhat more commonly, chief learning officer (CLO). In 1999, for example, the average salary for CLOs across seven industries (professional services; transportation, communications, and utilities; government; finance, insurance, and real estate; manufacturing; health care; and wholesale and retail sales) was $134,550. In management consulting firms, the average CLO salary that year was $225,000. Combining attractive stock options with these salaries, as is often the case, suggests the importance firms attach to the CLO's work—work that is completed to help their firms' employees learn how to acquire, develop, share, and exploit knowledge.

What is knowledge? As a social construct, knowledge emerges through interaction. Knowledge is not data, nor is it information. *Data* are objective facts, presented without any judgment or context. When categorized, analyzed, summarized, and placed into a context, data become *information.* As data that are endowed with relevance and purpose, information is of competitive value to organizations. Information develops into more competitively relevant knowledge when it is used to establish value-creating connections with the marketplace. *Knowledge,* then, is information that is laden with experience, judgment, intuition, and values. In the final analysis, most knowledge resides within individuals. Because of this, successful organizations provide continuous opportunities for employees to increase their stock of data and information.

At its core, knowledge management is concerned with identifying the valuable knowledge residing within the firm so that it can be catalogued for continuous and effective dissemination and use throughout the company. Developing the type of "corporate memory" that results from these activities is linked with the firm's ability to adapt and modify knowledge and its use in ways that are consistent with changing environmental conditions. Sometimes, as with Siemens, a firm's knowledge management process has a very specific customer focus. A global powerhouse in electrical engineering and electronics, Siemens argues that, for it, "knowledge management entails gathering in-depth information about customers' needs and immediately channeling the knowledge into development, production, logistics and sales processes to maximize customer benefit." To channel knowledge that is relevant to unique projects, Siemens must effectively disseminate catalogued information regarding its product development, production, logistics, and sales functions across the firm.

Two prominent researchers who study knowledge and its management, Ikujiro Nonaka and Hirotaka Takeuchi, believe that there are "four interrelated processes by which knowledge flows throughout the firm and transmutes into different forms." These four processes are the primary means through which firms can manage knowledge.

Socialization is the process of communicating an individual's tacit knowledge to others. Tacit knowledge is knowledge that can be acquired only through observation and practice. Using apprenticeships and assigning mentors to employees are knowledge management methods that firms employ to help people acquire another's skills by watching and practicing. *Externalization* is the process used to convert tacit knowledge into explicit concepts. Metaphors are used often for this purpose to express complex tacit knowledge in more easily understood terms. *Combination* involves the study of sets of knowledge that are held by different individuals. The purpose of combination is to integrate what are often unique tacit knowledge sets to create explicit knowledge that can be shared readily across the firm. Through *internalization*, people throughout the firm absorb explicit knowledge that has been created through socialization, externalization, and combination. This newly generated and explicit knowledge becomes the foundation from which employees are able to create new forms of tacit knowledge—knowledge that then initiates a new round of the fourfold knowledge management process.

SOURCES: J. Byrne, 1999, The search for the young and gifted, *Business Week*, October 4, 108–116; L. Empson, 1999, The challenge of managing knowledge, Mastering Strategy (Part Two), October 4, 9–10; B. Fryer, 1999, Get smart, *Inc. Tech 1999*, 3: 61–70; J. Pfeffer & R. L. Sutton, 1999, Knowing "what" to do is not enough: Turning knowledge into action, *California Management Review*, 42(1): 83–108; J. Webber, 1999, School is never out, *Business Week*, October 4, 164–168; Top Teachers, 1999, *Wall Street Journal*, November 30, B16; P. Clarke, 1998, Implementing a knowledge strategy for your firm, *Research-Technology Management*, March–April, 28–31; Siemens, 1998, Siemens Annual Report; I. Nonaka & H. Takeuchi, 1995, *The Knowledge Creating Company* (New York: Oxford University Press).

that, collectively, each employee will have command of as much organizational knowledge as possible.[90]

To help firms develop an environment in which knowledge is widely spread across all employees, organizations in many different industry settings (e.g., professional services, government, health care, and manufacturing) have created a new upper-level managerial position. As the chief learning officer (CLO), this person is expected to find ways for the organization to acquire, internalize, and share knowledge in competitively relevant manners. Another way of saying this is that the CLO is responsible for determining how the firm should manage knowledge to derive maximum competitive value from it. How to manage the capability called knowledge so it can be a source of competitive advantage is discussed in the Strategic Focus. Gaining an ability to manage knowledge is critical, in that 78 percent of U.S. companies indicated recently that they are moving toward becoming knowledge-based enterprises—enterprises that view knowledge as their primary source of competitive advantage.[91] In general, knowledge should be managed in ways that will support the firm's efforts to create value for customers.[92]

As illustrated in Figure 3.4 and Table 3.5, and as suggested by the description of Siemens in the Strategic Focus, capabilities are often developed in specific functional areas (e.g., manufacturing, R&D, marketing) or in a part (e.g., advertising) of a functional area. Research results suggest a relationship between distinctive competencies (or capabilities) developed in particular functional areas and the firm's financial performance at both the corporate and business-unit levels.[93] Thus, firms should seek to develop functional-area core competencies in individual business units and at the corporate level in the case of diversified firms (as explained in Chapter 6). Table 3.5

3.4 | Capabilities

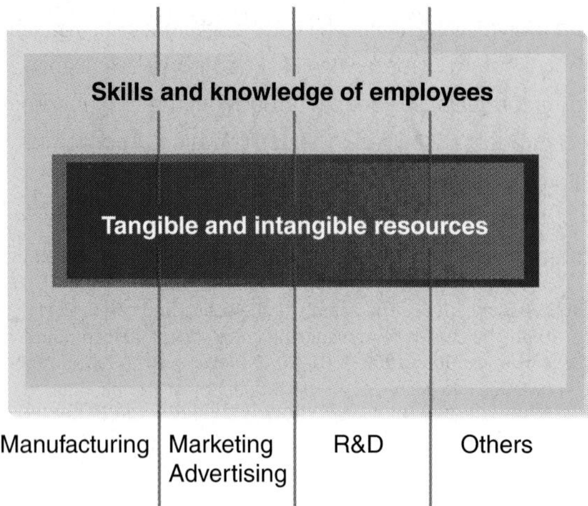

3.5 | Examples of Firms' Capabilities

Functional Areas	Capabilities	Examples of Firms
Distribution	Effective use of logistics management techniques	Wal-Mart
Human resources	Motivating, empowering, and retaining employees	AEROJET
Management information systems	Effective and efficient control of inventories through point-of-purchase data collection methods	Wal-Mart
Marketing	Effective promotion of brand-name products	Gillette Ralph Lauren Clothing McKinsey & Co.
	Effective customer service	Nordstrom Norwest Solectron Corporation Norrell Corporation
	Innovative merchandising	Crate & Barrel
Management	Effective execution of managerial tasks	Hewlett-Packard
	Ability to envision the future of clothing	Gap, Inc.
	Effective organizational structure	PepsiCo
Manufacturing	Design and production skills yielding reliable products	Komatsu
	Product and design quality	Gap, Inc.
	Production of technologically sophisticated automobile engines	Mazda
	Miniaturization of components and products	Sony
Research & development	Exceptional technological capability	Corning
	Development of sophisticated engineered elevator control solutions	Motion Control Engineering Inc.
	Rapid transformation of technology into new products and processes	Chaparral Steel
	Deep knowledge of silver-halide materials	Kodak
	Digital technology	Thomson Consumer Electronics

shows a grouping of organizational functions and the capabilities certain companies are thought to possess in terms of all or parts of those functions.

Core Competencies

Armed with knowledge about resources and capabilities, firms are prepared to identify their core competencies. Defined in Chapter 1, *core competencies* are resources and capabilities that serve as a source of competitive advantage for a firm over its rivals. As the source of competitive advantage for a firm, core competencies distinguish a company competitively and reflect its personality. Core competencies emerge over time through an organizational process of accumulating and learning how to deploy different resources and capabilities. As the capacity to take action, core competencies are the activities that the company performs especially well compared to competitors and through which the firm adds unique value to its goods or services over a long period of time.[94]

Not all of a firm's resources and capabilities are strategic assets—that is, assets that have competitive value and the potential to serve as a source of competitive advantage.[95] Some resources and capabilities may result in incompetence, because they represent competitive areas in which the firm is weak compared to competitors. Thus, some resources or capabilities may stifle or prevent the development of a core competence. Firms with insufficient financial capital, for example, may be unable to purchase facilities or hire the skilled workers required to manufacture products that yield customer value. In this situation, financial capital (a tangible resource) would be a weakness. Armed with an in-depth understanding of their resources and capabilities, firms must locate external environmental opportunities that can be exploited through their capabilities while avoiding competition in areas of weakness.

In addition, an important question is "How many core competencies are required for the firm to have a competitive advantage?" Responses to this question vary. McKinsey & Co. recommends that clients identify three or four competencies around which their strategic actions can be framed.[96] Trying to support and nurture more than four core competencies may prevent the firm from developing the focus it needs to fully exploit its competencies in the marketplace.

Many companies' actions are consistent with McKinsey's advice. With competencies in real estate, restaurant operations, marketing, and its global infrastructure, for example, McDonald's has exactly four competencies, as does Ford Motor Company. With the actual manufacturing of automobiles and trucks expected to become a declining part of its operations, Ford intends to frame its 21st-century competitive success around competencies in the areas of design, branding, sales, and service operations. Acquired recently by AlliedSignal, Honeywell, Inc., long relied on its technology and customer service core competencies to achieve strategic competitiveness. To restore its performance, Michael Capellas, Compaq Computer Corporation's newly appointed CEO and president, intends to use the firm's strong technology core and innovative culture. Brady Corporation is an international manufacturer and marketer of safety, graphics, specialty tape, and industrial identification products. Selling primarily to other companies rather than to end users, Brady relies on its expertise in adhesives and material conversion as the competencies through which it designs, manufactures, and sells a wide variety of special labels and tapes for many different industries. H. E. Butt Grocery Co. intends to use its product selection, pricing strategy, and store design and layout competencies to expand from its Texas base into Northern Mexico, a geographic market the firm finds attractive.[97]

As long as core competencies contribute to strategic competitiveness, it is important that the firm not deviate from their use. Sizzler International, Inc., for example, achieved initial success through competencies (e.g., expertise in purchasing products and the use of cost control systems) that allowed the firm to develop a low-cost steakhouse concept. Sizzler's performance declined as it abandoned the competencies on which this concept was developed and moved toward what eventually became an undistinguished buffet-court approach. To reverse its fortunes, the firm's CEO is taking actions so that Sizzler can return to its heritage of offering "a great streak grill concept and a great salad bar." Purchasing expertise and product storage and preparation skills are competencies to be emphasized in Sizzler's turnaround effort.[98]

Not all resources and capabilities are core competencies. The next section discusses two approaches for identifying core competencies.

Building Core Competencies

Two tools help the firm identify and build core competencies.[99] The first tool consists of four specific criteria that firms use to determine which of their resources and capabilities are core competencies. Because they have satisfied the four criteria of affording sustainable competitive advantage, the capabilities shown in Table 3.5 are core competencies for the firms possessing them. The second tool is the value chain analysis. Firms use this tool to select the value-creating competencies that should be maintained, upgraded, or developed and those that should be outsourced.

Criteria of Sustainable Competitive Advantage

As shown in Table 3.6, capabilities that are valuable, rare, costly to imitate, and nonsubstitutable are strategic capabilities. Strategic capabilities are also known as core competencies and hence serve as a source of competitive advantage for the firm over its rivals. Capabilities failing to satisfy the four criteria of sustainable competitive advantage are not core competencies. Thus, as shown in Figure 3.5, every core compe-

3.6 | Four Criteria for Determining Strategic Capabilities

Valuable Capabilities	• Help a firm neutralize threats or exploit opportunities
Rare Capabilities	• Are not possessed by many others
Costly-to-Imitate Capabilities	• Historical: A unique and a valuable organizational culture or brand name • Ambiguous cause: The causes and uses of a competence are unclear • Social complexity: Interpersonal relationships, trust, and friendship among managers, suppliers, and customers
Nonsubstitutable Capabilities	• No strategic equivalent

FIGURE 3.5 | Core Competence as a Strategic Capability

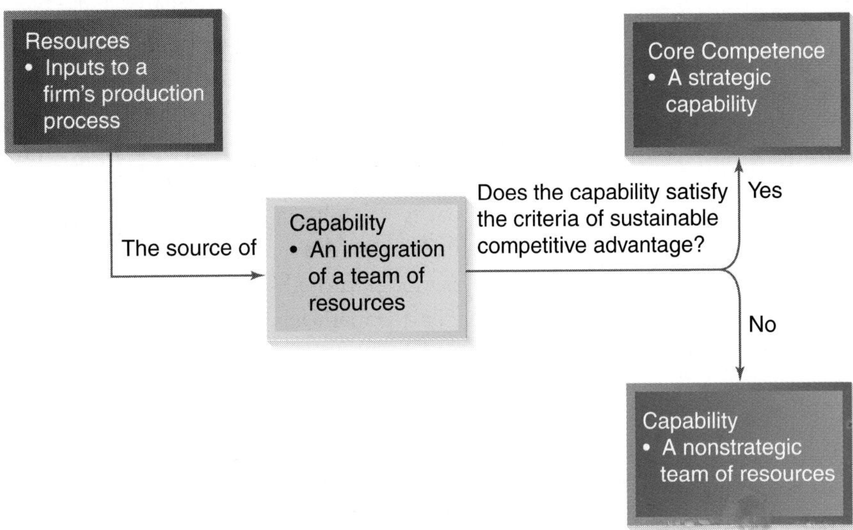

tence is a capability, but not every capability is a core competence. Operationally, for a capability to be a core competence, it must be "valuable and nonsubstitutable, from a customer's point of view, and unique and inimitable, from a competitor's point of view."[100]

A sustained competitive advantage is achieved only when competitors have tried, without success, to duplicate the benefits of the firm's strategy or when competitors lack the confidence to attempt imitation. For some period of time, the firm may earn a competitive advantage through the use of capabilities that are, for example, valuable and rare, but are imitable.[101] In such an instance, the length of time a firm can expect to retain its competitive advantage is a function of how quickly competitors can successfully imitate a good, service, or process. It is only through the combination of conditions represented by all four criteria that a firm's capabilities have the potential to create a sustainable competitive advantage.

Valuable

Valuable capabilities are those that create value for a firm by exploiting opportunities or neutralizing threats in the firm's external environment.

Valuable capabilities are those that create value for a firm by exploiting opportunities or neutralizing threats in the firm's external environment. Valuable capabilities enable a firm to formulate and implement strategies that create value for specific customers. Sony Corp. has used its valuable capabilities dealing with the designing, manufacturing, and selling of miniaturized electronic technology to exploit a range of marketplace opportunities, including those for portable disc players and easy-to-hold 8-mm video cameras. Identifying 21st-century opportunities that are a product of rapidly emerging technologies, Sony wants customers to enter its "digital world," whether that entry is through a television, PC, or cell phone.[102] Relying initially on its distribution capabilities to pursue an opportunity, Wal-Mart started its business by offering startlingly low prices on a vast selection of brand-name goods. Analysts believe that Wal-Mart changed the way consumers thought about value, letting them know that they did not have to pay the prices charged by most retailers.[103]

Rare

Rare capabilities are those possessed by a few, if any, current or potential competitors.

Rare capabilities are those possessed by few, if any, current or potential competitors. A key question managers seek to answer when evaluating this criterion is "How many rival firms possess these valuable capabilities?" Capabilities possessed by many rival firms are unlikely to be a source of competitive advantage for any one of them. Instead, valuable, but common (i.e., not rare), resources and capabilities are sources of competitive parity.[104] Competitive advantage results only when firms develop and exploit capabilities that differ from those they share with competitors. For example, Dell's business model through which it sells directly to customers allows it to be more efficient than its competitors and to record growth rates that outpace those of the industry. Thus, the capabilities Dell uses to shape and deploy its business model appear to be rare.[105]

Costly to Imitate

Costly-to-imitate capabilities are those that other firms cannot develop easily.

Costly-to-imitate capabilities are those that other firms cannot develop easily. Capabilities that are costly to imitate can occur because of one or a combination of three reasons (see Table 3.6).

First, a firm sometimes is able to develop capabilities because of *unique historical conditions*. "As firms evolve, they pick up skills, abilities and resources that are unique to them, reflecting their particular path through history."[106] Another way of saying this is that firms sometimes are able to develop capabilities because they were in the right place at the right time.[107]

A firm with a unique and valuable organizational culture that emerged in the early stages of the company's history "may have an imperfectly imitable advantage over firms founded in another historical period,"[108] one in which less valuable (or competitively useful) values and beliefs strongly influenced the development of the firm's culture. This may be the case for the consulting firm McKinsey & Co. Discussed briefly in Chapter 1, organizational culture is "something that people connect with, feel inspired by, think of as a normal way of operating. It's in their hearts and minds, and its core is voluntary behavior."[109] An organizational culture is a source of advantage when employees are held together tightly by their belief in it.[110]

McKinsey's culture is thought by competitors, clients, and analysts alike to be a primary source of competitive advantage. As testimony to the intangibility of culture—even to some of those familiar with it—consider the following description of culture as McKinsey's source of advantage: "It is that culture, unique to McKinsey and eccentric, which sets the firm apart from virtually any other business organization and which often mystifies even those who engage [its] services." Marvin Bower, the company's founder, established the historical foundation for McKinsey's culture. In fact, "much of what McKinsey is today harks back to the early 1930s," when Bower entered the consulting business. Bower's concept of how his consulting firm would operate was that it should provide advice about effective managerial practices to top-level executives. As guidance for McKinsey's consultants, Bower developed a set of principles. Cited frequently and intensely, these principles actually define what McKinsey was and is today. They are the backbone of the company's unique, and what some think is an enigmatic, culture. According to Bower's principles, a McKinsey consultant should (1) put the interests of the client ahead of increasing the company's revenues, (2) remain silent about the client's business operations, (3) be truthful and not fear challenging a client's opinion, and (4) perform only work that she or he believes is in the client's best interests and is something McKinsey can do well.[111] It would seem that McKinsey's culture is able to create a relentless, yet positive, dissatisfaction among those working within it to challenge themselves to perform in ways that will continuously generate greater levels of value for clients.

A second condition of being costly to imitate occurs when the link between the firm's competencies and its competitive advantage is *causally ambiguous*.[112] In these instances, competitors are unable to understand clearly how a firm uses its competencies as the foundation for competitive advantage. As a result, competitors are uncertain about the competencies they should develop to duplicate the benefits of a competitor's value-creating strategy. Gordon Forward, CEO of Chaparral Steel, allows competitors to tour his firm's facilities. In Forward's words, competitors can be shown almost "everything and we will be giving away nothing because they can't take it home with them."[113] Contributing to Chaparral Steel's causally ambiguous operations is the fact that in Forward's view, "We talk about 'mentomanufacturing' here—using our minds, as opposed to manufacturing—just using our hands."[114]

Social complexity is the third reason that capabilities can be costly to imitate. Social complexity means that at least some, and frequently many, of the firm's capabilities are the product of complex social phenomena. Examples of socially complex capabilities include interpersonal relationships, trust, and friendships among managers and between managers and employees and a firm's reputation with suppliers and customers. Firms such as GE, Hewlett-Packard, Merck, Sony, Wal-Mart, and Walt Disney Co. rely on their socially complex capabilities as the foundation for a vision of their role in the global economy, their responsibilities to stakeholders (including customers, suppliers, and local communities), and their commitment to employees. Important to how those firms operate, "these socially complex visions have profoundly affected the decisions made by these firms and the strategies they have pursued."[115]

Nonsubstitutable

Nonsubstitutable capabilities are those that do not have strategic equivalents.

Nonsubstitutable capabilities are those that do not have strategic equivalents. This final requirement for a capability to be a source of competitive advantage "is that there must be no strategically equivalent valuable resources that are themselves either not rare or imitable. Two valuable firm resources (or two bundles of firm resources) are strategically equivalent when they each can be exploited separately to implement the same strategies."[116] In general, the strategic value of capabilities increases the more difficult they are to substitute for.[117] The more invisible capabilities are, the more difficult it is for firms to find substitutes and the greater the challenge is to competitors trying to imitate a firm's value-creating strategy. Firm-specific knowledge and trust-based working relationships between managers and nonmanagerial personnel are examples of capabilities that are difficult to identify and for which finding a substitute is challenging. Additional comments about trust as a capability that can be a core competence are offered in the Strategic Focus.

Trust: Is It Valuable, Rare, Costly to Imitate, and Nonsubstitutable?

Trust has long been thought to have an important link with organizational success. When trust exists, for example, it is less necessary for firms to establish formal contracts to specify expected actions and interaction patterns. In addition, when parties trust one another, it is less necessary for the firm to rely on organizational structures (see Chapter 11 for study of different types of structures) to monitor and control individual and group behaviors. Thus, through trust-based working relationships, the firm's transaction costs, as measured by formal contracts and organizational structures, are reduced. Another way of saying this is that trust reduces the costs the firm incurs to manage or govern itself.

Various attributes are associated with trust. Perhaps the most prominent of these is risk. In terms of capabilities and core competencies, the study of trust is concerned with managerial and individual risk rather than organizational risk. *Managerial risk* speaks to the reality of uncertain outcomes that are associated with managerial decisions. In contrast, *organizational risk* is a characteristic of firms experiencing volatile and often unpredictable income streams. The logic of managerial risk applies at the level of each individual, in that "all trusting relationships have meaningful incentives at stake and the trusting party must understand the risks involved in the relationship." In essence, managerial risk creates vulnerability, because to trust another party makes a person vulnerable to the outcomes of that party's actions. Combining these perspectives with others about risk, Davis, Schoorman, Mayer, and Tan comprehensively define trust as "the willingness of a party (trustor) to be vulnerable to the actions of another party (trustee) based on the expectation that the trustee will perform an action important to the trustor, regardless of the trustor's ability to monitor or control the trustee."

Evidence is emerging to suggest that trust, as just explicated, is a source of competitive advantage for the firm when it exists between the general manager and her or his employees. This type of trust is based on the trustor's perception of the trustee's ability, benevolence, and integrity. *Ability* is the composite of skills and attributes through which a party is able to influence outcomes in a specific situation. *Benevolence* is the extent to which the trustee perceives that the trustor intends to perform in ways that serve the trustor's good in a particular situation. *Integrity* deals with the trustor's belief that the trustee will follow a set of principles that are not only acceptable, but also desirable, given the trustor's value set. A reputation for honesty and fairness influences the trustee's perception of the trustor's integrity.

As the foundation for a study that was conducted to determine whether trust could be a source of competitive advantage, Davis and his colleagues hypothesized that "the level of trust a general manager is able to garner from his/her employees is contingent upon the employee's perceptions of the general manager's ability, benevolence and integrity." The researchers found trust to be significantly related to sales, profits, and turnover in a corporation consisting of a chain of nine restaurants. More broadly, the study concluded that the ability of a general manager to earn higher trust from her or his employees likely creates a competitive advantage for a firm over its rivals.

Thus, the results from the Davis et al. study suggest that trust satisfies at least three, and seemingly all four, of the criteria of sustainable competitive advantage. Trust is *valuable* because it allows a firm (e.g., the restaurants in the study's sample) to better serve its customers and to improve its performance as a result. Trust is *rare* because few rivals have the relationship between managers and employees that trust denotes. Trust is *costly to imitate* because it is causally ambiguous and socially complex. As such, it is difficult for competitors to understand what trust is and how to establish it in their firms. Is trust *nonsubstitutable*? It may very well be, in that trust is a capability that is difficult for competitors to observe. As we have noted, capabilities that cannot be observed at least somewhat easily are hard to imitate. Although devices such as the use of strict performance benchmarks can be used to monitor employees' work, these mechanisms are costly relative to trust.

Placing these expectations about trust into the context of information included in Table 3.7 suggests that the firm that has trust as a valuable, rare, costly-to-imitate, and likely nonsubstitutable capability has a sustainable competitive advantage that can be expected to contribute to the earning of above-average returns. Thus, trust has the potential to reduce the costs that are required to monitor employees' behaviors, as well as to improve revenue streams through the efforts of employees who are motivated by the trust between themselves and their managers.

The suggestion that trust is a capability that can be a competitive advantage is supported by other firms' experiences. Anderson & Associates, for example, operates through what it calls "open-book management." Among other operational principles, this system is one through which all of the firm's financial information, including information about salaries, is placed on its intranet. The foundation on which open-book management is based is trust. As the firm's CEO says, "We do have a great deal of trust here, and our employees stick with us." In his view, the trust-based open-book management system contributes to the firm's profitability, although quantitative measures are not in place to verify this belief.

Radius, a restaurant in Boston serving French foods, believes that its success is attributable to four core competencies: superb cuisine, a special ambience, a chef with "presence," and excellent teamwork. Of these, the teamwork competence, the restaurant's personnel believe, is perhaps its most important source of competitive advantage. Sharing tasks at stations (e.g., the meat station, pastry station, fish station, etc.), personnel display high degrees of trust as they exchange their individual knowledge sets to benefit the entire operation. MTW Corp. provides software and Internet applications to the financial-services sector and to state governments. Critical to the firm's success are "expectation agreements," which establish a set of mutually agreed-on objectives between an individual, her or his boss, and a work team. These agreements are based largely on trust, in that the firm's personnel are spread out among its seven regional offices. This system results in situations where each person relies on others located in different settings to complete individual parts of consulting engagements for which several parties are held responsible.

Our discussion of these firms suggests that the abilities of Anderson & Associates, Radius, and MTW Corp. to earn above-average returns are increased because their respective trust capabilities are valuable, rare, costly to imitate, and nonsubstitutable.

SOURCES: J. H. Davis, F. David Schoorman, R. C. Mayer, & H. H. Tan, 2000, The trusted general manager and business unit performance: Empirical evidence of a competitive advantage, *Strategic Management Journal*, in press; G. Imperato, 2000, Their specialty? Teamwork, *Fast Company,* January–February, 54–56; K. Anderson, 1999, By the (open) book, *Inc. Tech 1999,* 3: 33–34; P. Martin, 1999, Lessons in humility, *Financial Times,* June 22, 18; T. B. Palmer & R. M. Wiseman, 1999, Decoupling risk taking from income stream uncertainty: A holistic model of risk, *Strategic Management Journal,* 20: 1037–1062; J. Rosenfeld, 1999, MTW puts people first, *Fast Company,* December, 86–88.

TABLE

3.7 | Outcomes from Combinations of the Criteria for Sustainable Competitive Advantage

Is the Resource or Capability Valuable?	Is the Resource or Capability Rare?	Is the Resource or Capability Costly to Imitate?	Is the Resource or Capability Nonsubstitutable?	Competitive Consequences	Performance Implications
No	No	No	No	Competitive disadvantage	Below-average returns
Yes	No	No	Yes/no	Competitive parity	Average returns
Yes	Yes	No	Yes/no	Temporary competitive advantage	Above-average returns to average returns
Yes	Yes	Yes	Yes	Sustainable competitive advantage	Above-average returns

To summarize this discussion, we reiterate that sustainable competitive advantage results only through the use of capabilities that are valuable, rare, costly to imitate, and nonsubstitutable. Table 3.7 shows the competitive consequences and performance implications resulting from combinations of the four criteria of sustainability. The analysis suggested by the table helps managers determine the strategic value of a firm's capabilities. Resources and capabilities falling into the first row in the table (that is, resources and capabilities that are neither valuable nor rare and that are imitable and for which strategic substitutes exist) are ones the firm should not emphasize to formulate and implement strategies. Capabilities yielding competitive parity and either temporary or sustainable competitive advantage, however, will be supported. Large competitors such as Coca-Cola and PepsiCo may have capabilities that can yield only competitive parity. In such cases, the firms will nurture these capabilities while simultaneously emphasizing those that can yield either a temporary or sustainable competitive advantage.

In the next section, we discuss another framework firms use to examine their resources and capabilities to identify their core competencies. Value chain analysis allows the firm to understand the parts of its operations that create value and those that do not. Understanding these issues is important because the firm earns above-average returns only when the value it creates is greater than the costs incurred to create that value.[118]

Value Chain Analysis

The value chain is a template that the firm uses to understand its cost position and to identify the multiple means that might be used to facilitate the implementation of its

FIGURE 3.6 | The Basic Value Chain

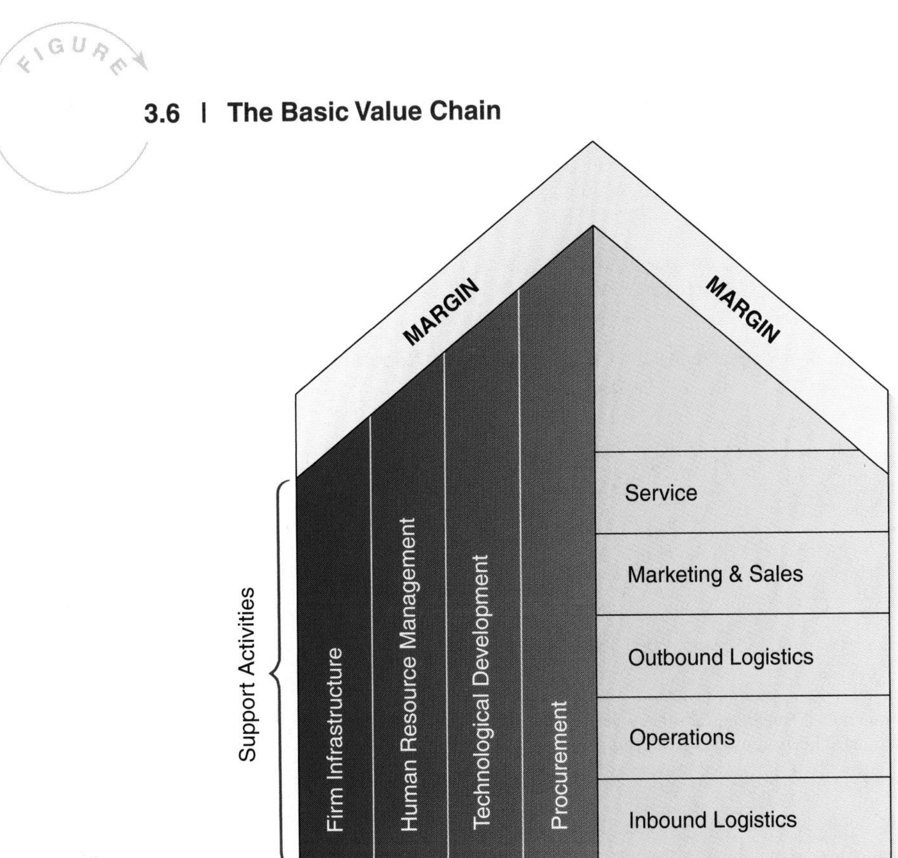

Primary activities are involved with a product's physical creation, its sale and distribution to buyers, and its service after the sale.

Support activities provide the support necessary for the primary activities to take place

business-level strategy.[119] As shown in Figure 3.6, a firm's value chain is segmented into primary and support activities. **Primary activities** are involved with a product's physical creation, its sale and distribution to buyers, and its service after the sale. **Support activities** provide the support necessary for the primary activities to take place. The value chain shows how a product moves from the raw-material stage to the final customer. For individual firms, the essential idea of the value chain "is to add as much value as possible as cheaply as possible, and, most important, to capture that value." In a globally competitive economy, "the most valuable links on the chain tend to belong to people who own knowledge—particularly about customers."[120] This locus of value-creating possibilities applies just as strongly to retail and service firms as it does to manufacturers. Thus, for organizations in all sectors, the effects of e-commerce make it increasingly necessary for companies to develop value-adding knowledge processes to compensate for the value and margin that the Internet strips from physical processes.[121]

Table 3.8 lists the items to be studied to assess the value-creating potential of primary activities. In Table 3.9, the items to consider when studying support activities are shown. As with the analysis of primary activities, the intent in examining these

3.8 | Examining the Value-Creating Potential of Primary Activities

Inbound Logistics

Activities, such as materials handling, warehousing, and inventory control, used to receive, store, and disseminate inputs to a product.

Operations

Activities necessary to convert the inputs provided by inbound logistics into final product form. Machining, packaging, assembly, and equipment maintenance are examples of operations activities.

Outbound Logistics

Activities involved with collecting, storing, and physically distributing the final product to customers. Examples of these activities include finished-goods warehousing, materials handling, and order processing.

Marketing and Sales

Activities completed to provide means through which customers can purchase products and to induce them to do so. To effectively market and sell products, firms develop advertising and promotional campaigns, select appropriate distribution channels, and select, develop, and support their sales force.

Service

Activities designed to enhance or maintain a product's value. Firms engage in a range of service-related activities, including installation, repair, training, and adjustment.

Each activity should be examined relative to competitors' abilities. Accordingly, firms rate each activity as *superior, equivalent,* or *inferior.*

Source: Adapted with the permission of The Free Press, a division of Simon & Schuster, Inc., from *Competitive Advantage: Creating and Sustaining Superior Performance,* by Michael E. Porter, pp. 39–40, Copyright © 1985,1998 by Michael E. Porter.

3.9 | Examining the Value-Creating Potential of Support Activities

Procurement

Activities completed to *purchase* the inputs needed to produce a firm's products. Purchased inputs include items fully consumed during the manufacture of products (e.g., raw materials and supplies, as well as fixed assets—machinery, laboratory equipment, office equipment, and buildings).

Technological Development

Activities completed to improve a firm's product and the processes used to manufacture it. Technological development takes many forms, such as process equipment, basic research and product design, and servicing procedures.

Human Resource Management

Activities involved with recruiting, hiring, training, developing, and compensating all personnel.

Firm Infrastructure

Firm infrastructure includes activities such as general management, planning, finance, accounting, legal support, and governmental relations that are required to support the work of the entire value chain. Through its infrastructure, the firm strives to effectively and consistently identify external opportunities and threats, identify resources and capabilities, and support core competencies.

Each activity should be examined relative to competitors' abilities. Accordingly, firms rate each activity as *superior, equivalent,* or *inferior.*

Source: Adapted with the permission of The Free Press, a division of Simon & Schuster, Inc., from *Competitive Advantage: Creating and Sustaining Superior Performance,* by Michael E. Porter, pp. 40–43, Copyright © 1985,1998 by Michael E. Porter.

Creating Value at FedEx and UPS

From the company's founding close to 30 years ago, FedEx's strategic competitiveness has been based on an obsession with, and careful nurturing of, delivery *speed* and *reliability* as its core competencies. These competencies have been critical to the pursuit of the opportunities that were associated with Frederick W. Smith's early vision of today's fast-cycle global economy. Believing that value could be added to business firms' operations if they were to receive urgently required materials on an overnight basis, Smith pioneered what is seen as a fast and reliable, yet pricey, delivery system.

Historically, the foundation of FedEx's successful business model has been customers' recognition that they were short of either key parts that were needed for their production processes or items being demanded by their customers. The reason this model worked is that for the first 20-plus years of FedEx's life, business firms "couldn't plan their needs particularly well, [so] they relied on FedEx to make up in speed what they lacked in precision." Today, however, both customers and competitors (e.g., UPS) are taking strategic actions that challenge the effectiveness of FedEx's business model. These challenges are largely a product of the opportunities being created by what is rapidly becoming a global, knowledge-based logistics business.

An increasing number of companies, some of which have been loyal FedEx customers that rely on the value FedEx's speed and reliability competencies create for them, are carefully studying the "supply" part of their value chains. By more effectively coordinating all of their inbound and outbound logistics activities, firms can reduce a number of their costs, including those associated with purchasing raw materials as well as expenses that are incurred to store component parts during the production process and to inventory finished goods. The actions the firm takes to increase the effectiveness of its inbound and outbound logistics activities are grouped into a system called *supply chain management*. An effective supply chain management system reduces the unpredictability of the firm's operations. In turn, increased predictability reduces the firm's need for the "kind of expensive, rapid-fire delivery FedEx excels at providing." Being able to create value by managing its own supply chain can result in a competitive advantage for the firm.

In response to changes in its external environment, as manifested by customers' actions, FedEx is trying to recast itself as a major provider of the type of supply-chain management systems that now threaten the firm's strategic competitiveness. Flowing from a newly designed strategic intent "to become the most compelling end-to-end supply-chain solution provider in the industry," FedEx wants to design networks that client organizations can use to replace their inefficient telephone and fax transactions with digital exchanges of information. These exchanges will address a number of supply-chain management issues, including those of product demand, production schedules, and the availability of raw materials. Using its systems, FedEx believes, would create more value for the client firm than would a decision to develop and use its own supply-chain management system. FedEx thinks that, working at maximum effectiveness and efficiency, its system could enable some companies to eliminate their warehouses. In general, the FedEx system is "planned to allow companies to outsource all or part of their supply-chain to a single provider, thus enabling them to concentrate on their core competencies while benefiting from cost-effective, globally synchronized distribution of their products."

Thus, through study of the value chain, FedEx believes that it has been able to design a supply-chain management system that can create value for a number of client organizations. The ability of supply-chain management systems to create value for organizations is being more widely recognized in a world that is increasingly being affected by the Internet's capabilities. In the context of the supply part of the value chain, the Internet has provided a host of new direct-ordering systems. Simultaneously, however, it has created a need for more efficient distribution capabilities. This need exists for the conduct of both business-to-consumer and business-to-business transactions.

Competitors are also challenging FedEx as the firm seeks to find ways to create value for customers. UPS, for example, has been very aggressive. The following comment from business analysts suggests the change UPS is completing to discover additional ways to create value for client organizations: "UPS used to be a trucking company with technology. Now it's a technology company with trucks." Largely responsible for this transformation of UPS is the $11 billion the firm poured into technology in the last decade. These funds were used to buy a host of products—mainframe computers, a vast array of networked PCs, handheld computers, wireless modems, and cellular networks, among others—and to hire and support 4,000 programmers and technicians. Founded in 1907, UPS relies on several core competencies, including those of operational efficiency and uniformity, to deliver over 3 billion parcels and documents annually. UPS has formed a core competency in operational efficiency through the development and consistent application of 340 precise methods that truck drivers are taught to use when delivering customers' products. The efficiencies generated by these methods contribute to UPS's net income and profit margins. In 1999, for example, the firm's net income was $2.3 billion, an amount that doubled 1996 earnings. Contributing to these earnings was an increase in the company's operating margin from 9.1 percent in 1996 to 14.7 percent in 1999.

As is the case for FedEx, UPS seeks to help customers create value by using its technological capabilities to facilitate improved management of clients' supply chains. The firm's working relationship with Fender International, maker of the world-famous Stratocaster electric guitar and other brands such as Guild and Squier, demonstrates how UPS does this. In fact, UPS actually manages Fender's supply-chain activities in Europe, the Middle East, and Africa. This relationship is specified in the formal contract between the two firms, which calls for UPS to "manage shipments coming into Europe by sea and land freight services from manufacturing sites around the world, inspect the products for quality, oversee inventory, fulfill distributor and dealer orders and manage multi-carrier deliveries to 22 countries in Europe and around 10 in the Middle East and Africa." One of the major benefits of this supply-chain management system is that Fender distributors, which no longer must hold substantial inventories, are able to focus more on areas of core competence, such as marketing activities, brand promotion, and sales support. Actions such as these to create value for customers are consistent with the UPS sales mantra: "We can help you move more than just packages. We can help manage your inventory and information."

Thus, FedEx and UPS are examples of firms that analyze the value chain to identify the core competencies they possess or can develop to create value for a customer or client. Increasingly, in a global economy in which some believe that the fundamental laws of pricing and distribution have changed, these firms' future strategic competitiveness may be linked to their ability to create value for customers through effective and efficient management of the customers' supply chains.

SOURCES: K. Barron, 2000, Logistics in brown, *Forbes*, January 10, 78–83; FedEx, 2000, FedEx Home Page, January 2, *www.fedex.com*; T. Petzinger, Jr., 2000, So long, supply and demand, *Wall Street Journal*, January 1, R31; R. S. Russell & B. W. Taylor, III, 2000, *Operations Management*, 3d ed. (Upper Saddle River, NJ: Prentice Hall, Inc.); United Parcel Service, 2000, United Parcel Service Home Page, January 2, *www.ups.com*; D. A. Blackmon, 1999, Overnight, everything changed for FedEx; Can it reinvent itself? *Wall Street Journal*, November 4, A1, A16; M. Budman, 1999, Getting it there, *Across the Board*, May, 37–40; P. Hastings, 1999, Another string to its bow, *Financial Times*, June 17, 18.

---

items is to determine areas where the firm has the potential to create and capture value. All items included in both tables are to be evaluated with competitors' capabilities in mind. To be a source of competitive advantage, a resource or capability must allow a firm (1) to perform an activity in a manner that is superior to the way competitors perform it, or (2) to perform a value-creating activity that competitors cannot complete. Only under these conditions does a firm create value for customers and have opportunities to capture that value. Sometimes, this requires firms to reconfigure or recombine parts of the value chain in unique ways. As shown in Figure 3.7, Federal Express (FedEx) changed the nature of the delivery business by reconfiguring both its outbound logistics (a primary activity) and its human resource management (a support activity) to originate the overnight delivery business, creating value for itself in the process of doing so. Further discussion about how FedEx and its major competitor, United Parcel Service (UPS), are trying to create value in the 21st-century competitive landscape appears in the Strategic Focus.

Rating a firm's capability to execute the primary and support activities is challenging. Earlier in the chapter, we noted that identifying and assessing the value of a firm's resources and capabilities requires judgment. Judgment is equally necessary in using value chain analysis. The reason for this is that there is no obviously correct model or rule available to help in the process. Moreover, most data that are available for these evaluations are largely anecdotal, sometimes unreliable, or difficult to interpret.

As with FedEx and UPS, an effective value chain analysis results in the identification of new ways to perform activities that create value. Recently, Pirelli SpA unveiled a tire-manufacturing process that it expects will eventually allow the company to reduce its production costs by 25 percent while simultaneously increasing product quality. Called a modular integrated robotized system, this new technology is an automated process through which Pirelli "will be able to reduce the steps in manufacturing a tire from 14 to just three, while cutting the lead time from six days to just 72 minutes."[122] Thus, this change is intended to help Pirelli create more value in the operation's primary activity. In the service sector, Rosenbluth International is altering how it creates value in terms of primary activities. As a small travel agent, Rosenbluth was being affected by airlines' efforts to encourage customers to make their own purchases via the Internet and by the reductions in commissions the company receives for bookings. Following a study of how it could reconfigure its value chain to create a different type of value, Rosenbluth decided to recast itself as a corporate travel adviser. This role is in contrast to its previous work as an intermediary between airlines and

FIGURE 3.7 | Increased Value in Human Resource Management and Outbound Logistics Created a Core Competence for Federal Express

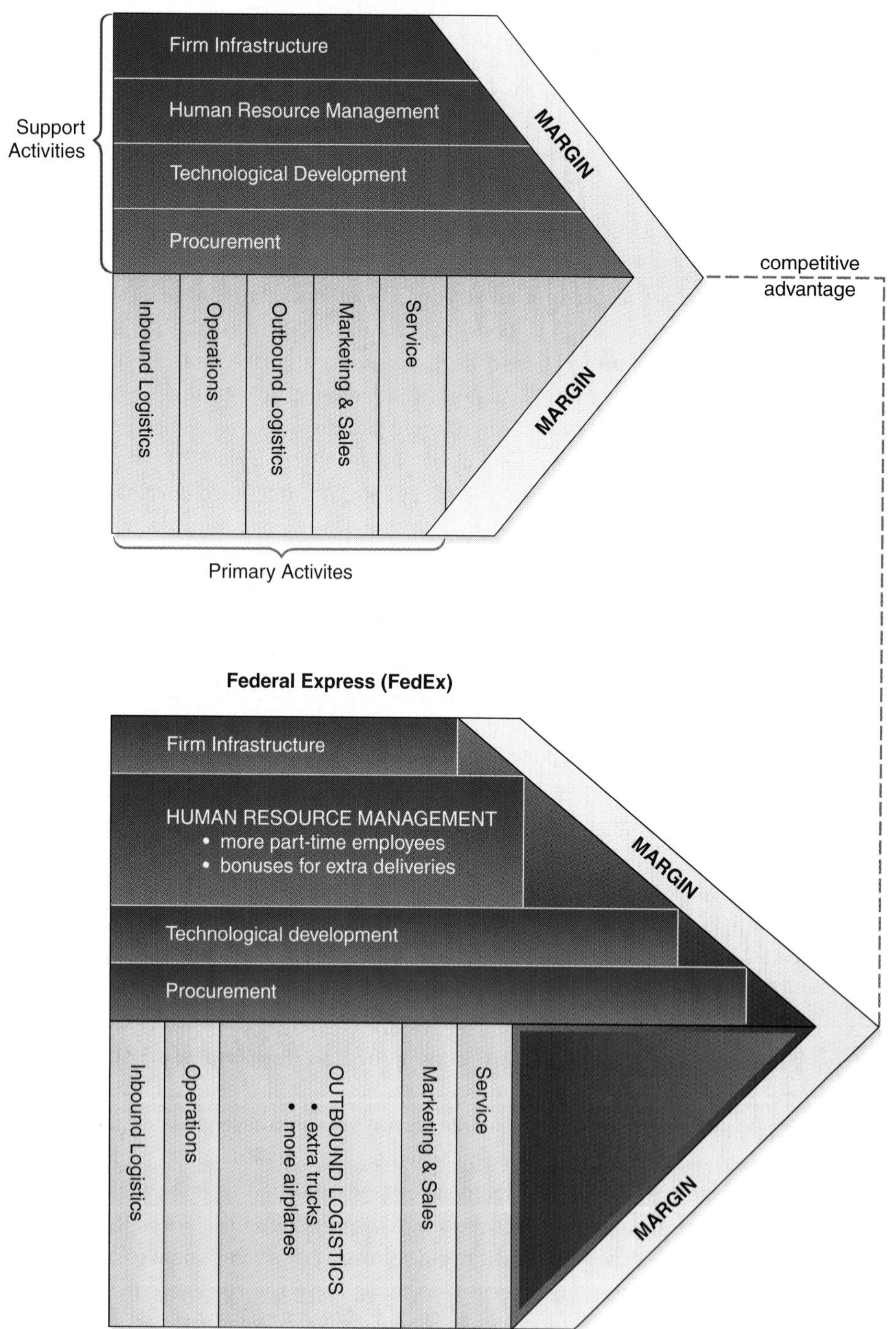

Firms use outsourcing because they do not possess the resources and capabilities needed to achieve competitive superiority in all primary and support activities. Outsourcing allows a firm to concentrate on its core competencies to create value.

passengers. Essentially, in its new value-creating role, Rosenbluth returns any commissions earned to its corporate client. The value Rosenbluth creates for corporations is to handle their travel requirements effectively and efficiently, sometimes offering videoconference links as an alternative to travel.[123]

What should a firm do with respect to primary and support activities in which its resources and capabilities are not a source of competence and competitive advantage? In these instances, firms should study the possibility of outsourcing the work associated with primary and support activities in which they cannot create and capture value.

Outsourcing

Outsourcing is the purchase of a value-creating activity from an external supplier.

Concerned with how components, finished goods, or services will be obtained, **outsourcing** is the purchase of a value-creating activity from an external supplier.[124] In multiple global industries, the trend toward outsourcing continues at a rapid pace.[125]

Sometimes, virtually all firms within an industry seek the strategic value that can be captured through effective outsourcing. The automobile-manufacturing industry is an example of this. Ford Motor Company, for example, has decided to outsource key parts of its final assembly operations. Initially, the plan is for machine tool suppliers and equipment manufacturers to take over assembly operations at Ford's new $1.3 billion Brazilian car plant. Although the outcome of Ford's move is too early to determine with certainty, some analysts suggest that this outsourcing foray may signal the firm's gradual withdrawal from final assembly activities as a core function. Nissan Motor Co. has signed a $1 billion contract with IBM. Covering a nine-and-one-half-year period, the arrangement calls for IBM to manage Nissan's North American computer systems. To fulfill its contractual obligations, IBM will handle software and hardware for various functions, including payroll, human resources, and car distribution. Nissan expects its outsourcing decision to reduce its costs.[126]

The major reason outsourcing is used prominently is that few, if any, firms possess the resources and capabilities required to achieve competitive superiority in all primary and support activities. With respect to technologies, for example, research suggests that few companies can afford to develop internally all the technologies that might lead to competitive advantage in the future. By nurturing a small number of core competencies, the firm increases its probability of developing a competitive advantage. In addition, by outsourcing activities in which it lacks capabilities, the firm can concentrate fully on those areas in which it can create value.[127] Dell Computer Corporation, for example, outsources most of its manufacturing and customer service activities, so it can concentrate on creating value through its distribution channels. Nike and Reebok both focus on design and marketing, areas in which those firms believe that they have core competencies. Outsourcing almost all of their manufacturing in order to control costs generates resources that can be used to nurture and support those firms' design and marketing competencies.[128]

Outsourcing by large firms such as Dell, Nike, and Reebok creates opportunities for smaller firms. Using focus business-level strategies (discussed fully in Chapter 4), these companies concentrate on providing superior service to their customers in terms of specific functions. Contract Chemicals, for example, is a small specialty chemicals producer based in Knowsley, United Kingdom. The firm specializes in handling and processing toxic, unstable, and corrosive materials for end users in the pharmaceuticals, detergents, photographic materials, foods, and agrochemicals industries. Its handling and processing core competencies are the foundation of the competitive success the firm has achieved as it has become the market leader in terms of some niche products and processes. Similarly, Stax Research, Inc., concentrates on providing business research and due-diligence support to its clients. Large companies contract with Stax to have the firm conduct the research needed for them to complete due-diligence processes related to possible merger and acquisition transactions. Unlike its competitors, Stax contracts with clients to conduct research only—it does not offer advice to its clients based on the results of its research. In the words of an analyst, "Stax has carved out a niche by stubbornly focusing on the research end of the business, packaging itself as an analyst group such as those at traditional consulting firms and investment banks—but without the advisory component and costs."[129]

When outsourcing, a firm seeks the greatest value. In other words, a company wants to outsource only to firms possessing a core competence in terms of performing the primary or support activity that is being outsourced. This is the case between Nissan and IBM. In fact, IBM's services division, the group to which Nissan outsourced some of its computer operations, is the fastest-growing part of the company.

IBM recently sold its Global Network division to AT&T at a price of $5 billion. As part of this transaction, IBM agreed to pay AT&T Solutions $5 billion to run its global telecom network through 2004. According to analysts, "This swap was a watershed in the corporate outsourcing world. IBM says it got fed up trying to maintain and understand a global telecom network." As a measure of the complexity of business operations in a technologically intensive global environment, the transaction is thought to allow AT&T and IBM to concentrate their efforts on different operations—operations in which the companies have core competencies.[130] For companies to whom others outsource, such as IBM from Nissan and AT&T Solutions from IBM, being able to create value is the pathway through which they achieve strategic competitiveness and earn above-average returns.

When evaluating resources and capabilities, firms must be careful not to outsource activities in which they can create and capture value. In addition, companies should not outsource primary and support activities that are used to neutralize environmental threats or complete necessary ongoing organizational tasks. Called a "nonstrategic team of resources" in Figure 3.5, firms must verify that they do not outsource capabilities that are critical to their success, even though the capabilities are not actual sources of competitive advantage.

Another risk that is part of outsourcing concerns the firm's knowledge base. As discussed earlier in the chapter, knowledge continues to increase in importance as a source of competence and competitive advantage for firms in the competitive landscape. In part, organizations learn through a continuous and integrated sharing of experiences that employees have as they perform primary and support activities. One reason for the success of a learning organization is that, with continuous and integrated sharing of experiences, the firm is able to evaluate thoroughly the ongoing validity of the key assumptions it holds about the nature and future of its business operations. Outsourcing activities in which the firm cannot create value can have the unintended consequence of damaging the firm's potential to continuously evaluate its key assumptions, learn, and create new capabilities and core competencies. Therefore, managers should verify that the firm does not outsource activities that stimulate the development of new capabilities and competencies.[131]

The next section discusses some important cautions about core competencies.

Core Competencies: Cautions and Reminders

An attractive attribute of a firm's core competencies is that, unlike physical assets, they tend to become more valuable through additional use. A key reason for this is that they are largely knowledge based.[132] Sharing knowledge across people, jobs, and organizational functions often results in an expansion of that knowledge in competitively relevant ways.[133] At Chaparral Steel, for example, the CEO believes that one of his firm's "core competencies is the rapid realization of new technology into steel products."[134] As a learning organization, Chaparral expends a significant effort on verifying that learning is shared across the entire firm. Thus, in a manner that is consistent with the most effective learning organizations, Chaparral Steel appears to have a healthy "disrespect" for the status quo. Resulting from this "disrespect" is a commitment to continuous self-examination and experimentation.[135]

Evidence and company experiences show that the value of core competencies as sources of competitive advantage should never be taken for granted. Moreover, the ability of any particular core competence to provide competitive advantage on a permanent basis should not be assumed. The reason for these cautions is the central dilemma that is associated with the use of core competencies as sources of competitive advantage; namely, that all core capabilities simultaneously have the potential to be *core rigidities*. This reality is captured by the following comment from Leslie Wexner, CEO of The Limited, Inc.: "Success doesn't beget success. Success begets failure because the more that you know a thing works, the less likely you are to think that it won't work. When you've had a long string of victories, it's harder to foresee your own vulnerabilities."[136] Thus, each capability is both a strength and a weakness—a strength because it is the source of competitive advantage and, hence, strategic competitiveness—and a weakness because, if emphasized when it is no longer competitively relevant, it can be a seed of organizational inertia.[137]

Events occurring in the firm's external environment create conditions through which core competencies can become core rigidities, generate inertia, and stifle innovation. "Often the flip side, the dark side, of core capabilities is revealed due to external events when new competitors figure out a better way to serve the firm's customers, when new technologies emerge, or when political or social events shift the ground underneath."[138] It really isn't changes in the external environment that cause core capabilities to become core rigidities; rather, it is strategic myopia and inflexibility on the part of a firm's managers that results in core competencies being emphasized to the point that strategic inertia strangles the firm's ability to grow and to adapt to environmental changes through innovations.[139]

Steelmakers, for example, need to approach major customers' intended actions with a great deal of flexibility. As suggested in other parts of the chapter, GM and Ford are launching Web-based networks that will force their suppliers to work together and cut costs. These two companies have aggressive objectives with their electronic networks: "Both automakers hope to save billions by replacing an elaborate network of personal contacts and triplicate forms with a global electronic forum where deals can be done almost instantly. And both want their suppliers to use the Web sites to make their own purchases or sell excess inventory."[140] Describing the potential effects of the electronic programs on steelmakers, a business writer suggested that the automakers' actions point "to yet another round of cost cuts and slimmer profits. Their best hope is to make up in volume what they will lose from lower prices."[141] Attempts by key customers to reduce their costs is an important issue to U.S. steelmakers, in that GM and Ford alone combine to buy roughly 17 percent of the industry's output. To cope with this environmental change, steelmakers may need to develop new competencies required to deal successfully with Web-based purchasing and delivery practices. Steelmakers' existing competencies may be less valuable, given the increase in the power of buyers (GM and Ford, for example) that the Internet is creating relative to the power of suppliers (e.g., steelmakers). Thus, domestic steel manufacturers should take actions necessary to prevent existing core competencies from becoming core rigidities in light of changes being brought to bear on their operations by major customers.

This chapter closes our discussion of strategic inputs as a primary part of the strategic management process. As shown in Figure 1.1, results gained from analyzing a firm's external and internal environments provide the strategic inputs the firm needs to develop its strategic intent and strategic mission. Beginning with the next chapter, our focus turns to explanations of the strategic actions firms take to achieve strategic competitiveness and earn above-average returns. However, before starting that important stream of discussions, we offer a few final comments on strategic intent and strategic mission. As mentioned in Chapter 1, the primary value of intent and mission is that they reflect what the firm wants to accomplish in light of its external opportunities and internal competencies.

Strategic Inputs and Strategic Actions

Defined in the first chapter, *strategic intent* is the leveraging of a firm's resources, capabilities, and core competencies (hereafter called capabilities for the purpose of this discussion) to accomplish the firm's goals in the competitive environment.[142] Recent evidence suggests that, indeed, successful companies competing in the global economy have learned how to leverage their capabilities to reach challenging goals.[143] How Chaparral Steel seeks to leverage its resources, capabilities, and competencies is suggested by the following statement: "[T]he goal for every hour, the criterion for every person's activity, is crystal clear: make ever more steel, increasingly better than anyone else."[144] The intent of the business magazine *Fast Company* is to "be the handbook of the business revolution." At 3M, the intent indicates that the firm "must be the company [that] innovates, [that] changes the basis of competition." For Southwest Airlines, the intent is to "deliver positively outrageous service at unbelievable low fares." Coca-Cola Company wants to leverage its competencies to have a "Coke within arm's reach of everyone on the planet."[145] The challenge expressed by strategic intent can also apply to individuals. Some upper-level executives believe that, when committed to the dreams and aspirations that are suggested by the firm's intent, "quite ordinary people consistently do extraordinary things."[146]

Strategic intent defines the framework for a firm's strategic mission, which is a statement of a firm's unique purpose and the scope of its operations in product and market terms.[147] The mission of the U.S. Internal Revenue Service is to "provide America's taxpayers top quality service by helping them understand and meet their tax responsibilities and by applying the tax law with integrity and fairness to all." Capital One Financial Corp.'s mission is to "deliver the right product, at the right price, to the right customer, at the right time."[148] An effective mission is formed when the firm has a very strong sense of what it wants to do and of the ethical standards that will guide behaviors in the pursuit of its goals.[149] Because it specifies the products a firm will offer in particular markets and presents a framework within which the firm will work, the strategic mission is an application of strategic intent.[150] In a small private school, the strategic intent is the vigorous pursuit of excellence. The strategic mission flowing from this intent is to use a curriculum that is grounded in the liberal arts to serve intellectually gifted or highly motivated students living within a six-county region who seek a college preparatory educational experience.

In the case of all firms and organizations, once formulated, the strategic intent and strategic mission are the basis for the development of business-level, corporate-level, acquisition, restructuring, international, and cooperative strategies (see Chapter 4 and Chapters 6 through 9). Business-level strategy is discussed in the next chapter.

Summary

- In the 21st-century landscape, traditional conditions and factors, including labor costs and superior access to financial resources and raw materials, can still create a competitive advantage for the firm. However, these factors now lead to a competitive advantage in a declining number of instances. In the new landscape, the resources, capabilities, and core competencies that make up the firm's internal environment may have a relatively stronger influence on the firm's performance than do conditions in the external environment. The most effective firms recognize that strategic competitiveness and above-average returns result only when core competencies (as identified through the study of the firm's internal environment) are matched with opportunities (as determined through the study of the firm's external environment).

- No competitive advantage lasts forever. Over time, rivals use their own unique resources, capabilities, and core competencies to form different, yet effective, value-creating propositions that duplicate the value-creating ability of the firm's competitive advantages. In general, the Internet's capabilities are reducing the sustainability of many competitive advantages. Thus, because competitive advantages are not sustainable on a permanent basis, firms must exploit their current advantages while simultaneously using their resources and capabilities to form new core competencies that can serve as relevant competitive advantages in the future.
- Effective management of core competencies requires careful analysis of the firm's resources (inputs to the production process) and capabilities (capacities for teams of resources to perform a task or activity in an integrative manner). To manage core competencies successfully, individuals must be self-confident, courageous, and willing both to hold others accountable for their work and to be held accountable for the outcomes of their own efforts.
- Individual resources are usually not a source of competitive advantage. Capabilities, which are groupings of tangible and intangible resources, are a more likely source of competitive advantages, especially sustainable ones. A key reason for this is that the firm's nurturing and support of core competencies that are based on capabilities is less visible to rivals and, as such, is harder to understand and imitate.
- Increasingly, employees' knowledge is viewed as perhaps the most relevant source of competitive advantage. To gain maximum benefit from knowledge, firms commit to finding ways for individuals' unique knowledge sets to be shared throughout the firm. The Internet's capabilities affect both the development and the sharing of knowledge.
- Only when a capability is valuable, rare, costly to imitate, and nonsubstitutable is it a core competence and a source of competitive advantage. Over time, core competencies must be supported, but they cannot be allowed to become core rigidities. Core competencies are a source of competitive advantage only when they allow the firm to create value by exploiting opportunities in the external environment. When this is no longer the case, attention shifts to selecting or forming other capabilities that do satisfy the four criteria of sustainable competitive advantage.
- Firms use value chain analysis to identify and evaluate the competitive potential of resources and capabilities. By studying their skills relative to those associated with primary and support activities, firms are able to understand their cost structure and identify the activities through which they can create value.
- When the firm cannot create value in either a primary or support activity, outsourcing is considered. Used commonly in the 21st-century landscape, outsourcing is the purchase of a value-creating activity from an external supplier. The firm must outsource only to companies possessing a competitive advantage in terms of the particular primary or support activity under consideration. In addition, the firm must verify continuously that it is not outsourcing activities from which it could create value.
- Results obtained from analyzing the external environment (see Chapter 2) and the internal environment provide the inputs needed for the firm to develop its strategic intent and strategic mission. With the intent and mission formed, the firm is prepared to choose the strategies it will follow to pursue strategic competitiveness and above-average returns.

Review Questions

1. Why is it important for a firm to study and understand its internal environment?
2. What is value? Why is it critical that a firm be able to create value, and how does it do so?
3. What are the differences between tangible resources and intangible resources? Why is it important for those making strategic decisions to understand these differences? Are tangible resources linked more closely to the creation of competitive advantages than are intangible resources, or is the reverse true? Why?
4. What are capabilities? What must firms do to create capabilities?
5. What are the four criteria firms use to determine which of their capabilities are core competencies? Why is it important for these criteria to be used?
6. What is value chain analysis? What insight or understanding does a firm gain when it uses this tool successfully?
7. What is outsourcing and why do firms engage in the practice? Will outsourcing's importance grow in the 21st century? If so, why?

8. What are core rigidities? Why is it vital that firms prevent core competencies from becoming core rigidities?
9. What is the relationship between strategic inputs and strategic actions and why is it important to understand it?

Application Discussion Questions

1. Several companies that have *brand* as a competitive advantage are discussed in the Opening Case. Given your knowledge about the global economy, which of these brands do you believe has the strongest likelihood of remaining as a source of advantage in the 21st century? Why? What effects do you believe the Internet's capabilities will have on this brand, and what should the owner of the brand do in light of them?
2. Visit the manager of a store with which you conduct business in your local community. Using the definition presented in the chapter, define *value* for the manager. Ask the manager if the definition is consistent with how her or his firm thinks of value. If there is a difference, ask the manager to assess why the difference exists.
3. Think of a group (e.g., a fraternity or sorority, Toastmaster's, or a voluntary organization) in which you hold membership. Using the categories shown in Tables 3.3 and 3.4, list what you believe are the group's tangible and intangible resources. Show the list to another member of your group. Does the person agree with your assessment of the group's resources? If not, what might account for the differences? If differences do exist between you and your colleague, what is the meaning of such differences in terms of trying to form the group's capabilities?
4. Refer to the third question. Was it easier for you to list the tangible or the intangible resources? Why? How confident are you with your assessments?
5. What competitive advantage does your university or college possess? What evidence can you provide to support your opinion? Share what you think the competitive advantages are with a colleague. Does this person agree with your assessment? If not, why not?
6. What effects do you believe the Internet will have on your university or college within the next five years as it seeks to develop new competitive advantages? In your view, do the strategic decision makers in your educational institution understand the Internet's capabilities? If not, why not?
7. Trust is identified in the chapter as a potential source of competitive advantage. Have you ever been involved in a situation in which trust was instrumental in accomplishing an organization's goals? If so, what outcomes were made possible because of trust?

Ethics Questions

1. Can efforts to develop sustainable competitive advantages result in employees using unethical practices? If so, what unethical practices might be used to compare a firm's core competencies with those held by rivals? How do the Internet's capabilities affect actions taken to form competitive advantages that will help the firm in efforts to outperform its rivals?
2. Do ethical practices affect a firm's ability to develop *brand* as a source of competitive advantage? If so, how does this happen? Can you think of brands that are a source of competitive advantage at least in part because of the firm's ethical practices?
3. What is the difference between exploiting a firm's human capital and using that capital as a source of competitive advantage? Are there situations in which the exploitation of human capital can be a source of advantage? If so, can you name such a situation? If the exploitation of human capital can be a source of competitive advantage, is this a *sustainable* advantage? Why or why not?
4. Are there any ethical dilemmas associated with outsourcing? If so, what are they? How would you deal with outsourcing ethical dilemmas you believe exist?
5. What ethical responsibilities do managers have if they determine that a set of employees has skills that are valuable only to a core competence that is becoming a core rigidity?
6. Through the Internet, firms sometimes make a vast array of data, information, and knowledge available to competitors as well as to customers and suppliers. What ethical issues, if any, are involved when the firm finds competitively relevant information on a competitor's Web site?
7. Firms are aware that competitors read information that is posted on their Web sites. Given this reality, is it ethical for a firm to include false information, for example, about its sources of competitive advantage on its Web site in hopes that the information will influence competitors to take certain actions as a result of viewing it?

Internet Exercise

A recent global development in the automobile industry has been the mergers and acquisitions going on among firms. These include the coupling of Daimler-Benz with Chrysler; VW with Audi, Rolls Royce, and Bentley; and GM with Saab; as well as, most recently, Ford's acquisition of Volvo. The new partnerships have allowed firms to combine resources and capabilities to build a new breed of universal car. Explore the Web sites of these firms. Do you still see a specific brand identification associated with each type of car? How important do you think branding will be in the future for these products?

***e-project:** Imagine that you are able to purchase your dream car from among the current year's models. Before buying, though, you would like to learn something about how the car is produced. (For example, is your Rolls Royce being assembled alongside a Beetle?) Using Internet sources, attempt to trace the origins of the car's major components, technology, and performance-testing resources, as well as the production and advertising or marketing facilities.

Notes

1. J. Clinton, 2000, Brand New Orleans, *Fast Company,* January/February, 33.
2. M. J. Rouse & U. S. Daellenbach, 1999, Rethinking research methods for the resource-based perspective: Isolating sources of sustainable competitive advantage, *Strategic Management Journal,* 20: 487–494.
3. D. Schendel, 1999, Fresh challenges for the future, Mastering Strategy (Part Twelve), *Financial Times,* December 13, 14.
4. C. K. Prahalad, 1999, Changes in the competitive battlefield, Mastering Strategy (Part Two), *Financial Times,* October 4, 3–4; W. J. Duncan, P. M. Ginter, & L. E. Swayne, 1998, Competitive advantage and internal organizational assessment, *Academy of Management Executive,* 12(3): 6–16.
5. J. Lee & D. Miller, 1999, People matter: Commitment to employees, strategy and performance in Korean firms, *Strategic Management Journal,* 20: 579–593; M. A. Huselid, S. E. Jackson, & R. S. Schuler, 1997, Technical and strategic human resource management effectiveness as determinants of firm performance, *Academy of Management Journal,* 40: 171–188.
6. G. Colvin, 1999, The ultimate manager, *Fortune,* November 22, 185–187.
7. J. G. Covin & M. P. Miles, 1999, Corporate entrepreneurship and the pursuit of competitive advantage, *Entrepreneurship: Theory and Practice,* 23(3): 47–64; D. J. Teece, G. Pisano, & A. Shuen, 1997, Dynamic capabilities and strategic management, *Strategic Management Journal,* 18: 509–534; R. G. McGrath, I. C. MacMillan, & S. Venkataraman, 1995, Defining and developing competence: A strategic process paradigm, *Strategic Management Journal,* 16: 251–275.
8. Colvin, The ultimate manager, 187.
9. G. Colvin, 1999, How to be a great eCEO, *Fortune,* May 24, 104–110.
10. C. Y. Coleman, 1999, Nordstrom tries to cut costs while maintaining service, *Wall Street Journal,* April 8, B4.
11. P. Sellers, 1996, Can Home Depot fix its sagging stock? *Fortune,* March 4, 139–146.
12. J. R. Hagerty, 2000, Home Depot strikes at Sears in tool duel, *Wall Street Journal,* January 24, B1, B4; B. Upbin, 2000, Profit in a big orange, *Forbes,* January 24, 122–127; N. Byrnes, W. C. Symonds, & D. Foust, 1999, The best performers, *Business Week,* March 29, 98–107.
13. P.-L. Yeoh & K. Roth, 1999, An empirical analysis of sustained advantage in the U.S. pharmaceutical industry: Impact of firm resources and capabilities, *Strategic Management Journal,* 20: 637–653; P. C. Godfrey & C. W. L. Hill, 1995, The problem of unobservables in strategic management research, *Strategic Management Journal,* 16: 519–533.
14. D. F. Abell, 1999, Competing today while preparing for tomorrow, *Sloan Management Review,* 40(3): 73–81; D. Leonard-Barton, 1995, *Wellsprings of Knowledge: Building and Sustaining the Sources of Innovation* (Boston: Harvard Business School Press); McGrath, MacMillan, & Venkataraman, Defining and developing competence, 253.
15. K. M. Eisenhardt, 1999, Strategy as strategic decision making, *Sloan Management Review,* 40(3): 65–72.
16. Rouse & Daellenbach, Rethinking research methods, 487–489; Godfrey & Hill, The problem of unobservables, 522.
17. J. B. Barney, 1999, How a firm's capabilities affect boundary decisions, *Sloan Management Review,* 40(3): 137–145; J. B. Barney, 1996, The resource-based theory of the firm, *Organization Science,* 7: 469–480; M. E. Porter, 1996, What is strategy? *Harvard Business Review,* 74(6): 61–78.
18. D. Stauffer, 1999, Why people hoard knowledge, *Across the Board,* September, 17–24; Changes in the competitive battlefield (Introduction), 1999, Mastering Strategy (Part Two), *Financial Times,* October 4, 1; A. Mehra, 1996, Resource and market based determinants of performance in the U.S. banking industry, *Strategic Management Journal,* 17: 307–322.
19. L. Thurow, 1999, *Creating Wealth* (London: Nicholas Brealey Publishing), 117.
20. Prahalad, Changes in the competitive battlefield, 3–4.
21. R. T. Pascale & A. H. Miller, 1999, The action lab: Creating a greenhouse for organizational change, *Strategy & Business,* 17: 64–72.
22. K. Kerwin, P. Burrows, & D. Brady, 1999, A new era of bright hopes and terrible fears, *Business Week,* October 4, 84–98.
23. S. Kirsner, 2000, Collision course, *Fast Company,* January/February, 118–144.
24. G. McWilliams & J. B. White, 1999, Dell to Detroit: Get into gear online! *Wall Street Journal,* December 1, B1, B4.
25. C. C. Markides, 1999, A dynamic view of strategy, *Sloan Management Review,* 40(3): 55–63; R. Henderson & W. Mitchell, 1997, The interaction of organizational and competitive influences on strategy and performance, *Strategic Management Journal,* 18(Summer Special Issue): 5–14; J. B. Barney, 1995, Looking inside for competitive advantage, *Academy of Management Executive,* IX(4): 59–60.
26. S. Ghoshal & C.A. Bartlett, 1995, Changing the role of top management: Beyond structure to processes, *Harvard Business Review,* 73(1): 96.

27. S. Wetlaufer, 1999, Driving change: An interview with Ford Motor Company's Jacques Nasser, *Harvard Business Review,* 77(2): 77–81.
28. K. Eddy, 1999, Bus group on road to success, *Financial Times,* May 26, 20.
29. V. P. Rindova & C. J. Fombrun, 1999, Constructing competitive advantage: The role of firm-constituent interactions, *Strategic Management Journal,* 20: 691–710; M. A. Peteraf, 1993, The cornerstones of competitive strategy: A resource-based view, *Strategic Management Journal,* 14: 179–191.
30. T. H. Brush & K. W. Artz, 1999, Toward a contingent resource-based theory: The impact of information asymmetry on the value of capabilities in veterinary medicine, *Strategic Management Journal,* 20: 223–250.
31. Porter, What is strategy?, 61–78.
32. T. J. Dean, R. L. Brown, & C. E. Bamford, 1998, Differences in large and small firm responses to environmental context: Strategic implications from a comparative analysis of business formations, *Strategic Management Journal,* 19: 709–728; K. E. Marino, 1996, Developing consensus on firm competencies and capabilities, *Academy of Management Executive,* X(3): 40–51.
33. Colvin, How to be, 107.
34. S. A. Zahra, R. D. Ireland, & M. A. Hitt, 2000, International expansion by new venture firms: International diversity, mode of market entry, technological learning and performance, *Academy of Management Journal,* in press.
35. D. Lei, M. A. Hitt, & R. A. Bettis, 1996, Dynamic core competencies through metalearning and strategic context, *Journal of Management,* 22: 247–267.
36. Deere & Company, 2000, Deere & Company Home Page, *www.deere.com,* January 21; T. A. Stewart, 1997, Does anyone around here know . . .? *Fortune,* September 29, 279.
37. G. Lorenzoni & A. Lipparini, 1999, The leveraging of interfirm relationships as a distinctive organizational capability: A longitudinal study, *Strategic Management Journal,* 20: 317–338; C. M. Christensen, 1997, Making strategy: Learning by doing, *Harvard Business Review,* 75(6): 141–156; C. E. Helfat, 1997, Know-how and asset complementarity and dynamic capability accumulation: The case of R&D, *Strategic Management Journal,* 18: 339–360; Lei, Hitt, & Bettis, Dynamic core competencies.
38. Pocket Strategy, 1998, Value, *The Economist Books,* 165.
39. M. Halkias, 2000, J.C. Penney hopes meeting lights fire, *Dallas Morning News,* January 14, D1, D11; M. Halkias, 1999, Penney to clarify its mission, *Dallas Morning News,* November 17, D1, D10.
40. R. Ramirez, 1999, Value co-production: Intellectual origins and implications for practice and research, *Strategic Management Journal,* 20: 49–65.
41. Herend Porcelain, 2000, Herend Brochure, 2.
42. S. W. Floyd & B. Wooldridge, 1999, Knowledge creation and social networks in corporate entrepreneurship: The renewal of organizational capability, *Entrepreneurship: Theory and Practice,* 23(3): 123–143; A. Campbell & M. Alexander, 1997, What's wrong with strategy? *Harvard Business Review,* 75(6): 42–51.
43. Allen-Edmonds Shoe Corporation, 2000, Allen Edmonds Brochure, 3.
44. M. A. Hitt, R. D. Nixon, P. G. Clifford, & K. P. Coyne, 1999, The development and use of strategic resources, in M. A. Hitt, P. G. Clifford, R. D. Nixon, & K. P. Coyne (eds.), *Dynamic Strategic Resources* (Chichester: John Wiley & Sons), 1–14.
45. Rouse & Daellenbach, Rethinking research methods, 49; C. Oliver, 1997, Sustainable competitive advantage: Combining institutional and resource-based view, *Strategic Management Journal,* 18: 697–713; D. J. Collis & C. A. Montgomery, 1995, Competing on resources: Strategy in the 1990s, *Harvard Business Review,* 73(4): 118–128; B. Wernerfelt, 1995, The resource-based view of the firm: Ten years after, *Strategic Management Journal,* 16: 171–174.
46. P. Chattopadhyay, W. H. Glick, C. C. Miller, & G. P. Huber, 1999, Determinants of executive beliefs: Comparing functional conditioning and social influence, *Strategic Management Journal,* 20: 763–789; J. H. Dyer, 1996, Specialized supplier networks as a source of competitive advantage: Evidence from the auto industry, *Strategic Management Journal,* 17: 271–291; R. L. Priem & D. A. Harrison, 1994, Exploring strategic judgment: Methods for testing the assumptions of prescriptive contingency theories, *Strategic Management Journal,* 15: 311–324; R. Amit & P. J. H. Schoemaker, 1993, Strategic assets and organizational rent, *Strategic Management Journal,* 14: 33–46.
47. R. Gertner & A. Rosenfield, 1999, How real options lead to better decisions, Mastering Strategy (Part Five), *Financial Times,* October 25, 14–15; H. R. Greve, 1998, Managerial cognition and the mimetic adoption of market positions: What you see is what you do, *Strategic Management Journal,* 19: 967–988; W. Boeker, 1997, Executive migration and strategic change: The effect of top manager movement on product-market entry, *Administrative Science Quarterly,* 42: 213–236; C. R. Schwenk, 1995, Strategic decision making, *Journal of Management,* 21: 471–493.
48. P. C. Nutt, 1999, Surprising but true: Half the decisions in organizations fail, *Academy of Management Executive,* 13(4): 75–90.
49. Eisenhardt, Strategy as strategic decision making, 70.
50. R. S. Dooley & G. E. Fryxell, 1999, Attaining decision quality and commitment from dissent: The moderating effects of loyalty and competence in strategic decision-making teams, *Academy of Management Journal,* 42: 389–402.
51. D. A. Aaker & E. Joachimsthaler, 1999, The lure of global branding, *Harvard Business Review,* 77(6): 137–144; R. G. McGrath, 1999, Falling forward: Real options reasoning and entrepreneurial failure, *Academy of Management Review,* 24: 13–30; McGrath, MacMillan, & Venkataraman, Defining and developing competence, 253.
52. Schendel, Fresh challenges, 15.
53. Colvin, The ultimate manager, 187.
54. Amit & Schoemaker, Strategic assets and organizational rent, 33.
55. W. S. Lovejoy, 1999, How many decisions should you automate? Mastering Strategy (Part Eleven), *Financial Times,* December 6, 12–13.
56. M. Farjoun & L. Lai, 1997, Similarity judgments in strategy formulation: Role, process and implications, *Strategic Management Journal,* 18: 255–273.
57. S. Bishop, 1999, The strategic power of saying no, *Harvard Business Review,* 77(6): 50–61; H. W. Vroman, 1996, The loyalty effect: The hidden force behind growth, profits and lasting value (book review), *Academy of Management Executive,* X(1): 88–90.
58. R. T. Pascale & A. H. Miller, 1999, The action lab: Creating a greenhouse for organizational change, *Strategy & Business,* 17: 64–72; W. Kiechel, 1993, Facing up to denial, *Fortune,* October 18, 163–165.
59. Colvin, The ultimate manager, 187; P. Sellers, 1996, What exactly is charisma? *Fortune,* January 15, 68–75.
60. Wetlaufer, Driving change, 79.
61. N. Tichy, 1999, The teachable point of view, *Harvard Business Review,* 77(2): 82–83.
62. J. G. Combs & D. J. Ketchen, Jr., 1999, Explaining interfirm cooperation and performance: Toward a reconciliation of predictions from the resource-based view and organizational economics, *Strategic Management Journal,* 20: 867–888; Teece, Pisano, & Shuen, Dynamic capabilities, 513–514; Barney, 1995, Looking inside for competitive advantage, 50.
63. D. L. Deeds, D. DeCarolis, & J. Coombs, 2000, Dynamic capabilities and new product development in high technology ventures: An empirical analysis of new biotechnology firms, *Journal of Business Venturing,* 15: 211–229; T. Chi, 1994, Trading in strategic resources: Necessary conditions, transaction cost problems, and choice of exchange structure, *Strategic Management*

Journal, 15: 271–290; R. Reed & R. DeFillippi, 1990, Causal ambiguity, barriers to imitation, and sustainable competitive advantage, *Academy of Management Review,* 15: 88–102.

64. Yeoh & Roth, An empirical analysis, 638; McGrath, MacMillan, & Venkataraman, Defining and developing competence, 252.
65. A. Goldstein, 1999, Dell outpaces Compaq in U.S. sales of PCs, *Dallas Morning News,* October 25, D1, D4.
66. K. Yung, 1999, An expanding palate, *Dallas Morning News,* October 15, D1, D12.
67. Deeds, DeCarolis, & Coombs, Dynamic capabilities, 213; Hitt, Nixon, Clifford, & Coyne, The development and use of, 2; M. de Miranda Oliveira, Jr., 1999, Core competencies and the knowledge of the firm, in M. A. Hitt, P. G. Clifford, R. D. Nixon, & K. P. Coyne (eds.), *Dynamic Strategic Resources* (Chichester: John Wiley & Sons), 17–42; P. R. Hall, 1991, The contribution of intangible resources to business success, *Journal of General Management,* 16(4): 41–52.
68. S. A. Zahra, A. P. Nielsen, & W. C. Bogner, 1999, Corporate entrepreneurship, knowledge, and competence development, *Entrepreneurship: Theory and Practice,* 23(3): 169–189; T. A. Stewart, 1996, Coins in a knowledge bank, *Fortune,* February 19, 230–233.
69. A. M. Webber, 2000, New math for a new economy, *Fast Company,* January/February, 214–224.
70. S. J. Marsh & A. L. Ranft, 1999, Why resources matter: An empirical study of knowledge-based resources on new market entry, in M. A. Hitt, P. G. Clifford, R. D. Nixon, & K. P. Coyne (eds.), *Dynamic Strategic Resources* (Chichester: John Wiley & Sons), 43–66.
71. Brush & Artz, Toward a contingent resource-based theory, 225; McGrath, MacMillan, & Venkataraman, Defining and developing competence, 252; Porter, What is strategy?
72. J. B. Quinn, P. Anderson, & S. Finkelstein, 1996, Making the most of the best, *Harvard Business Review,* 74(2): 71–80.
73. Webber, New math, 217.
74. Lee & Miller, People matter; Godfrey & Hill, The problem of unobservables, 522–523.
75. Webber, New math, 218.
76. V. Griffith, 1999, Branding.com: How bricks-and-mortar companies can make it on the Internet, *Strategy & Business,* 15: 54–59; S. I. Hill, J. McGrath, & S. Dayal, 1998, *Strategy & Business,* 11: 22–34.
77. S. Ward, L. Light, & J. Goldstine, 1999, What high-tech managers need to know about brands, *Harvard Business Review,* 77(4): 85–95.
78. D. P. Hamilton, 1999, H-P to relaunch its brand, adopt new logo, *Wall Street Journal,* November 16, B6.
79. G. Rifkin, 1998, How Harley-Davidson revs its brand, *Strategy & Business,* 9: 31–40.
80. Hitt, Nixon, Clifford, & Coyne, The development, 3.
81. C. L. Lengnick-Hall & J. W. Wolff, 1999, Similarities and contradictions in the core logic of three strategy research streams, *Strategic Management Journal,* 20: 1109–1132.
82. B. McEvily & A. Zaheer, 1999, Bridging ties: A source of firm heterogeneity in competitive capabilities, *Strategic Management Journal,* 20: 1133–1156.
83. W. C. Rappleye, Jr., 1999, Human capital management, *Fortune* (Special Advertising Section), October 14, S2.
84. D. G. Hoopes & S. Postrel, 1999, Shared knowledge: "Glitches," and product development performance, *Strategic Management Journal,* 20: 837–865; Lei, Hitt, & Bettis, Dynamic core competencies; J. B. Quinn, 1994, *The Intelligent Enterprise* (New York: Free Press).
85. Razorfish, 2000, Razorfish Home Page, January 3, *www.razorfish.com.*
86. Thurow, *Creating Wealth,* 117; Stross, 1997, Mr. Gates builds his brain trust; E. M. Davies, 1996, Wired for hiring: Microsoft's slick recruiting machine, *Fortune,* February 5, 123–124.
87. Thoughts on the business of life, 1999, *Forbes,* May 17, 352.
88. T. A. Stewart, 1999, Grab the knowledge and squeeze, *Fortune,* November 8, 322.
89. G. G. Dess & J. C. Picken, 1999, *Beyond Productivity* (New York: AMACOM).
90. D. Stauffer, 1999, Why people hoard knowledge, *Across the Board,* September, 17–24.
91. L. Empson, 1999, The challenge of knowledge management, Mastering Strategy (Part Two), October 4, 9–10.
92. M. T. Hansen, N. Nhoria, & T. Tierney, 1999, What's your strategy for managing knowledge? *Harvard Business Review,* 77(2): 106–116.
93. M. A. Hitt & R. D. Ireland, 1986, Relationships among corporate level distinctive competencies, diversification strategy, corporate structure, and performance, *Journal of Management Studies,* 23: 401–416; M. A. Hitt & R. D. Ireland, 1985, Corporate distinctive competence, strategy, industry, and performance, *Strategic Management Journal,* 6: 273–293; M. A. Hitt, R. D. Ireland, & K. A. Palia, 1982, Industrial firms' grand strategy and functional importance, *Academy of Management Journal,* 25: 265–298; M. A. Hitt, R. D. Ireland, & G. Stadter, 1982, Functional importance and company performance: Moderating effects of grand strategy and industry type, *Strategic Management Journal,* 3: 315–330; C. C. Snow & E. G. Hrebiniak, 1980, Strategy, distinctive competence, and organizational performance, *Administrative Science Quarterly,* 25: 317–336.
94. Hitt, Nixon, Clifford, & Coyne, The development, 3; Zahra, Nielsen, & Bogner, Corporate entrepreneurship, 171; D. Leonard-Barton, H. K Bowen, K. B. Clark, C. A. Holloway, & S. C. Wheelwright, 1994, How to integrate work and deepen expertise, *Harvard Business Review,* 72(5): 123; C. K. Prahalad & G. Hamel, 1990, The core competence of the corporation, *Harvard Business Review,* 68(3): 79–93.
95. Brush & Artz, Toward a contingent resource-based theory, 224–225; T. Chi, 1994, Trading in strategic resources: Necessary conditions, transaction cost problems, and choice of exchange structure, *Strategic Management Journal,* 15: 271–290.
96. C. Ames, 1995, Sales soft? Profits flat? It's time to rethink your business, *Fortune,* June 25, 142–146; S. Fatsis, 1993, Bigger is not necessarily better, *Waco Tribune-Herald,* January 17, B1, B6.
97. D. Fisher, 2000, Desktop battle plan, *Forbes,* January 10, 48–49; Brady Corporation, 1999, *Better Investing,* 48(1): 50; T. Burt, 1999, Ford to farm out key final assembly jobs to contractors, *Financial Times,* August 4, 1; A. Edgecliffe-Johnson, 1999, McDonald's buys pizza restaurant chain in Midwest, *Financial Times,* May 7, 19; K. Jacobs & G. Fairclough, 1999, Honeywell CEO faces challenge of melding corporate cultures, *Wall Street Journal,* December 3, B18; S. H. Lee & B. M. Case, 1999, Market Presence, *Dallas Morning News,* December 22, D1, D10; P. Taylor, 1999, Challenge for new man at the helm, *Financial Times,* October 6, III.
98. A. Palazzo, 1999, Sizzler restaurants are returning to their roots, *Wall Street Journal,* November 15, B13A.
99. This section is drawn primarily from three sources: Barney, How a firm's capabilities; Barney, Looking inside for competitive advantage; J. B. Barney, 1991, Firm resources and sustained competitive advantage, *Journal of Management,* 17: 99–120.
100. C. H. St. John & J. S. Harrison, 1999, Manufacturing-based relatedness, synergy, and coordination, *Strategic Management Journal,* 20: 129–145.
101. Barney, Looking inside for competitive advantage.
102. I. M. Kunii, W. Thornton, & J. Rae-Dupree, 1999, Sony's shakeup, *Business Week,* March 22, 52–53; Barney, Looking inside for competitive advantage, 50.
103. R. Tomkins, 1999, Marketing value for money, *Financial Times,* May 14, 18.
104. Barney, Looking inside for competitive advantage, 52.
105. L. B. Ward, 2000, Dell sales overtake Compaq, *Dallas Morning News,* January 24, D1–D2; A. Goldstein, 1999, Dell shareholders celebrate gains, *Dallas Morning News,* July 17, F1, F3.

106. Barney, Looking inside for competitive advantage, 53.
107. Barney, How a firm's capabilities, 141.
108. Barney, Firm resources, 108.
109. J. Kurtzman, 1997, An interview with Rosabeth Moss Kanter, *Strategy & Business,* 16: 85–94.
110. R. Burt, 1999, When is corporate culture a competitive asset? Mastering Strategy (Part Six), *Financial Times,* November 1, 14–15.
111. J. Huey, 1993, How McKinsey does it, *Fortune,* November 1, 56–81.
112. Reed & DeFillippi, Causal ambiguity.
113. Leonard-Barton, *Wellsprings of Knowledge,* 7.
114. Dess & Picken, *Beyond Productivity,* 213.
115. Barney, How a firm's capabilities, 141.
116. Barney, Firm resources, 111.
117. Amit & Schoemaker, Strategic assets, 39.
118. M. E. Porter, 1985, *Competitive Advantage* (New York: Free Press), 33–61.
119. G. G. Dess, A. Gupta, J.-F. Hennart, & C. W. L. Hill, 1995, Conducting and integrating strategy research at the international corporate and business levels: Issues and directions, *Journal of Management,* 21: 376; Porter, What is strategy?
120. T. A. Stewart, 1999, Customer learning is a two-way street, *Fortune,* May 10, 158–160; T. A. Stewart, 1995, The information wars: What you don't know will hurt you, *Fortune,* June 12, 119–121.
121. C. Batchelor, 1999, Logistics aspires to worldly wisdom, *Financial Times,* June 17, 13; Stewart, Customer learning, 158.
122. D. Ball, 1999, Pirelli expects new tire-making plan to lower costs, increase market share, *Wall Street Journal,* December 6, A29A.
123. M. Skapinker, 1999, Change of flight plan for corporate travel, *Financial Times,* March 21, 7.
124. J. Y. Murray & M. Kotabe, 1999, Sourcing strategies of U.S. service companies: A modified transaction-cost analysis, *Strategic Management Journal,* 20: 791–809.
125. S. Jones, 1999, Growth process in global market, *Financial Times,* June 22, 17.
126. Burt, Ford expects to farm out, 1; P. Landers, 1999, Nissan retains IBM to manage its computers, *Wall Street Journal,* October 29, A15.
127. B. H. Jevnaker & M. Bruce, 1999, Design as a strategic alliance: Expanding the creative capability of the firm, in M. A. Hitt, P. G. Clifford, R. D. Nixon, & K. P. Coyne (eds.). *Dynamic Strategic Resources* (Chichester: John Wiley & Sons), 266–298.
128. Dess & Picken, *Beyond Productivity,* 23.
129. Jones, Growth process, 17; K. Tan, 1999, Firms needing data in a hurry seek out Stax, *Wall Street Journal,* March 23, B10.
130. S. Woolley, 1999, Ma Bell at your service, *Forbes,* May 17, 54–55.
131. N. A. Wishart, J. J. Elam, & D. Robey, 1996, Redrawing the portrait of a learning organization: Inside Knight-Ridder, Inc., *Academy of Management Executive,* X(1): 7–20; D. Lei & M. A. Hitt, 1995, Strategic restructuring and outsourcing: The effect of mergers and acquisitions and LBOs on building firm skills and capabilities, *Journal of Management,* 21: 835–859.
132. Zahra, Nielsen, & Bogner, Corporate entrepreneurship, 171–177; J. C. Spender & R. M. Grant, 1996, Knowledge and the firm: Overview, *Strategic Management Journal,* 17(Winter Special Issue): 5–10.
133. Lei, Hitt, & Bettis, Dynamic core competences; Leonard-Barton, *Wellsprings of Knowledge,* 59–89.
134. Leonard-Barton, *Wellsprings of Knowledge,* 7.
135. Wishart, Elam, & Robey, Redrawing the portrait, 8.
136. G. G. Dess & J. C. Picken, 1999, Creating competitive (dis)advantage: Learning from Food Lion's freefall, *Academy of Management Executive,* 13(3): 97–111.
137. M. Hannan & J. Freeman, 1977, The population ecology of organizations, *American Journal of Sociology,* 82: 929–964.
138. Leonard-Barton, *Wellsprings of Knowledge,* 30–31.
139. Junior, Core competencies, 20–21; R. Sanchez & J. T. Mahoney, 1996, Modularity, flexibility, and knowledge management in product and organization design, *Strategic Management Journal,* 17(Winter Special Issue): 63–76; C. A. Bartlett & S. Ghoshal, 1994, Changing the role of top management: Beyond strategy to purpose, *Harvard Business Review,* 72(6): 79–88.
140. G. L. White, 1999, How GM, Ford think Web can make splash on the factory floor, *Wall Street Journal,* December 3, A1, A8.
141. R. G. Matthews, 1999, Steelmakers face online threat from auto industry, *Wall Street Journal,* November 26, B4.
142. G. Hamel & C. K. Prahalad, 1989, Strategic intent, *Harvard Business Review,* 67(3): 63–76.
143. R. Gulati, 1999, Network location and learning: The influence of network resources and firm capabilities on alliance formation, *Strategic Management Journal,* 20: 397–420; DeCarolis & Deeds, The impact of stocks and flows; P. Almeida, 1996, Knowledge sourcing by foreign multinationals: Patent citation analysis in the U.S. semiconductor industry, *Strategic Management Journal,* 17(Winter Special Issue): 155–165.
144. Leonard-Barton, *Wellsprings of Knowledge,* 8.
145. Action item, 2000, *Fast Company,* January/February, 86; 3M, 2000, 3M Home Page, January 16, *www.3m.com*; Herb Kelleher, 1998, *Financial Times,* November 30, 36; C. E. Smith, 1994, The Merlin factor: Leadership and strategic intent, *Information Access,* 5(1): 67–85.
146. M. M. Waldrop, 1996, Dee Hock on organizations, *Fast Company,* October, 84.
147. D. Roth, 1999, The value of vision, *Fortune,* May 24, 285–28; R. D. Ireland & M. A. Hitt, 1992, Mission statements: Importance, challenge and recommendations for development, *Business Horizons,* 35(3): 34–42.
148. C. Fishman, 1999, This is a marketing revolution, *Fast Company,* May, 204; U.S. Government, 1999, Your rights as a taxpayer, Department of the Treasury, Publication 1.
149. P. Martin, 1999, Lessons in humility, *Financial Times,* June 22, 18.
150. C. Marshall, 1996, A sense of mission, *The Strategist,* 7(4): 14–16.

PART 2
STRATEGIC ACTIONS: STRATEGY FORMULATION

CHAPTER **FOUR**

Business-Level Strategy

CHAPTER **FIVE**

Competitive Dynamics

CHAPTER **SIX**

Corporate-Level Strategy

CHAPTER **SEVEN**

Acquisition and Restructuring Strategies

CHAPTER **EIGHT**

International Strategy

CHAPTER **NINE**

Cooperative Strategy

BUSINESS-LEVEL STRATEGY

CHAPTER FOUR OBJECTIVES

After reading this chapter, you should be able to:

1. Define strategy and explain business-level strategies.
2. Describe the relationship between customers and business-level strategies.
3. Discuss the issues firms consider when evaluating customers in terms of who, what, and how.
4. Define the integrated cost leadership/differentiation strategy and discuss its increasing importance in the 21st-century competitive landscape.
5. Describe the capabilities necessary to develop competitive advantage through the cost leadership, differentiation, focused cost leadership, focused differentiation, and integrated cost leadership/differentiation business-level strategies.
6. Explain the risks associated with each of the five business-level strategies.

The Internet, Customer (Buyer) Power, and Business-Level Strategy

The Internet is spawning new companies and even new industries. Yahoo! Inc. is a start-up Internet-based venture. Initially, Yahoo! Inc. was thought by many to be an unusual name for a company that was founded by two graduate school dropouts. However, the firm's success is suggested by the fact that its recent market capitalization was approximately $40 billion, which is the amount CBS Corp. paid to acquire Viacom, Inc.

The Internet is a marketplace phenomenon that already features more than $1 trillion worth of network connections, computer power, and databases full of information. The Internet is largely free to anyone in the world who has a phone line and a personal computer. It can be used day or night, and it offers an opportunity to the founders of virtually any start-up venture to enter a range of industries and market segments within them. The Internet's significant effect is highlighted by the fact that Amazon.com's birth has been cited as one of the ten moments that shaped and defined the 1990s.

To date, the strategies that are being implemented by Internet companies are still undefined. Jacques A. Nasser, Ford Motor Company's CEO, joked recently that Amazon.com's strategy "boils down to buy at 100 and sell at 80." This comment hints at the fact that many Internet companies, including Amazon.com, are not profitable. However, the potential of e-commerce to generate above-average returns in the long term (see Opening Case in Chapter 1) encourages large firms, such as Ford, to pursue business through this medium.

Because of the immense flow of information through it, the Internet allows customers to have greater control over their buying behavior as never before. Prior to the Internet, buyers faced considerable obstacles when trying to make an optimal purchase. In addition, finding information about products was usually time consuming. Compounding the issue for buyers in pre-Internet days were sellers' efforts to guard against extensive distribution of product-related information. Restricting information flows tends to increase sellers' power relative to that of buyers (see Chapter 2). Today, however, buyers use the Internet to access a wealth of information about goods and services that are of interest to them.

The Internet also makes it possible for sellers to identify consumers and to collect an unprecedented amount of information about their purchasing patterns. Sophisticated software programs analyze this information and compare it with that of other customers. These sophisticated practices make it possible for companies to sell additional products to consumers. For example, based on a purchase profile, companies such as Amazon.com and barnesandnoble.com can suggest a specific book or CD for a customer to consider buying to complement the product that was ordered. This capability is generating significant levels of customer satisfaction for firms selling via the Internet and increases the viability of the differentiation and integrated cost leadership/differentiation business-level strategies (both strategies are discussed fully in the chapter).

The Internet is also creating different pricing options to which customers are responding favorably. Auctions, for example, traditionally resulted in pricing outcomes that favored sellers. In the Internet age, however, firms such as priceline.com organize the option in favor of the buyer. This allows buyers to pool as groups and purchase products at a lower price.

Amazon.com's Internet-based strategy has put traditional brick-and-mortar businesses such as Barnes & Noble at a significant cost disadvantage. Even virtual upstarts can reach customers faster than brick-and-mortar businesses with stores and full sales staffs can—and for a fraction of the cost. Amazon.com recently reached $1.2 billion in annual sales revenue. This amount equals the revenue Barnes & Noble generated from 200 of its superstores. While Barnes & Noble has spent $472 million to renovate and upgrade its 1,000-plus stores, Amazon.com carries only $56 million in fixed assets on its books. This amount of assets accounts primarily for the firm's warehouses and computers. Furthermore, the future portends an even worse situation for Barnes & Noble, because Amazon.com's new investment in warehouses can support $15 billion in sales. For these reasons, it has a $21.2 billion market capitalization, compared to $1.8 billion for Barnes & Noble. This suggests that the low-cost competitive advantage, an advantage that is pursued through the cost leadership business-level strategy, can shift from traditional brick-and-mortar stores to those pursuing cost leadership through an Internet-based strategy. In recognition of this shift, Barnes & Noble has formed an Internet operation (barnesandnoble.com) in partnership with Bertelsmann A.G., the German media giant that paid $200 million to purchase a 50 percent stake in the Web-based venture. Although, as suggested in a Strategic Focus in Chapter 2, the competition between Amazon.com and Barnes & Noble may be changing, it has still caused a significant shift in the business-level strategy of Barnes & Noble.

In addition, large traditional firms are being challenged on the cost side in terms of where value can be captured along the value chain (see Chapter 3). This challenge is a result of the fact that many firms are reconfiguring the value chain to generate additional value by purchasing through suppliers' Web-based business models. For instance, Cisco Systems handles 78 percent of its sales via the Internet, a practice that results in the firm never physically touching at least $4 billion in customers' orders. Cisco develops products and manufacturing and specifications but uses the Internet to forward orders directly to contract manufacturers. Cisco owns only 2 of the 30 plants that produce the networking switches and routers that are sold to its telecommunications customers.

As previously noted, many large traditional companies are responding to Web-based competition by establishing their own Internet presence. The main problem, however, is that these large firms' Web businesses have a tendency to cannibalize their company's existing businesses. In turn, cannibalization can increase rivalry inside the firm between those involved with "traditional" sales activities and those generating revenues via the newly formed Internet operation (see the Strategic Focus on Merrill Lynch later in the chapter). Notwithstanding the threat of cannibalization, Sears Roebuck Company has decided to establish a Web-based operation, Sears.com. But only products in which Sears has a competitive advantage are being sold initially through this channel. Appliances, parts, and tools are examples of products in which Sears believes it has competitive advantages that will contribute to success via Internet sales. Plans are for Sears.com to eventually sell lawn and garden accessories and home furnishings and allow customers to arrange for repair services. Because of the seasonality of the apparel business, and because it may not have a sustainable competitive advantage with this product line, Sears does not currently intend to make these goods available through Sears.com. Thus, with its Internet business, Sears has chosen a business-level strategy that fits in with its current approach and that will lead to less compromise.

However, using a different business-level strategy, Whirlpool Corporation has established a business-to-business (B2B) Web-based strategy. In the last several years, Whirlpool developed 3,300 customized Web pages for its dealers. By logging on to one of these pages, a dealer can order products and check on their delivery status. Whirlpool is also using the Internet to form start-up ventures. The initial concept is a venture called brandwise.com. This site serves as a portal to shop for appliances such as washing machines, clothes dryers, refrigerators, microwave ovens, and so forth. Featuring other brands in addition to its own, Whirlpool owns only 37 percent of brandwise.com. The risk that customers using brandwise.com will buy a competitor's product is acceptable, given Whirlpool's commitment to establishing a viable Internet distribution channel and given the firm's belief in the competitive superiority of its products. Another benefit from brandwise.com is the opportunity for Whirlpool to obtain valuable data that the company can use to design products in the future that can meet customers' emerging needs. Furthermore, the same data will allow Whirlpool to learn about buying patterns by tracking buyer demographics. Retailers who receive revenue referred from brandwise.com will pay a flat fee each time a sale is consummated that originated from the site. Revenues will also be generated through those advertising on the Web site and through commissions earned from sales of accessories, warranties, and service contracts. However, Whirlpool's rivals may be able to get the same information from the site and thereby compromise Whirlpool's differentiation business-level strategy. Thus, although there are opportunities, there are also significant risks involved with Whirlpool's decision to integrate the Internet into the formulation and implementation of its business-level strategy.

The strategic changes resulting from use of the Internet are profound. Firms such as Hewlett-Packard, IBM, Silicon Graphics, and others have sold plants because they were increasingly regarded as a liability. In fact, in 1998, firms outsourced 15 percent of all manufacturing. It is estimated that as much as 40 percent of manufacturing will be outsourced in 2000 and beyond. In addition, this approach allows much more customization in a shorter period of time: Instead of taking months or weeks to receive a customized car, Toyota and other Japanese automobile manufacturers, along with U.S. manufacturers such as GM, are pioneering the five-day car. This capability generates more value for customers and dealers. Customers receive products that satisfy their unique needs. Value is created for dealers in that the customized and direct sales approach prevents cars from being carried in their inventories for long periods of time.

In sum, the Internet has the potential to create more value for customers in the form of lower costs and additional differentiated features. Increasingly, the Internet is influencing a firm's choice of a business-level strategy. In other instances, the Internet affects

http://www.amazon.com

http://www.bn.com

http://www.cbs.com

http://www.cisco.com

http://www.ford.com

http://www.hp.com

http://www.sears.com

http://www.toyota.com

http://www.whirlpool.com

http//:www.yahoo.com

how companies implement a business-level strategy once it has been selected. Thus, as our discussion will show, the Internet is having major effects on business-level strategy, the topic of this chapter.

SOURCES: A. Goldstein, 2000, Online merchants seek to improve e-commerce, *Dallas Morning News,* January 14, D1–D2; E. Brown, 1999, Big business meets the e-world, *Fortune,* November 8, 88–98; R. D. Hof, K. Kerwin, P. Burrows, & D. Brady, 1999, A new year of bright hopes and terrible fears, *Business Week,* October 4, 84–98; B. Marvel, 1999, The '90s: Cultural trends that shaped a decade, *Dallas Morning News,* December 19, C1; O. Port, 1999, Customers move into the driver's seat, *Business Week,* October 4, 103–106; P. Timmers, 1998, Business models for electronic markets, in Y. Gadient, B. F. Schmid, & D. Selz, Electronic commerce in Europe, *EM - Electronic Markets,* 8, 2, July, *www.electronicmarkets.org/netacademy/publications.nsf/all_pk/949.*

It is clear from the Opening Case that the Internet's capabilities are yielding a rich array of opportunities for companies throughout the global economy. In terms of market potential, it is important to note that in the United States alone, it is estimated that three-fourths of all consumers have yet to make a purchase on the Internet.[1] This vast untapped market is enticing to both established firms and start-up ventures.

An established and dominant retailer, Wal-Mart is pursuing the Internet's opportunities largely through partnerships. One of the agreements it has formed is with Books-A-Million. The cooperative arrangement calls for Books-A-Million to supply and deliver books for Wal-Mart's on-line store, which will compete with Amazon.com and barnesandnoble.com, among others. Initial plans called for this venture to offer best-sellers at a 50-percent discount, with hardbacks being sold at a 30-percent discount. Wal-Mart intends to form alliances with still other companies to pursue its cost leadership business-level strategy through Internet sales. Fingerhut, for example, has agreed to form a partnership with Wal-Mart and will handle orders and ship some merchandise that is purchased at Wal-Mart's Web site.[2] In another venture, with a customer list that at any time includes almost 10 percent of all U.S. businesses—factories, garages, military bases, laundries, grocers and schools—W. W. Grainger, Inc., initially spent over $50 million to build its e-commerce systems. According to top-level executives, the reason for this activity is their assessment that business on the Web has an enormous upside for W. W. Grainger.[3] According to one analyst, "[B]usiness-to-business e-commerce is poised to soar, and GM and Ford are at the vanguard of this movement. Both companies are exercising their enormous buying power to jump start trading exchanges on the Internet."[4] As shown by the examples, the Internet is becoming an increasingly important aspect of firms' business-level strategies. Moreover, as noted previously, for firms in general, "the Internet is reshaping the global marketplace and it will continue to do so for some time to come."[5]

To achieve strategic competitiveness and earn above-average returns, a company analyzes its external environment, identifies opportunities in it, determines which of its internal resources and capabilities are core competencies, and selects an appropriate strategy to implement.[6] This array of actions is required of *all* companies—those competing through more traditional means, as well as those seeking above-average returns as Internet-based ventures.

A **strategy** is an integrated and coordinated set of commitments and actions designed to exploit core competencies and gain a competitive advantage.

A **strategy** is an integrated and coordinated set of commitments and actions designed to exploit core competencies and gain a competitive advantage. Strategies are purposeful, precede the taking of actions to which they apply, and demonstrate a shared understanding of a firm's strategic intent and mission.[7] An effectively formulated strategy marshals, integrates, and allocates the firm's resources, capabilities, and competencies so that it can cope successfully with its external environment.[8] An effective strategy also rationalizes the firm's strategic intent and strategic mission and what will be done to achieve them.[9] Information about a host of variables, including markets, customers, technology, worldwide finance, and the changing world economy, must be collected and analyzed to formulate and implement strategies properly.[10] As the Opening Case illustrates, the Internet creates a more competitive strategic situation in which to select strategies to use in the pursuit of strategic competitiveness and above-average returns.

Recall from Chapters 1 and 3 that *core competencies* are resources and capabilities that serve as a source of competitive advantage for a firm over its rivals. Strategic competitiveness and the earning of above-average returns hinge on a firm's ability to develop and exploit new core competencies faster than competitors can mimic the competitive advantages yielded by current ones.[11] Firms that focus on the continuous need to develop new core competencies are able to drive competition in the future as well as the present.[12] Thus, especially in the 21st-century competitive landscape, with its continuing globalization and rapid technological changes, only firms with the capacity to improve, innovate, and upgrade their competitive advantages over time can expect to achieve long-term success.[13]

As explained in this chapter, successful firms use their core competencies to satisfy customers' needs. The relationship between appropriate strategic actions and the achievement of strategic competitiveness is increasingly important in today's turbulent and competitive environment.[14] These relationships are shown in Figure 1.1. This figure shows that a firm's *strategic inputs* (gained through studying the external and internal environments) are used to select the *strategic actions* (the formulation and implementation of value-creating strategies) that will yield desired *strategic outcomes*.

At a broader level, companies that are committed to the importance of competing successfully in the global economy constantly scan developments in the world's markets to identify emerging opportunities to exploit their competitive advantages. The segments most closely linked with strategic competitiveness vary by the type of business-level strategy the firm is using.[15] Consider, for example, Taiwanese PC manufacturers. Collectively, PC manufacturers in Taiwan maintain the third-largest market share position behind the United States and Japan. The low-priced segment of the PC market is targeted by many of Taiwan's PC manufacturers. Competition among firms seeking to serve this segment through the use of the cost leadership business-level strategy is severe. To drive their costs lower and to exploit the competitive advantage their low cost structures provide, Taiwanese companies are relying more and more on suppliers from mainland China to supply low-priced components. Chinese component suppliers can offer less expensive parts to the Taiwanese PC manufacturers because of lower costs, made possible by relatively inexpensive land and labor expenses. Because the Taiwanese firms rely on export to fulfill global demand, completing business transactions with firms in China is not seen as risky: Taiwan does not rely on sales to Chinese customers and hence does not have to worry about the associated credit risks.[16]

Hungary's version of privatization of state-owned firms has helped to put it ahead of other Eastern European countries. Many Eastern European countries pursued a privatization process in which a voucher scheme was used to make each citizen an owner. Alternatively, Hungary chose to use initial public offerings (IPOs) and direct sales to strategically selected foreign investors. Most of the privatization sales became a combination of domestic and foreign interests. This was a much more difficult approach politically because of the fear of foreign investors and the potential for large-scale layoffs. The main difference was the opportunity to have cash for investment through stronger equity and debt markets relative to the voucher approach.

As a result of the success of its privatization approach, Hungary will likely be the first Eastern European country to join the European Union. In addition, it has management expertise from foreign owners that will allow it to have more cutting-edge technology. Ameritech, for example, in partnership with Deutsche Telekom, has put the Hungarian telecommunications company Matav on a par technologically with its Western European counterparts. Furthermore, through its significant investments, Electrolux has transformed Hungary's appliance industry such that the country is a leader in Eastern Europe. These companies have followed the strategic management process in that they have observed opportunities in the environment and have marshaled their resources in manners that allow them to implement particular business-level strategies in the pursuit of strategic competitiveness. In turn, the firms' strategic actions are creating a vibrant Hungarian economy, even though risks remain—for the country and for firms competing within its borders.[17]

A **business-level strategy** is an integrated and coordinated set of commitments and actions designed to provide value to customers and gain a competitive advantage by exploiting core competencies in specific, individual product markets.

Business-level strategy, this chapter's focus, is an integrated and coordinated set of commitments and actions designed to provide value to customers and gain a competitive advantage by exploiting core competencies in specific, individual product markets.[18] Thus, a business-level strategy reflects a firm's belief about where and how it has an advantage over its rivals.[19] The essence of a firm's business-level strategy is "choosing to perform activities differently or to perform different activities than rivals."[20] Related to the firm's competitive environment and the interactions the firm has with that environment is the necessity that all employees understand what the firm's advantage is relative to rivals.[21] Questions about the firm's strategy in the future and the competitive advantages on which it would be based should be resolved quickly to permit effective strategic actions.

Customers are the foundation of successful business-level strategies. Increasingly, firms are emphasizing the importance of the link between building relationships and delivering service to customers and the firm's financial performance. One CEO captures this sentiment by observing that in his firm, "the central question is, What kind of initiatives will help us strengthen the customer relationships we have and encourage new ones to form?"[22] This emphasis is consistent with the perspective that, at its core, business-level strategy is "the ability to build and maintain relationships to the best people for maximum value creation, both 'internally' (to firm representatives) and 'externally' (to customers)."[23]

Because of their strategic importance, we begin this chapter with a discussion of customers. Three issues are considered in this analysis. Each firm determines (1) *whom* it will serve, (2) *what* needs target customers have that it will satisfy, and (3) *how* those needs will be satisfied through the implementation of a chosen strategy. Following the discussion on customers, we describe four generic business-level strategies. These strategies are called *generic* because they are implemented in both manufacturing and service industries.[24] Our analysis of the generic strategies includes descriptions of how each one allows a firm to address the five competitive forces discussed in Chapter 2. In addition, we use the value chain (see Chapter 3) to show examples of primary and support activities that are necessary to implement each generic strategy. Risks associated with each generic strategy are also presented. Organizational structures and controls required for the successful implementation of business-level strategies are explained in Chapter 11.

A fifth business-level strategy that both manufacturing and service firms are implementing more frequently is considered in the chapter's final section. Some believe that this integrated strategy (a combination of attributes of the cost leadership and differentiation strategies) is essential to establishing and exploiting competitive advantages in the global economy—an economy with growth possibilities that are being expanded and changed because of the Internet's capabilities.[25]

Customers: Who, What, and How

Organizations must satisfy some group of customers' needs to be successful. *Needs* refer to the benefits and features of a good or service that customers want to purchase.[26] A basic need of all customers is to buy products that provide value.

A key reason that firms must be able to satisfy customers' needs is that, in the final analysis, returns earned from relationships with customers are the lifeblood of all organizations.[27] Relationships with customers are strengthened when the firm is committed to providing *superior* value to those it serves. Superior value is often created when a firm's product helps a customer enhance the business's own competitive advantage.[28]

The challenge of identifying and determining how to satisfy the needs of what some business analysts believe are increasingly sophisticated, knowledgeable, and fickle customers is difficult.[29] However, products are now available to assist companies in their efforts to better understand customers and suppliers and to manage their relationships with them. Through its acquisition of Smart Technologies, for example, i2Technologies offers software to companies that supports the management of Internet-based customer relationships. Additionally, i2's flagship product manages information related to manufacturers' customers and suppliers. GM's recent decision to use i2's software and services was seen by analysts as a significant affirmation of the firm's strategy to foster training hubs on the Internet.[30]

It is also important for firms to recognize that it is only through *total* satisfaction of their needs that customers develop the type of firm-specific loyalty companies seek. To improve the chances that its products will totally satisfy customers, Whirlpool now uses what it calls the "Real Whirled" training program. This program is intended to generate insights that can be passed on to the firm's sales trainers, personnel who work with employees at retail establishments such as Home Depot and Sears to teach them how to sell Whirlpool products. Real Whirled places eight company employees into a "retro-décor" house near a Lake Michigan beach. These people "spend two months living, baking, washing, cooking, and cleaning with the products their company sells. Then they take what they've learned as real-world consumers, and use those insights and experiences to train Whirlpool retailers to sell products in terms that buyers understand."[31] In addition to serving customers currently, being able to move toward total need satisfaction increases the likelihood that the firm will retain customers' interest and earn repeat business from them. It is also important to consider the strategic value of the finding that "companies reap far greater economic rewards from highly satisfied customers than they do from merely satisfied customer[s]."[32] This finding seems to offer important evidence of the need for the firm to provide goods or services through which customers will reach high levels of satisfaction. Increasingly, databases are linked with customer retention rates. Among other useful outcomes, information gleaned from these databases allows the firm to tailor its offerings more precisely to satisfy individualized customer needs.[33]

Evidence suggests that strategically competitive organizations in the 21st century—those that concentrate on customers in selecting and implementing business-level strategies—will (1) seek to solve customers' problems with the goods or services they sell, (2) remain focused on the need to innovate continuously, even when their current offerings are selling well, (3) determine how to use their core competencies in ways that competitors cannot imitate, and (4) design their strategies to allow them to satisfy customers' current, anticipated, and even unanticipated needs.[34] Consistent with these practices, Caterpillar, Inc., has developed a technology-based process that has customer needs as the starting point. As the driver of this process, customer needs are expected to help the firm remain a leader in developing innovative and customer-centered product technologies.[35] Similarly, to restore the competitive health of its brand, German automaker Adam Opel is committed to improving its understanding of customers' needs so that it can produce and deliver products that provide additional levels of satisfaction.[36]

However, to achieve strategic competitiveness in what seems to be a rapidly developing Internet-based economy, 21st-century firms will need to do even more than is called for by the four actions listed in the previous paragraph. The reason for this is that attention on the Internet is shifting from *claiming* virtual space to *defending* and *capturing* it. Three dimensions have been defined relative to customers that may facilitate competitive advantage in this context. The *reach* dimension is about access and connection to customers. For instance, the largest physical retailer in bookstores, Barnes & Noble, carries about 200,000 titles. By contrast, Amazon.com offers some 4.5 million titles and is located on roughly 25 million computer screens, with additional customer connections expected in the future. Thus, its reach is significantly magnified relative to that associated with Barnes & Noble's physical bookstores.

Reach is the most obvious difference between electronic and physical businesses. The second dimension, *richness,* is the depth and detail of information that the firm can deliver to customers, as well as collect from them. The richness dimension is causing traditional brokers to move on-line, because on-line brokers such as E*Trade and Charles Schwab are moving into the area that has been held by traditional brokerages (see the Strategic Focus on Merrill Lynch and other on-line brokers later in the chapter). Richness holds enormous potential for building close relationships with customers in a future dominated by e-commerce. Gaining access to rich information was prohibitively expensive before the e-commerce information era.

Affiliation is the third dimension and focuses on relationship with the customer. Navigators such as Microsoft CarPoint help on-line clients find and sort information. CarPoint provides car buyers with data and software that permit the comparison of different car models along 80 objective specifications. Microsoft is able to provide this service because Internet technology allows a great deal of information to be collected from a variety of sources at a very low cost. Once a consumer has selected a car as a result of studying the comparisons across different models, CarPoint can link the consumer with dealers that meet the customer's needs and purchasing requirements. Because a company represents its own products, the interests of an automobile manufacturer such as GM, Ford, or DaimlerChrysler can differ substantially from the consumer's interests. In contrast, CarPoint is representing the car buyer's interests, in that its revenues typically come from sources other than the customer (e.g., from those advertising on the navigator's Web site, from hyperlinks, and from the sale of associated products and services).[37]

Who: Determining the Customers to Serve

Market segmentation is a process through which people with similar needs are clustered into individual and identifiable groups.

Customers can be divided into groups based on differences in their needs. Called **market segmentation,** this is a process through which people with similar needs are clustered into individual and identifiable groups. Market segmentation is a two-step process of naming broad product markets and segmenting them in order to select target markets and develop suitable marketing mixes.[38] Compared to the decision that the firm will serve the needs of the "average customer," marketing segmentation creates a framework that is important to the selection of a business-level strategy. The reason for this is that averages sometimes do not provide the type of in-depth insights about issues that are relevant to the firm's strategic actions. Shown in Table 4.1 are characteristics of the average American, the average woman, and the average man. Although interesting, these descriptors are of less value to a company seeking to target customers than are attributes and needs associated with *specific* and *identifiable* customer market segments.

Almost any identifiable human or organizational characteristic can be used to subdivide a market into segments that differ from one another in terms of a given characteristic. In the ultraluxury automobile market, for example, Rolls-Royce Motor Cars, Ltd., suggests that its Bentleys and Rolls-Royces satisfy different customer needs, in that the Bentley is more of a car for people who want to drive the product while the Rolls is intended to serve those who have a need to be driven by a chauffeur.[39] Common characteristics on which customers' needs vary are illustrated in Table 4.2. These characteristics can be used as the basis for market segmentation.

Recently, some British pubs redesigned their facilities and the experiences offered within them in a manner that is intended to appeal to gender-related differences between customers (i.e., men's needs versus women's needs). Industry analysts observe that these actions, which are intended to better serve female customers' needs, have resulted in more "female friendly" outlets. In addition, start-up ventures have surfaced to meet women's needs. These pubs are viewed as quite "trendy." Thus, through their analysis of demographic variables, British pub operators concluded that two market segments exist. According to one pub manager, "[W]omen have higher expectations, and are more demanding and discerning. They want staff to be welcoming and

4.1 | Characteristics of the Average American

The Average American

- Watches television seven hours daily, makes 1,029 telephone calls annually, and eats 198 meals out a year.
- Wastes 150 hours a year sifting through clutter searching for things.
- Receives 49,060 pieces of mail in a lifetime. A third of it is junk.
- Charges $2,750 a year on credit cards.
- Owns 16 denim items, including seven pairs of jeans.
- Laughs 15 times daily. The average adult curses once every eight words at leisure and every 29 words at work.
- Eats 11,113 M&M's in a lifetime.
- Has 40 hours of leisure a week. In an average week, the average American parent spends six hours shopping and 40 minutes playing with the kids.

Average Woman

- Lives 78.6 years.
- Has a body with 28 percent fat.
- Owns 30 pairs of shoes.
- Tries on 16 pairs of jeans to find a perfect fit.
- Spends 15.7 minutes on her hair each morning.

Average Man

- Lives 71.6 years
- Has a body with 15 percent fat.
- Owns 15 dress shirts, six pairs of slacks, six sport shirts, five knit shirts, and three sweaters.
- Spends four hours a year tying his tie.
- Devotes 3,350 hours to shaving during his lifetime.

Sources: Columbus Dispatch; *In an Average Lifetime* and *On an Average Day* (Fawcett Columbine) by Tom Heymann; *Your Vital Statistics* (Citadel) by Gyles Brandreth; *American Averages* (Doubleday) by Mike Feinsilber & William B. Mead; *Statistical Abstract of the United States.*

4.2 | Basis for Customer Segmentation

Consumer Markets

1. Demographic factors (age, income, sex, etc.)
2. Socioeconomic factors (social class, stage in the family life cycle)
3. Geographic factors (cultural, regional, and national differences)
4. Psychological factors (lifestyle, personality traits)
5. Consumption patterns (heavy, moderate, and light users)
6. Perceptul factors (benefit segmentation, perceptual mapping)

Industrial Markets

1. End-use segments (identified by SIC code)
2. Product segments (based on technological differences or production economics)
3. Geographic segments (defined by boundaries between countries or by regional differences within them)
4. Common buying factor segments (cut across product market and geographic segments)
5. Customer size segments .

Source: Adapted from S. C. Jain, 2000, *Marketing Planning and Strategy* (Cincinnati: South-Western College Publishing), 120.

a pub to be clean and comfortable." To meet women's needs, pubs are now providing (1) toilets that are easy to find and that are clean, well lighted, and apportioned with a full-length mirror, (2) staff with a more positive attitude toward women, especially those entering the pub alone, (3) good ventilation, and (4) airy interiors. Data showing that the number of women entering pubs once a month or more increased 8 percent between 1991 and 1998 are seen by analysts and pub operators alike as evidence that the new approach to market segmentation has been successful.[40]

Increasing Segmentation of Markets

In the 21st-century competitive landscape, many firms are adept at identifying precise differences among customers' needs. Armed with this understanding, companies segment customers into *competitively relevant groups*, each with its own unique needs. Thus, General Motors believes that four of its automobile product groups serve the unique needs of four competitively relevant groups: "The Chevy is squarely aimed at people shopping for a low price. The Pontiac targets performance enthusiasts. The Olds is for upscale buyers who might normally shop for import sport sedans, and the Buick will appeal to older buyers who want premium cars with conservative styling and room for six riders."[41] In another attempt at segmentation, Title 9 Sports, named after a piece of legislation that was passed in the United States in 1972, sells athletic products to women of all ages. The firm's offerings are intended to support women's efforts to reach their personal fitness goals.[42] And New Balance shoes are targeted to meet baby boomers' unique needs for the availability of shoes in multiple width sizes.[43]

At 30.9 million, today's teenage population is the largest in U.S. history. After the baby boomers, teenagers are the most significant U.S. consumer group.

In the United States, teenagers are a large, competitively relevant group whose purchasing power continues to increase. Known today as Generation Y, G2000, or the new millennials, this group is the largest teen population in U.S. history—30.9 million between the ages of 12 and 19. These individuals appear to be living what Microsoft's Bill Gates calls the "Web lifestyle." Some Internet-based companies target children as young as five years of age.[44] Projections are that the 12-to-19-year-old age group will grow to 33.6 million by 2005. In 1998, this market segment spent $141 billion, compared to $122 billion the previous year. These purchases average $84 weekly per teenager, a mean expenditure that exceeds 1997's amount by $4 per teen and 1991's by $23. According to some analysts, the current teen group "is the most significant consumer group in America right now since the baby boomers. And what that means to companies is that if they want to stay in business, they'd best shift their attention from middle-aged concerns to those of this new group."[45]

Companies are responding to the challenge. To support its business-level strategy of focused differentiation when targeting the teenage market segment, JCPenney Co. developed its own fashion magazine called *Noise*. This publication features articles on the latest styles and trends in beauty and fashion and about music and sports-related events. According to a company executive, the magazine is seen "as a vehicle to create a strong, personal relationship with a very important customer—teenagers."[46] Although significant for all business-level strategies, personal relationships with specific customers are especially critical for firms implementing either the focused cost leadership or focused differentiation strategy (defined later in the chapter).

Observation of the array of unique goods (e.g., shoes to meet the unique needs of women and baby boomers in general) and services (e.g., Penney's publication for teenagers and those that are marketed to senior citizens by AARP) available in the United States suggests that segmenting markets into increasingly specialized niches continues to increase. The trend toward market segmentation is also occurring in many other nations' economies.

Particularly in instances in which focused business-level strategies are being used to serve unique market segments, companies may wish to capitalize on the fact that product uniqueness exists within categories, as well as in terms of the absolute number of available goods and services. For example, in comparison to the past's somewhat standardized soft drinks, consumers now choose from among different brands and different versions, sugar-free drinks, caffeine-free beverages, bottled water (flat or sparkling), and so forth. However, companies' efforts to create a huge set of goods and services that is intended to satisfy unique needs may be confusing to some customers. This confusion can result from the sheer number of goods and services that are available to consumers across the globe.[47] Selecting a business-level strategy that is called for by conditions in the firm's external and internal environments and then implementing that strategy effectively reduces the likelihood that the firm will confuse its customers through its product offerings.

What: Determining the Customer Needs to Satisfy

As a firm decides whom it will serve, it must simultaneously identify the targeted customer group's needs that its goods or services can satisfy. Top-level managers play a critical role in efforts to recognize and understand these needs. Their capacity to gain valuable insights from listening to and studying customers influences product, technology, and distribution decisions. For example, upper-level executives at Volkswagen AG heard concerns from customers about the firm's decision to base several Volkswagen and Audi models on the same chassis and to use the same transmissions. Some consumers asked the firm why they should pay for the premiere Audi brand when they could obtain much of the technology at a lower cost by purchasing a Volkswagen product. In response to these concerns, Volkswagen AG "intends to invest six billion marks ($3.32 billion) during the next few years to ensure that each of its brands retains a separate identity."[48]

An additional competitive advantage accrues to firms that are capable of anticipating and then satisfying needs that were unknown to target customers. Firms that are able to do this provide customers with unexpected value—that is, a product performance capability or characteristic they did not request, yet do value.[49] Moreover, anticipating customers' needs yields opportunities for firms to shape their industry's future and gain an early competitive advantage (called a **first-mover advantage** and discussed in Chapter 5). In some instances, a firm's formally stated strategy may be built on providing unexpected customer benefits and gaining first-mover advantages as a

First-mover advantage is an early competitive advantage that allows firms to anticipate customers' needs and shape their industry's future.

result of doing so. This appears to be the case for trendy retailer Williams-Sonoma. Implementing a focused differentiation business-level strategy, the firm concluded that shoppers expect to be surprised continuously when they purchase products at the high end of the apparel business.[50] Being able to positively surprise customers continuously allows the firm to earn above-average returns as it reinvents itself time and time again through its goods and services.

How: Determining Core Competencies Necessary to Satisfy Customers' Needs

Firms use their *core competencies* to implement value-creating strategies and satisfy customers' needs. One of the strategic imperatives at IBM is to convert the firm's technological core competence more quickly into commercial products that customers value. In addition, IBM's intensive knowledge of its customers' businesses has helped it turn its historical focus on customer service into a mainline business. In this context, since the beginning of Lou Gerstner's tenure as the firm's CEO, IBM has focused on providing customer "solutions" to clients. Historically, customer solutions were built around IBM's hardware. However, Gerstner has engineered a remarkable transformation, making services rather than products the firm's growth engine. For instance, fitting in with its focus, IBM's software division is competing quite effectively, earning in excess of 20-percent pretax profit margins. The computer sales division is now the one encountering performance problems. For example, IBM's PC division lost $992 million in 1998, although server computers were still yielding 25.7 percent pretax profit margins. Monitors, storage equipment, and memory chips were far less profitable, recording pretax profit margins of 5.8 percent. With increases of 22 percent in services revenue, this segment accounted for 28 percent of IBM's 1998 sales of $82 billion. It is also interesting to point out that IBM's services growth, which is expected to increase as the 21st century begins, has also helped the company sell its hardware. This suggests that a focus on customers' needs can help a business across a number of competitive dimensions.[51]

One of the most solid and trusted suppliers in the electronics and computer industries, Hewlett-Packard (HP), uses its engineering core competence to manufacture products that are renowned for their quality.[52] But changes such as those at IBM have sparked the interest of HP and other companies. In fact, HP has created an e-services division. Instead of selling multimillion-dollar computers, this division sells computing power over a network for a monthly fee. For purchasers, the value created by buying HP's services lies in avoiding the trouble and expense of operating their own systems. In running an e-commerce site for a client, HP can charge its customers a percentage of the client's transaction revenues. Ann Livermore, CEO of HP's $14-billion-dollar Enterprise Computing Solutions (the e-service division), estimates that such a fee may account for 80 percent of the division's revenues.[53]

Next, we discuss the business-level strategies firms use when pursuing strategic competitiveness and above-average returns.

Types of Business-Level Strategy

Business-level strategies are concerned with a firm's industry position relative to those of competitors.[54] Companies that have established favorable industry positions are better able to cope with the five forces of competition (see Chapter 2). To position itself, a firm must decide whether its intended actions will allow it to perform activities differently from the way its rivals do so or to perform different activities than those of its rivals.[55] Thus, favorably positioned firms may have a competitive advantage over their industry rivals. This is, of course, important in that the universal objective of all companies is to develop and sustain competitive advantages.[56] Improperly positioned firms encounter competitive difficulties and may fail to sustain competitive advantages. Ryder Systems, Inc., for example, recently faced a downturn in its core operations. Some argued that the firm's competitive advantages in its core businesses of truck leasing and third-party logistics were becoming less able to position the firm successfully vis-à-vis rivals.[57]

Earlier, we mentioned that firms choose from among four generic business-level strategies to establish and exploit a competitive advantage within a particular competitive scope: *cost leadership, differentiation, focused cost leadership,* and *focused differentiation* (see Figure 4.1). A fifth generic business-level strategy, the integrated cost leadership/differentiation strategy, has evolved through firms' efforts to find the most effective ways to exploit their competitive advantages.

FIGURE

4.1 | Four Generic Strategies

Competitive Scope		Competitive Advantage: Cost	Competitive Advantage: Uniqueness
	Broad target	Cost Leadership	Differentiation
	Narrow target	Focused Cost Leadership	Focused Differentiation

Source: Adapted with the permission of The Free Press, a Division of Simon & Schuster, Inc., from *Competitive Advantage: Creating and Sustaining Superior Performance,* by Michael E. Porter, Fig. 1–3, 12. Copyright © 1985, 1998 by Michael E. Porter.

In selecting a business-level strategy, firms evaluate two types of competitive advantage: "lower cost than rivals, or the ability to differentiate and command a premium price that exceeds the extra cost of doing so."[58] Having lower cost than rivals derives from the firm's ability to perform activities differently than rivals; being able to differentiate indicates a capacity to perform different activities.[59] Competitive advantage is achieved within some scope. Scope has several dimensions, including the group of product and customer segments served and the array of geographic markets in which a firm competes. Competitive advantage is sought by competing in many customer segments when implementing either the cost leadership or the differentiation strategy. In contrast, through the implementation of focus strategies, firms seek either a cost advantage or a differentiation advantage in a *narrow competitive scope* or *segment*. With focus strategies, the firm "selects a segment or group of segments in the industry and tailors its strategy to serving them to the exclusion of others."[60]

None of the five business-level strategies is inherently or universally superior to the others.[61] The effectiveness of each strategy is contingent on the opportunities and threats that exist in a firm's external environment *and* the possibilities permitted by the firm's unique resources, capabilities, and core competencies. It is critical, therefore, for the firm to select a strategy that is appropriate in light of its competencies and environmental opportunities; once selected, the strategy should be implemented carefully and consistently.

Cost Leadership Strategy

A **cost leadership strategy** is an integrated set of actions designed to produce or deliver goods or services at the lowest cost, relative to competitors, with features that are acceptable to customers.

A **differentiation strategy** is an integrated set of actions designed to produce goods or services that customers perceive as being different in ways that are important to them.

A **cost leadership strategy** is an integrated set of actions designed to produce or deliver goods or services at the lowest cost, relative to that of competitors, with features that are acceptable to customers. A **differentiation strategy** is an integrated set of actions designed to produce or deliver goods or services that customers perceive as being different in ways that are important to them.[62] The differentiation strategy calls for firms to sell nonstandardized products to customers with unique needs. With its Lexus product line, Toyota seeks to satisfy customers' unique needs for certain differentiated features (e.g., product quality) while delivering the firm's nonstandardized automobile to them at an acceptable cost. The cost leadership strategy should achieve low cost relative to that of competitors, while not ignoring means of differentiation that customers value. Firms seeking competitive advantage through this business-level strategy often sell no-frills, standardized goods or services to the industry's most typical customers. Alternatively, the differentiation strategy should consistently upgrade a good or service's differentiated features that customers value without ignoring costs to customers. Thus, although cost of leadership differentiation strategies differ, firms can create value and differentiation strategies through either one.[63]

Successful implementation of the cost leadership strategy requires a consistent focus on driving costs lower, relative to competitors' costs. Vanguard Group, the second largest mutual-fund company in the United States, follows the cost leadership strategy. Portraying fees and costs as an evil and extolling efficiency's worth, Vanguard has some believing that it is in the business of selling virtue. The passion in this firm appears to be to cut costs, but the company also seeks to provide excellent service to its clients. The low-cost producer in its industry, Vanguard had a 1998 average expense ratio for its actively managed domestic and international equity funds of

0.36 percent, actually down from 1993's 0.43 percent ratio. The average 1998 expense ratio across all equity funds was 1.56 percent. In the same year, the ratio was 1.18 percent for Fidelity, a major competitor of Vanguard. With a cost-cutting culture that is legendary in the industry, Vanguard is also committed to offering services to customers that they value. To save their time, for example, Vanguard's 2,000-plus telephone representatives are expected to answer all calls by the fourth ring. When representatives are in short supply, the firm's managers, including top-level executives, can be found answering customers' telephone queries. Continuous offers of innovative products such as index funds are an example of another differentiated feature that Vanguard provides to its customers. Following a study of Vanguard's operations, one analyst concluded that "no other company offers the highest-quality product and the lowest-possible price."[64]

However, as the description of Vanguard's strategy suggests, simply reducing costs is not equivalent to implementing the cost leadership strategy. For example, commenting about Avon's efforts to reduce its cost structure, a business analyst suggested that cost cuts could give the company "only a face-lift, not a full-body makeover." Other actions, fully consistent with conditions in the firm's external and internal environments, must be taken for Avon to improve its performance.[65] Some analysts believe that bankrupt PC manufacturer Packard Bell NEC, Inc., sold its products at low costs, but without levels of quality that were acceptable to customers.[66] Vanguard is implementing the cost leadership strategy while simultaneously attending to customer service and new product demands.

Firms that are fully committed to using the cost leadership strategy often drive their costs lower through investments in efficient-scale facilities, tight cost and overhead control, and cost minimizations in such areas as service, sales force, and research and development. One of the lowest-cost steel producers in the world, Nucor Corporation has relied on investments in efficient-scale facilities to achieve strategic competitiveness (the firm has operated profitably every year since 1966) through its cost leadership strategy.[67] Similarly, Unifi, Inc., a company that is one of the world's largest texturizers of filament polyester and nylon fiber, makes significant investments in its manufacturing technologies to drive its costs lower in an environment of upward pressure on prices for raw materials and packaging supplies. Already one of the most efficient producers in its industry, the company recently completed a modernization program for texturizing polyester. Unifi also intends to modernize and expand its nylon, covered-yarn, and dyed-yarn operations. Combined, these actions are expected to increase the firm's technological lead over its rivals and further reduce its production costs.[68]

Consolidated Stores, Inc., seeks to earn above-average returns by using the cost leadership strategy. One of the firm's strategic business units, the Closeout Division, is the largest U.S. retailer of closeout merchandise. According to the firm's CEO, as a discount retailer, Consolidated sells name-brand products at below discount prices.[69] Consolidated's buyers travel the country looking through manufacturer overruns and discontinued styles and buying the leftovers at well below wholesale. "We're the undertakers of the business," states CEO William Kelly. "We buy product when nobody else wants or needs it. We're the guys out there on February 15 buying red boxer shorts with little red hearts on them." Consolidated unloads these products at a deep discount at its outlets, which include Big Lots/Odd Lots and Kay-Bee Toy & Hobby shops. Recently, Consolidated acquired MacFrugal's, the second largest discount retailer in the United States. Acquiring the 326 MacFrugal units complemented Consolidated's existing closeout merchandise operations, gave the firm a national presence, and created a business unit with almost 1,100 total stores with locations in 40 states.[70]

As described in Chapter 3, firms use the value chain to determine the parts of the company's operations that create value and those that do not. Shown in Figure 4.2 are primary and support activities that allow a firm to create value through the cost leadership strategy. Companies that cannot link the activities mentioned in this figure lack the resources and capabilities (and hence the core competencies) that are required to use the cost leadership strategy successfully.

In using the cost leadership strategy, firms must be careful not to completely ignore sources of differentiation (e.g., innovative designs, service after the sale, product quality, etc.) that customers value. Emerson Electric Co. implements what it calls a best-cost producer strategy—"achieving the lowest cost consistent with quality."[71] Thus, the firm's products provide customers with a level of quality that at least meets, and often exceeds, their expectations relative to the purchase price.

Effective implementation of the cost leadership strategy allows a firm to earn above-average returns in spite of the presence of strong competitive forces.

Rivalry with Existing Competitors

Having the low-cost position serves as a valuable defense against rivals. Because of the cost leader's advantageous position, rivals hesitate to compete on the basis of price. Instead, competitors try to compete against cost leaders through some means of differentiation. In South America, for example, top-level executives at Disco SA concluded that they could not compete against giant retailers Wal-Mart and Carrefour of France on the basis of price alone. Offering products at prices nearly as low as its largest competitors, Disco believes that it provides more convenience and service to customers. Carrying a wide range of brands and perishables, Disco stores offer home delivery, telephone ordering, and child care. Strategically, the firm's executives believe that customers will accept a slight increase in the cost of the product in return for the store's conveniences and services.[72] However, if rivals challenge the firm to compete on the basis of price, the low-cost firm can still earn at least average returns while competitors may experience below average returns through competitive rivalry.[73]

Bargaining Power of Buyers (Customers)

Powerful customers can force the cost leader to reduce its prices, but price will not be driven below the level at which the next-most-efficient industry competitor is able to earn average returns. Although powerful customers could force the cost leader to reduce prices even below this level, they probably would not choose to do so. Still lower prices would prevent the next-most-efficient competitor from earning average returns, resulting in its exit from the market and leaving the cost leader in a stronger position. Customers lose their power and pay higher prices when they are forced to purchase from a firm operating in an industry without rivals.

Occasionally, a firm's bargaining power allows it to transfer increased costs to customers. For example, when Unifi incurred substantially higher costs for raw materials

FIGURE

4.2 | Examples of Value-Creating Activities Associated with the Cost Leadership Strategy

Firm Infrastructure	Cost-effective management information systems.	Relatively few managerial layers in order to reduce overhead costs.	Simplified planning practices to reduce planning costs.
Human Resource Management	Consistent policies to reduce turnover costs.	Intense and effective training programs to improve worker efficiency and effectiveness.	
Technology Development	Easy-to-use manufacturing technologies.	Investments in technologies in order to reduce costs associated with a firm's manufacturing processes.	
Procurement	Systems and procedures to find the lowest cost (with acceptable quality) products to purchase as raw materials.	Frequent evaluation processes to monitor suppliers' performances.	

MARGIN

Inbound Logistics	**Operations**	**Outbound Logistics**	**Marketing and Sales**	**Service**
Highly efficient systems to link suppliers' products with the firm's production processes.	Use of economies of scale to reduce production costs.	A delivery schedule that reduces costs.	A small, highly trained sales force.	Efficient and proper product installations in order to reduce the frequency and severity of recalls.
	Construction of efficient-scale production facilities.	Selection of low-cost transportation carriers.	Products priced so as to generate significant sales volume.	

MARGIN

Source: Adapted with the permission of The Free Press, a Division of Simon & Schuster, Inc., from *Competitive Advantage: Creating and Sustaining Superior Performance,* by Michael E. Porter. Copyright © 1985, 1998 by Michael E. Porter.

and packaging products, it was able to pass the costs on to customers because the firm is a dominant supplier in many of its markets (with up to a 70 percent share in some markets).[74]

Bargaining Power of Suppliers

The cost leader operates with margins greater than those of competitors. Among other benefits, higher margins relative to competitors' make it possible for the cost leader to absorb suppliers' price increases. When an industry is faced with substantial increases in the cost of its supplies, the cost leader may be the only one able to pay the higher prices and continue to earn either average or above-average returns. Alternatively, powerful cost leaders may be able to force suppliers to hold down their prices, reducing their margins in the process.

Potential Entrants

Through continuous efforts to reduce costs to levels that are lower than competitors', cost leaders become very efficient. Because they enhance profit margins, ever-improving levels of efficiency serve as a significant entry barrier to potential entrants. New entrants must be willing to accept no better than average returns until they gain the experience required to approach the efficiency of the cost leader. To earn even average returns, new entrants must have the competencies required to match the cost levels of other competitors.

The cost leader's low profit margins (relative to margins earned by firms implementing the differentiation strategy) make it necessary for the cost leader to sell large volumes of its product to earn above-average returns. Founded in 1976, headquartered in Taiwan, and selling its products in over 100 countries, Acer Computer Corporation follows the cost leadership strategy. In describing Acer's strategy, a business analyst noted that the firm's "core competency is building cutting edge personal computers faster and cheaper than the competition."[75] According to Acer's CEO, margins on his company's products, including its personal computers, are "shell-thin." "But sell enough of them," he believes, "and a formula emerges: Low margins and high turnover can be a recipe for success."[76] The cost leadership strategy and the resulting emphasis on high volume and low margins are the foundation for the firm's 20-plus-year effort to become Taiwan's first global brand-name powerhouse, similar to IBM or Sony Corp.[77] However, firms striving to be the cost leader must avoid pricing their products at a level that precludes them from earning above-average returns and encourages new industry entrants.

Product Substitutes

Compared to its industry rivals, the cost leader holds an attractive position in terms of product substitutes. When faced with the possibility of a substitute, the cost leader has more flexibility than its competitors. To retain customers, the cost leader can reduce the price of its good or service. With still lower prices and features of acceptable quality, the cost leader increases the probability that customers will prefer its product rather than a substitute. As an example, there are still millions of cassette tapes sold in world markets because of lower prices, even though CDs have taken over leadership as a substitute. MP3.com and other on-line distributors now sell music over the Internet through a digital-format substitute, but CDs are still dominant, partly because of legal and ownership problems that need to be resolved regarding the new format.[78]

Toyota's Lexus provides the unique characteristics of excellent quality, a quiet ride, and superior luxury touches. Because the vehicles satisfy customers' unique needs, the firm can charge premium prices for them.

Competitive Risks of the Cost Leadership Strategy

The cost leadership strategy is not risk free. One risk is that the cost leader's manufacturing equipment could become obsolete because of competitors' technological innovations. These innovations may allow rivals to produce at costs lower than those of the original cost leader.

A second risk is that too much focus on cost reductions may occur at the expense of trying to understand customers' needs or concerns regarding issues and other competitive dimensions. An emphasis on continuous cost reductions is somewhat legendary at Britain's Lloyds TSB Group, PLC. The chairman, Sir Brian Pitman, takes the second-class train to work, whereas his counterparts are driven to their offices. When traveling, employees from this bank are expected to book stays only at "cheap" hotel rooms. If a taxi is used, the employee, not the bank, pays for the service. According to analysts, though, the bank earns above-average returns through its use of the cost leadership strategy. Evidence for that assertion is provided by the fact that Lloyds's recently earned a net 33.5 percent return on shareholders' investments. This performance is quite attractive compared to those of major competitors Wells Fargo & Co. (17.4 percent) and Deutsch Bank AG (19.6 percent). However, Lloyds TSB Group may be risking an understanding of customer needs in that, according to analysts, some of the bank's customers "complain that they bear the brunt of Lloyds's bottom-line focus."[79] Note that, because of their focus on continuously driving costs lower, firms that follow the cost leadership strategy sometimes fail to detect significant changes in customers' needs or in competitors' efforts to differentiate what has traditionally been an undifferentiated, commoditylike product.

Before Orville Redenbacher and Charles Bowman launched Orville Redenbacher's Gourmet Popping Corn, popcorn was thought to be a humble, commoditylike product. Convinced that people would pay more for high-quality popcorn, Orville Redenbacher developed a popcorn hybrid that produced fuller popping corn. He also perfected harvesting and packaging techniques that minimized damage to kernels. In a tribute to Redenbacher, who died recently at the age of 88, the executive director of

The Popcorn Institute observed that "he pioneered the gourmet popcorn niche. He promoted it very effectively and helped bring popcorn to a new level of acceptance."[80]

A final risk of the cost leadership strategy concerns imitation. Using their own core competencies (see Chapter 3), competitors sometimes learn how to successfully imitate the cost leader's strategy. When this occurs, the cost leader must find ways to increase the value that its good or service provides to customers. Commonly, value is increased by selling the current product at an even lower price or by adding features that customers value while maintaining price. Even cost leaders must be careful when reducing prices to a still lower level. If the firm prices its good or service at an unrealistically low level (a level at which it will be difficult to retain satisfactory margins), customers' expectations about what they envision to be a reasonable price become difficult to reverse.

Differentiation Strategy

With the differentiation strategy, the *unique* attributes and characteristics of a firm's product (other than cost) provide value to customers. Some believe that the unique attributes and characteristics Toyota's Lexus gives to customers (including Bill Gates, Nicolas Cage, Master P, and Dennis Rodman) are excellent quality, a quiet ride, and superior luxury touches.[81] Because a differentiated product satisfies customers' unique needs, firms following the differentiation strategy usually charge premium prices. To do this successfully, a "firm must truly be unique at something or be perceived as unique."[82] The ability to sell a good or service at a price that exceeds what was spent to create the product's differentiated features allows the firm to outperform its rivals and earn above-average returns.

Rather than costs, the differentiation strategy's focus is on continuously investing in and developing features that differentiate a good or service in ways that customers value. Overall, a firm using the differentiation strategy seeks to be different from its competitors along as many dimensions as possible. The less similarity between a firm's goods or services and those of competitors, the more buffered the firm is from rivals' actions. Commonly recognized differentiated goods include Toyota's Lexus, Ralph Lauren's and Tommy Hilfiger's clothing lines, and Caterpillar's heavy-duty earth-moving equipment. Thought by some to be the world's most expensive and prestigious consulting firm, McKinsey & Co. is a well-known example of a firm that offers differentiated services.

A product can be differentiated in an almost endless number of ways. Unusual features, responsive customer service, rapid product innovations and technological leadership, perceived prestige and status, different tastes, and engineering design and performance are examples of approaches to differentiation. In fact, virtually anything a firm can do to create real or perceived value for customers is a basis for differentiation. The challenge is to identity features that create value for the customer.

For example, using full-service restaurants to provide food service to customers is a dimension along which some of General Cinema's movie theaters are trying to differentiate themselves from competitors'. In these theaters, 140 patrons at a time can dine on an array of culinary items such as prime ribs or salmon while watching a movie.[83] Barbie dolls may be the only ones in its product category with a line of personal computers associated with them. Through an agreement with Patriot Comput-

Sony Corporation's Use of the Differentiation Business-Level Strategy

Sony has long used differentiation as its business-level strategy. Frequently, the firm's core competence of product miniaturization is the foundation on which its products are differentiated. Miniaturized radios, televisions, transistors, the Camcorder, and the Walkman cassette recorder are examples of products that Sony developed through the use of this core competence. More recently, the miniaturization competence has been used to manufacture the firm's laptop computers. The success of Sony's laptop, the Vaio, is somewhat remarkable, considering that only four major PC brands remain on U.S. retailer shelves because of the intensity of rivalry among competitors (see Chapters 2 and 5). Furthermore, the company's success with this product is noteworthy in that Sony is the only firm with three digital devices—the PC, the TV, and the video-game machine—that are becoming wired into networks.

The most recent version of the Vaio, the 505 series, is slim and silvery in color with gray-toned accents. Teiyu Goto, a Sony engineer, originally designed the model so that it was 22 millimeters, or less than nine-tenths of an inch in thickness. Instead of using a standard plastic body, Goto designed the 505 series to be sheathed in a glossy magnesium alloy. To attract customers, Sony originally chose to sacrifice function for style. Ultimately, however, as the components advanced and became smaller, Sony was able to improve the Vaio's performance and memory capacity. The combination of the product's differentiated features, including style, then satisfied the needs of customers who were willing to pay a slightly higher price for the Sony PC.

The digital camera is another example of Sony's ability to design and produce products with differentiated features that customers value. Introduced in 1997, Sony's digital camera (called the Mavica) does not use film. As with competitors' offerings, the Mavica etches images onto electronic sensors, translating them into computer-readable binary data to create photos that can then be printed through the use of a PC. Digital cameras designed and sold by Eastman Kodak and Casio Computer Company were the original leaders in this segment of the photography market. The feature that differentiates the Mavica from competitors' products and that provides value to customers is ease of use. With the Mavica, the customer uses a standard floppy disk to take photographs. The disk is then removed from the camera and inserted into a PC to print pictures. Through this differentiated feature's capabilities, even novices are able to successfully use the Mavica. Also contributing to the product's ease-of-use feature is the fact that no additional cable hookups or adapters are required to view the images, in contrast to Kodak's and Casio's digital cameras.

Compared to Kodak's and Casio's digital cameras, the Mavica is more expensive and produces pictures that are not as clear. However, in 1998, sales of the Mavica were 50 percent higher on a year-to-year basis. This result suggests that customers value the ease-of-use differentiated feature more than the clarity-of-picture differentiated feature that is associated with Sony's competitors' digital cameras. The Mavica accounted for $1.1 million of the estimated $12 million point-and-shoot photographs sold in the United States in 1998 and helped Sony gain prominence as a brand name in digital cameras and as a major player in photography.

As noted earlier, the differentiation strategy yields long-term competitive success when the firm invests continuously to offer customers differentiated features that provide value to them. Now the market leader, Sony intends to improve the quality of the images that are generated by its digital cameras. One step the company already has taken is the introduction of a new camera that uses a "memory cap stick," a removable device with lots of storage space and higher resolution. Sony's intention is to reduce the value of competitors' clarity-of-picture differentiated feature by inducing current customers to purchase the firm's more advanced digital cameras. This strategic action is consistent with Sony's practices. For example, once consumers became familiar with the firm's camcorder, Sony began to move to the smaller, non-VHS format, with better picture and sound quality. Thus, Sony has effectively used the differentiation business-level strategy to design and sell multiple products.

SOURCES: P. Beamish, 1999, Sony's Yoshihide Nakamura on structure and decision making, *Academy of Management Executive* 13(4): 12–16; R. A. Guth & E. Ramstad, 1999, How Sony turned a skinny laptop into an unlikely PC success, *Wall Street Journal*, November 12, B1, B6; A. Klein, 1999, How Sony beat digital-camera rivals, *Wall Street Journal*, January 25, B1, B4.

---

ers, Barbie manufacturer Mattel, Inc., offers brightly colored PCs for sale at a price of $599, with Barbie doll included. At this price, the customer receives the PC, a monitor, and 20 software titles.[84]

The Strategic Focus on Sony Corporation shows how a firm can consistently creates value for customers by identifying and then providing desired features. Through this strategy, which is implemented through use of the firm's core competencies, Sony earns above-average returns.

As his next strategic challenge, Sony's CEO, Nobuyuki Idei, expects to make money by linking Web-based products and media to provide interactive versions of music, movies, and games that can be downloaded onto Sony-made devices. "The hardware business is peanuts," he says. "But the distribution of programs will be big."[85] However, such a strategy will require that Sony change its value chain significantly.

A firm's value chain can be used to determine whether it can link the activities required to create value through implementation of the differentiation strategy. Examples of primary and support activities that are commonly used to differentiate a good or service are shown in Figure 4.3. Companies without the core competencies needed to link these activities cannot expect to implement the differentiation strategy successfully.

As explained next, the successful use of the differentiation strategy allows a firm to earn above-average returns in spite of the presence of strong competitive forces.

Rivalry with Existing Competitors

Customers tend to be loyal purchasers of products that are differentiated in ways that are meaningful to them. As their loyalty to a brand increases, customers' sensitivity to price increases is reduced. This relationship between brand loyalty and price sensitiv-

4.3 | Examples of Value-Creating Activities Associated with the Differentiation Strategy

Firm Infrastructure	Highly developed information systems to better understand customers' purchasing preferences.	A company-wide emphasis on the importance of producing high-quality products.	
Human Resource Management	Compensation programs intended to encourage worker creativity and productivity.	Somewhat extensive use of subjective rather than objective performance measures.	Superior personnel training.
Technology Development	Strong capability in basic research.	Investments in technologies that will allow the firm to produce highly differentiated products.	
Procurement	Systems and procedures used to find the highest quality raw materials.	Purchase of highest quality replacement parts.	

Inbound Logistics	Operations	Outbound Logistics	Marketing and Sales	Service
Superior handling of incoming raw materials so as to minimize damage and improve the quality of the final product.	Consistent manufacturing of attractive products. Rapid responses to customers' unique manufacturing specifications.	Accurate and responsive order-processing procedures. Rapid and timely product deliveries to customers.	Extensive granting of credit buying arrangements for customers. Extensive personal relationships with buyers and suppliers.	Extensive buyer training to assure high-quality product installations. Complete field stocking of replacement parts.

MARGIN

MARGIN

Source: Adapted with the permission of The Free Press, a Division of Simon & Schuster, Inc., from *Competitive Advantage: Creating and Sustaining Superior Performance,* by Michael E. Porter, Fig. 4–1, 122. Copyright © 1985, 1998 by Michael E. Porter.

ity insulates a firm from competitive rivalry. Thus, McKinsey & Co. is insulated from its competitors, even on the basis of price, as long as it continues to satisfy the differentiated needs of what appears to be a loyal customer group. The same is true for the Tommy Hilfiger company, as long as its "classic preppy . . . with a twist" clothes[86] continue to satisfy the needs of customers for garments with unique features.[87]

Bargaining Power of Buyers (Customers)

The uniqueness of differentiated goods or services insulates a firm from competitive rivalry and reduces customers' sensitivity to price increases. On the basis of a combination of unique materials and brand image, "L'Oreal has developed a winning formula: a growing portfolio of international brands that has transformed the French company into the United Nations of beauty. Blink an eye, and L'Oreal has just sold 85 products around the world, from Mabelline eye makeup, Redken hair care and Ralph Lauren perfumes to Helena Rubinstein cosmetics and Vichy skin care." L'Oreal is finding success in markets stretching from China to Mexico when other consumer product companies are not doing so well. L'Oreal's differentiation strategy seeks to convey the allure of different cultures through its many products: "Whether it's selling Italian elegance, New York street smarts, or French beauty through its brands, L'Oreal is reaching out to more people across a bigger range of incomes and cultures than just about any other beauty-products company in the world."[88] L'Oreal seeks to satisfy certain customers' unique needs better than competitors' offerings do. A key reason that some buyers are willing to pay a premium price for the firm's cosmetic items is that, for them, other products do not offer a comparable combination of features and cost. The lack of perceived acceptable alternatives increases the firm's power relative to that of its customers.

Bargaining Power of Suppliers

Because a firm that is implementing the differentiation strategy charges a premium price for its products, suppliers must provide it with high-quality parts. However, the high margins the firm earns when selling effectively differentiated products partially insulate it from the influence of suppliers. Higher supplier costs can be paid through these margins. Alternatively, because of buyers' relative insensitivity to price increases, the differentiated firm might choose to pass the additional cost of supplies on to the customer by raising the price of its unique product.

Potential Entrants

Customer loyalty and the need to overcome the uniqueness of a differentiated product are substantial entry barriers faced by potential entrants. Entering an industry under these conditions typically demands significant investments of resources and a willingness to be patient while seeking the loyalty of customers.

Product Substitutes

Firms selling brand-name goods and services to loyal customers are positioned effectively against product substitutes. In contrast, companies without brand loyalty are more subject to their customers switching either to products which offer differentiated features that serve the same function as the current product (particularly if the substitute has a lower price) or to products which offer more features that perform more attractive functions.

Gap's Success and the Risk of Cannibalization by Its Own Offspring

Gap, Inc., built its reputation and achieved strategic competitiveness by using the differentiation strategy to sell to sophisticated customers who want to purchase moderately priced, high-fashion casual clothing. Gap's strategic success was largely a product of a segmentation strategy wherein the firm attempted to focus stores' offerings on the unique needs of different market segments. Continuing with its commitment to segmentation, Gap created the Old Navy store concept to serve the needs of customers desiring to purchase products at the low end of casual fashion. While they were designing Old Navy's concept, Gap officials concluded that the low-end casual fashion market segment was quite large. The company's Banana Republic stores were used for the purpose of serving the needs of those seeking to purchase higher end, more sharply differentiated casual clothing.

As president of the Gap's Old Navy chain, Jenny J. Ming, working in concert with her employees, has achieved a great deal of success in serving the needs of customers in Old Navy's market niche. Ming and her colleagues have demonstrated an uncanny knack for choosing the right fashion at the right moment. Across seasons, these fashion selections have appealed to Old Navy's large customer segment. Evidence of Old Navy's importance to the corporation's success is suggested by the fact that in 1999 Old Navy accounted for 35 percent of Gap's profits while generating only 16 percent of the corporation's $11.5 billion in total revenue.

In light of its growth and potential, some analysts anticipate that in just a few years Old Navy sales will surpass those of the original Gap chain. Contributing to this expectation is the fact that Old Navy's products are much less expensive compared to offerings featured in Gap and Banana Republic stores. An examination of the corporation's performance outcomes shows that Gap same-store sales declined from 1998 to 1999 while Old Navy's same-store sales increased at roughly a 20 percent rate over the 1998–1999 time period. The slow sales at the Gap chain contributed to Robert Fisher's decision to resign as Gap's CEO. The resignation of Fisher, 44-year-old son of Gap, Inc., chairman and founder Donald Fisher, is certainly not what was expected when he was appointed to the company's top managerial position. However, the market reacted favorably to Fisher's decision, in that the price of Gap, Inc., stock increased approximately 10 percent when the resignation was announced formally.

Some observers of this situation conclude, though, that Robert Fisher was "probably the victim of Old Navy and Banana Republic's success," in that the Gap chain requires a more focused product mix to reverse its fortunes. In this regard, one analyst commented, "I've got a problem when I see Gap trying to appeal to people age 12–60." The main problem for the new CEO, Millard Drexler, is to communicate to customers Gap's differentiated feature of higher levels of product quality relative to other offerings, including those of Old Navy. Successfully explaining this differentiated feature and its value to those in Gap's market segment is necessary to justify the higher costs of Gap's products compared to those for Old Navy goods. Furthermore, Gap has to contend with a number of increasingly competitive firms in its dominant segment, the fashion-conscious youth-oriented wearers of casual clothing.

Examples of important Gap competitors are Abercrombie & Fitch, J. Crew, and Web sites such as bluefly.com. Sales from these companies appear to be at least partly at the expense of Gap's revenues.

In sum, Gap's newly appointed CEO and his top-management team face several challenges as they seek strategic competitiveness and above-average returns through the use of the differentiation strategy. Is the price differential between Gap's and Old Navy's offerings beyond that which is acceptable to Gap's target customers? Is the combination of price and features offered by Old Navy more appealing to Gap's market segment than is the combination associated with Gap's clothing items? These are examples of the types of strategic questions that Gap's executives must examine as options are considered to improve the chain's performance.

SOURCES: C. Y. Coleman, 1999, Fisher resigns as president of Gap chain, *Wall Street Journal,* October 29, A3, A12; L. Lee, 1999, A savvy captain for Old Navy, *Business Week,* November 8, 130–136; L. Lee, 1999, Why Gap isn't galloping any more, *Business Week,* November 8, 136.

Competitive Risks of the Differentiation Strategy

Like the other business-level strategies, the differentiation strategy is not risk free. One risk is that customers might decide that the price differential between the differentiator's and the cost leader's product is too large. In this instance, a firm may be providing differentiated features that exceed customers' needs. When that happens, the firm is vulnerable to competitors that are able to offer customers a combination of features and price that is more consistent with their needs. Some of these problems are illustrated in the Strategic Focus about Gap, Inc.

In the case of Gap, its other concepts (e.g., Old Navy Stores) were its own worst enemy: The company experienced too much cannibalization. Gap has also lost sales to on-line retailers. Although recently Gap has tried to fend off on-line attacks by opening is own on-line store, this may contribute to the problem, unless Gap's "brick-and-mortar" stores can be used as an advantage.[89]

Another risk of the differentiation strategy is that a firm's means of differentiation no longer provide value for which customers are willing to pay. The differentiation strategy becomes less valuable if imitation by rivals causes customers to perceive that competitors offer the same good or service, sometimes at a lower price. For example, in the early 1990s, some health maintenance organizations (HMOs) were able to differentiate themselves by their unique and extensive physician networks. Today, in many markets, rival HMOs offer nearly identical plans with broadly overlapping hospital and physician networks. This commoditization of the service means that many health insurers are no longer able to differentiate themselves and now compete on price only.[90]

A third risk of the differentiation strategy is that learning can narrow customers' perceptions of the value of a firm's differentiated features. The value of the IBM name on personal computers was a differentiated feature for which some customers were willing to pay a premium price as the product emerged. However, as customers familiarized themselves with the standard features, and as a host of PC clones entered the market, IBM brand loyalty began to fail. Clones offered customers features similar to those of the IBM product at a substantially lower price, reducing the attractiveness of IBM's product. Even currently, IBM's relatively new Aptiva line is failing to meet company expectations. In assessing the situation, one dealer observed that while the Aptiva is a "cool" machine, it simply costs too much for the features that it provides relative to the combination of features and prices of products from competitors such as Compaq and HP.[91]

A fourth risk is concerned with counterfeiting. Increasingly, counterfeit goods—products that attempt to convey differentiated features to customers at significantly reduced prices—are a concern for many firms that use the differentiation strategy. In the United Kingdom, for example, "It has been estimated that the market for parallel imports—cars, toiletries and clothing imported to the UK without the brand owners' consent and sold at substantial discounts to retail prices—is worth 1.3 billion pounds a year."[92] Companies often seek help from governments and their import regulations to curb the problem that can surface because of this particular risk of the differentiation strategy.

Focus Strategies

In contrast to firms that employ the cost leadership and differentiation strategies, a company that implements a focus strategy seeks to use its core competencies to serve the needs of a certain industry segment: a particular buyer group (e.g., youths or senior citizens), a different segment of a product line (e.g., products for professional painters or those for "do-it-yourselfers"), or a different geographic market (the east or the west in the United States).[93] Thus, a **focus strategy** is an integrated set of actions that is designed to produce or deliver goods or services that serve the needs of a particular competitive segment. Although the breadth of a target is clearly a matter of degree, the essence of the focus strategy "is the exploitation of a narrow target's differences from the balance of the industry."[94] For example, to satisfy the interests of certain size companies that are competing in a particular geographic market, the Los Angeles-based investment-banking firm Grief & Company positions itself as "The Entrepreneur's Investment Bank." Grief & Company is a "leading purveyor of merger and acquisition advisory services to medium-sized businesses based in the Western United States."[95] As another example, Cisco Systems, Inc., mentioned in the chapter's Opening Case, has shifted increasing percentages of its sales to smaller companies—a particular buyer group.[96] Through successful implementation of a focus strategy, firms such as Grief & Company and Cisco Systems, Inc., can gain a competitive advantage in chosen target market segments, even though they do not possess an industry wide competitive advantage.[97]

A **focus strategy** is an integrated set of actions designed to produce or deliver goods and services that serve the needs of a particular competitive segment.

As our discussion implies, the foundation of the focus strategy is that a firm can serve a particular segment of an industry more effectively or efficiently than can industry wide competitors. Success with a focus strategy rests on a firm's ability either to find segments whose unique needs are so specialized that broad-based competitors choose not to serve them or to locate a segment being served poorly by the industrywide competitors.[98] For instance, the Station Inn serves the needs of a particular buyer group that does not appear to be of interest to industrywide competitors such as Hilton, Marriott, and Sheraton, among others. Through its focus strategy, the Station Inn serves the unique needs of railroad buffs. Instead of getting mints on their pillows and pay-per-view movies in their rooms, these railroad devotees stay in a hotel that is located a mere 125 feet from Conrail, Inc., tracks. Through the night, guests sleep "next to thundering freight trains—more than 60 of them every 24 hours."[99]

As noted at the beginning of the chapter, the Internet is having a significant influence on business-level strategies. This is clearly the case with focus business-level strategies. Some analysts believe that the Internet allows market segments to be refined with greater and greater specificity in terms of unique customer needs. In particular, start-up ventures seek to serve what often are very narrow market segments or niches. Frequently, the name of these companies gives the focus: Just-socks.com; Raremaps.com; Mustardstore.com; Uglies.com (ugly boxer shorts with a "no-wedgie" design), and Steelofthenight.com (steel drums).[100] For each of these ventures, as is the case for every company using the focus business-level strategy, the intention is to serve the needs of a specific market segment better than the industrywide competitor can.

Walnut Grove Press is another firm that uses the focus strategy. This company sells books through outlets other than major bookstores, generating 85 percent of its revenue through book sales to gift shops, convenience stores, and even car wash waiting rooms. Walnut Grove does not distribute its products through bookstore chains (e.g., Barnes & Noble) or New York mainstream publishers. The firm's primary author and owner is Criswell Freeman, whose books sold 330,000 copies in 1998. Sales volume is expected to double in 1999. Since 1995, Freeman has written 40 books, including *The Book of Stock Car Wisdom, The Book of New England Wisdom,* and *The Gardener's Guide To Life.* His books are filled with quotations. Freeman developed an interest in inspirational quotes when he lost his job in the real-estate business and began to try to recover psychologically by reading an inspirational quote each day. At the same time, he began work toward a degree in clinical psychology. Degree in hand, Freeman started seeing patients. However, he desired to affect the lives of people beyond his patient base. To reach this objective, he decided to publish a self-help book. While studying distribution possibilities, Freeman learned that the large traditional bookstore chains return unsold copies. In contrast, most gift shops, he discovered, buy books outright. Given the specialized nature of his initial product and those that followed, and given the practices of different types of retailers, Freeman decided to develop Walnut Grove Press to distribute his books. Freeman's products now sell in 5,000 locations, and sales have reached $1 million.[101]

Firms can create value for customers in specific and unique market segments by using one of two different focus strategies: focused cost leadership and focused differentiation.

Focused Cost Leadership Strategy

The global furniture retailer Ikea seeks to provide customers with "affordable solutions for better living" through use of the focused cost leadership strategy.[102] Young buyers desiring style at a low cost make up Ikea's market segment. For these customers, the firm offers home furnishings that combine good design, function, and quality with low prices. Several practices are used to keep costs low. For example, instead of relying primarily on third-party manufacturers, Ikea's engineers design low-cost, modular furniture that is ready for assembly by customers. Inside the stores, Ikea uses a self-service model rather than having sales associates trail customers from one room of furniture to the next. Typically, competitors' furniture stores display multiple varieties of a single item in single rooms. Thus, customers examine dining room tables in one room, living room sofas in another room, and beds in yet another room. In contrast to this approach, Ikea displays its products in roomlike settings. Viewing different living combinations (with sofas, chairs, tables, and so forth) eliminates the need for sales associates or decorators to help the customer imagine how a batch of furniture will look when placed in its setting (a living room, for example). Fewer sales personnel are required with this approach, allowing Ikea to keep its costs low. Expecting customers to pick up and deliver their purchased items also reduces the firm's costs. Although a cost leader, Ikea offers some features that appeal to customers in addition to products' low prices. Among these features are in-store child care and extended hours. These services, it is argued, "are uniquely aligned with the needs of Ikea's customers, who are young, are not wealthy, are likely to have children (but no nanny), and, because they work for a living, have a need to shop at odd hours."[103]

Focused Differentiation Strategy

Other firms implement the focused differentiation strategy. The number of ways products can be differentiated to serve the unique needs of particular market segments is virtually endless. Consider the following examples.

Upscale apartment buildings in various locations, including Manhattan in New York City, are being designed to serve the needs of technologically savvy city dwellers. Included as part of the these apartments' differentiated features are high-speed digital Internet access and other sophisticated telecommunications services. Having their needs satisfied by their differentiated features in an apartment is expensive. For instance, a one-bedroom apartment in Columbus One starts at $2,100 monthly.[104] In another use of this strategy, Batesville Casket Co. manufacturers personalized caskets. Shapes, sizes, and colors are among the choices from which customers can select to design their customized product. Although Batesville's caskets are expensive relative to standardized caskets, the firm is willing to personalize a customer's casket down to the smallest detail.[105] In yet another example, several auto manufacturers, including Ferrari, Aston Martin, and Lamborghini, compete in the tiny supercar category. With prices beginning at $150,000 and increasing to as high as $600,000, one company official suggested that these cars are about passion—not transportation.[106]

Firms must be able to complete various primary and support activities in a competitively superior manner to achieve strategic competitiveness and earn above-average returns when using a focus strategy. The activities that must be completed to implement the focused cost leadership and the focused differentiation strategies are virtually identical to those shown in Figures 4.2 and 4.3, respectively. Similarly, the manners in which the two focus strategies allow a firm to deal successfully with the five competitive forces parallel those described with respect to the cost leadership and the differentiation strategies. The only difference is that the competitive scope changes from an industrywide to a narrow industry segment. Thus, a review of Figures 4.2 and 4.3 and the text regarding the five competitive forces yields a description of the relationship between each of the two focus strategies and competitive advantage.

Competitive Risks of Focus Strategies

When using either type of focus strategy, the firm faces the same general risks as does the company pursuing the cost leadership or the differentiation strategy on an industrywide basis. However, focus strategies have three additional risks beyond these general ones. First, a competitor may be able to focus on a more narrowly defined competitive segment and "outfocus" the focuser. For example, Big Dog Motorcycles of Sun Valley, Idaho, is trying to outfocus another company, Harley-Davidson, that is pursuing a broader-focus differentiation strategy. While Harley focuses solely on producing heavyweight motorcycles, Big Dog builds motorcycles that target only the very high end of the heavyweight market. Big Dog's 55 employees currently produce about 300 motorcycles each year that generally look and sound like a Harley, but are highly customized to individual customer desires. Big Dog's customized motorcycles sell for upwards of $22,000, versus $16,000 for a Harley. Similarly, some analysts believe that, with its R 1200 C cycle, BMW has taken the concept of an American cruising machine and refined it with sophisticated German engineering. The product's seats are made of real leather, the cycle's engine is BMW's classic Boxer, and a unique telelever front suspension system yields a superior ride. This product may be another threat to Harley Davidson's offerings.[107]

Second, a firm that is competing on an industrywide basis may decide that the market segment being served by the focus-strategy firm is attractive and worthy of

Big Dog is trying to outfocus Harley-Davidson by building motorcycles that target only the very high end of the heavyweight market. Big Dog's motorcycles are highly customized for individual customers and sell at a premium price.

competitive pursuit. No longer content with its traditional customer group only, Home Depot now has plans to concentrate on more narrow segments that it has not tried to serve previously, such as people who make large-ticket home renovations. In addition, the firm has entered the institutional maintenance and cleaning business with its purchase of Maintenance Warehouse America Corp.[108] Because of its size and capabilities, firms now competing in focused market segments may be threatened by Home Depot's entrance into their market domains.

The third risk of a focus strategy is that the needs of customers within a narrow competitive segment may become more similar to those of customers as a whole. When this occurs, the advantages of a focus strategy are either reduced or eliminated. At some point, for example, the needs of those using what are elaborate and expensive resort-style hotels in Las Vegas (e.g., the Venetian, the newest swank hotel in Las Vegas, which cost $1.2 billion) may become aligned more closely with Las Vegas customers who prefer to spend their funds on entertainment other than hotel room accommodations.[109]

Integrated Cost Leadership/Differentiation Strategy

Particularly in global markets, a firm's ability to blend the cost leadership and differentiation approaches may be critical to sustaining competitive advantages. Compared to firms that rely on one dominant generic strategy for their success, a company that is capable of successfully using an integrated cost leadership/differentiation strategy should be in a better position to adapt quickly to environmental changes, learn new skills and technologies more quickly, and effectively leverage its core competencies across business units and product lines.

A growing body of evidence supports the relationship between the implementation of an integrated strategy and the earning of above-average returns.[110] Some time ago, for example, a researcher found that the most successful firms competing in low-profit-potential industries were able to effectively combine the low-cost and differentiation strategies.[111] In a more recent comprehensive study, it was discovered that "businesses which combined multiple forms of competitive advantage outperformed businesses that only were identified with a single form."[112] Other research found that the highest-performing companies in the Korean electronics industry were those that combined both the differentiation and cost leadership strategies, suggesting the viability of the integrated strategy in different nations.[113]

A key reason firms capable of successfully implementing the integrated strategy can earn above-average returns is that the benefits of this strategy are additive: "[D]ifferentiation leads to premium prices at the same time that cost leadership implies lower costs."[114] Thus, the integrated strategy allows firms to gain competitive advantage by offering two types of value to customers: some differentiated features (but fewer than those provided by the product-differentiated firm) and relatively low cost (but not as low as the products of the cost leader).

Kosmo.com is a start-up venture that is trying to achieve strategic competitiveness by using the integrated cost leadership/differentiation strategy. Through its Web site, Kosmo.com, this company delivers "junk food" and videos to customers. Founded and operated by CEO Joseph Park, the firm follows the tastes of New Yorkers in order to be able to satisfy their unique food needs through the click of a mouse. Oreos, popcorn, Twizzlers, and sodas, as well videos, books, DVDs, and magazines, are examples of items customers can order and have delivered to their door within an hour. Free delivery is one of the firm's primary differentiated features. Food items, however, are priced at levels that are equivalent to those seen in local grocery stores, because Kosmo.com does not have brick-and-mortar stores. The average order is $10; currently, the firm's annual revenue is approaching $4 million. Plans call for Kosmo.com to launch its operation soon in Boston and Washington, DC. These openings will follow those already completed in Seattle and San Francisco. Although videos are available from Amazon.com, they come at an increased price due to shipping and handling. *Shakespeare in Love,* a DVD from Amazon.com, costs $9, plus $9 shipping charges if you want it in a day or $3 for delivery within a week. Kosmo.com offers the product at the same price, but doesn't charge for delivery. Continuing with the integrated cost leadership/differentiation strategy, Park intends to blanket the country with 100 small Kosmos serving 100 cities. In contrast, giant Amazon.com is building a few massive warehouses to serve the entire nation. Thus, Kosmos.com's differentiated features include those of the convenience of on-line shopping with home delivery that yields instant gratification for the customer's video viewing and junk food needs. In compliance with the other half of this business-level strategy, Kosmo.com sells its products at prices that are comparable to those available through traditional stores. Thus, the firm's strategy creates value for the customer in terms of both differentiation and delivered costs.[115]

Firms must be strategically flexible to use the integrated cost leadership/differentiation strategy successfully. Discussed next are three approaches to organizational work that can increase the strategic flexibility that is associated with this strategy's use.

Flexible Manufacturing Systems

Made possible largely as a result of the increasing capabilities of modern information technologies, flexible manufacturing systems increase the "flexibilities of human, physical and information resources"[116] that are integrated to create differentiated products at low costs. A *flexible manufacturing system* (FMS) is a computer-controlled process used to produce a variety of products in moderate, flexible quantities with a minimum of manual intervention.[117]

The goal of an FMS is to eliminate the low-cost-versus-product-variety trade-off that is inherent in traditional manufacturing technologies. The flexibility provided by an FMS allows a plant to change quickly and easily from making one product to making another one.[118] Used properly, an FMS can help a firm become more flexible in response to changes in its customers' needs, while retaining low-cost advantages and consistent product quality. Because an FMS reduces the lot size needed to manufacture a product efficiently, a firm's capacity to serve the unique needs of a narrow competitive scope is increased. Thus, FMS technology is a significant technological advance that allows firms to produce a large variety of products at a low cost. Levi Strauss, for example, uses an FMS to make jeans for women that meet their exact measurements. Andersen Windows lets customers design their own windows through the use of proprietary software the firm has developed. And Motorola successfully uses an FMS to customize pagers in different colors, sizes, and shapes.[119]

The effective use of an FMS is linked with a firm's ability to understand the constraints these systems may create (in terms of materials handling and the flow of supporting resources in scheduling, for example) and to design an effective mix of machines, computer systems, and people.[120] As a result, this type of manufacturing technology facilitates the implementation of complex competitive strategies, such as the integrated cost leadership/differentiation strategy, that lead to strategic competitiveness in global markets.[121]

A *manufacturing execution system* (MES) is a type of FMS. An MES is able to simulate and model everything that takes place in a factory, including the routing of products and the direction of processes. With an MES, changes can be made quickly to alter how a product is manufactured. An MES is in use in Unifi, the producer of synthetic yarn discussed earlier in the chapter. With MES software that is available from Camstar, of Campbell, California, Unifi transformed its newest plant, in Yadkinville, North Carolina, from a commodity yarn producer to a maker of much more profitable specialty yarns. Importantly, this change was made without increasing the firm's costs. Unifi's marketing manager, Rob Rudder, observed that "MES software has created tremendous value for us at Yadkinville. It has increased our gross margin there by 69 percent, or $16 million a year."[122]

Information Networks across Firms

New information networks linking manufacturers with their suppliers, distributors, and customers are another technological development that increases a firm's strategic flexibility and responsiveness.[123] Companies have invested significant amounts of resources (in terms of dollars and people) to install elaborate enterprise resource planning (ERP) software systems that are intended to improve the firm's efficiency. These improvements result from the use of systems through which financial and operational data are moved rapidly from one department to another. In addition, the systems support the exchange of data between the firm and its suppliers and distributors.

The largest of the five major ERP software producers is SAP. This firm generated ERP revenue of $5 billion in 1998. The remaining four prominent ERP manufacturers with the amount of revenue they generated in 1998 are Oracle ($2.4 billion), PeopleSoft ($1.3 billion), J. D. Edwards ($979 million), and Baan ($743 million). However, these firms are encountering significant competition from product substitutes, in that many of their customers are using new ERP modules designed specifically for manufacturing companies. These dedicated systems have specialized features that contrast with those associated with the large, traditional ERP systems. Partly accounting for the differences between those systems could be the functional background of the companies' founders. Many SAP founders have expertise in financial software. In contrast, some of those developing the more specialized ERP modules come from manufacturing backgrounds. This is the case with Steve Haley, Pivotpoint's CEO who spent 17 years in manufacturing companies. Pivot.Man, Pivotpoint's principal ERP program, is built around a flexible business-modeling strategy that does not force a company to change its operations to suit the software.[124] This product, compared to its more generalized predecessors, may increase the ability of users to differentiate their products more sharply while driving costs lower. Thus, the new ERP generation of software may facilitate even more the implementation of the integrated cost leadership/differentiation strategy.

Total Quality Management Systems

Although total quality management (TQM) systems are sometimes difficult to implement,[125] many firms have established such systems (see also Chapter 5). Important objectives sought through the use of TQM systems include increases in the quality of a firm's product and the productivity levels of the entire organization.[126] Enhanced quality focuses customers' attention on improvements in the performance of products and on the utility and reliability of features. This allows a firm to achieve differentiation and, ultimately, higher prices and market share. An emphasis on quality in production techniques lowers manufacturing and service costs through savings in reworking, scrap, and warranty expenses. These savings can result in a competitive advantage for a firm over its rivals. Thus, TQM programs integrate aspects of the differentiation and cost leadership strategies.

Four key assumptions are the foundation of TQM systems. The first assumption is that "the costs of poor quality (such as inspection, rework, lost customers and so on) are far greater than the costs of developing processes that produce high-quality products and services."[127] The second assumption is that employees naturally care about their work and will take initiatives to improve it. These initiatives are taken only when the firm provides employees with the tools and training they need to improve quality and when managers pay attention to the employees' ideas. The third assumption is that "organizations are systems of highly interdependent parts."[128] Problems encountered in such systems often cross traditional functional (e.g., marketing, manufacturing, finance, etc.) lines. Solving interdependent problems requires integrated decision processes with participation from all affected functional areas. The fourth assumption is that the responsibility for an effective TQM system rests squarely on the shoulders of upper-level managers. These people must openly and totally support the use of a TQM system and accept the responsibility for an organizational design that allows employees to work effectively. In addition, managers must learn the rhetoric that facilitates the application of the rather clearly defined rules for using and analyzing information that constitutes TQM's technical aspects.[129]

Competitive Risks of the Integrated Cost Leadership/Differentiation Strategy

The potential of the integrated strategy, in terms of above-average returns, is significant, but this potential comes with substantial risk. Selecting a business-level strategy calls for firms to make choices about how they intend to compete.[130] Achieving the low-cost position in an industry or a segment of an industry (e.g., a focus strategy) demands that the firm be able to reduce its costs consistently relative to competitors' costs. The use of the differentiation strategy, with either an industrywide or a focused competitive scope (see Figure 4.1), results in above-average returns only when the firm provides customers with differentiated goods or services they value and for which they are willing to pay a premium price.

The firm that fails to establish a leadership position in its chosen competitive scope, as the cost leader or as a differentiator, risks becoming "stuck-in-the-middle."[131] Being stuck in the middle prevents the firm from dealing successfully with the five competitive forces and from earning above-average returns. Indeed, some research results show that the lowest performing businesses are those lacking a distinguishable

Merrill Lynch Compromises Its Differentiation Strategy by Implementing an On-line Strategy

As on-line competitors create lower cost structures in the retail brokerage industry, they force high-cost differentiators such as Merrill Lynch into a compromised position. Merrill Lynch and other full-service brokerage firms have been under siege from Internet firms such as E*Trade, as well as Charles Schwab & Co. In 1998, 20 percent of equity trading done by individuals was via Web-based brokers. It is expected that in the year 2000 49 percent of retail brokerage trades will be completed on-line. Because Merrill Lynch is the largest diversified brokerage company, it is taking the brunt of this swift change in consumers' approach to executing security trades. Merrill Lynch's recognition of the swift changes that have taken place and its realization that it let the competition jump ahead in the retail on-line market have led the company to reshape its strategy.

Merrill Lynch's traditional strategy has been to differentiate the company by customizing its research and products to allow it to price on a premium basis. The approach is a traditional broad differentiation business-level strategy. This strategy is based on the advantage that Merrill has had in the private information produced by its analysts, traders, and brokers. Against on-line brokers, the strategy suggests that at some point on-line technology will become ubiquitous and that the information produced by Merrill Lynch's people will become the battleground. At this point, however, Merrill Lynch faces the technological battle not only from portals such as Yahoo!, but also from other traditional brokers such as Morgan Stanley Dean Witter and Donaldson Lufkin & Jenrette, which have been rolling out on-line systems.

Besides the external competition from discount brokers such as Charles Schwab, portals such as Yahoo! using information that is available publicly, and other traditional brokers, Merrill Lynch has inside battles. In particular, the change necessary to meet the sweeping technological and cost focuses will be difficult to implement without significant disruption for the brokers and their client relationships. However, the internal momentum necessary to make the change inside occurred when Schwab's $25.5 billion market capitalization topped Merrill Lynch's $25.4 billion. This suggested to Merrill Lynch employees that the firm's current approach was coming up short. Merrill Lynch also has preached that it needs to gather assets so that customers will desire to put all their assets in accounts such as the cash management account (CMA) at the company. Even on this measure, however, Merrill Lynch was coming up short: Schwab increased its asset base by 39 percent in 1998, while Merrill Lynch's grew by only 18 percent. The message was clear: Merrill had to offer on-line-only accounts, or it would lose many assets, not to mention a whole generation of investors.

The main problem is that Merrill's 17,000 commissioned brokers would find it difficult to embrace the Internet, relative to the 7,000 salaried brokers at Schwab. The leaders at Merrill know that their brokers can go to another firm and take their clients with them. Without the support of the brokers to go on-line, it would be almost impossible to change to an on-line strategy without destroying the company's earnings and losing its sales force. Thus, to implement any Internet strategy, Merrill needs to enlist its brokers' support. If Merrill "hits a home run" on a low-cost on-line trading system and loses thousands of its best brokers in the process, it would be a Pyrrhic victory, with the battle won, but the war lost.

Merrill decided to roll out its retail on-line strategy with a $29.95 commission rate on transactions. To increase customer loyalty, it has also launched an elaborate e-commerce offering, signing on 40 electronic retailers from Barnes & Noble, Inc., to e-toys to sell through its portal. The firm wants customers to do some of their spending via Merrill Lynch, ideally through their Merrill Visa Signature cards, which gives credit or points toward discount purchases. In addition, Merrill is including business news and Merrill research reports to draw new customers and hold them.

The company is also building up the institutional side of its business. Represented are financial institutions (e.g., banks and insurance firms), corporations, and public organizations that operate retail or pension fund accounts. Merrill's strategy is to participate in a multidealer system, such as TradeWeb, wherein corporate clients see not only Merrill's offerings, but also those of competitors. With this new portal approach at the institutional level, Merrill's goal is to attract some 20,000 middle-market corporate accounts, well beyond its current 2,000 institutional clients, which are generally larger institutions. Merrill is currently not serving these middle-market companies, because it is not cost effective to hire conventional salespeople and traders to do so. Of course, the large institutions can pick up the phone and attract personal attention from Merrill traders and salespeople, and they have far more access to research on-line than do retail clients currently. Still, at the end of 1998, 26 percent of institutional customer trading was done electronically, and that amount was expected to rise to 44 percent in 2000. Thus, Merrill Lynch will need a better system for large traders anyway. Moreover, with the institutional customer portal, the firm would not only have the ability to reach the smaller institutional segment, but would also have the ability to attract new institutional clients overseas. In Internet-savvy countries such as Sweden and Japan, there is no reason why Merrill Lynch could not cover the medium-to-large institutional customers.

This approach, however, will deeply affect how Merrill Lynch is organized. Currently, the company is a loose confederation of "territories" from foreign exchange to municipal bonds. Each office has its own managers, computer systems, and clients. With the portal systems, both retail and institutional, Merrill Lynch will have to rationalize its products and services into a single system. The main risk of this approach is that in the transition period the company will cannibalize its thriving off-line business.

Firms such as Merrill Lynch that have used a differentiation strategy to build up their product image are confronting the new economics of information created by the Internet. Their customers have been able to exploit more direct information, which causes the firms to lower their pricing strategy. Furthermore, focused competitors are picking off the more profitable parts of their value chain. Alternatively, as in the Merrill Lynch case, the Internet opens new opportunities to markets that these companies have been unable to serve in the past using their current strategy. This opportunity is no more prevalent than the opportunity for Merrill Lynch to offer a broader range of products to smaller institutional investor clients such as small companies and foreign businesses. The main pitfalls to the changes are the internal systems that developed over time in these firms. The challenges will force significant changes upon the lives of the people involved if they are to be successful. Merrill's bureaucracy and culture will be hard to change as the firm tries to meet the low-margin on-line business, which will require deep cuts in company costs. Furthermore, the change will force cannibalization of Merrill Lynch's current strategies, which will also be difficult. However, all people in these companies realize that this strategy needs to take place for the company to meet the competition. Otherwise, an even worse disaster may follow.

SOURCES: R. Buckman, 1999, Merrill, an online skeptic, now plans an internet lure, *Wall Street Journal*, October 15, C1, C11; P. Evans & T. S. Wurster, 1999, Getting real about virtual commerce, *Harvard Business Review*, 77 6: 84–94; J. M. Laderman, 1999, Wall Street's frenzy over fees, *Business Week*, November 22, 140–141; L. N. Spiro, 1999, Merrill's E-Battle, *Business Week*, November 15, 256–268.

competitive advantage. Not having a clear and identifiable competitive advantage results from a firm being stuck in the middle.[132] Such firms can earn average returns only when an industry's structure is highly favorable or when the firm is competing against others that are in the same position.[133]

As is explained in the Strategic Focus, Merrill Lynch is at risk of becoming stuck in the middle. If this were to occur, the outcome would be primarily a product of the brokerage industry's competitive dynamics.

Once a firm has selected its business-level strategy, it must both anticipate and be prepared to respond to competitors' actions and responses. Merrill Lynch had to respond to the onslaught of on-line brokers. Although this change is difficult, it must take the risk. However, it has a very real risk of compromising its differentiation strategy in trying to implement the cost leadership strategy required to meet the on-line competition. In a similar way, Blockbuster, Inc., which offers video rentals, also has had to confront change. Although the firm currently sells movies, video games, and CD sound tracks at Blockbuster.com, it is now considering offering video rentals over the Internet. Currently, Blockbuster is a separate publicly traded unit of Viacom, Inc. Blockbuster is also considering delivering videos to consumers' homes in the way that Kozmo.com, the video and convenience food Internet delivery service mentioned earlier, has already been pursuing. Blockbuster is not backing away from its brick-and-mortar video retail outlets, but it is preparing for a future dominated by the electronic delivery of entertainment. As the company moves toward this future, any electronic strategy will cannibalize its current video rental approach. In addition to Internet movie transmission, Blockbuster is considering video-on-demand technologies similar to the pay-per-view offered by cable companies. This strategy may be carried out in collaboration with cable operators. Others worry that the cable operators, who are already offering video-on-demand services, will supplant the current strategy used by Blockbuster. Currently, Blockbuster differentiates its products through its in-store promotions and displays. If it is forced to create an Internet strategy and compete with Internet firms like Kosmo.com, which have a low-cost approach that includes free delivery and pay-per-view from cable companies, it may not be able to accomplish both strategies simultaneously and become stuck in the middle.[134]

Competitive dynamics between firms, such as those illustrated by Merrill Lynch and Blockbuster and their on-line competitors, are examined in the next chapter. These dynamics take place with respect to all types of strategies (see Chapters 6 through 9), but the majority of competitive actions and competitive responses are initiated in order to implement a firm's business-level strategy.

Summary

- A business-level strategy is an integrated and coordinated set of commitments and actions designed to provide value to customers and gain a competitive advantage by exploiting core competencies in specific, individual product markets. Five business-level strategies are examined in this chapter. The Internet's capabilities are affecting firms' strategic actions in terms of both selecting a business-level strategy and determining how to implement it. A firm's strategic competitiveness is enhanced when it is able to develop and exploit new core competencies faster than competitors can mimic the competitive advantages yielded by the firm's current competencies.
- Customers are the foundation of successful business-level strategies. When considering customers, a firm simultaneously examines three issues: who, what, and how. These issues respectively refer to the customer groups it will serve, the needs those customers have that the firm seeks to satisfy, and the core competencies the firm possesses that can be used to satisfy customers' needs. The increasing segmentation of markets now occurring throughout the world creates multiple opportunities for firms to identify unique customer needs.
- Firms seeking competitive advantage through the cost leadership strategy often produce no-frills, standardized products for an industry's typical customer. Above-average returns are earned when firms continuously drive their costs lower than those of their competitors, while providing customers with products that have low prices and acceptable levels of differentiated features.
- Competitive risks associated with the cost leadership strategy include (1) a loss of competitive advantage to newer technologies, (2) a failure to detect changes in customers' needs, and (3) the ability of competitors to imitate the cost leader's competitive advantage through their own unique strategic actions.
- The differentiation strategy enables firms to provide customers with products that have different (and valued) features. Because of their uniqueness, differentiated goods or services are sold at a premium price. Products can be differentiated along any dimension that is valued by some group of customers. Firms using this strategy seek to differentiate their products from competitors' goods or services along as many dimensions as possible. The less similarity with competitors' products, the more buffered a firm is from competition with its rivals.
- Risks associated with the differentiation strategy include (1) a customer group's decision that the differences between the differentiated product and the cost leader's good or service are no longer worth a premium price, (2) the inability of a differentiated product to create the type of value for which customers are willing to pay a premium price, (3) the ability of competitors to provide customers with products that have features similar to those associated with the differentiated product, but at a lower cost, and (4) the threat of counterfeiting, whereby firms produce a cheap "knock-off" of a differentiated good or service.
- Through the cost leadership and the differentiated focus strategies, firms serve the needs of a narrow competitive segment (e.g., a buyer group, product segment, or geographic area). This strategy is successful when firms have the core competencies required to provide value to a narrow competitive segment that exceeds the value available from firms serving customers on an industrywide basis.
- The competitive risks of focus strategies include (1) a competitor's ability to use its core competencies to "outfocus" the focuser by serving an even more narrowly defined competitive segment, (2) decisions by industrywide competitors to serve a customer group's specialized needs that the focuser has been serving, and (3) a reduction in differences of the needs between customers in a narrow competitive segment and the industrywide market.
- Firms using the integrated cost leadership/differentiation strategy strive to provide customers with relatively low-cost products that have some valued differentiated features. The primary risk of this strategy is that a firm might produce products that do not offer sufficient value—in terms of either low cost or differentiation. When this occurs, the company is "stuck in the middle." Firms stuck in the middle compete at a disadvantage.

Review Questions

1. What is a strategy and what are business-level strategies?
2. What is the relationship between a firm's customers and its business-level strategy? Why is this relationship important?
3. In studying customers in terms of who, what, and how, what questions are firms trying to answer?
4. What is the integrated cost leadership/differentiation strategy? Why is the number of firms using this strategy continuing to increase?
5. How is competitive advantage achieved through successful implementation of the cost leadership strategy? The differentiation strategy? The focused cost leadership strategy? The focused differentiation strategy? The integrated cost leadership/differentiation strategy?
6. What risks are associated with selecting and implementing each of the five strategies mentioned in question 5?

Application Discussion Questions

1. You are a customer of your university or college. What actions does your school take to recognize and satisfy your needs? Be prepared to discuss your views with your classmates.
2. Select a firm in your local community that interests you. Based on interactions with this company, which business-level strategy do you think the firm is implementing? What evidence can you provide to support your opinion? Is the Internet affecting the firm's strategic actions? If so, how?
3. Assume that you have decided to establish and operate a restaurant in your local community. What market segment would you intend to serve? What needs do these customers have that you could satisfy with your restaurant? How would you satisfy those needs? Be prepared to discuss your responses.
4. What business-level strategy is your school implementing? What core competencies are being used to implement this strategy?
5. Suppose you overheard the following comment: "It is impossible for a firm to produce a relatively low-cost, yet somewhat highly differentiated, product." Is this statement true or false? What is the reasoning behind your decision?
6. Is the Internet potentially of more value for firms implementing either the differentiation strategy or the focused differentiation strategy than for those using either the cost leadership or focused cost leadership strategy? If so, why?
7. Is it possible for a traditional firm to become too reliant on the Internet? If so, why? If not, why not?

Ethics Questions

1. Can a commitment to ethical conduct on issues such as the environment, product quality, and fulfilling contractual agreements affect a firm's competitive advantage? If so, how?
2. Is there more incentive for differentiators or cost leaders to pursue stronger ethical conduct? Think of an example to support your answer.
3. Can an overemphasis on cost leadership or differentiation lead to ethical challenges (such as poor product design and manufacturing) that create costly problems (e.g., product liability lawsuits)?
4. Reexamine the assumptions about effective TQM systems presented in the chapter. Do these assumptions urge top-level managers to maintain higher ethical standards than they now have? If so, how?
5. As discussed in Chapter 3, a brand image is one way a firm can differentiate its good or service. However, many questions are now being raised about the effect brand images have on consumer behavior. For example, considerable concern has arisen about brand images that are managed by tobacco firms and their effect on teenage smoking habits. Should firms be concerned about how they form and use brand images? Why or why not?
6. What ethical issues do you believe are associated with use of the Internet to implement the firm's business-level strategy?
7. If ethical issues do exist regarding Internet use, who do you believe should be responsible for addressing them—governments or companies themselves? Why?

Internet Exercise

Colleges and universities use different strategies to draw a wider customer base as well as to serve the needs of their current students and staff. Explore the Web sites of these diverse U.S. universities: University of Phoenix (**www.uophx.edu**), University of Chicago (**www.uchicago.edu**), Oglala Lakota College (**www.olc.edu**), the Ohio State University (*www.ohio-state.edu*), and Central Community College (*www.cccneb.edu*). Decide what types of strategy each pursues. How does each university or college determine its customer groups and utilize its core competencies to attract and retain its customers? With on-line course offerings increasing, do some of the institutions target markets overlap?

***e-project:** Go to the Web site of the school you currently attend. Based on your knowledge of students, staff, and curricula, what steps can be taken to improve customer satisfaction?

Notes

1. L. Franco, 1999, Internet buying increasing among U.S. consumers, *The Conference Board,* November 22, 4522A.
2. E. Nelson, 2000, Wal-Mart revamps its online stores for service in AOL Alliance, *Wall Street Journal,* January 13, A12; E. Nelson, 1999, Wal-Mart turns to Books-A-Million to supply, deliver books for Web store, *Wall Street Journal,* July 2, A3.
3. D. A. Blackmon, 1999, Selling motors to mops, unglamorous Grainger is a Web-sales star, *Wall Street Journal,* December 13, B8.
4. J. Pepper, 1999, GM and Ford are poised to take commanding lead in B2B e-commerce, *The Detroit News,* December 13, B3, B9.
5. C. V. Callahan & B. R. Pasternack, 1999, Corporate strategy in the digital age, *Strategy & Business,* 15: 10–14.
6. C. A. Lengnick-Hall & J. A. Wolff, 1999, Similarities and contradictions in the core logic of three strategy research streams, *Strategic Management Journal,* 20: 1109–1132; A. Campbell & M. Alexander, 1997, What's wrong with strategy? *Harvard Business Review,* 75(6): 42–51.
7. J. G. Covin & M. P. Miles, 2000, The strategic use of corporate entrepreneurship, Working Paper, Indiana University; D. P. Slevin & J. G. Covin, 1997, Strategy formation patterns, performance, and the significance of context, *Journal of Management,* 23: 189–209.
8. M. M. Crossan, H. W. Lane, & R. E. White, 1999, An organizational learning framework: From intuition to institution, *Academy of Management Review,* 24: 522–537; C. E. Helfat, 1997, Know-how and asset complementarity and dynamic capability accumulation: The case of R&D, *Strategic Management Journal,* 18: 339–360; A. Seth & H. Thomas, 1994, Theories of the firm: Implications for strategy research, *Journal of Management Studies,* 31: 167.
9. T. J. Dean, R. L. Brown, & C. E. Bamford, 1998, Differences in large and small firm responses to environmental context: Strategic implications from a comparative analysis of business formations, *Strategic Management Journal,* 19: 709–728; N. Rajagopalan & G. M. Spreitzer, 1997, Toward a theory of strategic change: A multi-lens perspective and integrative framework, *Academy of Management Journal,* 22: 48–79.
10. P. F. Drucker, 1999, *Management in the 21st Century* (New York: Harper Business); H. Courtney, J. Kirkland, & P. Viguerie, 1997, Strategy under uncertainty, *Harvard Business Review,* 75(6): 67–79.
11. D. Abel, 1999, Competing today while preparing for tomorrow, *Sloan Management Review,* 40(3): 73–81; C. C. Markides, 1999, A dynamic view of strategy, *Sloan Management Review,* 40(3): 55–72.
12. R. T. Pascale, 1999, Surviving the edge of chaos, *Sloan Management Review,* 40(3): 83–94.
13. P. Lane & M. Lubatkin, 1998, Relative absorptive capacity and interorganizational learning, *Strategic Management Journal,* 19: 461–478; W. Wiggenhorn, 1997, The evolution of learning strategies in organizations: From employee development to business redefinition, *Academy of Management Executive,* 11(4): 47–58; D. Lei, M. A. Hitt, & R. Bettis, 1996, Dynamic core competences through meta-learning and strategic context, *Journal of Management,* 22: 549–569.
14. R. A. D'Aveni, 1999, Strategic supremacy through disruption and dominance, *Sloan Management Review,* 40(3): 117–135; C. M. Christensen, 1997, Making strategy: Learning by doing, *Harvard Business Review,* 75(6): 141–156.
15. B. A. Walters & R. L. Priem, 1999, Business strategy and CEO intelligence acquisition, *Competitive Intelligence Review,* 10(2): 15–22.
16. R. Flannery, 1999, Taiwan PC makers rely more on China, *Wall Street Journal,* October 21, A16.
17. A. Bernasek, 1999, Hungarian rhapsody, *Fortune,* November 8, 46–48; Y. H. Youbir, 1999, Doing business in Hungary, *Thunderbird International Business Review,* 41, 6: 639–654.
18. V. P. Rindova & C. J. Fombrun, 1999, Constructing competitive advantage: The role of firm-constituent interactions, *Strategic Management Journal,* 20: 691–710; G. G. Dess, A. Gupta, J.-F. Hennart, & C. W. L. Hill, 1995, Conducting and integrating strategy research at the international, corporate, and business levels: Issues and directions, *Journal of Management,* 21: 357–393.
19. M. E. Porter, 1998, *On Competition* (Boston: Harvard Business School Press).
20. M. E. Porter, 1996, What is strategy? *Harvard Business Review,* 74(6): 61–78.
21. D. L. Deephouse, 1999, To be different, or to be the same? It's a question (and theory) of strategic balance, *Strategic Management Journal,* 20: 147–166.
22. R. A. Smith, 1999, Retailing: Confronting the challenges that face bricks-and-mortar stores, *Harvard Business Review,* 77(4): 164–165.
23. B. Lowendahl & O. Revang, 1998, Challenges to existing strategy theory in a postindustrial society, *Strategic Management Journal,* 19: 755–773.
24. M. E. Porter, 1980, *Competitive Strategy* (New York: The Free Press).
25. P. S. Adler, B. Goldoftas, & D. I. Levin, 1999, Flexibility versus efficiency? A case study of model changeovers in the Toyota production system, *Organization Science,* 10: 43–68.
26. D. A. Aaker, 1998, *Strategic Marketing Management* (5th edition) (New York: John Wiley & Sons), 20.
27. A. Afuah, 1999, Technology approaches for the information age, In Mastering Strategy (Part One), *Financial Times,* September 27, 8.
28. D. Peppers, M. Rogers, & B. Dorf, 1999, Is your company ready for one-to-one marketing? *Harvard Business Review,* 73(5): 59–72.
29. H. D. Rozanski, A. G. Baum, & B. T. Wolfsen, 1999, Brand zealots: Realizing the full value of emotional brand loyalty, *Strategy & Business,* 17: 51–63; T. A. Stewart, 1997, A satisfied customer isn't enough, *Fortune,* July 21, 112–113.

30. A. Goldstein, 2000, GM to use i2 software; stock soars, *Dallas Morning News,* January 20, D1–D2; A. Goldstein, 1999, i2 acquiring Smart for $68 million, *Dallas Morning News,* May 13, D2.
31. R. Balu, 1999, Whirlpool gets real with customers, *Fast Company,* December, 74–76.
32. N. G. Carr, 1999, The economics of customer satisfaction, *Harvard Business Review,* 77(2): 15–18.
33. P. Evans & T. S. Wurster, 1999, Getting real about virtual commerce, *Harvard Business Review,* 77(6): 84–94; S. F. Slater & J. C. Narver, 1999, Market-oriented is more than being customer-led, *Strategic Management Journal,* 20: 1165–1168.
34. W. Bounds & R. Quick, 1999, The secret of Ursula Andres's bikini, *Wall Street Journal,* November 10, B1, B6; T. Connor, 1999, Customer-led and market-oriented: A matter of balance, *Strategic Management Journal,* 20: 1157–1163.
35. A. Zadoks, 1997, Managing technology at Caterpillar, *Research-Technology Management,* January: 49–51.
36. K. L. Miller & K. Kerwin, 1999, GM's Mr. fixit really has his hands full, *Business Week Online,* March 8, *www.businessweek.com.*
37. Evans & Wurster, Getting real about virtual commerce.
38. S. C. Jain, 2000, *Marketing Planning and Strategy* (Cincinnati: South-Western College Publishing), 104–125.
39. Associated Press, 1999, Rolls Bentley targets U.S. drivers, *Dallas Morning News,* May 2, H5.
40. S. Jones, 1999, Women customers win warmer welcome at the bar, *Financial Times,* April 12, 7.
41. Associated Press, 1996, Automakers rolling out new models, *Dallas Morning News,* January 4, D2.
42. Title 9 Sports, 1999, *General Merchandise Catalog,* December, 10.
43. New Balance, 2000, New Balance Home Page, January 19, *www.newbalance.com.*
44. L. Kehoe, 1999, Teens mean new buyers, *Financial Times,* June 16, 26.
45. T. Gubbins, 1999, Tapping into teen power, *Dallas Morning News,* March 7, A1, A24.
46. M. Halkias, 1999, Penney brings in da *Noise, Dallas Morning News,* April 6, D1, D14.
47. V. Griffith, 1999, branding.com: How bricks-and-mortar companies can make it on the Internet, *Strategy & Business,* 15, Second Quarter: 54–59.
48. S. Miller, 1999, VW sows confusion with common pattern for models, *Wall Street Journal,* October 25, A25, A38.
49. J. Kurtzman, 1997, An interview with Gary Hamel, *Strategy & Business,* 9, Fourth Quarter: 89–97.
50. A. Linsmayer, 1999, When a napkin is a fashion statement, *Forbes,* September 20, 122–124.
51. D. Kirkpatrick, 1999, IBM: From big blue dinosaur to e-business animal, *Fortune,* April 26, 116–127.
52. Hewlett-Packard, 1999, Hewlett-Packard Home Page, *www.hp.com,* December 20.
53. P. Burrows, 1999, The hottest property in the valley? *Business Week,* August 30, 69–77.
54. M. E. Porter, 1985, *Competitive Advantage* (New York: The Free Press), 26.
55. Porter, What is strategy?
56. B. McEvily & A. Zaheer, 1999, Bridging ties: A source of firm heterogeneity in competitive capabilities, *Strategic Management Journal,* 20: 1133–1156.
57. D. A. Blackmon, 1999, Ryder System plans to make changes in management, *Wall Street Journal,* April 8, B2.
58. M. E. Porter, 1994, Toward a dynamic theory of strategy, in R. P. Rumelt, D. E. Schendel, & D. J. Teece (eds.), *Fundamental Issues in Strategy* (Boston: Harvard Business School Press), 423–461.
59. Porter, What is strategy? 62.
60. Porter, *Competitive Advantage,* 15.
61. G. G. Dess, G. T. Lumpkin, & J. E. McGee, 1999, Linking corporate entrepreneurship to strategy, structure, and process: Suggested research directions, *Entrepreneurship: Theory and Practice,* 23, 3: 85–102; P. M. Wright, D. L. Smart, & G. C. McMahan, 1995, Matches between human resources and strategy among NCAA basketball teams, *Academy of Management Journal,* 38: 1052–1074.
62. Porter, *Competitive Strategy,* 35–40.
63. Dess, Lumpkin, & McGee, Linking corporate entrepreneurship to strategy, 88–89.
64. A. Barrett & J. M. Laderman, 1999, That's why they call it Vanguard, *Business Week,* January 18, 82–86; T. Easton, 1999, The gospel according to Vanguard, *Forbes,* February 8, 115–119.
65. B. McLean, 1999, Not your mother's Avon, *Fortune,* May 24, 44–46.
66. Associated Press, 1999, Packard Bell pulling out of PC market, *Dallas Morning News,* November 11, D6.
67. Nucor Corporation, 1999, Nucor Home Page, December 20, *www.nucor.com*; Nucor Corporation, 1999, *Better Investing,* July, 76.
68. Unifi, Inc., 1999, Unifi Home Page, December 20, *www.unifi.com*; C. Sirois, 1997, Unifi, Inc., *Value Line,* August 22, 1640.
69. Consolidated Stores, 2000, Consolidated Stores Home Page, *www.cnstores.com,* January 20.
70. J. Pellet, 1997, Treasure hunt, *Chief Executive Magazine,* November, 22.
71. Emerson Electric Co., 2000. Emerson Electric Home Page, *www.emerson.com,* January 15; S. Lubove, 1994, It ain't broke, but fix it anyway, *Forbes,* August 1, 56–60.
72. J. Friedland, 1997, Latin American retailer fights giants, *Wall Street Journal,* September 19, A10.
73. Porter, *Competitive Strategy,* 36.
74. Sirois, Unifi, Inc., 1640.
75. Acer Computer Corporation, 2000, Acer Computer Corporation Home Page, January 12, *www.acer.com.*
76. L. Kraar, 1995, Acer's edge: PCs to go, *Fortune,* October 30, 192.
77. J. Moore & P. Burrows, 1997, A new attack plan for Acer America, *Business Week,* December 8, 82–83.
78. M. France, 1999, This lawsuit is cranking up the volume over MP3, *Business Week e-biz,* December 13, *www.businessweek.com.*
79. E. Portanger, 1999, One way Lloyds TSB earns so much money is by not spending it, *Wall Street Journal,* December 13, A1, A8.
80. T. Zorn, 1995, Orville Redenbacher leaves premium legacy, *Dallas Morning News,* September 24, H5.
81. A. Taylor, III, 1999, Chariot of the Gods of celebrity, *Fortune,* April 23, 16.
82. Porter, *Competitive Advantage,* 14.
83. D. Blank, 1999, The movie house is a steakhouse, *Business Week,* May 17, 8.
84. Associated Press, 1999, Barbie's newest accessory: A PC, *Dallas Morning News,* August 4, D2.
85. I. R. Kunii, 1999, Here comes the Sony netman, *Business Week e-biz,* November 1, *www.businessweek.com.*
86. Tommy Hilfiger, 2000, Tommy Hilfiger Home Page, March 10, *www.hilfiger.com*; It's Tommy's world, 1996, *Vanity Fair,* February, 110.
87. L. Goldstein, 1999, Tommy sings America, *Fortune,* September 6, 46.
88. G. Edmondson, E. Neuborne, A. L. Kazmin, E. Thornton, & K. N. Anhalt, 1999, L'Oreal: The beauty of global branding, *Business Week e-biz,* June 28, *www.businessweek.com.*
89. L. Lee, 1999, 'Click and mortar' at Gap.com, *Business Week Online,* October 18, *www.businessweek.com.*
90. K. H. Hammonds, 1999, Heathcare Prognosis 1999, *Business Week,* January 11, 108.
91. I. Sager & P. Burrows, 1997, I'm not gonna pay a lot for this Aptiva, *Business Week,* October 13, 59.
92. P. Hollinger, 1999, Big rise reported in counterfeiting of luxury goods, *Financial Times,* April 16, 3.
93. Porter, *Competitive Strategy,* 38.

94. Porter, *Competitive Advantage,* 15.
95. Lloyd Greif Center for Entrepreneurial Studies, 1999, Discussion of the Greif Center's founder.
96. S. Thurm, 1999, For Cisco, focus on smaller companies pays off, *Wall Street Journal,* May 27, B8.
97. Porter, *Competitive Advantage,* 15.
98. Ibid., 15–16.
99. D. Machalaba, 1999, There's a small hotel where happy guests see screamin' demons, *Wall Street Journal,* March 22, A1, A8.
100. E. De Lisser, 1999, Online retailers slice and dice niches thinner than Julienne fries, *Wall Street Journal,* November 29, B1, B6.
101. R. Ho, 1999, The little empire of quotes, *Wall Street Journal,* February 19, B1, B4.
102. Ikea, 2000, Ikea Home Page, January 14, *www.ikea.com.*
103. Porter, What is strategy? 65.
104. Associated Press, 1999, Key connection, *Dallas Morning News,* March 25, D11.
105. B. Smale, 1999, The customer is always dead, *Fast Company,* December, 314–326.
106. P. Lkebnikov, 1999, The $600,000 car, *Forbes,* May 17, 94–99.
107. K. L. Miller, 1999, On beyond "born to raise hell," *Business Week,* June 7, 96; K. Stevens, 1997, That vroom! you hear may not be a Harley, *Business Week,* October 20, 159.
108. J. R. Hagerty, 2000, Home Depot strikes at Sears in tool duel, *Wall Street Journal,* January 10, B1, B4; N. Harris, 1997, Home Depot: Beyond do-it-yourselfers, *Business Week,* October 20, 159.
109. R. Grover, 1999, Vegas' latest long shot, *Business Week,* April 12, 40–42.
110. Dess, Lumpkin, & McGee, Linking corporate entrepreneurship to strategy, 89.
111. W. K. Hall, 1980, Survival strategies in a hostile environment, *Harvard Business Review,* 58, 5: 75–87.
112. Dess, Gupta, Hennart, & Hill, Conducting and integrating strategy research, 377.
113. L. Kim & Y. Lim, 1988, Environment, generic strategies, and performance in a rapidly developing country: A taxonomic approach, *Academy of Management Journal,* 31: 802–827.
114. Porter, *Competitive Advantage,* 18.
115. A. L. Penenbert, 1999, Deliverance: The Internet may be global, but Kosmo is going local, *Forbes,* October 18, 164.
116. R. Sanchez, 1995, Strategic flexibility in product competition, *Strategic Management Journal,* 16 (Summer Special Issue): 140.
117. Ibid., 105.
118. L. J. Krajewski & L. P. Ritzman, 1999, *Operations Management: Strategy and Analysis,* 5th ed. (Reading, MA: Addison-Wesley), 161–163.
119. J. Martin, 1997, Give 'em exactly what they want, *Fortune,* November 10, 283–285.
120. R. S. Russell & B. W. Taylor, III, 2000, *Operations Management,* 3rd ed. (Upper Saddle River, NJ: Prentice-Hall), 262–264.
121. J. B. Dilworth, 2000, *Operations Management: Providing Value in Goods and Services,* 3rd ed. (Ft. Worth, TX: The Dryden Press), 286–289; D. Lei, M. A. Hitt, & J. D. Goldhar, 1996, Advanced manufacturing technology, organization design and strategic flexibility, *Organization Studies,* 17: 501–523.
122. G. Bylinsky, 1999, Challengers are moving in on ERP, *Fortune,* December 6, 250B–250D.
123. C. V. Callahan & J. Nemec, Jr., 1999, The C.E.O.'s information technology challenge: Creating true value, *Strategy & Business,* 14: 78–89.
124. Bylinsky, Challenges are moving in on ERP, 250C.
125. R. K. Reger, L. T. Gustafson, S. M. DeMarie, & J. V. Mullane, 1994, Reframing the organization: Why implementing total quality is easier said than done, *Academy of Management Review,* 19: 565–584.
126. J. D. Westphal, R. Gulati, & S. M. Shortell, 1997, Customization or conformity: An institutional and network perspective on the content and consequences of TWM adoption, *Administrative Science Quarterly,* 42: 366–394.
127. J. R. Hackman & R. Wageman, 1995, Total quality management: Empirical, conceptual, and practical issues, *Administrative Science Quarterly,* 40: 310.
128. Ibid., 311.
129. M. J. Zbaracki, 1998, The rhetoric and reality of Total Quality Management, *Administrative Science Quarterly,* 43: 602–636.
130. C. H. St. John & J. S. Harrison, 1999, Manufacturing-based relatedness, synergy, and coordination, *Strategic Management Journal,* 20: 129–145.
131. Porter, *Competitive Advantage,* 16.
132. A. Miller & G. G. Dess, 1993, Assessing Porter's (1980) model in terms of its generalizability, accuracy and simplicity, *Journal of Management Studies,* 30: 553–585.
133. Porter, *Competitive Advantage,* 17.
134. M. Peers, 1999, Blockbuster to offer Net video rentals, explores home-delivery technologies, *Wall Street Journal,* October 21, B16.

COMPETITIVE DYNAMICS

CHAPTER FIVE OBJECTIVES

After reading this chapter, you should be able to:

1. Define the conditions for undertaking competitive actions.
2. Identify and explain factors affecting the probability that a competitor will initiate a response to competitive actions.
3. Describe first, second, and late movers and the advantages and disadvantages of each.
4. Understand the factors that contribute to the likelihood of a response to a competitive action.
5. Explain the effects of the size of a firm, the speed with which it makes strategic decisions, and implementation, innovation, and quality on the firm's ability to take competitive action.
6. Understand three basic market situations as outcomes of competitive dynamics.
7. Discuss the types of competitive actions most relevant for each of the three stages of an industry evolution.

The Global Competitive Landscape Is Changing: Wal-Mart Is on the Move

Sam Walton defied conventional wisdom more than any other executive in the 20th century. He focused on locating large stores in rural areas, while rivals built large stores in urban cities and suburbs. In so doing, he built the largest retailing company in the world and the fourth largest of all companies behind GM, DaimlerChrysler, and Ford. Walton carefully chose the store sites and the company distributed its goods in a highly efficient manner. Essentially, Walton started a revolution in retailing. As noted in Chapter 3, prior to Wal-Mart's existence, most retailers carried the merchandise they were provided by suppliers, and consumers bought the merchandise that was available. However, Walton squeezed the suppliers for better prices on merchandise and gave the savings to the consumer. Most large competitors (e.g., Sears) ignored Wal-Mart, until it was so large and well established that it began to compete on their turf (in large cities and suburbs).

Wal-Mart's total annual sales of more than $160 billion and market capitalization of over $200 billion are both more than double the sales and capitalization of the closest rivals. This is why rivals in other parts of the world are worried about Wal-Mart's global expansion. In fact, analysts suggest that retailers across the European continent are running scared. Wal-Mart first entered Europe with the acquisition of 21 stores from Wertkauf GmbH in 1997. In 1998, Wal-Mart acquired 74 hypermarkets from Spar Handels AG in Germany. In 1999, it bought Asda of Great Britain with 229 supermarkets. Wal-Mart's entry into Europe has prompted price wars in Germany and England. Soon Wal-Mart is expected to make acquisitions in France and Italy as well. Wal-Mart already has operations in Canada, Mexico, and China and has targeted other global regions outside of North America. Thus, Wal-Mart is spreading its revolution to Europe and elsewhere around the world.

George Wallace, director of a prominent retail consulting firm based in London, suggests that "Wal-Mart's arrival will be the catalyst for a battle here [Europe] between the juggernauts of the industry." The rivalry is exemplified by British retailer Tesco's price reductions on goods amounting to $414 million. Metro AG, the largest retailer in Germany changed its logo, started opening earlier, and developed the slogans "honestly low prices" (similar to Wal-Mart's "everyday low prices") and "permanently reasonable." To reinforce its customer service, Real, another competitor, provides shoppers five marks if they have to wait more than five minutes at a cashier. German shoppers stated that they are encountering improved customer service.

http://www.ahold.com

http://www.asda.co.uk

http://www.carrefour.fr

In one of the boldest responses to Wal-Mart's European invasion, Carrefour acquired Promodes in late 1999. The merger of the two French firms created Europe's number-

http://www.daimler-chrysler.com
http://www.ford.com
http://www.gm.com
http://www.metro.de
http://www.promodes.com
http://www.sainsbury.co.uk
http://www.sears.com
http://www.spar.de
http://www.tesco.co.uk
http://www.walmart.com

one retailer and number two in the world behind Wal-Mart. In addition, Carrefour is now able to challenge Wal-Mart in global markets, with 8,800 stores in 26 countries. Carrefour has 20 percent of the Brazilian market, versus 1.4 percent for Wal-Mart. Carrefour has been operating in Latin America for 25 years. Its annual revenues are over $65 billion. Size is important in order to obtain lower prices from suppliers. To compete with Wal-Mart, Carrefour has reduced prices drastically, remodeled stores, and relocated other stores. One executive of a rival described Carrefour as "relentless—the toughest competitor I've ever seen anywhere." In addition to its presence in Latin America, Carrefour is strong in Asia.

The pressure is on other major European retailers, such as Royal Ahold, based in the Netherlands, and Great Britain's Sainsbury's. In fact, because of Wal-Mart's move into Great Britain, the stock prices of several of England's prominent retailers began to slide in late 1999. While Wal-Mart's road to success in Europe is not paved with gold, it is likely to revolutionize retailing there and in other regions of the world that it enters. Thus, Wal-Mart is spawning a global revolution.

SOURCES: A. Barrett & J. Carreyrou, 1999, French retailers Carrefour, Promodes agree to join in $16.3 billion accord, *Wall Street Journal Interactive,* August 30, *interactive.wsj.com/articles*; E. Beck & E. Nelson, 1999, As Wal-Mart invades Europe, rivals rush to match its formula, *Wall Street Journal Interactive,* October 6, *interactive.wsj.com/articles;* H. Dawley, 1999, Watch out Europe: Here comes Wal-Mart, *Businessweek Online,* June 28, *bwarchive.businessweek.com;* C. Matlack, I. Resch, & W. Zellner, 1999, Engarde, Wal-Mart, *Businessweek Online,* September 13, *bwarchive.businessweek.com;* E. Nelson & E. Beck, 1999, Wal-Mart seeks supermarket firm, *Wall Street Journal,* June 15, A3–A4; P. Sellers, 1999, Category killers: They left their competitors with nowhere to hide, *Fortune,* September 27, 223–226; S. Voyle, 1999, Wal-Mart casts shadow over gloomy retailers, *www.ft.com,* November 20, *www.ft.com/nbearchive;* D. Woodruff & J. Carreyrou, 1999, French retailers create new Wal-Mart rival, *Wall Street Journal,* August 31, A14, A19.

Wal-Mart's entry into European markets and competitors' reactions represent examples of changes in the 21st-century competitive landscape. Companies competing in this more volatile and unpredictable landscape must learn how to cope successfully with the challenges presented by discontinuous environmental changes, the increasing globalization of their industries, and the array of competitive actions and responses that are being taken by aggressive rivals.[1] In addition, top-level managers must be willing to make the type of difficult decisions that are called for by the nature of competitors' actions and responses. In fact, some believe that one of the most important skills that will be linked to strategic competitiveness in the 21st century will be managers' willingness, and perhaps even eagerness, to make significant and sometimes painful decisions.[2] Many of these decisions will be necessitated by the competitive dynamics affecting the firm's operations.

Wal-Mart's entry into European markets, along with its moves into Latin America and China, exemplify the globalization of markets. The competition's reactions, particularly the acquisition of Promodes by Carrefour, exemplify the trend toward consolidation in many industries to compete effectively in global markets. Wal-Mart's volume of sales provides tremendous leverage with suppliers because of large purchases of merchandise. Thus, Wal-Mart's market power continues to grow as it expands into global markets. Some fear Wal-Mart's power; thus, a few states in the United States, such as Arizona, California, and Nevada, have passed legislation limiting the size of retail establishments targeting supercenters.[3] However, Wal-Mart has responded by flexing its cybermuscles: It is starting to focus on selling merchandise through e-commerce. Granted that its sales over the Internet are considerably smaller than Amazon.com's, but with Wal-Mart's brand name, market power, and considerable resources, its e-commerce venture has a high probability of success.[4]

Increased Rivalry in the New Competitive Landscape

Conditions in the new competitive landscape are increasing competitive rivalry and require many companies to compete differently in order to achieve strategic competitiveness and earn above-average returns (recall the description of European retailers preparing to compete with Wal-Mart as it enters their markets). C. K. Prahalad refers to the environment as a competitive battlefield. He suggests that the strategic discontinuities a firm encounters can be positive. For example, the political changes in Eastern Europe opened markets and provided opportunities for firms from Western countries and Asia. And the Asian financial crisis represented a less-than-positive strategic discontinuity for many U. S. and Western European firms. Prahalad suggests that the competitive landscape in the 21st century requires a new strategic approach and managerial mind-set.[5] For instance, the increased competitive rivalry requires that firms bring new goods and services to the market more quickly.[6] Compaq has discovered this necessity. In the middle 1990s, Compaq won the competitive battle to become the number-one manufacturer and marketer of personal computers. However, in 1999, Dell overtook Compaq to become number one in this market (see the Strategic Focus in Chapter 1). In fact, Compaq reported a major loss in 1999. Compaq not only lost its leadership in the PC market, it also lost major users of Compaq servers to competitors (e.g., Volkswagen and America Online). In addition, Compaq was criticized for having an undeveloped Internet strategy. As a result, Compaq made a number of managerial changes and increased investment in the development of its product line.[7]

The competitive landscape is undergoing fundamental changes, with new entrants transforming industries, often by using new technology.[8] For example, a recent, but now classic, case of such change occurred with Amazon.com's entrance into the retail book market. In previous chapters, we saw the profound effects of Amazon.com on the retail book market, and indeed, the success of Amazon.com began the revolution in e-commerce. Before Amazon's entry into the market, analysts were predicting that Barnes & Noble would become the "master" of the retail book market. It had the most bookstores, the largest market share in the industry, and the promise of more growth. However, Barnes & Noble was "Amazoned," according to *Fortune* magazine. It was almost a year before Barnes & Noble responded with its own on-line book sales, and thus, its growth slowed.[9] Small bookstores are truly struggling, trying to compete against both Amazon.com and Barnes & Noble. Several have argued that it is a "jungle" in on-line book sales. Amazon.com offered 50 percent discounts on its books, forcing Barnes & Noble and other booksellers to match the prices at which they were selling the same items.[10] Amazon.com also obtained an injunction against Barnes & Noble, barring it from using Amazon.com's patented one-click system for on-line orders from its barnesandnoble.com.[11] Thus, it seemed that Amazon.com was continuing to keep Barnes & Noble at bay in their competitive battle.

Barnes & Noble recently expanded its on-line sales to include music as a catalyst to increase its growth.[12] But Amazon.com has been in the on-line music business for some time. In fact, Amazon now sells many products in addition to books. In 1999, it even purchased a stake in an on-line grocery firm.[13] Interestingly, Amazon.com may face its largest competition from Wal-Mart. Some have described Amazon.com as the Wal-Mart of the Internet. In fact, it is probably the significant presence of Amazon and other growing "e-tailers" that has led Wal-Mart and other brick-and-mortar retailers to respond to their growing presence. As noted in the Opening Case, however, Wal-Mart has moved into on-line sales of its merchandise. In late 1999, it announced an alliance with America Online to further its presence in on-line sales.[14]

Competitive advantages may come from nontraditional areas in the evolving competitive landscape. This is shown by the manner in which U-Haul dominated the consumer-truck rental business in the 1990s. The competitive battle in this industry was fierce. U-Haul was the first to recognize the profit potential in, and seize on, the accessories market. As a result, it maintained very low rental rates to attract many customers, who would then purchase profitable accessories. In contrast, competitors priced their rentals so as to maximize their return from the truck rental business. As a result, U-Haul increased its market share relative to the number-two competitor, Ryder, which ultimately abandoned the rental truck market.[15]

Another phenomenon in the 21st-century landscape is the consolidation of industries. There are many reasons for this, but among them is the need to be large in order to achieve economies of scale to compete effectively in global markets. With freer access to markets in many countries, foreign companies are entering at increasing rates. The enhanced competition has emphasized the need for efficiency, both to offer low prices and, at the same time, to differentiate a firm's products through innovation. Consolidation has occurred in industries ranging from the petroleum industry (e.g., the merger of Exxon and Mobil) and the communications industry (e.g., the merger of Carlton Communications and United News and Media, both from the United Kingdom) to the on-line computer electronics industry (e.g., the merger of Onsale and Egghead.com) and other e-commerce and Web-based markets (e.g., Excite At Home Corporation's acquisition of iMall, Inc.). On-line sales competition in the computer hardware industry had become so fierce that firms were selling products below their wholesale costs. Their only hope to make a profit was to sell on-line advertising. Thus, consolidation became necessary to reduce some of the competitive rivalry.[16]

On-line retailing is growing dramatically; on-line sales in 1999 were 2.5 times the amount in 1998. Some, such as CompUSA's former CEO James Halpin, still believe that there is a need and demand for physical stores where customers can see, feel, and operate the products as they desire. He also believes that the opportunity to have a salesperson work directly with the consumer provides an advantage to physical stores. However, analysts suggest that the environment is too different and uncertain to make definitive predictions at this time. Grupo Sanborns, a large Mexican retail company, recently acquired CompUSA, making predictions of how the firm will compete in the future even more difficult.[17]

Both significant advances in communication technologies that allow more effective coordination across operations in multiple markets and faster decision making and competitive responses facilitate the changes occurring in many industries' competitive landscapes.[18] In addition, new technology and innovations, particularly in the information technology and computer industries, have helped small and medium-sized businesses to compete effectively. Finally, the increasing number of agreements allowing free trade across country borders [such as the 1993 North American Free Trade Agreement (NAFTA)] is facilitating a growing cross-border focus.[19]

The changing competitive landscape even has former competitors cooperating in such areas as the development of new technology and forming strategic alliances to compete against other competitors (as discussed in Chapter 9).[20] For example, global alliances also have been formed among many of the world's telephone companies to pursue business in Europe. Increasingly, cooperative R&D arrangements are being developed in the competitive landscape as well. These arrangements are vehicles through which firms overcome their resource constraints by acquiring skills and capabilities from partners.[21]

This chapter focuses on competitive dynamics. The essence of this important topic is that a firm's strategies and their implementation (see Figure 1.1) are dynamic in nature. Actions taken by one firm often elicit responses from competitors that, in turn, typically result in responses from the original firm. This chain of events is illustrated by the Opening Case which is concerned with the competitive actions being taken by European retailers competing with Wal-Mart. The series of actions and responses among firms competing within a particular industry creates **competitive dynamics.** This competitive interaction often shapes the competitive position of firms undertaking the business-level strategies described in the previous chapter and, to some extent, the corporate strategies described in Chapters 6, 8, and 9. Thus, because of competitive dynamics, the effectiveness of any strategy is determined not only by the initial move, but also by how well the firm "anticipates and addresses the moves and countermoves of competitors and shifts in customer demands over time."[22]

Competitive dynamics results from a series of competitive actions and competitive responses among firms competing within a particular industry.

To more effectively explain competitive dynamics, we introduce a model of the phenomenon (see Figure 5.1). The remainder of the chapter then describes this model. After the overall model is introduced, we examine the factors that lead to competitive attack and potential responses. We follow this examination with a discussion of the incentives of market leadership (first-mover advantages) and its disadvantages. We also discuss the advantages and disadvantages of second and late movers. After a competitive action is taken, a number of factors affect the potential response. These factors are discussed, and we then examine firms' capabilities to attack and respond, including the size of the firms, the speed of decision making, innovation, and product and process quality. Following this analysis is a discussion of three different types of competitive markets (slow cycle, standard cycle, and fast cycle) that result from competitive interaction. In particular, we explore the nature of rivalry and propose strategies for competition in fast-cycle markets where competitive rivalry has escalated to an intense level. This discussion examines the strategy of competitive disruption, in which firms capitalize on temporary, compared to sustainable, competitive advantage by cannibalizing their past new-product entries to introduce the next product or process innovation. Finally, we describe competitive rivalry outcomes as industries move through the emerging, growth, and maturity stages.

FIGURE 5.1 | A Summary Model of Interfirm Rivalry: The Likelihood of Attack and Response

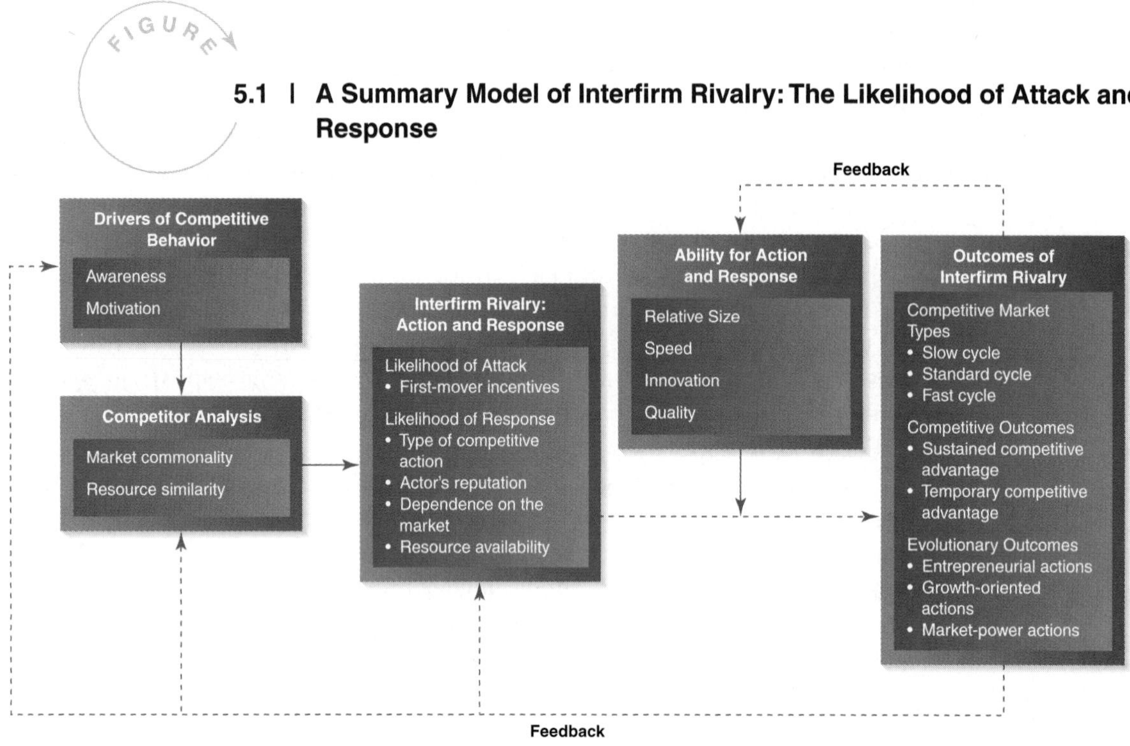

Source: Adapted from M. J. Chen, 1996, Competitor analysis and interfirm rivalry: Toward a theoretical integration, *Academy of Management Review*, 21: 100–134.

Model of Competitive Dynamics and Rivalry

Competitive rivalry exists when two or more firms jockey with one another in the pursuit of an advantageous market position.

Over time, firms competing in an industry employ a number of competitive actions and responses.[23] **Competitive rivalry** exists when two or more firms jockey with one another in the pursuit of an advantageous market position. Competitive rivalry takes place among firms because one or more competitors feel pressure or see opportunities to improve their market position. Rivalry is made possible by *competitive asymmetry,* which exists when firms differ from one another in terms of their resources, capabilities, and core competencies (see Chapter 3) and in terms of the opportunities and threats in their industry and competitive environments (see Chapter 2). Strategies—especially business-level ones—are formed to exploit the asymmetric relationships among competitors.[24]

In most industries, a firm's competitive actions have observable effects on its competitors and typically cause responses designed to counter the action.[25] In early 1998, for instance, Renault, France's largest car and truck manufacturer, announced plans to increase its output by 500,000 units a year through 2002. In addition, the carmaker indicated that it was committed to improving the efficiency of its manufacturing operations to reduce its overall costs. Renault's competitive decisions were made partly in response to Toyota's previously announced intention to build a new small-car manufacturing plant in France. Renault officials believed that the firm's response was required for it to become more competitive in its home market and to prevent Renault from falling behind more efficient rivals such as Toyota.[26] As noted in the Strategic Focus later in the chapter, Renault must respond to Toyota's strategic action. It is predicted that by the year 2010 only six major automakers will be operating globally. Although Renault will be a formidable competitor for any firm entering European markets, it is not expected to be among the surviving global six identified in the Strategic Focus.[27]

Competitive rivalry can have a major effect on a firm's profitability. As rivalry in an industry increases, the average profitability of firms competing in the industry decreases.[28] The intensity of the rivalry is affected not only by the number of competitors, but by many other factors as well. It is affected by the market structure and the firm's strategy. Thus, firms that develop and implement more effective strategies (recall the discussion of business-level strategies in Chapter 4) will fare better than others.[29] For example, Tultex, a manufacturer of casual apparel, experienced significant problems with competition, particularly from Asia and other regions outside of the United States. Unfortunately, Tultex was unable to compete effectively and filed for bankruptcy protection in late 1999.[30] Similarly, JCPenney's financial performance has suffered from competition since 1994. Penney's executives implemented a strategy of differentiation by marketing high-margin private labels as core brands. However, Penney failed to fully promote and thus capitalize on its private-label apparel. Its strategy was copied by numerous competitors (e.g., Sears, Roebuck & Co.), while others (e.g., Macy's) carried a more complete line of name-brand merchandise, such as Tommy Hilfiger and Ralph Lauren. In addition, discount retailers such as Target offered quality clothing comparable to Penney's, but at much lower prices. As a result, Penney's financial performance has trailed that of its competitors, and its stock price has suffered.[31]

Mutual interdependence among firms means that strategic competitiveness and above-average returns result only when companies recognize that their strategies are not implemented in isolation from their competitors' actions and responses.

As the example of the competitive actions and competitive responses among the retail apparel marketers demonstrates, firms and their competitors are mutually interdependent.[32] **Mutual interdependence** among firms means that strategic competitiveness and above-average returns result only when companies recognize that their strategies are not implemented in isolation from their competitors' actions and responses. Eastman Kodak Co. and Fuji Photo Film Co., for example, continue to engage in a series of competitive actions and responses in an effort to establish competitive advantage. Competition in the United States with Fuji has affected Kodak's performance. While the competitive dynamics between these two rivals has been continuous for the last several years, Fuji was clearly successful in 1999. Fuji continued to reduce the prices of its film, even during peak selling periods. Kodak reduced some prices, but most remained from 10 percent to 25 percent higher than Fuji's. As a result, Kodak's market share decreased by approximately 6 percent, and Fuji's increased by a similar percentage. Kodak's slide in the film market and its inability to develop highly competitive new products (e.g., in digital imaging) led to the resignation of George Fisher, CEO since 1993.[33] Thus, because they affect strategic competitiveness and returns, the pattern of competitive dynamics and the rivalry it creates are a major concern of firms.[34]

Figure 5.1 illustrates a summary model of interfirm rivalry and the likelihood of attack and response. As is seen in the figure, competitor analysis begins with an examination of competitor awareness and motivation to attack and respond to competitive action. *Awareness* refers to whether or not the attacking or responding firm is aware of the competitive market characteristics, such as the market commonality and the resource similarity of a potential attacker or respondent (these terms are defined in a subsequent section).[35] Managers may have "blind spots" in their industry and competitor analyses, due to underestimation or an inability to analyze these factors.[36] Of course, such errors are likely to harm the managers' firms and the industry as well. For example, this lack of awareness may lead to industry overcapacity and excessive competition.[37] Firms in an industry are likely to exhibit several different types of competitive responses. The reasons for these differences are several but include the number of common markets in which the firm competes with the firm to whose action it is responding, as well as its resources to respond. Also, the response may depend partially on the similarity of the resources among the competitors.[38] Market commonality and resource similarity both affect a firm's motivation to respond to a competitive action. *Motivation* relates to the incentives a firm has to attack and respond if attacked. A firm may perceive advantages to moving first, given the potential for interaction.

As Figure 5.1 suggests, both market commonality and resource similarity mediate the awareness and motivation to undertake actions and responses. The likelihood of action and response will result in the competitive outcomes which, however, will be moderated by a firm's ability to undertake strategic actions and responses. Furthermore, Figure 5.1 illustrates that feedback from the nature of a particular rivalry will also influence a competitor's awareness and motivation to take future actions or responses.

Market Commonality

Many firms—for example, those in the airlines, chemical, pharmaceutical, breakfast cereals, and electronics industries—compete in the same multiple markets. In the

The largest U.S. airlines compete in the same multiple markets, which can lead to multipoint competition. The firms must be continually aware of their competitors and be motivated to respond quickly to their competitive actions.

Air Wars: Competitive Rivalry among Airlines

Airlines compete in complex ways and yet offer a largely undifferentiated service. For example, most of the major airlines compete with one another in separate markets. While the overlap in markets is not perfect, oftentimes several major airlines compete on routes between major cities (markets). When that happens, reductions in fares by one airline in specific markets or, more generally, across the board are often met with swift responses by other airlines. As a result, airlines generally find it difficult to reduce prices. Alternatively, it is uncommon to match price increases, primarily because of multimarket competition between the major airlines. The situation suggests high rivalry. However, in many markets, customers complain about high fares. One airline may find it difficult to change its fares or even services without swift action by competitors, but sometimes in different markets. The one major exception to this "unwritten rule of competition" in the airline industry is Southwest Airlines. Southwest has offered low fares, and the other airlines have not been able to stall its success. Southwest has received considerable publicity about its success. Over the years, a number of firms have tried to imitate Southwest's strategy, but they have been unsuccessful. While Southwest was a regional carrier, most major airlines largely ignored it (except those that had large market shares in the regions served by Southwest). However, Southwest has grown and is no longer a regional airline. In 1999, it initiated its first transcontinental flight. The major airlines should be concerned about the expansion goals of Southwest. It is well known that Southwest has been able to create a successful strategy through strong leadership, a unique and favorable corporate culture, and excellent employees. These three largely tacit competencies make it difficult for competitors to imitate Southwest's strategy effectively. Given its attractive cost structure and the differentiated service created through its culture and employees, other larger airlines have largely given up trying to imitate it. Continental lost millions of dollars trying to compete directly with Southwest. The reason for its success is that Southwest enjoys a 59 percent cost advantage over other airlines on flights of 500 miles or longer and a 35 percent cost advantage on flights of 1,500 miles or longer. One airline executive described Southwest as "a huge threat."

Because of Southwest's advantage, most airlines search for unique ways to compete with each other while attempting to avoid Southwest. In recent years, several of the major airlines have focused on serving the business travel market, a market that Southwest does not reach well. For example, Continental has been particularly aggressive in the New York market, increasing its share there in the last few years, while United, American, Delta, and US Airways have all lost market share in New York. Continental has garnered over 100 new corporate accounts and expanded over 200 existing ones. To increase its business with Lucent Technologies, it changed its schedules from New York to Chicago, Denver, and Atlanta to accommodate Lucent executives' needs. It also added flights as Lucent grew.

Rival carriers are plotting new strategies to combat Continental. For example, American Airlines acquired Business Express to supplement its feed into New York. American also announced plans to spend $1 billion to double its capacity at JFK Airport to 59 gates. Delta is improving its international operations at JFK, too. Interestingly, Southwest Airlines recently moved into this market as well, with gates in Long Island.

Continental, however, is initiating other competitive actions and responses. It added flights between its Newark hub and Dallas, striking directly at American (Dallas is American's largest hub). Continental also began service to Lima, Peru; in contrast, American discontinued its direct flight between JFK and Lima. Continental is expanding its service to European cities as well.

Some airlines find it difficult to compete with these types of strategic actions. For example, British Airways is largely making internal moves to increase its efficiency. Once the most profitable airline, British Airways has encountered multiple problems in recent years. As a result, it is shrinking its number of routes and the size of its planes. The intent is to reduce the firm's cost of operations and increase its efficiency and profits.

Most larger airlines, including British Airways, have formed alliances to compete more effectively in international travel markets. For example, British Air formed a major alliance with American Airlines and Iberia Airlines. Continental has not been as successful in this regard. However, it has formed an alliance with Northwest Airlines and KLM, while Delta has an alliance with Air France. Although there are efficiencies to gain through alliances, the alliances are also developed in response to a competitive move of another airline (alliances are explained further in Chapter 9). In Europe, Virgin Atlantic Airways plays a role similar to that of Southwest in the U.S. domestic market. It is a part of a larger diversified firm, however, and thus does not receive the attention that is perhaps necessary to make it into an effective competitor of major European airlines. On the other hand, Virgin Atlantic and a continuous number of new airlines make this industry an intriguing one with significant rivalry.

SOURCES: BA first-half profits tumble 40%, 1999, *www.ft.com,* November 11, *www.ft.com/nbearchive*; British Airways takes a flier, 1999, *Fortune,* September 27, 214–220; J. Flynn, W. Zellner, L. Light, & Joseph Weber, 1999, Then came Branson, *Businessweek Online,* December 24, *bwarchive.businessweek.com*; T. Maxon, 1999, Prepared for takeoff: Southwest, American taking a turf fight to new airport, *Dallas Morning News,* May 22, F1, F11; S. McCartney, 1999, Continental is winning the battle for share in the New York market, *Wall Street Journal,* February 9, A1, A11; A. Robinson, 1999, Is Iberia ready for takeoff? *Businessweek Online,* December 24, *bwarchive.businessweek.com*; W. Zellner, 1999, Southwest's new direction, *Businessweek Online,* December 24, *bwarchive.businessweek.com.*

---

brewery industry, many beer producers compete in the same regional markets.[39] Regional competition is also evident in international markets through "triad" competition, or the necessity for multinational corporations to have businesses in Asia (traditionally, Japan), Europe, and North America.[40] Multimarket overlap presents opportunities for **multipoint competition,** a situation in which firms compete against each other simultaneously in several product or geographic markets.[41] In the airline industry, for instance, there are many opportunities for multipoint competition, as noted in the Strategic Focus. The largest U.S. airlines have substantial market overlap and therefore substantial awareness and motivation to respond to competitive actions. Research has shown that such commonality reduces the likelihood of competitive rivalry in the industry.[42] Because the major airlines operate in many common markets, peace will reign until one firm makes a competitive move; the competitive response is likely to be swift, as explained in the Strategic Focus.[43]

Multipoint competition occurs when firms compete against each other simultaneously in several product or geographic markets.

Continental's competitive actions in the New York market and American Airlines' competitive responses exemplify the competitive rivalry that exists in the airline industry. It also suggests that airlines try to compete on dimensions other than price. Continental's actions to increase its flights between New York and Dallas exemplify the multimarket competition that exists in the airline industry, because those actions were the direct result of American's actions in the New York market.

Interestingly, research suggests that market commonality and multimarket competition may begin almost by chance. However, the same research also suggests that after it begins, the multimarket competition becomes intentional.[44] Such intentional actions may provide incentives to reduce product lines and avoid entering certain markets.[45] Thus, multimarket competition can become a deterrent to competitive rivalry. However, most multimarket contact is highly complex, as in the airlines industry. As a result, competitive interactions are likely to be more complex than was even suggested in the Strategic Focus on the airlines.

Recent work suggests that firms may take one or more of three different actions in multimarket contact with competitors. First, they may make a *thrust,* which is a direct attack on a specific competitive market niche, forcing competitors to withdraw resources. Continental's action to increase flights from New York to Dallas could be categorized as a thrust to make American withdraw resources from the New York market. The second action that firms may take is a *feint,* which is an attack on a focal area that is important to a competitor, but not vital to the firm taking the action. The intent is to get the focal firm to commit more resources to the market in question. Given the absence of visible outcomes from the American and British Air alliance, it might have been intended as a feint by one or both firms. The final type of action firms may take is a *gambit,* from the game of chess. In a business gambit, a position is sacrificed to entice a competitor to divert resources to a certain niche.[46] Perhaps United Airlines used a gambit in New York to keep Continental out of its primary market. American Airlines' discontinuation of its flights to Lima, Peru, could also have been a gambit. Without knowing the intention behind the action, we can only speculate.

Resource Similarity

The intensity of competitive rivalry often is based on a potential response and is of great concern for an attacker. An attacker may not be motivated to target a rival that is likely to retaliate. This is especially true of firms with strategic resources similar to those of a potential attacker.[47] Resource similarity refers to the extent of resource overlap between two firms.[48] Resource dissimilarity also plays a vital role in a competitor's motivation to attack or respond. In fact, "the greater is the resource imbalance between the acting firm and competitors or potential responders, the greater will be the delay in response."[49] Although the degree of market commonality is obvious to both firms, strategic resources are difficult to identify because of their causal ambiguity and social complexity (as described in Chapter 3). The difficulty in identifying and understanding the competing firms' resources (including its capabilities and core competencies) also contributes to response delays, especially in instances of resource dissimilarity.

Coca-Cola and Pepsi's decisions to compete in the bottled-water market (as explained in a Strategic Focus later in the chapter) demonstrate an imbalance in resources between the acting firms (Coke and Pepsi) and their competitors (Perrier

Group, Suntory International, McKesson, Great Brands of Europe, and Crystal Geyser). However, the resource dissimilarity between firms such as the Perrier Group on the one hand and Coca-Cola and Pepsi on the other made it difficult for the smaller and less resource-rich companies to implement effective competitive responses.[50]

Because of the intense competition experienced in a number of industries, many firms have inadequate resources to be competitive. For example, Packard Bell NEC, owned jointly by NEC of Japan and Groupe Bull of France, announced in 1999 that it was closing most of its U.S. operations in the personal computer market. In 1995, Packard Bell was the largest retail PC marketer in the United States. However, its fortunes changed quickly with substantial competition from Hewlett-Packard and Compaq, particularly in the low-cost PC market. In 1998 and 1999, Packard-Bell NEC experienced significant net losses. As a result, it no longer had adequate resources to compete in that market.[51]

Inadequate resources, whether financial, technical, or important capabilities, have forced firms to form alliances to compete in specific markets. Thus, one of the primary reasons for strategic alliances is the opportunity for partners to share resources. Also, alliances help firms acquire certain types of resources. For instance, firms may enhance their capabilities by learning from partners, thereby improving their resource base.[52] NEC formed an alliance with Mitsubishi Electric with the purpose of improving the firm's ability to compete. The 50–50 joint venture is designed to develop, manufacture, and market computer monitors and displays. The venture is expected to sell 10 million units annually by 2002, generating revenue of 350 billion yen. NEC has also established a joint venture with GE to manufacture and market medical equipment.[53] Likewise, Global Crossing, based in Bermuda, has established a joint venture with Hutchison Whampoa, based in Hong Kong. The venture will integrate Hutchison's local fixed phone line network with Global Crossing's international telecommunications capabilities. Global Crossing has also formed a joint venture with Japan's Softbank and Microsoft to build a fiber-optic network in Asia.[54] In each of these ventures, both partners contribute a unique set of resources.

Competitive dynamics have caused firms to move beyond simple alliances to develop more complex networks of relationships. Networks of organizations can provide greater value to consumers, as well as draw on resources from multiple partners. Networks are particularly useful with smaller businesses and in international markets. In fact, the use of networks may allow smaller entrepreneurial businesses to compete with larger and more resource-rich firms. However, managing the networks of relationships is difficult: Firms must formulate and implement network strategies[55] (we discuss these network-based businesses further in Chapters 9 and 11). Next we examine the likelihood that firms will take strategic actions or respond to them from competitors.

Likelihood of Attack

Although awareness and motivation to respond are derived largely from competitors' analyses of market commonality and resource similarity, there are strong incentives to be the first mover in a competitive battle if the attacking firm believes it has the poten-

A **competitive action** is a significant competitive move made by a firm that is designed to gain a competitive advantage in a market.

tial to win. A **competitive action** is a significant competitive move made by a firm that is designed to gain a competitive advantage in a market.[56] Some competitive actions are large and significant; others are small and designed to help fine-tune or implement a strategy. The first mover in a competitive interaction may be able to gain above-average returns while competitors consider potential countermoves. Furthermore, the first mover may be able to deter a counterattack, given enough time. As a result, there are significant incentives to be a first mover, and the order of each competitive action and response influences an industry's competitive dynamics. Of greatest importance are first movers, second movers, and late movers.

First, Second, and Late Movers

A **first mover** is a firm that takes an initial competitive action.

A **first mover** is a firm that takes an initial competitive action. The concept of first movers has been influenced by the work of economist Joseph Schumpeter. In particular, he believed that firms achieve competitive advantage through entrepreneurial and innovative competitive actions.[57] In general, first movers "allocate funds for product innovation and development, aggressive advertising, and advanced research and development."[58] Through competitive actions such as these, first movers hope to gain a competitive advantage. For example, Disco SA was the first supermarket chain to offer on-line shopping in Argentina. Disco is jointly owned by Royal Ahold of the Netherlands and Velox Investment Co. of Argentina. The on-line service alliance represented a natural extension of Disco's shop-by-phone service initiated in 1996. Also in 1996, Disco had a Web site that clients in the company's frequent shopper program could consult about the points they had accumulated and their eligibility for prizes. Disco sells a minimum of 3 million pesos per month to nontraditional shoppers (by phone or on-line) and reached 2 billion pesos during 1999. Importantly, 72 percent of the on-line shoppers previously were customers of other supermarkets. Thus, the on-line service is attracting a significant new clientele to Disco. In addition, the average purchase of a Disco in-store shopper is 14 pesos, while the average purchase of an on-line customer is 100 pesos. As a result, the new service offered by Disco appears to be an unqualified success in all dimensions.[59]

Several competitive advantages can accrue to the firm that is first to initiate a competitive action. Successful actions allow a firm to earn above-average returns until other competitors are able to respond effectively. In addition, first movers have the opportunity to gain customer loyalty, thereby making it difficult for responding firms to capture customers. For instance, Harley-Davidson has been able to maintain a competitive lead in large motorcycles due to intense customer loyalty. Across time, though, the competitive advantage of a first mover begins to erode (recall from Chapter 1 that every competitive advantage can be imitated eventually). The advantages and their duration vary by the type of competitive action and industry. First-mover advantages also vary on the basis of the ease with which competitors can imitate the action. The more difficult and costly an action is to imitate, the longer a firm may receive the benefits of being a first mover. When core competencies are the foundation of a competitive action, first-mover advantages tend to last longer. Core competence-based competitive actions have a high probability of resulting in a sustained competitive advantage.

However, potential disadvantages may result from being the first firm to initiate a competitive action. Chief among these is the degree of risk taken by first movers. The risk of a first move is high, because it is not easy to predict the amount of success a particular competitive action will produce prior to its initiation.[60] Oftentimes, first movers have high development costs. Second movers can avoid these costs through reverse engineering (taking apart a new product and then reassembling it to learn how it works). Another potential disadvantage of being a first mover is the dynamic and uncertain nature of many markets in which a firm may compete. In other words, the extent and range of marketplace competition heighten the potential risk. In fact, in a highly uncertain market, it may be more appropriate to be a second or late mover.

A **second mover** is a firm that responds to a first mover's competitive action, often through imitation or a move designed to counter the effects of the action.

A **second mover** is a firm that responds to a first mover's competitive action, often through imitation or a move designed to counter the effects of the action. When the second mover responds quickly to a first mover's competitive action, it may earn some of the first-mover advantages without experiencing the disadvantages. For example, a fast second mover may gain some of the returns and obtain a portion of the initial customers and thereby customer loyalty, while avoiding some of the risks encountered by the first mover. The firm taking a second action as a competitive response to the first mover can do so after evaluating customers' reactions to the first mover's action.[61] To be a successful first mover or fast second mover, a company must be able to analyze its markets and identify critical strategic issues.[62] Firms have different capabilities of obtaining information on markets and analyzing that information after it is obtained. These differences explain why some firms are faster to adopt market innovations than are others.[63]

Bank One was a fast second mover in Internet banking. A few smaller banks established Internet banks before Bank One did. However, based on his analysis of these operations and the market's reaction to them, the CEO of Bank One at the time, John McCoy, decided that Internet banking would claim a significant market share. He also felt that only a few Internet banks would survive over time; thus, it was important to enter the market early and build customer loyalty. Therefore, Bank One started a new bank (not just a branch, as several banks have done) called Wingspan-Bank.com, accessible only on the Internet. This bank was independent of the parent bank, to allow it the flexibility to develop and change as needed to be a primary competitor in the virtual-banking market. Thus, Bank One entered the world of e-commerce.[64]

Being second to the market also allows a firm to conduct market research to learn the first mover's actions and improve on them. Thus, being a second mover allows a firm to introduce directed innovation to better meet consumer needs. A second mover has information that is unavailable to a first mover and thus can direct its strategy on the basis of observing what happens to the first mover. Furthermore, being second provides time to perfect the good or service, eliminating potentially irritating "bugs." Hence, the second-mover strategy gains time for R&D to develop a superior product.[65] Sometimes, being first to the market means that the firm will be the first to fail! It is difficult to conduct definitive market research before introducing a new good or service. First, it may be difficult to define precisely the market for a highly innovative product. Second, some market pioneers fail because they lack either sufficient vision for how the product can be used or the commitment to persist for the long term. Time may be required to convince consumers to accept a new good or service.[66]

In some instances, it may not be possible to move quickly in response to a first mover's action. For example, if the first mover introduces a sophisticated new product and competitors have not undertaken similar research and development, considerable time may be required to respond effectively. Therefore, some risks are involved in being a follower in the market. There are no blueprints for first-mover success. Followers may be able to respond without significant market development costs by learning from a first mover's successes and mistakes. Thus, the actions and outcomes of the first firm to initiate a competitive action may provide a more effective blueprint for second and later movers.[67]

New Balance, Inc., is a second mover in the athletic shoe industry. As mentioned in Chapter 2, accounting for New Balance's success as a second mover is its ability to satisfy baby boomers' needs. The firm's target market is demonstrated by customers' average ages—25 for Nike, 33 for Reebok, and 42 for New Balance. As a second mover's product, the firm's shoes are not particularly innovative compared to those of the industry leader, Nike. In contrast to many competitors that introduce new models roughly every six weeks, New Balance introduces a new one approximately every 17 weeks. New Balance's competitive success as a second mover appears to be based on its ability to offer high-quality products at moderate prices, but in multiple-sized widths. Unlike most companies, which produce shoes in two widths—medium and wide—New Balance offers customers multiple choices, ranging from a narrow AA to an expansive EEEE. The varying widths are a valued competitive feature, in that about 20 to 30 percent of the U.S. population has either narrower- or wider-than-average feet.[68]

A **late mover** is a firm that responds to a competitive action, but only after considerable time has elapsed after the first mover's action and the second mover's response.

A **late mover** is a firm that responds to a competitive action, but only after considerable time has elapsed after the first mover's action and the second mover's response. Although some type of competitive response may be more effective than no response, late movers tend to be poorer performers and often are weak competitors. Avon is a late mover in e-commerce. It implemented its Internet-based marketing and sales efforts in 2000, using IBM as a consultant to help in the design and implementation of its system. While analysts think that the change may be a good one for Avon in helping to attract a more upscale customer, Avon is alienating its direct-sales force. The company's Internet sales compete with its sales representatives who provide direct-sales' service. Furthermore, at least six major competitors established Internet sales before Avon did. It will be difficult for Avon to gain a reasonable share of this market with the formidable competition.[69]

Like Avon, Dell was a late mover in providing Internet access, but it has achieved a measure of success in the European market. Its free Internet access service probably benefits from the Dell brand name (see Chapter 2) that many other new ventures do not enjoy. In late 1999 and early 2000, Dell launched a free Internet access service in the United States as well.[70] Another successful late mover is Stewart Enterprises, which competes in the funeral home business. Essentially, Stewart allowed the two larger industry leaders to exhaust their resources competing against each other and then stepped in to claim market share when they could not effectively respond. Service Corporation International is now saddled with rising costs and decreasing profits, and the Loewen Group may have to declare bankruptcy. Both companies made increasing numbers of acquisitions even as prices escalated. The timing is good for Stewart, because it comes during a period in which the number of deaths in the United States is growing due largely to the aging baby boomers. Stewart also acquires firms and consolidates them in regions where they can share services that reduce their costs of operation. Thus, Stewart is making increasing investments to prepare for a growing market, while the other two firms are reducing their investments. However, as late movers, these firms are even more subject to innovation, which can happen even in industries such as funeral homes. Alton F. Doody, a retail consultant who helped Wal-Mart redesign its stores, has aided York Group, one of three large casket makers, in developing a new strategy for selling caskets that provided the industry a new way to sell and display caskets. The system shows only quarter, as opposed to whole, caskets, and the display has drawers that reveal swatches of interior fabric similar to sofa coverings. This method "not only makes it easier for consumers to buy caskets, but also increases the average sale by $200 to $400 per coffin." The strategy has helped the York Group associated funeral homes to maintain profits, even in the face of more cremations and dozens of Web sites that sell caskets, often at steep discounts.[71]

Likelihood of Response

A **competitive response** is a move taken to counter the effects of an action by a competitor.

After firms take a competitive action, the success of the action often is determined by the likelihood and nature of the response by competitors. A **competitive response** is a move taken to counter the effects of an action by a competitor. Firms considering offensive action need to evaluate the potential responses from competition in making their decision to act. An offensive action may escalate rivalry to a point where actions become self-defeating and an alternative strategy may be necessary. A *de-escalation strategy* is an attempt to reduce overly heated competition that has become self-defeating. As Figure 5.1 shows, the probability of a competitor's response to a competitive action is based on the type of action, the reputation of the competitor taking the action, the competitor's dependence on the market, and the availability of resources to the competitor.

Type of Competitive Action

A **strategic action** represents a significant commitment of specific and distinctive organization resources; it is difficult to implement and to reverse.

A **tactical action** is taken to fine-tune a strategy; it involves fewer and more general organizational resources and is relatively easy to implement and reverse.

The two types of competitive actions are strategic and tactical.[72] A **strategic action** represents a significant commitment of specific and distinctive organizational resources; it is difficult to implement and to reverse. Wal-Mart's entry into European markets, Continental's decision to introduce a new flight to Lima, Peru, and Bank One's implementation of an Internet banking company are examples of strategic actions.

In contrast to strategic actions, a **tactical action** is taken to fine-tune a strategy; it involves fewer and more general organizational resources and is relatively easy to implement and reverse. A price increase in a particular market (e.g., in airfares, as discussed in an earlier Strategic Focus) is an example of a tactical action. This action involves few organizational resources (e.g., communicating new prices and changing prices on products), its implementation is relatively easy, and it can be reversed (through a price reduction, for example) in a relatively short period of time.

Compared to a tactical action, responses to a strategic action are more difficult, because they require additional organizational resources and time. Compared to strategic actions, tactical actions usually have more immediate effects. The announcement of a price increase in a price-sensitive industry such as airlines could have immediate effects on competitors. Therefore, it is uncommon for airlines not to respond quickly to a competitor's price change, particularly if the announced change represents a price reduction, because without a response, the competing airline may lose market share.[73] In one case, American Airlines acquired another airline and planned to spend $1 billion to double its number of gates at JFK Airport to respond to Continental's actions to capture a larger share of the important New York business travel market. Both of the countermoves by American required substantial resources and were not accomplished quickly.

Not all competitive actions elicit or require a response from competitors. On the whole, there are more competitive responses to tactical than to strategic actions.[74] It is usually easier to respond to tactical actions, and sometimes it is necessary, at least in the short term. For example, responding to changes in a competitor's frequent-flier program is much easier and requires far fewer resources than responding to a major competitor's decision to upgrade its fleet of jets and to form strategic alliances to enter new markets.

Actor's Reputation

An action (either strategic or tactical) taken by a market leader is likely to serve as a catalyst to a larger number of and faster responses from competitors and to a higher probability of imitation of the action. In other words, firms are more likely to imitate the actions of a competitor that is a market leader. For instance, if Coca-Cola enters a new market or introduces a new product, competitors are likely to respond (if they have adequate resources to do so). Pepsi is the most likely competitor to respond, because it has adequate resources and because it is second behind Coca-Cola in most markets. Most market leaders have market power and enjoy special advantages because of their strong positive reputation.[75] Coca -Cola, for instance, enjoys a brand name that is well known globally and has considerable market power (as described in Chapter 3). These advantages create formidable barriers for competitors to overcome in trying to imitate Coca-Cola's actions. For example, Coca-Cola has an extensive bottling and distribution system. Many of the smaller competitors' products are bottled and distributed by Coca-Cola's bottlers (e.g., Dr. Pepper). Thus, a smaller competitor may have difficulty introducing a new product to the market that is competitive with Coca-Cola's products. Coca-Cola's distributors may refuse to distribute the new product. Coca-Cola remains strong even in light of its recent reductions in employment and announced restructuring.

Firms also often react quickly to imitate successful competitor actions. For example, in the personal computer market, IBM quickly dominated the market as a second mover, but was imitated by Compaq, Dell, and Gateway. By contrast, firms that take risky, complex, and unpredictable actions are less likely to solicit responses to, and imitations of, their actions.[76] Finally, firms that are known to be price predators (frequently cutting prices to hurt competitors and obtain market share, only to raise prices later) also do not elicit a large number of responses or imitation. In fact, there is less imitation and a much slower response to price predators than to either of the other two types of firms (market leader and strategic player).[77]

As suggested in the Strategic Focus on the auto industry, there is no single dominant company in the industry. GM was once dominant, but its share of the large U. S.

auto market decreased from 36 percent to 29 percent in the decade of the 1990s. GM, Ford, DaimlerChrysler, and Toyota have the strongest reputations globally. Any firm in the industry is likely to carefully observe a major strategic action by any of those four. If resources allow, other auto companies are likely to respond to the action. However, their response is not only because of the actor's reputation: Most auto firms are highly dependent on the industry, so they have no choice but to try to respond to strategic actions of competitors in order to remain viable.

Car Wars: The Battle for Survival

The number of automobile manufacturers continues to shrink. The acquisition of Chrysler by Daimler, Ford's purchase of Volvo, and GM's alliance with Honda may foretell the future of the industry. Toyota's CEO, Hiroshi Okuda, suggested that in the 21st century there will be only five or six major automakers. He proposes that a firm's sales volume needs to be at least 5 million vehicles annually in order for the company to compete in global markets. Consolidation is occurring in the auto industry, as it is in others. Most of the consolidation crosses country borders. Thus, national identity is becoming obsolete. It is predicted that by 2010, each major auto market in the world will have two automakers. Some analysts believe that six firms will remain: Ford and GM in the United States, DaimlerChrysler and Volkswagen in Europe, and Toyota and Honda in Asia. Currently, only GM and Ford sell more than 5 million vehicles annually.

The major firms will acquire the healthy, but smaller, firms in Europe (e.g., Renault) and the distressed firms in Asia (e.g., Nissan). Still, this is only speculation as the dynamism in the competitive landscape makes prediction difficult. As the likely survivors, the "big six" automakers noted above must continue to develop and implement effective strategies and respond effectively to competitors' strategic actions to be able to operate successfully and have the resources to acquire and win their battles with competitors. If they do not they will not survive. For example, DaimlerChrysler is desperately seeking an ally in Asia to help it penetrate Asian markets. Ford owns a significant interest in Mazda and GM is aligned with Honda. Both also have relationships with other Asian firms (e.g., GM is working on a deal to help improve Daewoo's auto unit). However, DaimlerChrysler does not have alliances with firms from this region—nor are there many available. Nissan has rejected Daimler's overtures. Of course, Renault owns a stake in Nissan, and Mitsubishi is engaged in talks with Volvo because of a previous relationship between the firms. But Daimler finally acquired a stake in Mitsubishi.

Toyota has announced that it is increasing its manufacturing capacity in North America. Toyota currently sells approximately 1.5 million vehicles in North America despite a capacity to produce only about 1.2 million vehicles. Such expansion may allow Toyota to better serve the lucrative North American market. The company is expected to increase its production of light trucks (e.g., SUVs), which account for about 50 percent of the North American market for motor vehicles. This is a highly contested market because of its popularity. In late 1999, for example, Ford and DaimlerChrysler both announced rebates on some of their most profitable light trucks. GM had already offered rebates on some of its light trucks (e.g., the

Chevrolet Venture minivan). The actions of all three firms have been prompted by competition, particularly from Japanese and European manufacturers.

Volkswagen is another concern in the survival war. While VW has about 19 percent of the Western European auto market, up from 15 percent in 1994, it is experiencing stagnation. Expectations are that it will continue to have problems over the foreseeable future and may be the most vulnerable of the "big six." Concerns grow as the European Union allows freer competition across European country borders and less control over auto dealers. GM's Opel expects to increase its market share in Germany, likely at the expense of VW, which may need a partner in Europe and elsewhere to be among the survivors. On the positive side, VW's sales in the large U.S. market are quite strong.

Thus, the 21st-century competitive landscape is likely to produce exciting battles and outcomes in the global auto industry.

SOURCES: J. Ball, 1999, Ford, DaimlerChrysler boost rebates on some very profitable light trucks, *Wall Street Journal Interactive,* November 17, *interactive.wsj.com/articles*; Chrysler in battle of minivan, 1999, *Houston Chronicle,* November 26, 4D; J. Ewing, K. Kerwin & K. N. Anhalt, 1999, VW: Spinning its wheels? *Businessweek Online,* November 22, *bwarchive.businessweek.com*; J. Ewing, E. Thornton, & M. Ihlwan, 1999, DaimlerChrysler: Desperately seeking an ally, *Businessweek Online,* December 13, *bwarchive.businessweek.com*; Ford: Faith in high prices, 1999, *www.ft.com,* December 24, *www.ft.com/sea*; K. Naughton, K. L. Miller, J. Muller, E. Thornton, & G. Edmondson, 1999, Autos: The global six, *Businessweek Online,* January 25, *bwarchive.businessweek.com*; N. Shirouzu, 1999, Toyota considers boosting capacity in North America, *Wall Street Journal Interactive,* June 29, *interactive.wsj.com/articles.*

Dependence on the Market

Firms with a high dependency on a market in which a competitive action is taken are more likely to respond to that action. For example, firms with a large amount of their total sales from one industry are more likely to respond to a particular competitive action taken in that industry than is a firm with businesses in multiple industries (e.g., a conglomerate). Thus, if the type of action taken has a major effect on them, firms are likely to respond, regardless of whether the action is strategic or tactical. The battle between McDonald's and Burger King exemplifies a pattern of competitive actions and responses occurring between two firms that are highly dependent on their core market. Burger King and McDonald's are both completely dependent on sales in the fast-food industry. Hence, it is not surprising that the two firms monitor each other's strategic and tactical actions quite carefully. Moreover, competitive actions taken by one of these companies, whether strategic or tactical, almost certainly will result in a competitive response. McDonald's and Burger King have battled over which has the crispest and best-tasting French fries and over 99-cent hamburgers, but have now decided that they need to be more creative and better serve the customer. In addition, they have decided against growing primarily through the development of more restaurants; rather, they are concentrating on growth through increases in average restaurant sales. To do so, Burger King returned to its flame-broiled hamburgers customized to each customer ("Have it your way"). The return to the older strategy has been successful. In addition, Burger King began to redesign all of its restaurants in 1999 and introduce innovations such as interactive video games at tables. In response, McDonald's implemented a "made for you" cooking system in each of its kitchens. The flexible kitchens allow McDonald's to experiment with new foods and recipes. For example, it has pilot tested such novelties as steak, egg, and cheese bagels for breakfast in some of its restaurants. The number-three hamburger restaurant chain, Wendy's, has also reorganized its kitchens to provide more flexible menus. The results have been positive; in 1999, McDonald's market share increased from 42.2 to 42.7 percent, Burger King increased its market share from 19.4 to 20.2 percent, and Wendy's market share increased from 11.3 to 11.5 percent. These increases have come at the expense of smaller chains such as Hardees and independent hamburger restaurants.[78]

Similarly, retail chains in Europe are responding to Wal-Mart's entry into their markets. For example, Tesco and Sainsbury have implemented initiatives to capture the home-shopping market. Tesco Direct, Tesco's e-commerce effort, is profitable and is predicted to become the world's largest Internet grocery business in 2000. The effort may be highly important for Tesco, because Wal-Mart's entry into Britain's grocery market has driven down prices, thereby reducing the margins earned from physical-store sales.[79]

Toys 'R' Us has responded to eToys' successful entry into the toy market with its own Internet toy market business. While Toys 'R' Us is the major competitor in the toy market and has some other businesses, it does not intend to be "Amazoned," according to analysts.[80] Likewise, Boeing has other businesses, but its core business is the manufacture and marketing of commercial aircraft. Its only global competitor, Airbus Industrie, has decided to develop a super jumbo aircraft that will hold up to 600 passengers. While a few years ago Boeing considered and decided against developing a larger version of its 747, it is now reconsidering this option as a competitive response to Airbus. Unfortunately, there are only six airlines that could use such a large aircraft profitably, thereby limiting the market size. Thus, one or both firms could lose money on a super jumbo aircraft.[81] Of course, Boeing has the resources to develop such an aircraft (said to cost about $3 billion) to respond to Airbus, but not all firms have the resources to respond effectively to competitors' strategic actions.

Competitors' Availability of Resources

A competitive response to a strategic or tactical action requires organizational resources. Firms with fewer resources are more likely to respond to tactical actions than to strategic ones, because responses to tactical actions require fewer resources and are easier to implement. In addition, a firm's resources may dictate the type of response it makes. For example, local video stores have relatively limited resources to respond to competitive actions taken by Blockbuster, the dominant firm in the video industry. Typically, a local store cannot imitate a Blockbuster strategic action to establish multiple units within a particular geographic area. In contrast, the smaller local firm is far more likely to respond to a Blockbuster tactical action of reduced prices. However, because of its lower volume and lack of purchasing power relative to the large chains, initiating a tactical price reduction can also be difficult for the local store. To compete against Blockbuster, the local video store often relies on personalized customer service and a willingness to stock or search for hard-to-find videos as the sources of its competitive advantage. Focusing instead on mass availability of the most popular titles and holding operating costs as low as possible, a large video chain such as Blockbuster is unlikely to respond to the local store's service-oriented competitive actions, even though it has the resources to do so.[82] However, given its new Web site, Blockbuster.com, Blockbuster may be able to customize rentals more easily for the consumer. As this example suggests, small firms can respond effectively to their larger counterparts' competitive actions, but this may be more difficult to accomplish in a future dominated by electronic markets.

In contrast, AT&T, SBC Communications, and MCI WorldCom are resource rich and directly compete against each other in many markets. Thus, they are likely to respond to one of the others' strategic actions. For example, in 1999, SBC Communications introduced a telephone service bundle targeted to compete with a similar package planned by AT&T. SBC's service bundles offer discounted packages that include local telephone, Internet, and entertainment services. AT&T is focused on developing its technological capabilities to gain a competitive advantage, particularly in digital communications. Alternatively, MCI WorldCom is trying to acquire the capabilities it needs, exemplified by its latest acquisition of Sprint. Thus, AT&T is undertaking technological risk, whereas MCI WorldCom is taking greater financial risk.[83]

Firms' Abilities to Take Action and Respond

As indicated earlier, resource availability and ability to respond affect the probability of a company's response to a competing firm's competitive actions. Firms' abilities therefore moderate the relationship between interfirm rivalry and the competitive outcomes (see Figure 5.1). In general, four characteristics of firms influence competitive interaction within a market or industry: (1) the relative size of the firm within a market or industry, (2) the speed at which competitive actions and responses are made, (3) the extent of innovation by firms in the market or industry, and (4) the quality of the firm's product.

Relative Size of Firm

The *size* of a firm can have two important, but opposite, effects on an industry's competitive dynamics. First, the larger a firm, the greater is its market power. Of course, the extent of any firm's market power is measured relative to the power of its competitors. Boeing Company (with roughly a 65 percent share of the world's commercial aircraft market) and Airbus Industrie (with approximately a 33 percent market share) both have substantial market power. Relatively, however, Boeing's market power exceeds that of Airbus. Thus, Boeing hopes that developing a larger 747 will limit the ability of Airbus to capture the super jumbo aircraft market niche.[84] In the global automobile manufacturing industry, the four major competitors identified earlier—GM, Ford, DaimlerChrysler, and Toyota—are large; hence, no individual firm has critical market power over the others. Nonetheless, it is difficult for small firms to enter the market because the sheer size of those four firms creates substantial entry barriers. Relative to them, Renault is smaller and has less market power, which is why it is predicted that the firm will not survive over the long term competing against the "big six."

Size usually reflects more than market power: Often, a firm's market share reflects the general level of its resources, which may even include its R&D capabilities and the perceived quality of its products.[85] The market power and resources of competitors also shape a focal firm's responses.[86] A firm competing against weaker competitors may ignore their actions. However, it may also take actions to which its competitors are unlikely to be able to respond. Indeed, it can even drive them out of the market. For example, in 1999, Intel implemented a tactical price reduction of 41 percent in the price of its Pentium III chips to take sales from its competitors. Actions like these caused National Semiconductor to exit the personal-computer microprocessor business. The company fell behind in the technology and did not have the resources to increase its technology development.[87]

Problems created by a firm's size are demonstrated by events—both historical and current—in the computer industry. Although the giant in the industry, IBM, was highly successful, it did not invent or even first introduce the microcomputer, which is the primary basis of the industry today. Entrepreneurial ventures, such as Apple Computer, Dell Computer, and Compaq, introduced the innovations in goods and services that revolutionized the industry. Small firms often do this by fostering what Joseph Schumpeter referred to as "creative destruction."[88] As Steven Jobs and his partner Steve Wozniak revolutionized the computer industry, Michael Dell, who was in high school when Apple introduced its computers, revolutionized the way computers were produced and distributed. The microcomputer market is highly dynamic. Compaq became the number-one manufacturer and seller of personal computers in the 1995–96 period. In 1999, however, Compaq was overtaken by Dell as the top producer of personal computers.[89] Thus, oftentimes the smaller competitor is more innovative and eventually overtakes the top firm. The moral is that it may not be best to grow too large, but rather to find a way to continue to operate using a small-firm culture even though the firm is actually large.

A quote attributed to Herbert Kelleher, cofounder and CEO of Southwest Airlines, best describes the approach needed by large firms. In Kelleher's words, "Think and act big and we'll get smaller. Think and act small and we'll get bigger."[90] This aphorism suggests that large firms should use their size to build market power, but that they must think and act like a small firm (e.g., move quickly and be innovative) in order to achieve strategic competitiveness and earn above-average returns over the long run. A commitment to the value of each employee and to the use of organizational structures that encourage individuals to demonstrate initiative appears to facilitate large firms' efforts to act entrepreneurially.[91] Thermo Electron, 3M, GTE, and Xerox are large companies that appear to be following Kelleher's prescription to overcome the liabilities of size through the creation and support of entrepreneurship.[92]

Pepsi and Coca-Cola's entry into the bottled-water market will make it difficult for the other firms in the industry to compete. Not only can Pepsi and Coca-Cola invest significant resources in promoting their brands of water, but they also have large and efficient distribution systems. Likely, the survivors of the battle among the small firms will be those that can claim a special niche in the market (e.g., Evian).

The following Strategic Focus explains two situations in which Pepsi acted much faster than Coca-Cola. In the Indian diet drink market, Pepsi moved Diet Pepsi to the market within two days of the Government's announcement allowing the use of artificial sweeteners in soft drinks. Coca-Cola was much slower. In addition, Coca-Cola entered the bottled-water market five years after Pepsi, only after the demand for bottled water began to grow significantly and Pepsi's product became number one in the market. Coca-Cola also is experiencing multiple problems that are only exacerbated by the firm's slowness to react to threats and opportunities.

Cola Wars, Water Wars, and Going for the Jugular Vein

Coca-Cola is the dominant firm in the global soft-drink market. It has the largest market share in the United States and in many other markets as well. For example, Coca-Cola has approximately 75 percent of the soft-drink market in Chile and just under 70 percent in Mexico. In fact, it has over 50 percent of the soft-drink market in many of the European countries (e.g., France, Germany, and Spain). Its share of the global soft-drink market is about 50 percent. Because of Coca-Cola's dominant position, along with those of several other competitors (mostly local or regional, except for Pepsi), many of these markets have become saturated. Thus, competitors can no longer enjoy a growing market and must target their competitors' market share. Competitors have largely targeted Coca-Cola.

Coca-Cola withdrew from the Indian market in 1987 because of a nationalist government that wanted it to sell to local firms. It returned to India in 1993, but by that time Pepsi was well entrenched without Coca-Cola as a competitor. A local cola firm also gained a major foothold in the market during Coca-Cola's absence. The stakes are high in India, because it is one of the few remaining large markets that is not saturated. Recently, the government approved the use of artificial sweeteners in carbonated drinks. Coca-Cola and Pepsi moved swiftly to introduce their diet colas. In fact, Pepsi introduced Diet Pepsi to the market within two days of the approval. Coca-Cola responded with prominent advertising announcing the arrival of Diet Coke. However, within a week, the Indian Health Ministry announced that it would enforce an old regulation requiring all carbonated drinks to contain at least 5 percent sucrose. Pepsi blamed Coca-Cola for bringing this regulation to the attention of the Indian government. Pepsi believed that Coca-Cola took its action to delay Pepsi so that Coca-Cola could catch up. Pepsi then sought and obtained a court waiver to avoid having to add the sucrose and also won a temporary injunction that allows it to keep selling Diet Pepsi until the court rules on its case. Coca-Cola also sought a waiver and then launched its Diet Coke into the market. Neither company may gain much, even if they win the right to sell their diet drinks: Indians generally do not like the taste of diet drinks and are suspicious of artificial sweeteners.

Pepsi and Coca-Cola are competing in another market as well. In 1994, Pepsi introduced its brand of bottled water, Aquafina. Since that time, Aquafina has become the top-selling brand of bottled water in convenience stores. Five years after Pepsi's introduction of bottled water, Coca-Cola announced that it was entering this market as well. In 1999, Coca-Cola declared that it would begin marketing bottled water under the brand name Dasani. The product will be purified, noncarbonated water fortified with minerals to enhance its taste. Coca-Cola was reluctant to add bottled water to its line of products, preferring instead to encourage consumption of its carbonated soft drinks. However, the popularity of bottled water and Pepsi's success probably lured Coca-Cola into the market, although belatedly. A large number of smaller competitors offer similar bottled-water products. Naya, another brand of water, is distributed by Coca-Cola, but probably will not be for much longer. Pepsi and Coca-Cola are expected to battle for sales of their water products. However, both will need to be careful not to substitute sales of water for soft-drink sales (because their margin is much higher on soft drinks).

In the 1990s, consumption of Pepsi's soft drinks increased by only 2 percent, while Coca-Cola's consumption increased by 30 percent in the same decade. Thus, Pepsi managers decided to invest heavily in advertising. In 1999, Pepsi spent almost as much as did Coca-Cola on advertising, even though Pepsi is much smaller, after spinning off its bottlers and restaurant operations, now called Tricon. Pepsi used the approximately $4 billion that it received from the spin-offs to help finance the new campaign.

While Coca-Cola is the clear global leader, all is not well in the company. In 1999, it experienced embarrassing and costly lapses in quality that caused short-term bans of its products in Belgium and France. It also had to withdraw 180,000 bottles of water in Poland after coliform bacteria were discovered in the drink. In addition, Italy's competition authority fined Coca-Cola for anticompetitive practices. Given all of these problems and slow and ineffective reactions to them, Coca-Cola's CEO, Douglas Ivestor, resigned his position. Coca-Cola also recently announced employee layoffs and a restructuring of its management. Managers at Pepsi are probably reveling over Coca-Cola's problems.

SOURCES: M. Benson, 1999, In New York, battle is over city-owned property, *Wall Street Journal Interactive,* September 29, *interactive.wsj.com/archive*; J. Blitz & B. Liu, 1999, Coca-Cola: $16 million fine from Italian authorities, *www.ft.com*, December 18, *www.ft.com/sea*; N. Deogun & E. Williamson, 1999, Coke, in new breakdown, recalls more water products in Poland, *Wall Street Journal Interactive,* July 6, *interactive.wsj.com/articles*; D. Foust, 1999, Coke and Pepsi want to make a splash in water, *Businessweek Online,* March 1, *bwarchive.businessweek.com*; D. Foust, G. Smith, & D. Rocks, 1999, Coke's man on the spot, May 3, bwarchive.businessweek.com; Going for broke, 1999, *The Economist,* August 16, *www.economist.com/editorial*; It's the real thing: Coca Cola preparing for dive into bottled water market, *Dallas Morning News,* February 20, F12; L. Light, 1999, The Pepsi generation, *Businessweek Online,* March 22, *bwarchive.businessweek.com.*

Speed of Competitive Actions and Competitive Responses

Time and speed are important in the 21st-century competitive landscape. The speed with which a firm can initiate competitive actions and competitive responses may determine its success. In the 21st-century competitive landscape, speed in developing a new product and moving it to the marketplace is becoming critical to establish a competitive advantage and earn above-average returns.[93]

Tesco and Sainsbury in Great Britain and Carrefours in France had to respond quickly to Wal-Mart's entry into their markets. Failure to do so could make them highly vulnerable to Wal-Mart's market power once it became established in their markets. In each country, the firms chose a different way to respond. Carrefour responded by acquiring a major competitor to increase its size, resource base, economies of scale, and breadth and depth of market power. In contrast, Tesco and Sainsbury chose to focus on a market niche in which Wal-Mart has not exhibited strength—e-commerce. Their actions were swift and helped the firms continue to be important competitors in their respective markets.

Speed in bringing their products to the marketplace is one of the problems U.S. automobile manufacturers have experienced in competing with Japanese firms. Some time ago, Japanese auto companies were able to design a new product and introduce it to the market within three years. In comparison, U.S. firms required between five and eight years to complete these activities. This time differential made it possible for Japanese firms to design two or three new automobiles and move them to the market in the same time it took a U.S. automaker to do one. Thereafter, Ford, GM, and DaimlerChrysler all reduced their development time to three to four years. However, Toyota responded by reducing its development time to a minimum of 15 months. In a global economy, although time is a critical source of competitive advantage, managing for speed requires more than attempting to have employees work faster. Essentially, it requires working smarter, using different types of organizational structures, and shortening the time it takes to bring a car to completion as primary work-related goals.[94] Research has shown that the pace of strategic decision making may be affected by an executive's cognitive ability, use of intuition, tolerance for risk, and propensity to act.[95] Executives who use intuition and have a greater tolerance for risk are predisposed to make faster strategic decisions than do those without such characteristics. Also, decisions are likely to occur faster in centralized organizations because they will not have to go through as many levels or get approval from as many people. More formalized and bureaucratic organizations, however, may find it difficult to make fast strategic decisions[96] because they require more layers of approval.

Jack Welch, former chairman and CEO of General Electric, states that speed is the ability sought by all of today's organizations.[97] He suggests that companies are striving to develop products faster, speed up production cycles in moving them to the market, and improve response time to customers. In Welch's opinion, having faster communications and moving with agility are critical to competitive success.

Innovation

In some industries, such as pharmaceuticals and computers, a third general factor, innovation, has long been known to have a strong influence on a firm's performance.[98] Innovation is increasing in importance in many industries in the 21st-century landscape. The strategic importance of innovation is explored further in Chapter 13. In today's global economy, research suggests that innovation, in both products and processes, is becoming linked with above-average returns in a growing number of industries.[99] One study, for example, found that companies with the highest performance also invested the most in research and development. In 1960, U.S. firms held more than two-thirds of the world market in 10 of the top 15 major industries. By 1970, the United States continued to dominate 9 of those 15 industries. However, by 1980, U.S. domination was limited to only 3 of the industries. The study found that this was due largely to changes in innovation: Firms from other countries were more innovative than U.S. firms in many of the industries.[100] In fact, a contributing factor to the productivity and technology problems experienced by U.S. firms has been managers' unwillingness to bear the costs and risks of long-term development of product and process innovations.[101]

In general, the dynamics of competition among firms in high-tech industries encourage significant allocations to each company's research and development operations.[102] In fact, as the number of competitors increases in an industry, so does the amount of innovation usually produced.[103] In particular, innovation is often a strength of small firms and acts to equalize the competitiveness between large and small firms (see Chapter 13). Innovation is especially important in the computer software industry. While there are different niches, and while separate companies have achieved significant market shares in these niches, Microsoft is probably the best-known and most dominant firm in the software industry. However, Sun Microsystems has targeted Microsoft. Sun acquired the Star Division Corporation, which makes a series of office software known as StarOffice. Sun's primary purpose in acquiring Star is to attack Microsoft with Web-based word-processing and spreadsheet applications. Sun plans to build StarOffice into a free Internet-based service that can be run directly with a Web browser, without the need to load large programs onto the PC. Sun's stated intention is to change the "rules of the game." Given that Microsoft earns approximately 40 percent of its revenue from sales of Office, this new challenge could present significant problems for the firm.[104] It also shows the need to continuously bring innovation to the market in the software industry.

In another industry in which innovation is important, mobile phones, Ericsson has fallen behind Nokia. Ericsson's problems stem primarily from being slow to bring innovations to the market. As a result, Nokia has moved ahead of the Swedish company. In 1999, the CEO of only 15 months was forced to resign. However, his supporters argue that he was treated unfairly because he was given a company with a poor product life cycle that could not be corrected in a short period of time. While Ericsson's problems can be solved, some analysts have predicted that the firm will need to embark on a process of managed decline.[105]

Firms competing in industries in which the pattern of competitive dynamics calls for innovation-related abilities should recognize that implementing innovations effectively can be difficult. Some researchers believe that a failure of implementation, not innovation, increasingly is the cause of many firms' inability to derive adequate competitive benefits from product and process innovations.[106] Among other capabilities, a firm requires executives who are able to integrate its innovation strategy with other strategies (such as the business-level strategies discussed in Chapter 4) and to recruit and select high-tech workers to successfully implement innovations.[107]

Procter & Gamble is a well-known company that has operated successfully in many global markets. However, it has suffered greatly from price competition and has been unable to differentiate itself through innovations. In fact, its new CEO in 1999, Durk Jager suggested that the firm's last important innovation was its feminine-hygiene product, Always, which was introduced in 1982. Thus, Jager has taken actions to triple the rate of Procter & Gamble's innovation and reduce the time it takes to introduce new products to the market by 50 percent. Of course, its competitors are likely to maintain or increase their own rates of innovation in response.[108]

Earlier, we suggested that large firms with significant market power that act like small firms—making strategic decisions and implementing them speedily—and that are innovative are strong competitors and are likely to earn above-average returns. However, no matter how large, fast, or innovative an organization is, the quality of its products and services also affects its industry's competitive dynamics and influences the firm's ability to achieve strategic competitiveness in domestic and global markets.

Quality

Product quality has become a universal theme in the global economy and continues to shape competitive dynamics in many industries.[109] Today, product quality is important in all industry settings and is a necessary, but not sufficient, condition for implementing a firm's strategy successfully. Without quality goods or services, strategic competitiveness cannot be achieved. Quality alone, however, does not guarantee that a firm will achieve strategic competitiveness or earn above-average returns. In the words of the president of the National Center for Manufacturing Sciences, a nonprofit research consortium, "Quality used to be a competitive issue out there, but now it's just the basic denominator to being in the market."[110]

This is the case in the café–bakery business, for example. Accepting product quality as a given, executives of competitors La Madeleine and Corner Bakery believe that their products are more than simply food. They suggest that their establishments and products contribute to a way of life for those interested in purchasing items from neighborhood bakeries with a family atmosphere.[111]

Quality involves meeting or exceeding customer expectations in the goods or services offered.

Quality involves meeting or exceeding customer expectations in the goods or services a firm offers.[112] The quality dimensions of goods and services are shown in Table 5.1. As a competitive dimension, quality is as important in the service sector as it is in the manufacturing sector.[113]

Quality begins at the top of the organization. Top management must create values for quality that permeate the entire organization.[114] These values should be built into strategies that reflect long-term commitments to customers, stockholders, and other important stakeholders.[115]

Quality and total quality management are closely associated with the philosophies and teachings of W. Edwards Deming (and, to a lesser extent, Armand Feigenbaum and Joseph Juran).[116] These individuals' contributions to the practice of

5.1 | Quality Dimensions of Goods and Services

Product Quality Dimensions

1. *Performance*—Operating characteristics
2. *Features*—Important special characteristics
3. *Flexibility*—Meeting operating specifications over some period of time
4. *Durability*—Amount of use before performance deteriorates
5. *Conformance*—Match with preestablished standards
6. *Serviceability*—Ease and speed of repair or normal service
7. *Aesthetics*—How a product looks and feels
8. *Perceived quality*—Subjective assessment of characteristics (product image)

Service Quality Dimensions

1. *Timeliness*—Performed in promised period of time
2. *Courtesy*—Performed cheerfully
3. *Consistency*—Giving all customers similar experiences each time
4. *Convenience*—Accessibility to customers
5. *Completeness*—Fully serviced, as required
6. *Accuracy*—Performed correctly each time

Source: Adapted from J. W. Dean, Jr., & J. R. Evans, 1994, *Total Quality: Management, Organization and Society* (St. Paul, MN: West Publishing Company); H. V. Roberts & B. F. Sergesketter, 1993, *Quality Is Personal* (New York: The Free Press); D. Garvin, 1988, *Managed Quality: The Strategic and Competitive Edge* (New York: The Free Press).

management are based on a simple, yet powerful, insight: the understanding that it costs less to make quality products than defect-ridden ones.

Total quality management is managerial innovation that emphasizes an organization's total commitment to the customer and to continuous improvement of every process through the use of data-driven, problem-solving approaches based on empowerment of employee groups and teams.

Total quality management (TQM) is a "managerial innovation that emphasizes an organization's total commitment to the customer and to continuous improvement of every process through the use of data-driven, problem-solving approaches based on empowerment of employee groups and teams."[117] Actually a philosophy about how to manage, TQM "combines the teachings of Deming and Juran on statistical process control and group problem-solving processes with Japanese values concerned with quality and continuous improvement."[118] Statistical process control (SPC) is a technique used to continually upgrade the quality of the goods or services a firm produces. SPC benefits the firm through the detection and elimination of variations in processes used to manufacture a good or service.[119]

Although there are skeptics, when applied properly, the principles of total quality management can help firms achieve strategic competitiveness and earn above-average returns.[120] Three principal goals sought when practicing total quality management are boosting customer satisfaction, reducing the amount of time required to introduce products into the marketplace, and cutting costs. These are accomplished in several ways, but most importantly, by empowering workers to achieve continuous improvements in all aspects of their tasks.[121] British Telecommunications (BT) uses a TQM system in order to be competitive with U.S. firms. In fact, BT implemented the system in 1986, so it has considerable experience with it. BT managers believe that the firm's TQM system has helped it to compete effectively in global markets.[122] Ironically, Deming's and Juran's ideas on quality and continuous improvement were adapted and implemented by Japanese firms long before many U.S. firms acknowledged their importance. For this reason, a host of Japanese companies developed a competitive advantage in product quality that was difficult for U.S. firms to overcome.[123] By implementing TQM systems effectively, many U.S. and Western European firms have overcome the original competitive advantage enjoyed by Japanese firms related to the quality of their products. Deming's 14 points for managing and achieving quality (see Table 5.2) have become a watchword in businesses around the world.

Embedded within Deming's 14 points for management is the importance of striving continuously to improve both the operation of a firm and the quality of its goods or services. In fact, Deming did not support use of the term "TQM," arguing that he did not know what total quality was and that it is impossible for firms to reach a goal of total quality. The pursuit of improvements in quality, Deming believed, should be a never-ending process.

Newer methods of TQM use benchmarking and emphasize organizational learning.[124] Benchmarking facilitates TQM by developing information on the best practices of other organizations and industries. This information is often used to establish goals for the firm's own TQM efforts. Benchmarking is a process by means of which a company can learn from the outcomes of other firms.[125] Because of the importance of quality (of both goods and services) in achieving competitive parity or a competitive advantage, many firms in the United States and around the world emphasize TQM and integrate it with their strategies.

In sum, relationships between each of the four general abilities (size, speed, innovation, and quality) influence a firm's competitive actions and outcomes. Those

TABLE 5.2 | Deming's 14 Points for Management

1. Create and publish to all employees a statement of the aims and purposes of the company or other organization. The management must demonstrate constantly their commitment to this statement.
2. Learn the new philosophy, top management and everybody.
3. Understand the purpose of inspection, for improvement of processes and reduction of costs.
4. End the practice of awarding business on the basis of price tag alone.
5. Improve constantly and forever the system of production and service.
6. Institute training.
7. Teach and institute leadership.
8. Drive out fear. Create trust. Create a climate for innovation.
9. Optimize toward the aims and purposes of the company—the efforts of teams, groups, staff areas.
10. Eliminate exhortations for the workforce.
11. (a) Eliminate numerical quotas for production. Instead, learn and institute methods for improvement. (b) Eliminate management by objective. Instead, learn the capabilities of processes and how to improve them.
12. Remove barriers that rob people of pride of workmanship.
13. Encourage education and self-improvement for everyone.
14. Take action to accomplish the transformation.

Source: Reprinted from *Out of the Crisis,* by W. Edwards Deming, by permission of MIT and The W. Edwards Deming Institute. Published by MIT, Center for Advanced Engineering Study, Cambridge, MA 02139. Copyright © 1986 by W. Edwards Deming.

responsible for selecting a firm's strategy should understand these relationships and anticipate that competitors will take competitive actions and competitive responses designed to exploit the positive relationships depicted in Figure 5.2. In the next section, we describe the different outcomes of competitive dynamics.

Outcomes of Interfirm Rivalry

Figure 5.1 illustrates various potential outcomes of interfirm rivalry. In some competitive environments, building a sustainable competitive advantage may be more likely than in others. As discussed in Chapter 3, one of the key determinants of sustainability is whether a firm's products are costly to imitate. Sustainability, therefore, might focus on different markets in which product imitability is largely or partially shielded.[126] In countries whose markets are largely open to international competitors, foreign rivals have made inroads into most major markets. However, even with strong rivalry and an increasing potential for imitability, some markets have been shielded from such competition. These markets are referred to as slow-cycle or sheltered markets. In other markets, product imitability is moderate, so they are labeled standard-cycle markets and are sometimes described as oligopolistic. In still other markets, firms operate in rapid, dynamic, and often entrepreneurial environments. These markets are identified as fast-cycle markets.[127]

FIGURE 5.2 | Effects of Firm Size, Speed of Decision Making and Actions, Innovations, and Quality on Sustainability of Competitor Actions and Outcomes

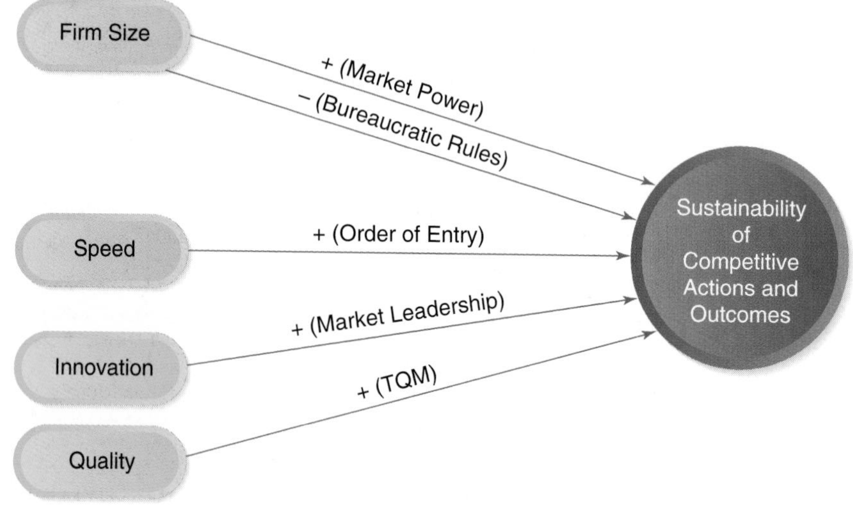

*Plus and minus signs indicate effects on performance.

Competitive Market Outcomes

Products in **slow-cycle markets** reflect strongly shielded resource positions wherein competitive pressures do not readily penetrate a firm's sources of strategic competitiveness.

Products in **slow-cycle markets** reflect strongly shielded resource positions wherein competitive pressures do not readily penetrate the firm's sources of strategic competitiveness. In economics, this situation is often characterized as a monopoly position. A firm that has a unique set of product attributes or an effective product design may dominate its markets for decades, as did IBM with large mainframe computers. This type of competitive position can be established even in markets where there is significant technological change; an example is Microsoft's position with respect to difficult-to-imitate, complex software systems. Of course, conditions have changed for IBM and also for Microsoft, as competitors such as Sun Microsystems close in on Microsoft and the government prosecutes the firm for anticompetitive practices. Other firms may be protected by regulations or laws prohibiting competition. For example, for a long time, the utilities industries were largely protected as legal monopolies. However, that stance has changed and competition is now allowed. In contrast, drug manufacturers still maintain a legally protected position under patent laws. Note that shielded advantages may be geographic; thus, the opening of huge emerging markets in Eastern Europe, Russia, China, and India offers strong motivation for firms to pursue such opportunities.

Although the idea of a monopoly, which has a single seller, restricted output, and high prices, is largely disallowed in the United States because of government policy restrictions, subtle and more complex variations are possible in local markets. This is exemplified by Wal-Mart's approach in its early years. The firm established a local monopoly in rural areas in the southwest United States and coupled it with an efficient distribution system to earn significantly above-average returns for its industry. Many airlines also seek to establish a shielded advantage through the innovation of hub control at airports. Examples are American Airlines' dominance in Dallas, Delta's hubs in Atlanta and Salt Lake City, and Continental's hubs in Newark (New York City), Houston, and Cleveland.

Effective product designs may enable the firms that produced them to dominate their markets for many years, as the examples of Microsoft and IBM show. These firms' advantages are drawn largely from their special core competencies, because their resources and capabilities are difficult to imitate. The sustainability of competitive action associated with a slow-cycle market is depicted in Figure 5.3. Because these markets (and hence the firms that operate in them) are largely protected, they usually enjoy the highest average price increase over time. Alternatively, price increases in standard-cycle markets often vary closely around zero.[128]

Products in **standard-cycle markets** reflect moderately shielded resource positions where competitive interaction penetrates a firm's sources of strategic competitiveness; but, with improvement of its capabilities, the firm may be able to sustain a competitive advantage.

Standard-cycle markets are more closely associated with the industrial organization economics approach exemplified in Porter's five forces model of competitive strategy (see Chapter 2). In these firms, strategy and organization are designed to serve high-volume or mass markets. The focus is on coordination and market control, as in the automobile and appliance industries.[129] Even though these firms may be able to sustain world-class products for decades (e.g., Coca-Cola), they may experience severe competitive pressures. Extended dominance and, in fact, world leadership are possible through continuing capital investment and superior learning, as was the case with Coca-Cola. However, as described in the last Strategic Focus, Coca-Cola is now experiencing substantial competitive pressures in several of its markets. In particular, Pepsi is taking strategic actions much more quickly than Coca-Cola. In contrast, less investment is made in innovation in protected markets. Although it may be difficult to enter

FIGURE

5.3 | Gradual Erosion of a Sustained Competitive Advantage

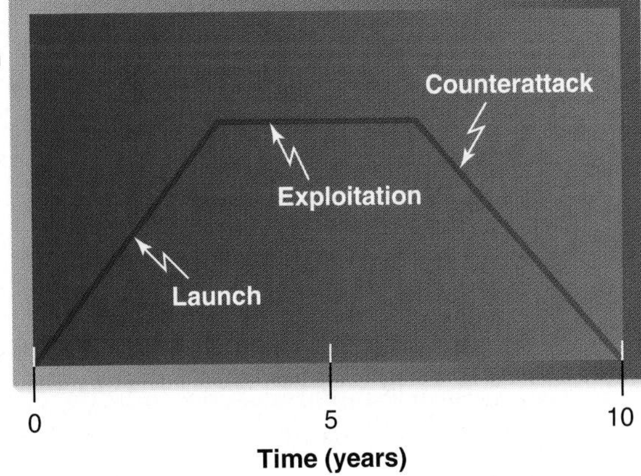

Source: Adapted from I. C. MacMillan, 1988, Controlling competitive dynamics by taking strategic initiative, *Academy of Management Executive*, II, 2: 111–118.

standard-cycle markets because of the competitive intensity, if a firm is successful and if its strategy is duplicated by competitors, more intense competitive pressures can be brought to bear. In that case, the competition may be similar to that found in fast-cycle markets.[130]

Standard-cycle markets that are intensely competitive may also require innovation (as discussed earlier). For example, a firm can capture market share in the standard-cycle market of brewing by offering innovative products. Anheuser-Busch recently introduced Tequiza beer to capture market share from the popular Mexican beer market in the United States. In 1998, imported beer sales increased by 15.5 percent in the nation, largely attributable to increased imports of Mexican beer. Some brands (e.g., Corona) increased sales by over 33 percent in 1998. In particular, Busch targeted Corona Beer, because it was the most popular Mexican beer. Corona is almost always served with a lime. Tequiza Beer has tequila and lime flavor added (but no tequila). Interestingly, Busch owns 50.2 percent of the firm that sells Corona. However, it is a noncontrolling interest. A spokesperson suggested that while Busch gained from sales of Corona, its distributors did not. Given the market power of Anheuser-Busch and its strong distribution system, analysts believe that Tequiza is likely to be a popular beer in the United States.[131]

Competing in Fast-Cycle Markets

In **fast-cycle markets** a competitive advantage cannot be sustained; firms attempt to gain temporary competitive advantages by strategically disrupting the market.

Achieving a sustained competitive advantage is possible in slow- and, possibly, standard-cycle markets. However, it is largely impossible to gain a sustained competitive advantage in a **fast-cycle market.** Figure 5.3 focuses on sustainable competitive advantage. Usually, there is an entrepreneurial launch stage of the strategy, then a period of exploitation, and, ultimately, a period of counterattack wherein the competitive advantage erodes. In fast-cycle markets, a competitive advantage can even create inertia and expose a firm to aggressive global competitors. Even though GM has economies of scale, a huge advertising budget, an efficient distribution system, cutting-edge R&D, and slack resources, many of its advantages have been eroded by global competitors in Europe and Japan. Fast-cycle markets are the most difficult to manage and are the most volatile. Such markets often experience average price reductions over time. For example, over a recent period, 10 fast-cycle markets experienced price reductions ranging from a minimum of 3.5 percent to a maximum of 29 percent.[132]

A new competitive advantage paradigm is emerging in which a firm seizes the initiative through a series of small steps, as illustrated in Figure 5.4. As the figure indicates, the idea is to create a counterattack before the advantage is eroded. The counterattack actually leads to cannibalizing a firm's own products through the next stage of product evolution and entry. Thus, the focus of this new paradigm is competitive disruption.[133] However, a firm can escalate competition in areas such as price and quality only so far before the dominant competitor seeks to achieve another level of competition focused on factors such as speed and know-how or innovation.

The telecommunications industry reflects a fast-cycle market. It is global in nature and highly dynamic. Firms in the industry have acquired cable companies and are now focusing on wireless communications companies. Most firms in the industry believe that the next generation of telecommunications will be based on wireless transmission. In 1999, Vodafone, a telecommunications firm based in Great Britain,

5.4 | **Obtaining Temporary Advantages to Create Sustained Advantage**

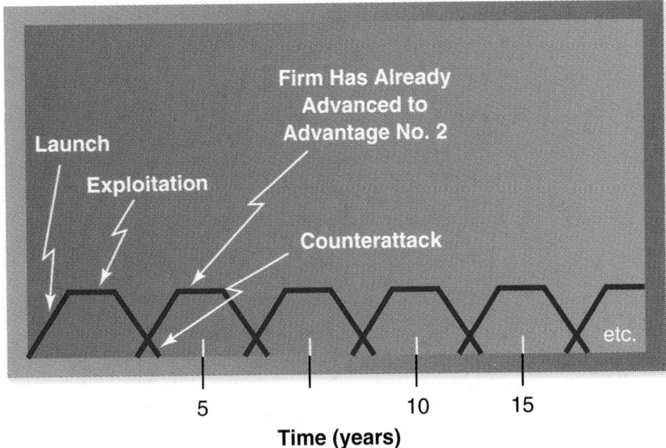

Source: Adapted from I. C. MacMillan, 1988, Controlling competitive dynamics by taking strategic initiative, *Academy of Management Executive*, II (2): 111–118.

acquired AirTouch Communications, a U.S.-based firm. Vodafone also has acquired Mannesman, a fast-growing wireless operator based in Germany. For similar reasons, MCI WorldCom acquired Sprint. The expectation is that telephone calls and access to the Internet are likely to be provided by wireless networks. Many of the firms in this industry are forming alliances to compete more effectively in global markets. An example is the alliance between AT&T and British Telecommunications to provide cellular communications.[134]

In an allied industry, telecommunications equipment, Nortel recently counterattacked Cisco Systems, which has been an especially effective competitor. Nortel announced that it was introducing new software and dramatically reducing hardware prices. The firm established licensing agreements with Intel and Microsoft. Cisco, a fast-growing data communications equipment manufacturer, developed the router that controls traffic on the Internet. Nortel was slow to respond to the Internet and is trying to make up lost ground. Cisco managers referred to Nortel's actions as a fire sale. They suggested that it indicated that the firm was desperate.[135]

The array of competitive actions and competitive responses occurring over time in the telecommunications industry demonstrates the four strategic steps shown in Table 5.3. At different times and with different products, several telecommunications firms have been able to (1) identify a competitive opportunity that disrupted the status quo, (2) create a temporary advantage that was eroded through aggressive responses by their competitors, (3) seize the initiative from their competitors through effective competitive actions, and (4) sustain their momentum by continually offering new products and entering new markets. Thus, firms must exhibit strategic flexibility if they are to be successful competing in fast-cycle markets. When operating under these mar-

5.3 | Strategic Steps for Seizing the Initiative in Fast-Cycle Markets

1. *Disrupting the status quo*	Competitors disrupt the status quo by identifying new opportunities to serve the customer and by shifting the rules of competition. These moves end the old pattern of competitive interaction between rivals. Disrupting the status quo requires speed and variety in approach.
2. *Create temporary advantage*	Disruption creates temporary advantages that are based on better knowledge of customers, technology, and the future. Derived from customer orientation and employee empowerment throughout the entire organization, these advantages are short lived and eroded by fierce competition.
3. *Seizing the initiative*	By moving aggressively into new areas of competition, acting to create a new advantage, or undermining a competitor's old advantage, the company seizes the initiative. This throws the opponent off balance and puts it at a disadvantage for a while. The opponent is forced to play catch-up, reacting rather than shaping the future with its own actions to seize the initiative. The initiator is proactive, whereas competitors are forced to be reactive.
4. *Sustaining the momentum*	Several actions in a row are taken to seize the initiative and create momentum. The company continues to develop new advantages and does not wait for competitors to undermine them before launching the next initiative. This succession of actions sustains the momentum. Continually offering new initiatives is the only source of sustainable competitive advantage in fast-cycle environments.

Source: Adapted from R. A. D'Aveni, 1995, Coping with hypercompetition: Utilizing the new 7's framework, *Academy of Management Executive*, IX (3): 45–60.

ket conditions, firms must learn how to respond quickly to technological change and market opportunities by offering more new products, broader product lines, and product upgrades more rapidly.[136]

Competitive Dynamics and Industry Evolution Outcomes

Because industries and markets evolve over time, so do the competitive dynamics between firms in an industry. We have examined how firms interact in a short span of time using an action–response framework, but we have not yet considered how competitive interaction evolves over longer periods of time. Three general stages of industry evolution are relevant to our study of competitive dynamics: the emerging, growth, and mature stages. These are shown in Figure 5.5.

Firms entering emerging industries attempt to establish a niche or an initial form of dominance within an industry. Competitive rivalry for the loyalty of customers is serious. In these industries, depending on the types of products, firms often attempt to establish product quality, technological superiority, or advantageous relationships with suppliers in order to develop a competitive advantage in the pursuit of strategic competitiveness. These firms are striving to build their reputation. As a result, a variety of different competitive strategies may be employed in such an industry. This diversity can be beneficial to many of the firms in the industry, helping them avoid direct competition and gain dominance in market niches.[137] Although speed is important in emerging industries, access to capital is often the critical issue. Therefore, it is not uncommon to have strategic alliances develop between a new firm entering the market and a more established firm that wishes to gain a foothold in the new industry.[138]

FIGURE

5.5 | An Action-Based Model of the Industry Life Cycle

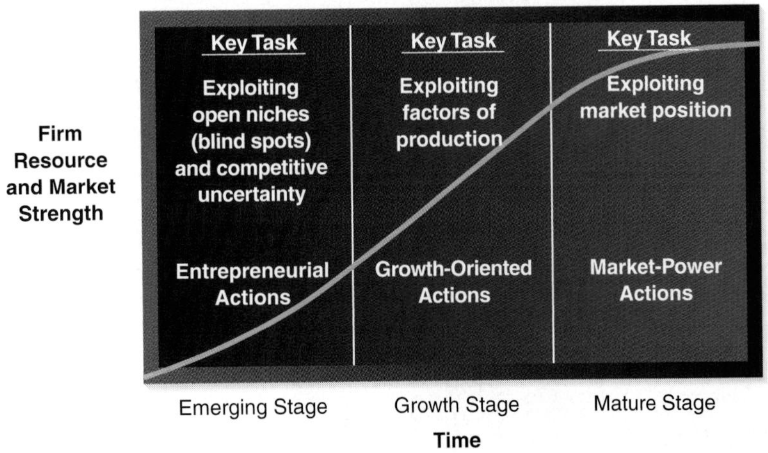

Source: Adapted from C. M. Grimm & K. G. Smith, 1997, *Strategy as Action: Industry Rivalry and Coordination* (St. Paul, MN: West Publishing Co.).

Firms in emerging industries often rely on top management to develop market opportunities. Steve Jobs and Bill Gates were able to foresee the future possibilities of the microcomputer and the standardized microcomputer operating system. Their vision of an uncertain environment gave rise to Apple Computer and Microsoft, respectively. Thus, firms in an emerging stage take *entrepreneurial actions* that focus on entrepreneurial discovery in uncertain environments.

Firms in growth-oriented industries are survivors from the emerging-industry stage. In the growth stage, *growth-oriented actions* are emphasized, which tend to create product standardization as consumer demand creates a mass market with growth potential. Thus, many of these firms are more established, but no less competitive. In fact, as the industry begins to mature, the variety of strategies that are implemented tends to decrease. Entrepreneurial actions are indeed still taking place, but there is more emphasis on growth-oriented actions. Oftentimes, groups of firms will follow a similar strategy and thus become directly competitive. However, the rivalry between groups may be more indirect.[139] In industries in which there is considerable rivalry both within strategic groups and between firms in separate strategic groups, firms frequently earn below-average returns.[140]

Some of these industries may also be fragmented. Fragmented markets, such as fast food restaurants, tend to offer standardized facilities and products, but leave decentralized decision making to the local units. The standardization allows for low-cost competition. The primary value added comes from the services that are provided. These markets offer a prime opportunity for franchising, because of the ability to standardize facilities, operations, and products.[141]

Steve Jobs of Apple Computer foresaw the future possibilities of the microcomputer and the need for user-friendly software.

The Internet access market has become relatively fragmented, but remains an emerging growth industry as well. America Online (AOL) is the market leader, particularly after acquiring its chief competitor, CompuServe. However, there is considerable rivalry in this market, with at least eight other major competitors, primary among which is Microsoft, with Microsoft Net (MSN), and Prodigy. While AOL is the dominant force in the Internet access business, Microsoft cannot be ignored. In particular, Bill Gates once threatened to buy or bury AOL. Although he has not been able to do that, Microsoft is a formidable foe. As stated by one author, "Microsoft's past is littered with the corpses of old enemies."[142] AOL is strengthened with its acquisition of Netscape and its alliance with Sun Microsystems, another old nemesis of Microsoft.

In response, Microsoft has devised a three-pronged attack on AOL. First, it has developed and brought to market an instant messaging system to compete directly with AOL's. Second, Microsoft is preparing the way for low-cost or free Internet access in the United States. This move could be particularly damaging to AOL, as the firm receives 77 percent of its revenues from Internet subscriptions. Third, Microsoft is trying to emphasize broadband communication to revolutionize the Internet as a platform for "infotainment" and commerce. Both firms are successful and powerful. AOL is in a good position in the markets it serves; however, it must be careful because Microsoft has the capability to win competitive battles and harm AOL.[143] AOL's recent merger with Time Warner has increased its strength and reduced the likelihood that Microsoft will be able to "bury it." In nonfragmented industries, the speed with which new products are developed and introduced to the marketplace becomes an important competitive weapon. Consumers tend to be more sophisticated and expect not only quality products, but also product designs that meet their needs. Firms that can move new products which better meet consumers' needs to the market more quickly than competitors are likely to gain a competitive advantage.

In mature industries, there are usually fewer surviving competitors. Those that do survive tend to be larger and hold dominant market share positions. Therefore, firms in the mature stage emphasize *market-power actions,* which focus the firm's attention on offering product lines that are profitable and producing those products in an efficient manner. Product innovations and entrepreneurial actions continue, but are greatly deemphasized. Process innovations are emphasized more, because they maintain dominance through cost efficiencies and the quality of the product manufactured and provided to customers.[144] Finally, firms in industries in the mature stage frequently seek to expand into international markets or increase their emphasis on international operations and sales to extend a product's life. Thus, growth-oriented actions also continue, even though the primary emphasis is on market-power actions.

In sum, once mature firms have a dominant market share, they seek to exploit their market power and extensive resources and capabilities to maintain dominance. The PC/server operating system market exemplifies a mature industry. Microsoft rather quickly became the dominant force in this industry and has held a virtual monopoly for the last decade. Because of its position, Microsoft provides incremental innovation of its Windows system (the latest version being Windows 2000). However, recently, a challenge to Microsoft's dominance developed from an operating system called Linux, which is distributed free by Red Hat and a few other entrepreneurial firms. These firms obtain their revenue by providing support operations for those who adopt the Linux operating system. Microsoft is concerned enough to develop an "attack team" designed to monitor and analyze Linux and its distributors. The purpose of this team, as described by Microsoft's director of marketing for Windows 2000, is "Getting inside the head of our competitor." Linux is targeted for the server market, of which it has captured approximately 17 percent, while Windows holds about 36 percent. The Linux advantage, besides the fact that the software is free, is that it is about 50 percent faster than Windows.[145] It will be interesting to observe the competitive battle between the rivals as it plays out.

This chapter concludes our emphasis on business-level strategy, although some business-level issues are discussed in subsequent chapters (e.g., Chapters 8, 9, and 11). The next chapter begins our discussion of corporate-level strategy.

Summary

- Competitive rivalry entails actions and responses to competitive actions taken by other firms. Competitive attack and response are more likely when awareness, motivation, and abilities to attack or respond are present.
- Market commonality, as determined by multimarket contact in such industries as airlines, is likely to lead to the dampening of a potential attack. However, if an offensive action is taken, a response is more likely in the presence of market commonality.
- Awareness of competitors' ability to attack or respond is facilitated by resource similarity among competitors. Those with similar resources are more likely to attack and respond than are those with less overlap in resources.
- First movers can gain a competitive advantage and customer loyalty in the market. First movers also take more risks; however, they often are higher performers. Second movers—particularly those that are larger and faster—can also gain a competitive advantage and earn at least average returns because they imitate first movers, but do not take some of the risk that first movers do. In fact, some second movers may gain significant market share and outperform the first movers. They do this when they carefully observe the market's reaction and are able to improve the product introduced by the first mover and correct or avoid its mistakes. However, the longer the time required for the second mover to respond, the higher is the probability that the first mover will enjoy strong performance gains. Late movers (those that respond a long time after the original action was taken) tend to be lower performers and much less competitive.
- The probability of a response by a competitor to a competitive action is based partially on the extent to which the competitor is dependent on the particular market in which the action was taken. In addition, the probability of response is based on the type of action, the reputation of the firm taking the strategic action (which affects the expectation of the firm's success), and the resources available to the competitor contemplating the response.
- The two types of competitive actions are strategic and tactical. Strategic actions are more long term in nature, require many specific resources, and are difficult to reverse. By contrast, tactical actions tend to be more short term in orientation, require fewer and more general resources, and can be reversed more easily. More tactical, rather than strategic, actions are taken, and more responses are made to tactical than to strategic actions. It is easier to respond to a tactical action, partly because doing so requires fewer resources. In addition, a tactical action is likely to have a shorter-term effect than a strategic action. Responses to strategic actions are more difficult, require more resources, and require a longer-term investment.
- When competitors are highly dependent on a market in which competitive actions are taken, there is a high probability that they will respond to such actions. However, firms

that are more diversified across markets are less likely to respond to a particular action that affects only one of the markets in which they compete.

- The highest probability of a response comes when an action is taken by a market leader. Furthermore, when a market leader takes an action, a competitor is more likely to imitate it. Alternatively, if the firm has a reputation for taking more complex and risky actions, there is a lower probability of response. A price predator is also less likely to elicit a response from competitors.
- Those with a larger resource base are more likely to respond to strategic actions than are those with fewer resources. Furthermore, the probability of response is determined not only by the amount of resources, but by the ability to use those resources in taking competitive actions.
- Characteristics important to engaging in competitive actions and responses include the relative size of the acting and responding firms, the function of speed in the market or industry, the importance of innovation in competitive moves, and the quality of the competing firms' products.
- Large firms often have strong market power. However, as firms grow larger, they frequently institute bureaucratic rules, procedures, and structures that have the effect of reducing the probability that a firm will take actions and respond to others' actions. In addition, they reduce the speed with which a firm may be able to implement an action or respond to competitors' actions.
- Speed is becoming increasingly important in many industries in order to gain and hold a competitive advantage. In fact, many large firms must act like small firms (i.e., be flexible and agile) to be competitive. This may require that they decentralize many responsibilities and decisions and that they create cross-functional teams in order to speed a number of processes (e.g., the innovation process).
- Both product and process innovation are becoming increasingly important in the competitive posture of many industries. Some research has shown that firms which invest more in R&D and create more innovation tend to have higher performance in multiple industries. Product innovation tends to be more important in emerging and growth industries, process innovation in mature industries.
- Product quality has become critical to maintaining competitive parity in most industries. Total quality management must be infused throughout the organization by top management and integrated with firm strategies. Benchmarking is used to help make comparative judgments about quality relative to other firms' best practices.
- There are three basic market outcomes of competitive rivalry among firms. Slow-cycle markets allow a firm to establish competitive advantage in a near-monopoly situation. Until recently, many utility firms were in this position. Standard-cycle markets allow market situations in which sustainability is possible. Firms that have multimarket contact may dampen competition somewhat. Fast-cycle markets create a situation in which only temporary competitive advantage is possible, such as that in the electronics and pharmaceutical industries.
- In fast-cycle markets, competitive disruption, a new paradigm of competitive action, may be necessary. This usually involves cannibalization of a previous product by reducing prices, while establishing a new product at the high end of the market, with increased performance at a premium price.
- Industry evolution is important in determining the type of competition and competitive actions that are emphasized by a firm. For example, firms in an emerging industry attempt to establish a reputation and develop a market niche in technology or the quality of products they provide. Their main task is to establish an entrepreneurial action, usually in an uncertain environment. In growth industries, the firm may place special emphasis on innovation to increase economies of scale. The speed of competitive actions taken is also important. The key task is to pursue growth-oriented actions by exploiting factors of production to increase the firm's dominance. In mature industries, with fewer competitors, special emphasis is placed on market-power actions designed to defend the most profitable product lines and processes in order to produce and distribute those products with the greatest efficiency (lowest cost). Entrepreneurial, growth-oriented, and market-power actions are taken at all stages, but the emphasis is different at each stage.

Review Questions

1. What two factors contribute to awareness, motivation, and ability in competitor analysis?
2. What are the advantages and disadvantages of being a first mover? a second mover? a late mover?

3. On what four factors is the likelihood of a response to a competitive action based?
4. What is the likelihood of response to a tactical action? a strategic action? actions taken by market leaders? Explain why in each of these cases.
5. How does size affect strategic actions and responses?
6. Why is speed important in many industries? What can firms do to increase their speed in making and implementing strategic decisions?
7. In what types of industries is innovation important in gaining competitive advantage? Explain the importance of product and process innovations for success in different industries.
8. What are the three types of markets and the nature of rivalry in each?
9. How does industry evolution affect interfirm rivalry? Identify three stages of industry evolution, and briefly explain the types of competitive actions emphasized in those stages.

Application Discussion Questions

1. Read the popular business press (e.g., *Business Week, Fortune, Fast Company*), and identify a strategic action and a tactical action taken by firms approximately two years ago. Next, use the Internet to search the popular business press to see if, and how, competitors responded to those actions. Explain the actions and the responses, linking your findings to the discussion in this chapter.
2. Why would a firm regularly choose to be a second mover? Likewise, why would a firm purposefully be a late mover?
3. How did Wal-Mart's strategic actions affect its primary European competitors? How will Wal-Mart's new e-commerce strategy affect competitors?
4. Choose a large firm and examine the popular business press to identify how its size, speed of actions, level of innovation, and quality of goods or services have affected its competitive position in its industry. Explain your findings.
5. Identify a firm in a fast-cycle market. What strategic actions account for its success or failure over the last several years? How has the Internet affected the firm?

Ethics Questions

1. Are there some industries in which ethical practices are more important than in other industries? If so, name the industries that are ethical, and explain how the competitive actions and competitive responses might differ for these industries compared with a typical industry?
2. When engaging in competitive rivalry, firms jockey for a market position that is advantageous, relative to competitors. In this jockeying, what types of competitor intelligence-gathering approaches are ethical? How has the Internet affected competitive intelligence activities?
3. A second mover is a firm that responds to a first mover's competitive actions, often through imitation. Is there anything unethical about how a second mover engages in competition? Why or why not?
4. Standards for competitive rivalry differ in countries throughout the world. What should firms do to cope with these differences? How do the differences relate to ethical practices?
5. Could total quality management practices result in firms operating more ethically than before such practices were implemented? If so, what might account for an increase in the ethical behavior of a firm using TQM principles?
6. What ethical issues are involved in fast-cycle markets?

Internet Exercise

With an offer of around 270 billion deutsche marks (U.S. $140 billion), Chris Gent, the head of Britain's telecommunications giant Vodafone, planned to acquire the traditional German firm, Mannesmann AG, by February 2000. In a last-minute effort in January 2000 to stave off the hostile takeover, Mannesmann attempted to acquire NetCologne to strengthen its position against Vodafone. Look up Vodafone (**www.vodafone.co.uk**) and Mannesmann (**www.mannesmann.de**) on the Web to see how the merger progressed and how each company's stocks reacted to the news. How did MCI WorldCom (**www.wcom.com**), Vodafone's lead competitor, respond to these competitive actions?

***e-project:** Discuss how the Internet has become a vital component in increasing the speed, ease, and frequency of today's large mergers and acquisitions.

Notes

1. J. Kurtzman, 1998, An interview with C. K. Prahalad, in J. Kurtzman (ed.), *Thought Leaders* (San Francisco: Jossey-Bass), 40–51; C. M. Grimm & K. G. Smith, 1997, *Strategy as Action: Industry Rivalry and Coordination* (Cincinnati: South-Western College Publishing); A. Y. Illinitch & R. A. D'Aveni, 1996, New organizational forms and strategies for managing in hypercompetitive environments, *Organization Science,* 7: 211–220.
2. G. Colvin, 1997, The most valuable quality in a manager, *Fortune,* December 29, 279–280.
3. Target: Wal-Mart, 1999, *Wall Street Journal Interactive Edition,* October 21, *www.interactive.wsj.com/articles.*
4. N. Byrnes & L. Armstrong, 1999, When Wal-Mart flexes its cybermuscles, *Business Week,* July 26, 82–83.
5. C. K. Prahalad, 1999, Changes in the competitive battlefield, Mastering Strategy (Part Two), *Financial Times,* October 4, 2–4.
6. J. Fox, R. Gann, A. Shur, L. Von Glahn, & B. Zaas, 1999, Process uncertainty: A new dimension for new product development, *Engineering Management Journal,* 10(3): 19–27.
7. G. McWilliams, 1999, Compaq's losses of big clients may foster plummeting profits, *Wall Street Journal Interactive Edition,* July 22, *www.interactive.wsj.com/articles.*
8. D. L. Deeds, D. DeCarolis, & J. Coobes, 2000, Dynamic capabilities and new product development in high technology adventures: An empirical analysis of new biotechnology firms, *Journal of Business Venturing,* 15: 211–229; C. V. Callhan & B. A. Pasterneck, 1999, Corporate strategy in the digital age, *Strategy & Business,* 15: 10–14; B. H. Clark, 1998, Managing competitive interactions, *Marketing Management,* 7(4): 8–20.
9. N. Munk, 1999, Title fight, *Fortune,* June 21, 84–94.
10. E. Noonan, 1999, Small booksellers struggle to beat out Internet retail, *Bryan-College Station Eagle,* June 14, A7.
11. S. Thurm & R. Quick, 1999, Amazon.com is granted an injunction in barnesandnoble.com patent dispute, *Wall Street Journal Interactive Edition,* December 3, *www.interactive.wsj.com/articles.*
12. P. M. Reilly, 1999, Barnesandnoble.com's redesign yields new online music store, *Wall Street Journal Interactive Edition,* July 7, *www.interactive.wsj.com/articles.*
13. G. Anders, 1999, Amazon.com buys 35% stake of Seattle online grocery firm, *Wall Street Journal,* May 18, B8.
14. B. Wysocki, Jr., 1999, The outlook, *Wall Street Journal Interactive Edition,* June 28, *www.interactive.wsj.com/articles*; W. Zellner, S. Anderson, & K. Morris, 1999, The big guys go online, *Business Week,* September 6, 30–32.
15. O. Gadiesh & J. L. Gilbert, 1998, Profit pools: A fresh look at strategy, *Harvard Business Review,* 76(3): 139–142.
16. N. Wingfield, 1999, Merger shows retailers can't cut prices forever, *Wall Street Journal Interactive Edition,* July 15, *www.interactive.wsj.com/articles*; J. Harding & P. T. Larsen, 1999, Carlton and United News set to merge, *www.ft.com,* November 25, www.ft.com/hippocampus; J. Bennett, 1999, A torrent of competition drives consolidation of Web companies, *Wall Street Journal Interactive Edition,* July 14, *www.interactive.wsj.com/articles.*
17. L. B. Ward, 2000, Mexican firm buys CompUSA *Dallas Morning News,* January 25, D1, D11; A. Goldstein, 1999, Rewiring plan: CompUSA to expand offerings amid rising competition, *Dallas Morning News,* March 11, D1, D11; R. Quick, 1999, Online-retailing revenue is seen totaling 2 1/2 times 1998's figures, *Wall Street Journal Interactive Edition,* July 19, *www.interactive.wsj.com/articles.*
18. E. K. Clemons, 1997, Technology-driven environmental shifts and the sustainable competitive disadvantage of previously dominant companies, in G. S. Day & D. J. Reibstein (eds.), *Wharton on Dynamic Competitive Strategy* (New York: John Wiley & Sons), 99–126.
19. B. S. Silverman, J. A. Nickerson, & J. Freeman, 1997, Profitability, transactional alignment, and organizational mortality in the U.S. trucking industry, *Strategic Management Journal,* 18 (Special Summer Issue): 31–52.
20. R. Gulati, 1999, Network location and learning: The influence of network resources and firm capabilities, *Strategic Management Journal,* 20: 397–420; A. C. Inkpen & P. W. Beamish, 1997, Knowledge, bargaining power, and the instability of international joint ventures, *Academy of Management Review,* 22: 177–202; J. Stiles, 1995, Collaboration for competitive advantage: The changing world of alliances and partnerships, *Long Range Planning,* 28: 109–112.
21. D. B. Holm, K. Eriksson, & J. Johanson, 1999, Creating value through mutual commitment to business network relationships, *Strategic Management Journal,* 20: 467–486; M. Sakakibara, 1997, Heterogeneity of firm capabilities and cooperative research and development: An empirical examination of motives, *Strategic Management Journal,* 18, Special Summer Issue: 143–164.
22. G. S. Day & D. J. Reibstein, 1997, The dynamic challenges for theory and practice, in G. S. Day & D. J. Reibstein (eds.), *Wharton on Competitive Strategy* (New York: John Wiley & Sons), 2.
23. S. J. Marsh, 1998, Creating barriers for foreign competitors: A study of the impact of anti-dumping actions on the performance of U.S. firms, *Strategic Management Journal,* 19: 25–37; K. G. Smith, C. M. Grimm, & S. Wally, 1997, Strategic groups and rivalrous firm behavior: Towards a reconciliation, *Strategic Management Journal,* 18: 149–157.
24. R. A. Klavans, C. A. Di Benedetto, & J. J. Prudom, 1997, Understanding competitive interactions: The U.S. commercial aircraft market, *Journal of Managerial Issues,* IX(1) 13–36.
25. Day & Reibstein, *Wharton on Competitive Strategy;* M. E. Porter, 1980, *Competitive Strategy* (New York: The Free Press), 17.
26. H. Simonian, 1998, Renault expands horizons, *Financial Times,* January 2, 10.
27. Autos: The Global Six, 1999, *BusinessWeek Online,* January 25, *www.businessweek.com/bwarchive.*
28. K. Cool, L. H. Roller, & B. Leleux, 1999, The relative impact of actual and potential rivalry on firm profitability in the pharmaceutical industry, *Strategic Management Journal,* 20: 1–14.
29. W. P. Putsis, Jr., 1999, Empirical Analysis of Competitive Interaction in Food Product Categories, *Agribusiness,* 15(3): 295–311.
30. D. Morse, 1999, Tultex seeks bankruptcy protection, plans to shut six plants, cut 2,600 jobs, *Wall Street Journal Interactive Edition,* December 6, *www.interactive.wsj.com/articles.*
31. S. A. Forest, 1999, A penney saved? *Business Week,* March 20, 64–66.
32. Porter, *Competitive Strategy.*
33. A. Klein, 1999, Shutter snaps on Fisher's leadership at Kodak, *Wall Street Journal,* June 10, B1, B4.
34. J. A. C. Baum & H. J. Korn, 1999, Dynamics of dyadic competitive interaction, *Strategic Management Journal,* 20: 251–278; C. R. Henderson & W. Mitchell, 1997, The interactions of organizational and competitive influences on strategy and performance, *Strategic Management Journal,* 18 (Special Summer Issue): 5–14.
35. W. Ocasio, 1997, Towards an attention-based view of the firm, *Strategic Management Journal,* 18 (Special Summer Issue): 187–206.
36. Grimm & Smith, *Strategy as Action,* 75–102; K. Krabuanrat & R. Phelps, 1998, Heuristics and rationality in strategic decision making: An exploratory study, *Journal of Business Research,* 41: 83–93.
37. G. P. Hodgkinson & G. Johnson, 1994, Exploring the mental models of competitive strategists: The case for a processual approach, *Journal of Management Studies,* 31: 525–551; J. F. Porac & H.

Thomas, 1994, Cognitive categorization and subjective rivalry among retailers in a small city, *Journal of Applied Psychology,* 79: 54–66.

38. N. J. Vilcassim, V. Kadiyali, & P. K. Chintagunta, 1999, Investigating dynamic multifirm market interactions in price and advertising, *Management Science,* 45(4): 499–518.
39. N. Houthoofd & A. Heene, 1997, Strategic groups as subsets of strategic scope groups in the Belgian brewing industry, *Strategic Management Journal,* 18: 653–666; G. P. Carroll & A. Swaminathan, 1992, The organizational ecology of strategic groups in the American brewing industry from 1975–1988, *Industrial and Corporate Change,* 1: 65–97.
40. L. C. Thurow, 1999, *Building Wealth: The New Rules for Individuals, Companies and Nationals in a Knowledge-Based Economy* (New York: Harper Collins); K. Ohmae, 1985, *Triad Power* (New York: The Free Press).
41. J. Gimeno & C. Y. Woo, 1999, Multimarket contact, economies of scope, and firm performance, *Academy of Management Journal,* 42(3): 239–259.
42. J. Gimeno, 1999, Reciprocal threats in multimarket rivalry: Staking out 'spheres of influence' in the U.S. airline industry, *Strategic Management Journal,* 20: 101–128; N. Fernandez & P. L. Marin, 1998, Market power and multimarket contact: Some evidence from the Spanish hotel industry, *Journal of Industrial Economics,* 46(3): 301–315.
43. M. J. Chen, 1996, Competitor analysis and interfirm rivalry: Toward a theoretical integration, *Academy of Management Review,* 21: 100–134.
44. H. J. Korn & J. A. C. Baum, 1999, Chance, imitative, and strategic antecedents to multimarket contact, *Academy of Management Journal,* 42: 171–193.
45. S. Javachandran, J. Gimeno, & P. R. Varadarajan, 1999, Theory of multimarket competition: A synthesis and implications for marketing strategy, *Journal of Marketing,* 63: 49–66.
46. R. G. McGrath, M. J. Chen, & I. C. MacMillan, 1998, Multimarket maneuvering in uncertain spheres of influence: Resource diversion strategies, *Academy of Management Review,* 23: 724–740.
47. J. A. Chevalier, 1999, When it can be good to burn your boats, Mastering Strategy (Part Four), *Financial Times,* October 25, 2–3; M. A. Peteraf, 1993, Intraindustry structure and response toward rivals, *Journal of Managerial Decision Economics,* 14: 519–528.
48. Grimm & Smith, *Strategy as Action,* 84; Chen, Competitor analysis.
49. Grimm & Smith, *Strategy as Action,* 125.
50. B. Horovitz, 1997, Coca-Cola, Pepsi tap bottled water market, *USA Today,* August 27, B10.
51. P. Abrahams & L. Kehoe, 1999, NEC and Bull pull out of US market, *www.ft.com,* November 4, *www.ft.com/hippocampus.*
52. W. Mitchell, 1999, Alliances: Achieving long-term value and short-term goals Mastering Strategy (Part Four), *Financial Times,* October 18, 6–11.
53. P. Abrahams, 1999, NEC/Mitsubishi: Competition forces joint venture, *www.ft.com,* October 1, *www.ft.com/hippocampus.*
54. Global crossing and Hutchison form telecom, web joint venture, 1999, *Wall Street Journal Interactive Edition,* November 15, *www.interactive.wsj.com/articles.*
55. K. P. Coyne & R. Dye, 1998, The competitive dynamics of network-based businesses, *Harvard Business Review,* 76(1): 99–109.
56. Smith & Grimm, *Strategy as Action,* 53–74.
57. A. A. Lado, N. G. Boyd, & S. C. Hanlon, 1997, Competition, cooperation, and the search for economic rents: A syncretic model, *Academy of Management Review,* 22: 110–141.
58. J. L. C. Cheng & I. F. Kesner, 1997, Organizational slack and response to environmental shifts: The impact of resource allocation patterns, *Journal of Management,* 23: 1–18.
59. M. Wallin, 1999, Supermarket chain to bring online shopping to Argentina, *Wall Street Journal Interactive Edition,* July 30, *www.interactive.wsj.com/articles.*
60. M. B. Lieberman & D. B. Montgomery, 1988, First-mover advantages, *Strategic Management Journal,* 9: 41–58.
61. K. G. Smith, C. M. Grimm, & M. J. Gannon, 1992, *Dynamics of Competitive Strategy* (Newberry Park, CA: Sage).
62. A. Ginsberg & N. Venkatraman, 1992, Investing in new information technology: The role of competitive posture and issue diagnosis, *Strategic Management Journal,* 13 (Special Summer Issue): 37–53.
63. H. R. Greve, 1998, Managerial cognition and the mimetic adoption of market positions: What you see is what you do, *Strategic Management Journal,* 19: 967–988.
64. R. Brooks, 1999, Bank One's strategy as competition grows: New, online institution, *Wall Street Journal,* August 25, A2, A8.
65. M. Zetlin, 1999, When it's smarter to be second to market, *Management Review,* March, 30–34.
66. G. J. Tellis & P. N. Golder, 1996, First to market, first to fail? Real causes of enduring market leadership, *Sloan Management Review Winter,* 57–66.
67. Smith, Grimm, & Gannon, *Dynamics of Competitive Strategy.*
68. New Balance Home Page, 2000, *www.newbalance.com,* February 1; I. Pereira, 1998, Sneaker company tags out-of-breath baby boomers, *Wall Street Journal,* January 16, B1, B2.
69. E. White, 1999, Avon tries to exploit internet without alienating its 'ladies', *Wall Street Journal Interactive Edition,* December 28, *www.interactive.wsj.com/articles.*
70. K. J. Delaney, 1999, Dell launches internet access free of charge in Europe, *Wall Street Journal Interactive Edition,* June 9, *www.interactive.wsj.com/articles.*
71. D. Morse, 2000, Breakthrough product visits funeral homes: Partial casket display, *Wall Street Journal,* January 7, A1, A10; D. Fisher, 1999, Grave dancer, *Forbes,* June 14, 77–78.
72. G. S. Day, 1997, Assessing competitive arenas: Who are your competitors? In G. S. Day & D. J. Reibstein (eds.), *Wharton on Competitive Strategy* (New York: John Wiley & Sons), 25–26.
73. K. Labich, 1994, Air wars over Asia, *Fortune,* April 4, 93–98.
74. Grimm & Smith, *Strategy as Action,* 134.
75. W. J. Ferrier, K. G. Smith, & C. M. Grimm, 1999, The role of competitive actions in market share erosion and industry dethronement: A study of industry leaders and challengers, *Academy of Management Journal,* 42: 372–388.
76. Smith, Grimm, & Gannon, *Dynamics of Competitive Strategy.*
77. Ibid.
78. Burger with fries and videos to go, 1999, *Financial Times,* April 18, 7.
79. N. Cope, 1999, Tesco and Sainsbury battle for home-shopping market, *Independent News,* December 1, *www.independent...inessother/tescoonline.*
80. W. Conard, 1999, Toys 'R' Us plans online challenge, *Dallas Morning News,* June 9, D11.
81. Boeing could make bigger 747 models, 1999, *Houston Chronicle,* September 21, 4C.
82. B. Pinsker, 1997, Rental block, *Dallas Morning News,* June 14, C5, C8.
83. S. N. Mehta, 1999, SBC Communications to launch service 'bundles' in two markets, *Wall Street Journal Interactive Edition,* August 24, *www.interactive.wsj.com/articles.*
84. J. Cole, 1999, Airbus prepares to 'bet the company' as it builds a huge new jet, *Wall Street Journal,* November 3, A1, A10; M. Skapinker, 1998, Airbus boasts year of record orders, *Financial Times,* January 8, 6.
85. L. Krishnamurthi & V. Shankar, *1998,* What are the options for later entrants? Mastering Marketing (Part Six), *Financial Times,* October 19, 4.
86. Baum & Korn, Dynamics of dyadic competitive interaction.

87. Intel reduces prices on Pentium III chips, 1999, *New York Times Online,* August 24, *www.nytimes.com/library.*
88. J. A. Schumpeter, 1961, *Theory of Economic Development* (New York: Oxford University Press).
89. M. A. Hitt, 2000, The new frontier: Transformation of management for the twenty-first century, *Organizational Dynamics,* 28 (Winter): 7–17.
90. B. A. Melcher, 1993, How Goliaths can act like Davids, *Business Week,* Special Issue, 193.
91. J. Kurtzman, 1998, An interview with Charles Handy, in J. Kurtman (ed.), *Thought Leaders* (San Francisco: Jossey-Bass), 134–149; J. Birkinshaw, 1997, Entrepreneurship in multinational corporations: The characteristics of subsidiary initiatives, *Strategic Management Journal,* 18: 207–229.
92. *Harvard Business Review Perspectives,* 1995, How can big companies keep the entrepreneurial spirit alive? *Harvard Business Review,* 73(6): 183–192.
93. R. E. Krider & C. B. Weinberg, 1998, Competitive dynamics and the introduction of new products: The motion picture timing game, *Journal of Marketing Research,* 35: 1–15.
94. C. E. Lucier & J. D. Torbilier, 1999, Beyond stupid, slow and expensive: Reintegrating work to improve productivity, *Strategy & Business,* 17: 9–13; R. R. Nayyar & K. A. Bantel, 1994, Competitive agility: A source of competitive advantage based on speed and variety, *Advances in Strategic Management,* 10A, 193–222.
95. S. Wally & J. R. Baum, 1994, Personal and structural determinants of the pace of strategic decision-making, *Academy of Management Journal,* 37: 932–956.
96. Ibid.
97. G. Colvin, 1999, The ultimate manager, *Fortune,* November 22, 185–187; T. Smart & J. H. Dobrzynski, 1993, Jack Welch on the art of thinking small, *Business Week,* Special Enterprise Issue, 212–216.
98. Kurtzman, An interview with Gary Hamel; J. Wind, 1997, Preemptive strategies, in G. S. Day & D. J. Reibstein (eds.), *Wharton on Dynamic Competitive Strategy* (New York: John Wiley & Sons), 256–276; S. C. Wheelwright & K. B. Clark, 1995, *Leading Product Development* (New York: The Free Press).
99. S. A. Zahra, A. P. Nielsen, & W. C. Bogner, 1999, Corporate entrepreneurship, knowledge, and competence development, *Entrepreneurship: Theory and Practice,* 23(3): 169–189; B. N. Dickie, 1998, Foreword, in J. Kurtzman (ed.), *Thought Leaders* (New York: Jossey-Bass), x–xvii; J. Kurtzman, 1998, An interview with Paul M. Romer, in J. Kurtzman (ed.), *Thought Leaders* (New York: Jossey-Bass), 66–83.
100. L. G. Franko, 1989, Global corporate competition: Who's winning, who's losing, and the R&D factor as one reason why, *Strategic Management Journal,* 10: 449–474.
101. R. E. Hoskisson & M. A. Hitt, 1994, *Downscoping: How to Tame the Diversified Firm* (New York: Oxford University Press).
102. D. L. Deeds, D. DeCarolis, & J. Coombes, 1999, Dynamic capabilities and new product development in high technology ventures: An empirical analysis of new biotechnology firms, *Journal of Business Venturing,* 18: 211–229; K. J. Klein & J. S. Sorra, 1996, The challenge of innovation implementation, *Academy of Management Review,* 21: 1055–1080.
103. N. Kim, E. Bridges, & R. K. Srivastava, 1999, A simultaneous model for innovative product category sales diffusion and competitive dynamics, *International Journal of Research in Marketing,* 16: 95–111.
104. D. P. Hamilton, 1999, Sun to challenge Microsoft's Office with purchase of software maker, *Wall Street Journal Interactive Edition,* August 31, *www.interactive.wsj.com/articles.*
105. N. George, 1999, Ericsson drifts in Nokia's wake, *Financial Times,* July 22, 13.
106. Klein & Sorra, The challenge of innovation implementation.
107. N. Dunne, 1998, American goldmine for high-tech workers, *Financial Times,* January 15, 4; V. Griffith, 1998, Learning to wear two hats, *Financial Times,* January 5, 20; N. Timmins, 1998, Manufacturers face skills shortfall, *Financial Times,* January 9, 4.
108. Procter's gamble, 1999, *The Economist Online,* December 6, *www.economist.com/editorial.*
109. J. W. Dean, Jr., & D. E. Bowen, 1994, Management theory and total quality: Improving research and practice through theory development, *Academy of Management Review,* 19: 392–419.
110. J. Aley, 1994, Manufacturers grade themselves, *Fortune,* March 21, 26.
111. M. Halkias, 1997, Rising competition, *Dallas Morning News,* November 13, D1, D12.
112. J. Heizer & B. Render, 1996, *Production and Operations Management,* 4th ed. (Upper Saddle River, NJ: Prentice Hall), 75–106.
113. M. van Biema & B. Greenwald, 1997, Managing our way to higher service-sector productivity, *Harvard Business Review,* 75(4): 87–95.
114. S. Chatterjee & M. Yilmaz, 1993, Quality confusion: Too many gurus, not enough disciples, *Business Horizons,* 36(3): 15–18.
115. J. Heizer & B. Render, 1999, *Operations Management,* 5th ed. (Upper Saddle River, NJ: Prentice Hall).
116. W. S. Sherman & M. A. Hitt, 1996, Creating corporate value: Integrating quality and innovation programs, in D. Fedor & S. Ghoshal (eds.), *Advances in the Management of Organizational Quality* (Greenwich, CT: JAI Press), 221–244.
117. J. D. Westphal, R. Gulati, & S. M. Shortell, 1997, Customization or conformity: An institutional and network perspective on the content and consequences of TQM adoption, *Administrative Science Quarterly,* 42: 366–394.
118. E. E. Lawler, III, 1994, Total quality management and employee involvement: Are they compatible? *Academy of Management Executive,* VIII(1): 68.
119. R. S. Russell & B. W. Taylor, III, 2000, *Operations Management,* 3d ed. (Upper Saddle River, NJ: Prentice Hall), 130–165.
120. A. M. Schneiderman, 1998, Are there limits to total quality management? *Strategy & Business,* 11: 35–45; R. Krishnan, A. B. Shani & G. R. Baer, 1993, in search of quality improvement: Problems of design and implementation, *Academy of Management Executive,* VII(3): 7–20.
121. S. Sanghera, 1999, Making continuous improvement better, *Financial Times,* April 21, 28.
122. Ibid.
123. H. V. Roberts & B. F. Sergesketter, 1993, *Quality Is Personal* (New York: The Free Press).
124. S. B. Sitkin, K. M. Sutcliffe, & R. G. Schroeder, 1994, Distinguishing control from learning in total quality management: A contingency perspective, *Academy of Management Review,* 19: 537–564.
125. J. R. Hackman & R. Wageman, 1995, Total quality management: Empirical, conceptualization and practical issues, *Administrative Science Quarterly,* 40: 309–342.
126. J. R. Williams, 1999, *Renewable Advantage: Crafting Strategy through Economic Time* (New York: The Free Press); J. R. Williams, 1992, How sustainable is your competitive advantage? *California Management Review,* 34, Spring: 29–51.
127. G. S. Day, 1997, Maintaining the competitive edge: Creating and sustaining advantages in dynamic competitive environments, in G. S. Day & D. J. Reibstein (eds.), *Wharton on Dynamic Competitive Strategy* (New York: John Wiley & Sons), 48–75.
128. J. R. Williams, 1999, Economic time, *Across the Board,* September, 11.
129. A. D. Chandler, 1990, The enduring logic of industrial success, *Harvard Business Review,* 68(2): 130–140.
130. J. L. Bower & T. M. Hout, 1988, Fast-cycle capability for competitive power, *Harvard Business Review,* 66(6): 110–118.
131. M. Wells, 1999, Tequiza beer takes on Corona, *USA Today,* February 8, B4.
132. Williams, Economic time.
133. K. R. Conner, 1995, Obtaining strategic advantage from being imi-

tated: When can encouraging "clones" pay? *Management Science,* 41: 209–225; R. A. D'Aveni, 1995, Coping with hypercompetition: Utilizing the new 7's framework, *Academy of Management Executive,* IX(3): 45–60; K. R. Conner, 1988, Strategies for product cannibalism, *Strategic Management Journal,* 9 (Special Summer Issue): 135–159.

134. S. N. Mehta, 1999, Phone companies expect wireless to usher in the telecom future, *Wall Street Journal Interactive Edition,* November 15, *www.interactive.wsj.com/articles.*
135. A. Cane, G. Bowley, & R. Taylor, 1999, Nortel counter attack launched against Cisco, *www.ft.com*, November 9, *www.ft.com/hippocampus.*
136. R. Sanchez, 1995, Strategic flexibility in product competition, *Strategic Management Journal,* 16 (Special Summer Issue): 9–26.
137. M. A. Hitt, B. B. Tyler, C. Hardee, & D. Park, 1995, Understanding strategic intent in the global marketplace, *Academy of Management Executive,* IX(2): 12–19.
138. M. A. Hitt, M. T. Dacin, E. Levitas, J. L. Arregle, & A. Borza, 2000, Partner selection in emerging and developed market contexts: Resource-based and organizational learning perspectives, *Academy of Management Journal,* in press.
139. R. E. Miles, C. C. Snow, & M. Sharfman, 1993, Industry variety and performance, *Strategic Management Journal,* 14: 163–177.
140. K. Cool & I. Dierickx, 1993, Rivalry, strategic groups and firm profitability, *Strategic Management Journal,* 14: 47–59.
141. S. A. Shane, 1996, Hybrid organizational arrangements and their implications for firm growth and survival: A study of new franchisers, *Academy of Management Journal,* 39: 216–234.
142. Pricks and kicks, 1999, *The Economist Online,* August 16, *www.economist.com/editorial.*
143. Ibid.
144. D. M. Schroeder, 1990, A dynamic perspective on the impact of process innovation upon competitive strategies, *Strategic Management Journal,* 11: 25–41.
145. L. Gomes, 1999, Upstart Linux draws interest of a Microsoft attack team, *Wall Street Journal Interactive Edition,* May 21, *www.interactive.wsj.com/articles.*

CORPORATE-LEVEL STRATEGY

CHAPTER SIX OBJECTIVES

After reading this chapter, you should be able to:

1. Define corporate-level strategy and discuss its importance to the diversified firm.
2. Describe the advantages and disadvantages of single-business and dominant-business strategies.
3. Explain three primary reasons why firms move from single-business and dominant-business strategies to more diversified strategies.
4. Describe how related diversified firms use activity sharing and the transfer of core competencies to create value.
5. Discuss the two ways an unrelated diversification strategy can create value.
6. Discuss the incentives and resources that encourage diversification.
7. Describe motives that can encourage managers to overdiversify a firm.

CMGI: A Diversified Internet Conglomerate

CMGI was named one of the top five best stocks of the 1990s (1990–1999), with a 57,191 percent increase in the value of a share. This increase in value was superseded only by that of Cisco Systems, AOL, Dell, and EMC shares. In fact, CMGI's performance was better than that of such well-known companies as Charles Schwab, Microsoft, Sun Microsystems, Yahoo!, and Qualcomm. The interesting aspect of CMGI's strategy, relative to most firms among the best performers, is that CMGI has used a classic diversification strategy to realize its increase in value. A NASDAQ 100 company, CMGI is in the business of creating and managing a diverse network of Internet companies focused in four areas: Internet advertising and marketing, content and Internet communities, e-commerce, and e-commerce enabling technologies.

CMGI's marketing and advertising companies offer state-of-the-art technologies to help firms establish interactive advertising and marketing. Engage Technologies, Inc., which is 80 percent owned by CMGI, is buying Flycast Communications, Inc., and AdSmart (already owned by the CMGI parent). These purchases will allow for more centralization of CMGI's advertising units and make the firm a strong competitor for DoubleClick, the leader in Internet advertising. AdSmart places Internet advertisements for media buyers across a network of 300 Internet sites, 90 percent of which come from CMGI properties. Adforce, another firm partly owned by CMGI, creates on-line ads for clients and measures their effectiveness. Flycast runs direct marketing campaigns on the Internet; it can run a test campaign and adjust it day by day to find what types of buyers should be targeted for specific products, such as golf clubs or winter vacations. Flycast gathers information from 1,700 sites, which will be combined with information from the 2,000 sites that Engage has signed up for collecting profile information.

CMGI's e-commerce companies sell directly to consumers or to businesses over the Web. Shopping.com sells everything from digital cameras to in-line skates. Mothernature.com is a purveyor of vitamins and health care supplements. Furniture.com, obviously, sells sofas, beds, and other furniture and furnishings. Carparts.com is a site used to find almost any car part imaginable. CMGI often owns a minority, but fairly large, percentage of these e-commerce companies.

Enabling technologies allow a firm to track Web traffic and create anonymous user profiles of those who surf the Web. With the information gathered by these technologies, firms can target their marketing to on-line users by tracking their proclivities for specific Internet sites. The new technologies and services help other e-commerce companies, as well as traditional corporations, exploit the Internet's full potential. Engage Technologies, for instance, a CMGI property, has allowed Lycos (a major portal associated with CMGI) to track and build a record of user behavior. Each time an Internet surfer arrives at a site, the site can automatically flash ads tailored to the surfer's interest. For example, a consumer who has repeatedly visited the National Park Service Web site automatically sees ads for tents and hiking boots when he or she visits an airline reservation site. Numberoneclickcharge is a payment software that allows on-line stores to charge customers a small transaction fee per click for reviews, music, or articles on-line. To help round out its Internet solutions offerings, CMGI also acquired an 80 percent interest in Tallan, Inc., which provides Internet consulting and software services.

Content and Internet community companies, however, are probably the main core engines of CMGI. These companies facilitate increases in traffic, the mainstay of the success of any Internet company. CMGI's main portals are Alta Vista and Lycos. The company wants to turn Alta Vista into a "megaportal" site that would be a showcase and jumping-off point for CMGI's other properties. The Raging Bull is one of the content companies that has increased traffic at CMGI. Compared to the e-commerce companies, CMGI owns larger percentages of the content and portal companies. CMGI owns 83 percent and 50 percent respectively, of Alta Vista and Raging Bull, for example.

Raging Bull is an example of what CMGI's CEO, David S. Wetherell, is trying to accomplish through his firm's diversification strategy. In August 1998, Wetherell was searching the Web and found a site called Raging Bull. Three college students who focused on investor chat rooms founded and ran the site from an apartment basement. Wetherell bought 50 percent for $2 million. Raging Bull's core technology operations were taken over and managed by the Web-site management company NaviSite, a CMGI Internet insight and infrastructure management company. NaviSite easily began generating ad revenues after receiving services from AdSmart, another CMGI company that provides on-line links for advertisers. All of these partnerships proved significant, as Raging Bull's audience exploded from 200,000 pages a day in January 1999 to over 5 million per day in September 1999. It now is the second most popular on-line investor forum behind Yahoo! Inc. Raging Bull is an example of CMGI's plan to harness the collective resources of its Internet partners by having them share customers and technology and create strategic partnerships to form a diversified firm composed of Internet companies.

Internet Capital Group (ICG) is another firm that uses a diversification strategy, one that is similar to CMGI's. ICG is a holding company that focuses exclusively on business-to-business (B2B) Internet operations. This is a somewhat different focus from CMGI's. ICG currently owns a percentage of over 50 on-line marketplaces where businesses can trade everything from chemicals, paper, and plastics to cattle and office supplies with other businesses. By the beginning of 2000, ICG's market capitalization had reached $30 billion. In September 1999, the company's shares were trading at $40; by the beginning of 2000, its shares were trading at $112. ICG's market capitalization rivals that of Merrill Lynch, and its stock price represented 40 percent of the market capitalization of the entire business-to-business Internet segment. Although it had only taken three of its companies (Breakaway Solutions, Rest Interactive, and Vertical Net) through the IPO process, a number of additional IPOs were planned during 2000.

http://www.aol.com

http://www.carparts.com

http://www.cisco.com

http://www.cmgi.com

http://www.dell.com

Firms such as CMGI and ICG are not risk-free ventures. These companies continue to show operating losses, and their market capitalization is based on highly valued stock prices that can disappear quite quickly, as was exemplified in the downturn of Internet stocks in early 1999. Only time will tell whether these business models will be successful in the long term.

http://www.internetcapital.com

SOURCES: W. M. Buckeley, 2000, GMGI's Engage will buy 2 other units of conglomerate for $2.5 billion in stock, *Wall Street Journal*, January 20, B10; M. Maremont, 2000, CMGI agrees to buy 80 percent of Tallan for about $715 million in cash, stock, *Wall Street Journal*, February 15, B6; E. Schonfeld, 2000, Investors still can't get enough of Internet capital group, *Fortune*, January 10, 212; C. Taylor, 2000, CMGI—the Internet catalyst, *www.cmgi.com/about/main.html*; J. G. Auerbach & G. McWilliams, 1999, How CMGI plans to make Alta Vista hot again, *Wall Street Journal*, June 30, B1, B4; T. C. Judge, 1999, Internet evangelists, *Business Week*, October 25, 141–150; T. C. Judge, 1999, One happy family—but for how long? *Business Week*, October 25, 148.

As indicated in the Opening Case, top-level managers at CMGI and Internet Capital Group decided that their firms should be more diversified than other Internet-related companies. CMGI is following a related linked diversification strategy (see Table 6.1) wherein the businesses function in a way that creates added value for each other. For example, the expertise of NaviSite greatly facilitated the success of Raging Bull's page views, and AdSmart facilitated links to Internet advertisers. Thus, the parent corporation, CMGI, and its affiliates significantly fostered the success of the newly added property, Raging Bull, which started as an investor's "chat room" site run by college students. Accordingly, by means of a corporate strategy, CMGI has been able to create increased market power and competitive advantage over other companies.

Disney, a large diversified entertainment company, has also sought to leverage its resources and capabilities to forge a set of on-line businesses. Its main portal, go.com, was seeking to compete with Yahoo!, Excite, and other major service portals. In 1999, Disney acquired the rest of Infoseek Corporation to incorporate the Infoseek search engine more fully with Disney's other on-line businesses. However, the firm was too late getting into the portal business to compete with Yahoo! and AOL, so it has shifted the focus of go.com to that of an entertainment and leisure site. ABC.com is the news and entertainment Web site associated with the Disney TV network. Disney.com is the main e-commerce site that sells Disney-associated products on-line. ESPN.com is the sports information and entertainment site associated with the Disney-owned cable sports network. Disney also has a stake in e-companies that serve as an incubator for Internet start-ups similar to NaviSite, a CMGI affiliate. Therefore, Disney is using its Internet diversification to build on the strengths that it already has in entertainment and associated products (e.g., toys created from its animated movie figures).[1]

Our discussions of different business-level strategies (Chapter 4) and the competitive dynamics associated with their use (Chapter 5) were focused primarily on firms competing in a single industry or product market.[2] When a firm chooses to diversify its operations beyond a single industry and to operate businesses in several industries, it is pursuing a corporate-level strategy of diversification. As is the case with business-level strategies, a corporate-level strategy of diversification allows a firm to adapt to conditions in its external environment.[3] As influential strategic choices that companies make, diversification strategies play a major role in the behavior of large firms.[4] Strategic choices regarding diversification are, however, fraught with uncertainty.[5]

A diversified company has two levels of strategy: a business-level (or competitive) strategy and a corporate-level (or companywide) strategy.[6] In diversified firms, each

A **corporate-level strategy** is an action taken to gain a competitive advantage through the selection and management of a mix of businesses competing in several industries or product markets.

business unit chooses a business-level strategy to implement to achieve strategic competitiveness and earn above-average returns. But diversified firms must also choose a strategy that is concerned with the selection and management of their businesses. Defined formally, a **corporate-level strategy** is an action taken to gain a competitive advantage through the selection and management of a mix of businesses competing in several industries or product markets. In essence, a corporate-level strategy is what makes "the corporate whole add up to more than the sum of its business unit parts."[7] Corporate-level strategy is concerned with two key questions: what businesses the firm should be in and how the corporate office should manage its group of businesses.[8] In the current complex global environment, top executives should view their firm's businesses as a portfolio of core competencies when seeking answers to these critical questions.[9]

Relating back to Figure 1.1, our focus herein is on the formulation of corporate-level strategy that evolves from the firm's strategic intent and mission. Also, as with business-level strategies, corporate-level strategies are expected to help the firm earn above-average returns (create value).[10] Some have suggested that few corporate-level strategies actually do create value.[11] In the final analysis, the value of a corporate-level strategy "must be that the businesses in the portfolio are worth more under the management of the company in question than they would be under any other ownership."[12] Thus, the corporate-level strategy should be expected to contribute a given amount to the returns of all business units that exceeds what those returns would be without the implementation of such a strategy.[13] When managed effectively, corporate-level strategies enhance a firm's strategic competitiveness and contribute to its ability to earn above-average returns.[14] In the 21st century, corporate-level strategies will be managed in a global business environment characterized by high degrees of risk, complexity, uncertainty, and ambiguity.[15]

A primary approach to corporate-level strategy is diversification, which requires corporate-level executives to craft a multibusiness strategy. One reason for the use of a diversification strategy is that managers of diversified firms possess unique general management skills that can be used to develop multibusiness strategies and enhance a firm's strategic competitiveness.[16] To derive the greatest benefit from their skills, managers must focus their energies on the tasks associated with managing a diversification strategy.[17] The prevailing theory of diversification suggests that firms should diversify when they have excess resources, capabilities, and core competencies that have multiple uses.[18] Multibusiness strategies often encompass many different industry environments and, as discussed in Chapter 11, require unique organizational structures.

This chapter begins by addressing the history of diversification. Included in that discussion are descriptions of the advantages and disadvantages of single-business and dominant-business strategies. Next, the chapter describes different levels of diversification (from low to high) and reasons firms pursue a corporate-level strategy of diversification. Two types of diversification strategies that denote moderate to very high levels of diversification—related and unrelated—are then examined.

Large diversified firms often compete against each other in several markets. This type of rivalry is called *multipoint competition*. For instance, RJR Nabisco competes against Philip Morris in both cigarettes and consumer foods. The chapter also explores vertical integration strategies designed to exploit market share and gain power over competitors. Closing the chapter is a brief discussion of issues firms should consider when examining the possibility of becoming more diversified.

History of Diversification

In 1950, only 38.1 percent of the *Fortune* 500 U.S. industrial companies generated more than 25 percent of their revenues from diversified activities. By 1974, the figure had risen to 63 percent. In 1950, then, more than 60 percent of the largest *Fortune* 500 industrial companies were either single-business or dominant-business firms; by 1974, the percentage had dropped to 37 percent.[19]

Beginning in the late 1970s and especially through the middle part of the 1980s, a significant trend toward refocusing on core businesses and divesting of business units unrelated to core business occurred in many firms. In fact, approximately 50 percent of the *Fortune* 500 companies refocused on their core businesses from 1981 to 1987.[20] As a result, by 1988, the percentage of single- or dominant-business firms on the *Fortune* 500 list of industrial companies had increased to 53 percent.[21] Although many diversified firms have become more focused, this trend is somewhat masked because extensive international diversification (as opposed to product diversification) has taken place that is not included in these statistics. As Chapter 8's discussion reveals, international strategy has been increasing in importance and has led to greater financial performance relative to product diversification.[22]

The trend toward product diversification has been most significant among U.S. firms. Nonetheless, large business organizations in Europe, Asia, and other parts of the industrialized world have also implemented diversification strategies. In the United Kingdom, the number of single- or dominant-business firms fell from 60 percent in 1960 to 37 percent in 1980. A similar, yet less dramatic, trend toward more diversification occurred in Japan: Among the largest Japanese firms, 60 percent were dominant- or single-business firms in 1958, compared with 53 percent in 1973.

These trends toward more diversification, which have been partially reversed due to restructuring (see Chapter 7), indicate that learning has taken place regarding corporate diversification strategies. The main lesson learned in the U.S. economy is that firms performing well in their dominant business may not want to diversify. Moreover, firms that diversify should do so cautiously, choosing to focus on a relatively few, rather than many, businesses.[23]

However, in some emerging economies, as well as in many industrialized countries, such as Germany, Italy and France, diversification has been the norm for the most successful firms (see the Strategic Focus later in this chapter). Subsequently, though, many of these diversified firms began to restructure. This sequence of diversification followed by restructuring mirrors actions of firms in the United States and the United Kingdom.[24]

In Germany, for example, many of the largest conglomerates are restructuring as a result of three elements' effects. First, deregulation both in Germany and across Europe is creating more competition, and the emergence of the European Union has caused firms to pursue pan-European strategies. Second, the realities of global competition are becoming prominent in Europe, and firms in several sectors are responding by restructuring. Finally, increasingly, shareholders are pressuring management to be more transparent and show separate business performances rather than reporting only overall results. One way to obtain this transparency is to spin off unrelated businesses and focus on core businesses. Two German conglomerates that have begun refocusing are Mannesman in mobile telephone networks and Sieman's, which makes multiple products from lightbulbs to locomotives and has now sold one-seventh of its operations. Hoechst, one of the large chemical producers, and utilities such as Viag and Veba also have restructured. Most of these restructurings are intended to streamline the companies, focusing on a narrow set of businesses and short-term cost-cutting objectives. As strategic actions, they are similar to the restructurings that took place earlier in the United States. Today, following refocusing of their businesses, many U.S. firms are positioned to pursue long-term growth in both sales revenue and profitability.[25]

Deciding to become more diversified in terms of both product offerings and geographic locations appears to have contributed to Cott Corporation's difficulties. Originally, Cott produced and sold (at discount prices) an array of private-label beverages, including soft drinks, New Age beverages, iced teas, juice drinks, sport drinks, and bottled water. Cott's customers were large retail chains such as Wal-Mart and Safeway. Through effective implementation of its strategy, this Toronto, Canada, company grew, in less than 10 years, from a small family business to a multinational corporation with annual sales of over $1 billion. Cott's growth resulted in the firm becoming the leading worldwide supplier of premium retailer branded beverages and the world's fourth-largest soft-drink company. Cott believes that product innovation, employee creativity, high-quality products, and world-class packaging are its core competencies.

However, as one analyst observed, the firm followed its initial success with expansions "into things it had no business expanding into, such as the Canadian beer market and faraway countries." In addition to these forays into new products and geographic areas, Cott also planned, but did not execute, a strategy that called for it to pattern a major line of private-label foods after the approach it used to sell its private-label soft drinks. Given the problems created by ill-advised diversification efforts, Cott Corporation sold its beer business and reorganized its international operations to cut costs.[26] Cott Corporation has continued its restructuring with the help of buyout specialist Thomas Lee, who has invested in the firm.[27] Thus, for Cott Corporation, diversification outside of its core business area did not result in additional financial returns.

As the foregoing examples about Cott and diversified business groups from Germany suggest, strategic competitiveness can be increased when firms pursue a level of diversification that is appropriate for their resources (especially financial resources) and core competencies and the opportunities and threats in their external environment.

Levels of Diversification

Diversified firms vary according to their level of diversification and the connections between and among their businesses. Figure 6.1 lists and defines five categories of businesses according to increasing levels of diversification. In addition to the single- and dominant-business categories, more fully diversified firms are classified into

6.1 | Levels and Types of Diversification

Low Levels of Diversification

Single business:	More than 95% of revenue comes from a single business.	
Dominant business:	Between 70% and 95% of revenue comes from a single business.	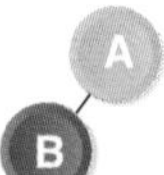

Moderate to High Levels of Diversification

Related constrained:	Less than 70% of revenue comes from the dominant business, and all businesses share product, technological, and distribution linkages.	
Related linked (mixed related and unrelated):	Less than 70% of revenue comes from the dominant business, and there are only limited links between businesses.	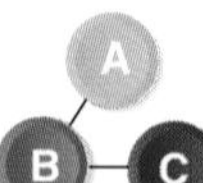

Very High Levels of Diversification

Unrelated:	Less than 70% of revenue comes from the dominant business, and there are no common links between businesses.	 

Source: Adapted from R. P. Rumelt, 1974, *Strategy, Structure and Economic Performance* (Boston: Harvard Business School).

related and unrelated categories. A firm is related through its diversification when there are several links between business units; for example, units may share products or services, technologies, or distribution channels. The more links among businesses, the more "constrained" is the relatedness of diversification. Unrelatedness refers to the absence of direct links between businesses.

Low Levels of Diversification

A firm pursing a low level of diversification focuses its efforts on a single or a dominant business. The Wm. Wrigley Jr. Company is an example of a firm with little diversification. Its primary focus is on the chewing-gum market.[28] A firm is classified as a single business when revenue generated by the dominant business is greater than 95 percent of the total sales.[29] Dominant businesses are firms that generate between 70 percent and 95 percent of their total sales within a single category. Because of the sales it generates from breakfast cereals, Kellogg is an example of a dominant business firm. Recently, Kellogg has been pushing its cereal products as a snack food, because sales have lagged in the breakfast cereal market.[30]

Hershey Foods Corp. (the largest U.S. producer of chocolate and nonchocolate confectionery items) is another dominant business firm. Although Hershey manufactures some food products (principally San Giorgio, American Beauty, Delmonico, Skinner, and Ronzoni pastas), the bulk of the firm's revenue is earned through the selling of its confectionery items.[31] To generate interest in its candies across time, the company introduces new products carefully and deliberately. Commenting about this approach, an analyst suggested that "Announcing that a new candy is on the way, then keeping it under wraps until it is ready increases sales and sparks a general feeling of enthusiasm for Hershey stock."[32]

Wal-Mart has focused narrowly on discount retailing. However, it recently bought Federal BankCentre, a small savings bank in Oklahoma, to add a "customer service" feature to its portfolio, noting that 20 percent of Wal-Mart's customers and many of its 780,000 employees lack "an established banking relationship." Wal-Mart currently leases space to banks in about 450 of its stores. The company indicated that it would learn about the business and then test-market its own branches in five stores.[33] Although Wal-Mart, as discussed in Chapter 5, is moving into foreign markets and creating a more competitive environment in Europe, it still has a very narrow scope in regard to product diversification. The move into financial services could signal that the firm is increasing its level of diversification.

Moderate and High Levels of Diversification

When a firm earns more than 30 percent of its sales volume outside a dominant business, and when its businesses are related to each other in some manner, the company is classified as a related diversified firm. With more direct links between the businesses, the firm is defined as related constrained. Examples of related constrained firms are Campbell Soup, Procter & Gamble, Xerox, and Merck & Company. If there are only a few links between businesses, the firm is defined as a mixed related and unrelated business, or a related linked firm (see Figure 6.1). Johnson & Johnson, General Electric, and Schlumberger are examples of related linked firms. Related constrained firms share a number of resources and activities between businesses. Related linked firms have less sharing of actual resources and assets and relatively more transfers of knowledge and competencies between businesses. Highly diversified firms, which have no relationships between businesses, are called unrelated diversified firms. Examples of firms pursuing an unrelated diversification strategy are Tenneco, Textron, and Samsung, which has been restructuring its operations after the Asian financial crisis.[34]

Although many unrelated diversified firms in the United States have refocused to become less diversified, a number continue to have high levels of diversification. General Electric is an example of a company that remains highly diversified. In Latin America and other emerging economies such as Korea and India, conglomerates (firms following the unrelated diversification strategy) continue to dominate the private sector.[35] For example, typically family controlled, these corporations account for more than two-thirds of the 33 largest private business groups in Brazil. Similarly, the largest business groups in Mexico, Argentina, and Colombia are family-owned, diversified enterprises.[36]

Consistent with a global trend of refocusing, some companies decide to become less diversified. Cited historically as perhaps the world's most successful follower of the unrelated diversification strategy, Hanson PLC nonetheless decided in the mid-1990s to become less diversified and streamline its operations. Thus, Hanson either sold or spun off a number of its operating businesses; those remaining were structured into four independent business units.[37]

As a more-than-100-year-old industrial manufacturer, Westinghouse Electric Corp. implemented a related linked diversification strategy for many years. The significant reduction in the amount of this firm's diversification began with its acquisition of CBS for $5.4 billion in cash in August 1995. Convinced that the firm's future was in broadcasting, then CEO Michael H. Jordan initiated a process that culminated in the official changing of the firm's name to CBS Corporation (CBS Corp.). To create its broadcasting focus, two business units, Thermo King and Westinghouse Power Generation, were sold in 1997. Jordan completed the sales of the remaining major business units—energy systems, process control, and government operations—by mid-1998.

During these divestitures, CBS Corp. acquired American Radio Systems' radio broadcasting operations. Calling the transaction "strategically attractive," a top-level CBS executive stated, "This investment will significantly strengthen CBS's position in the fast growing radio industry. It will enable CBS Radio to expand into new top 50 markets and increase its position in its existing markets." Thus, to expand its single product line of broadcasting—a line that includes the CBS Network, CBS radio, the TV station group, and cable and "other" broadcasting—CBS Corp. was committed to making selective acquisitions.

Ultimately, Mel Karmazin became CEO of CBS. In talking with Sumner M. Redstone, Viacom's 76-year-old CEO, about taking advantage of a Federal Communications Commission ruling that allowed one company to own two television stations in one market, these CEOs decided to merge their two firms. Viacom bought the assets of CBS and agreed to pay $37 billion in stock to combine the two companies into a new megamedia empire with capabilities comparable to Disney, News Corporation, and AOL Time Warner.[38] Thus, over time, Westinghouse first increased its diversification, then decreased its diversification and became CBS Corporation, and finally increased its diversification when it merged with Viacom.

Reasons for Diversification

Firms use a diversification strategy as their corporate-level strategy for many reasons. A partial list is shown in Table 6.1. These reasons are discussed throughout the remainder of the chapter in relation to related and unrelated diversification strategies, incentives, and managerial motives to diversify.

Most firms implement a diversification strategy to enhance the strategic competitiveness of the entire company. This reason describes strategic actions at CMGI, as explained in the Opening Case, and for Internet Capital Group as well. When a diversification strategy enhances strategic competitiveness, the firm's total value is increased. Value is created through either related diversification or unrelated diversification when that particular strategy allows a company's business units to increase revenues or reduce costs while implementing their business-level strategies. Another reason for diversification is to gain market power relative to competitors. As discussed later in more detail, this is often done through vertical integration.

Table 6.1 | Motives, Incentives, and Resources for Diversification

Motives to Enhance Strategic Competitiveness

- Economies of scope (related diversification)
  Sharing activities
  Transferring core competencies
- Market power (related diversification)
  Blocking competitors through multipoint competition
  Vertical integration
- Financial economies (unrelated diversification)
  Efficient internal capital allocation
  Business restructuring

Incentives and Resources with Neutral Effects on Strategic Competitiveness

- Antitrust regulation
- Tax laws
- Low performance
- Uncertain future cash flows
- Risk reduction for firm
- Tangible resources
- Intangible resources

Managerial Motives (Value Reduction)

- Diversifying managerial employment risk
- Increasing managerial compensation

Other reasons for implementing a diversification strategy may not enhance strategic competitiveness; in fact, diversification could have neutral effects or actually increase costs or reduce a firm's revenues. These reasons include diversification (1) to neutralize a competitor's market power (e.g., to neutralize the advantage of another firm by acquiring a distribution outlet similar to those of the competitors) and (2) to expand a firm's portfolio to reduce managerial employment risk (e.g., if one of the businesses fails, the top executive remains employed in a diversified firm). Because diversification can increase a firm's size and thus managerial compensation, managers have motives to diversify a firm. This type of diversification may reduce the firm's value. Diversification rationales that may have a neutral effect or that may reduce a firm's value are discussed in a later section.

To provide an overview of value-creating diversification strategies, Figure 6.2 illustrates the two dimensions as sources of relatedness. Researchers have studied these independent dimensions of relatedness[39] and have found that resources and key competencies are critical. The vertical dimension of the figure relates to sharing activities (operational relatedness), while the horizontal dimension represents corporate capabilities for transferring knowledge (corporate relatedness). The upper left quadrant has to do with the firm that has a high degree of capability in managing operational synergy, especially in sharing assets between its businesses. It also represents vertical sharing of assets through vertical integration. The lower right quadrant of the figure represents a highly developed corporate capability of transferring a skill to other businesses. This skill is located primarily in the corporate office. Whichever type of relat-

6.2 | Value-creating Strategies of Diversification: Operational and Corporate Relatedness

Related Constrained Diversification

Vertical Integration (Market Power)

Both Operational and Corporate Relatedness (Rare Capability and Can Create Diseconomies of Scope)

Unrelated Diversification (Financial Economies)

Related Linked Diversification (Economies of Scope)

High

Low

Sharing: Operational Relatedness Between Businesses

Low

High

Corporate Relatedness: Transferring Skills into Businesses Through Corporate Headquarters

edness is used, it is based on some kind of knowledge asset that the firm can either share or transfer.[40] Unrelated diversification may also be illustrated here, but its source of value does not come through either operational or corporate relatedness among business units; rather, it comes through financial economies or the restructuring of businesses the firm acquires. The next section examines related diversification.

Related Diversification

As suggested earlier in the chapter, related diversification is a strategy through which the firm intends to build upon or extend its existing resources, capabilities, and core competencies in the pursuit of strategic competitiveness.[41] Thus, firms that have selected related diversification as their corporate-level strategy seek to exploit economies of scope between business units. Available to firms operating in multiple industries or product markets,[42] **economies of scope** are cost savings attributed to transferring the capabilities and competencies developed in one business to a new business.

Economies of scope are cost savings attributed to transferring the capabilities and competencies developed in one business to a new business.

As illustrated in Figure 6.2, firms seek to create value from economies of scope through two basic kinds of operational economies: sharing activities (operational relatedness) and transferring skills or corporate core competencies (corporate relatedness). The difference between sharing activities and transferring competencies is based on how separate resources are used jointly to create economies of scope. Tangible resources, such as plant and equipment or other business-unit physical assets, often must be shared to create economies of scope. Less tangible resources, such as manufacturing know-how, also can be shared. However, when know-how is transferred between separate activities and there is no physical or tangible resource involved, a corporate core competence has been transferred, as opposed to operational sharing of activities having taken place.

Operational Relatedness: Sharing Activities

Sharing activities is quite common, especially among related constrained firms. At Procter & Gamble, a paper towels business and a baby diapers business both use paper products as a primary input to the manufacturing process. Having a joint paper production plant that produces inputs for both divisions is an example of a shared activity. In addition, these businesses are likely to share distribution sales networks, because they both produce consumer products.

In Chapter 3, primary and support value-chain activities were discussed. In general, primary activities, such as inbound logistics, operations, and outbound logistics, might possess multiple shared activities. Through efficient sharing of these activities, firms may be able to create core competencies. In terms of inbound logistics, the business units may share common inventory delivery systems, warehousing facilities, and quality assurance practices. Operations might share common assembly facilities, quality control systems, or maintenance operations. With respect to outbound logistics, two business units might share a common sales force and sales service desk. Support activities could include the sharing of procurement and technology development efforts. Among pharmaceutical producers, the importance of sharing of activities is driving a number of mergers and acquisitions of firms seeking to reduce their costs.

Jan Leschly, CEO of SmithKline Beecham PLC, and Richard Sykes, CEO of Glaxo Wellcome, both British pharmaceutical firms, have signaled that the two huge firms intend to merge. The merger is valued at $70 billion and will create the world's number-one drugmaker, to be called Glaxo SmithKline, PLC. This transaction is one of many that have been signaled among pharmaceutical firms recently. The anticipated acquisition of Warner-Lambert Co. by several suitor companies and the proposed merger of Monsanto Co. and Pharmacia & Upjohn, Inc., are two similar deals. The R&D costs of producing new drugs is forcing these firms to think about sharing laboratories and the capabilities they house. As one business writer said, "Part of what is driving companies to join together is the need to finance the enormous effort required to turn a revolution in human biology into a steady flow of new medicines."[43]

However, in 1996, when Swiss drugmakers Ciba-Geigy, Ltd., and Sandoz, Ltd., joined in a $63 billion merger to form Novartis, CEO Daniel Vasella stated that Novartis was "in a unique position to apply technologies learned from plant genetics to both pharmaceuticals and agricultural businesses." He staked the company's future on genetic engineering. But, especially in Europe, a backlash over genetically modified crops has been undermining the life-sciences concept upon which Novartis is based. In 1999, the whole firm required restructuring because of poor performance in its

Sandoz president Marc Monet (left) and Ciba president Alex Krauer (right) announced the merger of their firms on March 7, 1999. The new company, Novartis, is now one of the biggest drug and agrochemical concerns in the world.

agribusinesses.[44] Thus, there are risks associated with basing two businesses on a single value proposition to create economies of scope.

Firms expect the sharing of activities across units to result in increased strategic competitiveness and improved financial returns. Other matters, however, affect the degree to which these outcomes will be achieved through activity sharing. For example, firms should recognize that sharing activities requires sharing strategic control over business units. Moreover, one business-unit manager may feel that another is receiving more benefit from the activity sharing. Such a perception could create conflicts between division managers. Activity sharing also is risky because business-unit ties create links between outcomes. For instance, if demand for the product of one business is reduced, there may not be sufficient revenues to cover the fixed costs of running the joint plant. Shared activities create interrelationships that affect the ability of both businesses to achieve strategic competitiveness, as is illustrated in the aforementioned case of Novartis. Activity sharing may be ineffective if these costs are not taken into consideration.

The costs of activity sharing notwithstanding, research shows that the sharing of activities and resources across business units can increase the firm's value. For example, research examining acquisitions of firms in the same industry (referred to as horizontal acquisitions), such as the banking industry, has found that sharing resources and activities (thereby creating economies of scope) contributed to postacquisition increases in performance and higher returns to shareholders.[45] Research also found that firms which sold off related units in which resource sharing was a possible source of economies of scope produced lower returns than those which sold off businesses unrelated to the firm's core business.[46] Still other research found that firms with more related units had lower risk.[47] These results suggest that gaining economies of scope by sharing activities and resources across businesses within a firm may be important in reducing risk and in earning positive returns from diversification efforts. Further, more attractive results are obtained through the sharing of activities when a strong corporate office facilitates the sharing.[48]

Corporate Relatedness: Transferring of Core Competencies

Over time, a strategically competitive firm's intangible resources, such as its know-how, become the foundation for competitively valuable corporate capabilities and core competencies. Thus, as illustrated in Figure 6.2, corporate core competencies are complex sets of resources and capabilities that link different businesses, primarily through managerial and technological knowledge, experience, and expertise.[49]

Marketing expertise is an example of a core competence that could be used in this way. Because the expense of developing such a competence has already been incurred, and because competencies based on intangible resources are less visible and more difficult for competitors to understand and imitate, transferring these types of competencies from an original business unit to another one may reduce costs and enhance a firm's strategic competitiveness.[50] A key reason Philip Morris decided to acquire Miller Brewing Company was that it believed that a competitive advantage could be achieved by transferring its marketing core competence to Miller.

As a cigarette company, Philip Morris developed a particular expertise in marketing. When Philip Morris purchased Miller Brewing, the beer industry had efficient operations, but no firm in the industry had established marketing competence as a source of competitive advantage. The marketing competence that was transferred from Philip Morris to Miller resulted in the introduction of improved marketing practices to the brewing industry. These practices, especially in terms of advertising, proved to be the source of competitive advantage that allowed Miller Brewing to earn above-average returns for a period of time. In fact, several years passed before Anheuser-Busch, the largest firm in the brewing industry, developed the capabilities required to duplicate the benefits of Miller's strategy. A strong competitive response from Anheuser-Busch was predictable, however, in that beer is the firm's core business.

A number of firms have been exceptional in transferring skills across businesses. Besides Phillip Morris, in tobacco, food and beer, Virgin Industries has been able to transfer its marketing skills across travel, cosmetics, music, drinks, and a number of other businesses. Similarly, Thermo Electron has employed its entrepreneurial skills in starting up a number of new ventures and maintaining a new-venture network. Coopers Industries has been able to manage a number of manufacturing-related businesses. Tyco also has skills in managing similarly related manufacturing businesses and transferring manufacturing expertise from one to another. Honda has developed and transferred its expertise in small and now larger engines for a number of types of vehicles, from motorcycles and lawnmowers to its range of automotive products.[51] The Strategic Focus, on Williams Companies, shows how this firm has transferred its skills in building and operating natural-gas pipelines to building and operating fiber-optic Internet pipelines.

As the Strategic Focus suggests, Johnson & Johnson has discovered that some firms are either unable to transfer competencies, or they transfer competencies that do not

Williams Companies Transfers Its Skills from Natural-Gas Pipelines to Internet Pipelines

Williams Companies built its size and reputation on constructing large natural-gas pipelines. In the process, it learned how to manage large capital-intensive projects for a small number of vital business customers. Williams has now begun to transfer this skill to communication projects. Williams helps to connect businesses to other businesses in energy and communications. The company tries to deliver innovative, reliable products and services through its extensive networks of energy-distributing and high-speed fiber-optic cable pipelines. Williams also offers comprehensive services, including commodity trading and risk management on the energy side, and business communications systems and international satellite and fiber-optic video services through its communication business.

As it examined its wholesale role in energy and services, Williams found an analogous business in fiber-optic pipelines that were built to carry Internet traffic. The company felt that the two businesses were similar. As traffic increases in the pipeline, costs drop steeply. Williams felt that, as it had done in natural gas, it could ride this declining cost curve to profit from wholesale Internet traffic through a fiber-optic pipeline.

Accordingly, in the early 1980s, the firm started building a huge network of Internet pipelines that it ultimately sold to MCI WorldCom, Inc., in 1995. Williams is now in the process of building a second, more advanced 33,000-mile fiber-optic network. As it funded this network, Williams had a successful IPO that was partially financed by large potential customers who also became investors. Williams expects to complete this fiber-optic project by the end of 2000, one year ahead of schedule.

Even though telecommunication prices are declining, Williams believes that it can build volume and cut costs and still be "enormously profitable." Furthermore, its expertise in building pipelines will allow the company to move more rapidly and cheaply than other competitors who might produce similar large fiber-optic pipelines. Williams has already lined up SBC Communications (a large "Baby Bell"), Teléfonos de Mexico, and its own subsidiary company, Williams Communications, as customers. Furthermore, SBC Communications and Williams Communications are also investors in the project. Thus, through these ties with large customers (who also are committed through their investments), Williams expects to make the project successful.

Other firms have not been as effective as Williams in seeking to transfer their competencies. For instance, Johnson & Johnson (J&J) recently was criticized in this regard. J&J has three main businesses: professional health care devices, such as coronary stints and other wound-closure products associated with surgery; pharmaceuticals; and consumer health care products, such as Tylenol painkillers, Band-Aids, Johnson baby products, and Neutrogena skin products. Because J&J has not been very successful in keeping up its stock price in relationship to those of other pharmaceutical companies, investors and Wall Street analysts have been calling for a breakup of the firm into its three separate businesses.

The company's chief executive officer, Ralph Larsen, nonetheless argues that J&J is a health care company and not a pharmaceutical firm in particular. One of the problems is that

J&J's strategy is implemented through decentralization, an approach allowing each operating unit to manage itself independently. This makes it more difficult to transfer expertise from the corporate headquarters and between independent units. It is chiefly for this reason that many Wall Street analysts are suggesting that J&J should be broken up into three distinct units. In fact, to shore up its abilities in these separate areas, the company has been making acquisitions to allow each business to improve its competitiveness. Accordingly, J&J's approach has been to seek new knowledge from outside the firm, rather than trying to increase its ability to transfer knowledge from headquarters or across business units within the firm. Thus, relative to Williams Companies, J&J has been less successful in transferring its skills and knowledge within the company.

SOURCES: Williams Companies, Inc., 2000, Home Page, *www.williams.com*; R. King, 1999, Too much long distance, *Fortune,* March 15, 106–110; R. Langreth & R. Winslow, 1999, At J&J, a venerable strategy faces questions, *Wall Street Journal,* March 5, B1, B4; A. Stone, 1999, Why Williams Cos. mixes gas with fiberoptics, *Business Week Online,* March 11, *www.businessweek.com*; B. Wysocki, Jr., 1999, Corporate America confronts the meaning of a "core" business, *Wall Street Journal,* November 9, A1, A4.

help a business unit establish a competitive advantage. One way managers facilitate the transfer of competencies is to move key people into new management positions. Still, although Philip Morris accomplished a transfer of competence to Miller Brewing in this way, a business-unit manager of an older division may be reluctant to transfer key people who have accumulated corporate knowledge and experience. Thus, managers with the ability to facilitate the transfer of a core competence may come at a premium or may not want to transfer, and the top-level managers from the transferring division may not want the competencies transferred to a new division to fulfill the firm's diversification objectives. Research suggests that transferring expertise in manufacturing-based businesses often does not result in improved performance.[52] However, those businesses in which performance does improve often exhibit a corporate passion for pursing skill transfer and appropriate coordination mechanisms for realizing economies of scope.

Market Power

Market power exists when a firm is able to sell its products above the existing competitive level or reduce the costs of its primary and support activities below the competitive level, or both.

Related diversification can also be used to gain market power. **Market power** exists when a firm is able to sell its products above the existing competitive level or reduce the costs of its primary and support activities below the competitive level, or both.[53]

One approach to gaining market power through diversification is multipoint competition. *Multipoint competition* exists when two or more diversified firms compete in the same product areas or geographic markets.[54] For example, when Philip Morris moved into foods by buying General Foods and Kraft, RJR's competitive response was the acquisition of another food company, Nabisco.

If the diversified firms compete head to head in each market, multipoint competition will not create potential gains; instead, it will generate excessive competitive activity. Over time, if the firms refrain from competition and, in effect, realize mutual forbearance, they are engaged in a form of related diversification that creates value for each firm through less competitive activity (see Chapter 5). *Mutual forbearance* is a relationship between two or more firms in which excessive competition leads to a situation whereby the firms see that such competition is self-destructive and, without formal agreement, cease engaging in it.

Actions taken by Vodafone Airtouch and Mannesmann are an example of multipoint competition. Mannesmann began as a German producer of steel piping, but moved into telecommunications services in 1996 with the purchase of a telecommunications network formerly owned by the German railroad, Deutsche Bahn. By 1997, Mannesmann had more mobile-phone customers than Deutsche Telekom. In 1999, Mannesmann purchased a number of mobile assets across Europe. The company paid $1.2 billion for o.tel.o, owned by Veba and RWE, which exited the telecommunications business. Furthermore, Mannesmann purchased the cellular business of Olivetti, OmniTel, for $7.8 billion, because Olivetti was trying to take over Telecom Italia. Then, in a surprise move, Mannesmann acquired British mobile-phone company Orange for $34 billion in October 1999.

However, in November, 1999, Vodafone Airtouch launched a hostile bid for Mannesmann. Headquartered in Britain, Vodafone realized that it had to make this deal because Mannesmann would be the firm's biggest competitor in Europe, especially after it took over Orange, a leading mobile-phone service provider in Britain. Mannesmann paid a significant premium of $6,000 per subscriber for Orange, which is 70 percent above the industry average cost per subscriber. However, Mannesmann shares had increased 145 percent in 1999, a performance that satisfied shareholders.[55]

In 1998, Christopher Gent, Vodafone's CEO, paid $60 billion in stock and cash for San Francisco-based Airtouch, beating out a rival offer from Bell Atlantic. However, Gent later structured a transaction with Bell Atlantic, which had acquired GTE's cellular business. The partnership creates a network of 20 million cellular customers that would cover 90 percent of the U.S. population. AT&T would be in second place in market share, with 12 million wireless customers. As investors viewed the transaction, they not only approved of the U.S. deal, but also could see the cellular global strategy in the combination of Vodafone and Airtouch. Accordingly, the takeover price appreciated 25 percent. Bell Atlantic's stock price did not appreciate significantly, compared to the increases in Vodafone-Airtouch stock price. The reason for the difference is the international opportunity seen by shareholders in the Vodafone–Airtouch deal. Anticipating an advantage in the future of international cellular calls, Gent decided to pursue the Mannesmann deal.[56]

The preceding example illustrates the potential negative side of multipoint competition. Vodafone Airtouch actions represent a counterattack mode, an exceptional strategic action when multipoint competition exists.[57] Counterattacks are not common in multipoint competition because the threat of a counterattack may prevent strategic actions from being taken, or, more likely, firms may retract their strategic actions with the threat of counterattack.[58]

Vertical integration exists when a company is producing its own inputs (backward integration) or owns its own source of distribution of outputs (forward integration).

Another approach to creating value by gaining market power is the strategy of vertical integration (see Figure 6.2). **Vertical integration** exists when a company is producing its own inputs (backward integration) or owns its own source of distribution of outputs (forward integration). It is also possible to have partial vertical integration, wherein some inputs and outputs are sold by company units, while others are produced or sold by outside firms.

A company pursuing vertical integration is usually motivated to strengthen its position in its core business by gaining market power over competitors. This is done through savings on operations costs, avoidance of market costs, better control to establish quality, and, possibly, the protection of technology. It also happens when firms have strong ties between their assets for which no market prices exist. Establishing a market price would result in high search and transaction costs, so firms seek to vertically integrate rather than remaining separate businesses.[59]

In response to prominent threats from their external environment (such as changes in environmental regulations and third-party reimbursement practices) in the early to mid-1990s, some firms competing in the pharmaceutical industry pursued a strategy of vertical integration. More recently, these companies have completed horizontal acquisitions. (Recall the transaction between Glaxo and SmithKline.) However, in November 1993, Merck & Company, at the time the world's largest prescription drug manufacturer, paid $6.6 billion to acquire Medco Containment Services, Inc. (one of the largest mail-order pharmacy and managed care companies at the time of its purchase). With Medco, Merck controls a dominant supplier of its products. Contributing further to an increase in Merck's market power as a result of pursuing vertical integration was its opportunity to have detailed and immediate access to information regarding customers' marketing-related needs. In an identical fashion, the former SmithKline Beecham, PLC, attempted to increase its market power through forward vertical integration by purchasing United HealthCare's pharmacy-benefit services unit, Diversified Pharmaceutical Services, Inc.; Eli Lilly & Company's purchase of McKesson's PCS Health Systems unit was completed for the same strategic reason.[60] Important benefits accruing to Merck & Company, the former SmithKline Beecham, and Eli Lilly as a result of their separate decisions to vertically integrate in a forward direction include reductions in market transaction costs and some additional protection of proprietary technologies.

Of course, there are limits to vertical integration. For example, an outside supplier may produce the product at a lower cost. As a result, internal transactions from vertical integration may be expensive and reduce profitability. Also, bureaucratic costs are incurred in implementing this strategy. And because vertical integration can require that substantial sums of capital be invested in specific technologies, the strategy may be problematic when technology changes quickly. Finally, changes in demand create capacity balance and coordination problems. If one division of a firm is building a part for another internal division, but achieving economies of scale requires the first division to build the part at a scale beyond the capacity of the internal buyer to absorb demand, sales outside the company would be necessary. However, if demand slackens, overcapacity would result because the internal users cannot absorb the total demand. Thus, although vertical integration can create value and contribute to strategic competitiveness, especially in gaining market power over competitors, it is not without risks and costs.

Many manufacturing firms no longer pursue vertical integration. In fact, *de*integration is the focus of most manufacturing firms, such as Intel and Dell, and even among large auto firms, such as Ford and General Motors, as they develop independent supplier networks. However, in energy production, vertical integration still may be worthwhile and lead to strategic competitiveness and above-average returns. Duke

Vertical integration may still be worthwhile in energy production. Duke Power's construction arm built a power plant in Brownsville, Texas, which will be staffed by the firm's operating engineers and be provided with fuel by Duke's natural-gas pipelines.

Power has completed a 510-megawatt power plant near Brownsville, Texas. The plant was built through Duke's construction arm, will be staffed with the firm's operating engineers, and will be provided fuel through Duke's natural-gas pipelines. Furthermore, the power will be marketed through the firm's Houston-based power marketing division. Thus, Duke Energy's Texas operations are fully integrated through its energy supply chain.

As deregulation in the electric utility industry has progressed, other energy companies are also seeking to build their plant capacity to drive costs lower to compete in a more cost-conscious deregulated environment. However, many industry analysts predict that this approach will lead to overcapacity. To deal with that problem, Duke Energy's CEO has sought to distinguish himself as an energy asset trader. He acquired PanEnergy, a natural-gas supplier and pipeline operator, in 1998. Furthermore, he merged Duke's gas-gathering and -processing business with that of Phillips Petroleum in 1999. Duke has sold other assets in Ohio, Indiana, and Texas at prices higher than what the plants cost the company to build. CEO Richard Priory believes that Duke will have the ability to react and sell quickly if the market becomes overbuilt. With lower costs through its vertical integration strategy, and with the ability to react quickly through the astute buying and selling of assets, Duke Energy hopes to be well positioned for 21st-century competitive battles in the energy industry.[61]

As Figure 6.2 suggests, some firms may try to seek both operational and corporate forms of economies of scope.[62] Firms that attempt to do this often fail and create diseconomies of scope, because trying to manage two sources of knowledge is extremely difficult. However, if successful, this strategy can create value that is difficult for competitors to imitate. For example, through the leadership of Jack Welch, General Electric's famous former CEO, the firm has been successful both in realizing operational synergy and in transferring knowledge between business units. GE had long possessed the ability to develop operational synergies inside its business groups. Through the use of "sharing best practices" and "boundaryless behavior," techniques developed through Welch's leadership and support, the firm also possesses the ability to transfer knowledge among its units.[63] In describing the achievements resulting from these abilities, business analysts suggest that "GE is truly firing on all cylinders." For instance, "GE Capital, the world's largest nonbank finance company, boasts investments in 45 e-business companies. And NBC has allied with a host of Net players to capitalize on the convergence of the media, entertainment, and technology industries."[64]

Because knowledge management is so important in consulting firms such as McKinsey and Company and Andersen Consulting, each of these companies tries to manage both operational and corporate relatedness.[65] Andersen Consulting originally focused on consulting in the field of information system implementation, but now the company consults on information systems and technology and provides strategic services and outsourcing (wherein Andersen becomes the computer-processing department for a large firm). Andersen also has diversified industry lines of consulting businesses (financial services, government, oil and gas, etc.). The firm does a lot of sharing across these lines, but also has a large knowledge base from which consultants draw and seek to transfer information across lines of industry consulting engagements. Consulting is a business that requires both the sharing and transfer of skills in order to remain profitable, especially if business declines and consulting projects become more competitive.[66]

Disney has also been successful in using both operational and corporate relatedness. Disney's strategy is especially successful in comparison to that of Sony, at least as measured by revenues generated from blockbuster movies. Through the use of both operational and corporate relatedness, Disney made $3 billion on the 150 products that came out simultaneously with its movie, *The Lion King*. Sony's *Men in Black* was a super hit at the box office and earned $600 million, but box-office and video revenues were practically all of the success story. Disney was able to accomplish its great success by sharing knowledge within its movie and distribution divisions, while at the same time transferring knowledge into its retail and product divisions, creating a music CD, *Rhythm of the Pride Lands,* and producing a video, *Simba's Pride*. In addition, there were *Lion King* themes at Disney resorts and Animal Kingdom parks.[67]

The next corporate-level strategy considered, unrelated diversification, lacks both operational and corporate relatedness, but, when used appropriately, also creates value.

Unrelated Diversification

Financial economies are cost savings realized through improved allocations of financial resources based on investments inside or outside the firm.

An unrelated diversification strategy (see Figure 6.2) can create value through two types of financial economies. **Financial economies** are cost savings realized through improved allocations of financial resources based on investments inside or outside the firm.[68]

The first type of financial economy involves efficient internal capital allocations. This approach seeks to reduce risks among the firm's business units—for example, through the development of a portfolio of businesses with different risk profiles. The approach thereby reduces business risk for the total corporation. The second type of financial economy is concerned with purchasing other corporations and restructuring their assets. This approach allows a firm to buy and sell businesses in the external market with the intent of increasing the total value of the firm.

Efficient Internal Capital Market Allocation

Capital allocation is usually distributed efficiently in a market economy by capital markets. Capital is distributed efficiently because investors seek to purchase shares of firm equity (ownership) that have high future cash-flow values. Capital is allocated not only through equity, but also through debt, by means of which shareholders and debtholders seek to improve the value of their investment by investing in businesses with high growth prospects. In large diversified firms, however, the corporate office distributes capital to divisions to create value for the overall company. Such an approach may provide gains from internal capital market allocation, relative to the external capital market.[69] The corporate office, through managing a particular set of businesses, may have access to more detailed and accurate information regarding those businesses' actual and prospective performance.

Compared with corporate office personnel, investors have relatively limited access to internal information and can only *estimate* divisional performance and future business prospects. Although businesses that seek capital must provide information to those who will supply the capital (e.g., banks or insurance companies), firms with internal capital markets may have at least two informational advantages. First, information provided to capital markets through annual reports and other sources may not include negative information, but rather emphasize positive prospects and outcomes. External sources of capital have limited ability to know specifically what is taking place inside large organizations. Even owners who have access to information have no guarantee of full and complete disclosure.[70]

Second, although a firm must disseminate information, that information becomes available to potential competitors simultaneously. With insights gained by studying such information, competitors might attempt to duplicate a firm's competitive advantage. Without having to reveal internal information, a firm may protect its competitive advantage through an internal capital market.

If intervention from outside the firm is required to make corrections, only significant changes are possible, such as forcing the firm into bankruptcy or changing the dominant leadership coalition (e.g., the top-management team described in Chapter 12). Alternatively, in an internal capital market, the corporate office may fine-tune corrections by choosing to adjust managerial incentives or suggest strategic changes in a division. Thus, capital can be allocated according to more specific criteria than is possible with external market allocation. The external capital market may fail to allocate resources adequately to high-potential investments, compared with corporate office investments, because it has less accurate information. The corporate office of a diversified company can more effectively perform such tasks as disciplining underperforming management teams and allocating resources.[71]

Some firms still follow the unrelated diversification strategy.[72] Many of these large diversified business groups are found in southern European countries and throughout the emerging economies of the world. The Strategic Focus on diversified business

Refocusing Large Diversified Business Groups in Emerging Economies

Large firms with portfolios of unrelated businesses throughout the world's emerging economies, as well as in some developed economies, are seeking to refocus their portfolios on a "core." The intention of this type of strategic action is to improve performance. These large diversified business groups, known as the Chaebols in South Korea, are actually quite typical of those in capitalist countries that have industrialized since World War II. Many such firms from Asia and Latin America are using a model of Western corporate-level strategies and are refocusing their diversified operations: "Companies are mimicking Corporate America by refocusing, downsizing, merging, and spinning off faltering businesses to become globally competitive." But, at times, this refocusing may not be wholly appropriate in an emerging economy. Nonetheless, many of the firms have followed the pattern in the United States and the United Kingdom, where high levels of diversified operations have been refocused. A number of refocused firms specialize in managing businesses with core technology families to realize related diversification.

However, in emerging economies and in many highly developed economies such as France, Germany, and Italy, these diversified business groups have dominated the competitive landscape for several reasons. Some have argued that the underlying reason for having these conglomerates in the first place has not changed that much, especially in regard to emerging economies. Tarun Khanna and Krishna Palepu, accordingly, argue that the total restructuring of these diversified business groups is flawed. However, the recent financial crises in Asia and Latin America have reinforced the idea among politicians that these large business groups in emerging economies should refocus. In fact, in Korea, for instance, Kim Dae Jung, the president, pressed the Chaebols to downscope and invited foreign investors to help in the process by buying some of the assets that the Chaebols were forced to spin off.

Nevertheless, in a broad range of emerging economies, such as in Chile, India, and South Korea, it has taken longer than a decade to build institutions that support well-functioning infrastructure markets for capital, management, labor, and technology. The reason these diversified business groups evolved is that the markets for capital, management, labor, and international technology have been internalized in firms in those groups. The main problem is unequal (i.e., asymmetric) information and potential conflicts of interest between buyers and sellers in these markets. Where advanced markets exist, effective intermediaries, sound regulations, and contract laws can minimize the unequal information and any conflicts between buyers and sellers. For instance, in the U.S. financial market, investment bankers play an intermediary role in the allocation of capital to businesses. Furthermore, the Securities & Exchange Commission makes sure that investors can rely on corporate disclosure and, thereby, adequate information. In addition, well-developed contract law helps resolve conflicts between buyers and sellers, and hundreds of business schools provide graduates who possess the knowledge required to manage firms successfully through the use of the strategic management process.

However, in emerging economies, these institutional mechanisms are often missing, creating additional transaction costs between businesses. The existence of a "soft infrastructure" (laws, regulatory bodies, and financial intermediaries that facilitate the transactional environment) is as important as that of a hard physical infrastructure such as roads, ports, and telecommunications systems, because the former reduces transaction costs. China, for example, has invested heavily in its physical infrastructure, but has made little progress in creating a strong institutional infrastructure. Instead, China has been fostering large diversified business groups, such as the Baoshan Iron and Steel Group Corporation in steelmaking, the Haier Group in appliances, the Sichuan Chang Hong Group in televisions, the North China Pharmaceutical Group Corporation in drugs, the Jiangnan Shipyard Group Co. in shipbuilding, and the Peking University Founder Group Corp. in computer software. Although Western journalists have been disappointed with the formation of these large diversified corporations because unrelated diversification is often viewed as inefficient in more developed economies, they may be necessary because of the lack of a "soft infrastructure" in China. As in other emerging economies, these large diversified business groups serve as internal capital markets for the allocation of capital by a strong corporate headquarters. Furthermore, they function as a way to manage transactions, often through their own subsidiaries, when the country does not have a well developed legal infrastructure. The transactions are effective because the corporation has a way of managing them equitably within the firm and through family members or closely affiliated partners. In addition, these diversified companies serve as training grounds for managers in the labor market system, because educational institutions often are unable to train managers via distinctive business programs such as those found in Western educational institutions.

Although large diversified firms such as the Chaebols in Korea have been identified as the main cause of that country's economic problems, they in fact were necessary, given the absence of structure in the economy when those firms were first developing. Chile was one of the first emerging economies to seriously pursue market liberalization, and it has succeeded in developing one of the most efficient capital markets. However, the process of reform took more than 25 years and is still not complete. Although financial deregulation began in 1974 with the banking crisis, which was similar to the events in Asia in 1997, it was not until 1990 that the benefits of Chile's reforms started to take effect, when the first American Depository Receipt, La Compañía de Teléfonos de Chile, was listed on a U.S. exchange. In comparison, the Korean and Indian governments have both used banks as instruments of economic development, in a manner similar to bank lending policies in Malaysia and Indonesia. However, without a sharp-edged capital market such as that found in Chile, when a financial crisis develops, government interference has curtailed the development of basic financial intermediation expertise such as credit analysis.

As an example, Thai Petrochemical Industry, PCL, headquartered in Bangkok, Thailand, was recently forced to reorganize because of the Asian financial crisis and high levels of debt. This company and a number of others are sewn together in a large conglomerate owned by Prachai Leophairatana. Leophairatana was having a hard time understanding that when a company goes bankrupt, that its lenders, not its owners, have first claims over the remains of the firm. In Thailand, this sort of reasoning seemed unfair to the debtor and his employees. In fact, the government agreed, and the IMF relaxed the requirement to pass foreclosure legislation as part of a bailout package for Thailand. Without appropriate legislation and without suitable bankruptcy laws, it is unlikely that Thailand's financial difficulties can be resolved quickly. Traditionally, conglomerates in emerging economies have been controlled by families, and their main form of financing typically has been through debt, because debt allows family owners to control large business groups with a relatively small amount of equity capital. This approach has been used in Korean companies, and thus they are heavily indebted, even for very risky ventures. In theory, such risky ventures, such as diversifying into semiconductors, should be based on more long-term equity capital because debt requires short-term cash flow.

To restructure these firms in emerging economies, it may be necessary first to change their internal orientation rather than pursue drastic action, as was chosen by the Korean government. Most of these firms have adopted a growth orientation toward financial goals, forgoing some profits. Taking a stronger orientation toward profitability would help make individual firms or divisions more accountable for their operating performance. In addition, the corporate office should take a role in management development by delegating operational authority to large affiliate corporations. Groupwide recruiting, training, and job rotation programs would be helpful as well. These programs would allow executives to receive the training they need, but also enable them to be responsible for a greater profit orientation at the business or division level. Such an orientation would create better financial information internally and ultimately would lead to more transparent transactions in the economy. Rather than placing the blame on Korea's Chaebols, which have responded to government policy in the past, the Korean government should focus on building more effective institutions, a result of which would be a weeding out of inefficient groups. Simply blaming the Chaebols for the crisis is not helpful. The government should invite foreign competitors and, thereby, stronger product market competition. Effective intermediaries would then develop, and they would not be isolated from foreign competition. They could familiarize themselves with investment banking, venture capitalists, and new business school techniques. Thus, focusing on developing the "soft infrastructure" may be better for a government than blaming firms that helped them achieve the foundation of economic development, even though the current weaknesses have been exposed by the Asian financial crisis.

SOURCES: T. Khanna & K. Palepu, 1999, The right way to restructure conglomerates in emerging markets, *Harvard Business Review,* 77(4): 125–134; M. Schuman & J. L. Lee, 1999, Dismantling of Daewoo shows how radically Korea is changing, *Wall Street Journal,* August 17, A1, A10; J. Webber, H. Dawley, E, Malkin, M. Tanikawa, & I. Katz, 1999, International: As the world restructures, *Business Week Online,* June 14, *www.businessweek.com*; L. Chang, 1998, Big is beautiful, *Wall Street Journal,* April 30, R9; D. McDermott, 1998, Asian recovery focus shifts to Thailand, *Wall Street Journal,* December 9, A19.

groups in emerging economies speaks to how many of those business groups are becoming less diversified. As our discussion of these strategic actions suggests, choosing not to use the unrelated diversification strategy may actually decrease a firm's strategic competitiveness.

Implementing the unrelated business strategy continues to make sense in many economies of the world, as the Strategic Focus points out, especially among emerging economies such as that of China. But research also indicates that the conglomerate or unrelated strategy has not disappeared in Europe, where the number of firms using this strategy has actually increased.[73] Although many conglomerates (e.g., ITT and Hansen Trust) have refocused, other unrelated diversified firms have replaced them. The Achilles heel of the unrelated strategy is that conglomerates in developing economies have a fairly short life cycle because financial economies are more easily duplicated than in the case of operational and corporate relatedness. This is less of a problem in emerging economies, where the absence of a "soft infrastructure" (e.g., effective financial intermediaries, sound regulations, and contract laws) supports and encourages the pursuit of the unrelated diversification strategy.

Restructuring

Another alternative, similar to the internal capital market approach, focuses exclusively on buying and selling other firms' assets in the external market.[74] As in the real-estate business, profits are earned by buying assets low, restructuring them, and selling them as high as possible. This restructuring approach usually entails buying the firm, selling off its assets, such as corporate headquarters, and terminating corporate staff members.

Selling underperforming divisions and placing the remaining divisions under the discipline of rigorous financial controls is an additional restructuring action that is often used. Rigorous controls require divisions to follow strict budgets and account regularly for cash inflows and outflows to corporate headquarters. A firm that pursues this approach may have to use hostile takeovers or tender offers. Hostile takeovers have the potential to increase the resistance of the target firm's top-level managers. In these cases, corporate-level managers often are dismissed, while division managers are retained.

Creating financial economies through the purchase of other companies and the restructuring of their assets requires an understanding of significant trade-offs. Success usually calls for a focus on mature, low-technology businesses. Otherwise, resource allocation decisions become too complex because the uncertainty of demand for high-technology products requires information-processing capabilities that are beyond those of the smaller corporate staffs of firms employing the unrelated diversification strategy. Service businesses are also difficult to buy and sell in this way, because of their client or sales orientation. Sales staffs of service businesses are more mobile than those of manufacturing-oriented businesses and may seek jobs with a competitor, taking their clients with them. This is especially so in professional service businesses such as accounting, law, advertising, consulting, and investment banking. These businesses probably would not create value if they were acquired by a firm restructuring using an unrelated diversification strategy.

Through the strategic leadership of its CEO, L. Dennis Kozlowski, Tyco International, Ltd., completed 109 acquisitions between 1992 and the beginning of 1999. It is not unusual for this firm to conclude a dozen acquisitions per year. Accordingly, Tyco's revenues grew from $3 billion in 1992 to $23 billion in 1999. However, questions raised toward the end of 1999 resulted in a substantial decline in the value of the firm's stock. The main issue of inquiry revolved around concerns about accounting aberrations of the Bermuda-headquartered firm.[75]

Tyco focuses on buying and restructuring businesses in four market segments: disposable medical supplies, valves, fire protection and electronic security, and electrical and electronic components. Although those businesses are not highly profitable, "he [Kozlowski] squeezes the most out of these operations with ultra-lean and decentralized management. His headquarters staff numbers only about 70, centered around four worldwide managers."[76] As they dispose of larger headquarters staffs in acquired companies, streamline operations, and use Tyco financial control systems, Kozlowski and his small headquarters team improve the overall company performance of their diversified operations.

Diversification: Incentives and Resources

The economic reasons given in the last section summarize the conditions under which diversification strategies increase a firm's value. Diversification, however, is often undertaken with the expectation that doing so will prevent a firm from *losing* some of its value. Thus, there are reasons to diversify that are value neutral. In fact, some research evidence indicates that all diversification moves lead to trade-offs and some level of suboptimization.[77] Nonetheless, several incentives may lead a firm to pursue further diversification.

Incentives to Diversify

Incentives to diversify come from both the external environment and a firm's internal environment. The term "incentive" implies that managers have some choice regarding whether to pursue the incentive or not. Incentives external to the firm include antitrust regulation and tax laws. Internal firm incentives include low performance, uncertain future cash flows, and an overall reduction of risk for the firm.

Antitrust Regulation and Tax Laws

Government antitrust policies and tax laws provided incentives for U.S. firms to diversify in the 1960s and 1970s.[78] The application of U.S. antitrust laws to mergers that created increased market power (via either vertical or horizontal integration) was stringent in the 1960s and 1970s.[79] As a result, many of the mergers during that time were unrelated—that is, they involved companies pursuing different lines of business. Thus, the merger wave of the 1960s was "conglomerate" in character. Merger activity leading to conglomerate diversification was encouraged primarily by the Celler–Kefauver Act (which discouraged horizontal and vertical mergers). For example, in the 1973–1977 period, 79.1 percent of all mergers were conglomerate.[80]

The mergers of the 1980s, however, were different. Antitrust enforcement ebbed, permitting more and larger horizontal mergers (acquisitions of target firms in the same line of business, such as a merger between two oil companies).[81] In addition, investment bankers became more freewheeling in the kinds of mergers they would try to facilitate; as a consequence, hostile takeovers increased to unprecedented numbers.[82] The conglomerates or highly diversified firms of the 1960s and 1970s became more "focused" in the 1980s and 1990s as merger constraints were relaxed and restructuring was implemented.[83]

Tax effects on diversification stem not only from individual tax rates, but also from corporate tax changes. Some companies (especially mature ones) may have activities that generate more cash than they can reinvest profitably. Michael Jensen, a prominent financial economist, believes that such *free cash flows* (liquid financial assets for which investments in current businesses are no longer economically viable) should be redistributed to shareholders in the form of dividends.[84] However, in the 1960s and 1970s, dividends were taxed more heavily than ordinary personal income. As a result, before 1980, shareholders preferred that companies retained free cash flows for use in buying and building companies in high-performance industries. If the stock value appreciated over the long term, shareholders might receive a better return on those funds than through dividends, because they would be taxed more lightly under capital-gains rules.

In 1986, however, the top ordinary individual income tax rate was reduced from 50 percent to 28 percent, and the special capital-gains tax was changed, causing capital gains to be treated as ordinary income. These changes gave an incentive to shareholders to stop encouraging firms to retain funds for purposes of diversification. Moreover, the elimination of personal-interest deductions, as well as the lower attractiveness of retained earnings to shareholders, prompted the use of more leverage by firms, for which interest expense is tax deductible. These tax law changes also influenced an increase in divestitures of unrelated business units after 1984. Thus, although individual tax rates for capital gains and dividends created a shareholder incentive to increase diversification before 1986, they encouraged *less* diversification after 1986, unless it was funded by tax-deductible debt.

Regarding corporate taxation, acquisitions typically increase a firm's depreciable asset allowances. Increased depreciation (non–cash-flow expense) produces lower taxable income, thereby providing an additional incentive for acquisitions. Before 1986, acquisitions may have been the most attractive means for securing tax benefits,[85] but the 1986 Tax Reform Act diminished some of the corporate tax advantages of diversification.[86]

Recently, a loosening of federal regulations, coupled with a desire to expand product offerings in order to hold onto and build upon existing franchises, has provided incentives for large U.S. banks to become more diversified through the pursuit of related diversification. By acquiring securities firms, investment banks, and other financial services companies, some large banks have diversified their revenue streams considerably. For example, John McCoy became CEO of Bank One in 1986. "He transformed a family business into a national powerhouse by aggressively acquiring other regional banks," culminating with a $19 billion buyout of First Chicago NBD Corp. With this acquisition, Bank One became the fourth largest bank in the United States. However, such diversified growth recently led to the deterioration of Bank One's financial performance. As a result, Bank One's McCoy resigned and the bank itself may be a takeover candidate because of low valuations of its stock price.[87]

In another diversification move, Citigroup was formed from the merger of Travelers and Citibank. Travelers had formerly merged Solomon and Smith Barney, two investment bank and retail brokerage operations, with its insurance and other financial products divisions, once financial deregulation occurred. However, the merger creating Citigroup in mid-1999 was having some struggles dealing with the leadership and cultural integration of the banking, credit card, insurance, and investment businesses.[88]

In addition to the external incentive to diversify based on antitrust regulation and tax laws, a number of incentives internal to the firm increase the likelihood that diversification will be pursued.

Low Performance

It has been proposed that "high performance eliminates the need for greater diversification,"[89] as in the example of the Wm. Wrigley Jr. Co. Conversely, low performance may provide an incentive for diversification. Firms plagued by poor performance often take higher risks.[90] Interestingly, though, some researchers have found that low returns are related to greater levels of diversification.[91] Poor performance may lead to increased diversification, especially if resources exist to pursue that tack. Continued poor returns following additional diversification, however, may slow the pace of diversification and even lead to divestitures. Thus, an overall curvilinear relationship, as illustrated in Figure 6.3, may exist between diversification and performance.[92]

Lockheed Martin may have diversified beyond its capabilities to manage its level of diversification. The company is the largest defense contractor in the world, primarily because it chose to buy post-Cold War defense assets when other firms were selling them. However, the government has grown uncomfortable with so much power centered in one defense contractor. When Lockheed Martin was forced to drop its $11.6 billion bid for Northrop Grumman, another defense contractor, in the face of government objections, it sought to acquire Comsat Corporation, which launches and delivers satellites. Lockheed Martin has also been interested in General Electric, PLC, a British defense company, and other transatlantic deals, to diversify away from the United States. Financial analysts, however, have driven down Lockheed's stock as it ponders these potential deals, because the firm has become so diversified, that one analyst questioned, "Has this company just gotten too big and too complex?" In a period when the stock prices of most companies have been increasing, Lockheed Martin's price plummeted to a 52-week low at the beginning of the millennium. Although Lockheed's diversification creates strength when it can integrate its various

FIGURE

6.3 | The Curvilinear Relationship Between Diversification and Performance

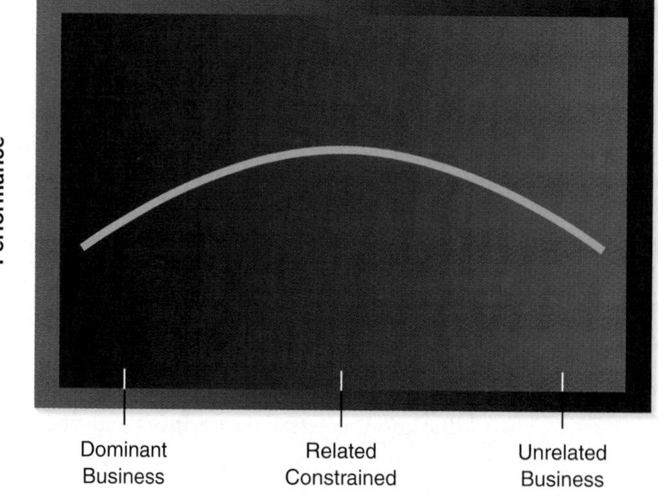

divisions to bid for contracts, Lockheed's CEO, Peter B. Teets, suggests, "My biggest challenge is to learn how to harness that strength." Evidence suggests that Lockheed Martin's diversification is currently on the downside of the diversification-performance curve in Figure 6.3.[93]

Recent evidence suggests that Jürgen Schrempp, CEO of DaimlerChrysler, is dealing successfully with the challenges that were created partly by the firm's failed attempts to diversify. Since assuming leadership of DaimlerChrysler, Schrempp has taken decisive actions. Money-losing operations, including the firm's electronics business and its 24 percent stake in Cap Gemini, the French software services company, were sold. Fokker, the Dutch airplane manufacturer, was liquidated (interestingly, when he was serving as head of Daimler's aerospace division, Schrempp himself orchestrated the acquisition of Fokker).[94] In addition, Schrempp eliminated a layer of upper-level executives and is trying to instill a culture of responsibility and entrepreneurship in the company. Thought of as a cultural revolution in which each of Daimler's 23 remaining business units is expected to earn at least 12 percent on its invested capital, innovation is the driving force being used to create the new culture.

With the resources from the sales of more diversified operations, Schrempp decided to focus on cars and proposed a revolutionary merger with Chrysler Corporation. The transaction set off a wave of consolidations in the global auto industry.[95] DaimlerChrysler is now at a more optimal level of diversification on the curve shown in Figure 6.3. However, DaimlerChrysler does not want to stop there; rather, the German–American company now hopes to be the "largest transportation company in the world." To achieve this it will need to overtake Volkswagen, Toyota, Ford, and General Motors, currently the fourth-largest through largest, respectively. This means that the

When Jürgen Schrempp (shown here) became CEO of Daimler-Benz, he had to take decisive actions to counteract the company's failed acquisitions. Money-losing operations were sold or liquidated and an upper layer of executives was eliminated. Deciding to focus on cars, Schrempp proposed a revolutionary merger with Chrysler Corporation.

firm will have to form one or two partnerships with other automakers or else acquire them outright. In fact, DaimlerChrysler had discussions with Honda Motor Co., Fiat SpA, and Peugot Citroën. In 2000, DaimlerChrysler acquired a percent stake in Mitsubishi Motors. The reasons for the purchase include the firm's need to be a prominent small-car manufacturer, given the increasing size of that market on a global basis. Thus, DaimlerChrysler will likely continue using focused diversified growth, and to gain access to the Asian Market.[96]

Uncertain Future Cash Flows

As a firm's product line matures or is threatened, diversification may be perceived as an important defensive strategy. Small firms and companies in mature or maturing industries sometimes find it necessary to diversify to survive over the long term.[97] Certainly, this was one of the dominant reasons for diversification among railroad firms during the 1960s and 1970s. Railroads diversified primarily because the trucking industry was perceived to have significant negative effects on the demand for rail transportation. Uncertainty, however, can be derived from both supply and demand sources.

Franco Tato is the CEO of ENEL, Italy's state-owned electricity company. Through Tato's leadership, ENEL has diversified its operation to the point where it has moved from a sole focus on electricity to the building of a diversified portfolio that includes telecommunications, water distribution, and Internet services. Accordingly, some have compared ENEL's acquisition spree to becoming a new version of the state-owned IRI, which once owned everything from Italy's telephone lines to Alitalia, the national airline. Furthermore, there are serious questions about whether ENEL is cross-subsidizing its acquisitions with revenues from the electricity side, which would be a questionable practice, because it is a consumer-oriented utility. However, Tato justifies the firm's diversification on the grounds that ENEL's grip on the Italian electricity market is threatened. Not only deregulation in Italy, but also deregulation across Europe, may mean that ENEL will have to cede 30 percent of its generating capacity to new rivals with cheaper electricity production. One of these rivals may be the state-owned Electricité de France, which is focused on selling its excess electricity across borders. With regard to electricity, ENEL's plans are to secure overseas contracts to build power stations, because that is a core competence of the company. However, the main thrust of the firm's diversification strategy is to develop a multiutility that focuses on a portfolio of services in electricity, water, gas, and Internet service, as well as mobile-phone customers. One analyst suggested that there may be five to seven large groups of electric producers in Europe. Thus, ENEL's future sources of revenue are threatened. ENEL has responded by using a corporate-level diversification strategy to compete in multiple segments of the utility market.[98]

For decades, Reuben Central Design Bureau was a secretive brain trust behind Russia's successful and renowned submarine industry. This Bureau created the *Typhoon*, the world's largest and most silent and lethal submarine. The group's work earned two coveted Orders of Lenin, which are still prominently displayed near the bust of the man himself. However, after 1989, this Soviet military design bureau needed to change. When it did change, the Bureau used a diversification strategy and became Russia's first international business center. With its world-class design engineers, it beat

Russian rivals competing to design an oil platform for a group of Russian companies working in the oil-rich waters around Sakhalin Island, off the nation's Pacific coast. With this success in 1992, the Bureau subsequently caught the eye of a consortium of firms, including Marathon Oil Company of Houston, Texas, and the Royal Dutch/Shell Group, which needed help customizing an enormous drilling platform transported from Alaska and used off Sakhalin. This work proved that the firm could do more than design submarines. Besides continuing its marine business, the Bureau was able to secure contracts in other areas, such as developing an experimental high-speed rail train and link. In addition, it won a contract to develop a floating sea launch for three rocket companies in Russia and Ukraine, with venture partners Boeing and a Norwegian company, Kvaerner ASA. In addition to executing these ventures and maintaining its focus on nonnuclear (e.g., diesel-powered) submarines, the Bureau has pursued real-estate development through its business center. The Bureau also has six restaurants and many other projects in St. Petersburg. It entered the tea business when tea was used as barter for some of its submarines sold in Asia. In many of these projects, the Bureau has used its connections with local and federal government leaders to gain the bureaucratic approvals needed. The Bureau's diversification strategy has allowed it to survive in the chaotic Russian economic environment.[99]

Firm Risk Reduction

Synergy exists when the value created by business units working together exceeds the value those same units create when working independently.

Because diversified firms pursuing economies of scope often have investments that are too inflexible to realize synergy between business units, a number of problems may arise. **Synergy** exists when the value created by business units working together exceeds the value those same units create working independently. But, as a firm increases its relatedness between business units, it also increases its risk of corporate failure, because synergy produces joint interdependence between business units and the firm's flexibility to respond is constrained. This threat may force two basic decisions.

First, the firm may reduce its level of technological change by operating in more certain environments. This behavior may make the firm risk averse to and thus uninterested in pursuing new product lines that have potential, but are not proven. Alternatively, the firm may constrain its level of activity sharing and forego the benefits of synergy. Either or both decisions may lead to further diversification. The former would lead to related diversification into industries in which more certainty exists. The latter may produce additional, but unrelated, diversification.[100] Research suggests that a firm which pursues a related diversification strategy is more careful in its bidding for new businesses, whereas a firm which pursues an unrelated diversification move may more easily overprice its bid. An unrelated bidder may not be aware of all the informational dilemmas that the acquired firm faces.[101]

Boeing, for example, has been diversifying to reduce its dependence on commercial airlines and the frequent cycles in this business line. In 1998, Boeing acquired Rockwell's space division and McDonnell Douglas. Both acquisitions were designed to help Boeing improve its position in commercial space activities. In 2000, Boeing agreed to purchase Hughes Electronics space operations. Hughes divested this unit so that it could better focus on DirectTV and other future Internet operations.[102] Boeing also invested in a long-range project with McCaw Cellular and Microsoft to create an Internet-in-the-sky satellite system called Teledesic. The Teledesic system would be the first satellite system with the capability of handling any kind of communication, from voice calls to Internet browsing to video and interactive multimedia. The system would be analogous to throwing a fiber-optic net around the world, but in space. Teledesic is different from Motorola's Iridium network, which has been in financial difficulty. The Iridium network was designed to handle only voice communication via mobile phones. These ventures are positioning Boeing as an aerospace firm for the next economic frontier—space. Once it has the Teledesic system in place, Boeing will be a world-class satellite producer and launcher.[103] However, the results of the firm's diversification strategy are as yet uncertain.

Resources and Diversification

Although a firm may have incentives to diversify, it must possess the resources required to make diversification economically feasible.[104] As mentioned earlier, tangible, intangible, and financial resources may facilitate diversification. Resources vary in their utility for value creation, however, because of differences in rarity and mobility; that is, some resources are easier for competitors to duplicate because they are not rare, valuable, costly to imitate, and nonsubstitutable. For instance, free cash flows may be used to diversify the firm. Because these resources are more flexible and common, they are less likely to create value compared with other types of resources.[105] The earlier-mentioned diversification on the part of steel firms was significantly facilitated by the presence of free cash flows.

Similarly, Anheuser–Busch was a very profitable company, and significant cash flows were created from the success of the brewery business. These resources were used to purchase the St. Louis Cardinals, to invest almost $400 million in the development and operation of the Eagle snack food business, and to acquire the Campbell Taggart bakery business. The use of the resources, however, did not produce significant positive returns for Anheuser–Busch, and as a result, the firm decided to spin off Campbell Taggart, sell the St. Louis Cardinals, and close the Eagle snacks business.[106] Still the world's largest brewing organization, Anheuser–Busch continues to use free cash flows to support its business interests in theme park operations, manufacturing and recycling aluminum beverage containers, rice milling, real-estate development, turf farming, railcar repair and transportation, and paper-label printing, among others.[107] It is the diversification created by this particular mix of businesses that the corporation's executives are able to manage in a way that creates value.

Tangible resources usually include the plant and equipment necessary to produce a product. Such assets may be less flexible: Any excess capacity often can be used only for very closely related products, especially those requiring highly similar manufacturing technologies. Excess capacity of other tangible resources, such as a sales force, can be used to diversify more easily. Again, excess capacity in a sales force would be more effective with related diversification, because it may be utilized to sell similar products. The sales force would be more knowledgeable about related-product characteristics, customers, and distribution channels. Tangible resources may create resource interrelationships in production, marketing, procurement, and technology, defined earlier as activity sharing.

Intangible resources are more flexible than tangible physical assets in facilitating diversification. Although the sharing of tangible resources may induce diversification, intangible resources could encourage even more diversification. Clearly, some potential intangible resource synergies could be achieved by Anheuser–Busch. For example, the firm's knowledge of yeast products may have been useful in the operation of Campbell Taggart. It did not, however, produce significant positive synergies between the brewery and bakery businesses, as was hoped by Anheuser–Busch executives.[108] Apparently, there was little sharing of tangible or intangible resources; thus, little value was created.

Extent of Diversification

If a firm has both the incentives and the resources to diversify, the extent of its diversification will be greater than if it has incentives or resources alone.[109] The more flexible, the more likely it is that the resources will be used for unrelated diversification; the less flexible, the more likely it is that the resources will be used for related diversification. Thus, flexible resources (e.g., free cash flows) are likely to lead to relatively greater levels of diversification.[110] Also, because related diversification requires more information processing to manage links between businesses, more unrelated units can be managed by a small corporate office.[111]

Managerial Motives to Diversify

Managerial motives for diversification may exist independently of incentives and resources and include managerial risk reduction and a desire for increased compensation.[112] For instance, diversification may reduce top-level managers' *employment risk* (the risk of job loss or income reduction). That is, corporate executives may diversify a firm in order to diversify their employment risk, as long as profitability does not suffer excessively.[113] Diversification also provides an additional benefit to managers that shareholders do not enjoy. Diversification and firm size are highly correlated, and as size increases, so does executive compensation.[114] Large firms are more complex and harder to manage; thus, managers of larger firms are better compensated.[115] This increased compensation may serve as a motive for managers to engage in greater diversification. Governance mechanisms, such as the board of directors, monitoring by owners, executive compensation, and the market for corporate control, may limit managerial tendencies to overdiversify. These mechanisms are discussed in more detail in Chapter 10.

On the other hand, governance mechanisms may not be strong, and in some instances managers may diversify the firm to the point that it fails to earn even average returns.[116] Resources employed to pursue each line of diversification are most likely to include financial assets (e.g., free cash flows), but may also involve intangible assets. Thus, this type of diversification is not likely to lead to improved performance. The loss of adequate internal governance may result in poor relative performance, thereby triggering a threat of takeover. Although this threat may create improved efficiency by replacing ineffective managerial teams, managers may avoid takeovers through defensive tactics (e.g., golden parachutes and poison pills). Therefore, an external governance threat, although having a restraining influence on managers, does not provide flawless control of managerial motives for diversification.[117]

Most large publicly held firms are profitable because managers are positive agents and many of their strategic actions (e.g., diversification moves) contribute to the firm's success. As mentioned, governance devices are designed to deal with *exceptions* to the norms of achieving strategic competitiveness and increasing shareholder wealth in the process. Thus, it is overly pessimistic to assume that managers usually act in their own self-interest as opposed to their firm's interest.[118]

Managers may also be held in check by concerns for their reputation in the labor market. If positive reputation facilitates power, a poor reputation may reduce power. Likewise, a market for managerial talent may deter managers from pursuing inappropriate diversification.[119] In addition, some diversified firms police other diversified firms, acquiring those poorly managed companies in order to restructure their asset base. Knowing that their firms could be acquired if they are not managed successfully, managers are encouraged to find ways to achieve strategic competitiveness.

In summary, although managers may be motivated to increase diversification, governance mechanisms are in place to discourage such action merely for managerial gain. However, this governance is imperfect and may not always produce the intended consequences. Even when governance mechanisms cause managers to correct a problem of overdiversification, these moves are not without trade-offs. For instance, firms that are spun off may not realize productivity gains, although spinning them off is in the best interest of the divesting firm.[120] Accordingly, the assumption that managers need disciplining may not be entirely correct, and sometimes governance may create consequences that are worse than those resulting from overdiversification.[121]

In general, the level of diversification the firm chooses should be based on the optimal levels indicated by market and strategic characteristics (resources) owned or available to each company. In turn, optimality may be judged in terms of resources, managerial motives, and incentives.

As shown in Figure 6.4, the level of diversification that can be expected to have the greatest positive effect on performance (i.e., strategic competitiveness and the earning of above-average returns) is based partly on how the interaction of resources, managerial motives, and incentives affects the adoption of particular diversification strategies. As indicated earlier, the greater the incentives and the more flexible the resources, the higher is the level of expected diversification. Financial resources (the most flexible) should have a stronger relationship to the extent of diversification than either tangible or intangible resources. Tangible resources (the most inflexible) are useful primarily for related diversification.

The model suggests that implementation issues are important to whether diversification creates value (see Chapter 11). The model also suggests that governance mechanisms are important to the level and type of diversification implemented (see Chapter 10).

As mentioned in this chapter, diversification strategies can enhance a firm's strategic competitiveness and help it to earn larger financial returns. However, as the model shows, diversification must be kept in check by governance devices, because managers also have motives (e.g., seeing their salaries increased) to grow the firm excessively through diversification. This appears to be the case, at least partially, with Philips Electronics NV.

FIGURE

6.4 | Summary Model of the Relationship Between Firm Performance and Diversification

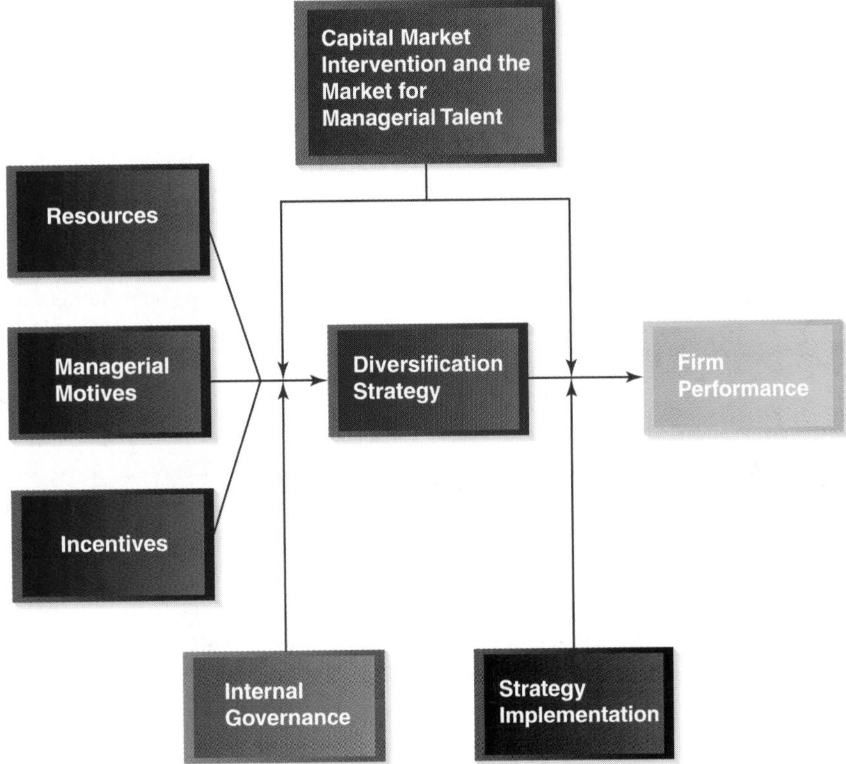

Source: R. E. Hoskisson & M. A. Hitt, 1990, Antecedents and performance outcomes of diversification: A review and critique of theoretical perspectives, *Journal of Management*, 16: 498.

Cor Boonstra has managed Philips, a large, widely diversified Dutch consumer electronics firm, since 1996. Although Boonstra has sold off or discontinued 40 of the company's businesses and has reorganized the company into eight groups called "building blocks," he has also added new businesses, such as ATL Ultrasound in medical equipment. Philips currently has 80 businesses, compared with 120 when Boonstra assumed the CEO position. However, some of the company's businesses continue to perform poorly. Philips recently had a charge against its earnings because of a failed cellular phone venture with Lucent Technologies. In this industry, Philips is a second-tier player behind leaders Nokia, Telefon ABLM Erikkson of Sweden, and Motorola of the United States. The firm's overall strategy is to compete in high-volume electronics businesses using the related linked diversification strategy. However, these businesses are very competitive, and Philips is competing against rivals such as Sony, which is much more focused and generates 44 percent more revenue than Philips with 59,000 fewer employees (Philips has a total of 234,000 employees). One analyst suggested

AOL's Diversification Merger with Time Warner

On January 11, 2000, a merger agreement was announced between AOL, an Internet service provider (ISP), and the media content company Time Warner, with businesses that include movies, magazines, and music, as well as significant cable TV operations. Both companies have resources and incentives to become more diversified, as Figure 6.4 suggests. In fact, additional levels of diversification solve a number of problems for each firm, but especially for AOL. First, there is much opportunity for resource synergy between the two firms. AOL will be able to advertise *Time* magazine and other Time Warner publications on AOL's Internet sites. Furthermore, Time Warner owns the Book-of-the-Month Club, which gives AOL an opportunity to connect with many new subscribers to its service. In addition, Time Warner music and movies could be made available over the Internet. However, the primary reason for the acquisition is the cable TV assets that provide AOL with broadband speed: Time Warner currently owns the Roadrunner cable modem ISP service. When AT&T bought MediaOne and developed TCI cable modem service, AOL's stock price decreased significantly, because, at the time, AOL did not appear to have a high-speed Internet service option. When the merger with Time Warner is complete, this problem will be solved. Accordingly, many resources will allow for synergistic improvement with both firms.

Some have questioned whether AOL and Time Warner are taking the best course of action. Because AT&T owns 25 percent of Time Warner, AOL must finalize an arrangement with AT&T to get more access to the broadband approach through AT&T's cable operations. The problem is that many service providers have been offering regular modem Internet service for free so that they can get households to spend money on bundled cable TV and local and long-distance telephone services. This development may be especially problematic for AOL because it generates most of its money from its ISP service.

At the time of the announcement of the AOL–Time Warner merger, Yahoo! did not feel that it would need to purchase a company like Disney; instead, Yahoo! decided that it would rather buy services from a *range* of media providers, such as Disney and News Corp., as well as from television stations and movie producers. Yahoo! believes that its media needs may be much cheaper to satisfy through purchase on the open market rather than through vertical integration. In addition, Yahoo! can achieve more flexibility that way. Yahoo! feels that the AOL–Time Warner merger is an unproved strategy for an ISP: "It may be more viable for AOL rivals to strike different contract and distribution deals with a number of companies rather than to tie themselves inextricably to one partner."

A number of implementation details also will influence the degree of success that is gained from the diversification created by the AOL–Time Warner merger. Gerald Levin, current CEO of Time Warner, will be the CEO of the new company, while Steve Case, current CEO of AOL, will be the chairman. Case apparently felt that the transaction would not be consummated unless Levin, a very powerful and politically astute individual, was in charge of operations. Fortunately, this plan fit in with Case's leadership style, in that he is more of a strategic thinker than an operations manager. It remains to be seen how successful the efforts to assimilate the two diverse cultures will be: AOL is quite entrepreneurial, while, in contrast, the culture at Time Warner is stodgier and not focused on running on "Internet time."

AOL's stock price depreciated considerably shortly after the merger was announced, while that of Time Warner increased significantly. This combination of events, in which the acquiring firm's stock price declines while that of the target increases, is not unusual. However, how the diverse set of investors will mesh is also an important issue, in that AOL and Time Warner investors have different investment criteria and risk preferences. Nonetheless, several analysts suggested that institutional investors supported the merger. The board of directors will also have an influence on what happens, but only time will tell how the situation will evolve. Eight directors from each firm will be on the board. AOL shareholders will own 55 percent of the newly formed company, Time Warner shareholders 45

In the long run, the product market and rivals' strategic positioning will influence the effectiveness of the merger. AT&T has said that it will not seek to get into media content through such an acquisition. However, the prices of its main products, telecommunications services, are rapidly decreasing, and one wonders whether the company may need to pursue content deals to earn higher profit margins. As mentioned, Yahoo! signaled that it would not get into content in the near future, preferring instead the flexibility to contract for opportunities in that regard with a broad range of providers.

In sum, a number of resources and incentives support the diversification merger between AOL and Time Warner. There also may be managerial motives, especially on the part of Ted Turner (Turner Broadcasting was purchased by Time Warner) and Gerald Levin, who own significant amounts of stock in the new company. Indeed, their net worth has increased with the acquisition. However, the success of the acquisition will depend on a number of leadership, cost, and restructuring issues. Furthermore, how well synergy is realized through the combination of resources will have a significant impact on the well-being of the firm. The reaction by capital and product market players will also play into the success or failure of the diversification move. Finally, whether the transaction is approved by regulators will influence the success or failure of the merger. Usually, media combinations take longer to pass through the regulatory process, creating at least short-term uncertainty for all parties.

SOURCES: G. Farrell, 2000, Deal forms multimedia marketer, *USA Today,* January 17, *www.usatoday.com*; M. Murray, N. Deogun, & N. Wingfield, 2000, Can Time Warner click with AOL? Here are eight things to watch, *Wall Street Journal,* January 14, A1, A16; M. Rose, 2000, Database of merged AOL brings cheers and chills, *Wall Street Journal,* January 14, B6; D. Solomon, 2000, AOL's path to broadband now clear, *USA Today,* January 11, *www.usatoday.com*; K. Swisher, 2000, Yahoo! posts a loud message: we're not next, *Wall Street Journal,* January 12, B1, B4.

---

that if Philips were headquartered in the United States, it "would have restructured more drastically many years ago."[122]

To understand why Philips has not restructured, one must understand the relationship between diversification strategy and corporate governance practices in the Netherlands. The board of directors at Philips is governed by a complex set of bylaws of the Philips Foundation, which includes most of the firm's directors and executives and gives them the power to make binding recommendations about appointments to the board. In effect, the foundation decides who runs Philips, and ordinary shareholders have little say in the matter. In fact, shareholders can do little to get rid of management if they feel that managers are not doing a good job. The main way that Philips investors have to express their concerns is to sell the company's stock. Corporate bylaws and custom in most Dutch-incorporated companies do not allow shareholders to vote for directors or fire underperforming managers. Neither do shareholders have the right to launch proxy fights and vote on takeover bids. Although pension funds and the Dutch government are starting to push for change, shareholders are still rarely consulted when it comes to large mergers or acquisitions. However, because Philips is internationally traded, analysts believe that it is still undervalued, although its shares have increased in value during Boonstra's tenure. In sum, Philips Electronics is overdiversified and undervalued primarily because there are no strong corporate governance procedures to force its restructuring.

To receive positive outcomes from a diversification strategy, a company must use a proper amount and type of diversification.[123] The chapter's final Strategic Focus is a recent example of diversification, with final outcomes that are yet to be determined. The transaction is between an Internet provider (AOL) and a media content provider (Time Warner).

As the Strategic Focus on the AOL–Time Warner merger suggests, a number of issues are involved in creating an effective diversification strategy. The firm must prepare forthright answers to questions of leadership, the synergistic use of combined resources, and competitive reactions in order for the strategy to improve the company's performance. If the answers to these questions are in the direction opposite that which suggests an ability to create value through diversification, then a decision *not* to become more diversified is required. At the corporate level, value is created through the selection and management of a particular group of businesses that is worth more under the ownership of the acquiring company than it would be under any other ownership.[124]

Summary

- Pursuing a single- or dominant-business, corporate-level strategy may be preferable to seeking a more diversified business strategy, unless a corporation can develop economies of scope or financial economies between businesses, or unless it can obtain market power through additional levels of diversification. These economies and market power are the main sources of value creation when the firm diversifies.
- The primary reasons a firm pursues increased diversification are value creation through economies of scope, financial economies, or market power; some actions are taken because of government policy, performance problems, uncertainties about future cash flow, or managerial motivations (e.g., to increase compensation).
- Managerial motives to diversify can lead to overdiversification. On the other hand, managers can also be good stewards of the firm's assets.
- The level of a firm's diversification is a function of the incentives the firm has to diversify, its resources, and the managerial motives to diversify.
- Related diversification can create value by sharing activities or transferring core competencies.
- Sharing activities usually involves sharing tangible resources between businesses. Transferring core competencies involves transferring the core competencies developed in one business to another business. It also may involve transferring competencies between the corporate office and a business unit.
- Sharing activities is usually associated with related con-

strained diversification. Activity sharing is costly to implement and coordinate, may create unequal benefits for the divisions involved in the sharing, and may lead to fewer managerial risk-taking behaviors.

- Successful unrelated diversification is accomplished by efficiently allocating resources or restructuring a target firm's assets and placing them under rigorous financial controls.

Review Questions

1. What is corporate-level strategy? Why is it important to a diversified firm?
2. What are the advantages and disadvantages of single- and dominant-business strategies, compared with those of firms with higher levels of diversification?
3. What are three reasons that firms choose to move from either a single- or a dominant-business position to a more diversified position?
4. How do firms share activities and transfer core competencies to obtain economies of scope while pursuing a related diversification strategy?
5. What are the two ways to obtain financial economies when a firm pursues an unrelated diversification strategy?
6. What incentives and resources encourage diversification in firms?
7. What motives might encourage managers to engage a firm in more diversification than seems appropriate?

Application Discussion Questions

1. This chapter suggests that there is a curvilinear relationship between diversification and performance. How can this relationship be modified so that the negative relationship between performance and diversification is reduced and the downward curve has less slope or begins at a higher level of diversification?
2. The *Fortune* 500 firms are very large, and many of them have significant product diversification. Are these large firms overdiversified? Do they experience lower performance than they should?
3. What is the primary reason for overdiversification? Is it industrial policies, such as taxes and antitrust regulation, or do firms overdiversify because managers pursue their own self-interest through increased compensation, and a reduced risk of job loss? Why? Explain.
4. One rationale for pursuing related diversification is to obtain market power. In the United States, however, too much market power may result in a challenge by the U.S. Justice Department (because it may be perceived as anticompetitive). Under what situations might related diversification be considered unfair competition?
5. Suppose you have two job offers, one from a dominant-business firm and one from an unrelated diversified firm (suppose the beginning salaries are virtually identical). Which offer would you accept and why?
6. Do you believe that by the year 2010 large firms will be more or less diversified than they are today? Why? Will the trends regarding diversification be identical in Europe, the United States, and Japan? Explain.
7. Will the Internet make it easier for firms to diversify? Why or why not?

Ethics Questions

1. Suppose you overheard the following statement: "Those managing an unrelated diversified firm face far more difficult ethical challenges than do those managing a dominant-business firm." Based on your reading of this chapter, is this statement true or false? Why?
2. Is it ethical for managers to diversify a firm rather than return excess earnings to shareholders? Provide reasoning in support of your answer.
3. What unethical practices might occur when a firm restructures? Explain.
4. Do you believe that ethical managers are unaffected by the managerial motives to diversify discussed in this chapter? If so, why? In addition, do you believe that ethical managers should help their peers learn how to avoid making diversification decisions on the basis of the managerial motives to diversify? Why or why not?

Internet Exercise

Search the Web sites of CMGI (**www.cmgi.com**), Cisco Systems (**www.cisco.com**), EMC (**www.emc.com**), and ICG (**www.internetcapital.com**). Compare their business models, and explain the type of strategy and level of diversification that describes each one. In the extremely fast-cycle Internet economy, these companies run exceptional risks. Track the success of each company's stocks over the past six months. Can you pinpoint changes within the industry that have affected the rise and fall of stock prices? What advancements in information technology and electronic commerce have had the greatest effect on the continuing strategies of these companies? Does this type of collaboration amongst Internet companies foster growth and value within the industry?

***e-project:** In the second Strategic Focus, the refocusing of large diversified groups in emerging economies was discussed. In late January 2000, the top three Chaebols in South Korea—Hyundai (**www.hyundai.com**), Samsung (**www.samsung.com**), and LG Group (**www.lg.co.kr**)—were fined by the government's Fair Trade Commission for illegally allocating funds to their failing subsidiaries. Using the information provided on the company Web sites, choose one of these companies, and provide alternative strategies for it to better compete in international markets.

Notes

1. B. Orwell, 2000, Disney to recast Go network Web property as entertainment destination, Dow Jones.com archives, January 27, *www.dowjones.com.*
2. M. E. Porter, 1980, *Competitive Strategy* (New York: The Free Press), xvi.
3. T. B. Palmer & R. M. Wiseman, 1999, Decoupling risk taking from income stream uncertainty: A holistic model of risk, *Strategic Management Journal,* 20: 1037–1062; K. Ramaswamy, 1997, The performance impact of strategic similarity in horizontal mergers: Evidence from the U.S. banking industry, *Academy of Management Journal,* 40: 697–715.
4. M. A. Hitt, R. E. Hoskisson, & H. Kim, 1997, International diversification: Effects on innovation and firm performance in product-diversified firms, *Academy of Management Journal,* 40: 767–798; W. G. Rowe & P. M. Wright, 1997, Related and unrelated diversification and their effect on human resource management controls, *Strategic Management Journal,* 18: 329–338.
5. D. D. Bergh & M. W. Lawless, 1998, Portfolio restructuring and limits to hierarchical governance: The effects of environmental uncertainty and diversification strategy, *Organization Science,* 9: 87–102; W. Boeker, 1997, Executive migration and strategic change: The effect of top manager movement on product-market entry, *Administrative Science Quarterly,* 42: 213–236; H. A. Haverman, 1993, Organizational size and change: Diversification in the savings and loan industry after deregulation, *Administrative Science Quarterly,* 38: 20–50.
6. M. E. Porter, 1987, From competitive advantage to corporate strategy, *Harvard Business Review,* 65(3): 43–59.
7. Ibid., 43.
8. Boeker, Executive migration and strategic change; C. A. Montgomery, 1994, Corporate diversification, *Journal of Economic Perspectives,* 8: 163–178.
9. B. Wysocki, Jr., 1999, Corporate America confronts the meaning of a "core" business, *Wall Street Journal,* November 9, A1, A4; J. Kurtzman, 1998, An interview with C. K. Prahalad, in J. Kurtzman (ed.), *Thought Leaders* (San Francisco: Jossey-Bass), 40–51; D. Lei, M. A. Hitt, & R. Bettis, 1996, Dynamic core competences through meta-learning and strategic context, *Journal of Management,* 22: 547–567.
10. C. C. Markides, 1997, To diversify or not to diversify, *Harvard Business Review,* 75(6): 93–99.
11. C. C. Markides & P. J. Williamson, 1996, Corporate diversification and organizational structure: A resource-based view, *Academy of Management Journal,* 39: 340–367; M. Goold & K. Luchs, 1993, Why diversify? Four decades of management thinking, *Academy of Management Executive,* VII(3): 7–25.
12. A. Roseno & C. Nokkentved, 1997, *Management Processes and Corporate-Level Strategy* (Copenhagen, Denmark: Management Process Institute); A. Campbell, M. Goold, & M. Alexander, 1995, Corporate strategy: The question for parenting advantage, *Harvard Business Review,* 73(2): 120–132.
13. T. H. Brush, P. Bromiley, & M. Hendrickx, 1999, The relative influence of industry and corporate on business segment performance: An alternative estimate, *Strategic Management Journal,* 20: 519–547; T. H. Brush & P. Bromiley, 1997, What does a small corporate effect mean? A variance components simulation of corporate and business effects, *Strategic Management Journal,* 18: 825–835.
14. J. B. Barney, 1997, *Gaining and Sustaining Competitive Advantage* (Reading, MA: Addison-Wesley).
15. M. A. Hitt, B. W. Keats, & S. DeMarie, 1998, Navigating in the new competitive landscape: Building strategic flexibility and competitive advantage in the 21st century, *Academy of Management Executive,* XII(4): 22–42; T. Mroczkowski & M. Hanaoka, 1997, Effective rightsizing strategies in Japan and America: Is there a convergence of employment practices? *Academy of Management Executive,* XI(2): 57–67.
16. D. J. Collis & C. A. Montgomery, 1998, Creating corporate advantage, *Harvard Business Review,* 76(3): 70–83.
17. R. Simons & A. Davila, 1998, How high is your return on management? *Harvard Business Review,* 76(1): 71–80.
18. B. S. Silverman, 1999, Technological resources and the direction of corporate diversification: Toward an integration of the resource-

based view and transaction cost economics, *Administrative Science Quarterly,* 45: 1109–1124.; D. Collis & C. A. Montgomery, 1995, Competing on resources: Strategy in the 1990s, *Harvard Business Review,* 73(4): 118–128; M. A. Peteraf, 1993, The cornerstones of competitive advantage: A resource-based view, *Strategic Management Journal,* 14: 179–191.

19. R. P. Rumelt, 1974, *Strategy, Structure and Economic Performance* (Cambridge, MA: Harvard University Press).
20. C. C. Markides, 1995, Diversification, restructuring and economic performance, *Strategic Management Journal,* 16: 101–118.
21. R. E. Hoskisson, M. A. Hitt, R. A. Johnson, & D. S. Moesel, 1993, Construct validity of an objective (entropy) categorical measure of diversification strategy, *Strategic Management Journal,* 14: 215–235.
22. Hitt, Hoskisson, & Kim, International diversification; M. A. Hitt, R. E. Hoskisson, & R. D. Ireland, 1994, A mid-range theory of the interactive effects of international and product diversification on innovation and performance, *Journal of Management,* 20: 297–326.
23. W. M. Bulkeley, 1994, Conglomerates make a surprising comeback—with a '90s twist, *Wall Street Journal,* March 1, A1, A6.
24. P. Ghemawat & T. Khanna, 1998, The nature of diversified business groups: A research design and two case studies, *Journal of Industrial Economics,* 46: 35–61.
25. *Financial Times,* 1999, Germany: The monoliths stir, September 29, *www.ft.com.*
26. M. Heinzl & N. Deogun, 1998, Cott loses sparkle due to price war, chairman's health, *Wall Street Journal,* January 6, B8; G. G. Marcial, 1998, Why Cott may bubble up, *Business Week,* March 2, 108; *Cott Corporation Home Page,* 1998, January 13, *www.cott.com.*
27. D. Westell, 1999, Taking the Cott challenge, *Canadian Business,* November 26, 27–28.
28. A. Bary, 1999, Who wants gum? *Barron's,* September 27, 21–22.
29. Rumelt, *Strategy, Structure, and Economic Performance;* L. Wrigley, 1970, Divisional autonomy and diversification (Ph.D. dissertation, Harvard Business School).
30. S. Thompson, 1999, Kellogg pushes portable snacks as cereal biz lags, *Advertising Age,* October 18(4), 78.
31. J. G. Brenner, 1999, *The Chocolate Wars: Inside the Secret Worlds of Mars and Hershey* (New York: HarperCollins Business).
32. Associated Press, 1997, Psst! Hershey's up to something, *Dallas Morning News,* October 14, D1.
33. E. Nelson, 1999, Wal-Mart, widening its focus, to buy tiny bank, *Wall Street Journal,* June 30, A3.
34. M. Ihlwan, P. Engardio, I. Kunii, & R, Crockett, 1999, Samsung: How a Korean electronics giant came out of the crisis stronger than ever, *Business Week Online,* December 20, *www.businessweek.com.*
35. T. Khanna & K. Palepu, 1997, Why focused strategies may be wrong for emerging markets, *Harvard Business Review,* 75(4): 41–50.
36. *The Economist,* 1997, Inside story, December 6, 7–9.
37. L. L. Brownlee & J. R. Dorfman, 1995, Birth of U.S. industries isn't without complications, *Wall Street Journal,* May 18, B4.
38. R. Siklos, 1999, Viacom-CBS: 'They Have It All Now', *Business Week Online,* September 20, *www.businessweek.com.*
39. M. Farjoun, 1998, The independent and joint effects of the skill and physical bases of relatedness in diversification, *Strategic Management Journal,* 19: 611–630.
40. R. Morck & B. Yeung, 1999, When synergy creates real value, Mastering strategy (Part 7), *Financial Times,* November 8, 6–7.
41. L. Capron, 1999, The long term performance of horizontal acquisitions, *Strategic Management Journal,* 20: 987–1018; D. J. Teece, G. Pisano, & A. Shuen, 1997, Dynamic capabilities and strategic management, *Strategic Management Journal,* 18: 509–533.
42. M. E. Porter, 1985, *Competitive Advantage* (New York: The Free Press), 328.
43. S. D. Moore, M. Waldholz & A. Raghavan, 2000, Glaxo Wellcome to buy SmithKline, *Wall Street Journal Interactive Edition,* January 17, *www.wsj.com.*
44. K. Capell & H. Dawley, 1999, Healing Novartis: As agribiz sours, it shifts to health care, *Business Week Online,* November 1, *www.businessweek.com.*
45. T. H. Brush, 1996, Predicted change in operational synergy and post-acquisition performance of acquired businesses, *Strategic Management Journal,* 17: 1–24; H. Zhang, 1995, Wealth effects of U.S. bank takeovers, *Applied Financial Economics,* 5: 329–336.
46. D. D. Bergh, 1995, Size and relatedness of units sold: An agency theory and resource-based perspective, *Strategic Management Journal,* 16: 221–239.
47. M. Lubatkin & S. Chatterjee, 1994, Extending modern portfolio theory into the domain of corporate diversification: Does it apply? *Academy of Management Journal,* 37: 109–136.
48. T. Kono, 1999, A strong head office makes a strong company, *Long Range Planning,* 32(2): 225.
49. Barney, *Gaining and Sustaining Competitive Advantage,* 367; A. Mehra, 1996, Resource and market based determinants of performance in the U.S. banking industry, *Strategic Management Journal,* 17: 307–322; S. Chatterjee & B. Wernerfelt, 1991, The link between resources and type of diversification: Theory and evidence, *Strategic Management Journal,* 12: 33–48.
50. N. Argyres, 1996, Capabilities, technological diversification and divisionalization, *Strategic Management Journal,* 17: 395–410.
51. M. Maremont, 2000, For plastic hangers, you almost need to go to Tyco International, *Wall Street Journal,* February 15, A1, A10; R. Whittington, 1999, In praise of the evergreen conglomerate, Mastering Strategy (Part 6), *Financial Times,* November 1, 4–6; W. Ruigrok, A. Pettigrew, S. Peck, & R. Whittington, 1999, Corporate restructuring and new forms of organizing: Evidence from Europe, *Management International Review,* 39(Special Issue): 41–64.
52. C. St. John & J. S. Harrison, 1999, Manufacturing-based relatedness, synergy, and coordination, *Strategic Management Journal,* 20: 129–145.
53. W. G. Shepherd, 1986, On the core concepts of industrial economics, in H. W. deJong & W. G. Shepherd (eds.), *Mainstreams in Industrial Organization* (Boston: Kluwer Publications).
54. J. Gimeno & C. Y. Woo, 1999, Multimarket contact, economies of scope, and firm performance, *Academy of Management Journal,* 42: 239–259; K. Hughes & C. Oughton, 1993, Diversification, multimarket contact and profitability, *Economica,* 60: 203–224.
55. R. Heller, 2000, The man with the big footprint, *Forbes,* January 24, 116–120.
56. J. Ewing & S. Reed, 2000, Can mannesmann wriggle away?, *Business Week,* January 17, 52–54.
57. A. Karnani & B. Wernerfelt, 1985, Multipoint competition, *Strategic Management Journal,* 6: 87–96.
58. f. i. smith & R. L. Wilson, 1995, The predictive validity of the Karnani and Wernerfelt model of multipoint competition, *Strategic Management Journal,* 16: 143–160.
59. O. E. Williamson, 1996, Economics and organization: A primer, *California Management Review,* 38(2): 131–146.
60. E. Karrer-Rueedi, 1997, Adaptation to change: Vertical and horizontal integration in the drug industry, *European Management Journal,* 15: 461–469.
61. C. Palmery, 1999, The integrated BTU, Forbes, January 24, 90.
62. K. M Eisenhardt & D. C. Galunic, 2000, Coevolving: At last, a way to make synergies work, *Harvard Business Review,* 78(1): 91–111.
63. J. A. Byrne, 1998, How Jack Welch runs GE, *Business Week Online,* June 8, *www.businessweek.com.*
64. *Business Week,* 2000, Live wire welch, *Business Week,* January 10, 71.
65. M. Sarvary, 1999, Knowledge management and competition in the consulting industry, *California Management Review,* 41(2), 95–107.

66. T. D. Schellhardt, E. McDonald, & P. Hennessey, 1998, Consulting firms get an unexpected taste of their own medicine, *Wall Street Journal*, October 20, A1, A10.
67. Eisenhardt & Galunic, 2000, Coevolving, 94
68. Bergh, Predicting divestiture of unrelated acquisitions; C. W. L. Hill, 1994, Diversification and economic performance: Bringing structure and corporate management back into the picture, in R. P. Rumelt, D. E. Schendel, & D. J. Teece (eds.), *Fundamental Issues in Strategy* (Boston: Harvard Business School Press), 297–321.
69. O. E. Williamson, 1975, *Markets and Hierarchies: Analysis and Antitrust Implications* (New York: Macmillan Free Press).
70. R. Kochhar & M. A. Hitt, 1998, Linking corporate strategy to capital structure: Diversification strategy, type, and source of financing, *Strategic Management Journal*, 19: 601–610.
71. Ibid.; P. Taylor & J. Lowe, 1995, A note on corporate strategy and capital structure, *Strategic Management Journal*, 16: 411–414.
72. D. J. Denis, D. K. Denis, & A. Sarin, 1999, Agency theory and the reference of equity ownership structure on corporate diversification strategies, *Strategic Management Journal*, 20: 1071–1076; R. Amit & J. Livnat, 1988, A concept of conglomerate diversification, *Journal of Management*, 14: 593–604.
73. Whittington, 1999, In praise of the evergreen conglomerate, 4.
74. S. J. Chang & H. Singh, 1999, The impact of entry and resource fit on modes of exit by multibusiness firms, *Strategic Management Journal*, 20: 1019–1035.
75. *Business Week*, 2000, Managers to watch in 2000, *Business Week*, January 10, 69.
76. *Business Week*, 1999, L. Dennis Kozlowski: Compulsive shopper, *Business Week*, January 11, 67.
77. S. Chatterjee & J. Singh, 1999, Are tradeoffs inherent in diversification moves? A simultaneous model for type of diversification and mode of expansion decisions, *Management Science*, 45: 25–41.
78. M. Lubatkin, H. Merchant, & M. Srinivasan, 1997, Merger strategies and shareholder value during times of relaxed antitrust enforcement: The case of large mergers during the 1980s, *Journal of Management*, 23: 61–81.
79. D. L. Smart & M. A. Hitt, 1998, A test of the agency theory perspective of corporate restructuring, working paper, Texas A&M University.
80. R. M. Scherer & D. Ross, 1990, *Industrial Market Structure and Economic Performance* (Boston: Houghton Mifflin).
81. A. Shleifer & R. W. Vishny, 1994, Takeovers in the 1960s and 1980s: Evidence and implications, in R. P. Rumelt, D. E. Schendel, & D. J. Teece (eds.), *Fundamental Issues in Strategy* (Boston: Harvard Business School Press), 403–422.
82. Lubatkin, Merchant, & Srinivasan, Merger strategies and shareholder value; D. J. Ravenscraft & R. M. Scherer, 1987, *Mergers, Sell-Offs and Economic Efficiency* (Washington, DC: Brookings Institution), 22.
83. P. L. Zweig, J. P. Kline, S. A. Forest, & K. Gudridge, 1995, The case against mergers, *Business Week*, October 30, 122–130; J. R. Williams, B. L. Paez, & L. Sanders, 1988, Conglomerates revisited, *Strategic Management Journal*, 9: 403–414.
84. M. C. Jensen, 1986, Agency costs of free cash flow, corporate finance, and takeovers, *American Economic Review*, 76: 323–329.
85. R. Gilson, M. Scholes, & M. Wolfson, 1988, Taxation and the dynamics of corporate control: The uncertain case for tax motivated acquisitions, in J. C. Coffee, L. Lowenstein, & S. Rose-Ackerman (eds.), *Knights, Raiders, and Targets: The Impact of the Hostile Takeover* (New York: Oxford University Press), 271–299.
86. C. Steindel, 1986, Tax reform and the merger and acquisition market: The repeal of the general utilities, *Federal Reserve Bank of New York Quarterly Review*, 11(3): 31–35.
87. P. L. Moore 1999, Will a sale be Bank One's salvation? *Business Week Online*, December 23, *www.businessweek.com*; M. Murray, 1997, Banks look afield to satisfy appetite for expansion, *Wall Street Journal*, July 9, B4.
88. G. Silverman, L. Nathans, J. Rossant, & O. Ullmann, 1999, Citigroup: Is this marriage working? *Business Week Online*, June 7, *www.businessweek.com*.
89. Rumelt, *Strategy, structure and economic performance*, 125.
90. R. M. Wiseman & L. R. Gomez-Mejia, 1998, A behavioral agency model of managerial risk taking, *Academy of Management Review*, 23: 133–153; E. H. Bowman, 1982, Risk seeking by troubled firms, *Sloan Management Review*, 23: 33–42.
91. Y. Chang & H. Thomas, 1989, The impact of diversification strategy on risk-return performance, *Strategic Management Journal*, 10: 271–284; R. M. Grant, A. P. Jammine, & H. Thomas, 1988, Diversity, diversification, and profitability among British manufacturing companies, 1972–1984, *Academy of Management Journal*, 31: 771–801.
92. L. E. Palich, L. B. Cardinal, & C. C. Miller, 2000, Curvilinearity in the diversification-performance linkage: An examination of over three decades of research. *Strategic Management Journal*, 21: 155–174.
93. S. Crock, 1999, A lean, mean fighting machine it ain't, *Business Week*, January 11, 41.
94. Taylor, Revolution at Daimler-Benz, 147.
95. *Business Week*, 1999, Jurgen E. Schrempp: Deal of the decade, *Business Week*, January 11, 61.
96. J. Ball & S. Miller, 2000, DaimlerChrysler is aiming for top spot, *Wall Street Journal*, January 14, A2, A10.
97. J. C. Sandvig & L. Coakley, 1998, Best practices in small firm diversification, *Business Horizons*, 41(3): 33–40; C. G. Smith & A. C. Cooper, 1988, Established companies diversifying into young industries: A comparison of firms with different levels of performance, *Strategic Management Journal*, 9: 111–121.
98. *Financial Times*, 1999, Enel: "Kaiser Franz" nears ambitious goal, September 29, *www.ft.com*; *Financial Times*, 1999, Germany: The monoliths stir, September 28, *www.ft.com*.
99. N. King, Jr., 1998, A Soviet defense giant saw the inevitable and decided: Diversify, *Wall Street Journal*, January 2, A4.
100. N. M. Kay & A. Diamantopoulos, 1987, Uncertainty and synergy: Towards a formal model of corporate strategy, *Managerial and Decision Economics*, 8: 121–130.
101. R. W. Coff, 1999, How buyers cope with uncertainty when acquiring firms in knowledge-intensive industries: Caveat emptor, *Organization Science*, 10: 144–161.
102. J. Cole & A. Pasztor, 2000, Boeing moves closer to satellite-based telecom niche, *Wall Street Journal*, January 14, B4.
103. D. Field, 1999, Boeing diversifies to avoid turbulence; February 28, *www.usatoday.com*; K. Maney & D. Field, 1999, Boeing joins Internet-in-the-sky venture, February 28, *www.usatoday.com*.
104. Chatterjee & Singh, Are tradeoffs inherent in diversification moves? S. J. Chatterjee & B. Wernerfelt, 1991, The link between resources and type of diversification: Theory and evidence, *Strategic Management Journal*, 12: 33–48.
105. R. Kochhar & M. A. Hitt, 1998, Linking corporate strategy to capital structure, *Strategic Management Journal*, 19: 601–610.
106. R. A. Melchor & G. Burns, 1996, How Eagle became extinct, *Business Week*, March 4, 68–69.
107. Anheuser-Busch Companies, Inc., Home Page, 2000, January 18, *www.anheuser-busch.com*.
108. R. Gibson, 1995, Anheuser-Busch will sell snacks unit, Cardinals, and the club's home stadium, *Wall Street Journal*, October 26, A3, A5; M. Quint, 1995, Cardinals and snack unit are put on block by Busch, *New York Times*, October 26, D2.
109. R. E. Hoskisson & M. A. Hitt, 1990, Antecedents and performance outcomes of diversification: Review and critique of theoretical perspectives, *Journal of Management*, 16: 461–509.
110. Chatterjee & Singh, Are tradeoffs inherent in diversification moves?

111. C. W. L. Hill & R. E. Hoskisson, 1987, Strategy and structure in the multiproduct firm, *Academy of Management Review,* 12: 331–341.
112. W. Grossman & R. E. Hoskisson, 1998, CEO pay at the crossroads of Wall Street and Main: Toward the strategic design of executive compensation, *Academy of Management Executive,* 12(1): 43–57; A. A. Cannella, Jr. & M. J. Monroe, 1997, Contrasting perspectives on strategic leaders: Toward a more realistic view of top managers, *Journal of Management,* 23: 213–237; S. Finkelstein & D. C. Hambrick, 1996, *Strategic Leadership: Top Executives and Their Effects on Organizations* (St. Paul, MN: West Publishing Company).
113. P. J. Lane, A. A. Cannella, Jr., & M. H. Lubatkin, 1998, Agency problems as antecedents to unrelated mergers and diversification: Amihud and Lev reconsidered, *Strategic Management Journal,* 19, 555–578; D. L. May, 1995, Do managerial motives influence firm risk reduction strategies? *Journal of Finance,* 50: 1291–1308; Y. Amihud and B. Lev, 1981, Risk reduction as a managerial motive for conglomerate mergers, *Bell Journal of Economics,* 12: 605–617.
114. S. R. Gray & A. A. Cannella, Jr., 1997, The role of risk in executive compensation, *Journal of Management,* 23: 517–540; H. Tosi & L. Gomez-Mejia, 1989, The decoupling of CEO pay and performance: An agency theory perspective, *Administrative Science Quarterly,* 34: 169–189.
115. S. Finkelstein & R. A. D'Aveni, 1994, CEO duality as a double-edged sword: How boards of directors balance entrechment avoidance and unity of command, *Academy of Management Journal,* 37: 1070–1108.
116. R. E. Hoskisson & T. Turk, 1990, Corporate restructuring: Governance and control limits of the internal market, *Academy of Management Review,* 15: 459–477.
117. J. K. Seward & J. P. Walsh, 1996, The governance and control of voluntary corporate spin offs, *Strategic Management Journal,* 17: 25–39; J. P. Walsh & J. K. Seward, 1990, On the efficiency of internal and external corporate control mechanisms, *Academy of Management Review,* 15: 421–458.
118. Finkelstein & D'Aveni, CEO duality as a double-edged sword.
119. E. F. Fama, 1980, Agency problems and the theory of the firm, *Journal of Political Economy,* 88: 288–307.
120. R. A. Johnson, 1996, Antecedents and outcomes of corporate refocusing, *Journal of Management,* 22: 439–483; C. Y. Woo, G. E. Willard, & U. S. Dallenbach, 1992, Spin-off performance: A case of overstated expectations, *Strategic Management Journal,* 13: 433–448.
121. H. Kim & R. E. Hoskisson, 1996, Japanese governance systems: A critical review, in S. B. Prasad (ed.), *Advances in International Comparative Management* (Greenwich, CT: JAI Press), 165–189.
122. J. Flynn & G. T. Zachary, 1999, Phillips, an innovator in electronic proves resistant to change, *Wall Street Journal,* September 10, A1, A6.
123. Markides, To diversify or not to diversify.
124. Collis and Montgomery, Creating corporate advantage.

ACQUISITION AND RESTRUCTURING STRATEGIES

HITT • IRELAND • HOSKISSON •

CHAPTER SEVEN OBJECTIVES

After reading this chapter, you should be able to:

1. Describe the popularity of acquisition strategies in firms competing in the global economy.
2. Discuss reasons firms decide to use an acquisition strategy to achieve strategic competitiveness.
3. Describe seven problems that work against developing a competitive advantage when a firm uses an acquisition strategy.
4. Name and describe attributes of acquisitions that increase the probability of competitive success.
5. Define the restructuring strategy and distinguish among its common forms.
6. Describe the short- and long-term outcomes resulting from the use of the different types of restructuring strategies.

The Internet: Driving Mergers and Acquisitions in the Global Economy

Now freed from many regulatory constraints in multiple global markets, telecommunications companies are using merger and acquisition strategies to develop the economies of scale that are important to their competitive success in rapidly changing and cost-sensitive markets and to enter new markets. For example, SBC Communications, Inc., the largest local telephone company in the United States, recently acquired Sterling Commerce, Inc., at a cost of $3.9 billion. The intent of the acquisition was to give SBC the capability it required to expand its reach into the business-to-business (B2B) electronic commerce market.

Others believe that "Internet fever" is also a primary driver of what is seen as a frenzy of merger and acquisition activity among telecommunications companies. For example, MCI WorldCom, Inc.'s proposed $115 billion acquisition of Sprint was necessary, according to MCI's CEO, for the combined company to be a viable competitor in a global arena in which size has an important relationship to profitability. In addition, the acquisition will allow the new firm to become an important participant in Internet-related business transactions. Interestingly, MCI WorldCom is a product of World Com's 1998 acquisition of MCI.

The price of MCI WorldCom's acquisition of Sprint paled in comparison to the cost of the proposed transaction between two of the world's leading wireless communications companies. In early 2000, at a cost of $190.5 billion, Vodafone AirTouch PLC of Britain was set to acquire Mannesmann AG of Germany. If the takeover is approved, the combined firm would dominate the European market with a global base of more than 50 million customers. Reviewing this proposed combination, an analyst stated that, "the power that this company will have to call the shots in wireless Internet is enormous."

The Internet's commercial potential is also one factor associated with America Online, Inc.'s intended acquisition of Time Warner (recall the discussion of this proposed merger in a Chapter 6 Strategic Focus). According to some analysts, the ability to bundle services together for customers may be the core reason for the acquisition. Describing this possibility, business writers suggested that "Time Warner's extensive cable network can help AOL compete with giants and fast-moving start-ups for the grand prize: the estimated $100 to $150 a month a middle-class household is willing to spend on cable TV, local and long-distance telephone service, and Internet access. Bundling all of that on a single network has become a central strategy of the country's biggest telecom and Internet companies." Moreover, it is likely that the commercial potential of bundling "will drive mergers and acquisitions across several industries."

The financial services industry is another industry in which merger and acquisition activity may be stimulated by bundling possibilities. If, as is expected, the financial services industry is modernized in the United States through regulation, a single company will have an opportunity to handle a customer's bank account, retirement savings, credit cards, home mortgage, auto loan, and insurance on a single monthly statement. All of these transactions can be completed via the Internet. Because acquisitions result in quicker market entry compared to developing a firm's capabilities internally (a point that is discussed in the chapter), it is likely that financial services firms will merge with or acquire other companies to have access to at least competitive, if not superior, Internet-based skills to facilitate customer-related transactions.

A second way the Internet is influencing merger and acquisition activity is through the large number of transactions taking place among Internet companies themselves. An interest in having first-mover advantages influences some of these transactions. By purchasing Internet ventures with strong brand names, the Internet-based firm that acquires them gains access to a critical mass of customers to whom products may be cross-sold. In addition, a firm with a strong brand name is harder to dislodge from its market share than are competitors without established brands. Examples of acquisitions involving Internet firms acquiring other Internet ventures include Yahoo! Inc.'s acquisition of Broadcast.com, Inc. (an Internet broadcaster), Excite@Home Corp.'s purchase of iMall, Inc. (an Internet retailer), and eBay, Inc.s' acquisition of Butterfield & Butterfield, Inc. (an auction house).

As discussed in earlier chapters, Amazon.com continues to acquire a host of Internet ventures, including Pets.com and Drugstore.com, to expand and diversify its operations. Facilitating high levels of acquisition activity among Internet ventures are the high valuations of many Internet-based companies, which allow the use of company stock as acquisition currency. In addition, venture capital funding is available at record rates to support growth via acquisitions. In general, experts predict that the torrent of merger and acquisition activity among Internet companies, as well as the number of transactions completed to gain access to an acquired firm's Internet capabilities, will likely continue, at least in the foreseeable future.

http://www.aol.com

http://www.glaxowellcome.com

http://www.mannesmann.com

http://www.sb.com

http://www.sbc.com

http://www.sprint.com

http://www.timewarner.com

http://www.vodafone.com

http://www.wcom.com

SOURCES: R. Blumenstein, 2000, MCI WorldCom seeks to demonstrate Sprint deal will boost competition, *Wall Street Journal,* January 13, B10; J. Files, 2000, SBC to pay $3.9 billion for Sterling Commerce, *Dallas Morning News,* February 23, D1, D7; J. Files, 2000, Competition rings in, *Dallas Morning News,* February 6, H1, H2; C. Hill & L. Landro, 2000, Does everybody have to own everything? *Wall Street Journal,* January 12, B1, B4; R. MacLean, 2000, What business is Amazon.com really in? *Inc.,* February, 86–88; Wire Reports, 2000, Mannesmann to accept Vodafone's takeover bid, *Dallas Morning News,* February 4, D1, D2; J. Harrison, 1999, Dynamics driving Internet deals, *Mergers & Acquisitions,* September/October, 49–51; R. Rivlin, 1999, Europeans lift M&A activity in US, *Financial Times,* July 28, 20.

In Chapter 6, we studied corporate-level strategies, focusing on types and levels of product diversification strategies that can build core competencies and create competitive advantage. As noted in that chapter, diversification allows a firm to create value by productively using excess resources.[1] For each strategy we discuss in this book, including diversification strategies and merger and acquisition strategies, the firm creates value only when its resources, capabilities, and core competencies are used productively.[2]

In this chapter, which is related closely to Chapter 6, we explore acquisitions as the dominant means firms use to develop a diversification strategy. In one sense, diversification is a risk management tool, in that its successful use reduces a firm's vulnerability to the consequences of competing in a single market or industry.[3] As suggested in Chapter 1, risk plays a role in the strategies a firm selects to earn above-average returns. In addition, continuous evaluations of risk are linked with a firm's ability to achieve strategic competitiveness.[4]

The purpose of this chapter is to explore acquisition and restructuring strategies. Firms from different industries decide to use an acquisition strategy for several reasons, some of which are mentioned in the following commentary: "Pharmaceutical companies are looking for new products, telecommunications companies are seeking faster ways to get into more households, finance companies want to burst into new services quickly, and high-tech money is constantly chasing creativity."[5] However, acquisition strategies are not without problems. Before describing attributes that evidence suggests are associated with effective acquisitions, we discuss the most prominent problems companies experience when using an acquisition strategy. When acquisitions contribute to poor performance, a firm may deem it necessary to restructure its operations. Closing the chapter are descriptions of three restructuring strategies, as well as the short- and long-term outcomes resulting from their use. Setting the stage for our consideration of all of these topics are brief descriptions of the differences among mergers, acquisitions, and takeovers.

The Increasing Use of Merger and Acquisition Strategies

Acquisitions have been a popular strategy among U.S. firms for many years. Some believe that the strategy played a central role in an effective restructuring of U.S. businesses during the 1980s and 1990s.[6] Increasingly, acquisition strategies are becoming more popular with firms in other nations and economic regions, including Europe.[7] In fact, in the third quarter of 1999, for the first time the dollar volume of merger and acquisition transactions announced in Europe exceeded the value announced in the United States.[8] As is the case with all strategies, acquisitions indicate a choice a firm has made regarding how it intends to compete.[9] Because each strategic choice affects a firm's performance, the possibility of diversification merits careful analysis.[10] The successful use of an acquisition strategy is another way a firm can differentiate itself from competitors.[11] Being differentiated effectively may benefit the firm in that less direct competition with competitors is experienced when this is the case.[12]

An indicator of the popularity of the acquisition strategy is the labeling of the 1980s as the "merger mania" decade. During that time, depending on whether only acquisitions of entire firms or partial (ownership) acquisitions are counted, the number of acquisitions completed in the United States varied from slightly over 31,000 to as many as 55,000. The total value of these acquisitions exceeded $1.3 trillion.[13] However, the merger and acquisition activity of the 1980s pales in comparison to what occurred in the 1990s.[14] In 1999 alone, $3.4 trillion was spent worldwide on mergers and acquisitions, up from $2.5 trillion in 1998 and $464 billion in 1990. In the United States in 1999, $1.75 trillion in deals were announced, compared to $1.6 trillion in 1998 and $195 billion in 1990. As discussed in the Opening Case, "the Internet is one key force driving this activity, merger experts say. With the Internet wrecking the traditional sales and distribution formulas for everything from cars to computers, even established companies believe they are at risk."[15] Recently, for example, Staples, Inc., decided to form alliances with some small Internet companies and acquire others, "to offer an array of small-business services on the Web including payroll management, insurance, and high-speed Internet connections and other phone services." In part, this strategic action was taken as a competitive response to competitor Office Depot, Inc.'s earlier entry into Internet sales, as well as because of the conviction within Staples's top management team that being able to sell on the Internet is "a matter of survival."[16]

Another trend in acquisition strategies is the rapid increase in the number of acquisitions completed between firms based in different countries.[17] These transactions are called *cross-border acquisitions.*[18] In Chapter 9, we discuss cross-border alliances. Sharing similar characteristics, cross-border acquisitions and cross-border alliances are strategic alternatives firms consider in the pursuit of strategic competitiveness and above-average returns, as are domestic alliances and acquisitions.

The strategic management process (see Figure 1.1) calls for an acquisition strategy to increase a firm's strategic competitiveness as well as its returns to shareholders. Thus, an acquisition strategy should be used only when the acquiring firm will be able to increase its economic value through ownership and the use of an acquired firm's assets.[19]

Evidence suggests, however, that at least for acquiring firms, acquisition strategies may not result in these desirable outcomes. Recently, for example, a survey by accounting and consulting firm KPMG estimated that 83 percent of mergers failed to increase shareholder value in acquiring firms; indeed, in 53 percent of the transactions, shareholder value in acquiring firms was actually reduced![20] In the words of KMPG personnel, "Mergers that didn't work out as promised have helped sink the stocks of Federal-Mogul Corp., Mattel Co., and Clorox Co., among others."[21] These results are consistent with those obtained through studies by academic researchers who have found that *shareholders of acquired firms* often earn above-average returns from an acquisition, while *shareholders of acquiring firms* are less likely to do so, typically earning returns from the transaction that are close to zero.[22] Apparently, investors anticipate this state of affairs, as is indicated by the fact that, in approximately two-thirds of all acquisitions, the acquiring firm's stock price falls immediately after the intended transaction is announced. This negative response is viewed by some as an indication of "investors' skepticism about the likelihood that the acquirer will be able both to maintain the original values of the businesses in question and to achieve the synergies required to justify the premium."[23]

Mergers, Acquisitions, and Takeovers: What Are the Differences?

A **merger** is a strategy through which two firms agree to integrate their operations on a relatively co-equal basis because they have resources and capabilities that together may create a stronger competitive advantage.

A **merger** is a strategy through which two firms agree to integrate their operations on a relatively co-equal basis because they have resources and capabilities that together may create a stronger competitive advantage. The transaction between Reckitt & Coleman of the U.K. and Benckiser of the Netherlands is an example of a merger. The deal joined firms with complementary products and geographical penetration. Because the merger created the world's leading household cleaning products group, the new firm had substantial market power that was expected to lead to significant cost reductions

An **acquisition** is a strategy through which one firm buys a controlling, or 100 percent interest in another firm with the intent of using a core competence more effectively by making the acquired firm a subsidiary business within its portfolio.

A **takeover** is a type of an acquisition strategy wherein the target firm did not solicit the acquiring firm's bid.

and improved profitability.[24] An **acquisition** is a strategy through which one firm buys a controlling, or 100 percent interest in another firm with the intent of using a core competence more effectively by making the acquired firm a subsidiary business within its portfolio.[25] Usually, the management of the acquired firm reports to its counterparts in the acquiring firm. Most mergers are friendly transactions, whereas acquisitions include unfriendly takeovers. A **takeover** is a type of an acquisition strategy wherein the target firm did not solicit the acquiring firm's bid. For example, Aetna, Inc., the large insurer whose recent performances were of concern to shareholders and financial analysts, received an unsolicited takeover bid from two corporations. Valued at $10.5 billion, the bid was offered by WellPoint Health Networks, Inc., a managed-care company, and ING America Insurance Holdings, Inc., a unit of Dutch financial company ING Group NV.[26]

In early 2000, a generally favorable worldwide economic climate and a strong stock market in the United States and some other countries created an environment in which few firms were safe from the possibility of a hostile takeover. According to some analysts, in the global economy, "the ability to use stock as a currency and finance enormous transactions means a company can run, but it can't hide" from an unsolicited takeover bid.[27] Even General Motors is not immune from takeover speculation. The reason for this is that, primarily because of the value of its majority stake in Hughes Electronics, GM's assets are worth substantially more than its market capitalization.[28]

On a comparative basis, acquisitions occur more commonly than mergers and takeovers. Accordingly, this chapter focuses on acquisitions.

Reasons for Acquisitions

In this section, we discuss reasons that support the active use of an acquisition strategy, as well as a decision to occasionally acquire another company.[29] In contrast to these appropriate reasons, managerial ego does not justify a decision to merge with or acquire another firm. For example, an out-of-control ego might cause a manager to acquire other companies to increase the firm's size, even when doing so may be at the expense of profitability. Hard to detect as a decision criterion in individual transactions, egos nonetheless may influence a number of merger and acquisition decisions, as the results of a survey by the U.S. Federal Trade Commission of Wall Street professionals suggests.[30]

Increased Market Power

A primary reason for acquisitions is to achieve greater market power.[31] Defined in Chapter 6, *market power* exists when a firm is able to sell its goods or services above competitive levels or when the costs of its primary or support activities are below competitors'. Many companies may have core competencies, but lack the size to exercise their resources and capabilities. Market power usually is derived from the size of the firm and its resources and capabilities to compete in the marketplace. Therefore, most acquisitions designed to achieve greater market power entail buying a competitor, a supplier, a distributor, or a business in a highly related industry to allow exercise of a core competence and gain competitive advantage in the acquiring firm's primary market. This is the case with RPM, Inc. Consisting of a group of specialty chemical companies, RPM relies on acquisitions to gain market power in its two major business units—industrial (e.g., coatings for commercial roofs and corrosion protection) and consumer products (e.g., Wolman wood treatments and DAP household caulks).[32]

Firms use horizontal, vertical, and related acquisitions to increase their market power.

Horizontal Acquisitions. The acquisition of a firm competing in the same industry that a competitor competes in is referred to as a *horizontal acquisition*.[33] Horizontal acquisitions increase a firm's market power by exploiting cost-based and revenue-based synergies.[34] For example, Taiwan Semiconductor Manufacturing Co.'s acquisition of competitor Worldwide Semiconductor Manufacturing Corp. is expected to increase the firm's manufacturing capacity by at least 14 percent (through revenue-based synergies) and preserve its "lead in a contract-manufacturing market that by 2003 will account for 12 percent of the semiconductor industry's total business."[35]

Research suggests that horizontal acquisitions of firms with similar characteristics result in higher performance than when firms with dissimilar characteristics combine their operations. Examples of important similar characteristics include strategy, managerial styles, and resource allocation patterns. Similarities in these characteristics make the integration of the two firms proceed more smoothly.[36] Sterling Software, Inc., and Computer Associates International, Inc., were rivals in the business of selling software solutions to corporations and governments. Recently, Sterling agreed to be acquired by Computer Associates in a $4 billion stock swap. Comments from the firms' executives suggested that the two formerly independent firms were similar in various respects, including their business philosophies.[37]

Vertical Acquisitions. A *vertical acquisition* refers to a firm acquiring a supplier or distributor of one or more of its goods or services. A firm becomes vertically integrated through this type of acquisition, in that it controls additional parts of the value chain (see Chapter 3). In the pharmaceutical industry, for example, Merck & Company purchased Medco Containment Services, Inc. A drug distribution firm, Medco allowed Merck to create more value by owning its own distribution source, in that, through Medco, Merck ensured that its products would be distributed as it managed prescription drug plans.[38] Although promising in terms of increasing the firm's performance, vertical acquisitions have the potential to alienate some of a company's customers. PepsiCo discovered this effect after acquiring Pizza Hut, Taco Bell, and KFC. One objective of these acquisitions was to use the three restaurant chains as distribution channels to sell Pepsi's drinks. Aware of this, Coca-Cola convinced Wendy's and other fast food chains that selling Pepsi in *their* stores indirectly benefited those of their competitors that PepsiCo owned.[39] Later, PepsiCo spun off its three food units to form Tricon, a separate entity. Thus, firms must balance anticipated benefits of a vertical acquisition with potential risks.[40]

Related Acquisitions. The acquisition of a firm in a highly related industry is referred to as a *related acquisition*. Carnival Corp., the large cruise-line firm, intended to acquire Fairfield Communities, Inc., a rapidly growing company competing in the time-share vacation business. The transaction was to be completed through a stock swap valued initially at $693 million. Carnival executives envisioned synergies by attaching the company's well-known brand name to Fairfield's properties in an effort

Sir John Browne, CEO of BP Amoco, announced the acquisition of Atlantic Richfield Co. for $26.6 billion in stock on April 1, 1999. If approved, the acquisition will give BP Amoco a dominant refining and marketing presence in the western United States.

to cross-sell products; cruise customers were to be offered time-share opportunities, while time-share customers were to be given chances to take a Carnival cruise. Also supporting Carnival's interest in this related acquisition was the belief that the firm faced a "dearth of opportunities in cruise-line acquisitions."[41]

However, roughly a month after the initial announcement, Carnival abandoned its attempt to acquire Fairfield. Influencing this decision was the stock market's reaction to Carnival's strategic intentions. Following the announcement that it sought to acquire Fairfield, the value of each firm's stock dropped dramatically (41 percent in Carnival's case, 27 percent for Fairfield). Thus, especially when stock swaps are involved, companies must anticipate a careful scrutiny of their merger and acquisition strategies by investors and financial analysts.[42] In this instance, investors apparently were not persuaded that an acquisition based on the firms' apparent relatedness would be in shareholders' best interests.

Acquisitions intended to increase market power are subject to regulatory review, as well as to analysis by financial markets (as in Carnival's intended acquisition of Fairfield). For example, in early 2000, the U.S. Federal Trade Commission voted to sue BP Amoco, PLC, to block its $30 billion acquisition of Atlantic Richfield Co. BP Amoco was the world's third-largest oil company when the intended acquisition was announced on March 30, 1999. BP Amoco was created when British Petroleum and Amoco merged in 1998. The foundation for the FTC's suit was the agency's assessment that the proposed transaction was anticompetitive and against consumers' interests, in that the combined company would dominate oil prices on the West Coast of the United States. Some analysts concluded that the suit showed the limits of the federal government's tolerance of steadily larger mergers. One observer suggested that monitoring agencies had seen the "merger wave just go on and on, get larger and larger and more and more complicated, and they feel they have to stop some of these things in order to have any ability to maintain a competitive economy."[43] Thus, firms seeking

BP Amoco and Atlantic Richfield Co.: A Case of Intentions and Realities in the World of Acquisitions

One of the world's three biggest oil companies and the largest company in the United Kingdom, BP Amoco has a reputation as an important and consistent driving force for change among the oil majors. Given its history, it is perhaps not surprising that BP Amoco announced in 1999 that it intended to acquire Atlantic Richfield Co. (Arco). The key purpose of the intended horizontal acquisition was to increase the acquiring firm's market power. In addition, buying Arco was thought of as an integral step in taking BP Amoco to the next level of becoming a "super major," wherein the firm would be in a position to compete directly against Exxon, Mobil, and Royal Dutch/Shell, the world's other super major oil companies.

The transaction was to be completed through an all-stock deal valued at approximately $25.6 billion. If completed, the acquisition will create the second-largest global oil firm, with 59 percent of refining capacity in the United States and 28 percent in Europe. In some analysts' view, this acquisition "would be the latest integration in a rapidly consolidating oil industry and the second acquisition for the former British Petroleum Co., which completed its $57.6 billion merger with Chicago-based Amoco Corp." in December 1998. Growing quickly, the intention of acquiring Arco was announced only 60 working days after British Petroleum concluded what was at the time one of the world's biggest industrial mergers with U.S. Amoco.

As a measure of the commitment between the acquiring and target firm, the parties agreed that the transaction was in the best interests of both companies' shareholders. From an industrywide perspective, the announcement of this intended acquisition should not have been too surprising, in that it was the eighth major merger or acquisition in the global oil and gas business in a six-month period during 1999. Partly driving these transactions were rapidly declining oil prices and increasing demands that energy companies produce and distribute cleaner fuels. Interestingly, shortly after the acquisitions were completed, the price of oil increased.

Although the transaction was of keen interest to BP Amoco officials, who thought that it was a logical decision to support the firm's growth and market power objectives, regulators took a contrary view: By a three-to-two vote, the U.S. Federal Trade Commission concluded that the market power that would result from the transaction was anticompetitive in nature (as we noted earlier). Describing the agency's position, the FTC's bureau of competition director said, "We will prove in federal court that BP has market power and that it has used that market power to maintain higher (crude oil) prices on the West Coast by exporting crude oil to the Far East." Thus, for U.S. regulatory officials, allowing BP Amoco to further increase its market power was undesirable, given the FTC's mandates. However, BP Amoco and Arco officials strongly disagreed with the regulators' assessment. Describing their position, executives from the two firms said, "We regret [that] the only course now open to us is to resolve the issue through litigation, but we believe we have a compelling case."

Time will determine the outcome of this intended acquisition. However, the situation among BP Amoco, Arco, and the U.S. Federal Trade Commission demonstrates the effect government policies and regulations have on horizontal acquisitions in particular and firms' efforts in general to use an acquisition strategy as a means of increasing their market power.

SOURCES: M. A. Hitt, J. S. Harrison, & R. D. Ireland, 2001, *Creating Value through Mergers and Acquisitions: A Complete Guide to Successful M&As* (New York: Oxford University Press); T. Barker & H. Durgin, 2000, BP Amoco: Company faces Arco battle, *Financial Times,* February 3, *www.ft.com,* H. Durgin, 2000, BP Amoco: US regulator moves to block Arco deal, *Financial Times,* February 4, *www.ft.com,* Associated Press, 1999, BP Amoco, Arco close to announcing merger, *Dallas Morning News,* March 29, D1, D4; R. Corzine, 1999, BP Amoco: UK's biggest company drills out of Alaskan trouble spot, *Financial Times,* November 9, *www.ft.com,* N. Know, 1999, Oil companies confirm talks, *Dallas Morning News,* March 30, D1, D4; V. Marsh, T. Barker, & H. Durgin, 1999, BP Amoco set to restructure to meet "aggressive" targets, *Financial Times,* July 16, M. White, 1999, Arco, BP make deal official, *Dallas Morning News,* April 2, D1, D11.

growth and market power through acquisitions must understand the political/legal segment of the external environment (see Chapter 2) in order to successfully use an acquisition strategy. Additional comments about BP Amoco PLC's intended acquisition of Atlantic Richfield Co. appear in the Strategic Focus.

Overcoming of Entry Barriers

Barriers to entry (introduced in Chapter 2) are factors associated with the market or firms operating currently in it that increase the expense and difficulty new ventures face when trying to enter a particular market. For example, well-established competitors may be producing their goods or services in quantities through which significant economies of scale are gained. In addition, enduring relationships with customers often create product loyalties that are difficult for new entrants to overcome. When facing differentiated products, new entrants typically must spend considerable resources to advertise their goods or services and may find it necessary to sell at a price below competitors' to entice customers. Facing the barriers created by economies of scale and differentiated products, a new entrant may find the acquisition of an established company to be more effective than attempting to enter the market as a competitor offering a good or service that is unfamiliar to current buyers. In fact, the higher the barriers to market entry, the greater is the probability that a firm will acquire an existing firm to overcome them. Although an acquisition can be expensive, it does provide the new entrant with immediate market access.

Entry barriers firms face when trying to enter international markets (i.e., markets outside of their home country) are often quite steep. In response, acquisitions are commonly used to overcome those barriers. Being able to compete successfully in international markets is becoming increasingly critical, in that in general, global markets are growing at more than twice the rate of domestic markets.[44] At least for large multinational corporations, another indicator of the importance of entering and then competing successfully in international markets is the fact that five emerging markets (China, India, Brazil, Mexico, and Indonesia) are among the 12 largest economies in the world, with a combined purchasing power that is already one-half that of the Group of Seven industrial nations (United States, Japan, Britain, France, Germany, Canada, and Italy).[45]

Cross-Border Acquisitions. Acquisitions made between companies with headquarters in different countries are called *cross-border acquisitions*. These kinds of acquisitions are often made to overcome entry barriers. In Chapter 9, we examine *cross-border alliances* and the reason for their use. Cross-border acquisitions and cross-border alliances are strategic alternatives firms consider while pursuing strategic competitiveness. Compared to a cross-border alliance, a firm has more control over its international operations through a cross-border acquisition.[46]

Historically, U.S. firms have been the most active acquirers of companies outside their domestic market. However, in the global economy, companies throughout the world are choosing this strategic option with increasing frequency. Based on what seems to be a general conviction among corporate executives—namely, that "if you are in the big leagues, you have to be big in the United States"—the activity through which foreign companies acquire U.S. firms is growing rapidly. During the first nine months of 1999, for example, non-U.S. companies acquired $256 billion of U.S. firm assets. In contrast, U.S. firms spent $121.9 billion to buy foreign entities during the same period. Because of relaxed regulations, the amount of cross-border activity among nations within the European community also continues to increase. Accounting for this growth in a range of cross-border acquisitions, some analysts believe, is the fact that "Many large European corporations seem to have come to the conclusion in recent years that they had reached the limits of growth within their domestic markets, and in order to preserve their strategic position, they had to be more aggressive in doing deals in foreign markets."[47] An example of the breadth of some nations' commitment to cross-border acquisitions of U.S. firms is the Netherlands' stock of direct investment in the United States. Recently, this amount exceeded the $100bn mark, equivalent to some 30 percent of the Netherlands' annual gross domestic product. That investment total placed the Dutch on course to pass Japan as the second-largest investor in the United States, ranking only behind Britain.[48]

Firms in all types of industries are completing cross-border acquisitions. For example, in the cosmetics industry, Japan's Shiseido created a new division to pursue mergers and acquisitions. With its growth long fueled by acquisitions, the firm is now committed to emphasizing the cross-border variety, especially with European companies. In another part of the consumer goods industry, Kimberly-Clark, the world's largest producer of tissue products, intends to acquire primarily non-U.S. companies to expand its disposable medical products lines and tissue and diaper businesses.[49]

Although used increasingly in multiple settings, financial services and telecommunications are industries in which cross-border mergers and acquisitions are prominent as a means of industry consolidation. For example, the Belgian–Dutch financial giant Fortis paid $2.6 billion to acquire American Bankers Insurance Group. At the time, analysts labeled the transaction the latest in a spate of cross-border mergers and acquisitions in the insurance industry.

European pension funds are also expanding rapidly in the global market. A great deal of this growth is occurring through cross-border transactions, with more than two-thirds of 1999's mergers and acquisitions among these firms involving companies outside a firm's domestic market. Analysts also anticipated that Europe's first major cross-border banking merger would take place in 2000. Unicredito SpA of Italy and

Banco Bilbao Vizcaya Argentaria, the recently merged Spanish bank, were top candidates for such a transaction.

Activity in the telecommunications industry is equally brisk. Speaking to this issue for U.S. firms, business writers suggested that "with the consolidations in the U.S. reaching a peak, big American companies are likely to turn their attentions across the Atlantic to become global providers of telephone and Internet services. But instead of forging joint ventures or making small investments in European operators as they had in the past, with mixed results, U.S. telephone companies increasingly are likely to make big acquisitions in Europe." Driving the interest in acquisitions is many companies' desire to own their networks rather than sharing or leasing them from competitors, as often is the case through joint ventures and other relationships. Ownership of network assets may help a firm reduce its costs of transporting voice and data traffic.[50]

The global automobile industry is also being consolidated through companies' strategic actions, including cross-border acquisitions. The Strategic Focus discusses what was reported as a merger between Daimler-Benz and Chrysler Corporation as an example of consolidation through cross-border acquisitions.

Cost of New-Product Development

Developing new products internally and successfully introducing them into the marketplace often requires significant investments of a firm's resources, including time, making it difficult to earn a profitable return quickly.[51] Also of concern to firms' managers are estimates that almost 88 percent of innovations fail to achieve adequate returns from the capital invested in them.[52] Perhaps contributing to these less-than-desirable rates of return is the fact that approximately 60 percent of innovations are successfully imitated within four years after patents are obtained. Because of outcomes such as these, managers often perceive internal product development as a high-risk activity.[53]

Acquisitions are another means through which a firm can gain access to new products and to current products that are new to the firm. Compared to internal product development processes, acquisitions provide more predictable returns as well as faster market entry. Returns are more predictable because the performance of the acquired firm's products can be assessed prior to completing the acquisition.[54] Pharmaceutical firms such as Watson Pharmaceuticals, Inc., frequently use acquisitions to enter markets quickly, to overcome the high costs of developing products internally, and to increase the predictability of returns on their investments. For example, acquiring TheraTech, Inc., gave Watson access to more than 50 patents in advanced drug-delivery systems. Watson intends to use these patented systems to help it create opportunities for new products.[55]

In a broader context, evidence shows that acquisition activity is extensive throughout the pharmaceutical industry. According to business analysts, "There's good reason" for this, in that "patents on stalwart drugs—generating $16 billion in annual revenue—are expiring" in the near future. Compounding the seriousness of this issue is the fact that "Some companies don't have adequate substitutes in their research pipelines." Without internally generated products, acquiring other firms, followed by cost reductions, is an attractive strategic option for many of these companies.[56]

strategic *focus*

INTERNATIONAL

Daimler-Benz and Chrysler Corporation: Will It Be a Successful Union?

At the time of its announcement, the merger between Daimler-Benz and Chrysler Corporation was the world's largest. A horizontal merger, this cross-border transaction was intended to create market power and generate synergies on which the world's preeminent automotive, transportation, and services company could be built. An immediate outcome of the merger was some additional consolidation of the global auto industry.

Each of the former competitors had needs that the merger was supposed to address. Chrysler lacked the infrastructure and management depth required to be a truly global automobile company. Daimler-Benz executives concluded that increasingly intense competitive rivalry in its core luxury-car segment made it necessary for their firm to diversify its product line and distribution channels. Recognizing these respective needs, some analysts believed that the two firms were a complementary fit for at least two reasons. First, Chrysler's dominant market position was in the United States, while Daimler's was in two regions—Europe and South America—where Chrysler lacked a meaningful presence. Second, the companies' product lines were complementary: The bulk of Chrysler's profitability was earned from sport utility vehicles and multipurpose vans, whereas luxury vehicles were the foundation of Daimler's automotive-based strategic competitiveness.

As discussed previously, horizontal acquisitions can create cost- and revenue-based synergies. Daimler and Chrysler expected to generate both types of synergies through their merger. For example, the integration of separate operations was expected to reduce costs by $1.3 billion in 1999 alone. The decision to build the Mercedes M-Class cars and the Jeep Grand Cherokee on the same production line in Graz, Austria, is one of the integration projects that was started immediately in the combined firm. In fact, DaimlerChrysler wants the Graz facility to showcase its ability to generate cost-based synergies by integrating previously independent manufacturing operations. On the revenue side, the new firm seeks cross-selling synergies by integrating Daimler-Benz's competencies in technological innovations with Chrysler's ability to rapidly introduce new products into the marketplace.

Although framed around anticipated benefits, the Daimler–Chrysler cross-border transaction has been questioned and criticized. Some thought that integrating the firms' computer systems would be quite difficult, as would determining how product development decisions were to be made. However, in the short run, it appeared that Daimler's style of making decisions enabled Chrysler to get products to the marketplace quickly. Still, critics also argued that the companies' estimates of cost- and revenue-based synergies were far too optimistic. Compounding these issues was the perception that an acquisition had occurred, rather than a merger. Actions witnessed in the combined firm indicated to some that in actuality, Daimler-Benz had acquired Chrysler Corporation. Regardless, the new firm's 1999 financial performance was encouraging: Operating profit for the year was approximately 11 billion euros ($10.72 billion), up from 8.6 billion euros in 1998. In addition, company officials were optimistic about the future, predicting that sales volume would climb from $151 billion in 1999 to at least $154 billion in 2000 and $168 billion by 2002.

Positions articulated by DaimlerChrysler in 2000 suggested confidence in the results of the cross-border acquisition that formed the company, as well as a commitment to continue growing by using the same strategic option. Currently, DaimlerChrysler is the world's fifth-largest automaker (behind General Motors, Ford, Toyota, and Volkswagen). Company executives noted that a key objective was for their firm to become the largest transportation company in the world by 2003. To reach this objective, DaimlerChrysler intended to acquire other companies and to form an array of strategic alliances. If completed, these transactions would almost certainly result in further consolidation of the world's auto industry.

SOURCES: M. A. Hitt, J. S. Harrison, & R. D. Ireland, 2001, *Creating Value through Mergers and Acquisitions: A Complete Guide to Successful M&As* (New York: Oxford University Press); J. Ball & S. Miller, 2000, Daimler profit accelerated 87 percent to $1.1 billion in 4th quarter, *Wall Street Journal,* February 29, A17, A19; J. Ball & S. Miller, 2000, DaimlerChrysler is aiming for top spot, *Wall Street Journal,* January 14, A10; S. Miller, 2000, Daimler results climbed to top of expectations for last year, *Wall Street Journal,* February 28, A21, A23; J. Flint, 1999, A letter to Jürgen Schrempp, *Forbes,* May 31, 168; R. Simison & S. Miller, 1999, Making "digital" decisions, *Wall Street Journal,* September 24, B1, B4.

Recently, large pharmaceutical companies have chosen to acquire a number of small biotechnology firms. For example, Warner-Lambert acquired Agouron, a California biotech company, and Pharmacia & Upjohn bought Sugen, a San Francisco–based biotech firm specializing in cancer drugs. In addition to citing attractive prices, analysts suggest that these acquisitions are a way for large pharmaceuticals to "fill their pipeline with projects from undervalued biotechnology companies and to get their hands on new products."[57]

Increased Speed to Market

As indicated previously, compared to internal product development, acquisitions result in more rapid market entries.[58] In two researchers' words, "Acquisitions remain the quickest route companies have to new markets and to new capabilities."[59] Using new capabilities to pioneer new products and to enter markets quickly can create advantageous market positions.[60] As discussed in Chapter 5, the durability of the advantage created by an attractive market position is determined largely by rivals' competitive responses.[61]

Firms seek rapid market entry in many different industries. British Telecommunications, PLC (BT), for example, recently spent $2.46 billion to acquire Esat Telecom Group, PLC, Ireland's second-largest phone company. The acquisition gives BT immediate access to "Ireland's rapidly growing telecommunications market, including in the area of high-speed broadband delivery."[62] In the home-building industry, D.R. Horton, Inc., uses an acquisition strategy aimed at growing by entering new markets quickly. Horton recently acquired Chicago-based Cambridge Properties, partly to gain an immediate strong position in the booming adult retirement market.[63] In the consumer foods industry, Kraft Foods acquired meat alternative producer Boca Burger. This acquisition gave Kraft an immediate presence in the rapidly expanding market for soy-based products as alternatives to traditional meat offerings. The attractiveness of soy-based goods gained steam in the United States when the U.S. Food and Drug Administration decided to allow companies to equate soy-protein consumption with a reduced risk of heart disease.[64] At a cost of $370 million, PC manufacturer Compaq Computer Corp. acquired the custom-assembly operations of Inacom Corp. Stimulating this purchase was new CEO Michael Capellas's conclusion that Compaq needed to be able to accelerate the speed with which it delivered products to major customers. According to Capellas, the "purchase gives us the right capability quickly and cost-effectively."[65] Increasing the speed of its distribution channel was necessary for Compaq to become more competitive with several rivals, especially Dell Computer Corp.

Lower Risk Compared to Developing New Products

As mentioned earlier, internal product development processes can be risky. Alternatively, because an acquisition's outcomes can be estimated more easily and accurately compared to the outcomes of an internal product development process, managers may view acquisitions as carrying lowering risk.[66]

The assessment of risk between an internal product development process and an acquisition may have taken place among managers at Procter & Gamble (P&G). Recently, P&G acquired premium dog- and cat-food manufacturer, Iams Co. Historically, Iams's customer base was pet-food chains and veterinary clinics. P&G intended to develop a first-time national advertising campaign for Iams to support the launch of its products into supermarket chains and mass merchandisers such as Wal-Mart. Company officials anticipated that broadening Iams's distribution channels would change the nature of competition in the pet-food industry.[67] Assessing Iams's performance before acquiring the company allowed P&G managers to have a reasonably high degree of confidence in the outcomes associated with their intended strategic actions. As a result, P&G managers may have considered entry into the premium pet-food market through acquisition to be less risky compared to entering the market through an internal product development process.

As with other strategic actions discussed in this book, caution must be exercised when a decision is made to acquire new products rather than to develop them internally. In the context of the issue of lower risk, for example, firms should be aware that research evidence suggests that acquisitions have become a common means of avoiding risky internal ventures (and therefore risky R&D investments). In fact, acquisition may become a substitute for innovation.[68] Thus, acquisitions are not a risk-free alternative to entering new markets through internally developed products.

Increased Diversification

Based on experience and the insights resulting from it, firms typically find it easier to develop and introduce new products in markets served currently by the firm. In contrast, it is harder for companies to develop products—ones that differ from their current lines—for markets in which they lack experience. Thus, it is uncommon for a firm to develop new products internally as a means of diversifying its product lines.[69] Instead, a firm usually opts to use acquisitions as the means to engage in product diversification. For example, CNET, Inc., acquired Internet comparison-shopping pioneer mySimon, Inc., at a price of $702.7 million in stock. The acquisition signaled CNET's interest in moving beyond its core technology-news market. According to analysts, the transaction reflects CNET's renewed interest in a broader consumer market, an area in which it has faced obstacles. Founded to provide computer users with comprehensive product data, including reviews by staff and customers, CNET decided to acquire other firms to enter related, but different, markets. To reflect its increased product diversity, the firm changed its name to CNET Networks, Inc.[70]

Both related diversification and unrelated diversification strategies can be implemented through acquisitions. In addition, as discussed in Chapter 8, acquisitions are the most frequently used means for firms to diversify their operations into international markets.[71] Using acquisitions to diversify a firm seems appropriate, in that evidence suggests that acquisitions are the quickest and, typically, the easiest way to change a firm's portfolio of businesses.[72] Nevertheless, acquisitions that diversify a firm's product lines must be undertaken only after careful study and evaluation, in that the more related the acquired firm is to the acquiring firm, the greater is the probability that the acquisition will be successful. Thus, horizontal acquisitions (through which a firm acquires a competitor) and related acquisitions tend to contribute more to strategic competitiveness than do those through which a firm acquires a company operating in product markets that are quite different from those in which it currently competes.[73] This evidence suggests the likelihood of a successful outcome from Philadelphia-based chemical company Rohm & Haas's acquisition of specialty-chemicals and salt manufacturer Morton International, Inc. The transaction involved companies offering similar products to similar, yet slightly different, markets. Business writers observed that this "acquisition offers Rohm & Haas multiple platforms for growth in coatings and electronic materials, provides complementary products lines and attractive financial returns, and is based on cultural compatibility of the companies."[74]

Reshaping the Firm's Competitive Scope

As discussed in Chapter 2, the intensity of competitive rivalry is an industry characteristic that affects a firm's profitability. To reduce the negative effect of an intense rivalry on its financial performance, the firm may use acquisitions as a way to restrict its dependence on a single or a few products or markets. Reducing a company's dependence on single products or markets alters the competitive scope of the company.

Increasingly, some of the world's automobile manufacturers are diversifying their operations to reduce their dependence on the intensely competitive global auto markets. DaimlerChrysler, for example, "is exploring opportunities to expand its presence in financial and computer services, aftermarket sales, and electronics and satellite systems." Company officials believe that, in addition to affording more desirable operating margins, growth possibilities in these areas are now more attractive than are either alliances or acquisitions in car manufacturing.[75] Similarly, Ford CEO Jacques Nasser wants to make his company the world's leading consumer services business that specializes in the automotive sector. Nasser wants Ford to tap all sectors in the after-sales market, including repairs, replacement parts, and product servicing. One of the first actions Ford took to reach this objective was the acquisition of Kwik-Fit, the U.K. automotive aftermarket group. To evaluate the success in its efforts to reshape the firm's competitive scope through diversification, "Ford will measure itself against world-class consumer businesses in whatever business they operate rather than the traditional yardsticks of rival automakers."[76]

Like DaimlerChrysler and Ford, Emerson Electric Co. is acquiring companies partly to reshape its competitive scope. A famous and highly profitable manufacturer of electric motors and electrical components, Emerson is using acquisitions to develop a focus on the electronics and telecommunications sectors. Jordan Industries, Inc., a firm competing in the telecommunications equipment business, is a recent acquisition Emerson completed to diversify its operations.[77] Japan's largest electronics manufacturer, Hitachi, Ltd., has $3 billion that it intends to use either to purchase U.S. and Japanese high-technology companies outright or to buy stakes in them. Recently, Hitachi studied 60 possible acquisitions, half in Japan and half in other nations. According to the president of the company, the acquisitions' primary purpose is to facilitate his objective of "remaking" a firm that he believed had become a sprawling giant in order to increase its competitiveness in the global economy.[78]

As we have described, there are legitimate reasons for firms to use acquisition strategies as part of their efforts to increase strategic competitiveness and to improve the likelihood of being able to earn above-average returns. However, also as we have said, acquisition strategies are not risk free. In fact, on the basis of company experience and research findings, it has been suggested that "less than 20 percent of all mergers and acquisitions are successful."[79] This success rate is consistent with the finding discussed earlier in the chapter that the average returns of acquisitions for acquiring firms hover close to zero.

Problems in Achieving Acquisition Success

Reasons supporting the use of acquisition strategies, as well as potential problems accompanying their use, are shown in Figure 7.1. The potential problems are discussed in the sections that follow. A reasonable conclusion to draw from those discussions is that "successful acquisitions involve a well thought out strategy in selecting the target, avoiding over-paying, and creating value in the integration process. [In addition], a good acquisition strategy combines the analytical with the intuitive, and the linear with the iterative."[80]

Integration Difficulties

Integrating two companies following an acquisition can be quite difficult.[81] Integration issues include those of melding two disparate corporate cultures,[82] linking different financial and control systems, building effective working relationships (particularly when management styles differ), and resolving problems regarding the status of the newly acquired firm's executives.[83]

The importance of a successful integration should not be underestimated. Without it, a firm achieves financial diversification, but little else. Thus, as suggested by a researcher studying the process, "managerial practice and academic writings show that the post-acquisition integration phase is probably the single most important determinant of shareholder value creation (and equally of value destruction) in mergers and acquisitions."[84] In addition, firms should be aware of the large number of activities associated with integration processes. For instance, Intel acquired Digital Equipment Corporation's semiconductors division. On the day Intel began to integrate the acquired division into its operations, six thousand deliverables were to be completed by hundreds of employees working in dozens of different countries.[85]

According to research completed by consulting firm Booz-Allen Hamilton, there is a positive relationship between the rapid integration of the acquiring and acquired

FIGURE 7.1 | Reasons for Acquisitions and Problems in Achieving Success

firms and overall acquisition success. Intentions at Honeywell (AlliedSignal kept the Honeywell name after acquiring it) are consistent with this relationship. According to analysts, "AlliedSignal and Honeywell have set an aggressive six-month timetable to merge their operations into a $24 billion industrial powerhouse that makes everything from aircraft landing systems to home thermostats."[86] To help integrate the two formerly independent firms within six months, Honeywell organized a team that was charged with developing and implementing an integration plan. Rapid integration is one of the guidelines that DaimlerChrysler CEO Jürgen Schrempp recommends companies follow to successfully integrate firms involved in a global merger or acquisition. Schrempp's other guidelines include dealing with unpopular issues immediately and being honest with people regarding the effects the integration will likely have on them.[87]

According to some business writers, Cisco Systems "wears the mantle of M&A king."[88] One reason for this is the firm's ability to quickly integrate its acquisitions into its existing operations. Focusing on small companies with products and services related closely to its own, some analysts believe that the day after the company acquires a firm, employees in that firm feel as though they have been working for Cisco for decades.[89] Additional information about Cisco's acquisition strategy and its ability to successfully avoid integration difficulties is provided in a Strategic Focus later in the chapter.

Inadequate Evaluation of Target

Due diligence is a process through which a firm evaluates a target firm for acquisition. An effective due-diligence process examines hundreds of items in areas as diverse as those of financing the intended transaction, differences in cultures between the acquiring and target firm, tax consequences of the transaction, and actions that would be necessary to successfully meld the two workforces. Due diligence is commonly performed by investment bankers, accountants, lawyers, and management consultants specializing in that activity, although firms actively pursuing acquisitions may form their own internal due-diligence team.

The failure to complete an effective due-diligence process often results in the acquiring firm paying a premium—sometimes an excessive one—for the target company. In fact, research shows that without due diligence, "the purchase price is driven by the pricing of other 'comparable' acquisitions rather than by a rigorous assessment of where, when, and how management can drive real performance gains. [In these cases], the price paid may have little to do with achievable value."[90] Premiums paid without effective due diligence may also account for research results indicating that the amount of the purchase premium does not predict acquisition success.[91]

The results of some acquisitions in a number of industries suggest a failure to perform adequate due diligence. In 1988, for example, British retailer Marks & Spencer spent $750 million to acquire Brooks Brothers of the United States. Even after more than 10 years, the acquisition remains unsuccessful. Initially, Marks & Spencer executives thought that renovating and "upscaling" Brooks Brothers would attract customers and improve the chain's deteriorating performance. These efforts proved unsuccessful, and indeed, some believe that the premium Marks & Spencer paid to acquire Brooks Brothers precluded success, almost irrespective of any actions taken to reverse the chain's fortunes. At twice the sales volume and 75 times the earnings, the acquisition price was the highest a certain retail analyst had seen paid for a U.S. retailer in his 35-year career. Another analyst called the purchase price "insane."[92] Effective due diligence might have resulted in a decision by Marks & Spencer not to buy Brooks Brothers. In the banking industry, First Union, the North Carolina–based superregional financial institution, "spent so much money for a couple of big acquisitions that even a sound, well-executed strategy hasn't been enough to keep the stock price up."[93] Again, due diligence might have led to different acquisition decisions at First Union.

An example of effective due diligence appears to be DaimlerChrysler's 1999 decision not to acquire Nissan Motor Company. DaimlerChrysler was interested in Nissan as a means of expanding Daimler's access to global auto markets, especially those in Southeast Asia. The primary concern for analysts and, apparently, for DaimlerChrysler executives was Nissan's $22 billion debt. Speaking to this possible acquisition, Robert Lutz, retired vice chairman of the former Chrysler Corporation, said that DaimlerChrysler "might as well take $5 billion in gold bullion, put it in a huge container, spray paint the word Nissan on the side and drop it into the middle of the Pacific Ocean."[94] An adequate evaluation of the target firm through DaimlerChrysler's due-diligence process appears to be the cause of the company's decision not to acquire Nissan.

Large or Extraordinary Debt

To finance a number of acquisitions completed during the 1980s and 1990s, some companies significantly increased their levels of debt. Partly making this possible was a financial innovation called *junk bonds,*[95] a financing option through which risky acquisitions are financed with money (debt) that provides a large potential return to lenders (typically called bondholders). Because junk bonds are unsecured obligations (that is, they are not tied to specific assets such as collateral), interest rates for these high-risk debt instruments sometimes reached between 18 and 20 percent during the 1980s.

Also supporting a decision to increase debt significantly during this period in order to acquire other companies was the belief that debt disciplined managers, causing them to act in shareholders' best interests. This view was grounded in work completed by finance scholars who argued that the constraints on spending possibilities created by the requirement to service debt obligations caused managers to be more prudent in allocating remaining funds and to behave less opportunistically. This logic resulted in managers sometimes being encouraged to utilize significant leverage to finance large acquisitions. Members of a firm's board of directors offered this type of encouragement, as did company finance officials.[96]

As the 21st century begins, junk bonds are being used less frequently to finance acquisitions. In addition, the conviction that debt disciplines managers is less strong than it was in the previous two decades. Nonetheless, some firms still take on too much debt to acquire companies. For example, AgriBioTech, Inc., recently acquired dozens of small seed firms. These acquisitions were used to gain access to the skills necessary to develop genetically enhanced alfalfa and turf grasses and to gain the economies of scope required to distribute products nationwide. But, the firm's "acquisition strategy got out of hand. AgriBioTech wound up issuing massive amounts of new shares. Debt, meanwhile, ballooned to $135 million compared to annual revenues of about $409 million." Analysts concluded that the first order of business to turn the firm around was to "clear up the debt mess."[97]

In spite of the issues associated with too much of it, debt can discipline managerial actions because when debt is high, principal and interest payments reach levels that preclude other investments, some of which might be in managers' best interests (e.g., greater amounts of diversification to reduce managerial employment risk). On the other hand, high debt levels increase the likelihood of bankruptcy, which can lead to a downgrade in the firm's credit rating from agencies such as Moody's and Standard & Poor's.[98] In addition, high debt precludes investments in activities that contribute to the firm's long-term success, including R&D, human resource training, and marketing.[99]

Therefore, we conclude that the use of debt has positive and negative effects. On the one hand, leverage can be a positive force in a firm's development, allowing it to take advantage of attractive expansion opportunities. However, too much leverage (e.g., extraordinary debt) can lead to negative outcomes, such as postponing or eliminating investments (e.g., R&D expenditures), that are necessary to maintain strategic competitiveness over the long term. Partly because of debt's potential disadvantages and partly because of a generally favorable global economy, cash and equity offerings were frequently used instead of significant amounts of debt to complete acquisitions during the latter part of the 1990s and into the 21st century. For example, in a transaction between two Canadian firms, Abitibi-Consolidated, Inc., acquired Donohue, Inc., for $4 billion in cash and stock. The transaction created market power for the new firm in that it became the world's largest newsprint maker, with 16.3 percent of global newsprint capacity (the next-largest market share holder had 8.2 percent).[100]

Inability to Achieve Synergy

Derived from the Greek word "synergos," which means "working together," *synergy* exists when the value created by units working together exceeds the value those units could create working independently (see Chapter 6). Another way of saying this is that synergy exists when assets "are worth more when used in conjunction with each other than separately. Synergies can involve physical and non-physical assets,"[101] such as human capital. For shareholders, synergy generates gains in their wealth that they could not duplicate or exceed through their own portfolio diversification decisions.[102] Being able to create synergy when using an acquisition strategy is important, in that doing so is a key justification for using such a strategy, which often results in a firm becoming more diversified.[103]

A firm develops a competitive advantage through an acquisition strategy only when a transaction generates *private synergy*, which is created when the combination and integration of the acquiring and acquired firms' assets yield capabilities and core competencies that could not be developed by combining and integrating either firm's assets with another company. Private synergy is possible when firms' assets are complementary in unique ways; that is, the unique type of asset complementarity is not possible by combining either company's assets with another firm's assets.[104]

Because of its uniqueness, private synergy is difficult for competitors to understand and imitate. However, private synergy is difficult to create. For example, Quaker Oats' executives believed that the company's ownership of Snapple, which came about through an acquisition, would create private synergy. The expectation was that integrating Quaker's own Gatorade products with Snapple's would create complementarities that could not be created through any other combination of each firm's assets with the assets of any other company. However, that expectation was not realized, and after struggling with the acquisition, Quaker Oats finally divested Snapple. Analysts suggested that there was a lack of complementarity between the sales and marketing activities required by Gatorade's and Snapple's drinks.

Firms experience several expenses when trying to create private synergy through acquisitions. Called transaction costs,[105] these expenses are incurred when firms use acquisition strategies to create synergy. Direct costs include legal fees and charges from investment bankers who complete due diligence for the acquiring firm. Managerial time to evaluate target firms and then to complete negotiations is an example of an indirect cost, as is the loss of key managers and employees following an acquisition.[106] Affecting an acquisition's success, in terms of whether synergy is created, is a firm's ability to account for costs that are necessary to create anticipated revenue- and cost-based synergies. Of the two types of costs, firms tend to underestimate the sum of indirect costs when the value of the synergy that may be created by combining and integrating the acquired firm's assets with the acquiring firm's assets is calculated.

Too Much Diversification

As explained in Chapter 6, when used properly, diversification strategies lead to strategic competitiveness and above-average returns. In general, firms using related diversification strategies outperform those employing unrelated diversification strategies. However, conglomerates, formed by using an unrelated diversification strategy, also can be successful. For example, Thermo Electron, a U.S. manufacturer of high-tech analytical instruments, is highly diversified, yet successful, as is Virgin Group, the U.K.-based firm with interests ranging from cosmetics to trains.[107]

At some point, firms can become overdiversified. The level at which this happens varies across companies. The reason for the variation is that each firm has different capabilities that are required to successfully manage diversification. Recall from Chapter 6 that related diversification requires more information processing than does unrelated diversification. The need for related diversified firms to be able to process more and more diverse information creates a situation in which they become overdiversified with a smaller number of business units, compared to firms using an unrelated diversification strategy.[108] Regardless of the type of diversification strategy implemented, however, declines in performance usually result from overdiversification,[109] after which different business units are divested. The pattern of excessive diversification followed by divestments of underperforming business units was observed frequently among U.S. firms during the 1960s through the 1980s.

Even when a firm is not overdiversified, a high level of diversification can have a negative effect on the firm's long-term performance. For example, the scope created by additional amounts of diversification often causes managers to rely on financial rather than strategic controls to evaluate business units' performances[110] (financial and strategic controls are defined and explained in detail in Chapters 11 and 12). Essentially, when top-level executives have the breadth and depth of information needed to understand each business unit's objectives and strategy, they are able to use strategic controls to monitor performance. Without such a rich understanding of business units' objectives and strategies, those same executives rely on financial controls to assess the performances of managers and their business units. Financial controls are based on objective evaluation criteria, such as the firm's return on investment (ROI). Executives' reliance on financial controls to judge managerial performance can cause

The costs associated with diversification may result in fewer allocations to innovative activities such as research and development. Without internal innovation skills, a firm may be forced to complete additional acquisitions to gain access to innovation.

individual business-unit managers to focus on short-term outcomes at the expense of long-term investments. When long-term investments are reduced to levels that jeopardize future success in order to boost short-term profits, a firm may have diversified to the point beyond which its diversification strategy can enhance overall strategic competitiveness.[111]

Another problem resulting from too much diversification is the tendency for acquisitions to become substitutes for innovation. Typically, managers do not intend acquisitions to be used in that way. However, a reinforcing cycle evolves. Costs associated with acquisitions may result in fewer allocations to activities (e.g., R&D) that are linked to innovation. But without adequate support, a firm's innovation skills begin to atrophy. Without internal innovation skills, the only option available to a firm is to complete still additional acquisitions to gain access to innovation. Across time, though, it is difficult for firms to rely continuously on other companies' innovations as an important source of strategic competitiveness. In fact, evidence suggests that a firm which uses acquisitions as a substitute for internally developed innovations eventually encounters performance problems.[112]

Managers Overly Focused on Acquisitions

Typically, a fairly substantial amount of managerial time and energy is required for acquisition strategies to contribute to a firm's strategic competitiveness. Activities with which managers become involved include (1) searching for viable acquisition candidates, (2) completing effective due-diligence processes, and (3) preparing for negotiations.

Top-level managers do not personally gather all data and information required to complete the activities that are part of an acquisition. However, upper-level executives do make final decisions regarding the firms to be pursued as targets, the nature of the negotiations to acquire a firm, and so forth. In a broader sense, the most important responsibility the top management team has in terms of acquisition strategies is to make certain that the firm is using them effectively. Company experiences show that being responsible for, and participating in, many of the activities that are part of an acquisition strategy can divert managerial attention from other matters (e.g., thinking seriously about the firm's purpose and interacting effectively with board members and external stakeholders) that are linked with long-term competitive success.[113]

Another issue that concerns some analysts centers on the possibility that managers who are overly focused on acquisitions may fail to objectively assess the value of outcomes achieved through the use of the firm's acquisition strategy, compared with outcomes that might be achieved by concentrating on using the firm's other strategies more effectively. For example, it has been suggested that Ford Motor Company's acquisition strategy may not be enhancing the firm's strategic competitiveness. Consider the words of an individual who studies the automobile industry: "Ford owns one-third of the stock of Mazda of Japan and essentially runs the company. There have been three Mazda presidents in three years (all from Ford). I wouldn't call that a sign of success. Ford pumped $6 billion into Jaguar over the past decade, and there are signs that this may work out one day, but it will take a decade to earn back the investment. And I don't think Ford will ever earn back its Volvo investment."[114] An option available to Ford is to rely on its technological skills to develop innovative engines, transmissions, suspension systems, and so forth. In other words, some believe that the firm might contribute more positively to its strategic competitiveness by focusing its time and attention on determining actions to take to increase the value of its own automobiles and trucks, instead of using managerial time and energy to expand the firm's product lines by acquiring competitors. Thus, upper-level executives should avoid focusing on the use of an acquisition strategy at the expense of a firm's long-term strategic competitiveness.

Acquisitions can consume significant amounts of managerial time and energy in target firms as well as in the companies that acquire them. Because of the uncertainty that an acquisition creates, some suggest that target firms find themselves in a state of virtual suspended animation during an acquisition.[115] For example, while the target firm's day-to-day operations continue, albeit sometimes at a slower pace, most of the company's executives are hesitant to make decisions with long-term consequences, choosing to postpone such decisions until negotiations have been completed. Thus, evidence suggests that the acquisition process can create a short-term perspective and a greater aversion to risk among top-level executives in a target firm.[116]

Too Large

Most acquisitions create a larger firm. In theory, the increased size should help a firm gain economies of scale in various organizational functions. These economies can then lead to more efficient operations. For instance, combining the R&D functions of two firms involved in an acquisition should create economies of scale that can be the stimulus to greater innovative output.

However, evidence suggests that a larger size creates efficiencies in various organizational functions only when the new firm is not *too* large. In other words, at some level, the additional costs required to manage the larger firm exceed the benefits of efficiency created by economies of scale. In addition, when faced with the complexities generated by the larger size, managers—especially those from the acquiring firm—typically decide that more bureaucratic controls should be used to manage the combined firms' operations. **Bureaucratic controls** are formalized supervisory and behavioral rules and policies that are designed to ensure consistency of decisions and actions across different units of a firm. Consistency in terms of decisions and actions can benefit the firm, primarily in the form of predictability and cost reductions. However, across time, relatively rigid and standardized managerial behavior tends to be the product of strict adherence to formalized rules and policies. Certainly, in the long run, the diminished degree of flexibility that accompanies rigid and standardized managerial behavior may produce less innovation. Because of innovation's importance to competitive success in the 21st-century landscape (see Chapters 1 and 2), the bureaucratic controls that are sometimes used when firms become too large through the use of an acquisition strategy can have a detrimental effect on performance.[117]

Bureaucratic controls are formalized supervisory and behavioral rules and policies that are designed to ensure consistency of decisions and actions across different units of a firm.

Effective Acquisitions

Earlier in the chapter, we noted that acquisition strategies do not consistently produce above-average returns for the acquiring firm's shareholders. Nonetheless, some companies are able to create value through the use of an acquisition strategy.[118] Results from a research study shed light on the differences between unsuccessful and successful acquisition strategies and suggest that there is a pattern of decisions and actions firms can follow which may improve the probability of acquisition strategy success.[119]

The study appears to show that when a target firm's assets are complementary to the acquired firm's assets, an acquisition is more successful. This is because, with complementary assets, integrating two firms' operations creates synergy. In fact, in the firms that were a part of the study, the researchers found that integrating two firms with complementary assets frequently produced unique capabilities and core competencies; a requirement for building strategic competitiveness, as previously described.[120] Thus, the acquisitions were generally highly related to the acquiring firm's businesses. In fact, the acquiring firm maintained its focus on core businesses and leveraged them with the complementary assets and capabilities from the acquired firm. Oftentimes, targets were selected and "groomed" by establishing a working relationship sometime prior to the acquisition. Using a cooperative strategy between the two firms is one way to determine whether firms can work together effectively over an extended period. As discussed in Chapter 9, strategic alliances are sometimes used to test the feasibility of firms trying to work together to pursue mutual interests.[121]

The study's results also show that friendly acquisitions facilitate integration of the firms involved in an acquisition. Through friendly acquisitions, firms work together to find ways to integrate their operations so that positive synergy can be created. In hostile takeovers, animosity often results between the two top-management teams, a condition that in turn often affects relationships and methods of working in the newly created firm. As a result, more key personnel in the acquired firm may be lost, and those who remain may resist the changes necessary to integrate the two firms and create synergy.[122] With effort, cultural clashes can be overcome, and fewer key managers and employees will become discouraged and leave.[123] Thus, successful acquisitions tend to be friendly, although there are exceptions.

Another finding from the study is that a successful acquiring firm generally has conducted effective due-diligence processes that, at a minimum, involve the deliberate and careful selection of target firms and an evaluation of how negotiations should be conducted. Having financial slack (in the form of debt equity or cash) in both the acquiring and acquired firms also frequently contributed to success in acquisitions. Relatedly, continuing to maintain a low to moderate amount of debt in the newly created firm is an important attribute of acquisition success. Indeed, maintaining low or moderate debt was shown to be critical to success even in instances when a substantial amount of leverage was used to finance the acquisition. When substantial debt is used to finance the acquisition, companies with successful acquisitions reduced the debt quickly, partly by selling off assets from the acquired firm. Often, the assets that are sold are not complementary to the acquiring firm's businesses or are performing poorly. Also, the acquiring firm may sell its own lower performing businesses after making an acquisition. In this way, high debt and debt costs are avoided. Therefore, the debt costs do not prevent long-term investments such as R&D, and managerial discretion in the use of cash flow is relatively flexible. Another attribute of successful acquisition strategies is an emphasis on innovation, as demonstrated by continuing investments in R&D activities. Significant R&D investments show a strong managerial commitment to innovation, a characteristic that is increasingly important to overall competitiveness, as well as acquisition success, in the 21st-century landscape.

Flexibility and adaptability are successful acquisitions' final two attributes. When both the acquiring and the target firms' executives have experience in managing change, they will be more skilled at adapting their capabilities to new environments. As a result, they will be more adept at integrating the two organizations, which is particularly important when firms have different organizational cultures. Adaptation skills allow the two firms to integrate their assets more quickly, efficiently, and effectively. In turn, rapid, efficient, and effective integration may quickly produce the desired synergy in the newly created firm.

The attributes and results of successful acquisitions are summarized in Table 7.1. Managers seeking acquisition success should emphasize the seven attributes that are listed. As explained in the Strategic Focus, Cisco Systems, Inc., uses an acquisition strategy quite successfully. While reading the Strategic Focus, notice how many of the attributes of effective acquisitions apply to this firm.

As we have learned, some acquisitions—particularly those characterized by the attributes shown in Table 7.1—enhance strategic competitiveness. Certainly, this is the case with Cisco Systems, Inc., which earned $2.1 billion in net income in fiscal-year 1999 on a sales volume of $12.1 billion.[124] However, the majority of acquisitions that took place from roughly the 1970s through the 1990s did not enhance firms' strategic competitiveness. In fact, some researchers observe that "history shows that anywhere between one-third [and] more than half of all acquisitions are ultimately divested or spun-off."[125] Thus, firms often use restructuring strategies to correct for the failure of a merger or an acquisition. According to Peter Drucker, restructuring strategies are being used more frequently. To support his view, he observes that, on a single, yet typ-

7.1 | Attributes of Successful Acquisitions

Attributes	Results
1. Acquired firm has assets or resources that are complementary to the acquiring firm's core business	High probability of synergy and competitive advantage by maintaining strengths
2. Acquisition is friendly	Faster and more effective integration; possibly lower premiums
3. Acquiring firm selects target firms and conducts negotiations carefully and deliberately	Firms with strongest complementarities are acquired and overpayment is avoided
4. Acquiring firm has financial slack (cash or a favorable debt position)	Financing (debt or equity) is easier and less costly to obtain
5. Merged firm maintains low to moderate debt position	Lower financing cost, lower risk (e.g., of bankruptcy), and avoidance of trade-offs associated with high debt)
6. Has experience with change and is flexible and adaptable	Faster and more effective integration facilitates achievement of synergy
7. Sustained and consistent emphasis on R&D and innovation	Maintain long-term competitive advantage in markets

ical, day in the business world, the *Wall Street Journal* reported that "Hewlett-Packard was spinning off its $8 billion business in test and measuring instruments, Procter & Gamble was selling its adult-incontinence business to a mid-sized company, and the Harris Co. was selling its entire semi-conductor business to a small company."[126]

Restructuring

The failure of an acquisition strategy is oftentimes the driver of a restructuring strategy.[127] Among the famous restructurings taken to correct for an acquisition failure are (1) AT&T's $7.4 billion purchase of NCR and subsequent spin-off of the company to shareholders in a deal valued at $3.4 billion, (2) Novell's purchase of WordPerfect for stock valued at $1.4 billion and its selling of the company to Corel for $124 million in stock and cash, and (3) SmithKline Beecham's purchase of Diversified Pharmaceutical Services for $2.3 billion and its sale of Diversified to Express Scripts for $700 million and $300 million in tax benefits.[128] In other instances, however, firms use a restructuring strategy because of changes in their external and internal environments. For example, different opportunities sometimes surface in the external environment that are particularly attractive to the diversified firm in light of the core competencies that have been developed in its internal environment. In such cases, restructuring may be appropriate to position the firm so that it can create more value for stakeholders, given the environmental changes. In the United States, restructuring strategies are also used to gain the support of financial analysts—individuals who value firms' efforts to operate efficiently and effectively in the challenging global economy.[129] Regardless of

Successful Acquisitions the Cisco Systems Way

Cisco Systems, Inc., provides end-to-end networking solutions that customers use to connect to someone else's network or to build a unified information infrastructure of their own. Essentially, Cisco provides the hardware and software that are behind state-of-the-art Internet networks. Cisco, the global leader in networking for the Internet, generates over $12 billion in annual sales, and, in early 2000, was recognized as the company creating the second highest amount of capital for its shareholders.

Contributing significantly to Cisco's strategic competitiveness and its ability to consistently earn above-average returns is the company's acquisition strategy. CEO John Chambers, architect of that strategy, believes that advancing technology precludes Cisco from doing everything itself. As a result, corporate growth is achieved by acquiring firms with products and technologies the firm cannot or does not want to develop internally.

Cisco is highly active with its acquisition strategy. For example, during the six-and-one-half-year period ending in March 2000, Cisco had acquired 51 companies, with 21 of the acquisitions completed in the last 12 months of that period. Midyear 2000 figures showed that the firm was on pace to complete at least 25 acquisitions in that year. Not every one of Cisco's acquisitions has been successful. CEO Chambers says that, of the dozens and dozens of acquisitions his firm has made, two or three have not met his expectations. But to prevent people who joined Cisco as part of a less-than-satisfactory acquisition experience from viewing their former top-level management team as a failure, Chambers chooses not to identify his acquisition disappointments. An overall evaluation of Cisco's acquisition strategy causes some analysts to suggest that "Cisco has succeeded repeatedly in using acquisitions to reshape itself and plug holes in its product line." Survey results identify Cisco as the most successful company using a merger and acquisition strategy. Yahoo! Inc. and US West, Inc., study Cisco's acquisition strategy, while competitors Lucent Technologies, Inc., and Nortel Networks Corp. attempt to mimic it.

What accounts for Cisco's successful acquisition strategy? Clearly, CEO Chambers deserves a great deal of credit. Appointed to the position in 1991, he conceived the strategy in 1993 and continues to fine-tune it today with the assistance of valued employees. With high expectations of those working with and for him, Chambers has been instrumental in the development of acquisition guidelines to which Cisco adheres rigorously. Although it is occasionally tempting to pass over one of the five inviolate guidelines to complete a prospective acquisition, Chambers says that "it takes courage to walk. It really does. You can actually get caught up in winning the acquisition rather than making the thing successful." Because of its commitment to the five acquisition guidelines, Cisco has refused to finalize a number of acquisitions.

Having a shared vision is the first of the five acquisition guidelines. Chambers believes that the acquiring company and the target firm must be in agreement regarding where the industry is going and the role each party is to play in the industry's anticipated future. Creating short-term wins for employees in the acquired firm is the second guideline. According to

Chambers, these people must "see a future. They've got to see a culture they want to be a part of. They have got to see an opportunity to really do what they were doing before or even more." A company strategy that blends with Cisco's is the third guideline. In this context, the target firm's strategy must be one that, when integrated with Cisco's operations, will create value for shareholders, employees, customers, and business partners. Cultural similarity and compatibility is the fourth guideline. Chambers and his colleagues are skeptical of efforts other companies take to integrate cultures that differ dramatically from one another. Last, target firms must be geographically proximate to parts of Cisco's current operations with which they would be most closely associated. Geographic dispersion between units prevents the development of operational efficiencies, in Cisco's view.

Facilitating compliance with the five guidelines is the work of Cisco's integration team. Approximately three dozen Cisco employees work full time "shepherding newcomers into the fold." Largely because of work this group completes before an acquisition is finalized, negotiations between Cisco and target companies tend to be brief. For example, only two-and-one-half hours of negotiations spread over three days were required for Cisco to finalize its $7.2 billion acquisition of Cerent Corp. At the time, this was the largest dollar transaction of all acquisitions Cisco had completed during Chambers's tenure.

SOURCES: Cisco Systems, Inc., 2000, Home Page, March 4, *www.cisco.com*, S. Thurm, 2000, Under Cisco's system, mergers usually work: That defies the odds, *Wall Street Journal*, March 1, A1, A12; J. Daly, 1999, John Chambers: The art of the deal, *Business 2.0*, October, 106–116; H. Goldblatt, 1999, Cisco's secrets, *Fortune*, November 8, 177–182; R. Karlgaard, 1999, Digital rules, *Forbes*, June 14, 43.

---

the reason for its use, a restructuring strategy changes the composition of a firm's business portfolio.[130]

Restructuring is a strategy through which a firm changes its set of businesses or financial structure.

Defined formally, **restructuring** is a strategy through which a firm changes its set of businesses or financial structure.[131] From the 1970s through the 1990s, divesting businesses from company portfolios and downsizing accounted for a large percentage of firms' restructuring strategies.[132]

Firms can adopt three types of restructuring strategies: downsizing, downscoping, and leveraged buyouts.

Downsizing

Downsizing is a reduction in the number of a firm's employees and, sometimes, in the number of operating units, but it may or may not change the composition of businesses in the company's portfolio.

Once thought to be an indicator of organizational decline, downsizing is now recognized as a legitimate restructuring strategy.[133] **Downsizing** is a reduction in the number of a firm's employees and, sometimes, in the number of its operating units, but it may or may not change the composition of businesses in the company's portfolio. Thus, downsizing is an intentional proactive management strategy, whereas "decline is an environmental or organizational phenomenon that occurs involuntarily and results in erosion of an organization's resource base."[134]

The late 1980s and the decade of the 1990s saw the loss of thousands of jobs in private and public organizations throughout the United States. For example, one study estimates that 85 percent of *Fortune* 1000 firms have used downsizing as a restructuring strategy.[135] Moreover, evidence suggests that, in spite of generally robust economic growth in many nations as the 21st century begins, "the organizational downsizing juggernaut continues unabated."[136]

Firms use downsizing as a restructuring strategy for different reasons. The most frequently cited reason is that the firm expects improved profitability from cost reductions and more efficient operations. For example, Bausch & Lomb, Inc., recently reduced its global workforce by 7 percent in order to consolidate or restructure its contact-lens operations. The company expected these actions to produce at least $30 million in payroll savings annually, beginning in 2001. Bausch & Lomb anticipated further savings through the phase out of older equipment in favor of more efficient machinery. To restore sales growth and to "revive a flagging culture of innovation," Procter & Gamble decided to cut 15,000 jobs from its operations. The cuts, called for by the firm's Organization 2005 restructuring plan, accounted for 13 percent of P&G's worldwide workforce. P&G expected annual savings of at least $900 million by 2004 as a result of its downsizing decision. In Japan, Malox, a logistics company and a unit of Mazda Motor Corp., tried for five years to restructure without layoffs. However, cost reductions and improvements in operational efficiency from these actions fell short of Mazda and Ford's expectations. Although downsizing was difficult because of the historical tradition in Japanese companies to avoid layoffs, Malox's executives finally decided to eliminate 100 of its 440 companywide jobs as a key part of the firm's overall restructuring strategy.[137]

Downscoping

Downscoping refers to divestiture, spin-off, or some other means of eliminating businesses that are unrelated to a firm's core businesses.

Compared to downsizing, downscoping has a more positive effect on firm performance.[138] **Downscoping** refers to divestiture, spin-off, or some other means of eliminating businesses that are unrelated to a firm's core businesses. Commonly, downscoping is described as a set of actions that causes a firm to strategically refocus on its core businesses. A firm that downscopes often also downsizes simultaneously.[139] However, it does not eliminate key employees from its primary businesses in the process, because such action could lead to a loss of one or more core competencies. Instead, a firm that is simultaneously downscoping and downsizing becomes smaller by reducing the diversity of businesses in its portfolio.

Following restructuring through downscoping, a firm can be managed more effectively by its top management team. Managerial effectiveness increases because the firm has become less diversified, allowing the top management team to better understand and manage the remaining businesses, primarily the core and other related businesses.[140]

In general, U.S. firms use downscoping as a restructuring strategy more frequently than do European companies. Highlighting this reality are research findings indicating that, "there is a powerful post-war trend towards the building of more conglomerates among the top 100 domestically-owned French, German and British industrial companies."[141] However, there has been an increase in downscoping by European firms. For example, RWE, the large German energy and industrial group, is restructuring through downscoping. Aiming to become a multienergy, multiutility company with a 15 percent share of the European energy market by 2010, RWE intends to hold stakes in "companies such as Hechtief, the construction group, E-Plus, the mobile telephone group, or Heidelberger printing machines, as pure financial investments, perhaps as a prelude to spin-offs." Thus, by downscoping, RWE is abandoning the unrelated diversification strategy that drove the firm's growth during the 1980s and 1990s.[142]

Walt Disney Co. is using downscoping as a restructuring strategy. The firm sold its Fairchild Publications unit and is seeking to divest its baseball and hockey teams.

Among the U.S.-based firms using downscoping as a restructuring strategy, Walt Disney Co. sold its Fairchild Publications unit to Advance Publications, Inc., for $650 million. Disney is also seeking to divest its baseball and hockey teams. As of the beginning of 2000, buyers had not been located for these units. According to analysts, sales of the sports teams and other operations (e.g., a magazine called *Los Angeles*) "would fit in with Disney's continuing drive to pare down or dispose of non-core operations. That drive [began in 1999], as Disney faced a deepening earnings slump."[143] ConAgra performed well in the 1980s through the use of an unrelated diversification strategy. Implemented through an acquisition strategy, the diversification strategy resulted in ConAgra becoming a conglomerate with roughly 90 independent companies that make products from fertilizers to Slim Jim meat snacks. Analysts argue that the firm's recent profitability problems indicate that it is due for a serious downscoping effort. In response to its difficulties, the firm's top-level managers are restructuring their company's operations into 10 product groups under three main divisions—food service (restaurants), retail (grocery stores), and agricultural products.[144]

Restructuring strategies may require a considerable amount of time before a firm is able to divest a sufficient number of operations so that it can refocus on its core business or businesses. This may or may not prove to be the case with Walt Disney Co. and ConAgra, though it has been for Ralston Purina, which intends to spin off its Eveready battery division, "leaving the once highly-diversified group focused entirely on pet food." However, Ralston has been restructuring almost since it purchased Eveready in 1986, and, analysts say, the firm's "long-running restructuring has seen it dispose of bakeries, baby food [manufacture], animal feed [production], and ski resorts."[145]

Leveraged Buyouts

A **leveraged buyout (LBO)** is a restructuring strategy whereby a party buys all of a firm's assets in order to take the firm private.

Commonly, leveraged buyouts (LBOs) are used as a restructuring strategy to correct for managerial mistakes or because managers are making decisions that primarily serve their own interests rather than those of shareholders.[146] A **leveraged buyout (LBO)** is a restructuring strategy whereby a party buys all of a firm's assets in order to take the firm private. Once the transaction is completed, the company's stock is no longer traded publicly. Usually, significant amounts of debt are incurred to finance an LBO. To support debt payments and to downscope the company so that managers can concentrate on the firm's core businesses, the owners of a firm created through an LBO may immediately sell, or attempt to sell, a number of assets.[147] It is not uncommon for those buying a firm through an LBO to restructure the firm to the point that it can be sold at a profit within a five- to eight-year period. A well-known finance scholar predicted that this restructuring strategy would become very prominent, but this has not proved to be the case.[148] In fact, as a percentage of the total U.S. merger and acquisition market in the United States, LBOs fell to 0.8 percent toward the end of 1999, compared with 4.1 percent in 1990.[149]

Management buyouts (MBOs), employee buyouts (EBOs), and whole-firm buyouts, in which one company or partnership purchases an entire company instead of a part of it are the three types of LBOs. In part because of managerial incentives, MBOs, more so than EBOs and whole-firm buyouts, have been found to lead to downscoping, an increased strategic focus, and improved performance.[150] As a case in point, Fender Musical Instruments, a unit of CBS, was performing poorly. In 1981, William Schultz was hired as the top-level executive and was charged with making decisions that would result in a turnaround at Fender. After four years of effort, Schultz decided to complete an MBO so that Fender could operate more independently than it was permitted to do under CBS ownership. Heavily leveraged at the outset, with $11 in debt for every $1 in equity, the firm's performance improved steadily after the MBO was executed in 1985. More than 10 years later, Fender's annual volume reached $300 million. In addition, Fender commanded almost 50 percent of the guitar market. The group Schultz assembled to complete the MBO thus saw its $500,000 investment grow to more than $100 million in value.[151]

Improvements at UAL (parent of United Airlines) and Avis Rent A Car are attributed to EBOs at those firms. The UAL arrangement appears to be working better than that at Avis. At UAL, there has been more of a cooperative spirit with gains in market share and above-average returns.[152] At Avis and other firms that have opted for EBOs, difficulties have surfaced between management and employees. Furthermore, few employee owners have been requested to sit on boards.[153] These problems are similar to problems experienced with EBOs in Russia: Needed restructuring is hard to accomplish because of employee job security fears,[154] and when change is needed, more problems usually occur between managers and employees.

Whole-firm LBOs, on the other hand, often produce improvements through downsizing and retrenchment. This approach is illustrated by a buyout of Dr Pepper by Forsmann Little, an LBO specialist. Dr Pepper was successful enough to receive a new infusion of capital through an initial public offering. Subsequently, the firm was purchased by Cadbury Schweppes, PLC.[155]

Restructuring Outcomes

The short- and long-term outcomes resulting from the three restructuring strategies are shown in Figure 7.2. As indicated, downsizing does not commonly lead to a higher firm performance. Commenting about this, two researchers noted that "annual surveys conducted by the American Management Association show that only 41 percent of downsizing companies have reported productivity increases, and only 37 percent have realized any long-term gains in shareholder value."[156] Still, in free-market-based societies at large, downsizing has generated a host of entrepreneurial opportunities for individuals to operate their own businesses. In fact, as discussed in Chapter 13, start-up ventures in the United States are growing at three times the rate of the national economy.[157]

Another researcher's findings about downsizing are also informative. This particular study showed that downsizing contributed to lower returns in both U.S. and Japanese firms in the group of companies that was examined. In effect, these findings indicate that the stock markets in the firms' respective nations evaluated the downsizings negatively (i.e., investors concluded that downsizing would have a negative effect

FIGURE 7.2 | Restructuring and Outcomes

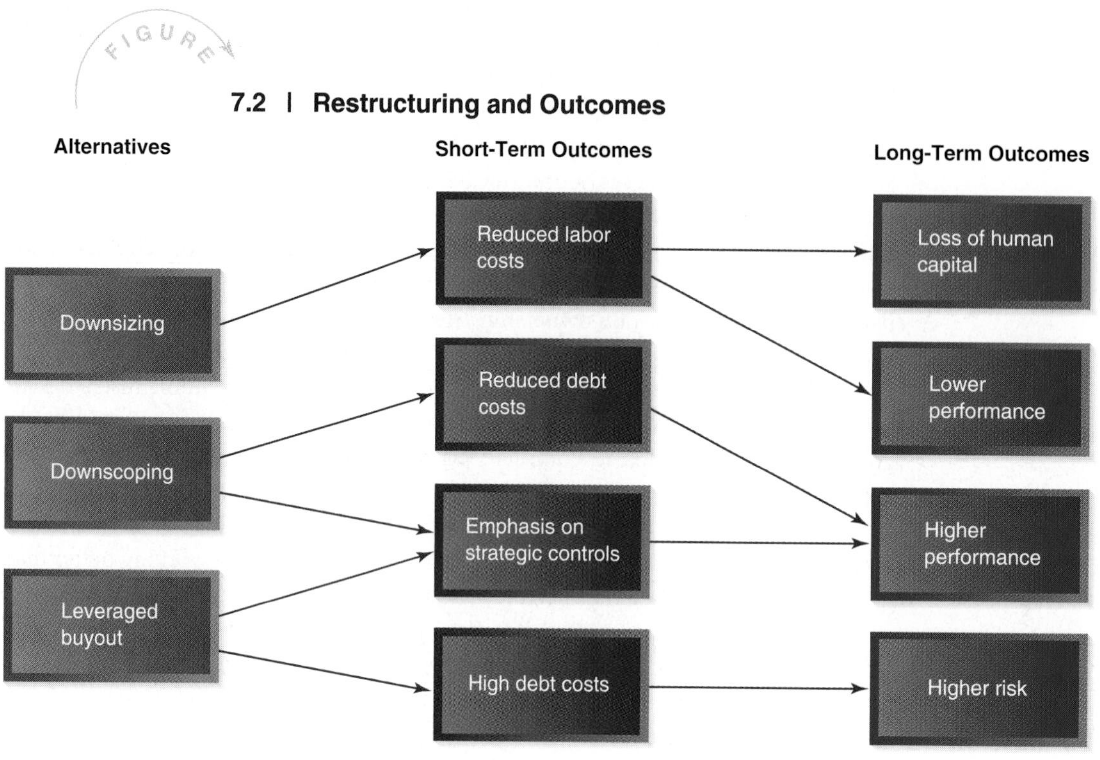

on companies' ability to achieve strategic competitiveness in the long term). An interpretation of the findings is that downsizing occurs as a consequence of other problems in a company.[158] As an example, in 2000, Coca-Cola announced a reduction of 21 percent of its 29,000-plus-strong global workforce, including what analysts saw as an "astonishing 40 percent at [the company's] headquarters." The largest downsizing in the firm's history, this decision was viewed by some as an admission "that the company had gone down the wrong road."[159]

Coca-Cola's decision to reduce its workforce may also demonstrate another concern that often surfaces when firms use downsizing as a restructuring strategy. As shown in Figure 7.2, downsizing tends to result in a loss of human capital in the long term. Losing employees with many years—perhaps even decades—of experience with a firm creates a vacuum in terms of knowledge. As noted in Chapter 3, knowledge is the foundation for the type of organizational learning that is vital to competitive success in the global economy.[160] As regards Coca-Cola, it has been noted that "analysts and company observers question whether [the firm] is cutting too many people in too many different places."[161] Thus, in general, research evidence and corporate experience suggest that downsizing may be of more tactical (i.e., short-term) than strategic (i.e., long-term) values (see Chapter 5).

As Figure 7.2 indicates, downscoping leads to more positive outcomes in both the short and the long term than does downsizing or engaging in an LBO. Downscoping's desirable long-term outcome of contributing to higher performance is a product of the positive short-term benefits of reduced debt costs and the emphasis on strategic controls that becomes possible once a firm restructures itself to concentrate on its core businesses—businesses that are less diverse in nature and that are more familiar to the top-management team. However, downscoping's positive short- and long-term outcomes are achieved only when the firm uses that restructuring strategy properly—that is, in ways which allow the company to refocus on its core business or businesses.[162]

While whole-firm LBOs have been hailed as a significant innovation in the financial restructuring of firms, there can be negative trade-offs. First, the large debt increases the financial risk of the firm, as is evidenced by the number of companies that filed for bankruptcy in the 1990s after having executed a whole-firm LBO. Sometimes, the intent of the owners to increase the efficiency of the bought-out firm and sell it within five to eight years creates a short-term and risk-averse managerial focus. As a result, many of these firms fail to invest in R&D or take other major actions designed to maintain or improve the company's core competence.[163] However, research suggests that in firms with an entrepreneurial mind-set, buyouts can lead to greater innovation.[164]

The strategic competitiveness spawned and above-average returns earned by GE during Jack Welch's tenure as CEO demonstrate the value that can be created by using restructuring strategies effectively. Downscoping was the primary restructuring strategy implemented by GE under Welch's leadership. Indicators of GE's success since Welch was appointed CEO in 1981 include the fact that the firm was at or near the top of *Fortune* magazine's "Most Admired Corporations" list while Welch was the firm's chief executive.[165] Toward the end of Welch's time as CEO, GE had become the ninth-largest and second-most-profitable company in the world. Between 1981, when Welch became CEO, and 1999, GE's sales rose 3.7 times (from $27.2 billion to $100.5 billion), while profits grew 5.7 times (from $1.6 billion to $9.2 billion). These outcomes indicate the significant increase in shareholders' wealth that was a product of strategic decisions made at GE while Welch was CEO.[166]

The GE of 1999 was substantially different from the GE of 1981, when Welch assumed the company's top executive position. Under Welch, GE was restructured almost continuously to create greater efficiencies, globalize operations, and develop world-class managers and top-level executives. During his final year as CEO, Welch was passionate about electronic commerce. Believing that electronic commerce was the biggest revolution in business in his lifetime, Welch thought that the Web would change how business was conducted on a global scale and how firms should be organized to compete successfully in light of those changes. Welch intended to include employees, suppliers, and customers in various activities to gather information required to determine how GE should restructure itself to exploit Web-based opportunities.[167]

As we discuss in Chapter 9 and as was mentioned earlier in this chapter, cooperative strategies, such as strategic alliances, are an alternative to merger and acquisition strategies. Citing statistics, Peter Drucker suggests that alliances of all kinds, "such as partnerships, a big business buying a minority stake in a small one, cooperative agreements in research or in marketing, joint ventures, and, often, handshake agreements with few formal and legally binding contracts behind them,"[168] are being completed with greater frequency. When used because of a match between opportunities in the firm's external environment and the competitive advantages formed through its internal resources and capabilities, both cooperative strategies and merger and acquisition strategies can lead to competitive success.

Before examining cooperative strategies in detail in Chapter 9, however, we turn our attention to an analysis of international strategies. Because of the rapidly expanding global economy, international strategies are becoming more important drivers of strategic competitiveness for firms competing in all industries and countries.

Summary

- Acquisition strategies are increasingly popular among the world's firms. Because of globalization, deregulation of multiple industries in many different economies, and favorable legislation, among other factors, the number and size of domestic and cross-border acquisitions continues to increase.
- Firms use acquisition strategies to (1) increase market power, (2) overcome entry barriers to new markets or regions, (3) avoid the costs of developing new products internally and bringing them to market, (4) increase the speed of new market entries, (5) reduce the risk of entering a new business, (6) become more diversified, and (6) reshape their competitive scope through developing a different portfolio of businesses.
- Among the problems associated with the use of an acquisition strategy are (1) the difficulty of effectively integrating the firms involved, (2) incorrectly evaluating the target firm's value, (3) creating debt loads that preclude adequate investments (e.g., R&D allocations) required for long-term success, (4) overestimating the potential for synergy between the companies involved, (5) creating a firm that is too diversified, given its core competencies and environmental opportunities, (6) creating an internal environment in which managers devote increasing amounts of their time and energy to analyzing and completing additional acquisitions, and (7) developing a combined firm that is too large, necessitating an extensive use of bureaucratic, rather than strategic, controls.
- Although potentially problematic, acquisitions can contribute to a firm's strategic competitiveness. They do so when (1) the target firm is selected and purchased through careful, detailed analyses and negotiations, (2) the acquiring and target firms have considerable slack in the form of cash or debt capacity, (3) the acquiring firm has a low or moderate level of debt, (4) the newly created firm reduces its debt obligations quickly (especially the debts that were incurred to complete the acquisition) by selling off portions of the acquired firm or some of the acquiring firm's poorly performing companies, (5) the acquiring and target firms have complementary resources that can be the basis of core competencies in the newly created firm, (6) the acquiring and acquired firms have experience in terms of adapting to change (such experience increases the likelihood that the companies' operations will be integrated successfully), and (7) R&D and innovation are emphasized in the new firm.
- In the late 1980s and continuing into the present, restructuring is a strategy firms use to improve their performance by correcting for problems that were created by inappropriate or excessive diversification. Downsizing, a set of actions through which a firm's number of employees and hierarchical levels are reduced, is a restructuring strategy. Although it can lead to short-term cost reductions, they may be realized at the expense of long-term success. The reason for this is that once downsizing begins, the firm is unable to prevent an exodus of employees with skills required for strategic success. These employees might leave the focal firm to obtain positions with less uncertainty in other companies.
- With the goal of reducing the firm's level of diversification, downscoping is a second restructuring strategy. Often, it is accomplished by divesting unrelated businesses. As a result, the firm and its top-level managers are able to refocus on the core businesses. Firms sometimes downsize and downscope simultaneously, a comprehensive process that often yields better results than does downsizing.
- Leveraged buyouts (LBOs) are the third restructuring strategy. Through an LBO, a firm is purchased so that it can become a private entity. LBOs usually are financed largely through debt. There are three types of LBOs: management buyouts (MBOs), employee buyouts (EBOs), and whole-firm LBOs. Because they provide clear managerial incentives, MBOs have been the most successful of the three. Although EBOs have the potential to improve cooperation throughout

the firm, power struggles are also a possibility. These struggles are more likely when significant change is required for a firm to improve its performance. In general, whole-firm LBOs have met with mixed success. Oftentimes, the intent is to improve efficiency and performance to point where the firm can be sold successfully within five to eight years. However, the cost of debt incurred to finance the whole-firm LBO makes it difficult for companies to perform in ways that make them attractive candidates for purchase.

- Commonly, restructuring's primary goal is gaining or reestablishing effective strategic control of the firm. Of the three restructuring strategies, downscoping is aligned the most closely with establishing and using strategic controls. Once refocused on core businesses, as downscoping allows, managers can more easily control the firm because it is less diverse (in terms or products or markets) and the businesses that remain are those about which managers tend to be the most knowledgeable.

Review Questions

1. Why are acquisition strategies popular in many firms competing in the global economy?
2. What specific reasons account for firms' decisions to use acquisition strategies as one means of achieving strategic competitiveness?
3. What are the seven primary problems that affect a firm's efforts to use an acquisition strategy successfully?
4. What are the attributes that have been found to be associated with the successful use of an acquisition strategy?
5. What is the restructuring strategy and what are its common forms?
6. What are the short- and long-term outcomes associated with the different restructuring strategies?

Application Discussion Questions

1. Evidence indicates that the shareholders of many acquiring firms gain little or nothing in value from the acquisitions. Why, then, do so many firms continue to use an acquisition strategy?
2. Of the problems that affect the success of an acquisition, which one do you believe is the most critical in the global economy? Why? What should firms do to make certain that they do not experience such a problem when they use an acquisition strategy?
3. Use the Internet to read about acquisitions that are currently underway. Choose one of these acquisitions. Based on the firms' characteristics and experiences and the reasons cited to support the acquisition, do you think it will result in increased strategic competitiveness for the acquiring firm? Why or why not?
4. Using the Internet, study recent merger and acquisition activity that is taking place throughout the global economy. Are most of the transactions you found between domestic companies or are they cross-border acquisitions? What accounts for the nature of what you found?
5. What is *synergy*, and how do firms create it through mergers and acquisitions? In your opinion, how often do acquisitions create *private synergy*? What evidence can you cite to support your position?
6. What can a top management team do to ensure that its firm does not become diversified to the point of earning negative returns from its diversification strategy?
7. Some companies enter new markets through internally developed products, while others do so by acquiring other firms. What are the advantages and disadvantages of each approach?
8. How do the Internet's capabilities influence a firm's ability to study acquisition candidates?

Ethics Questions

1. Some evidence suggests that there is a direct and positive relationship between a firm's size and its top-level managers' compensation. If this is so, what inducement does that relationship provide to upper-level executives? What can be done to influence the relationship so that it serves shareholders' interests?

2. When a firm is in the process of restructuring itself by divesting some assets and acquiring others, managers may have incentives to restructure in ways that increase their power base and compensation package. Does this possibility explain at least part of the reason for the less-than-encouraging outcomes of acquisitions for shareholders of the acquiring firm?
3. When shareholders increase their wealth through downsizing, does this come, to some degree, at the expense of loyal employees—those who have worked diligently to serve the firm in terms of accomplishing its strategic mission and strategic intent? If so, what actions would you take to be fair to both shareholders and employees if you were charged with downsizing or "smartsizing" a firm's employment ranks? What ethical base would you employ to make decisions regarding downsizing?
4. Are takeovers ethical? If not, why not?
5. Internet fever is mentioned in the Opening Case. Is it ethical for managers to acquire other companies just because industry competitors are doing so?

Internet Exercise

Many interesting Internet sites, including the U.S. Federal Trade Commission's official site at **www.ftc.gov.**, offer information on mergers and acquisitions. With the increasing number of cross-border mergers and acquisitions, the FTC has been required to work closely with other foreign antitrust enforcers to regulate the new era of the global transaction. For example, the United States and the European Union have a bilateral agreement on antitrust enforcement.

***e-project:** Trace the history of the some recent large mergers and acquisitions using the following Internet information sources: Daimler and Chrysler; BP Amoco and Arco; and Vodafone and Mannesmann. Use any other sources you find to obtain information on the official regulatory agencies that were involved in granting or denying permission for these mergers.

Notes

1. R. Whittington, 1999, In praise of the evergreen conglomerate, Mastering Strategy (Part Six), *Financial Times,* November 1, 4–6; M. A. Hitt, R. E. Hoskisson, R. D. Ireland, & J. S. Harrison, 1991, Effects of acquisitions on R&D inputs and outputs, *Academy of Management Journal,* 34: 693–706.
2. P. Moran & S. Ghoshal, 1999, Markets, firms, and the process of economic development, *Academy of Management Review,* 24: 390–412.
3. T. A. Stewart, 2000, Managing risk in the 21st century, *Fortune,* February 7, 202–206.
4. R. Simons, 1999, How risky is your company? *Harvard Business Review,* 77(3): 85–94.
5. S. Sugawara, 1999, Merger mania spawns powerhouses as world enters new century, *Dallas Morning News,* December 31, D11.
6. How M&A will navigate the turn into a new century, 2000, *Mergers & Acquisitions,* January, 29–35.
7. E. Portanger, 2000, Europe sets the stage for more megamergers, *Wall Street Journal,* January 4, A17.
8. How M&A will navigate, 30.
9. C. C. Markides, 1999, A dynamic view of strategy, *Sloan Management Review,* 40(3): 55–63.
10. H. R. Greve, 1998, Managerial cognition and the mimetic adoption of market positions: What you see is what you do, *Strategic Management Journal,* 19: 967–988.
11. B. Lowendahl & O. Revang, 1998, Challenges to existing strategy theory in a postindustrial society, *Strategic Management Journal,* 19: 755–773.
12. D. L. Deephouse, 1999, To be different, or to be the same? It's a question (and theory) of strategic balance, *Strategic Management Journal,* 20: 147–166.
13. M. A. Hitt, J. S. Harrison, & R. D. Ireland, 2001, *Creating Value through Mergers and Acquisitions: A Complete Guide to Successful M&As* (New York: Oxford University Press); Hitt, Hoskisson, Ireland, & Harrison, Effects of acquisitions, 693–706.
14. A. Rappaport & M. L. Sirower, 1999, Stock or cash? *Harvard Business Review,* 77(6): 147–158.
15. Sugawara, Merger mania, D11.
16. J. Pereira, 2000, Late to the Web, Staples forges dot-com links, *Wall Street Journal,* January 14, B1, B4.
17. M&A scorecard, 2000, *Mergers & Acquisitions,* January, 40–42.
18. Hitt, Harrison, & Ireland, *Creating Value*; K. C. O'Shaughnessy & D. J. Flanagan, 1998, Determinants of layoff announcements following M&As: An empirical investigation, *Strategic Management Journal,* 19: 989–999.
19. J. Anand, 1999, How many matches are made in heaven, Mastering Strategy (Part Five), *Financial Times,* October 25, 6–7.
20. B. Deener, 1999, Mega-deals stifle shares, survey implies, *Dallas Morning News,* November 30, D1, D6.
21. N. Deogun & S. Lipin, 1999, Cautionary tales: When big deals turn bad, *Wall Street Journal,* December 8, C1, C28.
22. M. C. Jensen, 1988, Takeovers: Their causes and consequences, *Journal of Economic Perspectives,* 1(2): 21–48.
23. Rappaport & Sirower, Stock or cash? 147–158.
24. E. Robinson, 1999, UK and Dutch cleaning products groups to merge, *Financial Times,* July 28, 13.
25. W. Mitchell, 1999, Recreating the company: Four contexts for change, Mastering Strategy (Part Ten), *Financial Times,* November 29, 4–7.
26. C. Gentry & R. L. Rundle, 2000, Aetna gets takeover bid for $10.5 billion, *Wall Street Journal,* March 2, A3, A12.

27. S. Lipin, 1999, More big firms are ripe for hostile takeover bids, *Wall Street Journal,* November 22, B10.
28. S. Tully, 2000, The new takeover target (Hint: It's in Detroit), *Fortune,* January 10, 28–30.
29. Mitchell, Recreating the company, 7; D. K. Datta, G. E. Pinches, & V. K. Naravyanan, 1992, Factors influencing wealth creation from mergers and acquisitions: A metaanalysis, *Strategic Management Journal,* 13: 67–84; P. C. Haspeslagh & D. B. Jemison, 1991, *Managing Acquisitions: Creating Value Through Corporate Renewal* (New York: The Free Press).
30. M. L. Marks, 2000, Egos can make—and unmake—mergers, *Wall Street Journal,* January 24, A26.
31. P. Haspeslagh, 1999, Managing the mating dance in equal mergers, Mastering Strategy (Part Five), *Financial Times,* October 25, 14–15.
32. RPM, Inc., 2000, *Better Investing,* February, 63–64.
33. L. Capron, 1999, Horizontal acquisitions: The benefits and risk to long-term performance, Mastering Strategy (Part Seven), *Financial Times,* November 8, 7–8.
34. L. Capron, 1999, The long-term performance of horizontal acquisitions, *Strategic Management Journal,* 20: 987–1018.
35. R. Flannery, 2000, Big Taiwan chip maker to acquire rival, *Wall Street Journal,* January 10, A7.
36. K. Ramaswamy, 1997, The performance impact of strategic similarity in horizontal mergers: Evidence from the U.S. banking industry, *Academy of Management Journal,* 40: 697–715.
37. L. B. Ward, 2000, Software companies to combine, *Dallas Morning News,* February 15, D1, D17.
38. J. Wyatt, 1995, Drug stocks—where M&A pays off, *Fortune,* October 30, 222.
39. Anand, How many matches, 6–7.
40. R. Gertner & M. J. Knez, 1999, Vertical integration: Make or buy decisions, Mastering Strategy (Part Ten), *Financial Times,* November 29, 12–13.
41. M. Brannigan, 2000, Carnival agrees to buy Fairfield for stock, debt, *Wall Street Journal,* January 25, A8.
42. M. Brannigan, 2000, Carnival, hit by stock dive, calls off talks to acquire Fairfield Communities, *Wall Street Journal,* February 28, A15.
43. J. Landers, 2000, Regulators increase scrutiny of mergers, *Wall Street Journal,* February 4, D1, D2.
44. T. Petzinger, Jr., 2000, So long, supply and demand, *Wall Street Journal,* January 1, R31.
45. J. A. Gingrich, 1999, Five rules for winning emerging market consumers, *Strategy & Business,* 15: 19–33.
46. Hitt, Harrison, & Ireland, *Creating Value,* Chapter 10; D. Angwin & B. Savill, 1997, Strategic perspectives on European cross-border acquisitions: A view from the top European executives, *European Management Review,* 15: 423–435.
47. N. Deogun, 1999, Made in U.S.A.: Deals from Europe hit record, *Wall Street Journal,* October 25, C1, C18.
48. G. Cramb, 1999, Off to New Amsterdam, 1999, *Financial Times,* July 21, 12.
49. Bloomberg News, 1999, Kimberly-Clark planning acquisitions, *Dallas Morning News,* December 1, D2; E. Robinson, 1999, Shiseido pursues M&A, *Financial Times,* July 27, 14.
50. E. Portanger, 2000, Europe sets the stage for more megamergers, *Wall Street Journal,* January 4, A17; Fortis to pay $2.6 billion for U.S. firm, *Wall Street Journal,* March 8, A4; J. Martinson, 1999, Mergers spur expansion, *Financial Times,* April 12, 3; S. Mehta & A. Raghavan, 1999, Europe is next frontier for U.S. telecom deals, *Wall Street Journal,* October 25, B12.
51. J. K. Shank & V. Govindarajan, 1992, Strategic cost analysis of technological investments, *Sloan Management Review,* 34(3): 39–51.
52. E. Mansfield, 1969, *Industrial Research and Technological Innovation* (New York: Norton).
53. Hitt, Harrison, & Ireland, *Creating Value*; L. H. Clark, Jr. & A. L. Malabre, Jr., 1988, Slow rise in outlays for research imperils U.S. competitive edge, *Wall Street Journal,* November 16, A1, A5; E. Mansfield, M. Schwartz, & S. Wagner, 1981, Imitation costs and patents: An empirical study, *Economic Journal,* 91: 907–918.
54. M. A. Hitt, R. E. Hoskisson, R. A. Johnson, & D. D. Moesel, 1996, The market for corporate control and firm innovation, *Academy of Management Journal,* 39: 1084–1119.
55. M. Elvekrog, 2000, Watson Pharmaceuticals, Inc., *Better Investing,* February, 32–34.
56. R. Wherry, 1999, Pfizer's surpriser, *Forbes,* November 29, 56.
57. D. Pilling, 1999, Big boys eye bite-sized bios, *Financial Times,* July 15, 14.
58. K. F. McCardle & S. Viswanathan, 1994, The direct entry versus takeover decision and stock price performance around takeovers, *Journal of Business,* 67: 1–43.
59. Rappaport & Sirower, Stock or cash? 147.
60. M. Song, A. A. Di Benedetto, & Y. L. Zhao, 1999, Pioneering advantages in manufacturing and service industries: Empirical evidence from nine countries, *Strategic Management Journal,* 20: 811–836.
61. H. Lee, K. G. Smith, C. M. Grimm, & A. Schomburg, 2000, Timing, order and durability of new product advantages with imitation, *Strategic Management Journal,* 21: 23–30.
62. S. Stecklow, 2000, BT rides in to buy Ireland's Esat, topping bid by Norway's Telenor, *Wall Street Journal,* January 12, A18.
63. D. R. Horton, Inc., 1999, *Better Investing,* July, 68–69.
64. Kraft Foods agrees to buy Boca Burger, a soy-products firm, 2000, *Wall Street Journal,* January 19, B7.
65. G. McWilliams, 2000, Compaq buying custom-PC lines of Inacom, with Dell in mind, *Wall Street Journal,* January 15, B2.
66. M. A. Hitt, R. E. Hoskisson, & R. D. Ireland, 1990, Mergers and acquisitions and managerial commitment to innovation in M-form firms, *Strategic Management Journal,* 11(Special Summer Issue): 29–47.
67. S. Branch, 2000, P&G is out to fetch distribution gains for Iams pet foods, *Wall Street Journal,* January 6, A6.
68. Hitt, Hoskisson, & Ireland, Mergers and acquisitions; J. Constable, 1986, Diversification as a factor in U.K. industrial strategy, *Long Range Planning,* 19: 52–60.
69. Hitt, Hoskisson, Ireland, & Harrison, Effects of acquisitions; Hitt, Hoskisson, & Ireland, Mergers and acquisitions.
70. J. Carlton, 2000, CNET agrees to buy mySimon in a $702.7 million stock deal, *Wall Street Journal,* January 21, B6.
71. J.-F. Hennart & S. B. Reddy, 2000, Digestibility and asymmetric information in the choice between acquisitions and joint ventures: Where's the beef? *Strategic Management Journal,* 21: 191–193.
72. D. D. Bergh, 1997, Predicting divestiture of unrelated acquisitions: An integrative model of ex ante conditions, *Strategic Management Journal,* 18: 715–731.
73. J. Anand & H. Singh, 1997, Asset redeployment, acquisitions and corporate strategy in declining industries, *Strategic Management Journal,* 18(Special Summer Issue): 99–118.
74. J. Harrison, 1999, Following the lead of a changing industry, *Mergers & Acquisitions,* May/June, 60–61.
75. T. Burt, 1999, DaimlerChrysler looks to diversify, *Financial Times,* August 3, 16.
76. J. Griffiths, 1999, Spotlight falls on Japanese, *Financial Times,* May 27, 1; J. Griffiths, 1999, Fitter future for Ford as Nasser takes the driving seat, *Financial Times,* April 13, 24.
77. J. P. Miller, 2000, Emerson Electric to announce pact to buy Ericsson division, *Wall Street Journal,* January 18, B6.
78. P. Landers & R. A. Guth, 2000, Japan's Hitachi plans high-tech shopping spree, *Wall Street Journal,* January 5, A19.
79. Marks, Egos can make, A26.
80. Anand, How many matches, 7.

81. Hitt, Harrison, & Ireland, *Creating Value*; D. K. Datta, 1991, Organizational fit and acquisition performance: Effects of post-acquisition integration, *Strategic Management Journal,* 12: 281–297
82. A. J. Viscio, J. R. Harbison, A. Asin, & R. P. Vitaro, 1999, Post-merger integration: What makes mergers work? *Strategy & Business,* 17: 26–33; H. Aaron, 1994, A poisoning of the atmosphere, *Wall Street Journal,* August 29, A10; P. M. Elsass & J. F. Veiga, 1994, Acculturation in acquired organizations: A force field perspective, *Human Relations,* 47: 453–471.
83. S. DeVoge & S. Spreier, 1999, The soft realities of mergers, *Across the Board,* December, 27–32; A. F. Buono & J. L. Bowditch, 1989, *The Human Side of Mergers and Acquisitions* (San Francisco: Jossey-Bass).
84. M. Zollo, 1999, M&A—the challenge of learning to integrate, Mastering Strategy (Part 11), *Financial Times,* December 6, 14–15.
85. Ibid., 14.
86. N. Knox, 1999, AlliedSignal, Honeywell plan rapid integration of companies, *Dallas Morning News,* June 8, D4.
87. R. L. Simison & S. Miller, 1999, Making 'digital' decisions, *Wall Street Journal,* September 24, B1, B4.
88. H. Goldblatt, 1999, Cisco's secrets, *Fortune,* November 8, 177–182.
89. Anand, How many matches, 7; K. Ohmae, 1999, The Godzilla companies of the new economy, *Strategy & Business,* 18: 130–139.
90. Rappaport & Sirower, Stock or cash?, 149.
91. Viscio, Harbison, Asin, & Vitaro, Post-merger integration, 27.
92. R. C. Morais, 2000, Takeover bait, *Forbes,* January 24, 74–75.
93. S. Tully, 1999, First Union buys retail—and pays the price, *Fortune,* June 21, 43.
94. Hitt, Harrison, & Ireland, *Creating Value.*
95. G. Yago, 1991, *Junk Bonds: How High Yield Securities Restructured Corporate America* (New York: Oxford University Press), 146–148.
96. M. C. Jensen, 1987, A helping hand for entrenched managers, *Wall Street Journal,* November 4, A6; M. C. Jensen, 1986, Agency costs of free cash flow, corporate finance, and takeovers, *American Economic Review,* 76: 323–329.
97. A. Osterland, 1999, False spring for a seed company, *Business Week,* June 12, 130.
98. M. A. Hitt & D. L. Smart, 1994, Debt: A disciplining force for managers or a debilitating force for organizations? *Journal of Management Inquiry,* 3: 144–152.
99. Hitt, Harrison, & Ireland, *Creating Value.*
100. C. J. Chipello, 2000, Abitibi agrees to purchase Donohue in $4 billion cash-and-stock accord, *Wall Street Journal,* February 14, A32.
101. T. N. Hubbard, 1999, Integration strategies and the scope of the company, Mastering Strategy (Part 11), *Financial Times,* December 6, 8–10.
102. Hitt, Harrison, & Ireland, *Creating Value.*
103. C. H. St. John & J. S. Harrison, 1999, Manufacturing-based relatedness, synergy, and coordination, *Strategic Management Journal,* 20: 129–145.
104. Hitt, Hoskisson, Ireland, & Harrison, Effects of acquisitions; J. B. Barney, 1988, Returns to bidding firms in mergers and acquisitions: Reconsidering the relatedness hypothesis, *Strategic Management Journal,* 9(Special Summer Issue): 71–78.
105. O. E. Williamson, 1999, Strategy research: Governance and competence perspectives, *Strategic Management Journal,* 20: 1087–1108.
106. Hitt, Hoskisson, Johnson, & Moesel, The market for corporate control.
107. Whittington, In praise of, 4.
108. C. W. L. Hill & R. E. Hoskisson, 1987, Strategy and structure in the multiproduct firm, *Academy of Management Review,* 12: 331–341.
109. R. A. Johnson, R. E. Hoskisson, & M. A. Hitt, 1993, Board of director involvement in restructuring: The effects of board versus managerial controls and characteristics, *Strategic Management Journal,* 14(Special Issue): 33–50; C. C. Markides, 1992, Consequences of corporate refocusing: Ex ante evidence, *Academy of Management Journal,* 35: 398–412.
110. R. E. Hoskisson & M. A. Hitt, 1988, Strategic control systems and relative R&D investment in large multiproduct firms, *Strategic Management Journal,* 9: 605–621.
111. Hitt, Hoskisson, & Ireland, Mergers and acquisitions.
112. Ibid.
113. Ibid.
114. J. Flint, No guts, no glory, *Forbes,* February 7, 88.
115. Hitt, Hoskisson, Ireland, & Harrison, Effects of acquisitions.
116. R. E. Hoskisson, M. A. Hitt, & R. D. Ireland, 1994, The effects of acquisitions and restructuring (strategic refocusing) strategies on innovation, in G. von Krogh, A. Sinatra, and H. Singh (eds.), *Managing Corporate Acquisitions* (London: Macmillan Press), 144–169.
117. Hitt, Hoskisson, & Ireland, Mergers and acquisitions.
118. K. Ohmae, 2000, The Godzilla companies of the new economy, *Strategy & Business,* 18: 130–139.
119. Hitt, Harrison, & Ireland, *Creating Value.*
120. J. S. Harrison, M. A. Hitt, R. E. Hoskisson, & R. D. Ireland, 1991, Synergies and post acquisition performance: Differences versus similarities in resource allocations, *Journal of Management,* 17: 173–190; Barney, Returns to bidding firms.
121. M. A. Lubatkin & P. J. Lane, 1996, Psst . . . The merger mavens still have it wrong! *Academy of Management Executive,* X(1): 21–39.
122. J. P. Walsh, 1989, Doing a deal: Merger and acquisition negotiations and their impact upon target company top management turnover, *Strategic Management Journal,* 10: 307–322.
123. L. S. Lublin, 1995, Strategies for preventing post-takeover defections, *Wall Street Journal,* April 28, B1, B8.
124. J. Daly, 1999, John Chambers: The art of the deal, *Business 2.0,* October, 106–116.
125. Anand, How many matches, 6.
126. P. F. Drucker, 2000, The unrecognized boom, *Across the Board,* January, 15–16.
127. R. E. Hoskisson, R. A. Johnson, & D. D. Moesel, 1994, Divestment intensity of restructuring firms: Effects of governance, strategy and performance, *Academy of Management Journal,* 37: 1207–1251.
128. Deogun & Lipin, Cautionary tales, C1.
129. S. R. Fisher & M. A. White, 2000, Downsizing in a learning organization: Are there hidden costs? *Academy of Management Review,* 25: 244–251.
130. R. A. Johnson, 1996, Antecedents and outcomes of corporate refocusing, *Journal of Management,* 22: 437–481.
131. J. E. Bethel & J. Liebeskind, 1993, The effects of ownership structure on corporate restructuring, *Strategic Management Journal,* 14 (Special Summer Issue): 15–31.
132. A. Campbell & D. Sadtler, 1998, Corporate breakups, *Strategy & Business,* 12: 64–73; E. Bowman & H. Singh, 1990, Overview of corporate restructuring: Trends and consequences, in L. Rock & R. H. Rock (eds.), *Corporate Restructuring* (New York: McGraw-Hill).
133. Fisher & White, Downsizing in a learning organization, 244.
134. W. McKinley, J. Zhao, & K. G. Rust, 2000, A sociocognitive interpretation of organizational downsizing, *Academy of Management Review,* 25: 227–243.
135. W. McKinley, C. M. Sanchez, & A. G. Schick, 1995, Organizational downsizing: Constraining, cloning, learning, *Academy of Management Executive,* IX (3): 32–44.
136. McKinley, Zhao, & Rust, A sociocognitive interpretation, 227.
137. N. Shirouzu, 2000, Driven by necessity—and by Ford—Mazda downsizes, U.S.-style, *Wall Street Journal,* January 5, A1, A8; A. Edgecliffe-Johnson, 1999, Procter & Gamble to cut 15,000 jobs in restructuring, *Financial Times,* June 10, 1; J. Hechinger, 1999, Bausch & Lomb to cut its work force, restructure contact-lens operation, *Wall Street Journal,* December 3, B14.
138. Hoskisson and Hitt, *Downscoping.*

139. J. S. Lublin, 1995, Spin offs may establish new companies, but they often spell the end of jobs, *Wall Street Journal,* November 21, B1, B8; J. Kose, H. P. Lang, & J. Netter, 1992, The voluntary restructuring of large firms in response to performance decline, *Journal of Finance,* 47: 891–917;
140. Johnson, Hoskisson, & Hitt, Board of directors involvement; R. E. Hoskisson & M. A. Hitt, 1990, Antecedents and performance outcomes of diversification: A review and critique of theoretical perspectives, *Journal of Management,* 16: 461–509.
141. Whittington, In praise, 4.
142. R. Atkins, 1999, German business giants evolve to meet new challenges, *Financial Times,* June 24, 23.
143. B. Orwall & M. Rose, 2000, Disney may sell Los Angeles magazine as it pares down noncore operations, *Wall Street Journal,* January 19, B7.
144. B. Copple, 2000, Synergy in ketchup? *Forbes,* February 7, 68–69.
145. A. Edgecliffe-Johnson & M. Marsh, 1999, Ralston plans to spin off Eveready arm, *Financial Times,* June 11, 18.
146. D. D. Bergh & G. F. Holbein, 1997, Assessment and redirection of longitudinal analysis: Demonstration with a study of the diversification and divestiture relationship, *Strategic Management Journal,* 18: 557–571; C. C. Markides & H. Singh, 1997, Corporate restructuring: A symptom of poor governance or a solution to past managerial mistakes? *European Management Journal,* 15: 213–219.
147. M. F. Wiersema & J. P. Liebeskind, 1995, The effects of leveraged buyouts on corporate growth and diversification in large firms, *Strategic Management Journal,* 16: 447–460.
148. M. C. Jensen, 1989, Eclipse of the public corporation, *Harvard Business Review,* 67(5): 61–74.
149. LBO signposts, 1999, *Mergers & Acquisitions,* November/December, 47–56.
150. A. Seth & J. Easterwood, 1995, Strategic redirection in large management buyouts: The evidence from post-buyout restructuring activity, *Strategic Management Journal,* 14: 251–274; P. H. Phan & C. W. L. Hill, 1995, Organizational restructuring and economic performance in leveraged buyouts: An ex-post study, *Academy of Management Journal,* 38: 704–739.
151. M. Matzer, 1996, Playing solo, *Forbes,* March 25, 80–81.
152. S. Chandler, 1996, United we own, *Business Week,* March 18, 96–100.
153. A. Bernstein, 1996, Why ESOP deals have slowed to a crawl, *Business Week,* March 18, 101–102.
154. I. Filatochev, R. E. Hoskisson, T. Buck, & M. Wright, 1996, Corporate restructuring in Russian privatizations: Implications for US investors, *California Management Review,* 38(2): 87–105.
155. B. Ortega, 1995, Cadbury seeking a new king of pop to oversee no. 3 soft-drink business, *Wall Street Journal,* January 30, B2.
156. Fisher & White, Downsizing in a learning organization, 244.
157. Petzinger, Jr., So long, R31.
158. P. M. Lee, 1997, A comparative analysis of layoff announcements and stock price reactions in the United States and Japan, *Strategic Management Journal,* 18: 879–894.
159. H. Unger, 2000, Coke cutbacks show company went down wrong path, *Wall Street Journal,* January 30, H6.
160. Fisher & White, Downsizing in a learning organization.
161. Unger, Coke cutbacks, H6.
162. Johnson, Antecedents and outcomes.
163. W. F. Long & D. J. Ravenscraft, 1993, LBOs, debt, and R&D intensity, *Strategic Management Journal,* 14(Special Issue, Summer): 119–135.
164. M. Wright, R. E. Hoskisson, L. W. Busenitz, & J. Dial, 2000, Entrepreneurial growth through privatizing: The upside of management tryouts. *Academy of Management Review,* in press.
165. Whittington, In praise, 6.
166. T. A. Stewart, 1999, See Jack. See Jack run, *Fortune,* September 27, 124–136.
167. Ibid.
168. Drucker, The unrecognized boom, 15.

INTERNATIONAL STRATEGY

CHAPTER EIGHT OBJECTIVES

After reading this chapter, you should be able to:

1. Explain traditional and emerging motives for firms to pursue international diversification.
2. Explore the four factors that lead to a basis for international business-level strategies.
3. Name and define generic international business-level strategies.
4. Define the three international corporate-level strategies: multidomestic, global, and transnational.
5. Discuss the environmental trends affecting international strategy.
6. Name and describe the five alternative modes for entering international markets.
7. Explain the effects of international diversification on firm returns and innovation.
8. Name and describe two major risks of international diversification.
9. Explain why the positive outcomes from international expansion are limited.

Technology and Globalization: A Changing Landscape in the 21st Century

As described in Chapter 1, technology and the globalization of business have created a new competitive landscape for the 21st century. In short, technology and globalization have interacted to create an ongoing revolution. In particular, the development and use of new technology facilitate increasing globalization. Two types of technology—the Internet and wireless communications—are having profound effects on the way business is conducted worldwide.

The Internet now allows rapid and effective communication and coordination of units and operations on a global basis. It also facilitates business-to-business (B2B) relationships (e.g., between supplier and customer) and increases the speed with which innovations are diffused throughout the world. While the Internet revolution largely emanated from the United States, the rest of the world is participating as well. For example, the United States accounted for approximately 75 percent of e-commerce in 1998, but is expected to account for only about 50 percent of global e-commerce by 2003. U.S. companies are projected to engage in approximately $2.8 trillion of e-commerce in 2003, whereas European firms' e-commerce is expected to reach E1.6 trillion by 2004 (a 140 percent annual growth rate). Consumer retailing purchases over the Internet are estimated to triple by 2003.

Likewise, mobile phones are becoming ubiquitous and used for multiple purposes. For example, it is becoming increasingly common for children in middle school (as young as 10 years old) to carry mobile phones in Sweden, and approximately 58 percent of all people in Finland own mobile phones. A company in Japan, DoMoCo, has developed and markets a mobile phone that allows people to connect to the Internet and perform many of the tasks normally confined to a computer. In fact, mobile phone technology will bring the Internet to locations throughout the world that have been slow to adopt computer-based connections. The number of mobile phones in use is growing at more than twice the rate of new fixed (wired) telephone connections annually. This third generation of mobile telephony will dramatically increase the speed of data transmission and greatly enlarge the number of users of such phones globally. Mobile phones are a cheaper and easier (i.e., more user-friendly) means of accessing the Internet than computers are and thus will be available to a larger number of people. Currently, the most wired nations are the United States and Western European countries, but the global potential for increased e-commerce is substantial. For example, although there were 4 million Internet users in China in 1999, it is predicted that by 2001 that country will have 27 million users. The potential for this rapid increase in the number of

Internet users in China rests with the introduction of mobile phone connections to the Internet.

For all of the preceding reasons, many firms are rushing to join the global e-commerce revolution. For instance, Seven-Eleven Japan is leading the development of an e-commerce joint venture with seven other firms to offer goods and services through the Internet and multimedia portals in 8,000 Japanese Seven-Eleven outlets. The goal is to expand this service to Seven-Eleven stores globally. Seven-Eleven Japan will hold the largest stake in the venture, followed by Sony, NEC, and Nomura Research Institute, each with a 13 percent share. Interestingly, prior to this joint venture formed in 2000, Seven-Eleven was the hub of e-commerce in Japan. Primarily domestic (e.g., Federated Department Stores) and multinational (e.g., Ford and GM) companies have joined the e-commerce revolution to extend their global reach. An example is GM's use of e-commerce to reach emerging markets. Firms in emerging-market countries such as Russia and Bulgaria in Eastern Europe are also increasing their use of e-commerce.

Another example is Ford and General Motor's competition to create increased global standardization of parts through Web-based systems. Both GM (via its TradeXchange system) and Ford (via its AutoXchange) are seeking to dominate the Web-based marketplace for automakers and suppliers. Volkswagen is also in talks with Toyota in Europe to join VW's system.

http://www.federated-fds.com

http://www.ford.com

http://www.gm.com

http://www.intel.com

http://www.nec.com

http://www.nri.co.jp

http://www.7dream.com or www.sej.co.jp

http://www.sony.com

http://www.vw.com

Evidence of the increasing importance of e-commerce is shown by Intel's recent decision to develop "server farms." These server farms are intended to provide companies with the capability of conducting e-commerce. Intel located its first server farm in Reading, Berkshire, England. This location houses 10,000 Internet servers and a staff of 170 people. These farms target small businesses that do not have the internal resources to support e-commerce activities. Intel projects that demand for servers will increase by 2,500 percent by 2005. Accordingly, Intel expects to locate server farms throughout Europe to meet the fast growing demand. Indeed, e-commerce activities will extend the reach of even small businesses across the globe.

In sum, two trends—the Internet and wireless telecommunication—as well as their combined use (Internet connections on mobile phones) are facilitating increased communications and e-commerce on a global basis. Although e-commerce initially spread rapidly in the United States and Western Europe because of those regions' dedicated telecommunication and computer infrastructures, it has now become a global revolution made possible by a broader availability and use of mobile communication devices.

SOURCES: N. Shirouzu, 2000, Toyota may join Ford's web system, *Wall Street Journal,* January 25, A13; S. Baker, 2000, Cell-phone central: Finland leads the wireless charge, *Businessweek Online,* January 6, *www.businessweek.com*; J. Borzo, 2000, Court ruling in Russia may mean more order in Internet industry, *Wall Street Journal Interactive,* January 6, *www.interactive.wsj.com.articles*; J. Dodge, 1999, Auto makers are shifting gears to accelerate a net revolution, *Wall Street Journal Interactive,* July 13, *www.interactive.wsj.com.articles*; C. Grande, 1999, E-commerce: U.S to retain global lead, *ft.com, www.ft.com.nbearchive*; C. Grande, 2000, Shopping: E-spending will triple by 2003, *ft.com*, January 17, *www.ft.com.nbearchive*; B. Groom, 2000, Intel: Berkshire hosts 90m server farm, *ft.com*, January 20, *www.ft,com,nbearchive*; R. Grover, 2000, Univision peers into Cyberspace, *Businessweek Online,* January 9, *www.businessweek.com*; A. Kaiser, 2000, Bulgaria, LVMH strike deal to team up for online sales, *Wall Street Journal Interactive,* January 6, *www.interactive.wsj.com.articles*; P. Landers, 1999, In Japan, the hub of E-Commerce is a 7-Eleven, *Wall Street Journal,* November 1, B1, B4; M. J. Mandel, 1999, The Internet economy: The world's next growth engine, *Businessweek Online,* September 27; C. Matlack, J. Ewing, G. Edmondson, & W. Echikson, 1999, Cashing in on an Internet bonanza, *Business Week,* December 13, 62; N. Nakamae, 2000, Seven-Eleven: Online arm to launch, *ft.com*, January 7, *www.ft.com.nbearchive*; R. Quick, 2000, Federated to invest up to $200 million in web business; 2000 Stock takes dive, *Wall Street Journal Interactive,* January 17, *www.interactive.wsj.com.articles*; Seven-Eleven Japan, NEC, Others JV called 7dream.com, 2000, *Wall Street Journal Interactive,* January 6, *www.interactive.wsj.com.articles*; Seven-Eleven Japan reveals e-commerce joint venture, 2000, *Wall Street Journal Interactive,* January 6, *www.interactive.wsj.com.articles*; The world in your pocket, 2000, *Economist.Com,* January 6, *www.economist.com/editorial*; F. Warner, 1999, GM tests e-commerce plans in emerging markets, *Wall Street Journal,* October 25, B4.

In the 1980s, the dramatic success of Japanese firms and products, such as Toyota and Sony, in the United States and other international markets provided a powerful jolt to U.S. managers and awakened them to the importance of international competition and global markets. In the 1990s, Russia and China represented potential major international market opportunities for firms from many countries, including the United States, Japan, Korea, and European nations.[1] They also represented potentially formidable competitors—particularly China, in low-technology manufacturing industries. However, concerns have been expressed about the relative attractiveness of the Russian and Chinese markets for companies competing in the global marketplace. The economic crises in Russia in the latter 1990s lent credibility to these concerns. Some believe that, for at least a period of time, foreign investors will continue to favor China, because China is more orderly while Russia remains full of risks. Russia's movement to more of a free-market economy now seems more likely to depend on homegrown developments instead of foreign direct investments (FDI) and other modes firms use to internationalize their operations.[2]

The 21st century may find less focus on a particular region of the world and more emphasis on truly global markets. An emphasis on global markets is facilitated by the developments in technology described in the Opening Case. Parallel developments in the Internet and mobile telephony facilitate communications all over the globe. Furthermore, these developments have led to the e-commerce revolution that is now prevalent in the business world. The information presented in the Opening Case suggests rapid growth of e-commerce globally. The global e-commerce phenomenon is exemplified by the venture led by Seven-Eleven in Japan, whereby portals to the Internet to offer goods and services for sale are available in 8,000 Seven-Eleven stores. The interface between the Internet and mobile telephony is evidenced in a popular Japanese firm, DoMoCo, that provides access to the Internet on mobile telephones. And DoMoCo is taking this service global.

E-commerce is not restricted to large firms. Intel's server farms provide the technology necessary for small firms to participate in e-commerce. Thus, even small firms can sell their goods and services globally without having (brick-and-mortar) facilities outside of their home location. Technology is promoting increasingly rapid globalization of markets and business. This revolution is evident all over the world. For example, Brazil's Internet market is expanding quickly. Recently, Terra Brasil, an Internet provider controlled by Telefónica of Spain, acquired ZAZ, the second-largest Internet provider in Brazil. This action followed an announcement by two of Brazil's largest private banks to offer free Internet services. Other free Internet services are expected to enter the Brazilian market, some by way of the current largest service providers.[3]

Clearly, the international arena features both opportunities and threats for firms seeking strategic competitiveness in global markets. This chapter examines opportunities facing firms as they seek to develop and exploit core competencies by diversifying into global markets. In addition, we discuss different problems and complexities that can be associated with the implementation of a firm's chosen international strategies. National boundaries, cultural differences, and geographical distances no longer pose barriers to business and entry into many markets. Business has become truly global, in markets ranging from drugs and tires to publishing and engineering.[4] Selecting and implementing appropriate international strategies allows the firm to become a global corporation. However, to mold their firms into truly global companies, managers must develop global mind-sets. Traditional means of operating with little cultural diversity and without global competition are no longer effective.[5] Developing a global mind-set among managers without international experience and with little experience with cultural diversity is challenging. Of course, firms experiencing these challenges are slower to change. Providing international experiences may be required to more quickly build global mind-sets among a firm's managers.[6] For example, Cemex rapidly changed from a domestic cement manufacturer in the Mexican market to a global producer of cement, largely through acquisitions of cement firms in Latin America, Asia, North America, and Europe. In fact, Cemex has played an important role in developing a global cement industry. For example, 60 percent of Asia's cement market is now served by multinationals, up from only 20 percent a few years ago. Cemex's managers had little experience with global markets, as its managers and those of the firms it acquired had focused primarily or solely on their domestic cement market. Thus, the company established an extensive management development program designed to help its managers build a global mind-set.[7]

As firms move into international markets, they develop relationships with suppliers, customers, and partners, and they learn from these relationships. In fact, partners learn from each other and begin to develop more similar policies over time. Firms also learn from their competitors in international markets. In effect, they begin to imitate the policies of each other in order to compete more effectively in those markets.[8] Such activity is evident in the drug industry as firms compete against each other in global pharmaceutical markets.[9] However, the Internet and e-commerce are likely to increase the standardization of practices and policies across industries and country borders as well. StarHub is an international communications company that recently developed a new venture designed to provide direct communication linkages between Singapore and China. Voice and data traffic between the two nations is growing at the rate of 20 percent annually, representing a potentially lucrative market. StarHub now has agreements with 16 international carriers across 12 countries. The company plans to establish standardized communications linkages with over 50 of the top global carriers in the next few years.[10]

In this chapter, as illustrated in Figure 1.1, we discuss the importance of international strategy as a source of strategic competitiveness and above-average returns. The chapter focuses on the incentives to internationalize. Once a firm decides to compete internationally, it must select its strategy and choose a mode of entry into international markets. It may enter international markets by exporting from domestic-based operations, licensing some of its products or services, forming joint ventures with international partners, acquiring a foreign-based firm, or establishing a new subsidiary. Such international diversification can extend product life cycles, provide incentives for more innovation, and produce above-average returns. These benefits are tempered by political and economic risks and the problems of managing a complex international firm with operations in multiple countries. Figure 8.1 provides an overview of the various choices and outcomes. The relationships among international opportunities, and the exploration of resources and capabilities that result in strategies and modes of entry that are based on core competencies, are explored in this chapter.

FIGURE 8.1 | Opportunities and Outcomes of International Strategy

Identifying International Opportunities: The Incentive to Pursue an International Strategy

An **international strategy** refers to the selling of products in markets outside a firm's domestic market.

An **international strategy** refers to the selling of products in markets outside a firm's domestic market.[11] One of the primary reasons for implementing an international strategy (as opposed to a strategy focused on the domestic market) is that international markets yield potential new opportunities. Raymond Vernon captured the classic rationale for international diversification.[12] He suggested that, typically, a firm discovers an innovation in its home-country market, especially in an advanced economy such as that found in the United States. Some demand for the product may then develop in other countries, and exports are provided by domestic operations. Increased demand in foreign countries justifies direct foreign investment in production capacity abroad, especially because foreign competitors also organize to meet increasing demand. As the product becomes standardized, the firm may rationalize its operations by moving production to a region where manufacturing costs are low. Vernon, therefore, suggests that firms pursue international diversification to extend a product's life cycle.

Another traditional motive for firms to become multinational is to secure needed resources. Key supplies of raw material—especially minerals and energy—are important in some industries. For instance, aluminum producers need a supply of bauxite, tire firms need rubber, and oil companies scour the world to find new petroleum reserves.

Others seek to secure access to low-cost factors of production. Clothing, electronics, watchmaking, and many other industries have moved portions of their operations to foreign locations in pursuit of lower costs. For example, to enhance its cost competitiveness, GE began shifting some of its appliance-manufacturing operations to various locations throughout the world. All of the firm's gas ranges are now made in San Luis Potosí, Mexico, through the firm's joint venture with Mabe, a Mexican company. In all, GE employs over 24,000 people in Mexico, primarily to manufacture appliances.[13]

Turkey's wage rates are among the lowest in Europe. In fact, the nation's hourly rates average one-half of those in Portugal, the poorest country in the European Union. Moreover, wages are lower than in some eastern European countries and many developing nations. Because of these wage rates, coupled with the fact that workers' productivity is increasing by 3.6 percent annually, compared to the OECD average of 2.8 percent, many multinational companies are establishing operations in Turkey. In fact, foreign investments have caused Turkey's economy to grow at a rate that has actually created labor shortages.[14]

Although these traditional motives persist, other emerging motivations have been driving international expansion (see Chapter 1). For instance, pressure has increased for a global integration of operations, mostly driven by more universal product demand. As nations industrialize, the demand for commodities appears to become more similar.[15] This nationless or borderless demand may be due to similarities in lifestyle in developed nations. Also, increases in global communication media facilitate the ability of people in different countries to visualize and model lifestyles in disparate cultures.[16]

In some industries, technology is driving globalization because economies of scale necessary to reduce costs to the lowest level often require an investment greater than that needed to meet domestic market demand.[17] There is also pressure for cost reductions, achieved by purchasing from the lowest-cost global suppliers. For instance, R&D expertise for an emerging business start-up may not exist in the domestic market.[18]

New large-scale markets, such as China and India, also provide a strong incentive because of the potential demand in those countries. And, because of currency fluctuations, firms may desire to have their operations distributed across many countries in order to reduce the risk of devaluation in one country.[19] This desire notwithstanding, the unique nature of emerging markets, such as China, presents major growth opportunities. The uniqueness of those markets presents both opportunities and challenges.[20] China, for example, differs from Western countries in many respects, including culture, politics, and the precepts of its economic system.[21] China, however, offers a huge potential market. While its differences from Western countries are numerous, many international firms perceive Chinese markets as almost virgin markets, without exposure to many modern and sophisticated products. With such exposure, these firms believe that demand will develop. However, the differences pose serious challenges for Western competitive paradigms that emphasize the need for possession of the skills to manage financial, economic, and political risks.

The vast percentage of U.S.-based companies' overseas business is in European markets. In addition, 60 percent of U.S. firms' assets that are located outside the domestic market are in Europe, and two-thirds of all foreign R&D spending by U.S. affiliates takes place in Europe.[22] Therefore, companies seeking to internationalize their operations should be aware of increased pressure on them to respond to local,

As an emerging market, China differs from Western countries in terms of culture, politics, and economic system. Many international firms believe that demand will develop when "virgin markets" are exposed to modern and sophisticated products.

national, or regional customs, especially where goods or services require customization because of cultural differences or effective marketing to entice customers to try a different product.[23] For example, food products often have to be adapted to local tastes. However, Danone, an international French provider of food products, either acquires local companies to meet local needs or uses marketing in an attempt to help local customers acquire new tastes. In recent years, Danone has acquired local water companies in Indonesia, China, and the United States. It has also acquired a number of local food providers in Latin America. In addition, the firm has attempted to overcome local dietary attitudes toward its products, such as yogurt, with marketing. Danone is the global leader in providing dairy products, with particularly strong sales of its yogurt worldwide. Because of its skill in adapting to international markets, Danone is among the top 10 food and beverage firms (in sales revenue) in the world.[24]

The frequent need for local repair and service is another factor influencing an increased desire for local country responsiveness. This localization may even affect industries that are seen as needing more global economies of scale, such as white goods (e.g., refrigerators and other appliances.)[25] Alternatively, it is becoming increasingly common for suppliers to follow their customers, particularly large ones, into international markets. When they do so, the need to find local suppliers is eliminated.[26] However, for large products, such as heavy earthmoving equipment, transportation costs are significant. Employment contracts and labor forces differ significantly as well. It is more difficult to negotiate employee layoffs in Europe than in the United States, because of employment contract differences. Often, host governments demand joint ownership, which allows the foreign firm to avoid tariffs. Also, host governments frequently require a high percentage of local procurements, manufacturing, and R&D. These issues increase the need for local investment and responsiveness compared to seeking global economies of scale.

Given the traditional and emerging motivations for expanding into international markets, firms may achieve four basic benefits from international diversification: (1) increased market size; (2) greater returns on major capital investments or on investments in new products and processes; (3) greater economies of scale, scope, or learning; and (4) a competitive advantage through location (e.g., access to low-cost labor, critical resources, or customers). These opportunities to enhance the firm's strategic competitiveness are examined relative to both the costs incurred to pursue them and the managerial challenges that accompany international diversification decisions. Higher coordination expenses, a lack of familiarity with local cultures, and limited access to knowledge about political influences in the host country are examples of costs firms incur when pursuing international diversification.[27]

Increased Market Size

Firms can expand the size of their potential market—sometimes dramatically—by moving into international markets. As part of its expansion efforts, BellSouth has entered multiple South American markets. Furthermore, the company is positioning itself to take advantage of the current and impending deregulation of telecommunications markets in that region of the world. In particular, BellSouth wants to become a one-stop telecommunications provider to businesses operating across Latin American markets. The firm was the first to introduce wireless roaming telephone communications in the Latin American markets that it serves. For example, customers in Argentina can use their mobile phones in Venezuela without dialing a special code or using a credit card number. About seven percent of BellSouth's total annual revenue comes from Latin American markets. While BellSouth is establishing a strong presence in those markets, it faces significant competition from Spain's Telefónica and Italy's Telecom Italia. Thus, it has significant opportunities, but also many challenges, as is common now in international markets.[28]

Changing consumer tastes and practices linked to cultural values or traditions is not simple. For example, when the cereal market in the United States stagnated, the U.S. cereal makers Kellogg and General Mills looked to international markets to revive their growth prospects. Initial efforts appeared to be successful. However, the dry cereal produced by these firms is not a staple in most European breakfasts. Thus, sales reached a peak, but then began to decline in the late 1990s. Kellogg had to close several manufacturing plants in Europe as its revenues and profits declined.[29]

Following an international strategy is a particularly attractive option to firms competing in domestic markets that have limited growth opportunities. For example, the U.S. soft-drink industry is relatively saturated. Most changes in market share for any single firm must come at the expense of competitors' shares. Given this situation, the two major soft-drink manufacturers, Coca-Cola and PepsiCo, entered international markets to take advantage of new growth opportunities. Pepsi moved into the former Soviet Union years ago; later, Coke entered China. Originally, each firm obtained an exclusive franchise in those countries; today, however, markets in Russia and China are more open. Coke gained competitive parity and has now surpassed Pepsi in Russia. Beyond this, Coke's volume exceeds Pepsi's in Europe, Latin America, and Asia. In terms of overall volume, Coke outsells Pepsi almost three to one outside the United States. Recently, however, Coke suffered problems in several of its international markets, particularly in Europe. Because of these problems, Coke's profitability has declined and the company has begun to restructure.[30]

The size of a particular international market also affects a firm's willingness to invest in R&D to build advantages in that market. Larger markets usually offer higher potential returns and thus generally pose less risk for a firm's investments. The strength of the science base in the country in question also can affect a firm's foreign R&D investments. Most firms prefer to invest more heavily in those countries with the scientific knowledge and talent to produce more effective new products and processes from their R&D.[31]

In Chapter 5, we described the current transformation of the global auto industry. As noted in that chapter, it is projected that only about six major auto manufacturers will survive over time. The surviving firms will be large and wield considerable market power, thereby driving out smaller competitors. In fact, Renault's much-criticized acquisition of the troubled automaker Nissan was completed because of the need to build adequate market power in order to maintain a measure of competitive parity with the other large global automakers (e.g., DaimlerChrysler, GM, Ford, and Toyota). Analysts predict that 8 to 10 years will be required before Renault realizes a return on its investment in Nissan. Furthermore, if Nissan fails to perform, this investment may eliminate Renault's chances to survive as an independent company. Because of the importance of Nissan to Renault's future, the company has assigned the task of reviving it to tough, but successful, Brazilian-born executive Carlos Ghosn. In turn, he developed and implemented a drastic restructuring of the Japanese automaker that was designed to greatly reduce costs and increase efficiency in its manufacturing operations. Interestingly, Renault is also seeking to acquire other companies, particularly in Asia (especially Korea).[32]

Market size and a firm's market power do not guarantee success, however. For example, analysts argue that the merger between France's Seita and Spain's Tabacalera is unlikely to be successful. They suggest that the combination of two small, inefficient, and poorly managed firms is likely to produce one large, inefficient, and poorly managed firm.[33]

Return on Investment

Large markets may be crucial for earning a return on significant investments, such as plant and capital equipment or R&D. Therefore, most R&D-intensive industries are international. For example, the aerospace industry requires heavy investments to develop new aircraft. To recoup their investments, aerospace firms may need to sell new aircraft in both domestic and international markets. This is the case for Boeing and Airbus Industrie. International sales are critical to the ability of each firm to earn satisfactory returns on its invested capital. Airbus is continuing to build its competitive ability. In fact, a merger in 1999 between two of its consortium owners, DASA (a DaimlerChrysler company) and Aerospatiale Matrais, was predicted to enhance the ability of Airbus to compete with Boeing in international markets. Boeing may need to take actions of its own, because Airbus captured more orders for civilian aircraft in 1999 than did Boeing.[34]

In addition to the need for a large market to recoup heavy investment in R&D, the development pace for new technology is increasing. As a result, new products become obsolete more rapidly. Therefore, investments need to be recouped more quickly. Beyond this, firms' abilities to develop new technologies are expanding, and because of different patent laws across country borders, imitation by competitors is more likely. Through reverse engineering, competitors are able to take apart a product, learn the new technology, and develop a similar product that imitates the new technology (see Chapters 5 and 13). Because of competitors' abilities to do this relatively quickly, the need to recoup new-product development costs rapidly is increasing. Consequently, the larger markets provided by international expansion are particularly attractive in many industries (e.g., computer hardware), because they expand the opportunity to recoup a large capital investment and large-scale R&D expenditures.[35] It must be emphasized, however, that the primary reason for making investments in international markets is to produce excellent returns on investments. Thus, expected returns from the investments represent a primary predictor of firms moving into international markets. Still, firms from different countries have different expectations and use different criteria to decide whether to invest in international markets.[36]

Economies of Scale and Learning

When firms expand their markets, they may be able to enjoy economies of scale, particularly in their manufacturing operations. Thus, to the extent that firms are able to standardize products across country borders and use the same or similar production facilities, thereby coordinating critical resource functions, they are likely to achieve more optimal economies of scale.[37] Economies of scale are critical in the global auto industry. As noted in Chapter 5 and earlier in the current chapter, only six global auto firms are expected to survive because of the need for market power and efficiency to compete effectively. For instance, Honda has been a largely successful firm with substantial competencies in the manufacture of engines. However, it has problems competing against several larger and more resource-rich automakers. Ford has $23 billion in cash, whereas Honda has only about $3.2 billion. GM invests approximately $9 billion annually in R&D, while Honda can only invest about $2.6 billion. As a result, Honda was not listed by PricewaterhouseCoopers as one of the expected surviving global six automakers. A consultant for the firm suggested that Honda would have a chance if it could become large enough (to have adequate resources and gain comparable economies of scale). Honda has achieved economies of scale in the development and sale of its engines. It sells about 2 million autos annually, but sells 10 million engines (including lawn mower engines). Honda recently formed an alliance with GM to produce engines for some of its vehicles. Thus, perhaps Honda will survive as an independent engine manufacturer.[38]

Firms may also be able to exploit core competencies across international markets. This allows resource and knowledge sharing between units across country borders.[39] It generates synergy and helps the firm produce higher-quality goods or services at lower cost. In addition, working across international markets provides an opportunity to learn. Multinational firms have substantial opportunities to learn from the different practices they encounter in separate international markets. Even firms based in developed markets can learn from operations in emerging markets.[40]

Location Advantages

Firms may locate facilities in other countries to lower the basic costs of the goods or services they provide.[41] For example, they may have easier access to lower-cost labor, energy, and other natural resources. Other location advantages include access to critical supplies and to customers. Once positioned favorably through an attractive location, firms must manage their facilities effectively to gain the full benefit of a location advantage.[42]

Telecommunications firms have sought specific location advantages in much of their international expansion efforts.[43] Likewise, U.S. agricultural-machinery manufacturers have made substantial investments in Latin American markets to take advantage of location advantages. Labor costs are significantly lower in Latin America than in the United States, and the markets for agricultural machinery are more promising as the economies become more robust. Some countries—particularly, Mexico—have well developed infrastructures and a skilled labor force.[44]

As described in the Strategic Focus, the European Union is changing the competitive landscape in Europe and the world. It provides a large and unified market for European and foreign firms that is attracting considerable investment from international companies. In addition, European markets and firms are undergoing substantial changes to take advantage of economies of scale, economies of learning, and advantages of location in the various European markets. The common currency and the integration of capital markets have reduced financial risks and made available significant amounts of capital that were previously unavailable in the separate country markets. Thus, European firms are growing in power and will challenge many of the world's prominent companies, including those from the United States and Asia.

International Strategies

In the previous section, we explored why international strategies may be important and examined some of their advantages. In this section, we describe the types and content of international strategies that might be formulated and then implemented.

An international strategy may be one of two basic types: business- or corporate-level strategy. At the business level, firms follow generic strategies: cost leadership, differentiation, focused cost leadership, focused differentiation, or integrated cost leadership/differentiation. At the corporate level, firms can formulate three types of strategy: multidomestic, global, or transnational (a combination of multidomestic and global). However, to create competitive advantage, each of these strategies must realize a core competence based on difficult-to-duplicate resources and capabilities.[45] As discussed in Chapters 4 and 6, firms expect to create value through the implementation of a business-level *and* a corporate-level strategy.[46]

International Business-Level Strategy

Each business must develop a competitive strategy focused on its own domestic market. We discussed business-level generic strategies in Chapter 4 and competitive dynamics in Chapter 5. However, international business-level strategies have some unique features. In pursuing an international business-level strategy, the home coun-

The Decade of Europe: 2000–2010

Europe is undergoing a substantial transformation. Only a little more than a decade since the dramatic "fall of the Berlin wall" and the collapse of the Socialist regimes in Eastern Europe, a new economic and political architecture is emerging. The transformation is being shaped by technology and the globalization of business, as described in Chapter 1. Economically, Europeans have made considerable gains. For instance, gross development product (GDP) in the new European Union (EU) increased by over 46 percent during the decade of the 1990s, and the future is even brighter. During the same decade, inflation in the EU decreased by 77 percent, autos per capita increased by 14.6 percent, and even life expectancy increased, from 73 to 74 years. The EU produced a seamless market of over 290 million people. The introduction of the common currency, the Euro, removed two barriers to economic development in Europe: the exchange-rate risk and limited access to capital. The Euro was introduced in 1999 and will be placed in full circulation in 2002. The use of the Euro helps European firms to compete more effectively in global markets. A strong Euro is welcomed in the rest of the world as well; it has helped to ease the economic crisis in Asia by increasing Asian firms' ability to compete in European markets. The strong Euro also reduced the pressure on the U.S. economy produced by the U.S. trade deficit by helping U.S. firms to compete more effectively in European markets. With the EU, Europe has joined the United States as a major driver of the world economy. Indeed, Europe has become a primary global growth engine. All but one of the EU members has adopted the Euro (England is the sole holdout). The EU has a $6.5 trillion economy representing approximately 8.1 percent of world trade.

The large pool and free flow of capital provides the means to finance large deals. Furthermore, to be competitive across the European markets and, externally, in global markets, firms needed to gain market power, achieve economies of scale, and realize synergies. The implementation of the EU and the Euro created and facilitated considerable incentives for large-scale mergers and acquisitions throughout Europe. In fact, one major business publication described the scene as consisting of mergers and acquisitions, American style, with hostile takeovers, substantial debt, and large fees for the investment bankers. Others described it as "buyout fever." European buyouts in 1999 were $100 billion more than in 1998. Consolidation is the watchword in industries ranging from banking to telecommunications, most occurring across country boundaries (e.g., the acquisition of Racal Electronics in the United Kingdom by the French firm Thomson-CSF). Consolidation also is exemplified by Cable & Wireless PLC's acquisition of eight Internet service providers throughout Europe. The companies that were acquired provide access primarily to business customers in Western Europe. The companies are located in Austria, Belgium, France, Italy, Spain, and Switzerland. Cable & Wireless is a multinational firm controlling approximately 28 percent of the Internet traffic in the United States as well.

While significant change engulfs most of Europe, resistance to change is also present. For example, four Italian top executives have forestalled change in their firms. These executives are well over the normal retirement age, and some refer to them as the "corporate gerontocracy." The four executives are Enrico Cuccia of Mediobanca, Cesare Romiti of Fiat,

Giovanni Bazoli of Banco Ambrosiano, and Alfonso Desiata of Assicurazioni Generali. These executives actually tightened their grip on power when analysts predicted changes that would likely reduce or even eliminate their power. However, their victory may be short lived as the EU comes into full bloom: These executives' firms may experience problems competing in the European markets, particularly against large, powerful, and nimble rivals.

In some cases, the new Europe and its firms are gaining significant strength. These gains are exemplified by Airbus Industrie's besting of Boeing in 1999. Airbus garnered orders for 470 new commercial aircraft, compared to Boeing's 391 orders. Thus, Airbus captured 55 percent of the global market for large commercial aircraft. In other sectors, the changes have not been kind to some venerable European competitors. For instance, Marks & Spencer, an old and formerly successful British retailer, is now experiencing significant problems. Marks & Spencer targets the "middle market." However, customers have been flocking to discounters and to the high-end market. Thus, Marks & Spencer's market has been shrinking, and the company has been unable to change its focus to other market niches. Marks & Spencer has tried to compete with the major discounters, but without success. It is also losing its traditional market to more attractive competitors, such as Gap and Next PLC. In European banking, there has been considerable consolidation as well. However, prominent banks, such as Deutsche Bank, have reached beyond Europe. For example, Deutsche Bank acquired Bankers Trust in the United States. Deutsche Bank's goal is to become a universal bank. Of course, to do so, it must compete with the large and formidable U.S. banks. In sum, there will be successes and failures in the new Europe. However, one can count on significant change, and, no doubt, the EU will be a prominent force in the world economy of the 21st century.

SOURCES: D. Ball, 2000, How old guard boardroom barons tightened their grip on new Italy, *Wall Street Journal Interactive,* January 13, *www.interactive.wsj.com.articles*; E. Beck, 2000, Dixons, Marks & Spencer post weak results in a tough year, *Wall Street Journal Interactive,* January 13, *www.interactive.wsj.com.articles*; P. Engardio & O. Ullmann, 1999, The Atlantic century, *Business Week,* February 8, 64–73; N. George, 2000, SDP backs Swedish entry to euro zone, *ft.com*, January 15, *www.ft.com.nbearchive*; T. Kamm, 1999, Europe's move into the free market spurs a massive corporate workout, *Wall Street Journal Interactive,* December 30, *www.interactive.wsj.com.articles*; D. Michaels & J. Cole, 2000, *Wall Street Journal Interactive,* January 13, *www.interactive.wsj.com.articles*; K. L. Miller, J. Ewing, S. Reed, & G. Silverman, 1999, Fixing Deutsche Bank, *Business Week,* July 19, 56–58; G. Naik, 2000, Cable & Wireless announces purchase of eight Internet providers in Europe, *Wall Street Journal Interactive,* January 13, *www.interactive.wsj.com.articles*; J. Peet, 1998, The year of Europe, *The Economist—The World in 1999,* 11–12; S. Reed, 1999, Buyout fever, *Business Week,* June 14, 60–61; S. Reed, 1999, We have liftoff! *Business Week,* January 18, 34–37; S. Reed, J. Rossant, & G. Edmondson, 1999, Deal, *Business Week,* April 5, 50–54; J. Rossant, 1999, Ten years after the wall, *Business Week,* November 8, 57–61; Thomson-CSF announces E1.32 bn Racal deal, 2000, *www.ft.com*, January 13, *www.ft.com.nbearchive.*

try of operation is often the most important source of competitive advantage.[47] The resources and capabilities established in the home country frequently allow the firm to pursue the strategy into markets located in other countries.

Michael Porter developed a model that describes the factors contributing to the advantage of firms in a dominant global industry and associated with a specific country or regional environment.[48] His model is illustrated in Figure 8.2. The first dimension in the model, *factors of production,* refers to the inputs necessary to compete in any industry, such as labor, land, natural resources, capital, and infrastructure (e.g., highway, postal, and communication systems). Of course, there are basic (e.g., natural and

8.2 | **Determinants of National Advantage**

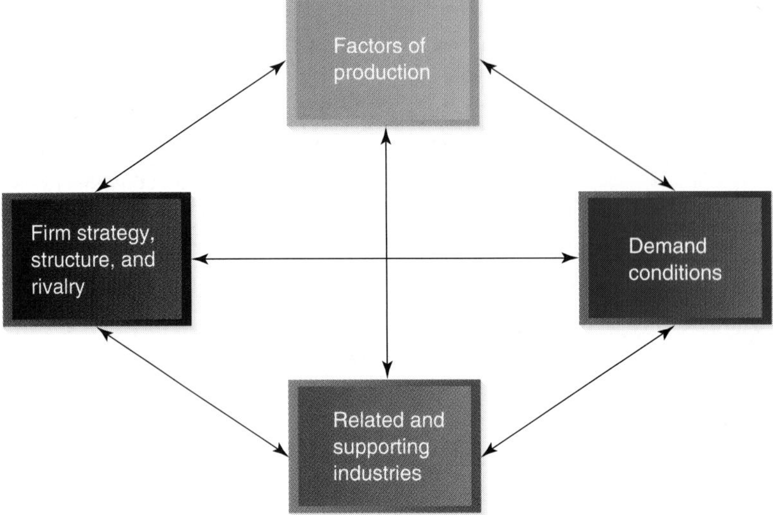

Source: Adapted with the permission of The Free Press, a Division of Simon & Schuster, Inc., from *The Competitive Advantages of Nations*, by Michael E. Porter, p. 72. Copyright © 1990, 1998 by Michael E. Porter.

labor resources) and advanced (e.g., digital communication systems and a highly educated workforce) factors. There are also generalized (highway systems and the supply of debt capital) and specialized factors (skilled personnel in a specific industry, such as the workers in a port that specializes in handling bulk chemicals). If a country has both advanced and specialized production factors, it is likely to serve an industry well in spawning strong home-country competitors that can be successful global competitors as well. Ironically, countries often develop advanced and specialized factors because they *lack* critical basic resources. For example, some Asian countries, such as South Korea, lack abundant natural resources, but the country's strong work ethic, large number of engineers, and systems of large firms have created an expertise in manufacturing. Similarly, Germany developed a strong chemical industry, partially because Hoechst and BASF spent years developing a synthetic indigo dye to reduce their dependence on imports. This was not the case in Britain, because large supplies of natural indigo were available in the colonies.[49]

The second dimension, *demand conditions,* is characterized by the nature and size of buyers' needs in the home market for the industry's goods or services. The sheer size of a market segment can produce the demand necessary to create scale-efficient facilities. This efficiency could also lead to domination of the industry in other countries. Specialized demand may also create opportunities beyond national boundaries. For example, Swiss firms have long led the world in tunneling equipment because of the need to tunnel through mountains for rail and highway passage in Switzerland. And

Japanese firms have created a niche market for compact, quiet air conditioners. Small, but quiet, units are required in Japan because homes are often small and located closely together.[50]

Related and supporting industries represent the third dimension in the model. Italy has become the leader in the shoe industry because of related and supporting industries. The leather supplies necessary to build shoes are furnished by a well-established leather-processing industry. Also, many people travel to Italy to purchase leather goods. Thus, there is support in distribution. In addition, supporting industries in leather-working machinery and design services contribute to the success of the shoe industry. In fact, the design services industry supports many of its own related industries, such as ski boots, fashion apparel, and furniture. In Japan, cameras and copiers are related industries. In Denmark, the dairy products industry is related to an industry focused on food enzymes.

Firm strategy, structure, and rivalry, the final country dimension, also fosters the growth of certain industries. The pattern of strategy, structure, and rivalry among firms varies greatly from nation to nation. Earlier, much attention was placed on examining U.S. and then Japanese enterprise managers. Because of the excellent technical training system in Germany, there is a strong emphasis on methodological product and process improvement. In Japan, unusual cooperative and competitive systems have facilitated the cross-functional management of complex assembly operations. In Italy, the national pride of the country's designers has spawned strong industries in sports cars, fashion apparel, and furniture. In the United States, competition among computer manufacturers and software producers has favored the development of these industries.

The four basic dimensions of the "diamond" model shown in Figure 8.2 emphasize the environmental or structural attributes of a national economy that contribute to national advantage. Government policy also clearly contributes to the success and failure of many firms and industries. This is exemplified in Japan, where the Ministry of International Trade and Investment has significantly affected the corporate strategies the country follows. Nevertheless, each firm must create its own success; not all firms survive to become global competitors—even those operating with the same country factors that spawned the successful firms. Therefore, the actual strategic choices managers make may be the most compelling reason for success or failure. Accordingly, the factors illustrated in Figure 8.2 are likely to produce competitive advantages for a firm only when an appropriate strategy is developed and implemented—one that takes advantage of distinct country factors. Hence, the next four subsections explain the cost leadership, differentiation, focused cost leadership, focused differentiation, and integrated cost leadership/differentiation generic strategies (discussed in Chapter 4) in an international context.

International Cost Leadership Strategy

The international low-cost strategy is likely to develop in a country with a large demand. Usually, the operations of such an industry are centralized in a home country, and obtaining economies of scale is the primary goal. Outsourcing of low-value-added operations may take place, but high-value-added operations are retained in the home country. Accordingly, products are often exported from the home country.

Through a variety of entry modes (entry modes are discussed in detail later in the chapter), Wal-Mart, too, follows an international cost leadership strategy as it continues to globalize its operations (explained in a Strategic Focus in Chapter 5).

The essence of Wal-Mart's international low-cost strategy is demonstrated by founder Sam Walton's words: "We'll lower the cost of living for everyone, not just in America." One of the keys to implementing its low-cost strategy, both domestically and internationally, is the firm's advanced retail technology, which enables Wal-Mart to have the correct quantities of goods in the appropriate place at the right time while minimizing inventory costs. The latest variation of this sophisticated system has employees carrying handheld computers that allow them to reorder merchandise. Simultaneously, backroom computers link each store with a sophisticated satellite system.

Wal-Mart started to internationalize its operations in 1991. Since then, the firm has already become the largest retailer in Canada and Mexico. Wal-Mart also operates stores in Argentina, Brazil, China, and Indonesia through joint ventures. To continue diversifying internationally, Wal-Mart decided to enter the European market, as explained in Chapter 5. The process was started with the purchase of the Wertkauf hypermarket company in Germany. Wal-Mart has moved heavily into the British market. Its means of entering European markets have been different than entering other international markets. Previously, Wal-Mart usually entered international markets via a joint venture. However, it entered some European markets by acquiring existing large retail operations in each country. Combining its volume with the firm's logistics skills and merchandising savvy will help Wal-Mart to achieve strategic competitiveness in the European markets. Also, Wal-Mart emphasizes customer service along with low prices, thereby changing the retailing culture in many European markets (e.g., England).[51] Many analysts believe that Wal-Mart will be successful in European markets. If so, its resources and skills, along with its international cost leadership strategy, will have changed the retailing landscape in Europe and perhaps globally.[52]

There are, of course, risks associated with implementing the international low-cost strategy. A major risk for Wal-Mart is learning quickly how to compete successfully in Europe's unique retailing environment. Does Wal-Mart have the confidence it needs to make small adjustments to satisfy local tastes while maintaining the discipline required to keep prices low? Will European retailers retain their customers by learning how to create value either through differentiation strategies or by driving their costs lower relative to Wal-Mart's? These issues pose strategic challenges to Wal-Mart's executives; but the fact that the company hopes to generate one-third of its profit growth annually through international sales suggests its intentions in Europe and other world markets.[53]

Volkswagen AG is attempting to implement an international cost leadership strategy in China. Volkswagen plans to produce a low-price "people's auto," reaching the huge mass market for autos in China. Few international manufacturers have been able to reach China's mass market, because most Chinese cannot afford expensive products such as autos. Foreign auto manufacturers have been selling their autos chiefly to the government and corporations, a relatively small market. There are about 13 million autos in China, with only 30 percent owned by individuals. However, Volkswagen built the original "people's auto" in Germany, lovingly referred to as the "bug" or "beetle." Volkswagen won approval from the Chinese government to produce a compact car over other hopeful firms, such as GM. The new auto will be developed and produced by Shanghai Volkswagen, a joint venture with Shanghai Automotive Industrial Corp. formed in 1984. The company already owns 46 percent of the Chinese market with its Santana model, used by many of the taxi fleets in China. The new car will have a small engine (1–1.6 liters) and sell for 100,000 yuan (about $12,000). It is expected on the market by 2002.[54]

International Differentiation Strategy

Firms based in a country with advanced and specialized factor endowments are likely to develop an international differentiation strategy. Germany has a number of world-class chemical firms, for example. The differentiation strategy followed by many of these firms to develop specialized chemicals was possible because of the country's favorable conditions with respect to this industry. The Kaiser Wilhelm (later, Max Planck) Institutes and university chemistry programs were superior in research and provided the best chemistry education in the world. Also, Germany's emphasis on vocational education fostered strong apprenticeship programs for workers.[55] Today, German companies competing in retailing consumer goods are learning how to improve their services to battle against competitors (e.g., Lands' End) implementing their international differentiation strategies in Germany.[56]

In the Opening Case for this chapter, we discussed the wireless Internet service offered by Japan's DoMoCo. DoMoCo has captured the Japanese market, but is planning to enter global wireless communication and Internet service markets. While Europeans and Americans can connect to the Internet using wireless technology with their Palm Pilots, the DoMoCo technology is ahead of all competitors. Clearly, DoMoCo is following a differentiation strategy. It offers the only i-mode in the world that allows continuous access to the Internet by using a cell phone. While some predict that DoMoCo may be the next global giant in wireless communications, it will have to continue to differentiate its product in ways that are attractive to the mass market, because it will face fierce competition in global markets from companies such as Vodafone Air-Touch, AT&T, and British Telecom. However, DoMoCo should have the resources to compete. In 1999, the company earned approximately $5 billion on sales of $36 billion, and it has access to the Japanese giant NTT, which owns 67 percent of DoMoCo. DoMoCo is working on a third-generation technology called 3G to continue its differentiation in the market. 3G is a set of wireless protocols that will permit much higher communication speeds. To maintain its competitive advantage, DoMoCo strongly emphasizes R&D.[57]

As described in Chapter 4, firms may differentiate their products and services through physical characteristics. However, they may also differentiate their products in the minds of the consumer. As the market for cigarettes in the United States has decreased, international markets have become critical to tobacco companies. Generally, greater percentages of the population smoke in countries outside of the United States, and they tend to be less litigious. In those countries, cigarette companies compete largely on brand differences established through advertising.[58]

International Focus Strategies

Many firms remain focused on small market niches as they pursue international focus strategies.[59] The ceramic tile industry in Italy contains a number of medium-sized and small fragmented firms that produce approximately 50 percent of the world's tile.[60] These firms, clustered in the Sassuolo area of the country, have formed a number of different focus strategies. Companies such as Marazzi, Iris, Cisa-Cerdisa, and Flor Gres invest heavily in technology to improve product quality, aesthetics, and productivity. The companies have close relationships with equipment manufacturers and tend to emphasize the focused cost leadership strategy, while maintaining a quality image. Another group, including Piemme and Atlas Concorde, attempts to compete more on image and design. Firms in this group invest heavily in advertising and showroom expositions. Because they try to appeal to selected customer tastes, they emphasize the focused differentiation strategy.[61]

The efficiency of the highly capitalized domestic institutions, coupled with their large branch networks and use of high-quality, sophisticated technologies, creates a retail banking environment in Spain in which it is difficult for foreign firms to compete successfully. Because of the domestic banks' competitive advantages, foreign rivals now concentrate on niche activities. Chase Manhattan, for example, focuses on a range of niches, including corporate finance, capital markets and derivatives businesses, and peseta- (euro) clearing activities. Based on its international focus strategy, Chase's recent performance in Spain is impressive—a return on earnings of 23 percent and a return on assets of 5.9 percent.

Because of what they envision as significant growth potential in terms of mutual and pension funds, U.K.-based Barclays and U.S.-based Citibank are focusing on the private banking sector. Citibank has converted the 83 branches it operates in Spain into product advisory centers. In each location, customers have access to computer systems that help them determine their desired risk levels; once these are known, a set of investment alternatives is recommended. Like Citibank, Barclays has "scaled back its retail operations in Spain, concentrated on the big cities and focused on asset management of medium to big private accounts according to a carefully elaborated segmentation of potential clients." Barclays operates 180 branches as it competes against Citibank and others to serve the unique needs of the private banking market segment in Spain.[62]

International Integrated Cost Leadership/Differentiation Strategy

The integrated strategy has become more popular because of flexible manufacturing systems, improved information networks within and across firms, and total quality management systems (see Chapter 4). Because of the wide diversity of markets and competitors, following an integrated strategy has become critical in many global markets.[63] Therefore, competing in global markets requires sophisticated and effective management.[64] Komatsu illustrates a classic case where this strategy was well executed. Komatsu was able to gain on a strong competitor, Caterpillar, by pursuing the integrated cost leadership/differentiation strategy. Caterpillar had a very strong brand image in world markets, but Komatsu was able to overcome this differentiation advantage by improving its image and reducing its costs. It was able to do this initially because of low labor costs and low steel prices. Then, in the 1970s, the dollar was strong, which allowed the company to implement a successful export strategy. Caterpillar continues to experience problems today because its competitors have been able to implement the integrated strategy more effectively than has Caterpillar. As a result, Caterpillar's competitors have been able to sell their differentiated products at lower prices than Caterpillar. Caterpillar's profits were down by 37.4 percent in 1999 over 1998. Analysts and company spokespersons suggested that the next few years would continue to be challenging for Caterpillar.[65]

Compaq also is attempting to employ an integrated cost leadership differentiation strategy. It needs to maintain low costs so that it can standardize its prices to compete with firms like Dell. Compaq is doing so by reducing the number of products in its product line and by using the Internet both to purchase supplies from across the globe and to manage the distribution of its products. But Compaq also must continue to differentiate its products and to meet U.S. and international market requirements.[66]

International Corporate-Level Strategy

The business-level strategies discussed previously are based at least partially on the type of international corporate-level strategy the firm is following. Some corporate strategies give individual country units the authority to develop their own business-level strategies; other corporate strategies largely dictate the business-level strategies used to accomplish standardization of products and sharing of resources across countries. International corporate-level strategy focuses on the scope of a firm's operations through both product and geographic diversification.[67] International corporate-level strategy is required when the firm operates in multiple industries and multiple countries or regions.[68] The strategy is guided by the headquarters unit, rather than by business or country managers. The three international corporate-level strategies are multidomestic, global, and transnational, as shown in Figure 8.3.

Multidomestic Strategy

A **multidomestic strategy** is one in which strategic and operating decisions are decentralized to the strategic business unit in each country in order to tailor products to the local market.

A **multidomestic strategy** is one in which strategic and operating decisions are decentralized to the strategic business unit in each country to allow the unit to tailor products to the local market.[69] A multidomestic strategy focuses on competition within each country. It assumes that the markets differ and therefore are segmented by country boundaries. In other words, consumer needs and desires, industry conditions (e.g., the number and type of competitors), political and legal structures, and social norms vary by country. Multidomestic strategies provide the opportunity to customize products to meet the specific needs and preferences of local customers. Therefore, they should be able to maximize a firm's competitive response to the idiosyncratic requirements of each market.[70] The use of multidomestic strategies usually expands the firm's local market share because of the attention paid to the needs of the local clientele. However, the use of these strategies also results in more uncertainty for the corporation as a whole, because of the differences across markets and thus the different strategies employed by local country units.[71] Moreover, multidomestic strategies do not allow for the achievement of economies of scale and thus can be more costly. As a result, firms employing a multidomestic strategy decentralize their strategic and operating decisions to the business units operating in each country. The multidomestic strategy has been more commonly used by European multinational firms because of the varieties of cultures and markets found in Europe.

8.3 | International Corporate-Level Strategies

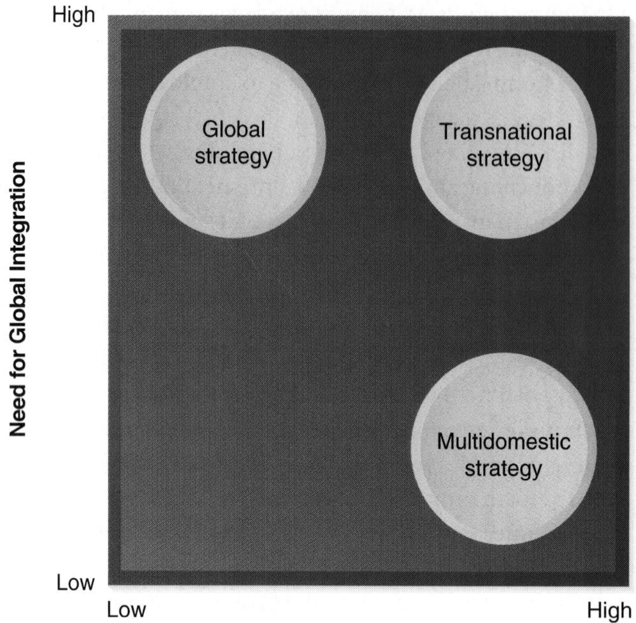

Sony's entertainment business recently changed its strategy from global to multidomestic, with positive results. Sony tried to penetrate the U.S. entertainment market but never succeeded. While attempting to penetrate this market, the company distributed television programs and films produced for the U.S. market to other markets across the world—the approach used by most large entertainment companies. Sony decided to change this approach and produce films and television programs itself for local markets around the world. To do so, Sony established production facilities and television channels in most larger Latin American and Asian countries. In 1999, Sony produced approximately 4,000 hours of foreign-language programs and about 1,700 hours of English-language programs. Sony now has 24 channels operating across 62 countries, and some of those channels are highly successful. In contrast, Sony's unit in China has lost money each of its three years of operation. Thus, this approach does not come without some uncertainty and risk.[72]

Global Strategy

A **global strategy** is one in which standardized products are offered across country markets and the competitive strategy is dictated by the home office.

In contradistinction to a multidomestic strategy, a global strategy assumes more standardization of products across country markets.[73] As a result, competitive strategy is centralized and controlled by the home office. The strategic business units operating in each country are assumed to be interdependent, and the home office attempts to achieve integration across these businesses. Therefore, a **global strategy** is one in which standardized products are offered across country markets and the competitive strategy is dictated by the home office. Thus, a global strategy emphasizes economies of scale and offers greater opportunities to utilize innovations developed at the corporate level or in one country in other markets. Accordingly, a global strategy produces lower risk, but may forego growth opportunities in local markets, either because those markets are less likely to identify opportunities or because opportunities require that products be adapted to the local market.[74] In effect, the strategy is not responsive to local markets and is difficult to manage because of the need to coordinate strategies and operating decisions across country borders. Consequently, achieving efficient operations with a global strategy requires the sharing of resources and an emphasis on coordination and cooperation across country boundaries, and these in turn require centralization and headquarters control. Many Japanese firms have often pursued this strategy with success.[75]

Aggreko, headquartered in England, has become the world's leading provider of power equipment through rentals. Currently, the company operates in 48 countries and employs a global strategy. The firm's fleet of equipment is integrated globally, which allows it to shift equipment to different regions of the world to meet specific needs. One of Aggreko's major competitors, Caterpillar, suffers because its dealers would rather sell than rent equipment. And Caterpillar's dealers are franchises, so the company cannot easily control their actions. Applying the global strategy, Aggreko designs and assembles its equipment in-house to meet the needs of its customers. Aggreko has been highly successful, earning approximately 18 percent on invested capital with a growth in earnings of 14 percent.[76]

Transnational Strategy

A **transnational strategy** seeks to achieve both global efficiency and local responsiveness.

A **transnational strategy** seeks to achieve both global efficiency and local responsiveness. Realizing these goals is obviously difficult, because one goal requires close global coordination while the other requires local flexibility. Thus, "flexible coordination"—building a shared vision and individual commitment through an integrated network—is required to implement the transnational strategy.[77] In reality, it is difficult to achieve a pure transnational strategy because of the conflicting goals. On the positive side, the effective implementation of a transnational strategy often produces higher performance than either of the other two corporate strategies alone do.[78]

Until the mid-1990s, Ford used a multidomestic strategy with separate, decentralized operations for North America and Europe. However, former CEO Alex Trotman implemented a global strategy in the middle 1990s. Applying this strategy, Ford attempted to build what it called a global auto. The Mondeo was Ford's global car. Unfortunately, both the auto and the strategy failed. The new CEO, Jacques Nasser, is now changing Ford's strategy to be transnational. Furthermore, Nasser is restructuring management so that it can respond flexibly to opportunities outside of the traditional auto-manufacturing business. Applying the transnational strategy, Ford is trying to standardize some of the components in its various automobiles—Ford, Lincoln, Jaguar, and Volvo—but yet allow design and other differences that appeal to the customers served in the market segments at which each of those brands of automobile is targeted. Ford is trying to become consumer oriented and be responsive to the various

After its attempt to build a global auto failed, Ford changed its strategy to be transnational instead of multidomestic. The firm is trying to become consumer oriented and responsive to various global markets.

markets across the globe that it serves.[79] The transnational strategy requires that managers think globally, but act locally.[80]

The next Strategic Focus describes the changes in Asia's economic landscape. The world's largest continent in both area and population is awakening again. Many Asian firms used a global strategy before the 1998 economic crisis. Most, however, will have to adopt a transnational strategy to be competitive in the 21st-century landscape.

Environmental Trends

Although the transnational strategy is difficult to implement, emphasis on the need for global efficiency is increasing as more industries begin to experience global competition. To add to the problem, there is also an increased emphasis on local requirements: Global goods and services often require some customization to meet government regulations within particular countries or to fit customer tastes and preferences. In addition, most multinational firms desire to achieve some coordination and sharing of resources across country markets to hold down costs. Furthermore, some products and industries may be better suited for standardization across country borders than others are. As a result, most large multinational firms with diverse products employ a multidomestic strategy with certain product lines and a global strategy with others. Perhaps this type of flexibility will be required in many Asian firms if they are to be strategically competitive in the coming years (see Strategic Focus for a discussion of the Asian transformation).

Awakening of the Asian Tiger

It looks as if the Asian tiger is awakening. Asia's economies are bottoming out and most are starting to grow again. For example, the economies in Malaysia, the Philippines, Korea, Japan, and China experienced growth. Furthermore, the stock markets in most of these countries are on the upswing, portending economic growth. Singapore largely avoided the severe problems experienced by most other Asian countries. For most countries, 1998 was the year in which they incurred their greatest losses. Singapore's economy grew, albeit only 1.5 percent. Still, Singapore is implementing reforms similar to those adopted by many of the other Asian countries to ensure continued economic prosperity. Asian countries must adapt as globalization continues and powerful forces shape the world economy. The two most prominent of these forces, the Internet and wireless communications, were discussed in the Opening Case.

Japan has the largest economy in Asia and also has suffered significantly. The suffering is greater there because Japan was considered the economic miracle at one time and was imitated by many countries around the world. But Japan had what was referred to as a "bubble economy," built on debt and interdependence, and the bubble eventually burst. Because of its economic difficulties, Japan has been subject to more outside influence than ever before. One of the best examples of Japan's fall is the problem experienced by Mitsubishi. The Mitsubishi kereitsu is huge and produces over 8 percent of Japan's total output. In the late 1980s, Mitsubishi companies were feared because of their economic power and potential domination of global markets. Today, most of Mitsubishi's companies are trying to stem the tide of losses. The organization had to obtain over $2 billion in capital from its member companies to keep some of the other member firms from going bankrupt. Japanese companies were harmed severely by the economic problems throughout Asia. However, these firms are beginning to enjoy growth again as the Asian economies grow. Many foreign firms—particularly financial institutions—are gaining a foothold in Japan. Furthermore, analysts argue that Japan's assets are largely undervalued; thus, they are of substantial value to foreign investors. Some of Japan's best firms, including Honda, Sony, Bridgestone, Canon, and Toyota, survived the crisis and even continued to achieve positive returns when many could not. In fact, these five firms experienced the largest growth in net profits among Japanese firms in 1999. Still, although most of them followed a global strategy, they will have to develop and implement a transnational strategy to compete effectively in global markets, because this strategy is being used increasingly by competitors from other regions of the world. Japan will have to become a larger participant in the Internet economy, particularly e-commerce. DoMoCo provides a good start, but more such firms are needed.

China has been the lone shining economic star in Asia, with a growing economy even during the crisis. In fact, China's economy is expected to grow at 7.5 percent annually for at least the foreseeable future. China's GDP grew at 7.1 percent in 1999, and the country is expected to enter the World Trade Organization in 2000. Interestingly, Chinese firms manufacture products sold globally, but few people know about them. For example, Haier, a firm that manufactures and sells household appliances, is one of a small number of companies from China that sell their products outside of the local domestic market. Still, there are many more products made in China, but marketed under non-Chinese brand names. China leads the world in the export of toys, kitchenware, and textile products. Magic Chef refrigerators, sold by Wal-Mart, are made by Haier. In many ways, China is undergoing an economic revolution. State enterprises are being transformed to private companies, and dynamic new entrepreneurial companies are growing dramatically. Some suggest that Chinese cities are flush with capital and entrepreneurs. While this is likely an overstatement, the economy does look bright. China has agreed to let many foreign firms enter Chinese markets, although usually requiring that they form a joint venture with a Chinese firm, similar to Volkswagen's venture with Shanghai Automotive Industrial Corp. The critical concern about China is the stability of its reforms. China still has an authoritarian Communist government, and if economic reforms stall, economic growth may come to a halt. In particular, if the government becomes too heavy handed, it could limit the inflow of foreign capital needed to fuel the country's economic growth. Also, many of the state firms have had problems privatizing and breaking government ties.

The last of the "big three" Asian economies is South Korea. A number of its companies suffered significant financial problems during the Asian economic crisis. In particular, Korean chaebols were caught with too much debt, were too diversified, and were not flexible enough (primarily due to the massive debt and cross shareholdings). Several of the chaebols have been "downscoping" (see Chapter 7)—ridding themselves of poorly performing diversified businesses. Samsung and Hyundai seem to be improving and likely will again become formidable competitors in global markets, but debate still surrounds the viability of Daewoo. In fact, Hyundai plans to be one of the six survivors in the global auto industry during this decade; however, the company must reduce its large debt and improve its market capitalization. Also, the South Korean economy remains fragile, and political problems—particularly those associated with dealing with the North Koreans—could spell trouble. South Korea would have difficulty absorbing North Korea in the way West Germany absorbed East Germany, and the German reunification was itself fraught with severe problems during the adjustment.

SOURCES: B. Bremner, S. Prasso, J. Veale, J. Moore, & J. Barnathan, 1999, Asia: How real is the recovery? *Business Week,* May 3, 56–58; B. Bremner, E. Thorton, & I. M. Kunii, 2000, Mitsubishi: Fall of a kereitsu, *Businessweek Online,* January 6, *www.businessweek.com*; B. Bremner, E. Thornton, I. M. Kunii, & M. Tanikawa, 1999, A new Japan, *Business Week,* October 25, 69–74;China at fifty: Can China change? 1999, *The Economist,* October 2, 23–25; China's economy is expected to expand by 7.5% in 2000, 2000, *Wall Street Journal Interactive,* January 13, *www.interactice.wsj.com.articles*; M. L. Clifford, M. Shari, & B. Einhorn, 2000, Remaking Singapore Inc., *Businessweek Online,* January 6, *www.businessweek.com*; P. Engardio, J. Veale, & M. L. Clifford, 1999, Boom or miracle? *Business Week,* November 8, 50–51; B. Fulford & T. Y. Jones, 1999, Up from Lemons, *Forbes,* June 14, 122–124; J. Grant, 1998, Why Japan is undervalued, *Wall Street Journal,* April 17, A14; J. E. Hilsenrath, 1999, The speed of change, *Wall Street Journal Interactive,* October 25, *www.interactive.wsj.com*; Japan's growth companies, 1999, *The Economist,* June 26, 69–70; J. L. Lee, 1999, South Korea checks big business groups, *Wall Street Journal,* July 23, A13; Out of the shadows, 1999, *The Economist,* August 28, 50–51; D. Roberts, 1999, China's new revolution, *Business Week,* September 27, 72–78; D. Roberts, 1999, Foreign carmakers get the green light, *Business Week,* July 19, 63; D. Roberts, J. Barnathan, J. Morre, and S. Prasso, 1999, Plans for reform are screeching to a halt as it enters a year of economic peril, *Business Week,* February 22, 48–50; J. Sapsford, 1999, U. S. financial firms delve deeper into Japan, *Wall Street Journal,* January 26, A13; The Koreas: Yesterday's war, tomorrow's peace, 1999, *The Economist,* July 10, 3–16; E. Thornton & M Shari, 1999, Japan's Asian comeback, *Business Week,* November 1, 58–59; P. Wonacott & I. Johnson, 2000, Petrochina prepares to go public: changes fail to break its state ties, *Wall Street Journal Interactive,* January 13, *www.interactive.wsj.com.*

Regionalization

Regionalization is becoming more common in world markets. A firm's location can affect its strategic competitiveness.[81] Firms must decide whether to compete in all (or many) world markets or to focus on a particular region(s).[82] The advantages of attempting to compete in all markets center on the economies that can be achieved because of the combined market size. However, if the firm is competing in industries where the international markets differ greatly (in which it must employ a multidomestic strategy), it may wish to narrow its focus to a particular region of the world. In so doing, it can better understand the cultures, legal and social norms, and other factors that are important for effective competition in those markets. For example, a firm may focus on Far East markets only, rather than attempting to compete in the Middle East, Europe, and the Far East simultaneously. Or the firm may choose a region of the world where the markets are more similar, and thus, some coordination and sharing of resources would be possible. In this way, the firm may be able not only to better understand the markets in which it competes, but also to achieve some economies, even though it may have to employ a multidomestic strategy.

Regional strategies may be promoted by countries that develop trade agreements to increase the economic power of their regions. The European Union (EU) and the Organization of American States (OAS, in South America) are collections of countries that developed trade agreements to promote the flow of trade across country boundaries within their respective regions.[83] Many European firms have been acquiring and integrating their businesses in Europe to better coordinate pan-European brands as the EU creates more unity in European markets. The North American Free Trade Agreement (NAFTA), signed by the United States, Canada, and Mexico, is designed to facilitate free trade across country borders in North America and may be expanded to include other countries in South America, such as Argentina, Brazil, and Chile.[84] NAFTA agreements loosen restrictions on international strategies within a region and provide greater opportunity to realize the advantages of international strategies. Contrary to what some might think, NAFTA does not exist for the sole purpose of U.S. businesses going north and south of the border. In fact, Mexico is the number-two trading partner of the United States, and NAFTA greatly increased Mexico's exports to this country. In December 1999, the U.S. trade deficit with Mexico increased to its highest level, $1.7 billion; the catalyst for Mexico's export boom was NAFTA.[85]

Most firms enter regional markets sequentially, beginning in markets with which they are more familiar. However, they also enter these markets with their largest and strongest lines of business first, followed by their other lines of business after the first ones are successful.[86] After firms decide on their international strategies and whether to employ them in regional or world markets, they must decide how to accomplish such international expansion.[87] Accordingly, the next section discusses how to enter new international markets.

Choice of International Entry Mode

International expansion is accomplished through exporting products, licensing arrangements, strategic alliances, acquisitions, and establishing new wholly owned subsidiaries. These means of entering international markets and their characteristics are shown in Table 8.1. Each has its advantages and disadvantages. Thus, choosing the appropriate mode of entering international markets is critical to the firms' financial performance in those markets.[88]

Exporting

Many industrial firms begin their international expansion by exporting goods or services to other countries.[89] Exporting does not require the expense of establishing operations in the host countries, but exporters must establish some means of marketing and distributing their products. Usually, exporting firms develop contractual arrangements with host-country firms. The disadvantages of exporting include the often high costs of transportation and possible tariffs placed on incoming goods. Furthermore, the exporter has less control over the marketing and distribution of its products in the host country and must either pay the distributor or allow the distributor to add to the price to recoup its costs and make a profit. As a result, it may be difficult to market a competitive product through exporting or to provide a product that is customized to each international market. However, evidence suggests that cost leadership strategies enhance the performance of exports in developed countries, whereas differentiation strategies are more successful in emerging economies.[90]

Firms export mostly to countries that are closest to their facilities, because of the lower transportation costs and the usually greater similarity between geographic neighbors. For example, the largest amount of exports from businesses located in Texas goes to Mexico, with which Texas shares a common border. In fact, exports from Texas to Mexico are greater than all of the other exports from Texas businesses combined.[91]

Small businesses are most likely to use the exporting mode of international entry. One of the largest problems with which small businesses must deal is currency exchange rates. Large businesses have specialists that help them manage the exchange rates, but small businesses rarely have this expertise. Thus, the change to a common currency in Europe actually is helpful to small businesses operating in European markets. Instead of trying to remain current with 12 different exchange rates (assuming that they are exporting to all EU countries), these firms only have to obtain information on one. However, small businesses still seem to have a concern about under-

TABLE

8.1 | Global Market Entry: Choice of Entry Mode

Type of Entry	Characteristics
Exporting	High cost, low control
Licensing	Low cost, low risk, little control, low returns
Strategic alliances	Shared costs, shared resources, shared risks, problems of integration (e.g., two corporate cultures)
Acquisition	Quick access to new market, high cost, complex negotiations, problems of merging with domestic operations
New wholly owned subsidiary	Complex, often costly, time consuming, high risk, maximum control, potential above-average returns

standing the Euro. Thus, U.S. small businesses continue to rely on the dollar, but often must pay prohibitive surcharges in doing so. In general, small businesses operating in international markets must try to understand those markets and manage the business with a knowledge of foreign exchange rates to reduce their overall costs and remain competitive.[92]

Licensing

A licensing arrangement allows a foreign firm to purchase the right to manufacture and sell the firm's products within a host country or set of countries.[93] The licenser is normally paid a royalty on each unit produced and sold. The licensee takes the risks and makes the monetary investments in facilities for manufacturing, marketing, and distributing the goods or services. As a result, licensing is possibly the least costly form of international expansion. As such, licensing is one of the forms of organizational networks that are becoming common, particularly among smaller firms.[94]

Licensing is also a way to expand returns based on previous innovations. For instance, Sony and Philips codesigned the audio CD and now license the rights to companies to make CDs. Sony and Philips collect 5 cents for every CD sold.[95] As this example demonstrates, many firms can earn good returns on their past innovations. A continual focus on research and patent licensing allows a firm to gain strong returns from its innovations for many years into the future.[96]

Today, however, the returns to Sony and Philips from CD sales are being threatened. Cheap counterfeit disks imitating the original products are a growth business. Sales of counterfeit disks in China alone are estimated to exceed $1 billion annually. Interestingly, technological advances are contributing to the severity of the problem. In fact, innovation makes it easier for counterfeiters to improvise. Pressing machinery used to manufacture disks is now so advanced and compact, that it can be operated in the smallest of quarters. Located commonly in housing tenements, counterfeiters' production lines are difficult for officials to find. Corporations are seeking legal remedies to this situation, but with limited success to date.[97]

Jakks Pacific has been named by *Forbes* magazine as one of the best 200 small companies to watch. Jakks's licensing strategy was developed by its two founders, Jack Friedman and Stephen Berman. On the basis of a 14-year licensing deal, the firm creates dolls representing World Wrestling Federation figures such as Stone Cold Steve Austin. The dolls are manufactured in China. Customers such as Wal-Mart, Toys "R" Us, and Kmart receive shipments directly from Chinese manufacturers, thereby keeping prices lower than those of comparable Mattel and Hasbro toys. Jakks, however, has been diversifying through licenses for toy cars with the National Hot Rod Association and the Indianapolis Motor Speedway, toy fishing rods with Bass (a sports equipment company), and toy hard hats and a matching tool belt with the Caterpillar logo. Through its licensing strategy, Jakks is close to becoming the fifth-largest toy company in the United States, and its stock price increased from $7 to $41 in 1999.[98]

Of course, licensing has its disadvantages. For example, it gives the firm very little control over the manufacture and marketing of its products in other countries. In addition, licensing provides the least potential returns, because returns must be shared between the licenser and the licensee. Worse, the international firm may learn the technology and produce and sell a similar competitive product after the license expires.

Komatsu, for example, first licensed much of its technology from International Harvester, Bucyrus-Erie, and Cummins Engine in order to enter the earthmoving equipment business to compete against Caterpillar. Komatsu then dropped these licenses and developed its own products using the technology it gained from the U.S. companies.[99]

Strategic Alliances

In recent years, strategic alliances have enjoyed popularity as a primary means of international expansion.[100] Strategic alliances allow firms to share the risks and the resources required to enter international markets.[101] Moreover, such alliances can facilitate the development of new core competencies that can contribute to a firm's future strategic competitiveness.[102] In addition, most strategic alliances are with a host-country firm that knows and understands the competitive conditions, legal and social norms, and cultural idiosyncrasies of the country, which should help the firm manufacture and market a competitive product. In return, the host-country firm may find its new access to technology and innovative products attractive. Each partner in an alliance brings knowledge or resources to the partnership.[103] Indeed, partners often enter an alliance with the purpose of learning new capabilities. Common among those desired capabilities are technological skills.[104]

Alliances are involved in providing many products that we use each day. For example, a consulting partner for McKinsey & Company recently observed that the gasoline he purchased for his auto came from a joint venture between Royal Dutch Shell and Texaco. Furthermore, the credit card that he used to pay for the purchase was co-branded by Royal Dutch Shell and Mastercard.[105]

British Telecommunications (BT) intends to create a virtual shopping mall in Spain through a joint venture with Banco Popular, a retail-focused Spanish bank with a strong client base of small and medium-sized enterprises (SMEs). The two firms will jointly develop a Web site for business-to-business transactions. They will use the Arrakis portal, BT's Internet operation in Spain. The goal is to develop a client base of 300,000 SMEs. BT will provide the common portal free of charge for the first year, and Banco Popular will charge only a nominal commission for brokering sales. In this way, the two firms expect to have 30,000 business clients within a year after the venture begins operating.[106]

Not all alliances are successful; in fact, many fail. The primary reasons include selecting an incompatible partner and conflict between the partners.[107] International strategic alliances are especially difficult to manage.[108] Trust between the partners is critical. Trust did not have time to develop in the much-publicized alliance, called Global One, among Deutsche Telecom, French Telecom, and MCI WorldCom. First, France Telecom became angry when it learned about Deutsche Telecom's attempt to take over Telecom Italia. When MCI WorldCom acquired Sprint without consulting its partners, the alliance was all but dead. Sprint is a member of another European alliance that is a rival of Global One.[109] Fortunately, research has shown that equity-based alliances, over which a firm has more control, tend to produce more positive returns[110] (strategic alliances are discussed in more depth in Chapter 9).

Acquisitions

With free trade expanding more and more in global markets, cross-border acquisitions have been increasing significantly.[111] In recent years, cross-border acquisitions have comprised over 40 percent of all acquisitions completed worldwide.[112] Acquisitions have been especially popular in Europe, as noted in an earlier Strategic Focus. Acquisitions are used by European firms to build their market power and extend their reach throughout the European Union. Also, foreign firms use acquisitions to enter the European Union and gain a foothold in its commerce. For example, GE completed 133 acquisitions of European firms during the 1990s. As a result, GE employs about 90,000 people in Europe, and its European operations produce approximately $24.4 billion in sales annually.[113] Similarly, Ford acquired Volvo in 1999 for about $6 billion. Ford's goal, however, was not so much entry into the European market as gaining access to assets and products that would make Ford more competitive in global markets in general.[114]

As explained in Chapter 7, acquisitions can provide quick access to a new market. In fact, acquisitions may provide the fastest and often the largest initial international expansion of any of the alternatives. Although acquisitions have become a popular mode of entering international markets, they are not without their costs. International acquisitions carry some of the same disadvantages as domestic acquisitions (see Chapter 7). In addition, they can be expensive and often require debt financing (which also carries an extra cost). International negotiations for acquisitions can be exceedingly complex—generally more complicated than for domestic acquisitions. For example, it is estimated that only 20 percent of the cross-border bids made lead to a completed acquisition, compared to 40 percent for domestic acquisitions.[115] Dealing with the legal and regulatory requirements in the host country of the target firm and obtaining appropriate information to negotiate an agreement frequently present significant problems. Finally, the problems of merging the new firm into the acquiring firm often are more complex than in the case of domestic acquisitions. The acquiring firm must deal not only with different corporate cultures, but also with potentially different social cultures and practices. Therefore, while international acquisitions have been popular because of the rapid access to new markets they provide, they also carry with them important costs and multiple risks.

Wal-Mart, the world's largest retailer, has used several entry modes to globalize its operations. For example, in China, the firm used a joint-venture mode of entry. To begin the firm's foray into Latin American countries, Wal-Mart also used joint ventures. But in some cases (e.g., Mexico), it acquired its venture partner after entering the host country's market. As described earlier, Wal-Mart has used acquisitions to enter European markets (e.g., in Germany and England). Thus, the most effective mode of entering a particular international market must be carefully considered and selected.

Interestingly, as mergers and acquisitions become more common in Europe, they are beginning to mirror such activity among U.S. firms. For instance, the number of hostile European takeover attempts has increased greatly in recent years. Olivetti made a hostile takeover bid for Telecom Italia, which tried to fend off the takeover with a restructuring plan. Olivetti was not deterred and made a larger offer. Telecom Italia then agreed to be acquired by Deutsche Telecom, but Olivetti entered into a bidding war and eventually won the bid to acquire Telecom Italia. Likewise, Vodafone AirTouch (based in England) actively pursued a hostile takeover of Mannesmann, a German firm. However, Mannesmann actively fought the takeover attempt in almost any way possible. Sometimes, takeover attempts become personal contests between the companies' executives, as opposed to taking the appropriate action for the shareholders.[116]

New Wholly Owned Subsidiary

A **greenfield venture** is one in which a new wholly owned subsidiary is established.

The establishment of a new wholly owned subsidiary is referred to as a **greenfield venture.** This is often a complex and potentially costly process, but it has the advantage of affording the firm maximum control and, therefore, if successful, has the most potential to provide above-average returns. This is especially true of firms with strong intangible capabilities that might be leveraged through a greenfield venture.[117] The risks are also high, however, because of the costs involved in establishing a new business operation in a new country. The firm may have to acquire the knowledge and expertise of the existing market by hiring either host-country nationals, possibly from competitive firms, or consultants (which can be costly). Still, the firm maintains control over the technology, marketing, and distribution of its products. Alternatively, the company must build new manufacturing facilities, establish distribution networks, and learn and implement appropriate marketing strategies to compete in the new market.

Kmart used a greenfield venture to establish a store in Guam. The 170,000-square-foot establishment was opened in 1995 and has been highly successful. Kmart took a risk, but research showed that the market was largely controlled by small retailers without the ability to carry the variety of merchandise handled by Kmart. Kmart's success in Guam continued even during the Asian economic crisis. The Kmart in Guam not only serves the residents of Guam, but also is a magnet for tourists. This Kmart sells more of Tengu beef jerky (made in California) than any other retailer in the world. Japanese tourists are particularly taken with the store. Thus, while Kmart took risks to establish its business in Guam, the investment has paid handsome dividends.[118]

Dynamics of Mode of Entry

A firm's choice of mode of entry into international markets is determined by a number of factors.[119] Initially, market entry will often be through export, because this requires no foreign manufacturing expertise and investment only in distribution. Licensing can facilitate the product improvement necessary to enter foreign markets, as in the Komatsu example. Strategic alliances have been popular because they allow a firm to connect with an experienced partner already in the targeted market. Strategic alliances also reduce risk through the sharing of costs. All three modes therefore are best for early market development tactics.

To secure a stronger presence in international markets, acquisitions, or greenfield ventures may be required. Many Japanese automobile manufacturers, such as Honda, Nissan, and Toyota, have gained a presence in the United States through both greenfield ventures and joint ventures. Toyota has particularly strong intangible production capabilities that it has been able to transfer through greenfield ventures.[120] Both acquisitions and greenfield ventures are likely to come at later stages in the development of an international diversification strategy. In addition, both strategies tend to be more successful when the firm making the investment has considerable resources, particularly in the form of valuable core competencies.[121] Large diversified business groups, often found in emerging economies, not only gain resources through diversification, but also have specialized abilities in managing differences in inward and outward flows of foreign direct investment. In particular, Korean chaebols have been adept at making acquisitions in emerging economies.[122]

Thus, to enter a global market, a firm selects the entry mode that is best suited to the situation at hand. In some instances, the various options will be followed sequentially, beginning with exporting and ending with greenfield ventures. In other cases, the firm may use several, but not all, of the different entry modes, each in different markets. The decision regarding the entry mode to use is primarily a result of the industry's competitive conditions, the country's situation and government policies, and the firm's unique set of resources, capabilities, and core competencies.

Strategic Competitiveness Outcomes

Once its strategy and mode of entry have been selected, a firm needs to be concerned about the overall success of its strategy. International expansion can be risky and may not result in a competitive advantage. This section examines a number of strategic competitiveness issues suggested by Figure 8.1.

International Diversification and Returns

International diversification is the primary international corporate-level strategy. In Chapter 6, we discussed the corporate-level strategy of product diversification. Through this strategy, the firm engages in the manufacture and sale of multiple diverse products. **International diversification** is a strategy through which a firm expands the sales of its goods or services across the borders of global regions and countries into different geographic locations or markets. The number of different markets in which it operates and their importance show the degree to which a firm is internationally diversified. The percentage of total sales is often used to measure a region's or country's importance to the firm.[123]

International diversification is a strategy through which a firm expands the sales of its goods or services across the borders of global regions and countries into different geographic locations or markets.

As noted earlier, firms have numerous reasons to diversify internationally. Because of its potential advantages, international diversification should be related positively to firms' returns. Research has shown that, as international diversification increases, firms' returns increase.[124] In fact, the stock market is particularly sensitive to investments in international markets. Firms that are broadly diversified into multiple international markets usually achieve the most positive stock returns.[125] There are also many reasons for the positive effects of international diversification, such as potential economies of scale and experience, location advantages, increased market size, and the opportunity to stabilize returns. The stabilization of returns helps reduce a firm's overall risk.[126] All of these outcomes can be achieved by smaller and newer ventures, as well as larger and established firms. Recently, it has been shown that new ventures can enjoy higher returns when they learn new technologies from their international diversification.[127]

Firms in the Japanese automobile industry have found that international diversification may allow them to better exploit their core competencies, because sharing knowledge resources between operations can produce synergy.[128] Also, a firm's returns may affect its decision to diversify internationally. For example, poor returns in a domestic market may encourage a firm to expand internationally in order to enhance its profit potential. In addition, internationally diversified firms may have access to more flexible labor markets, as the Japanese do in the United States, and may thereby benefit from global scanning for competition and market opportunities.[129] As a result, multinational firms with efficient and competitive operations are more likely to produce above-average returns for their investors and better products for their customers than are solely domestic firms.[130] However, as explained later, international diversification can be carried too far.

International Diversification and Innovation

In Chapter 1, we noted that the development of new technology is at the heart of strategic competitiveness. Michael Porter stated that a nation's competitiveness depends on the capacity of its industry to innovate and suggested that firms achieve competitive advantage in international markets through innovation. Eventually and inevitably, competitors outperform firms that fail to innovate and improve their operations and products. Therefore, the only way to sustain a competitive advantage is to upgrade it continually.[131]

International diversification provides the potential for firms to achieve greater returns on their innovations (through larger or more numerous markets) and thus lowers the often substantial risks of R&D investments. Therefore, international diversification provides incentives for firms to innovate. In addition, international diversification may be necessary to generate the resources required to sustain a large-scale R&D operation. An environment of rapid technological obsolescence makes it difficult to invest in new technology and the capital-intensive operations required to take advantage of it. Firms operating solely in domestic markets may find such investments problematic because of the length of time required to recoup the original investment. If the time is extended, it may not even be possible to recover the investment before the technology becomes obsolete.[132] As a result, international diversification improves a firm's ability to appropriate additional and necessary returns from innovation before competitors can overcome the initial competitive advantage created by the innovation. In addition, firms moving into international markets are exposed to new products and processes. If they learn about those products and processes and integrate this knowledge into their operations, further innovation can be developed.[133]

The relationship among international diversification, innovation, and returns is complex. Some level of performance is necessary to provide the resources to generate international diversification, which in turn provides incentives and resources to invest in research and development. The latter, if done appropriately, should enhance the returns of the firm, which then provides more resources for continued international diversification and investment in R&D.

Because of the potential positive effects of international diversification on performance and innovation, some have argued that such diversification may even enhance returns in product-diversified firms. International diversification would increase market potential in each of these firms' product lines, but the complexity of managing a firm that is both product diversified and internationally diversified is significant. Therefore, it is likely that international diversification can enhance the returns of a firm that is highly product diversified, but only when it is managed well.

Asea Brown Boveri (ABB) may demonstrate these relationships. This firm's operations involve high levels of both product and international diversification, yet ABB's performance is quite strong. Some believe that the firm's ability to effectively implement the transnational strategy contributes to its strategic competitiveness. To manage itself, ABB assembles culturally diverse corporate and divisional management teams, which are then used to facilitate the simultaneous achievement of global integration and local responsiveness. Evidence suggests that more culturally diverse top-management teams often have a greater knowledge of international markets and their idiosyncrasies[134] (top-management teams are discussed further in Chapter 12). Moreover, an in-depth understanding of diverse markets among top-level managers facilitates intrafirm coordination and the use of long-term, strategically relevant criteria to evaluate the performance of managers and their units. In turn, this approach facilitates improved innovation and performance.[135]

While many foreign firms experience risk in Latin American markets, they also find those markets attractive in which to invest, as explained in the Strategic Focus. Of course, the 33 different Latin American markets vary in attractiveness. A Latin American Union similar to the EU could be highly attractive and beneficial. However, given the differences in economic development, competition, and conflict among several of the countries, gaining the agreement necessary to establish such a union is likely to be difficult.

Complexity of Managing Multinational Firms

Although many benefits can be realized by implementing an international strategy, doing so is complex and can produce greater uncertainty.[136] For example, multiple risks are involved when a firm operates in several different countries. Firms can grow only so large and diverse before becoming unmanageable, or the costs of managing them exceed their benefits. Other complexities include the highly competitive nature of global markets, multiple cultural environments, potentially rapid shifts in the value of different currencies, and the possible instability of some national governments.

Risks in an International Environment

International diversification carries multiple risks.[137] International expansion is difficult to implement, and it is difficult to manage after implementation, because of these risks. The chief risks are political and economic. Taking these risks into account, highly diversified firms are accustomed to market conditions yielding competitive situations that differ from what was predicted. Sometimes, these situations contribute to the firm's strategic competitiveness; on other occasions, they have a negative effect on the firm's efforts.[138] Specific examples of political and economic risks are shown in Figure 8.4.

Political Risks

Political risks are related to instability in national governments and to war, both civil and international.

Political risks are related to instability in national governments and to war, both civil and international. Instability in a national government creates numerous problems. Among these are economic risks and uncertainty created by government regulation, the existence of many, possibly conflicting, legal authorities, and the potential nation-

LAU: Is There an Opportunity for a Latin American Union?

Currently, there are several trade groups among Latin American countries. The foremost is Mercosur, anchored by Brazil and Argentina (the organization also includes Bolivia, Chile, Paraguay, and Uruguay). The others are the Andean Community (Venezuela, Ecuador, Peru, Colombia, Bolivia, and Panama) and the Central American Common Market (Costa Rica, Guatemala, El Salvador, Honduras, and Nicaragua). However, there has been a push for a larger and more encompassing organization that would establish the Free Trade Area of the Americas that would include the United States. This alliance would create a common market among the 33 countries in Central and South America that some believe could become an economic powerhouse and be of great benefit to most Latin American countries and firms that do business in any of these 34 countries. The United States is the 34th country. However, it will be difficult to obtain agreement among the countries involved to establish such a common market: The separate trade groups may have trouble agreeing on a common format, as some of the groups already have trouble among themselves (e.g., between Brazil and Argentina in Mercosur), and there remain problems and disagreements within several of the countries as well (e.g., Ecuador).

Many companies from outside Latin America (e.g., from the United States, Europe, and Asia) find the region an attractive market in which to invest. In fact, even though some Latin American countries have experienced economic problems in recent years, many companies are increasing their investments in Latin America, thereby globalizing the region's markets. Companies such as Telefónica (Spain), ABN Amro (the Netherlands), CSFB (Switzerland), and Citigroup (the United States) have made substantial investments in Latin American countries in recent years. With NAFTA, Mexico has become a major investment target for many companies from the United States and Canada (and for some from Europe, Asia, and even other Latin American countries). Some of these firms look to their Mexican operations as a platform to reach South American markets.

Brazil is the largest country in both area and population in South America, and many believe that it has the most potential. Brazil recently experienced severe economic problems. However, Brazilian government officials and representatives from the International Monetary Fund reached an agreement to make changes in the Brazilian economy in exchange for a $41.5 billion rescue package of loans. The economic plan was designed to control inflation. Essentially, a new president of Brazil's central bank was appointed, and interest rates were increased to fight inflation. The new central-bank president impressed bankers in New York, London, and Paris, which caused Brazilian stocks to increase and made loans easier to obtain. Within two months after the interest rate hike, the rates were reduced to levels below those at the time of the increase. Analysts were amazed and pleased at the speed of Brazil's economic recovery. In addition, in 1999, many of Brazil's relatively autonomous states began to implement economic reforms. The result of these actions and the economic turnaround was increasing investment from foreign firms. For example, using Brazil as a global export base, Volkswagen will produce about 20 percent of its autos there. Another indication of

Brazil's economic recovery is shown in the increase in the number of subscribers for cellular service in the country. In 1998, before the privatization of Telebras, the Brazilian telecommunications company, the firm had fewer than 3 million subscribers for mobile phones. By early 2000, it had 14.4 million subscribers.

Brazil's economic recovery is creating problems for one of its important trading neighbors, however. Argentina began suffering economic problems in 1999, which were exacerbated by Brazil's actions to improve its economy. Brazil's devaluation of the *real* (Brazil's currency) created problems for Argentina: Suddenly, Argentina's products were more expensive, and the cost of doing business in Argentina was higher than in Brazil. The effects can be seen in the decision of Delphi Automotive Systems, Cica (a unit of Unilever), Goodyear Tire and Rubber, and Tupperware to close plants in Argentina and to focus on their operations in Brazil. Argentina cannot peg its peso to the dollar, as did Brazil with its *real,* because doing so could damage the country's businesses. Brazil's population base of 165 million people is five times the size of Argentina, making it an attractive market for foreign investors. Argentina has responded by increasing tariffs and placing quotas on Brazilian goods. And Brazil has retaliated with protectionist measures, too. As a result, two-way trade between the countries has decreased by 24 percent. The future of Mercosur may be in doubt. In 1998, Argentina's gross domestic product per capita was 19 percent higher than South Korea's, 72 percent higher than Brazil's, and almost twice that of Mexico. Indeed, Argentina was making progress until its latest crisis. The economy fell by 16 percent in 1999 and unemployment increased to 16 percent.

Similarly, Ecuador has been experiencing economic problems as well. Because of rampant inflation, the Ecuadorian president pegged the sucre to the U.S. dollar, at the rate of 25,000 to 1. The intent was to bring inflation under control and to increase the country's economic stability. Unfortunately, because of the economic problems, the president was driven

Brazil's economy underwent a major change to control inflation. As a result of the country's economic recovery, it is now more attractive to foreign investors.

from office by a coup and replaced with the vice president. With greater political support, the new president continued to peg the sucre to the U.S. dollar, after which interest rates on loans between banks decreased from 200 percent to about 20 percent. Also, the new president vowed to pursue free-market reforms. These actions are designed to woo foreign investors to Ecuador.

Colombia is also trying to lure foreign investors. Similar to its many Latin American neighbors, Colombia wants the infusion of foreign capital and employment for its citizens. In 1999, Colombia increased the number of firms privatized and did attract greater foreign investment. Several large U.S. firms, such as Exxon-Mobil and Procter & Gamble, already have investments in the country, but Colombia needs more.

Chile perhaps has had the best-performing economy in Latin America. It was the first to implement free-market reforms. Unfortunately, Chile is a small country, and as such, it was unable to greatly influence free-market reforms in other Latin American countries. Thus, while Latin American countries are enjoying some economic success and have much potential, they are unlikely to form a Latin American Union or Common Market for the Americas. However, they are at least moving in the right direction and represent much potential—as much or even more than China.

SOURCES: Brazilian cellular subscribers doubled to 14.4 million in 1999, 2000. *Wall Street Journal Interactive,* January 13, *www.interactive.wsj.com/articles*; Ecuador to switch to U.S. dollar for stability, 2000, *Houston Chronicle,* January 11, 16A; Ecuador's interbank rates drop after move toward U.S. dollar, 2000, *Wall Street Journal Interactive,* January 13, *www.interactive.wsj.com/articles*; I. Katz, 1999, A job half done, *Business Week,* August 30, 60–64; I. Katz, 2000, Adios, Argentina—hello, Brazil, *Business Week,* January 17, 56; I. Katz, 1999, Pulling Brazil back from the brink, *Business Week,* May 10, 50–52; I. Katz, 1999, Snapping up South America, *Business Week,* January 18, 60; J. Millman, 1999, U.S. food producers find growth recipe, *Wall Street Journal,* December 13, A28; S. Newport & R. Lapper, 2000, Ecuador's president faces battle over dollarisation, *www.ft.com,* January 11, *www.ft.com/nbearchive*; J. Otis, 2000, Ecuador's new president is sworn in, names cabinet, *Houston Chronicle,* January 24, 13A; M. M. Phillips, 1999, Brazil, IMF reach deal on new economic plan, *Wall Street Journal,* March 8, A12; C. Torres, 1998, U.S. aims to reassert influence over Latin trade, *Wall Street Journal,* April 14, A17 . T. Vogel, Jr., 1999, Colombia puts out welcome mat for foreign investors, *Wall Street Journal,* May 28, A15; Volkswagen is poised to create a global export base in Brazil, 2000, *Wall Street Journal Interactive,* January 6, *www.interactive.wsj.com/articles*; M. A. Warren, 1999, Brazilian states, once the problem, start to reform, *Wall Street Journal,* July 2, A13.

alization of private assets. For example, foreign firms that are investing in Russia may have concerns about the stability of the national government and what might happen to their investments or assets in that country should there be a major change in government. This concern remained as Yeltsin abruptly resigned at the beginning of 2000.

Different concerns exist for foreign firms investing in China. They are less worried about the potential for major changes in China's national government than about the uncertainty of China's regulation of foreign business investments. For example, some analysts suggest that China has an unclear foreign-investor policy. Some of China's leaders worry about the flood of foreign investment and the potential for the government to lose control over the country's economy. Unfortunately, all debate on the topic is conducted in secrecy within the Chinese government and thus, makes the situation even more unclear to potential foreign investors, creating further risk.[139]

Zeneca, a British chemical company, negotiated with Chinese government officials for five years for the right to build a large herbicide plant in the eastern province of

8.4 | Risks in the International Environment

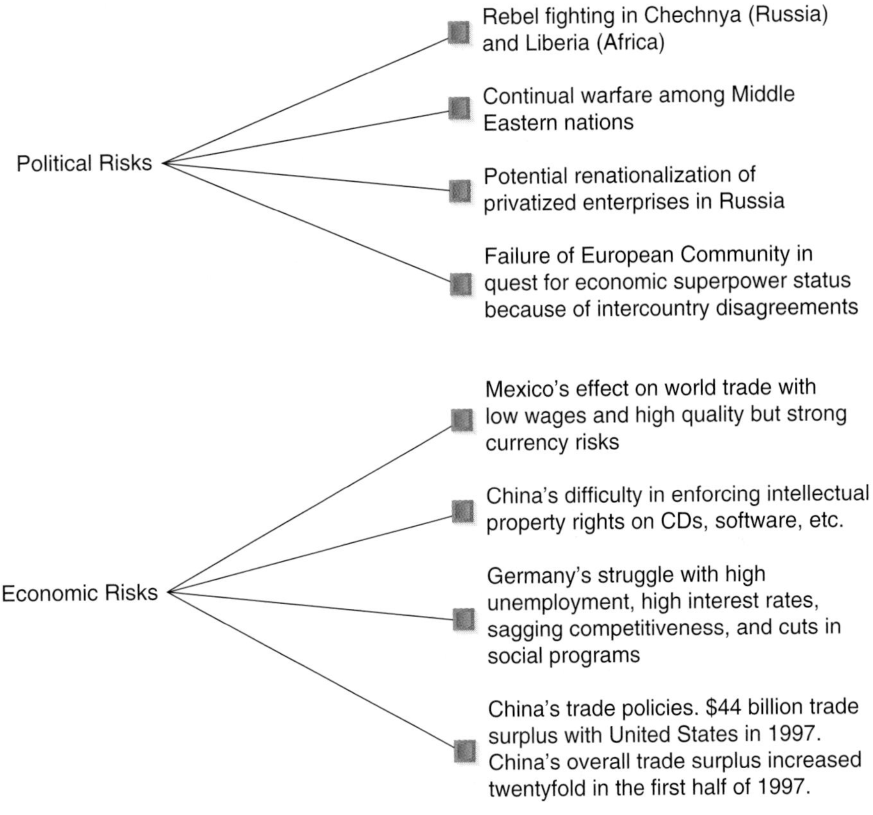

Source: N. Banerjee, 1996, Russia's many regions work to attract funds from foreign investors, *Wall Street Journal,* April 30, A1, A8; P. Engardio and D. Roberts, 1996, Rethinking China, *Business Week,* March 4, 57–64; R. S. Greenberger, 1996, U.S. sharply attacks China over intellectual property, *Wall Street Journal,* May 1, A3, A4; A. D. Marcus, 1996, Israel seems to target Lebanon economy, *Wall Street Journal,* April 17, A16; C. Rosett, 1996, Russian Communists target privatizers, *Wall Street Journal,* February 13, A11; P. Stein, 1996, Hong Kong feels heavy hand of China, *Wall Street Journal,* April 17, A16; J. Templeman, 1996, The economy that fell to earth, *Business Week,* January 15, 46.

Jiangsu. An even more direct example of political risk was the announced policy change in 1999 to reduce sales of cell phones by foreign companies. In addition, in 1999, a top Chinese official declared that ownership by a foreign company in the Chinese Internet was illegal.[140]

Economic Risks

Economic risks are interdependent with political risks, as noted earlier. Chief among the economic risks of international diversification are the differences and fluctuations in the value of different currencies. With U.S. firms, the value of the dollar relative to other currencies determines the value of their international assets and earnings; for example, an increase in the value of the U.S. dollar can reduce the value of U.S. multinational firms' international assets and earnings in other countries. Furthermore, the value of different currencies can, at times, dramatically affect a firm's competitiveness in global markets because of its effect on the prices of goods manufactured in different countries. An increase in the value of the dollar can harm U.S. firms' exports to international markets because of the price differential of the products.

Drypers experienced a strong decrease in sales due to the devaluation of Brazil's real in 1999. The devaluation reduced consumers' buying power and thus decreased Drypers' sales in Brazil. Its manufacturing facilities in Argentina became less viable, too, because they served the Brazilian market. The devaluation also hurt Argentina's economy, as described in the Strategic Focus on Latin America. As a result, Drypers moved some of its manufacturing facilities from Argentina to Malaysia and Mexico. Still, while losing money in Latin America, Drypers wants to stay the course because of a higher fertility rate in that region of the world (2.9 children per mother), where there is a strong demand for baby products.[141]

Limits to International Expansion: Management Problems

Research has shown that firms tend to receive positive returns on early international diversification, but they often level off and become negative as the diversification increases past some point.[142] There are several reasons for the limits to the positive effects of international diversification. First, greater geographic dispersion across country borders increases the costs of coordination between units and the distribution of products. Second, trade barriers, logistical costs, cultural diversity, and other differences by country (e.g., access to raw materials and different employee skill levels) greatly complicate the implementation of an international diversification strategy.[143]

Institutional and cultural factors often represent strong barriers to the transfer of a firm's competitive advantages from one country to another. Marketing programs often have to be redesigned and new distribution networks established when firms expand into new countries. In addition, they may encounter different labor costs and capital charges. In general, it is difficult to effectively implement, manage, and control a firm's international operations.[144]

Robert Shapiro, former CEO of Monsanto (now a part of Pharmacia), was once considered a genius for the development of NutraSweet and other positive strategic actions that he has taken. However, he made the fundamental mistake of assuming that Europe was similar to the United States. As a result of this miscalculation, Monsanto's genetically engineered seeds, such as herbicide-resistant soybeans, have been strongly rejected in Europe.[145] Similarly, Wal-Mart made significant mistakes in some Latin American markets. For example, Wal-Mart executives learned that giant parking lots do not draw huge numbers of customers in a country where the shoppers do not have autos. The lots were so far away from the bus stops used by many Mexicans for traveling and shopping that potential customers did not come to Wal-Mart stores because they could not easily get their goods home.[146]

The amount of international diversification that can be managed will vary from firm to firm and according to the abilities of each firm's managers. The problems of central coordination and integration are mitigated if the firm diversifies into more friendly countries that have cultures similar to its own country's culture. In that case, there are fewer trade barriers, the laws and customs are better understood, and the product is easier to adapt to local markets. For example, U.S. firms may find it less difficult to expand their operations into Canada and Western European countries than into Asian countries.[147]

Other Management Problems

One critical concern firms have is that the global marketplace is highly competitive. Firms that are accustomed to a highly competitive domestic market experience more complexities in international markets, caused not only by the number of competitors encountered, but also by the differences among those competitors. For instance, a U.S. firm expanding its operations into a European country may encounter competitors not only from Great Britain, Germany, France, and Spain, but also from countries outside of Europe, such as Hong Kong, Japan, Korea, Taiwan, Canada, and possibly even South America. Firms from each of these countries may enjoy different competitive advantages. Some may have low labor costs, others may have easy access to financing and low capital costs, and still others may have access to new high technology. Adapting to all these differences is neither simple nor easy. Finally, attempting to understand the strategic intent of a competitor is more complex because of all these different cultures and mind-sets.[148]

Another problem associated with international diversification focuses on the relationships between the host government and the multinational corporation. For example, while Japanese firms face few trade barriers in competing in U.S. markets, U.S. firms often encounter many barriers to selling their products and operating in Japanese markets.[149] These regulations have traditionally kept the yen high relative to the dollar by keeping out imports and reducing the value of Japanese exports. The latter, in turn, increases the price of Japanese products abroad. As noted earlier, the problem has been reversing itself somewhat, but much more remains to be done to reduce entry barriers. Many firms, such as Toyota and General Motors, are turning to strategic alliances to overcome those barriers. They do so to form interorganizational networks that allow firms to share resources and risks, but that also help to build flexibility.[150]

Summary

- International diversification is increasing not only because of traditional motivations, but also for emerging reasons. Traditional motives include extending the product life cycle, securing key resources, and having access to low-cost labor. Emerging motivations focus on the combination of the Internet and mobile telecommunications, which facilitates global transactions. Also, there is increased pressure for global integration as the demand for commodities becomes borderless, and yet pressure is also increasing for local country responsiveness.
- An international strategy usually attempts to capitalize on four important opportunities: an increased market size; the opportunity to earn a return on large investments, such as plant and capital equipment or research and development; economies of scale and learning; and advantages of location.
- International business-level strategies are similar to the generic business-level strategies and consist of international cost leadership, international differentiation, international focus, and international integrated cost leadership/differentiation strategies. However, each of these strategies is usually grounded in one or more home-country advantages, as Porter's diamond model suggests. The diamond model emphasizes four determinants: factors of production,

demand conditions, related and supporting industries, and patterns of firm strategy, structure, and rivalry.

- There are three types of international corporate-level strategies. A multidomestic strategy focuses on competition within each country in which a firm operates. Firms employing a multidomestic strategy decentralize strategic and operating decisions to the strategic business units operating in each country, so that each can tailor its goods and services to the local market. A global strategy assumes more standardization of products across country boundaries; therefore, competitive strategy is centralized and controlled by the home office. A transnational strategy seeks to combine aspects of both multidomestic and global strategies in order to emphasize both local responsiveness and global integration and coordination. This strategy is difficult to implement, requiring an integrated network and a culture of individual commitment.
- Although the transnational strategy is difficult to implement, environmental trends are causing many multinational firms to consider the need for both global efficiencies and local responsiveness. Many large multinational firms—particularly those with many diverse products—use a multidomestic strategy with some product lines and a global strategy with others.
- Some firms decide to compete only in certain regions of the world, as opposed to viewing all markets in the world as potential opportunities. Competing in regional markets allows firms and managers to focus their learning on specific markets, cultures, locations, resources, etc.
- Firms may enter international markets in one of several different ways, including exporting, licensing, forming strategic alliances, making acquisitions, and establishing new wholly owned subsidiaries, often referred to as greenfield ventures. Most firms begin with exporting or licensing, because of their lower costs and risks, but later may expand to strategic alliances and acquisitions. The most expensive and risky means of entering a new international market is through the establishment of a new wholly owned subsidiary. On the other hand, such subsidiaries provide the advantages of maximum control by the firm and, if they are successful, the greatest returns.
- International diversification facilitates innovation in a firm, because it provides a larger market to gain more and faster returns from investments in innovation. In addition, international diversification may generate the resources necessary to sustain a large-scale R&D program.
- In general, international diversification is related to above-average returns, but this assumes that the diversification is implemented effectively and that the firm's international operations will be well managed. International diversification provides greater economies of scope and learning, which, along with greater innovation, help produce above-average returns.
- Several risks are involved with managing multinational operations. Among these are political risks (e.g., instability of national governments) and economic risks (e.g., fluctuations in the value of a country's currency).
- There are also limits to the ability to manage international expansion effectively. International diversification increases coordination and distribution costs, and management problems are exacerbated by trade barriers, logistical costs, and cultural diversity, among other factors.
- Finally, international markets are highly competitive, and firms must maintain an effective working relationship with the host government.

Review Questions

1. What are the traditional and emerging motives that are causing firms to expand internationally?
2. What four factors provide a basis for international business-level strategies?
3. What are the generic international business-level strategies? How do they differ from each other?
4. What are the differences among the three corporate-level international strategies—multidomestic, global, and transnational?
5. What environmental trends are currently affecting international strategy?
6. What five modes of international expansion are available, and what is the normal sequence of their use?
7. What is the relationship between international diversification and innovation? How does international diversification affect innovation? What is the effect of international diversification on a firm's returns?
8. What are the risks involved in expanding internationally and managing multinational firms?
9. What are the factors that create limits to the positive outcomes of international expansion?

Application Discussion Questions

1. Given the advantages of international diversification, why do some firms choose not to expand internationally?
2. How can a small firm diversify globally using the Internet?
3. How do firms choose among the alternative modes for expanding internationally and moving into new markets (e.g., forming a strategic alliance versus establishing a wholly owned subsidiary)?
4. Does international diversification affect innovation similarly in all industries? Why or why not?
5. What is an example of political risk in expanding operations into Latin America or China?
6. Why do some firms gain competitive advantages in international markets? Explain.
7. Why is it important to understand the strategic intent of strategic alliance partners and competitors in international markets?
8. What are the challenges associated with pursuing the transnational strategy? Explain.

Ethics Questions

1. As firms attempt to internationalize, there may be a temptation to locate their facilities where product liability laws are lax in testing new products. What are some examples in which this motivation is the driving force behind international expansion?
2. Regulation and laws regarding the sale and distribution of tobacco products are stringent in the U.S. market. Use the Internet to investigate selected U.S. tobacco firms to identify if sales are increasing in foreign markets compared to domestic markets. In what countries are sales increasing and why? What is your assessment of this practice?
3. Some firms outsource production to foreign countries. Although the presumed rationale for such outsourcing is to reduce labor costs, examine the labor laws (for instance, the strictness of child labor laws) and laws on environmental protection in another country. What does your examination suggest from an ethical perspective?
4. Are there markets that the U.S. government protects through subsidies and tariffs? If so, which ones and why? How will the continuing development of e-commerce potentially affect these efforts?
5. Should the United States seek to impose trade sanctions on other countries, such as China, because of human rights violations?
6. Latin America has been experiencing significant changes in both political orientation and economic development. Describe these changes. What strategies should foreign international businesses implement, if any, to influence government policy in these countries? Is there a chance that the political changes will reverse?

Internet Exercise

As explained in the Opening Case, convenience stores in Japan, such as the corner Seven-Eleven, and supermarkets in Britain are capitalizing on Internet commerce by offering their customers easy access, e-service, and attractive prices and selections. Located at **www.7dream.com**, Seven-Eleven allows shoppers to surf, order, and pay for merchandise with cash, the most trusted method of payment in Japan, a country with a comparatively low crime rate. Locate the Web site of Britain's large supermarket chain, Tesco, at **www.tesco.com**. What types of services offered would appeal to you? What do you see as a deterrent to introducing these and other e-commerce services into supermarkets, hypermarkets, and convenience stores in the United States?

***e-project:** This chapter explains the different methods of entering foreign markets. Using sources on the Internet provided by your government's trade division, the U.S. State Department (**www.state.gov**), the U.S. Dept. of Commerce (**www.commerce.gov**), and private resources such as **www.china-venture.com**, plan the export of a new line of USA brand baseball hats to Shanghai and Beijing, China. Assume that you plan to manufacture the hats inside China and distribute them through local stores within those two cities.

Notes

1. T. Isobe, S. Makino, & D. B. Montgomery, 2000, Resource commitment, entry timing and market performance of foreign direct investments in emerging economies: The case of Japanese international joint ventures in China, *Academy of Management Journal,* in press.
2. I. Filatotchev, T. Buck T., & V. Zhukov, 2000, Downsizing in privatized firms in Russia, Ukraine and Belarus: Theory and empirical evidence, *Academy of Management Journal,* in press; P. Krantz, 2000, How Yeltsin blew Russia's big chance, *Business Week,* January 17, 50.
3. J. Wheatley, 2000, TERRA: Brazil ISP launches free access, *www.ft.com,* January 21, *http://news.ft.com/nbearchive.*
4. J. B. White, 1998, There are no German or U.S. companies, only successful ones, *Wall Street Journal,* May 7, A1, A11.
5. B. L. Kedia & A. Mukherji, 1999, Global managers: Developing a mindset for global competitiveness, *Journal of World Business,* 34(3): 230–251.
6. T. P, Murtha, S. A. Lenway, & R. P. Bagozzi, 1998, Global mind-sets and cognitive shift in a complex multinational corporation, *Strategic Management Journal,* 19: 97–114.
7. Bagged cement, 1999, *The Economist,* June 18, *www.economist.com/editorial.*
8. B. R. Koka, J. E. Prescott, & R. Madhaven, 1999, Contagion influence on trade and investment policy: A network perspective, *Journal of International Business Studies,* 30: 127–148.
9. J. Carey, 1999, This drug's for you, *Business Week,* January 18, 98–100.
10. S. McNutty, 2000, STARHUB: Telco agrees China deal, *www.ft.com,* January 11, *http://news.ft.com/nbearchive.*
11. C. W. L. Hill, 2000, *International Business: Competing in the Global Marketplace 3d ed.,* (Boston: Irwin/McGraw Hill), 378–380; B. J. Punnett & D. A. Ricks, 1997, *International Business,* 2d ed., (Cambridge, MA: Blackwell Publishers), 8.
12. R. Vernon, 1996, International investment and international trade in the product cycle, *Quarterly Journal of Economics,* 80: 190–207.
13. A. Bernstein, S. Jackson, & J. Byrne, 1997, Jack cracks the whip again, *Business Week,* December 15, 34–35.
14. *Financial Times,* 1997, Flexible and cheap, *Financial Times,* December 12, II.
15. J. N. Kapferer, 1998, Making brands work around the world, As business goes global, Part 1, *Financial Times,* February 12–13.
16. Punnett and Ricks, *International Business,* 334–337.
17. S. Batholomew, 1997, National systems of biotechnology innovation: Complex interdependencies in the global system, *Journal of International Business Studies,* 28: 241–266; A. Madhok, 1997, Cost, value and foreign market entry mode: The transaction and the firm, *Strategic Management Journal,* 18: 39–61.
18. W. Kuemmerle, 1997, Building effective R&D capabilities abroad, *Harvard Business Review,* 75(2): 61–70; B. J. Oviatt & P. P. McDougall, 1995, Global start-ups: Entrepreneurs on a worldwide stage, *Academy of Management Executive,* IX(2): 30–44.
19. J. J. Choi & M. Rajan, 1997, A joint test of market segmentation and exchange risk factor in international capital markets, *Journal of International Business Studies,* 28: 29–49.
20. R. E. Hoskisson, L. Eden, C. M. Lau, & M. Wright, 2000, Strategy in emerging economies. *Academy of Management Journal,* in press; D. J. Arnold & J. A. Quelch, 1998, New strategies in emerging markets, *Sloan Management Review,* 40: 7–20.
21. S. Lovett, L. C. Simmons, & R. Kali, 1999, Guanxi versus the market: Ethics and efficiency, *Journal of International Business Studies,* 30: 231–248; J. L. Xie, 1996, Karasek's model in the People's Republic of China: Effects of job demands, control, and individual differences, *Academy of Management Journal,* 39: 1594–1618.
22. J. P. Quinlan, 1998, Europe, not Asia, is corporate America's key market, *Wall Street Journal,* January 12, A20.
23. Y. Luo, & M. W. Peng, 1999, learning to compete in a transition economy: Experience, environment and performance, *Journal of International Business Studies,* 30: 269–295; M. A. Hitt, M. T. Dacin, B. B. Tyler, & D. Park, 1997, Understanding the differences in Korean and U.S. executives' strategic orientations, *Strategic Management Journal,* 18: 159–167.
24. G. Edmondson, 1999, Danone hits its stride, *Business Week,* February 1, 52–53.
25. Bernstein, Jackson, & Byrne, Jack cracks the whip again.
26. X. Martin, A. Swaminathan, & W. Mitchell, 1999, Organizational evolution in the interorganizational environment: Incentives and constraints on international expansion strategy, *Administrative Science Quarterly,* 43: 566–601.
27. S. Zaheer & E. Mosakowski, 1997, The dynamics of the liability of foreignness: A global study of survival in financial services, *Strategic Management Journal,* 18: 439–464.
28. S. N. Mehta, 1999, BellSouth pushes harder in Latin America, *Wall Street Journal,* May 24, B10.
29. E. Beck & R. Balu, 1998, Europe is deaf to snap! crackle! pop! *Wall Street Journal,* June 22, B1, B8.
30. B. Morris & P. Sellers, 2000, What really happened at Coke? *Fortune,* January 10, 114–116.
31. W. Kuemmerle, 1999, The drivers of foreign direct investment into research and development: An empirical investigation, *Journal of International Business Studies,* 30: 1–24.
32. K. L. Miller & J. Muller, 1999, Daimler Chrysler: The grace period is over, *Business Week,* March 29, 50; E. Thornton, 1999, Remaking Nissan, *Business Week,* November 15, 70–76; D. Owen, 1999, Renault lifted by news of interest in Korean carmaker, *www.ft.com,* December 30, *www.ft.com/nbearchive.*
33. Smoke gets in your eyes, 1999, *The Economist,* October 9, 83.
34. G. Edmondson, J. Rae-Dupree, & K. Capell, 1999, How Airbus could rule the skies, *Business Week,* August 2, 54; DASA, Aerospatiale to merge; Deal will also include Airbus, 1999, *Wall Street Journal Interactive,* November 14, *www.interactive.wsj.com/articles.*
35. W. Shan & J. Song, 1997, Foreign direct investment and the sourcing of technological advantage: Evidence from the biotechnology industry, *Journal of International Business Studies,* 28: 267–284.
36. L. G. Thomas, III & G. Waring, 1999, Competing capitalism: Capital investment in American, German and Japanese firms, *Strategic Management Journal,* 20: 729–748.
37. A. J. Venables, 1995, Economic integration and the location of firms, *The American Economic Review,* 85: 296–300.
38. E. Thornton, K. Kerwin, & K. Naughton, 1999, Can Honda go it alone? *Business Week,* July 5, 42–45.
39. H. Bresman, J. Birkinshaw, & R. Nobel, 1999, Knowledge transfer in international acquisitions, *Journal of International Business Studies,* 30: 439–462; J. Birkinshaw, 1997, Entrepreneurship in multinational corporations: The characteristics of subsidiary initiatives, *Strategic Management Journal,* 18: 207–229.
40. Luo & Peng, Learning to compete in a transition economy.
41. S. Makino & A. Delios, 1996, Local knowledge transfer and performance: Implications for alliance formation in Asia, *Journal of International Business Studies,* 27(Special Issue): 905–927.
42. K. Ferdows, 1997, Making the most of foreign factories, *Harvard Business Review,* 75(2): 73–88.
43. M. B. Sarkar, S. T. Cavusgil, & P. S. Aulakh, 1999, International expansion of telecommunication carriers: The influence of market structure, network characteristics, and entry imperfections, *Journal of International Business Studies,* 30: 361–382.

44. J. Millman, 1999, U.S. agricultural-machinery makers beef up their investments in Latin American factories, *Wall Street Journal,* June 24, B1.
45. D. J. Teece, G. Pisano, & A. Shuen, 1997, Dynamic capabilities and strategic management, *Strategic Management Journal,* 18: 509–533.
46. A. Campbell & M. Alexander, 1997, What's wrong with strategy? *Harvard Business Review,* 75(6): 42–51.
47. A. Rugman, 1998, Multinationals as regional flagships, as business goes global, Part 1, *Financial Times,* February 10–11, 6–9.
48. M. E. Porter, 1990, *The Competitive Advantage of Nations* (New York: The Free Press).
49. Ibid., 84.
50. Ibid., 89.
51. A. Edgecliffe-Johnson, 1999, A friendly store from Arkansas, *Financial Times,* June 19, 7.
52. N. D. Schwartz, 1998, Why Wall Street's buying Wal-Mart again, *Fortune,* February 16, 92–94.
53. Schwartz, Why Wall Street's buying Wal-Mart again, 94; Sam's travels, 1997, *Financial Times,* December 19, 13.
54. C. S. Smith, 1999, Volkswagen AG plans to build low-price car to sell in China, *Wall Street Journal,* June 30, A19.
55. Porter, *Competitive Advantage,* 133.
56. D. Woodruff, 1997, Service with a what? *Business Week,* September 8, 130F–130H.
57. I. M. Kunii & S. Baker, 2000, Amazing DoCoMo, *Business Week Online,* January 9, *www.businessweek.com.*
58. J. A. Byrne, 1999, Phillip Morris, *Business Week,* November 29, 176–192.
59. T. Burns, 1997, Niche goals bring away results, *Financial Times,* November 17, II; Oviatt & McDougall, Global start-ups.
60. Porter, *Competitive Advantage,* 210–225.
61. M. J. Enright & P. Tenti, 1990, How the diamond works: The Italian ceramic tile industry, *Harvard Business Review,* 68(2): 90–91.
62. Burns, Niche goals bring away results, 17.
63. D. Lei, M. A. Hitt, & J. D. Goldhar, 1996, Advanced manufacturing technology: The impact on organization design and strategic flexibility, *Organization Studies,* 17: 501–523.
64. R. D. Ireland & M. A. Hitt, 1999, Achieving and maintaining strategic competitiveness in the 21st century: The role of strategic leadership, *Academy of Management Executive,* 13(1): 43–57.
65. N. Tait, 2000, Caterpillar: Low demand pulls profits, *www.ft.com,* January 22, *www.ft.com/nbearchives.*
66. K. J. Delaney, 1999, Compaq boosts role of internet sales, plans single pricing for firms in Europe, *Wall Street Journal,* December 8, B2.
67. J. M. Geringer, S. Tallman, & D. M. Olsen, 2000, Product and international diversification among Japanese multinational firms, *Strategic Management Journal,* 21: 51–80.
68. M. A. Hitt, R. E. Hoskisson, & R. D. Ireland, 1994, A mid-range theory of the interactive effects of international and product diversification on innovation and performance, *Journal of Management,* 20: 297–326.
69. S. Ghoshal, 1987, Global strategy: An organizing framework, *Strategic Management Journal,* 8: 425–440.
70. J. Taggart & N. Hood, 1999, Determinants of autonomy in multinational corporation subsidiaries, *European Management Journal,* 17: 226–236.
71. T. T. Herbert, 1999, Multinational strategic planning: Matching central expectations to local realities, *Long Range Planning,* 32: 81–87.
72. The weakling kicks back, 1999, *The Economist,* July 2, *www.economist.com/editorial.*
73. Ghoshal, Global strategy.
74. Y. Luo, 1999, International strategy and subsidiary performance in China, *Thunderbird International Business Review,* 41: 153–178.
75. J. K. Johaansson & G. S. Yip, 1994, Exploiting globalization potential: U.S. and Japanese strategies, *Strategic Management Journal,* 15: 579–601.
76. From desert to tundra, becoming a global power in rental, 1999, *Financial Times,* October 20, 24.
77. C. A. Bartlett & S. Ghoshal, 1989, *Managing Across Borders: The Transnational Solution* (Boston: Harvard Business School Press).
78. Luo, International strategy and subsidiary performance in China.
79. J. B. White, 1999, Ford's CEO Nasser ponders giving more authority to regional units, *Wall Street Journal Interactive,* September 17, *www.interactive.wsj.com/articles.*
80. F. Rose, 1999, Think globally, script locally, *Fortune,* November 8, 157–160.
81. Govindarajan & Gupta, Setting a course; A. Saxenian, 1994, *Regional Advantage: Culture and Competition in Silicon Valley and Route 128* (Cambridge, MA: Harvard University Press).
82. Rugman, Multinationals as regional flagships, 6.
83. L. Allen & C. Pantzalis, 1996, Valuation of the operating flexibility of multinational corporations, *Journal of International Business Studies,* 27: 633–653.
84. J. I. Martinez, J. A. Quelch, & J. Ganitsky, 1992, Don't forget Latin America, *Sloan Management Review,* 33(Winter): 78–92.
85. H. Przybyla, 2000, Strong U.S. economy pushing trade deficit with Latin America, *Houston Chronicle,* January 21, 1C; 4C.
86. J. Chang & P. M. Rosenzweig, 1998, Industry and regional patterns in sequential foreign market entry, *Journal of Management Studies,* 35: 797–822.
87. V. Govindarajan & A. Gupta, 1998, How to build a global presence, in As business goes global, Part 1, *Financial Times,* February 10–11; Madhok, Cost, value and foreign market entry mode, 41.
88. Y. Pan & P. S. K. Chi, 1999, Financial performance and survival of multinational corporations in China, *Strategic Management Journal,* 20: 359–374.
89. Punnett & Ricks, *International Business,* 249–250; G. M. Naidu & V. K. Prasad, 1994, Predictors of export strategy and performance of small- and medium-sized firms, *Journal of Business Research,* 31: 107–115.
90. P. S. Aulakh, M. Kotabe, & H. Teegen, 2000, Export strategies and performance of firms from emerging economies: Evidence from Brazil, Chile and Mexico. *Academy of Management Journal,* in press.
91. A. Dworkin, 1999, Texas exports pinched by global slowdown, *Dallas Morning News,* March 10, D1, D10.
92. J. H. Prager, 1999, Many small businesses continue to have 'euro phobia', *Wall Street Journal,* April 6, B2.
93. Hill, *International Business,* 436–437.
94. M. A. Hitt & R. D. Ireland, 2000, The intersection of entrepreneurship and strategic management research, in D. L. Sexton & H. Landstrom (eds.) *The Blackwell Handbook of Entrepreneurship* (Oxford, UK: Blackwell Publishers, Ltd.).
95. B. Schlender, 1995, Sony on the brink, *Fortune,* June 12, 66.
96. J. R. Green & S. Schotchmer, 1995, On the division of profit in sequential innovation, *The Rand Journal of Economics,* 26: 20–33.
97. B. Einhorn, 1997, China's CD pirates find a new hangout, *Business Week,* December 15, 138F.
98. A. Marsh, 1999, Big Jakk attack, *Forbes,* November 1, 274–276.
99. C. A. Bartlett & S. Rangan, 1992, Komatsu limited, in C. A. Bartlett & S. Ghoshal (eds.), *Transnational Management: Text, Cases and Readings in Cross-Border Management* (Homewood, IL: Irwin), 311–326.
100. A. Jan & M. Zeng, 1999, International joint venture instability: A critique of previous research, a reconceptualization, and directions for future research, *Journal of International Business Studies,* 30: 397–414; A. C. Inkpen & P. W. Beamish, 1997, Knowledge, bargaining power, and the instability of international joint ventures, *Academy of Management Review,* 22: 177–202; S. H. Park & G. R. Ungson, 1997, The effect of national culture, organizational com-

plementarity, and economic motivation on joint venture dissolution, *Academy of Management Journal,* 40: 279–307.
101. Y. Pan & D. K. Tse, 1996, Cooperative strategies between foreign firms in an overseas country, *Journal of International Business Studies,* 27(Special Issue): 929–946.
102. M. A. Hitt, B. W. Keats, & S. M. DeMarie, 1998, Navigating in the new competitive landscape: Building strategic flexibility and competitive advantage in the 21st century, *Academy of Management Executive,* XII(4): 22–42.
103. B. L. Simonin, 1999, Transfer of marketing know-how in international strategic alliances: An empirical investigation of the role and antecedents of knowledge ambiguity, *Journal of International Business Studies,* 30: 463–490; M. A. Lyles & J. E. Salk, 1996, Knowledge acquisition from foreign parents in international joint ventures: An empirical examination in the Hungarian context, *Journal of International Business Studies,* 27(Special Issue): 877–903.
104. M. A. Hitt, M. T. Dacin, E. Levitas, J.-L. Arregle, & A. Borza, 2000, Partner selection in emerging and developed market contexts: Resource based and organizational learning perspectives, *Academy of Management Journal,* in press; J. A. Mathews & D. S. Cho, 1999, Combinative capabilities and organizational learning in latecomer firms: The case of the Korean semiconductor industry, *Journal of World Business,* 34: 139–156.
105. D. Sparks, 1999, The global rush to find partners, *Business Week Online,* October 25, *www.businessweek.com/bwarchive.*
106. T. Burns, 2000, BT: Spanish Internet venture for telecoms group, *www.ft.com,* January 21, *www.ft.com/nbearchive.*
107. C. R. Fey & P. W. Beamish, 1999, Strategies for managing Russian international joint venture conflict, *European Management Journal,* 17: 99–106.
108. M. T. Dacin, M. A. Hitt, & E. Levitas, 1997. Selecting partners for successful international alliances: Examination of U.S. and Korean Firms, *Journal of World Business,* 32: 3–16.
109. A. C. Inkpen, 1999, Case study: Global one, *Thunderbird International Business Review,* 41: 337–353.
110. Y. Pan, S. Li, & D. K. Tse, 1999, The impact of order and mode of market entry on profitability and market share, *Journal of International Business Studies,* 30: 81–104.
111. M. A. Hitt, R. E. Hoskisson, & H. Kim, 1997, International diversification: Effects on innovation and firm performance in product-diversified firms, *Academy of Management Journal,* 40: 767–798.
112. M. A. Hitt, J. S. Harrison, & R. D. Ireland, 2001, *Creating Value through Mergers and Acquisitions* (New York: Oxford University Press).
113. T. A. Stewart, 1999, See Jack. See Jack run, *Fortune,* September 27, 124–136.
114. K. Naughton & S. Reed, 1999, *Business Week,* February 8, 40.
115. French Dressing, 1999, *The Economist,* July 10, 53–54.
116. A. Raghavan & S. Lipin, 1999, Europeans are learning mergers the American way, *Wall Street Journal,* April 23, A12; J. Rossant, 1999, Germany is leading—in the wrong direction, *Business Week,* December 13, 66.
117. K. D. Brouthers & L. E. Brouthers, 2000, Acquisition or greenfield start-up? Institutional, cultural and transaction cost influences, *Strategic Management Journal,* 21: 89–97.
118. C. S. Smith, 1999, The exotic sound of Guam: 'Attention, Kmart shoppers', *Wall Street Journal,* July 12, A17, A20.
119. W. C. Kim & P. Hwang, 1992, Global strategy and multinationals' entry mode choice, *Journal of International Business Studies,* 23: 29–53.
120. D. K Sobek, II, A. C. Ward, & J. K. Liker, 1999, Toyota's principles of set-based concurrent engineering, *Sloan Management Review,* 40(2): 53–83.
121. H. Chen, 1999, International performance of multinationals: A hybrid model, *Journal of World Business,* 34: 157–170.
122. M. Guillen, 2000. Business groups in emerging economies: A resource-based view, *Academy of Management Journal,* in press.
123. Hitt, Hoskisson, & Kim, International diversification, 767.
124. A. Delios & P. W. Beamish, 1999, Geographic scope, product diversification, and the corporate performance of Japanese firms, *Strategic Management Journal,* 20: 711–727.
125. C. Y. Tang & S. Tikoo, 1999, Operational flexibility and market valuation of earnings, *Strategic Management Journal,* 20: 749–761.
126. J. M. Geringer, P. W. Beamish, & R. C. daCosta, 1989, Diversification strategy and internationalization: Implications for MNE performance, *Strategic Management Journal,* 10: 109–119; R. E. Caves, 1982, *Multinational Enterprise and Economic Analysis* (Cambridge, MA: Cambridge University Press).
127. S. A. Zahra, R. D. Ireland, & M. A. Hitt, 2000, International expansion by new venture firms: International diversity, mode of market entry, technological learning and performance, *Academy of Management Journal,* in press.
128. B. Bremner, L. Armstrong, K. Kerwin, & K. Naughton, 1997, Toyota's crusade, *Business Week,* April 7, 104–114.
129. S. J. Kobrin, 1991, An empirical analysis of the determinants of global integration, *Strategic Management Journal,* 12(Special Issue): 17–37.
130. M. Kotabe, 1989, Hollowing-out of U.S. multinationals and their global competitiveness, *Journal of Business Research,* 19: 1–15.
131. Porter, *Competitive Advantage.*
132. M. Kotabe, 1990, The relationship between off-shore sourcing and innovativeness of U.S. multinational firms: An empirical investigation, *Journal of International Business Studies,* 21: 623–638.
133. Y. Luo, 1999, Time-based experience and international expansion: The case of an emerging economy, *Journal of Management Studies,* 36: 505–533.
134. S. Finkelstein & D. C. Hambrick, 1996, *Strategic Leadership: Top Executives and Their Effects on Organizations* (St. Paul, MN: West Publishing Company).
135. Hitt, Hoskisson, & Kim, International diversification, 790.
136. W. G. Sanders & M. A. Carpenter, 1998, Internationalization and firm governance: The roles of CEO of compensation, top team composition and board structure, *Academy of Management Journal,* 41: 158–178.
137. D. M. Reeb, C. C. Y. Kwok, & H. Y. Baek, 1998, Systematic risk of the multinational corporation, *Journal of International Business Studies,* 29: 263–279.
138. C. Pompitakpan, 1999, The effects of cultural adaptation on business relationships: Americans selling to Japanese and Thais, *Journal of International Business Studies,* 30: 317–338.
139. D. Roberts, 1999, Logged on in limbo, *Business Week,* November 15, 64.
140. J. Harding, 1999, Zeneca's long march, *Financial Times,* March 16, 17; J. Kynge, 1999, Cell phone groups face big cut in China sales, *www.ft.com,* November 10, *www.ft.com/nbearchives*; M. Forney & L. Chang, 1999, Top Chinese official declares foreign net stakes are illegal, *Wall Street Journal Interactive,* September 15, *www.interactive.wsj.com/articles.*
141. J. Moreno, 2000, Pursuing the bottom line overseas, *Houston Chronicle,* January 23, 1D, 4D.
142. Hitt, Hoskisson, & Kim, International diversification; S. Tallman & J. Li, 1996, Effects of international diversity and product diversity on the performance of multinational firms, *Academy of Management Journal,* 39: 179–196; Hitt, Hoskisson, & Ireland, A mid-range theory of interactive effects; Geringer, Beamish, & daCosta, Diversification strategy.
143. Porter, *Competitive Advantage.*
144. Hitt, Hoskisson, & Kim, International diversification.
145. Grim reaper, 1999, *Economist Online,* December 23, economist.com/editorial.

146. A. Sanders, 1999, Yankee imperialist, *Forbes,* December 13, 56.
147. Hitt, Dacin, Tyler, & Park, Understanding the differences.
148. M. A. Hitt, B. B. Tyler, & C. Hardee, 1995, Understanding strategic intent in the global marketplace, *Academy of Management Executive,* IX(2): 12–19.
149. D. P. Hamilton, M. Williams, & N. Shirouzu, 1995, Japan's big problem: Freeing its economy from over regulation, *Wall Street Journal,* April 25, A1, A6.
150. N. Athanassiou & D. Nigh, 1999, The impact of U.S. company internationalization on top management team advice networks: A tacit knowledge perspective, *Strategic Management Journal,* 20: 83–92; P. C. Ensign, 1999, The multinational corporation as a coordinated network: Organizing and managing differently, *Thunderbird International Business Review,* 41: 291–322; M. J. H. Oomens & F. A. J. van den Bosch, 1999, Strategic issue management in major European-based companies, *Long Range Planning,* 32: 49–57.

COOPERATIVE STRATEGY

CHAPTER NINE OBJECTIVES

After reading this chapter, you should be able to:

1. Identify and define different types of cooperative strategy.
2. Explain the rationale for a cooperative strategy in three types of competitive situations: slow-cycle, standard-cycle, and fast-cycle markets.
3. Understand the advantages and disadvantages of using business-level cooperative strategies.
4. Describe uses of cooperative strategies at the corporate level.
5. Discuss why international cooperative strategies are used in the form of cross-border alliances.
6. Describe the competitive risks of cooperative strategies.
7. Understand why trust is a strategic asset when using cooperative strategies.
8. Describe the two basic approaches that are used to manage strategic alliances.

Using Cooperative Strategies in the Global Automobile Industry

Competition and competitive rivalry in the global automobile industry are dynamic and intense. Contributing to this situation is overcapacity on a global scale. With excess capacity, firms often seek to enter markets that are new to them or to expand sales in currently served, yet highly lucrative, markets. Both of these strategic decisions are made possible by excess resources in the firm's primary and support activities in which it creates value (see Chapters 6 and 7).

Using focus cost leadership strategies, Korean carmakers Hyundai Motors and Kia Motors Corp. announced intentions in 2000 to increase sales in the U.S. marketplace. Hyundai sought to increase its volume from 164,000 units in 1999 to 200,000 units in 2000. Kia is concentrating on its hot-selling sports utility vehicle (SUV), the Sportage. Sales for this vehicle in the United States grew 82 percent between 1998 and 1999. To increase sales in this general market segment, Kia introduced the Spectra, a four-door hatchback, into the U.S. market in April 2000. In total, Kia expected to sell 160,000 or more units in the United States in 2000—up from 1999's volume of 134,000. The target U.S. customers for these firms' products are ". . . lower-income and middle-income buyers with cars that come loaded with features for under $20,000, with some models starting well below $10,000." Analysts believe that for some customers, these cars, backed by long-term and comprehensive warranties, are substitutes for late-model used cars.

Increasingly, firms use cooperative strategies as one means of competing in the dynamic and challenging 21st-century competitive landscape. The nature and objectives of this type of strategy being used in the global auto industry are quite varied. For example, Renault SA, France's leading automaker, is investing $400 million over a seven-year period in a production alliance with Nissan Motor Co. Through this alliance, Renault expects to produce roughly 25,000 additional vehicles annually by 2003, all of which are to be sold in Mexico. For the long term, Renault hopes to manufacture 80,000 vehicles per year under its name through this joint venture. The relationship between Renault and Nissan is an example of a complementary strategic alliance.

To improve its competitiveness in the small-car segment, business analysts and company officials as well thought that DaimlerChrysler might be forced to form alliances with other firms to manufacture some parts and platforms for a small car. The primary objective of such complementary alliances is for DaimlerChrysler and partner firms to use their resources, capabilities, and core competencies to reduce development costs. Controlling product development costs is critical to operating profitably in the world's highly competitive small-car segment. In early 2000, PSA Peugeot Citroen was in talks with DaimlerChrysler regarding the possibility of forming an alliance to produce a small-car platform. It seems that collaborating with other companies to compete successfully in the small-car market segment against firms such as Korea's Hyundai Motors and Kia Motors might be an appropriate strategic direction for DaimlerChrysler to pursue.

General Motors (GM), the world's largest automobile manufacturer, is forming a number of alliances. With Toyota Motor Corp., GM has formed several technology development alliances. One of the objectives of this partnership is to cooperate on advanced environmental technology. In a more complicated cooperative arrangement, Honda Motor Co. and GM formed a basic agreement under which Honda sells low-emission gasoline engines to GM, and Isuzu (a Japanese manufacturer in which GM holds a 49 percent equity stake) supplies fuel-efficient diesel engines to Honda. In early 2000, GM purchased a 20 percent stake in Fuji Heavy Industries for approximately $1.4 billion. Fuji manufactures Subaru vehicles. When formed, this equity strategic alliance, one that is intended to reduce the uncertainty associated with GM's operations in Asia, involved the two companies exchanging technologies, including Fuji's four-wheel-drive systems and continuous variable transmission and GM's environmental technologies, such as its knowledge about fuel cell systems. According to analysts, these cooperative agreements are being developed because, "GM is trying to boost its share of the auto market in the Asia-Pacific region to 10 percent from just over 4 percent currently. But the number one auto maker has elected to do so partly by forming strategic alliances." Furthermore, an equity-based partnership with Fuji gives GM a presence in a different market segment as well as access to technologies such as the continuous variable transmission, which may be a source of competitive advantage for Fuji in the global automobile market. Thus, learning how to use cooperative strategies is becoming an important source of competitive advantage and strategic competitiveness for many of the world's automakers.

http://www.citroen.com

http://www.daimler chrysler.com

http://www.gm.com

http://www.honda.com

http://www.hyundai.com

http://www.kia.com

http://www.nissanmotors .com

http://www.renault.com

http://www.toyota.com

SOURCES: J. Flint, 2000, No guts no glory, *Forbes,* February 7, 88; S. Freeman, 2000, Auto firms see a boost in sales for Korean cars, *Wall Street Journal,* January 13, A6; G. L. White, 2000, GM stops making electric car, holds talks with Toyota, *Wall Street Journal,* January 12, A14; B. S. Akre, 1999, Toyota alliance could lead to bigger things, GM exec hints, *Dallas Morning News,* April 6, D6; A. Harney, 1999, Toyota seeks technology alliances, *Financial Times,* July 19, 18; S. Miller & J. Ball, 1999, Daimler faces big test in small-car market, *Wall Street Journal,* November 29, A20, A25; S. Miller & D. Woodruff, 1999, Peugeot is set to aid Daimler on small car, *Wall Street Journal,* December 10, A15; J. Millman, 1999, Renault to invest $400 million in Mexico in production alliance with Nissan, *Wall Street Journal,* December 13, A28; R. L. Simison, 1999, GM nears agreement to buy 20 percent stake in Japan's Fuji Heavy for $970.2 million, *Wall Street Journal,* December 8, A4; R. L. Simison & N. Shirouzu, 1999, GM may buy Honda gasoline engines: Both car makers consider other deals, *Wall Street Journal,* December 11, B5; R. L. Simison & N. Shirouzu, 1999, GM pursues new links with Japanese, *Wall Street Journal,* December 3, A3.

As discussed in different parts of the book's first eight chapters (especially in Chapter 3), the characteristics of the 21st-century's landscape make it necessary for firms to constantly re-create themselves to achieve competitive success.[1] Firms failing to do this risk decline and failure.[2] Enron Corp., the $30-plus billion dollar energy broker, is known as a company that has been able to continually reinvent itself with new products and by entering new markets.[3] According to some analysts, Enron's "audacious executives (now) think they can fundamentally alter the way the Internet works." Providing at least minimal support for belief in the firm's ability to achieve this objective is the fact that Enron has consistently been voted the Most Innovative Large Company in the Untied States in *Fortune* magazine's Most Admired Companies survey.[4] In general, how a firm re-creates itself is through use of newly developed competitive advantages and, more broadly, through the selection and implementation of different strategies or by using current strategies differently to increase the firm's effectiveness.

To this point in the book, competition among firms has been our focus. The previous chapters facilitate an understanding of competitive advantage and strategic competitiveness through strong positions against external challenges, maximizing of core competencies, and minimizing of weaknesses. This chapter focuses on gaining competitive advantage through cooperation with other firms.[5] This happens when firms find ways to combine their unique resources and capabilities to create core competencies that competitors find difficult to understand and imitate.[6]

Demonstrated by our discussion of the topics in this chapter is the fact that alliances are blurring the distinction between competitors and allies in some industries. For example, in the computer industry, IBM and Dell recently formed an alliance through which IBM will sell $16 billion in parts to frequent competitor Dell over a seven-year period. Analysts say that this alliance "positions IBM as a premier parts provider to one of the world's fastest growing computer firms. In exchange, people familiar with the matter said that Dell . . . receives reduced royalty rates on technology it currently licenses from IBM at what are believed to be steep prices."[7] Thus, the 21st-century's landscape involves a complex web of competitive interactions and dynamics (see Chapter 5).

Since roughly the mid-1980s, cooperative strategies have become increasingly popular as a way for a firm to at least partially re-create itself to use different competitive advantages to pursue strategic competitiveness.[8] Some refer to this trend as "coopetiton" in that major competitors are forming cooperative arrangements to compete against competitors, often those from other nations.[9] The Internet's capabilities provide an interesting medium through which effective cooperative strategies are being formed.[10] Wal-Mart, for example, is providing its own Internet service through an alliance with AOL, an Internet provider that is used widely by individual consumers. Through this alliance, Wal-Mart believes that it has access to a larger percentage of its giant customer base (data show that about one-third of Americans shop at Wal-Mart each week). Wal-Mart's comprehensive on-line shop includes "over 600,000 items from clothing to shampoo to computers to garden supplies, also offering services such as airline, hotel and car-rental booking, as well as a way to reorder a personal shopping list of essentials with one click."[11] The current plans are for the site to be updated quarterly with new items.

Strategic alliances are a primary form of cooperative strategies. Speaking to the increasing popularity of strategic alliances as an important cooperative strategy, two researchers note that an "unprecedented number of strategic alliances between firms are being formed each year. [These] strategic alliances are a logical and timely response to intense and rapid changes in economic activity, technology, and globalization, all of which have cast many corporations into two competitive races: one for the world and the other for the future."[12] Another indicator of the popularity of cooperative strategies is the fact that over 20,000 strategies alliances were formed in a recent two-year period on a worldwide basis; more than half of those alliances were between competitors.[13]

Although being used more frequently by companies headquartered within the same country, alliances are also increasingly popular with firms located in international markets. In this instance, alliances are formed between companies with headquarters in different countries. Discussed later in the chapter, these cooperative arrangements typically are called *cross-border alliances;* the arrangement between Electrolux and Toshiba is an example of a cross-border alliance. Through an alliance that is centered around white goods, the Swedish firm gains access to the Japanese market, while Toshiba hopes to gain the technical and marketing help it requires to improve the profitability of what is a loss-making business for it. In total, the alliance covers 15 projects in four main areas: technology, sourcing, marketing, and environmental issues.[14]

Even in light of the global economy's competitive realities, not all firms are positively predisposed to being involved with cooperative strategies. In the words of Takeshi Tanaka, president of Fuji Heavy Industries, "We will always build cars with our own distinctive features. We are not interested in putting our engine in Nissan's cars and selling bigger and bigger volumes. We would rather build cars using our own capabilities, pushing capacity to its fullest or increasing it in certain areas, and strengthen the Fuji Heavy and Subaru brand."[15] Shortly after articulating this position, Fuji entered into the strategic alliance with GM that we mentioned in the Opening Case. Thus, the realities of the 21st-century competitive landscape are such that firms may need to participate in cooperative strategies even if their preference is to avoid doing so.

As a prominent cooperative strategy, strategic alliances can serve a number of purposes. However, firms considering alliances must understand that managing them tends to be difficult.[16] Reflecting this difficulty is the fact that many alliances encounter trouble and that a number of them fail. In fact, evidence shows that two-thirds of all alliances have serious problems in their first two years and that as many as 70 percent of them fail.[17] A corporate alliance mind-set increases the probability of an alliance succeeding. Shared among all organizational members, an effective alliance mind-set is one through which *both* the strengths and risks of a firm's entire set of alliance relationships are recognized and understood by all involved with alliance formation and use.[18]

Types of Cooperative Strategies

Strategic alliances are partnerships between firms whereby their resources, capabilities, and core competencies are combined to pursue mutual interests in designing, manufacturing, or distributing goods or services.

As previously noted, strategic alliances are a primary type of cooperative strategy. **Strategic alliances** are partnerships between firms whereby their resources, capabilities, and core competencies are combined to pursue mutual interests in designing, manufacturing, or distributing goods or services.[19] An important attribute of strategic alliances is that they allow firms to leverage their resources.[20] Thus, one of the theoretical foundations of strategic alliances resides in the resource-based view of the firm.[21] In Chapter 3's discussion on the resource-based view, we talked about the importance of a firm being able to leverage resources to achieve its strategic intent—that is, to achieve what at first may seem to be unattainable goals. At a broader level, some believe that strategic alliances will play an increasingly important role in the consolidation of industries that is anticipated in the 21st century. A reason for this is that through alliances, companies overcome barriers (e.g., antitrust provisions) that sometimes prevent a firm's direct competitive entry into another nation's marketplace.[22]

A **joint venture** is when two or more firms create a independent company by combining parts of their assets.

Strategic alliances are explicit forms of relationships between firms. They come in three basic types. One type of strategic alliance is a **joint venture,** in which two or more firms create an independent company by combining parts of their assets. Joint ventures are effective in establishing long-term relationships and in transferring tacit knowledge, an important source of competitive advantage[23] (see discussion of this topic in Chapter 3). Commonly, partner firms own an equal percentage of a joint venture's equity. For example, Dan River, a U.S. manufacturer of bed sheets, home-textile goods and apparel fabrics has formed two joint ventures with Grupo Industrial Zaga, located in Mexico City. Through DanZa Textil—one of the ventures—the partners built a weaving plant that produces lightweight apparel fabrics. The second joint venture is producing sportswear. This particular venture represents Dan River's initial move into the actual manufacturing of garments. In both ventures, the firms are equal partners. In a 50/50 ownership of a joint venture (called Citistreet in the financial services sector), Citigroup Inc. and State Street Corp. entered the defined contribution market. This venture combines Citigroup's marketing core competence with State Street's "brand name" presence in the field.

Experience shows that joint ventures are framed around virtually any issue that is of common interest to involved parties. GM and DaimlerChrysler, for example, initiated talks in late 1999 about forming a charter aircraft joint venture. To be called Air Automotive, the purpose of the venture is to share a company aircraft fleet in order to cut costs and improve usage rates.[24]

An **equity strategic alliance** consists of partners who own different percentages of equity in a new venture.

A second type of strategic alliance is an **equity strategic alliance**; here, partners own different percentages of equity in a new venture. Many foreign direct investments are completed through equity strategic alliances, such as those by Japanese and U.S. companies in China.[25] Ford Motor Company and Mazda Motor Corporation formed an equity strategic alliance some time ago. Recently, four large Japanese companies formed this type of alliance to sell books through the Internet. Called e-shopping! Books, the partners hope to emulate Amazon.com's success by providing what they envision to be a Japanese version of that firm's operations. Softbank, a computer software and publishing company, holds the largest share (50 percent) of the venture, while Yahoo! Japan and Tohan, a leader publisher and book distributor, each own 10 percent. The remaining 30 percent equity position in this venture is held by Seven-Eleven Japan, the nation's largest convenience store operator.[26] Equity strategic alliances are considered more effective at transferring know-how between firms because they are closer to hierarchical control than are nonequity alliances.[27]

Nonequity strategic alliances are formed through contractual agreements given to a company to supply, produce, or distribute a firm's goods or services without equity sharing.

Nonequity strategic alliances are formed through contractual agreements given to a company to supply, produce, or distribute a firm's goods or services without equity sharing. Other types of cooperative contractual arrangements concern marketing and information sharing. Because they do not involve the forming of a separate venture or equity investments, nonequity strategic alliances are less formal and demand fewer commitments from partners than joint ventures and equity strategic alliances.[28] The attributes of nonequity alliances make them unsuitable for complex projects where success is to be influenced by effective transfer of tacit knowledge between partners.[29]

Tacit collusion exists when several firms in an industry cooperate tacitly to reduce industry output below the potential competitive level, thereby increasing prices above the competitive level.

Our focus in this chapter is on the explicit forms of strategic alliances just discussed. However, firms sometimes engage in implicit cooperative arrangements. Tacit collusion is an example of an implicit cooperative arrangement. **Tacit collusion** exists when several firms in an industry cooperate tacitly to reduce industry output below the potential competitive level, thereby increasing prices above the competitive level.[30]

Most strategic alliances, however, exist not to reduce industry output, but to increase learning, facilitate growth, or increase returns and strategic competitiveness.[31]

Cooperative agreements may also be explicitly collusive, which is illegal in the United States unless regulated by the government, as was the case in the telecommunications industries until recent deregulation. *Mutual forbearance* (another term for tacit collusion) is tacit recognition of interdependence, but it has the same effect as explicit collusion in that it reduces output and increases prices. Mutual forbearance is defined and explained in Chapter 6.

The following sections explain strategic alliances in depth. We first discuss reasons for engaging in strategic alliances. This is followed by examining strategic alliances at the business-unit level and then at the corporate and international levels. In addition, we describe network strategies where the cooperative relations among firms produce multiple alliances. Thus, we discuss how strategies among multiple alliance partnerships differ from those with two partner alliances. The major risks of pursuing the various alliance types are considered. Finally, we discuss the importance of trust as a strategic asset to foster cooperative strategies that create competitive advantage and approaches used to manage alliances.

Reasons Firms Develop Strategic Alliances

Different reasons support participation in strategic alliances.[32] The reasons for cooperation differ based on three types of basic market situations: slow cycle, standard cycle, and fast cycle.[33] All three types were discussed in Chapter 5. As noted in the earlier chapter, *slow-cycle* markets refer to markets that are sheltered or near monopolies, such as railroads and, historically, telecommunications companies and utilities. Often, these companies cooperate to develop standards (e.g., to regulate air or train traffic), but because they can also collude to reduce competition, the government usually provides significant regulation to avoid consumer price discrimination. *Standard-cycle* market cooperation can result from firms trying to avoid overcapacity, rather than attempting to increase their opportunities. These cooperative arrangements often focus on increasing firms' market power. *Fast-cycle* markets frequently involve entrepreneurial firms offering new goods or services with short life cycles that are imitated quickly. In these markets, a cooperative strategy is used to gain strategic competitiveness by increasing the speed of product development or market entry. The reasons for strategic alliances in each of these market types are listed in Table 9.1.

Slow-Cycle Markets

Firms in *slow-cycle markets* tend to seek entry into markets that are restricted or try to establish franchises in new markets. For instance, many firms in slow-cycle markets consider cooperative strategic alliances in emerging markets that usually have restricted entry. In emerging markets in Eastern Europe, Russia, Latin America, India, China, and elsewhere, utility firms from developed countries are strongly motivated to form strategic alliances with local partners. For example, as deregulation occurs in the United States, U.S. telecommunications firms have the opportunity to share in establishing a near-monopoly franchise in these emerging markets. Companies operating in emerging markets desire these alliances because they need the expertise and technological know-how that can be provided by firms from developed countries. For

Table 9.1 | Reasons for Strategic Alliances by Market Type

Market	Reason
Slow Cycle	• Gain access to a restricted market • Establish a franchise in a new market • Maintain market stability (e.g., establishing standards)
Standard Cycle	• Gain market power (reduce industry overcapacity) • Gain access to complementary resources • Overcome trade barriers • Meet competitive challenges from other competitors • Pool resources for very large capital projects • Learn new business techniques
Fast Cycle	• Speed up development of new goods or service • Speed up new market entry • Maintain market leadership • Form an industry technology standard • Share risky R&D expenses • Overcome uncertainty

instance, headquartered in France, Alcatel is the world's fourth largest telecommunications company with operations in over 130 countries. The company seeks to sell unique products to customers such as products associated with a fast-growing niche that carries voice and data calls over the same lines.[34] To reach its objectives, Alcatel has established strong market positions through joint ventures with local partners in Mexico and China.[35] It is also a leading telecommunications equipment supplier in South Africa and other emerging markets.

However, telecommunication companies also form alliances to compete in developed economies, as well as in emerging markets. In an equity strategic alliance, AT&T Corp. and British Telecommunications PLC took a combined 30 percent ownership position (worth $1.84 billion at the time) in Japan Telecom Co. This was the first joint investment the two firms completed since they announced their intention to participate as global partners "to serve international business customers and carriers."[36]

Utility firms participating in energy-related industries also use strategic alliances. In the petrochemical industry, for example, Petroleos de Venezuela and Petrobras of Brazil recently formed a joint venture that calls for cross-investments between the partners. The eventual goal of this cooperative arrangement is to form a pan-Latin American energy cooperative with other countries. To reach this ultimate goal, the initial partners seek to expand their venture to add other state-owned oil companies in the region, including Colombia's Ecopetrol and Petroleos Mexicanos.[37]

Experience shows that achieving cooperation among partner firms in slow-cycle markets can be difficult. Near monopolies usually seek to be self-sustaining rather than be maintained jointly by partners. For example, as competition for telecommunication services emerges in Europe, a number of telecommunication firms that were previously state monopolies have sought to cooperate and form strategic alliances.

The Global One Alliance, formed initially in 1994 by France Telecom SA, Sprint Corp., and Deutsche Telekom AG, has been plagued by disagreements among the partners. One reason for this is that the partners often compete in multiple markets against each other. In early 2000, expectations were that Sprint would sell its stake to its two European partners. Analysts believed that following this transaction, "The European companies would then conduct an auction in which each company places a bid for Global One with an independent party. The high bidder will buy out the remaining partner."[38] Thus, although alliance opportunities exist in slow-cycle markets, they are not without managerial challenges and corporate risk.

As shown by our discussion of strategic actions being taken by firms competing in the telecommunications and energy industries, the 21st-century's competitive landscape is one in which slow-cycle markets are becoming quite rare. The Internet's capabilities are a reason for this, as demonstrated by Enron's intention of fundamentally changing how the Internet is used (see the discussion at the beginning of the chapter). Firms that historically have competed in slow-cycle markets should recognize that their future is one that in all likelihood will require them to learn how to compete in standard-cycle market conditions at a minimum and perhaps even learn how to be successful in terms of fast-cycle market characteristics.

Standard-Cycle Markets

In *standard-cycle markets,* which are often large and oriented toward economies of scale (e.g., automobile and commercial aerospace), alliances are more likely to be between partners with complementary resources, capabilities, and core competencies (see Table 9.1). In markets where economies of scale are important for competitive parity or advantage, large international alliances are useful because national markets may be too small to support the scale-efficient nature of the businesses. Therefore, the increasing globalization of markets presents opportunities to combine resources, capabilities, and competencies. This is a primary reason for alliances between automobile firms such as the alliance formed by Ford and Mazda. However, recent evidence suggests that this alliance is not yielding totally positive strategic outcomes. Ford owns one-third of Mazda and essentially runs the company. Between 1997 and the end of 1999, Mazda had three presidents, all from Ford.[39] Nonetheless, because of potential synergies that are possible from this alliance, Ford remains committed to finding ways to derive the value it believes resides in the complementary resources possessed by the two companies.

Today, the Internet is shaping auto companies' international alliances. For example, in early 2000, GM held initial discussions with several companies, including Toyota and Honda, about joining its Internet marketplace for suppliers. Called GM TradeXchange, the Internet-based venture was intended to reduce costs for partner companies as they combined their purchases electronically to win larger discounts from suppliers.[40] Demonstrating the fluidity of alliances being considered by the world's automakers is the fact that less than a month after being contacted by GM, Toyota accepted an invitation from Ford to consider participating in its Web-based marketplace venture. Called AutoXchange, Ford's Internet operation was a competitor to GM's TradeXchange. As with the GM alliance, AutoXchange was designed to bring auto manufacturers and suppliers together in efforts to reduce costs through increased efficiencies.[41]

The Internet helps firms competing in standard-cycle markets gain economies of scale through cooperation. Humana Inc., the large managed-care concern, formed an alliance with Healtheon/WebMC Corp. The focus of the alliance is to process claims and other health-care transactions more efficiently by using the Internet. Increased cost efficiencies, Humana believes, will allow the firm to provide better service to both patients and physicians.[42]

Firms also may cooperate in standard-cycle markets to gain market power and pool resources to meet capital needs (see Table 9.1). These two reasons support the alliance formed between Goodyear Tire and Rubber of the United States and Sumitomo Rubber Industries of Japan. The cooperative arrangement calls for the firms to organize four joint-venture-operating companies and two global service and support operations. By pooling resources in these fashions, the partners believe that operating synergies would result in savings of between $300 and $360 million in the first three years of the alliance's life. In addition, the deal calls for Sumitomo to help Goodyear gain better access to the crowded Japanese original equipment and after-tire markets, while Goodyear is to facilitate Sumitomo's relaunch of its Dunlop brand into European markets.[43] To pool resources and enhance competitiveness, DuPont Co. is seeking partners "to bring its small pharmaceuticals business to critical mass through strategic alliances."[44] Finally, firms in standard-cycle markets also may form alliances to overcome trade barriers (see Chapter 8) and to learn new business techniques.

Fast-Cycle Markets

Fast-cycle markets, which have short product cycles, such as those among electronics firms, create incentives for cooperation because the development, manufacture, and distribution of a new good or service can happen more quickly. Alignment between a company and its customers requires more frequent redefinition than is the case in standard- and slow-cycle markets.[45] Thus, an important benefit of using alliances in fast-cycle markets is rapid entry into new markets. For example, Softbank Corporation sponsors a $1.2 billion venture fund called Softbank Capital Partners (SCP). The objective of this operation is to help capitalize Internet-based strategic alliances that cross industry and market-segment borders in fast-cycle markets. Currently, SCP has investment positions in approximately 120 Internet businesses. Through its 23 percent stake in Yahoo!, SCP has helped the company form its own alliances to expand its content and service offerings. Transformed into Yahoo Resume, Webhire was an on-line recruiting firm with which Yahoo formed an alliance. Even though AOL and CMGI's Alta Vista portals are Yahoo rivals, SCP is willing to coinvest in alliances with its competitors. Coinvestments such as these demonstrate the blurring of corporate identities as well as the increasing number of cases in which companies simultaneously cooperate and compete. The words of a business analyst indicate why concurrent cooperation and competition are becoming relatively common: "We're at a stage where there's a transformation of the economic infrastructure. It's too big a problem for any one company to solve. So you cooperate to create value."[46]

Other companies, such as Global Crossing and Hutchison Whampoa, a Hong Kong-based conglomerate, use cooperative arrangements to compete differently in fast-cycle markets. To speed entry into a new market, these firms formed a joint venture (with each partner having a 50 percent stake) called Hutchison Global Crossing (this venture is mentioned in Chapter 5). The venture's objective was to pursue fixed-line communications and Internet opportunities in Hong Kong and China, when permitted to do so by expected regulatory changes.[47] This means of competing differs from Softbank Corporation and CMGI (see the Opening Case in Chapter 6). These two firms use cooperative arrangements to sell Internet capacity and infrastructure equipment rather than to operate Internet portals or provide media content. This competitive approach is in response to the global frenzy of Internet traffic.

Cooperative arrangements between firms competing in fast-cycle markets where significant levels of uncertainty exist can also lead to the development of standard products.[48] For instance, Sematech, a cooperative strategic alliance formed by multiple electronic and semiconductor firms, was quite important in establishing the adoption of the UNIX standard operating system for workstation computer producers.[49] Today, firms are forming alliances such as the one between Intel and Hewlett-Packard to develop an entirely new kind of microprocessor chip with the potential to establish a new industry standard. The fact that the alliance to develop this new chip, dubbed the Merced, is now in trouble shows the complexity of firms using alliances to set industry standards in fast-cycle markets.[50]

Business-Level Cooperative Strategies

As our discussion shows, many reasons support a firm's use of strategic alliances when pursuing strategic competitiveness, including the desire to use them as a substitute for vertical integration.[51] In this section, we explain four types of business-level cooperative strategies: complementary strategies, competition reduction strategies, competition response strategies, and uncertainty reduction strategies (see Figure 9.1). Following our discussion of these four business-level cooperative strategies is an assessment of the potential competitive advantages associated with each one.

FIGURE 9.1 | Types of Business- and Corporate-Level Strategic Alliances

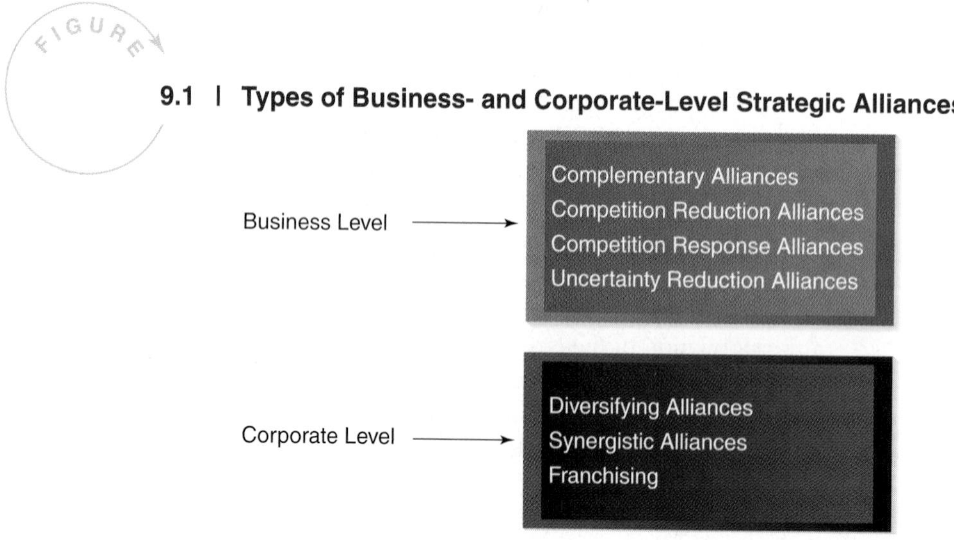

One type of cooperative arrangement used to engage in outsourcing is to contract with another firm to distribute goods or services. Manufacturers of computers and other hardware contract with CompUSA to sell their goods and provide services to customers.

Complementary Alliances

Complementary strategic alliances are designed to take advantage of market opportunities by combining partner firms' assets in complementary ways to create new value.

Complementary strategic alliances are designed to take advantage of market opportunities by combining partner firms' assets in complementary ways to create new value.[52] As shown in Figure 9.2, horizontal and vertical alliances are the two types of complementary strategic alliances.

Vertical Complementary Strategic Alliances

A *vertical complementary strategic alliance* is formed between firms that agree to use their skills and capabilities in different stages of the value chain to create value (see Figure 9.2). Retailer Benetton, for example, has developed a number of successful vertical complementary alliances. Benetton has core competencies in the marketing and sales primary activities. However, the firm chooses not to attempt to develop a core competence in the manufacture of clothing. Instead, Benetton uses a number of alliances with companies that are competitively skilled in terms of being able to create value when manufacturing the high-fashion, trendy clothing items for which Benetton is widely known. Partly because of the project's scale and size, Boeing Company formed vertical complementary alliances with several firms that are involved with different stages of the value chain to design and build its 777 plane. Among the partners in this venture were United Airlines and five Japanese companies that supplied a number of the plane's components. According to one of the partners involved with this project, "The development of the 777 was the fastest and most efficient construction of a new commercial aircraft ever."[53]

Discussed in Chapter 3, *outsourcing* is the purchase of a value-creating primary or support activity from another organization. A nonequity alliance, in which a contractual arrangement with another firm is developed to help in the design, manufacture, or distribution of the firm's good or service, is the particular type of cooperative

FIGURE

9.2 | Vertical and Horizontal Complementary Strategic Alliances

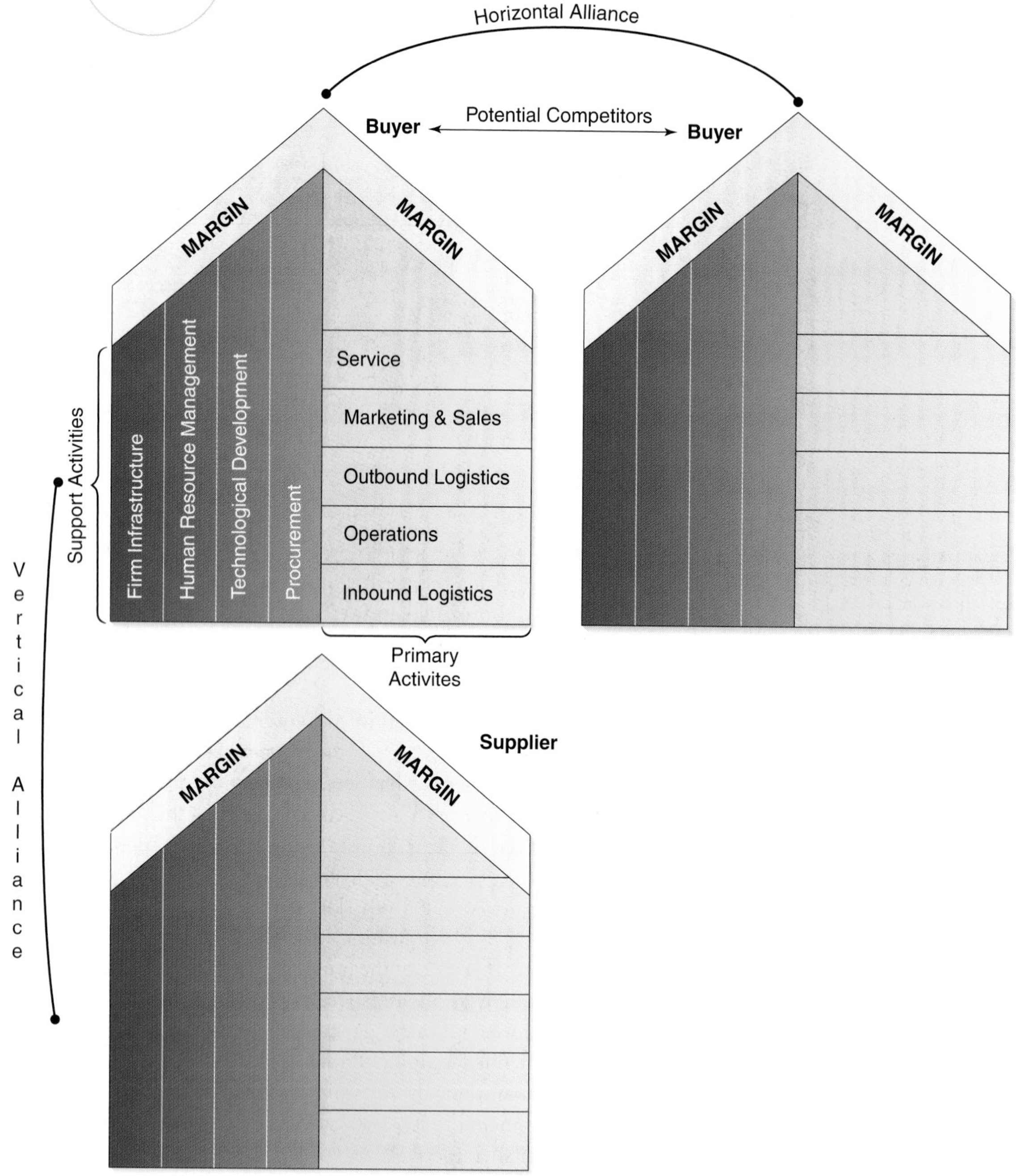

Horizontal Alliances Among Airline Companies: A Route to Increased Strategic Competitiveness?

As we noted in a Strategic Focus in Chapter 5, there is general consensus that the world's airline companies face difficult competitive conditions. Among the chief issues are the expenses associated with flying, maintaining, and updating aircraft and the stiff price competition among carriers that causes sales revenues to be under constant pressure. It is possible that through industry consolidation airline companies would be able to increase sales revenue through new routes they would acquire and would be able to use their larger size to reduce costs. However, because of laws and regulations, airline companies are prevented from using cross-border merger and acquisition strategies to consolidate their industry. The specifics of legal constraints vary by country or geographic regions. In the United States, for example, non-U.S. companies are not permitted to own more than 25 percent of a U.S. airline firm's stock. The ownership ceiling for foreign ownership of an airline based in a European Union country is 49.9 percent.

The realities of the political/legal segment of airline companies' general external environment (see Chapter 2) are a key driving force of the pattern of alliance activity occurring in the global airline industry. As previously noted, legal constraints prevent these companies from gaining economies of scale and economies of scope by using merger and acquisition strategies. Because they can result in some of the benefits of a merger or an acquisition, strategic alliances are a viable option for the world's airline companies. Describing the similarity of the benefits a firm can gain through a merger or acquisition and a strategic alliance, a business writer noted that through an alliance, "If an airline does not fly to a destination, it can instead sell seats on an alliance partner's flight that does go there. The alliance partners can also pool their frequent flyer programs, encouraging passengers not to desert them for other carriers." These practices are attempts to increase revenues for alliance partners with minimal capital investments; they also demonstrate airline companies' interest in being able to support their passengers' desire to reach a particular destination, even when they do not provide service to that destination.

Alliances formed among airline companies have changed the competitive dynamics in their industry. In one instance, a comprehensive alliance between two European-based airline firms is thought to be an initial step toward a merger. KLM of the Netherlands and Italy's Alitalia agreed to an alliance calling for them to combine their management staffs and marketing and sales organizations and to jointly purchase aircraft. Executives from the two firms anticipated that two to three years would be required to complete the merger, even if it were to be approved by the European Commission. The two main obstacles to a full merger "were that Alitalia was still not fully privatized and that Italy and the Netherlands had separate bilateral air agreements with the U.S. This meant that a half Dutch merged airline would not be able to fly from Italy to the U.S. A half Italian airline would have difficulty flying from the Netherlands."

Previous to KLM and Alitalia's efforts to merge, an attempt to form a comprehensive alliance between U.K.-based British Airways (BA) and U.S.-based American Airlines (AA) failed to gain regulatory approval. A key reason for this failure was a decision by U.S. authorities and the European Commission that BA would have to relinquish hundreds of take-off and landing slots at London's Heathrow airport for the alliance with American to receive regulatory clearance. Regulators believed that operating jointly, BA's and AA's dominance at Heathrow, an airport to which many carriers desire to fly, would stifle competition. Because BA declined the Commission's requirement, the alliance was not approved. Nonetheless, consistent with regulations, BA and AA continue to engage in code-sharing practices and cross-use of their frequent flyer programs.

While proceeding with its intentions of forming a merger, KLM and Alitalia also simultaneously teamed with U.S.-based Northwest and Continental in an alliance called Wings. Other global alliances among airline companies include (1) Oneworld (headed by BA and AA, but including other airlines—Cathay Pacific, Quantas, Finnair, LanChile, Iberia, and Canadian), and (2) Star (headed by Lufthansa of Germany and United Airlines of the United States and including SAS, Air Canada, Thai Airways, Varig, Air New Zealand, Ansett Australia, and All Nippon Airways). In late 1999 and early 2000, Air France and Delta, as primary partners, formed what at that time was an unnamed alliance with Sabena, Austrian, and Swissair. This was the fifth global horizontal alliance formed among airline companies since 1997. The fourth largest in the world, the alliance between Air France and Delta chose Havas Advertising's Euro RSCG Worldwide to receive a $30 million contract to establish an image for this alliance in the face of competition from the other airline global partnerships. The Air France/Delta alliance is expected to be a significant competitor of Oneworld, Star, and Wings. An important reason for this, analysts note, is that the alliance links Delta's Atlanta hub, the world's largest, with Paris-Charles de Gaulle, "the European hub offering the best potential for growth." Data show that this alliance joins together a European airline with 37 million passengers, 210 aircraft, roughly 50,000 employees, and $260 million in net income in 1998–1999 with a U.S. counterpart using 584 planes to serve 112 million passengers annually. Employing over 70,000 people, Delta had a 1999 net income of $1.1 billion.

Are these cooperative strategies, in the form of horizontal complementary strategic alliances, improving airline partners' strategic competitiveness? Evidence is mixed, but encouraging. Typically, performances expected from alliances run high. Air France chairman Jean-Cyril Spinetta anticipated that his firm's alliance with Delta (and the other partners) would add about FFr1 billion ($160 million) to the firm's results within two to three years—FFr700 million in revenue and FFr300 million from cost reductions. Studies of actual results from alliances indicate that partners' financial performances often do improve. Lufthansa, for example, generated an increase of DM500 million in 1998 through its participation in the Star alliance. However, alliances are proving less successful in terms of cost reductions. Stifling efforts among alliance partners to jointly purchase "everything from toilet paper to aircraft" is the airline companies' failure to establish common computer systems and similar service standards.

Although airline horizontal complementary strategic alliances may not be yielding the robust results companies want, the 21st-century landscape seems to demand their formation. Commenting about this, an airline executive suggested that, "In an environment of liberalized air transportation, every airline must be able to take advantage of the available chances." One of these opportunities is the Web site that almost two dozen airlines from across the globe formed to offer tickets, including discounted Internet-only special fares. United Airlines, Delta Air Lines, Northwest Airlines, and Continental Airlines created the Web site for this cooperative arrangement. The site is a competitive response to Travelocity.com, Expedia Inc., and other Web sites that appeal to independent-minded travelers—those willing to search Web sites to find the best fares. Thus, it appears that horizontal strategic alliances among airlines, ones through which complementary resources are combined to pursue mutual gains, will remain a viable and prominent strategic option in the 21st century for airline companies.

SOURCES: S. Carey, 2000, Nearly two dozen airlines will join planned Web site of four big carriers, *Wall Street Journal,* January 13, B4; Euro RSCG will promote Air France/Delta alliance, 2000, *Wall Street Journal,* January 25, B9; W. Hall, 1999, SAirGroup seeks promotion in global aviation league, *Financial Times,* June 28, 20; D. Owen & M. Skapinker, 1999, Delta and Air France form alliance, *Financial Times,* June 23, 8; D. Owen & M. Skapinker, 1999, Air France set to form fourth alliance, *Financial Times,* June 18, 8; M. Skapinker, 1999, BA fails to land its alliance with American, *Financial Times,* July 30, 3; M. Skapinker, 1999, KLM and Alitalia likely to merge, *Financial Times,* July 30, 3; M. Skapinker, 1999, Airlines bent on bigamy ruffle alliances, *Financial Times,* June 23, 8.

arrangement used to engage in outsourcing.[54] For example, to control costs and to remain abreast of the latest technologies, J.P. Morgan outsourced its Information Technology (IT) function to Pinnacle Alliance. Pinnacle is a consortium formed by Andersen Consulting, AT&T Solutions, Computer Sciences Corporation, and Bell Atlantic Network Integration. As J.P. Morgan's chairman, Douglas A. Warner III, explained, "Technology is critical to J.P. Morgan's success—so critical, and on so many specialized fronts, that no one firm can be a leader in all of them. . . . Teaming up with these firms will [increase] our ability to exploit new technologies, manage costs, and create competitive advantage."[55]

Horizontal Complementary Alliances

A *horizontal complementary strategic alliance* is formed between partners who agree to combine their resources and skills to create value in the same stage of the value chain. Commonly, firms form this type of an alliance to focus on long-term product and service technology development.[56] However, competing firms sometimes form horizontal complementary alliances to jointly market their goods or services. CSK Auto Inc. and Advance Auto Parts, for example, joined forces to establish a separate company called PartsAmerica.com. This Web-based venture allows consumers and repair shops to buy parts on-line. An interesting competitive feature to this alliance is that customers can pick up parts ordered on-line from either company's local stores (CSK operates stores under the trade names Checker Auto Parts, Shuck's Auto Supply, and Kragen Auto Parts; Advance Auto's stores are called Advance Auto). Customers can also use the stores to return or exchange products that were ordered on-line.[57] BMG Entertainment and Universal Music, two of the world's largest record companies, are expanding their joint Internet-based venture, called Getmusic.com. Operating initially in the United States, the partners' success with Getmusic.com encouraged expansion into international markets. This decision came at a time "when the established music industry is aggressively stepping up its investment in the Internet and other digital distribution vehicles."[58] As explained in the Strategic Focus, the world's airline companies are involved with a host of horizontal complementary strategic alliances in efforts to reduce costs and increase revenues.

A final observation about trust's role in horizontal and vertical complementary strategic alliances is useful. Company experiences show that perceptions about partner trustworthiness tend to be different between the two types of complementary alliances. Accounting for this difference is the fact that horizontal alliance partners are simultaneously competitors. This is not the case in vertical alliances where partners use their respective competitive advantages in different parts of the value chain to create mutually beneficial value. For example, the successful relationship Benetton has with the suppliers of its products is partly based on trust that has been developed across time as a result of positive outcomes from previous business transactions.

In contrast, the horizontal alliance between CSK Auto Inc. and Advance Auto Parts may prove less successful, simply because the firms compete directly with one another in bricks-and-mortar storefronts while cooperating through an Internet-based collaboration. In other words, simply because these two firms, as well as others involved in horizontal complementary alliances, are simultaneously cooperating and competing, there may be less of a basis for trust.

Similarly, the level of trust among the airline companies discussed in the Strategic Focus may be quite low because they continue to compete, even with their partners, on many routes. This may account in part for the evidence we mentioned previously about airline alliances; namely, that less than 30 percent of the alliances between international air carriers have been successful. Thus, in general, horizontal alliances tend to be shorter in duration than do vertical complementary alliances. As such, it is somewhat difficult to develop a sustainable competitive advantage through horizontal complementary strategic alliances, especially when cooperation is to occur between former competitors. This does not devalue the importance of this alliance type; rather, it suggests that companies should enter such an alliance with an understanding of the likelihood that it is an impermanent cooperative arrangement.

Competition Reduction Strategies

In the heat of rivalry, many firms may seek to avoid destructive or excessive competition. One means of avoiding such competition is tacit collusion, or mutual forbearance (see Chapter 6). This may be accomplished in some markets through cartels, such as OPEC, that seek to manage the price and output of companies (e.g., oil companies in member countries) in a specific industry. In countries around the world, governments develop policies that affect firms' efforts regarding competition reduction strategies. In the Untied States, for example, the federal government is committed to findings ways "to permit collaboration among rivals without violating antitrust laws."[59]

In general, governments seek to use competition-related policies that are consistent with the character of their nation's economics. This appears to be the case concerning a competitive situation in Russia. In the mid-1990s, Russia had a huge surplus of aluminum. When these aluminum-manufacturing firms were privatized, they began to export the metal in large quantities, an action that caused the world price to drop by as much as 50 percent. The Aluminum Association, a trade association of aluminum manufacturers, met and called for the United States to file antidumping trade charges, claiming that Russia was "dumping" aluminum below market rates. The Russians argued that they needed foreign hard currency to deal with a difficult transitional economy and to cut them off from foreign markets would create a difficult political problem. As a result, there was a meeting of government and industry officials in Brussels in 1994 that resulted in a government pact calling for "voluntary" cuts in production. Although the politicians claimed this was not a cartel, it had the same result: production cuts to sustain a world price.[60] Aluminum prices in the late 1990s increased. Prices rose from near 50 cents per pound to 65 cents in 1996 and 72 cents in 1997.[61]

Japan's economy entails a number of entrenched cartels and significant collusion. Even though economic and political forces have been working against cartels and collusion, approximately 50 percent of the manufacturing industries in Japan engage in some form of price fixing on a historical basis. Because some cartels date back to the 1600s, such anticompetitive activity in Japan is accepted and tolerated, which makes it difficult to change cartels and collusive practices. Although the situation is complex, Eastman Kodak argues that cartels and collusion reduce competition substantially, giving Japanese competitors excessive returns against which it is difficult for international firms to compete. As we discussed in Chapter 5, Kodak's market share for film in the United States continues to decrease while Fuji's increases. Partly in response to this competitive situation, Kodak is pursuing opportunities in other product areas. Early evidence from these actions is encouraging for Kodak, in that the firm's profits increased 75 percent during the fourth quarter of 1999.[62]

Recent evidence suggests that Japan's economy is now more open to foreign investment. One reason for this could be increasing acceptance of the finding that across countries, protected markets such as Japan's lead to inefficiencies throughout both the manufacturing and service sectors that contribute to poor performance in international markets.[63] Thus, the effects of competition-reducing policies may be counterproductive in the long term.

Because of eases in market entry restrictions, investors from around the world are forming a more positive image of investment opportunities in Japan. In early 2000, a study revealed that corporate investors ranked Japan their 16th-favorite investment opportunity, up from 21st in June 1999. Moreover, analysts believed that significant investments in Japan's economy would continue at least through the 21st century's first 10 years. However, this "doesn't mean it's always easy to do business (in Japan). There has been some domestic backlash recently against deregulation in (Japan's) financial services sector, and Americans still invest less here than Japanese do in the U.S." Thus, although caution is in order, global firms are becoming more confident of their ability to use their assets productively in Japan. Similarly, confidence in markets throughout Asia appears to be growing, at least as suggested by recent and dramatic increases in Asian equity markets. In 1999, for example, from "Tokyo to Singapore, markets performed as if they were on speed; Korea's Kosdaq, which is similar in composition to Nasdaq, more than quadrupled."[64]

Sometimes, firms collude directly to reduce competition. In a 1995 price-fixing scandal, three ADM executives were convicted and sentenced to jail terms for their role in fixing prices on farm commodities with other competitors.[65] Similarly, Toys "R" Us, a prominent toy retailer, was found to be in violation of U.S. federal trade laws by colluding with toy manufacturers to not sell popular toy lines to its primary competitors such as warehouse clubs Price/Costco and Sam's Club.[66] In addition to the ethical implications of collusive alliances, companies should not expect long-term competitive success through their use. Consider, for example, ADM's situation. Although not directly and totally attributable to the direct collusion just mentioned, it is interesting to note that ADM's "earnings have dropped by two-thirds to $266 million in the fiscal year that ended" on June 30, 1999.[67]

Competition Response Strategies

Companies also use strategic alliances to respond to competitors' strategic, but typically not tactical, competitive actions and reactions (see Chapter 5). For example, SAirGroup, owner of Swissair Airlines, recently bought a 20 percent stake in South African Airways. Although one of the top-quality airline names and recognized as a company with an effective top-level management team, Swissair, "unlike Air France, Lufthansa or British Airways, does not have a big home market on which it can rely to help reserve a prime position in the fast-changing world of global aviation alliances"—such as those discussed in a previous Strategic Focus. Also affecting the firm's competitive situation was Delta's decision to exit its alliance with Swissair in favor of forming one with Air France. In response to the pressures it feels from the array of strategic alliances its competitors are forming, Swissair considered other options in addition to the competitive possibilities that are associated with its investment in South African Airways, including the possibility of joining the One-World alliance dominated by AA and BA.[68]

Responding to increasing competition from Web-based ventures, some food companies are forming alliances with Internet companies. Pillsbury Co., Kellogg Co., Quaker Oats Co., General Mills, Inc., and the U.S. unit of Nestlé SA of Switzerland are participating in marketing-oriented alliances with Webvan Group Inc., a fast-growing Internet grocery store. An important benefit of such alliances is indicated by commentary from the director of e-business at Pillsbury: "We want to work with Webvan to understand how to relate to consumers that buy online." This is a critical objective, in that food manufacturers expect the 21st century to be a time during which the growth of on-line shopping will be explosive.[69] Similarly, to emulate Sun Microsystems Inc., its computer and server sales rival Hewlett-Packard (HP) formed an alliance with BEA Systems Inc. The two companies intend to work together to develop what is called middleware software products that firms can use to sell their goods or services via the Internet. Some analysts view the HP/BEA alliance "as a clear response to Sun's recent alliance with America Online Inc. In that deal, Sun and the enterprise-software unit of the former Netscape Communications Corp. plan to provide their own integrated suite of middleware and network applications."[70]

To improve its competitiveness in international mail operations, the U.S. Postal Service formed an alliance with DHL Worldwide Express Inc. Through this cooperative arrangement, the firms jointly offer a two-day delivery service between 11 major U.S. cities and any address in 18 European countries. The charges for these deliveries are significantly less than the prices of competitors' FedEx, UPS, and DHL's own trans-Atlantic operation. For the U.S. Postal Service, this alliance is a response to the rapid transformation of the world's major post offices. In particular, as private delivery companies such as FedEx and UPS expand their global delivery services, demand for "old-fashioned" international mail deliveries continues to decline.[71]

Uncertainty Reduction Strategies

Particularly in fast-cycle markets, strategic alliances are also used to hedge against risk and uncertainty.[72] Fearing the uncertainty of being able to obtain adequate exposure to a significant customer base, drkoop.com Inc. chose to pay AOL $89 million over a four-year period to become the firm's premiere health partner. Founded by former U.S. Surgeon General C. Everett Koop, drkoop.com provides consumer health information to consumers. It is competing with other new ventures to become the dominant provider of Internet-based health-care information and services. The firm's newly formed cooperative arrangement gives it access to AOL's large customer base. The investment community's positive response to the announcement of this alliance, as shown by a one-day increase of 56 percent in the value of drkoop.com's stock, seems to suggest that the future of the start-up venture is less uncertain as a result of its cooperative arrangement with AOL.[73]

Global overcapacity and fierce cost competition affected the ability of Siemens and Fujitsu to compete successfully in the world's PC business. To reduce their risk in the business line, the two firms formed a joint venture called Fujitsu Siemens Computers. Europe's second-largest computer operation was created by this cooperative arrangement. Siemens gained economies of scale required to be a leader in this industry, while Fujitsu thought the alliance would allow it to reach its long-held goal of being one of Europe's five biggest computer producers.[74] At virtually the same time that this alliance was developed, Acer, the world's third-largest PC manufacturer, formed an alliance with IBM. A multibillion-dollar seven-year procurement and technology development alliance, this arrangement was intended to strengthen Acer's relationship with its most important customer.[75]

Thus, the rapidly changing 21st-century competitive landscape may create uncertain outcomes for firms as they form and use cooperative strategies to reduce their risks. It is possible that in a competitive dynamics context (see Chapter 5), one firm's alliances can create risks and uncertainty for competitors. For example, Wal-Mart's intention of becoming a dominant Internet retailer was disconcerting to a host of firms. In a business writer's words, "Many online retailers are awaiting news of Wal-Mart's e-commerce plans with trepidation, given the unparalleled buying power of the Arkansas-based retail empire, its reputation for discount pricing and its well-established brand."[76]

In other instances, firms form alliances to reduce the uncertainty associated with developing new product or technology standards. For example, NEC, the Japanese electronics conglomerate and Hewlett-Packard are using an alliance to pool their expertise and technologies to further expand and develop their telecommunications applications. One purpose of the cooperative arrangement is to innovate the standard for next-generation communications networks.[77] In the global automobile industry, GM and Toyota formed a five-year R&D alliance that essentially makes the "no. 1 U.S. auto maker and the no. 1 Japanese auto maker partners in the competition to develop alternative-power green cars" for the 21st century. Through this alliance, the two firms expect to be able to set the industry standard for environmentally friendly vehicles.[78]

At the same time, GM and Toyota joined Ford, DaimlerChrysler, and Renault SA in an alliance to develop an industrywide standard through which their respective products would be able to accommodate the array of communications and entertainment equipment that the auto industry was developing.[79]

Assessment of Competitive Advantage for Business-Level Cooperative Strategies

Different competitive outcomes tend to be associated with the strategic alliances we have discussed. For example, alliances used to reduce competition are more likely to achieve competitive parity and average returns rather than competitive advantage and above-average returns. Firms anticipate these outcomes, in that, typically, they choose to use competition-reducing strategies on a short-term basis in efforts to reduce the negative effects of competitors' strategic or tactical competitive actions and responses. Compared with competition-reducing cooperative arrangements, complementary alliances (especially vertical ones) are more likely to create competitive advantage and contribute to the firm's earning of above-average returns. These positive strategic outcomes are possible when firms combine complementary resources in ways that reduce costs or create new competitive advantages.

Because one of their objectives is to buffer firms from the uncertainty of aggressive marketplace competition, uncertainty-reducing strategies historically have resulted in competitive parity and average returns for partners involved with this type of alliance. However, using the Internet in these partnerships, as increasingly is the case, allows firms to have full rapid access to a host of competitively relevant information. For example, drkoop.com will have opportunities to gain important insights about customers through the use of AOL's information-gathering and information-processing capabilities. Thus, the Internet's capabilities, combined with firms' growing understanding of how to properly use cooperative strategies, suggest a trend of increasing effectiveness, in terms of competitiveness and returns, across all types of business-level cooperative strategies.

Corporate-Level Cooperative Strategies

Strategic alliances designed to facilitate product and/or market diversification (see Chapter 6) are called **corporate-level cooperative strategies.** As shown in Figure 9.1, the corporate-level strategic alliances are called diversifying, synergistic, and franchising.

Strategic alliances designed to facilitate product and/or market diversification are called **corporate-level cooperative strategies.**

Diversifying Strategic Alliances

In order to grow, firms may choose to expand into new product or market areas. **Diversifying strategic alliances** allow a firm to expand into new product or market areas without completing a merger or an acquisition. A corporate-level strategic alliance is a viable strategic option for a firm that wants to grow, but chooses not to merge with or acquire another company to do so.[80]

Diversifying strategic alliances allow a firm to expand into new product or market areas without completing a merger or acquisition.

A reason that a diversifying strategic alliance is an attractive option to a merger or acquisition is that corporate-level alliances provide some of the potential synergistic benefits of a merger or acquisition, but with less risk and greater levels of flexibility.

These benefits accrue to a firm because exiting a strategic alliance is easier and costs less than divesting an acquisition that did not contribute expected levels of strategic success. In addition, some governments restrict acquisitions, especially horizontal ones (in which companies combine their assets to gain market share by creating still more value in the same stage of the value chain). This is the case in the United States, a nation in which regulators tend to think of horizontal acquisitions as an action that fosters explicit collusion when companies combine their like assets.

Gianni Versace SpA, the Italian fashion group, intends to diversify. Resort development is the first business area that is of interest to the firm's top-level management team. The firm has organized a business unit, Versace Hotel and Condominium Resort group, to focus on this business area. A corporate-level strategic alliance has been formed with Sunland Group, an Australian hotel developer, to help the Versace business unit begin its operations. The first hotel project to be completed by the alliance partners will be in the Gold Coast tourism strip of Queensland in northeast Australia.[81]

Firms might also form a diversifying alliance to determine whether a future merger would benefit both parties. For example, following the formation of one of the technology partnerships between GM and Toyota that we mentioned previously, Jack Pearce, GM's number-two executive, hinted that the cooperative arrangement could prove to be the prelude to a broader linkup between the automakers. In Pearce's words, "It would certainly be premature to talk about a merger. But I think it's important for both companies to have a very open mind in terms of where this kind of collaboration takes us."[82] The fact that a merged GM and Toyota would account for 25 percent of global automobile and truck sales demonstrates the market power the transaction would create. Sometimes, analysts think that a firm's alliance is an indication of a possible future merger when such may not be the case. Recently, Mitsubishi Motors formed an alliance with Fiat to jointly develop SUVs. In response to queries about the reason for this cooperative arrangement—especially in light of rumors that the two firms might merge their operations—a Mitsubishi executive observed that, "Mergers are not our priority. We continue to seek mutually beneficial business collaborations, without capital tie-ups."[83]

Synergistic Strategic Alliances

Synergistic strategic alliances create joint economies of scope between two or more firms. Similar to the horizontal complementary strategic alliance type that is used at the business level, synergistic strategic alliances create synergy across multiple functions or multiple businesses between partner firms. Two firms might, for example, create joint research and manufacturing facilities that they both use to their advantage and thus attain economies of scope without a merger.

Synergistic strategic alliances create joint economies of scope between two or more firms.

In the financial services sector, Rabobank and DG Bank, the Dutch and German cooperative institutions, have formed a joint venture called DG-Rabo International. This equally owned venture combines the banks' respective strengths in the corporate and investment banking businesses' areas. Viewed by some as "one of the most important cross-border partnerships yet seen in European banking," the organizations intended to meld their skills to cooperate in other areas (e.g., asset management transactions) in the future.[84] Through an array of technology-oriented synergistic alliances, Toyota is attempting to gain access to technologies that it has had difficulty develop-

Synergistic strategic alliances create synergy across multiple functions or multiple businesses between two or more partner firms.

ing on its own. Avoiding equity alliances, "the carmaker has linked with General Motors for joint development of electric, hybrid, and fuel cell vehicles (as mentioned in the Opening Case), and Volkswagen for intelligent transportation systems, recycling and marketing. It also has a tie-up with Panasonic EV Energy for batteries."[85]

Franchising

As discussed in Chapter 6, firms diversify when they can use excess resources, capabilities, and core competencies to create value in other product or geographic markets or to reduce the risk of operating in a single business area. As with diversifying strategic alliances, franchising is a cooperative strategy a firm uses to spread risk and to use resources, capabilities, and competencies productively, but without merging with or acquiring another company.[86]

As a cooperative strategy, franchising is based on a contractual relationship concerning a franchise that is developed between two parties: the franchisee and the franchisor. Thus, **franchising** is an alternative to diversification that is considered a cooperative strategy based on a contractual relationship. Defined more formally, a *franchise* is a "contractual agreement between two legally independent companies whereby the franchisor grants the right to the franchisee to sell the franchisor's product or do business under its trademarks in a given location for a specified period of time."[87]

Franchising is an alternative to diversification that is considered a cooperative strategy based on a contractual relationship.

The foundation for this cooperative strategy's success is the ability to gain economies of scale by forming multiple units while deriving operational efficiencies from the work of individual units competing in specific local markets.[88] Typically, the relationship between the franchisee and franchisor is seen as an entrepreneurial partnership, in that the parties work together to find new opportunities to achieve strategic competitiveness.[89] Franchising permits relatively strong centralized control and facilitates knowledge transfer without significant capital investment.[90] Brand name is thought to be the most effective competitive advantage for a franchise, in that, when powerful, it signals both tangible and intangible consumer benefits.[91]

Franchising is an increasingly popular strategic option on a global basis, accounting for 40 percent of retail volume in the United States, 32 percent in Great Britain, 25 percent in Australia, and 24 percent in Brazil. Overall, data show that U.S. companies dominate franchising internationally through the sheer number of franchisors and franchisees and that Canada, Japan, and Australia have franchising sectors that are as well established, although not quite as large as the U.S. franchising sector.[92] Food establishments (e.g., McDonald's, Burger King, Pizza Hut, and Dunkin' Donuts) and hotels (e.g., Hilton International) use franchising as a cooperative strategy as do a number of service firms. For example, the real estate firm Century 21 has created a nationwide chain through franchising. Examples of other firms using franchising include Charles Schwab in financial services and Service Corporation International in mortuaries. Increasingly, franchising is becoming popular in a different group of industries as well, including telecommunications (e.g., franchise systems of National Telecommunications of Bloomfield, New Jersey) and Internet-based businesses (e.g., franchise systems of Z Land of Santa Anna, CA, and First Internet Corp. of San Clamente, CA).[93]

As a cooperative strategy, franchising reduces financial risk, because franchisors commonly invest some of their own capital in the local venture. This capital investment motivates franchisors to perform well by reinforcing and emphasizing the quality, standards, and brand name that are associated with the franchisee's original business. Because of these potential benefits, franchising may provide growth at less risk than diversification. Of course, the franchising firm loses some control, but the franchise contract usually provides for performance and quality audits.

Assessment of Competitive Advantage for Corporate-Level Cooperative Strategies

As we have explained, firms use corporate-level cooperative strategies to develop competitive advantages and to reduce risk. However, corporate-level strategic decisions, such as cooperative strategies and diversification, can be influenced by managerial motives, as well as by the proper desire to achieve strategic competitiveness and earn above-average returns (see Chapter 6 for a related discussion).

In large diversified firms, incentives exist for managers to increase sales, particularly when firm performance falls short of the stakeholders' expectations. The incentive for managers is the increase in compensation that often is associated with larger firm size. A company's size can be increased through strategic alliances as it can be through diversification. Strong governance mechanisms (see Chapter 10) are required to verify that managerial use of cooperative strategies is in the best interests of shareholders in particular and other stakeholders as well. Without effective governance mechanisms in place to guard against opportunistic managerial behaviors, strategic alliances may be used for purposes that are inconsistent with shareholders' best interests and that do not contribute to enhanced strategic competitiveness.

Another risk of corporate-level cooperative strategies is that they may be based on an intricate set of relationships between members of a firm's top-level management team and their counterparts in other companies.[94] Managers, for example, may use the intricacy of alliance networks to enrich their own position in the firm. Alliances built on an upper-level manager's contacts and interpersonal relationships may be lost if that person leaves the company. He or she may be the only one who effectively understands the complex web of relationships existing in the corporate network of alliance partners.[95] These understandings can entrench the manager, making dismissal difficult.

Although risks exist, corporate-level cooperative strategies can also create value. We have described how this is done through our discussions of diversifying and synergistic alliances and of franchising. Beyond this, a firm can develop a competitive advantage at the corporate level through its ability to effectively manage a set of business-level and corporate-level cooperative strategies.

Recall from Chapter 6 that a corporate-level strategy is concerned with two key questions: what businesses the firm should be in and how the corporate office should manage its group of businesses. A competitive advantage is created when a firm selects an appropriate set of businesses and when that set is managed in a manner that is difficult for competitors to imitate. Similarly, through use of the alliance mind-set that we mentioned previously in this chapter, a firm can form an appropriate set of strategic alliances and manage that alliance set in ways that are difficult for competitors to imitate. In fact, research shows that firms capable of learning from their cooperative collaborations develop know-how that can be distinguished from mere experience with strategic alliances.[96] Although networks of alliances can be used to diversify the firm and to create a competitive advantage, the cost and difficulty of managing them should not be underestimated. Monitoring these relationships and maintaining cordial and trusting relations require time and effort. Such costs should be considered before entering into numerous strategic alliances.[97]

International Cooperative Strategies

Most strategic alliances are formed as either business-level or corporate-level cooperative strategies. This is because at the business level, cooperative strategies are used to help a firm create value for customers as it exploits its core competencies in specific, individual product markets. Firms use cooperative strategies at the corporate level as part of their process of selecting and managing a mix of businesses in a way that creates more value than would be created if the businesses were to operate as independent entities.

In addition to domestic collaborative arrangements, strategic alliances formed when using business-level or corporate-level cooperative strategies can involve a firm with companies that are headquartered in other countries[98] (as discussed in Chapter 8). Primarily because of increasing globalization, *cross-border alliances*—ones in which firms with headquarters in different nations form a partnership—continue to increase in number and are becoming more important sources of strategic competitiveness.[99] The business-level strategic alliances between Benetton and its suppliers are an example of a cross-border alliance, as is the corporate-level joint venture formed between RaboBank and DG Bank (these examples of alliances were discussed earlier in the chapter).

When using business-level and corporate-level cooperative strategies, the intent is to develop alliances that have a high probability of increasing the firm's strategic competitiveness. In this context, the interest is not to form only domestic or only cross-border alliances. Rather, either a domestic or a cross-border alliance is formed only when it is expected to contribute to successful use of the firm's business-level cooperative strategy or its corporate-level cooperative strategy. For four primary reasons, however, firms also choose to *focus* on forming cross-border alliances. When this happens, the firm has chosen explicitly to use an international cooperative strategy.

The first reason firms decide to use an international cooperative strategy to develop cross-border strategic alliances is that, in general, multinational corporations outperform firms operating on only a domestic basis.[100] In the context of cooperative strategies, this general evidence suggests that a firm can form cross-border strategic alliances to leverage core competencies that are the foundation of its domestic success to expand into international markets.[101] For example, U.S.-based Mellon Bank Corp. and France's Credit Lyonnais SA recently started discussions about forming an alliance in asset-management services. Commenting about this intended transaction, a business writer suggested that, "For a midsize U.S. bank, Mellon has been unusually aggressive in seeking joint ventures and alliances to gain wider international distribution for its stable of mutual fund companies, which includes Dreyfus Corp. and Boston Co. Asset Management."[102]

Sometimes, cross-border alliances are used when opportunities to grow through acquisitions or alliances are limited within a firm's home nation. This is the case for Belgo-Dutch financial group Fortis. Noting that occasions to grow in its home markets were quite limited, especially in the Netherlands, a Fortis official said that, "Our strength in Benelux has given us a strong platform to grow elsewhere." Three geographic regions in which Fortis intends to use cross-border strategic alliances to grow are Asia, the United Kingdom, and the United States. In the United States, Fortis is seeking alliances or acquisitions to concentrate on its successful niche market of funeral insurance.[103]

The third reason firms choose to form cross-border alliances revolves around government policies. As discussed in Chapter 8, some countries regard local ownership as an important objective of national policy. In general, western governments, though nervous about foreign ownership in some industries, are less concerned than many other governments. India, on the other hand, strongly prefers to license local companies, as opposed to foreign ownership and joint ventures with a local firm or wholly foreign-owned subsidiaries. Another example is South Korea, whose government recently increased the ceiling on foreign investment in South Korean firms from 15 to 18 percent.[104] Thus, in some countries, managers may not have the full range of entry mode choices that we described in Chapter 8. Investment by foreign firms may only be allowed through cooperative agreements such as a cross-border alliance. This is often true in newly industrialized and developing countries with emerging markets. Cooperative arrangements can be helpful to foreign partners because the local partner can provide information about local markets, capital sources, and management skills.

The fourth primary reason cross-border alliances are used is to help a firm transform itself in light of rapidly changing environmental conditions. GEC, a U.K.-based company, seeks to move from being "a broadly focused group deriving much of its revenues from the defence budget to a full range telecommunications and information systems manufacturer." Stimulating this intended transformation is the uncertainty associated with different nations' defense budgets. Relying on its status as a world leader in a number of technologies that are critical to the ongoing worldwide communications revolution, GEC is forming alliances as one means of transforming itself. One cross-border alliance completed in this regard is between GEC and NEC, the Japanese electronics giant. The alliance has both a commercial and technological focus in that NEC is distributing GEC products through its extensive marketing channels, while the two companies are collaborating in R&D efforts to develop new technologies.[105]

In general, cross-border alliances are more complex and risky than domestic ones. Partly because of this complexity and risk, cross-border alliances have higher dissolution rates than do other modes that are used to enter international markets, such as a greenfield venture, wherein the firm establishes a wholly owned subsidiary.[106] Although strategic alliances allow partner firms to share risks—and thus are less risky for each individual partner than a greenfield venture—they are difficult to manage.[107] The need to coordinate and cooperate to share skills and knowledge requires significant processing of information on the part of all partner managers.[108] When significant demands are placed on partners' managers to achieve quick returns, the alliance has less of a chance of succeeding. Although difficult to attain, evidence shows that cross-border alliance success can be achieved as a result of careful partner selection and value-creating managerial practices.[109]

Strategic Intent of Partner

In the context of cooperative strategies, strategic intent denotes the most critical and important objectives a firm wants to achieve through collaborative arrangements. The competitive conditions of the 21st-century's landscape—especially increasing globalization—create a large set of objectives that drives why a firm develops its alliances as well as how it intends to operate as an alliance partner. Some firms, for example, may intend to learn how to use a technology that belongs to a partner. Thus, it is important to assess potential partners' strategic intent when evaluating alliance possibilities. Many believe that Japanese firms "are particularly good at learning from their partners."[110] If a horizontal complementary alliance is the type through which knowledge about a technology is gained, the firm learning about the technology could become a competitor to the partner from whom it gained the insights required to successfully use that technology.[111] Other outcomes in these instances are for the firm that has acquired the knowledge it sought to exit the alliance quickly or to acquire its partner through a merger or an acquisition.[112] Thus, the probability of alliance success is increased when firms understand each other's strategic intent as alliance partners.[113] Understanding intent requires careful selection of alliance partners. Factors influencing the selection of partners are discussed further in the Strategic Focus.

Network Cooperative Strategies

The focus of our discussion up to this point has been on cooperative arrangements between two firms.[114] Sometimes, however, companies participate in an *alliance network,* which is a set of identifiable and competitively relevant links between more than two relatively comparable firms.[115] Because it involves a firm with many strategic partnerships, an alliance network is the foundation for a network strategy.

A **network strategy** is the alliance-related actions taken by a group of interrelated and comparable firms to serve the common interests of all partners.

A **network strategy** is the alliance-related actions taken by a group of interrelated and comparable firms to serve the common interests of all partners. The strategic intent of a network strategy is to serve the firms' common interests by increasing the performance of the alliance network itself.[116] Network strategies are particularly effective when formed among firms clustered together; this is the case in Silicon Valley in California and in Singapore' Silicon Island.[117] An alliance network's performance can be increased as a result of the mutual commitment partners make when a network is created and because of the mutual dependence the commitment creates, causing partners to work together to serve the common interests of all parties.[118] A network strategy can be used to form a stable network of alliances, a dynamic network of alliances, and even a network of alliances within an individual company.

The Relationship between Partner Selection and Strategic Alliance Success

Among the many factors influencing alliance success is partner selection. Choosing an appropriate partner calls for the firm to understand a great deal about another company, including the intent driving an interest to ally with the focal firm. Gaining these understandings typically requires multiple interpersonal interactions in that, in the final analysis, alliances are relationships between people, not institutions. As our discussion shows, one objective of virtually every alliance partner is to learn from its ally.

Several information sources can be of value to firms trying to better understand a potential partner's intent, historical methods of operating as an alliance partner, and trustworthiness (trust as an aspect of cooperative strategies is discussed further later in the chapter). Industry analysts have information about how companies operate as alliance partners and the strategies they implement, as well as their future competitive objectives. This knowledge is acquired by studying industry-specific data and through interactions with peers to interpret it in competitively relevant ways.

Executive recruiters are a second source of information. The foundation of these individuals' knowledge is the insights they gain about a company when researching it to understand the qualifications and characteristics prospective employees should possess. The richness of recruiters' knowledge increases when their searches are completed to fill top-management team positions in a client firm. One of the hiring criteria for an upper-level managerial position could be, for example, a person's ability to successfully develop the type of strategic alliances at the business, corporate, or international level that the firm uses as the core of its cooperative strategies. Business reporters and the articles they write are another source of information about firms and their intentions when they form strategic alliances.

Based on its experiences, Motorola Inc. developed a disciplined process that it uses to select alliance partners. The first step of the process calls for Motorola to specify the exact objectives it seeks through a possible alliance. The alliance objectives must be derived from the overall corporate or business unit objectives. In addition, the potential partner must possess complementary skills that can reinforce Motorola's value-creating capabilities, and it must have a strong desire to partner with Motorola. During discussions with potential partners, Motorola tries to gain a deep understanding of the potential partner's alliance intent.

Business Marketing Group Inc. (BMG) is a small firm specializing in strategic partnership matchmaking. Because of the founder's background, BMG focuses on helping startup ventures and smaller firms form strategic alliances with larger technology firms, especially Microsoft. Simultaneously, BMG looks for startup ventures that it believes could partner successfully with giant corporations such as Microsoft. Full Armor is one of the companies that BMG helped forge an alliance with Microsoft. Full Armor's software allows information-technology departments to customize the applications users can load at their desktops. But, for the product to be successful, it had to be compatible with Microsoft Windows 2000 (hence, the need for an alliance with Microsoft). Fully understanding each partner's strategic intent with the alliance is one of the issues BMG addresses when helping clients form a cooperative relationship. In addition to its alliance with Microsoft—one that it developed through assistance from BMG—Full Armor has formed a strategic alliance with Entex Information Services. The purpose of the alliance is to provide the latest services and solutions for Windows 2000.

Recent research findings inform our understanding of what firms can do to be aware of a potential alliance partner's strategic intent. In their study, Hitt, Dacin, Levitas, Arregle, and Borza found that alliance partners are selected largely so the focal firm can gain access to the ally's resources and to learn through participation in the alliance. Further refinement to this general expectation is also provided by the researchers' results. For example, when selecting partners, firms in emerging markets "more strongly emphasize partners' financial assets, technical capabilities, intangible assets and willingness to share expertise than do developed market firms." In contrast, firms in developed markets were found to emphasize partners' unique competencies and market knowledge and access more strongly than did emerging market firms. Thus, firms evaluating potential partners from emerging market countries can anticipate that the company likely will have strategic intentions that differ from the strategic intentions of possible allies from developed-market economies. These results provide additional evidence regarding the importance of trying to understand a potential partner's strategic intent before agreeing to form a cooperative strategy with it.

SOURCES: Full Armor Home Page, 2000, Full Armor and Entex announce strategic partnership, January 31, *www.fullarmour.com*; M. A. Hitt, M. T. Dacin, E. Levitas, J.-L. Arregle, & A. Borza, 2000, Partner selection in emerging and developed market conditions: Resource-based and organizational learning perspectives, *Academy of Management Journal*, in press; C. Caggiano, 1999, Hotlinks, Inc., October, 72–81; Y. L. Doz & G. Hamel, 1998, *Alliance Advantage: Creating the Art of Value through Partnering* (Boston: Harvard Business School Press); J. R. Harbison & P. Pekar, Jr., 1998, Institutionalizing alliance skills: Secrets of repeatable success, *Strategy & Business*, 11: 79–94.

Stable alliance networks are the foundation of a network strategy in mature industries that are characterized by largely predictable market cycles and demand. In Japan, these relationships usually include some shared ownership among the partners of the alliance network as part of a keiretsu.[119] This tends not to be the case in the United States in that firms form their own alliance networks. For example, in the athletic footwear and apparel business, Nike has long-established relationships with a network of global alliance partners to supply and distribute its products throughout the world.

Dynamic alliance networks are the basis for using a network strategy in industries where rapid technological innovations are introduced frequently. Driving this pattern of competitive dynamics are the relatively short life cycles of goods and services in what are rapidly changing industries. Apple Computer employed a dynamic network with its innovative Newton, a personal digital assistant. Although the product was developed by Apple, Newtons are manufactured almost entirely by Sharp Corporation. Apple is also involved in an alliance with Motorola and IBM to develop a new microprocessor.[120] IBM, Microsoft, Intel, Fujitsu, and NEC are examples of other technology firms that frequently form both individual alliances and alliance networks.

Internal alliance networks are formed within a company to facilitate the coordination of product and global diversity. For example, Asea Brown Boveri (ABB), the international electric products firm, buys and sells a wide range of products across many country boundaries. ABB has formed alliances inside the firm to coordinate its operations and to increase its efficiency as a result of doing so.[121]

Each of these network types has a focal *strategic center firm*. Positioned at the center of at least several bilateral alliances, the strategic center firm manages a network of alliance relationships.[122] Nike, Nintendo, Benetton, Apple, Sun Microsystems, and IKEA (a Swedish furniture maker) are examples of strategic center firms. Monsanto is a strategic center firm with alliance networks in many areas, including seeds and biotechnology.[123] Working at the center of an alliance network, these companies are not "virtual firms" where all central competence is outsourced;[124] instead, they have capabilities and core competencies that allow them to shift important activities to other companies, which creates value when these companies are better able to perform such activities.[125]

In the Strategic Focus, we offer additional insights about why alliance networks are formed as well as how to design and manage them.[126] The discussion is expanded in the analysis of organizational structure in Chapter 11.

strategic focus CORPORATE

Alliance Networks: Benefits and Issues

The number of firms involved with multiple alliances and partners continues to increase. Several reasons account for firms' interest in using alliance networks as the foundation of a network cooperative strategy. Examples of these reasons include an opportunity to (1) share complementary resources, capabilities, and core competencies, (2) remain abreast of emerging technologies, and (3) share the risk and expenses that are part of a major capital outlay.

Beyond the benefits that can accrue from alliances with a single partner, forming an alliance network can help a firm maintain pace with, and perhaps set, industry standards. This benefit is especially crucial for companies in the telecommunications, software, computer, and video game industries. Firms interested in these benefits are involved with dynamic alliance networks. As a researcher notes, "The importance of alliances in standards-based industries stems from an essential characteristic of competitive dynamics in such markets: these industries often end up being dominated by a single standard, for example, as the Microsoft/Intel platform known as Wintel controls the major share of the PC market." Partners in an alliance network that is committed to developing a new industry standard often have the influence and power to convince potential adopters of the probability that the standard produced by the alliance partners will likely dominate the market. A second reason for a firm to develop a network of alliances is to facilitate the introduction of major changes in the company's core activities. Through simultaneous cooperative relationships with multiple partners, a firm requiring change to remain competitive can be quickly exposed to an array of emerging technologies, allowing it to experiment with different strategic, technical, and operational options. Using a network strategy for this purpose illustrates an approach for a firm to continuously reinvent itself. This issue was addressed at the beginning of the chapter as an important one for companies committed to achieving strategic competitiveness in the 21st century.

Firms should analyze several key issues as an alliance network is being formed. Chief among these issues are (1) determining whether the alliance network will be horizontal (involving firms generating value in the same stage of the value chain) or vertical (involving companies generating value in different stages of the value chain), (2) assessing the number of firms that will foster the greatest levels of network effectiveness and efficiency, (3) identifying approaches to use to minimize conflicts among alliance partners, (4) specifying the alliance network's strategic intent in a manner that benefits all, and (5) determining how the network will be managed and selecting the strategic center firm. Failure to carefully and deliberately evaluate these issues reduces the probability that the alliance network will succeed.

Despite the challenges of alliance networks, the 21st-century landscape creates conditions that likely will stimulate their further use by companies competing throughout the different sectors of the global economy. Thus, firms seeking strategic competitiveness should devote resources to understanding alliance networks and how to use them as the foundation for development of an effective network cooperative strategy.

SOURCES: T. E. Stuart, 1999, Network positions and propensities to collaborate: An investigation of strategic alliance formation in a high-technology industry, *Administrative Science Quarterly,* 43: 668–698; T. E. Stuart, 1999, Alliance networks: View from the hub, Mastering Strategy (Part Eight), *Financial Times,* November 15, 4–7; K. P. Coyne & R. Dye, 1998, The competitive dynamics of network-based businesses, *Harvard Business Review,* 76(1): 99–109; Y. L. Doz & G. Hamel, 1998, *Alliance Advantage: The Art of Creating Value through Partnering* (Boston: Harvard Business School Press).

Competitive Risks with Cooperative Strategies

Cooperative strategies are not risk free, as shown by the risks included in Figure 9.3. One risk is that a partner may act opportunistically. Opportunistic behaviors surface either when formal contracts fail to prevent their occurrence or when an alliance is based on a perception of partner trustworthiness that does not exist. As mentioned earlier in the chapter, understanding a partner's actual strategic intent reduces the likelihood that a partner will or can operate opportunistically.

Recently, an arbitrator concluded that Caterpillar Inc. acted opportunistically as a joint venture partner with A-55 Inc., a small and closely held firm. Following an analysis of the two parties' positions, the arbitrator ruled that, "Caterpillar Inc. engaged in fraudulent and deceitful conduct by improperly patenting and then seeking to market clean-fuel technology for diesel engines belonging to (A-55), a former joint venture partner." In response to the judgment, a Caterpillar spokesperson stated that, "We're disappointed with the arbitrator's decision. Caterpillar upheld the terms of our joint venture and at all times acted in good faith toward A-55. We're evaluating our next steps."[127] A more effective formal contract might have prevented A-55's need to adjudicate outcomes from its joint venture with Caterpillar.

Some cooperative arrangements dissolve when it is discovered that a partner has misrepresented the competencies it can bring to the alliance. This happens most fre-

FIGURE 9.3 | Managing Competitive Risks in Cooperative Strategies

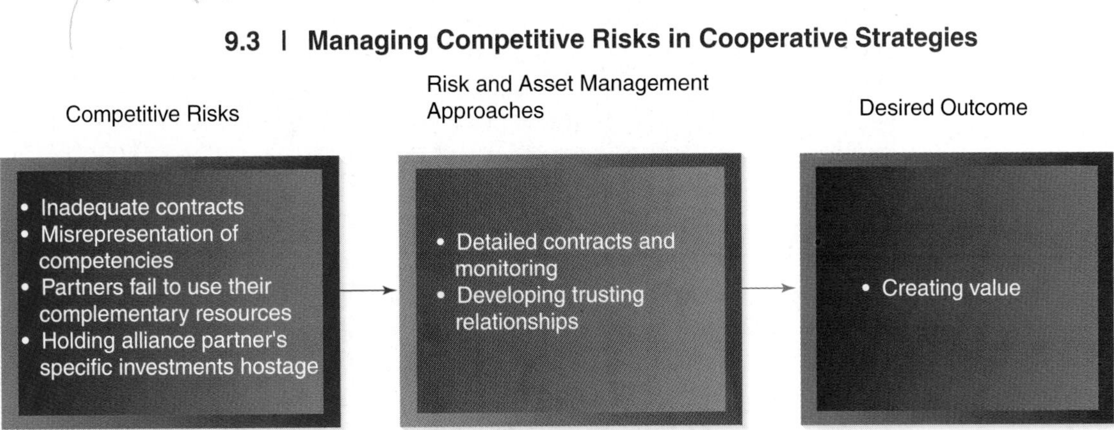

quently when a partner conveys an intention of relying on intangible assets as its contribution to a cooperative relationship. Superior knowledge of local conditions is an example of an intangible asset that partners often fail to deliver. In a related instance, a firm may decide to end a relationship in order to pursue a related option for which it believes that its competencies are even more valuable. Telefonos de Mexico and Sprint Communications, for example, ended their two-year partnership that was aimed at providing long-distance service to the U.S. Hispanic market. To finalize the relationship, Telmex purchased Sprint's 50 percent of the joint venture. According to a telecommunications analyst, Telmex may have ended the cooperative arrangement with Sprint "in case a more profitable partnership develops with another telecom giant."[128]

Failure to make its complementary resources available to a partner is another competitive risk of cooperative strategies. This risk surfaces most commonly between partners located in different nations. Contractual arrangements can sometimes discourage this form of adverse behavior. However, once a partner commits to and invests in a cooperative relationship with a firm located in a different global market, the local partner may hold those assets hostage if foreign countries do not have laws protecting the focal firm's investment.

Ineffective management skills or differences in managerial styles are a final risk to be mentioned. This issue caused the dissolution of a joint venture between Piaggio, the Italian scooter manufacturer and LML, its partner located in India. Formed in 1990, the venture lasted for almost 10 years. At one level, it was successful in that the venture was producing approximately 300,000 scooters annually for the Indian market. This sales volume earned a 27 percent market share for the venture. According to analysts, the venture ended because of "increasingly sour management differences."[129]

In addition to the moral hazards (potential cheating by partner firms), there are other risks. One of those risks is having the ability to form and manage a joint venture effectively. Prior experience, although obviously helpful, may not be adequate for collaborative strategies to endure.[130] Another risk is having the ability to collaborate.

Opportunistic behaviors surface when an alliance is based on a perception of partner trustworthiness that does not exist. An arbitrator found that Caterpillar Inc. acted opportunistically as a joint venture partner with A-55 Inc. when the firm patented and sought to market A-55's clean-fuel technology for diesel engines.

Alternatively, it may be difficult to identify trustworthy partners with which to collaborate.

Trust as a Strategic Asset

Trust between partners increases the likelihood that an alliance will succeed.[131] In fact, some believe that trust may be the most efficient mechanism for governing economic transactions.[132] Several conditions account for this efficiency. For example, trust creates confidence between partners that actions taken will serve both parties' interests. In addition, trust increases the probability that a firm will understand its partner's actual strategic intent as it participates in an alliance. Once intent is understood, it is also easier for a firm to predict the actions its partner will take as it encounters different situations requiring decisions to be made that will affect the alliance. When both partners are known to be trustworthy, an expectation of loyal behavior exists for the parties as a cooperative arrangement is formed. Because of this expectation, firms are able to allocate fewer resources to monitor and control the alliance. In contrast, greater amounts of resources are required to monitor and control an alliance formed with a firm whose previous behavior suggests that it can't be trusted.[133]

As explained in a Strategic Focus in Chapter 3, trust is valuable, rare, imperfectly imitable, and often nonsubstitutable.[134] Thus, firms known to be trustworthy have a competitive advantage when it comes to forming and using cooperative strategies. One reason for this is that it is impossible to specify all operational aspects of a cooperative arrangement in a formal contract. Confidence that its partner can be trusted reduces the firm's concern about the inability to control or influence each operational aspect of an alliance through a contractual agreement.

Especially in developing countries, a government's actions can affect the level of trust associated in some manner with the use of cooperative strategies. Events experienced by Adolph Coors, the U.S. Brewer, demonstrate this situation. To compete in the Korean market, Coors formed a joint venture called Jinro Coors. The venture had several partners, including the majority owner, Jinro Group. The South Korean government placed the venture up for auction following Jinro Group's bankruptcy in 1997. To maintain involvement with its joint venture, Coors submitted a bid to buy Jinro Coors. However, Coors dropped out of the auction at the end of July 1999 because of a "seriously flawed and unfair bidding process." Beyond this, Coors said that it "had no faith in the integrity of the process because of the questionable activities of a number of parties involved in the auction."[135] Thus, the absence of trust about the role of a country's government regarding a joint venture created an untenable situation for a firm (e.g., Adolph Coors) that wanted to engage in a cooperative strategy with partners in an international market.

Strategic Approaches to Managing Alliances

Two primary approaches are used to manage cooperative strategies[136] (see Figure 9.3). In one instance, the firm develops formal contracts with its partners. These contracts specify how the cooperative strategy is to be monitored and how partner behavior is to be controlled. The interest is to minimize the alliance's cost and to prevent opportunistic behavior by a partner. The focus of the second managerial approach is on maximizing value-creation opportunities as the partners participate in the alliance. In this instance, partners are prepared to take advantage of unexpected opportunities to learn from each other and to explore additional marketplace possibilities.[137] Trust-based relationships and complementary assets must exist between partners for this approach to be used successfully.

Although both managerial approaches can result in the creation of value, the amount of monitoring costs to partner firms differ. Writing detailed contracts and using extensive monitoring mechanisms is expensive. Furthermore, protective contracts and monitoring systems shield parts of the organization from both participating partners. Although monitoring systems can largely prevent opportunism and cheating by alliance partners, they also preclude positive responses to spontaneous opportunities that can surface as partners engage in alliance-related work. Thus, formal contracts and extensive monitoring systems tend to inhibit firms' efforts to maximize an alliance's value-creating potential. For example, if Adolph Coors were to form an additional alliance with a company in a developing economy, its previous experience, as described earlier, would likely influence the firm to develop formal contracts and use extensive monitoring systems. Such systems would be expensive and could be expected to stifle development of unexpected marketplace opportunities.

When trust exists, partners' monitoring costs are reduced and opportunities to create value through the cooperative relationship are maximized. This managerial approach is referred to as *opportunity maximizing* because alliance partners can pursue potential rent-generating opportunities that aren't available to partners in more contractually restricted alliances.[138] It is important, then, for firms to consider both the assets and liabilities of monitoring systems that will be used to manage the alliance.[139] For example, AT&T entered an alliance with a much smaller credit card technology firm to develop a new credit card service. To ensure secrecy so that the alliance could maintain a critical lead in the industry, no contract was used for the first several months of this relationship. During this time, the firms worked collaboratively, sharing information and resources while relying on the character and goodwill of each other to guide the relationship. In examining this relationship, AT&T was more concerned with maximizing the opportunities of the alliance than with the minimization of potential opportunism within it.[140]

Our focus in the next major section of the book (Part III) is the strategic actions firms take to implement the strategies they selected to pursue strategic competitiveness and above-average returns. Corporate governance, which is concerned with how firms align managers' interests with those of the shareholders and control managerial actions to assure alignment, is the first topic we address in Part III.

Proper alignment of managers' interests with those of shareholders is also an issue in terms of strategic alliances. Because of a separation of ownership and control in modern corporations, an agency problem exists (the agency problem is discussed in detail in the next chapter). When the two parties' interests are not aligned, "managers may enter strategic alliances when doing so may not be in the best interests of their firms. For example, managers may form alliances to protect jobs they might lose if there were a takeover, merger, or acquisition."[141] Thus, as this brief discussion shows, and as is discussed in detail in the next chapter, the effective governance of firms is linked with strategic competitiveness and the earning of above-average returns across a broad range of managerial actions.[142]

Summary

- Strategic alliances are the primary form of cooperative strategies. A strategic alliance is a partnership between firms whereby resources, capabilities, and core competencies are combined to pursue mutual interests. Joint ventures, equity strategic alliances, and nonequity strategic alliances are the three basic types of strategic alliances.

- Other types of cooperative strategies are implicit rather than explicit. These include mutual forbearance, or tacit collusion, in which firms in an industry tacitly cooperate to reduce industry output below the potential competitive output level, thereby raising prices above the competitive level. Firms might also explicitly collude, which is an illegal practice unless it is sanctioned through government regulations such as in the case of electric and telecommunications utilities. With increasing globalization, fewer government-sanctioned situations of explicit collusion are being observed.

- Four business-level cooperative alliances are frequently used. Through vertical and horizontal complementary alliances, companies combine their resources, capabilities, and core competencies in ways that create value. Vertical complementary strategic alliances result when firms creating value in different parts of the value chain combine their assets to create new value. When outsourcing to create value, the firm may choose to form a nonequity strategic alliance with a partner that is distinctively capable of creating value in a part of the value chain in which the focal firm lacks the skills needed to create that value. Horizontal complementary strategic alliances are developed when firms combine their assets to create additional value in the same stage of the value chain. Common examples of horizontal alliances include marketing agreements and joint product-development arrangements between competitors (e.g., domestic and international airlines).

- Competition reduction and competition response business-level cooperative strategies are formed in response to an industry's pattern of competitive dynamics among firms. Typically, with a short-term horizon, competition reduction alliances are used to avoid excessive competition while a firm marshals its resources to compete more successfully in light of changes in its competitive landscape. Competition response alliances are formed to deal directly with competitors' actions—especially strategic ones—rather than tactical competitive actions.

- Firms use uncertainty and risk reduction cooperative strategies to hedge their risks when competing in dynamic and volatile markets or when attempting to form a new industry standard (e.g., a new technology standard).
- Business-level cooperative strategies yield different strategic outcomes. In general, complementary strategic alliances are most likely to create strategic competitiveness, whereas competition reduction and competition response alliances are more likely to result in a firm achieving a condition of competitive parity with its competitors. Uncertainty reduction alliances may prevent a firm from experiencing below-average returns in the short run. However, when seeking to establish a new industry standard, an uncertainty reduction cooperative strategy can contribute to long-term strategic competitiveness.
- Corporate-level diversifying strategic alliances reduce risk, but, at the same time, tend to be highly complex. This alliance type can also be used when government policies prohibit or stifle horizontal mergers as an experimental step to determine whether a merger or an acquisition of an alliance partner would enhance the focal firm's strategic competitiveness.
- Corporate-level synergistic alliances create economies of scope. Such alliances facilitate the achievement of synergy across multiple businesses and functions at the corporate level.
- Franchising is an additional corporate-level cooperative strategy that provides an alternative to diversification. Firms following a franchising strategy can diversify their risk associated with a single business (even those in many markets) without adding new products.
- A number of firms use cross-border strategic alliances as the foundation for international cooperative strategy. These alliances are used for several reasons, including the performance superiority of firms competing in markets outside their domestic base and governmental restrictions on growth through mergers and acquisitions. International strategic alliances can be risky, especially when the firm fails to understand its partner's strategic intent in terms of being a party to an alliance.
- An alliance network is the foundation of a network cooperative strategy. Stable (primarily in mature industries), dynamic (witnessed mainly in rapidly changing industries), and internal (alliances within a single firm to coordinate its product and global diversity) are the three types of alliance networks. The strategic intent of a network strategy is for partners to serve their common good as they cooperate to reach agreed-upon alliance objectives.
- Cooperative strategies are not risk-free strategy choices. If a contract is not developed appropriately, or if a potential partner firm misrepresents its competencies or fails to make available promised complementary resources, failure is likely. Furthermore, a firm may be held hostage through asset-specific investments made in conjunction with a partner, which may be exploited.
- Trust is an important asset in alliances. Firms recognize the value of partnering with companies possessing a reputation for trustworthiness. When trust exists, an alliance is managed to maximize the pursuit of opportunities between partners. Without trust, formal contracts and extensive monitoring systems are used to manage an alliance.

Review Questions

1. What are the types of cooperative strategies that are described in this chapter, and how are they defined?
2. What are the different reasons that support a firm's use of cooperative strategies in slow-cycle, standard-cycle, and fast-cycle markets?
3. What are the advantages and disadvantages of using the four types of business-level cooperative strategies: complementary alliances, competition reduction alliances, competition response alliances, and uncertainty reduction alliances?
4. How are cooperative strategies used at the corporate level in a diversified firm? What are some potential problems when a firm uses cooperative strategies at the corporate level?
5. Why do firms use international cooperative strategies in the form of cross-border strategic alliances?

6. What are the four competitive risks of using cooperative strategies?
7. Why is trust important in cooperative strategies?
8. What are the differences between the cost-minimization approach and the opportunity-maximization approach to managing strategic alliances?

Application Discussion Questions

1. Using the Internet, go to the Web site for *Financial Times* (www.ft.com). Find three or four articles that discuss different firms' uses of cooperative strategies. What types of cooperative strategies are revealed in each article you found? What objective is each firm pursuing as it uses a particular cooperative strategy?
2. Use the Internet to find two articles describing firms' use of a cooperative strategy: one where trust is being used as a strategic asset and another where contracts and monitoring are being emphasized. What are the differences between the managerial approaches being used in the two companies? Which of the cooperative strategies you examined has the highest probability of being successful? Why?
3. Choose a *Fortune 500* firm that has a significant need to outsource a primary or support activity (such as information technology). Given the activity you believe the firm should outsource, can you justify a recommendation to the firm to form a nonequity strategic alliance to outsource the focal activity?
4. The possibility of DaimlerChrysler using cooperative strategies as the foundation for its small car strategy is discussed in the Opening Case. Use the Internet to determine whether the firm has formed strategic alliances to build its small cars. If these alliances have been formed, what factors caused this decision to be made? If alliances have not been formed for this purpose, why not?
5. Use the Internet to visit the home pages of Deutsche Telekom AG, Sprint, and France Telecom SA. What is the role each firm has now in terms of the Global One Alliance that is discussed in this chapter?

Ethics Questions

1. From an ethical perspective, how much information is a firm obliged to tell a potential strategic alliance partner about what it expects to learn from the cooperative arrangement?
2. "A contract is necessary because most firms cannot be trusted to act ethically in a cooperative venture such as a strategic alliance." In your opinion, is this statement true or false? Why? Does the answer vary by country? Why?
3. Ventures in foreign countries without strong contract law are more risky, because managers may be subjected to bribery attempts once their firms' assets have been invested in the country. How can managers deal with these problems?
4. The large number of international strategic alliances being formed by the world's airline companies is discussed in one of the chapter's Strategic Focus segments. Do these companies face any ethical issues as they participate in multiple alliances? If so, what are the issues? Are the issues different for airline companies headquartered in the United States than for those with European home bases? If so, what are the differences, and what accounts for them?
5. Firms with a reputation for ethical behavior in strategic alliances are likely to have more opportunities to form cooperative strategies than will companies that have not earned this reputation. What actions can firms take to earn a reputation for behaving ethically as a strategic alliance partner?

Internet Exercise

As explained in the first Strategic Focus in this chapter, many airlines are forming global cooperative alliances. Explore two of these major alliances on the Internet, the OneWorld Alliance, which includes American Airlines and British Airways (**www.oneworldalliance.com**), and the Star Alliance, which includes Lufthansa and United Airlines (**www.star-alliance.com**). How do these alliances share competitive resources? Review the four competitive risks associated with using cooperative strategies. How does each alliance avoid these risks?

***e-project:** Delta Airlines and its alliance partners commissioned an elite advertising firm to create an image for their airlines' network. As part of the team, you are hired to create the Web-based portion of the new advertising campaign. How would you design this new site? What features would you include to better define the alliance's strategic intent?

Notes

1. L. Capron, W. Mitchell, & J. Oxley, 1999, Recreating the company: Four contexts for change, Mastering Strategy (Part Ten), *Financial Times,* November 29, 4–7.
2. M. S. Kraatz, 1998, Learning by association? Interorganizational networks and adaptation to environmental change, *Academy of Management Journal,* 41: 621–643.
3. C. Palmeri, 1999, The watt hustlers, *Forbes,* September 20, 78–80.
4. D. Kirkpatrick, 2000, Enron takes its pipeline to the net, *Fortune,* January 24, 127–130.
5. J. G. Combs & D. J. Ketchen, Jr., 1999, Explaining interfirm cooperation and performance: Toward a reconciliation of predictions from the resource-based view and organizational economics, *Strategic Management Journal,* 20: 867–888; B. Gomes Casseres, 1996, *The Alliance Revolution: The New Shape of Business Rivalry* (Cambridge, MA: Harvard University Press).
6. J. H. Dyer & H. Singh, 1998, The relational view: Cooperative strategy and sources of interorganizational competitive advantage, *Academy of Management Review,* 23: 660–679.
7. J. G. Auerbach & G. McWilliams, 1999, IBM will sell Dell $16 billion of parts, *Wall Street Journal,* March 5, A3.
8. J. Kurtzman, 1999, An interview with Rosabeth Moss Kanter, *Strategy & Business,* 16: 85–94; J. Child & D. Faulkner, 1998, *Strategies of Cooperation: Managing Alliance Networks and Joint Ventures* (New York: Oxford University Press); Y. L. Doz & G. Hamel, 1998, *Alliance Advantage: The Art of Creating Value through Partnering* (Boston: Harvard Business School Press); S. E. Human & K. G. Provan, 1997, An emergent theory of structure and outcomes in small-firm strategic manufacturing networks, *Academy of Management Journal,* 40: 368–404.
9. A. N. Brandenburger & B. J. Nalebuff, 1996, *Co-opetition* (New York: Doubleday).
10. C. V. Callahan & B. A. Pasternack, 1999, Corporate strategy in the digital age, *Strategy & Business,* 15: 10–18.
11. E. Nelson, 2000, Wal-Mart revamps its online store, prepares for service in AOL alliance, *Wall Street Journal,* January 3, A12.
12. Doz & Hamel, *Alliance Advantage,* xiii.
13. J. R. Harbison & P. Pekar, Jr., 1998, Institutionalizing alliance skills: Secrets of repeatable success, *Strategy & Business,* 11: 79–94.
14. P. Abrahams, 1999, Electrolux, Toshiba link, *Financial Times,* May 27, 20.
15. A. Harney, 1999, Chief is slave to design, not fashion, *Financial Times,* June 4, 20; A. Harney, 1999, Fuji Heavy considers alliance, *Financial Times,* June 4, 21.
16. W. Mitchell, 1999, Alliances: Achieving long-term value and short-term goals, Mastering Strategy (Part Four), *Financial Times,* October 18, 6–7.
17. M. P. Koza & A. Y Lewin, 1999, Putting the S-word back in alliances, Mastering Strategy (Part Six), *Financial Times,* November 1, 12–13; S. H. Park & M. Russo, 1996, When cooperation eclipses competition: An event history analysis of joint venture failures, *Management Science,* 42: 875–890.
18. Mitchell, Alliances, 7.
19. Combs & Ketchen, Jr., Explaining interfirm cooperation and performance, 867–888.
20. Harbison & Pekar, Jr., Institutionalizing alliance skills, 79–94.
21. R. Gulati, 1999, Network location and learning: The influence of network resources and firm capabilities on alliance formation, *Strategic Management Journal,* 20: 397–420.
22. C. F. Freidheim, Jr., 1999, The trillion-dollar enterprise, *Strategy & Business,* 14: 60–66.
23. P. E. Bierly, III & E. H. Kessler, 1999, The timing of strategic alliances, in M. A. Hitt, P. G. Clifford, R. D. Nixon, & K. P. Coyne (eds.), *Dynamic Strategic Resources: Development, Diffusion and Integration* (Chichester: John Wiley & Sons), 299–345.
24. *Wall Street Journal Staff Reporter,* 2000, Dan River's ventures with Mexican textiler to eliminate U.S. jobs, *Wall Street Journal,* January 13, B17; T. Burt, 1999, Car giants plan to take wing, *Financial Times,* August 3, 16; J. Hechinger, 1999, Citigroup and State Street to form retirement-plan joint venture, *Wall Street Journal,* December 8, A4.
25. Y. Pan, 1997, The formation of Japanese and U.S. equity joint ventures in China, *Strategic Management Journal,* 18: 247–254.
26. N. Nakamae, 1999, Japanese giants join to sell books online, *Financial Times,* June 4, 20.
27. D. C. Mowery, J. E. Oxley, & B. S. Silverman, 1996, Strategic alliances and interfirm knowledge transfer, *Strategic Management Journal,* 17(Special Winter Issue): 77–92.
28. S. Das, P. K. Sen, & S. Sengupta, 1998, Impact of strategic alliances on firm valuation, *Academy of Management Journal,* 41: 27–41.
29. Bierly & Kessler, The timing of strategic alliances, 303.
30. J. B. Barney, 1997, *Gaining and Sustaining Competitive Advantage* (Reading, MA: Addison Wesley), 255.
31. Freidheim, Jr., The trillion-dollar enterprise; B. Kogut, 1988, Joint ventures: Theoretical and empirical perspectives, *Strategic Management Journal,* 9: 319–332.
32. D. Cyr, High tech-high impact: Creating Canada's competitive advantage through technology alliances, *Academy of Management Executive,* 13(2): 17–26; A. A. Lado, N. G. Boyd, & S. C. Hanlon, 1997, Competition, cooperation, and the search for rents: A syncretic model, *Academy of Management Review,* 22: 110–141; F. J. Contractor & P. Lorange, 1988, Why should firms cooperate? The strategic and economic bases for cooperative strategy, in F. J. Contractor & P. Lorange (eds.), *Cooperative Strategies in International Business* (Lexington, MA: Lexington Books).
33. J. R. Williams, 1998, *Renewable Advantage: Crafting Strategy Through Economic Time* (New York: Free Press); E. E. Bailey & W. Shan, 1995, Sustainable competitive advantage through alliances, in E. Bowman & B. Kogut (eds.), *Redesigning the Firm* (New York: Oxford University Press); J. R. Williams, 1992, How sustainable is your competitive advantage? *California Management Review,* 34(2): 29–51.
34. J. Files, 2000, Alcatel to focus on U.S. business market, *Dallas Morning News,* January 25, D6.
35. Alcatel Home Page, 2000, January 31, *www.alcatel.com,* M. A. Hitt, J. S. Harrison, & R. D. Ireland, 2001, (New York: Oxford University Press); J. C. Huertas & J. P. Chapon, 1997, Alcatel awarded major contract in South Africa, Alcatel Home Page, January 31, *www.alcatel.com,* J. Kahn, 1996, Alcatel's local call paying off in China, *Wall Street Journal,* January 15, A5.
36. Associated Press, AT&T, BT to buy Japan Telecom stake, *Dallas Morning News,* April 26, D4.
37. C. Hoag, 1999, Oil duo plan energy alliance, *Financial Times,* June 30, 17.

38. N. Harris & W. Boston, 2000, Three partners in Global One plan a statement, *Wall Street Journal,* January 21, B6; D. Owen, 1999, Future of Global One comes under spotlight, *Financial Times,* July 22, 17.
39. J. Flint, 2000, No guts, no glory, *Forbes,* February 7, 88.
40. G. L. White & F. Warner, 2000, GM in talks for Web plan with Honda, *Wall Street Journal,* January 12, A6.
41. N. Shirouzu, 2000, Toyota may join Ford's Web system, *Wall Street Journal,* January 25, A13.
42. A. Carrns, 2000, Humana agrees to an alliance with Web firm, *Wall Street Journal,* January 13, B2.
43. J. Griffiths, 1999, Tyre-makers sign up for strategic alliance, *Financial Times,* June 14, 22.
44. S. Warren & C. Tejada, 1999, DuPont plans tracking stock for life sciences, *Wall Street Journal,* March 11, A3.
45. Williams, *Renewable Advantage.*
46. B. Wysocki, 2000, Cyberspace Inc.: More companies cut risk by collaborating with their enemies, *Wall Street Journal,* January 31, A1, A10.
47. Global Crossing Home Page, 2000, Hutchison Whampoa and Global Crossing compete telecom joint venture in Hong Kong, January 12, *www.globalcrossing.com.*
48. C. W. L. Hill, 1997, Establishing a standard: Competitive strategy and technological standards in winner-take-all industries, *Academy of Management Executive,* XI(2): 7–25.
49. R. Axelrod, W. Mitchell, R. E. Thomas, D. S. Bennett, & E. Bruderer, 1995, Coalition formation in standard-setting alliances, *Management Science,* 41: 1493–1508; L. D. Browning, J. M. Beyer, & J. C. Shetler, 1995, Building cooperation in a competitive industry: Sematech and the semiconductor industry, *Academy of Management Journal,* 38: 113–151.
50. J. McHugh, 1999, No mercy for Merced, *Forbes,* September 20, 57–60.
51. J. T. Mahoney, 1992, The choice of organizational form: Vertical financial ownership versus other methods of vertical integration, *Strategic Management Journal,* 13: 559–584.
52. S. H. Park & G. R. Ungson, 1997, The effect of national culture, organizational complementarity, and economic motivation on joint venture dissolution, *Academy of Management Journal,* 40: 297–307; R. Johnston & P. Lawrence, 1988, Beyond vertical integration—The rise of the value adding partnership, *Harvard Business Review,* 66(4): 94–101.
53. Freidheim, The trillion dollar enterprise, 62.
54. M. Delio, 1999, Strategic outsourcing, *Knowledge Management,* 2(7): 62–68.
55. As quoted in P. Hapaaniemi, 1997, Side by side, *Chief Executive,* June: S4–S10.
56. M. Kotabe & K. S. Swan, 1995, The role of strategic alliances in high technology new product development, *Strategic Management Journal,* 16: 621–636.
57. D. Clark, 2000, CSK, Advance Auto for firm to allow customers to purchase parts online, *Wall Street Journal,* January 10, A8.
58. A. Rawsthorn, 1999, Internet music venture goes international, *Financial Times,* June 11, 9.
59. S. B. Garland & A. Reinhardt, 1999, Making antitrust fit high tech, *Business Week,* March 22, 34–36.
60. E. Norton & M. DuBois, 1994, Foiled competition: Don't call it a cartel, but world aluminum has forged a new order, *Wall Street Journal,* June 9, A1, A6.
61. C. Adams, 1998, Aluminum companies earnings increased in the fourth quarter, *Wall Street Journal Interactive Edition,* January 8, *www.wsj.com.*
62. A. Klein, 2000, Kodak posts gain of 75% in profit for fourth period, *Wall Street Journal,* January 25, A4; D. P. Hamilton & N. Shirouzu, 1995, Japan's business cartels are starting to erode, but change is slow, *Wall Street Journal,* December 4, Al, A6.
63. G. Hundley & C. K. Jacobson, 1998, The effects of the Keiretsu on the export performance of Japanese companies: Help or hindrance? *Strategic Management Journal,* 19: 927–937.
64. J. Rohwer, 2000, Get rich quick—in Asia, *Fortune,* January 24, 30–32.
65. M. Freedman, 2000, Planting seeds, *Forbes,* February 7, 62–64; H. S. Bryne, 1995, Damage control at ADM, *Barrons,* October 23, 14.
66. J. M. Broder, 1997, Toys 'R' Us led price collusion, judge rules in upholding F.T.C., *The New York Times on the Web,* October 1, *www.nytimes.com.*
67. Freedman, Planting seeds, 64.
68. W. Hall, 1999, SAirGroup seeks promotion in global aviation league, *Financial Times,* June 28, 20.
69. G. Anders, 2000, Several food companies to join Webvan in online grocery-marketing effort, *Wall Street Journal,* January 25, B4.
70. D. P. Hamilton, 1999, H-P sets alliance with BEA Systems to pursue Internet goals, *Wall Street Journal,* April 8, B9.
71. D. A. Blackmon, 1999, Postal service, DHL to form an alliance, *Wall Street Journal,* March 2, A3.
72. R. G. McGrath, 1999, Falling forward: Real options reasoning and entrepreneurial failure, *Academy of Management Review,* 24: 13–30; R. G. McGrath, 1997, A real options logic for initiating technological positioning investments, *Academy of Management Review,* 22: 974–996; B. Kogut, 1991, Joint ventures and the option to expand and acquire, *Management Science,* 37: 19–33.
73. A. Carrns, 1999, drkoop.com's shares jump on AOL link, *Wall Street Journal,* August 7, B6.
74. U. Harnischfeger, 1999, Siemens and Fujitsu set of computer deal, *Financial Times,* June 17, 26; U. Harnischfeger & B. Rahman, 1999, Fujitsu deal may give Siemens a computer break, *Financial Times,* June 18, 22; M. Rose, 1999, Siemens, Fujitsu sign world-wide co-operation accord, *Wall Street Journal,* June 17, A21.
75. M. Dickie, 1999, Acer agrees seven-year alliance with IBM, *Financial Times,* June 8, 20.
76. A. Edgecliffe-Johnson, 1999, Wal-Mart in online bookstore alliance, *Financial Times,* July 2, 19.
77. E. Kaneko, 1999, NEC, HP to extend alliance, *Financial Times,* June 29, 16.
78. J. Ball, 1999, To define future car, GM, Toyota say bigger is better, *Wall Street Journal,* April 20, B4.
79. J. Ball, 1999, Five of the world's top auto makers agree to develop technology standard, *Wall Street Journal,* April 28, B6.
80. S. Chaudhuri & B. Tabrizi, 1999, Capturing the real value in high-tech acquisitions, *Harvard Business Review,* 77(5): 123–130; J.-F. Hennart & S. Ready, 1997, The choice between mergers/acquisitions and joint ventures in the United States, *Strategic Management Journal,* 18: 1–12.
81. G. Robinson, 1999, Versace joins $2bn resorts venture, *Financial Times,* April 16, 17.
82. B. S. Akre, 1999, Toyota alliance could lead to bigger things, GM exec hints, *Dallas Morning News,* April 20, D6.
83. T. Burt, 1999, Mitsubishi Motors to slim range, *Financial Times,* July 26, 18.
84. C. Harris & G. Cramb, 1999, Seeking wider co-operation, *Financial Times,* October 19, 20.
85. A. Harney, 1999, Toyota seeks technology alliances, *Financial Times,* July 19, 18.
86. S. A. Shane, 1996, Hybrid organizational arrangements and their implications for firm growth and survival: A study of new franchisers, *Academy of Management Journal,* 39: 216–234.
87. F. Lafontaine, 1999, Myths and strengths of franchising, *Financial Times,* Mastering Strategy (Part Nine), November 22, 8–10.
88. P. J. Kaufmann & S. Eroglu, 1999, Standardization and adaptation in business format franchising, *Journal of Business Venturing,* 14: 69–85.
89. R. P. Dant & P. J. Kaufmann, 1999, Franchising and the domain of

entrepreneurship research, *Journal of Business Venturing,* 14: 5–16.

90. P. Ingram & J. A. C. Baum, 1997, Opportunity and constraint: Organizations' learning from the operating and competitive experience of industries, *Strategic Management Journal,* 18(Special Summer Issue): 75–98.
91. L. Wu, 1999, The pricing of a brand name product: Franchising in the motel services industry, *Journal of Business Venturing,* 14: 87–102.
92. Lafontaine, Myths and strengths, 10.
93. Kaufmann & Dant, Franchising, 14.
94. S. L. Brown & K. M. Eisenhardt, 1998, *Competing on the Edge: Strategy as Structural Chaos,* (Boston: Harvard Business School Press).
95. R. E. Hoskisson, W. P. Wan, & M. H. Hanson, 1998, Strategic alliance formation and market evaluation: Effects of parent firm's governance structure, in M. A. Hitt, J. E. Ricart I Costa, & R. D. Nixon, *Managing Strategically in an Interconnected World* (Chichester: John Wiley & Sons), 207–228.
96. B. L. Simonin, 1997, The importance of collaborative know-how: An empirical test of the learning organization, *Academy of Management Journal,* 40: 1150–1174.
97. P. J. Buckley & M. Casson, 1996, An economic model of international joint venture strategy, *Journal of International Business Studies,* 27: 849–876; J. E. McGee, M. J. Dowling, & W. L. Megginson, 1995, Cooperative strategy and new venture performance: The role of business strategy and management experience, *Strategic Management Journal,* 16: 565–580.
98. J. J. Reuer & K. D. Miller, 1997, Agency costs and the performance implications of international joint venture internalization, *Strategic Management Journal,* 18: 425–438.
99. M. A. Hitt, M. T. Dacin, E. Levitas, J.-L. Arregle, & A. Borza, 2000, Partner selection in emerging and developed market contexts: Resource-based and organizational learning perspectives, *Academy of Management Journal,* in press; L. K. Mytelka, 1991, *Strategic Partnerships and the World Economy* (London: Pinter Publishers).
100. M. A. Hitt, R. E. Hoskisson, & H. Kim, 1997, International diversification: Effects on innovation and firm performance in product diversified firms, *Academy of Management Journal,* 40: 767–798; R. N. Osborn & J. Hagedoorn, 1997, The institutionalization and evolutionary dynamics of interorganizational alliances and networks, *Academy of Management Journal,* 40: 261–278.
101. J. Hagedoorn, 1995, A note on international market leaders and networks of strategic technology partnering, *Strategic Management Journal,* 16: 241–250.
102. P. Beckett & C. Fleming, 1999, Mellon Bank, Credit Lyonnais discuss strategic alliance, equity investment, *Wall Street Journal,* March 8, A4.
103. I. Bickerton, 1999, Fortis seeks more link-ups, *Financial Times,* May 27, 18.
104. M. Schuman, 1996, South Korea raises limit to 18% on foreign investment in firms, *Wall Street Journal,* February 27, A12.
105. A. Cane, 1999, GEC and NEC in alliance talks, *Financial Times,* May 11, 20.
106. J.-F. Hennart, D.-J. Kim, & M. Zeng, 1998, The impact of joint venture status on the longevity of Japanese stakes in U.S. manufacturing affiliates, *Organization Science,* 9: 382–395; J. Li, 1995, Foreign entry and survival: Effects of strategic choices on performance in international markets, *Strategic Management Journal,* 16: 333–351.
107. J. M. Geringer, 1991, Measuring performance of international joint ventures, *Journal of International Business Studies,* 22(2): 249–263.
108. R. Madhavan & J. E. Prescott, 1995, Market value impact of joint ventures: The effect of industry information-processing load, *Academy of Management Journal,* 38: 900–915.
109. J. L. Johnson, J. B. Cullen, & T. Sakano, 1996, Setting the stage for trust and strategic integration in Japanese-U.S. cooperative alliances, *Journal of International Business Studies,* 27: 981–1004.
110. J.-F. Hennart, T. Roehl, & D. S. Zietlow, 1999, 'Trojan horse' or 'workhouse'? The evolution of U.S.–Japanese joint ventures in the United States, *Strategic Management Journal,* 20: 15–29.
111. M. T. Dacin, M. A. Hitt, & E. Levitas, 1997, Selecting partners for successful international alliances: Examinations of U.S. and Korean firms, *Journal of World Business,* 32(1): 3–16; M. A. Hitt, M. T. Dacin, B. B. Tyler, & D. Park, 1997, Understanding the differences in Korean and U.S. executives strategic orientations, *Strategic Management Journal,* 18: 159–168; G. Hamel, 1991, Competition for competence and inter-partner learning with international strategic alliances, *Strategic Management Journal,* 12: 83–103.
112. Hennart, Roehl, & Zietlow, 16.
113. C. Caggiano, 1999, Hotlinks, *Inc.,* October, 72–81; Koza & Lewin, Putting the S- word back, 12.
114. C. Jones, W. S. Hesterly, & S. P. Borgatti, 1997, A general theory of network governance: Exchange conditions and social mechanisms, *Academy of Management Review,* 22: 911–945; T. J. Rowley, 1997, Moving beyond dyadic ties: A network theory of stakeholder influences, *Academy of Management Review,* 22: 887–910.
115. Doz & Hamel, *Alliance Advantage,* 222.
116. Rugman & D'Cruz, 1997, The theory of the flagship firm; D. B. Holm, K. Eriksson, & J. Johanson, 1996, Business networks and cooperation in international business relationships, *Journal of International Business Studies,* 27: 1033–1053.
117. S. S. Cohen & G. Fields, 1999, Social capital and capital gains in Silicon Valley, *California Management Review,* 41(2): 108–130; J. A. Matthews, 1999, A silicon island of the east: Creating a semiconductor industry in Singapore, *California Management Review,* 41(2): 55–78; M. E. Porter, 1998, Clusters and the new economics of competition, *Harvard Business Review,* 78(6): 77–90; R. Pouder & C. H. St. John, 1996, Hot spots and blind spots: Geographical clusters of firms and innovation, *Academy of Management Review,* 21: 1192–1225.
118. D. B. Holm, K. Eriksson, & J. Johanson, 1999, Creating value through mutual commitment to business network relationships, *Strategic Management Journal,* 20: 467–486.
119. M. L. Gerlach, 1992, *Alliance Capitalism: The Social Organization of Japanese Business* (Berkeley, CA: University of California Press).
120. H. Bahrami, 1992, The emerging flexible organization: Perspectives from Silicon Valley, *California Management Review,* 34(3): 33–52.
121. J. Levine, 1996, Even when you fail, you learn a lot, *Forbes,* March 11, 58–62.
122. T. E. Stuart, 1999, Alliance networks: View from the hub, Mastering Strategy (Part Eight), *Financial Times,* November 15, 4–6; T. Nishiguchi & J. Brookfield, 1997, The evolution of Japanese subcontracting, *Sloan Management Review,* 39(1): 89–101.
123. Ibid., 4.
124. W. Davidow & M. Malone, 1992, *A Virtual Corporation: Structuring and Revitalizing the Corporation of the 21st Century* (New York: Harper Business).
125. G. Lorenzoni & C. Baden-Fuller, 1995, Creating a strategic center to manage a web of partners, *California Management Review,* 37(3): 146–163.
126. C. Shapiro & H. R. Varian, 1999, The art of standard wars, *California Management Review,* 41(2): 8–32.
127. A. Pasztor & M. Tatge, 2000, Caterpillar is found to have defrauded ex-partner over clean-fuel technology, *Wall Street Journal,* January 19, A6.
128. E. Rangel, 1999, Telmex, Sprint call of two-year joint venture, *Dallas Morning News,* May 5, D11.
129. K. Merchant, 1999, Piaggio pulls out of Indian venture, *Financial Times,* June 4, 20.
130. Simonin, The importance of collaborative know-how.

131. Cyr, High-tech, 19; Doz & Hamel, *Alliance Advantage,* 21–22; J. B. Barney & M. H. Hansen, 1994, Trustworthiness: Can it be a source of competitive advantage? *Strategic Management Journal,* 15 (Special Winter Issue): 175–203.
132. R. Gulati & H. Singh, 1998, The architecture of cooperation: Managing coordination costs and appropriation concerns in strategic alliances, *Administrative Science Quarterly,* 43: 781–814; R. Gulati, 1996, Social structure and alliance formation patterns: A longitudinal analysis, *Administrative Science Quarterly,* 40: 619–652.
133. M. J. Dollinger, P. A. Golden, & T. Saxton, 1997, The effect of reputation on the decision to joint venture, *Strategic Management Journal,* 18: 127–140; C. W. L. Hill, 1990, Cooperation, opportunism, and the invisible hand: Implications for transaction cost theory, *Academy of Management Review,* 15: 500–513.
134. J. H. Davis, F. D. Schoorman, R. C. Mayer, & H. H. Tan, 2000, The trusted general manager and business unit performance: Empirical evidence of a competitive advantage, *Strategic Management Journal,* in press; R. C. Mayer, J. H. Davis, & F. D. Schoorman, 1995, An integrative model of organizational trust, *Academy of Management Review,* 20: 709–734.
135. J. Burton, 1999, US brewer drops out of Korean auction, *Financial Times,* July 30, 17.
136. J. H. Dyer, 1997, Effective interfirm collaboration: How firms minimize transaction costs and maximize transaction value, *Strategic Management Journal,* 18: 535–556; M. Hansen, R. E. Hoskisson, & J. B. Barney, 1997, Trustworthiness in strategic alliances: Opportunism minimization versus opportunity maximization, Working paper, Brigham Young University.
137. Mitchell, Alliances, 7.
138. P. Moran & S. Ghoshal, 1996, Theories of economic organization: The case for realism and balance, *Academy of Management Review,* 21: 58–72.
139. A. Parke, 1993, Strategic alliance structuring: A game theoretic and transaction cost examination of interfirm cooperation, *Academy of Management Journal,* 36: 794–829.
140. C. S. Sankar, W. R. Boulton, N. W. Davidson, C. A. Snyder, & R. W. Ussery, 1995, Building a world-class alliance: The universal card—TSYS case, *Academy of Management Executive,* IX(2): 20–29.
141. Das, Sen, & Sengupta, Impact of strategic alliances, 30.
142. Hoskisson, Wan, & Hanson, Strategic alliance formation.

PART 3

STRATEGIC ACTIONS: STRATEGY IMPLEMENTATION

CHAPTER TEN

Corporate Governance

CHAPTER ELEVEN

Organizational Structure and Controls

CHAPTER TWELVE

Strategic Leadership

CHAPTER THIRTEEN

Corporate Entrepreneurship and Innovation

CORPORATE GOVERNANCE

CHAPTER TEN OBJECTIVES

After reading this chapter, you should be able to:

1. Define corporate governance and explain why it is used to monitor and control managers' strategic decisions.
2. Explain how ownership came to be separated from managerial control in the modern corporation.
3. Define an agency relationship and managerial opportunism and describe their strategic and organizational implications.
4. Explain how four internal corporate governance mechanisms—ownership concentration, the board of directors, executive compensation, and the multidivisional (M-form) structure—are used to monitor and control managerial decisions.
5. Discuss trends among the three types of compensation executives receive and their effects on strategic decisions.
6. Describe how the external corporate governance mechanism—the market for corporate control—acts as a restraint on top-level managers' strategic decisions.
7. Discuss the use of corporate governance in Germany and Japan.
8. Describe how corporate governance mechanisms can foster ethical strategic decisions and behaviors on the part of top-level executives.

Are CEOs Worth Their Weight in Gold?

Many years ago, Sultans were paid their weight in gold, thus beginning a traditional saying about individuals being worth their weight in gold. This statement is intended to be a positive assessment, and most of us would greatly value being paid our weight in gold. However, would most CEOs also value that opportunity? Most likely a CEO would not if he or she is the CEO of a large firm headquartered in the United States. Given the current price of gold and the average weight of most CEOs, they would receive approximately $750,000 per year. The average total compensation for U.S. CEOs was just under $10 million in 1999. Given that that amount is about 12 to 13 times a CEO's weight in gold, few would take this option. Furthermore, some would suffer severe losses taking their weight in gold. For example, Michael Eisner, CEO of Disney, had a total compensation over a recent five-year period of $631 million. Other five-year totals included Stephen Hilbert, CEO of Conseco, with $356 million; Stephen Case, CEO of America Online, with $220 million; and Jack Welch, CEO of GE, with $164 million. The new CEO of Hewlett-Packard, Carly Fiorina, is said to have received an annual compensation package of $80–$90 million.

Many U.S. executives also receive highly attractive pay and severance packages when they leave a firm. For example, Frank Newman received $74 million when he left Banker's Trust after Deutsche Telecom found no place for him following the firm's acquisition of Banker's Trust. David Coulter, former CEO of BankAmerica, received $29 million. Newman received a contract guaranteeing him $11 million per year, plus millions more in deferred compensation and additional compensation for five years, regardless of whether he stayed with the firm or not. He resigned approximately one month after the acquisition was finalized.

The exceptionally high compensation figure for U.S. executives is not copied outside of the country. The highest-paid executive outside of the United States is Edgar Bronfman, CEO of Seagrams, a Canadian Company, at $4.5 million annually. Jürgen Schrempp, CEO of DaimlerChrysler, is paid about $3 million annually. The CEO of Japan's second-largest firm, Nippon Telegraph and Telephone, is paid approximately $300,000 annually. Thus, foreign companies do not pay executives as much as U.S. companies do.

Stephen Jobs is the exception for U.S. executives, as he only takes $1 annually in pay. However, Apple's board of directors rewarded him for the strong performance of the company in recent years with approximately $90 million in perks and compensation in 1999. Part of his reward included a Gulfstream jet. He was remunerated handsomely because Apple's operating profit in 1999 was $178 million, or $1.00 per share, which

http://www.aol.com

http://www.apple.com

http://www.bankofamerica.com

http://www.conesco.com

http://www.daimlerchrsyler.com

http://www.disney.go.com

http://www.ge.com

http://www.hewlett-packard.com

http://www.nippon.com

http://www.seagrams.com

was much higher than the expected $0.89 per share, increasing from $0.29 per share in 1998. Jobs also received options to buy 10 million shares of Apple stock.

The action of Apple's board of directors is not that unique. The primary reason for the large differential in compensation between U.S. CEOs and non-U.S. CEOs is the stock or stock options awarded to U.S. CEOs based on the performance of their firms. There was a push in the late 1980s and into the 1990s to change the compensation of U.S. CEOs to be tied more directly to performance. Of particular importance was the linkage of their pay to the performance of the company's stock. Thus, it has become commonplace to award executives stock options, which represent an option to purchase a certain number of shares of the company's stock at a predetermined price. The intent is to provide the executive incentives to improve the performance of the stock. Also, the executive who exercises the options becomes an owner of the firm and has an incentive to maintain the performance of the firm at a high level, because it now affects her or his personal wealth as well. An increasing number of CEOs have received "mega-options" that are valued at over $10 million. Whereas options accounted for only 2 percent of the total compensation paid to CEOs in the 1980s, they accounted for approximately 26 percent of U.S. executives' compensation in 1994 and well over 50 percent of the total compensation paid to U.S. CEOs in 1998 and 1999. Therefore, stockholders and boards of directors have been trying to motivate CEOs to act in the owners' best interests by increasing the value of the company, which in turn increases shareholders' wealth. Thus, executive compensation is a tool of corporate governance.

SOURCES: G. Colvin, 2000, The big payoff: CEOs are getting pots of money just for getting out of the way, *Fortune*, February 22, 78; Share and share unalike, *The Economist*, February 7, *www.economist.com*; L. Kehoe, 2000, Jet for Jobs as Apple's profits surprise, *ft.com*, January 20, *www.ft.com/nbearchives*; T. W. Ferguson & J. Lee, 1999, Failing upward, *Forbes*, October 19, 52; D. P. Hamilton, 1999, H-P values CEO's package at $80 to $90 million, *Wall Street Journal Interactive*, September 22, *www.interactive.wsj.com/articles*; E. S. Hardy, S. DeCarlo, A. C. Anderson, & J. Chamberlain, 1999, Compensation fit for a king, *Forbes*, May 17, 202–207; Top-paid foreign CEOs lag far behind Americans, *Houston Chronicle*, May 5, 4C.

As the Opening Case illustrates, corporate governance is increasingly important as a part of the strategic management process.[1] If the board makes the wrong decision in compensating the firm's strategic leader, the CEO, the whole firm suffers, as do its shareholders. Compensation is used to motivate CEOs to act in the best interests of the firm—in particular, the shareholders. When they do so, the firm's value should increase. Of course, some question what a CEO's actions are worth. The Opening Case suggests that they are worth a significant amount in the United States (considerably more than the CEO's weight in gold). While some critics argue that U.S. CEOs are paid too much, the hefty increases in compensation they have received in recent years come from linking their pay to the performance of the firm. U.S. firms have performed well compared with many others from different countries. Some research suggests that CEOs receive excessive compensation when the corporate governance is the weakest.[2]

Corporate governance represents the relationship among stakeholders that is used to determine and control the strategic direction and performance of organizations.

Corporate governance represents the relationship among stakeholders that is used to determine and control the strategic direction and performance of organizations.[3] At its core, corporate governance is concerned with identifying ways to ensure that strategic decisions are made effectively.[4] In addition, governance can be thought of as a means used by corporations to establish order between parties (the firm's owners and its top-level managers) whose interests may be in conflict.[5] Thus, corporate gover-

Corporations around the world are making efforts to improve the performance of their boards of directors because corporate governance has failed to adequately monitor top managers' strategic decisions. A second reason is that a well-functioning governance and control system can result in a competitive advantage for a firm.

nance reflects and enforces the company's values.[6] In modern corporations—especially those in the United States and the United Kingdom—a primary objective of corporate governance is to ensure that the interests of top-level managers are aligned with the interests of the shareholders. Corporate governance involves oversight in areas where owners, managers, and members of boards of directors may have conflicts of interest. These areas include the election of directors, the general supervision of CEO pay and more focused supervision of director pay, and the corporation's overall structure and strategic direction.[7]

Corporate governance has been emphasized in recent years because some observers believe that corporate governance mechanisms have failed to adequately monitor and control top-level managers' strategic decisions.[8] This perspective is causing changes in governance mechanisms in corporations throughout the world, especially with respect to efforts intended to improve the performance of boards of directors.[9] This interest, however, is understandable for a second and more positive reason; namely, that evidence suggests that a well-functioning corporate governance and control system can result in a competitive advantage for an individual firm.[10] For example, one governance mechanism—the board of directors—has been suggested to be rapidly evolving into a major strategic force in U.S. business firms.[11] Thus, in this chapter, we describe actions designed to implement strategies that focus on monitoring and controlling mechanisms. When used properly, these actions help to ensure that top-level managerial actions contribute to the firm's strategic competitiveness and its ability to earn above-average returns.

Effective corporate governance is also of interest to nations. As stated by one scholar,

> Every country wants the firms that operate within its borders to flourish and grow in such ways as to provide employment, wealth, and satisfaction, not only to improve standards of living materially but also to enhance social cohesion. These aspirations cannot be met unless those firms are competitive internationally in a sustained way, and it is this medium- and long-term perspective that makes good corporate governance so vital.[12]

Corporate governance, then, reflects the standards of the company, which, in turn, collectively reflect the societal standards.[13] Thus, in many individual corporations, shareholders are striving to hold top-level managers more accountable for their decisions and the results they generate. As with individual firms and their boards, nations that govern their corporations effectively may gain a competitive advantage over rival countries.

In a range of countries, but especially in the United States and the United Kingdom, the fundamental goal of business organizations is to maximize shareholder value.[14] Traditionally, shareholders are treated as the firm's key stakeholders, because they are the company's legal owners. The firm's owners expect top-level managers and others influencing the corporation's actions (e.g., the board of directors) to make decisions that will result in the maximization of the company's value and, hence, of their own wealth.[15]

In the first section of this chapter, we describe the relationship providing the foundation on which the modern corporation is built; the relationship between owners and managers. The majority of this chapter is then devoted to an explanation of various mechanisms owners use to govern managers and ensure that they comply with their responsibility to maximize shareholder value.

Four internal governance mechanisms and a single external one are used in the modern corporation (see Table 10.1). The four internal governance mechanisms examined herein are (1) ownership concentration, as represented by types of shareholders and their different incentives to monitor managers, (2) the board of directors, (3) executive compensation, and (4) the multidivisional (M-form) organizational structure. Next, we consider the market for corporate control, an external corporate governance mechanism. Essentially, this market is a set of potential owners seeking to acquire undervalued firms and earn above-average returns on their investments by replacing ineffective top-level management teams.[16] The chapter's focus then shifts to the issue of international corporate governance. We briefly describe governance approaches used in German and Japanese firms whose traditional governance structures are being affected by the realities of competing in the global economy. In part, this discussion suggests the possibility that the structures used to govern global companies in many different countries, including Germany, Japan, the United Kingdom, and the United States, are becoming more, rather than less, similar. Closing our analysis of corporate governance is a consideration of the need for these control mechanisms to encourage and support ethical behavior in organizations.

Importantly, the mechanisms explained in this chapter have the potential to influence positively the governance of the modern corporation. The modern corporation has placed significant responsibility and authority in the hands of top-level managers. The most effective of these managers understand their accountability for the firm's per-

10.1 | Corporate Governance Mechanisms

Internal Governance Mechanisms
Ownership Concentration
• Relative amounts of stock owned by individual shareholders and institutional investors
Board of Directors
• Individuals responsible for representing the firm's owners by monitoring top-level managers' strategic decisions
Executive Compensation
• Use of salary, bonuses, and long-term incentives to align managers' interests with shareholders' interests
Multidivisional Structure
• Creation of individual business divisions to closely monitor top-level managers' strategic decisions
External Governance Mechanism
Market for Corporate Control
• The purchase of a firm that is underperforming relative to industry rivals in order to improve its strategic competitiveness

formance and respond positively to the requirements of the corporate governance mechanisms explained in this chapter.[17] In addition, the firm's owners should not expect any single mechanism to govern the company effectively over time. Rather, the use of several mechanisms allows owners to govern the corporation in ways that maximize strategic competitiveness and increase the financial value of their firm.[18] With multiple governance mechanisms operating simultaneously, it is also possible for some of the governance mechanisms to conflict.[19] Later, we review how these conflicts can occur.

Separation of Ownership and Managerial Control

Historically, U.S. firms were managed by the founder-owners and their descendants. In these cases, corporate ownership and control resided in the same person(s). As firms grew larger, "the managerial revolution led to a separation of ownership and control in most large corporations, where control of the firm shifted from entrepreneurs to professional managers while ownership became dispersed among thousands of unorganized stockholders who were removed from the day-to-day management of the firm."[20] These changes created the modern public corporation, which is based on the efficient separation of ownership and managerial control. Supporting the separation is a basic legal premise suggesting that the primary objective of a firm's activities is to increase the corporation's profit and, thereby, the financial gains of the owners (the shareholders).[21]

The separation of ownership and managerial control allows shareholders to purchase stock, which entitles them to income (residual returns) from the operations of the firm after expenses have been paid. This right, however, requires that they also take a risk that the firm's expenses may exceed its revenues. To manage this investment risk, shareholders seek to maintain a diversified portfolio by investing in several companies to reduce their overall risk.[22]

In small firms, managers often are the owners, so there is no separation between ownership and managerial control, but as firms grow and become more complex, owners–managers may contract with managerial specialists. These managers oversee decision making in the owner's firm and are compensated on the basis of their decision-making skills. Managers, then, operate a corporation through the use of their decision-making skills and are viewed as agents of the firm's owners.[23] In terms of the strategic management process (see Figure 1.1), managers are expected to form a firm's strategic intent and strategic mission and then formulate and implement the strategies that realize them. Thus, in the modern public corporation, top-level managers, especially the CEO, have primary responsibility for initiating and implementing an array of strategic decisions.

As shareholders diversify their investments over a number of corporations, their risk declines. The poor performance or failure of any one firm in which they invest has less overall effect. Thus, shareholders specialize in managing their investment risk, while managers specialize in decision making. Without management specialization in decision making and owner specialization in risk bearing, a firm probably would be limited by the abilities of its owners to manage and make effective strategic decisions. Therefore, the separation and specialization of ownership (risk bearing) and managerial control (decision making) should produce the highest returns.

Shareholder value is reflected by the price of the firm's stock. As stated earlier, corporate governance, such as the board of directors or compensation based on the performance of a firm, is the reason that CEOs show general concern about the firm's stock price. For example, the executives at DaimlerChrysler expressed considerable concern when the firm's stock price decreased by over 20 percent in 1999 after the merger between Daimler and Chrysler was completed. In particular, the firm has lost many U.S.-based shareholders, and this is reflected in the price of the stock.[24] In 2000, DaimlerChrysler's stock price increased, however. As such the market reacts to specific actions taken by firms. When Amazon.com announced that it was laying off 150 employees, the price of its stock declined 10 percent. The layoffs represented about 2 percent of the company's workforce. Investors did not view this as an action to increase the firm's efficiency, but rather saw it as a signal that the firm was experiencing problems. To forestall the negative reaction, top executives at Amazon announced that more employees would be hired in the United States later in the year.[25] In another situation, investors reacted positively to Ericsson's actions to overcome its internal problems in 1999, a year in which Ericsson's stock price doubled in value. The company initiated restructuring actions and announced a high-profile alliance with Microsoft during 1999. Also, early evidence suggested that its market position in mobile handsets had improved.[26]

An **agency relationship** exists when one or more persons (the principal or principals) hire another person or persons (the agent or agents) as decision-making specialists to perform a service.

Agency Relationships

The separation between owners and managers creates an agency relationship. An **agency relationship** exists when one or more persons (the principal or principals) hire another person or persons (the agent or agents) as decision-making specialists to perform a service.[27] Thus, an agency relationship exists when one party delegates decision-making responsibility to a second party for compensation (see Figure 10.1).[28] In addition to shareholders and top executives, other examples of agency relationships are consultants and clients and insured and insurer. Moreover, within organizations, an agency relationship exists between managers and their employees, as well as between top executives and the firm's owners.[29] In the modern corporation, managers must understand the links between these relationships and the firm's effectiveness.[30] Although the agency relationship between managers and their employees is important, in this chapter we focus on the agency relationship between the firm's owners (the principals) and top-level managers (the principals' agents), because this relationship is related directly to how strategies are implemented by managers.

Managerial opportunism is the seeking of self-interest with guile.

The separation between ownership and managerial control can be problematic. Research evidence documents a variety of agency problems in the modern corporation.[31] Problems can surface because the principal and the agent have different interests and goals or because shareholders lack direct control of large publicly traded corporations. Problems arise when an agent makes decisions that result in the pursuit of goals that conflict with those of the principals. Thus, the separation of ownership and control *potentially* allows divergent interests (between principals and agents) to surface, which can lead to managerial opportunism.[32] **Managerial opportunism** is the seeking of self-interest with guile (i.e., cunning or deceit).[33] Opportunism is both an

FIGURE 10.1 | An Agency Relationship

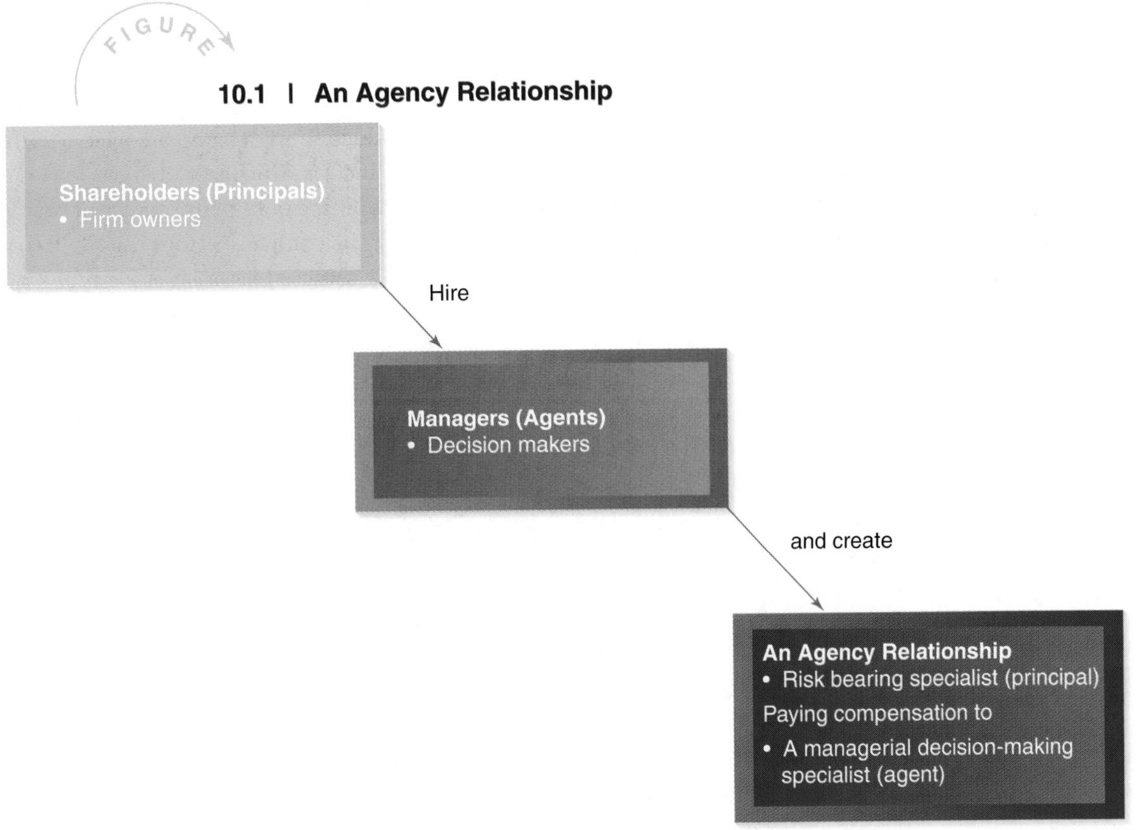

attitude (e.g., an inclination) and a set of behaviors (i.e., specific acts of self-interest).[34] However, it is not possible for principals to know beforehand which agents will or will not engage in opportunistic behavior. The reputations of top executives are an imperfect predictor, and opportunistic behavior cannot be observed until it has occurred. Thus, principals establish governance and control mechanisms to prevent agents from acting opportunistically, even though only a few are likely to do so.[35] Any time that principals delegate decision-making responsibilities to agents, the opportunity for conflicts of interest exist. Top executives, for example, may make strategic decisions that maximize their personal welfare and minimize their personal risk.[36] Decisions such as these prevent the maximization of shareholder wealth. Decisions regarding product diversification demonstrate these possibilities.

Product Diversification as an Example of an Agency Problem

As explained in Chapter 6, a corporate-level strategy to diversify the firm's product lines can enhance a firm's strategic competitiveness and increase its returns, both of which serve the interests of shareholders and the top executives. However, because product diversification can provide two benefits to managers that shareholders do not enjoy, top executives sometimes prefer more product diversification than do shareholders.[37]

Diversification usually increases the size of a firm, and size is positively related to executive compensation. Thus, increased product diversification provides an opportunity for top executives to increase their compensation through growth in firm size.[38]

In addition, product diversification and the resulting diversification of the firm's portfolio of businesses can reduce top executives' employment risk.[39] *Managerial employment risk* is the risk of job loss, loss of compensation, and loss of managerial reputation. These risks are reduced with increased diversification, because a firm and its upper-level managers are less vulnerable to the reduction in demand associated with a single or limited number of product lines or businesses. This risk is depicted clearly in the shareholders' strong expression of concern with the poor performance of Xerox in recent times and the precipitous loss in value of the company's stock. In 1999, the price of Xerox stock decreased by 65 percent. One shareholder, a large institutional investor, referred to an announcement by the board of directors supporting CEO Rick Thoman as a "kiss of death." Xerox competitors have been experiencing record sales. Thus, investors and shareholders are angry about the strategy implementation mistakes to which Thoman has admitted. According to a Goldman Sachs analyst, "The earnings problems they have been experiencing have been largely of their own making." Another analyst from J.P. Morgan stated, "To the extent that any CEO has any honeymoon, his is definitely over." Thus, Thoman faces significant employment risk.[40]

Furthermore, the firm may have free cash flows over which top executives have discretion. *Free cash flows* are resources generated after investment in all projects that have positive net present values within the firm's current product lines.[41] In anticipation of positive returns, managers may decide to use these funds to invest in products that are not associated with the current lines of business, even if the investments increase the firm's level of diversification. The managerial decision to use free cash flows to over-diversify the firm is an example of self-serving and opportunistic managerial behavior. In contrast to managers, shareholders may prefer that free cash flows be distributed to them as dividends, so they can control how the cash is invested.[42]

Curve *S* in Figure 10.2 depicts the shareholders' optimal level of diversification. Owners seek the level of diversification that reduces the risk of the firm's total failure while simultaneously increasing the company's value through the development of economies of scale and scope (see Chapter 6). Of the four corporate-level diversification strategies shown in Figure 10.2, shareholders likely prefer the diversified position noted by point *A* on curve *S*—a position that is located between the dominant business and related-constrained diversification strategies. Of course, the optimum level of diversification sought by owners varies from firm to firm. Factors that affect shareholders' preferences include the firm's primary industry, the intensity of rivalry among competitors in that industry, and the top management team's experience with implementing diversification strategies.

As with principals, upper-level executives—as agents—seek an optimal level of diversification. Declining performance resulting from too much product diversification increases the probability that a firm will be acquired in the market for corporate control. Once a firm is acquired, the employment risk for the firm's top executives increases substantially. Furthermore, a manager's employment opportunities in the external managerial labor market (discussed in Chapter 12) are affected negatively by a firm's poor performance. Therefore, top executives prefer diversification, but not to a point that it increases their employment risk and reduces their employment opportunities.

Curve *M* in Figure 10.2 shows that executives prefer higher levels of product diversification than shareholders. Top executives might prefer the level of diversification shown by point *B* on curve *M*. In general, shareholders prefer riskier strategies and more

10.2 | Manager and Shareholder Risk and Diversification

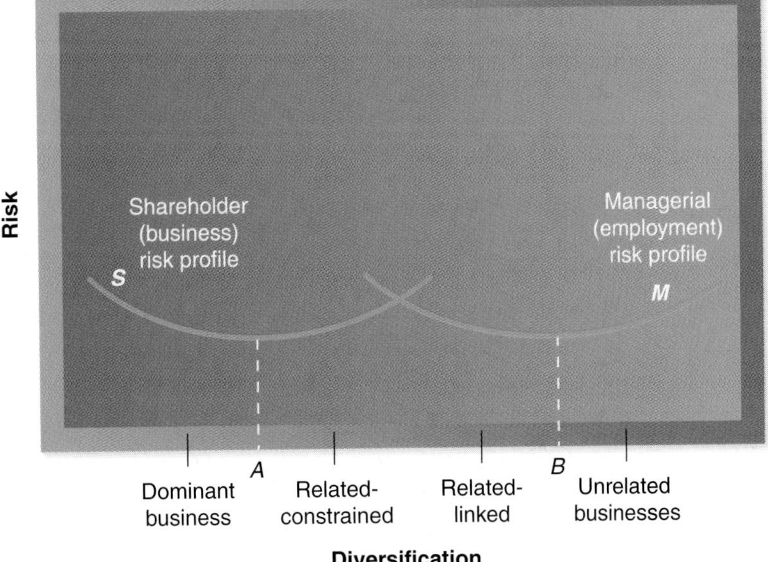

focused diversification. They reduce their risk through holding a diversified portfolio of equity investments. Alternatively, managers cannot work for a diverse portfolio of firms to balance their employment risk. Therefore, top executives may prefer a level of diversification that maximizes firm size and their compensation and that reduces their employment risk. Product diversification, therefore, is a potential agency problem that could result in principals incurring costs to control their agents' behaviors.

Agency Costs and Governance Mechanisms

The potential conflict illustrated by Figure 10.2, coupled with the fact that principals do not know which managers might act opportunistically, demonstrates why principals establish governance mechanisms. However, establishing and using the governance mechanisms create costs. **Agency costs** are the sum of incentive costs, monitoring costs, enforcement costs, and individual financial losses incurred by principals because it is impossible to use governance mechanisms to guarantee total compliance by the agent.[43]

Agency costs are the sum of incentive costs, monitoring costs, enforcement costs, and individual financial losses incurred by principals because it is impossible to use governance mechanisms to guarantee total compliance by the agent.

In general, managerial interests may prevail when governance mechanisms are weak, as is exemplified by allowing managers a significant amount of autonomy in making strategic decisions. If, however, the board of directors controls managerial autonomy, or if other strong governance mechanisms are used, the firm's strategies should better reflect the interests of the shareholders. However, recent research suggests that even using more governance mechanisms may produce major changes in strategies. This research showed, for example, that firms acquired unrelated businesses at approximately the same rate in the 1980s as they did in the 1960s, even though more governance mechanisms were employed in the 1980s. Thus, governance mechanisms represent an imperfect means of controlling managerial opportunism.[44] Alternatively, anecdotal evidence suggests that shareholders are not docile when they perceive that managers are not taking actions in their best interests. For example, Comair shareholders filed suit in late 1999 when the company's board of directors accepted a bid from Delta to buy the firm. The shareholders felt that the acquisition price was inadequate. Delta had threatened Comair with a reduction in the amount of revenue that it would receive from Delta's allied flights. Thus, Comair's board was faced with allowing Delta to reduce Comair's revenues significantly or accepting Delta's acquisition price for Comair stock. The shareholders named the board and Delta as defendants.[45] Likewise, shareholders in Japan are becoming more active. Recently, shareholders of Dai-Ichi Kangyo Bank filed suits over payments that the bank made to racketeers known as sokaiya. The sokaiya commonly disrupted annual shareholders' meetings by jeering unless the firm made payments to them not to attend the meeting. The banks and other firms are worried about this new shareholder activism.[46]

In the sections that follow, we explain the effects of various means of governance on managerial decisions to formulate and implement the firm's different strategies.

Ownership Concentration

Ownership concentration is defined by both the number of large-block shareholders and the total percentage of shares they own. **Large-block shareholders** typically own at least 5 percent of a corporation's issued shares. Ownership concentration as a gov-

Ownership concentration is defined by both the number of large-block shareholders and the total percentage of shares they own.

Large-block shareholders typically own at least 5 percent of a corporation's issued shares.

ernance mechanism has received considerable interest because large-block shareholders are increasingly active in their demands that corporations adopt effective governance mechanisms to control managerial decisions.[47]

In general, *diffuse ownership* (a large number of shareholders with small holdings and few, if any, large-block shareholders) produces weak monitoring of managerial decisions. Among other problems, diffuse ownership makes it difficult for owners to coordinate their actions effectively. An outcome of weak monitoring might be the diversification of the firm's product lines beyond the shareholders' optimum level. Higher levels of monitoring could encourage managers to avoid strategic decisions that do not create greater shareholder value. In fact, research evidence shows that ownership concentration is associated with lower levels of firm diversification.[48] Thus, with high degrees of ownership concentration, the probability is greater that managers' strategic decisions will be intended to maximize shareholder value.

Concentration of ownership is a natural consequence of deregulated industries. For example, after the airline industry was deregulated in the United States, the ownership of the airlines became more concentrated.[49] Much of this concentration often has come from increasing equity ownership by institutional investors.

The Growing Influence of Institutional Owners

A classic work published in the 1930s argued that the "modern" corporation had become characterized by a separation of ownership and control.[50] This change occurred as the growth of a firm prevented its founders–owners from maintaining their dual positions as owners and managers of their corporations. More recently, another shift has occurred: Ownership of many modern corporations is now concentrated in the hands of institutional investors rather than individual shareholders.[51]

Institutional owners are financial institutions such as stock mutual funds and pension funds that control large-block shareholder positions.

Institutional owners are financial institutions such as stock mutual funds and pension funds that control large-block shareholder positions. Because of their prominent ownership positions, institutional owners, as large-block shareholders, are a powerful governance mechanism.[52] Institutions of these types now own more than 50 percent of the stock in large U.S. corporations. Of the top 1,000 corporations, they own, on average, 59 percent of the stock.[53] Pension funds alone control at least one-half of corporate equity.[54] Some institutional investors even invest funds with other investment funds. For example, the California Public Employees Retirement System (CalPERS) announced plans to buy a 10 percent stake in Thomas Weisel Partners, a firm that focuses on investing in California's high-technology firms. CalPERS suggested that it will invest about $1 billion to purchase the 10 percent ownership interest and invest in several of the investment funds being organized by Weisel. CalPERS and Weisel managers call this action an alliance between the firms. It represents an interesting partnership and suggests the financial power of the large institutional investors.[55]

Thus, as the ownership percentages suggest, institutional owners have both the size and the incentive to discipline ineffective top-level managers and are able to influence significantly a firm's choice of strategies and overall strategic decisions.[56] Research evidence indicates that institutional and other large-block shareholders are becoming more active in efforts to influence a corporation's strategic decisions. Initially, the shareholders seemed to concentrate on the accountability of CEOs. After focusing on the performance of many CEOs, which has contributed to the ouster of a number of them, shareholder activists and institutional investors are targeting what they perceive as ineffective boards of directors.

CalPERS provides retirement and health coverage to more than one million current and retired public employees.[57] It is one of the largest public employee pension funds in the United States, and it has earned a reputation for bullying some U.S. companies into adopting its recommendations. CalPERS is generally thought to act aggressively to promote decisions and actions that it believes will enhance shareholder value in companies in which it invests. To pressure boards of directors to make what it believes are needed changes, CalPERS annually issues a target list of companies in which it owns stock that it believes are underachieving. This list is based on corporations' relative rates of shareholder return, their degree of responsiveness to CalPERS' inquiries, labor practices, and the percentage of shares owned by CalPERS. Once the list is published, CalPERS usually demands meetings with top-level managers from companies appearing on the list. CalPERS is known to flex its muscles and oust directors when its requests are denied.[58] According to CalPERS officials, the intent of these sessions is to persuade corporate boards to force management to initiate appropriate strategic changes inside the targeted company. The largest institutional investor, TIAA-CREF, has taken actions similar to those of CalPERS, but with a less publicly aggressive stance. To date, research suggests that these institutions' activism may not have a direct effect on firm performance, but that the influence may be indirect through effects on important strategic activities, such as innovation.[59]

The Strategic Focus examines how the actions by institutional investors affect companies' actions. It is also interesting to note that institutional investors are being targeted by shareholders with the purpose of getting the institutional investors to act in ways that fit in with their shareholders' interests.

Shareholder Activism: How Much Is Possible?

The U.S. Securities and Exchange Commission (SEC) has issued several rulings that support shareholder involvement and control of managerial decisions. One such action is the easing of the rule regarding communications among shareholders. Historically, shareholders could communicate among themselves only through a cumbersome and expensive filing process. With a simple notification to the SEC of an upcoming meeting, shareholders can now convene to discuss a corporation's strategic direction. If a consensus on an issue exists, shareholders can vote as a block. For example, the 20 largest shareholders of Philip Morris own approximately 25 percent of the firm's stock. Coalescing around a position and voting as a block can send a powerful message to Philip Morris's top executives and its board of directors. This voting capability has been referred to as *shareholder empowerment*.

Some argue that greater latitude should be extended to those managing the funds of large institutional investor groups. Allowing these individuals to hold positions on companies' boards of directors in which their organization has significant investments might enable fund managers to better represent the interests of those they serve.[60] As the Strategic Focus indicates, TIAA-CREF influences firms' decisions, but does so in a less public way. Serving on the board of directors of a firm in which it has significant investments would enable TIAA-CREF and other institutional investors to influence

Institutional Investors Carry a Big Stick

Large institutional investors have become quite powerful in their relationships with corporations in which they invest. The two largest public pension funds, TIAA-CREF and CalPERS, have been wielding their power with positive results. TIAA-CREF has been effective while pushing for changes, often more quietly than CalPERS. TIAA-CREF managers have been trying to use a less aggressive approach without substantial publicity. The company's focus has been on boards of directors. For example, it played a lead role in reshaping the board of directors at W. R. Grace in 1995. It also played a strong role in the attack on Heinz and Disney for the lack of independence of members of their boards of directors. After a meeting with the chairman of Heinz, Anthony O'Reilly, wherein O'Reilly declined to make any changes, TIAA-CREF filed a shareholder resolution with the SEC. After the first resolution was excluded from the Heinz proxy on a technicality, the firm filed another resolution. Eventually, it withdrew the proposal, as Heinz made substantial changes in its board. Eleven of Heinz's 19 directors are now outsiders. Disney has also made changes. It agreed to hold annual elections for directors and allowed a poison pill to expire. Disney also replaced inside board members with outside independent board members. The manager of shareholder affairs at Coca-Cola, Thomas Paris, referred to TIAA-CREF as "the Teddy Roosevelts of corporate governance. They speak softly but carry a big stick."

At times, however, TIAA-CREF does not speak softly. When the company managers or board ignore its requests, TIAA-CREF is willing to take more aggressive action. For example, it has strongly opposed "dead-hand" poison pills. This poison pill is a defense against a takeover that prevents an acquisition even if a majority of the shareholders favor it. Such a poison pill can be removed only by the incumbent directors. Thus, new board members cannot vote to remove these defense mechanisms. TIAA-CREFF managers suggest that the devices are used to entrench managers and directors. In suggesting this, they prepared shareholder resolutions for the removal of "dead-hand" poison pills at Lubrizol Corporation and Bergen Brunswig Corporation. They won 74 percent and 68 percent of the shareholders' support at these two companies, respectively. TIAA-CREFF also has taken similar action against Mylan Laboratories, issuing press releases on what they did.

CalPERS has found the Internet to be extremely helpful in its crusade for better firm governance. For example, it now posts its votes on proxy issues on its Web site. Since the company started posting these votes, its Web site has begun to receive over 30,000 hits per month. By accessing the Web site, investors found that CalPERS intended to withhold votes for the election of directors at Tyson Foods, Emerson Electric, and Micron Technology in January 2000 alone. The reasons for their actions were also posted. These directors had business or personal relationships with the company or top executives, and those relationships, CalPERS believed, could compromise the boards' decisions.

Recently, CalPERS expressed concern about two Disney board members who received consulting fees from Disney of $50,000 and $71,000, respectively. CalPERS questioned the independence of these board members, one of whom serves on the board audit review committee. CalPERS recommended that all shareholders withhold their votes for those two board members

Interestingly, institutional investors from both the United States and the United Kingdom have also begun to invest more of their money outside of their home markets. Accordingly, they have become increasingly interested in corporate governance practices in other countries. Of course, their potential actions complicate the governance activities in numerous other countries. However, their actions are constrained by the laws and accepted practices in those countries.

It is also interesting to note that these institutional investors are not immune to shareholder actions directed at them. For example, TIAA-CREF, with $268 billion invested in pension funds, recently had to react to activism directed toward its actions by a group of shareholders. This group, led by some of the company's investors (in particular, two professors) wants the pension fund to invest more of its money in socially responsible companies. TIAA-CREF managers are not responding to the group, however. Still, the effort has been gathering more supporters. Currently, more than 100 professors are supporting the efforts. In fact, TIAA-CREF's resistance is causing a negative reaction among some of its other investors, who argue that the money TIAA-CREF is investing is theirs, and thus, their opinions should count more. It is fascinating to observe this large institutional investor deal with some of its own "medicine."

SOURCES: B. Orwall & J. S. Lublin, 2000, Calpers will withhold votes for directors paid by Disney, *Wall Street Journal Interactive,* February 9, *www.interactive.wsj.com*; Now a gadfly can bite 24 hours per day, 2000, *Businessweek Online,* February, 6, *www.businessweek.com*; P.-W. Tam, 1999, TIAA-CREF resists heat from activist holders' group, *Wall Street Journal,* August 24, C1, C25; TIAA-CREF urges Mylan Laboratories shareholders to support removal of dead hand poison pills, 1999, *TIAA-CREF News Release,* June 15; J. A. Byrne, 1999, The Teddy Roosevelts of corporate governance, *Business Week,* May 31, 75–79; J. Martinson, 1999, A capital idea in search of consensus, *FT Director,* March 19, 1.

the firm's strategic decisions more effectively, but without external publicity. In addition, this capability would foster more direct disciplining of poorly performing or dissident top-level managers when that is needed. Such representation is allowed in other countries. For example, Telecom Italia proposed to spin off its wireless communications unit and compensate the shareholders with 1.5–1.65 shares in the new firm for every share they held in the parent company. Minority shareholders (Olivetti owns 40% of the stock) expressed dismay. Directors representing large Italian and U.S. investment funds objected and doomed the project.[61]

The type of shareholder and board-of-director activism used by CalPERS and other institutional investors sometimes provokes reactions from top executives. Unintended and not always anticipated, these reactions require still further attention by those monitoring the decisions being made by the firm's managers. A reaction articulated by one corporate CEO demonstrates this issue. When asked to evaluate results achieved through shareholder activism, the CEO suggested that at least some of the actions requested by shareholder activists exceeded the roles specified by the separation of ownership and managerial control. When this occurs, the CEO argued, owners and directors begin to micromanage the corporation, which is not their job. Faced with such a situation, executives have incentives to take actions that reduce their employment risk. Implementing strategies with greater diversification, as explained earlier, is one path top executives can pursue to achieve their objective. O'Reilly, for instance, did not increase Heinz's diversification, but he held ownership positions and board responsibilities in a number of other enterprises.[62] In so doing, he was less dependent on his chairman position with Heinz. Of course, having the additional positions reduced the time O'Reilly was able to spend on Heinz's strategic issues.

A number of CEOs are now declining to be outside directors on other firms' boards because CEOs have been criticized for serving on outside boards, taking time away from their CEO responsibilities. The National Association of Corporate Directors (NACD) has urged that CEOs hold no more than three directorships in publicly held firms. Gordon Bethune of Continental Airlines asks, "How much time do I want to spend doing somebody else's work?" Instead of serving on other firms' boards, top executives, such as those at Continental Airlines, increasingly desire to spend time improving their own firm's performance. Improved performance reduces the likelihood that a firm will become a takeover candidate, and, more generally, it reduces the risk that the CEO will lose her or his job.[63]

Executives may take actions to protect themselves against employment risks when institutional investors have major investments in their firm. Besides the proactive protection of doing a better job, they may seek defensive protection from a possible acquisition. Evidence suggests that the number of executives receiving such protection is increasing. A *golden parachute,* a type of managerial protection that pays a guaranteed salary for a specified period in the event of a takeover and the loss of one's job, is sought by many top-level managers, particularly the CEO. A number of other provisions also allow a firm to defend against an attempted takeover.[64] A more recently developed protection is called "the golden goodbye." A golden goodbye provides automatic payments to top executives if their contracts are not renewed, regardless of the reason for the nonrenewal. In the extreme, golden goodbyes are being offered in the case of acquisitions. In these cases, managers may receive compensation even if they personally decide to quit. For example, earlier we described the exit of Frank Newman after his firm was acquired. He had a golden-goodbye contract that paid him $11 million over the next five years, regardless of whether he worked for the firm or quit. He decided to resign only one month after the acquisition. He also received other payments during this five-year period as well. In theory, the golden-goodbye arrangement protects top-level managers whose long-term prospects are uncertain.

In general, though, the degree to which institutional investors can actively monitor the decisions being made in all of the companies in which they have invested is questionable. CalPERS, for instance, targets 12 companies at a time. The New York Teachers Retirement Fund, another activist institutional investor, focuses on 25 of the 1,300-plus companies in its portfolio. Given limited resources, even large-block shareholders tend to concentrate on corporations in which they have significant investments. Thus, although shareholder activism has increased, institutional investors face barriers to the amount of active governance they can realistically employ.[65]

Also, it is not only the large institutional investors that take actions against firms that fail to perform in the best interests of their shareholders. For example, David Corbin, manager of the Corbin Small-Cap Value Fund, has become an activist against Vtel, a manufacturer of videoconferencing products. In 1995, Vtel's stock sold for $26 per share, but, in 2000, it sold for $4.38 per share. Corbin believes that the firm's managers have missed opportunities and that the stock should be selling for $70 per share. Furthermore, he is upset because the board of directors has taken no action. He participated in a conference call to Vtel's board of directors and several other institutional investors in January 2000. Earlier, he expressed his concerns openly at the firm's annual stockholders' meeting. Rather than sell the shares, Corbin says, "I want them to go to bed at night thinking about what they're going to do to make me happy. And I want them to wake up in the morning and go do it."[66]

Typically, shareholders monitor the managerial decisions and actions of a firm through the board of directors. Shareholders elect members to their firm's board. Those who are elected are expected to oversee managers and to ensure that the corporation is operated in ways that will maximize its shareholders' wealth.

Institutional activism should create a premium on companies with good corporate governance. However, sometimes trustees for these funds—particularly large private pension funds—have other business relationships with companies in the fund's portfolio. This prevents effective monitoring.[67] In addition, a recent phenomenon is the increase in managerial ownership of the firm's stock. There are many positive reasons for managerial ownership, including the use of stock options to link managerial pay to the performance of a firm. However, an unexpected outcome has been reduced support for shareholder-sponsored proposals to repeal antitakeover provisions. Institutional owners generally support the repeal of these provisions, while managerial owners generally oppose their repeal. Thus, managerial ownership provides managers with power to protect their own interests.[68] This suggests that other means of governance are needed. Next, we examine the board of directors as a governance mechanism.

Board of Directors

As we have described, the practices of large institutional investors have resulted in an increase in ownership concentration in U.S. firms. Nonetheless, diffuse ownership still describes the status of most U.S. firms,[69] which means that monitoring and control of managers by individual shareholders is limited in large corporations. Furthermore, large financial institutions, such as banks, are prevented from directly owning stock in firms and from having representatives on companies' boards of directors. These conditions highlight the importance of the board of directors for corporate governance. Unfortunately over time, boards of directors have not been highly effective in monitoring and controlling top management's actions.[70] While boards of directors are imperfect, they can positively influence both managers and the companies they serve.

The **board of directors** is a group of elected individuals whose primary responsibility is to act in the owners' interests by formally monitoring and controlling the corporation's top-level executives.

The **board of directors** is a group of elected individuals whose primary responsibility is to act in the owners' interests by formally monitoring and controlling the corporation's top-level executives.[71] This responsibility is a product of the American legal system, which "confers broad powers on corporate boards to direct the affairs of the organization, punish and reward managers, and protect the rights and interests of shareholders."[72] Thus, an appropriately structured and effective board of directors protects owners from managerial opportunism. Board members are seen as stewards of their company's resources, and the way they carry out these responsibilities affects the society in which their firm operates.[73]

Generally, board members (often called directors) are classified into one of three groups (see Table 10.2). *Insiders* are active top-level managers in the corporation who are elected to the board because they are a source of information about the firm's day-to-day operations.[74] *Related outsiders* have some relationship with the firm—contractual or otherwise—that may create questions about their independence, but these individuals are not involved with the corporation's day-to-day activities. *Outsiders* are individuals elected to the board to provide independent counsel to the firm and may hold top-level managerial positions in another company or have been elected to the board prior to the beginning of the current CEO's tenure.[75]

Some argue that many boards are not fulfilling their primary fiduciary duty to protect shareholders. Among other possibilities, it may be that boards are a managerial tool: They do not question managers' actions, and they easily approve managers' self-serving initiatives.[76] In general, those critical of boards as a governance device believe that inside managers dominate boards and exploit their personal ties with them. A widely accepted view is that a board with a significant percentage of its membership from the firm's top executives tends to provide relatively weak monitoring and control of managerial decisions.[77] Critics advocate reforms to ensure that independent outside directors represent a significant majority of the total membership of a board.[78] In Great Britain, the Cadbury Report on Corporate Governance advocated improvements in board accountability and performance. Furthermore, the architect of this report, Sir Adrian Cadbury, suggests that the reform of corporate governance has become a worldwide movement, because of the growth of global markets.[79]

Boards have become more active in recent years because of the emphasis on reform, because of shareholder lawsuits, and because of active institutional investors such as TIAA-CREF and CalPERS. One criticism has been that some boards wait too long before taking action to replace CEOs who are not performing well. For example, in 1999, Compaq's board of directors asked its CEO to resign because of performance difficulties experienced by the large computer manufacturer and then hired a new CEO. However, critics argue that the board should have acted much sooner. They suggest that the board, ignoring warning signs of problems, failed to act until after a

TABLE

10.2 | Classifications of Boards of Directors' Members

Insiders

- The firm's CEO and other top-level managers

Related outsiders

- Individuals not involved with the firm's day-to-day operations, but who have a relationship with the company

Outsiders

- Individuals who are independent of the firm in terms of day-to-day operations and other relationships

number of other top executives departed and efforts to streamline the distribution system proved ineffective thereby resulting in several performance shortfalls. One former Compaq executive stated, "We lost vision, we lost empowerment and we lost speed."[80] Some argue that any time a board must replace a CEO, it has failed. The board must share the blame in the failure for two reasons. First, the board selected the CEO being replaced. Second, the board should be actively involved in the development of the firm's strategy. If the strategy fails, the board has failed.[81]

There is some disagreement over the most appropriate role of outside directors in a firm's strategic decision-making process.[82] Because of external pressures, board reforms have been initiated. To date, these reforms have generally called for an increase in the number of outside directors, relative to insiders, serving on a corporation's board. For example, in 1984, the New York Stock Exchange started requiring that listed firms have board audit committees composed solely of outside directors.[83] As a result of external pressures, boards of large corporations have more outside members. Research shows that outside board members can influence the strategic direction of companies. Thus, they play an important role on boards of directors.[84] Therefore, there are potential strategic implications associated with the movement toward having corporate boards dominated by outsiders.

Alternatively, a large number of outside board members can also present some problems. Outsiders do not have contact with the firm's day-to-day operations and thus do not have easy access to the rich information about managers and their skills that is required to evaluate managerial decisions and initiatives effectively. Valuable information may be obtained through frequent interactions with inside board members during board meetings. Insiders possess such information by virtue of their organizational positions. Thus, boards with a critical mass of insiders can be informed more effectively about intended strategic initiatives, the reasons for the initiatives, and the outcomes expected from them.[85] Without this type of information, outsider-dominated boards may emphasize financial, as opposed to strategic, evaluations. Such evaluations shift risk to top-level managers, who, in turn, may make decisions to maximize their interests and reduce their employment risk. Reductions in R&D investments, additional diversification of the firm, and the pursuit of greater levels of compensation are examples of managers' actions to achieve these objectives.

Enhancing the Effectiveness of the Board of Directors

Because of the importance of boards of directors in corporate governance, and as a result of increased scrutiny from shareholders—in particular, large institutional investors—the performances of individual board members and of entire boards are being evaluated more formally and with greater intensity.[86] This is shown by the actions of TIAA-CREF and CalPERS, as described in the previous Strategic Focus. Investors believe that directors fulfill their responsibilities more effectively when they act with prudence and integrity for the good of the entire firm and are committed to reaching independent judgments on an informed basis, rather than blindly supporting management's proposals.[87]

Given the demand for greater accountability and improved performance, many boards of directors have initiated voluntary changes. Among these changes are (1) increases in the diversity of the backgrounds of board members (e.g., a greater number of directors from public service, academic, and scientific settings; a greater percentage of boards with ethnic minorities; and more U.S. boards with members from different countries), (2) the strengthening of internal management and accounting control systems, and (3) the establishment and consistent use of formal processes to evaluate the board's performance. Changes such as these should enhance the effectiveness of the board of directors as a means of control.

McKinsey & Co., in a hypothetical survey, found that when companies in which outsiders constituted a majority of the board, owned significant amounts of stock, were subjected to formal evaluation, and were not personally tied to top management, institutional shareholders were willing to pay up to 11 percent more for their shares.[88]

Boards are now becoming more involved in the strategic decision-making process, so they must work collaboratively. Research shows that boards working collaboratively make higher-quality strategic decisions, and they make them faster.[89] Boards also are becoming more involved in decisions regarding succession, as opposed to blindly supporting the incumbent's choice. In general, however, boards have relied on precedence (past decisions) for guidance in the selection process. Also, they are most likely to consider inside candidates before looking for outside candidates.[90] Increasingly, outside directors are being required to own significant equity stakes as a prerequisite to holding a board position. A recent study also suggests that the performance of an inside director increases if she or he holds an equity position. The announcement of an inside director with less than 5 percent ownership decreases shareholder wealth, but an insider with ownership between 5 and 25 percent *increases* shareholder wealth. Therefore, an inside director's knowledge of the firm can be used appropriately. Finally, an inside director's relationship to the CEO does not necessarily lead to entrenchment of that CEO if the inside director has a strong ownership position.[91] Interestingly, the use of a nominating committee for the selection of new board members is less likely with boards that have more inside members, particularly when those members have greater ownership in the company. Alternatively, boards with more independent outside members are more likely to use nominating committees to select new directors.[92] The Strategic Focus examines some of the important characteristics of good and bad boards of directors. Furthermore, it provides examples of actions taken by good boards, thereby showing the importance of good boards of directors to effective corporate governance.

Next, we discuss a highly visible corporate governance mechanism: executive compensation.

Executive Compensation

As the Opening Case illustrates, the compensation of top-level managers, and especially of CEOs, generates a great deal of interest and strongly held opinions. The reason for this visibility and interest is depicted in the observations that while

> widespread interest in CEO pay can be traced to a natural curiosity about extremes and excesses . . . it also stems from a more substantive reason. Namely, to observe

strategic *focus*
CORPORATE

The Top and Bottom of Boards of Directors

In the summer of 2000, 18 people met to make a critical decision. They decided who will succeed Jack Welch of GE, who many feel is the best CEO among active top executives. Welch has been referred to as the CEO of the 20th century. The good news is that GE's board (making this critical decision) has been chosen as the best board of directors in the year 2000. The board was rated as the best through a survey conducted by *Business Week* of the largest investors on Wall Street and prominent experts in corporate governance. While GE's board received strong support as the best board, Disney's board was deemed the worst board of directors. For the reasons described in the Strategic Focus on institutional investors, Disney's board is not respected. It is not considered independent from Michael Eisner, and Disney's performance in recent years has been mediocre.

Some of the other top-rated boards are those of Johnson & Johnson, Campbell Soup, Compaq, Apria Healthcare, Intel, and Texas Instruments. Alternatively, some other poorly rated boards were those of Rite Aid, First Union, Cendant, Dilliards, Starwood Hotel, Warnaco, and Waste Management. The boards are rated on several criteria, including quality (e.g., allowing an open debate in meetings), independence (e.g., having a reasonable percentage of independent outside members), accountability (e.g., directors having an ownership stake in the company) and firm performance. An example of quality is evidenced by the GE board meeting regularly with lower-level managers without Jack Welch present. Welch himself suggested this practice. At Disney, Eisner has agreed to some changes, but still has refused to make major alterations in the board's composition. Because of the firm's mediocre performance, he is coming under increasing pressure, as the example of TIAA-CREF and CalPERS suggests.

Effective boards are action oriented. An example is the board's action at Baker Hughes, where the CEO was forced to resign because of several problems that culminated in poor company performance. While the CEO, Max Lukens, pledged to turn around the firm's performance, he was unable to do so in his three-year term in the job. Likewise, Coca-Cola's board encouraged its CEO of two years to resign, due to a series of disappointing problems and poorer-than-expected returns being reported. Warren Buffett argues that boards need to "put some bite in their audit committees." Buffett suggests that board audit committees cannot develop any meaningful knowledge of the firm's financial statements when they meet only a few hours annually. Rather, he suggests that they need to ensure that they know what the outside auditors know.

Others suggest that many board members do not understand their roles as directors. Thus, they advocate training for directors so that they are better prepared to perform their jobs as members of a board of directors. In other cases, new, independent and better-qualified directors are needed. After a number of large institutional investors banded together to file a suit against Columbia/HCA and its board for failing to exercise effective control, the company named three new board members. All are independent directors. GM's board was rated among the 25 worst boards in 2000. One of its members criticized the firm's unsuccessful efforts to restore its market share. He stated publicly that the firm's management had "absolutely not delivered" on the commitments it had made. GM's U.S. market share has continued to slide to about 27 percent, compared with its once 50 percent share of this market. Thus, stockholders have reason for concern. There is no magic formula; however, it is clear that the jobs of board members are more complex and challenging now than in previous years. The expectations from shareholders are high.

SOURCES: N. Antosh, 2000, Lukens is forced out at Baker Hughes, *Houston Chronicle,* February 1, 1C, 5C; B. McKay & J. S. Lublin, 2000, Behind Coke's massive cuts: An impatient board of directors, *Wall Street Journal Interactive,* January 27, *www.interactive.wsj.com*; J. A. Byrne, 2000, The best and the worst boards, *Business Week,* January 24, 142–152; J. B. White & G. L. White, 1999, GM's Pearce pans market-share efforts, *Wall Street Journal,* December 9, A3, A8; Competence: Growing legal complexities an issue, 1999, *FT Director,* October 28, *www.ft.com/ftsurveys*; Put bite into audit committees, 1999, *Fortune,* August 2, 90; L. Lagnado, 1999, Columbia/HCA names three to board in face of continuing Medicare probe, *Wall Street Journal Interactive,* March 27, *www.interactive.wsj.com/archive.*

CEO pay is to observe in an indirect but very tangible way the fundamental governance processes in large corporations. Who has power? What are the bases of power? How and when do owners and managers exert their relative preferences? How vigilant are boards? Who is taking advantage of whom?[93]

Executive compensation is a governance mechanism that seeks to align the interests of managers and owners through salaries, bonuses, and long-term incentive compensation such as stock options.

Executive compensation is a governance mechanism that seeks to align the interests of managers and owners through salaries, bonuses, and long-term incentive compensation such as stock options.[94] Stock options are a mechanism used to link executives' performance to the performance of their company's stock.[95] Increasingly, long-term incentive plans are becoming a critical part of compensation packages in U.S. firms. The use of longer-term pay helps firms cope with or avoid potential agency problems.[96] Because of this, the stock market generally reacts positively to the introduction of a long-range incentive plan for top executives.[97] Sometimes the use of a long-term incentive plan prevents major stockholders (e.g., institutional stockholders) from pressing for changes in the composition of the board of directors, because they assume that the long-term incentives will ensure that the top executives will act in the best interests of the shareholders. Alternatively, stockholders largely assume that top-executive pay and the permanence of a firm are more aligned when firms have boards that are dominated by outside members.[98] Effectively using executive compensation as a governance mechanism is particularly challenging in firms implementing international strategies. For example, preliminary evidence suggests that the interests of owners of multinational corporations are best served when there is less uniformity among the firm's foreign subsidiaries' compensation plans.[99] Developing an array of unique compensation plans requires additional monitoring and increases the firm's agency costs. Importantly, levels of pay vary by region of the world. For example, managers receive the highest compensation in the United States, as explained in the Opening Case of this chapter. Managerial pay is much lower in Asia. However, as firms acquire firms in other countries, the managerial compensation puzzle becomes more complex. For instance, when Daimler-Benz acquired Chrysler, the top executives of Chrysler made substantially more than the executives at Daimler-Benz. However, the Chrysler executives ended up reporting to the Daimler executives.[100]

A Complicated Governance Mechanism

For several reasons, executive compensation—especially long-term incentive compensation—is complicated. First, the strategic decisions made by top-level managers are typically complex and nonroutine, so direct supervision of executives is inappropriate for judging the quality of their decisions. Because of this, there is a tendency to link the compensation of top-level managers to measurable outcomes, such as the firm's financial performance. Second, an executive's decision often affects a firm's financial outcomes over an extended period, making it difficult to assess the effect of current decisions on the corporation's performance. In fact, strategic decisions are more likely to have long-term, rather than short-term, effects on a company's strategic outcomes. Third, a number of variables intervene between top-level managerial decisions and behavior and the firm's performance. Unpredictable economic, social, or legal changes (see Chapter 2) make it difficult to discern the effects of strategic decisions. Thus, although performance-based compensation may provide incentives to managers to make decisions that best serve shareholders' interests, such compensation plans alone are imperfect in their ability to monitor and control managers. Still, annual bonuses through incentive compensation represent a significant portion of many executives' total pay. For example, annual bonuses compose an average of about 60 percent of the CEO's total compensation in the United States, about 45 percent in the United Kingdom, approximately 30 percent in Canada, and only 19 percent in France.[101] These figures underscore the differences in compensation across countries described in the Opening Case in the chapter.

Although incentive compensation plans may increase the value of a firm in line with shareholder expectations, such plans are subject to managerial manipulation. For instance, annual bonuses may provide incentives to pursue short-run objectives at the expense of the firm's long-term interests. Supporting this conclusion, some research has found that bonuses based on annual performance were negatively related to investments in R&D, which may affect the firm's long-term strategic competitiveness.[102] Although long-term performance-based incentives may reduce the temptation to underinvest in the short run, they increase executive exposure to risks associated with uncontrollable events, such as market fluctuations and industry decline.[103] The longer the focus of incentive compensation, the greater are the long-term risks borne by top-level managers.

Interestingly, the CEO of GM, Jack Smith, received a bonus in 1998 that was 56 percent below his bonus in 1997, but his total compensation for the year increased by 12 percent over 1997. The bonus was lower because of poorer firm performance, but he was given an increase in his base salary and was granted stock options and stock under the firm's long-term incentive plan. His total compensation package in 1998 was $12.4 million, compared to $11 million in 1997.[104]

The Effectiveness of Executive Compensation

In recent times, many stakeholders, including shareholders, have been angered by the compensation received by some top-level managers, especially CEOs. For example, the top compensation received by an executive in 1998 was the $575.59 million awarded to Michael Eisner, CEO of Disney. In 1999, the highest reported top executive compensation was more than $696 million, for Charles Wang, CEO of Computer Associ-

Charles Wang, CEO of Computer Associates, received the highest reported top executive compensation—more than $696 million—in 1999.

ates. However, the firm lost a suit filed by a shareholder in which the award exceeded the amount provided by the company's long-range incentive compensation plan. The court ruled that Mr. Wang, along with the president and executive vice president of Computer Associates, had to return about $9.5 million shares of stock that were awarded. The value of the stock returned was about $558 million in total for the three executives. Interestingly, the 10th-highest-paid executive in 1997 was Douglas Ivestor, who was forced to resign his position as CEO of Coca-Cola in 2000.[105]

The primary component of such large compensation packages is stock options and stock. In fact, the average amount of the stock held by top executives and directors of firms reached 21 percent in the 1990s, partly because of the long-term incentive plans that compensate executives in stock options and stock.[106] The primary reasons for compensating executives in stock is that the practice affords incentives to keep the stock price high. Hence, it should align the interests of managers and owners. However, there may be some unintended consequences: Research has shown that managers who own greater than 1 percent of their firm's stock are less likely to be forced out of their jobs, even when the firm is performing poorly.[107]

Yahoo!'s CEO, Timothy Koogle, has unexercised stock options worth approximately $360 million and unvested options totaling about $184 million. Gap's CEO, Millard Drexler, has unvested stock options worth approximately $631 million. While these are large figures, many of the stockholders of firms whose CEOs have received large payoffs have seen their stocks gain significant value. For example, Gateway's CEO earned $147 million over a recent five-year period. However, the shareholders' stock value increased an average of 48 percent annually during this same period![108] Other CEOs who recently received substantial stock options are Michael Dell of Dell Computer, with about $90.7 million; Stephen Hilbert of Conseco, with $41.8 million; and Duane Burnham of Abbott Laboratories, with $24.1 million.[109] The stock option programs, while intended to tie executive compensation to firm performance, may be creating unintended benefits for executives. Some argue that executives with options have benefited by big increases in the overall value of their stocks, even though their firm's stock underperformed the market.

The compensation package for the CEO of Level (3) Communications may be an example of the future. For the CEO of Level (3) to exercise his options and earn a return, his firm must outperform the market. Graf Crystal, a compensation consultant, strongly supports this type of stock option program. He states, "The world of stock option accounting is utterly mad." Currently, if a firm ties its stock options to an index, as is done at Level (3), it must take a charge for the options against earnings, but if it does not, it only has to take a charge if the stock price is below the exercise price at the time options are exercised and the total shares are known.[110]

Interestingly, performance-based pay seems to be working. CEOs of the best-performing companies received substantial increases in their compensations, and CEOs in the poorest-performing companies experienced reductions in their compensation. In 1999, the top five companies ranked by increases in returns had changes in their stock returns averaging +234.40 percent. Their CEOs received increases in their compensation averaging 139 percent. Alternatively, the poorest-performing firms experienced a change in returns of –48.32 percent. The CEOs of these firms received a reduction of 48 percent in their compensation.[111]

A number of experts on executive pay were asked to predict the future compensation for top executives. Most all of them predicted that top executives' pay would be more closely aligned with their firm's performance in the future. In fact, one of the experts, B. Kenneth West, an institutional investor, predicted that future executive compensation packages would be likely to mirror the approach used at Level (3). Others predicted that the performance-based pay would eventually eliminate executive perks, because the executives who were left would be top performers and highly paid.[112]

Members of boards of directors are receiving more compensation as well. For example, the median base compensation for directors in the telecommunications industry is almost $90,000 annually.[113] In contrast, directors at Microsystems, Inc., receive an average compensation of about $410,000 annually, while directors at Compaq earned over $360,000. At Pfizer, they receive almost $260,000. On average, directors at the largest 200 firms received approximately $134,000 in 1999.[114] As with executives of a firm, there is a move by large institutional investors such as CalPERS to pay directors at least partially in stock. The rationale is the same as that for paying top executives in stock: If members of the board of directors hold equity in the company, it is assumed that they will make decisions that are in the best interests of the shareholders.[115] In fact, some estimate that approximately 50 percent of directors' pay will be in company stock by 2004.

A company's organizational structure also influences the alignment of principals' and agents' interests. As indicated in the next section, structure can be an especially valuable governance mechanism in diversified firms.

The Multidivisional Structure

An organizational structure, particularly the multidivisional (M-form) structure, serves as an internal governance mechanism by controlling managerial opportunism.[116] The corporate office that is a part of the M-form structure, along with the firm's board of directors, closely monitors the strategic decisions of managers responsible for the performance of the different business units or divisions of the corporation. Active monitoring of an individual unit's performance suggests a keen managerial interest in making decisions that will maximize shareholders' wealth. Still, while the M-form may limit division managers' opportunistic behaviors, it may not limit corporate-level managers' self-serving actions. For example, research suggests that diversified firms using the M-form structure are likely to implement corporate-level strategies that cause them to become even more diversified.[117] In fact, one of the potential problems with divisionalization in the M-form structure is that it is often used too aggressively.[118] Beyond some point, diversification serves managers' interests more than it serves shareholders' interests (see Chapter 6).

In addition, because of the diversification of product lines (breadth of businesses), top executives may not have adequate information to evaluate the strategic decisions and actions of divisional managers (depth). To complete their evaluations, they must focus on the resulting financial outcomes achieved by individual business units. While waiting for these financial outcomes, division managers may be able to act opportunistically.

Where internal controls are limited because of extensive diversification, the external market for corporate control and the external managerial labor market may serve as the primary controls on managers' decisions and actions, such as pursuing acquisitions to increase the size of their firm and their compensation.[119] Because external markets lack access to relevant information from inside the firm, they tend to be less efficient than internal governance mechanisms for monitoring the decisions and performance of top executives. Therefore, in diversified firms, corporate executive decisions can be controlled effectively only when other strong internal governance mechanisms (e.g., the board of directors) are used in combination with the M-form structure. When used as a single governance mechanism, the M-form structure may actually facilitate overdiversification and inappropriately high compensation for corporate executives.[120]

Market for Corporate Control

The **market for corporate control** is composed of individuals and firms that buy ownership positions in (or take over) potentially undervalued corporations so they can form new divisions in established diversified companies or merge two previously separate firms.

The market for corporate control is an external governance mechanism that becomes active when a firm's internal controls fail.[121] The **market for corporate control** is composed of individuals and firms that buy ownership positions in (or take over) potentially undervalued corporations so they can form new divisions in established diversified companies or merge two previously separate firms. Because they are assumed to be the party responsible for formulating and implementing the strategy that led to poor performance, that team is usually replaced. Thus, when operating effectively, the market for corporate control ensures that managers who are ineffective or act opportunistically are disciplined. In either case, the firm performs more poorly than it should.[122] This governance mechanism should be activated by a firm's poor performance relative to the competitors in its industry. A firm's poor performance, often demonstrated by the firm's earning below-average returns, is an indicator that internal governance mechanisms have failed; that is, their use did not result in managerial decisions that maximized shareholder value. This market has been active for some time. The 1980s were known as a time of merger mania, with approximately 55,000 acquisitions valued at approximately $1.3 trillion. However, there were many more acquisitions in the 1990s, and the value of mergers and acquisitions in that decade was more than $10 trillion.[123]

In 1999, Teleglobe's profits decreased for two consecutive quarters. The second reduction of 10 percent prompted analysts to speculate that the firm was an attractive takeover target. Teleglobe, Canada's largest telecommunications company, operates the third-largest undersea fiber-optic network. While analysts may speculate, a takeover is unlikely, because a few large shareholders (e.g., Bell Canada, Ameritech, and the US Group) own approximately 53 percent of the firm.[124]

Perhaps in more trouble is Ben & Jerry's, the well-known ice-cream maker. Both Unilever and Dreyer's Grand Ice Cream made overtures to the firm. Ben & Jerry's is socially conscious, and, should it be taken over, socially conscious investors fear that it would lose its focus. Those investors tried to obtain the funds to stop the takeover attempt by buying enough stock to make a takeover infeasible.[125] As a group, the investors are a form of a white knight that rescues takeover targets. But, Unilever acquired Ben & Jerry's in 2000. British Telecommunications served as a white knight for Esat, Ireland's second-largest telecommunications company.[126] In other cases, the firm may withstand the takeover without external help. This occurred when Philip Green, a retail entrepreneur, unsuccessfully tried to take over Marks & Spencer, the venerable British retailer. Green became concerned because of the likely fight that managers at Marks & Spencer would put up and the potential harm that a prolonged hostile takeover fight could have on the Marks & Spencer business.[127]

Hostile takeovers are the major activity in the market for corporate control. However, not all hostile takeovers are prompted by poorly performing targets. There may be other reasons, as explained in the Strategic Focus, which discusses hostile takeovers by Pfizer (Warner-Lambert) and Vodafone (Mannesmann).

Firms targeted for hostile takeovers may use multiple defense tactics to fend off the takeover attempt. Some of these actions are exemplified in the Strategic Focus. We discuss managerial defense tactics in the next section.

Managerial Defense Tactics

Historically, the increased use of the market for corporate control has enhanced the sophistication and variety of managerial defense tactics that are used to reduce the influence of this governance mechanism. The market for corporate control tends to increase risk for managers. As a result, managerial pay is often augmented indirectly through *golden parachutes* (wherein a CEO can receive up to three years' salary if his or her firm is taken over). Among other outcomes, takeover defenses increase the costs of mounting a takeover causing the incumbent management to become entrenched, while reducing the chances of introducing a new management team.[128] Some defense tactics require the type of asset restructuring that results from divesting one or more divisions in the diversified firm's portfolio. Others necessitate only changes in the financial structure of the firm, such as repurchasing shares of the firm's outstanding stock.[129] Some tactics (e.g., reincorporation of the firm in another state) require share-

Hostile Takeovers: The War between Corporations

Warner-Lambert and American Home Products (AHP) agreed to a merger and touched off a war. Pfizer had a co-marketing agreement with Warner-Lambert to market the blockbuster drug Lipitor, which reduces cholesterol. Pfizer was concerned that it would lose the agreement if Warner-Lambert was taken over by American Home Products. This and the fact that Pfizer's newly developed drugs were not achieving the success expected of them prompted the company's management to launch a hostile bid for Warner, even after the agreement with AHP was completed. The CEO of Warner, Lodewijk J. R. de Vink, was not interested in Pfizer's offer. While AHP was acquiring Warner-Lambert, de Vink was to be the CEO of the combined firm. Although Pfizer's offer was higher, Warner-Lambert's board of directors rejected it. Pfizer persisted, making a higher offer. However, Warner's board resisted and even entered talks with Procter & Gamble (P&G) regarding the possibility of a three-way merger among Warner, P&G, and AHP. Even in the face of these possibilities, Pfizer persisted, and, finally, given shareholder pressure, Warner's board agreed to listen to Pfizer's offer. Eventually, the two companies reached an agreement. The combined company would be the second-largest pharmaceutical company in sales, but have the largest capitalization among its competitors. Its market capitalization is approximately $220 billion, compared with that of second-place Merck, about $185 billion. Some refer to Pfizer's action not as a hostile takeover, but as a hostile intervention. The deal created a much higher return for Warner's shareholders. For example, the deal with AHP was worth approximately $58.6 billion, whereas the deal with Pfizer was valued at $84.4 billion. To win favor, Pfizer offered some board seats to Warner's current board members. However, de Vink will not remain with the merged firm. Also, AHP received a breakup fee of $1.8 billion from Warner-Lambert. In this case, the hostile bid and acquisition were not driven by the typical reasons cited for such actions. While Warner needed a partner, so did Pfizer.

Another hostile takeover also occurred for multiple reasons and generated substantial media attention. The largest hostile takeover bid in history was made by Vodafone AirTouch, based in England, for Mannesmann, based in Germany. Both firms are in the telecommunications industry. Until this takeover, Pfizer's takeover was the largest. As Warner-Lambert did with respect to Pfizer, Mannesmann rejected Vodafone's original offer and took several actions to avoid being taken over by Vodafone. For example, it agreed to a Web IPO, tried to acquire a Spanish telecommunications license, and developed an Internet joint venture with Deutsche Bank. Mannesmann also sought an acquisition partner in France. In addition, Germany was not in favor of the takeover (in fact, Germany generally looks on hostile takeovers with disfavor). Vodafone sweetened the offer, and the eventual value for the agreed takeover was approximately $180.95 billion, up from Vodafone's earlier offer of $134.5.

Vodafone, however, never gave up. Vodafone's goal was to establish a single global brand. The company revealed plans to develop a global mobile data and Internet operation. Thus, the acquisition of Mannesmann would help it implement these plans and achieve its goal. Interestingly, Mannesmann's CEO had no incentive to stop fighting the bid, because he knew that he would lose his job. However, his fight also ended up sweetening the deal for Mannesmann shareholders. Mannesmann was not a poorly performing firm—again, an atypical target in the market for corporate control. However, it was an important target for Vodafone in the struggle to be a major competitor in the global telecommunications industry.

SOURCES: Pfizer's prize. 2000, *The Economist,* February 17, *www.economist.com*; D. Piling & A. Michaels, 2000, Pfizer: Group seals Warner-Lambert deal, *ft.com*, February 17, *www.ft.com/nbearchive*; T. Burns, 2000, Mannesmann: Telcos fight for Spanish license, *ft.com*, February 8, *www.ft.com/nbearchive*; P. Galewitz & N. Knox, 2000, Pfizer wins war, must heal wounds, *Houston Chronicle,* February 8, 1C, 5C; P&G: Deal-making addiction, 2000, *ft.com*, February 8, *www.ft.com/nbearchive*; R. Langreth, 2000, Warner-Lambert agrees to a deal with Pfizer worth $90 billion, *Wall Street Journal Interactive,* February 7, *www.interactive.wsj.com*; Vodafone & Mannesmann-endgame, 2000, *The Economist,* February 7, *www.economist.com*; G. Naik & A. Raghavan, 2000, Mannesmann chief had no incentive to give up battle with Vodafone, *Wall Street Journal Interactive,* February 6, *www.interactive.wsj.com*; G. Naik & A. Raghavan, 2000, Vodafone, Mannesmann set takeover at $180.95 billion after long struggle, *Wall Street Journal Interactive,* February 6, *www.interactive.wsj.com*; S. Baker & K. Capell, 2000, How Vodafone aims to rule the wireless world, *Business Week,* January 25, 56; N. Deogun & R. Langreth, 2000, Procter & Gamble abandons talks with Warner-Lambert and AHP, *Wall Street Journal Interactive,* January 25, *www.interactive.wsj.com*; R. Langreth & N. Deogun, 2000, Drug firms continue talks on possible three-way deal, *Wall Street Journal Interactive,* January 20, *www.interactive.wsj.com*; G. Naik & A. Raghavan, 2000, Mannesmann plans Web IPO in bid to avert U.K. takeover, *Wall Street Journal Interactive,* January 17, *www.interactive.wsj.com*; Vodafone-Mannesmann: Some win, some lose, *ft.com*, January 17, *www.ft.com/nbearchive.*

---

holder approval, but the greenmail tactic (wherein money is used to repurchase stock from a corporate raider to avoid the takeover of the firm) does not. These defense tactics are controversial, and the research on their effects is inconclusive. Alternatively, most institutional investors oppose the use of defense tactics. As explained in an earlier Strategic Focus, TIAA-CREF and CalPERS have taken actions to have several firms' poison pills eliminated.[130] However, some defense tactics may be appropriate. For example, shareholders of Canadian Occidental Petroleum approved a poison pill designed to stop a takeover by the parent company, Occidental Petroleum. Canadian Occidental's managers claimed that the parent firm was trying to force Canadian Occidental to give it the Canadian affiliate's lucrative oil operations in Yemen. The parent firm threatened to take over the firm with several partners and then divide and sell its assets. However, with the poison pill, the parent company cannot take over the firm and is likely to sell its 29 percent stake in the Canadian firm.[131]

A potential problem with the market for corporate control is that it may not be totally efficient. A study of several of the most active corporate raiders in the 1980s showed that approximately 50 percent of their takeover attempts targeted firms with above-average performance in their industry—corporations that were neither undervalued nor poorly managed.[132] The targeting of high-performance businesses may lead to acquisitions at premium prices and to decisions by managers of the targeted firm to establish what may prove to be costly takeover defense tactics to protect their corporate positions.

Although the market for corporate control lacks the precision possible with internal governance mechanisms, the fear of acquisition and influence by corporate raiders is an effective constraint on the managerial-growth motive.[133] The market for corporate control has been responsible for significant changes in many firms' strategies and, when used appropriately, has served the interests of the corporate owners—the shareholders. But this market and other means of corporate governance vary by region of the world and by country. Accordingly, we next address the topic of international corporate governance.

International Corporate Governance

Understanding the corporate governance structure of the United Kingdom and the United States is inadequate for a multinational firm in today's global economy.[134] Accordingly, we briefly discuss the governance of German and Japanese corporations, and corporations in other countries, to illustrate that the nature of corporate governance throughout the world is being affected by the realities of that global economy and its competitive challenges.[135] Thus, while the stability associated with German and Japanese governance structures has historically been viewed as an asset, some believe that it may now be a burden.[136] And the governance in those two countries is starting to change, as it is changing in other parts of the world.

Corporate Governance in Germany

In many private German firms, the owner and manager may still be the same individual. In these instances, there is no agency problem. Even in publicly traded corporations, there is often a dominant shareholder. Thus, the concentration of ownership is an important means of corporate governance in Germany, as it is in the United States.[137]

Historically, banks have been at the center of the German corporate governance structure, as is also the case in many other European countries, such as Italy and France. As lenders, banks become major shareholders when companies they had financed earlier seek funding on the stock market or default on loans. Although the stakes are usually under 10 percent, there is no legal limit on how much of a firm's stock banks can hold (except that a single ownership position cannot exceed 15 percent of the bank's capital). Through their own shareholdings and by casting proxy votes for individual shareholders who retain their shares with the banks, three banks in particular—Deutsche, Dresdner, and Commerzbank—exercise significant power. Although shareholders can tell the banks how to vote their ownership position, they generally elect not to do so. A combination of their own holdings and their proxies results in majority positions for these three banks in many German companies. Those banks, along with others, monitor and control managers, both as lenders and as shareholders, by electing representatives to supervisory boards.

German firms with more than 2,000 employees are required to have a two-tiered board structure. Through this structure, the supervision of management is separated from other duties normally assigned to a board of directors, especially the nomination of new board members. Thus, Germany's two-tiered system places the responsibility for monitoring and controlling managerial (or supervisory) decisions and actions in the hands of a separate group.[138] While all the functions of direction and management are the responsibility of the management board—the *Vorstand*—appointment to the *Vorstand* is the responsibility of the supervisory tier—the *Aufsichtsrat*. Employees, union members, and shareholders appoint members to the *Aufsichtsrat*.

Banks have always been at the center of the German corporate governance structure. Through their shareholdings and proxy votes, three banks—Deutsche, Dresdner, and Commerzbank—exercise significant power.

Because of the power of banks in Germany's corporate governance structure, private shareholders rarely have major ownership positions in German firms. Large institutional investors, such as pension funds and insurance companies, are also relatively insignificant owners of corporate stock. Thus, at least historically, German executives generally have not been dedicated to the maximization of shareholder value that is occurring in many countries. But corporate governance in Germany is changing, at least partially because of the increasing globalization of business. Many German firms are beginning to gravitate toward the U.S. system. For example, SGL Carbon AG lost in excess of $71 million in the early 1990s. As a result, the corporation was restructured in an attempt to turn it around. In particular, the firm's governance structure was changed. Transparent accounting practices were adopted, and the goal of enhancing shareholder value was established. The firm's stock became listed on the U.S. stock exchange, and English was adopted as the official language. Thereafter, the firm's performance improved dramatically, with many attributing the improvement to its changed governance structure.[139]

Corporate Governance in Japan

Attitudes toward corporate governance in Japan are affected by the concepts of obligation, family, and consensus. In Japan, an obligation "may be to return a service for one rendered or it may derive from a more general relationship, for example, to one's family or old alumni, or one's company (or Ministry), or the country. This sense of particular obligation is common elsewhere but it feels stronger in Japan."[140] As part of a company family, individuals are members of a unit that envelops their lives; families command the attention and allegiance of parties throughout corporations. Moreover, a keiretsu is more than an economic concept; it, too, is a family. Consensus, an important influence in Japanese corporate governance, calls for the expenditure of significant amounts of energy to win the hearts and minds of people whenever possible, as opposed to issuing edicts from top executives. Consensus is highly valued, even when it results in a slow and cumbersome decision-making process.

As in Germany, banks in Japan play an important role in financing and monitoring large public firms. The bank owning the largest share of stocks and the largest amount of debt—the main bank—has the closest relationship with the company's top executives. The main bank provides financial advice to the firm and also closely monitors managers. Thus, Japan has a bank-based financial and corporate governance structure, whereas the United States has a market-based financial and governance structure.

Aside from lending money, a Japanese bank can hold up to 5 percent of a firm's total stock; a group of related financial institutions can hold up to 40 percent. In many cases, main-bank relationships are part of a horizontal keiretsu (a group of firms tied together by cross-shareholdings). A keiretsu firm usually owns less than 2 percent of any other member firm; however, each company typically has a stake of that size in every firm in the keiretsu. As a result, somewhere between 30 and 90 percent of a firm is owned by other members of the keiretsu. Thus, a keiretsu is a system of relationship investments.

As is the case in Germany, in Japan the structure of corporate governance is changing. For example, because of their continuing development as economic organizations, the role of banks in the monitoring and control of managerial behavior and firm outcomes is less significant than in the past.[141] The Asian economic crisis in the latter part of the 1990s made the governance problems in Japanese corporations transparent. The problems were readily evidenced in the large and once-powerful Mitsubishi kereitsu. Many of its core members lost substantial amounts of money in the late 1990s.[142] Toyota's president was ousted by its board of directors because he demanded changes in its governance system and argued against rescuing other firms in the Toyota kereitsu.[143]

Still another change in Japan's governance system has occurred. In past years, the market for corporate control was nonexistent. However, the first hostile bid for another firm was advanced by Cable & Wireless PLC of Great Britain in 1999 for International Digital Communications, Inc. In 2000, another hostile bid was made by a Japanese investment firm to take over Shoei Co., a large real-estate and electric parts firm. A 14 percent premium was offered, but Shoei's board quickly rejected it. The CEO of the investment company criticized the passivity of Japanese shareholders.[144]

Global Corporate Governance

The 21st-century competitive landscape (see Chapters 1 and 5) and the global economy are fostering the creation of a relatively uniform governance structure that will be used by firms throughout the world.[145] As markets become more global and customer demands more similar, shareholders are becoming the focus of managers' efforts in an increasing number of companies. Investors are becoming more and more active throughout the world. Changes in governance are evident in many countries and are moving the governance models closer to that of the United States. For example, in France, anger has been growing over the lack of information on top executives' compensation. A recent report recommended that the positions of CEO and chairman of the board be held by different individuals; it also recommended reducing the tenure of board members and disclosing their pay.[146] In South Korea, changes went much further: Principles of corporate governance were adopted that "provide proper incentives for the board and management to pursue objectives that are in the interests of the company and the shareholders and facilitate effective monitoring, thereby encouraging firms to use resources more efficiently."[147]

Even in transitional economies, such as those of China and Russia, changes in corporate governance are occurring. However, changes are implemented much slower in these economies. Chinese firms have found it helpful to use stock-based compensation plans, thereby providing an incentive for foreign companies to invest in China.[148]

Because Russia has reduced controls on the economy and on business activity much faster than China has, the country needs more effective governance systems to control its managerial activities.[149]

Governance Mechanisms and Ethical Behavior

The governance mechanisms described in this chapter are designed to ensure that the agents of the firm's owners—the corporation's top executives—make strategic decisions that best serve the interests of the entire group of stakeholders, as described in Chapter 1. In the United States, shareholders are recognized as a company's most significant stakeholder. Thus, the focus of governance mechanisms is on the control of managerial decisions to ensure that shareholders' interests will be served, but product market stakeholders (e.g., customers, suppliers, and host communities) and organizational stakeholders (e.g., managerial and nonmanagerial employees) are important as well.[150] Therefore, at least the minimal interests or needs of all stakeholders must be satisfied through the firm's actions. Otherwise, dissatisfied stakeholders will decide to withdraw their support from one firm and provide it to another (e.g., customers will purchase products from a supplier offering an acceptable substitute).

John Smale, an outside member of the board of directors at General Motors, believes that all large capitalist enterprises must be concerned with goals, in addition to serving shareholders. In Smale's opinion, "A corporation is a human, living enterprise. It's not just a bunch of assets. The obligation of management is to perpetuate the corporation, and that precedes their obligation to shareholders."[151] The argument, then, is that the firm's strategic competitiveness is enhanced when its governance mechanisms are designed and implemented in ways that take into consideration the interests of all stakeholders. Although the idea is subject to debate, some believe that ethically responsible companies design and use governance mechanisms that serve all stakeholders' interests. There is, however, a more critical relationship between ethical behavior and corporate governance mechanisms.

Evidence demonstrates that all companies are vulnerable to a display of unethical behaviors by their employees, including, of course, top executives. For example, HFS, Incorporated, acquired CUC International. Shortly after completing the transaction and attempting to merge the two businesses to create the newly named Cendant Corporation, significant accounting irregularities appeared in the figures provided by the former CUC executives. Investigations suggested fraud. When the accounting irregularities were announced, Cendant's stock price fell from over $47 per share to slightly more than $12 per share. The company had to restate its financial results, reducing profits by hundreds of millions of dollars. A class-action lawsuit was filed by stockholders, claiming negligence by Cendant's executives and board of directors. In late 1999, Cendant settled the suit for a record $2.83 billion. This is the primary reason that Cendant's board is rated as one of the worst, as reported earlier in the chapter.[152]

The decisions and actions of a corporation's board of directors can be an effective deterrent to unethical behaviors. In fact, some believe that the most effective boards participate actively in setting boundaries for business ethics and values.[153] Once formulated, the board's expectations related to ethical decisions and actions by all of the firm's stakeholders must be communicated clearly to the top executives. Moreover, these executives must understand that the board will hold them fully accountable for the development and support of an organizational culture that results in ethical decisions and behaviors. As explained in Chapter 12, CEOs can be positive role models for ethical behavior.

It is only when the proper corporate governance is exercised that strategies are formulated and implemented to achieve strategic competitiveness and above-average returns. As the discussion in this chapter suggests, corporate governance mechanisms are a vital, yet imperfect, part of firms' efforts to develop and implement successful strategies.

Summary

- Corporate governance is a relationship among stakeholders that is used to determine a firm's direction and control its performance. How firms monitor and control top-level managers' decisions and actions, as called for by governance mechanisms, affects the implementation of strategies. Effective governance that aligns the interests of managers with those of shareholders can produce a competitive advantage for the firm.
- In the modern corporation, there are four internal governance mechanisms—ownership concentration, the board of directors, executive compensation, and the multidivisional structure—and one external governance mechanism—the market for corporate control.
- Ownership is separated from control in the modern corporation. Owners (principals) hire managers (agents) to make decisions that maximize the value of the firm. As risk specialists, owners diversify their risk by investing in an array of corporations. As decision-making specialists, top executives are expected by owners to make decisions that will result in earning above-average returns. Thus, modern corporations are characterized by an agency relationship that is created when one party (the firm's owners) hires and pays another party (top executives) to use its decision-making skills.
- Separation of ownership and control creates an agency problem when an agent pursues goals that are in conflict with the principals' goals. Principals establish and use governance mechanisms to control this problem.
- Ownership concentration is based on the number of large-block shareholders and the percentage of shares they own. With significant ownership percentages, such as those held by large mutual funds and pension funds, institutional investors often are able to influence top executives' strategic decisions and actions. Thus, unlike diffuse ownership, which tends to result in relatively weak monitoring and control of managerial decisions, concentrated ownership produces more active and effective monitoring of top executives. An increasingly powerful force in corporate America, institutional owners are actively using their positions of concentrated ownership in individual companies to force managers and boards of directors to make decisions that maximize a firm's value. These owners (e.g., TIAA-CREF and CalPERS) have caused executives in prominent companies to lose their jobs because of their failure to serve shareholders' interests effectively.
- In the United States and the United Kingdom, a firm's board of directors, composed of insiders, related outsiders, and outsiders, is a governance mechanism that shareholders expect to represent their collective interests. The percentage of outside directors on many boards now exceeds the percentage of inside directors. The individuals from outside are expected to be more independent of a firm's top executives than are those selected from inside the firm.
- Executive compensation is a highly visible and often criticized governance mechanism. Salary, bonuses, and long-term incentives are used to strengthen the alignment between managers' and shareholders' interests. A firm's board of directors has the responsibility of determining the degree to which executive compensation controls managerial behavior.
- The multidivisional (M-form) structure is intended to reduce managerial opportunism and to align principals' and agents' interests. The M-form structure makes it possible for the corporate office to monitor and control managerial

decisions in the multiple divisions in diversified firms. However, at the corporate level, the M-form may actually stimulate managerial opportunism, resulting in top executives overdiversifying the firm.

- In general, evidence suggests that shareholders and boards of directors have become more vigilant in their control of managerial decisions. Nonetheless, these mechanisms are insufficient to govern managerial behavior in many large companies. Therefore, the market for corporate control is an important governance mechanism. Although it, too, is imperfect, the market for corporate control has been effective in causing corporations to combat inefficient diversification and to implement more effective strategic decisions.
- Corporate governance structures used in Germany and Japan differ from each other and from that used in the United States. Historically, the U.S. governance structure has focused on maximizing shareholder value. In Germany, employees, as a stakeholder group, have a more prominent role in governance. By contrast, until recently, Japanese shareholders played virtually no role in the monitoring and control of top-level managers. However, all of these systems are becoming increasingly similar, as are many governance systems in both developed countries, such as France and Italy, and transitional economies, such as Russia and China.
- Effective governance mechanisms ensure that the interests of all stakeholders are served. Thus, long-term strategic success results when firms are governed in ways that permit at least minimal satisfaction of capital market stakeholders (e.g., shareholders), product market stakeholders (e.g., customers and suppliers), and organizational stakeholders (managerial and nonmanagerial employees). Moreover, effective governance produces ethical behavior in the formulation and implementation of strategies.

Review Questions

1. What is corporate governance? What factors account for the considerable amount of attention corporate governance receives from several parties, including shareholder activists, business press writers, and academic scholars? Why is governance necessary to control managerial decisions?
2. What does it mean to say that ownership is separated from control in the modern corporation? Why does this separation exist?
3. What is an agency relationship? What is managerial opportunism? What assumptions do owners of modern corporations make about managers as agents?
4. How are each of the four internal governance mechanisms—ownership concentration, boards of directors, executive compensation, and the multidivisional (M-form) structure—used to align the interests of managerial agents with those of the firm's owners?
5. What trends exist regarding executive compensation? What is the effect of the increased use of long-term incentives on executives' strategic decisions?
6. What is the market for corporate control? What conditions generally cause this external governance mechanism to become active? How does the mechanism constrain top executives' decisions and actions?
7. What is the nature of corporate governance in Germany and Japan?
8. How can corporate governance foster ethical strategic decisions and behaviors on the part of managerial agents?

Application Discussion Questions

1. The roles and responsibilities of top executives and members of a corporation's board of directors are different. Traditionally, executives have been responsible for determining the firm's strategic direction and implementing strategies to achieve it, whereas the board of directors has been responsible for monitoring and controlling managerial decisions and actions. Some argue that boards should become more involved with the formulation of a firm's strategies. How would the board's increased involvement in the selection of strategies affect a firm's strategic competitiveness? What evidence can you offer to support your position?
2. Do you believe that large U.S. firms have been overgoverned by some corporate governance mechanisms and undergoverned by others? Provide an example of each.
3. How can corporate governance mechanisms create conditions that allow top executives to develop a competitive

advantage and focus on long-term performance? Use the Internet to search the business press and give an example of a firm in which this occurred.

4. Some believe that the market for corporate control is not an effective governance mechanism. What factors might account for the ineffectiveness of this method of monitoring and controlling managerial decisions?
5. Assume that you overheard the following comment: "As a top executive, the only agency relationship I am concerned about is the one between myself and the firm's owners. I think that it would be a waste of my time and energy to worry about any other agency relationships." What are these other agency relationships? How would you respond to this person? Do you accept or reject this view? Be prepared to support your position.

Ethics Questions

1. As explained in this chapter, using corporate governance mechanisms should establish order between parties whose interests may be in conflict. Do owners of a firm have any ethical responsibilities to managers in a firm that uses governance mechanisms to establish order? If so, what are those responsibilities?
2. Is it ethical for a firm's owner to assume that agents (managers hired to make decisions in the owner's best interests) are averse to risk? Why or why not?
3. What are the responsibilities of the board of directors to stakeholders other than shareholders?
4. What ethical issues surround executive compensation? How can we determine whether top executives are paid too much?
5. Is it ethical for firms involved in the market for corporate control to target companies performing at levels exceeding the industry average? Why or why not?
6. What ethical issues, if any, do top executives face when asking their firm to provide them with either a golden parachute or a golden goodbye?
7. How can governance mechanisms be designed to ensure against managerial opportunism, ineffectiveness, and unethical behaviors?

Internet Exercise

The use of the Internet for buying and selling stocks has opened up markets to an unprecedented number of people. With the click of a mouse, one can buy shares of the hottest stocks. Not always so, though, warns SEC Chairman Arthur Levitt. Orders are not necessarily processed at the moment they are sent, and by the time the stock is purchased, the price may have risen ten-fold. Read more about investing through the Internet and the SEC's efforts to combat growing Internet-based investment fraud at **www.sec.gov**.

e-project: Go to the Web sites of two on-line trading venues: the more traditional Merrill Lynch at **www.merrill-lynch.com** and the new, highly successful E*Trade at **www.etrade.com**. How effectively do these companies communicate the risks of a volatile market to their customers? Looking at the recommendations outlined by the SEC, how does each company rate?

Notes

1. R. D. Ward, 1997, *21st Century Corporate Board* (New York: John Wiley & Sons).
2. J. E. Core, R. W. Holthausen, & D. F. Larcker, 1999, Corporate governance, chief executive officer compensation, and firm performance, *Journal of Financial Economics,* 51: 371–406.
3. R. K. Mitchell, B. R. Agle, & D. J. Wood, 1997, Toward a theory of stakeholder identification and salience: Defining the principle of who and what really counts, *Academy of Management Review,* 22: 853–886.
4. J. H. Davis, F. D. Schoorman, & L. Donaldson, 1997, Toward a stewardship theory of management, *Academy of Management Review,* 22: 20–47.
5. M. M. Blair, 1999, For whom should corporations be run? An economic rationale for stakeholder management, *Long Range Planning,* 31: 195–200; O. E. Williamson, 1996, Economic organization: The case for candor, *Academy of Management Review,* 21: 48–57.
6. J. Magretta, 1998, Governing the family-owned enterprise: An in-

terview with Finland's Krister Ahlstrom, *Harvard Business Review,* 76(1): 112–123.

7. E. F. Fama & M. C. Jensen, 1983, Separation of ownership and control, *Journal of Law and Economics,* 26: 301–325.
8. Ward, *21st Century Corporate Board,* 3–144.
9. C. Arnolod & K. Breen, 1997, Investor activism goes worldwide, *Corporate Board,* 18(2): 7–12.
10. M. Kroll, P. Wright, L. Toombs, & H. Leavell, 1997, Form of control: A critical determinant of acquisition performance and CEO rewards, *Strategic Management Journal,* 18: 85–96; J. K. Seward & J. P. Walsh, 1996, The governance and control of voluntary corporate spinoffs, *Strategic Management Journal,* 17: 25–39.
11. J. D. Westphal & E. J. Zajac, 1997, Defections from the inner circle: Social exchange, reciprocity and diffusion of board independence in U.S. corporations, *Administrative Science Quarterly,* 42: 161–212; Ward, *21st Century Corporate Board.*
12. J. Charkham, 1994, *Keeping Good Company: A Study of Corporate Governance in Five Countries* (New York: Oxford University Press), 1.
13. A. Cadbury, 1999, The future of governance: The rules of the game, *Journal of General Management,* 24: 1–14.
14. Cadbury Committee, 1992, *Report of the Cadbury Committee on the Financial Aspects of Corporate Governance* (London: Gee).
15. C. K. Prahalad & J. P. Oosterveld, 1999, Transforming internal governance: The challenge for multinationals, *Sloan Management Review,* 40(3): 31–39.
16. M. A. Hitt, R. A. Harrison, & R. D. Ireland, 2001, *Creating Value through Mergers and Acquisitions: A Complete Guides to Successful M&As.* (New York: Oxford University Press); M. A. Hitt, R. E. Hoskisson, R. A. Johnson, & D. D. Moesel, 1996, The market for corporate control and firm innovation, *Academy of Management Journal,* 39: 1084–1119; J. P. Walsh & R. Kosnik, 1993, Corporate raiders and their disciplinary role in the market for corporate control, *Academy of Management Journal,* 36: 671–700.
17. Davis, Schoorman & Donaldson, Toward a stewardship theory of management.
18. C. Sundaramurthy, J. M. Mahoney, & J. T. Mahoney, 1997, Board structure, antitakeover provisions, and stockholder wealth, *Strategic Management Journal,* 18: 231–246; K. J. Rediker & A. Seth, 1995, Boards of directors and substitution effects of alternative governance mechanisms, *Strategic Management Journal,* 16: 85–99.
19. R. E. Hoskisson, M. A. Hitt, R. A. Johnson, & W. Grossman, 2000, Conflicting Voices: The effects of ownership heterogeneity and internal governance on corporate strategy, Paper presented at the Strategic Management Society, Vancouver, CA.
20. G. E. Davis & T. A. Thompson, 1994, A social movement perspective on corporate control, *Administrative Science Quarterly,* 39: 141–173.
21. M. A. Eisenberg, 1989, The structure of corporation law, *Columbia Law Review,* 89(7): 1461 as cited in R. A. G. Monks & N. Minow, 1995, *Corporate Governance* (Cambridge, MA: Blackwell Business), 7.
22. R. M. Wiseman & L. R. Gomez-Mejia, 1999, A behavioral agency model of managerial risk taking, *Academy of Management Review,* 23: 133–153.
23. E. E. Fama, 1980, Agency problems and the theory of the firm, *Journal of Political Economy,* 88: 288–307.
24. J. Ball, 1999, DaimlerChrysler frets over loss of U.S. shareholders, *Wall Street Journal,* March 24, B4.
25. A. Hill, 2000, Amazon.com: Investors jittery at staff cuts, *ft.com,* February 8, *www.ft.com/nbearchive.*
26. C. Brown-Humes, 2000, Ericsson: Clear message for Swedish Telco, *ft.com,* February 8, *www.ft.com/nbearchive.*
27. M. Jensen & W. Meckling, 1976, Theory of the firm: Managerial behavior, agency costs, and ownership structure, *Journal of Financial Economics,* 11: 305–360.
28. H. C. Tosi, J. Katz, & L. R. Gomez-Mejia, 1997, Disaggregating the agency contract: The effects of monitoring, incentive alignment, and term in office on agent decision making, *Academy of Management Journal,* 40: 584–602; P. C. Godfrey & C. W. L. Hill, 1995, The problem of unobservables in strategic management research, *Strategic Management Journal,* 16: 519–533.
29. P. Wright & S. P. Ferris, 1997, Agency conflict and corporate strategy: The effect of divestment on corporate strategy, *Strategic Management Journal,* 18: 77–83.
30. T. M. Welbourne & L. R. Gomez-Mejia, 1995, Gainsharing: A critical review and a future research agenda, *Journal of Management,* 21: 577.
31. P. Wright, S. P. Ferris, A. Sarin, & V. Awasthi, 1996, Impact of corporate insider, blockholder, and institutional equity ownership on firm risk taking, *Academy of Management Journal,* 39: 441–463.
32. P. B. Firstenberg & B. G. Malkiel, 1994, The twenty-first century boardroom: Who will be in charge? *Sloan Management Review,* Fall: 27–35, as cited in C. M. Daily, 1996, Governance patterns in bankruptcy reorganizations, *Strategic Management Journal,* 17: 355–375.
33. O. E. Williamson, 1996, *The Mechanisms of Governance* (New York: Oxford University Press), 6; O. E. Williamson, 1993, Opportunism and its critics, *Managerial and Decision Economics,* 14: 97–107.
34. S. Ghoshal & P. Moran, 1996, Bad for practice: A critique of the transaction cost theory, *Academy of Management Review,* 21: 13–47.
35. Godfrey & Hill, The problem of unobservables in strategic management research.
36. Y. Amihud & B. Lev, 1981, Risk reduction as a managerial motive for conglomerate mergers, *Bell Journal of Economics,* 12: 605–617.
37. R. E. Hoskisson & T. A. Turk, 1990, Corporate restructuring: Governance and control limits of the internal market, *Academy of Management Review,* 15: 459–477.
38. S. Finkelstein & D. C. Hambrick, 1989, Chief executive compensation: A study of the intersection of markets and political processes, *Strategic Management Journal,* 16: 221, 239; H. C. Tosi & L. R. Gomez-Mejia, 1989, The decoupling of CEO pay and performance: An agency theory perspective, *Administrative Science Quarterly,* 34: 169–189.
39. Hoskisson & Turk, 1990, Corporate restructuring.
40. D. Brady & P. L. Moore, 1999, Xerox: Investors turn up the heat on Rick Thoman, *BusinessWeek Online,* December 27, *www.businessweek.com.*
41. M. S. Jensen, 1986, Agency costs of free cash flow, corporate finance, and takeovers, *American Economic Review,* 76: 323–329.
42. C. W. L. Hill & S. A. Snell, 1988, External control, corporate strategy, and firm performance in research intensive industries, *Strategic Management Journal,* 9: 577–590.
43. A. Sharma, 1997, Professional as agent: Knowledge asymmetry in agency exchange, *Academy of Management Review,* 22: 758–798.
44. P. Lane, A. A. Cannella, Jr. & M. H. Lubatkin, 1999, Agency problems as antecedents to unrelated mergers and diversification: Amihud and Lev reconsidered, *Strategic Management Journal,* 19: 555–578.
45. M. Brannigan, 1999, Shareholders sue Comair and Delta over buyout price, *Wall Street Journal,* October 14, A15.
46. H. Sender, 2000, Japan grapples with shareholder suits, *Wall Street Journal,* January 7, A13.
47. J. A. Byrne, 1997, The CEO and the board, *Business Week,* September 15, 107–116.
48. R. E. Hoskisson, R. A. Johnson, & D. D. Moesel, 1994, Corporate divestiture intensity in restructuring firms: Effects of governance, strategy, and performance, *Academy of Management Journal,* 37: 1207–1251.
49. S. R. Kole & K. M. Lehn, 1999, Deregulation and the adaptation of

governance structure: The case of the U.S. airline industry, *Journal of Financial Economics,* 52: 79–117.
50. A. Berle & G. Means, 1932, *The Modern Corporation and Private Property* (New York: Macmillan).
51. M. P. Smith, 1996, Shareholder activism by institutional investors: Evidence from CalPERS, *Journal of Finance,* 51: 227–252.
52. J. D. Bogert, 1996, Explaining variance in the performance of long-term corporate blockholders, *Strategic Management Journal,* 17: 243–249.
53. M. Useem, 1998, Corporate leadership in a globalizing equity market, *Academy of Management Executive,* 43–59.
54. Hoskisson, Hitt, Johnson, & Grossman, Conflicting Voices; C. M. Dailey, 1996, Governance patterns in bankruptcy reorganizations, *Strategic Management Journal,* 17: 355–375.
55. R. Smith, 2000, CalPERS to buy 10% of Thomas Weisel, invest possibly $1 billion in firm, funds, *Wall Street Journal,* January 4, A8.
56. Useem, Corporate leadership in a globalizing equity market; R. E. Hoskisson & M. A. Hitt, 1994, *Downscoping: How to Tame the Diversified Firm* (New York: Oxford University Press).
57. E. Schine, 1997, CalPERS' grand inquisitor, *Business Week,* February 24, 120.
58. CalPERS highlights retailers in its list of underperformers, 1996, *Wall Street Journal,* February 7, Cl8.
59. J. S. Byrne, 1999, The Teddy Roosevelts of corporate governance, *Business Week,* May 31, 75–79.
60. M. J. Roe, 1993, Mutual funds in the boardroom, *Journal of Applied Corporate Finance,* 5(4): 56–61.
61. Y. Trofimov, 1999, Telecom Italia scuttles its split-off of wireless unit, bowing to pressure, *Wall Street Journal Interactive,* November 22, *www.interactive.wsj.com/articles.*
62. Byrne, The CEO and the board, 114.
63. J. S. Lublin, 1997, More CEOs decide: No time for seats, *Wall Street Journal,* October 28, A2.
64. Sundaramurthy, Mahoney, & Mahoney, Board structure, antitakeover provisions, and stockholder wealth; C. Sundaramurthy, 1996, Corporate governance within the context of antitakeover provisions, *Strategic Management Journal,* 17: 377–394.
65. B. S. Black, 1992, Agents watching agents: The promise of institutional investors voice, *UCLA Law Review,* 39: 871–893.
66. J. Weil, 2000, Heard in Texas: A gadfly investor admonishes Vtel to better serve its shareholders, *Wall Street Journal Interactive,* February 6, *www.interactive.wsj.com/articles.*
67. R. A. G. Monks, 1999, What will be the impact of active shareholders? A practical recipe for constructive change, *Long Range Planning,* 32(1): 20–27.
68. C. Sandaramurthy & D. W. Lyon, 1998, Shareholder governance proposals and conflict of interests between inside and outside shareholders, *Journal of Managerial Issues,* 10: 30–44.
69. Rediker & Seth, Boards of directors, 85.
70. D. R. Dalton, C. M. Daily, A. E. Ellstrand, & J. L. Johnson, 1998, Meta-analytic reviews of board composition, leadership structure, and financial performance, *Strategic Management Journal,* 19: 269–290; M. Huse, 1998, Researching the dynamics of board-stakeholder relations, *Long Range Planning,* 31: 218–226.
71. J. K. Seward & J. P Walsh, 1996, The governance and control of voluntary corporate spinoffs, *Strategic Management Journal,* 17: 25–39.
72. P. Mallete & R. L. Hogler, 1995, Board composition, stock ownership, and the exemption of directors from liability, *Journal of Management,* 21: 861–878.
73. D. P. Forbes & F. J. Milliken, 1999, Cognition and corporate governance: Understanding boards of directors as strategic decision-making groups, *Academy of Management Review,* 24: 489–505.
74. B. D. Baysinger & R. E. Hoskisson, 1990, The composition of boards of directors and strategic control: Effects on corporate strategy, *Academy of Management Review,* 15: 72–87.
75. E. J. Zajac & J. D. Westphal, 1996, Director reputation, CEO-board power, and the dynamics of board interlocks, *Administrative Science Quarterly,* 41: 507–529.
76. J. D. Westphal & E. J. Zajac, 1995, Who shall govern? CEO/board power, demographic similarity, and new director selection, *Administrative Science Quarterly,* 40: 60–83.
77. R. P. Beatty & E. J. Zajac, 1994, Managerial incentives, monitoring, and risk bearing: A study of executive compensation, ownership, and board structure in initial public offerings, *Administrative Science Quarterly,* 39: 313–335.
78. A. Bryant, 1997, CalPERS draws a blueprint for its concept of an ideal board, *New York Times,* June 17, C1.
79. A. Cadbury, 1999, What are the trends in corporate governance? How will they impact your company? *Long Range Planning,* 32: 12–19.
80. G. McWilliams & J. S. Lublin, 1999, Compaq could have averted missteps, *Wall Street Journal,* April 20, A3, A6.
81. J. A. Byrne, 1999, Commentary: Boards share the blame when the boss fails, *BusinessWeek Online,* December 27, *www.businessweek.com/articles.*
82. I. M. Millstein, 1997, Red herring over independent boards, *New York Times,* April 6, F10; W. Q. Judge, Jr. & G. H. Dobbins, 1995, Antecedents and effects of outside directors' awareness of CEO decision style, *Journal of Management,* 21: 43–64.
83. I. E. Kesner, 1988, Director characteristics in committee membership: An investigation of type, occupation, tenure and gender, *Academy of Management Journal,* 31: 66–84.
84. T. McNulty & A Pettigrew, 1999, Strategists on the board, *Organization Studies,* 20: 47–74.
85. S. Zahra, 1996, Governance, ownership and corporate entrepreneurship among the Fortune 500: The moderating impact of industry technological opportunity, *Academy of Management Journal,* 39: 1713–1735.
86. J. A. Conger, D. Finegold, & E. E. Lawler, III, 1998, Appraising boardroom performance, *Harvard Business Review,* 76(1): 136–148; J. A. Byrne & L. Brown, 1997, Directors in the hot seat, *Business Week,* December 8, 100–104.
87. H. Kaback, 1996, A director's guide to board behavior, *Wall Street Journal,* April 1, A14.
88. J. A. Byrne, 1997, Putting more stock in good governance, *Business Week,* September 15, 116; A. Bianco & J. A. Byrne, 1997, The rush to quality on corporate boards, *Business Week,* March 3, 34–35.
89. C. A. Simmers, 2000, Executive/board politics in strategic decision making, *Journal of Business and Economic Studies,* 4: 37–56.
90. W. Ocasio, 1999, Institutionalized action and corporate governance, *Administrative Science Quarterly,* 44: 384–416.
91. S. Rosenstein & J. G. Wyatt, 1997, Inside directors, board effectiveness, and shareholder wealth, *Journal of Financial Economics,* 44: 229–250.
92. N. Vafeas, 1999, The nature of board nominating committees and their role in corporate governance, *Journal of Business Finance & Accounting,* 26: 199–225.
93. D. C. Hambrick & S. Finkelstein, 1995, The effects of ownership structure on conditions at the top: The case of CEO pay raises, *Strategic Management Journal,* 16: 175.
94. L. Gomez-Mejia & R. M. Wiseman, 1997, Reframing executive compensation: An assessment and outlook, *Journal of Management,* 23: 291–374.
95. S. Finkelstein & B. K. Boyd, 1998, How much does the CEO matter? The role of managerial discretion in the setting of CEO compensation, *Academy of Management Journal,* 41: 179–199
96. W. G. Sanders & M. A. Carpenter, 1998, Internationalization and firm governance: The roles of ceo compensation, top team composition and board structure, *Academy of Management Journal,* 41: 158–178.

97. J. D. Westphal & E. J. Zajac, 1999, The symbolic management of stockholders: Corporate governance reform and shareholder reactions, *Administrative Science Quarterly,* 43: 127–153.
98. M. J. Conyon & S. I. Peck, 1998, Board control, remuneration committees, and top management compensation, *Academy of Management Journal,* 41: 146–157; Westphal & Zajac, The symbolic management of stockholders.
99. K. Roth & S. O'Donnell, 1996, Foreign subsidiary compensation: An agency theory perspective, *Academy of Management Journal,* 39: 678–703.
100. S. Fung, 1999, How should we pay them? *Across the Board,* June: 37–41.
101. C Peck, H. M. Silvert, & K. Worrell, 1999, Top executive compensation: Canada, France, the United Kingdom, and the United States, *Chief Executive Digest,* 3: 27–29.
102. R. E. Hoskisson, M. A. Hitt, & C. W. L. Hill, 1993, Managerial incentives and investment in R&D in large multiproduct firms, *Organization Science,* 4: 325–341.
103. K. A. Merchant, 1989, *Rewarding Results: Motivating Profit Center Managers* (Cambridge, MA: Harvard Business School Press).
104. GM chairman's pay drops 27%, 1999, *Dallas Morning News,* April 21, D2.
105. W. M. Bulkeley, 1999, Software firm executives ordered to return million in stock options, *Wall Street Journal Interactive,* November 10, *www.interactive.wsj.com/articles*; J. Reingold & R. Grover, 1999, Executive pay, *Business Week,* April 19, 72–118.
106. C. G. Holderness, R. S. Kroszner, & D. P. Sheehan, 1999, Were the good old days that good? Changes in managerial stock ownership since the Great Depression, *Journal of Finance,* 54: 435–469.
107. J. Dahya, A. A. Lonie, & D. A. Power, 1998, Ownership structure, firm performance and top executive change: An analysis of UK firms, *Journal of Business Finance & Accounting,* 25: 1089–1118.
108. E. S. Hardy, S. DeCarlo, A. C. Anderson, & J. Chamberlain, 1999, Compensation fit for a king, *Forbes,* May 17, 202–207.
109. R. E. Silverman & J. S. Lublin, 1999, The going rate: Mega options, *Dallas Morning News,* November 9, B20.
110. G. Crystal, 2000, Executive's pay sets top-flight example, *The Denver Post,* February 13, 5-1.
111. J. S. Lublin, 2000, CEO pay at best performers soared in 1999, study says, *Wall Street Journal Interactive,* February 28, *www.interactive.wsj.com.*
112. T. Hausman, 1999, Predicting Pay, *Wall Street Journal,* April 8, R9.
113. K. Worrell, 1999, Corporate directors' compensation in 1998, *Chief Executive Digest,* 3: 28–29.
114. T. D. Schellhardt, 1999, More directors are raking in six-figure pay, *The Wall Street Journal,* October 29, B1, B4.
115. C. M. Daily, S. T. Certo, & D. R. Dalton, 1999, Pay directors in stock? No, *Across the Board,* November/December, 47–50.
116. O. E. Williamson, 1985, *The Economic Institutions of Capitalism: Firms, Markets and Relational Contracting* (New York: Macmillan Free Press).
117. B. W. Keats & M. A. Hitt, 1988, A causal model of linkages among environmental dimensions, macro organizational characteristics, and performance, *Academy of Management Journal,* 31: 570–598.
118. O. E. Williamson, 1994, Strategizing, economizing, and economic organization, in R. P. Rumelt, D. E. Schendel, & D. J. Teece (eds.), *Fundamental Issues in Strategy* (Cambridge, MA: Harvard Business School Press), 380.
119. Hoskisson & Turk, Corporate restructuring: Governance and control limits of the internal market.
120. M. A. Hitt, R. E. Hoskisson, & R. D. Ireland, 1990, Mergers and acquisitions and managerial commitment to innovation in M-form firms, *Strategic Management Journal,* 11(Special Summer Issue): 29–47.
121. Hitt, Hoskisson, Johnson, & Moesel, The market for corporate control and firm innovation; Walsh & Kosnik, Corporate raiders.
122. Mallette & Hogier, Board composition, 864.
123. Hitt, Harrison, & Ireland, *Creating Value through Mergers and Acquisitions.*
124. S. Morrison, 1999, Teleglobe: Share fall opens takeover door, *ft.com,* October 1, *www.ft.com/nbearchive.*
125. J. Hechinger & J. Pereira, 2000, Socially conscious investors fear Ben & Jerry's could lose its flavor, *Wall Street Journal Interactive,* February 6, *www.interactive.wsj.com/articles.*
126. C. Daniel, J. M. Brown, & V. Skold, 2000, ESAT: Board supports $2.4bn BT bid, *ft.com,* February 3, *www.ft.com/nearchive.*
127. S. Voyle, 2000, M&S beats of Green threat, *ft.com,* February 17, *www.ft.com/nbearchive.*
128. Sundaramurthy, Mahoney, & Mahoney, Board structure, antitakeover provisions, and stockholder wealth.
129. R. A. Johnson, R. E. Hoskisson, & M. A. Hitt, 2000, The effects of environmental uncertainty on the mode of corporate restructuring, working paper, University of Missouri.
130. J. A. Byrne, 1999, Poison pills: Let shareholders decide, *Business Week,* May 17, 104.
131. T. Carlisle, 2000, Canadian oil firm sets defense against Occidental's takeover bid, *Wall Street Journal Interactive,* February 6, *www.interactive.wsj.com/articles.*
132. Walsh & Kosnik, Corporate raiders.
133. S. Johnston, 1995, Managerial dominance of Japan's major corporations, *Journal of Management,* 21: 191–209.
134. Useem, Corporate leadership in a globalizing equity market.
135. Our discussion of corporate governance structures in Germany and Japan is drawn from Monks and Minow, *Corporate Governance,* 271–299; Charkham, Keeping Good Company, 6–118.
136. H. Kim & R. E. Hoskisson, 1996, Japanese governance systems: A critical review, in B. Prasad (ed.), *Advances in International Comparative Management* (Greenwich, CT: JAI Press), 165–189.
137. E. R. Gedajlovic & D. M. Shapiro, 1998, Management and ownership effects: Evidence from five countries, *Strategic Management Journal,* 19: 533–553.
138. S. Douma, 1997, The two-tier system of corporate governance, *Long Range Planning,* 30(4): 612–615.
139. M. J. Rubach & T. C. Sebora, 1998, Comparative corporate governance: Competitive implications of an emerging convergence, *Journal of World Business,* 33: 167–184.
140. Charkham, *Keeping Good Company,* 70.
141. J. Fiorillo, 2000, While Tokyo's commitment to reform waivers, *Wall Street Journal Interactive,* January 12, *www.interactive.wsj.com/articles.*
142. B. Bremner, E. Thornton, & I. M. Kunii, 1999, Fall of a Keiretsu, *Business Week,* March 15, 87–92.
143. E. Thornton, 1999, Mystery at the top, *Business Week,* April 26, 52.
144. P. Landers, 2000, Hostile bid for Tokyo's Shoei marks a milestone for Japan, *Wall Street Journal Interactive,* February 6, *www.interactive.wsj.com/articles*; M. Almieda, 2000, Japanese hostile-takeover bid marks a departure from corporate model, *Wall Street Journal Interactive,* February 6, *www.interactive.wsj.com/articles.*
145. J. B. White, 2000, The company we'll keep, *Wall Street Journal Interactive,* January 17, *www.interactive.wsj.com/articles.*
146. S. Iskander, 1999, Salary disclosure in France: Transparency or voyeurism? *Financial Times,* July 26, 11–12.
147. C. P. Erlich & D.-S. Kang, 1999, South Korea: Corporate governance reform in Korea: The remaining issues—Part I: Governance structure of the large Korean firm, *East Asian Executive Reports,* 21: 11–14+.
148. L. Chang, 1999, Chinese firms find incentive to use stock-compensation plans, *The Wall Street Journal,* November 1, A2.; T. Clarke & Y. Du, 1998, Corporate governance in China: Explosive growth and new patterns of ownership, *Long Range Planning,* 31(2): 239–251.
149. T Buck, I. Filatotchev, & M. Wright, 1998, Agents, stakeholders and corporate governance in Russian firms, *Journal of Management Studies,* 35: 81–104.

150. E. Freeman & J. Liedtka, 1997, Stakeholder capitalism and the value chain, *European Management Journal,* 15(3): 286–295.
151. A. Taylor, III, 1996, GM: Why they might break up America's biggest company, *Fortune,* April 29, 84.
152. Hitt, Harrison, & Ireland, *Creating Value through Mergers and Acquisitions*; Cendant reaches preliminary agreement to settle common stock securities class action for $2.83 billion, 1999, *Cendant Press Release,* December 7.
153. R. F. Felton, A. Hudnut, & V. Witt, 1995, Building a stronger board, *McKinsey Quarterly* 1995(2): 169.

ORGANIZATIONAL STRUCTURE AND CONTROLS

CHAPTER ELEVEN OBJECTIVES

After reading this chapter, you should be able to:

1. Explain the importance of integrating strategy implementation and strategy formulation.
2. Describe the dominant path of evolution from strategy to structure to strategy again.
3. Identify and describe the organizational structures used to implement different business-level strategies.
4. Discuss organizational structures used to implement different corporate-level strategies.
5. Identify and distinguish among the organizational structures used to implement three international strategies.
6. Describe organizational structures used to implement cooperative strategies.

The New Structure of Microsoft

Although Microsoft has $257,000 of income per employee, versus the average of $17,000 for the Standard & Poor 500 stock index, the company's top executives are restructuring the firm in a way that will barely resemble the one that got them to that position. Microsoft had its largest market capitalization, $414 billion, in 1999 and has had a revenue growth of 30 percent annually. Why, then, does the firm feel that it must do something different to top this amazing performance for a 24-year-old company? In fact, Bill Gates is taking over as the chief software architect and stepping down as the CEO, and Steve Ballmer is taking over the top position.

In explaining why Microsoft is changing its leadership and structural arrangements, Bill Gates simply said, "The Internet has changed everything. In order to respond to these changes, Microsoft needs to give people the power to do anything they want, anywhere they want and on any device." Accordingly, the new vision, "Microsoft Vision 2.0," is directed at giving Microsoft programmers freedom to develop programs that don't revolve around Windows software, and for Microsoft, that's a significant change. For example, although Microsoft lost to AT&T in the bid for MediaOne Group, Inc., a large cable TV operation, it did receive a nonexclusive contract with MediaOne to provide set-top software for the interactive boxes that will facilitate using the Web through the home cable television platform, whereby consumers will also be able to hook up their PCs at lightning-fast speeds. In fact, MediaOne will have access to 8 percent of U.S. homes.

This Microsoft vision includes a new organizational structure that divides the company's product development into six different divisions. Two groups will target corporate leaders and knowledge workers. Two others emphasize home PC buyers and those who shop for computer and video games at stores. Still another is concerned with software developers. Finally, the last group is aimed at Web surfers and those who shop on the Web.

In the previous structure, products were split by technology, one focusing on Windows application software (such as Microsoft Word and associated software products) and the other on operating systems. The operating systems division focused on a range of systems, from Windows NT down to the stripped-down Win CE for handheld consumer devices. Accordingly, there was no distinction based on customers. Previously, this division had focused on technology for technology's sake and not on the basis of what consumers wanted. Thus, under the new structural arrangement, there will be fewer arcane technological features with the operating systems so that even less sophisticated consumers will obtain what they need and desire, without confusing them unnecessarily about technological aspects.

Previously, the power structure was such that Gates and Microsoft President Steven A. Ballmer made the division heads come to them for almost all decisions. With decisions large and small being funneled through this top pair, there was a decision-making bottleneck. Thus, the structure was functionally oriented (focused on technology) and centralized. With 30,000 employees, 183 different products, and at least five layers of management and staffers, there were significant complaints about bureaucratic red tape. Decision making was very slow, and many key employees were leaving because their ideas were not being heard. Additionally, there was little opportunity to develop them because of the centralized decision making. The new structure is closer to the multidivisional structure adoption which often follows increased product diversification.

Although the talent drain is one problem that Microsoft's restructuring is intended to slow down through more divisional independence and decentralization, the loss of key employees likely will continue to be a competitive challenge. The hope is that the new structure will give the company an opportunity for fresh ideas to take hold and develop. Along these lines, Microsoft has been considering offering a "tracking stock" (issues of stock focused on specific company assets) that would give its Internet properties a focus for investors. It would allow investors to cash in on the high Internet stock valuations, but also, protect their cash cow, the Windows software business, from wild price swings, because of the focus on the Internet. Furthermore, it would enable business-level managers to cash in on their entrepreneurial ideas. General Motors has had a tracking stock for Hughes that has risen much more rapidly than shares of General Motors common stock, because of the DirectTV assets targeted by the tracking stock. Thus, the tracking stock allows better market value adjustment, given information on the type of asset, and provides an incentive for up-and-coming creative management talent to stay with Microsoft.

Whether such a structural change will work and whether Gates and Ballmer will be able to give up control are questions that will be tested over time. Those two executives are used to delving into every decision, but that approach has slowed decision making. Another potential pitfall is that the different product groups might undertake conflicting strategies now that they are ostensibly independent. However, if the change helps Microsoft to stay focused on its customers, it is likely to increase its already outstanding performance.

http://www.att.com

http://www.gm.com

http://www.mediaone.com

http://www.microsoft.com

SOURCES: Microsoft Home Page, 2000, March 1, *www.microsoft.com*; D. J. Greene, 2000, A chat with the new guy in product development, *Business Week,* January 31, 43; D. Bank, 1999, Microsoft will split into five divisions that deal with customers and rivals, *Wall Street Journal Interactive Edition,* March 30, *www.wsj.com*; P. Gillin, 1999, Microsoft's Ballmer details reorg, *Computerworld,* April 5, 12; M. Moeller, S. Hamm, & T. J. Mullaney, 1999, Remaking Microsoft, *Business Week,* May 17, 106–114; M. Moeller & K. Rebello, 1999, Visionary-in-chief: A talk with Chairman Bill Gates on the world beyond Windows, *Business Week,* May 17, 114–116; E. Nee, 1999, Microsoft gets ready for a new game, *Fortune,* April 26, 107–112.

In the previous chapter, we described mechanisms companies use to govern their operations and to align various parties' interests—especially the interests of top-level executives—with those of the firm's owners. Governance mechanisms can influence a company's ability to implement formulated strategies successfully and thereby facilitate a competitive advantage.[1]

In this chapter, our focus is on the organizational structures and controls used to implement the strategies discussed previously (e.g., business level, Chapter 4; corporate level, Chapter 6; international, Chapter 8; and cooperative, Chapter 9). Moreover, as the discussion in the Opening Case about actions taken at Microsoft suggests, the proper use of an organizational structure and its accompanying integrating mechanisms and controls can contribute to the firm's strategic competitiveness.[2] In fact, the most productive global competitors are those with effective product innovation skills and an organizational structure in place that facilitates successful and timely applications of internal capabilities and core competencies.[3] Thus, a firm's organizational structure influences its managerial work and the decisions made by top-level managers.[4]

Organizational structure alone, however, does not create a competitive advantage; rather, a competitive advantage is created when there is a proper match between strategy and structure.[5] For example, it may be that what makes 3M's competitive advantage somewhat sustainable "is its unique blend of practices, values, autonomous structures, funding processes, rewards, and selection and development of product champions."[6] Similarly, the Acer Group, manufacturer of Acer personal computers, is known as an innovative competitor. Some analysts believe that a unique organizational structure (which the CEO labels "global brand, local touch") contributes significantly to the firm's strategic competitiveness.[7] On the other hand, ineffective strategy–structure matches may result in rigidity and failure, given the complexity and need for rapid changes in the 21st-century competitive landscape.[8] Thus, effective strategic leaders (see Chapter 12) seek to develop an organizational structure and accompanying controls that are superior to those of their competitors.[9] Using competitively superior structures and controls explains in part why some firms survive and succeed while others do not.[10] Bill Gates and Steve Ballmer, the executives at Microsoft who have implemented the new structure outlined in the Opening Case, expect that the organizational structure will contribute to the firm's future success. As with the other parts of the strategic management process, top-level managers bear the final responsibility to make choices about organizational structures that will enhance a firm's performance.[11] Following its acquisition of Digital Equipment Corporation (DEC), Compaq Computer Corporation executives, for example, did not make good structural decisions, and a successful integration of DEC's businesses into their own continues to cause problems (see Strategic Focus in Chapter 1).

Selecting the organizational structure and controls that will implement chosen strategies effectively is a fundamental challenge for managers, especially those at the top. A key reason is that in the global economy, firms must be flexible, innovative, and creative to exploit their core competencies in the pursuit of marketplace opportunities.[12] They also require a certain degree of stability in their structures so that day-to-day tasks can be completed efficiently. Accessible and reliable information is needed for executives to reach decisions regarding the selection of a structure that can provide the desired levels of flexibility and stability. By helping executives improve their decision making, useful information contributes to the formation and implementation of effective structures and controls.[13]

This chapter first describes a pattern of growth and accompanying changes in an organizational structure experienced by strategically competitive firms. For example, the success of Microsoft mentioned in the Opening Case necessitated the subsequent change in structural arrangement. The chapter's second major section discusses organizational structures and controls that are used to implement different business-level strategies.

The implementation of corporate-level strategy is then described, with the transition from the functional to the multidivisional structure highlighted. This major structural innovation took place in several firms during the 1920s, including DuPont. In fact, noted business historian Alfred Chandler cites DuPont as the innovator in both the strategy of diversification and the multidivisional structure.[14] Specific variations of the multidivisional structure are discussed in terms of their relationship with the effective implementation of the related and unrelated diversification strategies.

Because of the increasing globalization of many industries, the number of firms implementing international strategies continues to grow. The trend toward globalization is significant and pervasive. To cope successfully with the strategic challenges associated with discontinuous changes, the firm must develop and use organizational structures that facilitate meaningful conversations among all stakeholders regarding opportunities and threats facing the company at different points in time.[15] In the chapter's final two sections, we discuss the use of organizational structures to implement cooperative strategies and a few issues concerning organizational forms that should be of interest to those responsible for using a firm's strategic management process effectively.

Evolutionary Patterns of Strategy and Organizational Structure

All firms require some form of organizational structure to implement their strategies. Principally, structures are changed when they no longer provide the coordination, control, and direction managers and organizations require to implement strategies successfully.[16] The ineffectiveness of a structure typically results from increases in a firm's revenues and levels of diversification. In particular, the formulation of strategies involving greater levels of diversification demands structural change to match each strategy. Some corporate-level strategies require elaborate structures and strategic controls, while others focus on financial control.

Organizational structure is a firm's formal role configuration, procedures, governance and control mechanisms, and authority and decision-making processes.

Organizational structure is a firm's formal role configuration, procedures, governance and control mechanisms, and authority and decision-making processes.[17] Influenced by situational factors, including company size and age, organizational structure reflects managers' determinations of *what* the firm does and how it completes that work, given its chosen strategies.[18] Strategic competitiveness can be attained only when the firm's selected structure is congruent with its formulated strategy.[19] Consequently, a strategy's potential to create value is reached only when the firm configures itself in ways that allow the strategy to be implemented effectively. Thus, as firms evolve and change their strategies, new structural arrangements are required. In addition, existing structures influence the future selection of strategies.[20] Accordingly, the two key strategic actions of strategy formulation and strategy implementation continuously interact to influence managerial choices about strategy and structure.

Figure 11.1 shows the growth pattern many firms experience. This pattern results in changes in the relationships between the firm's formulated strategies and the organizational structures used to support and facilitate their implementation.

11.1 | Strategy and Structure Growth Pattern

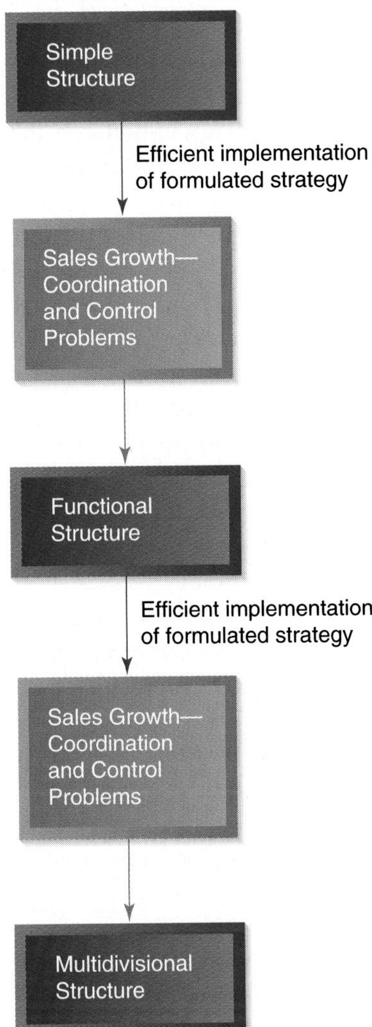

A **simple structure** is an organizational form in which the owner–manager makes all major decisions directly and monitors all activities, while the staff serves as an extension of the manager's supervisory authority.

Simple Structure

A **simple structure** is an organizational form in which the owner–manager makes all major decisions directly and monitors all activities, while the staff serves as an extension of the manager's supervisory authority. This structure involves little specialization of tasks, few rules, and limited formalization. Although important, information systems are relatively unsophisticated, and owner–managers participate directly in the firm's day-to-day operations. Typically, the simple structure is used by firms offering a single product line in a single geographic market. The simple structure is used frequently in firms implementing either the focused cost leadership or focused differentiation strategy. Restaurants, repair businesses, and other specialized enterprises are examples of firms whose limited complexity calls for the use of the simple structure. In this structure, communication is frequent and direct, and new products tend to be introduced to the market quickly, which can result in a competitive advantage. Because of these characteristics, few of the coordination problems that are common in larger organizations exist.

The simple structure, the operations it supports, and the strategies implemented in companies that use it play important roles in the success of various economies. Data on job creation are one indicator of this importance. In the United States, for example, companies with between 100 and 500 employees have become the largest job creators.[21] These small firms created approximately 85 percent of the new jobs in the United States in the latter 1990s. The value of small firms to the United Kingdom's economy has also been recognized: Some analysts believe that, in that country, the simple organizational structure may result in competitive advantages for some small firms relative to their larger counterparts. A broad-based openness to innovation, greater structural flexibility, and an ability to respond more rapidly to environmental changes are examples of these potential competitive advantages.[22] For example, large firms such as Nike have been overshadowed by a set of a dozen smaller firms at Super Show, the largest sporting-goods trade show in the United States. These smaller companies have endorsements by skateboarders, stunt bike riders and even rock stars, often with an extreme sports theme. "With kids more interested in shoes worn on MTV than those worn in the NBA, and many youngsters preferring the X Games to the World Series, industry giants focusing on traditional sports are slumping."[23] Nike's stock price has slumped because of its executives' inability to adapt to this change as quickly as the smaller firms can.[24] Thus, although large corporations are indeed vital to the health of the world's economies, the importance of small firms should not be overlooked. The simple organizational structure properly supports the implementation of the focused strategies that are chosen most often by small firms (see Chapter 4).

However, as the small firm grows larger and more complex, managerial and structural challenges emerge. For example, the amount of competitively relevant information requiring analysis increases substantially. The ensuing more complicated information-processing needs place significant pressures on the simple structure and the owner–manager. Commonly, owner–managers lack the organizational skills and experience required to manage effectively the specialized and complex tasks involved with multiple organizational functions. Owner–managers or the top-level managers employed by the small firm's owner bear the responsibility to recognize inadequacies in the firm's organizational structure and the need to change to one that is consistent with the firm's strategy.[25]

In fact, this is what has happened to Nike. Phil Knight, Nike's CEO, indicated, "We are becoming more of an international company than a U.S. company. That shift may be difficult to see for people who 'grew up' with the company as it exploded in the United States."[26] Nike's growth in Europe and Asia was 22 and 9.1 percent, respectively. In the Americas, including Latin America and Canada, Nike grew in the double-digit range, but the firm's growth in the United States is expected to be in the single-digit range. Furthermore, retail department store consolidation in the United States creates an uncertainty that has also affected Nike's stock price. Nike's growth has led to changes in the company's structure, as well as some inflexibility, as illustrated in the firm's failure to respond to the extreme-sports trend mentioned earlier. An appropriate structure for Nike in dealing with the pressures of growth would lead the company to move to a functional organizational structure or perhaps even one of the forms of the multidivisional structure, given that Nike has apparel in addition to shoe products.

Functional Structure

To coordinate more complex organizational functions, firms should abandon the simple structure in favor of the functional structure. The functional structure is used by larger firms implementing one of the business-level strategies and by firms with low levels of product diversification (for instance, companies implementing either the single- or dominant-business corporate-level strategy).

The **functional structure** consists of a chief executive officer and a limited corporate staff, with functional line managers in dominant organizational areas such as production, accounting, marketing, R&D, engineering, and human resources.

The **functional structure** consists of a chief executive officer and a limited corporate staff, with functional line managers in dominant organizational areas such as production, accounting, marketing, R&D, engineering, and human resources. This structure allows for functional specialization, thereby facilitating knowledge sharing and idea development.[27] Because the differences in orientation among organizational functions can impede communication and coordination, the central task of the CEO is to integrate the decisions and actions of individual business functions for the benefit of the entire corporation.[28] The functional structure also facilitates career paths and professional development in specialized functional areas.

An unintended negative consequence of the functional structure is the tendency for functional-area managers to focus on local versus overall company strategic issues. Such emphases cause specialized managers to lose sight of the firm's overall strategic intent and mission. When that happens, the multidivisional structure often is implemented to overcome the difficulty.

Another condition that encourages a change from the functional to the multidivisional structure is greater diversification. Strategic success often leads to growth and diversification. Deciding to offer the same products in different markets (market diversification) or choosing to offer different products (product diversification) creates control problems. The multidivisional structure provides the controls required to deal effectively with additional levels of diversification. In fact, the firm's returns may suffer when increased diversification is not accompanied by a change to the multidivisional structure, as shown in the Opening Case about Microsoft.

Multidivisional Structure

The CEO's limited ability to process increasing quantities of strategic information, the focus of functional managers on local issues, and increased diversification are primary causes of the decision to change from the functional to the multidivisional (M-form) structure. According to Alfred Chandler, "The M-form came into being when senior managers operating through existing centralized, functionally departmentalized . . . structures realized they had neither the time nor the necessary information to coordinate and monitor day-to-day operations, or to devise and implement long-term plans for the various product lines. The administrative overload had become simply too great."[29]

The **multidivisional (M-form) structure** is composed of operating divisions, each representing a separate business or profit center in which the top corporate officer delegates responsibilities for day-to-day operations and business-unit strategy to division managers.

The **multidivisional (M-form) structure** is composed of operating divisions, each representing a separate business or profit center in which the top corporate officer delegates responsibilities for day-to-day operations and business-unit strategy to division managers. Because the diversified corporation is the dominant form of business in the industrialized world, the M-form is being used in most of the corporations competing in the global economy.[30] However, only effectively designed M-forms enhance a firm's performance. Thus, for all companies—and perhaps especially for diversified firms—performance is a function of the goodness of fit between strategy and structure.[31]

Chandler's examination of the strategies and structures of large American firms documented the M-form's development.[32] Chandler viewed the M-form as an innovative response to coordination and control problems that surfaced during the 1920s in the functional structures then used by large firms such as DuPont and General Motors.[33] Among other benefits, the M-form allowed firms to greatly expand their operations.

Use of the Multidivisional Structure at DuPont and General Motors

Chandler's studies showed that firms such as DuPont began to record significant revenue growth through the manufacture and distribution of diversified products while using the functional structure. Functional departments (e.g., sales and production), however, found it difficult to coordinate the conflicting priorities of the firm's new and different products and markets. Moreover, the functional structures that were in use allocated costs to organizational functions, rather than to individual businesses and products. This allocation method made it virtually impossible for top-level managers to determine the contributions of separate product lines to the firm's return on its investments. Even more damaging for large firms trying to implement newly formulated product diversification strategies through the use of a functional structure that was appropriate for small companies and for those needing proprietary expertise and economies of scale[34] was the increasing allocation of top-level managers' time and energies to short-term administrative problems. Focusing their efforts on these issues caused executives to neglect the long-term strategic issues that were their primary responsibility.

To cope with similar problems, General Motors CEO Alfred Sloan, Jr., proposed a reorganization of the company.[35] Sloan conceptualized separate divisions, each representing a distinct business, that would be self-contained and have their own functional hierarchy. Implemented in 1925, Sloan's structure delegated day-to-day operating responsibilities to division managers. The small staff at the corporate level was responsible for determining the firm's long-term strategic direction and for exercising overall financial control of semiautonomous divisions. Each division was to make its own business-level strategic decisions, but because the corporate office's focus was on the outcomes achieved by the entire corporation, rather than the performance of separate units, decisions made by division heads could be superseded by corporate office personnel. Sloan's structural innovation had three important outcomes: "(1) it enabled corporate officers to more accurately monitor the performance of each business, which simplified the problem of control; (2) it facilitated comparisons between divisions, which improved the resource allocation process; and (3) it stimulated managers of poor[ly] performing divisions to look for ways of improving performance."[36]

The Use of Internal Controls in the Multidivisional Structure

The M-form structure holds top-level managers responsible for formulating and implementing overall corporate strategies; that is, they are responsible for the corporate-level acquisition and restructuring, international, and cooperative strategies we examined in Chapters 6 through 9.

Strategic and financial controls are the two major types of internal controls used to support the implementation of strategies in larger firms.[37] Properly designed organizational controls provide clear insights regarding behaviors that enhance the firm's competitiveness and overall performance.[38] Diversification strategies are implemented effectively when firms use both types of controls appropriately. For example, as the Opening Case illustrates, Microsoft is implementing a multidivisional structure. Currently, the company has good strategic control; however, it will need a better balance, with more of an emphasis on financial control, to create the appropriate incentives for managers of their new product-oriented divisions. If Ballmer and Gates do not allow division heads to develop stronger financial control of their divisions and evaluate the performance of those divisions with better financial controls (recall the idea of tracking stock, which could facilitate improved financial control and evaluation by the stock market), a control imbalance will remain, with Gates and Ballmer having too much centralized control.

Strategic control entails the use of long-term and strategically relevant criteria by corporate-level managers to evaluate the performance of division managers and their units.

Strategic control entails the use of long-term and strategically relevant criteria by corporate-level managers to evaluate the performance of division managers and their units. Strategic control emphasizes largely subjective judgments and may involve intuitive evaluation criteria. Behavioral in nature, strategic controls typically require high levels of cognitive diversity among top-level managers. *Cognitive diversity* captures the differences in beliefs about cause–effect relationships and desired outcomes among top-level managers' preferences.[39] Corporate-level managers rely on strategic control to gain an operational understanding of the strategies being implemented in the firm's separate divisions or business units. Because strategic control allows a corporate-level evaluation of the full array of strategic actions—those concerned with both the formulation and implementation of a business-unit strategy—corporate-level managers must have a deep understanding of a division's or business unit's operations and markets.[40] The use of strategic controls also demands rich exchanges of information between corporate and divisional managers. These exchanges take place through both formal and informal (i.e., unplanned) face-to-face meetings.[41] As diversification increases, strategic control can be strained.[42] Sometimes, the strain results in a commitment to reduce the firm's level of diversification. For example, Black & Decker's top-level managers decided recently to divest some divisions to reduce the firm's overall level of diversification. Units sold were the household products division in North America, Latin America, and Australia; Emhart Glass (a maker of equipment for the manufacture of glass containers); and True Temper Sports (a manufacturer of golf club shafts). Difficulties encountered when the firm attempted to use strategic controls to evaluate the performance of those units and of the individuals managing them may have contributed to the divestment decisions. Coupled with a reduction in force of 3,000 jobs (10 percent of the firm's workforce), the divestments were expected to generate annual savings of more than $100 million.[43]

Financial control entails objective criteria (e.g., return on investment) that corporate-level managers use to evaluate both the returns being earned by individual business units and the managers responsible for their performance.

Financial control entails objective criteria (e.g., return on investment) that corporate-level managers use to evaluate both the returns being earned by individual business units and the managers responsible for their performance. Because the units are oriented toward financial outcomes, an emphasis on financial controls requires each division's performance to be largely independent of that of other divisions.[44] Accordingly, when the firm chooses to implement a strategy calling for interdependence among the firm's different businesses, such as the related-constrained corporate-level strategy, the ability of financial control to add value to strategy implementation efforts is reduced.[45]

Implementing Business-Level Strategies: Organizational Structure and Controls

As discussed in Chapter 4, business-level strategies establish a particular type of competitive advantage (typically, either low cost or differentiation) in a particular competitive scope (either an entire industry or a narrow segment of it). The cost leadership, differentiation, and integrated cost leadership differentiation strategies are implemented effectively when certain modifications are made to the characteristics of the functional structure, based on the unique attributes of the individual business-level strategies.

Using the Functional Structure to Implement the Cost Leadership Strategy

The structural characteristics of specialization, centralization, and formalization play important roles in the successful implementation of the cost leadership strategy. *Specialization* refers to the type and number of job specialties that are required to perform the firm's work.[46] For the cost leadership strategy, managers divide the firm's work into homogeneous subgroups. The basis for these subgroups is usually functional areas, products being produced, or clients served. By dividing and grouping work tasks into specialties, firms reduce their costs through the efficiencies achieved by employees specializing in a particular and often narrow set of activities.

Centralization is the degree to which decision-making authority is retained at higher managerial levels. Today, the trend in organizations is toward decentralization—the movement of decision-making authority down to people in the firm who have the most direct and frequent contact with customers. However, to coordinate activities carefully across organizational functions, the structure used to implement the cost leadership strategy calls for centralization. Thus, in designing this particular type of functional structure, managers strive to push some decision-making authority lower in the organization, while remaining focused on the more general need for activities to be coordinated and integrated through the efforts of a centralized staff.

Because the cost leadership strategy is often chosen by firms producing relatively standardized products in large quantities, formalization is necessary. *Formalization* is the degree to which formal rules and procedures govern organizational activities.[47] To foster more efficient operations, R&D efforts emphasize improvements in the manufacturing process.

FIGURE 11.2 | Functional Structure for Implementation of a Cost Leadership Strategy

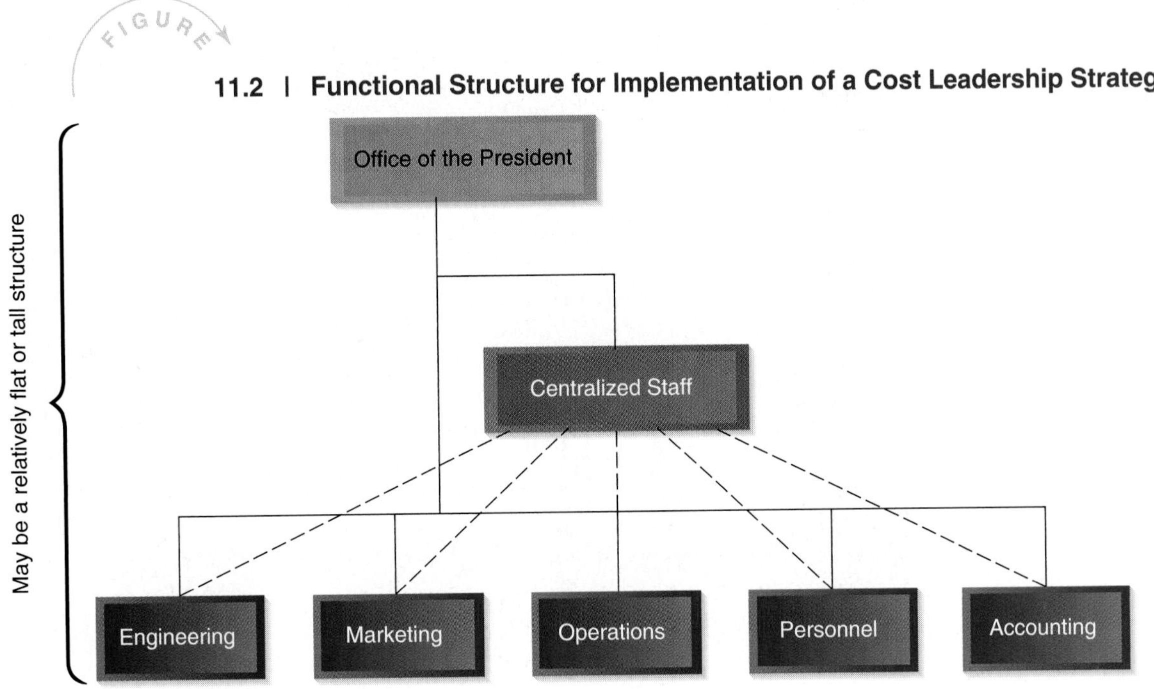

Notes:
- Operations is the main function
- Process engineering is emphasized, rather than new product R&D
- Relatively large centralized staff coordinates functions
- Formalized procedures allow for emergence of a low-cost culture
- Overall structure is mechanical; job roles are highly structured

As summarized in Figure 11.2, successful implementation of the cost leadership strategy requires an organizational structure featuring strong task specialization, the centralization of decision-making authority, and the formalization of work rules and procedures. This type of functional structure encourages the emergence of a low-cost culture—a culture in which all employees seek to find ways to drive their firm's or unit's costs lower than rivals' costs. Using highly specialized work tasks, cost leader Southwest Airlines strives continuously to increase the efficiency of its production and distribution systems. For example, Southwest was one of the first carriers to sell tickets on the Internet. A travel industry consultant concluded that Southwest's simple fares and schedule make it easy to sell travel directly to consumers on the Internet. For this reason, Southwest does not pay commissions to travel agents. Similarly, a number of European carriers have sprung up that follow Southwest's low-cost approach, including, for example, Virgin Express (www.virgin-express.com), Richard Branson's discount carrier, and EasyJet (www.easyjet.com).[48] In response, large U.S. airlines are forming a Web site to combat the discount airlines approach, as well as large Internet travel portals such as Expedia and Travelocity. Continental, Delta, United, and Northwest formed a new joint Web portal and also signaled a cut in base domestic commissions to travel agents, from 8 percent to 5 percent.[49]

Because L'Oreal is committed to continuous product innovation across all its operations, marketing and product R&D are emphasized in the company and in its recent acquisition of Maybelline. L'Oreal's CEO, Lindsay Owen-Jones is shown here at the far left.

Using the Functional Structure to Implement the Differentiation Strategy

The differentiation strategy is implemented successfully when a functional structure is used in which decision-making authority is decentralized. Unlike the cost leadership strategy, in which the coordination and integration of organizational function activities occurs through centralization of decision-making authority, the functional structure used to implement the differentiation strategy demands that people throughout the firm learn how to coordinate and integrate their activities effectively. In fact, the implementation of the differentiation strategy is facilitated if there is a consensus style of decision making among the top-management team members. Research suggests that the performance of an SBU pursuing a differentiation strategy increases if a consensus style is used. This is particularly true when a differentiation strategy is implemented in a stable environment; it is more difficult to implement a consensus style when the market being pursued by the firm is dynamic and changing.[50]

The marketing and R&D functions are often emphasized in the differentiation strategy's functional structure. For example, because of L'Oreal's commitment to continuous product innovation across all of its operations, marketing and product R&D are emphasized in the company and in its recent acquisitions in beauty products. Recently, L'Oreal, a French cosmetic firm, acquired Maybelline for $758 million and began a complete makeover of the brand, including moving the headquarters from Memphis, Tennessee, to New York City. L'Oreal created the theme of "urban American chic," which was posted on all Maybelline products to promote their U.S. origins. Maybelline rolled out a radical new makeup line, heavy on unusual colors such as yellow and green, dubbing it Miami Chill. When L'Oreal marketers discovered that the moderately successful Great Finish nail enamel dried in one minute, they changed the name to Express Finish—and sold it heavily as a product used by urban women on the go. Maybelline's share of the nail-enamel market in the U.S. has climbed from 3 percent to 15 percent since 1996.[51]

Often, R&D and marketing need to be coordinated in order to implement the differentiation strategy. For example, L'Oreal's CEO, Lindsay Owen-Jones, recognized two prominent beauty cultures: French and American. After buying Maybelline, he decided to galvanize L'Oreal's Paris R&D operations by setting up a second creative headquarters in New York, with R&D as well as marketing and advertising teams. "We set up a counter-power in New York with people that have a totally different mind-set, background, and creativity,"[52] said Owen-Jones.

Finally, to capitalize on emerging trends in key markets, the firm implementing the differentiation strategy often makes rapid changes based on ambiguous and incomplete information. Such changes demand that the firm use a relatively flat organizational structure to group its work activities (in a relatively flat structure, workers are likely to have a number of tasks included in their job descriptions). It is difficult to implement a differentiation strategy when the firm has extensive centralization and formalization, especially in a rapidly changing environment. Thus, the overall organizational structure needs to be flexible and job roles less structured. Additional characteristics of the form of the functional structure used to implement the differentiation strategy are shown in Figure 11.3.

FIGURE 11.3 | Functional Structure for Implementation of a Differentiation Strategy

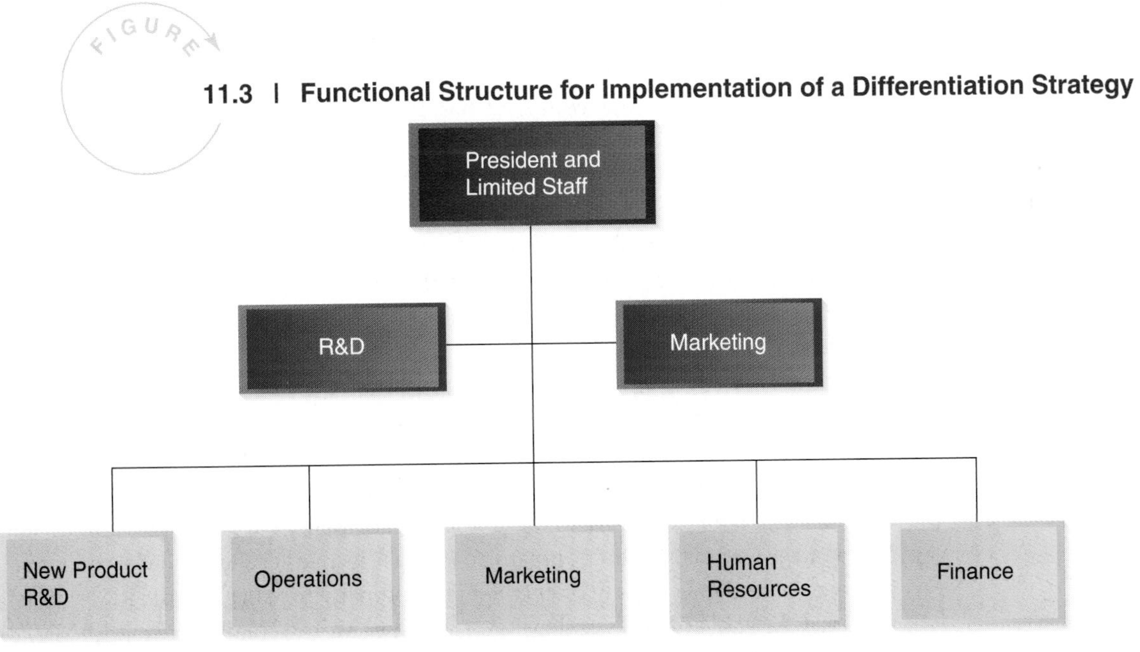

Using the Functional Structure to Implement the Integrated Cost Leadership/Differentiation Strategy

To implement the integrated cost leadership/differentiation strategy, companies seek to provide value which differs from that offered by the leader cost, and the differentiated firm—low cost, relative to the cost of the differentiated firm's product, and valuable differentiated features, relative to the features offered by the cost leader's product.

The integrated cost leadership/differentiation strategy is being formulated more frequently, especially by global firms, even though it is difficult to implement. The primary reason for this is that the strategic and tactical actions required to implement the cost leadership and the differentiation strategies are not the same. For example, to achieve the low-cost position, relative to rivals, emphasis is placed on production and manufacturing process engineering, with infrequent product changes. In contrast, to achieve a differentiated position, marketing and new-product R&D are emphasized. But, as explained earlier, the structural characteristics used to emphasize new-product development differ from those needed to stress process engineering. Thus, to implement the integrated cost leadership/differentiation strategy successfully, managers are challenged to form an organizational structure that allows the development of differentiated product features, while costs, relative to those of rivals, are reduced. Often, the functional structure has to be supplemented by horizontal coordination, such as cross-functional teams and a strong organizational culture, to implement this strategy effectively.

Toyota Motor Corporation has been able to be a world leader in the auto industry primarily because of its ability to implement cost leadership and differentiation simultaneously.[53] The key to Toyota's success has been the differentiated design and manufacturing process that the company has implemented concurrently through its integrated product design process. Toyota does this first by mapping the design space and defining feasible regions of overlap for product and process design. Second, it looks for intersections of feasible sets for this overlap. Finally, Toyota establishes the feasibility of the overlapping design before commiting to it. Overall, comparing the Toyota system to others, one author concluded: "Toyota considers a broader range of possible designs and delays certain decisions longer than other automotive companies, yet has what may be the fastest and most efficient vehicle development cycles in the industry."[54]

Similarly, Vanguard has been seeking to implement the integrated strategy. Although having originally focused on the cost leadership strategy, Vanguard has been attempting to differentiate itself through superior service. The average mutual fund in the industry has an expense ratio of 1.24 percent, compared to Vanguard's .28 percent. This strategy has enabled the company to increase its market share relative to its competitors. "No other company offers the highest-quality product and the lowest possible prices." Vanguard seeks to have exceptionally prompt mail reply, and its 2,000 phone representatives are trained to answer the service calls by the fourth ring. Its model is similar to that of Southwest Airlines. Costco, which sells high-quality goods, may be similar as well, but its retailing service is spartan. At Vanguard, you may get more service than you pay for, compared to Costco.[55]

Using the Simple Structure to Implement Focused Strategies

As noted earlier, many focused strategies—strategies through which a firm concentrates on serving the unique needs of a narrow part or scope of the industry—are implemented most effectively through the simple structure. At some point, however, the increased sales revenues resulting from success necessitate changing from a simple to a functional structure. The challenge for managers is to recognize when a structural change is required to coordinate and control the firm's increasingly complex operations.

In the summer of 1999, the U.S. Postal Service (USPS) allowed private firms to offer postage over the Internet. This regulatory change has spawned a number of small Internet operations, including Stamps.com, E-Stamp, and Neopost's Simply Postage. These companies allow a firm to print USPS-verified address labels on envelopes. The Postal Service is targeting 22 million home offices and 7.5 million small businesses with fewer than 100 employees. Although there are likely to be other start-ups and new entrants (one larger firm Pitney Bowes, is entering the business with its product, ClickStamp), because the market potential of these firms is high, they will have to adjust their structures as growth occurs. However, at present, they have flexible operations with low levels of specialization and formalization associated with the simple structure.[56]

Service Performance Corporation (SPC) also uses the simple organizational structure. Serving approximately 100 customers, SPC provides janitorial and facilities services in office buildings, malls, airports, laboratories, and manufacturing facilities. The firm's founder and CEO believes that service is his company's only product. To describe the character of SPC's organizational structure, the CEO noted that his nine-year-old company had retained its "aversion to bureaucracy." The simple structure is used to help all employees focus on what is believed to be the firm's key competitive advantage: superior customer service.[57]

Movement to the Multidivisional Structure

The above-average returns gained through the successful implementation of a business-level strategy often result in diversification of the firm's operations. This diversification can take the form of offering different products (product diversification) or offering the same or additional products in other markets (market diversification). As explained in Chapter 6, increased product or market diversification demands that firms formulate a corporate-level strategy, as well as business-level strategies for individual units or divisions. With greater diversification, the simple and functional structures must be discarded in favor of the more complex, yet increasingly necessary, multidivisional structure.

Implementing Corporate-Level Strategies: Organizational Structure and Controls

Effective use of the multidivisional structure helps firms implement their corporate-level strategy (diversification). In this section, we describe three M-form variations (see

FIGURE

11.4 | Three Variations of the Multidivisional Structure

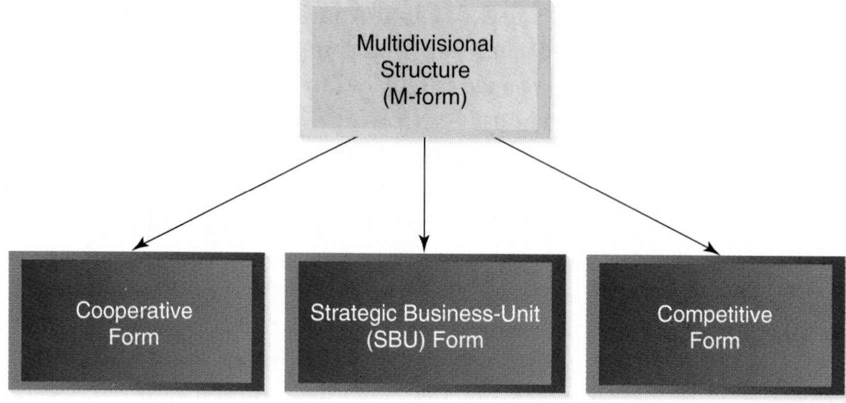

Figure 11.4) that are required to implement the related-constrained, related-linked, and unrelated diversification strategies.

Using the Cooperative Form to Implement the Related-Constrained Strategy

The **cooperative form** is an organizational structure that uses many integration devices and horizontal human resource practices to foster cooperation and integration among the firm's divisions.

To implement the related-constrained strategy, firms use the cooperative form of the multidivisional structure. The **cooperative form** is an organizational structure that uses many integration devices and horizontal human resource practices to foster cooperation and integration among the firm's divisions. The cooperative form (see Figure 11.5) emphasizes horizontal links and relationships more than the other two variations of the multidivisional structure described later in the chapter. Cooperation among divisions that are formed around either products or markets served is necessary to realize economies of scope and to facilitate the transfer of skills.[58] Increasingly, it is important for these links to allow and support the sharing of a range of strategic assets, including employees' "know-how," as well as tangible assets such as facilities and methods of operation.[59]

To facilitate cooperation among divisions that are either vertically integrated or related through the sharing of strategic assets, some organizational functions (e.g., human resource management, R&D, and marketing) are centralized at the corporate level. Work completed in these centralized functions is managed by the firm's central administrative, or headquarters, office. When the central office's efforts allow commonalties among the firm's divisions to be exploited in ways that yield a cost or differentiation advantage (or both) in the divisions, compared to undiversified rivals, the cooperative form of the multidivisional structure is a source of competitive advantage for the diversified firm.[60]

Besides centralization, a number of structural integration links are used to foster cooperation among divisions in firms implementing the related-constrained diversification strategy. Frequent direct contact between division managers encourages and

FIGURE 11.5 | Cooperative Form of the Multidivisional Structure for Implementation of a Related-Constrained Strategy

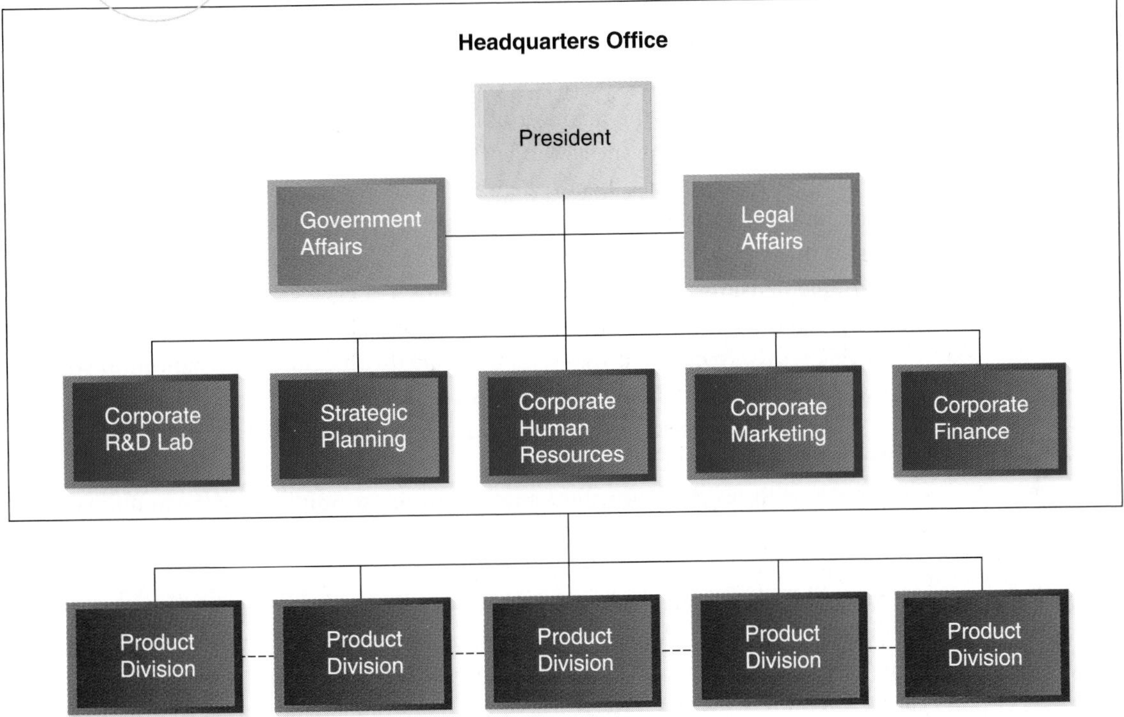

Notes:
- Structural integration devices create tight links among all divisions
- Corporate office emphasizes centralized strategic planning, human resources, and marketing to foster cooperation between divisions
- R&D is likely to be centralized
- Rewards are subjective and tend to emphasize overall corporate performance, in addition to divisional performance
- Culture emphasizes cooperative sharing

supports cooperation and the sharing of strategic assets. Sometimes, liaison roles are established in each division to reduce the amount of time division managers spend facilitating the integration and coordination of their units' work. Temporary teams or task forces may also be formed around projects and may require the efforts of many people from separate divisions to achieve desired levels of divisional coordination. Formal integration departments might be established in firms requiring the work of temporary teams or task forces on a continuous basis. Ultimately, a matrix organization may evolve in firms implementing the related-constrained strategy. A *matrix organization* is an organizational structure in which there is a dual structure combining both functional specialization and business product or project specialization.[61] Although complicated, effective matrix structures can lead to improved coordination among a firm's various divisions.[62]

As is implied by the horizontal procedures used for coordination that we described earlier, information processing must increase dramatically to implement the related-constrained diversification strategy successfully. But because cooperation among divisions implies a loss of managerial autonomy, division managers may not readily commit themselves to the type of integrative information-processing activities demanded by this organizational structure. Moreover, coordination among divisions sometimes results in an unequal flow of positive outcomes to divisional managers. In other words, when managerial rewards are based at least in part on the performance of individual divisions, the manager of the division that is able to derive the greatest marketplace benefit from the sharing of the firm's strategic assets might be viewed as receiving relative gains at others' expense. In these instances, performance evaluations are emphasized to facilitate the sharing of strategic assets. Furthermore, using reward systems that emphasize overall company performance, besides outcomes achieved by individual divisions, helps overcome problems associated with the cooperative form.

The use of the cooperative form of the multidivisional structure is illustrated in the Strategic Focus. Notice that IBM uses the related-constrained diversification strategy, which results in a match between strategy and structure within the firm.

When there are fewer links or less constrained links among a firm's divisions, the related-linked diversification strategy should be implemented. As explained next, this can be done through the use of the strategic-business-unit form of the multidivisional structure.

Using the Strategic-Business-Unit Form to Implement the Related-Linked Strategy

The **strategic business unit (SBU) form** of the multidivisional structure consists of at least three levels, the top level being corporate headquarters, the next, SBU groups, and the final level divisions grouped by relatedness (through either a product or a geographic market) within each SBU.

The **strategic business unit (SBU) form** of the multidivisional structure consists of at least three levels, the top level being corporate headquarters, the next, SBU groups, and the final level divisions grouped by relatedness (through either a product or a geographic market) within each SBU (see Figure 11.6). The firm's business portfolio is organized into those divisions related to one another within an SBU group and those unrelated to any division in other SBU groups. Thus, divisions within groups are related, but groups are largely unrelated to each other. Within the SBU structure, divisions with similar products or technologies are organized to achieve synergy. Each SBU is a profit center that is controlled by the firm's headquarters office. An important benefit of this structural form is that individual decision makers, within their strategic business unit, look to SBU executives rather than headquarters personnel for strategic guidance.

Nobuyuki Idei, CEO of Sony, is taking the opportunity to restructure the great Japanese consumer products firm, given the trend toward restructuring in Japan. In fact, the job cuts have led to a postwar unemployment peak of 4.4 percent in 1999. While Sony has had $50 million in revenues due to flat-screen TVs, digital video cameras, and many other differentiated products, its margins have not been significant relative to revenues. For example, Sony's PlayStation video games have contributed only 15 percent of Sony's total sales, but make up 42 percent of Sony's operating profits. Accordingly, Idei has been trying to shift the firm to make better use of software (e.g., music, films, and games) in its televisions and audio gear in order to increase Sony's profitability. To accomplish this, Sony's 10 internal companies are being regrouped

IBM Implements the Cooperative M-Form Structure, Facilitating E-commerce Services

Before Louis Gerstner took over the CEO position at IBM, John Akers had a strategic plan to break up IBM into a loosely affiliated network of "Baby Blues" built around different products. However, when Gerstner became the CEO, he determined that the company would be better off by keeping its businesses together. He felt that the corporation could offer the customers a lot more than just its name. Over the years since Gerstner has taken over, IBM has become the world's largest purveyor of technology services. The idea to pursue services was a "bet the company" decision made in 1993 that's paying off significantly now. Through its vast array of services and products, IBM "counsels customers on technology strategy, helps them prepare for mishaps, runs all their computer operations, develops their applications, procures their supplies, trains their employees, and even gets them into the dot com realm."

IBM has always been a digital solutions company. However, in the past, its solutions depended primarily on its hardware products as well as software. Now services are driving growth in the company. In 1998, services accounted for 28 percent of revenues. By 2003, it is expected that 46 percent of IBM's revenues will be derived from services. "It used to be that technology was strategic for IBM and services helped to sell technology. Now services-plus-software is more strategic. Services are IBM's primary form of account control."

Outsourcing is a primary service business for IBM, but it is a low-margin business in the services area. Few customers trust IBM with full-scale reengineering projects and prefer to use consultants like Andersen Consulting, Pricewaterhouse Coopers, and Ernst & Young. Thus, Sam Palmisano, who heads the services business, aims to move IBM's service focus into higher-margin businesses.

The whole system of interrelated businesses at IBM is held together by a cooperative M-form structure focused on serving e-commerce customers and providing total-solution services. The culture was supported early on by Gerstner, who shifted 25 percent of IBM's R&D budget into Internet and e-commerce projects. He declared that every IBM product or service must be Internet friendly. He also pushed the company's software development toward the Java programming language, which runs much of the software on the Web. Furthermore, he tried to tie Lotus Notes software tightly to the Web as well.

Gerstner saw early not just that the Internet was an information superhighway, but that it was about business—doing transactions, not looking up information. Moreover, Gerstner is not just out to help set up e-tailers or cyber shops; rather, he is focusing on creating Internet operations in supply chain management, consumer service, logistics, procurement, and even training, using Web technology. He divides companies into two types: "those who are above the e-line and those who are below it." Those who are above, such as Charles Schwab, Dell, and others who fully manage much of their operations through e-commerce techniques have not been the traditional customers of IBM. Those who are below the e-line, IBM's traditional customer group, use IBM services and products more often than those above the line. Accordingly, IBM is focusing on getting into the latter businesses.

For instance, although Sun and Hewlett-Packard have significantly more market share than IBM in Web servers, IBM has maintained a lead in mainframe computers that continues to grow. The problem with mainframes, however, is that their cost is coming down rapidly, which will cut into IBM's margins. For now, though, IBM's margins in mainframes are quite good, although revenues are staying relatively flat. IBM is hoping that its services business will foster better sales in Web servers.

With IBM's ability to implement its strategy through its cooperative M-form structure and its cooperative culture, it is likely to be successful at the next challenge of Internet products. This market appears to be developing a strategy centered on devices, software, and services that make the Internet accessible anywhere, anytime. It may be through a cell phone or a Palm device. To get the right people to develop these new Internet products, IBM has developed a Web design office in Atlanta that it will try to use to change its old-style culture into more of an Internet culture. The Atlanta center allows dogs, which are camped out alongside Web designers, and has an iguana. A Ping-Pong table doubles as a conference table, and there's a billiard table on an upper floor where workers can go to clear their heads after long hours toiling at their "Macintosh computers."

Like Intel and Cisco, IBM has invested $60 million in venture capital funding. For instance, IBM invested $45 million in Internet Capital Group, a holding company that funds B2B Internet companies. This investment took place just before the Internet Capital Group's public offering and is now worth $619 million. Thus, not only has IBM done a good job in focusing its organization and culture on Internet businesses, but it is also seeking to adjust this culture so that its future-oriented research center and also its venture capital fund will create new businesses for the corporation. Truly, the company could be renamed "Internet Business Machines."

SOURCES: IBM Home Page, 2000, March 1, *www.ibm.com*; P. Burroughs, D. Roks, & D. Brady, 1999, Inside IBM: Internet business machines, December 13, *Business Week e.biz*, eb20–eb38; D. Kirkpatrick, 1999, IBM: From Big Blue dinosaur to e-business animal, *Fortune*, April 26, 116–127; D. Lyons, 1999, Big iron, small iron, *Forbes.com*, April 19, *www.forbes.com*; I. Sager, 1999, Big Blue at your service, *Business Week*, June 21, 130–132.

"into four autonomous units focused on products and networks." In addition, Idei will cut headquarters staff from about 2,500 to several hundred over the next few years. Sony's global workforce of 170,000 will be cut by 10 percent, and factories will go from 70 to 55 by the year 2003. The restructuring now matches the SBU structure with its 10 internal companies organized into four strategic business units. Each such unit will receive research funds and will be required to justify its existence on the basis of profitability. The units will also be required to cooperate among themselves within each strategic group. For instance, Sony may build a new PlayStation that doubles as a video player or a high-capacity game feature on its notebook computers. Sony is well positioned to compete in this market because it is the only firm that has a successful computer, television producer, and video game player. Thus, Sony is one of the few companies that has the opportunity to integrate software and content across a broad range of consumer electronics products.[63] The company will implement this strategy through the SBU structure.

FIGURE 11.6 | SBU Form of the Multidivisional Structure for Implementation of a Related-Linked Strategy

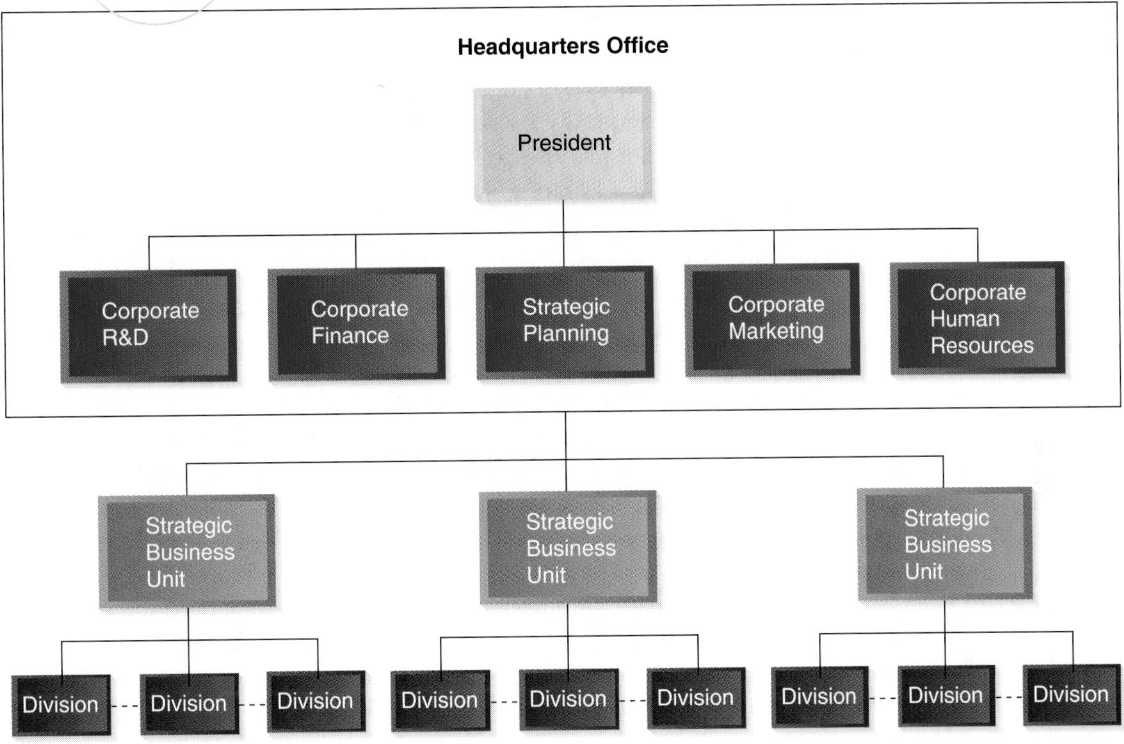

Notes:
- Structural integration among divisions within SBUs, but independence across SBUs
- Strategic planning may be the most prominent function in headquarters for managing the strategic planning approval process of SBUs for the president
- Each SBU may have its own budget for staff to foster integration
- Corporate headquarters staff serve as consultants to SBUs and divisions, rather than having direct input to product strategy, as in the cooperative form

Similar to Sony, ConAgra, a large food producer, has been in need of restructuring. Bruce Rhode, CEO at ConAgra, had difficulties with low increases in sales in both 1998 and 1999. During his tenure, shares of ConAgra have fallen 28 percent. His predecessor, Charles M. Harper, was a star on Wall Street because of the significant acquisitions he made, such as Hunt Wesson (tomato products and salad oil), Montfort (beef), Butterball (turkey), and Swift Premium (cold cuts). However, ConAgra wound up with 90 independent operating companies, and Harper gave them almost complete autonomy, which was significant because branded products in the industry had a burst of profitability. However, recently, price trends have not been in favor of branded products. Accordingly, Rhode has been trying to improve operating efficiencies. As such, he has been seeking better synergies across ConAgra's businesses. To achieve these synergies, he has been putting disparate units in three main SBUs: food service (restaurants), retail (grocery stores), and agricultural products. Furthermore, the extensive decentralization during Harper's reign created significant duplication and confusion for ConAgra's business customers. Big grocers like Kroger bought from a number of vendors without even knowing they were part of ConAgra. However, in a time of significant consolidation, large firms such as Wal-Mart will not tolerate many dozens of sales representatives. In 1998, 42 grocery store mergers were recorded. Thus, food producers like ConAgra were fighting defensively to deal with the power of buyers of their products, who are consolidating into larger and stronger retail powers.[64]

The organizational structure of large diversified firms such as Sony and ConAgra can be complex. Their complexity is a reflection of the size and diversity of a diversified firm's operations. Consider the case of General Electric (GE). Implementing the related-linked corporate-level strategy, the firm called for integration among divisions within SBUs, but independence between SBUs. GE managers expect to be able to "walk, think, and talk" like a small firm and to make decisions and introduce innovative products at a pace that is equivalent to its smaller competitors.[65]

Recently, GE's structure featured 10 major SBUs. The company's Aircraft Engines business unit is the world's largest producer of large and small jet engines for commercial and military aircraft. The Appliances business unit produces Monogram, Profile Performance, Profile, GE, and Hotpoint brands, as well as several private-label brands. Capital Services, a wholly owned subsidiary of GE, is a diversified financial services company that creates comprehensive solutions to increase client productivity and efficiency. Industrial Systems is a leading supplier of products used to distribute, protect, operate, and control electrical power and equipment, as well as a supplier of services for commercial and industrial applications. The Lighting business unit is a leading supplier of lighting products for global consumer, commercial, and industrial markets. Medical Systems is a world leader in medical diagnostic imaging technology, services, and health care productivity. NBC is a diverse global media company owned by GE. NBC in turn owns and operates the NBC Television Network, as well as 13 television stations. In the United States, NBC owns CNBC, operates MSNBC in partnership with Microsoft, and maintains equity interests in the A&E (Arts and Entertainment) Television Network and The History Channel. NBC also has an interest in Internet and new media businesses, holding equity stakes in CNET, Talk City, iVillage, Telescan, Hoover's, and 24/7 Media. Several of NBC's Internet assets have merged with Snap.com and XOOM.com, Inc., to form NBCi, the seventh largest Internet site and the first publicly traded Internet company integrated with a major broadcaster. GE's Plastics business unit is a world leader in versatile, high-performance engineered plastics used in the computer, electronics, data storage, office equipment, automotive, building and construction, and other industries. Power Systems is a world leader in the design, manufacture, and servicing of gas, steam, and hydroelectric turbines and generators for power production, pipeline, and industrial applications. Transportation Systems manufactures more than half of the diesel freight locomotives in North America, and its locomotives operate in 75 countries worldwide.[66]

NBC operates MSNBC in partnership with Microsoft. Several of NBC's Internet assets have merged with Snap.com and XOOM.com to form NBCi, the seventh largest Internet site and the first publicly traded Internet company integrated with a major broadcaster.

For firms as large as GE, structural flexibility is as important as strategic flexibility (recall the discussion in Chapter 5 indicating a need for firms to have strategic flexibility). Through a combination of strategic and structural flexibility, GE is able to respond rapidly to opportunities as they emerge throughout the world. Amidst the company's flexibility, Welch sets precise performance targets and monitors them throughout the year. Thus, GE is run such that the bureaucracy is removed so that the company has a small-firm culture, but managers are held accountable by a leader who seeks to understand its many businesses.[67] In sum, one analyst noted that GE is not so much a collection of businesses as it is "a repository of information and expertise that can be leveraged over a huge installed base."[68]

Using the Competitive Form to Implement the Unrelated Diversification Strategy

The **competitive form** is an organizational structure in which the controls used emphasize competition between separate (usually unrelated) divisions for corporate capital.

Firms implementing the unrelated diversification strategy seek to create value through efficient internal capital allocations or by restructuring, buying, and selling businesses.[69] The competitive form of the multidivisional structure is used to implement the unrelated diversification strategy. The **competitive form** is an organizational structure in which the controls used emphasize competition between separate (usually unrelated) divisions for corporate capital. To realize benefits from efficient resource allocation, divisions must have a separate, identifiable profit performance and must be held accountable for such performance. The internal capital market requires organizational arrangements that emphasize *competition* rather than *cooperation* between divisions.[70]

To emphasize competitiveness among divisions, the headquarters office maintains an arms-length relationship and does not intervene in divisional affairs, except to audit operations and discipline managers whose divisions perform poorly. In this situation, the headquarters office sets rate-of-return targets and monitors the divisional performance.[71] It allocates cash flow on a competitive basis, rather than automatically returning cash to the division that produced it. The competitive form of the multidivisional structure is illustrated in Figure 11.7.

A diversified supplier of hardware items to U.S. discount retailers, Newell Rubbermaid Company uses the competitive form of the multidivisional structure to implement its unrelated diversification strategy. "Newell Rubbermaid is a manufacturer and full-service marketer of consumer products sold through the mass-retailers." The company's basic strategy is to market a multiproduct offering of brand-name consumer products to mass retailers, "emphasizing excellent customer service."[72] Committed to growth by acquisition, Newell Rubbermaid added product lines to the firm's independent divisions that share no common characteristics. Supplying primarily large firms such as Wal-Mart, Newell Rubbermaid sells an array of products, including household products, hardware, and home-furnishing and office products. Newell Rubbermaid's competitive advantage is created at the corporate level. Using a small corporate headquarters staff, the firm has developed a sophisticated electronic logistics system. Allocated to each of its divisions, this system is used as the basis for each division's logistics with its customers. Although not related to each other, each of Newell Rubbermaid's divisions creates value from the lower cost and improved customer relations provided by the system.[73]

FIGURE

11.7 | Competitive Form of the Multidivisional Structure for Implementation of an Unrelated Strategy

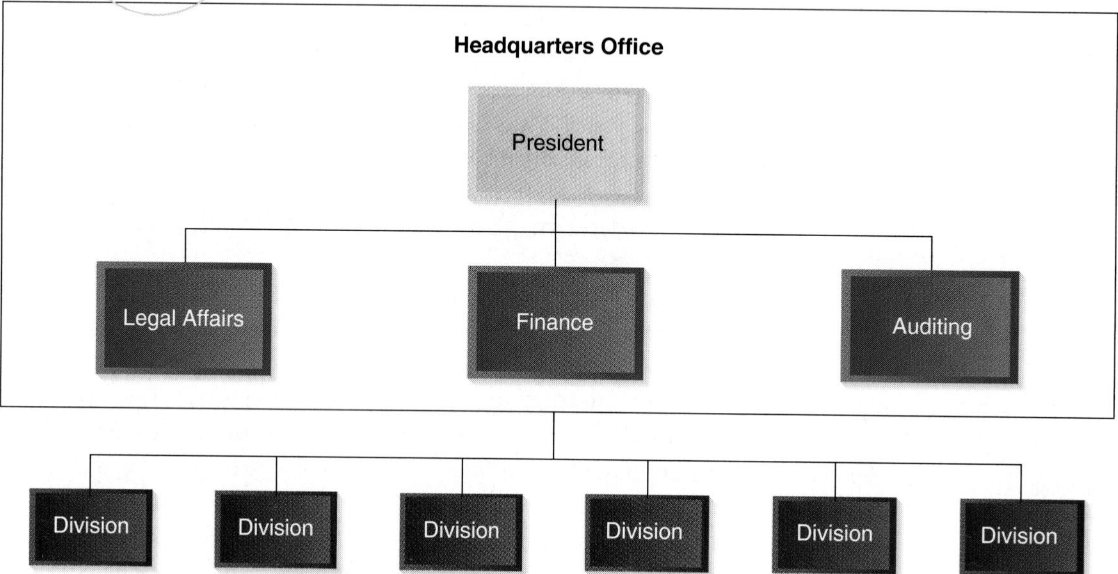

Notes:

- Corporate headquarters has a small staff
- Finance and auditing are the most prominent functions in the headquarters to manage cash flow and ensure the accuracy of performance data coming from divisions
- The legal affairs function becomes important when the firm acquires or divests assets
- Divisions are independent and separate for financial evaluation purposes
- Divisions retain strategic control, but cash is managed by the corporate office
- Divisions compete for corporate resources

Dennis L Kozlowski, CEO of Tyco international, Ltd., focuses on acquisitions in four market segments in which Tyco already has a major presence: disposable medical supplies, valves, fire protection and electronic security, and electrical and electronic components. As with many unrelated diversified firms that implement the competitive structure, these business are in mature product lines. However, Kozlowski "squeezes the most out of these operations with ultra-lean and decentralized management. In fact, he may have squeezed the operations too hard because there was a recent probe on the finances of Tyco by the SEC. His headquarters staff numbers only about 70, centered around four worldwide managers. Kozlowski hates meetings with a passion, preferring to keep in touch by PC and phone."[74]

In sum, there are three major forms of the multidivisional structure, each of which is related to a particular corporate-level strategy. Table 11.1 shows the characteristics of these structures. Differences are seen in the degree of centralization, the focus of the performance appraisal, the horizontal structures (integrating mechanisms), and the incentive compensation schemes necessary to implement the three corporate-level strategies, related-constrained, related-linked, and unrelated diversification, success-

TABLE 11.1 | Characteristics of the Structures Necessary to Implement the Related-Constrained, Related-Linked, and Unrelated Diversification Strategies

OVERALL STRUCTURAL FORM

Structural Characteristics	Cooperative M-form (Related-Constrained Strategy)[a]	SBU M-form (Related-Linked Strategy)[a]	Competitive M-form (Unrelated Diversification Strategy)[a]
Centralization of operation	Centralized at corporate office	Partially centralized (in SBUs)	Decentralized to divisions
Use of integrating mechanisms	Extensive	Moderate	Nonexistent
Divisional performance appraisal	Emphasizes subjective criteria	Uses a mixture of subjective and objective criteria	Emphasizes objective (financial or ROI) criteria
Divisional incentive compensation	Linked to overall corporate performance	Mixed linkage to corporate, SBU, and divisional performance	Linked to divisional performance

[a]Strategy implemented with structural form.

fully. The most centralized and most costly organizational form is the cooperative structure. The least centralized, with the lowest bureaucratic costs, is the competitive structure. The SBU structure requires partial centralization and involves some of the mechanisms necessary to implement the relatedness between divisions. Also, the divisional incentive compensation awards are allocated according to both SBUs and corporate performance. In the competitive structure, the most important criterion is divisional performance.

Earlier in the chapter, we indicated that, once formed, an organizational structure can influence a firm's efforts to implement its current strategy and the selection of future strategies. Using the multidivisional structure as the foundation for the discussion, the next section examines the relationship between structure and strategy.

The Effect of Structure on Strategy

As explained earlier, the M-form is a structural innovation that is intended to help managers deal with the coordination and control problems created by increasing product and market variety. Once established, however, the M-form structure has the potential to influence the firm's diversification strategy.[75] Strong and appropriate incentives that encourage managers to pursue additional marketplace opportunities, coupled with improved accountability and superior internal resource allocations from the corporate office, may stimulate additional diversification, which, in turn, can result in greater returns on the firm's investments.[76] Eventually, however, there is a tendency for the M-form to encourage inefficient levels of diversification. Following a comprehensive review, some researchers noted that there is a growing body of evidence which suggests that adoption of the M-form structure facilitates the pursuit of inefficient diversification.[77] Again, this cause–effect relationship—that is, the influence of the

M-form on a firm's pursuit of additional diversification—is not inherently negative; the complicating factor is that at some point, the additional amounts of diversification stimulated by the M-form become inefficient, thereby reducing the firm's strategic competitiveness and its returns.

Other research suggests that once the M-form influences the pursuit of more diversification that yields inefficient strategic outcomes, the relationship between structure and strategy may reverse direction.[78] In other words, firms that become inefficiently diversified implement strategies that result in less efficient levels of diversification. One study found, for example, that half of the diversified acquisitions made by unrelated diversified firms were later divested because of their lack of focus.[79] Another discovered that a decrease in the diversified scope of M-form firms was associated with an improvement in shareholder wealth. This finding, too, suggests that these firms' diversification had become inefficient.[80]

An example of a firm that recently changed its diversification strategy to increase its efficiency and strategic competitiveness is Sony Corporation, as described earlier. As Sony tied its array of electronic product offerings to software and content, it shifted its organizational structure to the SBU M-form, to create better links between its diversified set of businesses. Our discussion now turns to an explanation of organizational structures used to implement the three international strategies explained in Chapter 8.

Implementing International Strategies: Organizational Structure and Controls

Although important for many firms, competing successfully in global markets is perhaps especially critical for large companies. General Motors, for instance, is merging its manufacturing of cars and trucks in the United States. "For GM, the merger is the latest step in a long series of moves aimed at taking a company that for decades had been run largely as individual fiefdoms into a single global organization."[81] The move is designed to integrate the work of engineers with that of manufacturing and marketing personnel. International strategies such as those chosen by GM's top-level executives cannot be implemented successfully without using the proper organizational structure.[82]

Using the Worldwide Geographic Area Structure to Implement the Multidomestic Strategy

The *multidomestic strategy* is a strategy in which strategic and operating decisions are decentralized to business units in each country in order to tailor products to local markets. However, it is sometimes difficult for firms to know how local their products should or can become. Lands' End, for example, is one of the U.S. mail-order firms being lured by the promise of the European market for its products and services. Interested in adapting to local preferences, the firm's director of international operations observed that the most difficult part of achieving this objective is to know in which areas to be local.[83]

Firms implementing the multidomestic strategy often attempt to isolate themselves from global competitive forces by establishing protected market positions or by

The **worldwide geographic are structure** emphasizes national interests and facilitates managers' efforts to satisfy local or cultural differences.

competing in industry segments that are most affected by differences among local countries. The worldwide geographic area structure (see Figure 11.8) is used to implement the multidomestic strategy. The **worldwide geographic area structure** emphasizes national interests and facilitates managers' efforts to satisfy local or cultural differences.

The Body Shop, which pioneered the trend toward nature represented by "green" cosmetics, has been changing its centralized structure to create a stronger focus on regions of the world. This restructuring to the worldwide geographic area structure was proposed after Patrick Cournay took over the CEO position from the company's founder, Anita Roddick. The change includes "shifting centralized management from the company's base in Littlehampton [in the United Kingdom] to regional units in the U.K., Europe, the Americas and Asia."[84] Along with the structural change, the Body Shop is changing its approach to sourcing from local manufacturers linked to the regional centers. However, these manufacturers "would have to uphold the company's ban on animal testing, and other 'green' guidelines."

Because implementing the multidomestic strategy requires little coordination between different country markets, there is no need for integrating mechanisms

FIGURE 11.8 | Worldwide Geographic Area Structure for Implementation of a Multidomestic Strategy

Notes:

- The perimeter circles indicate decentralization of operations
- Emphasis is on differentiation by local demand to fit an area or country culture
- Corporate headquarters coordinates financial resources among independent subsidiaries
- The organization is like a decentralized federation

among divisions in the worldwide geographic area structure. Hence, formalization is low, and coordination among units in a firm's worldwide geographic area structure is often informal. Because each European country has a distinct culture, the multidomestic strategy and the associated worldwide geographic structure were a natural outgrowth of the multicultural European marketplace. This type of structure often was developed originally by friends and family members of the main business who were sent as expatriates into foreign countries to develop the independent country subsidiary. The relationship to corporate headquarters by divisions took place through informal communication among "family members."[85]

The primary disadvantage of the multidomestic strategy implemented through a worldwide geographic area structure is its inability to create global efficiency. As the emphasis on lower-cost products has increased in international markets, the need to pursue worldwide economies of scale and scope has also increased. These changes have fostered the use of the global strategy.

Using the Worldwide Product Divisional Structure to Implement the Global Strategy

The *global strategy* is a strategy in which standardized products are offered across country markets and the firm's home office dictates competitive strategy. International economies of scale and scope are sought and emphasized when the international strategy is implemented. Because of the important relationship between economies of scale and scope, on the one hand, and successful implementation of the global strategy, on the other, some activities of the firm's organizational functions are sourced to the most effective worldwide providers.

The **worldwide product divisional structure** is an organizational form in which decision-making authority is centralized in the worldwide division headquarters to coordinate and integrate decisions and actions among disparate divisional business units.

The worldwide product divisional structure (see Figure 11.9) is used to implement the global strategy. The **worldwide product divisional structure** is an organizational form in which decision-making authority is centralized in the worldwide division headquarters to coordinate and integrate decisions and actions among disparate divisional business units. This form is the organizational structure of choice for rapidly growing firms seeking to manage their diversified product lines effectively.[86] Integrating mechanisms also create effective coordination through mutual adjustments in personal interactions. Among such mechanisms are direct contact between managers, liaison roles between departments, temporary task forces or permanent teams, and integrating roles. As managers participate in cross-country transfers, they become socialized in the philosophy of managing an integrated strategy through a worldwide product divisional structure. A shared vision of the firm's strategy and structure is developed through standardized policies and procedures (formalization) that facilitate the implementation of this organizational form.

Two primary disadvantages of the global strategy and its accompanying worldwide product divisional structure are the difficulty involved with coordinating decisions and actions across country borders and the inability to respond quickly and effectively to local needs and preferences. As is explained in the Strategic Focus, Procter & Gamble is restructuring in order to use the worldwide product divisional structure to implement the global strategy. Notice that this structure is expected to contribute to the firm's efforts to improve its international operations and growth opportunities.

11.9 | Worldwide Product Divisional Structure for Implementation of a Global Strategy

Notes:
- The headquarters circle indicates centralization to coordinate information flow among worldwide products
- Corporate headquarters uses many intercoordination devices to facilitate global economies of scale and scope
- Corporate headquarters also allocates financial resources in a cooperative way
- The organization is like a centralized federation

Using the Combination Structure to Implement the Transnational Strategy

The **combination structure** has characteristics and mechanisms that result in an emphasis on both geographic and product structures.

The *transnational strategy* is an international strategy through which a firm seeks to provide the local responsiveness that is the focus of the multidomestic strategy and to achieve the global efficiency that is the focus of the global strategy. The **combination structure** has characteristics and mechanisms that result in an emphasis on both geographic and product structures; thus, it has the multidomestic strategy's geographic area focus and the global strategy's product focus. Ford is pursuing the combination structure to manage its international operations, as illustrated in the Strategic Focus.

The fit between the multidomestic strategy and the worldwide geographic area structure and between the global strategy and the worldwide product divisional structure is apparent. However, when a firm such as Ford seeks to implement both the multidomestic and the global strategy simultaneously through a combination structure, the appropriate integrating mechanisms for the two structures are less obvious. The structure used to implement the transnational strategy must be simultaneously

Procter & Gamble Restructures and Implements a Worldwide Product Divisional Structure

Durk Jager, the CEO at Procter & Gamble (P&G), has implemented a restructuring plan to facilitate increased growth, the lack of which has been a problem at P&G. When P&G introduced Pampers disposable diapers in the 1970s, it achieved 70 percent of the market. In 1998, P&G's diaper market share was down to near 40 percent, while that of Kimberly Clark, P&G's dominant competitor, was slightly above that mark. Also in the 1970s, P&G's Ivory brand soap had just under 50 percent of the market. In 1998, Unilever's Dove brand soap had overtaken P&G's dominant share. Similarly, Crest toothpaste was recently overtaken by the Colgate brand in market share. These three dominant brands signal the basic problem at P&G: The company has stopped growing; revenues have flattened out.

To overcome this problem, P&G has reorganized its structure into seven worldwide product divisions, including baby care, beauty care, fabric and home care, feminine protection, food and beverage, and tissues and towels. Previously, P&G was organized regionally through a multidomestic structure. Besides global product business units, P&G will have eight market development organizations that will work regionally to help prepare and market products created and managed by each global business unit. Jager hopes that this approach will move P&G from an obsession with perfection and risk aversion to one of risk taking. The structure will have to keep successful products (such as the laundry detergent Tide) growing while expanding globally and producing new brand-category products. P&G has had many decades of rigid conformity in its culture, which, over time, has squelched entrepreneurship, creative types, and freethinkers, who were labeled "troublemakers." Because of this culture, P&G may have lost some of the best business minds available. For instance, Steve Case at AOL, Bob Herbold at Microsoft, and Scott Cook at Intuit all began their careers at P&G. Now the company hopes that the decentralization to global product division structures will provide incentives for growth.

More than anything, P&G needs new products. The firm has a number of products with high potential, such as Termacare, a portable heat wrap; Fit, an antibacterial fruit-and-vegetable cleanser; Febreze, a spray-on odor eliminator; and its most recent and important entry, Dryel, a home dry-cleaning product that has been tested substantially and is now in supermarkets. P&G spends about 4 percent of its sales annually on R&D. Fifteen percent of its R&D budget is now devoted to major new projects involving products. Jager expects new products to generate another $1 billion in sales a year. For instance, he expects Dryel sales to reach $500 million, making it as big as Downy or Bounce. If these products are successful, they may create new global product divisions.

As part of its pursuit of growth, through an initiative of its beauty care division, P&G has launched a new Web site called reflect.com. The goal of this site was to introduce makeup and shampoos so personalized that no two individuals would get the same items. This strategy is similar to Dell's, which customizes its brand-name PCs. However, rather than research the issue itself, P&G chose to team with Institutional Venture Partners, a venture capital firm famous for backing Internet pioneers such as Excite, Inc. The Silicon Valley venture capital firm was used to closing a deal in a day, but with P&G lawyers involved, it took three weeks. Nonetheless, P&G hopes it has found a way to turn one of the nation's largest corporations into a significant on-line Internet competitor. The venture will be a learning experience for P&G. None of P&G's brand-name lines, such as Cover Girl and Oil of Olay, will be for sale on this site, which will sell only custom-made cosmetics. Women can log on and craft their own beauty products that will be individually mixed and packaged and shipped to their homes. P&G's sales of cosmetics on-line may be a significant shock to other on-line consumer product sellers, such as drugstore.com, ibeauty.com, and gloss.com.

P&G cannot afford to annoy its powerful retailer distributors, such as Wal-Mart, through this on-line selling initiative. Thus, reflect.com is only a small step in direct on-line selling. However, once someone figures out how to sell directly to somebody's home, the initiative may spread to other on-line projects by other global product divisions. Such initiatives are better carried out by global product divisions than by a geographic area structure, because on-line selling is not restricted by geographic markets.

In sum, P&G is seeking to reorganize itself into a worldwide product divisional structure wherein sales will be driven by growth in standard products, as well as new products such as Dryel. It is hoped that the "most far-reaching changes in the history of P&G" will result in "bigger innovation, faster speed to market, and greater growth." Along with this process, P&G is eliminating about 15,000 jobs and shutting 10 factories. Thus, not only is P&G trying to boost increased revenues through the growth of successful, innovative products, but it is also seeking to boost its earning power through reduced operating costs.

SOURCES: K. Brooker, 2000, Plugging the leaks at P&G, *Fortune,* February 21, 44–48; N. Deogun & E. Nelson, 2000, P&G is on the move, *Wall Street Journal,* January 24, A1, A16; Procter & Gamble Home Page, March 1, *www.pg.com*; K. Brooker, 1999, Can Procter & Gamble change its culture, protect its market share and find the next tide? *Fortune,* April 26, 146–152; G. Fairclough, 1999, P&G to slash 15,000 jobs, shut ten plants, *Wall Street Journal,* June 10, A3, A4; P. Galuszka, J. Ott, & D. Harbrecht, 1999, Procter and Gamble is set to shake itself up, *Business Week Online,* June 4, *www.businessweek.com*; L. Himelstein & P. Galuszka, 1999, P&G gives birth to a web baby, *Business Week Online,* September 27, *www.businessweek.com*; E. Neuborne, 1999, P&G could follow in Dell's net footsteps, *Business Week Online,* September 27, *www.businessweek.com.*

centralized and decentralized, integrated and nonintegrated, and formalized and nonformalized. These seemingly opposite characteristics must be managed by an overall structure that is capable of encouraging all employees to understand the effects of cultural diversity on a firm's operations. Accordingly, as in the case of Ford, there needs to be a strong educational component to change the whole culture of the organization. If the cultural change is effective, the combination structure should allow the firm to learn how to gain competitive benefits in local economies by adapting its capabilities and core competencies, which often have been developed and nurtured in less culturally diverse competitive environments. As firms globalize and move toward the combination strategy, the idea of a corporate headquarters has become increasingly important in fostering leadership and a shared vision to create a stronger company identity.[87]

Ford Implements the Combination Structure

Jacques Nasser, recently promoted to CEO at Ford, is seeking to implement a new structural arrangement in the firm that is aimed not only at changing the company's reporting relationships, but also at altering the mind-set of every employee. His vision is to reinvent the industrial giant into "a growth-oriented consumer powerhouse for the twenty-first century." As the battle for global market share continues, and only a few auto giants are expected to emerge at the end of the competition, Nasser wants his organization to be a nimble player in the global environment. "He envisions a company in which executives run independent units—cut loose from stifling bureaucracy and held more accountable for success and failure."

Nasser started his career in the Australian division of Ford, which he left in 1987 to run a struggling unit in the Philippines. Although his boss in Australia warned him that he would never come back from the Philippines, Nasser did return to help turn the Australian unit around in 1990. Next, he moved into Europe and was able to turn its large organizational unit around as well. In 1994, Nasser became the head of product development at Ford's Dearborn headquarters. By that time, he had become skilled at a nimble entrepreneurial decision-making style that was developed in peripheral Ford organizational units, where there was much more opportunity for making entrepreneurial decisions without a lot of bureaucratic oversight from headquarters. His focus today is to regenerate Ford's employees such that a new mind-set emerges in which this entrepreneurial spirit allows Ford to be a much more decentralized and value-creating enterprise (like a multidomestic structure). Nasser also views the market as valuing a global approach to business, where the company's units, divisions, teams, functions, and regions are all tightly integrated and synchronized across borders (like the world product structure).

Traditionally, however, Ford has been organized into a "collection of fiefdoms." Nasser suggests that this structure is due to Ford's history, which can be segmented into three stages of evolution. From 1905 to the 1920s, the organization was run by Henry Ford, who focused on building a single car for use throughout the world. Competition during that period was nonexistent and disorganized. The second period, from the late 1920s through the late 1950s, was a period of intense nationalism. Accordingly, Ford established companies in the United Kingdom, France, Germany, and Australia that built their own vehicles, tended toward nationalistic objectives, and were tailored to the policies of the host country. Foreign strategy was implemented through exports from independent European or U.S. operations. The third period, from the 1960s through the 1980s, was a period of regionalism, with the emergence of the European Common Market and NAFTA. Countries kept their own political systems and social values, but economic trading blocs were formed. Ford of Europe was fortunate to be evolving during this period. The units inside Ford decreased from 15 to 4 and competed in separate regions—one in Europe, one in the United States, one in Asia, and one in South America.

Currently, Nasser sees Ford in a fourth stage, in which the internationalization of capital, communications, economic policy, trade policy, human resources, marketing, advertising, and brands are forming around globally oriented markets or systems. Lately, globalization is not a choice, but is demanded by the current stage of the market. "You don't make money by downsizing or shutting plants or reducing your product line," he says. "You make money by building the company." Accordingly, he is out to rebuild Ford and change its basic cultural approach through a combination structure that simultaneously matches localization and global integration in the international automotive environment.

In Nasser's earlier days, the foreign units would get visitors from headquarters who would suggest new ways about thinking and doing things. The local managers would wine and dine them and nod yes at everything the visiting executives said. After the executives returned to Dearborn, the local managers would continue to run their division the way they saw fit. This can no longer be; there must be both decentralization *and* centralization to effect the integration that will meet the demands of the global marketplace. In the 1980s, Ford intended the Escort to be its first global product, and accordingly, the car was engineered on two continents—North America and Europe. This made it possible to capitalize on global sourcing for components. But because each country wants its own individual variety of product, the advertising and message heard in each country was devised by a different advertising agency in order to get Ford's message across in the local culture. In one country it was a limousine, in another a sports vehicle. In comparison, the Focus, the new Ford compact car, was engineered by one management team in Geneva and launched at one show in Paris. Journalists were brought in from all over the world, and there was only one advertising agency. The journalists who came all drove the Focus on the same roads in the same condition and got the same technological presentation from the same people. Therefore, they got the same brand and product positioning delivered to them from the same marketing people.

This integration and shift from a fiefdom approach to a combination structure is being implemented through an education program to help facilitate the change in mind-set. Using the GE program built by Jack Welch as a model, Nasser is following a "teachable point of view," in which a person writes out his or her version for the firm and teaches it to the leaders, who, in turn, teach it to their team members. Then the material becomes not just a manual for doing work, but a vision for why the business is approached the way it is. In the process of implementing the vision, managers and team members change their mind-set about how they have traditionally done their work at the company.

As part of the combination structure, Nasser hopes to package combinations of cars by using similar components, but still maintaining distinct brands. For example, he is seeking to combine the similar components of luxury cars in Lincoln, Jaguar, and Volvo, each of which has a different consumer appeal. He expects to do the same in the car divisions of Ford, Mercury, and Mazda. This is what Ford has done in its combinations of pickups and sport utility vehicles. Indeed, Ford has even used this platform to move into fancier versions, such as the SUV under the Lincoln brand. Such an approach can create significant savings on parts and drive costs down.

In sum, Ford has implemented the combination structure to change the centralized mind-set into one in which employees are taking more initiative. In addition, Ford is seeking to integrate across businesses to match these dual trends found in the automotive industry competitive environment. Besides the change in structure, Ford has brought in a lot of new outside management talent in key areas, such as design, and key regions, such as Europe, to manage the change. The focus is on education, as well as on the structural changes that have taken place. Managers are also receiving more incentive pay when they create value that will help realize an increased stock market capitalization.

SOURCES: K. Kerwin, M. Stepanek, & D. Welch, 2000, At Ford, e-commerce is job 1, *Business Week,* February 28, 74–78; *Economist,* 1999, Business: The revolution at Ford, *Economist,* August 7, 51–52; K. Kerwin & K. Naughton, 1999, Remaking Ford, *Business Week,* October 11, 132–140; N. Tichy, 1999, The teachable point of view: A primer, *Harvard Business Review,* 77(2): 82–83; S. Wetlaufer, 1999, Driving change: An interview with Ford Motor Company's Jacques Nasser, *Harvard Business Review,* 77(2): 77–81.

Implementing Cooperative Strategies: Organizational Structure and Controls

Increasingly, companies are developing multiple, rather than single, joint ventures or strategic alliances to implement cooperative strategies. Furthermore, the global marketplace accommodates many interconnected relationships among firms. Resulting from these relationships are networks of firms competing through an array of cooperative arrangements or alliances.[88] Managed effectively, cooperative arrangements can contribute to each partner's ability to achieve strategic competitiveness and earn above-average returns.

To facilitate the effectiveness of a *strategic network*—a grouping of organizations that has been formed to create value through their participation in an array of cooperative arrangements, such as a strategic alliance—a *strategic center firm* may be necessary. A *strategic center firm* facilitates management of a strategic network. Through its management, the center firm creates incentives that reduce the probability of any company taking actions that could harm its network partners. Also, the strategic center firm identifies actions that provide opportunities for each firm to achieve competitive success through its participation in the network.[89] Illustrated in Figure 11.10, the strategic center firm is vital to the ability of companies to create value and increase

FIGURE 11.10 | A Strategic Network

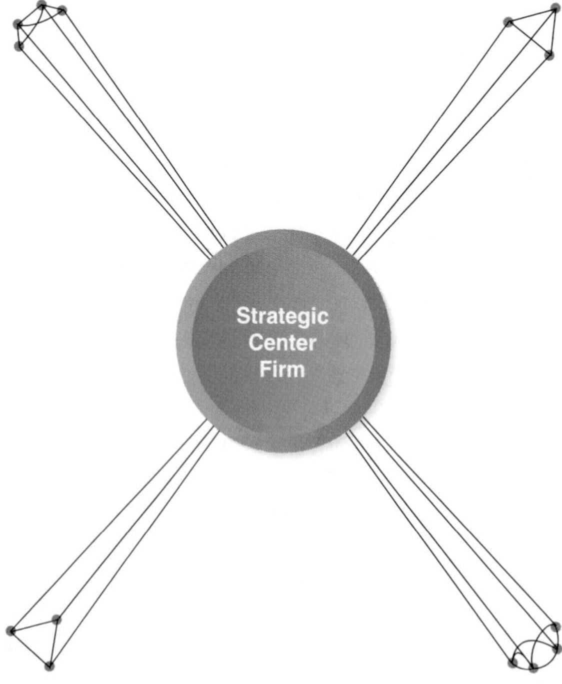

their strategic competitiveness. The four critical aspects of the strategic center firm's function are as follows:

Strategic outsourcing. The strategic center firm outsources and partners with more firms than do the other network members. At the same time, the strategic center firm requires partners to be more than contractors. Partners are expected to solve problems and to initiate competitive courses of action that can be pursued by the network.

Capability. The strategic center firm has core competencies that are not shared with all network partners. To increase the network's effectiveness, the center firm attempts to develop each partner's core competencies and provides incentives for network firms to share their capabilities and competencies with partners.

Technology. The strategic center firm manages the development and sharing of technology-based ideas among network partners.

Race to learn. The strategic center firm emphasizes to its partners that the principal dimensions of competition in competitive environments are between value chains and between networks of value chains. As a result, a strategic network is as strong as its weakest value-chain link and hence seeks to develop a competitive advantage in a primary or a support activity (see Chapter 3). The need for each firm to be strong for the benefit of the entire network encourages a friendly rivalry among the partners to learn rapidly and effectively.[90] The most effective strategic center firms learn how to manage the learning processes that occur among network members.

The dominant problem in single-venture cooperative arrangements is the difficulty they pose in controlling innovation and learning. However, a well-managed strategic network can overcome this problem. Therefore, as explained in the rest of this section, the managerial role of the strategic center firm is critical to the successful implementation of business-level, corporate-level, and international cooperative strategies.[91]

Implementing Business-Level Cooperative Strategies

As noted in Chapter 9, there are two types of complementary assets at the business level: vertical and horizontal. Vertical complementary strategic alliances are formed more frequently than horizontal alliances. Focused on buyer–supplier relationships, vertical strategic networks usually have a clear strategic center firm. Japanese vertical keiretsus such as those developed by Toyota Motor Company are structured this way. Acting as the strategic center firm, Toyota fashioned its lean production system around a network of supplier firms.[92]

A strategic network of vertical relationships in Japan, such as the network between Toyota and its suppliers, often involves a number of implementation issues. First, the strategic center firm encourages subcontractors to modernize their facilities and provides them with technical and financial assistance if necessary. Second, it reduces its transaction costs by promoting longer-term contracts with subcontractors, so that supplier–partners increase their long-term productivity. This approach is diametrically opposed to that of continually negotiating short-term contracts based on unit pricing. Third, the strategic center firm enables engineers in upstream companies (suppliers) to have better communication with contractee companies for services. As a result, both the upstream companies and the center firms become more interdependent and less independent.[93]

The lean production system pioneered by Toyota has been diffused throughout the Japanese and U.S. automobile industries. However, no automobile producer is able to duplicate the effectiveness and efficiency Toyota derives from the use of this manufacturing system.[94] A key factor accounting for Toyota's ability to derive a competitive advantage from the system is the cost other firms would incur to imitate the structural form used to support Toyota's application. In other words, Toyota's largely proprietary actions as the strategic center firm in the network it created are actions that competitors are unable to duplicate easily.[95]

In vertical complementary strategic alliances, such as the one between Toyota and its suppliers, the company that should function as the strategic center firm is obvious. However, this is not always the case with horizontal complementary strategic alliances. For example, the large airline alliances (discussed in a Strategic Focus in Chapter 9) have been quite unstable over the years, and a number of network partners have changed from one network to another or become partners in several networks.[96] Delta Airlines, for instance, recently changed allegiances in Europe from an affiliation with Swiss Air and Sabena to Air France.[97] This instability is usually caused by continuing rivalries among cooperating partners. A problem common to all of these ventures is the difficulty of selecting the strategic center firm. The distrust that formed among the network airline companies through years of aggressive competition prevented them from agreeing on which firm should function as the strategic center of a network. Thus, because who the dominant strategic center firm should be is not evident in horizontal complementary strategic alliances, they tend to be far less stable than vertical complementary strategic alliances.

Implementing Corporate-Level Cooperative Strategies

In some types of corporate-level cooperative strategies, it is difficult to choose a strategic center firm. For example, it is difficult for a strategic center firm to emerge in a centralized franchise network. McDonald's is an example.

McDonald's has formed a centralized strategic network in which its corporate office serves as the strategic center for its franchisees. Recently, McDonald's performance has been mediocre, and a new CEO, Jack M. Greenberg, has been trying to improve the network. Although McDonald's has had success with its Teenie Beanie Babies and Furby dolls promotions, without an improved menu and delivery system, the success is not likely to last. Long a favorite of children, McDonald's does not inspire the same degree of enthusiasm in their parents. Developed through the strategic center's centralized R&D function, a new product aimed at adults was introduced recently. Called the Arch Deluxe, this food item was pitched as "the burger with a grown-up taste." However, the Arch Deluxe was not successful, and one analyst suggested that McDonald's was a brand in need of "radical surgery, " which has been implemented by Greenberg.

To cope with its problems, McDonald's, as a strategic center firm, initiated a series of actions. Framed around the need to improve the quality of its products and speed up their delivery, the company developed a "just-in-time kitchen" concept for use by franchisees. This new production system is designed to move made-to-order sandwiches to customers without increasing the preparation time. As part of the system, a

NASCAR driver Bill Elliott celebrates his new multiyear contract from McDonald's, his primary sponsor. McDonald's characters Grimace and Hamburglar were on hand to present the contract.

computer-monitored machine dumps frozen fries into a basket that in turn is dunked into hot oil for cooking. The machine then shakes the fries and dumps them into bins for serving. Simultaneously, robot machines quickly prepare drinks ordered by the customer. Preventing the full use of the system's capabilities, however, was the delay in supplying all franchisees with the equipment. Thus, as the strategic center firm in its centralized franchise network, McDonald's still faces significant challenges.[98]

Unlike McDonald's corporate-level cooperative strategy, Corning's strategy has resulted in the implementation of a system of diversified strategic alliances that has required the company to implement a decentralized network. Over time, Corning has focused on intangible resources, such as a reliable reputation for being a trustworthy and committed partner, to develop competitively successful strategic partnerships. In this situation, the strategic network has loose connections between joint ventures or multiple centers, although Corning is typically the principal center. However, the joint ventures are less dependent on the strategic center firm and, consequently, require less managerial attention from it.[99]

Implementing International Cooperative Strategies

Competing in a number of countries dramatically increases the complexity associated with attempts to manage successful strategic networks formed through international cooperative strategies.[100] A key reason for this increased complexity is the differences among the various countries' regulatory environments. These differences are especially apparent in more regulated industries, such as telecommunications and air travel.

As shown in Figure 11.11, many large multinational firms form distributed strategic networks with multiple regional strategic centers to manage their array of cooperative arrangements with partner firms.[101] Among the large multinational firms, Swedish firms such as Ericsson (telecommunications exchange equipment) and Elec-

11.11 | A Distributed Strategic Network

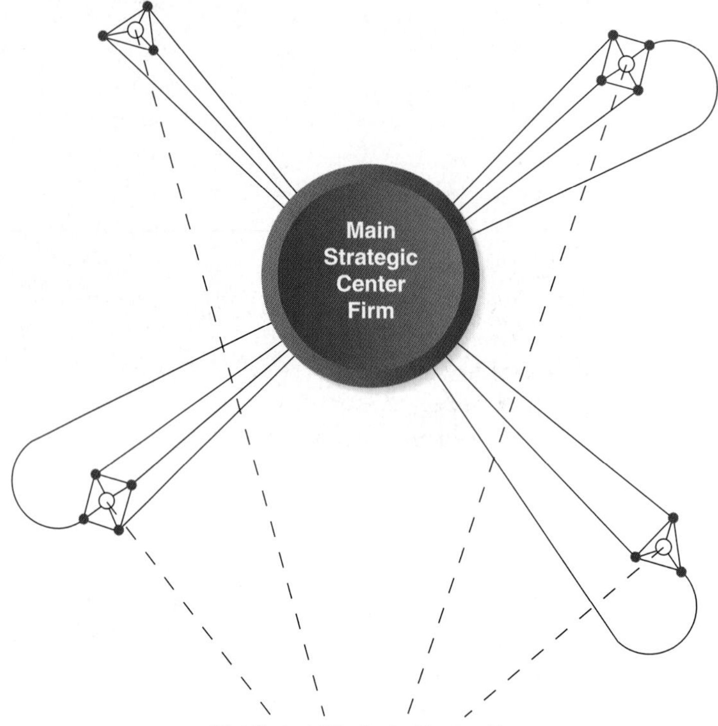

trolux (white goods, washing machines) have strategic centers located in countries throughout the world, instead of only in Sweden, where they are headquartered. Ericsson, for example, is active in more than 100 countries and employs over 85,000. Divided into five business areas (public telecommunications, radio communications, business networks, components, and microwave systems), the firm has cooperative agreements with companies throughout the world.

A world leader in electrical engineering, Asea Brown Boveri Group (ABB) is involved with a significant number of distributed strategic networks. Organized into four key business segments (power generation, power transmission and distribution, industrial and building systems, and financial services), ABB features 1,000 companies and 36 separate business areas. With a new global 11-member board of directors representing seven nationalities, ABB considers itself a truly global company—one that does not consider its home to be in any single country. The firm has formed strategic networks in five key world regions: the Americas, Europe (including the former Soviet Union), the Middle East and North Africa, sub-Saharan Africa, and the Asian Pacific rim.[102]

Contemporary Organizational Structures: A Cautionary Note

Contemporary organizational structures such as those used to implement international cooperative strategies emerge typically in response to social and technological advances.[103] However, the redesign of organizations throughout a society—indeed, globally—entails losses as well as gains.[104] For example, DuPont, the world's largest chemicals concern, decided recently to scrap most of its central support groups. Primarily, these groups provided information technology, communications, and other services to the company's main operating divisions. The gains expected from this decision included the elimination of some corporate bureaucracy and reductions in the amount of time required for product innovations to reach the marketplace. The primary loss associated with the decision concerned personnel: While some workers were transferred to other positions, many lost their jobs.[105]

With new organizational forms, many workers become de-skilled—that is, their abilities are not up to the challenge posed by a new structure that often demands constant innovation and adaptation. This may be the case with some of the workers assigned to new positions within DuPont. The attitude toward learning that is a part of a new organizational form requires that each worker become a self-motivated, continuous learner.[106] At least in the short run, a number of employees lack the level of confidence necessary to participate actively in organizationally sponsored learning experiences. Moreover, the flatter contemporary organizational structures can seem intrusive as a result of their demand for more intense and personal interactions with internal and external stakeholders. Combined, these conditions may create stress for many.

In the face of all this, managers need not abandon efforts to adopt organizational structures that have the greatest probability of facilitating the successful implementation of a firm's strategies. The challenge is to develop and use organizational structures that will enhance the productivity of individuals and the firm.[107]

Summary

- A firm's organizational structure is a formal configuration that largely determines what the firm will do and how it will complete its work. Different structures are required to implement different strategies. A firm's performance increases when strategy and structure are properly matched.
- Business-level strategies are usually implemented through the functional structure. The cost leadership strategy requires a centralized functional structure—one in which manufacturing efficiency and process engineering are emphasized. The differentiation strategy's functional structure decentralizes implementation-related decisions, especially those concerned with marketing, to those involved with individual organizational functions. Focus strategies, often used in small firms, require a simple structure until such time that a firm begins to compete in multiple markets or sells multiple products.
- The evolution from the functional structure to the three types of multidivisional structure (M-form) occurred from the 1920s to the early 1970s. The cooperative M-form, used to implement the related-constrained corporate-level strategy, has a centralized corporate office and extensive integrating mechanisms. Divisional incentives are linked to overall corporate performance. The related-linked SBU M-form structure establishes separate profit centers within the diversified firm. Each profit center may have divisions offering similar products, but the centers are unrelated to each other. The

competitive M-form structure, used to implement the unrelated diversification strategy, is highly decentralized, lacks integrating mechanisms, and utilizes objective financial criteria to evaluate each unit's performance.

- Initially, an organizational structure is chosen in light of the kind of support required to implement a firm's strategy. Once established, however, structure influences strategy. This is observed most prominently in the M-form structure, stimulating additional diversification in the diversified firm.
- The multidomestic strategy, implemented through the worldwide geographic area structure, emphasizes decentralization and locates all functional activities in the host country or geographic area. The worldwide product divisional structure is used to implement the global strategy. This structure is centralized in order to coordinate and integrate different functions' activities so as to gain global economies of scope and scale. Decision-making authority is centralized in the firm's worldwide division headquarters.
- The transnational strategy—a strategy through which the firm seeks the local responsiveness of the multidomestic strategy and the global efficiency of the global strategy—is implemented through the combination structure. Because it must be simultaneously centralized and decentralized, integrated and nonintegrated, and formalized and nonformalized, the combination structure is difficult to organize and manage successfully.
- Increasingly important to competitive success, cooperative strategies are implemented through organizational structures framed around strategic networks. Strategic center firms are critical to the management of such networks.

Review Questions

1. Why is it important that strategy implementation and strategy formulation be integrated carefully?
2. What is the meaning of the following statement? "In organizations, there is a consistent path of structure following strategy and then strategy following structure."
3. What organizational structures are used to implement the cost leadership, differentiation, integrated cost leadership-differentiation, and focused business-level strategies?
4. What organizational structures are used to implement the related-constrained, related-linked, and unrelated corporate-level diversification strategies?
5. What organizational structures should be used to implement the multidomestic, global, and transnational international strategies?
6. What is a strategic network? What is a strategic center firm? What roles do they play in organizational structures used to implement cooperative strategies?

Application Discussion Questions

1. Why do firms experience evolutionary cycles in which there is a fit between strategy and structure, punctuated with periods in which strategy and structure are reshaped? Provide examples of global firms that have experienced this pattern.
2. Select an organization (for example, an employer, a social club, or a nonprofit agency) of which you currently are a member. What is this organization's structure? Do you believe the organization is using the structure that is appropriate, given its strategy? If not, what structure should it use?
3. Use the Internet to find a firm that uses the multidivisional structure. Which form of the multidivisional structure is the firm using? What is there about the firm that makes it appropriate for it to use the M-form?
4. Through reading of the business press, locate one firm implementing the global strategy and one implementing the multidomestic strategy. What organizational structure is being used in each firm? Are these structures allowing each firm's strategy to be implemented successfully? Why or why not?
5. Identify a businessperson in your local community. Define strategic and financial controls for the person. Ask the businessperson to describe the use of each type of control in his or her business. In which type of control does the businessperson have the greatest confidence? Why?

Ethics Questions

1. When a firm changes from the functional structure to the multidivisional structure, what responsibilities does it have to current employees?
2. Are there ethical issues associated with the use of strategic controls? With the use of financial controls? If so, what are they?
3. Are there ethical issues involved in implementing the cooperative and competitive M-form structures? If so, what are they? As a top-level manager, how would you deal with them?
4. Global and multidomestic strategies call for different competitive approaches. What ethical concerns might surface when firms attempt to market standardized products globally? When they develop different products or approaches for each local market?
5. What ethical issues are associated with the view that the "redesign of organizations throughout a society—indeed, globally—entails losses as well as gains"?

Internet Exercise

Many retail industries, such as music sales, are ideal for Web-based organizational and selling structures. Visit the sites of some of the most popular venues: CDNow (**www.cdnow.com**), CD Quest (**www.cdquest.com**), CheckOut (**www.checkout.com**), Amazon.com (**www.amazon.com**), and European-based Front Stage (**www.frontstage.com**). Can you define the type of organizational structure each company uses? What attempts are being made by each to diversify and expand into other businesses?

***e-project:** Suppose you want to launch your own CD sales company on the Internet that will have an immense global reach to the large Spanish-speaking market around the world. Suppose further that you have hired a Web design firm to construct a site for you. Based on your research of top sites, how will you describe your Web design and business-level strategy for this project? What organizational structure is appropriate to implement the business-level strategy selected?

Notes

1. R. A. Johnson & D. W. Greening, 1999, The effects of corporate governance and institutional ownership on types of corporate social performance, *Academy of Management Journal,* 42: 564–756.
2. R. J. Kramer, 1999, Organizing for global competitiveness: The corporate headquarters design, *Chief Executive Digest,* 3(2): 23–28; D. J. Teece, G. Pisano, & A. Shuen, 1997, Dynamic capabilities and strategic management, *Strategic Management Journal,* 18: 509–533.
3. A. Sharma, 1999, Central dilemmas of managing innovation in large firms, *California Management Review,* 41(3): 146–164; C. Hales & Z. Tamangani, 1996, An investigation of the relationship between organizational structure, managerial role expectations and managers' work activities, *Journal of Management Studies,* 33: 731–756.
4. S. E. Human & K. Provan, 1997, An emergent theory of structure and outcomes in small-firm strategic manufacturing networks, *Academy of Management Journal,* 40: 368–403.
5. D. Miller & J. O. Whitney, 1999, Beyond strategy: Configuration as a pillar of competitive advantage, *Business Horizons,* 42(3): 5–17; K. J. Euske & A. Riccaboni, 1999, Stability to profitabilility: Managing interdependencies to meet a new environment, *Accounting, Organizations & Society,* 24: 463–481.
6. J. R. Galbraith, 1995, *Designing Organizations* (San Francisco: Jossey-Bass), 6.
7. J. Kurtzman, 1998, An interview with Stan Shih, in J. Kurtzman (ed.), *Thought Leaders* (San Francisco: Jossey-Bass), 85–93.
8. A. Y. Ilinitch, R. A. D'Aveni, & A. Y. Lewin, 1996, New organizational forms and strategies for managing in hypercompetitive environments, *Organization Science,* 7: 211–220.
9. D. A. Nadler & M. L. Tushman, 1997, *Competing by Design: The Power of Organizational Architecture* (New York: Oxford University Press).
10. E. F. Suarez & J. M. Utterback, 1995, Dominant designs and the survival of firms, *Strategic Management Journal,* 16: 415–430.
11. R. A. Heifetz & D. L. Laurie, 1997, The work of leadership, *Harvard Business Review,* 75(1): 124–134; R. H. Hall, 1996, *Organizations: Structures, Processes, and Outcomes* (6th ed.) (Englewood Cliffs, NJ: Prentice-Hall), 106–107.
12. H. W. Volberda, 1996, Toward the flexible form: How to remain vital in hypercompetitive environments, *Organization Science,* 7: 359–374.
13. D. Sull, 1999, Why good companies go bad, *Harvard Business Review,* 77(4): 42–52; Nadler and Tushman, *Competing by Design,* 9.
14. A. D. Chandler, Jr., 1990, *Scale and Scope: The Dynamics of Industrial Capitalism* (Cambridge: The Belknap Press of Harvard University Press), 182–183.
15. J. A. Chesley & M. S. Wenger, 1999, Transforming an organization: Using models to foster a strategic conversation, *California Management Review,* 41(3): 54–73.
16. C. H. Noble, 1999, The eclectic roots of strategy implementation research, *Journal of Business Research,* 45: 119–134.
17. Galbraith, *Designing Organizations,* 13; R. R. Nelson, 1994, Why do firms differ, and how does it matter? in R. P. Rumelt, D. E. Schendel, & D. J. Teece (eds.), *Fundamental Issues in Strategy* (Cambridge, MA: Harvard Business School Press), 259.
18. L. Donaldson, 1997, A positivist alternative to the structure-action approach, *Organization Studies,* 18: 77–92; Hales and Tamangani,

An investigation of the relationship, 738; Nelson, Why do firms? 259.

19. B. C. Esty, 1997, A case study of organizational form and risk shifting in the savings and loan industry, *Journal of Financial Economics,* 44: 57–76; C. W. L. Hill, 1994, Diversification and economics performance: Bringing structure and corporate management back into the picture, in R. P. Rumelt, D. E. Schendel, & D. J. Teece (eds.), *Fundamental Issues in Strategy* (Cambridge, MA: Harvard Business School Press), 297–321.
20. W. B. Werther, Jr., 1999, Structure driven strategy and virtual organization design, *Business Horizons,* 42(2): 13–18.
21. R. Waters, 1997, Return of the downsizers, *Financial Times,* December 19, 13.
22. V. Griffith, 1997, Lumbering giants, *Financial Times,* December 15, 10.
23. Associated Press, 2000, Smaller companies and extreme sports conquer the sporting-goods industry, *Wall Street Journal,* February 20, A9A.
24. P. Patterson, 2000, Market changes place demands on Nike Inc., *Wall Street Journal,* February 14, A9A.
25. J. J. Chrisman, A. Bauerschmidt, & C. W. Hofer, 1998, The determinants of new venture performance: An extended model, *Entrepreneurship Theory & Practice,* 23: 5–29; H. M. O'Neill, R. W. Pouder, & A. K. Buchholtz, 1998, Patterns in the diffusion of strategies across organizations: Insights from the innovation diffusion literature, *Academy of Management Review,* 23: 98–114.
26. Patterson, Market changes place demands on Nike, Inc.
27. Galbraith, *Designing Organizations,* 25.
28. P. Lawrence & J. W. Lorsch, 1967, *Organization and Environment* (Cambridge, MA: Harvard Business School Press).
29. A. D. Chandler, 1994, The functions of the HQ unit in the multibusiness firm, in R. P. Rumelt, D. E. Schendel, & D. J. Teece (eds.), *Fundamental Issues in Strategy* (Cambridge, MA: Harvard Business School Press), 327.
30. W. G. Rowe & P. M. Wright, 1997, Related and unrelated diversification and their effect on human resource management controls, *Strategic Management Journal,* 18: 329–338; D. C. Galunic & K. M. Eisenhardt, 1996, The evolution of intracorporate domains: Divisional charter losses in high-technology, multidivisional corporations, *Organization Science,* 7: 255–282.
31. G. G. Dess, A. Gupta, J.-F. Hennart, & C. W. L. Hill, 1995, Conducting and integrating strategy research at the international, corporate, and business levels: Issues and directions, *Journal of Management,* 21: 357–393.
32. A. D. Chandler, 1962, *Strategy and Structure: Chapters in the History of the American Industrial Enterprise* (Cambridge, MA: The MIT Press).
33. O. E. Williamson, 1994, Strategizing, economizing, and economic organization, in R. P. Rumelt, D. E. Schendel, & D. J. Teece (eds.), *Fundamental Issues in Strategy* (Cambridge, MA: Harvard Business School Press), 361–401.
34. Galbraith, *Designing Organizations,* 27.
35. J. Greco, 1999, Alfred P. Sloan, Jr. (1875–1966): The original "organization" man, *Journal of Business Strategy,* 20(5): 30–31.
36. R. E. Hoskisson, C. W. L. Hill, & H. Kim, 1993, The multidivisional structure: Organizational fossil or source of value? *Journal of Management,* 19: 269–298.
37. Rowe and Wright, Related and unrelated diversification.
38. C. M. Farkas & S. Wetlaufer, 1996, The ways chief executive officers lead, *Harvard Business Review,* 74(3): 110–122.
39. C. C. Miller, L. M. Burke, & W. H. Glick, 1998, Cognitive diversity among upper-echelon executives: Implications for strategic decision processes, *Strategic Management Journal,* 19: 39–58; D. J. Collis, 1996, Corporate strategy in multibusiness firms, *Long Range Planning,* 29: 416–418.
40. M. A. Hitt, R. E. Hoskisson, R. A. Johnson, & D. D. Moesel, 1996, The market for corporate control and firm innovation, *Academy of Management Journal,* 39: 1084–1119.
41. R. E. Hoskisson, M. A. Hitt, & R. D. Ireland, 1994, The effects of acquisitions and restructuring (strategic refocusing) strategies on innovation, in G. von Krogh, A. Sinatra, & H. Singh (eds.), *Managing Corporate Acquisitions* (London: Macmillan Press), 144–169.
42. R. E. Hoskisson & M. A. Hitt, 1988, Strategic control and relative R&D investment in large multiproduct firms, *Strategic Management Journal,* 9: 605–621.
43. R. Tomkins, 1998, Black & Decker plans to cut 3,000 jobs, *Financial Times,* January 28, 15.
44. Collis, Corporate strategy, 417.
45. M. A. Hitt, R. E. Hoskisson, & R. D. Ireland, 1990, Mergers and acquisitions and managerial commitment to innovation in M-form firms, *Strategic Management Journal,* 11(Special Summer Issue): 29–47.
46. S. Baiman, D. F. Larcker, & M. V. Rajan, 1995, Organizational design for business units, *Journal of Accounting Research,* 33: 205–229; Hall, Organizations, 13.
47. Ibid.; Hall, 64–75.
48. W. Echikson, 1998, Winging around Europe—cheaply, *Business Week,* September 14, 202.
49. A. Salkever, 1999, Dogfight in cyberspace: The online travel biz heats up, *BusinessWeek Online,* November 15, *www.businessweek.com.*
50. C. Homburg, H. Krohmer, & J.P. Workman, Jr., 1999, Strategic consensus and performance: The role of strategy type and market-related dynamism, *Strategic Management Journal,* 20: 339–357.
51. G. Edmondson, E. Neuborne, A. L. Kazmin, E. Thornton, & K. N. Anhalt, 1999, L'Oreal: The beauty of global branding, *BusinessWeek Online,* June 28, *www.businessweek.com.*
52. Ibid.
53. P. S. Adler, B. Goldoftas, & D. I. Levin, 1999, Flexibility versus efficiency? A case study of model changeovers in the Toyota production system, *Organization Science,* 10: 43–68.
54. D. K. Sobek, II, A. C. Howard, & J. K. Liker, 1999, Toyota's principles of set-based concurrent engineering, *Sloan Management Review,* 40(2): 67–83.
55. A. Barrett & J.M. Laderman, 1999, That's why they call it Vanguard, *Business Week,* January 18, 82–86; T. Easton, 1999, The gospel according to Vanguard, *Forbes,* February 8, 115–119.
56. D. Donovan, 2000, You just can't lick 'em, *Forbes,* January 10, 174.
57. Service Performance Corporation, 1998, *Fortune,* Special Advertising Section, February 2, S2.
58. C. C. Markides & P. J. Williamson, 1996, Corporate diversification and organizational structure: A resource-based view, *Academy of Management Journal,* 39: 340–367; C. W. L. Hill, M. A. Hitt, & R. E. Hoskisson, 1992, Cooperative versus competitive structures in related and unrelated diversified firms, *Organization Science,* 3: 501–521.
59. J. Robins & M. E. Wiersema, 1995, A resource-based approach to the multibusiness firm: Empirical analysis of portfolio interrelationships and corporate financial performance, *Strategic Management Journal,* 16: 277–299.
60. C. C. Markides, 1997, To diversify or not to diversify, *Harvard Business Review,* 75(6): 93–99.
61. Nadler & Tushman, *Competing by Design,* 99.
62. Hall, Organizations, 186; J. G. March, 1994, *A Primer on Decision Making: How Decisions Happen* (New York: The Free Press), 117–118.
63. I. M. Kunii, E. Thornton, & J. Rae-Dupree, 1999, Sony's shake-up, *Business Week,* 52–53.
64. B. Koppel, 2000, Synergy in ketchup?, *Forbes,* February 7, 68–69.
65. P. J. Frost, 1997, Bridging academia and business: A conversation with Steve Kerr, *Organization Science,* 8: 335.

66. GE HomePage, 2000, March 1, *www.ge.com*.
67. J. A. Byrne, 1998, How Jack Welch runs GE, *BusinessWeek Online*, June 8, *www.businessweek.com*.
68. T. A. Stewart, 1999, See Jack. See Jack run Europe. *Fortune*, September 27, 127.
69. R. E. Hoskisson & M. A. Hitt, 1990, Antecedents and performance outcomes of diversification: A review and critique of theoretical perspectives, *Journal of Management*, 16: 461–509.
70. C. W. L. Hill, M. A. Hitt, & R. E. Hoskisson, 1992, Cooperative versus competitive structures in related and unrelated diversified firms, *Organization Science*, 3: 501–521.
71. J. B. Barney, 1997, *Gaining and Sustaining Competitive Advantage* (Reading, MA: Addison-Wesley), 420–433.
72. Newell Rubbermaid homepage, 2000, February 24, *http://www.newellco.com*.
73. Collis, Corporate strategy, 418.
74. *Business Week*, 1999, L. Dennis Kozlowski: Compulsive shopper, *Business Week*, January 11, 67.
75. Williamson, Strategizing, economizing, 373.
76. B. W. Keats & M. A. Hitt, 1988, A causal model of linkages among environmental dimensions, macro organizational characteristics, and performance, *Academy of Management Journal*, 31: 570–598.
77. Hoskisson, Hill, & Kim, The multidivisional structure, 276.
78. R. E. Hoskisson, R. A. Johnson, & D. D. Moesel, 1994, Corporate divestiture intensity: Effects of governance strategy and performance, *Academy of Management Journal*, 37:1207–1251; R. E. Hoskisson & T. Turk, 1990, Corporate restructuring, governance and control limits of the internal capital market, *Academy of Management Review*, 15: 459–471.
79. S. J. Chang & H. Singh, 1999, The impact of entry and resource fit on modes of exit by multibusiness firms, *Strategic Management Journal*, 20: 1019–1035; M. E. Porter, 1987, From competitive advantage to corporate strategy, *Harvard Business Review*, 65(3): 43–59.
80. C. C. Markides, 1992, Consequences of corporate refocusing: Ex ante evidence, *Academy of Management Journal*, 35: 398–412.
81. G. L. White, 2000, GM to unify manufacturing of cars, trucks. *Wall Street Journal*, January 27, B22.
82. M. A. Hitt, M. T. Dacin, B. B. Tyler, & D. Park, 1997, Understanding the differences in Korean and U.S. executives' strategic orientations, *Strategic Management Journal*, 18: 159–167.
83. C. Rahweddeer, 1998, U.S. mail-order firms shake up Europe, *Wall Street Journal*, January 6, A15.
84. E. Beck, 1999, Body Shop gets a makeover to cut costs, *Wall Street Journal*, January 27, A18.
85. Bartlett & Ghoshal, *Managing Across Borders*.
86. Ibid.
87. Kramer, Organizing for global competitiveness.
88. B. Gomes-Casseres, 1994, Group versus group: How alliance networks compete, *Harvard Business Review*, 72(4): 62–74.
89. Werther, Structure driven strategy and virtual organization; G. R. Jones, 1998, *Organizational Theory* (Reading, MA: Addison-Wesley), 163–165.
90. P. Dussauge, B. Garrette, & W. Mitchell, 2000, Learning from competing partners: Outcomes and duration of scale and link alliances in Europe, North America and Asia, *Strategic Management Journal*, 21: 99–126; G. Lorenzoni & C. Baden-Fuller, 1995, Creating a strategic center to manage a web of partners, *California Management Review*, 37(3): 146–163.
91. S. Harryson, 1998, *Japanese Technology and Innovation Management* (Northhampton, MA: Edward Elgar).
92. J. H. Dyer, 1997, Effective interfirm collaboration: How firms minimize transaction costs and maximize transaction value, *Strategic Management Journal*, 18: 535–556.
93. T. Nishiguchi, 1994, *Strategic Industrial Sourcing: The Japanese Advantage* (New York: Oxford University Press).
94. W. M. Fruin, 1992, *The Japanese Enterprise System* (New York: Oxford University Press).
95. Sobek, Howard, & Liker, Toyota's principles of set-based concurrent engineering.
96. M. Skapinker, 1999, Airlines bent on bigamy ruffle alliances, *Financial Times*, June 23, 8.
97. D. Harbrecht, 1999, A talk with Air France's pilot as he hooks up with Delta, *BusinessWeek Online*, June 22, *www.businessweek.com*.
98. D. Leonhardt, A. T. Palmer, 1999, Getting off their McButts, *Business Week*, February 22, 84–88; S. Branch, 1997, What's eating McDonald's? *Fortune*, October 13, 122–125.
99. Corning homepage, 2000, February 24, *www.corning.com*; J. R. Houghton, 1990, Corning cultivates joint ventures that endure, *Planning Review*, 18(5): 15–17.
100. C. Jones, W. S. Hesterly, & S. P. Borgatti, 1997, A general theory of network governance: Exchange conditions and social mechanisms, *Academy of Management Review*, 22: 911–945.
101. R. E. Miles, C. C. Snow, J. A. Mathews, G. Miles, & J. J. Coleman, Jr., 1997, Organizing in the knowledge age: Anticipating the cellular form, *Academy of Management Executive*, XI(4): 7–20.
102. Kramer, Organizing for global competitiveness; Nadler and Tushman, *Competing by Design*, 89.
103. Chandler, *Scale and Scope*.
104. B. Victor & C. Stephens, 1994, The dark side of the new organizational forms: An editorial essay, *Organization Science*, 5: 479–482.
105. R. Waters, 1998, New DuPont shake-up to slash bureaucracy, *Financial Times*, January 8, 3; A. Barrett, 1997, At DuPont, time to both sow and reap, *Business Week*, September 29, 107–108.
106. M. A. Hitt, B. W. Keats, & S. M. DeMarie, 1998, Navigating in the new competitive landscape: Building competitive advantage and strategic flexibility in the 21st century, *Academy of Management Executive*, 12(4): 22–42.
107. R. D. Ireland & M. A. Hitt, 1999, Achieving and maintaining strategic competitiveness in the 21st century: The role of strategic leadership, *Academy of Management Executive*, 13(1): 43–57.

STRATEGIC LEADERSHIP

After reading this chapter, you should be able to:

1. Define strategic leadership and describe the importance of top-level managers as an organizational resource.
2. Define top management teams and explain their effects on the firm's performance and its ability to innovate and make appropriate strategic changes.
3. Describe the internal and external managerial labor markets and their effects on the development and implementation of a firm's strategy.
4. Discuss the value of strategic leadership in determining the firm's strategic direction.
5. Explain the role of strategic leaders in exploiting and maintaining core competencies.
6. Describe the importance of strategic leaders in developing a firm's human capital.
7. Define organizational culture and explain what must be done to sustain an effective culture.
8. Describe what strategic leaders can do to establish and emphasize ethical practices in their firms.
9. Discuss the importance and use of organizational controls.

Strategic Leaders: The Good, the Bad, and the Ugly

John F. (Jack) Welch, Jr., the renowned CEO of General Electric, is celebrated as one of the world's most effective CEOs because of the value that he has created for GE. Over the period from 1980 to 2000, more value has been created for GE shareholders than for any other company in the world. Early in his tenure as CEO of GE, Welch obtained the name "Neutron Jack" for his infamous efficiency moves, including significant downsizing of employees. However, while still considered decisive and demanding, Welch enjoys much respect for what he has done at GE, namely, create one of the most successful management development programs in the world. Many firms try to raid GE's management ranks because they know these people have strong management skills. Welch believes and invests in building human capital. In a recent ranking of companies worldwide by *Financial Times,* GE was ranked number one. He might be considered the master strategic leader. Welch retired on December 31, 2000. However, there are new, younger people to take Welch's place as excellent strategic leaders.

In the same ranking that GE received number-one status, Hewlett-Packard was ranked number 14 in the world. Interestingly, though, HP has not performed well in recent years, but has a new CEO, Carly Fiorina. During her tenure at Lucent Technologies, she was considered one of the world's most powerful women. In her current role, she *is* the most powerful woman. She has been described as having a silver tongue and an iron will. Fiorina has a challenge at HP: She must make the company more innovative without losing what made it great. She was chosen for HP's CEO position because of her ability to conceptualize and communicate sweeping strategies, her knowledge of operations to meet short- and long-term financial goals, her ability to create a need for change, and her capability to gain commitment to, and implement, a new vision for the company. Fiorina has the interpersonal skills that inspire loyalty from those who work with her. She also has savvy marketing skills and courts customers effectively. She can and will provide strong direction for HP.

Another new strategic leader is Jeff Bezos, the founder and CEO of Amazon.com. In 1999, Bezos was chosen as *Time*'s Person of the Year. Although a young firm, Amazon.com is a grandfather of the e-commerce age. Bezos developed a company selling books through the Internet, and at first, most paid little attention to him or his company. Those paying little attention included competitors Barnes & Noble and Borders. *Now* they pay attention. Barnes & Noble started barnesandnoble.com about two years after Amazon.com entered the market. However, Amazon.com had first-mover advantages (explained in Chapter 5). Bezos is innovative and willing to think entrepreneurially, a problem for some executives of large firms. Even as Amazon.com has grown, Bezos continues to think and act as an entrepreneur. He began expanding his on-line products by using the access to, and knowledge of, customers that he developed in the electronic business. In 1998, Amazon.com added music and films to its product offerings. Thereafter, the company began expanding into many product lines, such as pharmaceuticals and groceries. Today, Barnes & Noble is not considered Amazon.com's major competitor. Wal-Mart *is* a major competitor, but even it is scrambling to develop its Internet offerings to compete with Amazon.com. Clearly, Bezos has established a company with the best brand name in cyberspace.

Unfortunately, there are examples of less successful strategic leaders. Robert Shapiro is a thoughtful and likeable person who had a grand vision for Monsanto. Some refer to him as a genius. He was the "genius" behind the highly successful NutraSweet. He wanted Monsanto to integrate new genetics research and molecular design with drugs and food products. As a result, Monsanto developed genetically engineered seeds, such as herbicide-resistant soybeans. In undertaking this venture, Shapiro is described by some as revolutionizing agribusiness. But he did not envision market resistance to such products. In Europe especially, a major backlash against genetically engineered food products developed. Thus, there was a "blind spot" in Shapiro's vision. In addition, he was not entirely successful in selling Monsanto's employees on his vision. Some argued that he did not provide the strong leadership that was needed when the company was being attacked. As things turned out, the firm was acquired by Pharmacia & UpJohn, and Shapiro's vision is dead.

In 1999, John B. McCoy, CEO of Bank One Corporation, announced that he was taking early retirement at age 56. He had been CEO of the firm for 15 years and led the firm through years of tremendous growth, achieved primarily by acquisitions. He helped the bank become the fourth-largest bank in the United States. However, as opportunities to acquire other banks diminished, McCoy could not sustain Bank One's growth. Thus, while Welch transformed or "reinvented" GE several times during his leadership, McCoy was unable to do the same at Bank One. One analyst suggested that the company was in need of a change in leadership.

Other strategic leaders have been successful by some standards, but may not be highly regarded for other reasons. Perhaps the best known among these is Al Dunlap, sometimes referred to as "Chain-saw Al." Dunlap was known for taking the leadership reins of poorly performing companies and turning them around. He obtained his nickname because he often sold off businesses and laid off many employees. He seemed to be successful with these actions in several companies, including Scott Paper, until his last CEO role with Sunbeam. There, he also sold off many of Sunbeam's businesses and tried to jump-start new growth with some acquisitions. Unfortunately, the additional businesses did not improve the firm's performance, but their acquisition substantially increased the firm's debt (by $1.8 billion). The much higher debt led to a negative cash flow. With increased pressure from stockholders and creditors to improve the company's performance, Dunlap engaged in some highly questionable actions, and Sunbeam's board of directors requested his resignation.

Another person trying to gain respect is Charles Wang, CEO of Computer Associates. By most accounts, Computer Associates has flourished under his leadership. Wang has helped the company grow to a $5.6 billion software firm. Much of the growth

http://www.amazon.com
http://www.bankone.com
http://www.bn.com
http://www.borders.com
http://www.ge.com
http://www.hp.com
http://www.lucent.com
http://www.monsanto.com
http://www.wal-mart.com

has come from acquiring competitors and firms in complementary product markets. So, why wouldn't people give respect to this CEO? When asked why no executives from the acquired firm remain afterwards, Wang replied, "This dragon has only one head." Some use the term "ruthless" to describe both Wang and his actions. Overall, his methods can be described as harsh, but they produce positive results for the company. Wang doubled the size of the firm over a four-year period and, at the same time, maintained high profit margins. Computer Associates has approximately 31 percent of the client server market, with IBM second at slightly over 11 percent. In 1999, Computer Associates took a $1.1 billion write-off to fund a grant in that amount to its top three executives, a large share of which went to Wang. However, stockholders filed 10 separate suits, and a federal judge ruled that Wang had to give back approximately half of his $670 million share. The bottom line is that Wang has been successful, but his methods are questioned and generally disliked.

SOURCES: M. A. Hitt, J. S. Harrison, & R. D. Ireland, 2001, *Creating Value through Mergers and Acquisitions: A Complete Guide to Successful M&As*, New York: Oxford University Press; A. Bianco & Steve Hamm, 2000, Software's tough guy, *Business Week*, March 6, 133–144; Amazon.com, Inc., 2000, *Wall Street Journal Interactive*, February 15, *www.interactive.wsj.com/articles*; Grim reaper, 1999, *The Economist Online*, December 25, *www.economist.com*; J. B. Cahill, 1999, Bank One's McCoy is quitting his posts of chairman, chief, *Wall Street Journal Interactive*, December 22, *www.interactive.wsj.com/articles*; J. C. Ramo, 1999, Why the founder of Amazon.com is our choice for 1999, *Time Online*, December 21, *www.time.com*; Ranking: World's top companies, 1999, *ft.com*, October 18, *www.ft.com/ftsurveys*; P. Burrows & P. Elstrom, 1999, The boss, *Business Week*, August 2, 76–84.

The examples in the Opening Case show some of the significant strategic challenges with which CEOs are confronted and emphasize the importance and outcomes of effective strategic leadership. Some of the leaders are highly successful (e.g., Welch, Fiorina, and Bezos), while others may be successful for a while, but cannot sustain their success. Still others technically may be successful, but have less respect as leaders. It is difficult to build and maintain success over a sustained period of time. As this chapter makes clear, it is through effective strategic leadership that firms are able to use the strategic management process successfully (see Figure 1.1). Thus, as strategic leaders, top-level managers must guide the firm in ways that result in the formation of a strategic intent and strategic mission. This guidance may lead to goals that stretch everyone in the organization to improve their performance.[1] Moreover, strategic leaders are then challenged to facilitate the development of appropriate strategic actions and determine how to implement them. These actions culminate in strategic competitiveness and above-average returns[2] (see Figure 12.1).

This chapter begins with a definition of strategic leadership and its importance as a potential source of competitive advantage. Next, we examine top management teams and their effects on innovation, strategic change, and firm performance. Following this discussion is an analysis of the internal and external managerial labor markets from which strategic leaders are selected. Closing the chapter are descriptions of the six key components of effective strategic leadership: determining a strategic direction, exploiting and maintaining core competencies, developing human capital, sustaining an effective organizational culture, emphasizing ethical practices, and establishing balanced organizational control systems.

The impermanence of success is well documented by the change in leadership at Compaq Computer. Compaq's former CEO, Eckhard Pfeiffer, had been highly suc-

FIGURE 12.1 | **Strategic Leadership and the Strategic Management Process**

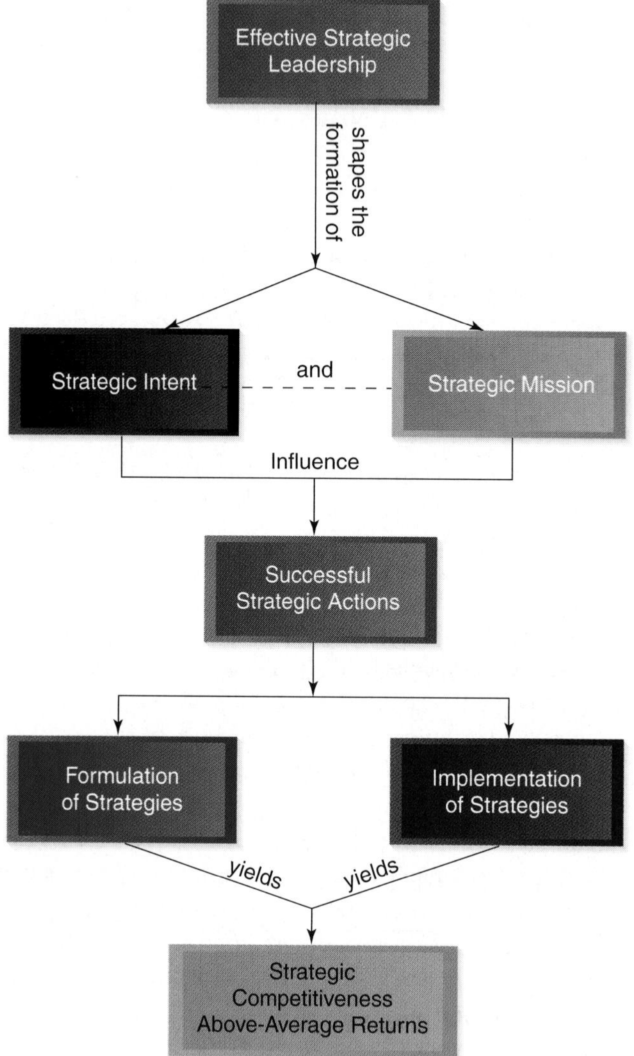

cessful in leading Compaq to the number-one position in the personal computer market. In 1998, Compaq seemed to be at the top of its game. However, problems ensued in 1999, and in a short period of time, Compaq became stagnant and was unseated as the number-one producer of personal computers by Dell. Compaq's board of directors forced Pfeiffer to resign. Pfeiffer's successor, Michael Capellas, is trying to reenergize the firm, to make it more innovative. He believes that this is necessary because, in the high-technology industry, the constant, substantial speed of change will relegate Compaq to a second-class seat. A short time after taking the job, Capellas made significant changes, restructuring the organization and eliminating redundant and overlapping programs. Analysts believe that his actions are on track. One analyst observed that Compaq executives must "start thinking outside the box and partner more with solution providers rather than box pushers." Capellas is trying to do just that.[3]

Strategic Leadership

Strategic leadership is the ability to anticipate, envision, maintain flexibility, and empower others to create strategic change as necessary.

Strategic leadership is the ability to anticipate, envision, maintain flexibility, and empower others to create strategic change as necessary. Multifunctional in nature, strategic leadership involves managing through others, managing an entire enterprise rather than a functional subunit, and coping with change that seems to be increasing exponentially in the current competitive landscape. Because of the complexity and global nature of this landscape, strategic leaders must learn how to influence human behavior effectively in an uncertain environment. By word or by personal example, and through their ability to envision the future, effective strategic leaders meaningfully influence the behaviors, thoughts, and feelings of those with whom they work.[4] The ability to manage human capital may be the most critical of the strategic leader's skills.[5] In the opinion of a well-known observer of leadership, the key to competitive advantage in the 1990s and beyond "will be the capacity of top leadership to create the social architecture capable of generating intellectual capital. . . . By intellectual capital, I mean know-how, expertise, brainpower, innovation [and] ideas."[6] Competent strategic leaders also establish the context through which stakeholders (e.g., employees, customers, and suppliers) are able to perform at peak efficiency.[7] The crux of strategic leadership is the ability to manage the firm's operations effectively and sustain a high performance over time.[8]

A **managerial mind-set** is the set of assumptions, premises, and accepted wisdom that bounds—or frames—a manager's understanding of the firm, the industry(ies) in which it competes, and the core competencies it uses in the pursuit of strategic competitiveness.

In the 21st century, many managers working in nations throughout the world will be challenged to alter their mind-sets to cope with the rapid and complex changes occurring in the global economy. A **managerial mind-set** is the set of assumptions, premises, and accepted wisdom that bounds—or frames—a manager's understanding of the firm, the industry(ies) in which it competes, and the core competencies it uses in the pursuit of strategic competitiveness[9] (see Chapter 3).

A firm's ability to achieve strategic competitiveness and earn above-average returns is compromised when strategic leaders fail to respond appropriately and quickly to changes in the complex global competitive environment. The failure to respond quickly prompted Eckhard Pfeiffer's problems at Compaq. Research suggests that a firm's "long-term competitiveness depends on managers' willingness to challenge continually their managerial frames" and that global competition is more than product versus product or company versus company: It is also a case of "mindset versus mindset, managerial frame versus managerial frame."[10] Competing on the basis of mind-sets demands that strategic leaders learn how to deal with diverse and cognitively complex competitive situations. One of the most challenging changes is overcoming one's own successful mind-set when that is required. Being able to complete challenging assignments that are linked to achieving strategic competitiveness early and frequently in one's career appears to improve a manager's ability to make appropriate changes to his or her mind-set.[11]

Effective strategic leaders are willing to make candid and courageous, yet pragmatic, decisions—decisions that may be difficult, but necessary in light of internal and external conditions facing the firm.[12] Effective strategic leaders solicit corrective feedback from peers, superiors, and employees about the value of their difficult decisions. Often, this feedback is sought through face-to-face communications. Unwillingness to accept feedback may be a key reason talented executives fail, highlighting the need for strategic leaders to solicit feedback consistently from those affected by their decisions.[13]

The primary responsibility for effective strategic leadership rests at the top, in particular, with the CEO. Other commonly recognized strategic leaders include members of the board of directors, the top management team, and divisional general managers. Regardless of their title and organizational function, strategic leaders have substantial decision-making responsibilities that cannot be delegated.[14]

Strategic leadership is an extremely complex, but critical, form of leadership. Strategies cannot be formulated and implemented to achieve above-average returns without effective strategic leaders. Because strategic leadership is a requirement of strategic success, and because organizations may be poorly led and overmanaged, firms competing in the 21st-century competitive landscape are challenged to develop effective strategic leaders.[15]

Managers as an Organizational Resource

As the introductory discussion suggests, top-level managers are an important resource for firms seeking to formulate and implement strategies effectively.[16] A key reason for this is that the strategic decisions made by top managers influence how the firm is designed and whether goals will be achieved. Thus, a critical element of organizational success is having a top-management team with superior managerial skills.[17]

Managers often use their discretion (or latitude for action) when making strategic decisions, including those concerned with the effective implementation of strategies.[18] Managerial discretion differs significantly across industries. The primary factors that determine the amount of a manager's (especially a top-level manager's) decision-making discretion include (1) external environmental sources (e.g., the industry structure, the rate of market growth in the firm's primary industry, and the degree to which products can be differentiated), (2) characteristics of the organization (e.g., its size, age, resources, and culture), and (3) characteristics of the manager (e.g., commitment to the firm and its strategic outcomes, tolerance for ambiguity, skills in working with different people, and aspiration levels) (see Figure 12.2). Because strategic leaders' decisions are intended to help the firm gain a competitive advantage, the way in which managers exercise discretion when determining appropriate strategic actions is critical to the firm's success.[19] Top executives must be action oriented; thus, the decisions that they make should spur the company to action. In fact, a renowned explorer, Robert Swan, once said that "complacency is death."[20]

In addition to determining new strategic initiatives, top-level managers develop the appropriate organizational structure and reward systems of a firm. In Chapter 11, we described how the organizational structure and reward systems affect strategic actions taken to implement different types of strategies. Furthermore, top executives have a major effect on a firm's culture. Evidence suggests that managers' values are critical in

FIGURE 12.2 | Factors Affecting Managerial Discretion

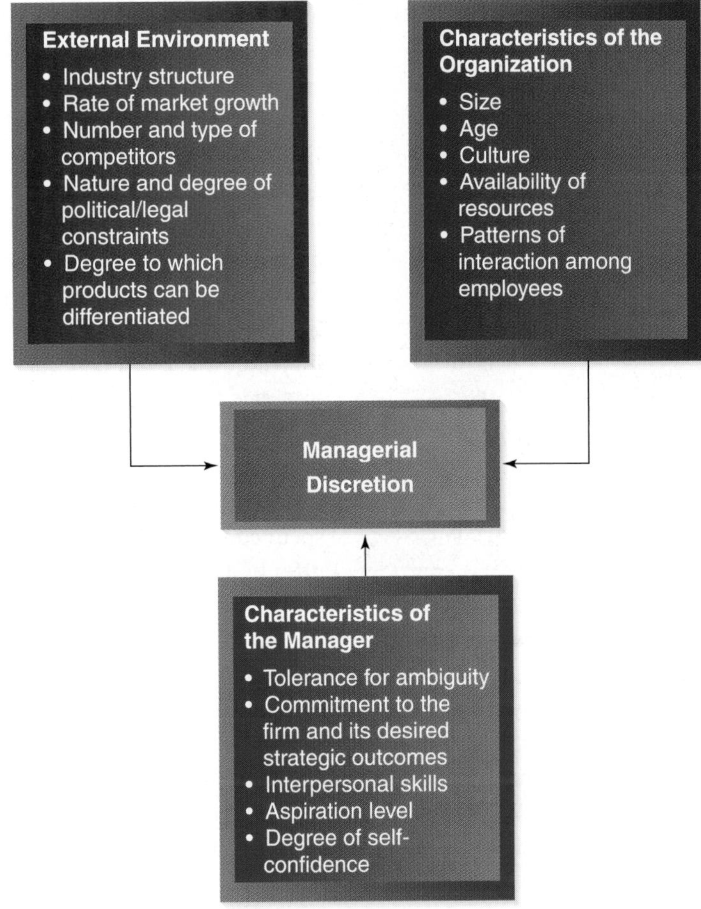

Source: Adapted from S. Finkelstein & D. C. Hambrick, 1996, *Strategic Leadership: Top Executives and Their Effects on Organizations* (St. Paul, MN: West Publishing Company).

shaping a firm's cultural values.[21] Accordingly, top-level managers have an important effect on organizational activities and performance.[22] The significance of this effect should not be underestimated.

D. Michael Abrashoff is a strategic leader comparable to any in the business world. However, he is a commander in the U.S. Navy. Abrashoff divides the world into "believers and infidels." Infidels, he suggests, are individuals who do not understand that innovation and empowerment produce highly positive results. Because of his beliefs, Abrashoff encourages innovation on his ships and practices empowerment by delegating substantial authority. His methods produce results: On average, only 54 percent of sailors reenlist in the Navy after their second tour of duty; however, 100 percent of Abrashoff's sailors reenlisted, translating into a savings of $1.6 million in recruiting and training costs for his ship alone.[23]

Peter I. Bijur, CEO of Texaco, acted quickly and strongly when the blatant discrimination practiced by managers in his firm was made public. He acknowledged that there was a problem and worked to change Texaco's corporate culture.

As the discussion that follows shows, the decisions and actions of some strategic leaders make those leaders a source of competitive advantage for their firm. In accordance with the criteria of sustainability discussed in Chapter 3, strategic leaders can be a source of competitive advantage only when their work is valuable, rare, costly to imitate, and nonsubstitutable.

Effective strategic leaders focus their work on the key issues that ultimately shape the firm's ability to earn above-average returns. For example, Peter I. Bijur, CEO of Texaco, was faced with blatant discrimination practiced by managers in his firm. When a tape recording of a key Texaco executive making disparaging racial remarks was made public, Bijur acted quickly and strongly. He acknowledged publicly that there was a problem within Texaco and that he intended to change it. He settled the lawsuit that prompted the public airing of discriminatory practices for $140 million. In addition, he fired one executive and eliminated benefits for two others who had retired. He also personally spent considerable time trying to change the corporate culture. In 1999, African Americans made up 23 percent of new employees, an increase of 53 percent over the previous year. Promotions for African Americans doubled. Today, after three years of Bijur's actions, many civil rights leaders suggest that Texaco has a model program to combat corporate discrimination. The Reverend Jesse Jackson stated, "In many ways, Peter Bijur saved Texaco."[24]

Managerial beliefs affect strategic decisions that in turn affect the firm's performance.[25] This causal chain is evident in Bijur's decisions and actions at Texaco. It is also evident that Carly Fiorina's self-confidence gives her the power to influence change in an organization. Managers use their discretion to develop and utilize strategic resources to create value for the shareholders and to meet the other stakeholders' requirements.[26] However, the complexity of the challenges faced and thus the need for substantial amounts of information and knowledge require the use of teams of executives to provide the strategic leadership in most firms.

Top Management Teams

The **top management team** is composed of the key managers who are responsible for formulating and implementing the organization's strategies.

The **top management team** is composed of the key managers who are responsible for formulating and implementing the organization's strategies. Typically, the top management team includes the officers of the corporation, as defined by the title of vice president and above or by service as a member of the board of directors.[27] The quality of the strategic decisions made by a top management team affects the firm's ability to innovate and engage in effective strategic change.[28]

Top Management Team, Firm Performance, and Strategic Change

The job of top-level executives is complex and requires a broad knowledge of the firm's operations, as well as the three key parts of the firm's external environment.

A **heterogeneous top management team** is composed of individuals with different functional backgrounds, experience, and education.

Therefore, firms try to form a top management team that has the appropriate knowledge and expertise to operate the internal organization, yet also deal with external stakeholders.[29] This normally requires a heterogeneous top management team. A **heterogeneous top management team** is composed of individuals with different functional backgrounds, experience, and education. The more heterogeneous a top management team is, with varied expertise and knowledge, the more capacity it has to provide effective strategic leadership in *formulating* strategy. Members of a heterogeneous top management team benefit from discussing the different perspectives advanced by team members. In many cases, these discussions increase the quality of the top management team's decisions, especially when a synthesis emerges out of the clash among diverse perspectives that is generally superior to any one individual perspective.[30] For example, heterogeneous top management teams in the airline industry have the propensity to take stronger competitive actions and reactions than do more homogenous teams.[31] The net benefit of such actions by heterogeneous teams was positive in terms of market share and above-average returns. Research shows that more heterogeneity among top management team members promotes debate, which often leads to better strategic decisions. In turn, better strategic decisions produce higher firm performance.[32]

It is also important that the top management team members function cohesively. In general, the more heterogeneous and larger the top management team is, the more difficult it is for the team to *implement* strategies effectively.[33] The fact that comprehensive and long-term strategic plans can be inhibited by communication difficulties among top executives who have different backgrounds and different cognitive skills may account for these implementation-related difficulties.[34] A group of top executives with diverse backgrounds may thus inhibit the process of decision making if it is not effectively managed. In these cases, top management teams may fail to comprehensively examine threats and opportunities, leading to a suboptimal strategic decision.[35] Having members with substantive expertise in the firm's core functions and businesses is also important to the effectiveness of a top management team. In a high-technology industry, it may be critical for a firm's top management team to have R&D expertise, particularly when growth strategies are being implemented.[36]

The characteristics of top management teams are related to innovation and strategic change.[37] For example, more heterogeneous top management teams are associated positively with innovation and strategic change. The heterogeneity may force the team or some of the members to "think outside of the box" and thus be more creative in making decisions.[38] Therefore, firms that need to change their strategies are more likely to do so if they have top management teams with diverse backgrounds and expertise. A top management team with various areas of expertise is more likely to identify environmental changes (opportunities and threats) or changes within the firms that require a different strategic direction.[39]

Diebold, Inc.'s new CEO, Walden O'Dell, is expected to form a heterogeneous top management team. Diebold is a basic manufacturer of hardware, but is now trying to add more diverse services and move into international markets to take advantage of opportunities and to react to an increasingly competitive environment. O'Dell himself has a diverse background. He has significant international experience in Hong Kong, China, Malaysia, the Middle East, Europe, and Canada. He has strong experience in technology development, along with sales service and distribution. While this diverse experience should be of considerable value to Diebold, still other members of the top management team with different managerial frames could enhance discussions of strategic decisions.[40]

The CEO and Top Management Team Power

As suggested in Chapter 10, the board of directors is an important mechanism for monitoring a firm's strategic direction and for representing the interests of stakeholders, especially shareholders. In fact, higher performance normally is achieved when the board of directors is involved more directly in shaping a firm's strategic direction.[41]

Boards of directors, however, may find it difficult to direct the strategic actions of powerful CEOs and top management teams. It is not uncommon for a powerful CEO to appoint a number of sympathetic outside board members or have inside board members who are on the top management team and report to the CEO. In either case, the CEO may have significant control over the board's actions. "A central question is whether boards are an effective management control mechanism . . . or whether they are a 'management tool,' . . . a rubber stamp for management initiatives . . . and often surrender to management their major domain of decision-making authority, which includes the right to hire, fire, and compensate top management."[42] This concern is evident with the board of directors of Disney and its CEO, Michael Eisner. As explained in Chapter 10, several institutional shareholders have taken actions to pressure Eisner to change Disney's board. Alternatively, recent research shows that social ties between the CEO and board members may actually increase board members' involvement in strategic decisions. Thus, strong relationships between the CEO and the board of directors may have positive or negative outcomes.[43]

CEOs and top management team members can also achieve power in other ways. Holding the titles of chairperson of the board and chief executive officer usually gives a CEO more power than one who is not simultaneously serving as chair of the firm's board.[44] Although the practice of CEO duality (i.e., when the CEO and the chairperson of the board are the same) has become more common in U.S. businesses, it has come under heavy criticism: Duality has been blamed for poor performance and slow response to change in a number of firms.[45]

DaimlerChrysler's CEO, Jürgen Schrempp, holds the dual positions of chairman of the board and CEO. And Schrempp has substantial power in the firm. In fact, insiders suggest that he is purging those individuals who are outspoken and who represent potential threats to his dominance. In particular, former Chrysler executives are leaving the firm. The loss of some of these key executives, such as Thomas Stallkamp, credited with being the spiritual leader of the company's U.S. operations and the leader of the integration efforts between the former Chrysler and Daimler operations, has worried investors. Without Stallkamp's leadership, investors worry that integration efforts may stall and the potential efficiencies and synergies may not be realized.[46]

Although it varies across industries, duality occurs most commonly in the largest firms. Increased shareholder activism, however, has brought CEO duality under scrutiny and attack in both U.S. and European firms. Historically, an independent board leadership structure in which one person did not hold the positions of CEO and chair was believed to enhance a board's ability to monitor top-level managers' decisions and actions, particularly in terms of the firm's financial performance.[47] Stewardship theory, on the other hand, suggests that CEO duality facilitates effective decisions and actions. In these instances, the increased effectiveness gained through CEO duality accrues from the individual who wants to perform effectively and desires to be the best possible steward of the firm's assets. Because of this person's positive orientation and actions, extra governance and the coordination costs resulting from an independent board leadership structure would be unnecessary.[48]

Top-management team members and CEOs who have long tenure—on the team and in the organization—have a greater influence on board decisions.[49] Long tenure is known to restrict the breadth of an executive's knowledge base. With the limited perspectives associated with a restricted knowledge base, long-tenured top executives typically develop fewer alternatives to evaluate in making strategic decisions.[50] However, long-tenured managers also may be able to exercise more effective strategic control, thereby obviating the need for board members involvement because effective strategic control generally produces higher performance.[51]

In the final analysis, boards of directors should develop an effective relationship with the firm's top management team. The relative degrees of power to be held by the board and top management team members should be examined in light of an individual firm's situation. For example, the abundance of resources in a firm's external environment and the volatility of that environment may affect the ideal balance of power between boards and top-management teams.[52] Through the development of effective working relationships, boards, CEOs, and other top management team members are able to serve the best interests of the firm's stakeholders.

Managerial Labor Market

The choice of top executives—especially CEOs—is a critical organizational decision with important implications for the firm's performance.[53] Moreover, the selection of new members for a top management team represents an opportunity for the firm to adapt to changes occurring in its external environment—that is, in its general, industry, and competitor environments (see Chapter 2).

Successful companies develop screening systems to identify those with managerial and strategic leadership potential. The most effective of these systems assesses people within the firm and gains valuable information about the capabilities of other firms' managers, particularly their strategic leaders. For current managers, training and development programs are provided in an attempt to preselect and shape the skills of people who may become tomorrow's leaders. As noted earlier, the management development program at GE is considered one of the most effective in the world.

An **internal managerial labor market** consists of the opportunities for managerial positions within a firm.

An **external managerial labor market** is the collection of career opportunities for managers in organizations outside of the one for which they work currently.

There are two types of managerial labor markets—internal and external—from which organizations select managers and strategic leaders. An **internal managerial labor market** consists of the opportunities for managerial positions within a firm, whereas an **external managerial labor market** is the collection of career opportunities for managers in organizations outside of the one for which they work currently. The discussion that follows focuses on how managerial labor markets are used to select CEOs.

Several benefits are thought to accrue to a firm when the internal labor market is used to select a new CEO. Because of their experience with the firm and the industry environment in which it competes, insiders are familiar with company products, markets, technologies, and operating procedures. Also, internal hiring produces lower turnover among existing personnel, many of whom possess valuable firm-specific knowledge. When the firm is performing well, internal succession is favored to sustain high performance. It is assumed that hiring from inside keeps the important knowledge necessary to sustain the performance. Given the phenomenal success of GE and its highly effective management development program, insiders are being considered for succeeding Jack Welch. The selection is likely to be one of two people: Jeffrey Immelt or James McNerney. Immelt has been in charge of the fast-growing medical systems business since 1997. The business's annual revenue has increased by about 44 percent during his tenure. While McNerney is not as aggressive as Welch, his aircraft engine business has enjoyed considerable success in recent times.[54] Similarly, the heir to the CEO position at IBM is likely to be an insider. Louis Gerstner was an outsider when he was chosen as IBM's CEO. However, IBM's performance was suffering at the time. Thus, a CEO was selected to change the strategic direction of the firm. However, IBM's performance has improved considerably. Hence, investors do not want a change in strategic direction. Samuel Palmisano, manager of IBM's computer server group, is viewed as the front-runner to succeed Gerstner when he retires in 2003.[55] For an inside move to the top to occur successfully, firms must develop and implement effective succession management programs. In that way, managers are developed such that one will eventually be prepared to ascend to the top.[56]

It is not unusual for employees to have a strong preference for using the internal managerial labor market to select top management team members and the CEO. The selection of insiders to fill top level management positions reflects a desire for continuity and a continuing commitment to the firm's current strategic intent, strategic mission, and chosen strategies. Thus, internal candidates tend to be valued over external candidates[57] in the selection of a firm's CEO and other top-level managers. In fact, outside succession to the CEO position "is an extraordinary event for business firms [and] is usually seen as a stark indicator that the board of directors wants change."[58]

Valid reasons exist for a firm to select an outsider as its new CEO. For example, research evidence suggests that executives who have spent their entire career with a particular firm may become "stale in the saddle."[59] Long tenure with a firm seems to reduce the number of innovative ideas top executives are able to develop to cope with conditions facing their firm. Given the importance of innovation for a firm's success in the competitive landscape (see Chapter 13), an inability to innovate or to create conditions that stimulate innovation throughout a firm is a liability for a strategic leader. In contrast to insiders, CEOs selected from outside the firm may have broader, less limiting perspectives, leading them to encourage innovation and strategic change. Carly Fiorina was selected from the outside to be Hewlett-Packard's CEO. One of the primary reasons for HP's selection of an outsider was the need to stimulate innovation. HP had become less innovative over the years, even though its initial strength came from innovation. The current organization seemed "fat and happy." Others referred to it as a bloated bureaucracy. Under Lew Platt's strategic leadership, it was unable to react effectively to changes in the industry caused by the Internet.[60] Figure 12.3 shows how the composition of the top management team and CEO succession (managerial labor market) may interact to affect strategy. For example, when the top-management team is homogeneous (e.g., its members have similar functional experiences and educational backgrounds) and a new CEO is selected from inside the firm, the firm's current strategy is unlikely to change.

On the other hand, when a new CEO is selected from outside the firm and the top management team is heterogeneous, there is a high probability that strategy will change. When the new CEO is from inside the firm, the strategy may not change, but with a heterogeneous top management team, innovation is likely to continue. An external CEO succession with a homogeneous team creates a more ambiguous situation.

To have an adequate number of highly qualified managers, firms must take advantage of a highly qualified labor pool, including one source of managers that has often been overlooked: women. Firms are beginning to utilize women's potential managerial talents with substantial success, as described in the Strategic Focus.

As noted earlier, the type of strategic leadership that results in the successful implementation of strategies is exemplified by several key actions. The most critical of these are shown in Figure 12.4. The remainder of this chapter is devoted to explaining each action. Note that many of the actions interact with each other. For example, developing human capital through executive training contributes to establishing a strategic direction, fostering an effective culture, exploiting core competencies, using effective organizational control systems, and establishing ethical practices.

Determining Strategic Direction

Determining the strategic direction of a firm involves developing a long-term vision of the firm's strategic intent.

Determining the strategic direction of a firm involves developing a long-term vision of the firm's strategic intent. Normally, a long-term vision looks at least 5 to 10 years into the future. A philosophy with goals, a long-term vision, is the ideal image and character the firm seeks.[61] The ideal long-term vision has two parts: a core ideology and an envisioned future. While the core ideology motivates employees through the company's heritage, the envisioned future encourages employees to stretch beyond their expectations of accomplishment and requires significant change and progress in order to be realized.[62] The envisioned future serves as a guide to many aspects of a firm's strategy implementation process, including motivation, leadership, employee empowerment, and organizational design. For firms competing in numerous industries, evidence suggests that the most effective long-term vision is one that has been accepted by those affected by it.[63]

To determine the firm's long-term vision, managers must take a sufficient amount of time to think about how it should be framed. Areas requiring executive thought include an analysis of the firm's external and internal environments and its current performance. Most top executives obtain inputs from many people with a range of skills to help them analyze various aspects of the firm's operations.

Irwin Jacobs had a vision of a new, technically complex, powerful digital wireless technology. Skeptics dismissed his vision as impractical. Jacobs is the founder and CEO of Qualcomm. His technology is now in millions of phones and is used in about 50 percent of the new digital handsets sold in the United States by such firms as Air-

strategic *focus* CORPORATE

Shattering the Glass Ceiling: Women Top Executives

Clearly, Carly Fiorina broke the glass ceiling in her ascent to the CEO position at Hewlett-Packard. While she represents only a few women CEOs, more women are moving into key positions within major companies. In fact, Lew Platt, the CEO of HP when Fiorina was hired, decided that a woman CEO was what HP needed. Harriet Rubin, author of *Princessa: Machiavelli for Women,* suggests that "we won't see great leaders until we see great women leaders." While this is overstated, there is little doubt that there are many women who have been, are, or will be great leaders. Margaret Thatcher and Golda Meir were both strong and great leaders. Lorraine Monroe is a less well known, but no less great, leader. When she became the principal of Harlem's School 10, it was a terrible place. The school was much better known for its violence and poor attendance than for its academics. However, within five years, Monroe had created a special place for education. The name of the school was changed to Frederick Douglass Academy, and students were educated and sent off to college and careers. Monroe first restored order and discipline. Then she emphasized learning. Now, her students are among the top ones in test scores in the New York public school system. Over 95 percent of the students who graduate from Frederick Douglass Academy now go on to college (a remarkable achievement in any school system).

Fewer women have been in business in the past only because of the glass ceiling, which, hopefully, is breaking. However, depending on who is counted, about 10–12 percent of the top executive positions in U.S. corporations are now held by women, an increase of approximately 48 percent over a five-year period. Debra Meyerson, from Stanford University, suggests that "It's not the ceiling holding women back; it's the whole structure of the organizations in which we work: the foundation, the beams, the walls, the very air." While this statement may seem a little extreme, it does reflect the reality of the past and the frustration felt by the many talented women leaders. Perhaps Carly Fiorina's selection to be HP's CEO will break the barrier. The first woman CEO of a *Fortune* 50 or Dow 30 firm, Fiorina does not seem to believe as strongly in the barriers as some others. She suggested that competitive industries do not have time for glass ceilings. Her advice is to "believe in yourself and invest in yourself and ignore the naysayers."

Arlene Blum, a mountain climber and consultant, states, "If you cannot picture it, you will not make it." Thus, leaders must know where they are and where they are headed. She also recommends "choosing your companions as if your life depended on it."

Several women executives have likely heeded Blum's and Fiorina's advice. For example, Captain Deborah McCoy is a senior vice president in charge of all of Continental's more than 5,200 pilots and approximately 8,700 flight attendants. She is the first woman to head a pilot group for a major airline. Other pilots said that McCoy overcame male chauvinism with humor and skill. She obviously has exceptional interpersonal skills, getting along with everyone. The first woman to serve as senior vice president of marketing at IBM is Abby Kohnstamm. She serves on IBM's elite 13-member corporate executive committee. She is credited with helping to transform IBM's global image from a stodgy old company to a cutting-edge corporation focused on electronic business. Because of this accomplishment, Kohnstamm is considered one of the most powerful women in advertising.

SOURCES: P. LaBarre, 2000, Here's how to make it to the top, *Fast Company Online,* March 1, *www.fastcompany.com*; L. Goldberg, 2000, A woman who became a high flier/Continental executive is still a pilot, *Houston Chronicle,* February 26, 1B; P. W. Lauro, 2000, Ad woman of year changed small planet's view of IBM, *Houston Chronicle,* January 1, 2B; Glass ceiling still difficult to break/Just 10 percent of senior managers for Fortune 500 are women, 2000, *Houston Chronicle,* January 7, 3B; H. Rubin, 2000, Living dangerously—Issue 31, *Fast Company Online,* January 7, *www.fastcompany.com*; P. Burrows & P. Elstrom, 1999, The boss, *Business Week,* August 2, 79–84; A. Orr, 1999, Hewlett-Packard picks Lucent exec as CEO, *Houston Chronicle,* July 20, 1B.

Touch and Sprint. In 1999, Qualcomm's stock price increased from $25 to $520, the best performance on the S&P 500 index that year.[64] Likewise, Minoru Arakawa, president of Nintendo's U.S. operations, had a vision. His vision was of U.S. enthusiasm for Pokémon, a Japanese video game with 150 collectible monsters. Market research produced conclusions that American kids did not like the game. Arakawa decided to import it anyway. Pokémon's sales in the U.S. exceeded $1 billion between 1998 and 2000.[65] Thus, both Jacobs and Arakawa followed a philosophy similar to the advice provided by Fiorina. They believed in their visions and ignored the naysayers. Once the vision is determined, CEOs must motivate employees to achieve it. Some, but not all, top executives are thought to be charismatic strategic leaders. Theory suggests that charisma comes through interactions between leaders and followers. Among these

12.3 | Effects of CEO Succession and Top Management Team Composition on Strategy

Top Management Team Composition	**Managerial Labor Market: CEO Succession** — Internal CEO succession	External CEO succession
Homogeneous	Stable strategy	Ambiguous: possible change in top management team and strategy
Heterogeneous	Stable strategy with innovation	Strategic change

FIGURE 12.4 | Exercise of Effective Strategic Leadership

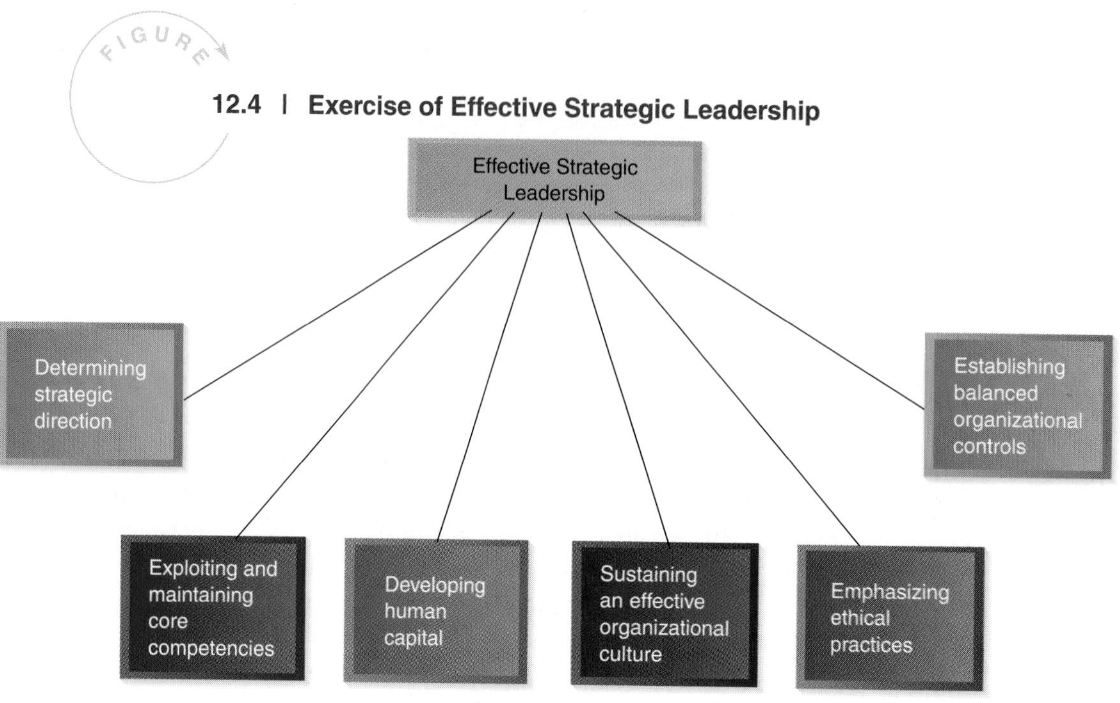

interactions is the creation and management of impressions, in which the strategic leader's framing, scripting, staging, and performing lead to being characterized as charismatic.[66] Although charisma is perceived as helpful, it is not a requirement for successful strategic leadership. Noncharismatic people often have other skills and traits—intelligence, vision, ambition, and toughness, for example—that provide benefits similar to those gained when one is thought to be charismatic.[67] In certain situations, charismatic CEOs might facilitate a better performance by followers; in others, charisma might diminish a leader's credibility. Jack Welch, General Electric's former CEO, combined outrageous self-confidence, a high-strung passion for ideas he unabashedly borrowed, and an unforgiving candor.[68] Christopher Gent, the CEO of Vodafone AirTouch, PLC, must operate in a similar fashion. He has made several aggressive acquisitions that surprised many when they were announced. He was a first mover in the global telecommunications industry. He boldly acquired AirTouch, a U.S. competitor, and followed that with even bolder moves, including a hostile takeover of Mannesman, a German telecommunications firm. He is willing to take risks and possesses strong self-confidence.[69]

A charismatic CEO may help gain employees' commitment to a new vision and strategic direction. Nonetheless, it is important not to lose sight of the strengths of the organization in making changes required by a new strategic direction. In addition, executives must structure the firm effectively to help achieve their vision.[70] The goal is to balance the firm's short-term need to adjust to a new vision while maintaining its long-term survivability by emphasizing its current and valuable core competencies.

Exploiting and Maintaining Core Competencies

Examined in Chapters 1 and 3, *core competencies* are resources and capabilities that serve as a source of competitive advantage for a firm over its rivals. Typically, core competencies relate to an organization's functional skills, such as manufacturing, finance, marketing, and research and development. As shown by the descriptions that follow, firms develop and exploit core competencies in many different functional areas to implement their strategies. Strategic leaders must verify that the firm's competencies are emphasized in strategy implementation efforts. Intel, for example, has core competencies of competitive agility (an ability to act in a variety of competitively relevant ways) and competitive speed (an ability to act quickly when facing environmental and competitive pressures).[71]

In many large firms, and certainly in related diversified ones, core competencies are exploited effectively when they are developed and applied across different organizational units (see Chapter 6). Alternatively, Amazon.com, built by Jeff Bezos, has a core competence that creates synergies across its multiple and diversified *product lines*. Amazon's core competencies are in its customer knowledge base that in turn contributes to another competence: customer service. These competencies translate into a significant asset for a diversified e-commerce business: 17 million customers. Also, because of the company's knowledge of its customers and emphasis on customer service, 73 percent of Amazon.com's sales is repeat business.[72]

In making a number of acquisitions, managers at GE Capital, a large business unit of General Electric, have become skilled at integrating the new businesses into the firm's operating culture. In the process, they have developed a new management position, that of *integration manager*.[73] Core competencies, however, cannot be developed or exploited effectively without developing the capabilities of human capital.[74]

Developing Human Capital

Human capital refers to the knowledge and skills of a firm's entire workforce.

Human capital refers to the knowledge and skills of a firm's entire workforce. From the perspective of human capital, employees are viewed as a capital resource that requires investment. Much of the development of U.S. industry can be attributed to the effectiveness of its human capital. In support of this conclusion, it is noted that "as the dynamics of competition accelerate, people are perhaps the only truly sustainable source of competitive advantage."[75] This statement suggests that the role of human resource management should be increasing in importance.[76] In turn, the effective development and management of the firm's human capital—that is, of all of the firm's managerial and nonmanagerial personnel—may be the primary determinant of a firm's ability to formulate and implement strategies successfully.[77]

Finding the human capital necessary to run an organization effectively is a difficult problem that many firms attempt to solve by using temporary employees. Other firms try to improve their recruiting and selection techniques. Solving the problem, however, requires more than hiring temporary employees; it requires building effective commitment to organizational goals as well. Hiring star players is also insufficient; rather, a strategic leader needs to build an effective organizational team committed to achiev-

Amazon.com, founded by Jeff Bezos (shown here with a Pokémon doll), has a core competence that created synergies across its multiple product lines. Amazon.com's core competencies are in its customer knowledge base and customer service and they translate into a significant asset of 17 million customers.

ing the company's vision and goals, as the Strategic Focus indicates.

Actively participating in company-sponsored programs to develop one's abilities is highly desirable, because upgrading one's skills continuously leads to more job and economic security.[78] Increasingly, part of the development necessary for strategic leaders is international experience. As one business analyst noted, "With nearly every industry targeting fast-growing foreign markets, more companies are requiring foreign experience for top management positions."[79] Thus, companies committed to the importance of competing successfully in the global economy are wise to provide opportunities for their future strategic leaders to work in locations outside of their home nation. Also, because international management capabilities are becoming important, managing "inpatriation" (the process of transferring host-country or third-country national managers into the domestic market of multinational firms) has become an important means of building global core competencies.[80]

Effective training and development programs increase the probability that a manager will be a successful strategic leader. These programs have grown progressively important as knowledge has become more integral to gaining and sustaining a competitive advantage.[81] Additionally, such programs build knowledge and skills, inculcate a common set of core values, and offer a systematic view of the organization, thus promoting the firm's strategic vision and organizational cohesion. The programs also contribute to the development of core competencies.[82] Furthermore, they help strategic leaders improve skills that are critical to completing other tasks associated with effective strategic leadership (e.g., determining the firm's strategic direction, exploiting and maintaining the firm's core competencies, and developing an organizational culture that supports ethical practices). Thus, building human capital is vital to the effective execution of strategy.[83]

Strategic leaders must acquire the skills necessary to help develop human capital in their areas of responsibility. This is an important challenge, given that most strategic leaders need to enhance their human resource management abilities. For example, firms that place value on human resources and have effective reward plans for employees obtained higher returns on their initial public offerings.[84] When human capital investments are successful, the result is a workforce capable of learning continuously. Continuous learning and leveraging the firm's expanding knowledge base are linked with strategic success.[85] When asked to specify what accounts for Johnson & Johnson's competitive success, the firm's CEO answered that his company was "not in the product business, [but] in the knowledge business."[86]

Programs that achieve outstanding results in the training of future strategic leaders become a competitive advantage for a firm. As noted in the Opening Case, General Electric's system of training and development of future strategic leaders is comprehensive and thought to be among the best.[87] Accordingly, it may be a source of competitive advantage for the firm.

Competitive Advantage Powered by Human Capital

Consolidated Diesel's manufacturing plant does not look extraordinary. The equipment is the same as its competitors'. However, Consolidated produces exceptional results, powered by the firm's human capital, which is captured and released through its team-based system. To ensure the effective use of the company's human capital, employees are cross-trained on several jobs. Furthermore, employees are involved in developing solutions to problems. For example, with customer demand high, the plant had to add significant overtime and a third shift. However, after enlisting the aid of team leaders to help resolve the problem, Consolidated developed a more flexible scheduling system that cut the shifts back to eight hours, but the work continued to be completed. Similarly, MTW, an e-commerce applications firm, places high importance on its employees' needs. Like Consolidated Diesel, it uses teams. In addition, MTW attempts to create an environment in which people like to work. In so doing, the company has grown from a firm with 50 employees and $8 million in annual sales to one with 200 employees and $31 million in sales. In this environment, teams of employees make many of the operational decisions that affect the whole company. While decisions take longer in teams, the company gains the employees' confidence, trust, and commitment.

Warren Buffet is known as one of the world's most successful investors. One of the criteria he uses in investing in firms is their managerial talent and human capital. The firms in which he invests heavily, such as Coca-Cola, American Express, and Disney, are known to rely heavily on their human capital.

The importance of human capital also is shown in mergers and acquisitions, many of which are not successful (see Chapter 7). There are a number of reasons for these failures, a prime one of which is the loss, or failure to take advantage, of human capital from the acquired firm. Oftentimes, there is significant turnover in the acquired firm before and after the two firms are merged. Frequently, the most talented managers and employees leave because they have attractive opportunities and are uncertain whether they will have the same opportunities in the new company. Certainly, they are unlikely to have opportunities if their firm is acquired by Computer Associates, Charles Wang's company. Wang is notorious for firing many of the managers and technical talent of a firm he acquires immediately after the acquisition is consummated. Dennis Kozlowski, CEO of Tyco, analyzes the managerial talent of potential target firms in his quest for acquisitions. He targets only those firms with substantial managerial skills and capabilities. In fact, he considers his review of the human capital of a firm a part of the due-diligence process.

Among the substantial number of underutilized sources of human capital are underrepresented groups, such as women and minorities. We discussed women in managerial roles in the previous Strategic Focus. According to Luci Li, partner of Wang & Li Asia Associates, there is a glass ceiling for many expatriate Chinese and Chinese Americans as well. These workers have many technical and other skills and a host of capabilities that can be developed, but frequently are not. Some suggest that the new types of distance learning using Internet courses can help firms develop their human capital without significant costs. Clearly, the real-time environment of Internet instruction could revolutionize the means of developing human capital, particularly by promoting continuous learning within companies. In large and small firms, there are tremendous economic returns to human capital. In fact, human capital is critical to the implementation of various of a firm's strategies.

SOURCES: G. Gendron, 2000, Editors tackle the question, what makes a good start-up? *Wall Street Journal Interactive,* February 16, *www.interactive.wsj.com/archive*; J. Rosenfeld, 1999, MTW puts people first, *Fast Company Online,* December, *www.fastcompany.com*; C. Sittenfeld, 1999, Powered by the people, *Fast Company Online,* July–August, *www.fastcompany.com*; G. S. Becker, 1999, How the web is revolutionizing learning, *Business Week Online,* July 5, *www.businessweek.com*; J. Pfeffer & J. F. Veiga, 1999, Putting people first for organizational success, *Academy of Management Executive,* 13(2): 37–48; J. Reingold & P. Elstrom, 1999, Big headhunter is watching you, *Business Week Online,* March 1, *www.businessweek.com*; J. O'C. Hamilton, 1999, Have tech business, will travel, *Business Week Online,* February 8, *www.businessweek.com.*

A number of interesting changes are occurring in the corporate education market. Most training and development is conducted in-house, but firms are increasingly outsourcing this activity to private companies and to university outreach programs. Many of the firms have been pleased with the results.[88] Another trend is an increasing demand for on-line education programs. For example, GM has developed an on-line training program for its 175,000 employees at 7,500 dealerships. This program will save GM millions of dollars (e.g., in travel, housing, and food costs for the normal training programs at corporate headquarters). The program also saves time, as all employees can be reached in less than one week, whereas the normal training process required at least four months to include all of them.[89]

In the 1990s, millions of managers, strategic leaders, and nonmanagerial personnel lost jobs through restructuring and downsizing in many companies (see Chapter 7). These processes are continuing into 2000, with Unilever announcing that it will downsize by 25,000 employees—10 percent of its workforce—and close as many as 100 of its plants.[90] Unilever's stated goals are to increase its rate of growth and earn greater profits. The move should reduce the firm's costs and thus increase its profits over time. However, it is not clear how this action will increase the firm's growth, because, regardless of the cause, layoffs can result in a significant loss of knowledge that is possessed by a firm's human capital. Although it is also not uncommon for restructuring firms to reduce their expenditures on, or investments in, training and development programs, restructuring may be an important time to *increase* investments in these programs. Restructuring firms have less slack and cannot absorb as many errors; moreover, many employees may be placed into positions without all of the skills or knowledge necessary to perform the required tasks effectively.[91] In the final analysis, a view of employees as a resource to be maximized, rather than a cost to be minimized, facilitates the successful implementation of a firm's strategies. The implementation of such strategies also is more effective when strategic leaders approach layoffs in a manner that employees believe is fair and equitable.[92]

As described next, human capital is an important part of a firm's ability to develop and sustain an effective organizational culture.

Sustaining an Effective Organizational Culture

An **organizational culture** consists of a complex set of ideologies, symbols, and core values that is shared throughout the firm and influences the way it conducts business.

An **organizational culture** consists of a complex set of ideologies, symbols, and core values that is shared throughout the firm and influences the way it conducts business. Evidence suggests that a firm can develop core competencies both in terms of the capabilities it possesses and the way the capabilities are used to produce strategic actions. In other words, because it influences how the firm conducts its business and helps regulate and control employees' behavior, the organizational culture can be a source of competitive advantage.[93] Thus, shaping the context within which the firm formulates and implements its strategies—that is, shaping the organizational culture—is a central task of strategic leaders.[94]

James Halpin, former CEO at CompUSA, believed that CompUSA had an effective corporate culture. When asked to what he attributes his firm's substantial growth, he replied, "It's our culture. McKinsey & Company does consulting for us, and they say that they've never seen a culture like ours. Companies win or lose based on the culture they create. . . . We have a lot of fun but its highly disciplined. You can do almost anything in this company—except lie. . . . As long as you tell the truth, it's OK. And you don't have to see just your boss if you have a problem; you can see your boss' boss. An incredibly important thing is that, in our company, we all trust each other."[95] CompUSA also tries to instill an entrepreneurial orientation. The managers want people to take actions and not be afraid to make decisions. If there is a problem, CompUSA managers prefer that it be caused by something an employee did, rather than something she or he did not do.

Entrepreneurial Orientation

An organizational culture often encourages (or discourages) the pursuit of entrepreneurial opportunities, especially in large firms. IBM produces a handbook designed to infuse an entrepreneurial spirit into its culture. The handbook is called *Changing the World* and is filled with tips designed to break mental barriers and to enable employees to be more creative in their jobs. For example, one tip states, "Remember, if you don't exceed your authority at least once a week, you probably aren't doing your job." Another tip states, "Brainstorm with someone 10 years older and someone 10 years younger."[96]

Gerald Haman has developed a process to help firms build a stronger entrepreneurial orientation and creativity in their employees. He refers to it as the Thinkubator. According to Haman, the Thinkubator is designed to help people rediscover their gifts for creativity. At the Thinkubator, a person may be placed in a chair called the Symmetron that moves and reclines so that the person's back is parallel to the floor and the feet are in the air. Also, the person wears headgear referred to as the Orion Brain machine. It sounds silly, but Haman's clients include such firms as AT&T, BP Amoco, American Express, and Kraft Foods, among many others. Also, Haman claims that brainstorming sessions at the Thinkubator have produced over 260,000 ideas in 10 years. He suggests that most people experience "cubicle thinking," in which their production of ideas is directly proportional to the space in which they have to think. His goal is to open individuals' intellectual spaces.[97]

Successful outcomes derived through employees' pursuit of entrepreneurial opportunities are a major source of growth and innovation for firms.[98] These benefits are exemplified by the culture and activities at Oakley, Inc., manufacturer of sunglasses and sneakers. The company's culture combines "a passion for design with a lust for combat." The culture places a strong importance on being entrepreneurial, to challenge the norms. Oakley's sales flourished in the late 1990s, growing substantially. The company continues to introduce wild and different designs in its products—and it finds a market for them.[99]

Five dimensions characterize a firm's entrepreneurial orientation.[100] In combination, these dimensions influence the activities a firm uses in efforts to be innovative and launch new ventures. Discussed in Chapter 13, one of the key ways new ventures are launched in large firms is through corporate entrepreneurship. Particularly for firms seeking first-mover advantages (see Chapter 5), an entrepreneurial orientation among employees is critical.

Autonomy is the first of an entrepreneurial orientation's five dimensions. An active part of a firm's culture, autonomy allows employees to take actions that are free of stifling organizational constraints and permits individuals and groups to be self-directed. The second dimension, *innovativeness*, "reflects a firm's tendency to engage in and support new ideas, novelty, experimentation, and creative processes that may result in new products, services, or technological processes."[101] Cultures with a tendency toward innovativeness encourage employees to think beyond existing knowledge, technologies, and parameters in efforts to find creative ways to add value. *Risk taking* reflects a willingness by employees and their firm to accept risks in the pursuit of marketplace opportunities. These risks can include assuming significant levels of debt and allocating large amounts of other resources (e.g., people) to projects that may not be completed. Often, a firm accepts risks in order to seize marketplace opportunities that can substantially increase the firm's strategic competitiveness and its returns. The fourth dimension of an entrepreneurial orientation, *proactiveness*, describes a firm's ability to be a market leader rather than a follower. Proactive organizational cultures constantly use processes to anticipate future market needs and to satisfy them before competitors learn how to do so. Finally, *competitive aggressiveness* is a firm's propensity to take actions that allow it to outperform its rivals consistently and substantially. In summary, the key dimensions that characterize an entrepreneurial orientation are autonomy, a willingness to innovate and take risks, and a tendency to be aggressive toward competitors and proactive relative to marketplace opportunities.[102]

Martha Stewart Living Omnimedia's IPO in 1999 was a phenomenal success. While the IPO made Martha Stewart (shown at center) a billionaire, she continues to work toward the company's goal to teach a mass market to plan weddings and parties and to create the "perfect home."

Martha Stewart Living Omnimedia went public in 1999, and its initial public offering

(IPO) was a phenomenal success. The company mirrors many of the characteristics of an entrepreneurial orientation. While the IPO made Martha Stewart a billionaire, she continues to work toward the company's goal of building an organization that teaches a mass market the fine details of planning weddings and parties, along with a method of developing the "perfect home." The firm produces a monthly magazine, radio and television segments, and a newspaper column and markets merchandise for the home through Kmart, which is expected to sell more than $1 billion of Martha Stewart products in 2000.[103]

Changing the Organizational Culture and Business Reengineering

Changing a firm's organizational culture is more difficult than maintaining it, but effective strategic leaders recognize when change is needed. Incremental changes to the firm's culture typically are used to implement strategies.[104] However, more significant and, sometimes, even radical changes to a company's organizational culture are designed to support the selection of strategies that differ from the ones the firm has implemented historically. Regardless of the reasons for change, shaping and reinforcing a new culture requires effective communication and problem solving, along with the selection of the right people (those who have the values desired for the organization), effective performance appraisals (establishing goals and measuring individual performance toward goals that fit in with the new core values), and appropriate reward systems (rewarding the desired behaviors that reflect the new core values).[105]

Evidence suggests that cultural changes succeed only when they are supported actively by the firm's CEO, other key top management team members, and middle-level managers.[106] In fact, for large-scale changes, approximately one-third of middle-level managers need to be effective change agents possessing "a nice balance of capabilities: They are technically skilled people who are also very capable in personal relationships. They're an odd combination. On the one hand, they're tough decision-makers who are highly disciplined about performance results. But they also know how to get lots of people energized and aligned in the same direction."[107]

One catalyst for changing an organization's culture, particularly for critical changes, is the selection of new top management team members from outside the corporation. Dell Computer Corporation founder and CEO Michael Dell, who pioneered direct marketing of computers to customers, recruited executives from companies such as Motorola, Hewlett-Packard, and Apple Computer to deal with problems the firm encountered in late 1993 and early 1994.[108]

Transforming an organization and its culture is challenging. For example, in 1997, top executives at Sara Lee decided to change the firm from a capital-intensive manufacturer to a less asset-intensive brand manager. Thus, the company had to sell its manufacturing facilities, find excellent suppliers to replace products manufactured in-house, and change the firm's internal culture to focus on brand management. However, by 2000, Sara Lee had reduced its ratio of fixed assets to net working capital from 31 percent to 24 percent. Also, it had become an unwieldy conglomerate, unable to capture many synergies across product lines. Local managers are suspicious of managers in other product units or profit centers and thus will not cooperate with them to gain economies. The decentralized culture that developed at Sara Lee disallowed any centralization (e.g., of payroll or computer systems). Worse, the firm has not yet developed brand management as a core competence. Thus, the changes that accrued from the culture and strategy have not produced the end results desired; a different culture evolved than was intended.[109]

Alternatively, Continental Airlines successfully changed its culture, building a system of teamwork that has paid handsomely through increased returns. Gordon Bethune, Continental's CEO, describes the importance of the teamwork culture that he and his managers have created at the company. Bethune suggests that Continental is not composed of cross-functional teams. Rather, he compares Continental's operation to that of a watch: If one part fails, the whole watch quits working. He notes that the firm is composed of multiple functions that have value when they all work cooperatively. In this way, all functions are important. Thus, Continental managers made cooperation a part of everyone's job, and employees are rewarded for cooperating and working as a team. Continental also developed a means of rewarding specific behaviors that it desired. For example, it provided bonuses to all employees each month that the company met its deadline. Prior to Bethune, Continental had suffered through 10 CEOs and two bankruptcies.[110] Essentially, a company's reputation is linked to its culture and its strategy,[111] and in that regard, Continental's reputation has been vastly improved.

Emphasizing Ethical Practices

The effectiveness of processes that implement strategy increases when the processes are based on ethical practices. Ethical companies encourage and enable people at all organizational levels to exercise ethical judgment. Alternately, if unethical practices evolve in an organization, they become like a contagious disease.[112] To properly influence employees' judgment and behavior, ethical practices must shape the firm's decision-making process and be an integral part of an organization's culture. In fact, research has found that a value-based culture is the most effective means of ensuring that employees comply with the firm's ethical requirements.[113] As discussed in Chapter 10, in the absence of ethical requirements, *managerial opportunism* allows managers to take actions that are in their own best interests, but not in the firm's best interests. In other words, managers take advantage of their positions and therefore make decisions that benefit them to the detriment of the owners (shareholders).[114] Problems that have been documented include questionable hiring practices and a willingness to commit fraud by understating write-offs that reduce corporate returns.[115] Sometimes, very high CEO compensation is a sign of opportunism being pursued by those in top management (i.e., the court order to Charles Wang to return almost 50 percent of the $670 million compensation awarded him in 1999).[116]

Another set of studies sheds light on these issues. Research examining managers' ethical values and beliefs in the mid-1980s and again in the early 1990s showed little change. In both of those years, managers emphasized utilitarian goals—that is, the achievement of economic gains for the organization's stakeholders. In fact, the earlier survey found that one of the primary reasons managers emphasized ethical practices was to achieve greater profits. Some argue that the managerial and organizational gains are mutually beneficial. In other words, firms that establish and maintain ethical practices are more likely to achieve strategic competitiveness and earn above-average returns. A key reason for this relationship is that a reputation for ethical practices attracts loyal customers.[117]

On the other hand, other evidence suggests that at least some individuals from different groups—including top-level executives and business students—may be willing to commit either illegal actions (e.g., fraud) or actions that many think are unethical. In one study, researchers found that 47 percent of upper-level executives, 41 percent of controllers, and 76 percent of graduate-level business students expressed a willingness to commit fraud (as measured by a subject's willingness to misrepresent his or her company's financial statements). Moreover, these researchers discovered that 87 percent of the managers made at least one fraudulent decision in seven situations requiring a decision. Another of their findings is that the more an individual valued a comfortable life or pleasure, and the less he or she valued self-respect, the greater was the probability that a fraudulent decision would be made.[118]

Another study's results appear to have important implications for organizations and those who manage them.[119] The study found that, although cheating was observed, there was reluctance to report it. An unwillingness to report wrongdoing calls for the development of comprehensive organizational control systems to assure that individuals' behaviors are consistent with the firm's needs and expectations.

These studies' findings suggest the need for firms to employ ethical strategic leaders—leaders who include ethical practices as part of their long-term vision for the firm, who desire to do the right thing, and for whom honesty, trust, and integrity are important.[120] Strategic leaders who consistently display these qualities inspire employees as they work with others to develop and support an organizational culture in which ethical practices are the expected behavioral norms.

Unfortunately, not all people in positions of strategic leadership display the ethical approach described. The actions explained in the next Strategic Focus suggest the need for vigilance in guarding against unethical actions taken by those in key managerial positions within companies.

Strategic leaders are challenged to take actions which increase the probability that an ethical culture will prevail in their organization. One means of doing this that is gaining favor in companies is to institute a formal program to manage ethics in the organization. While such programs operate much like control systems, they help inculcate values throughout the organization as well.[121] Therefore, when these efforts are successful, the practices associated with an ethical culture become institutionalized in the firm; that is, they become the set of behavioral commitments and actions accepted by most of the firm's employees and other stakeholders with whom employees interact. Further actions that strategic leaders can take to develop an ethical organizational culture include (1) establishing and communicating specific goals to describe the firm's ethical standards (e.g., developing and disseminating a code of conduct), (2) continuously revising and updating the code of conduct, based on inputs from people throughout the firm and from other stakeholders (e.g., customers and suppliers), (3) disseminating the code of conduct to all stakeholders to inform them of the firm's ethical standards and practices, (4) developing and implementing methods and procedures to use in achieving the firm's ethical standards (e.g., using internal auditing practices that are consistent with the standards), (5) creating and using explicit reward

Lies, Managed Earnings, and Conflicts of Interest—the Ethics of Strategic Leaders

Fran Tarkenton, the former professional football star, settled a case brought by the U.S. Securities and Exchange Commission (SEC) claiming fraudulent inflation of his company's earnings. The SEC accused the company, KnowledgeWare, Inc., of increasing sales figures and profit growth through the reporting of $8 million in phony software sales. The results likely facilitated the sale of the company to Sterling Software, Inc. Essentially, the sales were recorded even though the customers were told that they were not obligated to pay for the software and it could be returned at any time. Tarkenton neither admitted nor denied any wrongdoing in the settlement, but paid the SEC a $100,000 fine and $54,187 of the bonus he received on the basis of the company's results.

Another case of "managed earnings" occurred at Sunbeam Corporation, where the problems involved Al Dunlap, a well-known and often controversial CEO. Dunlap had been successful in turning around the performance of several companies (although his methods had been criticized) prior to his role with Sunbeam. He took actions similar to those he took with previous firms, such as selling off assets and laying off employees, but was unable to reach the performance targets desired by Sunbeam investors. He attempted to sell the company, but could not find a buyer. So instead, he acquired three other firms in an effort to jump-start Sunbeam's performance. Partly because of a massive accrual of debt to finance the acquisitions (and because of the accompanying cost of the debt), Sunbeam's performance deteriorated even further. The company reported a net loss in the first quarter of 1998. However, close examination suggested that the books had been "cooked" in 1997 to create a false turnaround. Most believe that this was done to facilitate the sale of Sunbeam. Unfortunately for Dunlap, the firm did not sell, and he had to live with the consequences. The results for 1997 were restated, and it was discovered that Sunbeam actually incurred a loss of $6.4 million in that year. Sunbeam's board of directors fired Al Dunlap for his actions.

A similar incident occurred at Cendant Corporation, but it was discovered several months after an acquisition was completed. HFS Incorporated had acquired CUC International to form Cendant. A review of the accounts revealed that CUC executives had been overstating the firm's profits for approximately three years prior to the acquisition. The earnings had to be restated by $511 million less than previously reported. Upon the announcement of the restatement, Cendant's stock price fell from $41 to less than $10, and the company lost $29 billion in value. Later, stockholders settled with Cendant for the largest shareholder settlement in history to that point, $335 million.

In 2000, it was reported that the SEC accused PricewaterhouseCoopers of over 8,000 violations. The most serious of the allegations was having employees and officers owning stock in companies that were auditing clients of the firm. Five percent of the firm's employees, including 31 of 43 senior partners, were charged with violations. Five partners were asked to resign, and five managers and other staff were also dismissed.

Other examples involving ethical concerns include a price-fixing investigation at Sotheby's, an auctioneering company, and managers at British Nuclear Fuels (BNFL) who overlooked safety violations. Sotheby's stock price declined significantly after the investigation was announced, and the firm's top two officers resigned. BNFL fired managers whom it suspected of ignoring safety violations in order to meet the company's timetable for privatization. These actions of questionable ethics and their outcomes suggest that they are undertaken with considerable risk. The consequences may be great if the practices are uncovered.

SOURCES: M. A. Hitt, J. S. Harrison, & R. D. Ireland, 2001, *Creating Value Through Mergers and Acquisitions: A Complete Guide to Successful M&As,* New York: Oxford University Press; K. Brown & M. Jones, 2000, BNFL to cull managers in fall-out from safety scandal, *ft.com,* February 29, *www.ft.com*; J. Chaffin, 2000, Sotheby's shares slide amid scandal, *ft.com,* February 23, *www.ft.com*; A. Peers & D. Costello, 2000, Top executives quit Sotheby's amid price-fixing investigation, *Wall Street Journal Interactive,* February 23, *www.interactive.wsj.com/archive*; P. L. Moore, 2000, The PWC scandal changes everything, *Business Week Online,* February 28, *www.businessweek.com*; M. Schroeder & E. MacDonald, 1999, SEC enforcement actions target accounting fraud, *Wall Street Journal Interactive,* September 29, *www.interactive.wsj.com/articles.*

systems that recognize acts of courage (e.g., rewarding those who use proper channels and procedures to report observed wrongdoings), and (6) creating a work environment in which all people are treated with dignity.[122] The effectiveness of these actions increases when they are taken simultaneously, thereby making them mutually supportive. When managers and employees do not engage in such actions—perhaps because an ethical culture has not been created—problems are likely to occur. These problems are exemplified in the Strategic Focus on ethically questionable practices. Formal organizational controls may then be needed to prevent further problems.

Establishing Balanced Organizational Controls

Organizational controls have long been viewed as an important part of strategy implementation processes. Controls are necessary to help ensure that firms achieve their desired outcomes of strategic competitiveness and above-average returns.[123] Defined as the "formal, information-based . . . procedures used by managers to maintain or alter patterns in organizational activities," controls help strategic leaders build credibility, demonstrate the value of strategies to the firm's stakeholders, and promote and support strategic change.[124] Most critically, controls provide the parameters within which strategies are to be implemented, as well as corrective actions to be taken, when implementation-related adjustments are required. In this chapter, we focus on two organizational controls—strategic and financial—that were introduced in Chapter 11. Our discussion of organizational controls here emphasizes strategic and financial controls because strategic leaders are responsible for their development and effective use.

Evidence suggests that, although critical to the firm's success, organizational controls are imperfect. Consider the example of PricewaterhouseCoopers, in which many of the partners and employees owned stock in companies that the firm audited. This conflict of interest could provide incentives for taking an inappropriate action in audits. If, for example, an audit discovered a major impropriety in which the profits were overstated, revealing the problem could harm the firm's stock price. A clear example of this harm was evident with Cendant, described in the Strategic Focus. The problem at PricewaterhouseCoopers could be described as a *control failure*. Control failures such as this have a negative effect on the firm's reputation and divert managerial attention from actions that are necessary to use the strategic management process effectively.

As explained in Chapter 11, financial control is often emphasized in large corporations. Financial control focuses on short-term financial outcomes. In contrast, strategic control focuses on the *content* of strategic actions, rather than their *outcomes*. Some strategic actions can be correct, but poor financial outcomes may still result because of external conditions, such as a recession in the economy, unexpected domestic or foreign government actions, or natural disasters.[125] Therefore, an emphasis on financial control often produces more short-term and risk-averse managerial decisions, because financial outcomes may be due to events beyond managers' direct control. Alternatively, strategic control encourages lower-level managers to make decisions that incorporate moderate and acceptable levels of risk because outcomes are shared between the business-level executives making strategic proposals and the corporate-level executives evaluating them.

Successful strategic leaders balance strategic control and financial control (they do not *eliminate* financial control), with the intent of achieving more positive long-term returns.[126] In fact, most corporate restructuring is designed to refocus the firm on its core businesses, thereby allowing top executives to reestablish strategic control of their separate business units.[127] Thus, both types of controls are important. The former CEO of Lightbridge was credited with establishing better financial controls, thereby increasing the firm's financial performance.[128]

The effective use of strategic control by top executives frequently is integrated with appropriate autonomy for the various subunits so that they can gain a competitive advantage in their respective markets. Strategic control can be used to promote the sharing of both tangible and intangible resources among interdependent businesses within a firm's portfolio. In addition, the autonomy provided allows the flexibility necessary to take advantage of specific marketplace opportunities. As a result, strategic leadership promotes the simultaneous use of strategic control and autonomy.[129]

Diversified business firms often have trouble in balancing the two types of control. Because large diversified firms have not maintained this balance, many throughout the world are restructuring their operations. For instance, the currency crisis in Southeast Asia has revealed significant problems in the diversification strategies of large diversified firms in South Korea. Among the South Korean chaebols that had to restructure are Samsung, Daewoo, LG Group, Hyundai, and Sangyong.

Family-owned companies of expatriate Chinese run many of the business groups in Southeast Asia. Traditionally, these firms have been in consumer industries that are nontechnical, such as shipping; commodity trading; hotel, real estate, and financial services; and other light industries. As these firms sought to move into high-tech industries, such as chemicals and electronics, they have had to move away from the family-managed business concept to more professional managerial techniques. This adjustment was partly due to the change in capital markets, where more transparency is now required and where contracting law is becoming more prominent. Strategic leaders of those firms, mostly family members and friends, ran the business operations before the economic shocks occurred. They are now being forced to implement better and more professional control systems, as have other diversified business groups throughout the world.[130]

As our discussion in this chapter suggests, organizational controls establish an integrated set of analyses and actions that reinforce one another. Through the effective use of strategic controls, strategic leaders increase the probability that their firms will gain the benefits of carefully formulated strategies, but not at the expense of the financial control that is a critical part of the strategy implementation process. Effective organizational controls provide an underlying logic for strategic leadership, focus attention on critical strategic issues, support a competitive culture, and provide a forum that builds commitment to the firm's strategic intent.

Summary

- Effective strategic leadership is required to use the strategic management process successfully, including the strategic actions associated with the implementation of strategies. Strategic leadership entails the ability to anticipate events, envision possibilities, maintain flexibility, and empower others to create strategic change.
- Top executives are an important resource for firms to develop and exploit competitive advantages. In addition, these strategic leaders can be a source of competitive advantage.
- The top management team is composed of key managers who formulate and implement strategies. Generally, they are officers of the corporation or members of the board of directors.
- There is a relationship among the top management team's characteristics, a firm's strategy, and a firm's performance. For example, a top management team that has significant marketing and R&D knowledge often enhances the firm's effectiveness in the implementation of growth strategies. Overall, most top management teams are more effective when they have diverse skills.
- When boards of directors are involved in shaping firms' strategic direction, those firms generally improve their strategic competitiveness. Alternatively, boards may be less involved in decisions regarding strategy formulation and implementation when CEOs have more power. CEOs obtain power when they appoint people to the board and when they simultaneously serve as the CEO and board chair.
- Strategic leaders are selected from either the internal or the external managerial labor market. Because of their effect on firm performance, the selection of strategic leaders from these markets has implications for a firm's effectiveness. Valid reasons exist to use both labor markets when selecting strategic leaders and managers with the potential to become strategic leaders. In the majority of cases, the internal market is used to select the firm's CEO. Outsiders often are selected to initiate needed change.
- Effective strategic leadership has six components: determining the firm's strategic direction, exploiting and maintaining core competencies, developing human capital, sustaining an effective organizational culture, emphasizing ethical practices, and establishing balanced organizational controls.
- A firm must develop a long-term vision of its strategic intent. A charismatic leader can help realize that vision.
- Strategic leaders must ensure that their firm exploits its core competencies, which are used to produce and deliver products that create value for customers, through the implementation of strategies. In related diversified and large firms in particular, core competencies are exploited by sharing them across units and products.
- A critical element of strategic leadership and the effective implementation of strategy is the ability to develop a firm's human capital. Effective strategic leaders and firms view human capital as a resource to be maximized, rather than as a cost to be minimized. Resulting from this perspective is the development and use of programs intended to train current and future strategic leaders to build the skills needed to nurture the rest of the firm's human capital.
- Shaping the firm's culture is a central task of effective strategic leadership. An appropriate organizational culture encourages the development of an entrepreneurial orientation among employees and an ability to change the culture as necessary.

- In ethical organizations, employees are encouraged to exercise ethical judgment and to behave ethically at all times. Ethical practices can be promoted through several actions, including setting specific goals to describe the firm's ethical standards, using a code of conduct, rewarding ethical behaviors, and creating a work environment in which all people are treated with dignity.
- The final component of effective strategic leadership is the development and use of effective organizational controls. It is through such controls that strategic leaders provide the direction the firm requires to flexibly, yet appropriately, use its core competencies in the pursuit of marketplace opportunities. The best results are obtained when there is a balance between strategic and financial controls.

Review Questions

1. What is strategic leadership? In what ways are top executives considered important resources for an organization?
2. What is a top-management team, and how does it affect a firm's performance and its abilities to innovate and make appropriate strategic changes?
3. What are the differences between the internal and external managerial labor markets? What are the effects of each type of labor market on the formulation and implementation of firm strategy?
4. How does strategic leadership affect the determination of the firm's strategic direction?
5. Why is it important for strategic leaders to make certain that their firm exploits its core competencies in the pursuit of strategic competitiveness and above-average returns?
6. What is the importance of human capital and its development for strategic competitiveness?
7. What is organizational culture? What must strategic leaders do to develop and sustain an effective organizational culture?
8. As a strategic leader, what actions could you take to establish and emphasize ethical practices in your firm?
9. What are organizational controls? Why are strategic controls and financial controls an important part of the strategic management process?

Application Discussion Questions

1. Choose a CEO of a prominent firm you believe exemplifies the positive aspects of strategic leadership. What actions does this CEO take that demonstrate effective strategic leadership? What are the effects of those actions on the firm's performance?
2. Select a CEO of a prominent firm you believe does *not* exemplify the positive aspects of strategic leadership. What actions did this CEO take that are inconsistent with effective strategic leadership? How have those ineffective actions affected the firm's performance?
3. What are managerial resources? What is the relationship between managerial resources and a firm's strategic competitiveness?
4. Examine some articles in the popular press, and select an organization that recently went through a significant strategic change. Collect as much information as you can about the organization's top management team. Is there a relationship between the top management team's characteristics and the type of change the organization experienced? If so, what are the nature and outcome of that relationship?
5. Read some articles in the popular press and identify two new CEOs, one from the internal managerial labor market and one from the external labor market. Why do you think these individuals were chosen? What do they bring to the job, and what strategy do you think they will implement in their respective organizations?
6. Based on your reading of this chapter and accounts in the popular press, select a CEO you feel has exhibited vision. Has this CEO's vision been realized? If so, what have its effects been? If the vision has not been realized, why not?
7. Identify a firm in which you believe strategic leaders have emphasized and developed human capital. What do you believe are the effects of this emphasis and development on the firm's performance?
8. Select an organization you think has a unique organizational culture. What characteristics of that culture make it unique? Has the culture had a significant effect on the organization's performance? If so, what is that effect?
9. Why is the strategic control exercised by a firm's strategic leaders important for long-term competitiveness? How do strategic controls differ from financial controls?

Ethics Questions

1. As discussed in this chapter, effective strategic leadership occasionally requires managers to make difficult decisions. In your opinion, is it ethical for managers to make these types of decisions without obtaining feedback from employees about the effects of those decisions? Be prepared to justify your response.
2. As an employee with less than one year of experience in a firm, what actions would you pursue if you encountered unethical practices by a strategic leader?
3. Are firms ethically obligated to promote employees from within, rather than relying on the external labor market to select strategic leaders? What reasoning supports your position?
4. What ethical issues, if any, are involved with a firm's ability to develop and exploit a core competence in the manufacture of goods that may be harmful to consumers (e.g., cigarettes)?
5. As a strategic leader, would you feel ethically responsible for developing your firm's human capital? Why or why not? Do you believe that your position is consistent with the majority or minority of today's strategic leaders?
6. Select an organization, social group, or volunteer agency of which you are a member that you believe has an ethical culture. What factors caused this culture to be ethical? Are there any events that would cause the culture to become less ethical? If so, what are they?

Internet Exercise

As pointed out in a Strategic Focus in this chapter, women in the United States are advancing to top positions in some of America's leading firms. With a 48 percent increase since 1995 and a 10 to 12 percent representation overall in the top executive jobs, the advancement of women in this area sounds promising. Go to the Working Woman Web site at **http://www.workingwoman.com/25cos** to see which companies were rated as leaders in hiring women executives. What practices in these companies promote the selection of women for managerial roles?

***e-project:** Amazon.com has revolutionized the Internet shopping industry, a fact that can, in large part, be accredited to Jeff Bezos, America's number-one CEO of an Internet-based company. Learn about Bezos's background through the Amazon home page and other Web resources. What was his initial strategy in creating Amazon? Was he able to implement the strategy effectively? What successes spurred him to expand and diversify his Web-based business?

Notes

1. K. R. Thompson, W. A. Hochwarter, & N. J. Mathys, 1997, Stretch targets: What makes them effective? *Academy of Management Executive,* XI(3): 48–59.
2. R. D. Ireland & M. A. Hitt, 1999, Achieving and maintaining strategic competitiveness in the 21st century: The role of strategic leadership, *Academy of Management Executive,* 12(1), 43–57; D. Lei, M. A. Hitt, & R. Bettis, 1996, Dynamic core competencies through meta-learning and strategic context, *Journal of Management,* 22: 547–567.
3. D. Silverman, 2000, CEO brings new life to stagnant Compaq/Capellas moves firm back to profitability, *Houston Chronicle,* January 25, 1B.
4. Ireland and Hitt, Achieving and maintaining strategic competitiveness.
5. M. A. Hitt, B. W. Keats, & S. DeMarie, 1998, Navigating in the new competitive landscape: Building competitive advantage and strategic flexibility in the 21st century, *Academy of Management Executive,* XI(4), 22–42; J. B. Quinn, P. Anderson, & S. Finkelstein, 1996, Managing professional intellect: Making the most of the best, *Harvard Business Review,* 74(2): 71–80.
6. M. Loeb, 1994, Where leaders come from, *Fortune,* September 19, 241–242.
7. M. F. R. Kets de Vries, 1995, *Life and Death in the Executive Fast Lane* (San Francisco: Jossey-Bass).
8. T. Kono, 1999, A strong head office makes a strong company, *Long Range Planning,* 32: 225–246.
9. R. Nixon, M. A. Hitt, & J. E. D., Ricart I Costa, 1998, New managerial mindsets and strategic change in the new frontier, in M. A. Hitt, J. E. Ricart, and R. D. Nixon, (eds.), *New Managerial Mindsets* (New York: John Wiley & Sons).
10. G. Hamel & C. K. Prahalad, 1993, Strategy as stretch and leverage, *Harvard Business Review,* 71(2): 75–84.
11. R. Calori, G. Johnson, & P. Sarnin, 1994, CEOs' cognitive maps and the scope of the organization, *Strategic Management Journal,* 15: 437–457.
12. U. S. Daellenbach, A. M. McCarthy, & T. S. Schoenecker, 1999, Commitment to innovation: The impact of top management team characteristics, *R&D Management,* 29: 199–208.
13. M. Hammer & S. A. Stanton, 1997, The power of reflection, *Fortune,* November 24, 291–296.

14. S. Finkelstein & D. C. Hambrick, 1996, *Strategic Leadership: Top Executives and Their Effects on Organizations* (St. Paul, Minn.: West Publishing Company), 2.
15. E. Weldon & W. Vanyhonaker, 1999, Operating a foreign-invested enterprise in China: Challenges for managers and management researchers, *Journal of World Business,* 34: 94–107; J. A. Byrne & J. Reingold, 1997, Wanted: A few good CEOs, *Business Week,* August 11, 64–70.
16. H. P. Gunz & R. M. Jalland, 1996, Managerial careers and business strategy, *Academy of Management Review,* 21: 718–756.
17. C. M. Christensen, 1997, Making strategy: Learning by doing, *Harvard Business Review,* 75(6): 141–156; M. A. Hitt, B. W. Keats, H. E. Harback, & R. D. Nixon, 1994, Rightsizing: Building and maintaining strategic leadership and long-term competitiveness, *Organizational Dynamics,* 23: 18–32; R. L. Priem & D. A. Harrison, 1994, Exploring strategic judgment: Methods for testing the assumptions of prescriptive contingency theories, *Strategic Management Journal,* 15: 311–324.
18. M. J. Waller, G. P. Huber, & W. H. Glick, 1995, Functional background as a determinant of executives' selective perception, *Academy of Management Journal,* 38: 943–974; N. Rajagopalan, A. M. Rasheed, & D. K. Datta, 1993, Strategic decision processes: Critical review and future directions, *Journal of Management,* 19: 349–384.
19. Finkelstein & Hambrick, Strategic Leadership, 26–34; D. C. Hambrick & E. Abrahamson, 1995, Assessing managerial discretion across industries: A multimethod approach, *Academy of Management Journal,* 38: 1427–1441; D. C. Hambrick & S. Finkelstein, 1987, Managerial discretion: A bridge between polar views of organizational outcomes, in B. Staw & L. L. Cummings (eds.), *Research in Organizational Behavior* (Greenwich, CT: JAI Press), 369–406.
20. C. Sittenfeld, 2000, Leader on the edge, *Fast Company Online,* March 1, *www.fastcompany.com.*
21. R. C. Mayer, J. H. Davis, & F. D. Schoorman, 1995, An integrative model of organizational trust, *Academy of Management Review,* 20: 709–734.
22. D. A. Waldman & F. Yammarino, 1999, CEO charismatic leadership: Levels of management and levels of analysis effects, *Academy of Management Review,* 24: 266–285. N. Rajagopalan & D. K. Datta, 1996, CEO characteristics: Does industry matter? *Academy of Management Journal,* 39: 197–215.
23. P. LaBarre, 2000, The agenda—grassroots leadership, *Fast Company Online,* March 1, *www.fastcompany.com.*
24. Rooting out racism. 2000, *Business Week Online,* January 10, *www.businessweek.com/articles.*
25. P. Chattopadhyay, W. H. Glick, C. C. Miller, & G. P. Huber, 1999, Determinants of executive beliefs: Comparing functional conditioning and social influence, *Strategic Management Journal,* 20: 763–789.
26. M. A, Hitt, R. D. Nixon. P. G. Clifford, & K. P. Coyne, 1999, The development and use of strategic resources, in M. A. Hitt, P. G. Clifford, R. D. Nixon, and K. P. Coyne (eds.) *Dynamic Strategic Resources* (New York: John Wiley & Sons).
27. H. A. Krishnan, 1997, Diversification and top management team complementarity: Is performance improved by merging similar or dissimilar teams? *Strategic Management Journal,* 18: 361–374; J. G. Michel & D. C. Hambrick, 1992, Diversification posture and top management team characteristics, *Academy of Management Journal,* 35: 9–37.
28. A. L. Iaquito & J. W. Fredrickson, 1997, Top management team agreement about the strategic decision process: A test of some of its determinants and consequences, *Strategic Management Journal,* 18: 63–75; K. G. Smith, D. A. Smith, J. D. Olian, H. P. Sims, Jr., D. P. O'Bannon, & J. A. Scully, 1994, Top management team demography and process: The role of social integration and communication, *Administrative Science Quarterly,* 39: 412–438.
29. N. Athanassiou & D. Nigh, 1999, The impact of U.S. company internationalization on top management team advice networks: A tacit knowledge perspective, *Strategic Management Journal,* 20: 83–92.
30. D. Knight, C. L. Pearce, K. G. Smith, J. D. Olian, H. P. Sims, K. A. Smith, & P. Flood, 1999, Top management team diversity, group process, and strategic consensus, *Strategic Management Journal,* 20: 446–465.
31. D. C. Hambrick, T. S. Cho, & M. J. Chen, 1996, The influence of top management team heterogeneity on firms' competitive moves, *Administrative Science Quarterly,* 41: 659–684.
32. T. Simons, L. H. Pelled, & K. A. Smith, 1999, Making use of difference, diversity, debate, and decision comprehensiveness in top management teams, *Academy of Management Journal,* 42: 662–673.
33. Finkelstein & Hambrick, *Strategic Leadership,* 148.
34. C. C. Miller, L. M. Burke, & W. H. Glick, 1998, Cognitive diversity among upper-echelon executives: Implications for strategic decision processes, *Strategic Management Journal,* 19: 39–58.
35. Ibid.
36. D. K. Datta & J. P. Guthrie, 1994, Executive succession: Organizational antecedents of CEO characteristics, *Strategic Management Journal,* 15: 569–577; M. A. Hitt & R. D. Ireland, 1986, Relationships among corporate-level distinctive competencies, diversification strategy, corporate structure, and performance, *Journal of Management Studies,* 23: 401–416; M. A. Hitt & R. D. Ireland, 1985, Corporate distinctive competence, strategy, industry, and performance, *Strategic Management Journal,* 6: 273–293.
37. W. Boeker, 1997, Strategic change: The influence of managerial characteristics and organizational growth, *Academy of Management Journal,* 40: 152–170; W. Boeker, 1997, Executive migration and strategic change: The effect of top manager movement on product-market entry, *Administrative Science Quarterly,* 42: 213–236.
38. A. Tomie, 2000, Fast Pack 2000, *Fast Company Online,* March 1, *www.fastcompany.com.*
39. M. E. Wiersema & K. Bantel, 1992, Top management team demography and corporate strategic change, *Academy of Management Journal,* 35: 91–121; K. Bantel & S. Jackson, 1989, Top management and innovations in banking: Does the composition of the top team make a difference? *Strategic Management Journal,* 10: 107–124.
40. P. Beckett, 1999, Diebod expected to name O'Dell as its new president and CEO, *Wall Street Journal Interactive,* October 26, *www.interactive.wsj.com/articles.*
41. W. Q. Judge, Jr. & C. P. Zeithaml, 1992, Institutional and strategic choice perspectives on board involvement in the strategic decision process, *Academy of Management Journal,* 35: 766–794; J. A. Pearce II & S. A. Zahra, 1991, The relative power of CEOs and boards of directors: Associations with corporate performance, *Strategic Management Journal,* 12: 135–154.
42. J. D. Westphal & E. J. Zajac, 1995, Who shall govern? CEO/board power, demographic similarity, and new director selection, *Administrative Science Quarterly,* 40: 60.
43. J. D. Westphal, 1999, Collaboration in the boardroom: Behavioral and performance consequences of CEO-board social ties, *Academy of Management Journal,* 42: 7–24.
44. Ibid., 66; E. J. Zajac & J. D. Westphal, 1995, Accounting for the explanations of CEO compensation: Substance and symbolism, *Administrative Science Quarterly,* 40: 283–308.
45. B. K. Boyd, 1995, CEO duality and firm performance: A contingency model, *Strategic Management Journal,* 16: 301.
46. J. Muller, K. Kerwin, & J. Ewing, 1999, DaimlerChrysler's Schrempp: Man with a plan, *Business Week Online,* October 4, *www.businessweek.com.*
47. C. M. Daily & D. R. Dalton, 1995, CEO and director turnover in failing firms: An illusion of change? *Strategic Management Journal,* 16: 393–400.

48. R. Albanese, M. T. Dacin, & I. C. Harris, 1997, Agents as stewards, *Academy of Management Review,* 22: 609–611; J. H. Davis, F. D. Schoorman, & L. Donaldson, 1997, Toward a stewardship theory of management, *Academy of Management Review,* 22: 20–47.
49. J. D. Westphal & E. J. Zajac, 1997, Defections from the inner circle: Social exchange, reciprocity and diffusion of board independence in U.S. corporations, *Administrative Science Quarterly,* 161–183; A. K. Buchholtz & B. A. Ribbens, 1994, Role of chief executive officers in takeover resistance: Effects of CEO incentives and individual characteristics, *Academy of Management Journal,* 37: 554–579.
50. Rajagopalan & Datta, CEO characteristics, 201.
51. R. A. Johnson, R. E. Hoskisson, & M. A. Hitt, 1993, Board involvement in restructuring: The effect of board versus managerial controls and characteristics, *Strategic Management Journal,* 14(Special Summer Issue): 33–50.
52. B. K. Boyd, 1995, CEO duality and firm performance: A contingency model, *Strategic Management Journal,* 16: 301–312.
53. T. A. Stewart, 1998, Why leadership matters, *Fortune,* March 2, 71–82.
54. M. Murray, 1999, At General Electric, two insiders vie for Jack Welch's CEO title, *Wall Street Journal Interactive,* September 9, *www.interactive.wsj.com/articles.*
55. J. G. Auerbach, 1999, Likely heir to Gerstner is tapped to run IBM's computer-server unit, *Wall Street Journal Interactive,* September 21, *www.interactive.wsj.com/articles.*
56. W. C. Byham, 1999, Grooming leaders, *Executive Excellence,* 16: 18.
57. Datta & Guthrie, Executive succession, 570.
58. Finkelstein & Hambrick, *Strategic Leadership,* 180–181.
59. D. Miller, 1991, Stale in the saddle: CEO tenure and the match between organization and environment, *Management Science,* 37: 34–52.
60. P. Burrows & P. Elstrom, 1999, The boss, *Business Week,* August 2, 76–84.
61. J. E. Ettlie, 1996, *Review of the Perpetual Enterprise Machine: Seven Keys to Corporate Renewal through Successful Product and Process Development,* in E. Bowman (ed.), (New York: Oxford University Press), appearing in *Academy of Management Review,* 21: 294–298; Hitt et al., Rightsizing, 20.
62. J. C. Collins & J. I. Porras, 1996, Building your company's vision, *Harvard Business Review,* 74(5): 65–77.
63. C. M. Falbe, M. P. Kriger, & P. Miesing, 1995, Structure and meaning of organizational vision, *Academy of Management Journal,* 39: 740–769.
64. Qualcomm's wizard, 2000, *Businessweek Online,* January 10, *www.businessweek.com.*
65. Pokemon patriarch, 2000, *Businessweek Online,* January 10, *www.businessweek.com.*
66. W. L. Gardner & B. J. Avolio, 1998, The charismatic relationship: A dramaturgical perspective, *Academy of Management Review,* 23: 32–58.
67. Finkelstein & Hambrick, 1996, *Strategic Leadership,* 69–72; P. Sellers, 1996, What exactly is charisma? *Fortune,* January 15, 68–75.
68. T. Smart, 1996, Jack Welch's encore, *Business Week,* October 28, 154–160.
69. Voracious at Vodaphone, 2000, *Businessweek Online,* January 10, *www.businessweek.com.*
70. R. M. Hodgetts, 1999, Dow Chemical's CEO William Stavropoulos on structure and decision making, *Academy of Management Executive,* 13(4): 29–35.
71. P. R. Nayyar & K. A. Bantel, 1994, Competitive agility: A source of competitive advantage based on speed and variety, in P. Shrivastava, A. Huff & J. Dutton (eds.), *Advances in Strategic Management,* 10A, (Greenwich, CT: JAI Press), 193–222.
72. R. D. Hof, H. Green, & D. Brady, 2000, Suddenly, Amazon's books look better, *Business Week,* February 21, 78–84.
73. R. N. Askenas, L. J. DeMonaco, & S. C. Francis, 1998, Making the deal real: How GE Capital integrates acquisitions, *Harvard Business Review,* 76(1): 165–178.
74. C. A. Lengnick-Hall & J. A. Wolff, 1999, Similarities and contradictions in the core logic of three strategy research streams, *Strategic Management Journal,* 20: 1109–1132.
75. S. A. Snell & M. A. Youndt, 1995, Human resource management and firm performance: Testing a contingency model of executive controls, *Journal of Management,* 21: 711–737.
76. D. Ulrich, 1998, A new mandate for human resources, *Harvard Business Review,* 76(1): 124–134.
77. Snell & Youndt, Human resource, 711; K. Chilton, 1994, *The Global Challenge of American Manufacturers* (St. Louis, MO: Washington University, Center for the Study of American Business); J. Pfeffer, 1994, *Competitive Advantage through People* (Cambridge, MA: Harvard Business School Press), 4.
78. H. W. Jenkins, Jr., 1996, What price job security? *Wall Street Journal,* March 26, AI9.
79. J. S. Lublin, 1996, An overseas stint can be a ticket to the top, *Wall Street Journal,* January 29, BI, B2.
80. M. G. Harvey & M. R. Buckley, 1997, Managing inpatriates: Building a global core competency, *Journal of World Business,* 32(1): 35–52.
81. D. M. DeCarolis & D. L. Deeds, 1999, The impact of stocks and flows of organizational knowledge on firm performance: An empirical investigation of the biotechnology industry, *Strategic Management Journal,* 20: 953–968.
82. J. Sandberg, 2000, Understanding human competence at work: An interpretative approach, *Academy of Management Journal,* 43: 9–25.
83. J. Lee & D. Miller, 1999, People matter: Commitment to employees, strategy and performance in Korean firms, *Strategic Management Journal,* 20: 579–593.
84. T. M. Welbourne & L. A. Cyr, 1999, The human resource executive effect in initial public offering firms, *Academy of Management Journal,* 42: 616–629.; J. Pfeffer & J. F. Veiga, 1999, Putting people first for organizational success, *Academy of Management Executive,* 13(2): 37–48.
85. DeCarolis & Deeds, The impact of stocks and flows of organizational knowledge.
86. H. Rudnitsky, 1996, One hundred sixty companies for the price of one, *Forbes,* February 26, 56–62.
87. Live Wire Welch, 2000, *Business Week,* January 10, 71; L. Grant, 1995, GE: The envelope, please, *Fortune,* June 26, 89–90.
88. W. C. Symonds, 2000, Education, *Business Week,* January 10, 138–140.
89. Log on for company training, 2000, *Business Week,* January 10, 140.
90. J. Bains, 2000, Unilever overhaul includes 25,000 job cuts, *ft.com,* February 22, *www.ft.com.*
91. M. A. Hitt, R. E. Hoskisson, J. S. Harrison, & B. Summers, 1994, Human capital and strategic competitiveness in the 1990s, *Journal of Management Development,* 13(1): 35–46; C. R. Greer & T. C. Ireland, 1992, Organizational and financial correlates of a contrarian human resource investment strategy, *Academy of Management Journal,* 35: 956–984.
92. C. L. Martin, C. K. Parsons, & N. Bennett, 1995, The influence of employee involvement program membership during downsizing: Attitudes toward the employer and the union, *Journal of Management,* 21: 879–890.
93. C. M. Fiol, 1991, Managing culture as a competitive resource: An identity-based view of sustainable competitive advantage, *Journal of Management,* 17: 191–211; J. B. Barney, 1986, Organizational culture: Can it be a source of sustained competitive advantage? *Academy of Management Review,* 11: 656–665.
94. S. Ghoshal & C. A. Bartlett, 1994, Linking organizational context and managerial action: The dimensions of quality of management, *Strategic Management Journal,* 15: 91–112.

95. S. M. Puffer, 1999, CompUSA's CEO James Halpin on technology, rewards, and commitment, *Academy of Management Executive,* 13(2): 29–36.
96. L. Zack, 1999, How IBM gets unstuck, *Fast Company Online,* October, *www.fastcompany.com.*
97. C. Sittenfeld, 1999, What's the big idea? *Fast Company Online,* April, *www.fastcompany.com.*
98. C. A. Bartlett & S. Ghoshal, 1997, The myth of the generic manager: New personal competencies for new managerial roles, *California Management Review,* 40(1): 92–116.
99. P. Roberts, 1999, The empire strikes back, *Fast Company Online,* February, *www.fastcompany.com.*
100. G. T. Lumpkin & G. G. Dess, 1996, Clarifying the entrepreneurial orientation construct and linking it to performance, *Academy of Management Review,* 21: 135–172.
101. Ibid., 142.
102. Ibid., 137.
103. Martha's World, 2000, *Business Week Online,* January 10, *www.businessweek.com.*
104. FT.com, 1999, Gradual process: One that cannot be pushed, October 28, *www.ft.com.*
105. Ireland & Hitt, Achieving and maintaining strategic competitiveness.
106. J. E. Dutton, S. J. Ashford, R. M. O'Neill, E. Hayes, & E. E. Wierba, 1997, Reading the wind: How middle managers assess the context for selling issues to top managers, *Strategic Management Journal,* 18: 407–425.
107. S. Sherman, 1995, Wanted: Company change agents, *Fortune,* December 11, 197–198.
108. A. E. Serwer, 1997, Michael Dell turns the PC world inside out, *Fortune,* September 8, 76–86.
109. Branded goods 2-Fashion victim, 2000, *Economist Online,* February 26, *www.economist.com.*
110. S. M. Puffer, 1999, Continental Airlines' CEO Gordon Bethune on teams and new product development, *Academy of Management Executive,* 13(3): 28–35.
111. E. R. Gray & J. M. Balmer, 1998, Managing corporate image and corporate reputation, *Long Range Planning,* 31: 695–702.
112. D. J. Brass, K. D. Butterfield, & B. C. Skaggs, 1998, Relationships and unethical behavior: A social network perspective, *Academy of Management Review,* 23: 14–31.
113. L. K. Trevino, G. R. Weaver, D. G. Toffler, & B. Ley, 1999, Managing ethics and legal compliance: What works and what hurts, *California Management Review,* 41(2): 131–151.
114. C. W. L. Hill, 1990, Cooperation, opportunism, and the invisible hand: Implications for transaction cost theory, *Academy of Management Review,* 15: 500–513.
115. D. Blalock, 1996, Study shows many execs are quick to write off ethics, *Wall Street Journal,* March 26, CI, C3; A. P. Brief, J. M. Dukerich, P. R. Brown, & J. F. Brett, 1996, What's wrong with the Treadway Commission Report? Experimental analysis of the effects of personal values and codes of conduct on fraudulent financial reporting, *Journal of Business Ethics,* 15: 183–198; G. Miles, 1993, In search of ethical profits: Insights from strategic management, *Journal of Business Ethics,* 12: 219–225.
116. Zajac & Westphal, Accounting for the explanations of CEO compensation.
117. S. R. Premeaux & R. W. Mondy, 1993, Linking management behavior to ethical philosophy, *Journal of Business Ethics,* 12: 219–225.
118. Brief et al., What's wrong?
119. B. K. Burton & J. P. Near, 1995, Estimating the incidence of wrongdoing and whistle blowing: Results of a study using randomized response technique, *Journal of Business Ethics,* 14: 17–30.
120. J. Milton-Smith, 1995, Ethics as excellence: A strategic management perspective, *Journal of Business Ethics,* 14: 683–693.
121. G. R. Weaver, L. K. Trevino, & P. L. Cochran, 1999, Corporate ethics programs as control systems: Influences of executive commitment and environmental factors, *Academy of Management Journal,* 42: 41–57.
122. Brief et al., What's wrong? 194; P. E. Murphy, 1995, Corporate ethics statements: Current status and future prospects, *Journal of Business Ethics,* 14: 727–740.
123. L. J. Kirsch, 1996, The management of complex tasks in organizations: Controlling the systems development process, *Organization Science,* 7: 1–21.
124. R. Simons, 1994, How new top managers use control systems as levers of strategic renewal, *Strategic Management Journal,* 15: 170–171.
125. K. J. Laverty, 1996, Economic "short-termism": The debate, the unresolved issues, and the implications for management practice and research, *Academy of Management Review,* 21: 825–860.
126. M. A. Hitt, R. E. Hoskisson, & R. D. Ireland, 1990, Mergers and acquisitions and managerial commitment to innovation in M-form firms, *Strategic Management Journal,* 11(Special Summer Issue): 29–47.
127. R. A. Johnson, 1996, Antecedents and outcomes of corporate refocusing, *Journal of Management,* 22: 437–481; R. E. Hoskisson & M. A. Hitt, 1994, *Downscoping: How to Tame the Diversified Firm* (New York: Oxford University Press).
128. T. Corcoran, 2000, Lightbridge shares tumble after financial chief resigns, *Wall Street Journal Interactive,* February 18, *www.interactive.wsj.com/articles.*
129. Ireland & Hitt, Achieving and maintaining strategic competitiveness.
130. M. Weidenbaum, 1996, The Chinese family business enterprise, *California Management Review,* 38(4): 141–156.

CORPORATE ENTREPRENEURSHIP AND INNOVATION

CHAPTER THIRTEEN OBJECTIVES

After reading this chapter, you should be able to:

1. Define and describe the importance of innovation, entrepreneurship, corporate entrepreneurship, and entrepreneurs.
2. Discuss the three stages of the innovation process.
3. Discuss the two forms of internal corporate venturing: autonomous strategic behavior and induced strategic behavior.
4. Discuss how the capability to manage cross-functional teams facilitates the implementation of internal corporate ventures.
5. Explain how strategic alliances are used to produce innovation.
6. Discuss how a firm creates value by acquiring another company to gain access to that company's innovations or innovative capabilities.
7. Explain how large firms use venture capital to increase the effectiveness of their innovation efforts.
8. Describe the resources, capabilities, and core competencies of small versus large firms in producing and managing innovation.

Innovation, Competition, and Competitive Success in the Global Automobile Industry

Innovation drives competitive success in many companies, including global automobile manufacturers. However, when thinking about innovations, we typically recall product innovations. But organizations can be innovative in other ways, such as with their organizational structure. For example, as discussed in Chapter 11, the multidivisional organizational structure that was developed by Alfred Sloan during his tenure as General Motors' CEO was an innovative response to coordination and control problems. These difficulties surfaced during the 1920s in a number of large firms (e.g., DuPont and GM) that were using the functional structure. For many years, most of the world's dominant automobile firms, including General Motors, Ford Motor Company, and Chrysler Corporation, among others, used the multidivisional structure as an innovative way of coordinating and controlling their diversified operations.

In part, the merger or acquisition between Daimler-Benz and Chrysler Corporation (see Chapter 7) was an innovative structural response to the need to create economies of scope to compete successfully in global automobile markets. Another objective of that transaction was to integrate the R&D functions of the formerly independent Daimler-Benz and Chrysler Corporation to enhance the quality and innovativeness of each product the combined firm produces. Innovation is especially critical to DaimlerChrysler's minivan. Developed initially by Chrysler, the minivan has a large profit margin that plays a key role in DaimlerChrysler's attempts to earn above-average returns.

Innovations are viewed as the pathway to reverse a decline in DaimlerChrysler's share of the U.S. minivan market, from 40.3 percent in 1998 to 36 percent in 1999. Analysts note that DaimlerChrysler's 2001 model "will up the ante in the minivan-gadget game, adding features such as a power-lift tailgate, an electrified console that can power a cellular phone and can be moved between the front and middle seats, and side doors that aren't merely powered, but are equipped with sensors that stop the doors in their tracks if they detect that an object—say, a child's head—is in the way." By contrast, minivan competitors Honda Motor Company, General Motors, and Mazda Motor Co. believe that these innovations are relatively risk free and fail to provide customers with functions or capabilities that create significant value. Incremental innovations, such as those planned for Chrysler's 2001 minivan, are less risky, but also have a lower probability of contributing substantially to a firm's strategic competitiveness.

Historically, General Motors' Cadillac is a product line in which new technologies have been used as a source of innovation. Night Vision is a recent example of an innovation that is a $2,000 option on the Cadillac DeVille DTS. Night Vision is based on thermal-imaging technology. Developed initially by Raytheon Systems for the U.S. military, this technology was adapted for GM after being declassified in 1993. Through the use of 76,800 infrared detectors mounted in a camera on the middle of the DTS's grille, the nighttime driving conditions are improved—and for a good reason, according to analysts: "You're three times as likely to die driving at night—and this is one case where the usual rule that younger drivers are more dangerous does not hold. A 40-year-old needs ten times as much light to see a given object as a 20-year old." Other innovations in the auto industry that are expected to facilitate nighttime vision include infrared beams, ultrasonic pulses, xenon gas-filled headlights that emit a purplish hue, and headlights that emit ultraviolet rays.

Innovative trucks, such as Chevrolet's Avalanche, are also being introduced to consumers. "Part pickup truck and part sport-utility vehicle, the Avalanche is a 'crossover' that combines the interior roominess of a full-size SUV with the convenience of a small pickup in the back." The Avalanche competes with Ford's SuperCrew. Both products are built on a pickup-truck chassis with bodies stretched to accommodate four doors and an upscale sport-utility-type interior.

Hybrid vehicles are an example of a radical, rather than an incremental, product innovation. Unlike Chrysler's minivan, Cadillac's Night Vision product, and the Avalanche and SuperCrew, Ford Motor Company's TH!NK, a new brand for cars and bicycles, uses clean-battery and fuel-cell propulsion technology. Norwegian made, the TH!NK City car was to become available to consumers during 2001's fourth quarter, through Ford Electric-vehicle dealerships in California and New York. Already being sold in Norway, the City is a battery-powered electric two-seater that has a top speed of 90 kilometers (roughly 56 miles) per hour and a maximum cruising range of 85 kilometers. Among other TH!NK products, two electric-powered bicycles, retailing for $1,000 to $1,200, were introduced in June 2000. These products are sold directly to consumers through TH!NK Mobility, an Internet-based electronic-commerce system, as well as through Ford dealers.

http://www.chevrolet.com

http://www.daimler chrylser.com

http://www.dupont.com

http://www.ford.com

http://www.ge.com

http://www.gm.com

http://www.honda.com

http://www.mazda.com

As these examples suggest, innovation is a vital dimension on which global auto companies compete. Innovation is also critical to start-up ventures in the industry, such as the one trying to reintroduce the once-mighty Packard. The prototype for the new Packard is all aluminum in its construction, with a 440-horsepower engine that propels the 3,740-pound car from zero to 60 miles per hour in 4.8 seconds. The following opinion from a business writer suggests a link between innovation and strategic competitiveness in the global auto industry: "The numbers don't lie. Detroit's single greatest failure has been its unwillingness to innovate. It is less risky to simply develop a new version of an existing product than to pioneer a new category. Despite what you may read and hear about new Detroit iron over the next few months, the imports are poised to lengthen their lead in innovation." Thus, for firms in this industry, resources must be devoted to develop and support innovation and the skills that make it possible.

SOURCES: J. Ball, 2000, DaimlerChrysler fights to retain minivan dominance, *Wall Street Journal,* January 11, B4; T. Box, 2000, A new breed, *Dallas Morning News,* January 11, D1, D4; S. Freeman, 2000, Ford introduces TH!NK brand for cars, bikes, *Wall Street Journal,* January 11, A10; M. Murphy, 2000, Boogies lights, *Forbes,* February 7, 208; M. Murphy, 2000, The Packard is back, *Forbes,* February 7, 108–110; T. Powers, 2000, Auto company merger good idea, *Newswire,* March 13, *www.newswise.com*; A. Taylor, III, 2000, Detroit: Every silver lining has a cloud, *Fortune,* 92–93.

The Opening Case suggests that innovation is related to a firm's strategic competitiveness and ability to earn above-average returns. In many industries, including the world's automobile industry, conditions of the global economy make it increasingly easy to commoditize products. Overcapacity, multiple competitors, intense competitive rivalries, rapidly changing technologies and market conditions, and the ability to standardize production methods in manufacturing firms and delivery mechanisms in service businesses are examples of these conditions.[1] Innovations are critical to companies' efforts to differentiate their goods or services from competitors in ways that create additional or new value for customers.[2] Thus, as a corporate capability, innovation can be a vital source of competitive advantage as firms seek to compete in the arenas created by the global economy's characteristics.[3] For example, the automobile company that is able to use innovation as the foundation to manufacture fuel-efficient, environmentally friendly products may be able to establish a competitive advantage over its rivals in the 21st century's first few years.

As our discussion in this chapter suggests, and as is indicated in Figure 1.1, producing and managing innovation is a capability that is vital to a firm's efforts to successfully implement its strategies. For example, this is the case in terms of two business-level strategies, as product innovations are linked with the successful use of the product differentiation strategy, while process innovations are linked to the effective use of the cost leadership strategy. In addition to the role they play in strategy implementation, innovations developed by a firm in the course of using its strategies may affect its choice of future strategies. This possibility is shown by the feedback loop in Figure 1.1. Moreover, as suggested by the events described in the Opening Case, innovation has a strong effect on an industry's competitive dynamics.[4]

To describe how firms produce and manage innovation, we examine several topics in this chapter. To set the stage, we speak about innovation in general; then we define terms that are central to the chapter: innovation, entrepreneurship, corporate entrepreneurship, and entrepreneurs. In defining these terms, we examine their importance and link to a firm's strategic competitiveness. Next, we discuss international entrepreneurship, a phenomenon reflecting the increased use of entrepreneurship in countries throughout the world. Internally, firms innovate through either autonomous or induced strategic behavior. After our descriptions of these internal corporate venturing activities, we discuss actions firms take to implement the innovations resulting from those two types of strategic behavior. In addition to innovating through internal activities, firms can gain access to other companies' innovations or innovative capabilities through strategic alliances and acquisitions. Following our discussion of these topics is a description of entrepreneurship in start-up ventures and smaller firms. This section closes both the chapter and our analysis of actions firms take to successfully implement strategies.

Innovation, Entrepreneurship, Corporate Entrepreneurship, and Entrepreneurs

Peter Drucker argues that "innovation is the specific function of entrepreneurship, whether in an existing business, a public service institution, or a new venture started by a lone individual in the family kitchen." Moreover, Drucker suggests that innovation is "the means by which the entrepreneur either creates new wealth-producing resources or endows existing resources with enhanced potential for creating wealth."[5] Thus, entrepreneurship and the innovation resulting from it are important for large and small firms, as well as start-up ventures, as they compete in the 21st-century competitive landscape. In the words of several researchers, "Entrepreneurship and innovation are central to the creative process in the economy and to promoting growth, increasing productivity and creating jobs."[6]

Innovation is as vital to the development of competitive advantages in the service sector as it is in the manufacturing sector. Data processing, health care, transportation, financial planning, and telecommunications are examples of service areas that are growing in size and in which firms are able to develop competitive advantages through innovation.[7] Telecommunications giant, Deutsche Telekom, suggests that innovation is the firm's competitive advantage: "Innovation—we use it to our advantage. Today, our innovation pipeline is full. From 50-megabit transfers in the telephone network, to applications for the intelligent home, to our pioneering work in wireless/Internet integration, innovation is at the heart of our competitive strategy."[8]

Although certainly important today, innovation has long been recognized as vital to competitive success. For example, Henry Ford, founder of Ford Motor Company, observed that "Competition whose motive is merely to compete, to drive some other fellow out, never carries very far. The competitor to be feared is one who never bothers about you at all, but goes on making his own business better all the time. Businesses that grow by development and improvement do not die. But when a business ceases to be creative, when it believes it has reached perfection and needs to do nothing but produce—no improvement, no development—it is done."[9]

Partly because it is intended to disrupt the status quo, entrepreneurship is not risk free.[10] However, the characteristics of the 21st-century competitive landscape (see Chapters 1 and 2) generate significant risks that firms cannot avoid while competing in the global economy. In fact, not seeking to innovate through entrepreneurship may be riskier than are actions taken to match a firm's capabilities and core competencies with its external environmental opportunities in order to innovate. In one sense, decisions some auto manufacturers make about the Formula One racing season demonstrate the risk of innovating and competing on the basis of that innovation with the risks of not innovating. According to companies involved with Formula One racing, developing a losing car can actually damage a brand. To avoid this outcome, companies sometimes spend "a fortune trying to give their entries a technological edge." In describing this matter, the head of Ford's Premier Auto Group states, "This sport is about perfection. Formula One is the No. 1 communication tool if you have the right brand. But it can backfire if you show that you tried to do something and failed."[11]

Thus, in the rapidly changing global economy, firms simultaneously encounter risk and opportunity in terms of innovation. The Internet is an instructive example of these twin conditions. Dell Computer Corp.'s chairman Michael Dell suggests that, for almost all firms, the Internet will be their business. Describing the risk the Internet creates for many businesses, Dell observes that "If your business isn't enabled by information, if your business isn't enabled by customers and suppliers having more information and being able to use it, you're probably already in trouble." Moreover,

According to Michael Dell, "The Internet is like a weapon sitting on a table ready to be picked up by either you or your competitors." For a firm that is committed to innovation, the Internet is an incredible source of opportunity and competitive advantage.

Dell believes that "the Internet is like a weapon sitting on a table ready to be picked up by either you or your competitors."[12] However, for the agile and responsive firm that is committed to innovation and the change that it brings, the Internet is an incredible source of opportunity and competitive advantage. In this book's first 12 chapters, we have offered numerous examples of firms that are innovating through the Internet's capabilities and moving toward competitive success as a result of doing so.

Innovation

As noted earlier, innovation is a key outcome firms seek through entrepreneurship and is often the source of competitive success for firms competing in the global economy. In Rosabeth Moss Kanter's words, "Winning in business today demands innovation. Companies that innovate reap all the advantages of a first mover."[13] Thus, innovation is intended to enhance a firm's strategic competitiveness and financial performance.[14] Academic studies also highlight innovation's importance. For example, research results show that firms competing in global industries that invest more in innovation also achieve the highest returns.[15] In fact, investors often react positively to the introduction of a new product, thereby increasing the price of a firm's stock. Innovation, then, is an essential feature of high-performance firms.[16] The fact that firms differ in their propensity to produce value-creating innovations, as well as in their ability to protect innovations from imitation by competitors, is an another indicator of innovation's ability to be a source of competitive advantage.[17] In other words, because "innovation is relatively rare in organizations, compared to normal administrative routines," the firm that is able to innovate consistently and effectively is well positioned to rely on its innovative skill as a competitive advantage.[18]

Invention is the act of creating or developing a new product or process.

In his classic work, Joseph Schumpeter argued that firms engage in three types of innovative activity.[19] **Invention** is the act of creating or developing a new product or

Innovation is the process of creating a commercial product from an invention.

process. **Innovation** is the process of creating a commercial product from an invention. In the 21st-century competitive landscape, "innovation may be required to maintain or achieve competitive parity, much less a competitive advantage in many global markets."[20] Moreover, innovation success is influenced by a firm's ability to absorb and evaluate external environmental information.[21] Because they typically are built by integrating knowledge and skills from multiple sources, every innovation creates opportunities for additional innovations.[22] Thus, an invention brings something new into *being,* while an innovation brings something new into *use.* Accordingly, technical criteria are used to determine the success of an invention, whereas commercial criteria are used to determine the success of an innovation.[23] For some time, Enron has been voted the most innovative large U.S. company in *Fortune* magazine's Most Admired Companies survey. As mentioned in an earlier chapter, one of Enron's current innovation-based efforts is to use the Internet so that the firm can become the preferred platform for e-commerce around the world.[24] Finally, **imitation** is the adoption of an innovation by similar firms. Imitation usually leads to product or process standardization, and products based on imitation often are offered at lower prices, but without as many differentiated features.

Imitation is the adoption of an innovation by similar firms.

The array of innovative products that have been and may be created from invention is intriguing. Previous product innovations, as well as future ones, are described in the Strategic Focus, which also discusses the importance of R&D as the source of all product innovations.

In the United States in particular, innovation is the most critical of the three types of innovative activity that occur in firms. Many companies are able to create ideas that lead to inventions, but commercializing those inventions through innovation has, at times, proved difficult. This may be the case at the *Washington Post.* Some analysts believe that the *Post* has established one of the most successful Internet newspaper operations. Recently, the washingtonpost.com Web site reached 20 percent of Washington-area Internet users. This penetration is quite favorable compared with the typical local reach of 5 to 10 percent for newspapers. However, similar to other Internet provider newspapers, the *Post* hasn't been able to innovate a successful Internet business model. In the words of a business writer, "The business model of offering news and getting ads isn't enough to thrive on—especially when specialized Internet rivals are clawing at newspapers' dominance of local offerings such as classified advertising, sports scores and weather."[25] Thus, competitive success requires the *Post* to develop an innovation that will result in more effective commercialization of a Web site that is based on the Internet—a powerful invention.

Entrepreneurship

Schumpeter viewed entrepreneurship as a process of "creative destruction," through which existing products or methods of production are destroyed and replaced with new ones.[26] Thus, entrepreneurship is "concerned with the discovery and exploitation of profitable opportunities."[27] Formerly, *entrepreneurship* was defined as "any attempt at new business or new venture creation, such as self-employment, a new business organization, or the expansion of an existing business, by an individual, a team of individuals, or an established business."[28] As this definition suggests, entrepreneurship is an important mechanism for creating changes, as well as for helping firms adapt to

Surprise, Surprise, Surprise! What Might Be Tomorrow's Innovative Products, and What Will Be the Source of Their Development?

As defined in the text, innovation is the process of creating a commercial product or process from an invention. Thus, in terms of creating value, an invention's potential is reached only when a firm develops and sells a product that satisfies customers' current or unmet needs.

One way to think of the value created by previous product innovations is to group them by functionality. For example, some innovative products have created value for consumers in their homes. The vacuum cleaner, invented by James Murray Spangler in 1907, 1918's Frigidaire refrigerator, Permacel duct tape in 1942, and the 1946 introduction of Tupperware products are recognized as important innovations in the home environment. RCA's radio in 1921 and television in 1939 were significant innovations in communication that history may show pale in comparison to the value created by 1991's establishment of the World Wide Web. The paper clip, Xerox's photocopier and fax machine, Intel's microprocessor, and Apple's Macintosh personal computer all changed the nature of work. Each of these products was the commercialization of an invention.

What about the future? With regard to the energy sector of the economy, environmentally friendly products are expected to become more prominent. A diversified energy provider, TXU Corp. is trying to develop products from renewable energy sources through which significant amounts of energy can be delivered to customers. Currently, TXU is devoting considerable efforts to windmills and solar-powered energy sources as the foundation of its future delivery mechanisms. For personal residences, future home appliances probably will be linked through tethered and wireless connections. Experts believe that "the day will come when you can order a book from a restaurant, preheat the oven from the office and start the dishwasher over the telephone." As regards financial investments, individual consumers will have access to vast quantities of data and information that were once the purview of professional advisors only. In addition, investors will be able to use videoconferencing to attend stockholders' meetings and to cast their ballots on a real-time basis, rather than by submitting a written proxy through the mail. Even toilets are undergoing innovation: Japan's Matsushita has developed a high-tech toilet that reads an individual's weight, body temperature, and blood pressure. By 2003, the product will also be able to check the amount of glucose and protein in a user's urine.

It is interesting to recall earlier product innovations and to think about those to come. But from a strategic management perspective, it is more important to recognize that, in some form or fashion, R&D activities are the source of all innovations. This fact is widely accepted in many Japanese corporations. For example, Samsung Electronics Co., Ltd., tripled its investment in R&D in 2000 to support the development of new products. Viewing the company's actions, a business writer suggested that "If you are beginning to think that Japan has lost its flair for product innovation and global marketing, think again. No matter how far down Japan's economy may be, its R&D divisions and factories are far from out." Supported by national policies and firm-level commitments to R&D, Japanese companies continue to develop innovations that yield a large number of patents, an important indicator of R&D productivity. In 1998, the U.S. Patent Office granted 32,119 U.S. patents to Japanese firms, an increase of 32 percent over the 1997 figure. The competitive dynamics created by this situation are fascinating. For example, the chairman of the U.S. National Research Council's Committee on Japan observes that "Japanese companies are just as strong as ever in many key technologies. If the U.S. is complacent and underestimates Japan, we could find ourselves facing the same problems we faced in the early 1980s, when complacency was rampant."

Evidence shows, however, that companies throughout the world, not just those in Japan, are committed to innovation through R&D. U.S.-based Xerox and Hewlett-Packard are two examples of those companies, as is the U.K.'s AEA Technology. AEA "seeks to be recognized as the world's most successful innovation business" as it uses its knowledge and skills to provide innovative solutions to customers' problems. Thus, companies committed to innovation must be willing to devote considerable resources to R&D. Indeed, the most successful of these firms develop R&D as a source of competitive advantage.

SOURCES: AEA Technology, 2000, Who we are, AEA Technology Home Page, March 10, *www.aeat.com*; K. Fairbank, 2000, Beyond 2000, *Dallas Morning News,* January 2, H1, H2; Staff Reports, 2000, TXU to expand wind, solar power program, *Dallas Morning News,* January 25, D7; C. Chen & T. Carvell, 1999, Products of the century, *Fortune,* November 22, 134–140; A. Paul, 1999, Made in Japan, *Fortune,* December 6, 190–200; E. Ramstad, 1999, Samsung to pour money into R&D, new ad campaign, *Wall Street Journal,* November 11, B6.

---

changes created by others.[29] Firms that encourage entrepreneurship are risk takers, are committed to innovation, and act proactively[30] (i.e., they try to create opportunities rather than waiting to respond to those created by others).

Corporate Entrepreneurship

Corporate entrepreneurship is a process whereby an individual or group in an existing organization creates a new venture or develops an innovation.

An organizational process that contributes to a firm's survival and performance, **corporate entrepreneurship** is a process whereby an individual or a group in an existing organization creates a new venture or develops an innovation.[31] Another important perspective is that corporate entrepreneurship is the sum of a firm's innovation, renewal, and venturing efforts.[32] Evidence suggests that corporate entrepreneurship practices are facilitated through the effective use of a firm's strategic management process.[33] One of the issues addressed when a firm uses the strategic management process to facilitate corporate entrepreneurship is determining how to harness the ingenuity of a firm's employees and reward them for it while retaining some of the rewards of the entrepreneurial efforts for the shareholders' benefit.[34]

Entrepreneurs

Evidence shows that entrepreneurs are primary agents of economic growth, introducing new products, new production methods, and other innovations that stimulate economic activity.[35] Seeking to create the future, organizational entrepreneurs, engaging in corporate entrepreneurship, take risks and act aggressively and proactively in their firms.[36] Moreover, entrepreneurs sense opportunities before others do and take risks in the face of uncertainty to establish new markets, develop new products, or form innovative production processes or service delivery mechanisms.[37] These charac-

Entrepreneurs are individuals, acting independently or as part of an organization, who create a new venture or develop an innovation and take risks entering them into the marketplace.

teristics and evidence suggest that **entrepreneurs** are individuals, acting independently or as part of an organization, who create a new venture or develop an innovation and take risks entering them into the marketplace.[38]

Entrepreneurs surface at any organizational level. Thus, top-level managers, middle- and first-level managers, staff personnel, and those producing the company's good or service can all be entrepreneurs. Suggesting the importance of each person in a firm acting as an entrepreneur is the following opinion expressed by a corporate executive: "In the future—the not-too-distant future—only two groups of people will be in the world of work: entrepreneurs and those who think like entrepreneurs."[39]

Although all members of a firm can be entrepreneurs, expectations of their entrepreneurship vary by organizational level. Top-level managers, for example, should try to establish an entrepreneurial culture that inspires individuals and groups to engage in corporate entrepreneurship.[40] Apple Computer's Steve Jobs is committed to this effort, believing one of his key responsibilities is to help Apple become "more entrepreneurial and start-up like."[41] Top-level executives at 3M have emphasized innovation through entrepreneurship for years. Speaking about this, George Allen, retired vice president of research and development at 3M, states, "3M innovates for the same reason that cows eat grass. It is a part of our DNA to do so."[42] Middle- and first-level managers are promoters and caretakers of organizational efficiency. Their work is especially important once an idea for a product has been commercialized and the organization necessary to support and promote the product has been formed.[43] Because of their close contacts with customers, suppliers, and other sources of external information, first-level managers are vital to efforts to absorb and evaluate information from outside the firm that signals insights about potentially successful innovations. Because they work with procedures, staff personnel have the knowledge required to develop innovative processes that can increase organizational efficiency. Similarly, those producing a good or service have the experience necessary to propose process innovations, as well as the knowledge of customers' needs required to facilitate a firm's efforts to design and produce product innovations.

Accordingly, innovation, entrepreneurship, corporate entrepreneurship (as one form of entrepreneurship), and the work of entrepreneurs affect a firm's efforts to achieve strategic competitiveness and earn above-average returns. As we shall see in the next section, entrepreneurship and corporate entrepreneurship are being practiced more commonly in countries throughout the global economy.

International Entrepreneurship

Entrepreneurship is at the top of public policy agendas in many of the world's countries, including Finland, Germany, Israel, Ireland, and France, among others. In Northern Ireland, for example, the minister for enterprise, trade, and investment told businesspeople that their current and future commercial success would be affected by the degree to which they decided to emphasize R&D and innovation (critical components of entrepreneurship).[44]

According to some researchers who study economies throughout the world, virtually all industrial nations "are experiencing some form of transformation in their economies, from the dramatic move from centrally planned to market economies in East-central Europe . . . to the efforts by Asian countries to return to their recent high growth levels."[45] Entrepreneurship and corporate entrepreneurship can play central roles in those transformations, in that they have strong potential to fuel economic growth, create employment, and generate prosperity for citizens.[46] For example, in a comprehensive study in which entrepreneurial activity was assessed in 10 countries (Canada, Denmark, Finland, France, Germany, Israel, Italy, Japan, the United Kingdom, and the United States), researchers discovered that "variation in rates of entrepreneurship may account for as much as one-third of the variation [in countries'] economic growth."[47]

A society's cultural characteristics influence a nation's rate and practice of entrepreneurship. In the late 1970s, for example, Chinese economic reforms facilitated the use of market forces as an important, but not exclusive, driver of economic activity. With increased economic freedom, some businesspeople used entrepreneurship as the foundation to initiate and then operate a start-up venture. In other cases, corporate entrepreneurship was introduced into existing companies to improve their performance.[48]

However, tension surfaced among Chinese workers regarding the need for individualism to promote entrepreneurship and the more traditional Chinese cultural characteristic of collectivism: "Individualism refers to a self-orientation, an emphasis on self-sufficiency and control...and a value system where people derive pride from their own accomplishments. [In contrast, collectivism] involves the subordination of personal interests to the goals of the larger work group, an emphasis on sharing, . . . a concern with group welfare, and antipathy towards those outside the group."[49] How the tension between individualism and collectivism is handled is important, because research shows that entrepreneurship declines as collectivism is emphasized. Simultaneously, however, research results suggest that exceptionally high levels of individualism might be dysfunctional for entrepreneurship. Viewed collectively, these results appear to call for a balance to be established between individual initiative and the spirit of cooperation and group ownership of innovation. For firms to achieve corporate entrepreneurship, they must provide appropriate autonomy and incentives for individual initiative to surface, but also promote cooperation and group ownership of an innovation if it is to be implemented successfully. Thus, corporate entrepreneurship often requires teams of people with unique skills and resources, especially perhaps with cultures in which collectivism is a valued historical norm.[50]

The importance of balancing individualism and collectivism for entrepreneurship is exemplified by the success of Asian entrepreneurs in North America. Some have argued that the success of those of Chinese and Korean origin in North America is due to their industriousness, perseverance, frugality, and emphasis on family. Research shows, however, that other traits also promote their success. In North America, these individuals are allowed the autonomy necessary for creativity and entrepreneurial behavior. In addition, the emphasis on collectivism afforded by their cultural background helps them promote cooperation and group ownership of innovation.[51]

Interestingly, Chinese entrepreneurs operating in China have several character traits that are similar to those of U.S. entrepreneurs, including ambitiousness, independence, and self-determination. But the two sets of entrepreneurs also have different characteristics, particularly those most influenced by Confucian social philosophy.[52] Entrepreneurs of Chinese and Korean descent who operate in the United States exhibit differences from all other entrepreneurs in the country. For example, Chinese and Korean entrepreneurs conducting business in the United States invest more equity, obtain more capital from family and friends, and receive fewer loans from financial institutions. Furthermore, they achieve higher profits than their non-Asian counterparts.[53] In contrast, a study of Israeli women showed that industry experience, business skills, and achievement were related to their performance, much the same as with other entrepreneurs in the United States and Europe. But, unlike those other entrepreneurs, Israeli women entrepreneurs could attribute their success to their affiliation with a network for support and advice. When they were affiliated with multiple networks, by contrast, their performance suffered, possibly because of too much and potentially conflicting advice.[54]

Internal Corporate Venturing

Internal corporate venturing is the set of activities used to create inventions and innovations through internal means.

Internal corporate venturing is the set of activities used to create inventions and innovations through internal means.[55] Spending on R&D is linked to success in internal corporate venturing. Put simply, firms are unable to invent or innovate without significant R&D investments.

As the 21st century begins, evidence suggests that U.S. firms are committed to the importance of supporting R&D. In fact, the amount of funds allocated to R&D by U.S. firms during 2000 was projected to increase by 10 percent compared with the 1999 figure. Driving these investments, some experts believe, is the fact that "companies are looking at where they need to be in five to 10 years to remain competitive. They have to spend the money now to get there."[56] However, as noted in a previous Strategic Focus, companies in other countries, including Japanese firms, also are devoting significant resources to R&D in recognition of innovation's relationship to competitive success in the 21st century.[57]

As shown in Figure 13.1, there are two forms of internal corporate venturing: autonomous strategic behavior and induced strategic behavior. We discuss each form separately.

Autonomous strategic behavior is a bottom-up process in which product champions pursue new ideas, often through a political process, by means of which they develop and coordinate the commercialization of a new good or service until it achieves success in the marketplace.

A **product champion** is an organizational member with an entrepreneurial vision of a new good or service who seeks to create support for its commercialization.

Autonomous Strategic Behavior

Autonomous strategic behavior is a bottom-up process in which product champions pursue new ideas, often through a political process, by means of which they develop and coordinate the commercialization of a new good or service until it achieves success in the marketplace. A **product champion** is an organizational member with an entrepreneurial vision of a new good or service who seeks to create support for its commercialization. Evidence suggests that product champions play critical roles in moving innovations forward.[58] Autonomous strategic behavior is based on a firm's wellsprings of knowledge and resources that are the sources of the firm's innovation. Thus, a firm's capabilities and competencies are the basis for new products and processes.[59]

GE is a company in which autonomous strategic behavior occurs regularly. Essentially, "the search for marketable services can start in any of GE's myriad businesses.

13.1 | Model of Internal Corporate Venturing

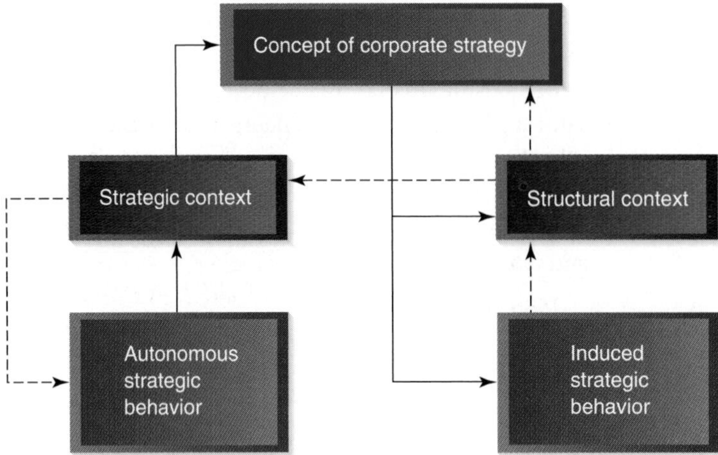

Source: Adapted from R. A. Burgelman, 1983, A model of the interactions of strategic behavior, corporate context, and the concept of strategy, *Academy of Management Review*, 8: 65.

[For example], an operating unit seeks out appropriate technology to better do what it already does. Having mastered the technology, it then incorporates it into a service it can sell to others." In response to frequent crisis calls and requests from customers, GE's Industrial Systems division took six months to develop a program that uses artificial intelligence to help assign field engineers to customer sites. Quite sophisticated, the program handles thousands of constraints while making assignments. The division's customer relationship manager was a champion for this product. The manager observed that the program "reduced the average time to dispatch an engineer from 18 hours to 4 hours."[60] In addition to facilitating the operations of one of GE's units, the program is being sold as a marketable item that developed through autonomous strategic behavior.

Changing the concept of corporate-level strategy through autonomous strategic behavior results when a product is championed within strategic and structural contexts (see Figure 13.1). The strategic context is the process used to arrive at strategic decisions (often requiring political processes to gain acceptance). The best firms keep changing their strategic context and strategies because of the continuous changes in the 21st-century competitive landscape (see Chapter 1). Thus, some believe that the most competitively successful firms reinvent their industry or develop a completely new one across time as they engage in competition with current and future rivals.[61]

Callaway Golf Co. may be a firm with a capability to reinvent the industry in which it competes. For example, Callaway reinvented the oversized club part of the golf club industry through the introduction of its "Big Bertha." Callaway now seeks to reinvent the golf ball segment of the golfing industry. Using state-of-the-art-technology and relying in part on autonomous strategic behavior among some of the firm's personnel, Callaway claims that its golf ball, introduced in February 2000, "will be as revolutionary to balls as the Big Bertha was to clubs." Called the Rule 35, two versions (the Firmfeel and the Softfeel) of Callaway's golf ball were introduced initially. Callaway engineers and scientists spent more than three years in R&D activities to innovate the Rule 35 golf ball.[62]

Induced Strategic Behavior

Induced strategic behavior is a top-down process whereby the firm's current strategy and structure foster product innovations that are associated closely with that strategy and structure.

The second of the two forms of internal corporate venturing, **induced strategic behavior,** is a top-down process whereby the firm's current strategy and structure foster product innovations that are associated closely with that strategy and structure. In this situation, the strategy in place is filtered through a matching structural hierarchy. Innovations developed or being developed through induced strategic behavior as a form of internal corporate venturing are described in the Strategic Focus.

Product Innovations and Induced Strategic Behaviors: Personal Computers, Video Games, and Other Delights

According to analysts, competitors likely chuckled to themselves, at least privately, when they heard in 1996 that Sony Corp. intended to introduce another PC line, called the Vaio series. One reason for this reaction was that the firm had endured four previous short-lived efforts to establish Sony in brand-name computers. Today, however, through the success of the Vaio line of PCs, Sony is one of four major PC brands remaining on U.S. retailers' shelves. An edict from Sony CEO Nobuyuki Idei to "build a Sony-style personal computer" was the foundation through which the firm's current strategy fostered a product innovation. Managers listening to their CEO heard a challenge to develop a PC "whose design would be as distinctive as Sony's televisions, Walkman and digital cameras." The product evolved from work completed at Sony's main research facility in Japan. Engineer Susumu Ito and designer Teiyu Goto combined their visions and efforts to develop what has become a successful product innovation. Observers believe that the Vaio's sleek looks and design compensate for what the product lacks in cutting-edge technical performance.

Sony's current strategy and structure also induced strategic behaviors through which the PlayStation 2 came into being. Introduced into Japan in March 2000 and into Europe and North America in the fall of that year, the PlayStation 2 was viewed by Sony officials "as a sort of Trojan horse that will enter the house as a videogame player and then become a secret weapon to access the Internet, play movies and download music, rivaling the PC as the hub of entertainment in the home." The PlayStation 2's introduction into Japan was nothing short of sensational, with 980,000 initial units sold in record time. Ken Kutaragi, CEO of Sony Computer Entertainment, the video-game unit of Sony Corp., stimulated the innovation of the PlayStation. This strategic leader's objective was to use the firm's current strategy and structure to develop a product that would move Sony to a position of being able to dominate a new wave of Internet gadgets and services. Thus, Sony views its PlayStation 2 as a viable entertainment platform for the home. Interestingly, Sony is currently the world's only company that offers consumers all three devices—the PC, television, and video-game machine—around which homes could be wired with networks of digital products. Moreover, the firm's penetration in markets around the world through these three products is impressive. In the United States, for example, one of every five American households owns a PlayStation.

Executives at Nissan Motor Co. are not abandoning their firm's innovation strategy. Instead, they intend to continue to rely on Nissan's internal innovation capabilities to develop and introduce four new products into North America, a market that is vital to Nissan's success. By 2003, plans call for Nissan to launch a large sport-utility vehicle, a new minivan, a new Z-series sports car, and a fourth vehicle that had not yet been specified by mid-2000. In addition, Nissan executives decided to use the firm's innovation skills to complete changeovers of six other models, including major changes to the Altima sedan to enable the product to become a more viable competitor of Toyota's Camry and Honda's Accord.

SOURCES: R. A. Guth, 2000, Inside Sony's Trojan horse, *Wall Street Journal,* February 25, B1, B4; C. Taylor, 2000, Game wars, *Time,* March 20, 44–45; Nissan Motor Co., 2000, March 15, *www.nissan.com*; N. Shirouzu, 2000, Nissan may launch new SUV, minivan for North America in product revamp, *Wall Street Journal,* February 14, A18; Sony Home Page, 2000, March 13, *www.sony.com*; R. A. Guth & E. Ramstad, 1999, How Sony turned a skinny laptop into an unlikely PC success, *Wall Street Journal,* November 12, B1, B6.

Implementing Internal Corporate Ventures

Innovation is a necessary, but insufficient, condition for competitive success. Having processes and structures in place through which a firm can successfully implement the outcomes of internal corporate ventures is as vital as the innovations themselves. The successful introduction of innovations into the marketplace reflects implementation effectiveness. In the context of internal corporate ventures, processes are the "patterns of interaction, coordination, communication, and decision making employees use"[63] to convert the innovations resulting from either autonomous or induced strategic behaviors into successful market entries. Organizational structures are the sets of formal relationships supporting organizational processes.

To facilitate the implementation of product innovations and to identify opportunities to engage in still more innovation that can create value for customers, IBM is creating a network of innovation centers. Devoted to IBM's e-commerce services, these centers are locales "where business customers can visit with Web designers, software engineers, business strategists and marketing people under the same roof." The purpose of the centers is to foster collaborative relationships among IBM personnel, technologists, business experts, and customers to develop and implement product innovations.[64]

Effective integration among the various functions involved with either autonomous or induced strategic innovation behavior processes—from engineering to manufacturing and, ultimately, market distribution—is required to implement (i.e., to effectively use) the innovations that result from internal corporate ventures. Increasingly, product development teams are being used as a means of integrating the activities associated with different organizational functions. The outcome sought by using product development teams is commonly called *cross-functional integration,* a concept that is concerned with coordinating and applying the knowledge and skills of different functional areas in order to maximize innovation.[65]

Using Product Development Teams to Achieve Cross-Functional Integration

Cross-functional integration's importance has been recognized for some time.[66] Cross-functional teams facilitate efforts to integrate activities associated with different organizational functions, such as design, manufacturing, and marketing. In addition, new product development processes can be completed more quickly when cross-functional teams work effectively.[67] Through the work of cross-functional teams, product development stages are grouped into parallel or overlapping processes. Doing this allows the firm to tailor its product development efforts to its unique core competencies and to the needs of the market. In addition, the cross-functional integration that results from the work of such teams helps a firm learn how to mass-produce a successful new product.[68]

Horizontal organizational structures support the use of cross-functional teams in their efforts to integrate innovation-based activities across organizational functions. In a *horizontal organization,* managing changes in organizational processes across functional units is more critical than managing up and down functional hierarchies.[69] Therefore, instead of being built around vertical hierarchical functions or departments, the organization is built around core horizontal processes that are used to produce and manage innovations. As noted earlier, processes are the patterns of interaction, coordination, communication, and decision making personnel use to transform resources into outputs (e.g., product innovations). Some of the core horizontal processes that are critical to innovation efforts are formal—defined and documented as procedures and practices. More commonly though, these processes are informal: "They are routines or ways of working that evolve over time."[70] Often invisible, infor-

Cross-functional teams facilitate efforts to integrate activities associated with different organizational functions, such as design, manufacturing, and marketing. Effective cross-functional teams also expedite new product development processes.

mal processes are critical to successful product innovations and are supported properly through horizontal organizational structures more so than through vertical organizational structures.

As we discuss next, barriers sometimes exist that must be overcome for a firm to use cross-functional teams as a means of integrating organizational functions.

Barriers to Integration

The two primary barriers that may prevent the successful use of cross-functional teams as a means of integrating organizational functions are independent frames of reference of team members and organizational politics.[71]

Personnel working within a distinct specialization (i.e., a particular organizational function) typically have common backgrounds and experiences. Because of these similarities, people within individual organizational functions tend to view situations similarly and are likely to use the same decision criteria to evaluate issues such as those having to do with product development efforts. In fact, research results suggest that departments around which organizational functions are framed vary along four dimensions: time orientation, interpersonal orientation, goal orientation, and formality of structure.[72] Thus, individuals from different functional departments that have different orientations on these dimensions can be expected to understand separate aspects of product development in different ways. Accordingly, they place emphasis on separate design characteristics and issues. For example, a design engineer may consider the characteristics that make a product functional and workable to be the most important of the product's characteristics. Alternatively, a person from the marketing function may hold characteristics that satisfy customer needs most important. These different orientations can create barriers to effective communication across functions.[73] Although functional specialization may be damaging to the horizontal relationships necessary to successfully implement innovations produced from internal corporate venturing efforts, such specialization has an important purpose in creating an efficient organization. Therefore, eliminating functional specialization to overcome barriers to cross-functional integration may do more harm than good to the organization.

Organizational politics is the second potential barrier to the effective integration of organizational functions through use of cross-functional teams. In some organizations, considerable political activity may center on allocating resources to different functions. Interunit conflict may result from aggressive competition for resources among those representing different organizational functions. Of course, dysfunctional conflict between functions creates a barrier to their integration.[74] Methods must be found through which cross-functional integration can be promoted without excessive concurrent political conflict and without simultaneously changing the basic structural characteristics necessary for task specialization and efficiency.

Facilitating Integration

Shared values are the first of four methods firms use to achieve effective cross-functional integration.[75] Highly effective shared values are framed around the qualities that make the firm unique compared to its rivals.[76] Moreover, when linked clearly with a firm's strategic intent and mission, shared values reduce political conflict and become the glue that promotes coupling among functional units. Hewlett-Packard, for example, has remained an accomplished technological leader because it has established the "HP way." In essence, the HP way refers to the firm's esteemed organizational culture that promotes unity and internal innovation.

Leadership is a second method of achieving cross-functional integration. Effective strategic leaders remind organizational members continuously of the value of product innovations. In the most desirable situations, this value-creating potential becomes the basis for the integration and management of functional department activities. During his tenure as GE's CEO, Jack Welch frequently highlighted the importance of integrated work among business units and different functions. To frame this message consistently, Welch helped to establish a management-training center that focuses on relationships among all levels of the company's management structure.

A third method of achieving cross-functional integration is concerned with *goals and budgets*. This method calls for firms to formulate goals and allocate the budgetary resources necessary to accomplish them. These goals are specific targets for the integrated design and production of new goods and services. Effective horizontal organizations—those in which accomplishments are expected in terms of processes as well as outcomes such as product innovations—reinforce the importance of integrating activities across organizational functions.

An *effective communication system* is a fourth method used to facilitate cross-functional integration. Some key beneficial outcomes of effective communication are increased motivation, more and better information, and the sharing of knowledge among cross-functional team members.[77] Free-flowing communications between those working within different organizational functions is important, but effective communication within cross-functional teams is critical to the successful implementation of a new product. Without such communication, members of a cross-functional team would find it difficult to integrate their individual function's activities in ways that create synergy. Shared values and leadership practices shape the communication systems that are developed to support the work of cross-functional product development teams.

Appropriating (Gaining) Value from Innovation

Internal corporate-venturing implementation efforts are designed to help a company gain competitive benefits from its product innovations. Another way of saying this is that implementation efforts are used to help a firm appropriate or gain value from activities undertaken to innovate (i.e., commercialize) inventions.

The model in Figure 13.2 shows how value can be appropriated, or gained, from internal corporate-venturing processes. As mentioned earlier, cross-functional integration is required for innovation's value to be tapped fully. Cross-functional teams increase the likelihood of cross-functional integration, in that their effective use helps to overcome barriers to integration. Also helping a firm's efforts to overcome these barriers are four facilitators of integration: shared values, visionary leadership, supportive budgets and allocations, and effective communication systems.

The model highlights three desirable outcomes of achieving cross-functional integration: time to market, product quality, and the creation of customer value. In several earlier chapters, we described the competitive value of the rapid entry of a product into the marketplace; we highlighted evidence which suggests that a firm can gain a com-

FIGURE 13.2 | Appropriating (Gaining) Value from Internal Firm Innovation

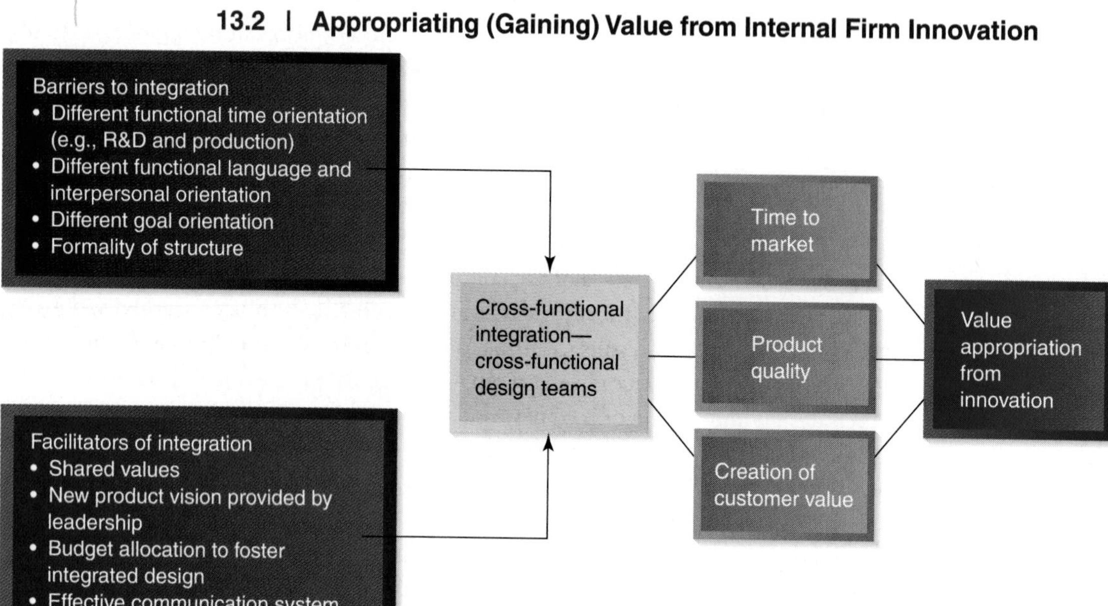

Source: Adapted from M. A. Hitt, R. E. Hoskisson, & R. D. Nixon, 1993, A mid-range theory of interfunctional integration, its antecedents and outcomes, *Journal of Engineering and Technology Management*, 10: 161–185.

petitive advantage when it is able to develop innovative goods or services and transfer them to the marketplace faster than competitors can.[78] In fact, some argue that developing products rapidly in the global economy has a strong and positive effect on a firm's profitability.[79] But product quality is also important.[80] Although shorter time-to-market cycles that result from the rapid entry of a product into a marketplace have the potential to help a firm appropriate value from its innovations, unacceptable levels of product quality may contribute to expensive recalls, product performances that fail to meet customers' expectations, and exposure to product liability charges. In the final analysis, customer value is created when product innovations *with acceptable levels of quality* are introduced rapidly into the marketplace. Thus, as our discussion of the model in Figure 13.2 suggests, internal corporate ventures must be effectively managed to facilitate cross-functional integration so that a firm will be able to appropriate maximum value from its product design and commercialization efforts.[81]

Strategic Alliances: Cooperating to Produce and Manage Innovation

It is difficult for a firm to possess all the knowledge required to compete successfully in its product areas over the long term. Complicating this matter is the fact that the knowledge base confronting today's organizations is not only vast, but also increasingly specialized. As such, the knowledge needed to commercialize inventions is frequently embedded within different corporations located in various parts of the global economy.

In Chapter 9, we discussed why and how firms use *strategic alliances* (partnerships between firms whereby resources, capabilities, and core competencies are combined to pursue common interests and goals)[82] to gain either competitive parity or competitive advantage relative to rivals. Used with increasing frequency,[83] alliances are often formed to produce or manage innovations. To innovate through a cooperative relationship such as a strategic alliance, firms share their knowledge and skills.[84] Forming alliances for this purpose is appropriate, in that value is created through the effective formation and use of an alliance.[85]

Porsche AG and Volkswagen AG recently formed an alliance to develop an innovative sport-utility vehicle that was to appear as a year-2002 model. Because of a conviction that their product had to be unique compared to existing SUVs, both firms committed significant resources to R&D activities. Although some components (e.g., a core platform) were to be shared, the partners also were seeking to produce their own individualized versions of the jointly developed product. For example, a Porsche executive noted that his firm was "going to great lengths to differentiate the two versions and [to] guard Porsche's brand image." The historically cooperative relationship between the two companies was expected to enhance the probability of the alliance's success.[86]

In the United States, a major alliance was formed between industry and the federal government. Called Partnership for a New Generation of Vehicles (PNGV) and featuring participation between GM, Ford, and DaimlerChrysler and the federal government, this alliance was developed to improve the U.S. auto industry's competitive position compared to the Japanese auto manufacturers which had increased their share of the U.S. auto market during the 1980s with cars that were fuel-efficient and desired by customers.

The three automobile manufacturers involved in PGNV showed test cars in 2000 and announced that they would have ready-to-build prototypes in 2004. All of the parties to the alliance hoped that innovative products would be developed from these prototypes that could achieve marketplace success. However, at least in terms of rapid market entry, the initial results were not encouraging. In early 2000, for example, Honda Motor Co. introduced its Insight into the marketplace. The Insight is a two-seat hybrid car that uses an auxiliary electric motor to achieve a fuel economy rating of 76 miles per gallon. Similarly, Toyota Motor Corp. intended to launch its Prius hybrid in the United States in the latter part of 2000. Rated at approximately 55 miles per gallon, this car had been sold in Japan for two years prior to its slated introduction into the U.S. market.[87] As noted earlier in the chapter, the rapid introduction of product innovations into the marketplace helps firms appropriate, or gain, value from their innovations. Thus, PNGV participants were already at a disadvantage relative to Japanese competitors with respect to this performance criterion.

Although the final results of the PNGV alliance are not known at this time, experience shows that alliances can be used successfully to produce and manage innovations. The cooperative relationship between Porsche and Volkswagen described earlier may help both firms create value for their customers. However, alliances formed for the purpose of innovation are not without risks. An important risk is that a partner will appropriate a firm's technology or knowledge and use it to enhance its own competitive abilities. To prevent or at least minimize this risk, a firm—particularly a start-up venture—needs to select its partner carefully.[88] The ideal partnership is one in which the firms have complementary skills, as well as compatible goals and strategic orientations.[89] Two other risks include a firm becoming dependent on its partner for the development of core competencies and the loss of skills that can result when they are not used regularly to produce or manage innovations.

In sum, building successful strategic alliances to produce and manage innovation requires focusing on knowledge, identifying core competencies, and developing strong human resources to manage those core competencies. Expecting to gain financial benefits in the short run may lead to unintended consequences in the long run. Also, firms may view their collaboration with other companies as an indirect form of competition for knowledge.[90]

Acquisitions and Venture Capital: Buying Innovation

In this section, we focus on acquisitions and venture capital, activities representing the third approach firms use to produce and manage innovation.

Acquisitions

Meritor Automotive, Inc., is emerging as an ambitious and competitively successful participant in the global auto parts-manufacturing industry, an industry that is being consolidated rapidly. A spin-off from Rockwell International Corp., Meritor has a strategy built around specialization, modular assembly operations, innovation, acquisitions, and globalization.

Recently, Meritor designed an integrated roof system that DaimlerChrysler is using in Europe with its Smart car. According to analysts, Meritor's design is unique because the car goes through the entire assembly process without a roof. This gives assembly-line workers greater access to the car's interior. The roof is bolted on at the end of the process. Other recent Meritor product innovations include a fully integrated door module and a modular assembly that incorporates struts, brakes, and other suspension components in a single package.

To continuously strengthen its ability to innovate, Meritor completes strategic acquisitions. The purchases of Euclid Industries, a supplier of replacement parts for trucks, the European heavy-truck axle business of Sweden's AB Volvo, and the heavy-vehicle brake business of LucasVarity, PLC, of the United Kingdom are three of Meritor's recent acquisitions. By integrating the capabilities of these acquisitions with those of companies it owns already, Meritor intends to continue producing and managing innovations in ways that create value for customers. As an indication that firms often seek innovation through more than one of the three approaches available to produce and manage innovations (i.e., internal corporate ventures, alliances, and acquisitions), we note that Meritor also formed a joint venture with Germany's ZF Friedrichshafen AG to produce transmissions.[91] Thus, the firm is using alliances and acquisitions in efforts to appropriate what it hopes will be full value from its innovation activities.

Similar to internal corporate venturing and strategic alliances, acquisitions are not a risk-free approach to producing and managing innovations. A key risk of acquisitions is that a firm may substitute an ability to buy innovations for an ability to produce innovations internally. As discussed next, research results suggest that this substitution may not be in the firm's best interests.[92]

Figure 13.3 shows that firms gaining access to innovations through acquisitions risk reductions in both R&D inputs (as measured by investments in R&D) and R&D outputs (as measured by the number of patents received). The curves indicate that the R&D-to-sales ratio drops after acquisitions have been completed and that the patent-to-sales ratio drops significantly after companies have been involved with large acquisitions. Additional research shows that firms engaging in acquisitions introduce fewer new products into the market.[93] Thus, firms appear to substitute acquisitions for internal corporate-venturing processes. This substitution may take place because firms lose strategic control and emphasize financial control of original, and especially of acquired, business units.[94] Although reduced innovation may not always result, managers of firms seeking to make acquisitions should be aware of this potential outcome.

Venture Capital

Venture capital is a resource that is typically allocated to entrepreneurs who are involved in a project with high growth potential. The intent of venture capitalists is to

FIGURE 13.3 | **Evidence of R&D Inputs (Expenditures) and Outputs (Number of Patents) per Dollar of Sales before and after Large Acquisitions**

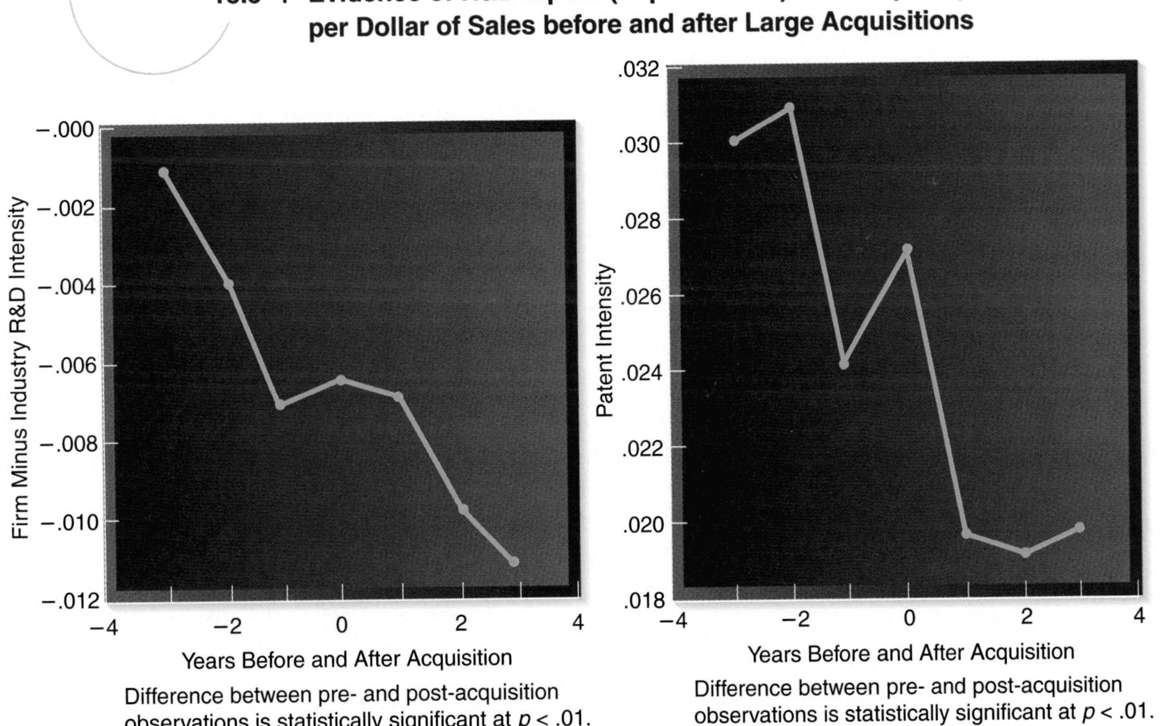

Source: M. A. Hitt, R. E. Hoskisson, R. D. Ireland, & J. S. Harrison, 1991, Are acquisitions a poison pill for innovation?, *Academy of Management Executive*, 5(4): 24–25.

help achieve a high rate of return on the funds they invest.[95] Increasingly, venture capital is being used to facilitate the earning of high rates of return by supporting the acquisition of innovations. To provide such support, some firms establish their own venture-capital divisions. These divisions carefully evaluate other companies to identify those with innovations or innovative capabilities that might yield a competitive advantage. In other instances, a firm might decide to serve as an internal source of capital for innovative product ideas that can be spun off as independent or affiliated firms. New enterprises that are backed by venture capital provide an important source of innovation and new technology. Furthermore, they are a major source of new wealth in the United States. For example, such firms account annually for about one-third of all initial public offerings of stock. On average, these venture-capital-backed new enterprises create approximately 230,000 new jobs and spend about $5 billion on R&D each year.[96]

Historically, the venture-capital business has been associated primarily with independent venture-capital firms, but both domestic and foreign corporations have discovered that investing in venture capital adds a new dimension to their corporate development strategies and can produce an attractive return on their investments.[97] A major strategic benefit to a corporation is the ability to invest early and observe what happens to the new venture. This may lead to subsequent acquisitions, the licensing of technology, product marketing rights, and, possibly, the development of international opportunities. Large firms often view venture capital as a window on future technological development. Participation by corporations can take many forms, but usually begins with investment in several venture capital funds as a limited partner and evolves into direct investments in new business ventures. Many firms begin this strategy by forming a venture development division.

The disdain of large corporations by outside entrepreneurs can be a potential pitfall. Entrepreneurs may be wary of large corporations that seek to dominate fledgling companies. The syndication of venture funds to reduce risk may also be a factor limiting potential gains from venture-capital investments. Other large firms may become part of the syndication and reduce the potential returns for the large corporate partner (through the sharing of knowledge).[98] With corporate restructuring and downsizing continuing, executives seem willing to try more entrepreneurial ventures. Apparently, venture capital is one way to participate, and it may be less risky than internal development.[99]

Our focus has been on corporate entrepreneurship. But entrepreneurship may be practiced successfully in small firms as well, especially those that are entrepreneurial ventures. In fact, both company experiences and research results suggest that small businesses and entrepreneurial ventures may have superior product innovation skills, while larger corporations may have superior innovation management skills (i.e., the skills required to maximize the marketplace return of product innovations).

Entrepreneurship in Small Businesses and Entrepreneurial Ventures

Small businesses and entrepreneurial ventures based in countries throughout the global economy are awarded a large number of U.S. patents.[100] Although 80 percent of the world's R&D activity in developed nations is concentrated in firms with 10,000 or more employees, these large firms account for under half of the world's technological activity, as measured by U.S. patents awarded. The data suggest that, while large firms are important for technological advances, small businesses, entrepreneurial ventures, and individual entrepreneurs account for a significant share of today's innovative activity and the technological progress resulting from it. Concurrently, smaller nations are contributing meaningfully to the global economy's innovative activity. One business writer observed recently that "Many of the most important innovations in cellphone technology have come from some of the smallest economies in the developed world, in Scandinavia. Even though a pharmaceutical company may spend billions shepherding a new product through the regulatory process, the spark of innovation behind new drugs comes increasingly from college labs and biotech start-ups."[101]

It is also interesting to observe that the proportions between large and small companies in terms of several key indicators of economic activity are shifting. In the United States, for example, small and midsize companies have been responsible for nearly all of the new jobs created since 1987.[102] In fact, "since 1980, *Fortune* 500 companies have lost more than five million jobs, but more than 34 million new jobs have been created (mostly by small firms and entrepreneurial ventures). [In addition], small firms, those with fewer than 500 people, employ 53 percent of the private workforce and account for 47 percent of sales and 51 percent of private sector Gross Domestic Product (GDP)."[103]

Among the factors accounting for the growth of job creation and economic productivity in small businesses and entrepreneurial ventures are the greater amounts of flexibility, resourcefulness, and agility that these enterprises have, compared to large organizations. Partly because of those desirable job attributes, a substantial shift toward self-employment and entrepreneurial ventures is occurring, especially in Canada, Israel, and the United States.[104]

Executives and women are two categories of workers who are changing their employment venue in large numbers. Evidence suggests, for example, that "Executives leaving large companies are taking jobs with smaller firms, including Internet start-ups. The latest figures from outplacement firm Challenger, Gray & Christmas show that seven out of 10 job-switching executives and managers are signing on with smaller firms."[105] Moreover, at least in developed countries, "the greatest and most rapid gain in firm start-ups will be achieved by increasing the participation of women in the entrepreneurial process."[106] In the United States, Phoenix, Arizona, recently was rated the best city in the nation for starting and growing a company, a fact that current and would-be small-business managers and entrepreneurs should consider in deciding where to locate their firms.[107] Collectively, these data suggest that small businesses and entrepreneurial ventures are rapidly becoming an important part of the mainstream economy and business activity, most certainly in developed countries.[108] As mentioned earlier in the chapter, entrepreneurship and corporate entrepreneurship are assuming increasing levels of importance in emerging economies as well.

Previously, we stated that small businesses and entrepreneurial ventures tend to outperform large organizations in terms of *producing* innovations. A reason for this is that entrepreneurs have been found to be more innovative than managers of large firms. The increased level of innovative capability that entrepreneurs possess is at least partly a function of their tendency to use more heuristics in making decisions than do those managing large organizations.[109] However, successfully *managing* innovations is more difficult for small firms and entrepreneurial ventures than it is for large established companies. Integrating and coordinating the work required to fund the introduction of an innovation to the marketplace (work that includes writing a strategic plan as well as a marketing plan and establishing effective production and distribution systems) typically challenges what are often constrained resources in small and entrepreneurial firms. The disadvantages notwithstanding, small and entrepreneurial ventures are proving vital to the growth of several industries, such as semiconductors, communications, biotechnology, and the entire Internet phenomenon, among others.[110] In these industry settings, some small businesses and entrepreneurial ventures seem to be demonstrating their capacity to excel in terms of producing *and* managing innovation.

Innovation as a Key Source of Value Creation

In Chapter 4, we discussed the relationship between value creation and strategic competitiveness. As we noted there, *value* consists of the performance characteristics and attributes that a company offers in the form of a good or service for which customers are willing to pay. Thus, the ability to create value is at the core of a firm's competitive success. In this chapter, the importance of innovation to a firm's success in the global economy has been emphasized. In fact, innovation, which is the process of creating a commercial good or service from an invention, is *critical* to competitive success for today's firms.

Combining value with innovation yields an interesting term called *value innovation.* According to researchers Kim and Mauborgne, "Value innovation makes the competition irrelevant by offering fundamentally new and superior value in existing markets and by enabling a quantum leap in buyer value to create new markets." Through value innovation, a firm seeks to commercialize each invention so that a new good or service is able to offer performance characteristics to customers that exceed their expectations or that actually create a new market through the use of unique product characteristics or attributes. Thus, effective value innovation creates radically different or greater value for customers, rather than producing incremental value enhancements. To make this possible, a firm must learn consistently and effectively and must be able to convert what is learned into knowledge that can become the foundation for developing new core competencies.

The actions of firms in numerous industries have resulted in value innovation. In the manufacturing tools and equipment industry, for example, SolidWorks Corporation developed the SolidWorks 2000, which is the leading mainstream computer-aided-design (CAD) solution for various design problems. Some argue that this product has allowed customers to substantially reduce errors and the amount of rework they must perform, as a result of its ability to permit rapid and simple changes to parts, drawings, and assemblies simultaneously through modeling techniques. Earlier, we learned about Callaway Golf Company's Big Bertha golf club, which created, at a minimum, fundamentally new and superior buyer value. The Big Bertha was unlike competitors' golf clubs at the time of its introduction. Essentially, Callaway Golf Company innovated a product with a larger head that made playing golf less difficult and more enjoyable. Through this value innovation, Callaway's product captured a large share of existing players *and* drew new players into the market. Other companies recognized for their value innovations include Wal-Mart in discount retailing, CNN in news broadcasting, Southwest Airlines in short-haul air travel, and IKEA in the retailing of home furnishings. Product development teams can be instrumental in helping a firm appropriate or gain maximum value from its value innovations.

In the final analysis, value innovation challenges firms to develop their knowledge-generating capabilities. With knowledge as the foundation for the shaping and nurturing of core competencies, a firm has the capacity to produce and manage innovations that have the potential to create new markets or significantly expand current ones.

SOURCES: Callaway Golf Company, 2000, Callaway Golf Company Home Page, March 22, *www.callaway.com*; SolidWorks, 2000, *SolidWorks 2000,* March 16; M. A. Hitt, R. D. Nixon, R. E. Hoskisson, & R. Kochhar, 1999, Corporate entrepreneurship and cross-functional fertilization: Activation, process and disintegration of a new product design team, *Entrepreneurship: Theory and Practice,* 23(3): 147–167; W. C. Kim & R. Mauborgne, 1999, Strategy, value innovation, and the knowledge economy, *Sloan Management Review,* 40(3): 41–44; S. A. Zahra, A. P. Nielsen, & W. C. Bogner, 1999, Corporate entrepreneurship, knowledge, and competence development, *Entrepreneurship: Theory and Practice,* 23(3): 169–189.

Producing More Innovation in Large Organizations

Full value from innovation is achieved when a firm is able to produce *and* manage innovation effectively. As we have mentioned, large organizations are less effective than small and entrepreneurial ventures in producing innovations. Given their deficiency relative to smaller and more entrepreneurial ventures, what can large firms do to act small and improve their ability to produce innovations?

Several actions can be taken to deal with this issue. First, greater levels of individual autonomy can be created through the restructuring of a firm into smaller and more manageable units (see Chapter 7). The additional amounts of creativity and innovation that tend to be witnessed among those granted more autonomy stimulates autonomous strategic behavior when a firm purses innovation through internal corporate ventures.[111] Simultaneously, a firm can reengineer its operations to develop more efficient work-related processes and to form channels through which customers' interests can be expressed with greater clarity and intensity.[112] The cross-functional work teams described earlier also provide opportunities for personnel to think and act creatively. Handled effectively, even downsizing (see Chapter 7) can create arrangements through which a firm is able to better focus its efforts on key tasks, such as those required to produce innovations.[113] Other actions a firm can take to stimulate the production of innovations are allocating significant levels of resources to R&D and using cooperative arrangements effectively.

Thus, both large and small firms can innovate. Until the skills required to both produce and manage innovation are mastered by either large organizations or small businesses and entrepreneurial ventures, cooperative arrangements will be an attractive option. Through effective collaborations, the small partner has an opportunity to concentrate on producing an innovation that the large partner can manage to marketplace success.[114] As the Strategic Focus shows, regardless of the approach used to produce and manage innovations, a firm may be able to appropriate or gain the greatest amount of value when its innovations create exceptional value for customers.

Summary

- Firms engage in three types of innovative activity. *Invention* is the act of creating and developing an idea for a new product or process. *Innovation* is the process of commercializing the products or processes that surfaced through invention. *Imitation* is the adoption of an innovation by others, often the firm's competitors. Imitation usually leads to product or process standardization and market acceptance.
- Increasingly, entrepreneurship and corporate entrepreneurship are being practiced in many countries. As used by entrepreneurs, entrepreneurship and corporate entrepreneurship are strongly related to a nation's economic growth. This relationship is a primary reason for the increasing use of entrepreneurship and corporate entrepreneurship in countries throughout the global economy.
- Three basic approaches are used to produce and manage innovation: internal corporate venturing, strategic alliances, and acquisitions. Autonomous strategic behavior and induced strategic behavior are the two processes of internal corporate venturing. Autonomous strategic behavior is a bottom-up process through which a product champion facilitates the commercialization of an innovative good or service. Induced strategic behavior is a top-down process in which a firm's current strategy and structure facilitate product or process innovations that are associated with them. Thus, induced strategic behavior is driven by the organization's current corporate strategy, structure, and reward and control systems.
- Increasingly, cross-functional integration is vital to a firm's efforts to appropriate or gain value from its internal corporate venturing efforts. Facilitated by cross-functional teams, cross-functional integration can reduce the time a firm needs to introduce innovative products into the marketplace. Cross-functional integration also can improve product quality and, ultimately, create value for customers.
- In the complex global economy, it is difficult for an individual firm to possess all the knowledge needed to innovate consistently and effectively. To gain access to the kind of specialized knowledge that often is required to innovate, firms may form a cooperative relationship such as a strategic alliance with others—sometimes even with competitors.
- Acquisitions are the third basic approach firms use to produce and manage innovation. Innovation can be acquired either through direct acquisition or through indirect investment. Examples of indirect investment are the formation of a wholly owned venture-capital division and the use of private placement of venture capital. Buying innovation, however, comes with the risk of reducing a firm's internal invention and innovative capabilities.
- Small firms are particularly well suited for fostering innovations that do not require large amounts of capital. Small firms have therefore become a vibrant part of industrialized nations, accounting for more job creation than large firms during the last decade.
- Large firms are needed to foster innovation due to capital requirements. Small firms are often found to be better at creating specialty products and diffusing the innovation through spin-offs from large corporations. Thus, collaborations between large and small firms often lead to successful product innovation processes.

Review Questions

1. What is innovation? What is entrepreneurship? What is corporate entrepreneurship? Who are entrepreneurs? What is the importance of these terms for firms competing in the global economy?
2. What are the three stages of the innovation process and why are the differences among them important?
3. What is autonomous strategic behavior? What is induced strategic behavior?

4. Some believe that, when managed successfully, cross-functional teams facilitate the implementation of internal corporate ventures and a firm's innovation efforts. How should cross-functional teams be managed to achieve these desirable outcomes?
5. How do firms use strategic alliances to help them produce innovation?
6. How can a firm create value when it acquires another company to gain access to its innovations or its ability to produce innovations?
7. How do large firms use venture capital to produce innovations and to identify new product opportunities?
8. What are the differences in the resources, capabilities, and core competencies of large and small firms to produce and manage innovation?

Application Discussion Questions

1. During the 1980s and 1990s, the number of acquisitions grew, as did the amount of money available as venture capital. Is there a relationship between the wave of acquisitions and the increase in available venture capital?
2. In your opinion, is the term "corporate entrepreneurship" an oxymoron? In other words, can corporations—especially large ones—be innovative?
3. Have you observed a product champion supporting an innovation in a corporation? If so, what were the results of the champion's efforts?
4. The economies of countries such as Russia and China have historically been operated through centralized bureaucracies. What can be done to infuse such economies with a commitment to corporate entrepreneurship and the innovation resulting from it?
5. Use the Internet to find an example of two corporate innovations—one brought about through autonomous strategic behavior and one developed through induced strategic behavior. Which innovation do you believe holds the most promise for commercial success and why?
6. Are strategic alliances a way to enhance a firm's technological capacity, or are they used more commonly to maintain pace with technological developments in a company's industry? In other words, are strategic alliances a tool of firms that have a technological advantage, or are they a tool of technologically disadvantaged companies?

Ethics Questions

1. Is it ethical for a company to purchase another firm to gain ownership of its product innovations and innovative capabilities? Why or why not?
2. Do firms encounter ethical issues when they use internal corporate-venturing processes to produce and manage innovation? If so, what are these issues?
3. Firms that are partners in a strategic alliance may legitimately seek to gain knowledge from each other. At what point does it become unethical for a firm to gain additional and competitively relevant knowledge from its partner? Is this point different when a firm partners with a domestic firm as opposed to a foreign firm? If so, why?
4. Small firms often have innovative products. When is it appropriate for a large firm to buy a small firm for its product innovations and new product ideas?

Internet Exercise

The World Wide Web has made it both possible and necessary for many traditional businesses to market and sell their goods and services on-line. Consumer goods and services such as banking, clothing, vacations, and grocery items can be ordered through the Internet. Creating new, safe, and reliable methods to access, pay for, and deliver goods and services via the Web has added to the list of innovations and management strategies that corporate entrepreneurs need to explore to be successful. To find out more about entrepreneurship and innovation, explore the following Web sites:

- Babson College's Center for Entrepreneurial Studies at **http://www.babson.edu/entrep**
- EGOPHER, a site produced by St. Louis University at

http://www.slu.edu/eweb/egopher.html

- The Kauffman Foundation's EntreWorld at

  http://www.entreworld.org

***e-project:** America's most successful pizza delivery chains, including Domino's, Pizza Hut, and other regional businesses, have long since relied on phone orders for delivery. How can the Internet's capabilities be integrated into their business? Weighing the pros and cons of ordering pizza on-line, make a list of 10 management concerns and techniques that you would need to consider to successfully promote, develop, and run an on-line business in this lucrative market.

Notes

1. A. Taylor, III, 2000, Detroit: Every silver lining has a cloud, *Fortune,* January 24, 92–93.
2. R. D. Ireland & M. A. Hitt, 1999, Achieving and maintaining strategic competitiveness in the 21st century: The role of strategic leadership, *Academy of Management Executive,* 13(1): 43–57; M. D. Nevins & S. A. Stumpf, 1999, 21st century leadership: Redefining management education, *Strategy & Business,* 16: 41–51.
3. M. A. Hitt, R. D. Nixon, P. G. Clifford, & K. P. Coyne, 1999, The development and use of strategic resources, in M. A. Hitt, P. G. Clifford, R. D. Nixon, & K. P. Coyne (eds.), 1999, *Dynamic Strategic Resources: Development, Diffusion and Integration* (Chichester: John Wiley & Sons, Ltd.), 1–14.
4. H. Lee, K. G. Smith, C. M. Grimm, & A. Schomburg, 2000, Timing, order and durability of new product advantages with imitation, *Strategic Management Journal,* 21: 23–30.
5. P. F. Drucker, 1998, The discipline of innovation, *Harvard Business Review,* 76(6): 149–157.
6. P. D. Reynolds, M. Hay, & S. M. Camp, 1999, *Global Entrepreneurship Monitor, 1999 Executive Report* (Babson Park, MA.: Babson College).
7. M. H. Meyer & A. DeTore, 1999, Product development for services, *Academy of Management Executive,* 13(3): 64–76.
8. Deutsche Telekom, 2000, The new millennium with a capital "T," *Forbes,* January 24, 81.
9. H. Ford, 2000, Noteworthy quotes, *Strategy & Business,* 18: 154.
10. S. A. Zahra, D. F. Kuratko, & D. F. Jennings, 1999, Guest editorial: Entrepreneurship and the acquisition of dynamic organizational capabilities, *Entrepreneurship: Theory and Practice,* 23(3): 5–10.
11. S. Miller, 2000, Formula One racing gets riskier—for its sponsors, *Wall Street Journal,* February 25, B1, B4.
12. D. Roth, 1999, Dell's big new act, *Fortune,* December 6, 152–155.
13. R. M. Kanter, 1999, From spare change to real change: The social sector as Beta site for business innovation, *Harvard Business Review,* 77(3): 122–132.
14. M. A. Mone, W. McKinley, & V. L. Barger, III, 1998, Organizational decline and innovation: A contingency framework, *Academy of Management Review,* 23: 115–132.
15. R. Price, 1996, Technology and strategic advantage, *California Management Review,* 38(3): 38–56; L. G. Franko, 1989, Global corporate competition: Who's winning, who's losing and the R&D factor as one reason why, *Strategic Management Journal,* 10: 449–474.
16. G. T. Lumpkin & G. G. Dess, 1996, Clarifying the entrepreneurial orientation construct and linking it to performance, *Academy of Management Review,* 21: 135–172; K. M. Kelm, V. K. Narayanan, & G. E. Pinches, 1995, Shareholder value creation during R&D innovation and commercialization stages, *Academy of Management Journal,* 38: 770–786.
17. P. W. Roberts, 1999, Product innovation, product-market competition and persistent profitability in the U.S. pharmaceutical industry, *Strategic Management Journal,* 20: 655–670.
18. Mone, McKinley, & Barker, Organizational decline, 117.
19. J. Schumpeter, 1934, *The Theory of Economic Development* (Cambridge, MA: Harvard University Press).
20. M. A. Hitt, R. D. Nixon, R. E. Hoskisson, & R. Kochhar, 1999, Corporate entrepreneurship and cross-functional fertilization: Activation, process and disintegration of a new product design team, *Entrepreneurship: Theory and Practice,* 23(3): 145–167.
21. D. L. Deeds, D. DeCarolis, & J. Coombs, 2000, Dynamic capabilities and new product development in high technology ventures: An empirical analysis of new biotechnology firms, *Journal of Business Venturing,* 15: 211–229.
22. T. Petzinger, Jr., 2000, So long, supply and demand, *Wall Street Journal,* January 1, R31.
23. P. Sharma & J. L. Chrisman, 1999, Toward a reconciliation of the definitional issues in the field of corporate entrepreneurship, *Entrepreneurship: Theory and Practice,* 23(3): 11–27; R. A. Burgelman & L. R. Sayles, 1986, *Inside Corporate Innovation: Strategy, Structure, and Managerial Skills* (New York: Free Press).
24. D. Kirkpatrick, 2000, Enron takes its pipeline to the Net, *Fortune,* January 24, 127–130.
25. E. White, 2000, Washington Post stays the course with Web operations, *Wall Street Journal,* February 2, B4.
26. Schumpeter, *The Theory of Economic Development.*
27. S. Shane & S. Venkataraman, 2000, The promise of entrepreneurship as a field of research, *Academy of Management Review,* 25: 217–226.
28. Reynolds, Hay, & Camp, *Global Entrepreneurship Monitor,* 3.
29. A. Zacharakis, P. D. Reynolds, & W. D. Bygrave, 1999, *Global Entrepreneurship Monitor, National Entrepreneurship Assessment, United States of America* (Babson Park, MA.: Babson College).
30. B. R. Barringer & A. C. Bluedorn, 1999, The relationship between corporate entrepreneurship and strategic management, *Strategic Management Journal,* 20: 421–444.
31. Sharma & Chrisman, Toward a reconciliation, 18.
32. S. A. Zahra, 1995, Corporate entrepreneurship and financial performance: The case of management leveraged buyouts, *Journal of Business Venturing,* 10: 225–247.
33. Barringer & Bluedorn, The relationship between, 421.
34. S. D. Sarasvathy, 2000, Seminar on research perspectives in entrepreneurship (1997), *Journal of Business Venturing,* 15: 1–57.
35. Barringer & Bluedorn, The relationship between, 422; R. W. Smilor, 1997, Entrepreneurship: Reflections on a subversive activity, *Journal of Business Venturing,* 12: 341–346.
36. Lumpkin and Dess, Clarifying the entrepreneurial orientation construct.
37. Reynolds, Hay, & Camp, *Global Entrepreneurship Monitor,* 7.
38. Sharma & Chrisman, Toward a reconciliation, 17.
39. *Fast Company,* 2000, March 8, *www.fastcompany.com.*
40. J. Birkinshaw, 1999, The determinants and consequences of subsidiary initiative in multinational corporations, *Entrepreneurship: Theory and Practice,* 24(1): 9–36.
41. B. Schlender, 2000, Jobs' Apple, *Fortune,* January 24, 66–76.

42. J. Bowles, 1997, Best practices: Driving growth through innovation, alliances, and stakeholder symbiosis, *Fortune,* November 14, S3–S24.
43. S. W. Floyd & B. Wooldridge, 1999, Knowledge creation and social networks in corporate entrepreneurship: The renewal of organizational capability, *Entrepreneurship: Theory and Practice,* 23(3): 123–143; J. P. Kotter, 1990, *A Force for Change* (New York: The Free Press).
44. Staff reporter, 2000, Business innovation urged, *Irish Times,* 23.
45. J. E. Jackson, J. Klich, & V. Kontorovich, 1999, Firm creation and economic transitions, *Journal of Business Venturing,* 14: 427–450.
46. Reynolds, Hay, & Camp, *Global Entrepreneurship Monitor,* 7.
47. Ibid., 3.
48. F. N. Pieke, 1995, Bureaucracy, friends and money: The growth of capital socialism in China, *Comparative Studies in Society and History,* 37: 494–518.
49. M. H. Morris, 1998, *Entrepreneurial Intensity: Sustainable Advantages for Individuals, Organizations, and Societies* (Westport, CT: Quorum Books), 85–86.
50. Ibid.; M. H. Morris, D. L. Davis, & J. W. Allen, 1994, Fostering corporate entrepreneurship: Cross-cultural comparisons of the importance of individualism versus collectivism, *Journal of International Business Studies,* 25: 65–89.
51. P. S. Li, 1993, Chinese investment and business in Canada: Ethnic entrepreneurship reconsidered, *Pacific Affairs,* 66: 219–243.
52. D. H. Holt, 1997, A comparative study of values among Chinese and U.S. entrepreneurs: Pragmatic convergence between contrasting cultures, *Journal of Business Venturing,* 12: 483–505.
53. T. Bates, 1997, Financing small business creation: The case of Chinese and Korean immigrant entrepreneurs, *Journal of Business Venturing,* 12: 109–124.
54. M. Lerner, C. Brush, & R. Hisrich, 1997, Israeli women entrepreneurs: An examination of factors affecting performance, *Journal of Business Venturing,* 12: 315–339.
55. R. A. Burgelman, 1983, A model of the interaction of strategic behavior, corporate context, and the concept of strategy, *Academy of Management Review,* 8: 61–70.
56. M. Guidera, 2000, Report: Research funds to surge, *Waco Tribune-Herald,* January 2, B4.
57. A. Paul, 1999, Made in Japan, *Fortune,* December 6, 190–200.
58. R. Leifer & M. Rice, 1999, Unnatural acts: Building the mature firm's capability for breakthrough innovation, in M. A. Hitt, P. G. Clifford, R. D. Nixon, & K. P. Coyne (eds.), *Dynamic Strategic Resources: Development, Diffusion and Integration* (Chichester: John Wiley & Sons), 433–453.
59. M. A. Hitt, R. D. Ireland, & H. Lee, 2000, Technological learning, knowledge management, firm growth and performance, *Journal of Engineering and Technology Management,* in press; D. Leonard-Barton, 1995, *Wellsprings of Knowledge: Building and Sustaining the Sources of Innovation* (Cambridge, MA: Harvard Business School Press).
60. S. S. Rao, 2000, General Electric, software vendor, *Forbes,* January 24, 144–146.
61. G. Hamel, 1997, Killer strategies that make shareholders rich, *Fortune,* June 23: 70–88.
62. F. M. Biddle, 2000, Fore! Callaway Golf, maker of Big Bertha clubs, tees up a new ball, *Wall Street Journal,* February 4, B1; Callaway Golf Co., 2000, The history of Callaway Golf Company, March 13, *www.callawaygolf.com.*
63. C. M. Christensen & M. Overdorf, 2000, Meeting the challenge of disruptive change, *Harvard Business Review,* 78(2): 66–77.
64. A. Goldstein, 1999, IBM plans e-commerce network, *Dallas Morning News,* November 16, D1, D11.
65. P. S. Adler, 1995, Interdepartmental interdependence and coordination: The case of the design/manufacturing interface, *Organization Science,* 6: 147–167.
66. B. L. Kirkman & B. Rosen, 1999, Beyond self-management: Antecedents and consequences of team empowerment, *Academy of Management Journal,* 42: 58–74.
67. A. R. Jassawalla & H. C. Sashittal, 1999, Building collaborative cross-functional new product teams, *Academy of Management Executive,* 13(3): 50–63.
68. Hitt, Nixon, Hoskisson, & Kochhar, Corporate entrepreneurship, 146.
69. J. A. Byrne, 1993, The horizontal corporation: It's about managing across, not up and down, *Business Week,* December 20, 76–81.
70. Christensen & Overdorf, Meeting the challenge, 68.
71. Hitt, Nixon, Hoskisson, & Kochhar, Corporate entrepreneurship, 149–150.
72. A. C. Amason, 1996, Distinguishing the effects of functional and dysfunctional conflict on strategic decision making: Resolving a paradox for top management teams, *Academy of Management Journal,* 39: 123–148; P. R. Lawrence & J. W. Lorsch, 1969, *Organization and Environment* (Homewood, IL: Richard D. Irwin).
73. D. Dougherty, L. Borrelli, K. Muncir, & A. O'Sullivan, 2000, Systems of organizational sensemaking for sustained product innovation, *Journal of Engineering and Technology Management,* in press; D. Dougherty, 1992, Interpretive barriers to successful product innovation in large firms, *Organization Science,* 3: 179–202; D. Dougherty, 1990, Understanding new markets for new products, *Strategic Management Journal,* 11(Special Summer Issue): 59–78.
74. Hitt, Nixon, Hoskisson, & Kochhar, Corporate entrepreneurship, 150.
75. E. C. Wenger & W. M. Snyder, 2000, Communities of practice: The organizational frontier, *Harvard Business Review,* 78(1): 139–144; J. D. Orton & K. E. Weick, 1990, Loosely coupled systems: A reconsideration, *Academy of Management Review,* 15: 203–223.
76. J. Champy, 2000, Only a few sea turtles survive, *Forbes,* February 21, 96.
77. G. Rifkin, 1998, Competing through innovation: The case of Broderbund, *Strategy & Business,* 11: 48–58.
78. K. M. Eisenhardt, 1999, Strategy as strategic decision making, *Sloan Management Review,* 40(3): 65–72.
79. B. B. Flynn & E. J. Flynn, 2000, Fast product development, *Newswise,* March 23, *www.newswise.com.*
80. S. A. Zahra & W. C. Bogner, 2000, Technology strategy and software new ventures' performance: Exploring the moderating effect of the competitive environment, *Journal of Business Venturing,* 15: 135–173.
81. S. W. Fowler, A. W. King, S. J. Marsh, & B. Victor, 2000, Beyond products: New strategic imperatives for developing competencies in dynamic environments, *Journal of Engineering and Technology Management,* in press.
82. P. Kale, H. Singh, & H. Perlmutter, 2000, Learning and protection of proprietary assets in strategic alliances: Building relational capital, *Strategic Management Journal,* 21: 217–237.
83. R. Gulati, N. Nohria, & A. Zaheer, 2000, Strategic networks, *Strategic Management Journal,* 21(Special Issue): 203–215.
84. Hitt, Ireland, & Lee, Technological learning.
85. B. N. Anand & T. Khanna, 2000, Do firms learn to create value? The case of alliances, *Strategic Management Journal,* 21(Special Issue): 295–315.
86. S. Miller, 1999, Porsche profits may leave the fast lane, *Wall Street Journal,* December 9, A21.
87. J. Ball, 1999, Japanese auto makers outpace U.S. in race for super-efficient cars, *Wall Street Journal,* December 30, B1, B3.
88. J. A. C. Baum, T. Calabrese, & B. S. Silverman, 2000, Don't go it alone: Alliance network composition and startups' performance in Canadian biotechnology, *Strategic Management Journal,* 21(Special Issue): 267–294.
89. M. T. Dacin, M. A. Hitt, & E. Levitas, 1997, Selecting partners for successful international alliances: Examination of U.S. and Korean

firms, *Journal of World Business,* 32, 1: 3–16; M. A. Hitt, M. T. Dacin, B. B. Tyler, & D. Park, 1997, Understanding the differences in Korean and U.S. executive's strategic orientations, *Strategic Management Journal,* 18: 159–167.

90. G. Hamel, 1991, Competition for competence and interpartner learning within international strategic alliances, *Strategic Management Journal,* 12: 83–103.
91. M. Yost, 1999, Innovation lifts Meritor's profile in auto-parts business, *Wall Street Journal,* November 15, B4.
92. M. A. Hitt, R. E. Hoskisson, R. A. Johnson, & D. D. Moesel, 1996, The market for corporate control and firm innovation, *Academy of Management Journal,* 39: 1084–1119; M. A. Hitt, R. E. Hoskisson, R. D. Ireland, & J. S. Harrison, 1991, Effects of acquisitions on R&D inputs and outputs, *Academy of Management Journal,* 34: 693–706.
93. Hitt et al., The market for corporate control.
94. M. A. Hitt, J. S. Harrison, & R. D. Ireland, 2001, *Creating Value through Mergers and Acquisitions: A Complete Guide to Successful M&As* (New York: Oxford University Press); M. A. Hitt, J. S. Harrison, R. D. Ireland, & A. Best, 1998, Attributes of successful and unsuccessful acquisitions of U.S. firms, *British Journal of Management,* 9: 91–114.
95. J. A. Timmons, 1999, *New Venture Creation: Entrepreneurship for the 21st Century* (5th ed.) (New York: IRWIN/McGraw-Hill), 440.
96. D. S. Cable & S. Shane, 1997, A prisoner's dilemma approach to entrepreneur-venture capitalist relationships, *Academy of Management Review,* 22: 142–176.
97. T. E. Winters & D. L. Murfin, 1988, Venture capital investing for corporate development objectives, *Journal of Business Venturing,* 3: 207–222.
98. G. F. Hardymon, M. J. DeNino, & M. S. Salter, 1983, When corporate venture capital doesn't work, *Harvard Business Review,* 61(3): 114–120.
99. U. Gupta, 1993, Venture capital investment soars, reversing four-year slide, *Wall Street Journal,* June 1, B2.
100. Paul, Made in Japan, 190–200.
101. Petzinger, Jr., So long, R31.
102. Timmons, *New Venture Creation,* 4–6.
103. Reynolds, Hay, & Camp, *Global Entrepreneurship Monitor,* 7.
104. Ibid., 3.
105. R. Poe & C. L. Courter, 2000, Small is beautiful again, *Across the Board,* January, 9.
106. Reynolds, Hay, & Camp, *Global Entrepreneurship Monitor,* 4.
107. J. A. Tannenbaum, 1999, Phoenix tops list of fertile areas for small companies, *Wall Street Journal,* December 7, B2.
108. A. L. Anna, G. N. Chandler, E. Jansen, & N. P. Mero, 2000, Women business owners in traditional and non-traditional industries, *Journal of Business Venturing,* 15: 279–303.
109. L. W. Busenitz, 1997, Differences between entrepreneurs and managers in large organizations: Biases and heuristics in strategic decision making, *Journal of Business Venturing,* 12: 9–30.
110. A. Goldstein, 2000, Culture of money, *Dallas Morning News,* January 30, H1, H2.
111. R. A. Melcher, 1993, How Goliaths can act like Davids, *Business Week* (Special Bonus Issue): 192–201.
112. Champy, Only a few, 96.
113. M. A. Hitt, B. W. Keats, H. F. Harback, & R. D. Nixon, 1994, Rightsizing: Building and maintaining strategic leadership and long-term competitiveness, *Organizational Dynamics,* 23(2): 18–32.
114. M. A. Hitt, B. W. Keats, & S. M. DeMarie, 1998, Navigating in the new competitive landscape, *Academy of Management Executive,* 12(4): 22–42.

CASE STUDIES

INTRODUCTION

Preparing an Effective Case Analysis

In most strategic management courses, cases are used extensively as a teaching tool.[1] A key reason is that cases provide active learners with opportunities to use the strategic management process to identify and solve organizational problems. Thus, by analyzing situations that are described in cases and presenting the results, active learners (i.e., students) become skilled at effectively using the tools, techniques, and concepts that combine to form the strategic management process.

The cases that follow are concerned with actual companies. Presented within the cases are problems and situations that managers and those with whom they work must analyze and resolve. As you will see, a strategic management case can focus on an entire industry, a single organization, or a business unit of a large, diversified firm. The strategic management issues facing not-for-profit organizations also can be examined using the case analysis method.

Basically, the case analysis method calls for a careful diagnosis of an organization's current conditions (as manifested by its external and internal environments) so that appropriate strategic actions can be recommended in light of the firm's strategic intent and strategic mission. Strategic actions are taken to develop and then use a firm's core competencies to select and implement different strategies, including business-level, corporate-level, acquisition and restructuring, international, and cooperative strategies. Thus, appropriate strategic actions help the firm to survive in the long run as it creates and uses competitive advantages as the foundation for achieving strategic competitiveness and earning above-average returns. The case method that we are recommending to you has a rich heritage as a pedagogical approach to the study and understanding of managerial effectiveness.[2]

As an active learner, your preparation is critical to successful use of the case analysis method. Without careful study and analysis, active learners lack the insights required to participate fully in the discussion of a firm's situation and the strategic actions that are appropriate.

Instructors adopt different approaches in their application of the case analysis method. Some require active learners/students to use a specific analytical procedure to examine an organization; others provide less structure, expecting students to learn by developing their own unique analytical method. Still other instructors believe that a moderately structured framework should be used to analyze a firm's situation and make appropriate recommendations. Your professor will determine the specific approach you take. The approach we are presenting to you is a moderately structured framework.

We divide our discussion of a moderately structured case analysis method framework into four sections. First, we describe the importance of understanding the skills active learners can acquire through effective use of the case analysis method. In the second section, we provide you with a process-oriented framework. This framework can be of value in your efforts to analyze cases and then present the results of your work. Using this framework in a classroom setting yields valuable experiences that can, in turn, help you successfully complete assignments that you will receive from your employer. The third section is where we describe briefly what you can expect to occur during in-class case discussions. As this description shows, the relationship and interactions between instructors and active learners/students during case discussions are different than they are during lectures. In the final section, we present a moderately structured framework that we believe can help you prepare effective oral and written presentations. Written and oral communication skills also are valued highly in many organizational settings; hence, their development today can serve you well in the future.

SKILLS GAINED THROUGH USE OF THE CASE ANALYSIS METHOD

The case analysis method is based on a philosophy that combines knowledge acquisition with significant involvement from students as active learners. In the words of Alfred North Whitehead, this philosophy "rejects the doctrine that students had first learned passively, and then, having learned should apply knowledge."[3] In contrast to this philosophy, the case analysis method is based on principles that were elaborated upon by John Dewey:

> *Only by wrestling with the conditions of this problem at hand, seeking and finding his own way out, does [the student] think. . . . If he cannot devise his own solution (not, of course, in isolation, but in correspondence with the teacher and other pupils) and find his own way out he will not learn, not even if he can recite some correct answer with a hundred percent accuracy.*[4]

The case analysis method brings reality into the classroom. When developed and presented effectively, with rich and interesting detail, cases keep conceptual discussions grounded in reality. Experience shows that simple fictional accounts of situations and collections of actual organizational data and articles from public sources are not as effective for learning as fully developed cases. A comprehensive case presents you with a partial clinical study of a real-life situation that faced managers as well as other stakeholders including employees. A case presented in narrative form provides motivation for involvement with and analysis of a specific situation. By framing alternative strategic actions and by confronting the complexity and ambiguity of the practical world, case analysis provides extraordinary power for your involvement with a personal learning experience. Some of the potential consequences of using the case method are summarized in Exhibit 1.

As Exhibit 1 suggests, the case analysis method can assist active learners in the development of their analytical and judgment skills. Case analysis also helps you learn how to ask the right questions. By this we mean questions that focus on the core strategic issues that are included in a case. Active learners/students with managerial aspirations can improve their ability to identify underlying problems rather than focusing on superficial symptoms as they develop skills at asking probing yet appropriate questions.

The collection of cases your instructor chooses to assign can expose you to a wide variety of organizations and decision situations. This approach vicariously broad-

1 | Consequences of Student Involvement with the Case Method

1. Case analysis requires students to practice important managerial skills—diagnosing, making decisions, observing, listening, and persuading—while preparing for a case discussion.
2. Cases require students to relate analysis and action, to develop realistic and concrete actions despite the complexity and partial knowledge characterizing the situation being studied.
3. Students must confront the *intractability of reality*—complete with absence of needed information, an imbalance between needs and available resources, and conflicts among competing objectives.
4. Students develop a general managerial point of view—where responsibility is sensitive to action in a diverse environmental context.

Source: C. C. Lundberg and C. Enz, 1993, A framework for student case preparation, *Case Research Journal*, 13 (Summer): 134.

ens your experience base and provides insights into many types of managerial situations, tasks, and responsibilities. Such indirect experience can help you make a more informed career decision about the industry and managerial situation you believe will prove to be challenging and satisfying. Finally, experience in analyzing cases definitely enhances your problem-solving skills, and research indicates that the case method for this class is better than the lecture method.[5]

Furthermore, when your instructor requires oral and written presentations, your communication skills will be honed through use of the case method. Of course, these added skills depend on your preparation as well as your instructor's facilitation of learning. However, the primary responsibility for learning is yours. The quality of case discussion is generally acknowledged to require, at a minimum, a thorough mastery of case facts and some independent analysis of them. The case method therefore first requires that you read and think carefully about each case. Additional comments about the preparation you should complete to successfully discuss a case appear in the next section.

STUDENT PREPARATION FOR CASE DISCUSSION

If you are inexperienced with the case method, you may need to alter your study habits. A lecture-oriented course may not require you to do intensive preparation for *each* class period. In such a course, you have the latitude to work through assigned readings and review lecture notes according to your own schedule. However, an assigned case requires significant and conscientious *preparation before class*. Without it, you will be unable to contribute meaningfully to in-class discussion. Therefore, careful reading and thinking about case facts, as well as reasoned analyses and the development of alternative solutions to case problems, are essential. Recommended alternatives should flow logically from core problems identified through study of the case. Exhibit 2 shows a set of steps that can help you familiarize yourself with a case, identify problems, and propose strategic actions that increase the probability that a firm will achieve strategic competitiveness and earn above-average returns.

Gaining Familiarity

The first step of an effective case analysis process calls for you to become familiar with the facts featured in the case and the focal firm's situation. Initially, you should become familiar with the focal firm's general situation (e.g., who, what, how, where, and when). Thorough familiarization demands appreciation of the nuances as well as the major issues in the case.

Gaining familiarity with a situation requires you to study several situational levels, including interactions between and among individuals within groups, business units, the corporate office, the local community, and the society at large. Recognizing relationships within and among levels facilitates a more thorough understanding of the specific case situation.

It is also important that you evaluate information on a continuum of certainty. Information that is verifiable by several sources and judged along similar dimensions can be classified as a *fact*. Information representing someone's perceptual judgment of a particular situation is referred to as an *inference*. Information gleaned from a situation that is not verifiable is classified as *speculation*. Finally, information that is independent of verifiable sources and arises through individual or group discussion is an *assumption*. Obviously, case analysts and organizational decision makers prefer having access to facts over inferences, speculations, and assumptions.

Personal feelings, judgments, and opinions evolve when you are analyzing a case. It is important to be aware of your own feelings about the case and to evaluate the accuracy of perceived "facts" to ensure that the objectivity of your work is maximized.

Recognizing Symptoms

Recognition of symptoms is the second step of an effective case analysis process. A symptom is an indication that something is not as you or someone else thinks it should be. You may be tempted to correct the symptoms instead of searching for true problems. True problems are the conditions or situations requiring solution before the performance of an organization, business unit, or individual can improve. Identifying and listing symptoms early in the case analysis process tends to reduce the temptation to label symptoms as problems. The focus of your analysis should be on the *actual causes* of a problem, rather than on its symptoms. Thus,

2 | An Effective Case Analysis Process

Step 1: *Gaining Familiarity*	a. In general—determine who, what, how, where, and when (the critical facts of the case). b. In detail—identify the places, persons, activities, and contexts of the situation. c. Recognize the degree of certainty/uncertainty of acquired information.
Step 2: *Recognizing Symptoms*	a. List all indicators (including stated "problems") that something is not as expected or as desired. b. Ensure that symptoms are not assumed to be the problem (symptoms should lead to identification of the problem).
Step 3: *Identifying Goals*	a. Identify critical statements by major parties (e.g., people, groups, the work unit, etc.). b. List all goals of the major parties that exist or can be reasonably inferred.
Step 4: *Conducting the Analysis*	a. Decide which ideas, models, and theories seem useful. b. Apply these conceptual tools to the situation. c. As new information is revealed, cycle back to substeps a and b.
Step 5: *Making the Diagnosis*	a. Identify predicaments (goal inconsistencies). b. Identify problems (discrepancies between goals and performance). c. Prioritize predicaments/problems regarding timing, importance, etc.
Step 6: *Doing the Action Planning*	a. Specify and prioritize the criteria used to choose action alternatives. b. Discover or invent feasible action alternatives. c. Examine the probable consequences of action alternatives. d. Select a course of action. e. Design an implementation plan/schedule. f. Create a plan for assessing the action to be implemented.

Source: C. C. Lundberg and C. Enz, 1993, A framework for student case preparation, *Case Research Journal,* 13 (Summer): 144.

it is important to remember that symptoms are indicators of problems, subsequent work facilitates discovery of critical causes of problems that your case recommendations must address.

Identifying Goals

The third step of effective case analysis calls for you to identify the goals of the major organizations, business units, and/or individuals in a case. As appropriate, you should also identify each firm's strategic intent and strategic mission. Typically, these direction-setting statements (goals, strategic intents, and strategic missions) are derived from comments made by central characters in the organization, business unit, or top management team as described in the case and/or from public documents (e.g., an annual report).

Completing this step successfully sometimes can be difficult. Nonetheless, the outcomes you attain from this step are essential to an effective case analysis because identifying goals, intent, and mission helps you to clarify the major problems featured in a case and to evaluate alternative solutions to those problems. Direction-setting statements are not always stated publicly or prepared in written format. When this occurs, you must infer goals from other available factual data and information.

Conducting the Analysis

The fourth step of effective case analysis is concerned with acquiring a systematic understanding of a situation. Occasionally cases are analyzed in a less-than-thorough manner. Such analyses may be a product of a busy schedule or the difficulty and complexity of the issues described in a particular case. Sometimes you will face pressures on your limited amounts of time and may believe that you can understand the situation described in a case without systematic *analysis* of all the facts. However, experience shows that familiarity with a case's facts is a necessary, but insufficient, step in the development of effective solutions—solutions that can enhance a firm's strategic competitiveness. In fact, a less-than-thorough analysis typically results in an emphasis on symptoms, rather than problems and their causes. To analyze a case effectively, you should be skeptical of quick or easy approaches and answers.

A systematic analysis helps you understand a situation and determine what can work and probably what will not work. Key linkages and underlying causal networks based on the history of the firm become apparent. In this way, you can separate causal networks from symptoms.

Also, because the quality of a case analysis depends on applying appropriate tools, it is important that you use the ideas, models, and theories that seem to be useful for evaluating and solving individual and unique situations. As you consider facts and symptoms, a useful theory may become apparent. Of course, having familiarity with conceptual models may be important in the effective analysis of a situation. Successful students and successful organizational strategists add to their intellectual tool kits on a continual basis.

Making the Diagnosis

The fifth step of effective case analysis—diagnosis—is the process of identifying and clarifying the roots of the problems by comparing goals to facts. In this step, it is useful to search for predicaments. Predicaments are situations in which goals do not fit with known facts. When you evaluate the actual performance of an organization, business unit, or individual, you may identify over- or underachievement (relative to established goals). Of course, single-problem situations are rare. Accordingly, you should recognize that the case situations you study probably will be complex in nature.

Effective diagnosis requires you to determine the problems affecting longer term performance and those requiring immediate handling. Understanding these issues will aid your efforts to prioritize problems and predicaments, given available resources and existing constraints.

Doing the Action Planning

The final step of an effective case analysis process is called action planning. Action planning is the process of identifying appropriate alternative actions. In the action planning step you select the criteria you will use to evaluate the identified alternatives. You may derive these criteria from the analyses; typically, they are related to key strategic situations facing the focal organization. Furthermore, it is important that you prioritize these criteria to ensure a rational and effective evaluation of alternative courses of action.

Typically, managers "satisfice" when selecting courses of action; that is, they find *acceptable* courses of action that meet most of the chosen evaluation criteria. A rule of thumb that has proved valuable to strategic decision makers is to select an alternative that leaves other plausible alternatives available if the one selected fails.

Once you have selected the best alternative, you must specify an implementation plan. Developing an implementation plan serves as a reality check on the feasibility of your alternatives. Thus, it is important that you give thoughtful consideration to all issues associated with the implementation of the selected alternatives.

WHAT TO EXPECT FROM IN-CLASS CASE DISCUSSIONS

Classroom discussions of cases differ significantly from lectures. The case method calls for instructors to guide the discussion, encourage student participation, and solicit alternative views. When alternative views are not forthcoming, instructors typically adopt one view so students can be challenged to respond to it thoughtfully. Often students' work is evaluated in terms of both the quantity and the quality of their contributions to in-class case discussions. Students benefit by having their views judged against those of their peers and by responding to challenges by other class members and/or the instructor.

During case discussions, instructors listen, question, and probe to extend the analysis of case issues. In the course of these actions, peers or the instructor may challenge an individual's views and the validity of alternative perspectives that have been expressed. These challenges are offered in a constructive manner; their intent is to help students develop their analytical and communication skills. Instructors should encourage students to be innovative and original in the development and presentation of their ideas. Over the course of an individual discussion, students can develop a more complex view of the case, benefiting from the diverse inputs of their peers and instructor. Among other benefits, experience with multiple-case discussions should help students increase their knowledge of the advantages and disadvantages of group decision-making processes.

Student peers as well as the instructor value comments that contribute to the discussion. To offer *relevant* contributions, you are encouraged to use independent thought and, through discussions with your peers outside of class, to refine your thinking. We also encourage you to avoid using "I think," "I believe," and "I feel" to discuss your inputs to a case analysis process. Instead, consider using a less emotion-laden phrase, such as "My analysis shows." This highlights the logical nature of the approach you have taken to complete the six steps of an effective case analysis process.

When preparing for an in-class case discussion, you should plan to use the case data to explain your assessment of the situation. Assume that your peers and instructor know the case facts. In addition, it is good practice to prepare notes before class discussions and use them as you explain your view. Effective notes signal to classmates and the instructor that you are prepared to engage in a thorough discussion of a case. Moreover, thorough notes eliminate the need for you to memorize the facts and figures needed to discuss a case successfully.

The case analysis process just described can help you prepare to effectively discuss a case during class meetings. Adherence to this process results in consideration of the issues required to identify a focal firm's problems and to propose strategic actions through which the firm can increase the probability that it will achieve strategic competitiveness.

In some instances, your instructor may ask you to prepare either an oral or a written analysis of a particular case. Typically, such an assignment demands even more thorough study and analysis of the case contents. At your instructor's discretion, oral and written analyses may be completed by individuals or by groups of two or more people. The information and insights gained through completing the six steps shown in Exhibit 2 often are of value in the development of an oral or written analysis. However, when preparing an oral or written presentation, you must consider the overall framework in which your information and inputs will be presented. Such a framework is the focus of the next section.

PREPARING AN ORAL/WRITTEN CASE STRATEGIC PLAN

Experience shows that two types of thinking are necessary to develop an effective oral or written presentation (see Exhibit 3). The upper part of the model in Exhibit 3 outlines the *analysis* stage of case preparation.

In the analysis stage, you should first analyze the general external environmental issues affecting the firm. Next your environmental analysis should focus on the particular industry (or industries, in the case of a diversified company) in which a firm operates. Finally, you should examine the competitive environment of the focal firm. Through study of the three levels of the external environment, you will be able to identify a firm's opportunities and threats. Following the external environmental analysis is the analysis of the firm's internal environment, which results in the identification of the firm's strengths and weaknesses.

As noted in Exhibit 3, you must then change the focus from analysis to *synthesis*. Specifically, you must *synthesize* information gained from your analysis of the firm's internal and external environments. Synthesizing information allows you to generate alternatives that can resolve the significant problems or challenges facing the focal firm. Once you identify a best alternative, from an evaluation based on predetermined criteria and goals, you must explore implementation actions.

Exhibit 4 and Exhibit 5 outline the sections that should be included in either an oral or a written strategic plan presentation: introduction (strategic intent and mission), situation analysis, statements of strengths/

EXHIBIT 3 | Types of Thinking in Case Preparation: Analysis and Synthesis

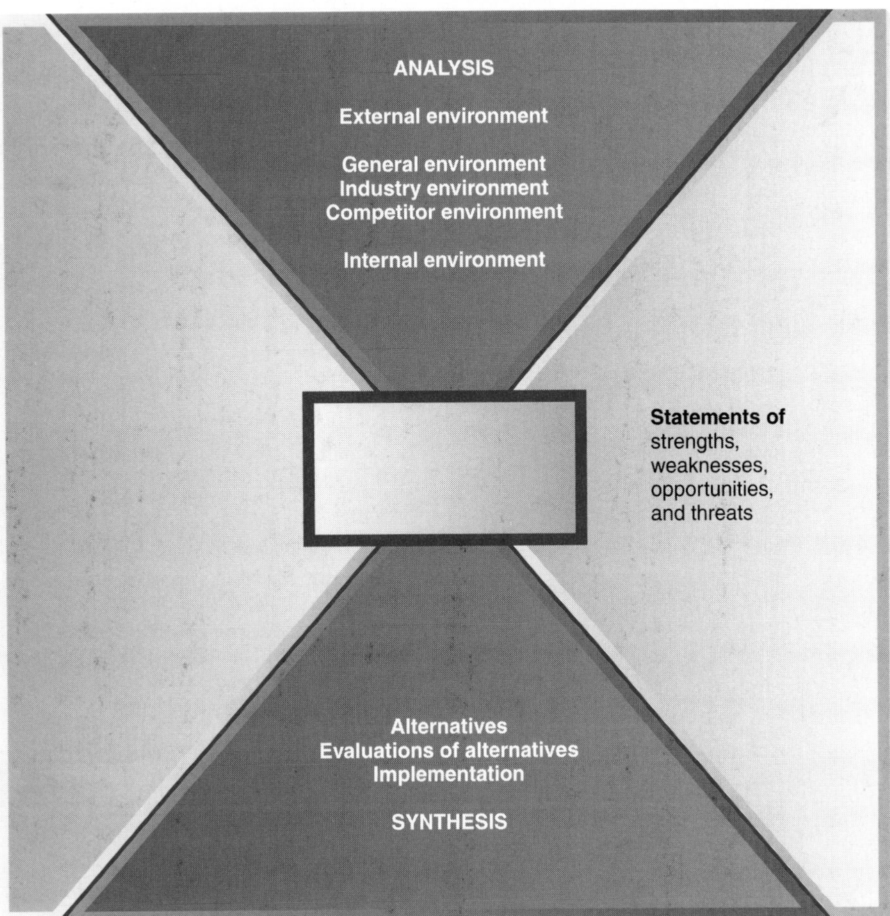

weaknesses and opportunities/threats, strategy formulation, and implementation plan. These sections, which can be completed only through use of the two types of thinking featured in Exhibit 3, are described in the following discussion. Familiarity with the contents of your book's 13 chapters is helpful because the general outline for an oral or a written strategic plan shown in Exhibit 5 is based on an understanding of the strategic management process detailed in those chapters.

External Environment Analysis

As shown in Exhibit 5, a general starting place for completing a situation analysis is the external environment. The *external environment* is composed of outside (external) conditions that affect a firm's performance. Your analysis of the environment should consider the effects of the *general environment* on the focal firm. Following that evaluation, you should analyze the *industry and competitor environmental* trends.

These trends or conditions in the external environment shape the firm's strategic intent and mission. The external environment analysis essentially indicates what a firm *might choose to do*. Often called an *environmental scan*, an analysis of the external environment allows a firm to identify key conditions that are beyond its direct control. The purpose of studying the external environ-

EXHIBIT 4 | Strategic Planning Process

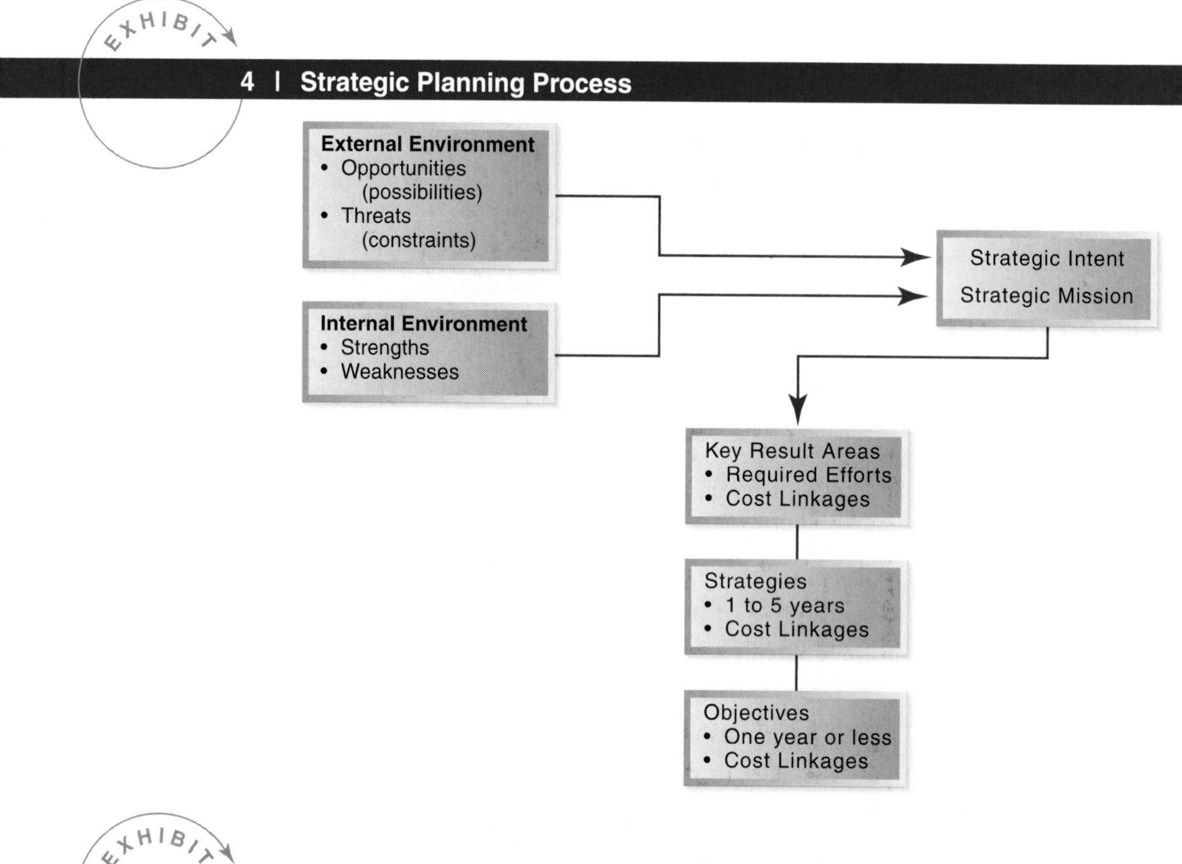

EXHIBIT 5 | Strategic Planning and Its Parts

- *Strategic planning* is a *process* through which a firm determines what it seeks to accomplish and the actions required to achieve desired outcomes
  - ✓ *Strategic planning*, then, is a *process* that we use to determine *what* (outcomes to be reached) and *how* (actions to be taken to reach outcomes)
- The effective *strategic plan* for a firm would include statements and details about the following:
  - ✓ *Opportunities* (possibilities) and *threats* (constraints)
  - ✓ *Strengths* (what we do especially well) and *weaknesses* (deficiencies)
  - ✓ *Strategic intent* (an indication of a firm's ideal state)
  - ✓ *Strategic mission* (purpose and scope of a firm's operations in product and market terms)
  - ✓ *Key result areas* (KRAs) (categories of activities where efforts must take place to reach the mission and intent)
  - ✓ *Strategies* (actions for each KRA to be completed within one to five years)
  - ✓ *Objectives* (specific statements detailing actions for each strategy that are to be completed in one year or less)
  - ✓ *Cost linkages* (relationships between actions and financial resources)

ment is to identify a firm's opportunities and threats. *Opportunities* are conditions in the external environment that appear to have the potential to contribute to a firm's success. In essence, opportunities represent *possibilities*. *Threats* are conditions in the external environment that appear to have the potential to prevent a firm's success. In essence, threats represent potential *constraints*.

When studying the external environment, the focus is on trying to *predict* the future (in terms of local, regional, and international trends and issues) and to *predict* the expected effects on a firm's operations. The external environment features conditions in the broader society *and* in the industry (area of competition) that influence the firm's possibilities and constraints. Areas to be considered (to identify opportunities and threats) when studying the general environment are listed in Exhibit 6. Many of these issues are explained more fully in Chapter 2.

Once you analyze the general environmental trends, you should study their effect on the focal industry. Often the same environmental trend may have a significantly different impact on separate industries. Furthermore, the same trend may affect firms within the same industry differently. For instance, with deregulation of the airline industry, older, established airlines had a significant decrease in profitability, while many smaller airlines such as Southwest Airlines, with lower cost structures and greater flexibility, were able to aggressively enter new markets.

Porter's five forces model is a useful tool for analyzing the specific industry (see Chapter 2). Careful study of how the five competitive forces (i.e., supplier power, buyer power, potential entrants, substitute products, and

EXHIBIT 6 | Sample General Environmental Categories

Technology	■ Information technology continues to become cheaper and have more practical applications. ■ Database technology allows organization of complex data and distribution of information. ■ Telecommunications technology and networks increasingly provide fast transmission of all sources of data, including voice, written communications, and video information.
Demographic Trends	■ Computerized design and manufacturing technologies continue to facilitate quality and flexibility. ■ Regional changes in population due to migration ■ Changing ethnic composition of the population ■ Aging of the population ■ Aging of the "baby boom" generation
Economic Trends	■ Interest rates ■ Inflation rates ■ Savings rates ■ Trade deficits ■ Budget deficits ■ Exchange rates
Political/Legal Environment	■ Anti-trust enforcement ■ Tax policy changes ■ Environmental protection laws ■ Extent of regulation/deregulation ■ Developing countries privatizing state monopolies ■ State-owned industries
Sociocultural Environment	■ Increasing number of women in the work force ■ Awareness of health and fitness issues ■ Concern for the environment ■ Concern for customers
Global Environment	■ Currency exchange rates ■ Free trade agreements ■ Trade deficits ■ New or developing markets

rivalry among competitors) affect a firm's strategy is important. These forces may create threats or opportunities relative to the specific business-level strategies (i.e., differentiation, cost leadership, focus) being implemented. Often a strategic group's analysis reveals how different environmental trends are affecting industry competitors. Strategic group analysis is useful for understanding the industry's competitive structures and firm constraints and possibilities within those structures.

Firms also need to analyze each of their primary competitors. This analysis should identify competitors' current strategies, strategic intent, strategic mission, capabilities, core competencies, and a competitive response profile. This information is useful to the focal firm in formulating an appropriate strategic intent and mission. Sources that can be used to gather information about a general environment, industry, and companies with whom the focal firm competes are listed in Appendix 1. Included in this list is a wide range of Web sites; publications, such as periodicals, newspapers, bibliographies, and directories of companies; industry ratios; forecasts; rankings/ratings; and other valuable statistics.

Internal Environment Analysis

The *internal environment* is composed of strengths and weaknesses internal to a firm that influence its strategic competitiveness. The purpose of completing an analysis of a firm's internal environment is to identify its strengths and weaknesses. The strengths and weaknesses in a firm's internal environment shape the strategic intent and strategic mission. The internal environment essentially indicates what a firm *can do*. Capabilities or skills that allow a firm to do something that others cannot do or that allow a firm to do something better than others do it are called strengths. *Strengths* can be categorized as something that a firm does especially well. Strengths help a firm take advantage of external opportunities or overcome external threats. Capabilities or skill deficiencies that prevent a firm from completing an important activity as well as others do it are called weaknesses. *Weaknesses* have the potential to prevent a firm from taking advantage of external opportunities or succeeding in efforts to overcome external threats. Thus, *weaknesses* can be thought of as something the firm needs to improve.

Analysis of the primary and support activities of the value chain provides opportunities to understand how external environmental trends affect the specific activities of a firm. Such analysis helps highlight strengths and weaknesses (see Chapter 3 for an explanation of the value chain). For purposes of preparing an oral or written presentation, it is important to note that strengths are internal resources and capabilities that have the potential to be core competencies. Weaknesses, on the other hand, have the potential to place a firm at a competitive disadvantage relative to its rivals.

When evaluating the internal characteristics of the firm, your analysis of the functional activities emphasized is critical. For instance, if the strategy of the firm is primarily technology-driven, it is important to evaluate the firm's R&D activities. If the strategy is market-driven, marketing functional activities are of paramount importance. If a firm has financial difficulties, critical financial ratios would require careful evaluation. In fact, because of the importance of financial health, most cases require financial analyses. Appendix II lists and operationally defines several common financial ratios. Included are exhibits describing profitability, liquidity, leverage, activity, and shareholders' return ratios. Other firm characteristics that should be examined to study the internal environment effectively include leadership, organizational culture, structure, and control systems.

Identification of Strategic Intent and Mission

Strategic intent is associated with a mind-set that managers seek to imbue within the company. Essentially, a mind-set captures how we view the world and our intended role in it. Strategic intent reflects or identifies a firm's ideal state. Strategic intent flows from a firm's opportunities, threats, strengths, and weaknesses. However, the major influence on strategic intent is a firm's *strengths*. Strategic intent should reflect a firm's intended character and reflects a commitment to "stretch" available resources and strengths in order to reach what may seem to be unattainable strategies and objectives in terms of Key Result Areas (KRAs). When established effectively, strategic intent can cause each employee to perform in ways never imagined possible. Strategic intent has the ability to reflect what may be the most worthy goal of all: to unseat the best or to be the best on a regional, national, or even international basis. Examples of strategic intent include:

- The relentless pursuit of perfection (Lexus).
- It's our strategic intent that customers worldwide view us as their most valued pharmaceutical partner (Eli Lilly).
- To be the top performer in everything that we do (Phillips Petroleum).
- To become a high performance multinational energy company—not the biggest, but the best (Unocal Corporation).
- We are dedicated to being the world's best at bringing people together (AT&T).
- Ben & Jerry's is dedicated to the creation and demonstration of a new corporate concept—linked prosperity.
- Our intent is to be better than the best (Best Products).
- The Children's Defense Fund exists to provide a strong and effective voice for the children of America who cannot vote, lobby, or speak for themselves.
- We build homes to meet people's dreams (Kaufman & Broad).
- We will be a leader in the emerging energy services industry by challenging conventional wisdom and creating superior value in a safe and environmentally responsible manner (PSI Energy, Inc.).
- We intend to become the single source of information technology for the home (Dell Computer Corporation).
- To be a premier provider of services and products that contribute to the health and well-being of people (MDS Health Group Limited).
- We seek to set the standard for excellence, leadership and integrity in the utility industry (New York State Electric & Gas Corp.).

The strategic mission flows from a firm's strategic intent; it is a statement used to describe a firm's unique intent and the scope of its operations in product and market terms. In its most basic form, the strategic mission indicates to stakeholders what a firm seeks to accomplish. An effective strategic mission reflects a firm's individuality and reveals its leadership's predisposition(s). The useful strategic mission shows how a firm differs from others and defines boundaries within which the firm intends to operate. Examples of strategic missions include:

- To make, distribute and sell the finest quality all-natural ice cream and related products in a wide variety of innovative flavors made from Vermont dairy products (Ben & Jerry's).
- To serve the natural and LP needs of the customers in the Clearwater and surrounding Florida SunCoast area in the most safe, reliable and economical manner possible while optimizing load growth, customer satisfaction, financial return to the City of Clearwater and the equity value of the Clearwater Gas System (Clearwater Gas System).
- Public Service Company of Colorado is an energy company that primarily provides gas, electricity and related services to present and potential markets.
- Our mission is to understand and satisfy customer expectations for quality and energy and energy-related products and services and profitably serve Oklahoma markets (Public Service Company of Oklahoma).
- Children's Hospital Medical Center is dedicated to serving the health-care needs of infants, children, and adolescents and to providing research and teaching programs that ensure delivery of the highest quality pediatric care to our community, the nation, and the world (Children's Hospital Medical Center).
- To provide services and products which will assist physicians, health care institutions, corporations, government agencies, and communities to improve the health and well-being of the people for whom they are responsible (MDS Health Group Limited).
- The William Penn Foundation is a private grant making organization created in 1945 by Otto Haas and his wife, Phoebe. The principal mission of the Foundation is to help improve the quality of life in the Delaware Valley (William Penn Foundation).

Key Result Areas (KRAs)

Once the strategic intent and mission have been defined, the analysis can turn to defining KRAs to help accomplish the intent and mission. *Key result areas* are categories of activities that must receive attention if the firm is to achieve its strategic intent and strategic mission. A rationale or justification and specific courses of action for each KRA should be specified. Typically, a firm should establish no more than six KRAs. KRAs should suggest (in broad terms) a firm's concerns and intended directions.

Flowing from the nature of a firm's KRAs, *strategies* are courses of action that must be taken to satisfy the requirements suggested by each KRA. Strategies typically have a one-, two-, or three-year time horizon (although it can be as long as five years). Strategies are developed to describe approaches to be used or methods to follow in order to attain the strategic intent and strategic mission (as suggested by the KRAs). Strategies reflect a group's action intentions. Flowing from individual strategies, *objectives* are specific and measurable statements describing actions that are to be completed to implement individual strategies. Objectives, which are more specific in nature than strategies, usually have a one-year or shorter time horizon.

Strategic planning should also result in cost linkages to courses of action. Once key cost assumptions are specified, these financial requirements can be tied to strategies and objectives. Once linked with strategies and objectives, cost or budgetary requirements can be related back to KRAs.

HINTS FOR PRESENTING AN EFFECTIVE STRATEGIC PLAN

There may be a temptation to spend most of your oral or written case analysis on results from the analysis. It is important, however, that you make an equal effort to develop and evaluate KRA alternatives and to design implementation for the chosen alternatives. In your presentation, the *analysis* of a case should not be overemphasized relative to the *synthesis* of results gained from your analytical efforts (see Exhibit 3).

Strategy Formulation: Choosing Key Result Areas

Once you have a formulated a strategic intent and mission, choosing among alternative KRAs is often one of the most difficult steps in preparing an oral or written presentation. Each alternative should be feasible (i.e., it should match the firm's strengths, capabilities, and especially core competencies), and feasibility should be demonstrated. In addition, you should show how each alternative takes advantage of the environmental opportunity or avoids/buffers against environmental threats. Developing carefully thought out alternatives requires synthesis of your analyses and creates greater credibility in oral and written case presentations.

Once you develop strong alternative KRAs, you must evaluate the set to choose the best ones. Your choice should be defensible and provide benefits over the other alternatives. Thus, it is important that both the alternative development and evaluation of alternatives be thorough. The choice of the best alternative should be explained and defended.

Key Result Area Implementation

After selecting the most appropriate KRAs (that is, those with the highest probability of enhancing a firm's strategic competitiveness), you must consider effective implementation. Effective synthesis is important to ensure that you have considered and evaluated all critical implementation issues. Issues you might consider include the structural changes necessary to implement the new strategies and objectives associated with each KRA. In addition, leadership changes and new controls or incentives may be necessary to implement these strategic actions. The implementation actions you recommend should be explicit and thoroughly explained. Occasionally, careful evaluation of implementation actions may show the strategy to be less favorable than you originally thought. A strategy is only as good as the firm's ability to implement it effectively. Therefore, expending the effort to determine effective implementation is important.

Process Issues

You should ensure that your presentation (either oral or written) has logical consistency throughout. For example, if your presentation identifies one purpose, but your analysis focuses on issues that differ from the stated purpose, the logical inconsistency will be apparent. Likewise, your alternatives should flow from the configuration of strengths, weaknesses, opportunities, and threats you identified through the internal and external analyses.

Thoroughness and clarity also are critical to an effective presentation. Thoroughness is represented by the comprehensiveness of the analysis and alternative generation. Furthermore, clarity in the results of the analyses, selection of the best alternative KRAs, and design of implementation actions are important. For example, your statement of the strengths and weaknesses should flow clearly and logically from the internal analyses presented.

Presentations (oral or written) that show logical consistency, thoroughness, and clarity of purpose, effective analyses, and feasible recommendations are more effective and will receive more positive evaluations. Being able to withstand tough questions from peers after your presentation will build credibility for your strategic plan presentation. Furthermore, developing the skills necessary to make such presentations will enhance your future job performance and career success.

APPENDIX I: SOURCES FOR INDUSTRY AND COMPETITOR ANALYSES

STRATEGIC MANAGEMENT WEB SITES

Search Engines (may be the broadest sources of information on companies and industries)

Alta Vista—*http://www.altavista.digital.com*
Excite—*http://www.excite.com*
InfoSeek—*http://www.infoseek.com*
Lycos—*http://www.lycos.com*
WebCrawler—*http://www.webcrawler.com*
Yahoo!—*http://www.yahoo.com*

Professional Societies

Academy of Management <*http://www.aom.pace.edu*> publishes *Academy of Management Journal, Academy of Management Review*, and *Academy of Management Executive*, three publications that often print articles on strategic management research, theory, and practice. The Academy of Management is the largest professional society for management research and education and has a large Business Policy and Strategy Division.

Strategic Management Society <*http://www.smsweb.org*> publishes the *Strategic Management Journal* (a top academic journal in strategic management).

Government Sources of Company Information and Data

Census Bureau <*http://www.census.gov*> provides useful links and information about social, demographic, and economic information.

Federal Trade Commission <*http://www.ftc.gov*> includes discussion on several antitrust and consumer protection laws useful to businesses looking for accurate information about business statutes.

Free EDGAR <*http://www.freeedgar.com*> provides free, unlimited access to real-time corporate data filed with the Securities and Exchange Commission (SEC).

Better Business Bureau <*http://www.bbb.org*> provides a wide variety of helpful publications, information, and other resources to both consumers and businesses to help people make informed marketplace decisions.

Publication Web Sites

Business Week <*http://www.businessweek.com*> allows search of *Business Week* magazine's articles by industry or topic, such as strategy.

Forbes <*http://www.forbes.com*> provides searching of *Forbes* magazine business articles and data.

Fortune <*http://www.fortune.com*> allows search of *Fortune* magazine and other articles, many of which are focused on strategy topics.

Financial Times <*http://www.ft.com*> provides access to many *Financial Times* articles, data, and surveys.

Wall Street Journal <*http://www.wsj.com*> *The Wall Street Journal* Interactive edition provides an excellent continuing stream of strategy-oriented articles and announcements.

ABSTRACTS AND INDEXES

Periodicals

ABI/Inform
Business Periodicals Index
InfoTrac (CD-ROM computer multidiscipline index)
Investext (CD-ROM)

Predicasts F&S Index United States
Predicasts Overview of Markets and Technology (PROMT)
Predicasts R&S Index Europe
Predicasts R&S Index International
Public Affairs Information Service Bulletin (PAIS)
Reader's Guide to Periodical Literature

Newspapers	*NewsBank*

Business NewsBank
New York Times Index
Wall Street Journal Index
Wall Street Journal/Barron's Index
Washington Post Index

BIBLIOGRAPHIES

Encyclopedia of Business Information Sources
Handbook of Business Information

DIRECTORIES

Companies—General	*America's Corporate Families and International Affiliates* *Hoover's Handbook of American Business* *Hoover's Handbook of World Business* *Million Dollar Directory* *Standard & Poor's Corporation Records* *Standard & Poor's Register of Corporations, Directors, and Executives* *Ward's Business Directory*
Companies—International	*America's Corporate Families and International Affiliates* *Business Asia* *Business China* *Business Eastern Europe* *Business Europe* *Business International* *Business International Money Report* *Business Latin America* *Directory of American Films Operating in Foreign Countries* *Directory of Foreign Firms Operating in the United States* *Hoover's Handbook of World Business* *International Directory of Company Histories* *Moody's Manuals, International* (2 volumes) *Who Owns Whom*
Companies—Manufacturers	*Manufacturing USA: Industry Analyses, Statistics, and Leading Companies* *Thomas Register of American Manufacturers* U.S. Office of Management and Budget, Executive Office of the President, *Standard Industrial Classification Manual* *U.S. Manufacturer's Directory*
Companies—Private	*Million Dollar Directory* *Ward's Directory*

Companies—Public	Annual Reports and 10-K Reports
	Disclosure (corporate reports)
	Q-File
	Moody's Manuals:
	  Moody's Bank and Finance Manual
	  Moody's Industrial Manual
	  Moody's International Manual
	  Moody's Municipal and Government Manual
	  Moody's OTC Industrial Manual
	  Moody's OTC Unlisted Manual

Moody's Public Utility Manual
Moody's Transportation Manual
Standard & Poor Corporation, *Standard Corporation Descriptions:*
Standard & Poor's Handbook
Standard & Poor's Industry Surveys
Standard & Poor's Investment Advisory Service
Standard & Poor's Outlook
Standard & Poor's Statistical Service

Companies—Subsidiaries and Affiliates

America's Corporate Families and International Affiliates
Ward's Directory
Who Owns Whom
Moody's Industry Review
Standard & Poor's Analyst's Handbook
Standard & Poor's Industry Report Service
Standard & Poor's Industry Surveys (2 volumes)
U.S. Department of Commerce, *U.S. Industrial Outlook*

INDUSTRY RATIOS

Dun & Bradstreet, *Industry Norms and Key Business Ratios*
Robert Morris Associates Annual Statement Studies
Troy Almanac of Business and Industrial Financial Ratios

INDUSTRY FORECASTS

International Trade Administration, *U.S. Industrial Outlook Predicasts Forecasts*

RANKINGS & RATINGS

Annual Report on American Industry in *Forbes*
Business Rankings and Salaries
Business One Irwin Business and Investment Almanac
Corporate and Industry Research Reports (CIRR)
Dun's Business Rankings
Moody's Industrial Review
Rating Guide to Franchises
Standard & Poor's Industry Report Service
Value Line Investment Survey
Ward's Business Directory

STATISTICS

American Statistics Index (ASI) Bureau of the Census, U.S. Department of Commerce, *Economic Census Publications*
Bureau of the Census, U.S. Department of Commerce, *Statistical Abstract of the United States*
Bureau of Economic Analysis, U.S. Department of Commerce, *Survey of Current Business*
Internal Revenue Service, U.S. Treasury Department, *Statistics of Income: Corporation Income Tax Returns*
Statistical Reference Index (SRI)

APPENDIX II: FINANCIAL ANALYSIS IN CASE STUDIES

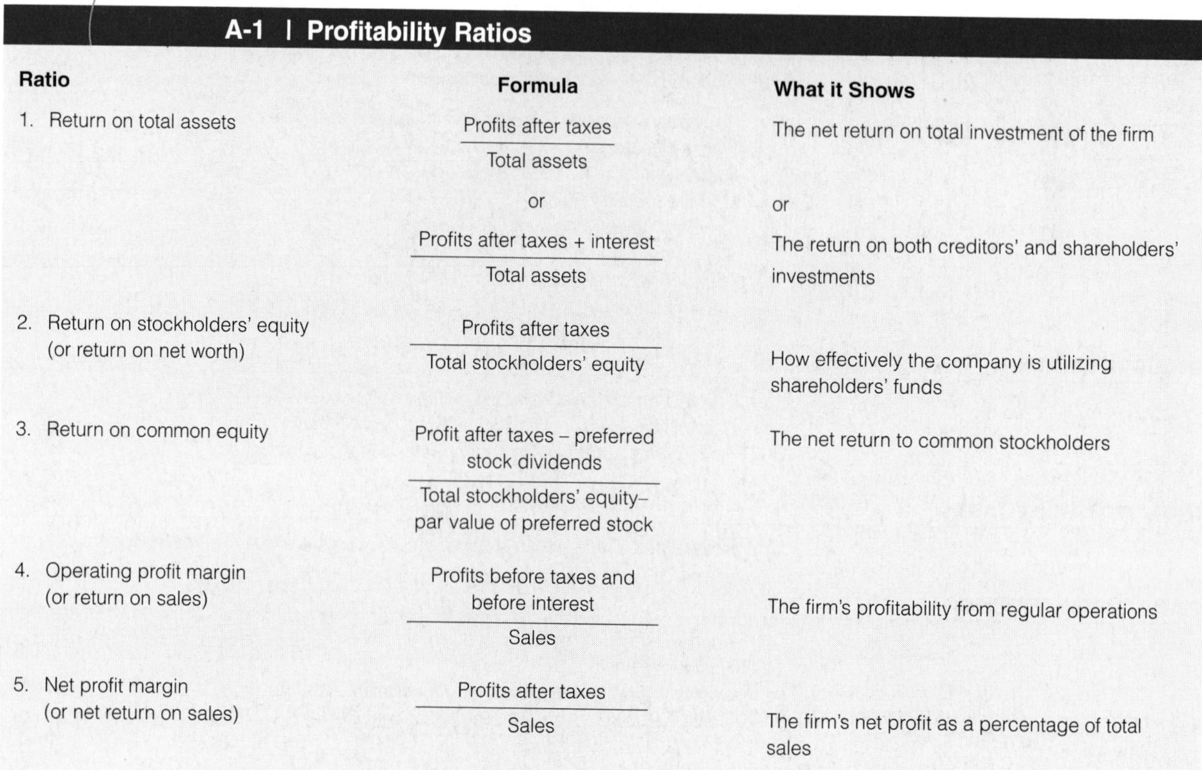

EXHIBIT A-1 | Profitability Ratios

Ratio	Formula	What it Shows
1. Return on total assets	$\frac{\text{Profits after taxes}}{\text{Total assets}}$	The net return on total investment of the firm
	or	or
	$\frac{\text{Profits after taxes + interest}}{\text{Total assets}}$	The return on both creditors' and shareholders' investments
2. Return on stockholders' equity (or return on net worth)	$\frac{\text{Profits after taxes}}{\text{Total stockholders' equity}}$	How effectively the company is utilizing shareholders' funds
3. Return on common equity	$\frac{\text{Profit after taxes – preferred stock dividends}}{\text{Total stockholders' equity– par value of preferred stock}}$	The net return to common stockholders
4. Operating profit margin (or return on sales)	$\frac{\text{Profits before taxes and before interest}}{\text{Sales}}$	The firm's profitability from regular operations
5. Net profit margin (or net return on sales)	$\frac{\text{Profits after taxes}}{\text{Sales}}$	The firm's net profit as a percentage of total sales

EXHIBIT A-2 | Liquidity Ratios

Ratio	Formula	What it Shows
1. Current ratio	$\frac{\text{Current assets}}{\text{Current liabilities}}$	The firm's ability to meet its current financial liabilities
2. Quick ratio (or acid-test ratio)	$\frac{\text{Current assets – inventory}}{\text{Current liabilities}}$	The firm's ability to pay off short-term obligations without relying on sales of inventory
3. Inventory to net working capital	$\frac{\text{Inventory}}{\text{Current assets – current liabilities}}$	The extent of which the firm's working capital is tied up in inventory

A-3 | Leverage Ratios

Ratio	Formula	What it Shows
1. Debt-to-assets	Total debt / Total assets	Total borrowed funds as a percentage of total assets
2. Debt-to-equity	Total debt / Total shareholders' equity	Borrowed funds versus the funds provided by shareholders
3. Long-term debt-to-equity	Long-term debt / Total shareholders' equity	Leverage used by the firm
4. Times-interest-earned (or coverage ratio)	Profits before interest and taxes / Total interest charges	The firm's ability to meet all interest payments
5. Fixed charge coverage	Profits before taxes and interest + lease obligations / Total interest charges + lease obligations	The firm's ability to meet all fixed-charge obligations including lease payments

A-4 | Activity Ratios

Ratio	Formula	What it Shows
1. Inventory turnover	Sales / Inventory of finished goods	The effectiveness of the firm in employing inventory
2. Fixed assets turnover	Sales / Fixed assets	The effectiveness of the firm in utilizing plant and equipment
3. Total assets turnover	Sales / Total assets	The effectiveness of the firm in utilizing total assets
4. Accounts receivable turnover	Annual credit sales / Accounts receivable	How many times the total receivables have been collected during the accounting period
5. Average collection period	Accounts receivable / Average daily sales	The average length of time the firm waits to collect payments after sales

A-5 | Shareholders' Return Ratios

Ratio	Formula	What it Shows
1. Dividend yield on common stock	$\frac{\text{Annual dividends per share}}{\text{Current market price per share}}$	A measure of return to common stockholders in the form of dividends.
2. Price-earnings ratio	$\frac{\text{Current market price per share}}{\text{After-tax earnings per share}}$	An indication of market perception of the firm. Usually, the faster-growing or less risky firms tend to have higher PE ratios than the slower-growing or more risky firms.
3. Dividend payout ratio	$\frac{\text{Annual dividends per share}}{\text{After-tax earnings per share}}$	An indication of dividends paid out as a percentage of profits.
4. Cash flow per share	$\frac{\text{After-tax profits + depreciation}}{\text{Number of common shares outstanding}}$	A measure of total cash per share available for use by the firm.

ENDNOTES

1. M. A. Lundberg, B. B. Levin, & H. I. Harrington, 2000, *Who Learns What From Cases and How? The Research Base for Teaching and Learning with Cases* (Englewood Cliffs, New Jersey: Lawrence Erlbaum Associates).
2. L. B. Barnes, A. J. Nelson, & C. R. Christensen, 1994, *Teaching and the Case Method: Text, Cases and Readings* (Boston: Harvard Business School Press); C. C. Lundberg, 1993, Introduction to the case method, in C. M. Vance (ed.), *Mastering Management Education* (Newbury Park, Calif.: Sage); C. Christensen, 1989, *Teaching and the Case Method* (Boston: Harvard Business School Publishing Division).
3. C. C. Lundberg, & E. Enz, 1993, A framework for student case preparation, *Case Research Journal*, 13 (Summer): 133.
4. J. Solitis, 1971, John Dewey, in L. E. Deighton (ed.), *Encyclopedia of Education* (New York: Macmillan and Free Press).
5. F. Bocker, 1987, Is case teaching more effective than lecture teaching in business administration? An exploratory analysis, *Interfaces*, 17(5): 64–71.

CASE 1

ABB in China: 1998

Suzanne Uhlen
Lund University

Michael Lubatkin
University of Connecticut

"I want to make ABB a company that encourages and demands innovation from all of its employees, and a company that creates the environment in which teamwork and innovation flourish," declares ABB's CEO Göran Lindahl. In seeking new growth, CEO Göran Lindahl is escaping the long shadow of his predecessor Percy Barnevik. The former CEO of ABB, Percy Barnevik, was argued to be one of the most successful international managers in Europe.

ABB, the world leader in electrical engineering, is a US$35 billion electrical engineering group, with companies all over the globe. It operates primarily in the fields of reliable and economical generation, transmission and distribution of electrical energy.[1] Much has been written about the worldwide company. In 1996 ABB was ranked in the top 40 listed by *Fortune* 500. Recently, the company announced its newest reorganization making it more up-to-date with the global world, as the current CEO, Göran Lindahl, expressed.[2] In 1997, Göran Lindahl took over from Percy Barnevik as CEO of the technology giant ABB, and is feeling the demanding market and shareholder pressures.

ABB has different priorities in different markets. Western Europe and North America are the company's biggest markets. However, the high-potential markets are the Middle East, Africa, Latin America and Asia. These markets are growing fast and ABB expects to have half of its customers in these regions not long into the next century. The priority is on building local manufacturing, engineering and other forms of added value. ABB wants to integrate these operations into the global networks to obtain full synergy effects and economies of scale.

During 1998 it was shown that the industrial production in OECD countries, in which ABB performs about 75 percent of its total business, continues to grow, although at a slower pace than the strong growth rates a year ago. Overall, industrial production in Europe is lower than a year ago, but still high compared with historical levels. Current economic activity in North America is slowing compared with the strong economy of recent years. In Latin America, high interest rates are delaying the financial closing of projects in an environment of reduced economic activity. The Indian economy is slowing due to reduced exports as a result of its strong currency compared with others in the region. Southeast Asia is gradually stabilizing at a low level, with reduced consumption and investments.

As a result of the ongoing economic uncertainty, overall global demand is forecast to remain soft in the near future. ABB expects to benefit with its well-established local presence around the world from higher demand in various industries and world markets. Appropriate cost cutting, continued selective tendering and successful working capital reduction programs are expected to continue contributing positively to the ABB Group results. The company recognizes the world to be rapidly changing and increasingly unpredictable. Efforts have paid off and the Group has taken its opportunities in Asia and positioned itself for future growth in what is seen to be "the world's most dynamic market over a long term—China."[3]

This case is to serve as a basis for classroom discussion rather than to illustrate either effective or ineffective handling of an administrative situation.

The interest in China is growing steadily and companies in Japan, the western European countries, the United States and elsewhere today view the Chinese market as having enormous potential. With a population of a billion and a growing economy, it seems to be worthwhile to gain a foothold in the market.[4] On the one hand, China represents a huge and largely untapped market. The Chinese market alone is potentially bigger than that of the United States, the European Community, and Japan combined! On the other hand, China's new firms are proving to be very competitive, and China's culture is quite different from that of the West. However, the Chinese market growth remains relatively good for enterprises such as Procter & Gamble, Motorola, Nestlé and ABB. This market acts as a lifeboat to many of worldwide companies suffering from the financial crisis in the rest of South East Asia. Nevertheless, discussions exist about China devaluating its currency, which might also drag China down into the crisis. Yet the country has not shown any visible scratches from the surrounding crisis. China seems to be unshakable and analysts are still valuing China as the country of the future.[5] Thus, the changes in China are creating both opportunities and threats for established worldwide companies. This is a country that, according to *Management Today,* will be one of the top 10 economies in the world by the year 2010.[6]

CHINESE INFLUENCE

> *China will enter the next century as the rising power in Asia after two decades of astonishing economic growth that has transformed the country and that has given rise to new challenges.*[7]

Many cities in China have more than five million inhabitants. It is a country that has had a growing economy which cannot be compared to that of any other country during almost three decades.[8] It is argued that China is not like any other developing country, due to the rapid changes that are taking place in certain areas. In some areas, such as with home electronics,[9] the development has surpassed the development in Western countries, while in other areas, China lags far behind.

The Chinese culture and society is more than five thousand years old with a unique cultural heritage of philosophy, science and technology, societal structures and traditional administrative bureaucracy.[10] With this in mind it is no wonder, according to researchers, that conflicts often occur between Chinese and foreign cultures. This is caused by foreign managers being accustomed to other values and norms, some of which are not acceptable in China.[11]

In the current half-year reports from worldwide companies, a distinct trend is noticed, according to Dagens Industri.[12] The more focus that the companies have put on basic industry, the more the Asian crisis tends to affect these companies. However, China can save these companies and others, especially those companies operating in the business of infrastructure.[13] Now that the Cold War with China has ended, economic growth is stabilizing and the country is demanding a speedy reconstruction. The country has begun to enjoy unprecedented strategic latitude for the first time in 200 years, and it no longer faces the threat of aggression from superior powers.[14] This has enabled the country to focus on economic developments as the driving force of both its domestic and foreign policies. According to Professor Yahuda, China's leaders are basing their legitimacy on providing stability and continued high levels of prosperity. The need for economic development is fueled by many other factors, such as providing employment for a vast population that increases by some 15 million people a year. In addition, there are significant regional inequalities that can be addressed only by further economic development.[15]

China is expected to evolve into a hybrid system of authoritarianism, democracy, socialism, and capitalism. Also recognized are the internal problems the country faces, such as environmental disasters, political struggles, and tensions between the emerging entrepreneurial economy and the vast parts of China still under state control.[16] Today China receives the most direct investment and foreign aid of any developing country. Many companies are eager to establish their presence in China, which, it is argued, attracts more than its proportionate share of investments.[17] However, "westerners cannot expect to know how China will develop and need to expect that the Chinese will always be different from them. Instead of trying to change China, they should look for positive steps that take their differences into account."[18]

According to China's Premier, Zhu Rongji, China is indeed the largest market in the world. However, due to the problem of duplicate construction, there is a problem of oversupply in some areas. Nevertheless, the Premier states that the market is far from being saturated.[19] Since China opened up its doors to the outside world in the late 1970s, a large number of foreign investors have gained rich returns from their investments, yet some have ended in failure. Some guiding keys to ensuring successful business in China, according to *China Daily*, include:[20]

- Making long-term strategies for the Chinese market. Competition is intensifying and market exploitation needs time and patience. Foreign companies eager to get a quick return are usually disappointed at the results.
- Localizing staff. They are familiar with the local business environment.
- Being aware of changes in policies and regulation. China is in a process of transforming from a planned economy to a market economy. Various policies and regulations are being revised and replaced, while new ones are being issued. Foreign investors must keep informed of the ongoing changes.
- Undertake practical market research. Due to social, economic, and cultural differences, practical and down-to-earth market research is a must before and during investment in China.

CHINESE CULTURAL INFLUENCE

There is a consensus among several authors that China has a traditional respect for age, hierarchy and authority.[21] This originates from the Confucian concept of *li* (rite, proprietary), which plays an important role in maintaining a person's social position. *Li* can be seen today in the existing traditional bureaucracy and in vertical relationships concerning centralization of decision-making, and in corruption to some extent, which is acceptable in such a cultural context.[22]

Second, the family is viewed as an essential social unit and there is a strong tendency to promote the collective or the group. Members within the family or group must maintain harmonious relationships and these social relations are seen as more important than the individual.[23] Thus, the family or clan norms are adopted as the formal code of conduct, and members are bound to these standards. Other research found that in modern China, business and industrial enterprises were perceived as an extension of the family system.[24]

Third, the concept of "face" (*mianzi*) is seen as an important characteristic. As Ju noted, the general idea of *mianzi* is related to "a reputation achieved through getting on in life through success and ostentation."[25] *Mianzi* also serves to enhance harmony within the family or group, so that the positive is expressed publicly and any conflicts remain private.[26] Hong has found that the concept of *mianzi* still plays an important role in social relationships and organizational behavior.[27] However, Yuan points out that there are two sides to this concept.[28] The first includes the individual's moral character, and the strong fear of losing this limits the person's behavior. The second aspect of *mianzi* involves assertions about a person, which is not seen quite as seriously as the former type of loss of face.[29]

The importance of personal relations (*guanxi*) is the fourth characteristic. According to Hong, persons with *guanxi* usually share a common birthplace, lineage, surname or experience, such as attending the same school, working together or belonging to the same organization.[30] A comparative study of decision-making in China and Britain has revealed that Chinese managers use their personal *guanxi* more widely to exchange information, negotiate with planning authorities and accelerate decision-making processes than do managers from British firms.[31] As it is, the network transmits information, and because contacts and cooperation are built on trust, it is seen as very serious if that trust is broken. If a trust is broken, the whole network will soon know about the incident and it is maintained that the person involved will have a hard time doing business again.[32]

A company that has been doing business on the Chinese market since 1919 is ABB. At that time this was the first product delivery to China, and it was not until 1979 that ABB established its first permanent office. Almost 11 years later, the heart of almost every chairman of an energy company started to pound with excitement if it heard the words "Asia" and "electricity." There were billions to be had from the booming demand for electricity in Asia.[33] But in recent years, the emerging Asian market has slowed down due to the financial crisis in the area. At the moment it seems as if China is the only country not affected by this financial crisis, and consequently, there are many companies that are now trying to be successful in China.

ABB is argued to be a company with a good position on the Chinese market, due to good performance, delivery, autonomy and its good name. Today the company has 9 representative offices and 15 joint ventures, and the number of employees has grown in four years from approximately 1,000 to 6,000 employees in China.

LOCAL ROOTS

The strategy of ABB is to use its global strength to support the needs of its local customers around the world. However, in China, ABB has a fairly high import duty on its products, which limits how much the company can sell. The idea of setting up local production in China was to increase the market share, as most Chinese customers do not have foreign currency[34] and are consequently forced to buy locally produced goods with the local currency. Furthermore, the reason for ABB to localize in China was not to achieve lower production costs, as some locally supplied components are actually more expensive in China than elsewhere. It was rather to be closer to the local market, and therefore facilitate a few local modifications to the products and provide shorter delivery times to the customer.

The phase "think global, act local" is said to reflect ABB's fundamental idea of strong local companies working together across borders to gain economies of scale in many areas.[35] In spite of ABB's claims to respond swiftly and surely to market conditions,[36] some of the products in China are not truly adapted to the local market. Most of the products are designed for the IEC—international standard association based in Europe. The company manufactures products that have to be tested according to different norms and standards. For example, North America ABB follows the ANSI-standard, and Canada ABB follows the CSA-standard.

However, some of ABB's products would not pass a type test based on the Chinese standards. That is not because the quality is too low; on the contrary, the quality of ABB products is sometimes too high. The quality of some of the products has evolved far beyond the requirements of Chinese standards; therefore these ABB products cannot meet local Chinese standards. The Chinese standards are based on what the local manufacturer can produce, because the country does not have much other information. As one manager at ABB in China stated,

> *We are not going to redesign our products in order to meet the standards, for the obvious reasons: Why should we take our quality out? Why shall we take the advances out? It does become an issue from time to time. Chinese are very risk averse, if we have not done the type test in China. It is more to cover themselves in case something goes wrong.*

Some managers feel that when ABB tries to adapt the products to the Chinese local standard, there is a negative response. The customer regards Western standards as superior and are actually asking for the superior product. The Chinese customers are seen as tough and sometimes demand more tests than ABB's products have gone through. Another reason put forward is insufficient feasibility studies when setting up new joint ventures in China. This delays the work when new information has to be collected about the market conditions. This aspect originates from the speed of changes in China and the difficulty for the company to catch up with what is going on.

However, when the so-called "type tests" of the product have been done, the company cannot change the design, due to the high costs involved in this test. Some criticism has been heard that ABB should adapt more to the Chinese situation, which the company cannot respond to concerning the technical design, because then the tests have to be done all over again. Of course, it is different from product to product; for some of the products, as one manager said,

> *We have to adapt to the configurations the customers have a demand for, because they have an option—go to the competitor.*

Still in most cases, the local ABB companies in China are not allowed to change the products other than according to agreements with the licensee. The reason for that is that the technology partners[37] have the overall view of the quality and performance. The ABB corporation definitely does not want to have different product performance from different countries. The products must have the same descriptions, so that they are seen as the same product all over the world. Consequently the local ABB company can only do a few modifications to the standard product for the specific customer and cannot change the technology involved. The technology partners have a few alternatives that meet the demands of the Chinese customers, and these products are also tested, but do not necessarily meet the Chinese standards.

The local ABB company tries to follow the ABB Group's policy, to be close to the customer and responsive to his or her needs.[38] In China, however, contracts are not commonly used, and this frequently obstructs satisfying many customer demands.

> *They keep on saying this is China and you should adapt to the Chinese way: Ok, if you want to buy a Chinese product that's fine, but this is our product—here are the terms and conditions. You can't just give in to that; otherwise you will kill your company, because they expect you to accept unlimited liability and lifetime warranty, and the risks to which you would expose your company would eventually lead to its shutting down, so you just cannot do that.*

ABB feels that to be close to the customer is the best guarantee that local requirements are met.[39] However, the headquarters in Zurich has also set up some rules about the kind of contracts that the local subsidiaries shall sign worldwide. In China contracts are something rather new, and many Chinese customers do not want it that way. The consequence is that some ABB companies in China do not use the standard ABB contract and are actually responsive to the customers' needs. When another ABB company comes to the same customer to set up a standard contract, the customer will refer them to the previous ABB company who did not seem to find the contract necessary. The question asked by the confused customer is said to be,

> *Why do you then have to use a standard contract when the other ABB didn't?*

PROFIT CENTERS

ABB's strategy is to take full advantage of its economies of scale and at the same time be represented by national companies in many home markets where some 5,000 entrepreneurial profit centers are attentive to every local customer. These companies are independent and have to stand on their own economically. The individual company's profit can easily be compared to revenue. The individual ABB company is measured on its own performance and needs. It is recognized that the profit centers are efficient for decentralization and that the organization can act relatively fast. This enables the company to be sensitive and responsive to potential problems. Each company has a fair amount of autonomy, making the individual company flexible. Even though ABB brochures state that the strategy of having profit centers enables the easy transfer of know-how across borders,[40] the direction is pretty much one way—from the technology partners, Business Areas and Country level to the subsidiary—rather than a two-way exchange.

Nevertheless, some conflicts of interest have occurred because the local ABB company and all other licensees are more or less dependent on their licensors in Europe.[41] In the local ABB company's case, one of their technology partners is measured like the others, on performance and profit. If it gives the local ABB company support, it will cost the former money, and likewise, if it sells the local ABB company components, it wants to make a profit. The consequence is that it is charging the local ABB company 25–100 percent over and above the cost of its parts.

> *So in the end you end up calling them as little as possible and we end up buying parts from local suppliers that probably we should not buy from local suppliers. And we reduce our quality. They have great profit figures, we have some profit figures but there are some real serious problems along the way.*

The technology partner argues that the prices are high because first it has to buy from its supplier and then sell to the local ABB company. This makes the products more expensive. The technology partners also pay for the "type tests" and all the product development.[42]

Conflicts of this sort have been occurring for a long time within ABB, but nobody has yet found a solution. It is difficult for a company like ABB, which is working with so many different products, markets, and in different cultures, to have anything other than sole profit centers. If the profit centers did not aim for a profit when selling within the ABB Group, then the companies would no longer be independent companies. Being independent is seen as a strength, and therefore it would be against the laws of nature if the companies were not always aiming for a profit. Nonetheless, between these independent companies with profit centers there are some extreme examples:

Our partner in Y-country was selling the finished product in China before. Now he sells the parts to the joint venture in China and wants to charge more for the parts than he did for the finished product, and that is because it is in his interest and he will be evaluated on his performance. If he does not do that, his profits will be too low and he will be blamed for it. So he has got to do what he has got to do. That is what he is motivated to do and that is what he is going to do.

To some extent the technology partners are selling indirectly to the Chinese market using non-official agents to avoid a high import tax and the high market price that exists on the Chinese market. ABB China is trying to force ABB companies to use only two official channels for ABB goods into the Chinese market—the locally produced by the local ABB company and the directly imported from a technology partner.

STRUCTURE

ABB is a huge enterprise with dispersed business areas, which encompass the three segments: Power Generation, Transmission & Distribution and Industrial Building systems. However, this recently has been changed and divided into six segments. Before the reorganization, every country had its national ABB head office, dealing with all the company business in that particular country. The other dimension of the matrix structure reflects the clustering of the activities of the enterprise into 36 Business Areas (or BAs). Each Business Area represents a distinct worldwide product market. Simplified, each BA is responsible for worldwide market allocation and the development of a worldwide technical strategy for that specific product line. Additional responsibilities for the BA are to coordinate who shall supply or deliver where, and also to work as a referee in potential disagreements between companies within the ABB Group.

However, in China, as in most developing countries, there is no BA in place and the decision-power of the country management is consequently closer at hand. The power of the decision-making tends to rest more heavily on the country level than on the BA level. Disagreements between licensees in Western countries and subsidiaries in China have been, and are occurring, due to different business orientations. The local subsidiary in China has two or more licensors in western countries, from which they buy components. Some of the licensees sold these components themselves before the local subsidiary was set up in China. In some cases the licensee feels that the market in China was taken from them and that they therefore can compensate for potentially lost sales only by charging the Chinese subsidiary a higher cost. Consequently, if the disagreeing partner seeks the BA as a referee in this kind of case, the following happens and is explained by one manager:

The BA are looking at the global business—we can increase our global business if we set up a joint venture in China. But the technology partner can't increase their business if we set up a joint venture in China. If we set up a joint venture in China the technology partner wants to increase its business also, they are going to do some work, and of course want something for it. The BA is really powerless to push those along.

To date, the licensors have been paying for all the technology development, which is the reason for charging a higher price for the components they are selling. Since the enterprise is divided into 5,000 profit centers and because each of these profit centers wants a profit when selling a component or product, there have been some shortcomings in the coordination and cooperation between the licensors and the local Chinese subsidiary.

The licensor in X-country makes the same breakers that the local ABB company does and faces the same problems with quality. For example, in Germany, they do not inform their licensee in China, who will also run into the same problem with quality in the near future. The problem is also discussed at the local ABB company, but if it suggests changes to the licensor, the licensor will evaluate on the basis of benefits to itself. Since they are going to invest their own resources, they are, of course, going to invest in areas beneficial to themselves first, or else charge the local ABB company extra. The consequences are thus summarized as follows:

> *We have had some things that would really help us here in China. But I don't even bother, because I know the reaction.*

Over 80 percent of what the Centers of Excellence produce is going to be exported,[43] making it important that the partners of the licensor manage the contemporary challenges and opportunities that can emerge. However, the BA divides the world markets into different areas in which the specific ABB companies are to be a first source.[44] Between some of the licensors and the local ABB company, this has resulted in certain disputes. For example,

> *We are responsible for the Peoples Republic of China's market and are supposed to be the sole source (or rather first source) because we have the expertise for this market. Our technology partner in X-country quotes into this market on a regular basis, does not inform us, and competes against us, and takes orders at a lower price. This can destroy our position in the marketplace.*

According to the licensor, it does not quote in the local ABB company's market because a customer with foreign currency will prefer imported products. The licensor argues that it does not go into the Chinese market and offer its products, but does get inquiries from ABB in Hong Kong and deliver to it. Hong Kong sells the products directly to the Chinese customer after having increased the original price several times higher in China than in Europe. It is a decision of the ABB China management that the Hong Kong coordinated sales force shall sell the local ABB company's products on the Chinese market among imported products and locally joint venture produced products. It helps to have sales coordination when deciding whether the products should be imported or not.

The technology is owned today by the Centers of Excellence in Europe or so-called licensors who pay for all the product development. ABB has chosen these licensees to be responsible for the company's world source of this specific technology. These units are responsible for developing new products and look after the quality. They arrange technical seminars about the technology, and by keeping special technology parts at only their factory. The strategic decision to keep special parts and the drawings of these parts at only one chosen factory enables the company to secure itself against competitors copying its products. Consequently, these parts will not be localized or purchased in China. However, for one products group (THS) there has been an organizational change, including the establishment of a unit called CHTET, which shall now own all new technology that is developed and also pay for the product development. This change now involves all product groups.

MULTICULTURAL

The current fashion, exemplified by ABB, is for the firms to be "multicultural multinationals" and be very sensitive to national differences.[45] Barnevik did debate that a culturally diverse set of managers can be a source of strength. According to Barnevik, managers should not try to eradicate these differences and establish a uniform managerial culture. Rather, they should seek to understand these cultural differences, to empathize with the views of people from different cultures, and to make compromises for such differences. Barnevik believes that the advantage of building a culturally diverse cadre of global managers is to improve the quality of managerial decision making.[46]

ABB in China is typified by a culturally diverse set of managers with a mixture of managerial ideas, derived from the different managers' national backgrounds, different values, and different methods of working. It then depends on which stage in personal development the manager has reached if he or she is going to be influenced and absorb the new climate. Or as one manager said,

> *If you are close to being retired you might not change so much, there isn't much point. But you can't work in the same way as you do at home—it just wouldn't work.*

According to another manager, ABB is a very international company with a great deal of influence from Scandinavian culture. However, it is a mixture of many cultures and it really depends on where the ABB company is located. In China the ABB culture is influenced by Chinese culture, by the environmental circumstances and by the laws. It is stricter in China than it is, for example, in Europe, because there are more rules. In spite of that, the managers do not feel that the result is a subculture of the ABB culture, rather a mixture of managers from different cultures—"we are a multidomestic company."

However, the top level of the ABB management is seen to be far away from the daily life at the subsidiary level in China, such as at the Local ABB company. Or as one manager expressed, "between that level and here, it's like the Pacific Ocean." All the managers agree that what the top level, including Barnevik and Lindahl,[47] says sounds very good and that is how it should be. Some managers continued the discussion and expressed this difference:

> *Sounds like I'm working for a different ABB than these guys are. What they talk about is really good and that is how it should be. But then when I sit back and go into the daily work and say that's not at all how it is. Somewhere along the line something gets lost between the theory and ideas at that level which is quite good. But when you get down to the working level and have to make it work something really gets lost along the way.*

EXPATRIATES

It is the BA with its worldwide networks that recommends, after suggestions from local offices, who is going to be sent as an expatriate to China or any other country. Thereafter, it is a cooperation between the BA and the country level, but it is the latter that finally decides which potential foreign expatriate is appropriate. However, it is important that an expatriate be able to fit into the system when coming to China with the high costs involved in being there. It is estimated that an expatriate costs the company about $0.25 million a year, due to the high taxes the company is paying to have a foreign employee.

ABB's identity is supported by a coordinating executive committee and an elite cadre of 500 global managers, which the top management shifts through a series of foreign assignments. Their job is intended to knit the organization together, to transfer expertise around the world, and to expose the company's leadership to differing perspectives.[48]

However, ABB in China is not yet a closely tied country unit for several reasons. First, the expatriates come from the outside and most of their contacts are back in the home country. Most expatriates feel that the home office does not understand how difficult it can be to work abroad and that they need support. "Sometimes it just feels like I'm standing in the desert screaming," one expatriate expressed. The home office feels that the expatriates can be a burden because they need so much support. It is the home office, along with the BA, that selects candidates for foreign placement, even though it has brief or no knowledge, of how it is to work in that country. However, it would be impossible to have insights into how the working conditions are in the other operating countries.

Concerning growing a strong country unit, the expatriates are stationed in China on assignments for a relatively short time period, and are thus less able to build up informal networks. Few efforts are put into establishing an informal network, because the few contact persons the managers have today will eventually return home after a while and there is no formal way of contacting the replacing person. Of course, there is the formal LOTUS Notes®, which is a computer-based network with all managers worldwide included, but it is said to be deficient in building the preferred strong country unit within China. Finally, the managers do not feel they can offer the time to establish informal networks to be rebuilt due to the replacement of expatriates every two to three years. A worldwide policy within the company limits the expatriates to operating as such for not more than five years at a time. Executives have questioned this policy, saying that

> *It is during the first year you learn what is going on and get into your new clothes. During the second year you get to know the people and the system, the third year you apply what you learned and the fourth year you start to make some changes—and this is very specific for developing countries.*

Three years ago the expatriates did not get any information or education about the country-specific situation before being sent out to ABB's subsidiaries in China. Today, when there are about 100 expatriates with 25 different nationalities in China, it has changed, but it is mostly up to the individual to collect material and prepare for the acclimatization. Within the worldwide corporation there is no policy of formal training before one is sent out as an expatriate; rather, it is up to the home office of the expatriates to prepare the managers for the foreign assignments. Some argue that "you could never prepare for the situation in China anyway, so any education wouldn't help." Others say that this has resulted in a lot of problems with the expatriates, which results in even higher costs for the company if the expatriate fails.

When the contract time as an expatriate is finished, he or she may feel unsure about placement for him or herself back home. Thus, it is important for the expatriate to have close contact with the home office and make use of the free trips home. In most cases the expatriates do not know what will happen when the contract expires and they are to return back home.

THE CHINESE CHALLENGE

According to ABB they prefer to send out managers with 10–15 years of experience. However, the task is difficult when the location may be in a rural area overseas and most managers with 10–15 years experience have families who are less likely to want to move to these areas. Sometimes a manager gets sent to China when the company does not want to fire him.

> *So instead they send the manager to where the pitfalls are greater and challenges bigger and potential risks are greater.*

It is found throughout the research that most expatriates have strong feelings about living in and adapting to the new environment in China. Newly arrived expatriates seem to enjoy the respect they get from the Chinese, and several managers delightedly expressed,

> *I love it here, and how could you not, you get a lot of respect just because you're a foreigner and life is just pleasant.*

Other expatriates that have stayed a bit longer disliked the situation to a great extent and a number of expatriates have asked to leave because their expectations about the situation in China have not been fulfilled.[49]

One country-specific situation is how to teach the Chinese employees to work in teams. The worldwide company ABB is especially focusing on creating an environment that fosters teamwork and promotes active participation among its employees.[50] This is a big challenge for Western managers (the expatriates) because the Chinese employees have a hard time working in a group, due to cultural and historical reasons. Some of the local ABB companies have failed in their attempt with team working, *ad hoc* groups and the like, because they have been in too much of a hurry. Or, as one manager said,

> *Here in China the management needs to encourage the teamwork a little bit, because it is a little against the culture and the nature of the people. This is not a question of lack of time for the managers, but I do not think we have the overall commitment to do it. Some of us feel strongly that we should, others that we can't.*

Another consequence is expatriate management does not have the understanding or the commitment to teach local employees the company values, a situation that has resulted in unacceptable quality at some companies.

ABB has a great advantage in comparison to other worldwide companies due to its top priority of building deep local roots by hiring and training local managers who know their local markets.[51] Replacing expatriates with local Chinese employees, where the local employees are set to be successors to the expatriates after a certain number of years, shows the commitment to the philosophy of having a local profile. However, as the Chinese employees are coming from an extremely different system from the western expatriates, it takes quite a long time for the former to get exposed to western management practices. To ease this problem and to teach western management style, ABB China, among other companies, has recently set up an agreement with a business school in Beijing to arrange training for Chinese employees with good management potential. This is specific for ABB China because in developed countries the employees are responsible for their own development.[52] Recently ABB had its own school in Beijing for Chinese employees to learn ABB culture and management. Unfortunately, this school had to close due to the profit-center philosophy, where even the school had to charge the individual ABB companies for teaching their employees.

ABB is sending about 100 local Chinese employees to an ABB company in a Western country every year. After problems with several employees quitting after training, ABB has set up precautions with a service commitment. The employee (or new employer) has to pay back the training investment if he or she quits or that the employee signs an agreement that he or she will continue working for ABB for a certain number of years. The problem with local employees quitting after ABB's investment in training also has been experienced in India and Thailand. It is shown in the personnel turnover rate, approximately 22 percent within ABB China, that many local employees are aiming for the experience of working for an international company such as ABB and then move on to a better-paying job.

However, by having local employees, the local ABB company is responsive to local conditions and sensitive to important cultural objectives such as the Chinese "guanxi."[53] It has been decided that the local employees should take care of the customer contact, since the expatriates are usually stationed for only a few years at one location and are consequently not able to build up strong connections with customers.

REORGANIZATION

The organization is decentralized based on delegated responsibility and the right to make decisions in order to respond quickly to customers' requirements. In the core of this complex organization are two principles: decentralization of responsibility and individual accountability. These principles have been very relevant in China, which is a relatively young country for ABB to be operating in.[54] Decentralization is highly developed and the expatriate[55] managers have a wide responsibility that would normally demand more than one specialist in a western company. However, in some instances the organization is criticized for being too centralized.

The changes in China happen very fast, and according to ABB brochures, the greatest efficiency gains lie in improving the way people work together.[56] Within the ABB China region, communication has its shortcomings. Companies with overlapping products or similar products do not exchange information to any large degree or coordinate their marketing strategies. On the technical side, communication is used frequently, which can be seen when a manager usually receives up to 100 e-mails per day from other ABB employees. However, tactics for building up effective informal communication are lacking between most ABB companies operating in China. The distances are large, and accordingly, a meeting demands greater efforts than in almost any other country in the world.

According to the former CEO, Percy Barnevik, the purpose with the matrix organization is to make the company more bottom heavy than top heavy—"clean out the headquarters in Zurich and send everybody out, have independent companies operating in an entrepreneurial manner," as one respondent mentioned. It is further maintained in the company brochures that these entrepreneurial business units have the freedom and motivation to run their own business with a sense of personal responsibility.[57]

However, the result from the matrix organization in China is ABB subsidiaries have ABB China's objectives (the country level) and the Business Areas' (BA) objectives to follow. ABB China is measuring how the different companies are performing within China. The BA, on the contrary, is measuring how the specific products are performing on a worldwide basis and what the profitability is for the products. Each BA has a financial controller, and each country level has one also.

> *Rarely are the two coordinated, or do they meet. So you end up with one set of objectives from each . . . Duplication! Which one shall you follow?*

According to the ABB Mission Book, the roles in the two dimensions of the ABB matrix must be complementary.[58] It demands that both the individual company and the headquarter level are flexible and strive for extensive communication. This is the way to avoid the matrix interchange becoming cumbersome and slow. It is seen to be the only way to "reap the benefits of being global (economies of scale, technological strength, etc.) and of being multidomestic (a high degree of decentralization and local roots in the countries in which we operate)."

For many years ABB was widely regarded as an exemplary European company, yet it is undergoing a second major restructuring within four years. CEO Göran Lindahl says that restructuring is aimed at making the organization faster and more cost efficient.[59] Due to the demands of a more global market, there are reasons for getting rid of the regional structure and to concentrate more on the specific countries. The reorganization has basically dismantled one half of the matrix: the country management. Henceforth, the BAs will manage their businesses on a worldwide basis and there will no longer be the confusion caused by BA and country management setting different objectives. At the same time, segments are split up (many BAs form a segment) to make them more manageable (e.g., the Transmission and Distribution segment has been split into two segments: Transmission and Distribution). To conclude, the general managers of the individual joint ventures and other units will have only one manager above them in the organization that has a global view of the business. In China, it also means the dismantling of the Hong Kong organization as well as the Asia Pacific organization.

According to Göran Lindahl, the reorganization is preparation for a much faster rate of change on the markets and for the company to be able to respond more effectively to the demands of globalization. It is seen as an aggressive strategy to create a platform for future growth.

FUTURE VISION

CEO Göran Lindahl was appointed in 1997 to be the new president and chief executive of ABB. His view of the future is that it can no longer be extrapolated, but can be forecast by creativity, imagination, ingenuity, innovation—action based not on what was, but on what could be. The corporate culture needs to be replaced by globalizing leadership and corporate values. ABB is focusing on this by creating a unified organization across national, cultural, and business borders.

On the path towards the next century, ABB is going to focus on several essential elements: a strong local presence; a fast and flexible organization; the best technology and products available; and excellent local managers who know the business culture, are able to cross national and business borders easily, and who can execute your strategy faster than the competition.[60]

> *We are living in a rapidly changing environment, and our competitors will not stand still. In the face of this great challenge and opportunity, enterprises that adapt quickly and meet customer needs will be the winner, and this is the ultimate goal of ABB.*[61]

APPENDIX

Motorola

Motorola was involved in Russia and faced some problems with Glasnost and decline of the country. At that time the founder of the company, Galvin, realized that there was no future in Russia and declared that China was the country where the growth was to be. Consequently, Motorola established its first representative office in China in 1987 and has grown very fast ever since. Today, China generates more than 10 percent of Motorola's sales and the company has its major businesses in China.

Motorola has found that modernization in China happens quickly and all their competitors are present in the country. They still predict China to be the potential leader in Asia for their business. The customers also have high expectations on the products Motorola is offering, because the products are regarded to be very expensive. However, the problem the company is facing in China is that the company is growing too fast, or as expressed another way,

> *The problem we have is that Motorola is growing very fast and it is like chasing a speeding train and trying to catch up with it.*

Presently, Motorola has 12,000 employees and 200 expatriates in China, where the goal is that Chinese successors will take over the jobs of the expatriates. The expatriates are sent out on assignments for two to three years, with the possibility of renewal with a one–two rotation, but limited to a maximum of six years as an expatriate. High demands are set on the expatriates, especially concerning the difficulties experienced teaching teamwork to local employees. This is very important within the company, since all the strategy planning is done in teams. When the contract time for the expatriate has expired, the following is expressed:

> *You have done your job when the time comes and you have left the company and everything is working smoothly, but if everything is falling apart, you are a failure as an expatriate and have not taught a successor.*

However, progress has been made in developing the company's local employees. Motorola has set up training abroad. The training, nevertheless, is preferably held within China, with rotation assignments and training at Motorola University. This company university was set up in 1994 when the company found that the Chinese universities did not turn out sufficiently well trained students. Within the company there is, however, a requirement that every employee worldwide shall have at least 40 hours of training, which is exceeded in China. There must be a combination of good training and mentor development. Motorola admits that it does not provide enough training for foreign expatriates before they come to China.

You get more understanding if you look like a foreigner and make some mistakes than if you don't. Overseas Chinese are measured through other standards than other foreigners.

Some expatriates just cannot handle the situation in China. If an expatriate fails, it has to be handled with care, otherwise the person loses face when coming back to the home office. The company also has pointed out that it needs expatriates with 10–15 years of experience in order to teach the local employees the company values and to transfer company knowledge. However, the people that are willing to change addresses and move to China are the younger employees with less than five years of experience.

The expatriates are often responsible for transferring technology knowledge and helping start projects, especially the newly set-up Center of Excellence in Tianjin, where $750 million was invested. This was Motorola's first manufacturing research laboratory outside the United States. The company has invested $1.1 billion in China and has plans to invest another $1–1.5 million. Motorola has also set up two branches of worldwide training universities to educate customers, suppliers, and government officials, as well as its own employees. The invested money in China is from the earnings within the whole enterprise, with the motivation that the Chinese market is going to be huge. Sincere commitment has been made and the present CEO, Gary Tucker, expressed the following:

When Motorola has come to your country they never leave . . . We manufacture in China, because this is where our market is. We get wealth by going to a lot of countries around the world and then doing well in that country.

The expansion strategy in China is through joint ventures. However, it is important that the Chinese partners bring something of value, which means that the partners have to be approved by the CEO. The company has become "so decentralized that it has become bad" and that the company desires to reorganize more along customer than product lines. A practical reorganization has taken place to move everybody operating in Beijing to the same newly built headquarters. However, entrepreneurial activities are also of importance, but difficult, due to financial motivation and autonomy.

In China the products are localized with Chinese characters on the cellular phones and pagers. In 1987 Motorola started selling pagers and thought there would not be a big market because the telephone-net was not well established. The company invented codebooks, which enabled two-way communication. Fortunately this also worked in Hong Kong, Singapore, and Taiwan. After five years of operation in China, the company does not have deep roots in the market. Motorola has invested huge sums in sponsoring environmental protection, providing scholarships to students, building labs at universities, and donating money to primary schools in rural areas.[62]

The worldwide organization is a "pyramid," with the corporate on top and Business Units underneath—"then put the apex at the bottom." The Corporate office works as the glue that holds the organization together. In 1997 Motorola conducted a reorganization to better reflect the global nature of the business.[63] The coordination is safeguarded by this new formal structure. However, the informal information flow is better, but it is overused. The information flow is mostly through e-mails. A manager gets approximately 70–100 per day, of which less than 30 percent are really useful. Regarding communication, the following was expressed:

Some days it feels like we have all these opportunities and we do not really communicate.

All the controllers or general managers in the joint ventures get together quarterly to counsel, to solve problems and give support to each other. Information is encouraged, but no system is developed to track what is going on in all the six districts in China where the company is operating. Competition between the different units is a common problem Motorola is experiencing, which results in the customers getting confused. This is a problem that has no solution due to the matrix organization, or as expressed another way,

> *We do not have the answers, because if we are too centralized then we miss new opportunities. How do you encourage creativity and yet keep people from competing with each other?*

What makes Motorola a worldwide company is a set of key common beliefs or guiding principles from the role model and father figure of the company, Galvin: "uncompromising integrity and constant respect for people—that is what makes us Motorola." This is the principal code of conduct that Motorola practices, and which the management has to reread and sign every two years.

Motorola notes it "obviously" has to change because it is operating in the Chinese market—for example, show face, build relations, and go to ceremonial meetings. It is essential that the partner is reliable, that the business makes sense, and that it is legal. However, Motorola always looks the same all over the world, but it is the expatriates and their families that have made an effort to adapt to the surrounding changes.

The challenge for Motorola is doing business in China. China is very difficult for a company like Motorola, or as said another way, Motorola has trouble in China

> *because they would like to control the system and everything takes a long time because they will make sure that you are not cheating. You must be able to work with all the people that come from different departments and to let them trust you. Ordinary things like getting water, electricity, etc., is a huge problem. Doing business in the Chinese system is a challenge and therefore creates pressure because you get frustrated.*

Procter & Gamble

In August 1998 China's largest international employer had been in China for ten successful years. Procter and Gamble, or P&G, has approximately 5,000 employees and 100 expatriates spread in 11 joint ventures and wholly owned enterprises in the country. P&G was ranked this year on *Fortune* magazine's "World's Most Admired Companies" list. Currently, the biggest market for the company is China, where new companies are being established. However, before companies were established in China, a feasibility study was done. As with most other feasibility studies done in China, the information was outdated even though it was only one year old, and people were criticized for not having sufficient knowledge about the country's specific situation.

The expatriates sent to China for the P&G account are no more prepared for the situation, except for knowing that the company has a deep culture that will support them. Furthermore, a continuous effort exists within the company to put different cultural backgrounds together. Cultural values are also written down and are consistent all over the world. However, the different expatriates have a wide variety of cultural backgrounds, and their culture is colored by their management style. This mixture of management styles might confuse the local Chinese employees.

The main benefit gained for an expatriate is the one offered in the daily work. One exception is made, for the expatriate sales people, who get a whole year of orientation training and language training. In line with the localization demands, the number of expatriates is decreasing. Due to the high costs involved in having expatriates, who are mostly 3–4 levels up in the organization, one key strategy is to develop local employees. Everybody who is an expatriate for P&G has a sponsor back home, a contact. It is essential to keep contact with the sponsor so that it is not just a name on a paper, and people are encouraged to go back home once a year at the company's cost. There is no official limit in expatriate policy within the company; however, most expatriates are on a three-year contract. The expatriate network is not yet an issue; however the expatriates are said to be a very close group—"we are all in this together and we have a common vision."

The optimal goal for P&G is to develop the organization so that it can be a Chinese-run company. Today, everything is made in the Chinese P&G factories for internal use and the company opened up a research center in Beijing, in cooperation with a prominent university.[64] If the company has developed a good idea in China, the company will analyze how to re-apply the idea in the rest of the world.

Counterfeits are the greatest competition for the company and an extensive problem. However, not all the products from P&G are sold in China and the quality of the products sold is not as high as it is in Western countries. The Chinese customers are unable to pay for better value; nevertheless, the company is trying to offer a consistency of quality to Chinese consumers.

In the Chinese P&G organization, fewer layers are developed and the decision-making takes a shorter time within the organization. Because the company evolved very quickly and the market is so dynamic and changing, it has not had the time to implement the layers—"only tried to understand the market." Consequently, the Chinese organization and structure are not the same as in other countries, but the Chinese organization is more efficient. P&G will implement some of the ideas from China in other countries. At the current time a reorganization is taking place within the world-wide P&G group where the organization is being changed along with the culture and reward system—all to make the company more flexible.[65]

As for the Chinese situation, "*guanxi*" is mentioned, which is difficult for the expatriates to establish, and consequently the company relies on the local staff. On the contrary, the local employees get an immense amount of education at P&G's own school. Also, some of the company's expatriates have an explicit responsibility to deal with company principles, values, and all the technical specifics for P&G. The company falls short with the expatriates, because "they are so into running the business that sometimes the coaching of the locals is not possible."

One of the challenges Procter & Gamble faces in China is the difficulty in dealing with the government. The company has dealt with this by searching for a sophisticated government-relations manager who shall report not only to the head of operations in China but also to the chief executive of the company.[66]

NESTLÉ

In the beginning of the 1980s China asked the world's largest food company—Nestlé—to come and build "milk streets" in the country. China was unfamiliar with how to produce milk and turned to Nestlé, whose core business is actually milk powder. From that time the company has grown strongly in China and now has almost 4,000 employees, where 200 of them are foreign expatriates.

Today Nestlé is regarded as having come from Swiss roots and turned into a transnational corporation.[67] Nestlé is argued to have its foundation in its history for being locally adaptive. During the first world war, Nestlé gave its local managers increasing independence to avoid disruptions in distribution.[68] This resulted in a great deal of Nestlé's operations being established at other locations than its headquarters in Switzerland. Another cause was the company's belief that the consumers' tastes were very local and that there were no synergy effects to be gained by standardizing the products. However, in 1993 the company started to rethink its belief in localization, due to the increasing competition in the industry. Nestlé has acquired several local brands, influenced by its own country's culture, causing Nestlé to standardize where it is possible.[69]

However, although the company is growing in China, it is not always selling products with as much margin as desired. The downside is that they must have lower margins in order to be competitive, which might not always be profitable. On the question, "Why does Nestlé have to be in China?", the following was expressed:

> *It is because China is a large country and if you have a company that is present in more than 100 countries, you see it as a must for all international companies to be present there. We supply all over the world and it is our obligation to bring food to the people—which is the Company's priority.*

Nestlé entered China with a long-term strategy to focus on the long-run perspective. Nestlé's overall approach is stated to be "Think global and act local!" The Company's strategy is guided by several fundamental principles, such as the following:

> *Nestlé's existing products will grow through innovation and renovation while maintaining a balance in geographic activities and product lines.*[70]

With regard to the local Chinese employees, they receive a few days of Nestlé education to learn about the

Nestlé culture, but the expatriates have less training going to another country. It is up to the home country to decide if it is necessary to train expatriates before sending them on an often three-year foreign assignment. However the leadership talent is highly valued within the company and consequently Nestlé has developed courses for this. The managers can independently develop their leadership talent without any connection with the specific company style or culture. Community centers have been developed to help expatriates with their contacts, supporting these expatriates psychologically and even offering language training.

In 1997 Nestlé's *The Basic Nestlé Management and Leadership Principles* was published, aimed to make "the Nestlé spirit" of the company generally known throughout the organization by discussions, seminars, and courses.[71] According to the CEO of Nestlé China, Theo Klauser, this publication is the key factor in Nestlé's corporate culture and started the company's international expansion 130 years ago.[72]

Within the organization of Nestlé China, the company has developed a specific structure, due to the joint-venture configuration. The information flow is easy and smooth between these regions, thanks to the company concentrating its activities in only three regions in China. However, communication is said to be on a high level; yet, it is not even necessary to get all levels involved. As an example, only one unit in China takes care of all the marketing. At the same time, each Nestlé company in China is responsible for its own turn-over rate, which creates the flexible and decentralized company Nestlé is today. Quite unique for a world-wide company, Nestlé does not have any external e-mail network, believed to concentrate the flow of information within the company.

A major challenge indicated for Nestlé in China is in building long relationships to establish Nestlé as the leading food company. Difficulties are to bring the products to a more acceptable level in terms of profitability. Legal difficulties are also more important than in any other country. Other challenges are the issues concerning change, about which the following was expressed:

> *Change happens every couple of months here, that is how the environment is, a lot of employees come from other more stable countries and sometimes find it difficult with all the changes. Change is how things are in China—it is normal. It is when something doesn't change, that is when you get worried! It is expected to change! Different from other countries where changes can be difficult to get.*

ENDNOTES

1. *100 years of experience ensures peak technology today,* ABB STAL AB, Finspong.
2. *Dagens Industri,* August 13, 1998, p. 25.
3. Ibid.
4. Usunier, Jean-Claude, *Marketing across Cultures.*
5. *Dagens Industri,* July 2, 1998.
6. *Management Today,* April 1996, by David Smith, p. 49.
7. Ahlquist, Magnus as editor, *The recruiter's guide to China,* by preface of Professor Michael Yahuda.
8. *Bizniz,* Sept. 30, 1997.
9. Examples include VCD-player, CD-ROM player, mobile telephones, beepers, and video cameras.
10. Garten, Jeffrey E., "Opening the Doors for Business in China," *Harvard Business Review,* May–June, 1998, pp. 160–172.
11. *Månadens Affärer,* Nov. 11, 1996, searched through AFFÄRSDATA via http://www.ad.se/bibsam/.
12. *Dagens Industri,* August 19, 1998, searched through AFFÄRSDATA via http://www.ad.se/bibsam/.
13. Ibid.
14. Ahlquist, Magnus as editor, *The recruiter's guide to China,* by preface of Professor Michael Yahuda.
15. Ibid.
16. Garten, Jeffrey E., "Opening the Doors for Business in China," *Harvard Business Review,* May–June, 1998, pp. 167–171.
17. See a recent report from *The Economist,* www.economist.com, in October 1998.
18. Hong Yung Lee, "The implications of reform for ideology, state and society in China," *Journal of International Affairs,* vol. 39, no. 2, pp. 77–90.
19. An interview with Premier Zhu Rongji in *China Daily,* March 20, 1998, p. 2.
20. *China Daily, Business Weekly,* Vol. 18, No. 5479, March 29–April 4, 1998, p. 2.
21. Hoon-Halbauer, Sing Keow, *Management of Sino-Foreign Joint Ventures;* Yuan Lu, *Management Decision-Making in Chinese Enterprises.*
22. Ibid.
23. Ma, Jun, *Intergovernal relations and economic management in China.*
24. Laaksonen, Oiva, *Management in China during and after Mao in enterprises, government, and party.*

25. Ju, Yanan, *Understanding China,* p. 45.
26. Hwang, Quanyu, *Business decision making in China.*
27. Hong Yung Lee, "The implications of reform for ideology, state and society in China," *Journal of International Affairs,* Vol. 39, No. 2, pp. 77–90.
28. Yuan Lu, *Management decision-making in Chinese enterprises.*
29. Yuan Lu, *Management decision-making in Chinese enterprises.*
30. Hong Yung Lee, "The implications of reform for ideology, state and society in China," *Journal of International Affairs,* Vol. 39, No. 2, pp. 77–90.
31. Yuan Lu, *Management decision-making in Chinese enterprises.*
32. *Månadens Affärer,* Nov. 11, 1996.
33. *The Economist,* Oct. 28, 1995, searched from http://www.economist.com.
34. Due to China still being a quite closed country, Chinese people are not able to obtain foreign currency, other than in very limited amounts.
35. ABB, "The art of being Local," ABB Corporate Communications, Ltd., printed in Switzerland.
36. ABB Brochure, "You can rely on the power of ABB." ABB Asea Brown Boveri, Ltd., Department CC-C, Zurich.
37. Technology partner (in this case) = Center of Excellence (CE), = Licensors.
38. ABB's Mission, Values, and Policies.
39. HV Switchgear, ABB, ABB Business Area H. V. Switchgear, Printed in Switzerland.
40. ABB Asea Brown Boveri, Ltd., You can rely on the power of ABB, Department CC-C, Zurich.
41. Licensing is defined here as a form of external production where the owner of technology or proprietary right (licensor) agrees to transfer this to a joint venture in China which is responsible for local production (licensee).
42. During the study this has changed to some degree, due to a unit called CHTET being introduced.
43. http://www.abb.se/swg/switchgear/index.htm in November 1997.
44. First source = you are the first source, but if you cannot meet the customers' requirements, the second source steps in.
45. *The Economist,* Jan. 6, 1996, searched from http://www.economist.com.
46. Ibid.
47. Göran Lindahl is the present CEO, Chairman of the Board.
48. *The Economist,* Jan. 6, 1996, searched from http://www.economist.com.
49. There are two types of common, but false, expectations expatriates have when coming to China. Either they believe they are going to make a lot of money or they are going to experience the old Chinese culture—a culture that, most of the time, does not correspond to the culture of today in China.
50. ABB's Mission, Values, and Policies, Zurich, 1991.
51. ABB, "The art of being Local," ABB Corporate Communications, Ltd., printed in Switzerland.
52. ABB's Mission, Values, and Policies, Zurich, 1991.
53. *Guanxi* = connections, relations.
54. ABB set up its first office, a representative office, in 1979.
55. An expatriate is a person who has a working placement outside the home country.
56. ABB Asea Brown Boveri, Ltd., *You can rely on the power of ABB,* Department CC-C, Zurich.
57. ABB Asea Brown Boveri, Ltd., *You can rely on the power of ABB,* Department CC-C, Zurich.
58. ABB's Mission, Values, and Policies.
59. *Dagens Industri,* August 13, 1998, p. 25.
60. "Meeting the Challenges of the Future," Presentation given to the Executives Club of Chicago, October 16, 1997.
61. ABB, "Leading the way in efficient and reliable supply of electric power," ABB Transmission and Distribution, Ltd., Hong Kong.
62. Garten, Jeffrey E., "Opening the Doors for Business in China," *Harvard Business Review,* May–June, 1998, pp. 174–175.
63. Motorola Annual Report, 1997.
64. Qinghua University.
65. Procter & Gamble Annual Report, 1998.
66. Garten, Jeffrey E., "Opening the Doors for Business in China," *Harvard Business Review,* May–June, 1998, pp. 173–175.
67. http://www.Nestlé.com/html/home.html, September 1998.
68. Quelch, J. A., & Hoff, E. J., "Customizing Global Marketing," *Harvard Business Review,* 1986, May–June, No. 3, pp. 59–60.
69. Brorsson, Skarsten, Torstensson, *Marknadsföring på den inre markanden—Standardisering eller Anpassning,* Thesis at Lund University, 1993.
70. http://www.Nestlé.com/html/h2h.html, in September 1998.
71. Nestlé Management Report, 1997.
72. Interview with CEO of Nestlé China, Theo Klauser, *Metro,* July 1998, p. 27.

CASE 2

Adidas

Giana Boissonnas
Ursula Hilliard
Jacques Horovitz
International Institute for Management Development

It was April 1993 and Robert Louis-Dreyfus had just become the majority shareholder of Adidas, after purchasing 15 percent of the company. Pioneer in the sporting goods industry, Adidas had once ridden the waves of great success but had now sunk to its lowest ebb. Louis-Dreyfus was now confronted with the challenge of how to turn around the company, currently faced with a deficit of close to US$100 million.

There were numerous hurdles on Louis-Dreyfus's road to creating the best sports brand in the world. The company was losing market share in some of its major European markets and had neglected the vast American market, where Nike and Reebok were now firmly established. Nike and Reebok had outmarketed Adidas. They had developed brash marketing campaigns supported by huge budgets and begun targeting teenagers and women with lower quality, more fashionable leisure products.

Adidas had struggled through turbulent organizational and management changes after the death of its founder Alfred "Adi" Dassler in 1978. (Refer to Exhibit 1 for the Adidas company history.) The company had remained in the family until 1990, at which point Bernard Tapie, a French business tycoon and populist politician, bought it. Tapie had since been jailed following his involvement in a soccer-fixing scandal. Adidas had subsequently been declared bankrupt and left to a number of French banks who, in turn, approached Louis-Dreyfus for help.

The company was in economic and organizational disarray. It was, however, just the type of challenge Louis-Dreyfus liked. He seized the opportunity to save Adidas and give it a new lease on life.

THE SPORTING GOODS INDUSTRY AND KEY INFLUENCING FACTORS

The first thing Louis-Dreyfus did as CEO was analyze the sporting goods industry. He knew little about it, apart from being a fanatical soccer fan. His past career had been in advertising, pharmaceutical market research and his family's banking business. (Refer to Exhibit 2 for details on Louis-Dreyfus's career.)

Market Overview

In 1992, the world sporting goods market was estimated at $43 billion.[1] The top three geographical markets were the US, accounting for approximately 50 percent followed by Western Europe with approximately 25 percent, and Japan with 10 percent. Industry analysts expected the market to grow by 28 percent to $55 billion by 1998. (Refer to Exhibit 3 for worldwide sporting goods industry statistics.)

The market was divided into three segments: clothing, footwear, and equipment. Given the recent trends for using sports clothing both for leisure and sport, the clothing segment accounted for over half of sales. The footwear segment accounted for a third of sales, and sports equipment accounted for the remaining 13 percent of sales.[2]

This case was prepared as a basis for class discussion rather than to illustrate either effective or ineffective handling of a business situation. Copyright © 1998 by **IMD**—International Institute for Management Development, Lausanne, Switzerland. All rights reserved. Not to be used or reproduced without written permission directly from **IMD**, Lausanne, Switzerland.

1 | The History of Adidas, 1920–1993

It all began just after World War I in 1920 in Herzogenaurach, a small village in the south of Germany. Alfred "Adi" Dassler, a German amateur athlete, and his brother Rudolph began making slippers with soles made from old tires. Adi converted the slippers into gymnastics shoes and soccer shoes with nailed-on studs or cleats. At the 1928 Amsterdam Olympics, German athletes first showcased Dassler shoes to the world. In 1936, the brothers achieved a major breakthrough when Jesse Owens agreed to wear their shoes in the Berlin Olympics, where he won four gold medals. By 1937, the Dassler brothers were manufacturing shoes for more than 11 different sports.

In 1949, however, the two brothers quarreled, and Rudolph left to establish the Puma sports company, while Alfred registered Adidas and the now-famous three diagonal stripes. Alfred was the innovator and used his connections in the athletic arena not only to promote Adidas, but also to develop new materials and techniques. Adidas grew from strength to strength, and athletes continued to wear the company's products at the Olympic games and soccer World Cup.

The first samples of Adidas footwear were used at the 1952 Helsinki Olympics. In 1954, Germany won the World Cup, wearing the new screw-in studs on their soccer shoes. In 1963, the first Adidas soccer ball was produced. And in 1967, clothing was added to the product range. Alfred continued to use the Olympic Games as a forum to promote his shoes. By the Montréal Olympics in 1976, over 80% of medal winners were Adidas-equipped athletes. Business was booming, and Adidas had become a household name in the sporting arena, synonymous with sporting achievement.

In the 1970s, however, two major changes affected the fortunes of Adidas. Nike entered the American market in 1972, with low-quality, fashionable products and was followed by Reebok in 1979. Nike targeted teenagers with leisure wear; Adidas continued to focus on performance shoes for athletes and the middle-aged category. Then, in 1978, Adolph Dassler died.

Adidas struggled through the 1980s. It had to deal with major management changes and was quickly outrun by changes in the industry. The street popularity of Adidas faded as newer, more aggressive companies like Nike and Reebok took control.

Footwear. North America accounted for approximately 50 percent of worldwide sales of branded athletic footwear. In 1992, Nike was the leader with 32 percent of the market, followed by Reebok with 21 percent. Adidas held a mere 4 percent market share in 1992 (compared with a previous high of 70 percent) and was ranked seventh.

The European market represented 31 percent of worldwide sales. Adidas was the leader in its home market, Germany, and Italy. However, the company had lost its leadership position to Nike and Reebok in France, Spain and the UK.

(Refer to Exhibit 4 and Exhibit 5 for statistics on the athletic footwear market and major-player market shares.)

The Trends in Sports in the 1990s

The market was undergoing many changes in the early 1990s. It was developing fast and was increasingly being affected by fashion trends:

2 | Robert Louis-Dreyfus's Background

Robert Louis-Dreyfus (47) was appointed chairman of the management board of Adidas on April 7, 1993.

Prior to his appointment, he was CEO of Saatchi & Saatchi, London. He restructured and recapitalized the company, sold businesses and cut 4,000 jobs. In 1993, the company returned to profitability.

With IMS International, a market research company that serviced the pharmaceutical industry in over 70 countries, he held the position of COO from 1982–1983 and CEO from 1984–1988. He built the company up from a market capitalization of $400 million to $1.7 billion and then, in 1988, sold the company to Dun & Bradstreet.

From 1974 to 1981, he was managing director for diversification with Louis-Dreyfus SA, his family's company and one of France's largest privately held companies.

He also worked in finance at the merchant bank S.G. Warburg in London.

3 | Geographical Breakdown of Wholesale Volume of World Sporting Goods Market (US$ billion)

				ESTIMATED			
WORLD	**1990**	**1991**	**1992**	**1995e**	**1996e**	**1997e**	**1998e**
North and South America	**22**	**23**	**24**	**28**	**29**	**30**	**30**
U.S.	20	21	22	25	26	26	27
Canada	1	1	1	1	1	1	1
Central America	1	1	1	1	1	1	1
South America	1	1	1	1	1	1	1
Europe	**11**	**11**	**11**	**12**	**13**	**13**	**14**
Western Europe	10	10	10	11	12	12	12
Eastern Europe	1	1	1	1	1	1	1
Asia	**4**	**5**	**5**	**5**	**6**	**6**	**7**
Japan	4	4	4	4	4	4	4
Others	1	1	1	1	2	2	3
Pacific	**1**	**1**	**1**	**1**	**2**	**1**	**1**
Australia	0	1	1	0	1	1	1
New Zealand	0	0	0	0	0	0	0
Africa	**0**	**0**	**0**	**1**	**1**	**1**	**1**
Others	**1**	**2**	**2**	**2**	**2**	**3**	**3**
Total	**40**	**41**	**43**	**49**	**52**	**53**	**55**

Source: "Adidas: A Star in Stripes," *UBS Global Research*, October 1995.
Note: Figures are rounded up.

4 | Worldwide Athletic Footwear Market

1992 BRANDED ATHLETIC FOOTWEAR SALES BY REGION AT WHOLESALE PRICES (US$ Million)

	Total	Europe	North America	Latin America	Asia Pacific
Sales	13,700	4,300	6,500	1,200	1,700
% of sales		31%	47%	9%	12%
Pairs of shoes (millions)	612	124	391	44	53

Source: Harvard Business School, Planet Reebok, Case number 9-594-074.

1993 USA ATHLETIC ADULT SHOE MARKET (US$ at Wholesale Prices)

1993	US$ million	%
Basketball	1,600	26%
Cross-training/fitness	1,150	18%
Walking	800	13%
Hiking/outdoor	650	10%
Running/jogging	525	8%
Aerobic	380	6%
Tennis	325	5%
Golf	280	4%
Cleated/studded shoes	275	4%
Other	225	4%
Other court	40	1%
Total	**6,250**	

Source: Merrill Lynch, Adidas Report, Jan. 14, 1997.

5 | Market Shares in the US and European Athletic Footwear Market

1984–1992 MARKET SHARE % US ATHLETIC FOOTWEAR MARKET (Primary Sport Retail Chains)

%	1984	1985	1986	1987	1988	1992
Nike	33	30	20	18	23	32
Reebok	3	14	31	30	27	21
Adidas	10	8	6	5	4	4

Sources: "Adidas: A Star in Stripes," *UBS Global Research,* October 1995; Athletic Footwear—Industry Report, "U.S. Branded Athletic Footwear," Salomon Brothers, Inc., Steinberg, H.R., Figure 3, New York, May 1, 1989.

1993 MARKET SHARE % EUROPEAN ATHLETIC FOOTWEAR MARKET (Primary Sport Retail Chains)

%	Adidas	Nike	Reebok
UK	13	26	32
France	21	27	24
Germany	32	19	17
Italy	17	15	16
Spain	13	14	21

Source: Nielsen published in *International Management,* July/August 1994.

1990–1992 MARKET SHARE IN GERMANY (Adidas's home market)

%	Jan-90	Jan-91	Jan-92	Nov-92
Adidas	47	41	35	33
Nike	9	12	19	20
Puma	17	17	13	14
Reebok	5	7	10	12
Asics	5	5	6	6

Source: Adidas/UBS estimates.

- People, and in particular women, were taking more interest in health and sports. They gave leisure time more attention, especially in Europe and the US, as more positive attitudes towards health emerged, characterized by the development of aerobics and other fitness sports.
- Young people were changing the philosophy of sport and setting the trends. Sport was no longer reserved for an elite group of gifted people. New "fun" sports that involved everyone were developing: street sports such as street basketball and soccer, mountain biking, and sliding/gliding activities.
- Athletic footwear was no longer reserved for professional exercise and competition but had also become a part of leisurewear, particularly for the under-25 age group. Eighty percent of sports shoes were now used for casual wear.[3]
- The development of outdoor recreation sports, such as skiing, golfing, jogging and hiking, was encouraging growth of functional outdoor clothing. Less prone to fashion changes than the more youthful "street" and "fun" sports, outdoor recreation sports required authentic, performance products.
- In parallel to this movement, casual footwear was also expanding outdoors with the growth in popularity of brands like Timberland. The casual shoe

market in the US was estimated to be worth over $5 billion. Timberland's sales had increased by over 40 percent to $420 million in 1993.

- Traditional sports, such as soccer in Europe and basketball in the US remained, nevertheless, extremely popular.

Product Research and Development

Although fashion and design were important factors in the sporting goods industry, particularly for the under-25 age group, technology was a key element of success and provided manufacturers with their key differentiation factors. Unlike fashion, technological advances gave companies a lasting competitive edge over their rivals.

For the sports footwear sector, 1 to 3 percent of annual footwear sales was reinvested in the development of new products and technology that were designed to provide increased comfort and performance for the consumer.

Production

By 1992, most sporting goods companies outsourced the main part of their footwear production to the Far East for cost reasons, although some of the clothing production was still maintained in Europe or the US. In-house company-owned factories manufactured approximately 10 percent of production. Sourcing and production lead-times for footwear were 5–8 months. Depending on the quality of the shoe, between 20 and 40 percent of production costs were related to personnel costs, 20 to 40 percent to material costs, and 20 to 30 percent to other costs. Price differences between regions resulted mainly from a difference in personnel costs.

Retail Product Cycles

There were two distinct seasons in the sporting goods industry that dictated the timeline of the production process: summer/spring and autumn/winter. Sixty percent of the footwear production and 75 percent of the textile production were renewed each year and replaced by new models and/or colors. Tight control of inventory and production planning was critical.

Distribution

The distribution process depended largely on the size of the company and the market. The bigger the manufacturer and the more important the market, the more likely it was that the company would bypass distributors and sell directly to a retailer.

In Europe, manufacturers tended to distribute via a wholesaler or local distributor who, in turn, distributed to the different retailers. The distributor was responsible for warehousing, distribution and marketing of the product. It was estimated that wholesale distribution, when used by the manufacturer, represented 20 percent of the final customer price.

In the US, on the other hand, manufacturers tended to sell directly to retailers who, in turn, sold to the customers. Retail distribution added an additional 100 percent to the manufacturer's price.

Many of the retailers were former athletes or coaches who had shifted into the business side of sports at the end of their sporting careers. The 1990s, however, was the era of change in retailing. Rapid consolidation took place, and old-line sporting goods stores went bankrupt or were sold off to major regional chains.

There were four kinds of retailers:

1. Independent specialized chains of sporting goods retailers, which accounted for approximately 60 percent of the distribution of sporting goods:
    - In the US: Foot Locker, Sport Authority, and Foot Action.
    - In Germany: Intersport, and Sport 2000.
    - In France: Decathlon, Intersport, and Go Sport.
2. Department stores and hypermarkets: Hypermarkets were particularly popular in France.
3. Shoe shops.
4. Mail order. Mail order was more popular in the UK than in other countries.

ADIDAS AND THE COMPETITIVE ENVIRONMENT

The next challenge for Louis-Dreyfus was to analyze his two major competitors: Nike and Reebok. Although the industry had been monopolized by Adidas since the early 1920s, all this had changed in the 1970s when first Nike and then Reebok entered the US market and started to aggressively attack Adidas in Europe.

Nike was now clearly established as the worldwide

leader, with sales of over $3.4 billion in 1992. Two-thirds of Nike's sales were generated in the US, and over 75 percent of sales were in footwear.

Reebok was in second position, with $3 billion in 1992 worldwide sales. Like Nike, the US was Reebok's single biggest market, representing over two-thirds of sales. Approximately 90 percent of Reebok sales were in the footwear segment.

Adidas was now in third position, with $1.7 billion in sales in 1992. It was not surprising that, as a European company, 75 percent of Adidas sales were generated in Europe, with only 15 percent in North America. Furthermore, unlike its direct competitors, Adidas had a broad portfolio, with 55 percent of sales generated by footwear, 40 percent by clothing, and the remaining 5 percent by equipment.

(Refer to Exhibits 6 to 9 for financial information on Nike, Reebok and Adidas.)

Nike's Key Strategies

Phil Knight, an amateur runner, and his one-time coach Bill Bowerman founded Nike in Oregon, USA, in 1964. The company's principal business activity, according to its annual report, involved the "design, development

EXHIBIT

6 | Nike Financial Information

EVOLUTION OF NIKE FINANCIALS 1990–1992
(US$ million; Year ended May 31)

	1990	1991	1992
Total Revenues	2,235	3,004	3,405
Cost of sales	1,384	1,850	2,089
Gross profit	851	1,154	1,316
Gross profit margin	38%	38%	39%
Selling, general and admin	455	664	761
Operating profit	396	490	555
Other expenses, interest and taxes	154	202	225
Net income	242	288	330
Net profit margin	11%	10%	10%
Geographical Revenues			
US	1,755	2,141	2,271
Europe	334	665	920
Asia/Pacific	29	56	76
Canada, Latin America and other	116	141	139

Source: Nike Annual Reports.

BREAKDOWN OF NIKE SALES BY SEGMENT 1990–1992 (US$ million)

	1990	1991	1992
US footwear	1369	1676	1,748
US clothing	266	326	361
Other brands	120	139	162
Total US	**1,755**	**2,141**	**2,271**
	79%	71%	67%
International footwear	369	652	868
International clothing	110	210	267
Total International	**480**	**863**	**1,134**
Total Nike	**2,235**	**3,004**	**3,405**

Source: Nike Annual Reports.

7 | Reebok Financial Information

EVOLUTION OF REEBOK FINANCIALS 1990–1992 (US$ million; Year ended December 31)

	1990	1991	1992
Total revenues	2,160	2,734	3,023
Cost of goods	1,288	1,645	1,809
Gross profit	872	1,089	1,214
Gross profit margin	40%	40%	40%
Selling, general and admin	556	666	807
Operating profit	316	423	407
Other expenses, interest and taxes	138	188	331
Net income	178	235	76
Net profit margin	8%	9%	3%
Geographical Revenues			
U.S.	1,655	1,883	1,982
UK	0	380	415
Other Europe	385	296	425
Rest of world	120	175	201

Source: Reebok 1993 Annual Report, Edgar Online.
Note: In 1992, there were important restructuring changes related to the write-down of Avia and estimated losses from the planned sales of Ellesse and Boston Whaler.

BREAKDOWN OF REEBOK SALES BY SEGMENT 1990–1992 (US$ million)

	1990	1991	1992
US footwear	1,172	1,336	1,472
US clothing	43	53	60
International	475	833	1,008
Other brands (including Avia, Rockport, Boston Whalers and Ellesse)	470	512	483

Source: Reebok 1993 Annual Report, Edgar Online.

and worldwide marketing of high quality footwear, apparel and accessory products."

It also sold a line of dress and casual footwear and accessories for men, women and children under the brand "Cole Haan."

Nike: Market Positioning and Segmentation. While Nike associated itself with top athletes and portrayed itself as a serious brand for world-class athletes, the company broadened its image to appeal to teenagers and young adults. Knight had said,

> *The secret of the business is to build the kind of shoes professional athletes will wear, then put them on the pros. The rest of the market will follow.*[4]

Nike dominated the basketball, American football and baseball shoe categories because of the success of the "Air Jordan" basketball shoe and clothing campaign.

Nike: Product Research and Development. In-addition to the company's own staff of specialists, Nike used research committees and advisory boards made up of coaches, athletes, trainers, and other experts to review designs, materials, and concepts for product improvement.

Nike had developed the "Air-Sole" technology with the help of Frank Rudy, a NASA engineer who developed the idea of using air in athletic shoes to reduce the shock of impact. The process used pressurized gas encapsulated

8 | Adidas Financial Information*

ADIDAS FINANCIALS 1989–1992 (US$ million; Year ended December 31)

	1989	1990	1991	1992
End of year exchange rate US$/DEM	*0.59*	*0.67*	*0.66*	*0.62*
Total sales	1,887	2,229	2,208	1,704
Change in inventory	4	–15	–21	–24
Other operating income	61	49	74	77
Total revenues	1,952	2,263	2,261	1,758
Cost of materials	1,264	1,400	1,411	1,094
Gross profit	688	864	849	664
Gross profit margin	35%	38%	38%	38%
Personnel costs	258	297	287	242
Depreciation and amortization	36	33	33	27
Other operating expenses**	386	440	466	407
Operating profit	8	93	64	–13
Other expenses, interest and taxes	84	58	53	79
Net income	–77	35	11	-92
Net profit margin	–4%	2%	0.5%	-5%
Number of Employees	9,532	9,067	8,329	6,401

**Includes advertising, promotion and travel expenses, services, rent and lease, legal and advisory fees, and commissions.

	1989	1990	1991	1992
End of year exchange rate US$/DEM	*0.59*	*0.67*	*0.66*	*0.62*
Fixed assets	139	149	139	132
Current assets	846	995	872	669
Total assets	985	1,144	1,011	800
Equity	127	169	178	168
Equity as % of total assets	13%	15%	18%	21%
Investments in tangible assets	37	31	34	38
Depreciation of tangible assets	34	31	31	25

Source: Adidas annual reports.
*Note that Adidas financial data were reported in German DM. For the purposes of the case, the financial data have been converted to US$.

in polyurethane. Nike claimed that Nike-Air cushioning allowed athletes to train longer and feel more comfortable while reducing their potential of injury.

Nike: Marketing and Advertising. Nike leveraged athlete endorsements as the key element in its advertising strategy. The company chose top-class athletes with brash personalities—John McEnroe and André Agassi (tennis), Ronaldo (soccer), Michael Jordan (basketball)—which particularly appealed to the young market and was consistent with the image Nike wanted to promote.

Nike had created Nike Sports Management with the objective of creating a coherent portfolio of marketing agreements for the company's endorsement activities. Nike also moved into career management of its sports stars. "We are not a shoe company, we are a sports company," said Liz Dolan, vice president of corporate communications. As of early 1993, a new venture had also been created with Creative Artists Agency and Michael

8 | Adidas Financial Information *(Continued)*

ADIDAS GEOGRAPHICAL REVENUES 1989–1992
(US$ million; Year ended December 31)

Geographical Revenues	1989	1990	1991	1992
Total	1,887	2,229	2,208	1,704
Europe	1,265	1,652	1,660	1,258
% total	67%	74%	75%	74%
North America	442	370	347	258
% total	23%	17%	16%	15%
Asia Pacific	80	84	92	93
% total	4%	4%	4%	5%
Latin America	41	56	66	70
% total	2%	3%	3%	4%
Africa	59	67	43	25
% total	3%	3%	2%	1%

Source: Adidas annual reports.

BREAKDOWN OF ADIDAS SALES BY SEGMENT (US$ million)

	1989	1990	1991	1992
End-of-year exchange rate, US$/DEM	*0.59*	*0.67*	*0.66*	*0.62*
Footwear	1,014	1,163	1,179	900
% total	54%	52%	53%	53%
Clothing	686	846	823	651
% total	36%	38%	37%	38%
Equipment, royalties, and other	188	220	206	153
% total	10%	10%	9%	9%

Source: Adidas annual reports.

Ovitz to "redefine and expand the world of sports entertainment."

The company invested most of its advertising budget in television spots targeted at young customers, and on new television and cable television (MTV). The spots sold lifestyle, a combination of sports and music, fashion, and fun. With a small agency in the US, Weiden and Kennedy, Nike developed a series of hundreds of short, creative spots using the sponsored athletes, with one single slogan, "Just do it," that were also run in overseas markets with minimal adaptation.

On average, Nike's advertising budget accounted for an estimated 10 percent of sales. In 1992, Nike spent $180 million in the US and between $80 million and $100 million in Europe.

Nike: Production. Nike behaved like a marketing and design group and had totally outsourced its footwear production primarily to Indonesia, China, South Korea, Taiwan, and Thailand. The company also had manufacturing agreements with independent factories in Brazil, Hungary, Italy, and Mexico.

Approximately 40 percent of apparel production for sale in the US was manufactured in the US. All of the non-US apparel was manufactured outside the US.

Nike: Distribution. Nike sold its products to approximately 14,000 retail accounts in the US and through a mix of distributors, licenses, and subsidiaries in approximately 80 other countries.

Nike would help distributors by giving them sales

9 | Comparison of Total Worldwide Revenues and Net Income (US$ million)

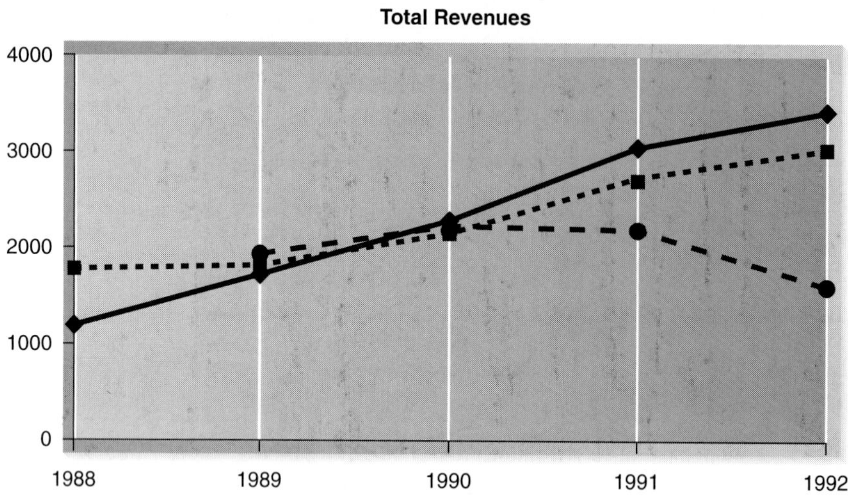

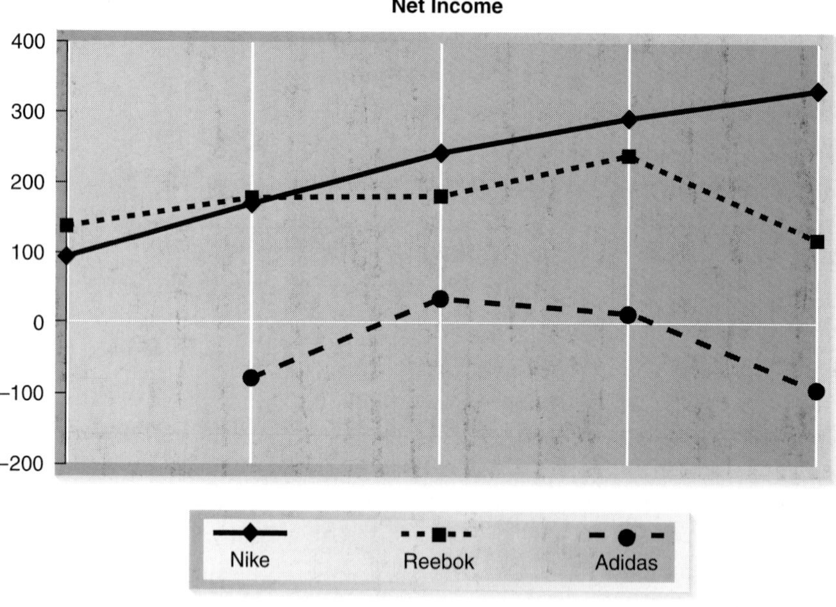

Source: 1988–1992 company annual reports.

support and training. Over the last five years, Nike had bought back previous distributors in Denmark, Belgium, Spain, Switzerland, Italy, Finland, Portugal, and the Netherlands. There were still independent distributors in Austria, Ireland, Greece, Turkey, and Eastern Europe.

Nike's retail strategy was to sell shoes through different channels to different target segments. Nike sold shoes for athletes in specialized shops, for sportspeople in sports stores, for amateur sportspeople in department stores, and for the mass consumer in shoe stores. Nike had pioneered the "futures," or pre-ordering, process. Due to the strong demand for Nike products among retailers, Nike held a commanding brand position. Consequently, 77 percent of Nike footwear products were pre-ordered in 1992. This strategy had considerable impact on inventory management, production planning, and securing retail accounts.

In 1990, Nike opened its first Nike Town store in Portland, Oregon, a 20,000-square-foot mall with 14 stores that sold equipment for 25 sports. In 1992, the company opened its second Nike Town store in Chicago. Nike was expecting to open 10 to 12 other Nike Towns all over the US.

Reebok's Key Strategies

Reebok had two major divisions: Reebok and the Specialty Business Group. The Reebok Division was responsible for

> *designing, producing and marketing sports and fitness footwear, apparel and accessories that combine the attributes of athletic performance with style, including footwear for basketball, running, soccer, tennis, track and field, volleyball, football, baseball, aerobics, cross training and walking activities, as well as athletic apparel and accessories.*[5]

The division's athletic apparel and accessories included Reebok-branded products, the "Above the Rim" brand of basketball clothing and accessories, and the "Tinley" brand of running and cycling performance clothing. The division also produced clothing and accessories for toddlers and infants under the brand "Weebok."

The Specialty Business Group consisted of Reebok-brand outdoor products and golf products under the "Greg Norman" brand, along with the company's other major brands, including "BOKS" casual footwear, "Avia" women's fitness products, and "Rockport" outdoor and casual clothing.

Reebok: Market Positioning and Segmentation. Reebok was a fashion-oriented sports company whose goal was to become the number one performance sports and fitness brand. The company was organized by product group, with fitness (aerobics, cross training, walking) generating 52% of sales, followed by sports (running, basketball, tennis, football, baseball, soccer, etc.) with 44 percent of sales, and casual footwear with 4 percent of sales.

Reebok's rise to success was fueled by the launch in 1982 of "FreeStyle," the first aerobic/dance shoe designed for women. Freestyle had captured the vast majority of the female sporting market and branded Reebok as a fitness company rather than a performance sports company. Although it had also developed its own technology, Reebok had never really been accepted as an authentic sporting goods producer. The company's strength lay in trendy shoes.

Reebok: Product Research and Development. Reebok had developed "pump" technology, which was an integrated system of one or more inflatable air chambers that could be adjusted to fit the instep of the foot and hence allow athletes to achieve a customized fit.

"Instapump" technology was Reebok's latest development, a new inflatable technology that used the features and benefits of the pump technology in lightweight performance shoes. An inflator containing a carbon dioxide cartridge was used to inflate the chambers instantly. This technology was tested at the 1992 Olympic Summer Games in Barcelona and the 1992 US Tennis Open.

Reebok had also recently developed the "Hexalite" and "Graphlite" technologies that helped improve shoe comfort, stability, and strength.

Reebok: Marketing and Advertising. In 1991, Reebok had invested most of its advertising budget in the "Pump Up and Air Out" campaign in direct competition to Nike's "Air" technology. In 1992, Reebok's media advertising budget was $85 million in the US, $25 million in Asia, and $10 million in Europe. Sixty percent of its advertising was used in television spots and the remaining 40 percent in print media.

The company's objective was to develop its image as a serious sports company, not simply as a fitness company. Reebok had recently made a strong strategic push in the sports market, gaining increased visibility on playing fields and sports arenas worldwide through endorsement arrangements. The company signed Shaquille O'Neal, a 21-year-old basketball player, and developed a campaign targeted to males aged 12 to 34. The objective was to enhance the company's performance image in basketball. Other athlete endorsements included Michael Chang, Michael Stich, and Jimmy Connors (tennis), Arturo Barrios (running), Emmitt Smith (cross training), and Ryan Giggs (UK soccer).

Reebok had also just launched its first global marketing campaign. The objective of the "Planet Reebok" campaign was to build a stronger global brand for Reebok and position it as a global company, present in all areas of sport and fitness. Reebok also adopted a new performance logo that provided a single, easily recognizable symbol for Reebok products around the world.

Advertising accounted for 60 percent of Reebok's marketing budget, followed by sponsorships (20 percent), promotions (10 percent), merchandising (10 percent), and public relations (5 percent).

Reebok: Production. Like Nike, Reebok had outsourced most of its production, although some of the clothing and footwear component parts were still sourced in the US. Indonesia, China, Thailand, and South Korea accounted for over 80 percent of the company's overall footwear production.

Reebok: Distribution. Reebok's products were distributed and marketed in 140 countries. The company's US distribution strategy emphasized high-quality retailers and sought to avoid lower margin mass merchandisers and discount outlets. Reebok's footwear was distributed primarily through specialty athletic retailers, sporting goods stores, and department stores. Distribution of clothing was predominately through professional shops, health clubs, and department sporting goods and specialty stores.

In the early 1990s, Reebok's growth had been driven by expansion outside the US, especially in Europe. Reebok had wholly owned subsidiaries in Austria, Belgium, Canada, Chile, France, Germany, the Netherlands, Italy, Russia, and the UK and majority-owned subsidiaries in Japan and Spain. Reebok also marketed through 32 independent distributors and joint ventures.

Reebok also had "concept" stores located in Boston, Santa Monica, and New York that sold a selection of Reebok's footwear and clothing, and it had also opened a retail store in Moscow in Spring 1993. Reebok operated 30 factory-direct stores.

ADIDAS: CURRENT POSITION AND FUTURE STRATEGIES

Adidas: Market Positioning and Segmentation

Adidas had established an image of seriousness, performance, and quality. Customers associated Adidas with authenticity and regarded Adidas as a genuine sporting goods company, not a fashion company. As a result, the company was more popular with middle-aged categories than with teenagers.

Adidas was also essentially a man's brand. This was primarily because the company's heritage had been in men's shoes, and the share of sports articles used for leisure purposes in the early 1990s was higher among men than women.

The company's five core categories of products were soccer, tennis, cross-training, basketball, and running, which accounted for approximately 90 percent of turnover. Each country chose the range of products most suitable for sales in its market.

Adidas and Soccer. The cornerstone of Adidas was soccer. The first Adidas soccer shoe was created in 1925. The German soccer team, which won the 1954 World Cup, wore the first pair of Adidas soccer shoes with screw-in studs. Adidas was now the worldwide leader in soccer footwear, apparel, and hardware, with market shares up to 60 percent in Germany, 48 percent in the US, and 45 percent in France. Hardware consisted essentially of sales of bags and balls. The first Adidas football was used at the 1970 World Cup, and the first collection of Adidas clothing was used at the 1974 World Cup.

Footwear. Footwear accounted for over half of Adidas sales. In 1992, Adidas had 2,000 different footwear models.

The Adidas premium brand, "Adidas Equipment" products, was sold on average at $62, and all other products were sold at $57. Prices were much lower than those of Nike and Reebok. For example, Nike could sell premium-brand shoes for more than $115.

Adidas clearance sales accounted for 30 percent of sales, which was much higher than the average for competitors, which rarely exceeded 10 percent.

Adidas: Product Research and Development

Adidas was the inventor of the so-called "Torsion Technology." The torsion system consisted of a pair of cross supports running from the front to the back of the shoe, allowing movement and at the same time maintaining shoe stability and strength.

Adidas research and development was focused on the creation of new footwear and textiles. Footwear and textile creation, which had previously been attached to the production department, had been integrated into the marketing and sales department.

Adidas: Marketing and Advertising

The strength of Adidas was in international and Olympic events in which participants were amateurs, and endorsement contracts were made with national sporting associations rather than individuals. The Adidas brand had been built through event marketing rather than individual athlete endorsements. Adidas promoted the Olympic games and major sports events in soccer, tennis, running, basketball, and outdoor activities. The company supplied team athletes with Adidas products and benefited from the resulting coverage in press and television. This strategy and the quality of its products had in the past enabled Adidas to win leadership in the athletic, professional, and semi-professional sports class and position its brand as a "professional," high-quality brand among customers. (Refer to Exhibit 10, which illustrates the different major sports events sponsored by Adidas between 1990 and 1992.)

In 1992, Adidas had spent $60 million on advertising in Europe, of which $28 million was spent in Germany. On average, the advertising and promotion budget accounted for 6 percent of sales, and 75 percent of the marketing budget was spent on promotion. TV advertising was covered by a single spot, which stressed the quality of Adidas products and would be shown all year long without change. A major American advertising company created the advertising.

EXHIBIT

10 | Major Sports Events Sponsored by Adidas in 1990–1992 by Sport Category

Soccer	In the 1990/91 season, over 20 teams wearing Adidas products won major-league or cup honors in national and international competition.
Tennis	Steffi Graf and Stefan Edberg wore Adidas-brand shoes and clothing.
Running	Adidas was the dominant supplier in the shoe and textile sector for the Track and Field World Championships in Tokyo. In 1992, Adidas supplied the most prestigious marathon events in the world, such as Boston, London, and Berlin.
Basketball	Dikembe Mutombo, number 55 of the National Basketball Association's Denver Nuggets and new player in the US National Basketball League, wore Adidas-brand shoes and clothing.
	Adidas was also well represented on the basketball court during the 1992 Olympics, having equipped teams such as China, the CIS, Spain, and Germany.
	In NCAA basketball, the organization of US college basketball teams, Adidas supplied two of the leading teams—The University of Indiana and rival Duke University.
Outdoor Activities	In 1992, Adidas sponsored the first Adidas Adventure Cup—an outdoor spectacular in which participants competed in mountain biking, climbing, and cross-country running. Many television channels broadcast this event. In Germany alone, six television channels covered the Adidas Adventure Cup.

Adidas: Production

In the mid-80s, Adidas owned 20 textile factories and footwear factories in Germany, France, Austria, North Africa, and the US. At that time, 60 percent of the footwear and 25 percent of clothing were produced in-house. Since 1986, however, Adidas had begun restructuring and had significantly decreased the amount of in-house production. More than 20 factories employing 6,000 employees had been closed or sold. By 1991, only 12 percent of the footwear and 7 percent of textiles were produced in-house.

Nevertheless, Adidas wanted to maintain a certain level of company-owned production to ensure high manufacturing quality standards, which had made the Adidas reputation in sporting goods. One factory was maintained in Alsace, France; one in Scheinfeld, Germany; and a joint venture in Morocco.

Outsourcing of the footwear production was divided between Asian countries and Europe, 70 and 30 percent, respectively. An organization for distribution and sourcing activities was set up in Hong Kong.

Adidas: Distribution

Adidas sales markets were divided among subsidiaries and licensees. Germany, France, the US, and the UK were the most important subsidiaries, representing, respectively, 17, 11, 9 and 6 percent of total turnover. In countries where Adidas was not represented by subsidiaries, distributors were responsible for the sale and distribution of Adidas products.

Licenses were given in countries with restricted imports. The largest licensees were in Argentina and Japan, which generated 10 percent and 8 percent, respectively, of total turnover. Licensees paid royalties to manufacture and distribute the Adidas brand. Adidas expected a licensee to have a solid financial background, to produce according to Adidas specifications, and to represent the Adidas brand in terms of market share, brand coverage, and image. Normally, Adidas would also propose production support from Adidas technicians. Adidas provided pricing guidelines, but licensees were free to fix their own prices. Marketing and sales people regularly visited licensees to monitor how the Adidas brand was represented. Financial audits were done to control the calculation of royalties.

Adidas also had its own brand shops in Eastern European countries—in Budapest, Prague, Moscow, Warsaw, Brno, and Riga.

Adidas delivered to its subsidiaries with a seven-month leadtime, resulting from considerable sourcing and production in Asia. In order to minimize inventory risk, incentives were given to the retailers to encourage them to pre-order. In general, retailers pre-ordered about 50 percent of Adidas products, and the remaining 50 percent consisted of on-demand re-ordering during the year. Adidas, however, was not considered a reliable brand; half of the pre-ordered stock consistently arrived late.

Adidas: The Culture and Organization

Although Adidas was an international company, most of the employees and management in the headquarters were from Germany, and the official language was German. The culture was very formal and hierarchical, and decision-making was centralized.

Adidas was organized around four departments: Marketing, Sourcing & Logistics, Finance, and General Services & Human Resources. In addition, each country reported directly to the CEO.

- René Jäggi, a 44-year-old Swiss, was the CEO. Prior to this appointment, he had been head of marketing of Adidas.
- Rob Strasser, a 48-year-old American, was head of Marketing. He had been marketing director for Nike and had been part of the original five-member team that had built Nike and developed the highly successful Air Jordan campaign. Strasser had had a falling out with Phil Knight, CEO of Nike, in the 1980s and left to establish his own marketing consulting business.
- Michel Perraudin, a 45-year-old Swiss, was head of Sourcing & Logistics. He had been a partner and a principal at McKinsey.
- Axel Markus, a 45-year-old German, was head of Finance. He had come from Grundig, where he had been head of finance.
- Willy Meinders, a 45-year-old German, was head of General Services & Human Resources. Previous to joining Adidas, he had been head of human resources for a leading German ceramic and porcelain manufacturer.

(Refer to Exhibit 11 for an illustration of the Adidas organizational structure.)

EXHIBIT 11 | Organizational Structure of Adidas

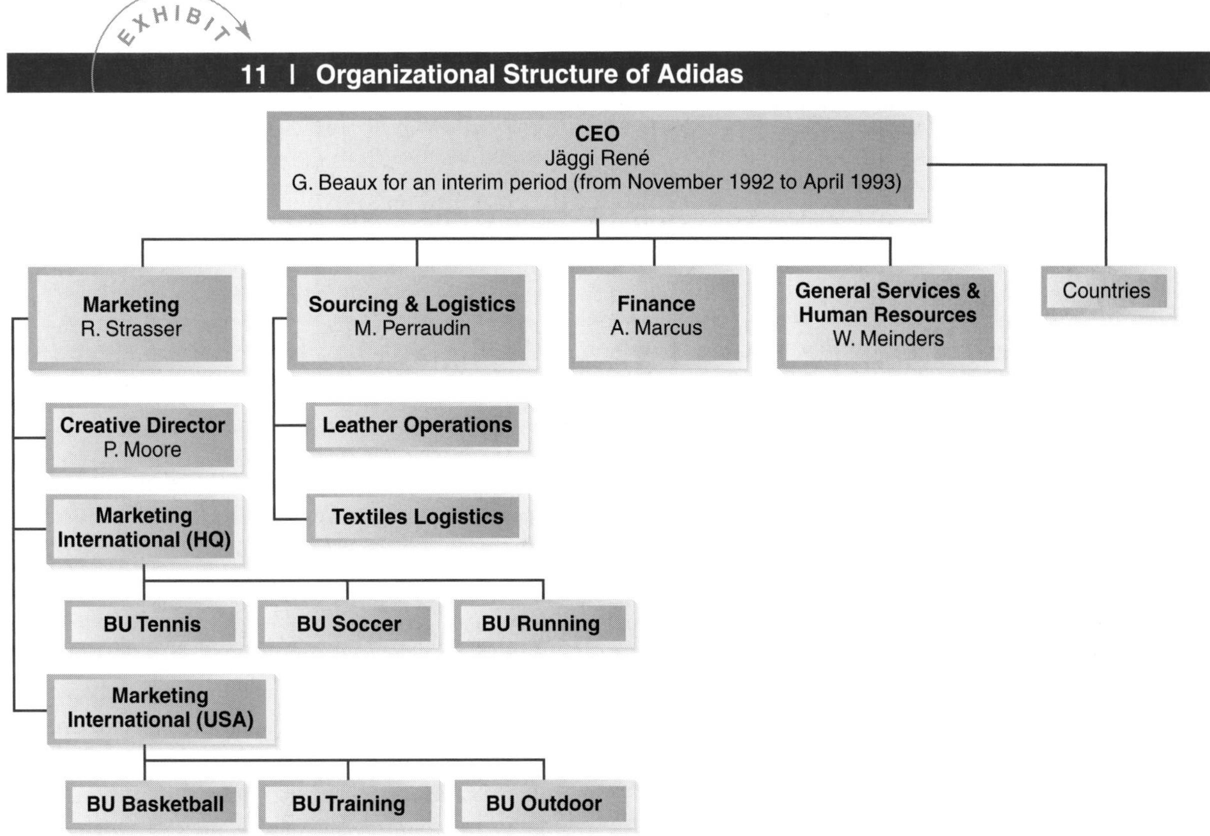

Source: Adidas.

Robert Louis-Dreyfus and Future Strategies

What decisions should Louis-Dreyfus take?

- Should he enter directly in competition with Nike and Reebok?
- Should he change the Adidas image, or should he reinforce its reputation as an authentic sporting goods company?
- What should he change in the Adidas marketing strategy?
- Which products and sports should he keep, eliminate, or develop?
- Should he outsource the rest of the production, with the risk of losing control over the high manufacturing quality standards, which had made the Adidas reputation?
- What other decisions should he take to get Adidas out of the red? Could he improve his distribution strategy? What other information was missing to make the right decisions?

ENDNOTES

1. Source: UBS Global Research, October 1995.
2. Source: Adidas estimates, 1994.
3. *International Management*, "Best of the Rest," July/August 1994: 30.
4. *Forbes*, "Nike's Fast Track," November 23, 1981: 59–62.
5. Reebok 1993 Annual Report, Edgar Online.

CASE 3

Banking on the Internet:

The Advance Bank in Germany

Tawfik Jelassi
Euro-Arab Management School

Albrecht Enders
Leipzig Graduate School of Business

Walking through the bank's call center in Munich on March 28, 1998, the two-year anniversary day of the bank, Volker Visser was wondering what suggestions he could make to the other members of the Executive Board of Advance Bank at their next business strategy meeting. As he observed some agents answering customer calls, he wondered how to better manage customer relationships and whether new technological capabilities could be effectively used to create value in an electronic world. He knew that with the intensifying competition in the branchless banking sector, "his" direct bank needed to further customize the financial advice it offered, especially if it wanted to achieve its goal of 250,000 customers by the year 2001. While recognizing the tasks that lay ahead to achieve that goal, he thought that the uniqueness of the Advance Bank concept would still be a strong competitive weapon in the market place:

> *Marketing and winning over customers who fit our target profile is our key challenge. We are not afraid of current competitors or new entrants because we believe [that] we have a niche and a differentiated quality service. . . . Brick-and-mortar branches don't have a future. Why should the customer keep paying for their fancy branches in prime locations and for their large staff payroll, while dealing with restricted opening hours and lousy service quality?*

This case is intended to be used as the basis for class discussion rather than to illustrate either effective or ineffective handling of a management situation.

The case was made possible by the co-operation of Advance Bank (Germany).

© 1999 T. Jelassi, Euro-Arab Management School, Granada, Spain.

1. THE BANKING INDUSTRY IN GERMANY

The banking industry in Germany is dominated by large universal banks that offer comprehensive banking services to both private and corporate customers. Unlike in other financial systems such as those in the United States, German universal banks are allowed to offer both commercial and investment banking services. In order to exploit economies of scale and synergies and to build global scale, many German banks have merged with one another. The largest bank merger in Germany took place in 1997 when the two Bavarian banks Vereinsbank and Bayerische Hypotheken and Wechselbank (Hypo-Bank) decided to join forces and create a single bank. Today, there are four major universal banks operating in Germany: Deutsche Bank, Vereinsbank/Hypo-Bank, Dresdner Bank, and Commerzbank.

A central feature of the German banking industry is the strong link between banks and companies from other industries. For example, Deutsche Bank owns over 20 percent of Daimler Benz (valued at DM15 billion) and 10 percent of the insurance company Allianz (valued at DM10 billion). Allianz, on the other hand, owns 22 percent of Dresdner Bank.

Two important events have marked recent developments in the German banking industry. The first event, which took place on July 1, 1990, was the federal monetary union which integrated the states of the former

German Democratic Republic into the West German monetary system. The inclusion of the five new *Bundeslaender* (states) opened up new market opportunities and motivated almost all banks to open branches in these states. The second important event is the launch of the European Monetary Union (EMU) which will establish, on January 1, 1999, the Euro as the single currency within the eleven European Union member states that have so far been admitted in the EMU.[1]

A second major trend in the banking industry in Germany is the rationalization of bank branches and the staff reduction that often results from it. Deutsche Bank, for instance, intends to cut the number of employees by 4,100 by the year 2001 and to close 200 to 300 of its current 1,600 branches. The German Employees Union foresees that overall staff reductions might amount to a loss between 100,000 and 140,000 positions during the coming years. To a large extent, this trend results from an increasing use of technology in banking, which is illustrated by the widespread use of automatic teller machines (ATMs), money transfer terminals, and direct banking institutions.

2. THE COMPETITIVE ENVIRONMENT IN DIRECT BANKING

In 1996, the direct banking market in Germany was divided into two categories. First, traditional banks offered telephone banking delivery channels, built as extensions to their branch network, which provided increased availability for the customer beyond traditional business hours. Already in 1989, Citibank had launched a telephone banking service, and other banks (such as Postbank and Vereinsbank) had followed with a similar service. In 1994, the Direkt Anlage Bank started a discount brokerage, offering cheap transactions with only limited advice to the knowledgeable investor. The discount brokerage service was also appealing to other banks with a branch network since the risk of cannibalization was considered to be low, thus allowing the branch network to coexist with the new direct banking channel. Therefore, many traditional German retail banks, such as Commerzbank (with Comdirect), Berliner Bank (with Bank Girotel), and Deutsche Bank (with Bank 24), started a direct banking service limited to discount brokerage services. In order to get a full range of banking services, customers still had to go to a traditional branch-based bank.

The strategic intent of Vereinsbank's new direct bank (called Advance Bank) was to go beyond the above-mentioned categories. It aimed instead at offering instead a full range of banking services and extensive investment advice, through the telephone and later through the Internet.

In early 1998, direct banks in Germany have cumulatively 1.8 million customers. Market studies suggest that out of the current 63 million customers of German banks, 10 million of them are interested in direct banking; however, only 3 million customers intend to switch to direct banking in the near future. Commenting on this competitive environment, Hans Jürgen Raab, member of the executive board at Advance Bank said:

> *The direct banking market is growing quickly, but not as fast as there are new competitors entering the market. In the spring of 1996, there were eight direct banks; today [in January 1998] there are already 39. About one third of them won't survive.*

3. VEREINSBANK'S DIRECT BANKING STRATEGY

Vereinsbank is a large, regional bank in Germany with 22,000 employees and 770 branches nationwide. The branches are mainly located in Bavaria (the southern part of the country) and in the Hamburg area (in the northern part), and a few are scattered in the rest of the country (see Exhibit 1). In 1993, the Vereinsbank board decided that, in order to stay competitive and attract a larger customer base, it was necessary to expand the scope of the bank's operations to other parts of Germany. One possible option to achieve this goal was to physically expand the branch network to the central part of Germany; however, this option was discarded because of the high costs associated with it (a single branch would have cost DM1–3 million annually). The additional branch network of 100–200 branches needed to reach enough customers would have been too expensive. A second problem that needed to be addressed was the "over-age" customer base of Vereinsbank with a disproportionately large number of customers aged 50 years and above (see Exhibit 2).

1 | Vereinsbank's Branch Network in Germany

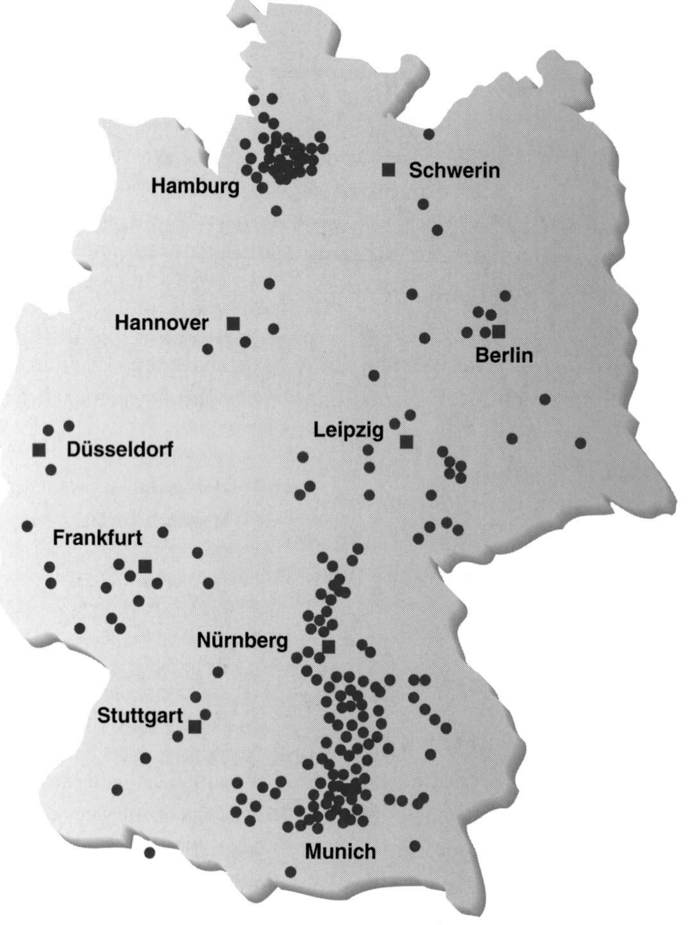

Source: Advance Bank.

In order to address these issues, Vereinsbank decided to launch a direct (branchless) bank to offer ubiquitous access throughout Germany (via the telephone, letter, fax, PC, and Internet) and to attract a younger customer base. In 1994, a feasibility study for the direct bank project was conducted, and it was agreed that the design and implementation of the new bank should be completed in just two years. Andersen Consulting was then selected to provide the required know-how and personnel. The three main challenges were: (1) to build from scratch a completely new banking system, (2) to align this system with the newly defined business processes, and (3) to implement this system within a completely new organization. Tasks allocated to Andersen Consulting included conducting a pre-study, designing the system, acting as general contractor for the system implementation, and training the personnel. Because of the new banking concept, Andersen consultants had to design by themselves large parts of the required software and hardware. During peak periods in the development process, over 100 Andersen consultants worked on the direct bank project at a total cost of over DM50 million.

In December 1996, the new direct bank employed

EXHIBIT 2 | Vereinsbank's Customer Base

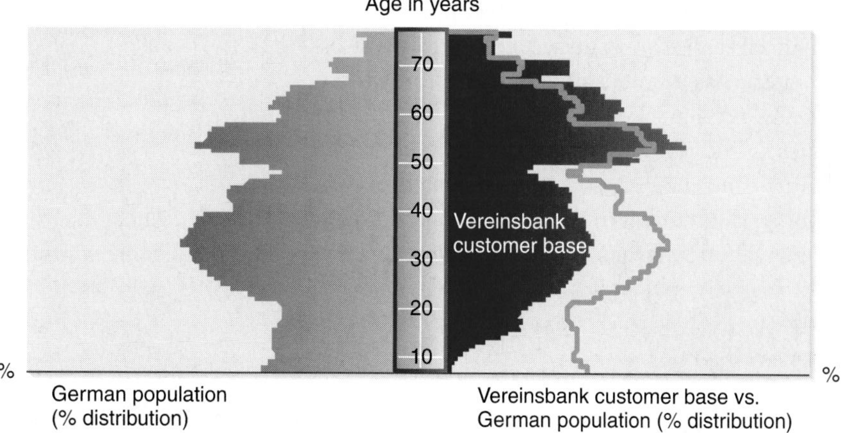

Source: Adapted from Advance Bank material.

269 people,[2] 40 percent of which had an academic degree and 55 percent a banking or business educational background. In 1997, after the merger of the parent company Vereinsbank and Hypo-Bank, Advance Bank was sold to Dresdner Bank, which is now the sole owner of Advance Bank.

4. THE ADVENT OF A VIRTUAL BANK

We wanted to be the first direct bank in Germany that offers value-added service in terms of price-performance, [customer advice] objectivity, and convenience.

—Frank Spreier, Manager, Organization and IT, Advance Bank

4.1. Choosing a Name for the Virtual Bank

When looking for a name for the new bank, many possibilities were considered, including "First Choice" and "Bank High 3." However, they had to be discarded later because the name was either already patented, not accepted outside Germany, or there were some laws against using a particular name. Eventually, the bank's marketing group was left with only two choices: "Quantum" and "Advance Bank." Volker Visser commented:

During the first two years of the project, we thought it would be easy to find the right name for the bank, so we didn't think too much about it. That was a mistake.

Finally, the name selected was "Advance Bank" because the word *Advance* (which was an artificially created word since it is missing the "d" at the end), was thought to best convey the new bank's philosophy of being future oriented and forward looking. Another important advantage was that the first two letters of the name (i.e., "A" followed by a "d") put the name at the beginning of almost any alphabetically ordered list. This characteristic will become more important as the Internet expands since WWW browsers typically sort their hits alphabetically.

The name for the new bank was then protected worldwide to keep open the possibility for an eventual international expansion of the business.

4.2. Key Features of Advance Bank

An important feature distinguishing Advance Bank from other direct banks is that it was designed and built from scratch without relying on the banking infrastructure and products of the parent company. This independence, combined with advanced information technology, enabled Advance Bank to create a virtual bank that could source its services and products from different financial services providers spread out all over Germany (see Exhibit 3). When choosing a partner, Advance Bank looks throughout Germany for the best provider of a given financial service or product. Applying this best-of-breed strategy has resulted in having the individual parts of Advance Bank service assembled by different companies spread out all over the country. The bank's headquarters and main call center are located in Munich; another call center is in Wilhelmshaven (in northern Germany), an area where the unemployment rate is at 16 percent.[3] Furthermore, the accent which is spoken in that area of Germany is easy to understand, which facilitates the search for well-suited call agents. Regarding the selection of Wilhelmshaven, Volker Visser said:

> *There is no reason to have all the call centers in Munich. Because of the high unemployment rate in Wilhelmshaven, the call agent salary is on average 29 percent lower than in Munich. This makes a big difference when we talk about costs.*

IBB, a subsidiary of IBM, in Schweinfurt maintains the mainframe computer data.[4] Eurocom Printing (in

EXHIBIT 3 | Advance Bank: A Virtual Organization

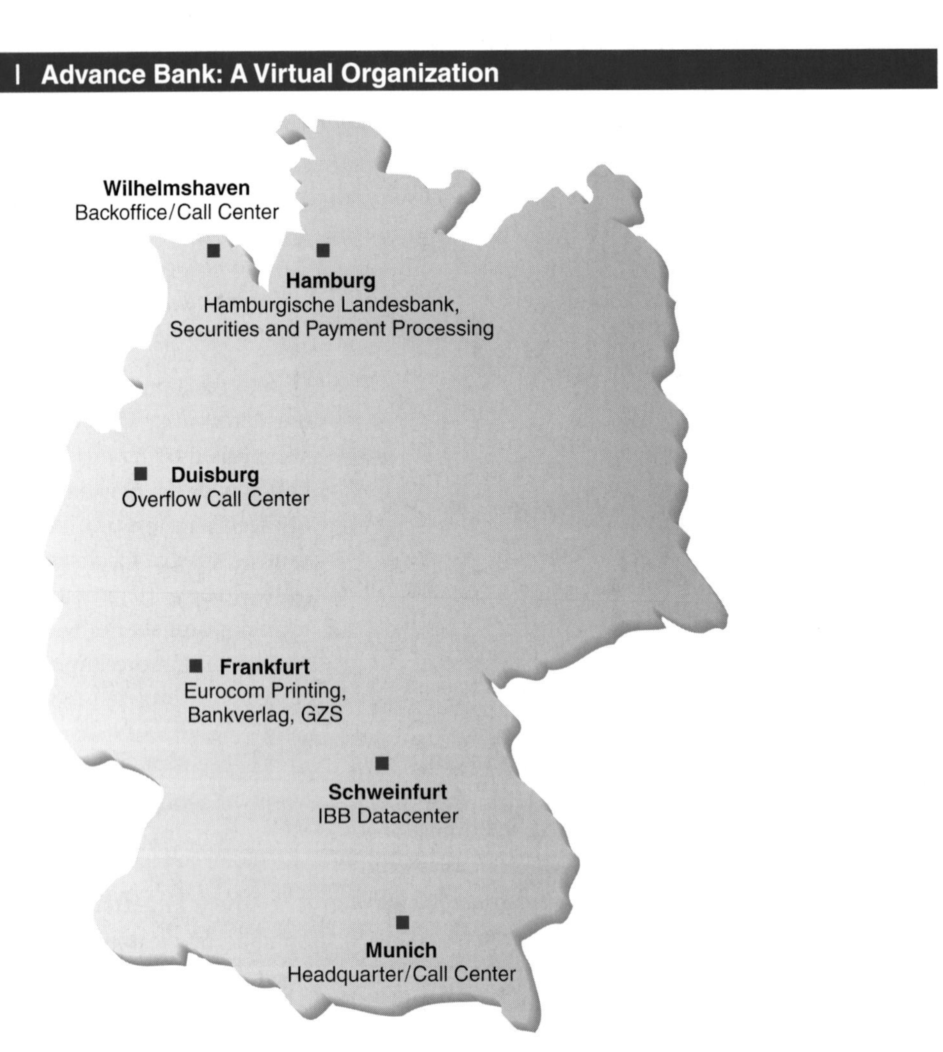

Source: Advance Bank.

Frankfurt) prints all letters and statements and distributes them together with brochures and leaflets. GZS (also located in Frankfurt) processes all incoming Euro-card statements, while the Hamburgische Landesbank (HaLaBa) in Hamburg processes securities and payments.

In order to integrate all the above-listed services provided by the different companies, a custom-designed front-end of Advance Bank was necessary. A high integrated seamless interface with the customer has therefore been created, which gives him/her the impression of dealing with just one institution.

4.3. Security System

In order to ensure that customer information is kept confidential and secure at all times, Advance Bank relies on a complex security system. Upon opening an account with the bank, the customer receives a personal identification number (PIN) and a computer generated six-digit secret code. Every time the customer accesses his account by telephone or Internet, he is first requested to provide his PIN; then, the bank's computer system randomly asks for three numbers from the customer's secret six-digit code (e.g., the first, the fourth, and the fifth digits). Marc Hemmerling, an Advance Bank customer, explained:

> *I am more concerned about security when I leave my credit card number with the waiter in a restaurant or with the cashier at the gas station. I believe that the Advance Bank security system is reasonably safe.*

This security system is used for two reasons. First, to ensure that even if someone were to intercept the customer message to the bank, he/she wouldn't have all the required information allowing him to access the account. Second, this system ensures also that even the call center agent handling the customer's call cannot know the customer's complete authorization code. An illustrative phone conversation between a call center agent and a customer, with the relevant identification procedure, is shown below:

Claudia (Advance Bank agent): Advance Bank. Good evening. How may I help you?

Hr. Schmitt (customer): Hello. This is Herr Schmitt. I would like to make a transaction.

Claudia: Would you please tell me your personal number, Herr Schmitt?

Hr. Schmitt: My [personal] number is 92466503.

Claudia: Thank you. Then I also need the first, second, and fourth digits of your authorization code.

Hr. Schmitt: 9, 4, and 2.

Claudia: Thank you. Your account information is now being loaded into my PC, this will take a second. [. . .] How much money would you like to transfer?

Hr. Schmitt: 200 Marks.

Claudia: 200 Marks. Which account do you want to transfer this money to?

Hr. Schmitt: Account number: 1800 252191.

Claudia: And the number of the corresponding bank?

Hr. Schmitt: 860 555 92.

Claudia: Who is the recipient?

Hr. Schmitt: Thomas Schmitz.

Claudia: Thank you. 200 Marks will be credited to account number 1800 252191 at the Stadt und Kreissparkasse Leipzig. The recipient is Thomas Schmitz.

Hr. Schmitt: Excellent. Thank you very much.

Claudia: Is this all you need?

Hr. Schmitt: Actually, I also need 1,000 U.S. dollars in traveller's checks.

Claudia: No problem. Shall I send the [traveller's] checks to your home address?

Hr. Schmitt: Yes, provided that I get them before my trip to New York which will be at the end of next week.

Claudia: You should receive them in 3 to 4 days. Do you need something else, Herr Schmitt?

Hr. Schmitt: No, thank you.

Claudia: You're welcome. Good bye!

A few weeks later, Herr Schmitt called Advance Bank again. After being greeted by the Call Center agent and being authenticated through the identification procedure (explained above), the following dialogue took place:

Peter (Advance Bank agent): I hope that your visit to the U.S. went well, Herr Schmitt. I heard that there was lately a major snow storm on the East Coast [of the United States].

Hr. Schmitt: Yes, indeed. However, I was quite lucky since I left New York before the start of that storm.

Peter: I am glad you did! How can I help you this morning?

Within the bank, there are also various security systems to ensure that only authorized personnel can obtain and manipulate customer data. Depending on his/her user class, every Call Center agent works at a desktop with access to specific software applications. Every time he wants to use one of these applications, he has to enter his user ID number and his personal password. When a Call Center agent wants to contact a customer, he must first provide a word code (already specified by the customer) to prove his identity to the customer.[5]

The above-mentioned security system seems to work well, since two years after its launch, Advance Bank has had no security-related incident in carrying out its operations. However, in case a customer authorization code falls into wrong hands, Advance Bank is liable for 100 percent of all damages, provided the customer informs the bank about it as soon as it happens. In case the customer does not find out about the misuse or does not notify the bank on time, his/her maximum liability is only 10 percent of the caused damage; thus personal risk is minimized.

5. ADVANCE BANK'S MARKETING STRATEGY

5.1. Market Positioning

We need to differentiate our bank from our competitors. Eventually, we will only be able to capture our target customer group if we can establish a well-known brand with a differentiated appearance and a clear profile.

—Hans Jürgen Raab

An important marketing issue was to define the customer group that Advance Bank should target. The options were either to offer products that do not require financial advice (such as discount brokerage) or those that necessitate the bank's expertise. A marketing study showed that only 500,000 potential customers would be able to do their personal banking without any advice. Furthermore, the discount brokerage market was already crowded with players such as Bank24 and Comdirect Bank. Advance Bank has thus carved a niche for itself by offering investment advice, hence targeting customers who are interested in joining a direct bank and who want to receive personalized advice.

Advance Bank targets the so-called "individual customer" (IK) who typically earns more than DM5,000 per month, owns or rents a house, lives in an urban area, enjoys sports and culture, and is either self-employed, a freelancer, or an executive (see Exhibit 4). Although this group represents only 17 percent of the potential customer population, it generates for the bank an average annual profit of DM2,400 per customer. The

4 | Profile of the "Typical" Advance Bank Customer

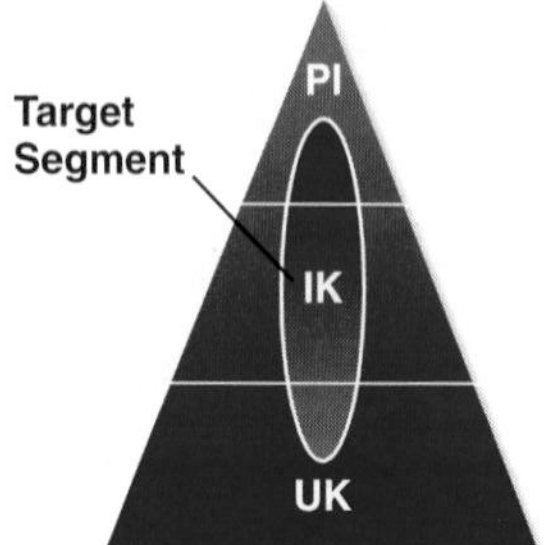

Age: 25–49 years
Education: high school graduate and higher qualifications
Profession: self-employed, freelancer, executive
Income: >5,000 DM net/month
Resident: urban areas (>200,000 population)
Housing conditions: tenant/owner of a house
Hobbies: sports, culture
Other characteristics: high mobility (frequent traveler, etc.)

Source: Adapted from Advance Bank material.

other two groups consist of "universal customers" (UK) who represent 80 percent of potential customers but only generate an average profit of DM650 annually, and "private investors" (PI) who generate an annual average profit of DM5,000 but represent a mere 2 percent of the potential customer population. Additional information on the profiles of Advance Bank customers (in terms of age as well as employment status and sector) is provided in Exhibit 5.

5.2. Promotion and Advertisement Campaigns

In order to attract its target customer group, Advance Bank first started a direct mailing campaign to potential customers informing them in detail about the bank's product line. Besides being very expensive (due to the printed material and postage), these campaigns did not achieve much impact since the "Advance Bank" brand name was not yet known to the public. In the fall of 1996, the bank had to stop all advertisement campaigns due to budgetary constraints. This action did not help strengthen the brand name, especially at a time when the public had just started to take notice of the bank. In total, DM44 million were spent on marketing in 1996, out of which DM22 million went into traditional advertising.

Having learned from its mistakes, Advance Bank devised a new marketing strategy along two dimensions. First, a brand image campaign was launched to make the name better known to the public. Part of this campaign was based on the sponsoring of the weather forecast during the nightly news program "Heute" on ZDF,[6] one of the most popular news broadcasts in Germany. The advertisement consisted of a short cartoon focusing only on the Advance Bank brand name; including more information would have been too expensive for the bank. Similar advertisements also appeared in other programs (such as N-TV) which are popular among the above-mentioned target group. Second, a content advertisement campaign was launched through several high-quality German newspapers and news magazines aiming at conveying the benefits customers can accrue through Advance Bank.

5 | Advance Bank Customer Profiles (as of January 1997)

Average Account Balances
Cash-Management Account: US $52,000
Portfolio: US $63,000

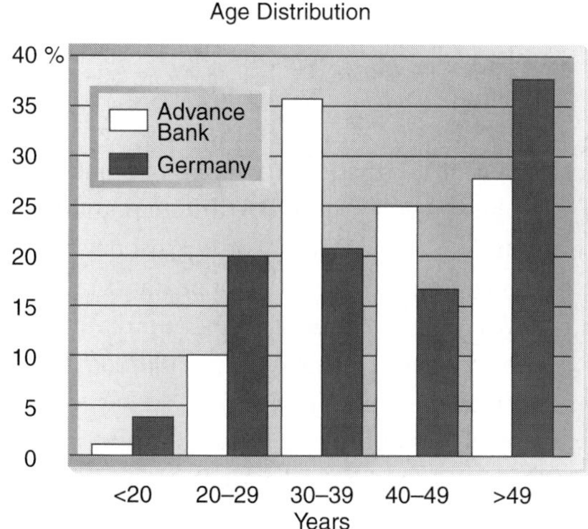

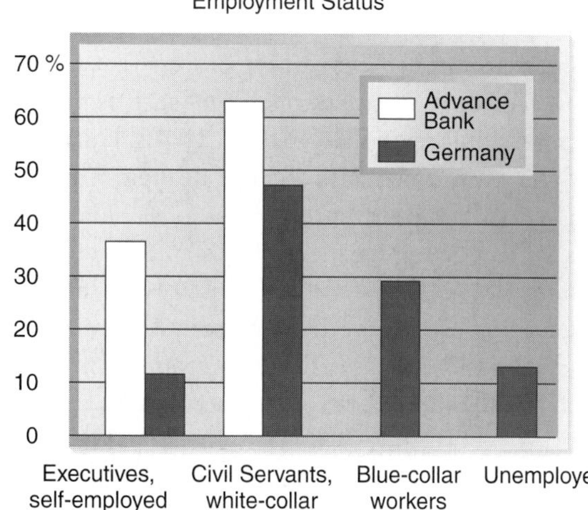

Source: Advance Bank.

5.3. Acquiring New Customers at Advance Bank

As of May 1998, Advance Bank had a customer base of 79,000 people. This relatively small number of customers partly results from the difficulty of pitching promotion campaigns at the desired target group and the high advertising costs involved.[7] To overcome these problems, Advance Bank has considered new ways of reaching potential customers such as offering special rates to companies whose employees match the profile of the Advance Bank target customer. Companies that were first considered included those that were already cooperating with Advance Bank such as Andersen Consulting and CompuNet.[8] This offer was later extended to other companies with similar employee profiles like McKinsey, Microsoft, and Oracle.

Another approach has consisted of cooperating with other nonbank companies that offer products complementary to Advance Bank's financial products; this included the technology retailer TELIS and the Internet Service Provider AOL.[9] Through this cooperation, customers are offered a low-priced package solution (containing an ISDN[10] card, a modem, and the Internet service) for online banking. This package is subsidized by Advance Bank as to make online banking more attractive and accessible.

6. OPENING AN ACCOUNT AT ADVANCE BANK

In order to open an account at Advance Bank, prospective customers go through a screening process that assesses their creditworthiness. Personal data (such as the income tax form, information from the SCHUFA,[11] marital status, and employment) are used to rate them. This rating is necessary to reduce the loan default risk of new customers who, upon joining the bank, instantly receive a credit line of DM30,000.[12] Of all applicants 94 percent pass the screening process; of the remaining 6 percent, half of them typically choose to make the required time deposit of DM30,000 and become customers of the bank.

Upon requesting the application material (either through the Internet, phone, fax, or postal mail), prospective clients receive a package including information about Advance Bank's products and services as well as the application form. Walter Klein, a new customer at Advance Bank, commented:

> *Before choosing my direct bank, I requested information packages from both Advance Bank and Bank 24. In the end, I found the Advance Bank offer more convincing.*

They then fill out the application form, attach the income tax file as proof of income, and put these documents into a blue envelope (included in the package) and seal it. This envelope is then given to the post office where the prospective customer presents his/her passport to a clerk (as a proof of identity). The post office forwards this envelope to Advance Bank.[13] Upon passing the above-mentioned screening, the customer receives from Advance Bank a confirmation letter containing the six-digit secret code (mentioned above).

7. ADVANCE BANK PRODUCT PORTFOLIO AND PRICE/PERFORMANCE

Advance Bank's product line consists of two main products: the cash management account and the investment-fund service. In addition to these products, Advance Bank also offers insurance and retirement funds.

7.1. The Cash Management Account

The cash management account is the central piece of the Advance Bank service. This account provides the combined features of a current (checking) account and those of a savings account; i.e., availability of customer funds at all times and an interest-bearing account.[14] The customer can subdivide his/her main account into up to nine subaccounts used for different purposes (e.g., household, car, rent, etc.). For interest payments, these accounts are automatically totaled and the customer receives (or pays) interest on the cumulative balance of both accounts. During the first quarter of 1998, the interest that the bank applied was 3.3 percent on deposits and 8.75 percent on loans. Philip Torsten, who has been a customer at Advance Bank since its creation, explained:

> *Advance Bank charges more but also offers more service than other direct banks. I don't want to be check-*

ing the balance of my current account every two weeks to make sure that I don't have money sitting idle there that should better be put into an interest-bearing account. At the same time, I don't lose any interest whatsoever, and I don't end up paying interest for overdrawing one of my subaccounts. This [service] is very important for me.

Customers can choose between the standard cash management account (which allows up to 50 free transactions per quarter) and the cash management account plus (which allows up to 150 free transactions per quarter). A Eurocard Gold or a VISA Gold credit card (offering withdrawals of up to DM6,000 per week) and a Euro-Check card (with withdrawals of up to DM5,000 per week) are given free of charge once the account is opened.

Following an agreement with a group of German private banks (including Deutsche Bank and Commerzbank), Advance Bank allows its customers to use all the automatic teller machines (which total 6,000 in Germany) of these banks free of charge. In addition, Advance Bank customers have free access to all the ATMs of Vereinsbank, Hypo-Bank, and Dresdner Bank. Furthermore, customers can also withdraw cash at any ATM in Germany (in total, there are 38,000 ATMs in the country), and Advance Bank will reimburse each customer up to DM30 of ATM fees per quarter

At the end of each month, each Advance Bank customer receives by postal mail a financial report (DIN A4 format) containing detailed information on all transactions as well as changes in his/her main account and subaccounts. Additionally, the customer is immediately informed when an incoming transfer (that exceeds DM20,000) or an outgoing transfer (of more than DM10,000) is made.

Every month, Advance Bank charges its customers a flat fee of DM16 if they hold a cash management account and DM28 if they have a cash management plus account. However, if a customer has a cumulative annual charge to his credit card of over DM8,000, the monthly fee is reduced to respectively DM13.50 and DM25. If this cumulative annual charge exceeds DM25,000, then the fee is waived for the cash management account holder while it is lowered to DM12 for the cash management plus account holder.

7.2. Investment Fund Service

Through its investment fund selection service, Advance Bank offers "objective" advice for selecting investment funds. In contrast with most other banks, which primarily sell their own funds to their customers, Advance Bank uses the expertise and experience of the "Feri Trust" investment specialists. Based on the information they receive, Advance Bank's financial consultants first select the 50 best-performing funds out of a group of 2,700. They then recommend to the customer an individual portfolio strategy that takes into account personal investment goals, return and risk preferences as well as the customer's tax situation, to maximize after-tax returns. Customers can choose from five different strategies:

- DM conservative
- Germany conservative
- International growth
- International chance
- Europe growth

In addition to sending its customers a monthly market assessment and a personalized analysis of their portfolio, Advance Bank also sends up-to-date buying and selling recommendations. The fee the bank charges for managing the customer's asset portfolio is DM79 per year, regardless of the portfolio size. In January 1997, the average balance of a customer portfolio was the equivalent of US$63,000. Volker Visser commented on the average balances of the portfolio and of the cash management account:

When you look at these average balances, you see that we are doing fine quality-wise. But we are not doing so well quantity-wise, and we need to increase the number of [Advance Bank] customers.

7.3. Advance Bank Price/Performance

To compensate for the fees it charges, which are higher than those of other direct banks, Advance Bank aims at offering a uniquely differentiated value through its all-inclusive banking services as well as its high customer service satisfaction. For example, prior to a trip abroad, a customer may deposit at the bank copies of important personal documents (such as his/her passport). In case one of these documents were lost or stolen, Advance Bank would fax the customer a copy of it and also provide money within 24 hours. If a customer gets ill while abroad, he can contact the bank's medical consultation service where multilingual doctors are on call around the clock to give advice over the phone and, if necessary, to arrange for transportation back to Germany. Furthermore, to cover emergencies while abroad, customers receive up to 62 days of free insurance coverage, which fully covers treatment and medication costs and allows the customer to consult the doctor of his choice. All of the above-listed services are free for customers with a cash management account at the Advance Bank.

Advance Bank also decided to give the same benefits, including a free Euro-Check card, to heterosexual as well as homosexual couples when they open a joint current account.[15] The bank's service quality is constantly monitored and each customer complaint is answered within 24 hours. If the latter is not met, then the bank sends the customer a compensation gift (e.g., a Jazz compact disc). In order to enhance service quality further, complaints are tracked for each customer and aggregated under six categories: service, bank's appearance, competence, reliability, customer treatment, and product range. These complaint records are also analyzed when designing new applications and processes or training Call Center agents.

Volker Visser elaborated on the price/performance issue at Advance Bank:

> *We offer quality to our customers. We have to pay for quality and our customers are willing to pay us for this quality because in the end they profit from it. Our customers are not so much interested in low fees. They want the best information they can get to help them make money [by] investing into the funds we recommend to them. They don't care about the extra three marks that we charge for our services. If they did, they would do discount brokerage with another bank.*

8. THE CALL CENTER: THE HEART OF ADVANCE BANK

Since the Call Center agent is the only Advance Bank employee who has direct contact with the customer, special attention was given to the set-up of the Call Center during the bank's design and implementation stages. The goal was to reach a high level of service quality by combining well-trained Call Center agents and sophisticated information technology to make the customer's banking experience as convenient, pleasant, and efficient as possible.[16] This was done in order to remedy problems of traditional brick-and-mortar branches such as the ones described below by Susanne Meier, another Advance Bank customer:

> *When I was still a customer of a brick-and-mortar bank, I had to deal with lots of incompetent people, who weren't able to help me out. In order to get a hold of competent bank agents, I was often sent from one branch to the next before I got the service I wanted. Restricted opening hours also really got to me, especially during weekends when I would have had the time to sit down and do my banking. Now, every time I call up Advance Bank, on the other hand, I receive good and qualified service quickly.*

Key features of the Call Center architecture include:

- **Availability:** Supports operations 24 hours a day, seven days a week (actual availability is at 99.91 percent of the time).
- **High service level:** 85 percent of all calls answered within 15 seconds.
- **Personalized service:** Human contact offered at all times.
- **Assured security:** All customer calls are recorded, secure customer verification.
- **Open architecture:** Use of standard hardware and software components.
- **Scale-ability of the system:** Supports up to 250,000 customers and beyond.
- **Interconnected Call Centers:** Incoming calls are routed automatically to available call center agents independent of location.
- **Adequate technical support:** On-site service within four hours for critical components.
- **Outbound dialing.**
- **Management reports.**

8.1. IT Support for the Call Center

We spend about 20 to 30 percent of the bank's budget on IT. This may sound exaggerated but it is not.

—Frank Spreier

Advance Bank Call Centers, located in Munich and in Wilhelmshaven (with a staff of 100 and 150 call agents, respectively), receive all incoming calls from current and prospective customers from 7 A.M. to 10 P.M., seven days a week.[17] Depending on availability, the Automatic Call Distributor (ACD) routes the incoming call to the least occupied Call Center. In order to optimize the Call Centers' utilization while reducing the wait time for incoming calls, Advance Bank designed a support system for the Call Centers that provides information on typical call frequencies (e.g., the breakdown of calls per day, week, or month). The system also forecasts changes in call frequencies caused by special promotions, TV advertisements, mailings, or newspaper/magazine articles, thus allowing the human resources manager to efficiently schedule personnel and to foresee possible bottlenecks.

Call Center agents work in teams of five to six members, with each agent using a multitask workstation (with a large display screen) to access all relevant data while talking to the customer. The workstation integrates the functions of a PC and those of a telephone through a UNIX-based CTI[18] platform. It allows the Call Center agent to receive calls without having to pick up the receiver and to simultaneously transfer calls and call-related information to other agents in the Call Center. Furthermore, the agent can place calls without having to dial but just by clicking on the customer name on his screen. He can then talk to him through a headphone-speaker set which is connected to the computer workstation.[19]

8.2. Customer Information

Upon receiving a call, the Call Center agent first enters the customer's personal identification number and the three digits (provided by the customer) from his/her security code. A pop-up menu is then displayed on the screen which allows the agent to access and, if need be, modify the customer's personal account information (see Exhibit 6). The information includes:

- *Customer contact information* such as home/office and e-mail addresses, phone and fax numbers, as well as his/her preferred contact times.
- *Customer credit rating* that Advance Bank assigns to each customer in order to determine his/her credit line and the interest rate at which he/she can borrow money. This rating is first given to the customer when he/she opens an account; it is then monthly updated based on the customer's transactions and other account activities.
- *Record of previous contacts:* When talking to the customer, the Call Agent can also view a detailed list of the past contacts the customer had with the bank. This list shows the time and date of each contact, the name of the Call Center agent who handled the call, the issue discussed, and any other relevant comments that the agent deemed important to record.
- *Customer life style:* The Call Center agent may also record customer lifestyle information. For instance, if a customer tells the agent that he needs to withdraw DM3,000 for a vacation in the U.S., the Call Center agent notes (in the lifestyle information column) that this customer likes traveling. Similarly, there are columns for musical taste, other cultural preferences, etc. Another column informs the call agent about individual customer characteristics (e.g., a hearing problem), so that each agent can take these characteristics into account when dealing with that customer the next time.
- *Customer likes and dislikes:* At the end of the first three months with the bank, every new customer receives the "honeymoon" questionnaire asking him to rate his satisfaction with the bank, its Call Center agents, the account opening procedure, and the intelligibility of the information material sent to him. Another survey is sent annually to the bank's customers aiming at tracking their satisfaction level and finding new ways to improve the service quality and offerings. All surveys are scanned into the customer database and thus added to the already recorded customer information. When next talking to a customer, the call center agent can, from his workstation, instantly access this scanned information. Furthermore, to avoid "annoying" a given customer by repeatedly offering him/her a certain product or service, the Call Center agent has the option to block certain capabilities. For instance, if he finds out from a phone conversation that a given customer would rather not receive direct mailings from Advance Bank, he can block this permanently by crossing out this function in the customer database record. Likewise, if a customer turns down a Call agent's offer

(over the phone) to open a cash management account, the agent makes a note of this refusal in the corresponding database record as to take into account future contacts with that customer.

8.3. Maintaining the Human Touch

We can also talk about non-banking matters during our conversation with the customer. In fact, we are even encouraged to ask one question aside from banking to make things more human. By doing so, I create a positive atmosphere, where the customer gets the feeling that I am there to help him make a decision and not to push him over. Once I establish this atmosphere, the customer usually opens up and tells me more personal information which then makes it easier to suggest the right product to him.

—Klaus Eutin
Call Center Agent
Advance Bank

Making the customer feel comfortable and at ease while banking over the phone is one of the crucial challenges faced by a direct bank. Advance Bank tries to meet this challenge by authorizing its Call Center agents to also talk to customers about topics that are not banking related. Klaus Eutin further elaborated on this matter:

> *Some customers also ask personal questions, about your age, for example, or your hobbies. There are some call agents here in the office who met their future spouses while working.*

Furthermore, Call Center agents were trained to keep the customer's best interest in mind. They are advised to make the decision with the customer instead of trying to "push him/her over" and make the sale at any cost. The guiding principle of Advance Bank is to pull the customer and not to push him to buy a product. Marc Hemmerling elaborated on this point:

> *It is important to build up a personal trusting relationship with a call [center] agent; this can only happen over time. When you think that you've really received excellent service and advice from a call agent, you'd like to come back to him and build on this good initial understanding. It's very much a psychological thing. I want an excellent product, but I also need to have the trust that the call agent is not trying to sell me something [that] I don't need.*

8.4. The Call Center Agent

Initially, we thought that we needed to hire [for the bank's call center] telemarketeers and give them banking training. That turned out to be a mistake. Now we hire first-rate bankers and we give them a telemarketing training.

—Volker Visser

Since Call Center agents are the crucial interface between customers and a direct bank, Advance Bank carefully selects then trains and motivates its call agents. Before getting invited to an assessment center, applicants for Call Agent positions are first interviewed over the phone. During this interview, the recruiter has the opportunity to test the applicant's telephone "appearance," which is the call agent's most important qualification. Besides having a warm and welcoming voice, a call agent must be able to communicate clearly and intelligibly over the telephone. Regional dialects are irrelevant as long as the call agent can make himself well understood to the customer. Although call agents have varying educational backgrounds, they must have a service mentality when joining Advance Bank. Many of them have completed a banking apprenticeship, but there are also university students, former restaurant employees, and housewives. After passing the telephone interview, applicants are invited to an assessment center where they have to demonstrate, over two days, that they are stress-resistant and also somewhat persistent, especially with regard to sales conversations.

Before starting their work, new Call Center agents undergo a six- to seven-week, full-time training program during which they first get to know Advance Bank's philosophy, computer system, and product portfolio. Call agents are then trained as to how to handle a phone conversation with a customer and how to talk to him/her. For example, instead of saying "no problem" which might suggest to the customer that he is a problem, call agents are trained to say, "I will gladly do so" or similar nonjudgmental sentences. During the final part of the initial training which focuses on sales, call agents learn how to sell the bank's products to the customers using the following steps. First the agent needs to establish a personal contact with the customer and create a rapport of trust with him/her. Second, the call agent needs to inquire about the customer's needs and then make the appropriate offer. The final step is closing the deal.

In order to improve the training quality, experienced call agents model the "optimal call process" with its most frequently recurring parts such as needs analysis, necessary explanations, and possible customer objections. They then develop a script for the new call agents which they can refer to. After the call agent starts his/her work, a team trainer provides coaching on the job, listens to customer conversations and gives instant feedback afterwards.

9. WHAT NEXT?

9.1. Internet-Based Banking

I switched to Advance Bank because I want to be able to do my banking anytime and anywhere, as long as there is a phone or an Internet connection available.

—Rudolf Pfitzer
Advance Bank customer

From the start, Advance Bank recognized the importance of the Internet as an additional information, communication, marketing, and sales channel as well as customers' willingness to use it to perform financial operations (see survey results in Exhibit 7). The bank strategy stipulated the use of this technology-driven media to offer banking services. An Internet web site was set up to inform prospective customers about the bank's products and services (see Exhibit 8). Since summer 1997, customers have been able to also access their main and subaccounts through Advance Bank's Internet Web site (without having to purchase any additional banking software) and perform all banking operations online (e.g., transactions, standing orders and funds management) from any computer with Internet access. As of April 1998, 42 percent of all money transfers were conducted through Advance Bank's Web site. Susanne Meier added:

With many other Internet banks, you need to install specialized software packages on your PC to access

6 | User Interface of the Integrated Computer/Telephony Application

Zielgruppenbank User-Interface

File Customer Assets CM Correspondence Interessent Contact Help

07.01.97 22:34 rteschner 015 mainframe offline Length of call: 00:00

Dr. Johanna Kirchgang Status: Customer Since: 05/95 Corporate Business
Remarks Profession: Businesswoman
City: München

Creditworthiness: 7 Potential: 2 Member-Chips: 300
Customer-Position: 2 Purchase behavior: Spontaneous
Credit line: DEM

CMK:	1222000010	Balance:	5.600,21 DEM	Interest earning dispo:	5.00000
External Limit:	10.000 DEM	Ext Available:	11.310,42 DEM	Interest on credit (%):	7.30000
Internal Limit:	50.000 DEM	Int Available:	51.310,42 DEM	Overdraft interest (%):	14.90000

Customer Panel

Type	Number	Description	Lock	Balance
CMK	1222000010	Current account		5.600,21 DM
SA	1222000011	Pocket money draughts		0.210,21 DM
SA	1222000012	Building society sav		–4.600,00 DM
SA	1222000013	Housekeeping money		100,00 DM
InvAcct	2222000014	Lombard account	Lombard	–5.684,00 DM
InvAcct	2222000015	Deposit	Deposit	6.000,00 DM
InvAcct	2222000016	Deposit	Deposit	20.000,00 DM
Depot	5222000010	Securities Lombard		48.931,00 DM
Depot	5222000014	Securities daughter		12.092,50 DM

Contact History Johanna Kirchgang

No.	Date	Time	Subject	Type	Age
1	12.11.1995	10:07	First contact/Acquisition	TI	AQ
2	14.12.1995	16:31	Consultation	TI	WP
3	18.01.1996	19:54	Follow up contact/Acquisition	TO	WP
4	07.01.1997	22:37	Actual contact	BI	KS

EXHIBIT 7 | Survey of Internet Users

What kind of financial information would you like to access through the Internet?

Based on 8,435 responses from Internet users:	Total	Women	Men	AGE (IN YEARS) <19	20–29	30–39	40–49	>50	EMPLOYMENT STATUS: Civil servants	Self-employed	Other employees	High School students/ apprentices	University students
Information about stocks and investment opportunities	52.1%	41.3%	53.4%	46.7%	53.7%	52.9%	48.6%	52.7%	44.9%	55.4%	52.9%	46.5%	53.9%
Information about insurance (prices, premiums, services)	36.1%	33.7%	36.5%	16.7%	36.5%	39.9%	36.7%	34.0%	38.4%	38.8%	40.7%	18.5%	30.1%
Information about mortgages and real estate financing	19.6%	17.6%	19.8%	9.7%	18.2%	23.8%	21.3%	14.5%	20.5%	22.3%	22.9%	11.9%	14.2%
Databases with general financial information	38.1%	32.7%	38.8%	22.2%	37.9%	41.2%	38.4%	38.0%	30.5%	44.0%	40.5%	25.1%	34.5%
Articles about general financial topics	32.0%	27.4%	32.6%	25.9%	32.5%	33.9%	30.2%	29.6%	30.2%	35.0%	32.3%	26.8%	32.8%
Statistical tables and graphical displays	332.2%	22.0%	34.6%	32.5%	35.6%	33.0%	29.7%	30.1%	26.7%	36.7%	32.1%	32.7%	37.5%
Stock quotations	48.1%	38.1%	49.3%	48.6%	51.1%	47.8%	44.4%	42.6%	37.0%	49.5%	47.9%	47.3%	52.1%

(Source: Fittkau & Maaß, 1997)

Would you perform the following financial tasks through the Internet?

Based on 6,292 responses from Internet users:	Total	Women	Men	AGE (IN YEARS) <19	20–29	30–39	40–49	>50	EMPLOYMENT STATUS: Civil servants	Self-employed	Other employees	High School students/ apprentices	University students
Online Banking (account management)	95.4%	93.2%	95.6%	96.5%	95.8%	94.8%	95.7%	95.8%	96.5%	95.1%	95.7%	95.7%	95.1%
Purchasing shares	56.1%	39.3%	57.7%	50.7%	58.4%	55.6%	53.0%	56.1%	50.2%	59.5%	56.0%	50.7%	58.1%
Purchasing real-estate mortgage	14.9%	13.0%	15.0%	10.0%	13.7%	16.6%	23.8%	13.5%	17.1%	15.3%	16.8%	9.4%	10.4%
Purchasing car insurance	39.8%	29.5%	40.9%	16.1%	35.3%	44.9%	41.2%	43.9%	42.0%	46.2%	44.2%	17.1%	29.0%
Purchasing liability insurance	34.6%	28.8%	35.3%	12.0%	29.9%	40.0%	33.9%	36.1%	38.1%	39.7%	39.2%	12.8%	23.2%
Purchasing home insurance	33.3%	29.5%	33.7%	11.1%	28.3%	38.7%	33.0%	37.1%	35.8%	37.3%	38.2%	11.1%	21.7%
Purchasing accident insurance	28.4%	23.2%	28.9%	10.9%	24.5%	32.8%	47.8%	30.4%	29.2%	32.5%	32.0%	12.0%	18.8%
Purchasing life insurance	20.2%	17.0%	20.5%	10.0%	17.3%	22.9%	47.8%	19.8%	23.3%	23.3%	22.0%	9.4%	13.2%

(Source: Fittkau & Maab, 1997)

8 | Advance Bank Internet Web Site

Source: Advance Bank.

your banking account online. This limits the usage [of Internet-banking] to your home PC. With Advance Bank, I have universal access to my account as long as I can get a hold of a PC with Internet access. I could conceivably check my account in the US during vacation and make a transaction in case I have forgotten to pay my rent, for example.

However, for security reasons, the bank put a DM10,000 ceiling on transactions and transfers done through the Internet. Volker Visser explained:

Our Internet transactions are very secure. For each transaction, we provide the customer with a transaction authentication number and a confirmation receipt. However, if something goes wrong, for example a customer transfer does not reach its destination, we bear the cost and pay for it.

9.2. Toward a Two-Channel Distribution System: Integrating Telephone and Internet Banking

Banking through the Internet, without any human interaction, works well for selling standardized or simple financial products. However, for highly customized or complex products (such as a mortgage or a life insurance policy), the provision of customer advice is highly desirable, if not even required, by the client. For the latter case and in order to meet customer demands and expectations, Advance Bank intends to integrate the telephone into its Internet banking service as to offer simultaneous voice and data communication between its call center agents and the bank customers (see Exhibit 9).

For example, when choosing a real-estate mortgage, the customer first provides through the Advance Bank Internet Web site some personal data (e.g., duration, amount, rate, etc.). This data is then used to instantaneously produce some "what-if" analyses and scenarios. If the customer wishes to receive some personal advice, he/she then clicks on a specific icon on the screen. Subsequently, an Advance Bank call agent calls up that customer and discusses the matter with him/her; both parties have the possibility to look at the same document while talking and, if need be, modify the mortgage data the customer has entered on the Advance Bank Internet Web site. The resulting communication is very similar to the traditional form of communication at a

9 | Integrated Internet and Telephone Banking

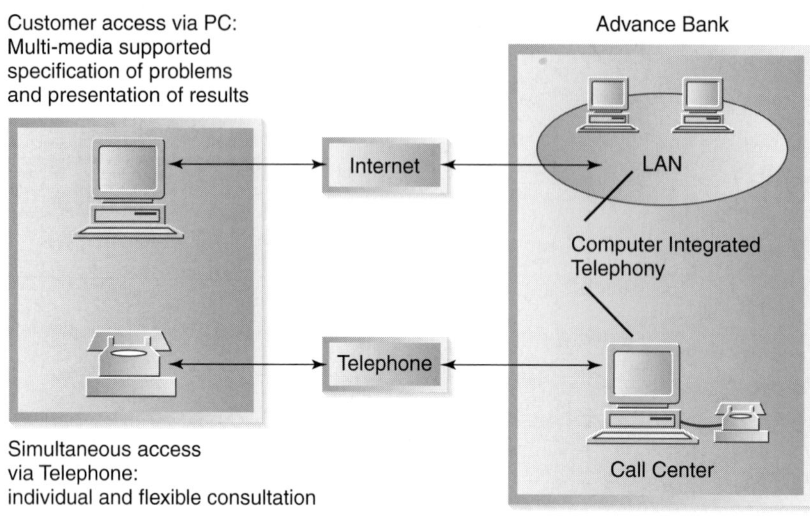

Source: Adapted from Buhl and Wil (1998).

bank branch; for instance, the call agent can suggest over the phone changing parts of the mortgage (e.g., the duration or the deposit) to obtain a better offer. Simultaneously, the agent can show on the Web document what impact the change will have on the mortgage. Compared to traditional phone conversations, such an integrated telephone-Internet sales channel allows a reduction of call time since the customer now enters the request parameters by himself, hence also reducing the number of possible entry errors.

In order to further enhance its customer relationship, Advance Bank plans to install video cameras on top of the call agents' workstations, thus allowing the customer to see the call agent on his/her PC screen while talking to him/her. In order to provide these complex services, the transmission speed of the Internet will have to increase greatly. Already today, customers are complaining about slow Internet connections to the Advance Bank Web site, as illustrated by Marc Hemmerling's comment:

> *The main problem of Internet banking is that it takes too long to download the web site. The initialization process [i.e.; the online identification of the customer] also takes too long. When I think about the online fees, it is almost cheaper to do my banking over the phone or even to fill out a form and send it in by mail.*

9.3. Internationalization

Having gained good experience and expertise in offering direct banking services through its business operations in Germany, Advance Bank plans to expand its geographical presence by penetrating other European countries. This ambition to go international is not new at the bank as stated by Volker Visser:

> *Advance Bank is not a German bank. If we had wanted to be a German bank, we wouldn't have called ourselves "Advance Bank" because Advance is not a German word. We would have called ourselves Hermann or Schmidt Bank. We chose an English name because we expect to expand throughout Europe.*

9.4. Challenges Ahead

Preparing for his next board meeting, Volker Visser was pondering the evolution of direct banking in Germany and in Europe, and the future of Advance Bank in the increasingly global and competitive business environment. What should Advance Bank do next in order to further attract new customers and build loyalty among existing ones? Should the bank broaden its business scope and extend its product portfolio? Should it go ahead at this stage with its plans to enlarge the geographical scale of its operations by launching its direct banking concept in other European countries?

Volker Visser is well aware that embarking on such ambitious projects is at the same time an opportunity and a threat for the survival and growth of Advance Bank. However, since the bank needs to achieve its goal of 250,000 customers by the year 2001 in order to break even, can it afford not to pick up the opportunity and take the risk that comes with it?

ENDNOTES

1. These member states are Austria, Belgium, Finland, France, Germany, Ireland, Italy, Luxembourg, the Netherlands, Portugal, and Spain.
2. This number includes part time workers.
3. Before choosing Wilhelmshaven, Advance Bank considered for its second call center 29 possible locations which were assessed based on 220 quantitative and qualitative criteria including: availability of qualified personnel, wages, government subsidies, and real estate prices.
4. Initially, Advance Bank considered using the data center of its parent company Vereinsbank. However, since this center could not provide the required 24-hour accessibility, Advance Bank looked for another provider.
5. Upon dialing the customer's telephone number, the Call Center agent can access on his PC that customer's password if and only if the customer picks up the phone. The call agent then asks whether he has the customer him/herself on the phone; only then, he identifies himself as an Advance Bank employee and gives the customer the word code.
6. ZDF is one of the two public television networks in Germany.
7. Each newly acquired customer costs on average DM600.
8. CompuNet delivers computer hardware equipment to Advance Bank.
9. AOL stands for America Online.
10. ISDN (Integrated Services Digital Network) is capable of handling data, voice, text, and image transmission over the same communication line.
11. SCHUFA, which stands for "Schutzgemeinschaft für allgemeines Kreditwesen," records the credit history of bank customers and provides this information to banks when customers want to open up a new account.
12. DM10,000 for each account, the VISA card, and the EuroCheck card.
13. The German law requires every bank to confirm the customer's identity before opening an account.
14. In January 1997, the average account balance was the equivalent of US $52,000.
15. The bank does not require from homosexual couples to provide a proof of their relationship.
16. Advance Bank was awarded the Grand Prix Customer Service Award for being the best call center in Germany in 1997.
17. Calls coming in during night hours are rerouted to an overflow call center located in Duisburg.
18. Through CTI (Computer Telephony Integration), databases are linked to the incoming call, allowing the call center agent to quickly access the file of the customer at hand.
19. For security reasons, all customer calls are automatically recorded.

CASE 4

Alcoholes de Centroamerica, S.A. de C.V.

Richard L. Priem
The University of Texas at Arlington

K. Matthew Gilley
James Madison University

On a summer afternoon in 1995, Sr. Emin Barjum watched the faded-yellow Toyota pickup truck pull away from his loading dock in Tegucigalpa, Honduras. Sr. Barjum, founder and president of the Honduran liquor manufacturer *Alcoholes de Centroamerica* (ALDECA), wondered if his plan would work. The truck was laboring under a load of *Yuscaran,* a competitor's brand of *aguardiente*. Sr. Barjum had purchased the *Yuscaran* for delivery to his most important customers, the large liquor distributors in San Pedro Sula, a major industrial city in northern Honduras.

Sr. Barjum was doing this because *Grupo Cobán,* a large conglomerate that had been able to establish a virtual monopoly in the Guatemalan *aguardiente* market, was planning to expand its business into Honduras. As an initial step in this process, *Grupo Cobán* had begun offering incentives to the largest San Pedro Sula liquor distributors in exchange for carrying its brands. Sr. Barjum was attempting to send a subtle message to these distributors. He wanted them to believe that ALDECA, which accounted for up to 80 percent of their business, could distribute its own brands, as well as those of the competition, directly to retailers. Sr. Barjum felt that this warning would provide leverage in his dealings with the distributors and might discourage them from doing business with *Grupo Cobán*. To make his message even stronger, Sr. Barjum was providing the *Yuscaran* to his distributors at a very low price. The distributors did not realize that ALDECA was actually losing money on each bottle of *Yuscaran* it delivered to San Pedro Sula.

Sr. Barjum also faced other problems in August 1995. In addition to the *Grupo Cobán* threat, the market for *aguardiente* was shrinking slowly, because Honduran preferences were shifting to lighter alcohols like wine and beer. Also, *Licorera de Boaco,* A Nicaraguan distillery with production facilities in Honduras, had proposed a merger. After a year of study, a decision had to be made soon. The merger would give ALDECA additional capacity and could help fight the *Grupo Cobán* threat, but it would result in less direct control over marketing and operations. Was the additional capacity worth the loss of control? What other strategies might work? Sr. Barjum went back inside his office to speak with his son, Salomon "Tony" Barjum, about their company's future.

HISTORY OF *ALCOHOLES DE CENTROAMERICA*

Emin Barjum returned home in 1965 to Tegucigalpa, the capital city of Honduras, after receiving a B.B.A. from the University of Pennsylvania and an M.B.A. from the University of California at Berkeley. He began looking for business opportunities while working for the Honduran government's Economics Ministry. Sr. Barjum noticed that there was a lack of good quality industrial alcohol in Honduras. To fill this gap, he founded ALDECA in 1967, with initial financing from

---

We thank Emin and Tony Barjum for their cooperation during the field research for this case, which was written solely for the purpose of student discussion. All data are based on field research and all incidents and individuals are real. The names of some ALDECA competitors have been disguised.

Copyright © 1999 by the *Case Research Journal* and Richard L. Priem and K. Matthew Gilley.

the Barjum family and a group of friends. The plant was designed with the help of a Mexican consulting firm. Because the minimum efficient scale was greater than the local demand for industrial alcohol, Sr. Barjum had to go into the liquor business to make the project feasible. He obtained technical advice on fermentation, distillation, and other aspects of alcohol manufacturing from a retired Cuban distiller who lived in Miami, Florida. ALDECA then began producing small quantities of rum, vodka, gin, Scotch, and an inexpensive liquor called *aguardiente*.

With production established, Sr. Barjum began marketing his liquor by loading as many cases as possible into his car and driving northward from Tegucigalpa. Those early sales trips were very difficult because Honduras had only 1,000 kilometers of roads (barely 100 kilometers were paved). At first, Sr. Barjum sold only a few cases per trip. However, his marketing efforts soon began showing results. He persuaded the owners of many northern cantinas to begin carrying ALDECA's rum and *aguardiente*. Sr. Barjum was successful in part because he was the only distillery owner who called directly on customers; other distilleries used sales people. ALDECA's sales grew each year.

When Sr. Barjum began producing alcohol, there were about sixteen distilleries in Honduras, most of which were relatively small in terms of output and market share. Sr. Barjum believed that "it was easier for us to compete then, since we had many small competitors instead of a few very large ones." ALDECA's entry into the market changed liquor manufacturing in Honduras. Most of the competitors had been using raw sugar in the fermentation process, which was quite expensive. ALDECA, however, produced lower-priced products made with black-strap molasses. In 1995, only eight distilleries remained in Honduras; the rest had gone out of business. About half of the survivors were forced to change to molasses to remain cost competitive.

ALDECA prospered until 1972, when a large Nicaraguan distillery, *Licorera de Boaco*, entered the Honduran rum market. Hondurans preferred internationally produced rums, and sales of ALDECA's rum declined rapidly. As a result, ALDECA changed its focus to *aguardiente* production. By the early 1990s, the company had developed a presence in the *aguardiente* market throughout the country and had captured approximately 50 percent of the market share. However, northern Honduras was ALDECA's most important market, comprising nearly 85 percent of its sales.

THE HONDURAN *AGUARDIENTE* INDUSTRY

The Product, Its Consumers, and Place of Consumption

Aguardiente is a clear, inexpensive, very strong liquor that is generally purchased by the glass in small cantinas by poor, uneducated males between the ages of 26 and 45. The small, family-owned cantinas usually have a maximum of six tables and a small bar. "The cantinas are traditionally the place where men meet after work to have a few drinks," states Sr. Barjum. "They are basically a haven for men." Women traditionally avoided consumption of *aguardiente* because those women who drank it were considered immoral. The serving size is typically 125 milliliters (approximately one-half cup), and the average consumer drinks three servings per cantina visit. About 60 percent of *aguardiente* consumers drink it straight, while roughly 40 percent follow it with lemon, salt, or a sip of a soft drink.

The product is traditionally sold to the cantinas in 750-milliliter and one-liter bottles, from which the bartenders pour drinks for their customers. A trend is developing, however, toward smaller, 125-milliliter bottles. Some customers prefer the small bottles because, when they purchase one, they are guaranteed that the bartender did not "water down" the product. However, production of *aguardiente* in the smaller bottles is quite expensive, and price is an important factor in the purchase decision. The "best" combination of taste (smoothness) and strength (alcohol content) typically determine a consumer's brand preference.

The Competitors

There were three major players in the Honduran *aguardiente* market in the mid-1990s: ALDECA, which sold approximately 2.5 million liters of its brands per year; *Destilleria Buen Gusto*, which sold approximately 2.5 million liters of *Yuscaran* per year; and *Licorera de Boaco*, which sold 700,000 liters of its brands per year. There were several smaller competitors in Honduras, as well as many black-market operations.

Although ALDECA commanded nearly half of the legal Honduran *aguardiente* market, the company did not fare well "brand-to-brand" with *Destilleria Buen Gusto*'s *Yuscaran* brand. A recent ALDECA marketing survey revealed that, in the city of San Pedro Sula (within ALDECA's core northern market), 57 percent of the respondents preferred *Yuscaran* over ALDECA's *Caña Brava*. Sr. Barjum notes that, "If we combine all of our brands, then we win. But, brand against brand, they have a better share."

The General Environment in Honduras

Honduras is located in Central America between Guatemala, El Salvador, and Nicaragua. Although the Honduran political environment has been stable in recent years, more than 150 internal rebellions, civil wars, and governmental changes have occurred in Honduras since 1900. Its six million people live in a country that is approximately the size of Louisiana (see Exhibit 1) and depend primarily on agriculture for employment. In the mid-1990s, Honduras was among the poorest countries in the western hemisphere, with per capita income of approximately $630 (U.S.). The country suffered from high population growth, high unemployment (15 percent) and under-employment (36 percent), high interest rates (approximately 36 percent), and high inflation (averaging 22 percent between 1990 and 1994). A weak infrastructure was also a problem. For example, there were only 1,700 kilometers of paved roads in 1995, and water and electric service were very unreliable.

A lack of hard currency for foreign exchange was also a problem. In 1994, the Honduran Central Bank mandated that commercial banks, exchange houses, and businesses could not retain foreign currency. Rather, they were required to sell foreign currency to the Central Bank within 24 hours of its acquisition in exchange for *lempiras*, the Honduran currency. The Central Bank then auctioned the foreign currency on the open market, but quotas limited the amount anyone could purchase per day. It took businesses quite some time, therefore, to obtain the currency necessary for foreign transactions.

EXHIBIT 1 | Regional Map of Central America

ALCOHOLES DE CENTROAMERICA IN 1995

Personnel

In 1995, Sr. Barjum was joined by his son, Tony, who was "learning the business" after completing a B.B.A. and an M.B.A. at The University of Texas at Arlington. Sr. Barjum's daughter, Patricia, provided some marketing advice to ALDECA as needed. Other top managers at ALDECA included Armando Leonel Aguilar, Production Manager; Ileana Zelaya, Head of Laboratory; Lesbia Argentina Nunez de Flores, Head of Accounting; and Julio Valladares, Sales Manager. Exhibit 2 highlights the education and experience of ALDECA's top managers. The remainder of the 84 employees filled clerical and production positions. ALDECA had little trouble filling these lower-level positions because of the high Honduran unemployment and underemployment rates, as well as ALDECA's higher-than-average pay scale.

EXHIBIT 2 | ALDECA's Top Management Team

Name and Position	Age	Years at Company	Education	Experience
Emin Barjum Owner and General Manager	53	28	M.B.A., University of California at Berkeley and B.B.A., University of Pennsylvania	Company President
Salomon "Tony" Barjum Assistant General Manager	23	1	M.B.A. and B.B.A., The University of Texas at Arlington	Started here
Armando Leonel Aguilar Production Manager	26	2	Chemical Engineer and M.B.A., Honduras University	Assistant production manager at a sugar mill
Ileana Zelaya Head of Laboratory	24	1	Chemical Engineer, Currently getting M.B.A., Honduras University	Head of lab at another company
Lesbia Argentina Nunez de Flores Head of Accounting	41	21	CPA, Honduras University	Started here
Julio Valladares Sales Manager	40	4	High School Graduate	10 years in sales (liquor)

EXHIBIT 3 | Liters of *Aguariente* Sold by ALDECA, 1987–1994

1987	1,944,000
1988	2,177,000
1989	2,342,000
1990	2,449,000
1991	2,801,000
1992	2,711,000
1993	2,554,000
1994	2,445,000

EXHIBIT 4 | ALDECA *Aguardiente* Prices, 1990–1995 (In Lempiras per 12-bottle Case)

	1990	1991	1992	1993	1994	1995
Caña Brava	104	Not Available	116	122	152	156
Tic-Tac	86	Not Available	98	110	132	138
Catrachito	91	Not Available	103	110	128	124
Costeño	95	Not Available	107	114	129	115
Torero	99	Not Available	111	117	135	124
Favorito	85	Not Available	97	104	121	115
Bambu	85	Not Available	97	104	116	93

The importance of having a qualified, in-house chemical engineer was highlighted in the early 1990s, when Sra. Zelaya discovered a virus living in the fermentation tanks. The elimination of this virus enhanced the efficiency of the fermentation process and increased ALDECA's production capacity by nearly one-third.

Product Lines

ALDECA produced seven brands of *aguardiente: Caña Brava* (its highest-quality and best-selling brand), *Tic-Tac, Catrachito, Costeño, Torero, Favorito,* and *Bambu*. The multi-brand strategy was developed in part, Sr. Barjum notes, because "each cantina will carry only two or three brands. That's one of the reasons we're trying to get a lot of brands into the market, to confuse the markets. That way, our brands could stock a whole cantina."

ALDECA also manufactured small amounts of vodka and wine on a manual production line. A separate Barjum-controlled company produced a line of cosmetics (perfumes, deodorants, and lotions) made from excess alcohol. *Aguardiente* production, however, remained ALDECA's specialty.

Production Process

ALDECA produced all of its alcohol from black-strap molasses, which was obtained from a few large sugarcane plantations in northern Honduras. Sr. Barjum signed contracts with these producers each year at the beginning of the harvest to ensure that ALDECA had enough molasses to last the entire year. However, since the molasses producers often promised more than they could manufacture, shortages were common toward the end of the year. ALDECA's attempts to resolve this problem were ineffective. Transportation costs prohibited the company from acquiring molasses from other countries, and large-capacity tanks, pipelines, and pumps would be very costly. Furthermore, it was impossible for ALDECA to build additional storage tanks in its current location because the land adjacent to the distillery had become developed in recent years.

Upon receiving the molasses from the manufacturers, ALDECA mixed the molasses with yeast and stored it in tanks, where it was allowed to ferment. After ALDECA's chemical engineer, Ileana Zelaya, determined that the mixture had achieved the proper level of fermentation, the molasses was pumped into distilling units, where it was converted into alcohol. The alcohol was then pumped into large vats, where it awaited the bottling process.

Following a standard practice in Honduras, ALDECA recycled all of its bottles. The bottling process began at an enormous bottle-washing machine. Once the used bottles were washed, they were moved one by one through the filling machine, to the capping machine, and on to the labelling machine. They were then placed in boxes of twelve and were stored for shipment.

Although it may appear that ALDECA's production process was highly automated, it was still relatively labor-intensive. The bottles returned by the distributors were loaded manually into the bottle washer. After each bottle was filled, it was visually inspected for purity. Then, each bottle cap was started by hand before being tightened by the capping machine. Next, safety seals were secured by hand. Finally, the full bottles were boxed and stored manually.

In 1995, ALDECA was still using most of the same

equipment with which it had begun production. Despite its age, the equipment remained simple, safe, efficient, flexible, and trouble-free. The bottling line was seldom interrupted by mechanical failures, and the interruptions that took place were usually solved within a few minutes.

Marketing

Marketing ALDECA's *aguardiente* was difficult. Nearly all *aguardiente* consumers were illiterate, so common vehicles for advertising, such as newspapers and magazines, were ineffective. Advertising on television was also ineffective because the customers generally had no access to television. ALDECA used some radio advertising, since many cantinas (and some customers) had radios.

Most of ALDECA's marketing efforts, however, involved point-of-sale advertising. Each year, ALDECA developed a poster featuring a female model in a bathing suit. A twelve-month calendar appeared at the bottom of the poster so that, according to Sr. Barjum, "the cantina owners will leave the poster on the wall all year." One year, ALDECA's advertising company failed to put the year itself on the calendar. As a result, that particular calendar remained on the walls of many cantinas for several years, even though the day/date designations were wrong! ALDECA also distributed to the cantinas, free of charge, disposable plastic cups with ALDECA's various product logos on the front and the serving sizes marked on the sides. Less successful marketing campaigns, such as neon signs for distributors and metal signs for cantinas, had been attempted at various times in the past.

ALDECA tried to improve the effectiveness of its advertising campaigns by hiring a well-respected local marketing firm to evaluate and revise its advertising. ALDECA gave this firm detailed information that included consumer demographics as well as frequency, amount, and location of consumption. The marketing firm then developed a multimedia campaign (television, radio, and print) that focused on a man consuming *aguardiente* at home. Sr. Barjum was disappointed with the result of the marketing firm's work because "we had given them all of the marketing information we had, but they came out with a campaign which was completely out of the environment where people drink *aguardiente*."

New product testing and introduction were handled through ALDECA's sales department. A sales representative typically visited the cantinas with the new *aguardiente* and offered the cantina owners several free bottles in exchange for permission to conduct a brief taste test. The free bottles were provided to the cantina owner as a show of goodwill and to offset revenues lost by the cantina during the test. The salesperson then offered cantina patrons free samples of the new product and asked for their opinions on how the new product compared to their favorite brands. A follow-up sales call was made later to secure the cantina's order.

Financial Performance

A cursory look at ALDECA's sales figures might lead one to believe that its bottom line had been suffering. Total factory sales dropped from 22 million *lempiras* in 1991 to 12 million *lempiras* in 1994. This drop, however, reflected an intentional response by ALDECA to changes in the taxation of *aguardiente* by the Honduran government. Until April 1992, the factory price of ALDECA's *aguardiente* included a flat tax of 4.5 *lempiras* per liter. In April 1992, the Honduran government implemented a new tax system requiring that tax be paid on a *percentage* of the selling price at the factory.

To remain competitively priced, ALDECA altered its transfer pricing. The company began selling its *aguardiente* to an in-house distributor at a lower price, thereby reducing the effect of taxes on the final price to wholesalers. The in-house distributor then provided ALDECA with the dividends shown at the bottom of ALDECA's income statement. Exhibits 5 and 6 provide more detailed information about ALDECA's financial performance.

THE HONDURAN *AGUARDIENTE* MARKET IN 1995

In the early 1990s, demand for *aguardiente* began to shrink after 15 years of relative stability. As a result, ALDECA produced only 2.4 million liters in 1994, compared to 2.8 million liters in 1991. Sr. Barjum explains the possible reason for this decline:

> *We feel that there is a market for softer, or less alcoholic, beverages, like wine or beer. We found out that*

5 | Alcoholes de Centroamerica Balance Sheet, 1990–1995 (in lempiras)

ACTIVO CIRCULANTE	**(SHORT-TERM ASSETS)**	**1990**	**1991**	**1992**	**1993**	**1994**
Caja Chica	(Petty Cash)	500	500	500	500	500
Caja General	(Cash on Hand)	8,266	133,771	128,265	3,586	17,111
Cuentas de Banea	(Bank Accounts)	1,580,559	1,299,762	2,231,299	1,574,759	1,088,872
Total	(Total Cash)	1,589,325	1,434,033	2,360,064	1,578,845	1,106,483
Cuentas a Cobrar	(Accounts Receivable)	505,077	453,648	1,370,009	1,723,785	2,500,668
Provision Cuentas in Cobrables	(Loss Provision for A/R)	58,914	58,914	137,000	172,378	250,066
	(Total A/R)	446,163	394,734	1,233,009	1,551,407	2,250,602
Anticipos	(Employee Advances)	159,795	59,588	80,127	48,003	220,489
Prestamos a Cobrar	(Loans Receivable)	36,489	37,916	79,604	451,794	329,723
Reparos a Cobrar	(Dividends Receivable)	1,308	1,308	1,308	1,308	1,308
	(Total)	197,592	98,812	161,039	501,105	551,520
Materias Primas	(Raw Materials)	247,656	449,741	486,839	626,792	569,605
Envases	(Containers)	330,825	388,210	721,474	835,297	1,300,724
Timbres y Casquetes	(Caps, Labels, Etc.)	6,079	9,754	0	0	0
Combustibles	(Fuel)	16,661	30,416	16,606	28,003	47,960
Producto En Proceso	(Work in Progress)	130,471	171,738	215,949	190,000	192,097
Producto Terminado	(Finished Goods Inventory)	35,663	245,240	49,522	53,995	104,000
Total Inventarios	(Total Inventory)	767,355	1,295,099	1,490,309	1,734,087	2,214,386
Accesorarios	(Accessories)	35,996	29,487	114,846	118,433	127,897
Inv. En Transito	(Goods in Transit)	0	0	0	0	0
Seguros Diferidos	(Prepaid Insurance)	6,162	2,942	11,917	9,963	11,033
Publicidad Diferida	(Prepaid Advertising)	4,924	0	9,057	18,911	5,234
Misc. Diferidos	(Prepaid Misc.)	33,507	15,393	4,623	5,511	5,632
Impuestos Pagados	(Prepaid Taxes)	8,233	9,094	26,662	5,300	25,562
Depositos Garanta	(Guaranteed Deposits)	31,525	140,394	6,180	6,180	6,580
Envases En Circulacion	(Bottles in Circulation)	179,989	266,131	353,205	370,306	350,222
Inversiones	(Short-Term Investments)	714,911	714,911	798,191	758,926	406,240
	(Total Other)	1,015,247	1,178,352	1,324,681	1,295,367	938,400
Total/Activo Circulante	(Total Short-Term Assets)	4,015,682	4,401,030	6,569,183	6,660,811	7,061,391
ACTIVO FIJO	**(LONG-TERM ASSETS)**					
Terrenos	(Land)	297,004	297,400	297,004	317,246	317,246
Edificios	(Buildings)	485,880	485,880	485,880	595,949	595,949
Desp. Acum. Edificios	(Accumulated Depr.—Bldgs.)	151,411	163,486	175,561	197,195	224,160
Total	(Total)	631,473	619,398	607,323	716,000	689,035

5 | Alcoholes de Centroamerica Balance Sheet, 1990–1995 *(Continued)*

ACTIVO FIJO	(LONG-TERM ASSETS)	1990	1991	1992	1993	1994
Maquinaria	(Machinery)	1,582,256	1,824,121	2,180,582	2,386,341	2,884,602
Depr. Acum.—Maquinaria	(Accumulated Depr.—Mach.)	1,024,297	1,120,029	1,246,176	1,410,718	1,603,770
Total	(Total)	557,959	704,092	934,406	975,623	1,280,832
Otras Instalaciones	(Other Installations)	193,708	248,695	285,469	398,005	455,890
Depr. Accum.—Instalaciones	(Accumulated Depr.—Install.)	141,288	156,841	173,404	195,991	228,021
Total	(Total)	52,420	91,854	112,065	202,014	227,869
Mobiliario y Equipo Oficina	(Office Equipment)	187,016	124,292	175,752	220,418	231,584
Depr. Acum.—Mobil. y Equipo Oficina	(Accumulated Depr. —Off. Equip.)	114,983	92,025	102,134	118,466	138,593
Total	(Total)	72,033	32,267	73,618	101,952	92,991
Vehiculos	(Vehicles)	464,976	428,404	658,497	644,147	732,647
Depr. Acum.—Vehiculos	(Accumulated Depr. —Veh.)	353,718	353,298	416,043	466,158	516,949
Total	(Total)	111,258	75,106	242,454	177,989	215,698
Otros Activos Fijas	(Other Long-Term Assets)	2,657	2,657	2,657	2,657	2,657
Depr. Accu.—Other Activos Fijas	(Accumulated Depr.—L/T Assets)	2,451	2,451	2,451	2,451	2,451
Total	(Total)	206	206	206	206	206
Activos	(Total Assets)	5,441,031	5,923,953	8,539,255	8,834,595	9,568,022
PASIVO CIRCULANTE	**LIABILITIES**					
Pasivo Circulante	(Accounts Payable)	210,435	137,030	73,186	113,791	214,013
Documentos Por Pagar	(Documents Payable)	0	0	0	0	0
Prestamos Por Pagar	(Loans Payable)	483,325	0	0	166,672	0
Imp. S Ventas Recaudado	(Taxes Payable)	202,211	247,576	1,779,839	1,695,078	1,845,644
Retencion Empleados	(Employee Benefits Payable)	3,266	4,580	6,796	4,545	9,192
Imp. S Renta a Pagar	(Income Taxes Payable)	346,005	427,230	4,206	2,958	(12,861)
Dividendos Por Pagar	(Dividend Payable)	3,476	3,476	454,781	3,476	3,476
Depositos de Clientes	(Client Deposits)	160,241	160,241	160,241	160,241	160,241
Total Pasivo Circulante	(Total Liabilities)	1,408,959	980,133	2,479,049	2,146,761	2,219,705
CAPITAL Y RESERVAS	**EQUITY**					
Capital Social	(Owner's Equity)	2,000,000	2,000,000	2,000,000	2,000,000	2,000,000
Reserva Legal	(Legal Reserves)	441,543	17,127	611,690	688,818	774,696
Otras Reservas	(Other Reserves)	0	0	0	0	0
Utilidades no distribuidas	(Retained Earnings)	522,553	915,001	1,556,925	2,476,507	4,573,621
Perdidas y Ganancias	(Net Income)	1,068,048	1,511,692	1,891,591	1,542,506	0
Total Capital y Reservas	(Total Equity)	4,032,144	4,934,820	6,060,206	6,707,831	7,348,317
Total Pasivo, Capital, y Reservas	(Total Liabilities and Equity)	5,441,103	5,923,953	8,539,255	8,854,592	9,568,022

6 | Alcoholes de Centroamerica Income Statements, 1990–1995 (in lempiras)

VENTAS	SALES	1990	1991	1992	1993	1994	1995 THROUGH 4/30
Aguardientes y Rones	Aguardiente and Rum	16,166,341	20,412,604	13,309,216	8,638,207	9,448,812	3,759,387
Otras Bebidas	(Other Drinks)	87,702	157,122	182,237	131,180	123,080	74,440
Vinos	(Wines)	49,720	38,880	97,268	118,564	95,642	56,230
Otros Productos	(Other Products)	860,260	115,764	1,062,047	1,262,978	1,959,433	844,051
Otros Ingresos	(Other Income)	438,591	512,147	364,106	454,011	484,937	225,735
Total Ventas	(Total Income)	17,602,614	22,276,507	15,014,874	10,604,940	12,111,904	4,959,844
Devoluciones y Rebajas S/Ventas	(Returned Sales)	29,154	15,979	11,369	12,321	7,913	1,957
Total Ventas E Ing Netos	(Net Sales)	17,573,460	22,260,528	15,003,505	10,592,619	12,103,991	4,957,887
Costo de Ventas	(Cost of Goods Sold)	13,826,979	16,957,738	8,591,248	4,898,314	6,397,587	2,798,326
Utilidad Bruta	(Gross Income)	3,746,481	5,302,790	6,412,257	5,694,305	5,706,404	2,159,561
GASTOS DE FABRICATION	**(MANUFACTURING COSTS)**						
Salarios	(Salaries)	212,244	330,425	403,930	407,991	437,602	134,938
Sueldos	(Wages)	93,656	132,244	126,339	110,098	166,959	85,331
Vacaciones	(Vacation)	12,390	15,751	20,265	21,782	27,876	10,820
Prestaciones Sociales	(Severance Pay)	39,000	16,057	57,873	55,215	50,972	38,184
Depr. Maquinaria	(Depr. of Equip.)	76,369	95,731	126,147	164,541	193,052	64,357
Depr. Otras Instalaciones	(Depr. of Installations)	10,304	15,553	16,562	22,587	32,030	10,677
Mantenimiento	(Maintenance)	155,334	225,031	232,628	177,324	223,830	39,741
Combustibles	(Fuels)	4,110	70	8,128	2,776	64,275	13,328
Miscelanea	(Misc.)	6,027	13,768	14,286	13,413	17,488	5,360
Materiales	(Materials)	30,671	48,230	10,909	14,725	5,586	1,171
Herramientas	(Tools)	2,668	8,066	3,877	1,573	4,316	181
Energia Electrica	(Electricity)	75,737	145,582	183,817	215,922	213,482	72,745
Agua	(Water)	71	3,382	10,206	11,279	4,145	2,114
Vigilancia	(Security)	64,408	155,468	199,906	218,460	220,762	96,396
Regalias	(Licensing Fees)	38,282	28,569	48,144	36,882	6,019	0
Marcas de Registros	(Brand Registration Fee)	2,499	1,419	2,501	22,187	3,338	1,171
Total	(Total)	823,770	1,235,346	1,465,518	1,496,755	1,671,732	576,507
GASTOS DE VENTAS	**(SELLING EXPENSES)**						
Sueldos	(Wages)	8,423	20,256	43,616	46,600	49,050	12,700
Comisiones	(Commissions)	76,713	0	0	0	0	0
Vacaciones	(Vacations)	466	566	1,566	1,833	2,300	800
Prestacioines Sociales	(Severance Pay)	0	0	0	0	0	0
Depr. Vehiculos	(Depreciation of Vehicles)	34,609	32,296	62,475	77,954	70,791	23,597
Combustibles	(Fuels)	62,499	103,425	89,378	112,819	126,278	38,182
Mantenimiento	(Maintenance)	39,855	125,614	129,591	77,034	108,265	58,199
Seguros	(Insurance)	25,981	37,705	37,716	33,701	38,014	39,733
Otros Gastos Vehiculos	(Other Vehicle Expense)	23,966	24,634	32,441	31,864	38,950	11,484
Fletes	(Transportation Fees)	187,674	265,800	103,092	155,563	225,189	93,456
Cuentas Incobrales	(Bad Dept Exp.)	0	0	93,197	35,377	77,688	0
Gastos de Viaje	(Travel Expense)	11,438	16,479	23,473	28,001	20,175	2,405

6 | Alcoholes de Centroamerica Income Statements, 1990–1995 *(Continued)*

GASTOS DE VENTAS	**(SELLING EXPENSES)**	**1990**	**1991**	**1992**	**1993**	**1994**	**1995 THROUGH 4/30**
Promocion	(Advertising)	254,662	351,225	520,997	506,214	622,613	43,151
Otros Gastos de Venta	(Other Selling Expenses)	48,258	77,305	61,251	54,486	43,542	7,878
Miscelaneos	(Misc. Expenses)	475	599	2,682	586	484	136
Impuestos Distr. S/Ventas	(Taxes)	23,436	46,990	55,088	54,982	60,353	21,218
Total	(Total)	797,915	1,102,894	1,256,563	1,216,814	1,483,692	352,939
GASTOS ADMIN. Y GRALES	**(ADMINISTRATIVE EXPENSES)**						
Sueldos	(Wages)	189,707	219,926	238,788	246,322	284,979	115,513
Vacaciones	(Vacations)	6,663	5,341	5,305	5,169	8,172	1,689
Prestaciones Sociales	(Severance Pay)	27,066	0	0	0	566	0
Benef. Empleados	(Empl. Benefits)	96,926	133,039	133,962	168,490	195,830	52,610
Depr. Edificios	(Building Exp.)	12,075	12,075	12,075	21,634	26,965	8,988
Depr. Mobiliario	(Depr.—Furniture)	12,880	9,360	10,108	16,331	20,127	6,709
Mantenamiento	(Maintenance)	11,426	22,565	23,931	15,676	28,142	10,106
Seguro	(Insurance)	22,232	28,731	34,626	29,532	29,532	24,359
Arrendamiento Equipos	(Lease-Buyback Expense)	0	20,060	60,979	53,123	39,193	0
Gastos de Viaje	(Travel Exp.)	0	34,905	34,928	25,892	38,254	10,072
Honorarios Profesionales	(Legal Fees)	15,061	52,524	33,625	20,870	19,210	56,308
Dietas y Gastos de Repres.	(Representation Fees)	32,100	47,600	56,000	63,600	78,600	30,900
Papeleria y Utiles	(Office Supplies)	22,133	21,037	20,717	17,634	29,493	16,779
Correro, Telgrafo, Telefono	(Telephone and Mail)	11,909	18,157	25,771	19,907	38,008	11,827
Donaciones	(Donations)	22,300	35,989	46,650	17,850	21,235	11,028
Miscelaneos	(Miscellaneous)	19,551	43,496	39,444	44,719	41,104	13,192
Otros Impuestos Distritales	(Taxes)	5,776	11,043	11,089	10,639	11,813	0
Otros Gastos	(Other Expenses)	0	0	0	0	0	0
Total	(Total)	507,805	715,848	787,998	777,388	911,223	370,082
Gastos Financieros	(Financial Exp.)						
Interese Pagados	(Interest Paid)	75,589	56,668	51,884	53,852	6,722	83,887
Gastos Bancarias	(Bank Comms.)	103,185	10,462	50,286	1,169	0	9,728
Total	(Total)	178,774	67,130	102,270	55,021	6,722	74,159
GASTOS NO DEDUCIBLES	**(NON-DEDUCTIBLE EXPENSES)**						
Aportaciones INFOP	(Training Institute Tuition)	5,819	7,791	9,157	9,168	11,369	1,911
Multas, Reparos, y Otros	(Penalties)	378	989	423	352	128	0
Total	(Total)	6,197	8,780	9,580	9,520	11,497	1,911
Total Gastos	(Total Expenses)	2,314,461	3,129,998	3,621,929	3,555,498	4,084,866	1,375,598
Utilidad Antes Del I/S/Renta	(Net Income Before Taxes)	1,432,020	2,171,792	2,790,328	2,138,807	1,621,538	783,963
Impuestos S Renta Estimado	(Taxes)	523,876	823,073	1,071,835	809,715	597,306	0
Utilidad Despues Del I/S/Renta	(Net Income After Taxes)	908,144	1,349,719	1,718,493	1,329,092	1,024,232	783,963
Dividendos Recibidos	(Dividends Received)	159,904	161,973	173,098	213,414	693,365	423,000
UTILIDAD NETA	(Net Income)	1,068,048	1,511,692	1,891,591	1,542,506	1,717,597	1,206,963

the demand for beer in Honduras is 260 million 12-ounce bottles per year. Wine imports have increased considerably. We don't have the exact figures because they aren't published, but we feel certain that these products have been taking some overall market share.

There were indications that demand for *aguardiente* was declining throughout Central America. As a result, competition within the industry was becoming more intense by the mid-1990s, as distilleries looked for ways to maintain profitability. Because of this, ALDECA was faced with a potential new competitor from Guatemala, as well as a merger offer from another Honduran distillery.

A New Threat

A Guatemalan conglomerate, *Grupo Cobán*, had recently made attempts to enter the Honduran *aguardiente* market. Sr. Barjum believed that *Grupo Cobán* was a major threat to ALDECA because it "has a monopoly on the Guatemalan *aguardiente* market, producing 15 million liters per year. They have total control in Guatemala. They own a bank and a sugar mill. They also have an interest in the Pepsi Cola™ manufacturing facilities in Guatemala, as well as beer. In addition, they have a cost advantage with respect to raw materials; both molasses and fuel oils are cheaper in Guatemala."

Grupo Cobán purchased a small distillery in Honduras, as well as the rights to use several brands of *aguardiente* that have been popular there. Sr. Barjum explains,

They [Grupo Cobán] *have purchased relatively new facilities. That is a disadvantage because they had to put up a lot of money for them. Right now, they are testing the market and testing what competitive reactions will be. If they give credit to distributors, for example, what are we going to do? If they give away bottles, how will we react? They are at that stage. They have not really come in full-strength. I think they are just at the initial testing stage.*

Grupo Cobán's initial attempts to enter the Honduran market came in the form of enticements to ALDECA's distributors. *Grupo Cobán* executives offered one particularly attractive incentive; for initial orders, and for orders expanding a distributor's volume, *Grupo Cobán* would provide the reusable bottles free of charge. Normally, distributors wishing to carry a new manufacturer's *aguardiente* were required either to pay for the bottles up front or to provide acceptable used bottles for exchange. This represented a large initial cost for the distributors. *Grupo Cobán*'s incentive shifted this cost from the distributor to the manufacturer. After the initial order was sold, the distributor would simply exchange the empty bottles to cover the bottle cost for the next order. However, while the bottles of most *aguardiente* manufacturers were interchangeable, thus minimizing the distributors' switching costs, *Grupo Cobán*'s bottles were unique. Therefore, the distributors could recover the value of these bottles only by reordering *Grupo Cobán* brands.

Recently, *Grupo Cobán* invited ALDECA's four largest distributors in the San Pedro Sula area to visit *Grupo Cobán*'s facilities in Guatemala. Two of the four declined that offer. The two distributors that accepted the offer reported some of the details of the meetings to Sr. Barjum. They were informed that *Grupo Cobán* was in the initial marketing stages in Honduras, confirming Sr. Barjum's suspicions. Later, *Grupo Cobán* was planning to introduce two new *aguardiente* brands into the Honduran market, each having a traditional Honduran name.

Unknown to ALDECA's distributors, *Grupo Cobán* had a history of entering markets in this way, then bypassing local distributors after its brands became established. Several of ALDECA's distributors indicated that they were considering *Grupo Cobán*'s proposal, and Sr. Barjum was very concerned. He had been gathering and analyzing information on *Grupo Cobán*'s entry into the Honduran market and identified several alternative courses of action for ALDECA. He explains,

We can respond in-kind. To a certain extent, we can give credit to the wholesalers. We can also lower our prices. But, I'm trying to figure out some unique way to respond. One way might be to go to our distributors and tell them that they cannot take on different brands. If they choose to go with Grupo Cobán, *then they can forget about us; we will begin selling directly to the cantinas. But, that would require a lot of changes in our marketing department. We don't have too much experience with retailing.*

An Opportunity

ALDECA also had the opportunity to merge with another Honduran distillery, *Licorera de Boaco*, which had recently approached Sr. Barjum with a merger proposal. *Licorera de Boaco* was also concerned about *Grupo Cobán*'s entry into the Honduran *aguardiente* market and felt that a merger was the best way to handle the situation. According to Sr. Barjum,

> *We have been off and on for about two years with the possibility of closing down our plant and manufacturing all of our products in their facility, under our supervision, but using their technical procedures. We would give them all of our equipment, but we would keep the land and buildings. But, we are used to making decisions without talking too much with our board of directors. This merger would mean that any decision would have to be mutually agreed upon. They have been in the market for about fifteen years and haven't really been successful. They have good marketing and distribution, but they have not done a good job with the product.*

In 1995, ALDECA was running at 80 percent of capacity. ALDECA's plot of land was surrounded by other development and was too small for additional construction. Any large increase in output would require a shift in production to a different location. *Licorera de Boaco*, however, had the ability to produce three times more alcohol than ALDECA, and they had the potential to produce it at 15 to 20 percent lower cost. Sr. Barjum notes,

> *If we united with* Licorera de Boaco, *that would mean that we would have larger storage facilities, or we could build larger storage facilities because they have more land than we have. That would give us an advantage of being able to get better prices for molasses because, at certain times of the year, the sugar mills are really pressed for storage. At that time, you will find two or three of them competing with each other. The thing is, though, I'll be frank with you. If I'm going to merge, I don't want more problems than I had to begin with. I'm going to have to look closely at their operation from the start and see what problems they are having. It is going to be more difficult for us, because I'm going to have their production problems. Tony cannot take care of that, because he is just starting to learn. I'll have to worry about that myself. I'll also have to be concerned with their marketing problems.*

A major marketing problem was that *Licorera de Boaco* had not been able to establish a strong brand name for its *aguardiente*. If ALDECA chose not to merge, however, *Licorera de Boaco* might have continued to try to build strong brands themselves. Says Sr. Barjum,

> *They have their own sugar mill, they have 85 percent control of the Nicaraguan market, they have the technical know-how, and they have banks in the United States. So, they are a very powerful company. They also own the franchise for MasterCard™ in Central America. Financially, I think they may be more powerful than* Grupo Cobán, *and we are in the middle. We are like the cheese between the two slices of bread . . . everyone is trying to get us. So that's one of the reasons we thought about the possible merger with these people. But, that would mean we would have to close down shop here. Some of our personnel would be taken over there, and some of them would not. So, we would have to pay approximately 1.2 million* lempiras *in workers' compensation.*

Some of the conditions of the merger proposal were as follows:

1. ALDECA would shift all of its production equipment to the *Licorera de Boaco* distillery.
2. The consolidated firm would have exclusive rights to the brand names of both ALDECA and *Licorera de Boaco* for 99 years.
3. The board of directors of the new firm would have seven members, three from ALDECA and four from *Licorera de Boaco*.

Details of the proposed equity arrangement for the merged company are provided in Exhibit 7. Additional portions of ALDECA's initial merger analysis are shown in Exhibit 8.

SR. BARJUM'S VIEW OF THE FUTURE

Sr. Barjum sat in his office with his son, Tony, late into the night trying to come to some conclusions about their situation. "I am reacting on a day-to-day basis," Sr. Barjum explained. "I have not determined where I want the company to go in, say, five years. How are we going

7 | ALDECA's Merger Analysis

ALDECA Sales (2,491,000 its/year)	L 28,694,112.00
Licorera de Boaco Direct Costs (if produced 2,491,000 lts.)	
Alcohol	L 5,762,513.33
Bottle Caps	L 498,200.00
Labels	L 163,990.83
Flavorings	L 207,583.33
Security Seal	L 78,560.00
Direct Labor	L 398,560.00
Indirect Expenses	L 1,668,970.00
Total Costs	L 8,778,377.49
Profit Margin Distillery	L 4,151,666.67
Sale Price at the Factory (2,491,000 lts.)	L 12,930,365.83
Add:	
44% Elaboration Tax	L 5,689,360.97
20% Consumption Tax	L 2,586,073.17
10% Sales Tax	L 2,120,580.00
Cost To Distribution Co.	L 23,326,379.96
Dist. Gross Margin	L 5,367,732.04
Less:	
Advertising (L 4.00/box)	L 830,333.33
Administration Costs	L 600,000.00
Sales Exp.	L 360,000.00
Transportation (L 4.00/box)	L 830,333.33
Other Costs	L 400,000.00
Total Costs	L 3,020,666.66
NI Distribution Co.	L 2,347,065.37
NI Liquor Manufacturing	L 4,151,666.68
ALDECA contribution	L 6,498,732.04
Licorera de Boaco Contr. (Their NI)	L 1,100,000.00
TOTAL	L 7,598,732.04
45% Participation ALDECA	L 3,419,429.42
1994 ALDECA	L 3,592,181.26

to meet the new competition that is coming into the country? Maybe the way we've operated in the past is not correct for today."

They decided to call a meeting of their most important distributors to discuss the issue. Tony wanted to tell the distributors directly of *Grupo Cobán*'s usual form of market entry and then give them an ultimatum: "Our brands or theirs, but not both." But what if the distributors did not believe that ALDECA could enforce the ultimatum? Sr. Barjum favored discussing the problem with the distributors and explaining to them some of the options that ALDECA was considering, like distributing *aguardiente* directly to the cantinas themselves. The implied threat should be enough to persuade the distributors to avoid *Grupo Cobán*'s brands. Sr. Barjum hoped that the distributors did not know that ALDECA could only ship competitors' products, like the pickup-load of *Yuscaran,* at a loss.

8 | Consolidation Analysis

1. The equity structure of *Licorera de Boaco S.A.* and *Distribuidora de Boaco S.A.* is as follows:

Investor #1	10.2%
Investor #2	5.3%
Investor #3	5.3%
Familia Cortez	79.2%

Note: Investor #3 is the general manager of *Licorera* and *Distribuidora de Boaco.*

2. *Distribuidora de Boaco S.A.* has 39% ownership of *Distribuidora Puerto Barrias S.A.*, a large distribution company which had sales of 53 million lempiras last year.

Consolidation Proposal

1. ALDECA will transfer to *Licorera de Boaco* all its production machinery and equipment, including storage tanks and the electrical plant.
2. ALDECA will give *Licorera de Boaco* the exclusive authorization to produce and distribute its brand name products (a period of 99 years).
3. The owners of the brands that *Licorera de Boaco* currently manufactures and distributes would give the same authorization to the consolidation firm.
4. ALDECA would receive stock totaling 45% of the capital of *Licorera de Boaco* and *Distribuidora de Boaco.* The new capital structure would be the following:

Familia Cortez	45.0%
ALDECA	45.0%
Investor #1	5.0%
Investor #3	5.0%

5. The capital structure of *Distribuidora Puerto Barrias* will not be altered.
6. The board of directors will be chosen as follows:

Familia Cortez	3 directors
ALDECA	3 directors
Investor #1	1 director

7. The bylaws and articles of the corporation would be modified so that important decisions could be adopted with 90% of the stockholders approving a motion (for the General Assembly) and only with the vote of 6 of the 7 directors for the decisions pertaining to the Administrative Council.
8. The administration of *Distribuidora de Boaco* will correspond to Emin Barjum (CEO ALDECA).
9. The consolidated operations would yield the estimated income before taxes (taking into account current sales prices and costs):

For the fabrication and distribution of ALDECA products:	L 6.5 million
For the fabrication and distribution of *L de Boaco* products:	L 1.1 million
Total	L 7.6 million

Note: The contribution by ALDECA seems substantially superior due to the fact that it has been calculated as a marginal contribution and the fixed costs are absorbed by the production of *Licorera de Boaco* products.

The income before taxes of ALDECA in 1994 was L 3.6 million, with distributorship alcohol manufacturing and sales.

Advantages

- Currently ALDECA has very little capability of increasing its production capacity without a substantial investment in equipment and buildings. The production capacity of ALDECA is 5,000 liters of ethyl alcohol (12.5000 liters of liquor) in 24 hours (currently operating at 80% of capacity).
- The production capacity of *Licorera de Boaco* is 15,000 liters of ethyl alcohol (37,500 liters of liquor) in 24 hours.
- Due to superior technology, the direct fabrication costs of *Licorera de Boaco* are 10% lower than ALDECA's costs.
- The consolidation would strengthen ALDECA's competitive situation against *Grupo Cobán,* which currently bought a distillery in the north part of the country. (They want to produce not only rum, but also *aguardientes,* attacking ALDECA's core market.)
- The consolidated sales would represent 40% of the liquor market in Honduras.
- ALDECA would have a 17.5% (45% of 39%) direct participation in *Distribuidora Puerto Barrias'* operations.
- The very valuable location where ALDECA is currently located could be developed for housing or commercial purposes.

Disadvantages

- Administrative autonomy would be lost.
- ALDECA would have to lay-off many workers and pay approximately L 900,000 as compensation. (This cost will be recovered by asking *Licorera de Boaco* to pay ALDECA L 6.00 for every box of liquor produced for a period of 2–3 years.)
- The merger agreement would have to be drafted carefully, with a lot of emphasis on detail, to protect both parties, to avoid paralyzing the operations due to disagreement, etc.
- There is always risk of bad faith in the actions of the other party.

Financial

ALDECA	
Machinery and Equipment	L 1,281,000.00
Other Installments	L 228,000.00
Replacement Parts and Accessories	L 129,000.00
Total	L 1,638,000.00
Owners Equity and Retained Earnings	
Licorera de Boaco	L 4,720,000.00
Distribuidora de Boaco	L 4,054,000.00
Total	L 8,774,000.00

REFERENCES

United Nations Economic Commission for Latin America and the Caribbean, 1996 *Report.*

U.S. Central Intelligence Agency. 1995. *World Fact Book.*

U.S. Department of Commerce. 1996. *National Trade Data Bank.*

U.S. International Trade Administration. 1995. *Country Commercial Guide: Honduras.*

Panet, J-P., Hart, L., and Glassman, P. 1994. *Honduras and Bay Islands Guide (2nd edition).* Washington, D.C.: Open Road Publishing.

CASE 5

Amazon.com

Expanding Beyond Books

Suresh Kotha
University of Washington

Jeff Bezos, the CEO of Amazon.com, was pleased that his three-year-old online start-up, www.amazon.com, had gone from being an underground sensation for book-lovers on the World Wide Web (WWW) to one of the most admired Internet retailers on Wall Street. To date, his attempts to transform the traditional book-retailing format through technology that taps the interactive nature of the Internet has been very successful. Although his company garnered rave reviews from respected Wall Street analysts, Bezos clearly understood that this was not the moment to dwell on the past. In the fast-moving world of the Internet, he and his firm continued to face many formidable challenges.

This case describes how Bezos has managed to build a rapidly growing retail business on the Internet and the challenges he and his top management currently face as other industry giants such as Barnes & Noble and Bertelsman, the German publishing conglomerate, attempt to imitate his model of competition.

COMPANY BACKGROUND

In 1994, Jeffrey Bezos, a computer science and electrical-engineering graduate from Princeton University, was the youngest senior vice-president in the history of D.E. Shaw, a Wall Street-based investment bank. During the summer of 1994, one important statistic about the Internet caught his attention and imagination—Internet usage was growing at 2300 percent a year. His reaction: "Anything that's growing that fast is going to be ubiquitous very quickly. It was my wake-up call."

He left his job at D.E. Shaw and drew up a list of 20 possible products that could be sold on the Internet. He quickly narrowed his prospects to music and books. Both shared a potential advantage for online sale: far too many titles for a single store to stock. He chose books.

> *There are so many of them! There are 1.5 million English-language books in print, 3 million books in all languages worldwide. This volume defined the opportunity. Consumers keep demonstrating that they value authoritative selection. The biggest phenomenon in retailing is the big-format store—the "category killer"—whether it's selling books, toys, or music. But the largest physical bookstore in the world has only 175,000 titles. . . . With some 4,200 US publishers and the two biggest booksellers, Barnes & Noble and Borders Group Inc., accounting for less than 12 percent of total sales, there aren't any 800-pound gorillas in book selling.*[1]

In contrast, the music industry had only six major record companies that controlled the distribution of records and CDs sold in the United States. With such control, these firms had the potential to lock out a new business threatening the traditional record store format.

To start his new venture, Bezos left New York City to move west, either to Boulder, Seattle, or Portland. As he drove west, he refined and fine-tuned his thoughts as well as his business plan. In doing so, he concluded that Seattle was his final destination. Recalls Bezos:

This case was prepared as the basis for class discussion rather than to illustrate either effective or ineffective handling of an administrative situation. Copyright © 1998 Kotha. All rights reserved.

It sounds counterintuitive, but physical location is very important for the success of a virtual business. We could have started Amazon.com anywhere. We chose Seattle because it met a rigorous set of criteria. It had to be a place with lots of technical talent. It had to be near a place with large numbers of books. It had to be a nice place to live—great people won't work in places they don't want to live. Finally, it had to be in a small state. In the mail-order business, you have to charge sales tax to customers who live in any state where you have a business presence. It made no sense for us to be in California or New York. . . . Obviously Seattle has a great programming culture. And it's close to Roseburg, Oregon, which has one of the biggest book warehouses in the world.[2]

Renting a house in Bellevue, a Seattle suburb, Bezos started working out of his garage. Ironically, he held meetings with prospective employees and suppliers at a nearby Barnes & Noble superstore. Bezos also raised several million dollars from private investors. Operating from a 400-square-foot office in Bellevue, he launched his venture, Amazon.com, on the Internet in July 1995.

As word about his new venture spread quickly across the Internet, sales picked up rapidly. Six weeks after opening, Bezos moved his new firm to a 2,000-square-foot warehouse. Six months later, he moved once again, this time to a 17,000-square-foot building in an industrial neighborhood in Seattle. To fund further expansion, Bezos attracted $8 million from Kleiner, Perkins, Caufield & Byers, a venture-capital firm based in the Silicon Valley that has funded firms such as Sun Microsystems and Netscape.

By the end of 1996, his firm was one of the most successful Web retailers, with revenues reaching $15.6 million. (Revenues for a large Barnes & Noble superstore amount to about $5 million on average per year.) With revenues surging quarter after quarter. Bezos decided to take his company public. However, just days before the firm's initial public offering (IPO) of three million shares, Barnes & Noble—the nation's largest book retailer—launched its online store and sued Amazon.com for claiming to be the world's largest bookstore. To entice customers to visit its Web store, Barnes & Noble offered deeper discounts. Bezos retaliated with a counter lawsuit of his own.[3]

On May 14, 1997, Bezos took Amazon.com public. *The Wall Street Journal* noted that: "Amazon's May 1997 debut on the Nasdaq Stock Market came with no small amount of hype. On the first day of trading, investors bid the price of shares up to $23.50 from their offering price of $18. But the shares then fell, and within three weeks of the IPO they were below their offering price."

Despite this, customers have continued to flock to Amazon.com's Web site. By October 1997 Amazon.com served its millionth "unique" customer. To keep pace with such growth, the firm expanded its Seattle warehouse and built a second 200,000-square-foot, state-of-the-art distribution center in New Castle, Delaware. With these additions Amazon.com successfully increased its stocking and shipping capabilities to nearly six times its 1996 levels.

As the firm has continued to expand its customer base, sales revenues have surged. The firm's revenues increased from $15.7 million in 1996 to $147 million in 1997 (see Exhibit 1 for the firm's income statement and balance sheet). Sales are now on pace to top $550 million for fiscal 1998. In response to this revenue growth, the company's stock and market capitalization have proceeded to rise as well. As of July 1998, the company's capitalization was around $6.4 billion, a number that represents the combined value of the nation's two largest retailers, Barnes & Noble and Borders Books & Music, whose combined sales are about 10 times that of Amazon.com's.

THE BOOK PUBLISHING INDUSTRY

The United States is the world's largest market for books, with retail book sales accounting for $20.76 billion in 1997. With over 2,500 publishers in the US, the book publishing industry is one of the oldest and most fragmented industries.[4] Exhibit 2 shows the structure of the US publishing industry.

Publishers Publishers sell books on a consignment basis and assume all the risk in this industry. They also accept returns on unsold books, thus guaranteeing their distributors a 100 percent refund on all unsold books. They provide money and contracts to prospective authors and decide how many copies of a book to print. Typically a "first-run" print for a book varies

EXHIBIT 1 | Amazon.com, Inc.—Consolidated Balance Sheets (unaudited) (in thousands, except share and per share data)

	June 30, 1998	December 31, 1997
Assets		
Current assets:		
Cash	$ 2,523	$ 1,567
Marketable securities	337,396	123,499
Inventories	17,035	8,971
Prepaid expenses and other	12,487	3,298
Total current assets	369,441	137,335
Fixed assets, net	14,014	9,265
Deposits and other	284	166
Goodwill and other purchased intangibles, net	52,398	—
Deferred charges	7,622	2,240
Total assets	$ 443,759	$ 149,006
Liabilities and Stockholders' Equity		
Current liabilities:		
Accounts payable	$ 47,556	$ 32,697
Accrued advertising	9,971	3,454
Other liabilities and accrued expenses	13,713	6,167
Current portion of long-term debt	684	1,500
Total current liabilities	71,924	43,818
Long-term portion of debt	332,225	76,521
Long-term portion of capital lease obligation	181	181
Stockholders' equity:		
Preferred stock, $0.01 par value:		
Authorized shares—10,000,000 issued and outstanding shares—none		
Common stock, $0.01 par value:		
Authorized shares—300,000,000 issued and outstanding shares—49,669,601 and 47,874,338 shares, resp.	497	479
Additional paid-in capital	104,368	63,552
Deferred compensation	(1,301)	(1,930)
Other gains (losses)	(35)	—
Accumulated deficit	(64,100)	(33,615)
Total stockholders' equity	39,429	28,486
Total liabilities and stockholders' equity	$ 443,759	$ 149,006

(Continues)

from 5,000 to 50,000 copies. However, best-selling authors' first-run prints are generally set at around 300,000 copies.

In practice, however, trade (adult and juvenile books) and paperback publishers print far more copies than will be sold. About 25 percent of all books distributed to wholesalers are returned and at times these percentages run as high as 40 percent for mass-market paperbacks. According to industry experts, 20–30 percent for hardcover book returns is considered acceptable and 30–50 percent is generally considered high. Anything above 50 percent is considered disastrous. In a process

EXHIBIT 1 | *(Continued)* Amazon.com, Inc.—Consolidated Statements of Operations (Unaudited) (in thousands, except per share data)

	Quarter Ended June 30		Six Months Ended June 30	
	1998	1997	1998	1997
Net sales	$ 115,977	$ 27,855	$ 203,352	$ 3,860
Cost of sales	89,786	22,633	157,840	35,117
Gross profit	26,191	5,222	45,512	8,743
Operating expenses:				
Marketing and sales	26,452	7,773	45,955	11,679
Product development	8,060	2,808	14,789	4,383
General and administrative	3,262	1,708	5,225	2,850
Amortization of goodwill and other purchased intangibles	5,413	—	5,413	—
Total operating expenses	43,187	12,289	71,382	18,912
Loss from operations	(16,996)	(7,067)	(25,870)	(10,169)
Interest income	3,334	366	4,974	430
Interest expense	(7,564)	(4)	(9,589)	(4)
Net interest income (expense)	(4,230)	362	(4,615)	426
Net loss	$ (21,226)	$ (6,705)	$ (30,485)	$ (9,743)
Basic and diluted loss per share	$ (0.44)	$ (0.16)	$ (0.64)	$ (0.24)
Shares used in computation of basic and diluted loss per share	47,977	42,634	47,299	40,719

EXHIBIT 2 | Book Publishing Market Structure

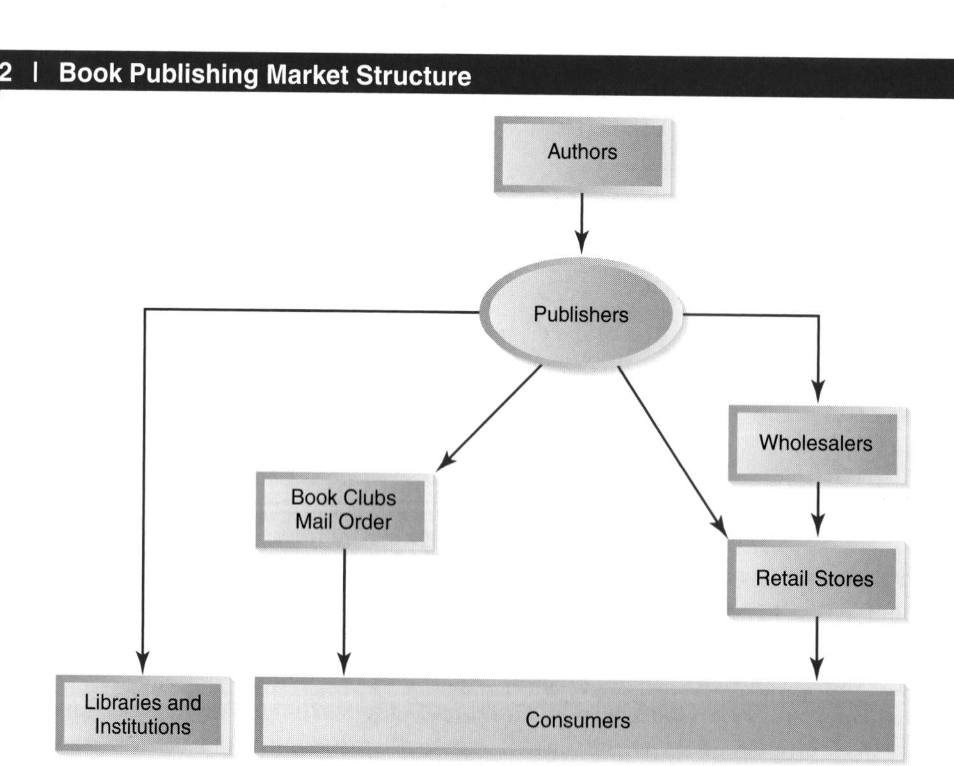

known as "remaindering" (offering books to discount stores, jobbers, and other vendors) publishers drastically reduce the price after a certain period. Apart from the material cost of returns and the lost revenue they represent, publishers spend millions of dollars each year transporting books back and forth. In this industry profit margins are driven by book volume, which in turn hinges on the size of each print run. Generally about 10 percent of titles make a profit, with 90 percent barely breaking even. Exhibit 3 illustrates the margins on a typical hardcover book.

The "big three"—Warner Books, Simon & Schuster and Pearson—accounted for 21 percent of sales in 1995. The 20 largest book-publishing companies in the US command over 60 percent of all retail sales. Warner Books, a subsidiary of Time Warner, the U.S. entertainment giant, was the largest publisher, with sales of $3.7 billion in 1995. Simon & Schuster, a division of Viacom Corporation, ranked second with sales reaching $2.17 billion, and Pearson, a group that owns the *Financial Times,* ranked third with revenues of $1.75 billion.

Wholesalers Wholesalers distribute books. They take orders from independent booksellers and chains, and consolidate them into lot-orders for publishers. Publishers supply wholesalers who in turn supply the thousands of retail bookstores located throughout the United States. Wholesalers accounted for almost 30 percent of publishers' sales in 1996. Unlike publishing and retailing, wholesalers are highly concentrated, with firms like Ingram Book Co. and Baker and Taylor commanding over 80 percent of the market.

Competition in wholesaling revolves around the speed of delivery and the number of titles stocked. Ingram, for instance, receives more than 70 percent of its orders electronically and offers one-day delivery to about 82 percent of its US customers. In 1994 the average net profit per book for wholesalers was less than 1.5 percent. This figure was down from the traditional margin of about 2 percent a few years earlier.[5]

Technological advances have made warehouse operations more efficient which in turn has made it possible for wholesalers to provide attractive discounts to retailers. Also, the types of books wholesalers are supplying to retailers are changing. Bookstores are increasingly relying on wholesalers for fast-selling titles and less-popular backlist books.[6] However, with the emergence of superstores, such large retailers as Barnes & Noble and Borders Books & Music are no longer using wholesalers for initial orders of major titles. For example, Borders Books & Music currently buys over 90 percent of its titles directly from publishers.

Retail Bookstores Retail bookstores, independents and general retailers accounted for between 35–40 percent of industry revenues (see Exhibit 4). From 1975 to 1995, the number of bookstores in the United States increased from 11,990 to 17,340. According to industry sources, the total sales for the nation's four largest bookstore chains—Barnes & Noble, Borders Books & Music, Books-A-Million, and Crown Books—rose 14.3 percent to $5.68 billion for the fiscal year ended January 1998. This figure represented about 24 percent of all book sales (see Exhibit 5). Industry analysts point out that

EXHIBIT

3 | Profit Margins for a "Typical" Book

Book List Price	**$19.95**	
Revenue to Publisher (i.e., price paid by wholesaler or bookstore)	$10.37	48% discount off suggested retail price
Manufacturing cost	$ 2.00	Printing, binding, jacket design, composition, typesetting, paper, ink
Publisher overhead	$ 3.00	Marketing, fulfillment
Returns and allowances	$ 3.00	
Author's royalties	$ 2.00	
Total publishing costs	$10.00	
Publisher's operating profit	$ 0.37	Returns amount for 3.7%

EXHIBIT

4 | Book Sales in 1994 by Various Distribution Channels

Channel	% of Total sales
Bookstore chains, independents and general retailers	35%–40%
Mail order and book clubs	21%
Sales to college book stores	17%
Schools	15%
Libraries and other institutions	10%

from 1992 through 1995, superstore bookstore sales grew at a compounded rate of 17 percent while non-superstore sales grew at a rate of 4 percent.

With the increasing growth of these superstores, experts cautioned that in smaller markets a shakeout was inevitable.[7] Also, 1995 marked the first year in which bookstore chains sold more books than independents (see Exhibit 6).[8] A spokesperson for the *American Booksellers Association* noted:

> *In the three years from 1993 to 1995, 150 to 200 independent-owned bookstores went out of business—50 to 60 in 1996 alone. . . . By contrast in the same period, approximately 450 retail superstore outlets opened, led by Barnes & Noble and the Borders Group, with 348 openings.*[9]

Independent booksellers believed the growth of superstores might be reaching a saturation point. But even as Barnes & Noble and Borders entered city after city, as many as 142 U.S. metropolitan markets still did not have a book superstore. According to Amy Ryan, a Prudential Securities analyst, the current rate of expansion could continue at least through the year 2000. This is because the United States could support about 1,500 such stores.

Institutions and Libraries There are more than 29,000 private, public, and academic libraries in the United States.[10] This market is crucial to publishers because of its stability and size. Since libraries order only what they want, this lowers the overhead costs associated with inventory and return processing, making this segment a relatively profitable one for publishers. Moreover, as hardcover trade books have become relatively expensive, many readers now borrow them from libraries rather than purchase them outright. Industry experts observed that about 95 percent of general titles published in any year sold less than 20,000 copies; of that amount, about 55 percent were purchased by li-

EXHIBIT

5 | Bookstore Chain Sales ($ millions)

Chain	1998*	1997	% Change
Barnes & Noble	$2,797.0	$2448.0	14.2%
Borders Group	2,266.0	1,958.8	15.7
Books-A-Million	324.8	278.6	16.5
Crown Books	297.5	287.7	3.4
Total	$5685.3	$4,973.1	14.3%

Source: *Publishers Weekly,* March 23, 1998, p. 17.
*Estimates.

EXHIBIT 6 | Growth of Independents vs. Chain Stores

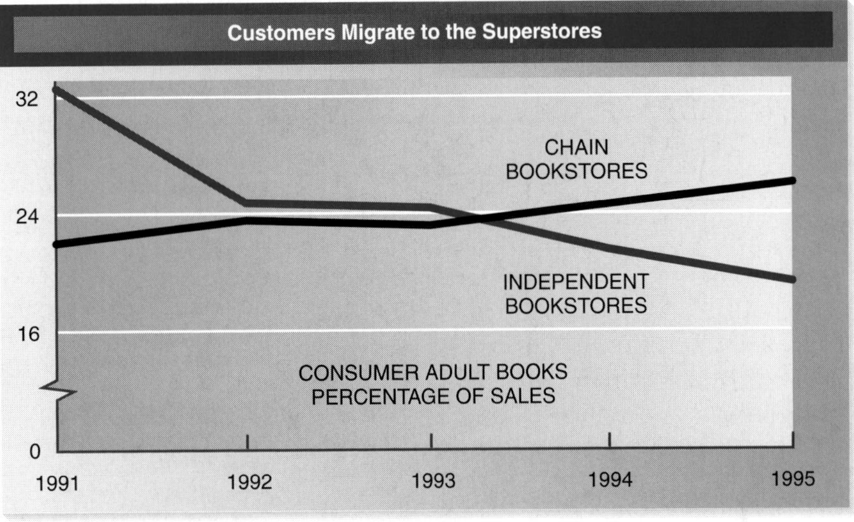

Source: *Business Week*, 1998

braries. Libraries also frequently repurchase titles to replace worn-out and stolen books. By doing so, they keep the "backlist" sales healthy.

Mail Order and Book Clubs The industry is witnessing a significant drop in the mail order book business. This drop in sales was attributed to the growth of large discount-sale retailers. Publishers' book club sales, on the other hand, have risen steadily, gaining 9 percent in 1994 and in early 1995. This growth was attributed to the increasing popularity of specialized book clubs that focus on favorite baby-boomer interests such as gardening and computers.

The industry sells a variety of books that include trade, professional, mass market, El-Hi (elementary-high school) and college-textbooks, and others, and each of these categories varied in terms of sales, competition, profitability, and volatility (see Exhibits 7 and 8).

A survey commissioned by American Booksellers Association found that some 106 million adults purchased about 456.9 million books in any given quarter. The survey, which looked at book-buying habits of consumers during the calendar year 1994, revealed that six in 10 American adults say they purchased at least one book in the last three months. Annually that corresponds to 1.8 billion books sold, an average of 17 books per book-buying consumer a year. The average amount paid for the three most recent books purchased by consumers in the last 30 days was about $15. According to another report by *Book Industry Study Group*, "1996 was a year of major transition and flux in the publishing industry with buyer and seller alike reexamining standard operating procedures to work together in order to adapt to recent changes including growth of retail space and the impact of the Internet."

The Growing Presence of "Virtual" Bookstores

The two hardest challenges for book selling—physically distributing the right number of books to bookstores and getting the word about serious books out to potential readers—are getting a more than trivial assist from the new online technologies. The rapid growth of the online businesses is spreading to book publishing and retailing. According to Larry Daniels, director of information technologies for the National Association of College Stores:

> *Booksellers' concern revolves around the potential for publishers to deal directly with consumers and the*

7 | The Various Product Categories

Trade Books. This segment includes general interest hardcover and paperback books sold to adults and juveniles. Trade books accounted for almost 25% of book revenues in 1997. According to industry reports, books sold to adults increased by more than 30% between 1991 and 1995. However, juvenile hardcover book sales represented a 2.3% increase in 1997 over the previous year and juvenile paperback book sales fell by as much as 18.6% during the same time period. This slow growth was attributed to a decline in the number of popular titles and increased spending by children on toys and games.

Random House Inc., Bantam Doubleday Dell, Simon & Schuster, HarperCollins, and Penguin are some of the leading firms that competed in this product category.

Professional Books. Over 165 million professional books were sold in 1997 accounting for $4.15 billion. Since 1991 professional book sales have grown at a compound annual rate of 3.0% (in units). Legal publishing was the largest segment of the professional-books category, with the scientific and technical category coming in second place. The long-term outlook for this category was good because employment in the medical, legal, scientific, and business professions was expected to grow strongly.

Thomson Corp's was the largest professional-books publisher with sales of $1.99 billion. Professional book revenues comprised of 31% of Thomson's total revenues. Reed Elsevier ranked second with 1994 sales of $1.63 billion, and was followed by Wolters Kluwer and Times Mirror with $1.07 billion and $775 million in sales, respectively.

Mass Market Books. A large proportion of these books are sold through magazine wholesalers and outlets such as newsstands and drugstores. This category includes best-sellers that have shelf lives of about three to six weeks and in 1997 they accounted for about 7% of all books sold. Although the cost of acquiring the paperback rights to a best-selling hardcover title can cost millions of dollars, the per-unit fixed costs for printing are small because print runs were as large as 500,000. However, when return rates, which typically exceed 40%, are factored in, profit margins tend to be less than 12%.

The largest publishers are Random House, Bantam Doubleday Dell, Simon & Schuster, and HarperCollins.

El-Hi Textbooks. El-Hi or Elementary-High school books accounted for 14% of all books sold in 1997 (they used to represent 30% of all books sold in 1994). Sales in this segment rose nearly 14% in 1997 and forecasts suggest that they are likely to increase by 4.8% in 1998. El-Hi is driven by state adoption and enrollment levels and books are sold to school systems on a contract basis. The development of materials for schools is a capital-intensive process that typically takes up to five years to develop for most new programs. Per-pupil expenditures as well as the number of students are expected to grow through the year 2000, implying moderate growth (3 to 4%) for this segment.

The big publishers are owned by media conglomerates such as News Corp. Times Mirror and Paramount. The largest El-Hi publisher is McGraw-Hill, followed by Paramount (the parent company of Prentice Hall and Silver Burdett), Harcourt Brace, and Houghton Mifflin.

College Textbooks. College publishing is the most profitable category. The cost of producing a college text is lower than in the El-Hi market, because the texts are typically prepared by university faculty members and used individually. However, the unit sales tend to be small and used textbook sales generally accounted for 20–40% of total sales. College textbook sales represented 12.8% of all book sales in 1997. Sales are estimated to increase 6.9% to $2.85 billion in 1998.

Prentice Hall (owned by Paramount) is the largest college publisher, followed by HB College (owned by Harcourt General), International Thomson, McGraw-Hill, and Irwin (a division of Times Mirror).

> *media on the Internet. . . . The phenomenon could mean the elimination of middlemen such as bookstores.*[11]

Moreover, Daniels notes that there is also the potential for publishers to be "disintermediated," because computer-literate writers can now publish and distribute their own works online. However, the leading publishing houses are skeptical of electronic book-publishing capabilities and remain uncertain about the Internet's future with regard to physical books.

Despite industry skepticism and concern, a plethora of "virtual" bookstores are now selling books on the Internet. A cursory search on an Internet search engine such as Yahoo! produced a listing of 475 online bookstores operating on the Web (as of August 1998). A search on Buyers Index (www.buyersindex.com), a mail order buyers' search engine, lists over 234 online bookstores. Many of these firms are relatively unknown compared to such online retailers as Amazon.com and Barnes & Noble. These two firms in particular have been growing at the self-reported double-digit rates and are

EXHIBIT 8 | Unit Sales (in millions) and Dollar Sales (in millions) by Product Category

Product Category	1997 Units	1997 ($mill)	1998* Units	1998* ($mill)	Profit Margins in 1993
Trade Books					
Adults (hardcover and paperbacks)	441.8	$4095.2	438.9	$4160.0	13.7%**
Juvenile (hardcover and paperbacks)	343.8	1358.0	355.9	1437.6	7.7%
Mass Market	473.2	1433.8	472.3	1480.3	3.1%
Book Clubs	137.7	1145.3	141.3	1207.2	
Mail Order	85.7	521.0	81.8	504.7	
Religious	166.6	1132.7	170.3	1178.0	12.4%
Professional (business, medical, scientific, and technical)	165.2	4156.4	169.6	4404.6	8.0%
University Press	17.8	367.8	18.0	382.1	
El-Hi (Elementary-High school)	286.5	2959.6	282.8	3102.4	14.9%
College (textbook and materials)	168.2	2669.7	173.7	2852.8	15.8%
Standard Tests	—	191.4	—	204.3	
Subject Reference	1.2	736.5	1.2	766.9	
Total	**2287.7**	**$20,767.4**	**2305.8**	**$21,680.9**	

Source: Book Industry Study Group Trends, 1998.
*Projected sales.
**For hardcover books.

fast becoming a formidable presence on the Web. Book and music sales online accounted for $156 million in 1997. Although this amount represented a small percentage of the overall retail book sales in 1997, it is projected to reach about $1.1 billion in 2001.

COMPETING ON THE WORLD WIDE WEB

Operating a Virtual Bookstore

At Amazon.com, unlike traditional bookstores, there are no bookshelves to browse. All contact with the company is either through its Web site [www.amazon.com] or by e-mail. At the firm's Web site, customers can search for a specific book, topic, or author, or they can browse their way through a book catalog featuring numerous subjects. Visitors can also read book reviews from other customers, *The New York Times*, the *Atlantic Monthly*, and Amazon.com's staff. Customers can browse, fill up a virtual shopping basket, and then complete the sale by entering their credit card information or by placing their order online and then phoning in their credit card information. Customer orders are processed immediately. Books in stock (mostly best-sellers) are packaged and mailed the same day. When their order has been shipped, customers are notified by e-mail. Amazon.com places orders for non-best-sellers with the appropriate book publisher immediately.

Shunning the elaborate graphics that clutter many Web sites on the Internet, the firm loads up its customers with information instead. For many featured books, it offers capsule descriptions, snippets of reviews, and "self-administered" interviews posted by authors. The firm has found a way to use the technology to offer services that a traditional store or catalog can't match. Notes Bezos:

> *An Amazon customer can romp through a database of 1.1 million titles (five times the largest superstore's inventory), searching by subject or name. When you select a book, Amazon is programmed to flash other related titles you may also want to buy. If you tell Amazon about favorite authors and topics, it will send you by electronic mail a constant stream of recommendations. You want to know when a book comes out in paperback? Amazon will email that too.*[12]

Additionally, the firm offers space for readers to post their own reviews and then steps out of the way and lets its customers sell to each other. Notes Bezos:

> *There are so many things we can do on-line that can't be done in the real world. We want customers who enter Amazon.com to indicate whether they want to be "visible" or "invisible." If they choose "visible," then when they're in the science fiction section, other people will know they're there. People can ask for recommendations—'read any good books lately?'—or recommend books to others. I'm an outgoing person, but I'd never go into a bookstore and ask a complete stranger to recommend a book. The semi-anonymity of the on-line environment makes people less inhibited.*[13]

Value Propositions and Customer Service

When asked why people come to their site, Bezos responds:

> *Bill Gates laid it out in a magazine interview. He said, "I buy all my books at Amazon.com because I'm busy and it's convenient. They have a big selection, and they've been reliable." Those are three of our four core value propositions: convenience, selection, service. The only one he left out is price: we are the broadest discounters in the world in any product category. . . . These value propositions are interrelated, and they all relate to the Web.*[14]

At Amazon.com almost all books are discounted. Bestsellers are sold at a 30 to 40 percent discount and the other books at a 10 percent discount. Bezos points out:

> *We discount because we have a lower cost structure than physical stores do and we turn our inventory 150 times a year. That's like selling bread in a supermarket. Physical bookstores turn their inventory only 3 or 4 times a year.*

The firm's Seattle and Delaware warehouses are used to stock popular book items, and to consolidate and repack customer orders. Moreover, only after the firm receives a paid customer order does it request the appropriate publisher to ship the book to Amazon.com. The firm then ships the book to the customer.[15] The firm owns little expensive retail real estate and its operations are largely automated. Its distribution center in Delaware, for example, uses state-of-the-art technology to consolidate and package books for shipment.

To keep customers interested in Amazon.com, the firm offers two forms of e-mail-based service to its registered customers. "Eyes" is a personal notification service, in which customers can register their interests in a particular author or topic. Once customers register with Amazon.com, they receive information about new books published by their favorite author. "Editor's service" provides editorial comments about featured books via e-mail. Three full-time editors read book reviews, pore over customer orders, and survey current events to select the featured books. These, and other free-lance editors employed by the firm, provide registered users with e-mail updates on the latest and greatest books they've been reading. These services are automated and are available free of charge and customers subscribing to these services have certain guaranteed rights (see Exhibit 9 for "Customer Bill of Rights").

9 | Amazon.com's Customer Bill of Rights

Amazon.com's Bill of Rights claims that as a customer there is:

1. **No obligation.** Eyes & Editors Personal Notification Services are provided free of charge, and you are under no obligation to buy anything.
2. **Unsubscribing.** You can unsubscribe or change your subscriptions at any time.
3. **Privacy.** We do not sell or rent information about our customers. If you would like to make sure we never sell or rent information about you to third parties, just send a blank email message to never@amazon.com.

According to Bezos, such services are vital for success on the Internet:

> *Customer service is a critical success factor for online merchants. If you make customers unhappy in the physical world, they might each tell a few friends. If you make customers unhappy on the Internet, they can each tell thousands of friends with one message to a newsgroup. If you make them really happy, they can tell thousands of people about that. I want every customer to become an evangelist for us. About 63 percent of the book orders come from repeat customers.*

Additionally, the firm's employees compile a weekly list of the 20 most obscure titles on order, and Bezos awards a prize for the most amusing. Amazon.com drums up all these orders through a mix of state-of-the-art software and old-fashioned salesmanship. When asked to differentiate his firm from potential rivals, Bezos notes:

> *People who just scratch the surface of Amazon.com say—"oh, you sell books on the Web"—don't understand how hard it is to actually be an electronic merchant. We're not just putting up a Web site. We do 90% of our customer service by email rather than by telephone. . . . There are very few off-the-shelf tools that help do what we're doing. We've had to develop lots of our own technologies. There are no companies selling software to manage email centers. So we had to develop our own tools. In a way this is good news. There are lots of barriers to entry.*[16]

Culture and Philosophy

Amazon.com had 800 employees in August 1998. A significant portion of the firm's employees manage "content" on the firm's Web site, including such tasks as Web page updating and formatting book reviews for display. The firm also employs a large number of people to develop software tools for operating on the Internet and a large group of employees do nothing but answer e-mails from customers. Notes Bezos:

> *Amazon.com is committed to ingenuity and problem-solving. Almost nothing is off-the-shelf at Amazon .com: Our software engineers are developing programs that are the first of their kind; our editors create original content; our site team designs features that can't be found anywhere else. . . . Also, we have some of the best programmers, and the best servers in the world.*

According to Amazon.com insiders: "This is a very driven place. Hours are typically 8 to 8 and many people work weekends. Jeff spends every waking hour on this business." Adds Bezos:

> *Everyone at Amazon.com works hard, long, and smart. We act like owners because we are owners—stock options give each of us an equity stake in the company. We are passionate about what we're doing. Because of that, we have fun at work, and it makes it easy for us to work hard. What we're building is unprecedented. We're not aspiring to a corporate model—we are creating the model. This to me is the most compelling reason for people to come to work here.*

Continues Bezos:

> *There is no Amazon.com "type." There are Amazon.com employees who have three master's degrees and some who speak five languages. We have people who worked at Procter & Gamble and Microsoft, and people who worked at* Rolling Stone *and* The Village Voice. *We have a professional figure skater, two racecar drivers, a Rhodes scholar, a set of twins, a husband and wife, and their dog. We wear jeans to work, have meetings in the hallway, and we get excited about HTML-enabled email.*

Bezos describes his firm's corporate philosophy as follows:

> *The Amazon.com corporate philosophy is simple: If it's good for our customers, it's worth doing. Our company mission is to leverage technology and expertise to provide the best buying experience on the Internet. Put another way, we want people to come to Amazon.com, find whatever they want, discover things they didn't know they wanted, and leave feeling they have a new favorite place to shop.*

Operating Philosophy

The firm's operating philosophy is unlike traditional bookstores. At Amazon.com there are no salespeople.

The firm is open for business 24 hours a day and has a global presence. Over 3 million customers from 160 countries have purchased books from the firm. The firm is devoid of expensive furnishings, and money is spent sparingly. Notes Bezos:

> *We made the first four desks we have here ourselves—all our desks are made out of doors and four-by-fours. . . . My monitor stand is a bunch of old phone books. We spend money on the things that matter to our customers and we don't spend money on anything else.*[17]

Amazon.com spends a substantial amount on Web advertising and marketing. According to Jupiter Communications, the firm spent over $340,000 for the first half of 1996 and ranked 34th in Web ad spending. Since then, however, these expenses have gone up significantly. This is partly because Amazon.com has entered into multi-year advertising agreements with Internet aggregators, such as Yahoo!, Excite, and AOL. For the most recent quarter ending June 1998, the firm spent $26.5 million on marketing, equivalent to 23 percent of sales.

Since Amazon.com is an Internet-only retailer, Web advertising gives it a unique opportunity to track the success of an ad by the number of click-throughs to the store's Web site and the number of Internet surfers who actually purchase something. Industry analysts estimate that between 2 percent and 3 percent of people who see an ad on the Web will actually click-through to see more.

The firm advertises mainly in such large-circulation newspapers as *The Wall Street Journal, New York Times,* and *San Jose Mercury News,* and on Internet search-engine sites such as Yahoo!, Lycos, the Microsoft Network (MSN), and Microsoft's *Slate* magazine. Amazon.com keeps its banner ads simple, with just a few words and a Web address. Recently, the firm has started advertising on radio and television (e.g., CNN). It also hands out discount coupons in several cities to entice customers to use its services.

The decision to locate Amazon.com in Seattle appears to be paying off. The firm has been able to attract some Microsoft veterans and many highly qualified executives. See Exhibit 10 for an illustration of how the firm is organized and Appendix A for a brief description of the firm's top management.

Growth via Micro-Franchising

The firm is currently growing at a rapid pace each quarter. Parts of the reason for this rapid growth is the firm's

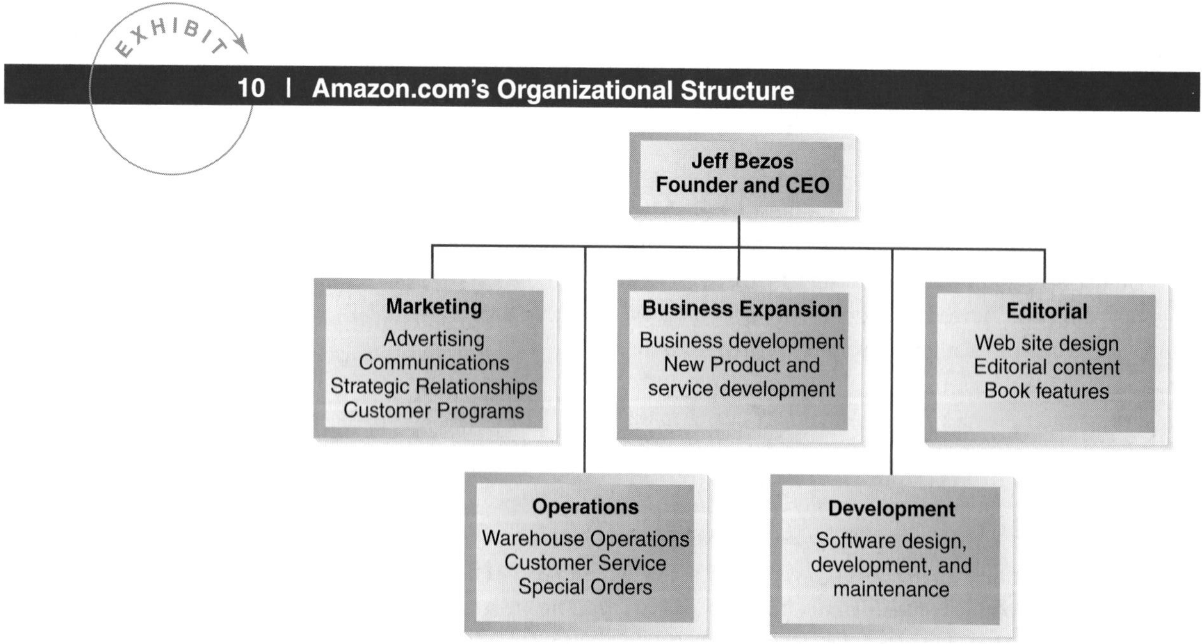

Associates Program. The program was designed to increase traffic to Amazon.com by creating a referral service from other Web sites to Amazon.com's 2.5-million book catalog. An associates Web site, such as Starchefs—which features cookbook authors—recommends books and makes a link from its Web page to Amazon.com's catalog page for the books. The associated Web site then earns referral fees for sales generated by these links. Partners receive weekly referral fee statements and a check for the referral fees earned in that quarter. More than 90,000 sites have already signed up under this program and earn a commission sometimes up to 15 percent of the value of books bought by the referred customer. Notes Bezos, "[The] Web technology has made it possible to set up microfranchises, and with zero overhead."[18]

Since July 1995 Amazon.com has doubled in size every 2.4 months.[19] By August 1996, sales were growing at 34 percent a month. The firm posted revenues of $147.8 million for 1997, an 838 percent increase over the previous year. However, the net loss for fiscal 1997 was $27.6 million, compared to a net loss in fiscal 1996 of $5.8 million. When the company was founded in 1995, the plan was to be profitable in five years. The firm claims to have exceeded expectations and has made its business plan more aggressive. Despite continuing losses, Wall Street's interest in the new venture has remained strong. Further, based on cybershare (and revenues), the firm is currently acknowledged to be the largest online bookstore on the Web.

Moreover, Bezos is focused on expanding Amazon.com: "In the year 2000, our goal is to be one of the world's leading bookstores." Adds Bezos:

> *We believe we're expanding the market for books. With this new way of selling books on the Web we can expose people to far more books than before. People buy books from us that they won't find in bookstores. And we're growing rapidly in this stagnant market.*

CHALLENGES FACING AMAZON.COM

Although Bezos is pleased that Amazon.com is well regarded by analysts on Wall Street, he acknowledges that many strategic challenges remain. Particularly, a few important challenges demand his immediate attention. They include: finding creative ways to fend off formidable new competitors, leveraging the firm's brand name to expand beyond just books, and meaningfully integrating the new acquisitions made by the firm.

Fending Off Formidable Competitors

Competition between online book merchants is likely to become even more intense, with a growing number of publishers and retailers going online. For example, Ingram and other large publishers have begun experimenting with the WWW. Notes *The Wall Street Journal:* "In addition to Amazon and Barnes & Noble, publisher Random House Inc. sells books online and Viacom Inc.'s Simon & Schuster unit launched an Internet bookselling site grandly called "The SuperStore."[20]

Barnes & Noble, the largest US book retailer, launched its online store in May 1997, a little less than two years after Amazon.com opened for business. Although Barnes & Noble finds itself in the unusual position of trailing a competitor, it claims that it holds the unique distinction of operating in four different channels—retail stores, the Internet, 1-800-THE-BOOK, and mail order. Notes Stephen Riggio, vice chairman of Barnes & Noble, who is presiding over the new online venture:

> *How big is it [online sales] going to get? We're looking at $100 million in sales this year [1998]. We're not being speculative about that range. We're going to be there. It's going to be bigger than a billion dollar business.*

Barnes & Noble online sales for the year ending in 1997 amounted to $14 million, a small fraction of the firm's overall retail book sales. However, according to a report in *Business Week,* Leonard Riggio, CEO of Barnes & Noble, is dead serious about the online segment:

> *Riggio plans to spend $40 million to ballyhoo the service in 1998. . . . Riggio is already thinking ahead of how to integrate this technology into the shelves of Barnes & Noble. In the bookstore of the future, he says, customers could tap into millions of titles and print any part from these works on the spot. He talks about software programs that could point customers to specific lines in various books, threaded by a single topic, or ones that could ferret out and print ob-*

scure texts that never made it into book form. In short, Riggio envisions modifying what constitutes a published work.[21]

In July 1998, Borders Group Inc. (the parent corporation of Borders Books & Music) entered the fray with Borders.com, a newly formed subsidiary. At the Borders' Web site, customers can purchase books, music CDs, and videos. The firm's Web site described Borders' late entry as follows:

We're not content with being just another online bookseller. We want to do it right. Anyone who's been to a Borders store knows that selling books, music, and videos isn't just a business, it's a passion. . . . At Borders.com, we aim to provide the same high level of expertise and vast selection customers have come to associate with the Borders name. No other online bookseller can offer 10 million books, CDs, and videos—in stock and available now.

In late 1997 Ingram, the largest U.S. distributor of books, began experimenting with online retailing. It began testing an experimental service to create new online retailers. Notes *Business Week:* "All the would-be retailers had to do was lure the shoppers. Ingram handled everything else, from maintaining the Web site to taking orders, processing credit-card billings, and shipping the books. In effect the virtual bookshops became little more than a retail façade of Ingram. However, after six months of test-marketing, Ingram quietly pulled the plug in early October."[22]

Undaunted by Ingram's failure, Bertelsman, the German media conglomerate, announced in February 1998 that it planned to open an online store (tentatively called BooksOnline) that will sell books in English, French, Spanish, German and Dutch.[23] Bertelsman hoped to ship books to customers in Europe and the United States through its extensive distribution in both countries. In October 1998, however, the firm announced it was buying a 50 percent share in Barnesandnoble.com for $200 million and both Bertelsman and Barnes & Noble are expected to spend another $100 million each to strengthen their joint operation. Further, Bertelsman will abandon the U.S. rollout of its BooksOnline service. Observes Maria Latour-Kadison, an online retail analyst at *Forrester Research:*

This is a real powerhouse combination: the retail power of Barnes & Noble and the fulfillment power of Bertelsman. . . . They already have what Amazon is spending millions to acquire [a brand name and infrastructure]. There's a very steep learning curve associated with doing online retailing well, and Bertelsman will be able to leapfrog some of it because of Barnesandnoble.com's experience.[24]

Acknowledges Bezos: "Bertelsman can be a formidable competitor. They have 50 percent stake in AOL's German operations, over 35 million active book and music club members and significant warehousing and book distribution assets spread out internationally." However, he notes:

We are not competitor focused but customer focused. Figuring out what the customer wants is a never ending process. We differentiate along the following dimensions: selection (we are still the largest); ease of use; price; and discovery. Scale is important in e-commerce and so is "ease of use." Our innovations like "1-Click shopping" continue to make our Web site far more attractive than competitors. We are working with interesting features such as "book matcher," using the latest collaborative filtering technology that we acquired from Net Perceptions. We believe such things greatly enhance the customer experience at our store. Discovery means understanding customers as individuals and finding ways to accelerate their discovery process while they are at the store. We are working on software that increases the odds that customers will find the right book that they are looking for when searching in our store. Discovery is powerful for customers.

Bezos's immediate concern therefore revolves around finding innovative ways to stay ahead of his competitors and he acknowledges that this will remain a continuing challenge.

Leveraging the Amazon.com Brand Name

In June 1998, Amazon.com expanded its product line to include music. The music store offers more than 125,000 titles, 10 times the CD selection of the typical music store, and everyday savings of up to 40 percent. The new music store features expert and customer reviews, interviews, an essentials list, a list of the hottest

CDs from around the country and the world, music news, and recommendations. Music fans can search for their favorite music by CD title, artist, song title, or label. Bezos describes the new venture as follows:

> *You can browse through nearly 300 styles ranging from Alternative to Zydeco (everything but Classical, which is on the way) or use "Essentials" (my favorite feature) to learn about the best CDs to help you start or build a collection in a particular style. And you can reduce guesswork by listening to some of our 225,000 song clips. . . . It's a music discovery machine. Using the power of technology and the Internet, we're enriching the music experience for everyone, from casual to devoted listeners alike.*

More importantly, he adds:

> *The music store was designed with the help of more than 20,000 customers who responded to our invitation to "build the music store of your dreams." Many of the features in our new music store are the direct result of these suggestions. Our customers told us they wanted a site that is as rich in musical selection and content as the Amazon.com bookstore—with the same great prices, features, and customer service.*

The launch of Amazon.com's music store was accompanied by a major update of the firm's Web site. Bezos describes the changes thus:

> *We didn't focus only on music. We've also redesigned our store to make it even easier to find the books you want. . . . The new store design permits customers to move easily between the book and music areas, making it fast and simple to find what they are looking for and to discover new titles. We now provide an integrated shopping cart, 1-Click ordering, and consolidated shipping across both books and music.*

Unlike book retailing, many online music stores such as cdnow.com (*www.cdnow.com*) and n2k.com (*www.n2k.com*) have been in operation for more than a few years. Cdnow.com, for example, claims it is the world's leading online music store by offering over 250,000 music-related items. N2k.com operates many music sites (called channels) including Music Boulevard on the WWW (see Exhibit 11 for a partial listing of online

11 | A Partial Listing of Online Music Stores

Cdnow*—The idea for this store was conceived in the summer of 1994 and was started by twin brothers Jason and Matt Olim in their parents' basement in 1994. In 1997, the firm posted sales of $15 million. It reported averages of about 18% in operating margins.

Music Boulevard (*www.musicboulevard.com*)—Owned by n2k, Music Boulevard operates transaction sites in English, French, German, Japanese, and Spanish. Started in September of 1996, n2k.com bills itself as "the premier online music entertainment company and the Internet's only complete source for music content, community and comment." In 1997 it reported revenues of $11.7 million.

Musicspot (*www.musicspot.com*)—According to a recent 10,000-household PC-Meter survey, CUC's Musicspot ranked top among the top "Hot Storefronts."

Tunes.com (*www.tunes.com*)—Berkeley, California-based Tunes.com, launched in November 1996, features 200,000 30-second music clips backed by collaborative filter, which matches visitors' music interests to profiles created by people with similar tastes. The company plans to have 1 million samples online by mid-1998, which will make it the largest music sampling source online.

Record Clubs—Record clubs are shaping up to be the Web's most powerful retailers. An estimated 16.5 million customers belong to record clubs in the U.S. Columbia House and BMG both debuted Web sites in 1995. Their sites now handle all club chores including administration, buying, status checking, and the commendable job of cyber-retailing.

*Cdnow and Music Boulevard signed an agreement on October 8, 1998, to merge their two companies.

music stores). In response to Amazon.com's entry into the music business, Cdnow and N2K signed an agreement in October to merge their two companies.

Notes Bezos: "We don't really view existing online music stores as our direct competitors. We are more focused on parties that already have a large portion of music sales." Some analysts are, however, skeptical about whether Amazon.com should compete in the music business. Notes a report in *The Wall Street Journal:*

> *But the move [to offer music CDs] is risky too; Cyberspace is increasingly crowded with on-line superstores set up by Amazon's physical-world counterparts, companies with more marketing clout and track records of profitability. And Amazon could lose cachet with bibliophiles if its forays into other media dilute its reputation as a destination for booklovers. . . . [M]ail-order giants Columbia House, a joint venture of Time Warner Inc. and Sony Corp., and Bertelsmann AG's BMG Entertainment have made Internet selling a top priority. Columbia House is taking orders from music-club members on one site; on a separate super-store site, Total E, it's moving straight into Amazon territory with plans to add books and CD-ROMs to its existing catalogue of videos and CDs.*[25]

Some analysts point out that the music business is "somewhere between a no-margin and a low-margin business" and therefore question the firm's recent move. But notes Bezos:

> *Amazon.com brand has to stand for something. For us the brand name means price, convenience, customer service, and a great selection. There is a huge advantage in expanding to other product categories. The customer acquisition costs are significantly lower and so are the costs related to the lifetime value of that customer. If we can successfully expand the brand, as we think we can, then there are significant economic benefits to expansion. . . . We recognize that the music business is a different environment than books. About half-a-dozen players control the entire distribution of music in this country and the likely implication of such control is lower margins. However, we like to emphasize the incremental dollar value of music sales to our existing customers.*

International Expansion and Acquisitions

Capitalizing on increased market value, Amazon.com acquired three companies, Bookpages Ltd., Telebook Inc., and Internet Movie Database Ltd. in April 1998. Notes Bezos:

> *With these we have accelerated our expansion into European e-commerce and acquired a foundation for a best-of-breed video store. These acquisitions will enable Amazon.com to offer a new set of consumers the same combination of selection, service and value that we now provide our US book customers. Fortunately, we were able to build an international brand name as a byproduct of operating on the Internet. People in Japan, Germany, and UK are very familiar with the Amazon.com name (about 22 percent of the firm's sales come from outside the United States currently).*

Although Bezos remains quiet about his intentions regarding Internet Music Database Ltd., analysts speculate that The Internet Movie Database is likely to form the key underpinning for Amazon.com's eventual entry into online video sales.

In July 1998, Amazon.com signed agreements to acquire two additional firms. They include Junglee Corp and PlanetAll. PlanetAll is a Cambridge, Massachusetts, firm that provides a unique Web-based address book, calendar, and reminder service. Junglee Corp., based in Sunnyvale, Calif., is a leading provider of advanced Web-based virtual database (VDB) technology that can help shoppers find millions of products on the Internet (see Exhibit 12). Discussing his firm's intention to acquire these two firms Bezos noted:

> *PlanetAll is the most innovative use of the Internet I've seen. It's simply a breakthrough in doing something as fundamental and important as staying in touch. The reason PlanetAll has over 1.5 million members—and is growing even faster than the Internet—is simple: it creates extraordinary value for its users. I believe PlanetAll will prove to be one of the most important online applications. . . . Junglee has assembled an extraordinary team of people. Together we'll empower customers to find and discover the products they want to buy.*

Bezos, commenting on the recent expansion and acquisitions, argues:

12 | Recent Acquisitions by Amazon.com

Bookpages (www.bookpages.co.uk). As one of the largest online bookstores in the United Kingdom, the firm provides access to all 1.2 million UK books in print.*

Telebook (www.telebuch.de). This firm, operating through its ABC Bücherdienst subsidiary, is Germany's number-one online bookstore, with a catalog of nearly 400,000 German-language titles.

Internet Movie Database (www.imdb.com). Originally launched in 1990, Internet Movie Database is a comprehensive repository for movie and television information on the Internet and is an excellent example of genuine community on the Internet.

PlanetAll.com (www.PlanetAll.com). Launched in November 1996, the firm reportedly has 1.5 million members, and reports that thousands of new members are joining each day to use the secure, free service to organize and automatically update information about friends, business associates, relatives, and alumni. Users accessing PlanetAll service have complete control over their own contact information and decide what information they want to share with others on a person-by-person basis. Moreover, PlanetAll's service is compatible with personal information managers (PIMs) and personal digital assistants (PDAs), such as Microsoft Outlook and 3Com Palm Pilot. Also, it has integrated its service within the sites of a number of Internet leaders, including Lycos and GeoCities, as well as numerous universities and professional associations. Amazon.com intends to operate PlanetAll as a wholly owned subsidiary located in Cambridge. Savage and the two cofounders will remain with the company.**

Jungle Corp (www.junglee.com). The firm was founded in June 1996. The firm's breakthrough virtual database (VDB) technology is based on founders' doctoral research carried out at Stanford University. Junglee's first deployment was CareerPost.com, the Washington Post Company's online recruitment site, in January 1997. Junglee carries more than 15 million items in the Junglee Shopping Guide and over 90,000 job listings in its Job Canopy. Junglee has developed breakthrough database technology that can dramatically enhance customers' ability to discover and choose from among millions of products online. To date, two of the markets it has targeted have been online retailing and online recruitment. Junglee's customers and partners in these markets include Yahoo!, Compaq, Snap!, six of the top seven newspaper companies, and many other new-media companies. All founders of Junglee are expected to remain with the company.

*Each of the acquisitions—Bookpages, Telebook, and Internet Movie Database—will be accounted for under the purchase method of accounting. The company will incur total charges of approximately $55 million in connection with all three transactions. Consideration was comprised of cash and common stock, and the company anticipates issuing an aggregate of approximately 540,000 shares of common stock as a result of these transactions.

**Amazon.com will acquire 100% of the outstanding shares and assume all outstanding options of Junglee and PlanetAll in exchange for equity having an aggregate value of approximately $280 million. Amazon.com will issue approximately 800,000 shares and assume all outstanding options in connection with the acquisition of PlanetAll and anticipates accounting for this transaction as a pooling of interests. Amazon.com will issue approximately 1.6 million shares and assume all outstanding options in connection with the acquisition of Junglee and anticipates accounting for this transaction under the purchase method of accounting.

> *Our product extension and geographic expansion is better late than early. Why better late than early? We had to first focus on the book business and grow that until we were comfortable with it. There are always numerous opportunities to expand. We try to err on the side of being slow. Fortunately, we are not capital constrained, but we are definitely people constrained. We only pursue opportunities when the people bandwidth is not constrained. . . . The single most important criterion that we use to acquire a new company is this: Who are the people behind this venture, and what is the people bandwidth of the acquired company going to be? We are looking for business athletes indoctrinated in this space and companies that have a culture that is common with ours.*

However, notes a report in *The Wall Street Journal:*

> *In the end, though, neither specialization nor branding may determine who succeeds in the on-line sales game. In the physical world, hardcore-comparison shopping has been left to a highly motivated faction of consumers willing to trudge between stores. But on the Web, it's become almost effortless. Today, a user can enter a title of a book on Yahoo! Inc.'s Visa Shopping Guide site which then queries multiple booksellers for prices and displays the result in a table. Hyperlink next to book prices lets users order the*

cheapest one at the click of a mouse. With comparison services proliferating elsewhere on the Web—and for dozens of other products—it's unclear whether a sterling brand like Amazon's will ultimately sway consumers when rock-bottom prices are so easy to spot.[26]

Bezos concedes that many challenges still confront him and his top management team as they ponder the future moves by his firm. Acknowledges Bezos:

It is hard to provide great customer service and experience for the customer. It is hard to grow the business. But when you combine these two, the complexity of operating increases exponentially. We are expanding our product line and broadening our geographic reach simultaneously, and there is a lot of execution risk when you try to do this. Moreover, many of our new initiatives will continue to require aggressive investment and entail significant execution challenges. However, that is the nature of this business.

ENDNOTES

1. "Who's writing the book on web business?" *Fast Company,* October-November, 1996, p. 132–133.
2. *Fast Company,* October-November, 1996.
3. In October 1997, Barnes & Noble and Amazon.com settled their respective lawsuits by saying that they would prefer to get back to business and compete in the marketplace rather than in the courtroom.
4. Much of the information discussed in this section, and the section that follows, is drawn from *Amazon.com,* a Washington University Business School Case, by Suresh Kotha and Emer Dooley, 1997.
5. *Publishers Weekly,* January 1, 1996.
6. Although the best-selling books get the bulk of the attention and marketing dollars, "backlist" books are considered the "bread and butter" of the industry. A backlist is the publishing company's catalog of books that have already appeared in print. Estimates indicated that as much as 25 to 30 percent of a publisher's revenues come from this source. Backlisted books have predictable sales with occasional bumps, such as when a subject matter loses favor with consumers or when an author dies. Since these books require no editing and little promotion, they are generally profitable. Moreover, print runs are easier to predict, resulting in fewer returns to publishers.
7. *Publishers Weekly,* March 11, 1996. Superstores, originally confined to big metropolitan areas, were increasingly entering markets with populations of 150,000 or less. Industry estimates indicated that superstores had to make around $200 a square foot to turn a profit. For example, a typical Barnes & Noble superstore needed $3 to $4 million in sales revenues to break even. Some industry observers questioned whether such cities can support these mammoth stores and whether superstores in these locations could sell enough books to turn a profit.
8. *Philadelphia Business Journal,* September 27, 1996.
9. "A Nonchain Bookstore Bucks the Tide." *The New York Times,* September 8, 1996.
10. *Standard and Poors Industry Surveys,* July 20, 1995.
11. *The Christian Science Monitor,* September 18, 1996.
12. *The Wall Street Journal,* Thursday, May 16, 1996.
13. *Fast Company,* October-November, 1996.
14. *Fast Company,* October-November, 1996.
15. Industry observers note that although Amazon discounts most books, it levies a $3 service charge per order, plus 95 cents per book. And it can take Amazon a week to deliver a book that isn't a best-seller, and even longer for the most esoteric titles. Also, some people don't like providing their credit card number over the Internet.
16. *Fast Company,* October-November, 1996.
17. *Upside,* October, 1996.
18. "Amazon.com forges new sales channel," *Web Week,* August 19, 1996.
19. *Financial Times,* October 7, 1996.
20. *The Wall Street Journal,* October 21, 1997.
21. "The baron of books," *Business Week,* June 29, 1998.
22. The reason why Ingram's experimental foray into online retailing floundered was because many of the new online entrants were unable to attract enough customers. Notes *Business Week,* "Ingram stirred a backlash among its existing clientele, who were clearly not happy with the prospect of having to compete with other low-cost clones."
23. Bertelsman AG is the world's third largest media conglomerate with $14 billion in sales in 1997. In July 1998, Bertelsman acquired US-based Random House Publishing. This single largest publisher of English language books owns Doubleday, Bantam Books, Dell Publishing, and several other publishing companies.
24. *Internet World,* October 12, 1998.
25. "In looking to branch out, Amazon goes out on a limb," *The Wall Street Journal,* May 12, 1998.
26. *The Wall Street Journal,* May 12, 1998.

APPENDIX A: AMAZON.COM'S TOP MANAGEMENT TEAM

Jeffrey P. Bezos, *Founder and Chief Executive Officer*

Jeff Bezos has always been interested in anything that can be revolutionized by computers. Intrigued by the amazing growth in use of the Internet, Jeff created a business model that leveraged the Internet's unique ability to deliver huge amounts of information rapidly and efficiently. In 1994 he founded Amazon.com, Inc., an Internet retailer of books and other information-based products that offers services that traditional retailers cannot: lower prices, authoritative selection, and a wealth of product information. Before heading West to start Amazon.com, Jeff worked at the intersection of computer science and finance, leading the development of computer systems that helped manage more than $250 billion in assets for Bankers Trust Company. He also helped build one of the most technically sophisticated quantitative hedge funds on Wall Street for D. E. Shaw & Co. Jeff received a degree in electrical engineering and computer science, summa cum laude, from Princeton University in 1986. He is a member of Phi Beta Kappa.

George T. Aposporos, *Vice President, Business Development*

George Aposporos joined Amazon.com in May 1997 as vice president of business development and is responsible for identifying and negotiating key strategic relationships for the company. Prior to joining Amazon .com, George was founder and president of Digital Brands, a strategic consulting and interactive marketing firm that has served clients such as Starbucks Coffee, Sybase, American Express, and BMG Entertainment. While at Digital Brands, he placed Starbucks in the first campaign to use animated advertising on America Online. From March 1994 to August 1995, George was vice president of I.C.E., a Toronto-based multimedia developer and corporate communications firm, where he spearheaded involvement in interactive media, including development of the company's interactive television and Internet capabilities. From 1989 to 1994, George was an independent producer in a variety of media, including television, video, and CD-ROMs. George was an Olin Scholar at Wesleyan University.

Rick Ayre, *Vice President and Executive Editor*

Rick Ayre joined Amazon.com in September 1996 as vice president and executive editor and is responsible for the editorial content and design of the Amazon.com Web site. Rick comes to Amazon.com from *PC Magazine,* the popular Ziff-Davis publication, where he served as executive editor for technology. Rick launched *PC Magazine* on the World Wide Web in March 1995. He was responsible for the print coverage of online technology, and he ran *PC Magazine*'s online services, including the PC Magazine Online Web site and PC MagNet, part of ZD Net on CompuServe. During his five years at *PC Magazine,* Rick also held positions as the magazine's executive editor for software and as technical director for software in PC Magazine Labs, where he supervised all software product testing. Before joining *PC Magazine,* Rick served as chief of information resources management at the Highland Drive VAMC, a 750-bed hospital in Pittsburgh. He began his technology career while a Ph.D. candidate in psychiatric epidemiology at the University of Pittsburgh in the early 1980s. There he learned to program in Fortran to manipulate large data sets on an early DEC time-sharing system. When the IBM PC was born, he quickly adopted one and taught himself to program in Pascal and to use dBASE. He was soon logging on to local BBS systems, and he's been working online ever since.

Joy D. Covey, *Chief Financial Officer*

Joy Covey joined Amazon.com in December 1996 as chief financial officer and vice president of finance and administration. She is responsible for financial and management systems and reporting, and she also manages planning and analysis, legal, administrative, investor relations, and human relations activities. Before joining Amazon.com, Joy was vice president of business development and vice president of operations, broadcast division, of Avid Technology, a leader in the digital media industry. From 1991 to 1995, she was the CFO of Digidesign, where she managed a successful IPO and eventual merger with Avid Technology. During her tenure, Digidesign achieved more than 50% annual growth and strong and consistent profitability and cash flow, and strengthened its dominant position in the digital audio production systems market. Before she worked at Digidesign, Joy was a mergers and acquisitions associate at the investment bank of Wasserstein Perella & Co. and a certified public accountant with Arthur Young & Co. (currently Ernst & Young). She holds both a J.D. and an M.B.A. from Harvard, where she was a Baker Scholar, and a B.S. in business administration, summa cum laude, from California State University, Fresno.

Richard L. Dalzell, *Chief Information Officer*
Richard Dalzell joined Amazon.com in August 1997 as chief information officer and is responsible for all Amazon.com information systems, including corporate networks, logistics, electronic buying, accounting, and data warehousing. Before joining Amazon.com, Rick was vice president of information systems for Wal-Mart Stores. He managed all merchandising and logistics systems, led the development of world-class supply chain systems, set the standard for international retailing and merchandising systems, and was instrumental in establishing the world's largest commercial decision-support and data-mining systems. From 1990 to 1994, Rick held several management positions within the information systems division at Wal-Mart. Prior to that, he spent three years as the business development manager for E-Systems and seven years as a teleprocessing officer in the U.S. Army. Rick received a B.S. in engineering from the U.S. Military Academy, West Point, in 1979.

Mary Engstrom Morouse, *Vice President, Merchandising*
Mary Engstrom Morouse joined Amazon.com in February 1997 as vice president of publisher affairs and became vice president of merchandising in April 1998. She is responsible for managing supplier relationships and direct purchasing. Before joining Amazon.com, Mary served as general manager of the security business unit and vice president of product marketing at Symantec Corporation, a developer of information management and productivity enhancement software. In these roles, she managed the development, production, testing, manufacturing, distribution, and marketing of Symantec's line of antivirus and security products, including the Norton AntiVirus line. From July 1989 to September 1994, Mary held several management positions at Microsoft Corporation, including group product manager for Microsoft Access, group product manager for Microsoft Project, and director of marketing in strategic relations. Mary received her B.A. in economics from the University of California, Berkeley, in 1984 and her M.B.A. from the Anderson Graduate School of Management at the University of California, Los Angeles, in 1989.

Sheldon J. Kaphan, *Chief Technology Officer*
Shel Kaphan has served as Amazon.com's vice president and chief technology officer since March 1997. In this role, Shel is responsible for technical architecture and directing technical efforts. From October 1994 to March 1997, Shel was vice president of research and development for the company and was responsible for developing Amazon.com's core software and maintaining the company's Web site. Shel brings more than 20 years of experience in designing hardware and software systems and services to Amazon.com. Prior to joining the company, he held senior engineering positions at Kaleida Labs, Frox, and Lucid. Shel received a B.A. in mathematics, cum laude, from the University of California, Santa Cruz, in 1980.

John David Risher, *Senior Vice President, Product Development*
David Risher joined Amazon.com in February 1997 as vice president of product development, responsible for developing new products and services. He was promoted to senior vice president of product development in December 1997 and now has overall responsibility for product development, marketing, editorial, and content licensing. Before joining Amazon.com, David served as founder and product unit manager for Microsoft Investor, Microsoft Corporation's Web site for personal investment. From 1991 to 1995, he held a variety of marketing and project management positions within the Microsoft Access product team, including Microsoft Access team manager. In this role he managed all aspects of the product development team including design, development, branding, advertising, and customer research to produce Microsoft Access 95. From 1987 to 1989 David was an associate at the LEK Partnership, a corporate management consulting firm. David holds a B.A. in comparative literature, magna cum laude, from Princeton University and an M.B.A. from Harvard Business School.

Joel R. Spiegel, *Vice President, Engineering*
Joel Spiegel joined Amazon.com in March 1997 as vice president of engineering and is responsible for all Web site software. From March 1995 to March 1997, Joel held several positions with Microsoft Corporation, including Windows 95 Multimedia development manager, Windows Multimedia group manager, and product unit manager for information retrieval. From June 1986 to March 1995, he held a variety of positions at Apple Computer, most recently as senior manager, and was responsible for new product development in the Apple Business Systems Division. Prior to that he held software product development positions at a number of companies, including Hewlett-Packard and VisiCorp. During his career, Joel has had a hand in the development and delivery of a wide range of software products, including Windows 95 Multimedia, Direct X, Macintosh System 7 File Sharing, several versions of MacDraw, AppleSearch, Smalltalk-80 for the Macintosh, and VisiON. Joel holds a B.A. in biology, with honors, from Grinnell College.

Jimmy Wright, *Chief Logistics Officer*
Jimmy Wright joined Amazon.com in July 1998 as vice president and chief logistics officer. He is responsible for all global supply chain activities, including managing the company's distribution centers, product purchasing, distribution, and shipping. Jimmy comes to Amazon .com with more than 26 years of experience in logistics management. He was recognized as one of the key logistics leaders within Wal-Mart Stores, the world's largest retailer and a company globally known for its logistics excellence. He joined Wal-Mart in 1985 and served as vice president of distribution from 1990 to his retirement in 1998. During that time he was responsible for more than 30 regional and specialty distribution centers, which accounted for 38 million square feet of retail distribution space, staffed by more than 32,000 employees. Jimmy's career in logistics management began at the Fina Oil and Chemical Company, a branch of Petrofina S.A. based in Brussels. From 1972 to 1985, he held a variety of positions, most recently as general manager of distribution. He received a B.B.A. in personnel management from the University of Texas in 1976.

CASE 6

Beano's Ice Cream Shop

Todd A. Finkle
University of Akron

Terry Smith has spent the last six months preparing to purchase a Beano's Ice Cream franchise. Because his personal assets were limited, Smith needed a partner who could finance the purchase. After Smith found a prospective partner, Barney Harris, they negotiated a purchase price with Beano's. Then, Harris gave Smith a partnership proposal. As the case opens, Smith is evaluating the partnership proposal. His three choices are: to accept Barney Harris's partnership proposal, to make a counter proposal, or to try to find a new partner.

Two months ago, Terry Smith had been so confident that he would soon own his own Beano's Ice Cream franchise, that he had put an "I LOVE BEANO'S ICE CREAM" bumper sticker on his Honda. As he looked at it now, he noticed how faded it had become in such a short time. He wondered if in fact it had been a short time—or a lifetime.

Until recently, Smith had rarely second-guessed himself. After carefully researching an issue, he would base his decision on the facts and then proceed—without looking back.

Now, however, he knew he had to put all of the momentum from the past six months to one side. He had to forget about the months spent investigating franchises, selecting Beano's, writing his business plan, and looking for financing. He had to forget about the fact that he had found only one prospective partner who could finance the deal—Barney Harris—and that he and his partner had spent several more months negotiating to purchase the franchise. He had to push away his own emotional investment in the deal now and make one more critical decision: should he go into partnership with Harris?

If he signed the partnership proposal that Barney Harris had given him, Smith would get his franchise. If he did not sign the agreement, he may or may not ever see his dream come to life. It depended on whether he decided to make a counter offer, to look for a new partner, or to walk away from the deal altogether. It was that simple: sign it and get all the marbles, or risk everything for the chance to get something better.

Now, as Smith looked at his faded bumper sticker, he realized that he had to evaluate the proposal in the context of the whole franchise deal. The question was not just, "Is this a good partnership proposal?" The real question was, "Given the potential of this particular franchise, and given my financial and managerial needs, will this proposal help me reach my goals?"

SMITH'S BACKGROUND

In the fall of 1995, Terry Smith, a 36-year-old marketing representative for a Fortune 500 telecommunications firm in Cleveland, was among the thousands of employees who were downsized.

At first, he investigated the possibility of working for other major corporations in Cleveland. His education (a B.S. in biology and an MBA) and experience made him very marketable. During the seven years he had spent with the telecommunications firm, he had developed a solid reputation in his field. In a relatively short time, he received several job offers for about $60,000 per year.

And yet . . . Smith felt reluctant to jump back into a

Copyright © 1999 by Todd A. Finkle

large corporation. He realized that as a new employee, he would be among the first to be cut, if his employer experienced a downturn. Did he want to go through *that* again?

Smith had had a positive experience as an entrepreneur during the years he was in college getting his degrees. He had started a successful mobile music company. While it had not made him a millionaire, it had paid for his education and living expenses, even though he had worked only when he could take time away from his studies.

One day, he found himself captivated by an article in *Entrepreneur* magazine. It pointed out that the number of downsized executives who were turning to entrepreneurship had doubled over the past two years. In 1993, between six and eight percent started their own businesses; in 1995, over twelve percent did so.

Smith decided that he needed to explore his options as an entrepreneur. He knew the down sides of owning a business: the long hours, the stress, problems with employees, paperwork, and a lack of benefits. However, he felt that these could be outweighed by the opportunity to make all of the important decisions himself.

After several months of research, he decided to seriously explore the purchase of an ice cream franchise in Gainesville, Florida, called Beano's Ice Cream Shoppe, which cost $275,000 (see Exhibits 1–3 for the estimated costs and financial statements for a Beano's franchise). Smith had a net worth of $50,000 and a liquidity of $20,000, which meant that he had to obtain financing.

BEANO'S ICE CREAM SHOPPE, INC.'S BACKGROUND

Beano's was founded by Bill Hogan, Jeff Pricer, and Annie Aubey, three former executives who had grown weary of the corporate world. In 1968, they founded Beano's based on a secret ice cream recipe.

Since opening its first ice cream shop, Beano's has become one of the most respected ice cream companies in the U.S., selling superpremium ice cream, low-fat and non-fat frozen yogurt, and ice cream novelties. Sales and net income for Beano's have been increasing in recent years. Net sales have increased from $48 million in 1989 to $120 million in 1993. Net income has increased from $1.5 million to $6.7 million over the same time period. In the last quarter of 1994, net sales totaled $27,193,000, up 2 percent from $26,532,000. Overall, 1994 net sales went up from $120,328,000 to $128,802,000, an increase of 7 percent.

The company used the finest, high-quality, all natural ingredients. They have differentiated themselves from the competition with: (1) superior ingredients, (2) new product development, (3) new market development, and (4) environmentally conscious behavior. These strategies have allowed Beano's several competitive advantages over the competition in the frozen dessert industry. Beano's has held the number three market position in sales within the U.S.'s superpremium ice cream market for the past few years behind Haagen-Dazs and Ben and Jerry's. The company has two primary

EXHIBIT 1 | Investment Breakdown of a Beano's Ice Cream Shoppe Franchise

Expenditure	Dollars
Franchise Fee	$ 30,000
Design & Architecture Fees	15,000
Real Estate & Improvements	80,000
Professional Fees	2,000
Equipment	40,000
Signage & Graphics	15,000
Miscellaneous Opening Costs	7,000
Initial Inventory	11,000
Working Capital	75,000
Total	$275,000

2 | Pro Forma Income Statement/Cash Flow Summary For the Years 1997–2001 Expected Scenario (in 000s)

	1997		1998		1999		2000		2001	
	$	% Sales	$	% Sales	$	% Sales	$	% Sales	$	% Sales
Sales	$300.0	100.0%	$400.0	100.0%	$450.0	100.0%	$490.0	100.0%	$500.0	100.0%
Cost of Sales	105.0	35.0	140.0	35.0	157.5	35.0	171.5	35.0	175.0	35.0
Gross Profit	195.0	65.0%	260.0	65.0%	292.5	65.0%	318.5	65.0%	325.0	65.0%
Operational Expenses										
Employee Wages	21.0	7.0%	28.0	7.0%	31.5	7.0%	34.3	7.0%	35.0	7.0%
Management Wages	30.0	10.0	31.5	7.9	33.1	7.4	34.8	7.1	36.5	7.3
Health Insurance	3.0	1.0	3.3	0.8	3.6	0.8	3.9	0.8	4.2	0.8
Rent	37.5	12.5	39.3	9.8	41.4	9.2	43.5	8.9	45.6	9.1
Utilities	5.3	1.8	5.4	1.3	5.6	1.2	6.2	1.3	6.5	1.3
Prop/Liability Insurance	4.5	1.5	5.2	1.3	5.1	1.1	5.5	1.1	5.9	1.2
Marketing	13.6	4.5	15.4	3.9	17.4	3.9	19.6	4.0	20.0	4.0
Accounting/Legal	2.0	0.7	2.4	0.6	2.6	0.6	2.8	0.6	2.9	0.6
Supplies	4.2	1.4	0.7	0.2	1.0	0.2	1.0	0.2	1.2	0.2
Repairs/Maintenance	1.4	0.5	1.8	0.5	2.1	0.5	2.4	0.5	2.8	0.6
Telephone	1.8	0.6	2.1	0.5	2.4	0.5	2.7	0.6	2.7	0.5
Bank Charges	0.3	0.1	0.3	0.1	0.6	0.1	0.7	0.1	0.8	0.2
Association/Chamber Dues	0.5	0.2	0.5	0.1	0.5	0.1	0.5	0.1	0.5	0.1
Auto	—	0.0	4.5	1.1	4.5	1.0	5.0	1.0	5.0	1.0
Depreciation	12.0	4.0	12.0	3.0	12.0	2.7	12.0	2.4	12.0	2.4
Miscellaneous Expenses	8.0	2.7	3.0	0.8	4.8	1.1	5.0	1.0	5.5	1.1
Total Operating Expense	145.0	48.3%	157.3	39.3%	168.2	37.4%	179.8	36.7%	186.6	37.3%
EBIT	50.0	16.7%	102.7	25.7%	124.7	27.7%	138.7	28.3%	138.4	27.7%
Interest Income	0.6	0.2	1.2	0.3	1.2	0.3	2.0	0.4	2.0	0.4
Interest Expense	$15.0	5.0	$12.1	3.0	$9.1	2.0	$5.7	1.2	$2.1	0.4
Earnings before Taxes	34.4	11.5	91.8	23.0	116.8	26.0	135.7	27.7	138.3	27.7
Add: Depreciation Expense	12.0	4.0	12.0	3.0	12.0	2.7	12.0	2.4	12.0	2.4
Cash From Operations	46.4	15.5	103.8	26.0	128.8	28.6	147.7	30.1	150.3	30.1
Debt Service	0	0.0	31.7	7.9	34.7	7.7	38.1	7.8	41.7	8.3
DISTRIBUTIONS	$46.4	15.5%	$72.1	18.0%	$94.1	20.9%	$109.6	22.4%	$108.6	21.7%

growth strategies: (1) international expansion and (2) increased domestic penetration.

Beano's had 300 franchises located all over the world, with the majority located in the United States. Five percent of the franchises were company-owned and 75 percent of the franchises were located in the Washington D.C.–Boston corridor and Southern California. More recently, the company has targeted warmer climates such as Florida, Texas, and Georgia.

The company has not had a franchise failure since 1991. Overall, only five percent of its franchises have failed. The average franchise had $350,000 in sales a year. However, in more successful markets, average sales were closer to $500,000. The company's domestic franchise agreements were generally for a ten-year term with an option for renewal. The agreements grant the franchisee an exclusive area to sell bulk ice cream and frozen yogurt, which the franchisee is required to purchase directly from the company.

Beano's provided the following to its franchisees: (1) a seven-day training seminar, (2) on-going operational support, which included access to a territory fran-

3 | Pro Forma Financial Statement Assumptions 1997–2001

General: Projections are made on one store location in Gainesville, Florida. The projections do not include additional store openings projected in the business plan. It appears that cashflow from first store operation is adequate for additional store(s) after Year 3. The timing of first store opening would affect the timing of the projections but would not adversely affect the revenues and expenses used in the forecast.
Depreciation: Equipment purchased of $40,000 is depreciated over a five-year life. Real Estate improvements and expenditures of $80,000 are depreciated over 31.5 years, consistent with IRS tax depreciation laws.
Charitable/Advertising: Four percent of sales after sales tax.
EBIT: Earnings Before Interest and Taxes
Interest Expense: Estimated at 9.25% applied to average outstanding debt balance.
Fixed Assets: Recorded at Historical Cost.
Debt Service: Initial borrowings of $275,000 at assumed rate of 9.25%. Payoff of debt service assumed to be made from internally generated funds and is forecasted to conclude in 2002. Extra funds will be used to pay off debt early.

chise consultant, (3) phone support, and (4) help with real estate and site selection. An input committee, comprised of five of the most successful franchisees, was developed to assist existing franchisees. There was also an annual franchisees' meeting, which included workshops. Finally, Beano's sent field consultants to visit each franchise four times a year.

INDUSTRY ENVIRONMENT

In 1995, the U.S. Frozen Dairy Dessert Industry was in its mature stage of the industry life-cycle, with the market segmented into the retail (dipping store-franchises) sector and the supermarket (take-home) sector. Estimated sales for 1998 were $12.8 billion, an increase of about 20 percent over 1993 sales. Two contrasting trends had developed in recent years: a movement towards full-fat products (which appeal to indulgent consumers) and a movement towards fat-free products (which appeal to health-conscious consumers). Brands such as Healthy Choice, which were able to offer both rich taste and low-fat content, prospered.

The following trends characterized the environment: the fastest growing age group was the 45-54-year-olds; more two-income families; the U.S. annual population growth rate was expected to average 0.9 percent per year through the remainder of the decade; aging population; enhanced disclosure requirements for food labeling; more single-occupant and single-parent households; and more health-conscious eating.

Ice cream has historically been one of the most popular dessert items. However, increased competitive pressures from entrants into supermarkets (Starbucks, Colombo, TCBY, and Swensen's) and new product development (novelty items like Haagen-Dazs's frozen yogurt bars) made the industry fiercely competitive.

Due to the fierce competitive environment, Baskin-Robbins, International Dairy Queen, Haagen-Dazs, and TCBY have increased their advertising. Finally, there has been a movement towards locating stores in non-traditional locations like airports, grocery stores, and in other franchises (such as Baskin-Robbins and Dunkin' Donuts).

LOCAL ENVIRONMENT

Gainesville is located in north-central Florida. The city was ranked as *Money Magazine's* "Best Place to Live" in the U.S. for 1995. It had been ranked among Florida's most livable cities since 1991.

Employment growth in the 1990s had averaged 6.2 percent, which was nearly double the national average. Gainesville also had a low cost of living component compared to other cities of similar size in the U.S. In

EXHIBIT

4 | Statistics for Gainesville, Florida

Gainesville population (excluding students)	91,000
Area Population (Alachua County)	191,000
Total Labor Force	114,346
Cost of a Three-Bedroom House	$82,000
Property Tax	$1,618
Retail Sales Tax (excluding food and medicine)	6%
State Personal Income Tax	0%
Franchise and Inventory Tax	0%
Unemployment	2.8%
Robberies/100,000	301
Annual Sunny Days:	242
Mean Temperature (degrees F)	70.1
Average Sunshine/Day (hrs)	7.8
Annual Rainfall (inches)	49.9
Percent of population over 65	9.3%

Source: Gainesville/Alachua County Community Overview 1994, produced by The Council for Economic Outreach, Gainesville, Florida

1994, the unemployment rate was 2.8 percent, while the national average was 5.9 percent. In the past three years, Florida's economy has surpassed the national average. Florida was also one of nine states without a state income tax. Some of the statistics of Gainesville can be seen in Exhibit 4.

Prior marketing research efforts in Gainesville showed wide acceptance for Beano's products. Beano's had two promotional events in Gainesville, in which ice cream was given to consumers. The feedback about the quality of the products was very positive, and the company had experienced success at selling products in local supermarkets.

Additionally, research showed that franchises located in college towns had sales averages that were surpassed only by resort areas. This made Gainesville very appealing, because the largest university in the South was located there. The University of Florida had an enrollment of 38,000 students and employed 15,500 people. Other institutions of higher education of Gainesville had a total enrollment of 20,000 students.

The population for Gainesville and Alachua County has increased 26 percent since 1980, an average increase of two percent a year (see Exhibit 5).

Exhibit 6 shows the Median Household Effective Buying Income Groups for Gainesville and Alachua County. The total effective buying income for Gainesville has risen from $627,766,000 in 1981 to $1,041,191,000 in 1992, an average increase of six percent a year. The average household income for Gainesville was $29,073.

LOCAL COMPETITION

Fifteen local dipping store competitors are listed in Exhibit 7, which includes information about each store's age, number of employees, and estimated sales. It should be noted that of these fifteen, three stores have sales of $500 thousand to one million.

In addition to these dipping stores, the local market also included supermarkets, convenience stores, restaurants, and an ice cream truck that parked near campus. Of these sources, three were seasonal. The ice cream truck, the campus food court, and a campus Freshen's Yogurt all operated only during the school year.

Four features were missing from the local competition. First, there were no national competitors of *super-premium* desserts in Gainesville. Second, no competitor had a place for customers to sit outside. Third, no com-

5 | Area Population Trends

Year	Gainesville	Alachua County
1970	64,510	107,764
1980	81,370	151,369
1990	84,770	181,596
1995	91,000	191,000
2000	NA	208,900
2005	NA	221,600
2010	NA	233,900
2015	NA	245,200
2020	NA	256,200

Source: Gainesville/Alachua County Demographics 1994, produced by The Council for Economic Outreach, Gainesville, Florida.

6 | Median Household Effective Buying Income Groups

Group	Gainesville	Alachua County	Florida
Under $10,000	21.8%	20.7%	12.6%
$10,000–19,999	20.6	19.7	18.0
$20,000–34,999	22.1	22.7	25.4
$35,000–49,999	14.2	15.1	18.8
$50,000–Over	21.3	21.8	25.2

Source: Gainesville/Alachua County Demographics 1994, produced by The Council for Economic Outreach, Gainesville, Florida.

7 | Dipping Store Competitors in Gainesville

Store	Age	Employees	Sales
Dairy Queen	5 yrs	10–19	$500–1M
Dairy Queen	1	Unknown	Unknown
Baskin-Robbins	Pre 85	10–19	< $500K
Baskin-Robbins	7	Unknown	Unknown
TCBY	10	5–9	$500–1M
TCBY	9	5–9	$500–1M
TCBY	5	5–9	<$500K
Bresler's	5	5–9	<$500K
Doug's Dairy Twirl	5	5–9	<$500K
Fast Eddie's	7	1–4	<$500K
Laurie's Cafe	3	10–19	<$500K
Laurie's Cafe	2 months	Unknown	Unknown
Gator Ice Cream	1	5–9	<$500K
Ice Cream Club	1	5–9	<$500K
Real Italian Ice	Unknown	Unknown	Unknown

petitor had a policy of "giving back to the community." Fourth, there were no Haagen-Dazs stores. This was significant because Haagen-Dazs had been one of the first and strongest competitors, with sales peaking at $560 thousand at one location. A decline in sales prompted their withdrawal from the market.

A discussion of the four largest players in the local market follows.

Laurie's Cafe

Laurie's Cafe was a locally owned competitor that served superpremium ice cream, low-fat frozen yogurt, bagels, gourmet coffee, sandwiches, and salads. They had two stores and offered delivery services. The first store was located directly across from the university and had been there for three years. The second store was new and larger than the first.

TCBY

The city had three TCBY stores. Two of the franchises had sales between $500,000 and $1,000,000. These were located in the upper-income areas of Gainesville. The other store was younger (five years old) and located near campus. The stores sold soft-serve frozen yogurt and superpremium ice cream products along with novelty items. Currently, TCBY was marketing their "Treats" program heavily. Their Treats program featured candy mixed into the ice cream and frozen yogurt.

International Dairy Queen

Two successful Dairy Queen franchises were located in Gainesville. Dairy Queen sold hamburgers, hot-dogs, barbecue, fish and chicken sandwiches, french fried potatoes, and onion rings. Their desserts consisted of cones, shakes, malts, sundaes and sodas, hardpacked products, and frozen ice cream cakes and logs.

Baskin-Robbins

Baskin-Robbins had two stores in Gainesville. One was located directly across from the main campus. It had standing room only. They recently remodeled this store and signed a ten-year lease. The other store was located one mile west of the university. Baskin-Robbins was known for their variety of flavors. They served both frozen yogurt and other ice cream products.

SMITH'S GOALS AND FINANCIAL OBJECTIVES

Smith saw an opportunity to obtain a franchise that had brand-name recognition and a history of success. Florida already had four Beano's franchises in Miami, Fort Lauderdale, Jacksonville, and Orlando. However, there were ample opportunities to open other stores in Florida.

Smith's goals were:

- Phase I: Open one franchise in the Gainesville area in the fall of 1996. For the first two years of operation, the focus would be on the success of that store;
- Phase II: Open a second store in Tallahassee in early 1998;
- Phase III: Open a third, fourth, and fifth store in consecutive years (1999, 2000, and 2001) in Orlando.

The financial objectives were:

Objective 1: Pay off any loans to each store by the sixth year.

Objective 2: Maintain an average return on investment of 20 percent for each store.

Objective 3: Maintain a positive cash flow starting in year one for each store.

Objective 4: Have sales of 2.5 million at the end of ten years.

THE SEARCH FOR INVESTORS

Because Smith had already founded one company, he knew how difficult raising capital could be. He developed a list of people to talk with, and then proceeded as follows:

SBA Consultant

The Small Business Administration (SBA) consultant, Tom Hughes, was impressed with Smith's education, work experience, and detailed business plan. He stated that Smith would have no problem getting a loan of $175,000 as long as he had one-third of the loan amount in liquid assets. For example, if Smith wanted a loan of $175,000, he would need approximately $58,000 in liquid assets. However, Smith's liquidity had dropped to $7,000 over the past few months, due to living expenses. Consequently, he needed an investor(s).

Mr. Hughes also asserted that if Smith got an investor who owned 20 percent or more of the company, the SBA required that person to sign on the note. Smith realized that this could pose a problem because the investor(s) would be at risk for the entire investment of $275,000 if they put up $100,000. That could decrease their desire to invest in the venture. Mr. Hughes also explained that Smith could not receive an SBA loan in the state of Ohio. He would have to go through an SBA branch office located in Florida.

Banker

Smith's banker was Mike Tork, a casual friend. Tork was also impressed with Smith's credentials and affirmed that he should not have a problem getting an SBA loan for $175,000 if he got an investor(s) to put in $100,000. Tork stated the bank preferred to see the following before granting a loan: (1) quality management team, (2) likelihood of success, and (3) financial projections. Tork also stated that obtaining a loan would be easier due to Beano's successful track record.

The bank required Smith to submit his business plan, tax returns for the past three years, and a current copy of his personal financial statement. Tork sent a copy of the business plan to the branch manager in Orlando, Florida, Don Pelham. Pelham told Smith that he might be willing to give him a conventional loan, which would exclude the SBA. Pelham stated, "We want you to be successful, and we will do whatever it takes. The more successful you become, the more successful we become." Pelham gave Smith two scenarios from which to choose.

The first scenario was an SBA loan guaranteed by the federal government. This would involve a lot of paperwork. Pelham estimated the interest rate to be around 9.25–9.5% or 1–1.5% above prime, plus a closing cost of $3,300. The terms of the loan would be worked out later, but Smith figured he would pay off the loan over six or seven years.

The second scenario would be a conventional loan from the bank. The time frame to obtain this loan was similar to the SBA's. However, the terms of this loan would be much more conducive to the needs of Smith's company. The loan would be broken down into operating and reducing lines of credit (both using variable interest rates). The exact interest rate percentages were not discussed. However, Smith learned through friends that these loans were usually structured at five points above prime.

The operating line of credit would be oriented towards short-term operations (working capital, inventory, and payroll). Pelham told Smith that they were very flexible on the terms. For instance, Pelham said that he was willing to let Smith pay interest-only for up to 36 months. However, the loan would have to be paid off over six-to-eight years.

The reducing line of credit would be used for equipment, renovation, and other fixed asset allocations. For this line, Pelham also stated that he would allow Smith to pay interest-only for up to two or three years, and Smith would have to pay off the note at the end of six or seven years.

SCORE Counselor

Smith's last meeting was with the local Service Corps of Retired Executives (SCORE) counselor, George Willis. Willis had worked for Dupont for 30 years in various marketing positions and had owned his own executive search franchise for 14 years. Willis had also consulted with several franchisees in the frozen dessert industry.

Willis told Smith to obtain two partners with an equity interest of 20 percent or less because having one partner with a 33 or 40 percent interest would put you at his or her mercy if, for instance, the partner decided not to do the deal or if something happened to the partner. Also, that partner would have too much control because he or she has the money. If you have two partners, you would have much more control. If one partner drops out, then you could get another. Smith stored this information and began his search for capital.

Family, Friends and Savings

Remembering his days in graduate school, Smith sought out the number one source of financing for most start-ups: friends, family, and savings. He failed at finding resources there.

Business Professionals

Smith's next step was networking through his database of business professionals in the Cleveland area. The first person he contacted was an acquaintance, Barney Harris, whom he had met a year earlier through a friend. Harris was a very successful restaurateur. Smith called Harris to arrange a meeting. Harris agreed, but wanted a copy of the business plan a week in advance. Smith dropped off a copy of the plan and a confidentiality agreement contract the next day.

A week later, Smith and Harris met. Harris stated, "You know, Terry, most of the people who come to see me with business deals just talk. They do not have a business plan, and they expect me to invest hundreds of thousands of dollars with them. Your business plan is excellent. I like how you examined the business from broad and narrow perspectives. This is exactly what I like to see." Harris was also impressed with Smith's intensity and ambition. Harris stated that he knew Smith had what it takes to become successful—"a fire in the belly." Harris told Smith that he was interested in becoming a potential partner, not an investor, and would be willing to put up $100,000.

After four months of hard work, Smith was excited at the opportunity of obtaining a partner. In his excitement, Smith stated that he was willing to give up 33 percent of the company in exchange for an investment of $100,000. No further business professionals were contacted.

BEANO'S SELECTION PROCESS

The selection process at Beano's required the potential franchisee(s) to send in an application form, psychological questionnaire, and personal financial statement. The next step was an independent phone interview that lasted one hour, followed by another half-hour for questions from the applicant. After this stage, there was a personal interview at the company's corporate headquarters in Phoenix, Arizona. The interview focused on the specifics of running a small business.

This process lasted approximately six weeks. After Smith and Harris passed, they received a letter with a password that allowed them to contact any franchisee. Beano's also sent the potential franchisee a copy of their Uniform Franchise Offering Circular (UFOC), a legal document containing information on the company's history, management, finances, operations, and franchisees.

Smith quickly took advantage of this opportunity to gather more information by making a list of questions. He contacted ten franchises and learned about sales, profitability, successful and unsuccessful marketing strategies, employees, and horror stories of partnership agreements. One of the franchisees from Tucson, Arizona, was kind enough to send Smith a copy of his financial statements from the previous year. After examining the differences between the franchisee's numbers and his projected proformas, Smith made some changes (see Exhibit 8 for revised expected scenario).

One of the most significant changes that Smith noticed was the cost of the franchise. Early in the negotiation process, Smith estimated the cost of a franchise at $275,000. After talking with several franchisees in similar college towns, he estimated the cost of starting a franchise in Gainesville at $220,000, including working capital.

Smith also noticed that he initially overestimated the profitability of the business. In his original financial statements, Smith estimated the expected net income of the business at: $34,400, $91,800, $116,800, $135,700, and $138,300 for the years 1997–2001. He revised his figures to be: $29,000, $49,000, $67,600, $87,100, and $87,800. There was a significant difference, primarily due to his failure to include employee wages in the financial statements. This was a gross oversight.

Smith realized that he needed to get the partnership agreement out of the way as soon as possible. After all, they had been negotiating with Beano's for over five months now. Beano's had given Smith and Harris the green light. Now it was time for them to fulfill their side of the deal, to produce a partnership agreement and then to move forward with the construction of the franchise.

HARRIS'S PARTNERSHIP PROPOSAL

Smith went to Harris and told him that it was time for them to draw up a partnership agreement. They had previously talked about a partnership proposal where Harris's percentage of the business would be 33 percent

8 | Revised Pro Forma Income Statement/Cash Flow Summary For the Years 1997–2001 Expected Scenario (in 000's)

	1997		1998		1999		2000		2001	
	$	**% Sales**	**$**	**% Sales**	**$**	**% Sales**	**$**	**% Sales**	**$**	**% Sales**
Sales	$340.0	100.0%	$385.0	100.0%	$435.0	100.0%	$490.0	100.0%	$500.0	100.0%
Cost of Sales	119.0	35.0	134.8	35.0	152.3	35.0	171.5	35.0	175.0	35.0
Gross Profits	221.0	65.0%	250.3	65.0%	282.8	65.0%	318.5	65.0%	325.0	65.0%
Operational Expenses										
Employee Wages	46.9	13.8%	52.0	13.5%	57.6	13.3%	64.9	13.3%	66.8	13.4%
Management Wages	30.0	8.8	31.5	8.2	33.1	7.6	34.8	7.1	36.5	7.3
Payroll Taxes	10.0	2.9	11.2	2.9	12.4	2.9	14.0	2.9	14.3	2.9
Worker's Compensation	1.2	0.4	1.5	0.4	1.5	0.4	1.7	0.4	1.8	0.4
Health Insurance	3.0	0.9	3.3	0.9	3.6	0.8	3.9	0.8	4.2	0.8
Rent	37.5	11.0	39.3	10.2	41.4	9.5	43.5	8.9	45.6	9.1
Utilities	5.3	1.6	5.4	1.4	5.6	1.3	6.2	1.3	6.5	1.3
Prop/Liability Insurance	4.5	1.3	5.2	1.4	5.1	1.2	5.5	1.1	5.9	1.2
Marketing	13.6	4.0	15.4	4.0	17.4	4.0	19.6	4.0	20.0	4.0
Accounting/Legal	2.0	0.6	2.4	0.6	2.6	0.6	2.8	0.6	2.9	0.6
Supplies	4.2	1.2	0.7	0.2	1.0	0.2	1.0	0.2	1.2	0.2
Repairs/Maintenance	1.4	0.4	1.8	0.5	2.1	0.5	2.4	0.5	2.8	0.6
Telephone	1.8	0.5	2.1	0.5	2.4	0.6	2.7	0.6	2.7	0.5
Bank Charges	0.3	0.1	0.3	0.1	0.6	0.1	0.7	0.1	0.8	0.2
Association/Chamber Dues	0.5	0.1	0.5	0.1	0.5	0.1	0.5	0.1	0.5	0.1
Auto	—	0.0	4.5	1.2	4.5	1.0	5.0	1.0	5.0	1.0
Depreciation	12.0	3.5	12.0	3.1	12.0	2.8	12.0	2.4	12.0	2.4
Miscellaneous Expenses	8.0	2.4	3.0	0.8	4.8	1.1	5.0	1.0	5.5	1.1
Total Operating Expenses	181.5	53.4%	192.9	50.1%	217.7	50.0%	226.6	46.2%	234.3	46.9%
EBIT	39.5	11.6%	57.4	14.9%	74.6	17.1%	91.8	18.7%	90.7	18.1%
Interest Income	0.6	0.2	1.2	0.3	1.2	0.3	2.0	0.4	2.0	0.4
Interest Expense	$10.9	3.2	$9.6	2.5	$8.2	1.9	$6.7	1.4	$5.0	1.0
Earnings Before Taxes	29.0	8.5	49.0	12.7	67.6	15.5	87.1	17.8	87.8	17.6
Add: Depreciation Expense	12.0	3.5	12.0	3.1	12.0	2.8	12.8	2.4	12.0	2.4
Cash From Operations	41.0	12.1	61.0	15.8	79.6	18.3	99.1	20.2	99.8	20.0
Debt Service	0	0.0	12.7	3.3	13.9	3.2	15.3	3.1	16.8	3.4
DISTRIBUTIONS	$41.0	12.1%	$48.3	12.5%	$65.7	15.1%	$83.8	17.1%	$83.0	16.6%

for an investment of $100,000. Smith offered to write up the proposal. However, Harris insisted that he would write up the initial proposal. Two weeks later, Smith received it (see Exhibit 9) in the mail.

Smith found three surprises in this proposal. First, Harris changed the structure of the deal. Second, Harris charged him for accounting services, when Smith could do the book work himself. Third, the buy-out clause proposed three times the cash flow of the business, averaged over the number of years they were in business, divided by the ownership percentage. Cash flow was not defined.

Smith was stunned. Quickly, he sketched out the proposal that he had expected to receive, so that he could compare them side by side (see Exhibit 10).

9 | Barney Harris's Partnership Proposal

Short-term goal:	1 Store by fall 1996
Long-term goal:	5 Stores
Incorporation:	Limited Liability Corporation
Harris's Investment:	$100,000 with $5,000 going to equity in the company and $95,000 as a loan to the company. The loan would be repaid over the next five years with Harris receiving quarterly interest at the prime rate for the loan. Also Harris's equity position would increase to 49% of the company.
Scoop Shop Operations:	Terry Smith agrees to spend 100% of his time operating the store.
Book Work:	Harris's accountant would do all of the book work. Her fees are as follows: $2,000 to set up the books and $600/month thereafter, not including franchise reports, budgets, and forecasts.
Buy-Out Arrangement:	Three times the cash flow of the business, averaged over the number of years the franchise is in business. This figure would then be divided by the seller's ownership percentage. For example, if the partnership developed cash flows of $100,000/year and Smith wanted to purchase Harris's interest, the $100,000 would be multiplied by three and by Harris's ownership percentage of .49, meaning the purchase price would be $147,000.

10 | Expected Proposal From Harris

Short-term goal:	1 Store by fall 1996
Long-term goal:	5 Stores
Incorporation:	Limited Liability Corporation
Your Investment:	Harris's investment would be $100,000, with $100,000 going towards a 33% equity position. The other $120,000 will be obtained through an SBA loan. All debt service must be current prior to distributions paid out to partners. The expansion of future stores will occur at a later date.
Scoop Shop Operations:	All day-to-day operations will be performed by Smith.
Bookwork:	Smith will do the bookwork and have a payroll service do the taxes.
Buy-Out Arrangement:	Two formulas will be used to estimate the value of the company: Price-to-Sales Discounted Cash Flow Purchase price will be repaid over a five-year period while the seller holds the note to the debt. The loan will be repaid on a quarterly basis at the current prime rate for that quarter (as quoted in the *Wall Street Journal*). Both partners would have a first right of refusal to purchase the stock of the other party and neither party has the right to sell until after three years.

CONCLUSIONS

Terry Smith winced as he turned away from his "I LOVE BEANO'S ICE CREAM" bumper sticker. He knew he had three choices: take what Harris had offered in the proposal, even though it was not the proposal Smith had expected; give Harris a counter proposal that included the three changes Smith wanted, knowing that there was a chance that Harris could back away from the deal altogether; or, start looking for a new partner. Smith started to walk across the parking lot, knowing it was time to make his next move.

REFERENCES

Answers to frequently asked questions about franchising (1995). *Franchising in the Economy.* International Franchise Association (IFA).

Hill, T. & Jacobs, M. (1995). Franchise turnover ratio below nine percent. Frandata Corp. for the International Franchise Association's Education Foundation.

Top 50 franchisers ranked by system-wide sales. (1995). *Restaurant Business,* November 1.

Vaughn, B. (1976). The international expansion of U.S. franchise systems: Status and strategies. *Journal of International Business,* Spring, 65–72.

NOTE

Special thanks to James Chrismon, Reinhold Lamb, Phil Greenwood, and three anonymous reviewers for their assistance.

CASE 7

Ben & Jerry's Homemade Inc.: "Yo! I'm Your CEO!"

Katherine A. Auer
Indiana University

Alan N. Hoffman
Bentley College

"Ben & Jerry's Grows Up"—The Boston Globe
"Ben, Jerry Losing Their Values?"—The Washington Times
"Ben & Jerry's Melting Social Charter"—The Washington Post
"Life Won't Be Just a Bowl of Cherry Garcia"—Business Week
"Say It Ain't So, Ben & Jerry"—Business Week

The headlines said it all. Ben & Jerry's, the company that built its success as much on its down-home image and folksy idealism as on its super-rich ice cream, was at a crossroads. Having been started in 1978 in a renovated Vermont gas station by childhood friends Ben Cohen and Jerry Greenfield, the unconventional company soon grew into a $140 million powerhouse that was rivaled only by Haagen-Dazs in the superpremium category of the ice cream market. With its many donations and policies promoting corporate responsibility, Ben & Jerry's took great pride in its success combining social activism with financial viability. But in mid-1994, the outlook was not so rosy. Sales were flat, profits were down, and the company's stock price had fallen to half of what it was at the end of 1992. In its 1993 annual report, Ben & Jerry's admitted that some flavors of its "all natural" ice cream included ingredients that were not, in fact, all natural. And staffers within the company reportedly criticized it for lack of leadership.

On June 13, 1994, Ben & Jerry's announced that Ben was stepping down as CEO, and that it would abandon its longtime cap on executive salaries in order to help it find a new one. The message was clear: Ben & Jerry's was no longer the company it once was. For many, the question then was, what would it become?

THE CONTEST

With a marketing flair befitting its tradition of wacky promotional tactics, Ben & Jerry's set out to find its new leader by announcing the "Yo! I'm Your CEO!" contest. Customers were asked to send in a lid from a container of their favorite Ben & Jerry's ice-cream flavor along with a 100-word essay explaining "Why I Would Be a Great CEO for Ben & Jerry's." The winner would become the new CEO, the runner-up would receive a lifetime supply of ice cream, and the losers would receive a rejection letter "suitable for framing."

"We have never had an experienced CEO and we have reached the point in our life when we need one," said Ben, adding that he planned to continue with the company as chairman and concentrate on "fun stuff" like product development.

But the search wasn't all fun and games. Ben & Jerry's also announced that it would abandon its longtime policy that no executive be paid more than seven times the salary of the lowest paid employee, and hired an executive recruiting firm to help find the right person. Under the old policy, Ben was paid $133,212 in 1993 and no bonuses; the going rate for executives at companies of like size was $300,00 to $500,000.

"I think we are looking for a rare bird," said Ben. "I guess there are about five or ten executives who will be

Source: D. Canedy, 1996. Ben & Jerry's is losing chief, in addition to market share. *The New York Times*, September 28. http://www.nytimes.com/yr/mo/day/news/financial/ben-jerry.html

interested and have the skills." The key, he added, is experience in keeping "everyone aligned and moving the same direction" as the company grows—something he admitted he was learning but not good at. "I haven't found the happy medium between autocratic and laissez-faire," he explained.

Some 22,500 aspiring leaders around the world flooded the company with their responses, which were as varied as the flavors in its ice cream line. Entries came from places as far away as Australia, Thailand, East Africa, and Saudi Arabia. An entire fifth-grade class sent in letters, with offers from some of the students to develop new flavors. One woman sent in a near-nude photo of herself, while an advertising executive attached his resume to a Superman costume.

An Indiana schoolteacher scrawled her essay on a painting of a woman reading a book, while Allen Stillman, head of New York restaurant chain Smith & Wollensky, put a full-page ad in *The New York Times*. "I propose a whole new line of flavors," he wrote. "Red Meat Swirl, Potato Gravy Chunk, Starchie Bunker." Stillman also proposed a merger and a new name: Ben Smith & Jerry Wollensky Steaks and Shakes.

Other response tactics included a resume written entirely on a giant sheet cake, another engraved on a brass plaque and mounted on marble, and one written in crayon by a hopeful couple's 2½-year-old son. A Milwaukee car salesman sent a mock two-foot-wide lid of a New York Super Fudge Chunk carton, folded in half. When the lid was unfolded an electronic device made a sound like a telephone ring; the opener then read "Please call me—I'm the one you want to be your CEO."

"Some of them may not be right for the CEO's job, but they sure would be right for marketing jobs," Ben said. "We may not have to advertise for people for the next several years."

THE WINNER

On February 2, 1995, Ben & Jerry's announced that they found the leader they wanted: Robert Holland Jr., a former partner at management consultancy McKinsey & Co. By taking the helm of Ben & Jerry's, the 55-year-old MBA became one of the most visible African-American chief executives among the nation's publicly traded corporations.

Holland was selected not through the essay contest, but through New York executive recruiter Russell Reynolds. Some 500 candidates were initially considered by that firm, and Ben & Jerry's board members ultimately reviewed about 15 applicants. The race was eventually narrowed to six competitors (one of which came from the essay contest), and from there, it came down to two finalists, both of whom spent considerable time over dinner and ice cream with Ben, Jerry, and board members. Rumor had it that his competitor preferred frozen yogurt, while Holland was a passionate ice cream fan.

Having grown up in Michigan, Holland spent 13 years as an associate and partner at McKinsey, where he worked with consumer and industrial clients including the soft drink division of Heineken. He left McKinsey in 1981 to become an independent consultant and businessman. Among his subsequent roles were chairman of Gilreath Manufacturing Inc., a plastic injection-molding company, and chairman and CEO for Rokher-J Inc., a White Plains, New York, consulting and takeover firm. Holland earned his MBA at Baruch College in New York.

His experience in turning troubled companies around was important, however, more important were Holland's social values. He was chairman of the board of trustees at Spelman College in Atlanta, a school traditionally attended by black women, as well as the founder of a dropout-prevention program for Detroit high school students and a board member of the Harlem Junior Tennis program for inner city youth.

"We were very impressed not only with Bob's operational expertise, but with his social commitment, as expressed in both his business experience and his active involvement with the nonprofit sector," said Ben.

Holland's salary was set at $250,000 plus options on 180,000 shares of stock and a bonus of up to $125,000 if he met certain financial goals. Though significantly higher than what Ben had been earning, it is low compared to the pay scale for CEOs at midsized manufacturers, and reportedly less than what Holland had been earning as a management consultant.

Though he didn't submit an essay as part of the contest, Holland did submit something—a poem—upon request after he was chosen. The poem, entitled "Time, Values and Ice Cream" (see Exhibit 1), reflected his background in poor, working-class, south central Michi-

1 | Time, Values and Ice Cream* **by Robert Holland**

Born before the baby boom
as war drums raged cross distant waters—way
beyond my family's lore since our 1600s coming to this far off land called
America.

T'was a simple time, as I grew tall.
Shucks! Uncle Sam really wanted you (so the poster said)—pride
in work, parades and proms, company picnics 'tween eve'ns spent with "Suspense,"
"The Shadow," and everybody's "Our Miss Brooks."
Good ole days in the summertime, indeed! . . . in
America.

Yet, some nostalgia stayed 'yond one's grasp,
like Sullivans,
the ice cream place on Main—swivel stools, cozy booths, and sweet,
sweet smells with no sitting place for all of some of us.
Could only dream such humble pleasure. Sometimes, dear 'Merica,
of thee I simply hum.

Much, so much has changed in twenty springs. Sputnik
no longer beeps so loud;
Bay of Pigs, Vietnam and contentions in Chicago . . .
come and gone . . .
All that noise almost drowning out "One small step for man . . ."
and ". . . Willie, time to say goodbye to baseball."
Confusing place, this melodious mix,
called America.

Now I sit by eyeing distance twilight,
Engineer and MBA,
smiling wide on M.L.K.'s day,
CEO of Cherry Garcia and Peace Pops' fountain
having not forgotten the forbidden seats of Sullivans',
with miles to go before we sleep . . .
and time left yet to get there.
Only in America!

*Only 100 words before translation from the language of Chunky Mandarin Orange with Natural Wild Brazil Nuts.

gan. Though his appointment at Ben & Jerry's made Holland one of just a few African-American CEOs at public companies, Holland declined to be called a role model for other blacks, calling the term "too presumptuous." Nevertheless, he said, "I'm looking forward to dispelling whatever concerns people have."

Holland faced a formidable challenge at Ben & Jerry's, however. The company posted its first quarterly loss for the fourth quarter of fiscal 1994, and when Holland's appointment was announced, Chuck Lacy, the company's longtime president, resigned.

While Holland won the executive slot, what some may say was the better prize—a lifetime supply of ice cream—went to three runners-up. Among them was Taylor James Caldwell, the toddler, by then three years old, who had submitted an entry for his parents. In addition, about 100 honorable mentions received limited edition T-shirts.

THE "GOOD OLD DAYS"

The birth of Ben & Jerry's can be traced to a $5 correspondence course in ice cream making taken by Ben Cohen and Jerry Greenfield. The duo, friends since early childhood in Merrick, New York, then gathered $12,000 ($4,000 of which was borrowed), and in May 1978 opened an ice cream shop in a renovated Burlington, Vermont, gas station. Featuring an antique rock-salt ice cream freezer and a Volkswagen squareback for its delivery van, the shop soon became popular for its innovative flavors made from fresh Vermont milk and cream.

At the heart of Ben & Jerry's is the distinct business philosophy shared by its founders. In essence, they believe that companies have a responsibility to do good for society, not only for themselves. This philosophy is best explained by the company's three-part mission statement, formally stated in 1988 and reproduced here in its entirety:

> *Ben & Jerry's is dedicated to the creation and demonstration of a new corporate concept of linked prosperity. Our mission consists of three interrelated parts: Product Mission: To make, distribute, and sell the finest quality, all-natural ice cream and related products in a wide variety of innovative flavors made from Vermont dairy products.*
>
> *Social Mission: To operate the company in a way that actively recognizes the central role that business plays in the structure of society by initiating innovative ways to improve the quality of life of a broad community—local, national, and international. Economic Mission: To operate the company on a sound financial basis of profitable growth, increasing value for our shareholders, and creating career opportunities and financial rewards for our employees.*
>
> *Underlying the mission of Ben & Jerry's is the determination to seek new and creative ways of addressing all three parts, while holding a deep respect for the individuals, inside and outside the company, and for the communities of which they are a part.*

This unconventional philosophy touched everything the company did, from the way it treated its employees to the way it dealt with its suppliers.

The company enjoys a strong team- and family-oriented atmosphere; for example, it has progressive family leave, health insurance, and other benefit plans. Reasoning that happy employees reduce stress and improve the workplace in general, Ben & Jerry's kept the culture extremely casual and relaxed, and formed a "Joy Committee" to spread joy among their employees. Some of the spontaneous events coordinated by the Joy Committee include an Elvis Presley recognition day, with an Elvis look-alike contest, a Barry Manilow appreciation day, and a car race derby in which employees raced their own toy cars. Pranks abounded at all gatherings, including the annual shareholders' meetings, and most were followed by entertainment such as 1960s musicians Richie Havens, Livingston Taylor, and dozens of other bands. In essence, Ben and Jerry truly seemed to live by their motto: "If it's not fun, why do it?"

Yet in their desire to create a healthy and equitable workplace, Ben & Jerry's did more than just promote fun and games: Their longtime cap on executive salaries required that no executive be paid more than seven times the salary of the lowest paid employee. Typical staff meetings included all employees, and issues affecting women, minorities, and gays in their workforce were always discussed openly.

In choosing suppliers for the ingredients of their products, Ben & Jerry's tried to be equally responsible. For example, the brownies used in its Chocolate Fudge Brownie ice cream are brought from a bakery in Yonkers, New York, that hires undertrained and underskilled workers and uses its profits to house the homeless and teach them trades. Ben & Jerry's Rainforest Crunch ice cream features nuts grown in South American rain forests; the firm pays the harvesters directly, and donates a portion of the proceeds from sales of the ice cream to environmental preservation causes. Wild Maine Blueberry ice cream is made with blueberries grown and harvested by the Passamaquoddy Indians of Maine. Fresh Georgia Peach ice cream is made from Georgia-grown peaches as part of the company's policy of supporting family farms.

Similarly, for the milk and cream that forms the bulk of its products, Ben & Jerry's is committed to buying from Vermont dairy farms, to whom it pays above-market prices. When rBGH, a genetically engineered drug to increase cows' milk production, was approved by the FDA, Ben & Jerry's declared it would buy only from farms not using the drug, citing health concerns and a desire to protect smaller farms. To ensure that its products remain wholesome and pure, the company pays a premium to suppliers in exchange for their written assurance that they will not use rBGH.

Finally, the company also established the Ben & Jerry's Foundation, which donates 7.5 percent of its pretax profits to nonprofit organizations. These causes included the American Wildlands in Montana; Burch House in New Hampshire (a safe house); the Burlington Peace and Justice Coalition in Vermont; the Citizens Committee for Children in New York (aid for drug-addicted pregnant women); Natural Guard (an environmental group for school-age children and teens); the Brattleboro Area AIDS Project (providing free services to HIV-positive individuals and their families); and the Massachusetts Coalition for the Homeless.

Such efforts won the hearts of scores of like-minded consumers, many of whom had grown up in the same socially conscious generation as Ben and Jerry. Indeed, because of its values and its unconventional nature, the company has done very little marketing: Media coverage of its various antics has been virtually guaranteed on a regular basis, providing free publicity for the company, its products, and its values. Thanks in part to the size of the "baby boomer" generation of which its leaders were a part, Ben & Jerry's flourished in the 1980s, growing to more than 100 franchises. In 1984 the company went public in Vermont, and by 1986 it had achieved 100 percent growth.

RECENT TROUBLES

While Ben & Jerry's thrived during the 1980s, the 1990s presented a very different picture. One of the primary reasons was that the baby boomer generation—Ben & Jerry's primary target market—was entering middle age and becoming more health conscious. Whereas, during the 1980s these consumers enjoyed the socially conscious self-indulgence of Ben & Jerry's ice cream, they became averse to high-fat goods such as superpremium ice cream. At the same time, new labeling requirements imposed by the FDA meant that customers could see with painful clarity the amount of fat each scoop of Ben & Jerry's ice creams contained, thus showing their less-than-healthful nature.

To respond Ben & Jerry's introduced a reduced-fat, reduced-calorie ice milk, called Ben & Jerry's Lite. That line failed, reportedly due to poor quality, but the subsequent introduction of a low-fat low-cholesterol frozen yogurt line met with much better success. In addition, the company introduced the first flavors in its nonfat yogurt line in the summer of 1995. Nevertheless, the fact remains that ice cream sales are slowing.

Ben & Jerry's also faced increased competition from the deep-pocketed Haagen-Dazs, which expanded its selection of flavors to better rival Ben & Jerry's (including its chunky "Extraas," a low-fat ultrapremium ice cream as well as frozen yogurt) and started a price war by reducing its prices and offering a variety of promotions and discounts. During the weakened economy of the 1990s, competing on price was common.

Indeed, the superpremium category as a whole witnessed increased competition from lower cost, lower fat premium ice creams. Among those are Edy's, manufactured by Dreyer's, which produces roughly half of Ben & Jerry's output. Also, Dreyer's recently received a huge cash infusion from Nestle, giving it increased competitive muscle.

Despite the fact that U.S. ice cream exports had tripled in recent years, and that Haagen-Dazs had begun exporting (even opening a factory in France), Ben & Jerry's paid little attention to markets outside the United States. Chuck Lacy, the company's president, stated "It's something that we're starting to think about, but we've got a lot of work to do here in the U.S." Sales to restaurants was another option for growth outside of the heated grocery store market, but again, Lacy said, while "there's huge potential, it's a completely different business. It requires completely different distributors and sales staff, a completely different head."

Software glitches, meanwhile, repeatedly delayed the opening of Ben & Jerry's new $40 million ice cream plant in St. Albans, which was planned to increase production significantly. But with sales down, it was not clear that the company would be able to use much of the plant's capacity when it opened.

Management problems also plagued the firm, reducing morale and drawing criticism from employees, who said there was a lack of direction. By the end of 1994, the mood reportedly became so dark that the company asked author Milton Moskowitz to remove them from the most recent edition of *The 100 Best Companies to Work for in America.*

Finally, on December 19, 1994, Ben & Jerry's announced an expected loss of $700,000 to $900,000 for the fourth quarter of 1994—its first since going public in 1984.

THE INDUSTRY LANDSCAPE

The packaged ice cream industry includes ordinary, premium, and superpremium products. These types are distinguished primarily by their butterfat content and density, as well as the freshness of their ingredients and the way they were blended and treated.

Ordinary ice creams typically contain the minimum of 10 to 12 percent butterfat and the maximum proportion of air; one four-ounce scoop contained 150 calories or less. Premium ice creams contain 12 to 16 percent butterfat and less air than regular types; a four-ounce scoop usually contained 180 calories. Superpremium ice creams, which include Ben & Jerry's, generally contain about 16 to 20 percent fat (excluding add-ins) and less than 20 percent air. The caloric value of a four-ounce scoop is generally about 260 calories. This type of ice cream is characterized by a greater richness than the other types, and is sold in packaged pints priced between $2.29 and $2.89 each.

The total annual sales in U.S. supermarkets for the ice cream and frozen yogurt market as a whole were more than $3.6 billion in 1994. The superpremium market (ice cream, frozen yogurt, ice milk, and sorbet) accounted for about $415 million. Ninety-three percent of American households consumed ice cream, but demand is seasonal, with summer levels as much as 30 percent higher than those in the winter. Sales for frozen yogurt (superpremium and regular) were $550 million in supermarkets in 1994; at this time, Ben & Jerry's was clearly ahead of Haagen-Dazs in the superpremium frozen yogurt market.

Gross margins in the ice cream industry as a whole are about 30.6 percent, compared with only 20 percent for the frozen food department as a whole. Premium and superpremium varieties outperform other ice cream types, accounting for 45.8 percent of sales and 45.9 percent of profits of the ice cream category as a whole, and earning a gross margin of 31.5 percent.

The superpremium ice cream and frozen yogurt business is highly competitive. Ben & Jerry's principal competitor is The Haagen-Dazs Company, Inc., which roughly matches Ben & Jerry's 42 percent share of the market; others, including Columbo, Dannon, Healthy Choice, Simple Pleasures, Elan, Frusen Gladje, Yoplait, Honey Hill Farms, and Steve's, constituted less than 10 percent of the market.

Haagen-Dazs is owned by The Pillsbury Company, which in turn is owned by Grand Metropolitan PLC, a British food and liquor conglomerate with resources significantly greater than those of Ben & Jerry's. Haagen-Dazs entered the market well before Ben & Jerry's, and also became well established in certain markets in Europe and the Pacific Rim. And to compete with Ben & Jerry's, it introduced in 1992 its Extraas line of products that included a variety of add-ins like cookies, candies, and nuts.

Ben & Jerry's also competed with several well-known brands in the ice cream novelty segment, including Haagen-Dazs and Dove Bars, which are manufactured by a division of Mars, Inc. Both Haagen-Dazs and Dove Bars achieved significant market share before Ben & Jerry's entered their markets.

MARKET SHARE

The total U.S. sales for superpremium ice cream, frozen yogurt, ice milk, and sorbet were more than $415 million in 1994. The market was dominated by Haagen-Dazs and Ben & Jerry's: In 1993, the former held 62 percent of the market while Ben & Jerry's held 36 percent, but by early 1995, both held roughly 42 percent.

Haagen-Dazs entered the superpremium market back in 1961. Though success was not achieved overnight, the brand remained on the market and became the industry leader. Early success was linked to word-of-mouth advertising, but by 1983 Haagen-Dazs spent $14 million on advertising, while average ice cream manufacturers spent less than one percent of sales on advertising.

When new competitors began entering the market in the early 1980s, namely, Ben & Jerry's, Haagen-Dazs attempted to keep them out by threatening distributors. Ben & Jerry's fought back with a lawsuit and a campaign including bumper stickers and T-shirts displaying the statement, "What's the Pillsbury Doughboy Afraid of?" The litigation was settled and the campaign brought to an end within about a year.

Between 1989 and 1993, overall growth in the market was sluggish, increasing by only 14 percent. During that same time period, however, Ben & Jerry's market share rose by 120 percent, while Haagen-Dazs' share decreased by 10 percent. In 1992, Ben & Jerry's increased its U.S. market share by 10 percent; Haagen-Dazs, on the other hand, lost 8 percent. Thus, while Ben & Jerry's entered late into the mature, low-growth ice cream market, it gained substantial market share, primarily at the expense of Haagen-Dazs.

Ben & Jerry's products are distributed primarily by independent regional ice cream distributors. With certain exceptions, only one distributor was appointed to each territory. In some areas, subdistributors are used. Ben & Jerry's trucks also distributes some of the ice cream and frozen yogurt sold in Vermont and upstate New York. Ben & Jerry's has a distribution agreement with Dreyer's whereby Dreyer's has exclusivity, in general, for sales to supermarkets and similar accounts of Ben & Jerry's products in most of its markets outside New England, upstate New York, Pennsylvania, and Texas. Net sales to Dreyer's accounted for about 54 and 52 percent of Ben & Jerry's net sales for 1993 and 1994, respectively.

While Dreyer's markets its own premium ice cream, as well as frozen dessert products made by other companies, it does not produce or market any other superpremium ice cream or frozen yogurt. Were it to begin doing so, Dreyer's would lose its exclusivity as a Ben & Jerry's distributor.

Because of instances of legal action over distribution agreements, manufacturers and distributors generally opted for verbal rather than written contracts. In recent years, two independent distributors claimed that Ben & Jerry's and Dreyer's had squeezed them out of the business, and at least three others claimed they had lost access to the brand after building it for years. Furthermore, Amy Miller, founder of Amy's Ice Creams in Austin, Texas, claimed that Ben & Jerry's pressured the best distributor in that area to not carry Amy's pints or risk losing the immensely popular Ben & Jerry's. But Ben and Jerry categorically denied any such involvement, and were supported by the distributor. There were also a few other instances in which distributors claimed that they had been pressured not to carry brands competing with Ben & Jerry's. Said one retailer, who sued Ben & Jerry's after it stopped sales to his firm, "corporately, they are absolutely vicious."

Ben & Jerry's admitted that while its relationships with Dreyer's and other distributors have been generally satisfactory, they were not always easy to maintain. But alternatives are few: According to the company, the loss of one or more of the related distribution agreements could have a material adverse effect on the company's business.

When it came to choosing suppliers, Ben & Jerry's insistence on social responsibility earned it much acclaim, but developing such relationships was not always easy. Its search for the perfect coffee bean, for example, took more than five years and led to one of its most complex, yet successful, supplier relationships. The company's goal is to give much of the profits back to the grower, rather than to a middleman broker; accomplishing this requires a significant commitment of time and resources to learn each party's needs and expectations.

Because working directly with suppliers requires so much energy, Ben & Jerry's plan to establish only one or two new relationships each year. The R&D, quality assurance, finance, and manufacturing departments all are involved in the evaluation and education of each new supplier. Although the work involved is much more than would have been required if it simply made calls to existing suppliers, Ben & Jerry's felt the result made it worthwhile.

FINANCE

Ben & Jerry's sales steadily increased from 1988 through 1992, but then slowed dramatically in 1993. Sales increased by about 30 percent annually from 1990 to 1992, but that dropped to 6 percent in 1993. Furthermore, the company indicated that virtually all of its growth in 1993 came from its frozen yogurt line the sales of which increased by 35 percent during that year. Sales for fiscal 1993 were $140 million and $149 million for fiscal 1994.

Net income grew steadily along with sales growth, and exceeded that pace during 1991 and 1992. While sales grew at 26 and 36 percent during 1991 and 1992, respectively, net income grew at 42 and 81 percent. During 1993, sales grew 6 percent while net income grew at 7 percent. For 1994, however, the company reported a net loss of $1.87 million (see Exhibits 2 and 3).

The company's net profit margin was 5.1 percent, compared with the industry average of 3.4 percent. The net loss per share for 1994 was ($0.26); during previous years, earnings per share had risen steadily, from $0.32 in 1988 to a high of $1.07 in 1992, then falling to $1.01 in 1993. Consequently, its stock price fell nearly 50 percent from its 1993 high of $32 by investors impatient with the company's lack of momentum. On February 1, 1995, the company's stock price was $12,125.

MARKETING

Product

Ben & Jerry's "product" is a carefully orchestrated combination of premium ice cream products and social consciousness—"Caring Capitalism"—created through bottom-up management and cause-generated marketing and public relations efforts. The physical products include superpremium ice cream, in both chunky and smooth flavors, low-fat frozen yogurt, and ice-cream novelties. The company operates in the focused niche of superpremium ice cream products, with the driving competitive factor traditionally being diversity and uniqueness of flavor.

As such, the primary marketing goal at Ben & Jerry's is to develop and deliver great new products and flavors.

EXHIBIT 2 | Five-Year Financial Highlights (In thousands except per share data)

	YEAR ENDED				
Summary of Operations	**12/31/94**	**12/25/93**	**12/26/92**	**12/28/91**	**12/29/90**
Net sales	$148,802	$140,328	$131,969	$96,997	$77,024
Cost of sales	109,760	100,210	94,389	68,500	54,203
Gross profit	39,042	40,118	37,580	28,497	22,821
Selling, general and administrative expenses	36,253	28,270	26,243	21,264	17,639
Asset write-down	6,779				
Other income (expense)-net	229	197	(23)	(729)	(709)
Income (loss) before income taxes	(3,761)	12,045	11,314	6,504	4,473
Income taxes	(1,893)	4,845	4,639	2,765	1,864
Net income (loss)	(1,868)	7,200	6,675	3,739	2,609
Net income (loss) per common share[1]	$(0.26)	$1.01	$1.07	$0.67	$0.50
Weighted average common shares outstanding[1]	7,148	7,138	6,254	5,572	5,225

	YEAR ENDED				
Balance Sheet Data:	**12/31/94**	**12/25/93**	**12/26/92**	**12/28/91**	**12/29/90**
Working capital	$37,456	$29,292	$18,053	$11,035	$8,202
Total assets	120,295	106,361	88,207	43,056	34,299
Long-term debt	32,419	18,002	2,641	2,787	8,948
Stockholders' equity[2]	72,502	74,262	66,760	26,269	16,101

[1]The per share amounts and average shares outstanding have been adjusted for the effects of all stock splits, including stock splits in the form of stock dividends.
[2]No cash dividends have been declared or paid by the Company on its capital stock since the Company's organization. The Company intends to reinvest earnings for use in its business and to finance future growth. Accordingly, the Board of Directors does not anticipate declaring any cash dividends in the foreseeable future.

3 | Consolidated Balance Sheets

ASSETS	12/31/94	12/25/93
Current assets:		
Cash and cash equivalents	$20,777,746	$14,704,795
Accounts receivable, less allowance for doubtful accounts: $504,000 in 1994 and $229,000 in 1993	11,904,844	11,679,222
Inventories	13,462,572	13,452,863
Deferred income taxes	3,146,000	1,689,000
Income taxes receivable	2,097,743	
Prepaid expenses	534,166	847,851
Total current assets	51,923,071	42,373,731
Property, plant and equipment, net	57,980,567	40,261,538
Investments	8,000,000	22,000,000
Other assets	2,391,465	1,725,316
	$120,295,103	$106,360,585

LIABILITIES & STOCKHOLDERS' EQUITY	12/31/94	12/25/93
Current liabilities:		
Accounts payable and accrued expenses	$13,914,972	$12,068,424
Income taxes payable		344,519
Current portion of long-term debt and capital lease obligations	552,547	669,151
Total current liabilities	14,467,519	13,082,094
Long-term debt and capital lease obligations	32,418,565	18,002,076
Deferred income taxes	907,000	1,014,000
Commitments and contingencies		
Stockholders' equity:		
$1.20 noncumulative Class A preferred stock—$1.00 par value, redeemable at the Company's option at $12.00 per share; 900 shares authorized, issued and outstanding, aggregate preference on voluntary or involuntary liquidation—$9,000	900	900
Class A common stock—$.033 par value; authorized 20,000,000 shares; issued: 6,290,580 shares at December 31, 1994 and 6,266,772 shares at December 25, 1993	208,010	207,224
Class B common stock—$.033 par value; authorized 3,000,000 shares; issued: 932,448 shares at December 31, 1994 and 947,637 shares at December 25, 1993	30,770	31,271
Additional paid-in capital	48,366,185	48,222,445
Retained earnings	25,316,309	27,185,003
Unearned compensation		(19,815)
Treasury stock, at cost: 69,032 Class A and 1,092 Class B shares at December 31, 1994 and 66,353 Class A and 1,092 Class B shares at December 25, 1993	(1,420,155)	(1,364,613)
Total stockholders' equity	72,502,019	74,262,415
Total liabilities and stockholders' equity	$120,295,103	$106,360,585

It maintains a full-time R&D team dedicated to the development of unconventional, cutting-edge flavors. It is this strength that has placed Ben & Jerry's at the forefront of the superpremium ice cream market, with 6 of the Top 10 and 13 of the Top 20 Best Selling Flavors.

In its traditional line, Ben & Jerry's distinguishes its flavor and products through "chunkiness," maintaining specifications not only for chunk size, but for number per spoonful and quality of the fruits and nuts they contain. Although such requirements add a great deal more to the cost of the finished product, the enhancement in taste differentiates Ben & Jerry's product from the competition.

The company also distinguishes its product by its use of pure, natural, and socially conscious milk from Vermont dairy farmers who agree not to use rBGH. The FDA allowed the voluntary labeling of dairy products made from non-rBGH treated cows, so Ben & Jerry's aggressively promotes its products' purity on its packaging.

Ben & Jerry's products are sold by the pint in recycled paper board cups, a standard practice in the superpremium market. Ben & Jerry's arrived at that strategy based on the demographics of its target market: 25- to 40-year-old consumers in the upper middle class sector who had no children. People in this segment do not need to purchase larger quantities of ice cream at one time.

Ice cream pints accounts for only about 13 percent of supermarket ice cream sales. Nonetheless, Ben & Jerry's strategy has been to obtain an increasingly large piece of shrinking pie, but that is becoming more difficult as the competitive landscape has changed.

It became apparent that the company would have to work harder to continue success based on its "new flavor" strategy because competitors are increasingly imitating its flavors. While originally it could count on about six months before imitations arrived, Ben & Jerry's now solely "owned" a flavor for only about 60 days. As a result, the company revised its marketing goal to establish a standard of product quality that cannot be imitated, to introduce more "euphoric" new flavors and to improve the selection of the company's flavors in grocery stores.

In March 1994, Ben & Jerry's introduced its line of Smooth, No Chunks flavors in response to market research indicating that a large portion of the superpremium market did not like chunks. The company targeted the segment that was "just too tired to chew" at the end of a busy day and who would rather "experience their ice cream without having to exert too much energy." That move placed Ben & Jerry's in a fortified position in its battle with Haagen-Dazs.

Other product innovations include novelty items such as Brownie Bars, which failed, and Peace Pops, which were marginally successful. Peace Pops were wrapped in a message to redirect one percent of the military budget to social programs; they did well only at convenience stores, suggesting to the company that they were primarily impulse buys. Recently, 70 percent of Peace Pops were sold in convenience stores.

Place

Ben & Jerry's markets its superpremium ice cream products to supermarkets, grocery stores, convenience stores, and restaurants that demonstrate corporate consciousness in the way they do business. Roughly 105 Ben & Jerry's franchises or licensed "scoop shops" exist across the United States, in addition to some in Canada and Israel and a 50–50 joint venture in Russia. In addition, in March 1994 the company began shipping a small amount of its products to small specialty stores in the United Kingdom.

The company also attempted to increase its distribution channels by offering gifts by mail. This concept featured a brochure advertising earthy, tie-dyed gifts, as well as ice cream, coffee, and candy, and offered consumers the ability to have the ice cream dry-ice packed and delivered overnight anywhere in the country. The concept met with limited success, due in part to limited promotion.

Restaurants represent another venue the company explored to maintain growth, but to date, Ben & Jerry's has not made this opportunity a primary goal. The same is true for global expansion. The company was successful abroad, but efforts had been haphazard and outcomes were based solely on luck. The company admitted that it did not have an international strategy and that true commitment to global exporting would require that it learn much more about the market—something it had not made a current priority.

Price

Ben & Jerry's ice cream products are premium priced at the high end of the ice cream market. A pint of its ice cream retails for approximately $2.69. Although this pricing strategy worked extremely well within the exploding market of the late 1980s and early 1990s, it experienced some difficulty in recent years, as demand shifted toward lower priced and/or private-label products in grocery stores. Price elasticity declined, whereas in the past, Ben & Jerry's could impose significant price increases (8 percent in 1991, 4 percent in early 1993).

Pricing pressure also resulted from the apparent consolidation of sales in a few players' hands and the stagnation of the market, with new forms of pricing competition coming into play. Until recently, all superpremium ice cream and frozen yogurt makers had roughly equivalent prices for their products. But Haagen-Dazs, the "sleeping giant" that allowed Ben & Jerry's to gain market share at its expense during the late 1980s, recently awakened and began "throwing dollars and incentives at the marketplace."

Haagen-Dazs is much larger than Ben & Jerry's and is capable of waging a significant price war without fear of any lasting harm. The result was 2-for-1 sales and discounts in certain parts of the country. Ben & Jerry's guardedly followed suit with price discounts and store coupons for $1.49 pints, recognizing that the battle had become primarily financial.

Promotion

Ben & Jerry's product promotion relies primarily on cause-generated marketing. It is the company's belief that marketing should not be performed simply to sell the product, but to have an effect on society. This marketing theory is called "Edible Activism."

The company's cause-related events included such things as traveling vaudeville shows in buses with solar-powered freezers—the more unconventional and politically correct, the better. The largest part of Ben & Jerry's promotion budget goes to major music festivals around the country, including the Newport Folk Festival in Rhode Island. In addition, the company's own plant is the largest tourist attraction in Vermont, hosting 275,000 visitors annually; thus, just by opening its own doors, Ben & Jerry's is promoting its products.

The company's socially conscious practices also earned it regular publicity, thereby saving it millions in public expenditures annually. As Ben once said, "The media can supply the ink and Ben & Jerry's will supply the wackiness."

Responsibility for marketing is not farmed out to outside design and advertising firms. Rather, the company maintains control of this function in-house. In March 1994, for example, Ben & Jerry's created its first 30-second commercial to sell its new Smooth, No Chunks flavors; directed by Spike Lee, the ad featured socially minded stars who received nothing but a lifetime supply of ice cream for their efforts. The $6 million campaign to launch the line also included print ads featuring high-profile activists such as Carlos Santana, Bobby Seal, and Pete Seeger.

As competitive pressures increased and market growth slowed, Ben & Jerry's was forced to reexamine its exclusive use of socially oriented promotion. Many publicity events were abandoned so that funds could be diverted to promotional priorities such as store coupons and price discounts. While apparently rational, such a shift also garnered criticism that the company was simply using the "world's ills and social needs to sell a product."

OPERATIONS

In February 1995, Ben & Jerry's had two manufacturing plants located in Waterbury and Springfield, Vermont; its St. Albans plant, whose opening had been delayed several times, was scheduled to come on line in the second half of 1995. The company's main factory, in Waterbury, is located just over the hill from company headquarters, and generally operates two shifts a day, six days a week. Production averages about 4.7 million gallons a year. The Springfield plant is used for the production of ice cream novelties, bulk ice cream and frozen yogurt, and packaged pints; its production averages about 1.2 million dozen novelties, 2.3 million gallons of bulk ice cream and frozen yogurt, packaged pints and quarters per year. It, too, operates six days a week. Overall, the company has a maximum manufacturing capacity at its own facilities of about 10.2 million gallons per year of packaged pints.

During 1992 and 1993, Ben & Jerry's increased its manufacturing capacity to support its phenomenal sales growth. After a surge in sales in the winter of 1991, the company added pint production lines at its Springfield plant and at the St. Albans Cooperative Creamery, in space loaned to the company by the site's family farmer owners.

The new St. Albans plant has a maximum ice cream and yogurt production capacity of about 17 million gallons per year when operated six days a week. It was built with energy-efficient lighting, motors, and compressors to reduce the total amount of energy required for production. At the same time, Ben & Jerry's invested $2 million in the Waterbury plant to improve efficiency. In the early 1990s the company was fined for dumping too much waste into the Waterbury system; since then, it launched a pilot cleanup product using a solar greenhouse to treat sewage.

The production equipment used at Ben & Jerry's is not highly efficient; in fact, the only new machine added in recent years is a wrapping machine, which replaced an antiquated predecessor. The company felt that increased automation might eliminate jobs, which would undermine its philosophy of social responsibility. In discussing the labor-intensive nature of the packaging line, the company stated that it would choose versatility over speed, should the choice be necessary. Executives admitted that there were several faster machines available than what they currently used: It took the company about two hours to change from one size packaging capability to another.

Until the new plant was finished, Ben & Jerry's had a manufacturing and warehouse agreement with Edy's Grand Ice Cream, a subsidiary of Dreyer's Grand Ice Cream Inc., to manufacture certain pint ice cream flavors at its plant in Fort Wayne, Indiana. The agreement was in accordance with Ben & Jerry's quality control specifications, and used dairy products shipped from Vermont. About 5 million gallons, or 40 percent of the packaged pints, were manufactured under this agreement in 1994, compared with about 37 percent in 1993. For 1995, the company expected it to be 2 million gallons.

HUMAN RESOURCES

Since its inception, Ben & Jerry's has been managed entrepreneurially by Ben and Jerry and "built on the cult of these two counter-cultural personalities." As the company grew to almost 600 employees, the challenge was to maintain the original spirit while managing an increasingly large organization.

The key to Ben & Jerry's human resources success is keeping employees at all levels involved in the decision making. The company attempts to create ownership at all levels and follows the New Age management model of worker empowerment. Because they have the power to make decisions and influence how things were done, employees are energized and committed.

Of course as the company grew, it became difficult to preserve the small company atmosphere in which people matter amid the firm's transformation into an immense corporate entity. Both Ben and Jerry receive considerable praise from those inside as well as outside the company for their efforts to achieve this, and are viewed by many as the company's two biggest assets.

At the same time, however, there are those who criticize the company for "not walking its talk" in terms of employee treatment. Despite the firm's much hailed and publicized politically correct culture, for instance, employees nonetheless hold less than half of one percent of company stock. And while Ben and Jerry frequently drew attention to the fact that their own salaries are a relatively paltry $130,000 per year, they failed to note that their combined stock is worth in excess of $50 million.

Finally, known for occasionally getting bored with the daily grind and going off on some sabbatical, Ben and Jerry do not enjoy an untarnished reputation on Wall Street. The company's stock consistently underperforms the market and irritates many investors, largely as a result of the firms' insistence on putting its principles—the promotion of charity, peace, and environmental preservation—ahead of its public shareholders.

The benefits offered to employees at the company are widely regarded as cutting edge. Tuition reimbursement, flexible spending accounts, opinion surveys, evaluate-your-boss polls, paid health club fees, 12 unpaid weeks of maternity, paternity, and adoption leave, child care centers, free body and foot massages, sabbatical leave, profit sharing, paid adoption expenses, wellness plans, an insurance plan covering unmarried heterosexual and homosexual domestic partners, and free ice cream are among the offerings employees have. Ben & Jerry's management also reflects a commitment to minorities and women: Of the five senior positions filled in 1990, four were women or minorities.

Minimum wage at Ben & Jerry's is $8 per hour. While top salaries were capped at roughly $150,000 (the sum earned in 1993 by Charles Lacy, president and COO), that policy was abandoned with the hiring of Holland. Nevertheless, while the average per capita income of Vermont residents was $17,436, the lowest paid employee at Ben & Jerry's earned salary and benefits worth roughly $22,000.

Not surprisingly, the result of all its attention to employees has earned Ben & Jerry's a generally happy workforce; its turnover rate is only 12 percent.

THE CHALLENGE

When Robert Holland took the helm as CEO, Ben & Jerry's future direction was far from clear. While the company built its success by selling high-fat ice creams to consumers who were willing to pay more for the unique flavors and for Ben & Jerry's social causes, those days are gone. Health concerns, increased competition, pressure on prices and its own massive size suggest that Ben & Jerry's had to change. For Holland, the question is not "if" but "how."

EPILOGUE

After the highly publicized and unusual search and hiring process for Ben & Jerry's new CEO, Robert Holland, another change is in the offing. Robert Holland announced his resignation from the CEO position effective October 31, 1996. Holland had been CEO for only two years but stated that he had taken the firm as far as he could.

Earnings were down from the previous year as Ben & Jerry's faced increasing competition and challenges in marketing its products. While the stock price reached a high of $20.00 per share in 1995, the share price closed at $12.50 on the day of Holland's resignation announcement. Holland stated that the firm now needs a CEO with expertise in consumer products. Unfortunately, because of the slowing sales and marketing problems, large investors (e.g., institutional investors) have been unloading their holdings in Ben & Jerry's.

SELECTED SOURCES

Allen, Robin Lee. "Demographics Changing, Shaping Industry." *Nation's Restaurant News,* October 28, 1991, p. 42.

Annual Report, Ben & Jerry's Homemade Inc.

"Ben & Jerry's: A Firm with a View." *Packaging Digest,* January 1993, p. 50.

"Ben & Jerry's Finally Scoops Up New CEO." *The Chicago Tribune,* February 2, 1995, p. 1.

"Ben & Jerry's Names Cream of the Crop." *The Washington Post,* February 2, 1995, p. D11.

"Ben & Jerry's Projecting Loss for Fourth Quarter." *Ice Cream Reporter,* January 20, 1995, p. 1.

"Ben, Jerry Losing Their Values?" *The Washington Times,* June 27, 1994, p. A17.

Bittman, Mark. "Ben & Jerry's Caring Capitalism." *Restaurant Business Magazine,* November 20, 1990, p. 132.

Britt, Bill. "Haagen-Dazs Pushes Cold Front Across World." *Marketing (UK),* October 4, 1990, pp. 30–31.

Bryant, Adam. "Ding-a-Ling Marketing; an Ice Cream Truck Not Just for Kids." *The New York Times,* August 21, 1992, p. 3.

Calta, Marialisa, "Ice Cream Sorcerer." *The New York Times,* March 21, 1993, p. 66.

Carlin, Peter. "Pure Profit; For Small Companies That Stress Social Values as Much as the Bottom Line, Growing Up Hasn't Been an Easy Task." *The Los Angeles Times,* February 5, 1995, p. 12.

Carton, Barbara. "A Ben & Jerry's Principle Hits a Melting Point; Seeking New CEO, Firm To Scrap Pay Ceiling." *The Boston Globe,* June 14, 1994, p. 1.

Collins, Glenn. "Ben & Jerry's Talent Hunt Ends." *The New York Times,* February 2, 1995, p. D1.

Feder, Barnaby J. "Ben Leaving as Ben & Jerry's Chief." *The New York Times,* June 14, 1994, p. D1.

Forseter, Murray. "Ben & Jerry's Caring Capitalism." *Chain Store Age Executive with Shopping Center Age,* December 1991, p. 12.

Glassman, James K. "Inside Scoop." *The Washington Post,* June 19, 1994, p. H1.

Henriques, Diana B. "Ben & Jerry's—and Dreyer's?" *The New York Times,* June 16, 1991, p. 27.

Hitchner, Earl. "We All Scream for Ice Cream; Ben and Jerry's Homemade Inc. *National Productivity Review,* December 22, 1994, p. 114.

Horwich, Andrea. "Ice Cream Still America's Favorite Dessert?" *Dairy Foods,* August 1990, p. 42.

Hwang, Suein L. "Marketscan: While Many Competitors See Sales Melt, Ben & Jerry's Scoops Out Solid Growth." *The Wall Street Journal,* May 25, 1993, p. 1.

"Ice Cream Firm Names New CEO; Ben & Jerry's Uses Traditional Search." *The Houston Chronicle,* February 2, 1995, p. 2.

"The Ice Cream Market Grows Up." *Frozen and Chilled Foods,* April 1992, p. 25.

Katz, David M. "How Ben & Jerry's Mingles Conscience with Profit Motive." *Property & Casualty/Risk & Benefits Management Edition,* June 3, 1991, p. 9.

Kuhn, Mary Ellen. "Ben & Jerry's Suffers Some Growing Pains; Ben & Jerry's Homemade Inc." *Food Processing,* September 1994, p. 56.

Laabs, Jennifer J. "Ben & Jerry's Caring Capitalism; Ben & Jerry's Homemade Inc." *Personnel Journal Optimas Award,* November 1992, p. 20.

LaFranchi, Howard. "Haagen Dazs Invades Europe, Sans Bowl." *The Christian Science Monitor,* August 19, 1993, p. 7.

Lager, Fred "Chico." *Ben & Jerry's: The Inside Scoop.* New York: Crown Publishers, 1994.

Larrabbe, Kathryn. "Ben Cohen Runs a Business with a Mission." *Business Insurance,* T27, April 1990.

Linsen, Mary Ann. "Slow Going for Ice Cream." *Progressive Grocer,* March 1991, p. 117.

Lowery, Mark. "Sold on Ice Cream." *Black Enterprise,* April 1995, p. 60.

Mann, Ernest J. "Ice Cream, Part 1." *Dairy Industries International,* July 1991, p. 15.

Manor, Robert. "Ben, Jerry Aren't Above Making a Profit." *Star Tribune,* July 5, 1994, p. 6B.

Maremont, Mark. "Say It Ain't So, Ben & Jerry." *Business Week,* June 13, 1994. p. 6.

Maremont, Mark. "They're All Screaming for Haagen Dazs." *Business Week,* October 14, 1991, p. 121.

Mathews, Jay. "Ben & Jerry's Melting Social Charter; Ice Cream Maker Abandons Progressive Pay Policy to Find New CEO." *The Washington Post,* June 14, 1994, p. D3.

"More than an Ice Cream . . . Ben & Jerry's Is Social Responsibility." *Chain Store Age Executive,* August 1991, p. 81.

Norris, Floyd. "Market Place: Low-Fat Problem at Ben & Jerry's." *The New York Times,* September 9, 1982, p. 6.

O'Donnell, Claudia Dziuk. "The Story Behind the Story: Two Dairy Processors Tell a Tale of Fruits, Flavors and Nuts; Dean Foods Co.; Ben & Jerry's Homemade Inc." *Dairy Foods Magazine,* May 1993, p. 53.

Palmer, Thomas. "News in Advertising." *The Boston Globe,* November 11, 1990, p. A4.

Pandya, Mukul. "The Executive Life: Ice-Cream Dream Job Is Tempting Thousands." *The New York Times,* July 10, 1994, p.21.

Pereira, Joseph, and Joann S. Lublin. "Ben & Jerry's Appoints Holland President, CEO." *The Wall Street Journal,* February 2, 1995.

Rosenberg, John S. "Growing Pains: After a Remarkable Adolescence, Is Ben & Jerry's Settling into Middle Age?" *Vermont Magazine,* November–December 1993, p. 44.

Ryan, Nancy Ross. "Frozen Assets." *Restaurants & Institutions,* March 25, 1992, pp. 118–126.

Saulnier, John M. "Ice Cream Serves Up Sweetest Profits of All in Retail Frozen Food Cabinet." *Quick Frozen Foods International,* January 1992, p. 134.

Seligman, Daniel, and Patty de Llosa. "Ben & Jerry Save the World." *Fortune,* June 3, 1991, p. 247.

Shao, Maria. "A Scoopful of Credentials: CEO Holland Brings an Activist's Blend to Ben & Jerry's." *The Boston Globe,* March 1, 1995, p. 1.

Shao, Maria. "Ben & Jerry's Grows Up." *The Boston Globe,* July 3, 1994, p. 65.

Shao, Maria. "The New Emperor of Ice Cream." *The Boston Globe,* February 2, 1995, p. 35.

Smith, Geoffrey. "Life Won't Be Just a Bowl of Cherry Garcia." *Business Week,* July 18, 1994, p. 42.

Sneyd, Ross. "Ben & Jerry's Set to Appoint New CEO." *The Associated Press,* January 31, 1995.

Stableford, Joan. "Ben & Jerry's Sweetens Its Success by Helping Others." *Fairfield County Business Journal,* March 4, 1991, p. 1.

Wallace, Anne. "Ben Cohen to Step Down as CEO of Ben & Jerry's." *The Associated Press,* June 13, 1994.

Windle, Rickie. "Ben & Jerry's Creams Amy's." *Austin Business Journal,* October 4, 1993, p. 1.

"World Screams for America's Ice Cream." *The Christian Science Monitor,* September 28, 1990, p. 8.

CASE 8

Benecol

Raisio's Global Nutriceutical

Michael H. Moffett
Stacey Wolff Howard
Thunderbird, The American Graduate School of International Management

The discovery and launch of a revolutionary new margarine—Benecol—scientifically proven to cut cholesterol without known side-effects, has transformed Raisio into the hottest stock on the Finnish stock exchange. When Benecol was launched in Finland early in 1996, it sold out quickly, even though it cost seven times more than ordinary margarine. As talk of "miracle margarine" began to filter out of Finland, Raisio's slumbering share price jumped. It has risen 16-fold since Benecol's launch, helped by a surge of foreign ownership. Overseas investors held 10 percent of the shares at the start of 1996. Today the proportion is 63 percent.

"Benecol's Spread of Riches,"
The Financial Times, July 9, 1998.

The share price of Raisio Oy, a Finnish grain and chemicals company, had recently exhibited all the characteristics of a roller-coaster ride. The ride up had been on the back of Benecol *neutriceutical,* a human nutrient-based product with pharmaceutical qualities. The firm had rolled out its new margarine product in Finland under the patented Benecol name in November 1995 with enormous success and fanfare. Sales had grown rapidly, but global interest in both Raisio and Benecol had grown even faster. The share price had skyrocketed, rising from 6.2 Finnish marks (FIM) in December 1995 to 64.7 in December 1997. Kenza Medici, food and pharmaceutical analyst for Sinagua Capital, had picked and promoted Raisio.

But 1998 had proved difficult for both Raisio and Kenza. The share price continued upward in the spring with the signing of an international licensing agreement with the U.S. consumer and pharmaceutical conglomerate, Johnson & Johnson (J&J). But forces out of Raisio's control inflicted severe damage to the firm's earnings potential in late summer and early fall. First, two of Raisio's four major business units had been seriously hit by the Russian economic and financial collapse in August. Both the margarine and grain divisions were expected to end the year at a loss. The second hit was worse: the U.S. Food and Drug Administration (FDA) blocked J&J's McNeil Consumer Products Group from test-marketing Benecol in the United States. All bets on earnings for Benecol-based products were off. As 1998 drew to a close, Kenza revisited her valuation of Raisio.

RAISIO OY

The Raisio Group was a Finnish foodstuffs, animal feed, paper, and chemicals conglomerate. Founded in 1939, Raisio had grown from a single flour mill to a FIM4.9 billion firm in 1997 ($912 million at FIM5.37/$) with more than 2,800 employees working in 17 countries. Raisio characterized its various business lines as being linked by their common input—renewable natural resources—and took pride in its continued investment in research, innovation, and development. Raisio's strategy was to improve the quality, reduce the cost, increase the availability, and expand the uses of all products in its value chain.

Sales growth and profitability at Raisio had been quite volatile in the 1990s. As illustrated by Exhibit 1,

Copyright © 1999 Thunderbird, The American Graduate School of International Management. All rights reserved. This case was prepared by Professor Michael H. Moffett and Stacey Wolff Howard for the purpose of classroom discussion only, and not to indicate either effective or ineffective management.

the turnover of the traditional business lines of Raisio, heavily chemical and foodstuff in composition, had grown rapidly in 1992 and 1993, falling dramatically in 1994 and 1995, only to resume a rapid growth path in 1996 and 1997. Sales growth for 1998 was expected to be flat. That was, however, before Benecol. Although Benecol's actual sales were not yet significant, contributing only 2 percent of total Group sales in 1997, the earnings potential for the product globally was thought to be enormous. The growth in corporate earnings and prospects in 1996 and 1997 had led the share price to increase ten-fold.

Raisio first listed on the Helsinki Stock Exchange in 1989. Raisio's free shares of the parent company (Series V) are quoted on the Helsinki Exchanges (RAIVV) and the firm's restricted shares (Series K) on the brokers' list (RAIKV). Restricted shares of the company, limited to qualified buyers according to the firm's Articles of Association, possess 20 votes per share, while the free shares, sold to all buyers (both domestic and foreign), possess one vote per share. Acquisition of restricted shares must be approved by the firm's Board of Directors, with the exception of that by Finnish citizens. Both kinds of shares were entitled to equal amounts of profits.

BENECOL

Raisio's scientists had started searching for a cholesterol-decomposing food product in the late 1980s. The firm's knowledge and background in wood- and plant-based sterols led it to believe it could be found (the potential for plant sterols to inhibit cholesterol absorption was known as early as 1950). Raisio became the first to successfully isolate and manufacture *stanol ester,* a by-product of wood and vegetable pulping. *Stanol ester* had been shown in clinical trials in Finland to reduce total blood serum cholesterol in the human blood stream by up to 15 percent. Benecol could be ingested from within a product like margarine and actually inhibit cholesterol absorption.

Fats (lipids) are generally insoluble in water. Lipids are therefore transported through the human blood stream via proteins—lipoproteins—that are water soluble. Water-soluble lipoproteins are classified according to density, and fall into three primary categories: very low-density lipoproteins (VLDL), a relatively rare complex; low-density lipoproteins (LDL), often termed "bad cholesterol," making up roughly 60 percent of the average cholesterol in the human blood stream; and high-density lipoproteins (HDL), "good cholesterol," which transport excess cholesterol from the body's cells to the liver for excretion. It was Benecol's impact on LDL which was of value.

The human digestive tract receives cholesterol from two sources, ingested food and the body itself. Once cholesterol enters the digestive tract, roughly half is eliminated and half is absorbed by the body. *Stanol ester,* the active ingredient in Benecol, inhibits the body's abil-

EXHIBIT 1 | Selected Financial Results, The Raisio Group (million Finnish marks)

	1992	1993	1994	1995	1996	1997
Turnover (sales)	3,070	3,549	3,518	3,224	3,928	4,947
Percent change	33%	16%	−1%	−8%	22%	26%
Profit before extraordinary items	158	199	165	141	166	209
Percent of sales	5.1%	5.6%	4.7%	4.4%	4.2%	4.2%
Return on equity (ROE)	14.6%	19.7%	10.8%	7.5%	4.5%	7.8%
Return on investment	15.5%	13.5%	11.1%	9.2%	9.2%	10.1%
Share price (eoy), FIM	40.3	83.9	70.2	61.9	280.0	647.0
Earning per share (EPS)	8.0	11.0	9.4	6.2	6.0	10.0
Price/EPS ratio	5.0	7.6	7.5	10.0	46.7	64.7

Source: The Raisio Group and Handelsbanken Share price and EPS on a pre-split basis. The Raisio Group approved a 10 to 1 split in June 1998.
eoy = end-of-year.

ity to absorb this cholesterol. Specifically, it reduces the body's absorption of LDL, which the body compensates for by increasing its own production of cholesterol. The net result is a reduction in LDL, a reduction in VLDL (a precursor to some LDL), leaving the levels of good cholesterol (HDL) unchanged. Clinical studies in Finland indicated that total blood serum cholesterol was reduced by 10 percent and LDL reduced by 15 percent.[1]

Benecol—the margarine product—was launched in November 1995 in Finland. Though the product was initially priced at about seven times the average margarine product, store shelves were emptied in days. Although hoping for such success, Raisio had not anticipated the level of demand. Nearly a year passed before sufficient quantities for stanol ester could be produced to meet the Benecol product demands simply within Finland itself.

DEVELOPING A GLOBAL STRATEGY

Time was the critical element. Raisio had a unique product with enormous market potential, but, if it could not be brought to the global market quickly, competitors would succeed in reaping many of the gains from Raisio's long and expensive research and development process.[2] Unilever already was thought to be nearing a very similar product. Time to penetrate the global market was running short. Tor Bergman, Director of the Benecol Division, estimated Raisio had an 18- to 24-month lead on the competition. The problem, however, was that Raisio had little experience with a business line like that of Benecol.

In late 1996, Raisio had formed a 12-person panel to aid in formulating a five-year development plan for Benecol. The panel, comprising current and former executives from Nestlé, Kraft, and Heinz, among others, provided valuable insights into food products that Raisio did not possess. Together, they worked to develop an understanding of the potential Benecol value-chain, and where Raisio should position itself in the chain. The resulting strategy focused on international licensing, requiring Raisio to find a global partner for market penetration. Raisio itself, however, would maintain the control of stanol ester production, which was consistent with the company's traditional core businesses.

Raisio, as a result of its determination to maintain productive control over stanol ester, launched a global effort both to increase production of stanol ester (esterification) and to secure increasing supplies of stanol ester's primary component, plant sterol. In addition to the existing production facility in Finland, four new sterol production facilities were now under construction: in France with a joint-venture partner, DRT; in Chile via a joint venture (named Detsa S.A.) with one of Chile's largest private companies, Harting S.A.; in the United States via a joint venture with Westvaco Corporation in Charleston, South Carolina; and a second facility in Finland itself. Even with this build-up in production capacity, if the global distribution of Benecol was anywhere near as successful as thought possible, there would be insufficient production capacity of stanol ester.

THE J&J AGREEMENTS

Johnson & Johnson's McNeil Consumer Products group had proposed a comprehensive production, promotion, and distribution strategy. Kenza, like all segment ana-

EXHIBIT

2 | Margarine Prices in Finland (August 1998, per 250-gm container)

Margarine Brand	FIM	US$
Benecol	24.90	4.61
Becel (reduced cholesterol)	4.94	0.91
Keiju (table margarine)	3.33	0.62
Flora (table margarine)	4.06	0.75
Soila (table margarine)	2.88	0.53

Note: U.S. dollar prices at FIM5.40/US$

lysts, had pieced together what she could find out (neither Raisio nor McNeil was talking). First, J&J would purchase all stanol ester from Raisio. Second, it would make a number of lump-sum payments to Raisio, *milestone* payments, based on unspecified product or sales goals. Third, J&J would pay Raisio a royalty on sales of all products containing Benecol. Kenza was unsure of the exact royalty rate; it was also unclear whether the milestone payments were payable only upon specific stanol ester capacity or upon the attainment of production goals. Kenza did know that royalties were to be based on the final product retail price, not on the cost or internal transfer price associated with the stanol ester input. Although the milestone payments were thought to be substantial in 1998 and 1999, they were expected to quickly become minor in magnitude relative to the royalty payments arising from J&J's prospective global sales (see Appendix 2 for additional detail).

McNeil's proposed product strategy included the introduction of two different varieties of Benecol margarine and a line of four Benecol-based salad dressings, all to be introduced by March of 1998.[3] In January of 1999, McNeil would introduce boxes of 21 individually wrapped servings of light and regular margarine containing Benecol. The four Benecol-based salad dressings, 8-ounce bottles of French, Creamy Italian, Russian, and Thousand Island, would retail for $5.99 per bottle.[4] This was a significant price increase over normal salad dressings, and reflected the underlying product strategy shared by Raisio and McNeil: low population penetration rates with high margin product sales. Raisio estimated that approximately 40 percent of the Finnish population had tried Benecol, and 3.5 percent of the population continued to use the product on a regular basis. The product-packaging and marketing strategy was to use the green coloration or *better-for-you products* to help rationalize the higher prices.

In addition to the product commitment was the promotional commitment: McNeil had slated over US$80 million in national television, print, radio, and free-standing inserts (FSIs) to promote the new product lines, in addition to substantial educational promotions for doctors and pharmacists. Saatchi & Saatchi had been retained to handle the advertising campaign. The promotional campaign would combine the general health benefits of Benecol usage with an explicit recommendation to use Benecol three times per day to lower cholesterol (hence the individually wrapped servings). McNeil, a firm with extensive experience in healthcare-based product promotion and distribution, planned to use retail brokers to get the products into supermarket and grocery chains.

Raisio signed an exclusive North American marketing rights agreement with J&J in July of 1997 (the United States, Canada, and Mexico), and a similar global marketing agreement in March 1998.[5] In June 1998, the share price reached its peak at just over FIM1,000 (pre-split basis). The strategic plan was to introduce Benecol in the United States and Continental Europe in 1999, followed by Japan in 2000. Raisio moved quickly to assure adequate production capacity of stanol ester was available in the United States and Europe for 1999.

Exhibit 3 depicts the Benecol value-chain and Raisio's now assembled corporate partners. Raisio wished to focus the majority of its actual equity interest and control in the middle phase, the production of stanol esters, and partner with those possessing existing capabilities and resources for the initial sterol supply and final Benecol production and distribution.

POTENTIAL COMPETITORS

One potential competitive product was under development by Unilever, trade-named *New Flora*, but slated for U.S. distribution by Unilever's Lipton subsidiary as *Take Control*. Although Unilever planned to introduce *Take Control* as a cholesterol-reducing margarine, it was actually *sterol ester*, not a *stanol ester*. Sterol esters are also colorless, odorless, and fat-soluble, but clinical studies indicated LDL cholesterol reduction of only 7–8 percent. This was only half of that thought achievable by Benecol. A second, but potentially more serious, concern for Unilever was the possibility that some human bodies absorb sterol esters. Absorption could possibly lead to the development of arteriosclerosis. Benecol, a stanol ester, was not subject to absorption. Analysts expected Unilever to introduce *New Flora* to the European Union's (EU) regulatory process sometime in early 1999, but given its potential side-effects of absorption, the timing of regulatory approval was uncertain. The primary ad-

3 | The Benecol Value-Chain and Raisio's Corporate Partners

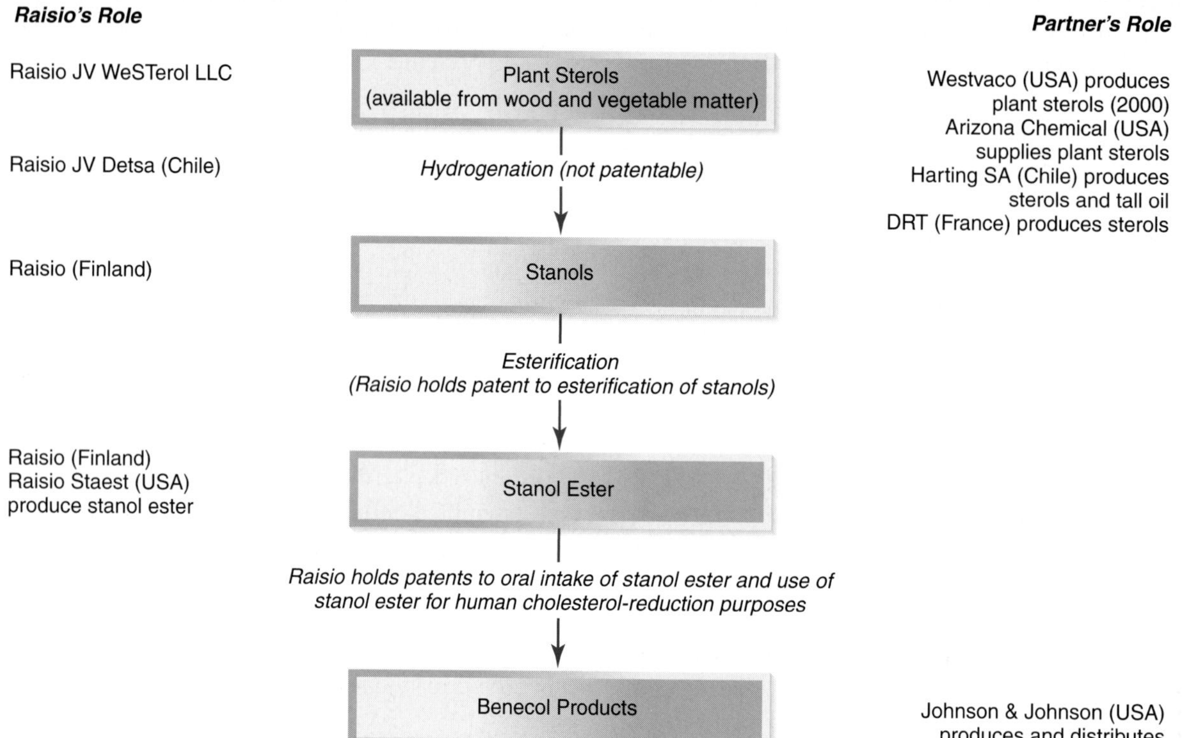

vantage to Unilever was its well-established brand name in Europe.

A number of other competitive products were also on the horizon. Forbes Medi-Tech, a Vancouver-listed firm, was studying the possibility of marketing *CardioRex,* a blend of plant sterols derived from wood pulp. Novartis, a Swiss-based pharmaceutical firm, had taken an equity stake of C$7 million in Forbes in early 1998 to aid in the product's development and to position itself for potential global marketing. While *CardioRex* was thought to have some LDL cholesterol-reducing benefits and was relatively cheap to produce, its efficacy was still much less than Benecol. Like *New Flora,* it was based on sterol esters, which could be absorbed. Very limited clinical tests had been completed.

Monsanto Life Sciences (U.S.) was studying the possibility of extracting sterols from maize products, but the development process was still in its infancy. An added complexity for Monsanto in 1998 had been its preoccupation with its attempted merger with American Home Products (which failed). Fytokem (Canada) was rumored to be investigating extracting sterols from rapeseed oil, but no information was currently available on their success. Nabisco (U.S.) was similarly experimenting with sterol derivation from wheat.

Kenza and other analysts had concluded that Unilever posed the greatest competitive threat. Tor Bergman, Director of the Benecol Division, was quoted in the *Financial Times* as saying "Benecol patents will run 15–20 years. We are sleeping well at night."[6]

REGULATORY HURDLES

There were, however, substantial regulatory hurdles facing Benecol in both Europe and the United States.

Europe In Europe, functional foods like Raisio's Benecol and Unilever's *New Flora* were regulated by the

Novel Foods Regulation. In effect since May of 1997, it specified that *functional foods* must follow one of two potential regulatory development paths prior to commercial sale, a *fast-track process* or a *full-assessment track. Fast-track approval* was available to new functional foods which were "substantially equivalent to a counterparty," meaning that if the food was similar to other food products already in the marketplace, it could enter the EU market immediately. The local food authority of the member state in which the functional food's firm is established was still required to forward its opinion and relevant data to the central Novel Foods Commission in Brussels for approval. This would not likely apply to Benecol simply because it was the first nutriceutical of its kind. Benecol had been registered in Finland as a *dietary product,* according to both Finnish and European Union (EU) legislation.

Full-assessment track approval was a much more complex and time-consuming process. The representative member-state food authority must file an application with the Novel Foods Commission and submit a detailed report within 90 days of the application filing. This report was then distributed to all other 15 members states for evaluation, the results of which must be returned to the Commission within 60 days. If there were no substantial queries or objections, the Standing Committee of the Novel Commission could issue a permit for the food to be sold within the EU immediately. If, however, there were objections arising from the member states, the questions were referred back to the member state authority and the individual firm for evaluation and potential testing or explanation. The firm then resubmitted to the same permit process until all concerns were resolved.

Benecol might, however, fit through a regulatory loop-hole. Benecol had been sold in Finland since November 1995, meeting the food authority regulatory needs in Finland, an EU member state, *prior* to the inception of the Novel Foods Commission. It was possible that the Commission's authority did not apply, and Benecol would only need apply to each individual member state's food authority for commercial approval.

United States The regulatory process was different in the United States, and arguably more difficult. Benecol or McNeil Consumer Products had three basic paths: 1) *food-additive path;* 2) *pharmaceutical path,* and 3) *dietary-supplement path.*

1. **Food-additive path.** Acquiring approval directly from the Food and Drug Administration (FDA) for commercial sale of a food additive was a lengthy and costly process.[7] This process could, however, be superceded if the food was *generally regarded as safe* (GRAS). This standing could be acquired through the firm's own self-affirmation, in which it assembles a panel of independent experts that declares the product safe, and then informs the FDA of its findings. Barring any exceptional objections to submitted data and clinical studies, the product may be introduced commercially in 60 days.
2. **Pharmaceutical path.** Once approved as a pharmaceutical, Benecol could potentially be marketed in a variety of ways (as a drug, a food additive, or a dietary-supplement), giving substantial flexibility to exploiting its profit potential. It required, however, an arduous, costly, and time-consuming process of clinical testing. This would take several years.
3. **Dietary-supplement path.** This was by far the easiest and fastest of the three approval paths, although it represented a significant level of risk if questions arose over product properties or claims. To register Benecol as a dietary-supplement, the sponsoring firm must simply file a notification letter with the FDA 60 days prior to commercial rollout.[8] Firms would typically file complete data and clinical studies following the notification letter. The dietary supplement was not considered either a drug or a food under this path.

McNeil had chosen the third alternative, to introduce Benecol as a dietary supplement. This would allow the fastest route to market in order to maximize profit and market-growth opportunities. (Introduction of Benecol as a dietary supplement would not preclude a subsequent application as a pharmaceutical.) Although clearly the cheapest and most expeditious, this approach posed significant additional risks to Benecol's profit potential. Marketers would have to walk a fine line in outlining and promoting Benecol. Dietary supplements had traditionally been sold as pills, powders, and tonics. As a dietary supplement, it was unclear whether

McNeil could promote Benecol's cholesterol-reducing effects or its added benefits in reducing heart disease.

What troubled Kenza was the possibility that the dietary-supplement/food approach was leaving too much money on the table. If Raisio or Raisio's agent was able to guide Benecol through the troubled waters of FDA approval as a pharmaceutical, it was possible that the value-margins could be substantially larger. On-going clinical tests were not only showing stronger and stronger cholesterol-reducing benefits, but also the clear competitiveness of Benecol with the cholesterol-reducing pharmaceuticals on the market.

The second question was whether Benecol would be promoted for the reduction of coronary heart disease (CHD). CHD, considered one of the top two or three causes of death in most industrialized countries, is principally caused by arteriosclerosis.[9] Arteriosclerosis is the condition in which *fibrous plaques,* fatty streaks, adhere to the walls of blood vessels. This reduces blood flow to the brain and heart. These fibrous plaques are created when free radicals (chemical compounds) cause LDL cholesterols to peroxidize (a process called *lipid peroxidization*). If the LDL levels in the blood serum are reduced, so are the probable levels of fibrous plaques.

The medical profession has tended to focus on three ways to reduce the risk of CHD: (1) reduction of serum cholesterol, via diet or medication; (2) stopping smoking; and (3) increased exercise, which not only encourages HDL cholesterol production but also reduces weight and stress. Reduction of serum cholesterol is considered fundamental to true risk-reduction. Benecol could potentially fall into a very discrete but valuable niche between a low cholesterol diet (the cheapest alternative) and prescribed pharmaceuticals (the most expensive).

FALL 1998 EVENTS

The August crisis in Russia greatly reduced the profitability of grain and margarine sales, dominated by Russian buyers. Raisio reported in October that Benecol sales in Finland were essentially flat, even with the introduction of a lighter version. This implied the new light product had simply replaced existing Benecol sales. Raisio's share price appeared to be headed toward a year-end close of FIM60.

One bit of good news had come from Dr. Tu T. Nguyen of the Mayo Clinic in Rochester, Minnesota, who reported in October that McNeil's slightly altered recipe of Benecol performs comparably to that studied and marketed in Finland. LDL concentrations were reduced by 14 percent on average. According to Nguyen, "we got the same response in eight weeks that [the Finnish study] got at one year."[10]

In late October, however, the FDA notified McNeil of its objections:

> *The purpose of this letter is to advise you that marketing this product with the prototype label that the agency was shown at the meeting would be illegal under the Federal Food, Drug and Cosmetic Act (FD&C Act). . . . The label for the Benecol spread, through statements that the product replaces butter or margarine, vignettes picturing the product in common butter and margarine uses, statements promoting the texture and flavour of the product, and statements such as ". . . help(s) you manage your cholesterol naturally through the food you eat," represents this product for use as a conventional food. Therefore, the product is not a dietary supplement.*

Kenza and other analysts had interpreted this to mean that if McNeil wished to distribute Benecol as a dietary supplement, it must be that—a *supplement*—and not a food like margarine (a yellow-colored *spread* applied to food much like butter or margarine).

Although it was known that the FDA and McNeil had a number of additional meetings in November, the impasse was still without official resolution. The FDA argued that Benecol in margarine form was a *food,* not a *dietary supplement.* And the FDA had the rights and responsibilities of regulating foods with additives which had not yet been approved as safe. Several analysts had speculated that if McNeil had introduced Benecol in tablet form, it would not have been a problem. McNeil countered FDA arguments with the contention that consumers were not likely to pay $16 a pound for a food (the planned price of the margarine product to be test-marketed). McNeil spokeswoman Amy Weiselman noted that this distinction makes Benecol "less a food substitute than a supplement delivered in the guise of a food."

Kellogg's, in a surprise announcement on November 2nd, unveiled a line of products under the *Ensemble* name containing psyllium, a cholesterol-reducing substance. *Ensemble* would include a variety of food products (cookies, bread, breakfast cereals, among others), and was already approved by the FDA to be marketed as a dietary supplement. Similar to Unilever's *Take Control,* cholesterol reduction was estimated at 8–9 percent, relative to Benecol's 10 percent. *Ensemble* was slated for a March 1999 launch.

RAISIO'S VALUATION REVISITED

The key to Raisio's value rested on both the global volume and value of Benecol sales. Given the timing delays of FDA approval and the entry of new competitors, forecasts for Benecol sales and Raisio's share price were all over the map. Kenza reviewed various analysts' opinions on Raisio's shares over the past year (Appendices 2 and 3), and returned to her own valuation (Appendices 4–11).

APPENDIX 1. REUTERS ITEM ON RAISIO

April 3, 1998. Credit Suisse First Boston (CFSB) has upped its 12-month target price for Finnish food, animal feeds and chemicals group Raisio to 1,200 markka from 900 markka in a report dated January 28. It said it is maintaining its buy recommendation on the stock because it expected the company's cholesterol reducing agent Benecol to get wider application in the second half of 1998.

"We are looking to announcements of Benecol subcontracts with food manufacturers during the second half of 1998," it said. CSFB said it believes there is a possibility of Benecol being launched in 1998 without full approval, with very limited medical claims.

"Assuming that the 2.5 percent market penetration could be reached after four years in every country, and that the total penetration of the western world could reach 3.5 percent in ten years, our model points to a stock-price target of FIM 1,200," it said. It forecast earnings per share of 10.9 markka in 1997, 20.7 markka in 1998 and 32.9 markka in 1999.

"If the product is a clear success once commercialization in large countries has started, we believe penetration rates could rise further and, as consequence, our target price could also rise," it said.

CSFB said Raisio would face competition from others trying to develop agents similar to Benecol, such as Swiss drug maker Novartis. Novartis agreement with Forbes Medi-Tech to have an exclusive option on a worldwide license to use Forbes' plant-based sterol composition, FCP, in nutritional products is a cheap way of entry into Benecol's potential market, it said.

"If Novartis succeeds in developing FCP with 'scientifically proven benefits,' we believe it will take a share of the market a few years from now," it said. This would, however, stimulate the cholesterol-lowering food market as a whole and therefore not be detrimental to Raisio, it added.

APPENDIX 2. A SURVEY OF INVESTMENT BANKERS' OPINIONS ON RAISIO

Analyst	Date of Analysis	Recommendation	Title	Current Price	12 Month Price
Credit Suisse	June 1998	Strong Buy		100	
First Boston	September 1998	Strong Buy		67	107.5–55
	October 21, 1998	Buy	"A Buoyant Market Before Birth"	84	107.5–55
	November 9, 1998	Upgrade to Strong Buy	"Market Overreaction"	50	107.5–50
	December 1998	Strong Buy		60	107.5–49.2
Merrill Lynch	October 6,1998	Neutral: Long Term Neutral		76	96
	October 20, 1998	Reduce: Long Term Neutral	"Cholesterol Klondike?"	91	76
	November 9, 1998	Neutral: Long Term Neutral		53	45
Dresdner Kleinwort	June 1998	Buy	"Benecol Goes from Strength to		
Benson	October 6, 1998	Buy (unchanged)	Strength"	96	135
			"Benecol Goes Pan-US on 7 January"	83	
Warburg Dillon	October 8, 1998	Buy	"It's Not Over Until the Fat Lady Sings"	82	57–108
Read	April 15, 1998	Buy	"Fear Not the Free Market"	90	175
Nordic Equities	October 14, 1998	Outperform/Medium Risk	"Unilever Meets the Misery of EU"	77	
	September 3, 1998	Outperform/High Risk	"Benecol Fears Overrated"	62	
Handelsbanken	December 1998	Reiterate Strong Buy	"Greasing for US Launch"	58	120

APPENDIX 3. RAISIO'S HISTORICAL PERFORMANCE

Millions of FIM	**1992**	**1993**	**1994**	**1995**	**1996**	**1997**
Turnover (Net Sales)	3,070	3,549	3,518	3,224	3,928	4,947
Percent change	33%	16%	−1%	−8%	22%	26%
Earnings Before Interest & Taxes	252	294	230	183	196	246
Percent change	5%	17%	−22%	−20%	7%	26%
Shares, Earnings & Dividends						
Average Shares Outstanding (000s):						
Free shares	4,447	4,626	7,060	9,174	10,690	11,709
Restricted shares	8,092	7,914	6,676	5,848	5,200	4,624
Total shares	12,539	12,540	13,736	15,022	15,890	16,333
Share Price (free shares):						
Share price, average (FIM)	29.40	69.54	101.65	59.25	228.01	497.65
Share price, December 31 (FIM)	40.33	82.32	69.98	61.48	290.81	646.82
EPS (FIM)	10.32	18.74	9.68	6.16	4.08	8.27
Dividend per share (FIM)	1.13	1.40	4.58	1.76	2.00	3.00
Price to Earnings Ratio free shares (PE)	3.9	4.4	7.2	10.0	71.2	78.2

APPENDIX 4. RAISIO'S BENECOL SALES IN FINLAND

Individual use of Benecol	Size (grams)	Stanol Ester (grams)	Price (FIM)	Daily Need (grams)	Days per Package	Price/day (FIM)		
One package of Benecol margarine	250.0	20.0	25.00	2.0	10.0	2.50		
Per kilogram	1,000.0	80.0	100.0	2.0	40.0	2.50		
Raisio's Finnish Market	**1998e**	**1999e**	**2000e**	**2001e**	**2002e**	**2003e**	**2004e**	**2005e**
Population: Finland	5,100,000	5,100,000	5,100,000	5,100,000	5,100,000	5,100,000	5,100,000	5,100,000
Penetration rate	3.50%	3.60%	3.70%	3.80%	3.90%	4.00%	4.00%	4.00%
Consumption population	178,500	183,600	188,700	193,800	198,900	204,000	204,000	204,000
Gross revenue per person per year (FIM)	912.50	912.50	912.50	912.50	912.50	912.50	912.50	912.50
Accruing to Raisio after distribution costs	593.13	593.13	593.13	593.13	593.13	593.13	593.13	593.13
Raisio's revenues in FIM	105,872,813	108,897,750	111,922,688	114,947,625	117,972,563	120,997,500	120,997,500	120,997,500
Sales price, Benecol margarine (FIM/kg)	100	100	100	100	100	100	100	100
Less distribution costs	35	35	35	35	35	35	35	35
Net revenue accruing to Raisio (FIM/kg)	65	65	65	65	65	65	65	65
Cost of margarine input per kg	10	10	10	10	10	10	10	10
Cost of stanol ester input	27	22	20	15	15	15	15	15
Total cost of inputs in Benecol per kg	37	32	30	25	25	25	25	25
Raisio's gross profit per kg of Benecol	28	33	35	40	40	40	40	40
Gross margin	43%	51%	54%	62%	62%	62%	62%	62%
Raisio's costs of Benecol (FIM)	60,266,063	53,611,200	51,656,625	44,210,625	45,374,063	46,537,500	46,537,500	46,537,500

APPENDIX 5. RAISIO'S GLOBAL MARKET PENETRATION

Individual use of Benecol	Size (grams)	Stanol Ester (grams)	Price (FIM)	Daily Need (grams)	Days per Package	Price/day (FIM)
One package of Benecol margarine	250.0	20.0	25.00	2.0	10.0	2.50
Per kilogram	1,000.0	80.0	100.0	2.0	40.0	2.50

North America	**1998e**	**1999e**	**2000e**	**2001e**	**2002e**	**2003e**	**2004e**	**2005e**
North American population	284,000,000	284,000,000	284,000,000	284,000,000	284,000,000	284,000,000	284,000,000	284,000,000
NA penetration rate, all products	0.0%	1.0%	2.0%	2.5%	3.0%	3.5%	3.5%	3.5%
Benecol market share		70.0%	65.0%	60.0%	50.0%	40.0%	40.0%	40.0%
Benecol consumers		1,988,000	3,692,000	4,260,000	4,260,000	3,976,000	3,976,000	3,976,000
Retail price of Benecol, kilo (USD)	$20.00	$20.00	$20.00	$20.00	$20.00	$20.00	$20.00	$20.00
Gross revenue per person per year (USD)	$182.50	$182.50	$182.50	$182.50	$182.50	$182.50	$182.50	$182.50
Gross revenue, NA market (USD)		362,810,000	673,790,000	777,450,000	777,450,000	725,620,000	725,620,000	725,620,000
Distribution costs (% of retail)	30.0%	30.0%	30.0%	30.0%	30.0%	30.0%	30.0%	30.0%
Revenues accruing to J&J (USD)		253,967,000	471,653,000	544,215,000	544,215,000	507,934,000	507,934,000	507,934,000
European Union								
European population (EU11)	372,000,000	372,000,000	372,000,000	372,000,000	372,000,000	372,000,000	372,000,000	372,000,000
European penetration rate, all product		0.2%	0.5%	1.0%	1.5%	2.0%	2.5%	3.0%
Benecol market share		50.0%	45.0%	40.0%	40.0%	40.0%	40.0%	40.0%
Benecol consumers		372,000	837,000	1,488,000	2,232,000	2,976,000	3,720,000	4,464,000
Retail price of Benecol, kilo (USD)	$20.00	$20.00	$20.00	$20.00	$20.00	$20.00	$20.00	$20.00
Gross revenue per person per year (USD)	$182.50	$182.50	$182.50	$182.50	$182.50	$182.50	$182.50	$182.50
Gross revenue, EU market (USD)		67,890,000	152,752,500	271,560,000	407,340,000	543,120,000	678,900,000	814,680,000
Distribution costs (% of retail)	30.0%	30.0%	30.0%	30.0%	30.0%	30.0%	30.0%	30.0%
Revenues accruing to J&J (USD)		47,523,000	106,926,750	190,092,000	285,138,000	380,184,000	475,230,000	570,276,000
Japan								
Japanese population	126,000,000	126,000,000	126,000,000	126,000,000	126,000,000	126,000,000	126,000,000	126,000,000
Japanese penetration rate, all products			0.2%	0.4%	0.5%	0.8%	1.0%	1.5%
Benecol market share			100%	75%	50%	50%	50%	50%
Benecol consumers			252,000	378,000	315,000	504,000	630,000	945,000
Retail price of Benecol, kilo (USD)	$20.00	$20.00	$20.00	$20.00	$20.00	$20.00	$20.00	$20.00
Gross revenue per person per year (USD)	$182,50	$182,50	$182,50	$182,50	$182,50	$182,50	$182,50	$182,50
Gross revenue, Japanese market (USD)			45,990,000	68,985,000	57,487,500	91,980,000	114,975,000	172,462,500
Distribution costs (% of retail)	35.0%	35.0%	35.0%	35.0%	35.0%	35.0%	35.0%	35.0%
Revenue accruing to J&J (USD)			29,893,500	44,840,250	37,366,875	59,787,000	74,733,750	112,100,625

APPENDIX 6. RAISIO'S PROCEEDS FROM GLOBAL AGREEMENT WITH JOHNSON & JOHNSON

Individual use of Benecol	**Size (grams)**	**Stanol Ester (grams)**	**Price (FIM)**	**Daily Need (grams)**	**Days per Package**	**Price/day (FIM)**		
One package of Benecol margarine	250.0	20.0	25.00	2.0	10.0	2.50		
Per kilogram	1,000.0	80.0	100.0	2.0	40.0	2.50		
J&J Agreement: Royalties	**1998e**	**1999e**	**2000e**	**2001e**	**2002e**	**2003e**	**2004e**	**2005e**
Gross revenues, US market (USD)	—	362,810,000	673,790,000	777,450,000	777,450,000	725,620,000	725,620,000	725,620,000
Gross revenues, EU market (USD)	—	67,890,000	152,752,500	271,560,000	407,340,000	543,120,000	678,900,000	814,680,000
Gross revenues, Japanese market (USD)	—	—	45,990,000	68,985,000	57,487,500	91,980,000	114,975,000	172,462,500
Total revenues (USD)	—	430,700,000	872,532,500	1,117,995,000	1,242,277,500	1,360,720,000	1,519,495,000	1,712,762,500
Exchange rate (FIM/USD)	5.0000	5.0000	5.0000	5.0000	5.0000	5.0000	5.0000	5.0000
Revenue base for royalties (FIM)		2,153,500,000	4,362,662,500	5,589,975,000	6,211,387,500	6,803,600,000	7,597,475,000	8,563,812,500
Royalty rate to Raisio for Benecol products	5%	5%	5%	5%	5%	5%	5%	5%
Royalty payments to Raisio (FIM)	—	107,675,000	218,133,125	279,498,750	310,569,375	340,180,000	379,873,750	428,190,625
J&J Agreement: Stanol ester								
Sales price of stanol ester to J&J (FIM/tonne)	600	600	600	600	600	600	600	600
Cost price of stanol ester	300	244	222	167	167	167	167	167
Gross profit on stanol ester (FIM/tonne)	300	356	378	433	433	433	433	433
Gross margin	50%	59%	63%	72%	72%	72%	72%	72%
Stanol ester per person per year (kg)	0.730	0.730	0.730	0.730	0.730	0.730	0.730	0.730
Total consumers (US, EU, Japan)	—	2,360,000	4,781,000	6,126,000	6,807,000	7,456,000	8,326,000	9,385,000
Total stanol ester, kilograms		1,722,800	3,490,130	4,471,980	4,969,110	5,442,880	6,077,980	6,851,050
Total stanol ester, tons		1,723	3,490	4,472	4,969	5,443	6,078	6,851
Sales of stanol ester to J&J (FIM)	—	1,033,680	2,094,078	2,683,188	2,981,466	3,265,728	3,646,788	4,110,630
J&J Agreement: Milestone payments								
Payments to Raisio from J&J (FIM)	110,000,000	150,000,000	100,000,000	50,000,000				

APPENDIX 7. RAISIO'S DIVISION RESULTS (IN MILLIONS OF FIM)

Chemical division	1996	1997	1998e	1999e	2000e	2001e	2002e	2003e	2004e	2005e
Revenue	1,360	1,634	1,733	1,819	1,910	2,006	2,106	2,211	2,322	2,438
Revenue growth	24%	20%	6%	5%	5%	5%	5%	5%	5%	5%
EBIT	101	93	90	102	107	112	118	124	130	137
EBIT margin	7.4%	5.7%	5.2%	5.6%	5.6%	5.6%	5.6%	5.6%	5.6%	5.6%
Implied cost of sales	1,259	1,541	1,642	1,717	1,803	1,893	1,988	2,087	2,192	2,301
Margarine division										
Revenue	864	1,678	1,309	1,322	1,361	1,402	1,444	1,488	1,532	1,578
Revenue growth	45%	94%	–22%	1%	3%	3%	3%	3%	3%	3%
EBIT	12	106	7	20	27	35	43	45	46	47
EBIT margin	1.4%	6.3%	0.5%	1.5%	2.0%	2.5%	3.0%	3.0%	3.0%	3.0%
Implied cost of sales	852	1,572	1,302	1,302	1,334	1,367	1,401	1,443	1,486	1,531
Grain division										
Revenue	1,627	1,725	1,725	1,759	1,812	1,866	1,922	1,980	2,039	2,100
Revenue growth	45%	6%	0%	2%	3%	3%	3%	3%	3%	3%
EBIT	79	58	60	69	78	80	83	85	88	90
EBIT margin	4.9%	3.4%	3.5%	3.9%	4.3%	4.3%	4.3%	4.3%	4.3%	4.3%
Implied cost of sales	1,548	1,667	1,664	1,691	1,734	1,786	1,840	1,895	1,952	2,010
Benecol										
Revenue	—	99	216	368	432	447	432	464	505	553
Revenue growth	na	na	118%	70%	18%	3%	–3%	8%	9%	10%
Revenue summary										
Benecol	—	99	216	368	432	447	432	464	505	553
Chemicals	1,360	1,634	1,733	1,819	1,910	2,006	2,106	2,211	2,322	2,438
Margarine	864	1,678	1,309	1,322	1,361	1,402	1,444	1,488	1,532	1,578
Grain	1,627	1,725	1,725	1,759	1,812	1,866	1,922	1,980	2,039	2,100
Total Sales	3,851	5,136	4,982	5,268	5,516	5,721	5,904	6,143	6,398	6,670
Benecol	0%	2%	4%	7%	8%	8%	7%	8%	8%	8%
Chemicals	35%	32%	35%	35%	35%	35%	36%	36%	36%	37%
Margarine	22%	33%	26%	25%	25%	25%	24%	24%	24%	24%
Grain	42%	34%	35%	33%	33%	33%	33%	32%	32%	31%
Total Sales	100%	100%	100%	100%	100%	100%	100%	100%	100%	100%

APPENDIX 8. RAISIO'S PRO FORMA INCOME STATEMENT (MILLIONS OF FIM)

Year-end (December)	1996	1997	1998e	1999e	2000e	2001e	2002e	2003e	2004e	2005e
Benecol, Raisio's sales	—	69	106	109	112	115	118	121	121	121
Benecol, milestones	—	30	110	150	100	50	—	—	—	—
Benecol, stanol ester	—	—	—	1	2	3	3	3	4	4
Benecol, royalties	—	—	—	108	218	279	311	340	380	428
Benecol revenues	—	99	216	368	432	447	432	464	505	553
As percent of total	0%	2%	4%	7%	8%	8%	7%	8%	8%	8%
Chemicals	1,360	1,634	1,733	1,819	1,910	2,006	2,106	2,211	2,322	2,438
Margarine	864	1,609	1,309	1,322	1,361	1,402	1,444	1,488	1,532	1,578
Grain	1,627	1,725	1,725	1,759	1,812	1,866	1,922	1,980	2,039	2,100
Other income	77	68	—	—	—	—	—	—	—	—
Non-Benecol revenues	3,928	5,036	4,766	4,900	5,083	5,274	5,473	5,679	5,893	6,117
As percent of total	100%	98%	96%	93%	92%	92%	93%	92%	92%	92%
Total revenues	3,928	5,135	4,982	5,268	5,516	5,721	5,904	6,143	6,398	6,670
Percent growth	22%	31%	–3%	6%	5%	4%	3%	4%	4%	4%
Cost of sales	(3,535)	(4,604)	(4,277)	(4,356)	(4,472)	(4,596)	(4,770)	(4,950)	(5,139)	(5,335)
As % of Cost-Revenue	90.0%	92.1%	91.0%	90.0%	89.0%	88.0%	88.0%	88.0%	88.0%	88.0%
EBITDA	393	531	705	912	1,044	1,125	1,134	1,193	1,259	1,335
Gross margin	10.0%	10.3%	14.2%	17.3%	18.9%	19.7%	19.2%	19.4%	19.7%	20.0%
Depreciation	(212)	(229)	(249)	(263)	(276)	(286)	(295)	(307)	(320)	(333)
Goodwill amortization	(12)	(22)								
EBIT	169	281	456	648	768	839	839	886	940	1,002
Operating margin	4%	6%	10%	13%	15%	16%	15%	16%	16%	16%
Associates	3	10	12	12	12	12	12	12	12	12
Investment income & other	19	3	3	3	3	3	3	3	3	3
Net interest	(51)	(50)	(72)	(46)	(30)	(30)	(30)	(30)	(30)	(30)
EBT	140	244	399	618	753	824	825	872	925	987
Extraordinary income	(4)	(90)	—	—	—	—	—	—	—	—
Tax	(63)	(64)	(132)	(204)	(249)	(272)	(272)	(288)	(305)	(326)
Minorities	(8)	21	(9)	(10)	(10)	(10)	(10)	(10)	(10)	(10)
Net profit	66	110	258	404	495	542	542	574	610	651
EPS	0.40	0.67	1.57	2.44	3.00	3.28	3.28	3.48	3.69	3.94
Tax rate			33%	33%	33%	33%	33%	33%	33%	33%
Distribution rate	50%									
Dividends	32.76	55.22	129.24	201.89	247.36	271.13	271.23	286.96	304.79	325.59
Retained earnings	32.76	55.22	129.24	201.89	247.36	271.13	271.23	286.96	304.79	325.59

Notes:

1 "Cost-Revenue" refers to all revenues which possess actual production costs; it excludes milestone and royalty payments.

2 Cost of sales line item includes differing cost assumptions by the following categories: traditional product lines; stanol ester sales to J&J; Benecol sales by Raisio.

3 The line item "change in deferred tax liability" included in Raisio's Finnish income statement (just prior to net profit) is excluded here.

4 As a result of the differences between Finnish accounting standards and US GAAP, these 1996 and 1997 results may not match those reported by Raisio exactly.

5 Depreciation assumed to be 5% of sales throughout.

APPENDIX 9. RAISIO'S PRO FORMA BALANCE SHEET (MILLIONS OF FIM)

Year-end (December)	1996	1997	1998e	1999e	2000e	2001e	2002e	2003e	2004e	2005e
Cash & marketable securities	306	247	582	604	769	1,016	1,266	1,525	1,800	2,094
Receivables	677	668	682	722	756	784	809	842	876	914
Inventory	669	775	797	843	883	915	945	983	1,024	1,067
Current assets	1,652	1,690	2,062	2,168	2,407	2,715	3,020	3,350	3,700	4,075
Intangible	556	529	529	529	529	529	529	529	529	529
Net fixed assets	1,385	1,491	1,491	1,491	1,491	1,491	1,491	1,491	1,491	1,491
Investments	86	116	116	116	116	116	116	116	116	116
Total assets	3,679	3,826	4,198	4,304	4,543	4,851	5,156	5,486	5,836	6,211
Payables	431	450	498	527	552	572	590	614	640	667
Other creditors	347	617	498	474	441	458	472	491	512	534
Current liabilities	778	1,067	996	1,001	993	1,030	1,063	1,106	1,152	1,201
Total debt (long term)	928	988	800	700	700	700	700	700	700	700
Equity	1,098	1,611	1,740	1,942	2,189	2,461	2,732	3,019	3,324	3,649
Minorities & provisions	875	161	161	161	161	161	161	161	161	161
Total equity	1,973	1,772	1,901	2,103	2,350	2,622	2,893	3,180	3,485	3,810
Total liabilities & equity	**3,679**	**3,827**	**3,698**	**3,804**	**4,043**	**4,351**	**4,656**	**4,986**	**5,336**	**5,711**
Sales	3,928	5,135	4,982	5,268	5,516	5,721	5,904	6,143	6,398	6,670
Days sales outstanding	63	47	50	50	50	50	50	50	50	50
Inventory as % of sales	17%	15%	16%	16%	16%	16%	16%	16%	16%	16%
Payables days outstanding	40	32	40	40	40	40	40	40	40	40
As % of sales	11%	9%	10%	10%	10%	10%	10%	10%	10%	10%
Other credits % of sales	9%	12%	10%	9%	8%	8%	8%	8%	8%	8%

APPENDIX 10. RAISIO'S PRO FORMA STATEMENT OF CASH FLOWS (MILLIONS OF FIM)

Year-end (December)	1997	1998e	1999e	2000e	2001e	2002e	2003e	2004e	2005e
Net income	110	258	404	495	542	542	574	610	651
Add back depreciation	229	249	263	276	286	295	307	320	333
Add back goodwill amortization	22	—	—	—	—	—	—	—	—
Increases in A/R	9	(14)	(39)	(34)	(28)	(25)	(33)	(35)	(37)
Increases in stocks	(106)	(22)	(46)	(40)	(33)	(29)	(38)	(41)	(44)
Increases in A/P	19	48	29	25	21	18	24	25	27
Increases in credit	270	(119)	(24)	(33)	16	15	19	20	22
Other	(10)								
Operating cash flows	543	400	587	689	804	816	853	900	953
Capital expenditure	(106)	(249)	(263)	(276)	(286)	(295)	(307)	(320)	(333)
Investing cash flows	(106)	(249)	(263)	(276)	(286)	(295)	(307)	(320)	(333)
Dividends paid	(55)	(129)	(202)	(247)	(271)	(271)	(287)	(305)	(326)
Change in net debt	60	(188)	(100)	—	—	—	—	—	—
Financing cash flows	5	(317)	(302)	(247)	(271)	(271)	(287)	(305)	(326)
Cash (boy)	306	748	582	604	769	1,016	1,266	1,525	1,800
Change in cash flow	442	(166)	21	166	247	250	259	275	294
Cash (eoy)	748	582	604	769	1,016	1,266	1,525	1,800	2,094

APPENDIX 11. VALUATION OF THE RAISIO GROUP (MILLIONS OF FIM)

YEAR OF DCF		1	2	3	4	5	6	7	Terminal
Calendar Year	**1998**	**1999**	**2000**	**2001**	**2002**	**2003**	**2004**	**2005**	**Value**
EBIT	456	648	768	839	839	886	940	1,002	1,032
Less calculated taxes	(151)	(214)	(253)	(277)	(277)	(293)	(310)	(331)	(340)
EBIT after-tax	306	434	515	562	562	594	630	671	691
Plus depreciation	249	263	276	286	295	307	320	333	383
Less capital expenditure	(249)	(263)	(276)	(286)	(295)	(307)	(320)	(333)	(383)
Less added working capital	(107)	(80)	(82)	(28)	(29)	(30)	(32)	(34)	(34)
Free cash flows	198	354	433	534	533	564	598	637	657
Terminal value								**13,386**	
CFs for discounting		354	433	534	533	564	598	14,023	
Discount factor (WACC)		0.9267	0.8588	0.7958	0.7375	0.6834	0.6333	0.5869	
Discounted CF @ WACC		328	372	425	393	385	378	8,230	
Cumulative PV of cashflows	10,513								

Valuation

Firm value	10,513
Less debt	(800)
Equity value	9,713
Shares outstanding	165.15
Equity value per share	59

Note: Terminal Value makes up the following percentage of total valuation: 75%

FCF compound growth rate, 1999 to 2005: 10.3%

WACC calculation

Cost of equity	8.30%	Atx Cost of debt	4.36%	Debt	800	7%
Risk premium	4.00%	Borrowing rate	6.50%	Equity	10,239	93%
Beta for Raisio	1.00	Tax rate	33.0%	Firm Value	11,039	100%
Long bond (risk-free rate)	4.30%	L.T. growth	3.00%			
Current share price	62	Shares out (m)	165.15	WACC	7.91%	

Notes:

1. Recalculation of taxes on EBIT eliminates the tax shields associated with interest, which are in turn eventually included in the discounting by the WACC.
2. Depreciation and CAPEX are assumed equal into the future.

APPENDIX 12. RAISIO'S SHARE PRICE, 1993–1998 (FIM)

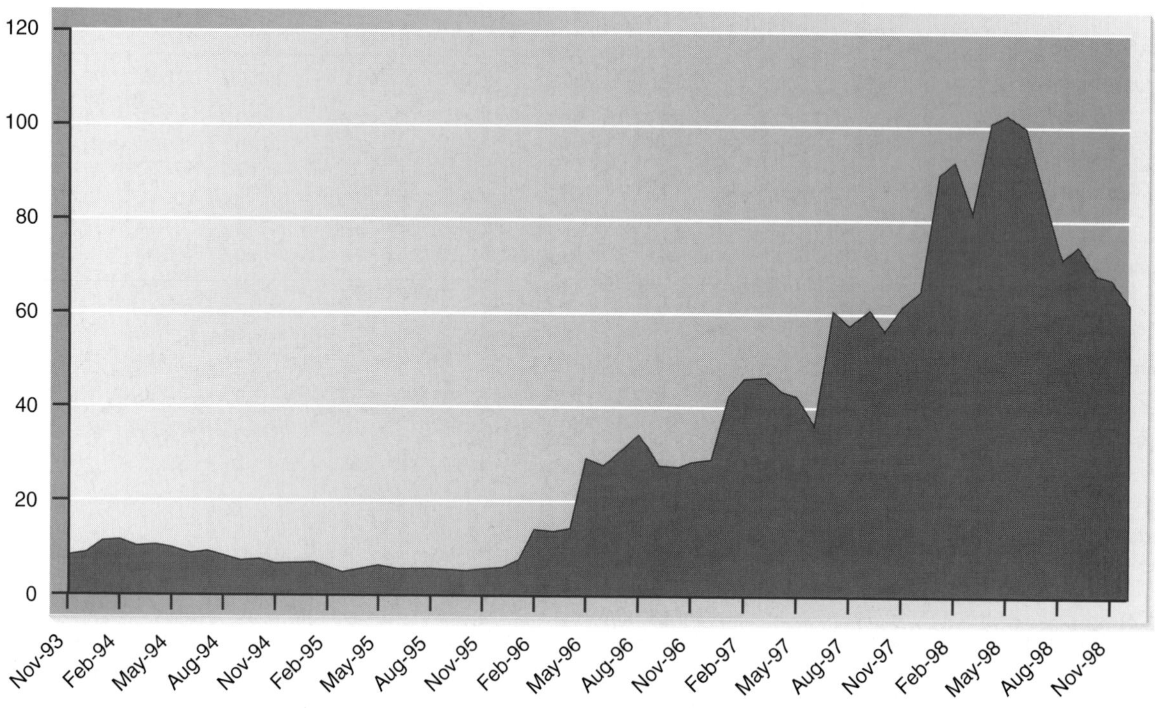

ENDNOTES

1. A study published in the *New England Journal of Medicine* (T. A. Miettinen, H. Gylling, H. Vanhanen, and E. Vartiainen, "Reduction of serum cholesterol with sitostanol-ester margarine in a mildly hyper-cholesterolemic population," *New England Journal of Medicine,* 1995, 333, 1308–1312) documented a 10 percent reduction in total blood-serum cholesterol levels and a 14 percent reduction in low-density lipoprotein (LDL) levels among Finnish consumers who used Benecol margarine regularly.
2. Raisio's U.S. patent for stanol ester, Benecol7, was initiated in 1992 and awarded in March 1996. The patent will expire in the year 2008, 17 years after the initiation of patent request protection.
3. McNeil planned to introduce a slightly altered form of Benecol which contained even more cholesterol-lowering mono-unsaturated fats and less cholesterol-raising saturated fats than the original Finnish version. Additional product deliveries of Benecol currently under study by J&J included mayonnaise and ice cream.
4. McNeil Loads Up $80M Warchest for Benecol," *Brandweek,* New York, October 5, 1998.
5. Although the J&J agreement provided specific detail over individual responsibilities, the partners agreed to share joint responsibilities on continuing clinical studies and product development.
6. "Benecol's Spread of Riches," *The Financial Times,* July 9, 1998.
7. For example, Johnson & Johnson received FDA approval in early 1998 for a product first submitted for direct FDA approval in 1987, 11 years earlier.
8. Although the U.S. Congress largely exempted dietary supplements from FDA regulation in 1994, the FDA still retained the right to pursue additional investigation and study at future dates if health questions arose.
9. The risk factors for coronary heart disease, in rank-order, are: 1. smoking; 2. serum cholesterol (LDL-based); 3. high blood pressure; 4. obesity; 5. lack of exercise; 6. stress; 7. sex at advancing age; 8. genetics.
10. *Science News,* November 14, 1998, Volume 154, Issue 20, p. 311.

CASE 9

The Boeing Company

The Merger with McDonnell Douglas

Isaac Cohen
San Jose State University

On December 10, 1996, Boeing CEO Philip Condit and McDonnell Douglas CEO Harry Stonecipher met in a hotel suite in Seattle to negotiate what *Fortune* magazine called "the sale of the century." Approved by both boards four days later, the merger of Boeing and McDonnell Douglas ended the longest running rivalry in the aerospace industry. Boeing offered McDonnell Douglas's shareholders a stock swap that amounted to a premium of 21 percent over the price of McDonnell stock on the New York Stock Exchange—the equivalent of $14 billion in company stock. McDonnell Douglas's shareholders readily accepted the offer.[1]

To Stonecipher, the merger with Boeing represented an opportunity. With only one-third of its revenues and almost no earnings derived from its commercial products, McDonnell Douglas's commercial aircraft business was fast declining. With the rapid consolidation of the defense business in the hands of a few large corporations (Lockheed Martin, Raytheon, Northrop Grumman, Boeing), coupled with the steady shrinkage of the defense budget, McDonnell Douglas's defense business was seriously threatened. To survive, McDonnell Douglas had to merge with other defense firms. Stonecipher, therefore, was faced with a difficult decision: Should McDonnell Douglas buy other defense businesses and pay a premium to the seller, or should it merge with the leading commercial aircraft maker and one of the largest defense companies and be paid a premium by the buyer? Clearly, the high premium offered by Boeing tipped the balance in favor of a Boeing-McDonnell Douglas merger. Following the deal Stonecipher became president of Boeing.[2]

To Condit, the takeover of McDonnell Douglas also represented an opportunity. Because the commercial aircraft industry was subject to deep cyclical movement of booms and busts, and because the demand for defense products was relatively stable, Boeing could have benefited from the acquisition of a major military aircraft maker. Recalling two major slumps in Boeing's history, Condit explained: "We found ourselves moving in a direction . . . of 80 percent commercial 20 percent defense and space, and at 20 percent, defense doesn't provide much pad for the next downturn on the commercial side."[3]

Condit acquired McDonnell Douglas just four months after he made a successful bid to purchase Rockwell's military and space division for $3.2 billion. He made both acquisitions during his first year at Boeing's helm. Departing from Boeing's long-standing tradition of relying on in-house expansion rather than outright acquisition,[4] Condit continued serving as Boeing CEO following the takeover of McDonnell Douglas.

Although top management at Boeing and McDonnell Douglas had been discussing the possibilities of a merger for nearly three years, Condit's decision represented a strategic gamble. Would the Boeing Aircraft Company gain or lose from the merger with McDonnell Douglas? Would the merger enhance Boeing's worldwide competitive position relative to Airbus Industrie (a consortium formed by aerospace firms in four

This case was presented in the October 1999 annual meeting of the North American Case Research Association at Santa Cruz, California. Copyright Isaac Cohen, 1999.

European countries), its only remaining rival? Or would it instead result in climbing costs and diminishing profits, stemming from the difficulties in integrating the two companies?

THE AEROSPACE INDUSTRY: COMMERCIAL AIRCRAFT

The structure of the commercial aircraft industry resembled that of a pyramid with a few airframe integrators at the top, dozens of primary subcontractors at the middle, and thousands of secondary subcontractors at the base. Subcontracting of aircraft production had grown in importance as aircraft components became more and more complex. In the 1930s, subcontracting made up less than 10 percent of the industry's operation; in the 1950s, 30–40 percent; and by the 1970s subcontractors fabricated between 60 and 70 percent of the value of American airframes.[5] As aircraft production became increasingly more risky, subcontracting became associated with risk sharing. Over time, aircraft manufacturers extended subcontracting throughout the world, partly as a result of the demand made by foreign customers and their governments. As overseas carriers bought aircraft, their governments required airframe integrators to share design work and production with overseas firms.[6]

Entry into the business of manufacturing large commercial aircraft had always been very limited. One barrier to entry into the industry was the high and increasing cost of product development. The Boeing 747, for example, cost $1 billion to develop, the Boeing 767 cost $1.5 billion, the Airbus A320 cost $2.5 billion, and the total cost of developing the Boeing 777 in the early 1990s was in excess of $5.5 billion.[7]

Another entry barrier was the need to establish learning curves and achieve economies of scale. To break even on an entirely new aircraft, it took sales of 400 to 500 units and a minimum of 50 sales per year. Not only was it necessary for a company to wait up to 10 years in order to reach the break-even point, but there was no guarantee that the company would ever break even, let alone make profits. As one group of industry analysts concluded, "Economic failure is the norm in the civil aircraft business."[8]

The need to control costs gave rise to the "family concept" in aircraft design. Producing families of planes rather than single models, aircraft manufacturers built flexibility into the design of a given aircraft so that the fuselage could be stretched in the future to add more passenger seats in the cabin. Pioneered by Boeing, model stretching did play an important role in enhancing aircraft productivity.

Notwithstanding these cost-cutting measures, commercial aircraft makers were unable to survive without government support. In the past, military contracts were extremely beneficial to commercial aircraft and engine makers, especially insofar as expensive new technologies such as jet propulsion and swept wings were concerned. Since the mid-1960s, however, military and commercial developments had diverged, and consequently, government support to commercial projects declined. The Department of Defense continued to fund research with potential military implications, but by the late 1980s such funding amounted to less than 5 percent of Boeing's research and development. NASA also provided some direct funding, but again, only for technology development, not commercial product development.[9]

An additional factor that influenced the dynamics of the aircraft industry was airline deregulation. Deregulation of the domestic airlines in 1978 resulted in a substantial increase in air travel, intense airfare competition among carriers, the entry of new low-cost, low-capacity airlines into the industry, and the growing utilization of the hub-and-spoke system by the major carriers. On the one hand, the explosion in air travel led to a steep growth in demand for new aircraft of all kinds. On the other hand, the proliferation of low-cost, short-haul airline companies (i.e., Southwest Airlines, American West), combined with the extensive use of hubs by the large carriers, brought about an increased demand for short-range, single-aisle airplanes such as the Boeing 737, the McDonnell Douglas MD80, and the Airbus A320. Additionally, the deregulatory environment shifted the focus of airline competition from performance to cost and from service to price. As Frank Shrontz, Boeing CEO between 1988 and 1996 observed, "In the old days airlines were infatuated with technology for its own sake. Today the rationale for purchasing a new plane is cost savings and profitability."[10]

In Europe, similarly, the airline industry experienced progressive deregulation during the 1980s and 1990s. By 1998, about one-half of all worldwide air travel took place within a competitive, deregulated environment.[11] Such a trend—which was expected to continue—was likely to encourage foreign air carriers to become more cost-conscious and more profit-oriented in the future. In both the domestic and foreign markets, the economic deregulation of airline travel promoted increased competition among aircraft manufacturers.

THE AEROSPACE INDUSTRY: DEFENSE AND SPACE

The defense and space industry differed from the commercial aircraft industry in three important respects. First, the U.S. government was the only primary customer for noncommercial aerospace products and services, and consequently, the total output of the industry was determined by political considerations. On the one side, the production of domestic military aircraft, missiles, and space products and services was subject to congressional debate over the budget; on the other, foreign military sales were restricted by the administration's foreign policy.[12]

Second, the defense and space industry operated under favorable contractual arrangements with the government. Unlike investments in commercial aircraft manufacturing, investments in defense and space were not subject to excessive risks or to volatile changes in market demand. The potential for unforeseen obstacles in developing defense and space products was so large that cost estimates prior to production were almost impossible to obtain. Accordingly, the government provided contractors with a special shelter—a contractual arrangement known as "cost plus" under which a defense contractor was guaranteed fixed profits regardless of the level of the final costs. Contractors competed over projects by submitting bids, but such bids were later supplemented by additional funds to cover overrun costs.[13] To control cost overrun, the U.S. government introduced "fixed-price contracts" in the late 1980s, but as a result of intense lobbying efforts on the part of the defense contractors, the fixed-price contracts were replaced again by "cost reimbursement contacts" in the early 1990s.[14]

Third, the government's importance as a customer for aerospace products and services had diminished (Exhibit 1). With the break-up of the Soviet Union in 1990, the Cold War was over and projected defense spending plummeted. Between 1987 and 1997, the Pentagon budget declined by 30 percent and its weapon procurement budget declined by 54 percent in 1997 dollars.[15] The shrinking defense budget led to large-scale mergers and acquisitions among defense contractors and to the growing consolidation of the industry (Exhibit 2). Following the merger of Boeing and McDonnell Douglas, four defense and space conglomerates ruled the aerospace industry: Lockheed Martin, Boeing-McDonnell Douglas, Raytheon, and Northrop Grumman. All four competed for leadership, and all were joined in a dense web of alliances and subcontracting arrangements that allowed each to prosper.[16]

EXHIBIT 1 | U.S. Aerospace Industry Sales by Customer, 1982–1996, Selected Years

Year	Total Sales ($ billion)	% of Total Sales to U.S. Government	% of Total Sales to Other Customers
1982	56.4	69.0%	31.0%
1984	69.6	74.9	25.1
1986	88.5	73.9	26.1
1988	95.5	72.6	27.4
1990	112.0	63.9	36.1
1992	115.5	55.7	44.3
1994	92.1	60.5	39.5
1996	93.9	54.6	45.4

Source: Aerospace Facts and Figures, 1997–98 (Washington, D.C.: Aerospace Industries Association of America, 1997), p. 13.

2 | The Ten Largest Defense Mergers and Acquisitions, 1992–1996

March 1993	Lockheed acquired General Dynamics' aircraft and military businesses for $1.52 billion.
April 1993	Martin Marietta acquired General Electric's aerospace assets for $3.05 billion.
December 1993	Loral Corporation Acquired IBM's Federal Systems' Division for $1.57 billion.
May 1994	Northrop Corporation acquired Grumman Corporation for $2.17 billion.
December 1994	Martin Marietta merged with Lockheed in a transaction valued at more than $10 billion.
April 1995	Raytheon Company acquired E-Systems for $2.3 billion.
March 1996	Northrop Grumman acquired the defense electronics business of Westinghouse for $3.2 billion.
April 1996	Lockheed acquired most of the assets of the Loral Corporation for more than $9 billion.
August 1996*	Boeing acquired the defense business of Rockwell International Corporation for $3.2 billion.
Dec. 1996**	Boeing acquired McDonnell Douglas for $14 billion.

Sources: Wall Street Journal, December 16, 1996, **New York Times*, December 16, 1997; ***Business Week*, December 30, 1996, p. 38.

HISTORY OF THE BOEING-DOUGLAS RIVALRY

In 1917, William Boeing founded the Boeing Airplane Company in Seattle, Washington. Three years later, Donald Douglas established what would become in 1926 the Douglas Aircraft Company. During the early 1920s, both the Boeing and Douglas companies were building a variety of flying machines—made of wood and fabric—for the military. The market for commercial aircraft evolved during the 1930s. As Boeing supplied United Airlines with its first 60 B-247s, Douglas went ahead with the development and production of a similar but superior aircraft: the DC1 (Douglas Commercial). The DC1 served as a prototype, but the larger DC2 outclassed the B-247, and the improved DC3 established Douglas as the world's largest manufacturer of commercial aircraft.[17]

Unable to compete with Douglas in the commercial aircraft business, Boeing redirected its efforts toward the military. Boeing's principal success during WWII was the development and production of the B-17 "Flying Fortress"—a giant four-engine bomber. Douglas also put its resources into the war effort, building attack bombers (A-20 Havoc) and Navy bombers (SBD Dauntless) and suspending its commercial production.[18]

The steep decline in military orders at the end of the war placed the aircraft industry on the verge of collapse. Douglas met the crisis by reestablishing itself as the world's largest manufacturer of commercial aircraft, producing the last great American piston transport: the DC6 and DC7. Boeing survived the downturn by producing an early generation of jet aircraft for the military: the B-47 and B-52 strategic bombers.[19] Having been out of civil aviation for more than 10 years,[20] Boeing reentered the air transport market only after the jet had become operational for commercial use.

Boeing's first jet, the 707, followed closely the design of the military tanker KC-135 which Boeing had first produced under government contract. Douglas had no such advantage. By contrast to the Boeing 707, Douglas's first jet, the DC8, was a financial disaster: The company did not sell a sufficient number of units to recover its development cost.[21] Douglas's second jet, the smaller DC9, also failed to compete successfully with its rival, the Boeing 727. Altogether, twice as many 727s as DC9s were delivered (Exhibit 3), Douglas's expenses were higher than Boeing's, and Douglas was selling the DC9 below cost. As a result of growing financial difficulties, Douglas merged in 1967 with the stronger McDonnell Aircraft Corporation (a defense contractor) to avoid bankruptcy.[22]

3 | Total Number of Best Selling Commercial Airplanes Delivered by Boeing and McDonnell Douglas, 1959–1997

BOEING		MCDONNELL DOUGLAS	
B-707	1,010 (retired)	DC-8	556 (retired)
B-727	1,831 (retired)	DC-9	976 (retired)
B-737	2,975	MD80/90	1,221
B-747	1,136	DC-10	446 (retired)

Source: Boeing, Commercial Airplane Group, *Announced Orders and Deliveries as of 12/31/97*

The newly formed McDonnell Douglas Corporation became the U.S.'s largest manufacturer of military aircraft. McDonnell's premier aircraft in the 1960s and early 1970s was the F-4 Phantom, the Air Force's top fighter in Vietnam. To replace the Phantom, the McDonnell Douglas Corporation developed and produced the Air Force F-15 Eagle Attack fighter (1972) and the Navy F/A-18 Hornet strike fighter (1978). Both fighters were still in production in the 1990s, both were used in the Persian Gulf (1991) and Kosovo (1999), and both were principal contributors to McDonnell Douglas's revenues on the eve of the merger with Boeing. On the eve of the merger, the McDonnell Douglas Corporation also produced the C-17 Globemaster, the Air Force's most advanced military transport, first introduced in 1995. Other defense products manufactured by McDonnell Douglas at the time of the merger included attack jump jets for the Marines (AV-8B Harrier), training aircraft for the Navy (T-45 Goshawk), attack helicopters (AH-64 Apache), and guided missiles (Harpoon, Cruise, and Tomahawk Cruise). In 1993 and 1994, respectively, foreign orders of F/A-18s (Switzerland) and F-15s (Israel) boosted the company's military business.[23]

By contrast to its defense sector, McDonnell Douglas's commercial business lagged far behind Boeing's. Between 1959 and 1996, Boeing produced 8,200 commercial jetliners and Douglas only 3,300. Defined by range of travel, Boeing families of airframes included the 737 for short-range, the 757 and 767 for medium-range, and the 747 and 777 for medium- to long-range travel. Boeing's most successful models were the 737 and 747 series. Going into service in 1967, the B-737 had become the top selling commercial jetliner in history with 3,300 units delivered by early 1999. Boeing offered the 737 in a variety of models of different ranges (2,000 to 3,200 miles) and different seat capacities (108–189 seats).[24]

The 747 family was introduced in 1970. Its development and tooling costs had almost bankrupted the company, but by 1978 sales reached the break-even point and thereafter the 747 became Boeing's most profitable aircraft.[25] Responding to Boeing's challenge, both the McDonnell Douglas and the Lockheed Corporations launched a new wide-body aircraft and both failed. The DC10, like the L1011, carried only two-thirds of the passenger load of the 747, cost two-thirds as much, had one-half the travel range of the 747, and the market for such an airplane could not sustain two competing models. Lockheed exited the market in 1981 after selling only 244 units, and Douglas rolled out the last passenger version of the DC10 in 1980, unable to recover the airplane's high development costs.[26]

Still, McDonnell Douglas introduced two other commercial aircraft models. To compete with the B-737, Douglas upgraded and stretched the DC9 into the MD-80 (1980) and MD-90(1995). Although an initial success, the MD-80/90 series did not generate sufficient orders to sustain sales (Exhibit 4). By 1996, less than 150 units were on order (against more than 750 B-737 units on order),[27] sales were slowing down, costs were going up, and the MD program was losing money (Exhibit 4). Following the merger with McDonnell Douglas, the Boeing company decided to discontinue manufacturing the two MD models, effective 1999.[28]

4 | Shipments of Large (over 33,000 lbs) U.S.-manufactured Civil Transport Aircraft during the Five Years Preceding the Boeing-McDonnell Douglas Merger, 1992–1996

COMPANY & MODEL	1992	1993	1994	1995	1996
B 737	218	152	121	89	76
B 747	61	56	40	25	26
B 757	99	71	69	43	42
B 767	63	51	40	36	42
B 777	—	—	—	13	32
Boeing Total	**441**	**330**	**270**	**206**	**218**
MD-11	42	36	17	18	15
MD-80	84	42	22	18	12
MD-90	—	—	—	14	24
McDonnell Douglas Total	**126**	**78**	**39**	**50**	**51**
Total	**567**	**408**	**309**	**256**	**269**

Source: Aerospace Facts and Figures, 1997–98, p. 34.

Finally, McDonnell Douglas made one last effort to enter the market for large wide-body aircraft. In 1989, the company put into service the three-engine ("tri-jet") MD-11, a derivative of the DC10.[29] Again, sales of the MD-11 languished, and Douglas soon faced competition from Boeing's newest jetliner, the 777. Entering into service in 1995, the 777 outsold the MD11 by a margin of 2 to 1 within a year (Exhibit 4). Following the merger with McDonnell Douglas, Boeing management decided to limit future production of the MD11 to its freighter version.[30]

PRODUCT DEVELOPMENT

Product development in the commercial aircraft industry had long been the preferred growth strategy undertaken by competing manufacturers. The occasional development of a new family of planes was essential for securing market share in the future, and accordingly, both Boeing and McDonnell Douglas undertook such a strategy in the 1990s. Yet only Boeing managed to deliver the new product.

Early in 1996, McDonnell Douglas announced a plan to develop a new twin-engine, wide-body aircraft. Named the MD-XX, the new jetliner (8,000 mile range/300–400 seats) was intended to broaden McDonnell Douglas's product line and thereby reestablish the company's role as a major player in the commercial aircraft industry in the 21st century. During the spring and summer of 1996, engineers at Douglas facilities in Long Beach, California, worked on the design of the MD-XX, the company received orders for 40–50 units from customers, and Douglas made preparations to launch the new aircraft at the end of the year. Yet, on October 24, the company decided to terminate the project. Harry Stonecipher, McDonnell Douglas's CEO, urged the company board to forego the development of the MD-XX because of its prohibitive cost: The project would have required an initial investment of $3 billion and an additional capital of $12 billion spent over a 10-year period. "Fundamentally, it wasn't an MD-XX decision," Stonecipher admitted, "it was a question of how far, how fast, and at what rate" Douglas could compete in the commercial aircraft business. "The market may be too tough for us to battle through" and "I have . . . other alternatives." Six weeks later, Stonecipher negotiated with Philip Condit the sale of McDonnell Douglas to Boeing.[31]

Condit led the 777 program to completion. Condit's role in developing the 777 paved his way to the top. Midway through the 777 development program, Boeing's board of directors elected Condit as president and gave him a seat on the board. Four years later, in 1996, the board promoted Condit to CEO.

Launching the 777 in 1990, Boeing management sought to ensure the company's future. "This is an offensive, not a defensive strategy," Condit noted, predicting that the 777 family would remain in production for 50 years. A wide-body aircraft with two gigantic jet engines ("the most powerful ever built"), the 777 went into service two years after Airbus had introduced its own new wide-body models: the two-engine A320 and the four-engine A340.[32]

COMPETITION—AND COOPERATION—IN SPACE

Boeing and McDonnell Douglas had long competed over NASA contracts, but such competition did not rule out partnership. On the contrary, the typical NASA project was extremely demanding and therefore required the joint efforts of several competing contractors. In the 1960s, Boeing built the Lunar Orbiters that circled the moon and the first stage of the rockets used in the Apollo space program; McDonnell created the Mercury and Gemini capsules; and Douglas developed the Delta expendable launch vehicle, the world's most reliable space launcher. Following the successful moon mission, both Boeing and McDonnell Douglas competed over NASA's contract to build Skylab, America's first space station, and McDonnell Douglas won. In the 1980s, the Rockwell Corporation led the development of the Space Shuttle program with Boeing and McDonnell Douglas as key partners. Boeing produced the upper stage of the shuttle and McDonnell Douglas provided the structural parts for the booster that lifted the shuttle into space. In the 1990s, Boeing was in charge of leading the development of the International Space Station—the largest and most complex structure ever assembled in space—and McDonnell Douglas served as a subcontractor to Boeing, responsible for producing the station's structural backbone. As the two companies merged in 1997, the International Space Station contract was a major contributor to Boeing's revenues, just as the Delta II space launcher contract was a principal contributor to McDonnell Douglas's revenues. Following its merger with Rockwell (1996) and McDonnell Douglas, the new Boeing had become NASA's single largest contractor.[33]

THE CHALLENGE OF AIRBUS COMPETITION

The new Boeing had one formidable rival: Airbus Industrie. While Airbus's production rates in the 1980s were still low, its booking of new aircraft orders skyrocketed, and subsequently, the consortium was quickly expanding its capacity. Airbus orders surpassed those of McDonnell Douglas in 1986, and its deliveries exceeded those of McDonnell Douglas in 1991. As Airbus gained, Boeing's new orders fell below the 50 percent mark for the first time in more than two decades. In 1990, the 777 launch year, Boeing booked 45 percent of the total industry orders, Airbus 34 percent, and McDonnell Douglas 21 percent. In 1996, the year in which Boeing announced its merger with McDonnell, Airbus booked nearly 50 percent of the worldwide industry orders, and delivered close to one-third of the worldwide output of commercial jetliners (Exhibit 5). The merger created a duopoly that was supposed, in theory, to reduce competition and give each of the two companies a price advantage in a seller's market. On the contrary, however, the merger intensified the battle between Boeing and Airbus, leading each company to slash aircraft prices by as much as 20 percent.[34]

In 1970 aerospace companies in France, Germany, Britain, and Spain formed Airbus. Pooling their resources to create a consortium, the participating companies served as both shareholders of and subcontractors to Airbus. The participating companies competed with each other over the development and production of particular aircraft components, and thus different shares of a given program were distributed among the partners. The partners, in addition, received generous subsidies from their governments to finance Airbus projects and ensure the consortium's long-term survival. Airbus received nearly $10 billion in government assistance for the development and manufacture of its first three models, and an additional $4–5 billion for initial work on its A330/340 models. These subsidies led to a trade war. The U.S. government, together with representatives of Boeing and McDonnell Douglas, claimed that Airbus's subsidies violated the General Agreement on Tariffs and Trades (GATT), and called for their removal. Again and again, the parties failed to reach a compromise. In 1992, at long last, Airbus and Boeing signed a bilateral agree-

5 | Market Share of Actual (1992–1998) and Forecast (1999–2000) Shipments of Commercial Aircraft, Boeing, McDonnell Douglas (MD), Airbus

	1992	1993	1994	1995	1996	1997	1998	1999	2000
Boeing	61%	61%	63%	54%	55%	67%	71%	68%	61%
MD	17	14	9	13	13				
Airbus	22	25	28	33	32	33	29	32	39

Sources: Aerospace Facts and Figures, 1997–98, p. 34; *Wall Street Journal,* December 3, 1998, and January 12, 1999; *The Boeing Company 1997 Annual Report,* p. 19; Data supplied by Mark Luginbill, Airbus Communication Director, November 16, 1998.

ment that limited government subsidies to 33 percent of Airbus's total development costs. In exchange, the agreement limited federal indirect R&D funds to 3 percent of the total revenues received by American aircraft manufacturers. In 1995, following 25 years of losses, Airbus finally generated profits.[35]

Although government assistance helped Airbus stay in the aircraft industry for the long haul, the consortium's success was impossible to understand without considering its strategy. In developing its long-term plans, Airbus sought to build on Boeing's rich experience, mimicking three elements of the old Boeing strategy: technological leadership, cost controls, and the development of families of planes.

Technological Leadership

"You cannot compete with a dominant . . . player if you don't offer something different," former Airbus President Roger Beteille said. To persuade the major airlines to switch to a new supplier, Airbus had to differentiate itself from Boeing by incorporating the most advanced technology into its planes. Among Airbus technological firsts, the fly-by-wire system was perhaps the most famous. Introduced in 1988, the A-320 was the world's first fly-by-wire commercial aircraft, controlled by a pilot transmitting commands to the rudder and flaps electrically, not mechanically.[36]

Cost Controls

As competition with Boeing intensified during the recession of the early 1990s, Airbus sought to reduce costs through deep cuts in jobs, streamlining the production process, and the speed-up of deliveries. Each of the consortium's partner companies participated in these cost-cutting efforts. In Britain, British Aerospace cut its wing-production time by 50 percent in two years while trimming its Airbus workforce from 15,000 to 7,000 in five years. In Germany, Daimler-Benz (later Daimler-Chrysler), which built fuselages, reduced its production costs by 33 percent and production time by 50 percent in six years (1992–1998). And in France, state-owned Aerospatiale, which produced cockpits, reduced its workforce by 17 percent between 1993 and 1996.[37]

Families of Planes

Boeing was the first company to use the family concept in aircraft design. Airbus made the concept the foundation of its manufacturing and marketing strategy. A family of planes was made up of derivative jetliners built around a basic model. Since all derivatives of a given model shared maintenance, training, and operation procedures, as well as replacement parts and components, the use of such derivative airplanes to serve different markets enabled airline carriers to cut costs. Airbus used this family-based strategy in two ways. First, it produced and marketed derivative jetliners, and second, it introduced common design features ("commonalities") across the entire range of its models, not just the members of a single family, thus providing airline carriers with additional sources of savings.[38]

Airbus's strategy served the consortium well. By the mid-1990s, Airbus competed with Boeing in every travel market except the one served by the 747. The A320 family challenged the 737 in the short-range 120+ seat market, the A300/A310 family competed with the 757 and 767 in the medium-range 200+ seat market, and the A330/A340 family went after the market for medium- to long-range travel, anticipating the coming of the 777.

THE RESULTS OF THE MERGER

The Boeing-McDonnell Douglas merger was completed on August 1, 1997, eight months after Condit and Stonecipher had originally announced it. Upon the completion of the merger, Boeing became the world's largest producer of military aircraft and the second largest supplier to the U.S. Department of Defense (DOD). The newly merged company quickly consolidated its holdings. It turned McDonnell's St. Louis headquarters into Boeing's headquarters for military aircraft and missile program, put Boeing's space division (based in Seal Beach, California) in charge of all Boeing and McDonnell-Douglas space-related programs, and developed detailed plans to phase out McDonnell-Douglas's commercial aircraft business.[39]

Yet the merger failed to produce the expected results. In 1997, Boeing recorded a net loss of $178 million, the worst financial performance in 50 years. In 1998, a United Airlines executive called Boeing a "dysfunctional organization,"[40] a *Wall Street Journal* reporter described Boeing's revised projections for 1999–2000 (Exhibit 6) as "shock[ing]," and Boeing President Harry Stonecipher conceded that the crisis was likely to last from "two to five" years.[41] Over a two-year period following the announcement of the merger, Boeing shares lost one-third of their value.[42] What, then, was the source of Boeing's post-merger difficulties?

Defense and Space

Boeing's defense and space business units had performed well from the early days of the merger. Defense and space revenues accounted for 39 percent of the total company sales in 1997, up from 25 percent in 1996, 23 percent in 1994, and 20 percent in 1992.[43] The DOD was Boeing's largest customer, spending nearly four times as much as NASA (Exhibit 7). Boeing's Defense and Space Group was profitable in 1997, generating a 7.3 percent return on sales and thus offsetting, almost entirely, the large loss incurred by the company's Commercial Airplane Group. As shown in Exhibit 6, Boeing's defense and space business units were profitable in 1998, and were expected to continue generating profits through the year 2000 with the group's margins steadily improving.

Boeing Defense and Space Group gained from recent changes in the defense budget. Following a decade-long decline in U.S. military spending, the defense budget stabilized in 1997 at about $250 billion and was

EXHIBIT 6 | Highlights of Boeing's Financial and Operation Data: Actual (1997–1998) and Projected (1999–2000)

	1997	1998	1999	2000
Operating revenues (bm)	$46	$56	$58	$50
R&D spending (bm)	$1.9	$1.9	$1.6–1.8	$1.5–1.7
Comm. aircraft shipped	374	559	620	490
Employment (thousands)	238	231	200–210	185–195
Profit margins:*				
Comm. aircraft	–6.6%	0%	2–3%	1–3%
Defense and space**	7.3%	7.7%	7–9%	8–10%

*Operating Earnings Returns on Sales
**Including "Information."
Sources: For 1997, 1998, *The Boeing Company 1997 Annual Report*, pp. 19, 24, 35, 72, and *The Boeing Company 1998 Annual Report*, pp. 35, 51, 76. For 1998–2000: Frederick M. Biddle and Andy Pasztor, "Boeing May Be Hurt Up to 5 Years," *Wall Street Journal*, December 3, 1998.

7 | Boeing's Defense and Space Group:* Sales by Customer, 1997

Air Force	30%
Navy	18
Army	6
NASA	15
Foreign	22
Other	9
Total	$18 Billion

*Including Information.
Source: The Boeing Company 1997 Annual Report, p. 24.

expected to increase moderately between 1998 and 2003. NASA's budget was expected to remain flat on an inflationary-adjusted basis.[44] With no further spending cuts projected in either defense or space, and with a slight increase in the military procurement budget, the prospects of the industry were fast improving. Lockheed Martin, Raytheon, and to a lesser extent, the Northrop Grumman Corporation, were Boeing's principal competitors in this segment.

The largest defense contractor, Lockheed Martin was a highly diversified company, producing a well-balanced mix of aircraft, electronics, and missiles. Lockheed held the most lucrative DOD contract in the 1990s: the development and production of the Raptor fighter jet (F-22), a successor to McDonnell Douglas's "still unchallengeable" F-15. The Pentagon ordered 340 F-22s at a "minimum" cost of $75 million each. In 1997, Lockheed delivered the first test model to the Air Force but the Raptor was not expected to go into full production until 2004. Although Lockheed was the project's prime contractor, Boeing served as a subcontractor to Lockheed, producing about one-third of the Raptor, including the wings and the aft fuselage.[45]

Raytheon was Boeing's major competitor in aerospace electronics. Of the total cost of a given fighter aircraft, electronics made up one-third and airframe and engine accounted for the remaining two-thirds. Raytheon had acquired Hughes Electronics in 1997, and as a result became a powerful rival to Boeing, specializing in the development and production of radar systems, night vision equipment, avionics gear, and missiles.[46]

Northrop Grumman was a much smaller company than either Lockheed or Raytheon. Building one of the last B-2 stealth bombers in 1997, Northrup had become the industry's principal subcontractor and Boeing's single largest supplier. Northrop manufactured the aft fuselage for the Navy's Super Hornet fighter and the tail assembly and surface controls for the C-17 military transport, both produced by McDonnell Douglas, later owned by Boeing. Northrop, in addition, served as a major supplier to Boeing Airplane Commercial Group, building half of the 747's fuselage and the doors for most of Boeing's passenger jetliners, including the 747.[47]

Boeing's position in the industry was unique. The company had no recent experience in building fighter jets, and therefore its merger with McDonnell Douglas was critical, especially insofar as long-term government contracts were concerned. First, McDonnell held the second largest DOD contract in the industry: the production of the Super Hornet F/A18E/F aircraft fighter, the latest addition to the Navy fleet. The Navy ordered a total of 500 Super Hornets at a cost of $45 million each. Production of the F/A18E/F had begun in 1997 and was expected to continue until the year 2010.[48]

More important, the merger strengthened Boeing's competitive position in the contest over the richest military aircraft contract ever: the development and production of the Joint Strike Fighter (JSF), a successor to Lockheed's F-16. In October 1996, the DOD selected Boeing and Lockheed, not McDonnell, to compete over the JSF project. The exclusion of McDonnell Douglas played a key role in Stonecipher's decision to sell the company to Boeing. A multipurpose low-end fighter, the JSF was expected to cost less than half as much as the high-end Raptor, yet the sheer size of the Pentagon's projected order was staggering: 2,850 JSFs in three different versions (Air Force, Navy, and Marine models) at the total estimated cost of over $200 billion. The fly-off contest between Boeing and Lockheed was scheduled for 2001, and according to defense analysts, Boeing had the edge both because it was better equipped to master the complex manufacturing process required, and because it was able to control costs better, having had the discipline of the commercial marketplace. In 1999, Lockheed reported a $150 million cost overrun for work on the design of an "entrant" to the JSF fly-off competition, a problem that was likely to hurt the company's prospects of winning the contract.[49]

Finally, the merger with McDonnell Douglas provided Boeing with ample engineering and manufacturing resources. In the long run, the potential of transferring technological know-how back and forth between commercial and military business units gave Boeing an enormous advantage over its rivals, as even the company's competitors acknowledged. Boeing, to mention one example, had developed expertise in composite materials while working on the B-2 bomber and then used that expertise to build the tail-wing of the 777, which, in turn, was used to develop its advanced wing design for the proposed JSF jet.[50]

Commercial Aircraft

Boeing Commercial Aircraft Group lost $1.8 billion in 1997, the first year of the merger. In 1998, the group barely generated any profits, and during the next two years (1999–2000), its profits were expected to remain low, with the margins ranging from 1 to 3 percent (Exhibit 6).

One source of Boeing's post-merger troubles was its acquisition of McDonnell Douglas's MD model series. At the time of the merger, McDonnell's commercial jetliner business was losing money, and consequently, Boeing's management decided to phase it out, taking a special $1.4 billion pre-tax charge[51] that resulted in a larger than expected reported loss in 1997 (Exhibit 8).

Another source of difficulties was Condit's neglect of Boeing's commercial aircraft business. A newly promoted CEO, Condit focused almost exclusively on expanding Boeing's military business. He developed a long-term strategy of turning Boeing into the world's largest aerospace and defense company and implemented it at once, buying Rockwell's military units first, and the McDonnell Douglas Corporation second. Eager to complete the deal with McDonnell and preoccupied with lobbying the U.S. government for its approval, he overlooked mounting assembly-line problems that crippled Boeing Commercial Airplane Group. As it became apparent in the summer of 1997 that Boeing's assembly line was falling behind, Condit still underestimated the problem, acknowledging just a month-long delay in deliveries of commercial jets.[52]

But Boeing production problems were serious. A rapid ramp-up in aircraft production led to shortages of raw materials (aluminum, titanium, and other composites) and to delays in deliveries of parts and subassemblies. The hiring of thousands of inexperienced, "green" workers resulted in productivity inefficiencies.[53] So severe were the shortages and inefficiencies that the company was forced to shut down its 737 and 747 production line for one month in order "to bring work back into sequence."[54] Although largely unrelated to the Boeing-McDonnell Douglas merger, these problems did affect the post-merger results.

Other problems affected the post-merger results as well. Increased competition with Airbus drove Boeing's management to protect the company's market share at almost any cost. Caught in the competition, Boeing's management overlooked expenses, slashed prices, and gave up technological leadership. In the market for single-aisle, narrow-body aircraft, for example, Boeing competed with Airbus on price rather than technology, often selling the B-737 below cost. Because the A-320 was slightly more advanced than the B-737 (and its cabin a bit larger), a growing number of airline carriers favored the first over the second, citing passengers' preferences as the reason. United Airlines' 1996 decision to extend an Airbus A-320 order was a case in point.[55]

Still, Boeing's most pressing problem was cost escalation. In 1998, Boeing used 20–30 percent more labor hours to produce a jetliner than it had in 1994.[56] As the company's four-year efforts to contain costs had stalled, Boeing lost $1 billion on the sale of its first 400 new-model 737s.[57] Although Boeing had launched a two-year program to modernize production, the company continued to operate 400 separate computer systems that were not linked together.[58] While Airbus had already adopted a flexible, lean-production manufacturing system, Boeing was still utilizing a standardized, mass-production system that had barely changed since WWII. Hence the gap in labor productivity. In 1998, Boeing employed 211 workers for every commercial aircraft (560 jets made by 119,000 employees) and Airbus just 143 (230 jets produced by 33,000 workers).[59]

Finally, the merger of Boeing and McDonnell Douglas coincided with the Asian economic slump. The slump prompted the Asian airlines to cancel, or defer, aircraft orders. The slump affected both Airbus and Boeing, but not in the same way. On the one hand, Asian orders of wide-body jets were the most vulnerable and the first to be canceled; on the other, Airbus booked fewer such orders than did Boeing. Since Boeing, unlike Airbus, was highly dependent on the Asian market for the sale of its wide-body jets, the 747 and 777, Boeing's potential losses were greater than Airbus's.[60]

CULTURE AND LEADERSHIP

The merger of Boeing and McDonnell Douglas posed a related challenge to the new Boeing, namely, the integration of the corporate cultures and leadership styles of the two companies. To be sure, both Boeing and McDonnell Douglas were aerospace firms dominated by an engineering culture. Their respective corporate images embodied the values and attitudes of engineers, that is, logic, precision, professionalism, and authority. Their professional workforce was made up, first and foremost, of engineers, and their skilled workforce of aircraft mechanics.

Still, there was a difference. According to industry analysts, McDonnell had long been known for its top-down management style that was formed in close alliance with the defense industry. Its organizational structure was rigid, its decision making procedure centralized, and its chain of command quasi-military. Boeing, by contrast, had developed a more progressive management structure based partly on teamwork and partly on employees' participation in decision making.[61] Boeing's management practices were shaped, above all, by the need to compete in the marketplace.

Philip Condit's leadership style reflected Boeing's managerial tradition. An inspirational leader endowed with exceptional social skills, Condit led by example. Always preferring to work in groups, he regularly assigned tasks to teams rather than individuals. To promote camaraderie, loyalty, and a strong sense of bonding among Boeing's executives, he developed a ritual. Periodically, he would invite a new group of managers to his house to sit around the fire and tell anecdotes about their experience at Boeing. Each executive would then write on a piece of paper a positive and a negative story about Boeing, toss the paper with the negative story into the fire, and keep the paper with the positive story to carry it around and show others.[62]

Harry Stonecipher's style was different, reflecting, to some extent at least, McDonnell's managerial philosophy. A strong executive with a track record of corporate turnaround, downsizing, and outsourcing, Stonecipher was a blunt talker, aggressive leader, feared by his subordinates, and highly respected on Wall Street. A non-player, he led by explicit command rather than persuasion. Asked (1998) to compare his managerial style to that of Condit, he replied, "I'm more likely to shoot you and then ask your name; Phil is likely to ask your name and then shoot you."[63]

Condit had joined Boeing in 1965 after receiving a master's degree in aeronautical engineering from Princeton University. A gifted engineer, he rose quickly at Boeing, becoming vice president in 1983, president in 1992, and CEO in 1996.[64] Stonecipher had spent 27 years at General Electric, rising through the ranks to become head of GE's jet engine division. He subsequently spent seven years at the Sunstrand Corporation (a military contractor making aerospace components), turning the company around, and three years at McDonnell Douglas, improving the firm's financial performance before selling it to Boeing.[65] At Boeing, Stonecipher served as president and as a director of the board.

The contrast between Condit and Stonecipher's leadership styles raised an interesting question: Would the two executives cooperate successfully during the post-merger years or would they clash? Apparently, as Boeing's financial performance worsened, Stonecipher had gained power relative to Condit. Stonecipher was now one of Boeing's largest shareholders—Condit owned a relatively small amount of stock—and he enjoyed wide support among the company's investors. Nevertheless, he had two handicaps. First, he lacked the backing of Boeing's board of directors. Only four of Boeing's 13 board members (including Stonecipher and John F. McDonnell, son of the company's founder) were McDonnell Douglas affiliates, and eight directors represented the old Boeing and were loyal to Condit. Second, he was 63 years old (1999) and Boeing's top executives were required to retire at 65.[66]

TURNAROUND

As Boeing's crisis deepened, Condit, Stonecipher, and other top executives laid out a turnaround strategy. The strategy was based on a combination of four elements: the reorganization of Boeing's two major product groups, the replacement of the executive responsible for running the company's commercial airplane division, the introduction of radical cost-cutting measures, and the hiring of a new chief financial officer from outside the company.

On September 1, 1998, Condit ousted Ronald Woodward, head of Boeing's Commercial Airplane Group who was next in line to become CEO, and replaced him with Alan Mulally. Mulally had served as Condit's chief engineer on the 777 project, had a reputation as a skillful team leader, and headed Boeing's Defense and Space Group, following the merger with McDonnell Douglas.

In consolidating the businesses of Boeing and McDonnell, Mulally quickly reorganized the Defense and Space Group. Taking a page from Alfred Sloan's reorganization of General Motors in the 1920s, he grouped all products and services into separate, autonomous divisions, drew carefully the divisional boundaries, and rendered each division responsible for its own financial performance. He then took charge of Boeing Commercial Airplane Group and did the same. He reorganized the commercial group into three independent divisions: one responsible for single-aisle (narrow-body) planes, one for twin-aisle (wide-body) planes, and one for customer service. Again, each division was expected to generate its own profits and each was responsible for its own losses. In the past, Boeing's executives rarely knew the exact cost of the planes they produced. Now they were fully accountable.[67]

Next, Boeing undertook several steps to cut costs, the most significant of which was downsizing. During the two-year period 1999–2000, Boeing planned to cut 30,000 to 50,000 jobs (Exhibit 8), most of them in the commercial aircraft division. Early in 1999, Boeing introduced a new computerized system designed to control the supply and stock of parts and components, and thereby reduce inventory costs. At the same time, Boeing renewed its efforts to build a flexible, integrated production-management system that would link its separate computer systems together. Boeing, in addition, was trying to reduce the number of special features it introduced into a variety of aircraft models sold to different airlines, and by so doing, cut its expenses further (without, of course, turning away customers).[68]

Finally, in December 1998, in a move initiated by Stonecipher, Deborah Hopkins, former chief financial officer at General Motors, Europe, replaced Boeing's chief financial officer for 32 years, Boyd Givan. A 44-year-old financial analyst, Hopkins was the youngest senior executive at Boeing, and the only woman occupying such a high position. She spelled out her plans at once. To help Boeing recover, she sought first to obtain more accurate cost data and deliver the data to line supervisors in a timely fashion; second, to determine the risks of undertaking large projects in a more methodical way; third, to discontinue unprofitable projects; and fourth, to increase Boeing's reliance on the outsourcing of aircraft components, systems, and equipment. "Teaching the business" to Boeing managers and workers, she had quickly proved she could deliver, helping the company improve its financial results.[69]

Hopkins' early success at Boeing raised the issue of succession. On the one side, Alan Mulally represented the traditional CEO candidate. A Boeing engineer groomed and promoted by Condit, he occupied the immediate position leading directly to the top. On the other, Deborah Hopkins embodied anything but the traditional. An outsider brought in by another outsider, she was a woman working in a company dominated by a tribal culture of white male engineers. An ambitious and outspoken executive, she said she was interested in running the company following Condit's retirement, a statement that created some tension within the leadership.[70] Whoever succeeded Condit, the rivalry between Mulally and Hopkins was likely to underlie Boeing's difficult journey to recovery and comeback.

FUTURE CONCERNS

Despite its initial promise, Boeing's turnaround strategy failed to adequately address two major concerns that could have affected its recovery. One pertained to the state of labor relations, the other to the prospects of product development.

Labor Relations

Following the merger of Boeing and McDonnell Douglas, about half of all Boeing's employees were covered by collective bargaining agreements. Boeing's two largest unions were the International Association of Machinists (IAM), representing 30 percent of its employees, and the Seattle Professional Engineering Employees Association (SPEEA), representing 12 percent of its employees. In 1999, Boeing was expected to negotiate new union contracts with 54,000 machinists, 24,000 engineers, and 8,000 other workers, the vast majority of whom were employees of the old Boeing, working in four states (Washington, Oregon, California, and Kansas). In 2001, Boeing was scheduled to negotiate an additional IAM contract with 10,000 machinists, all of whom were former employees of McDonnell Douglas in the St. Louis area.[71]

During the 1995–96 round of union negotiations, just before the merger, both Boeing and McDonnell Douglas experienced bitter and costly strikes. In 1995, the Boeing machinists struck for 69 days, and a year later, the McDonnell machinists struck for 99 days. The two strikes erupted over the issue of job security.

At Boeing, the machinists had voted down two proposed contracts before ratifying a third with an approval rating of 87 percent. Described by analysts as "overly generous," the Boeing IAM 1995 agreement provided the machinists with the best job security provisions in the industry (management was required to discuss outsourcing decisions with the union before implementing them) and with excellent health benefits. Financially weak, Boeing was unwilling to undergo another lengthy strike by the engineers. Instead, it offered the SPEEA a labor agreement closely modeled after the IAM's.[72]

At McDonnell Douglas, the striking machinists ratified the contract with only 68 percent of the vote. Described by some analysts as "rich," the McDonnell Douglas-IAM agreement, like Boeing's contract a year earlier, contained several clauses restricting the company's ability to subcontract jobs. In addition, the agreement required McDonnell management to compensate displaced workers with adequate job training and/or limited severance pay.[73]

Following the strikes of the mid-1990s, negotiations in 1999 were particularly difficult owing to Boeing's commitment to produce a record 620 commercial jets throughout the year, a goal that enhanced the union's bargaining power relative to management's. Still, as the IAM contract expired in the summer of 1999, Condit and his team managed to avoid a Boeing strike, reaching an agreement with the machinists on a three-year contract. Ratified by the majority of the membership, the agreement provided the machinists with job security (no layoffs as a result of outsourcing) while granting the company the right to decide which jobs should be outsourced. Both the union president and a Wall Street analyst praised Condit for the successful negotiation of the agreement, yet in the long run, the contentious issue of outsourcing had not been resolved.[74] Because the Boeing company was fast increasing its reliance on subcontracting, on the one hand, and because Boeing management was reluctant to give union leaders a greater voice in outsourcing decisions, on the other, labor relations at Boeing were likely to remain strained as the company entered the 21st century.

Product Development

Similarly, Boeing's decision not to develop a new aircraft had far-reaching implications on the company's long-term competitive advantage. Historically, the aviation industry had rewarded risk taking. On the eve of the jet age, Boeing upstaged Douglas with the 707, gambling the entire company on the success of jet technology. In the 1970s, Boeing revolutionized air travel with the introduction of the 747, taking another huge risk, and leaving McDonnell Douglas further behind. At the dawn of the 21st century, Boeing suddenly turned conservative. Not only was the company reluctant to develop a new family of planes, but its R&D budget was shrinking: Between 1998 and 2000, Boeing's research and development spending was projected to decline from $1.9 billion to as low as $1.5 billion (Exhibit 8).

Airbus, in the meantime, was developing an entirely

8 | Highlights of Financial and Operating Data for Boeing before the Merger with McDonnell Douglas (1994–96) and after the Merger (1997–98)

Dollars in Millions except Per Share Data

	AFTER MERGER		BEFORE MERGER		
	1998	**1997**	**1996**	**1995**	**1994**
Sales and other Operating revenues					
Commercial jets	$35,545	$26,929	$16,904	$13,933	$16,851
Defense & space	19,872	18,125	5,777	5,582	5,073
Other revenues	730	745			
Total	56,154	45,800	22,681	19,515	21,924
Net earnings (loss)	$1,120	($178)	$1,095	$393	$856
Earnings per share (loss)	1.16	(0.18)	3.19	1.15	2.51
R & D expense	1,895	1,924	1,200	1,267	1,704
No. of employees	231,000	238,000	112,000	109,000	119,000

Source: Boeing Annual Report for 1996, p. 64; *Boeing Annual Report for 1998*, p. 78.
*Including Information

new aircraft, the "super jumbo" A3XX. A giant double-decker designed to carry 550–650 passengers, or 230 more than the largest standard 747, the A3XX was projected to go into production in 2000 and into service in 2005, at the earliest. Airbus intended to use the A3XX to compete with the 747 "from above."[75]

During the 20-year period 1999–2019, Airbus management forecasted a need for 1,400 "super jumbos" valued at $300 billion. Boeing disputed these figures, contending that about three-quarters of Airbus's projected demand for the "super jumbo" was, in fact, a demand for the 747. Given its projections, Boeing management concluded that there was no justification for spending more than $10 billion (Airbus's estimate of the project's cost) on replacing the jumbo. Instead, Boeing decided to introduce derivative airplanes built around the 747. Looking for ways to stretch and upgrade the 30-year-old jumbo, Boeing engineers were examining a 550-seat 747 equipped with improved wing aerodynamics and a fly-by-wire technology.[76]

Finally, Boeing decided to delay another project, its most ambitious one: the development and production of a supersonic jet. In November 1998, Boeing postponed until the year 2020 the date on which its projected supersonic jetliner would enter service. A 300-foot-long mockup built in 1970—now under restoration in a San Francisco museum—represented the most advanced progress Boeing had ever made toward completing the project.[77]

NOTES

1. David Whitford, "Sale of the Century," *Fortune*, February 17, 1997, p. 100; Andy Reinhardt, "Three Huge Hours in Seattle," *Business Week*, December 30, 1996, p. 38; Jeff Cole, "Air Power: Boeing Plan to Acquire McDonnell Douglas Bolsters Consolidation," *Wall Street Journal*, December 16, 1996.
2. *Fortune*, February 17, 1997, pp. 96, 98, 100; Anthony Velocci, "Vertical Integration looming larger at McDonnell Douglas," *Aviation Week and Space Technology*, March 6, 1996, pp. 58–59.
3. Quoted in *Fortune*, February 17, 1997, p. 96.
4. Lawrence Fisher, "Boeing Chairman Offers 'Exuberance and Dynamism,'" *New York Times*, December 16, 1996.
5. David C. Mowery & Nathan Rosenberg, "The Commercial Aircraft Industry" in Richard R. Nelson, ed., *Government and Technological Progress: A Cross Industry Analysis* (New York: Pergamon Press, 1982), p. 116; Michael L. Detrouzos, Richard K.

Lester, & Robert M. Solow, *Made in America: Regaining the Productive Edge* (New York: Harper-Perennial, 1990), p. 204.

6. Mowery & Rosenberg, "The Commercial Aircraft Industry," p. 116; Dertouzos et al., *Made in America*, p. 204.
7. David C. Mowery & Nathan Rosenberg, *Technology and the Pursuit of Economic Growth* (New York: Cambridge University Press, 1989), p. 172. For the Boeing 777, see Eugene Rodgers, *Flying High: The Story of Boeing* (New York: Atlantic Monthly Press, 1996), p. 431; and for the A320: Eric Vayle. "Collision Course in Commercial Aircraft: Boeing—Airbus—McDonnell Douglas, 1991 (A)," Harvard Business School, Case No. 9-391-106, October 1993, p. 3.
8. Dertouzos et al., *Made in America*, p. 203.
9. Ibid., pp. 206, 214.
10. Quoted in Janet Simpson, Lee Field, & David Garvin, "The Boeing 767: From Concept to Production," Harvard Business School, Case No. 9-688-040, p. 6.
11. *The Boeing Company 1998 Annual Report*, p. 45.
12. For more on this argument see Barry Bluestone, Peter Jordan, & Mark Sullivan, *Aircraft Industry Dynamics: An Analysis of Competition, Capital, and Labor* (Boston: Auburn House, 1981), pp. 9–10.
13. Bluestone et al., *Aircraft Industry Dynamics*, pp. 163–164.
14. *Form 10-K of the Boeing Company for the Year Ended December 1, 1997*, p. 3.
15. Lee Smith, "Air Power: Warplane Contracts Give a Lift to the New Aerospace Conglomerates," *Fortune*, July 7, 1997, p. 136.
16. Ibid., p. 135.
17. John B. Rae, *Climb to Greatness: The American Aircraft Industry, 1920–1960* (Cambridge Mass.: MIT Press, 1958), pp. 9–11, 63–72, 171; Boeing Commercial Airplane Group, *Backgrounder*, August 1997, p. 2.
18. Irving B. Holley, *Buying Aircraft: Material Procurement for the Army Air Force* (Washington: GPO, 1964), pp. 550, 576–77.
19. Rae, *Climb to Greatness*, p. 206.
20. Almarin Phillips, *Technology and Market Structure: A Study of the Aircraft Industry* (Lexington, Mass.: D.C. Heath, 1971), p. 110.
21. Rodgers, *Flying High*, p. 199.
22. Ibid., pp. 225–26.
23. Rae, *Climb to Greatness*, pp. 187–188; *Aerospace Facts and Figures, 1997–98*, pp. 47, 52–54; Boeing, *Backgrounder*, August 1997, pp. 5, 7–8; *Hoover's Handbook of American Business, 1997* (Austin: Hoover's Business Press, 1997), pp. 892–93.
24. Boeing, *Commercial Airplane Group, Announced Orders and Deliveries as of 12/31/97*, p. 1. in conjunction with *The Boeing Company 1997 Annual Report*, p. 19; and *Aerospace Facts and Figures* 1997–98, p. 35.
25. Rodgers, *Flying High*, p. 287–88; Boeing, *Backgrounder*, August 1997, p. 6.
26. Rodgers, *Flying High*, p. 284–85.
27. *Aerospace Facts and Figures 1997–98*, p. 33.
28. *The Boeing Company Annual Report*, p. 23.
29. Rodgers, *Flying High*, p. 413.
30. *The Boeing Company 1997 Annual Report*, p. 35.
31. Anthony L. Velocci, "MD-XX Termination May Seal Douglas' Fate," *Aviation Week and Space Technology*, November 4, 1996, pp. 24–25. See also *Fortune*, February 17, 1997, p. 98; and Bruce Smith, "Douglas Looks at Twin-engine Design," *Aviation Week and Space Technology*, September 2, 1996, p. 78.
32. The quotations are from Jeremy Main, "Betting on the 21st Century Jet," *Fortune*, April 20, 1992, pp. 103–104, but see also Rodgers, *Flying High*, p. 420.
33. *Hoover's Handbook of American Business, 1997*, pp. 272–73, 892–93; Boeing, *Backgrounder*, August 1997, pp. 8–9; Rodgers, *Flying High*, p. 327; *Form 10-K of the Boeing Company for the Year Ended December 31, 1997*, p. 3.
34. Rodgers, *Flying High*, p. 422; Dertouzos et al., *Made in America*, p. 208; Vayle, "Collision Course in Commercial Aircraft," p. 18.
35. Dertouzos et al., *Made in America*, pp. 210–214; Rodgers, *Flying High*, Ch. 12; "Airbus 25 Years Old," *Le Figaro*, October 1997 (reprinted in English translation by Airbus Industrie), p. 6.
36. Equally important, Airbus made an aggressive use of composite materials to reduce the aircraft's weight and simplify the aircraft's construction (for example, it used composites to build a vertical fin, reducing the fin's parts-count from 2,000 to 100). Similarly, in the area of aerodynamics, Airbus designed a wing that featured a distinct twist at the root to reduce drag, and a gust alleviation system to improve efficiency in cruise as well as reduce passenger discomfort in turbulence. "Airbus Industrie: 25 Flying Years," Airbus Industrie, 1997, pp. 13, 14, 17; Dertouzos et al., *Made in America*, pp. 212–213.
37. Together, these efforts enabled Airbus to slash its delivery "lead time" (the period lasting from the time a customer gave specifications until delivery) from 15 to 9 months (single-aisle) and from 18 to 12 months (wide-body), and thereby reduce costly inventories by 30 percent. Charles Goldsmith, "Re-engineering: After Trailing Boeing for Years Airbus Aims at 50% of the Market," *Wall Street Journal*, March 16, 1998.
38. Dertouzos et al., *Made in America*, p. 212. A typical Airbus ad read: "Airbus' unique use of the latest fly-by-wire technology . . . enables airlines to operate . . . a whole set of aircraft types ranging from 120 to over 400 seats in capacity . . . with a single pool of pilots" at a saving of "$1 million per aircraft per year." "Airbus: the Airbus Family," Airbus Industrie, 1997.
39. *The Boeing Company 1997 Annual Report*, p. 3; Jeff Cole, "Boeing Names New Managers, Alters Structure," *Wall Street Journal*, August 7, 1997.

40. Lawrence Zuckerman, "Boeing's Man in the Line of Fire," *New York Times,* November 8, 1998.
41. Frederick Biddle & Andy Paszor, "Boeing May Be Hurt Up to 5 Years," *Wall Street Journal,* December 3, 1998.
42. "Fearful Boeing," *Economist,* February 27, 1999, p. 59.
43. The *Boeing Company 1997 Annual Report,* p. 72.
44. Jeanne Cummings, "President, in State of the Union Address, Offers Most Ambitious Agenda Since 1995," *Wall Street Journal,* January 20, 1999; *The Boeing Company 1997 Annual Report,* p. 27; *Fortune,* July 7, 1997, p. 134.
45. *Fortune,* July 7, 1997, pp. 133–136.
46. Ibid., p. 136.
47. Ibid., p. 136.
48. *The Boeing Company 1997 Annual Report,* p. 25; *Fortune,* July 7, 1997, p. 136.
49. *Fortune,* February 17, 1999, p. 100; July 7, 1997, p. 136; Jeff Cole, "Lockheed Warplane Has Racked Up Cost Overruns," *Wall Street Journal,* February 5, 1999.
50. Adam Bryant, "Boeing Offering $13 Billion to Buy McDonnell Douglas," *New York Times,* December 16, 1996.
51. *The Boeing Company 1997 Annual Report,* p. 36; Frederick Biddle, "Boeing Is Still Waiting for the Merger Results to Take Off," *Wall Street Journal,* March 2, 1998.
52. Frederick Biddle & John Helyar, "Flying Low: Behind Boeing's Woes: Clunky Assembly Line, Price War with Airbus," *Wall Street Journal,* April 24, 1998.
53. *Form 10-K of the Boeing Company for the Year Ended December 31, 1997,* p. 4; *Form 10-O of the Boeing Company for the Quarterly Period Ended June 30, 1998,* pp. 14–15.
54. "Out-of-sequence work is an especially costly problem on an aircraft assembly line," says the *Boeing Company 1997 Annual Report* (p. 3), "as it causes efficiency to plummet to a small fraction of what it should be." See also p. 37.
55. "Bouncing Boeing," *Economist,* June 13, 1998, p. 72; *Wall Street Journal,* April 24, 1998.
56. According to Harry Stonecipher, cited in *The New York Times,* December 3, 1998.
57. "Aircraft Making: Boeing Woeing," *Economist,* August 8, 1998, p. 55; June 13, 1998, p. 72.
58. *Wall Street Journal,* April 24, 1998.
59. "Aerospace: Hubris at Airbus, Boeing Rebuilds," *Economist,* November 28, 1998, p. 65. My figures are slightly different than those of the *Economist* because I used the actual number of jets produced and the *Economist* used the projected number.
60. *Wall Street Journal,* December 3, 1998.
61. *Business Week,* December 30, 1996, p. 39.
62. Rodgers, *Flying High,* pp. 428–430.
63. Laurence Zuckerman, "Boeing's Leaders Loosing Altitude," *New York Times,* December 13, 1998.
64. Rodgers, *Flying High,* pp. 427–28.
65. *New York Times,* December 13, 1998.
66. *New York Times,* December 13, 1998; Seanna Brower, "Comeback: Boeing Breathes Easier," *Business Week,* May 3, 1999.
67. *New York Times,* November 8, 1998; *Economist,* November 28, 1998, p. 65.
68. *Economist,* November 28, 1998, p. 65.
69. Jeff Cole, "New CEO's Assignment: Signal a Turnaround," *Wall Street Journal,* January 26, 1999.
70. Ibid.
71. *The Boeing Company 1998 Annual Report,* p. 39; Jeff Cole, "Boeing Co. May Give Unions Say on Subcontracts," *Wall Street Journal,* April 5, 1999.
72. Rodgers, *Flying High,* pp. 449–62; for the quotation see Anthony Velocci, "Healing Begins at McDonnell Douglas as Strikers Return to Work," *Aviation Week and Space Technology,* September 16, 1996, p. 90.
73. Robert Rafalko & James Fisher, "Business as Warfare at McDonnell Douglas Corporation." Paper presented in the 1998 meeting of the North American Case Research Association, Durham, New Hampshire, pp. 1–7. For the quotation, see *Aviation Week and Space Technology,* September 16, 1996, p. 90.
74. *Wall Street Journal,* April 5, 1999; Ann Marie Squeo, "Boeing, Union Leaders Reached Pact on Contract," *Wall Street Journal,* August 30, 1999.
75. Frederic Biddle, "Pulled Off Its Cloud, Boeing Suspends Quest for the Next Generation Jumbo Jet," *Wall Street Journal,* December 3, 1998; "Airbus May Be About to Challenge the Jumbo Jet's 30 Year-Old Monopoly," *Economist,* March 27, 1999, pp. 61–62.
76. *Economist,* March 27, 1999, pp. 61–62.
77. *Wall Street Journal,* December 3, 1998.

CASE 10

BP-MOBIL and the Restructuring of the Oil Refining Industry

Karel Cool
Jeffrey Reuer
Ian Montgomery
Francesca Gee
INSEAD

On February 29, 1996, British Petroleum (BP) and Mobil surprised investors and competitors with an unexpected announcement: After six months of secret talks, the two oil companies had agreed to merge their refining and retail sales operations in a pan-European joint venture.

The move was a new approach to confronting longstanding problems in the European oil market. In refining, international companies had been confronted with low returns, excess capacity and high exit costs; in retail, competition was heating up, especially from a new category of players: supermarkets. For years, major players had practiced increasingly stringent cost-cutting. Yet, none had attempted anything as ambitious as Mobil and BP.

When presenting the deal, Mobil and BP stressed their shared focus on financial performance and discipline and said that the combination provided an excellent fit in terms of geographic spread and quality of assets which would give them leadership in key markets. By pooling their $5 billion in European assets, BP and Mobil figured they could save $400–500m a year. They said their combined market share in Europe would amount to 12 percent in fuels, hard on the heels of market leaders Exxon and Shell, and 18 percent in lubricants.

While oil industry analysts praised BP and Mobil for acting decisively, they also expressed some doubts with the joint venture. Was an alliance the best response to the industry's troubles at a time when other players were leaving the market altogether? "It's an original deal," said an investment banker, "but it puts them right in the middle: They are not niche players but they are not the leaders either. I wonder whether they are quite big enough." To reap the dramatic savings they were announcing, Mobil and BP would have to close down more refineries and petrol stations and lay off thousands—an unpopular move in unemployment-stricken Europe.

THE OIL INDUSTRY VALUE CHAIN

Oil was the world's main source of energy. Its end products were used in a variety of ways: transport by land, water and air (petrol[1], diesel, jet propulsion fuels), heating (heating oil), lubricants (mainly in rolling mills, car engines, machinery, and precision instruments), building materials (asphalt), etc. About 12 percent of crude oil was converted into plastics and synthetic fibers. Crude oils varied substantially in looks, composition, density, and flow properties due to their different formation conditions. Crude from Libya and Algeria, for instance, was thin-bodied and yellowish with virtually no sulphur content. Venezuelan heavy oils, by contrast, were viscous, almost solid and dark black in color with a lot of sulphur. Normal petroleum products could be made from all oils but good crude (thin-bodied, low-sulphur) was easier to refine.

This case is intended to be used as a basis for classroom discussion rather than to illustrate either effective or ineffective handling of an administrative situation.

Copyright © 1999 INSEAD, Fontainebleau, France. All rights reserved.

Upstream Operations

Upstream operations, the generic name for all activities related to crude oil before refining, included exploration and production. Oil was found in underground reservoirs, surrounded by rock formations which geologists studied to identify the presence of oil. They used increasingly sophisticated and expensive tools, from surface mapping and aerial surveys to seismic soundings. Advanced drilling techniques had made it possible to explore new areas such as the seabeds of the Gulf of Mexico and the North Sea. Exploratory wells could reach 2,500 meters below the surface of the ocean. By 1996 world production averaged 65m barrels per day (bpd).[2] While the world's largest oil fields were in the Middle East, part of production had moved to the North Sea and the Americas, the result of a switch to politically safer areas.

After a series of nationalizations, mostly in the 1970s, the upstream industry became dominated by major producers which owned most of the world's proven reserves. Aramco of Saudi Arabia was the biggest; other important players were Petroleos de Venezuela, Pemex of Mexico, the Kuwait Petroleum Company and Statoil of Norway. Exhibit 1 shows their share in world production.

Downstream Operations

Downstream included transportation and storage of crude oil, processing, refining and marketing of final products to customers. Refining (described in Exhibit 2)

EXHIBIT 1 | Distribution of Control of World Oil Production and Refining

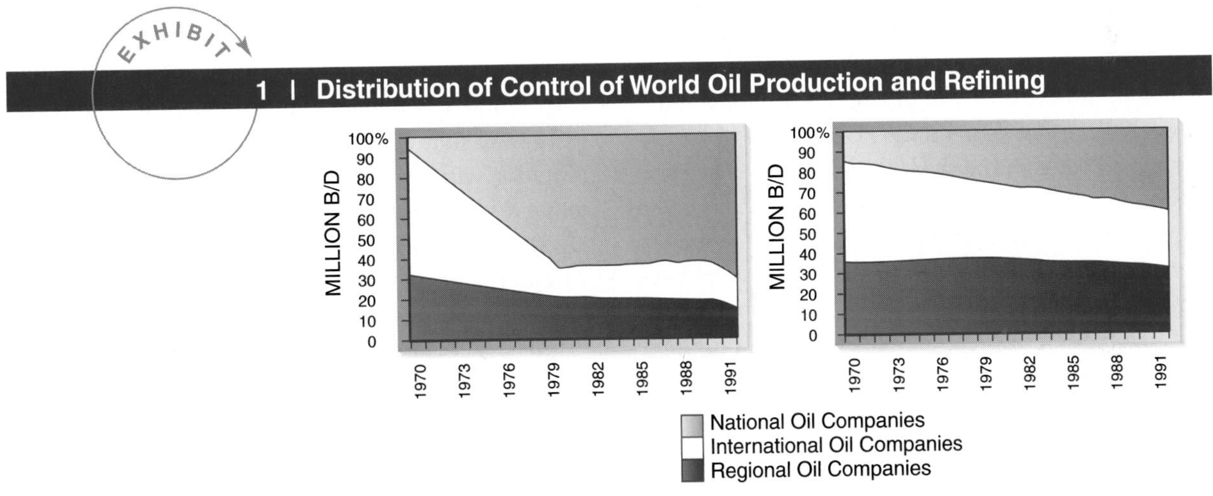

Source: Booz-Allen & Hamilton ("Dinosaurs Can Fly")

EXHIBIT 2 | Refining Processes and Product Flows

	Input	Intermediate	Output
Products	Crude oil	Kerosene, naphtha, gas oils, distillate	Gasoline, distillate, jet fuel, liquefied petroleum gas (LPG), and residuals
Processes	Crude distillation	Coker, hydrotreater, catalytic cracker, alkylation, hydrocracker, reformer	Distribution and retailing

essentially breaks down crude into various components which are then reconfigured into new products. While refineries could handle different qualities of crude and produce various end products, the more sophisticated refineries were better able to upgrade crude into high-value products. Although the product mix could not be changed completely, the way plants were configured and the quality of crude afforded some flexibility.

Global refining capacity in 1996 stood at 78m bpd. Refining was carried out in about 700 refineries which were evenly distributed between North America, Europe, Asia, and the rest of the world. The average capacity was 100,000 bpd.[3] Most of these plants had been planned before the 1973 oil shock when demand had been expected to grow almost indefinitely. Opening a new refinery took a long time and cost billions of dollars. Running it was comparatively inexpensive but closing it down entailed substantial clean-up costs (estimated to be as high as $100m) and redundancy costs. For these reasons, owners usually operated existing plants, even in a situation of over-capacity. Exhibit 3 shows the worldwide trend in refining.

In marketing, the largest volumes sold were petrol at the pump. Initially, service stations had been operated by large oil companies and by small independent operators. Lately, large out-of-town supermarkets had been joining the fray. Profitability was determined by the number and location of service stations and by supply logistics. Oil companies also offered specific services to industrial customers, supplies of jet fuel and bunkering (marine fuels, diesel oil, and gas oil). These were usually delivered directly from the refinery.

Large integrated companies were dominating downstream operations. These included Shell, BP, Texaco, Gulf, Exxon, Mobil, and Chevron. The last three had been formed after an antitrust decision to break up John D. Rockefeller's Standard Oil in 1911. These giant multinationals engaged in all aspects of the oil and gas business, from exploration and production to refining and marketing. Exhibit 4 shows their relative position in terms of reserves, output, and sales.

Customer Demand

Historically, the main driver of demand for oil had been the rate of economic growth. Demand also followed an annual cycle, peaking during the Northern Hemisphere's winter and falling in summer and stood at about 65m bpd in 1996. The global oil market was still growing, albeit at a slower pace than in the sixties and seventies. After World War II, demand had surged from 10m bpd in 1945 to 60m bpd in 1970. This had encouraged exploration which soon unveiled large, accessible reserves in the Middle East.

The oil shock caused by OPEC's embargo in 1973–74 and the second shock in 1979 wrought such havoc to Western economies that governments embarked on long-term programs to reduce oil dependence. Coal, liquefied natural gas, and nuclear power were developed as

EXHIBIT 3 | World Refining Capacity (Millions of Tonnes)

Region	1980	1993	1994	1995	1996 (est.)
Western Europe	1,000.0	704.5	706.7	701.4	704.1
Middle East	205.8	255.0	266.2	264.8	269.8
Africa	107.4	145.9	144.2	144.1	145.3
North America	1,025.0	851.1	861.3	860.1	864.2
Latin America	436.3	375.4	367.8	371.0	372.6
Far East	572.0	682.9	720.9	740.2	814.3
Eastern Europe and FSU	769.7	642.3	642.6	636.6	632.5
Total	4,116.2	3,657.1	3,709.7	3,718.2	3,802.8

Source: Union Francaise des Industries Petrolieres (Bilan 1996).

4 | Relative Positions of Large Companies at Various Stages of the Oil Industry Value Chain

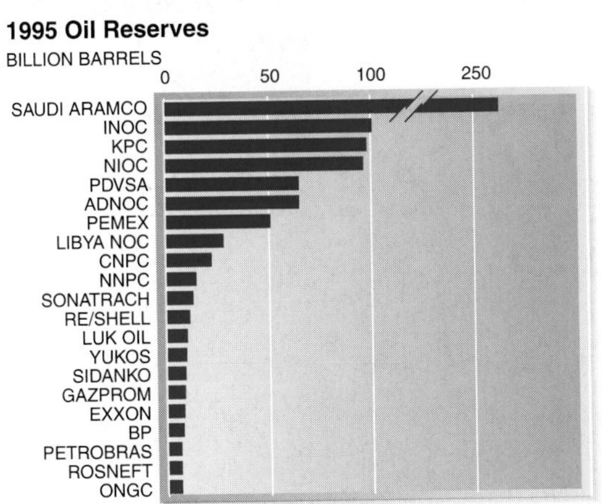

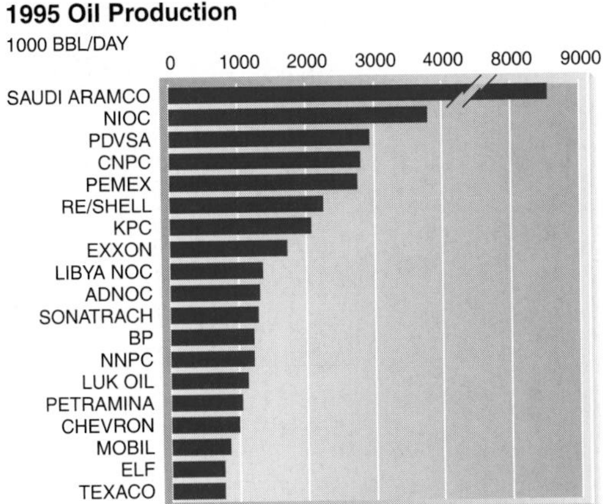

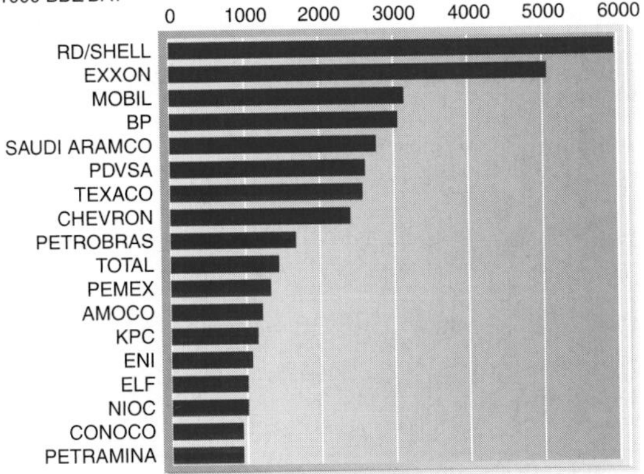

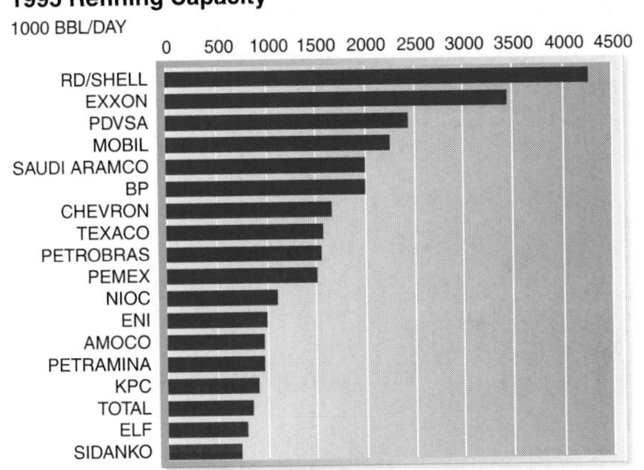

Source: National statistics, oil company annual reports.

substitutes; energy conservation and efficiency gains were encouraged. (Exhibit 5 shows the expected shift away from oil until 2005; Exhibit 6 shows fuel savings achieved by car manufacturers.) The result was that between 1978 and 1985, oil's share of the total energy market in industrial countries fell to 43 percent from 53 percent.

The oil shocks, government programs, and the cyclical nature of demand caused wide swings in oil prices. After the 1973 shock, the price per barrel increased from $2.9 in the summer to $11.65 in December. By 1979, it had shot up to $34. In 1985, OPEC stopped protecting its prices to regain demand. The bellwether West Texas Intermediate futures contract immediately lost two-thirds of its value to trade below $10. Internal conflict within OPEC and cheating on quotas led to overproduction. While more volatility ensued, prices stabilized in the mid-nineties within a $15–18 range. Exhibit 7 plots spot prices in the 1990s.

5 | European Energy Market (Existing and Projected)

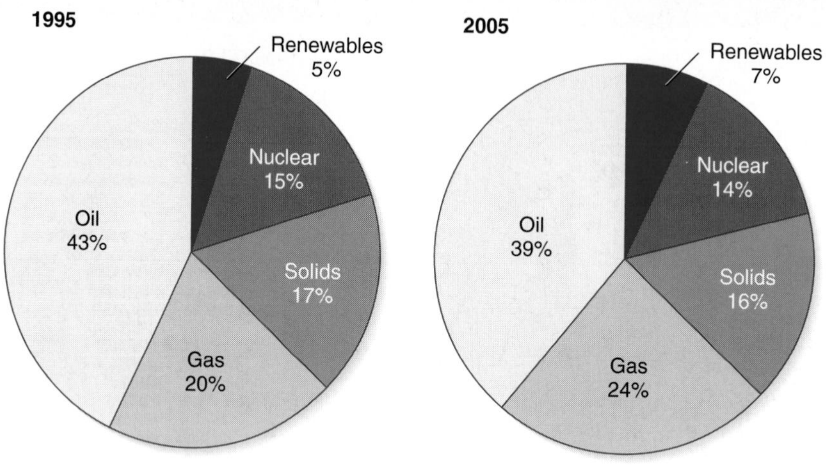

Source: Internal Marakon Analysis.

6 | Increase in Automobile Fuel Efficiency

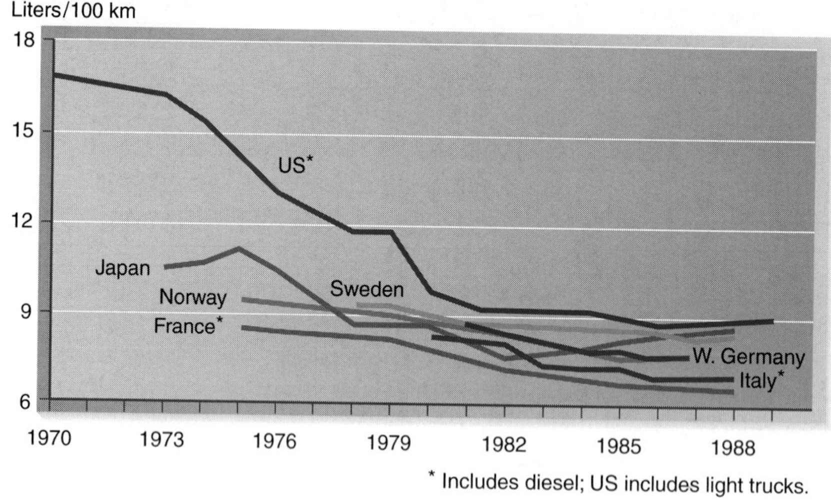

Source: International Energy Studies, LBL. Incl. diesel; US includes light trucks.

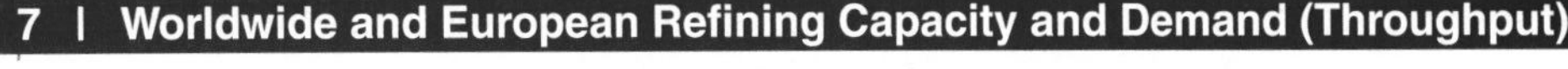

EXHIBIT 7 | Worldwide and European Refining Capacity and Demand (Throughput)

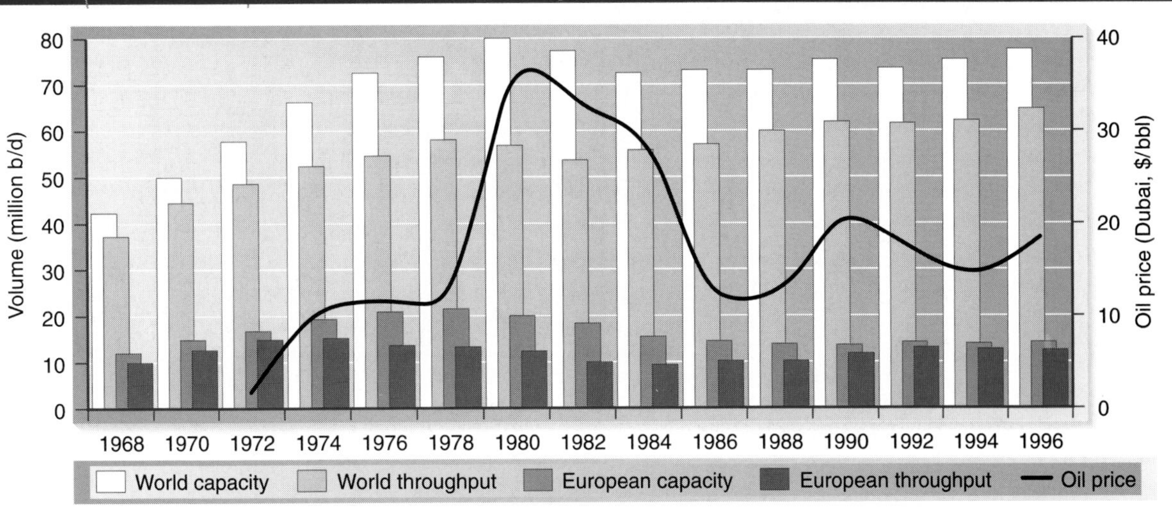

Source: BP Statistical Review of World Energy, 1997.

THE EUROPEAN DOWNSTREAM INDUSTRY

Refining

In recession-hit Europe in the mid-nineties, demand was nearly flat with growth forecasts of 0.5 percent p.a. until 2005. The market was depressed by fuel efficiency gains, higher duties, taxes (which governments often justified on environmental grounds), and increased supplies of nuclear power and natural gas. This stagnation was in stark contrast with the optimistic development programs prior to 1973 when demand had been expected to grow exponentially. Because of the long lead times for planning and building refineries, new plants had come onstream, resulting in significant overcapacity in some parts of Europe. Exhibit 8 shows margins during the nineties.

High exit costs as well as governments' industrial and employment policies were often blamed for the industry's failure to tackle overcapacity. There also was fragmented ownership of firms. The European refining industry had a mix of state-owned, integrated, and independent companies. In most national markets, up to a dozen of these companies shared half the total capacity.

Overcapacity was also exacerbated by productivity improvements. Until 1991, capacity utilization and margins had grown in parallel but this was no longer true, as Exhibit 9 shows. Demanding new regulations,

EXHIBIT 8 | European Refining Margins

DOLLAR MARGIN ON A BARREL OF COMPLEX NWE BRENT

	1991	1992	1993	1994	1995	1996
Quarter 1	6.28	2.2	1.81	2.17	1.35	1.56
Quarter 2	3.37	1.92	2.26	1.43	1.67	1.75
Quarter 3	2.88	1.94	2.34	1.74	1.64	
Quarter 4	–2.89	1.92	2.4	1.67	1.46	

Source: Woods Mackenzie.

9 | European Refining Margins and Utilization

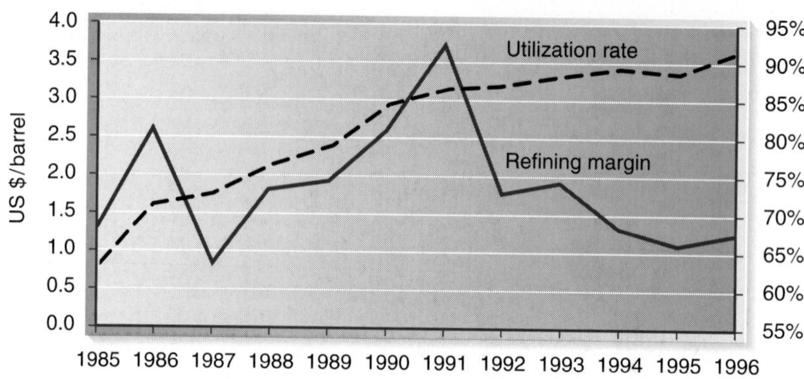

Source: Woods Mackenzie.

often dictated by environmental concerns, had resulted in capacity creep. As margins declined, all producers were working to incrementally increase their capacity. Exhibit 10 shows capacity utilization for major European oil companies.

The problem of overcapacity was aggravated by mismatches between the configuration of refineries (which had been planned for heavy Middle East crude) and actual supplies (often, lighter North Sea oil). Demand for diesel also had grown much faster than expected so that many refineries operating at capacity for diesel had spare capacity for petrol. Demand for fuel oil also had declined as supplies of natural gas became available. Exhibit 11 shows changes in the European demand mix.

Although oil companies generally aggregated into their published accounts their refining and marketing results, it was known that refining was far less profitable than marketing. Geographic differences in refining margins persisted. Margins had been higher in Asia where refining units were larger and yielded greater market power. In Europe, they were lower than in the United States where cheap prices for divested plants had enabled independent refiners to acquire assets which they operated at about 15 percent return on capital. (Tosco, for instance, had bought refineries and retail sites from both Exxon and BP). More lenient environmental laws, a flexible labor market, less price competition in a more consolidated industry, and the absence of direct central

10 | Refining Capacity Utilization Rate

	EUROPEAN REFINERS UTILIZATION RATE			
	1993	**1994**	**1995**	**1996**
Agip	78%	79%	74%	75%
Exxon	86	84	79	89
Repsol	86	87	87	84
Shell	100	100	98	102
Total	89	94	90	104
BP-Mobil	95	92	99	94
European average	86	88	88	91

Source: Woods Mackenzie.

11 | Demand Mix

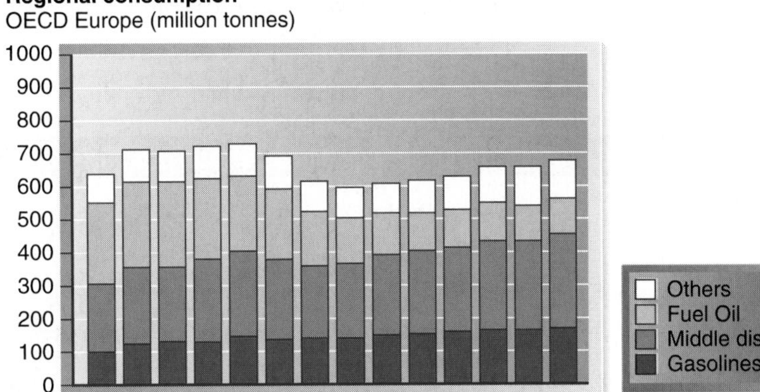

Note: "Middle distillates" refers to diesel.
Source: BP Statistical Review of World Energy, 1997.

government control also helped make U.S. downstream players more profitable than European ones.

Beyond these concerns, the European downstream industry was bracing itself for a huge bill following the European Commission's 1993 Auto-Oil program, which aimed at reducing levels of urban atmospheric pollution by the year 2010. The industry would probably need huge investments to improve the quality of diesel and petrol. This was likely to cost the industry a total of $16b over a 15-year period.

Marketing

Some 300 billion liters of petrol and other retail products were sold every year in Western Europe. The leaders, Shell and Exxon, each had about 12 percent market share. There were some 120,000 service stations operated by the major integrated companies, supermarkets, and independent retailers. Their number was falling rapidly (as shown in Exhibit 12). In France, there were 18,000 petrol stations left, compared with 47,000 in 1976, and a further 5,500 were expected to close. Ger-

12 | The Trend in Petrol Retailing Sites

	AVERAGE NUMBER OF RETAIL SITES			
	United Kingdom	Germany	France	Benelux
1987	20197	20751	31100	15510
1988	20016	20198	29000	15150
1989	19756	19802	27700	14699
1990	19465	19351	25700	13937
1991	19247	18898	23700	13211
1992	18549	18836	21700	12668
1993	17969	18464	20000	11820
1994	16971	18300	19013	11022
1995	16244	17957	18406	10490
1996	14748	17660	17974	10030

Source: Woods Mackenzie.

many too had 18,000, down from a peak of 46,700. In the UK, their number was forecast to fall below 10,000 by 2005, from 16,000 in 1996.

The Western European market was characterized by weak brands and by changes in distribution channels where supermarkets increasingly displaced small dealer networks while integrated companies and national players were trying to turn service station forecourts into convenience stores. (Exhibits 13 to 20 describe various characteristics of national markets). Petrol was increas-

EXHIBIT 13 | Comparative Average Throughput per Site (1995)

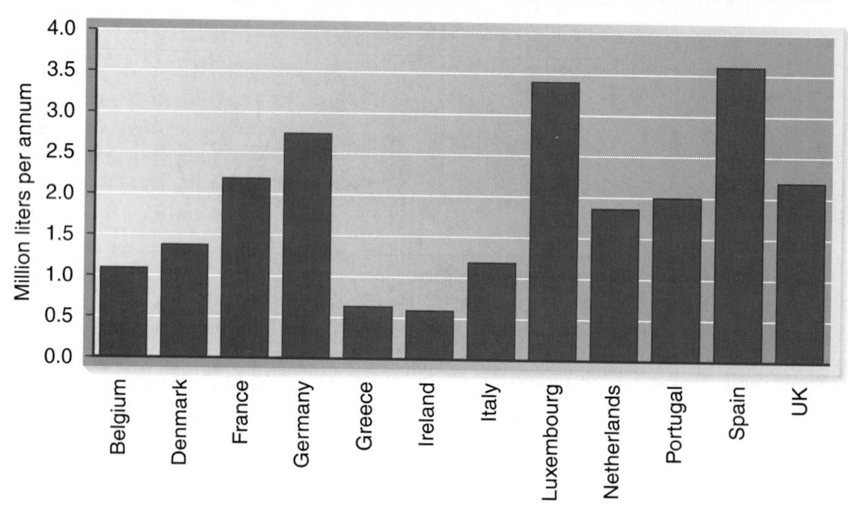

Source: Woods Mackenzie.

EXHIBIT 14 | Retail Petrol Margins

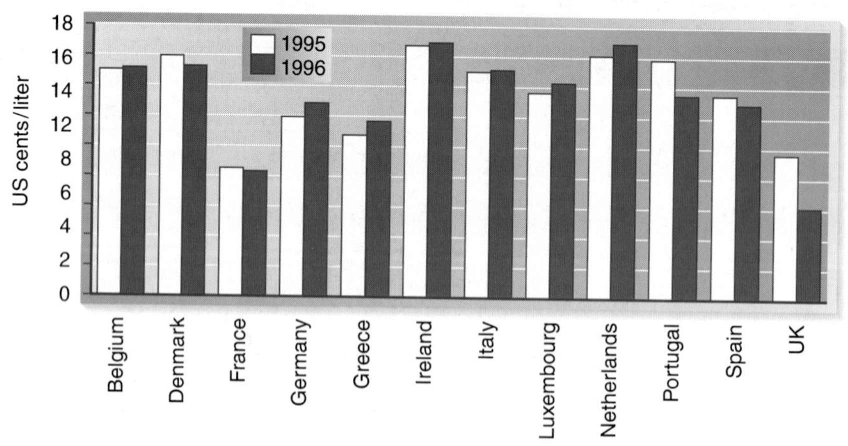

Source: Woods Mackenzie.

ingly perceived as a commodity product with gross sales margins of 2–4 percent. Consumers bought mainly on convenience (proximity) and price. Even the "majors" now competed on price. Brands remained weak and undifferentiated despite efforts to build them up; independent surveys showed that brand value, measured by the additional margin compared with an unbranded product, was minimal.

The weakness of brands had favored the entry and growth of supermarkets. Huge shopping centers had

EXHIBIT 15 | Retail Diesel Margins

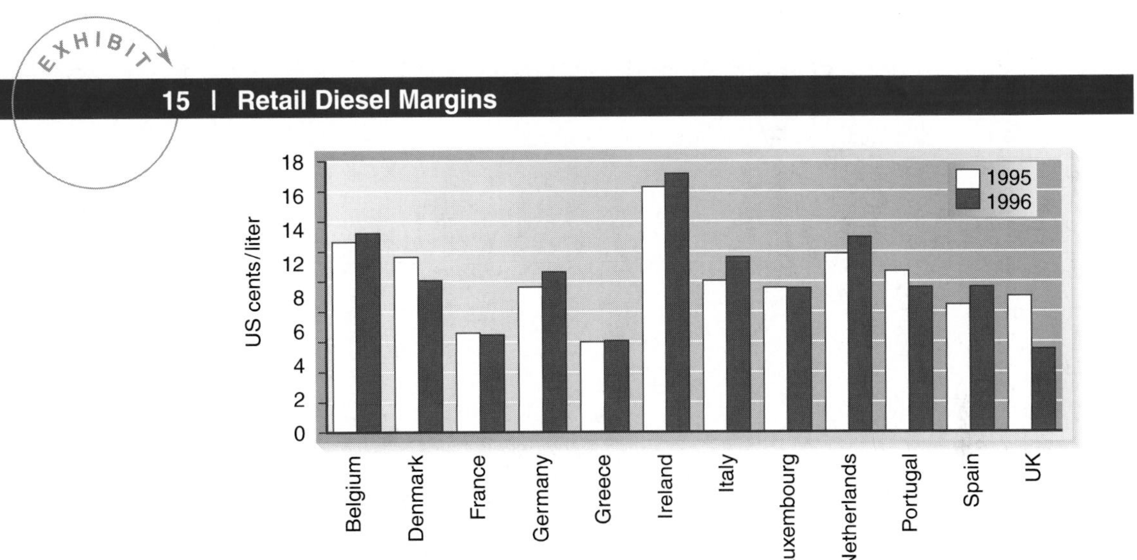

Source: Woods Mackenzie.

EXHIBIT 16 | Comparative Total Gross Margin per Site (1995)

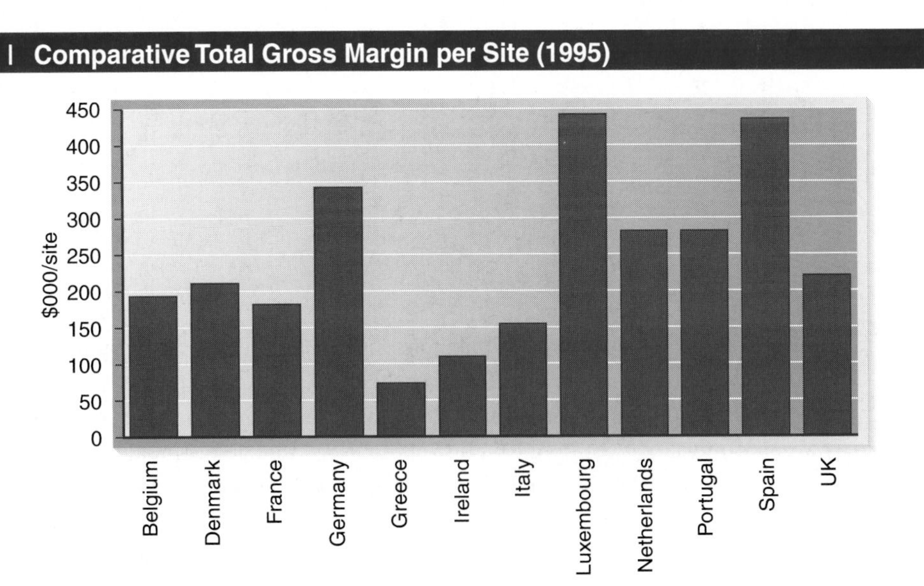

Source: Woods Mackenzie.

17 | Comparison of European Countries—Selected Variables

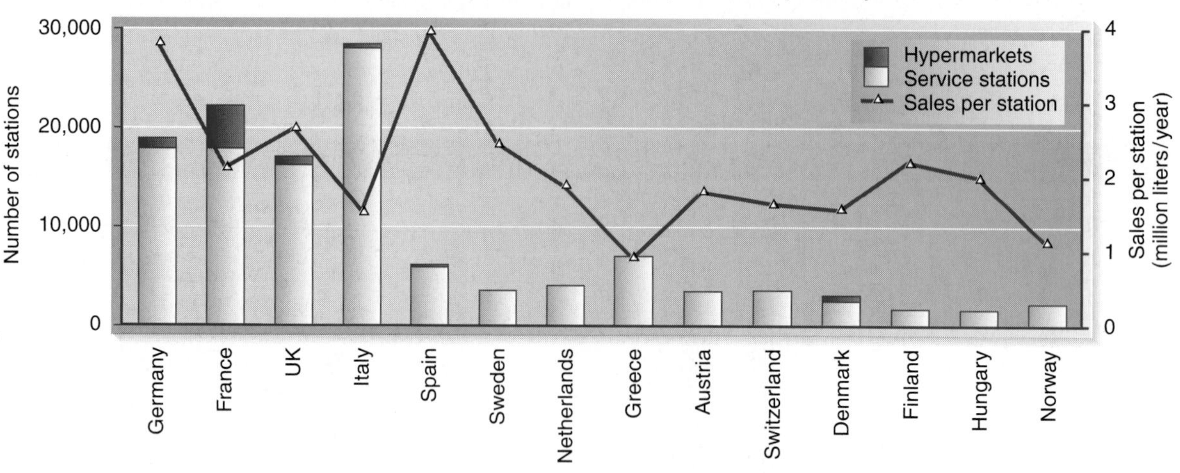

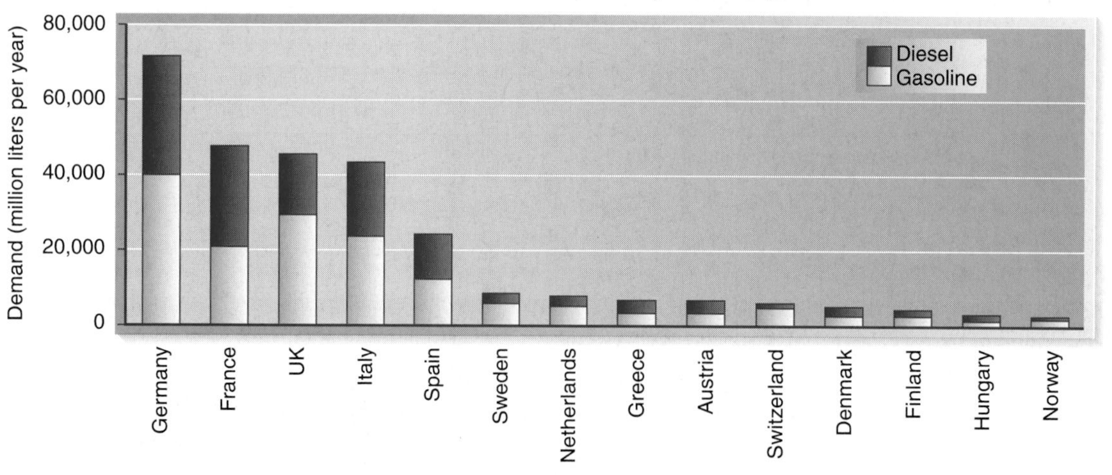

Sources: Petroleum Review June 1997 / UFIP/ national oil industry associations.

sprung up near major cities and enjoyed many advantages. They had acres of free parking and customers had become used to visiting them every week. Filling up was just part of "one-stop shopping." In 1996 their market share was already high in France (over 50 percent), the UK (over 20 percent), and Germany (over 10 percent).

The average supermarket service station sold much more fuel than other service stations. In Britain, for example, the 664 supermarket stations had 20 percent of the whole market. As "bulk" buyers, they could negotiate lower prices for supplies. They could also take advantage of imbalances between supply and demand in their region. As a result, the supermarkets often paid lower wholesale prices than the integrated oil companies' own marketing divisions.

Supermarkets also seemed to operate on smaller margins than traditional service stations. Competitors

EXHIBIT 18 | The Economics of Selling Petrol across Europe

REFINING NET PROFITABILITY ANALYSIS

	United Kingdom	Italy	Germany	France
Retail costs				
Distribution	0.8	23.5	2.2	8
Advertising and promotion	0.5	15	1.4	4.5
Other marketing	1.3	33.5	3.4	11.5
Retail site costs	3.4	66	8.5	19
Retail revenue				
Unit margin	6.2	223	17.8	43
Nonfuel sources	1.5	12	4.3	4.5
	pence/liter	lire/liter	pfenning/liter	centimes/liter

Source: Woods Mackenzie.

EXHIBIT 19 | Market Share Data

ESTIMATED OVERALL MARKET SHARE (1996)

	United Kingdom	Italy	Germany	France	Benelux
Exxon	16%	10%	11%	11%	16%
Shell	16	3	13	12	19
Total	5	n/a	2	21	6
Elf	3	n/a	6	21	n/a
Agip	n/a	19	2	1	n/a

Source: Woods Mackenzie.

grumbled that supermarkets didn't hesitate to sell at a loss in order to capture market share. In fact, French supermarkets had increased their prices as soon as they had established a degree of market power. While the growth of out-of-town supermarkets seemed to have peaked in the UK and France, it continued in Germany and Italy and was only starting up in Spain, Portugal, and Ireland.

Independent retailers that could no longer compete went out of business. Other retailers tried to rise to the challenge: They consolidated their networks, keeping only the more profitable locations, and engaged in price wars. Others tried to turn old rivals into allies, opening their own branded outlets on supermarket premises. This was Repsol's strategy in Spain with El Corte and Shell's in the Netherlands with Ahold.

Another strategy was to develop convenience stores in existing service stations. Taking advantage of long opening hours and dedicated car parks, these new "corner shops" offered goods and services such as cigarettes, newspapers, food and drinks, automated bank tellers, fax, photocopiers, post office, lottery, and photo shops, reducing the dependence of retailers on petrol sales. It was hoped that, in the longer term, forecourts would become shopping areas in their own right, maybe in partnership with established food retailers.

Opportunities in Eastern Europe

The stagnation of the Western European retail market was encouraging oil companies to look east. The collapse of communism in 1989 had left a dilapidated infrastructure and limited distribution networks, but

20 | Western European Oil Consumption (1987–1996)

	1987	1988	1989	1990	1991	1992	1993	1994	1995	1996
Austria	9,359	9,145	8,948	9,489	10,158	9,913	9,984	10,074	10,136	10,816
Belgium	17,486	17,788	17,205	17,022	18,559	19,240	18,656	19,188	18,884	21,262
Denmark	8,997	8,351	7,898	7,704	7,879	7,648	7,665	8,100	7,847	8,128
Finland	9,810	9,561	9,410	9,371	9,058	8,786	8,541	8,913	8,664	8,960
France	77,528	77,616	80,518	79,636	84,124	84,337	82,718	82,984	84,234	85,871
Germany	120,020	120,172	112,954	117,617	125,062	126,134	127,451	126,102	126,210	128,358
Greece	10,351	10,948	11,379	11,328	12,133	12,190	12,072	12,541	13,273	14,212
Ireland	3,895	3,675	3,715	4,199	4,419	4,678	4,655	5,112	5,266	5,454
Italy	82,842	82,126	85,593	85,412	84,224	85,686	83,841	84,279	86,865	85,694
Luxembourg	1,285	1,316	1,450	1,585	1,848	1,897	1,892	1,884	1,736	1,808
Netherlands	17,902	18,680	18,293	17,537	18,038	17,840	16,923	17,365	18,264	17,295
Portugal	8,208	8,566	10,993	10,776	10,940	12,192	11,475	11,335	12,267	11,841
Spain	36,415	41,060	41,063	40,672	40,570	41,882	44,997	48,504	50,613	49,272
Sweden	15,032	16,119	15,122	13,735	13,941	14,570	14,161	15,058	15,330	17,719
United Kingdom	67,703	72,316	73,029	73,941	74,507	75,472	75,790	74,957	73,836	75,241
EU total	**486,833**	**497,439**	**497,570**	**500,024**	**515,460**	**522,465**	**520,821**	**526,396**	**533,425**	**541,931**
Island	608	596	538	540	565	561	718	729	731	780
Norway	7,402	7,087	6,909	6,737	6,599	6,560	6,147	6,407	6,442	7,171
Switzerland	12,211	12,247	11,774	12,612	12,790	12,969	12,117	12,508	11,577	11,923
Turkey	20,387	20,436	20,763	21,326	20,905	22,020	25,412	24,016	26,725	27,889
Western Europe Total	**527,441**	**537,805**	**537,554**	**541,239**	**556,319**	**564,575**	**565,215**	**570,056**	**578,900**	**589,694**

Thousands of metric tonnes
Source: National statistics.

upbeat forecasts for economic growth suggested that the downstream oil market would grow quickly. Oil companies could enter this new market in two ways. First, existing oil assets could be purchased at bargain-basement rates. However, their low prices often reflected poor quality and underinvestment; cleaning up the sites and meeting potential environmental liabilities could turn out to be enormously costly. Second, firms could build new refineries and retail networks. This was less uncertain but it would take a long time and be hugely expensive. While these risks had made investment slower than expected, all the integrated oil companies had plans for Eastern Europe, with Shell, Exxon, and Total leading the pack.

BP AND MOBIL'S COMPETITORS IN EUROPE

Historically, integrated companies had been able to mitigate the impact of price variations as upstream and downstream hedged each other's risk. Traditionally, high crude prices depressed downstream results and boosted upstream profits. Low oil prices supposedly had the opposite effect. However, from the mid-1980s, profitability fell both upstream (with lower crude prices) and downstream, where overcapacity and flat demand eroded margins.

Faced with these various challenges, downstream companies had taken steps to restructure, often in alliance with competitors. Overall, however, restructuring in Europe had remained less ambitious than in North America. The European players tended to only sell or swap assets. Their profitability was also lower as illustrated in Exhibit 21.

Royal Dutch/Shell

Royal Dutch/Shell, the European market leader, had been founded in 1907 by merging a British and a Dutch group in order to counter the dominance of Standard Oil. With time, the group had become one of the

21 | Comparative Financial Data

	ROACE (91–96)	ROE (91–96)	Average NI (91–96)	Average CAPEX (91–96)	Average Market Cap (91–96)	Average P/E (91–96)	Price to Book (91–96)	Net Income 1996	Balance Sheet 1996	
British Petroleum	6.8%	8.2%	1501	5092	38,378	15.4	2.1	3,025	12,914	(£ mln)
Mobil	8.6	10.2	1823	4288	34,886	21.7	2.0	3,043	19,118	(£ mln)
Royal Dutch/Shell	20.6	10.7	6028	9848	100,752	18.1	1.8	5,591	39,299	(£ mln)
Exxon	12.1	15.4	5788	7081	87849	15.3	2.3	6,975	45,456	($ mln)
Agip	6.9	9.1	1289	874	34,487	12.1	2.2	4,829	27,407	(LIT bn)
Elf	4.3	4.6	744	4167	19,592	24.0	1.3	7,518	99,709	(FF mln)
Total	7.0	7.7	713	2028	12,918	20.4	1.3	4,795	61,479	(FF mln)
Repsol	13.9	15.7	769	1332	8,967	12.1	1.9	120,932	986,886	(Ptas mln)
Norsk Hydro	8.4	11.1	548	1182	7681	1.9	1.7	6,991	42,808	(NKR mln)
Tosco	8.3	7.5	60	123	4127	34.9	6.1	146	1070	($ mln)
Lyondell	26.2	61.9	167	342	1858	37.4	4.1	96	1040	($ mln)
			($mln)	($mln)	($mln)					

world's largest corporations. Its operations in over 100 countries covered exploration and production of oil and natural gas, refining, marketing and chemicals, as well as coal mining, polymers, crop protection products, and various metals.

In Europe, Shell was the second largest refiner after Exxon, with annual capacity of 70m tons and sales of 65m tons. In marketing, it had been the leader with a 12 percent market share and 8,500 retail sites. After the 1990–91 Gulf War, Shell had found itself with large inventories just as prices fell. The drop in profits had prompted a round of internal restructuring that had left analysts generally unimpressed. In 1996 Shell was planning to sell its Swiss refinery, close down lubricant plants, and reduce its retail workforce.

An early mover into central and eastern Europe, Shell had formed a joint venture with Agip and Conoco to take a 49 percent stake in two Czech refineries. In 1996, it had swapped 38 of its sites in western Germany for 44 total sites in eastern Germany. It had also invested in some smaller markets such as Romania, Bulgaria, and Slovenia.

Two recent public relations crises had damaged Shell's image. In 1995, it was forced to shelve plans to dump its used Brent Spar oil installation into the North Sea after vocal complaints led by Greenpeace and consumer boycotts orchestrated across Germany and the rest of Europe. And when Nigeria executed a leading dissident, human rights campaigners accused Shell of supporting a military dictatorship in contempt of minority rights.

Exxon

Exxon, the former Standard Oil of New Jersey (Esso), was the world's largest oil company in terms of revenue. After many of its Middle Eastern oil fields and facilities had been nationalized, Exxon had aggressively expanded exploration and production in safer regions in the 1980s. It suffered a major setback in 1989 when the *Exxon Valdez* tanker ran aground in Alaska, spilling 11m gallons of oil. The initial clean-up bill was $3.6b with a lawsuit seeking $16.5b in compensatory and punitive damages still pending.

In Europe, Exxon had a retail market share of about 11 percent. It had cut back on refining investments and was focusing on reducing costs. In refining, the size and integration of its assets gave it a cost advantage. In marketing, it had started a fierce price war in Britain with its "Price Watch" campaign, which promised to match any competitor's prices within five kilometers.

Eastern Europe was a major area of new investment for Exxon. It had formed marketing joint ventures in

Hungary (with state company AFOR) and in Poland (with a German partner). By 1996, 35 Esso stations were operating in Hungary, Poland, the Czech Republic, and Slovakia.

National Companies

Agip, the leading Italian integrated oil company, was part of the ENI Group. It had production and downstream activities in 13 countries and downstream activities only in a further 13 countries. However most of its refining and marketing operations were in Italy (which accounted for 41 percent of 1995 sales). Agip's strategy was to maintain a strong presence in the attractive Italian market while gradually expanding elsewhere in Europe. In Italy, it wanted to increase return on capital by reducing excess capacity in refining and by closing down less profitable retail sites.

Elf Aquitaine, France's largest industrial company, had been formed in 1965 by merging several small state companies. It was gradually being privatized; the government still had a 13.3 percent stake. Elf was a diversified conglomerate with interests in health and hygiene products and was refocusing on oil. Under a new chief executive, explicit goals had been set in terms of cost savings, debt reduction, and return on capital; noncore assets were sold, resulting in a \$1b net loss of 1994 from write-downs. Its new strategy was to focus on the upstream business, limiting downstream operations to France, Spain, and Germany where Elf had a strong position. There were plans to leave the British market. Elf was expanding in eastern Europe, although with mixed success. A joint venture with a Russian consortium and German public authorities to acquire 1,000 petrol stations in eastern Germany had proven expensive and unprofitable and Elf now wanted to sell.

Repsol, Spain's largest industrial company, had a 60 percent share of the domestic oil market. The government, which had formed Repsol in 1987 to consolidate the fragmented Spanish oil industry, retained a 10 percent stake. The company was expanding its natural gas business through acquisitions, mostly, but not solely, in Spain. Repsol's strategy was to defend its domestic position while expanding natural gas exploration and production. Targets for international expansion included Latin America as well as Portugal, southern France, and northern Africa.

Total, Europe's fourth largest oil and gas producer, had over 10,000 retail stations across the continent. It was listed on the New York Stock Exchange. Yet the French government retained a 5 percent stake. The company had invested aggressively upstream in exploration, especially in the former Soviet Union. Efforts to restore downstream profitability had included cost-cutting and selling off less profitable assets (e.g., refineries in Portugal and the Czech Republic were sold in 1995). In France, competition from the supermarkets had hurt profitability, prompting the company to trim retailing costs and to launch an aggressive effort to regain market share.

Total wanted to expand in high-growth regions such as central and eastern Europe, Portugal, and Turkey, with a focus on marketing and distributing motor fuel. Total had invested FF 700m in Hungary and the Czech Republic between 1992–94. A joint venture with Benzina, owned by the Czech government, had been disappointing in terms of sites and market share. In Hungary, Total had 25 percent of the LPG market after acquiring two marketing companies, Egaz and Kogaz, in 1993.

BP AND MOBIL

British Petroleum

One of the world's largest petroleum and petrochemical groups, BP had operations in some 70 countries, more than 56,000 employees, and annual revenues of \$79b. It had been fully privatized in 1987 when the British government sold its 51 percent stake and had gradually become more diversified and decentralized.

Upstream, BP focused on oil exploration, with production facilities in Alaska, the Gulf of Mexico, Colombia, and the North Sea. (Exhibit 22 summarizes BP's upstream activities.) Downstream, BP had a weak position in the United States. Aggressive restructuring and asset disposals had not quite solved the problem of high costs and asset quality.

The company, however, had forced the admiration of industry watchers by staging a remarkable recovery under the successive CEOs David Simon and John Browne. In 1992 an unprecedented quarterly loss had caused it to nearly default on interest payments. Since then, BP increased earnings to \$3.2b (from \$900m), while the share price had more than doubled (see Ex-

22 | BP's Upstream Activities

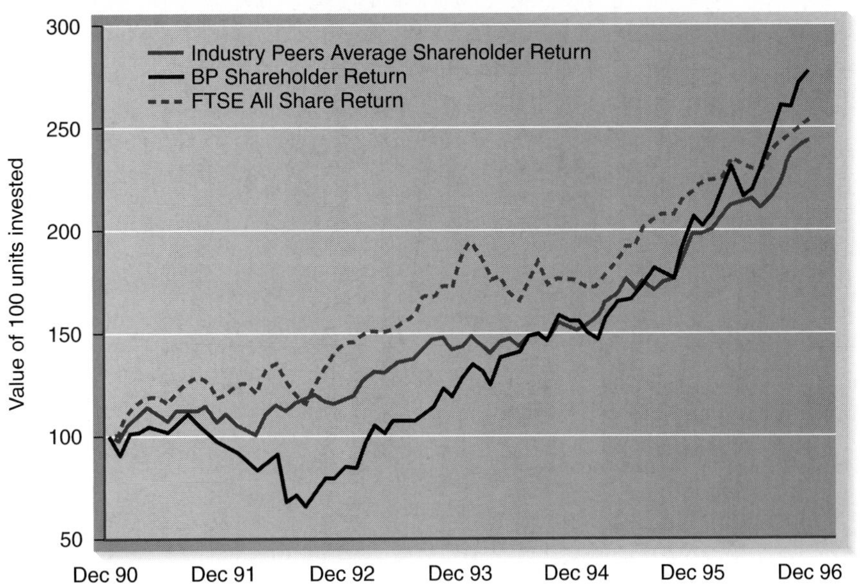

hibit 22 for an overview of cumulative returns). By 1995, dividend payments were back above their 1992 level. (Exhibits 23 and 24 give financial data.) Analysts expected financial improvement to continue until at least the year 2000, thanks to higher output (by 5 percent p.a. on average) and a better product mix.

BP was seen as a leader in cutting costs: It had halved its total workforce to 56,500 in 1995 from 111,900 four years earlier. The company also sought greater efficiency through consolidation, reorganization, and optimization of storage and logistics. In refining, its strategy was to sell or close unprofitable refineries, upgrade others, and generally improve operating reliability. It had recently spent £171m on a five-year, worldwide rebranding effort, with mixed success.

Europe was BP's main market with 48 percent of refinery capacity and 49 percent of sales. The company had downstream operations in 18 countries. It employed some 15,500 people, including 4,000 service station staff, and owned wholly or in part, eight European refineries with combined capacity of 760,000 bpd (the planned sale of the Lavera plant in southern France would reduce this to 575,000 bpd). BP and partner Texaco had also announced the closure of their Pernis refinery and the consolidation of their joint refining at BP's Europort plant in Holland. (Exhibit 25 has data on BP's refineries.)

BP sold 825,000 bpd of oil products through 5,600 retail sites. Its market share, 8 percent in both fuels and lubricants, had been steady for years. (Exhibit 26 shows BP's market performance.)

In marketing, its two-pronged strategy was to upgrade facilities at prime retail sites to improve petrol throughput and increase nonfuel revenue and to pursue expansion in eastern Europe where it planned to quadruple its 100 service stations. In the last two years, BP had sold 90 service stations in southwestern France to Repsol, 60 other French sites to PetroFina, and eight Austrian sites to Shell. In the UK, it had acquired independent fuel distributor Charringtons.

BP's success in cost-cutting had spawned imitators and had not produced notable gains in its market share. Analysts believed that European oil companies (including BP) had cut "all the fat and some of the muscle" and doubted whether any further cost reductions were possible.

23 | British Petroleum Earnings Summary

	1991	1992	1993	1994	1995	1996E
Exploration & Production						
UK	870	795	1086	1527	1492	1636
Rest of Europe	423	483	399	257	330	304
US	1673	1607	1277	920	1251	1246
Rest of World	54	91	123	169	386	437
Total	3020	2976	2885	2873	3459	3623
Refining and Marketing						
UK	115	−132	36	119	92	13
Rest of Europe	407	175	245	189	−22	280
US	211	2	270	173	43	250
Rest of World	586	416	582	509	528	591
Total	1319	461	1133	990	641	1134
Chemicals						
US	−19	64	26	35	216	175
Non-US	76	−106	−128	350	−216	750
Total	57	−42	−102	385	0	925
Other & Corporate	−199	−60	−164	−79	−61	−13
Replacement cost operating profit	4197	3335	3752	4169	4039	5669
Gain/(loss) from asset sales	428	124	−60	55	−5	−11
Restructuring costs	−103	−1884	−300	0	−1525	0
Inventory gain/(loss)	−1113	−187	−426	95	4	95
Historical cost operating profit	3409	1388	2966	4319	2513	5753
Interest expense	−1280	−1190	−1013	−829	−787	−600
Pretax income	2129	198	1953	3490	1726	5153
Income tax	−1451	−1000	−1027	−1059	−1310	−1476
Minority interest	57	−9	−7	−18	8	−20
Historical cost income	735	−811	919	2413	424	3657
Exploration & Production						
US capital employed	7639	7237	7064	7017	7124	7480
US adjusted earnings	931	883	682	546	828	674
Foreign capital employed	11199	9912	9787	10594	11502	12422
Foreign adjusted earnings	843	784	969	1042	1322	1441
Refining and Marketing						
US capital employed	3697	3482	2802	2775	1571	1602
US adjusted earnings	139	1	176	112	59	162
Foreign capital employed	6317	5784	5476	5947	5663	5890
Foreign adjusted earnings	720	308	578	577	553	592

All numbers are in millions of dollars.
Source: "BP and Mobil—Similar in Size but Different in the Way They Are," Merrill Lynch, 1996.

Mobil

Mobil, founded as Standard Oil of New York, was the world's third largest oil company after Exxon and Shell. It operated in over 100 countries with 50,000 employees and annual revenues of $73b; it owned 21 refineries and 28 tankers and shared ownership in over 36,000 miles of pipeline. Its response to the 1970s oil shock had been to diversify. This had culminated in the acquisition of the Montgomery Ward department stores. Mobil later sold that business to concentrate once more on oil.

The company had worldwide earnings of $2.9b in 1995, nearly double the 1992 level of $1.5b. It had not suffered as badly as BP from the Gulf War but its performance had not improved as dramatically either. Analysts saw potential for more cost-cutting and increased

EXHIBIT

24 | BP Refining and Marketing Profitability

	1992	1993	1994	1995	1996	Average
Net profit after tax (£ million)						
Refining	20	180	6	–68	194	66.4
Marketing	240	575	640	474	485	482.8
Total	260	755	646	406	679	549.2
Operating capital (£ million)						
Total	6,137	5,593	5,591	4,637	5,137	5,419
Refining	53%	56%	61%	54%	43%	53.4%
Marketing	47%	44%	39%	46%	57%	46.6%
Return on average capital employed (ROACE)						
Refining	0.6%	5.6%	0.2%	–2.3%	8.2%	2.5%
Marketing	8.3	21.5	27.6	22.0	19.2	19.7
Total	4.2	12.9	11.6	7.9	13.9	10.1

Source: BP Financial and Operating Information 1992–1996.

25 | Summary BP Downstream Activity

Crude Oil Sources[i]	thousand barrels per day				
	1991	**1992**	**1993**	**1994**	**1995**
Produced from own reserves[ii]					
UK	359	364	370	429	403
Rest of Europe	81	87	88	81	69
USA	738	688	627	605	572
Rest of World	37	23	32	32	56
	1,215	1,162	1,117	1,147	1,100
Produced from associated undertakings					
Abu Dhabi	141	131	125	118	113
Total Production	**1,356**	**1,293**	**1,242**	**1,265**	**1,213**
Purchased					
USA	358	427	568	572	728
Rest of World	1,474	2,016	2,087	2,434	2,648
	1,832	2,443	2,655	3,006	3,376
Total	**3,188**	**3,736**	**3,897**	**4,271**	**4,589**

[i]Crude oil in respect of which royalty is taken in cash is shown as a purchase: royalty oil taken in kind is excluded from both production and purchased oil.
[ii]Oil production includes natural gas liquids and condensate.

Crude Oil Sales	thousand barrels per day				
	1991	**1992**	**1993**	**1994**	**1995**
UK	1,167	1,301	1,378	1,860	**2,004**
Rest of Europe	40	88	82	90	116
USA	391	479	497	534	693
Rest of World	27	33	30	15	24
Total	1,625	1,901	1,987	2,499	**2,837**

(Continues)

25 | Summary BP Downstream Activity *(Continued)*

REFINERY THROUGHPUTS AND UTILIZATION

Refinery Throughputs[(i)]	thousand barrels per day				
	1991	**1992**	**1993**	**1994**	**1995**
UK	194	185	184	183	193
Rest of Europe	525	570	617	593	661
USA	701	711	717	621	713
Rest of World	297	307	327	339	332
	1,717	1,773	1,845	1,736	1,899
For BP by others	21	13	11	9	10
Total	1,738	1,786	1,856	1,745	1,909
Crude distillation capacity at December 31	2,066	2,020	1,963	2,004	2,000
Crude distillation capacity utilization[(ii)]	90%	94%	97%	94%	104%

[(i)]Includes actual crude oil and other feedstock input both for BP and third parties.
[(ii)]Crude distillation capacity utilization is defined as the percentage utilization of capacity per calendar day over the year after making allowance for average annual shutdowns at BP refineries (net rated capacity).

Crude Oil Input	thousand barrels per day				
	1991	**1992**	**1993**	**1994**	**1995**
Low sulphur crude	69%	62%	63%	72%	**71%**
High sulphur crude	31	38	37	28	**29**

Refinery yield[(i)]	thousand barrels per day				
	1991	**1992**	**1993**	**1994**	**1995**
Aviation fuels	171	186	184	192	194
Gasolines	659	712	676	668	704
Middle distillates	530	549	603	574	548
Fuel oil	220	245	282	214	215
Other products	212	218	230	196	286
Total	1,792	1,910	1,975	1,844	1,947

[(i)]Refinery yields exceed throughputs because of volumetric expansion

production. Exhibit 27 summarizes Mobil's financial results.

Upstream, Mobil was a major player in both oil and natural gas. Output, which had dropped in 1994, was expected to increase 2–3 percent annually in the medium term. A significant share of Mobil's revenue came from international exploration and production in Indonesia, Qatar, Nigeria, the North Sea, and Canada where it had a share in the Hibernia offshore oil field.

Mobil had a strong downstream position in the United States, especially in terms of market share and retail network. It was the world's leader in finished lubricants, with large market share in all regions. As part of its global strategy, Mobil had made considerable R&D investments in lubricants, and it was recognized as a quality brand in this business.

In Europe, Mobil's downstream operations had remained relatively weak despite extensive rationalization. Analysts wondered whether it would have to leave the market. Mobil owned, wholly or in part, six European refineries with capacity of 350,000 bpd (about 16 percent of its total capacity) but was planning to close its Woerthe plant in Germany. It made 25 percent of its sales in Europe where its market share in fuels was only

EXHIBIT 26 | BP's Prealliance Market Share

	ESTIMATED MARKET SHARE					
	1991	1992	1993	1994	1995	Rank
Benelux	12.1%	12.2%	12.0%	12.3%	12.6%	4
France	7.8	8.1	8.0	8.5	8.0	5
Germany	8.2	8.6	8.5	8.8	8.8	6
Italy						
Spain/Portugal	8.4	8.1	6.9	6.9	6.7	3
UK	12.5	12.0	11.9	11.5	11.5	3
Ireland	12.6					
Austria	9.4	8.9	9.1	9.2	9.3	4
Switzerland	13.5	13.1	12.4	18.0	18.6	2
Denmark						
Norway						
Sweden	7.1	2.6	2.0	0.1	0.1	
Finland						
Greece	12.8	13.2	13.4	13.0	13.5	1
Turkey	8.0	8.0	8.0	8.1	8.1	

Source: Woods Mackenzie.

EXHIBIT 27 | Mobil Earnings Summary

	1991	1992	1993	1994	1995	1996E
US Petroleum						
Exploration & Production	189	348	363	125	–107	444
Refining & Marketing	116	–145	151	241	226	448
Total	305	203	514	366	119	892
Foreign Petroleum						
Exploration & Production	1094	1042	1289	951	952	1150
Refining & Marketing	819	329	554	–33	447	846
Total	1913	1371	1843	918	1399	1996
Total Petroleum	2218	1574	2357	1284	1518	2888
Chemicals	217	136	44	102	1164	375
Financing	–385	–316	–127	–209	–295	–240
Other & Corporate	–130	–86	–190	–98	–11	–150
Accounting changes	0	–446	0	0	0	0
Net Income	1920	862	2084	1079	2376	2873
Exploration & Production						
US capital employed	6443	5670	4925	4420	4035	4116
US adjusted earnings	189	423	432	306	332	444
Foreign capital employed	3760	3621	3836	4076	4474	4832
Foreign adjusted earnings	1045	1066	1098	1018	1065	1150
Refining and Marketing						
US capital employed	4705	5286	5071	5155	5128	5231
US adjusted earnings	212	–17	296	273	330	448
Foreign capital employed	7362	7193	7464	7356	7770	8159
Foreign adjusted earnings	805	370	792	681	805	846

All numbers are in millions of dollars
Source: "BP and Mobil—Similar in Size but Different in the Way They Are," Merrill Lynch, 1996.

28 | Mobil's Prealliance Market Share

	ESTIMATED MARKET SHARE					
	1991	1992	1993	1994	1995	Rank
Benelux	2.3%	2.2%	2.2%	2.3%	2.9%	8
France	5.5	5.3	4.5	4.6	4.3	6
Germany	7.1	7.4	7.5	7.3	7.1	7
Italy						
Spain/Portugal	2.2	2.0	2.1	2.8	2.6	6
UK	5.0	5.2	4.9	5.2	5.3	6
Ireland						
Austria	12.0	12.4	12.2	13.0	12.9	3
Switzerland	2.7	2.8	2.8	2.6	2.0	8
Denmark						
Norway	6.6	3.1	0.1	0.1	0.1	
Sweden						
Finland						
Greece	11.9	12.2	11.2	11.1	11.4	3
Turkey	10.9	10.8	12.6	12.9	12.6	3

Source: Woods Mackenzie.

4 percent. In lubricants, however, it had 10 percent share (Exhibit 28 has details). In 1996, Mobil's 8,000 workforce sold 550,000 bpd of oil products. About 2,000 service station staff operated 3,300 service stations in 22 European countries. In the last two years, Mobil had swapped 18 of its French service stations for eight Repsol stations in southern Spain.

In Germany, Mobil did not sell any retail fuels under its own brand but it was a major supplier to Aral, a joint venture with German group Veba Oel in which Mobil had a 28 percent stake. Aral, which had by far the largest network of service stations in Germany, with a 20 percent market share, had been one of the first German retailers to open convenience stores. It was energetically expanding nonfuel retailing and considered selling McDonald's hamburgers. For some products, however, and in other countries, Mobil competed with Aral.

The Alliance

Discussions between Mobil and BP had begun in the summer of 1995; lawyers had become involved in October. The two companies had decided to form a partnership, with no changes in ownership of assets or equity. Setting up a traditional joint venture would have taken much longer because of the complex business of valuing assets, technologies, and trademarks. Both BP and Mobil were familiar with using partnerships in their upstream activities.

The partnership would operate refineries, buy crude oil and other feedstocks for these refineries, refine and convert downstream products such as lubricants, and market them, both to retail and to industrial and commercial customers, in western and eastern Europe (including west Russia) as well as in Turkey and Cyprus. The deal did not extend to international operations such as exploration and production, international trading, and basic research and development. Aviation fuels and lubricants, marine fuels and lubricants, and shipping, as well as natural gas marketing and chemicals, were also excluded.

In each country, Mobil and BP would combine their fuel and lubricant businesses through two separate partnerships, one for fuels, one for lubricants. BP would operate the fuels business as a whole, while Mobil would operate the lubricants business. All 8,000 service stations in the combined network would be rebranded with BP colors. They would display the alliance's logo and distribute Mobil oils.

EXHIBIT 29 | Structure of the BP-Mobil Alliance

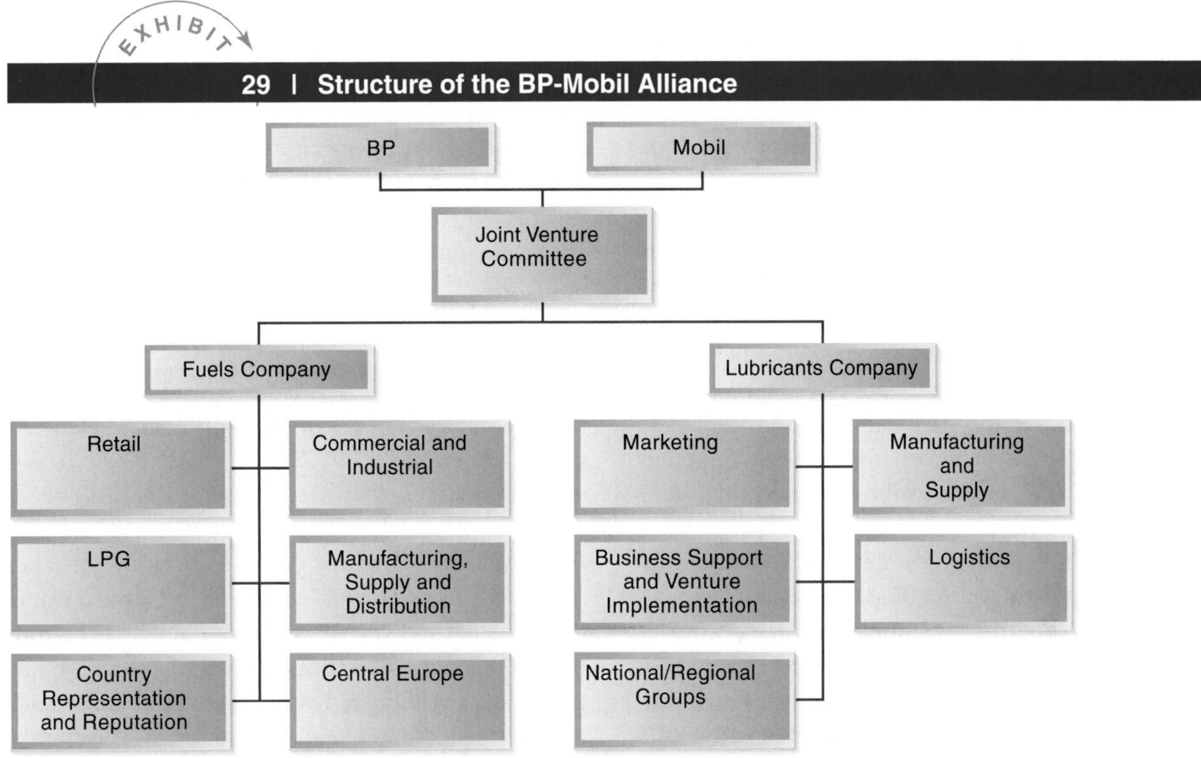

BP as Fuels Operator and Mobil as Lubricants Operator would be controlled by a Supervisory Committee which would approve business plans, major acquisitions, closures, disposals, and investments and oversee the national Fuels and Lubricants partnerships. BP and Mobil would have the power to veto any of the Committee's decisions. Exhibit 29 shows the alliance's organizational design.

BP and Mobil would have different equity stakes in each business: in fuels, BP would have 70 percent and Mobil 30 percent in lubricants, Mobil would hold 51 percent and BP 49 percent. This reflected the value of the two partners' assets in February 1996 as well as their strength and expertise across Europe. Profits and losses in each partnership would be shared in the same proportion as the firms' equity stakes. If either partner contributed less assets than the agreed ratio in a given country, it would have to bridge the gap through cash.

BP and Mobil would hand over all relevant fuels and lubricants assets to the joint venture (including 10 refineries, terminals, retail sites, pipelines, and truck fleets). BP would transfer its lubricants activities to Mobil and Mobil would transfer its fuels activities to BP. Even though the ownership of assets would not be transferred, the joint venture would enjoy indefinite and exclusive use of those assets. Employees would transfer from one company to the other where appropriate. Central services (such as IT, human resources, legal, and accounting management) would be merged under BP management. The new structure was expected to be fully implemented by mid-1998.

The Expected Benefits

The alliance would have $5b assets ($3.4b from BP) and sales of $20b, with an estimated 12 percent market share in fuel retail (10 percent according to the European Commission) and 18 percent in lubricants. Combining the two retail networks would lead to redundant sites which could be sold without affecting overall sales volume. This and other asset disposals would produce one-off revenues of $200m. However, this one-off benefit would be more than offset by exceptional charges to cover the costs of the alliance in its first year ($490m for BP and $330m for Mobil). The deal was also expected to produce annual savings of $400–500m (most would come in the five largest markets) from three main sources:

Eliminating Duplication (60% of Expected Savings) Most of the savings would come from operating as one business instead of two. This included operating a single accounting organization and computer system. In refining, BP and Mobil would consolidate their portfolio, selling assets where there was a clear overlap in capacity (this was the case for three refineries in Bavaria, among others), a move that would maximize capacity utilization. Both companies had found it difficult to find buyers for individual refineries in the past, but they hoped that a range of assets would be easier to sell.

Synergies (25%) These would arise from the complementarity of the two partners' downstream organizations. In terms of geography, a bigger network of stations with the right spread across Europe would cut distribution costs. In the UK, for instance, Mobil's network in the south of England complemented BP's strong presence in Scotland. In terms of product range, BP's strength in fuels complemented Mobil's leadership in lubricants. Duplicated storage and distribution facilities would be eliminated. The alliance would manage fuel storage at a pan-European level, ensuring a better balance relative to demand and reducing dependence on expensive external storage.

Thousands of jobs across Europe were earmarked for cuts, many from closing down overlapping service stations. In particular, between 2,000 and 3,000 non-service-station jobs (out of a total 17,500) would be cut. BP and Mobil were already the industry's cost leaders in petrol retailing; they had built increasingly large self-service stations and their combined network had lower costs than the small operators. Many competitors (especially national companies like Total, Elf, Agip, and Repsol) were thought to be unable to match those cuts. Their governments, opposed to layoffs and fearing to lose control of a "strategic" industry, were unlikely to let them merge or enter cost-cutting alliances.

Scale (15%) More refineries spread across major markets would reduce high transport costs to the retail site (shown in Exhibit 30). In many cases, this would obviate the need to buy from competitors.[4] In the United Kingdom, BP had been forced to buy from other refiners because its refinery at Grangemouth, in Scotland, was too far from its retail network concentrated in the south of England. The alliance would now source from Mobil's refinery at Coryton. In France, the situation was similar: BP's refinery at Lavera served southern France and the Mediterranean market, but most of its petrol stations were in the Paris area. This forced it to buy from competitors. The alliance could use Mobil's refinery at Gravenchon to supply the Paris region. If buying from competitors was still necessary, at least BP and Mobil would have a stronger hand to negotiate.

The alliance could deliver better logistics, streamlined management processes, more efficient procurement, and economies of scale which BP saw as vital in the downstream industry. Together, Mobil and BP would be able to compete on prices with the largest Eu-

EXHIBIT 30 | Transportation costs of petrol

Transportation	Cost
German rail	$4.34 per mt + $0.034 per km per mt
Polish rail	$2.38 per mt + $0.028 per km per mt
German road	$0.046 per km per mt
Czech pipe	$0.02 per km per mt
United Kingdom pipeline	$0.013 to $0.02 per km per mt
Rhine barge	$0.022 to $0.04 per km per mt

Mt = metric tonne
Source: BP.

ropean players. In particular, greater power in procurement, especially in lubricants packaging and nonfuel retail site supplies, was an obvious benefit.

Beyond Cash Savings The two partners also expected other advantages from combining their operations. "The key issue is competitive performance," said John Browne, CEO of BP. "BP and Mobil were number three and four in the European market; now we will be up there with the big players." Together, they would be able to enter new markets, especially in central and eastern Europe. They would achieve economies of scale in investment and logistics to enter these attractive markets. They would be in a better position to buy privatized companies, since governments favored large investors.

A larger distribution network would also help attract food-retailing partners in new forecourt convenience stores and be better able to counter the supermarkets' negotiating power. Additional capacity to implement environmental investments would also be welcome. Finally, a wider geographic spread would make the joint venture less vulnerable to cyclical downturns as market conditions differed across Europe. For example, a strong, diversified pan-European player would be less affected by price wars in the UK or domineering supermarkets in France. Size was seen as an important advantage since it could smooth out some of the competitive conditions across Europe.

THE UNCERTAIN FUTURE

Analysts' initial reaction to the deal was largely favorable. Most saw the alliance as an innovative response to the industry's problems; they underlined the advantages in terms of market power and brand power as well as the complementariness of the two businesses. Both partners would gain from the deal: BP would be able to further cut costs and continue its expansion. For Mobil, it was an opportunity to reaffirm its position in the European market. "The subtext of this BP-Mobil deal is that you need a 10 percent market share to survive in the European market," commented investment bank Morgan Stanley.

But there were some negative interpretations as well. In a sense, the alliance was an admission of failure: BP and Mobil were acknowledging their inability to achieve economies of scale on their own. Since neither could grow big enough and neither wanted to leave the market, they had to compromise. Another concern was that the deal still left Mobil and BP in a middle position, stuck between the national players (each strong in its own domestic market) and overall leaders Shell and Exxon. Some analysts also questioned the extent of possible synergies, considering that the two companies were not a perfect fit. "A merger isn't a catch-all solution for the industry's fundamental problems," said one. "When you combine weak resources and low-quality assets, you do not make a strong company."

While BP and Mobil had deliberately avoided an acquisition, the partnership still raised governance issues. Both partners had to give up a measure of control and flexibility. The Supervisory Committee had considerable operational independence but it remained subject to a veto from either company. While Mobil and BP both had a lot of experience in managing upstream alliances, no oil company ever had attempted such an ambitious deal downstream. Initially, their interests seemed aligned, but questions about the longer term remained.

There was also the tricky Aral issue. Mobil was now allied with two competing groups. Given the strength of the BP-Mobil marketing network, Aral was the clear loser. Some analysts felt that Mobil should sell its stake to enable Aral to find another partner. Others criticized Mobil's ability to manage complex alliances as the European Commission began investigating the two joint ventures.

The daunting task of actually merging operations still lay ahead. BP and Mobil executives were aware that most large mergers, no matter their strategic logic, failed to create value for shareholders. The challenges involved in bringing together different products, services, management systems, and culture as well as workforces while competing in the marketplace often precluded benefits. These issues could be even more problematic in this deal because BP and Mobil continued to compete as independent corporations in petrol and other businesses elsewhere in the world.

Analysts also wondered how the relationship between the two partners would evolve over time. What if the deal turned out to be a half-hearted compromise that neither side was fully satisfied with? Neither was there a guarantee that EU regulators would approve the deal. The combined market share of the two companies gave them a strong presence in several countries. Determined to root out anticompetitive behavior, the European Commission was targeting large, headline-grabbing mergers. If the alliance was shown to establish a dominant position which significantly restricted competition, the Commission could stop the deal. To overcome this hurdle, BP and Mobil had to provide enough information for the Commission to make a quick decision and they had to demonstrate that there was no threat to competition.

Commentators were already speculating about how BP and Mobil's competitors would respond to the move. Was it the beginning of industry-wide realignment? The next few years could be crucial. What would the two companies have to do to turn their deal into a success? Was the deal a masterstroke or insufficient as some claimed? What would Mr. Browne have to do to keep the performance of BP on track?

ENDNOTES

1. Known as gasoline in the United States. We use the word "petrol" throughout to refer to retail motor fuels (petrol, diesel, and other refinery products), unless otherwise specified.
2. One barrel equals 42 U.S. gallons, or 159 liters.
3. The world's largest refinery was at Yukong in South Korea (770,000 bpd).
4. Because even the integrated oil companies didn't have refineries near all their major markets, they were often faced with a difficult choice: Either they bought fuels internally and paid the cost of shipment, or they purchased from competitors. For this reason major refining players such as Shell and Exxon often managed to extract high prices from retailers.

CASE 11

British Airways: Latin America

David T. A. Wesley
Henry W. Lane
Richard Ivey School of Business

On August 21, 1998, an approaching storm, as if to signal the impending hurricane season, was clearly visible from Mark Dunkerley's downtown Miami office. Yet, the British Airways general manager for Latin America and the Caribbean (LACAR) scarcely noticed it as he prepared for the next meeting with his country managers. Although British Airways (BA) had been lagging behind other carriers in the region, in his opinion the company had the potential to be the leading European airline in the region.

Latin America had never been considered an important market for British Airways and Dunkerley believed that the managers would be delighted to see LACAR move ahead. After six months of visiting all the offices in Latin America, Dunkerley was beginning to feel as though the country managers of some key South American countries were not supporting the changes that he was proposing. Perhaps he had been "naïve." After all, several managers had passed through the Miami regional headquarters in the past and little had changed. Dunkerley wondered how to get his managers to buy into his plan.

COMPANY PROFILE

British Airways traced its roots to the pioneering days of civil aviation following the First World War, providing air service from London to Paris using single-engine biplane bombers that had been converted to civilian use. Imperial Airways, as it was then known, was nationalized by the British government in 1939 and was renamed the British Overseas Airways Corporation (BOAC). South American routes were operated by British South American Airways, which merged with BOAC in 1949. When BOAC was merged with British European Airways (BEA) in 1974, the company was renamed British Airways. BA was successfully privatized in 1987 with simultaneous public offerings in London, Toronto and New York.

By the early 1990s, when the world's airlines racked up record losses totalling more than $16 billion, BA was among the very few that remained profitable. The airline carried 24 million passengers a year on international flights, making BA the largest international carrier in the world.

Circumstances of geography worked in BA's favor. In the U.S., major carriers made great efforts to establish a hub system. Flights converged at these locations from throughout the world, allowing convenient connections for passengers. London's Heathrow Airport served much

IVEY David T. A. Wesley prepared this case under the supervision of Professor Henry W. Lane solely to provide material for class discussion. The authors do not intend to illustrate either effective or ineffective handling of a managerial situation. The authors may have disguised certain names and other identifying information to protect confidentiality.

Ivey Management Services prohibits any form of reproduction, storage or transmittal without its written permission. This material is not covered under authorization from CanCopy or any reproduction rights organization. To order copies or request permission to reproduce materials, contact Ivey Publishing, Ivey Management Services, c/o Richard Ivey School of Business, The University of Western Ontario, London, Ontario, Canada, N6A 3K7; phone (519) 661-3208, fax (519) 661-3882, e-mail cases@ivey.uwo.ca.

Copyright © 1999, Ivey Management Services. One-time permission to reproduce Ivey cases granted by Ivey Management Services on February 15, 2000.

the same purpose, acting as a North Atlantic hub for Europe and the Americas. Heathrow was the world's busiest international airport, serving nearly 45 million passengers a year, of which 39 percent were scheduled on BA flights. Much of BA's premium international services, which represented some 94 percent of the company's business, was served out of Heathrow. In the 1990s, more flights began to use Gatwick Airport due to congestion at Heathrow, and as a result, slots at both Gatwick and Heathrow became increasingly scarce.

The company's three most important markets were Europe, North America and Asia. In 1995, air traffic within and between these three regions accounted for 90 percent of Revenue Passenger Kilometres (RPKs)[1] for the world's major airlines. The U.S. market was the largest in the world, representing approximately 50 percent of RPKs on domestic and transatlantic routes.

A key constraint for any major airline was the acquisition of slots.[2] Applying for new slots was a slow, bureaucratic and costly process. To get around this, airlines in the U.S. traded slots between them, but this practice was not permitted in the U.K. Another, more costly, way of obtaining slots was to purchase another airline.

The 1990s saw a trend towards mega-alliances between major carriers in different countries. Such alliances were an alternative to increasing the number of slots on international routes by providing instant access to an extended network of connecting flights. Member airlines typically offered code-sharing[3] and the transferability of frequent flyer awards. BA strategists believed that mega-alliances would become a key success factor in the future. In 1998, the company had established, or was in the process of establishing, formal links with Quantas, American Airlines, Canadian Airlines, Deutsche BA, Air Liberté, America West, LOT Polish Airlines, Iberia and Finnair. This would be by far the largest airline alliance in the world, allowing passengers to fly seamlessly to virtually any destination in the world.

The company's alliance with American Airlines was intended to not only provide important access to the large U.S. market, but also to open up the number of destinations BA could offer to Latin America. With a hub in Miami, American Airlines was the most important international carrier in Latin America.

British Airways' fleet of 300 large aircraft, including seven Concordes and 50 Boeing 747s, served more than 170 destinations in 80 countries. As such, BA had the distinction of operating the largest international route network of any airline.

In 1998, BA unveiled plans to purchase a further 220 aircraft valued at more than £8 billion. Early model 747s purchased by BA in 1970 were scheduled to be retired from service in 1998 after travelling more than 51 million miles, clocking up to 102,000 hours of service and carrying six million passengers on almost 21,000 flights. In 1996, BA posted record pre-tax profits of £585 million. The following year, *Fortune* magazine ranked BA as the most admired airline in the world.[4]

THE ASIA CRISIS

In 1997, airline industry analysts predicted strong growth in the Asia Pacific region:

> *The strong correlation between economic growth and air traffic growth implies that at least until the year 2010, air traffic will grow faster in higher growth Asia Pacific economies than in any other region of the world.*[5]

Then, in October 1997, the Honk Kong Hang Seng index fell by 23 percent in only four days, while currencies and stock markets across Asia and Latin America experienced record declines.

While Latin American markets quickly recovered from the initial shock, Asian economies continued to experience currency devaluations and severe market losses. Japan fell into recession. As a result, international airlines, including BA, experienced a sharp decline in demand for air travel within the region and shareholders began voicing concerns over the impact on profitability.

BA LATIN AMERICA

In 1988, British Airways acquired British Caledonian Airlines (BCal). BCal operated a number of routes to South America and, until the Falkland Islands War between Britain and Argentina in 1982, these routes had been some of the company's most profitable.

By BA standards, BCal was a fat company with high salaries and fewer on-time departures. About half of BCal's management positions were cut, while those remaining were required to take salary cuts. Peter Owen, BA's director of operations at the time recalled:

> *We found there was a seven percent chance of BCal long-haul services not operating as scheduled. In BA, this same chance is one percent. On the people side, they were facing a 40 percent cut in pay.*[6]

Meanwhile, Latin America was just beginning its worst economic crisis of the century. Following on the heels of a global recession in the early 1980s, Latin America's export-driven economies experienced a worldwide decline in demand for their products. At the same time, Latin American currencies became overvalued and trade surpluses quickly turned into trade deficits. The region's governments turned to external debt to finance the imbalances, but rising interest rates around the world led many governments to print money in order to meet their obligations. Sharp declines in commodity prices in 1985 only helped to exacerbate the problem, as state-owned energy companies experienced serious shortfalls in revenue. Such factors, along with a bloated and inefficient civil service, gave rise to hyperinflationary pressures during the latter half of the decade.

Brazil and Argentina, two of Latin America's largest economies and the two most important South American destinations for BA, experienced inflation in excess of 1,000 percent. Mexico and other countries followed with less spectacular, but nonetheless high, rates of inflation.

In the 1990s, inflation was reduced to single digits and most economies in the region began to stabilize. Many attributed the turnaround to heightened pressure from international funding organizations such as the International Monetary Fund (IMF), which resulted in most Latin American countries privatizing state industries and liberalizing trade. Regional trade agreements, such as the North American Free Trade Agreement (NAFTA) and Mercosur,[7] helped to further stimulate international investment.

Flights between Latin America and Europe accounted for 2.2 percent of RPKs, or approximately five million of the 273 million passengers carried worldwide that year on the world's major airlines. In 1997, BA carried 380,000 passengers between Latin America and Europe, generating £190 million in revenue.

THE AIRLINE BUSINESS

Profitability

The airline industry was characterized by high fixed costs, with large capital outlays going to purchase aircraft.[8] Therefore, it was important to keep aircraft flying as much as possible and as such, most of BA's aircraft averaged around 12 hours per day in flight. North American airlines typically averaged around 10 hours per day, while many airlines in developing countries had much lower utilization at about five hours per day.

Labor, which accounted for 25 percent of BA's operating costs and as much as 40 percent of some U.S. airlines' costs, was considered by most industry analysts to be fixed. (A revenues and expenses summary is provided in Exhibit 1). Safety requirements determined how many ground crew were needed for such functions as engineering and refuelling. However, through cross-functional training, BA had shown that labor costs could be dramatically reduced, while actually improving service. For example, BA was able to cut staff by more than 72 percent in its domestic Highlands Division in 1982, while increasing services by more than 25 percent on some routes.

Fuel, which accounted for approximately 10 percent of BA's operating costs, was considered a semi-variable cost. While it could be reduced by purchasing more efficient aircraft, or by reducing the number of flights, on any given flight the fuel cost was the same, regardless of whether the flight was full or empty. For this reason, it was important to have a high load factor (the percentage of available seats occupied by passengers).

In 1996, most major European Airlines, including BA, had load factors in excess of 70 percent, while in the U.S. this figure dropped to around 65 percent. Many airlines from developing countries had load factors as low as 40 percent. Short-haul flights were generally more expensive with a larger portion of fuel consumption going to take offs and landings. Landing at congested airports was particularly expensive as aircraft hovered in holding patterns above the airport, waiting for clearance to land.

In the U.S., concern over load factors had led to severe discounting, as airlines attempted to fill empty seats. By providing fewer services to passengers, no frills airlines, such as Southwest Air, were able to spend less time loading passengers on the ground and offered fares

1 | Summary Consolidated Statements of Income Audited For the year to March 31, 1998

REVENUE	£ MILLION
Income from passengers flying on scheduled services, plus excess baggage	7,233
Freight and mail carried on scheduled services	595
Revenue from charter flights	53
Total Traffic Revenue	7,881
Other activities, largely aircraft maintenance and other airline services provided to third parties	761
Total Group operating revenue	8,642
EXPENSES	
Pay, pension contributions and other employee costs	2,211
Depreciation of fixed assets	551
Operating leases	127
Fuel and oil	790
Engineering and other aircraft costs	614
Airport landing fees and air traffic control charges	703
Handling charges, catering and other operational costs	1,152
Selling costs	1,217
Accommodation, ground equipment costs and currency differences	773
Total Group operating expenses	8,138
Group operating income	504
Associated undertakings	61
Other charges and income	19
Net profit on sale of fixed assets	164
Net interest payable	(168)
Group income before tax	580
Tax	(133)
Group net income for the period	447
Minority shareholder losses	13
Group profit attributable to shareholders	460
Interim and proposed dividends	(176)
Retained Income	284
INCOME PER ORDINARY SHARE*	44.7p

*The standard measure of a company's profitability was calculated by dividing net income for the period by the average number of ordinary shares in issue during the year. Fees, salaries, performance bonuses and benefits payable to board members during the year totalled £1,228,000.

that competed more with buses and trains than with major airlines. In the mid-1990s, several airlines began offering discount services between the U.K. and continental Europe, prompting BA to set up its own no frills airline in 1998.

Network Development

Operating the world's largest route network entailed a certain amount of reliance on others within that network. One senior manager in London noted:

> *It is the man on the spot who knows best what the customer wants, whether he lives in Bangkok or Birmingham. Yet, there is a danger that one part of the organization can pursue a policy, which is good for the local market, but which seriously cuts across what their colleagues are trying to achieve in another part of the airline.*[9]

In order to co-ordinate routes across its worldwide network, BA had a Network Development department in London. Using three-year forecasts, Network Development staff organized flight schedules and allocated company resources. They accounted for market variability and made appropriate adjustments on an almost constant basis. To optimize all of BA's constraints, such as ground and air crews, slots and aircraft, Network Development staff were required to have an "encyclopedic knowledge" of the company's resources and schedules. The number of external variables involved made the process "infinitely complex."

In 1996, BA operated four flights per week to Brazil. Flights would leave London at night and arrive in Brazil in the morning. The flights would then continue to Santiago, Chile, where they would remain on the ground for five hours awaiting a return flight, also overnight. Flights to Buenos Aires spent even more time on the ground. Unlike the Brazil flights, these flights did not have secondary destinations and, therefore, remained on the ground for the greater part of the day. Furthermore, the schedules mandated that some flight crews remain 16 days on the ground in Latin America. The overall result was significantly higher costs.

Managers in Latin America understood that having aircraft sitting in airports all day was a poor use of company resources, but they did not feel that it was their place to influence the decisions made by the Network Development office in London. In addition, changing flights to return during the day would entail considerable risk, as many passengers preferred to arrive early in the morning in London.

Revenue Management

Revenue Management (RM) relied on actuarial and other predictive methods to optimize future revenue. Seats on any given flight were assigned to "buckets," with each bucket representing a specific fare category, such as economy discount, economy full-fare, or first, as demonstrated by the following simplified example.[10]

On a flight with a capacity of 400 seats and a departure date 90-days hence, RM would assign 200 seats to economy discount, 50 seats to economy full-fare, 50 seats to first and another 100 seats to other fare categories. The number allocated to each fare category was based on historical data, current demand and other factors that were incorporated into sophisticated models. Each and every day, the buckets would be adjusted based on demand, such that if the economy full-fare bucket was being exhausted at a faster rate than expected, discount seats would be shifted into the higher fare category, which generated more revenue for the same cost.

An increased level of complexity was added through the trading of seats between the various regions of the world. A BA representative in Hong Kong, for example, not only sold seats to London, but also to other destinations that used London as a hub. A passenger wanting to go from Hong Kong to Bogota would purchase only one ticket and as a result, RM needed to determine how much of that fare would be allocated to the Hong Kong portion and how much to the Bogota portion. In order to secure the seat, the Hong Kong representative needed to ensure that the fare offered for the Bogota portion was the same or higher than the normal fare for that bucket, or the representative for Bogota would likely refuse the offer in order to hold the seat for a higher paying passenger. As a result, there was no guaranteed consistency in prices across regions and the same ticket could be purchased in one country for a different price than another country.

Revenue Management was highly dependent on the information provided by the different countries and was considered the center point of information sharing within the BA network. This was especially true when external factors, such as international sporting events, economic crises and political unrest, rendered RM's predictive models obsolete.

On the Bogota to London route, for example, flights stopped in Caracas, Venezuela, to pick up passengers before proceeding to London. In the summer of 1997, Lufthansa quit Venezuela and Viasa, the local carrier, declared bankruptcy. These two carriers accounted for 23 weekly flights between Caracas and Europe, resulting in a sudden increase in demand for flights on other carriers. When BA Venezuela offered a summer seat sale, as they had customarily done in the past, sale seats were obtained through Revenue Management and sold at a discount to passengers. The route quickly became sold out and Colombian passengers who were willing to pay higher fares were forced to book flights with other carriers. In this circumstance, seats in the economy discount bucket should have been shifted to the full-fare category in order to accommodate the increased demand, but the information needed by RM to make this adjustment was not communicated.

The relationship between local offices and the Revenue Management office in London was clearly in need of improvement. LACAR managers continued to perceive that Revenue Management was underselling the market by selling the Americas portion of various routes for less than the price that could be obtained locally.

However, managers from Latin America did not communicate these concerns to Revenue Management, nor did they offer advice on pricing. Carlos Carbonell, country manager for Colombia, noted, "Communication did not flow either way, and there was aggravation between both parties."

Dunkerley arranged for LACAR managers to meet with Revenue Management in London, but noted, "There is a considerable amount of antagonism between local managers and Revenue Management for underselling flights. They have no sense of shared responsibility."

Information Technology

British Airways was viewed as a leader in the area of information technology (IT). Before the Second World War, the airline established its own telecommunication system, known as the Overseas Fixed Telecommunications System Network (OFTS). It was also the first European airline to introduce a computerized reservations system in 1965. By the early 1970s, the British Airways Business System (BABS) was one of the largest and most sophisticated information technology systems in the world. Eventually, BABS expanded beyond a reservations system to permeate virtually every area of the company, from meal inventory planning, to human resources, to flight planning.

In 1989, BA's IT director predicted:

> *Virtually everybody in BA within the next five years will have to use a computer at some time in their day-to-day job, in addition to the high percentage of our staff who use them now . . . companies that are going to be successful in the future are the ones that get their managers to be systems and technology aware.*[11]

While this prediction held true for Europe, North America and Asia, information technology was sorely lacking in Latin America. In 1997, most staff still did not have access to computers and some countries had 747s flying into their airports, yet lacked such basic tools as e-mail.

LACAR was at least 10 years behind the rest of the company in the area of IT. Therefore, even with the support of London, bringing LACAR up to company standards would be a costly process in terms of training and infrastructure.

BREAKING THE UNVIRTUOUS CYCLE

Mark Dunkerley, who held a degree in economic theory, joined British Airways in 1989. In 1993, after serving the company in a variety of capacities, including governmental affairs, investor relations and strategy, he was called upon to help negotiate the purchase of U.S. Air. He later served as the country manager for the Czech Republic. And, although born in Colombia, he spent most of his childhood in Washington, DC and the United Kingdom. As a result, he did not speak Spanish.

When Dunkerley arrived in Latin America in April 1997, BA's performance in the region lagged well behind the rest of the company. He noted:

> *Latin America was put on the bottom of the pile in terms of priorities for the corporation. This was reflected in almost everything we did in the region.*

When it came to investment in the region, what we got was what was left over.

The attitude in London was "Latin America is breaking even, so there is no real need to solve the problem." The word 'volatile' ran around the hallways of London. Professionally, "Latin America is where you get burned!"

Lack of Institutional Comfort

This attitude was reinforced by BA's recent entry into Mexico. In 1994, BA had inaugurated a new service to Mexico City. Within the year, BA fell victim to *The Tequila Effect,*[12] and by the following year, had decided to withdraw the new service. Some believed they had made a mistake by entering in the first place. After all, Mexico had never been part of the former British Empire and perhaps BA did not have an institutional comfort for the area. While BA had been flying to routes in other parts of the world for a very long time, Latin America was relatively new territory.

Dunkerley, on the other hand, believed that BA's poor performance was "a function of an absence of vision, focus and investment." There was nothing intrinsic to Latin America that mandated lower levels of performance, he believed. "It was not because of a lack of opportunity," he noted.

Some managers, however, became accustomed to blaming poor performance on economic and political instability. The country manager for Colombia, Carbonell, observed:

People weren't focused. Decisions were taken that were short term. There was no clear sales and marketing strategy. There was no teamwork between different functional areas.

I started in Colombia in June 1996, the fiscal year started in April, and we were down 30 percent from our target. And summer is the peak season! I had meetings with everyone involved and was told that we were not doing well because the economy was not doing well. Meanwhile, other carriers had twice as many passengers. The market had grown by 15 percent, but we had shrunk.

A Self-Reinforcing Problem

For the first few months after arriving in Latin America, Dunkerley travelled extensively to the regions where BA had flights in order to try and understand the market. The view of Latin America that he developed was very different from the one held by his compatriots in London. He believed the market had all the characteristics in which BA had traditionally been most strong. Nearly all flights were long-haul, Latin Americans were very brand-conscious and status was important. From his perspective, BA should have been the leading European carrier in the region. Instead, it was the weakest.

In terms of routes, BA was the smallest major European carrier in all the markets the company served in Latin America. "This became a self-reinforcing problem," Dunkerley noted. All the routes provided less than daily service. Since slots into Heathrow and Gatwick airports in London were BA's major constraint, routes that had less than daily service were given leftover slots.

This created unusual and often inconvenient, flight schedules. In Brazil, for example, BA operated four flights per week and, over a period of six months, had made six schedule changes. Tour operators, such as those that offered Eco-tours of the Amazon, became frustrated by the frequent schedule changes, which created serious logistical problems with respect to the ground portion. Under such circumstances, many customers simply chose other carriers.

In order to avoid such problems in the future, Latin American flights needed to have secure slots at Heathrow. This meant increasing investment to provide daily service. However, without better returns, the corporation was reluctant to increase spending in the region. Thus, the cycle continued.

Infectious Optimism

Communication was also a concern. During his first six months, Dunkerley met regularly with his senior managers to develop plans to move Latin America forward. Managers readily agreed to follow through on Dunkerley's recommendations and he was initially very pleased with the amount of cooperation that was offered. However, weeks would pass without any progress toward the implementation of the points agreed upon. He noted:

I became infectiously optimistic . . . My shortcoming was in assuming that people would automatically pick up where these meetings left off. The first six months was spent on decisions. The focus in the second six to eight months has been, "How do you get people to follow in behind you and follow through on the decisions being made?"

COUNTRY MANAGERS

Colonial Style

When Dunkerley began his new post as head of LACAR, he found an old style management structure. "It had a colonial feel to it," he recalled.

> *Country managers are powerful figures. In many cases, the separation between them and staff is enormous.*

The country manager was responsible for the entire staff in his country. There was no delegation of decision-making responsibilities to department managers. Information was usually not shared with lower-level managers, who had little or no information about budgets or individual pay scales. Airport managers did not even know how much they were paying their staff. Line managers were also rarely involved in strategic decisions. BA's airport manager for Bogota noted:

> *People wouldn't share information because it could put your job in jeopardy. To share information would be to share power.*
>
> *We had briefings before flights, but nothing else. We had nothing like a mission, values or goals. If we did, at least nobody knew about them.*
>
> *To us, it didn't matter if an aircraft left on time. We needed clear goals and for everyone to know what the goals are.*

Even simple decisions, such as authorizing bill payments or handling passenger complaints, had to go through the country manager. Carbonell explained:

> *People had to ask for permission for everything. They hadn't been pressured in the past or advised on the effect their work had on the organization.*

The division between country managers and other BA employees was thought to be limiting the amount of ideas that came from the rank and file. The airport manager for Bogota explained:

> *We had a meeting once a month where the country manager and the sales manager would tell everyone the yields, targets and other figures. But the people wouldn't understand the commercial issues. They didn't understand what they meant by "yields." They would simply give an update of how we are doing from their point of view. None of the other staff would say what was going on in their departments. People felt that these meetings were a waste of time.*

A Life of Luxury

Carbonell described the lifestyle of a LACAR country manager:

> *BA was paying for a luxury apartment. There were maids and a life of affluence.*
>
> *Many of those who have been overseas for a number of years have a difficult time returning to headquarters. They cannot adapt to life back home and mix with the people in their own country.*
>
> *A lot of country managers that have been in Latin America for many years are losing touch with the head office. The country manager's main role has been public relations and there was much less focus on the business.*

Carbonell voluntarily gave up some of the perks, such as the luxury apartment. "I don't need all that," he noted.

Dunkerley was pleased with the changes undertaken by the Colombian office and planned to introduce similar changes across the region. However, some of the country managers, those who had been in their posts for many years, were used to the lifestyle. They strongly resisted any changes to their lifestyle even when it seemed to be in the company's best interest.

Dealing with Customers

Carbonell noted:

> *I am Mr. BA in Colombia. I meet with ambassadors and heads of companies. It is very different from England, where you are the same as everyone else. I have to be involved in these functions and I even know the president of Colombia.*

While public relations with a country's elite was part of the daily routine, country managers also found themselves dealing with individual customers. For example, Carbonell described how he dealt with one irate customer:

This man flew with us from London and then connected to a flight on Aces.[13] *Aces lost his bags, and now he wants us to pay for them. He has phoned several times, and now he has written a letter. I have told him that we are not responsible for the other airline, but he thinks that because he booked the ticket through us, we are responsible. We will send him a polite letter saying that his complaint has been sent to Aces.*

I do not take many calls from businesspeople myself, but it is important in this culture for the senior businessman to speak to the 'person in charge.' I am used to making judgments about when it is appropriate for me to deal directly with customers, or personally introduce them to other members of my team.

Country Manager Evaluation

Country managers were evaluated on a number of areas thought to measure performance. These included costs, revenue targets, sales margins and customer service. While BA was clear in communicating the targets to be met by managers, there was some flexibility in the evaluation, with consideration given to external influences such as economic downturns and political unrest.

One key performance indicator (KPI) was on-time departure. With some Latin American points experiencing problems in this area, a debate between Dunkerley and the country managers ensued with regard to how much a country manager can influence on-time departures. Carbonell noted:

We debated how to differentiate between what we are responsible for and what we inherit. This is not as straightforward as it might appear, as only one or two stations in this area have direct non-stop services from London.

Flights departing London for Bogota, for example, left at approximately 10:00 a.m., which coincided with peak activity at the airport. As a result, flights were often delayed in London and consequently arrived late in Bogota. This made the process of preparing the aircraft to leave on-schedule out of Bogota more difficult. Clearly, delays in London were out of the control of managers in Bogota and they wondered why this should affect their KPI.

Colombia—A Model for Change?

In 1997, Carbonell introduced a number of changes to the Colombian office. A first step toward narrowing the gap between the country managers and their subordinates was to dissolve symbolic differences. An open floor plan was developed that allowed easier access to the country manager and enhanced interdepartmental communication. Large country manager offices were converted to meeting rooms. As a European of Spanish descent, Carbonell noted:

Many Colombians are used to a much more hierarchical managerial style than I am and usually say "yes" even if they think the contrary . . . It is important to "walk the talk" and to encourage people to share information with each other. Changing the office to an open-plan style—and leading the way on this—has certainly helped.

BA's finance manager for Colombia agreed:

Before we went to an open-plan, we had three people in the finance department and nobody knew what the others in the office were doing. When we were asked why we were doing something a certain way, the answer was "because we have always done it that way," with no idea as to why. Now everyone in the office can see what we are doing and evaluate the processes.

THE DEAD MAN'S SHOES

Managers who had been inherited from British Caledonian saw little opportunity for advancement under BA. The only opportunities came when one's direct superior resigned or retired. Dunkerley referred to this as "the Dead Man's Shoes."

Moving from one country to another was uncommon and with 30 to 50 staff per country, opportunities within one's own country were limited. The most talented managers moved to other companies, while less able managers remained with BA. On the other hand, Dunkerley believed that line staff were highly competent and only needed proper direction.

Dunkerley wanted to break the "Dead Man's Shoes" mentality and circumvent further defections by the company's most talented employees. He thought about making all vacancies available to any BA employee in the region, not just those working in the same country. He also thought about transferring high potential individuals between departments, allowing sales managers to become head of finance or marketing and vice versa. In his view, personal suitability and team leadership skills were more important than technical skill, which could be acquired on the job.

London believed such promotions would be very risky. Having someone lead a department in which the person has little or no technical expertise greatly increased the possibility of decision-making errors, they believed. At least some LACAR country managers agreed with London's assessment.

GENERAL SALES AGENTS

In Latin America, most of BA's sales were generated through general sales agents (GSAs). GSAs were usually travel agencies that provided functions such as ticketing. Some GSAs represented other airlines, but most did not. In Colombia, GSAs provided hotel bookings and other travel services, with BA accounting for approximately 25 percent of their business. In 1996, BA had contracts with 58 GSAs throughout Latin America, with coverage divided geographically between them.

They were expected to generate new sales for the airline and, in return, were given a three percent commission on sales. However, most GSAs rarely did anything to increase business, but would "simply collect the three percent on whatever sales walked through the door." Carbonell described the situation in Colombia:

> *Most GSAs weren't effective and had a high turnover in staff. They were happy with the status quo and did not know what competitors offered or what BA offers over the others. They were receiving easy money. With a little bit of effort we could have doubled our sales.*

Local laws tended to favor GSAs, making it difficult for BA to withdraw from contracts without paying significant compensation. Dunkerley explained:

> *They view us as the big corporation taking advantage of small local companies. Even when contracts expire, we can be asked to pay compensation if the contract is not renewed. Each country has different laws in this regard.*

Local courts determined the amount of compensation and thus, BA had no way of identifying in advance the cost effectiveness of terminating the contracts.

In total, 41 GSAs were identified that were not providing adequate service. Contracts for many GSAs were due to expire and in most cases, not renewing the contracts would result in a lower court settlement than cancelling the contracts.

SALES

Measuring performance in the airline industry was made difficult by factors, such as the economy, that were beyond a manager's control. The hyperinflationary environment that dominated in Latin America in the late 1980s demanded a transactional-based strategy. The most important thing was getting tickets in customers' hands in exchange for U.S. currency. This practice became institutionalized over the years, such that when the economy improved, the company continued to deal with customers in the same way. Often this meant visiting a sales shop in a major city where, after passing through heavy security, tickets were issued directly to passengers.

For example, the Colombia office operated a telesales reservations desk in Bogota. Passengers would call in and make a reservation or inquiry, and the BA staff would process the request. Lost calls ran as high as 50 percent compared to the company average of five percent.

In early 1998, training was implemented in order to reduce the lost call rate and to improve telephone etiquette. Telesales agents learned to listen to the passengers needs and to offer less restrictive (higher priced) fares that served the passenger better and provided higher returns for BA. Following the training, agents were given the freedom to offer discounts to passengers without requesting the manager's approval.

In addition to telesales, BA had sales agents that visited travel agencies and other organizations to promote BA products. Agents were evaluated purely on revenue.

No consideration was given to the cost of sales. In Colombia, the sales team had a marketing budget of $200,000 to $300,000 per year. This was typically spent on advertising seat sales that occurred during peak sales times. Before Carbonell arrived, the sales team ensured that the entire budget was spent every year, even when a full budget was not needed, as this ensured that the head office would not reduce the budget for the next fiscal year. In addition, seat sales were offered to counter similar sales by competing airlines, such as Avianca, even when projections indicated that demand would exceed capacity.

CONCLUSION

Brazil was BA's most important market in Latin America. In 1996, it accounted for 50 percent of BA's Latin America business (80,000 passengers) and with the necessary investment in resources and personnel, Dunkerley believed BA's service to Brazil could be further doubled within three years. Over the past year, Dunkerley made 10 visits to Brazil.

> *For the Brazil trips, I needed to be visible. My role during these visits was not to make operational decisions, but rather to demonstrate the focus and priority I was placing on Brazil.*

Despite his visibility, Brazil remained perhaps the most resistant to the changes Dunkerley wanted to see implemented across the region. Dunkerley explained:

> *I was preaching revolution. I believed that people were shackled, but key members liked things the way they were. Their attitude was that "I am young, ambitious and just passing through."*

With the Mexican *Tequila Effect* still on everyone's mind, he also had to contend with London's understandable skepticism about the region's potential. Dunkerley considered the challenge facing him.

> *How do you break out of this unvirtuous cycle? How do you convince an organization that such a poor area is worth investing in?*

ENDNOTES

1. RPKs are calculated from the number of revenue passengers carried multiplied by the distance flown.
2. Slots were spaces allocated by government transportation authorities that limited the number of flights any particular airline could have into or out of a given airport.
3. Code-sharing is an arrangement in which one airline sells its seat inventory under the airline code of another airline, usually a marketing partner.
4. "The World's Most Admired Companies," *Fortune*, Oct. 27, 1997.
5. Oum, T. H. and Yu, C., *Winning Airlines*, Kluwer Academic Publishers, Norwell, MA, 1998.
6. Reed, Arthur, *Airline, The Inside Story of British Airways*, BBC Books, London, 1990.
7. The Southern Common Market, known as Mercosur, included Argentina, Paraguay, Uruguay and Brazil and represented a total population of 190 million individuals. NAFTA included Canada, Mexico and the United States.
8. In 1997, a new Boeing 747 cost more than $160 million to purchase and had an expected service life of more than 25 years. At the end of a 747's useful life, it was typically sold for a write down price of $3 million, to be used either for spare parts or converted to haul cargo.
9. Corke, Alison, *British Airways: The Path to Profitability*, Frances Pinter, London, 1986.
10. These three buckets are given only as a simplified example. In reality, there was a very wide range of buckets.
11. Reed, Arthur, *Airline, The Inside Story of British Airways*, BBC Books, London, 1990.
12. The Tequila Effect refers to Mexico's economic crisis, which also affected the rest of Latin America. Mexico devalued its peso on Dec. 20, 1994 and triggered a seven percent drop in its gross domestic product as well as sharp declines in stocks and currency. The effects were felt well into 1995.
13. Aces, a Colombian regional airline, was owned by Continental Airlines.

CASE 12

Circus Circus Enterprises, Inc., 1998

John K. Ross, III
Mike Keeffe
Bill Middlebrook
Southwest Texas State University

We possess the resources to accomplish the big projects: the know-how, the financial power and the places to invest. The renovation of our existing projects will soon be behind us, which last year represented the broadest scope of construction ever taken on by a gaming company. Now we are well-positioned to originate new projects. Getting big projects right is the route to future wealth in gaming; big successful projects tend to prove long staying power in our business. When the counting is over, we think our customers and investors will hold the winning hand.

—(Annual Report, 1997)

Big projects and a winning hand. Circus Circus does seem to have both. And big projects they are, with huge pink and white striped concrete circus tents, a 600-foot-long river boat replica, a giant castle, and a great pyramid. Their latest project, Mandalay Bay, will include a 3,700 room hotel/casino, an 11-acre aquatic environment with beaches, a snorkeling reef and a swim-up shark exhibit.

Circus Circus Enterprises, Inc. (hereafter "Circus") describes itself as in the business of entertainment and has been one of the innovators in the theme-resort concept popular in casino gaming. Its areas of operation are the glitzy vacation and convention meccas of Las Vegas, Reno and Laughlin, Nevada, as well as other locations in the U.S. and abroad. Historically, Circus's marketing of its products has been called "right out of the bargain basement" and has catered to "low rollers." Circus has continued to broaden its market and now aims more at the middle-income gambler and family-oriented vacationers as well as the more upscale traveler and player.

Circus was purchased in 1974 for $50,000 as a small and unprofitable casino operation by partners William G. Bennett, an aggressive cost-cutter who ran furniture stores before entering the gaming industry in 1965, and William N. Pennington. (See Exhibit 1 for the Board of Directors and top managers.) The partners were able to rejuvenate Circus with fresh marketing, went public with a stock offering in October 1983, and experienced rapid growth and high profitability over time. Within the five-year period between 1993 and 1997 the average return on invested capital was 16.5 percent and Circus had generated over $1 billion in free cash flow. Today, Circus is one of the major players in the Las Vegas, Laughlin, and Reno markets in terms of square footage of casino space and number of hotel rooms—despite the incredible growth in both markets. For the first time in company history, casino gaming operations in 1997 provided slightly less than one half of total revenues, and that trend continued into 1998. (See Exhibit 2.) On January 31, 1998, Circus reported a net income of approximately $89.9 million on revenues of $1.35 billion. This was done slightly from 1997's more than $100 million net income on revenues of $1.3 billion. During that same year Circus invested over $585.8 million in capital expenditures, and another $663.3 million was invested in fiscal year 1998.

This case was prepared for classroom purposes only and is not designed to show effective or ineffective handling of administrative situations.

EXHIBIT 1 | Directors and Officers of Circus Circus Enterprises, Inc.

Directors

Name	Age	Title
Clyde T. Turner	59	Chairman of the Board and CEO Circus Circus Enterprises
Michael S. Ensign	59	Vice Chairman of the Board and COO Circus Circus Enterprises
Glenn Schaeffer	43	President, CFO Circus Circus Enterprises
William A. Richardson	50	Vice Chairman of the Board and Executive Vice President Circus Circus Enterprises
Richard P. Banis	52	Former President and COO Circus Circus Enterprises
Arthur H. Bilger	44	Former President and COO New World Communications Group International
Richard A. Etter	58	Former Chairman and CEO Bank of America–Nevada
William E. Bannen, M.D.	48	Vice President/Chief Medical Officer, Blue Cross Blue Shield of Nevada
Donna B. More	40	Partner, Law Firm of Freeborn & Peters
Michael D. McKee	51	Executive Vice President The Irving Company

Officers

Name	Title
Clyde T. Turner	Chairman of the Board and Chief Executive Officer
Michael S. Ensign	Vice Chairman of the Board and Chief Operating Officer
Glenn Schaeffer	President, Chief Financial Officer and Treasurer
William A. Richardson	Vice Chairman of the Board and Executive Vice President Circus Circus Enterprises
Tony Alamo	Senior Vice President, Operations
Gregg Solomon	Senior Vice President, Operations
Kurt D. Sullivan	Senior Vice President, Operations
Steve Greathouse	Senior Vice President, Operations
Yvett Landau	Vice President, General Counsel and Secretary
Les Martin	Vice President and Chief Accounting Officer

Source: Annual Report 1998; Proxy Statement May 1, 1998.

EXHIBIT 2 | Circus Circus Enterprises, Inc. Sources of Revenues as a Percentage of Net Revenues

	1998	1997	1996	1995
Casinos	46.7%	49.2%	51.2%	52.3%
Food & Beverage	15.9	15.8	15.5	16.2
Hotel	24.4	22.0	21.4	19.9
Other	10.5	11.0	12.2	14.2
Unconsolidated	7.3	6.5	3.5	.5
Less: Complimentary Allowances	4.8	4.5	3.8	3.1

Source: Circus Circus 10-K, January 31, 1995–1998.

CIRCUS CIRCUS OPERATIONS

Circus defines entertainment as pure play and fun, and it goes out of the way to see that customers have plenty of opportunities for both. Each Circus location has a distinctive personality. Circus Circus–Las Vegas is the world of the Big Top, where live circus acts perform free every thirty minutes. Kids may cluster around video games, while the adults migrate to nickel slot machines and dollar game tables. Located at the north end of the Vegas strip, Circus Circus–Las Vegas sits on 69 acres of land with 3,744 hotel rooms, shopping areas, two specialty restaurants, a buffet with seating for 1,200, fast-food shops, cocktail lounges, video arcades, 109,000 square feet of casino space, and the Grand Slam Canyon, a five-acre glass-enclosed theme park including a four-loop roller coaster. Approximately 384 guests may also stay at nearby Circusland RV Park. For the year ending January 31, 1997, $126.7 million was invested in this property for new rooms and remodeling, with another $35.2 million in fiscal year 1998.

Luxor, an Egyptian-themed hotel and casino complex, opened on October 15, 1993, when 10,000 people entered to play the 2,245 slot and video poker games and 110 table games in the 120,000-square-foot casino in the hotel atrium (reported to be the world's largest). By the end of the opening weekend 40,000 people per day were visiting the 30-story bronze pyramid that encases the hotel and entertainment facilities.

Luxor features a 30-story pyramid and two new 22-story hotel towers, including 492 suites, and is connected to Excalibur (see later) by a climate-controlled skyway with moving walkways. Situated at the south end of the Las Vegas strip on a 64-acre site adjacent to Excalibur, Luxor features a food and entertainment area on three different levels beneath the hotel atrium. The pyramid's hotel rooms can be reached from the four corners of the building by state-of-the-art "inclinators" that travel at a 39-degree angle. Parking is available for nearly 3,200 vehicles, including a covered garage that contains approximately 1,800 spaces.

The Luxor underwent major renovations, costing $323.3 million during fiscal 1997 and another $116.5 million in fiscal 1998. The resulting complex contains 4,425 hotel rooms, extensively renovated casino space, an additional 20,000 square feet of convention area, an 800-seat buffet, a series of IMAX attractions, five theme restaurants, seven cocktail lounges and a variety of specialty shops. Circus expects to draw significant walk-in traffic to the newly refurbished Luxor and is one of the principal components of the Masterplan Mile.

Located next to the Luxor, Excalibur is one of the first sights travelers see as they exit interstate highway 15. (Management was confident that the sight of a giant, colorful medieval castle would make a lasting impression on mainstream tourists and vacationing families arriving in Las Vegas.) Guests cross a drawbridge, with moat, onto a cobblestone walkway where multicolored spires, turrets and battlements loom above. The castle walls are four 28-story hotel towers containing a total of 4,008 rooms. Inside is a medieval world complete with a Fantasy Faire inhabited by strolling jugglers, fire eaters and acrobats, as well as a Royal Village complete with peasants, serfs, and ladies-in-waiting around medieval theme shops. The 110,000-square-foot casino encompasses 2,442 slot machines, more than 89 game tables, a sports book, and a poker and keno area. There are 12 restaurants, capable of feeding more than 20,000 people daily, and a 1,000-seat amphitheater. Excalibur, which opened in June 1990, was built for $294 million and was financed primarily with internally generated funds. In the year ending January 31, 1997, Excalibur contributed 23 percent of the organization's revenues, down from 33 percent in 1993. Yet 1997 was a record year, generating the company's highest margins and over $100 million in operating cash flow. In fiscal 1998 Excalibur underwent $25.1 million in renovations and was connected to the Luxor by enclosed, moving walkways.

Situated between the two anchors on the Las Vegas strip are two smaller casinos owned and operated by Circus. The Silver City Casino and Slots-A-Fun depend primarily on the foot traffic along the strip for their gambling patrons. Combined, they offer more than 1,202 slot machines and 46 gaming tables on 34,900 square feet of casino floor.

Circus owns and operates 10 properties in Nevada, 1 in Mississippi and has a 50-percent ownership in 3 others. (See Exhibit 3.)

All of Circus's operations do well in the city of Las Vegas. However, Circus Circus's 1997 operational earnings for the Luxor and Circus Circus–Las Vegas were off 38

Exhibit 3 | Circus Circus Enterprises, Inc. Properties and Percent of Total Revenues

Properties	1998	1997	1996	1995
	PERCENT REVENUES			
Las Vegas				
Circus Circus–Las Vegas	25[1]	24[1]	27[1]	29[1]
Excalibur	21	23	23	25
Luxor	23	17	20	24
Slots-A-Fun and Silver City				
Reno				
Circus Circus–Reno				
Laughlin				
Colorado Bell	12[2]	12[2]	13[2]	16[2]
Edgewater				
Jean, Nevada				
Gold Strike	6[3]	6[3]	4[3]	NA
Nevada Landing				
Henderson, Nevada				
Railroad Pass				
Tunica, Mississippi				
Gold Strike	4	4	5	3
50% ownership:				
Silver Legacy, Reno, Nevada	7.3	6.5[4]	3.5[4]	.5[4]
Monte Carlo, Las Vegas, Nevada				
Grand Victoria Riverboat Casino, Elgin, Illinois				

[1]Combined with revenues from Circus Circus–Reno.
[2]Colorado Bell and Edgewater have been combined.
[3]Gold Strike and Nevada Landing have been combined.
[4]Revenues of unconsolidated affiliates have been combined.
Note: Revenues from Slots-A-Fun and Silver City, management fees and other income were not separately reported.

percent from the previous year. Management credits this decline to the disruption in services due to renovations.

However, Circus's combined hotel room occupancy rates had remained above 90 percent, due, in part, to low room rates ($45 to $69 at Circus Circus–Las Vegas) and popular buffets. Each of the major properties contain large, inexpensive buffets that management believes make staying with Circus more attractive. Yet, recent results show a room occupancy rate of 87.5 percent, due in part to the building boom in Las Vegas.

The company's other big-top facility is Circus Circus–Reno. With the addition of Skyway Tower in 1985, this big top now offers a total of 1,605 hotel rooms, 60,600 square feet of casino, a buffet that can seat 700 people, shops, video arcades, cocktail lounges, midway games and circus acts. Circus Circus–Reno had several marginal years, but has become one of the leaders in the Reno market. Circus anticipates that recent remodeling, at a cost of $25.6 million, will increase this property's revenue-generating potential.

The Colorado Belle and The Edgewater Hotel are located in Laughlin, Nevada, on the banks of the Colorado River, a city 90 miles south of Las Vegas. The Colorado Belle, opened in 1987, features a huge paddlewheel riverboat replica, a buffet, cocktail lounges and shops. The Edgewater, acquired in 1983, has a southwestern motif, a 57,000-square-foot casino, a bowling center, a buffet and cocktail lounges. Combined, these two properties contain 2,700 rooms and over 120,000 square feet of casino. These two operations contributed 12 percent of the company's revenues in the year ended January 31, 1997, and again in 1998, down from 21 percent in 1994. The extensive proliferation of casinos throughout the region, primarily on Indian land, and the development of mega-resorts in Las Vegas have seriously eroded outlying markets such as Laughlin.

Three properties purchased in 1995 and located in Jean and Henderson, Nevada, represent continuing investments by Circus in outlying markets. The Gold Strike and Nevada Landing service the I-15 market between Las Vegas and southern California. These properties have over 73,000 square feet of casino space, 2,140 slot machines and 42 gaming tables combined. Each has limited hotel space (1,116 rooms total) and depends heavily on I-15 traffic. The Railroad Pass is considered a local casino and is dependent on Henderson residents as its market. This smaller casino contains only 395 slot machines and 11 gaming tables.

Gold Strike–Tunica (formally Circus Circus–Tunica), a dockside casino located in Tunica, Mississippi, opened in 1994 on 24 acres of land located along the Mississippi River, approximately 20 miles south of Memphis. In 1997 operating income declined by more than 50 percent, due to the increase in competition and lack of hotel rooms. Circus decided to renovate this property and add a 1,200 room tower hotel. Total cost for all remodeling was $119.8 million.

Joint Ventures

Circus is currently engaged in three joint ventures through the wholly owned subsidiary Circus Participant. In Las Vegas, Circus joined with Mirage Resorts to build and operate the Monte Carlo, a hotel–casino with 3,002 rooms designed along the lines of the grand casinos of the Mediterranean. It is located on 46 acres (with 600 feet on the Las Vegas strip) between the New York-New York casino and the soon-to-be-completed Bellagio, with all three casinos to be connected by monorail. The Monte Carlo features a 90,000-square-foot casino containing 2,221 slot machines and 95 gaming tables, along with a 550-seat bingo parlor, high-tech arcade rides, restaurants and buffets, a microbrewery, approximately 15,000 square feet of meeting and convention space and a 1,200-seat theater. Opened on June 21, 1996, the Monte Carlo generated $14.6 million as Circus's share in operating income for the first seven months of operation.

In Elgin, Illinois, Circus is in a 50-percent partnership with Hyatt Development Corporation in The Grand Victoria. Styled to resemble a Victorian riverboat, this floating casino and land-based entertainment complex includes some 36,000 square feet of casino space, containing 977 slot machines and 56 gaming tables. The adjacent land-based complex contains two movie theaters, a 240 seat buffet, restaurants and parking for approximately 2,000 vehicles. Built for a total of $112 million, The Grand Victoria returned to Circus $44 million in operating income in 1996.

The third joint venture is a 50-percent partnership with Eldorado Limited in the Silver Legacy. Opened in 1995, this casino is located between Circus Circus–Reno and the Eldorado Hotel and Casino on two city blocks in downtown Reno, Nevada. The Silver Legacy has 1,711 hotel rooms, 85,000 square feet of casino, 2,275 slot machines and 89 gaming tables. Management seems to believe that the Silver Legacy holds promise; however, the Reno market is suffering and the opening of the Silver Legacy has cannibalized the Circus Circus–Reno market.

Circus engaged in a fourth joint venture to penetrate the Canadian market, but on January 23, 1997, announced it had been bought out by Hilton Hotels Corporation, one of three partners in the venture.

Circus has achieved success through an aggressive growth strategy and a corporate structure designed to enhance that growth. A strong cash position, innovative ideas, and attention to cost control have allowed Circus to satisfy the bottom line during a period when competitors were typically taking on large debt obligations to finance new projects. (See Exhibits 4, 5, 6, and 7.) Yet the market is changing. Gambling of all kinds has spread across the country; no longer does the average individual need to go to Las Vegas or New Jersey. Instead, gambling can be found as close as the local quick market (lottery), bingo hall, many Indian reservations, the Mississippi River and others. There are now almost 300 casinos in Las Vegas alone, 60 in Colorado and 160 in California. In order to maintain a competitive edge, Circus has continued to invest heavily in renovation of existing properties (a strategy common to the enter-

EXHIBIT 4 | Selected Financial Information

	FY98	FY97	FY96	FY95	FY94	FY93	FY92	FY91
Earnings Per Share	0.40	0.99	1.33	1.59	1.34	2.05	1.84	1.39
Current Ratio	0.85	1.17	1.30	1.35	0.95	0.90	1.14	0.88
Total Liabilities/Total Assets	0.65	0.62	0.44	0.54	0.57	0.48	0.58	0.77
Operating Profit Margin	17.4%	17%	19%	22%	21%	24.4%	24.9%	22.9%

Source: Circus Circus Annual Reports and 10K's, 1991–1998.

EXHIBIT 5 | Twelve-Year Summary

	Revenues (in '000s)	Net Income
FY98	$1,354,487	$89,908
FY97	1,334,250	100,733
FY96	1,299,596	128,898
FY95	1,170,182	136,286
FY94	954,923	116,189
FY93	843,025	117,322
FY92	806,023	103,348
FY91	692,052	76,292
FY90	522,376	76,064
FY89	511,960	81,714
FY88	458,856	55,900
FY87	373,967	28,198
FY86	306,993	37,375

Source: Circus Circus Annual Reports and 10K's, 1986–1998.

tainment/amusement industry) and continues to develop new projects.

New Ventures

Circus currently has three new projects planned for opening within the near future. The largest project, named "Mandalay Bay," is scheduled for completion in the first quarter of 1999 and is estimated to cost $950 million (excluding land). Circus owns a contiguous mile of the southern end of the Las Vegas strip that it calls its "Masterplan Mile" and that currently contains the Excalibur and Luxor resorts. To be located next to the Luxor, Mandalay Bay will aim for the upscale traveler and player and will be styled as a South Seas adventure. The resort will contain a 43-story hotel–casino with over 3,700 rooms and an 11-acre aquatic environment. The aquatic environment will contain a surfing beach, swim-up shark tank and snorkeling reef. A Four Seasons Hotel with some 400 rooms will complement the remainder of Mandalay Bay. Circus anticipates that the remainder of the Masterplan Mile will eventually comprise at least one additional casino resort and a number of stand-alone hotels and amusement centers.

Circus also plans three other casino projects, provided all the necessary licenses and agreements can be obtained. In Detroit, Michigan, Circus has combined with the Atwater Casino Group in a joint venture to build a $600 million project. Negotiations with the city

6 | Circus Circus Enterprises, Inc. Annual Income

Year ended January 31, (in thousands of dollars)

Fiscal year ending	**1/31/98**	**1/31/97**	**1/31/96**	**1/31/95**	**1/31/94**
Revenues					
Casino	$632,122	$655,902	$664,772	$612,115	$538,813
Rooms	330,644	294,241	278,807	232,346	176,001
Food and beverage	215,584	210,384	201,385	189,664	152,469
Other	142,407	146,554	158,534	166,295	117,501
Earnings of unconsolidated affiliates	98,977	86,646	45,485	5,459	—
	1,419,734	1,393,727	1,348,983	1,205,879	984,784
Less complimentary allowances	(65,247)	(59,477)	(49,387)	(35,697)	(29,861)
Net revenue	1,354,487	1,334,250	1,299,596	1,170,182	954,923
Costs and expenses					
Casino	316,902	302,096	275,680	246,416	209,402
Rooms	122,934	116,508	110,362	94,257	78,932
Food and beverage	199,955	200,722	188,712	177,136	149,267
Other operating expenses	90,187	90,601	92,631	107,297	72,802
General and administrative	232,536	227,348	215,083	183,175	152,104
Depreciation and amortization	117,474	95,414	93,938	81,109	58,105
Preopening expense	3,447	—	—	3,012	16,506
Abandonment loss		48,309	45,148	—	—
	1,083,435	1,080,998	1,021,554	892,402	737,118
Operating profit before corporate expense	271,052	223,252	278,042	277,780	217,805
Corporate expense	34,552	31,083	26,669	21,773	16,744
Income from operations	236,500	222,169	251,373	256,007	201,061
Other income (expense)					
Interest, dividends and other income (loss)	9,779	5,077	4,022	225	(683)
Interest income and guarantee fees from unconsolidated affiliate	6,041	6,865	7,517	992	—
Interest expense	(88,847)	(54,681)	(51,537)	(42,734)	(17,770)
Interest expense from unconsolidated affiliate	(15,551)	(15,567)	(5,616)	—	—
	(88,578)	(58,306)	(45,614)	(41,517)	(18,453)
Income before provision for income tax	147,922	163,863	205,759	214,490	182,608
Provision for income tax	58,014	63,130	76,861	78,204	66,419
Income before extraordinary loss		—	—	—	116,189
Extraordinary loss		—	—	—	—
Net income	89,908	100,733	128,898	136,286	116,189
Earnings per share					
Income before extraordinary loss	.95	.99	1.33	1.59	1.34
Extraordinary loss		—	—	—	—
Net income per share	.94	.99	1.33	1.59	1.34

Source: Circus Circus Annual Reports and 10K's, 1994–1998.

7 | Circus Circus Enterprises, Inc. Consolidated Balance Sheets

(in thousands of dollars)

Assets	1/31/98	1/31/97	1/31/96	1/31/95	1/31/94
Current assets					
Cash and cash equivalents	$ 58,631	$ 69,516	$ 62,704	$ 53,764	$ 39,110
Receivables	33,640	34,434	16,527	8,931	8,673
Inventories	22,440	19,371	20,459	22,660	20,057
Prepaid expenses	20,281	19,951	19,418	20,103	20,062
Deferred income tax	7,871	8,577	7,272	5,463	
Total current	142,863	151,849	124,380	110,921	87,902
Property, equipment	2,466,848	1,920,032	1,474,684	1,239,062	1,183,164
Other assets					
Excess of purchase price over fair market value	375,375	385,583	394,518	9,836	10,200
Notes receivable	1,075	36,443	27,508	68,083	
Investments in unconsolidated affiliates	255,392	214,123	173,270	74,840	
Deferred charges and other assets	21,995	21,081	17,533	9,806	16,658
Total other	653,837	657,230	612,829	162,565	26,858
Total assets	3,263,548	2,729,111	2,213,503	1,512,548	1,297,924
Liabilities and stockholders' equity					
Current liabilities					
Current portion of long-term debt	3,071	379	863	106	169
Accounts and contracts payable					
Trade	22,103	22,658	16,824	12,102	14,804
Construction	40,670	21,144	—	1,101	13,844
Accrued liabilities					
Salaries, wages and vacations	36,107	31,847	30,866	24,946	19,650
Progressive jackpots	7,511	6,799	8,151	7,447	4,881
Advance room deposits	6,217	7,383	7,517	8,701	6,981
Interest payable	17,828	9,004	3,169	2,331	2,278
Other	33,451	30,554	28,142	25,274	25,648
Income tax payable					3,806
Total current liabilities	166,958	129,768	95,532	82,008	92,061
Long-term debt	1,788,818	1,405,897	715,214	632,652	567,345
Other liabilities					
Deferred income tax	175,934	152,635	148,096	110,776	77,153
Other long-term liabilities	8,089	6,439	9,319	988	1,415
Total other liabilities	184,023	159,074	157,415	111,764	78,568
Total liabilities	2,139,799	1,694,739	968,161	826,424	737,974
Redeemable preferred stock		17,631	18,530		
Temporary equity		44,950			
Commitments and contingent liabilities					
Stockholders' equity					
Common stock	1,893	1,880	1,880	1,607	1,603
Preferred stock					
Additional paid-in capital	558,658	498,893	527,205	124,960	120,135
Retained earnings	1,074,271	984,363	883,630	754,732	618,446
Treasury stock	(511,073)	(513,345)	(185,903)	(195,175)	(180,234)
Total stockholders' equity	1,123,749	971,791	1,226,812	686,124	559,950
Total liabilities and stockholders' equity	3,263,548	2,729,111	2,213,503	1,512,548	1,297,924

Source: Circus Circus Annual Reports and 10K's, 1994–1998.

to develop the project have been completed; however, the remainder of the appropriate licenses will need to be obtained before construction begins.

Along the Mississippi Gulf, at the north end of the Bay of St. Louis, Circus plans to construct a casino resort containing 1,500 rooms at an estimated cost of $225 million. Circus has received all necessary permits to begin construction; however, these approvals have been challenged in court, delaying the project.

In Atlantic City, Circus has entered into an agreement with Mirage Resorts to develop a 181-acre site in the Marina District. Land title has been transferred to Mirage; however, Mirage has purported to cancel its agreement with Circus. Circus has filed suit against Mirage, seeking to enforce the contract, while others have filed suit to stop all development in the area.

Most of Circus's projects are being tailored to attract mainstream tourists and family vacationers. However, the addition of several joint ventures and the completion of the Masterplan Mile will also attract the more upscale customer.

THE GAMING INDUSTRY

By 1997 the gaming industry had captured a large amount of the vacation/leisure time dollars spent in the United States. Gamblers lost over $44.3 billion on legal wagering in 1995 (up from $29.9 billion in 1992), including wagers at racetracks, bingo parlors, lotteries and casinos. This figure does not include dollars spent on lodging, food, transportation and other related expenditures associated with visits to gaming facilities. Casino gambling accounts for 76 percent of all legal gambling expenditures, far ahead of second-place Indian reservation gambling, at 8.9 percent, and lotteries, at 7.1 percent. The popularity of casino gambling may be credited to a more frequent and somewhat higher payout as compared to lotteries and racetracks; however, as winnings are recycled, the multiplier effect restores a high return to casino operators.

Geographic expansion has slowed considerably, as no additional states have approved casino-type gambling since 1993. Growth has occurred in developed locations, with Las Vegas, Nevada, and Atlantic City, New Jersey, leading the way.

Las Vegas remains the largest U.S. gaming market and one of the largest convention markets, with more than 100,000 hotel rooms hosting more than 29.6 million visitors in 1996, up 2.2 percent from 1995. Casino operators are building to take advantage of this continued growth. Recent projects include the Monte Carlo ($350 million), New York-New York ($350 million), Bellagino ($1.4 billion), Hilton Hotels ($750 million), and Project Paradise ($800 million). Additionally, Harrah's is adding a 989-room tower and remodeling 500 current rooms, and Caesar's Palace has expansion plans to add 2,000 rooms. Las Vegas's hotel and casino capacity is expected to continue to expand, with some 12,500 rooms opening within a year, beginning fall of 1998. According to the Las Vegas Convention and Visitor Authority, Las Vegas is a destination market with most visitors planning their trip more than a week in advance (81 percent), arriving by car (47 percent) or airplane (42 percent), and staying in a hotel (72 percent). Gamblers are typically return visitors (77 percent), averaging 2.2 trips per year, who like playing the slots (65 percent).

Besides geographical location, the primary differences between the Atlantic City market and the Las Vegas market reflect the different types of consumers frequenting these markets. While Las Vegas attracts overnight resort-seeking vacationers, Atlantic City's clientele are predominantly day-trippers traveling by automobile or bus. Gaming revenues are expected to continue to grow, perhaps to $4 billion in 1997 split between 10 casino/hotels currently operating. Growth in the Atlantic City area will be concentrated in the Marina section of town, where Mirage Resorts has entered into an agreement with the city to develop 150 acres of the Marina as a destination resort. This development will include a resort wholly owned by Mirage, a casino/hotel developed by Circus, and a complex developed by a joint venture between Mirage and Boyd Corp. Currently, in Atlantic City, Donald Trump's gaming empire holds the largest market share, with Trump's Castle, Trump Plaza and the Taj Mahal. (Total market share is 30 percent.) The next closest in market share are Caesar's (10.3 percent), Tropicana and Bally's (9.2 percent each), and Showboat (9.0 percent).

There remain a number of smaller markets located around the U.S., primarily in Mississippi, Louisiana, Illinois, Missouri, and Indiana. Each state has imposed various restrictions on the development of casino operations within their states. In some cases—for example, in Illinois, where there are only 10 gaming licenses available, this has severely restricted the growth opportunities and hurt revenues. In other states—Mississippi and Louisiana—revenues are up 8 percent and 15 percent, respectively, in riverboat operations. Native American casinos continue to be developed on federally controlled Indian land. These casinos are not publicly held, but do tend to be managed by publicly held corporations. Overall, these other locations present a mix of opportunities and generally constitute only a small portion of overall gaming revenues.

MAJOR INDUSTRY PLAYERS

Over the past several years there have been numerous changes as mergers and acquisitions have reshaped the gaming industry. As of year end 1996, the industry was a combination of corporations ranging from those engaged solely in gaming to multinational conglomerates. The largest competitors, in terms of revenues, combined multiple industries to generate both large revenues and substantial profits. (See Exhibit 8.) However, those engaged primarily in gaming could also be extremely profitable.

In 1996 Hilton began a hostile acquisition attempt of ITT Corporation. As a result of this attempt, ITT has merged with Starwood Lodging Corporation and Starwood Lodging Trust. The resulting corporation is one of the world's largest hotel and gaming corporations, owning the Sheraton, The Luxury Collection, the Four Points Hotels, and Caesar's, as well as communications and educational services. In 1996 ITT hosted approximately 50 million customer nights in locations worldwide. Gaming operations are located in Las Vegas, Atlantic City, Halifax and Sydney (Nova Scotia), Lake Tahoe, Tunica (Mississippi), Lima (Peru), Cairo (Egypt), Canada, and Australia. In 1996 ITT had net income of $249 million on revenues of $6.579 billion. In June 1996, ITT announced plans to join with Planet Hollywood to develop casino/hotels with the Planet Hollywood theme in both Las Vegas and Atlantic City. However, these plans may be deferred as ITT becomes fully integrated into Starwood and management has the opportunity to refocus on the operations of the company.

Hilton Hotels owns (as of February 1, 1998) or leases and operates 25 hotels and manages 34 hotels partially or wholly owned by others, along with 180 franchised hotels. Eleven of the hotels are also casinos, six of which are located in Nevada and two in Atlantic City, with the other three in Australia and Uruguay. In 1997 Hilton had net income of $250.0 million on $5.31 billion in revenues. Hilton receives some 38 percent of total operating revenues from gaming operations and continues to expand in the market. Recent expansions

EXHIBIT 8 | Major U.S. Gaming, Lottery & Pari-mutuel Companies 1996 Revenues and Net Income (in millions of dollars)

	1997 Revenues	1997 Income	1996 Revenues	1996 Net Income
Starwood/ITT			$6597.0	$249.0
Hilton Hotels	5316.0	250.0	3940.0	82.0
Harrah's Entertainment	1619.0	99.3	1586.0	98.9
Mirage Resorts	1546.0	207	1358.3	206.0
Circus Circus	1354.4	89.9	1247.0	100.7
Trump Hotel and Casino, Inc.	1399.3	–42.1	976.3	–4.9
MGM Grand	827.5	111.0	804.8	74.5
Aztar	782.3	4.4	777.5	20.6
Int. Game Technology	743.9	137.2	733.5	118.0

Source: Individual companies' annual reports and 10K's, 1996.

include the Wild Wild West theme hotel casino in Atlantic City, the completed acquisition of all the assets of Bally's, and construction on a 2,900-room Paris Casino resort located next to Bally's Las Vegas.

Harrah's Entertainment, Inc., is primarily engaged in the gaming industry, with casino/hotels in Reno, Lake Tahoe, Las Vegas, and Laughlin, Nevada, and Atlantic City, New Jersey; riverboats in Joliet, Illinois, Vicksburg and Tunica, Mississippi, Shreveport, Louisiana, and Kansas City, Kansas; two Indian casinos; and a casino in Auckland, New Zealand. In 1997 it operated a total of approximately 774,500 square feet of casino space, with 19,835 slot machines and 934 table games. With this and some 8,197 hotel rooms, it had a net income of $99.3 million on $1.619 billion in revenues.

All of Mirage Resorts, Inc.'s gaming operations are currently located in Nevada. It owns and operates the Golden Nugget–Downtown, Las Vegas, the Mirage on the strip in Las Vegas, Treasure Island, and the Golden Nugget–Laughlin. In addition, it is a 50-percent owner of the Monte Carlo with Circus Circus. Net income for Mirage Resorts in 1997 was $207 million on revenues of $1.546 billion. Current expansion plans include the development of the Bellagio in Las Vegas ($1.6 billion estimated cost) and the Beau Rivage in Biloxi, Mississippi ($600 million estimated cost). These two properties would add a total of 265,900 square feet of casino space to the current Mirage inventory and an additional 252 gaming tables and 4,746 slot machines. An additional project is the development of the Marina area in Atlantic City, New Jersey, in partnership with Boyd Gaming.

MGM Grand Hotel and Casino is located on approximately 114 acres at the northeast corner of Las Vegas Boulevard, across the street from New York-New York Hotel and Casino. The casino is approximately 171,500 square feet in size and is one of the largest casinos in the world, with 3,669 slot machines and 157 table games. Current plans call for extensive renovation costing $700 million. Through a wholly owned subsidiary, MGM owns and operates the MGM Grand Diamond Beach Hotel and a hotel/casino resort in Darwin, Australia. Additionally, MGM and Primadonna Resorts, Inc., each own 50 percent of New York-New York Hotel and Casino, a $460 million architecturally distinctive themed destination resort that opened on January 3, 1997. MGM also intends to construct and operate a destination resort hotel/casino, entertainment and retail facility in Atlantic City on approximately 35 acres of land on the Atlantic City Boardwalk.

THE LEGAL ENVIRONMENT

Within the gaming industry all current operators must consider compliance with extensive gaming regulations as a primary concern. Each state or country has its own specific regulations and regulatory boards requiring extensive reporting and licensing requirements. For example, in Las Vegas, Nevada, gambling operations are subject to regulatory control by the Nevada State Gaming Control Board, the Clark County Nevada Gaming and Liquor Licensing Board, and city government regulations. The laws, regulations and supervisory procedures of virtually all gaming authorities are based upon public policy concerned primarily with the prevention of unsavory or unsuitable persons from having a direct or indirect involvement with gaming at any time or in any capacity, and the establishment and maintenance of responsible accounting practices and procedures. Additional regulations typically cover the maintenance of effective controls over the financial practices of licensees, including the establishment of minimum procedures for internal fiscal affairs and the safeguarding of assets and revenues, requirements for reliable record keeping and the filing of periodic reports, the prevention of cheating and fraudulent practices, and requirements for providing a source of state and local revenues through taxation and licensing fees. Changes in such laws, regulations and procedures could have an adverse effect on any gaming operations. All gaming companies must submit detailed operating and financial reports to authorities. Nearly all financial transactions, including loans, leases and the sale of securities, must be reported. Some financial activities are subject to approval by regulatory agencies. As Circus moves into other locations outside of Nevada, it will need to adhere to local regulations.

FUTURE CONSIDERATIONS

Circus Circus states that it is "in the business of entertainment, with . . . core strength in casino gaming," and that it intends to focus its efforts in Las Vegas, Atlantic City and Mississippi. Circus further states that the "future product in gaming, to be sure, is the entertainment resort" (Circus Circus 1997 Annual Report).

Circus was one of the innovators of the gaming resort concept and has continued to be a leader in that field. However, the mega-entertainment resort industry operates differently than the traditional casino gaming industry. In the past, consumers would visit a casino to experience the thrill of gambling. Now they not only gamble, but expect to be dazzled by enormous entertainment complexes that cost in the billions of dollars to build. The competition has continued to increase at the same time that growth rates have been slowing.

For years, analysts have questioned the ability of the gaming industry to continue high growth in established markets as the industry matures. Through the 1970s and 1980s the gaming industry experienced rapid growth. Through the 1990s the industry began to experience a shakeout of marginal competitors and a consolidation phase. Circus Circus has been successful through this turmoil, but now faces the task of maintaining high growth in a more mature industry.

BIBLIOGRAPHY

"Circus Circus Announces Promotion," *PR Newswire,* June 10, 1997.

Industry Surveys—Lodging and Gaming, *Standard and Poors Industry Surveys,* June 19, 1997.

"Casinos Move into New Areas," *Standard and Poors Industry Surveys,* March 11, 1993, pp. L35–L41.

Circus Circus Enterprises, Inc., *Annual Report to Shareholders,* January 31, 1989; January 31, 1990; January 31, 1993; January 31, 1994; January 31, 1995; January 31, 1996.

Circus Circus Enterprises, Inc., *Annual Report to Shareholders,* January 31, 1997.

Circus Circus Enterprises, Inc., *Annual Report to Shareholders,* January 31, 1998.

Corning, Blair, "Luxor: Egypt Opens in Vegas," *San Antonio Express News,* October 24, 1993.

Lalli, Sergio, "Excalibur Awaiteth," *Hotel and Motel Management,* June 11, 1990.

"Economic Impacts of Casino Gaming in the United States," by Arthur Anderson for the American Gaming Association, May 1997.

"Harrah's Survey of Casino Entertainment," Harrah's Entertainment, Inc., 1996.

"ITT Board Rejects Hilton's Offer as Inadequate, Reaffirms Belief that ITT's Comprehensive Plan is in the Best Interest of ITT Shareholders," Press Release, August 14, 1997.

Mirage Resorts, Inc., *1997 and 1998 10K,* retrieved from EDGAR Data Base, http://www.sec.gov/Archives/edgar/data/.

Hilton Hotels Corp., *1997 and 1998 10K,* retrieved from EDGAR Data Base, http://www.sec.gov/Archives/edgar/data/.

Aztar Corp., *1997 and 1998 10K,* retrieved from EDGAR Data Base, http://www.sec.gov/Archives/edgar/data/.

ITT Corp., *1997 10K,* retrieved from EDGAR Data Base, http://www.sec.gov/Archives/edgar/data/.

Harrah's Entertainment, Inc., *1997 and 1998 10K,* retrieved from EDGAR Data Base, http://www.sec.gov/Archives/edgar/data/.

MGM Grand, Inc., *1997 and 1998 10K,* retrieved from EDGAR Data Base, http://www.sec.gov/Archives/edgar/data/.

CASE 13

Cisco Systems, Inc.

Michael I. Eizenberg
Donna M. Gallo
Irene Hagenbuch
Alan N. Hoffman
Bentley College

COMPANY BACKGROUND

Internet giant, Cisco Systems Inc., had its humble beginnings in 1984 as the brainchild of Leonard Bosack and Sandy Learner, a husband and wife team, both of whom were computer scientists at Stanford University. Together they had designed a new networking device that made it dramatically easier for computers to communicate data with each other. It was their plan to integrate this technology into local area and wide area networks (LANs and WANs). Their vision was to bring the ideas and technology they had used in developing the campuswide computer network at Stanford to a broader marketplace.

Cisco's original customers were universities, the aerospace industry, and governmental agencies. Bosack and Learner hired John P. Morgridge to run their growing company. Morgridge, who is now chairman of the board, established a culture at Cisco that stressed frugality and rapid ongoing innovation (see Exhibit 1). In 1986, the company shipped its first multiprotocol router and, in 1987, revenues reached $1.5 million.

Since 1987, Cisco has pioneered development of router and switch technology that has enabled the development and connectivity of larger and larger computer networks, which over a period of ten short years have combined to form the burgeoning World Wide Web of today. Throughout a period of rampant Internet and intranet development, Cisco has remained the market leader and holds either number one or number two market share in almost every segment in which it participates. Today, in 1998, Cisco stands at the threshold of a sea of unparalleled opportunities as all forms of communication—whether data, voice, or video—are converging on the Internet as the multimedia superhighway of the future.

Cisco's key to growth is its position as the innovative leader in providing an ever broader and more powerful range of intranet and Internet products, primarily routers and switches, and related services. Expandability is a critical aspect as customers move from small office networks to huge intranet- and Internet-based network solutions that transmit data as well voice and full-motion video. Potential prospects now see Cisco's Systems as forming the strategic backbone of their enterprises with completely integrated end-to-end solutions that are capable of expanding as business requirements change or networking capabilities increase.

JOHN CHAMBERS, CEO

Within one year of Cisco going public, Morgridge hired John T. Chambers as Senior Vice President of Worldwide Operations. Chambers is the son of two physicians and had thoughts of entering the medical field himself, but opted for "running his own business." He holds a JD (law degree) as well as BS and BA degrees in business from West Virginia University and an MBA from Indiana University. His career in the computer industry began with IBM in 1977 where he spent six years. Subsequently, he worked at Wang Laboratories for eight years.

Printed by permission of Michael I. Eizenberg and Dr. Alan N. Hoffman, Bentley College.

1 | Cisco Systems Board of Directors

Ms. Bartz, 50, has been a member of the Board of Directors since November 1996. She has been Chairman and Chief Executive Officer of Autodesk, Inc. since September 1996. From April 1992 to September 1996 she was Chairman, Chief Executive Officer, and President of Autodesk, Inc. Prior to that, she was with Sun Microsystems from August 1983 to April 1992 most recently as Vice President of Worldwide Field Operations. Ms. Bartz also currently serves on the Board of Directors of Airtouch Communications, Inc., BEA Systems, Inc., Cadence Design Systems, Inc., and Network Appliance, Inc.

Ms. Cirillo, 51, has been a member of the Board of Directors since February 1998. She has been at Bankers Trust as Executive Vice President and Managing Director since July 1997. Prior to joining Bankers Trust, she was with Citibank for 20 years, most recently as Senior Vice President. Ms. Cirillo also currently serves on the Board of Directors of Quest Diagnostics, Inc.

Mr. Chambers, 49, has been a member of the Board of Directors since November 1993. He joined the company as Senior Vice President in January 1991 and became Executive Vice President in June 1994. Mr. Chambers became President and Chief Executive Officer of the company as of January 31, 1995. Prior to his services at Cisco, he was with Wang Laboratories for eight years, most recently as Senior Vice President of U.S. Operations.

Dr. Gibbons, 67, has been a member of the Board of Directors since May 1992. He is a Professor of Electrical Engineering at Stanford University and also Special Consul to the Stanford President for Industrial Relations. He was Dean of the Stanford University School of Engineering from 1984 to 1996. Dr. Gibbons also currently serves on the Board of Directors of Lockheed Martin Corporation, Centigram Communications Corporation, El Paso Natural Gas Company, and Raychem Corporation.

Mr. Kozel, 43, has been a member of the Board of Directors since November 1996. He joined the company as Director, Program Management in March 1989. In April 1992, he became Director of Field Operations and in February 1993, he became Vice President of Business Development. From January 1996 to April 1998 he was Senior Vice President and Chief Technical Officer. In April 1998, Mr. Kozel became Senior Vice President, Corporate Development of the company. Mr. Kozel currently serves on the Board of Directors of Centigram Communications Corporation.

Mr. Morgan, 60, has been a member of the Board of Directors since February 1998. He has been Chief Executive Officer of Applied Materials, Inc. since 1977 and also Chairman of the Board since 1987. He was President of Applied Materials, Inc. from 1976 to 1987. He was previously a senior partner with West Ven Management, a private venture capital partnership affiliated with Bank of America Corporation.

Mr. Morgridge, 65, joined the company as President and Chief Executive Officer and was elected to the Board of Directors in October 1988. Mr. Morgridge became Chairman of the Board on January 31, 1995. From 1986 to 1988 he was President and Chief Operating Officer at GRiD Systems, a manufacturer of laptop computer systems. Mr. Morgridge currently serves on the Board of Directors of Polycom, Inc.

Mr. Puette, 56, has been a member of the Board of Directors since January 1991. He has been President, Chief Executive Officer, and on the Board of Directors of Centigram Communications Corporation since September 1997. Prior to this, he was Chairman of the Board of Directors of NetFRAME Systems, Inc. from January 1996 to September 1997 and was President, Chief Executive Officer, and on the Board of Directors of NetFRAME Systems, Inc. from January 1995 to September 1997. He was a consultant from November 1993 to December 1994. Prior to that, he was Senior Vice President of Apple Computer, Inc. and President of the Apple USA Division from June 1990 to October 1993. Mr. Puette also currently serves on the Board of Directors of Quality Semiconductor, Inc.

Mr. Son, 41, has been a member of the Board of Directors since July 26, 1995. He has been the President and Chief Executive Office of SOFTBANK Corporation since September 1981.

Mr. Valentine, 66, has been a member of the Board of Directors of the company since December 1987 and was elected Chairman of the Board of Directors in December 1988. He became Vice Chairman of the Board on January 31, 1995. He has been a general partner of Sequoia Capital since 1974. Mr. Valentine currently serves as Chairman of the Board of Directors of C-Cube Microsystems Inc., a semiconductor video compression company, and Chairman of the Board of Network Appliance, Inc., a company in the network file server business.

Mr. West, 43, has been a member of the Board of Directors of the company since April 1996. He has been President and Chief Executive Officer of Hitachi Data Systems, a joint venture computer hardware services company owned by Hitachi, Ltd. and Electronic Data Systems Corporation, since June 1996. Prior to that, Mr. West was at Electronic Data Systems Corporation from 1984 to June of 1996, most recently as President of Electronic Data Systems Corporation Infotainment Business Unit.

Since 1994, Chambers has been President and CEO of Cisco Systems Inc. He has led Cisco through a time period of huge expansion in the face of extremely tough competition. His personal and corporate business philosophy has remained customer oriented.

Chambers spends as much as 40 percent of his working hours dealing directly with Cisco's customers. He sees at least two and as many as twelve customers every day. He says, "The two things that get companies into trouble is that they get too far away from their customers and too far away from their employees." Chambers is committed to staying close to customers and employees. His method is simple. Every employee associated with a Cisco account marks an account critical when there is an upcoming decision that might go against Cisco. Chambers still personally checks out each of the company's critical accounts every day, always with the employee, and often with the company itself.

JOHN CHAMBERS GOES TO CHINA

In September 1998, John Chambers embarked on a five-day tour of Asia that included meetings with Prime Minister Goh Chok Tong of Singapore, Prime Minister Mahathir Mohamad of Malaysia, and Chief Executive Tung Chee Hwa of the Hong Kong SAR. On September 21, 1998, Chambers met with China's President Jiang Zemin at the Diaoyutai State Guesthouse in Beijing, the final stop of his Asia tour.

During the 90-minute meeting, President Jiang and Chambers exchanged views on a broad range of topics, including development of the China market economy, the importance of IT and education on the future development of China, the impact of networking technology on the globalization of economies, and China's leadership role during the Asian financial crisis.

President Jiang expressed his desire to see more multinational companies such as Cisco Systems cooperate with and invest in China. However, he further stressed that while investment in manufacturing is important, even greater synergy would arise from intellectual exchange. To this end, he said the Chinese government would set legislation and policies to create a beneficial environment to facilitate the technology transfer process.

Said Chambers, "Rapid innovations in networking and telecommunications technologies have accelerated the pace of globalization of the emerging Internet economy. These technological innovations have created unprecedented opportunities for companies in emerging nations such as China to compete globally by leveling the playing field.

At a time when multinational corporations are withdrawing from Asia due to the recent financial crisis, Cisco Systems is taking a long-term view and increasing our investment in Asia, leveraging our position as the worldwide leader in networking for the Internet and the converging telecommunications market."

Chambers noted, "As a business leader I would like to express my thanks to President Jiang for his leadership role in the recent Asian financial crisis. I would also like to reaffirm Cisco Systems' long-term commitment to China, with continued investments in the form of technology laboratories, Cisco Networking Academy education programs, joint research and development programs, and local manufacturing alliances. Through these investments, we aim to cooperate with the Chinese government in training a new generation of knowledge workers who can take on the challenges of the emerging Internet economy." In conclusion, President Jiang Zemin wished Cisco continued success in China, and re-emphasized his desire to see further cooperation between the Chinese government and Cisco Systems, as part of his government's efforts to strengthen the IT industry and further accelerate the pace of modernization.

Cisco is the largest networking company in China, and has enjoyed tremendous growth in this market, achieving a year-on-year revenue growth of over 100 percent for the past two years. Over the last 12 months, Cisco has increased its China staff by 500 percent and continues to invest heavily in this country.

CISCO'S BUSINESS PLAN

During the past three-and-a-half years as president and CEO of Cisco Systems, Chambers has increased Cisco Systems' revenue from $1.2 billion to its current size of more than $8.5 billion in annual revenues (see Exhibits 2 and 3). Cisco is the fastest growing company in the history of the computer industry.

Unlike most technology companies, Cisco has never taken a restrictive approach that favors one technology over another. The company's philosophy is to pay close attention to its customers' requests, monitor all technological alternatives, and provide customers with a range of options from which to choose. Cisco designs and develops its products to encompass all widely accepted industry standards. Some of its technological solutions are so broad that they have become industry standards themselves.

Cisco is the world's largest supplier of high performance computer Internet working systems. Its rout-

EXHIBIT 2 | Consolidated Balance Sheets

(in thousands, except per value)	July 25, 1998	July 26, 1997
Assets		
Current assets:		
Cash and equivalents	$ 534,652	$ 269,608
Short-term investments	1,156,849	1,005,977
Accounts receivable, net of allowances for doubtful accounts of 539,842 in 1998 and 522,340 in 1997	1,297,867	1,170,401
Inventories, net	361,986	254,677
Deferred income taxes	344,905	312,132
Prepaid expenses and other current assets	65,665	88,471
Total current assets	$3,761,924	$3,101,266
Investments	3,463,279	1,267,174
Restricted investments	553,780	363,216
Property and equipment, net	595,349	466,352
Other assets	542,373	253,976
Total assets	$8,916,705	$5,451,984
Liabilities and shareholders' equity		
Current liabilities:		
Accounts payable	$ 248,872	$ 207,178
Income taxes payable	410,363	256,224
Accrued payroll and related expenses	390,542	263,269
Other accrued liabilities	717,203	393,438
Total current liabilities	$1,766,980	$1,120,109
Commitments and contingencies		
Minority interest	$ 43,107	$ 42,253
Shareholders' equity:		
Preferred stock, no par value, 5,000 shares authorized: none issued or outstanding in 1998 and 1997		
Common stock and additional paid-in capital, $0.001 par value (no par value—July 26, 1997) 2,700,000 shares authorized: 1,562,582 shares issued and outstanding in 1998 and 1,509,252 shares in 1997	3,220,205	1,763,200
Retained earnings	3,828,223	2,487,058
Unrealized gain on investments	78,314	49,628
Cumulative translation adjustments	(20,124)	(10,264)
Total shareholders' equity	7,106,618	4,289,622
Total liabilities and shareholders' equity	$8,916,705	$5,451,984

3 | Consolidated Statements of Operations

(in thousands, except per-share amounts)

Years ended	**July 25, 1998**	**July 26, 1997**	**July 28, 1996**
Net sales	$8,458,777	$6,440,171	$4,096,007
Cost of sales	2,917,617	2,241,378	1,409,862
Gross margin	$5,541,160	$4,198,793	$2,686,145
Expenses:			
Research and development	1,020,446	698,172	399,291
Sales and marketing	1,564,419	1,160,269	726,278
General and administrative	258,246	204,661	159,770
Purchased research and development	593,695	508,397	
Total operating expenses	$3,436,806	$2,571,499	$1,285,339
Operating income	2,104,354	1,627,294	1,400,806
Realized gains on sale of investment	5,411	152,689	
Interest and other income, net	192,701	108,889	64,019
Income before provision for income taxes	2,302,466	1,888,872	1,464,825
Provision for income taxes	952,394	840,193	551,501
Net income	$1,350,072	$1,048,679	$ 913,324
Net income per share—basic	$ 0.88	$ 0.71	$ 0.64
Net income per share—diluted	$ 0.84	$ 0.68	$ 0.61
Shares used in per-share calculation—basic	1,533,869	1,485,986	1,437,030
Shares used in per-share calculation—diluted	1,608,173	1,551,039	1,490,078

ers and other communication products connect and manage local and wide area networks (LANs and WANs). It entails many protocols, media interfaces, network topologies, and cabling systems, which allow customers to connect different computer networks by using a variety of hardware and software across offices, countries, and continents. Cisco's products are sold in 90 countries through a direct sales force, distributors, and value-added resellers. They are supported through a worldwide network of direct sales representatives and business partners. Their products include backbone and remote access routers, LAN and asynchronous transfer mode (ATM) switches, dial-up access servers, and network management software.

All these products uphold multiprotocol multiple media connectivity in a multitude of vendor environments. Cisco's Gigabit Switch Router (GSR), which provides Internet routing and switching at gigabit speed, was introduced to answer criticism that routers create bottlenecks in the Internet backbone, the network's core. It is targeted at the Internet service provider market and was designed to substantially outperform Ascend Technologies GRF high-speed router. The GSR supports several hundred thousand routes compared to the GRF, which is limited to supporting about one hundred fifty thousand routes.

CISCO'S TARGET MARKET

Cisco sells to three target markets: large enterprises, service providers (SPs), and small/medium businesses. Enterprises that use Cisco's products are large corporations, government agencies, utilities, and educational institutions that have complex networking requirements. In these environments Cisco's products connect multiple locations and types of computer systems into one large network. SPs are companies that provide information services such as telecommunications carriers, Internet service providers, cable companies, and wireless communication providers. The small and medium-sized businesses that Cisco targets need data networks for connections to the Internet and their business partners.

Selling to these target markets has become more complex as technology has developed. The industry trend during the mid-1990s has been for high-tech companies to provide consultation services when selling their products. For Cisco this has meant that each sale has the potential of becoming a technical consulting assignment. This will often result in a system integration issue to be addressed from the level of overall business strategy. Cisco consultants would become an integral part of this process. Selling becomes a highly value added service where a company cannot solely depend "on selling the box." In response to this demand, Cisco has begun to build its network application consulting service. This service, headed by Sue Bostrom, who came to Cisco with extensive consulting experience from McKinsey, consists of the Networked Application Group of twelve people that began expanding in late 1997.

CISCO'S STOCK

Cisco's stock has been a strong point of the company's history. Cisco Systems went public on February 16, 1990, in an initial public offering underwritten by Morgan Stanley & Co. with Smith Barney, Harris Upham & Co., of 90.4 million shares at a split adjusted price of $0.5625 per share. Cisco's annual revenues increased from $69 million in 1990 to $6.44 billion in fiscal 1997. This represents a nearly one hundred-fold growth in seven years. Cisco is the third largest company on NASDAQ and among the top 40 in the world measured by market capitalization. The stock has split six times since the initial public offering. A share of Cisco common stock sold on February 16, 1990, for $18.00. That single share of stock on November 18, 1997, was worth $53.42 and the split history would yield 48 shares of stock for a total value of $2,564.16. In short, an investment of $1,000 in 1990 grew nearly 150 times to a value of slightly more than $142,000 by 1997. The fundamental challenge for Cisco's management is to maintain the phenomenal growth rate in revenue as well as profitability in the future. Where will the continuing growth opportunities come from?

GLOBALLY NETWORKED BUSINESSES

In the 1990s, the rapid emergence of networking technologies has changed the pace at which individuals and companies communicate. The speed of conducting business accelerates daily. A dynamic environment like this forces companies to vastly increase accessibility to all its relevant information in order to remain competitive.

Chris Sinton, director of Cisco Connection, is convinced that "the first challenge is moving beyond viewing the network only as an information-sharing tool to using the network as a foundation for applications linked to core business systems that serve all business constituents."

Cisco has transformed itself using its own technology to its fullest advantage into a leading example of a Globally Networked Business. Cisco has positioned its network together with its core business systems and operational information and opened this information to prospects, customers, partners, suppliers, and employees. The company now works in an open, collaborative environment that transcends the traditional corporate barriers in business relationships. There are no communication channels for customers, employees, or suppliers to make their way through. Virtually all operational and business information is open to everybody online all the time, no matter their geographic location or business relationship to Cisco. Through being globally networked, Cisco saved $250 million in 1997 business expenses by reducing servicing costs and improving customer/supplier relationships.

According to John Chambers, the Global Networked Business model is based on three core assumptions:

- The relationships a company maintains with its key constituencies can be as much of a competitive differentiation as its core products or services.
- The manner in which a company shares information and systems is a critical element in the strength of its relationships.
- Being "connected" is no longer adequate. Business relationships and the communications that support them must exist in a "networked" fabric.

John Chambers believes that Globally Networked Business will set new standards on efficiency and productivity within business relationships by simplifying network infrastructures and deploying a unifying software fabric that supports end-to-end network services. This will allow companies to automate the fundamental ways in which they work together.

Global network applications provide Cisco Systems with a wide range of business opportunities. Cisco's prospects are presented with several attractive alternatives when they are considering purchase of a network system. Cisco noted that a key competitive differentiator is the ease with which prospects can access company information that simplifies and facilitates the purchasing processes. Hence, Cisco provides its prospects with the Cisco Connection Online (CCO) Web site. CCO is the foundation of the Cisco Connection suite of interactive, electronic services that provide immediate, open access to Cisco's information, resources, and systems anytime, anywhere, allowing all constituents to streamline business processes and improve their productivity. Using CCO, prospects have immediate access to information on Cisco's products, services, and partners. CCO allows potential customers to buy promotional merchandise and Internet software, read technical documentation, and download public software files. Almost a quarter of a million prospects log on to CCO monthly.

Cisco's fast growth forced the company to find alternatives to traditional sales ordering methods. With rising expenses and a shortage in qualified salespeople in the industry, Cisco created the Internetworking Product Center (IPC), part of CCO. IPC serves as an online ordering system for direct customers as well as partners. It creates better access to support capabilities that enable the customers to solve problems in less time. Within six months of operation, IPC processed more than $100 million in orders. It led to an immense increase in the percentage of orders received by Cisco via the Web. Between September 1996 and September 1997, the number of orders increased by 800 percent. At the same time, the annualized dollar run rate of orders received climbed from $30 million to $2.734 billion, a 9,013 percent increase. At present, the company receives more than $9 million in orders per day. Through IPC, Cisco also assists its direct customers and partners to configure equipment. This leads to shorter delivery intervals and more precise orders than using traditional sales methods. In short, customers receive exactly what they want in less time.

Cisco also assists its worldwide clientele with technical support through the CCO. The online support service looks at over 20,000 support cases each month. The service speeds the resolution of problems, betters the support process, and gives immediate global access to Cisco's engineers and support systems around the clock.

For its partners, Cisco has a Partner-Initiated Customer Access (PICA) program. They have access to information and interactive applications that support them in selling more effectively. PICA helps its partners to in turn provide their customers with real-time access to the latest software releases. It lifts the resources of Cisco's partners and brings up higher levels of customer satisfaction and loyalty. Through CCO, partners are able to address difficult customer questions and problems more quickly by using the self-help support solutions.

Being a globally networked company, Cisco relies heavily on successful partnerships with suppliers. In order to do that, Cisco created the Cisco Supplier Connection. This is an extranet application that increases the productivity and efficiency in the supply function. The Cisco Supplier Connection enables suppliers and manufacturers to dial into Cisco's manufacturing resource planning. It allows them to use this connection to reduce the order fulfillment cycle. Through the link, they can monitor orders and see them almost at the same time Cisco's customers place them. The suppliers then can assemble the parts needed from stock and ship them directly to the specific customer. After that, the system reminds Cisco to pay for the parts used. Through Cisco Supplier Connection, the company was able to reduce the time and labor-intensive functions of purchase ordering, billing, and delivery. The application allows the suppliers to better manage their manufacturing schedules, improve their cash management, and respond more quickly to Cisco's needs which in turn benefits Cisco's customers. Cisco has gained real-time access to suppliers' information, experienced lower business costs in processing orders (an estimated $46 per order), improved the productivity of its employees involved in purchasing (78 percent increase), and seen order cycles reduced substantially.

For its employees, Cisco created Cisco Employee Connection (CEC), an intranet Web site which allows them to fulfill their tasks more proficiently. The site contains the unique needs of its 10,000 networked employees and provides users with immediate access to current services and information and instant global communications. All of Cisco's employees can access the same information simultaneously through the power of networking regardless of where they are located. The CEC has been the primary mechanism for decreasing Cisco's communication cost and time to market.

Overall, by becoming a Globally Networked Business, Cisco has been able to react more quickly and compete more effectively. Becoming a Globally Networked Business provided Cisco with a scalable (the ability to add on to), manageable business system that enabled it to do more with less. The technology allowed Cisco to reach the goals of improved productivity, reduced time to market, greater revenue, lower expenses, and stronger relationships. It will prosper as other businesses adopt the model it has successfully pioneered. As indicated by the market researcher International Data Corporation (IDC), sales on the Internet will grow to $116 billion by the year 2000. More than 70 percent of that amount will be from business-to-business transactions which indicates that the Internet will become one of the key distribution channels for companies. Ultimate business success depends on the ability of companies to become online businesses, and to leverage their networks and cultivate their interactive relationships with prospects, customers, partners, suppliers, and employees.

THE CONVERGENCE OF DATA, VOICE, AND VIDEO

In 1994, there were 3,000 Web sites in the world, 3.2 million host computers, and 30 million Internet users. Four short years later, there are 2.5 million sites, 36.7 million hosts, and 134 million Internet users. During this time of rapid expansion, the question of which communication protocol would be the standard for linking the increasingly vast numbers of computer systems and networks has been resolved. Internet Protocols (IP) is now the one fundamental language used in every type of interconnected computing. There are two important unresolved questions: (1) how pervasive will Internet-based communication become? and (2) will it become the predominant means of converging data, voice, and video? That public communications in the year 2002 will be synonymous with the Internet, at this juncture, seems more realistic than strained.

The world is now experiencing exponential growth of communication via the Internet. This rapid rate of growth is accelerating because of the daily increase in the number of Internet users and the fact that transmissions over the Internet have evolved from just text and data to include multimedia, audio, and full-motion video.

Traditional phone companies, using proven and highly stable circuit switching, continue to make impressive technological gains. Northern Telecom's DMS stored program switch has been able to double its performance every six-and-one-half years without any increase in cost. IP routers and frame relay packet switches, such as the ones provided by Cisco, have been able to double their performance every 10 to 20 months without cost increases. IP routers and switches now are able to transfer a higher number of bits per second at a lower cost than traditional circuit switches.

Tom Steinert-Threlkeld states in his *Internet 2002* article that if you follow this trend to its most reasonable conclusion, the Internet will soon provide the underlying structure for all communication networks including multimedia transmissions between individuals and businesses, local and long distance phone service, and television broadcasts via cable or satellite. Given this perspective, we are barely at the beginning of the growth cycle in the networking industry.

Cisco executives are already talking about the day when the cost of moving data, voice, and video along IP networks is so inexpensive that the price of bundled IP data services will include both long distance and local phone calls at a price substantially lower than what customers pay now for telephone services alone. Other included features will be as diverse as videoconferencing, feature film, and audio downloading, and voice mail messaging including lengthy video and audio clips.

Cisco itself continues to provide fundamental solutions that will enable data to move more efficiently along IP networks. Its new Tag Switching technology allows data packets of various sizes to flow substantially faster and more reliably through routers directly past switches using the same unique Tag. This new technology enables networks to handle more traffic, users, media rich data, and bandwidth-intensive applications.

The opportunities in the networking industry are becoming vast as the Internet takes its place as the platform for all forms of traditional and innovative communication. Cisco is positioned to be a major innovative force in the future generations of Internet technology. Many experts predict a one hundred-fold increase in Internet usage within the next five years.

KEY COMPETITIVE ISSUES

Customers of the computer networking industry are seeking access to information that will set higher standards of efficiency and productivity, leading to higher profits. The objective is to heighten their competitive capabilities and give them a competitive advantage over their rivals. Central to this is the ability to manage constituent relationships through the sharing of critical information and the open exchange of resources and services. The need for seamless transmission of data and voice is important to the customer base. Accomplishing this necessitates broad-based suppliers of networking products. Competitors in the networking industry are shifting their focus toward becoming full-service providers in this rapidly growing industry in order to meet the needs of their growing customer base. Correctly assessing the current and, most importantly, the future informational needs of customers is a key factor to a firm's survival or extinction. Presently, Cisco Systems, Lucent Technologies, 3Com, Ascend Communications, and Bay Networks are the strongest forces in the push to dominate the market.

Industry growth is so dramatic that analysts and investors are having difficulty determining continuing and future growth rates. This leaves competitors scrambling to gain as much market share as their organizations can maintain and manage. High growth and profitability lead to intense competitive challenges. New entrants are possible from many segments of the high-tech community. New competitors could be from the telecommunications, data networking, software, and semiconductors industries. Companies from these industries are likely to enter based on their strengths in brand name recognition, technological knowledge and capabilities, and a strong financial background. Globalization and the growing strength of both domestic and foreign competitors in all these industries makes the competitive pressure even greater for existing companies.

THE CHALLENGERS

Commanding approximately 80 percent of its market puts Cisco in an enviable competitive position. However, formidable competitors exist and as the industry growth rates continue to accelerate, maintaining this market share could be a daunting task. As the industry moves toward convergence of voice and data systems, it is anticipated that competitors will be positioning for growth through merger, acquisition, and/or joint venture partnering. End users are driving industry competitors to provide a full range of services as well as a high level of customization. The ability to create a total system that enables the customer to access information and enhances their ability to efficiently facilitate their own business and communication processes with their vendors and customers will be a key factor for success. Escalating industry growth leaves Cisco faced with the decision of how much internal growth it can sustain in order to hold its current percentage of a growing market. Its top competitors are sure to be opportunistic of any weakness within Cisco.

Ascend Communications

Founded in 1989, Ascend Communications has been the leading supplier of remote access solutions, supporting in excess of 30 million Internet connections daily. The company operates in over 30 countries worldwide through a distribution system comprised of direct sales, OEM relationships, strategic alliances, distributors, and VARs. Ascend's extensive service program, Ascend Advantage Services, is enhanced through an alliance with IBM's Availability Services, a segment of IBM Global Services. This allows Ascend and its participating resellers to utilize the resources of IBM's worldwide service network for support of Ascend products. Quality is an important strength for Ascend. The company holds the prestigious Quality System Certificates ISO 9000 and ISO 9001 covering design, manufacture, sale, and service of data networking products.

Fiscal year 1997 proved to be prosperous for Ascend. Net sales increased 31 percent from $890.3 million in 1996 to $1.167 billion in 1997. Strengthening its competitive position and maintaining a leadership status in networking products and technologies is a high priority of top management. Several acquisitions throughout the year have been in support of the company's transition from recognition as the leading supplier of remote access solutions to a broad-based supplier of wide area networking products. The acquisition of Cascade Communications proved to be a significant link to becoming a full-service provider for global communications. Cascade's strength as a leader in broadband data communications products enabled Ascend to extensively broaden its product base. The company also acquired Whitetree, Inc., a pioneer in local area network switching technology, and InterCon, a developer of client software products for both the corporate and ISP markets. These two smaller acquisitions filled gaps in building a seamless networking system for their customers. Strong research and development, strategic alliances, and key acquisitions are the strategies Ascend is using to position itself as a strong competitor in providing integrated networking solutions for its service provider customers and its enterprise customers.

Lucent Technologies

On February 1, 1996, AT&T transformed Lucent Technologies into a stand-alone entity by separating it from the parent corporation. The independent organization competes in three core businesses. The largest is network operating systems followed by business communications systems and microelectronics products. Their technologies connect, route, manage, and store information across networks. In 1997 net income was reported as $541 million, compared to a net loss of $793 million for the previous 12 months.

Lucent faces serious challenges both from the intense competitive nature of the industry and from its internal organization. Two significant factors play a role in the company's performance. The first is its heavy reliance on a limited number of large customers for a material portion of its revenues. One of its largest customers is the former parent AT&T. Increasingly, Lucent's customer base is purchasing from fewer suppliers. Therefore, the contracts from these buyers are very large and tend to be highly seasonal, which is the second significant factor impacting Lucent's performance. Delaying capital expenditures until the fourth quarter of the calendar is typical purchasing behavior for Lucent's large customers. With a fiscal year ended September 30, the result is that a disproportionate share of Lucent's revenue stream is recognized in its first quarter. On a calendar year basis, profitability is lower in each of the first three-quarters than in the fourth quarter. Consequently, investors may have concerns regarding the value of the stock throughout the year. In addition to fluctuations in its revenue stream, Lucent faces stringent demands from its large customers in terms of favorable pricing, financing, and payment terms that extend over multiyear contracts. Recognition of revenue from large cost outlays in the development of large-scale systems for its customers reflects harshly on the company's financial statements. The company encounters a material risk factor should any of its large purchasers reduce orders or move to a competitor.

To reduce the overall risk of dependence on a few large buyers, Lucent is beginning to diversify its customer base by pursuing customers from other industries such as cable television network operators, access providers, and computer manufacturers. However, management does not anticipate that the company's customer base will broaden significantly in the near future. Beginning fiscal year 1997 the company embarked on an acquisition strategy aimed at strengthening its core businesses and smoothing out the revenue stream. The first transaction in October 1996 was for Agile Networks, Inc., a provider of advanced intelligent data switching products that support both ethernet and ATM technology. In September 1997 Lucent embarked on a major transaction with the $1.8 million purchase of Octel Communications Corporation, a provider of voice, fax, and electronic messaging technologies. The products of Octel were viewed as complementary to the products and services Lucent was offering. Fiscal year 1998 began with two transactions. The company sought to further enhance and broaden R&D knowledge and the capabilities gained from the previous transactions. The acquisition of Livingston Enterprises, Inc., a global company that provides connection equipment to Internet service providers was a strategic step in this direction. Lucent continued to follow a strategic direction of strengthening its core businesses in a joint venture with Philips Electronics N.V. The joint venture, 40 percent owned by Lucent, is a global conveyor of personal communications products. The complete range of products includes digital and analog wireless phones, corded and cordless phones, answering machines, screen phones, and pagers.

In an effort to focus on its core businesses, Lucent sold off some of its businesses. The subsidiary Paradyne and the company's interconnect products and Custom Manufacturing Services were sold in 1996. The company's Advanced Technology Systems unit was sold in October 1997. By the end of fiscal 1997, Lucent had positioned itself as a leader in the design, development, and manufacture of integrated systems and software applications for network operators and business enterprises.

3Com

3Com Corporation was the first organization to develop technology for networking personal computers. In the 20 years following its introduction of this new technology the industry has grown to be one of the largest in the world. 3Com has remained one of the top industry competitors. Revenues in 1997 were approximately $3.2 billion, up from $2.3 billion in 1996. Net income rose from $177 million in 1996 to $373 million in 1997. Growth in fiscal 1997 focused on the introduction of new products to expand and strengthen its product breadth and establish the company in emerging market segments. New products were developed in its systems business, switching technology, client across business, and networking software. The new product introductions were supported through the bolstering of the company's sales and support functions and acquisition activity.

The first acquisition of 1997 was OnStream Networks, a leading provider of solutions for integrated video, voice, and data. This addition to 3Com's business portfolio strengthened its ATM/broadband wide-area focus. The most significant event of 1997 was the announcement of a merger between 3Com and U.S. Robotics, creating a $5.6 billion company. U.S. Robotics is a leader in remote access concentrators, modems, and connected handheld organizers. The addition of U.S. Robotics' products and technology to 3Com's product portfolio gives it strong representation in key business areas. Once the transaction was completed in early fiscal 1998 it was one of two networking companies with revenues over $5 billion. These acquisitions enabled the 3Com to gain leverage as a full-service provider in each of the four key markets of the networking industry: enterprise networks, Internet service providers, business systems, and the consumer market. Further, the combined companies comprise a wider distribution channel allowing for greater reach to the customer base. 3Com's management believes that flexible, faster, and simpler access to networks will be the most important features a networking company can offer and believes that through these acquisitions the company is in a superior competitive position to its nearest competitors. They see the way to achieve this is by providing low-cost solutions to customers for fully integrated end-to-end connectivity that extends across local and wide area networks. 3Com is solidly positioned to provide that extensive service to the networking market.

Bay Networks

Bay Networks is a global company offering networking solutions to enterprise networks and Internet and telecommunications service providers. The company's fiscal position has remained steady from 1996 to 1997 with little growth. Revenues in each year were just over $2.0 billion. The company adopted a strategy called Adaptive Networking to meet the changes and challenges of the high growth Internet services and networking segments of the industry. Its focus has been on key technologies in switching/ATM services and network management. As with most of its competitors, Bay Networks used a merger and acquisition strategy to bolster its competitive position and become a full-service provider. However, the strategy failed to change the company's position. By the end of fiscal 1997 net income fell with a loss of $1.46 per share. A few months later the company made a blockbuster announcement that would have a drastic effect on the competitive environment in the industry. Executives of the communications giant Northern Telecom and Bay Networks announced a merger of the two organizations, to be called Nortel. This merger would combine telecommunications with the data equipment used to move information across networks, giving the combined entity a significant competitive advantage that no other competitor comes close to matching. Estimates set the value of Nortel at almost $18 billion, by far the largest company in the industry.

Niche Competitors

Cisco also faces competition from smaller networking companies specializing in specific niches of the industry. Company estimates place the number of competitors in the ATM switching, frame relay, and workgroups segments to be between 30 and 50 in each segment. Customers with the need for specialties in these areas might find doing business with a small expert organization to be advantageous. However, as the industry moves toward mergers and consolidations competitors from this segment are not a formidable threat.

The key challenge for Cisco Systems will be its ability to remain on top of a critical and growing industry in light of increasing competitive challenges and continuing weakness from foreign markets.

REFERENCES

www.ebmag.com/registered/issues/9712/1297ceo.html

www.cisco.com

www.cisco.com/warp/public/756/gnb_gen/gnb_wp.htm

www.cisco.com/warp/public/756/gnb/ncom_wp.htm

www.cisco.com/warp/public/750/corpfact.html

www.cisco.com/warp/public/749/ar97—Cisco Systems 1997 Annual Report

www.cbs.marketwatch.com/news/current/csco.htx?source=htx/http2_mw

www.eb.com

cisco.com/warp/public/756/gnb_gen/gnb_wp.htm

cbs.marketwatch.com/news/current/csco.htx?source+htx/http2_mw

"Computing's Net Superpower," *Fortune,* May 12, 1997.

"Financial Profile," Dow Jones & Company Inc., November 13, 1997.

Internet 2002: The Future of Communications by Tom Steinert-Threlkeld, ZDNet.

www.Ascend.com

www.Lucent.com

www.Baynetworks.com

www.Nortel.com

www.3com.com

CASE 14

Cognex Corporation

"Work Hard, Play Hard"

Marilyn T. Lucas
Alan N. Hoffman
Bentley College

"To preserve and enhance vision," recited Bill Silver with his hand held vertically on the bridge of his nose, as he entered the office of Robert Shillman. With his usual smile, the CEO looked up from the Cognex Corporation's 1998 Annual Report and returned the corporate salute, adopted from "The Three Stooges." Silver, the Vice-President of Research and Development, joined Shillman to discuss the future of Cognex Corporation, the company they started together 18 years ago. In spite of its leading position as a manufacturer of machine vision systems, Cognex has hurdled over changes in the industry in recent years. It has survived an industry shakeout of competitors in the early 1990s and managed to sustain stable growth during the slump of the semiconductor industry. However, competitors have recently begun to tap into the OEM (original equipment manufacturer) market, the cornerstone of Cognex's business, and have beaten Cognex to the punch in the international marketplace. Finally, the 1998 Annual Report shows that Cognex's revenues and profits have fallen from the peak levels they had reached in 1997 (Exhibit 1).

Robert Shillman, Bill Silver, and their fellow executives must decide which direction the company should take to realize growth and remain the number-one manufacturer of machine vision systems.

COMPANY BACKGROUND

Two brand-new bicycles and $100,000 constituted the initial investment made by Robert Shillman to start Cognex Corporation. A professor in human visual perception at Massachusetts Institute of Technology (MIT), near Boston, Shillman had a vision for the future of machine imaging analysis. In the summer of 1981, with the help of the bicycles, he convinced two graduate students, Marilyn Matz and Bill Silver, to work for him. This small group of artificial-intelligence experts went on to form the Cognex Corporation and develop machine vision devices.

The machine vision technology works by capturing an image of a part through a video camera, converts it to digital data and, via software, analyzes the data and derives answers about the image, such as where an object is located and whether or not it is defective. This information can then be sent to other equipment—such as a robotic arm to remove the defective part—and/or fed to an automated feedback loop.

In the early days of the company, machine vision technology was limited to black-and-white image analysis. Although reliable, this technology was slow to process, and the systems used were extremely expensive to develop and implement. In 1982, harnessing the use of algorithms written by Silver, Cognex pioneered the industry's first optical character-recognition system and built the company's first machine vision system, called DataMan. This system was able not only to quickly process grayscale image data to locate patterns and shapes, but also to reliably read numbers. Priced at approximately $30,000, this revolutionary product was sold directly to end-users on the factory floor, and its

The authors would like to thank Joseph Breen, Nan MacSwan, Lawrence Isaac, Kerry Armstrong, Nancy Manley, and Kendra Schoentag for their valuable comments and suggestions.

EXHIBIT 1 | Cognex Corporation—*Financial Highlights* (In thousands, except per-share amounts)

	1998	1997	1996	1995	1994
For the year:					
Revenue	$121,844	$155,340	$122,843	$104,543	$ 62,484
Net income	20,203	40,536	30,369	23,034	16,072
Diluted net income per share	.47	.91	.69	.55	.43
At year-end:					
Working capital	184,363	199,570	152,817	119,402	88,619
Total assets	247,928	261,840	201,253	162,172	112,946
Long-term debts	—	—	—	—	—
Stockholders' equity	222,875	236,142	182,689	143,916	103,608

success attracted many investors, allowing Cognex to grow rapidly in the early 1980s. This machine vision market, however, became quickly flooded with competitors, all looking to find a place in this new profitable segment.

In the mid-1980s, Cognex modified its strategy and decided to target OEMs, which had the technical expertise for systems integration. The company designed the first machine vision system built on a single printed circuit board, called the Cognex 2002, specifically to support OEMs. Two years later, Cognex also introduced the world's first custom vision chip, the VC-1, which quadrupled the processing power of the company's machine vision system without increasing their size.

In 1989, the company had its initial public offering. Within one year, the price of the company's stock jumped from $2.75 per share to $33.50 per share. In the following five years, Cognex successfully introduced many products, including the Cognex 5000, the first machine vision system designed to plug into a personal computer, and in 1994, after $5 million in research and development, a revolutionary user-friendly machine vision system—the Checkpoint vision system.

DR. BOB

Dr. Robert Shillman enjoyed life in academia—his research on the study of human visual perception was innovative, and his unique style gave him a reputable presence among the community at MIT. However, he had the idea that artificial intelligence could replicate the accurate process of human vision to make computers that can "see." With such an innovative technology, he could introduce new manufacturing applications and open the doors to the machine vision industry. With a life savings of $100,000 and two top students, he left MIT to start Cognex in the summer of 1981.

In his management style, Robert Shillman has instilled the philosophical attitude that "work is the meaning of life." He is theatrical and believes in the "work hard, play hard" attitude. Cognex's employees, from the newest to the vice-presidents, all recognize that those who work hard will be rewarded. But "Dr. Bob," as he is referred to around the office, has also designated Halloween to be the official company holiday, requiring that all employees wear a costume to work on that day. His unique style has contributed to international recognition. Now President, Chief Executive Officer, and Chairman of Cognex, Shillman was named *Inc. Magazine's* Entrepreneur of the Year in 1990 and received the Achievement Award in Leadership from the Automated Imaging Association in 1992.

THE "COGNOID" SPIRIT

Cognex, derived from **Cogni**tion **Ex**perts, has a corporate culture that is as unique as its highest ranking officer. The "work hard, play hard" attitude fosters as environment of people dedicated to the cause of the Cognex mission: to remain the number-one manufacturer of machine vision systems. Only the best and the brightest are recruited to work for the company. A recent advertisement in the *Boston Globe* extended an invitation to those who liked candy to apply to Cognex Corporation. (A ritual at Cognex is to give out free Goobers candy to all employees on the company's monthly movie night). Once initiated into the employee roll book, employees are fondly referred to as "Cognoids."

A 110 percent effort is expected, but the company acknowledges the importance of its human capital. It proposes many highly innovative reward programs designed to recognize and thank its employees for their hard work and dedication. Payback includes fringe benefits like those of no other company. In every other paycheck, all employees receive a coupon for a free car wash. Friday evening socials are regular events, offering an array of food and beverages for employees to gather and relax with each other. Every other month, Cognex rents a local movie theater and invites each employee and a guest to enjoy a free movie and open concession stand. Once a year, Dr. Shillman gives out the President's award to all employees who surpass the company's high expectations and who demonstrate superior job performance, a positive attitude, and a commitment to excellence. The award consists of a plaque and a bonus check ranging from $1,000 to $10,000. Finally, Cognex commemorates employees' 3, 5, 10, and 15-year anniversaries with Perseverance Awards. After three years of service, each employee receives a Seiko watch engraved with his or her start date. After five years of service, employees receive a gold Cognex pin and an all-expense paid weekend getaway to a choice of locations. On their 10-year anniversaries, employees receive an extravagant one-week vacation in addition to a beautiful Atmos clock. And on the milestone of a 15-year anniversary, "Cognoids" receive a 10-day vacation of their choice of one of the Wonders of the World.

COGNEX'S PRODUCTS

Cognex designs products, referred to as machine vision systems, to improve the speed and quality of inspection in manufacturing processes. The complexity, higher volume and lower cost of consumer items have made it virtually impossible to use human operators to perform the task of detecting errors and irregularities in those items. Machine vision is basically an electronic and computer-based method of inspecting materials during production. Its use enables companies to reduce manufacturing costs, with a decrease in the number of defective products, a gain in efficiency, and increased productivity. Industrial applications of machine vision include tasks such as inspecting, measuring, verifying, identifying, recognizing, grading, sorting, counting, locating and manipulating parts, monitoring/controlling production processes, and more. In short, machine vision is a substitute for the human eye in a number of inspecting processes that occur during manufacturing applications with tight limits on speed, cost, reliability, size or safety.

Machine vision systems consist of software and hardware components that are customized for specific manufacturing needs. Cognex's family of products offers a choice of hardware platforms, development modes and price/performance points. Customers typically choose systems that are programmable in C or programmable with a "point and click" interface and specify deployment options on either set or integrated board level machines or on a stand-alone, rack mountable system. For example, the revolutionary Checkpoint series of vision systems, introduced in 1994, offers a "point and click" development environment with a flexible graphical user interface (GUI) based on Microsoft Windows. This system drastically simplifies the implementation of automated visual inspection, since it does not require in-depth knowledge of vision technology or programming expertise from the automation engineers to customize for their specific needs. With Checkpoint, a computer can inspect parts on an assembly line in as few as 10 milliseconds and measure each part precisely; this results in inspection speeds 10 to 100 times faster than with conventional methods.

New-Product Introduction

To maintain its leadership position in the machine vision industry, Cognex's team of expert engineers has traditionally developed and introduced new products. The new products of the last few years have helped the company not only to expand on existing markets, but also to venture in new application areas for machine vision.

In 1997, Cognex introduced a new product known as PatMax. This software technology represented an entirely new method of pattern finding, which fundamentally changed the way machine vision systems locate objects. This ability to locate, with very high accuracy, just about any object has enormous potential applications in a variety of new areas. In 1998, Cognex introduced the next generation of programmable machine vision systems, the MVS-8000™ product family, based on INTEL-MMX. Prior to this year, all of Cognex's softwares ran only on proprietary hardware, based on the Motorola 68K line of microprocessors. With this ability to run directly on the customer's own PC, the MVS-8000™ series became the most successful product introduction ever for Cognex, with more than 1,000 systems shipped in its first year. Finally, an addition to the product line in 1998 was a new surface-inspection vision system. The SmartView™ Modular Camera Network (MCN) was the world's first modular surface-inspection vision system for detecting, measuring, and classifying defects on products made in continuous processes. It allows for more complex applications for machine vision.

THE MACHINE VISION INDUSTRY

There are two basic segments in the machine vision market: OEMs and the factory-floor customers.

The OEMs are companies that manufacture standard products sold as capital equipment for the factory floor. These customers possess the technical expertise necessary to build Cognex's machine vision systems directly into their products, which are then sold to end-users.

The factory-floor customers can be further subdivided between system integrators and end-users. System integrators are companies that create complete, automated inspection solutions for end-users on the factory floor. For example, in designing a custom inspection system for, say, examining sneakers or aspirin bottles, they combine proper lighting, robotics, machine-vision devices, and other necessary components. Because of the wide variety of automation problems they encounter, system integrators typically purchase a wide variety of Cognex products, ranging from programmable systems to application-specific solutions tailored to solving particular manufacturing tasks.

End-users are companies that "build" products—such as phones, metal, pens and paper—on the factory floor. This market includes all high-volume product manufacturers who are interested in increasing the quality of their products and lowering their manufacturing costs. End-users include companies in industries such as automotive (e.g., gauging dimensions on automotive brake pads), medical devices (e.g., inspecting heart catheters), banking and financing (e.g., performing detailed inspection of financial cards), keyboard and display (e.g., inspecting the LCD on a cellular phone), consumer products (e.g., color inspection of eyeliner pencils), computer printing (e.g., ink jet and laser printer inspection), and packaging (e.g., inspecting caps and lids on cans). While they may purchase capital equipment containing machine vision or contract a system integrator to build an inspection system, many end-users choose to purchase machine vision directly to solve specific applications on their product lines. Unlike OEMs and system integrators, these customers typically have little or no computer programming or machine vision experience and are interested in a more user-friendly product.

Cognex's Early Days

In 1981, the company's initial strategy was to sell and install customized vision systems directly to end-users. However, within four years, it became clear to Cognex's management that the strategy of providing turnkey vision systems to end-users was not profitable. In this arena, over 100 competitors were vying for business, and all were being hampered by the cost of custom engineering each system to individual customer needs. As a result, Cognex turned to OEMs. Its new strategy was to develop and sell high volumes of standard machine vision hardware and software products to OEMs, who would have the technical expertise to configure Cognex's machine vision systems directly into their products, which would then be sold to end-users. This strategy allowed the company to focus its strength in research, development and engineering.

In the 1980s, Cognex's focus was on OEMs in the semiconductor and electronics industries. These were two industries strongly affected by miniaturization, and this made the use of machine vision technology essential. The semiconductor industry originally adopted this technology to perform wafer identification, alignment and dicing, while the electronics industry used it to align printed circuit boards for screen printers/paste dispensers, guide surface-mount device robots and inspect surface-mount devices, disk drives and keyboards.

Cognex was first to enter the semiconductor market with a product that contained the VC-1 chip and quadrupled the processing power of the existing machines. In late 1986, Cognex struck a deal with General Signal's Electroglas division, which made test equipment for silicon wafers. Cognex had attempted to acquire General Signal as a customer before this new direction, but the product was rejected as too costly. This time, General Signal was so interested that it bought a piece of Cognex to get access to the technology.

In 1990, Cognex had two-thirds of the market for vision systems bought from outside vendors by makers of semiconductors and electronic equipment. Some of Cognex's customers included IBM, NEC, and Hewlett-Packard, which helped sales grow 50 percent in 1989 to $16 million; profits jumped 56 percent to $3.7 million. Cognex also found success by selling to its competitors (OEMs who build their own machine vision systems), which represented about half of the approximately $200 million machine vision market of the late 1980s.

The Early and Mid-1990s

The North American consumption of machine vision systems over 1990–96 showed annual increases of 15 percent or better. The industry performance in 1996 saw a revenue gain of 16.3 percent, from $894 million in 1995 to $1040 million in 1996. Similarly, the number of units shipped grew 21.3 percent, from 16,372 in 1995 to a total of 19,868 units in 1996.

In 1995, 75 percent of Cognex's customer base represented the OEM market, and the corporation claimed the leading market share at 38 percent. In fact, the company grew its OEM market by 60 percent, with 50 new customers. The factory-floor customer base represented 25 percent with a second-place finish with a market share of 14 percent behind Rockwell International. Cognex, however, grew its factory-floor market by 96 percent, with the addition of 140 new customers. In 1995, both of these markets were growing at a rapid pace.

In the OEM market segment Cognex's closest competitors were ICOS and AISI, who had a combined market share of 32 percent. The remaining market (30 percent) comprised in-house developers. On the factory-floor side of the business, the market was more fragmented, with the clear leader being Rockwell International, grabbing only 16 percent of the share. It appeared as though this market was growing at a more rapid pace than the OEM market. However, the revenue potential and gross margins (77 percent) were lucrative enough to make both market segments extremely attractive.

The 1998 Market

In 1998, the majority of Cognex's customers are still OEMs. Although Cognex lists metals, papers, and plastics as other materials for machine vision inspection markets, the overwhelming application base still lies in semiconductor and electronics inspection. However, easy-to-use products, such as the Checkpoint vision system, have enabled Cognex to further penetrate the end-user market, which shows great promise for machine vision. In fact, while analysts estimate the current OEM market to be worth $170 million and the end-user (or factory floor) market to be worth $150 million, many believe that the factory-floor market potential is in excess of $1 billion, a figure that creates many exciting prospects for Cognex. Opportunities for machine vision applications have been identified in industries such as the following:

- Aerial/satellite image analysis
- Agriculture
- Document processing
- Forensic science, including fingerprint recognition
- Health screening
- Medicine
- Military applications
- Publishing
- Research, particularly in physics, biology, astronomy, materials engineering, etc.
- Security and surveillance
- Traffic control

Cognex wants to capitalize on this large growth area by reducing its exposure to the cyclical semiconductor and electronic industries. In 1998, Cognex grew its end-user business by 6 percent to $3,112,000, due to increased volume from customers in general manufacturing industries; meanwhile, business in Europe has increased 14 percent over the previous year. Due to its devotion of additional sales and marketing resources to grow its end-user customer base, the company saw end-user revenue grow to 43 percent of its total revenue in 1998, from 32 percent of total revenue in 1997.

TROUBLED TIMES . . .

The company's revenues for 1998, however, decreased by 22 percent to nearly $122 million from $155 million. This decrease of revenue from the previous year is due primarily to decreased volume from the company's OEM customers. Sales to OEM customers, most of whom make capital equipment used by manufacturers in the semiconductor and electronics industries, decreased by 34 percent from the previous year. Geographically, revenues decreased nearly $14 million, or 23 percent, in North America and $20.5 million, or 30 percent, in Japan from the previous year, as most of the company's large OEM customers are based in these regions, while they increased $3 million, or 14 percent, in Europe.

This worldwide slowdown in the production and use of chips, resulting in a slowdown in the purchase of capital equipment for both semiconductor and electronics products, began in early 1996. Naturally, when customers slowed down their rate of purchasing, they delayed orders for vision systems until they had better "visibility," and consequently, Cognex's domestic and global sales revenue decreased and its growth slowed. From 1995–1996, domestic OEM sales revenues decreased 24 percent, from $21 million to $17 million. Similarly, global sales revenue to Japanese OEM customers also decreased, from nearly $14 million to $9 million, during this period. Cognex was forced to write off $4.2 million of obsolete inventory as a result of overproduction and reduced its production plans for 1996. Lower sales order fulfillment rates in these industries reduced Cognex's profitability, and in the fall of 1996, the value of Cognex's stock plummeted. This was no surprise, as 35 percent of its annual sales stem from these troubled semiconductor and electronics markets (see Exhibits 2 and 3).

Cognex has since made a deliberate attempt to begin to diversify into other industries, through both acquisition and product innovation. In 1995, Cognex acquired Acumen, Inc., a developer of wafer identification products, which allowed the company to penetrate the factory-floor market with 143 new end-user customers. Later, in 1996, Cognex acquired Isys Controls, Inc., known for its surface inspection technology. On July 31, 1997, Cognex acquired Mayan Automation, Inc. (Mayan), a developer of low-cost machine vision systems used for surface inspection. Finally, in 1998, Cognex formed a business relationship with Rockwell Automation, a leading supplier of factory automation products (e.g., components and systems), which also sells machine vision and has an extensive global distribution network to many Fortune 100 companies. This *preferred supplier* relationship with Rockwell Automation allowed Cognex to be introduced to all Rockwell's customers worldwide, in industries such as automotive, consumer products, and pharmaceutical manufacturing, where Cognex previously had little name recognition or market penetration.

A Changing Market

The focus of the machine vision industry is changing from technology to applications. Machine vision systems provide the most value-added benefits to operations through application engineering. In addition, machine vision tends to be demand inelastic. Since the product is less differentiated than the full solution, price reductions will have little impact on demand. From 1985–1995 there has been a 75 percent decline in the cost of hardware and software associated with machine vision systems. Falling prices have caused pressure in all segments of the real-time image processing systems industry. This industry is expected to surpass $5 billion by the year 2002.

Moreover, current trends in the personal-computer and machine vision industries do not complement each other. For example, on one hand, the speeds of central processor units on standard computers advance monthly. On the other hand, production leadtimes on high-performance vision processor boards are 18 to 24 months. Since machine vision systems need to operate on diverse hardware platforms, their application software could be customized and updated for different hardware platforms.

Competition

The increased use and availability of information technology has also resulted in increased competition. For example, Nikon, Inc., introduced the Veritas CNC to assist OEMs and end-users in computer chip inspection.

2 | Cognex Corporation—*Consolidated Balance Sheets*

December 31, (all amounts in thousands)	1998	1997
Assets		
Current assets:		
Cash and investments	$158,458	$178,014
Accounts receivable, less reserves of $2,583 and $1,940 in 1998 and 1997, respectively	20,987	25,095
Revenues in excess of billings	4,945	3,723
Inventories	10,812	7,784
Deferred income taxes	3,936	3,453
Prepaid expenses and other	8,141	5,937
Total current assets	207,279	224,006
Property, plant, and equipment, net	34,255	32,995
Deferred income taxes	2,237	1,377
Other assets	4,157	3,462
	$247,928	$261,840
Liabilities & stockholders' equity		
Current liabilities:		
Accounts payable	$ 2,488	$ 3,332
Accrued expenses	11,653	13,712
Accrued income taxes	916	2,684
Customer deposits	4,894	3,112
Deferred revenue	2,965	1,596
Total current liabilities	22,916	24,436
Other liabilities	2,137	1,262
Commitments		
Stockholders' equity:		
Common stock, $.002 par value— Authorized: 120,000,000 shares, issued: 42,453,980 and 41,859,395 shares in 1998 and in 1997, respectively	85	84
Additional paid-in capital	97,531	91,082
Treasury stock, at cost, 2,307,140 and 103,139 shares in 1998 and 1997, respectively	(41,353)	(1,436)
Retained earnings	166,571	146,368
Accumulated other comprehensive income	41	44
Total stockholders' equity	$222,875	$236,142
	$247,928	$261,840

Electro Scientific Industries acquired Applied Intelligent Systems, Inc., to further its expertise in developing process control and visual inspection systems for the assembly of semiconductor chips. As competition increases to provide the highest quality machine vision systems at the lowest prices, existing operating margins of approximately 75 percent could be affected as industry players compete for market share.

EXHIBIT 3 | Cognex Corporation—*Consolidated Statements of Income*

Year Ended December 31, (in thousands, except per-share amounts)	1998	1997	1996
Revenue	$121,844	$155,340	$122,843
Cost of revenue	37,296	42,273	38,855
Gross margin	84,548	113,067	83,988
Research, development & engineering expenses	24,662	22,481	19,434
Selling, general & administrative expenses	37,973	35,810	26,261
Charges for acquiring technology	2,100	3,115	
Income from operations	19,813	51,661	38,293
Investment income	6,756	5,947	4,726
Other income	733	718	678
Income before provision for income taxes	27,302	58,326	43,697
Provisions for income taxes	7,099	17,790	13,328
Net income	$ 20,203	$ 40,536	$ 30,369
Net income per common and common equivalent share:			
Basic	$ .49	$ .98	$ .75
Diluted	$ .47	$ .91	$ .69
Weighted-average common and common equivalent shares outstanding			
Basic	40,978	41,322	40,594
Diluted	43,203	44,702	43,814

OPPORTUNITIES FOR GROWTH

Machine vision is not widely known outside of the semiconductor and electronic industries. The business climate in the U.S. and throughout the world is reaching a highly hypercompetitive stage in which companies need to continually cut costs by streamlining processes to remain viable. The use of machine vision in the production process accomplishes this. It is Cognex's challenge to communicate these advantages and benefits to other industries in pursuit of diversification.

Cognex's sales are generated predominately from two economies: the U.S., at 41 percent, and Japan, at 46 percent. Its penetration into the European market is virtually untapped at 11 percent. Since its core business has always been in the OEM segment of the semiconductor industry, it is understandable as to why the geographic distribution would appear as such. However, there are limitless opportunities for machine vision technology throughout manufacturing processes across geographic and industry boundaries, as noted by the President: "Our goal is to exploit every available opportunity for our machine vision technology." The opportunities become limitless with global implications. Cognex has taken the first steps into the pharmaceutical (11 percent of total revenue) and automotive (9 percent of total revenue) industries. They have also established satellite offices in Singapore and South Korea to break into the manufacturing bases there, as the Pacific Rim, because of its low labor rates and favorable incentives, offers many opportunities.

A solid reputation, a strong sales force, a commitment to customer service, and research and development are the factors that contributed to the number-one position Cognex captured and maintained in the OEM market. Cognex was the first to introduce efficient machine vision processing into the production of semiconductor components and entered the market with a viable product, which it continually tweaked to meet the ever-changing needs of its customer base. Its highly trained technical sales force, comprising top-quality and experienced engineers, focused not only on understanding the needs and requirements of its customers in such a highly technical market (OEM), but also on developing and nurturing potential and existing relationships. The purchase of OEM equipment is an expensive undertaking in which the face of the manufacturing process is forever altered. As a result, the relationships that are established are longer in duration and require a solid foundation.

In being the first to introduce efficient machine vision processing into the production of semiconductor components, Cognex quickly established a solid name with a reliable reputation, which fostered its leading position. However, this has not been the case in the factory-floor market segment, for it is a fragmented market. Cognex still intends to increase its sales to these customers by 50 percent. Without a reputation, or a leading position to drive this objective, Cognex needs to develop a solid strategy for clearly identifying itself as the optimum solution. The factory-floor applications provide a challenge to create differentiated products that are specific enough to end-users' needs in diverse manufacturing processes, but yet still standardized enough to make them profitable to produce. This requires depth and flexibility in the design and application process.

CUSTOMER SERVICE AND RESEARCH & DEVELOPMENT

Building a solid relationship with the potential customer prior to signing any agreement is quite an extensive process undertaken by the engineers at Cognex. This commitment to the relationship is maintained throughout the life of the contract, as set forth by the culture within the company. This emphasis on customer service contributes to the loyalty of Cognex's customer base. Cognex's company directives state that all customer inquiries be responded to within a 24-hour time frame by a group of technicians who are on call at all times. Additionally, educational services are offered by Cognex to its customers to train their workforce. For its global customers, regional sales and distribution facilities exist to respond more quickly to these customers' needs, with all written or verbal support presented in the native language.

A direct output of the tight relationship between the Cognex engineers and their customers is the feedback provided by customers on product quality and enhancements. Since the sales force comprises mainly engineers, the discussions with customers can be quite technical in nature. This information is then funneled to the research and development staff at Cognex. The company regards research and development as a top priority. This is one of the ways in which Cognex has developed and maintained its leadership position in the machine vision industry. For nearly two decades, it has invested tens of millions of dollars in R&D expense to invent and improve its products.

In order to focus all of its financial and labor resources on R&D, Cognex chose to outsource its manufacturing operation by January of 1997. The in-house manufacturing operations created a strain on its management and financial resources, due to the large monetary outlays for capital equipment and the day-to-day operations. This forced the company to re-evaluate its business in terms of manufacturing, and it chose to outsource in order to lower costs, increase profitability, and focus on its core business—Cognex is unique among its competitors in terms of its decision. This was done in an attempt to give strength to the R&D department in terms of developing products to compete effectively in the factory-floor marketplace, which is more relevant to diversified industries like aerospace, automotive and pharmaceuticals.

Cognex's commitment to new-product development and to the creation and nurturing of potential or existing relationships is evident in the composition of its workforce. Thirty-nine percent of the total staff is dedicated to sales and marketing efforts, while 34 percent is focused on R&D. Cognex protects its investment in R&D with the use of patents, copyrights and trade agreements. Full-disclosure agreements are signed by all Cognex employees, suppliers, consultants and customers. In situations when computer codes need to be disclosed to the customer, legal confidentiality agreements are instituted.

COGNEX'S *"VISION"* OF THE FUTURE . . .

Having survived the 1996–1997 crash of the semiconductor industry, Cognex needs to insulate itself against this kind of industry-wide volatility in the future. There are several corporate strategies to choose from. They range from expanding globally to diversifying its target markets.

One strategic alternative for Cognex would be to diversify away from OEMs and compete more aggressively in the factory-floor marketplace. Although Cognex benefited greatly from its first-mover advantage, a dysfunctional consequence was that it never fully developed an effective marketing campaign. This will leave Cognex vulnerable as its first-mover advantage erodes.

Because the general manufacturing factory-floor market is so competitive, Cognex will need to strengthen its marketing capabilities. More widely recognized names such as Allen-Bradley have already established themselves in this market. A significantly larger investment in training is required for factory-floor workers than is needed for OEMs, as the OEM customers have a more technical background. However, Cognex's new graphical user interface reduces the need for training and offers a better match for the factory-floor worker. With this product innovation Cognex has inadvertently positioned itself for a whole new market. Factory-floor customers, who already have hardware platforms and yet are in the market for an upgrade on software, represent a large target market.

Finally, Cognex never had to be concerned with decoupling its hardware and software solutions, and therefore offers only bundled packages to its customers. It should be noted that Cognex's competitors, however, are successful with selling hardware and software solutions separately. And that flexibility and compatibility are crucial to meet the diverse needs of the customer base.

Another strategic alternative would be to expand into Europe to minimize the company's dependence on Japan. Unlimited opportunities exist for Cognex's core products globally, because of the rapid expansion of manufacturing outside the U.S., due to lower labor rates and lucrative incentives. Although Cognex has established itself as a leader in the industry through its strength in engineering, it lacks strong marketing to complement its expertise in technology. Outside the semiconductor industry, the use of machine vision to enhance production processes is still in its infancy. Yet, manufacturing inspection processes involving high speed and small parts are hardly unique to the semiconductor industry. There exist many industries with a variety of applications that Cognex can explore as potential opportunities to expand its business. But, if a strategy to expand geographically is pursued, reverse engineering becomes an even stronger threat, since intellectual property laws are weak abroad.

The Pacific Rim represents yet another untapped growth expansion opportunity. Cognex maintains a strong presence in Japan, and its name recognition should help it penetrate the Pacific Rim. In pursuing rapid geographical expansion, two viable strategic vehicles are acquisitions and strategic alliances. If Cognex could find a complementary business to align itself with, this alliance could enable a transfer of technology, which may lead to diversification. But, as in any alliance, the company would risk sharing its technical know-how with this transfer of technology.

Finally, the high profit margins in the machine vision industry continue to attract new competitors, and Cognex must prepare itself for this heightened level of competition. To stay on top, Cognex needs to make some serious strategic decisions.

BIBLIOGRAPHY

"An Adventurer's Guide to Machine Vision," Cognex Corporation, Annual Report 1998.

"Activity Book," Cognex Corporation, Annual Report 1997.

Barrow, Tom, "Eye on Machine Vision: New Technologies, Old Markets Fuel Vision Field's Growth," *Robotics World*, (5) Summer 1998, p. 30.

"Machine-Vision Industry Eyes Future Growth," *Machine Design*, (5) August 20, 1999, p. 80.

"North American Machine Vision Market Tops $1.5 Billion; Worldwide Market Hits $4.6 Billion," *Robotics World*, May/June 1999, p. 12.

Stevens, Tim, "Shill the showman: CEO Dr. Robert Shillman's unique management style and dogged drive for perfection have powered Cognex Corporation to explosive growth," *Industry Week*, (4) Nov. 7, 1994, v. 243, n. 20, p. 26.

Teresko, John, "New Eyes in Manufacturing," *Industrial World*, (4) April 19, 1999, p. 47.

CASE 15

Compaq in Crisis

Adrian Elton

Eckhard Pfeiffer was named CEO of Compaq Computer Corporation in 1991. Since 1991, Compaq's annual revenues have increased almost ten times (see Exhibit 1) and its stock price increased 1,072 percent.[1] Compaq became the world's largest PC vendor in 1994—two years ahead of schedule. In 1998, it was named Company of the Year by *Forbes* magazine. "As long as Pfeiffer is at the wheel, Compaq will continue to execute with relentless efficiency," said *Fortune* magazine in 1996.[2] In 1998, *The Economist* declaimed, "Compaq's rivals now fall into two categories: those it is leaving behind and those whose corporate markets it threatens."[3]

On April 18, 1999, Eckhard Pfeiffer was unceremoniously fired by Compaq's board of directors. How did the man who turned Compaq around in 1991 and built it into the premier PC vendor end up in such a position? What strategic decision during his tenure led to his downfall? What problems has he bequeathed to the CEO who follows him?

COMPANY HISTORY

Compaq was founded in 1982 by three former Texas Instruments executives, Rod Canion, Jim Harris, and Bill Murto. Their guiding idea was to build a "portable" version of the IBM PC. They persuaded Benjamin Rosen of Sevin Rosen Management Company to fund a prototype and later the company, and Compaq was born. Rod Canion was its first president and Rosen became chairman of the board.

Compaq had two major advantages. First, it built an IBM-compatible machine that could run IBM software right out of the box. Demand for PCs was so great that IBM couldn't keep up, and dealers were happy to have Compaq fill the gaps.[4] Second, Compaq didn't develop its own sales force and so its dealers didn't have any direct competition from the company. This was in stark contrast to the other major computer makers of the time, IBM and Apple.[5]

Compaq began setting records its first year of operation with sales of $111 million. This was a record in first-year sales for a new business in any industry. In 1983 it began to sell in Europe and shipped its 100,000th PC. In 1985, the company began trading on the New York Stock Exchange and earned a place on the Fortune 500 list. No other company has grown so fast.

In 1986, Compaq became a serious threat to IBM by introducing a computer that used Intel's new 386 processor nine months before IBM did. Sales continued to increase, breaking $1 billion in 1987. Compaq introduced the first battery-powered laptop in 1988, and revenues that year were $2.1 billion, twice what they were the previous year. In 1990, international sales topped U.S. sales for the first time, making Compaq a truly global corporation. Total sales were $3.2 billion, second only to IBM. All this in less than a decade.

In 1991, Compaq experienced its first hard times. There was a general industry downturn, and Compaq had the first layoffs in its history, releasing 12 percent of its workforce. On October 24, a day after reporting

This case was prepared under the direction of Professor Robert E. Hoskisson. The case is intended to be used as the basis for class discussion rather than to illustrate either effective or ineffective handling of an administrative or strategic situation.

EXHIBIT 1 | Compaq's Revenue Growth (in millions of dollars)

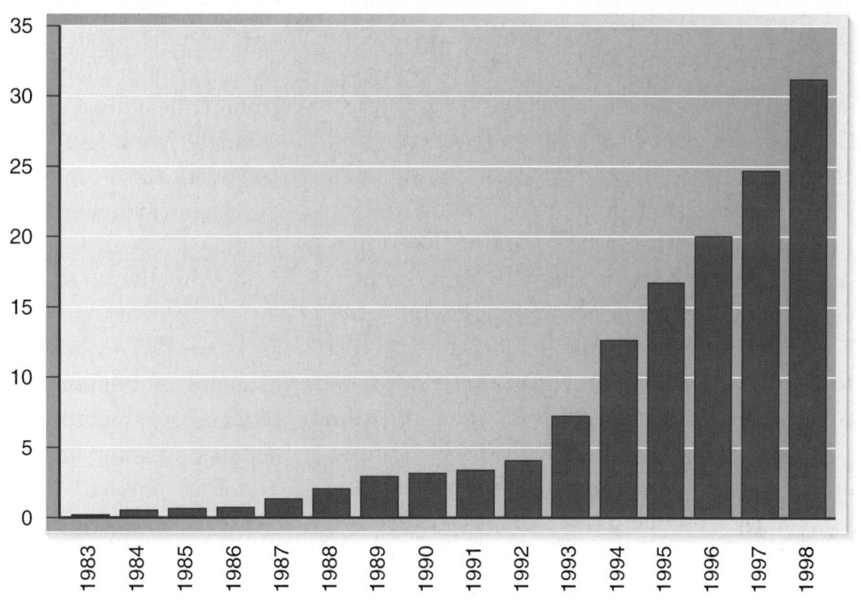

Sources: Compaq home page, Financial Highlights, www.compaq.com/corporate/1998ar; Burrows, P., 1994, Compaq Stretches for the Crown, *Business Week*, July 11, p. 140; Compaq reports record 1992 sales, *Business Wire,* 1993, January 26; Compaq's History, 1991, *The Atlanta Journal and Constitution*, p. C3; Compaq Computer Financial Results, 1989, *Business Wire*, February 1; Compaq Computer Financial Results, 1986, *Business Wire*, February 1; Compaq Computer Financial Results, 1985, *Business Wire*, February 11; *Christian Science Monitor*, 1984; Compaq wins by thinking big, *The San Diego Union-Tribune*, April 19, D6.

Compaq's first quarterly loss, Rod Canion was "unexpectedly removed"[6] from his position as CEO, and Eckhard Pfeiffer succeeded him.

Ben Rosen indicated that Canion's dismissal was not a knee-jerk reaction to bad quarterly results. He indicated that the board had been discussing creating an "office of the president" to be shared by Canion and Pfeiffer but Canion was not pleased by the idea. Forced to choose between them, the board opted in favor of Pfeiffer, mainly because of his international experience in a rapidly globalizing industry.[7]

Michael Swavely, former president of Compaq's North American operations who retired in July 1991, commented, "Change was overdue at Compaq." Past success had generated a "self-satisfied view of the world" that produced a reluctance to change, a fatal attribute in any industry, but especially in computer technology.[8] The reasons Rosen gave for Compaq's falling sales and declining market share were tardiness in lowering prices and not enough emphasis on its core market, desktop PCs.[9] Rod Canion had believed that Compaq could sell at a higher price based on its brand reputation for quality, and the company quickly found that was a fallacy.[10]

COMPAQ UNDER ECKHARD PFEIFFER

Eckhard Pfeiffer began his career at Compaq in 1983 when he left Texas Instruments to launch Compaq's European operation. He was very successful, opening 20 subsidiaries and increasing sales in Europe accounting for 54 percent of Compaq's revenues in 1990.[11] Rod Canion brought Pfeiffer to Houston in January 1991 to be chief operating officer, and he succeeded Canion as CEO in October of 1991.

The first thing Pfeiffer did as CEO was cut the gross margins from 35 to 27 percent[12] by slashing prices and effectively declaring war on the companies who built clones, which at that time held 60 percent of the market.[13] He also fired 25 percent of the workforce and increased the number of resellers.[14] Even amid restructuring, Compaq still managed to finish the year with increased revenue of $3.3 billion, slightly up from $3.1 billion the year before. Pfeiffer, with vision and determination, set a goal: Compaq will be the world's biggest PC producer in 1997—in only six years. Industry analysts didn't think he could do it in such a short time.[15]

The first Compaq computers were high performance and high price, and they sold well until competitors introduced lower priced machines with fewer extras.[16] Compaq regrouped and in 1992 introduced a new low-cost PC called the ProLinea. There was "a lot of doubt," Pfeiffer recalls. "Would we . . . bastardize the Compaq name?"[17] Instead, the ProLinea put Compaq back on track for continued growth, rapidly becoming the company's best-selling PC.[18] Compaq nearly doubled its U.S. market share to 23 percent, surpassing both IBM and Apple. It also emerged as the favored PC supplier in Europe, holding 10.3 percent market share.[19] Revenues continued to rise, reaching $4.1 billion at the end of the year.[20]

In August 1993, Compaq took another giant stride forward and introduced the Presario, another PC directed toward individual consumers, especially those with little or no previous computing experience. The Presario broke all the records at Compaq, selling twice as fast as the ProLinea in the first 60 days.[21] The Presario quickly became, and has remained, Compaq's mainstay, and the company finished the year with $7.2 billion in revenues.

In January 1994 the business world was shocked when Compaq announced that it would no longer exclusively use Intel's microprocessor chips in its computers. In explaining the choice to buy from Advanced Micro Devices, Compaq told the press that AMD was more than just an Intel clone; it also had products that would potentially fill some holes where Intel did not compete.[22] Compaq also began to sell the Presario in Japan in 1995, traditionally a tough market for American companies.

Pfeiffer convened a company meeting in an arena in Houston in January 1995 where in front of 16,000 employees and their families, he announced, "We are No. 1! We made it in 1994! We've replaced IBM as the world's top PC vendor!"[23] Compaq had reached a six-year goal in only two years. Although Compaq products were not all that original, it had realized this accomplishment through exceptional execution. When Pfeiffer took over, he began by cutting prices and costs, not by looking for brilliant new engineering. He said, "A ground rule is to set very aggressive cost goals to get very attractive entry-level products."[24] Compaq finished 1994 with $10.9 billion in sales.

Having conquered the PC market, Compaq shifted its strategic focus slightly in 1995. It began to add value to the computers it sold, emphasizing built-in networking and system management features.[25] The company also launched a worldwide service and support system to assure information technology workers that Compaq systems could reliably run business-critical applications and that the company could deliver the service and support they required. This brought Compaq one step closer to becoming a computer company rather than just a PC company.[26] Deciding to operate in the service sector as well as the hardware sector put the company in more direct competition with industry giants Hewlett-Packard and IBM.

Compaq also decided to move into the networking business and signed a joint venture deal with Cisco Systems to build low-cost gear to connect servers to networks. Likewise, it signed a marketing agreement with Germany's ITK, which produces modems that link portable PCs to servers. It also closed a deal with Thomas-Conrad Co., a manufacturer of local-network cards for PCs. The final transaction in November 1995 was the acquisition of NetWorth, Inc., a company that makes high-speed network gear. All of this gave Compaq the technology to offer a complete networking package to its customers.[27] Revenues continued to rise, and the company finished the year with $14.8 billion in sales.[28]

In 1996, Compaq landed two big contracts, one with SmithBarney and the other with General Motors. The contracts included purchase of both PCs and servers, a major step forward for enterprisewide client-server computing.[29] Compaq's ProLiant server captured nearly 80 percent of the Pentium server market, and Compaq shipped its 1,000,000th server in November 1996, the first company in the industry to reach this milestone.[30]

However, things were beginning to strain. In March, Pfeiffer had to warn analysts that Compaq might not meet its first-quarter earnings estimates, and the stock plunged. He acted quickly, ordering incentives for dealers and price cuts to lift demand. Revenues for the quarter jumped 42 percent, and the stock recovered. This should have been cause for celebration, but the cost to the company of hitting the growth target was a drop in profit margin to 20 percent—the lowest it had ever been. A troubling fact emerged: Compaq had been running twice as fast just to stay in place. Sales and revenues had increased, but profits hadn't moved. Pfeiffer wanted the company to continue growing at the rapid rate of the past years and reach $40 billion in revenues by the year 2000. Following a meeting with managers from around the world, a new strategy was forged: Move aggressively into new product areas that will make Compaq a full-line information-technology company, capable of competing with IBM and Hewlett-Packard.[31] Also, a new strategic approach was needed because IBM had reversed the trend and begun to take PC market share from Compaq.[32]

In May 1997, Compaq announced another step into the networking business by acquiring Microcom, Inc., a company that makes networking gear. The line between the networking business and the computer business had become increasingly blurry, as computer companies rushed to increase sales in the lucrative industry. Also, in June, Compaq announced that it was expanding by purchasing Tandem Computers, another computer maker, which helped the company expand its line to include more powerful servers and parallel commercial systems.[33]

More symptoms of internal problems cropped up in 1997, as Pfeiffer had to make an extra effort to soothe its resellers after Compaq officials said they wanted a "more direct relationship with customers." Because of the inroads that Dell Computer had made into Compaq's sales, many resellers interpreted the remark to mean that Compaq was seriously considering turning to the direct online business model practiced by Dell. Pfeiffer had to summon distributors to the company's Houston headquarters and reassert his commitment to Compaq's traditional distribution channels.[34]

In October 1997, Compaq paid its first dividend and finished the year with sales of $24.5 billion.[35] However, its next move surprised the industry; in 1998, Compaq acquired Digital Equipment Company (DEC) for $9.6 billion—the largest computer buyout in history.[36] Digital, which was founded in 1957, was one of IBM's original competitors. It helped bring computers out of back offices and into the hands of the general public, giving birth to the minicomputer market. When Compaq was formed, Digital was second only to IBM. However, bad leadership and bad technology decisions had made Digital into a second-tier player.[37]

The acquisition of Digital considerably filled out Compaq's product line. Digital specialized in higher-end computers: workstations and Internet servers. More important, Digital brought to Compaq an excellent, large service and support organization used to working with big companies and provided Compaq with the entrance into an upper scale big business market that it had been trying to achieve for several years.[38] Additional assets were the Alta Vista Web search engine (which was later sold to KPMG) and the blazingly fast Alpha 64 bit processor chip. Analysts expected Compaq to bring its low-cost no-holds-barred PC economics into the high-end computing markets that were dominated by IBM, Hewlett-Packard, and Sun Microsystems. Such an approach could have potentially revolutionized the high-end computing business, and would make Compaq's regular PC business more competitive with Dell and Gateway 2000. Although some commentators raised concerns about the difference between the corporate cultures at Digital and Compaq, the merger moved forward and was finalized on June 11, 1998.

At the 1998 PC Expo tradeshow, Pfeiffer was invited to give the keynote address. In his speech, he discussed the five key areas that Compaq's strategy was focused on and what it was doing to accomplish each:

- *Industry Standard Computing:* "Anywhere there is standards-based computing, Compaq wants to be the driver, whether it's in your home, your business or your car."
- *Business Critical Computing:* Compaq will continue to invest in high-performance 64-bit computing with its Alpha chip.
- *Global Service and Support:* Compaq now has more than 25,00 service professionals around the world who can give customers support and availability

services, systems integration, and operations management. This gives customers a single point of accountability and lowers the cost and risk of ownership.

- *Cost-Effective Solutions for the Enterprise:* "We will focus on solutions that build on our leadership in enterprise platforms, expertise in key markets, service capabilities, and partnerships with industry-leading companies."
- *Customers:* Compaq will leverage the account-based customer relationships nurtured by Digital and Tandem and combine them with Internet-based selling to provide customers the most flexibility and choice. Compaq wants to be "a strategic partner whose mission is to give you what you need, when you need it, and how you want it, at the lowest total cost."[39]

At the end of 1998, Compaq had $31.2 billion in sales revenues and, with the acquisition of Digital, was one of the largest computer companies in the world. It had a definite strategy and although build-to-order companies were beginning to take away market share, it still had commanding market share.

THE FIRING

On April 9, 1999, Pfeiffer announced to Wall Street that Compaq would probably not meet earnings expectations for the quarter; that they would in fact be about half of what analysts predicted. Compaq's stock plummeted on the news.[40]

Benjamin Rosen, chairman of Compaq's board of directors, called a board meeting without Pfeiffer, and the board voted him out. On April 18, Pfeiffer handed in his resignation to Compaq's board of directors. Rosen and two other board members, Frank P. Doyle and Robert T. Enloe, formed the Office of the Chief Executive to run the company while they searched for another CEO. This office was not intended to be a passive caretaker of the company. Rosen said, "The board is committed to move quickly to select the right Chief Executive Officer to lead the next era of Compaq's growth and development. In the interim, we will move decisively to take those actions that are indicated."[41]

So where did Pfeiffer go wrong? What grave mistakes did he make that merited his removal as CEO? When he announced the quarterly results (or lack thereof), he attempted to blame Compaq's poor performance on a generally weak demand in the PC industry, lower profit margins, and competitive pricing.

As with Rod Canion, he was not removed for simply having a bad quarter. The bad quarterly results were merely symptomatic of larger internal problems. Pfeiffer's complaints about weak demand, lower profit margins, and competitive pricing were valid, but the other major PC makers (IBM, Dell, Hewlett-Packard, and Gateway) were not struggling in the same way as Compaq. Even Rosen had said as much when he commented that Compaq itself was largely at fault for its disappointing financial performance.[42] He also added that problems at Compaq were more severe than at first glance, and he wished they'd replaced Pfeiffer a year earlier.[43]

To arrive at this point, Pfeiffer had begun to isolate himself from employees, even some of his own vice presidents and higher executives. He oversaw the construction of an executive parking garage at a company where parking places had never been reserved, visibly separating himself from the other employees. Security on the executive floor was repeatedly increased and access increasingly restricted. Pfeiffer and his inner circle worked out the acquisition of Digital, and the rest of the senior executives only found out about it the night before it was announced to the press. Apparently, Pfeiffer had become too insular, not open to feedback and new ideas from those below.[44]

When he replaced Canion as CEO in 1991, his aggressive initiatives changed Compaq's fortunes and turned the company around. But he seemed to have become less definite about making decisions. "He was paralyzed by the speed with which the market was changing, and he couldn't make the difficult decisions," says one former executive.[45]

As a result of his indecision, there was a failure to execute as effectively as Compaq had in the past. "Pfeiffer is not supposed to be the guy who fails on implementation," says Jonathon Eunice, an analyst at Illuminata Inc. "Everyone talks about keeping the CEO accountable; almost no one does it. But [Rosen's] not afraid to fire his main guy and move on." Eunice continues, "the operations have been so sloppy for the second year in a row that it's almost staggering how off those numbers have been."[46] The reason the office is called "Chief Executive Officer" is because the CEO should execute strategy. Pfeiffer was no longer following through, getting things done, delivering on commitments. Benjamin Rosen told the press, "The change [will not be in] our fundamental strategy—we think that strategy is sound—but in execution. Our plans are to speed up decision-making and make the company more efficient."[47]

Over time, Pfeiffer began to focus on being number one and forgot about understanding the customer. Longtime chief strategist Robert Stearns, who left Compaq in June 1998, says, "In his quest for bigness, he lost an understanding of the customer and built what I call empty market share—large but not profitable."[48] The acquisitions of Tandem Computers and especially of Digital Equipment were indicative of this flaw. Against the advice of some of the senior executives, Pfeiffer and his tiny inner circle negotiated for Digital and presented it to the rest of the company after it was already completed. "Buying Digital played into Eckhard's fantasy, but it's turning out to be a beast that's consuming the company," said one former executive.[49] Digital had proved to be tougher to integrate than predicted: The corporate cultures were more incompatible than first thought, and Compaq seemed to have lost its way, although it was likely to reach Pfeiffer's ambitious goal of $40 billion in earnings by 2000.

While Pfeiffer bears extensive blame for the company's poor performance, he should also be given a great deal of credit. Since becoming CEO in 1991, he turned Compaq around more than once and helped it grow into a tremendous power in the PC industry. "Eckhard Pfeiffer oversaw a period of stunning growth in Compaq's history," said Rosen. "All those who benefited from that growth owe him a debt of gratitude."[50] (See Exhibit 2 for Compaq's financial performance from 1994–1998.)

WANTED: CEO FOR A LARGE FORTUNE 500 COMPANY

The board's search for a new CEO went on for three months. Rumors were rampant as many different people were considered for the job. Finally, on July 22, 1999, Rosen called a press conference and announced that Michael A. Cappellas, the chief operating officer at Compaq, had been offered the job and accepted.

Cappellas joined Compaq in August 1998 as the chief information officer and became the acting chief operating officer in June 1999. Before coming to Compaq, he had worked at Schlumberger, an oil service company, for 15 years as an executive which included the company's first corporate director for information systems. In 1996, he moved to SAP America as the director

EXHIBIT 2 | Compaq Consolidated Income Statement (Year Ended December 31)

	1998	1997	1996	1995	1994
Revenue					
• Products	$27,372	24,122	19,611	16,308	12,274
• Services	3,797	462	398	367	331
Total:	31,169	24,684	20,009	16,675	12,605
Cost of Sales					
• Products	$21,383	17,500	14,565	12,026	8,671
• Services	2,597	333	290	265	214
Total:	23,980	17,833	14,855	12,291	8,885
Other Total Costs	$ 9,851	3,993	3,271	3,058	2,367
Income (Loss) Before Taxes	(2,662)	2,758	1,883	1,326	1,353
Income Taxes	81	903	565	43	365
Net Income (Loss)	(2,743)	1,855	1,318	893	988

Source: Compaq home page, 1998 Annual Report, www.compaq.com/corporate/1998ar/financials/5yr_summary_nf.html.

of supply chain management, and in 1997 he joined Oracle Corporation as senior vice president before moving to Compaq.[51]

One of the first problems Cappellas faced as CEO was convincing shareholders and customers that he was capable of filling the job. Industry analysts were concerned by the appointment of an "insider" who had been at the company for less than a year and who did not have any CEO experience. Many shared concerns about his ability to lead a large company like Compaq.[52] This issue didn't bother Cappellas, who told the press, "Strategy is about solving business problems. I've been in IT for many years, [so] I'm confident that I can do that."[53]

On the other hand, others were glad to see someone with a great deal of information technology experience appointed CEO. "The companies that put marketing and sales people in as CEO never had to run a full enterprise infrastructure, and they have no idea what our [IT] problems are," says Mike May, vice president of IT at Teknion Furniture Systems, a Compaq customer.[54] And an analyst at J.P. Morgan & Co. comments, "He is not well-known, but in terms of his qualifications, he's as credible as any of the other candidates we were hearing about."[55] Cappellas's experience in information technology could prove to be an asset for Compaq. However, he faces a set of strong rivals.

COMPETITION

Compaq competes with four other major competitors: Dell, IBM, Hewlett-Packard, and Gateway. These companies will challenge Cappellas's capabilities in strategic leadership. (See Exhibit 3 for the PC market shares of Compaq and its dominant competition.)

Dell Computer

Dell was founded in 1985 by Michael Dell in Round Rock, Texas, with a unique premise: selling directly to the customer and bypassing resellers. Because it sells direct,

EXHIBIT 3 | PC Market Share (First Quarter 1999)

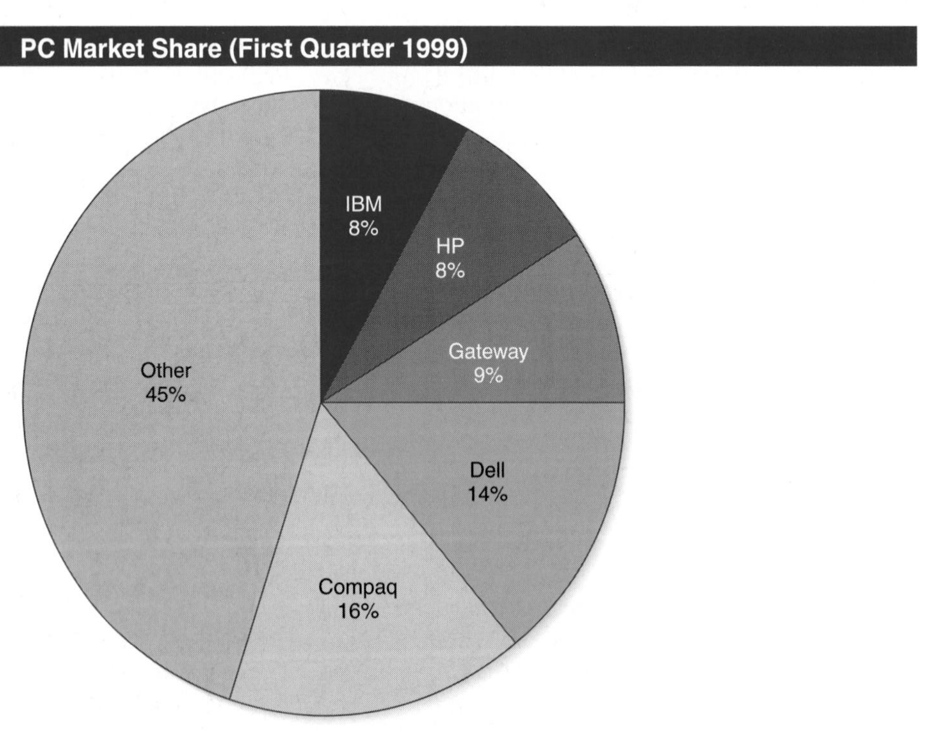

Source: PC Week Online, Archives, www.zdnet.com/pcweek/stories/jumps/0.4270,2263744,00.html.

Dell has greatly reduced inventory cost and turnover time. (Currently, turnover is every six days.) In 1996, Dell began to sell directly over the Internet, which now accounts for approximately 50 percent of orders. Dell has used the Internet to offer specially catered customer service to its large corporate customers by constructing a personal Web page for each. Dell has been increasing its high-profit product line for big business. Corporate sales account for most of Dell's revenue. In October 1999, Dell outsold Compaq for the first time in the PC market, increasing its market share to 18.1 percent while Compaq's fell to 15.9 percent.[56]

IBM (International Business Machines)

IBM was incorporated in 1911. It was the first and biggest computer company, and pioneered the introduction of the PC in 1981. IBM faltered in the mid-1980s when confronted with Compaq and other rivals. In 1996, IBM began to regain market share in the PC market and came back to be second in the U.S., after Compaq.[57] In 1999, it had $81.7 billion in revenues.

Despite its turnaround in the PC sector, IBM has shifted its focus to its more profitable services division and is marketing itself as an "e-business," emphasizing how it can help other companies get their companies online to take advantage of the Internet. This allows it to emphasize services such as high-end servers which also drives its hardware sales into a higher profit margin than PCs.[58] Currently it holds 7.5 percent of the PC market share in the United States.[59]

Hewlett-Packard

Hewlett-Packard (HP) was founded by two engineers, Bill Hewlett and Dave Packard, in 1938 in a garage in Palo Alto, California. Hewlett-Packard was incorporated the following year and has never stopped growing. Hewlett and Packard developed a remarkable corporate culture that encouraged communication and innovation, and their company has performed accordingly. HP began by building oscillators and evolved with the technology, building the scientific calculator that made slide rules obsolete, and eventually computers and other hardware.[60]

HP gradually diversified into many areas, including communications and medical technology. In 1999, HP launched a new company, Agilent, consisting of its industry-leading test-and-measurement products, semiconductor products, and chemical-analysis medical businesses. HP could now focus on its core business of computers and hardware, including printers. HP had computer-related revenue of $39.5 billion in its 1998 fiscal year,[61] and had 8 percent of the PC market.[62]

Gateway Computers

Gateway Computers was founded in 1985 by Ted Waitt. Like Dell, Gateway's business model is based on direct customized selling. In 1996, it began to sell computers on the Internet. Gateway has begun experimenting with various ways to earn more revenues from its customers. It opened "Gateway Country Stores," brick and mortar stores that are owned by the company; the stores carry no inventory but provide customer service and facilitate shopping for first-time customers by giving them the opportunity to test machines before buying. Gateway has also started up its own Internet service provider, which has taken off this past year, with half a million subscribers. At 9 percent[63] Gateway has more U.S. PC market share than either IBM or HP.

FUTURE CHALLENGES

Michael Cappellas has quite a formidable task in front of him. Although Compaq has many problems, it has just as many opportunities. The merger with Digital must be completed and assimilated into Compaq.[64] Buying Digital was to help Compaq grow into a full-line computer company offering a large range of products that would be driven by service solutions. Cappellas said, "We underestimated the cultural issues and just the hard work it takes to integrate two companies like Compaq and Digital. And that drains a lot of energy in the field. . . . The core PC business was coming under attack, and the market was shifting just as the integration was draining management attention. So the timing was really bad."[65]

Completing Digital's integration will allow Compaq to expand into the profitable services business by leveraging Digital's admirable services arm. This will put it into direct competition with Hewlett-Packard and IBM.

Business users are buying all-in-one packages of products and services. However, the solutions business at Compaq is not functioning well, while at the same time, margins in the PC business are falling.[66]

To compete with Dell, Compaq must develop a better online strategy.[67] PCs depreciate approximately one percent per week, and Company mustn't continually be caught with back inventory on its hands. To reduce the costs of back inventory, it needs to move to a more direct sales model.[68] When IBM tried selling direct, its dealers complained and IBM backed off; the company currently doesn't sell online. Compaq may need to find a happy medium between online and retail selling.

In May, a month after Pfeiffer's departure, Compaq announced a restructuring of the sales channel, reducing the number of places that it ships to from 29 to 4. This new "Distributor Alliance Program" will reduce shipping and transaction costs.[69] It will also reduce inventories and thus cut the associated costs. All this will boost the bottom line, as well as open up many more opportunities and make Compaq a more viable competitor with Dell.

Cappellas stated, "We did not do a good job of telling our story. We had fragmented marketing messages. Compaq had stood for the world's most powerful personal computing brand. Then we added the very high-end Tandem side, and then we brought in Digital. The customer lost track of who we were."[70] Compaq has the opportunity to reinvent itself once more as a comprehensive computer company that can offer an enormous services benefit to its customers, instead of just being the "world's top PC vendor."[71] This is a chance to realign the company's focus and become a computing behemoth like IBM.

In an interview, Cappellas was asked, "Who do you worry about more, Dell or IBM?" He responded, "I worry about IBM. They have done a very good job of positioning themselves around e-business. They sell the entire suite. They have a great solutions mindset. I have a great respect for them as a competitor."[72] At first glance, an observer would think that surely Dell should be Cappellas's big worry. However, as the quote indicates, Mr. Cappellas may seek to pursue a strategy similar to IBM's. Whatever strategic approach is taken, Cappellas has a significant challenge.

ENDNOTES

1. Eckhard's gone but the PC rocks on: Compaq's CEO blames his ouster on a savagely competitive industry, 1999, *Fortune*, May 24, p. 153.
2. Kirkpatrick, David, 1996, Fast times at Compaq, *Fortune*, April 1, p. 121–128.
3. Compaq goes after Big Blue, 1998, *The Economist*, January 31, p. 66.
4. How Compaq's portable leaped ahead of the pack, 1983, *Business Week*, August 15, p. 89.
5. Ibid.
6. Richards, Evelyn, 1991, Compaq ousts president who founded firm, *The Washington Post*, October 26, p. C1.
7. Kehoe, Louise, 1991, Compaq founder fired because board "had to make choice," *Financial Times*, October 28, p. 19.
8. Ibid.
9. Ibid.
10. And the losers are . . . , 1994, *The Economist*, September 17, p. 6.
11. Kirkpatrick, David, 1996, Fast times at Compaq, *Fortune*, April 1, p. 121–128; Preston, Holly, 1994, Compaq's winning ways, *International Business*, September, p. 56.
12. Nee, Eric, 1998, Company of the year—Compaq Computer Corp., *Forbes*, January 12, p. 90.
13. Selling computers is easy—the hard bit is making a profit, *The Economist*, 1994, p. 6.
14. Nee, Eric, 1998, Company of the year—Compaq Computer Corp., *Forbes*, January 12, p. 90.
15. Loeb, Marshall, 1995, Leadership lost—and regained, *Fortune*, April 17, p. 217.
16. Jones, John, 1993, Compaq builds sales, profits with aggressive price policy, *Investor's Business Daily*, May 27, p. 32.
17. Higgins, Steve, 1993, Executive update, *Investor's Business Daily*, June 7, p. 4.
18. Compaq Presario 425 is fastest-selling new PC in company's history, 1993, *Business Wire*, October 26.
19. Compaq's Pfeiffer sees significant growth opportunities for U.S. computer industry, 1992, *Business Wire*, December 7.
20 Compaq reports record 1992 sales, 1993, *Business Wire*, January 26.
21. Reuters, 1993, Compaq says its new PC set sales record, *The New York Times*, October 27, p. D3.
22. Burgess, John, 1994, Compaq goes with clone over Intel chip, *The Washington Post*, January 27, p. D11.
23. Loeb, Marshall, 1995, Leadership lost—and regained, *Fortune*, April 17, p. 217.
24. Burrows, Peter, 1994, Compaq stretches for the crown, *Business Week*, July 11, p. 140.

25. Spiegelman, Lisa & Mehler, Mark, 1995, Compaq's new PCs mark a shift in strategic focus, *Investor's Business Daily*, March 9, p. A6.
26. Compaq launches world-class enterprise service and support capability, 1995, *Business Wire*, October 16.
27. McWilliams, Gary, 1995, Compaq hooks up with a networking wizard, *Business Week*, November 20, p. 48.
28. Compaq Home page, 1999, 1995 Annual Report, www.compaq.com/corporate/1995ar, November 17.
29. Compaq, Microsoft announce major contracts with EDS to revolutionize General Motors dealer service, 1996, *Business Wire*, June 4; Compaq, Microsoft awarded $17 Million contract to supply PCs, servers, software to Smith Barney, 1996, *Business Wire*, April 17.
30. Compaq first company in world to ship one million industry-standard servers, 1996, *Business Wire*, November 19.
31. McWilliams, Gary, 1996, Compaq at the "crossroads," *Business Week*, July 22, p. 70.
32. Alster, Norm, 1996, IBM's silver-medal win: Sign of a PC power shift?, *Investor's Business Daily*, August 5, p. A6.
33. Compaq Company Home Page, Press Release Archives, 1997, www.compaq.com/newsroom/pr/1997/pr230697a, November 18.
34. Britt, Russ, 1997, Compaq soothes resellers, but will the détente last?, *Investor's Business Daily*, June 3, p. A6.
35. Compaq Home page, 1999, 1995 Annual Report, www.compaq.com/corporate/1995ar, November 17; Silverman, Dwight, 1997, Compaq Computer to pay first dividend, *Investor's Business Daily*, October 17.
36. Abrahms, Doug, 1998, Compaq agrees to purchase Digital in largest computer buyout in history, *The Washington Times*, January 27.
37. Ramstad, Evan & Auerbach, Jon, 1998, Behind Digital's downfall: It's the story of modern computing, and how a mega-giant has stumbled in recent years, *The Ottawa Citizen*, January 28, C3.
38. Quinlan, Tom, 1998, Texas-Based Compaq to acquire Digital for $9.6 billion, *San Jose Mercury News*, January 27; McWilliams, Gary, 1998, Power play, *Business Week*, February 9, p. 90.
39. Compaq president and CEO Pfeiffer outlines vision for "new world of computing", 1998, *Business Wire*, June 16.
40. Einstein, David, 1999, Compaq stock tumbles on profit warning, *The San Francisco Chronicle*, April 13, C1.
41. Compaq board of directors forms office of the chief executive under leadership of chairman Benjamin Rosen; Eckhard Pfeiffer and Earl Mason Resign as CEO and CFO, 1999, *Business Wire*, April 18.
42. Balfour, Gail, 1999, Pfeiffer: How Compaq's mighty CEO has fallen, *ComputerWorld Canada*, May 7, p. 1.
43. Company profile, 1999, The lion in winter, *Business Week*, July 26, p. 108; "I was an asset . . . rather than a meddler," *Business Week*, July 26, p. 116.
44. Eckhard's gone but the PC rocks on: Compaq's CEO blames his ouster on a savagely competitive industry, 1999, *Fortune*, May 24, p. 153; DiCarlo, Lisa, 1999, Eye of the storm: Compaq executive turmoil traced to Pfeiffer's inner circle, *PC Week*, May 24, p. 1.
45. DiCarlo, Lisa, 1999, Eye of the storm: Compaq executive turmoil traced to Pfeiffer's inner circle, *PC Week*, May 24, p. 1.
46. Balfour, Gail, 1999, Pfeiffer: How Compaq's mighty CEO has fallen, *ComputerWorld Canada*, May 7, p. 1.
47. Charan, Ram and Colvin, Geoffrey, 1999, Why CEOs fail, *Fortune*, June 21, p. 69.
48. Eckhard's gone but the PC rocks on: Compaq's CEO blames his ouster on a savagely competitive industry, 1999, *Fortune*, May 24, p. 153.
49. DiCarlo, Lisa, 1999, Eye of the storm: Compaq executive turmoil traced to Pfeiffer's inner circle, *PC Week*, May 24, p. 1.
50. Compaq board of directors form office of the chief executive, 1999, *Business Wire*, April 18.
51. Darwin, Jennifer, 1999, Surprising week shakes up Compaq, *Houston Business Journal*, July 30, p. 1.
52. Kehoe, Louise and Taylor, Roger, 1999, Compaq faces "Internet speed" change, *The Financial Times*, July 26, p. 20; Dicarlo, Lisa, 1999, New Compaq, HP CEOs: A contrast, *PC Week*, July 26, p. 1; Darwin, Jennifer, 1999, Surprising week shakes up Compaq, *Houston Business Journal*, July 30, p. 1; Dicarlo, Lisa, and Zimmerman, Michael R., 1999, Initial reactions vary on new Compaq CEO, *PC Week*, August 2, p. 40; Hawkins, Lori, 1999, Compaq Computer selects company insider as CEO, *Knight Ridder/Tribune Business News*, July 23; Taylor, Roger, 1999, Compaq promotes Cappellas to top job, *The Financial Times*, July 23, p. 21.
53. Dicarlo, Lisa, 1999, New Compaq, HP CEOs: A contrast, *PC Week*, July 26, p. 1.
54. Ibid.
55. Dicarlo, Lisa, and Zimmerman, Michael R., 1999, Initial reactions vary on new Compaq CEO, *PC Week*, August 2, p. 40.
56. Dell Home Page, www.dell.com, 1999; Goldstein, Alan, 1999, Dell outpaces Compaq in U.S. sales of personal computers, *Knight-Ridder/Tribune Business News*, October 25; Eckhard's gone but the PC rocks on: Compaq's CEO blames his ouster on a savagely competitive industry, 1999, *Fortune*, May 24, p. 153.
57. Alster, Norm, 1999, IBM's silver-medal win: Sign of PC power shift?, *Investor's Business Daily*, August 5, p. A6.
58. IBM Home Page, 1998 Annual Report, www.ibm.com/annualreport/1998/letter/ibm98arlsen01.

59. PC Week Online, Archives, http://www.zdnet.com/pcweek/stories/jumps/0,4270,2263744,00.html; Eckhard's gone but the PC rocks on: Compaq's CEO blames his ouster on a savagely competitive industry, 1999, *Fortune*, May 24, p. 153.
60. Hewlett-Packard Home Page, History, http://www.hp.com/abouthp/history.
61. Hewlett-Packard Home Page, Press Releases, http://www.hp.com/pressrel/jul99/28jul99.htm.
62. PC Week Online, Archives, http://www.zdnet.com/pcweek/stories/jumps/0,4270,2263744,00.html.
63. Eckhard's gone but the PC rocks on: Compaq's CEO blames his outer on a savagely competitive industry, 1999, *Fortune*, May 24, p. 153; Gateway Home Page, History, www.gateway.com/about/info, 1999; PC Week Online, Archives, http://www.zdnet.com/pcweek/stories/jumps/0,4270,2263744,00.html.
64. Gibson, Stan, 1999, Compaq, customers need common ground, *Fortune*, May 10, p. 85.
65. Kirkpatrick, David, 1999, Superior performance is the key to independence, *Fortune*, August 16, p. 126.
66. Deck, Stewart, 1999, Compaq counts its losses, *Computerworld*, June 28, p. 30.
67. Compaq looks inside for salvation: Can Michael Capellas make the PC giant into a Web master?, 1999, *Fortune*, August 16, p. 124.
68. Ibid.
69. Campbell, Tricia, 1999, Compaq tries to reboot, *Sales & Marketing Management*, July, p. 20.
70. Kirkpatrick, David, 1999, Superior performance is the key to independence, *Fortune*, August 16, p. 126.
71. Loeb, Marshall, 1995, Leadership lost—and regained, *Fortune*, April 17, p. 217.
72. Kirkpatrick, David, 1999, Superior performance is the key to independence, *Fortune*, August 16, p. 126.

CASE 16

Enersis

Global Strategy in the Electric Power Sector

Robert Grosse
Thunderbird,
The American Graduate School of International Management

Carlos Fuentes
Universidad Gabriela Mistral

I. INTRODUCTION

Enersis the Chilean multinational electricity company, had grown into a $US 3.7 billion (market capitalization) leader in the South American market by December of 1997. Beginning as the privatized version of the Santiago regional power distribution company, Enersis has become a true multinational, with major operating subsidiaries in Argentina, Peru, Brazil, and Columbia, along with those in Chile.

As the company prepares for the next century, conditions are either opportune for additional growth and profitability, or threatening with the possible arrival of major multinational electric companies from North America and Europe in the region. As the process of privatization of the spector proceeds throughout Latin America, Enersis is encountering increasing challenges from companies such as EDF (France), AES (US) and Iberdrola (Spain). Mr. Pablo Ihnen, CEO of Enersis, has a clear vision of the need for Enersis to expand through the region and to build a portfolio of businesses around the core electric generation and distribution activities.

At the same time that Enersis is exploring expansion opportunities abroad, the company is experiencing limitations on its ability to expand at home. As the largest electric power company in Chile, Enersis is always under public scrutiny for its pricing, service quality, and environmental protection issues. As one of the largest companies in the country, Enersis again is subject to constant public discussion. This reality makes it difficult for the company to pursue expansion activities in Chile, though recently Enersis did bail out a failing water utility (Lo Castillo), and other power generation projects have been started (such as a natural gas–powered plant in Atacama, in northern Chile).[1]

Perhaps the greatest limitation on growth in the domestic market is its size; Chile's population of 14 million people is already fairly well supplied with hydroelectric power and some coal/has thermoelectric power. The limit to domestic growth is very relative, however. In North American terms, the economic growth rate of Chile, at more than 6 percent annually, with power needs at least matching the rate, is fairly attractive. Still, the need for increased electric power supply within Chile is expected to grow less rapidly than the demand elsewhere in Latin America.

Total capital investment in power generation in Latin America was growing at a value of about $US 10 billion per year during the 1990s. Chile's investment in power generation grew at about $US 600 million per year during that time, and appears likely to continue at this rate for the next five years. As Enersis expands in the rest of the region, capital investment needs are growing almost exponentially. Exhibit 1 depicts this environment.

If privatizations of state-owned power generation and distribution companies continue on the current path, the need for capital investment is expected to reach $US 100 billion over the course of the next five years. To continue its role as the largest, highly prof-

Copyright © 1999 Thunderbird, The American Graduate School of International Management. All rights reserved. This case was prepared for the purpose of classroom discussion only, and not to indicate either effective or ineffective management.

1 | Installed Capacity (MW)

	1998	1999	2000	2001	2002	2003	% Participation
Argentina	20,799	22,284	23,875	25,579	27,406	29,362	13
Bolivia	877	939	1,007	1,078	1,155	1,238	1
Brazil	61,591	65,988	70,700	75,748	81,156	86,950	37
Chile	6,712	7,191	7,705	8,255	8,845	9,476	4
Colombia	11,287	12,093	12,956	13,881	14,872	15,934	7
Ecuador	2,934	3,143	3,368	3,608	3,866	4,142	2
México	36,997	39,638	42,469	45,501	48,750	52,230	22
Perú	6,795	4,066	4,356	4,667	5,001	5,538	2
Venezuela	20,225	21,669	23,216	24,874	26,650	28,553	12
Total	165,216	177,012	189,651	203,192	217,700	233,244	

itable private power company in the region, Enersis needs a huge amount of additional resources.

The global (or regional) strategy being developed by Enersis was simply unthinkable only ten years ago. With the Latin American region in the late stages of an enormous external debt crisis and prolonged recession, the economic conditions were singularly unfavorable. The electric power industry at that time was almost entirely government-owned throughout Latin America. Chile was the first country in the region to privatize both the electric power generation industry and also the electricity distribution industry.

In December of 1997, as the leaders of Enersis considered the whirlwind process that had led the company to its current level of activities and internationalization, they realized that the process could not stop now. The competition in electric power generation was heating up in Brazil, in Colombia, and in other target markets for Enersis. The possible entry of foreign power providers was very real, and even in Chile competition was possible from providers in Argentina and Brazil. The distribution business was less subject to market entry, since all countries in the region had nonoverlapping power grids, and thus, new entrants would have to build an entire infrastructure to compete. Nevertheless, even in distribution Enersis wanted to compete with other firms to buy privatizing companies in South America, and the bidding was often cutthroat. Mr. Ihnen and other Enersis top managers began to wonder if the process that they had begun was really sustainable.

In addition to the competitive pressures, Enersis felt constrained by the government of Chile, which was very concerned about the monopoly power held by the company. With Enersis 47 percent share in electric power generation and 45 percent share of electricity distribution in Chile, this was a very real concern. Thus far, Enersis had avoided any anti-trust violations, but the risk of becoming subject to a complicated investigation was significant.

II. BACKGROUND ON ENERSIS

Enersis is the Chilean energy company that was formed from the dismantling of the Compañia Chilena de Electricidad in 1981. In that year three new companies were formed, including the Compañia Chilena de Generacion de Electricidad, Chilgener; the Compañia Chilena Metropolitana de Distribucion Electrica, Chilectra; and the Compañia de Electricidad de la Quinta Region, Chilquinta. These new companies were than privatized in 1987 in separate auctions.

The new owners of Chilectra included Chilean pension funds, company employees, institutional investors, and thousands of small shareholders. In 1988 the company changed its name to Enersis, which was structured to operate as a holding company. The principal operating subsidiary of Enersis was and is Chilectra, which is the main electricity distribution company in Santiago, the capital of Chile.

Soon after the privatization, Enersis began to move aggressively into a diversification program, mainly in other electricity-related activities. A major shareholding in Endesa, the largest electric power generating company in Chile, was taken in 1990. Today Enersis owns 25 percent of Endesa, and is the largest single shareholder. A computer equipment and services subsidiary, Synapsis, was established to provide these services to the Enersis group. Manso de Velasco, a real estate and construction company, was acquired to be the main vehicle for buying land and building facilities for both Endesa and Chilectra throughout the country. The company's organization chart appears in Exhibit 2 below. The various operating companies are described in the next section.

Enersis in 1997 has become the largest privately-owned electric power generation and distribution company in Latin America. The company has operations that it manages in Chile, Argentina, Brazil, Colombia, and Peru. While focused principally on the electric power sector, Enersis is also active in real estate ventures through its subsidiary, Manso de Velasco.

To finance its growth, Enersis sold shares in the Chilean stock exchange, borrowed domestically and internationally, and sold ADRs in the US market, bringing its total financial structure in 1996 to 75 percent equity/25 percent debt, and a total asset value of $US 9.736 billion—December 1996. The distribution of shareholdings is shown in Exhibit 3.

III. OPERATING COMPANIES AND AFFILIATES

The initial business of Enersis, and still its single largest activity, is electricity distribution in the Santiago region of Chile through the operating company ***Chilectra***. Chilectra Metropolitana was created in 1981 as part of the dismantling of the Compañia Chilena de Electricidad. In 1985, the company was placed into a privatization process, which resulted in Chilectra being 100 percent privately owned by 1987. The name of the overall company, as previously noted, was changed to Enersis in 1988, and Chilectra became its main distribution subsidiary.

Chilectra today is owned 74 percent by Enersis and the rest by individual and institutional shareholders through the Chilean stock exchange. Exhibit 4 shows the distribution of ownership of Chilectra, and demonstrates that this affiliate of Enersis has its own international capital structure, with ADRs issued in New York and a broad base of ownership among pension funds, foreign investment funds, and individual shareholders.

Chilectra purchases most of its electric power from domestic generating companies, led by Endesa (which also belongs to Enersis). Endesa provided 30.1 percent of Chilectra's electricity in 1997, followed by Chilgener with 24.1 percent, Pehuenche with 16.9 percent, Pangue with 14 percent, Colbun with 10.6 percent, and others with 4.3 percent. This portfolio of energy sources is expected to shift with the arrival of imported natural gas from Argentina. The natural gas will replace some of the Chilean system's use of coal for thermoelectric power generation.

Rio Maipo

Rio Maipo is Enersis' second largest distribution system in Chile. This company was created from a division of Chilectra, with the goal of serving the Maipo Valley region. After sale of shares on the stock exchange, Enersis maintains 85 percent ownership of Rio Maipo.

Rio Maipo had approximately 255,000 customers at year end 1997 and sold about 955 GWh of power during the year.

Edesur (Argentina)

Electricidad del Sur (Edesur) is the power distribution company for the southern half of the city of Buenos Aires, Argentina. Initially, in 1992, Enersis purchased 20 percent of the shares of Edesur in the privatization process. In 1995 Enersis purchased another 39 percent of Edesur, such that today Enersis holds 59 percent of the outstanding shares. As with the other distribution and generation companies, Enersis holds a majority of seats on the board of directors of Edesur, and thus is assured management control of the firm.

In 1997 Edesur had approximately 2,042,000 customers in the Buenos Aires region, producing revenues of about $US 66.9 million for the year. Edesur distributed 11,160 GWh of power during the year.

Edelnor (Peru)

In 1994 Enersis bought 33 percent of the Peruvian firm, Empresa de Distribucion Electrica del Norte, Edelnor, in a public auction. This investment gave Enersis control of the firm and the right to place a majority of directors on Edelnor's board.

2 | Enersis

Electricity Distribution
- Chilectra 74%
- Rio Maipo 85%
- Edesur (Argentina) 58%
- Edelnor (Peru) 33%
- Codensa (Colombia) 22%
- CREJ (Brazil) 42%
- Coelce (Brazil) 21.43%

Electric Power Generation
- Endesa 25.3%
  - ARGENTINA: Costanera – Central Buenos Aires – El Chocon
  - CHILE: Pehuenche – Pangue – Celta – Transelec (Transmission) – San Isidro – Pacific
  - COLOMBIA: Betania – Emgesa
  - PERU: Edegel
  - BRAZIL: Cachoeira Dorada
  - Infra-Estructura 2000 – Tunel El Melon – Autopista Del Sol – Ingendesa
  - Electrogas – Gas Atacama – Gasoducto Tal Tal

Related Services
- Manso De Velasco 100%
  - Elenet (Argentina)
- Synapsis 100%
- Diprel 100%
- Aquas Cordillera 100%

EXHIBIT 3 | Ownership of Enersis, December 1997

Shareholder	Number of Shareholders	Number of Shares	%
Pension Funds	13	2,164,892,601	31.84
Employee Companies	5	1,981,587,840	29.16
ADRs	1	1,132,239,300	16.65
Foreign Equity Funds	19	150,909,038	2.20
Other Shareholders	13,153	1,370,371,221	20.15
Total	13,191	6,800,000,000	100.00

Source: Enersis Annual Report, 1997.

EXHIBIT 4 |

Main Shareholders	% Dec. 97
Enersis S.A.	74.12
Morgan G.T.C. (A.D.S.)	11.35
Deposito Central de Valores (Dcv)	3.44
Stockbrokers, Insurance Companies, Mutual Funds	2.66
Foreign Funds	2.41
Others	6.02
Total Shares (11,051 Shareholders)	100.00

Source: Enersis Annual Report, 1997.

Distribution of Ownership in Chilectra S. A.

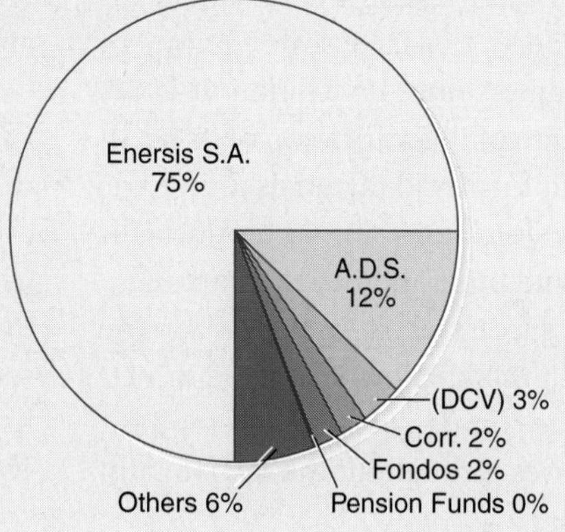

Edelnor served about 805,000 customers in the northern district of Lima in 1997 and sold 3,256 GWh of electricity during the year.

Aguas Cordillera

This company is the main provider of drinking water and also of wastewater treatment in several districts of Santiago, Chile. Aguas Cordillera produces and distributes drinking water, and collects and disposes of wastewater, for a population of 310,000 people in the communities of Lo Barnechea, Vitacura, and part of Las Condes.

Compañia Electrica de Rio de Janeiro (CERJ-Brasil)

This company was acquired in 1996, and it distributes electricity through the state of Rio de Janeiro in Brazil. CERJ had 4.4 million customers at the end of 1997. During 1997, after one year under the management of Enersis, CERJ sold 6,424 GWh of electric power, 12 percent more than in the previous year. Energy losses were reduced by 4 percentage points, remaining at 25.3 percent at year end 1997. CERJ had 1,340,573 clients at the end of the year, growth of 10.1 percent over the previous year.

Distribuidora de Productos Electricos SA (Diprel)

The main business of Diprel is distribution and marketing of materials, products, and large-scale equipment to electric power companies. Since its creation in 1989, Diprel has followed a path of diversification of its products. In addition to equipment and materials for electric companies, Diprel now distributes similar products for construction, mining, and other industrial companies.

Dipres has been successful in penetrating the Chilean market through establishment of a major network of sales offices. The company is also developing a network of representatives throughout the rest of Latin America.

Condensa (Colombia)

Codensa distributes electricity to 1,536,035 clients in the city of Bogota; this constitutes about 24 percent of the entire country. The volume of power sold during 1997 was 7, 929 GWh, with an energy loss of 23.8 percent.

Central Hidroelectica de Betania (Colombia)

This was Enersis' first investment in Columbia, in 1996. Betania has an installed capacity of 540 MW, and in 1997 generated 2,070 GWh.

Emgesa (Colombia)

Emgesa is the largest electric power generating company in Colombia. It has eight generating plants with a total of 2,458 MW of capacity. Emgesa produced 11,200 GWh of power during 1997.

Endesa (Chile)

The Empresa Nacional de Electricidad, S. A. ***Endesa***, is the main electric power generating company in Chile. The government sold partial ownership to the private sector in 1989, when Enersis bought a 5 percent interest. Subsequently, additional share purchases have given Enersis a 25.3 percent holding in Endesa by 1995, and the right to place a majority of directors on Endesa's board. Endesa is now reported as a consolidated affiliate of Enersis on the holding company's books.

Endesa's main business is the generation of electric power, which it then transmits mainly through the Central Interconnected System (SIC). In addition, Endesa participates in the generating system in the northern part of the country as a part owner and operator of the Interconnected System of Norte Grande (SING). Exhibit 5 describes the production of electricity in Chile in 1996 and Endesa's role in it.

An interesting twist to Endesa's leadership in the Chilean power generation market is that it utilizes mainly hydroelectric power sources (i.e., rivers coming down from the Andes mountains). In the mid-1990s, Chile experienced a prolonged drought, which reduced the generating capacity of the hydroelectric plants and caused the country to become more dependent on thermoelectric power (from coal, oil, or natural gas). This drought caused Endesa to lose market share, since competitors were more able to deliver thermoelectric power during this time. Paradoxically, Endesa enjoys a major cost advantage when weather conditions are normal, since hydro power costs approximately one-tenth as much as thermo power to generate.

Endesa made its first foreign investment in Argentina in 1992, where it purchased the power plant,

EXHIBIT 5 | Installed Electric Power Capacity in Chile

	CAPACITY (MW)				PRODUCTION (GWH)		
	Endesa	Total	% Endesa		Endesa	Total	%
SIC	2,641	4,594	57.5	SIC	12,868	22,421	57.4
SING	97	1,131	8.6	SING	30	5,545	0.5
Total	2,738	5,725	47.8	Total	12,898	27,996	46.1

Source: Endesa Annual Report, 1996.

Central Costanera. With three plants operating in 1996, Endesa produced 9,513 GWh of electricity, constituting about 16 percent of total Argentine production.

In 1995 Endesa invested in Peru, buying 60 percent of the Empresa de Generacion Electrica de Lima, Edegel. Edegel has installed capacity of 689 MW of electricity, representing about 24 percent of total installed capacity in Peru. In 1995 Edegel produced about 2,650 GWh of electricity.

Ingenieria e Inmobiliaria Manso de Velasco

One of the key activities in generating and distributing electric power is the construction of power plants, transmission lines, and connections to users. While plant construction is contracted out to major construction firms, the engineering and construction of electric distribution lines and links was originally carried out within Chilectra. This last activity in 1988 was placed into the wholly-owned subsidiary, Manso de Velasco.

Manso de Velasco continues to be the engineering and construction firm used by Chilectra for constructing electricity distribution facilities. In addition, Manso de Velasco has contracted to offer services to a wide range of outside users, such as constructing lighting and power facilities for the Santiago metro system and also installing lighting for public parks and gardens in the city.

Synapsis

Enersis has extensive activity in information technology to operate its power generation and distribution businesses. This activity has been placed into the subsidiary Synapsis, which in addition sells information technology services to outside clients.

Financial statements for Enersis and each of the major subsidiaries are presented in the Appendix.

IV. THE CHILEAN CONTEXT

Chile is one of the most industrialized countries in Latin America. With a per capita income of over $US 3,000 per year, Chile ranks at the top of the Latin American region. Its population is highly educated, with adult illiteracy at just 5 percent of the population. The country has embraced a free-market capitalist economic model since the overthrow of the Marxist regime of Salvador Allende in 1973. Initially under the military regime of Augusto Pinochet, Chile began to liberalize its economy long before this policy framework became popular in the region. The 'Chicago Boys,' trained by the University of Chicago free-market economists such as Arnold Harberger and Milton Friedman, followed a highly successful set of policies to reduce barriers to competition and to stimulate investment. Tariffs were gradually lowered to a uniform 10 percent ad valorem by 1976, the least restrictive in Latin America. The door was opened to foreign direct investment in 1976, when Chile withdrew from the protectionist Andean Pact integration group and implemented its own liberal foreign investment regime.

The results of this economic opening in the 1970s were clearly very positive. To a certain extent they were assisted unintentionally by the rise in raw-materials prices that accompanied the oil crises. Chile's main export product has long been copper, and copper prices rose dramatically in the late 1970s. This alone produced solid economic growth in the country during those years. When oil and other raw-materials prices dropped in the early 1980s, and when the foreign debt crisis hit the region in 1982, Chile unfortunately was dragged down as well, and it took several years until the economy rebounded. In comparison with other Latin American countries, however, Chile did pull out of the crisis more rapidly. By 1986 GDP was growing by a positive 6½ percent per year, and this continued through the rest of the decade. In the early 1990s Chile's economy remained near the top of the Latin American list, with an average growth rate of 7.4 percent per year.

Chile's government began in the 1970s a process of *privatization*, or sell-off of state-owned companies, that has been followed in various degrees throughout the rest of Latin America in the late 1980s and 1990s. At a time when the economic model of import-substituting industrialization was widely followed in the region, Chile turned its back to that view and aggressively began a process of open markets and export-led growth. Since the government participated in the economy as owner of well over half of industry, a major step to opening markets was the denationalization of companies. This was begun with the sale of Compañía de Cervecerías Unidas (beer), Cemento Melón (cement), and Celulosa Arauco (paper) in the late 1970s, and with subsequent sales of electric power, telephone, airline, and other government-owned businesses in the 1980s.

In the 1990s the Chilean model used the government as regulator and overseer of the economy, much as in the industrial countries of Europe and North America—with a few key exceptions, such as the national copper company, Codelco, which still remains in state hands.

Interestingly, there has been a very considerable consensus in Chile on the free-market economic policies that have been followed. This policy framework was closely associated with the Pinochet military regime, which, as any such government, was criticized for being authoritarian. Without debating that issue, it can be concluded that the Pinochet regime did indeed strongly support the open-market policy framework, and consistently maintained it through economic booms and recessions. When Pinochet stepped down as President in 1988, the elected government of Patricio Alwyn continued the economic policy framework, as have subsequent Chilean governments. The result was an economic performance (e.g., growth, inflation, balance of payments) superior to all other countries in Latin America from 1975–1995.

V. RECENT HISTORY OF CHILE'S ELECTRICITY SECTOR

The electric power sector in Chile is divided into three stages: generation, transmission, and distribution. The generation sector consists of companies that generate electricity from hydroelectric and thermal electric sources and sell their production to distribution companies, other regulated and unregulated customers, and other generation companies. The transmission sector consists of companies that transmit high-voltage electricity from the generating companies. These companies are all subsidiaries of the main generation and distribution companies. Distribution companies purchase electricity from generating companies at the nodes of the countrywide system, typically at low voltage (23 kV or less), and then distribute it for sale to the public. Each of these segments is privately owned, with government regulation on pricing and oversight on service quality. Exhibit 6 describes the system.

The national electricity industry is divided into two large geographic grids, the Central Interconnected System (SIC) and the Interconnected System of Norte Grande (SING). In addition there are several other systems, including systems owned and operated by individual industrial companies (e.g., copper companies) for their own use, typically in remote areas.

As discussed above, Endesa dominates power generation in Chile, with approximately a 50 percent market share. Endesa owns and operates 16 power plants connected to the SIC and another three power plants connected to the SING.

At the level of distribution, there are eight major companies and several smaller ones. Their characteristics are described in Exhibit 7.

Chilectra and Rio Maipo are both part of the SIC network, which provides power to Santiago and to about 90 percent of Chile's total population.

Legal Framework

Chile's electricity law essentially allows private ownership of all stages of electric power production and distribution, with public-sector regulation and price

EXHIBIT 6 | Stages in the Electric Power System

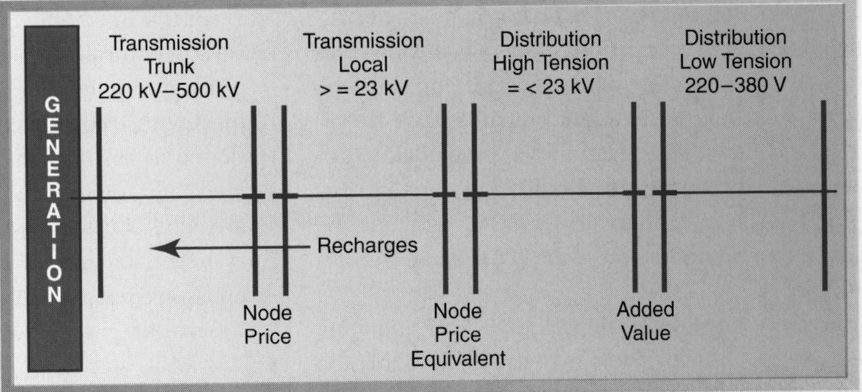

EXHIBIT 7 | Distribution of Electricity in Chile by Company

Company	Number of Customers	%	Sales GWh	%
Chilectra (ENERSIS)	1,099	36	6,676	50
CGE	498	16	1,918	15
Chilquinta	335	11	1,122	9
Rio Maipo (ENERSIS)	230	7	763	6
Saesa (COPEC)	319	10	939	7
Emec	151	5	426	3
Frontel (COPEC)	149	5	336	3
Emel	130	4	169	1
Others	170	6	759	6
Total	3,081	100	13,108	100

Source: Comision Nacional de Energia, 1995.

controls. The National Electricity Commission (CNE) sets prices and plans expansion of the system. The SEF sets and enforces technical standards for the system. And finally, the Ministry of Economy has final authority over electricity prices, and it regulates the granting of concessions to electric generation, transmission, and distribution companies.

Probably one of the key continuing problems faced by Enersis was the complex system of price controls placed on the electricity sector. Negotiation of prices of power generation for sales to distributors and of power distribution for sale to final customers takes place on a four-year cycle, and in general prices fall behind costs by the end of each cycle. Endesa and Chilectra regularly seek to keep their output prices in a profitable range, but the negotiation process often is drawn out and leads to periods of very low profit.

The electricity law seeks to provide objective criteria for electricity pricing and resource allocation. The regulatory system is designed to provide a competitive rate of return on investments in order to stimulate private investment, while ensuring electricity to all who request it. Under the law, companies engaged in electric power generation must coordinate their activities through the association of power suppliers, CDEC (Centro de Despacho Economico de Carga), for either the SIC or the

SING, to minimize the operating costs of the electric system. Generation companies meet their contractual sales requirements with power that they either generate themselves or buy or on the open market. Because Endesa's production in the SIC is primarily hydroelectric, its marginal cost of production is generally the lowest in the system, and therefore Endesa generates most of the power it sells there. Generation companies have to balance their contractual obligations with their delivery of power by buying any needed electricity at the spot market price, which is set hourly by the CDEC based on the marginal cost of production of the last generation facility utilized.

The main purpose of the two CDECs in operating the power assignment system is to ensure that only the most efficiently-produced electricity reaches customers. The CDECs also seek to ensure that every generation company has enough installed capacity to produce the electricity needed by its customers.

Sales of electric power may be made through short-term or long-term contracts, or between generation companies, or the spot market. Generation companies may also contract to deliver power among themselves at negotiated prices. Generation companies are free to determine whether and with whom to contact, the duration of contracts, and the amount of electricity to be sold.

Sales of electricity to distribution companies for resale to regulated customers (customers with demand for capacity less than equal to 2 megawatts) must be made at the node prices then in effect at the relevant locations, or nodes, on the interconnected system. Two node prices are paid by distribution companies: node prices for capacity and node prices for energy consumption. Node prices for capacity are calculated based on the annual cost of installing a new diesel fuel gas turbine generation facility. Node prices for energy are calculated based on the projected short-term marginal cost of satisfying the demand for energy at a given point in the interconnected system, quarterly during the succeeding 48 months in the SIC and monthly during the succeeding 24 months in the SING. To calculate the marginal costs, a formula is used that takes into account 10-year projections of the principal variables in the cost of energy, such as water reservoir levels, fuel costs for thermoelectric power, maintenance, demand levels, etc.

A generation company may need to purchase or sell energy or capacity in the spot market at any time, depending on its contractual requirements in relation to the amount of electricity that it is able to produce. These purchases and sales are transacted at the 'spot marginal cost' of the interconnected system, which is the marginal cost of the last generation facility to be dispatched.

Energy supply prices are unregulated for final customers with a connected capacity greater than 2 MW (referred to as "large customers"), for temporary customers, and for customers that have special quality requirements. Customers not subject to regulated prices may negotiate prices freely with distribution and/or generation companies. All other customers are subject to the maximum prices established by the tariffs.

As far as electric power **distribution** is concerned, tariffs are established to allow distribution companies to recover their costs of operation, including allowed losses, and a return on investment. The operational costs include selling, general and administrative costs of distribution; maintenance and operating costs of distribution assets; cost of energy and capacity losses; and expected return on investment of 10 percent per year in real terms, including the cost of renewing all the facilities and physical assets used to provide the distribution services, including interest costs, intangible assets and working capital. The various costs are based on an average of those incurred by electricity distribution companies operating in Chile. Thus, more efficient companies may earn more than 10 percent returns, and less efficient ones less.

Key Competitors in Chile

The main competitor in Chile is Chilgener. Chilgener is a major competitor in power generation, with thermoelectric plants in Santiago, Valparaiso, and Copaipo. In addition, Chilgener owns several electricity distribution companies operating in both the central and the northern power grids. Chilgener consistently bids for electric power projects in Chile and elsewhere in Latin America (especially Argentina) against Chilectra and Endesa. In a highly publicized recent duel for construction of a natural gas-pipeline between Argentina and Chile, a consortium led by Chilgener beat Enersis and gained a major new power source. Other smaller electric companies such as Chilquinta also compete domestically and abroad with Enersis.

Separate from the two major electric distribution grids, the electric companies serve 'non-regulated clients,' which are large-volume electricity users that are permitted to buy electricity directly from generating companies. The nonregulated clients are customers that use more than 2 megawatt[2] hours of power—typically large industrial companies such as copper mines.

VI. GLOBAL STRATEGY AT ENERSIS

According to company documents, "The company's business strategy is to use its accumulated utility experience and expertise to improve the profitability of its existing electric distribution and generation businesses in Chile, Argentina, Peru, Brazil, and Colombia, and to enhance the value of other businesses it may acquire in Latin America. The company believes it has proven expertise in managing privatized utilities, including experience in reducing energy losses of distribution businesses, constructing and operating generation facilities, implementing proprietary billing and accounts receivable management systems, improving labor relations, increasing work force productivity, streamlining information systems, and operating under tariff and regulatory frameworks that reward efficient operations."

Following this broad statement in 1995, Enersis has continued to expand its activities in Latin America with the purchase of controlling interest in the Rio de Janeiro power distribution company, CERJ, and the Colombian power generation company, Betania. In addition the company has diversified more widely in Chile, with the purchase of the water utility Lo Castillo in Santiago in 1996 and various real-estate activities through the Endesa subsidiary, Infraestructura 2000.

VII. STRATEGIC ALLIANCES OF ENERSIS

Enersis has used strategic alliances frequency in its short history. When building the information systems part of its business, Enersis formed Synapsis as a joint venture with Unisys Corporation of the United States. After three years of operation, Enersis bought the partner's interest and now runs Synapsis as a wholly owned subsidiary.

In overseas ventures Enersis has worked exclusively with local partners in each country, as well as with other foreign investors on some occasions. For its initial foray into Argentina, a joint venture (Distrilec) was formed with Perez Companq (a large Argentine conglomerate) and PSI (from the US) to own the power distribution company, Edesur. Likewise, when entering Peru to buy the power generation company, Edelnor, the company formed a joint venture with Endesa of Spain, Compañia Peruana de Electricidad, and Banco del Credito del Peru. Subsequently, when bidding for and winning the ownership of CERJ in Brazil, Enersis formed a joint venture with Endesa (Spain) and Electricidad de Portugal. No Brazilian partner participated in the consortium with Enersis on this occasion, but the consortium itself has Electrobras as a local partner in the total shareholding of CERJ. For capital and technology resources, Enersis has found the Spanish electric company Endesa to be a valuable partner in these and other projects.

As a policy, Enersis management asserts that strategic alliance partners will continue to be sought in each foreign venture undertaken, to assure knowledge of the local market and treatment as a local (at least partly local) company. The bias against foreign companies is particularly strong in Enersis' situation, for example because Argentine companies and government agencies often view Chilean firms smaller, less capable competitors, and because Peruvian companies and government agencies often view Chilean firms as antagonists, given the history of conflicts between the two countries. To defuse some of this opposition, in addition to gaining local market knowledge, Enersis will continue to work with local partners in future Latin American ventures.

Even as Enersis continues to actively use strategic alliances in its international ventures, the company maintains a clear policy of seeking to exert the highest possible degree of managerial influence in the business undertaken. It always follows an intention of long-term ownership, and generally obtains majority control of the board of directors (i.e., operational control) of affiliates.

VIII. DIVERSIFICATION STRATEGY

Enersis management has defined the strategy of the firm to be focused on the electric power industry and on related activities. These related activities began with the establishment of a subsidiary for information technology and one for real estate and construction activities. Since that time, additional activities have largely fallen into the categories of electric power generation and distribution outside of Chile and diversification into other sectors inside Chile. In 1996 the water company, Lo Castillo, was purchased. This move was justified as a step into additional infrastructure that accompanies electric power. In fact much of the distribution and physical facilities' construction is quite similar between the two businesses, so the diversification may be reasonably related to the core business after all.

Enersis, through Manso de Velasco, has spread its activities far from electric power, investing in construction of apartment buildings in Viña del Mar, a highway tunnel connecting Santiago with the coast (El Melón), and other ventures that have much to do with real estate and construction but virtually nothing to do with electricity other than relating to infrastructure development. While the real-estate/infrastructure ventures do move the company away from power generation, these activities constitute well under 10 percent of the total business, and the intention is to keep this type of diversification limited to a small percentage of total Enersis activity.

IX. THE CHALLENGE OF OPERATING MULTINATIONALLY

Enersis has been involved in business outside of Chile since 1992. This experience has not been without some missteps. For example, when expanding into Argentina, Enersis faced the inability to reduce staffing at the Edesur electricity distribution company, due to local labor rules. As well, there was a relatively low level of motivation of the labor force there, due to a history of state ownership of the electricity sector and the lack of performance-related incentives for the workers. It took Enersis managers more than two years to carry out the needed staffing reductions and to install modern performance measures and incentives.

As the Latin American region became more attractive for foreign investment during the 1990s, electric power utilities became important targets for foreign companies in the region. Once the threat of the external debt crisis had been extinguished, by about 1991, interest began to pick up. At the beginning of the decade, Enersis had very few competitors when it bid for power companies that were being privatized in Argentina, Peru, and Brazil. By the middle of the decade, American companies such as Houston Energy, AES, Duke Power, and others had entered the bidding in Brazil, Mexico, and elsewhere. At the same time European power companies such as Iberdrola (Spain), Éléctricité de France, ENE (Italy), and Electricidad de Portugal also entered the fray.

Enersis found that the most useful strategy for dealing with the foreign competition, and being a foreign company itself outside of Chile, was to ally with a local power company in the target market and with one or more industrial-country companies. This package of Enersis management skills, local knowledge held by the local partner, and capital plus technology contributed by the U.S. or European partner, turned out to be a winning combination in bids for Edelnor in Peru, CERJ in Brazil, and Betania in Colombia.

A continuing problem for Enersis in overseas business is the fact that most electric power business remains in government hands throughout Latin America. This problem extends as well to the generation of electricity, where, for example, Argentine government-owned companies operate nuclear power plants that compete with Endesa to supply power to the distribution networks.

ENDNOTES

1. This project is actually fairly complex, including the construction of a natural-gas pipeline across the Andes from Salta in Argentina to Mejillones in northern Chile, building a power plant in Mejillones, and connecting it to the national power grid (SING) at Atacama. Enersis is co-owner of both the pipeline and the power plant, along with partner CMS. CMS operates the gas pipeline, and Enersis operates the power plant which is connected to both the SIC and SING distribution networks.
2. See, for example, "El Precio de una Derrota," *Que Pasa*, July 22, 1995, pp. 52–56.

APPENDIX A. ENERSIS S. A. AND SUBSIDIARIES

Consolidated Statements of Income
Years Ended December 31, 1997 and 1996 (Expressed in Thousands of Chilean Pesos—M$)

	1997	1996
Operating Results		
Revenue from Operations	1,334,976,829	1,233,788,841
Cost of Operations	(857,443,897)	(763,248,909)
Gross Profit	477,532,932	470,539,932
Administrative and Selling Expenses	(115,128,805)	(124,625,967)
Net Operating Income	362,404,127	345,913,965
Other Income (Deductions)		
Interest Income	37,867,295	31,892,890
Equity in Income of Related Companies	31,999,177	17,610,537
Other Income	59,736,909	72,550,465
Equity in Loss of Related Companies	(987)	(9)
Amortization—Goodwill	(35,006,194)	(24,132,148)
Financial Expenses	(158,395,649)	(108,835,106)
Other Expenses	(43,947,488)	(29,052,406)
Monetary Correction	41,053,618	24,285,123
Non-Operating Income	(66,693,319)	(15,780,654)
Income Before Income Taxes and Minority Interest	295,710,808	330,133,311
Income Taxes	(57,002,970)	(40,701,164)
Income Before Minority Interest	238,707,838	289,432,147
Minority Interest	(157,945,493)	(179,094,920)
	80,762,345	110,337,227
Amortization—Negative Goodwill	22,753,925	2,307,295
Net Income	103,516,270	112,644,522
Liabilities and Stockholders' Equity Current Liabilities		
Due to Banks and Financial Institutions—Short-Term	56,328,049	79,321,790
Due to Banks and Financial Institutions—Current Installments	56,185,075	81,251,887
Bond Issues	39,622,264	52,059,672
Long-Term Obligation–Current Installment	6,097,099	9,682,682
Dividends Payable	18,714,200	48,621,825
Accounts Payable	80,828,450	62,828,616
Notes Payable	359,140	794,334
Miscellaneous Payables	43,054,841	44,174,656
Notes and Accounts Payable to Related Companies	7,519,838	5,337,297
Provisions	39,198,551	33,500,327
Withholdings	58,220,021	32,738,280
Deferred Income	6,253,329	19,733,523
Deferred Taxes	167,726	182,949
Other Current Liabilities	19,571,116	19,602,614
Total Current Liabilities	432,119,719	489,930,452
Long-Term Liabilities		
Due to Banks and Financial Institutions	1,707,736,423	969,611,840
Bond Issues	963,287,650	611,034,148
Notes Payable	28,725,949	24,893,286
Miscellaneous Payables	7,712,680	3,784,433
Provisions	19,301,360	8,558,077
Other Long-Term Liabilities	43,157,727	43,455,860
Total Long-Term Liabilities	2,769,921,789	1,661,327,644
Minority Interest	2,272,352,449	1,558,254,355

(continues)

APPENDIX A. ENERSIS S. A. AND SUBSIDIARIES *(Contuinued)*

Consolidated Statements of Income
Years Ended December 31, 1997 and 1996 (Expressed in Thousands of Chilean Pesos—M$)

	1997	1996
Stockholders' Equity		
Paid-In Capital	372,505,262	372,505,262
Premium on Sale of Own Shares	22,600,111	22,600,111
Other Reserves	21,594,889	22,163,444
Retained Earnings:		
Prior Years	232,469,742	196,759,783
Net Income for the Year	103,516,270	112,644,522
Interim Dividends	(46,665,681)	(43,883,980)
Total Retained Earnings	289,320,331	265,520,325
Total Stockholders' Equity	706,020,593	682,789,142
Total Liabilities and Stockholders' Equity	6,180,414,550	4,392,201,593

Source: Enersis Annual Report, 1997.

APPENDIX B. OWNERSHIP OF ENERSIS AS OF 12/31/97

SHAREHOLDER	NUMBER OF SHAREHOLDERS	NUMBER OF SHARES	%
ENDESA Spain	5	1,981,587,840	29.16
Pension Funds	13	2,164,892,601	31.84
ADRs (Citibank as Depository Bank)	1	1,132,239,300	16.65
Foreign Equity Funds	19	150,909,038	2.20
Stockbrokers, Mutual Funds, and Insurance Companies	97	364,098,443	5.35
Other Shareholders	12,665	1,006,272,778	14.80
Total	12,800	6,800,000,000	100.00

As of December 31, 1997, Enersis S. A. was owned by 12,800 shareholders of record. The twelve largest shareholders of the company were as follows:

NAME OF SHAREHOLDER	NUMBER OF SHARES	%
Citibank N. A. (Depository Bank)	1,132,239,300	16.65
A. F. P. Provida S. A.	424,999,771	6.25
Compañia de Inversiones Luz y Fuerza S. A.	445,061,585	6.55
Compañia de Inversiones Chispa dos S. A.	445,061,585	6.55
A. F. P. Habitat S. A.	439,578,489	6.46
Compañia de Inversiones Los Almendros S. A.	445,061,585	6.55
Compañia de Inversiones Chispa Uno S. A.	445,061,585	6.55
A. F. P. Santa Maria S. A.	297,490,170	4.37
A. F. P. Proteccion S. A.	224,955,672	3.31
A. F. P. Cuprum S. A.	264,364,775	3.89
Endesa Desarollo S. A.	201,341,500	2.96
Compañia de Inversiones Luz S. A.	194,412,126	2.86
Subtotal (12)	4,959,628,143	72.95
Other Shareholders (12,788)	1,840,371,857	27.05
Total Shareholders (12,800)	6,800,000,000	100,00

Source: Enersis Annual Report, 1997.

APPENDIX C. ENERSIS SUBSIDIARIES

Compared Balance Sheets for the Years Ended 1996 & 1997
Consolidated Financial Statements (in th ch$)

Company	Chilectra S. A.		Compañia Électrica Del Rio Maipo S. A.		Ingenieria e Inmobiliaria Manso de Velasco S. A.	
	1996	1997	1996	1997	1996	1997
Assets						
Current Assets	95,932,965	113,655,826	6,905,251	5,103,062	80,165,281	57,556,408
Fixed Assets	164,847,753	178,162,696	23,685,481	26,250,384	59,234,937	61,332,698
Other Assets	379,964,688	437,704,746	744,612	633,057	68,835,658	71,321,779
Total Assets	640,745,406	729,523,268	31,335,344	3,198,650	208,235,876	190,220,885
Liabilities						
Short-Term Liabilities	58,650,663	82,328,872	7,339,729	6,480,372	100,203,749	83,691,072
Long-Term Liabilities	306,420,814	349,552,396	7,780,720	8,172,423	13,411,853	8,332,892
Minority Interest	123,453,124	12,323,641	0	0	16,522,817	18,695,577
Equity and Reserves	223,769,192	231,755,351	14,156,363	15,223,794	10,287,095	10,094,723
Subsidiary's Organization Cost	0	0	0	0	(104,700)	(155,125)
Accumulated Profits/Losses	11,628,679	23,463,597	906,555	908,673	57,375,144	60,480,194
Net Income	75,613,700	81,219,326	7,679,842	8,008,277	19,208,102	19,386
Less Interim Dividends	(47,682,766)	(51,119,915)	(6,527,865)	(6,807,036)	(8,671,184)	638
Total Liabilities and Equity	640,745,406	729,523,268	31,335,344	31,986,503	208,235,876	(10,304,986)

Compared Income Statements for Years Ended 1996 & 1997

Company	Chilectra S. A.		Compañia Électrica Del Rio Maipo S. A.		Ingenieria e Inmobiliaria Manso de Velasco S. A.	
	1996	1997	1996	1997	1996	1997
Operating Income						
Operating Reserves	292,409,961	278,601,779	36,909,063	35,611,809	55,715,923	61,322,185
Operating Costs	(204,231,674)	(189,633,558)	(26,344,032)	(25,452,716)	(33,144,910)	(38,505,737)
Operating Margin	88,178,287	88,968,221	10,565,031	10,159,093	22,751,013	22,816,448
Administrative and Selling Expenses	(27,950,367)	(22,585,093)	(3,635,883)	(2,653,949)	(5,834,837)	(4,168,383)
Operating Income	60,227,920	66,433,128	6,929,148	7,505,144	16,736,176	18,648,065
Non-Operating Income						
Non-Operating Revenues	64,013,747	74,206,722	3,781,890	3,456,969	9,132,738	7,365,254
Non-Operating Costs	(35,929,075)	(49,392,093)	(1,935,881)	(1,933,976)	(8,493,689)	(8,404,216)
Monetary Adjustment	458,642	3,231,872	146,227	642,586	2,744,554	3,394,882
Non-Operating Income	28,543,314	28,046,501	2,092,236	1,865,579	3,383,603	2,355,920
Income Tax	(11,296,447)	(11,569,453)	(1,341,542)	(1,362,446)	(1,499,578)	(2,192,476)
Minority Interest	(1,861,087)	(1,690,850)	0	0	(1,320)	(22,037)
Negative Goodwill Amortization	0	0	0	0	58,922	597,166
Net Income	75,613,700	81,219,326	7,679,842	8,008,277	19,208,102	129,386,638

(continues)

APPENDIX C. ENERSIS SUBSIDIARIES *(Continued)*

Compared Balance Sheets for the Years Ended 1996 & 1997
Consolidated Financial Statements (in th ch$)

Company	Synapsis S. A.		Distribuidora de Productos Electricos S. A.		Enersis Argentina S. A.	
	1996	1997	1996	1997	1996	1997
Assets						
Current Assets	5,298,555	7,315,617	5,300,799	6,182,065	1,419	76,797
Fixed Assets	1,303,521	971,981	401,102	412,784	1,466	1,172
Other Assets	36,818	5,798	62,053	47,484	327	288
Total Assets	6,638,894	8,293,396	5,763,954	6,642,333	3,212	78,257
Liabilities						
Short-Term Liabilities	3,120,286	4,426,779	3,946,667	4,842,934	2,563	998
Long-Term Liabilities	97,082	60,452	129,139	106,039	0	0
Minority Interest	326	196	0	0	0	0
Equity and Reserves	3,519,754	3,519,754	1,374,800	1,374,800	65,987	69,561
Subsidiary's Organization Cost	0	0	0	0	0	0
Accumulated Profits/Losses	(1,236,720)	(98,554)	2,982	5,011	(62,432)	(65,338)
Net Income	1,138,166	2,060,079	2,043,231	2,088,050	(2,906)	5,082,808
Less Interim Dividends	0	(1,675,310)	(1,732,865)	(1,774,501)	0	(5,009,772)
Total Liabilities and Equity	6,638,894	8,293,396	5,763,954	6,642,333	3,212	78,257

Compared Income Statements for Years Ended 1996 & 1997

Company	Synapsis S. A.		Distribuidora de Productos Electricos S. A.		Enersis Argentina S. A.	
	1996	1997	1996	1997	1996	1997
Operating Income						
Operating Revenues	9,960,829	11,163,764	21,133,538	20,201,295	0	0
Operating Costs	(6,795,779)	(7,132,759)	(15,706,397)	(15,115,664)	0	0
Operating Margin	3,165,050	4,031,005	5,427,141	5,085,631	0	0
Administrative and Selling Expenses	(1,914,044)	(2,009,342)	(3,005,473)	(2,583,994)	(2,848)	(3,286)
Operating Income	1,251,006	2,021,663	2,421,668	2,501,637	(2,848)	(3,286)
Non-Operating Income						
Non-Operating Revenues	526,984	770,727	273,882	146,180	60	5,088,892
Non-Operating Costs	(316,216)	(169,111)	(192,207)	(226,786)	0	(4)
Monetary Adjustment	(95,182)	(199,020)	(48,717)	(14,779)	(118)	(2,794)
Non-Operating Income	105,586	402,596	32,958	(95,385)	(58)	5,086,094
Income Tax	(218,389)	(364,196)	(411,395)	(318,202)	0	0
Minority Interest	(37)	16	0	0	0	0
Negative Goodwill Amortization	0	0	0	0	0	0
Net Income	1,138,166	2,060,079	2,043,231	2,088,050	(2,906)	5,082,808

Source: Enersis Annual Report, 1997.

CASE 17

Internal Entrepreneurship at Ericsson:

Finding Opportunities and Mobilizing Talent

Ulf Mimer
Ericsson

Richard M. McErlean, Jr.
Els van Weering
International Institute for Management Development

In 1993, it was clear to Jan Uddenfeldt—vice president of research and development at Ericsson Radio Systems—that in the near future, Ericsson risked losing its leading edge in mobile telecommunications transmission systems. Ericsson's offering would soon become too expensive and not very competitive. Clients, the operators of mobile telephone systems, were going to ask for different and more flexible transmission products and services for their stations. With this in mind, Uddenfeldt initiated a project to find a solution for the future. Leader of this project would be Tsviatko Ganev. Some considered Ganev an "entrepreneur" who could get a new business going, yet others found him impossible to work with.

ERICSSON AT A GLANCE

Ericsson was founded in Sweden in 1876. Through its exceptional ability to adapt to the changing times, the company that originally started as a telegraph equipment repair shop had grown to become a world-leading supplier in telecommunications.

Since 1992, Ericsson's net sales have risen 356.75 percent from SEK 47,020 million to SEK 167,740 million in 1997. Income before taxes has jumped 1,387 percent, from SEK 1,241 million to SEK 17,218 million in the same time period. At year end 1997, Ericsson employed a total of 100,774 people worldwide.

In 1988, Ericsson produced advanced systems and products for wired and mobile telecom systems in private and public networks. In the field of mobile telephone systems, Ericsson had nearly 40 percent of the world market share. Present in more than 130 countries, Ericsson had developed the world's largest customer base in telecommunications, with telecom customers on all continents. Compared with competitors such as Nokia, Lucent, Siemens, Alcatel, and Motorola, Ericsson maintained the highest percentage of international sales.

To stay ahead of the competition, Ericsson invested 15 percent to 20 percent of sales in technical development and had more than 23,000 employees in 23 countries working in research and development.

Ericsson was divided into three major business areas: radio mobile systems, infocom systems and mobile phones, and terminals. Each of these business areas was supported by major local companies. (Refer to Exhibit 1 for a partial, simplified view of the Ericsson organizational structure.)

A NEW ERICSSON STRATEGIC PLAN PROPOSAL

At the beginning of 1994, Uddenfeldt initiated an Ericsson strategic plan (ESP) project to:

- Establish a deeper understanding in Business Area Radio of the problems related to the fixed transmission of the mobile cellular network.

This case was prepared as a basis for class discussion rather than to illustrate either effective or ineffective handling of a business situation.

Copyright © 1999 by **IMD**—International Institute for Management Development, Lausanne, Switzerland. All rights reserved. Not to be used or reproduced without written permission directly from **IMD**, Lausanne, Switzerland.

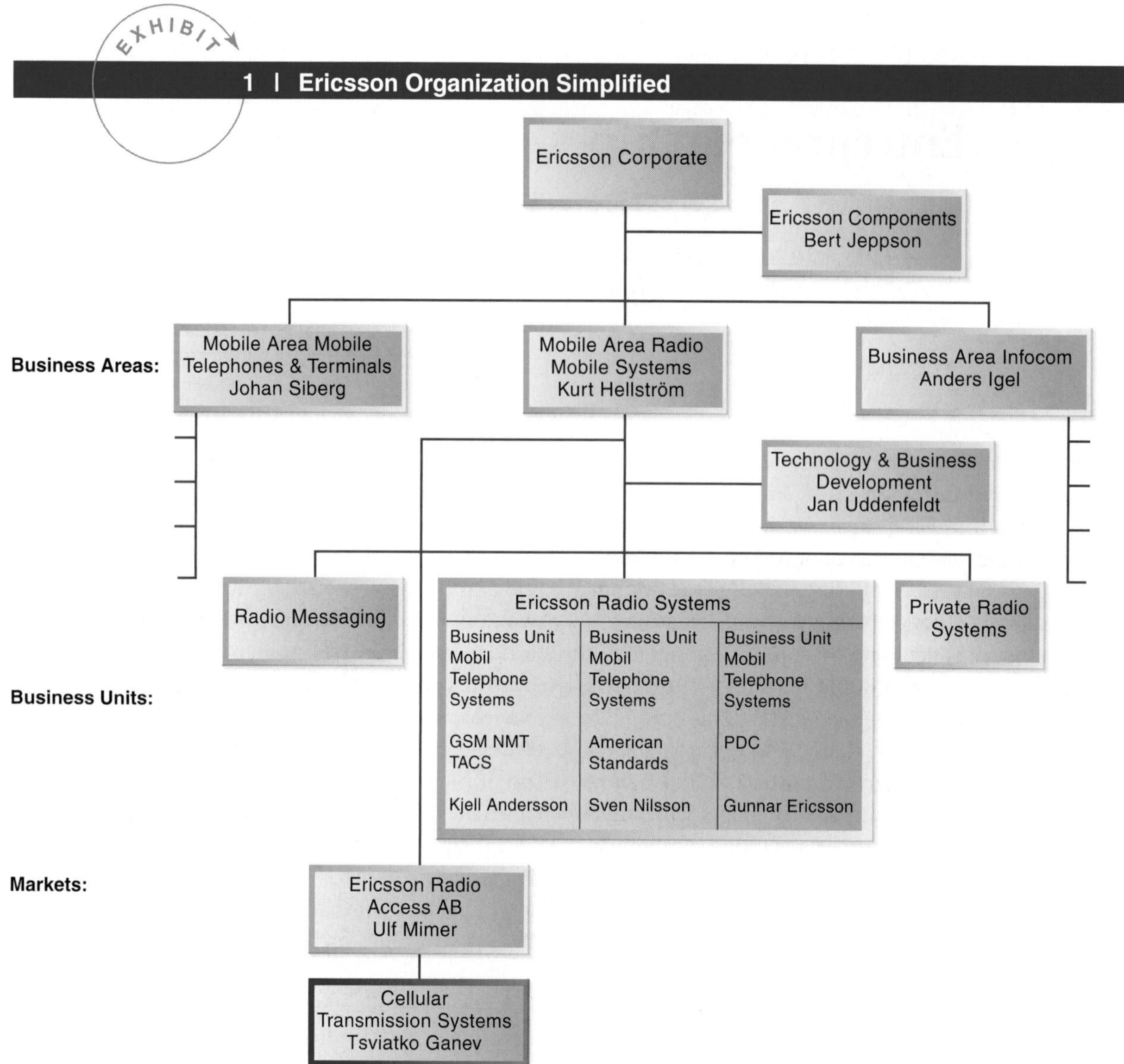

- Increase Business Area Radio's competence in this field.
- Suggest suitable actions.

Ganev, who had been recruited to Business Area Radio/R&D by Uddenfeldt during late 1993, was appointed project manager for the ESP project. The project work was performed in a "working group" of five experts, and the results were reported and discussed in a "steering group." The steering group consisted of Jan Uddenfeldt and the head of strategic business development and its role was to legitimize the project and to open doors where needed.

To support Ganev and the working group, a "reference group" consisting of people involved in infrastructure product development was appointed.

ASSESSING CUSTOMERS' NEEDS

The reference group established that the customers needed not only low-cost hardware, but also tools to manage the fixed transmission system most efficiently.

Not surprisingly, customers wanted to buy and operate the system for the lowest possible overall cost.

Ganev met with representatives from Bell South, Mannesman, PTT Ireland, One-2-One/Mercury, and Telia Mobitel to discuss the customers' needs and requirements regarding the fixed transmission part of the cellular network.

Historically, Ericsson's business in the transmission field had been weak. Different Ericsson units had tried to accommodate their Telecom customers' various transmission needs. This had created a number of similar products from different organizational units *inside* Ericsson.

In 1994, one common opinion among telecom operators was that Ericsson did not offer an efficient and cost-effective fixed network. Even though the Ericsson products had a lot of capacity—in the opinion of customers—they were not optimal for each country and/or each operator. Additionally, due to their high quality and large capacity, Ericsson's fixed transmission systems were expensive. What the operators needed were flexible hardware units with which they could build and manage their own networks.

THE ESP FINDINGS

Ganev presented his findings to the management of Business Area Radio on two occasions. The first was at a management meeting in March/April 1994. The main conclusions and recommendations of the report stated:

- The future success of Business Area Radio depends on its ability to offer customized design of the fixed part of the network.
- The current product development projects neglect the importance of network functionality.
- Ericsson's future competitiveness is threatened by insufficient functionality and the lack of integrated operation and management systems in the product offering. Additionally, our offering does not cater to operators' future needs.
- If we get it right, Ericsson's cellular transmission market will exceed an accumulated value of US $500 million by the year 2000.

The report also contained a vision of future Ericsson offerings to customers (refer to Exhibit 2).

The team recommended creating a new organization responsible for product development and supply of transmission products to Business Area Radio's cellular customers. The new organization would use internal or external partners as suppliers.

Ganev and his team recommended preparation of a business plan and a sourcing strategy for approval by Business Area Radio management. They also saw a need for a strong coordination council on a working level with representatives from all business units.

The report was approved, and the management of Business Area Radio decided to go ahead without too much further consideration.

LAUNCHING THE NEW ORGANIZATION

After the decision by Business Area Radio management to start this new activity, Uddenfeldt and Ganev had many discussions about the location of the new transmission unit. They wanted to get full support and commitment from all business units in Business Area Radio, even if it was not organized within Ericsson Radio Systems. The discussions revealed that Ericsson Radio Access AB (a local business based in Stockholm), which was organized by business segments, turned out to be the best host. Whether or not the new organization would get the necessary support from the business units still remained a question.

During these discussions, Ganev did not consider himself a candidate for the job as head of the new operation. However, Uddenfeldt and others believed that Ganev would be the best person to run the new business. As a result, Ganev was appointed head of the new unit. He was given a budget of SEK 50 million for the first year.

Ericsson Radio Access president Ulf Mimer looked back on the beginning of the project and on Ganev's appointment:

> *When Jan Uddenfeldt approached me and asked if my company would take on the project, I was quite pleased. It was a good sign. I was told that Ganev would be heading up the project. I wasn't given a choice. Jan Uddenfeldt had scooped Ganev up when he had to leave Ericsson Components because of*

2 | The Cellular Transmission Vision

In the ESP report, Ganev describes the vision of the CTS business as follows:

During the second half of the 1990s, Ericsson Radio is still the world leading supplier of cellular radio systems. The competitive strength of the company is its unique competence in offering total cost optimized solutions for mobile network systems with superior quality.

Ericsson's technological approach in implementing the most optimal network topology includes supply of intelligent network products enabling the administration of the mobile network as a single entity.

Ericsson's operational system offers the operator ability for configuration of the network in "real time," achieving maximum performance at the lowest cost. Graphical representation on the network elements level and administration reports will provide comprehensive inputs for daily network planning as well as future network expansion.

The functionality and capabilities of Ericsson's network product will be optimized to meet the specific demands of mobile access networks cost efficiently. The configuration will be dictated by the customers' network and service requirements—rather than vice versa.

A common, standardized network unit will be a technological platform for implementing a long-term product strategy for transport nodes in radio cellular networks worldwide.

The successful development of our own transport technology, optimized to the mobile network requirements in time, is the best guarantee for Ericsson to stay a world leader, offering the most advanced systems with best total economy for the operators.

Source: Company document.

managerial differences with the president, Bert Jeppson. I'd heard about Ganev being difficult to handle, that he wasn't easy to understand and deal with. But I'd also heard good things about him. However, before I took on the project and Ganev, Bert Jeppson came to see me to warn me about working with him. I listened . . . and then I made my decision to go ahead anyway. I figured I would just give it a try.

In June 1994, Ganev moved from Ericsson Radio Systems to Ericsson Radio Access as head of a new division named Cellular Transmission Systems (CTS). Ganev reported directly to Mimer. Together they wrote the official announcement of the new organization, which was then signed by Business Area Radio president Kurt Hellström and distributed at Ericsson on June 15, 1994.

Reactions from Business Units at Business Area Radio

Within a week after the announcement of the new organization, Claes Gyllencreutz, head of Access Networks, another organization in Business Unit Mobile Systems GSM, contacted Ganev. Gyllencreutz was very upset about the new organization and claimed that he and his organization had the responsibility for transmission products to the cellular systems.

This was the first time Ganev had ever heard of the Access Network organization in the Mobile Telephone Systems GSM business unit. Neither the working group nor the reference group knew that Gyllencreutz's organization even existed. Obviously, the issue of creation of a "transmission organization" within Business Area Radio had not been discussed with the marketers of Mobile Telephone Systems GSM.

Ganev and Gyllencreutz had a meeting in order to establish a common platform and look at ways they could cooperate. With each manager's interest in his own product, the conflict was obvious.

THE BUILD-UP PHASE

Business Area Radio Steering Group

For CTS and Ganev, it was very important to have the Business Area Radio business units fully committed to the new organization. Ganev and Mimer had to make sure that all activities of the new organization were in line with the strategies and plans of the different business units.

For this reason, the Business Area Radio steering group was established. The first meeting was held on August 25, 1994. The participants of this meeting consisted of representatives from each of the three business units and Ganev and Mimer from Ericsson Radio Access. Ganev wrote the minutes of the meeting, which were later distributed to the steering group members.

The steering group meetings continued quarterly; however, the members changed continuously. The business unit managers delegated their participation to managers at lower organizational levels. In the end, participants were unable to make any commitments on behalf of their business units. After eight months, Ganev did not call for the next meeting—no one objected.

THE CONSIDERATION OF POSSIBLE SUPPLIERS

In the project phase, Ganev's goal was to create a product portfolio of existing Ericcson products and additional in-house development. Among the Ericsson products and organizations discussed were:

- ASCOM, a Swiss/Ericsson venture and existing supplier with the UMUX transmission product.
- DIAX, an Ericsson company in Denmark and supplier of small switches with DIAMUX as their transmission product.

There was also an external supplier—Tellabs—with a transmission product called DXX. Initially, this supplier was not discussed in the transmission strategic plan; it was only used as a reference for other products.

After the start of CTS, discussions were held with ASCOM management. ASCOM had very advanced and aggressive development plans for UMUX. However, when Ganev and CTS asked for support and adaptation of UMUX to meet the special needs of the cellular systems, ASCOM rejected the idea.

Peter Fischer, president of ASCOM, expressed his feelings about establishing a relationship with CTS:

> *UMUX is ready and complete; we only need to make minor mechanical changes in UMUX in order to meet the needs of Business Area Radio. We have our own contacts with Business Area Radio, and we do not regard CTS as their representative.*

This corresponded with Gyllencreutz's opinion of UMUX. He rejected the DXX product Ganev had suggested because "it was not the right product for Business Area Radio." He and his organization had better alternatives in mind, such as UMUX.

The result of these discussions was that Ganev and CTS deemed it very difficult to work with ASCOM.

Discussions were also held with DIAX. However, its solution did not meet the basic requirements of the cellular transmission system. The lack of a network management system was one important reason why the DIAX product was rejected.

Within Ericsson, CTS tried to set up a cooperation between Business Area Radio and Infocom in the transmission field. As the discussions with Infocom progressed very slowly, Ganev decided to start talking to external supplier Tellabs about incorporating DXX into the Ericsson cellular system. In May 1994, Ganev informed the head of Business Area Infocom Transmission that CTS had started discussions with an external supplier. (Refer to Exhibit 3 for a short background on Tellabs.)

Evaluation of DXX and Discussions with Tellabs

To evaluate Tellabs' DXX system, business unit Mobile Telephones American Standard in the USA borrowed a system from Tellabs. During March and April of 1994, experts form Ericsson US and Ericsson Canada evaluated the system. One reason for performing these tests in the United States, rather than in Sweden, was that business unit Mobile Telephones American Standard

3 | Background of Tellabs

Tellabs/Martis and Harald Devik

Harald Devik, presently responsible for Tellabs operations in Scandinavia, started to work as a Tellabs representative in Sweden in 1991. Before that, he worked with transmission products for Ericsson US. He had several contacts in Ericsson, and had great knowledge of the transmission products that Ericsson offered. Devik recognized the vast potential for Tellabs transmission products in Ericsson.

Devik worked with different Ericsson organizations to sell different products from Tellabs. He also had solid contacts with other Ericsson managers to implement sales of transmission products to the cellular systems.

In autumn 1993, Tellabs bought Martis OY, a Finnish entrepreneurial company working in the transmission field.

Martis started the design of its transmission/network product called DXX in 1988. Later, at the time of the transmission ESP at Business Area Radio, the system was in use of Telia Mobitel and some other operators. It was a known product, and Ganev had already had some early discussions with Tellabs during the transmission ESP.

was very open and free of prejudice regarding the selection of transmission products. Another reason for performing the tests in the United States was that Harald Devik—director marketing and sales Tellabs Scandinavia—had good contacts within Ericsson US (due to his earlier association with Ericsson), and therefore promoted the DXX at Ericsson US. The evaluation showed the DXX was technically outstanding and superior to both UMUX and DIAMUX.

In June 1994, a letter of intent was signed with Tellabs giving Ericsson the possibility to conduct an in-depth evaluation of the management system. Ericsson experts were sent to Finland for the evaluation. Finding the system satisfactory, CTS started contract negotiations with Tellabs. Throughout the negotiations, Ganev's objective was to arrive at an agreement that would be beneficial to both parties, thus creating a win-win situation from the beginning.

With the exception of Devik, practically no one at Tellabs believed that a cooperation with Ericsson would be successful. This feeling was based on a bad experience from an earlier business relationship with Ericsson Infocom. A great amount of work had resulted in less than US$2 million of business.

During the negotiations with Tellabs, it was difficult for Ganev to get support from Business Area Radio's mother company, Ericsson Radio Systems, which did not perceive him as a representative of Business Area Radio.

At the first meeting of the steering group in August 1994, Ganev presented a proposal for "mission and goals," a budget for 1994 and 1995, a recruitment plan, and strategies for product development—what to design in house and what to buy from external sources or partners. Two suppliers were discussed: ASCOM and Tellabs. At the meeting regarding these issues and plans, few questions were raised before they were approved.

Despite difficulties on both sides, the first agreement with Tellabs was signed September 1994. Unsure of the situation, Tellabs agreed to an initial test period of two years. The contract enabled Ericsson to integrate Tellabs' product with other Ericsson products and market it under the Ericsson name (OEM: original equipment manufacturing contract). In the agreement there were to be no modifications to the products whatsoever.

Devik of Tellabs spoke about his working relationship with Ganev:

> *When Ganev appeared on the scene things began to happen really fast. He was very eager to have an*

agreement with Tellabs because he wanted his business to move forward. Ganev pushed very hard that the Ericsson requirements were both for an OEM agreement and a collaboration agreement.

When Ganev has a goal or a plan, he pushes it until he gets a result or he finds that he cannot reach his goal. When he realizes he can't reach his goal, he changes the plan, and the action. By the same token, he is very good at understanding the problems and difficulties on both sides, and works toward finding a solution that satisfies the counterpart. If, for instance, Tellabs had difficulty meeting a requirement from Ericsson, it could openly put it on the table and Ganev would try to find a creative solution.

CTS: BUILDING THE ORGANIZATION

In the beginning, CTS was a pure supplier of Tellabs products. In order to succeed with the business, Ganev felt Ericsson had to create added value by offering additional services to the customer. Therefore, Ganev needed to create an organization that had a profound, technical understanding of customers' needs. He felt it was also very important to be able to thoroughly answer the "requests for quotations" (RFQs) and speak with the customers at their level of expertise. For this, he wanted employees who were not influenced by the "history" of Ericsson in the transmission field.

Ganev sought out people who were experts in the transmission field and had experience working for cellular systems operators. Among the first employees were Ib Andersen from Comvik (Comvik was a cellular operator and Ericsson customer), Fredrik, Alm from Telia (a Comvik competitor), and three people from Ericsson Components.

Ganev contacted Andersen on recommendation from a colleague. Before joining Comvik, Andersen had worked for Ericsson Radio Systems as a project manager. Ganev described the work, and Andersen easily recognized the different issues. He had studied many Ericsson proposals for Comvik and knew that the Ericsson offering in the area of transmission for the fixed part of the cellular system was usually very weak. He found the work presented by Ganev very interesting and challenging. For Andersen, accepting the job offer was an easy decision.

As a division manager at his former company, Ericsson Components, Ganev had a loyal following. To get CTS up and running (much to the chagrin of the senior management at Ericsson Components), Ganev took advantage of Ericsson's policy of freedom to transfer and recruited five people for Ericsson Components. Subsequently, Ganev's boss, Mimer, met with the senior management for lunch to smooth things over and assured them that Ganev was finished poaching talent.

Ann Catherine Planstedt, human resources director at Ericsson Radio Access, reflected on Ganev's hiring demands and attitude toward his employees:

Most people Ganev employs stay in his organization for quite a long time and are very loyal and enthusiastic to that organization they've created. People who join him with a big interest only *in R&D don't tend to stay long.*

Ganev shows a genuine interest and devotion to his employees. This also includes their social and private lives. When hiring people, Ganev does not look that much for formal competence. He looks more for people who are interested in the work, people who will fit the organization. It is very important to him that his employees be enthusiastic about their work and find it to be both interesting and fun.

Ganev demands a lot of his employees . . . he pushes them to work hard and to accomplish what is needed to meet the promises they've made to the customers.

Planstedt had this to say about Ganev's style:

Ganev was born in Bulgaria and lived there under the communist regime for a number of years before he moved to Sweden. In my opinion, I'd say this has had an impact on his reaction to directives that come from his superiors. He likes to work in a flat organization, or with as few levels as possible. He involves himself in all kinds of issues on different levels. I suppose this could be difficult for some of his subordinate managers to deal with.

Ideally, Ganev wants an organization with ample room for new ideas, while at the same time he is emotional and quick to react, never tolerating what he thinks is wrong. He needs a lot of "living space" and the freedom to create a business and an organization according to his own ideas. For example, he didn't accept the limitations to his business regarding the company's policy on overtime restriction. Therefore, he had to agree to a special financial compensation to many of his employees so as not to restrict their work time. The fact that Ericsson Radio Access AB was a separate legal company from Business Area Radio implied neutral, commercial, and businesslike borders to the transmission business, and created a situation where an entrepreneur like Ganev could be successful.

By the end of 1994, CTS had 11 employees: one network designer, two project managers for implementations, two logistics experts, two software support people, one secretary, one finance person and one technical marketing support person. Ganev himself focused on visiting potential clients and made sure he knew what was going on in all parts of his organization.

THE FIRST BUSINESS OPPORTUNITIES

Ganev added value to the Tellabs product by integrating DXX in an entire solution package for his customers. He made his position as a price/service leader clear. "The customer shall be prepared to pay 10 percent more when buying from Ericsson instead of Tellabs or other suppliers." The Ericsson solution focused on lowering the ultimate longer term "total costs of ownership" for the operators. In fact, the initial investment in Ericsson switches and systems cost 5 percent to 10 percent of total costs of ownership after a period of around five years of average growth for the operator. The other cost centers consisted of lease costs for infrastructure, operational costs, and marketing costs, each around 30 percent on average. With the Ericsson solution these costs could be reduced.

Mannesman: An Opportunity Missed/A Lesson Learned

The first business opportunity for CTS was Mannesman in Germany. Mannesman had issued an RFQ for transmission equipment at the beginning of October 1994. The very same day the agreement was signed with Tellabs, Ganev flew to Germany to present Ericsson's offer to Mannesman. Despite a very late entrance, Ericsson was invited for discussions and added to the short list. This proved that CTS was on the right track.

Ultimately, the business went to Bosch. Ganev believed he had missed the opportunity for the following reasons:

- CTS was not ready with the market message and market strategy.
- Too much was thrown together at the last minute.
- CTS had to depend on Ericsson Germany for its knowledge of the local market and customer situation. Unfortunately, CTS learned that Ericsson Germany's knowledge and expertise in the transmission field was insufficient.
- In the past, Mannesman and Ericsson had had several multivendor discussions. In this case, Ericsson was presenting one more proprietary product. This was not acceptable to Mannesman in those days.
- According to Devik of Tellabs, Mannesman lacked sufficient knowledge to fully understand the benefits of the DXX system and its software. Mannesman, it seemed, was thinking too much in terms of just "boxes" and not in terms of a complete operating and management package.
- Including Tellabs in the negotiations made it impossible to find fast, flexible solutions to the customer's needs.

Ganev regarded this experience as a good lesson for CTS on how to present itself to a customer and how to work with a local Ericsson company.

Vodafone: The First Success

Shortly after missing out on the Mannesman deal, the second business opportunity came from Vodafone in Australia. A friend outside Ericsson informed Ganev that Vodafone in Australia had issued an RFQ for transmission equipment. The RFQ had not been sent to Ericsson Australia because, at the time, it did not offer any transmission systems.

Ganev contacted Ericsson Australia and its cellular systems marketing manager, Dave Colbeck, and asked him to request the RFQ from Vodafone. Having neither experience nor competence in transmission systems, Ericsson Australia was very hesitant. In 1994, Ericsson Australia had no possibilities to support a system in

Australia. If they were going to handle a DXX contract and system, they wanted 100 percent support from Sweden.

In the meantime, Tellabs salespeople made several presentations to Vodafone. Vodafone knew the DXX system and was convinced it was the system it needed. Believing it did not have the resources to support a contract that far away from Finland, Tellabs management rejected the idea of a direct sale. Vodafone had very good relations with Ericsson Australia and knew about the agreement between Ericsson and Tellabs. Trusting Ericsson's reputation, Vodafone wanted to buy DXX through Ericsson Australia.

In a meeting between Colbeck, Ganev and Mimer in Sundbyholm, Sweden on November 27, Ericsson Australia got the necessary commitment from Ericsson Radio Access to whom CTS belonged. Without involving Tellabs, Ericsson Australia and CTS then made an offer to Vodafone. A contact worth SEK 22 million was signed December 13, 1994.

Mimer on Ganev and the growth of CTS:

> *Ganev has a real entrepreneurial spirit, but I wouldn't exactly call him an entrepreneur. By working at Ericsson, he can draw freely from our resources. Money, personnel, and R&D support are easy to get here and he can get them quickly. He appreciates that.*
>
> *People have told me that I must be quite a special manager to be able to handle him. It is true that he is not so easy to deal with, he is a superstar, and they are usually not too easy to deal with. Ganev is emotional and can be very stubborn. But he can be understood. He is emotional because he throws himself entirely into his job and serving our clients, and he's stubborn when he is sure the customer is being mistreated or cheated. So why don't we call it conviction instead of being stubborn? Ganev is all for the customer, and they love that, and so do his employees, even if it can be hard on them sometimes.*
>
> *When the CTS business was up and running, things took off fast. I was concerned about putting together an organizational structure that could support our growth. Ganev was only concerned with sales and marketing and getting more support for sales and marketing. He didn't see the need for organization and administration. But there, in the conflict, was the essence of the balance we brought each other. The balance that ultimately led to our success. We had our moments, believe me. And he left me with my fair share of fires to put out and bruised egos to mend, but it was worth it. In the end, it was worth it.*

Since its start-up in mid-1994 until the end of 1998, CTS generated accumulated Ericsson sales of nearly SEK 1.2 billion. During the same period, the consolidated Ericsson profit from CTS was SEK 250 million, with a positive accumulated cash flow exceeding SEK 150 million. Order intake grew from SEK 95 million in 1995 to SEK 1.2 billion in 1998. By the end of 1998, CTS had sold over 50 networks in more than 40 countries around the world. It had achieved this with 120 CTS staff.

CASE 18

E*Trade, Charles Schwab and Yahoo!

The Transformation of On-line Brokerage

Nassim Dagher
Soumitra Dutta
Arnoud De Meyer
INSEAD

INTRODUCTION

The Internet is giving individual investors access to more resources than they've ever had before.

—Smith Barney analyst Jonathan Cohen[1]

With a few mouse clicks, an experienced Net navigator can today tap into Wall Street research reports on publicly traded companies, view up-to-the-minute stock quotes, gather reams of performance data on thousands of mutual funds, check out the latest rates on bank loans, and save up to 80 percent on traditional brokerage commissions by trading securities on the Web.

Pioneered by E*Trade, Internet stock trading service providers have mushroomed since early 1996. The user-friendliness, accessibility, speed, and low fees of online trading have challenged established full-service and discount brokers and changed the way people invest. Even Charles Schwab, a firm that practically invented the concept of a discount broker, has not gone unchallenged. More than 60 online brokerage firms have emerged within the last two years. Within this fast growing segment which holds about 3 million of the approximately 80 million accounts managed by full-service brokers and traditional discounters, the marketshare war is on with some early winners: Charles Schwab leads with 35 percent market share; next comes E*Trade with a 15 percent market share, beating a traditional giant such as Fidelity, which commands 13 percent of the market.

Thanks to the Internet, stock-broking seems destined to change in fundamental ways. Retail trading by new Internet-based brokers such as E*Trade is challenging traditional giants such as Merrill Lynch. A recent study by Forrester Research predicts that by 2002, online accounts will total more than 14 million and hold nearly $700 billion in assets.[2] However, the end scenario is far from clear. The idea of fully automated agents running people's portfolios in linked electronic financial markets is no longer far-fetched; it is merely far off.[3] Internet-based bulletin boards for secondary trading are rapidly emerging and challenging the role of the broker-dealer, both traditional and Internet-based. Advances in security and reliability on the Internet are lowering the barrier to using the Net for direct trading among investors. Banking on the global access provided by the Internet, many firms are launching Direct Public Offerings (DPOs) to sell equities directly to interested investors without the traditional intermediary of an underwriter or a syndicate of underwriters.

In this case, we will focus on E*Trade—the pioneer, Charles Schwab—the leader, and Yahoo!—a potential new entrant, to understand the rapidly changing dynamics of the online brokerage business.

This case is intended to be used as a basis for class discussion, rather than to illustrate either effective or ineffective handling of an administrative situation.

Copyright © 1998 INSEAD, Fontainebleau, France. All rights reserved.

E*TRADE[4]

*A slick interface, a solid portfolio manager and a wide variety of access options put E*Trade at the top of a growing heap of on-line investment services.*[5]

—PC COMPUTING while announcing the winner of the Most Valuable Product Award for 1997 Internet Financial Services.

E*Trade is one of the largest—and fastest growing—Internet brokerage firms in the business, adding 500 new accounts daily to its 125,000-strong customer list. That, plus additions to existing accounts, works out to $10 million a day in new business. E*Trade's customers—predominantly young and male—have lately been conducting upwards of 14,000 trades a day, with 7.8 million shares changing hands. And that's equivalent to roughly 1.5 percent of a typical day's trading volume for the entire New York Stock Exchange. During the first quarter of 1998, E*Trade's Web site hosted 22.2 million total visits from an average of 50,000 unique visitors daily. Customer retention remained strong, at a annualized rate of 95 percent.

E*Trade's CEO, Christos Cotsakos commented:

A full 8 percent of all visits result in revenue generating transactions. . . . We're changing the entire DNA of the industry. When companies like Merrill Lynch start talking about themselves as if they were national icons, that's when you know you've got them.[6]

Indeed, E*Trade's profit margins give it a price advantage hard to be matched by a traditional broker (see Exhibit 1). But what really sets E*Trade apart from a traditional broker is the quality of the investment research it provides its customers free of charge. After logging onto E*Trade, customers enter a world of user-friendly stock and market analysis equivalent to what a broker has access to. They are offered real-time price-and-volume quotes and news stories for any stock. They can track the action on any stock market, follow trend alerts for any sector, and perform sophisticated investment analysis using option models. When customers decide to buy or sell a stock, they just have to click to the "transaction" page and type in the order, and E*Trade's computers in California take over. The system will query the computers of, typically, four different market makers in the stock, searching for the lowest price (if buying) or the highest (if selling).

The Balance of Power Has Shifted

*E*Trade is changing the entire value proposition of the financial services industry by applying the power of*

EXHIBIT 1 | Comparison of Rates

	E*Trade	e.Schwab	Schwab	Fidelity	Merrill Lynch
Mutual funds with no loads/no transaction fees	YES	YES	YES	YES	YES
Transaction fee on applicable funds (based on $15,000 purchase)	$24.95	$84	$105	$28.95 Minimum	$150 annual account fee
Mutual fund research & Morningstar ratings on-line	YES	YES	YES	YES	NO
Trade stocks by phone 800 shares @ $20	$14.95 Listed $19.95 Nasdaq	$117.36	$117.36	$101.56	$319.00
Trade stocks via PC (Web) 800 shares @ $20	$14.95 Listed $19.95 Nasdaq	$29.95	$104.32	$28.95	Not Available
10 options contracts @ $2	$38.00	$48.80	$48.80	$45.56	$144.00
30 options contracts @ $3	$73.00	$96.80	$96.80	$90.56	$373.00
Breaking news, charts, fundamental data, and earnings estimates	Free	Free	Free	Free	Free
Customer service	Free	Fees may apply	Free	Free	Free

Source: www.etrade.com

*technology and the power of the Internet to the business of investing. Technology enables E*Trade to offer more value to the self-directed investor. E*Trade has shifted the balance of power—from the temples of finance to customers. . .*

—E*Trade Online Documentation

E*Trade gives its customers direct control over their investment activities, offering them an integrated and customized access not only to their portfolios, but also to data, research, and analysis as well as information on their holdings and the markets. E*Trade offers a broad array of investment opportunities, including listed and OTC stocks, options, and (as of November 1997) more than 3,500 mutual funds. E*Trade also offers to its customers margin lending and check writing services and a full range of account types, including individual, joint, partnership, corporate, trust, investment club, and retirement accounts. Exhibit 2 provides a summary of E*Trade's products and services.

2 | E*Trade: Services and Products

E*Trade's existing services and product offerings are described below:

- **Stocks, Options, and Mutual Funds Trading:** Customers can directly place orders to buy and sell NASDAQ and exchange-listed securities, as well as equity and index options and mutual funds through the E*Trade automated order processing system. E*Trade supports a range of order types, including market orders, limit orders (good-till-canceled or day), stop orders, and short sales. System intelligence automatically checks the parameters of an order, together with the customer's available cash balance and positions held, prior to executing an order. All listed market orders (subject to certain size limitations) are executed at the National Best Bid/Offer ("NBBO") or better at the time of receipt by the third market firm or exchange. The NBBO is a dynamically updated representation of the combined highest bid and lowest offer quoted across all United States stock exchanges and market makers registered in a specific stock.
- **Market Data and Financial Information:** During trading hours E*Trade continuously receives a direct feed of detailed quote data, market information, and news. Customers can create their own personal lists of stocks and options for quick access to current pricing information. E*Trade provides its customers free access of 20-minute-delayed quotes, including stocks, options, major market indices, most active issues, and largest gainers and losers for the major exchanges. Users are alerted when there is current news on an identified stock or when a stock has reached a user-defined price threshold. Through its alliances, the company also provides immediate access to breaking news, charts, market commentary and analysis, and company financial information. Upon placing an order, the customer is provided with a real-time bid or ask quote at no extra charge. For $30 per month, individual investors can obtain unlimited real-time quotes and market data.
- **Portfolio Tracking and Records Management:** Customers have online access to a listing of all their portfolio assets held at E*Trade, including data on the date of purchase, cost basis, current price, and current market value. The system automatically calculates unrealized profits and losses for each asset held. Detailed account balance and transaction information includes cash and money fund balances, buying power, net market portfolio value, dividends paid, interest earned, deposits, and withdrawals. Brokerage history includes all orders, executions, changes, and cancellations. Tax records include total short-term or long-term gain/loss and commissions paid. Customers can also create "shadow" portfolios to include most financial instruments a customer is interested in tracking—for example, assets held at another brokerage firm. These shadow portfolios can include stocks, options, bonds, and most mutual funds.
- **Cash Management Services:** Customer payments are received through the mail, federal wire system, or the Internet and are credited to customer accounts upon receipt. The company also provides other cash management services to its customers. For example, uninvested funds earn interest in a credit interest program or can be invested in one of five money market funds. In addition, the company provides free check-writing services with no minimum through a commercial bank and is exploring the expansion of these services. The company, through its strategic relationship with National Processing Company, has expanded its cash management offerings to include electronic funds transfer via the Internet and an automatic deposit program to allow scheduled periodic transfers of funds into customers' E*Trade accounts.

2 | E*Trade: Services and Products *(Continued)*

- **Account Security:** Customers are assigned unique account numbers, user identifications, and trading passwords that must be used each time they log onto the system. The company relies on encryption and authentication technology, including public key cryptography technology, to provide the security and authentication necessary to effect the secure exchange of information. In addition the company uses Secure Socket Layers ("SSL") technology for data encryption. Touch-tone telephone transactions are secured through a personal identification number ("PIN"). In addition, the company has agreement to provide digital certification and authentication services for electronic commerce through its alliance with VeriSign, Inc.
- **Access and Delivery of Services:** The company's services are widely accessible through multiple gateways, with automated order placement available 24 hours a day, seven days a week by personal computer. In addition, customers can access E*Trade by touch-tone telephone and, in a limited number of markets, through interactive television.
  1. *Personal Computer.* Customers using personal computers can access the E*Trade system through the Internet, online service providers (America On-line, AT&T WorldNet, CompuServe, Microsoft Network, and Prodigy), or direct modem access. The company's Web site combines an easy-to-use graphical user interface with the trading capabilities that experienced investors demand. Alternatively, accessing E*Trade by dialing directly through a modem offers a method for connecting to the trading system independent of either the Internet or a proprietary online service.
  2. *Touch-tone Telephone.* TELE*MASTER, E*Trade's interactive investing system, provides customers with a convenient way to access quotes, place orders, and access portfolio information using their voice or touch-tone telephone keypad. E*Trade is the first online investing service to offer its customers a fully speech-enabled telephone investing system.
  3. *Interactive Television.* GTE MainStreet, an interactive television system operated by GTE Corporation, is available as a gateway to the company's investing services.

Source: Form 10-K

E*Trade's customers can access their accounts any day, any time, and virtually anywhere via the Internet or major online services (AOL, CompuServe, Prodigy Internet, Microsoft Investor), by direct modem or interactive TV, or by telephone. Customer trades are confirmed immediately and executed orders are posted to customer accounts immediately. Further, E*Trade's account data can be automatically integrated into most popular personal finance programs.

To help customers, E*Trade has developed a fun, online game to help them learn about investing and trading online. Online help is available at each step of a transaction and on every screen on the Web site. E*Trade offers fax-on-demand and interactive voice response systems to answer frequently asked questions. Customer service associates are also available to answer questions.

A Personalized Window on Wall Street

Based on strategic alliances with some of the most respected suppliers of news and market data on the Internet, E*Trade's Web site gathers everything from company profiles to consensus earnings estimates, from the latest news to the latest stock prices, provided by resources like First Call, BASELINE Financial Services, Quote.com, Reuters, and InvestorsEdge.com. Exhibit 3 summarizes some of the content available to E*Trade's customers.

E*Trade's customers can choose exactly what news and information they're interested in—and access it on-demand. They can create a customized Personal Market Page that provides a snapshot view of the news and other stock-related information they want whenever they access their account. They can get dynamic, Java-based pricing charts and other technical data. Options traders can apply the Black-Scholes pricing model online, and check prices, premium, and any data on the underlying stocks.

E*Trade's on-line documentation summarizes the benefit to customers as:

In a market where information is power, professional investors paid, a few years ago, large amounts for

3 | E*Trade: Content Available to Customers

Content such as news, quotes, charts, and fundamental data helps provide investors with the information necessary to make investment decisions. The company's partnerships with leading content providers fulfill customers' information needs and help drive transaction volume.

- **BASELINE Financial Services:** To provide customers with access to a wide array of investment fundamentals, First Call earnings estimates, and historical prices on over 6,500 stocks. Available to customers free of charge from the "Investor Tools" area of the E*Trade Web site, BASELINE information can be used to examine a company's statistics prior to making investment decisions.
- **Briefing.com:** To provide market commentary and analysis to E*Trade customers free of charge. Updates are posted throughout the day to keep investors informed of important developments affecting the markets.
- **INVESTools:** To provide E*Trade customers with direct access to 25 branch-name research reports and newsletters plus stock screening tools on a pay-per-use basis.
- **QUOTE.com:** To provide current news and charts that are directly linked to E*Trade customers' Stock Watch portfolio and quote lookup features. News provided includes Reuters News, PR Newswire, and BusinessWire. Charts provided include intra-day, daily, and weekly price graphs.
- **IDD Enterprises:** To provide E*Trade customers with access to mutual fund profiles and two types of screening tools (Quick Fund Search and Advanced Fund Search) within the E*Trade Mutual Fund Center.
- **InUnity Corporation:** To provide customers with access to electronic prospectuses for funds offered within the E*Trade Mutual Fund Center.
- **Morningstar Inc.:** To provide performance information and proprietary "star" ratings on mutual funds within the E*Trade Mutual Fund Center.
- **MSNBC Business Video:** To provide E*Trade customers with direct access to exclusive audio and video coverage of news events worldwide, as well as an archive of more than 8,000 audio and video segments at a preferred customer discount.

Source: Form 10-K

*some of these tools and resources, which helped them make a decision. E*Trade has changed the rule of the game thanks to the Internet, by putting the intelligence directly into the hands of customers.*

Technology and Operations

Technology gives E*Trade the power to offer a better value proposition to its customers. Mindful of security concerns over the Net, E*Trade uses Netscape's Secure Server to process transactions over the Internet (accessible though Netscape and Microsoft Internet Explorer browsers), which automatically encrypts data and protects it from hackers. It intends to provide encryption and verification technology from VeriSign.

Partnerships with leading technology providers support E*Trade's products and services with up-to-date features. Its agreement with National Processing Company allows customers to initiate fund transfers from checking accounts at third-party institutions into their E*Trade accounts over the Internet. Neural's Java-based intelligent process optimization solutions and data management systems will be incorporated into E*Trade's Java-based charting and quote applications. Telesphere provides E*Trade with real-time market data on some internationally traded securities, in addition to data on domestically traded securities. VeriSign enhances the electronic commerce by authenticating the individuals, organizations, and content involved in an electronic transaction.

E*Trade implemented equities of self-clearing operations in July 1996 and options self-clearing operations in April 1997. Clearing operations include the confirmation, receipt, settlement, custody, and delivery functions involved in securities transactions. Performing its own clearing operations allows E*Trade Securities to retain customer free credit balances and securities for use in margin lending activities subject to SEC rules. The company has an agreement with Beta Systems for the provision of computer services to support order entry, order routing, securities processing, customer statements, tax reporting, regulatory reporting, and other services necessary to the management of a brokerage clearing business.

An International Financial Destination

By listening to our customers and continuing to innovate, we strive to give them what they want when they want it. We are focused on creating a business that's built to last, as we build our destination brand for the long term.

—Christos M. Cotsakos, President and CEO, E*Trade

As of March 31, 1998, E*Trade had over 400,000 accounts (with assets under management in excess of $10 billion). E*Trade's Web site continued to increase its share of the company's business, with a total of 980,000 transactions, or 62 percent of total transactions, during the first quarter of 1998. One year ago, total Web transactions were only 316,000, or 46 percent, of total transactions.[7] Exhibit 4 summarizes selected financial data for E*Trade.

E*Trade has secured or is actively pursing alliances with (i) Internet access and service providers, (ii) Inter-

EXHIBIT 4 | E*Trade: Selected Financial Data

Years Ended September 30, (in thousands, except per share amounts)	1997	1996	1995	1994	1993
CONSOLIDATED STATEMENT OF OPERATIONS DATA					
Revenues					
Transactions revenues	$109,659	$44,178	$20,835	$9,548	$2,158
Interest, net of interest expense	25,265	4,813	1,004	302	17
International	4	—	—	—	—
Computer services and other	3,813	2,604	1,501	1,055	799
Net revenues	142,737	51,595	2,334	10,905	2,974
Cost of services					
Cost of services	66,507	34,268	1,334	7,646	1,973
Registration charge	4,334	—	—	—	—
Self-clearing start-up costs	—	224	141	—	—
Total cost of services	70,841	36,508	13,481	7,646	1,973
Operating expenses					
Selling and marketing	24,193	76	2,466	998	282
Technology development	10,761	2,792	943	335	216
General and administrative	13,612	6,078	2,141	1,682	400
Total operating expenses	48,566	1,647	555	3,015	898
Total cost of services and operating expenses	119,407	52,978	19,031	10,661	2,871
Pretax income (loss)	2,333	-1,383	4,309	244	103
Income tax expense (benefit)	9,425	-555	1,728	-541	4
Net income (loss)	$13,905	$(828)	$2,581	$785	$99
Net income (loss) per share	$.40	$(0.03)	$0.10	$0.03	$-
Weighted average number of common and common equivalent shares outstanding	34,574	28,564	26,481	26,186	26,677

September 30, (in thousands)	1997	1996	1995	1994	1993
CONSOLIDATED BALANCE SHEET DATA					
Cash and equivalents	$21,814	$14,641	$9,624	$692	$36
Total assets	989,903	294,881	14,164	2,163	728
Long-term obligations	—	—	45	64	131
Shareholders' equity (deficiency)	281,275	69,304	11,148	-92	-788

net content providers, (iii) providers of home and on-line banking services, and (iv) electronic commerce companies. These alliances (see Exhibit 5) are intended to increase the Company's core customer base, transaction volume, and operational efficiency and to further enhance its brand-name recognition.

E*Trade also makes loans to customers collateralized by customer securities. In April 1998, E*Trade announced an alliance with E-Loan Inc., to give E*Trade customers comprehensive information on mortgages, the ability to shop for the best rates (both locally and nationally), and apply for a home loan. Christos Cotsakos commented:

> *Adding mortgages to the portfolio of financial products and services E*Trade offers its customers is a significant step towards the development of an on-line destination where customers can conduct their personal financial business. Because of our all-electronic model, E*Trade is able to continually innovate and increase personalization of our offerings for our customers.*

All of the above efforts are directed at making E*Trade the financial destination of choice for customers. During the second quarter of 1998, E*Trade started a major push into international markets, partic-

5 | E*Trade: New Account Development and Distribution

E*Trade has developed alliances with key channels in the online medium to increase account development and expand distribution. These channels include proprietary online services, Internet service providers, and popular destination Web sites such as search engines or financial content providers. These channels attract significant numbers of users, and the company's relationships provide access to expanded market opportunities. Set forth below are descriptions of certain of the company's key alliances:

- **America On-line:** To place E*Trade in America On-line's new online Brokerage Area, giving America On-line's approximately 10 million subscribers access to E*Trade's Web site.
- **CompuServe:** To permit the approximately 5.3 million CompuServe customers to open accounts with E*Trade and access those accounts either through CompuServe or any of the company's other channels of access.
- **Intuit:** To allow customers to download E*Trade account information into Quicken 98 for Windows using the Open Financial Exchange (OFX) communications protocol. In addition, users can directly access E*Trade's Web site from Quicken 98 and the Excite Business and Investing channel by Quicken.com.
- **Microsoft:** To integrate E*Trade's online investing services into the Microsoft Investor online trading area of the Microsoft Network. E*Trade also supports the OFX standard allowing customers to download information from their E*Trade account into Microsoft Money 98 and the Microsoft Investor Portfolio Manager.
- **Prodigy Services Corporation:** To offer Prodigy Internet's members direct access to E*Trade's products and services.
- **USA Today:** To provide direct access to E*Trade's services through USA Today On-line's Financial Marketplace, a commercial area that includes personal finance services and products.
- **Yahoo!:** To provide direct access from the Quotes area of Yahoo! Finance to E*Trade's Web site.
- **PointCast:** To provide PointCast viewers with BASELINE Company Profiles through links from the PointCast Business Network's Companies Channel to a special E*Trade Web site.
- **Banc One:** Combining the popularity of Internet investing with a full range of banking services, the company and BANC ONE CORPORATION, headquartered in Columbus, Ohio, established co-branded Web sites this fall to market each other's financial services.
- **SinaNet:** The company has an exclusive agreement to promote its Internet-based investing services to Chinese-speaking investors in the United States through SinaNet, Inc., a media company that has created a popular Chinese-language Web site in North America.

Source: Form 10-K

ularly in Europe, Southeast Asia, and North Asia. Master licensing agreements have been signed for the formation of E*Trade Asia, E*Trade Germany, E*Trade France, and E*Trade Israel. For example, on April 16 1998, E*Trade announced an alliance with two leading financial services firms in Germany, the New York Broker Group and the Berliner Freiverkehr Group, for the formation of E*Trade Germany and E*Trade Central Europe. Expansion in these markets is clearly seen as part of the long-term strategy of E*Trade.

CHARLES SCHWAB

Schwab is the only place where people and the Internet come together to serve and empower investors. Our mission is to help every investor enjoy the benefits of a complete investing experience, with extensive access to information and trading, and no conflict of interest, both electronically and in-person. We think this combination of technology, service and people is beyond the scope of what other brokerage firms provide.[8]

—David S. Pottruck, co-CEO and President, Charles Schwab

Company Background

The Charles Schwab Corporation (CSC) was incorporated in 1986 and engages, through its subsidiaries, in securities brokerage and related financial services to individual investors, independent investment managers, retirement plans, and institutions. CSC is one of the nation's largest financial services companies, serving 5 million total active accounts with over $400 billion in client assets.[9]

CSC's principal subsidiary, Charles Schwab & Co., Inc. (Schwab), is a securities broker-dealer. Schwab was incorporated in 1971, and entered the discount brokerage business in 1974. It began with a very simple idea: "to provide investors with the most useful and ethical brokerage services in America."[10] Initially established as a full-service broker, Schwab competed with traditional brokerage firms such as Merrill Lynch and Salomon Smith Barney, which made the bulk of their profit from interest on loans to margin customers, fees for underwriting securities sales, and other investment-banking activities. Schwab became a discount brokerage after the SEC outlawed fixed commissions in 1975. While most brokers defiantly raised commissions, Schwab drastically cut its rates. Schwab changed the focus of its business to executing trades for clients who make their own investment decisions at a discount price. This strategy proved to be very profitable. Schwab increased its client list thirty-fold while tripling its revenue from 1977 to 1983. Today, Schwab controls roughly 50 percent of the discount brokerage industry with its closest competitors only half of its size.

During the nineties, Schwab has faced increasing competition from other discount brokerage firms such as National Discount Brokers. Schwab has differentiated itself by offering a great amount of educational investment materials and analytical tools. As a result, it has been able to attract a new wave of more sophisticated investors, including independent financial advisors, who defected from traditional full-service brokerage firms and mutual-fund companies. Schwab has placed a new emphasis on guidance and advice. This new focus is also an attempt to set Schwab apart from the new pack of deep-discount trading firms that have sprung up in the past few years. In many ways, Schwab is expanding into a full-service firm once again, only this time at a discount price.

Schwab's total customer assets exceeded $350 billion by year end 1997 as customers brought almost $69 billion in net new assets to the firm and 1.2 million new accounts were opened. Revenues surpassed $2 billion just three years after reaching $1 billion in 1994. The company achieved a 12.8 percent after-tax margin for 1997, its fifth consecutive year of margins in excess of 12 percent. Exhibit 6 provides a summary of selected financial data for Charles Schwab.

Schwab On-line

Schwab is reaching the mass market of Web investors by providing them with information, access, and control combined with the powerful combination of technology and people to serve their needs. Customers want the convenience of multiple ways to conduct business—whether it be through the Internet, in 270 branch offices, access to brokers 24 hours a day, or through speech recognition or touch-tone trading telephone services.[11]

—Gideon Sasson, EVP of Electronic Brokerage

Technology has always played an important role in Schwab's success. The company was one of the first

6 | The Charles Schwab Corporation: Financial and Operating Highlights (Unaudited)

Consolidated Operating Results (in millions, except per share amounts)	1997				1996		
	Fourth Quarter	Third Quarter	Second Quarter	First Quarter	Fourth Quarter	Third Quarter	Second Quarter
REVENUES							
Commissions	$315.0	$322.7	$261.4	$274.9	$241.9	$210.1	$261.2
Mutual fund service fees	119.0	112.2	101.8	94.7	86.8	80.3	75.4
Principal transactions	100.4	61.3	63.6	69.1	64.7	57.4	73.2
Interest revenue, net of interest expense	64.0	94.0	82.5	76.7	69.7	64.0	62.4
Other	22.2	21.6	21.4	20.3	19.4	18.2	19.6
Total	620.6	611.8	530.7	535.7	482.3	430.0	491.8
EXPENSES EXCLUDING INTEREST							
Compensation and benefits	261.7	255.1	224.2	220.8	198.6	171.6	200.5
Communications	45.7	45.8	45.5	45.7	37.3	40.2	44.3
Occupancy and equipment	41.0	39.3	38.5	35.4	34.2	33.2	33.1
Depreciation and amortization	38.5	34.9	29.7	27.8	26.0	24.2	23.3
Advertising and market development	32.3	29.3	26.0	35.8	27.5	16.5	17.8
Commissions, clearance and floor brokerage	20.9	26.3	22.3	22.4	20.7	18.7	21.8
Professional services	19.3	19.8	16.6	13.9	17.7	10.8	10.2
Other	56.9	33.4	22.1	23.6	21.1	18.2	22.1
Total	516.3	484.9	424.9	425.4	383.1	333.4	373.1
Income before taxes on income	104.3	126.9	105.8	110.3	99.2	96.6	118.7
Taxes on income	41.2	50.4	41.8	43.6	39.5	39.5	48.6
Net Income	$63.1	$76.5	$64.0	$66.7	$59.7	$57.1	$70.1
Weighted-average number of common and common equivalent shares outstanding (1,2)	263.8	273.0	271.6	271.2	269.8	269.4	268.9
Primary/Fully diluted earnings per share (2,3)	$.23	$.28	$.23	$.25	$.22	$.21	$.26
Dividends declared per common share (2)	$.040	$.033	$.033	$.033	$.033	$.033	$.027
CONSOLIDATED FINANCIAL CONDITION (at quarter end)							
Cash and investments required to be segregated (in billions)	$6.8	$6.6	$7.0	$7.5	$7.2	$6.2	$5.2
Receivable from customers (in billions)	$7.8	$7.1	$5.9	$5.4	$5.0	$4.5	$4.7
Total assets (in billions)	$16.5	$15.6	$14.7	$14.6	$13.8	$12.1	$11.2
Payable to customers (in billions)	$13.1	$12.3	$11.8	$11.8	$11.2	$9.7	$9.1
Borrowings (in millions)	$361	$320	$289	$283	$284	$294	$300
Stockholders' equity (in millions)	$1,145	$1,078	$993	$938	$855	$814	$757
OTHER							
Return on stockholders' equity (4)	23%	30%	27%	30%	29%	29%	39%
Revenue growth over prior year's quarter	29%	42%	8%	20%	22%	12%	43%
After-tax profit margin	10.2%	12.5%	12.1%	12.5%	12.4%	13.3%	14.3%
Full-time equivalent employees (at quarter end, in thousands)	12.7	12.0	11.2	11.1	10.4	9.6	9.4
Capital expenditures – cash purchases of equipment, office facilities and property, net (in millions)	$36.3	$33.6	$36.9	$32.7	$49.1	$31.7	$10.3

6 | The Charles Schwab Corporation *(Continued)*

Consolidated Operating Results (in millions, except per share amounts)	1997				1996		
	Fourth Quarter	Third Quarter	Second Quarter	First Quarter	Fourth Quarter	Third Quarter	Second Quarter
CUSTOMERS' DAILY AVERAGE TRADING VOLUME (in thousands)							
Daily average revenue trades [(5)]	77.5	77.4	64.0	68.2	55.9	48.7	57.5
Mutual Fund OneSource® trades [(6)]	33.1	34.8	32.5	36.4	26.1	27.0	28.9
Daily average trades	110.6	112.2	96.5	104.6	82.0	75.7	86.4
Average Commission Per Revenue Trade [(5)]	$63.38	$64.61	$63.59	$65.55	$66.89	$66.88	$71.79

Source: © 1998 Charles Schwab & Co., Inc. All rights reserved. Member SIPC/New York Stock Exchange, Inc.
[(1)]Amounts shown are used to calculate primary earnings per share.
[(2)]Reflects the three-for-two common stock split declared July 16, 1997, distributed September 15, 1997.
[(3)]Basic and Diluted Earnings Per Share are presented in accordance with SFAS No. 128.
[(4)]Calculated based on annualized quarterly net income and average stockholders' equity for the quarter.
[(5)]Effective with the first quarter of 1997, revenue trades have been restated for all quarters presented to include all customer trades (both domestic and international) that generate either commission revenue or revenue from principal markups.
[(6)]Primary mutual fund trades executed through Schwab's Mutual Fund OneSource service.

firms to introduce 24-hour touch-tone trading service. Schwab first offered online trading in 1984. Customers conducted PC-based trading through the proprietary Equalizer software. Today Schwab offers a number of electronic brokerage services including telephone and PC-based distribution channels (see Exhibit 7).

There are two telephone-based online services: TeleBroker and VoiceBroker. The TeleBroker system, which is a touch-tone trading service, allows Schwab's clients to place trades, to check the status of a trade, to get quotes, and to check account balances. The VoiceBroker system, which was introduced in the third quarter of 1996, uses voice recognition technology to provide real-time quotes to the customer. Schwab's automated telephone channels handled 73 percent of total customer calls received in 1997.

Schwab's PC-based online services have evolved over the years. StreetSmart, which was established in 1994, allowed customers to dial into the Schwab system to execute trade and research, to review accounts, and to use portfolio management tools. Trades executed through StreetSmart received a 10 percent discount on Schwab's regular commission. E-Schwab, which was established in June 1996, was Schwab's first Internet service and offered the same services as StreetSmart. The customer, however, was expected to conduct most of his business online.

SchwabNow is offered through the Schwab home page and was introduced in 1997. This Web service is positioned as a "value-added" service that supplies market data and a comprehensive set of financial tools for clients. Similar to a virtual branch it allows customers to communicate with Schwab and to execute trades. In January 1998, Schwab extended its home page to include investment ideas, research, guidance, and decision-making tools never before offered by Schwab, and beyond the scope of what full-commission brokers have traditionally provided, including the Asset Allocation Toolkit for portfolio allocation guidance, the Mutual Fund OneSource On-line, and Market Buzz sites for research and information. Exhibit 8 provides a summary of selected Schwab products and services.

Schwab surpassed 1.6 million active online accounts at month end March 1998. Online customer assets reached $112 billion in March 1998. During the first quarter of 1998, 48 percent of total customer trades were executed through online channels, versus 33 percent a year ago and 41 percent in the fourth quarter of

7 | Charles Schwab: Multichannel Delivery Systems

The company differentiates itself with multichannel delivery systems that allow customers to choose how they prefer to do business with the company. In addition to its branch office network, the company maintains four regional customer telephone service centers as well as electronic brokerage channels.

- **Branch Office Network:** On December 31, 1997, Schwab operated 272 domestic branch offices in 47 states, as well as branches in the Commonwealth of Puerto Rico and the United Kingdom. In addition, in 1997, the company opened new offices in Hong Kong and the Cayman Islands. The company's office network plays a key role in building its business. With the customer service support of regional customer telephone service centers and electronic brokerage channels, branch personnel are focusing a significant portion of their time on business development. Customers can use branch offices to open accounts, deliver and receive checks and securities, obtain market information, place orders, and obtain related customer services in person, yet most branch activities are conducted by telephone and mail.
- **Regional Customer Telephone Service Centers:** Schwab's four regional customer telephone service centers, located in Indianapolis, Denver, Phoenix, and Orlando, handle customer trading and service calls 24 hours a day, seven days a week. Customer orders placed during nonmarket hours are routed to appropriate markets the following business day. The capacity of the service centers allows the branch office network to be maintained at lower staffing levels and to focus on business development.

The company's customer service approach is to use teams led by registered representatives in the service centers who work closely with branch office network personnel. Additionally, certain teams at these centers provide specialized services to active and affluent investors. Each registered representative has immediate access to the customer account and market-related information necessary to respond to customer inquiries.

- **Electronic Brokerage Channels:** Customers are able to obtain financial information and execute trades on an automated basis through the company's electronic brokerage channels that provide both online and automated telephonic access. These channels are designed to provide added convenience for customers and minimize Schwab's costs of responding to and processing routine customer transactions. To assist customers in using online channels, the company maintains two online customer support centers that operate both during and after normal market hours.

Online channels include PC-based services such as SchwabLink and the Charles Schwab Web site (formerly known as SchwabNOW!)—an information and trading service on the Internet. The company's online channels handled 37% of total trades in 1997. Automated telephonic channels include TeleBroker—Schwab's touch-tone telephone trading service, and VoiceBroker—Schwab's voice recognition quote service. Schwab's automated telephonic channels handled 73 percent of total customer calls received in 1997. Trades placed through electronic brokerage channels provide discounts from the company's standard commission rates.

Source: Form 10-K

1997. Gideon Sasson, Enterprise President of Electronic Brokerage, commented.:

> *On-line investing is evolving. Phase one was about early adopters getting on the Internet and a fragmented marketplace of firms fighting a price war at the cost of providing service, quality information and quick access. Phase two is about providing millions more investors with access to an Internet experience where investing smart at a good value is paramount, and where high levels of customer service support and unbiased information, with value pricing, are the competitive differentiators. Phase two is here.*[12]

CIO Dawn Lepore added:

> *If you wait until a technology is widely adopted before you try it, you've lost your market advantage. That is why we were early entrants on the Web and we have such a big share of that market.*[13]

Schwab has also focused on providing innovative services to independent fee-based financial advisors.

8 | Charles Schwab: Products and Services

Schwab offers both a broad range of products and services tailored to meet customers' varying investment and financial needs, as well as access to extensive investment news and information.

The offer lists the purchase and sale of securities which include exchange-listed, NASDAQ and other equity securities, options, mutual funds, unit investment trusts, variable annuities, and fixed income investments, including United States Treasuries, zero-coupon bonds, listed and OTC corporate bonds, municipal bonds, GNMAs, and CDs. Customers approved for margin transactions may borrow a portion of the price of certain securities purchased through Schwab, or may sell securities short. A customer may receive additional services by qualifying for and opening a Schwab One brokerage account. For cash balances awaiting investment, Schwab pays interest to Schwab One customers. In Schwab IRAs, cash balances are swept daily into one of three SchwabFunds money market funds.

Customers' securities transactions are conducted on either a cash or margin basis. Interest on margin loans to customers provides an important source of revenue to Schwab. During 1997, Schwab's outstanding margin loans to customers averaged $6.4 billion. Schwab may use cash balances in customer accounts to extend margin credit to other customers. To the extent Schwab's customers elect to have cash balances in their brokerage accounts swept into certain SchwabFunds money market funds, the cash balances available to Schwab for investments or for financing margin loans are reduced. However, Schwab receives mutual fund service fees from such funds based on the daily average invested balances.

On December 31, 1997, Schwab's Mutual Fund OneSource service enabled customers to trade 825 mutual funds in 121 fund families without incurring transaction fees. Customer assets held by Schwab that have been purchased through the Mutual Fund OneSource service, excluding Schwab's proprietary funds, totaled $56.6 billion at the end of 1997.

Schwab's Mutual Fund Marketplace (including Mutual Fund OneSource) provides customers with the ability to invest in nearly 1,400 mutual funds in 219 fund families sponsored by third parties. Schwab charges a transaction fee of trades placed in the funds included in the Mutual Fund Marketplace (except on trades through the Mutual Fund OneSource service).

Schwab's proprietary funds, collectively referred to as the SchwabFunds, include money market funds, equity index funds, bond funds, asset allocation funds, and funds that primarily invest in stock, bond, and money market funds. Qualifying Schwab customers may elect to have cash balances in their brokerage accounts automatically invested in certain SchwabFunds money market funds.

M&S provides trade execution services in NASDAQ and other securities to broker-dealers, including Schwab, and institutional customers. Schwab has specialist operations on the Pacific Exchange and the Boston Stock Exchange to make markets in exchange-listed securities. The majority of trades originated by the customers of Schwab in exchange-listed securities for which Schwab makes a market, are directed to these operations.

Schwab also offers SchwabPlan, a comprehensive 401(k) retirement plan, which enables employers to offer a wide range of investment options as well as employee education to their 401(k) retirement plan participants.

Source: Form 10-K

Schwab introduced the new SchwabLink Web site, which has made it easier for advisors to communicate with Schwab and receive news and information tailored to their needs. Customer assets managed by advisors reached $106 billion by year end 1997, up 45 percent from December 1996.

Schwab continued to expand its branch network during 1997 by opening a record 40 new offices. Schwab also expanded its international branch network, opening offices in Hong Kong and the Cayman Islands during 1997. In addition, Schwab created the first online marketplace for international customers to trade third-party mutual funds. Over 200 funds are now available through http://www.schwab-worldwide.com. Schwab believes that for the retail investor, the combination of multiple service channels, technology, access to information and guidance, and value pricing offered by Schwab is unequaled in the industry.[14]

TECHNOLOGY AND OPERATIONS[15]

Through the creative use of technology, Schwab is able to offer investors greater depth of services than was previously available. With unbiased and quick access to real-time information on the Web, combined with the support of Schwab's people, investors benefit from guidance both electronically and in person. We believe this combination of technology, service, and people places Schwab in a category by itself.[16]

—Art Shaw, SVP of Electronic Brokerage Product Development

To support its multichannel delivery systems, as well as other applications such as clearing functions, account administration, record keeping, and direct customer access to investment information, Schwab maintains a sophisticated computer network connecting all of the branch offices and regional customer telephone service centers. Schwab's computers are also linked to the major registered United States securities exchanges, M&S, the National Securities Clearing Corporation, and The Depository Trust Company. The company handles both telephone and online trades from all over the world through six different call centers located throughout the United States.

Schwab also puts a great emphasis on rapid technology deployment. It took a mere ten weeks for its Web site to go from concept to final testing in 1996. In the final quarter of last year, the team put out more than 20 production releases of its Web presence. Management prefers to work with in-house experts who have a "marrow-deep" understanding of the business, rather than outside consultants. Gideon Sasson notes:

> *We're trying to create a Web experience in an environment that changes extremely fast. You can't control that experience very well with a vendor.*[17]

To enhance the reliability of the system and integrity of data, Schwab maintains monitored backup and recovery functions. These include logging of all critical files intraday, duplication and storage of all critical data outside of its central computer site every 24 hours, and the maintenance and periodic testing of a disaster recovery plan. To reduce the exposure to system failures caused by external factors, including earthquakes, the primary data center is located in Phoenix.

Global Presence

With the success of its U.S. online business, Schwab is acting on its global ambitions. In 1997, Schwab began moving the manually conducted business of its subsidiary, UK-based Sharelink, into cyberspace. Schwab's Senior Vice-President of International Technology Bob Duste notes that Schwab's Web strategy is ultimately designed to create a borderless business:

> *That makes it easier for anyone, anywhere in the world, to access Schwab and its subsidiaries over the Internet.*

Nevertheless, the firm faces significant legal and regulatory challenges as it moves abroad. For example, in some places, as Bob Duste observes:

> *Putting up a Web site is seen as an unsolicited sale, and it's frowned upon. It takes a lot of time and effort to be sure that we don't run foul of a country's rules and regulations.*[18]

Another challenge is setting up an international communications infrastructure that is faster and more reliable than the current setup. Today, a Web order placed by a customer located in Germany passes first to the company's Internet service provider in Phoenix, then back to Schwab's London office for processing. This may not be best strategy for the future and Duste concedes that Schwab may eventually have to put a data center on the Continent.

The virtual nature of cyberspace is one reason why Schwab insists on keeping doors of its 254 U.S. domestic and international branches open, and 5,000 human brokers among a total of 11,000 employees. The company envisions its physical branches in the U.S., London, Hong Kong, and the Cayman Islands as a kind of backup, a reassuring presence that reminds customers that even if the wires aren't working, they can still walk into a building to get a check. Duste comments:

> *The branches represent the physical reality of the company. It tells people we won't disappear next week.*[19]

YAHOO!

Company Background[20]

Yahoo! is a global Internet media company that offers a network of branded World Wide Web programming to service millions of users daily. As the first online navigational guide to the Web, www.yahoo.com is the single largest guide in terms of traffic, advertising, and household and business user reach, and is one of the most recognized brands associated with the Internet.

Yahoo! was developed and first made available in 1994 by the company's founders, David Filo and Jerry Yang, while they were graduate students at Stanford University. Yahoo! started to sell advertisements on its Web pages in August 1995. In April 1996, it completed its initial public offering. By late 1997, Yahoo! had advertising contracts with more than 2,600 clients. Exhibit 9 depicts selected financial data for Yahoo!.

Customers can access Yahoo! for free. The traffic on Yahoo! reached a record of 95 million page views per day during the month of March 1998. In addition, Yahoo! has the largest audience of any online service or site on the Web with more than 30 million unique users per month in the United States. Jeff Mallett, chief operating officer, comments:

> *We have relentlessly continued to add valuable content, communication tools, and commerce services, and as a result, Yahoo!'s users are using our service more frequently and are very loyal. And, our audience is growing as more new Internet users make Yahoo! the place they go to meet all of their online information and entertainment needs.*

Yahoo! the Site

The company's principal offering, Yahoo!, provides the flagship product for its global Internet media network that offers branded programming and services used by millions of people each day. Yahoo! offers a comprehensive, intuitive, and user-friendly online guide to Web navigation, aggregated information content, communi-

EXHIBIT 9 | Yahoo! Inc. Condensed Consolidated Statement of Operations (in thousands, except per share amounts) (unaudited)

	THREE MONTHS ENDED MARCH 31,	
	1998	**1997**
Net revenues	$30,206	$10,065
Cost of revenues	3,917	1,437
Gross profit	26,289	8,628
Operating expenses:		
Sales and marketing	16,096	7,415
Product development	4,534	2,249
General and administrative	1,992	1,297
Total operating expenses	$22,622	$10,961
Income (loss) from operations	3,667	(2,333)
Investment income, net	1,446	1,391
Minority interests in operations of consolidated subsidiaries	243	202
Income (loss) before income taxes	5,356	(740)
Provision for income taxes	1,071	—
Net income (loss)	$ 4,285	$ (740)
Diluted net income (loss) per share	$ 0.08	$ (0.02)
Weighted average common shares and equivalents used in diluted per share calculation	53,374	42,231

Source: http://www.yahoo.com/docs/pr/1q98balance.html

cation services, a strong user community, and commerce. Yahoo! includes a hierarchical, subject-based directory of Web sites, which enables Web users to locate and access desired information and services through hypertext links included in the directory.

As of December 1997, Yahoo! organized over 750,000 Web site listings under the following 14 principal categories: Arts and Humanities, Business and Economy, Computers and Internet, Education, Entertainment, Government, Health, News and Media, Recreation and Sports, Reference, Regional, Science, Social Science, and Society and Culture. Web sites are further organized under these major headings by hierarchical subcategories. Users can browse the directory listings by subject matter through a rapid keyword search request that scans the contents of the entire directory or any subcategory within Yahoo!.

Yahoo! also incorporates a rich set of current and reference information from leading content providers, including real-time news (provided by Reuters News Media), stock quotes (Reuters), corporate earnings reports (Zacks), mutual fund holdings (CDA/Wiesenberger), stock investing commentary (Motley Fool), sports scores (ESPN SportsTicker), sports commentary (The Sporting News), weather information (Weathernews, Inc.), and entertainment industry gossip (E! On-line). Yahoo! also organizes hypertext links to Web sites featuring current events and issues of interest, such as elections, holidays, political issues and major weather conditions, organized in a topical format and updated regularly. Other content offered by Yahoo! includes Yellow Pages, maps, driving directions, and classifieds listings.

Yahoo! has also established itself as a leading communications hub on the Internet. Through its integrated chat service and message boards, Yahoo! members can contact each other as well as communicate with the Web community at large. Yahoo! has built a community of members who register with Yahoo!, establish a personalized version of Yahoo!, use Web-based Yahoo! Mail for e-mail and submit classified advertisements.

In addition, one of the company's primary strategies is to provide a marketplace for commerce on the Web. Through sponsorship arrangements with premier merchants, Yahoo! offers its members the opportunity to purchase goods and services such as books (Amazon.com), music (CDNow), videos (Reel.com, Videoserve), automotive services (Autoweb, Microsoft Carpoint), mortgages (E-Loan), and brokerage services (DLJ direct, E*Trade, Ameritrade, Datek).

Strategic Alliances

Yahoo! has entered into several strategic relationships with business partners who offer content, technology, and distribution capabilities. These strategic alliances include leading providers such as Ziff-Davis, SOFTBANK, Rogers Communications, Reuters, Granite Broadcasting, Sporting News, ESPN SportsTicker, E! On-line, MSNBC, MTV, and the Motley Fool—which permit Yahoo!-branded, targeted media products to be marketed more quickly, while avoiding the cost of producing original editorial content.

In order to broaden Yahoo!'s user base, co-promotional relationships with commercial online services, Internet access providers, and operators of leading Web sites have been established. For example, Yahoo! is one of the premier navigational guides distributed through Microsoft Internet Explorer, the Microsoft home page, and the Microsoft Network.

Yahoo! also has relationships with companies such as AT&T, MCI, @Home, MediaOne, Roadrunner, US West, and WebTV, and under which these Internet access providers feature Yahoo! as a key navigational tool. Yahoo! has established distribution agreements with Compaq and Gateway whereby links to Yahoo! services are offered on the desktop of new computers. My Yahoo!, Yahoo! Search, Yahoo! Weather, and My Yahoo! NewsTicker are integrated into customized versions of Microsoft Internet Explorer.

In the first quarter of 1998, Yahoo! and MCI agreed to launch a new co-branded, co-marketed online service—Yahoo! On-line—powered by MCI Internet and designed to provide consumers with an integrated and simple solution to easily explore the Internet with nationwide dial-up access coverage.

Yahoo! Around the World

Yahoo!'s successful growth in the United States is being duplicated in international sites. Yahoo! Korea (www.yahoo.co.kr), the newest of Yahoo!'s sites in Asia, has already reached approximately one million page views per day since being launched in 1997. In Europe,

Yahoo!'s U.K./Ireland site (www.yahoo.co.uk) was recently ranked the most popular among all U.K. Web sites with three times more traffic than the next closest site (*New Media Age*, February 1998). Yahoo! Deutschland (www.yahoo.de) is ranked No. 1 in reach (44.5 percent) and is the most regularly used navigational guide on the Internet in Germany (GfK On-line Monitor, February 1998). Yahoo! France (www.yahoo.fr) is ranked No. 1 in reach among all Web sites in France, with 55.3 percent of all Internet users using the site in a one-week period (Etude Motivation On-line, January 1998).[21]

Finance Center

Yahoo! operates one of the most popular financial destination sites on the Internet: Yahoo! Finance (quote.yahoo.com). At this site, customers can access, free of charge, a wealth of financial information and tools.

Yahoo! Finance allows customers to create customized portfolios and track their holdings, obtain information about stock price movements, observe earnings surprises and collate buy/sell recommendations from a number of industry analysts. A number of chat-forums allow investors to participate in online discussions about different sectors and/or firms. A Java-based portfolio manager was added to the site in April 1998. Exhibit 10 provides a summary of the features of Yahoo! Finance.

In March 1997, analysis conducted by PC Meter found Yahoo!'s finance area to be the most popular source for up-to-the-minute financial information on the Web. Yahoo! Finance had an audience reach of 3.1 percent—surpassing the reach of other leading finance sites (Galt.comwith 1.6 percent, DBC.com with 1.4 percent, Quote.com with 1.4 percent, and CNNfn.com with 1.4 percent).

Through an agreement with E-Loan, the Yahoo! Finance Loan Center (http://loan.yahoo.com) offers consumers comprehensive features for securing a home loan including custom mortgage quotes, rare monitoring, and loan prequalification, and provides resources to save time and money when applying for and researching loans.

In February 1998, Yahoo and First USA unveiled the Yahoo platinum Visa card with a special 9.99 percent APR and no annual fee.[22] Cardmembers have exclusive

10 | Current Yahoo! Finance Features

- **High Performance Quotes:** Quotes for stocks (United States and Canada), mutual funds, currencies, and indices plus United States and international market summary information.
- **Portfolios:** Users can create multiple portfolios to track performance of their holdings.
- **Charts:** Three-month, one-year, two-year, and five-year charts.
- **The Motley Fool:** Financial editorial and advice.
- **Zacks Investment Research:** Earnings estimates and brokerage recommendations on more than 6,000 companies, plus industry rankings and daily earnings surprises.
- **EDGAR On-line:** Summaries of SEC electronic corporate filings for quarterly and annual reports with management's discussions.
- **Financial News:** Company-specific and general business news from wire services such as Reuters, PR Newswire, and Business Wire.
- **Morningstar Mutual Fund Profiles:** Fund descriptions with rating, risk, and return information.
- **Hoover's Profiles:** Profiles on more than 6,000 companies with company business overviews, officer rosters and links to additional resources.
- **Legg Mason Economic & Treasury Calendar:** Highlights of upcoming events significant to the market.
- **Stock Chat:** Chat area with integrated stock quotes for users to discuss investment ideas with others.

Source: http://www.yahoo.com/docs/pr/release82.html

online access to their credit card account and rewards program information 24-hours-a-day through the Yahoo! Visa Web site (visa.yahoo.com).

Yahoo! Finance, in conjunction with InsWeb, announced in April 1998 a service that lets users compare quotes and estimates for automobile, life, health, homeowners', and renters' insurance.[23] InsWeb only provides insurance quotes and estimates at this point, but company spokesman Greg Berardi noted that there are plans to sell insurance online in the future:

> *Our goal is to do end-to-end insurance sales, but now we're focused on what consumers really want, and that's comparison shopping. Payment takes a pretty short time in the process, and what's really important is the ability to get quotes without having to spend the time making phone calls.*

InsWeb is free, as is the Yahoo Insurance Center. InsWeb and the Yahoo Insurance Center offer auto quotes from eight insurance carriers; life insurance quotes from three carriers; health insurance from two carriers in two states; and homeowner and renter insurance estimates. Quotes for homeowners and renters will be added in the near future. Additional health insurance information is also slated for the future. Yahoo! users will get a few extra features, including a health insurance needs analyzer to help users determine what kind of health plan they require.

CONCLUSION

The Internet has transformed the rules of the brokerage industry. In mid-1998, there are at least 70 online trading firms in North America. The giant cybersecurities mall, Stockhouse at www.stockhouse.com, not only provides links to these online firms but also provides connections to over 50 stock markets around the world. It is certain that many more such new entrants shall emerge in the global arena in the coming years. These new entrants are changing the rules of the game and forcing traditional players such as Schwab and Merrill Lynch to reevaluate their strategic options.

But the long-term impact of the Internet on the brokerage industry is going to be far more dramatic. Certain trends for future developments can already be observed:

- *Customer Gatekeepers:* Companies such as Yahoo! are rapidly positioning themselves as gatekeepers to cyber-customers. Today, these gatekeepers provide customers with free access to a wealth of value-adding information on a variety of topics. If these organizations emerge as the cyber-destination of choice for a large segment of cyber-customers, then their roles vis-a-vis customers and content providers will change significantly. For example, Yahoo! is slowly entering the domain of providing financial (and other) services. How far will Yahoo! go in such a direction? What does this mean for firms such as E*Trade and Charles Schwab?
- *Direct Public Offerings (DPOs):* Unlike traditional Initial Public Offerings (IPOs), a DPO is a "best-efforts" offering made directly by the issuer itself without the help of any underwriter as an intermediary. Several sites for DPOs have been established over the last years. For example, see the Web site of IPO Data Systems (www.ipodata.com). DPOs represent an approach by companies to reach investors directly. Several additional sites (such as IPOnet at www.zanax.com/iponet) have emerged to form databanks of potential investors for DPOs. It is certain that the influence of DPOs will increase as the penetration of the Internet increases in society.
- *Bulletin Boards for Secondary Trading:* Large institutional investors have used closed electronic networks (such as the Island System and "POSIT"—Portfolio System for Institutional Trading) to trade shares among themselves since the early 1980s. As security and reliability concerns on the Net are addressed, such closed trading will expand to include small investors via the Internet. Already bulletin boards are emerging where investors can trade stocks among themselves. Examples include Real Goods (www.realgoods.com), PerfectData Corporation (www.perfectdata.com), and Internet Capital Exchange (www.inetcapital.com).

There are several open questions:

- Who will be the key players in the online brokerage industry five years from now?
- What will the industry look like in ten years' time?
- How will emerging customer gatekeepers such as Yahoo! change the brokerage business?

- What kind of a role will traditional brokerage players play in the industry?
- Do new entrants like E*Trade risk becoming obsolete themselves?
- What kind of a role should banks play in this scenario of dramatic changes?

Where it will all end is hard to predict.

ENDNOTES

1. "Surfing the Net to Make More Money," *MONEY* Magazine, 11-Nov-96 (http://www.etrade.com/news/m1196.html).
2. "Trade Fast, Trade Cheap" *Fortune*, 2-Feb-98 (http://www.pathfinder.com/fortune/1998/980202/bro.html).
3. "A Survey of Technology in Finance: Turning Digits into Dollars—Fixing What Is Broken (Part 5 of 8)," *The Economist*, 26-Oct-96.
4. The following description of E*Trade is partially based on the following sources: (a) E*Trade Press Release: http://www.etrade.com/visitor/press/pr111897.html; (b) On-line document: http://www.etrade.com/visitor/annual/action/balance.html; (c) On-line document: http://www.etrade.com/visitor/annual/action/window.html; (d) On-line document: http://www.etrade.com/visitor/annual/action/value.html; and (e) E*Trade 10-K Report: http://www.sec.gov/Archives/edgar/data/1015780/0001012870-97-002529.txt
5. E*Trade Press Release: http://www.etrade.com/visitor/press/pr111897.html
6. "Money Talks: Flame Your Broker!" *Esquire*, 5-May-97 (http://www.etrade.com/news/eq042997.html)
7. E*Trade Press Release: http://www.etrade.com/visitor/press/pr040798.html
8. Schwab News Release: 13-Jan-98: http://www.prnewswire.com/gh/cnoc/comp/154881.html
9. Schwab News Release: 15-Apr-98: http://www.prnewswire.com/gh/cnoc/comp/154881.html
10. Schwab Annual Report 1995: http://www.schwab.com/SchwabNOW/SNLibrary/SNLib030/1995/viscomm3.html
11. Schwab News Release: 12-Feb-98: http://www.prnewswire.com/gh/cnoc/comp/154881.html
12. Schwab News Release: 16-Dec-98: http://www.prnewswire.com/gh/cnoc/comp/154881.html
13. "Betting the Bank," *Information Strategy*, Sep-97.
14. Schwab News Release: 14-Jan-98: http://www.prnewswire.com/gh/cnoc/comp/154881.html
15. This section is adapted from: Schwab Annual Report Form 10-K (EDGAR Archives): http://www.sec.gov/Archives/edgar/data/316709/0001047469-98-012181.txt
16. Schwab News Release: 13-Jan-98: http://www.prnewswire.com/gh/cnoc/comp/154881.html
17. "Betting the Bank," *Information Strategy*, Sep-97.
18. "Betting the Bank," *Information Strategy*, Sep-97.
19. "Betting the Bank," *Information Strategy*, Sep-97.
20. The description of Yahoo! is partially adapted from Yahoo! Annual Report Form 10-K (EDGAR Archives): http://www.sec.gov/Archives/edgar/data/1011006/0001047469-98-009651.txt
21. Yahoo! Press Release, 8-Apr-98: http//www.yahoo.com/docs/pr/release169.html
22. Yahoo! Press Release, 23-Feb-98: http://www.yahoo.com/docs/pr/release150.html
23. "Yahoo! launches Insurance Center," News.com, 6-Apr-98.

CASE 19

FEMSA Meets The 21st Century

Felipe Gonzalez y Gonzalez
Universidad Panamericana

A CENTENARIAN BUSINESS

October 28th of 1998, a FEMSA manager is interviewed to see how he perceived the company at that point in time. Without hesitating he answers, "We're doing fine. But we're not yet where the corporation ought to be. It has to reach a point where the best investors, the best professionals in each field, the best sales people, the best in each of the areas the company is involved in, want to belong to FEMSA. And right now, that is not the case."

Due to the changes made at FEMSA, he feels the Group is quite far from what it longs to become. The organization is just getting ready to make the change that will lead to that. "What we are looking at is not a change, we're making way for the change. We are alerting the organization, trying to arouse an awareness, and in many cases we are startling people. Our organization aims to stand out and do important things: to become an organization that attracts the best people in all fields. But there is a huge gap between what we are now doing and what we intend to be doing. We want to promote a mentality whereby managers seek excellence in all orders. We don't like complacency, or that other very similar attitude that justifies keeping someone in a managerial position because of their past performance. We are preparing the organization for a differential leap."

For FEMSA the turn of the century means more than turning over a leaf of the calendar. It means being a 20th century company that becomes a company of the 21st century. According to its managers, this makes a big difference. Rather than changing the firm, it's a matter of reinventing it. They are seeking a new mentality and a new way to do business and to conduct their business, which is what is truly paramount when it comes to the permanence of a company that is over a century old.

Historically speaking, the current *Fomento Económico Mexicano, S.A.*, group (FEMSA) began with the founding of *Cervecería Cuauhtémoc* brewery in 1890. As time went by, related businesses were added, allowing for a certain degree of integration (Appendix A).

These businesses were practically divisions of the brewery in the early stages, but were later structured as individual companies, under the umbrella of *Valores Industriales, S.A.* (VISA), founded in 1936 as their holding company.

Capitalizing on the benefits of a closed economy that only slightly communicated with other countries, the holding was able to engage in several ventures and grow into one of the strongest business groups in Mexico.

VISA's strategy was to aggressively diversify from the 1940s to 1980, engaging the Group in a wide variety of ventures that ranged from fishing or large-scale hotels to

---

Case written by Prof. Felipe Gonzalez y Gonzalez, Instituto Panamericano de Alta Dirección de Empresa, Graduate School of Business, Mexico. This case is provided as a baseline to discuss—not illustrate—the proper or improper way to manage a given situation.

Copyright © 1999 by *Sociedad Panamerica de Estudios Empresariales, A.C. (Instituto panamericano de Alta Dirección de Empresa, IPADE)*

No part of this document may be reproduced by any means, including electronic, without permission in writing from the copyright holder.

For copies hereof, contact:

Mexico City:	5 354-18-00	Fax: 5 354-18-52
Guadalajara:	(3)627-15-50	Fax: (3)627-15-61
Monterrey:	(8)335-80-25	Fax: (8)335-80-15

agricultural endeavors, naturally including financial concerns—creating first a private investment company and later a bank with nationwide coverage. It was a worldwide trend throughout the 1970s to diversify.

The takeover of the third-largest brewery in the country was added to these operations in 1985. This involved new challenges: handling a broader portfolio of brands, losing Moctezuma's market share, consolidating two previously antagonistic groups of people into one single team, and improving their skills to manage the new portfolio. A considerable portion of this diversification was financed with liabilities in U.S. dollars (especially in the late 1970s and early 1980s). In 1981 the expansion came to a halt.

This left the whole domestic beer market to just two breweries.

The corporation was seriously affected by several events in 1982, such as the macroeconomic crisis, which led to the peso devaluating 100 percent to the dollar, and a severe slump in the domestic market, due to the debt crisis. The whole decade turned out to be a heavy setback for growth expectations in Mexico and all of Latin America.

The organization dealt with the ordeal of those years on two fronts. On the one hand it divested all unrelated businesses; and on the other, a whole financial strategy was devised to restructure the organization's liabilities and enable it to cope with the new circumstances that were placing Mexico in a new light on the international business scene.

The care personnel received at the *Cauhtémoc* brewery from its founding in 1890 became a tradition to be later maintained by the VISA group. Its promoters and founders not only had great entrepreneurial vision, but were also humanitarians. This led them to create a whole social welfare system for their workers. They developed schools, professional training centers and even a college. They created a system whereby their workers could afford to purchase decent housing, and they founded a first-rate medical center to meet their employees' health care needs. Other pursuits included cultural and recreational efforts organized by what was known as *Sociedad Cauhtémoc y Famosa*.

This care and consideration extended to its personnel led the company to develop a very strict tradition in selecting employees, and a welfare policy that was comprehensive, visionary and early for the country's stage of development. Stable jobs became a Group hallmark. With such a personnel policy and the success achieved in the different businesses it went into, the people's loyalty and identification with the company became proverbial.

On *Cervecería*'s first centennial in 1990, the firm seemed to be in top shape to face the last decade of the century. Having restructured its finances and taken over *Cervecería Moctezuma*, plus *Coca-Cola para el Valle de México* in 1978, and with the beverage market tightly targeted, letting go of all businesses except those related to packaging, logistics and the distribution, the Group seemed to be standing on an enviable launching pad.

THE CHALLENGES OF LIBERALIZATION

In the late '80s Mexico faced not only the high point in a process of soaring inflation, a crisis in public finances marred by a budgetary deficit and a staunch contraction of the domestic market, but also misgivings about whether a whole policy of domestic development should be based on import substitution and dependence on the single-exportation system.

With all its advantages and drawbacks, the stabilizing development model was on its way out. Protectionist policies were falling by the wayside, along with the communist and socialist regimes. The world was getting ready to open its doors everywhere to a free-market economy, regarded as the indispensable sire of wealth and growth. As protectionism waned, outdone by the might of globalization, the model had to be upgraded. This implied opening up the economy, which basically amounted to tougher domestic and foreign competition, and the need to export to other markets.

This was a new scenario for the FEMSA group, as for all major Mexican businesses. It was like having to relearn how to walk, and do so as you went along. There was no restarting the meter. Switching over to the new rules of the game would have to be done on the way. The choice was clear: either the Group continued to pursue its financial strategy as the key to the vault of expansion, or it had to start focusing on other aspects of the business. A tradition nurtured over a whole century could be either a liability or an asset. The process of reorganizing its financial status and divesting non-related businesses had created procedures and ways of proceeding that would be put to the test by the new circumstances that the firm was up against.

One of the managers with the firm in 1990 spoke of the outlook at FEMSA (one of VISA's main subsidiaries) as follows: "We did a magnificent job in the '80s. The *Valores Industriales* group managed to create an impressive launching pad, thanks to its great talent and strenuous effort in restructuring the finances of the firm. We have worked with exemplary dedication to turn the firm into a group of related businesses strictly geared to beverages and are sustaining a very promising integration with packaging and distribution. The problem lies in whether concentrating almost exclusively on our financial status will enable us to consolidate the Group for the next 100 years."

In divesting, taking over *Cervecería Moctezuma,* and renegotiating liabilities, the Group developed impressive financial skills. Its intellectual capital was moving in those circles, for during those years a good financial strategy was crucial for survival.

On the other hand, thanks to its highly conservative financial policy, the competition in the beer sector had managed to move into the domestic market and more than remarkably increase its exports during those years. While *Cuauhtémoc–Moctezuma* was scrambling out of the disaster induced by the debt crisis, the competition—unencumbered by such concerns—was busy developing strategies and skills in other areas that were yielding not only sound profits, but a market position hard to equal, given the head start afforded by a carefree financial status.

Notwithstanding its grand reputation as caring employers, the VISA group had to cut back on spending in every area. Training was no exception and even became critical. Other than a few exceptions, no training at all was provided throughout the entire restructuring process, which took practically ten years. Even people in charge of key areas such as quality control simply had to make do with the experience accumulated over long years of having been with the different businesses, because they couldn't be provided any specific or formal training.

"Our experience," commented a former manager, "is based on a totally different set of rules, unlike those you see nowadays. We may have even incurred in isolationism, partly due to the fact that our company is firmly established in a local community that hardly ever receives ideas or people from outside. The globalization that we are witnessing makes us particularly vulnerable, since the nature of our products involves our reaching the ultimate consumer with very specific brands."

In a time of great changes, globalization was taking shape as a situation that brings markets and competition together, calling for more essential skills, other than financial controls, keeping within the budget, or the traditional operational systems. In addition, globalization required making managerial adjustments to transform a family-run business into an institutional one. This involved simplifying the firm's stock structure.

Business management criteria had to be revised in light of the new circumstances that were arising. It seemed clear that there was a need for an internal change and a change of outlook. The new competition scheme pressed the corporation to revise its priorities and working procedures. Some managers were concerned mainly with preventing the change from taking place. It had to be defined and implemented.

The dramatic changes the world was undergoing were leading large firms to share their know-how and strengths. A new type of skills was called for to approach a globalized market. It was nothing new for hundred-year-old companies to be sharing functions. Even the domestic competition had managed to forge an alliance with one of the leading world producers. With their exports, they had attained unquestionable international standing, much more so than *Cervecería Cuauhtémoc–Moctezuma,* whose productivity was comparatively lower.

The financial restructuring issue had been so absolutely vital that operations seemed to have become incidental. The Group was not—as an American would say—on top of the business in its key endeavors. This involved, first of all, defining its strategy. Management had to decide where it wanted the businesses to go. No one questioned the fact that the Group had the elements to become a first-class player on the international scene. The issue was how. The structural part and the portfolio had already been defined. What was still lacking was to define the organization's new style of behavior. The corporate role, among other things, had to be defined. Must the corporate headquarters merely define a few general policies and see that they were enforced? Did it have to get involved in the operations? Answering those questions required delving deeply into the business, the market, the consumers, the industry in general, technology and performance trends.

In short, the businesses' critical success factors had to be defined. Up until then the results of the several operators were given in terms of their contribution to the Group, but their vision of the firm was reduced to their sphere of influence.

"In a nutshell, they've got to have something that is very hard to define. They have to have a knack for doing business. Basically it's not a matter of techniques or methods, but a knack that only comes with judgment based on plenty of experience. We want them to have the ability and commitment of someone involved in making the business thrive, with a broad overall vision. It's also a matter of balancing the time you devote to certain activities and to others."

THE CHANGE

Against this backdrop, Jose Antonio Fernandez became Chief Executive Officer of the Group in January of 1995. A change was in order and was encouraged by voices within the very organization. The subsidiaries' restrictions, their need to be independent, and the need to value each individual business in terms of what it contributed to the Group were all obvious.

For example, at one point the OXXO chain was regarded as the "ugly duckling" of the organization. It was treated like an appendix of the brewery, but its potential was overlooked as such. Certain results were expected, but not achieved. The chain's demand for greater independence had to be dealt with; new products had to be introduced in the convenience stores, products that up until then were regarded as inappropriate, but were actually products offered at any of the stores run by the competition. All sorts of problems had to be solved, ranging from the poor location of several retail outlets all the way to the key points in determining where to place the point of sales. The number of retail outlets needed to build up business in a given location was later identified. Retail outlets in places where prospects looked good were opened, and those where the locations wouldn't yield a minimum profit were shut down. One bit of significant negotiating led to the pricing policy, whereby vendors were required to provide the same treatment as competitors in the same line of business.

"At that time," says one manager, "I realized that perhaps there was also somewhat of a personality cult in the company. This ranged from unnecessary assistants who functioned more as private secretaries to what at the time I called 'the route to the director.' There was a whole program of activities scheduled at the location to be visited, just for show, but without the detail work that makes a business take roots and be sustainable. I also discovered what you might call a subculture of nonconfrontation, which actually amounts to concealing negative aspects, and magnifying results that may momentarily seem brilliant, but are not necessarily relevant for the consolidation of a business.

"My diagnosis could definitely be summarized by saying that we were very good then at financial processes, but we had not developed the same skills to run the businesses."

"The time had come to pay more attention to operations. We had to change not only to stay in business, but also to increase the bottom line and position the Group as one of the leading companies in the field."

"Although the Group had been defined as one striving for maximum satisfaction of beverage consumers," says one of those interviewed, "we were yet to be convinced that excellence these days requires being very mindful of the market and its processes, as well as of the operations that make our products items of excellence. We had to gain renown not only for our skills to buy up and sell businesses, but also for the level of excellence achieved in our own operations. This involved a challenge for the whole organization, all the way from the corporate headquarters, who had to initiate the process of revising our identity, down to the subsidiaries, who had to redefine their role and manage to add up to the Group as a whole, which in turn would be reflected, among other things, in the value of each share of FEMSA stock."

There was a great sense of urgency in some, but not all, of the operators. The Chief Executive Office's first injunction was to listen, to go to the meetings to hear. Participation was not to be inhibited. The idea was to propitiate an atmosphere where all voices were heard. It took some time to make the decision, but it could no longer be postponed. The Chief Executive Office's future and that of the company depended on it. The refrain was and will continue to be the following: manage processes, formulate and identify successful practices, reproduce them, revive businesses with their own dynamics and duplicate them.

Initial Diagnosis

The consensus drawn from several interviews sustained with the managers is that, compared with others, the corporation is clearly average. Viewed from any standpoint this is clearly not good enough.

"The organization is not aligned," affirms one executive. "Not even the top managers are aligned. There are managers with the attitude that they own the job. They roost on their power, rather than rely on it as a tool for advancement. We aren't aligned yet. We're working at it. With some people you struggle more and with other people you struggle less.

"You're driven by present crises or by future ones. The process lies in anticipating issues. If you don't do something today you'll be facing a crisis tomorrow. The need for change can be internal or external. It's internal when those involved see the need and make up their minds to do something about it. External changes are motivated by environmental circumstances that force you to adjust."

A simile was referred to at a meeting with the planning team: the famous Toby Club, where no girls are allowed. This is fine when the members have similar interests that are fully met with the current organization, but when the individuals grow up and their needs and interests change, the Toby Club structure evidently collapses. Either those involved change or they're forced to change. Setting this example aside, in this last case the promoters of change establish the need, they invite people to change, and encourage people to change, but the actual change is ultimately up to the people.

As another executive put it, "Change has a price. It's easy to sell the benefits of change, but the price you pay isn't that clear or whether you're willing to pay it. There are those who postpone paying it and therefore postpone the change itself. Motivation for change may be kindled by people's dissatisfaction with results and aspiring to something better. Or someone in the organization may become aware of the need for change. So they point out that we are not very ambitious, and the generator of change induces us to change, gives us the opportunity to change and the help we need to do so. But people have to interiorize the need for change, and that at times is difficult, either because of their mental blocks, because they're too comfortable or they're too scared to face a new reality."

Making a change can at times face very strong and trying resistance. It's got to be captivating and exciting. And if the change is not made, ever greater resistance will arise, until perhaps you'll reach the conclusion that what needs to be changed is the person. The task is to give you a chance to change. If you don't, then you have to be changed.

Change is always going to involve some risk. It can fail. Changes in the environment aren't always perceived as a vital threat to organizations, and this can inhibit the sense of crisis, which is one of the strongest motivators to change. When this happens management must be able to throw the organization into a crisis, so it will be prepared to put up a fight against new competitors and confront new challenges.

"So far U.S. breweries are not in Mexico," affirms one of those interviewed, "but tomorrow they will be. As for other fields, public television will not be exclusively Mexican in the future. Most likely the U.S. networks will be coming in and foreign companies will be competing on the domestic market. Perceiving all this, the need for change becomes evident, so why not play the lead in that change and start by standing up to our competition at home in the domestic market. We're talking about change all the time at FEMSA, but we've got to do less talking and more working. And that's where we get a trifle jittery.

"The opportunity to change can be brought on by an external crisis, but that isn't the only factor that leads to change. We are more interested in change that comes from within individuals. And here we have to apply this formula: Point out the need. Give people a chance to learn and make the change. If it doesn't take place they will have to review their situation and choose to either put up a fight or change. If they choose the former, they are going to be overtaken and will probably have to leave.

"The need to change has to be heard," he goes on to say. "An example has to be set, starting with managerial positions, where a real change can be made. And last of all change has to be demanded. If executives don't do these two things—set an example and demand the change—the change is going to take quite some time."

There is a need for changes throughout the whole organization, from *Cervecería,* where profits are the highest they have been in 15 years, to Coca-Cola FEMSA, in the Valley of Mexico, where sales reached a record high in all Latin America, but where the flow generated in terms of investment must be examined.

"When it comes to change," comments one manager, "I believe we should let the investors judge us, let them want to invest with us. Let them find us the best executives and show it by wanting to do business with us. We have the potential to bear an impact on Mexico and on the world. But the organization has not generated the personnel it needs. We have to bring in people from abroad. I find this embarrassing, because it is a sign that we haven't done things right. We haven't been able to generate the managerial staff we need."

The personnel policy strongly inhibited change for over 100 years, not because of its obvious benefits, but because of the feeling it gave the personnel that they had it made in the company. All they had to do was behave according to the book. But there seemed to be no need to be proactive. As a current manager says, "A personnel policy can be a competitive edge if handled properly, or it can become a burden if misused. Any extreme is bad. And I think we had gone to extremes. The policy had degenerated to such an extent that people actually considered that we were in business to provide all sorts of aid, ranging from personal help to all kinds of social activities. I even had the opportunity to see such a strategic plan drawn up by *Sociedad Cuauhtémoc y FAMOSA*. People were helped for the sake of being helped, often without evaluating the importance of the projects or what the company might expect in exchange both from its employees and from institutions that have been given aid.

"I consider," he continues, "that our state-of-the-art personnel policy should be upheld, as it has been a company tradition to do, but pointing out to our male and female staff alike that FEMSA is a splendid place to work, provided the relationship is reciprocal. We give in exchange for what we expect, and our expectations have a clear purpose: we want our people and our organization to grow. Paternalism, in the worst sense of the word, is not our goal. We don't want our personnel policy to consist of merely keeping people happy by creating an undemanding work environment. It's now perfectly clear to everyone that we are no longer going to reward mere effort. We need results. I am so sorry, but it's time to put a stop to years of 'giving it all you've got,' as people say. If we want to achieve outstanding results we must have outstanding human resources."

One of the fundamental elements for change at FEMSA has been implementing a human resources stoplight. Everyone is given a chance to change, but those who stall on a red light will have to leave the company, if for no other reason than for their own sake. Those who are stuck at a yellow light will be given help and trained, to develop the required new skills. Where we are especially careful is with our values. If people don't embrace our values in their daily practice, they won't be able to stay with the Group. Today the companies and their personnel will have to understand that the new conditions of world competition involve a risk that must be acknowledged, must be explicitly stated and must be shared. There is no such thing as absolute security, for anyone.

As the early analyses came forth, it became evident that the Group had not developed a mentality focused on operations. Competitive market structures were not contemplated. There was no benchmarking. There were no industry-specific appeal or competency surveys. Outsiders with an understanding of the new business approach had to be brought in, or personnel had to migrate from one operator to another. At the corporate level executives tended to have a background in business, law or finance, but there was hardly anyone with a degree in any of the engineering areas.

The new top management intended to become involved in the businesses. That alone was unusual. The gap from one department to another could be huge, such as between sales and management. Some managers even expressed that there was a non-confrontational culture. Disagreeing with the boss was perceived as inappropriate. Stating different points of view was not necessarily viewed as a way to enrich a dialogue.

The New Corporate Role

Likewise, there was the challenge of defining the new corporate role, and at the corporate headquarters they embarked on the task of drawing up their profile. Studies say the corporate role is determined by the group's vocation. A very diversified group will be fundamentally oriented to its financial role. On the other hand, one more related to a business portfolio must adopt more of a hands-on approach. After months of study, it was concluded that the new corporate role would that of a group made up of integrated businesses with common competencies, where the corporate headquarters' participation had to be strategic and synergetic, because the different businesses were closely related.

The next challenge was to sell the idea to the organization, and especially to the subsidiary operators. Resistance came forth at once. The new corporate role was not understood. It took long months of hard work to convince people that there was a need for change. The idea was to steer their mentality toward a new type of management, not only with a different managerial style, but one with different goals that required new skills.

The challenge of throwing the organization into a crisis had to be met, starting with the corporate headquarters, which was no easy task. Having decided to focus on operations, the need arose for a keen corporate headquarters readily able to respond with business know-how. A new Planning and Strategic Control division was added to the Finance and Human Resource divisions. This aroused suspicion, for there were—and still are—some operators who claim, "I don't understand strategies; all I understand is growth." However, this hasn't stopped the work from being done in the corporate headquarters; and now all projects are questioned. Investment costs are addressed and ways to reduce them are sought.

The lines of change are clearly outlined by the corporate headquarters. The goal is an organization willing to learn, whose personnel is firmly motivated to achieve excellence, and operators who are strongly identified with FEMSA.

The planning division plays an essential role in this process, ensuring that all the departments, areas and subsidiaries are willing to follow FEMSA's course and are able to prove it with hard facts borne out in their daily practice. This had required defining the subsidiaries' role and their integration in the business portfolio. The company's mission statement has several implications for the subsidiaries, in terms of growth guidelines, and skills they must either have or develop in the business endeavor. At this point we had to establish a hierarchy of skills. Which is most important and vital for the organization? Which are necessary although they don't involve any competitive edge? And which are obsolete? Identifying these skills—and this is the breaking point in the corporate strategy—no longer lies in what each subsidiary can or should do on its own, but in making the most of a whole body of knowledge generated within the entire organization and turning this body of knowledge into the main fountainhead of know-how for the organization itself. Synergies are what the Chief Executive Office is focusing on as one of the strategic advantages to be achieved if FEMSA is to reach the position it envisions.

The corporate headquarters has defined the company's mission statement as follows: to satisfy beverage consumers with excellence. Now it's a matter of giving the mission an economic twist, developing it to create value. The mission statement has made it possible to classify the businesses in core, strategic and peripheral endeavors. *Cervecería* and soft drinks are core businesses. Strategic businesses are those that offer advantages, reduce risks, or develop specific skills to be used in the core businesses. Peripheral activities are those that are not essential to the company, but offer important complementary advantages.

The corporate headquarters is thus growing more familiar with the business portfolio, gaining a better understanding of its individual business processes, and expediting the development of key skills for the Group. We definitely want to better understand the businesses and their operations, so the corporate headquarters can challenge them to higher levels of performance.

This new vision is not free of tension. For as new possibilities open up, whoever is not aligned with the organization's values, mission statement and vision is shut down. Along these lines the subsidiaries are not always going to perceive the value generated for them by the corporate headquarters. There will be businesses you are not interested in developing and would prefer to sell. The value generated is for FEMSA's shareholders. On the other hand, opportunities will arise because there will be a chance for subsidiaries to make deals with each other, far beyond mere bargain and sale contracts.

"However, not everything is rose-colored in the businesses," comments one of those interviewed on the subject. "If you decide certain skills are no longer needed or that others are required, if you decide that certain businesses no longer have priority, that will cause stress, and it will be negative stress. You'll cause pain and there are going to be strong emotional reactions. This is why you have to engage in a process of convincing people throughout the structure, giving them a chance to change and offering whatever support is needed. But there must be no compromise in the changes. Otherwise you will lose the motivation of the most skillful people in the organization. Perhaps pain must be regarded as inevitable. Those who want changes will be in pain if they are not made. And there will be pain among those who don't want to see changes. We must avoid the first and give the latter a chance to turn their fears and reluctance into attitudes that will draw them forward."

The rules of the game thus look very clear: FEMSA, as the head of the Group, sets down the guidelines; makes plenty of room for dialogue, preventing the organization from becoming excessively vertical; seeks ways to afford operators the freedom to make their own decisions within the corporate framework; and hopes that its guidelines are followed by everyone.

The role of the subsidiaries is still the company's touchstone, for it is in the subsidiaries where competitive skills are bred, where business opportunities arise, where projects grow roots and become market business. This is why the task of the corporate headquarters is merely to guarantee that efforts are united, point out the synergies that add up for the whole Group, encourage change, and promote among all participants a state of permanent dissatisfaction and a passion for excellence.

Process Orientation

Change was essential. Now we had to not only address the financial side, which is a *sine qua non*, but also completely delve into the processes. Both the corporate headquarters and the operators had to pay more attention to issues such as transfer price decisions among the different businesses. On top of this, however, was the mistrust among operators, who were suspicious of each another, perhaps because they lacked a really practical vision of the overall picture.

All the above in a corporation in which the different subsidiary managers had never discussed their respective businesses with each other; in an organization where there was practically no communication among the different divisions, and therefore no common language or shared practices.

"The attitude developed in the organization was a mixture of haughty pride and seclusion," tells one manager. "Comparisons of the company with what was going on outside, with the competition and changes posed by a new environment, were not well taken. We weren't listening. Our feelings of superiority led us to overprotect the corporation. As far as our employment policy, the business was preferably kept in the family. When it came to hiring new personnel, relatives or friends were more valued than skills needed to fill the position. The change here involved finding competent people, wherever they came from. This aroused criticism and misinterpretations. Outsiders were hired because that was what the organization required, and the results are right there. This crucial issue was defended with cloak-and-dagger, but the outcome was very positive.

"The policy, however, has been that if there is anyone with the required qualifications within the organization, they are certainly given the opportunity to take on new responsibilities. But the main concern has been to get the right people, the people qualified to solve the problems and make the company grow. People are not given a promotion just because of their seniority, or because we assume—or they actually do—identify with the company. Internal promotions are most worthy, but not to the extent of secluding the corporation or developing hemophilia. Besides, the results of the outsiders whom we have hired are self-evident. Their job experience is very enriching and shows up in better results. Innovation and change are paramount for the new organization that we are developing. The most important values are innovation and change."

Being process-oriented also leads us to first look at the internal resources available, at successful practices that can be replicated, and most definitely at building upon our know-how, which fundamentally consists of detecting and discovering synergies.

In this regard a senior manager establishes that "it would be a misinterpretation to simply consider our designed synergies already determined by the integration of the business portfolio. Nor must we think our synergies are limited to the purchasing among the Group producers. Sometimes the idle capacity of third parties can be used, because it is more profitable. The key to synergies is that they all add up, for the benefit of all. We don't want some parts to grow at the expense of the whole organization."

Some have understood the above, yet others have not. The operators feel they are being evaluated only on what they are doing down below, but corporate headquarters looks at the whole picture, and there are synergies that can be used and others that are not so useful. The new FEMSA is an organization that has to add up, and this can cause problems among the subsidiaries and the operators. However, we're determined to face those issues.

Participation and Personal Commitment

The organization was definitely being launched on a process of change, to become more open to learning. This had to be discussed with everyone, but the problem was the lack of a common language.

All levels had to be addressed with a personal commitment. Everyone—starting with the CEO, all the way down to the bottom-rung executive—had to understand the issues of each individual business, and the challenges and goals of the Group as such. This required delving further into each business area. It was necessary to find out what makes some businesses successful and others not so successful, what was required to compete on the domestic and international market.

Achieving the above required an atmosphere of participation, which in turn involved learning how to lay your cards on the table, and to often question ideas, policies and modus operandi. "Here," says one of those interviewed, "I found other problematic factors of the organization, and that are yet to be eradicated from the corporation. We shun confrontation to the extreme. We dropped into a *'laissez-faire, laissez passe'* mode. People's attitudes, abilities or performance were never questioned. It was very painful and very sad to come across people who had been with the company for many years, and who had been receiving their yearly bonus without anyone ever pointing out their weaknesses to them. Many underwent a painful eye-opening process.

"That lack of confrontation exists at all levels and in all divisions. I became aware of it long ago. People would say to me, 'Hey, you can't say that in front of the boss.' They would say that to me, when I wasn't the boss. Now we're trying to change all that."

To get top management involved the Chief Executive Office–generated guidelines, which enabled the executives to freely state their points of view, so they could see that confrontation was not only welcome, but was being encouraged from the higher ranks; so they, in turn, would encourage such an atmosphere of participation in meetings with their subordinates, where the key lies in listening and learning from others. Putting the organization through this growth crisis made everyone see that situations have to be met head on, face to face, stating things as they were. The purpose was not only to learn from one's mistakes, but basically to generate the building processes to share the know-how collected in the different areas and divisions. Headway has been made, but there is undoubtedly "still a lot of fear to deal with," comment some of those interviewed. Hunting within and outside the organization for successful practices meant focusing on the people, unlike what had been done traditionally in the Group. Each person had to assume responsibility for his or her own development. The organization had to be reinvented, making people, in turn, reinvent themselves, by talking, getting involved and confronting ideas.

Leading the Change

A course had to be set. Management had to take the lead. But once the course was set, the task became to reach the commitment, based on very specific competencies, which in most cases were yet to be developed.

"You have to make the organization's problems your own, and then their solution appears, as a personal commitment," states one of the Group's managers. "This meant foregoing anonymity, and rather than being an organization where you mostly hear 'we,' becoming one where everybody speaks in the first person, and is starting to assume risks."

This amounted to telling a hundred-year-old organization that it had to change. That the old patterns and the old skills were history. The company had to go forward with the century about to begin.

In a structure where participation is welcome and opinions are shared, you have to *have* an opinion. Thus, the Chief Executive Office's first injunction to the management team was: "Listen. Don't speak." Find out how others feel. You don't want to impose top management's ideas. There are unsuspected resources among the operators.

For a top management that welcomes participation, the clue is the know-how. The idea is to learn who has the answers to a problem or a business, not wield your powers. Learning calls for an open team, free of fears, and the abilities to cope with new situations. But listening to the perpetrators of change can be unappreciated in an organization bogged down by traditions.

A common language was required to initiate the change, but such a language had to be learned, and it wasn't going to be found within the organization. Managers had to be exposed and defied by the actual business world. They had to leave their cozy desks and jobs, to face the challenges that make a business either succeed or fail.

"The dialogue process has begun," continues our interviewee, "not only do you have to talk to the CEO, but you have to participate in discussions with other managers."

The Challenge: The Organization of the 21st Century

What the Chief Executive Office has proposed is to transform a traditional competitive organization into a visionary one (Appendix B). This calls for revising the Group's mission statement, its vision, and its values, for the organization's structure and people must be aligned with the new challenges. This means entering into a new corporate pact, in which people are actually being rehired.

In a reactive organization, problems are dealt with as they occur. In a proactive situation, you try to foresee them before they arise. As one manager put it, "The results appear to be the consequence of decisions made long before. These decisions are the ones that should be made with expertise. What needs to be stressed is the cause of the results, not the last-minute correction of mistakes. Results are a consequence of the systems that make them possible. This involves changes in the infrastructure, in the operating systems, in the people, in the way they work, in the processes. The most important part of the change process lies in the human factor. There is no point in making technological and managerial progress if the personnel aren't aligned with those changes, for it's the people who most definitely produce the results. You have to go to the cause."

Another major topic suggested by the top management was how to best use the strengths entailed in being a large group. The idea was to find out "how to make the most of the learning experiences of a large group, without losing sight of the local markets, without losing the speed and strength generated there. This entailed a whole process of determining the competitive edge of each business and of the organization as a whole. The challenge definitely lay in a new corporate culture that strongly stresses synergy."

The whole organization has gone into a tuning process. Incentive systems were revised and adjusted to the new circumstances. As for results, people usually are interested in two fundamental aspects: market share and profitability. They may occasionally conflict, and one or the other is sacrificed. But both definitely have to be achieved. It's not acceptable to forego one for the other, because market share and profitability are the two feet that a business stands on. Profitability is a short-term goal; market share is a long-term one.

To achieve a proper balance between the two, the Chief Executive Office has instructed the corporate headquarters to implement an incentive system, which strives to unequivocally join these two poles, rewarding results rather than efforts. It is a strategic steering system in line with the new business vision of the organization.

As in any change process, one of the factors to be dealt with is resistance, which usually comes from people. A few managers commented that "there are CEOs who want to make big changes and others who don't, or who want to make just slight changes. There is a lot of inflexibility within the organization, and this is the first obstacle to overcome. You can see it at the quarterly meetings, which are very open, because we are very much involved in the processes, and we attend those meetings with results in our hands."

Another person interviewed commented that "there are very good bosses and many mediocre ones. If they have values and potential, they must be helped. The problem is that if they're unwilling to get beyond their mediocrity, they become defensive and will fight the changes. We have found that the more insecure executives are, the harder it is to communicate with them, because deep down inside they are afraid. They are literally scared to death. In other cases we have come across bosses who were indeed capable of changing, but they didn't need to change—or weren't aware of the need. Now they are very satisfied, for they have discovered a new horizon in their development.

"It has been discovered that those executives who put up the most resistance have trouble opening up. They are more used to competing against one another than against outside competition. They are the type who—in soccer terms—don't pass the ball. They want to score all the goals and show off to the team. In business terms this means that they conceal their successful practices and don't readily pass them on to others." "Deep down inside," said another manager, "what that attitude reveals is a lack of the maturity needed to want to get to know yourself, with your particular strengths and weaknesses. In FEMSA we don't intend to put people on pedestals. Everyone has their good points and their bad points. The idea is to try and learn to deal with them. I think there are people who don't see change as an opportunity to get to know themselves and improve, but rather as a threat to their job."

The new environment of world competition requires people and businesses to be more focused, with skills that really meet the new challenges. Up until now, the executives interviewed feel that the measures implemented to encourage executives to change have not been drastic measures. They have attempted to persuade them to gradually change, yet clearly conveying the message that the organization's businesses, divisions, competencies, skills and people must eventually be perfectly aligned.

Another major topic is that of information. The channels are provided, the systems are operating, and efforts are being made for the communication to be as broad and as direct as possible. "The first step," they tell us, "has been to institutionalize information. But then—and this is what is most important—you have to be open to the information and you have to be honest with it, you have to rely on the data as it is displayed. The improvement in the availability of information is of no use without the willingness to learn, and full acknowledgment of this improvement."

COMMUNICATION MECHANISMS

The Values

In order to achieve a corporate culture in line with the trends of the new century, it was necessary to establish open communication processes, which would in turn require not only communication channels, but also an underlying common language to make communication possible. However, the corporate belief is that no matter how useful and sophisticated state-of-the-art technology may be, what is most important in a business is its basic blueprint, which involves the corporate values, the mission it aims to carry out, and the long-term vision that enables it to generate strategies and align them with its objectives.

Instituting the new corporate culture did not require starting from scratch, but it did have to be brought in line with the times. As for FEMSA's values, the firm is heir to a long tradition, for its founder Eugenio Garza Sada drew up the Cuauhtémoc Ideology back in 1928, stating a number of values that were the rules of behavior to be followed by everyone belonging to the organization. These are not only of historical value, but also express the company's commitment and that of those who work for it. However, the Cuauhtémoc Ideology, attached herewith under Exhibit 1, was not that practical, for it was written in 17 descriptive paragraphs. The new management was committed to newly enforcing those values, but they had to be reworded, and summarized into a both manageable and operative statement. Through the communication channels described below, the Chief Executive Office promoted a broad and sustained effort to achieve first the acceptance of certain basic values and then the commitment to incorporate them into daily activities, so they could inspire worker behavior in each action. A list of the organization's values is found in Appendix C, comparing the original version, the subsequent revisions, and their current format.

The Chief Executive Office is absolutely and cate-

1 | FEMSA Values, October 1998 (Current)

- A Passion to Serve and Focus on the Customer/Consumer. We strive for all our activities to be focused on identifying and meeting the needs of both our internal and external customers and consumers, by means of the products and services we offer. Customers and consumers are our reason for being in business.
- Innovation and Creativity. We want innovation and creativity to be indispensable in our businesses, since betterment, growth and continuity largely depend on these two key elements. Everything we implement must begin with an innovative and creative idea, which—with a lot of work—will yield excellent results. We want our company to stand out for its creativity and ability to innovate.
- Quality and Productivity. We understand this to mean doing things right the first time, while continually improving and optimizing resources, processes and technology, since this is the means to be domestically and internationally competitive.
- Respect, Comprehensive Development, and Excellence of Personnel. We promote respect and comprehensive development of people and their families, as we seek to expand their learning, skills and vision. Our goal is to have a staff of excellent, world class employees, affording them better opportunities, and thus propitiating financial, cultural and moral betterment.

  We seek to integrate these elements in people, because we want them to look on the demands of globalization and competition with a broader perspective more geared to success. This company's greatest asset is its people! That is why we consider ourselves, above all, a humanistic firm.
- Honesty, Integrity, and Austerity. We demand honesty and integrity of our people, understanding this to mean respect for the firm's ethical and moral principles. Consistency is expected in each person's thoughts, words and actions. Austerity, as a performance variable, is understood as making rational and efficient use of firm resources. The "work and save" slogan must be a way of life in our organizations.

gorically committed to observing and enforcing these values, to the extent that the assessment of all executives begins by looking at how they are working those values into their performance. "We wanted to make sure," explains one manager, "that the values weren't merely used for decorative purposes. They are not a set of paradigms for public relations, but a commitment without which you can't belong to the organization.

"It's hard to live up to these values. We talk of them all the time, but that is not enough. We want to see them implemented." He explains that, in this regard, there must be no slack, for the values must be an asset to the people in the firm. This can be illustrated by a few cases. There are certain types of behavior that are simply unacceptable. Such was the case of a senior executive who indulged in sexual harassment, and to save everyone any further problems, he himself decided to resign. Another case was that of a very efficient manager who was producing good results, until it was discovered that he had taken a bribe from a client. When the latter reported this, the manager was forced to return the money and apologize to the client for having violated one of the company's fundamental rules. That person was allowed to stay on with the company, because it was an exceptional incident, but eventually he had to leave. The reason was quite clear for those who learned of the incident: internally he had never really identified with the corporate values. Another manager was distorting information. He had to be dismissed because he was sowing mistrust. And this is top management's goal in implementing the values: to generate trust in the organization and in the individuals working there, so that all conduct is ruled by very well defined parameters. This trust is making it possible to persuade everyone that there is no room for backbiting, whispering, unshared information, gossip or devious behavior, even among executive groups. "Yes," categorically affirms the person interviewed, "we are committed to the values."

There is still a bit of resistance, but this is becoming increasingly easier to overcome, as confidence and trust grow. A direct mailbox has even been put up for those who wish to communicate with the CEO.

PARTICIPATIVE PROCESSES

Once the values were defined, and based on our fundamental purpose (Exhibit 2), the Group's mission statement and vision had to be outlined (Exhibits 3

2 | FEMSA Purpose

"Create Value for the Community by Developing Businesses and Institutions."

3 | FEMSA Mission Statement

FEMSA MISSION STATEMENT

The FEMSA mission statement is a brief statement describing what we are and why we exist as a business, which we must always bear in mind in everything that we undertake.

"Satisfy and please beverage consumers with excellence."

FEMSA KEY RULES OF BEHAVIOR

FEMSA is formed by men and women trained and motivated to continually improve, set an example, and be outstanding members of the companies they work for, and the communities where they live.

Key rules of behavior:

- Seek out and use learning
- Continuously strive to better results
- Promote risk taking
- Delegate, empower, trust
- Serve and provide guidance for customers

4 | FEMSA Vision

Our commitment on the threshold of the new millennium is stated in the "FEMSA Vision." The fundamental intent expressed therein is to share future scenarios as the 21st century begins.

It is relevant to clarify that in establishing scenarios, phrases must be worded in the present or present progressive tense, to imply that this vision has been achieved or that it is already a reality. Thus the FEMSA vision contemplates the following:

- Doubling the value of the business every five years.
- FEMSA revenues come from markets and exchange currencies outside of Mexico.
- FEMSA pays a handsome yield to stockholders.
- FEMSA businesses are leaders in their respective industries.
- Contributing to social development.

and 4). This called for engaging in a broad and extensive participative process, which would involve as many people as possible, pooling whatever talent, skills, and experience might benefit the process and make it operational.

This was when it was decided to ask one of the country's major schools of business to design a program for executives from all the operations. The objective set down by the Chief Executive Office was to give them all an overview of the managerial skills that make a difference on a daily basis; to give them both those required in their special field and a comprehensive vision needed to integrate with the other divisions of their operator, the subsidiaries and the corporate headquarters. The Business Management program began in 1995. It's an intensive study program based on different types of case studies and business situations, which require participants to become highly involved, for the cases are discussed in depth by all participants, who must diagnose the situation and come up with a solution to the identified problem. The pilot group began with nearly 80 executives, has grown since, and to date continues. Thanks to the intensive personal participation training provided by this program, many executives are able to participate in several management meetings.

In terms of communication channels and information systems, The Chief Executive Office decided to establish the following mechanisms: the Monthly Meeting of the Management Team, the Annual Management meeting, and the Annual Operations Congress. TOPS, standing for The One Page System, was chosen as the information system to be used by executives throughout the entire organization.

Monthly Meeting of the Management Team

These meetings began under the new management and are attended by managers from the corporate headquarters and each of the subsidiaries. All types of issues may be discussed, but the main agenda is to review compliance of the Chief Executive Office's objectives for the Group. Members are invited to get away from the specific problems of their businesses to look at those of the organization as a whole. It is also a chance for operator managers to listen to each other and reinforce communication.

Annual Management Meetings

The one hundred top executives of the organization are summoned to these meetings to interact with the whole management team. The leading topic at the first meeting was the issue of corporate values. At that time they were itemized in 45 paragraphs, and an attempt was made to condense them into five or six workable definitions. Likewise a whole project was undertaken with the above-mentioned school of business. This project, summarized in the phrase "FEMSA MEETS THE 21ST CENTURY," was the beginning of the process of concreting a new corporate culture. A famous guest attended the meeting: Jerry I. Porras, who is on the faculty at Stanford University's Graduate School of Business. His metaphor that a manager's importance lies not in timetelling, but in clock-building, conveyed to the organization the type of leadership wanted to face the future.

The leading topic at the meeting held in 1997 was *"What's Our Business's Business?"* This led to a change of policy. No longer would the best ideas be rewarded, but rather the successful implementation of the best ideas, regardless of their source. "We are no longer going to reward the one who dreams up the idea. The hero in the organization will be the one who is able to implement it." Another major item on the agenda was to continue working with the values, seeking a way for them to have bearing on the daily work done throughout the Group, creating a process of cultural infrastructure. The "FEMSA Award for Innovation and Creativity" was established.

The next year—in 1998—the device used was the catchphrase "clockbuilding." More than 50 questions were prepared for discussion and analysis and then put to vote, using green-for-yes and red-for-no sign cards, to thus establish the company vision. All those attending signed the document containing that vision. The topic of results was discussed—results, as consequences of the causes by which they are produced—so as to instill in executives the importance of a long-term, overall vision. They were thus able to appreciate that the process is just as important as the outcome. It was stated that the goal was to achieve results consistent with the vision agreed upon at the meeting.

Operations Congress

Conceived as a channel of interaction for the various divisions involved in the processes, the Operations Congress, held annually since 1997, brings together the 500 top executives of the organization. The first year they focused on topics related to flexibility and leadership. And they also discussed integrative and disjunctive motivation, to demonstrate that the organization's bottom line ultimately lies in its people. The Operations Congress is meant to be a forum, where the company's best practices are presented, in order to evaluate the possibility of their being replicated by the other operators. The idea is to fan out the broad array of synergies offered by a group such as this.

The 1998 Congress focused on presenting useful practices to discover synergies. Cases from other companies illustrated ways to develop and spread skills among different operators. The Chief Executive Office also presented the new typical characteristics that must be in force in the organization.

TOPS

The One Page System represents the technological aspect of the new vision that management wishes to establish in FEMSA. TOPS is a system whereby a single computer sheet tells how all the critical factors and vital competencies are aligning, as well as how much empowerment is being conferred upon anyone in their job.

This has entailed concomitant changes in titles and office space in the workplace, brought about by the intent to make the organization more horizontal, more equalitarian. Other changes resulting from the same effort include, for example, no longer having an executive dining room, but one for all the personnel.

The objectives, goals and skills to be achieved by the company's 600 executives are all visible on-line with TOPS. The critical success factors are clearly determined there. Systems, culture and technology interrelate with optimum efficiency, to generate the desired performance in terms of their consequence.

TOPS is a way to generate and maintain a common language in the organization. "It is based on three basic factors," reports one of the interviewees. "Once the strategic goals of any business are defined (first factor), everyone must see how the critical success factors (second factor) and personal competencies (third factor) are aligned to achieve the company goals. It is a comprehensive process of accountability."

TOPS is designed for each executive to keep these three basic factors on-line: the objectives to be achieved, the critical factors to achieve them, and the development of necessary skills. The system assimilates all the data provided by the executives and produces an immediate follow-up of the results.

In referring to the system, one manager states that "it's a methodology we are learning to use. Some 60 percent of the executives are training in this discipline. Some—even senior executives—have expressed their difficulty in finding the right measurement model and are being helped to do so. Operators are at different stages of implementation. One operator uses TOPS simultaneously with the previous system, while another's implementation is at 40 percent, and yet another's has reached 95 percent. A lateral review consisting of a customer evaluation process has already begun in the latter's case. They have developed the INEX, which is a rate of excellence index in vendor customer service. Operators in other countries, such as Argentina, are also using the system."

The Core of the Follow-Up System

TOPS provides the basic follow-up on tasks and objectives, which is supplemented with the individual evaluations, and the monthly and quarterly meetings, as the case may be.

The individual review (also called the vertical review) consists of a monthly meeting, which may be "virtual," between a staff member and his or her immediate boss. The Chief Executive Office sets up the structure of this meeting. It lasts one hour and is divided into four 15-minute sections. The first one deals with the progress being made in the culture. The point is to identify specific behavior that might indicate how the staff member is experiencing FEMSA values. The second phase of the meeting is spent reviewing the critical success factors and the objectives set in each case. Viewed by TOPS, the review can be very swift, for the measurement systems determine the percentage of progress made and visually identified in green, yellow and red. "The status indicator rates the progress either minimum, satisfactory or excellent. Only those areas rated below minimum are discussed. Those rated excellent may be touched upon for replication purposes." Results are entered in a management report, which remains integrated in TOPS.

The third part of the meeting is devoted to developing the key competencies identified for that person. Competency parameters range from apprentice to expert. The goal is to bring all competencies up to the expert level. In company jargon these are usually referred to as "my vitals," for example one senior executive needs to develop the following competencies: his counseling skill, his financial skills, his awareness of business strategies, how to operate one in particular, and his external exposure.

The last 15 minutes of the meeting are devoted to sundry matters, under the heading "miscellaneous."

The team meetings are the other pillar of the follow-up methodology. There are established by the subsidiaries and the corporate management team. The first take place on a monthly basis and the latter on a quarterly basis.

Objectives and skills to be developed are set at the team meetings. In these meetings all members involved present their respective proposals, which are then voted upon by the attending members. Proposals can thus be added or withdrawn on the individual sheets. At the end, the staff member and their boss both sign the report, thereby indicating their acceptance and commitment.

An innovative agenda was designed for the team meetings. "In these meetings we want people to spend 80% of the time discussing how they might solve the issues posed and what opportunities they foresee in the future and spend 20% of the time discussing what has been done in the past. If people talk about the past, you have a poor agenda. The team meets to decide how to achieve the objectives set down by the team leader, not to look at each one's particular issues. The point is to deal with the things everyone has in common, not the differentials. Those are discussed in private. What we discuss at the team meetings are the boss's demands. This is the paradigm. Bonus systems depend on results achieved by the team. Individuality gives it a certain factorization, indicates how the critical success factors have been met, but more important is what they add up to, and their bearing on the Group.

"What we are definitely seeking in opening new channels of communication and using TOPS to meet our information needs is to enhance our efficiency in making decisions. The project aims to give the Group a more horizontal structure. Aligning the mission, the vision and the values of the Group entails a number of bold objectives in terms of personal performance. We have to decide which types of performance are more conducive to turning the Group vision into a reality. The strategy to achieve this involves an intensive communication process. The yearly meetings and congresses, the value promotion campaign, the satellite communication and TOPS, consistency between the magazines and the media, all this has a very definite purpose, which is to align the whole organizational architecture."

LOOKING AHEAD

"We are very fond of our history," says one manager, "and so often do we reminisce that it curbs our need to change. We keep recalling how we founded the Institute of Technology in Monterrey, how we created the *Cuauhtémoc y Famosa* Clinic, how we created a project to provide housing for our workers. We're always blowing the same old horn. That horn belonged to other people. It's high time the people who are now working for FEMSA do our own thing and boast of new accomplishments that this generation can be just as proud of, as past generations were of theirs. We don't want to live in the past. We want to do this for the future, always remembering that those of us who work for FEMSA are merely passing through, for the organization must live on for another 100, 200 or 300 years."

Top management has envisioned the objective clearly. Seek out leading businesses. But leadership in business means market share, quality and profitability. For the Chief Executive Office, FEMSA's future lies in "our having four, five or six highly focused divisions." And that is precisely what is difficult: being a very diversified organization with highly focused divisions, monitoring their own development, yet also the whole picture "to make sure it all adds up" (Appendix D).

Leadership in business naturally involves communication and information, developing skills and talent. "But you also need the ability to implement ideas. There is a point we don't want to ever forget: 90 percent of the success of a project lies in its effectiveness, in the consistency of implementing it. Our competition has been very good at that. They have just a few practices, but they are key practices and effective ones and have been implemented with mastery. We, on the other hand, have gone the other way, trying to implement many things that are very sophisticated, with highly developed technology. But we still have to find simpler processes, those that make a difference in the market place, where we're facing the consumer. Sometimes they're very simple things, but they have to be discovered. I am not implying—and I mean this very emphatically—that we are going to neglect technological innovation. Technology is quite necessary, but it must become so much a part of us that we can use and develop it creatively. Looking ahead, priority must be given to invention, and even to generating patents. Almost everything is yet to be done in this field. We need not only good ideas, but also that they be perfectly well implemented and generate differential know-how that will effectively position the organization, regardless of whether or not we patent the ideas. We must be assertive enough, not only to give birth to the baby, but also to nurture it until it can fend for itself."

The serious effort to enhance professional relationships within the corporation has been a trying experience. But its future shimmers clearly as a global enterprise operating in several countries with several highly focused divisions led by the Group. From 40 percent to 45 percent of the company's revenue will be generated outside Mexico. This will not only protect the firm against the ups and downs of the Mexican economy, but is a fundamental strategy to ensure the Group's presence in the global market place, at a time when doing business with other markets is imperative for survival.

"The FEMSA group that we see is a global organization well within our reach of achieving. It is somewhat like diving into a swimming pool. We just have to decide when."

A | FEMSA History

For over a century, the companies of *Grupo Fomento Económico Mexicano, S.A. de C.V.* (FEMSA), have been able to successfully compete in their various markets, achieving consumer preference, business expansion and new market penetration, while creating more and more jobs, offering their shareholders adequate yields and spurring the socioeconomic development of the communities where they operate.

FEMSA is the largest strategically integrated beverage group in Latin America. Besides manufacturing beverages, beer and soft drinks, as well as high quality packaging products, it owns the most successful chain of convenience stores in Mexico. Approximately 40,000 people work for FEMSA.

The group's six divisions are

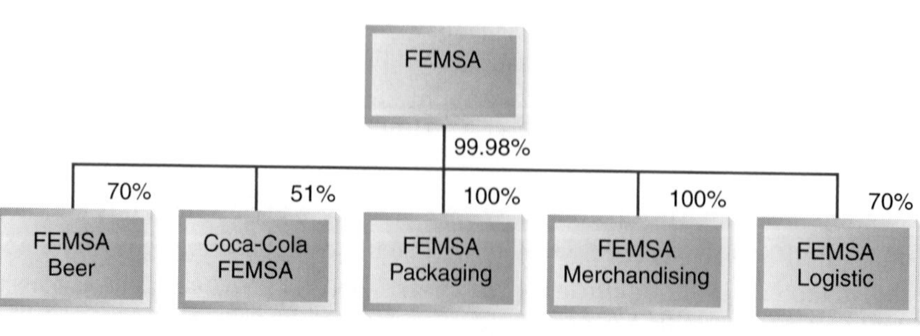

A | FEMSA History *(Continued)*

FEMSA BEER

In 1943, Eugenio Garza Sada, at that time director of *Cervecaría Cuauhétemoc*, set out to found the institute *Cervecería Cuauhtémoc Moctezuma*, the cornerstone of the FEMSA group, which was founded in 1980 by Isaac Garza and Jose Calderon, two distinguished gentlemen known for their work ethic and entrepreneurial spirit. These visionaries were later joined by Jose A. Muguerza, Joseph M. Schnaider [sic] and Francisco Sada.

The brewery *Cervecería Gillermo Hasse y Cía* was founded in the city of Orizaba, Veracruz, in 1894. This was the first step toward what would two years later be renamed *Cervecería Moctezuma*, for in 1896 a brewery in Guadalajara, Jalisco, operated at the time by foreign investors, was dissolved, and it became *Moctezuma, S.A.* The brewery became a 100 percent Mexican operation when purchased by Raul Bailleres in 1941. In 1985 the consolidation of *Cervecería Cuauhtémoc* and *Cervecería Moctezuma* gave rise to the largest brewery groups worldwide.

Cervecería's efficient market strategies have enabled it to make a place for itself in the growing international market, exporting products to a wide variety of countries on the five continents. Of its 400 brands Tecate is the leading canned beer and Dos Equis the leading amber beer imported in the United States, the company's main export market. Sol continues to be the most popular Mexican beer in Europe.

Upgrading and innovation have distinguished the company's philosophy for over a century. With consumer satisfaction as its prime goal, the brewery has offered top quality products and excellent customer service. As a result, many of the beer brands that *Cervecería* manufactures have earned renown for their excellence in prestigious international contests. Gold medals and awards date back to 1893, only three years after the brewery was founded.

Consistent with its principles and values, *Cervecería Cuauhtémoc Moctezuma* has undertaken many a project to improve the well-being of its staff members and their families. The company has thus created institutions devoted to raising the cultural and educational level of the communities where it operates: *Sociedad Cuauhtémoc y Famosa* (1981), including the Recreational Center and the Clinic; the Mexican Baseball Hall of Fame (1973); the Monterrey Sports Museum (1977); and the Monterrey Museum (1977).

In 1943, Eugenio Garza Sada, at that time director of *Cervecería Cuauhétemoc*, set out to found the Institute of Technology and Higher Studies of Monterrey (ITESM), currently acknowledged to be one of the best institutions of middle and higher education in Latin America, with 26 campuses throughout Mexico. In 1993, *Cervecería* also established the Eugenio Garza Sada Award, inspired by this great man's example. The objective of this award is to honor and foster exceptional activities undertaken by individuals and institutions on behalf of Mexico's cultural, economic and social development.

As of 1994, *Cervecería* established a strategic alliance with the Canadian brewery John Labatt, thus joining a more competitive market and consolidating its share in more demanding world markets.

Due to its commitment to the community, *Cervecería* aims to protect the environment by providing waste water treatment on the premises of its facilities, implementing environmental control and protection programs, and further investing in the preservation of the environmental equilibrium.

Main Businesses:
Cervecería Cuauhtémoc Moctezuma

Main Brands:

Tecate	Tecate Light
Carta Blanca	Superior
Bohemia	XX Lager
Dos Equis	Indio
Sol	Nochebuena (only during Christmas holidays)

Location:
Six breweries in Mexico are located in:

Guadalajara	Monterrey
Navojoa	Orizaba
Tecate	Toluca

35 distribution centers throughout the Mexican Republic

COCA-COLA FEMSA

In terms of the soft drink sector, Coca-Cola FEMSA is one of the largest Coca-Cola franchises in the world, with 13 plants in the Valley of Mexico and southeastern Mexico, plus two in Buenos Aires, Argentina. For over 20 years this company has excelled among several other bottling companies, due to its high sales volume, leadership, continuous innovation and quality service.

To meet the needs of its different markets, Coca-Cola FEMSA has innovatively increased its variety of flavors and packaged its products in cans, half liter, 1 liter, 1.5 liter and 2 liter bottles, thus catering to consumer convenience.

A | FEMSA History *(Continued)*

In 1993, The Coca Cola Company purchased 30% of Coca-Cola FEMSA shares, reinforcing its competitive position in several markets. As a result of this strategic association Coca-Cola FEMSA has been appointed the anchor bottling company for Latin America and as such in 1994 engaged in various transactions that led to the 1997 purchase of the Coca Cola bottling company in Buenos Aires, Argentina. It is now the goal of Coca-Cola FEMSA to uphold its lead in sales, quality and innovation, consolidating its strategic position in the Mexican and Latin American markets.

Main Businesses:

Industria Embotelladora de México
Embotelladora de Tlalnepantla
Embotelladora del Istmo
Refrescos de Oaxaca
Embotelladora sin Rival
Distribuidora de Bebidas del Valle de México
Distribuidora Sureña
Coca-Cola FEMSA de Buenos Aires

Main Brands:

Coca-Cola	Sprite
Fanta	Coca-Cola Light
Diet Sprite	Freska
Delaware Punch	Lift
Ciel	

In Argentina:

Coca-Cola	Coca-Cola Light
Sprite	Diet Sprite
Fanta	Cherry Coke
Quatro	Kin

Location:

13 plants in Mexico
Valley of Mexico (7)
Southeastern Mexico (6):

Villahermosa	Oaxaca
Juchitán	Minantitlán
San Cristóbal de las Casas	Tapachula

Two plants in Buenos Aires, Argentina

FEMSA PACKAGING

FEMSA Packaging supplies the food and beverage industries with several different packaging products. Operations are backed by the latest technology and excellent service.

With state-of-the-art technology and an ongoing effort to develop more skilled human resources, the company has been able to successfully compete in Mexico and abroad. As a result, FEMSA Packaging continues growing, maintaining its leadership in production processes, quality and service, continually developing new and better products to meet the needs of domestic and international markets. Sales to outside customers and exports have increased, by offering top quality products and excellent service at internationally competitive prices.

Evidence of continuous improvement are the awards won by this division, particularly by FAMOSA Monterrey, which took two major prizes in 1995: Premium Vitae for Human Quality, the Nuevo Leon Award for Quality and ISO 9002 Certification. FAMOSA is an example to be followed nationwide, due to the advances reflected in all its operational, technological and management processes. Operations began in Buenos Aires, Argentina, in 1998, with the opening of a crown cap plant.

Main Businesses:

Fábricas Monterrey
Grafo Regia
Plásticos Técnicos Mexicanos
Vendo de México
Sílices de Veracruz
Corrugados de Tehuacán
Quimoproductos

Main Products:

Beer, soft drink and food cans
Crown caps and S.O.T. ends
Labels
Cartons and plastic crates
Chemical products
Glass bottles
Flexible packaging
Containers
Coolers

Location:

14 plants in Mexico:
Ensenada
Mexico City
Orizaba
Ixtaczoquitlán
Jalapa
Acayucan
Toluca
Monterrey (3)
San Juan del Río, Querétaro (2)
Tehuacán
Nogales
One plant in Buenos Aires, Argentina

A | FEMSA History *(Continued)*

FEMSA MERCHANDISING

OXXO is the largest chain of convenience stores in Mexico, with more than 1000 outlets in major metropolitan areas. The company has been the forerunner in operating convenience stores in Mexico and is currently the leader in this commercial field. OXXO continues expanding its quality coverage at a sound rate, in Mexico City, Guadalajara, Monterrey and Veracruz.

The OXXO chain of stores is a total quality operation, staffed by obliging and friendly personnel that offer customers the best possible service, at convenient and accessible locations in each city.

Furthermore, OXXO is steadily becoming the number-one purchaser and marketer of FEMSA products.

The OXXO chain is focused on meeting the needs of its customers, in a quest for constant improvement that leads to a higher quality of service.

Main Businesses:

OXXO convenience stores

Main Products:

Fast consumer goods

Location:

Northwest	213
North	118
Northeast	239
West	137
Center	293

AMOXXO

A new business called *Empresas AMOXXO* was formed in August of 1995. FEMSA associated with Amoco Oil Co. of Chicago, Illinois, which shall manage and invest in OXXO Express Service Centers. Premium products and services will be sold at competitive prices, by personnel especially trained to provide customers fast service in a pleasant atmosphere.

Service centers will be geared to customers in cars and will include an OXXO convenience store, a PEMEX filling station, possibly offering customers a jiffy lube and car wash, fast food and spare parts, among other services.

This alliance is one more step in the FEMSA strategy to more actively participate in the merchandising sector, offering consumers convenience stores and filling stations in Mexico.

The two partners pooled their experience in the convenience store and filling station sector. *Empresas AMOXXO* will offer current and future PEMEX licensees several technical building, management and marketing services, which will enable them to enhance their image and facilities, optimize the quality of their service and boost their profits.

Likewise, this association with Amoco reasserts the recent FEMSA strategy. Over the last few years, it has sought to forge alliances with top level multinational partners that have state-of-the-art technology, management capability and experience, to thus continue improving its businesses and their strategic position.

Location:

Aguascalientes	4
Guadalajara	5
León	3
Mexico City	1
Monterrey	8
Saltillo	3
San Luis Potosí	1
Torreón	2

FEMSA LOGISTICS

FEMSA Logistics was established as a new business in 1998. The main objective is to make the most of FEMSA's opportunity to generate value participating in this industry.

This company is founded on a capability to design and operate logistic solutions, which align the companies' operational processes, their ongoing customer orientation and familiarity with the Mexican shipping market with an ability to innovate vehicle development and good maintenance systems.

Its products are the following:

- *Integrated Logistics:* Total or partial management services are provided throughout the entire supply chain, from collecting raw material to distributing finished goods, with the option of including warehouse management.

  Technological innovations and advanced logistic systems are developed to better coordinate, align and integrate efforts and resources used in the companies' procurement and distribution procedures.
- *Financial Leasing with Maintenance.* Financial elements are structured in such a way that customers may lease a vehicle, with maintenance included for a monthly fee.

  Companies thus need not invest in these sorts of assets to ensure top level maintenance for their

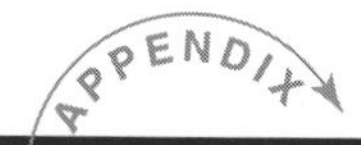

APPENDIX A | FEMSA History *(Continued)*

shipping fleet, which is renewed within a time frame most suitable to the characteristics of the operation.

Location:

Seven service centers:

Monterrey	Orizaba
Toluca	Mexico City
Guadalajara	Navojoa
Tecate	

Main Customers:

FEMSA Beer	82%
Coca-Cola FEMSA	10%
FEMSA Packaging	8%

APPENDIX B | A Visionary Organization

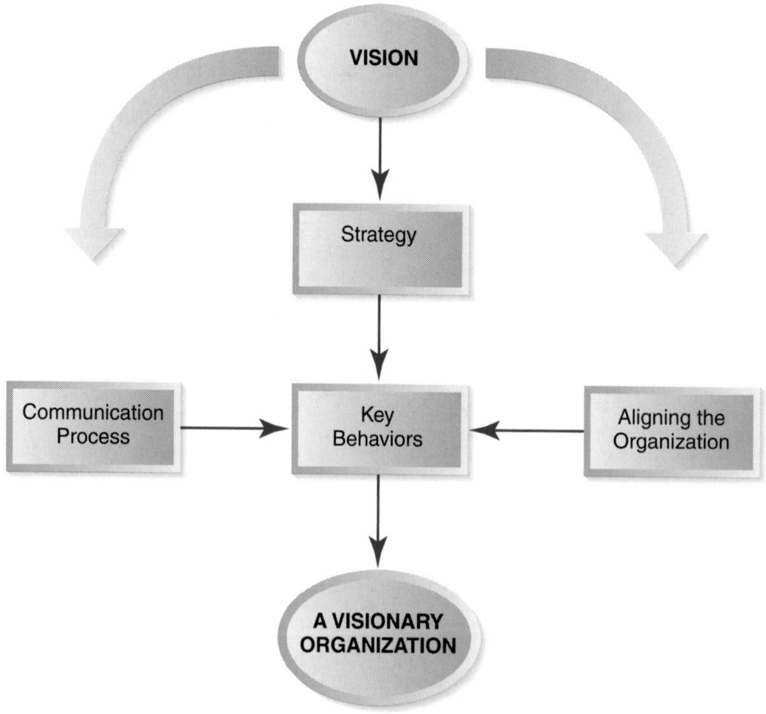

B | A Visionary Organization *(Continued)*

COMPETITIVE TRADITIONAL		A VISIONARY ORGANIZATION
Leadership		
✔ The leader of the moment	➡	✔ The leader builds the clock.
✔ The manager is afraid to go out "because there are many decisions to be made."	➡	✔ There is empowerment and key areas to provide them without the need of the leader.

COMPETITIVE TRADITIONAL		A VISIONARY ORGANIZATION
Conflicts/Communication		
✔ The conflict becomes uneasy.	➡	✔ Different viewpoints are considered a source of wealth.
✔ It doesn't look "good" to disagree with the boss.	➡	✔ It's good we differ in the way we see the world. If we agree on the direction, we will have learned something.

COMPETITIVE TRADITIONAL		A VISIONARY ORGANIZATION
Values		
✔ They're lived in isolation.	➡	✔ They're ways of life. ✔ The clock will work because it will be based on values.

COMPETITIVE TRADITIONAL		A VISIONARY ORGANIZATION
Ways of Seeing Results		
✔ The past is spoken of more than the future.	➡	✔ Eighty percent of the time they talk about building the future.
✔ Pressure is put on and results are pursued on a daily basis.	➡	✔ They change the causes that produce results. ✔ Talent is applied for structural change.

COMPETITIVE TRADITIONAL		A VISIONARY ORGANIZATION
How People Are Viewed		
✔ They are trained in key areas.	➡	✔ They are also developed as full individuals.
✔ They know their critical factors of success; they analyze the progress made.	➡	✔ They are also clients of the organization. ✔ Individuals know they are responsible for their own development.

COMPETITIVE TRADITIONAL		A VISIONARY ORGANIZATION
Innovation and Learning		
✔ Individuals with ideas are sought and rewarded.	➡	✔ Individuals who implement ideas, wherever they come from, are sought and rewarded.
✔ There is constant improvement.	➡	✔ The quantitative leap is sought.
✔ I devote myself fully to my specialty, my industry, and try to be the best in my field.	➡	✔ I observe other industries, other specialties to discover new learning.
✔ There are excellent work practices in each area.	➡	✔ The institution immediately takes advantage of successful practices.
✔ Focused on total quality.	➡	✔ It is focused on reinventing itself.

B | A Visionary Organization *(Continued)*

Fomento Económico Mexicano, S.A. de C.V. and Subsidiaries

Millions of Pesos	1998 Dollars	1998	1997	% Var	1996	% Var
Total Earnings	3393	33,530	29,329	14.3	26,544	10.5
Operation Profit	478	4,722	4,214	12.1	2,589	62.8
Net Profit	206	2,038	2,805	−27.3	2,996	−6.4
Total Assets	3704	36,595	35,079	4.3	33,485	4.8
Total Liabilities	1515	14,967	17,270	−13.3	16,691	3.5
Accounting Capital	2189	21,628	17,809	21.4	16,794	6
Fixed Investment	421	4,155	3,733	11.3	3,374	10.6
Value in Books per Share[1]	0.279	2,7579	—	—	—	—
Net Profit per Share[1]	0.026	0.255	—	—	—	—
Staff	—	39,770	37,202	6.9	35,694	4.2

[1]Information in pesos was determined based on 5,341,340,450 shares in circulation.

	% Contribution	Total Assets (Millions of pesos)
▶ FEMSA Beer	46.3	33,595
▶ Coca-Cola FEMSA	29.6	
▶ FEMSA Packaging	18.4	
▶ FEMSA Merchandising (OXXO)	4.1	
▶ FEMSA Logistics	1.6	

	% Contribution	Total Income (Millions of pesos)
▶ FEMSA Beer	35.6	33,530
▶ Coca-Cola FEMSA	34.1	
▶ FEMSA Packaging	16.8	
▶ FEMSA Merchandising (OXXO)	11.2	
▶ FEMSA Logistics	2.3	

	% Contribution	Operation Profit (Millions of pesos)
▶ FEMSA Beer	42.9	4,722
▶ Coca-Cola FEMSA	31.6	
▶ FEMSA Packaging	21.0	
▶ FEMSA Merchandising (OXXO)	3.1	
▶ FEMSA Logistics	1.4	

B | A Visionary Organization *(Continued)*

FEMSA Beer

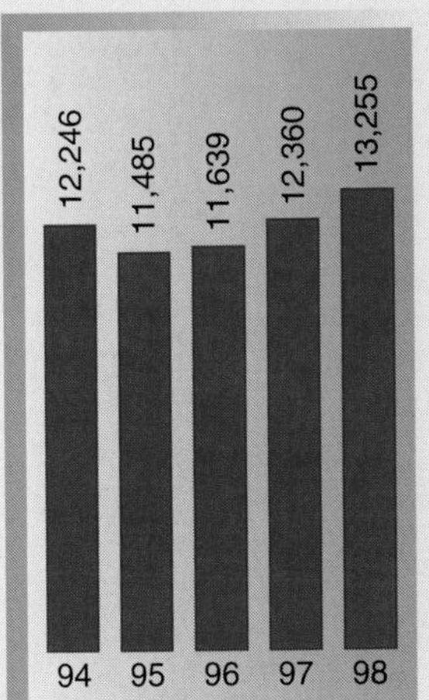

Total Sales
96–97 6.2%
97–98 7.2%

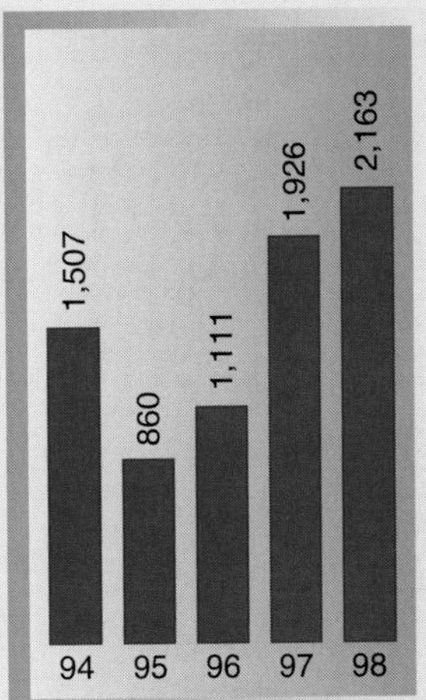

Operation Profit*
96–97 73.4%
97–98 12.3%

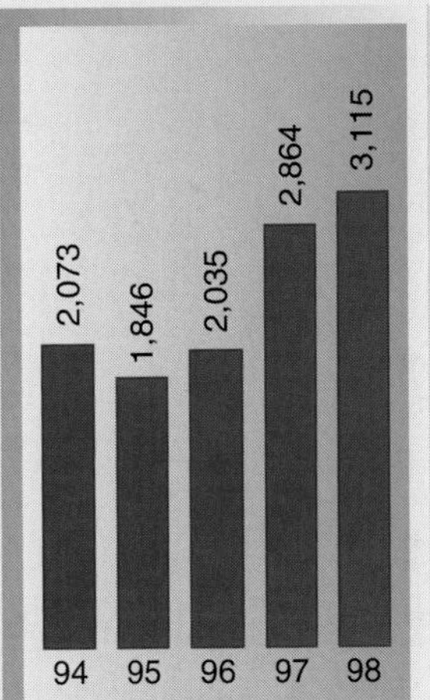

Operation Flow*
96–97 40.7%
97–98 8.7%

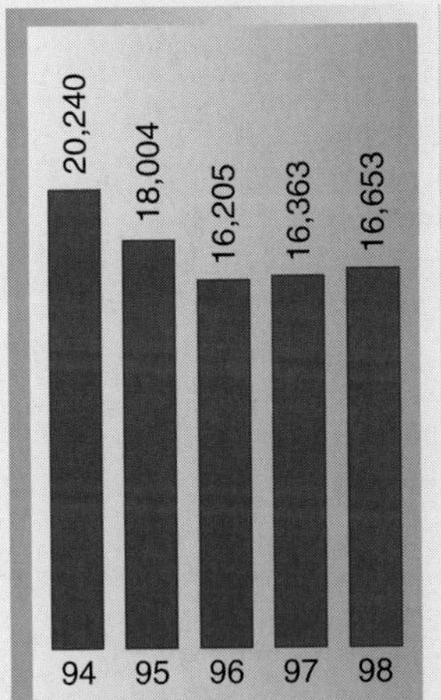

Total Assets
96–97 1.0%
97–98 1.8%

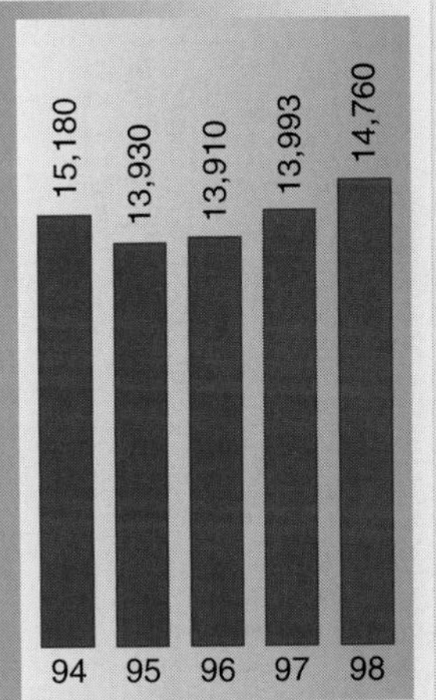

Staff
96–97 0.6%
97–98 5.5%

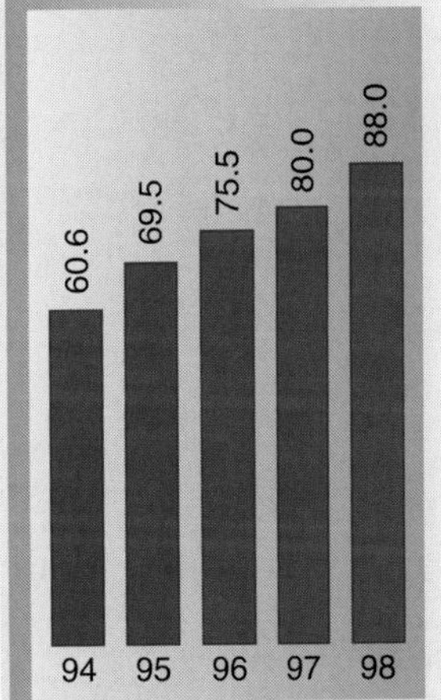

Exports FEMSA Beer
(millions of dollars)

All financial figures in millions of pesos.
*Before payment of corporate services.

Coca-Cola FEMSA

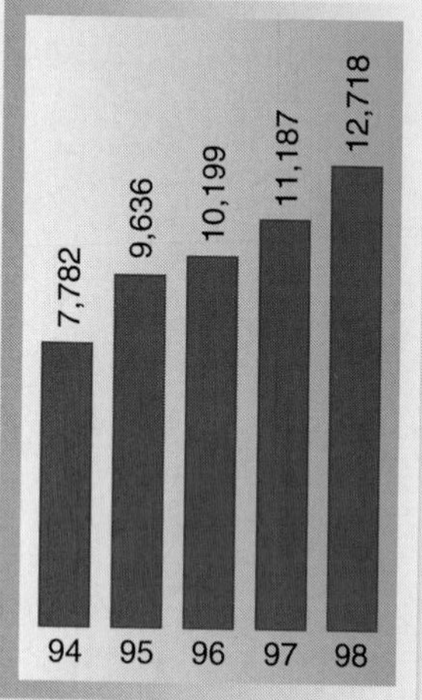

Total Sales
96–97 9.7%
97–98 13.7%

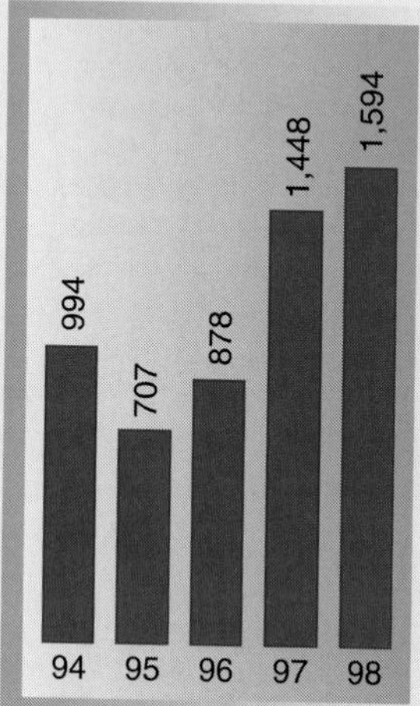

Operation Profit*
96–97 64.9%
97–98 10.1%

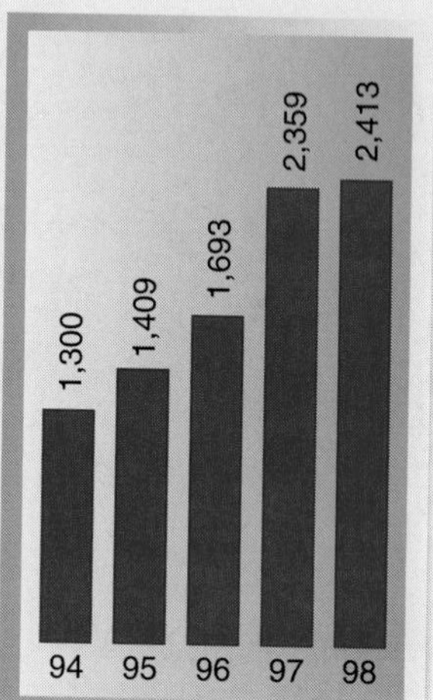

Operation Flow*
96–97 39.3%
97–98 2.3%

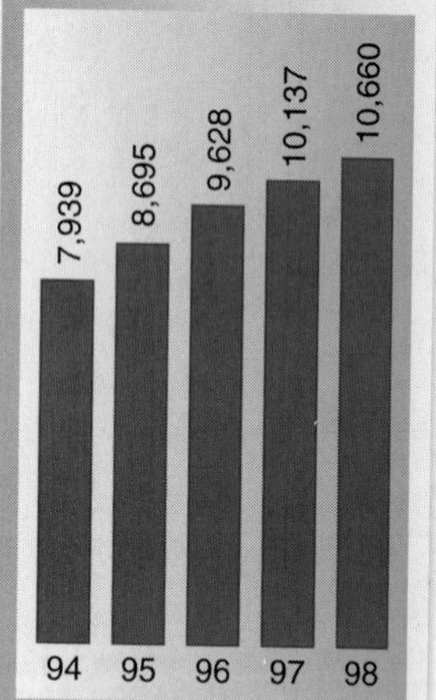

Total Assets
96–97 5.3%
97–98 5.2%

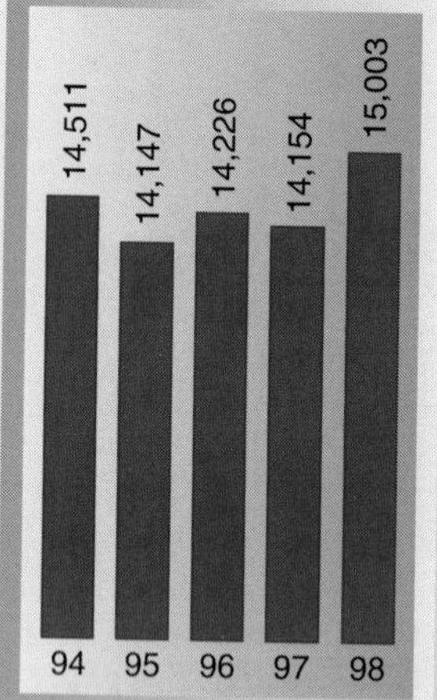

Staff
96–97 1.3%
97–98 6.0%

All financial figures in millions of pesos.
*Before payment of corporate services.

B | A Visionary Organization *(Continued)*

FEMSA Packaging

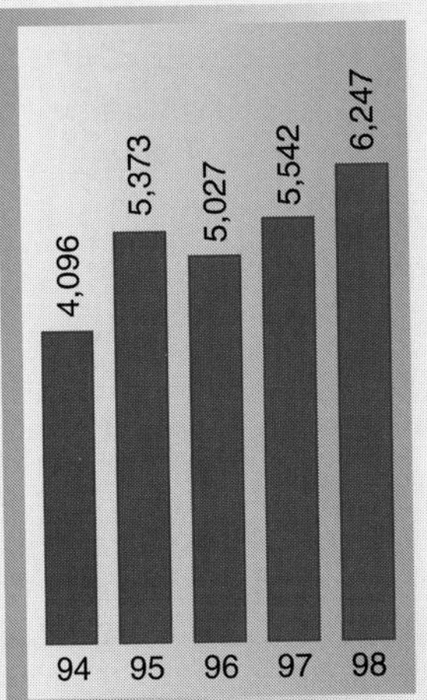

Total Sales
96–97 10.2%
97–98 12.7%

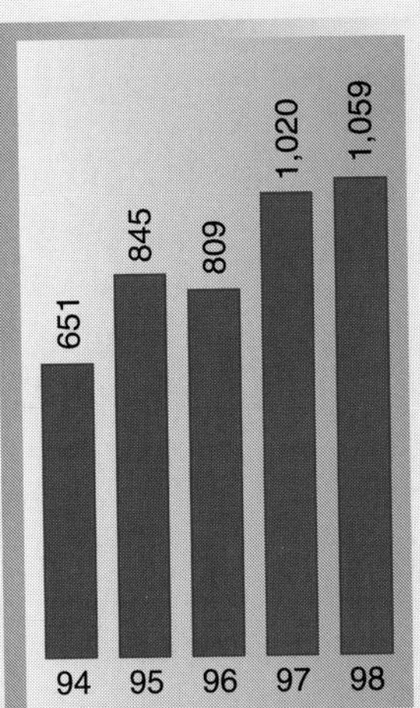

Operation Profit*
96–97 26.1%
97–98 3.8%

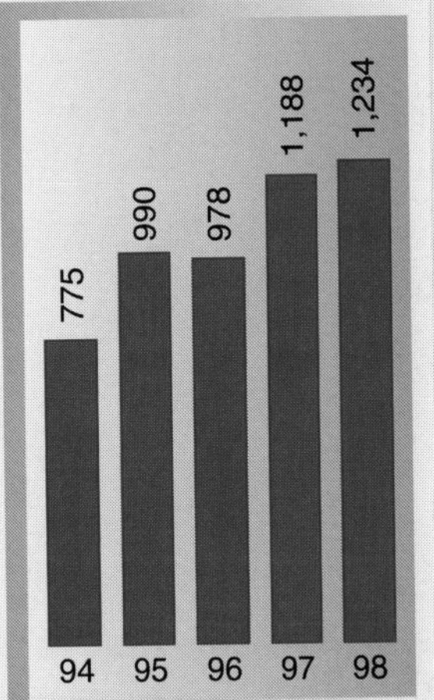

Operation Flow*
96–97 21.5%
97–98 3.9%

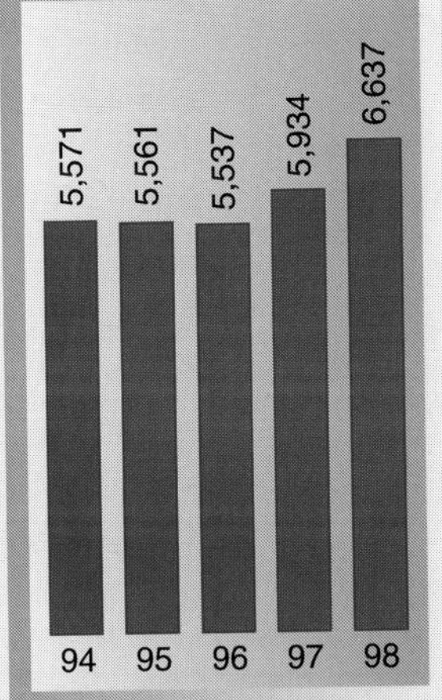

Total Assets
96–97 1.0%
97–98 1.8%

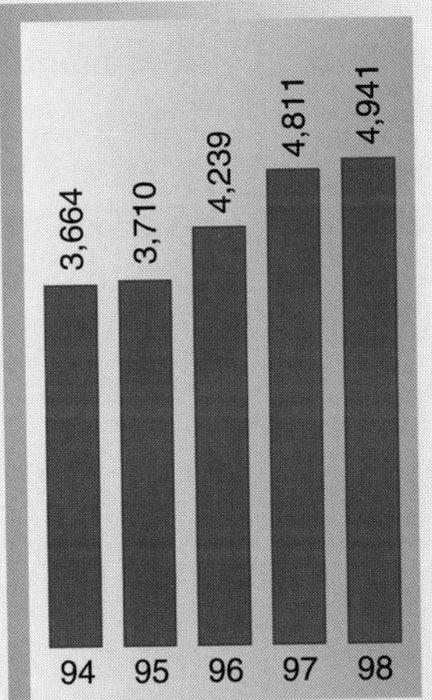

Staff
96–97 0.6%
97–98 5.5%

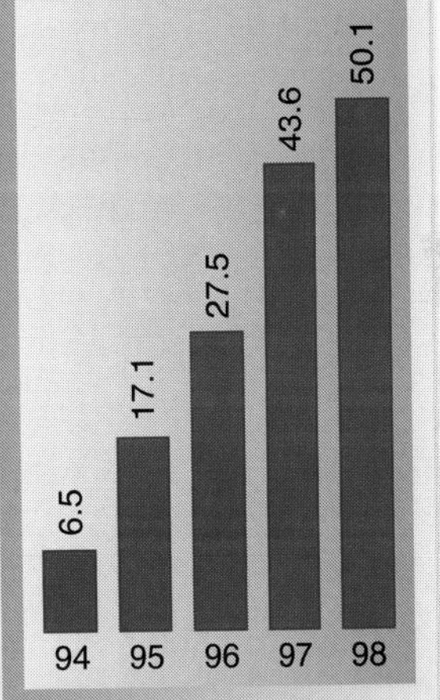

Exports FEMSA Packaging
(millions of dollars)

All financial figures in millions of pesos.
*Before payment of corporate services.

B | A Visionary Organization *(Continued)*

FEMSA Merchandising (OXXO)

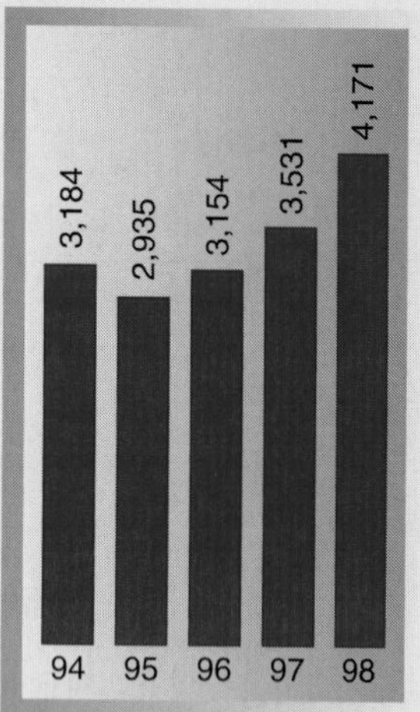

Total Sales
96–97 12.0%
97–98 18.1%

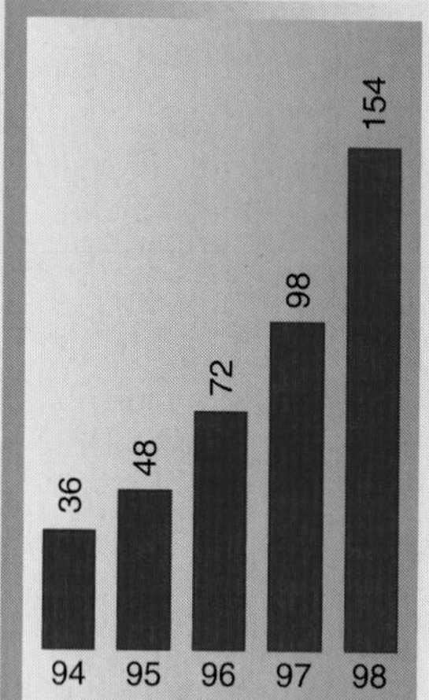

Operation Profit*
96–97 36.1%
97–98 58.0%

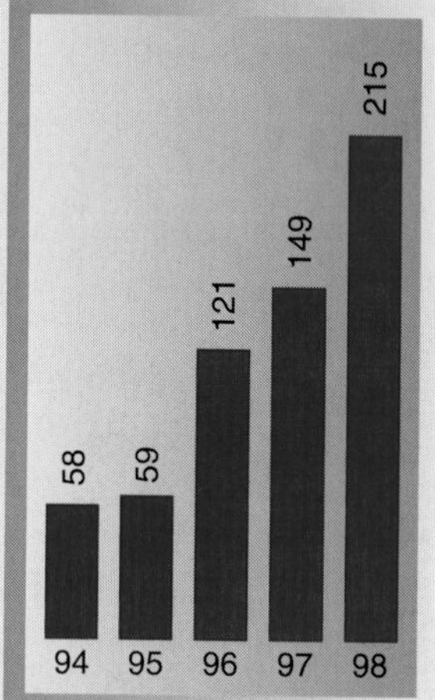

Operation Flow*
96–97 23.1%
97–98 44.3%

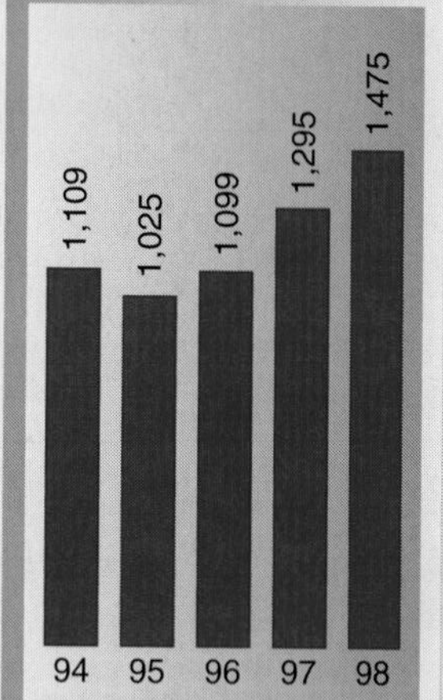

Total Assets
96–97 17.8%
97–98 13.9%

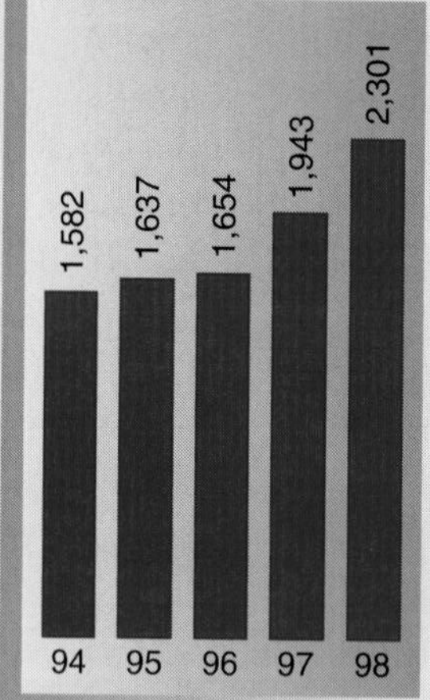

Staff
96–97 17.5%
97–98 18.4%

All financial figures in millions of pesos.
*Before payment of corporate services.

B | A Visionary Organization *(Continued)*

All Subsidiaries Combined

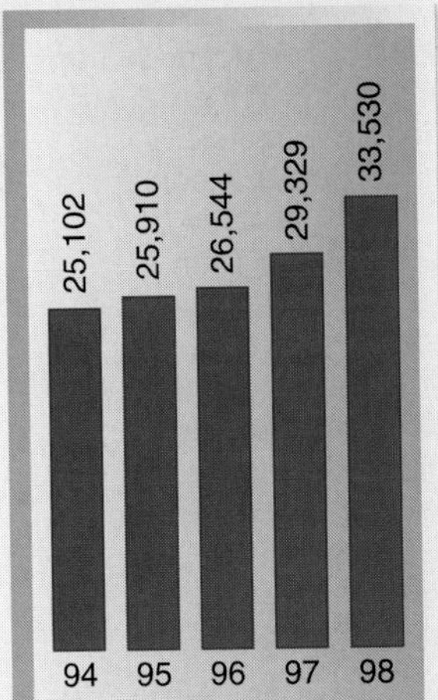

Total Sales

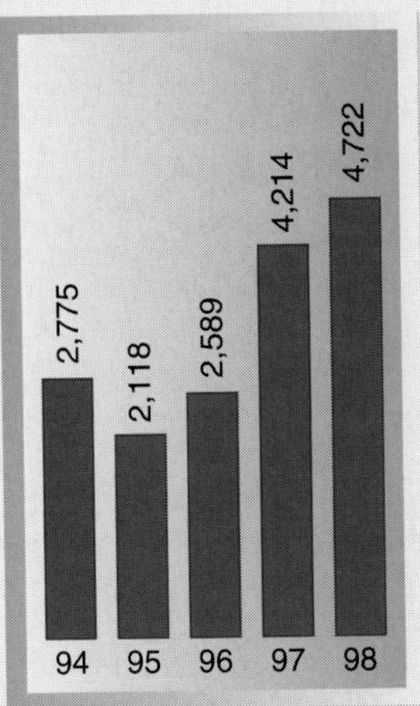

Operation Profit

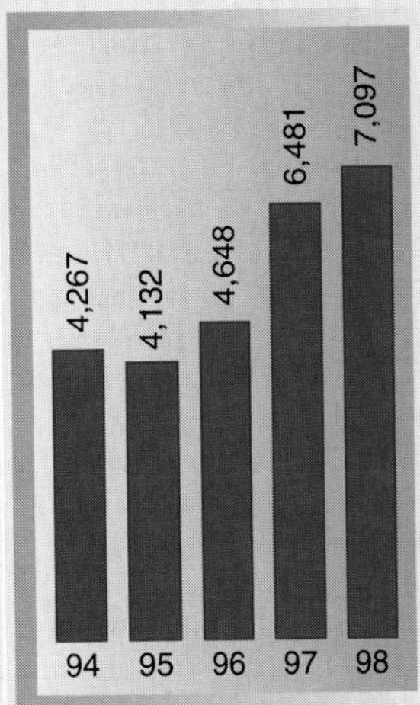

Operation Flow

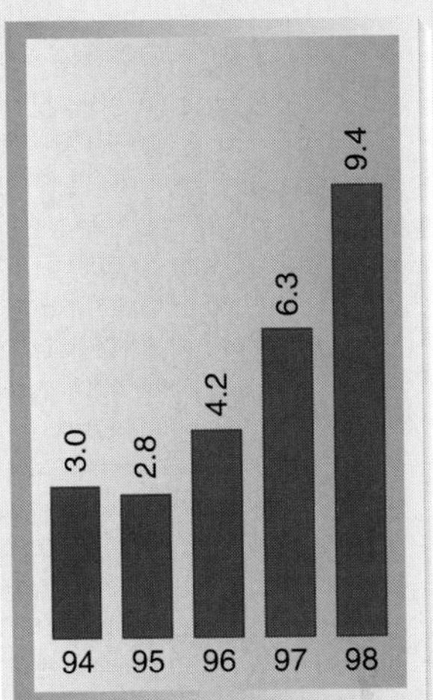

Interest Coverage

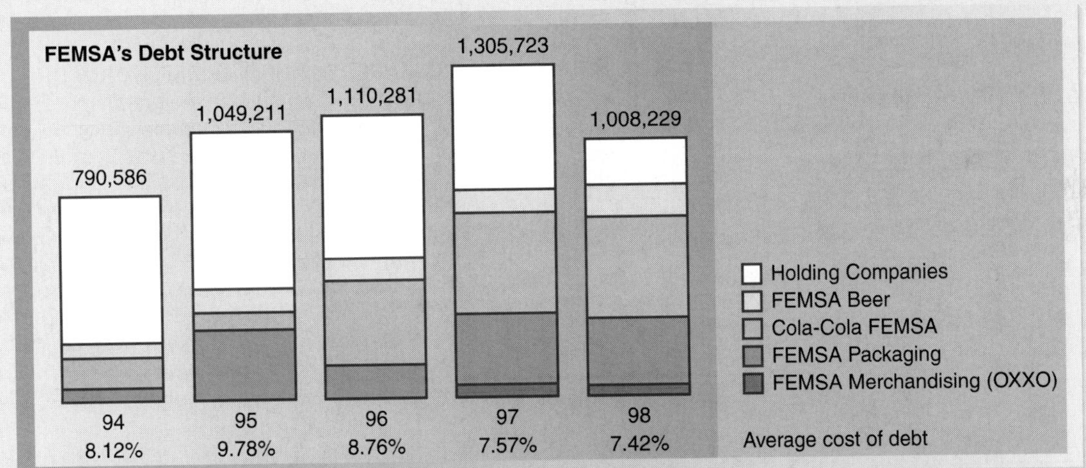

All financial figures in millions of dollars.

C | Cuauhtémoc Ideology

I. GIVE PEOPLE CREDIT for their role in the company's success, and do so spontaneously, soon and in public. Taking credit for the accomplishments of your subordinates would be unworthy, would snip the source of affection, and prevent you from conducting yourself as behooves an executive.

II. CONTROL YOUR TEMPER. You must be capable of peacefully and rationally settling any problem or situation, no matter how annoying the provocations you have to tolerate may seem. Anyone who has no command over his own impulses and means of expression is unqualified as a company manager. A true executive foregoes his right to rage.

III. NEVER MAKE FUN of anyone or anything. Avoid hurtful or double meaning jokes. Bear in mind that sarcasm lands wounds that never heal.

IV. BE POLITE. You need not be formal, but do be mindful that others enjoy the moments spent in your company.

V. BE TOLERANT of the shortcomings that might be found in another's race, color, manners, upbringing or idiosyncrasy.

VI. BE PUNCTUAL. People who cannot keep appointments very soon become a hindrance.

VII. IF YOU ARE VAIN, KEEP IT TO YOURSELF, as though it were your deepest secret. An executive cannot be arrogant or self-complacent. How often does the failure of a well-known man confirm the adage "Pride precedes their downfall." When people start saying that other employees are clumsy or that customers are stingy fools, they are in for trouble.

VIII. DO NOT ALTER THE TRUTH. Think things out before you make a statement; and keep your promises. Telling half the truth can hide a mistake, but not for long. Lies work like a boomerang.

IX. LET OTHERS TALK WITH ABANDON, especially subordinates. Let them come to the real crux of the matter, even if you have to listen to them for an hour. It takes a poor manager indeed to hog the conversation rather than stick to guiding it.

X. BE BRIEF, clear and thorough, especially when giving instructions. It never hurts to keep a good dictionary on hand.

XI. CLEAN UP YOUR VOCABULARY. Eliminate interjections. Vulgar words and slang weakens your speech and leads to misunderstandings. The great speakers of parliament never used a single vulgar word to demolish their foes.

XII. MAKE SURE YOU ENJOY YOUR JOB. It is quite legitimate to have hobbies and outside interests, but if you regard coming to work on Saturday or staying after hours when necessary as an imposition, then you need a rest or should be working for another company.

XIII. ACKNOWLEDGE THE ENORMOUS VALUE OF THE MANUAL WORKER, whose productivity makes the manager's job possible and upholds the future of both.

XIV. THINK MORE ON BEHALF OF THE BUSINESS THAN ON YOUR OWN. It is a good tactic. Loyalty to your company fosters your own benefit.

XV. ANALYSIS OUTWEIGHS INSPIRATION OR INTUITION. This must be the precursor of action.

XVI. DEVOTION TO THE JOB benefits the individual, the company and the entire community. In this it resembles priesthood.

XVII. BE MODEST. A person's value has nothing to do with the size of their car, or their home, or how many friends they have and clubs they belong to, or the price of their wife's fur, or the title on their office door. If you cherish these things more than a task well done and quietly fulfilled, more than the learning and spiritual refinement acquired, then you need to change your attitude or find yourself another job.

D | Statistical Data

Beer

Thousands of Hectoliters	Year through December 31				
	1998	1997	1996	1995	1994
Domestic shipments	21.218	20.549	19.515	18.358	19.108
Export shipments	1.322	1.235	1.027	1.021	.840
Total shipments	22.540	21.784	20.542	19.379	19.948

Source: INEGI and estimates from FEMSA Beer.

Coca-Cola
Comparison of Sales Volume by Territory

Millions of Unit Boxes	Year through December 31				
Territory	1998	1997	1996	1995	1994
Valley of Mexico	304.6	259.6	213.7	201.2	199.8
Southeast	96.7	75.6	65.3	65.6	70.0
Argentina	118.4	103.6	101.5	88.2	

Source: Estimates from Coca-Cola FEMSA.
Note: A unit box holds 24 8-ounce bottles.

Packaging

Millions of Units	Years through December 31				
Product	1998	1997	1996	1995	1994
Cans	3.020	2.376	2.014	1.955	2.009
Crown caps	11.048	10.488	10.570	9.825	10.342
Cans food	401	457	380	358	417
Glass bottles	990	949	604	568	507
Corrugated cardboard boxes (1)	98.283	88.075	67.503	58.704	49.106
Labels	3.651	3.342	3.367	3.207	3.594
Flexible packaging (2)	7.363	6.928	6.373	5.883	5.971

(1) Thousands of square meters.
(2) Tons.
Source: Estimate from packaging.

FEMSA Merchandising

Thousands of Pesos in 1998	Years through December 31				
Concept	1998	1997	1996	1995	1994
Average sales by store.	363.1	323.3	315.9	329.2	391.4
Average monthly sale by store.	22.9	20.9	19.9	19.0	19.9
Beer boxes sold in OXXO stores.	9.90	9.10	8.70	7.70	7.40
% of beer sold in OXXO stores.	14.5%	15.3%	14.2%	14.3%	14.7%
Total OXXO stores.	1,000	892	823	767	677
% growth of OXXO stores.	12.1%	8.4%	7.3%	13.3%	8.5%

Source: Estimate from OXXO stores.
(1) Millions of cans.

D | Statistical Data *(Continued)*

Market Share FEMSA Beer

Region	1998	1997	1996	1995	1994
	Years through December 31				
Northeast	59.7%	59.4%	59.2%	59.7%	59.9%
Southeast	56.2%	56.1%	56.2%	56.5%	55.9%
Center	23.7%	23.3%	23.6%	23.9%	24.9%
Total	45.1%	45.2%	45.2%	45.2%	45.2%

Source: Estimate from FEMSA Beer.

Coca-Cola FEMSA

Territory	1998	1997	1996	1995
	Years through December 31			
Valley of Mexico	56.1%	52.7%	46.1%	41.5%
Southeast	65.7%	66.1%	65.2%	64.1%
Argentina	60.5%	58.2%	58.7%	58.3%

Source: Information from Argentina and SIRSA.

FEMSA Packaging

Product	1998	1997	1996	1995	1994
	Years through December 31				
Cans[(1)]	54.3%	51.2%	49.0%	48.1%	50.6%
Crown caps[(2)]	37.8%	37.9%	36.2%	32.0%	32.7%

[(1)]Includes market share in exports.
[(2)]Does not include exports.
Source: FEMSA Packaging.

D | Statistical Data *(Continued)*

Fomento Económico Mexicano, S.A. De C.V. y Subsidiarias (before known as Valores Industriales, S.A. y Subsidiarias)

The figures presented in this summary correspond to the financial statements of Fomento Económico Mexicano, S.A. de C.V. y Subsidiarias ("FEMSA"), before known as Valores Industriales, S.A. de C.V. ("VISA"). Therefore, figures for years from 1993 to 1997 are not comparable with the financial statements of Grupo Industrial Emprex, S.A. de C.V. (before FEMSA), presented in previous annual reports (see note 1 on the financial statements).

	1998	1997	1996	1995	1994	1993
FINANCIAL STATEMENT						
Total earnings	33,530	29,329	26,544	25,910	25,102	21,797
Gross profit	15,160	13,277	10,901	10,603	11,717	10,130
Operation profit	4,722	4,214	2,589	2,118	2,775	2,223
Consolidated net profit	2,038	2,805	2,996	331	(1,390)	2,016
Majority net profit	1,360	1,174	1,434	(225)	(961)	975
Minority net profit	678	1,631	1,562	586	(429)	1,040
Ratios to Sale (%)						
Gross margin	45.5	45.7	41.2	41.1	47	46.8
Operation margin	14.1	14.4	9.8	8.2	11.1	10.2
Net profit	6.1	9.6	11.3	1.3	(5.5)	9.2
Other Information						
Operation flow	7,097	6,481	4,648	4,132	4,267	3,505
Investments on fixed assets	4,155	3,733	3,374	2,948	2,211	2,558
Balance						
Total assets	36,595	35,079	33,485	35,709	37,764	34,203
Liabilities						
Short term debt	2,656	3,287	4,490	1,951	4,524	1,550
Other liabilities	12,311	13,983	12,201	16,903	11,084	12,701
Total liabilities	14,967	17,270	16,691	18,854	15,608	14,251
Accounting capital	21,628	17,809	16,794	16,855	22,156	19,952
Financial Ratios (%)						
Money supply	2.07	2.06	2.13	2.19	2.17	2.48
Leverage	0.69	0.97	0.99	1.12	0.7	0.71
Capitalization	0.35	0.46	0.5	0.49	0.38	0.37
Number of employees	39,770	37,202	35,694	34,840	36,512	36,720

Figures are in millions of constant pesos through December 31, 1998.

CASE 20

Fleming Companies, Inc.

Year 2000 ("Y2K") Compliance: The Communications Debacle

Laura Callahan
Chris Huston
John Millar
R. Glenn Richey
The University of Oklahoma

September 1, 1998. Tom Zaricki, vice president of Retail Services for Fleming, Inc., a food distribution company, ponders recent problems. Pricing lawsuits, the Teamsters strike and turbulent acquisitions all come to mind as problems of the past. For the company to be proactive, he realizes that Fleming must circumnavigate the largest obstacle of this decade, the Year 2000 (Y2K) information technology crisis.

Fleming's history of information technology leadership and strong customer communications network helps Zaricki maintain confidence. He believes in his people and the market strength of Fleming as the nation's leading grocery wholesaler/retailer. "We are a diverse group of people working toward a common goal," he says proudly.[1] To maintain communications cohesiveness, Zaricki spends four of every five days on the road meeting with retailers and managers. Those he cannot reach physically are invited to attend his monthly videoconference. Zaricki's leadership is the glue that binds the Fleming Retail Services Division. He is committed to superior corporate communications tools and techniques.

Fleming's 283 company-owned retail outlets are the products of multiple acquisitions. The market focus has been to keep local facilities intact, decentralized and autonomous. In addition, Fleming services some 3,100 independent supermarkets across 42 states and in several foreign countries. The customer base comprises hundreds of independent grocers with highly fragmented information technology systems. Several months ago, Fleming tested a customer's system by forwarding the date to January 1, 2000. In five minutes, the retailer's entire system was inoperative.

Fleming operates at both the wholesale and retail levels. It must assure that all wholesale facilities, company-owned retail outlets and related independent retail outlets, which rely on Fleming for products and services, are Y2K compliant by the end of 1999. While internal systems and company owned retail outlets are expected to be compliant, there is less certainty about independent retailers. Now, Fleming has sixteen months to integrate all of these fragmented systems. Zaricki considers, "We have worked at this for nearly three years. Do we have the resources to get it done?"[2] Furthermore, because Fleming has followed an alliance partnering system strategy, instead of strict vertical integration, it does not have direct control over the compliance of its retail partners.

HISTORY OF FLEMING

Fleming was founded in 1915 in Topeka, Kansas. Ned Fleming's small wholesale produce company focused on serving area retailers. Even in the earliest days of the company's existence, its founder knew that the company's success would be derived from its commitment to the success of its retail customers.[3]

This case was prepared under the direction of Professor Robert E. Hoskisson. The case is intended to be used as the basis for class discussion rather than to illustrate either effective or ineffective handling of an administrative or strategic situation.

Copyright © 1999 by South-Western College Publishing and Thomson Learning Custom Publishing (ISBN: 0-324-01766-9). For information regarding this and other CaseNet® cases, please visit CaseNet® on the World Wide Web at **casenet.thomson.com**.

In 1927, Fleming was instrumental in establishing the Independent Grocers Alliance (IGA) for the first time west of the Mississippi. The intent was to establish a partnership/alliance system between the wholesalers and the retailers that would permit economies of scale through lower costs, stronger identity, and better marketing and merchandising. It would also allow small retailers to compete with chains. IGA today is an independent organization headquartered in Chicago. It is owned by Fleming and 22 other wholesalers and continues to license the IGA name to retailers throughout the country. The IGA Board of Directors includes CEOs from Fleming and other wholesalers in the ownership group. Its mission today remains essentially the same as that envisioned by the founders.

In 1941, Fleming expanded from Kansas to Oklahoma. Over time, Fleming's involvement in the operations of its customers expanded to include assistance with site selection, financing and leasing arrangements for capital requirements. Innovation in warehousing allowed the company and its retail partners to be more productive and profitable. Today, the typical Fleming 700,000 square foot warehouse turns $705 million in inventory per year.[4]

The company went public in 1959, and during the 1960s aligned itself with IBM to develop the industry's first computerized inventory management system.[5] An interest in cutting-edge technological innovation was also evidenced by Fleming's active involvement in the development of the Universal Product Code (UPC) during the late 1960s. The UPC was the basis for computer tracking of grocery items and eventually all products for inventory and pricing applications.

The company continued to expand during the 1970s and 1980s, becoming the largest food distributor in the United States in 1988. During the 1990s, Fleming continued to emphasize technological innovation with the goal of improved productivity. Leading change in this area from 1994 to July 1998 was Robert E. Stauth, who served as CEO during this period.

Recent Position and Performance

Fleming has chosen to grow the business through captive customers, resulting in the Retail Division, managed by Tom Zaricki. The food and general merchandise products of more than 3,000 manufacturers, vendors, and brokers flow through Fleming to more than 3,400 retailers and millions of consumers, helped by Fleming's 39,000 employees.

Fleming consists of four main business segments—Fleming Food & General Merchandise Distribution, Fleming Brands, Fleming Retail Services and the Fleming Retail Group (see Exhibit 1). It is currently the second largest food products distributor in the United States with net annual sales of $14.1 billion, $2 billion of which were through the Retail Division, in fiscal 1997. Fleming owns 283 supermarkets, which are operated under various regional names. This segment contributed $3.5 billion of total sales during the fiscal year ended December 1997.

The food distribution segment offers both national brands and private Fleming brands in the various grocery, meat, dairy, produce, bakery, deli and general merchandise categories. The objective behind providing private brands is that both Fleming and the retailer should be able to generate improved margins over national brands.

The company has been successful in reducing its debt-to-capital ratio from 62.3 percent in 1995 to 58.9 percent since 1997, but nevertheless continues to exceed its targeted 50 percent to 55 percent goal (see Exhibit 2).

RETAIL GROUP BACKGROUND AND OPERATIONS

A major part of the Retail Group's strategy was implemented with the acquisition of Scrivner, another grocery chain, in 1994 (Exhibit 3). The acquisition allowed Fleming to greatly expand its market coverage and increase Retail Division sales from 6 percent to 17 percent of total sales. Fleming's recent retail acquisitions raised this percentage to 21 percent by 1996, with the company's near term goal to increase it to 25 percent.[6]

Company stores are grouped under various trade names, including *ABCO Markets* (Arizona), *Baker's* (Nebraska & Oklahoma), *Boogaarts Food Stores* (Kansas), *Consumer Markets* (Missouri), *Festival Foods* (Pennsylvania), *Hyde Park Markets* (Florida), *Market Basket and Jubilee* (New York), *Rainbow Foods* (Minnesota), *SuPeRSaVeR and Sentry Foods* (Wisconsin) and *Thompson Food Basket* (Illinois).[7] Expansion of Fleming in-store/private label brands is also a priority. Current of-

EXHIBIT 1 | Fleming's Four Main Business Segments

Business Segment	Task	Scope
Fleming Food & General Merchandise	Provide customers with valuable, competitively priced goods through wholesale distribution.	Offers a wide selection of groceries, meat, produce, beauty care and specialty items.
Fleming Brands	Growth and profitability through marketing and packaging of private label brands.	Five-Brand Consolidation: Best Yet, Piggly Wiggly, Rainbow, IGA, & Marquee
Fleming Retail Services	Management of independent retail relationships and programs.	Retail Programs: Advertising, Education, Financial Services, Technological Services, Development, Pricing, Operations, Category Management, Franchising, Insurance, VISIONET, Promotions, Loyalty Marketing Services
Fleming Retail Group (Retail Food)	Management of 12 different Fleming owned retail stores.	ABCO Markets, Baker's Supermarkets, Boogaarts, Consumer's Markets, Festival Foods, Jubilee Foods, Market Basket, Rainbow Foods, SuPeRSaVeR, Sentry Foods, Thompson Food Basket

Source: Http:/www.fleming.com

Sales of Retail vs. Wholesale Distribution (in Thousands)

Net Sales	1997	Est. 1998
Food Distribution	$11,914	$11,400 to $11,700
Retail Food	$ 3,459	$3,500 to $3,600

Source: Fleming 8K Report, 12/7/98, p. 2.

ferings include *BestYet, Marquee, Piggly Wiggly, Rainbow* and *IGA,* as well as a line of upscale specialty products.[8]

Fleming's Retail Services segment has also expanded to include assistance in advertising, training, finance, insurance, promotions, franchising, technology, store development, operations, inventory management, and pricing for both company-owned and independent food retailers.

Fleming's pricing methodology is an evolving concept. Historically, Fleming actually sold much of its products at or below its invoice cost. Just as car dealers would not stay in business selling at below invoice, it was no secret among customers that Fleming was able to sell at its cost based on receipt of manufacturer rebates. The other part of the equation was that historically, the retailers paid a fixed percentage fee for Fleming services such as delivery and storage. Over time, Fleming created system efficiencies (i.e., backhauling live loads where possible) that resulted in a "profit" on actual expenses versus the fixed fee customarily charged to retailers.

Independent retailers were aware of the above-described system, but pricing, or alleged overcharging, was at the core of recent litigation (which is discussed later in this case) and ultimately, the decision was made to rationalize the pricing approach.[9] The new approach was to sell to retailers at Fleming's cost less applicable discounts and then charge a fee based on the cost plus a reasonable profit on services provided by Fleming. Every component of Fleming cost is factored into the equation. Retailers are then given the option to purchase lesser degrees of service from Fleming, which in turn reduces their net cost. The program is a basic form of activity-based costing offering five levels of value added services.

Even retailers generally are in agreement with the theory behind the new system. The problem, from the retailer's point of view, is that the system, as currently administered, is too complex. The perception is that no one really understands the system. One longtime retail customer explained that, on average, he finds approximately $500 per week in mistaken overcharges on Flem-

2 | Consolidated Financial Statement

40 weeks ended October 3, 1998, and October 4, 1997 (in thousands)

	1998	**1997**
Net sales	$11,511,835	$11,755,946
Costs and expenses:		
Cost of sales	10,385,064	10,670,361
Selling and administrative	959,389	911,420
Interest expense	124,411	124,129
Interest income	(28,172)	(36,410)
Equity investment results	9,506	11,027
Litigation charge	7,385	19,218
Total costs and expenses	11,457,583	11,699,745
Earnings before taxes	54,252	56,201
Taxes on income	27,668	28,602
Earnings before extraordinary charge	26,584	27,599
Extraordinary charge from early retirement of debt (net of taxes)		13,330
Net earnings	$26,584	$14,269
Earnings per share:		
Basic and diluted before extraordinary charge	$.70	$.73
Extraordinary charge		$.35
Basic and diluted net earnings	$.70	$.38
Dividends paid per share	$.06	$.06
Weighted average shares outstanding:		
Basic	37,848	37,803
Diluted	38,058	37,825

Source: Fleming 10-Q Report, p. 2, 11/6/98

Year	**1995**	**1996**	**1997–Q3**	**1997–Q4**	**1998–Q1**	**1998–Q2**
Debt % of Tot. Capital	62.3%	59.8%	58.9%	58.9%	58.2%	57.5%

Source: Fleming 10-Q Report, Summary Fact Sheet, p. 2, 7/31/98.

ing invoices. He simply calls his Fleming contact to receive credit but is "in the dark" about the substance behind many of the numbers on his invoice.[10]

THE Y2K PROBLEM

The Y2K problem exists in nearly all areas of information systems and technology, including hardware platforms, software applications, operating systems, low-level micro-code, files and databases. It is a result of decisions made during the 1950s and 1960s when the computer was in its development stages. At that time, memory was expensive, so it seemed logical to designate the year date in a two-digit format instead of a four-digit format. This action, however, has resulted in computer systems being unable to distinguish between the years 2000 and 1900.

It has been suggested that failure to update computer systems to become Y2K compliant may result in scenarios where computer systems slightly malfunction or stop completely, resulting in delays, costly mistakes and/or business failures. Also, Y2K system initiatives are complex, and the danger is that an attempted fix will cause other problems.

3 | Fleming's Acquisition/Growth History

1950s	Fleming acquired Ryley-Wilson Grocery Company in Kansas.
1960s	Fleming acquired companies and facilities in the Midwest and Southwest. Growth also expanded to the East Coast with the purchase of Thriftway in Pennsylvania and to the West Coast with the purchase of Kockos Brothers, Ltd., in California.
1970s	Fleming grew its East Coast business with moves into New York and New Jersey.
1980s	Fleming acquired distribution centers in Texas, Oregon, Utah, Tennessee, California, Arizona, Pennsylvania, Wisconsin and Hawaii.
1990s	Fleming acquired Scrivner, Inc., which strengthened Fleming's customer base throughout the Midwest and East and established the company's first facilities in seven markets—Iowa, North Carolina, South Carolina, western Pennsylvania, New York, Illinois and Minnesota.

Source: http://www.fleming.com/history.htm.

Technology experts note that there is not a simple, cost-effective solution to the problem. Globally, an estimated 180 billion lines of program code are currently in use, and approximately 93 percent are date sensitive and will require repair or replacement.[11] While the costs of corrective action vary from company to company, some companies report a cost of $1.10 per line of source code to correct the date field problem.[12] Furthermore, Gartner Group, Inc., an information technology research firm, estimates the worldwide impact of Y2K compliance—including corrective action and litigation and damages—will cost between $300 billion and $600 billion worldwide.[13]

To help alleviate some of the legal problems that could be incurred as a result of Y2K problems, Congress recently passed legislation that would make it easier for companies to share information about fixing their Y2K problems without fear of a lawsuit. The legislation provides companies with limited protection from the use of statements concerning Y2K remedies or companies' progress in correcting problems. The bill results from some companies' reluctance to share information about how to repair the problem or provide status reports on their efforts to fix their own systems because of fear that the information could be used against them in a lawsuit by disgruntled customers or competition. The bill protects companies from liability for statements made that are alleged to be false, inaccurate or misleading unless it is proven the company knew it was false, inaccurate or misleading and made it with an intent to deceive or mislead.[14]

IMPACT OF Y2K PROBLEMS ON FLEMING

The food distribution industry depends heavily on information systems and technology for warehousing and distribution, point-of-sale, merchandising and operations. Although the average grocery information system operating expenses of 0.44 percent of sales is fairly low for the wholesale food industry and significantly less than other industries, the impact of Y2K technology on the food distribution industry will still be considerable for a number of reasons.[15]

For Fleming, the impact of Y2K may be felt not only internally, but also in dealings with suppliers, subsidiaries, recently acquired stores, and independent retailers who order groceries from Fleming. In addition, retail customers could experience lower levels of customer service because of Y2K problems. Accordingly, this is a core strategic issue facing Fleming.

For example, most of Fleming's suppliers either manufacture a product in a factory environment or distribute perishables. Any automatic production control system or just-in-time ordering system could be compromised by a Y2K problem.[16] Also, a Y2K failure in

Fleming's order processing and invoicing system could result in Fleming's shipping subsidiaries and independent retail grocery stores the wrong products and incorrect quantities due to date errors in complex calculation routines.[17]

In addition, stores currently being acquired by Fleming are not likely to be Y2K compliant. As such, these stores become part of Fleming's retail group, and it must add the costs required to install the company's predefined store equipment configuration to the cost of the acquisition. If the acquired store will be sold to one of Fleming's customers, the company must take time to inventory the equipment and advise the purchaser that certain technologies need to be replaced or upgraded to avoid liability.[18]

In turn, technology at Fleming's retail and independent stores could, by its failure, result in

- appearance of ads for special sales on the wrong days, resulting in stock-outs and customer dissatisfaction;
- failure of accounting systems, causing more time-consuming and error-prone manual bookkeeping methods to be used;
- failure of credit card processing and automated check writing;
- incorrect marking of expiration dates on perishables, causing potential illness and/or increase shrink;
- malfunctioning produce misters, either staying on continuously or stopping entirely;
- breakdown of computerized scales, and
- general disruption of everything on a timer, including safes, security systems, energy management and temperature controls, lighting, phone systems, elevators, refrigerators and freezers.[19]

While these retail problems may not force noncompliant grocers to close their business, it could have a negative impact on the stores' level of customer service and increase their cost of doing business. These potential effects are of great concern to Fleming because even a one-percentage point drop in sales in the grocery business is significant.[20]

Y2K problems also present a number of legal issues. For example, as noted above, the failure of corporate computer systems could lead to breached contracts, delivery of defective products and services, and business interruptions. Affected companies may sue the computer consultants that advised them on the design of the companies' computer systems.[21] However, according to Bob Stauth, the legal implications are a non-issue for Fleming. "Fleming will be compliant, it will make sure systems sold to retailers are compliant, and it will attempt to communicate the urgency of the situation to its customers. It does not have the time nor the resources to fix the independent stores' systems even if it wanted to," he says.[22]

FLEMING'S BUDGET FOR ITS Y2K INITIATIVES

A core competence of Fleming is its information technology leadership, as indicated earlier. Fleming's Retail Services Division invests heavily in creating new innovative IT products designed to give retailers a competitive systems edge. Products include point-of-sale equipment purchasing and leasing, systems evaluations, electronic payment systems, direct store delivery, various software applications, electronic shelf labels, in-store file managers and total store technology solutions.

However, short-term concerns regarding profitability have resulted in a corporate decision not to increase the normal budget for information technology to pay the anticipated $10 million cost per year ($35 to $38 million over the four-year period) of Y2K compliance. The corporate goal is for the project not to exceed 12.5 percent of the $80 million per year operating budget. While management asserts that only noncritical development and support will be impacted or delayed, it will be difficult to continue on the leading technology edge with a significantly reduced expenditure for normal development activity. The following is an excerpt from the SEC Filings found in the 10Q for the period ended July 11, 1998:

> *Program costs to comply with year-2000 requirements are being expensed as incurred. Total third party expenditures in 1997 through completion in 1999 are not expected to exceed $10 million, none of which is incremental. Through the end of the third quarter of 1998, these third party expenditures totaled over $5 million. To compensate for the dilutive effect on results of operations, the company has de-*

layed other non-critical development and support initiatives. Accordingly, the company expects that annual information technology expenses will not differ significantly from prior years.[23]

FLEMING'S COMPANY-WIDE AND RETAIL SERVICES Y2K PLANS

Noting that few companies are as pivotal in maintaining America's food supply chain, Fleming believes it owes its stakeholders, associates and customers the duty of not only repairing its systems, but also assuring that the entire food supply chain will not be disrupted.

In 1997, Fleming created a Y2K Project Office to undertake a comprehensive plan to position Fleming as an industry leader in Y2K compliance and as a resource to the food distribution industry—especially to its 3,100 retail customers. The Project Office consists of seven people that oversee the enterprise-wide effort of 76 project leaders, their teams, and more than 50 information technology experts. (Exhibit 4) Guiding the project are the Chief Financial Officer Harry Winn, Senior Vice President of Information Technology Arlyn Larson, and Project Director Mike McCormick. Since Y2K poses business risks as well as technical problems, Fleming also assigned an attorney, an auditor, a member of Fleming's Risk Management Department and a knowledge coordinator to provide guidance. Also, in early 1998, Fleming named a full-time retail Y2K manager, Mike Sweeney, to direct a marketing campaign to increase awareness in the retail community, as well as to manage the internal activities to ensure the compliance of Fleming and Fleming's customers.[24]

Fleming's Company-Wide Initiatives

Touting the motto "Don't Wait, Fix it in '98," the Project Office strove to address the Y2K issue on a company-wide basis by completing the inventory, assessment and planning phases of the project and beginning renovation of mission critical systems in the first half of 1997.[25] Fleming believed this timeline would allow it to complete the renovations, replacements and hardware/software upgrades as well as to test and finalize compliance in 1998. During 1999, Fleming could work on less critical systems, do more testing and actual simulations of Y2K scenarios and ensure that systems with dates that look ahead into the future are ready and would not fail in mid-1999.

More specifically Fleming focused on the Fleming Operational Online Distribution System (FOODS) in 1997. FOODS is the proprietary core operating software information system that allows Fleming to efficiently process billing and service marketing activities for its retail customers. In December 1996, Fleming contracted with Information Management Resources (IMR), a firm specializing in Y2K remediation, for the assessment phase of the FOODS Y2K compliance. The assessment was completed in April 1997, and Fleming contracted with the company to do the code repairs and accomplish testing and implementation phases.[26]

Before Fleming could begin Y2K repairs, it had to upgrade its operating systems and language and convert FOODS to Y2K compliant levels. With the help of another outside firm, Automated Migration Services, this was accomplished from May 1997 through August 1997. IMR then took some of the programs offshore to its "software factory" in India to make the code repairs and tests. The software was ready by December 1997 for Acceptance Testing and Year 2000 Certification Testing, packaging and release for internal use by Fleming.[27]

This was the first time Fleming had ever completely released the entire FOODS system and Fleming thought this process would help it refine the process for other Y2K remediation systems.[28] Other Fleming mainframe systems were handled in-house by Fleming's Information Technology Development group. The systems include all of the corporate systems, such as payroll and general ledger.[29] As a result, all of Fleming's mission critical systems became compliant in the fourth quarter of 1998.[30]

In addition, Fleming executives noted that most of the Y2K issues relating to suppliers and trading partners had been addressed. The main interface between Fleming and its suppliers and partners is through Electronic Data Interchange, an industry standard communications format administered by the Uniform Code Council (UCC). The UCC specified a transaction method for handling dates for Y2K and beyond that is being used by Fleming and its suppliers.[31]

Fleming's Retail Services Y2K Initiatives

Fleming's subsidiaries are required to have the same technology configuration, and all the micro-chip driven

EXHIBIT 4 | Year 2000 Project Office

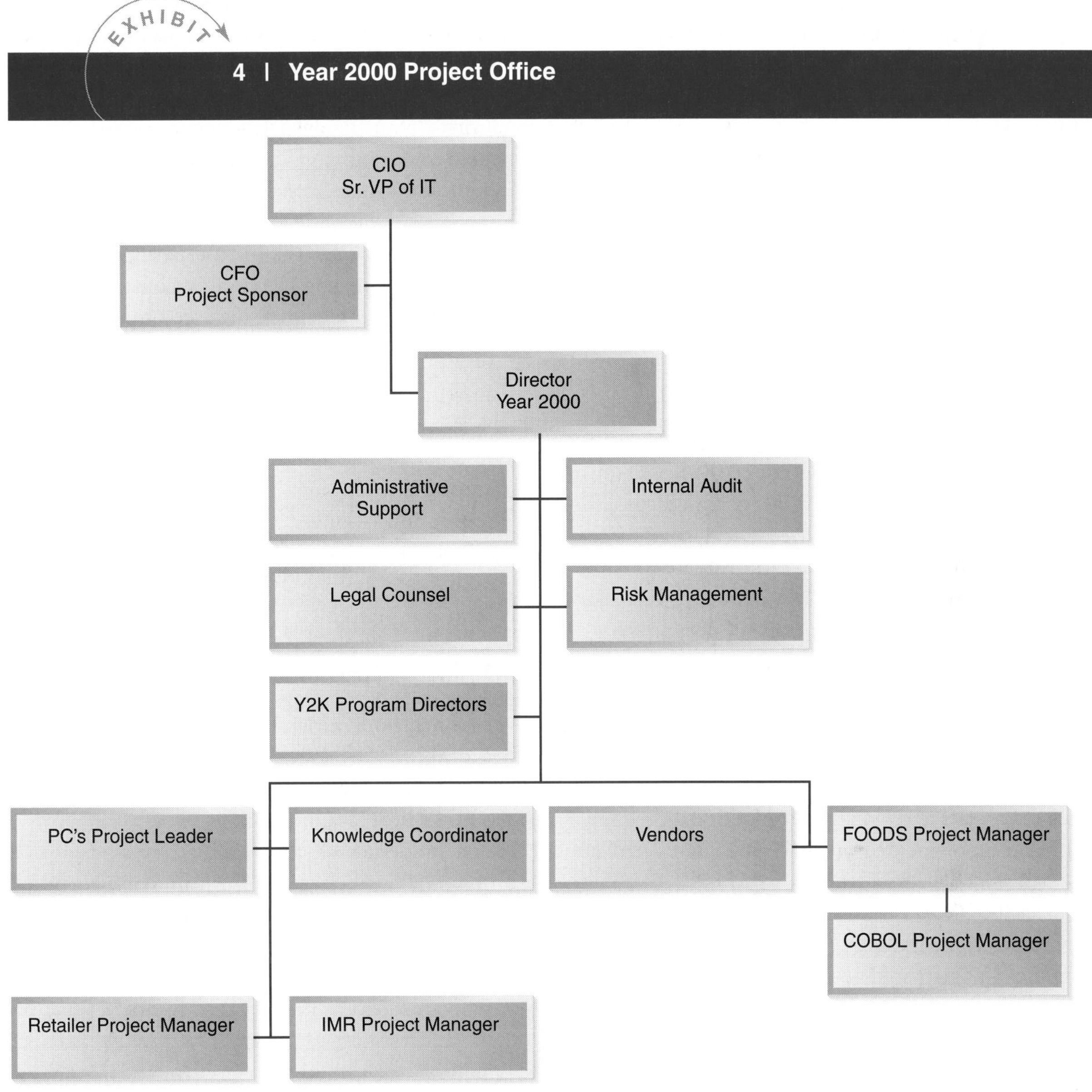

Source: Year 2000 Project Office, December 1997.

systems are known, allowing a single fix to be applied in a production-like sequence. Therefore, Fleming subsidiaries are already in compliance. However, the majority of the independent retailers—which use a diverse mixture of systems, cobbled together over years, even decades—are still not Y2K compliant. Fleming executives knew that it would be difficult to convince independent storeowners that a risk really did exist and to motivate them to action.

Bob Stauth confirms that the level of independent retailer sophistication is from "A to Z." Few of the independent stores have a detailed inventory of all non-Fleming supplied computer systems that note the make, model, and version of their hardware and software.

Many of them also do not have information systems support on site, but outsource this function as needed. Essentially, technology upgrades are driven by future profitability increases, not by any need or desire to be cutting-edge.[32]

Fleming has supplied many of the systems in place in retailers' stores. However, Fleming acts only as a pass-through for the equipment, leaving service and support to the original manufacturer. Equipment is either leased or sold outright to the stores. Fleming also carries the note on purchases for retailers that expect difficulty in obtaining financing elsewhere.

To assist Fleming's independent retailers in dealing with Y2K issues, the company's Retail Services Y2K Division kicked off a Y2K Awareness Campaign in January 1998.[33] Through a series of publications and newsletters, presentations at gatherings of grocers around the nation, and personal visits with independent storeowners, the division tried to explain the problem, the possible solutions and the urgency of the situation.

At a conference of Fleming's top 100 customers, audience comments proved Fleming's fear that few retailers were remediating Y2K issues. Less than 5 percent of the retailers were in compliance, 5 percent had done nothing at all, and the majority had some plan but had not started implementation.[34] As a follow-up, Fleming wrote to retailers and requested copies of their compliance plan, implemented or not. Few retailers had responded several weeks later.

To facilitate the process of developing a plan, Fleming then compiled an exhaustive list of grocery store equipment it had placed in each store, with compliance level and contacts for those systems not in compliance. Fleming sent these documents via registered mail, with return receipt (Exhibit 5).[35] Several weeks later, at a gathering of Fleming customers, Fleming asked how many of them had received the packet. No one claimed knowledge of it. Recently, Fleming used its *Technology Update* newsletter in an attempt to scare retailers into compliance.[36]

On February 11, 1998, Fleming and IBM offered a Y2K information seminar. Joe Jurich of IBM presented the program with the hope that independent grocers would recognize the importance of Y2K compliance. Jurich suggested that problems existed in hardware; system software such as databases, traction processors and operating systems; and application software. He stressed that no one could sit still. Grocers must fix existing systems or replace outdated systems with Y2K compliant software and hardware.

Jurich's plan involved five phases: awareness, assessment, renovation, validation and implementation. His approach called for six different project teams per grocer—The Development Team, The Program Team, The Applications Team, The In-Store Systems Team, The Infrastructure Team, and The Quality Control Team. The following is a schedule Jurich suggested grocers observe:

1. **Awareness**—Define the problem, gain executive support, establish teams, develop a strategy (Completed April 1997)
2. **Assessment**—Determine impact, prioritize conversions, secure resources (Completed August 1997)
3. **Renovation**—Conversion, replacement, retirement (Completed August 1999)
4. **Validation**—Test applications, databases and utilities (Completed August 1999)
5. **Implementation**—Place into production and conduct training (Completed August 1999)

In conclusion, Jurich begged the grocers to get started if they had yet to move on the crisis. He asked them to review the potential problems and focus on "Mission Critical" applications.[37]

After undertaking these initiatives and several months of talking to retailers, the team sensed continuing resistance to education efforts and reluctance to acknowledge the problem. Many retailers were too overwhelmed with the daily operations of their stores to worry about an event that was nearly two years away. Others were resistant to Fleming's overtures for fear that Fleming was exaggerating the problem and simply trying to sell something else to them. Company personnel confirm that trust is an issue.

Interestingly, one of the company's recent official pronouncements with respect to Y2K compliance states that, "Although responses (from vendors and customers) have not been conclusive, they have been encouraging."[38] This report goes on to say that the company's greatest concern is for potential disruption at the customer level. Some contingency plans are in place to deal with lost sales that may result from the

Exhibit 5 | Selected Product Listing from January 1998 Technology Update

Product	Version	Year 2000 Ready	Comments
Point of Sale			
IBM 4683 Hardware	All	Yes	
IBM 4693.4694	All	Yes	
IBM 4680 Supermarket	All	No	Upgrade to 4690
IBM 4680 OS	All	No	Upgrade to 4690
IBM 4690 Supermarket		Yes	
IBM 4690 OS		Yes	
NCR: 1255		No	
NCR: 2126		No	
NCR: 227		No	
NCR: 7000		No	
NCR: Scanmaster			
ICL ISS45	7.4&8.0	Yes	
ICI S18	14.9.3 & Above	Yes	
TEC	All	No Vendor Response	
Casio: 2100	5.4.18 & Above	Yes	
SASI	All	No Vendor Response	
Back Office Applications			
Tomax	All	Yes	
ASSET	All	Yes w/comment	
Malone & Hyde ASSET	All	No	Replace
TCI	3.X & Above	Yes w/comment	
Time Clocks			
Time Star	Dos 10.0, Windows	Yes	Upgrade Old
Accounting Applications			
FIRST Accounts Payable		No	
FIRST Accounts Receivable		No	
FIRST Store Report		No	
FIRST Return Clerk		No	
FIRST Payroll		No	
FIRST General Ledger		No	
Personal Computers			
All: Model			
Pricing Programs			
FIRST POS		No	Replace
FIRST Retail Connection		No	Replace

Source: Fleming Year 2000 Technology Assessment Guide, p. 4, January 1998.

anticipated disruptions. The following is an excerpt from the SEC Filings found in the 10Q for the period ended July 11, 1998:

Fleming has numerous computer systems which were developed employing six digit date structures (i.e., two digits each for month, day and year). Where date logic requires the year 2000 or beyond, such date structures may produce inaccurate results. Management has implemented a program to comply with year-2000 requirements on a system-by-system basis including both information technology (IT) and non-IT systems, e.g., microcontrollers. Fleming's plan includes extensive systems testing and is expected to be substantially completed by mid-1999. Code for the company's largest and most comprehensive system, FOODS, has been completely remediated and bench tested and is being reinstalled throughout the company for final testing. Although the company believes contingency plans will not be necessary based on progress to date, contingency plans have been developed for each critical system. The content of the contingency plans varies depending on the system and the assessed probability of failure and such plans are modified periodically based on remediation and testing. The plans are comprised of activities such as reallocating internal resources, obtaining additional outside resources, implementing temporary manual processes or temporarily rolling back the internal clocks. Although the company is developing greater levels of confidence regarding its internal systems, ultimate success must still be verified through extensive testing. Failure to ensure that the company's computer systems are year-2000 compliant could have a material adverse effect on the company's operations. The company is also assessing the status of its vendors' and customers' year-2000 readiness through meetings, discussions, notices and questionnaires. Vendor and customer responses and feedback are encouraging, but not conclusive. Failure of the company's suppliers or its customers to become year-2000 compliant might also have a material adverse impact on the company's operations.[39]

Another Y2K concern is that perhaps even "fixed" systems will not work properly when integrated with other systems. Testing all systems in concert is obviously the only way to ensure Y2K problems are corrected. The degree to which Fleming's independent retail customers are at risk depends largely on their historical approach to using Fleming systems versus third-party providers.

Wrights IGA of Norman, Oklahoma, for example, has generally shunned Fleming systems based on a preference to purchase rather than lease its hardware. The extent to which Fleming has provided financial help to the independents through lease guarantees and working capital bears some correlation with the percentage of Fleming systems that the retailer must lease from Fleming. Wrights, therefore, believes that its systems are generally not interdependent with Fleming systems and that, therefore, the testing issue will not be a problem. Obviously, many retailers have acquired their equipment from Fleming and therefore can be effectively targeted and made compliant.[40] Unfortunately, Fleming has limited knowledge of what its independent retail partners have purchased from third-party system suppliers or what related compliance issues may arise in the systems.

RECENT LITIGATION

Partnerships are partly dependent on the trust found among partners, which is an issue related to partners' responses to Fleming's Y2K initiatives. Fleming's stated philosophy, as set forth in the February 1997 Statement of Corporate Governance Policy, confirms the commitment to ". . . operate pursuant to the highest possible ethical standards with integrity, propriety, and fairness, and in full compliance with the law . . . every action . . . will be taken with full consideration for the interests and well-being, first, of all company stockholders and second, of all other company stakeholders. . . ."[41]

The impact of the trust issue is evident in recent litigation against Fleming. Over the course of the past six years, Fleming has been forced to deal with significant customer litigation involving allegations of fraudulent practices.[42] In 1993, David's, a Texas based retail partner, won a jury verdict of $211 million based on allegations of fraudulent overcharges and deceptive trade practices.[43] Two major customers, Randall's and Furr's, initially rejected overtures of attorney William D. Sims, who represented David's, to file similar suits. After the David's judgment, these customers filed similar overcharge suits in what appears to have been an effort to free themselves of long-term distribution contracts with Fleming. The fact is that major retailers are penalized by the financial markets if they choose not to self distribute. It is believed that this Wall Street requirement for retailers considering sale or public offering was the major motivation for Randall's and Furr's to reconsider their initial rejection of litigation.

In a related development, Sims and other attorneys recently filed a federal class-action lawsuit against Fleming on behalf of retailers in Utah, Idaho, Nevada and Wyoming. The lawsuit alleges violation of the federal Racketeer Influenced and Corrupt Organization Act (RICO) based on an assertion that Fleming charged inflated prices under its distribution agreements. Speculation is that damage claims will exceed $100 million. Given that the current legal action only involves customers in four states, it is reasonable to speculate that other similar actions will follow.[44]

Continuing litigation threatens the future relationships between Fleming and its independent retail partners. Can retail customers trust Fleming's Y2K compliance program, when they do not trust Fleming's current pricing programs? If independent retail partners make compliance decisions based on trust, current Y2K compliance suggestions may be completely disregarded.

TODAY: THE UPDATED STATUS OF THE Y2K DEBACLE

Zaricki, Simpson, Sweeney and Stauth all share one common perspective. They view the Fleming Y2K crisis as a debacle that could hinder corporate operations and damage sales starting Jan. 1, 2000, and thereafter. Still, their views of the retail landscape differ.

Zaricki, vice president of Retail Services, recognizes the problem as critical. He has placed his confidence in the hands of a very capable staff. He is concerned about the number of programmers available but knows that the company has successfully dealt with adversity in the past and will overcome this problem as well. His biggest concern is retail motivation and the time available to correct the problem. Can Fleming convince its customers to make the investment and become compliant in time?[45]

Simpson, senior vice president of Retail Services, is a strong company man. Simpson must walk a fine line between assisting customers and profiting from the Y2K compliance issue. It is Simpson's mission to find common ground between customer service and profitability. Fleming's Y2K compliance programs are a service that required extensive R&D expenditures and years to complete. Retail partnerships often include R&D costs, requiring customers to help "foot the bill." Simpson hopes to protect Fleming's investment in the service business.[46]

Sweeney, manager of Information Technology, sees the issue as one that may not incorporate profit for Fleming. He claims that customers understand the importance of the problem, but lack trust in Fleming's plan due to the capital required in updating systems. Most customers have been through computer problems before and have expectations that local computer technicians will be able to iron out any potential Y2K problems. These customers lack a sense of urgency and therefore refuse to buy into Fleming's plans despite Sweeney's best efforts. Sweeney is convinced that upper level management is aware of the number of customers who will hold out, but he is still having difficulty motivating customers to address the problem.[47]

Stauth, former CEO, views the Fleming Y2K situation as a timing and awareness issue. "The fourth quarter is historically the busiest time for retailers . . . there simply will not be enough time, if retailers wait (until the fourth quarter of 1999)," he says.[48] Historically, small independents expect to be taken care of and blame Fleming for mistakes. No retailer will be truly Y2K compliant until the entire system has been tested. Fleming has diverted a number of resources to cover the Y2K project. Stauth sees Fleming's efforts as lost opportunities in other areas and therefore believes that the company deserves to be paid for the service provided.[49]

Stauth also questions the future direction of Fleming. Fleming is still searching for a CEO. Stauth hopes to see Fleming hire a replacement CEO who is respected by "Wall Street and has a strong financial background."[50] It will be this individual's job to decide if Fleming should pursue additional acquisitions, hold the retail business at 25 percent or focus on becoming the most dominant wholesaler. This individual must have a strong grocery background and Wall Street appeal. The company will likely have difficulty finding this combination in one person.

Experts have described the Y2K issue as being the

largest single problem ever faced by mankind. Due to the close interrelationship with its customers, Fleming is faced with a task of a significantly greater magnitude than most companies. In addition to getting its own house in order, Fleming's very survival may well depend on the extent to which Fleming customers recognize and react to the problem.

ENDNOTES

1. Interview with Tom Zaricki, vice president of Retail Services, Fleming Companies, Inc., Sept. 1, 1998.
2. Ibid.
3. http://www.fleming.com/history.htm.
4. Interview with Bob Stauth, former CEO, Fleming Companies, Inc., Nov. 2, 1998.
5. http://www.fleming.com/history.htm.
6. Ibid.
7. http://www.fleming.com/retailgroup.htm.
8. http://www.fleming.com/brands.htm.
9. http://www.fleming.com/news97.htm.
10. Interview with Larry Wright, owner, Wright's IGA, Norman, Oklahoma, Nov. 4, 1998.
11. R. Hemphill, May 1997, The Millennium Crisis: A Year 2000 White Paper, IV.
12. J. Jinnett, September 1998, Legal Issues Concerning the Year 2000 Computer Problem: An Awareness Article for the Private Sector, http://www.year2000.com/archive/legalissues.html, 2.
13. R. Hemphill, The Millennium Crisis: A Year 2000 White Paper, 5.
14. J. Gruenwald, 1998, Year 2000 Liability Shield Bill Clears, *CQ Weekly*, October 3, 1663.
15. R. Hemphill, The Millennium Crisis: A Year 2000 White Paper, 3.
16. Interview with Mike Sweeney, manager of Information Technology, Fleming Companies, Inc., Oct. 9, 1998.
17. Ibid.
18. Ibid.
19. Ibid.
20. Interview with Dick Simpson, senior vice president of Retail Services, Fleming Companies, Inc., Oct. 2, 1998.
21. J. Jinnett, September 1998, Legal Issues Concerning the Year 2000 Computer Problem: An Awareness Article for the Private Sector, http://www.year2000.com/archive/legalissues.html, 2.
22. Interview with Bob Stauth.
23. SEC Filings found in the 10Q for the period ended July 11, 1998, p. 14.
24. Fleming, Dateline Fleming newsletter, January 1998, p. 3.
25. Ibid., p. 1.
26. Ibid., p. 1.
27. Ibid., p. 1.
28. Ibid., p. 2.
29. Ibid., p. 2.
30. Ibid., p. 2.
31. Interview with Mike Sweeney.
32. Interview with Bob Stauth, former CEO, Fleming Companies, Inc., Nov. 2, 1998.
33. Interview with Dick Simpson, senior vice president of Retail Services, Fleming Companies, Inc., Oct. 2, 1998.
34. Interview with Mike Sweeney.
35. Ibid.
36. Fleming Technology Update: Special January Addition, pp. 1–8.
37. National Grocers Association Presentation, Joe Jurich, IBM, February 11, 1998.
38. Found in the 10Q for the period ended July 11, 1998 states that "Although responses have not been conclusive, they have been encouraging . . . (therefore) no contingency plans will be developed regarding the purchase of products from vendors or the sale and delivery of products to customers."
39. SEC Filings found in the 10Q for the period ended July 11, 1998, p. 14.
40. Interview with Larry Wright.
41. Exhibit B, Schedule 14A, Proxy Statement Pursuant to Section 14(a) of the Securities Exchange Act of 1934 filed March 24, 1998.
42. http://www.fleming.com/history.htm.
43. Interview with Bob Stauth.
44. G. Hogan, "Another Lawsuit Targets Fleming," *Daily Oklahoman*, Nov. 11, 1998, http://www.oklahoman.com.
45. Interview with Tom Zaricki.
46. Interview with Dick Simpson.
47. Interview with Mike Sweeney.
48. Interview with Bob Stauth.
49. Ibid.
50. Ibid.

CASE 21

Gillette and the Men's Wet-Shaving Market

Lew G. Brown
Jennifer M. Hart
University of North Carolina at Greensboro

SAN FRANCISCO

On a spring morning in 1989, Michael Johnson dried himself and stepped from the shower in his San Francisco Marina District condominium. He moved to the sink and started to slide open his drawer in the cabinet beneath the sink. Then he remembered that he had thrown away his last Atra blade yesterday. He heard his wife, Susan, walk past the bathroom.

"Hey, Susan, did you remember to pick up some blades for me yesterday?"

"Yes, I think I put them in your drawer."

"Oh, okay, here they are." Michael saw the bottom of the blade package and pulled the drawer open.

"Oh, no! These are Trac II blades, Susan, I use an Atra."

"I'm sorry. I looked at all the packages at the drugstore, but I couldn't remember which type of razor you have. Can't you use the Trac II blades on your razor?"

"No. They don't fit."

"Well, I bought some disposable razors. Just use one of those."

"Well, where are they?"

"Look below the sink. They're in a big bag."

"I see them. Wow, ten razors for $1.97! Must have been on sale."

"I guess so. I usually look for the best deal. Seems to me that all those razors are the same, and the drugstore usually has one brand or another on sale."

"Why don't you buy some of those shavers made for women?"

"I've tried those, but it seems that they're just like the ones made for men, only they've dyed the plastic pink or some pastel color. Why should I pay more for color?

"Why don't you just use disposables?" Susan continued. "They are simpler to buy, and you just throw them away. And you can't beat the price."

"Well, the few times I've tried them they didn't seem to shave as well as a regular razor. Perhaps they've improved. Do they work for you?"

"Yes, they work fine. And they sure are better than the heavy razors if you drop one on your foot while you're in the shower!"

"Never thought about that. I see your point. Well, I'll give the disposable a try."

HISTORY OF SHAVING

Anthropologists do not know exactly when or even why men began to shave. Researchers do know that prehistoric cave drawings clearly present men who were beardless. Apparently these men shaved with clamshells or sharpened animal teeth. As society developed, primitive men learned to sharpen flint implements. Members of the early Egyptian dynasties as far back as 7,000 years

Engraph Corporation provided a grant to UNCG to support development of the case. Gillette's management cooperated in the field research for the case, which was written solely for the purpose of stimulating student discussion; the authors also drew from secondary sources. All incidents and events are real, but individual names were disguised at Gillette's request.

Copyright © 1992 by the *Case Research Journal* and Lew G. Brown.

ago shaved their faces and heads, probably to deny their enemies anything to grab during hand-to-hand combat. Egyptians later fashioned copper razors and, in time, bronze blades. Craftsmen formed these early razors as crescent-shaped knife blades, like hatchets or meat cleavers, or even as circular blades with a handle extending from the center. By the Iron Age, craftsmen were able to fashion blades that were considerably more efficient than the early flint, copper, and bronze versions.

Before the introduction of the safety razor, men used a straight-edged, hook-type razor and found shaving a tedious, difficult, and time-consuming task. The typical man struggled through shaving twice a week at most. The shaver had to sharpen the blade (a process called stropping) before each use and had to have an expert cutler hone the blade each month. As a result, men often cut themselves while shaving; and few men had the patience and acquired the necessary skill to become good shavers. Most men in the 1800s agreed with the old Russian proverb: "It is easier to bear a child once a year than to shave every day." Only the rich could afford a daily barber shave, which also often had its disadvantages because many barbers were unclean.

Before King C. Gillette of Boston invented the safety razor in 1895, he tinkered with other inventions in pursuit of a product which once used would be thrown away. The customer would have to buy more, and the business would build a long-term stream of sales and profits with each new customer.

"On one particular morning when I started to shave" wrote Gillette about the dawn of his invention, "I found my razor dull, and it was not only dull but beyond the point of successful stropping and it needed honing, for which it must be taken to a barber or cutler. As I stood there with the razor in my hand, my eyes resting on it as lightly as a bird settling down on its nest, the Gillette razor was born." Gillette immediately wrote to his wife who was visiting relatives, "I've got it; our fortune is made."

Gillette had envisioned a "permanent" razor handle onto which the shaver placed a thin, razor "blade" with two sharpened edges. The shaver would place a top over the blade and attach it to the handle so that only the sharpened edges of the blade were exposed, thus producing a "safe" shave. A man would shave with the blade until it became dull and then would simply throw the used blade away and replace it. Gillette knew his concept would revolutionize the process of shaving; however, he had no idea that his creation would permanently change men's shaving habits.

SHAVING IN THE 1980s

Following the invention of the safety razor, the U.S. men's shaving industry grew slowly but surely through World War I. A period of rapid growth followed, and the industry saw many product innovations. By 1989, U.S. domestic razor and blade sales (the wet-shave market) had grown to a $770 million industry. A man could use three types of wet shavers to remove facial hair. Most men used the disposable razor—a cheap, plastic-handled razor that lasted for 8 to 10 shaves on average. Permanent razors, called blade and razor systems, were also popular. These razors required new blades every 11 to 14 shaves. Customers could purchase razor handles and blade cartridges together, or they could purchase packages of blade cartridges as refills. The third category of wet shavers included injector and double-edge razors and accounted for a small share of the razor market. Between 1980 and 1988, disposable razors had risen from a 22 percent to a 41.5 percent market share of dollar sales. During the same period cartridge systems had fallen from 50 percent to 45.8 percent and injector and double-edge types had fallen from 28 percent to 12.7 percent. In addition, the development of the electric razor had spawned the dry-shave market, which accounted for about $250 million in sales by 1988.

Despite the popularity of disposable razors, manufacturers found that the razors were expensive to make and generated very little profit. In 1988 some industry analysts estimated that manufacturers earned three times more on a razor and blade system than on a disposable razor. Also, retailers preferred to sell razor systems because they took up less room on display racks and the retailers made more money on refill sales. However, retailers liked to promote disposable razors to generate traffic. As a result, U.S. retailers allocated 55 percent of their blade and razor stock to disposable razors, 40 percent to systems, and 5 percent to double-edge razors.

Electric razors also posed a threat to razor and blade systems. Unit sales of electric razors jumped from 6.2 million in 1981 to 8.8 million in 1987. Low-priced imports from the Far East drove demand for electric razors up and prices down during this period. Nonetheless, fewer than 30 percent of men used electric razors, and most of these men also used wet-shaving systems.

Industry analysts predicted that manufacturers' sales of personal care products would continue to grow. However, the slowing of the overall U.S. economy in the late 1980s meant that sales increases resulting from an expanding market would be minimal and companies would have to fight for market share to continue to increase sales.

The Gillette Company dominated the wet-shave market with a 60 percent share of worldwide razor market revenue and a 61.9 percent share of the U.S. market as of 1988. Gillette also had a stake in the dry-shave business through its Braun subsidiary. The other players in the wet-shave market were Schick with 16.2 percent of market revenues, BIC with 9.3 percent, and others, including Wilkinson Sword, with the remaining 12.6 percent.

THE GILLETTE COMPANY

King Gillette took eight years to perfect his safety razor. In 1903, the first year of marketing, the American Safety Razor Company sold 51 razors and 168 blades. Gillette promoted the safety razor as a saver of both time and money. Early ads proclaimed that the razor would save $52 and 15 days shaving time each year and that the blades required no stropping or honing. During its second year, Gillette sold 90,884 razors and 123,648 blades. By its third year, razor sales were rising at a rate of 400 percent per year, and blade sales were booming at an annual rate of 1,000 percent. In that year, the company opened its first overseas branch in London.

Such success attracted much attention, and competition quickly developed. By 1906, consumers had at least a dozen safety razors from which to choose. The Gillette razor sold for $5, as did the Zinn razor made by the Gem Cutlery Company. Others, such as the Ever Ready, Gem Junior, and Enders sold for as little as $1.

With the benefit of a 17-year patent, Gillette found himself in a very advantageous position. However, it was not until World War I that the safety razor gained wide consumer acceptance. One day in 1917, King Gillette had a visionary idea: have the government present a Gillette razor to every soldier, sailor, and marine. In this way, millions of men just entering the shaving age would adopt the self-shaving habit. By March, 1918, Gillette had booked orders from the U.S. military for 519,750 razors, more than it had sold in any single year in its history. During World War I, the government bought 4,180,000 Gillette razors as well as smaller quantities of competitive models.

Although King Gillette believed in the quality of his product, he realized that marketing, especially distribution and advertising, would be the key to success. From the beginning, Gillette set aside 25 cents per razor for advertising and by 1905 had increased the amount to 50 cents. Over the years, Gillette used cartoon ads, radio shows, musical slogans and theme songs, prizes, contests, and cross-promotions to push its products. Perhaps, however, consumers best remember Gillette for its Cavalcade of Sports programs that began in 1939 with the company's sponsorship of the World Series. Millions of men soon came to know Sharpie the Parrot and the tag line. "Look Sharp! Feel Sharp! Be Sharp!"

Because company founder King Gillette invented the first safety razor, Gillette had always been an industry innovator. In 1932, Gillette introduced the Gillette Blue Blade, which was the premier men's razor for many years. In 1938, the company introduced the Gillette Thin Blade; in 1946, it introduced the first blade dispenser that eliminated the need to unwrap individual blades; in 1959, it introduced the first silicone-coated blade, the Super Blue Blade. The success of the Super Blue Blade caused Gillette to close 1961 with a commanding 70 percent share of the overall razor and blade market and a 90 percent share of the double-edge market, the only market in which it competed.

In 1948, Gillette began to diversity into new markets through acquisition. The company purchased the Toni Company to extend its reach into the women's grooming-aid market. In 1954, the company bought Paper Mate, a leading marker of writing instruments. In 1962, Gillette acquired the Sterilon Corporation, which manufactured disposable hospital supplies. As a result of these moves, a marketing survey found that the public associated Gillette with personal grooming as much as, or more than, with blades and razors.

In 1988, the Gillette Company was a leading producer of men's and women's grooming aids. Exhibit 1 lists the company's major divisions. Exhibits 2 and 3

1 | Gillette 1988 Product Lines by Company Division

Blades and Razors	Stationery Products	Toiletries and Cosmetics	Oral B Products	Braun Products
Trac II	Paper Mate	Adorn	Oral B Toothbrushes	Electric Razors
Atra	Liquid Paper	Toni		Lady Elegance
Good News	Flair	Right Guard		Clocks
	Waterman	Silkience		Coffee Grinders and Makers
	Write Bros.	Soft and Dri		
		Foamy		
		Dry Look		
		Dry Idea		
		White Rain		
		Lustrasilk		
		Aapri Skin Care Products		

2 | Gillette's Sales and Operating Profits by Product Line (in Millions)

	1988		1987		1986	
Product Line	Sales	Profits	Sales	Profits	Sales	Profits
Blades and razors	$1,147	$406	$1,031	$334	$ 903	$274
Toiletries and cosmetics	1,019	79	926	99	854	69
Stationery products	385	56	320	34	298	11
Braun products	824	85	703	72	657	63
Oral B	202	18	183	7	148	8
Other	5	(0.1)	4	2	48	(1)
Totals	$3,582	$643	$3,167	$548	$2,908	$424

Source: Gillette Company Annual Report, 1985–1988.

3 | Gillette's Net Sales and Profit by Business (by Percent)

	Blades and Razors		Toiletries and Cosmetics		Stationery Products		Braun Products		Oral B Products	
Year	Sales	Profits	Sales	Profits	Sales	Profits	Sales	Profits	Sales	Profits
1988	32	61	28	14	11	9	23	13	6	3
1987	33	61	29	18	10	6	22	13	6	2
1986	32	64	30	16	11	3	20	15	5	2
1985	33	68	31	15	11	2	17	13	6	3
1984	34	69	30	15	12	3	17	12	3	2

Source: Gillette Company Annual Report, 1985–1988.

show the percentages and dollar volumes of net sales and profits from operations for each of the company's major business segments. Exhibits 4 and 5 present income statements and balance sheets for 1986–1988.

Despite its diversification, Gillette continued to realize the importance of blade and razor sales to the company's overall health. Gillette had a strong foothold in the razor and blade market, and it intended to use this

EXHIBIT 4 | Gillette Income Statements (in Millions Except for Per Share Data)

	1988	1987	1986
Net sales	$3,581.2	$3,166.8	$2,818.3
Cost of sales	1,487.4	1,342.3	1,183.8
Other expenses	1,479.8	1,301.3	1,412.0
Operating income	614.0	523.2	222.5
Other income	37.2	30.9	38.2
Earnings before interest and tax	651.2	545.1	260.7
Interest expense	138.3	112.5	85.2
Non-operating expense	64.3	50.1	124.0
Earnings before tax	448.6	391.5	51.5
Tax	180.1	161.6	35.7
Earnings after tax	268.5	229.9	15.8
Earnings per share	2.45	2.00	.12
Average common shares outstanding, 000	109,559	115,072	127,344
Dividends paid per share	$0.86	$0.785	$0.68
Stock price range			
High	$49	$45 7/8	$34 1/2
Low	$29 1/8	$17 5/8	$17 1/8

Source: Gillette Company Annual Report, 1986–1988.

EXHIBIT 5 | Gillette Balance Sheets (in Millions)

		1988	1987	1986
Assets	Cash	$ 156.4	$ 119.1	$ 94.8
	Receivables	729.1	680.1	608.8
	Inventories	653.4	594.5	603.1
	Other current assets	200.8	184.5	183.0
	Total current assets	1,739.7	1,578.2	1,489.7
	Fixed assets, net	683.1	664.4	637.3
	Other assets	445.1	448.6	412.5
	TOTAL ASSETS	2,867.9	2,731.2	2,539.5
Liabilities and Equity	Current liabilities*	965.4	960.5	900.7
	Long-term debt	1,675.2	839.6	915.2
	Other long-term liabilities	311.9	331.7	262.8
	Equity†	$ (84.6)	$ 599.4	$ 460.8

*Includes current portion of long-term debt: 1988 = $9.6, 1987 = $41.0, 1986 = $7.6.
†Includes retained earnings: 1988 = $1,261.6, 1987 = $1,083.8, 1986 = $944.3.
Source: Gillette Company Annual Report, 1986–1988.

dominance to help it achieve the company's goal—"sustained profitable growth." To reach this goal, Gillette's mission statement indicated that the company should pursue "strong technical and marketing efforts to assure vitality in major existing product lines; selective diversification, both internally and through acquisition; the elimination of product and business areas with low growth or limited profit potential; and strict control over product costs, overhead expenses, and working capital."

Gillette introduced a number of innovative shaving systems in the 1970s and 1980s as part of its strategy to sustain growth. Gillette claimed that Trac II, the first twin-blade shaver, represented the most revolutionary shaving advance ever. The development of the twin-blade razor derived from shaving researchers' discovery that shaving causes whiskers to be briefly lifted up out of the follicle during shaving, a process called "hysteresis" by technicians. Gillette invented the twin-blade system so that the first blade would cut the whisker and the second blade would cut it again before it receded. This system produced a closer shave than a traditional one-blade system. Gillette also developed a clog-free, dual-blade cartridge for the Trac II system.

Because consumer test data showed a 9-to-1 preference for Trac II over panelists' current razors, Gillette raced to get the product to market. Gillette supported Trac II's 1971 introduction, which was the largest new product introduction in shaving history, with a $10 million advertising and promotion budget. Gillette cut its advertising budgets for its other brands drastically to support Trac II. The double-edge portion of the advertising budget decreased from 47 percent in 1971 to 11 percent in 1972. Gillette reasoned that growth must come at the expense of other brands. Thus, it concentrated its advertising and promotion on its newest shaving product and reduced support for its established lines.

Gillette launched Trac II during a World Series promotion and made it the most frequently advertised shaving system in America during its introductory period. Trac II users turned out to be predominantly young, college-educated men who lived in metropolitan and suburban areas and earned higher incomes. As the fastest-growing shaving product on the market for five years, Trac II drove the switch to twin blades. The brand reached its peak in 1976 when consumers purchased 485 million blades and 7 million razors.

Late in 1976, Gillette, apparently in response to BIC's pending entrance into the U.S. market, launched Good News!, the first disposable razor for men sold in the United States. In 1975, BIC had introduced the first disposable shaver in Europe; and by 1976 BIC had begun to sell disposable razors in Canada. Gillette realized that BIC would move its disposable razor into the United States after its Canadian introduction, so it promptly brought out a new blue plastic disposable shaver with a twin-blade head. By year's end, Gillette also made Good News! available in Austria, Canada, France, Italy, Switzerland, Belgium, Greece, Germany, and Spain.

Unfortunately for Gillette, Good News! was really bad news. The disposable shaver delivered lower profit margins than razor and blade systems, and it undercut sales of other Gillette products. Good News! sold for much less than the retail price of a Trac II cartridge. Gillette marketed Good News! on price and convenience, not performance; but the company envisioned the product as a step-up item leading to its traditional high-quality shaving systems.

This contain-and-switch strategy did not succeed. Consumers liked the price and the convenience of disposable razors, and millions of Trac II razors began to gather dust in medicine chests across the country. Many Trac II users figured out that for as little as 25 cents, they could get the same cartridge mounted on a plastic handle that they had been buying for 56 cents to put on their Trac II handle. Further, disposable razors created an opening for competitors in a category that Gillette had long dominated.

Gillette felt sure, however, that disposable razors would never gain more than a 7 percent share of the market. The disposable razor market share soon soared past 10 percent, forcing Gillette into continual upward revisions of its estimates. In terms of units sold, disposable razors reached a 22 percent market share by 1980 and a 50 percent share by 1988.

BIC and Gillette's successful introduction of the disposable razor represented a watershed event in "commoditization"—the process of converting well-differentiated products into commodities. Status, quality, and perceived value had always played primary roles in the marketing of personal care products. But consumers were now showing that they would forego performance and prestige in a shaving product—about as close and personal as one can get.

In 1977, Gillette introduced a new blade and razor system at the expense of Trac II. It launched Atra with a $7 million advertising campaign and over 50 million $2 rebate coupons. Atra (which stands for Automatic Tracking Razor Action) was the first twin-blade shaving cartridge with a pivoting head. Engineers had designed the head to follow a man's facial contours for a closer shave. Researchers began developing the product in Gillette's United Kingdom Research and Development Lab in 1970. They had established a goal of improving the high-performance standards of twin-blade shaving and specifically enhancing the Trac II effect. The company's scientists discovered that moving the hand and face was not the most effective way to achieve the best blade-face shaving angle. The razor head itself produced a better shave if it pivoted so as to maintain the most effective shaving angle. Marketers selected the name "Atra" after two years of extensive consumer testing.

Atra quickly achieved a 7 percent share of the blade market and about one-third of the razor market. The company introduced Atra in Europe a year later under the brand name Contour. Although Atra increased Gillette's share of the razor market, 40 percent of Trac II users switched to Atra in the first year.

In the early 1980s, Gillette introduced most new disposable razors and product enhancements. Both Swivel (launched in 1980) and Good News! Pivot (1984) were disposable razors featuring movable heads. Gillette announced Atra Plus (the first razor with the patented Lubra-smooth lubricating strip in 1985 just as BIC began to move into the United States from Canada with the BIC shaver for sensitive skin. A few months later, Gillette ushered in Micro Trac—the first disposable razor with an ultra-slim head. Gillette priced the Micro Trac lower than any other Gillette disposable razor. The company claimed to have designed a state-of-the-art manufacturing process for Micro Trac. The process required less plastic, thus minimizing bulk and reducing manufacturing costs. Analysts claimed that Gillette was trying to bracket the market with Atra Plus (with a retail price of $3.99 to $4.95) and Micro Trac (99 cents), and protect its market share with products on both ends of the price and usage scale. Gillette also teased Wall Street with hints that, by the end of 1986, it would be introducing yet another state-of-the-art shaving system that could revolutionize the shaving business.

Despite these product innovations and introductions in the early 1980s, Gillette primarily focused its energies on its global markets and strategies. By 1985, Gillette was marketing 800 products in more than 200 countries. The company felt a need at this time to coordinate its marketing efforts first regionally and then globally.

Unfortunately for Gillette's management team, others noticed its strong international capabilities. Ronald Perelman, Chairman of the Revlon Group, attempted an unfriendly takeover in November, 1986. To fend off the takeover, Gillette bought back 9.2 million shares of its stock from Perelman and saddled itself with additional long-term debt to finance the stock repurchase. Gillette's payment to Perelman increased the company's debt load from $827 million to $1.1 billion, and put its debt-to-equity ratio at 70 percent. Gillette and Perelman signed an agreement preventing Perelman from attempting another takeover until 1996.

In 1988, just as Gillette returned its attention to new product development and global marketing, Coniston Partners, after obtaining 6 percent of Gillette's stock, engaged the company in a proxy battle for 4 seats on its 12-person board. Coniston's interest had been piqued by the Gillette-Perelman $549 million stock buyback and its payment of $9 million in expenses to Perelman. Coniston and some shareholders felt Gillette's board and management had repeatedly taken actions that prohibited its stockholders from realizing their shares' full value. When the balloting concluded, Gillette's management won by a narrow margin—52 to 48 percent. Coniston made $13 million in the stock buyback program that Gillette offered to all shareholders, but Coniston agreed not to make another run at Gillette until 1991. This second takeover attempt forced Gillette to increase its debt load to $2 billion and pushed its total equity negative to ($84,600,000).

More importantly, both takeover battles forced Gillette to "wake up." Gillette closed or sold its Jafra Cosmetics operations in 11 countries and jettisoned weak operations such as Misco, Inc. (a computer supplies business), and S.T. Dupont (a luxury lighter, clock, and watchmaker). The company also thinned its work force in many divisions, such as its 15 percent staff reduction at the Paper Mate pen unit. Despite this pruning, Gillette's sales for 1988 grew 13 percent to $3.6 billion, and profits soared 17 percent to $268 million.

Despite Gillette's concentration on fending off takeover attempts, it continued to enhance its razor and blade products. In 1986, Gillette introduced the Contour Plus in its first pan-European razor launch. The company marketed Contour Plus with one identity and one strategy. In 1988, the company introduced Trac II Plus, Good News! Pivot Plus, and Daisy Plus—versions of its existing products with the Lubra-smooth lubricating strip.

SCHICK

Warner-Lambert's Schick served as the second major competitor in the wet-shaving business. Warner-Lambert, incorporated in 1920 under the name William R. Warner & Company, manufactured chemicals and pharmaceuticals. Numerous mergers and acquisitions over 70 years resulted in Warner-Lambert's involvement in developing, manufacturing, and marketing a widely diversified line of beauty, health, and well-being products. The company also became a major producer of mints and chewing gums, such as Dentyne, Sticklets, and Trident. Exhibit 6 presents a list of Warner-Lambert's products by division as of 1988.

Warner-Lambert entered the wet-shave business through a merger with Eversharp in 1970. Eversharp, a long-time competitor in the wet-shave industry, owned the Schick trademark and had owned the Paper Mate Pen Company prior to selling it to Gillette in 1955. Schick's razors and blades produced $180 million in revenue in 1987, or 5.2 percent of Warner-Lambert's worldwide sales. (Refer to Exhibit 7 for operating results by division and Exhibits 8 and 9 for Income Statement and Balance Sheet data.)

In 1989, Schick held approximately a 16.2 percent U.S. market share, down from its 1980 share of 23.8 percent. Schick's market share was broken down as follows: blade systems, 8.8 percent; disposable razors, 4.1 percent; and double-edged blades and injectors, 3.3 percent.

Schick's loss of market share in the 1980s occurred for two reasons. First, even though Schick pioneered the injector razor system (it controlled 80 percent of this market by 1979), it did not market a disposable razor until mid-1984—eight years after the first disposable razors appeared. Secondly, for years Warner-Lambert had been channelling Schick's cash flow to its research and development in drugs.

In 1986, the company changed its philosophy; it allocated $70 million to Schick for a three-year period and granted Schick its own sales force. In spite of Schick's loss of market share, company executives felt

EXHIBIT 6 | Warner-Lambert 1988 Product Lines by Company Division

Ethical Pharmaceuticals	Gums and Mints	Non-prescription Products	Other Products
Parke-Davis drug	Dentyne	Benadryl	Schick razors
	Sticklets	Caladryl	Ultrex razors
	Beemans	Rolaids	Personal Touch
	Trident	Sinutab	Tetra Aquarium
	Freshen-up	Listerex	
	Bubblicious	Lubraderm	
	Chiclets	Anusol	
	Clorets	Tucks	
	Certs	Halls	
	Dynamints	Benylin	
	Junior Mints	Listerine	
	Sugar Daddy	Listermint	
	Sugar Babies	Efferdent	
	Charleston Chew	Effergrip	
	Rascals		

7 | Warner-Lambert's Net Sales and Operating Profit by Division (in Millions)

Division		Net Sales				Operating Profit (LOSS)			
		1988	1987	1986	1985	1988	1987	1986	1985
Health Care	Ethical products	$1,213	$1,093	$ 964	$ 880	$ 420	$ 351	$ 246	$ 224
	Nonprescription products	1,296	1,195	1,077	992	305	256	176	177
	Total health care	2,509	2,288	2,041	1,872	725	607	422	401
	Gums and mints	918	777	678	626	187	173	122	138
	Other products*	481	420	384	334	92	86	61	72
	Divested businesses								(464)
	R&D					(259)	(232)	(202)	(208)
	Net sales and operating profit	3,908	3,485	3,103	3,200	745	634	599	(61)

Source: Warner-Lambert Company Annual Report, 1987 and *Moody's Industrial Manual.*
*Other products include Schick razors, which accounted for $180 million in revenue in 1987.

8 | Warner-Lambert Income Statements (in Thousands)

		1988	1987	1986
	Net sales	$3,908,400	$3,484,700	$3,102,918
	Cost of sales	1,351,700	1,169,700	1,052,781
	Other expenses	2,012,100	1,819,800	1,616,323
	Operating income	544,600	495,200	433,814
	Other income	61,900	58,500	69,611
	Earnings before interest and tax	606,500	553,700	503,425
	Interest expense	68,200	60,900	66,544
	Earnings before tax	538,300	492,800	436,881
	Tax	198,000	197,000	136,297
	Nonrecurring item	...	...	8,400
	Earnings after tax	340,000	295,800	308,984
	Retained earnings	1,577,400	1,384,100	1,023,218
	Earnings per share	5.00	4.15	4.18
	Average common shares outstanding, 000	68,035	71,355	73,985
Dividends paid	Stock price range	2.16	1.77	1.59
Per Share	High	79 1/2	87 1/2	63 1/8
	Low	$59 7/8	$48 1/4	$45

Source: Moody's Industrial Manual.

they had room to play catch up, especially by exploiting new technologies. In late 1988, Schick revealed that it planned to conduct "guerrilla warfare" by throwing its marketing resources and efforts into new technological advances in disposable razors. As a result, Warner-Lambert planned to allocate the bulk of its $8 million razor advertising budget to marketing its narrow-headed disposable razor, Slim Twin, which it introduced in August, 1988.

Schick believed that the U.S. unit demand for disposable razors would increase to 55 percent of the market by the early 1990s from its 50 percent share in 1988.

9 | **Warner-Lambert Balance Sheets (in Thousands)**

		1988	1987	1986
Assets	Cash	$ 176,000	$ 24,100	$ 26,791
	Receivables	525,200	469,900	445,743
	Inventories	381,400	379,000	317,212
	Other current assets	181,300	379,600	720,322
	Total current assets	1,264,500	1,252,600	1,510,068
	Fixed assets, net	1,053,000	959,800	819,291
	Other assets	385,300	263,500	186,564
	Total assets	2,702,800	2,475,900	2,515,923
Liabilities and Equity	Current liabilities*	1,025,200	974,300	969,806
	Current portion long-term debt	7,100	4,200	143,259
	Long-term debt	318,200	293,800	342,112
	Equity	$ 998,600	$ 874,400	$ 907,322

Source: Moody's Industrial Manual.
*Includes current option of long-term debt.

Schick executives based this belief on their feeling that men would rather pay 30 cents for a disposable razor than 75 cents for a refill blade. In 1988, Schick held an estimated 9.9 percent share of dollar sales in the disposable razor market.

Schick generated approximately 67 percent of its revenues overseas. Also, Schick earned higher profit margins on its nondomestic sales—20 percent versus its 15 percent domestic margin. Europe and Japan represented the bulk of Schick's international business, accounting for 38 percent and 52 percent, respectively, of 1988's overseas sales. Schick's European business consisted of 70 percent systems and 29 percent disposable razors, but Gillette's systems and disposable razor sales were 4.5 and 6 times larger, respectively.

However, Schick dominated in Japan. Warner-Lambert held over 60 percent of Japan's wet-shave market. Although Japan had typically been an electric shaver market (55 percent of Japanese shavers use electric razors), Schick achieved an excellent record and reputation in Japan. Both Schick and Gillette entered the Japanese market in 1962; and their vigorous competition eventually drove Japanese competitors from the industry, which by 1988 generated $190 million in sales. Gillette's attempt to crack the market flopped because it tried to sell razors using its own salespeople, a strategy that failed because Gillette did not have the distribution network available to Japanese companies. Schick, meanwhile, chose to leave the distribution to Seiko Corporation. Seiko imported razors from the United States and then sold them to wholesalers nationwide. By 1988, Schick generated roughly 40 percent of its sales and 35 percent of its profits in Japan. Disposable razors accounted for almost 80 percent of those figures.

BIC CORPORATION

The roots of the BIC Corporation, which was founded by Marcel Bich in the United States in 1958, were in France. In 1945, Bich, who had been the production manager for a French ink manufacturer, bought a factory outside Paris to produce parts for fountain pens and mechanical lead pencils. In his new business, Bich became one of the first manufacturers to purchase presses to work with plastics. With his knowledge of inks and experience with plastics and molding machines, Bich set himself up to become the largest pen manufacturer in the world. In 1949, Bich introduced his version of the modern ballpoint pen, originally invented in 1939, which he called "BIC," a shortened, easy-to-remember version of his own name. He supported the pen with memorable, effective advertising; and its sales surpassed even his own expectations.

Realizing that a mass-produced disposable ballpoint pen had universal appeal, Bich turned his attention to the U.S. market. In 1958, he purchased the Waterman-Pen Company of Connecticut and then incorporated as Waterman-BIC Pen Corporation. The company changed its name to BIC Pen in 1971 and finally adopted the name BIC Corporation for the publicly owned corporation in 1982.

After establishing itself as the country's largest pen maker, BIC attacked another market—the disposable lighter market. When BIC introduced its lighter in 1973, the total disposable lighter market stood at only 50 million units. By 1984, BIC had become so successful at manufacturing and marketing its disposable lighters that Gillette, its primary competitor, abandoned the lighter market. Gillette sold its Cricket division to Swedish Match, Stockholm, the manufacturer of Wilkinson razors. By 1989, the disposable lighter market had grown to nearly 500 million units, and BIC lighters accounted for 60 percent of the market.

Not content to compete just in the writing and lighting markets, BIC decided to enter the U.S. shaving market in 1976. A year earlier, the company had launched the BIC Shaver in Europe and Canada. BIC's entrance into the U.S. razor market started an intense rivalry with Gillette. Admittedly, the companies were not strangers to each other—for years they had competed for market share in the pen and lighter industries. Despite the fact that razors were Gillette's primary business and an area where the company had no intention of relinquishing market share, BIC established a niche in the U.S. disposable-razor market.

BIC, like Gillette, frequently introduced new razor products and product enhancements. In January, 1985, following a successful Canadian test in 1984, BIC announced the BIC Shaver for Sensitive Skin. BIC claimed that 42 percent of the men surveyed reported that they had sensitive skin, while 51 percent of those who had heavy beards reported that they had sensitive skin. Thus, BIC felt there was a clear need for a shaver that addressed this special shaving problem. The $10 million ad campaign for the BIC Shaver for Sensitive Skin featured John McEnroe, a highly ranked and well-known tennis professional, discussing good and bad backhands and normal and sensitive skin. BIC repositioned the original BIC white shaver as the shaver men with normal skin should use, while it promoted the new BIC Orange as the razor for sensitive skin.

BIC also tried its commodity strategy on sail boards, car-top carriers, and perfume. In 1982, BIC introduced a sail board model at about half the price of existing products. The product generated nothing but red ink. In April, 1989, the company launched BIC perfumes with $15 million in advertising support. BIC's foray into fragrances was as disappointing as its sail board attempt. Throughout the year, Parfum BIC lost money, forcing management to concentrate its efforts on reformulating its selling theme, advertising, packaging, and price points. Many retailers rejected the product, sticking BIC with expensive manufacturing facilities in Europe. BIC found that consumers' perceptions of commodities did not translate equally into every category. For example, many women cut corners elsewhere just to spend lavishly on their perfume. The last thing they wanted to see was their favorite scent being hawked to the masses.

Despite these failures, BIC Corporation was the undisputed king of the commoditizers. BIC's success with pens and razors demonstrated the upside potential of commiditization, while its failures with sail boards and perfumes illustrated the limitations. BIC concentrated its efforts on designing, manufacturing, and delivering the "best" quality products at the lowest possible prices. And although the company produced large quantities of disposable products (for example, over 1 million pens a day), it claimed that each product was invested with the BIC philosophy: "maximum service, minimum price."

One of BIC's greatest assets was its retail distribution strength. The high profile the company enjoyed at supermarkets and drugstores enabled it to win locations in the aisles and display space at the checkout—the best positioning.

Even though BIC controlled only the number three spot in the wet-shaving market by 1989, it had exerted quite an influence since its razors first entered the U.S. market in 1976. In 1988, BIC's razors generated $52 million in sales with a net income of $9.4 million; BIC held a 22.4 percent share of dollar sales in the disposable razor market. Exhibit 10 presents operating data by product line, and Exhibits 11 and 12 give income statement and balance sheet data.

The introduction of the disposable razor revolutionized the industry and cut into system razor profits. However, despite the low profit margins in disposable razors and the fact that the industry leader, Gillette, emphasized razor and blade systems, BIC remained bullish on the disposable razor market. In 1989, a spokesperson for BIC claimed that BIC "was going to stick to what

EXHIBIT 10 | BIC Corporation's Net Sales and Income Before Taxes (in Millions)

		1988	1987	1986
Net Sales	Writing instruments	$118.5	$106.7	$91.7
	Lighters	113.9	120.0	115.0
	Shavers	51.9	47.1	49.6
	Sport	10.6	16.8	11.3
	Total	294.9	290.6	267.6
Profit (loss) Before Taxes	Writing instruments	$16.7	$17.5	$15.0
	Lighters	22.9	28.2	28.5
	Shavers	9.4	8.5	8.0
	Sport	(4.7)	(3.5)	(3.6)
	TOTALS	44.3	50.7	47.9

Source: BIC Annual Report, 1986, 1987 and 1988.

EXHIBIT 11 | BIC Corporation Consolidated Income Statements (in Thousands)

		1988	1987	1986
	Net sales	$294,878	$290,616	$267,624
	Cost of sales	172,542	165,705	147,602
	Other expenses	81,023	73,785	67,697
	Operating income	41,313	51,126	52,325
	Other income	4,119	1,836	7,534
	Earnings before interest and tax	45,432	52,962	59,859
	Interest expense	1,097	2,301	11,982
	Earnings before tax	44,335	50,661	47,877
	Tax	17,573	21,944	24,170
	Extraordinary credit	...	...	2,486*
	Utilization of operating loss carry forward	2,800	...	...
	Earnings after tax	$ 29,562	$ 28,717	$ 26,193
	Retained earnings	159,942	142,501	121,784
	Earnings per share	2.44	2.37	2.16
	Average common shares outstanding, 000	12,121	12,121	12,121
	Dividends paid per share	0.75	0.66	0.48
Stock Price Range	High	$30 3/8	$34 7/8	$35
	Low	$24 3/8	$16 1/2	$23 1/4

Source: Moody's Industrial Manual and *BIC Annual Reports.*
*Gain from elimination of debt.

EXHIBIT

12 | BIC Corporation Balance Sheets (in Thousands)

		1988	1987	1986
Assets	Cash	$ 5,314	$ 4,673	$ 5,047
	Certificates of deposit	3,117	803	6,401
	Receivables, net	43,629	41,704	32,960
	Inventories	70,930	59,779	50,058
	Other current assets	37,603	47,385	34,898
	Deferred income taxes	7,939	6,691	5,622
	Total current assets	168,532	161,035	134,986
	Fixed assets, net	74,973	62,797	58,385
	Total assets	243,505	223,832	193,371
Liabilities and Equity	Current liabilities*	55,031	54,034	45,104
	Current portion long-term debt	157	247	287
	Long-term debt	1,521	1,511	1,789
	Equity	$181,194	$164,068	$142,848

Source: Moody's Industrial Manual.
*Includes current portion of long-term debt.

consumers liked." The company planned to continue marketing only single-blade, disposable shavers. BIC stated that it planned to maintain its strategy of underpricing competitors, but it would also introduce improvements such as the patented metal guard in its BIC Metal Shaver. Research revealed that the BIC Metal Shaver provided some incremental, rather than substitute, sales for its shaver product line. BIC executives believed that the BIC Metal Shaver would reach a 5 to 8 percent market share by 1990.

WILKINSON SWORD

Swedish Match Holding Incorporated's subsidiary, Wilkinson Sword, came in as the fourth player in the U.S. market. Swedish Match Holding was a wholly owned subsidiary of Swedish Match AB, Stockholm, Sweden. The parent company owned subsidiaries in the United States that imported and sold doors, produced resilient and wood flooring, and manufactured branded razors, blades, self-sharpening scissors, and gourmet kitchen knives (Exhibits 13 and 14 present income statement and balance sheet data on Swedish Match AB.)

A group of swordsmiths founded Wilkinson in 1772, and soldiers used Wilkinson swords at Waterloo, the charge of the Light Brigade, and in the Boer war. However, as the sword declined as a combat weapon, Wilkinson retreated to producing presentation and ceremonial swords. By 1890, Wilkinson's cutlers had begun to produce straight razors, and by 1898 it was producing safety razors similar to King Gillette's. When Gillette's blades became popular in England, Wilkinson made stroppers to resharpen used blades. Wilkinson failed in the razor market, however, and dropped out during World War II.

By 1954, Wilkinson decided to look again at the shaving market. Manufacturers used carbon steel to make most razor blades at that time, and such blades lost their serviceability rapidly due to mechanical and chemical damage. Gillette and other firms had experimented with stainless steel blades; but they had found that despite their longer-lasting nature, the blades did not sharpen well. But some men liked the durability; and a few small companies produced stainless steel blades.

Wilkinson purchased one such small German company and put Wilkinson Sword blades on the market in 1956. Wilkinson developed a coating for the stainless blades (in the same fashion that Gillette had coated the Super Blue Blade) that masked their rough edges, al-

EXHIBIT 13 | Swedish Match AB Income Statements (in Thousands of U.S. Dollars)

		1988	1987	1986
	Net sales	$2,814,662	$2,505,047	$1,529,704
	Cost of sales	N/A	N/A	N/A
	Operating expenses	2,541,128	2,291,023	1,387,360
	Other expenses	108,206	95,420	48,711
	Earnings before interest	165,328	118,604	93,633
	Interest expense	5,386	19,084	21,618
	Earnings before tax	159,942	99,520	72,015
	Tax	57,612	29,996	39,165
	Earnings after tax	102,330	69,554	32,850
	Dividends paid per share	0.53	0.51	1.75
Stock Price Range	High	22.53	19.65	66.75
	Low	$ 15.00	$ 11.06	$ 22.00

Source: Moody's Industrial Manual.

EXHIBIT 14 | Swedish Match AB Balance Sheets (in Thousands)

		1988	1987	1986
Assets	Cash and securities	$ 159,616	$ 117,027	$323,993
	Receivables	611,372	561,479	297,321
	Inventories	421,563	415,116	258,858
	Total current assets	1,192,551	1,093,622	880,172
	Fixed assets, net	707,664	671,409	397,411
	Other assets	161,085	132,799	93,211
	Total assets	2,061,300	1,897,830	370,794
Liabilities and Equity	Current liabilities	996,214	905,778	576,534
	Current portion long-term debt			
	Long-term debt	298,505	316,542	244,118
	Equity			

Source: Moody's Industrial Manual.

lowing the blades to give a comfortable shave and to last two to five times longer than conventional blades. Wilkinson called the new blade the Super Sword-Edge. Wilkinson introduced the blades in England in 1961 and in the United States in 1962, and they became a phenomenon. Schick and American Safety Razor followed a year later with their own stainless steel blades, the Krona-Plus and Personna. Gillette finally responded in late 1963 with its own stainless steel blade; and by early 1964 Gillette's blades were outselling Wilkinson, Schick, and Personna combined. Wilkinson, however, had forever changed the nature of the razor blade.

In 1988, Wilkinson Sword claimed to have a 4 percent share of the U.S. wet-shave market; and it was predicting a 6 percent share by mid-1990. Industry analysts, however, did not confirm even the 4 percent share; they projected Wilkinson's share to be closer to 1 percent. Wilkinson introduced many new products over the years, but they generally proved to be short-lived. The company never really developed its U.S. franchise.

However, in late 1988, Wilkinson boasted that it was going to challenge the wet-shave category leader by introducing Ultra-Glide, its first lubricating shaving system. Wilkinson designed Ultra-Glide to go head-to-head with Gillette's Atra Plus and Schick's Super II Plus and Ultrex Plus. Wilkinson claimed that Ultra-Glide represented a breakthrough in shaving technology because of an ingredient, hydromer, in its patented lubricating strip. According to Wilkinson, the Ultra-Glide strip left less residue on the face and provided a smoother, more comfortable shave by creating a cushion of moisture between the razor and the skin.

Wilkinson introduced Ultra-Glide in March 1989 and supported it with a $5 million advertising and promotional campaign (versus the Atra Plus $80 million multimedia investment in the United States). Wilkinson priced Ultra-Glide 5 to 8 percent less than Atra Plus. Wilkinson was undaunted by Gillette's heavier advertising investment, and it expected to cash in on its rival's strong marketing muscle. Wilkinson did not expect to overtake Gillette but felt its drive should help it capture a double-digit U.S. market share within two to three years.

Many were skeptical about Wilkinson's self-predicted market share growth. One industry analyst stated, "Gillette dominates this business. Some upstart won't do anything." One Gillette official claimed his company was unfazed by Wilkinson. In fact, he was quoted as saying in late 1988 that, "They [Wilkinson] don't have a business in the U.S.; they don't exist."

Nonetheless, Gillette became enraged and filed legal challenges when Wilkinson's television ads for Ultra-Glide broke in May 1989. The ads stated that Ultra-Glide's lubricating strip was six times smoother than Gillette's strip and that men preferred it to the industry leader's. All three major networks had reservations about continuing to air the comparison commercials. CBS and NBC stated that they were going to delay airing the company's ads until Wilkinson responded to questions they had about its ad claims. In an 11th-hour counterattack, Wilkinson accused Gillette of false advertising and of trying to monopolize the wet-shave market.

GILLETTE'S SOUTH BOSTON PLANT

Robert Squires left his work station in the facilities engineering section of Gillette's South Boston manufacturing facility and headed for the shave testlab. He entered the lab area and walked down a narrow hall. On his right were a series of small cubicles Gillette had designed to resemble the sink area of a typical bathroom. Robert opened the door of his assigned cubicle precisely at his scheduled 10 A.M. time. He removed his dress shirt and tie, hanging them on a hook beside the sink. Sliding the mirror up as one would a window, Robert looked into the lab area. Rose McCluskey, a lab assistant, greeted him.

"Morning, Robert. See you're right on time as usual. I've got your things all ready for you." Rose reached into a recessed area on her side of the cubicle's wall and handed Robert his razor, shave cream, aftershave lotion, and a clean towel.

"Thanks, Rose. Hope you're having a good day. Anything new you've got me trying today?"

"You know I can't tell you that. It might spoil your objectivity. Here's your card." Rose handed Robert a shaving evaluation card (see Exhibit 15).

Robert Squires had been shaving at the South Boston Plant off and on for all of his 25 years with Gillette. He was one of 200 men who shaved every work day at the plant. Gillette used these shavers to compare its products' effectiveness with competitors' products. The shavers also conducted R&D testing of new products and quality control testing for manufacturing. An additional seven to eight panels of 250 men each shaved every day in their homes around the country, primarily conducting R&D shave testing.

Like Robert, each shaver completed a shave evaluation card following every shave. Lab assistants like Rose entered data from the evaluations to allow Gillette researchers to analyze the performance of each shaving device. If a product passed R&D hurdles, it became the responsibility of the marketing research staff to conduct consumer-use testing. Such consumer testing employed 2000 to 3000 men who tested products in their homes.

From its research, Gillette had learned that the average man had 30,000 whiskers on his face that grew at the rate of 1/2 inch per month. He shaved 5.8 times a week and spent 3 to 4 minutes shaving each time. A man with a life span of 70 years would shave more than 20,000 times, spending 3350 hours (130 days) removing 27½ feet of facial hair. Yet, despite all the time and effort in-

15 | Gillette Shaving Evaluation Card

NUMB.	CODE	STA	TEST #	NAME	EMP.#	DATE

IN-PLANT SHAVE TEST SCORECARD

INSTRUCTIONS: Please check one box in each column

Overall Evaluation of Shave	Freedom from Nicks and Cuts	Caution	Closeness	Smoothness	Comfort
☐ Excellent	☐ Excellent	☐ Exceptionally Safe	☐ Exceptionally Close	☐ Exceptionally Smooth	☐ Exceptionally Comfortable
☐ Very Good	☐ Very Good	☐ Unusually Safe	☐ Very Close	☐ Very Smooth	☐ Very Comfortable
☐ Good	☐ Good	☐ Average	☐ Average	☐ Average Smoothness	☐ Average Comfort
☐ Fair	☐ Fair	☐ Slight Caution Needed	☐ Fair	☐ Slight Pull	☐ Slight Irritation
☐ Poor	☐ Poor	☐ Excessive Caution Needed	☐ Poor	☐ Excessive Pull	☐ Excessive Irritation

Source: The Gillette Company

volved in shaving, surveys found that if a cream were available that would eliminate facial hair and shaving, most men would not use it.

Robert finished shaving and rinsed his face and shaver. He glanced at the shaving head. A pretty good shave, he thought. The cartridge had two blades, but it seemed different. Robert marked his evaluation card and slid it across the counter to Rose.

William Mazeroski, Manager of the South Boston shave test lab, walked into the lab area carrying computer printouts with the statistical analysis of last week's shave test data.

Noticing Robert, William stopped. "Morning, Robert. How was your shave?"

"Pretty good. What am I using?"

"Robert, you are always trying to get me to tell you what we're testing! We have control groups and experimental groups. I can't tell you which you are in, but I was just looking at last week's results, and I can tell you that it looks like we are making progress. We've been testing versions of a new product since 1979, and I think we're about to get it right. Of course, I don't know if we'll introduce it or even if we can make it in large quantities, but it looks good."

"Well, that's interesting. At least I know I'm involved in progress. And, if we do decide to produce a new shaver, we'll have to design and build the machines to make it ourselves because there is nowhere to go to purchase blade-making machinery. Well, I've got to get back now; see you tomorrow."

THIRTY-SEVENTH FLOOR, THE PRUDENTIAL CENTER

Paul Hankins leaned over the credenza in his 37th-floor office in Boston's Prudential Center office building and admired the beauty of the scene that spread before him. Paul felt as though he were watching an impressionistic painting in motion. Beyond the green treetops and red brick buildings of Boston's fashionable Back Bay area, the Charles River wound its way towards Boston Harbor. Paul could see the buildings on the campuses of Harvard, MIT, and Boston University scattered along both sides of the river. Soon the crew teams would be out practicing. Paul loved to watch the precision with which the well-coordinated teams propelled the boats up and down the river. If only, he thought, we could be as coordinated as those crew teams.

Paul had returned to Boston in early 1988 when Gillette created the North Atlantic Group by combining what had been the North American and the European operations. Originally from Boston, he had attended Columbia University and earned an MBA at Dartmouth's Tuck School. He had been with Gillette for 19 years. Prior to 1988, he had served as marketing director for Gillette Europe from 1983–84, as the country manager for Holland from 1985–86, and finally as manager of Holland and the Scandinavian countries.

During this 1983–87 period, Paul had worked for Jim Pear, Vice President of Gillette Europe, to implement a pan-European strategy. Prior to 1983, Gillette had organized and managed Europe as a classic decentralized market. To meet the perceived cultural nuances within each area, the company had treated each country as a separate market. For example, Gillette offered the same products under a variety of sub-brand names. The company sold its Good News! disposable razors under the name "Blue II" in the United Kingdom, "Parat" in Germany, "Gillette" in France and Spain, "Radi e Getta" (shave and throw) in Italy, and "Economy" in other European markets.

Jim Pear believed that in the future Gillette would have to organize across country lines, and he had developed the pan-European idea. He felt that shaving was a universal act and that Gillette's razors were a perfect archetype for a "global" product.

Gillette had launched Contour Plus, the European version of Atra Plus, in 1985–86 and had experienced greater success than the U.S. launch which took place at the same time. The pan-European strategy seemed to be both more efficient and more effective. Colman Mockler, Gillette's chairman, noticed the European success and asked Pear to come to Boston to head the new North Atlantic Group. Paul had come with him as vice president of marketing for the Shaving and Personal Care Group.

Paul turned from the window as he heard people approaching. Sarah Kale, vice president, Marketing Research; Brian Mullins, vice president of marketing, Shaving and Personal Care Group; and Scott Friedman, business director, Blades and Razors, were at his door.

"Ready for our meeting?" Scott asked.

"Sure, come on in. I was just admiring the view."

"The purpose of this meeting," Paul began, "is to begin formulating a new strategy for Gillette North Atlantic, specifically for our shaving products. I'm interested in your general thoughts and analysis. I want to begin to identify options and select a strategy to pursue. What have you found out?"

"Well, here are the market share numbers you asked me to develop," Scott observed as he handed each person copies of tables he had produced (see Exhibit 16 and Exhibit 17). Like Paul, Scott had earned an MBA from the Tuck School and had been with Gillette for 17 years.

EXHIBIT 16 | Gillette Market Share of Dollar Sales 1981–1988 (by Percent)

Product or Category	1981	1982	1983	1984	1985	1986	1987	1988
Atra blades	15.4	17.3	19.4	18.7	20.2	20.9	20.0	20.5
Trac II blades	17.5	16.4	15.2	14.6	14.1	13.5	11.8	11.4
Gillette blades	47.3	48.9	52.1	54.2	55.8	57.1	54.1	56.0
Gillette disposables	14.3	15.4	17.4	20.0	21.1	22.7	22.2	24.0
All disposables	23.0	23.2	27.0	30.6	32.7	34.9	38.5	41.1
Gillette disposables as % of all disposables	67.9	66.9	64.7	65.7	64.6	64.2	57.6	58.4
Gillette razors	50.3	52.5	54.9	58.8	62.2	67.6	64.1	61.0

Source: Prudential-Bache Securities.

17 | Gillette System Cartridges (Dollar Share of U.S. Blade Market)

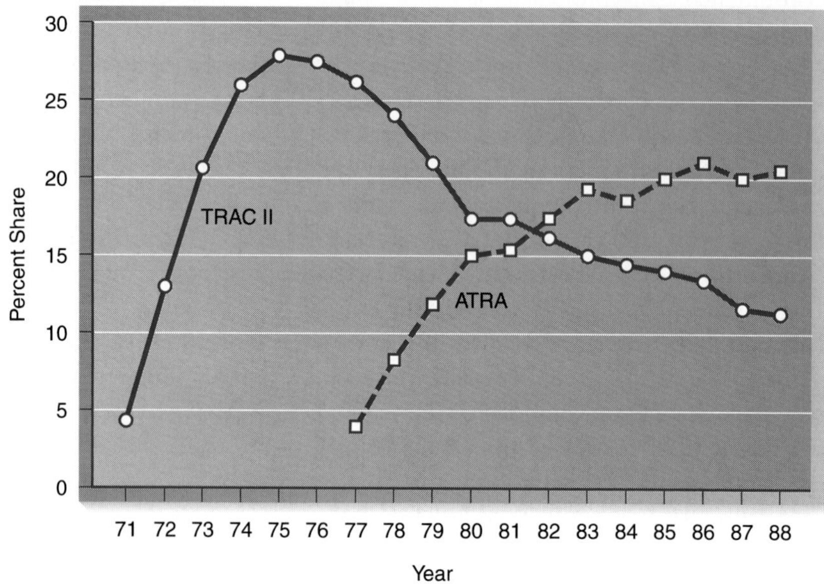

Source: The Gillette Company and Prudential-Bache Securities.

"These are our U.S. share numbers through 1988. As you can see, Atra blades seem to have leveled off and Trac II blades are declining. Disposable razors now account for over 41 percent of the market, in dollars, and for over 50 percent of the market in terms of units. In fact, our projections indicate that disposable razors will approach 100 percent of the market by the mid to late 1990s given current trends. Although we have 56 percent of the blade market and 58 percent of the disposable razor market, our share of the disposable razor market has fallen. Further, you are aware that every 1 percent switch from our system razors to our disposable razors represents a loss of $10 million on the bottom line."

"I don't think any of this should surprise us," Sarah Kale interjected. Sarah had joined Gillette after graduating from Simmons College in Boston and had been with the firm for 14 years. "If you look back over the 1980s, you'll see that we helped cause this problem."

"What do you mean by that?" asked Paul.

"Well, as market leader, we never believed that the use of disposable razors would grow as it has. We went along with the trend, but we kept prices low on our disposable razors which made profitability worse for both us and our competition because they had to take our price into consideration in setting their prices. Then, to compensate for the impact on our profitability from the growth of the disposable razor market, we were raising the prices on our system razors. This made disposable razors even more attractive for price-sensitive users and further fueled the growth of disposable razors. This has occurred despite the fact that our market research shows that men rate system shavers significantly better than disposable razors. We find that the weight and balance contributed by the permanent handle used with the cartridge contributes to a better shave."

"Yes, but every time I tell someone that," Paul added, "they just look at me as if they wonder if I really believe that or if it is just Gillette's party line."

"There's one other thing we've done," Scott added. "Look at this graph of our advertising expenditures in the U.S. over the 1980s (see Exhibit 18). In fact, in constant 1987 dollars, our advertising spending has fallen from $61 million in 1975 to about $15 million in 1987. We seem to have just spent what was left over on adver-

18 | Blade and Razor Media Spending—United States

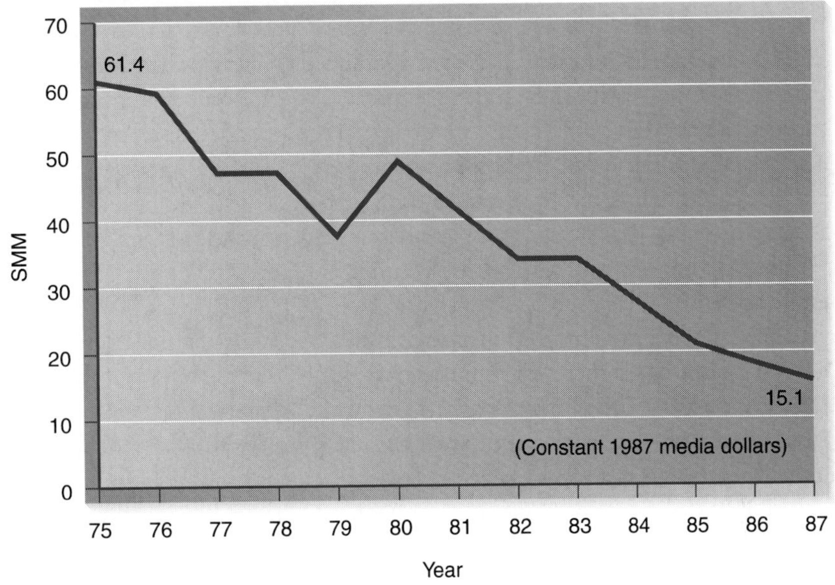

Source: The Gillette Company

tising. We are now spending about one-half of our advertising on Atra and one-half on Good News!. Tentative plans call for us to increase the share going to Good News!. Our media budget for 1988 was about $43 million. Further, we've tried three or four themes, but we haven't stuck with any one for very long. We're using the current theme, "The Essence of Shaving," for both system and disposable products. Our advertising has been about 90 percent product-based and 10 percent image-based."

"Well, Scott's right," Sarah noted, "but although share of voice is important, share of mind is what counts. Our most recent research shows a significant difference in how we are perceived by male consumers based on their age. Men over 40 still remember Gillette, despite our reduced advertising, from their youth. They remember Gillette's sponsorship of athletic events, like the Saturday Baseball Game of the Week and the Cavalcade of Sports. They remember "Look Sharp! Feel Sharp! Be Sharp" and Sharpie the Parrot. They remember their fathers loaning them their Gillette razors when they started shaving. There is still a strong connection between Gillette and the male image of shaving."

"How about with younger men?" asked Brian. Brian had joined Gillette in 1975 after graduating from Washington and Lee University and earnings a master's degree in administration from George Washington University.

"Younger men's views can be summed up simply—twin blade, blue, and plastic," Sarah reported.

"Just like our disposable razors!" Paul exclaimed.

"Precisely," Sarah answered. "As I say, we've done this to ourselves. We have a 'steel' man and 'plastic' man. In fact, for males between 15 and 19, BIC is better known than Gillette with respect to shaving. Younger men in general—those under 30, these 'plastic' men—feel all shavers are the same. Older men and system users feel there is a difference."

"Yes," Paul interjected, "and I've noticed something else interesting. Look at our logos. We use the Gillette brand name as our corporate name, and the brand name is done in thin, block letters. I'm not sure it has the impact and masculine image we want. On top of that, look at these razor packages. We have become so product-focused and brand-manager-driven that we've lost focus on the brand name. Our brands look tired:

there's nothing special about our retail packaging and display."

"Speaking of the male image of shaving, Sarah, what does your research show about our image with women?" asked Brian.

"Well, we've always had a male focus and women identify the Gillette name with men and shaving, even those who use our products marketed to women. You know that there are more women wet shavers than men in the U.S. market, about 62 million versus 55 million. However, due to seasonability and lower frequency of women's shaving, the unit volume used by women is only about one-third that of the volume used by men. Women use about 8 to 12 blades a year versus 25 to 30 for men. It is still very consistent for us to focus on men."

"Well, we've got plenty of problems on the marketing side, but we also have to remember that we are part of a larger corporation with its own set of problems," Brian suggested. "We're only 30 percent or so of sales but we are 60 percent of profits. And, given the takeover battles, there is going to be increased pressure on the company to maintain and improve profitability. That pressure has always been on us, but now it will be more intense. If we want to develop some bold, new strategy, we are going to have to figure out where to get the money to finance it. I'm sure the rest of the corporation will continue to look to us to throw off cash to support diversification."

"This can get depressing," Paul muttered as he looked back at the window. "I can sense the low morale inside the company. People sense the inevitability of disposability. We see BIC as the enemy even though it is so much smaller than Gillette. We've got to come up with a new strategy. What do you think our options are, Scott?"

"Well, I think we're agreed that the 'do-noting' option is out. If we simply continue to do business as usual, we will see the erosion of the shaving market's profitability as disposable razors take more and more share. We could accept the transition to disposable razors and begin to try to segment the disposable razor market based on performance. You might call this the 'give up' strategy. We would be admitting that disposable razors are the wave of the future. There will obviously continue to be shavers who buy based on price only, but there will also be shavers who will pay more for disposable razors with additional benefits, such as lubricating strips or movable heads. In Italy, for example, we have done a lot of image building and focused on quality. Now, Italian men seem to perceive that our disposable razors have value despite their price. In other words, we could try to protect the category's profitability by segmenting the market and offering value to those segments willing to pay for it. We would deemphasize system razors.

"Or, we could try to turn the whole thing around. We could develop a strategy to slow the growth of disposable razors and to reinvigorate the system razor market."

"How does the new razor system fit into all this?" Paul asked.

"I'm pleased that we have continued to invest in R&D despite our problems and the takeover battles," Brian answered. "Reports from R&D indicate that the new shaver is doing well in tests. But it will be expensive to take to market and to support with advertising. Further, it doesn't make any sense to launch it unless it fits in with the broader strategy. For example, if we decide to focus on disposable razors, it makes no sense to launch a new system razor and devote resources to that."

"What's the consumer testing indicating?" asked Scott.

"We're still conducting tests," Sarah answered, "but so far the results are very positive. Men rate the shave superior to both Atra or Trac II and superior to our competition. In fact, I think we'll see that consumers rate the new shaver as much as 25 percent better on average. The independently spring-mounted twin blades deliver a better shave, but you know we've never introduced a product until it was clearly superior in consumer testing on every dimension."

"Okay. Here's what I'd like to do," Paul concluded. "I'd like for each of us to devote some time to developing a broad outline of a strategy to present at our next meeting. We'll try to identify and shape a broad strategy then that we can begin to develop in detail over the next several months. Let's get together in a week, same time. Thanks for your time."

REFERENCES

Adams, Russell B., Jr. *King Gillette: The Man and His Wonderful Shaving Device.* Boston: Little, Brown, 1978.

BIC Annual Report, 1989.

Caminiti, Susan. "Gillette Gets Sharp." *Fortune,* 8 May 1989: 84.

Dewhurst, Peter. "BICH = BIC." *Made in France International,* Spring 1981: 38–41.

Dunkin, A., Baum, L., and Therrein, L. "This Takeover Artist Wants to Be a Makeover Artist, Too." *Business Week,* 1 December 1986: 106, 110.

Dun's Million Dollar Directory, 1989.

Fahey, Alison, and Sloan, Pat. "Gillette: $80M to Rebuild Image." *Advertising Age,* 31 October 1988: 1, 62.

——— and ———. "Kiam Gets Some Help: Grey Sharpens Remington Ads." *Advertising Age,* 13 November 1989: 94.

——— and ———. "Wilkinson Cuts In." *Advertising Age,* 28 November 1988: 48.

Gillette Annual Corporate Reports, 1985–1988.

Hammonds, Keith. "At Gillette Disposable Is a Dirty Word." *Business Week,* 29 May 1989: 54–55.

———. "How Ron Perelman Scared Gillette into Shape." *Business Week,* 12 October 1987: 40–41.

Jervey, Gay. "Gillette and BIC Spots Taking on Sensitive Subject." *Advertising Age,* 18 March 1985: 53.

———. "Gillette, Wilkinson Heat up Disposable Duel." *Advertising Age,* 10 June 1985: 12.

———. "New Blade Weapons for Gillette-BIC War." *Advertising Age,* 5 November 1984: 1, 96.

Kiam Victor. "Remington's Marketing and Manufacturing Strategies." *Management Review,* February 1987: 43–45.

———. "Growth Strategies at Remington." *Journal of Business Strategy,* January/February 1989: 22–26.

Kummel, C. M., and Klompmaker, J. E. "The Gillette Company—Safety Razor Division." In D. W. Cravens and C. W. Lamb (eds.). *Strategic Marketing: Cases and Applications.* Homewood, Ill.: Irwin, 1980, pp. 324–345.

McGeehan, Patrick. "Gillette Sharpens Its Global Strategy." *Advertising Age,* 25 April 1988: 2, 93.

Newport, John Paul. "The Stalking of Gillette." *Fortune,* 23 May 1988: 99–101.

North American Philips Corporation Annual Report, 1987.

Pereira, Joseph. "Gillette's Next-Generation Blade to Seek New Edge in Flat Market." *The Wall Street Journal,* 7 April, 1988: 34.

Shore, Andrew. "Gillette Report." Shearson Lehman Hutton, New York. (19 October 1989).

———. "Gillette Company Update." New York: Prudential-Bache Securities, May 18, 1990.

Raissman, Robert. "Gillette Pitches New Throwaway." *Advertising Age,* 9 July 1984: 12.

"Razors and Blades." *Consumer Reports,* May 1989: 300–304.

Rothman, Andrea. "Gillette, in a Shift, to Emphasize Cartridge Blades Over Disposables." *The Wall Street Journal,* 18 November 1988: B6.

Sacharow, Stanley. (1982). *Symbols of Trade.* New York: Art Direction Book Company.

Shore, Andrew. "Gillette Report." Shearson Lehman Hutton, New York. (19 October 1989).

Sloan, Pat. "Marschalk Brains Land Braun." *Advertising Age,* 18 March 1985: 53.

———. "Remington Gets the Edge on Gillette." *Advertising Age,* 16 May 1988: 3, 89.

Sutor, Ruthanne. "Household Personal Care Products." *Financial World,* 27 December 1988.

The Europa World Year Book 1990, vol. II.

Trachtenberg, Jeffery A. "Styling for the Masses." *Forbes,* 10 March 1986: 152–153.

Warner-Lambert Annual Corporate Report, 1987.

Weiss, Gary. "Razor Sharp: Gillette to Snap Back from a Dull Stretch." *Barron's,* 25 August 1986: 15, 37.

CASE 22

Kiwi Travel International Airlines Ltd.

Jared W. Paisley
The University of Manitoba

In recognition of his "raw determination and tenacity" in cutting through red tape and surmounting huge obstacles to set up an airline—in the face of direct competition from industry giants Qantas and Air New Zealand—Ewan Wilson (29) was awarded the *1996 Young Entrepreneur of the Year Award.*

Accepting the award, Ewan remarked, "It's been a bumpy flight for the past couple of years, but we've changed the way New Zealanders will fly across the Tasman. If people won't concede anything else, they have to acknowledge that fares have been influenced by Kiwi International. People still make the mistake of saying I can't do something, but that only adds fuel to the fire and some of those people must be feeling pretty silly now. If I asked you to give me $1,000 because I had a good idea for a business, it would be smart to give it to me."

EWAN WILSON, CEO

The son of a psychiatrist and a nurse, Ewan Wilson was born in the small South Island town of Timaru, New Zealand. His two brothers have five university degrees between them, one sister is a newspaper editor, and his other sister a lab technician. Family members suspect Ewan's drive to succeed stems in part from the fact that, in a highly academic family, he had his share of problems at school. According to one of his sisters, "It would have been very hard in my family, where everybody else who went through school sort of soared. He's the youngest and always felt like he had to run to keep up with the rest of us. Although he is not an academic, he's proved that he's got a business acumen that I can only describe as startling."

"For a while they thought I was dyslexic," stated Ewan, "Obviously I'm not, but even today I will avoid at all costs having to write." After leaving school at age 16, he worked as an Air Force Steward and as a "go-fer" for a small regional airline. He says he inherited his love for ports and airports from his father, and managed to get his Pilot's License ("I had a terrible job passing all the academic exams"). Ewan worked for a short time in Australia and at a pub in Yorkshire, and he spent six months washing cars in Montreal where, in 1986, he married his French Canadian wife, Monique.

KIWI TRAVEL

Ewan finally found his thing—selling airline tickets and arranging charter flights. He set up his own Montreal travel agency in 1988 and ran escorted tours to the Brisbane Expo. Shortly thereafter he sold the business to his brother-in-law, and, with his wife and twin daughters, moved from Montreal to Hamilton, New Zealand where his parents lived.

This case was prepared as a basis for classroom discussion rather than to illustrate either effective or ineffective handling of an administrative situation. The cooperation of Kiwi Travel International Airlines and the Department of Strategic Management and Leadership—University of Waikato is gratefully acknowledged. Some of the historical information presented in this case was obtained from an article by Paul Panckhurst in the November 1995 issue of *North and South* magazine. Used with permission.

Copyright © 1998 by South-Western College Publishing and Thomson Learning Custom Publishing (ISBN: 0-324-03795-3). For information regarding this and other CaseNet® cases, please visit CaseNet® on the World Wide Web at **casenet.thomson.com**.

Fresh from the cutthroat competition of North America, Ewan set about establishing his own Hamilton-based travel agency, *Kiwi Travel*, in 1990. "I was not exactly Mr. Popularity with the other travel agents," commented Ewan, "We were quite aggressive in our retail operation. We discounted; we *really* discounted." Unlike the vast majority of the country's travel agents, Kiwi Travel was not a member of the Travel Agents' Association of New Zealand, which demanded a bond, qualified staff, and financial reporting.

According to Ewan, the Association refused him membership because he and his staff did not have the required qualifications. "That was b—- s—-! I was a bloody good travel agent who learned at the coalface, as did every one of my employees." Always looking for his main chance, Wilson hooked up with three other young strivers and set up a company called *Kiwi Travel Air Charters Ltd.*, later renamed *Kiwi Travel International Airlines Ltd.*

THE AIR CHARTER BUSINESS TAKES OFF

Besides Ewan Wilson and his wife Monique, the Directors of the new airline company were:

- Mike Tournier (30), an Air Traffic Controller, ex-army, formerly from Hamilton but now living and working in Auckland;
- Mike Park (29), a friend of Tournier's and a pilot for Air New Zealand. Park later resigned his position as Director of Kiwi Airlines, because his employer was "not comfortable" with him holding a management position with a rival business; and
- Patrick Pruett (29), a University of Tennessee business graduate, formerly a travel agent in the United States. Pruett met Ewan Wilson when they roomed together for an airline computer reservation course in Houston, Texas, and later traveled to New Zealand for a "working holiday" in Wilson's travel agency with, he says, "US$400 and a lot of ambition." Wilson calls Pruett "level headed and conservative—everything that I'm not—and my best friend."

Each of the partners chipped in about $1,000, and with a grand total of $5,000, chartered an old DC3 in June 1994 to transport passengers from Auckland and Wellington to Hamilton's National Agricultural Fieldays. In Ewan's words: "We made no money, but we had a hell of a lot of fun."

In August and September 1994, they decided to "go international," and offered flights on four consecutive Sundays from Hamilton to Brisbane, using a chartered *Air Nauru* plane. In December 1994, the group offered what Ewan termed a series of "hugely profitable" charter flights to Western Samoa and Tonga. "These were what really set us up," said Pat Pruett, "We could make $30,000 on each of those flights."

RED TAPE & TIGHT DEADLINES

In March 1995, New Zealand's Ministry of Transport advised Ewan that he could not run weekly charter flights indefinitely without an *Air Service License*, because they effectively amounted to a scheduled service. But the Ministry was not in a hurry to close down the fledgling airline and gave him until January 1996 to make the switch. That extension allowed Kiwi Travel to start offering weekly Sunday charter flights from Hamilton to Brisbane, and sometimes other Australian destinations such as Cairns, Rockhampton, Coolangatta, and Townsville. On the subject of market research, Ewan had this to say: "We didn't do any. I just had a gut feeling it would work."

Shortly thereafter, Ewan closed his travel agency so he could concentrate on the airline business. A couple of months later, he decided to work towards launching a scheduled air service, and initially planned a fairly "relaxed" implementation schedule, to meet the Ministry's January 1996 deadline. However, in early June 1995, Ewan and his partners got wind of a Boeing 737 available for lease from Adelaide-based National Jet Systems. It was a cargo plane which could be reconfigured to take passengers.

To proceed with the deal and to convince the Ministry of Transport that Kiwi Travel was "a sound and viable operator", the four shareholders (Monique is not a shareholder), had to come up with more money. Pruett, Tournier, and Park each set out to raise another $64,000. Pat Pruett had to borrow from his family in Nashville. By using funds from the sale of his house in Canada, and borrowing from his parents' life savings, Wilson was able to come up with $250,000. Altogether,

1 | Kiwi Travel International Airlines Ltd.

Summary of Shareholders
June 1995

Shareholder	$ Holdings	Paid Capital
Ewan Wilson	49%	$381,220
Mike Park	17	$132,260
Patrick Pruett	17	$132,260
Mike Tournier	17	$132,260
TOTAL	100%	$778,000

including profits from charter operations, the group was able to increase Kiwi Travel International Airlines' paid-up capital from $200 to $778,000. This took three weeks. A summary of each shareholder's stake is shown in Exhibit 1.

The Bank of New Zealand provided an overdraft account on the strength of a registered security over the company, making the bank first in line if the company went broke. The BNZ did not, however, provide any start-up capital. In late June 1995, with the tentative National Jet Systems agreement in hand, Kiwi Travel began advertising and selling tickets for their scheduled Hamilton–Dunedin to Sydney–Brisbane flights to commence August 23rd. Unfortunately, the deal fell through in July, when it became clear that National Jet Systems would not be able to convert the plane to passenger use in time for the August 23, 1995 launch date. "I guess we should have looked at that deal more carefully," commented Pat Pruett. So there they were—six weeks before their first scheduled flight and no aircraft. Ewan recalled the rush that ensued:

> *We started faxing everywhere in the Pacific looking for a plane. At the end of July, I went off to the States and Europe and met with four or five operators. They said they needed 90 days, and I said I don't have bloody 90 days, I have less than five weeks!*

Ewan finally came across a family-owned aircraft charter company called AvAtlantic, in Savannah, Georgia (*Forrest Gump* territory). They were willing to supply a Boeing 727, which could carry about 50 more passengers than the 737 but had a significant disadvantage in that it would have to refuel in Auckland before heading across to Australia. This extra 30-minute wait that passengers would have to endure was not something that Kiwi Airlines had planned on or mentioned in their advertisements. Returning to Hamilton from Georgia, Ewan interviewed prospective flight attendants over a weekend in early August, hired them on Monday, and four days later, sent them packing off to Savannah for training.

With three weeks to go before their inaugural flight, Ewan Wilson had managed to line up an aircraft, but he still didn't have the licenses his airline needed to fly. This involved negotiations with government organizations in the United States, Australia, and New Zealand. As for the political approval, Kiwi Airlines required an *Air Service License* from the New Zealand Ministry of Transport (MOT). AvAtlantic needed an *Air Service Certificate* from New Zealand's Civil Aviation Authority (CAA) as the safety approval. The International Air Services Licensing Act required, among other things, an investigation of Kiwi Airlines' financial viability.

According to the head of the CAA:

> *At times the relationship was not easy. Mr. Wilson did not really understand the depth and breadth of the safety requirements to get a license, and would not sit still long enough to find out. We suggested Kiwi spend a day with us to allow full explanations of what was required of them, but Mr. Wilson spent just 15 minutes.*

The CAA was faced with the extra hassle of dealing with the media, with what it says were Wilson's unfounded claims of unfair treatment. Wilson acknowledged:

> *I hyped it up and put so much pressure on them, they decided to be very thorough with their investigations of AvAtlantic's application. They came over as arrogant as I am. I now know why it's so frustrating dealing with people like me, but it's not every day you get somebody calling you up saying you want to start a second international airline, and of course you take it as a joke. They think I'm pulling their leg, but I'm not. The feeling was "look, you're a travel agent, you're wasting our time," and I said, "Well hold on, you're a government department and I'm a taxpayer, that's what you get paid for."*

Ewan claims that he would have loved to have spent a day with the CAA, but didn't know the invitation existed.

There was doubt within the CAA as to whether the license would be issued in time. Altogether, they had less than four weeks to complete investigations which normally take two to three months. They sent a staff member to Savannah and Ft. Lauderdale to check on AvAtlantic's charter operations and maintenance facilities, and Ewan made sure he was on the same flight.

On August 22, 1995, the day before Kiwi's first scheduled flight, Ewan Wilson arrived back in Hamilton aboard the freshly painted Boeing 727. A crowd of several hundred spectators cheered as Patrick Pruett ran up the steps of the aircraft waving the CAA approval which had just come in. The final international approval from the Australian authorities came in a short time later, and New Zealand's Transport Minister had already promised that an Air Service License would be granted, subject to CAA approval.

When asked whether it was responsible of Kiwi Travel to take bookings before the airline had a plane or the required licenses, Ewan had this to say:

> *I knew I was going to have a plane and I knew the licenses to fly would be granted. We had faith. If the licenses had not been granted in time, we would have operated the scheduled flights as charter flights.*

August 23, 1995, the morning of Kiwi Travel's inaugural flight to Australia, Hamilton's airport was buzzing with excitement. Ewan Wilson had paint on his trousers and the newly built check-in counter was still not completely dry. Behind the counter were Ewan's wife Monique (known within the company as "fluffy") working long days for no pay, and Pat Pruett, with bags under his eyes. Finally, everyone was loaded aboard, and the big silver bird sporting the new "KIWI" logo took off over Hamilton amid applause and cheers from the passengers. New Zealand now had *two* international airlines. A chronology of events in Kiwi Travel's brief history is summarized in Exhibit 2.

PEANUTS AND COLA

Ewan Wilson came up with the idea of offering at least 50 seats per flight at bargain-basement return fares of $349 (Hamilton–Sydney) and $399 (Hamilton–Brisbane), when other airlines were charging $629 (e.g., Auckland). He dubbed these no-meal, no-bar service fares as "Peanuts and Cola" class, which turned out to be a stroke of marketing genius. The media quickly latched onto the term, which gained national publicity and jammed the phone lines at Kiwi Travel's office.

In the early days, Kiwi Travel International Airlines wasn't getting much support from local travel agents, and they showed very little interest in booking Kiwi flights. Perhaps this was because they wanted to see if Kiwi would survive, or perhaps they were getting pressure from the major airlines; probably both. To get around this problem, Kiwi took the innovative step of setting up their own toll-free 800 number to handle bookings directly, which also meant they didn't have to pay commissions to travel agents. Kiwi set up their own reservations center with an initial compliment of 30 staff.

All went well until October 18, 1995, when two tires blew out as the Boeing 727 landed in Hamilton. Damage to the aircraft was minimal, and under terms of their lease, AvAtlantic was to provide all service and repairs. Unfortunately there were delays, caused in part by AvAtlantic's failure to provide parts locally, and Ewan even traveled to Georgia to personally escort the required parts back to New Zealand. In all, the plane was grounded for ten days, at a cost to Kiwi of $500,000, as they had to book their passengers on other airlines.

Kiwi Travel attempted to sue AvAtlantic to recover their loss, and as a result, their business relationship

2 | Kiwi Travel International Airlines Ltd.

CHRONOLOGY OF EVENTS (1990–APRIL 1996)

1990 Ewan Wilson establishes a travel agency called Kiwi Travel in Hamilton, N.Z.

June 1994 Ewan, his wife Monique, and three partners set up a company called Kiwi Travel Air Charters Ltd. They charter a DC3 to transport passengers from Auckland and Wellington to Hamilton's Agricultural Fieldays.

August 1994 The company charters an *Air Nauru* jet. Offers four Sunday flights from Hamilton to Brisbane.

December 1994 A series of charter flights is offered to Western Samoa and Tonga.

March 1995 Ministry of Transport advises Kiwi that it required an *Air Service License* if it wished to offer scheduled flights. Extension granted until January 1996.

April 1995 Scheduled weekly charters are offered from Hamilton to various destinations in Queensland: Brisbane, Cairns, Rockhampton, Coolangatta, and Townsville.

May 1995 Ewan closes the travel agency to concentrate on the airline business. Company name changed to *Kiwi Travel International Airlines Ltd.*

June 1995 Ewan signs a lease for a Boeing 737 from National Jet Systems in Adelaide.

Advertising begins for trans-Tasman service, scheduled to commence August 23.

July 1995 National Jet Systems deal falls through. Kiwi scrambles to find another plane.

Boeing 727 leased from Georgia-based charter company AvAtlantic.

August 1995 Flight attendants interviewed, hired, and sent to Georgia for training.

CAA operating approval granted one day before scheduled flights to begin.

August 23 Kiwi's inaugural flight to Australia takes off on schedule.

October 1995 Boeing 727 blows two tires on landing. AvAtlantic is unable to supply parts and the plane is grounded for ten days, at a cost to Kiwi of $500,000.

November 1995 Kiwi leases a nearly-new Boeing 757 from British-based charter company *Air 2000* and sends the 727 back to AvAtlantic.

February 1996 Services begin from Dunedin.

March 1996 Kiwi Airlines' staff compliment grows to almost 200, including 60 reservations staff, and Company profits are described as "stunning". Competition heats up as Air New Zealand subsidiary Freedom Air offers more flights on Kiwi's routes.

April 1996 Air 2000 requests an early return of the Boeing 757. In its place, Kiwi leases a 737–400 and a 737–300.

soured. In November 1995, Ewan was able to source a nearly-new Boeing 757 from the British-based charter company *Air 2000*, and sent AvAtlantic's older 727 back. This new arrangement had several advantages for Kiwi:

1. The 757 could fly direct to Australia without having to stop in Auckland to fill up;
2. Their "ACMI" lease required Air 2000 to assume all aircraft, crew, maintenance and insurance costs. This included provision of some NZ $5 million in spare parts in New Zealand, four flight crews, three aircraft maintenance engineers, and an operations supervisor; and
3. As a large northern-hemisphere operator, Air 2000 had the flexibility to provide Kiwi Travel with additional aircraft that might be required to cope with demand during the southern hemisphere's "high season."

Within one year (April 1995–March 1996), Kiwi Travel International Airlines had grown from five staff to almost 200. In their first ten months of operation, Kiwi's before-tax profit of $1.2 million was almost double their earlier forecasts. One airline analyst considered the company's financial performance "stunning" (refer to Exhibit 3). Meanwhile, their chief rival Air New Zealand announced a four percent *decline* in profit to $135 million for the six months ending December 1995, compared to $140 million for the same period the previous year.

Kiwi Travel's passenger movements increased from 256 per week in August 1994, to 1,500 in August 1995,

3 | Kiwi Travel International Airlines Ltd.

Kiwi Airline's Profit "Stunning" Says Analyst

by Andrea Fox

A $1.2 million before-tax profit announced by Hamilton's new Kiwi trans-Tasman airline is a "stunning" result, says an aviation financial analyst.

The one-aircraft privately owned, no-frills airline yesterday said it had almost doubled its forecast profit of $700,000 for the 10 months from April 1995 to January.

In this period Kiwi's gross sales from tickets were $13.5 million—$2.5 million better than the airline's own predictions.

Chief executive Ewan Wilson said Kiwi had flown more than 50,000 people.

The broking house analyst, who would not be named because of possible repercussions from Air New Zealand, said if the announcement was correct, the recorded profit was stunning because Kiwi only had shareholder funds of $700,000 the result was stunning.

The analyst took a "cautious" approach to announcements from any company wanting to list on the Stock Exchange. Kiwi is preparing a prospectus for a possible September public share issue.

Kiwi, which started as a trans-Tasman charterer in 1994, became a scheduled international carrier last August. Today it has 155 staff in New Zealand and Australia.

The analyst said a small "start-up" airline faced several perils, and Kiwi had encountered and apparently survived some of them.

"You can go out the back door very quickly if things go wrong. From the start he (Ewan Wilson) said he didn't intend to be a price setter. And it's clear Air New Zealand and Qantas (his trans-Tasman competitors) decided to drop their fares very quickly (to match) so things could have gone very wrong if he didn't get the yields."

Another peril was only having one jet when mechanical failures struck. Kiwi was grounded for 10 days shortly after launching as a scheduled airline because of a serious tyre blowout. Mr. Wilson said if not for the grounding the profit could have been $500,000 higher.

Kiwi had also been involved in rows—another peril. It's recent run-in with a Cook Islands agency over charters to Rarotonga could have cost it dearly.

Another risk was growing too quickly. The analyst was concerned at Kiwi's plan to build an $8 million building after its sharefloat.

Waikato Times, February 17, 1996.

to 3,500 in December 1995. Cargo grew from nothing in August 1995, to 14 tons per week in December of the same year. Managing this exponential growth has been no small feat for Ewan and his General Manager, Patrick Pruett.

The organizational structure was viewed internally as being "fairly flat, project oriented, and floating." For example, someone might be given the task of organizing an in-flight magazine and would be responsible for that project from start to finish, reporting directly to Ewan or Patrick. Someone else might be put in charge of setting up an office in Christchurch. A general organization chart (subject to change) is shown in Exhibit 4. The average age of Kiwi's employees was 27. "Ours is a very young company," stated Pat Pruett, "I've been here almost two years—which makes me one of the old-timers."

Many of Kiwi Travel's operations were contracted out, which allowed the airline to minimize capital investments while maximizing their ability to expand quickly. The aircraft came with three flight crews and maintenance staff as part of the lease agreement. Catering and ground services, including baggage handling, were contracted. Flight Attendants (40–50 per aircraft) were Kiwi's employees, as were about 60 staff at their Hamilton reservation center.

Kiwi planned to lease a second aircraft in June 1996—an Airbus A320, which, at 180 seats, was slightly smaller than the Boeing 757 but still capable of direct trans-Tasman service. The A320 was to be leased through *Orix*, a Japanese bank and leasing firm, and was, according to Ewan, "the most modern passenger aircraft in the world." In New Zealand, a Christchurch destination was to be added with a feeder service[1] to

EXHIBIT 4 | Kiwi Travel International Airlines Ltd.

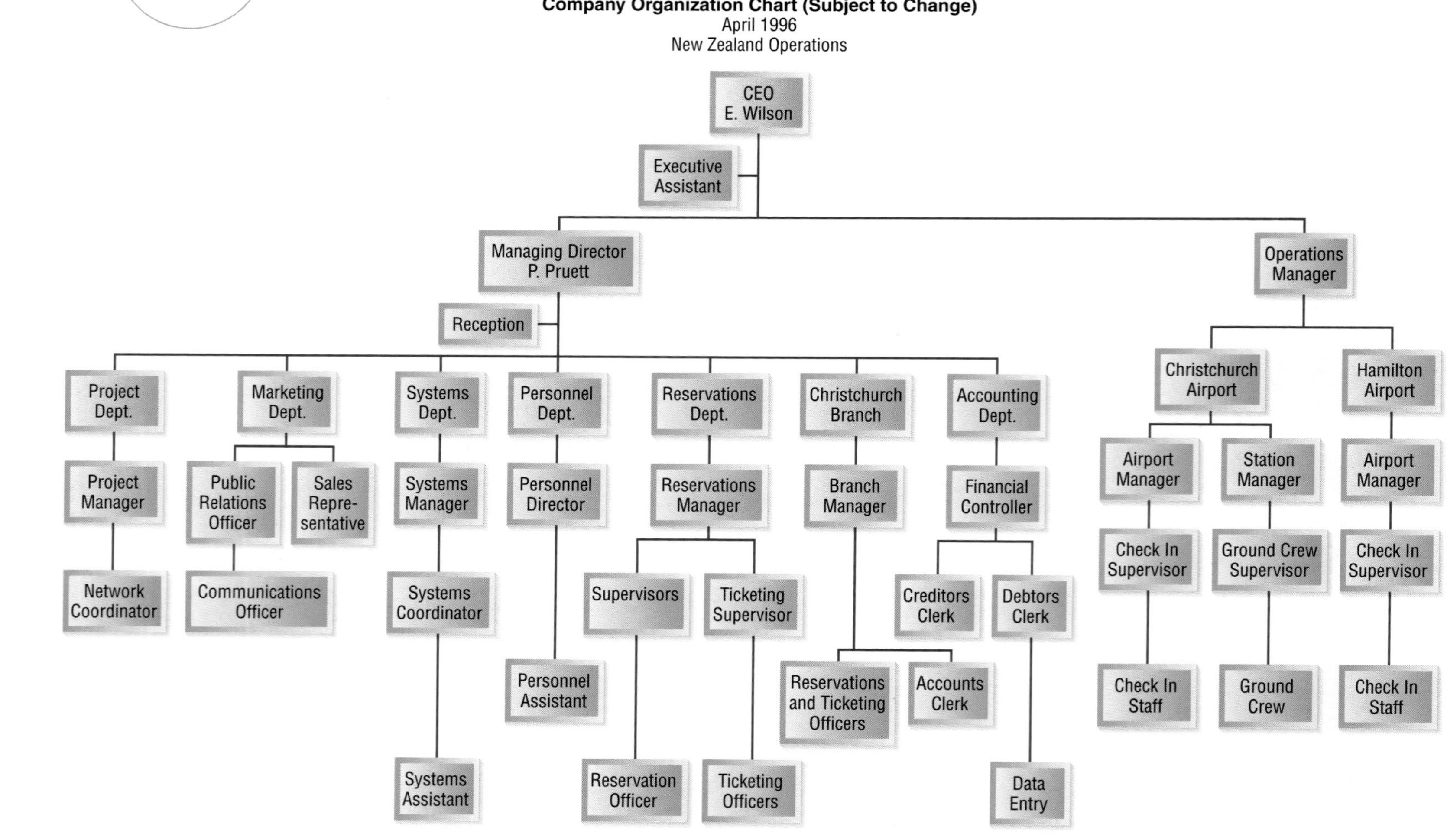

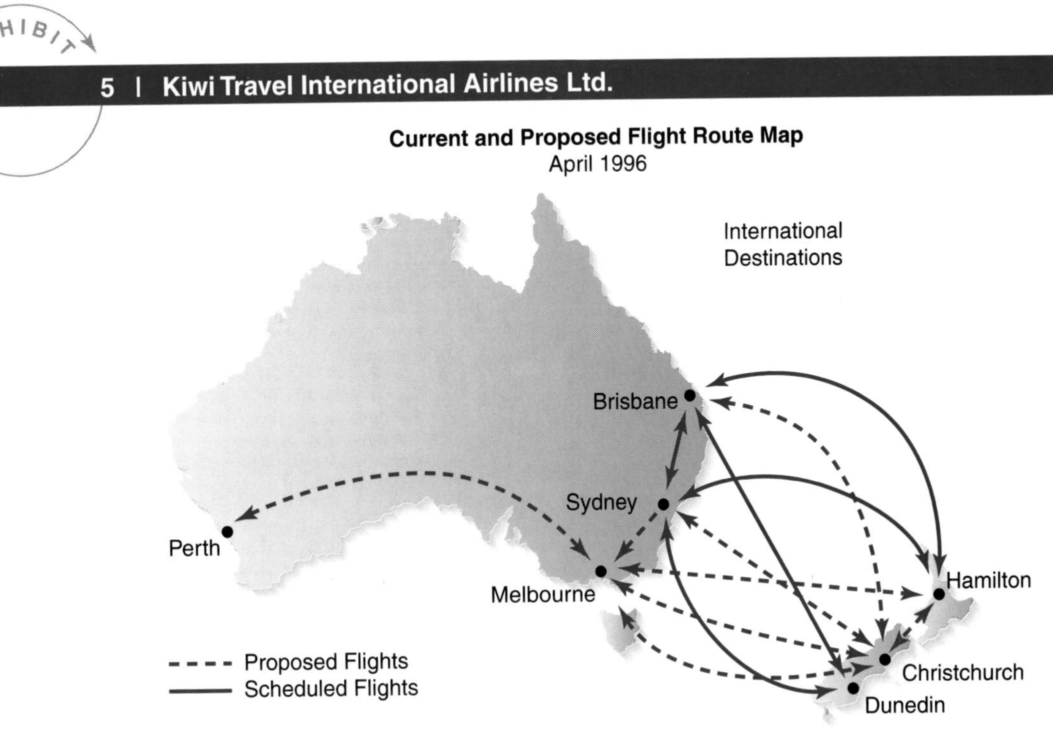

EXHIBIT 5 | Kiwi Travel International Airlines Ltd.

Current and Proposed Flight Route Map
April 1996

Important: All information is subject to change without prior notice and information in this timetable was correct at time of printing. All flight times must be confirmed with Kiwi Travel International Airlines Ltd.

Hamilton. Melbourne and Perth would be added to their Australian destinations (refer to Exhibit 5).

THE COMPETITION HEATS UP

"She's a tough old world out there, and we don't intend to let the grass grow under our feet in terms of addressing them or any other competitor," were the words of Bob Matthew, Chairman of Air New Zealand, when asked in a television interview for his thoughts on Kiwi Travel—New Zealand's second international airline.

There was no doubt in anybody's mind that the big airlines like Air New Zealand and Qantas could, as one aviation analyst put it, "squash Kiwi like a bug," should a price war develop. Ewan recognized this risk but remained philosophical:

> *If it gets too hot in the kitchen, we'll just get out of that kitchen. We'll keep coming up with new niches such as flying out of other provincial airports, but I believe we have a trump card—public support for the little guy. People still support* The Spirit of Entrepreneurship. *I think the public appreciates what is likely to happen to airfares if we're forced out of the market.*

By early 1996, the kitchen was certainly getting warm (refer to Exhibit 6). *Freedom Air*, a subsidiary of Air New Zealand, was competing head-on with Kiwi Travel, by offering direct flights from Hamilton to Sydney for $299, or to Brisbane for $349. This compared to $329 (Sydney) and $379 (Brisbane) for Kiwi's *Nuts and Cola* flights. In addition, Freedom's customers could, for an additional $9, choose between two nights accommodation or two days car rental in Australia.

Ewan Wilson filed a complaint with New Zealand's Commerce Commission, citing "predatory pricing by Air New Zealand in an attempt to blast Kiwi out of the skies." In response, legal counsel for Air New Zealand categorically denied that it had been involved in unlawful predatory pricing "on certain Tasman routes, or

6 | Kiwi Travel International Airlines Ltd.

Freedom Air Turns Up Heat on City Rival

by Andrea Fox

Crunch time is looming for Hamilton's trans-Tasman airline industry.

Air New Zealand-connected Freedom Air yesterday announced it was increasing its limited Hamilton-transtasman operations to seven days a week with low fares. It signals the acid test on Waikato's ability to support two high-frequency trans-Tasman airlines and keep the city's own airline Kiwi flying.

Freedom started in December, flying charters to Brisbane and Sydney from Hamilton, Dunedin, Auckland, Christchurch and Wellington.

Yesterday it announced a new schedule from late April, with more flights from Hamilton and Dunedin, and introducing Palmerston North as a gateway.

Auckland, Christchurch and Wellington would now be served on special dates with specific fares.

Introductory return fares between all Freedom's New Zealand gateways and Sydney would be $299 and Brisbane $349.

Kiwi chief executive Ewan Wilson, who pioneered Hamilton-trans-Tasman flights, said today Freedom's move was "very nasty". Kiwi's outlook was bleak without regional support.

"I can tell you now we can't match those fares if they continue them until the end of the year."

Kiwi's Hamilton-Sydney return is $329, rising to $349 next month. Hamilton-Brisbane return is $379, rising to $399 next month.

May to September was the traditional money-spinning period for a trans-Tasman airline, before the low season of October–November, he said.

Freedom management did not respond to *Waikato Times* calls.

Regional aviation sources said Freedom loadings have been small, with sometimes only 12 people flying out on its 233-seat Boeing 757. The sources said Kiwi's Boeing 757 has had minimum loads of 150.

Freedom spokesman Stuart Eastman recently said Hamilton was the airline's "soft spot".

Hamilton airport chief executive Barry O'Connor said whether the region could support two full-time trans-Tasman airlines was "anybody's guess."

Waikato Development Foundation chief, Frank van der Velden said Freedom's move was a "classic case" of a big company "using predatory tactics to take out competition that is hurting its bottom line".

Consumers' Institute spokesman Peter Sutton said competition was good provided it was sustained. Waikato Chamber of Commerce president Gail Jones predicted Freedom would pull out immediately if Kiwi failed.

Air NZ last week reported a slight decline in its six-monthly financial result on the corresponding period last year. It cited trans-Tasman trade as a contributing factor.

Source: Waikato Times, March 1, 1996.

indeed other predatory behavior designed to eliminate a competitor." Ewan disagreed, citing information on lease costs and passenger loadings which, he said, clearly showed that Freedom Air was operating well below cost.

To make matters worse, in April 1996 Ewan accused Freedom Air of "poaching" his staff by offering flight attendants an expense allowance of $55 per flight in addition to their regular salary of $24,00 to $30,000 per year. He commented on this new development:

> *It's a case of Freedom deliberately targeting every one of our flight attendants. They want our staff because they are well trained and well qualified. I really feel hurt. Four of our flight attendants quit to work for Freedom Air, and three of them were from our original group.*

Ewan was quick to point out that his airline's initial marketing strategy was based upon *location* rather than price. They were trying to appeal to a niche market by offering direct air service to Australia from cities (such as Hamilton and Dunedin) which were not served by the other airlines. For example, prior to the arrival of Kiwi, Hamilton residents had no choice but to travel to Auckland if they wanted to catch a plane to Australia. The company's initial target market was the Central North Island region (approximate population of 650,000), and the Lower South Island region (approximately 250,000 people).

When Kiwi Travel announced its plans to expand service to Christchurch, Freedom Air responded by offering its own Australia-direct discount fares from that city. Christchurch was different from Hamilton and Dunedin in that it was already served by Qantas and Air New Zealand. This was clearly moving away from Kiwi's initial strategy of operating out of centers that did not have direct trans-Tasman air service. This move was explained by Rodney Macdonald, Kiwi's Communication's Officer:

> *Moving into Christchurch is moving into Air New Zealand's territory, but they've already moved into our territory by offering Freedom Air flights out of Hamilton. But they have actually shot themselves in the foot. In Christchurch, Air New Zealand staff complained that Freedom Air was taking their customers!*

In effect, Air New Zealand ended up competing with themselves in the Christchurch market through their subsidiary Freedom Air.

MARCH 1996

Considering that Kiwi Travel International Airlines and its competitive environment were changing, almost on a daily basis, the traditional exercise of "long-range strategic planning" was almost impossible. Nevertheless, a major accounting firm was given the task of developing financial projections for the twelve-month period from June 1, 1996 to May 31, 1997. These projections were made using historical information available at the time (if you consider seven months of scheduled airline operation "historical") and other assumptions based upon company and industry experience. Refer to Exhibits 7–13 for a summary of these projections and related assumptions.

The projections mentioned above assume the lease of an Airbus A320 aircraft commencing July 1996, to compliment the existing aircraft, and the addition of new routes to include Christchurch, Melbourne, and Perth. A net profit of NZ $9.3 million on total revenue of NZ $72.4 million was forecast for the period. According to Ewan Wilson:

> *We aim to become the number one independent airline in New Zealand, operating a variety of low-cost services and taking travel to a wide sector of the world market. Synergy will be sought with other airline and tour operators worldwide, to capitalize on seasonal reciprocity and global asset management. Part of our aims are to establish a strong presence in Hamilton, and develop vertical integration of our business in areas such as ground handling, catering, cargo, and hanger facilities.*

APRIL 1996

In true Kiwi Airlines fashion, the company's situation once again "changed overnight." Their British leasing company, Air 2000, requested an early return of the Boeing 757. Instead of extending the lease as Kiwi had originally planned, Air 2000 wanted it back at the end of April. Ewan commented on this latest development:

> *Kiwi has an excellent relationship with Air 2000, so when they asked for the return of the 757 earlier than originally agreed, to accommodate a busier European summer than expected, we felt obliged to work with them.*

In short order, Ewan managed to source *two* more aircraft to replace the 757. A 126 seat *Air Nauru* Boeing 737–400, scheduled to arrive at the end of April, and a 148 seat Boeing 737–300 from a leasing company called *Aviareps*, to commence service June 1, 1996.

> *This is yet another exciting time for Kiwi. We are going from our current one aircraft with a seat capacity of 233 passengers, to a total of three aircraft with a seat capacity of 454. Life does not get any easier in the airline business, and we have to be proactive to keep our customers happy. The additional aircraft will allow us to offer a wider variety of flight schedules, including special flights for major events, and will give us greater depth in the area of aircraft backup. These changes will give Kiwi more flexibility to combat competition from Freedom Air.*

Over the "long term", Kiwi Airlines was considering a number of new initiatives:

- Establishment of New Zealand's first on-line booking system, which would allow Kiwi's customers to book their own flights using a home computer and

7 | Kiwi Travel International Airlines Ltd.

Assumptions Used in Financial Projections
Twelve Months Ending 31 May 1997

Aircraft

1.	Boeing B757	
	Capacity:	192 passengers
	ACMI Lease Cost:	US$3,235 per hour for the first 250 hours, US$2,805 per hour thereafter
	Fuel Consumption:	10.24 liters per mile
	Airbus A320	
	Capacity:	180 passengers. In service commencing 1 July 1996
	ACMI Lease Cost:	US$3,361 per hour for first 250 hours, US$2,726 per hour thereafter
	Fuel Consumption:	825 gallons per hour
2.	Fuel Cost:	US$0.90 per gallon
3.	Landing Fees:	New Zealand = NZ$585 per landing Australia = AUS$731 per landing
	Terminal Charges:	New Zealand = NZ$1 per passenger Australia = AUS$10 per passenger
4.	Aircraft Ferry Costs:	US$50,000 delivery and return charge per aircraft
5.	Supplementary Aircraft Rental:	Payable at US$65,000 per month for the first six months of the A320 lease term

Revenue

6.	Passenger:	50% of passengers on Nuts & Cola fares
7.	Cargo:	B757 = 3,000 kg per sector at NZ$0.50 per kg A320 = 2,000 kg per sector at NZ$0.50 per kg
8.	Duty Free Sales:	NZ$11.00 per passenger per flight

Other Costs

9.	Catering:	NZ$6.60 per person per rotation
	Beverages:	NZ$2.58 per person per rotation
10.	GST:	12.5%. Applicable to domestic (NZ) expenses and income only
	Income Tax:	33%

Other Assumptions

11.	Exchange Rates:	NZ$1.00 = US$0.647 NX$1.00 = AUS$0.871
12.	Depreciation:	Office Equipment = 35% DV Motor Vehicles = 26% DV Furniture & Fittings = 9.5% DV

EXHIBIT 8 | Kiwi Travel International Airlines Ltd.

Proposed Flight Schedules
Twelve Months Ending 31 May 1997

AIRBUS A320

Destination	Mon	Tues	Wed	Thur	Fri	Sat	Sun
4. HLZ→BNE→HLZ→MEL→HLZ				✈			
3. BNE→HLZ→SYD→HLZ			✈				
5. HLZ→SYD→DUD→SYD→HLZ					✈		
2. BNE→SYD→HLZ→SYD→BNE		✈					
6. HLZ→SYD→HLZ→MEL→PER						✈	
1. BNE→DUD→BNE	✈						
7. PER→MEL→HLZ→BNE→HLZ→BNE							✈

BOEING B757 (or alternate)

Destination	Mon	Tue	Wed	Thur	Fri	Sat	Sun
8. HLZ→CHC→SYD→CHC	✈						
9. CHC→MEL→PER→MEL→CHC		✈					
10. CHC→BNE→CHC→MEL→CHC			✈				
11. CHC→SYD→MEL→CHC				✈			
12. CHC→BNE→CHC					✈		
13. CHC→BNE→DUD→BNE→CHC						✈	
14. CHC→SYD→DUD→SYD→CHC→HLZ							✈

Destination Codes: BNE—Brisbane; CHC—Christchurch; DUD—Dunedin; HLZ—Hamilton; MEL—Melbourne; PER—Perth; SYD—Sydney.

a credit card number. The company had recently launched their own World Wide Web site,[2] which was proving extremely popular.

- A public share float on the New Zealand Stock Exchange. Ewan had recently sold 10,000 of his shares to some friends, which had the effect of lowering his holdings from 49% to about 47%. Kiwi's own employees were considered good potential customers for some shares.
- Obtaining its own Air Operating Certificate, and purchasing two new aircraft in May 1997.

ENDNOTES

1. It is important to note that Kiwi Travel's Air Service License did not, at present, permit them to operate scheduled flights between points within New Zealand. They were only permitted to ferry their own international passengers to connection points for overseas flights. Kiwi planned to offer "free" flights between Christchurch and Hamilton for their Kiwi Class (full economy) passengers booked on international flights.
2. As of October 1997, Kiwi's www address was: http://www.kiwi-travel.co.nz/

9 | Kiwi Travel International Airlines Ltd.

Projected Balance Sheet
31 May 1997

Assets	
Current assets	
Cash	$22,588,346
Deposits with suppliers	2,508,953
GST balance	1,533,705
Prepayments	25,000
Shareholders' current accounts	233,428
	$26,889,432
Fixed assets (depreciated value)	
Furniture & fittings	6,145
Motor vehicles	39,731
Office equipment	204,288
Total fixed assets	$ 250,164
Total assets	$27,139,596
Liabilities & equity	
Current liabilities	
Bond-Flight attendants	$ 45,000
Flight deposits	6,979,742
Taxation balance	5,767,754
Accounts payable	1,784,993
Total current liabilities	$14,577,489
Term liabilities	
Hire-purchase account payable	21,165
Authorized, issued, & paid up capital	778,000
Retained earnings	11,762,942
Total liabilities & equity	$27,139,596

Source: **Unaudited company records.**

C-366

10 | Kiwi Travel International Airlines Ltd.

Projected Statement of Income and Expenses
Twelve Months Ending 31 May 1997

Income		
Sales		$87,328,380
Less: direct costs		66,115,668
Gross profit		$21,212,712
Expenses		
ACC levy		$ 18,000
Accounting & legal fees		18,000
Advertising & promotion		1,575,004
Aircraft ferry expenses		308,892
Cleaning & maintenance		24,000
Communication		379,500
Computer expenses		96,000
Contingency		200,004
Depreciation		124,606
Flight consumable		114,000
Freight		18,000
Fringe benefit tax		10,000
Insurance		996
Interest & bank charges		48,648
Miscellaneous expenses		24,000
Office costs:	Brisbane office	456,000
	Sales office	666,000
	General expenses	22,800
Rent		54,300
Salaries, wages, benefits		1,805,928
SITA reservation system fees		276,000
Staff recruitment, seminars, training		346,000
Stationery & subscriptions		38,400
Supplementary aircraft rental		602,316
Travel & entertainment		54,000
Utilities		12,000
Vehicle expenses		36,000
Total expenses		$ 7,329,394
Profit before taxation		$13,883,318
Taxation (33%)		4,581,495
Net profit after tax		$ 9,301,823

Source: Unaudited company records.

Exhibit 11 | Kiwi Travel International Airlines Ltd.

Projected Monthly Income and Expenses
Twelve Months Ending 31 May 1997

	June	July	Aug	Sept	Oct	Nov	Dec	Jan	Feb	March	April	May	Total
Total sales	3,588,394	8,243,234	8,243,234	8,000,786	7,588,092	7,364,912	8,243,234	8,243,234	6,495,099	7,177,085	6,965,994	7,177,085	87,328,380
Less: direct costs	2,824,377	5,873,231	5,873,231	5,763,299	5,785,072	5,677,732	5,873,231	5,873,231	5,411,687	5,755,685	5,649,159	5,755,685	66,115,668
Gross profit	762,017	2,370,003	2,370,003	2,237,487	1,803,020	1,687,180	2,370,003	2,370,003	1,083,412	1,421,400	1,316,785	1,421,400	21,212,712
Less: expenses	599,851	595,851	674,051	703,050	701,051	637,050	532,665	556,415	556,415	569,665	602,665	600,665	7,329,394
Profit before taxation	162,166	1,774,152	1,695,952	1,534,437	1,101,969	1,050,130	1,837,338	1,813,588	526,997	851,735	714,120	820,735	13,883,318
Less: tax @ 33%	55,515	585,470	559,664	506,364	363,650	346,543	606,322	598,484	173,909	281,073	235,660	270,843	4,581,495
Net profit after tax	108,651	1,188,682	1,136,288	1,028,073	738,319	703,587	1,231,016	1,215,104	353,088	570,662	478,460	549,892	9,301,823

Note: One additional aircraft projected to commence July 1996. June figures reflect the operation of only one aircraft.

Exhibit 12 | Kiwi Travel International Airlines Ltd.

Projected Current Account Summary
Twelve Months Ending 31 May 1997

	June	July	Aug	Sept	Oct	Nov	Dec	Jan	Feb	March	April	May
Opening bank balance	5,364,760	10,591,181	11,612,425	13,538,345	13,932,775	15,681,968	16,803,118	19,413,338	18,778,308	20,857,004	20,784,872	22,513,688
Total net cash movement	5,226,421	1,021,244	1,925,919	394,430	1,749,193	1,121,151	2,610,220	(635,030)	2,078,696	(72,132)	1,728,816	74,658
Closing bank balance	10,591,181	11,612,425	13,538,345	13,932,775	15,681,968	16,803,118	19,413,338	18,778,308	20,857,004	20,784,872	22,513,688	22,588,346

13 | Kiwi Travel International Airlines Ltd.

Projected Statement of Contribution to Profit per Destination
Twelve Months Ending 31 May 1997

Rotation Destination	1	2	3	4	5	6	7	8	9	10	11	12	13	14	Total
Avg. aircraft costs per rotation															
ACMI	27,945	34,687	36,012	53,551	48,991	54,837	68,166	28,577	55,572	52,024	31,160	26,648	54,299	52,988	
Fuel	11,097	12,273	13,940	18,806	18,696	18,150	18,806	14,161	18,751	20,771	14,511	11,097	22,194	21,088	
Handling	4,018	12,114	7,010	9,079	8,958	9,809	9.079	7,448	13,102	10,436	8,666	5,218	10,436	12,896	
Landing charges	1,331	3,522	1,992	2,859	2,492	2,471	2,859	3,046	3,298	3,980	2,588	2,102	3,980	4,695	
Airway charges	3,968	8,997	4,810	6,759	6,932	7,154	6,759	3,564	7,888	7,562	3,594	3,968	7,562	7,188	
Aircrew	918	1,709	1,183	1,759	1,609	1,801	1,753	1,423	2,767	2,590	1,551	1,327	2,703	2,638	
Total	**49,277**	**73,302**	**64,947**	**92,813**	**87,678**	**94,222**	**107,422**	**58,219**	**101,378**	**97,363**	**62,070**	**50,360**	**101,174**	**101,493**	
Other costs per year															
Commission	280,449	358,488	392,235	556,751	519,840	461,311	625,826	282,631	386,159	513,504	294,782	258,814	513,504	496,614	5,940,908
Catering	97,346	194,693	149,020	194,693	194,693	194,693	243,366	134,598	179,464	179,464	134,598	89,732	179,464	224,330	2,387,154
Beverages	38,054	76,107	57,080	76,107	76,107	76,107	95,134	52,616	70,154	70,154	52,616	35,077	70,154	87,693	933,160
Total	**415,849**	**629,288**	**595,335**	**827,551**	**790,640**	**732,111**	**964,326**	**469,845**	**635,777**	**763,122**	**481,996**	**383,623**	**763,122**	**808,637**	**9,261,222**
Flight hours per rotation	7.17	8.9	9.24	13.75	12.57	14.07	17.49	7.41	14.41	13.49	8.08	6.91	14.08	13.74	
Number of rotations	52	52	52	52	52	52	52	48	48	48	48	48	48	48	
Avg. capacity loading	78.58%	78.58%	78.58%	78.58%	78.58%	78.58%	78.58%	74.0%	74.0%	74.0%	74.0%	74.0%	74.0%	74.0%	
Total seat capacity	180	180	180	180	180	180	180	192	192	192	192	192	192	192	
Avg. ticket income per head	$532.33	$680.33	$744.33	$1,056.33	$986.33	$875.33	$1,187.33	$582.09	$795.09	$1,057.09	$607.09	$533.09	$1,057.09	$1,086.09	
Other Revenue															
Duty free sales	81,122	81,122	81,122	81,122	81,122	81,122	74,777	74,777	74,777	74,777	74,777	74,777	74,777	74,777	1,091,293
Net cargo revenue	104,200	208,400	156,300	208,400	208,400	208,400	260,500	215,145	286,890	286,860	215,145	143,430	286,860	358,575	3,147,505
Contribution summary:															
Total revenue	4,107,687	5,303,346	5,723,229	8,076,243	7,560,013	6,741,418	9,094,432	4,242,799	5,762,462	7,543,505	4,412,746	3,837,988	7,543,505	7,379,007	87,328,380
Total direct costs	2,982,291	4,290,953	3,977,899	5,661,423	5,357,050	5,639,377	6,559,205	3,253,720	5,480,756	5,416,299	3,448,548	2,790,442	5,598,459	5,659,246	66,115,668
Gross profit	**1,125,396**	**1,012,393**	**1,745,330**	**2,414,820**	**2,202,963**	**1,102,041**	**2,535,227**	**989,079**	**281,706**	**2,127,206**	**964,198**	**1,047,546**	**1,945,046**	**1,719,761**	**21,212,712**

Source: Unaudited company records.

CASE 23

KUVO Radio

Marketing an Oasis

Joan Winn
Christina Móntez
University of Denver

Florence Hernandez-Ramos, KUVO radio's President/CEO, reflected on the Hispanic-owned jazz radio station with pride. For over ten years the station had broadcast up to 23 1/2 hours of classic jazz every day of every week. Special weekend programming included Blues, Latin jazz, Tejano, Salsa, Native American rhythms, and a Brazilian Fantasy (see Exhibits 1 and 2 for a terminology list and the programming schedule). These sounds were peppered with hourly National Public Radio (NPR) news and information, and book reviews by local authors and bookstore owners. Hernandez-Ramos believed that KUVO's unique programming mix justified its tag line "Oasis in the City," a refreshing escape from the rock and country commercial radio stations.

But as the 1996 spring membership drive was coming to a close, her pride turned to concern over the future of the station. KUVO, a licensed educational broadcasting station, was a 501(c)(3) non-profit organization and a member of both NPR and Public Radio International (PRI). As such, it relied largely on donations of "members," rather than commercial sales, for its operating budgets. During this 9-day membership campaign, the first of three during the year, 1,457 members had pledged $79,928, five percent less than the $84,247 pledged in the fall membership drive and eight percent less than the $86,000 spring-drive goal. With the threat of cuts in federal funding for public radio, the station would not have enough funds to sustain its current operations if membership contributions did not increase. (See Exhibit 3 for operating expenses.) KUVO also relied on sponsorship from profit and non-profit organizations, but legal restrictions regarding advertising on public radio stations deterred many corporate sponsors. Without increased support from listeners, donors, and volunteers, the station's future was uncertain. As the Latin rhythms filtered in from the studio, Florence Hernandez-Ramos hoped her goals were realistic and that the station would be able to meet the expenses that loomed on the horizon.

THE ORGANIZATION AND ITS HISTORY

The story of KUVO becoming a player in the Denver metropolitan broadcast area was, in the words of Florence Hernandez-Ramos, one of "[t]rying to find people who would essentially believe in a pipedream." More so, KUVO's birth was, in large part, the result of efforts by the Hispanic[1] community to increase its presence in the American media, an often difficult task for minorities.

In 1982, of the 300 public radio stations in the continental United States (including Indian Reservations) and Alaska, African-Americans controlled 16, Hispanics 12, and Native Americans 9. The Hispanic controlled stations composed the National Federation of Community Broadcasting (NFCB), an organization dedicated to increasing Hispanic access to media. In the western United States, Hugo Morales of Fresno, California, managed the Western Community of Bilingual Radio and Radio Bilingue, the regional arms of the NFCB. Only one Spanish language station operated in Denver (KBNO, an AM station), despite the fact that 13

©1996 by Joan Winn and Christina Móntez, University of Denver.

1 | Terminology Guide to Radio, Jazz, and the KUVO Format

Blues	A 12-bar song form that evolved from black spirituals and work songs; unique elements are blue notes, speechlike inflection, and emotional expression (*Jazz for Beginners*, 1995).
Brazilian Fantasy	This programming format included bossa nova and other Brazilian music with jazz influences.
Chicano	A person of Mexican descent born and raised in the U.S. (*American Heritage Dictionary*, 1985).
Classic Jazz	Refers to the various types (big band, swing, be-bop, cool, modal) of jazz music produced between approximately 1920 and 1970.
Format	Programming broadcast over 20 hours weekly (*Broadcasting and Cable Yearbook*, 1995).
Fusion	Classic jazz themes electrified and rock influenced; produced between 1970 and the present.
Hispanic	Of or pertaining to the language, people, and culture of Spain, Portugal, or Latin America (*American Heritage Dictionary*, 1985).
Latin jazz	Latin rhythms combined with jazz.
Latino	A native or descendant of Latin America, including the Caribbean (*American Heritage Dictionary*, 1985).
Native American rhythms	This programming includes music from various Native American tribes from the United States.
Salsa	Literally the word means "sauce" or "juice" in Spanish; with regard to music, it refers to the encounter of Afro-Cuban and Puerto Rican music with big band jazz in the Latin barrios of New York; one unifying theme in salsa is the reference to the syncretic Afro-Catholic religions (*World Music Rough Guide*, 1994).
Smooth jazz	Classic jazz themes with pop music influences; produced between 1975 and the present.
Special programming	Programming broadcast from 1–20 hrs. weekly (*Broadcasting and Cable Yearbook*, 1995).
Straightahead jazz	Synonym for classic jazz.
Tejano	A modern, urban version of conjunto (an accordion-led style of Tex-Mex music), using synthesizers and other electric instruments (*World Music Rough Guide*, 1994).

percent—approximately 378,000 people—of the Denver metropolitan area's population was of Hispanic origin (Accola, 1996). By 2020, Colorado's Hispanic population is expected to reach 20 percent (Schwab, 1996). See Exhibit 4 for statewide population growth information.

In November 1982, the owners of the 89.3 FM frequency were forced to relinquish their rights to the station, having failed to raise enough money to air their planned "alternative, community-action"-broadcast. At that time, National Public Radio had two subscriber stations in Colorado, both through university-owned affiliates, one at the University of Denver (KCFR, which became independent in 1988), and the other at Colorado State University in Ft. Collins (KCSU), 60 miles north of Denver.

A group of concerned Hispanic, Denver citizens, led by Hugo Morales and the NFCB, attended the bid meeting of the Federal Communications Commission (FCC) to forestall sale of the station to the highest bidder. NPR was concerned about the low participation of minorities in public radio and supported Morales' group in its re-

2 | Programming Guide

	Sunday	Monday	Tuesday	Wednesday	Thursday	Friday	Saturday
2–5 am				Jazz			
5–7 am							
7–8 am	Alternative Voices			KUVO Morning Show Music & Features w/ Carlos Lando			Jazz
8–9 am	La Nueva Voz	Latino USA				Telling It Like It Was w/ Lou Rawls	
9–1 pm	Cancion Mexicana						
1–3 pm	Latin Musicians				Jazz		
3–4 pm	Salsa on Sunday						
4–6 pm	Brazilian Fantasy			Marketplace News			
6–7 pm		Jazz Smithsonian w/ Lena Horne	Making the Music w/ Wynton Marsalis	Piano Jazz w/ Marian McPartland	Jazzset	Jazz at the Kennedy Center w/ Dr. Billy Taylor	JazzTown
7–10 pm				Jazz			All Blues 7–9 pm
10–1 am							
1–2 am		Jazz Smithsonian w/ Lena Horne	Making the Music w/ Wynton Marsalis	Piano Jazz w/ Marian McPartland	Jazzset	Jazz at the Kennedy Center w/ Dr. Billy Taylor	So What? Acid Jazz

Source: KUVO, 1996.

quest for FCC approval of the transfer of the rights to the station.

After having won the rights to the frequency, two immediate tasks faced the new licensees: to raise money for broadcasting equipment and to name a Chief Executive Officer and Board of Directors. Morales, Hernandez-Ramos, and Mark Hand (a friend of Morales) decided to draw upon the national pool of Hispanics in radio for the Board and then gradually replace them with locals as the station became more well-known. A solution to

3 | KUVO/Denver Educational Broadcasting, Inc.

Statement of Revenue and Expenses for the Years Ended December 31,

Revenues	**1990**	**1991**	**1992**	**1993**	**1994**	**1995**
Underwriting	$88,689	$178,568	$83,813	$105,458	$128,777	$135,886
Memberships	$159,736	$180,718	$194,326	$228,184	$232,104	$320,790
Grants	$129,195	$156,826	$243,628	$262,476	$310,033	$183,125
Channel charges	$44,488	$46,712	$49,248	$51,500	$54,296	$57,578
Misc	$10,650	$11,261	$13,271	$23,811	$36,094	$16,316
Total cash	$432,758	$574,085	$584,286	$671,429	$761,304	$713,695
In-kind[1]	$71,195	$161,231	$84,869	$85,941	$52,679	$31,909
Trade[2]	$44,956	$44,631	$105,451	$38,928	$35,497	$7,418
Volunteer[3]	$153,575	$191,122	$194,892	$213,706	$217,644	$239,969
Total noncash	$269,726	$369,984	$385,212	$338,575	$305,820	$279,296
Total revenues	$702,484	$971,069	$969,498	$1,010,004	$1,067,124	$992,991
Expenses						
Salaries	$185,840	$216,463	$227,953	$256,953	$260,031	$286,625
Profess. services	$90,220	$155,134	$99,444	$102,016	$90,105	$81,122
Programming	$183,948	$232,450	$326,019	$287,286	$407,676	$368,348
Rent/util.	$59,195	$56,384	$50,135	$46,842	$54,150	$55,587
Ad & promo	$88,192	$175,893	$203,324	$197,339	$88,899	$53,918
General/admin.	$64,640	$80,465	$74,981	$79,286	$126,323	$101,988
Deprec/amort.	$30,799	$21,034	$31,925	$29,279	$25,255	$25,256
Interest	$4,878	$9,620	$5,770	$6,655	$0	$0
Total expenses	$707,712	$947,443	$1,019,551	$1,005,656	$1,052,439	$972,844
Loss of abandonment of lease					$20,555[+]	
Surplus/deficit	($5,228)	$23,626	($50,053)	$4,348	($5,870)	$20,147

[1]"In-kind" donations are goods and services, recorded at "fair market value."
[2]KUVO "trades" air time for goods and services. Revenue is recorded at the "fair market value" of the related goods and services or the air time given.
[3]Volunteer services are valued at hourly rates established by the Corporation for Public Broadcasting.
[4]KUVO entered into a 20-year lease for the facilities at the Five Points Media Center Building in July 1994.

the search for a CEO was not so easy: there were few Hispanic media personalities in Denver. Of those few, all had highly remunerative positions; running a start-up radio station for a non-competitive salary was not in their plans.

In 1982, Florence Hernandez-Ramos was engaged in a career as a paralegal for the State Attorney General's Office. A native of Lamar, Colorado, Hernandez-Ramos had graduated from the University of Colorado in Boulder and had moved to Denver in 1968. Morales was impressed with Hernandez-Ramos's professionalism and her involvement in cultural activities in the Denver area. Consequently, Morales encouraged Hernandez-Ramos to apply for the position. Shortly thereafter, she had a new job and spent her first day in Washington, D.C., learning the ins-and-outs of public radio.

The capitalization issue remained: the station needed at least $200,000 to acquire the equipment necessary to broadcast. The station eventually obtained a one-year, federally funded operating and technical grant of $326,000, with the stipulation that an additional $117,000 be raised for hiring a staff. Hernandez-Ramos was elated and overwhelmed—these numbers, pocket change for many companies, appeared astronomically high and unachievable. Nevertheless, she faced the challenge by turning to the very people for whom the station

4 | Demographic Trends

While the KUVO footprint reaches a 60 mile radius from its location atop Lookout Mountain in Golden, Colorado, the majority of the listener membership is found in the Denver metropolitan area. The U.S. Census data shown below refers to the Denver–Boulder Consolidated Metropolitan Statistical Area (CMSA) which includes the following seven counties (within approximately a 30 mile radius from the transmitter): Adams, Arapahoe, Boulder, Denver, Douglas, Gilpin, and Jefferson.

	1980	1990	% Change
Total Population Denver–Boulder CMSA	1,620,902	1,848,319	14.0
Persons of Hispanic Origin	173,773	223,361	28.5
(% of Total Population)	(10.7%)	(12.1%)	
By Country/Region of Origin			
Mexico	108,697	150,483	38.4
Puerto Rico	2,067	4,246	105.4
Cuba	1,169	1,609	37.6
All others	61,840	67,023	8.4
By Race			
White	89,679	124,212	38.5
Black	1,183	2,902	145.3
All others	82,911	96,247	16.1
Number of Households Speaking Spanish or Spanish Creole at Home	45,965	102,010	121.9
Number of Households Speaking Portuguese or Portuguese Creole at Home	367	352	-4.1

Source: U.S. Bureau of the Census, 1980, 1990.

was intended, the Hispanic community. For 22 months, Hernandez-Ramos and Morales sponsored every grassroots fundraising campaign they could think of, from break-dancing contests to social dances to bake-outs. They enlisted the community to make colorful paper flowers to sell during the annual Cinco de Mayo celebration and Posados (a mid-December Mexican Christmas tradition). Hernandez-Ramos recalled with humor and pride the Adopt-A-Watt doll campaign: youth groups from a local recreation center made dolls that were awarded to individuals who donated $10 or more towards obtaining a 25,000 watt transmitter. The fundraising efforts were not in vain. On August 29, 1985, the 89.3-frequency station went on the air as KUVO.

THE MISSION

As politically and socially active members of the community, both Hernandez-Ramos and Morales saw the opportunity to own a radio station as a vehicle for establishing a voice for the Latino community. From the beginning, the radio's programming was intended to serve Denver's Hispanic community. Hence, the station was named "KUVO," the shortened version of "¿Qué (hu)vo?" ("What's going on?"). "KPSA" ("¿Qué pasa?") had already been assigned to an AM station in Alamogordo, New Mexico. The station owners had envisioned that the station would play Spanish-language music, because it was a common language heritage that united "la raza bronce," the bronze-colored race. But through the casual marketing research conducted during the fundraising efforts, the organizers noticed that the majority of the surveys, completed in English, expressed a preference for jazz programming, which was conspicuously absent from Denver radio at the time. So, KUVO decided to play jazz and Spanish-language music, at first glance a rare mix.

Once on the air, listeners happily welcomed the jazz selections, but something was amiss: few of those who called in "sounded Hispanic." "What are *they* doing listening to our station?!" The question was asked not with prejudice, but with perplexity. To confuse everyone more, listeners who called in during Spanish language programming spoke English and requested Tejano and similar musical genres produced along the Mexican-American border and in the southwest United States, rather than traditional Mexican music. This diversity of the listening audience was critical in establishing the station's current mission:

> *The mission of Denver Educational Broadcasting, KUVO, is to provide alternative educational, informational, and entertainment opportunities that enrich, maintain, reflect, and institutionalize a multilingual, multicultural perspective and foster appreciation for cultural diversity with an emphasis on the Chicano/Hispanic experience.*

RADIO: A NATIONAL OVERVIEW

In spite of the advent of television in 1946, its steady popularity, and the relatively recent explosion of cable and direct-TV satellites, American radio has continued to grow. According to the *Broadcasting and Cable Yearbook 1995*, both AM and FM radio authorizations and broadcasts continued to rise. Between 1984 and 1994, Adult Contemporary, Country and Western, Top 40 and Album oriented Rock dominated commercial radio.

The national growth in public radio was reflected in the number of contributors. In 1970, when public radio was first established, approximately 33,000 individuals donated. By 1980, the number had grown to 487,000, and up to 1,275,000 in 1990. As the number of contributors to public radio grew, so had the average contribution. In 1990, the mean gift amount was $57.44.

Public radio had evolved into a source for in-depth news coverage and programming not found on commercial radio stations. While most public radio stations featured classical music, many ventured into alternative music venues not viewed as commercially viable. Jazz, for example, had experienced significant challenges in spite of its steady growth. According to John Corbett in *Down Beat Magazine*, "[t]he road for jazz broadcasting has been rocky since World War II, passing out of network radio in the 50s, moving into a world of increased specialization and fragmentation." In fact, in late 1994, classic jazz formats ceased to exist on commercial radio, when Alameda, California-based KJAZ went off the air.

There was some debate about whether jazz was commercially viable. On the one hand, advertisers looked away from the "straightahead" classic jazz stations because their Arbitron ratings for market share were low. Meanwhile, advertisers turned to the smooth jazz stations, which attracted a larger mainstream audience. For example, Ron Cowan, CEO/Chairman of KJAZ, a satellite station that had broadcasted in both northern California and New York, pointed out that advertisers also turned away from jazz stations because ". . . the highly educated jazz listener has different listening habits than the typical 'drive-time" public. Our audience listened to KJAZ at home or in the office . . . Our heaviest listening began at five or six in the evening. We had a little 1,900-watt license, and we got up to a 5.5 share between 6 PM and midnight. Those hours don't mean anything to an advertising buyer who's looking at drive time." According to Cowan, "[t]he mainstream jazz aficionado, by and large, was the best educated and makes the highest income. It's the most desirable demographic for advertisers to reach. That does not hold true for what I would call New Age jazz or Yuppie Jazz." In 1993, 367 radio stations featured jazz programming as part of their weekly schedule. Of these, 92 percent (337) were FM broadcasts, and 80 percent (295) were on noncommercial, or public radio, stations.

Industry insiders believed that there was little money to be made by record companies in jazz radio. Bob Rusch of North County Distribution, which handled over 800 jazz labels, commented that record companies and distributors did not see financial benefits in sending promo copies to radio stations. Rusch claimed that "labels who spend thousands of dollars sending it out, tracking it, . . . find almost no impact." Local stores often failed to carry specialized jazz labels, reinforcing the perception that radio promotions were ineffective marketing tools.

Legislative changes placed niche stations at a further competitive disadvantage. The Telecommunications Act of 1996 allowed companies to own up to eight stations in a single market, spurring a wave of radio industry consolidation. In March 1996, the *Wall Street Journal* reported over $2 billion in radio acquisition deals in one month alone. In Denver, Jacor Communications, one of the largest radio-broadcasting companies in the U.S., acquired Noble Broadcasting Group, holder of four Denver radio stations, thereby doubling its Denver-area presence. While some industry insiders believed that consolidation would curtail program diversity, others saw the increase in advertising leverage by these large companies contributing to more program diversity as stations could experiment with alternative programming without compromising market share (Lippman, 1996).

DENVER'S RADIO MARKET

In 1995, there were 109 AM stations and 75 FM stations in Colorado. One hundred fifty-four stations were commercial and 30 were non-commercial (*Broadcasting and Cable Yearbook*, 1995). By 1991, the FCC had granted 47 FM licenses to the Denver area "in what many considered to be an already over-radioed area" (Wehner, 1991). Industry analysts saw this as the first signs of a rebounding economy and the herald of what would be called a "broadcast boom" by 1993. By 1995, Denver ranked 23rd of 131 radio markets nationwide, with approximately 1,705,800 listeners. Not including KUVO, listeners could tune into one of three AM Spanish language stations, two public radio stations and one station that had special jazz and blues programming. Exhibit 5 provides an overview of Colorado radio programming. Though other stations played occasional jazz selections, none matched KUVO in its jazz focus. KUVO thus assumed a unique position in the Denver radio market.

When KUVO went on the air in 1985, the local radio scene included one FM jazz station, KADX based in Castle Rock, 30 miles south of Denver, and one Spanish language station, KBNO, an AM frequency. KDKO, an African-American–owned station with a weak AM frequency, played rhythm, blues, and soul. Over the next ten years, two major changes regarding Denver's jazz radio presence occurred. KADX went off the air in 1987. Between November 1994 and January 1995, eight stations changed ownership hands, including KHIH (co-owned with KHOW-AM), which eventually began to promote itself as "Smooth Jazz Colorado Style" (Steers, 1993). The new owners set out to make KHIH worth $5 million, the amount for which several other stations had recently been sold or traded.

KHIH was KUVO's main competitor. To music purists, the comparison was weak: KHIH played a bastardization of the classics—jazz themes electrified and "pop" influenced. Many dedicated classic jazz aficionados scoffed at KHIH. Yet, for those who didn't know the difference between classic jazz and its newer mutations, KUVO was viewed as the maverick. Predictions on the genre's radio future were divided, but the bottom line was that jazz was hard to sell. However, jazz audiences were loyal listeners and generous supporters.

THE KUVO STUDIO AND STAFF

KUVO's headquarters was located in a predominantly African-American area northeast of downtown Denver in the Five Points Media Center, a newly-refurbished building owned by the Piton Foundation. The Mayor's Office of Economic Development, TCI, and The Boettcher Foundation had contributed over $2.6 million for renovations. The building was occupied by three public media concerns: KUVO, KBDI Channel 12 television (a Corporation for Public Broadcasting affiliate), and Denver Community Access Television, a cable studio where community members could produce shows for public broadcast. All three organizations provided internship programs to university students. The Center's Executive Director, Jeff Hirota, explained that the Center's mission was to use media ". . . as a means of positive social change . . . where we [can] help women and minorities get jobs in the [media] industry . . . Our contribution is to give them hands-on experience in broadcast media" (Mora, 1995).

KUVO's second-floor suite reflected the corporate culture and provided an environment that encouraged quality service delivery. One was welcomed into the Media Center by the clear sounds of KUVO's live programming. The elevator opened into a comfortable waiting space where a glass façade with a single door handsomely displaying the KUVO logo opened into a receptionist area. The walls were decorated with framed prints of famous jazz musicians and Chicano art.

The Resource Room and the offices of the Advertising Underwriters, Volunteer Coordinator, and Business Manager had large windows that faced directly west, offering a sweeping view of downtown Denver and the Rocky Mountains. Hernandez-Ramos' office featured

EXHIBIT

5 | Format Distribution of Colorado Radio Stations

Format	Number
Country	53
Adult Contemporary	36
Rock/AOR	20
Variety/Diverse	14
Religious	14
Oldies	14
News/Talk	13
News	13
Talk	9
Classical	8
Progressive	7
Sports	7
Spanish	7
Contemporary Hits/Top 40	7
Jazz	5
Middle of the Road (MOR)	4
Big Band	3
Educational	3
Agricultural & Farm	3
Classic Rock	3
Children	2
Beautiful Music	2
Black	2
Foreign Language/Ethnic	1
Nostalgia	1
Urban Contemporary	1
New Age	1

Note: The Broadcasting and Cable Yearbook recognizes 71 different formats.
Source: Broadcasting and Cable Yearbook, 1995.

Mexican-American folklore items reminiscent of those displayed during Dia de los Muertos, Day of the Dead (the Mexican equivalent of Halloween, though a far more meaningful and elaborate holiday). *Gato Guerrero* and other books in the *Luis Montez Mystery Series* by Hernandez-Ramos' husband, Manuel Ramos, added to the cultural decor.

The station was overseen by a nine-member Board of Directors. The KUVO staff was made up of 13 employees, 9 full-time and 4 part-time (see the organizational chart in Exhibit 6). Unlike the staff of the early years, in 1996 KUVO employees had extensive experience in radio, public broadcasting, or non-profits. The collective experience and enthusiasm for both jazz and the organizational mission made the staff one of KUVO's most valuable assets.

In addition to the paid staff, KUVO also benefited from over 400 volunteers. Approximately 2/3 of this group was involved in programming, with the remaining 1/3 in administration. According to Sandra Solimando, Volunteer Program Administrator, the volunteers were a loyal and dedicated group. Forty of the volunteers served as on-air hosts who brought their own style and flavor to programming. Most volunteers offered clerical skills and performed customer (member) service functions such as assisting membership drives, mailing premiums, correcting premium notices, handling phone calls from listeners and members, responding to member letters, and "talking up" the station.

KUVO showed its appreciation for its volunteers in several ways. The *Scat Sheet*, a bi-monthly newsletter, highlighted volunteer accomplishments and was sent to

6 | Organizational Chart

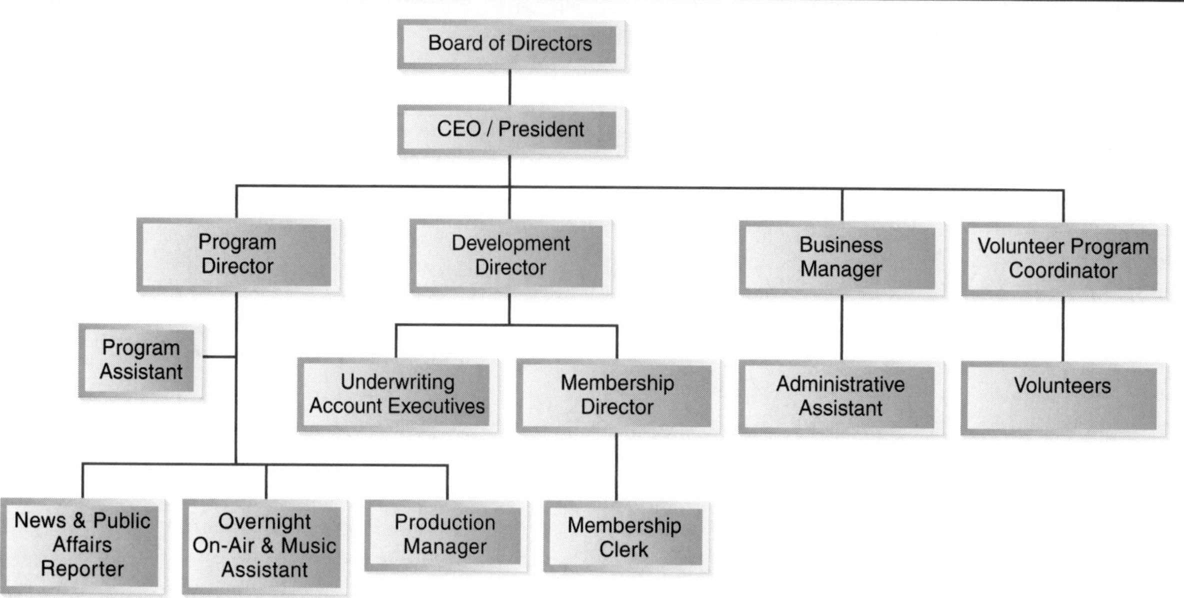

all volunteers. Each issue featured a cover story and photograph of two or three volunteers. The *Scat Sheet* also listed upcoming volunteer opportunities and solicited help, printed letters from volunteers temporarily out of the Denver area, and offered general reminders relevant to the group. Volunteers were also recognized at an annual party, replete with food, drink, and music, of course! The Resource Room was available for use by volunteers and paid staff alike. It contained books, KUVO archives, a computer, and audio-visual equipment. KUVO also rewarded volunteers with pins and other memorabilia.

KUVO LISTENER PROFILE

KUVO's target audience was Denver's Hispanic community. As part of KUVO's mission to "foster appreciation for cultural diversity with an emphasis on the Chicano/Hispanic experience," the station was a voice for the community. Many of the Denver Hispanic community cultural events were announced on KUVO. The station organized "The Milagro Tours," an expedition to New Mexico to explore Native American and southwestern culture. The Hispanic community remained a focal point for KUVO. Paid and volunteer staff included a significant number of Hispanics.

However, the Latino community was not KUVO's primary listening market. KUVO listeners in 1996 composed an audience far different from the one that the station originally set out to serve. A listener profile study completed for KUVO by NPR in 1994 revealed that KUVO's audience fell squarely in the middle class. Specifically, the typical KUVO listener was 42 years old; had an average annual income of $44,000; had completed college; and was a white-collar worker and/or a management employee. Additionally, the listener was likely to have a passport, make investments, and belong to a health club. The study by NPR was the first ever completed for KUVO. Advertising Underwriting and Membership Management used this listener profile information to solicit business contributions.

According to Arbitron, the most widely used measure of radio listenership, KUVO attracted between 1.4 and 1.5 percent of the Denver radio market (estimated at 1,705,800). KHIH's market share was estimated to be around 5 percent. These numbers indicated the percentage of the listening audience tuned in at a particular time of day. Using a diary method, Arbitron determined the demographics and the number of people listening. These numbers were reported on a weekly basis.

MEMBERSHIP DRIVES AND GOALS

Three times a year, the serene KUVO studio was transformed into a frenzied fund drive with phones ringing, people moving about in every available space, and premiums littering the floor. These membership drives were the major effort to solicit money for KUVO. Listeners were urged to pledge, i.e., donate money for the programming that KUVO delivered. By 1996, membership had grown to over 5,300.

The on-air membership drives occurred each year in February, June, and October, the months when most public broadcasting entities conducted fundraising. Membership drives were held for nine days, from Saturday through the following Sunday. The membership drives sought to attract new members, retain current members, increase the number of pledges made by credit card, upgrade members from one level to another, lower the amount of direct mail, and improve the customer service.

There were seven designated membership levels, each accompanied by premiums, such as coffee mugs and t-shirts, bearing the KUVO logo. Members also received a KUVO membership card which entitled them to discounts at over 30 retail businesses in the Denver Metropolitan area and a subscription to the KUVO newsletter, published quarterly.

Prior to the membership drives, KUVO staff and volunteers engaged in extensive business-to-business marketing. The station acquired premiums from retail and restaurant establishments which the target audience was likely to patronize. Premiums had been offered by organizations such as the Colorado Latino Dance Festival, The Shrine Circus, and Los Cabos Mexican Restaurant. Different premiums were offered for certain hours and contribution levels as inducements to call in pledges. The most popular premium was the KUVO t-shirt which bore the logo of various special programming shows. There had been numerous designs over the years, all created by local artists.

An aggressive direct marketing campaign was employed both before and after a membership drive to encourage renewals. Members who had not renewed continued to receive the *Oasis Member Newsletter* as a reminder that they hadn't pledged again. After five notices were mailed, the member was telemarketed.

After a pledge was received, KUVO immediately mailed a pledge form confirming the donation and requesting payment. Members could pay by cash, check, credit card, or through electronic funds transfer (EFT). The KUVO membership director maintained a membership database which contained members' name, address, phone number, premium, and pledge and renewal dates.

SPONSORS AND ALLIANCES

One sixth of KUVO's operating budget came from federal funding. Public broadcasting entities referred to the Republican "Contract with America" as the "Contract *on* America" as the 1995 Republican congress pushed to eliminate federal funding for public broadcasting. Despite an amendment by Rep. Dan Miller (R–Fla.) to sustain funding until 1998, public radio and public television were increasingly forced to be self-sustaining. KUVO was one of the few all-jazz stations not supported by an academic institution. Because of KUVO's small size and lack of academic sponsorship, it was particularly vulnerable to cuts in funds. Industry analysts believed that ". . . without state assistance, the diversity and depth of public radio will be staring down the long, cold barrel of commercial compromise" (Corbett, June 1995).

Corbett's assessment rang true for Hernandez-Ramos. KUVO had already taken steps to make up for the anticipated loss in federal support. One step was the replacement of "Morning Edition," an expensive NPR broadcast, with a 6 AM–9 AM "drive time" music, news and information program "à la Lando" created by KUVO Program Director Carlos Lando, in November 1995.

Another step was a conscientious effort to increase donations from corporate underwriters. Corporate underwriting was public radio's answer to advertising. Underwriting was the solicitation of companies to sponsor, i.e., underwrite, certain programming. KUVO promoted underwriting to corporations by pointing out that "[r]ecent surveys indicate that listeners remember your company name, think positively about the fact that your business supports public radio, and are influenced by this association in their decision to purchase your products or services" (KUVO, 1996). In 1994 and 1995, KUVO underwriting dollars had fallen short of expectations and the new underwriting director was concerned about the lack of funds available for promotion material to solicit additional corporate sponsors for 1996.

KUVO targeted corporations that employed KUVO members or were likely to desire an affiliation with an organization such as KUVO. Approximately 30 percent of underwriting came *from* businesses that called KUVO directly; the remainder were solicited by KUVO staff. There were 40–50 companies that consistently supported the station. Local performing arts organizations, food vendors, bookstores, and automobile dealerships were also notable sponsors, offering discounts to KUVO members. While Denver" [r]adio stations have seen the biggest windfall [in advertising], increasing revenues 39% in the past five years to an estimated $102 million in 1995" (Conklin, 1995), most of this money went to commercial stations. Nevertheless, KUVO's business contributions averaged $300-$400 each, considerably more than the base amount KUVO requested from sponsors in its solicitations.

As a non-profit organization, KUVO also maintained alliances with its struggling counterparts. For numerous non-profit organizations, KUVO provided Public Service Announcements (PSAs), free announcements about events sponsored by the non-profit. KUVO benefited by being named as a media sponsor. These and the underwriting efforts were critical to KUVO, especially as dollars became harder to come by.

KUVO maintained significant business-to-business relationships with both profit and non-profit organizations. In return for sponsoring a KUVO program, an underwriter was entitled to a 20-second spot (in commercial radio, a spot was generally 30 seconds). Legal restrictions regarding advertising on public radio stations severely restricted the potential number of corporate underwriters because these rules were seen as a deterrent to potential sponsors.

The Communications Act required noncommercial licensees to identify sponsors and limited the content and scheduling of those announcements:

> acknowledgments may not promote the for-profit underwriter, its services, facility, or product;
>
> acknowledgments may not contain comparative or qualitative language;
>
> acknowledgments may not contain 'non-identifying verbosity;'
>
> acknowledgments may not contain price information;
>
> acknowledgments may not contain calls to action; and
>
> acknowledgments may not contain inducements to buy, sell, or lease (NFCB, 1994).

KUVO also solicited "partnerships" with local retailers where KUVO members were likely to shop. These businesses offered discounts to KUVO members. Recently, KUVO teamed up with the Wild Oats natural food store to promote its new location. In the *Oasis Member Newsletter*, the store publicly thanked KUVO for making its grand opening a smash. These sort of arrangements served as an effective vehicle for exposing KUVO to the public. KUVO also teamed up with local jazz clubs to promote itself and the partner through remote broadcasts.

KUVO CHALLENGES

KUVO believed that it faced a significant challenge in programming to "stay true" to the Hispanic community. The station was founded with this community in mind and in its mission statement reflected the emphasis on the Chicano experience as key to its success. But jazz music was, in many ways, far from the Hispanic culture. Latin jazz, the fusion of Latin rhythms with jazz, continued to make stronger ties with this culture, but this music was not considered "classic" jazz and was greeted with disdain by many of KUVO's listeners "concerned about the possible loss of REAL jazz radio to the salsa and other non-jazz programs that have been showing up on KUVO . . ." (letter to *Oasis Member Newsletter*, 1996). Despite the listener complaints directed at the Sunday Latin jazz focus, membership drive pledges were highest on Sunday. During the February 1996 membership drive, 1,492 new or renewing members pledged. During the first week, 300 were received on Sunday, and 200 on the second Sunday. This indicated that over one third of all pledges came during programming that accounted for less than 10 percent of the total format hours. In addition to member enthusiasm, KUVO had won a $20,000 grant from the National Endowment for the Humanities to use for "Ritmo Latino," a 13-hour series on African–Cuban music.

While member and sponsor donations continued to increase, operating expenses were expected to rise at a faster pace. In the past, the station had provided informal sales training for the on-air hosts for the membership drives, but lack of money had eliminated further training programs. KUVO volunteers were a dedicated and competent crew, but there was no one currently on KUVO's staff responsible for training and supervision. Though few volunteer tasks required "hand-holding" per se, there was a need for overseeing that a job was done correctly and in a timely manner.

Increased funding was also needed for maintenance of KUVO's transmission equipment. KUVO's transmitter was located on Lookout Mountain, in the city of Golden to the west of Denver, which was the location of numerous Denver radio station transmitters. The power (watts) of a transmitter was a critical component in the distance and quality of radio service delivered. KUVO's signal from the studio was amplified to 25,000 watts of power, guaranteed to deliver KUVO's sounds 60 miles in all directions. Based on member calls, the KUVO signal reached as far north as Cheyenne, Wyoming. However, as KUVO's transmission equipment aged, there were increasing complaints of weak signaling, static, and erratic program transmission in outlying cities and counties. As cable and satellite companies increased their music and entertainment offerings, radio stations were under increased pressure to update their transmission technology to match the clear sound from satellite signals.

Florence Hernandez-Ramios believed that KUVO's ultimate challenge was marketing. KUVO's 1996 budget allocated $35,000 for marketing, most of which was expected to pay for membership premiums such as mugs and t-shirts. Despite the obvious lack of money to support fundraising efforts, all of the department heads expressed confidence as they set to work on a marketing plan for the remainder of the year. Florence Hernandez-Ramos looked at the latest returns and wondered if the station would be able to meet its upcoming expenses. She hoped they were headed in the right direction.

ENDNOTES

1. This term is used interchangeably with "Latin." See Exhibit 1 for definitions.

REFERENCES

Accola, J. (1996, Sept. 20). 'Huge' Hispanic market ignored, consultant says. *Rocky Mountain News*, 2B.

Broadcasting & Cable Yearbook 1995. Volume 1. New Providence, NJ: A Broadcasting and R. R.. Bowker Publication.

Conklin, M. (1995, July 20). Area advertising market is glutted and still growing. *The Rocky Mountain News*, 52A.

Corbett, J. (1995, June). The sorry-assed state of jazz radio: Can it be fixed? *Down Beat*, 30–35.

Farhi, P. (1995, July 13). Big bird taken off death row; Congress may soften on public broadcasting. *The Washington Post*, C0l.

Jacor buys four radio stations in Denver's biggest acquisition. (l996, July 18). *Rocky Mountain News*, 3B.

KUVO. (1995, October, November, December). Future is so bright we need shades! *The Oasis Member Newsletter*.

Lippman, J. (1996, March 18). New telecom law spurs wave of radio-station deals. *The Wall Street Journal*, B1.

Millman, J. (1996, March 5). Infinity is buying 12 radio stations from KKR for total of $410 million. *The Wall Street Journal*, B1.

Mora, P. (1995, July 22). Live from Five Points Media Center puts minorities in broadcasting: Bilingual live-wire KUVO turns 10. *The Denver Post*, E-14.

NFCB, National Federation of Community Broadcasters. (1994, October). *NFCB's Guide to Underwriting For Public Radio*. NFCB: Washington, D.C.

Schwab, R. (1996, Sept. 1996). Hispanic chamber gains new clout. *The Denver Post*, 1G, 20G.

Steers, S. (1993, January 8). New rules prompt flurry of radio sales. *The Denver Business Journal*, 1.

Wehner, P. (1991, November). Over-radioed Denver gets another station. *Colorado Business*, 10.

CASE 24

LEGO

Idunn Eir Jonsdottir
Pedro Nueno
University of Navarra

At LEGO A/S, the board of directors was meeting to discuss the years ahead and LEGO's vision of the future. The company was facing many changes and competition was more intense than ever before in its trading history. As LEGO's design for manufacturing its bricks had inspired companies in many other countries, competition from imitators was also very aggressive. A new management system, Compass Management, had been put into practice; some departments had been merged; and some employees had been transferred to new, unfamiliar surroundings and circumstances. At LEGO, people knew that maintaining the popularity of the brick might prove to be more of a challenge in the future. Competition from child-oriented computer entertainment was growing and the market was coming to be dominated by fashion products. Children too were changing; they were getting older more quickly, a phenomenon known as KGOY. Attracting children who were used to the boundaries of computer games was a marketing challenge.

Although LEGO was a widely known toy brand name, the company's goal was to do better and have the LEGO logo and name known as the strongest brand in the world by the year 2005. To reach that goal it was necessary to keep pace with changing tastes. In recent years, the company had moved from supplying the bricks as raw material to selling themed sets and branded themed ranges. Some felt that in doing so the brand was losing its way. They said there was a danger of LEGO forgetting what had made the brand famous—the fact that it allowed children free expression.

Another thing that needed to be discussed was the fact that LEGO's overall sales in 1996 had not lived up to expectations and LEGO was losing market share in some countries. LEGO's consumer sales—sales by retailers to their customers—had risen by only 2 percent in 1996, compared with almost 4 percent in 1995 and even more in 1994.

THE HISTORY—"ONLY THE BEST IS GOOD ENOUGH"

The LEGO Group Today

In 1997 the LEGO Group was one of the world's top ten toy manufacturers; it was the only European company on the list, and a leader in the construction toy sector. It had 9,200 employees in 50 companies in 29 countries, of whom 4,210 worked in Denmark. The company was based in Billund, Denmark, and was fully owned and managed by Kjeld Kirk Kristiansen and his wife and two children. There were LEGO factories in five countries: Denmark, Switzerland, the USA, Brazil, and Korea. In Brazil and Korea, production was for the local market. The factory in the USA served the large North American market, including Canada and Mexico. The LEGO Group also had three mold factories, in Switzerland and Germany. In 1996 LEGO products were sold in about 130 countries throughout the world in more than 60,000 retail outlets. There were 25 LEGO sales companies and 82 distributors all over the world. Over the previous 40 years, around 400 million children had played

This case is intended to be used as a basis for class discussion rather than to illustrate either effective or ineffective handling of an administrative situation.

Copyright © 1998, IESE.

with LEGO bricks. The 1997 product line consisted of 515 sets, put together from 1,964 different elements. There were six product lines and nearly all the elements were compatible with each other, even with the elements dating back to the 1950s.

Early History of the LEGO Group

The history of the LEGO company can be traced back to 1932, when Ole Kirk Christiansen, the LEGO Group's founder, set up his business in Billund, a little village with only a handful of houses located in the middle of southern Jutland in Denmark. The firm manufactured stepladders, ironing boards, and wooden toys and had seven employees. Ole's son Godtfred Kirk Christiansen started actively working in the business from the beginning, although he was only 12 years old at the time.

The depression of the 1930s, which began with the Wall Street crash in 1929, had an impact on the entire industrial world. Times were hard for Denmark's main industry at that time, agriculture. Local farmers were Ole Kirk Christiansen's most important customers and the greatly reduced demand for his services almost pushed him into bankruptcy.

Ole Kirk did not give up. He believed that, although people could not afford to build houses, there was—in the short term—business potential in producing wooden toys. He realized that children always needed toys, so in 1932 he began producing wooden toys by hand in his small workshop.

In 1934 the company and its products were given a new name, LEGO, which is formed from the Danish words "Leg Godt," which in English mean "play well." Later it was discovered that in Latin the word "lego" means "I study," "I put together." A few years later, Ole Kirk's motto hung on the wall of the workshop: "Only the best is good enough." With this motto to guide it, the business eventually became successful, selling high-quality, robust toys to toyshops all over Denmark. It was a struggle in the early years, but it was during this period that the foundations were laid for the worldwide success the company was later to achieve. Exhibit 1 shows some interesting landmarks in the history of LEGO from 1932 to 1996.

New Material, New Methods

In 1944 the company was converted into a family-owned limited company, which it still was in 1997. In 1947 the LEGO company was Denmark's first company to buy a plastics injection-molding machine for making toys. At that time, the company produced 200 different plastic and wooden toys, including Automatic Binding Bricks, a forerunner of the LEGO bricks that we know today. The factory had a total area of 2,300 m^2 and approximately 50 employees. The products were sold only in Denmark. Six years later, Godtfred Kirk Christiansen was appointed junior director on his 30th birthday.

The LEGO System of Play

The word "LEGO" was officially registered in Denmark on May 1, 1954. A year later, after further developing its LEGO bricks, the company launched the revolutionary "LEGO System of Play" and started exporting it to Sweden and Norway. The first proper sales company outside Denmark was founded in Germany in 1956. Sales companies in a number of other European countries, including Great Britain, France, Switzerland, and Sweden, were established in 1960. In 1958 the definitive LEGO stud-and-tube coupling system (the brick) was invented and patented. The new coupling principle ensured that models were stable and allowed all possible combinations, running into astronomical figures. In 1958 Ole Kirk Christiansen died and Godtfred Kirk Christiansen became the head of the company. In 1960 the wooden-toy warehouse was destroyed by fire. The company's management decided to cease production of wooden toys and concentrate exclusively on plastics. The Danish LEGO companies now employed 450 people, with factory/office premises totaling 6,000 m^2. In 1967 the DUPLO brick was invented and a patent applied for. The DUPLO series was eight times bigger than basic LEGO bricks—twice as long, twice as wide, and twice as high—so it was easier for small hands to manipulate.

In 1970 LEGO opened a new production organization in Billund and a production area of 18,000 m^2 was built, with new facilities that included raw material warehousing, a molding shop, and assembly and packing departments. There were 975 employees at the LEGO headquarters and close to 30,000 m^2 under cover. In the following years LEGO launched new models and series every year and, among other things, presented a new concept, the LEGO family. The set immediately be-

1 | Interesting World and LEGO Events, 1932–1995

1932:

Ole Kirk Christiansen starts his own toy-manufacturing company. There are 7 employees at the Billund workshop.

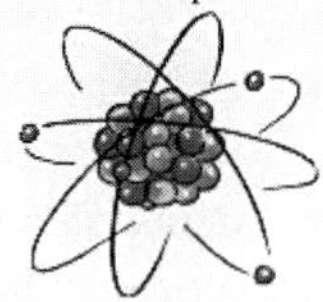

The atom is split for the first time.

1934:

LEG GODT!

The words "leg godt" (play well) are contracted to form the word LEGO, which becomes the name of the company and its wooden toys.

Launch of the "Queen Mary", the world's largest ship.

1947:

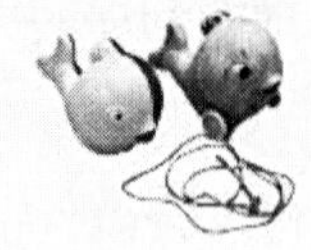

The first plastic LEGO products are introduced in Denmark.

The sound barrier is broken by aircraft for the first time.

1949:

Automatic Binding Bricks–forerunners of LEGO bricks–are launched in Denmark.

1955:

"The LEGO System of Play" is launched.

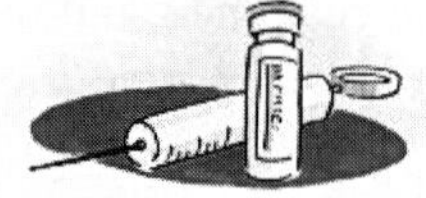

The first polio vaccine.

1958:

The LEGO clutch principle is invented by Godtfred Kirk Christiansen.

Inauguration of the first North Atlantic non-stop scheduled air service.

1960:

Fire at the Billund wood-products warehouse. Production of wooden toys stops.

1966:

LEGO Train and 4.5 V motors introduced.

First synthetic protein (insulin).

1967:

The DUPLO brick is developed and a patent application is filed.

The first battery-powered, cordless telephone.

1968:

LEGOLAND Park opens in Billund.

1973:

Introduction of the present LEGO logo.

1 | Interesting World and LEGO Events, 1932–1995 *(Continued)*

1974:

The first LEGO figures join the range. LEGO production extends outside Denmark–first in Switzerland.

The first direct TV transmission via satellite.

1977:

Launch of LEGO TECHNIC.

1979:

Launch of LEGO Space. Kjeld Kirk Kristiansen becomes President of the LEGO Group's international management company.

Nuclear accident at Three Mile Island.

1982:

Technic I is launched in the schools programme.

1986:

British schoolchildren are the first to get LEGO Technic Computer Control.

1987:

The LEGO storage bucket is introduced.

1989:

Introduction of the Pirate line.

1990:

The biggest Model Team set contains the elements to make such models as a truck, a trailer and a helicopter.

Hubble telescope is launched.

1992:

DUPLO Toolo is the year's new line.

1994:

The LEGO TECHNIC Super Car (with almost 1,300 elements) is launched.

The first genetically engineered food–a tomato–is now on sale.

1995:

DUPLO Primo is launched for the very young.

1996:

LEGOLAND Windsor opens.

came a huge commercial hit and was equally popular with boys and girls. In 1977 Kjeld Kirk Kristiansen—third generation—joined the LEGO Group's management. Since 1980 he has been the President and CEO of LEGO A/S, the LEGO Group's international management company.

LEGOLAND

Other important events in the history of the LEGO Group include the opening of the LEGOLAND parks. The first was opened in Billund in June 1968, then came LEGOLAND Windsor in the spring of 1996. The third LEGOLAND park was to be in Carlsbad, California, opening in 1999.

After its opening in 1968, LEGOLAND soon became Denmark's most popular tourist attraction outside Copenhagen, with 1.3 million visitors in 1996 and 25 million visitors since it started. LEGOLAND was a family park containing LEGO models of buildings and scenes from many countries. More than 45 million LEGO bricks were used to build the models, which were made by the LEGO model builders. Visitors could wander through a wealth of miniature versions of famous buildings or entire districts from almost every corner of the globe. Every year large new LEGO Theme Shows were on display in the park's indoor exhibitions. LEGOLAND Billund also had several collections, such as old mechanical toys and antique dolls.

The LEGOLAND parks had nine characteristics:

- the child was the focal point
- enthusiasm and interaction between adult and child
- a world of fun and learning
- participation and creation
- all LEGO brands were shown at their best
- Miniland—attractive landscaping and gardening
- intimacy
- highest standards of safety and quality
- positive contribution to the local community

THE TOY INDUSTRY

Figures

In 1996 the child population was 53.85 million in the USA, 21.37 million in Japan, 12.2 million in Germany, 10.9 million in Britain, 11.3 million in France, and 9.6 million in Italy. In these countries, around 51 percent of children were male and 49 percent female. With the decline in the birth rate, 1995 marked the peak of the market's expansion.

Consumption per child under 15 years old was highest in the USA. Of the European countries, consumption was highest in France. Worldwide, infant, and preschool children had been receiving a bigger share, per person, of toy spending than other children. The average spending per child of up to four years was estimated to be about 207 ECU a year in 1996, compared with about 177 ECU for children aged 5–9, and a mere 55 ECU for children aged 10–14.

The Consumer

Children up to the age of 15 were the toy industry's consumers. Each age had its own games and its own toys. Exhibit 2 shows how the people at LEGO's Marketing Department had defined four stages through which children passed in the way they played with toys.

A lot of research, including research carried out at LEGO, had shown that when children were very small, there were no big differences in the things that boys and girls liked to play with. This situation could change surprisingly early on in life, and children could become aware of their gender as early as 18 months. The things that girls and boys found important were usually very different. Research at LEGO had shown that while boys loved the actual process of building, girls were more interested in doing something with the product once it had been made. They attached importance to such concepts as sweet, pretty, soft, "like mummy," transformation, dreams, and hope. For boys, important concepts were "can do something," "can be done," hard, big, and strong identity.

Buying Decision

Mothers were considered to be the overwhelming influence on purchasing for their children. The younger the child, the more sensitive a toy purchase was likely to be. This had important implications for branding and for the retail outlets where such toys were sold. In 1996 about 45 percent of mothers were first-time mothers, while 55 percent had already had a baby. Some of the toys bought for first-born children would still be around for their siblings and this could restrict sales in some

2 | The LEGO Consumer

At LEGO's marketing department, the "five ages of childhood" were defined as follows:

- **From birth to toddler.** The first transition is from baby to toddler at 15–18 months. Until that age, children do not play; they work really hard to find out what they can do with their hands and bodies. They knock over everything they get their hands on, and all objects go straight "from hand to mouth." The next phase is when their attention focuses on their immediate surroundings, especially on what they can do with an object: what is "inside," "under," and "behind" it, and how it "works." Objects do not always do exactly what the child wants, so frustration and "defiance" are characteristic of this age group. But everything the little child does is still an intensive working and learning process, not play.
- **The three-year-old.** The second distinct age threshold is at about age three. Now the child wants to play with other children and exchange knowledge and experiences. He or she chooses playmates, seeks company, and is open and free from prejudice. They become very interested in everyday life, the many interesting roles it involves, and the way things are done. They want realistic explanations, use questions to stimulate conversation, and enjoy being given simple tasks. Daily life is described through stories and drawings.
- **Now we are six.** The third transition comes at about the age of six. It involves both chaos and growing pains. The urge to be active is enormous and children try to be independent to show that they are "big." However, as they are neither big nor little, there are often small crises in their relationships with friends and family. They begin to develop a sense of morality and discuss what is permitted and what is not. Open-mouthed parents sometimes find themselves on the receiving end of very thorough lessons in "right" and "wrong." A sense of time begins to be acquired, and children start to turn away from the down-to-earth and toward the imaginative and fictitious.
- **Children of 10–11 years.** The fourth threshold occurs at about the age of 10 or 11, as children steadily increase their competence in reading and writing. They become "alphabetized" and symbol-oriented, and become aware that adults give a higher priority to skills in this area than to drawing or spontaneous talk and song.

  The child seeks harmony and security. He or she is harmonious and independent, so irony and ridicule hurt deeply. Challenges are sought, limits are tested, and the child starts to learn how to manipulate his or her surroundings.

  But at last! By this time, childhood is almost over and just a year later the world changes catastrophically for many children when they experience puberty.
- **The disappearance of spontaneity.** These four distinctive "thresholds" do actually occur between birth and puberty. Each age has its own form of play and its own toys. Together, these periods form an entire life, or universe, in themselves. But with the fourth threshold, the last of childhood's spontaneity disappears, however sad a thought this may be for us adults who have been through the process.

  Play nevertheless remains an enormously strong impulse in human nature; it is essential if the individual is to achieve a meaningful existence in his or her relationships with other people. Fortunately, for most people, play continues into adulthood and, it is to be hoped, for the rest of their lives.

cases. Some much more important factors, however, operated in favor of giving each new child its full "entitlement" of new toys:

- Working mothers who left their children with nannies and childminders might try to assuage feelings of guilt by buying toys.
- The high divorce rate created a growing number of friends and relatives per child, and thus more toys.
- The average age of mothers was rising, so they and their household had more earning power and could buy more toys.

LEGO's Market Share

In 1996 LEGO was the fifth biggest toy manufacturer in the world, with a turnover of ECU 1,027 million. LEGO's market share in the traditional toy market was 9.1 percent in Europe, 1.7 percent in the USA, and 1 percent in Japan. In the construction toy sector LEGO was the leader in all of its markets.

Competitors

The biggest toy manufacturing company in the world was the American company Mattel, with a turnover of

ECU 3,411 million in 1996. Mattel had achieved success by manufacturing Disney toys and Barbie dolls, but it also had products such as Fisher-Price (since 1994), Hot Wheels, and Frisbees. Mattel had recently expanded by buying up Tyco, one of the companies that was imitating LEGO's products.

Hasbro Inc. was another U.S. company, with a turnover of ECU 2,698 million. It was best known for its film toys, such as Star Wars, Batman, Jurassic Park, etc.

Sega Enterprises (Japan, turnover ECU 2,452 million) and Nintendo (Japan, ECU 2,137 million) had both found their place in the toy industry with computer games. Nintendo, which in late 1995 was the biggest in the toy industry, was planning to launch a computer game that used 64-bit instead of 32-bit technology.

According to LEGO, the competition in recent years was stiffer than ever, with numerous new digital products making their breakthrough into the markets. Competition from LEGO's imitators was also more aggressive.

The competition in the construction segment of the toy market was also increasing. Two of LEGO's competitors in this sector had been growing fast. K'NEX was a company that was determined to make a success of the construction market, and 1997 was proving to be a good year. In 1996 K'NEX had taken its highest ever share (19 percent) of the U.K. construction toy market. The company's new toy ranges had proved a clear winner, with year-on-year sales growth of over 35 percent. In 1997 K'NEX was planning to break into the educational market, launching its first new sets for schools. Exhibit 3 shows an advertisement for K'NEX in a toy magazine. Ritvik was another company in the construction toy sector. It was the world's second largest marketer of building blocks. It had posted record sales in 1996, with 25 percent growth worldwide.

Distribution

There had been intense competition in the retail sector throughout the world and retailer financing had been tough in recent years, resulting in price competition and late ordering. Large retailers, such as Toys 'R' Us and Wal-Mart, were getting larger and larger and therefore more dominant. There had been big changes in the distribution channels, especially in the USA, where the small local retailers had been losing sales to the chains. For the last five years the percentages of LEGO sales that went through the largest five retailer chains had grown from 65 percent to 74 percent. In Europe, the changes in distribution had not been so rapid, except in Holland, where LEGO was starting to sell its products through only five big chains.

LEGO had developed a strong and mutually beneficial relationship with Toys 'R' Us, which was developing a new store concept, making its stores more consumer-friendly. Part of the store was handed over to selected vendors, including LEGO, who were given the opportunity to create in-store boutiques in their own traditional format. Toys 'R' Us would then hire outside store-design agencies to help it create the store of the future, the Concept 2000.

UK Toy News, one of the leading toy trade magazines in Great Britain and Ireland, runs an annual survey in which retailers are asked what they think about the toy industry. The survey conducted in March 1997 had four questions. First, retailers were asked to score suppliers, on a scale of 1 to 10 (with 10 being the highest), for their "product performance" in 1996. A similar question was asked about "service performance." The third question asked, "How seriously do you rate the threat of the retailers listed?" And the last question asked, "How strong do you think the various toy categories will be in 1997?"

The results are shown in Exhibit 4.

Another survey carried out by *UK Toy News* in April 1997 asked retailers in the U.K. to rank the top-selling items by units. The results are shown in Exhibit 5.

The Market Situation

Seasonal sales have always been a feature of the toy industry, with 60 percent of sales in the last six weeks before Christmas.

LEGO's consumer sales, i.e., sales by retailers to their customers, rose by 2 percent in 1996 compared with almost 4 percent in 1995. There were both increases and decreases in this area. In North America, total consumer sales rose by around 9 percent. In Europe, in spite of a 40 percent rise in sales in the East European countries, there was only a very modest overall advance compared with 1995. To the great surprise of LEGO's managers, there was a 20 percent fall in the company's sales to end-consumers in Japan.

EXHIBIT

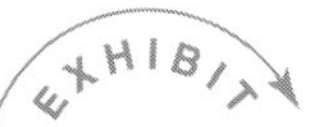

3 | LEGO Construction Toys

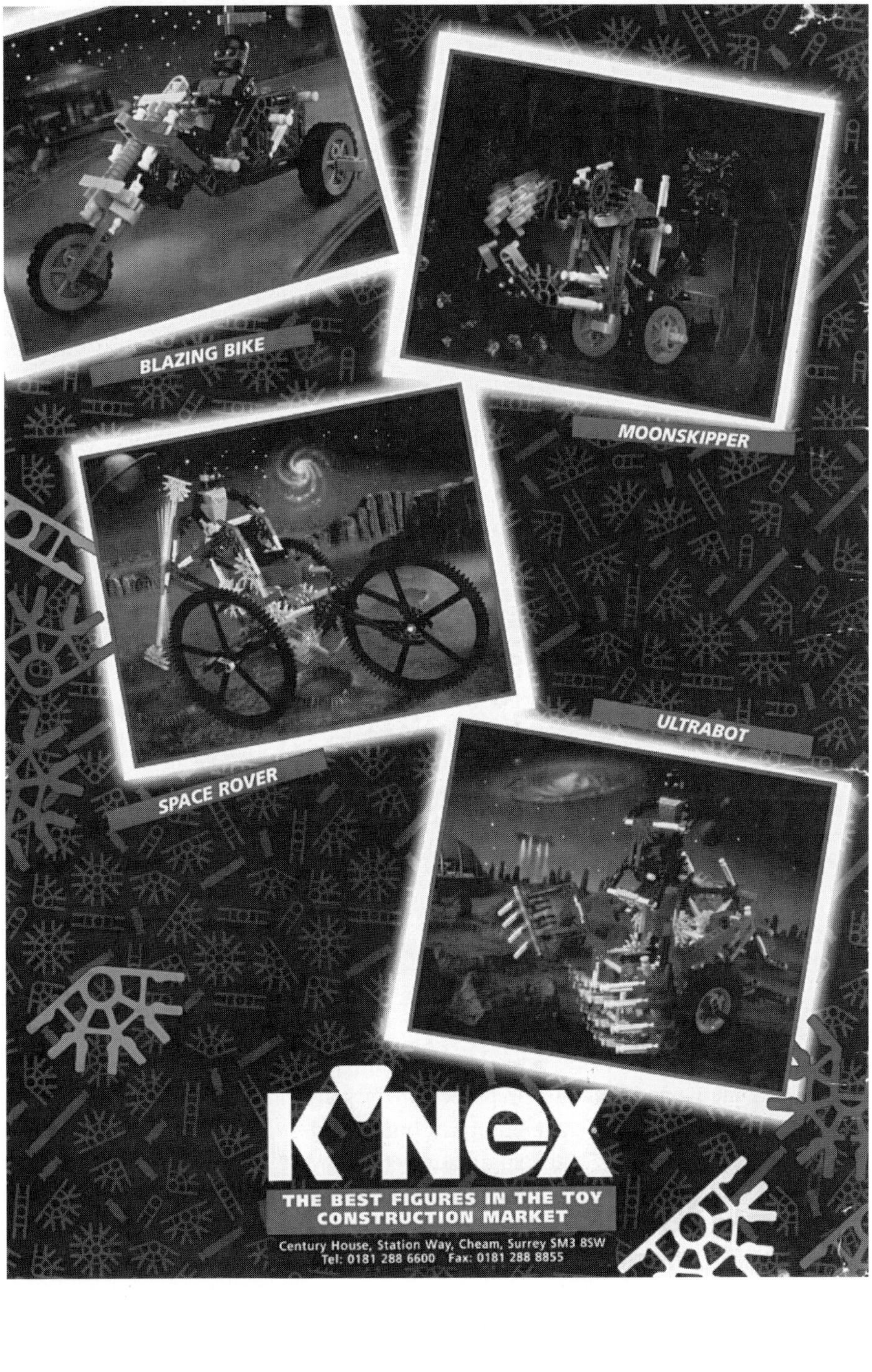

BLAZING BIKE
MOONSKIPPER
SPACE ROVER
ULTRABOT
K'NEX
THE BEST FIGURES IN THE TOY CONSTRUCTION MARKET
Century House, Station Way, Cheam, Surrey SM3 8SW
Tel: 0181 288 6600 Fax: 0181 288 8855

EXHIBIT 4 | UK Toy News Survey Results, March 1997

Top Ten Suppliers by Product Performance	Top Ten Suppliers by Service Performance
1. LEGO Great Britain	1. LEGO Great Britain
2. Toy options	2. Playmobil
3. Mattel	3. Tomy
4. Playmobil	4. K'Nex
5. Hasbro	5. TP Activity Toys
6. TP Activity Toys	6. Toy Options
7. Corinthian	7. Dekkertoys
8. K'Nex	8. Hornby
9. Tomy	9. Meccano
10. United Overseas	10. Goliath

Top Retail Threats	Top Product Categories
1. Woolworths	1. Male action figures
2. Argos	2. Fashion dolls
3. Toys 'R' Us	3. Games

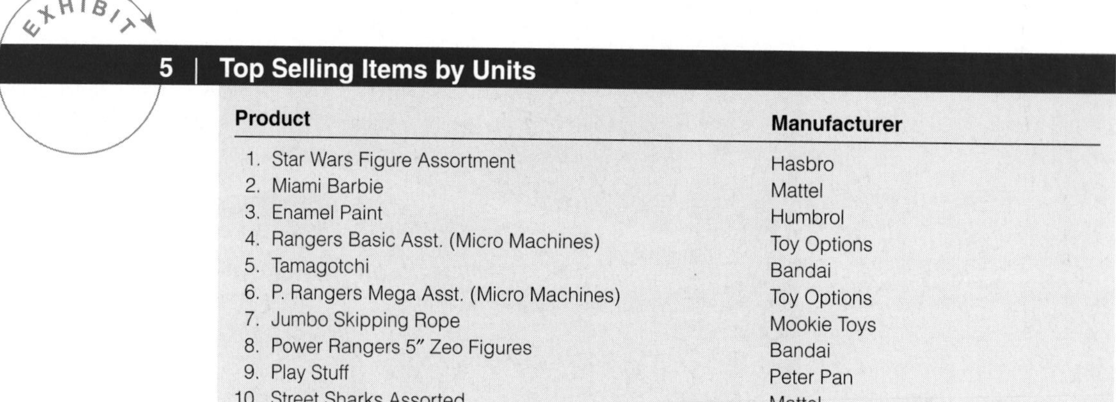

EXHIBIT 5 | Top Selling Items by Units

Product	Manufacturer
1. Star Wars Figure Assortment	Hasbro
2. Miami Barbie	Mattel
3. Enamel Paint	Humbrol
4. Rangers Basic Asst. (Micro Machines)	Toy Options
5. Tamagotchi	Bandai
6. P. Rangers Mega Asst. (Micro Machines)	Toy Options
7. Jumbo Skipping Rope	Mookie Toys
8. Power Rangers 5" Zeo Figures	Bandai
9. Play Stuff	Peter Pan
10. Street Sharks Assorted	Mattel

There were thought to be several reasons for the modest growth in consumer sales. In particular, the general consumption of the average European household was falling. Germany and Switzerland had been hit by unemployment in recent years, which had influenced toy purchases. In addition, the fight for the time and favor of children and their parents was intensifying.

LEGO's 1996 league table for the ten largest markets measured by retail sales was, in descending order: Germany, the USA, France, Benelux, Great Britain, Japan, Korea, Italy, Austria, and Russia.

LEGO'S ORGANIZATIONAL STRUCTURE

LEGO was divided into two business areas: core business and new business. Exhibit 6 shows the organizational chart. The core business area, which included construction toys, was further divided into three areas:

- Sales and marketing
- Manufacturing
- Product development (LEGO Futura)

6 | LEGO Corporate Management Organization

Country	Company	Established
Denmark	LEGO A/S	1975

Core Business

Product Development

Country	Company	Established
Denmark	LEGO Futura A/S	1959
Great Britain	LEGO Futura A/S, London Branch	1997
Italy	LEGO Futura A/S, Milano Branch	1997
Japan	LEGO Futura A/S, Tokyo Development Center	1991
USA	LEGO Futura A/S, Boston Branch	1989

Manufacturing

Country	Company	Established
Brazil	LEGO do Brasil Ltda. Manaus	1986
Denmark	LEGO System A/S	1932
	LEGO Engineering A/S	1991
Germany	LEGO Werkzeugbau GmbH	1958
	Hohenwestedt, Holstein	1958
Hong Kong	LEGO Company Ltd. (Purchasing)	1994
Hungary	LMM Kft., Budapest	1992
Korea	LEGO Korea Co., Seoul	1985
Switzerland	INTERLEGO AG (Technical research and development), Hagendorn Züg	1974
	LEGO Produktion AG, Baar, Züg Willisau, Lucerne	1974
	LEGO Werkzeugbau Steinhausen, Züg	1974
	LEGO Werkzeugbau AG, Au. St. Gallen	1985
USA	LEGO Systems, Inc., Enfield, Connecticut	1975

Sales and Marketing

Country	Company	First Sale	Founded
Argentina	LEGO Overseas A/S, Branch Argentina*	1967	1996
Australia	LEGO Australia Pty. Limited	1962	1962
Austria	LEGO Handelsges. mbH	1957	1963
Belgium	LEGO Benelux B.V.**	1958	1959
Brazil	LEGO do Brasil Ltda.	1986	1984
Canada	LEGO Canada Inc.	1961	1988
Czech Republic	LEGO Trading S.R.O.	1972	1997
Denmark	LEGO Denmark A/S	1932	1944
	LEGO System A/S	1932	1973
	LEGO Trading A/S	1980	1980
	LEGO Overseas A/S	1962	1974
Finland	Oy Suomen LEGO Ab	1959	1960
France	LEGO S.A.	1956	1959
Germany	LEGO GmbH	1956	1956
Great Britain	LEGO U.K. Limited	1959	1959
Hungary	LEGO Hungaria Kft.	1973	1992
Italy	LEGO S.p.A.	1958	1961
Japan	LEGO Japan Ltd.	1962	1978
Korea	LEGO Korea Co., Ltd.	1985	1984
Mexico	LEGO Mexico S.A. de C.A.	1987	1995
Netherlands	LEGO Benelux B.V.**	1957	1960
New Zealand	LEGO New Zealand Ltd.	1971	1995
Norway	LEGO Norge AS	1953	1962
Poland	LEGO Polska Sp.Zo.o.	1973	1995
Portugal	LEGO, LDA	1957	1976
Russia	LEGO Trading A/S*	1987	1996
Singapore	LEGO Singapore, Private Limited	1962	1979
	LEGO Asia Pte. Ltd.		1997
South Africa	LEGO South Africa (Pty.) Limited	1962	1993
Spain	LEGO S.A.	1965	1974
Sweden	LEGO Sverige AB	1955	1959
Switzerland	LEGO Vertrieb AG	1957	1957
Turkey	LEGO Trading A/S*	1983	1997
USA	LEGO Systems, Inc.	1961	1973

Some dates refer to the year the company was established, while others refer to the start of current activities.
*Representative offices
**LEGO Benelux B.V. was established in 1996

New Business Areas

Family Parks

Country	Company	Established
Denmark	LEGOLAND Development A/S	1991
	LEGOLAND A/S	1968
Great Britain	LEGOLAND Park Windsor UK Ltd.	1992
	LEGO Park Design Ltd.	1994
USA	LEGOLAND Carlsbad, Inc.	1996

Preschool and school products

Country	Company	Established
Denmark	LEGO Dacta A/S	1980
	LEGO Dacta Procurement A/S	1989
France	LEGO Dacta A/S, Chartres Sales branch	1996
Germany	LEGO Dacta Lernmittel GmbH	1992
Great Britain	LEGO Dacta A/S, Wrexham Sales branch	1996
Italy	LEGO Dacta A/S, Lainate Sales branch	1996
USA	LEGO Dacta A/S, Development and sale of school products, Enfield	1995

Software for Children

Country	Company	Established
Great Britain	LEGO Media Int. Ltd.	1996

Licensed Products

Country	Company	Established
Denmark	LEGO Licensing A/S	1991
Great Britain	LEGO Licensing International Ltd.	1994

The new business area had four subareas:

- **LEGO DACTA.** Since 1980. The objective of this area was to meet the particular needs of childcare institutions and schools for learning systems and educational materials that combined play, entertainment, and learning.
- **LEGOLAND Parks.** Since 1968. This business area aimed to provide an attractive day out for families with children aged 2–13.
- **LEGO Licensing.** Since 1993. This business area entered into cooperation agreements with companies that targeted quality products at children and families with children, allowing them to use the LEGO brand name. An important objective for these activities was to increase brand visibility and relevance. It was also an independent profit center which had to contribute to the LEGO Group's profits. The range of licensed products included children's clothing, watches, and bags.
- **LEGO Media.** This was a new business area established in mid-1996 to develop software, music, video, and film projects for children. Its activities were intended to build on close relationships with carefully selected top-quality developers and publishers of products in the children's media sector. There were six people working at LEGO Media, all of whom had a background in computer games or licensing. It was not clear when they would be in a position to make the results of their work public.

Each business area had to develop its own competitive and globally optimized business system, which had to fulfill the following requirements:

- Strong and close consumer contact
- Strong commitment to research and product development
- Efficient management systems
- Well-educated, qualified, and motivated employees
- An efficient, flat organization without overlapping functions
- Focus on what the company is, or ought to be, good at.

These were LEGO's core skills and core processes—i.e., they added value for the benefit of LEGO's consumers. In other areas it was becoming increasingly necessary to ask whether it would not be more appropriate to let others do the work for LEGO, unless strategic considerations justified LEGO's carrying out these tasks itself.

While each business area had to operate independently, it was important to exploit the benefits of joint coordination and close cooperation between business areas. These benefits were obtained by ensuring a common perception and strengthening of the LEGO brand, the sharing of ideas and experiences between business areas, cooperation in product and system development, quality systems, access to consumers, and development of human resources.

In recent years LEGO had been conducting a number of development projects, two of which were of strategic importance: DARWIN and LEGO MINDSTORMS. DARWIN involved researching and developing new digital media products and designing a database to hold all the elements and boxes produced by the LEGO Group in digital form. LEGO MINDSTORMS was aimed at developing a number of robots and an educational program for use in the home.

CORPORATE CULTURE AND PHILOSOPHY—"CHILDREN ARE OUR VITAL CONCERN"

For a company like LEGO it was vital to take children's interests and needs seriously. LEGO considered its basic task to be to stimulate children's imagination and creativity, encouraging them to explore, experience, and express their own world—a world without limits.

LEGO had three guiding principles: To be a good corporate citizen, to be a global business that traded everywhere in accordance with the interests and culture of the local community, and to be a workplace in which employees were safe and healthy and had the opportunity for personal development.

The LEGO culture was built on respect for the individual employee, the customers, and the consumers. The corporate culture was rooted in the history of the LEGO Group, its unique product and concept, the attitudes of the Kirk Christiansen family, and the company's long-term objective of remaining financially independent. As one manager at LEGO said,

> *The fact that the LEGO company is a family company that is drawn to traditions has influenced its devel-*

opment in a big way. There have been lots of times when everybody knew everything about everything, but gradually the company is growing and growing, and you see that there's a serious need to change things. That's what is happening right now, with Compass Management, with all its pros and cons, because there are so many people who've worked here for over 20 years, and they're not so keen on changes.

LEGO wanted the following principles to be active ingredients of its corporate culture:

Consumer focus: LEGO's consumers are the starting point and the end goal for all the company's activities—from the moment a product is developed to the moment it is played with.

Openness: Exchange of information, internally as well as externally. Easy access to information, cooperation, and personal dialogue—spontaneous and planned.

Market leadership: The LEGO Group must set the standard in meeting the genuine requirements of children and of families with children. It must offer quality products that stimulate children's imagination and creativity and motivate them to explore, experience, and express their own world—a world without limits.

Results: A prerequisite for progress and attainment of goals is an ongoing evaluation of LEGO's results against the objectives that are set at the company.

Action orientation: To lead the way implies taking certain risks—but to act and to learn from one's actions is better than doing nothing.

Shared mindset: Empowerment and quick, efficient decision-making depend on having a common understanding based on the same values. LEGO must be in agreement over its direction and how best to achieve the company's objectives.

Simplicity: The less complicated the organization, the more efficient its actions in an increasingly complex world.

Employees

At LEGO the importance of there being coherence between the corporate objectives, the objectives of individual business areas, and those of employees was emphasized. "We should all have a clear idea of what we are building together, while at the same time, of course, having specific tasks in the overall process. Only if we have the same understanding of where we've come from, where we are today and which direction we must take in the future can we work closely together to realize our plans," said Kjeld Kirk Kristiansen, LEGO's president. To help build up a common understanding, employees were given a booklet that summarized LEGO's strategic platform with all kinds of general information about the company and its products.

LEGO considered its employees to be its most important resource. The following was LEGO's personnel policy:

- We must create a working climate in which employees regard change and adaptation as a way to personal development and realizing their potential.
- We must develop a workplace that has clearly expressed expectations and requirements. This will best enable employees to perform their jobs effectively.
- We must develop management systems and managers' qualifications in order to ensure the best possible business system based on process orientation and teamwork.
- We must maintain good physical and psychological working conditions for all our employees.

When one of LEGO's managers was asked how the company attracted and selected individuals to the company, he replied:

We've often thought that it would be very difficult to attract employees to a place like Billund, in the middle of nowhere, but it has never been a problem. I think that what attracts people to the company is its reputation. It is highly regarded, it stands for quality from top to bottom, and everybody knows they can learn a lot. And if they've been here for some years, they can always find a job somewhere else. Part of it has to do with a professional reputation, and part of it with the company's reputation for treating its people very well. I think that's an important factor, because it's definitely not the salaries. We've always told our employees that we're not a leading company as far as salaries are concerned, but we have other ways of treating people. I think, originally, it all comes from the owner. The way he used to treat people and the way his son is now treating people. It's not a bossy organization but a very human one; when top management act the way they do at LEGO, where the doors are always open and the atmosphere is relaxed, it influences the whole organization. The other aspect is the specific things we do. We do things for people's welfare; for example, we offer lectures, concerts, tickets to the LEGOLAND park. We have a certain day in the summer when ice-cream is bought for everyone, and another day when there's an open day at the factory, so employees can invite their family and children to come and visit the LEGO factory; people get Christmas presents, etc. All this gives you the feeling that the company cares for you.

Do you look for people with many years of work experience or do you recruit people straight from school?

We take people right out of school, certainly. We have lots of educational programs. We take a lot of young people and train them. We very rarely hire experienced top managers; there are a few examples, but usually we recruit from within the company.

Are there many young people in the company?

We've recently taken in a lot of young people. For the time being, we also have a big group of people in the 50–60 age bracket, especially at presidential level, people who have grown within the company. But in general it's a young company.

Do you look for a certain profile in people?

Of course, quality for the job; but a certain profile, yes, people must fit into the organization. We look for people who are well qualified, but at the same time people who have the personal qualities that will help them fit into the company. For example, it's very important that employees, especially those working in the development department, should like children. We take in ambitious people, but probably not the most aggressive ones (this isn't a policy, though, more a question of culture).

How do you ensure that employees are clear about their responsibilities?

We have a job description for every job, and it is a management responsibility to make sure that every employee knows his job. We also have what we call a conversation with the employees every year; even though we have a philosophy of talking openly about things whenever they come up, this yearly thing gives us a chance to talk about career plans and ambitions, what's good and bad in the company, suggestions for improvements in the department, the job profile, and so on; plus, you get feedback and set targets for the following year.

COMPASS MANAGEMENT

At the end of 1995, in response to the decline in sales and profits in that year and in order to speed up decision-making, the LEGO Group began to implement a philosophy known as Compass Management. A manager at LEGO made the following observations about the company before Compass Management: "We used to be an organization where we discussed everything, and everything had somehow to go up to top management. It was very important to have consensus, maybe a little bit Japanese."

The purpose of Compass Management was to change the organizational structure from a traditional division along functional lines to one that enabled optimal interplay between and within all the business processes and that increased competitiveness. Compass Management gave directions, but people had to find their own way to reach their goals within the company's framework. It was about being willing to explore new paths, accept risks, believe in simplicity, and trust in individual employees' efficiency and willingness to assume responsibility, their pioneering spirit, initiative, and energy.

LEGO used Compass Management to help reach the following goals:

- Strengthen the company's ability to react more quickly and efficiently to meet the demands of its market and consumers.
- Shift from being functionally oriented toward being a process-oriented company.
- Make things simpler and more transparent.
- Focus on the core processes and fundamental skills.
- Make decisions/take action faster.

Five focus areas were defined:

- Clarification of the corporate center and the roles and responsibilities of corporate staff.
- Streamlining of the service organization and application of ideas globally wherever appropriate.
- Establishment of a flexible/responsive European and global supply chain.
- Strengthening of the sales/marketing processes, particularly with regard to the European market area and marketing activities at Billund.
- Simplification of the company's legal structure in Billund.

Compass Management had led to greater collaboration between departments. A manager at LEGO said that although people had always worked together even before Compass Management, they were now working more in a project way. He also said that it took time to change a company's management style and that the process was still evolving and finding its way.

THE PRODUCT—"LIMITLESS OPPORTUNITIES FOR PLAY"

LEGO had both simple, basic elements and specialized composite elements, large components for small, unschooled and curious fingers and tiny ones for the very complex models. The various LEGO components were divided into five independent product programs: LEGO PRIMO, LEGO DUPLO, LEGO SCALA, LEGO SYSTEM, and LEGO TECHNIC. Most of the elements in each product line could be used in combination with the elements in the other lines.

LEGO PRIMO. This program, in existence since 1995, had been specially designed for babies and toddlers, for the early years in which children's development is at its fastest. The range was made up of multifunctional elements that were easy to combine. The jolly, brightly colored elements were designed to stimulate small children's senses, develop their motor skills, and satisfy their need for challenges. The elements could be stacked, spun round, and pushed along.

LEGO DUPLO. Since 1967. The figures and bricks were easy to hold, put together, and separate. They formed a building system in which the elements were large enough for handling them not to be a problem. As children grow up, their appetite for using toys in more complicated settings and role-play games increases. This was why LEGO had developed different themes within the LEGO DUPLO program. Houses and trains had been added to make up the kind of "world" that children love to build around themselves. The LEGO DUPLO products encouraged children to use their imagination and natural curiosity in active, enjoyable, positive, and healthy play.

LEGO SCALA. Test launching in 1997 (see Exhibit 7). This was a product for girls, developed on the basis of their own tastes. It was a flexible doll's house system that was capable of infinite variation, combining the doll's house and role-play with the characteristic flexibility and creativity of LEGO construction. The atmosphere was warm and friendly and was centered on the family. There were many new aspects to LEGO SCALA: the system for building the doll's house was brand new, and a new stud design had been developed, the flower stud, which fitted other LEGO elements but gave a very different visual impression. One flower stud fitted an ordinary 2×2-stud LEGO SYSTEM brick, and vice versa.

LEGO SYSTEM. The LEGO SYSTEM product program was the biggest in the LEGO range. It had various product lines, catering to almost every conceivable interest: from the drama and action of pirates to the romance of the Belville and Paradise figures. The FreeStyle line in the LEGO SYSTEM (since 1955) consisted of bricks without any particular theme or building style.

LEGO TECHNIC. Since 1977. This line offered the chance to find out how complex technical products were constructed and how they worked. A motorcycle or a helicopter, for example, or a machine based on pure fantasy. In August 1997 a CD-ROM containing building instructions and other information was to be added to the LEGO TECHNIC line.

Exhibit 8 shows examples of some of these product lines.

EXHIBIT 7 | LEGO SCALA

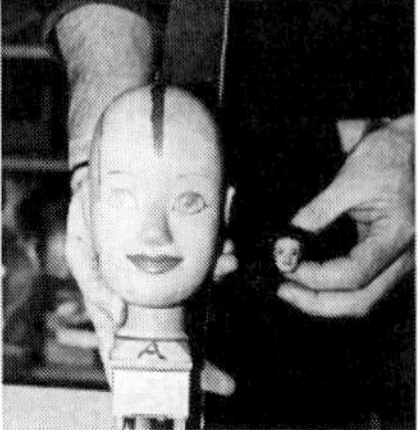

The doll's appearance, especially their faces, is important. But making faces is difficult–a small detail can change them completely. A face six times larger than the final version may look fine but look quite wrong when reduced in size. The head is first shaped in clay or plastics; then a copy is made in a CNC machine tool–e.g. at six times the final size. It is then reduced to a 1:1 scale.

The studs on the building plates are shaped like flowers. One flower stud fits an ordinary 2x2-stud LEGO SYSTEM brick. And all SCALA elements have a matt finish.

The textiles have to be specially designed to suit the dolls' size. It would look quite wrong if ordinary small patterns were used.

Examples of the many details: set no. 3243 (kitchen) and set no. 3242 (bathroom).

Carsten Michaelsen, who has been involved in the development of LEGO SCALA, demonstrates how the doll's house is assembled. The wall system is designed in such a way that things that hang on the walls can be moved around very easily. The cupboards are flexible–they can be hung on the walls, be put up against the walls or be used as free-standing furniture. They can also be transformed into other types of furniture by switching various elements–e.g. a cupboard can become a cooker or refrigerator. And a single set can naturally be used for various layouts and interior decoration options.

The 10 LEGO SCALA sets are being launched in March.

8 | LEGO DUPLO and Various LEGO Product Lines

INNOVATION

At LEGO, innovation was a high priority, and an enormous amount of work and substantial financial resources were invested before any new LEGO product reached the shelves of stores on every continent. Continuous renewal was one of the hallmarks of the LEGO Group: new ideas, new themes, new sets, new elements. As a result, children always had new ways to build, new ways to play, and new ways to think and learn. Every year, many new LEGO sets were added to the LEGO line, elements and play themes resulting from the hundreds of ideas that were constantly being worked on at LEGO's four product development departments in Europe, the USA, and Japan. The products that reached the shops were the cream skimmed from this process. A large number of designs and prototypes were developed and tried out. Some were dropped for one reason or another, while others were selected for inclusion in future product lines after further development. To be approved for sale, every LEGO product had to meet certain requirements. It had to give unlimited play opportunities and inspire enthusiasm in people of all ages. It had to appeal to and stimulate children's sense of shape and color; be suited to and develop their motor skills; allow them to exploit their creativity; and offer fun and experience that would strengthen their intellect and thereby contribute to their development.

Behind every LEGO set and each individual LEGO toy element lay a great deal of research, development, designing, and testing. On average, the LEGO Group introduced 100 new sets and about 100 different new elements each year. Many, many more designs and prototypes for elements were developed. Some were abandoned for various reasons; others were chosen to become parts of future product lines requiring further development.

Several hundred LEGO designers, engineers, and technicians were occupied solely with developing new elements, trying out their uses, and turning their experience into new play themes and product lines—a process that usually stretched over several years. The designers and model developers drew inspiration from the world around them.

The bricks and other elements made more than a generation earlier still fitted with those made in 1997. LEGO believed that it was important that elements in new product lines could be used together with elements bought earlier. One 8-stud LEGO brick could be combined in 102,891,500 different ways.

DEVELOPING A NEW PRODUCT

The Ten Characteristics

In developing LEGO toys in the old days, a set of ten characteristics was established that every LEGO product should stand up to:

- unlimited play potential
- for girls and boys
- fun for every age
- year-round play
- healthy, quiet play
- long hours of play
- development, imagination, creativity
- the more LEGO, the greater the value
- extra sets available
- quality in every detail

These ten guidelines were still used at LEGO when developing new products.

From the Initial Idea to the Product

At LEGO there were many ways to get new ideas for a product. The product development people had to think in unconventional ways. A rule of thumb was that about 20 percent of the creative effort was devoted to "wild ideas." One manager at the Product Development Department said that brainstorming was one method that was often used to generate new ideas. He said that an idea could come from different places: from within the design groups in Billund, from the marketing department, or from concept groups in other places (Tokyo, Milan, Windsor, Boston, Copenhagen).

In developing new products, people from different departments in the Product Development area (LEGO Futura) worked together in project groups. In the development process LEGO used a systematic method called the "Stage Gate Method," developed by Robert C. Cuber. Lene Bach, a Product Development Manager, described the method in the following terms:

> *If you have an idea for a product, you divide the development process into different stages and steps.*

Then you have gates and milestones in between, where you make decisions. The idea of the method is to start with concept development, then move on to the assortment development, and finally on to finalizing every last detail.

According to Lene Bach the development time of a product was one to five years, depending on market needs and the company's decision. Sometimes, the company decided to develop a product in a very short time, but usually longer planning was needed. She said that every product had to appeal to children's tastes, stimulate their imagination, and satisfy their desire to create something new. Inspiration from children, parents, and teachers was what shaped new LEGO products.

The Life Cycle

The life cycle of LEGO products had shrunk from three years to two years. In 1997 the international LEGO product range would consist of 385 sets (divided between the five product programs: LEGO PRIMO, LEGO DUPLO, LEGO SCALA, LEGO SYSTEM, LEGO TECHNIC). Of those 385 sets, around 183 would be new product sets, put on the market in 1997.

Children's Needs

LEGO considered the starting point of every LEGO toy to be its knowledge of children. It emphasized the need to learn as much as possible about what children find stimulating and challenging. The designers, product developers, and market researchers observed children at play for hours on end and talked to their parents and teachers. Developing each product raised different questions, to which the product development team sought to find answers. A common way of learning about children was to bring a group of children into the company and give them the prototype toy to play with, or to have teachers try the toys out in their schools. It was then from the ways the children played, from the ways they solved specific tasks, and from their self-defined role-play that children's wants and limitations were discovered.

Product Development Facility

At the beginning of 1997 all the product development departments in Billund were put under the same roof in a new building, LEGO Futura. New objectives were set, demanding that more new concepts be found and more new products created every year.

The development groups were located in the middle of the building, where they could enjoy the architectural splendour of the roof of the old factory, built in 1958. The light from above and the airy, open feeling gave a sense of well-being. The existing product programs sent out their color signals in each area, reinforced by the exuberant colors and shapes of the future. The office landscape also included "meeting islands" and the individual workplaces where employees could spread their creative wings and let their imagination take flight.

In principle, everything to do with LEGO Futura was a "closed book," so it was very difficult to get into the product development department. Entry was in several stages, following a carefully thought-out security procedure which involved repeated use of the visitor's security card. There were lots of doors, passages, and staircases, making people feel in danger of losing their sense of direction as they moved around the complex. A guide was an essential accessory if one wanted to avoid getting lost.

Around 200 members of the Futura family worked in Billund, including those in the administration, staff, and central service functions. Then there was the Model Completion department and the development departments for LEGO SYSTEM, LEGO TECHNIC, and LEGO SCALA. Development work on LEGO PRIMO and LEGO DUPLO took place in Copenhagen. There were around 100 people in the satellites, including the Copenhagen departments. Futura also developed the LEGO DACTA products, apart from the software.

Product Development—LEGO Futura

LEGO Futura's job was to develop new concepts, new models, and new elements. Futura also had to ensure the consistency that was essential in the production process; that is to say, that the permissible elements were used, that the packaging designers received accurate information about each model, that Engineering got the necessary sketches and notes of packs and bag concepts, etc. The material had a packing code that stated how many bricks there were in the model; a mistake over one tiny element in a pack could turn things upside down in the

Packing Department. Reference cards were prepared for each model. If there was any query about a particular design, it was always possible to refer back to the model prototype, which was kept in the Product Refinement section. The model prototype was the only standard for comparisons and was not scrapped until the model was withdrawn from the range. That required a lot of storage space, given that there were about 250 new models each year.

The elements archive was also very impressive. There were around 3,500 different elements[1] in the product range, and there were a further 6,000 prototype elements that did not leave Futura. That meant there were almost 10,000 different elements to keep in order. "We have to make sure that the development groups have access to the newly developed elements," said Niels Otto Nielsen, head of Model Completion. Everything had to be visible and easy to get at. The new products for 1997 involved 1,600 new product numbers, when the color variations and different decorations on the elements were taken into account. That was a whole lot of elements to organize so that they were in the right place and readily available.

Staff from the central functions and designers sat on Futura's Internal Model and Element Committees. They had to ensure that the "correct LEGO construction principles" were applied for the elements, and that the colors, shapes, and modularity of the elements fitted in with the overall system. The seven people who prepared the building instructions were also involved in the process.

Ole Vestergaard Poulsen, chief designer in LEGO TECHNIC development, had the following to say about product development: "We must have products that are more narrowly targeted, for more specific markets, and those markets must have them more quickly."

Poulsen said that, in contrast to previous practice, before Compass Management, when the developers had narrowly defined individual areas, people now had to be ready to be flexible—e.g., by participating in a number of limited projects, while at the same time devoting some of their energy to developing new ideas.

9 | LEGO Coupling Now and in 1958

The LEGO coupling principle as we know it today is shown on the left. To the right is the LEGO brick as it was invented and patented in 1958.

10 | Examples of LEGO Elements

Technology

There were 30 toolmakers and machinists in Futura's central workshops. They were also very aware of the increasing number of new products, including some with a shorter development time. Jörn Pedersen, head of the department, explained that they worked in two ways: "If only around 15 units are needed of a particular item, we vacuum-mold, using silicon-rubber molds. Prototype tooling is made when 100 or more units are to be produced."

Advances in technology were changing work procedures in the department. "In a few years' time, we shall be totally reliant on computer-aided tooling design," said Jörn. "We have always coordinated our work with Engineering, but the project groups mean that the collaboration is now even closer."

LEGO SCALA—An Example of the Development of a New Product

The development of LEGO SCALA began in Copenhagen in 1992 and was moved to Billund in 1994, when the final stage of the process began. Exhibit 7 shows the LEGO SCALA product.

To arrive at the final product, LEGO undertook no fewer than 32 consumer tests during the development period. First, the basic concept was tested. Having established that it was of interest, various designs (color, shape, style, models, appearance, packaging) were tested and comparisons were invited between the product and those of competitors. Play tests were also performed; for example, the way girls play at the ages of five, seven, and so on. One of the things that became clear was that girls did not want furniture and houses in the classical designs of famous designers and architects. They found these styles cold, sterile, and lacking in atmosphere. They wanted designs that were more romantic, styles that would help them to act out their dreams.

Tests were carried out, both among girls' mothers and among girls themselves, in France, Germany, Great Britain, the USA, and Japan. All these tests helped make the right decisions about the LEGO SCALA product line. In addition, there was close cooperation throughout the development process among all the departments involved. According to Lene Bach, Product Development Manager of the SCALA project, this was absolutely crucial to the project's success.

All the way along, the process was veiled in secrecy. For example, the development group used a room to which access was barred for everyone not involved in the project. LEGO Engineering set up a special group to work on LEGO SCALA, and so on. Even Production established a closed area, which was only opened up once the product was ready.

In the first instance, LEGO SCALA will be launched in six test markets: Austria, Switzerland, Germany, Sweden, Denmark, and France. After test marketing, LEGO SCALA will be developed further.

Bricks were not used in the LEGO SCALA product. LEGO developed a new stud, known as the flower stud, although the flower stud in fact combined perfectly well with the traditional brick, so it was basically the same system. SCALA did not focus on building and construction; it was more a changing toy than a construction toy. It was made in such a way that it was very easy to make a house or a different environment.

Quality

For the LEGO Group, quality had always been key. LEGO divided quality into three types:

Technical quality—properties such as durability, genuine color, stability, and product safety.

Utility quality—the fact that the toy was versatile and could be used in a variety of ways.

Development quality—that the toy attracted children and retained their interest year after year—stimulating and developing their senses, dexterity, imagination, creativity, and intellect.

To ensure quality, LEGO had an organization that allowed it to check every link in the chain, every process, from the production of raw materials to the design of packaging and the development of marketing strategy. LEGO worked closely with the companies that manufactured the raw materials to LEGO's specifications. This guaranteed consistently high quality and ensured characteristics such as color match, nontoxicity, and a production process that had the least possible impact on the environment. The next step in the processing was injection-molding in molds designed and produced at LEGO's three mold factories in Switzerland and Germany. After that, LEGO used advanced, state-of-the-art manufacturing and control processes, frequently purpose-built to its own specifications. The company had an ISO 9000-certification that was part of its quality management procedures. For example, in Denmark alone, random spot checks were carried out on almost 10 million elements each year. The robots in LEGO's fully automated molding factories collected the finished elements at the machines when a certain quantity had been molded. The full boxes received a special bar code giving details of their contents and were then sent via an automatic transport system to the warehouse. The various factory departments in which the products were assembled or packed ordered from the warehouse exactly the elements they needed. The orders were picked automatically and then transported by truck. Everything was controlled electronically and staff members only intervened if something went wrong.

Since November 1995, LEGO System, Inc.'s Storage Container Moulding operation (SCM) had been producing at zero defects; that is, no defective elements had been found in the outgoing quality audit. The team responsible for this result had achieved a remarkable milestone in the history of molding at LEGO Systems, Inc. They had made possible what was once thought to be impossible. Over the previous few years, Peter Sibley, the SCM Production Coordinator, had worked closely with each member of the team to build their skills, focus their energies, and organize and align every step in the operation. With such large-scale molds and machinery, as well as robotics equipment, it was a challenge to make this marvel of technology pay off in productivity and quality. In 1996, the SCM team clearly met the challenge of full production utilization and zero defects, with just 5.8 percent downtime and 0.7 percent scrap.

With determination, consistent follow-through of the quality system, a focus on each step in the operation, and a high level of workmanship, all the members of the SCM team made it their daily mission to let no defects out of their door. Throughout the year, they watched as the number of days producing at zero defects accumulated on the scoreboard hanging in the department.

In December 1996, when 365 days had passed without defects, the success was celebrated. A huge banner was hung in front of the building and the team was treated to a surprise lunch and ceremony.

LEGO—THE BRAND

For the LEGO company, the LEGO brand was its most valuable asset. The company's objective for the LEGO brand was to make it the most powerful brand in the world among families with children by the year 2005. An international analysis—the Brand Asset Valuator—carried out by the advertising agency Young & Rubicam said that the LEGO brand was currently number eleven when it came to Familiarity/Esteem and number three in Relevance/Differentiation.

In building the brand, LEGO considered it important to look at the following things:

Familiarity: How well-known the brand is

Esteem: How highly regarded the brand is

Relevance: How the brand meets individual needs and wishes

Differentiation: To what degree the brand is distinctive, what characteristics set it apart from other brands

LEGO's efforts to secure and maintain a leading, global position for the brand were based on the company's vision; but Kjeld Kirk Kristiansen said that, at the end of the day, it was what the company could offer consumers and the way it conducted itself that decided what families with children associated with the LEGO brand.

At the beginning of 1997, LEGO adopted a policy of using the brand name LEGO in the names of all of its product lines. Thus, the names of two product lines, DUPLO and PRIMO, were changed to LEGO DUPLO and LEGO PRIMO. Exhibit 11 shows all of the LEGO brands.

In a French opinion poll, conducted by the research organization Brule Ville & Associés (BVA) between November 21 and December 18, 1996, the LEGO brand was awarded the title of "Brand of the Century" in the Toys and Games category, beating 19 major competitors in the process. The objective of the poll was to assess the major brands of the 20th century. The group questioned was a representative selection of French households, 5,694 in all, with a total of 11,438 people aged from 15 years upwards.

The four criteria on which consumers were asked to judge the brands were:

Reputation: known by everyone and used as a reference

Quality: better than all competitors

Innovation: a pioneer in its field, changing people's lives

Confidence: a lasting brand, with a past, present and future

The following were the results:

The Best-Known, Most Famous Brands

1. Monopoly
2. Barbie
3. LEGO

The Brand with the Most Consistent Quality

1. LEGO
2. Fisher Price
3. Meccano

EXHIBIT 11 | LEGO Brands

The Product Which Has Done Most to Change People's Lives

1. LEGO
2. Scrabble
3. Barbie

The Product That Inspires the Most Confidence for the Future

1. LEGO
2. Fisher Price
3. Nathan (educational toys of various kinds)

THE PATENT

Illegal copying of LEGO designs was a problem. Every year LEGO brought a number of lawsuits against companies or individuals that were misusing the LEGO brand or products in one way or another. As LEGO no longer had the patent for manufacturing the bricks, other companies had imitated them and put the product onto the market with only minor changes, in an attempt to mislead the consumer. Some copies were imitations down to the smallest detail, changing only the LEGO name. One manufacturer, for example, called its brick elements LIGO. Exhibit 12 shows some copies of LEGO products. National patent, design, and trademark laws, not to mention the degree of observance of such laws and associated regulations, varied quite substantially from one country to another. In a number of countries, laws against unfair competition did not even exist.

Even if consumers were not aware that they were being deceived when they bought a LEGO look-alike product, the shortcomings would become obvious soon enough. The child for whom it was intended would discover that his or her new toy did not live up to LEGO standards. Obvious qualities such as accuracy and clutch power would be lacking. A child that received a box of building blocks would almost certainly add them to the LEGO collection she or he already had. If the fake elements did not come up to LEGO's quality standards, the user's disappointment would automatically be directed toward the LEGO product, because of LEGO's position as a market leader in the construction toy category.

Generally, the LEGO Group was confronted with problems in the following areas:

12 | LEGO Copies

- **Product copying.** A large proportion of the more than 3,000 different elements of the LEGO product programs were protected by the laws of a substantial number of countries. Imitation products were made and marketed in an attempt to mislead consumers, and the aim of many copyists was to present their products as genuine LEGO products.
- **Misuse of trademarks.** Product names, graphic images, and product shapes that obviously imitated the LEGO Group's registered trademarks and designs were frequently used to mislead consumers into thinking that they were buying genuine LEGO products.
- **Association with unrelated activities.** LEGO elements had often been used by other companies to illustrate all kinds of modular services and products. It was against the LEGO Group's general policy to permit others to make such use of LEGO products in

EXHIBIT 13 | LEGOs Used with Unrelated Activities

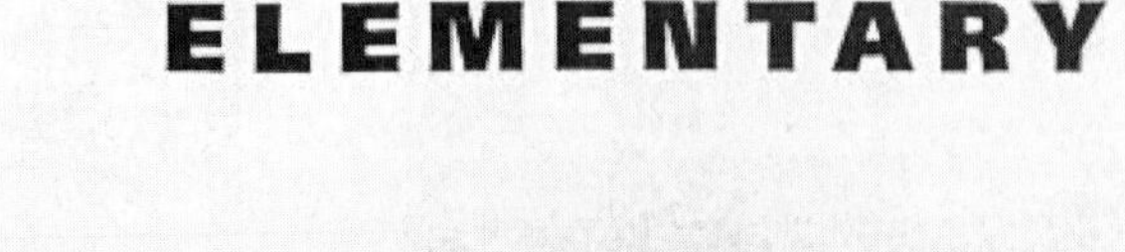

What are LEGO toy elements doing in this setting? The answer is: Nothing at all. Since the product offered has nothing whatsoever to do with LEGO bricks, we insist on being left out.

their marketing. Exhibit 13 shows an example where LEGO elements have been used to this end.

FINANCE

At the end of 1995, the emphasis had been on achieving higher profits in 1996 and the years to come. Even though, in overall terms, there had been a positive trend in sales in 1996, this had not led to an improvement in results. Exhibit 14 shows some key figures from LEGO's annual report. Total sales of all LEGO Group business areas were ECU 1,027 million, an increase of 10 percent over the 1995 figure. Turnover was positively influenced by exchange-rate movements. LEGOLAND Windsor's turnover was also included in the total. The profit before tax was ECU 95 million, 3 percent more than in 1995.

EXHIBIT 14 | The LEGO Group in 1996—Key Figures (ECU million)

Key Figures	1996	Percentage	1995	Percentage
Results				
Turnover	1,032	100	937	100
Profit before tax	95	9.3	92	9.9
Profit after tax	64	6.2	59	6.3
Balance sheet				
Total assets	1,378	100	1,306	100
Equity capital	810	58.8	816	62.5
Investment activities				
Investments in tangible fixed assets	204		102	
Employment				
Persons	9,450		9,660	
Converted to full-time employment	8,178		8,535	
Key ratios				
Return on assets (profit before tax × 100)/assets		6.9		7.1
Return on equity capital (profit after tax ×100)/equity capital		7.9		7.2
Equity capital as proportion of total assets (equity capital × 100)/total assets)		58.8		62.5

This small rise was in part attributable to higher investment in product development.

The company was not satisfied, given its long-term objective of self-financing operations and investments out of earnings. In 1996, the LEGO Group completed investments in operating equipment and buildings amounting to just under ECU 204 million, a markedly higher level than in 1995. An important contributory factor was the start of operations at LEGOLAND Windsor.

The LEGO A/S Group, which comprised the 23 LEGO Group companies owned by LEGO A/S, had a turnover of ECU 794 million in 1996, an increase of 11 percent over the previous year. Profit before tax was ECU 52 million, 8 percent down from 1995. Profit after tax, however, was 8 percent higher than the previous year, owing to dividends from abroad and the resulting tax refunds.

The turnover of the LEGO Group in 1996 was only ECU 233 million higher than that of the LEGO A/S Group. This was explained primarily by the fact that the Swiss factories sold their product via LEGO System A/S. Because these sales were internal Group transactions, when the accounts for the entire LEGO Group were prepared, they had to be eliminated.

THE FUTURE—TOWARD 2005

Looking to the future, LEGO still had the same objective as in the early years, namely to be the best, not the biggest. To be a leader in terms of quality and coverage, in its particular area, LEGO wanted continuous, controlled growth that would secure the LEGO Group's financial independence as a family-owned, family-run company. LEGO considered it very important to be a "good corporate citizen" and to fulfil its global responsibilities by doing its utmost to minimize resource consumption and pollution.

LEGO had set ambitious targets for the development of the LEGO Group in the years to 2005: To strengthen growth and make the LEGO brand the strongest in the world among families with children.

The objectives for the future were to increase growth within the main business areas as well as to establish and strengthen new business areas. Total turnover, in consumer sales, was targeted to grow by an average of approximately 10 percent a year up to the year 2005. The driving force would continue to be the core business, but new business areas would also contribute to growth. A 10-year growth objective envisaged that the current turnover would increase almost threefold.

An important general theme for LEGO was to set goals in such a way that it was possible to monitor whether or not they were reached, and whether they were moving in the right direction. As Kjeld Kirk Kristiansen put it, "It's the same in sport: If you don't keep scores or measure the results, all you do is practice. But in sport, and in business too, the ultimate purpose is to succeed, without forgetting to have fun in the process."

Ever since the company had lost the patent on the brick, the competition from imitators had been more intense than ever. What should LEGO do? Competition from so-called fashion toys had also risen and they were getting more and more popular among children. Should LEGO do anything about it?

In spite of LEGO's policy of being both a girls' and a boys' toy, LEGO had always been stronger in the boys' toy market. This had to change. Launching LEGO SCALA would be a first step, but there were still more steps to be taken.

The company had been undergoing many changes and was moving toward the digital world. At the end of 1997 the company was planning to create a new department in their headquarters in Billund. The purpose of the department would be to develop digital key technologies based on the LEGO concept, "Generation LEGO." The plan was to market the finest software in the world for kids. Would this mean big changes at LEGO? Was it a good decision? Was the company moving from the construction toy area to the traditional toy market? There were examples in the toy industry where successful companies in one category had moved to a completely new category. Nintendo, for example, had gone from being the biggest card producer to being the biggest producer of computer games.

NOTE

1. In each product set there is a different number of elements. The elements are the contents of the set. Exhibit 9 shows coupling now and in 1958. Exhibit 10 shows some LEGO elements.

CASE 25

The Lincoln Electric Company, 1996

Arthur Sharplin
Waltham Associates, Austin, Texas

John A. Seeger
Bentley College

It was February 29, 1996. The Lincoln Electric Company, a leading producer of arc welding products, had just celebrated its centennial year by reporting record 1995 sales of over $1 billion, record profits of $61.5 million, and record employee bonuses of $66 million. This performance followed two years of losses—the only losses in the company's long history—stemming from a seemingly disastrous foray into Europe, Asia, and Latin America. (Exhibits 1 and 2 tabulate operating results and ratios for recent years.)

Headquartered in the Cleveland suburb of Euclid, Ohio, Lincoln Electric was widely known for its Incentive Management System. According to the *New York Times,* thousands of managers visited Lincoln's headquarters each year for free seminars on the system, which guaranteed lifetime employment, paid its production people only for each piece produced, and paid profit-sharing bonuses which had averaged 90 percent of annual wages or salary for the sixty years from 1934 to 1994.[1] James Lincoln, the main architect of the Incentive Management System, had been dead 30 years by 1995, but he remained a dominant influence on the company's policies and culture.

Record sales and profits, however, were not a cause for complacence. Lincoln Electric had gone public during 1995 to reduce the substantial debts it incurred during its two losing years; now the company was subject to public scrutiny and such publications as the *New York Times* and *Business Week* questioned whether the famous Incentive Management System was consistent with the firm's obligations to its public stockholders. Dividends for 1995 amounted to $9.1 million, while bonuses had totalled $66 million. Even at $66 million, however, bonuses equalled only 56 percent of employees' annual pay. Some workers complained loudly that the average $21,000 payment in December was far short of what it should have been.

Lincoln's hometown newspaper, the Cleveland *Plain Dealer,* saw the worker complaints as a sign of increasing strain between management and workers. Characterizing Lincoln's work pace as ". . . brutal, a pressure cooker in which employees are constantly graded and peer pressure borders on the fanatical," reporter Thomas Gerdel said Lincoln "faces growing discontent in its workforce."[2] *Business Week* said, ". . . Lincoln increasingly resembles a typical public company. With institutional shareholders and new, independent board members in place, worker bonuses are getting more of a gimlet eye." Chairman and CEO Donald F. Hastings had set up a committee and hired Price Waterhouse to study the bonus program and the company's productivity.

"If Lincoln can adapt to new times without sacrificing employee good will," said *Business Week,* "another model pay plan may yet emerge."[3]

The authors thank Richard S. Sabo of Lincoln Electric for help in the field research for this case, which is written solely for the purpose of stimulating student discussion. Management exerted no editorial control over content or presentation of the case. All events and individuals are real.

Copyright © 1997 by the *Case Research Journal* and Arthur Sharplin and John A. Seeger.

EXHIBIT

1 | Five-Year Operating Results

	Year Ended December 31				
	1995	1994	1993	1992	1991
	(in thousands of dollars, except per share data)				
Net sales	$1,032,398	$906,604	$845,999	$853,007	$833,892
Income (loss) before cumulative effect of accounting change	61,475	48,008	(40,536)	(45,800)	14,365
Cumulative effect of accounting change			2,468		
Net income (loss)	$ 61,475	$ 48,008	$ (38,068)	$ (45,800)	$ 14,365
Per share:					
Income (loss) before cumulative effect of accounting change	$ 2.63	$ 2.19	$ (1.87)	$ (2.12)	$ .67
Cumulative effect of accounting change			.12		
Net Income (loss)	$ 2.63	$ 2.19	$ (1.75)	$ (2.12)	$ .67
Cash dividends declared	$ .42	$ .38	$ .36	$ .36	$ .30
Total assets	$ 617,760	$556,857	$ 559,543	$ 603,347	$ 640,261
Long-term debt	$ 93,582	$194,831	$ 216,915	$ 221,470	$ 155,547

A HISTORICAL SKETCH

In 1895, having lost control of his first company, John C. Lincoln took out his second patent and began to manufacture an improved electric motor. He opened his new business with $200 he had earned redesigning a motor for young Herbert Henry Dow (who later founded the Dow Chemical Company). In 1909, John Lincoln made his first welding machine (Exhibit 3 describes the welding process). That year, he also brought in James, his younger brother, as a salesman. John preferred engineering and inventing to being a manager, and in 1914 he appointed James vice president and general manager (Exhibit 4 shows a condensed history of the firm).

James Lincoln soon asked the employees to form an "Advisory Board." At one of its first meetings, the Advisory Board recommended reducing working hours from 55 per week, then standard, to 50. This was done. In 1934, the famous Lincoln bonus plan was implemented. The first bonus averaged 25 percent of base wages. By 1940, Lincoln employees had twice the average pay and twice the productivity of other Cleveland workers in similar jobs. They also enjoyed the following benefits:

- An employee stock purchase plan providing stock at book value,
- Company-paid life insurance,
- An employees' association for athletic and social programs and sick benefits,
- Piece rates adjusted for inflation,
- A suggestion system with cash awards,
- A pension plan,
- A policy of promotion from within,
- A practice, though not in 1940 a guarantee, of lifetime employment,
- Base pay rates determined by formal job evaluation,
- A merit rating system which affected pay, and
- Paid vacations.

During World War II, the company suspended production of electric motors as demand for welding products escalated. Employee bonuses averaged $2,250 in 1942 (about $20,000 in 1995 dollars). Lincoln's original bonus plan was not universally accepted: the Internal Revenue Service questioned the tax deductibility of em-

EXHIBIT 2 | Financial Ratios, 1992–1995

Fiscal Year Ending December 31:	1995	1994	1993	1992
Quick Ratio	0.89	0.95	0.74	0.89
Current Ratio	2.12	2.17	1.85	2.16
Sales/Cash	102.35	86.97	41.51	41.35
SG&A/Sales	0.28	0.29	0.33	0.35
Receivables: Turnover	7.33	7.19	7.66	7.66
Receivables: Day's Sales	49.11	50.04	47.02	46.98
Inventories: Turnover	5.65	5.84	5.89	4.98
Inventories: Day's Sales	63.77	61.66	61.14	72.27
Net Sales/Working Capital	5.48	5.35	5.65	4.94
Net Sales/Net Plant & Equipment	5.02	4.92	4.99	4.09
Net Sales/Current Assets	2.89	2.89	2.60	2.66
Net Sales/Total Assets	1.67	1.63	1.51	1.41
Net Sales/Employees	172,066	159,249	140,159	134,714
Total Liability/Total Assets	0.46	0.64	0.73	0.64
Total Liability/Invested Capital	0.67	0.92	1.13	0.92
Total Liability/Common Equity	0.87	1.90	3.01	2.13
Times Interest Earned	9.07	6.09	–1.66	–0.84
Long-Term Debt/Equity	0.28	1.00	1.51	1.11
Total Debt/Equity	0.29	1.02	1.58	1.19
Total Assets/Equity	1.87	2.87	3.90	3.04
Pre-Tax Income/Net Sales	0.10	0.09	–0.06	–0.04
Pre-Tax Income/Total Assets	0.16	0.14	–0.08	–0.06
Pre-Tax Income/Invested Capital	0.24	0.21	–0.13	–0.08
Pre-Tax Income/Common Equity	0.31	0.43	–0.35	–0.19
Net Income/Net Sales	0.06	0.05	–0.04	–0.05
Net Income/Total Assets	0.10	0.09	–0.07	–0.08
Net Income/Invested Capital	0.15	0.12	–0.11	–0.11
Net Income/Common Equity	0.19	0.26	–0.28	–0.25
R & D/Net Sales	NA	NA	NA	NA
R & D/Net Income	NA	NA	NA	NA
R & D/Employees	NA	NA	NA	NA

Source: Disclosure, Inc., Dow-Jones On-Line News Service.

ployee bonuses, arguing they were not "ordinary and necessary" costs of doing business, and the Navy's Price Review Board challenged Lincoln's high profits. But James Lincoln overcame the objections, loudly refusing to retract the firm's obligations to its workers. Also during World War II, Lincoln built factories in Australia, South Africa, and England.

In 1951, Lincoln completed a new main plant in Euclid, Ohio; the factory remained essentially unchanged in 1995. In 1995, Lincoln again began making electric motors, but they represented only a small percentage of the company's revenue through 1995.

Executive Succession

William Irrgang, an engineer and longtime Lincoln protégé, was president when James Lincoln died in 1965. By 1970, Lincoln's annual revenues had grown to $100 million, and bonuses were averaging about $8,000 per employee each year (about $30,000 in 1995 dollars). Irrgang was elevated to chairman in 1972 and Ted Willis, also an engineer and protégé of James Lincoln, became president. In 1977, Lincoln completed a new electrode plant a few miles from Euclid, in Mentor, Ohio; this doubled the capacity for making welding wire and rods.

3 | What Is Arc-Welding?

Arc-welding was the standard joining method in shipbuilding for decades and remained so in 1995. It was the predominant way of connecting steel in the construction industry. Most industrial plants had their own welding shops for maintenance and construction. Makers of automobiles, tractors, and other items employed arc-welding. Welding hobbyists made metal items such as patio furniture and barbecue pits. The popularity of welded sculpture was growing.

Arc-welding employs electrical power, typically provided by a "welding machine" composed of a transformer or solid-state inverter connected to a building's electrical system or to an engine-driven generator. The electrical output may vary from 50 to 1,000 amps at 36–60 volts (for comparison, a hair dryer may use 10 amps at 120 volts) and may be alternating or direct current (AC or DC) of varying wave patterns and frequencies. The electrical current travels through a welding electrode and creates an arc to the item being welded. This melts the actual surface of the material being welded, as well as the tip of the electrode, resulting in deposit of the molten metal from the electrode onto the surface. When the molten metal re-freezes, the pieces being joined are fused into one continuous piece of steel.

Welding electrodes—called "consumables" because they are used up in the welding process—are of two main types: short pieces of coated wire (called "stick" electrodes or "welding rods") for manual welding and coils of solid or tubular wire for automatic and semiautomatic processes. The area of the arc must be shielded from the atmosphere to prevent oxidation of the hot metal. This shielding is provided by a stream of inert gas which surrounds the arc (in "MIG," or metallic-inert gas welding) or by solid material called "flux" which melts and covers the liquefied metal surface. Flux often contains substances which combine with the molten metal or catalyze chemical reactions. The flux may be affixed as a coating on welding rods, enclosed inside tubular welding wire, or funneled onto the weld area from a bin (in "submerged-arc" welding). Arc-welding produces sparks, heat, intense light, and noxious fumes, so operators usually wear face, body, and eye protection and, if ventilation is inadequate, breathing devices.

Other types of welding include oxy-fuel welding, which uses a flame to melt metals together; tungsten-inert gas (TIG) welding, which employs a tungsten electrode to create an arc to melt a welding rod; induction welding, which uses electrical coils to induce currents in the metal being welded, thereby heating it; resistance welding, which heats the weld joint by passing current directly through it; and plasma-arc welding, which is similar to arc-welding but involves higher temperatures and a more tightly constrained arc. Related processes include cutting metals with oxy-fuel torches, laser beams, and plasma-arc systems.

Lincoln's net sales were $450 million in 1981, and employee bonuses averaged $20,760 (about $34,000 in 1995 dollars) that year. But sales fell by 40 percent in the next two years owing, Lincoln management said, to "the combined effects of inflation, sharply higher energy costs, and a national recession." By 1983, the firm's net income and bonuses had collapsed to less than half their 1981 levels. (Exhibit 5 lists bonus amounts from 1981 to 1995.)

But there was no layoff. Many factory workers volunteered to do field sales work and customer assistance. Others were reassigned within the plants, some repairing the roof of the Euclid factory, painting, and cleaning up. The work week, previously averaging about 45 hours, was shortened to 30 hours for most nonsalaried workers. Several new products, that had been kept in reserve for just this kind of eventuality, were brought to market. Sales, profits, and bonuses began a slow recovery.

Bill Irrgang died in 1986. Ted Willis took over as chairman and Don Hastings became president, taking primary responsibility for domestic operations.

4 | Condensed History of Lincoln Electric Company

1895	Company founded by John C. Lincoln.
1909	James Lincoln joins as salesman. (General Manager, 1914)
1934	Bonus plan implemented, at 25 percent of base earnings.
1940	Employees earning double the area's average wage.
1942–1945	Factories built in South Africa (later closed), England (later sold to employees), and Australia. Motor production discontinued.
1951	Main factory built in Euclid, Ohio.
1955	Motor production resumed.
1958	Historic guaranteed employment policy formalized.
1965	James Lincoln's death. William Irrgang named president.
1970	Annual revenues reach $100 million for the first time.
1972	Irrgang named chairman/CEO. Ted Willis becomes president.
1977	New electrode factory built in Mentor, Ohio.
1982–1983	Recession slashes revenues. Employees on 30-hour weeks. ESAB begins global expansion.
1986	Willis named chairman/CEO. Don Hastings becomes president. International operations include five plants in four countries.
1992	Foreign operations include 21 plants in 15 countries. Long-term debt at $220 million. Hastings named chairman/CEO. Fred Mackenbach named president.
1992–1993	Global recession. First losses in Lincoln's history. International retrenchment begins.
1995	International operations include 16 plants in 11 countries. Public stock issue provides funds for debt reduction. New motor factory built.

5 | The Lincoln Electric Company Bonus History

Year	Total $ Millions	Number Employees	% of Wages	Average Gross Bonus	W-2 Average Earnings Factory Worker
1981	59.0	2684	99.0	22,009	
1982	41.0	2634	80.1	15,643	
1983	26.6	2561	55.4	10,380	
1984	37.0	2469	68.0	15,044	
1985	41.8	2405	73.2	17,391	
1986	37.7	2349	64.8	16,056	
1987	44.0	2349	70.5	18,791	
1988	54.3	2554	77.6	21,264	
1989	54.5	2633	72.0	20,735	47,371
1990	56.2	2701	71.2	20,821	47,809
1991	48.3	2694	65.0	17,935	39,651
1992	48.0	2688	61.9	17,898	40,867
1993	55.0	2676	63.9	20,585	48,738
1994	59.0	2995	60.2	19,659	55,.757
1995	64.4	3396	55.9	*21,168	57,758

Source: Lincoln Electric Company document.
*Employees with more than 1 year of service.

THE LINCOLN PHILOSOPHY

Throughout the tenures of these CEOs, the business philosophies first articulated by James Lincoln remained in effect, forming the foundation of the company's culture and providing the context within which the Incentive Management System worked. Lincoln's own father had been a Congregationalist minister, and the biblical Sermon on the Mount, with Jesus' praise of meekness, mercifulness, purity of heart, and peacemaking, governed his attitudes toward business. James never evangelized his employees, but he counseled truthfulness in speech, returning evil with good, love of enemies, secret almsgiving, and quiet trust and confidence.[4]

Relationships with Customers

In a 1947 speech, James Lincoln said, "Care should be taken . . . not to rivet attention on profit. Between 'How much do I get?' and 'How do I make this better, cheaper, more useful?' the difference is fundamental and decisive." He later wrote, "When any company has achieved success so that it is attractive as an investment, all money usually needed for expansion is supplied by the customer in retained earnings. It is obvious that the customer's interests, not the stockholder's, should come first." He added,

> *The Christian ethic should control our acts. If it did control our acts, the savings in cost of distribution would be tremendous. Advertising would be a contact of the expert consultant with the customer, in order to give the customer the best product available when all of the customer's' needs are considered. Competition then would be improving the quality of products and increasing efficiency in producing and distributing them; not in deception, as is now too customary. Pricing would reflect efficiency of production; it would not be a selling dodge that the customer may well be sorry he accepted. It would be proper for all concerned and rewarding for the ability used in producing the product.*

Lincoln's pricing policy, often stated, was "Price on the basis of cost and keep downward pressure on cost." C. Jackson Graham, founder of The American Productivity Institute, said prices of Lincoln products, on average, grew at only one-fifth the rate of inflation in the decades after 1930. Some prices actually went down. For example, Lincoln welding electrodes which sold for $0.16 per pound in 1929 were $0.05 in 1942. And Lincoln's popular SA-200 welder decreased in price from 1958–1965.

Until the 1990s, Lincoln was the dominant U.S. producer of arc-welding products and was able to keep market prices low, especially for consumables. That changed after Miller Welding Co. grew to match Lincoln in U.S. sales of machines, and ESAB became the world's largest supplier of consumables and materials. In 1984, Don Hastings said,

> *Right now we are paying the price of not having enough capacity in Mentor [Ohio] to supply our customer demand. We are spending money now. But if we had spent it last year, we would not be having the shortages that we're having right now. We're also allowing our competition to raise prices because there's nothing we can do about it without more capacity.*

Lincoln quality was legendary. In the refinery and pipeline industries, where price was seldom the main consideration in purchasing, Lincoln welders and electrodes were almost universally specified for decades. Warranty costs at Lincoln typically averaged under one-fourth of one percent of sales. A Lincoln distributor in Monroe, Louisiana, said he had sold hundreds of Lincoln welders and had never had a warranty claim.

Lincoln sold its products directly to major customers and indirectly through distributors, most of which were welding supply stores. Lincoln also licensed hundreds of service centers and trained their personnel to do maintenance and warranty work on Lincoln machines. The company maintained a system of regional sales offices, which serviced both direct customers and distributors. In keeping with James Lincoln's principle that salespersons should be "expert consultants," sales jobs at Lincoln were open only to graduate engineers until about 1992, when Hastings changed the policy; he began to recruit majors in liberal arts, business, and other disciplines into the sales force.

Hastings instituted Lincoln's Guaranteed Cost Reduction (GCR) program in 1993. Under GCR, Lincoln sent teams of engineers, technical representatives, and distributors to customer facilities with a goal to "find ways to improve the customer's fabrication procedures and product quality as well as methods to increase its productivity." Hastings promised, "The Lincoln Electric Company will guarantee in writing that your company's annual arc welding fabrication costs will be reduced by a specified amount when you use Lincoln products and methods. If you don't save that amount, a check will be written for the difference." Lincoln cited these "successes" in its literature promoting GCR:

> *A fabricator of steel buildings found GCR savings of $25,000/year and, as a result of the program, developed an improved welding cost analysis system. A manufacturer of heavy grading equipment verified savings in excess of $50,000/year and productivity gains from 50 to 90 percent. An automotive manufacturer produced productivity increases, in specific welding operations, exceeding 20 percent. Resultant savings totaled over $1,000,000 a year.*

Relationships with Employees

The company professed to still adhere to the basic precepts James Lincoln set down early in his development of the incentive system:

> *The greatest fear of the worker, which is the same as the greatest fear of the industrialist in operating a company, is the lack of income . . . The industrial manager is very conscious of his company's need of uninterrupted income. He is completely oblivious, evidently, of the fact that the worker has the same need.*
>
> *He is just as eager as any manager is to be part of a team that is properly organized and working for the advancement of our economy . . . He has no desire to make profits for those who do not hold up their end in production, as is true of absentee stockholders and inactive people in the company.*
>
> *If money is to be used as an incentive, the program must provide that what is paid to the worker is what he has earned. The earnings of each must be in accordance with accomplishment.*
>
> *Status is of great importance in all human relationships. The greatest incentive that money has, usually, is that it is a symbol of success . . . The resulting status is the real incentive . . . Money alone can be an incentive to the miser only.*
>
> *There must be complete honesty and understanding between the hourly worker and management if high efficiency is to be obtained.*

"I don't work for Lincoln Electric; I work for myself," said Lester Hillier in the 1994 *New York Times* article. "I'm an entrepreneur," added Hillier, a welder at Lincoln for 17 years. Other workers, asked in April of 1995 about why people worked so hard and what motivated them, responded:

Joe Sirko, machine operator since 1941:

> *People want their bonus. And a decent job. No layoffs. I wanted a job where I could spend all the money I make all year and then I get the bonus. I still do that. I go out and live it up. I go to the races. I go everywhere.*
>
> *When I came here—under James Lincoln—the jobs were given to family. Almost everybody in here was family. My brother got me in. Somebody else's brother got them in or their dad got them in. It was all family. And J.F. backed that a hundred percent. Family, right on down. If you had someone in your family, they were in. Now, they have three different interviewers down there. They all interview.*
>
> *They hired a lot of people once, to reduce the overtime, remember, and they had all them people when it slowed down. They were sweeping and cleaning—and they didn't know what to do with them. When James Lincoln was alive, he always got up when he gave the bonus and told them—they would be complaining about overtime—he told them that they would either work, because he didn't want to over hire all them extra people. He believed in all the overtime.*

Kathleen Hoenigman, wiring harness assembler hired in 1977:

> *I worked in factories before and the factories I worked at either went out of business or moved to another state. I will have to say that my money is more here, but I did always make good money. This is much more, because of the bonus. I invest. I also bought a house. Right now, I give my mother money.*
>
> *I feel that people here that are making all this money, they work so hard for it that they don't want to spend it stupidly and what they do is invest, for the future. And they also, you know, take care of their family.*
>
> *I like the challenge. I also like the money and the*

fact that the money is tied to my own output. You have to be motivated yourself. You want the company to succeed, so you want to do better. By having guaranteed employment, the company has to be strong. To me, guaranteed employment means if there's a slowdown you always have a job. Like they'll always take care of you. Back in 1982, when sales slumped, they put me on the roof carrying buckets of tar.

Scott Skrjanc, welder hired in 1978:

Guaranteed employment is in the back of my mind. I know I'm guaranteed a job. But I also know I have to work to get paid. We don't come in and punch a card and sit down and do nothing.

Linda Clemente, customer service representative hired in 1986:

Well, I guess the biggest thing is guaranteed employment. And I think most people want to be the best that they can be. For other people, maybe the motivation is the money, because they are putting kids through college and things like that. I mean, it's definitely a benefit and something everybody works for.

Relationships with Unions

There had never been a serious effort to organize Lincoln employees. While James Lincoln criticized the labor movement for "selfishly attempting to better its position at the expense of the people it must serve," he still had kind words for union members. He excused union excesses as "the natural reactions of human beings to the abuses to which management has subjected them." He added, "Labor and management are properly not warring camps; they are parts of one organization in which they must and should cooperate fully and happily."

Several of the plants Lincoln acquired during 1986–1992 had unions, and the company stated its intention to cooperate with them. No major Lincoln operation had a union in 1995, although 25 of the Ohio employees did attend a union presentation by the United Auto Workers in December, after the announcement of the 1995 bonus rate. "The attendance, out of a total of 3,400 workers, was disappointing even to organizers," said the Cleveland *Plain Dealer.* Lincoln spokesman Bud Fletcher said, "The secret to avoiding those types of situations is that management has to work twice as hard to provide all the elements that membership in an organization like a union would have. We've got to listen, we've got to sit down, we've got to take our time."

Relationships with Stockholders

Through 1992, Lincoln shareholders received dividends averaging less than 5 percent of share price per year, and total annual returns averaged under 10 percent. The few public trades of Lincoln shares before 1995 were at only a small premium over book value, which was the official redemption price for employee-owned stock.

"The last group to be considered is the stockholders who own stock because they think it will be more profitable than investing money in any other way," said James Lincoln. Concerning division of the largess produced by Incentive Management, he wrote, "The absentee stockholder also will get his share, even if undeserved, out of the greatly increased profit that the efficiency produces."

Under Hastings, Lincoln Electric gave public shareholders more respect. Dividends, while limited under certain credit agreements, were increased in 1994 in preparation for the public issue, and again in 1995. And the presence of new outside directors on the Lincoln board (see Exhibit 6) seemed to protect public shareholder interests.

THE LINCOLN INCENTIVE MANAGEMENT SYSTEM

Lincoln's Incentive Management System was defined by the firm's philosophy and by the rules, regulations, practices, and programs that had evolved over the 60 years since its origination.

Recruitment. Every job opening at Lincoln was advertised internally on company bulletin boards and any employee could apply. In general, external hiring was permitted only for entry-level positions. Often, applicants were relatives or friends of current employees. Selection for these jobs was based on personal interviews—there was no aptitude nor psychological testing and no educational requirement—except for engineering and sales positions, which required a college degree. A committee consisting of vice presidents and supervisors interviewed candidates initially cleared by the

6 | Officers and Directors of Lincoln Electric Company

DIRECTORS

Donald F. Hastings, 67, *1980
Chairman of the Board and
Chief Executive Officer

Frederick W. Mackenbach, 65, *1992
Retired President and Chief Operating Officer

Harry Carlson, 61, *1973
Retired Vice Chairman

David H. Gunning, 53, *1987
Chairman, President and Chief Executive Officer of Capitol American Financial Corp.

Edward E. Hood, Jr., 65, *1993
Former Vice Chairman of the Board and Executive Officer of The General Electric Co.

Paul E. Lego, 65, *1993
President of Intelligent Enterprises

Hugh L. Libby, 70, *1985
Retired Chairman of the Board and Chief Executive Officer of Libby Corp.

David C. Lincoln, 70, *1958
Retired Chairman of the Board and Chief Executive Officer of Lincoln Laser Co. and President of Arizona Oxides LLC

Emma S. Lincoln, 73, *1989
Retired Attorney in private practice

G. Russell Lincoln, 49, *1989
Chairman of the Board and Chief Executive Officer of Algan, Inc.

Kathryn Jo Lincoln, 41, *1995
Vice President of The Lincoln Foundation, Inc. and Vice Chair/Secretary of The Lincoln Institution of Land Policy

Anthony A. Messaro, 52, *1996
President and Chief Operating Officer

Henry L. Meyer, III, 46, *1994
Chairman of the Board of Society National Bank and Senior Executive Vice President and Chief Operating Officer of KeyCorp

Lawrence O. Selhorst, 63, *1992
Chairman of the Board and Chief Executive Officer of American Spring Wire Corporation

Craig R. Smith, 70, *1992
Former Chairman and Chief Executive Officer of Ameritrust Corporation

Frank L. Steingass, 56, *1971
Chairman of the Board and President of Buehler/Steingass, Inc.

*Date elected as a director.

OFFICERS

Donald F. Hastings, 67, *1953
Chairman and Chief Executive Officer

Anthony A. Massaro, 52, *1993
President and Chief Executive Officer

David J. Fullen, 64, *1955
Executive Vice President
Engineering and Marketing

John M. Stropki, 45, *1972
Executive Vice President
President, North America

Richard C. Ulstad, 56, *1970
Senior Vice President,
Manufacturing

H. Jay Elliott, 54, *1993
Senior Vice President,
Chief Financial Officer and Treasurer

Frederick G. Stueber, 42, *1995
Senior Vice President,
General Counsel and Secretary

Frederick W. Anderson, 43, *1978
Vice President,
Systems Engineering

Paul J. Beddia, 62, *1956
Vice President,
Government and Community Affairs

Dennis D. Crockett, 53, *1965
Vice President,
Consumable Research and Development

James R. Delaney, 47, *1987
Vice President
President, Lincoln Electric Latin America

Joseph G. Doria, 46, *1972
Vice President
President and Chief Executive Officer, Lincoln Electric Company of Canada

Paul Fantelli, 51, *1970
Vice President,
Business Development

Ronald A. Nelson, 46, *1972
Vice President,
Machine Research and Development

Gary M. Schuster, 41, *1978
Vice President,
Motor Division

Richard J. Seif, 48, *1971
Vice President,
Marketing

S. Peter Ullman, 46, *1971
Vice President
President and Chief Executive Officer, Harris Calorific Division of Lincoln Electric

Raymond S. Vogt, 54, *1996
Vice President,
Human Resources

John H. Weaver, 57, *1961
Vice President
President, Lincoln Africa, Middle East and Russia

*Year joined the Company.

Personnel Department. Final selection was made by the supervisor who had a job opening. From over 3,500 applicants interviewed by the Personnel Department in 1988, fewer than 300 were hired. The odds were somewhat better in 1995, as Lincoln scrambled to staff its new electric motor factory and to meet escalating demand for its welding products.

Training and Education. New production workers were given a short period of on-the-job training and then placed on a piecework pay system. Lincoln did not pay for off-site education unless specific company needs were identified. The idea behind this policy was that not everyone could take advantage of such a program, and it was unfair to spend company funds for a benefit to which there was unequal access. Recruits for sales jobs, already college graduates, were given an average of six months on-the-job training in a plant, followed by a period of work and training at a regional sales office.

Sam Evans, regional manager for international, described the training program when he joined Lincoln in 1953 as an electrical engineering graduate:

> *A few months into the training, I decided to move to sales. During those days, the training program was about a year—several months learning to weld, several months on the factory floor, and in other departments. I got the MBA while I was working in Buffalo as a Sales Engineer.*

Merit Rating. Each manager formally evaluated subordinates twice a year using the cards shown in Exhibit 7. The employee performance criteria—"quality," "dependability," "ideas and cooperation," and "output"—were considered independently of each other. Marks on the cards were converted to numerical scores, which were forced to average 100 for each specified group, usually all the subordinates of one supervisor or other manager. Thus, any employee rated above 100 would have to be balanced by another rated below 100. Individual merit rating scores normally ranged from 80 to 110. Any score over 100 required a special letter to top management. These scores (over 110) were not considered in computing the required 100 point average for each evaluator. Point scores were directly proportional to the individual's year-end bonus.

Welder Scott Skrjanc seemed typical in his view of the system. "You know, everybody perceives they should get more. That's natural. But I think it's done fairly."

Under Lincoln's early suggestion program, employees were given monetary awards of one-half of the first year's savings attributable to their suggestions. Later, however, the value of suggestions was reflected in merit rating scores. Supervisors were required to discuss performance marks with the employees concerned. Each warranty claim was traced to the individual employee whose work caused the defect, if possible. The employee's performance score was reduced, or the worker could repay the cost of servicing the warranty claim by working without pay.

Compensation. Basic wage levels for jobs at Lincoln were determined by a wage survey of similar jobs in the Cleveland area. These rates were adjusted quarterly in response to changes in the Cleveland Area Wage Index, compiled by the U.S. Department of Labor. Wherever possible, base wage rates were translated into piece rates. Practically all production workers—even some fork truck operators—were paid by the piece. Once established, piece rates were charged only if there was a change in the methods, materials, or machinery used in the job. Each individual's pay was calculated from a daily Piecework Report, filled out by the employee. The payroll department, responsible for paying 3,000 employees, consisted of four people; there was no formal control system for checking employees' reports of work done.

In December of each year, bonuses were distributed to employees. Lincoln reported that incentive bonuses from 1934 to 1994 averaged about ninety percent of annual wages; the total bonus pool typically exceeded after-tax (and after-bonus) profits. Individual bonuses were determined by merit rating scores. For example, if the Board of Directors authorized a bonus equal to 80 percent of total base wages paid, a person whose performance score averaged 95 in the two previous evaluation periods received a bonus of 76 percent (0.80×0.95) of base wages.

Because of company losses in 1992 and 1993, the bonus was about 60 percent of base wages, and management was forced to borrow $100 million to pay it. After Lincoln's turnaround in 1994, the 60-percent

EXHIBIT 7 | Lincoln's Merit Rating Cards

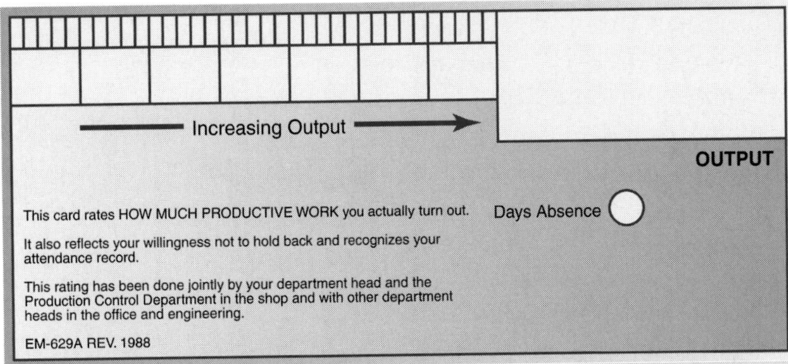
Increasing Output

OUTPUT

Days Absence

This card rates HOW MUCH PRODUCTIVE WORK you actually turn out.

It also reflects your willingness not to hold back and recognizes your attendance record.

This rating has been done jointly by your department head and the Production Control Department in the shop and with other department heads in the office and engineering.

EM-629A REV. 1988

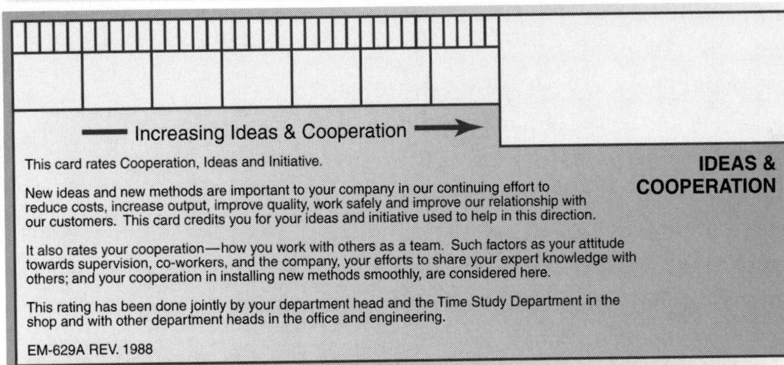
Increasing Ideas & Cooperation

IDEAS & COOPERATION

This card rates Cooperation, Ideas and Initiative.

New ideas and new methods are important to your company in our continuing effort to reduce costs, increase output, improve quality, work safely and improve our relationship with our customers. This card credits you for your ideas and initiative used to help in this direction.

It also rates your cooperation—how you work with others as a team. Such factors as your attitude towards supervision, co-workers, and the company, your efforts to share your expert knowledge with others; and your cooperation in installing new methods smoothly, are considered here.

This rating has been done jointly by your department head and the Time Study Department in the shop and with other department heads in the office and engineering.

EM-629A REV. 1988

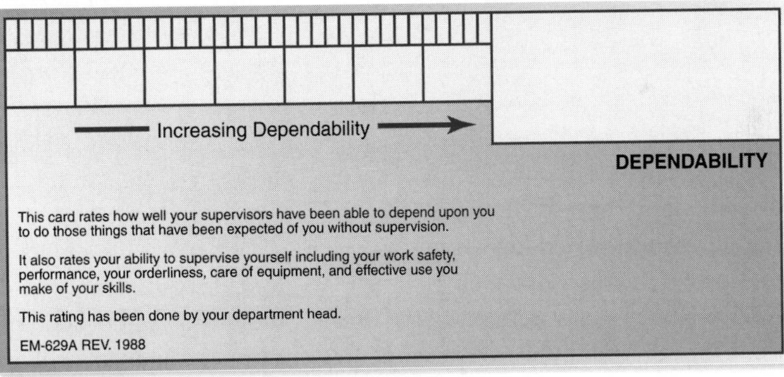
Increasing Dependability

DEPENDABILITY

This card rates how well your supervisors have been able to depend upon you to do those things that have been expected of you without supervision.

It also rates your ability to supervise yourself including your work safety, performance, your orderliness, care of equipment, and effective use you make of your skills.

This rating has been done by your department head.

EM-629A REV. 1988

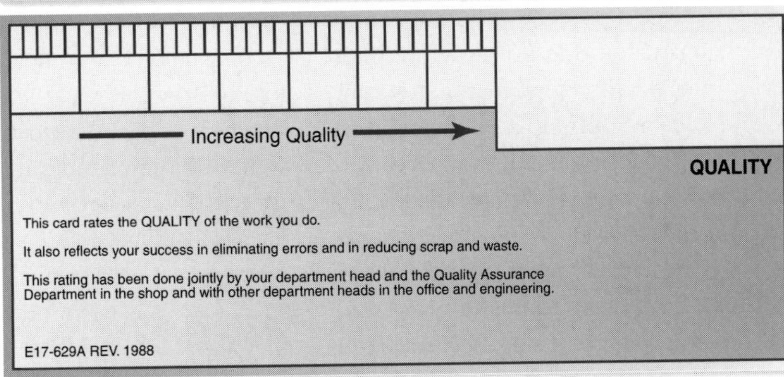
Increasing Quality

QUALITY

This card rates the QUALITY of the work you do.

It also reflects your success in eliminating errors and in reducing scrap and waste.

This rating has been done jointly by your department head and the Quality Assurance Department in the shop and with other department heads in the office and engineering.

E17-629A REV. 1988

bonus rate was continued as $63 million was used to repay principal and interest on the borrowed money. Average compensation of Lincoln's Cleveland employees in 1994 was about $35,000 before bonuses, and the average bonus was $20,000—$12,000 less than if the 90 percent average had applied. Some felt that employees were paying for management's mistakes.

Continuous Employment. In 1958 Lincoln formalized its guaranteed continuous employment policy, which had already been in effect for many years. Starting in 1958, every worker with over two years' longevity was guaranteed at least 30 hours per week, 49 weeks per year. The requirement was changed to three years' longevity in the recession year of 1982, when the policy was severely tested. In previous recessions the company had been able to avoid major sales declines. However, sales plummeted 32 percent in 1982 and another 16 percent the next year. Management cut most of the nonsalaried workers back to 30 hours a week for varying periods of time. Many employees were reassigned, and the total workforce was slightly reduced through normal attrition and restricted hiring. The previous year had set records, and some employees grumbled at their unexpected misfortune, to the surprise and dismay of some Lincoln managers.

Among employees with a year or more of service, employee turnover ran only four percent at Lincoln Electric. Absenteeism, too, was extremely low; critics in the press noted this was understandable, since workers were not paid for sick days. They noted, too, that 25 to 30 percent of new hires quit in their first six months of work, in spite of Lincoln's intensive interview process. In 1995, Lincoln's Cleveland workers were averaging over 45 hours a week on the job. Employee turnover after the first year was under 1 percent per year, excluding retirements. "The vast majority that quit do so before their first bonus," said Dick Sabo, director of corporate communications. "Once they see the dollars, they realize they are extremely well paid for their efforts." The average length of service of Lincoln's Cleveland workers in 1995 was approximately 14 years.

Stock Ownership by Employees. James Lincoln said that financing for company growth should come from within the company—through initial cash investment by the founders, through reinvestment of earnings, and through stock purchases by those who work in the business. He claimed this approach gave the following advantages:

1. Ownership of stock by employees strengthens team spirit. "If they are mutually anxious to make it succeed, the future of the company is bright."
2. Ownership of stock provides individual incentive because employees feel they will benefit from company profitability.
3. "Ownership is educational." Owner-employees "will know how profits are made and lost; how success is won and lost."
4. "Capital available from within controls expansion." Unwarranted expansion would not occur, Lincoln believed, under his financing plan (which did not allow for borrowing capital for growth).
5. "The greatest advantage would be the development of the individual worker. Under the incentive of ownership, he would become a greater man."
6. "Stock ownership is one of the steps that can be taken that will make the worker feel that there is less of a gulf between him and the boss."

Under Lincoln's Employees' Stock Purchase Plan, each employee could buy a specified number of shares of restricted common stock from the company each year, with company financing. The stock was priced at "estimated fair value" (taken to be book value), and the company had an option to repurchase it. Lincoln had always exercised its option to repurchase shares tendered by employees, and many employees felt it was obligated to do so. In 1992, approximately 75 percent of the employees owned over 40 percent of the total stock of the company. Lincoln family members and former Lincoln executives owned about half the remainder.

As Lincoln was preparing to report its first quarterly loss in August 1992, the directors voted to suspend repurchases under the Stock Purchase Plan in order to prevent wholesale tendering of shares by employees at a time when Lincoln was short of cash. The change in policy meant that employees could sell their stock in the open market as unrestricted stock if they wished to convert it to cash. At that time, book value (and therefore market value) was about $19 per share. As it turned out, only 11 percent of the restricted shares were converted.

In preparation for the public issue of stock in 1995, the Employees' Stock Purchase Plan was terminated on March 30, automatically converting all shares issued under it to unrestricted stock. Market value of the shares at that time was about $40. After the public issue, shareholders approved a new stock purchase plan permitting employees to purchase up to $10,000 per year in open-market shares without brokers' commissions.

Vacations. Lincoln's plants were closed for two weeks in August and two weeks during the Christmas season for vacations, which were unpaid. Employees with over 25 years of service got a fifth week of vacation at a time acceptable to superiors. When Lincoln was unable to meet its customers' orders in 1994, most employees agreed to work overtime through the August vacation period. Some of the employees were given vacations at alternate times.

Fringe Benefits. Lincoln sponsored a medical plan (with the cost deducted from the annual bonus pool) and a company-paid retirement program. At the main plant, a cafeteria operated on a break-even basis, serving meals at about sixty percent of outside prices. The Employee Association, to which the company did not contribute, provided disability insurance and social and athletic activities. Dick Sabo commented.

> *The company maintains traditional fringe benefits which include life insurance, health care, paid vacations, an annuity program (401K), and a variety of employee participation activities. All of these programs, of course, reduce the amount of money which otherwise could be received by the employees as bonus. Each employee is, therefore, acutely aware of the impact of such benefit items on their overall earnings in each year.*

He also cautioned,

> *When you use "participation," put quotes around it. Because we believe that each person should participate only in those decisions he is most knowledgeable about. I don't think production employees should control the decisions of the chairman. They don't know as much as he does about the decisions he is involved in.*

The primary means of employee participation beyond an employee's immediate work environment were the suggestion program and the Advisory Board. Members of the Advisory Board were elected by employees and met with President Fred Mackenbach every two weeks. Unlike James Lincoln and Bill Irrgang, CEOs Willis and Hastings did not regularly attend these meetings. Responses to all Advisory Board items were promised by the following meeting. Exhibit 8 provides excerpts from minutes of the Advisory Board meeting of March 14, 1995 (generally typical of the group's deliberations).

The Advisory Board could only advise, not direct, although its recommendations were taken seriously. Its influence was shown on December 1, 1995, when Lincoln reversed a two-year-old policy of paying lower wages to new hires. Veteran workers had complained loudly. *Business Week* quoted Joseph Tuck, an inspector with 18 years' service: "If an individual shows he can handle the workload, he should be rewarded" with full pay.[5]

INTERNATIONAL EXPANSION

Internationally, the welding equipment industry was highly fragmented but consolidating. No global statistics reported total economic activity or companies' market shares in various countries, but many developed economies had local suppliers. Two U.S. producers—Lincoln and Miller Electric—and one European firm, ESAB (the largest welding firm in the world by 1996), were present in most markets. (Exhibit 9, adapted from the 1995 annual report, shows Lincoln's recent sales by region.)

Until 1986, Lincoln Electric held to James Lincoln's original policy toward international ventures, according to Sam Evans, regional manager of international and a 40-year Lincoln veteran. James Lincoln had felt his company could manufacture in any English-speaking country. Otherwise, he let others promote Lincoln products internationally. Evans described the approach:

> *We dealt with Armco International, which was a division of Armco Steel. Lincoln licensed Armco to manufacture and market our products in Mexico, Uruguay, Brazil, Argentina, and in France. It was electrodes, but included assembly of machines in Mexico. Armco also marketed Lincoln products along*

8 | Excerpts from Advisory Board Minutes, March 14, 1995

Mr. Mackenbach opened the meeting by welcoming three new members to the Board. He called on Mr. Beddia to inform the Board about the Harvest for Hunger food drive.

Prior Items

1. Could all air-cooled engines be covered when we receive them? Answer: The Material Handling Department will cover the top pallet of each stack when the engines are unloaded.
2. Could the 401K contributions from bonus be included in the year-to-date totals on the remaining regular December pay stubs? Answer: Yes, it will be.
3. An employee was almost hit by a speeding electric cart in Bay 16. Could a slow speed sign be posted? Answer: Signs cautioning pedestrians regarding Towmotor traffic have been installed. Additional changes are being reviewed.

New Business

1. Why was an employee of the Motor Division penalized for a safety issue when he performed his job as instructed? Answer: Referred to Mr. Beddia.
2. Has our total percent of market share increased? Answer: In the past, we could provide a precise answer. Some of our competitors no longer provide the required information to NEMA. However, in our judgment, we are increasing our percent of market share in both consumables and equipment.
3. Could an additional microwave unit be installed in the Bay 24 vending area? Answer: Referred to Mr. Crissey.
4. Could we consider buying an emergency vehicle instead of paying between $300 and $500 per ambulance run to the hospital? Answer: When we use the services of the Euclid Fire and Rescue Squad, there is a charge of approximately $350. While in general this charge is covered by hospitalization insurance, we will ask Mr. Trivisonno to review this with city officials.
5. When will the softball field be completed? Answer: A recreational area on the EP-3 site will become a reality, although certain issues with the city must be resolved first. We will show the preliminary layout at the next meeting.
6. Is a member of the Board of Directors being investigated for fraud? Answer: We are not aware of any investigation of this type.
7. Is our investment in Mexico losing value? Could we have an update as to how our Mexican operation is doing? Answer: Yes. An update will be provided at the next meeting.
8. Could something be done to eliminate the odor created when the septic tank is cleaned? Answer: Referred to Mr. Hellings.

the Pacific Rim and in a few other areas of the world. At one point, we also had a joint venture with Big Three Corporation in Scotland.

In 1986, Lincoln Electric faced a newly aggressive Scandinavian competitor, ESAB Corporation, part of the Swiss-Swedish engineering/energy group Asea Brown Boveri. ESAB had bought up welding products manufacturers throughout the world during the industry downturn of 1982–1985. Starting in 1986, ESAB began to penetrate the U.S. market, buying several U.S. welding products companies (trade names acquired by ESAB included Oxweld, Genuine Heliarc, Plasmarc, Allstate Welding Products, Alloy Rods, and the former Lindy Division of Union Carbide). ESAB opened an electrode plant less than a mile from Lincoln's Cleveland headquarters.

In the global recession of the early 1980s, ESAB's movement toward consolidation threatened to give the firm a volume base large enough to provide economies of scale for research and development programs. Dick Sabo said Lincoln's CEO, Ted Willis, was concerned

9 | Financial Results by Geographic Sector, 1993–1995 (in thousands of dollars)

	United States	Europe	Other Countries	Total*
1995				
Net Sales to Unaffiliated Customers**	$711,940	$201,672	$118,786	$1,032,398
Pre-Tax Profit (Loss)	79,737	10,171	10,956	99,584
Identifiable Assets	404,972	194,319	80,921	617,760
1994				
Net Sales to Unaffiliated Customers	$641,607	$156,803	$108,194	$906,604
Pre-Tax Profit (Loss)	68,316	7,891	4,062	80,168
Identifiable Assets	350,012	165,722	76,129	556,857
1993				
Net Sales to Unaffiliated Customers	$543,458	$211,268	$91,273	$845,999
Pre-Tax Profit (Loss)	42,570	(68,865)	(22,903)	(46,950)
Identifiable Assets	389,247	172,136	69,871	559,543

*Totals for Profit/Loss and Identifiable Assets will not cross-add due to elimination of intercompany transactions.
**Net Sales reported for the United States include materials exported to unaffiliated customers, amounting to $81,770 in 1995; $64,400 in 1994; and $58,100 in 1993. Net Sales excludes intracompany sales to Lincoln's overseas branches.

and met with the chairman of ESAB in 1986, hoping "that we could work together." The relationship soon soured, however, and Willis decided to challenge ESAB internationally.

From 1986–1992, Lincoln purchased controlling interests in manufacturing and marketing operations in 16 countries. It took over most of the operations previously licensed to Armco and Big Three. It put a factory in Brazil, where ESAB had an estimated 70-percent market share. Lincoln expanded into gas welding and cutting by buying Harris Calorific Corporation, which made oxyacetylene cutting and welding equipment in the U.S., Italy, and Ireland. Lincoln's largest new investment was the purchase of Messer Griesheim's welding products business in Germany, considered ESAB's most profitable territory. Altogether, Lincoln opened or expanded plants in England, France, the Netherlands, Spain, Norway, Mexico, Venezuela, and Japan. The expansion required heavy borrowing; for the first time, James Lincoln's conservative financial policies were discarded. Long-term debt rose from zero in 1986 to over $220 million in 1992. (Exhibit 10 summarizes Lincoln financial statements for 1986–1995.)

Separate Lincoln-type incentive management plans remained in place at the company's factories in Australia, Mexico, and the U.S., but attempts to implement such plans in other countries were largely unsuccessful. Sabo said the main problem was that Europe lapsed into recession. He added, "Germany started to fail within two months after we purchased Griesheim. The country had 27-percent unemployment. So we didn't implement the system at all. We didn't get a chance to." In Brazil, Willis learned that regulations defined incentive bonuses to be part of base salaries, which could not be reduced during downturns, so the Lincoln system was not installed there.

Welder Scott Skrjanc, a 17-year veteran of the production force, had another idea about why the system did not work out overseas:

> *Their culture, as I understand it, was so much different from ours. Their work ethic and work habits, I*

10 | Summaries of Lincoln Financial Statements, 1986–1995*

Balance Sheets	**12/86**	**12/87**	**12/88**	**12/89**	**12/90**	**12/91**	**12/92**	**12/93**	**12/94**	**12/95**
Assets										
Cash and Equivalents	47.0	61.0	23.9	19.5	15.5	20.3	20.6	20.4	10.4	10.1
Receivables	46.0	61.7	90.9	100.8	127.3	118.0	111.3	110.5	126.0	140.8
Inventories	52.3	74.7	116.3	120.5	164.4	206.3	171.3	143.7	155.3	182.9
Other Current Assets	9.4	9.1	12.0	14.4	14.5	17.5	18.0	51.1	21.7	23.3
Total Current Assets	154.8	206.4	243.1	255.1	321.7	362.1	321.2	325.7	313.4	357.1
Gross Plant	153.2	195.7	274.8	328.2	387.7	422.9	435.2	406.7	444.5	490.6
Accumulated Depreciation	93.4	121.2	148.6	170.2	193.1	213.3	226.8	237.0	260.3	285.0
Net Plant	59.8	74.5	126.3	158.0	194.7	209.6	208.4	169.7	184.2	205.6
Long-Term Investments	11.5	0.3	0.0	0.0	0.0	0.0	0.0	0.0	0.0	0.0
Intangible and Other Assets	13.1	13.4	33.8	42.6	55.9	68.6	73.7	64.1	59.2	55.1
Total Assets	239.2	294.7	403.2	455.8	572.2	640.3	603.3	559.5	556.9	617.8
Liabilities & Equity										
Short-Term Debt	4.6	6.6	39.2	41.6	40.6	50.7	27.1	33.4	18.1	29.8
Accounts Payable	11.2	23.4	36.8	40.0	44.3	46.6	44.2	43.5	54.8	53.9
Other Current Liabilities	25.1	32.7	38.1	41.0	52.4	61.3	77.2	99.0	71.2	85.0
Total Current Liabilities	41.0	62.7	114.2	122.6	137.3	158.6	148.5	175.9	144.1	168.7
Long-Term Debt	0.0	5.7	17.5	30.2	109.2	155.5	221.5	216.9	194.8	93.6
Other Long-Term Liabilities	11.7	9.7	15.3	16.6	24.0	20.3	17.8	15.3	17.0	20.1
Minority Interests	4.0	11.9	31.4	42.6	47.4	41.7	16.8	7.9	6.8	5.5
Total Liabilities	56.7	90.0	178.4	211.9	317.9	376.1	404.6	416.0	218.6	287.9
Common Equity	182.6	204.7	224.8	243.8	254.3	264.1	198.7	143.5	194.1	329.9
Total Equity Capital	182.6	204.7	224.8	243.8	254.3	264.1	198.7	143.5	194.1	329.9
Total Liabilities & Capital	239.2	294.7	403.2	455.8	572.2	640.3	603.3	559.5	556.9	617.8
INCOME STATEMENTS										
Net Sales	370.2	443.2	570.2	692.8	796.7	833.9	853.0	846.0	906.6	1,032.4
Cost of Goods Sold	245.4	279.4	361.0	441.3	510.5	521.8	553.1	532.8	556.3	634.6
Gross Profit	124.8	163.8	209.2	251.5	286.2	312.1	299.9	313.2	350.3	397.8
SG&A Expense	100.3	119.7	165.2	211.1	259.2	270.5	280.3	273.3	261.7	289.8
Operating Profit	24.5	44.1	44.0	40.4	27.0	41.6	19.6	39.9	88.6	108.0
Restructuring Charge	0	0	0	0	0	0	–23.9	–70.1	2.7	0
Non-Recurring Oper. Exp.	0	0	0	0	0	0	–18.9	–3.7	0	0
Other Income	6.1	7.1	14.4	15.7	14.4	8.5	7.5	4.5	4.5	3.9
EBIT	30.6	51.2	58.4	56.1	41.4	50.1	–15.7	–29.4	95.9	111.9
Interest Expense	1.0	1.3	2.6	7.6	11.1	15.7	18.7	17.6	15.7	12.3
Pre-tax Earnings	29.6	49.9	55.9	48.5	30.4	34.4	–34.4	–47.0	80.2	99.6
Income Taxes	13.7	22.3	21.5	21.0	19.3	20.0	11.4	–6.4	32.2	38.1
Accounting Change	0	0	0	0	0	0	0	2.5	0	0
Net Income	15.8	27.6	34.4	27.6	11.1	14.4	–45.8	–38.1	48.0	61.5

*Source of Data, McDonald and Company and SEC reports.

guess, aren't like the United States. They have a saying in German that means, "slowly, slowly, but good." And I guess that's how they perceive it. Here, we do high-quality work, but we work fast—and smart. As you get older, you get wiser and work smarter.

Sam Evans, who managed Lincoln's operations in Eastern Europe until cancer forced his return to Cleveland for successful treatment, gave his view of CEO Willis' performance in the international expansion:

Ted Willis' belief—and I think it was a very good belief, although he is often criticized by Lincoln people—was that we needed a stronger world organization. The welding industry was consolidating in the world market, much like the steel industry did in the 1930s. He felt we needed this larger sales base so that we could invest in the research and development to maintain our position in the industry. I think that has succeeded. Even though we have had failures internationally, we have grown with our base.

We are coming out with a lot of new items—the new square-wave machines, which control the actual wave form, the new stainless products, the inverter technology in motors and machines. We are moving rapidly ahead of the industry. That was Mr. Willis' vision, and it was a good one. His financial vision wasn't so good—perhaps.

Retrenchment and Turnaround under Hastings

Willis retired in 1992 and Don Hastings became chief executive officer. Hastings set about "consolidating and reorganizing" the foreign operations. He agreed with ESAB to close the Lincoln factory in Brazil and to license ESAB to make Lincoln products there. Similarly, ESAB closed its Spanish electrode plant, and Lincoln used its excess capacity in that country to supply ESAB's needs. Lincoln mothballed its German plant, losing an estimated $100 million there. It also shut down factories in Venezuela and Japan. Practically all of Lincoln's international operations that were not closed were scaled back. By 1996 ESAB, now owned by Britain's Charter Group, was recognized as the largest welding vendor in the world, with key markets in East and Western Europe, South America, and the Far East; it had the "leading position in stick electrodes (a declining market) and an even bigger position in fluxed core wires (a rapidly growing market)."[6]

In 1992 and 1993, Lincoln wrote off approximately $130 million of its foreign assets and reported its first-ever net losses—$46 million and $38 million respectively. Citing the profitable performance of the firm's U.S. workers, Hastings convinced the Board of Directors to give them incentive bonuses averaging $19,000 each year in spite of the overall losses. Dividends were cut by nearly 40 percent from the 1991 level. In 1994, Hastings told the U.S. employees, "We went from five plants in four countries in 1986 to 21 plants in 15 countries in 1992. We did it too fast, we paid too much, we didn't understand the international markets or cultures, and then we got hit by a tremendous global recession." By mid 1995, Lincoln was down to 16 plants in 11 countries. Dick Sabo described the company's new relationship with ESAB:

So the animosity has ended. We're still competitors, but we are more like the U.S. competitors. In the U.S., we've always had a competitive situation, but we're friendly competitors. So, overall, the strategy that Ted Willis originated was good. The implementation was poor. That's where the problem was.

Rank and file employees commented on the results of the attempt at international expansion. Stenographer Dee Chesko, a 27-year employee, said she had heard no bitterness voiced about the losses:

What I was hearing was people were disappointed—that they felt upper management should know, per se, what they're doing. You know, how could this happen? Not bitterness . . . a little frustration. But, if companies are to expand and be global, this has to be expected.

Assembler Kathleen Hoenigman, hired in 1997, added:

They say, "We want to be number one. We want to be number one." So we are going to keep buying and buying and buying. I think we will be investing more overseas. And I think we are going to be number one internationally, not just in the U.S., but the manufacturing will be done here. The expansion helped. We lost money, but I think it helped. You know what, if we didn't do as we did, we wouldn't be known as well as we are right now. Because we were staying just like a little . . . a little pea, while everybody was building up around us.

Sabo said Lincoln expected to continue expanding internationally, "But we're going at it a little differently." He explained,

> *Under Willis, we bought a manufacturing site with the intent of creating the marketing demand. Under Hastings, we're developing the marketing demand with the anticipation that we'll build the manufacturing site to meet the demand. So what we're trying to do is take the existing facilities that we have and sell a lot of product and create enough demand so that we have to buy—or build—more facilities to service that demand.*
>
> *We're just getting there in terms of being global. We're global to the extent that we market in 123 countries. We're global to the extent that we have distributors in 86 different countries. We're global because we have manufacturing sites in ten countries. Are we global in our management style? No. We're just starting to develop that.*

THE U.S. WELDING PRODUCTS INDUSTRY IN 1995

The welding products market of the mid 1990s was classified as "mature and cyclical." In the United States, annual sales volume had ranged between \$2.5 and \$2.7 billion since 1988 (see Exhibit 11). The main arc-welding products were power sources and welding machines; consumable items such as welding electrodes; accessories such as protective clothing; automated wire feeding systems; and devices to manipulate or position the electrodes, such as robots.

After the downturn in 1982–1983, when industry sales fell 30–40 percent, the U.S. welding products industry consolidated. By 1995, at least 75 percent of machine and consumables sales could be attributed to just four companies: Lincoln, Miller Electric Company (which did not sell consumables), ESAB Corporation, and Hobart Brothers, Inc. ESAB was now owned by Britain's Charter Group; both Miller and Hobart had recently been acquired by Illinois Tool Works, Inc. Lincoln and Miller were thought to have about equal unit sales of machines and power supplies, about double Hobart's volume. Hundreds of smaller companies marketed various niche products, and several international firms sold limited lines of transformer- and inverter-based machines in the U.S. and elsewhere. Over 600 exhibitors were registered to show their wares at the 1996 annual Welding Show in Chicago, where 25,000 potential customers would attend.

Starting in the early 90s, Lincoln, Miller, and Hobart each began buying similar articulated-arm robots and adapting them to welding applications. The size of the robotics segment of the welding products market was unclear in 1995, but Chet Woodman, head of Lincoln Automation, said his unit had robotics sales of about \$7 million in 1994 and predicted \$50 million annual revenue by the year 2000.

ESAB, Lincoln, and Hobart each marketed a wide range of continuous-wire and stick electrodes for welding mild steel, aluminum, cast iron, and stainless and special steels. Most electrodes were designed to meet the standards of the American Welding Society (AWS) and were thus essentially the same as to size and composition from one manufacturer to another. Price differences for similar products among the three companies amounted to only a percent or two. Low-price competitors were well represented in the market, however, as imported consumables that purported to meet AWS standards were commonly available. There was no testing system to confirm a product's conformance to the standards.

Every electrode manufacturer had a limited number of unique products, which typically constituted only a small percentage of its total sales. There were also many producers of specialized electrodes for limited applications, such as welding under water and welding space-age alloys, and several international companies marketed general-purpose electrodes. Wire for gas-shielded (MIG) welding was thought to be the biggest-selling welding consumable. ESAB claimed to have the largest share of the global welding consumables and materials market.

LINCOLN'S MANUFACTURING PROCESSES

Lincoln made about twice as many different products in 1995 as it had ten years earlier. Its net sales per em-

EXHIBIT 11 | Trends and Forecasts: Welding Apparatus (SIC 3548) (in millions of dollars except as noted)

	1987	1988	1989	1990	1991	1992[1]	1993[2]	1994[3]
Industry Data								
Value of shipments[4]	2,105	2,498	2,521	2,684	2,651	2,604	2,576	—
Total employment (000)	18.7	19.7	19.0	19.2	19.5	19.4	19.5	—
Production workers (000)	11.5	12.3	11.6	12.0	11.8	11.7	11.7	—
Average hourly earnings ($)	12.10	12.45	12.67	13.15	13.07	—	—	—
Capital expenditures	45.4	49.3	59.1	67.7	50.5	—	—	—
Product Data								
Value of shipments[5]	1,918	2,263	2,298	2,475	2,434	2,374	2,340	—
Value of shipments (1987 $)	1,918	2,135	2,077	2,154	2,034	1,935	1,874	1,954
Trade Data								
Value of imports	—	—	480	365	478	381	458	458
Value of exports	—	—	491	566	597	621	661	671

	Percent Change (1989–1994)					
	88–89	89–90	90–91	91–92	92–93	93–94
Industry Data						
Value of shipments[4]	0.9	6.5	–1.2	–1.8	–1.1	—
Value of shipments (1987 $)	–3.3	2.5	–5.2	–4.1	–3.0	3.9
Total employment (000)	–3.6	1.1	1.6	–0.5	0.5	—
Production workers (000)	–5.7	3.4	–1.7	–0.8	0.0	—
Average hourly earnings ($)	1.8	3.8	–0.6	—	—	—
Capital expenditures	19.9	14.6	–25.4	—	—	—
Product Data						
Value of shipments[5]	1.5	7.7	–1.7	–2.5	–1.4	—
Value of shipments (1987 $)	–2.7	3.7	–5.6	–4.9	–3.2	4.3
Value of exports	747.0	15.3	5.5	4.0	8.1	11.3

Source: U.S. Department of Commerce: Bureau of the Census; International U.S. Industrial Outlook January, 1994.
[1]Estimate, except exports and imports.
[2]Estimate.
[3]Forecast.
[4]Value of all products and services sold by establishments in the welding apparatus industry.
[5]Value of products classified in the welding apparatus industry produced b.

ployee in 1994 were $159,248. For U.S. employees only, the number was approximately $225,000. About two-thirds of net sales was represented by products made in the Cleveland area.

Fortune magazine declared Lincoln's Euclid operation one of America's ten best-managed factories, and compared it to a General Electric plant also on the list:

> *Stepping into GE's spanking new dishwasher plant, an awed supplier said, is like stepping "into the Hyatt Regency." By comparison, stepping into Lincoln Electric's 33-year-old, cavernous, dimly lit factory is like stumbling into a dingy big-city YMCA. It's only when one starts looking at how these factories do things that similarities become apparent. They have found ways to merge design with manufacturing, build in quality, make wise choices about automation, get close to customers, and handle their work forces.*[7]

As it had for decades, Lincoln required most suppliers to deliver raw materials just as needed in production. James Lincoln had counseled producing for stock when necessary to maintain employment. For many years after his death, however, the firm manufactured only to customer order. In the late 1980s, Hastings decided to resume maintaining substantial finished goods inventories. Lincoln then purchased its finished goods warehouse.

Outsourcing

It was James Lincoln's policy to keep Lincoln as insulated as possible from work stoppages in supplier plants, especially unionized ones. He also felt Lincoln quality was higher than that most suppliers could provide. So instead of purchasing most components from outsiders, Lincoln made them from basic industrial raw materials such as coils of steel sheet and bar, pieces of metal plate, spools of copper and aluminum wire, and pallets of paints and varnishes. Lincoln even made its own electronic circuit boards, to assure their performance in outdoor, cold, dirty conditions; commercial suppliers were accustomed to making circuit boards for warm, clean computers. At one point the firm had contemplated buying its own steel rolling mill. President Ted Willis, however, was concerned over the mill's union affirmation, and the purchase was not completed.

As an exception to on-site manufacture of components, gasoline and diesel engines for the engine-driven machines were purchased. Like its main competitors, Lincoln used Wisconsin-Continental, Perkins, and Deutz engines in 1995.

Welding Machine Manufacture

In the machines area, most engine-driven welders, power supplies, wire feeders, and so forth, were assembled, tested, and packaged on conveyor lines. Almost all components were made by numerous small "factories within a factory." Various of these small factories—mostly open work areas—made gasoline tanks, steel shafts, wiring harnesses, and even switches, rheostats, and transformers. The shaft for a certain generator, for example, was made from round steel bar by two men who used five machines. A saw cut the bar to length, a digital lathe machined different sections to varying diameters, a special milling machine cut a slot for the keyway, and so forth, until a finished shaft was produced. The operators moved the shafts from machine to machine and made necessary adjustments and tool changes. Nearby, a man punched, shaped and painted sheet metal cowling parts. In another area, a woman and a man put steel laminations onto rotor shafts, then wound, insulated, and tested the rotors. Many machines in the factory appeared old, even obsolete; James Lincoln had always insisted on a one-year payback period for new investments, and it appeared the policy was still in effect.

Consumables Manufacture

The company was secretive about its consumables production, and outsiders were barred from the Mentor, Ohio plant (which made only electrodes) and from the electrode area of the main plant. Electrode manufacture was highly capital intensive, and teams of Lincoln workers who made electrodes shared group piece rates. To make electrodes, rod purchased from metals producers, usually in coils, was drawn down to make wire of various diameters. For stick electrodes, the wire was cut into pieces, most commonly 14" long, and coated with pressed-powder "flux." Dick Sabo commented,

> *The actual production of a stick electrode has not changed for at least forty years. Bill Irrgang designed that equipment. As to the constituents which make up the electrodes, that may change almost daily. There are changes in design from time to time. And every new batch of raw material has a little different consistency, and we have to adjust for that. We make our own iron oxide [a main ingredient of many fluxes]. We have had that powder kiln in operation since about the 1930s. We may have the largest production facility for iron oxide pellets in the world. At first, we contemplated selling the pellets. But we decided not to give our competition an edge.*

Stick electrodes were packaged in boxes weighing two to 50 pounds. Continuous-wire electrode, generally smaller in diameter, was packaged in coils and spools, also two to 50 pounds each, and in drums weighing up to half a ton. Some wire electrode was coated with copper to improve conductivity. Lincoln's Innershield wire, like the "cored" wire of other manufacturers, was hollow and filled with a material similar to that used to coat stick electrodes.

The New Electric Motor Factory

In 1992, Lincoln saw an opportunity to become a major factor in the electric motor business by purchasing the assets of General Motors' AC-Delco plant in Dayton, Ohio. New government regulations on motors' energy efficiency made it necessary to redesign whole product lines; GM decided instead to exit the industry. Lincoln's intent was to combine AC-Delco's technology and product line with Lincoln's manufacturing expertise and cost structure in the Dayton plant. Don Hastings offered to involve the existing union in its operation of the plant if it were retained. Dick Sabo described the implementation efforts:

> *We asked the AC-Delco employees if they wanted to adopt the Lincoln Incentive System and keep their plant open—and their jobs. They voted overwhelmingly not to adopt the system. And they knew all about us. We put a lot of effort into telling them about Lincoln, even brought some employees up here to tour our plant and talk to Lincoln people. What struck Mr. Hastings as odd was that people would vote themselves out of work rather than knuckle down and put in the effort that it takes to be in the motor business. That was sort of an eye opener for Lincoln Electric.*

In mid-1995, Lincoln's new electric motor factory, close to the main plant, was near completion and in partial operation. The plant was designed to make motors from one-third to 1,250 horsepower, in custom configurations as well as standard specifications, with shipment six days after customer orders. Lincoln's net sales of electric motors in 1994 totalled about $50 million, and the goal was $100 million in sales by the year 2000.

Robotics

Adjacent to the electric motor factory was a smaller building housing Lincoln's Automation unit. There, work teams of two or three put together robotic welding units that combined Fanuc (Japanese) articulated arms with Lincoln automatic welders. In operation, the robot arm manipulated the wire electrode much as a human operator would, but faster and more accurately. The system priced at about $100,000, could be purchased with a laser "eye" to track irregular seams and could be programmed to follow any three dimensional path within the arm's reach. Chet Woodman, head of Lincoln Automation, was a former Hobart executive with over a decade of experience in robotics manufacturing and marketing.

MANAGEMENT ORGANIZATION

James Lincoln stressed the need to protect management's authority. "Management in all successful departments of industry must have complete power," he said, "Management is the coach who must be obeyed. The men, however, are the players who alone can win the game." Examples of management's authority were the right to transfer workers among jobs, to switch between overtime and short time as required, and to assign specific parts to individual workers. As to executive perquisites, there were few—crowded, austere offices, no executive washrooms or lunchrooms or automobiles, and no reserved parking spaces, except for visitors. Even CEO Hastings and President Mackenbach paid for their own meals, normally in the employee cafeteria.

James Lincoln never allowed preparation of a formal organization chart, saying this might limit flexibility. Irrgang and Willis continued that policy. During the 1970s, Harvard Business School researchers prepared a chart reflecting the implied management relationships at Lincoln. It became available within the company, and Irrgang felt this had a disruptive effect. Only after Hastings became CEO was a formal chart prepared. (Exhibit 12 shows the official chart in 1995 and Exhibit 6 lists officers and directors.) Two levels of management, at most, existed between supervisors and Mackenbach. Production supervisors at Lincoln typically were responsible for 60 to over 100 workers. Hastings, who was 67, had recruited experienced managers from outside the company and appointed a number of new, young vice presidents, mainly from the field, so they could compete for the top jobs.

Promotion from Within

Until the 1990s, Lincoln had a firm policy of promotion from within and claimed to hire above the entry level "only when there are no suitable internal applicants." In 1990, all senior managers at Lincoln were career Lincoln employees—and all directors were present or former employees or Lincoln family members. However, when Lincoln purchased Harris Calorific in 1992, its CEO, Paul F. Fantelli, was retained and later became vice

12 | Lincoln Organization Chart, 1995

- **D. Hastings** — Chairman and Chief Executive Officer
  - **Vice Chairman** — *H. Carlson*
  - **Corporate Communications & Investor Relations** — *R. Sabo*
  - **Executive Assistant** — *M. Baller*
  - V.P., President Lincoln Europe — *A. Massaro*
  - V.P., CFO & Treasurer Acting Secretary — *J. Elliot*
  - President & COO — *F. Mackenbach*
    - Manager Administration — *J. Hach*
    - Manager Customer Logistics — *R. Trivisonno*
    - President Lincoln Canada — *J. Daria*
    - Senior V.P. Sales — *J. Stropki*
    - V.P. Machine R&D — *R. Nelson*
    - V.P. Marketing — *R. Seif*
    - V.P. Consumable R&D — *D. Crockett*
    - Senior V.P. Consumable Division — *R. Ulstad*
    - Senior V.P. Machine & Motor Divisions — *D. Fullen*
    - V.P., President Lincoln Latin America — *J. Delaney*
    - Managers Quality Assurance, Machine, Motor & Consumables — *W. Downing/G. Skerl*
    - President Lincoln Australia — *J. Twyble*
    - President Harris Division — *P. Ullman*
  - V.P. Human Resources — *P. Beddia*
  - V.P., General Counsel & Secretary — *F. Stueber*
  - V.P. Business Development — *P. Fantelli*

president, business development of Lincoln. A number of other acquired company officials were integrated into Lincoln's management structure.

Lincoln's CFO in 1996, H. Jay Elliott, came from Goodyear in 1993; General Counsel Frederick Stueber came from a private law firm in 1995; and Anthony Massaro, the nominated successor to Fred Mackenbach as president, joined Lincoln from his position as group president of Westinghouse Electric Co. in 1993. Several outside directors were also elected, including the CEO of Capitol American Financial Corporation, a former vice chairman of General Electric, a former CEO of Westinghouse, and the CEO of Libby Corporation. Still, there were no announced plans to hire more managers from outside. And insiders and Lincoln family members retained a clear majority on the board.

Lincoln managers received a base salary plus an incentive bonus. The bonus was calculated in the same way as for workers. The only exceptions were the three outsiders Hastings hired as managers in 1993–1995 and the chairman and chief executive officer. The former outsiders had special employment contracts. Sabo explained how the CEO was compensated:

> *James Lincoln set the chairman's salary at $50,000 plus 0.1 percent of sales. After Willis became chairman, it was based on a percentage of sales plus a percentage of profit. It became apparent that when the*

company started losing money it was difficult to pay someone based on losses. So they changed the approach for Don Hastings. [Through the lean years] Don has somewhere around $600 thousand base salary plus incentives.

For 1995, Hastings was paid $1,003,901.[8]

LOOKING TO THE FUTURE

When Lincoln announced plans in the spring of 1995 to raise capital with a public issue of stock, Dick Sabo said that certain Lincoln family members were afraid the family would lose control of the company. "Paranoid, I guess, is the proper term," he remarked. Sam Evans added,

I hope the public issue is handled in such a manner that those public owners understand that the success of this company is based on the incentive system. For sixty or seventy years, that has been our success—through the contribution of the employees. We have succeeded because we had a good product, good R&D, and excellent management for most of that period. But we've also had great contribution from the employees.

With the public issue accomplished and a record year in the books, noted *Business Week*,

. . . executives are now considering ways to move toward a more traditional pay scheme and away from the flat percentage-bonus formula. "The bonus is a good program, and it has worked well, but it's got to be modified some," says Director David C. Lincoln, whose father John C. Lincoln founded the company in 1895. Adds Edward E. Lawler, who heads the University of Southern California's Center for Effective Organizations: "One of the issues with Lincoln is how [its pay plan] can survive rapid growth and globalization."

NOTES

1. Feder, Barnaby J. "Rethinking a Model Incentive Plan," *The New York Times*, September 5, 1994, Section I, p. 33.
2. Gerdel, Thomas W. "Lincoln Electric Experiences Season of Worker Discontent," *Plain Dealer*, December 10, 1995.
3. Schiller, Zachary, "A Model Incentive Plan Gets Caught in a Vise," *Business Week*, January 22, 1996, p. 89.
4. Eiselen, F.C., E. Lewis, and D.G. Downey, eds. *The Abingdon Bible Commentary*, Nashville, TN: The Abingdon Press, Inc., 1929, pp. 960–969.
5. Schiller, *op. cit.*
6. Utley, N., *et al.*, Greig Middleton & Co., Ltd. Company report number 1674211, *Charter 12/12/95*. Investext 02/23.
7. Bylinsky, Gene. "America's Best-Managed Factories," *Fortune*, May 28, 1984, p. 16.
8. Baltimore, MD, Disclosures, Inc. (Via Dow Jones News Service).

CASE 26

The Loewen Group

Ariff Kachra
Mary Crossan
The University of Western Ontario

On September 17, 1996, Ray Loewen, Chairman and CEO of the Loewen Group, North America's second largest funeral home consolidator, was seeking approval from his Board for the purchase of the largest cemetery in the U.S., Rose Hills Memorial Park in California. As he was speaking about the $240 million[1] acquisition, one of the investment bankers at the meeting responded to a 911 on his beeper display. He returned with a news wire bulletin announcing the launch of a hostile take-over bid by SCI (Service Corporation International), the world's largest funeral consolidator. What began as a meeting seeking approvals for acquisitions had turned into a war council. The entire Board turned to Mr. Loewen for his reaction. Should Loewen Group fight the takeover, or should it accept SCI's offer? (See Exhibit 1 for a copy of the letter sent by William Heiligbrodt to Ray Loewen, outlining the parameters of the proposed bid.)

IVEY Ariff Kachra prepared this case under the supervision of Professor Mary Crossan solely to provide material for class discussion. The authors do not intend to illustrate either effective or ineffective handling of a managerial situation. The authors may have disguised certain names and other identifying information to protect confidentiality.

Ivey Management Services prohibits any form of reproduction, storage or transmittal without its written permission. This material is not covered under authorization from CanCopy or any reproduction rights organization. To order copies or request permission to reproduce materials, contact Ivey Publishing, Ivey Management Services, c/o Richard Ivey School of Business. The University of Western Ontario, London, Ontario, Canada, N6A 3K7; phone (519) 661-3208; fax (519) 661-3882; e-mail cases@Ivey.uwo.ca.

Copyright © 1997, Ivey Management Services. One-time permission to reproduce Ivey cases granted by Ivey Management Services on November 18, 1999.

THE FUNERAL SERVICE INDUSTRY

Typically, when a person passed away and had not made provisions for a pre-planned funeral, the process began with a phone call to book a meeting with the funeral director at a home. The funeral director used this meeting to grasp initial perceptions and thoughts of the bereaved family. The family had many choices including anything from a simple disposition to a traditional, full visitation service. With the help of the funeral director, the family made decisions on the elements of the funeral service, such as embalming, visitation, music, chapel, etc. As required by law, the funeral director reviewed the fee schedule with the family. The family then purchased merchandise such as caskets and urns. The family was then referred to a local cemetery, where they purchased a burial plot and any other related merchandise like vaults, markers, and headstones. After obtaining the family's legal authorization, the funeral director proceeded with the arrangements. Typically, a few weeks after the service, the funeral home made an after-care call to determine if the family needed additional support or had any bereavement-related concerns.

Exhibit 2 maps out the industry players that made up the funeral industry's business system.

Funeral Homes

Funeral homes did everything from selling pre-need insurance[2] to arranging a cremation, a simple burial and, more often than not, a traditional funeral service. Sources of revenue for a funeral home included professional services, facility and automotive rentals, and cas-

1 | Heiligbrodt Letter to Loewen

L. William Heiligbrodt
President
September 17, 1996

Mr. Raymond L. Loewen
Chairman of the Board and Chief Executive Officer
The Loewen Group Inc.
4126 Norland Avenue
Burnaby, British Columbia, Canada

Dear Mr. Loewen:

As you know, I have tried to reach you several times since September 11. While your office has assured me that you received my messages, my calls have not been returned. In view of that, and in view of the importance of this matter, I am sending this letter.

I would like to discuss with you a combination of our two companies. The combination would involve a stock-for-stock exchange accounted for as a pooling which values Loewen Group at US$43 per share. We believe that this transaction can be structured in a manner that is tax-free to both companies and (except for a relatively nominal amount in the case of U.S. stockholders) to the U.S. and Canadian stockholders of Loewen Group.

I think you and your Board and stockholders would agree that our proposal is a generous one, resulting in the following premiums for Loewen Group stockholders:

- 48.9% above the price at which Loewen Group stock traded 30 days ago;
- 39.3% above the price at which Loewen Group stock traded one week ago; and
- 27.4% above the price at which Loewen Group stock is currently trading.

This represents an opportunity for your stockholders to realize excellent value, by any measure, for their shares. In addition, and importantly, since your stockholders would be receiving stock, they would continue to participate in Loewen Group's business as well as share in the upside of our business.

Thus, in essence, your stockholders would:

- continue their investment in our industry;
- get an immediate, and very significant, increase in the market value of their investment;
- get that immediate and substantial increase on an essentially tax free basis; and
- diversify their risk by participating in a much larger number of properties.

This is a "win-win" situation for you and your stockholders.

Finally, with respect to consideration, I would note also that our proposal is based on public information. After a due diligence review, we may be in a position to increase the consideration that your stockholders would receive.

We, of course, recognize that our businesses overlap in various locations. We have carefully reviewed this matter and are convinced that competition issues can be cured by selecting divestitures without impairment of the values that a combination would achieve for the stockholders of our two companies.

I would very much like to discuss any and all aspects of our proposal with you and your Board of Directors. We believe you and they will recognize the tremendous benefit to your stockholders of our proposal. Our proposal is conditioned upon approval of our Board and upon negotiation of mutually satisfactory agreements providing for a combination on a pooling basis.

We hope that after you meet with us, you will similarly determine that the transaction should be pursued. We look forward to hearing from you.

In view of the importance of this matter, we are simultaneously releasing this letter to the press.

Sincerely,

William Heiligbrodt
President

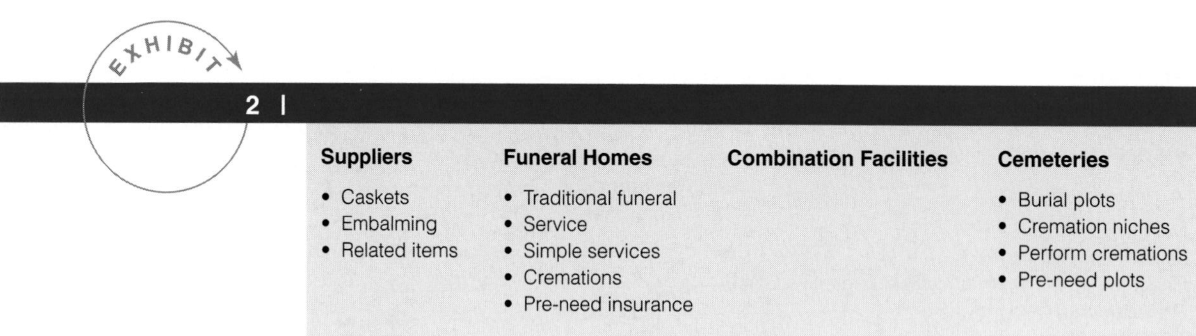

ket and urn sales. Expenses were made up of personnel, automotive equipment, promotion, business services, supplies, after-sale expenses and sundry items (See Exhibit 3). The funeral home was usually the customer's first point of contact. Whether the customer wanted a simple burial or a traditional funeral, the funeral home had the first opportunity to sell all related services and supplies.

Suppliers

Funeral home consolidators had consistently put a great deal of pressure on suppliers to reduce prices. This had a negative impact on the profitability of suppliers because they were very dependent on funeral homes. The potential threat to the casket producers and embalming suppliers was that as the funeral industry gave way to more and more consolidation, they would become increasingly dependent on a few large customers. With this dependence would come decreased margins and potential consolidation in the supply side of the industry.

Cemeteries

The sources of revenue for cemeteries included the sales of at-need[3] and pre-need burial plots, cremation niches,[4] burial stones and plaques and professional services related to cremation and burial. Expenses consisted of personnel, maintenance of facilities, and sales and promotion (see Exhibit 4). Historically in Canada and the U.S., the vast majority of cemeteries had been privately owned. At the beginning of 1996, in Canada alone, there were over 10,000 private cemeteries. There were two key benefits of purchasing a cemetery. The first was that cemeteries offered a secure revenue stream for about 30 to 50 years. This revenue stream slowly began increasing as cemeteries concentrated on merchandising. The second was that cemeteries accrued pre-need revenues upon receipt, and used the money for investment purposes. This was a legal use of the funds, as long as 10 to 15 percent of the revenues were invested in a perpetual care fund.[5] This represented a marked advantage over funeral homes, whose pre-need sales revenues had to be placed in trust until the time when the beneficiary passed away.

Combination Facilities

A recent development in the industry was the concept of combination facilities. Combination facilities afforded consumers the very attractive option of one-stop shopping, i.e., both the funeral home and the cemetery were located in one facility. The growth opportunities were vast in terms of combinations because industry statistics indicated that "within six to eight years of opening, the average funeral home operating within a cemetery should perform the number of funerals approximately equivalent to 80 percent of the number of interments at that cemetery." (The Death Care Industry, July 16, 1996, Darren Martin, TD Securities Inc.)

IMPORTANT INDUSTRY TRENDS

Consolidation

The North American funeral industry was very large and fragmented (see Exhibit 5 for industry structure). This made it ripe for consolidation. Consolidators felt that there were many opportunities for growth and profitability. With an increasing death rate (see Exhibit 6)

3 | Typical Income Statement of an Independent Funeral Home ($)

	1986	1991	1992	1993	1996
Average "Regular Adult Funeral" Services & Casket	2766.26	3507.19	3663.49	3819.17	4287.14
Operation Cost per Adult Funeral	2015.75	2597.69	2717.2	2823.03	3160.33
Percentage of Operating Cost to Selling Price	72.87%	74.07%	74.17%	73.92%	73.72%
Casket Cost	469.99	606.04	627.7	652.18	729.68
Percentage of Casket Cost to Selling Price	16.99%	17.28%	17.13%	17.08%	17.02%
Profit Before Federal Income Tax	280.52	303.46	318.59	343.96	397.13
Percentage of Profit to Selling Price	10.14%	8.65%	8.70%	9.01%	9.26%

Using data from Federated Funeral Directors of America.

Breakdown of Operational Expenses for a Typical Independent Funeral Home ($)

	1986	% of Rev.	1991	% of Rev.	1992	% of Rev.	1993	% of Rev.	1996	% of Rev.
Personnel	913.33	33.02	1209.51	34.49	1266.75	34.58	1347.55	35.28	1507.2	35.16
Cost of Facilities	602.78	21.79	789.55	22.51	811.81	22.16	830.13	21.74	919.32	21.44
Automotive Equipment	207.43	7.50	213.11	6.08	222.42	6.07	223.2	5.84	256.5	5.98
Promotion	118.48	4.28	146.72	4.18	157.1	4.29	159.12	4.17	173.06	4.04
Business Service	65.06	2.35	86.49	2.47	90.12	2.46	93.52	2.45	107.46	2.51
Supplies	59.51	2.15	74.69	2.13	79.35	2.17	83.08	2.18	92.32	2.15
After Sale Expenses	41.05	1.48	66.9	1.91	78.5	2.14	75.49	1.98	93.57	2.18
Sundry	8.11	0.29	10.72	0.31	11.15	0.30	10.94	0.29	10.9	0.25
Total Operating Expenses	2015.75		2597.69		2717.2		2823.03		3160.33	

Using data from Federated Funeral Directors of America.

4 | Typical Income Statement of a Cemetery

	$	%
Revenues		
Pre-Need Sales	$1,173,000	65.9%**
At-Need Sales	213,000	11.9%**
Other	395,000	22.2%**
	1,781,000	100.0%**
Cost & Expenses		
Cost of Sales	313,000	22.6%*
Selling	446,000	32.1%*
Cemetery Maintenance	259,000	14.5%**
G&A	215,000	12.1%**
	1,233,000	69.2%**
Cemetery Gross Margin	**$548,000**	**30.8%****

*Percentage of P/N + A/N Sales.
**Percentage of Total Revenues.

5 | Ownership Distribution in the Industry

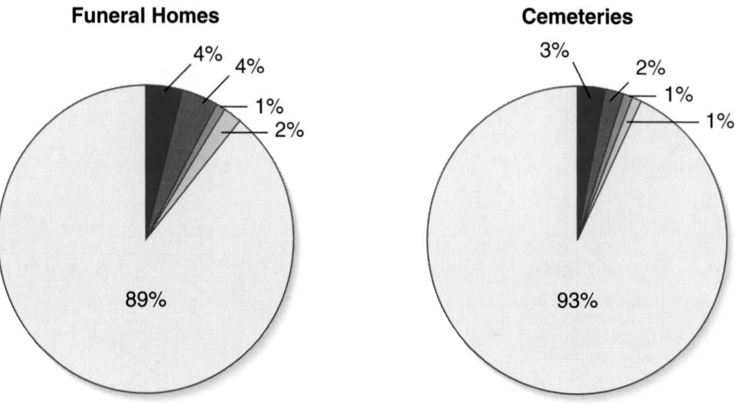

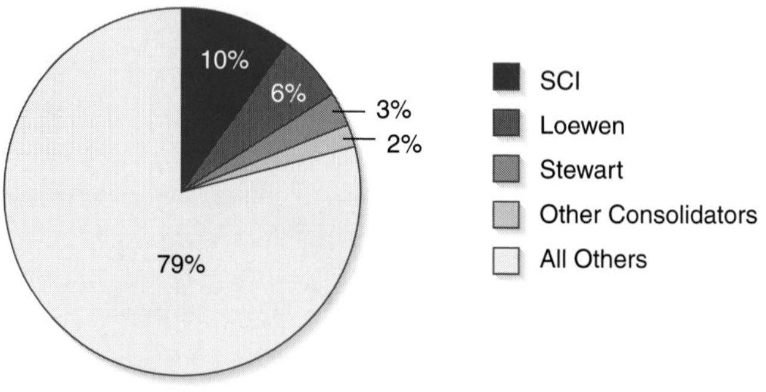

Source: From Darren Martin, "The Death Care Industry," TD Securities, 1996.

and more funeral homes being typically family-run businesses, there was great potential for increased revenue generation and cost cutting.

One industry characteristic that directly affected consolidation was the succession crisis. Independent funeral homes needed to deal with the issue of succession, since the average age of a funeral home owner was older than 50. Most independently owned funeral homes were family businesses. As with many family businesses, there was often no one who was interested in taking on the succession responsibility. Generally, only 30 percent of family businesses made it to the second generation, and 10 percent to the third generation.

Consolidators were typically the only buyers who had access to enough capital to make a market price offer to purchase a funeral home. Obtaining a fair price was crucial to funeral home owners because the equity in their business was, often, their only form of savings.

With issues like a succession crisis, and an increasing death rate, it would seem that there would be a number of new funeral facilities in the market. This was not the case because there were many barriers to entry associated with establishing new facilities. These included elements such as high fixed costs, lack of history in the local community, zoning regulations, and "not-in-my-backyard" protests.

6 | Projected Death Rate

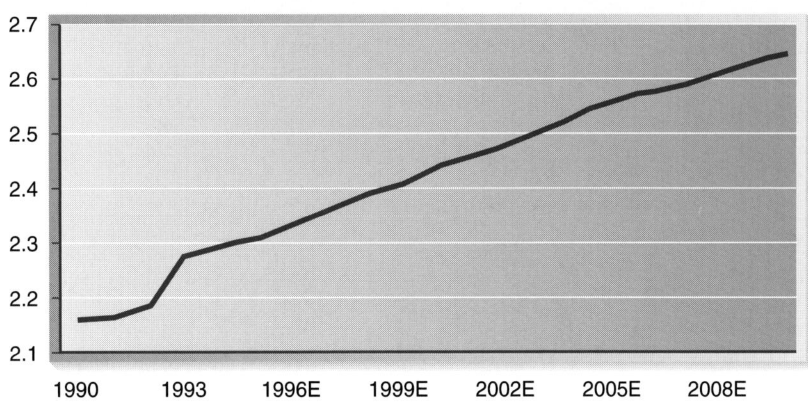

Source: From Darren Martin, "The Death Care Industry: TD Securities, 1996.

Increasing Consumer Price Sensitivity

There were indications in the market that consumers were looking for lower priced products and services. In response to this demand, there was an increase in "no frills" funeral homes. "No frills" referred to companies that specialized in simple funerals, grave-side services, limited or no visitation and frequently no embalming. Another reaction to the demand for lower priced products and services was the casket shop. Most major cities had casket shops that exclusively sold caskets at prices much lower than those offered by the funeral home. These shops, although in their infancy, had the potential of decreasing casket sales revenues for funeral homes.

Pre-Need Funerals

Pre-need planning was gaining in popularity with consumers. This was because it afforded individuals peace of mind that, upon their death, their loved ones would not be faced with the often-difficult task of making funeral arrangements. In addition to emotional security, pre-need planning also offered financial security. It allowed individuals to determine which types of products and services they were willing to pay for when it came time for them to pass on. It also allowed them to lock into present-day prices.

Pre-need plans were usually financed through trust funds or the purchase of pre-need insurance. Money placed in trust was usually invested in bonds, stocks and other investments; these decisions were very strongly regulated. Money placed in insurance was typically placed with a third-party insurance provider who guaranteed a fixed rate of return, typically four to six percent. The very conservative approach to investing pre-need dollars did not afford the seller any real opportunities for revenue generation. In fact, with every pre-need contract sold, there was a threat that when the contract came due, on average after 10 to 12 years, the amount of money available would not cover the at-need price of the service. Despite all of these risks, consolidators were very actively selling pre-need contracts.

Cremations

According to the CANA (Cremation Association of North America), cremation rates in the year 2000 would be 35.72 percent and in the year 2010, they would be 41.80 percent. The increasing rate of cremations could be attributed to the increasing income and education levels, immigration rates, environmental concerns and the perception of cost savings.

There were significant differences in the way that funeral homes treated cremations relative to traditional funeral services. A traditional service involved a casket,

7 | Typical Charges for a Funeral Service ($)

Itemized Charges	Home1 Traditional Service	Home2 Traditional Service	Home3 Traditional Service	Average Traditional Service	Average Simple Cremation
Professional Services					
Basic Service	730	255	1,070	685	NA
Visitation	370	365	0	245	NA
Day of Service	300	275	0	192	NA
Documentation	130	155	145	143	NA
Embalming	60	150	285	165	NA
Other Preparation	50	0	0	17	NA
Facilities and Equipment					
Basic Facility	450	275	625	450	NA
Visitation	130	300	0	143	NA
Day of Service	200	0	0	67	NA
Preparation Room	90	110	150	117	NA
Retaining Room	140	0	0	47	NA
Motor Vehicles					
Initial Transfer	260	120	195	192	NA
General Purpose Vehicle	100	85	125	103	NA
Funeral Coach	205	195	195	198	NA
Total Charges	3,215	2,285	2,790	2,763	827
Casket	3,500	2,500	2,700	2,900	288
Urn					567
Total	**6,715**	**4,785**	**5,490**	**5,663**	**1,682**

Using Data from Consumer Funeral Home Information Packages, July 1996.

visitation, and a burial ceremony. Traditional cremations had typically been marketed with no visitation, an extremely simple casket, and an urn (see Exhibit 7).

Combination Facilities

Cemeteries had traditionally been considered as suppliers to funeral homes. They supplied burial plots, stones, plaques, etc. With an increase in cremations and combination facilities, cemeteries were very well poised to take a larger role than that of a simple supplier. This represented a threat to the traditional funeral home on many levels. First, the cemetery culture was a sales-oriented culture, i.e., cemeteries had been actively selling pre-need plots for decades and, therefore, had access to an extensive list of sales leads, if they decided to sell full pre-need funeral services. Second, with an increase in cremations, items such a crematory niches and cremation viewing facilities (a necessary part of many cultures) represented opportunities for potentially high margins. It was plausible that with increased combination facilities, cremations could become solely a cemetery phenomena. This would steal market share away from the funeral homes and then pose a barrier to entry for new funeral homes. In addition to all of this, combination facilities were able to offer real one-stop-shopping, a definite advantage to the consumer.

Cost Control

Consolidators maintained a cost advantage over independent funeral homes because they were able to take advantage of economies of scale. By using "clustered locations," consolidators were able to significantly reduce their operational costs. Clustering involved centralizing vehicle fleets, embalming operations and corporate management, in addition to buying supplies in bulk and sharing staff.

Competitors

Consolidators in the funeral service industry could be classified by size. The first group consisted of large public companies such as Service Corporation International (SCI), The Loewen Group (Loewen) and Stewart Enterprises (Stewart), whose current equity market capitalization and public float by company did not exceed $1 billion. The second group consisted of small companies such as Arbor Memorial Services, Equity Corporation International and Carriage Services, whose current equity market capitalization and public float by company did not exceed $1 billion.

SERVICE CORPORATION INTERNATIONAL

SCI, located in Houston, Texas, was the largest funeral service provider in the world with 2,795 funeral homes and 324 cemeteries. In 1996, SCI was expected to have an equity market capitalization of $6.04 billion and revenues of $2.4 billion. Establishments that it owned performed 9, 29, 14 and 24 percent of the funeral services in North America, France, the UK and Australia, respectively. SCI was also active in the funeral service industries of Malaysia and Singapore. Finally, it was becoming active in the funeral industries of six European countries in addition to France and the UK.

SCI had initiatives in response to all the major industry trends. For example,

- SCI had the second largest backlog (1.5 years) of pre-need funeral services.[6] It also consistently tried to increase its pre-need revenue base. In 1995, 22 percent of all funerals performed by SCI were prearranged. This was the highest percentage in the industry.
- SCI was increasing its presence in the area of combination facilities.
- In response to the potential threat of a more price-sensitive consumer, SCI started its own chain of discount operators called Family Funeral Care.

SCI was successful at leveraging its size through its aggressive use of clustering. At SCI, clustering drove the decisions on where to locate new homes and where to purchase existing ones. SCI was so committed to the concept of clustering that it had developed maps showing death rate projections by zip code and by the company's market share in different areas. Analysts believed that clustering was one of the key drivers of SCI's profitability. Although costs were an important element of operational management, sometimes equally as important, for a consolidator, was the facility with which it integrated new acquisitions. Of all of the large capital companies, SCI seemed to be the most aggressive in terms of integrating its existing acquisitions. This was clearly seen in the following comments made by Robert Waltrip, Chairman of the SCI Board of Directors:

> *What many in this industry don't seem to understand or want to believe is that when we make a purchase, we have to introduce our way of doing business. You can't spend $100 million to buy a business of that size and just go on doing business the old way. ("Robert Waltrip Takes on His Critics," Mortuary Management, May 1993)*

SCI's approach to integration was aggressive and detail oriented. Previous owners and managers were often asked to step aside. Owners who were retained worked solely in public relations on a part-time basis. This allowed SCI to benefit from the owners' community presence and network. SCI used a decentralized approach to manage its network of homes. SCI had recently changed its organizational structure from eight regions to 17 regions. This was done to allow regional managers to be more in touch with their areas and to be able to make decisions in more proximity to their respective homes.

In terms of acquisitions, SCI tended to concentrate on urban homes. It prided itself on owning quality institutions. Like most industry players it retained the original names of its acquisitions to benefit from the goodwill. However, SCI claimed that goodwill was not the only factor that kept its customers coming back. Excellent service levels and quality personnel also played a key role in customer retention. SCI acquired many of its homes based on referrals from Provident. Provident was SCI's financial subsidiary. It lent money to independent funeral home operators. Provident played an important role in allowing SCI to keep its finger on the pulse of the industry.

MR. LOEWEN AND THE LOEWEN GROUP

Ray Loewen

In 1961, Ray Loewen graduated from Briercrest Theological College before joining his father in the family funeral home in Steinbach, Manitoba. He left the family firm, along with his wife, Anne, to purchase their own funeral home in Fort Frances, Ontario, and subsequently another home in the Lower Mainland of B.C. Times were good and by 1975, Loewen owned a number of different funeral homes. He turned to politics to serve one term as the Social Credit MLA for Burnaby-Edmonds in the B.C. legislature. In 1979, he returned to his business career. More and more, the owners of funeral homes whose children were either unable or unwilling to take over the family business were searching for an answer to the question of their own succession. This represented an excellent opportunity for the Loewen Group. Loewen knew that by raising money on the stock exchange and using it to acquire these homes, while enabling local owner families to remain as active in the business as they would like, he could make Loewen Group a national presence. In 1987, fueled by Loewen Group's first public offering, Ray Loewen acquired $24 million in funeral establishments and acquired its first U.S. property.

Mr. and Mrs. Loewen owned 15 percent of the company's voting shares and, in his capacity as CEO and Chairman of the Board of Directors, Ray Loewen played an active role in guiding senior management. He took a real interest in the operations of the company and had a grass roots understanding of the business, given his background. This meant he was sensitive to the needs of funeral directors.

Mr. Loewen looked on his growing complement of employees as part of a family and felt they should all be able to participate in the company. This led to the introduction of "Sharing The Vision," an employee stock plan with employees receiving five free shares and being offered a stock purchase program. This reflected Mr. Loewen's vision of having a company in which every employee was a shareholder. When he described his management philosophy, he liked to use the analogy of an eagle's flight: one wing was the care-giving at the heart of funeral service, the other, fiscal responsibility. The eagle needed both wings to soar. Mr. Loewen was passionate about the Loewen Group and he counted on his management and employees for their full support.

Acquisitions Group

Since 1992, the acquisition growth rates for Loewen, SCI and Stewart had all been greater than 50 percent (see Exhibit 8). Loewen attributed its position to four key competitive advantages. First and foremost, it had an acquisition group that was very skilled and very dedicated to identifying and closing the sale. Second, Loewen's Regional Partnership Program had often accounted for more than 50 percent of its yearly acquisitions. This program allowed Loewen to capitalize on the skills and network contacts acquired through its acquisitions by partnering up with the previous owners. These owners helped Loewen initiate new acquisitions in return for a

EXHIBIT 8 | Dollar Values of Acquisitions as Estimated by Loewen (000's)

	Loewen	SCI	Stewart
1992	83,200	203,774	33,962
1993	148,000	226,415	95,094
1994	265,000	815,094	178,868
1995	487,900	1,138,868	149,434
1996	1,154,600	498,113	201,509
1997E	600,000	498,113	249,057
1998E	840,000	647,547	336,226
1999E	1,680,000	874,189	470,717
2000E	3,780,000	1,223,864	682,540

10 percent ownership stake in every successful referral. Loewen participated in about 20 of these types of partnerships. Third, Loewen had built a reputation for doing its utmost to satisfy the needs of sellers. Fourth, with its acquisition of Osiris Holdings, a large and successful cemetery management company, Loewen was building its in-house expertise in cemetery management.

Competition around acquisitions was not entirely price-based, since all major industry consolidators were amply capable of matching each other's price offers. Instead, competition was based on the more intangible nature of acquisitions. Loewen claimed it had one of the most customer-focused approaches and a genuine concern for sellers' needs. In every single acquisition, Loewen maintained the funeral home's name. It also strove to increase the brand equity of this name by offering excellent service, being involved in the community, and improving the facilities. When Loewen purchased a home, it tended to keep all employees in place. This allowed seamless service during the acquisition process and was in line with preserving the home's heritage and community appeal. Also, the salaries and benefits it introduced were usually an improvement over what had previously been offered. Owners and their families could remain active in the management of the business. In terms of capital gains and other financial issues, Loewen was extremely flexible. It did anything from paying a large cash portion up front, usually 75 percent, to a share for share stock issue. In some cases it had even agreed to lease a home, although this was not common practice.

Given Loewen's penchant for smaller homes, it has a reputation as the "country bumpkin" of funeral home acquirers. This was a misnomer because like its competitors, Loewen also acquired large, urban funeral homes in the $10 million to $50 million range. However, given that these opportunities were not commonplace, Loewen had developed an infrastructure that allowed it to identify and purchase smaller, yet very profitable, homes in more rural areas.

As the number of acquisitions grew, Loewen became increasingly strategic in its expansion planning. This was explained by Mr. J. P. Gabille, Loewen's Vice President of Corporate Development: "We use many different criteria to evaluate a home. For example, we prefer larger operations, reputable operations, profitability, good staff, etc. Until about two or three years ago we just bought funeral homes that met our criteria. Now we are much more strategic, i.e., trying to build hubs, consolidating existing properties to create new, more high quality properties, building new homes to fill the gaps. We currently have 20 to 25 new homes in progress."

Loewen believed that its reputation as "the preferred acquirer" was a significant advantage in attracting high quality acquisitions. Loewen endeavoured to develop this image by paying competitive prices for homes and cemeteries, being very flexible in the integration of these establishments, and going the extra mile to satisfy the needs and concerns of sellers. Many independent funeral establishments indicated that they would prefer selling to the Loewen Group rather than to other consolidators, a position that saw many holding on until Loewen's 1995 Mississippi court case problems were resolved in early 1996. The company planned to sign or close a record number of acquisitions that year. However, for every funeral director that preferred Loewen Group, there seemed to be a funeral director that preferred SCI.

Operations Management

Mr. Harry Rath, VP of Loewen–Eastern Canada, described how Loewen integrated its acquisitions: "Loewen does not have homogeneous operating guidelines for the various homes we own. We understand the importance of local culture and allow our homes a great deal of leeway in operations. We make one very important change, i.e., we impose the utilization of budgets[7] that can be agreed upon together, and we insist on regular accountability and encourage accountability. Our expectations are clear. We are also very interested in helping funeral homes achieve their goals, i.e., you don't only see us during budget time. For example, as VP Operations of Eastern Canada, I oversee 62 funeral homes, with the help of some regional managers. All my homes know me personally. I am available to them for guidance and assistance."

One of the challenges faced by Loewen was the balancing act between operational profitability and commitment to its corporate culture. Loewen paid close attention to cost control and efficiency improvement. However, with the pressures for continual growth and with the various events in the life of the company,

Loewen found the balancing act more and more difficult to manage.

Marketing Orientation

In terms of pre-need, Loewen's unfulfilled prearranged funeral contracts amounted to $750 million. This equated to a backlog of just under 1.5 years of services. Loewen realized the importance of increasing its pre-need sales and hoped to be more aggressive in the future. At present, 16 percent of all funeral services performed by the Loewen Group were pre-arranged. It was hoped that by 1997, Loewen would increase its pre-need funeral revenues by five to 10 percent.

In terms of cremations, Loewen expected that by the year 2000, its cremation rate would jump from 26 percent, in 1995, to 28.21 percent. To deal with the industry's gradual shift towards cremations, Loewen had increased its acquisition of cemeteries and had developed a "Celebration of Life" program. This program allowed Loewen to sell cremations in such a way that they were almost as profitable and often more profitable than the traditional funeral service. Traditionally, cremations were treated in the same way as dispositions. No effort was made to provide families with visitation, a memorial service, a reception, etc. This was because funeral homes did not understand their cremation customers. When a customer chose cremation, he or she was not choosing a less dignified funeral service; he or she was only choosing not to be buried. Loewen's "Celebration of Life" program trained its funeral directors to sell cremations just like traditional funerals. Brian Falvey, Loewen's Celebration of Life program coordinator for Cape Cod, explained:

> *The family had never had a cremation before . . . but they wanted to respect the mother's wishes . . . They also wanted to have some type of religious service and a final chance to say good-bye to her. (VISION Magazine, November/December 1996, The Loewen Group, Inc.)*

By explaining the Celebration of Life philosophy, Brian assured the couple that together they could tailor arrangements to include a private family viewing at the funeral home, followed by a religious service conducted by a local minister. Furthermore, he would personally supervise the burial of the cremated remains at an out-of-state family plot.

> *They were surprised that all this could take place. Like many people, they didn't realize that these arrangements could be made in conjunction with a cremation. (VISION Magazine, November/December 1996, The Loewen Group, Inc.)*

Organizational Culture

> *Stock at funeral home-owner Loewen Group has risen nearly $5, to a recent 35 1/4, since a recent promotion that carried the message: Exercise, Eat Well, Stay Healthy—We Can Wait. (Forbes, July 3, 1995.)*

Loewen's organizational culture was truly captured in the above few lines. The key tenet of the Loewen culture was that employees believed that the company was doing something good, something beyond just making money. The Loewen Group insisted that they were not solely a funeral consolidator or a funeral service operator, they were both. This belief provided a strong sense of purpose to employees.

Shareholder Relations

From 1990 to 1994, when Loewen was experiencing high growth levels and good profitability, there was never a need for formal shareholder relations. However, with the loss of a major legal battle[8] causing share prices to fall from $41 to $18, shareholder relations became crucial. After this immense drop in share price, Loewen's financial people became very active and for two months they never stopped talking to investors. Their goal was to communicate the key message that Loewen's stock was undervalued and, with a little time, would be trading at its previously high multiples. These trips were very successful, as the market saw some active purchasing of Loewen stock and an increase in stock prices. Other methods by which shareholders were kept abreast of Loewen's activities included a detailed annual report, Loewen's *VISION Magazine*,[9] and conference calls between Mr. Loewen and the company's major shareholders. However, despite all of these tactics, the most important link to shareholders was that, notwithstanding any crises, Loewen maintained its acquisition pace and operational profitability.

Finance

Every year since 1990, Loewen had successfully raised funds from the public. Loewen had a very innovative finance group that regularly developed new types of issues that allowed increased fund raising and increased returns for potential buyers. For example, even after coming close to bankruptcy after the Mississippi trial, Loewen's financial people, with the assistance of Nesbitt Burns and RBC Dominion Securities, designed a convertible preferred security with a seven-year term to raise funds for increased acquisitions. Funds were placed in trust to ensure that they would be used for acquisitions and not legal obligations. This financing tool helped Loewen raise US$200 million.

Another innovative tactic used by Loewen was a partnership with Blackstone Capital Partners II Merchant Banking Fund LP. This partnership allowed Loewen to make strategic acquisitions off the balance sheet. The first was Prime Succession, Inc., a consolidator that had 16 cemeteries and 146 funeral homes in the U.S. Prime Succession was purchased for $295 million. Loewen paid $72 million and held 20 percent of the shares, with an option to buy the remaining 80 percent after four years. Until that time, the 80 percent would be held by Blackstone. Loewen's holdings were primarily preferred shares and Blackstone's holdings were common shares. Its partnership with Blackstone allowed Loewen to make strategic deals, while leaving enough capital free to continue to make other acquisitions.

Competitive Rivalry

The two largest competitors in the North American market were Loewen and SCI. Nationally, they competed with each other in terms of acquisitions and regionally for market share. Increasing acquisitions and ensuring their successful integration were fundamental to the success of both companies. However, both Loewen and SCI approached acquisition and integration in different ways, as shown in Exhibit 9.

These different approaches were very important to potential funeral home sellers. Funeral home sellers were not only interested in selling to the highest bidder, but typically had a number of criteria that had to be met before a sales deal could be signed. For example, funeral home owners were very concerned with:

- preservation of the funeral home's name and heritage
- job security of their managers and non-management staff
- fair staff remuneration
- maintenance of the home's community involvement
- the maintenance of a service to the community image as opposed to a corporate business image

Of these owners, those who were selling larger establishments involving stock trades were also concerned with issues related to

- the company's acquisition growth rate
- historical and future growth in the stock price
- meeting industry trends head on
- company cost structures and profitability

See Exhibit 10 for a comparison of SCI and Loewen along some key financial indicators.

Strategy

Loewen's strategic direction had not significantly changed in the last few years. It was clearly and simply stated in its 1995 annual report as follows:

> *The company capitalizes on these attractive industry fundamentals through a growth strategy that emphasizes three principal components (i) acquiring a significant number of small, family-owned funeral homes and cemeteries; (ii) acquiring strategic operations consisting predominantly of large, multi-location urban properties that generally serve as platforms for acquiring small, family-owned businesses in surrounding regions; and (iii) improving the revenue and profitability of newly-acquired and established locations. The first element of the Company's growth strategy is the acquisition of small, family-owned funeral homes and cemeteries. Management believes the Company has a competitive advantage in this market due to its culture and its well-known and understood reputation for honoring existing owners and staff. The final element of the Company's growth strategy is its focus on enhancing the revenue and profitability of newly-acquired and established locations.*

9 | Acquisition Methods of Loewen and SCI.

Business Activity	SCI	Loewen
Personnel	Almost all of the homes purchased by SCI were part of a clustering strategy. Clustering allowed the company to decrease operational costs by pooling and sharing resources among regionally proximate homes. Clustering saved personnel costs because it allowed homes to operate with a skeletal staff while being able to call upon floater employees for assistance.	It was part of Loewen's integration strategy not to make significant changes to the staffing levels of a newly acquired funeral home. The preservation of a funeral establishment's brand equity was very important to Loewen and it viewed personnel as a key component.
Facilities	Clustering allowed SCI to centralize functions such as embalming and preparing the body.	Loewen did not centralize its embalming or preparation facilities.
Automotive Equipment	Typically at SCI, every cluster shared one fleet of cars.	Loewen did not actively centralize its use of automobiles. However, some homes often shared automobiles.
Management	SCI offered a great deal of training and had a large number of managers available to assist homes with specific problems. From an organizational perspective, a home was about four management tiers away from the head office.	Training was an important component of Loewen's integration process. Funeral home managers worked closely with the Regional Vice Presidents to develop budgets together. Budgeting was done on an individual home level, taking into account factors in each home's micro-environment. All Regional Vice Presidents reported directly to the Head Office.
Locations of Acquisitions	The driver behind SCI's growth strategy was clustering. Rarely were homes purchased that did not fit into one cluster or the other.	Loewen tended to acquire profitable homes that showed the potential for sustainable and/or increasing future profits and growth. It focused on smaller "mom & pop" operations with larger returns on investment. Loewen developed greater regional market share in some areas via strategic (large, urban) acquisitions.
Purchasing	SCI used a centralized purchasing program, both at the regional and national levels. Purchases of vehicles, caskets, cremation urns, grave markers were centralized at the national level.	Loewen often allowed funeral establishments to keep their suppliers intact, especially if relationships were profitable. However, Loewen had established large volume contracts for most of its supply needs.
Legal Counsel/Insurance	Centralized	Centralized

EXHIBIT

10 | Key Financial Indicators

	1995	1994	1993	1992	1991	1990	1989	1988
Gross Profit Margins on Funeral Homes for Loewen	41.4%	40.5%	39.4%	39.3%	39.8%	40.2%	43.7%	42.2%
Gross Profit Margins on Cemeteries for Loewen	27.8%	24.3%	24.4%	24.8%	25.8%	39.9%	28.8%	37.6%
Gross Profit Margins on Funeral Homes for SCI	25.3%	29.5%	29.4%	28.8%	28.7%	29.4%	28.2%	28.5%
Gross Profit Margins on Cemeteries for SCI	34.6%	32.1%	28.4%	24.4%	22.9%	20.0%	18.8%	19.7%
EPS for Loewen (US$)	−1.69	0.97	0.76	0.58	0.46			
EPS for SCI (US$)	1.70	1.43	1.17	1.07	1.00			
Growth Per Year in EPS at Loewen	−274.2%	27.6%	31.0%	26.0%				
Growth Per Year in EPS at SCI	18.9%	22.2%	9.4%	7.0%				
Share Price at Loewen (US$)	25.31	26.50	25.38	15.50	13.38			
Share Price at SCI (US$)	33.17	25.56	22.00	17.38	16.09			
Growth Per Year in Share Price at Loewen	−4.5%	4.4%	63.7%	15.8%				
Growth Per Year in Share Price at SCI	29.8%	16.2%	26.6%	8.0%				
Return on Sales for Loewen	−12.8%	9.2%	9.3%	9.0%	8.9%	9.6%	9.5%	
Return on Sales for SCI	11.1%	11.7%	11.5%	11.2%	11.4%	10.7%	9.0%	
Return on Total Assets for SCI	2.4%	2.5%	2.8%	3.3%	3.5%	3.6%	2.9%	
Return on Total Assets for Loewen	−3.4%	2.9%	3.1%	2.9%	2.8%	2.4%	2.8%	
Return on Equity for Loewen	−12.4%	9.4%	8.7%	8.4%	8.4%	8.7%	9.1%	
Return on Equity for SCI	9.3%	11.0%	11.7%	12.7%	11.9%	13.9%	8.4%	

Source: Annual Reports of the Loewen Group and Service Corporation International.

Cemeteries were going to play a major role in Loewen's strategy over the next few years. Loewen executives forecasted that from 1997 onwards, 30 to 40 percent of all revenues would come from cemeteries (see Exhibits 11 and 12).

THE FAMOUS MISSISSIPPI CASE

In 1990, Loewen made two major purchases in Mississippi. The first was an insurance company and funeral homes from the Riemann Family of Gulfport, Mississippi, and the second was a Jackson-based funeral home from Wright & Ferguson funeral directors. A large funeral home operator in the Gulfport area was Jerry O'Keefe, who owned Gulf National Life Insurance Company and some funeral homes and cemeteries. Prior to Loewen's acquisition of the Wright & Ferguson funeral homes, Gulf National had an exclusive contract with Wright & Ferguson, to exclusively sell its "burial insurance" as this product was defined in Mississippi. Gulf National also had an unexclusive representation contract with Wright & Ferguson to sell "pre-need" insurance (a different product than burial insurance) on behalf of Wright & Ferguson. O'Keefe commenced a court action, following Loewen's acquisition of Wright & Ferguson, claiming that since the Loewen acquisition, Wright & Ferguson had not been honoring the exclusivity agreement with respect to burial insurance. O'Keefe sued Loewen for breach of contract. In reply, Loewen's position was that it had at all times scrupulously honored the exclusivity contract with burial insurance; however, burial insurance had become out of date, and most funeral insurance being sold was of the pre-need variety, and Gulf National had no exclusivity provision with respect to pre-need insurance.

The parties subsequently entered into a settlement agreement settling the litigation, whereby Loewen agreed to sell to Gulf National its insurance company (purchased from Riemann) and O'Keefe would sell to Loewen two of its funeral homes. The settlement agreement was clearly made subject to subsequent agreement on the valuation of the funeral homes; the valuation of the insurance company; mutually satisfactory design of a new insurance product; and mutually satisfactory

11 | Income Statement (US$ 000s)

Income Statement	1995	1994	1993	1992	1991	1990	1989	1988
Revenue								
Funeral	441,352	353,904	275,106	202,748	150,943	92,391	52,856	35,566
Cemetery	143,577	63,424	27,905	16,159	11,662	8,565	4,427	1,987
Insurance	13,564		0	0	0	0	0	0
Total revenues	598,493	417,328	303,011	218,907	162,605	100,956	57,283	37,553
Costs and expenses								
Funeral	258,872	210,471	166,782	123,044	90,861	55,237	29,759	20,557
Cemetery	103,726	48,003	21,111	12,155	8,657	5,152	3,152	1,240
Insurance	10,533	0	0	0	0	0	0	0
Cost of goods sold	373,131	258,474	187,893	135,199	99,518	60,389	32,911	21,797
Revenues—Costs of goods sold	225,362	158,854	115,118	83,708	63,087	40,567	24,372	15,756
Expenses								
General and administrative expenses	67,652	34,751	28,225	17,086	12,981	7,495	4,278	2,101
Depreciation and amortization	40,103	28,990	21,196	16,059	11,053	5,876	3,254	2,166
Total expenses	107,755	63,741	49,421	33,145	24,034	13,371	7,532	4,267
Earnings from operations	117,607	95,113	65,697	50,563	39,053	27,196	16,840	11,489
Interest on long-term debt	50,913	34,203	21,801	19,083	14,913	10,914	7,177	4,916
Legal settlements	184,914	0	0					
Earnings (loss) before undernoted items	−118,220	60,910	43,896	31,480	24,140	16,282	9,663	6,573
Dividends on preferred securities of subsidiary	7,088	2,678	0					
Earnings (loss) before income taxes and undernoted items	−125,308	58,232	43,896	31,480	24,140	16,282	9,663	6,573
Total income taxes	−47,178	19,738	15,714	11,714	9,715	6,549	4,215	3,152
Net Income not including equity & earnings from assoc. companies	−78,130	38,494	28,182	19,766	14,425	9,733	5,448	3,421
Equity and other earnings of associated companies	1,446	0						
Net earnings (loss) for the year	−76,684	38,494	28,182	19,766	14,425	9,733	5,448	3,421
Basic earnings (loss) per common share	−1.69	0.97	0.77	0.59	0.46	0.39	0.31	0.23
Dividend per common share	0.050	0.070	0.045	0.032	0.017	0.000	0.000	0.000
Dividend per preferred share	0.000	0.000	0.000	0.000	0.000	0.288	0.586	0.327
Number of common shares at year-end (in thousands)	48,168	41,015	38,647	35,534	32,754	28,391	19,977	12,849
Common share price at year-end ($Cdn.)	34.38	36.75	33.25	19.63	15.63	12.50	9.31	5.31
Common share price at year-end ($U.S.)	25.31	26.50	25.38	15.50	13.38	10.63	n/a	n/a

agreement on a new agency representation agreement. A number of these "subject to" provisions were never satisfied, and the settlement agreement therefore did not complete. O'Keefe then amended his lawsuit to claim that Loewen breached the settlement agreement and acted in bad faith.

The litigation took place in Jackson, Mississippi, before judge and jury. With respect to the settlement agreement, the total value of the assets involved (the insurance company and two funeral homes) was approximately $6 million. Close to trial, O'Keefe hired Willie Gary, a renowned Plaintiff's contingency fee lawyer in the United States. Many people felt that, as a result, the case was not based on facts in law but rather on an emotional, "theatre of mind" approach to the jury.

The jury's verdict was in favor of O'Keefe for an amount of US$500 million which amounted to 20 times the damages stated by the Plaintiff in pre-trial motions. Loewen wished to appeal the result, but under Mississippi court rules, a pre-condition of the appeal

EXHIBIT

12 | Balance Sheet (US$ 000s)

	1995	1994	1993	1992	1991	1990	1989	1988
Current assets								
Cash and term deposits	39,454	15,349	18,167	12,176	16,035	9,706	17,940	3,180
Receivables, net of allowances	115,953	70,547	51,684	37,211	27,451	25,063	10,574	5,882
Inventories	27,489	19,673	15,952	12,323	8,165	6,381	2,919	1,805
Prepaid expenses	8,185	4,299	4,941	3,974	2,248	785	956	645
Total current assets	191,081	109,868	90,744	65,684	53,899	41,935	32,389	11,512
Prearranged funeral services	245,854	178,982	175,216	146,109	127,086	104,413	49,524	33,343
Long-term receivables, net of allowances	167,367	67,895	30,059	11,460	5,725	2,319		
Investments	86,815	78,269	3,749	1,338	915	921		
Insurance invested assets	97,024							
Cemetery property at cost	369,022	114,861	48,158	24,135	15,939	15,230	3,160	2,859
Property and equipment	551,965	426,038	346,244	284,654	216,851	159,438	79,417	52,442
Names and reputations	424,944	314,599	199,514	126,156	87,547	72,982	25,363	17,910
Deferred income taxes	61,959							
Other assets	66,949	35,763	19,977	15,575	10,530	6,881	2,845	4,091
Total assets	2,262,980	1,326,275	913,661	675,111	518,492	404,119	192,698	122,157
Liabilities and shareholders' equity								
Current liabilities								
Current indebtedness	38,546	3,700	4,435	3,558		5,404		
Accrued settlements	53,000							
Accounts payable and accrued liabilities	80,058	48,436	37,952	22,715	13,601	14,013	6,504	4,188
Income taxes payable				446	730		589	1,582
Long-term debt, current position	69,671	45,529	6,572	7,553	6,073	6,088	4,431	2,990
Total current liabilities	241,275	97,665	48,959	34,272	20,404	25,505	11,524	8,760
Long-term debt	864,838	471,125	335,405	239,162	187,780	141,072	61,280	44,613
Subordinated debentures						8,956	8,571	8,240
Other liabilities	136,433	83,678	22,327	16,439	9,415	5,956	375	458
Insurance policy liabilities	84,898							
Deferred income taxes		8,686	5,864	2,812	1,413	385	1,364	1,485
Deferred prearranged funeral services revenue	245,854	178,982	175,216	146,109	127,086	104,413	49,524	33,343
Preferred securities of subsidiary	75,000	75,000						
Total non-current liabilities	1,407,023	817,471	538,812	404,522	325,694	260,782	121,114	88,139
Shareholders' equity								
Common shares	490,055	282,560	227,968	172,133	139,151	98,031	42,418	11,828
Common shares issuable under legal settlements	72,000							
Preferred shares							7,566	7,566
Retained earnings	36,439	115,492	79,867	53,382	34,651	20,720	11,275	6,414
Foreign exchange adjustment	16,188	13,087	18,055	10,802	−1,408	-919	-1,199	-550
Total shareholders' equity	614,682	411,139	325,890	236,317	172,394	117,832	60,060	25,258
Total liabilities and shareholders' equity	2,262,980	1,326,275	913,661	675,111	518,492	404,119	192,698	122,157
Number of funeral homes	815	640	533	451	365	268	131	98
Number of cemeteries	179	116	70	38	23	21	7	5
Number of funeral services	114,000	94,000	7,900	64,000	52,000	34,000	22,000	18,000
Number of employees	10,000	7,000	5,000	4,000	3,000	2,000	1,000	1,000
Business acquisitions in million	487.9	265.6	148.0	83.2	68.5	140.2	31.5	30.8

was that Loewen post a full-cash bond in the amount of US$625 million. Accordingly, Loewen's lawyers began making preparations to voluntarily file for Chapter 11, since a filing in Chapter 11 would permit the appeal to go forward without the necessity of filing the $625 million bond.

In the result, the Company was able to settle with O'Keefe on an after-tax basis to the Company of US$85 million, consisting of a combination of cash, shares, and a promissory note.

The initial result of the bizarre jury award was to send Loewen's share price spiralling down from CDN$41.00 to CDN$18.00 per share. The process of dealing with the aftermath of the Mississippi jury award, and the consequent need to refinance the Company, left management tired after a challenge that lasted many months. About six months after the settlement of the case, SCI announced its hostile takeover bid.

Options Facing the Loewen Group

As Mr. Loewen read the letter, sent by SCI's President, William Heiligbrodt, several thoughts ran through his head:

- Was the price being offered for Loewen shares a fair value?
- Was selling the Loewen Group in the best interest of shareholders and other stakeholders?
- Could the Loewen Group guarantee that dollar for dollar it would be able to generate a better return than SCI?

ENDNOTES

1. All dollar values in the case are in U.S. dollars unless otherwise noted.
2. The consumer who wished to pre-plan and pre-pay for his or her funeral purchased pre-need insurance.
3. Sales of at-need burial plots referred to sales that occurred when someone had died.
4. When a body was cremated, the remains were usually stored in an urn. If the family chose not to scatter the ashes, the urn could be placed in the family home, buried in a cemetery or stored in a cremation niche. Usually, cremation niches were structures in cemeteries that allowed families to store the cremation remains of loved ones. Niches afforded family members an alternative to burying cremation remains while retaining the benefit of having a place where they could visit and remember the departed.
5. A perpetual care fund was a perpetual annuity that ensured that cemeteries would always have funds for up-keep of the cemetery.
6. A backlog of 1.5 years in pre-need funeral services was interpreted a follows: If all the company's pre-need funerals came due, the company would be able to run at full capacity for 1.5 years without performing any at-need services.
7. Once a home had been acquired, the use of Loewen's legal counsel and insurance provider was non-negotiable.
8. The major legal battle in question was the Mississippi case. Details of the Mississippi case are provided later on.
9. *VISION Magazine* was a publication that Loewen sent to all its funeral establishments, industry analysts, shareholders and other industry stakeholders. It allowed Loewen to explain what was going on in the company, from the perspective of an individual funeral home right up to major issues like the Mississippi case.

CASE 27

Madd Snowboards—1999

Melissa A. Schilling
Amy Eng
Mayra Velasquez
Boston University

John Gilmour wandered through his makeshift warehouse of snowboards, looking at the eclectic jumble of parts, equipment, and boards that had not yet been sold. He stopped to run his hand down the steel edge of a high-performance racing board, and found himself asking aloud, "Where do we go from here?" Should he and his partners try to make Madd Snowboards a large company, like Ride or Burton, or remain a very small niche player, making a handful of boards each year? If they decided to grow, how would they raise enough money to fund the cost of more inventory, more supplies, more wages? Would they need to build their own manufacturing facilities or continue to outsource production to Italy? How would they position themselves? Would they be able to secure retail space with their high-end alpine niche boards? Or should they try to find other channels of distribution?

The snowboard market was still growing quickly and could be quite profitable. This combined with the "glamour" of snowboarding would attract large numbers of new entrants every year. However most of those new entrants failed, or were swallowed up by larger companies. The snowboard industry could be a fickle market; new boards could soar into fashion, only to have their sales wither away within a couple of years. It could also be difficult for a company to establish credibility among financial backers and distribution channels, because so many young, entrepreneurial snowboard companies had earned sporadic returns, and had been unreliable in delivering their product to stores. Most entrants into the field were snowboarders themselves, and while they knew the sport and knew the equipment, translating that knowledge into a successful business had proven to be a difficult task.

THE SNOWBOARD INDUSTRY

Snowboarding traces its history back to 1965, when Sherman Poppen attached two skis together into what he called a "snurfer." By the early seventies, several other entrepreneurs were experimenting with "skiboards" or other surfboard-like innovations designed to glide over snow. Dimitrije Milovich set up one of the earliest snowboard companies, Winterstick, in 1975 to sell his swallow-tailed snowboards based on a surfboard design. He gained considerable exposure when *Newsweek* covered him in March of that same year, and *Powder Magazine* gave him a two-page photo spread.[1] Around the same time, Jake Burton, Mike Olson, Bob Webber, and Chuck Barfoot each began their own snowboard prototypes, which would evolve to become the snowboard lines of Burton, Gnu, Sims and Barfoot.

Snowboarding became a fast growing industry, with sales climbing consistently in the double-digit rates. This rapid growth provided a greatly needed economic boost to a slumping ski industry. While the total number of alpine skiers decreased 38 percent from 12,400,000 in 1988, to 7,700,000 in 1998, the number of snowboarding participants rose dramatically from 1,300,000 to 3,600,000 (a 177 percent increase) (see

This case was developed for the purpose of classroom discussion and is not intended to demonstrate either effective or ineffective management of an administrative situation.

Exhibit 1). In 1998, snowboarders accounted for 21 percent of visitors to winter sports resorts, reflecting a 20.7 percent annual rate of growth since 1994.[2] Analysts predicted that snowboarding would surpass skiing as the No. 1 winter sport by the year 2000.[3]

Though part of snowboarding's growth appears to have come at the expense of the ski industry (the crossover rate between skiing and snowboarding is very high), total consumer purchases of skis and snowboards have been on the increase (see Exhibits 2 and 3).

Demographics

When snowboarding first started gaining popularity in the 1980s, the sport was dubbed as a sport for rebel-

EXHIBIT 1 | Ski and Snowboard Participants, 1988–1998 (millions)

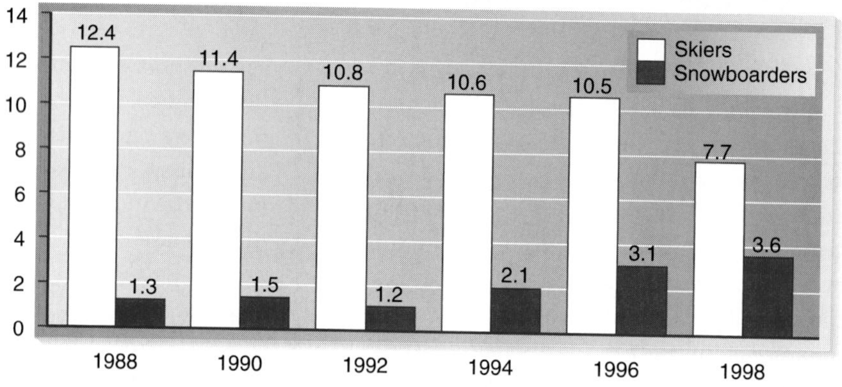

Source: National Sporting Goods Association.

EXHIBIT 2 | Ski and Snowboard Purchases, 1997–1999 (millions of US$)

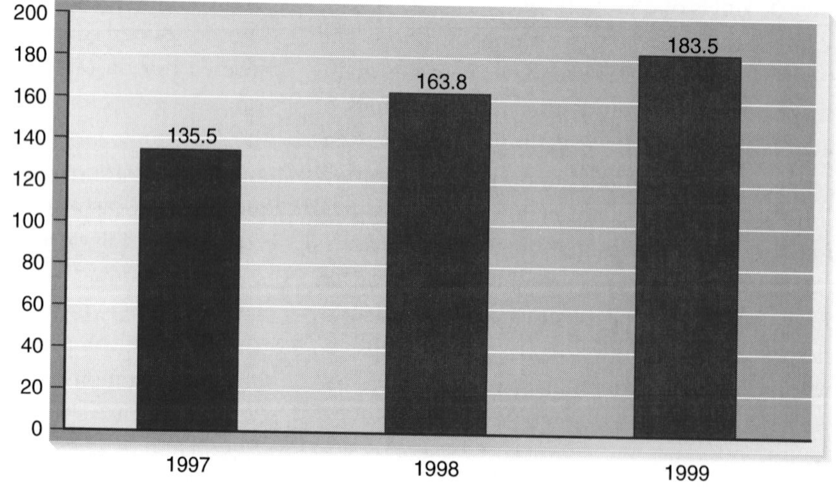

Source: National Sporting Goods Association.

Exhibit 3 | Winter Sports Equipment Orders by Type, 1997–1999

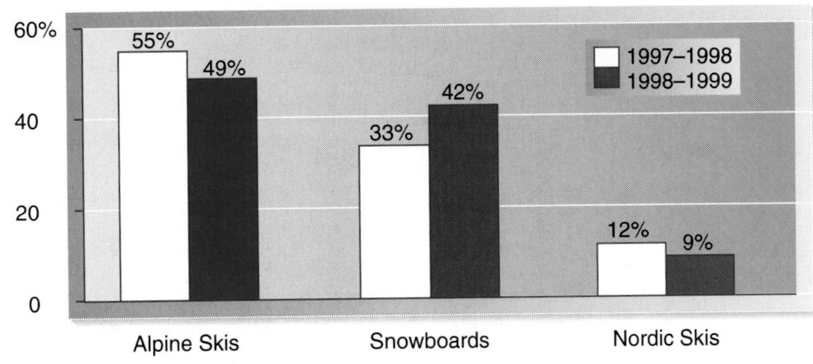

Source: 1998 Statistics on Snow Sports. *SnowLink Media Center.*

lious, pierced and tattooed young males; however, the sport's increased visibility helped to attract new boarders of a greater diversity (see Exhibit 4). Women and children have become growing markets for the sport, and children often lure their parents into giving snowboarding a try. In 1998, more than half of the snowboarders in the U.S. were aged 24 or older. Snowboard sales to 24–36 year-olds increased 270 percent in 1998, while purchases by 36-to-45 year-olds increased 99 percent.[4] Another favorable trend for snowboarding has been the apparent rise in the downhillers' income. In 1997, 17.8 percent of snowboard participants earned between $35,000–49,999, 20.3 percent earned between $50,000–74,999 and 20.3 percent earned over $75,000.[5]

Historically snowboarding had been most popular in the Pacific region, however the New England and Mid-Atlantic regions have experienced fast growth in the last few years. Snowboard participation is lowest in the West North Central, the West South Central and the East South Central regions (see Exhibit 5).

Market Segments

Most snowboards fall into three categories—freeride, freestyle, and alpine. These snowboard types vary according to materials, stiffness, length, weight, and shape.

Exhibit 4 | 1998–1999 Winter Sports Participation Breakdown

The Snowboard Consumer Market

	Kids (Ages 7–11)	The "Core" (Men 14–24)	The Employed (24 or older)	Women (All Ages)	Beginners (All Ages)
Growth Trend	Modest	Substantial	Substantial	Modest	Moderate
% of Snowboard Population	17%	56%	30%	24%	45%
Buying Power (in Millions)	$3.47	$9.5	$6.6		

Source: Transworld Snowboarding Vol. 10, No. 5, Feb. 1999.

5 | Snow Sports Participation by U.S. Regions

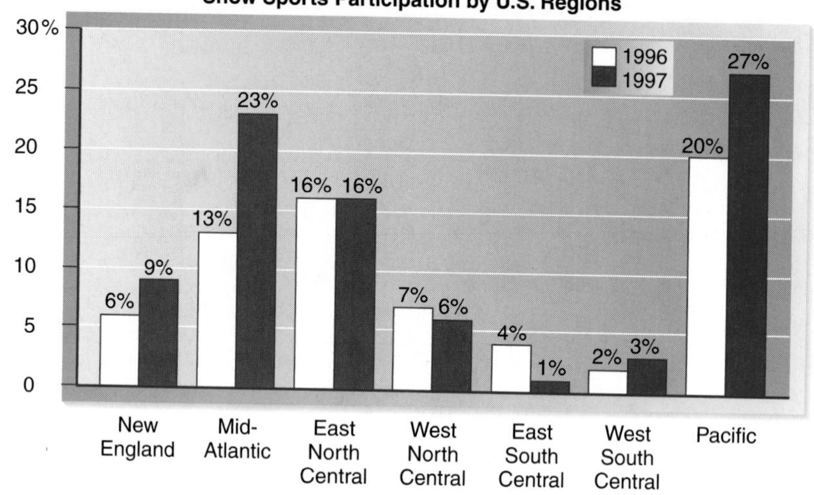

Source: 1998 Statistics on Snow Sports, SnowLink Media Center.

Freeride boards, also known as "directional designs," are the most commonly sold boards and made up over 60 percent of the market in 1998. This type of board is suitable for several riding purposes including performing tricks, "carving" (long, smooth turns, typically at high speeds), and riding on hardpack or powder snow. Freeride boards are very good for introducing a novice to snowboarding and thus are the most frequent first-time board purchase. *Freestyle* boards occupied 30 percent of the market in 1998. These boards are more flexible, and are used primarily for jumping and performing tricks. *Alpine* boards, made up less than 10 percent market share in 1998,[6] are designed mainly for detailed, high speed turns. These boards tend to be stiff and narrow and are not usually used for performing tricks or free riding.

Since its inception, the snowboard industry has been bombarded with companies entering the market, and the majority of these entrants produce freestyle or freeride boards that are suitable for beginner to advanced riders. By contrast, Madd Snowboards produces only premium performance snowboards, targeting the alpine market niche. Because of its small market size (relative to other snowboard market segments) and the high performance specifications required, many snowboard manufacturers do not compete in the alpine market. During the 1997–1998 season, there were approximately 150,960 alpine participants. These participants purchased 12,830 alpine boards for a total of $8,100,000 in snowboard sales.

Madd's secondary target is an even smaller niche, the boardercross segment. In a boardercross race, six riders push out of a gate at the same moment. At high speeds, riders are pitted against each other and the course. Boardercross boards allow riders to combine every riding style—freeride, freestyle, and alpine—into one big ride. The boardercross segment is a quickly growing market due to the broadening MTV and ESPN coverage of the sport.

Competitors

The snowboarding market is highly competitive. In 1997 over 350 brands existed in the growing snowboard market.[7] However, from 1997 to 1999, this number shrunk dramatically (to approximately 75 snowboard brands) in an industry-wide shakeout in which *Snow-*

boarding Business expected only 30 to 40 brands to survive.[8] Smaller brands were acquired by larger brands, causing an overall market consolidation.

In the past few years, the overproduction of snowboards also caused a drop in prices. For example, in the late 1980s, snowboards often sold for prices close to $400; by 1995 prices had dropped to an average of $325 and $273 in specialty stores and chain stores, respectively, and by 1998, boards averaged $260 at specialty stores and $163 at chains.[9]

Burton Snowboards is the undisputed leader in snowboard sales, while other brands continue to scramble for positions two, three, and four. Currently the top eight brands in the market account for about 85 percent of the snowboarding business (see Exhibit 6).

A major distinction that may be made between snowboard companies is whether they compete as producers and marketers, or solely as marketers. Many companies, categorized as "marketing companies," outsource all board production (primarily to a small group of manufacturers in Austria and Italy), and then transfer graphics onto generic board designs. A company that has successfully chosen this track is Sims Snowboards. In contrast, other brands own their production facilities. This allows them to control R&D in terms of product and design changes, and control manufacturing quality. Madd does not fit neatly into either category; it does its own board design and develops the primary molds and construction processes used for its boards in-house, but then outsources production to other high quality lamination houses.

Madd's closest competitors include Coiler Snowboards, Prior Snowboards, and Palmer USA. Each of these competitors competes in the high-end specialty snowboard market. These companies vary in product offerings but are dedicated to providing custom built high performance snowboards to riders.

Coiler Snowboards. Coiler offers boards for freecarve, slalom, giant slalom and Super G, focusing primarily on race and alpine snowboards. It offers consumers 18 different boards and recently introduced four new boards including two models for young riders and a board specifically designed for women. Coiler sells its boards factory direct to its consumers and offers a one-year warranty on its boards that cover material and workmanship defects. The average price of a Coiler Snowboard is $580 Canadian Dollars.

Prior Snowboards. Prior has been providing riders with boards since 1992. It offers a total of 21 boards for alpine carving, technical freestyle performances, halfpipe/snowboard park boards and a freeride board designed for female riders. Prior has 13 dealers in five countries—Australia, Canada, Japan, Korea and the United States. It also sells directly to consumers and offers custom-built boards. Prior offers a one-year warranty on its boards. The price of its boards average between $550–$660 Canadian Dollars.

Palmer USA. Palmer was established in 1995 and offers 16 different boards in four categories, in addition to bindings and rider gear. Palmer USA, in conjunction with Swatch, formed a team dedicated solely to boardercross—Board-X Team. The Palmer Snowboard Team

EXHIBIT 6 | Top Snowboard Brands in 1997

Company	Sales (in 000s)	Market Share	Manufacturing Capabilities
Burton Snowboards	$49,275	36.5%	Yes
K2, Inc.	24,975	18.5%	Yes
Morrow Snowboards, Inc.	12,825	9.5%	Yes
Ride Inc.	9,450	7.0%	Yes
Sims Sports	4,050	3.0%	No
Others	33,075	24.5%	Varies

has won major boardercross races in the past three years—1997 and 1998 Swatch World Tour, 1998 US Open, and the 1997 and 1998 ESPN Winter Games. Palmer has a worldwide network of retailers. The price of its boards average between $442–$555 US Dollars.

MADD SNOWBOARDS

John Gilmour had been in the snowboard industry since 1983 when he acted as a representative and product tester for Sims Snowboard Corporation, and he also served as a representative for Winterstic. In 1982 he helped to develop and introduce the high back binding system that allowed the use of soft boots in snowboarding, and in 1985, he helped to develop the world's first step-in binding system. Both an active snowboarder and skateboarder, John served as the U.S. coordinator for skateboard slalom and won a silver medal in Jeux Pyrennes D'Aventure, an adventure game organized by the French and Spanish Olympic committees for speed skateboarding. John had also assisted in the launch of two other snowboarding companies—Lizard and Bond.

In 1993, Gilmour founded Madd Snowboards. He got initial funding from Michael Banker, the previous owner of Madd Mike's, a sailboard and snowboard retail shop that specialized in mail order. Under Mike's direction, Madd Mike's had evolved into one of the largest mail order houses of its kind in the 1980s and 1990s. Madd Mike's was well-known throughout the snowboard industry because many snowboarders had bought their first boards through Madd Mike's.

Gilmour handled all product design, testing, sales, marketing and materials specification. Gilmour brought on a partner in 1995, Michael Cappelletti, to serve as controller of day-to-day activities, and to manage the finances. Cappelletti also acted as a Madd-to-retailer liaison, information systems controller, and product procurer.

In 1999, Madd offered four race, three alpine, three freecarve, two boardercross, one half-pipe, and two directional boards. Madd snowboards are primarily manufactured for racing and for highly skilled snowboard riders. A high performance board can increase a rider's acceleration and performance, and Madd strived to maximize this performance enhancement through producing the highest quality boards. In its 1998 production run, four out of five Madd boards won industry awards—more than any other snowboard manufacturer.

Manufacturing

Until recently, many snowboarders based their purchasing decisions primarily on the board graphics and company reputation. However, customers have become more sophisticated about board technology, and many customers are now able to assess a board's performance features. This shift benefits Madd and other manufacturers that have focused on using the best materials and high performance design.

Madd snowboards are made of the best materials available. Its boards are made of P-Tex 5000, 90 full-length vertically laminated wood strips, Triaxial braided fiberglass, and high sheer epoxy. These materials allow for flexibility and strength while resisting fragmentation and lessening the vibrations of the board.

The most critical part of a snowboard is its core. The most popular materials used for the core of a board are foam and wood. The core of a Madd board embodies over 90 full-length hardwood strips covering the entire surface area of the board. While foam allows for a lighter weight board, it lacks the durability and vibration-absorbing characteristics of wood. Madd's vertically laminated hardwood core utilizes the most advanced lightweight epoxies available, giving it exceptional strength. The core weighs 2 lbs. 4 oz. which makes it one pound heavier than the typical board. Madd uses poplar and birch wood to provide a maximum weight-to-response ratio that allows for a stronger, snappier flex pattern.

The wood core is sandwiched between two layers of fiberglass. The graphics on Madd boards are screened into Triaxial-Balance fiberglass. Typical boards utilize a ABS plastic topsheet to screen the graphics onto the board; however, by imbedding the graphics into the fiberglass itself, Madd graphics are shielded against scratching without the added weight of a topsheet and the glue holding it together (1/6 of the board weight).

The P-Tex 5000 base is a super-durable, almost indestructible material. It has over twice the durability of P-Tex 2000 (commonly used by other snowboard manufacturers) and is usually only found on custom boards used by pro riders. The P-Tex 5000 base is stone ground absolutely flat with a fine rill pattern for speed. Its boards are "competition flat." A stone ground board that is not flat has little advantage over a board that is not stone ground, except for reducing the suction of the board on wet snow. Truly flat boards ride faster, edge better, and turn easier. The edges on Madd snowboards are inlaid by hand and Madd uses only noncorrosive 4×4 inserts to prevent rusting.

Madd subcontracts its manufacturing to an independent snowboard manufacturer, Lucio Longoni of Funky Snowboards, in Italy. Lucio has been manufacturing snowboards since 1981 and has accumulated over 15 years of lamination experience in the snowboard industry. His designs, while considered radical by many, have proven themselves to be first-rate and have quickly found imitators. Lucio sources fiberglass locally and owns his own Computer Numerically Controlled (CNC) production machines and laminating presses. In the event of larger production runs, Madd has used Damsco, another Italian laminating shop, to produce its boards.

Through visual inspection, Madd checks each board for any manufacturing oversights. The high quality materials utilized in the production of Madd boards allow for minimal defects, and though each board comes with a 30-day no-hassle return policy and a one-year warranty, as of 1999, no board had ever been returned.

Marketing

Distribution. Madd sells its snowboards primarily through specialty snowboard retail shops under the "Madd Snowboards" brand name (see Exhibit 7). Specialty retailers cater to snowboard riders, skiers and other winter sport enthusiasts. In 1999, all of Madd's retailers carried the 158 *race board* and *boardercross* board models. Direct selling is utilized on a limited basis in areas not serviced by Madd retailers.

In the past, most specialty snowboard retailers were only willing to carry approximately 25 models manufactured by the six most well known brands to reduce the risk of excess inventory. Due to the increasing popularity of the sport throughout all ages and genders, retailers have been forced to carry a wider selection of brands and designs to accommodate the different consumer segments. This trend has allowed smaller, lesser-known snowboard companies to successfully enter the retail outlets and establish their presence within the market. Utilizing specialty retail outlets for product distribution allows Madd to achieve the higher margins associated with the premium snowboard market while enhancing the appeal of the "Madd Snowboards" brand name.

One recent trend in snow sport retailing is a shift in market share between off-site and resort-based snow shops. As of 1998, 21 percent of all retail dollars were generated by resort shops, an increase of five percent in just two years.[10] Having recognized this trend towards resort shops, in 1998 Madd secured a distribution relationship with a retail shop at Stowe Mountain in Vermont. This retail shop generates the most traffic from Stowe resort visitors due to its close proximity to the mountain (it is the closest resort shop to Stowe). Madd also has a representative at Out Of Bounds, the recognized alpine specialty retailer at Killington ski resort in Vermont. Stowe and Killington Mountains are two of the most frequented ski resorts in the New England area.

Products are shipped from its manufacturer to Madd, and from Madd to its retailers via regular mail. When retailers are close to the Boston area, John Gilmour will occasionally deliver product personally to retailers to further develop that customer relationship.

EXHIBIT 7 | Madd Snowboards Orders by Shop Size in 1988

Madd Snowboards Orders by Shop Size (# of Units)

	Race	Alpine	Boarder-X	Half-Pipe	Freeride	Freestyle
Small	—	—	1	—	2	1
Medium	8	2	3	—	2	4
Large	16	4	6	—	4	8

Pricing. Madd determines its prices based on two factors. Initially, Madd looks at the unit cost of each board and then applies a specific mark-up percentage to set its price. Following along with the industry standards, Madd applies a 50 percent mark-up at the manufacturing level and a 40 percent mark-up at the retail level. After its optimal selling price is determined, Madd adjusts the price based on what it believes the market will bear. The average price of Madd snowboards sold to retailers during the 1998–1999 season was $260, and the average price of snowboards sold direct to consumers was approximately $400.

Promotion. Through its promotional efforts Madd attempts to gain name awareness and recognition, identification as a performance product, identification as a status product, and to put forth a strong, committed image. High performance boards are usually sold following consumer trial, therefore Madd's most immediate goal was to gain the awareness that would prompt consumer trial. To enable consumer trial, Madd planned to establish permanent shared demo centers located at ski resorts throughout the Northeast. Madd would provide its chosen on-site retail shops with two boards that would be displayed and offered for test rides for interested riders.

Madd Snowboards is fairly well known in New England, Italy, and the elite World Cup circuit. To help strengthen its reputation, Madd attempts to recruit well-recognized professional snowboarders to endorse its snowboards. In 1999, five U.S. Snowboard team members (Anton Pogue, Rob Berney, Jeff Greenwood, and Eric Hotstetter) and several other competitive riders (e.g., Kevin Blages and Eric Schnorrbusch) rode Madd boards.

As of 1999, Madd had a company Web site, **www.maddsnowboards.com**, that acted mainly as a showcase for its boards. Recognizing the growing popularity of the Internet, Gilmour was considering implementing a Web shopping cart that would allow site visitors to directly purchase Madd boards at a straight retail price plus shipping and handling charges.

Madd also intended to offer tips on board tuning, waxing, and turning on the website, and feature interviews with World Cup riders and other riders reviewing the product. To keep consumers returning to its site, Madd's site would offer a forum for riders to communicate with each other through either a chat room or a community bulletin board, and provide links to other related snowboard Web sites and offer a list of recommended readings.

Research & Development

Gilmour worked continuously to discover fresh ideas and innovative ways to improve on Madd's boards. An inventor at heart, Gilmour had developed a modified version of Luciano's "butterfly pattern" that enhanced the performance of the board. The butterfly pattern is a fiberglass design in which the outer sides of the center of the board are shaved inwards to create a "butterfly" shape. This design allows for the manufacturing of boards with a snappier flex pattern, while minimizing the excess weight that slows down a rider's speed. Gilmour also developed several innovative binding designs, however he did not pursue patent rights on any of his innovations. As of 1999, John Gilmour also had several other new product designs underway, including a click-in binding system.

THE FUTURE

Though Madd had been successful in establishing a premium product reputation, the company was still very small, producing and selling between 75–200 boards a year (see Exhibit 8 for financial details). Though John Gilmour had ample experience with snowboarding design and manufacturing, and a pretty broad knowledge of the market, he had much less knowledge of how to grow a business. How big should the company strive to become? As the company grew, he would also need to decide whether to establish local manufacturing facilities. Many large snowboard companies had their own manufacturing facilities, but to perform in-house production would require a major increase in working capital (for financials of a typical large snowboard company, Ride Inc., see Exhibit 9). Gilmour had considered moving production to the Route 128 area of Boston once the cost of production within the U.S. became feasible given its production scale.

Gilmour also realized that Madd would need a larger-scale marketing plan. He had considered buying an RV to call the "Madd motor coach," which would serve

EXHIBIT

8 | Madd's Summary Financial Statements

	1996	1997	1998
Summary income statement			
Sales	$220,000	$73,750	$48,750
Cost of goods sold	$ 87,200	$37,750	$26,250
General selling and administrative expenses	$ 50,400	$20,400	$ 8,000
R&D expense	$ 2,000	$ 5,000	$ 3,000
Other expenses: trade shows, etc.	$ 76,020	$15,000	$ 2,000
Earnings before interest and taxes	$ 4,380	($4,400)	$9,500
Interest expense	0	0	$ 5,000
Income taxes	$ 1,445	0	$ 1,300
Net income	$ 2,935	($4,400)	$ 3,200
Consolidated balance sheet data			
Working capital	$ 60,000	$49,250	$ 6,400
Total assets	$ 60,000	$51,750	$ 6,400
Long-term obligations	$ 60,000	$49,250	$38,500

9 | Ride Inc., Selected Financial Information (in Thousands)

	1993	1994	1995	1996
Net sales	$5,877.00	$25,349.00	$74,850.00	$75,728.00
COGS	$3,879.00	$18,398.00	$54,988.00	$61,641.00
Gross Profit	$1,998.00	$ 6,951.00	$19,862.00	$14,087.00
Administrative expenses	$1,373.00	$ 4,022.00	$10,868.00	$20,487.00
Restructuring charges				$ 2,500.00
Operating income (loss)	**$ 625.00**	**$ 2,929.00**	**$ 8,994.00**	**($8,900.00)**
Interest expense	($130.00)	($1.00)	($18.00)	($268.00)
Interest income	$ 2.00	$ 72.00	$ 406.00	$ 333.00
Gain on sale of subsidiary				$ 482.00
Income (loss) before income taxes and extraordinary item	$ 497.00	$ 3,000.00	$ 9,382.00	($8,353.00)
Income taxes provision (benefit)		$ 1,134.00	$ 3,427.00	($2,863.00)
Income (loss) before extraordinary item	$ 497.00	$ 1,866.00	$ 5,955.00	($5,490.00)
Extraordinary item	($83.00)			
Net income (loss)	**$ 414.00**	**$ 1,866.00**	**$ 5,955.00**	**($5,490.00)**
Consolidated Balance Sheet Data				
Working capital	$1,046.00	$ 7,663.00	$26,104.00	$20,941.00
Total Assets	$2,431.00	$15,718.00	$57,599.00	$50,655.00
Long-term obligations				$ 832.00
Shareholders equity	$1,152.00	$11,524.00	$46,495.00	$42,309.00

as a travelling demo center. The motor coach would travel to ski resorts, trade shows, exhibitions and competitions throughout the nation to act as a temporary demo center. It could also be used to aid in the distribution of Madd snowboards, and help build relationships with retailers.

Madd was also considering using national print advertising. Other snowboard manufacturers placed ads in magazines such as *Transworld Snowboard Life, Transworld Snowboard, Blunt, Skiing, Snowboarder, Women's Sport + Fitness* and *Mountain Biking Magazine.* Placing national ads was expensive, but would allow Madd to get exposure to a much wider market.

Gilmour also wondered if he should expand Madd's product line. Possibilities included offering a women's or children's line of snowboards, or producing apparel items such as T-shirts, hats, gloves, pants, and jackets. Many snowboard companies had expanded their lines into other goods such as gear bags, tuning kits, and snowboard boots. John was even considering producing a new line of ski boards. This was a relatively untapped market that John felt might nicely complement Madd's line of snowboards.

However to grow the company and expand its product line meant that the company would need a large infusion of capital. How would Madd fund the development costs and increase in working capital that such expansion and product line enhancements would require?

NOTES

1. Transworld Snowboarding, Snowboard History Timeline, www.twsnow.com.
2. Jim Emerson, Snowboarders; statistics on snowboarding, *Cowles Business Media, Inc.* 1 Feb. 1999:133.
3. Cyndee Miller, Stoked over snowboarding, *Marketing News* 18 Nov. 1996: 24.
4. Adult boarders create silver lining for maturing sport, *USA Today* 29 Jan. 1999.
5. Slope and slide, *Sporting Goods Business* Aug. 1997.
6. David E. Schultz, Thoughts for the First-Time Buyer, *Monmouth* Nov. 1998.
7. Leigh Gallagher, Balance of powder, *Sporting Goods Business* 24 Feb. 1997 26–27.
8. Jim Emerson, Snowboarders; statistics on snowboarding, *Cowles Business Media, Inc.* 1 Feb. 1999:133.
9. 1998 Statistics on Snow Sports, *SnowLink Media Center.*
10. Kristin Carpenter, Resorts lifting retail sales with off-site acquisitions, *Sporting Goods Business* 24 July 1998:12.

Mendocino Brewing Company, Inc.—1996

Armand Gilinsky
Sonoma State University

Well, I made beer in the garage. And we got pretty good at it. We started a fad. Brewpubs are everywhere now. California is nice to small brewers. The microbrewery industry is a good one to be in now. It's exciting, there's romance, it's the American dream. Brewing is art and science. The art is creating a stable product; the science is to maintain quality throughout the distribution system. Big brewers can do this because they preserve shelf life with no problems.

—Michael Laybourn, President & CEO, Mendocino Brewing Company

On September 6, 1996, the Mendocino Brewing Company (MBC) announced that it had been forced to postpone the opening of its new brewery until early 1997. The new brewery, which would immediately allow MBC to quadruple its production of beer, was scheduled to commence operations in the third quarter of 1996. The company's Marketing Director, Michael Lovett, had high hopes for the new brewery:

> *We are building a state-of-the-art brewery using the latest knowledge in order to become more "efficient." We also need to control costs in the distribution and management areas. We have developed controls for production and processes, using industry benchmarks. As we get better at doing these things, we will automatically make money without spending more.*

This case study was prepared as a basis for class discussion rather than to illustrate either effective or ineffective handling of an administrative situation.

Copyright © 1998 by Armand Gilinsky and *Case Research Journal*. All rights reserved.

However, costs of the previously estimated $8.2 million capacity expansion had risen to $9.2 million, and the project had been delayed by a combination of setbacks. These setbacks included a longer-than-expected environmental impact review process; the August 1995 departure of its proponent, Ukiah city manager Charles Rough, Jr.; heavy winter rains in early 1996 that postponed construction; and unexpected soil conditions that hampered installation of a wastewater treatment system. The expansion project also underwent last-minute changes in design, consolidating two construction phases into one.

Lovett wondered whether or not MBC had waited too long to begin its capacity expansion project. He explained the rationale behind ramping up capacity faster than originally planned:

> *That was a market-driven decision. We just felt that the market was dictating that we move faster . . . Our biggest regrets are (1) we lost market share by not responding to changes in the market; (2) we didn't get on-line like Sierra Nevada; and (3) we didn't raise money in 1990 for expansion. We're too small for NASDAQ. Our stock price is overvalued now. With regard to selling off the brewery to someone else, we have been approached in the past, but not approached recently. Capitalization and managing growth are our biggest problems. We are learning. In the meantime, it's trial and error.*

When the postponement of the new brewery's opening was announced, MBC's President and Chief Executive Officer, Michael Laybourn, remarked,

We could fall behind because of improper market positioning, insufficient resources, or lack of invested capital. We are currently evaluating several options to strengthen our market position: (1) continuing product quality, (2) product line extension, (3) geographical expansion, (4) improving distribution via entry into new distribution channels, and (5) adding product awareness promotion to brand loyalty promotion. Choosing any of these strategies requires access to capital on favorable terms, could incur additional costs, and represents a tradeoff between remaining a small, manageable high-margin business and becoming a larger, more impersonal, and less profitable business.

Over the past ten years MBC had grown from a small business run by entrepreneurs with traditional beer recipes into a regional microbrewery. (See Exhibit 1 for a classification of brewing companies by size.) In 1983 California became the first state to change its laws to allow the operation of brewpubs. Laybourn, MBC's founder, seized this opportunity, opening the Hopland Brewery, restaurant and gift shop in Hopland, about 100 miles north of San Francisco. MBC thus became the first new brewpub in California and the second in the United States since Prohibition. Like other pioneers in the microbrewing industry, MBC faced several disadvantages associated with its small size and lack of business experience.

By 1996, microbreweries accounted for nearly 2 percent of total U.S. beer sales. By the 21st century, microbreweries were expected to reach a 5 percent–6 percent share of this market. Industry observers considered management skills, quality control and adequate capital to be essential to survival in the microbrewing business. The necessary state-of-the-art equipment alone required substantial capital infusions. Funds were needed for plant capacity expansions and marketing.

1 | Classification of Breweries

The brewing industry uses the terms of kegs, barrels (bbls.) and cases to measure and sell beer. A keg of beer equals 15.5 gallons, a barrel of beer equals 2 kegs, or 31 gallons, and a barrel of beer produces 13.8 24-unit cases of 12-ounce bottles.

A **microbrewery** is defined as a brewery that produces less than 15,000 bbls. of beer per year. Microbreweries typically sell their production via the following methods: (1) the traditional three-tier system (brewer to wholesaler to retailer to consumer); (2) the two-tier system (brewer acting as wholesaler to retailer to consumer); and (3) in some cases, directly to the consumer through carryouts, on-site tap-room or brewery restaurant sales.

A **brewpub** is defined as a restaurant-brewery that brews and sells the majority of its beer on site. Beer is brewed for sale and consumption in an adjacent restaurant and/or bar. Beer is often dispensed directly from a brewery's storage tanks. Where allowed by law, brewpubs often sell beer "to go" and/or distributed products to off-site accounts. When off-site beer sales exceed 50 percent of total production, then a brewpub can be reclassified as a microbrewery.

A **regional brewery** is defined as having an annual capacity of 15,000 to 500,000 bbls. Although its distribution could be limited in scope to a specific geographical area, for categorization purposes "regional" refers to the brewery's size only.

A **regional specialty brewery** is defined as a regional brewery with its largest selling brand being a micro or specialty beer.

A **large brewery** typically produces more than 500,000 bbls. annually.

Source: Institute for Brewing Studies, Boulder, CO.

Without such funding, brewpubs and microbreweries typically failed at an annual rate of 14 percent and 16 percent, respectively, according to the Institute for Brewing Studies in Boulder, Colorado.

Latecomers with large marketing and financial resources were introducing microbrewed beers aimed toward the mass market. With deeper pockets and greater economies of scale, these large competitors could be expected to lower prices to capture greater market shares and thus squeeze out the pioneers. George Johnson, Professor of Business and Director of the Craft Brewing Business Institute at Sonoma State University, remarked in 1995:

> *The big guys have already started to do it. Anheuser-Busch, Coors and Miller's are trying to market beer into this 'craft' beer market. Will the public buy them? Craft beer buyers are loyal to their brands. People move into the craft brewing market and stay there. But where do these small companies get the money to grow? That's the big question.*

Some microbreweries sought conventional bank loans; some, strategic alliances as contract manufacturers for the large national brewing companies. Other microbreweries, hoping to remain independent while increasing volume and sales, resorted to equity or "creative financing," noted Jack Erickson, the publisher of the *Erickson Report,* a microbrewing industry newsletter. In some cases, with brewers hawking shares "like penny stocks over the radio," these schemes seemed as much about marketing as raising money, Erickson said. At a time when a beer's popularity could be measured in weeks, persuading a customer to invest in a brewery was seen by many entrepreneurs as a means for raising funds as well as a way to help ensure customer loyalty. Several microbreweries went public with their stock in 1994 and 1995 via Initial Public Offerings (IPOs). "However," Julie Tilsner wrote in the January 16, 1995, issue of *Business Week,* "it's not easy to invest (in microbreweries). None of these IPOs are large enough to be on any (major) public exchanges. The companies are selling the shares directly, without benefit of an underwriter, and no brokers handle later trading."

By the end of 1995, the IPOs of several large microbreweries had nevertheless gained national attention and their stocks were actively being traded on public exchanges. Notable examples included the Boston Beer Company in Massachusetts, Redhook Ale Brewery and Hart Brewing, both of the state of Washington, and Pete's Brewing Co. in Palo Alto, California. (See Exhibit 2 for a list of recent IPOs.)

COMPANY HISTORY

In February 1982, Laybourn, Norman Franks, and John Scahill began home brewing as a hobby. They then took the legal steps and provided initial capital to start a commercial brewery. In January 1983, MBC acquired the assets of New Albion Brewing Co., located in Sonoma, CA. Founded by Jack McAuliffe in 1976, New Albion had been the first new microbrewery to commence operations in the U.S. since Prohibition. The venture team also hired McAuliffe, Donald Barkley (New Albion's master brewer), and Michael Lovett. The five founders were also principal shareholders. (See Exhibit 3 for a profile of MBC's current venture team.)

Michael Lovett recalled the early days:

> *We evolved from the first microbrewery in California, New Albion. Because of local opposition to expansion of New Albion's original site, we then picked a new location for a brewpub in Hopland (about an hour's drive north of Sonoma), then hired New Albion Brewing Company staff. We decided to produce beer because we loved it ourselves. We saw a market for other styles of beer. Beer, after all, is associated with benefits like the "happy side" of life.*
>
> *The original three founders are still with the company. I expect all three founders will still be involved with the brewery in five years, as we bring it up to capacity. We are team players and will stick with the company until the end. The rewards to us for completing MBC are great. We like seeing the growth process, receiving financial rewards, and ensuring that our investment is secure.*

In March 1982, the company leased a 100-year-old brick building, known since the early 1900s as the "Hopvine Saloon," located along U.S. Highway 101 in the center of Hopland, a historic region for hop growing. The building was renovated and, behind it, a hop kiln brewhouse was built. Mendocino Brewing Company, a California limited partnership, was formed in

2 | Recent Initial Public Offerings by Microbreweries

Brewery	History	IPO Information
Boston Beer Co. (Boston, MA)	Nation's number one microbrewery; primarily engaged in contract brewing; sold 961,000 barrels in 1995.	Raised $60 million in 1995 DPO: Samuel Adams label mainly brewed by Pittsburgh Brewing and Blitz-Weinhard (owned by Stroh).
Buffalo Brewing (Buffalo, NY)	New York's number-one microbrewery; ranked the 17th largest microbrewery in the U.S.	Raised more than $1 million by going public in 1994; proceeds will be used for new product lines and additional equipment.
Hart Brewing (Seattle, WA)	Washington's second largest brewery; began as a microbrewery and grew into a regional brewery before going public.	Raised $35 million in December 1995 for capacity and geographical expansion.
Mile High Brewing (Denver, CO)	Venture between Ron Smith, founder and CEO of Vail Valley Vintners, and Jim Bernau, president of Willamette Valley Brewing of Oregon; began brewing in November 1993.	First public microbrewery in Colorado; raised approximately $1.8 million on its first public offering in 1994.
Portland Brewing (Portland, OR)	Founded in 1986 by home brewers Fred Bowman & Art Larrance; later partnered with Robert MacTarnahan, who contributed $2 million in capital.	First microbrewery to go public (1993); has raised nearly $4 million in three offerings.
Red Hook Brewing (Seattle, WA)	Founded in '81 by Paul Shipman and Gordon Bowker (Starbucks Coffee) as Independent Ale Brewery; long-term, exclusive distribution agreement with Anheuser-Busch (owns 25 percent stake) in '94; sales $26 million, net profits of $3.1 million in '95.	1,956,614 shares of common stock were offered at $17 per share in 1995; proceeds used to build a $30 million, 250,000-barrel brewery in New Hampshire.
Rock Bottom Restaurants (Boulder, CO)	Incorporated April 1993; one of the first brew-restaurants to be publicly traded; operates in Colorado, Minnesota and Texas.	First offering netted approximately $16.5 million in proceeds, mostly used to build new restaurants.
Seattle Brewing Co. (Seattle, WA)	Founded by Jim Bernau; brewery construction began in early 1995.	Raised $2.4 million in its first stock offering (8/94) to build a new microbrewery.
Willamette Valley Brewing (Portland, OR)	Founded by Jim Bernau; company began brewing in November 1993.	Raised $2.4 million on its 1993 IPO and raised an additional $1.2 million on its second offering.

Source: Sonoma State University Craft Brewing Business Institute.

March 1983. Because of its remote location, the founding venture team expected that the brewery's future retail sales growth would be limited to local customers and drive-by tourist traffic on Highway 101. According to Lovett,

We were customer-oriented from the beginning. We built MBC in Hopland along the tourist route, hoping that the positive image from visiting the brewpub would translate into buying products on the retail shelf. We added a full kitchen and restaurant along

Exhibit 3 | Mendocino Brewing Co.—Venture Team Profiles

Michael Laybourn, 58, CEO, President and Director (co-founder and officer since 1982). Prior to MBC, Laybourn co-owned and operated Thunder Road Design and Construction. He is the VP of the California Small Brewers Association and was elected Chairman of the Brewers Association of America in 1995. Laybourn has a B.F.A. from Arizona State University.

Norman Franks, 49, CFO, VP, Treasurer and Director has been an officer since 1982. Prior to MBC, Franks co-owned and operated Thunder Road Design and Construction. He has a B.S. in mechanical engineering from UC Berkeley.

Michael Lovett, 49, Marketing Director, Secretary and Director, joined MBC in 1983 as Assistant Master Brewer and became Marketing Director in 1987. Between 1980 and 1983, he was VP Quality Control of New Albion Brewing Co. From 1976–1980, Lovett was Production Superintendent at Farm Foods in San Francisco. He is Membership Chairman and past Technical Chairman of the Master Brewers Association of the Americas. He has a B.A. in psychology from San Francisco State College.

Eric G. Bradley, 58, Director, became Director in 1994 and will serve until 1995. Bradley has been a business and financial consultant since 1988. He was employed 20 years with Kaiser Aluminum & Chemical Corp. in positions rising from Division Controller to Business Manager. He is a Fellow of the Institute of Chartered Accountants (UK) and a Certified Personal Financial Planner.

Dan Moldenhauer, 62, Director, is a management consultant. He was president of Conex Products, Inc., of Dublin, CA, from 1988–1990, a company formed from assets divested by Kaiser Aluminum & Chemical Corp. and later sold to Coleman Cable Systems. Moldenhauer served in several capacities with Kaiser Aluminum from 1971–1988, most recently as president of the subsidiary.

John Scahill, 58, Facilities Manager, has served MBC since its inception. Scahill used to be a self-employed rancher. He has a background in construction and counseling and has a B.S. degree in sociology from UC Berkeley.

Donald Barkley, 43, Master Brewer, joined in 1983. Prior to joining MBC, Barkley was Head Brewer and Plant Manager at New Albion Brewing Co. from 1981 to 1983. Barkley joined New Albion in 1978 and held several positions. He has a BS degree in fermentation science from UC Davis.

Sources: Mendocino Brewing Company, 10-K filing, 12/31/95 and direct public offering prospectus.

> *with a retail merchandise store. We relied solely on word-of-mouth advertising, which gave us a cult following. Our original customer profile included wine connoisseurs with culinary interests who liked beer and were either white- or blue-collar workers. We have been copied by other microbreweries and they still come to us for ideas.*

Brewing began in July 1983. On August 14, the partners opened The Hopland Brewery. In December 1983, the partners began hand-bottling Red Tail Ale in 1.5-liter champagne magnums to satisfy off-premises demand. Lovett recalled,

> *They sold immediately as 42-lb six packs. Because large glass bottle manufacturers were unwilling or unable to do so, Fritz Maytag (CEO of the Anchor Steam Brewing Company in nearby San Francisco) sold us glass bottles in the smaller quantities that we needed. Maytag has helped to maintain the industry*

as a "labor of love" and to save it, among other things.

By 1984 the company had expanded production by 67 percent and doubled the size of The Hopland Brewery.

From 1986 to 1987, additional limited partnership units were sold to private investors to finance the purchase of new brewing equipment and fermenting tanks. MBC began shipping Red Tail Ale in 12-oz bottles to wholesale distributors, who in turn sold to retail accounts. Wholesale distribution was at the time the principal means of expanding sales to the mass market. Lovett explained that demand for Red Tail Ale soon surpassed production capacity, and MBC then implemented a policy of allocating limited supply to distributors.

In 1990, MBC acquired a 120-bottle-per-minute bottling machine. Also in that year the company hired a consultant to help management begin the transition from the entrepreneurial stage to the growth stage. Laybourn instituted a total quality management training program and structured the company into teams:

> *We began realizing problems from growth. Total Quality Management issues were raised, as well as needs to improve Human Resources Management. We knew back then that we would have to become a corporation and, as a result of these changes, the partners wouldn't be equal shareholders anymore.*

In 1993, sales increased 1.5 percent to $3,363,908 over $3,314,199 in 1992. Growth was attributed to brewing operations, which increased wholesale bottled beer shipments by 5.5 percent in 1993. Red Tail Ale, the company's flagship brand, now represented 84 percent of production. Retail sales showed a decline as draft sales decreased by 5.6 percent, which was almost offset by an increase in food and merchandise sales at the brewpub. Gross profit from brewing operations decreased 3.8 percent to $1,051,291 (from $1,091,828 in 1992), largely due to increases in labor costs (primarily wages, production hours, and training costs) of $38,000, and a 6 percent increase in the cost of bottles. A reduction in food costs and improvements in inventory control resulted in a gross profit increase of 1.7 percent to $525,752 in 1993.

By 1993, wholesale distribution accounted for 72 percent of MBC's total sales, of which 85 percent were to eight Northern California distributors. Products were sold in over 1,500 retail outlets in Northern California. The single largest retail outlet, in terms of volume sold, was The Hopland Brewpub, which was highly dependent upon tourist traffic for sales. The brewery's two largest Northern California distributors, Bay Area Distributing (25 percent) and Golden Gate Distributing (20 percent), accounted for 45 percent of 1993 wholesale distributions. In 1993, retail sales, as a percentage of total sales, were 12 percent for draft and bottled beer and 16 percent for food and merchandise.

On January 1, 1994, the Partnership incorporated by transferring all of its assets, including its name, to a newly formed California corporation in exchange for 100 percent of the Common and Preferred Stock of the corporation. The Partnership distributed these shares to its partners on January 3.

Lovett explained that by 1994, MBC had reached the point

> *where we couldn't store everything we needed to brew and package our beer. You see, cost is a factor with our suppliers for storing and delivering raw materials. Labels are a more controllable factor for us in terms of cost and availability, but glass is costly because we use very little, compared with competitors, and we tend to get the end of a production run from bigger suppliers. We expected that our leverage with suppliers would naturally increase as we grew larger.*

MBC decided it needed to raise money to build another brewery to churn out more of its Red Tail Ale. Typically, a company hired an underwriter when it decided to offer shares to the public in an Initial Public Offering (IPO). But looking to save $200,000 in underwriters' fees, MBC chose to market the stock directly to consumers in a Direct Public Offering (DPO). Lovett described this process:

> *We were running at 100% capacity and were constrained by this. We could not meet demand. Insufficient capacity also constrained the expansion of our product line. So, we hired Drew Fields (a San Francisco–based securities lawyer and author of* Taking Your Company Public*) to advise us on how to go public via a DPO, which is really an extended private placement of stock to customers and affinity groups.*

Fields had also advised our neighbors in Ukiah, Real Goods Trading Company, on how to do a DPO. We used multi-phased marketing to raise capital: pitching to our customers in our 13,000-reader circulation newsletter, The Brewsletter; *stuffing tombstone notices into each of our six-packs; and advertising in the local papers. All of the funds raised would be used for the capacity expansion.*

In February 1995, the company closed its DPO of 600,000 shares of common stock for $6 per share, raising gross proceeds of $3.6 million and net proceeds of $3.3 million. Funds were earmarked primarily for the acquisition of land and equipment and construction of a new brewery in nearby Ukiah. MBC's expansion plans also included long-term debt and equipment financing commitments from bank loans of approximately $4.7 million and the use of $200,000 from internally generated funds.

The new brewery was expected to have enough capacity to produce 50,000 barrels (bbls.) of beer for shipment within four to eight weeks after start-up, and additional space was available to permit incremental capacity expansions to brew up to 200,000 bbls. annually. MBC was listed on the Pacific Stock Exchange, and during its first year as a public company, its shares traded steadily in the $7½ to $8½ range, but without much upward movement. Laybourn later said publicly that he had been pleased with the result of the first DPO.

On Friday, May 12, 1995, MBC held its first annual shareholder meeting at the nearby Ukiah Conference Center. At that annual meeting Laybourn told shareholders that the company hoped to close purchase of the land for the new brewery as soon as the necessary environmental impact studies were completed and that there was no known opposition to the project. He also said that the company intended to purchase a new fermentation tank to increase production at the existing Hopland facility. The new tank was expected to increase existing capacity, beginning around August 1995. Laybourn observed that, because the Hopland brewery had been operating at full capacity for several years. it possessed little ability to increase revenues for 1995 without these measures. Meanwhile, costs associated with being a public company resulted in increased operating expenses. (See Exhibits 4–7 for company financial in-

EXHIBIT

4 | Mendocino Brewing Company—Comparative Income Statements, 1993–1996

	Quarterly report for:		Fiscal year ending:		
	06/30/96	**03/31/96**	**12/31/95**	**12/31/94**	**12/31/93**
Net sales	$1,209,290	$ 631,034	$3,566,500	$3,365,600	$3,363,908
Cost of goods	545,711	324,739	1,846,500	1,840,900	1,786,865
Gross profit	663,579	306,295	1,720,000	1,524,700	1,577,043
Sell gen & admin exp	579,612	429,531	1,537,300	1,324,700	1,375,771
Operating profit	83,967	(123,236)	182,700	200,000	201,272
Non-operating inc	(43,274)	11,219	147,600	29,000	25,541
Interest expense	—	—	3,700	4,200	6,088
Income before tax	40,693	(112,017)	326,600	224,800	220,725
Prov for inc taxes	(21,500)	800	152,900	71,500	0
Net income	$ 62,193	$ 112,817)	$ 173,700	$ 153,300	$ 220,725
Outstanding shs.	2,322,222	2,322,222	2,322,222	2,220,445	—

Segment data, FY 1995	**Sales**	**Op. Income**
Brewing operations	$2,775,500	$758,400
Hopland Brewery	$ 959,600	$ 34,600

Sources: Mendocino Brewing Company, 10-K filing, 12/31/95 and direct public offering prospectus.

5 | Mendocino Brewing Company—Comparative Balance Sheets, 1994–1996

	Quarterly report for:		Fiscal year ending:	
	06/30/96	**03/31/96**	**12/31/95**	**12/31/94**
Assets				
Cash	$ 21,226	$ 523,410	$1,696,100	$2,900,800
Receivables	550,382	250,075	458,900	293,900
Inventories	463,532	448,709	256,200	202,000
Notes receivable	110,088	67,843	—	—
Other current assets	—	—	62,600	25,300
Total current assets	1,145,228	1,290,037	2,473,800	3,422,000
Prop, plant & equip	—	—	3,954,100	301,000
Accumulated dep	6,947,661	5,197,818	—	—
Net prop & equip	—	—	3,954,100	301,000
Other non-cur assets	23,575	14,344	—	—
Deferred charges	—	—	15,100	60,500
Deposits, other assets	98,413	94,672	71,000	254,600
Total assets	$8,214,877	$6,596,871	$6,514,000	$4,038,100
Liabilities & Net Worth	**06/30/96**	**03/31/96**	**12/31/95**	**12/31/94**
Notes payable	$ 360,000	$ 400,000	—	—
Accounts payable	367,982	138,131	$ 105,700	$ 144,700
Cur long term debt	10,021	8,104	10,400	7,900
Accrued expenses	2,532,522	1,164,192	1,364,400	149,800
Income taxes	—	—	34,200	12,400
Total current liab	3,270,525	1,710,427	1,514,700	314,800
Deferred charges/inc	20,200	20,200	20,200	—
Long-term debt	550,652	554,937	554,900	—
Total liabilities	3,841,377	2,285,564	2,089,800	314,800
Preferred stock	227,600	227,600	227,600	227,600
Common stock net	3,869,569	3,869,569	3,869,600	3,342,400
Retained earnings	276,331	214,138	327,000	153,300
Shareholder's equity	4,373,500	4,311,307	4,424,200	3,723,300
Tot liab & net worth	$8,214,877	$6,596,871	$6,514,000	$4,038,100

Sources: Mendocino Brewing Company, 10-K filing, 12/31/95 and direct public offering prospectus.

formation and financial ratios and Exhibit 8 for selected comparative financial ratios for microbreweries.)

U.S. BREWING INDUSTRY AND COMPETITION

Domestic brewing has its foundations entwined with the establishment of the original 13 colonies. Many of the country's founding fathers were either brewers or had some connection with breweries. In 1870, there were over 3,000 breweries in the U.S. Most were small scale—in the back room of a pub—or free-standing small local breweries serving their surrounding communities. In 1887, the average brewery produced 10,000 bbls. Mass production and marketing, along with improved technologies, increased competition among brewers, and larger brewers either bought competing breweries or forced them out of business. By 1990, the number of domestic brewing companies had decreased to 1,751. As Prohibition gained momentum, and as sev-

6 | Mendocino Brewing Company—Statement of Cash Flows Provided by Operations, 1995

	FYE 12/31/95
Cash provided by (used in) operations	
Net income (loss)	$ 173,700
Depreciation/amortization	49,300
Net increase (decrease) in assets/liabilities	(237,700)
Other adjustments, net	21,100
Net cash provided by (used in) operations	$ 6,400
Cash from investments	
(Increase) decrease in property & plant	$(2,922,800)
Other cash inflow (outflow)	(27,800)
Net cash provided by (used in) investments	$(2,950,600)
Cash flows from financing	
Issuances (purchases) of equity security	$ 568,900
Increase (decrease) in bank, other borrowings	(11,700)
Other cash inflow (outflow)	1,182,300
Net cash provided by (used in) financing	$ 1,739,500
Net change of cash/cash equivalents	(1,204,700)
Cash/cash equivalents at start of year	2,900,800
Cash/cash equivalents at year end	$ 1,696,100

Source: Mendocino Brewing Company, 10-K filing, 12/31/95.

7 | Mendocino Brewing Company—Selected Comparative Financial Ratios, 1993–1995

	Fiscal year ending		
	12/31/95	12/31/94	12/31/93
Current ratio	1.63	10.87	2.63
Quick ratio	1.42	10.15	1.96
Days receivables	46.32	31.44	28.78
Inventory turnover	13.92	16.66	18.93
Times interest earned	89.27	54.52	37.26
Fixed asset turnover	0.90	11.18	16.26
Total asset turnover	0.55	0.83	3.12
Total debt: total assets	0.32	0.08	0.27
Total debt: common equity	0.50	0.09	0.38
Sales/cash	2.10	1.16	11.37
SG&A/sales	0.43	0.39	0.41
Inventories: days sales	25.86	21.61	19.02
Net sales/working capital	3.72	1.08	7.17
Net income/net sales	0.05	0.05	0.07
Net income/total assets	0.03	0.04	0.20
Net income/invested capital	0.03	0.04	0.28
Net income/common equity	0.04	0.04	0.28
Net sales/employee	$49,535	$45,481	—

Source: Disclosure On-Line.

8 | Selected Comparative Financial Ratios for Microbreweries

	Ownership	
	Public (*n* = 16)	Private (*n* = 6)
Current	2.58 times	1.76 times
Quick	.88 times	.92 times
Days receivables	35.02 days	37.87 days
Inventory turnover	53.02 days	105.19 days
Days payables	53.43 days	64.23 days
Times interest earned	6.80 times	1.82 times
Debt coverage indicator	3.89 times	12.32 times
Assets to equity	.88 times	1.31 times
Liabilities to equity	.43 times	.98 times
Return on equity	5.50%	−8.83%
Return on assets	3.88%	−2.18%
Fixed assets turnover	1.54 times	2.12 times
Total assets turnover	.90 times	.99 times

Source: Sonoma State University Craft Brewing Business Institute survey of microbrewers, Fall 1996.

eral states adopted dry laws, the number of brewers further decreased so that by 1914, there were 1,250 domestic brewing companies. Fewer than 600 of these resumed production after Prohibition, as the competitive nature of the industry increased, with the larger national brewers gaining a greater market share by buying or forcing smaller brewers out of business. By the mid-1960s, fewer than 100 domestic brewing companies remained in operation.

In the late 1960s and early 1970s, wine-drinking patterns and culinary trends changed to more diversified and up-scale products. This trend continued into the beer market and increased demand for distinctive, full-flavored beers, primarily brewed by foreign brewers and a few of the remaining small domestic brewers. The gradual renaissance for the small domestic specialty brewer began in 1965, when a Stanford University graduate, Fritz Maytag, bought and began resurrecting San Francisco's Anchor Brewing Co. (originally founded in 1896). The number of small brewers, meanwhile, continued to decline, as fewer than 40 domestic brewing companies were in operation by the late 1970s.

While the U.S. beer market's sales volume grew at an average rate of 3 percent annually from 1970 to 1980, the market experienced a .9 percent average growth rate from 1981 to 1991. Domestic beer sales fell by .4 percent in 1992, increased by .5 percent in 1993, were flat in 1994, and declined by 1.1 percent in 1995. By then, beer sales in the U.S. had reached $51.1 billion and the market was dominated by the top five domestic beer producers, ranked by their 1993 sales: Anheuser-Busch Cos. (the world's largest brewer with 46.6 percent of the U.S. beer market); Miller Brewing Co. (owned by tobacco and food conglomerate Philip Morris, with a 22.7 percent share), Adolph Coors Co. (10.5 percent), Stroh Brewery Co. (7.6 percent) and G. Heileman Brewing Co. (6.2 percent). In early 1996, Stroh Brewery purchased the Heileman Brewing Co. for an estimated $275 million.

The remaining 7.5 percent of the U.S. beer market was shared by imported beers and some smaller brands such as Pabst, Keystone and Henry Weinhard's. According to The Institute for Brewing Studies, just under one percent of this specialty niche was shared by over 570 microbreweries, regional specialty breweries and brewpubs. The import/domestic specialty segment, by contrast, had grown steadily from the mid '80s to the mid '90s, with annual rates of growth approaching the 40–50 percent range. By 1995, there were over 90 brewpubs, microbreweries, and regional specialty brewers in California alone (more than any other state) and approximately 745 nationwide, according to the Institute for Brewing Studies. There was a 7.6 percent increase in

1995 sales of imported beers and an increase of approximately 40 percent in domestic specialty beers. In that year, sales of domestic specialty beers made up approximately 1.5 percent of the U.S. beer market, up from less than 1.0 percent in 1994.

This rapid growth of small specialty brewers did not go unnoticed by the large brewers. Having experienced less than 1 percent annual growth over the last decade, large brewers were now researching specialty beer products and entering either niche markets or markets that could be segmented to provide an added source of growth. These segments included

1. Low-priced (Busch, Milwaukee's Best, Old Milwaukee)—20 percent U.S. market share
2. Premium (Budweiser, Miller Lite, Bud Light, Coors Light)—60 percent share
3. Super-Premium (Michelob, Lowenbrau)—15 percent share
4. Import/Domestic Specialty—5 percent share, including
   - Foreign Imports (Guinness, Pilsner Urquell, Bass Pale Ale, Harp, Heineken, Amstel Light, Beck's, St. Pauli Girl)
   - Regional Specialty/Contract Brewers (Bridgeport Pale Ale, Red Tail Ale, Anchor Steam Beer, Pyramid Pale Ale, Full Sail Ale, Red Hook ESB, Pete's Wicked Ale, Sierra Nevada Pale Ale, Samuel Adams Boston Lager)
   - Large Brewer Specialty Products (Killian's Irish Red, Henry Weinhard's Private Reserve, Miller Reserve Amber, Rolling Rock Extra Ale)

Sales of domestic specialty beers were highest on the West Coast. In California approximately 300,000 bbls. were sold in 1993, of which MBC sold 12,500 bbls. In Oregon, sales of domestic specialty beers accounted for 4 percent (29,000 bbls.) of that state's total beer sales. Of that amount, 23,000 bbls. were sold as draft beer. Portland had more microbreweries and brewpubs than any other city in the U.S. Oregon and Washington had approximately 50 brewpubs and microbreweries and were considered mature markets for specialty beers.

As the domestic specialty beer segment continued to grow, the number and availability of specialty beers were also expected to proliferate as regional specialty brewers and microbrewers expanded their capacity and as new brewers entered the market. MBC competed directly with other small local microbreweries and brewpubs, foreign brewers, contract brewers (such as Boston Beer Co. and Pete's Brewing Co.), regional specialty brewers (such as Anchor Brewing Co., Sierra Nevada Brewing Co., and Redhook Ale Brewery), and large brewers. Several of MBC's competitors were known to be expanding their production capacity to meet increasing demand. These competitors typically had a substantially greater critical mass of financial resources, marketing strength and distributor influence than did MBC.

Similarly, the nation's largest brewers showed interest in the emerging market niche by introducing their own specialty products, purchasing the rights to specialty products, and investing in regional specialty brewers. By 1995, Miller Brewing Company was producing Reserve Lager, Amber Ale, and Velvet Stout. It also acquired Jacob Leinenkugel Brewing Company in 1987 and was distributing Leinenkugel Red Lager, Leinie Light and Leinie Limited. In February 1995, Miller bought a controlling share in Celis Brewery, Inc., of Austin, Texas. Similarly, Coors began a subsidiary company brewing Killian Red in 1981. The brand went national in 1989 and was experiencing annual growth of about 40 percent. Stroh Brewery Co. made Augsburger Octoberfest and Doppelbock and produced a regional brew called Red River Valley Select Red Lager. Anheuser-Busch developed its own microbrews named Red Wolf, Elk Mountain, Amber Ale and Red Lager. In 1995, Anheuser joined forces with Redhook via a 25 percent equity investment and distribution rights for Redhook Ale.

BARRIERS TO ENTRY

Entry into the regional specialty beer market segment was, compared with entering the mass market, relatively easy. Each year, a growing number of small brewers entered the segment, while the established segment leaders increased sales and, in certain cases, production capabilities and market share. MBC expected competition in its segment to intensify further, as regional specialty brewers increased production and became more sophisticated in marketing.

Still, the manufacture and sale of alcoholic beverages was a highly regulated and taxed business. If alcohol taxes were increased, MBC would have to raise prices to maintain present profit margins. MBC did not believe that this would reduce sales, but it could depend on the amount of increase, general economic conditions, and other factors. MBC believed that its position as a high-quality specialty brewer and its penetration into the market segment would enable it to continue to withstand tax increases in the near-term. Higher taxes could reduce overall demand for beer. More restrictive regulations relating to environment, plant safety or product advertising could also increase operating costs.

MBC was licensed to manufacture and sell beer by the California Department of Alcoholic Beverage Control (ABC). A "Small Beer Manufacturer's License" allowed MBC to brew up to 1,000,000 bbls. per year, to conduct wholesale sales, and to conduct on-premise sales of the brewery's beers in The Hopland Brewery. An "Off Sale Beer and Wine License" issued by ABC allowed off-premises sales of beer and wine. A federal permit from the Bureau of Alcohol, Tobacco, and Firearms (BATF) allowed MBC to manufacture fermented malt beverages.

To keep these licenses and permits in force, MBC paid annual fees and submitted timely production reports and excise tax returns. Prompt notice of any changes in the operations, ownership, or company structure also had to be made to these regulatory agencies. BATF approved all product labels, which needed to include an alcohol use warning. These agencies required that individuals owning equity securities in aggregate of 10 percent or more in MBC be investigated as to their suitability (these individual owners included Laybourn, Franks, and Scahill).

MBC also paid Federal excise taxes of $7.00 per bbl. for up to 60,000 bbls. of production per year and $18.00 per bbl. for production in excess of 60,000 bbls. The California tax rate as of 1994 was $6.20 per bbl. Beginning with the six-month period ended June 30, 1995, MBC began classifying federal and state excise taxes as a reduction of gross sales in order to be consistent with industry standards.

The Hopland Brewery's restaurant was regulated by the Mendocino County Health Department, which required an annual permit and inspections. MBC was also subject to various federal, state, and local environmental laws that regulated the use, storage, handling, and disposal of substances. Production operations had to comply with OSHA standards.

MBC planned to operate water treatment facilities at its new brewery site to assist in degrading proteins present in wastewater discharges. Permits were required from the California State Water Quality Management Agency in connection with the treatment facilities operation. The possibility existed that MBC could be held liable for contamination of the earth beneath its brewing operations.

Shortages or increased costs of fuel, water, raw materials, power, or building materials, or allocations by suppliers or governmental regulatory bodies, could materially delay the expansion of the brewery, restrict the operations of the existing brewery and/or brewpub, or otherwise adversely affect the ability of MBC to meet its objectives. Certain supplies that MBC used for production were subject to risks inherent in agriculture, and MBC had experienced minor delays in shipment of bottles, which were at the time available from only two manufacturers. All supplies needed to be transported and were subject to work stoppages and other risks. (See Exhibit 9 for a comparison of suppliers' inputs.)

None of MBC's products were heat pasteurized, irradiated, or chemically treated. The brewing operations were subjected to hazards such as contamination. MBC maintained product liability insurance. No such claims had been filed in its 13-year history.

MBC's business was subject to variations as a result of seasonality, which management believed was typical in the brewing industry. Beer consumption historically increased by approximately 20 percent during the summer months. Since MBC's wholesale distributors had always been on an allocation basis, seasonality had little effect on wholesale sales. Retail sales, which depended largely on tourist traffic, were historically higher in the third and fourth quarters. MBC also brewed three seasonal beers: Springtide Ale in March, Eye of the Hawk Special Ale from July through October, and Yuletide Porter in November and December. (See Exhibit 10 for a list of MBC's products.)

Although all of MBC's brands were protected by Federal and California trademark laws, the processes and equipment used to brew its beer were not considered to be proprietary and could not be protected. A licensing agreement with Bridgeport Brewing Co. in Portland, Oregon, prevented Mendocino Brewing from marketing Blue Heron Pale Ale in the states of Washington,

EXHIBIT

9 | Inputs for Malt Beverages

Economic Sector or Industry Providing Inputs	%
Metal cans	31.5
Glass containers	15.8
Malt	7.6
Advertising	7.4
Imports	6.8
Paperboard containers & boxes	3.6
Motor freight	1.7
Miscellaneous crops (rice, barley, wheat, hops)	1.7
Electric services	1.5
Gas production	1.4
Feed grains (corn, sorghum, soy bean)	1.0
Crowns & closures	1.0

Source: US Department of Commerce, *Benchmark Input–Output Accounts for the US Economy,* July 1991.

10 | Mendocino Brewing Company—Product Description

The Company brews three ales and a stout year-round, as well as two seasonal ales and a seasonal porter:

Red Tail Ale, a full flavored amber ale, is the flagship brand of Mendocino Brewing. It has a long lasting complex character created by a blend of pale and caramel malted barley and balanced to a somewhat dry finish with Yakima Valley whole hops.

Blue Heron Pale Ale is a golden ale, with a full body and a distinctive hop character. Tending toward the "India Pale Ale" style, this ale leaves a fresh, clean hoppy aftertaste. Named for the Great Blue Heron, which has nesting areas in the Hopland area, this ale is made with 100 percent pale malted barley and Cluster and Cascade hops.

Eye of the Hawk Ale is a high gravity deep amber ale. It is a rich flavored, smooth ale which is brewed in the summer and fall. Caramel and pale malted barley are used. The brew is then balanced with Cluster and Cascade hops to make a very drinkable, strong ale.

Black Hawk Stout is the fullest in flavor and body of the Company's brews. It is a dry, crisp stout with a rich taste achieved by blending fully roasted black malt and caramel malts along with two-row pale malt. It is then balanced with Cluster and Cascade hops.

Yuletide Porter is a deep brown ale made during November and December with 100% malted barley, using pale, caramel, and black malts. With the traditionally rich, creamy flavor balanced with Cluster and Cascade whole hops, the ale has a slightly dry, yet rich finish and a delicate spiciness. Yuletide Porter has been a tradition at Mendocino Brewing since 1987.

Peregrine Pale Ale is brewed for a more delicate flavor and character. It is named for the Peregrine Falcon. This ale is a classic golden ale brewed with 100 percent pale malt and Cascade hops. This ale is featured exclusively at the Hopland Brewery.

Springtide Ale is brewed around St. Patrick's Day and is always an unusually flavored pale ale. The spices vary from year to year and the ale appears as a fresh, flowery, spicy golden ale. It is on tap only at The Hopland Brewery in the springtime.

Oregon, and Idaho. Bridgeport produced Blue Heron Bitter Ale and was likewise prevented from marketing that product throughout the rest of the U.S.

AWARDS AND HONORS

MBC was dedicated to quality graphic design of its packaging as a means to enhance the value of its products. The company's philosophy was that the quality of the package must meet and reflect the quality of what's inside. Nationally known wildlife artists, including Randy Johnson and Lee Jayred, were retained to design labels and promotional materials.

MBC's products and packaging won several awards. Eye of the Hawk Select Ale won the silver medal in the Strong Ale category at the 1990 Great American Beer Festival, a gold medal in 1991, and a bronze medal in 1992. MBC's Blue Heron Pale Ale won a bronze medal in the Pale Ale category in 1991. MBC received the Paperboard Packaging Council's Silver Award for Excellence in Packaging and Award for Excellence in Graphic Design and Northern California Advertising and Design Council's "ADDY" Award for its Red Tail Ale packaging in 1990. The design team also won Northern California ADDY award for its new Blue Heron label design in 1996.

MBC hoped that its award-winning packaging and point-of-sale materials would become an even stronger influence, not only on the buying decisions of consumers who faced an increasing number of products, but also on distributors and retailers, who realized the importance of superior package graphic design, making the products easier for the distributor and retailer to promote.

HUMAN RESOURCES

By 1994, MBC had grown to 32 full-time and 33 part-time employees, of which 10 were in management and administration, 19 in brewing operations, and 36 in retail, restaurant, and brewpub operations. By late 1995, when the company had grown to nearly 80 full- and part-time employees, MBC brought in a networked computer system. Management also purchased a sophisticated accounting program, but "we didn't have the time to learn all of its functions," Lovett said. Upon completion of its expansion, MBC hoped to upgrade four employees to full-time status and hire five additional management and administrative employees, three marketing employees and five employees in brewing operations. None of MBC's workforce was unionized. Lovett commented on the company's human resources plans:

> *Currently, we are organized by profit center: brewing operations and retail operations. In the next 7–10 years, we may have a "next generation" management team running the company. We are currently grooming that next generation. In the beginning, we (the founders) were self-motivated. A problem is having to motivate new employees. They see it as a job. New employees have to buy into our mission and values; otherwise we won't hire them. Employees have the possibility of becoming owners and we are in the process of accomplishing this. We like to get together and celebrate success.*

MISSION AND VALUES

MBC was committed to brewing the highest quality beers it could and marketing them profitably, while maintaining high standards of customer service and satisfaction and social responsibility. MBC believed that customers required products with high intrinsic value. It was not sufficient to just have a quality product; a product must distinguish itself from the competition by carrying other values. These values included a commitment to employees, community involvement, and environmental responsibility. An unstated part of MBC's mission was to have the community view it as an asset and as a positive example of how a business should be operated. (See Exhibit 11 for MBC's mission statement.)

The venture team instilled these values in employees via weekly team meetings and a monthly newsletter (*The Brewsletter*), using the newsletter to pass along to its customers a commitment to act responsibly. While MBC's strategy was to grow through expanded production and increased wholesale distributions, it promoted its beers as beverages of moderation by producing beers whose distinctive taste and high quality, not quantity, provided customer satisfaction. By adhering to these commitments, the venture team believed that it had captured and could continue to develop a defensible niche in the domestic specialty segment.

11 | Mendocino Brewing Company's Mission Statement

Mission: Our mission is to create distinctive beers of the highest quality we can and market them profitably, realizing that the customer is the number one priority. We have a reputation for high quality natural products, and we believe that the company can continue that tradition, after our initial expansion, by focusing on four areas of production: (1) new modern brewing equipment installed in a custom designed brewing facility; (2) traditional brewing methods, (3) carefully selected ingredients including a unique strain of yeast (we have developed a yeast management program that includes pure culturing and propagation techniques, yeast analysis in our laboratory, continual monitoring of yeast performance and a yeast maintenance plan to ensure yeast viability—we maintain samples of the strain at two offset locations); and (4) brewing experience and expert knowledge along with a passion for brewing high quality beers.

Position: We compete primarily on the basis of quality; therefore, to ensure that our brewing standards are among the highest in the industry, we use carefully selected ingredients, traditional brewing methods, and specially trained craftsmen to brew high quality beers. We use a unique strain of yeast (first introduced in New Albion Brewing Co. in the late 1970s and purchased by the company in 1983 and not commercially available) that produces distinctive tasting beers, and we strive to maintain the fresh quality of our beers after distribution by conducting field sampling and through distributor and retailer education. As part of our initial expansion plan, we intend to acquire new brewing equipment and build a custom-designed brewing facility, both of which, we believe, will increase the consistency and further enhance the quality of our beers as well as make our brewing operations more efficient.

Expansion: We believe that consumer demand already exists for our initial expansion to a production capacity of 50,000 bbls. per year. Working with various consultants, we have developed an initial expansion plan which provided the basis for our capital budgeting decisions. Also, both new equipment and the new facilities have been designed to permit future production capability expansion.

Wholesale Distribution: A factor critical to our post-expansion success and long-term growth is our ability to maintain positive relationships with and attract new distributors and retail outlets. We plan to implement a distributor management program and competitive pricing strategy.

Marketing: Our promotional strategies are designed to create brand awareness and to reinforce a distinct brand image built on quality products, customer service, and social responsibility. We build our product identity and positioning as a leader in the industry by utilizing high quality graphics in its packaging and marketing materials and through our presence at selected promotional events.

Brand Loyalty through Customer Service, Interaction and Satisfaction: We believe that achieving and maintaining brand loyalty not only through product excellence but also through customer service, interaction and satisfaction are primary keys to our success.

Social Responsibility: We strive to be a leader among all businesses in addressing areas of social concern. MBC remains committed to acting in a responsible manner that provides value to our shareholders, customers, employees, the community and the environment.

Source: Mendocino Brewing Company, Direct Public Offering Prospectus.

MARKETING AND DISTRIBUTION

MBC based its marketing strategy on the expectation that demand in the specialty draft market would increase. Historically, the introduction of draft products in restaurants and other establishments had driven bottle sales, which in turn created an increased demand for draft products in areas not serviced. MBC measured customer satisfaction and monitored changing consumer preferences via surveys in its newsletter, *The Brewsletter,* and via interviews with customers, retailers, and distributors. MBC hoped to use survey data to educate and train staff in customer service and satisfaction. According to Lovett,

> *We fostered our image by allowing direct interaction between our employees and customers through The Hopland Brewery and through participation in community events and beer festivals. By providing product sampling, information, and education, these direct interaction marketing tools were designed to provide customers with a positive and lasting memory of MBC, which we believed would carry over and influence customers' future buying decisions at retail outlets and restaurants. In 1987, we expanded into the wholesale distribution market. There wasn't the competition as there is now. It was easier to get the product on the shelf. We had a nice margin at the case level. We watched Fetzer the most as a "marketing company" to get ideas from, in terms of how to price quality beer right. We revise our marketing plan at least once each year.*
>
> *Today, our audience includes 21 to 30-year olds, trendy, social users, not product educators, not brand loyal, but experimenters. We need to sell them an "image." We tell them they made the right choice buying this beer. In return, customers will tell us what they want. For example, although we don't have organic growers for suppliers now, we would have to survey customers to "push" for this. Our shareholders are starting to give us ideas, too. In the future, we'll work with shareholders on how to sell and use word-of-mouth advertising more effectively. We also view our shareholders as a source of market intelligence. From what we've heard (from them) recently, we will need to have a Web page soon.*

To accommodate growth, MBC planned to expand its Marketing Department from one (Michael Lovett) to four persons. Lovett's sales and marketing team would initially focus on building relationships with new distributors to gain retail shelf space, next on attracting new customers with a broader line of beers in the Northern California market, and then on identifying and entering potential new regional markets. MBC's wholesale pricing strategy was to position its beers near the top of their segment, which allowed a 25 percent markup with an additional 25 percent markup by the distributors' retail accounts. MBC believed this strategy was supported by the quality and reputation of its products and could also be sustained by customer demand, so long as demand exceeded current production capacity. Lovett recognized that MBC's wholesale pricing strategy could become more sensitive to downward pressure as direct competitors increased capacity and began to saturate the market with specialty beers. (See Exhibit 12 for a table comparing the increases in production capacity by direct competitors.)

Distributors were eager to increase their exposure in the domestic specialty market, as large brewers continued to battle for market share in flat growth segments and as price wars in those segments continued to decrease margins. Laybourn commented,

> *Major brewers have determined to take some of this market and they will. "Real" small brewers will have to keep the public aware of who brews what. It will be our job to communicate to our customers the distinction of our products and company. MBC has decided to move quickly to implement a national marketing plan. Market share and profits will not only rely on producing a quality product, but will also require that we find the marketing expertise to design and implement a national marketing plan.*

Some large brewers attempted to open distribution channels directly with large retail accounts, using their market power in order to capture higher margins. As a counter-move, MBC initiated a distributor management program. This program entailed understanding the needs of the distributor through market research, surveying current and potential distributors to develop a criteria list and standards of performance, developing comprehensive sales agreements, and maintaining a

EXHIBIT 12 | Capacity Increases by Competitors in the Microbrewing Segment

Company Name	Location	Capacity, thousand bbls. 1992	1993	Annual Growth %
Boston Beer Co.	Boston, MA	273	450	65
Sierra Nevada Brewing Co.	Chico, CA	68	104	53
Anchor Brewing Co.	San Francisco, CA	82	92	11
Pete's Brewing Co.	Palo Alto, CA	36	75	110
Redhook Ale Brewery	Seattle, WA	49	73	49
Widmer Brewing Co.	Portland, OR	28	41	47
Full Sail Brewing Co.	Hood River, OR	29	38	34
Hart Brewing Co.	Kalma, WA	18	32	83
Portland Brewing Co.	Portland, OR	9	17	85
Bridgeport Brewing Co.	Portland, OR	13	16	20
Mendocino Brewing Co.	Hopland, CA	13	13	0

Source: Institute for Brewing Studies, *1993 Beer and Brewery Statistics, Estimated Total Removals*

clear understanding of the standards expected of distributors and standards of brewery support.

CAPACITY EXPANSION PLANS

In 1992, MBC hired consultants to design and develop a "Master Brewery Plan." MBC then developed an initial expansion plan that provided the basis for its capital budgeting decisions and included budgeted initial costs for the proposed acquisition of equipment and land and facilities construction as well as projected cash flows.

The plan involved the acquisition of a new turn-key brewery along with new fermenting tanks, kegs, packaging and other miscellaneous equipment, all to be installed with the company's existing bottling line at a new 52,000 sq. ft. custom-designed brewing facility to be built on an eight-acre parcel of land in Ukiah, CA, approximately 10 miles from the existing brewery. The initial expansion plan called for the purchase of wastewater treatment equipment and construction of facilities to house the treatment plant. The new facilities were originally designed and the property and equipment had been chosen to allow for future expansion in several stages.

Net proceeds to MBC from the sale of its Direct Public Offering of shares were estimated to be $3,350,000 after expenses. MBC hoped to use the proceeds over a 12-month period for land ($200,000 for down payment on a $700,000, eight-acre parcel in Ukiah), facilities ($670,000 as down payment on a 52,000 sq. ft. brewery and wastewater facility, the balance financed by the Savings Bank of Mendocino County), equipment ($3.9 million to acquire a new turn-key brewery along with new fermenting tanks, kegs, packaging, and water treatment, the balance to be financed by bank loans), and working capital ($339,000 for pre-expansion debt servicing, inventory purchases, accounts payable, or other purposes).

Changeover to the new facility was expected to take place after the new equipment was tested, ensuring that no lapse in production would occur. MBC intended to keep The Hopland Brewery on line as a channel for developing greater customer interaction, for research and development and test marketing of new specialty brews, and as a possible future brewing education and training site.

Lovett reflected on the fact that once MBC had succeeded in its capacity expansion efforts, its culture would have to change.

Our greatest strength is that we got to this growth point. We know the product and the company. Our greatest weakness is that we have no experience in growth processes to take the company to the next level. It's a risk. Shifting from a partnership to a corporation to going public has made us more formalized and structured, and now functional experts have to be hired. We now have a mission, organization chart and objectives, but we will also need to hire management who knows the industry, has marketed new-age beverages, knows more than we do and shares our vision that this is an exciting industry. Our vision is to build the Ukiah brewery. In order to do so, we will have to learn government regulations as we grow.

ECONOMIC DEVELOPMENT ISSUES

In June 1996, Julie Meier Wright, the Secretary of the California Trade and Commerce Agency, announced that the City of Ukiah Redevelopment Agency has been awarded a loan for $758,000 through California's Rural Economic Development Infrastructure Program (REDIP). In an article in the *Santa Rosa Press Democrat,* Wright remarked,

We live in an ever-changing economy. REDIP gives communities the opportunity to make the changes necessary to bring new industries to these rural areas. Mendocino County will greatly benefit from the expansion of the Mendocino Brewing Company.

The REDIP program provided financing for the construction, improvement or expansion of public infrastructure, with the intent of creating jobs in cities and counties having an unemployment rate either equal to or above the state's average unemployment rate. The City of Ukiah's Redevelopment Agency had applied for funds for an extension of Airport Boulevard, including construction of more than 2,000 feet of road, storm drains and overhead electrical work to the Airport Industrial Park. These improvements were needed for MBC's capacity expansion.

In addition to its capacity expansion, MBC planned to add a total of 24 new jobs by 1997. Due to its heavy reliance on the timber industry for economic growth, Mendocino County had suffered tremendous job losses in recent years. Mendocino County's unemployment rate for April 1995 was 9.2 percent, compared with 7.3 percent for the state.

THE FUTURE

MBC's growth strategy was to expand its production capabilities and to increase its wholesale distribution through further penetration of existing and targeted regional markets with a broader line of specialty beers. "We compete primarily on the basis of quality, not price. Quality includes the taste of the products, ingredients, packaging, and the company's image as a responsible member of the community," said Lovett. "As our products become more widely available as the result of the planned capacity expansion, we may be required to compete on the basis of price to a greater extent than we do at present," he continued.

Similarly, the quality of domestic specialty beers being brewed by regional specialty brewers and microbrewers was improving, as many domestic specialty brewers won awards for their beers at competitions here and abroad. Lovett expected that competition at the product quality level would also continue to increase:

I predict that in 7–10 years, the microbrewery market will become saturated. Shelf space is already dwindling, and there will be consolidations and buyouts. Brew pubs aren't affected yet. Yes, they'll survive, but they won't become large companies. The tradeoff is that we will lose our mystique as we expand, but we'll have to continue to create an "image." The packaging of the company, not just its quality products, will be how we—and others—will compete in the future.

CASE 29

Nucor Corp. and the U.S. Steel Industry

Brian K. Boyd
Steve Gove
Arizona State University

Darlington, South Carolina, 1969. Making steel is a technically demanding, complex, and dangerous process. Nucor Corp.'s initial foray into steel production was the latter. Instead of staffing the plant with seasoned steel veterans, Nucor hired farmers, mechanics, and other intelligent, motivated workers. Those employees along with company executives and dignitaries in attendance at Nucor's mill opening fled the plant as the inaugural pour resulted in molten steel pouring onto the mill floor and spreading toward the crowd. Onlookers and employees alike were left wondering if Nucor would ever successfully produce steel.[1]

The steel industry, a classic example of a market in the late stages of maturity, traces its roots to colonial era blacksmiths who forged basic farm and household equipment. The industry grew (and consolidated) rapidly in the first half of the 20th century, with worldwide demand growing throughout the 1960s. However, a series of shifts in market dynamics led to dramatic industrywide declines in growth and profitability. The dominant players faced the same problems as leaders of other mature industries—Ford and General Motors, for example: obsolete production facilities, bureaucratic management systems, heavily unionized workers, and hungry foreign competitors. Due to its centrality in the economy, the decline of the steel industry was cited by some observers as evidence of the decline of the overall U.S. economic system.

While foreign competition played a significant role in changing the U.S. steel industry, an even larger factor emerged during the 1970s: minimill technology. Traditional "integrated mills" rely on large-scale vertical integration including integrated coke and ore production. "Minimills" used a new technology to recycle scrap steel and quickly stole most of the commodity steel market away from integrated producers. This enabled minimills to enter a geographic market with a distinct cost advantage: they typically require a capital investment of \$300 to \$500 million or 5 to 10 percent of that required for an integrated mill. The minimill revolution has resulted in a dramatic dispersion of the steel manufacturers from the "rust belt" to the primary population and growth areas of the U.S. The impact of minimills on the industry is best demonstrated by looking at the former industry leader US Steel (now USX Corp.). In 1966 US Steel controlled 55 percent of the American steel market; in 1986 it controlled only 17 percent.

Despite its inauspicious foray into steel, Nucor Corp. has become the benchmark for both the U.S. steel industry and U.S. industry in general. Nucor is one of the fastest growing and most efficient steel producers in the world. Despite declining demand for steel, Nucor's growth has been phenomenal. Since pouring its first batch of steel in the 1960s to support in-house operations, the company has become one of the top five producers of steel in the United States. Without an R&D department, Nucor has repeatedly achieved technological feats other steel producers thought impossible. Their hourly pay is among the lowest in the industry, yet they have the highest productivity per worker of any steel producer in the U.S. and near zero employee turnover. How has Nucor achieved such phenomenal success? Can it continue to do so?

1 | Comparative Trends: GDP, Steel Industry Output, and Nucor Output

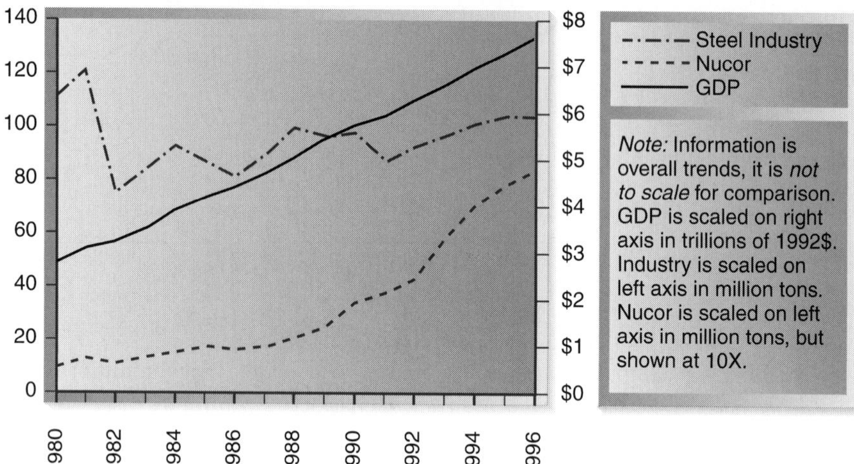

U.S. STEEL INDUSTRY HISTORY

Steel has been a part of the domestic economic system since the Colonial Era when iron (the parent of steel) was smelted and forged. The early 19th century, with the advent of steam engines, cotton gins, and farming combines, advanced iron as a commodity of progress. The addition of carbon to iron yielded a material with additional strength, elasticity, toughness, and malleability at elevated temperatures. The Civil War provided the impetus for the industry to organize, consolidate, expand, and modernize to supply the vast quantities of steel required for warfare.

Following the Civil War, the construction of new transportation systems, public works projects, automobiles, bridges, ships, and large buildings all fueled a torrid expansion of the industry lasting through the turn of the century. Domestic economic expansion and two world wars maintained an unquenchable appetite for steel both in the United States and around the world in the first half of the 20th century. Even in the aftermath of World War II, America's steel industry prospered as it supplied an ever expanding domestic economy and the rebuilding of war-ravaged infrastructures. This windfall for the domestic industry was in actuality one of the root causes for its eventual decline. U.S. plants, left idle by the end of the war, were reactivated to support the Marshall Plan and MacArthur's rebuilding of Japan. The war-torn nations of the world, however, rebuilt their industrial facilities from the ground up, incorporating the latest production technology. Conversely, domestic producers were content with older, formerly inactivated facilities.

Global demand for steel expanded continuously throughout the 1960s; domestic producers elected not to meet this demand, choosing only to match domestic consumption requirements. This presented an opportunity for up-start foreign producers to rejuvenate and strengthen themselves without directly competing against U.S. producers. Throughout this expansion, the relationship between management and labor soured. In 1892, Henry Clay Frick's Pinkerton guards attacked striking workers, setting the stage for a contentious relationship between management and labor. Labor, represented by the United Steel Workers of America (USWA), and management began negotiating three-year collective bargaining agreements beginning in 1947. These negotiations frequently collapsed and strikes following the third year of a contract became commonplace. Firms dependent on steel soon initiated a pattern of accumulating 30-day "strike hedge" inventories to feed operations during strike shutdowns. In 1959, the

2 | World Capacity, Production, and Idle Capacity, 1970–1991

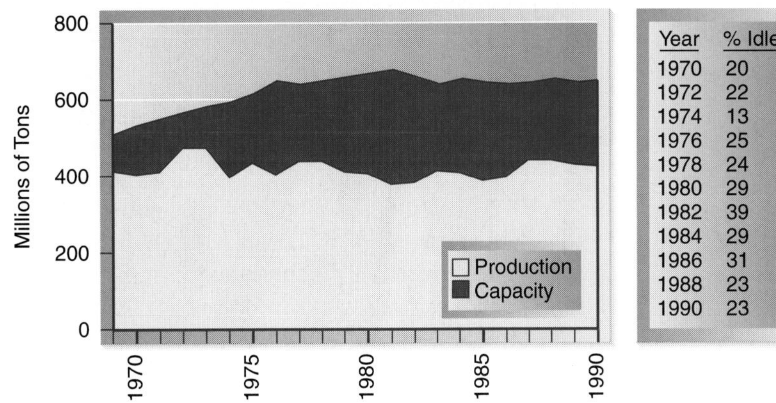

USWA walked out for 116 days. In 1964, another strike required presidential intervention. The impact of these strikes reverberated throughout the economy. Major customers began to look for stable supplies of steel from foreign producers who, in 1959, met only 3 percent of domestic demand. Fueled by excess capacity and strike-induced demand, foreign producers were providing 18 percent of domestic demand by the time a long-term labor accord was reached in the early 1970s. Foreign producers currently supply 20–25 percent of the steel used in the United States.

Protectionists are quick to blame the Japanese for the decimation of the American steel industry. However, other countries have an even stronger presence in the U.S. market: since 1991, for example, Canada has exported more steel to the United States than has Japan. By 1994, Europe and other regions accounted for the bulk of steel imports. While foreign producers maintain a strong presence in the United States, the same cannot be said for American steel firms abroad. Exports by U.S. firms have traditionally been minuscule, 1 percent of production in the mid-1980s, but have grown to 3 to 5 percent of production during the 1990s.

While the labor accords reached in the 1970s stabilized the supply of domestic steel, the cost of living adjustments (COLAs) and automatic wage adjustments included in the accords would prove to be detrimental to the industry's cash position during periods of reduced demand for steel. Such a situation was experienced in the 1970s when the domestic auto industry, historically the largest consumer of steel in the United States began to decline. Domestic producers attempted to remedy the resulting cash flow crisis with layoffs and price hikes, but the price hikes came at the expense of further market share erosion to low-cost foreign producers. While the industry claimed productivity improvements, these were often the result of layoffs and shutdowns as opposed to process efficiency improvements.

The slowdowns and closures of the 1970s set the stage for the steel industry's "dark ages"—the period from 1980 to 1986 when steel output declined from 115 to 80 million tons despite an increase in real GDP. The energy crisis led to demand for smaller, lighter cars which require less steel, also resulting in less required tonnage. R&D in the steel industry led to stronger blends of steel. New materials, such as petroleum-based materials (plastics), organics (wood/pulp), and synthetic materials (fiberglass, epoxies) became significant threats in several applications customarily met by steel. Overall employment in steel fell from 535,000 in 1979 to 249,000 in 1986.

Despite this decline, this was also a period of shake-out and dynamic activity in the industry. Slowly, and with the help of the federal government (primarily in tax and regulatory relief and enforcement of Uruguay Trade Agreements/Voluntary Restraining Agreements), some

3 | U.S. Production: 1974 & 1994

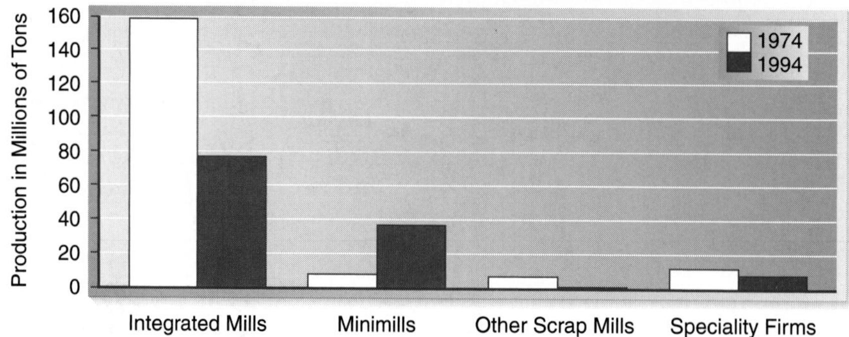

	1974	1994	% Change
Integrated Mills	158	77	–51
Minimills	8	37	363
Other Scrap Mills	7	1	–86
Specialty Firms production in million of tons	12	8	–33

firms were able to revitalize their operations by streamlining production, selecting better markets, focusing production (minimills), improving facilities, stabilizing labor contracts, and reducing labor content through plant modernization, dollar devaluation, and a reprieve from the onslaught of substitute materials. This gave the surviving firms an opportunity to recover and prosper.

Historically, demand for steel fluctuates in both the U.S. and international markets due to its close ties to durable and capital goods, markets which suffer more acutely during austerity and are more prosperous during economic expansions. Economic swings notwithstanding, there has been little appreciable growth in steel demand between the 1950s and the 1990s. Current domestic production is approximately 100 million tons per year, far less than the 120 million tons of 1981. Decline in demand has led to substantial excess capacity. In 1980, for example, domestic producers had 25 percent idle capacity. While the industry now operates at 90 percent of capacity, this has come as a result of reduced capacity, not increased output; total domestic capacity declined by 30 percent between 1980 and 1994. Capacity reduction in the steel industry is expensive, particularly for integrated producers. USX Corp., for example, eliminated 16 percent of its capacity in 1983 at a cost of $1.2 billion. Still, by 1987, USX had 40 percent idle capacity.

While large-scale, integrated producers such as USX were shedding excess capacity, a new type of competitor, "minimills," was entering the market. Minimills utilize recycled steel (in the form of junk cars, scrap, etc.) as a primary ingredient. Unlike the integrated producers, minimills are less capital intensive, smaller, and have historically focused on producing low-technology, entry-level products. Unlike integrated mills which have seen production decline, minimills have seen explosive growth with numerous plants opening in the late 1980s and 1990s.

Overall, the steel industry has all of the characteristics of a highly competitive market: stagnant demand, excess capacity, and numerous global competitors. The ability of the largest firm to use its power to set prices is gone. Above average industry margins are quickly targeted by other firms. These factors are compounded by a largely commodity-like product which minimizes switching costs and customer loyalty. Not surprisingly, the profit performance of the industry has been weak; the industry as a whole lost money during much of the

1980s. In 1987, the first (albeit small) industrywide profit in eight years was posted. With the exception of the 1990–91 recession, domestic producers have gradually improved the return on assets to a value of 6.1 percent in 1994. A flurry of exits and Chapter 11 reorganizations led to an improved profit potential for remaining firms by the mid-1990s. The success is more pronounced in the minimill sector, although the integrated producers are presently healthy and now represent a new threat to the minimills.

EMERGING INDUSTRY TREND

While in many ways the industry appears to have stabilized, a number of emerging trends threaten to cause further disruption within the industry to both integrateds and minimills.

Minimill Overcapacity. Starting in 1989, only one company, Nucor, was capable of producing flatrolled steel using minimill technology. However, competing firms have started using similar technology and there were expected to be 10 new flat-roll minimills online by 1997, adding 13 million tons of production capacity—about 10 percent of 1996 production—to the industry. This new capacity should become available just as steel consumption is expected to decline.

Scrap Prices. Due to growing demand for scrap metal, its cost has become increasingly volatile in the 1990s. In 1994, for example, prices climbed as much as $50/ton to $165–170/ton while 10 million tons of American scrap were exported to offshore customers. In 1996 prices reached $200/ton, and were expected to climb, but instead declined to $170–180/ton by the end of 1997.

Euro Production. While growth has improved in recent years, demand for steel is still weak in much of Europe, particularly in Eastern European nations. Western Europe alone had 20 million tons of excess capacity in 1994, and Russian mills were operating at 65 percent of capacity. Additionally, many European mills are state-owned and subsidized. Faced with weak performance and idle capacity, many of these mills are aggressively pursing export opportunities in China and other parts of Asia. Russian steel exports approached $4 billion in 1993, double their 1992 level.

Antidumping Rulings. U.S. integrated steel producers filed 72 charges of dumping against foreign competitors—primarily the Germans and Japanese. In 1993, the International Trade Commission concluded that there was some justification for these charges, but not for others and ruled that foreign steel caused no harm in 40

EXHIBIT 4 | Domestic Capacity and Production

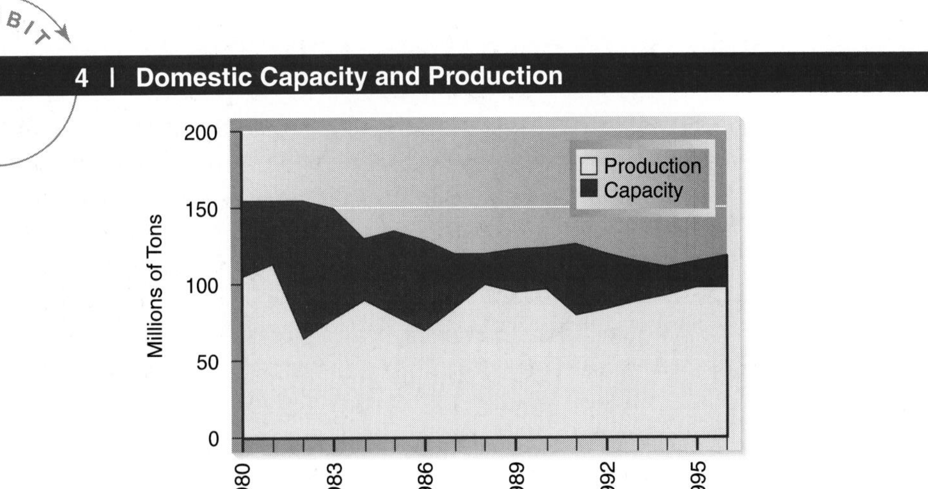

of the 72 cases. Stock prices for U.S. producers (in aggregate) declined $1.1 billion in the 90 minutes following the announcement of the ruling.

INDUSTRY ECONOMIC STRUCTURE

The domestic steel industry, until recent technological changes, was essentially composed of two vertically integrated sectors. The first was the raw steel production sector which encompassed steel-making operations from the unearthing of ores and coke to the basic ore reduction and smelting. The outcome or product of this sector was ingots, billets, and slabs which are standard steel shapes. These products were then sent to finishing mills (the second sector) which conducted various heat treating and shaping processes to produce finished steel products such as bars, tubes, castings, forgings, plates, sheets, and structural shapes. These two sectors were typically housed under a single facility but as two distinct operations in what was termed the "integrated" producer. Traditionally, steel manufacturers used batch processing which involved heating a furnace of steel and pouring the entire furnace full of molten steel into billets, ingots, and slabs. These intermediate products were then processed and the process was repeated. The onset of continuous casting technology (a process in which ores are reduced and poured into final shapes without the intermediate production of slabs and ingots) in the late 1970s has blurred the classical two-sector demarcation. Most producers today use the continuous casting process for producing isometric shapes, but raw steel must still be shipped to finishing mills for manufacture of more complex products.

The suppliers to the steel industry can be broadly assigned to three major classes: ore, energy, and transportation. Since a preponderance of the final production cost is tied up in these input items, many producers have vertically integrated backwards by acquiring ore and coal/coke mining firms and transportation networks (rail and barge). The supply factors of production (transformation factors) are labor to operate plants, capital facilities, and land. Recent modernization has significantly substituted technology for labor in steel production.

Minimills are a significant force of change in the industry as their supplier and customer requirements differ from the integrated mills. First, ore supplies are, to differing degrees, replaced by a need for access to large quantities of scrap steel. Second, minimills, while still large consumers of electricity, consume far less power than their integrated mill counterparts. This, along with the lower output capacity of each plant, allows for placement of the mills closer to the third factor: the changing customer base. This has resulted in a radical shift in steel production in recent years from western Pennsylvania and Ohio to a much broader dispersion of steel mills

EXHIBIT 5 | Steel Demand by Market Sector

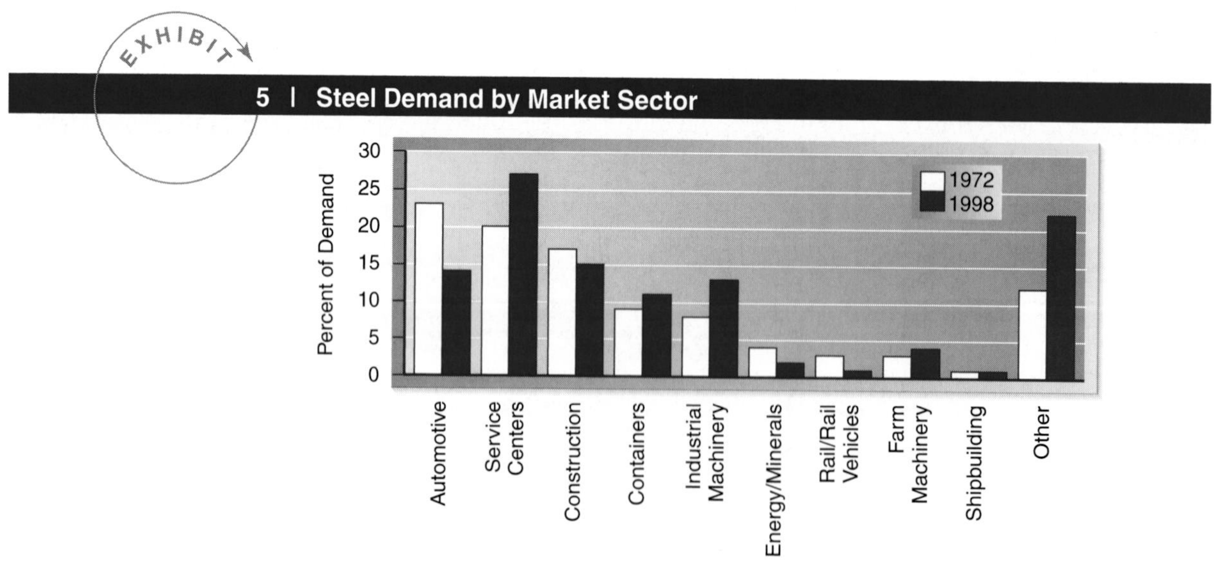

throughout the United States. By one estimate, steel mills can now be found in over half of the U.S. states.

The principal markets and customers for steel are the classical markets. Some sectors are on the decline while others are fairly stable. The automotive sector was historically the largest consumer of steel in peacetime. Construction materials is now the largest sector, followed by the auto and container industries, energy equipment, industrial machinery, farming equipment, car/rail production, and various military applications. The reduced demand by the auto industry is the result of the lower steel content in a modern automobile, a trend steel producers are aggressively trying to counter by banding together to form the Steel Alliance which is running a $100 million advertising campaign targeted at consumers touting the advantages of steel for automobile design (and house construction).

Service centers are playing an increased role in the industry, acting as major distributors and wholesalers for finished steel products to steel consumers (construction firms, shipbuilders, machine fabricators, etc.). With the exception of the auto and auto part manufacturers (who contract directly with producers), most finished steel is delivered to end users via the steel service center, moving some of the inventory management burden to the service centers for a marginal markup to the end user. This presents a forecasting complication to planners and strategists as all demand for steel is a derived demand. The forecaster must be able to look into the macro forces affecting an economy and project steel's role in the broader economic system from which a consumer demand pattern could be ascertained.

STEEL PRODUCTION TECHNOLOGY

Any attempt to consolidate steel and steel production technology into a few paragraphs would be doing the topic a disservice. However, two major issues deserve additional attention: production factors and substitutes. Automation has improved the competitive position of the industry by reducing its exposure to volatile labor markets and labor costs. It has also increased the flexibility of producers to shift product output and to the incorporation of the continuous casting process. Closely related is the elimination of the old open-hearth furnace in favor of the blast-oxygen furnace and electric arc furnaces which are far more efficient, more easily automated, and require less manpower. These furnaces also reduce stack emissions, a critical environmental requirement (and a concern which many foreign producers do not face). While technology has been a driver of change, labor agreements and relations have not always made it possible to fully exploit the benefits of technological improvements.

The proliferation of substitute materials is an important issue. It is important to note, however, that while substitutes have made significant inroads into steel markets over the last 30 years, they will likely never replace steel as the commodity of choice for many applications. Steel will not be displaced (with very minor exceptions) as a material in strength applications: Plastic is not strong enough; graphite-reinforced plastics and epoxies lack steel's thermal resistance properties; wood is not as strong or environmentally resistant as steel; and titanium remains a rare, expensive, strategically controlled material. Furthermore, steel comes in many different compositions (stainless, tool, high-strength, galvanized). The industry's R&D efforts have continued to evolve steel to meet the demands of customers. In short, steel remains and is likely to remain *the* material of choice in most applications.

NUCOR CORPORATION

Nucor Corp. began life as the Nuclear Corporation of America. The latter was a highly diversified and marginally profitable company; its products included instruments, semiconductors, rare earths, and construction. One of its potential acquisitions was Coast Metals, a family-owned producer of specialty metals. When the acquisition fell through, Nuclear hired one of Coast's top engineers as a consultant to recommend other acquisition targets. The engineer—Ken Iverson—had strong technical skills (including a graduate degree in metallurgy from Purdue University) and general management experience. Based on Iverson's recommendation, Nuclear acquired a steel joist company in South Carolina. Subsequently, Iverson joined Nuclear as a vice president in 1962. Nuclear built a second joist plant in Nebraska the following year. Iverson was responsible for supervising the joist operations as well as the research, chemical, and construction segments. By 1965, the diversified company had experienced another string of losses, although the joist operations were profitable, and Iverson was promoted to president.

Recognizing that its most valuable skills lay in its joist operations, Nuclear became Nucor Corp. and divested nonjoist operations. New joist plants soon followed, including one in Alabama in 1967 and another in Texas in 1968. As a joist company, Nucor was dependent on American and foreign steel producers for its key input. Iverson decided to integrate backwards into steel making in the hopes of stabilizing supply and lowering input costs for the joist business. So, Nucor began construction on its own steel mill in Darlington, South Carolina—a location close to an existing joist operation. The Darlington plant used the then new minimill technology. When the plant opened on October 12, 1969, the pouring of the first batch of steel resulted in molten steel cascading out of the mold and across the floor of the plant. Despite the mishap, Nucor quickly became adept at minimill technology. In addition to supplying its own joist operations, it began competing with integrateds and other minimills in the commodity steel business. Iverson and Nucor soon became recognized as the "Southwest Airlines" of steel: a simple, no-frills organization, with a unique culture, highly motivated workers, and the lowest cost structure of the industry. Some indicators of Nucor's success include:

- It is the only major player in the industry that can boast of 22 years of uninterrupted quarterly dividends (Nucor began paying quarterly dividends in 1973) and 30 years of continuous quarterly profits, despite numerous slumps and downturns in the industry. (See Exhibits 6–14.)
- Between 1980 and 1990, Nucor doubled in size. In comparison, the six main integrated producers reduced their steel making capacity from 108 to 58 million tons during this period.
- In 1990, Nucor had six steel plants and a total annual capacity of 3 million tons. By 1995, it had added a seventh plant, and its overall capacity neared 8 million tons.
- In 1994, Nucor generated $1.50 in sales for every dollar in property, plant, and equipment. The industry average was $0.95 before depreciation expenses. After depreciation, these ratios are $2.18 and $1.83 respectively.
- Nucor continues to be the industry leader in cost efficiency. In 1990, Nucor produced 980 tons of steel per employee each year, at a net cost of $60/ton compared to the industry average of 420 tons per employee at a cost of $135/ton. In 1994, Nucor's conversion cost was $170/ton, roughly $50–75 less than competitors.

Nucor has primary mills located in Arkansas, Nebraska, Utah, South Carolina, Texas, Indiana, and South Carolina. Additional operating facilities located in Fort Payne, Alabama; Conway, Arkansas; Saint Joe and Waterloo, Indiana; Wilson, North Carolina; and Swansea, South Carolina are all engaged in the manufacture of steel products. During 1997, the average utilization rate of all operating facilities was more than 85 percent of production capacity. Nucor competes in a number of distinct product segments and the emphasis on these segments has changed substantially in recent years. Historically, the largest segment was the Nucor Steel division, which produces bar and light structural steel products. In 1991, this was its largest segment (measured by product volume). However, by 1995, sheet steel, once considered to be an exclusive product of integrated producers, accounted for the largest production volume. Heavy structural beams from a joint venture with Yamato Steel of Japan were the third largest segment, followed by the Vulcraft joist division. Remaining products—including grinding balls, fasteners, ball bearings, and prefabricated steel buildings—each account for relatively small proportions of total output.

While Nucor's first experience with steel was the result of backward integration by the Vulcraft joist division, the manufacture of steel has become the central focus of the firm. That focus has broadened to include sheet steel (1989) and heavy structural beams (1988). The company has also extended its focus to several downstream products, including fasteners and ball bearings (both in 1986) and prefabricated metal buildings (1988). With the exception of the ball bearings mill, which was acquired, new business segments are developed internally. Roughly 15 percent of steel output is used internally for downstream operations. More recently, Nucor has chosen to integrate backwards from

EXHIBIT

6 | Historical Data, 1955 to 1996

Year	Net Sales	Earnings			Earnings Per Share			Total Assets	Stockholders' Equity			Common Stock	
		Operations	Other	Net	Operations	Other	Net		Amount	Per Share	Shares Outstanding	Per Share	Amount
PRIOR MANAGEMENT													
1955	415,658	(39,359)	—	(39,359)	LOSS	—	LOSS	1,630,644	930,188	0.06	16,355,402	0.48	7,850,593
1956	1,653,007	(355,293)	—	(355,293)	LOSS	—	LOSS	1,881,385	848,934	0.04	20,573,241	0.23	4,731,845
1957	1,925,462	(546,270)	—	(546,270)	LOSS	—	LOSS	1,908,337	1,052,664	0.03	33,803,241	0.17	5,746,551
1958	2,020,886	(521,827)	—	(521,827)	LOSS	—	LOSS	1,717,335	672,638	0.02	35,628,981	0.21	7,482,086
1959	1,859,034	(260,161)	—	(260,161)	LOSS	—	LOSS	1,783,598	502,454	0.01	36,532,149	0.28	10,229,002
1960	2,182,204	(367,149)	(261,829)	(628,978)	LOSS	LOSS	LOSS	1,837,102	647,565	0.01	44,023,275	0.44	19,370,241
1961	4,014,416	379,006	(16,021)	362,985	0.01	LOSS	0.01	5,630,178	2,307,566	0.04	55,267,743	0.43	23,765,129
1962	9,100,958	24,095	(683,323)	(659,228)	—	LOSS	LOSS	7,184,395	1,952,764	0.03	56,646,415	0.23	13,028,675
1963	15,374,487	260,710	240,000	500,710	0.01	0.00	0.01	8,324,759	2,453,474	0.04	56,646,415	0.18	10,196,355
1964	17,485,319	33,264	30,000	63,264	—	—	—	10,337,955	2,796,719	0.05	57,809,552	0.18	10,405,719
1965	22,310,595	(431,013)	(1,803,748)	(2,234,761)	LOSS	LOSS	LOSS	6,937,251	762,380	0.01	58,695,962	0.26	15,260,950
Present Management													
1966	23,006,483	698,900	635,000	1,333,900	0.01	0.01	0.02	8,109,190	2,239,882	0.04	59,310,011	0.23	13,641,303
1967	23,600,093	822,424	880,832	1,703,256	0.01	0.02	0.03	11,546,498	6,581,876	0.10	66,836,275	0.64	42,775,216
1968	35,544,913	1,002,954	1,235,982	2,238,936	0.01	0.02	0.03	16,501,866	9,288,771	0.14	68,078,687	0.78	53,101,376
1969	46,321,797	1,210,083	1,125,000	2,335,083	0.02	0.01	0.03	24,655,801	11,938,178	0.17	68,935,656	0.45	31,021,045
1970	50,750,546	1,140,757	—	1,140,757	0.02	—	0.02	28,800,183	13,101,313	0.19	69,001,709	0.27	18,630,461
1971	64,761,634	2,740,694	—	2,740,694	0.04	—	0.04	33,168,014	15,892,357	0.23	69,245,150	0.41	28,390,512
1972	83,576,128	4,668,190	—	4,668,190	0.07	—	0.07	47,537,247	20,929,525	0.30	70,353,577	0.54	37,990,932
1973	113,193,617	6,009,042	—	6,009,042	0.09	—	0.09	67,550,110	26,620,195	0.38	70,302,597	0.41	28,824,065
1974	160,416,931	9,680,083	—	9,680,083	0.14	—	0.14	82,038,748	37,103,939	0.50	73,712,586	0.30	22,113,776
1975	121,467,284	7,581,788	—	7,581,788	0.10	—	0.10	92,639,413	44,549,735	0.59	75,010,113	0.41	30,754,146
1976	175,768,479	8,696,891	—	8,696,891	0.11	—	0.11	119,095,581	54,084,970	0.70	77,790,707	0.74	57,565,123
1977	212,952,829	12,452,592	—	12,452,592	0.16	—	0.16	128,010,982	66,295,405	0.84	78,807,784	1.02	80,383,940
1978	306,939,667	25,848,849	—	25,848,849	0.33	—	0.33	193,454,693	92,129,119	1.15	80,261,028	1.74	139,654,189
1979	428,681,778	42,264,537	—	42,264,537	0.52	—	0.52	243,111,514	133,257,816	1.64	81,046,524	3.32	269,074,460
1980	482,420,363	45,060,198	—	45,060,198	0.55	—	0.55	291,221,867	177,603,690	2.16	82,199,964	5.82	478,403,790
1981	544,820,621	34,728,966	—	34,728,966	0.42	—	0.42	384,782,127	212,376,020	2.54	83,562,084	4.98	416,139,178
1982	486,018,162	22,192,064	—	22,192,064	0.27	—	0.27	371,632,941	232,281,057	2.77	83,951,292	5.21	437,386,231
1983	542,531,431	27,864,308	—	27,864,308	0.33	—	0.33	425,567,052	258,129,694	3.05	84,541,086	7.13	602,777,943
1984	660,259,922	44,548,451	—	44,548,451	0.53	—	0.53	482,188,465	299,602,834	3.53	84,966,474	5.38	457,119,630
1985	758,495,374	58,478,352	—	58,478,352	0.68	—	0.68	560,311,188	357,502,028	4.16	85,890,030	8.98	771,292,469
1986	755,228,939	46,438,888	—	46,438,888	0.54	—	0.54	571,607,644	383,699,454	4.54	84,525,192	7.72	652,534,482
1987	851,022,039	50,534,450	—	50,534,450	0.60	—	0.60	654,090,139	428,009,367	5.05	84,784,352	9.91	840,212,928
1988	1,061,364,009	70,881,020	38,558,822	109,439,842	0.83	0.46	1.29	949,661,710	532,281,449	6.25	85,150,764	11.94	1,016,700,122
1989	1,269,007,472	57,835,844	—	57,835,844	0.68	—	0.68	1,033,831,512	584,445,479	6.83	85,598,480	15.06	1,289,113,109
1990	1,481,630,011	75,065,261	—	75,065,261	0.88	—	0.88	1,035,886,060	652,757,216	7.59	85,950,696	15.50	1,332,235,788
1991	1,465,456,566	64,716,499	—	64,716,499	0.75	—	0.75	1,181,576,798	711,608,991	8.23	86,417,804	22.34	1,930,573,741
1992	1,619,234,876	79,225,703	—	79,225,703	0.92	—	0.92	2,507,382,255	784,230,713	9.04	86,736,700	39.19	3,399,211,273
1993	2,253,738,311	123,509,607	—	123,509,607	1.42	—	1.42	1,829,268,322	902,166,939	10.36	87,073,478	53.00	4,614,894,334
1994	2,975,596,456	226,632,844	—	226,632,844	2.60	—	2.60	2,001,920,165	1,122,610,257	12.85	87,333,313	55.50	4,846,998,872
1995	3,462,045,648	274,534,505	—	274,534,505	3.14	—	3.14	2,296,141,333	1,382,112,159	15.78	87,598,517	57.13	5,004,503,276
1996	3,647,030,387	248,168,948	—	248,168,948	2.83	—	2.83	2,619,533,406	1,609,290,193	18.33	87,795,947	51.00	4,477,593,297

Source: Nucor Corporation Web Page (http://www.nucor.com/h_historicaldata.htm) 04/09/98.

7 | Annual Balance Sheets, 1977 to 1996

Note—all $ Millions

	Dec-96	Dec-95	Dec-94	Dec-93	Dec-92	Dec-91	Dec-90	Dec-89
Assets								
Cash & equivalents	104.40	201.80	101.93	27.26	25.55	38.30	51.65	32.55
Net receivables	292.64	283.21	258.13	202.18	132.14	109.46	126.75	106.95
Inventories	385.80	306.77	243.03	215.02	206.41	186.08	136.64	139.45
Prepaid expenses	0.00	0.00	0.00	0.00	0.00	0.00	0.00	0.00
Other current assets	45.54	38.97	35.61	23.79	0.52	0.47	0.09	1.08
Total current assets	828.38	830.74	638.70	468.23	364.62	334.29	315.13	280.03
Gross plant, property & equipment	2,698.75	2,212.89	1,977.58	1,820.99	1,574.10	1,261.53	1,086.37	1,048.01
Accumulated depreciation	907.60	747.49	614.36	459.95	448.34	414.25	363.12	294.22
Net plant, property & equipment	1,791.15	1,465.40	1,363.22	1,361.04	1,125.77	847.28	723.25	753.80
Investments at equity	0.00	0.00	0.00	0.00	0.00	0.00	0.00	0.00
Other investments	0.00	0.00	0.00	0.00	0.00	0.00	0.00	0.00
Intangibles	0.00	0.00	0.00	0.00	0.00	0.00	0.00	0.00
Deferred charges	0.00	0.00	0.00	0.00	0.00	0.00	0.00	0.00
Other assets	0.00	0.00	0.00	0.00	0.00	0.00	0.00	0.00
Total assets	2,619.53	2,296.14	2,001.92	1,829.27	1,490.38	1,181.58	1,038.38	1,033.83
Liabilities								
Long-term debt due in one year	0.75	0.15	0.25	0.20	0.20	2.00	2.21	2.27
Notes payable	0.00	0.00	0.00	0.00	0.00	0.00	0.00	0.00
Accounts payable	224.37	214.56	182.85	165.74	119.30	93.76	78.72	89.75
Taxes payable	10.29	11.30	15.51	14.27	10.46	11.07	10.65	13.20
Accrued expenses								
Other current liabilities	230.25	221.12	183.86	170.29	142.02	122.34	134.00	88.34
Total current liabilities	465.65	447.14	382.47	350.49	271.97	229.17	225.58	193.56
Long-term debt	152.60	106.85	173.00	352.25	246.75	72.78	28.78	155.98
Deferred taxes	50.00	51.00	63.00	53.00	18.82	21.10	25.82	18.82
Investment tax credit	0.00	0.00	0.00	0.00	0.00	0.00	0.00	0.00
Minority interest	265.71	220.66	175.99	143.09	140.50	124.05	105.44	81.02
Other liabilities	76.28	88.38	84.86	28.27	28.11	22.87	0.00	0.00
Total liabilities	1,010.24	914.03	879.31	927.10	706.15	469.97	385.62	449.39
Equity								
Preferred stock—redeemable	0.00	0.00	0.00	0.00	0.00	0.00	0.00	0.00
Preferred stock—nonredeemable	0.00	0.00	0.00	0.00	0.00	0.00	0.00	0.00
Total preferred stock	0.00	0.00	0.00	0.00	0.00	0.00	0.00	0.00
Common stock	35.95	35.90	35.80	35.70	17.78	8.86	8.82	8.78
Capital surplus	55.05	48.67	39.27	29.91	39.41	42.81	37.67	34.23
Retained earnings	1,535.95	1,315.85	1,065.80	854.86	745.26	678.16	624.66	559.90
Less: treasury stock	17.66	18.30	18.26	18.31	18.23	18.23	18.39	18.46
Common equity	1,609.29	1,382.11	1,122.61	902.17	784.23	711.61	652.76	584.45
Total equity	1,609.29	1,382.11	1,122.61	902.17	784.23	711.61	652.76	584.45
Total liabilities & equity	2,619.53	2,296.14	2,001.92	1,829.27	1,490.38	1,181.58	1,038.38	1,033.83
Common shares outstanding	87.80	87.60	87.33	87.07	86.74	86.42	85.95	85.60

Source: Compusta.

Dec-88	Dec-87	Dec-86	Dec-85	Dec-84	Dec-83	Dec-82	Dec-81	Dec-80	Dec-79	Dec-78	Dec-77
26.38	72.78	128.74	185.14	112.71	79.06	44.89	8.71	21.75	36.65	27.42	7.10
97.43	80.08	61.27	70.87	66.87	58.17	38.34	48.70	43.52	40.21	31.90	23.39
123.22	81.50	105.60	78.64	73.80	56.56	48.83	73.00	49.60	40.01	41.55	30.41
0.00	0.00	0.00	0.00	0.00	0.00	0.00	0.00	0.00	0.00	0.00	0.00
0.74	0.36	0.14	0.11	0.08	0.11	0.48	0.98	0.49	0.50	0.25	0.26
247.76	234.72	295.74	334.77	253.45	193.89	132.54	131.38	115.37	117.36	101.11	61.16
942.27	618.54	452.26	376.23	359.97	338.66	322.85	318.86	219.10	160.46	115.25	86.67
240.37	199.16	181.43	150.95	131.87	107.36	83.78	66.25	46.02	35.88	26.72	20.73
701.90	419.37	270.83	225.28	228.10	231.31	239.07	252.62	173.07	124.58	88.53	65.94
0.00	0.00	0.00	0.00	0.00	0.00	0.00	0.00	0.00	0.00	0.00	0.00
0.00	0.00	0.00	0.00	0.00	0.00	0.00	0.00	0.00	0.00	0.00	0.00
0.00	0.00	0.00	0.00	0.00	0.00	0.00	0.00	0.00	0.00	0.00	0.00
0.00	0.00	0.00	0.00	0.00	0.00	0.00	0.00	0.00	0.00	0.00	0.00
0.00	0.00	5.04	0.27	0.63	0.37	0.02	0.78	2.78	1.17	3.81	0.92
949.66	654.09	571.61	560.31	482.19	425.57	371.63	384.78	291.22	243.11	193.46	128.01
2.21	2.21	3.05	2.40	2.40	2.40	1.60	1.66	1.70	1.25	0.46	0.44
0.00	0.00	0.00	0.00	0.00	0.00	0.00	0.00	0.00	0.00	0.00	0.00
93.17	68.46	53.17	35.47	32.69	37.14	22.95	32.24	36.64	26.42	24.15	12.08
35.80	24.34	14.31	27.60	23.71	14.81	12.54	10.73	4.36	15.91	15.64	4.44
84.92	52.46	47.91	55.78	41.74	34.14	29.02	28.41	23.79	19.96	15.54	13.35
216.11	147.47	118.44	121.26	100.53	88.49	66.10	73.03	66.49	63.54	55.79	30.30
113.25	35.46	42.15	40.23	43.23	45.73	48.23	83.75	39.61	41.40	41.47	28.13
15.32	19.32	27.32	41.32	38.82	33.22	25.02	15.62	7.52	4.92	4.02	2.62
0.00	0.00	0.00	0.00	0.00	0.00	0.00	0.00	0.00	0.00	0.00	0.00
72.71	23.83	0.00	0.00	0.00	0.00	0.00	0.00	0.00	0.00	0.00	0.00
0.00	0.00	0.00	0.00	0.00	0.00	0.00	0.00	0.00	0.00	0.04	0.66
417.38	226.08	187.91	202.81	182.59	167.44	139.35	172.41	113.62	109.85	101.33	61.72
0.00	0.00	0.00	0.00	0.00	0.00	0.00					
0.00	0.00	0.00	0.00	0.00	0.00	0.00	0.00	0.00	0.00	0.00	0.00
0.00	0.00	0.00	0.00	0.00	0.00	0.00	0.00	0.00	0.00	0.00	0.00
8.74	8.70	8.67	5.73	5.67	5.64	2.80	2.79	2.74	2.70	1.78	1.25
30.54	27.38	25.19	24.30	18.99	17.02	17.70	16.24	12.91	10.67	10.41	9.55
511.46	410.51	367.58	327.82	275.04	235.57	211.92	193.36	161.95	119.89	79.94	55.50
18.46	18.58	17.73	0.35	0.09	0.10	0.14					
532.28	428.01	383.70	357.50	299.60	258.13	232.28	212.38	177.60	133.26	92.13	66.30
532.28	428.01	383.70	357.50	299.60	258.13	232.28	212.38	177.60	133.26	92.13	66.30
949.66	654.09	571.61	560.31	482.19	425.57	371.63	384.78	291.22	243.11	193.46	128.01
85.15	84.78	84.52	85.89	84.97	84.54	83.95	83.57	82.20	81.05	80.26	78.80

8 | Annual Cash Flow Statement, 1977 to 1996

Note—all $ Millions

	Dec-96	Dec-95	Dec-94	Dec-93	Dec-92	Dec-91	Dec-90	Dec-89
Indirect operating activities								
Income before extraordinary items	248.17	274.54	226.63	123.51	79.23	64.72	75.07	57.84
Depreciation and amortization	182.23	173.89	157.65	122.27	97.78	93.58	84.96	76.57
Extraordinary items and disc. operations	0.00	0.00	0.00	0.00	0.00	0.00	0.00	0.00
Deferred taxes	(8.00)	(15.00)	(2.00)	1.00	(3.00)	(4.00)	7.00	3.50
Equity in net loss (earnings)	0.00	0.00	0.00	0.00	0.00	0.00	0.00	0.00
Sale of property, plant, and equipment and sale of investments—loss (gain)	0.00	0.00	0.00	0.00	0.00	0.00	0.00	0.00
Funds from operations—other	82.57	48.18	17.67	9.75	23.17	26.11	29.71	8.32
Receivables—decrease (increase)	(9.43)	(25.07)	(55.96)	(70.03)	(22.69)	14.80	(19.80)	(9.52)
Inventory—decrease (increase)	(79.03)	(63.75)	(28.01)	(8.61)	(20.33)	(49.43)	2.81	(16.24)
Accounts payable and accrued liabs—inc (Dec)	9.81	31.72	17.11	46.44	25.53	11.54	(11.03)	(3.43)
Income taxes—accrued—increase (decrease)	(1.01)	(4.21)	1.24	3.81	(0.61)	0.42	(2.55)	(22.60)
Other assets and liabilities—net change	25.30	26.87	90.60	43.67	26.32	15.66	48.16	3.56
Operating activities—net cash flow	450.61	447.16	424.95	271.79	205.41	173.40	214.33	98.00
Investing activities								
Investments—increase	0.00	0.00	0.00	0.00	0.00	0.00	0.00	0.00
Sale of investments	0.00	0.00	0.00	0.00	0.00	0.00	0.00	0.00
Short-term investments—change	0.00	0.00	0.00	0.00	0.00	0.00	0.00	0.00
Capital expenditures	537.44	263.42	185.32	364.16	379.12	217.72	56.75	130.20
Sale of property, plant, and equipment	1.59	0.92	5.22	1.30	2.12	0.55	0.83	1.26
Acquisitions	0.00	0.00	0.00	0.00	0.00	0.00	0.00	0.00
Investing activities—other	0.00	0.00	0.00	0.00	0.00	0.00	0.00	0.00
Investing activities—net cash flow	(535.84)	(262.50)	(180.11)	(362.86)	(377.00)	(217.17)	(55.92)	(128.95)
Financing activities								
Sale of common and preferred stock	7.07	9.67	9.50	8.51	5.60	5.35	3.59	3.86
Purchase of common and preferred stock	0.00	0.22	0.00	0.17	0.08	0.00	0.04	0.14
Cash dividends	28.06	24.49	15.69	13.91	12.13	11.22	10.30	9.40
Long-term debt—issuance	46.50	24.00	0.00	105.70	183.90	46.00	0.00	45.00
Long-term debt—reduction	0.15	90.25	179.20	0.20	11.73	2.20	127.27	2.21
Current debt—changes				0.00				
Financing activities—other	(37.52)	(3.51)	15.22	(7.16)	(6.73)	(7.51)	(5.29)	0.00
Financing activities—net cash flow	(12.16)	(84.79)	(170.17)	92.77	158.84	30.42	(139.31)	37.11
Exchange rate effect	0.00	0.00	0.00	0.00	0.00	0.00	0.00	0.00
Cash and equivalents—change	(97.40)	99.87	74.68	1.71	(12.75)	(13.35)	19.10	6.17
Direct operating activities								
Interest paid—net	6.95	9.21	16.06	10.74	9.14	3.42	8.58	16.03
Income taxes—paid	152.90	176.50	124.37	57.52	40.82	34.68	31.70	46.90

Source: Compustat.
@CF—combined figure
@NA—not available
@NC—not calculable

Dec-88	Dec-87	Dec-86	Dec-85	Dec-84	Dec-83	Dec-82	Dec-81	Dec-80	Dec-79	Dec-78	Dec-77
70.88	50.53	46.44	58.48	44.55	27.86	22.19	34.73	45.06	42.27	25.85	12.45
56.27	41.79	34.93	31.11	28.90	27.11	26.29	21.60	13.30	9.71	7.46	5.93
0.00	0.00	0.00	0.00	0.00	0.00	0.00	0.00	0.00	0.00	0.00	0.00
(4.00)	(8.00)	(14.00)	2.50	5.60	8.20	9.40	8.10	2.60	0.90	1.40	0.80
0.00	0.00	0.00	0.00	0.00	0.00	0.00	0.00	0.00	0.00	0.00	0.00
0.00	0.00	@NA	@NA	@NA	@NA	@NA	@NA	@NA	@NA	@NA	@NA
0.00	0.00	0.00	0.00	0.00	0.00	0.00	0.00	0.00	0.00	0.00	0.00
(18.93)	@NA	@NA	@NA	@NA	@NA	@NA	@NA	@NA	@NA	@NA	@NA
(44.65)	@NA	@NA	@NA	@NA	@NA	@NA	@NA	@NA	@NA	@NA	@NA
25.36	@NA	@NA	@NA	@NA	@NA	@NA	@NA	@NA	@NA	@NA	@NA
(8.54)	@NA	@NA	@NA	@NA	@NA	@NA	@NA	@NA	@NA	@NA	@NA
71.33	@NA	@NA	@NA	@NA	@NA	@NA	@NA	@NA	@NA	@NA	@NA
147.71	@NA	@NA	@NA	@NA	@NA	@NA	@NA	@NA	@NA	@NA	@NA
0.00	0.00	0.00	0.00	0.00	0.00	0.00	0.00	0.00	0.00	0.00	0.00
0.00	0.00	0.00	0.00	0.00	0.00	0.00	0.00	0.00	0.00	0.00	0.00
0.00	@NA	@NA	@NA	@NA	@NA	@NA	@NA	@NA	@NA	@NA	@NA
345.63	188.99	81.43	29.07	26.08	19.62	14.79	101.52	62.44	45.99	31.59	15.95
0.40	3.69	0.94	0.79	0.38	0.27	2.05	0.38	0.65	0.23	1.54	0.02
0.00	0.00	0.00	0.00	0.00	0.00	0.00	0.00	0.00	0.00	0.00	0.00
78.50	@NA	@NA	@NA	@NA	@NA	@NA	@NA	@NA	@NA	@NA	@NA
(266.73)	@NA	@NA	@NA	@NA	@NA	@NA	@NA	@NA	@NA	@NA	@NA
3.33	2.34	3.96	5.39	2.01	2.20	1.46	3.37	2.29	1.33	1.52	1.02
0.0	0.96	17.52	0.27	0.00	0.00	0.12	0.00	0.00	0.16	0.13	0.22
8.49	7.60	6.68	5.70	5.08	4.22	3.63	3.33	3.00	2.31	1.41	1.04
80.00	0.00	4.91	0.00	0.00	0.00	7.50	46.40	0.00	1.14	13.90	0.00
2.21	6.69	3.00	3.00	2.50	2.50	43.02	2.25	1.79	1.21	0.56	3.54
	0.84	(0.65)	0.00	@NA	@NA	@NA	@NA	@NA	@NA	@NA	@NA
0.00	@NA	@NA	@NA	@NA	@NA	@NA	@NA	@NA	@NA	@NA	@NA
72.62	@NA	@NA	@NA	@NA	@NA	@NA	@NA	@NA	@NA	@NA	@NA
0.00	@NA	@NA	@NA	@NA	@NA	@NA	@NA	@NA	@NA	@NA	@NA
(46.40)	(55.96)	(56.41)	72.43	33.66	@CF	@CF	@CF	@CF	@CF	@CF	@CF
3.65	@NA	@NA	@NA	@NA	@NA	@NA	@NA	@NA	@NA	@NA	@NA
49.24	@NA	@NA	@NA	@NA	@NA	@NA	@NA	@NA	@NA	@NA	@NA

9 | Annual Income Statement, 1977 to 1996

Note—all $ Millions

	Dec-96	Dec-95	Dec-94	Dec-93	Dec-92	Dec-91	Dec-90	Dec-89
Sales	3,647.03	3,462.05	2,975.60	2,253.74	1,619.24	1,465.46	1,481.63	1,269.01
Cost of goods sold	2,956.93	2,726.28	2,334.11	1,843.58	1,319.60	1,209.17	1,208.12	1,028.68
Gross profit	690.11	735.77	641.49	410.16	299.64	256.29	273.51	240.33
Selling, general, & administrative expense	120.39	130.68	113.39	87.58	76.80	66.99	70.46	66.99
Operating income before deprec.	569.72	605.09	528.10	322.57	222.84	189.30	203.05	173.34
Depreciation, depletion, & amortization	182.23	173.89	156.65	122.27	97.78	93.58	84.96	76.57
Operating profit	387.49	431.20	370.45	200.31	125.06	95.73	118.09	96.77
Interest expense	7.55	9.28	14.59	14.32	9.03	2.60	8.10	16.88
Non-operating income/expense	7.84	10.41	1.08	1.12	1.30	2.69	1.23	5.74
Special items	0.00	0.00	0.00	0.00	0.00	0.00	0.00	0.00
Pretax income	387.77	432.34	356.93	187.11	117.33	95.82	111.22	85.64
Total income taxes	139.60	157.80	130.30	63.60	38.10	31.10	36.15	27.80
Minority interest								
Income before extraordinary items & discontinued operations	248.17	274.54	226.63	123.51	79.23	64.72	75.07	57.84
Preferred dividends	0.00	0.00	0.00	0.00	0.00	0.00	0.00	0.00
Available for common	248.17	274.54	226.63	123.51	79.23	64.72	75.07	57.84
Savings due to common Stock equivalents	0.00	0.00	0.00	0.00	0.00	0.00	0.00	0.00
Adjusted available for common	248.17	274.54	226.63	123.51	79.23	64.72	75.07	57.84
Extraordinary items	0.00	0.00	0.00	0.00	0.00	0.00	0.00	0.00
Discontinued operations	0.00	0.00	0.00	0.00	0.00	0.00	0.00	0.00
Adjusted net income	248.17	274.54	226.63	123.51	79.23	64.72	75.07	57.84

	Dec-96	Dec-95	Dec-94	Dec-93	Dec-92	Dec-91	Dec-90	Dec-89
Earnings per share (primary)—excluding extra items & disc op	2.83	3.14	2.60	1.42	0.92	0.75	0.88	0.68
Earnings per share (primary)—including extra items & disc op	2.83	3.14	2.60	1.42	0.92	0.75	0.88	0.68
Earnings per share (fully diluted) excluding extra items & disc op	2.83	3.13	2.59	1.41	0.91	0.75	0.87	0.68
Earnings per share (fully diluted) including extra items & disc op	2.83	3.13	2.59	1.41	0.91	0.75	0.87	0.68
EP from operations	2.83	3.14	2.60	1.42	0.92	0.75	0.88	0.68
Dividends per share	0.32	0.28	0.18	0.16	0.14	0.13	0.12	0.11

Source: Compustat.

Dec-88	Dec-87	Dec-86	Dec-85	Dec-84	Dec-83	Dec-82	Dec-81	Dec-80	Dec-79	Dec-78	Dec-77
1,061.36	851.02	755.23	758.50	660.26	542.53	486.02	544.82	482.42	428.68	306.94	212.95
832.88	671.55	575.45	569.69	510.83	434.62	382.32	434.61	356.12	305.98	220.50	162.32
228.49	179.47	179.78	188.80	149.43	107.91	103.70	110.21	126.30	122.71	86.44	50.63
62.08	55.41	65.90	59.08	45.94	33.99	31.72	33.53	38.16	36.72	28.66	19.73
166.40	124.06	113.88	129.72	103.49	73.93	71.98	76.69	88.14	85.98	57.78	30.90
56.27	41.79	34.93	31.11	28.90	27.11	26.29	21.60	13.30	9.71	7.46	5.93
110.14	82.27	78.95	98.62	74.59	46.82	45.69	55.09	74.84	76.27	50.33	24.98
9.18	3.94	5.32	4.36	4.62	4.80	8.41	10.67	3.53	4.30	2.87	2.82
6.63	4.91	10.61	11.92	8.58	5.55	0.52	0.42	4.75	2.79	1.00	0.10
0.00	0.00	0.00	0.00	0.00	0.00	0.00	0.00	0.00	0.00	0.00	0.00
107.58	83.23	84.24	106.18	78.55	47.56	37.79	44.83	76.06	74.77	48.45	22.25
36.70	32.70	37.80	47.70	34.00	19.70	15.60	10.10	31.00	32.50	22.60	9.80
70.88	50.53	46.44	58.48	44.55	27.86	22.19	34.73	45.06	42.27	25.85	12.45
0.00	0.00	0.00	0.00	0.00	0.00	0.00	0.00	0.00	0.00	0.00	0.00
70.88	50.53	46.44	58.48	44.55	27.86	22.19	34.73	45.06	42.27	25.85	12.45
0.00	0.00	0.00	0.00	0.00	0.00	0.00	0.00	0.00	0.00	0.00	0.00
70.88	50.53	46.44	58.48	44.55	27.86	22.19	34.73	45.06	42.27	25.85	12.45
0.00	0.00	0.00	0.00	0.00	0.00	0.00	0.00	0.00	0.00	0.00	0.00
38.56	0.00	0.00	0.00	0.00	0.00	0.00	0.00	0.00	0.00	0.00	0.00
70.88	50.53	46.44	58.48	44.55	27.86	22.19	34.73	45.06	42.27	25.85	12.45

Dec-88	Dec-87	Dec-86	Dec-85	Dec-84	Dec-83	Dec-82	Dec-81	Dec-80	Dec-79	Dec-78	Dec-77
0.83	0.60	0.54	0.69	0.53	0.33	0.27	0.42	0.55	0.52	0.33	0.16
1.29	0.60	0.54	0.69	0.53	0.33	0.27	0.42	0.55	0.52	0.33	0.16
0.83	0.60	0.54	0.68	0.53	0.33	0.27	0.42	0.54	0.52	0.32	0.16
1.28	0.60	0.54	0.68	0.53	0.33	0.27	0.42	0.54	0.52	0.32	0.16
0.83											
0.10	0.09	0.08	0.07	0.06	0.05	0.04	0.04	0.04	0.03	0.02	0.01

10 | Annual Ratios, 1977 to 1996

Note—all ratios	Dec-96	Dec-95	Dec-94	Dec-93	Dec-92	Dec-91	Dec-90	Dec-89
Liquidity								
Current ratio	1.78	1.86	1.67	1.34	1.34	1.46	1.40	1.45
Quick ratio	0.85	1.08	0.94	0.65	0.58	0.64	0.79	0.72
Working capital per share	4.13	4.38	2.93	1.35	1.07	1.22	1.04	1.01
Cash flow per share	4.90	5.12	4.40	2.82	2.04	1.83	1.86	1.57
Activity								
Inventory turnover	8.54	9.92	10.19	8.75	6.72	7.49	8.75	7.83
Receivables turnover	12.67	12.79	12.93	13.48	13.40	12.41	12.68	12.42
Total asset turnover	1.48	1.61	1.55	1.36	1.21	1.32	1.43	1.28
Average collection period (days)	28.00	28.00	28.00	27.00	27.00	29.00	28.00	29.00
Days to sell inventory	42.00	36.00	35.00	41.00	54.00	48.00	41.00	46.00
Operating cycle (days)	71.00	64.00	63.00	68.00	80.00	77.00	70.00	75.00
Performance								
Sales/net property, plant & equip	2.04	2.36	2.18	1.66	1.44	1.73	2.05	1.68
Sales/stockholder equity	2.27	2.50	2.65	2.50	2.06	2.06	2.27	2.17
Profitability								
Operating margin before depr (%)	15.62	17.48	17.75	14.31	13.76	12.92	13.70	13.66
Operating margin after depr (%)	10.62	12.46	12.45	8.89	7.72	6.53	7.97	7.63
Pretax profit margin (%)	10.63	12.49	12.00	8.30	7.25	6.54	7.51	6.75
Net profit margin (%)	6.80	7.93	7.62	5.48	4.89	4.42	5.07	4.56
Return on assets (%)	9.47	11.96	11.32	6.75	5.32	5.48	7.23	5.59
Return on equity (%)	15.42	19.86	20.19	13.69	10.10	9.09	11.50	9.90
Return on investment (%)	12.24	16.06	15.40	8.84	6.76	7.12	9.54	7.04
Return on average assets (%)	10.10	12.77	11.83	7.44	5.93	5.83	7.24	5.83
Return on average equity (%)	16.59	21.92	22.39	14.65	10.59	9.49	12.13	10.36
Return on average investment (%)	13.28	17.26	15.80	9.62	7.62	7.63	9.33	7.51
Leverage								
Interest coverage before tax	52.35	47.60	25.46	14.07	13.99	37.85	14.73	6.07
Interest coverage after tax	33.87	30.59	16.53	9.63	9.77	25.89	10.27	4.43
Long-term debt/common equity (%)	9.48	7.73	15.41	39.04	31.46	10.23	4.41	26.69
Long-term debt/shrhldr equity (%)	9.48	7.73	15.41	39.04	31.46	10.23	4.41	26.69
Total debt/invested capital (%)	7.56	6.26	11.77	25.22	21.08	8.23	3.94	19.26
Total debt/total assets (%)	5.85	4.66	8.65	19.27	16.57	6.33	2.98	15.31
Total assets/common equity	1.63	1.66	1.78	2.03	1.90	1.66	1.59	1.77
Dividends								
Divident payout (%)	11.31	8.92	6.92	11.26	15.31	17.34	13.72	16.25
Divident yield (%)	0.63	0.49	0.33	0.30	0.36	0.58	0.77	0.73

Source: Compustat.
@NC—not calculable

Dec-88	Dec-87	Dec-86	Dec-85	Dec-84	Dec-83	Dec-82	Dec-81	Dec-80	Dec-79	Dec-78	Dec-77
1.15	1.59	2.50	2.76	2.52	2.19	2.01	1.80	1.74	1.85	1.81	2.02
0.57	1.04	1.60	2.11	1.79	1.55	1.26	0.79	0.98	1.21	1.06	1.01
0.37	1.03	2.10	2.49	1.80	1.25	0.79	0.70	0.59	0.66	0.56	0.39
1.49	1.09	0.96	1.04	0.86	0.65	0.58	0.67	0.71	0.64	0.41	0.23
8.14	7.18	6.25	7.47	7.84	8.25	6.28	7.09	7.95	7.50	6.13	@NC
11.96	12.04	11.43	11.01	10.56	11.24	11.17	11.81	11.52	11.89	11.10	@NC
1.32	1.39	1.33	1.46	1.45	1.36	1.29	1.61	1.81	1.96	1.91	@NC
30.00	30.00	31.00	33.00	34.00	32.00	32.00	30.00	31.00	30.00	32.00	@NC
44.00	50.00	58.00	48.00	46.00	44.00	57.00	51.00	45.00	48.00	59.00	@NC
74.00	80.00	89.00	81.00	80.00	76.00	90.00	81.00	77.00	78.00	91.00	@NC
1.51	2.03	2.79	3.37	2.89	2.35	2.03	2.16	2.79	3.44	3.47	3.23
1.99	1.99	1.97	2.12	2.20	2.10	2.09	2.57	2.72	3.22	3.33	3.21
15.68	14.58	15.08	17.10	15.67	13.63	14.81	14.08	18.27	20.06	18.83	14.51
10.38	9.67	10.45	13.00	11.30	8.63	9.40	10.11	15.51	17.79	16.40	11.73
10.14	9.78	11.15	14.00	11.90	8.77	7.78	8.23	15.77	17.44	15.78	10.45
6.68	5.94	6.15	7.71	6.75	5.14	4.57	6.37	9.34	9.86	8.42	5.85
7.46	7.73	8.12	10.44	9.24	6.55	5.97	9.03	15.47	17.38	13.36	9.73
13.32	11.81	12.10	16.36	14.87	10.79	9.55	16.35	25.37	31.72	28.06	18.78
9.87	10.37	10.91	14.70	12.99	9.17	7.91	11.73	20.74	24.20	19.35	13.19
8.84	8.25	8.21	11.22	9.81	6.99	5.87	10.27	16.87	19.36	16.08	@NC
14.76	12.45	12.53	17.80	15.97	11.36	9.98	17.81	28.99	37.50	32.63	@NC
11.76	11.07	11.28	15.79	13.78	9.54	7.70	13.53	23.00	27.42	22.67	@NC
12.72	22.11	16.83	25.35	18.00	10.91	5.49	5.20	22.55	18.40	17.86	8.88
8.72	13.82	9.73	14.41	10.64	6.81	3.64	4.25	13.77	10.84	9.99	5.41
21.28	8.29	10.98	11.25	14.43	17.72	20.76	39.44	22.30	31.07	45.02	42.44
21.28	8.29	10.98	11.25	14.43	17.72	20.76	39.44	22.30	31.07	45.02	42.44
16.08	7.73	10.61	10.72	13.31	15.84	17.77	28.84	19.01	24.42	31.39	30.26
12.16	5.76	7.91	7.61	9.46	11.31	13.41	22.20	14.18	17.54	21.68	22.32
1.78	1.53	1.49	1.57	1.61	1.65	1.60	1.81	1.64	1.82	2.10	1.93
11.98	15.04	14.38	9.74	11.41	15.13	16.34	9.58	6.66	5.46	5.46	8.38
0.84	0.91	1.03	0.74	1.12	0.70	0.83	0.80	0.63	0.86	1.03	1.30

11 | Comparative Income Statements SIC 3312

	NUCOR CORP Dec-96	BETHLHM STL Dec-96	BIRM STEEL Jun-96	CARPNTR TCH Jun-96	CHAPARR STL May-96	INLAND STL Dec-96	STEEL DYNAM Dec-96	USX-US STL Dec-96
Sales	3,647.0	4,679.0	832.5	865.3	607.7	2,397.3	252.6	6,547.0
Cost of goods sold	2,956.9	4,168.2	730.4	601.6	480.6	2,156.1	201.2	6,005.0
Gross profit	690.1	510.8	102.0	263.8	127.1	241.2	51.5	542.0
Selling, general, & administrative expense	120.4	105.5	37.7	112.9	26.1	54.7	13.8	–169.0
Operating income before deprec.	569.7	405.3	64.3	150.9	101.0	186.5	37.6	711.0
Depreciation, depletion, & amortization	182.2	268.7	34.7	35.2	29.5	124.6	19.4	292.0
Operating profit	387.5	136.6	29.6	115.6	71.5	61.9	18.2	419.0
Interest expense	7.6	60.3	18.5	19.3	10.0	50.7	23.7	97.0
Non–operating income/expense	7.8	12.9	10.4	–3.8	4.3	2.5	2.9	51.0
Special items	0.0	–465.0	–23.9	2.7	0.0	–26.3	0.0	–6.0
Pretax income	387.8	–375.8	–2.4	95.2	65.8	–12.6	–2.6	367.0
Total income taxes	139.6	–67.0	–0.2	35.0	23.8	–3.5	0.0	92.0
Minority interest	@CF	@CF	0.0	0.0	@CF	0.0	0.0	@CF
Income before extraordinary items & discontinued operations	248.2	–308.8	–2.2	60.1	42.0	–9.1	–2.6	275.0
Preferred dividends	0.0	41.9	0.0	1.6	0.0	25.8	0.0	22.0
Available for common	248.2	–350.7	–2.2	58.6	42.0	–34.9	–2.6	253.0
Savings due to common Stock equivalents	0.0	0.0	0.0	0.0	0.2	0.0	0.0	0.0
Adjusted available for common	248.2	–350.7	–2.2	58.6	42.2	–34.9	–2.6	253.0
Extraordinary items	0.0	0.0	0.0	0.0	0.0	–8.8	–7.3	–2.0
Discontinued operations	0.0	0.0	0.0	0.0	0.0	0.0	0.0	0.0
Adjusted net income	248.2	–350.7	–2.2	58.6	42.2	–43.7	–9.8	251.0

Source: Compustat.
Note—all $ Millions

EXHIBIT 12 | Comparative Balance Sheets SIC 3312

	NUCOR CORP Dec-96	BETHLHM STL Dec-96	BIRM STEEL Jun-96	CARPNTR TCH Jun-96	CHAPARR STL May-96	INLAND STL Dec-96	STEEL DYNAM Dec-96	USX-US STL Dec-96
Assets								
Cash & equivalents	104.4	136.6	6.7	13.2	20.0	0.0	57.5	23.0
Net receivables	292.6	311.6	111.6	137.1	49.5	225.6	32.5	580.0
Inventories	385.8	1,017.3	196.8	160.5	121.8	182.0	65.9	648.0
Prepaid expenses	0.0	0.0	1.4	0.0	7.8	0.0	0.0	0.0
Other current assets	45.5	22.9	11.6	13.8	0.0	18.6	1.6	177.0
Total current assets	828.4	1,488.4	328.0	324.5	199.1	426.2	157.4	1,428.0
Gross plant, property, & equip.	2,698.8	6,344.0	678.2	809.7	493.5	4,011.4	356.1	8,347.0
Accumulated depreciation	907.6	3,924.2	134.2	390.2	279.4	2,642.7	16.8	5,796.0
Net plant, property & equipment	1,791.2	2,419.8	544.0	419.5	214.1	1,368.7	339.3	2,551.0
Investments at equity	0.0	50.0	0.0	9.8	0.0	221.4	0.0	412.0
Other investments	0.0	@NA	0.0	0.0	0.0	0.0	0.0	209.0
Intangibles	0.0	160.0	46.1	18.8	59.2	0.0	0.0	39.0
Deferred charges	0.0	0.0	@CF	91.5	2.0	@CF	12.4	1,734.0
Other assets	0.0	991.7	9.9	48.0	1.0	326.5	13.2	207.0
TOTAL ASSETS	2,619.5	5,109.0	928.0	912.0	475.3	2,342.8	522.3	6,580.0
Liabilities								
Long-term debt due in one year	0.8	49.3	0.0	7.0	12.4	7.7	11.2	73.0
Notes payable	0.0	0.0	0.0	19.0	0.0	272.5	0.0	18.0
Accounts payable	224.4	410.4	83.2	75.8	34.1	217.7	41.2	667.0
Taxes payable	10.3	67.9	0.4	13.7	0.0	69.2	0.0	154.0
Accrued expenses	@CF	313.3	32.8	56.5	15.9	73.3	9.2	387.0
Other current liabilities	230.2	116.5	0.0	0.0	0.0	3.9	0.0	0.0
Total current liabilities	465.7	957.4	116.4	172.0	62.4	644.3	61.6	1,299.0
Long-term debt	152.6	497.4	307.5	188.0	66.7	307.9	196.2	1,014.0
Deferred taxes	50.0	0.0	50.3	84.5	@CF	0.0	0.0	0.0
Investment tax credit	0.0	0.0	0.0	0.0	0.0	0.0	0.0	0.0
Minority interest	265.7	@CF	0.0	0.0	@CF	0.0		
Other liabilities	76.3	2,689.1	5.6	158.4	51.3	1,179.8	0.0	2,637.0
Equity								
Preferred stock—redeemable	0.0	0.0	0.0	0.0	0.0	0.0	0.0	0.0
Preferred stock—nonredeemable	0.0	14.1	0.0	5.8	0.0	0.0	0.0	7.0
Total preferred stock	0.0	14.1	0.0	5.8	0.0	0.0	0.0	7.0
Common stock	36.0	113.9	0.3	97.7	3.0	0.0	0.5	85.0
Capital surplus	55.0	1,886.3	331.4	13.5	178.5	1,194.5	303.8	@NA
Retained earnings	1,535.9	(988.6)	137.6	256.6	126.9	(983.7)	(39.8)	@NA
Less: treasury stock	17.7	59.7	21.1	64.5	13.4	0.0	0.0	0.0
Common equity	1,609.3	951.9	448.2	303.3	295.0	210.8	264.6	1,559.0
TOTAL EQUITY	1,609.3	66.0	448.2	309.1	295.0	210.8	264.6	1,566.0
TOTAL LIABILITIES & EQUITY	2,619.5	5,109.9	928.0	912.0	475.3	2,342.8	522.3	6,580.0

Source: Compustat.
Note—all $ Millions.

EXHIBIT 13 | Comparative Ratios—SIC 3312

	BETHLHM STL Dec-96	BIRM STEEL Jun-96	CARPNTR TCH Jun-96	CHAPARR STL May-96	INLAND STL Dec-96	IPSCO INC Dec-96	NUCOR CORP Dec-96	STEEL DYNAM Dec-96	USX-US STL Dec-96	WEIRTON Dec-96
Liquidity										
Current ratio	1.55	2.82	1.89	3.19	0.66	2.98	1.78	2.56	1.10	2.14
Quick ratio	0.47	1.02	0.87	1.12	0.35	1.92	0.85	1.46	0.46	0.98
Working capital per share	4.75	7.40	9.18	4.76	–218099.97	9.48	4.13	2.01	1.52	7.31
Cash flow per share	–0.36	1.14	5.74	2.49	115499.99	2.76	4.90	0.35	6.68	0.32
Activity										
Inventory turnover	4.22	3.95	4.78	4.31	11.33	4.17	8.54	5.06	9.62	4.99
Receivables turnover	13.64	7.48	6.76	12.01	10.27	8.18	12.67	15.51	10.97	9.08
Total asset turnover	0.87	0.99	0.99	1.29	1.02	0.62	1.48	0.60	1.00	1.06
Average collection per (days)	26.00	48.00	53.00	30.00	35.00	44.00	28.00	23.00	33.00	40.00
Days to sell inventory	85.00	91.00	75.00	84.00	32.00	86.00	42.00	71.00	37.00	72.00
Operating cycle (days)	112.00	139.00	129.00	114.00	67.00	130.00	71.00	94.00	70.00	112.00
Performance										
Sales/net PP&E	1.93	1.53	2.06	2.84	1.75	1.07	2.04	0.74	2.57	2.27
Sales/stockholder equity	4.84	1.86	2.80	2.06	11.37	1.02	2.27	0.95	4.18	8.25
Profitability										
Oper. margin before depr (%)	8.66	7.73	17.44	16.61	7.78	15.78	15.62	14.89	10.86	4.24
Oper. margin after depr. (%)	2.92	3.56	13.36	11.76	2.58	13.39	10.62	7.21	6.40	0.05
Pretax profit margin (%)	–8.03	–0.28	11.00	10.82	–0.53	15.13	10.63	–1.01	5.61	–4.00
Net profit margin (%)	–6.60	–0.26	6.95	6.91	–0.38	10.35	6.80	–1.01	4.20	–3.22
Return on assets (%)	–6.86	–0.23	6.42	8.83	–1.49	5.93	9.47	–0.49	3.84	–3.42
Return on equity (%)	–36.84	–0.49	19.31	14.23	–16.56	10.53	15.42	–0.97	16.23	–29.83
Return on investment (%)	–23.96	–0.29	11.78	11.61	–6.73	7.08	12.24	–0.56	9.57	–7.43
Return on average assets (%)	–6.49	–0.26	6.72	8.88	–1.49	6.37	10.10	–0.61	3.86	–3.40
Return on average equity (%)	–32.23	–0.48	20.78	14.86	–15.31	11.01	16.59	–1.56	17.47	–25.59
Return on average invest.(%)	–21.59	–0.32	12.26	11.78	–5.95	7.62	13.28	–0.69	10.17	–7.29
Leverage										
Interest coverage before tax	–5.23	0.87	5.92	7.57	0.75	6.27	52.35	0.89	4.78	–0.22
Interest coverage after tax	–4.12	0.88	4.11	5.19	0.82	4.60	33.87	0.89	3.84	0.02
Long-term debt/common eq. (%)	52.25	68.61	61.99	22.61	146.06	48.73	9.48	74.15	65.04	288.89
Long-term debt/shrhldr eq. (%)	51.49	68.61	60.83	22.61	146.06	48.73	9.48	74.15	64.75	256.97
Total debt/invested cap. (%)	37.36	40.69	43.05	21.86	113.38	32.89	7.56	45.00	41.79	71.99
Total debt/total assets (%)	10.70	33.14	23.47	16.63	25.10	27.57	5.85	39.70	16.79	33.12
Total assets/common equity	5.37	2.07	3.01	1.61	11.11	1.77	1.63	1.97	4.22	8.72
Dividends										
Dividend payout (%)	0.00	–524.80	37.10	13.88	0.00	15.62	11.31	0.00	33.60	0.00
Dividend yield (%)	0.00	2.42	4.13	1.37	@NA	1.26	0.63	0.00	3.19	0.00

Source: Compustat.
Note: All ratios.

14 | Steel Companies (SIC 3312) Sorted by Sales

Company Name	SIC	1996 Sales	1996 Assets
Broken Hill Proprietary -ADR	3312	$15,260.90	$28,113.50
British Steel PLC -ADR	3312	$11,882.00	$12,939.60
Pohang Iron & Steel Co -ADR	3312	$11,140.60	$18,967.60
USX-US Steel Group	3312	$6,547.00	$6,580.00
Bethlehem Steel Corp	3312	$4,679.00	$5,109.90
LTV Corp	3312	$4,134.50	$5,410.50
Allegheny Teledyne Inc	3312	$3,815.60	$2,606.40
Nucor Corp	3312	$3,647.03	$2,619.53
National Steel Corp -CL B	3312	$2,954.03	$2,547.06
Inland Steel Co	3312	$2,397.30	$2,342.80
AK Steel Holding Corp	3312	$2,301.80	$2,650.80
Armco Inc	3312	$1,724.00	$1,867.80
Weirton Steel Corp	3312	$1,383.30	$1,300.62
Rouge Steel Co -CL A	3312	$1,307.40	$681.95
WHX Corp	3312	$1,232.70	$1,718.78
Texas Industries Inc	3312	$985.67	$847.92
Lukens Inc	3312	$970.32	$888.75
Grupo IMSA SA DE CV -ADS	3312	$953.00	$1,404.00
Algoma Steel Inc	3312	$896.47	$983.47
Quanex Corp	3312	$895.71	$718.21
Carpenter Technology	3312	$865.32	$911.97
Birmingham Steel Corp	3312	$832.49	$927.99
Oregon Steel Mills Inc	3312	$772.82	$913.36
Republic Engnrd Steels Inc	3312	$746.17	$640.58
Geneva Stl Co -CL A	3312	$712.66	$657.39
Highvld Stl & Vanadium -ADR	3312	$695.36	$957.28
Northwestern Stl & Wire	3312	$661.07	$442.52
Tubos de Acero de Mex -ADR	3312	$645.16	$1,027.85
Titan International Inc	3312	$634.55	$558.59
Florida Steel Corp	3312	$628.40	$554.90
J & L Specialty Steel	3312	$628.02	$771.93
Chaparral Steel Company	3312	$607.66	$475.34
Ipsco Inc	3312	$587.66	$1,025.00
Talley Industries Inc	3312	$502.70	$280.39
NS Group Inc	3312	$409.38	$300.03
Laclede Steel Co	3312	$335.38	$331.11
Keystone Cons Industries Inc	3312	$331.18	$302.37
Huntco Inc -CL A	3312	$264.09	$222.44
Steel Dynamics Inc	3312	$252.62	$522.29
Roanoke Electric Steel Corp	3312	$246.29	$167.02
Grupo Simec-Spon ADR	3312	$214.64	$509.72
Bayou Steel Corp -CL A	3312	$204.43	$199.27
New Jersey Steel Corp	3312	$145.21	$151.37
China Pacific Inc	3312	$123.50	$114.33
Kentucky Electric Steel Inc	3312	$98.32	$78.43
Steel of West Virginia	3312	$95.33	$79.30
UNVL Stainless & Alloy Prods	3312	$60.26	$42.10
Consolidated Stainless Inc	3312	$50.82	$51.25
Stelax Industries Ltd	3312	$0.73	$16.76

15 | Nucor Annual Sales, 1986–1997

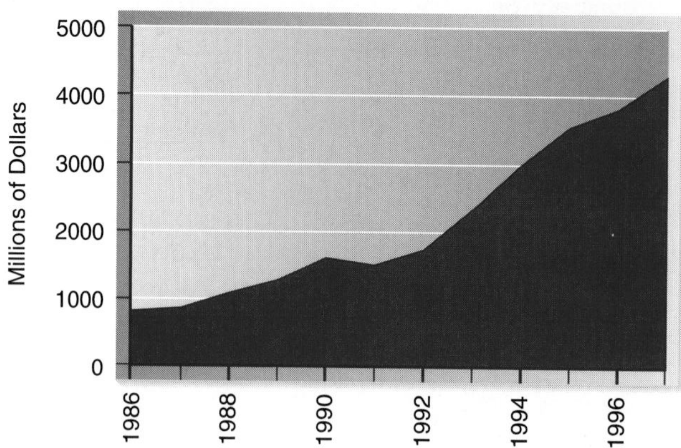

steel with a plant in Trinidad. This backward integration is aimed at lowering production costs; the plant produces iron carbide, which is expected to become an alternative to scrap in the minimill process.

Nucor's Strategy

Nucor has chosen to avoid the formalized planning processes that are typically found in *Fortune 500* firms. This lack of formalization also extends to the company's mission statement, which is nonexistent but known to all employees. The company does not have a *formal* mission statement as management believes that most mission statements are developed in isolation, never seen or conveyed to employees, and have little in common with what the firm really does and how it operates. Nonetheless, all Nucor employees can tell you what their job entails and what the objective of the organization is: the production of high volumes of quality, low-cost steel.[2] Nucor and its employees recognize that all the steel produced must meet industry standards for quality. In fact, Nucor frequently exceeds quality standards. High levels of production per man hour result in low-cost and, subsequently, prices among the lowest in the industry.

Nucor's strategic intent is clearly known by employees, customers, and its competitors. Each year, the business review of the annual report gives this succinct description of its scope of operations: "Nucor Corporation's business is the manufacture of steel products." The annual letter to shareholders gives this picture of the company:

EXHIBIT

16 | Nucor's Principal Manufacturing Locations (1997)

Location	Size (ft^2)	Products
Blytheville-Hickman, Arkansas	2,880,000	Steel shapes, flat-rolled steel
Norfolk-Stanton, Nebraska	2,280,000	Steel shapes, joists, deck
Brigham City-Plymouth, Utah	1,760,000	Steel shapes, joists
Darlington-Florence, South Carolina	1,610,000	Steel shapes, joists, deck
Grapeland-Jewett, Texas	1,500,000	Steel shapes, joists, deck
Crawfordsville, Indiana	1,410,000	Flat-rolled steel
Berkeley, South Carolina	1,300,000	Flat-rolled steel

Your management believes that Nucor is among the nation's lowest cost steel producers. Nucor has operated profitably for every quarter since 1966. Nucor's steel products are competitive with those of foreign imports. Nucor has a strong sense of loyalty and responsibility to its employees. Nucor has not closed a single facility, and has maintained stability in its work force for many years . . . Productivity is high and labor relations are good.[3]

As with the mission, goals at Nucor are equally streamlined. Iverson has noted that in some companies planning systems are as much ritual as reality, resulting in plans and budgets that are inappropriate and unrealistic.[4] Nucor has both long- and short-range goals. However, they are handled differently than at many firms. Short-term plans focus on budget and production for the current and next fiscal year. The plans are zero-based—created from actual needs and estimates for specific projects—not an updated copy of a prior year's budget. Long-range plans are a combination of the plans of different divisions and plant—a bottom-up approach to planning. The long-range plans are seen as guides—not gospel. The plans incorporate relative goals instead of specific milestones that the firm expects managers to achieve. Division and plant managers set their target goals knowing that they will be rewarded for meeting them, but not punished if for unexpected reasons they are not met.

Similarly, even plans for specific projects are minimalist. For example, the company handles new mill construction largely internally. Many aspects of the plant design are done "on the fly" to save time. The company does not create finely detailed construction plans for new plants. Instead, it uses this experience as a guide for starting construction. It then fills in the details as construction proceeds.[5] This approach allows Nucor to construct plants both faster and at less cost than their competitors. The Hickman, Arkansas, mill was completed six months ahead of schedule, going from groundbreaking to first commercial shipment in a mere 16 months.

By 1995, Nucor had become the fourth largest domestic steel producer. CEO John Correnti targets annual growth between 15 and 18 percent—substantially above the 1 to 2 percent rate of growth for the industry. Given Nucor's size and the industry's maturity, growth for Nucor requires taking market share away from the integrated producers. Most experts agree that Nucor is well positioned to achieve such growth and sustain profitability, given its industry leading cost structure. Steel industry analysts attribute Nucor's ability to grow in a constricting market to the firm's aggressive style of management, its innovative and revolutionary technologies, and a solid understanding of the dynamics and cost-drivers of the steel industry.

Nucor can trace its low-cost position to a combination of three factors: *technological innovation*, continuous *process refinement*, and a strong *corporate culture*. Investments in any of the three alone is insufficient; the three elements must work together for the firm to be productive and successful.

Technological Innovation at Nucor

Historically, the main distinction between minimills and integrated producers has been the range of products offered. While minimill technology is less capital intensive, the production process is also limited to commodity steel products: bars, angles, and structural steel beams. Integrated producers largely retreated from these commodity products and concentrated on sheet steel, which was presumably safe from encroachment by the minis. Strategically, though, Nucor more closely resembles the integrated producers versus other minimills in terms of product offerings. Innovative use of technology is key to this strategy.

A prime example of Nucor's innovation was its foray into sheet steel. By the mid-1980s, Iverson had anticipated the coming shake-out among minimills; the lure of easy pickings from dinosaurs like Bethlehem Steel had drawn many firms into the minimill business, resulting in oversupply. Integrated mills produce steel sheet by starting with 10-inch-thick slabs of steel and repeatedly processing the slab through rollers to reduce thickness and increase width. Multiple rolling machines result in a production line hundreds of yards long. Conventional wisdom said that it was impossible to produce the 10-inch-thick steel slabs needed to roll sheet steel in a minimill; their small electric arc furnaces simply did not have the same capability as the blast furnace used by an integrated mill. Nucor carefully researched emerging technology. Rather than develop a proprietary system, they licensed and modified a new German caster and began a $270 million experiment. This new plant—in Crawfordsville, Indiana—started up in 1987. The process was very different from making sheet steel in an integrated plant. Nucor's system involves the highly controlled continuous pouring of molten steel into a narrow mold and onto a conveyor belt to form a continuous two-inch-thick ribbon of semisolid steel—pouring steel much in the same manner as frosting an endless cake using a pastry tube. The process requires sophisticated computer technology and monitoring to ensure constant quality and avert costly and dangerous spills. This precisely sized ribbon of steel is then rolled to the specific thickness using a few, smaller sized rolling machines. This results in a much smaller and less expensive plant than a traditional mill for the production of sheet steel.

The technical challenges of producing steel using this method are the basic requirements of entry into the minimill market. Profitability, however, is achieved through efficiency. Labor costs constitute a large portion of the cost of steel. Integrated producers can take up to 4–5 manhours per ton to produce sheet steel, with 3 hours/ton on a productivity benchmark. In comparison, Nucor's Crawfordsville plant took only 45 man-minutes per ton. Such efficiency gave Nucor a $50–75 cost advantage per ton, a savings of nearly 25 percent compared to their competitor. By 1996, Nucor had production time down to 36 minutes per ton with additional savings expected. A second sheet plant was added in 1992, and capacity was expanded at both plants in 1994. Production capacity was one million tons in 1989, and 3.8 million tons in 1995.

Not content with the sheet steel market, Nucor chose to enter a new strategic segment in 1995: specialty steel. The Crawfordsville plant was modified to produce thin slab stainless steel—another "impossible" feat for a minimill. Through experimentation, it was able to produce 2-inch-thick stainless steel slabs. It shipped 16,000 tons in 1995, 50,000 tons in 1996, and expect to hit a production capacity of 200,000 tons annually. Coincidentally, perhaps, its projected capacity mirrors the volume of stainless sheet imported to the United States—about 10 percent of stainless steel demand in the United States.

Another example of technological innovation was Nucor's entry into the fastener steel segment. Fasteners include hardware such as hex and structural bolts and socket cap screws, which are used extensively in an array of applications, including construction, machine tools, farm implements, and military applications. Dozens of American fastener plants shuttered their doors through the 1980s, and foreign firms captured virtually all of this business segment. After a year of studying the fastener market and available technology, Nucor built a new fastener plant in Saint Joe, Indiana. Productivity was substantially higher than that at comparable U.S. plants, and a second fastener plant came online in 1995. The fastener plants receive most of their steel from the Nucor Steel division. With a production capacity of 115,000 tons—up substantially from 50,000 tons in 1991—Nucor has the capacity to supply nearly 20 percent of this market.

A final example of technological innovation concerns upstream diversification. Scrap steel is a critical input for minimills. Quality differences in scrap types coupled with insufficient supply have led to large fluctuations in scrap costs. Frank Stephens, a mining engineer, had developed a technology to improve the efficiency of steel making through the use of iron carbide. Stephens had tried—unsuccessfully—to sell this process to US Steel, National Steel, and Armco, among others.[6] In comparison, to Nucor, iron carbide appeared to be an opportunity to reduce its reliance on the increasingly volatile scrap steel market. After speaking with the inventor of the process and touring an iron carbide pilot plant in Australia, Nucor made preliminary plans to construct an iron carbide pilot plant.[7] The location selected—Trinidad—would provide the large quantities of low-cost natural gas needed for iron carbide production. Nucor estimated that establishing the pilot plant would require $60 million. However, as the process was unproven, Nucor would, in essence, be making a gamble that would yield an industry-revolutionizing process or be investing $60 million in a plant that would be virtually worthless. To Nucor, the investment constituted a measured risk; while the investment to determine the feasibility was significant, if the process failed it would not cripple the firm. In 1994, Nucor opened the iron carbide pilot plant at a cost of $100 million—almost double expectations. At the end of 1995, the plant was operating at only 60 percent of capacity. Still, Nucor was betting big on this opportunity. Nucor estimates that the use of iron carbide would allow them to reduce their steel making costs by $50 per ton— 20 percent reduction. Additionally, Nucor is working on joint venture with US Steel to manufacture steel directly from iron carbide which could revolutionize the steel industry.

Process Refinement at Nucor

Much of the business press focuses on the high-profile quantum advances made at Nucor, such as the creation of flat-rolled steel in an electric arc furnace and the use of iron carbide as a substitute for scrap. However, an emphasis on continuous innovation is felt throughout the organization and is equally important. A manager from Nucor's Crawfordsville mill observed that most of the innovation comes not from management, but from equipment operators and line supervisors. The job of management, says the manager, is to make sure the innovations can be implemented.[8] For example, workers discovered that they could fine tune surface characteristics of their galvanized steel (a benefit valued by many customers) simply by making small adjustments to the air pressure of a coating process. Changes such as these do not require management review or approval. Instead, equipment operators and line supervisors are authorized to innovate and implement processes that improve production. Such innovation is routine enough at Nucor that management does not track individual improvements. Rather, Nucor tracks innovation by looking at the end result—reductions in the amount of labor required to produce each ton of steel.

Employee innovation is driven by two factors. First, the company's bonus system means that any substantial improvements to efficiency will contribute to both the plant's performance and individual paychecks. Second, the corporate culture emphasizes how experiments—even failed ones—keep Nucor as the perennial benchmark for industry productivity. Experiments are conducted both at the time of mill start-up and on an ongoing basis. Typical of most mill start-ups, the start-up of Nucor's Hickman plant was fraught with problems. The high rate of the production line resulted in "breakouts"—bad pours—of the "ribbon" of steel for thin-slap casting. Though initially occurring at the rate of several per day, breakouts have been declining since the plant became operational. The high rates of production still result in two to five breakouts per week and Nucor continues to make modifications to the equipment to reduce this level.

Focusing on clean-steel practices, the melt-shop people are developing mold powders that can handle the high-speed, thin-slab casting. Mold powders insulate, lubricate, aid uniform heat transfer, and absorb inclusions, all of which makes for cleaner steel. Unfortunately, no existing mold powders can handle hot steel at the rate Nucor could potentially produce it: 200 inches a minute. To reduce inclusions (impurities in the steel), Nucor is working to standardize all operating practices in the two furnaces and two ladle furnaces.

The Nucor philosophy toward innovation is that attempts at improvement will be accompanied by failures. Tony Kurley, a Nucor plant manager, recalls Nucor Chairman Ken Iverson's expectation that success is making the correct decision 60 percent of the time. What's important isn't the mistakes that are made, says Iverson, but the ability to learn from the 20 percent that are truly mistakes and the 20 percent that are sub-optimal decisions.[9]

This willingness to modify on the fly and "shoot from the hip," as one melt-shop supervisor puts it, makes Nucor an exciting place to work. The lean, flexible workforce is continually trying new things, doing different jobs. Employees continue to engage in risk taking because the company rewards success and does not punish for failures. The result is employees, from top managers to hourly personnel, being willing to take risks to achieve innovation and take ownership in their jobs.

At Nucor, the tolerance levels for failure are apparently high. In the 1970s, a Nucor plant manager was considering the replacement of the electric arc furnace in the plant with an induction furnace. At Nucor, the plant manager has the authority to select the type of furnaces used in his plant. There was no clearly right or wrong answer. A discussion yielded strong arguments in favor of the switch from some plant managers and equally enthusiastic arguments against the switch from others. The plant manager elected to make the switch at a cost to Nucor of $10 million. From the start, the new furnaces failed to live up to expectations and resulted

17 | Nucor Annual Worker Productivity

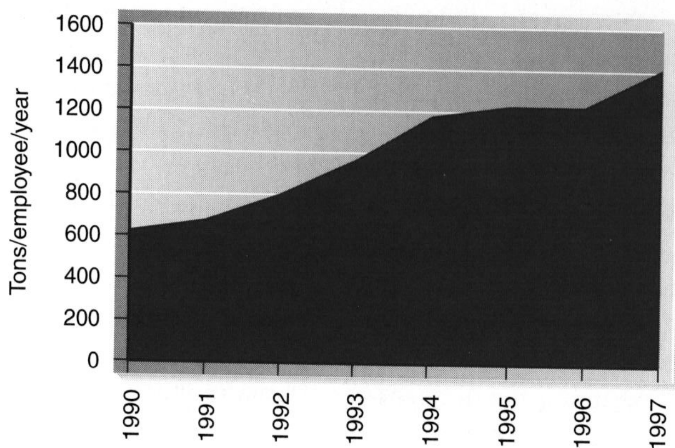

in repeated shutdowns. Discussion shifted to the plusses and minuses of removing the furnace and within a year the furnace was removed. Upon telling Iverson of his decision, Iverson supported the manager saying he had made the right decision—no sense in leaving the reminder of a bad decision laying around.[10]

Despite the price tag on this particular learning experience, management was unfazed. Iverson's comment on this failure was that the true problem is people not taking risks. Nucor has a saying: Don't study an idea to death in a dozen committee meetings; try it out and make it work.

Through incremental advances, employees are continually able to streamline and refine the steel-making process. The data suggests that Nucor employees have not come close to exhausting these enhancements. Productivity, as measured in tons produced per employee, doubled from 1990 to 1995 (626 tons/worker and 1,269 tons/worker, respectively) and continues to climb. In 1997, productivity exceeded 1,400 tons/worker. How is Nucor able to realize such productivity gains in this mature industry? The following examples highlight incremental innovations.

Preventive Maintenance. Preventive maintenance is a crucial but time-consuming task at a minimill. At Nucor-Yamato, a joint venture between Nucor and Yamato Kogyo, a Japanese steel producer, the plant had week-long shutdowns three times a year. During these periods, outside contractors—as many as 800 at a time—would strip, service, and replace worn machinery. The outages could involve as many as 800 contractor personnel—a difficult task to manage. Further exacerbating the situation was the level of skill and low level of productivity of some contractor personnel. Aside from the challenges of hunting down missing contractors, the plant (and employees) suffered from the three weeks without production. The company addressed both of these concerns by eliminating the week-long shutdowns, instead tackling specific areas of the mill in focused, 24-hour shutdowns. This new process has several advantages, including spreading the maintenance costs over a wider window and being able to use a smaller in-house staff that operates continually. Some maintenance jobs are large enough to still require multiple-day shutdowns, but the number of outside contractors has been reduced from 800 to 150. Through this program, downtime at the plant has fallen from 10 percent to near 1 percent. Some improvements are less dramatic, but significant nonetheless. A young engineer at a Nucor plant was concerned that too much was being spent to lubricate and maintain a series of supporting screws under a rolling line. He had a better idea. The screws, part of the original manufacturer's design, were replaced with metal shims, achieving an annual savings of over $1 million.

Reduced Melt Times. At the Crawfordsville plant, workers made a series of small changes such as replacing an exhaust pipe and tinkering with the chemistry of the melt. By doing so, they reduced the melt time from 72 minutes to 65 minutes. While this may seem a small improvement, it meant that an additional 25 tons of steel could be poured in a single shift.

Revitalization of Outdated Equipment. When Nucor bought a casting line from a German supplier, an obsolete reversing mill, which is used to reduce the thickness of steel, was thrown in as an afterthought to sweeten the deal. The capacity of the reducing mill was rated as 325,000 tons a year by the supplier. Nucor employees immediately began fiddling with the mill; the following are among the improvements and results:

- Changing the way the steel was fed into the machine increased capacity from 360 to 1,960 feet per minute.
- Changes reduced the time to thread the machine from five minutes to 20 seconds.
- Nucor changed the type and grade of lubricating oil and installed a bigger motor.

With these changes, Nucor processed 650,000 tons of steel during the first year the equipment was in operation—twice the machine's capacity as rated its manufacturer. Nucor anticipates that an additional 10 percent increase can be achieved.[11]

New Galvanizing Line. At one point, Nucor decided to install a galvanizing line that coats finished steel to enhance its durability. Engineers from $17.8-billion USX Corp. visited the plant before the foundation for the line had even been poured, and Nucor engineers told them they'd have the line running by year's end. The USX visitors laughed because they had started building a similar line a year earlier and it still wasn't operational. The day after Christmas, USX ran its first coil through its new galvanizing line. Twelve hours later, Nucor's $25 million galvanizing line was operational. No other firm had constructed such a line for less than $48 million.[12]

Continuous Production. In most minimills, the conversion of scrap to a finished product is a discontinuous process. Scrap is converted to ingots, for instance, which are then stockpiled for further conversion. When building their new Hickman plant in the early 1990s, Nucor tried an experiment: continuous production. All steps of the steel-making process are coordinated, from picking up the raw scrap, to melting it, forming it, and laying down a finished coil. Continuous production is both faster (3–4 hours from inputs to finished product) and more efficient. The downside? This just-in-time approach eliminates all slack or buffers in the process; problems at any point in the production line shut the entire operation down. How well has this new process worked? As with other Nucor plants, virtually none of the employees had ever worked in a steel mill before. Still, plant performance within one year of start-up was competitive with more established mills: 0.66 man-hours per ton, and a 91 percent yield (percent of scrap converted to finished product, a measure of efficiency). In late July 1993, the Hickman plant shipped 8,804 tons, setting a new Nucor record for the most tons shipped from a single plant in a day.[13]

Culture at Nucor

A key ingredient in any effective corporate culture is people. It is not surprising that many organizations, especially manufacturing firms, have dysfunctional cultures given the fear and distrust experienced by many workers, frequent layoffs, and an "us versus them mentality." Executives of Bethlehem Steel, for example, constructed a golf course using corporate funds, then built a second and third course for middle managers and employees, respectively. Ken Iverson questioned how a company with a culture so dysfunctional as to require the construction of three golf courses to maintain the hierarchical distinction between executives, managers, and line employees could ever expect to improve its operations.[14]

Nucor differs dramatically from its competitors. At Nucor, "us versus them" clearly implies management and workers united against competitors. One melt-shop supervisor described a sense of personal responsibility not only for his own job but also for the firm. He described his position at Nucor as being much like running his own company—a typical comment given the entrepreneurial environment Nucor has created. Decentralized authority and sense of individual responsibility are a key part of that structure. John Correnti explains that he does not want to micromanage the firm's operations.

Doing so, he feels, would result in employees placing blame when things go wrong instead of taking responsibility and finding solutions. This, Correnti feels, results in line personnel having a realistic ability to control their own job environment, increase productivity, and increase their pay.[15]

Still, Nucor is anything but a "workers paradise." The standards for employee productivity are extremely high, and there are a number of painful reminders of this emphasis. For example, the steelworker who is 15 minutes late loses his production bonus for the day—as much as half of the day's pay. Thirty minutes late and the bonus for the entire week is forfeited. Workers are not paid for sicknesses less than three days, or for production downtime due to broken machinery. However, by most measures, Nucor is the employer of choice. There is extreme competition for new positions. The Darlington plant has routinely received 1,000 applications from a single job posting in the newspaper. Similarly, the new plant in Jewett, Texas (population 435), received 2,000 applications. Employee turnover rates are among the lowest in the industry. For example, the Crawfordsville, Indiana, plant lost a total of four employees between 1988 and 1994: two for drug use and two for poor performance. Nucor is a nonunion shop with much of the opposition to unions coming from Nucor employees who feel that union rules would hurt productivity and subsequently their paychecks. According to company folklore, there has been one labor dispute outside the mill gates and plant supervisors had to protect union pamphleteers from angry employees!

How does Nucor achieve such levels of motivation and dedication? Iverson suggests that corporate America has confused the ideas of motivation and manipulation. Manipulation stipulates one-sided relationship wherein management convinces employees to do things in the interest of management. Motivation involves getting employees to do things that are in the best interest of both parties. In the long term, Iverson says motivation yields a strong company whereas manipulation destroys a company. With this in mind, Nucor has identified the following elements as critical to effective employee motivation:

1. Everyone must know what is expected of them and goals should not be set too low.
2. Everyone must understand the rewards, which must be clearly delineated and not subjective.
3. Everyone must know where to go to get help. The company must have a system that clearly tells the employee who to talk to when confused or upset.
4. Employees must have real voices. They must participate in defining the goals, determining the working conditions, and establishing production processes.
5. The company must provide a feedback system so that employees always know how they, their group, and the company are doing.[16]

The approach appears to work. A long-time Nucor employee recalls when the Darlington, South Carolina, plant could produce 30 tons of steel a day. The same plant now produces a hundred tons of steel *an hour.* The worker says that given the can-do attitude of employees and the focus on constant improvement, the "sky is the limit" for additional improvements.[17]

While Nucor is a merit-oriented company, it also makes it clear that there are no "classes" of employees. Top managers receive the same benefits as steelmakers on everything from vacation time to health insurance. There are no preferred parking spaces, and the "executive dining room" is the delicatessen across the street. Incidentally, the corporate headquarters is located in a dowdy strip mall in Charlotte, North Carolina. Not surprisingly, there is no corporate jet or executive retreat in the Caymans. Officers travel in coach class on business trips, and the organization is rife with legends of corporate austerity—such as Iverson traveling via subway when on business in New York City (true, incidentally). This emphasis on egalitarianism is an integral part of the Nucor culture. Iverson, wanting to eliminate even the smallest distinctions between personnel, ordered everyone to wear the same color hardhat. In many plants, the color of your hardhat is a highly visible signal of your level in the company hierarchy. Even at Nucor, some mangers thought that their authority rested not in their expertise and management ability, but in the color of their hat. This goal of egalitarianism has not been completely without problems. When it was brought to Iverson's attention that workers needed to be able to quickly identify maintenance personnel, Iverson admitted his mistake and at Nucor plants everyone wears green hardhats except maintenance personnel who wear yellow so that they can be easily spotted.[18]

This approach appears transferrable and the motivational effects are contagious. Iverson recalls when Nucor purchased a plant and immediately sold the limousine and eliminated executive parking spaces in favor of a first-come, first-serve system. Iverson greeted employees on their way into the plant and recalls one employee who parked in what was the boss's reserved spot and commented that the simple changes in the parking system made him feel much better about the company.[19]

Compensation and Bonus System. Leadership by example can only induce so much behavior; one of the more visible aspects of Nucor's culture is its compensation system, particularly the prominent bonus system. "Gonna make some money today?" is a common greeting on the plant floor, and discussion of company financials is as common in the lunchroom as basketball scores. The bonus system is highly structured, consisting of no special or discretionary bonuses. The company is divided based on production teams of 25–50 individuals who are responsible for a complete task (such as a cold rolled steel fabrication line). The group includes everyone on that line from scrap handlers to furnace operators, mold and roller operators, and even finish packagers. Managers get together and, based on the equipment being used, set a standard for production. This standard is known to everyone in advance and doesn't change unless the company makes a significant investment in capital equipment. With the standard in mind, employees make whatever changes they see fit to increase production. A bonus is paid for all production over the standard and there is no limit as to how much bonus can be paid. The only qualifier is that the production must be good, that is, of sufficient quality for sale. No bonus is paid for bad production. At the end of the week, all employees on a particular line get the same production bonus which is issued along with their weekly checks.[20]

With bonuses, Nucor employees typically earn as much as their unionized counterparts in the integrated plants. Weekly bonuses have, in recent years, averaged 100 to 200 percent of base wages. Typical production workers earn $8 to $9 in base pay plus an additional $16 per hour in production bonuses and averaged $60,000 in 1996, making them the highest paid employees in the industry. Since Nucor locates its plants in rural locations, employee salaries are well above the norm for any specific area, making Nucor jobs highly desirable.

Nucor also offers several other benefits to help motivate and retain employees. In the 1980s, it shifted to a work week of four 12-hour days. Workers take four days off and then resume another intensive shift—a practice borrowed from the oil industry. While this practice results in a lot of expensive overtime—Crawfordsville alone paid out an extra half million dollars in 1995 due to the compressed work week—management feels that the ensuing morale and productivity gains pay for themselves. The company has also disbursed special $500 bonuses (four times in the last 20 years) in exceptionally good years. They also provide four years' worth of college tuition support (up to $2,000/year) for each child of each employee—excluding only the children of corporate officers.

Job Security. Listening to Nucor managers, it is difficult to determine which fact they are most proud of: 30 years of uninterrupted quarterly profits or 20 years since they have last had to lay off an employee. Nucor locates in rural areas and there are often few other employment opportunities, let alone other jobs at similar pay scales, so Nucor feels a strong responsibility for keeping workers employed, even during economic downturns.

Popular impressions aside, Iverson is clear to note that Nucor does not have a no-layoff policy. He cautions that Nucor will lay off employees as a last resort if the survival of the company is at stake.[21] But during prior downturns, the company has chosen to ride out slowdowns with its "Share the Pain" program, which involves reduced workweeks and plant lowdowns instead of layoffs. What is most unusual with the program is that the brunt of poor performance is felt most heavily at upper parts of the organization, particularly as long-term compensation is an integral part of the executive pay system. During a period of reduced demand for steel, the plants reduce their operations. For line personnel and foremen, this reduces their income by about 20 percent. For department heads, who are covered by a bonus plan based on the profitability of their plant, slowdowns result in a reduction of about one-third of their pay. Nucor's top managers have their pay based largely on return on stockholders' equity—the measure most important to shareholders. This is hit the hardest and top managers see their pay decline the most—as much as two-thirds or three-quarters of their income is lost.[22] This structure serves a number of purposes. First, the line personnel don't feel that they are bearing the brunt of a downturn. Second, there is a great deal of motivation to further reduce the cost per ton so that Nucor can underprice any other producer and keep its mills active even during an economic downturn. Lastly, while the shareholders may not be happy with a reduced ROI, they at least know that management has an incentive to improve company performance. As an example, Iverson notes that in 1961—a good year—he made $460,000 including bonuses. In 1982, though, Nucor fell shy of its 8 percent return on equity and Iverson earned only $108,000.[23]

SUMMARY

How important is the corporate culture to Nucor's success? Management is free to point out that their advantage does not stem from proprietary technology. After all, most of their innovations—including thin-slab casting and the use of iron carbide—are based on technology developed by other firms. While they pioneered the modifications to make thin-slab casting possible, numerous other minimills are hot on their heels in this product segment. Nucor's plants are open to firms seeking to benchmark their operations, including other steel producers. When other firms tour a plant they may see the same equipment as in their plant. Many comment on the culture of the plant. One visitor from an integrated producer commented that at his plant the culture is adversarial, management versus employee, with no trust between the parties. "Us versus them" refers to workers versus management and production. In contrast, at Nucor workers are seen striving together as a team, helping each other, and working toward a common goal: the production of a high volume of low-cost, quality steel.[24]

Iverson explains Nucor's success as being based on a combination of the technology used and the culture of the organization. He's unsure if technology is 20, or 30, or even 40 percent—but he's sure it is less than half of the formula for Nucor's achievements. The culture that Nucor instills is focused primarily on the long-term health of the organization. For example, debt is avoided, start-up costs are not capitalized but rather are expensed in the current period, and depreciation and write-offs lean toward the detriment of short-term earnings. Iverson is adamant about not bowing to short-term pressures to manage earnings or spread dividends evenly over a quarterly basis. He refuses to do it. He compares companies that try endlessly to meet short-term projec-

18 | Nucor Profitability vs. Industry

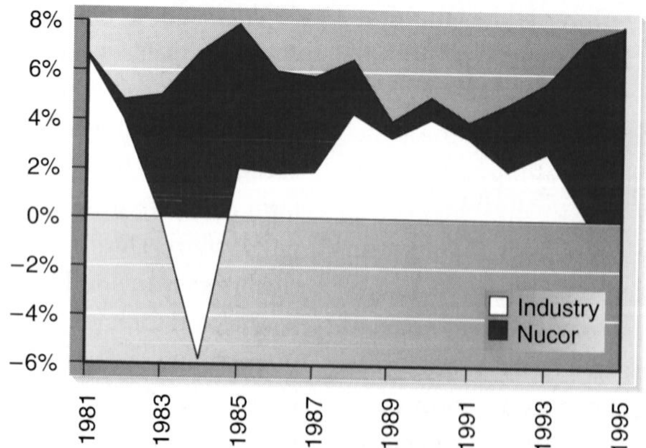

tions at the expense of a long-term approach to dogs on a leash—trying to make perform a trick to satisfy the stock market. He admonishes short-term stock speculators to stay away from the company. He compares Nucor to an eagle and invites long-term investors to soar with the company.[25]

ENDNOTES

1. McCarthy, J. L. (1996) Passing the torch at big steel. *Chief Executive*, 111: 22.
2. Iverson, K. (1993) Changing the rules of the game. *Planning Review*, 21(5): 9–12.
3. Nucor Corp. 1996 Annual Report.
4. Iverson, K. (1993) Effective leaders stay competitive. *Executive Excellence*, 10(4): 18–19.
5. McManus, G. (1992) Scheduling a successful startup. *Iron Age New Steel*, 8(7): 14–18.
6. Carey, S., & Norton, E. Blast from the past: Once scorned, a man with an idea is wooed by the steel industry. *Wall Street Journal*, Dec 29, 1995: Sec A, p 1, col. 6.
7. Ahlbrandt, R. S., Fruehan, R. J., & Giarratani, F. (1996) *The Renaissance of American Steel*. Oxford University Press: New York.
8. Kuster, T. (1995) How Nucor Crawfordsville works. *Iron Age New Steel*, 11(12): 36–52.
9. Berry, B. (1993) Hot band at 0.66 manhours per ton. *Iron Age New Steel*, 1(1): 20–26.
10. Iverson, K. (1998) *Plain Talk: Lessons from a Business Maverick*. New York: John Wiley & Sons.
11. Welles, E. O. (1994) Bootstrapping for billions. *Inc.*, 16(9): 78–86.
12. Welles, E. O. (1994).
13. Berry, B. (1993).
14. Iverson, K. (1998).
15. Ahlbrandt, R. S., Fruehan, R. J., & Giarratani, F. (1996).
16. Iverson, K. (1993).
17. Iverson, K. (1993).
18. Isenberg, J. (1992) Hot steel and good common sense. *Management Review*, 81(8): 25–27.
19. Iverson, K. (1998).
20. Iverson, K. (1993).
21. Iverson, K. (1998).
22. Isenberg, J. (1992).
23. Iverson, K. (1993).
24. Berry, B. (1996) The importance of Nucor. *Iron Age New Steel*, 12(7): 2.
25. Iverson, K. (1998).

CASE 30

Odwalla, Inc., and the *E. Coli* Outbreak

Anne T. Lawrence
San Jose State University

October 30, 1996, was a cool, fall day in Half Moon Bay, California, a coastal town an hour's drive south of San Francisco. At the headquarters of Odwalla, Inc., a modest, two-story wooden structure just blocks from the beach, company founder and chairman Greg Steltenpohl was attending a marketing meeting. Odwalla, the largest producer of fresh fruit and vegetable-based beverages in the western United States, had just completed its best-ever fiscal year, with sales of $59 million, up 40 percent over the past twelve months.

The company's CEO, Stephen Williamson, urgently knocked on the glass door and motioned Steltenpohl into the hall. Williamson, 38, a graduate of the University of California at Berkeley and a former investment banker, had served as president of Odwalla from 1992 to 1995, when he became CEO.

It was unlike him to interrupt a meeting, and he looked worried. "I just got a call from the King County Department of Health," Williamson reported. "They've got a dozen cases of *E. Coli* poisoning up there in the Seattle area. A number of the families told health officials they had drunk Odwalla apple juice." *E. coli* O157:H7 was a virulent bacterium that had been responsible for several earlier outbreaks of food poisoning, including one traced to undercooked Jack-in-the-Box hamburgers in 1993.

This case was written with the cooperation of management solely for the purpose of stimulating student discussion. All individuals and events are real. Support for this research by the San Jose State University College of Business is gratefully acknowledged. An earlier version of this case was presented at the 1997 annual meeting of the North American Case Research Association.

Copyright © 1999 by the *Case Research Journal* and Anne T. Lawrence.

Steltenpohl was puzzled. "What do they know for sure?"

"Right now, not a whole lot. It's just epidemiology," Williamson replied. "They don't have any bacteriological match-ups yet. They said it might be a while before they would know anything definitive."

"We'd better see what else we can find out."

Steltenpohl and Williamson returned to their offices, where they began placing calls to food safety experts, scientists at the Food and Drug Administration and the Centers for Disease Control, and the company's lawyers. A while later, Steltenpohl came out to speak to his next appointment, who had been waiting in the lobby for over an hour. "I'm awfully sorry," the chairman said apologetically. "I'm not going to be able to see you today. Something important's happening that I've got to deal with right away."

HISTORY OF ODWALLA, INC.

Odwalla, Inc., was founded in 1980 by Steltenpohl, his wife Bonnie Bassett, and their friend Gerry Percy. Steltenpohl, then 25, was a jazz musician and Stanford graduate with a degree in environmental science. The group purchased a used hand juicer for $200 and began producing fresh-squeezed orange juice in a backyard shed in Santa Cruz, California. They delivered the juice to local restaurants in a Volkswagen van. Steltenpohl later said that he had gotten the idea from a book, *100 Businesses You Can Start for Under $100*. His motivation, he reported, was simply to make enough money to support his fledgling career as a musician and producer of educational media presentations. The company's name came from a jazz composition by the Art Ensemble of Chicago, in which Odwalla was a mythical figure who led the "people of the sun" out of the "gray haze," which the friends chose to interpret as a reference to overly processed food.

During the 1980s, Odwalla prospered, gradually extending its market reach by expanding its own distribution and production capabilities and by acquiring other juice companies. In 1983, the company moved into a larger production facility and added carrot juice to its product line. In 1985—the same year Odwalla incorporated—the company purchased a small local apple juice company, Live Juice. With apple added to the line, the company expanded its distribution efforts, moving into San Francisco and further north into Marin County. In 1986, Odwalla purchased Dancing Bear Juice Company in Sacramento and assimilated that company's juice products and distribution network in central California.

The company financed its rapid growth in its early years through bank loans and private stock offerings in 1991, 1992, and 1993. In December 1993, the company went public, offering for sale one million shares of common stock at an initial price of $6.375 a share. The proceeds of the initial public offering were used in part to construct a 65,000 square foot state-of-the-art production facility in Dinuba, in California's agricultural Central Valley.

The company also made additional acquisitions. In June 1994, the company acquired Dharma Juice Company of Bellingham, Washington, to distribute its products in the Pacific Northwest. In January 1995, Odwalla purchased J.S. Grant's, Inc., the maker of Just Squeezed Juices, which became the distributor for Odwalla products in the Colorado market. The strategy appeared to be successful. By 1996, Odwalla, which already controlled more than half the market for fresh juice in northern California, had made significant inroads in the Pacific Northwest and Colorado and was poised to extend its market dominance into New Mexico, Texas, and southern California.

PRODUCT LINE

The company considered its market niche to be "fresh, minimally processed juices and juice-based beverages." The company produced a range of products from fresh juice, some single strength and some blended. Odwalla chose fun, clever names, such as Strawberry C-Monster (a vitamin C-fortified fruit smoothie), Femme Vitale (a product formulated to meet women's special nutritional needs), and Guava Have It (a tropical fruit blend). Packaging graphics were brightly colored and whimsical. Pricing was at the premium level; a half gallon of fresh-squeezed orange juice retailed for around $5.00; a 16-oz. blended smoothie for $2.00 or more.

Odwalla was committed to making a totally fresh product. In the company's 1995 annual report, for example, the letter to shareholders stated:

> *Our juice is FRESH! We believe that fruits, vegetables and other botanical nutrients must be treated with respect. As a result, we do not heat-treat our juice, like the heavily processed products made by most other beverage companies.*

The company's products were made without preservatives or any artificial ingredients, and the juice was not pasteurized (heat treated to kill microorganisms and to extend shelf life). Unpasteurized juice, the company believed, retained more vitamins, enzymes, and what Steltenpohl referred to as the "flavor notes" of fresh fruits and vegetables.

Although Odwalla did not pasteurize its juice, it took many steps in the manufacturing process to assure the quality and purity of its product. To avoid possible contamination, the company did not accept ground apples, only those picked from the tree. Inspectors checked field bins to see if there was any dirt, grass, or debris; and bins with evidence of ground contact were rejected. The company's manufacturing facility in Dinuba was considered the most advanced in the industry. The plant operated under a strict code of Good Manufacturing Practices. At Dinuba, apples were thoroughly washed with a sanitizing solution of phosphoric acid and scrubbed with whirling brushes. All juice was produced under extremely strict hygienic standards.

MARKETING

Odwalla marketed its products through supermarkets, warehouse outlets, specialty stores, natural food stores, and institutions such as restaurants and colleges.

Slightly over a quarter of all sales were with two accounts—Safeway, a major grocery chain, and Price/Costco, a discount warehouse.

A distinctive feature of Odwalla's strategy was the company's direct store distribution, or DSD, system. Most sites, from supermarkets to small retailers, were provided with their own stand-alone refrigerated cooler, brightly decorated with Odwalla graphics. Accounts were serviced by route sales people (RSPs), who were responsible for stocking the coolers and removing unsold juice that had passed its "enjoy by" date. RSPs kept careful records of what products were selling well, enabling them to adjust stock to meet local tastes. As an incentive, salespeople received bonuses based on their routes' sales, in addition to their salaries.

Although the DSD system was more expensive than using independent distributors, it allowed the company to maintain tight control over product mix and quality. Moreover, because the company assumed responsibility for ordering, stocking, and merchandising its own products within the store, Odwalla in most cases did not pay "slotting" and other handling fees to the retailer.

CORPORATE CULTURE

The fresh juice company was always, as Steltenpohl put it, "values driven." In 1992, around 80 Odwalla employees participated in a nine-month process that led to the creation of the company's vision, mission, and core values statements (Exhibit 1). These focused on nourishment, ecological sustainability, innovation, and continuous learning.

Concerned that rapid growth might erode common commitment to these values, in 1995 the company ini-

1 | Odwalla's Vision Statement, Mission Statement, and Core Values

Vision
Odwalla
a breath of fresh
intoxicating rhythm
living flavor
soil to soul
people to planet
nourishing the body whole

Mission Statement
Lead in the culture's access to a
restorative vision through nourishment delivery
systems and artful presentation.

Core Values
Honesty, integrity and respect
leadership through creativity and innovation
nourishment and sustainability
empowerment of the individual and personal responsibility
effective communication
learning and improvement
striving for the essence
ecological awareness and response-ability
cultivating community and diversity
agreed upon standards and goals
"resonating on the alignment thang"

tiated annual three-day training sessions, known as Living Vision Conferences, held at multiple locations, for employees to talk about the application of the vision to everyday operating issues. An internal process the company called Vision Link sought to link each individual's job to the Odwalla vision. Managers were expected to model the company's values. The company called its values a "touchstone (for employees) in assessing their conduct and in making business decisions."

In addition, Odwalla instituted a "strategic dialogue" process. A group of 30 people, with some fixed seats for top executives and some rotating seats for a wide cross-section of other employees, met quarterly in San Francisco for broad discussions of the company's values and strategic direction.

Social responsibility and environmental awareness were critical to Odwalla's mission. Community service efforts included aid to farm families in the Central Valley, scholarships to study nutrition, and gifts of cash and juice to many local community organizations. The company instituted a recycling program for its plastic bottles. It attempted to divert all organic waste away from landfills—for example, by selling pulp for livestock feed, citrus peel for use in teas, and condiments and past-code juice for biofuels. In the mid-1990s, the company began the process of converting its vehicle fleet to alternative fuels. Odwalla's corporate responsibility extended to its employees, who received innovative benefits that included stock options, extensive "wellness" programs, and an allowance for fresh juice. The company won numerous awards for its environmental practices, and in 1993, *Inc.* Magazine honored Odwalla as Employer of the Year.

During these years, the Odwalla brand name became widely identified with a healthful lifestyle, as well as with California's entrepreneurial business climate. In an oft-repeated story, Steve Jobs, founder of Apple Computer, was said to have ordered unlimited quantities of Odwalla juice for all employees working on the original development of the Macintosh computer.

THE *E. COLI* BACTERIUM

The virulent strain of bacteria that threatened to bring down this fast growing company was known in scientific circles as *Escherichia coli, E. coli* for short. The broad class of *E. coli* bacteria, microscopic rod-shaped organisms, are common in the human intestinal tract, and few pose a danger to health. In fact, most *E. coli* play a beneficial role by suppressing harmful bacteria and synthesizing vitamins. A small minority of *E. coli* strains, however, cause illness. One of the most dangerous of these is *E. coli* 0157:H7. In the intestine, this strain produces a potent toxin that attacks the lining of the gut. Symptoms of infection include abdominal pain and cramps, diarrhea, fever, and bloody stools. Most cases are self-limiting, but approximately 6 percent are complicated with hemolytic uremic syndrome, a dangerous condition that can lead to kidney and heart failure. Young children, the elderly, and those with weakened immune systems are most susceptible.

E. coli 0157:H7 lives in the intestines of cows, sheep, deer, and other animals. The meat of infected animals may carry the infection. *E. coli* is also spread to humans through fecal contamination of food. For example, apples may be contaminated when they fall to the ground and come in contact with cow or deer manure. Secondary infection may also occur, for example, when food is handled by infected persons who have failed to wash their hands after using the toilet. Unfortunately, only a small amount of "157"—as few as 500 bacteria—is required to cause illness. As one epidemiologist noted, "It does not take a massive contamination or a major breakdown in the system to spread it."

E. coli 0157:H7 is known as an *emergent* pathogen, meaning that its appearance in certain environments is viewed by researchers as a new phenomenon. The organism was first identified in 1982, when it was involved in several outbreaks involving undercooked meat. Since then, poisoning incidents have increased dramatically. By the mid-1990s, about 20,000 cases of *E. coli* poisoning occurred every year in the United States; about 250 people died. Most cases were believed to be caused by undercooked meat. Although a serious threat, *E. coli* was not the most common food-borne illness. In the United States, five million cases of food poisoning were reported annually, with 4,000 of these resulting in death. Most cases were caused by mistakes in food preparation and handling, not by mistakes in food processing or packaging.

E. COLI IN FRESH JUICE

It was widely believed in the juice industry that pathogens like *E. coli* could not survive in an acidic environment, such as citrus and apple juice. Odwalla apple juice had a pH (acidity) level of 4.3. (On the pH scale, 7 is neutral, and levels below 7 are increasingly acidic.) Odwalla did conduct spot testing of other, more pH-neutral products. The Food and Drug Administration (FDA), although it did not have specific guidelines for fresh juice production, indicated in its Retail Food Store Sanitation Code that foods with a pH lower than 4.6 were *not* "potentially hazardous."

In the early 1990s, however, scattered scientific evidence emerged that *E. coli* 0157:H7 might have undergone a critical mutation that rendered it more acid-tolerant. In 1991, an outbreak of *E. coli* poisoning sickened 23 people in Massachusetts who had consumed fresh, unpasteurized apple cider purchased at a roadside stand. A second, similar incident occurred in Connecticut around the same time. In a study of the Massachusetts outbreak published in 1993, the *Journal of the American Medical Association* reported that *E. coli* 0157:H7, apparently introduced by fecal contamination of fresh apples, had unexpectedly survived in acidic cider. The journal concluded that *E. coli* 0157:H7 could survive at a pH below 4.0 at the temperature of refrigerated juice. The journal recommended strict procedures for sanitizing apples used to make fresh juice, all of which Odwalla already followed.

Although the FDA investigated both instances in New England, it did not issue any new regulations requiring pasteurization of fresh juice, nor did it issue any advisories to the industry. At the time of the Odwalla outbreak, neither the FDA nor state regulators in California had rules requiring pasteurization of fresh apple juice.

CONSIDERING THE OPTIONS

In the company's second-floor conference room, later in the day of October 30, Steltenpohl and Williamson gathered the company's senior executives to review the situation.

King County officials had identified about a dozen cases of *E. coli* infection associated with Odwalla apple juice products. But, as Steltenpohl later described the situation, "It was all based on interviews. They didn't yet have bacteriological proof." Washington health officials had not yet made a public announcement, nor had they ordered or even recommended a product recall.

Conversations with federal disease control and food safety specialists throughout the day had turned up troubling information. From them, Odwalla executives had learned of the two earlier outbreaks of *E. coli* illness associated with unpasteurized cider in New England. And they had been told that "157" could cause illness in very minute amounts, below levels that would reliably show up in tests. The FDA had indicated that it planned to launch in investigation of the incident but did not suggest that Odwalla had broken any rules.

Management understood that they had no *legal* obligation to order an immediate recall, although this was clearly an option. Another possibility was a nonpublic recall. In this approach, the company would quietly pull the suspect product off the shelves and conduct its own investigation. If a problem was found, the company could then choose to go public with the information.

The company carried general liability insurance totaling $27 million. It had little debt and about $12 million in cash on hand (Exhibit 2). The cost of various options, however, was hard to pin down. No one could be sure precisely how much a full or partial product recall would cost, if they chose that option, or the extent of the company's liability exposure.

In the midst of their consultations with various experts, company officials had been frantically collecting all the data they could. The conference room was littered with laptops and printouts. "We were just trying to get all the information, all our MIS data," Steltenpohl later recalled of that afternoon. "What lots were affected? What product was out there? What was on the shelves? What was on the trucks? We were just trying to figure out where it all was."

A decision would need to be made very quickly. Steltenpohl and Williamson both knew that the company could not afford to delay, even for one day.

2 | Odwalla, Inc.: Selected Financial Data, 1992–1996

	Year Ended August 31,				
	1996	1995	1994	1993	1992
	(in thousands, except per share data)				
Statement of Operations Data:					
Net sales	$ 59,197	$ 35,869	$ 18,153	$ 12,551	$ 9,594
Cost of sales	29,889	18,425	8,984	6,342	4,835
Gross Profit	29,308	17,444	9,169	6,209	4,759
Operating expenses:					
Sales and distribution	20,158	11,588	6,212	4,133	3,206
Marketing	2,257	891	484	469	264
General and administrative	6,206	3,576	1,973	1,458	1,026
Total Operating Expenses	28,621	16,055	8,669	6,060	4,496
Income from operations	687	1,389	500	149	263
Other income (expenses), net	346	108	(199)	(575)	(218)
Income (loss) before income taxes	1,033	1,497	301	(426)	45
Provision for income taxes	400	500	—	1	6
Net income (loss)	$ 633	$ 997	$ 301	$ (427)	$ 39
Net income (loss) per share	$ 0.12	$ 0.22	$ 0.08	$ (0.15)	$ 0.02
Weighted average common and common equivalent shares outstanding	5,420	4,472	3,623	2,889	2,111

	August 31,				
	1996	1995	1994	1993	1992
	(in thousands)				
Balance Sheet Data:					
Cash, cash equivalents and short-term investments	$12,413	$18,496	$ 2,137	$ 715	$ 96
Working capital (deficit)	14,655	17,918	2,516	(295)	2,118
Total assets	37,700	35,481	12,072	8,038	6,691
Long-term liabilities	501	736	872	2,467	1,901
Total shareholders' equity	29,574	29,499	8,719	2,822	3,408

Source: Odwalla, Inc., *1996 Annual Report*, p. 15.

CASE 31

Outback Goes International

Marilyn L. Taylor
University of Missouri at Kansas City
George M. Puia
Indiana State University
Krishnan Ramaya
University of Southern Indiana
Madelyn Gengelbach
University of Missouri at Kansas City

In early 1995 Outback Steakhouse enjoyed the position as one of the most successful restaurant chains in the U.S. Entrepreneurs Chris Sullivan, Bob Basham, and Tim Gannon, each with more than 20 years experience in the restaurant industry, started Outback Steakhouse with just two stores in 1988. In 1995 the company was the fastest growing U.S. steakhouse chain with over 200 stores throughout the United States.

Outback achieved its phenomenal success in an industry that was widely considered as one of the most competitive in the U.S. Fully 75 percent of entrants into the restaurant industry failed within the first year. Outback's strategy was driven by a unique combination of factors atypical of the foodservice industry. As Chairman Chris Sullivan put it, "Outback is all about a lot of different experiences that have been recognized as entrepreneurship." Within six years of commencing operations, Outback was voted as the best steakhouse chain in the country. The company also took top honors along with Olive Garden as America's favorite restaurant. In December 1994, Outback was awarded *Inc's* prestigious Entrepreneur of the Year award. In 1994 and early 1995 the business press hailed the company as one of the biggest success stories in corporate America in recent years.

In late 1994 Hugh Connerty was appointed President of Outback International. In early 1995, Connerty, a highly successful franchisee for Outback, explained the international opportunities facing Outback Steakhouse as it considered its strategy for expansion abroad:

> *We have had hundreds of franchise reports from all over the world. (So) it took about two seconds for me to make that decision (to become President of Outback International). . . . I've met with and talked to other executives who have international divisions. All of them have the same story. At some point in time the light goes off and they say, "Gee, we have a great product. Where do we start?" I have traveled quite a bit on holiday. The world is not as big as you think it is. Most companies who have gone global have not used any set strategy.*

Despite his optimism, Connerty knew that the choice of targeted markets would be critical. Connerty wondered what strategic and operational changes the company would have to make to assure success in those markets.

HISTORY OF OUTBACK STEAKHOUSE, INC.

Chris Sullivan, Bob Basham, and Tim Gannon met in the early 1970s shortly after they graduated from college.

The authors express deep appreciation to the following individuals at the Ewing Marion Kauffman Foundation, which underwrote the expenses for the development of the case and a video on the company: Dr. Ray Smilor, Vice President, and Dr. Mabel Tinjacha, Program Specialist for the Center for Entrepreneurial Leadership. In addition, the authors also wish to express special appreciation to Outback executives Bob Merritt, CFO and Treasurer; Nancy Schneid, Vice President of Marketing; and Hugh Connerty, President (of Outback International), who contributed special time and attention to this particular case. The research team has had sustained commitment from all the senior executives, including Chris Sullivan, Chairman and CEO; Bob Basham, President and COO; Tim Gannon, Sr. Vice President; and Ava Forney, Assistant to the Chairman and CEO; as well as other Outback officers, executives, and employees. Numerous "Outbackers" have given generously of time, knowledge, and skills to make this case study possible.

The three joined Steak & Ale, a Pillsbury subsidiary and restaurant chain, as management trainees as their first post-college career positions. During the 1980s Sullivan and Basham became successful franchisees of 17 Chili's restaurants in Florida and Georgia with franchise headquarters in Tampa, Florida.[1] Meanwhile Tim Gannon played significant roles in several New Orleans restaurant chains. Sullivan and Basham sold their Chili's franchises in 1987 and used the proceeds to fund Outback, their start-from-scratch entrepreneurial venture. They invited Gannon to join them in Tampa in fall 1987. The trio opened their first two restaurants in Tampa in 1988.

The three entrepreneurs recognized that in-home consumption of meat, especially beef, had declined.[2] Nonetheless, upscale and budget steakhouses were extremely popular. The three concluded that people were cutting in-home red meat consumption, but were still very interested in going out to a restaurant for a good steak. They saw an untapped opportunity between high priced and budget steakhouses to serve quality steaks at an affordable price.

Using an Australian theme associated with the outdoors and adventure, Outback positioned itself as a place providing not only excellent food but also a cheerful, fun, and comfortable experience. The company's Statement of Principles and Beliefs referred to employees as "Outbackers" and highlighted the importance of hospitality, sharing, quality, fun, and courage.

Catering primarily to the dinner crowd,[3] Outback offered a menu that featured specially seasoned steaks and prime rib. The menu also included chicken, ribs, fish, and pasta entrees in addition to the company's innovative appetizers.[4] CFO Bob Merritt cited Outback's food as a prime reason for the company's success. As he put it,

> *One of the important reasons for our success is that we took basic American meat and potatoes and enhanced the flavor profile so that it fit with the aging population . . . Just look at what McDonalds and Burger King did in their market segment. They (have) tried to add things to their menu that were more flavorful. (For example) McDonald's put the Big Mac on the menu. . . . as people age, they want more flavor . . . higher flavor profiles. It's not happenstance. It's a science. There's too much money at risk in this business not to know what's going on with customer taste preferences.*

The company viewed suppliers as "partners" in the company's success and was committed to work with suppliers to develop and maintain long term relationships. Purchasing was dedicated to obtaining the highest quality ingredients and supplies. Indeed, the company was almost fanatical about quality. As Tim Gannon, Vice President and the company's chief chef, put it, "We won't tolerate less than the best." One example of the company's quality emphasis was its croutons. Restaurant kitchen staff made the croutons daily on site. The croutons had 17 different seasonings, including fresh garlic and butter. The croutons were cut by hand into irregular shapes so that customers would recognize they were handmade. At about 40 percent of total costs, Outback had one of the highest food costs in the industry. On Friday and Saturday nights customers waited up to two hours for a table. Most felt that Outback provided exceptional value for the average entree price of $15 to $16.

Outback focused not only on the productivity and efficiency of "Outbackers" but also their long term well-being. Executives referred to the company's employee commitment as "tough on results, but kind with people." A typical Outback restaurant staff consisted of a general manager, an assistant manager and a kitchen manager plus 50 to 70 mostly part time hourly employees. The company used aptitude tests, psychological profiles, and interviews as part of the employee selection process. Every applicant interviewed with two managers. The company placed emphasis on creating an entrepreneurial climate where learning and personal growth were strongly emphasized. As Chairman Chris Sullivan explained,

> *I was given the opportunity to make a lot of mistakes and learn, and we try to do that today. We try to give our people a lot of opportunity to make some mistakes, learn, and go on.*

In order to facilitate ease of operations for employees, the company's restaurant design devoted 45% of restaurant floor space to kitchen area. Wait staff were assigned only three tables at any time. Most Outback restaurants were only open 4:30–11:30 PM daily. Outback's wait staff enjoyed higher income from tips than in restaurants that also served lunch. Restaurant management staff worked 50–55 hours per week in contrast to the 70 or more common in the industry. Company executives felt that the dinner-only concept had led to effective utilization of systems, staff, and management. "Outbackers" reported that they were less worn out working at Outback and that they had more fun than when they worked at other restaurant companies.

Outback executives were proud of their "B-locations (with) A-demographics" location strategy. They deliberately steered clear of high-traffic locations targeted by companies that served a lunch crowd. Until the early 1990s most of the restaurants were leased locations, retrofits of another restaurant location. The emphasis was on choosing locations where Outback's target customer would be in the evening. The overall strategy payoff was clear. In an industry where a sales-to-investment ratio of 1.2-to-1 was considered strong, Outback's restaurants generated $2.10 for every $1 invested in the facility. The average Outback restaurant unit generated $3.4 million in sales.

In 1995 management remained informal. Headquarters were located on the second floor of an unpretentious building near the Tampa airport. There was no middle management—top management selected the joint venture partners and franchisees, who reported directly to the President. Franchisees and joint venture partners in turn hired the general managers at each restaurant.

Outback provided ownership opportunities at three levels of the organization: at the individual restaurant level, through multiple store arrangements (joint venture and franchise opportunities), and through a stock ownership plan for every employee. Health insurance was also available to all employees, a benefit not universally available to restaurant industry workers. Outback's restaurant-level general managers' employment and ownership opportunities were atypical in the industry. A restaurant general manager invested $25,000 for a 10% ownership stake in the restaurant, a contract for five years in the same location, a 10% share of the cash flow from the restaurant as a yearly bonus, opportunity for stock options, and a 10% buyout arrangement at the end of the five years. Outback store managers typically earned an annual salary and bonus of over $100,000 as compared to an industry average of about $60,000–70,000. Outback's management turnover of 5.4% was one of the lowest in its industry, in which the average was 30–40%.

Community involvement was strongly encouraged throughout the organization. The corporate office was involved in several non-profit activities in the Tampa area and also sponsored major national events such as the Outback Bowl and charity golf tournaments. Each store was involved in community participation and service. For example, the entire proceeds of an open house held just prior to every restaurant opening went to a charity of the store manager's choice.

Early in its history the company had been unable to afford any advertising. Instead, Outback's founders relied on their strong relationships with local media to generate public relations and promotional efforts. One early relationship developed with Nancy Schneid, who had extensive experience in advertising and radio. Schneid later became Outback's first Vice President of Marketing. Under her direction, the company developed a full-scale national media program that concentrated on television advertising and local billboards. The company avoided couponing and its only printed advertising typically came as part of a package offered by a charity or sports event.

Early financing for growth had come from limited partnership investments by family members, close friends, and associates. The three founders' original plan did not call for extensive expansion or franchising. However, in 1990 some friends, disappointed in the performance of several of their Kentucky-based restaurants, asked to franchise the Outback concept. The converted Kentucky stores enjoyed swift success. Additional opportunities with other individuals experienced in the restaurant industry arose in various parts of the country. These multi-store arrangements were in the form of franchises or joint ventures. Later in 1990 the company turned to a venture capital firm for financing for a $2.5M package. About the same time, Bob Merritt joined the company as CFO. Merritt's previous IPO[5] experience helped the company undertake a quick succession of three highly successful public equity offerings. During 1994 the price of the company's stock ranged from $22.63 to a high of $32.00. The company's income statements, balance sheets, and a summary of the stock price performance appear as Exhibits 1, 2, and 3, respectively.

1 | Outback Steakhouse, Inc., Consolidated Statements of Income

	YEARS ENDED DECEMBER 31,		
	1994	**1993**	**1992**
Revenues	$451,916,000	$309,749,000	$189,217,000
Costs and expenses			
Costs of revenues	175,618,000	121,290,000	73,475,000
Labor and other related expenses	95,476,000	65,047,000	37,087,000
Other restaurant operating expenses	93,265,000	64,603,000	43,370,000
General & administrative expenses	16,744,000	12,225,000	9,176,000
(Income) from oper. of unconsol. affl.	(1,269,000)	(333,000)	
	379,834,000	262,832,000	163,108,000
Income from operations	72,082,000	46,917,000	26,109,000
Nonoperating Income (expense)			
Interest income	512,000	1,544,000	1,428,000
Interest expense	(424,000)	(369,000)	(360,000)
	88,000	1,175,000	1,068,000
Income before elimination			
Minority partners' interest and income taxes	72,170,000	48,092,000	27,177,000
Elimination of minority partners' interest	11,276,000	7,378,000	4,094,000
Income before provision for income taxes	60,894,000	40,714,000	23,083,000
Provision for income taxes	21,602,000	13,922,000	6,802,000
Net income	$39,292,000	$26,792,000	$16,281,000
Earnings per common share	$0.89	$0.61	$0.39
Weighted average number of common shares outstanding	43,997,000	43,738,000	41,504,000
Pro forma:			
Provision for income taxes	22,286,000	15,472,000	8,245,000
Net income	$38,608,000	$25,242,000	$14,838,000
Earnings per common share	$0.88	$0.58	$0.36

OUTBACK'S INTERNATIONAL ROLLOUT

Outback's management believed that the U.S. market could accommodate at least 550–660 Outback steakhouse restaurants. At the rate the company was growing (70 stores annually), Outback would near the U.S. market's saturation within four to five years. Outback's plans for longer-term growth hinged on a multi-pronged strategy. The company planned to roll out an additional 300–350 Outback stores, expand into the lucrative Italian dining segment through its joint venture with the successful Houston-based Carrabba's Italian Grill, and develop new dining themes.

At year-end 1994 Outback had 164 restaurants in which the company had direct ownership interest. The company had six restaurants which it operated through joint ventures in which the company had a 45% interest. Franchisees operated another 44 restaurants. Outback operated the company-owned restaurants as partnerships in which the company was general partner. The company owned from 81 to 90 percent. The remainder was owned by the restaurant managers and joint venture partners. The six restaurants operated as joint ventures were also organized as partnerships in which the company owned 50 percent. The company was responsible for 50 percent of the costs of these restaurants.

The company organized the joint venture with Carrabba's in early 1993. The company was responsible for 100 percent of the costs of the new Carrabba's Italian Grills although it owned a 50 percent share. As of

2 | Outback Steakhouse, Inc., Consolidated Balance Sheets

	DECEMBER 31,				
	1994	1993	1992	1991	1990
Assets					
Current assets					
Cash and cash equivalents	$18,758,000	$24,996,000	$60,538,000	$17,000,700	$2,983,000
Short-term municipal securities	4,829,000	6,632,000	1,316,600		
Inventories	4,539,000	3,849,000	2,166,500	1,020,800	319,200
Other current assets	11,376,000	4,658,000	2,095,200	794,900	224,100
Total current assets	39,502,000	40,135,000	66,116,700	18,816,400	3,526,300
Long-term municipal securities	1,226,000	8,903,000	7,071,200		
Property, fixtures, and equipment, net	162,323,000	101,010,000	41,764,500	15,479,000	6,553,200
Investments in and advances to Unconsolidated affiliates	14,244,000	1,000,000			
Other assets	11,236,000	8,151,000	2,691,300	2,380,700	1,539,600
	$228,531,000	$159,199,000	$117,643,700	$36,676,100	$11,619,100
Liabilities and stockholders' equity					
Current liabilities					
Accounts payable	$10,184,000	$1,053,000	$3,560,200	$643,800	$666,900
Sales taxes payable	3,173,000	2,062,000	1,289,500	516,800	208,600
Accrued expenses	14,961,000	10,435,000	8,092,300	2,832,300	954,800
Unearned revenue	11,862,000	6,174,000	2,761,900	752,800	219,400
Current portion of long-term debt	918,000	1,119,000	326,600	257,000	339,900
Income taxes payable			369,800	1,873,200	390,000
Total current liabilities	41,098,000	20,843,000	16,400,300	6,875,900	2,779,600
Deferred income taxes	568,000	897,000	856,400	300,000	260,000
Long-term debt	12,310,000	5,687,000	1,823,700	823,600	1,060,700
Interest of minority partners in consolidated partnerships	2,255,000	1,347,000	1,737,500	754,200	273,000
Total liabilities	56,231,000	28,774,000	20,817,900	8,753,700	4,373,300
Stockholders equity					
Common stock, $0.01 par value, 100,000,000 shares authorized for 1994 and 1993; 50,000,000 authorized for 1992 42,931,344 and 42,442,800 shares issued and outstanding as of December 31, 1994 and 1993, respectively. 39,645,995 shares issued and outstanding as of December 31, 1992.	429,000	425,000	396,500	219,000	86,300
Additional paid-in capital	83,756,000	79,429,000	74,024,500	20,296,400	4,461,100
Retained earnings	88,115,000	50,571,000	22,404,800	7,407,000	2,698,400
Total stockholders' equity	172,300,000	130,425,000	96,825,800	27,922,400	7,245,800
	$228,531,000	$159,199,000	$117,643,700	$36,676,100	$11,619,100

3 | Outback Steakhouse, Inc., Selected Financial and Stock Data

Year	Systemwide Sales	Co. Revenues	Net Income	EPS	Co. Stores	Franchises & JVS	Total
1988	2,731	2,731	47	0.01	2	0	2
1989	13,328	13,328	920	0.04	9	0	9
1990	34,193	34,193	2,260	0.08	23	0	23
1991	91,000	91,000	6,064	0.17	49	0	49
1992	195,508	189,217	14,838	0.36	81	4	85
1993	347,553	309,749	25,242	0.58	124	24	148
1994	548,945	451,916	38,608	0.88	164	50	214

Outback Stock Data

1991	High	Low
Second Quarter	$4.67	$4.27
Third Quarter	6.22	4.44
Fourth Quarter	10.08	5.5
1992		
First Quarter	13.00	9.17
Second Quarter	11.41	8.37
Third Quarter	16.25	10.13
Fourth Quarter	19.59	14.25
1993		
First Quarter	22.00	15.50
Second Quarter	26.16	16.66
Third Quarter	24.59	19.00
Fourth Quarter	25.66	21.16
1994		
First Quarter	29.50	23.33
Second Quarter	28.75	22.75
Third Quarter	30.88	23.75
Fourth Quarter	32.00	22.63

year end 1994 the joint venture operated ten Carrabba's restaurants.

The franchised restaurants generated 0.8 percent of the company's 1994 revenues as franchise fees. The portion of income attributable to restaurant managers and joint venture partners amounted to $11.3M of the company's $72.2M 1994 income.

By late 1994 Outback's management had also begun to consider the potential of non-U.S. markets for the Outback concept. As Chairman Chris Sullivan put it,

> *We can do 500–600 (Outback) restaurants, and possibly more over the next five years. . . . (However) the world is becoming one big market, and we want to be in place so we don't miss that opportunity. There are some problems, some challenges with it, but at this point there have been some casual restaurant chains that have gone (outside the United States) and their average unit sales are way, way above the sales level they enjoyed in the United States. So the potential is there. Obviously, there are some distribution issues to work out, things like that. But we are real excited about the future internationally. That will give us some potential outside the United States to continue to grow as well.*

In late 1994 the company began its international venture by appointing Hugh Connerty as president of Outback International. Connerty, like Outback's three founders, had extensive experience in the restaurant industry. Prior to joining Outback he developed a chain of successful Hooter's restaurants in Georgia. He used the proceeds from the sale of these franchises to fund the development of his franchise of Outback restaurants in Northern Florida and Southern Georgia. Connerty's success as a franchisee was well recognized. Indeed, in 1993 Outback began to award a large crystal trophy with the designation "Connerty Franchisee of the Year" to the company's outstanding franchisee.

Much of Outback's growth and expansion were generated through joint venture partnerships and franchising agreements. Connerty commented on Outback's franchise system:

> *Every one of the franchisees lives in their areas. I lived in the area I franchised. I had relationships that helped with getting permits. That isn't any different than the rest of the world. The loyalties of individuals that live in their respective areas (will be important). We will do the franchises one by one. The biggest decision we have to make is how we pick that franchise partner. . . . That is what we will concentrate on. We are going to select a person who has synergy with us, who thinks like us, who believes in the principles and beliefs.*

Outback developed relationships very carefully. As Hugh Connerty explained,

> *Trust . . . is foremost and sacred. The trust between (Outback) and the individual franchisees is not to be violated. . . . Company grants franchises one at a time.*[6] *It takes a lot of trust to invest millions of dollars without any assurance that you will be able to build another one.*

However, Connerty recognized that expanding abroad would present challenges. He described how Outback would approach its international expansion:

> *We have built Outback one restaurant at a time. . . . There are some principles and beliefs we live by. It almost sounds cultish. We want international to be an opportunity for our suppliers. We feel strongly about the relationships with our suppliers. We have never changed suppliers. We have an undying commitment to them and in exchange we want them to have an undying commitment to us. They have to prove they can build plants (abroad).*

He explained,

> *I think it would be foolish of us to think that we are going to go around the world buying property and understanding the laws in every country, the culture in every single country. So, the approach that we are going to take is that we will franchise the international operation with company-owned stores here and franchises there so that will allow us to focus on what I believe is our pure strength, a support operation.*

U.S. RESTAURANTS IN THE INTERNATIONAL DINING MARKET

Prospects for international entry for U.S. restaurant companies in the early 1990s appeared promising. Between 1992 and 1993 alone international sales for the top fifty restaurant franchisers increased from U.S. $15.9 billion to U.S. $17.5 billion. Franchising was the most popular means for rapid expansion. Exhibit 4 provides an overview of the top U.S. restaurant franchisers including their domestic and international revenues and number of units in 1993 and 1994.

International expansion was an important source of revenues for a significant number of players in the industry. International growth and expansion in the U.S. restaurant industry over the 1980s and into the 1990s was largely driven by major fast food restaurant chains. Some of these companies, for example, McDonald's, Wendy's, Dairy Queen, and Domino's Pizza, were public and free-standing. Others, such as Subway and Little Caesars, remained private and free-standing. Some of the largest players in international markets were subsidiaries of major consumer products firms such as Pepsico[7] and Grand Metropolitan plc.[8] In spite of the success enjoyed by fast food operators in non-U.S. markets, casual dining operators were slower about entering the international markets. (See Appendix A for brief overviews of the publicly available data on the top ten franchisers and casual dining chains that had ventured abroad as of early 1995.)

One of the major forces driving the expansion of the U.S. food service industry was changing demographics. In the U.S. prepared foods had become a fastest-growing category because they relieved the cooking burdens on working parents. By the early 1990s, U.S. consumers were spending almost as much on restaurant fare as for prepared and non-prepared grocery store food. U.S.

4 | Top 50 U.S. Restaurant Franchises Ranked by Sales

Rank	Firm	Total Sales		International Sales		Total Stores		International Stores	
		1994	1993	1994	1993	1994	1993	1994	1993
1	McDonald's	25986	23587	11046	9401	15205	13993	5461	4710
2	Burger King	7500	6700	1400	1240	7684	6990	1357	1125
3	KFC	7100	7100	3600	3700	9407	9033	4258	3905
4	Taco Bell	4290	3817	130	100	5615	4634	162	112
5	Wendy's	4277	3924	390	258	4411	4168	413	377
6	Hardee's	3491	3425	63	56	3516	3435	72	63
7	Diary Queen	3170	2581	300	290	3516	3435	628	611
8	Domino's	2500	2413	415	275	5079	5009	840	550
9	Subway	2500	2201	265	179	9893	8450	944	637
10	Little Caesar's	2000	2000	70	70	4855	4754	155	145
Average of firms 11–20		1222	1223	99	144	2030	1915	163	251
Average of firms 21–30		647	594	51	26	717	730	37	36
Average of firms 31–40		382	358	7	9	502	495	26	20
Average of firms 41–50		270	257	17	23	345	363	26	43

NON-FAST FOOD IN TOP 50

Rank	Firm	Total Sales		International Sales		Total Stores		International Stores	
		1994	1993	1994	1993	1994	1993	1994	1993
11	Denny's	1779	1769	63	70	1548	1515	58	63
13	Dunkin' Donuts	1413	1285	226	209	3453	3047	831	705
14	Shoney's	1346	1318	0	0	922	915	0	0
15	Big Boy	1130	1202	100	0	940	930	90	78
17	Baskin-Robbins	1008	910	387	368	3765	3562	1300	1278
19	T.G.I. Friday's	897	1068	114	293	314	NA	37	NA
20	Applebee's	889	609	1	0	507	361	2	0
21	Sizzler	858	922	230	218	600	666	119	116
23	Ponderosa	690	743	40	38	380	750	40	38
24	Int'l House of Pancakes	632	560	32	29	657	561	37	35
25	Perkins	626	588	12	10	432	425	8	6
29	Outback Steakhouse	549	348	0	0	NA	NA	NA	NA
30	Golden Corral	548	515	1	0	425	425	2	1
32	TCBY Yogurt	388	337	22	15	2801	2474	141	80
37	Showbiz/Chuck E. Cheese	370	373	7	8	332	NA	8	NA
39	Round Table Pizza	357	340	15	12	576	597	29	22
40	Western Sizzlin'	337	351	3	6	281	NA	2	NA
41	Ground Round	321	310	0	0	NA	NA	NA	NA
42	Papa John's	297	NA	0	NA	632	NA	0	NA
44	Godfather's Pizza	270	268	0	0	515	531	0	0
45	Bonanza	267	327	32	47	264	NA	30	NA
46	Village Inn	266	264	0	0	NA	NA	NA	NA
47	Red Robin	259	235	27	28	NA	NA	NA	NA
48	Tony Roma's	254	245	41	36	NA	NA	NA	NA
49	Marie Callender	251	248	0	0	NA	NA	NA	NA

NA: Not ranked in the top 50 for that category
Source: "Top 50 Franchises," Restaurant Business, November 1, 1995, pp. 35–41

food themes were very popular abroad. U.S. food themes were common throughout Canada as well as Western Europe and East Asia. As a result of the opening of previously inaccessible markets like Eastern Europe, the former Soviet Union, China, India, and Latin America, the potential for growth in U.S. food establishments abroad was enormous.

In 1992 alone, there were more than 3000 franchisers in the U.S. operating about 540,000 franchised outlets—a net outlet of some sort opened about every 16 minutes. In 1992, franchised business sales totaled $757.8 billion, about 35% of all retail sales. Franchising was used as a growth vehicle by a variety of businesses including automobiles, petroleum, cosmetics, convenience stores, computers, and financial services. However, food service constituted the franchising industry's largest single group. Franchised restaurants generally performed better than free-standing units. For example, in 1991 franchised restaurants experienced per-store sales growth of 6.2% versus an overall restaurant industry growth rate of 3.0%. However, despite generally favorable sales and profits, franchisor–franchisee relationships were often difficult.

Abroad franchisers operated an estimated 31,000 restaurant units. The significant increase in restaurant franchising abroad was driven by universal cultural trends, rising incomes, improved international transportation and communication, rising educational levels, an increasing number of women entering the work force, demographic concentrations of people in urban areas, and the willingness of younger generations to try new products.[9] However, there were substantial differences in these changes between the U.S. and other countries and from country to country.

FACTORS IMPACTING COUNTRY SELECTION

Outback had not yet formed a firm plan for its international rollout. However, Hugh Connerty indicated the preliminary choice of markets targeted for entry:

> *The first year will be Canada. . . . Then we'll go to Hawaii. . . . Then we'll go to South America and then develop our relationships in the Far East, Korea, Japan, . . . the Orient. At the second year we'll begin a relationship in Great Britain and from there a natural progression throughout Europe. But we view it as a very long-term project. I have learned that people think very different than Americans.*

There were numerous considerations which U.S. restaurant chains had to take into account when determining which non-U.S. markets to enter. Some of these factors are summarized in Exhibit 5. Issues regarding infrastructure and demographics are expanded below. Included are some of the difficulties that U.S. restaurant companies encountered in various countries. Profiles of Canada, South Korea, Japan, Germany, Mexico, and Great Britain appear as Appendix B.

Infrastructure

A supportive infrastructure in the target country is essential. Proper means of transportation, communication, basic utilities such as power and water, and locally available supplies are important elements in the decision to introduce a particular restaurant concept. A restaurant must have the ability to get resources to its location. Raw materials for food preparation, equipment for the manufacture of food served, employees, and customers must be able to enter and leave the establishment. The network that brings these resources to a firm is commonly called a supply chain.

The level of economic development is closely linked to the development of a supportive infrastructure. For example, the U.S. International Trade Commission said,

> *Economic conditions, cultural disparities, and physical limitations can have substantial impact on the viability of foreign markets for a franchise concept. In terms of economics, the level of infrastructure development is a significant factor. A weak infrastructure may cause problems in transportation, communication, or even the provision of basic utilities such as electricity. . . . International franchisers frequently encounter problems finding supplies in sufficient quantity, of consistent quality, and at stable prices. . . . Physical distance also can adversely affect a franchise concept and arrangement. Long distances create communication and transportation problems, which may complicate the process of sourcing supplies, overseeing operations, or providing quality management services to franchisees.*[10]

5 | Factors Affecting Companies' Entry into International Markets

External Factors

Country Market Factors: Size of target market, competitive structure—atomistic, oligopolistic to monopolistic, local marketing infrastructure (distribution, etc.)

Country Production Factors: Quality, quantity and cost of raw materials, labor, energy and other productive agents in the target country, as well as the quality and cost of the economic infrastructure (transportation, communications, port facilities and similar considerations)

Country Environmental Factors:

- Political, economic and sociocultural character of the target country—government policies and regulations pertaining to international business.
- Geographical distance—impact on transportation costs.
- Size of the economy, absolute level of performance (GDP per capita), relative importance of economic sectors—closely related to the market size for a company's product in the target country.
- Dynamics, including rate of investment, growth in GDP, personal income, changes in employment. Dynamic economies may justify entry modes with a high break-even point even when the current market size is below the break-even point.
- Sociocultural factors—cultural distance between home country and target country societies. Closer the cultural distance, quicker entry into these markets, e.g., Canada.

Home Country Factors: Big domestic market allows a company to grow to a large size before it turns to foreign markets. Competitive structure. Firms in oligopolistic industries tend to imitate the actions of rival domestic firms that threaten to upset competitive equilibrium. Hence, when one firm invests abroad, rival firms commonly follow the lead. High production costs in the home country are an important factor.

Internal Factors

Company Product Factors:

- Products that are highly differentiated with distinct advantages over competitive products give sellers a significant degree of pricing discretion.
- Products that require an array of pre- and post-purchase services makes it difficult for a company to market the product at a distance.
- Products that require considerable adaptation.

Company Resource/Commitment Factors: The more abundant a company's resources in management, capital, technology, production skills, and marketing skills, the more numerous its entry mode options. Conversely, a company with limited resources is constrained to use entry modes that call for only a small resource commitment. Size is therefore a critical factor in the choice of an entry mode. Although resources are an influencing factor, they must be joined with a willingness to commit them to foreign market development. A high degree of commitment means that managers will select the entry mode for a target from a wider range of alternative modes than managers with a low commitment.

The degree of a company's commitment to international business is revealed by the role accorded to foreign markets in corporate strategy, the status of the international organization, and the attitudes of managers.

Source: Franklin Root, *Entry Strategies for International Markets* (Lexington, MA: D.C. Heath, 1987).

Some food can be sourced locally, some regionally or nationally, and some must be imported. A country's transportation and distribution capabilities may become an element in the decision regarding the country's suitability for a particular restaurant concept.

Sometimes supply chain issues require firms to make difficult decisions that affect the costs associated with the foreign enterprise. Family Restaurants, Inc., encountered problems providing brown gravy for its CoCo's restaurants in South Korea. "If you want brown gravy in South Korea," said Barry Krantz, company president, "you can do one of two things. Bring it over, which is very costly. Or, you can make it yourself. So we figure out the flavor profile and make it in the kitchen." Krantz concedes that a commissary is "an expensive proposition but the lesser of two evils."[11]

In certain instances a country may be so attractive for long term growth that a firm dedicates itself to creating a supply chain for its restaurants. An excellent illustration is McDonald's expansion into Russia in the late 1980s:

> *Supply procurement has proved to be a major hurdle, as it has for all foreign companies operating in Russia. The problem has several causes: the rigid bureaucratic system, supply shortages caused by distribution and production problems, available supplies not meeting McDonald's quality standards. . . . To handle these problems, McDonald's scoured the country for supplies, contracting for such items as milk, cheddar cheese, and beef. To help ensure ample supplies of the quality products it needed, it undertook to educate Soviet farmers and cattle ranchers on how to grow and raise those products. In addition, it built a $40 million food-processing center about 45 minutes from its first Moscow restaurant. And because distribution was (and still is) as much a cause of shortages as production was, McDonald's carried supplies on its own trucks.*[12]

Changing from one supply chain to another can affect more than the availability of quality provisions—it can affect the equipment that is used to make the food served. For example,

> *Wendy's nearly had its Korean market debut delayed by the belatedly discovered problem of thrice-frozen hamburger. After being thawed and frozen at each step of Korea's cumbersome three-company distribution channel, ground beef there takes on added water weight that threw off Wendy's patty specifications, forcing a hasty stateside retooling of the standard meat patty die used to mass-produce its burgers.*[13]

Looking at statistics such as the number of ports, airports, quantity of paved roads, and transportation equipment as a percentage of capital stock per worker can give a bird's eye view of the level of infrastructure development.

Demographics

Just like the domestic market, restaurants in a foreign market need to know who their customers will be. Different countries will have different strata in age distribution, religion, and cultural heritage. These factors can influence the location, operations, and menus of restaurants in the country.

A popular example is India, where eating beef is contrary to the beliefs of 80 percent of the population which is Hindu.[14] Considering India's population is nearly one billion people, companies find it hard to ignore this market even if beef is a central component of the firm's traditional menu. "We're looking at serving mutton patties," says Ann Connolly, a McDonald's spokeswoman.[15]

Another area where religion plays a part in affecting the operation of a restaurant is the Middle East. Dairy Queen expanded to the region and found that during the Islamic religious observance of Ramadan no business was conducted; indeed, the windows of shops were boarded up.[16]

Age distribution can affect who should be the target market. "The company [McDonald's in Japan] also made modifications [not long after entering the market], such as targeting all advertising to younger people, because the eating habits of older Japanese are very difficult to change.[17] Age distribution can also impact the pool of labor available. In some countries over 30 percent of the population is under 15 years old; in other countries over 15 percent is 65 or older. These varying demographics could create a change in the profile for potential employees in the new market.

Educational level may be an influence on both the buying public and the employee base. Literacy rates vary, and once again this can change the profile of an employee as well as who makes up the buying public.

Statistics can help compare countries using demographic components like literacy rates, total population and age distribution, and religious affiliations.

Income

Buying power is another demographic that can provide clues to how the restaurant might fare in the target country, as well as how the marketing program should position the company's products or services. Depending on the country and its economic development, the firm may have to attract a different segment than in the domestic market. For example, in Mexico,

> *Major U.S. firms have only recently begun targeting the country's sizable and apparently burgeoning middle class. For its part, McDonald's has changed tactics from when it first entered Mexico as a prestige brand aimed almost exclusively at the upper class, which accounts for about 5 percent of Mexico's population of some 93 million. With the development of its own distribution systems and improved economies of scale, McDonald's lately has been slashing prices to aid its penetration into working-class population strongholds. "I'd say McDonald's pricing now in Mexico is 30 percent lower, in constant dollar terms, than when we opened in '85," says Moreno [Fernando Moreno, now international director of Peter Piper Pizza], who was part of the chain's inaugural management team there.*[18]

There are instances where low disposable income does not translate to a disinterest in dining out in a Western-style restaurant. While Americans dine at a fast food establishment such as McDonald's one or two times per week, lower incomes in the foreign markets make eating at McDonald's a special, once a month occurrence. "These people are not very wealthy, so eating out at a place like McDonald's is a dining experience."[19] China provides another example:

> *At one Beijing KFC last summer, [the store] notched the volume equivalent of nine U.S. KFC branches in a single day during a $1.99 promotion of a two-piece meal with a baseball cap. Observers chalk up that blockbuster business largely to China's ubiquitous "spoiled-brat syndrome" and the apparent willingness of indulgent parents to spend one or two months' salaries on splurges for the only child the government allows them to rear.*[20]

Statistics outlining the various indices describing the country's gross domestic product, consumer spending on food, consumption and investment rates, and price levels can assist in evaluating target countries.

Trade Law

Trade policies can be friend or foe to a restaurant chain interested in expanding to other countries. Trade agreements such as NAFTA (North American Free Trade Agreement) and GATT (General Agreement on Tariffs and Trade) can help alleviate the ills of international expansion if they achieve their aims of "reducing or eliminating tariffs, reducing non-tariff barriers to trade, liberalizing investment and foreign exchange policies, and improving intellectual property protection. . . . The recently signed Uruguay Round Agreements [of GATT] include the General Agreement on Trade in Services (GATS), the first multilateral, legally enforceable agreement covering trade and investment in the services sector. The GATS is designed to liberalize trade in services by reducing or eliminating governmental measures that prevent services from being freely provided across national borders or that discriminate against firms with foreign ownership."[21]

Franchising, one of the most popular modes for entering foreign markets, scored a win in the GATS agreement. For the first time franchising was addressed directly in international trade talks. However, most countries have not elected to make their restrictions on franchising publicly known. The U.S. International Trade Commission pointed out,

> *Specific commitments that delineate barriers are presented in Schedules of Commitments (Schedules). As of this writing, Schedules from approximately 90 countries are publicly available. Only 30 of these countries specifically include franchising in their Schedules. . . . The remaining two-thirds of the countries did not schedule commitments on franchising. This means that existing restrictions are not presented in a transparent manner and additional, more severe restrictions may be imposed at a later date. . . . Among the 30 countries that addressed franchising in the Schedules, 25 countries, including the United States, have committed themselves to maintain no limitations on franchising except for restrictions on the presence of foreign nationals within their respective countries.*[22]

Despite progress, current international restaurant chains have encountered a myriad of challenges because of restrictive trade policies. Some countries make the import of restaurant equipment into their country difficult and expensive. The Asian region possesses "steep tariffs and [a] patchwork of inconsistent regulations that impede imports of commodities and equipment."[23]

OUTBACK'S GROWTH CHALLENGE

Hugh Connerty was well aware that there was no mention of international opportunities in Outback's 1994 Annual Report. The company distributed that annual report to shareholders at the April 1995 meeting. More than 300 shareholders packed the meeting to standing room only. During the question and answer period a shareholder had closely questioned the company's executives as to why the company did not pay a dividend. The shareholder pointed out that the company made a considerable profit in 1994. Chris Sullivan responded that the company needed to reinvest the cash that might be used as dividends in order to achieve the targeted growth. His response was a public and very visible commitment to continue the company's fast-paced growth. Connerty knew that international had the potential to play a critical role in that growth. His job was to help craft a strategy that would assure Outback's continuing success as it undertook the new and diverse markets abroad.

APPENDIX A: PROFILES OF CASUAL DINING AND FAST FOOD CHAINS[24]

This appendix provides summaries of the 1995 publicly available data on (1) the two casual dining chains represented among the top 50 franchisers that had operations abroad (Applebee's and T.G.I. Friday's/Carlson Companies, Inc.) and (2) the top ten franchisers in the restaurant industry, all of which are fast food chains (Burger King, Domino's, Hardee's, International Dairy Queen, Inc., Little Caesar's, McDonald's, Pepsico including KFC, Taco Bell and Pizza Hut, Subway, and Wendy's).

Casual Dining Chains with Operations Abroad

Applebee's. Applebee's was one of the largest casual dining chains in the United States. It ranked 20th in sales and 36th in stores for 1994. Like most other casual dining operators, much of the company's growth had been fueled by domestic expansion. Opening in 1986, the company experienced rapid growth and by 1994 had 507 stores. The mode of growth was franchising, but in 1992 management began a program of opening more company-owned sites and buying restaurants from franchisees. The company positioned itself as a neighborhood bar and grill and offered a moderately priced menu including burgers, chicken, and salads.

In 1995 Applebee's continued a steady program of expansion. Chairman and CEO Abe Gustin set a target of 1,200 U.S. restaurants and had also begun a slow push into international markets. In 1994 the company franchised restaurants in Canada and Curaçao and signed an agreement to franchise 20 restaurants in Belgium, Luxembourg, and the Netherlands.

T.G.I. Friday's/Carlson Companies, Inc. T.G.I. Friday's was owned by Carlson Companies, Inc., a large, privately held conglomerate that had interests in travel (65 percent of 1994 sales), hospitality (30 percent) plus marketing, employee training and incentives (5 percent). Carlson also owned a total of 345 Radisson Hotels and Country Inns plus 240 units of Country Kitchen International, a chain of family restaurants.

Most of Carlson's revenues came from its travel group. The company experienced an unexpected surprise in 1995 when U.S. airlines announced that they would put a cap on the commissions they would pay to book U.S. flights. Because of this change, Carlson decided to change its service to a fee-based arrangement and expected sales to drop by US $100 million in 1995. To make up for this deficit, Carlson began to focus on building its hospitality group of restaurants and hotels through expansion in the U.S. and overseas. The company experienced significant senior management turnover in the early 1990s and founder Curtis Carlson, age 80, had announced his intention to retire at the end of 1996. His daughter was announced as next head of the company.

T.G.I. Friday's grew 15.7% in revenue and 19.4% in stores in 1994. With 37 restaurants overseas, international sales were 12.7% of sales and 11.8% of stores systemwide. Carlson operated a total of 550 restaurants in 17 countries. About one third of overall sales came from activities outside the U.S.

The Top Ten Franchisers in the Restaurant Industry

Burger King. In 1994 Burger King was number two in sales and number four in stores among the fast food

EXHIBIT

6 | Applebee's

Year	1989	1990	1991	1992	1993	1994
Sales*	29.9	38.2	45.1	56.5	117.1	208.5
Net income*	0.0	1.8	3.1	5.1	9.5	16.9
EPS ($)	(0.10)	0.13	0.23	0.27	0.44	0.62
Stock price—close ($)	4.34	2.42	4.84	9.17	232.34	13.38
Dividends ($)	0.00	0.00	0.01	0.02	0.03	0.04
# Employees	1,149	1,956	1,714	2,400	16,600	8,700

*$M. of Sterling 1994: Debt ratio 20.1%; ROE 19.2; Cash $17.2M; Current ratio 1.13; LTD $23.7

competitors. Burger King did not have the same presence in the global market as McDonald's and KFC. For example, McDonald's and KFC had been in Japan since the 1970s. Burger King opened its first Japanese locations in 1993. By that time, McDonald's already had over 1,000 outlets there. In 1994 Burger King had 1,357 non-U.S. stores (17.7 percent of systemwide total) in 50 countries, and overseas sales (18.7 percent) totaled US$1.4 billion.

Burger King was owned by the British food and spirits conglomerate Grand Metropolitan plc. Among the company's top brands were Pillsbury, Green Giant, and Haagen-Dazs. Grand Met's situation had not been bright during the 1990s, with the loss of major distri-

EXHIBIT

7 | T.G.I. Friday's/Carlson Companies, Inc.

Year	1985	1986	1987	1988	1989	1990	1991	1992	1993	1994
Sales*	.9	1.3	1.5	1.8	2.0	2.2	2.3	2.9	2.3	2.3

*$B; no data available on income; excludes franchisee sales

EXHIBIT

8 | Burger King

Year	1985	1986	1987	1988	1989	1990	1991	1992	1993	1994
Sales*	5,590	5,291	4,706	6,029	9,298	9,394	8.748	7,913	8,120	7,780
Net income*	272	261	461	702	1,068	1,069	432	616	412	450
EPS ($)	14	16	19	24	28	32	33	28	30	32
Stock price—close ($)	199	228	215	314	329	328	441	465	476	407
Dividend/share ($)	5.0	5.1	6.0	7.5	8.9	10.2	11.4	12.3	13.0	14.0
Employees (K)	137	131	129	90	137	138	122	102	87	64

*M of Sterling; 1994: debt ratio 47.3%; R.O.E. 12.4%; Cash (Ster.) 986M; LTD (Ster.) 2,322M.
1994 Segments sales (profit): North America 62% (69%); U.K. & Ireland 10% (10%); Africa & Middle East 2% (1%); Other Europe 21% (18%); Other Countries 5% (2%).
Segment Sales (Profits) by Operating Division: Drinks 43% (51%); Food 42% (26%); Retailing 14% (22%); Other 1% (1%).

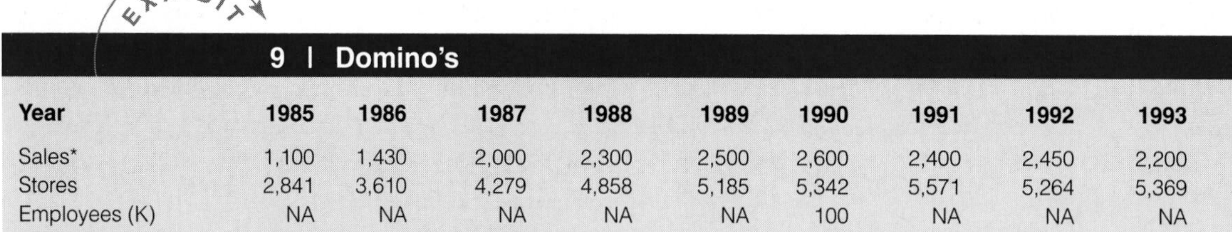

EXHIBIT 9 | Domino's

Year	1985	1986	1987	1988	1989	1990	1991	1992	1993	1994
Sales*	1,100	1,430	2,000	2,300	2,500	2,600	2,400	2,450	2,200	2,500
Stores	2,841	3,610	4,279	4,858	5,185	5,342	5,571	5,264	5,369	5,079
Employees (K)	NA	NA	NA	NA	NA	100	NA	NA	NA	115

*$M

bution contracts like Absolut vodka and Grand Marnier liqueur, as well as sluggish sales for its spirits in major markets. Burger King was not a stellar performer either, and undertook a major restructuring in 1993 to turn the tide, including reemphasis on the basic menu, cuts in prices, and reduced overhead. After quick success, BK's CEO James Adamson left his post in early 1995 to head competitor Flagstar Corporation.

Domino's Domino's Pizza was eighth in sales and seventh in stores in 1994. Sales and store unit growth had leveled off; from 1993 to 1994 sales grew 3.6 percent, and units only 1.4 percent. The privately held company registered poor performance in 1993, with a 0.6 percent sales decline from 1992. Observers suggested that resistance to menu innovations contributed to the share decline. In the early 1990s the company did add deep dish pizza and buffalo wings.

Flat company performances and expensive hobbies were hard on the owner and founder Thomas Monaghan. He attempted to sell the company in 1989 but could not find a buyer. He then replaced top management and retired from business to pursue a growing interest in religious activities. Company performance began to slide, and the founder emerged from retirement to retake the helm in the early 1990s. Through extravagant purchases of the Detroit Tigers, Frank Lloyd Wright pieces, and antique cars, Monaghan put the company on the edge of financial ruin. He sold off many of his holdings (some at a loss), reinvested the funds to stimulate the firm, and once again reorganized management.

Despite all its problems, Domino's had seen consistent growth in the international market. The company opened its first foreign store in 1983 in Canada. Primary overseas expansion areas were Eastern Europe and India. By 1994 Domino's had 5,079 stores with 823 of these in 37 major international markets. International stores brought in 17 percent of 1994 sales. Over the next 10–15 years the company had contracts for 4,000 additional international units.[25] These units would give Domino's more international than domestic units. International sales were 16.6 percent of total, and international stores were 16.5 percent of total in 1994.

Hardee's. Hardee's was number six in sales and eleven in stores for 1994. In 1981 the large diversified Canadian company Imasco purchased the chain. Imasco also owned Imperial Tobacco (Player's and du Maurier, Canada's top two sellers), Burger Chef, two drug store chains, the development company Genstar, and CT Financial.

Hardee's had pursued growth primarily in the U.S. Of all the burger chains in the top 10 franchises, Hardee's had the smallest international presence, with 72 stores generating US$63 million (1.8 percent and 2.0 percent of sales and stores, respectively) in 1994.

Hardee's sales grew by about 2 percent annually for 1993 and 1994. A failed attempt by Imasco to merge its Roy Roger's restaurants into the Hardee's chain forced the parent company to maintain both brands. Hardee's attempted to differentiate from the other burger chains by offering an upscale burger menu, which received a lukewarm reception by consumers.

International Diary Queen, Inc. Diary Queen was one of the oldest fast-food franchises in the United States: the first store was opened in Joilet, Illinois, in 1940. By 1950, there were over 1,100 stores, and by 1960 Dairy Queen had locations in 12 countries. Initial

EXHIBIT

10 | Hardee's

Year	1985	1986	1987	1988	1989	1990	1991	1992	1993	1994
Sales*	3,376	5,522	6,788	7,311	8,480	9,647	9,870	9,957	9.681	9.385
Net income*	262	184	283	314	366	205	332	380	409	506
EPS ($)	1.20	0.78	1.12	1.26	1.44	1.13	0.64	0.68	0.74	0.78
Stock Price—Close ($)	13.94	16.25	12.94	14.00	18.88	13.81	18.25	20.63	20.06	19.88
Dividends ($)	0.36	0.42	0.48	0.52	0.56	0.64	0.64	0.68	0.74	0.78
Employees (K)	na	na	na	na	190	190	180	na	200	200

*$M–all $ in Canadian; 1994: Debt ratio 38.4%; R.O.E. 16.1%; Current ratio 1.37; LTD (M) $1,927.
1994 Segment Sales (Operating Income): CT Financial Services 47% (28%); Hardees 32% (11%); Imperial Tobacco 16% (10%); Shoppers Drug Mart 2% (9%); Genstar Development 1% (2%).

EXHIBIT

11 | International Diary Queen, Inc.

Year	1985	1986	1987	1988	1989	1990	1991	1992	1993	1994
Sales*	158	182	210	254	282	287	287	296	311	341
Net income*	10	12	15	20	23	27	28	29	30	31
EPS ($)	0.33	0.42	0.51	0.70	0.83	0.97	1.05	1.12	1.79	1.30
Stock Price—Close ($)	5.20	7.75	8.00	11.50	14.75	16.58	21.00	20.00	18.00	16.25
Dividends ($)	-0-	-0-	-0-	-0-	-0-	-0-	-0-	-0-	-0-	-0-
Employees (K)	430	459	503	520	549	584	592	672	538	564

*$M; 1994: Debt ratio 15.3%; R.O.E. 24.4%; Current ratio 3.04; LTD $23M.

1994 Restaurants: U.S. 87%; Canada 9%; Other 4%; Restaurants by type: DQ's: franchised by company 62%; franchised by territorial operators 27%; foreign 3%; Orange Julius 7%; Karmelkorn 1%; Golden Skillet less than 1%; Sales by Source: Good supplies & equipment to franchises 78%; service fees 16%; franchise sales & others fees 3%; real-estate finance & rental income 3%.

franchise agreements focused on the right to use the DQ freezers, an innovation that kept ice-cream at the constant 23 degrees (F) necessary to maintain the soft consistency. In 1970 a group of investors bought the franchise organization; but the group has been only partly successful in standardizing the fast-food chain. In 1994 a group of franchisees filed an antitrust suit in an attempt to get the company to loosen its control on food supply prices and sources. DQ franchises cost $30,000 initially plus continuing payments of 4 percent of sales.

The company's menu consisted of ice cream, yogurt, and Brazier (hamburgers and other fast food) items. Menu innovations had included Blizzard (candy and other flavors mixed in the ice cream). The company had also acquired several companies, including the Golden Skillet (1981), Karmelkorn (1986) and Orange Julius (1987).

In 1994, Diary Queen ranked number seven in sales and six in stores. By that same year the company had expanded its presence into 19 countries with 628 stores and US$300 million in international sales. 1994 was an excellent year for DQ: sales were up 22.8 percent over 1993. This dramatic change (1993 scored an anemic 3.0 percent gain) was fueled by technology improvements for franchisees and international expansion. In 1992 Dairy Queen opened company-owned outlets in Austria, China, Slovenia, and Spain. DQ announced in 1995 that it had a plan to open 20 stores in Puerto Rico over a four year period.

Little Caesar's. Little Caesar's ranked 10th in sales and eighth in stores for 1994. Sales growth had slowed to a halt: a 1992–93 increase of 12.2 percent evaporated into no increase for 1993–94.

These numbers were achieved without a significant overseas presence. Of the top ten franchises, only Hardee's had a smaller number of stores in foreign lands. Little Caesar's received 3.5 percent of sales from foreign stores. Only 3.2 percent of the company's stores were in non-U.S. locations, namely, Canada, Czech and Slovak Republics, Guam, Puerto Rico, and the U.K.

McDonald's. At the top in 1994 international sales and units, McDonald's, Inc., was the most profitable retailer in the U.S. during the 1980s and into the 1990s. The company opened its first store in California in 1948, went public in 1965, and by 1994 had over 20 percent of the U.S. fast food business. McDonald's opened its first international store in Canada in 1967. Growing domestic competition in the 1980s gave impetus to the company's international expansion. By 1994 there were over 15,000 restaurants under the golden arches in 79 countries. The non-U.S. stores provided about one third of total revenues and half of the company's profits. McDonald's planned to open 1,200–1,500 new restaurants in 1995—most outside the U.S. International markets had grown into an attractive venue for the burger giant because there was "less competition, lighter market saturation, and high name recognition" in international markets.

The company's growth was fueled by aggressive franchising. In the early 1990s two thirds of the McDonald's locations were franchised units and franchisees remained with the company an average of 20 years. McDonald's used heavy advertising ($1.4B in 1994) and frequent menu changes and other innovations (1963: Filet-O-Fish sandwich and Ronald McDonald; 1968: Big Mac and first TV ads; 1972: Quarter Pounder, Egg McMuffin (breakfast); 1974: Ronald McDonald House; 1975: drive thru; 1979: Happy Meals; 1983: Chicken McNuggets; 1986: provided customers with list of products' ingredients; 1987: salads; 1980s: "value menus,"

EXHIBIT

12 | Little Caesar's

Year	1985	1986	1987	1988	1989	1990	1991	1992	1993	1994
Sales*	340	520	725	908	1,130	1,400	1,725	2,050	2,150	2,000
# of stores	900	1,000	1,820	2,000	2,700	3,173	3,650	4,300	5,609	4,700
Employees	18,000	26,160	36,400	43,600	54,000	63,460	73,000	86,000	92,000	95,000

*$M

EXHIBIT

13 | McDonald's

Year	1985	1986	1987	1988	1989	1990	1991	1992	1993	1994
Sales*	3,695	4,144	4,894	5,566	6,142	6,640	6,695	7,133	7,408	8,321
Net income*	433	480	549	656	727	802	860	959	1,083	1,224
EPS ($)	0.56	0.63	0.73	0.86	0.98	1.10	1.18	1.30	1.46	1.68
Stock price—close ($)	9.00	10.16	11.00	12.03	17.25	14.56	19.00	24.38	28.50	29.25
Dividend ($)	0.10	0.11	0.12	0.14	0.16	0.17	0.18	0.20	0.21	0.23
Employees (K)	148	159	159	169	176	174	168	166	169	183

*$M; 1994: Debt ratio 41.2%; R.O.E. 20.7%; Cash $180M; Current ratio 0.31: LTD $2.9M; Market Value: $20B

1991: McLean DeLuxe, a low-fat hamburger (not successful) and experimentation with decor and new menu items at local level; 1993: first restaurants inside another store (Wal-Mart). The company planned to open its first restaurants in India in 1996 with menus featuring chicken, fish sandwiches, and vegetable nuggets. There would be no beef items.

From 1993–1994, McDonald's grew 10.2 percent in sales and 8.7 percent in stores. Because of its extensive experience in international markets, international sales had grown to 42.5 percent of total revenues, and half its profits. Indeed, McDonald's was bigger than the 25 largest full-service chains put together.

Pepsico: KFC and Taco Bell—also includes Pizza Hut (Latter Is Not in the Top 50).

Pepsico owned powerful brand names such as Pepsi-Cola and Frito-Lay and was also the world's #1 fast-food chain, with its ownership of KFC, Taco Bell, and Pizza Hut. Pizza Hut and KFC had operations in over 60 countries while Taco Bell had operations in 11 countries.

KFC was third in sales and stores of the top 50 franchises in 1994. Active in the international arena since the late 1960s, KFC had been a major McDonald's competitor in non-U.S. markets. In 1994, the company had US$3.6 billion in sales and 4,258 stores in other countries. McDonald's had been commonly number one in each country it entered, but KFC had been number two in international sales and had the number one sales spot in Indonesia. In 1994, KFC international revenues were 50.7 percent of sales, with 45.3 percent of stores in international locations.

Taco Bell was fourth in sales and fifth in stores of the top 50 franchises in 1994. This ranking had been achieved with minimal international business to date. Taco Bell had $130 million USD sales and 162 stores internationally. The company attempted to enter the Mexican market in 1992 with a kiosk and cart strategy in Mexico City. The venture did not fare well, and Taco Bell soon pulled out of Mexico.[26] In 1994, international revenues were 3.0 percent of sales and 2.9 percent of stores were international locations.

Subway. Founded more than 29 years ago, Subway remained privately held in 1994.[27] The company had experienced explosive growth during the 1990s. It ranked ninth in sales and second in stores for 1994. Sales grew 13.6% from 1993 to 1994, and 26 percent from 1992 to 1993. Stores grew 17.1 percent from 1993 to 1994, and 15.3 percent from 1992 to 1993. In 1994, Subway overtook KFC as the number two chain in number of stores behind McDonald's. The company attributed its growth at least partially to an exceptionally low-priced and well-structured franchise program. In addition, store sizes of 500–1500 square feet were small. Thus, the investment for a Subway franchise was modest.

The company's growth involved a deliberate strategy. The formula involved no cooking on site, except for the baking of bread. The company promoted the "efficiency and simplicity" of its franchise and advertised its food as "healthy, delicious, (and) fast.[27] The company advertised regularly on TV with a $25M budget and planned to increase that significantly. All stores contributed 2.5 percent of gross sales to the corporate ad-

EXHIBIT 14 | PepsiCo: KFC and Taco Bell (plus Pizza Hut)

Year	1985	1986	1987	1988	1989	1990	1991	1992	1993	1994
Sales*	8,057	9,291	11,485	13,007	15,242	17,803	19,608	21,970	25,021	28,474
Net income*	544	458	595	762	901	1,077	1,080	1,302	1,588	1,784
EPS ($)	0.65	0.58	0.76	0.97	1.13	1.35	1.35	1.61	1.96	2.22
Stock price—close ($)	8.06	8.66	11.11	13.15	21.31	26.00	22.88	3.40	40.88	36.25
Div./share ($)	0.15	0.21	0.22	0.25	0.31	0.37	0.44	0.50	0.58	0.68
Employees (K)	150	214	225	235	266	308	338	372	423	471

*$M; 1994: Debt ratio 48.1%; R.O.E. 27.)%; cash (M) $1,488; Current ratio 0.96; LTD (M) $8,841
1994 Segment Sales (Operating Income): Restaurants 37% (22%); Beverages 34% (37%); Snack foods 29% (41%)

vertising budget. Subway's goal was to equal or exceed the number of outlets operated by the largest fast food company in every market that it entered. In most cases the firm's benchmark was burger giant McDonald's.

International markets played an emerging role in Subway's expansion. In 1994, international sales were 10.6 percent of sales, compared to 8.9 percent the previous year. International stores were 9.5 percent of total in 1994, and 7.5 percent in 1993. Subway boasted a total of 9,893 stores in all 50 states and 19 countries.[28]

Wendy's. Wendy's was number five in sales and number nine in stores for 1994. In 1994, after 25 years of operation, Wendy's had grown to 4,411 stores. This growth had been almost exclusively domestic until 1979, when Wendy's ventured out of the U.S. and Canada to open its first outlets in Puerto Rico, Switzerland, and West Germany. Wendy's granted J.C. Penney the franchise rights to France, Belgium, and Holland, and had one store opened in Belgium by 1980.

Wendy's still saw opportunities for growth in the U.S. Industry surveys had consistently ranked Wendy's burgers number one in quality, but poor in convenience (Wendy's had one store for every 65,000 people while McDonald's, in contrast, had one for every 25,000). Growth was driven primarily by franchising. In 1994 71 percent of the stores were operated by franchises and 29 percent by the company. Company restaurants provided 90 percent of total sales while franchise fees provided 8 percent. The company had made menu and strategic changes at various points in its history. For example in 1977 the company first began TV advertising; 1979 introduced its salad bar; 1985 experimented with breakfast; 1986 and 1987 introduced Big Classic and SuperBar buffet (neither very successful); 1990 introduced the grilled chicken sandwich and 99 cent Super Value Menu items; and 1992 introduced packaged salads.

Wendy's planned to add about 150 restaurants each year in foreign markets. With a presence of 236 stores in 33 countries in 1994, international was 9.1 percent of sales and 9.4 percent of stores in 1994.

APPENDIX B: COUNTRY SUMMARIES[29]

Canada

In the 1990s Canada was considered an ideal first stop for U.S. business seeking to begin exporting. Per capita output, patterns of production, market economy, and business practices were similar to the U.S. U.S. goods and services were well received in Canada: 70 percent of all Canadian imports were from the United States. Canada's market conditions were stable, and U.S. companies continued to see Canada as an attractive option for expansion.

Canada had one of the highest real growth rates among the OECD during the 1980s, averaging about 3.2 percent. The Canadian economy softened during the 1990s, but Canadian imports of U.S. goods and services were expected to increase about 5 percent in fiscal year 1996.

Although Canada sometimes mirrored the U.S.,

EXHIBIT 15 | Wendy's

Year	1985	1986	1987	1988	1989	1990	1991	1992	1993	1994
Sales*	1,126	1,140	1,059	1,063	1,070	1,011	1,060	1,239	1,320	1,398
Net income*	76	(5)	4	29	24	39	52	65	79	97
EPS ($)	0.82	(0.05)	0.04	0.30	0.25	0.40	0.52	0.63	0.76	0.91
Stock price—close ($)	13.41	10.25	5.63	5.75	4.63	6.25	9.88	12.63	17.38	14.38
Div./share ($)	0.17	0.21	0.24	0.24	0.24	0.24	0.24	0.24	0.24	0.24
Employees (K)	40	40	45	42	39	35	39	42	43	44

*$M; 1994: Debt ratio 36.6%; R.O.E. 5.2%; Current ratio 0.98; LTD(M) $145.

there are significant cultural and linguistic differences from the U.S. and between the regional markets in Canada. These differences were evident in the mounting friction between the English- and French-speaking areas of Canada. The conflict had potential for splitting of territory between the factions, slicing Canada into two separate countries. The prospect of this outcome left foreign investors tense.

Germany

In the mid-1990s Germany was the largest economy in Europe, and the fifth largest overall importer of U.S. goods and services. Since reunification in 1990, the eastern part of Germany had continued to receive extensive infusions of aid from western Germany, and these funds were only just beginning to show an impact. The highly urbanized and skilled Western German population enjoyed a very high standard of living with abundant leisure time. In 1994, Germany emerged from a recession, and scored a GDP of US$2 trillion.

A unique feature of Germany was the unusually even distribution of both industry and population—there was no single business center for the country. This was a challenge for U.S. firms. They had to establish distribution networks that adequately covered all areas of the country. In Germany there was little opportunity for regional concentration around major population centers as in the United States.

The country was a good market for innovative high tech goods and high quality food products. Germans expected high quality goods, and would reject a less expensive product if quality and support were not in abundance. Strongest competition for U.S. firms were the German domestic firms, not only because of their home-grown familiarity of the market, but also because of the consumers' widely held perception that German products were "simply the best."

A recurring complaint from Germans was the prevalent "here today, gone tomorrow" business approach of American firms. Germans viewed business as a long term commitment to support growth in markets, and did not always receive the level and length of attention necessary from U.S. companies to satisfy them.

Conditions in the area of former East Germany were not the doomsday picture often painted, nor were they as rosy as the German government depicts. It would take 10–15 years for the eastern region of the country to catch up to the western region in terms of per capita income, standard of living, and productivity.

Japan

Japan had the second largest economy in the world. Overall economic growth in Japan over the past 35 years had been incredible: 10 percent average annual growth during the 1960s, 5 percent in the 1970s and 80s. Growth ground to a halt during the 1990s due to tight fiscal policy. The government tightened fiscal constraints in order to correct the significant devaluation of the real estate markets. The economy posted a 0.6 percent growth in 1994 largely due to consumer demand. The overall economic outlook remained cloudy, but the outlook for exports to Japan remained positive.

Japan was a highly homogeneous society with business practices characterized by long-standing close relationships among individuals and firms. It took time for Japanese businessmen to develop relationships and for non-Japanese business people the task of relationship building in Japan was formidable. It was well known that Japan's market was not as open as the United States but the U.S. government had mounted multi-faceted efforts to help U.S. business people to "open doors." While these efforts were helpful, most of the responsibility in opening the Japanese market to U.S. goods or services remained with the individual firm. Entering Japan was expensive and generally required four things: 1) financial and management capabilities and a Japanese-speaking staff residing within the country, 2) modification of products to suit Japanese consumers, 3) a long term approach to maximizing market share and achieving reasonable profit levels, and 4) careful monitoring of Japanese demand, distribution, competitors, and government. Despite the challenges of market entry, Japan ranked as the second largest importer of U.S. goods and services.

Historically Japanese consumers were conservative and brand conscious, although the recession during the '90s nurtured opportunities for "value" entrants. Traditional conformist buying patterns were still prominent, but more individualistic habits were developing in the younger Japanese aged 18–21. This age cohort had a population of 8 million people, and boasted a disposable income of more than US$35 billion.

Japanese consumers were willing to pay a high price for quality goods. However, they had a well-earned reputation for having unusually high expectations for quality. U.S. firms with high quality, competitive products had to be able to undertake the high cost of initial market entry. For those that were willing, Japan could provide respectable market share and attractive profit levels.

Mexico

Mexico had experienced a dramatic increase in imports from the United States since the late 1980s. During 1994 the country experienced 20 percent growth over 1993. In 1994, Mexico's peso experienced a massive devaluation brought on by investor anxiety and capital flight. Although the Mexican government implemented tight fiscal measures to stabilize the peso, their efforts could not stop the country from plunging into a serious recession.

Inflation rose as a result of the austerity policies and it was expected to be between 42 and 54 percent in 1995. Negative economic growth was anticipated in 1995 as well. The U.S. financial assistance package (primarily loans) provided Mexico with nearly US$50 billion and restored stability to the financial markets by mid-1995. The government was taking measures to improve the country's infrastructure. Mexico's problems mask that its government had, on the whole, practiced sound economic fundamentals.

Mexico was still committed to political reform despite the current economic challenges. After ruling the government uninterrupted for 60 years, the PRI party had begun to lose some seats to other political parties. Mexico was slowly evolving into a multi-party democracy.

Despite the economic misfortunes of recent years, Mexico remained the United States' third largest trading partner. Mexico still held opportunities for U.S. firms able to compete in the price-sensitive recessionary market. Mexico had not wavered on the NAFTA agreement since its ratification and in the mid-1990s 60 percent of U.S. exports to Mexico entered duty free.

South Korea

South Korea had been identified as one of the U.S. Department of Commerce's 10 "Big Emerging Markets." The country's economy overcame tremendous obstacles after the Korean War in the 1950s left the country in ruins. The driving force behind South Korea's growth was export-led development and energetic emphasis on Entrepreneurship. Annual real GDP growth from 1986–1991 was over 10 percent. This blistering pace created inflation, tight labor markets, and a rising current account deficit. Fiscal policy in 1992 focused on curbing inflation and reducing the deficit. Annual growth, reduced to a still enviable 5 percent in '92, rose to 6.3 percent in 1993. Fueled by exports, 1994's growth was a heady 8.3 percent. S. Korea's GDP was larger than that of Russia, Australia, or Mexico.

The American media had highlighted such issues as student demonstrations, construction accidents, and the North Korean nuclear problem and trade disputes. Investors needed to closely monitor developments related to North Korea. However, the political landscape in S. Korea had been stable enough over the 1980s to fuel tremendous economic expansion. The country was undertaking significant infrastructure improvements. Overall, S. Korea was a democratic republic with an open society and a free press. It was a modern, cosmopolitan, fast-paced and dynamic country with abundant business opportunities for savvy American businesses.

There had been staggering development of U.S. exports to S. Korea: US$21.6 billion in 1994 and over US$30 billion expected in 1995. While S. Korea was 22 times smaller than China in terms of population, it imported two times more U.S. goods and services than China in 1994!

Although S. Korea ranked as the United State's sixth largest export market, obstacles for U.S. firms still remained. Despite participation in the Uruguay Round of GATT and related trade agreements, customs clearance procedures and regulations for labeling, sanitary standards, and quarantine often served as significant non-tariff barriers.

The United Kingdom (or Great Britain)

The United Kingdom (UK) was the United States' fourth largest trading partner and the largest market for U.S. exports in Europe. Common language, legal heritage, and business practices facilitated U.S. entry into the British market.

The UK had made significant changes to its taxation, regulation, and privatization policies that changed the structure of the British economy and increased its overall efficiency. The reward for this disciplined economic approach had been sustained, modest growth during the 1980s and early 1990s. GDP grew 4.2 percent in 1994, the highest level in six years. The UK trimmed its deficit from US$75 billion in fiscal 1994 to $50 billion in fiscal 1995.

The UK had no restrictions on foreign ownership and movement of capital. There was a high degree of labor flexibility. Efficiencies had soared in the UK and in the mid-1990s the country boasted the lowest real per unit labor cost of the Group of Seven (G7) industrialized countries.

The UK's shared cultural heritage and warm relationship with the United States translated into the British finding U.S. goods and services as attractive purchases. These reasons, coupled with British policy emphasizing free enterprise and open competition, made the UK the destination of 40 percent of all U.S. investment in the EU.

The U.K. market was based on a commitment to the principles of free enterprise and open competition. Demand for U.S. goods and services was growing. The abolition of many internal trade barriers within the European Common market enabled European-based firms to operate relatively freely. As a result, U.S. companies used the UK as a gateway to the rest of the EU. Of the top 500 British companies, one in eight was a U.S. affiliate. Excellent physical and communications infrastructure combined with a friendly political and commercial climate were expected to keep the UK as a primary target for U.S. firms for years to come.

ENDNOTES

1. All three Outback founders credited casual dining chain legend and mentor Norman Brinker with his strong mentoring role in their careers. Brinker played a key role in all of the restaurant chains Sullivan and Basham were associated with prior to Outback.
2. American consumption of meat declined from the mid-1970s to the early 1990s primarily as a result of health concerns about red meat. In 1976 Americans consumed 131.6 pounds of beef and veal, 58.7 pounds of pork, and 12.9 pounds of fish. In 1990 the figures had declined to 64.9 pounds of beef and veal, 46.3 pounds of pork, and 15.5 pounds of fish. The dramatic decrease was attributed to consumer attitudes toward a low fat, healthier diet. Menu items that gained in popularity were premium baked goods, coffees, vegetarian menu items, fruits, salsa, sauces, chicken dishes, salad bars, and spicy dishes. [George Thomas Kurian, *Datapedia of the United States* 1790–2000 (Maryland: Bernan Press, 1994) p. 113.]
3. Outback's original Henderson Blvd. (Tampa, Florida) Restaurant was one of the few open for lunch. By 1995 the chain had also begun to open in some locations for Sunday lunch or for special occasions such as Mother's Day lunch.
4. Outback's signature trademark was its best-selling "Aussie-Tizer," the "Bloomin' Onion." The company expected to serve nine million "Bloomin' Onions" in 1995.
5. Merritt had worked as CFO for another company which had come to the financial markets with its IPO (initial public offering).
6. Outback did not grant exclusive territorial franchises. Thus, if an Outback franchisee did not perform the company could bring additional franchisees into the area. Through 1994 Outback had not had territorial disputes between franchises.
7. PepsiCo owned Kentucky Fried Chicken, Taco Bell, and Pizza Hut.
8. Grand Met owned Burger King.
9. Ref. AME 76 (KR).
10. "Industry and Trade Summary: Franchising," U.S. International Trade Commission, Washington, DC, 1995, pp. 15–16.
11. "World Hunger," Restaurant Hospitality, November 1994, p. 97.
12. *International Business Environments and Operations*, seventh edition, 1995, pp. 117–119.
13. U.S. restaurant chains tackle challenges of Asian expansion," Nation's Restaurant News, February 14, 1994, p. 36.
14. *CIA World Factbook*, India, 1995.
15. "Big McMuttons," Forbes, July 17, 1995, p. 18.
16. Interview with Cheryl Babcock, Professor, University of St. Thomas, October 23, 1995.
17. "Franchise management in East Asia," *Academy of Management Executive*, Vol. 4, No. 2, 1990, p. 79.
18. "U.S. operators flock to Latin America," *Nation's Restaurant News*, October 17, 1994, p. 47.
19. Interview with Cheryl Babcock, Professor, University of St. Thomas, October 23, 1995.
20. "U.S. restaurant chains tackle challenges of Asian expansion," *Nation's Restaurant News*, February 14, 1994, p. 36.
21. "Industry and Trade Summary: Franchising," U.S. International Trade Commission, Washington, DC, 1995, p. 30.
22. Ibid.
23. "U.S. restaurant chains tackle challenges of Asian expansion," *Nation's Restaurant News*, February 14, 1994, p. 36.
24. Unless otherwise noted, the information from this appendix was drawn from "Top 50 Franchisers," *Restaurant Business*, November 1, 1995, pp. 35–41, and Hoover's Company Profile

Database, 1996, The Reference Press, Inc., Austin, TX (from American Online Service), various company listings.

25. "Big News Over There!", *Restaurants and Institutions,* July 1, 1994.
26. "US Operators Flock to Latin America," *Nation's Restaurant News,* November 17, 1994.
27. There is, thus, no publicly available financial data on Subway.
28. Subway's site on the Internet, accessed March 24, 1996.
29. Note: The material in this appendix is adapted from the Department of Commerce Country Commercial Guides and the CIA World Fact Book.

CASE 32

Philip Morris

Rhonda Fronk
Bill Pilgrim
Bill Prosser
Regan Urquhart
Monte Wiltse
University of Oklahoma

INTRODUCTION

After the second quarter of 1998, Philip Morris Chairman and Chief Executive Officer Geoffrey C. Bible could look back upon both positive and negative occurrences within the tobacco industry that had an impact on his company during the first half of the year. In its favor, the industry avoided comprehensive federal tobacco legislation in 1998. Such legislation was avoided primarily for two reasons. First, an advertising campaign linking the legislation to tax increases for government spending, which spurred conservative opposition to the proposed legislation. Second, the president was involved in an investigation regarding possible felony violations. The investigation forced the president to focus his energies on events other than the tobacco legislation.

Philip Morris, however, was still concerned with the continued prospect of future federal legislation that might have a severe impact upon the profitability of the firm's domestic operations. Additionally, there were significant and numerous legal actions being taken against Philip Morris by parties claiming damages caused by tobacco products. On the operations side, the company had seen a decline of almost six percent in cigarette shipments in the second quarter due in part to price increases and consumer promotions.[1]

Given this background, there are a number of ethical, legal, and operational issues facing Philip Morris. As the health risks associated with the use of tobacco have become more evident, public sentiment against tobacco companies is becoming increasingly negative. Many feel that the companies have a responsibility to eliminate nicotine from their products and to discontinue marketing to minors. Others claim that management's only responsibility is to shareholders and not to the public at large. How can Philip Morris continue its success in the midst of pending and threatened litigation and negative public sentiment both in the United States and abroad?

This case begins with an overview of the tobacco industry and a brief history of Philip Morris Company to provide background for the current legal situation. The case will also discuss current Philip Morris competitors such as B.A.T. Industries PLC and Gallaher Group PLC. Philip Morris business units will be discussed and their financial performance will be addressed. Once the current competitive and internal situations are described, the case will end with a discussion of the legal issues facing Philip Morris and a summary of the future strategic issues the company will face.

OVERVIEW OF THE TOBACCO INDUSTRY

The Mayan people first introduced tobacco to Native North Americans in the 15th century. Tobacco use quickly spread throughout Europe and Russia, and by the 17th century it had reached China, Japan, and the western coast of Africa.[2] Early proponents claimed medicinal properties could be found in tobacco.

Tobacco fields were found in Colonial America as early as 1615. Tobacco quickly became the staple crop

This case was prepared under the direction of Professor Robert E. Hoskisson. The case is intended to be used as the basis for class discussion rather than to illustrate either effective or ineffective handling of an administrative situation.

and principal currency in the colony of Jamestown. After 1776, the tobacco business spread to North Carolina and as far west as Missouri. By the late 1880s, the United States was the second largest tobacco producer after China and was responsible for about 9 percent of world production.[3]

About 50 million people in the United States currently smoke a total of 570 billion cigarettes each year.[4] For the first part of the 20th century, society's general attitude was that smoking relieved tensions and produced no ill effects. As recently as the 1940s, smoking was considered harmless, but laboratory and clinical research have proven that smoking can be harmful.[5]

Because of a dramatically noticeable rise in previously rare lung cancer, the American Cancer Society and other organizations began studies comparing death among smokers and nonsmokers over a period of several years. All such studies found increased mortality among smokers. As a result of this information, the government became involved in the early 1960s and ongoing reports and warnings have been issued since that time. All cigarette advertising was banned from radio and television starting in 1971.[6] Research suggests that smokers crave the effect of nicotine. In a 1988 report, the Surgeon General declared nicotine to be an addictive drug comparable to other addictive substances in its ability to induce dependence.[7] A 1989 report stated that smoking definitely did cause cancer and therefore warranted substantial investigation.[8]

Medical studies have established that the overall mortality rate is twice as high among middle-aged men who smoke as among those who do not. The American Cancer Society estimated that cigarettes are responsible for 30 percent of all U.S. cancer mortality. Cigarette smoke is also estimated to be responsible for 83 percent of all lung cancer mortality in the United States. Lung cancer is seven times as likely to strike a smoker as a nonsmoker. Smoking can also be tied to a number of other forms of cancer and disease, such as strokes and emphysema. While this information, combined with awareness campaigns, has reduced the number of male smokers, there has been a rise in female and teenage smokers despite the Surgeon General's reports.

Cigarette consumption, which accounts for most tobacco use in the United States, dropped slightly after 1964, when a special report to the U.S. Surgeon General linked cigarette smoking with lung cancer, coronary artery disease, and other ailments. Since 1987, U.S. cigarette consumption has been slipping by about 2 percent per year (also see Exhibit 1).[9] This has resulted in two

EXHIBIT 1 | Tobacco Products—U.S. Per-Capita Consumption

	Units		Pounds			
Year	Cigarettes	Large Cigars and Cigarillos#	Smoking Tobacco#	Chewing Tobacco#	Snuff*	Total Tobacco Products*
1996P	2482	32.7	0.1	0.6	0.31	4.70
1995R	2505	27.5	0.1	0.7	0.31	4.70
1994R	2524	25.3	0.2	0.7	0.32	4.90
1993R	2543	23.4	0.2	0.7	0.30	5.37
1992	2641	24.5	0.2	0.8	0.29	5.30
1991	2720	25.1	0.2	0.8	0.28	5.54
1990	2826	26.4	0.2	0.8	0.28	5.62
1989	2926	27.9	0.2	0.8	0.27	5.68
1988	3096	29.1	0.3	0.9	0.26	6.11
1987	3197	31.7	0.3	0.9	0.25	6.30

Source of Information: Department of Agriculture.
Source: Standard and Poor's, 1997, Alcoholic Beverages and Tobacco, *Standard and Poor's Industry Survey*, September 11, 12.
*Consumption per capita, 18 years and over.
#Consumption per male, 18 years and over.
PPreliminary.
RRevised.

major industry strategies: diversify at home and pursue international business. According to Robert Miles, author of *Coffin Nails and Corporate Strategies*, diversification was the most substantial strategy implemented by the tobacco companies in response to the decreasing consumption.[10] The companies pursuing international business found the formerly communist regions of Eastern Europe and China to be ideal markets for American cigarette makers. Also, tobacco consumption is rising rapidly in developing countries, where tobacco use is projected to increase 2.8 percent annually. This is supported by a 1974 to 1987 U.S. tobacco export increase from $650 million to $3.4 billion.[11]

The U.S. tobacco industry is highly profitable. It is estimated that one in four Americans smoke, and the average smoker spends $260 per year on tobacco products.[12] Leaders in the market maintain a monopolistic position because of extremely difficult barriers to entry. Tobacco companies also enjoy almost no capital, research, or advertising costs. The product sells as is, leaving no incentive for change. The demand for the product has driven itself, resulting in minimal advertising requirements. Social consciousness alone has greatly reduced the industry's advertising budgets.

BRIEF HISTORY OF PHILIP MORRIS

In 1847, Philip Morris opened a tobacco shop in London. It was in this London shop that he began making cigarettes. After Morris's death before the turn of the century, the company was sold to William Thomson. Mr. Thomson introduced cigarettes to the United States in 1902.

During this same period the American Tobacco Trust controlled 92 percent of the world's tobacco.[13] A 1911 U.S. Supreme Court decision broke the trust into four separate companies. Those companies would become American Tobacco (now B.A.T. Industries), R. J. Reynolds, Loews' Lorillard unit, and Liggett & Meyers (now Brooke Group subsidiary Liggett Group).

In 1919, American investors purchased Philip Morris and U.S. production began in 1929. Shortly thereafter, the original companies of the American Tobacco Trust began to raise their prices. Philip Morris successfully took advantage of this situation by offering its product at a lower price.

Philip Morris's success can be attributed to its expertise in sales and marketing. The company's early growth was tied to its close alliances with tobacco wholesalers and retailers along the East Coast. As the market evolved, Philip Morris became more dependent on its advertising campaigns. Early on, Philip Morris was promoted as a milder cigarette. Later the company claimed that its English blend did not cause something referred to as "cigarette hangover."[14] The company's 1955 introduction of the "Marlboro man" enabled it to capitalize on the American cowboy image.

Today Philip Morris is the world's largest cigarette maker. The company leads the cigarette industry in market share, followed by RJR Nabisco and B.A.T. subsidiary, Brown & Williamson. Marlboros account for about a third of all U.S. sales. At the same time, the company gets almost half of its revenues (but only one-third of its profits) from food and beer subsidiaries that include Kraft and Miller Brewing Company. Miller is ranked number two among U.S. beer makers after Anheuser-Busch (see Exhibit 2). The company also operates a financial service and operated a real estate investment division until its sale in 1997.

OVERVIEW OF COMPETITORS

The following overview provides a description of each of Philip Morris's major competitors. Ultimately, this will provide a background to discuss how individual firms might respond to the legal threat considered later.

B.A.T. Industries PLC

B.A.T. Industries PLC is the world's second largest tobacco company. It owns both Brown & Williamson (the third largest tobacco company in the United States) and British-American Tobacco. B.A.T. controlled 16 percent of the U.S. cigarette market share in 1997.[15] It is planning to spin off the tobacco portion of its business in September or October. In 1997, sales by segment were as follows: tobacco, 71 percent (53 percent operating profit); insurance, 29 percent (47 percent operating profit).[16] BAT owns 40 percent of Imasco, which is a Canadian business centered around tobacco and banking. The company has 164,000 employees.[17] Return on equity for the five years including 1993–1997 has ranged from 25.2 to 30.0 percent.[18] Its major tobacco

2 | Philip Morris Products

Tobacco

Marlboro
Benson & Hedges
Virginia Slims
Merit
Parliament
Cambridge
Basic
*Selected International Brands**
Bond Street
Caro
Chesterfield
Diana
f6
Klubowe
Lark
L&M
Longbeach
Multifilter
Muratti
Next
Peter Jackson
Petra
Philip Morris

Food

Grocery Aisles

Beverages

Coffee
- Maxwell House
- Sanka
- Yuban
- General Foods International Coffees
- Maxim

Soft Drinks
- Country Time
- Crystal Light
- Kool-Aid
- Tang
- Capri Sun

Post Cereals
- Alpha-Bits
- Banana Nut Crunch
- Blueberry Morning
- Cranberry Almond Crunch
- Frosted Shredded Wheat
- Fruit & Fiber
- Grape-Nuts
- Great Grains
- Honey Bunches of Oats
- Honeycomb
- Honey Nut Shredded Wheat
- Natural Bran Flakes
- Pebbles
- Raisin Bran
- Shredded Wheat
- Shredded Wheat 'n Bran
- Spoon Size Shredded Wheat
- Toasties
- Waffle Crisp
- 100% Bran

Condiments & Sauces
- Kraft mayonnaise
- Kraft barbecue sauces
- Miracle Whip
- Bull's-Eye barbecue and grilling sauces
- Sauceworks cocktail, horseradish, sweet 'n sour and tarter sauces

Confectioneries
- Altoid's mints
- Callard & Browser toffees
- La Vosgienne
- Toblerone and Tobler chocolates

Dry Desserts
- D-Zerta
- Jell-O
- Minute brand tapioca

Dry Grocery
- Baker's chocolate and coconut
- Calumet baking powder
- Oven Fry coatings
- Shake 'N Bake
- Sure-Jell and Certo pectins

Ethnic Foods
- Taco Bell dinner kits, salsa and meal components

Meals/Side Dishes
- Kraft macaroni & cheese
- Minute rice
- Stove Top
- Velveeta shells & cheese

Salad Dressings
- Good Seasons mixes
- Kraft
- Seven Seas

Snacks
- Handi-Snacks

Toppings
- Dream Whip whipped topping mix
- Kraft dessert toppings

Refrigerated Case

Cheese

Parmesan/Romano
- Kraft
- Kraft Free
- Di Giorno

Natural
- Cracker Barrel
- Harvest Moon

Processed American Cheese
- Kraft Deluxe
- Kraft Singles
- Kraft Super Slice
- Kraft Cheez Whiz
- Light n' Lively
- Old English
- Velveeta

Cream Cheese
- Philadelphia
- Philly Flavors
- Temp-Tee

Other Cheeses
- Althenos
- Chumy
- Di Giorno
- Hoffman
- Polly-O

Dairy Products
- Breakstone's sour cream and cottage cheese
- Breyer's yogurt
- Jell-O yogurt
- Knudsen sour cream and cottage cheese
- Light n' Lively low-fat cottage cheese, yogurt
- Sealtest cottage cheese, dips, and sour cream

Desserts
- Ready-to-eat Jell-O

Fresh Pasta & Sauces
- Di Giorno

Processed Meats
- Oscar Mayer hot dogs, cold cuts and bacon
- Oscar Mayer Lunchables
- Louis Rich turkey products (hot dogs, cold cuts and bacon).
- Louis Rich Carving Board sliced meats

Pickles & Sauerkraut
- Claussen

Freezer Case

Desserts
- Cool Whip

Pizza
- Di Giorno
- Jack's
- Tombstone

*Selected International Brands**

Cheese
- Dairylea
- El Caserio
- Eden
- Invernizzi
- Philadelphia
- Sottilette
- P'tit Quebec

Coffee
- Blendy
- Carte Noire
- Gevalia
- Grand' Mere
- Kaffee HAG
- Jacobs Kronung
- Jacobs Monarch
- Jacques Vabre
- Kenco
- Maxim
- Nabob
- Saimaza
- Splendid

Confectioneries
- Aladdin
- Africana
- Cote d'Or
- Daim
- Figaro
- Freia
- Hollywood
- Korona
- Marabou
- Milka
- Peanott
- Poiana
- Prince Polo
- Suchard
- Sugus
- Terry's of York
- Toblerone

Other
- Estrella snacks
- Frisco beverages
- Kraft ketchup, peanut butter
- Magic Moments
- Miracle Whip
- Miracoli
- Simmenthal
- Vegemite

2 | Philip Morris Products (Continued)

Beer				
Miller Lite	Miller High Life	Best	Molson	non-alcohol
Miller Lite Ice	Miller Beer	Meister Brau	Foster's	brew
Miller Genuine	Red Dog	Leinenkugel's	Asahi	Magnum
Draft	Icehouse	Celis	Presidente	malt liquor
Miller Genuine	Lowenbrau	Shipyard	Sharp's	
Draft Light	Milwaukee's			

Source: Philip Morris Annual Report inside back cover.
*Not generally available in the U.S. as Philip Morris products.

brands are GPC Approved, Kool, and Lucky Strike. The Chief Executive Officer (CEO) is Martin Broughton and the company is headquartered in London, England. Stocks are traded on the American Stock Exchange (ASE) under the symbol BTI.

Gallaher Group PLC

Gallaher Group PLC is the largest manufacturer of tobacco products in the United Kingdom (U.K.), with 39.6 percent of the market in 1997.[19] In 1997, sales by region were as follows: U.K., 87 percent (84 percent operating profit); outside U.K., 13 percent (16 percent operating profit).[20] The company currently has about 3,600 employees.[21] Its major tobacco brands are Silk Cut, Berkeley, Mayfair, Sovereign, and Sobraine. Gallaher's lower priced offerings, Mayfair and Sovereign, are selling well mostly because consumers faced with higher prices due to increased taxation are switching to less expensive brands. The CEO is Peter Wilson and the company is headquartered in the U.K. Stocks are traded on the New York Stock Exchange (NYSE) under the symbol GLH.

Imasco Ltd.

Imasco Ltd. is the dominant company in the Canadian cigarette industry with almost 65 percent of the Canadian market.[22] Tobacco accounts for more than 50 percent of the company's operating profit.[23] Return on equity for the five years including 1993–1997 ran between 13.7 and 17.3 percent.[24] The company's major tobacco brands are the Players and du Maurier. These brands continue to do well even with the virtual ban on tobacco advertising in Canada, which confirms an industry belief that advertising restrictions "freeze" market positions. Restrictions make it harder for smaller rivals or new entrants to persuade consumers to switch brands. The CEO is Brian Levitt and the company is headquartered in Montreal, Canada.

RJR Nabisco Holdings Corporation

RJR Nabisco, formerly R. J. Reynolds, is the second largest U.S. producer of cigarettes with about 25 percent of the market.[25] The company has major positions in both the food and tobacco industries. Food products include Oreo, Chips Ahoy!, Ritz, Wheat Thins, Cream of Wheat, and LifeSavers. The company has approximately 80,000 employees.[26] Return on equity for the four years including 1994–1997 ran between 7.0 and 9.5 percent.[27] Its major tobacco brands include Winston, Salem, Camel, Doral, and Vantage & More. RJR is test marketing a new tobacco brand named Eclipse in several markets in the United States. Eclipse—which primarily heats tobacco rather than burning it—reduces second-hand smoke by 80 percent and leaves practically no ash, stains, or lingering odor.[28] The CEO is Steven Goldstone and the company is headquartered in New York City. Stocks are traded on the NYSE under the symbol RN.

Loews Corporation

Loews is a diversified investment company. Its primary business segments are a multiline insurance company (85 percent of 1997 revenues, 81 percent operating profit)[29] and tobacco segment (12 percent of 1997 revenues, 29 percent operating profit).[30] In 1997, Loews held around 8 percent of the U.S. cigarette market.[31] The company employs approximately 35,000 people.[32] Return on equity for the five years including 1993–1997 ran between 5.0 and 21.4 percent.[33] The company's major tobacco brands include Newport, Kent, and True. The CEO is L. A. Tisch and the company is headquartered in New York City. Stocks are traded on the NYSE under the symbol LTR.

UST Inc.

UST Inc. is the leading U.S. producer of smokeless tobacco with approximately a 75 percent share of the moist smokeless segment.[34] Smokeless tobacco products accounted for 86 percent of sales as well as 97 percent of the company's profits.[35] The company has approximately 4,500 employees.[36] Return on equity for the five years including 1993–1997 ran between 74.9 and 164.5 percent.[37] Its major brands include Copenhagen, Skoal, Borkum Riff, and Don Tomas pipe tobacco. The company has been able to price its products at a premium to the market. It is now beginning to face serious competition from discounters that can deliver similar products for about one-half the price UST is charging. UST is reluctant to compete in the discount market for fear of cannibalizing sales from their premium brands. UST has started a promotional initiative that puts a "made date" on cans of Copenhagen that indicates the freshness of the product to the consumer. This has led to an increase in the number of cans being returned. The CEO is Vincent Gierer, Jr., and the company is headquartered in Greenwich, Connecticut. Stocks are traded on the NYSE under the symbol UST.

Universal Corporation

Universal Corporation, formerly known as Universal Leaf Tobacco, is the largest leaf tobacco exporter/importer in the world. It purchases, processes, and sells tobacco to manufacturers. Because many of the other competitors are vertically integrated, Universal is a direct competitor in supply and otherwise indirectly affects competition. The company has approximately 25,000 employees.[38] Return on equity for the five years including 1993–1997 was between 9.3 and 21.5 percent.[39] The CEO is A. B. King and the company is headquartered in Richmond, Virginia. Stocks are traded on the NYSE under the symbol UVV.

PHILIP MORRIS'S BUSINESS UNITS

Philip Morris understood the need to diversify long before the introduction of the current formal tobacco litigation. Philip Morris and R. J. Reynolds were among the first to begin a serious program of diversification only a few years after the 1964 Surgeon General's Report.[40] Major acquisitions began in 1969 with the purchase of Miller Brewing Co. and continued through the late 1980s with the acquisition of Kraft Foods. After the 1985 acquisition of General Foods, former Philip Morris CEO Hamish Maxwell said, "We wanted to lessen our dependence on cigarettes as our earnings source, and to spur growth."[41] By making several major diversification efforts, Philip Morris was able to invest a portion of its cash and diversify the risk of what it perceived to be an inevitable tobacco liability. The resulting family of products created by these acquisitions is delineated in Exhibit 2.

Tobacco

Philip Morris USA (PMUSA) holds the nation's largest market share in retail tobacco sales with 51.0 percent. According to *The Maxwell Consumer Report* issued by Wheat, First Securities, Inc., Philip Morris USA has been the leading cigarette company in the United States market since 1983.[42] This claim is founded upon the strength of the brand name of its leading cigarette, Marlboro. Marlboro itself holds 35.2 percent market share in domestic sales.[43] Other Philip Morris tobacco brand names include Basic, Merit, Benson & Hedges, Parliament, and Virginia Slims. In 1997, domestic tobacco provided 38 percent of domestic operating revenue, while providing for 47 percent of domestic operating income. Operating income margins were 24 percent in 1997, down significantly from 33 percent in 1996.

Philip Morris International (PMI) has a cigarette market share of at least 15 percent in more than 40 markets, including Argentina, Australia, Belgium, the Canary Islands, the Czech Republic, Finland, France, Germany, Hong Kong, Italy, Japan, the Netherlands, the Philippines, Poland, Singapore, Spain, Switzerland, and Turkey.[44] Marlboro is the largest selling brand internationally as well, with 6 percent of the world market. Philip Morris maintains brands internationally that include Bond Street, Parliament, L&M, and Chesterfield.

PMI utilizes a practice of expanding into new international markets by acquiring existing local brands.[45] This practice has recently been used in Poland, Portugal, and Mexico. PMI operating revenues are much more dependent upon tobacco, with 70 percent of operating revenues coming from tobacco sales, but it has much lower profitability than its domestic counterpart, with only a 17 percent operating income margin.

Food

Kraft Foods, Inc. (KFI) is the largest processor and marketer of retail packaged food in the United States. KFI is a combination of General Foods Corp., which was acquired in September 1985 for $5.75 billion,[46] and Kraft Foods, Inc., which was acquired through a hostile takeover in December 1988 for $12.9 billion.[47] The investment community questioned Philip Morris at the time of these acquisitions for investing in businesses with significantly smaller operating income margins than the traditional tobacco margins. At the time of the General Foods acquisition, analyst David A. Goldman of Dean Witter was quoted as saying, "Those turkeys, . . . this is dumb."[48] Philip Morris has been able to increase the operating margins on the food business by utilizing superior marketing skills, capitalizing on the industry knowledge of key personnel from both Kraft and General Foods, and reducing expenses by leveraging common resources across the entire food business.

KFI owns trademarks to major brand names, which include Jell-O, Oscar Mayer, Maxwell House, Post Cereals, Kool-Aid, DiGiorno Pizza, and Altoids. In 1997 the domestic division of KFI generated 48 percent of domestic operating revenues and 41 percent of domestic operating margins. KFI has shown significant growth in operating income margins, from 14 percent in 1995 to 17 percent in 1997.

Internationally, the food business unit has been a globalization of the existing Kraft and General Foods brand names as well as the acquisition of large international brands. Subsidiaries and affiliates of KFI manufacture and market a wide variety of coffee, confectionery, cheese, grocery, and processed meat products in Europe, the Middle East, Africa, and the Asia/Pacific region. The international portion of the food business provided an operating income margin of 12 percent in 1997.

Beer

Philip Morris acquired Miller Brewing in 1969 from W. R. Grace.[49] In 1969, Miller sales placed seventh in the domestic beer market. In less than six years Miller moved from seventh to fourth place in domestic beer sales and it currently holds the number two position behind Anheuser-Busch. This growth is attributed to the superior marketing expertise of Philip Morris and the overlapped target customer segments for both product categories.

In 1997, the Miller Brewing Company provided Philip Morris with only 3.7 percent of operating income at a margin of 11 percent, significantly less than both the tobacco and food business units. The international portion of this business represents only 6 percent of the volume of the beer business. Philip Morris has decided to keep the beer business mainly domestic. This was demonstrated when Miller sold its 20 percent equity stake in Molson Breweries in Canada, but retained majority ownership of Molson USA, LLC, in order to maintain importing, marketing, and distribution rights for Molson and Foster's brands in the U.S.

PHILIP MORRIS'S FINANCIAL PERFORMANCE

The diversification practices of Philip Morris Companies Inc., combined with its ongoing market dominance of the tobacco industry, have yielded tremendous growth in earnings for the company. Exhibit 3 highlights selected financial data of Philip Morris Companies Inc. during the past 11 years. One illustration of the company's growth is its increase in net earnings. This number grew from $1.8 billion in 1987 to $6.3 billion in 1997, with an average annual increase of 25 percent.

Exhibits 4 and 5 show the Philip Morris Companies Inc. balance sheets and results of operations for the six months ending June 30, 1998, and for the years ended December 31, 1995, through December 31, 1997. Comparisons of operating results between reporting periods and items of significant impact on operating results are discussed in the following three sections. The discussion will highlight general (consolidated) operations, discuss operating results of the domestic tobacco and international tobacco business segments, and conclude with summary results.

3 | Philip Morris Companies Inc. and Subsidiaries Selected Financial Data—Eleven-Year Review (in millions of dollars, except per share data)

	1997	1996	1995	1994	1993	1992	1991	1990	1989	1988	1987
Operating revenues	$72,055	$69,204	$66,071	$65,125	$60,901	$59,131	$56,458	$51,169	$44,080	$31,273	$27,650
Cost of sales	$26,689	$26,560	$26,685	$28,351	$26,771	$26,082	$25,612	$24,430	$21,868	$13,565	$12,183
Operating income	$11,663	$11,769	$10,526	$9,449	$7,587	$10,059	$8,622	$7,946	$6,789	$4,397	$3,990
Net earnings (including cumulative effect of accounting changes)	$6,310	$6,303	$5,450	$4,725	$3,091	$4,939	$3,006	$3,540	$2,946	$2,337	$1,842
Total assets	$55,947	$54,871	$53,811	$52,649	$51,205	$50,014	$47,384	$46,569	$38,528	$36,960	$21,437
Total long-term debt	$12,430	$12,961	$13,107	$14,975	$15,221	$14,583	$14,213	$16,121	$14,551	$16,812	$5,983
Stockholders' equity	$14,920	$14,218	$13,985	$12,786	$11,627	$12,563	$12,512	$11,947	$9,571	$7,679	$6,823
United States export sales	$6,705	$6,476	$5,920	$4,942	$4,105	$3,797	$3,061	$2,928	$2,288	$1,863	$1,592
Federal excise taxes on products	$3,596	$3,544	$3,446	$3,431	$3,081	$2,879	$2,978	$2,159	$2,140	$2,127	$2,085
Foreign excise taxes on products	$12,345	$11,107	$9,486	$7,918	$7,199	$6,157	$5,416	$4,687	$3,608	$3,755	$3,331
Basic EPS (including per-share cumulative effect of accounting changes	$2.61	$2.57	$2.17	$1.82	$1.17	$1.82	$1.08	$1.28	$1.06	$0.84	$0.65
Diluted EPS (including per-share cumulative effect of accounting changes)	$2.58	$2.54	$2.15	$1.81	$1.17	$1.80	$1.07	$1.27	$1.05	$0.83	$0,64
Dividends declared per share	$1.60	$1.47	$1.22	$1.01	$0.87	$0.78	$0.64	$0.52	$0.42	$0.34	$0.26
Book value per common share outstanding	$6.15	$5.85	$5.61	$5.00	$4.42	$4.69	$4.53	$4.30	$3.43	$2.77	$2.40
Market price per common share at year end	$45.25	$37.67	$30.08	$19.17	$18.54	$25.71	$26.75	$17.25	$13.88	$8.50	$7.13

Source: Philip Morris Companies Inc. 1998, Exhibit 13, *Annual 10-K Report to Security Holders for 1997*, March 6, 35.

EXHIBIT

4 | Philip Morris Companies Inc. and Subsidiaries Consolidated Balance Sheets (in millions of dollars)

	(a) June 30, 1998	(b) December 31, 1997	(b) December 31, 1996
ASSETS			
Consumer Products:			
Cash and cash equivalents	$ 4,605	$ 2,282	$ 240
Receivables, net	5,293	4,294	4,466
Inventories:			
Leaf tobacco	4,166	4,348	4,143
Other raw materials	1,910	1,689	1,854
Finished product	3,043	3,002	3,005
Total inventories	9,119	9,039	9,002
Other current assets	1,840	1,825	1,482
Total current assets	20,857	26,479	24,192
Property, plant and equipment, at cost:			
Land and land improvements		666	664
Buildings and building equipment		5,114	5,168
Machinery and equipment		12,667	12,481
Construction in progress		1,555	1,659
Sub-total	20,595	20,002	19,972
Less accumulated depreciation	(8,740)	(8,381)	(8,221)
Total property, plant and equipment	11,855	11,621	11,751
Goodwill and other intangible assets, net of accumulated amortization of $5,087; $4,814; and $4,391)	17,557	17,789	18,998
Other assets	3,023	3,211	3,015
Total consumer products assets	53,292	50,061	48,954

	(a) June 30, 1998	(b) December 31, 1997	(b) December 31, 1996
LIABILITIES			
Consumer Products:			
Short-term borrowings	$ 847	$ 157	$ 260
Current portion of long-term debt	1,577	1,516	1,846
Accounts payable	2,505	3,318	3,409
Accrued liabilities:			
Marketing	2,148	2,149	2,106
Taxes, except income taxes	1,667	1,234	1,331
Employment costs		1,083	942
Accrued settlement charges	1,790		
Other	3,467	3,780	2,726
Income taxes	1,000	862	1,269
Dividends payable	975	972	978
Total current liabilities	15,976	15,071	14,867
Long-term debt	12,289	11,585	11,827
Deferred income taxes	920	889	731
Accrued postretirement health care costs	2,506	2,432	2,372
Other liabilities	6,630	6,218	5,773
Total consumer products liabilities	38,321	36,195	35,570
Financial services and real estate:			
Short-term borrowings	103		173
Long-term debt	838	845	1,134
Deferred income taxes	3,933	3,877	3,636
Other liabilities	146	110	140
Total financial services and real estate liabilities	5,020	4,832	5,083
Total Liabilities	43,341	41,027	40,653

(Continues)

EXHIBIT 4 | Philip Morris Companies Inc. and Subsidiaries Consolidated Balance Sheets (in millions of dollars) *(Continued)*

	(a) June 30, 1998	(b) December 31, 1997	(b) December 31, 1996
Financial services and real estate:			
Finance assets, net	5,900	5,712	5,345
Other assets	171	174	572
Total financial services and real estate assets	6,071	5,886	5,917
TOTAL ASSETS	$59,363	$55,947	$54,871

	(a) June 30, 1998	(b) December 31, 1997	(b) December 31, 1996
STOCKHOLDERS' EQUITY			
Common stock, par value $0.33–1/3 per share (2,805,961,317 shares issued)	935	935	935
Earnings reinvested in the business	26,111	24,924	22,478
Currency translation adjustments	(1,330)	(1,109)	192
Sub-total	25,716	24,750	23,605
Less cost of repurchased stock $374,902,778; 380,474,028; and 374,615,043 shares)	(9,694)	(9,830)	(9,387)
Total stockholders' equity	16,022	14,920	14,218
TOTAL LIABILITIES AND STOCKHOLDERS' EQUITY	$59,363	$55,947	$54,871

[a] *Source:* Philip Morris Companies Inc. 1998, *Form 10Q Quarterly Report for the Quarterly Period Ended June 30, 1998*, July 31, 2–3.
[b] *Source:* Philip Morris Companies Inc. 1998, Exhibit 13, *Annual 10-K Report to Security Holders for 1997*, March 6, 36–38.

5 | Philip Morris Companies Inc. and Subsidiaries Consolidated Statements of Earnings (in millions of dollars, except per share data)

	(a) Six Months Ended June 30, 1998 (Unaudited)	(b) For the years ended December 31, 1997	1996	1995
Operating revenues	$37,361	$72,055	$69,204	$66,071
Cost of sales	13,590	26,689	26,560	26,685
Excise taxes on products	8,419	15,941	14,651	12,932
Gross profit	15,352	29,425	27,993	26,454
Marketing, administration and research costs	8,354	15,720	15,630	15,337
Settlement charges	1,005	1,457		
Amortization of goodwill	290	585	594	591
Operating income	5,703	11,663	11,769	10,526
Interest and other debt expense, net	482	1,052	1,086	1,179
Earnings before income taxes and cumulative effect of accounting changes	5,221	10,611	10,683	9,347
Provision for income taxes	2,103	4,301	4,380	3,869
Earnings before cumulative effect of accounting changes	3,118	6,310	6,303	5,478
Cumulative effect of accounting changes	0	0	0	(28)
Net earnings	$3,118	$6,310	$6,303	$5,450
Per-share data:				
Basic earnings per share before cumulative effect of accounting changes	$1.28	$2.51	$2.57	$2.18
Cumulative effect of accounting changes				(0.01)
Basic earnings per share	$1.28	$2.61	$2.57	$2.17
Diluted earnings per share before cumulative effect of accounting changes	$1.28	$2.58	$2.54	$2.16
Cumulative effect of accounting changes				(0.01)
Diluted earnings per share	$1.28	$2.58	$2.54	$2.15

[a]Source: Philip Morris Companies Inc. 1998, *Form 10Q Quarterly Report for the Quarterly Period* Ended June 30, 1998, July 31, 4.
[b]Source: Philip Morris Companies Inc. 1998, Exhibit 13, *Annual 10-K Report to Security Holders for 1997*, March 6, 39.

Results of Operations—General

As Exhibit 5 illustrates, for the first six months of 1998, operating revenues were in excess of $37 billion. This represented a 2 percent increase over the comparable 1997 period for the combined Philip Morris Companies Inc. This increase was primarily the result of an increase in sales of domestic tobacco, international tobacco, and North American food operations. Financial services and real estate operating revenues decreased due to the sale of the real estate business in 1997.[50]

Several unique events affected income during the first six months of 1998. In February 1998, the company announced voluntary early retirement and separation programs for salaried and hourly employees, which resulted in pretax charges of $327 million. During the same six-month period, the company recorded pretax charges of $806 million related to the settlement of health care cost recovery litigation in Minnesota and $199 million related to "Most Favored Nation" clauses in previous state settlement agreements with the states of Mississippi and Texas. Excluding these charges, as well as results from operations divested in 1997, underlying operating income increased 7.4 percent, or $484 million, over the first six months of 1997.[51]

Operating revenues in 1997 were approximately $72 billion, as seen in Exhibits 5 and 6. This was an increase of $2.9 billion, or $4.1 percent, over 1996. This improvement was due primarily to sales increases in domestic and international tobacco and North American food operations. Operating profit, however, showed a slight decline of 0.2 percent, or $25 million, in comparison to the 1996 results.[52]

Operating results in 1997 were also affected by several singular events. The operating profit decrease was the result of several pretax charges. These included $1.5 billion paid by Philip Morris Incorporated, the company's domestic tobacco subsidiary, for settlement of health care cost recovery litigation in Mississippi, Florida, and Texas; a one-time charge from a Florida class action suit settlement; and a $630 million charge for realignment of the international food operations. Operating profit included a $774 million pretax gain on the sale of ice cream businesses in Brazil and a $103 million pretax gain on the sale of real estate operations.[53]

Results of Operations—Domestic Tobacco

During the first six months of 1998, operating revenues of $7.01 billion for Philip Morris Inc. represented an increase of 10.1 percent over 1997, due to pricing and improved product mix, partially offset by lower volume. In the same 1998 period, this segment recorded pretax charges of over $1 billion related to tobacco litigation settlements (mentioned previously), and $309 million related to voluntary early retirement and separation programs for salaried and hourly employees. Operating income decreased 53.6 percent from the comparable 1997 period, due primarily to the aforementioned tobacco litigation settlement charges; higher marketing, administration, and research costs; charges for the voluntary early retirement and separation programs; and lower volume.[54]

In 1997, operating revenues of $13.5 billion in this business segment (Exhibit 6) represented an increase of 8.2 percent over 1996 because of pricing, higher volume and an improved product mix. This category sustained the $1.5 billion charge for litigation settlement mentioned previously. Operating profit for 1997 decreased 22.3 percent from 1996, due to litigation charges; higher marketing, administration, and research costs; higher fixed manufacturing costs; higher volume; and the improved product mix. Excluding the impact of litigation settlement charges, Philip Morris Inc.'s operating profit for 1997 increased 12.3 percent over 1996.[55]

Results of Operations—International Tobacco

During the first six months of 1998, operating revenues of Philip Morris International were $14.3 billion, an increase of 4.5 percent over the comparable 1997 period, including excise taxes. Increases were caused by price increases, favorable volume/mix, and the consolidation of previously unconsolidated subsidiaries. Operating income for this period increased 11.1 percent over the comparable 1997 period for primarily the same reasons.[56]

During 1997, tobacco operating revenues of this segment were $26.3 billion (Exhibit 6) which is $2.2 billion over 1996, including a $1.2 billion increase in excise taxes. Excluding excise taxes, operating revenues increased $1.0 billion, due primarily to price increases; favorable volume/mix; and the consolidation of previously unconsolidated and newly acquired subsidiaries. Operating profit for 1997 increased 12.6 percent over 1996, because of these same factors.[57]

Summary Results

A summary of operating results for Philip Morris Companies, Inc. indicates that the tobacco business segment provides a substantial portion of the company's revenues. For the six months ended June 30, 1998, domestic tobacco sales of $7.011 billion represented 32.9 percent of tobacco revenues and 18.8 percent of operating revenues, while international tobacco sales of $14.325 billion represented 67.1 percent of tobacco revenues and 38.3 percent of total operating revenues.[58] For the year ended December 31, 1997, domestic tobacco sales of $13.485 billion represented 33.9 percent of tobacco revenues and 18.7 percent of total operating revenues, while international tobacco sales of $26.339 billion represented 66.1 percent of tobacco revenues and 36.6 percent of total operating revenues.[59]

6 | Philip Morris Companies Inc. and Subsidiaries Consolidated Operating Results

	Operating Revenues (in millions)(a)			Operating Revenue %		
	1997	1996	1995	1997	1996	1995
Tobacco						
Domestic	$13,485	$12,462	$11,493	18.7%	18.0%	17.4%
International	26,339	24,087	20,823	36.6%	34.8%	31.5%
Total Tobacco	39,824	36,549	32,316	55.3%	52.8%	48.9%
Food	27,690	27,950	29,074	38.4%	40.4%	44.0%
Beer	4,201	4,327	4,304	5.8%	6.3%	6.5%
Financial Services	340	378	377	0.5%	0.5%	0.6%
Operating Revenues	$72,055	$69,204	$66,071	100.0%	100.0%	100.0%

	Operating Income (in millions)(b)			Operating Income %			Operating Income Margins %		
	1997	1996	1995	1997	1996	1995	1997	1996	1995
Tobacco	$7,830	$8,263	$7,177	64.1%	67.4%	65.4%	19.7%	22.6%	22.2%
Food	3,647	3,362	3,188	29.8%	27.4%	29.1%	13.2%	12.0%	11.0%
Beer	456	437	444	3.7%	3.6%	4.0%	10.9%	10.1%	10.3%
Financial Services	296	192	164	2.4%	1.6%	1.5%	87.1%	50.8%	43.5%
Operating Income	$12,229	$12,254	$10,973	100.0%	100.0%	100.0%			

	Assets(c) (in millions)			Return on Assets %		
	1997	1996	1995	1997	1996	1995
Tobacco	$14,820	$13,314	$11,196	52.8%	62.1%	64.1%
Food	$30.926	$32,934	$33,447	11.8%	10.2%	9.5%
Beer	$1,455	$1,707	$1,751	31.3%	25.6%	25.4%
Financial Services	$5,886	$5,917	$5,632	5.0%	3.2%	2.9%

(a)Source: Philip Morris Companies Inc. 1998, Exhibit 13, *Annual 10-K Report to Security Holders for 1997*, March 6, 20.
(b)Source: Philip Morris Companies Inc. 1998, Exhibit 13, *Annual 10-K Report to Security Holders for 1997*, March 6, 26.
(c)Source: Philip Morris Companies Inc. 1998, Exhibit 13, *Annual 10-K Report to Security Holders for 1997*, March 6, 48.

PHILIP MORRIS LEGAL ISSUES

In recent years, tobacco companies have been faced with significant legal threats, as noted in the previous financial results section. In the past, tobacco companies were able to maintain defense. Things started to change in 1988, when Liggett was ordered to pay the first award in a liability suit.[60] Later, in 1994, Florida passed a law making it legal to sue cigarette makers for reimbursement of Medicaid expenses from smoking-related illnesses. A total of 39 states have filed suit seeking compensation for health care costs. Adding to tobacco firms' potential problems, the President declared nicotine a drug and placed it under the jurisdiction of the Federal Drug Administration.[61]

Philip Morris faces a tremendous amount of tobacco-related litigation both in and outside the United States. The pending legal proceedings pertain to many different issues, but generally fall into three basic categories: individual smoking and health cases, class action smoking and health care cost recovery cases.[62]

The smoking and health cases vary according to the

7 | Overview of Pending Tobacco-Related Litigation Against Philip Morris Companies Inc. as of August 1, 1998

Category	Approximate Number of Cases Pending: In the United States	Approximate Number of Cases Pending: Outside the United States
(1) Smoking and health cases alleging personal injury brought on behalf of INDIVIDUAL plaintiffs	400	20
(2) Smoking and health cases alleging personal injury brought on behalf of a CLASS of individual plaintiffs	65	4
(3) Health care cost recovery cases brought by state and local governments and similar entities seeking reimbursement for health care expenditures allegedly caused by cigarette smoking	140	1

Source: This information was obtained from the *Philip Morris Companies Inc. Form 10Q Quarterly Report for the Quarter Ended June 30, 1998* and filed July 31, 1998. For a detailed listing of the pending litigation for categories (2) and (3) above, please refer to Exhibit 99 of the aforementioned Form 10Q.

claim being made. Claims such as negligence, gross negligence, strict liability, fraud, misrepresentation, design defect, failure to warn, breach of express and implied warranties, breach of special duty, conspiracy, concert of action, violations of deceptive trade practice laws and consumer protection statutes, and claims under the federal and state Racketeer Influenced and Corrupt Organization Act (RICO) statutes are common among the pending legal proceedings.[63] Currently, approximately 400 smoking and health cases have been filed and served against Philip Morris in the United States and approximately 25 cases are pending outside of the United States. Of the 400 cases, only 22 allege personal injuries as a result of exposure to environmental tobacco smoke.[64]

The health care cost recovery cases mostly seek reimbursement for Medicaid and/or other health care related costs allegedly incurred through the fault of tobacco companies. Some of the recovery cases seek future damages as well (Exhibit 7).[65] Approximately 140 health care cost recovery cases are currently pending against Philip Morris. Of the 140 cases, 37 were filed by states, 70 were filed by unions, six were filed by HMOs, eight were filed by city and county governments, five by Native American tribes, and five by federal and state taxpayers.[66]

Other tobacco-related claims are also common. For instance, one claim asserts that Philip Morris allegedly failed to manufacture a fire-safe cigarette when they possessed knowledge of a technology that would produce a cigarette that was less likely to cause fires. Cigarette price-fixing claims and suits filed by former asbestos manufacturers also add to the list of tobacco-related cases against Philip Morris.[67]

In an effort to increase stability and decrease uncertainties in the tobacco industry, Philip Morris and other tobacco companies have adopted a Memorandum of Understanding (referred to as the Resolution). The purpose of the Resolution is to address the majority of the legal and regulatory issues that the tobacco industry faces. Issues discussed in the Resolution include: advertising and marketing, product warning and labeling, underage smoking reduction goals, enforcement of no sales to underage consumers by the states, and surcharges against the industry for failure to reduce underage smoking.[68]

Philip Morris has proposed its own form of legislation safeguarding against sales to minors. Steve Parrish, Philip Morris's senior vice president of corporate affair, and Richard H. Verheij, UST executive vice president and general counsel, presented the plan. The plan includes a ban of outdoor advertising within 1,000 feet of a school or playground and also calls for a minimum age of 18 for the sale of tobacco products. The plan would

8 | Actual and/or Proposed Regulations on the Tobacco Industry

- Excise tax increases
- Federal regulatory controls
- Requirements regarding disclosure of cigarette ingredients and other proprietary information
- Requirements regarding disclosure of the yields of tar, nicotine, and other components of cigarette smoke
- Governmental and grand jury investigations
- Increased smoking and health litigation
- Federal, state, and local governmental and private bans and restrictions on smoking
- Restrictions on tobacco manufacturing, marketing, advertising, and sales
- Legislation and regulations to require substantial additional health warnings on cigarette packages and in advertising
- Elimination of the tax deductibility of tobacco advertising and promotional costs
- Legislation or other governmental action seeking to ascribe to the tobacco industry responsibility and liability for the purported adverse health effects associated with smoking

Source: Philip Morris Companies Inc., 1998, *Form 10Q Quarterly Report for the Quarterly Period Ended June 30, 1998,* July 31, 26.

ban vending sales by requiring face-to-face sales and would ban the sale of single cigarettes and mini packs (fewer than 20 cigarettes to a pack). Cigarette sampling would also be banned in areas where minors are allowed to enter.[69]

It is difficult for Philip Morris to predict the uncertain outcome of the litigation it is facing, and it is unable to estimate potential losses that may result from an unfavorable outcome. It is also hard to predict the effect that the pending litigation will have upon current smokers and cigarette sales. The company does feel that it has valid and concrete defenses against the pending litigation and the officers stress their willingness to continue to defend the company.[70]

THE FUTURE

What must Philip Morris Companies, Inc. do in the future to maintain its financial success in light of ongoing tobacco litigation, proposed legislation, and increasing public sentiment against smoking? A recent comment from *The Wall Street Journal* states: "Even as the 30 stocks making up the Dow Jones industrial average have been pummeled over the past month, one company has managed to stand out: Philip Morris Co.'s."[71] Philip Morris continues to outdistance its competitors in the tobacco industry and to show marked success in its beer and packaged food divisions.

In the United States and abroad, many actual and/or proposed regulations are pending. These regulations (listed in Exhibit 8), along with the aforementioned potential liabilities arising from unfavorable outcomes of litigation, could have negative effects on the future operating results of Philip Morris Companies, Inc. as well as its competitors.

How will the current litigation affect the nature of competition? How will competitors choose to manage their own litigation threat?

How can Philip Morris balance social responsibility with business success? Do legislation and litigation present imminent threats to the company's tobacco segment? What business strategies can Philip Morris use to hedge against possible adverse effects on or elimination of this segment of its operations?

ENDNOTES

1. P. H. Roth, 1998, Investment Survey, *Value Line Publishing, Inc.,* August 14, 1581.
2. *Microsoft Encarta 96 Electronic Encyclopedia on CD-ROM,* Microsoft Corporation, 1996, search Life Science, Plants, Tobacco, History.

3. Ibid.
4. Ibid; search Life Science, Medicine, Smoking, Introduction.
5. Ibid.
6. Ibid; search Life Science, Medicine, Smoking, History.
7. Ibid; search Life Science, Medicine, Smoking, Smoking Cessation.
8. R. M. Jones, 1997, Strategic Management in a Hostile Environment, *Lessons from the Tobacco Industry*, Greenwood Publishing Group, Westport, Connecticut, 12.
9. Ibid.
10. R. H. Miles, 1982, *Coffin Nails and Corporate Strategy*, Prentice Hall, New Jersey, 138.
11. Ibid; search Life Science, Plants, Tobacco, Use.
12. Byron Sachs, Industry Zone, Industry Snapshot: Tobacco, *Hoover's Online*, 2.
13. Byron Sachs, Industry Zone, Industry Snapshot: Tobacco, 2.
14. Philip Morris Companies Inc; *International Directory of Company Histories*, 1998, p. 417.
15. New Content Copyright 1998 PBS Online, accessed 9/28/98, *http://www.pbs.org/wgbh/pages/frontline/shows/settlement/big/owns.html*, 2.
16. N. Primavera, 1998, Investment Survey, *Value Line Publishing, Inc.*, August 14, 1578.
17. New Content Copyright 1998 PBS Online.
18. N. Primavera, 1998, Investment Survey, 1578.
19. Ibid, 1579.
20. Ibid.
21. Ibid.
22. P. H. Roth, Investment Survey, 1580.
23. Ibid.
24. Ibid.
25. New Content Copyright 1998 PBS Online.
26. Market Guide, Inc., accessed 11/98, http://research.web.aol.com/data/marketguide/stock/r/rn.htm
27. N. Primavera, 1998, Investment Survey, 1582.
28. RJR Nabisco 1997, *Annual Report*, http://www.rjrnabisco.com/annual97/whatsup.htm.
29. J. W. Milner, 1998, Investment Survey, *Value Line Publishing, Inc.*, September 4, 2151.
30. Ibid.
31. New Content Copyright 1998 PBS Online.
32. Ibid.
33. J. W. Milner, 1998, Investment Survey, *Value Line Publishing, Inc.*, September 4, 2151.
34. P. H. Roth, Investment Survey, 1583.
35. Ibid.
36. New Content Copyright 1998 PBS Online.
37. P. H. Roth, Investment Survey, 1583.
38. N. Primavera, 1998, Investment Survey.
39. Ibid.
40. R. H. Miles, 1982, *Coffin Nails and Corporate Strategy*, 138.
41. J. Sasseen, 1985, The General Foods Deal May Not Be So Sweet, *Business Week*, October 14, 40–41.
42. Philip Morris 1994 10K, 2.
43. Philip Morris 1997 Annual Report, 6.
44. Philip Morris 1996 10K, 3.
45. Philip Morris 1997 Annual Report, 9.
46. J. Sasseen, 1985, The General Foods Deal May Not Be So Sweet, 40–41.
47. S. P. Sherman, 1989, How Philip Morris Diversified Right, *Fortune*, October 23, 120–122.
48. J. Sasseen, 1985, The General Foods Deal May Not Be So Sweet, 40–41.
49. Make Way for Miller, *Forbes*, May 15, 1976, 45–47.
50. Philip Morris Companies Inc. 1998, Form 10Q Quarterly Report for the Quarterly Period Ended June 30, 1998, July 31, 24.
51. Ibid.
52. Philip Morris Companies Inc. 1998, Exhibit 13, Annual 10-K Report to Security Holders for 1997, March 6, 21.
53. Ibid.
54. Philip Morris Companies Inc. 1998, Form 10Q Quarterly Report for the Quarterly Period Ended June 30, 1998, July 31, 33.
55. Philip Morris Companies Inc. 1998, Exhibit 13, Annual 10-K Report to Security Holders for 1997, March 6, 27–28.
56. Philip Morris Companies Inc. 1998, Form 10Q Quarterly Report for the Quarterly Period Ended June 30, 1998, July 31, 34.
57. Philip Morris Companies Inc. 1998, Exhibit 13, Annual 10-K Report to Security Holders for 1997, March 6, 28.
58. Philip Morris Companies Inc. 1998, Form 10Q Quarterly Report for the Quarterly Period Ended June 30, 1998, July 31, 33.
59. Philip Morris Companies Inc. 1998, Exhibit 13, Annual 10-K Report to Security Holders for 1997, March 6, 27.
60. Byron Sachs, Industry Zone, Industry Snapshot: Tobacco, *Hoover's Online*, 2.
61. Ibid.
62. Philip Morris 1997 *Annual Report*, 51.
63. Ibid, 52–53.
64. http://www.sec.gov/Archives/edgar/data/764180/0001047469-98-031299.txt, accessed 10/4/98, 10–11.
65. Philip Morris 1997 *Annual Report*, 54.
66. http://www.sec.gov/Archives/edgar/data/764180/0001047469-98-031299.txt, accessed 10/4/98, 15.
67. Ibid, 56.
68. Ibid, 57.
69. A. Kaplan, 1998, Tobacco Cos. Propose Federal Legislation, *CS News Online*, accessed 10/4/98, http://macfadden.com/csnews/news/bn_52.html.
70. Ibid, 20–21.
71. Philip Morris a Bright Spot in Dow Industrials, 1998, *WSJ Interactive Edition*, August 31, accessed 8/31/98, *www.wsj.com*.

CASE 33

Southwest Airlines, 1996

Andrew Inkpen
Valerie DeGroot
Thunderbird, The American Graduate School of International Management

In January 1996, Southwest Airlines (Southwest) entered the Florida and southeastern U.S. markets. The company planned to operate 78 daily flights to Tampa, Fort Lauderdale, and Orlando by August of the following year. With the expansion into Florida, the northeast remained the only major U.S. air traffic region where Southwest did not compete. The northeast U.S. market had generally been avoided by low-fare airlines such as Southwest because of airport congestion, air traffic control delays, frequent inclement weather, and dominance by a few major airlines. Airports such as Logan International in Boston, J. F. Kennedy International in New York, and Newark International were among the busiest and most congested airports in the country. Continental Airline's attempt to introduce widespread, low-fare operations in the East during 1994–1995 was a financial disaster.

With the move into Florida and the potential challenges associated with the northeastern market, questions were being raised about Southwest's ability to maintain its position as America's most consistently profitable airline. In particular, there were concerns whether Southwest was growing too fast and deviating from its proven strategy. Would entry into the Florida market and possibly the northeastern market jeopardize 25 years of success? Success resulted in a focused strategy based on frequent flights, rapid turnarounds at airport gates, and a careful selection of markets and airports that avoided ground and air traffic control delays. Herb Kelleher, the charismatic president, co-founder, and chief executive officer of the airline, wrote to his employees in 1993: "Southwest has had more opportunities for growth than it has airplanes. Yet, unlike other airlines, it has avoided the trap of growing beyond its means. Whether you are talking with an officer or a ramp agent, employees just don't seem to be enamored of the idea that bigger is better."[1]

Copyright 1997 Thunderbird, The American Graduate School of International Management. All rights reserved. This case was prepared for the basis of classroom discussion only and is not intended to illustrate either effective or ineffective management.

THE U.S. AIRLINE INDUSTRY

The nature of the U.S. commercial airline industry was permanently altered in October 1978 when President Jimmy Carter signed the Airline Deregulation Act. Before deregulation, the Civil Aeronautics Board regulated airline route entry and exit, passenger fares, mergers and acquisitions, and airline rates of return. Typically, two or three carriers provided service in a given market, although there were routes covered by only one carrier. Cost increases were passed along to customers, and price competition was almost nonexistent. The airlines operated as if there were only two market segments: those who could afford to fly and those who couldn't.[2]

Deregulation sent airline fares tumbling and allowed many new firms to enter the market. The financial impact on both established and new airlines was enormous. The fuel crisis of 1979 and the air traffic controller's strike in 1981 contributed to the industry's difficulties, as did the severe recession that hit the United States during the early 1980s. During the first decade of deregulation, more than 150 carriers, many of them new start-up airlines, collapsed into bankruptcy. Eight of the major 11 airlines dominating the industry in 1978 ended up filing for bankruptcy, merging with other carriers, or simply disappearing from the radar screen. Collectively, the industry made enough money during this period to buy two Boeing 747s (Exhibit 1).[3] The three major carriers that survived intact—Delta, United, and American—ended up with 80 percent of all domestic U.S. air traffic and 67 percent of trans-Atlantic business.[4]

Competition and lower fares led to greatly expanded demand for airline travel. By the mid-1990s, the airlines were having trouble meeting this demand. Travel increased from 200 million travelers in 1974 to 500 million in 1995, yet only five new runways were built during this time period. During the 1980s, many airlines acquired significant levels of new debt in efforts to service the increased travel demand. Long-term debt-to-capitalization ratios increased dramatically: Eastern's went from 62 to 473 percent, TWA's went from 62 to 115 percent, and Continental's went from 62 to 96 percent. In contrast, United and Delta maintained their debt ratios at less than 60 percent, and American Airline's ratio dropped to 34 percent.

Despite the financial problems experienced by many fledgling airlines started after deregulation, new firms continued to enter the market. Between 1992 and 1995, 69 new airlines were certified by the FAA. Most of these airlines competed with limited route structures and lower fares than the major airlines. The new low-fare airlines created a second tier of service providers that save consumers billions of dollars annually and provided service in markets abandoned or ignored by major carriers. One such startup was Kiwi Airlines, founded by former employees of the defunct Eastern and Pan Am airlines. Kiwi was funded largely by employees: pilots paid $50,000 each to get jobs and other employees paid $5,000.

Despite fostering competition and the growth of new airlines, deregulation created a significant regional disparity in ticket prices and adversely affected service to small and remote communities. Airline workers generally suffered, with inflation-adjusted average employee wages falling from $42,928 in 1978 to $37,985 in 1988. About 20,000 airline industry employees were laid off in the early 1980s, while productivity of the remaining employees rose 43 percent during the same period. In a variety of cases, bankruptcy filings were used to diminish the role of unions and reduce unionized wages.

Industry Economics

About 80 percent of airline operating costs were fixed or semivariable. The only true variable costs were travel agency commissions, food costs, and ticketing fees. The operating costs of an airline flight depended primarily on the distance traveled, not the number of passengers on board. For example, the crew and ground staff sizes were determined by the type of aircraft, not the passenger load. Therefore, once an airline established its route structure, most of its operating costs were fixed.

Because of this high fixed-cost structure, the airlines developed sophisticated software tools to maximize capacity utilization, known as *load factor*. Load factor was calculated by dividing RPM (revenue passenger miles—the number of passengers carried multiplied by the distance flown) by ASM (available seat miles—the number of seats available for sale multiplied by the distance flown).

On each flight by one of the major airlines (excluding Southwest and the low-fare carriers), there were typically a dozen categories of fares. The airlines analyzed historical travel patterns on individual routes to determine how many seats to sell at each fare level. All of the major airlines used this type of analysis and flexible pricing practice, known as a *yield management system*. These systems enabled the airlines to manage their seat inventories and the prices paid for those seats. The objective was to sell more seats on each flight at higher yields (total passenger yield was passenger revenue from scheduled operations divided by scheduled RPMs). The higher the ticket price, the better the yield.

Although reducing operating costs was a high priority for the airlines, the nature of the cost structure limited cost-reduction opportunities. Fuel costs (about 13 percent of total costs) were largely beyond the control of the airlines, and many of the larger airlines' restrictive union agreements limited labor flexibility. Although newer aircraft were much more fuel efficient than older models, most airlines had sharply lowered their new aircraft orders to avoid taking on more debt. At the end of June 1990, U.S. airlines had outstanding orders to buy 2,748 aircraft. At the end of June 1996, orders had fallen to 1,111.[5] (A new Boeing 737 cost about $28 million in 1995.)

EXHIBIT 1 | Airline Operating Data, 1986–1994

Seat-Miles Flown

	American	America-West	Continental	Delta	Eastern	Northwest	Pan-American	SouthWest	TransWorld	United	USAir	Total All Majors
1994	110,658	17,852	49,762	98,104		52,110	0	29,624	27,938	95,965	58,311	540,324
1993	117,719	16,980	49,690	99,852		52,623	0	34,759	25,044	98,652	55,918	551,237
1992	114,418	18,603	49,143	100,904		52,430	0	21,371	30,483	89,605	56,027	532,984
1991	104,616	19,460	48,742	94,350		48,847	9,042	18,440	29,684	88,092	56,470	517,743
1990	102,864	18,139	48,385	87,748	25,299	47,210	12,157	16,456	33,942	86,085	58,014	536,299
1989	98,638	13,523	47,107	82,440	15,489	44,372	11,670	14,788	35,246	82,758	40,652	486,683
1988	88,620	11,994	53,343	79,719	41,126	39,349	10,331	13,370	35,024	84,240	28,234	485,350
1987	77,724	10,318	54,626	71,504	50,156	41,499	8,217	11,457	33,566	86,246	20,014	465,327
1986	66,901	4,296	27,778	50,448	52,556	27,561	8,901	9,712	29,534	78,568	18,254	374,509
Total	882,158	131,165	428,576	765,069	184,626	406,001	60,318	169,977	280,461	790,211	391,894	4,490,456

Revenue per Passenger-Miles (RPMs) (in cents)

	American	America-West	Continental	Delta	Eastern	Northwest	Pan-American	SouthWest	TransWorld	United	USAir
1994	13.11	10.81	11.50	13.93		13.93	0	11.65	12.67	11.81	15.92
1993	13.65	11.13	11.97	14.66		13.06	0	11.92	12.78	12.49	17.94
1992	12.03	10.36	11.01	14.02		12.21	0	11.78	11.13	11.88	16.97
1991	13.11	10.00	11.79	14.30		12.79	10.02	11.25	11.31	12.21	16.93
1990	12.86	11.14	12.48	14.21		13.24	11.65	11.48	12.34	12.71	16.37
1989	12.27	11.84	12.04	13.91	11.71	13.02	11.98	10.49	12.10	12.18	15.83
1988	11.92	10.52	10.61	13.52	12.00	12.54	10.94	10.74	11.47	10.86	15.33
1987	11.06	9.66	9.34	131.10	11.02	11.73	9.97	10.02	11.02	10.10	14.91
1986	10.23	9.90	8.56	13.54	11.26	10.48	10.12	10.59	10.07	9.87	14.93

Passenger Load Factor (percent)

	American	America-West	Continental	Delta	Eastern	Northwest	Pan-American	SouthWest	TransWorld	United	USAir
1994	62.35	67.99	62.48	64.68		64.88	0.00	66.80	62.73	69.80	62.02
1993	59.21	65.56	62.20	61.52		63.51	0.00	68.09	62.38	63.80	58.59
1992	63.12	61.62	63.14	60.59		62.24	0.00	64.52	62.94	66.15	58.60
1991	60.86	64.94	61.80	59.95		62.90	60.53	61.14	60.94	64.23	58.22
1990	61.48	60.99	58.42	57.98	60.80	62.53	60.00	60.60	58.90	63.85	59.54
1989	63.6	57.7	60.3	63.6	61.9	60.9	61.2	62.7	59.4	65.4	61.2
1988	63.1	57.9	58.8	57.6	61.8	61.8	63.4	57.7	59.9	67.4	61.3
1987	63.7	56.1	60.7	55.5	65.3	61.8	64.1	58.9	62.0	65.0	65.3
1986	65.6	61.0	62.7	57.4	60.6	54.9	51.4	58.3	59.5	65.6	61.1

1 | Airline Operating Data, 1986–1994 *(Continued)*

Operating Revenues, in millions of dollars

	American	America-West	Continental	Delta	Eastern	Northwest	Pan-American	SouthWest	TransWorld	United	USAir	Total All Majors
1994	10,631	1,414	4,091	9,514		5,325		2,417	2,555	8,966	6,394	51,307
1993	10,828	1,332	4,128	9,653		4,928		2,067	2,325	8,794	6,364	50,419
1992	9,902	1,281	3,840	9,164		4,464		1,685	2,510	7,861	5,974	46,681
1991	9,429	1,359	4,014	8,593		4,356	596	1,314	2,464	7,790	5,895	45,810
1990	9,203	1,322	4,036	7,697		4,298	946	1,187	2,878	7,946	6,085	45,598
1989	8,670	998	3,896	7,780	1,295	3,944	957	1,015	2,918	7,463	4,160	43,096
1988	7,548	781	3,682	6,684	3,423	3,395	804	860	2,777	7,006	2,803	39,763
1987	6,369	577	3,404	5,638	4,054	3,328	625	699	2,668	6,500	2,070	35,932
1986	5,321	330	1,676	4,245	4,093	1,815	553	620	2,064	5,727	1,787	28,231
Total	77,901	9,394	32,767	68,968	12,865	35,853	4,481	11,864	23,159	68,053	41,532	

Net Operating Income (Loss), in millions of dollars

	American	America-West	Continental	Delta	Eastern	Northwest	Pan-American	SouthWest	TransWorld	United	USAir	Total All Majors
1994	432	146	(145)	123		725		290	(81)	262	(466)	1,286
1993	357	121	56	335		268		281	(63)	184	(143)	1,396
1992	(251)	(64)	(183)	(225)		(203)		182	(191)	(354)	(397)	(1,686)
1991	40	(79)	(218)	(115)		17	(186)	62	(233)	(412)	(233)	(1,357)
1990	103	(32)	(191)	(176)		(132)	(280)	82	(134)	(34)	(437)	(1,231)
1989	709	48	124	677	(666)	57	(118)	98	10	302	(239)	1,002
1988	794	18	(87)	441	(187)	19	(181)	86	113	461	144	1,621
1987	483	(35)	(56)	383	66	72	(260)	41	79	97	263	1,133
1986	378	4	91	212	61	(25)	(283)	81	(77)	51	164	657
Total	3,045	127	(609)	1,655	(726)	798	1,308	1,203	(577)	557	(1,344)	

Source: Department of Transportation.

To manage their route structures, all of the major airlines (except Southwest) maintained their operations around a "hub-and-spoke" network. The spokes fed passengers from outlying points into a central airport—the hub—where passengers could travel to additional hubs or their final destination. For example, to fly from Phoenix to Boston on Northwest Airlines, a typical route would involve a flight from Phoenix to Northwest's Detroit hub. The passenger would then take a second flight from Detroit to Boston.

Establishing a major hub in a city like Chicago or Atlanta required an investment of as much as $150 million for gate acquisition and terminal construction. Although hubs created inconveniences for travelers, hub systems were an efficient means of distributing services across a wide network. The major airlines were very protective of their so-called "fortress" hubs and used the hubs to control various local markets. For example, Northwest controlled more than 78 percent of the local traffic in Detroit and 84 percent in Minneapolis. When Southwest entered the Detroit market, the only available gates were already leased by Northwest. Northwest subleased gates to Southwest at rates 18 times higher than Northwest's costs. Southwest eventually withdrew from Detroit, one of only three markets the company had abandoned in its history. (Denver and Beaumont, Texas, were the other two.)

Recent Airline Industry Performance

U.S. airlines suffered a combined loss of $13 billion from 1990 to 1994 (Exhibit 1).[6] High debt levels plagued the industry. In 1994, the earnings picture began to change with the industry as a whole reducing its losses to $278 million.[7] Overall expansion and health returned to the industry in 1995 and 1996. In 1996, net earnings were a record $2.4 billion (see Exhibit 2 for 1995 airline performance and Exhibit 3 for 1995 market share ratings). For 1996, revenue forecasts were $7.2 billion with a net profit of $3 billion.

In 1996, for the first time in 10 years, the industry had a profitable first quarter ($110 million). Numerous statistics indicated that the industry was in good shape:

EXHIBIT 2 | Airline Performance

	Revenue (in $000s)	Net Profit (in $000s)	RPM (in 000s)	ASM (in 000s)
American	15,501,000	167,000	102,900,000	155,300,000
United	14,943,000	349,000	111,811,000	158,569,000
Delta	12,194,000	510,000	86,400,000	130,500,000
Northwest	9,080,000	392,000	62,500,000	87,500,000
USAir	7,474,000	119,000	37,618,000	58,163,000
Continental	5,825,000	224,000	40,023,000	61,006,000
TWA	3,320,000	(227,400)	25,068,683	38,186,111
Southwest	2,872,751	182,626	23,327,804	36,180,001
America West	1,600,000	53,800	13,300,000	19,400,000
Alaska	1,417,500	17,300	9,335,000	15,299,000
American Trans Air	715,009	8,524	4,183,692	5,951,162
Tower Air	490,472	10,689	1,208,001	1,455,996
Mesa	454,538	14,012	1,179,397	2,310,895
Conair	418,466	N/A	1,187,706	2,274,695
ValuJet	367,800	67,800	2,600,000	3,800,000
Hawaiian	346,904	(5,506)	3,171,365	4,238,320
Atlantic Southeast	328,725	51,137	763,000	1,700,000
Midwest Express	259,155	19,129	1,150,338	1,794,924
Reno Air	256,508	1,951	2,090,017	3,322,475

Source: Business Travel News, May 27, 1996, and *Air Transport World*, March 1996.

3 | Airline Market Shares

1995 Company Rankings	% Market Share	1985 Company Rankings	% Market Share
United	21.0	American	13.3
American	19.3	United	12.5
Delta	16.0	Eastern	10.0
Northwest	11.7	TWA	9.6
Continental	7.5	Delta	9.0
USAir	7.2	Pan Am	8.1
TWA	4.7	NWA	6.7
Southwest	4.4	Continental	4.9
America West	2.5	People Express	3.3
American Trans Air	1.2	Republic	3.2
Others	4.5	Others	19.4
Total	100.0	Total	100.0

Sources: Department of Transportation and Standard & Poor's, cited by *Industry Surveys*, February 1, 1996.

load factors were up to 68–69 percent in 1996; fares were up 5 percent; and yields were up to 13.52 cents per passenger mile. The break-even load factor fell 2.5 points to about 65 percent and unit costs dropped by 0.4 percent in 1995.[8] The expiration of a 10 percent domestic ticket tax resulted in net lower-priced tickets to customers despite increased fares. Traffic growth outpaced the 1.7 percent industry rise in capacity.

Future Pressures on the Industry

Despite the recent positive financial performance, concerns over fare wars, overcapacity in some markets, increased fuel prices, and the possibility of economic recession created significant uncertainty about the future. In particular, cost pressures were expected from several factors:

1. *Labor costs.* The average salary per airline employee from 1987 to 1996 rose at a rate faster than the increase in the CPI index (4.4 percent increase in labor costs compared with a 3.7 percent CPI increase over the same period).[9] Pressure from labor was expected to increase as employees sought a share of the airlines' recent record profits. The possibility of new federal regulations concerning aircrew flight and duty time requirements were also an issue. It was estimated that the potential costs from regulation changes could be as high as $1.2 billion in the first year and $800 million in each subsequent year.
2. *Aircraft maintenance.* The aging of the general aircraft population meant higher maintenance costs and eventual aircraft replacement. The introduction of stricter government regulations for older planes placed new burdens on those operating them.
3. *Debt servicing.* The airline industry's debt load of approximately 65 percent greatly exceeded U.S. industry averages of about 40 percent.
4. *Fuel costs.* Long-term jet fuel cost was uncertain. Prices had risen 11 cents per gallon from July 1995 to May 1996. Proposed fuel taxes could cost the industry as much as $500 million a year.
5. *Air traffic delays.* Increased air traffic control delays caused by higher travel demand and related airport congestion were expected to negatively influence airlines' profitability.

SOUTHWEST AIRLINES BACKGROUND

In 1966, Herb Kelleher was practicing law in San Antonio when a client named Rollin King proposed starting a short-haul airline similar to California-based Pacific Southwest Airlines. The airline would fly the "Golden

Triangle" of Houston, Dallas, and San Antonio and by staying within Texas, avoid federal regulations. Kelleher and King incorporated a company, raised initial capital, and filed for regulatory approval from the Texas Aeronautics Commission. Unfortunately, the other Texas-based airlines, namely Braniff, Continental, and Trans Texas (later called Texas International) opposed the idea and waged a battle to prohibit Southwest from flying. Kelleher argued the company's case before the Texas Supreme Court, which ruled in Southwest's favor. The U.S. Supreme Court refused to hear an appeal filed by the other airlines. In late 1970, it looked as if the company could begin flying.

Southwest began building a management team and purchased three surplus Boeing 737s. Meanwhile, Braniff and Texas International continued their efforts to prevent Southwest from flying. The underwriters of Southwest's initial public stock offering withdrew and a restraining order against the company was obtained two days before its scheduled inaugural flight. Kelleher again argued his company's case before the Texas Supreme Court, which ruled in Southwest's favor a second time, lifting the restraining order. Southwest Airlines began flying the next day, June 18, 1971.[10]

When Southwest began flying to three Texas cities, the firm had three aircraft and 25 employees. Initial flights were out of Dallas' older Love Field airport and Houston's Hobby Airport, both of which were closer to downtown than the major international airports. Flamboyant from the beginning, original flights were staffed by flight attendants in hot pants. By 1996, the flight attendant uniform had evolved into khakis and polo shirts. The "Luv" theme was a staple of the airline from the outset and became the company's ticker symbol on Wall Street.

Southwest management quickly discovered that there were two types of travelers: convenience, time-oriented business travelers and price-sensitive leisure travelers. To cater to both groups, Southwest developed a two-tiered pricing structure. In 1972, Southwest was charging $20 to fly between Houston, Dallas, and San Antonio, undercutting the $28 fares of the other carriers. After an experiment with $10 fares, Southwest decided to sell seats on weekdays until 7:00 P.M. for $26 and after 7:00 P.M. and on weekends for $13.[11] In response, in January 1973, Braniff Airlines began charging $13 for its Dallas-Houston Hobby flights. This resulted in one of Southwest's most famous ads, which had the caption "Nobody's going to shoot Southwest out of the sky for a lousy $13." Southwest offered travelers the opportunity to pay $13 or $26 and receive a free bottle of liquor. More than 75 percent of the passengers chose the $26 fare and Southwest became the largest distributor of Chivas Regal scotch whiskey in Texas. In 1975, Braniff abandoned the Dallas-Houston Hobby route. When Southwest entered the Cleveland market, the unrestricted one-way fare between Cleveland and Chicago was $310 on other carriers; Southwest's fare was $59.[12] One of Southwest's problems was convincing passengers that its low fares were not just introductory promotions but regular fares.

SOUTHWEST OPERATIONS

Although Southwest grew to be one of the largest airlines in the United States, the firm did not deviate from its initial focus: short-haul (less than 500 miles), point-to-point flights; a fleet consisting only of Boeing 737s; high-frequency flights; low fares; and no international flights. In 1995, the average Southwest one-way fare was $69. The average stage length of Southwest flights was 394 miles, with flights of 600 miles making up less than 2.5 percent of the airline's capacity. Kelleher indicated in an interview that it would be unlikely that the company's longer flights (those more than 600 miles) would ever exceed 10 percent of its business.[13] On average, Southwest had more than 40 departures per day per city, and each plane flew about 10 flights daily, almost twice the industry average.[14] Planes were used an average of 11.5 hours a day, compared with the industry's 8.6 hours per day average.[15] Southwest's cost per available seat mile was the lowest in the industry (Exhibit 4) and the average age of its fleet in 1995 was 7.9 years, the lowest for the major carriers. Southwest also had the best safety record in the airline business.

Southwest was the only major airline to operate without hubs. Point-to-point service provided maximum convenience for passengers who wanted to fly between two cities, but insufficient demand could make such nonstop flights economically unfeasible. For that reason, the hub-and-spoke approach was generally assumed to generate cost savings for airlines through op-

4 | Cost Per Available Seat Mile Data

Short-Haul Costs*
(Based on standardized seating, 500-mile hop)

Company	Plane	Cost (in cents)	Percent
American	F-100	12.95	202
USAir	F-100	12.05	187
USAir	737-300	11.49	179
United	737-300	11.17	174
American	MD-80	11.02	171
Continental	737-300	10.18	158
Northwest	DC-9-30	10.18	158
TWA	DC-9-30	9.67	150
Continental	MD-80	9.58	149
Delta	MD-80	8.77	136
Northwest	MD-80	8.76	136
TWA	MD-80	8.29	129
America West	737-300	7.96	124
Alaska	MD-80	7.59	118
ValuJet	DC-9-30	6.58	102
Reno Air	MD-80	6.53	102
Southwest	737-300	6.43	100

Long-Haul Costs
(Based on standardized seating, 1,400-mile hop)

Company	Plane	Cost (in cents)	Percent
USAir	757	6.72	134
American	757	6.70	134
United	757	6.51	130
Northwest	757	5.83	116
Continental	757	5.70	114
Delta	757	5.61	112
American Trans Air	757	5.40	108
America West	757	5.02	100

Source: Roberts Roach & Associates, cited in *Air Transport World*, June 1996, p. 1.
*Second Quarter 1995 data.

erational efficiencies. However, Southwest saw it another way: hub-and-spoke arrangements resulted in planes spending more time on the ground waiting for customers to arrive from connecting points.

Turnaround time—the time it takes to unload a waiting plane and load it for the next flight—was 15 minutes for Southwest, compared with the industry average of 45 minutes. This time savings was accomplished with a gate crew 50 percent smaller than that of other airlines. Pilots sometimes helped unload bags when schedules were tight. Flight attendants regularly assisted in the cleanup of airplanes between flights.

Relative to the other major airlines, Southwest had a "no frills" approach to services: reserved seating was not offered and meals were not served. Customers were handed numbered or color-coded boarding passes based on their check-in order. Seating was first come, first served. As a cost-saving measure, the color-coded passes were reusable. As to why the airline did not have assigned seating, Kelleher explained: "It used to be we only had about four people on the whole plane, so the idea of assigned seats just made people laugh. Now the reason is you can turn the airplanes quicker at the gate. And if you can turn an airplane quicker, you can have it fly more routes each day. That generates more revenue, so you can offer lower fares."[16]

Unlike some of the major carriers, Southwest rarely offered delayed customers a hotel room or long-distance telephone calls. Southwest did not use a computerized reservation system, preferring to have travel agents and customers book flights through its reservation center or vending machines in airports. Southwest was the first national carrier to sell seats from an Internet site. Southwest was also one of the first airlines to use ticketless travel, first offering the service on January 31, 1995. By June 1996, 35 percent of the airline's passengers were flying ticketless, at a cost savings of $25 million per year.[17] The company was a 1996 Computerworld Smithsonian Awards Finalist for the rapid development and installation of its ticketless system within a four-month time frame.

Over the years, Southwest's choice of markets resulted in significant growth in air travel at those locations. In Texas, traffic between the Rio Grande Valley (Harlingen) and the "Golden Triangle" grew from 123,000 to 325,000 within 11 months of Southwest's entering the market.[18] Within a year of Southwest's arrival, the Oakland-Burbank route became the 25th largest passenger market, up from 179th. The Chicago-Louisville market tripled in size 30 days after Southwest began flying that route. Southwest was the dominant carrier in a number of cities, ranking first in market share in more than 50 percent of the largest U.S. city-pair markets. Exhibit 5 shows a comparison of Southwest in 1971 and 1995.

Southwest's Performance

Southwest bucked the airline industry trend by earning a profit in 23 consecutive years (see Exhibit 6 for Southwest's financial performance). Southwest was the only major U.S. airline to make a profit in 1992. Even taking into account the losses in its first two years of operation, the company averaged an annual 12.07 percent return on investment. In 1995, for the fourth year in a row, Southwest received the coveted Triple Crown award given by the U.S. Department of Transportation for having the best on-time performance, best luggage handling record, and fewest customer complaints. No other airline achieved that record for even one month.

Southwest accomplished its enviable record by challenging accepted norms and setting competitive thresholds for the other airlines to emulate. The company had established numerous new industry standards. In 1991, Southwest flew more passengers per employee (2,318 versus the industry average of 848) than any other airline, while at the same time having the fewest number of employees per aircraft (79 at Southwest compared with the industry average of 131).[19] Southwest maintained a debt-to-equity ratio much lower than the industry average. The ratio was 50 percent in 1995, with

EXHIBIT 5 | Southwest 25-Year Comparison

	1971	1995
Size of fleet	4	224
Number of employees at year-end	195	19,933
Number of passengers carried	108,554	44,785,573
Number of cities served	3	45
Number of trips flown	6,051	685,524
Total operating revenues	2,133,000	2,872,751,000
Net income (losses)	(3,753,000)	182,626,000
Stockholders' equity	3,318,000	1,427,318,000
Total assets	**22,083,000**	**3,256,122,000**

Source: K. Freiberg and J. Freiberg, 1996. *Nuts: Southwest Airlines Crazy Recipe for Business and Personal Success*, Austin, TX, Band Press, p. 326.

6 | Southwest Airlines 10-Year Financial Summary

Selected Consolidated Financial Data[1]
(in thousands except per share amounts)

	1995	1994	1993	1992	1991	1990	1989	1988	1987	1986
Operating revenues:										
Passenger	$2,760,756	$2,497,765	$1,144,421	$973,568	$1,267,897	$1,144,421	$973,568	$828,343	$751,649	$742,287
Freight	65,825	54,419	42,897	33,088	26,428	22,196	18,771	14,433	13,428	13,621
Charter and other	46,170	39,749	37,434	146,063	84,961	70,659	65,390	17,658	13,251	12,882
Total operating revenues	2,872,751	2,591,933	2,296,673	1,802,979	1,379,286	1,237,276	1,057,729	860,434	778,328	768,790
Operating expenses	2,559,220	2,275,224	2,004,700	1,609,175	1,306,675	1,150,015	955,689	774,454	747,881	679,827
Operating income	313,531	316,709	291,973	193,804	72,611	87,261	102,040	85,980	30,447[9]	88,963
Other expenses (income), net	8,391	17,186	32,335	36,361	18,725	(6,827)[6]	(13,696)[7]	620[8]	1,374[10]	23,517
Income before income taxes	305,140	299,523	259,637	157,443	53,886	80,434	115,736	85,360	29,073	65,446
Provision for income taxes[3]	122,514	120,192	105,353	60,058	20,738	29,829	41,231	27,408	8,918	15,411
Net income[3]	$182,626	$179,331	$154,284[4]	$97,385[5]	$33,148	$50,605	$74,505	$57,952	$20,155	$50,035
Income per common and common equivalent share[3]	$1.23	$1.22	$1.05[4]	$.68[5]	$.25	$.39	$.54	$.41	$.14	$.34
Cash dividends per common share	$.04000	$.04000	$.03867	$.03533	$.03333	$.03223	$.03110	$.02943	$.02890	$.02890
Total assets	$3,256,122	$2,823,071	$2,576,037	$2,368,856	$1,854,331	$1,480,813	$1,423,298	$1,308,389	$1,042,640	$1,061,419
Long-term debt	$661,010	$583,071	$639,136	$735,754	$617,434	$327,553	$354,150	$369,541	$251,130	$339,069
Stockholders' equity	$1,427,318	$1,238,706	$1,054,019	$879,536	$635,793	$607,294	$591,794	$567,375	$514,278	$511,850
Consolidated financial ratios[1]										
Return on average total assets	6.0%	6.6%	6.2%[4]	4.6%[5]	2.0%	3.5%	5.5%	5.1%	1.9%	4.8%
Return on average stockholder's equity	13.7%	15.6%	16.0%[4]	12.9%[5]	5.3%	5.4%	12.9%	10.3%	4.0%	10.3%
Debt as a percentage of invested capital	31.7%	32.0%	37.7%	45.5%	49.3%	35.0%	37.4%	39.4%	32.8%	39.8%

Consolidated Operating Statistics[2]										
Revenue passengers carried	44,785,573	42,742,602[11]	36,955,221[11]	27,839,284	22,669,942	19,830,941	17,958,263	14,876,582	13,503,242	13,637,515
RPMs (000s)	23,327,804	21,611,266	18,827,288	13,787,005	11,296,183	9,958,940	9,281,992	7,676,257	7,789,376	7,388,401
ASMs (000s)	36,180,001	32,123,974	27,511,000	21,366,642	18,491,003	16,411,115	14,796,732	13,309,044	13,331,055	12,574,484
Load factor	64.5%	67.3%	68.4%	64.5%	61.1%	60.7%	62.7%	57.7%	58.4%	58.8%
Average length of passenger haul	521	506	509	495	498	502	517	516	577	542
Trips flown	685,524	624,476	546,297	438,184	382,752	338,108	304,673	274,859	270,559	262,082
Average passenger fare	$61.64	$58.44	$59.97	$58.33	$55.93	$57.71	$54.21	$55.68	$55.66	$54.43
Passenger revenue yield per RPM	11.83¢	11.56¢	11.77¢	11.78¢	11.22¢	11.49¢	10.49¢	10.79¢	9.65¢	10.05¢
Operating revenue yield per ASM	7.94¢	8.07¢	8.35¢	7.89¢	7.10¢	7.23¢	6.86¢	6.47¢	5.84¢	6.11¢
Operating expenses per ASM	7.07¢	7.08¢	7.25¢[12]	7.03¢	6.76¢	6.73¢	6.20¢	5.82¢	5.61¢	5.41¢
Fuel cost per gallon (average)	55.22¢	53.92¢	59.15¢	60.82¢	65.69¢	77.89¢	59.46¢	51.37¢	54.31¢	51.42¢
Number of employees at year end	19,933	16,818	15,175	11,397	9,778	8,620	7,760	6,467	5,765	5,819
Size of fleet at year end[13]	224	199	178	141	124	106	94	85	75	79

[1]The Selected Consolidated Financial Data and Consolidated Financial Ratios for 1992 through 1989 have been restated to include the financial results of Morris. Years prior to 1989 were immaterial for restatement purposes.

[2]Prior to 1993, Morris operated as a charter carrier; therefore, no Morris statistics are included for these years.

[3]Pro forma for 1992 through 1989 assuming Morris, an S-Corporation prior to 1993, was taxed at statutory rates.

[4]Excludes cumulative effect of accounting changes of $15.3 million ($.10 per share).

[5]Excludes cumulative effect of accounting changes of $12.5 million ($.09 per share).

[6]Includes $2.6 million gains on sales of aircraft and $3.1 million from the sale of certain financial assets.

[7]Includes $10.8 million gains on sales of aircraft, $5.9 million from the sale of certain financial assets, and $2.3 million from the settlement of a contingency.

[8]Includes $5.6 million gains on sales of aircraft and $3.6 million from the sale of certain financial assets.

[9]Includes TranStar's results through June 30, 1987.

[10]Includes $10.1 million net gains from the discontinuance of TranStar's operations and $4.3 million from the sale of certain financial assets.

[11]Includes certain estimates for Morris.

[12]Excludes merger expenses of $10.8 million.

[13]Includes leased aircraft.

cash holdings of $400 million. In addition, Southwest had a credit rating of "A," with a $460 million line of credit in 1995. Southwest was the only airline with an investment-grade credit rating.

Southwest's fleet of 737s had grown to 224 by 1995, up from 106 in 1990 and 75 in 1987. New aircraft deliveries were expected to average 22 per year until 2000, split equally between purchases and leases.[20] Revenues more than doubled between 1987 and 1995. Profits grew even faster during the same period. In 1994, Southwest tripled annual capacity growth, measured by available seat miles, to 30 percent and flew to 46 cities in 22 states. The number of flights per day in 1995 was 2,065 serving 46 cities, up from 1,883 flights in 1994.

HERB KELLEHER

Southwest's CEO, Herb Kelleher, managed the airline with a leadership style of flamboyance and fun and a fresh, unique perspective. Kelleher played Big Daddy-O in one of the company videos, appeared as the King of Rock (Elvis Presley) in in-flight magazine advertisements, and earned the nickname "High Priest of Ha-Ha" from *Fortune* magazine.[21] Although Kelleher was unconventional and a maverick in his field, he led his company to consistently new standards for itself and for the industry. Sincerely committed to his employees, Kelleher generated intense loyalty to himself and the company. His ability to remember employees' names and to ask after their families was just one way he earned respect and trust. At one point, Kelleher froze his salary for five years in response to the pilots agreeing to do the same. Often when he flew, Kelleher would help the ground crew unload bags or help the flight crew serve drinks. His humor was legendary and served as an example for his employees to join in the fun of working for Southwest. He was called "a visionary who leads by example—you have to work harder than anybody else to show them you are devoted to the business."[22]

Although Kelleher tried to downplay his personal significance to the company when questions were raised about succession, many analysts following Southwest credited the airline's success to Kelleher's unorthodox personality and engaging management style. As one analyst wrote, "the old-fashioned bond of loyalty between employees and company may have vanished elsewhere in corporate America, but it is stronger than ever at Southwest."[23]

THE SOUTHWEST SPIRIT

Customer service far beyond the norm in the airline industry was not unexpected at Southwest and had its own name—Positively Outrageous Service. Some examples of this service included: a gate agent volunteering to watch a dog (a Chihuahua) for two weeks when an Acapulco-bound passenger showed up at the last minute without the required dog crate; an Austin passenger who missed a connection to Houston, where he was to have a kidney transplant operation, was flown there by a Southwest pilot in his private plane. Another passenger, an elderly woman flying to Phoenix for cancer treatment, began crying because she had no family or friends at her destination. The ticket agent invited her into her home and escorted her around Phoenix for two weeks.[24]

Southwest Airlines customers were often surprised by "Southwest Spirit." On some flights, magazine pictures of gourmet meals were offered for dinner on an evening flight. Flight attendants were encouraged to have fun: songs, jokes, and humorous flight announcements were common. One flight attendant had a habit of popping out of overhead luggage compartments as passengers attempted to stow their belongings, until the day she frightened an elderly passenger who called for oxygen.[25] Herb Kelleher once served in-flight snacks dressed as the Easter Bunny.

Intense company communication and camaraderie were highly valued and essential to maintaining the *esprit de corps* found throughout the firm. The Southwest Spirit, as exhibited by enthusiasm and extroverted personalities, was an important element in employee screening conducted by Southwest's People Department. Employment at Southwest was highly desired. When the company held a job fair in Oklahoma City, more than 9,000 people attended in four days.[26] In 1995, 5,444 employees were hired from the 124,000 applications received and 38,000 interviews held.[27] Once landed, a job was fairly secure. The airline had not laid off an employee since 1971. Employee turnover hovered around 7 percent, the lowest rate in the industry.[28] More than half of Southwest's 22,000 employees had been hired after 1990. In 1990, Southwest had only 8,600 employees and less than 6,000 in 1987.

During initial training periods, efforts were made to share and instill Southwest's unique culture. New employee orientation, known as the new-hire celebration, included Southwest's version of the Wheel of Fortune, scavenger hunts, and company videos including the "Southwest Airlines Shuffle" in which each department introduced itself, rap style, and in which Kelleher appeared as Big Daddy-O.

Advanced employee training regularly occurred at the University of People at Love Field in Dallas. Various classes were offered, including team building, leadership, and cultural diversity. Newly promoted supervisors and managers attended a three-day class called "Leading with Integrity." Each department also had its own training department focusing on technical aspects of the work. "Walk-a-Mile Day" encouraged employees from different departments to experience first hand the day-to-day activities of their co-workers. The goal of this program was to promote respect for fellow workers while increasing awareness of the company.[29]

Employee initiative was supported by management and encouraged at all levels. For example, pilots looked for ways to conserve fuel during flights, employees proposed designs for ice storage equipment that reduced time and costs, and baggage handlers learned to place luggage with the handles facing outward to reduce unloading time.

Red hearts and "Luv" were central parts of the internal corporate culture, appearing throughout the company literature. A mentoring program for new hires was called CoHearts. "Heroes of the Heart Awards" were given annually to one behind-the-scenes group of workers, whose department name was painted on a specially designed plane for a year. Other awards honored an employee's big mistake through the "Boner of the Year Award." When employees had a story about exceptional service to share, they were encouraged to fill out a "LUV Report."

Southwest placed great emphasis on maintaining cooperative labor relations. Within the firm, almost 90 percent of all employees were unionized. The company encouraged the unions and their negotiators to conduct employee surveys and to research their most important issues prior to each contract negotiation. Southwest had never had a serious labor dispute. The airlines' pilot union, SWAPA, represented 2,000 pilots. At its 1994 contract discussion, the pilots proposed a 10-year contract with stock options in lieu of guaranteed pay increases over the first five years of the contract. In 1973, Southwest was the first airline to introduce employee profit sharing.

SOUTHWEST IMITATORS

Southwest's low-fare, short-haul strategy spawned numerous imitators. By the second half of 1994, low fares were available on more than one-third of the industry's total capacity.[30] Many of the imitators were new start-up airlines. The Allied Pilots Association (APA) claimed that approximately 97 percent of start-ups resulted in failures. According to the APA, only 2 of 34 start-up airlines formed between 1978 and 1992 were successful, with success defined as surviving 10 years or longer without bankruptcy. The two successful firms, Midwest Express and America West, had both been through Chapter 11 bankruptcy proceedings. APA's prognosis for newer airlines was equally pessimistic, with only Frontier and Western pacific of the 19 start-ups formed since 1992 perceived as having good prospects for long-term survival.[31] Three of the 19 had already folded by 1996, and ValuJet was grounded after its May 1996 crash in the Florida Everglades.

The major airlines had also taken steps to compete directly with Southwest. The Shuttle by United, a so-called "airline with an airline," was started in October 1994. United's objective was to create a new airline owned by United with many of the same operational elements as Southwest: a fleet of 737s, low fares, short-haul flights, and less restrictive union rules. Although offering basically a no-frills service, the Shuttle provided assigned seating and offered access to airline computer reservation systems. United predicted that the Shuttle could eventually account for as much as 20 percent of total United U.S. operations.

United saturated the West Coast corridor with short-haul flights on routes such as Oakland-Seattle, San Francisco-San Diego, and Sacramento-San Diego. Almost immediately, Southwest lost 10 percent of its California traffic. Southwest responded by adding six aircraft and 62 daily flights in California. In April 1995, United eliminated its Oakland-Ontario route and proposed a $10 fare increase on other flights. By January 1996, United had pulled the Shuttle off routes that did not feed passengers to its San Francisco and Los Angeles hubs. In early 1995, United and Southwest competed directly on 13 percent of Southwest's routes. By 1996, that number was down to 7 percent.[32]

Cost was the major problem for United in competing with Southwest. The Shuttle's cost per seat mile remained at about 8 cents, whereas Southwest's cost was close to 7 cents. Two factors were largely responsible for the Shuttle's higher costs. First, many passengers booked their tickets through travel agents, which resulted in commission fees. Second, many of the Shuttle's flights were in the San Francisco and Los Angeles markets, both of which were heavily congested and subject to costly delays. In addition, the Shuttle was unable to achieve the same level of productivity as Southwest. Nevertheless, by launching the Shuttle, United was able to gain market share in the San Francisco and Los Angeles markets, largely at the expense of American, USAir, and Delta.

Continental Lite (CALite) was an effort by Continental Airlines to develop a low-cost service and revive the company's fortunes after coming out of bankruptcy in April 1993. CALite began service in October 1993 on 50 routes, primarily in the Southeast. Frequency of flights was a key part of the new strategy. Greenville-Spartanburg got 17 flights a day and in Orlando, daily departures more than doubled. CALite fares were modeled after those of Southwest and meals were eliminated on flights less than 2.5 hours.

In March 1994, Continental increased CALite service to 875 daily flights. Continental soon encountered major operational problems with its new strategy.[33] With its fleet of 16 different planes, mechanical delays disrupted turnaround times. Various pricing strategies were unsuccessful. The company was ranked last among the major carriers for on-time service and complaints soared by 40 percent. In January 1995, Continental announced that it would reduce its capacity by 10 percent and eliminate 4,000 jobs. By mid-1995, Continental's CALite service had been largely discontinued. In October 1995, Continental's CEO was ousted.

Delta was developing its "Leadership 7.5" campaign, intended to cut costs by $2 billion by mid-1997 and lower its ASM costs to 7.5 cents. Western Pacific (WestPac) was one of the newest domestic start-up airlines building on Southwest's formula, while adding its own twists. WestPac began flying out of a new airport in Colorado Springs in April 1995. WestPac's fleet consisted of 12 leased Boeing 737s. The airline started with 15 domestic destinations on the West Coast, East Coast, Southwest and Midwest, and all medium-length routes. Offering an alternative to the expensive Denver International Airport, business grew quickly. The company made a profit in two of its first four months of operation. Load factors averaged more than 60 percent in the first five months of operation, and were 75.9 percent in August. Operating cost per available seat mile averaged 7.37 cents during the early months and dropped to 6.46 cents within five months. The Colorado Springs airport became one of the country's fastest growing as a result of WestPac's market entry. WestPac had one-third of the market share and had flown almost 600,000 passengers during its first seven months.

One of WestPac's most successful marketing efforts was the "Mystery Fare" program. As a way to fill empty seats, $59 round-trip tickets were sold to one of the airline's destinations, but which one remained a mystery. Response greatly exceeded the airline's expectations; thousands of the mystery seats were sold. "Logo jets," also known as flying billboards, were another inventive approach by the start-up company. Jets painted on the outside with client advertising raised more than $1 million in fees over a one-year period. The airline also benefited from recent advances in ticketless operations. A healthy commission program to travel agents and a diverse, nonunion work force were other features of WestPac operations.[34]

Morris Air, patterned after Southwest, was the only airline Southwest had acquired. Prior to the acquisition, Morris Air flew Boeing 737s on point-to-point routes, operated in a different part of the United States than Southwest, and was profitable. When Morris Air was acquired by Southwest in December 1993, seven new markets were added to Southwest's system.

SOUTHWEST'S MOVE INTO FLORIDA

In January 1996, Southwest began new flights from Tampa International to Fort Lauderdale, Nashville, New

Orleans, St. Louis/Lambert International Airport, Birmingham, Houston/Hobby Airport, and Baltimore/Washington International Airport. Saturation and low initial fares were part of Southwest's expansion strategy. Some of the routes would have as many as six daily flights. In April, service began from Orlando International airport, with 10 flights headed to five different airports. Southwest's goal was to operate 78 daily flights to Tampa, Ft. Lauderdale, and Orlando.

Availability of assets and staff was a potential restriction on the airline's expansion possibilities. Ground crews were being transferred from other Southwest locations, with pilot and flight attendants coming from Chicago and Houston bases to cover the Florida expansion. Ten new Boeing jets were on order for the Florida routes.

EXPANSION INTO THE NORTHEAST

With Southwest established as a leader in many aspects of the industry, continued success was hard to doubt. Yet, Southwest had shown itself to be vulnerable, at least for a short time, to the well-planned competition from Shuttle by United on the West Coast. New airlines, such as WestPac, had also proved capable of innovating and quickly becoming profitable.

The proposed entry into the northeastern region of the United States was, in many respects, the next logical move for Southwest. The Northeast was the most densely populated area of the country and the only major region where Southwest did not compete. New England could provide a valuable source of passengers to Florida's warmer winter climates. Southwest's entry into Florida was exceeding initial estimates. Using a low-fare strategy, ValuJet had, until its crash, built a strong competitive base in important northeastern markets.

Despite the large potential market, the Northeast offered a new set of challenges for Southwest. Airport congestion and air traffic control delays could prevent efficient operations, lengthening turnaround time at airport gates and wreaking havoc on frequent flight scheduling. Inclement weather posed additional challenges for both air service and car travel to airports. Southwest had already rejected some of the larger airports as too crowded, including LaGuardia, JFK International, and Newark International airports. Some regional airports lacked facilities required by a high-volume airline. For example, Stewart International Airport, near Newburgh, New York and north of New York City lacked basic facilities such as gates and ticket counters.

The critical question for Southwest management was whether expansion to the Northeast, and particularly New England, was premature. Or, would the challenge bring out the best in a firm with a history of defying conventional wisdom and doing things its own way?

ENDNOTES

1. K. Freiberg and J. Freiberg, 1996, *Nuts: Southwest Airlines, Crazy Recipe for Business and Personal Success*, Austin: TX: Bard Press, p. 61.
2. Ibid., p. 28.
3. P. S. Dempsey, 1984, Transportation Deregulation: On a Collision Course, *Transportation Law Journal* 13: 329.
4. W. Goralski, 1996, Deregulation Deja Vu, *Telephony*, June 17: 32–36.
5. A. Bryant, 1996, U.S. Airlines Finally Reach Cruising Speed, *New York Times*, October 20, Section 3: 1.
6. *Business Week*, August 7, 1995, p. 25.
7. C. A. Shifrin, 1996, Record U.S. Airline Earnings Top $2 Billion, *Aviation Week & Space Technology*, January 29: 46.
8. P. Proctor, 1996, ATA Predicts Record Year for U.S. Airline Profits, *Aviation Week & Space Technology*, May 13: 33.
9. Ibid., p. 33.
10. Freiberg and Freiberg, pp. 14–21.
11. Ibid., p. 31.
12. Ibid., p. 55.
13. More City Pairs Await Southwest, 1995, *Aviation Week & Space Technology*, August 7: 41.
14. K. Labich, 1994, Is Herb Kelleher America's Best CEO?, *Fortune*, May 2: 47.
15. Freiberg and Freiberg, p. 51.
16. Herb Kelleher, http://www.iflyswa.com/cgi-bin/imagemap/swagate 530.85.
17. *Computerworld*, June 23, 1996, p. 98.
18. Freiberg and Freiberg, p. 29.
19. Southwest Airlines Charts a High-Performance Flight, 1995, *Training & Development*, June: 39.
20. A. L. Velocci, 1995, Southwest Adding Depth to Short-Haul Structure, *Air Transport*, August 7: 39.
21. Labich, p. 45.
22. 24th Annual CEO Survey: Herb Kelleher, Flying His Own Course, 1995, *IW*, November 20: 23.
23. Labich, p. 46.

24. *IW*, p. 23.
25. B. O'Brian, 1992, Flying on the Cheap, *Wall Street Journal*, October 26: A1.
26. B. P. Sunoo, 1995, How Fun Flies At Southwest Airlines, *Personnel Journal*, June: 66.
27. Freiberg and Freiberg, p. 72.
28. *Training & Development*, June p. 39.
29. A. Malloy, 1996, Counting the Intangibles, *Computerworld*, June: 32–33.
30. Industry Surveys, 1996, *Aerospace & Air Transport*, February 1: A36.
31. E. H. Phillips, 1996, GAO Study: Demographics Drive Airline Service, *Aviation Week & Space Technology*, May 13: 37.
32. S. McCartney and M. J. McCarthy, 1996, Southwest Flies Circles Around United's Shuttle, *Wall Street Journal*, February 20: B1.
33. B. O'Brian, 1995, Heavy Going: Continental's CALite Hits Some Turbulence in Battling Southwest, *Wall Street Journal*, January 10: A1, A16.
34. Rapid Route Growth Tests WestPac's Low-Fare Formula, 1995, *Aviation Week & Space Technology*, December 4: 37–38.

CASE 34

Starbucks

Ariff Kachra
Mary Crossan
University of Western Ontario

Mr. Howard Schultz, the Chairman and CEO of Starbucks Corporation, had just given a speech on the future of the coffee industry at a well-known business school. As he left the lecture hall, he stopped at the University's most popular coffee shop, the Brewery. The shop's sign indicated that it was "Now Serving Starbucks Coffee." As Mr. Schultz ordered the House Blend, he noticed that the Brewery was a far cry from any Starbucks coffeehouse. The shop was messy, the service was poor, and the coffee was average. As Mr. Schultz was leaving the Brewery, Orin Smith, Starbucks President and COO, called him on his cellular phone. McDonald's, whom Starbucks had turned down a number of times, was once again petitioning for a contract to serve Starbucks coffee. On the plane back to Seattle, Washington, Mr. Schultz's thoughts drifted back to his experience at the Brewery and the call from McDonald's. He asked himself two questions: Was Starbucks growing in the best way possible? Was Starbucks overextending in its quest for growth?

IVEY The authors do not intend to illustrate either effective or ineffective handling of a managerial situation. The authors may have disguised certain names and other identifying information to protect confidentiality.

Ivey Management Services prohibits any form of reproduction, storage or transmittal without its written permission. This material is not covered under authorization from CanCopy or any reproduction rights organization. To order copies or request permission to reproduce materials, contact Ivey Publishing, Ivey Management Services, c/o Richard Ivey School of Business, The University of Western Ontario, London, Ontario, Canada, N6A 3K7; phone (519) 661-3208; fax (519) 661-3882; e-mail cases@ivey.uwo.ca.

Copyright © 1997, Ivey Management Services. One time permission to reproduce granted by Ivey Management Services on November 18, 1999.

SPECIALTY-COFFEE INDUSTRY

Coffee was the second most traded commodity next to oil. It was divided into two categories: specialty coffee and basic coffee. Specialty coffee was the highest echelon of quality coffee available in the world. Many people described it as gourmet coffee. There was no one accepted definition in the industry; however, everyone agreed that specialty coffee was of higher quality than basic supermarket brand coffee.

It was estimated in 1994 that the specialty-coffee industry was growing at a rate of 15 percent per year and that the basic-coffee industry was suffering. Although most consumers only saw this division at the retail level, specialty vs. basic coffee was a concept that originated with the coffee grower.

SUPPLIERS

Specialty-coffee companies did not typically deal with suppliers, i.e., coffee farmers, directly. They dealt with exporters instead. About a third of the coffee farms in the world were less than three acres. These farmers did not have the desire, the volume, the money, the expertise, or the connections to export coffee themselves because most countries regulated coffee sales. Coffee processors or exporters regularly visited smaller farmers and bought their coffee[1] either in cherry or parchment.[2] The coffee would then be moved to a mill where there would be other farmers' production from the same or different regions. After husking the parchment, the millers sold it to the exporter(s). It was commonplace

1 | Specialty Coffee Sales as a Percentage of Total Coffee Sales

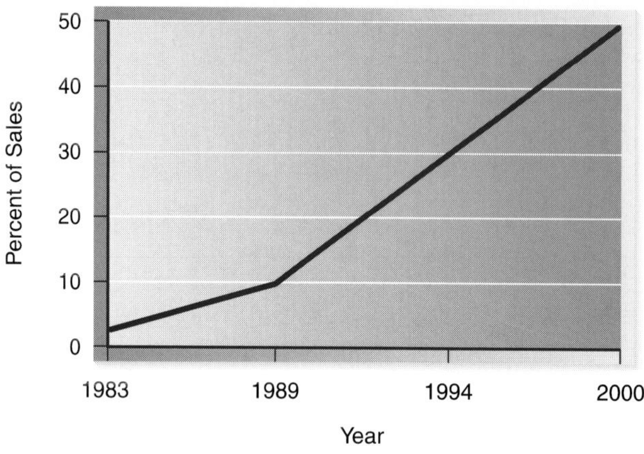

Source: Specialty Coffee Association of America, Montgomery Securities, Volume 27.

for coffee to change hands as many as five times before it reached a specialty-coffee seller. Typically, coffee was moved from the farmer, to the collector, to the miller, to the exporter, to the importer, and finally, to the specialty-coffee seller.

The bean suppliers that managed this process well typically concentrated on high quality Arabic beans for which they could command premium prices. Lower quality bean suppliers concentrated on Robusta beans. This quality division was somewhat congruent to the way the industry was divided, i.e., lower quality beans were harvested for the commercial industry and higher quality beans for the specialty coffee industry. (Industry experts estimated that specialty coffee made up 31 percent of the total coffee consumption. See Exhibit 1.)

The price of certain coffee was a direct reflection of the quality and quantity of coffee available at a particular time. It was very difficult to get price confirmations because a successful coffee harvest was dependent on so many different factors. These included weather conditions, health of the coffee trees, harvesting practices, disease and infection caused by insects, and the social, political, regulatory and economic environments of the coffee-producing countries. For example, the 1975 Brazilian frost drove the price of coffee up, and U.S. coffee consumption never recovered from the 18.5 percent decline.

CONSUMERS

Coffee consumption patterns had changed in the U.S. In 1996, the per capita consumption of coffee was 1.7 cups per day per person, a significant decrease from the two to three cups daily consumption in the '60s and '70s. The National Coffee Association attributed this decrease to poor product development, packaging, and position (price focused) by the industry's leading coffee producers. However, now it seemed that coffee consumption was on the rise. The following compares U.S. consumption rates to global consumption rates:

> *In terms of kilograms of coffee per person consumed in 1985, the United States at 4.7 ranked tenth, behind Sweden (11.6), Denmark (11.0), Finland (10.0), Holland (9.5), Germany (6.8), France (5.5), and Italy (4.9) among the coffee-consuming nations and behind Costa Rica (6.5) and Brazil (5.5) among the coffee-producing nations. Overall, in the decade between 1975 and 1985, Europe's level of imported coffee rose significantly, those of Japan doubled, while those of the United States remained steady despite increased population.*[3]

The recent popularity of specialty coffee was the result of four consumer trends: (1) the adoption of a healthier lifestyle had led North Americans to replace alcohol with coffee; (2) coffee bars offered a place where people could meet; (3) people liked affordable luxuries and specialty coffee fit the bill; and (4) consumers were becoming more knowledgeable about coffee.

Profile

According to *Avenues for Growth—A 20-Year Review of the U.S. Specialty Coffee Industry*,[4] 22 percent of the U.S. consumers purchased specialty coffee. This 22 percent of the population typically lived and worked in urban areas, and had an annual income over $35,000. Research had shown that two-parent families with a stay-at-home mother purchased 41 percent more specialty coffee than the average. Single people purchased 39 percent more than the average and consumers with college degrees purchased 49 percent more than the average. Females purchased slightly more specialty coffee than men and coffee consumption was higher among individuals aged 30 to 59 than those aged 20 to 29.[5] Research by many coffee companies had found that once a consumer learned to appreciate a high-quality specialty coffee, he or she did not go back to his or her favorite average-quality brew.

Community Gathering Place

Consumers' patterns of socializing had changed since the '80s. While the mid-'80s were characterized by the pursuit of entertainment outside the home, in the early nineties, people wanted to stay home. There was a move away from restaurants and dance clubs. Now, in the second part of the decade, there seemed to be a resurgence of outside-the-home entertainment. Coffeehouses were able to fill this need and were more accessible than bars. Coffee's image had changed from being purely a breakfast drink to a beverage that could be enjoyed any time and as a social catalyst. Coffee purchasers wanted more than just a place where they could get a higher quality cup of coffee. They wanted a place that answered a lifestyle need. Increasingly, coffee shops were turning into living rooms, where people sat back and enjoyed a cup of coffee or something else and relaxed with their friends or business associates. Coffeehouses had become community gathering places.

COMPETITION

Product-Based Competition

In retail coffee-house sales, specialty coffee not only competed with basic coffee, it also competed with tea, juice, soft drinks, alcohol and other coffee and non-coffee-related drinks. However the consumption of all of these beverages relative to specialty coffee was declining.

Specialty coffee could be divided into flavored coffee which represented 25 percent of all specialty coffee sold, and non-flavored coffee. Flavored coffee referred to coffee that was flavored with a variety of essences during the roasting process. Popular flavors included hazelnut, amaretto, raspberry, etc. Flavored coffee was not offered by specialty-coffee companies like Starbucks, Peet's, Caribou Coffee and The Coffee Station, but the opposite was true for Timothy's and The Second Cup. Flavored coffee was popular among traditional non-coffee drinkers, younger coffee drinkers, and those interested in a low calorie substitute for desserts or snacks. For a comparison of retail sales of different types of coffee, see Exhibit 2.

Another important product substitute was specialty coffee originating from basic-coffee companies in the grocery chain. To respond to the phenomenal growth in speciality coffee in the grocery chain, many large, basic-coffee manufacturers were moving into more speciality brands by introducing upscale versions of already popular supermarket brands. However, industry analysts forecasted that there would be a shift in consumer purchasing of specialty coffee. Currently, grocery stores were responsible for 81 percent of specialty coffee sales; this figure was expected to fall to 46 percent in 1999. This shift would result in greater amounts of coffee being purchased from specialty stores: 19 percent currently to 54 percent in 1999.

Retail-Based Competition

The Specialty Coffee Association of America estimated there would be room for about 10,000 coffee retail outlets in the United States and Canada by 1999. But only 5,500 of those would be coffee bars and cafes; the rest would be carts.[6] Exhibit 3 depicts the amount of room for growth in the retail coffee industry.

Given the low barriers to entry in the retail specialty-coffee market, there were more than 3485 competitors in the market.[7] However, most of these were one-store establishments with no real plans for growth. Exhibit 4 describes those companies that had developed a strong regional and/or national presence.

EXHIBIT 2 | Comparing the Retail Sales of Coffee (US$ millions)

	1990	1994	1998E	1990–1994 Growth	1994–1998E Growth
Ground regular	2,050	1,240	800	−11.8%	−10.4%
Ground decaffeinated	650	575	450	−3.0%	−5.9%
Ground specialty	810	1,315	1,635	12.9%	5.6%
Instant regular	1,175	1,010	780	−3.7%	−6.3%
Instant decaffeinated	385	295	170	−6.4%	−12.9%
Whole bean	255	380	500	10.5%	7.1%
Ready-to-drink	5	250	1,255	165.9%	49.7%
Total	5,330	5,065	5,590	−1.3%	2.5%

Source: Yorkton Securities Inc., March 25, 1997.

SECOND CUP

The Second Cup was primarily a franchiser (90 percent of all locations), and as a result, the company was consistently cash flow positive and had the benefit of taking little operating risk at the store level. Traditionally, the Second Cup was mall-based, but in the past few years it had moved into more stand-alone locations. These locations were established rather quickly and were not always on prime real estate. In its retail concept, the Second Cup offered specialty coffee drinks, varietals, flavored coffee and snack items.

The Second Cup was very growth-oriented and believed strongly in growth via acquisitions. One of its major acquisitions included Gloria Jean's (247 locations), in the U.S. Including its own 243 stores, the Second Cup was the second largest player in the specialty coffee industry. Where the Second Cup's revenues came from liquid coffee and snack food items, Gloria Jean's obtained a high percentage of sales from coffee mugs, related items and coffee beans.

In recent times, the Second Cup had become quite active in developing alliances with other food service companies. Through its alliance with Cara Operations

EXHIBIT 3 | Growth Potential in Retail Coffee Industry

Location	Population (missions)	Number of Starbucks Stores	Current Population /Store	Population necessary to support a coffee house	Maximun number of coffee stores supportable by market	Total Starbucks Stores as a percentage of total possible stores
Top 50 U.S. Markets	144.9	914	158,581	54,470	2,661	34%
Vancouver, Toronto, Ottowa, Montreal, Calgary	11.3	113	99,611	56,000	201	56%
Top 100 U.S. & major Canadian markets	180.2	1,074	167,784	55,000	3,276	33%
Total U.S. & Canadian markets	276.2	1,074	257,128	56,000	4,931	22%

Source: William Blair & Company, Starbucks Corporation, June 20, 1997.

EXHIBIT 4 | Companies with a Strong Regional and/or National Presence

Diedrich's Coffee
- Made with its own freshly roasted beans
- Sold light food items and whole bean coffee
- A few wholesale customers
- Operated a total of 32 coffeehouses in Texas, Colorado, and California
- 1996 sales: $10.2 million

Green Mountain Coffee Inc.
- Primarily a wholesaler of specialty coffee (3,000 customers)
- Small number of retail operations with in-store roasting facilities
- Roasted over 25 high quality Arabica coffees to produce over 70 varieties
- 1996 sales: $38.3 million

Coffee People
- Located in suburban neighborhoods and business districts, averaging about 1,500 to 2,000 square feet in size
- Used specialty kiosks located in high traffic locations such as airports and shopping malls
- Hoped to have 100 locations by 1998

A.L. Van Houtte
- Offered 36 types of ground coffee, nine types of flavored coffee and 54 types of whole beans
- Sold its coffee through restaurants, including its own network of 107 cafe-bistros (only 4 corporate stores)
- Good reputation as a vendor of coffee to offices, hotels, etc.
- 1996 sales: $164.1 million

Barnie's Coffee & Tea Company
- Focused on the merchandising aspect of coffee retailing; it offered 400 different branded products
- Typically seated about 50 people and was located in malls
- Its newest innovation was a restaurant, La Venezia Cafe; seated 200 people and offered 47 different coffees

Caribou
- Wanted to be the 3rd place between work and home where people could socialize
- Implemented a very American feel to its coffeehouses rather than a European feel
- Offered very fast service, magazines, newspapers, free refills, and seating
- Had 50 stores; analysts predicted that it would be a growth leader

Coffee Beanery
- Franchiser who operated 175 units across the U.S.
- Coffee beverages and food accounted for 80% of the sales and 20% came from merchandise
- Focus had always been on malls but it was now shifting its focus to free-standing locations
- Began franchising coffee carts

Chock Full O'Nuts
- Operated as a coffee supplier to the restaurant industry
- Enough contracts with restaurants to warrant its own fleet of 150 trucks
- Recently, company had begun diversifying into different coffeehouse formats like double drivethroughs and sit-down retail outlets, about 3,000 square feet in size

Cafe Appasionato
- Small but aggressive player in the industry
- Primarily a coffee roaster
- Sold its coffee in its own retail outlets, franchised stores, wholesale coffee to specialty stores and restaurants, grocery division, direct mail, exports to the Pacific Rim, private label coffee production and co-label ventures with fast food chains, such as Taco Bell

Ltd., the Second Cup hoped to gain access to a number of its partner's institutional and retail sites such as Harvey's and Swiss Chalet. The Second Cup also held a 30 percent interest in the Great Canadian Bagel, which operated 120 stores in 1996 and was planning to own 175 by the end of 1997. Finally, the company had also struck a deal to serve its coffee on Air Canada flights. Revenues for 1996 amounted to $63.3 million.

See Exhibit 5 for a comparison of the industry competitors using different financial and growth measures.

STARBUCKS' STRATEGY

Starbucks' strategy for the future was presented in the following extracts of a letter to Starbucks' shareholders. This letter, from Howard Schultz, Chairman and CEO, and Orin Smith, President and Chief Operating Officer, appeared in the company's 1996 Annual Report:

> *We have firmly established our leadership position, ending fiscal 1996 with more than 1000 retail locations in 32 markets throughout North America and two new stores in Tokyo, Japan. With more than 20,000 dedicated partners (employees), we are creating opportunities every day for millions of customers around the world to enjoy the Starbucks Experience. From selecting the finest Arabica beans to hiring the most talented people, we are committed to applying the highest standards of quality in everything we do. . . . When you walk into a Starbucks store, when you open a mail order package, when you*

5 | Coffee Chains' Stock Prices and Market Capitalizations

Company	Year High ($)	Year Low ($)	Market Cap. ($mm)
U.S. Companies			
Brothers	4.63	2.13	30.8
Coffee People	9.38	6.00	21.4
Diedrich	12.00	3.00	23.6
Green Mountain	7.50	6.88	24.8
Starbucks	40.25	21.50	2,438.5
Canadian Companies			
Cara	4.80	3.30	440.2
Van Houtte	28.35	18.50	225.6
Second Cup	13.35	9.15	137.2

COMPARING THE COFFEE CHAINS

Company	TEV[1]/EBITDA[2]	Net Margin
U.S. Companies		
Brothers	6.0	–14.0%
Coffee People	8.4	1.7%
Diedrich	15.6	1.2%
Green Mountain	7.3	3.3%
Starbucks	25.1	6.0%
Average	14.5	
Canadian Companies		
Cara	7.7	5.8%
Van Houtte	7.8	4.7%
Second Cup	13.2	-3.7%
Average	17.9	

Source: Yorkton Securities Inc., March 25, 1997.

[1]TEV is total enterprise value defined as current market cap plus debt less cash. Debt and cash are as latest available balance sheet date.

[2]EBITDA for Brothers and Diedrich is trailing twelve months.

drink our coffee on United Airlines, it is our goal to offer more than just a great cup of coffee—we want to offer a memorable experience . . . We are excited about the global possibilities as more new customers embrace our business, and we know that we have many brand-building opportunities ahead of us. In 1994, when we entered into a joint venture agreement with Pepsi-Cola to develop ready-to-drink coffee products, we knew that we wanted to redefine the category. . . . We look forward to the positive reception of bottled Frappuccino . . . but most importantly, we know that we have developed a platform for bigger product innovations. During fiscal 1996, we installed proprietary, state-of-the-art roasting and manufacturing equipment to create a world-class logistics and manufacturing organization. . . . Our specialty sales and marketing team has continued to develop new channels of distribution . . . our direct response group launched a new America Online Café Starbucks store . . . we continue to work towards our long-term goal of becoming the most recognized and respected brand of coffee in the world. . . . We believe more strongly than ever that at the heart of our continuing success lie the company's two cornerstones, coffee and our people. . . . Twenty-five years from now, when we look back again, if we an say that we grew our company with the same values and guiding principles that we embrace today, then we will know we have succeeded.

STARBUCKS' BUSINESS SYSTEM

Sourcing

Starbucks sourced approximately 50 percent of its beans from Latin America, 35 percent from the Pacific Rim, and 15 percent from East Africa. Having a diversified portfolio allowed Starbucks to offer a greater palette of coffees to its customers while being able to maintain a hedged position.

Starbucks maintained close relationships with its exporters by working directly with them and providing them with training. Mary Williams, Senior Vice-President of Coffee at Starbucks, described what it took to be considered an official Starbucks' exporter:

If I am working with a dealer who has sold me 5000 bags of Guatemalan for January's shipment and he knows that he is not going to be able to deliver, I don't want to hear about it in January. I want him to call me in September and say, 'Mary, we are going to have trouble with this January. What can we do? How can we work this problem out? What can I do to help you? Shall we switch it to another coffee?' If I have a quality problem, I expect to be able to call up the person I bought the coffee from and say: 'Sorry, I have to reject this; it doesn't meet our standards.' I expect them to say: 'OK, we will take it back, no problem and we will replace it.' Both the customer service and consistency are the things we look for over time.

Exporters of high quality coffee were very anxious to become Starbucks suppliers because Starbucks purchased more high quality coffee than anyone else in the world. Starbucks' relationship with its suppliers was so good that if Supplier 'A' sold to a number of different buyers and it had only one container of a certain coffee, Starbucks would be the first to get it.

To ensure quality, Starbucks extracted three different samples of coffee from every shipment of 250 bags. Sample one was an offer sample sent by an exporter trying to make a sale to Starbucks. Sample two was taken just before the shipment was due to be sent. Sample three was extracted from the shipment, which arrived at the coffee roasting plant. At every stage of sampling, Starbucks reserved the right to reject the coffee if it was not in line with its quality standards.

Starbucks hoped to double volumes over the next three years. This could make the ability to find coffees that would meet its quantity/quality requirements difficult. Starbucks needed to offer an increasing number of blends to deal with its increasing volumes, since blends provided more flexibility around components. Mary Williams explained:

When you blend coffee, it's like baking a cake; you need to put lots of different kinds of spices in a spice cake; you don't necessarily have to have cinnamon, nutmeg and allspice. You can have other kinds of spices, and the consumers of that cake will not know the difference, because it tastes like a spice cake. So a House Blend with a particular flavor profile can have different types of the same quality components to reach the same flavor profile. Moving towards offering more blends and revolving varietals is one of the most important things Starbucks can do to ensure the quality/quantity mix of the coffee we buy.

Despite Starbucks' large supply needs, growing its own, high-quality coffee was an option that was never seriously considered.

ROASTING AND BLENDING

Roasting was a combination of time and temperature. Recipes were put together by the coffee department once all the components had been tested and were up to standard. Despite computerized roasters which guaranteed consistency, roasting was not a complete science; it was more of a technological art. This was because the people roasting the coffee had to understand the properties of the roasting process, i.e., managing temperature and being able to roast coffees along different roast curves. Roasting was essential to Starbucks, because how a coffee was roasted could change its entire taste.

Starbucks undertook a great deal of research by roasting its coffees in many different ways, under many different temperature and time conditions to ensure that it was getting as much as possible from the bean. These trial and error sessions allowed Starbucks to build signature roasting curves. These roasting curves were then built into proprietary computer software. The method by which they were developed was as much a result of the technology as the art. This ensured that even if a roaster were to defect to another competitor, he/she would not be able to duplicate Starbucks' signature roasts.

After roasting and air cooling, the coffee was immediately vacuum-sealed in one-way valve bags. This packaging was unique in its ability to ensure freshness, since it allowed gases naturally produced by fresh roasted beans out without letting oxygen in. This one-way valve technology extended the shelf life of Starbucks coffee to 26 weeks. However, Starbucks did not keep any coffee on its shelves for more than three months and for the coffee it used to prepare beverages in the store, the shelf life was limited to seven days after the bag was opened.

SUPPLY CHAIN OPERATIONS

Starbucks Supply Chain Operations (SCO) claimed it had the best transportation rates in the industry, a complex bakery distribution model, a forecasting process for 'who will need coffee when' that was generally very accurate, strong inventory turns for the specialty-coffee industry, and a fully integrated manufacturing and distribution process that protected the coffee beans from oxygen from the time beans were roasted to the time they were packaged (closed loop system). Starbucks had developed these skills and benefits because it benchmarked against its competitors, hired experts, and believed strongly in the concept of integrated supply.

Starbucks tried to build its supply chain operations in order to eliminate redundancy and maximize efficiency. Supply chain operations served four business units: the retail store units, the specialty sales and wholesale channels, the mail order business and the grocery channel. According to Ted Garcia, Starbucks' Executive Vice President, Supply Chain Operations, the phenomenal growth in these business units was posing challenges to supply chain operations:

> *Supporting four business units in an integrated, effective, efficient, cost-effective method is a challenge. We are trying new and innovative things. We are not afraid to enter into agreements or challenge our suppliers such as United Parcel Service (UPS) to do things in new and innovative ways.*

RETAIL SALES

The retail outlet had been Starbucks' fundamental growth vehicle. For many customers Starbucks was not only a place to drink coffee but also an experience. Howard Schultz's vision for Starbucks was a place that offered interesting coffee-related drinks in a theatrical kind of atmosphere, which pivoted around an espresso machine:

> *You get more than the finest coffee when you visit Starbucks. You get great people, first-rate music, a comfortable and upbeat meeting place, and sound advice on brewing excellent coffee at home. At home, you're part of a family. At work you're part of a company. And somewhere in between there's a place where you can sit back and be yourself. That's what a Starbucks store is to many of its customers—a kind of 'third place' where they can escape, reflect, read, chat or listen.*[8]

Starbucks' formula was firmly based in its coffee, its employees, its merchandising, its ownership philosophy, its real-estate approach, its image, and its innovativeness.

Employees

Starbucks' store employees (baristas) tended to be either in college or university. They received a great deal of training and were able to talk about a variety of different coffees and processes. Having baristas that had a strong coffee education was essential because Starbucks' consumers were becoming more and more knowledgeable about coffee. Mary Williams, SVP Coffee for Starbucks, outlined the nature of the questions asked of the baristas at Starbucks:

> *We have very educated consumers. They ask very interesting questions of the people who work in our stores, such as, 'I am having chocolate mousse for dessert, what kind of coffee should I serve?' or 'I am having shrimp scampi for dinner and a fruit salad for*

dessert; what kind of coffee should I serve?' So we have to give the baristas some kind of a basis and background so that they can answer these difficult questions.[9]

Developing coffee knowledge and service expertise demanded a great deal of effort from employees, and as Starbucks grew, finding enough good people that could replicate the values, culture and service experiences was an ongoing challenge.

Merchandising

Starbucks only carried the highest quality merchandise. In terms of coffee-making equipment, it purchased its machines from manufacturers like Krups, Gaggia and Bodum. It also offered accessory items bearing the Starbucks Logo such as coffee mugs, grinders, coffee filters, storage containers and other items. In terms of merchandising, Starbucks faced challenges related to the design of a nationally consistent merchandising program, since many of its stores dealt with individual suppliers.

Real-Estate Approach

Starbucks considered itself to be real-estate opportunistic. It did not always wait for the perfectly designed location, i.e., a box. It had a design team that could fit a location in many retail spaces, be it a corner, a trapezoid, or triangle. This flexibility, in addition to Starbucks' concept of store clustering, which often placed retail outlets across from one another or on the same block, allowed Starbucks to maximize its market share in given areas of a city and to begin building a regional reputation.

To meet its growth needs Starbucks had approximately 20 real-estate managers across the country. These managers worked with 'street sniffers,' i.e., professionals who specialized in identifying the best retail locations. Their commissions were paid either by the landlord or by Starbucks. These real-estate brokers were guaranteed a minimum commission per location. If the landlord's brokerage commission did not cover the minimum, Starbucks paid the difference. This engendered a very loyal relationship between Starbucks and the real-estate network.

Starbucks was very disciplined about its entire approach to real estate:

Discipline is the difference between locating a store in a targeted demographic area this year, in order to get in there and gain market share, versus being disciplined enough to wait for the corner or the mid-block with a parking lot. Discipline is rooted in the ability to understand the differences and business issues involved with taking a store today that may do $750,000 vs. waiting for a store that may do $1 million. Understanding and acting upon location issues such as corners, parking lots and co-tenants; that's the discipline of it.[10]

As Starbucks grew and the number of 'A' sites in 'A' markets decreased, one of the key challenges faced by Starbucks was to constantly motivate its real-estate staff to continue to generate 20 to 40 solid stores per month. Starbucks had to meet this challenge if it was going to meet its goal of 2,000 stores by the year 2000. Traditionally, Starbucks had been focused on the retail store on Main and Main of every major North American city. Now it was expanding to the Main and Main of different regions within a city. See Exhibit 6 for the actual and forecasted income statement of a typical store.

Another way in which Starbucks hoped to reach a new customer base was through the introduction of its new espresso carts or kiosks. By introducing Starbucks Espresso Carts, the company had succeeded in branding the coffee cart, which had always been a brandless, grassroots type of specialty-coffee retailer. Starbucks called its version of the espresso cart Doppio. The Doppio was an 8×8-foot cube that unfolded into a larger stand with sides, counters, and Starbucks' trademark finishes. It would allow the company to take advantage of sales areas such as train stations, street corners, malls, etc. Starbucks was in the initial stages of its Doppio strategy.

Domestic vs. International Retail Image

The retail system is the base or anchor of the brand-building strategy, the essence of the company's passion for quality coffee, and the showcase for the lifestyle that Starbucks is defining. It is this lifestyle attribute of the brand that could catapult the company beyond its roots as a speciality retailer/restaurant with a few closely associated brand extensions.[11]

Starbucks decided to enter the international market place to prevent competitors from getting a head start, to build upon the growing desire for Western brands, and to take advantage of higher coffee consumption rates in different countries. It focused on Asia Pacific simply because it did not have the resources to go into different areas of the globe at once and because one half of the world's population lived a five and a half hour flight from the area. It was expected that in the next five to ten years, international retail's contribution would be sizeable. See Exhibit 7 for a forecast of International Retail's potential contribution to Starbucks' earnings. Also see Exhibit 8 for a forecast of Starbucks' growth in the Pacific Rim.

EXHIBIT

6 | Analysis of Unit Economic Trends (US$ thousands)

	1994	1995	1996	1997E	1998E	1999E
Cash investment:						
Store build out[1]	330	357	315	310	305	300
Pre-opening	16	23	21	20	20	20
Beginning inventory	17	20	24	20	20	20
Total cash investment	363	400	360	350	345	340
Average sales/store[2]	820	820	850	825	790	765
Average sales/investment	2.3x	2.1x	2.4x	2.4x	2.3x	2.3x
EBIT margin[3]	18.9%	17.5%	16.5%	18.0%	17.8%	17.6%
EBIT	155	144	140	150	141	135
ROI (EBIT/cash invested)	43.0%	36.0%	39.0%	43.0%	41.0%	40.0%

Source: William Blair & Company, 1997.
[1]Estimated investment per store opened during the fiscal year.
[2]Estimated average sales and EBIT for units open at least one year.
[3]EBIT includes marketing and field level overhead expenses.

7 | Projected Avenues of Growth-Estimated Contribution from Joint Ventures (US$ millions)

	1995	1996	1997E	1998E	1999E
Annual investment					
Ice cream	0.0	0.9	2.0	1.0	0.5
Bottled beverages	1.2	2.7	18.0	15.0	10.0
Whole bean	0.0	0.0	3.0	5.0	9.5
Total	1.2	6.0	30.0	33.0	35.0
Retail revenues					
Ice cream	0.0	15.0	40.0	45.0	50.0
Bottled beverages	0.0	0.0	65.0	250.0	300.0
Whole bean	0.0	0.0	1.3	43.8	78.8
Total	0.0	15.0	114.8	368.8	501.3
Contribution to Starbucks earnings					
Ice cream	0.0	–0.7	0.5	2.4	3.0
Bottled beverages	–1.2	–0.4	–0.5	4.4	7.9
Whole bean	0.0	0.0	–0.5	1.6	4.5
Total	–1.2	–1.1	–1.5	8.4	15.4
Joint venture contributions	–1.2	–1.1	–1.5	8.4	15.4

Source: William Blair & Company, 1997.

SPECIALTY SALES

Specialty sales were agreements with retailers, wholesalers, restaurants, service providers, etc. to carry Starbucks coffee. Specialty sales not only provided Starbucks with revenue growth potential but also with increased name recognition. Starbucks partnered with companies that were leaders in their field, companies that had stellar reputations for success and quality. Partnerships existed with many different companies, some of which included

- **United Airlines**—Starbucks was served on all domestic and international flights.
- **Nordstrom**—Starbucks had developed a special blend for Nordstrom.
- **Barnes & Noble Bookstores**—Starbucks operated individual but attached locations. Many of these locations had separate entrances that allowed them to stay open even after Barnes & Noble closed.
- **PepsiCo**—Starbucks and PepsiCo had jointly developed the Frappuccino product, a milk-based cold coffee beverage in a bottle.
- **PriceCostco**—Starbucks had developed a special brand name, Meridian, for PriceCostco.
- **Red Hook Breweries**—Starbucks provided coffee concentrate as an ingredient for one of the brewery's beers, Double Black Stout.
- **Dreyers' Ice Cream**—In this joint venture, Starbucks had its own brand of ice cream that Dreyers' promoted via its grocery channels.
- **ARAMARK**—This was the world's leading provider of a broad range of services to businesses, reaching 10 million people a day at more than 400,000 locations. Through ARAMARK, Starbucks coffee was now being served at over one hundred of those locations, including college campuses such as the University of Florida and Boston University, corporations such as Boeing and Citicorp, and hospitals such as St. Vincent's in New York. ARAMARK also had a few licensed locations.

Some of these partnerships involved serving Starbucks coffee, some were for product development and others were for store development. Starbucks was actively increasing its participation in specialty sales contracts.

NEW VENTURES

Three of Starbucks' newest business ventures included its contract with Dreyers' Ice Cream, its bottled Frappuccino product with Pepsi and its penetration into the grocery channel.

It was estimated that Starbucks' ice cream would perhaps reach $40 million at retail and contribute at

EXHIBIT 8 | **Starbucks Corporation Projected Pacific Rim Development[1] (US$ millions)**

	1997E	1998E	1999E	2000E
New units	13	30	55	100
Ending units	15	45	100	200
Average unit volume	$1.0	$1.0	$1.0	$1.0
Total sales[1]	$9	$30	$73	$150

Source: William Blair & Company, 1997.

[1]Note that total sales reflect sales of joint ventures, partnerships, and licensees. We expect additional partnership agreements in the Pacific Rim to be disclosed before year-end. In fact, an executive of President Foods (the largest food company in Taiwan and a 7-Eleven franchisee) was recently quoted saying that the company expected to develop Starbucks stores in Taiwan, and perhaps China. Given the magnitude of the opportunity in the Pacific Rim, we do not anticipate development in Europe until at least 1999. Whereas the long-term potential of international development is tremendous, we expect expenses of building infrastructure and growing rapidly will be a drag on Starbucks profits at least through 1999. Depending on the structure of future international ventures, this business could become a significant consumer of Starbucks investment capital.

least $500,000 to earnings during fiscal 1997. Although the return was somewhat limited (see Exhibit 6), it opened Starbucks to an entirely new customer base, reinforced its premium-quality image, and built its reputation with supermarket chains.

Bottled Frappuccino was Starbucks' attempt to introduce a quality ready-to-drink coffee beverage into the North American market place. Starbucks' viewed this bottled beverage as a $1 billion opportunity. These estimates were from Pepsi, who said that it had never seen a product test quite as well as bottled Frappuccino, where 70 percent of testers became repeat purchasers. Other products that had hit the billion dollar mark with less favorable test results were Ocean Spray Juices and Lipton Iced Teas. The product might even do better in countries where there was already a market for cold coffee beverages, like the Pacific Rim. Bottled Frappuccino was currently being offered in all Starbucks retail stores and had begun to be distributed via PepsiCo's national distribution channels. See Exhibit 6 for a forecast of bottled Frappuccino's contribution to Starbucks' future earnings.

In penetrating the grocery market, Starbucks met with a great deal of success when it began test marketing in the Portland area. Now it was test marketing the Chicago market. If it were successful in Chicago, then it would consider initiating a national roll out with the expectation that in five years it would be nationally available. See Exhibit 6 for an estimate of the impact of a national roll out on Starbucks' earnings. Mr. Orin Smith, Starbucks President and COO, explained how he viewed the importance of Starbucks' penetration into the grocery chain:

> *Presence in supermarkets is not essential to Starbucks' survival or prosperity. However, in the interest of being a major player in coffee for the home, we have to be available in supermarkets. This is because convenience plays a key role in the decision to purchase coffee for the home. Therefore, no matter how many stores we open, we will never overcome the 'convenience' advantage of supermarkets. For us, the choice is clear: Are we going to allow supermarkets to continue to capture 70 to 80 percent of the home coffee business or are we going to join up and take our piece of that? Supermarkets are very interested in carrying Starbucks Coffee because we can offer them greater margins; we can grow their business and we will help pull consumers out of the lower priced categories into our category.*[12]

Other areas of opportunity included the introduction of Starbucks coffee to the higher echelon restaurants and day-part chains. Day-part chains are retail outlets catering to the day-time trade. Examples are bagel shops, juice bars, lunch counters, etc.

MAIL ORDER

For a long time, mail order had allowed Starbucks to meet the needs of its customers not located near a Starbucks retail store and its regular home users. The company had a direct mail program entitled Encore. Encore customers received a monthly shipment of a different type of either ground or whole bean coffee. This program helped boost sales by increasing transaction size, and introducing customers to a wider range of company products.

HOWARD SCHULTZ

Howard Schultz began his coffee career with Starbucks Coffee Company in 1982, when it used to be a retailer solely of whole bean coffees. On a buying trip to Italy, in 1983, the vast number of coffee bars in Milan inspired Mr. Schultz. He returned to Starbucks and presented his idea to expand the whole bean retailer into a coffee bar. The Board of Directors rejected his idea and two years later, Mr. Schultz left Starbucks to start his own coffee bar company which he named Il Giornale. After two years of great success, Il Giornale purchased the Starbucks name and assets and changed the names of all of its retail outlets to Starbucks.

Howard Schultz came from rather humble beginnings. He remembered how his father used to work hard for little money and no respect. He said his upbringing instilled in him "not a fear of failure but a fear of mediocrity." He was the first in his family to get a college degree and had always been an over-achiever. He was young and energetic at 45 and very hands-on in the company. "Howard is very creative, he is very inspiring, he is exceptionally demanding, he is tremendously competitive, exceptionally ambitious, and has very high standards in everything we can do and he is always ratcheting the bar up. He really cares about people; anything anyone would do to damage the culture—he would be right on it."[13]

Howard Schultz played a very important and unique role at Starbucks. "The barista's interpretation of the vision is the engine of the company, Howard is the onboard computer, and to some extent he is also the fuel that drives through it. People around here feel very much that they are following Howard up some mountain with a flag clenched under their teeth and they give 110 percent."[14]

HUMAN RESOURCES

Starbucks had a very flat organizational structure. Everyone from the CEO to a barista was a partner and not an employee. Starbucks placed a great deal of effort into seeking the thoughts and opinions of its baristas, because they were in direct contact with Starbucks' customers. Starbucks' retail management, at headquarters, kept in regular contact with field people. Many people in the stores knew Deidra Wager, the Executive Vice-President of Retail, and would not hesitate to call her directly to talk about the retail group's decisions. The head office managers had sessions with people in the field, standard mission reviews where they collected questions from anyone about any topic and then responded, and open forums where they heard from and listened to the partner base.

The coffee service system was built on three principles: hospitality, production and education. Starbucks expected baristas to be customer-service oriented by being hospitable, effective in making exactly the type of drink the customer requested and able to answer the customers' coffee-related questions. This demanded a great deal of effort on behalf of the baristas. To prepare them for the challenge, they all underwent 24 hours of training before they were allowed to serve a cup of coffee to a Starbucks customer. Every employee, even those that were hired for executive positions, went through the same training program, which included a two-week term in a store.

In addition to training, Starbucks paid its partners a slightly higher wage than most food service companies. Also, all employees received health insurance (vision, dental, medical), disability and life insurance, and a free pound of coffee each week. All company employees also received "Bean Stock," an employee stock option plan. This was quite profitable for some employees.

From its baristas to its senior managers, Starbucks took great care in recruitment. For baristas, turnover rates were about 60 percent; this was less than half of the industry average (150 to 300 percent). Many of the senior managers came from companies like Taco Bell, Nike, McDonalds, Hallmark, Wendy's, and Blockbuster. These managers knew how to manage a high growth retailer.

ORGANIZATIONAL CULTURE

The following six guiding principles, from the company's 1995 Annual Report, helped Starbucks measure the appropriateness of its decisions:

1. Provide a great work environment and treat each other with respect and dignity.
2. Embrace diversity as an essential component of the way we do business.
3. Apply the highest standards of excellence to the purchasing, roasting, and fresh delivery of our coffee.
4. Develop enthusiastically satisfied customers all of the time.
5. Contribute positively to our community and our environment.
6. Recognize that profitability is essential to our future success.

The following statements captured employee sentiments about Starbucks' culture.

> *When people ask me what I do for a living, I say: I drink coffee and talk about it. That's my job—not too shabby. I have a lot to learn, and a lot of places I can go if I wanted to leave Starbucks, but it's so interesting and I've met the neatest people that work here. I have a lot of passion for it. You know you go through bumps and grinds because we've changed a lot but it's like being in any kind of relationship. You fall in love, it's all great, everything is beautiful and then you find out that there are some things like wrinkles or bad habits. You work on those and then you're in puppy love again. I love working at Starbucks; my*

husband thinks it's pretty twisted. I mean I was a store manager and I lived at my store . . . people would say that you do such a great job and I would say that I couldn't do it without these people—I can't do it alone—none of us can. I totally rely on the wealth and depth of knowledge that other people have, the background they bring to Starbucks, their support and work ethic. And I just embrace that hugely; I can bring my weird ideas and be as goofy as I want one day or as serious as I need to be another day and it's OK. When I started at Starbucks someone told me: you tell me what you want to do and I will help you.[15]

In a day offsite, with Jim Collins (author of Built to Last*), the senior management team of 40 people or so was divided into 10 groups of four. First, we identified our own set of values and then we broke into groups of four people and combined our lists of values. It was absolutely mind-boggling that we all came back and had exactly the same list of values. Collins had never seen anything like that. Everyone is passionate about what they do, about life, about everything. Everybody has a sense of integrity, that we want to succeed but we want to do it in a fair, equitable, ethical way. We care about winning; you know we aren't ashamed to admit that we want to be successful, that we do care about people and do respect our partners. The fifth value was our entrepreneurial spirit. We don't want this to become a big company; we want to continually strive to be innovative and continually rejuvenate the company.*[16]

FINANCIAL

Starbucks' stock price and EPS had been rapidly increasing over the last five years (See Exhibit 9). In the span of six months from January to June 1997, four prominent investment companies had rated the company as a "BUY" in their report to investors. See Exhibit 10 for a forecast from each of these companies regard-

EXHIBIT 9 | Income Statement (US$ thousands)

	1994	1995	1996	1997E	1998E	1999E
Net revenues						
Retail	248453	402874	600367	827003	1053796	1276840
Specialty sales	26498	47917	78702	110331	148612	193552
Direct response	9972	14422	17412	22066	25792	30008
Total net revenues	284923	465213	696481	959400	1228200	1500400
Store operating expenses	90087	148757	210693	296200	368700	441800
Other operating expenses	8698	13932	19787	24200	31800	40200
Cost of sales and related occupancy costs	162840	262408	409008	548800	687000	827700
Operating income	23298	40116	56993	90200	140700	190700
Other expenses	–5544	3027	11508	3600	–2600	–7000
Earnings before income taxes	17754	43143	68501	93800	138100	183700
Income taxes	7548	17041	26373	36100	53200	70700
Net Eearnings	10206	26102	42128	57700	84900	113000
Preferred stock dividends accrued	–270	0	0			
Net earnings available to common shareholders	9936	26102	42128	57700	84900	113000
Net earnings per share	0.17	0.36	0.47	0.70	1.00	1.30
Weighted average shares outstanding	57575	71909	80831	88600	89500	90400
Average share price	25	15	24			
Price earnings ratios	148	42	51	51	36	28

Sources: Starbucks Annual Reports & William Blair & Company.
Note 1: The $0.47 EPS in 1996 excludes the gains from the sale of Noah's Bagels.
Note 2: The $0.17 EPS in 1994 would be $0.22 without the one-time charges associated with the acquisition of Coffee Connection.
Note 3: On December 1, 1995, the company recorded a 2 for 1 stock split to holders of record on November 1, 1995. Net earnings per share for all years have been restated to reflect the stock split.

10 | Investment Companies' Rating of Starbuck's Earnings

Robinson-Humphrey Company Inc.	1996	1997E	1998E	
Earnings per share	$0.54*	$0.70	$1.00	
Price earnings ratio	55.6 times	42.9 times	30.0 times	
Forecasted share price			$49.00	
Alex. Brown & Sons	**1996**	**1997E**	**1998E**	
Earnings per share	$0.48	$0.70	$0.98	
Price/earnings ratio		39.0 times	27.8 times	
Forecasted share price			$45.00	
Painewebber Inc.	**1996**	**1997E**	**1998E**	
Earnings per share	$0.47	$0.70	$0.95	
Price/earnings ratio		40.5 times	30.0 times	
Forecasted share price			$42.00	
William Blair and Company	**1996**	**1997E**	**1998E**	**1999E**
Earnings per share	$0.47	$0.70	$1.00	$1.30
Price/earnings ratio	76.1 times	51.1 times	35.8 times	27.5 times

*Includes a one-time gain on the Sale of Noah's Bagels.

ing EPS, P/E ratios and share price. One investment company that rated Starbucks as a long-term buy stated,

> *Since its 1992 IPO, Starbucks has executed its strategy to near perfection, achieving its initial goal of building the country's leading branded retailer of specialty coffees. As growth in its North American retail business decelerates from unsustainably rapid rates, the company is now in the early stages of pursuing a more ambitious goal—to build the most recognized and respected coffee brand in the world. Current initiatives include the development of Starbucks stores with local partners in the Pacific Rim, domestic brand extensions into packaged ice cream and bottled beverages, and test-marketing Starbucks whole bean coffees in the supermarket channel. While greatly enhancing the company's long-term growth potential, we believe these new pursuits also raise the risk profile of the stock. With SBUX shares trading at 33 times our estimate of calendar 1998 EPS, we believe extraordinary intermediate-term appreciation relies upon the successful execution of these ventures. Given the strength of the brand, our confidence in management, and impressive joint-venture partners, we are optimistic that these activities, in the aggregate, will contribute significantly to Starbucks' profitability over the next three to five years. We conclude that Starbucks remains a core holding for long-term growth stock investors, albeit with higher risk, as it transitions from a category-dominant domestic branded retailer into a global consumer brand.*[17]

In North America, Starbucks owned all of its retail outlets other than host licensing arrangements. However, owning all of its stores, Starbucks was faced with the prospect of depending heavily on equity and debt financing to grow. Its competitors like Seattle's Best Coffee and the Second Cup were all franchised, and consequently, needed less internal financing to roll out stores. For Starbucks' balance sheet, see Exhibit 11. For the income statement, see Exhibit 9.

11 | Balance Sheet (US$ thousands)

	1994	1995	1996	1997E	1998E	1999E
Assets						
Current assets						
Cash and cash equivalents	8,394	20,944	126,215	128,900	53,200	21,000
Accounts receivable	5,394	9,852	17,621	24,300	31,100	38,000
Inventories	56,064	123,657	83,370	122,500	149,600	178,100
Other current assets	14,728	50,897	112,335	12,500	16,100	19,600
Total current assets	84,580	205,350	339,541	288,200	250,000	256,700
Property and equipment, net	140,754	244,728	369,477	496,700	617,600	733,600
Other assets	6,087	18,100	17,595	43,100	78,100	121,100
Total assets	231,421	468,178	726,613	828,000	945,700	1,111,400
Liabilities and shareholders' equity						
Current liabilities						
Accounts payable	9,128	28,668	38,034			
Other current liabilities	31,290	42,378	63,057			
Total current liabilities	40,418	71,046	101,091	134,100	165,800	198,100
Other liabilities	81,105	84,901	173,862			
Shareholders' equity:						
Common stock	89,861	265,679	361,309	519,400	604,300	717,200
Retained earnings	20,037	46,552	90,351			
Total shareholders' equity	109,898	312,231	451,660			
Total liabilities	231,421	468,178	726,613	828,000	945,700	1,111,400

Sources: Starbucks Corporation Annual Reports & William Blair & Company.

MARKETING

Of key concern in Starbucks' marketing department was its brand equity. The retail business had historically been Starbucks' source of brand equity. This had meant that Starbucks was never just about the coffee; it was about a place, an experience.

Starbucks now wanted to develop its brand beyond being the preferred outlet from which to purchase coffee to becoming the preferred consumer brand. Scott Bedbury, Starbucks' Senior Vice-President of Marketing, explained its brand:

> *We are transitioning from a very retail centric view about the brand to a view that will allow us to say that Starbucks' role is to provide uplifting moments to people every day. I didn't say coffee! If you go beyond coffee, you can get to music, you can get to literature, you can get to a number of different areas. It can also become a license to dilute the brand. Therefore our goal is to remain true to our core, coffee. After all we are the protectors of something that is 900 million years old. Just like when you drop a rock in a pond there will be ripples that come outside that core, Starbucks is not just a pound of coffee, but a total coffee experience.*

One of the key challenges faced by Starbucks was trying concretely to define its brand image. Company executives felt that this was essential before Starbucks started mounting grand-scale national-advertising campaigns and other brand leveraging activities. Liz Sickler, Starbucks Director of Special Projects, commented:

> *I don't think that we leverage our size well enough. Very often we have strong competition in local markets from Caribou, to Seattle's Best Coffee to the Second Cup in Canada. And it's always mind-bog-*

gling how they can be so competitive in their local markets despite the fact that our national brand image is so much stronger. We need to take advantage of our national presence. We need to compete on our brand recognition. I think that's why we started to do some national advertising this year to see if that's how we can leverage our size. I think going into different distribution channels and leveraging the brand is the answer.

OPTIONS

Howard Schultz and the senior management at Starbucks were committed to the company's strategy. It was felt that Starbucks' current strategic direction would allow it to sustain growth by continuing the development of the Starbucks brand image and by increasing its presence in different markets. Starbucks was growing very rapidly and was consistently evaluating new opportunities in its domestic and international retail markets, new specialty sales partners, penetration in the grocery channel and the future potential of its mail order business. How the company should react to all of these opportunities was one of Mr. Schultz's key concerns.

ENDNOTES

1. This process varied by country.
2. Once the coffee cherry had been washed and dried, what remained was the coffee bean in some sort of husk.
3. *Encyclopaedia of American Industries,* Volume 1, *Manufacturing Industries,* SIC 2095, Roasted Coffee.
4. *Montgomery Securities,* April 30, 1996, Vol. 27.
5. *1995 Winter Coffee Drinking Study,* National Coffee Association of the U.S.A. & Montgomery Securities, Volume 27.
6. *Chicago Tribune,* Sunday, March 10, 1996.
7. "Caffeine Rush: Customers are High on Gourmet Coffee and so are Operators," *Restaurant Business,* January 1, 1996.
8. 1995 Annual Report, Starbucks Corporation.
9. Mary Williams, SVP Coffee, Starbucks Corporation.
10. Arthur Rubinfeld, Senior Vice-President Real Estate, Starbucks Corporation.
11. Merrill Lynch Capital Markets, *Starbucks Company Report,* September 16, 1996.
12. Orin Smith, Chief Operating Officer, Starbucks Corporation.
13. Orin Smith, Chief Operating Officer, Starbucks Corporation.
14. Scott Bedbury, Senior Vice-President, Marketing, Starbucks Corporation.
15. Aileen Carrell, Coffee Taster, Starbucks Corporation.
16. Liz Sickler, Director, Special Projects, Starbucks Corporation.
17. William Blair and Company on June 20, 1997.

C-586

CASE 35

The Stone Group's Diversification Strategy: "Caught Between a Rock and a Hard Place"

Pascale M. Brunet
INSEAD

In 1997, the Stone Group's senior management outlined the following strategies for the future: (a) reorganization of the group's mainstay enterprises; (b) cooperation with well-known large electronics manufacturers to become their primary distributor and to develop new products and open markets together with them inside and outside China; (c) diversification, to free Stone from its dependence on few products and markets and to strive to acquire a certain superiority in other technical fields and markets by forming alliances with other (Chinese and foreign) enterprises; and (d) contribution to China's welfare. It also intended to offer more services, improve the information system that provided economic data about the country, develop its marketing and distribution plans, improve its sales method, control its costs, and enhance its market development.[1]

It was an ambitious plan for Stone's senior executives who, in the 1980s, had dreamed of turning the company into China's IBM (see Exhibit 1 for historical highlights). Back then, the Group had revolutionized the Chinese-language printer and word-processor industry and was seen as one of the most promising domestic high-tech companies. That was before competition intensified in the Middle Kingdom and, in 1992, forced Stone to move from being a high-tech company to a holding group now diversifying into unrelated businesses such as chocolate pies and vitamin C. Whereas in the West, after a boom in the 1970s, diversification had declined, based on the need to rationalize operations and stick to core competencies, in Asia, this type of diversification was common; it was often based on the claim that market size and untapped potential constituted an opportunity no one could forego. Chinese firms were quick to understand that privileged relationships with government officials were beneficial in more than one industry and these would weigh significantly in their negotiations with foreigners to obtain technological knowledge.

Given this context, how could diversification strategies be shaped so as to ensure a competitive edge that came from concentrating on core competencies as well as reaping the incommensurable first-mover advantages in unrelated areas?

ABOUT THE COMPANY

Stone (Sitong in Chinese) was founded in 1984 by a group of alumni from Qinghua University. Co-founder Mr. Shen Guojun had been Chairman of the Group since 1992. Mr. Duan Yongji, who had joined the company soon after its creation, had been Vice Chairman and President of the Group since 1992 (see Exhibit 2 for Stone's organizational structure).

The principal activity of the Stone Group was investment holding (see Exhibit 3 for the Group's structure). The main activities of the subsidiaries (more than 50) were sourcing, distribution, and sales of computer-

This case was developed as a basis for class discussion rather than to illustrate either effective or ineffective handling of an administrative situation.

The case is based on publicly available information. Financial support was provided by CEIBS.

Copyright © 1999 INSEAD/CEIBS, France-China. All rights reserved.

1 | Stone's Historical Highlights

Year	Events
1997	Distribution agreement with Lexmark for distribution of inkjet printers; agreement with a MNE to develop products for postal services.
1996	The establishment of Mitsubishi Stone Semiconductor Co., Ltd. Stone was listed 5th among 100 Electronic Enterprises of China.
1995	Stone was credited as one of the National Large Industrial Enterprises; the establishment of Beijing Unistone Pharmaceutical Co., Ltd.
1994	The establishment of Anhui Stone Pharmaceutical Co., Ltd.
1992	Stone commenced its Business Recreation with the aim of Share-holding, Conglomeration, Industrialization, and Internationalization; the establishment of Beijing Stone Matsushita Electric Works, Ltd.
1991	The establishment of Shenzhen Shentong Printing Equipment Co., Ltd.
1990	The introduction of MS-2406 Chinese-foreign languages word processor; Stone officially signed the Madrid Agreement on International Registration of Trade Marks; the production of the 100,000th unit of the Stone MS series.
1989	The introduction of MS-2403 Chinese-foreign languages word processor; the establishment of Shenzhen SOTEC Electronic Co., Ltd.
1988	The establishment of Beijing Stone New Technology Industry Co., Ltd.
27 May 1987	The introduction of MS-2401 word processor; the establishment of Beijing Stone Office Equipment Co., Ltd. (SOTEC); the establishment of Stone Electronic Technology Co., Ltd. (Hong Kong); the establishment of Stone Finance Co. under the approval of the People's Bank of China.
1986	The establishment of Beijing Stone Group Corporation; the birth of the first generation of the Stone MS word processor, the Stone MS-2400; the beginning of the development of a nationwide sales network.
1985	The establishing of Stone Tong Ren Foundation; the completion of the second development of M1570 color printer.
1984	The establishment of Beijing Stone New Industrial Development Company; the success of the second development of M2024 printer and its introduction in the market; the establishment of Beijing Stone General Company.

ized word-processors, computers, and peripheral equipment; software and system integration; industrial control; measurement and meters; telecommunications; illumination; and electrical appliances, business machinery, electrical devices and materials, and, more recently, biological medicines and food. Stone had also begun to show an interest in finance and securities. The Group primarily operated in the PRC, but also sourced computers, electronic and electric products, and component parts in Hong Kong for distribution and sale in China.

The Stone Group was a nongovernmental high-tech enterprise group, collectively owned by its employees. It could make decisions on its own about the Group's organizational structure and fund raising. The Group kept independent accounts and was responsible for its own profits and losses. Stone enjoyed exclusive rights of ownership, use, profits, and disposal of all its properties, but could not liquidate its assets or conduct a share offering that would result in the transfer of majority control into private hands. All employees, including Mr. Shen and Mr. Duan, collectively owned interests in the

Exhibit 2 | Stone Group's Organizational Structure

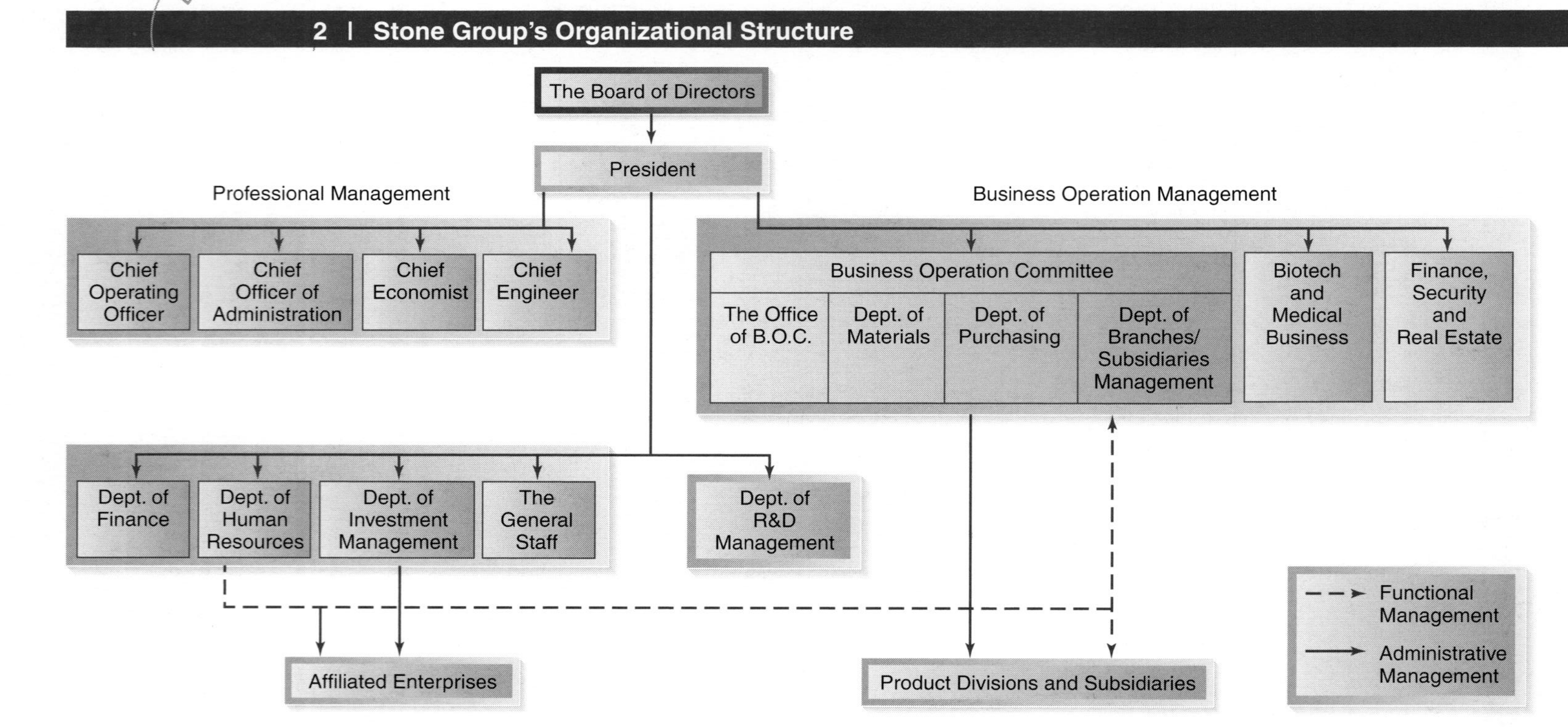

Source: www.china-stone.com.

EXHIBIT 3 | Structure of Stone Group

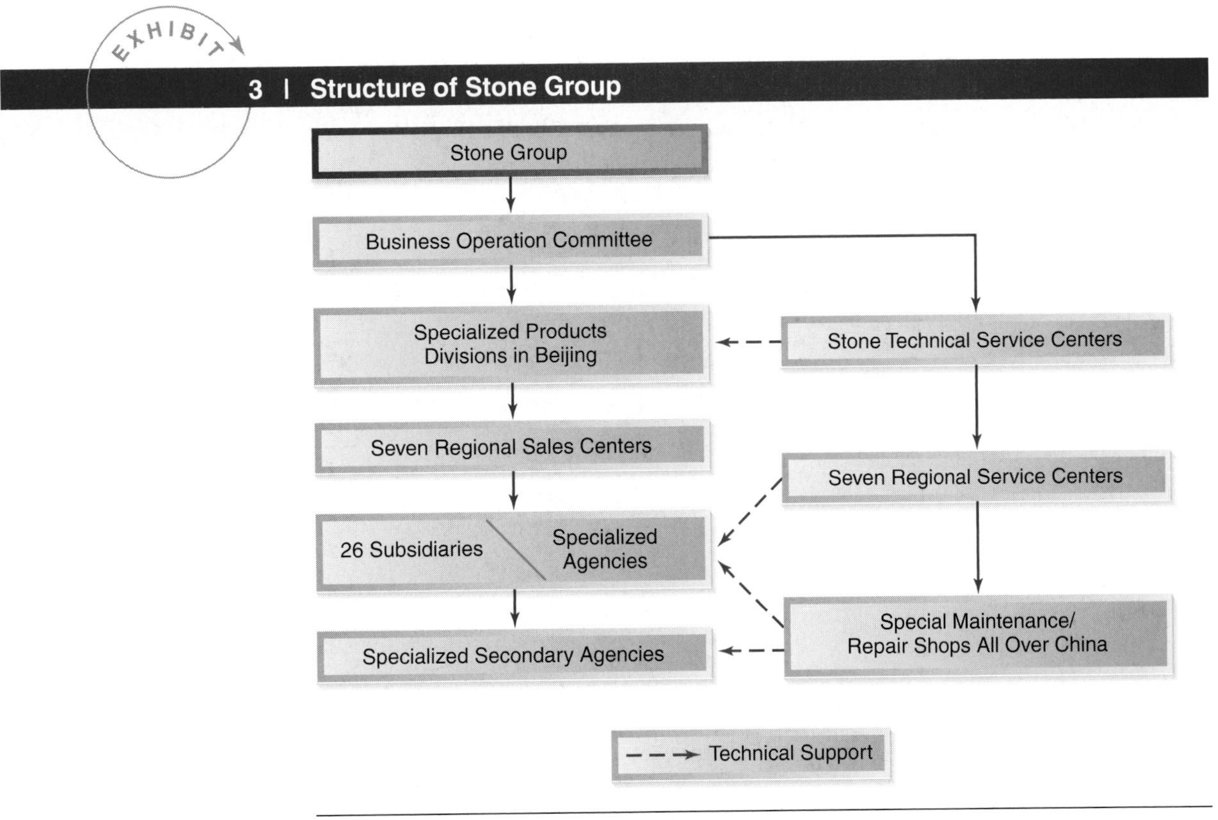

Source: www.china-stone.com.

assets of the Stone Group, but none of them had any private interests in the Group. The Stone Group was the majority shareholder of the Hong Kong-listed company, Stone Electronic Technology Ltd. A share option scheme had been adopted whereby the directors of the listed company, at their discretion, were authorized to invite employees to take up options to subscribe for shares not exceeding 10 percent of the issued share capital of the listed company.

In 1996, total revenues of Stone Group Holding (including the listed company and the subsidiaries) was HK$ 1,510 million with an after-tax profit of about HK$ 30 million,[2] up 76 percent from 1995. With a current ratio of 1.46, Stone had the resources to build its core competences (see Exhibits 4 and 5 for performance measures). The products sold by the Stone Group (see Exhibit 6) could be classified as manufactured products (i.e., products produced by Stone subsidiaries or the Group's joint ventures) and traded products (i.e., products manufactured abroad by foreign companies and then imported and distributed by Stone; see Exhibit 7 for a breakdown of the income by product).

The sales of manufactured products, such as integrated word processors, printers, electronic cash registers, Chinese platform software (RichWin), and fluorescent electronic ballasts accounted for 24 percent of the company's 1996 revenues. Integrated word processors still accounted for the largest revenue share. However, as personal computers were becoming more affordable, they would eventually take over the market of stand-alone word processors. In 1996, the sales of Stone's word processors had decreased by 45 percent from 1995 to HK$ 85 million. On the other hand, Stone had recorded an increase in sales of printers, commercial machinery, industrial controllers, computer auxiliary design, and lighting equipment. The Group had launched a new se-

4 | Consolidated Balance Sheet (at 31st December, 1996, Expressed in Hong Kong $)

	1996 $'000	1995 $'000
Fixed assets	278,534	150,810
Interest in associated companies	25,256	26,191
Investments	2,977	2,996
Current assets	881,808	906,553
Current liabilities	604,887	616,189
Net current assets	276,921	290,364
Long-term bank loans	(103,833)	(8,956)
Deferred taxation	(2,554)	(2,577)
	477,301	458,828
Representing		
Share capital	60,591	60,591
Reserves	353,249	332,735
Shareholders' funds	413,840	393,326
Minority interests	63,461	65,502
	477,301	458,828

Source: Stone Annual Report, 1996.
Note: The consolidated accounts include the accounts of the listed company and all of its subsidiaries made up to 31st December each year.

ries of OKI printers under its own brand name with production of these printers carried out in plants in Shenzhen.

The balance of the revenues (76 percent) came from the sales of traded goods. In 1996, Beijing Stone Matsushita Electric Works Ltd., a joint venture with Matsushita, distributed HK$ 109 million worth of Matsushita's electronic appliances and products, a 230 percent increase from the previous year. Other products distributed by Stone were Compaq and AT&T computers. Facing fierce competition, however, the sales of these computers had dropped by 48 percent to HK$ 74 million. In addition, Compaq's diminished reliance on Stone to distribute its products had contributed to a decrease in revenues. Other traded products included Motorola pagers, Roland draft plotters, Selex copy machines, and other office automation equipment.

Stone was the exclusive distributor of the OKI printer series, Roland DG products, Genicom high-speed printers, the Omron series of industrial control computers, 3M diskettes, and Hewlett-Packard (HP) laser printers. The Stone Group was also a distributor of Dysan diskettes, Philips chips, Panasonic telephone sets and fax machines, and Santak and UPS products.

SUCCESS FACTORS AND PERFORMANCE

Several factors contributed to Stone's past success. First, Stone had the capability to convert institutional technologies into applications that could fulfill the market's needs. Like its home-grown competitors, Legend and Founder, Stone was able to translate the technological potential of the state sector into commercial success by hiring its employees from the Chinese Academy of Sciences (CAS), the top research institute in China.

The ability to develop a successful distribution network was another element of Stone's success story. With over 3,000 sales agencies spread all over China, Stone had a competitive advantage over its competitors, espe-

5 | Performance of Stone Electronic Technology Ltd.

	Six months ended 30th June	
	1997 HK$'000	1996 HK$'000
Turnover	836,731	755,698
Operating profit	26,529	18,385
Share of (losses)/profits of associated companies	(190)	412
Profit before taxation	26,339	18,797
Taxation (Note 1)	(5,094)	(4,753)
Profit after taxation	21,245	14,044
Minority interests	(3,158)	(3,822)
Profit attributable to shareholders	18,087	10,222
Earnings per share (Note 2)		
Basic	2.98 cents	1.69 cents

Notes:

1. Taxation

	Six months ended 30th June	
	1997 HK$'000	1996 HK$'000
Hong Kong Profits tax	1,973	1,900
PRC income tax	3,054	2,738
Share of associated companies PRC	67	115
Income tax	5,094	4,753

Hong Kong profits tax is calculated at the rate of 16.5% of the estimated assessable profit for the period. PRC income tax is calculated in accordance with the applicable rates on the estimated taxable income in the PRC.

2. Earnings per share

The calculation of the basic earnings per share is based on the profit after taxation and minority interests of HK$18,087,000 (1996: HK$10,222,000) and on the weighted average number of 605,993,009 shares (1996: 605,907,600) in issue during the period.

Source: Stone Electronic Technology Ltd.: Interim Results, *South China Morning Post*, September 29, 1997, p. 4.

cially foreign companies, in distribution. Meanwhile, Stone was one of the first Chinese companies to initiate user training and after-sales services, which became an added value for Stone's products. In 1995, it had over a hundred training and maintenance centers around the country.

Good relationships with government officials are a critical success factor in China. Despite Stone's founders' involvement in the democracy movement in 1989,[3] Stone maintained good contacts with officials in both the central and local governments. For example, Stone was one of the few manufacturers approved to produce the value-added tax (VAT) electronic cash register (ECR) to be installed in every retail store in China.

Finally, Stone was a pioneer in corporate culture development. The company stressed the importance of individual employees and encouraged them to develop their own ideas. The company's compensation system was linked with the employees' performance. All employees were given one-year employment contracts and

EXHIBIT 6 | Stone's Star Products

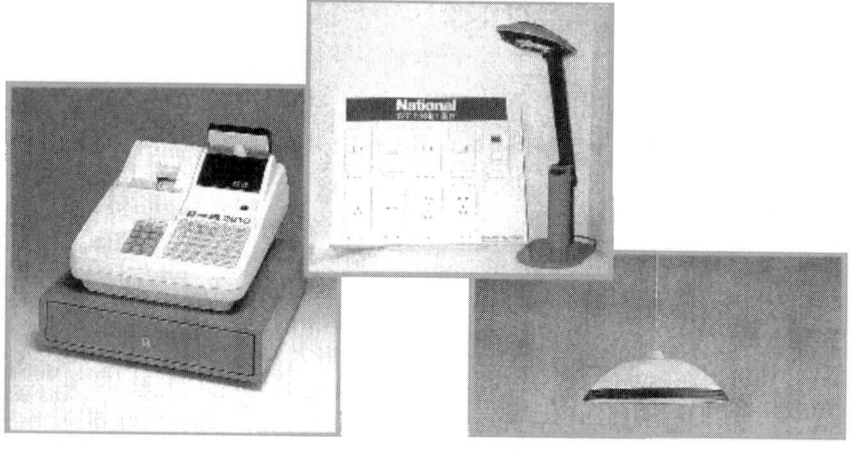

Source: www.china-stone.com.

directors were given three-year contracts. The reward system helped attract many excellent researchers in the early years and cultivated a sense of responsibility and ownership inside the corporation.

STONE'S ACTIVITIES

In May 1987, the first of Stone's manufacturing joint ventures was set up to turn out Chinese-foreign language word processors designed and developed by the group itself. A number of other joint venture factories (e.g., Shenzhen SOTEC Electronic Co., Ltd., Shenzhen Shentong Printing Equipment Co., Ltd.) were also established and formed a preliminary industrial manufacturing base.

In order to industrialize the Group further, Stone set up a number of joint ventures with foreign and local companies—from Beijing Stone Office Equipment Technology, a joint venture with Mitsui producing electronic cash registers and word processors, to the newly formed Mitsubishi Stone Semiconductor Co., a joint venture expected to become the largest semiconductor manufacturer in China.

Stone also participated in other businesses. During 1994 and 1995, it formed four joint ventures in the medical and pharmaceutical fields. In 1994, Stone, Mit-

EXHIBIT 7 | Stone's Activities and Importance of Subsidiaries

Composition of Stone Group's Income in 1995

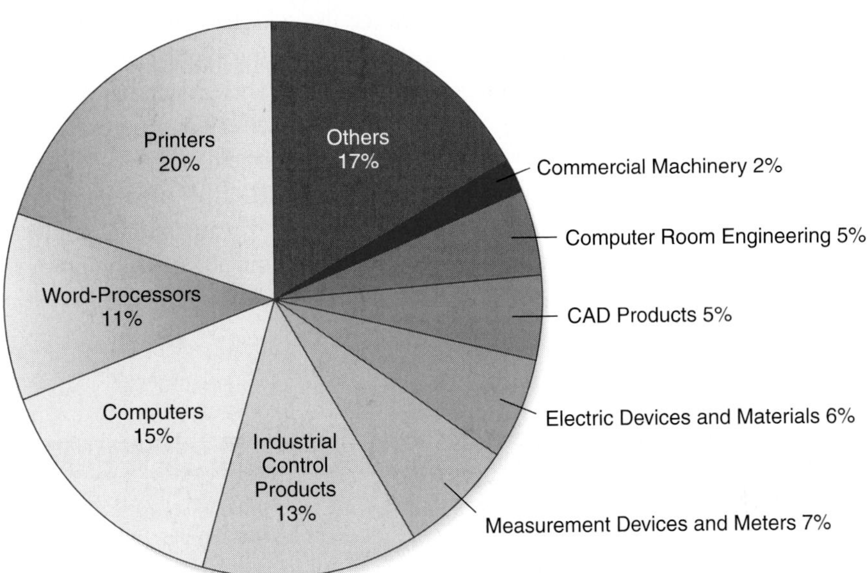

Stone Subsidiaries' Position in the Stone Group's Sales System

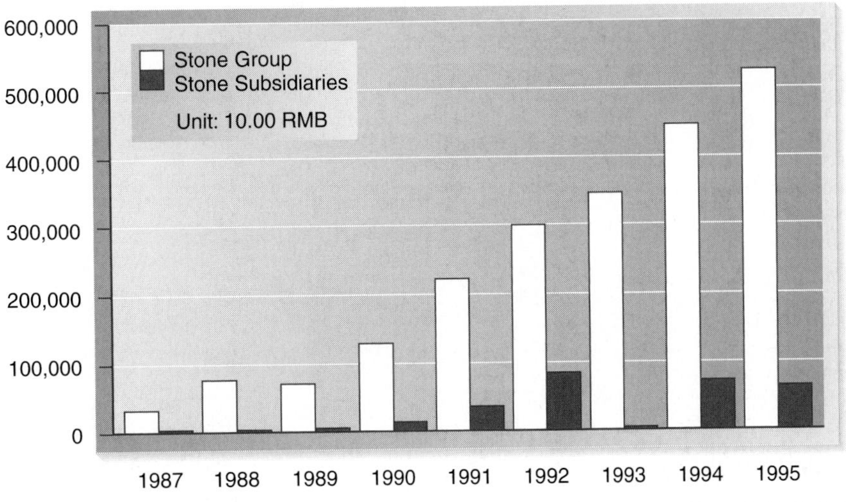

Source: www.china-stone.com.

sui, and Lotte, a Korean candy company, formed Lotte Stone Food Co., Ltd. in Beijing and started to produce chocolate cakes. By 1997, Stone handled about 20,000 products and was involved in about 25 joint ventures. Unlike other Chinese joint venture partners, Stone contributed more than labor and land to the projects; its proprietary software technology was a major contribution to many of the ventures (see Exhibits 8 and 9 for details on Stone's joint ventures).

By 1997, Stone's activities (either manufacturing or trading) covered three product areas: electronics (mainly word processors, ECRs, invoice processors, and computer hardware and software), food and pharmaceuticals (mainly confectionary products and vitamins), and electrical appliances and lighting equipment.

1. Electronics

China's electronics industry had been predicted to grow at least 20 percent annually until the year 2000, reaching a total output of RMB 700 billion (US$ 83 billion). This growth has represented an interesting opportunity for both foreign and domestic companies. Japanese manufacturers (mainly Matsushita, Sanyo, Toshiba, and Hitachi) invested heavily in the early 1990s, and South Korean companies (mainly Samsung and LG) were quickly catching up. A small number of American and

EXHIBIT 8 | Major Industrial Investment Projects of the Stone Group in Recent Years

	Joint Venture Partners	Total Investment (US$ million)	Stone's Interest	Inauguration Date
Anhui Stone: Vitamin C (pharmaceuticals)	Bangpu No. 2 Pharmaceuticals	29.9	75%	March 1994
Compaq Computer Technologies Personal Computers (pats and kits)	Compaq	10	10%	May 1994
Lotte Stone Foods	Mitsui, Lotte (Korea)	20	25%	August 1994
VAT cash registers	Omron, Great Wall, Qingdao TV	5	25%	January 1995
Beijing Unistone Pharmaceuticals Co.	Beijing University, Medy Corporation	7.8	51%	May 1995
Lighting equipment	Matsushita, Mitsui	40	40%	May 1995
Beijing Stone Tianli Biopharmaceutical		.6	100%	October 1995
Beijing Unipharm Medicine	Beijing Municipal General Pharmaceutical Corporation	.6	80%	December 1995
Mitsubishi Stone Semiconductor: (MCU, MPU, ASIC, MEMORY)	Mitsubishi, Mitsui	90.64	30%	June 1997 (planned)

Source: Stone.

9 | A Few Stone Joint Ventures

1. Electric Appliances and Lighting

Beijing Stone Matsushita Electric Works, Ltd. Electric Works and Illumination was inaugurated in January 1993 as a joint venture with the Japanese Matsushita Electric Works, Ltd. and Mitsui & Co., Ltd. With a total investment amounting to USD $40 million, Stone holds 40 percent of the shares. The main products are illumination devices, accessories to electrical appliances, automatic sliding door controllers, and health devices. The company went into production in May 1995.

2. Electronics

Beijing Stone Office Equipment Technology Co. Ltd. (SOTEC) was formally inaugurated on 27 May 1987 as a joint venture with Mitsui & Co., Ltd., Japan, in which Stone holds 75 percent of the shares. The company's main products are MS series of computerized Chinese-foreign language word processors and ECRs in 1995.

Shenzhen SOTEC Electronic Co., Ltd. is a joint venture with Mitsui & Co., Ltd., initiated on 1 April 1989. Stone holds 75 percent of the shares. Its main products are Chinese-foreign language word processors, editing machines, fast printing machines, and bar code reading and writing equipment.

Tianjin Stone Computer Equipment Co., Ltd. was inaugurated on 27 November 1987. It is a joint venture with Kingsun Computer Holdings Ltd. (Hong Kong) and Stone holds 75 percent of the shares. Its main product was electronic ballasts.

Shenzhen Shentong Printing Equipment Co., Ltd. was inaugurated on 11 October 1991 as a joint venture with the Japanese companies Fujitsu Co., Ltd., Fujitsu ISOTEC Co., Ltd. and Mitsui & Co., Ltd. Stone holds 51 percent of the shares. Its main products are frames for word processors, printers, air-conditioner controllers, and printing heads.

Compaq Computer Technologies (China) Co., Ltd. was inaugurated in Shenzhen in May 1994. It is a joint venture with Compaq Computer Company, USA, with a joint investment of US$ 10 million. Stone holds 10 percent of the shares. Its main products are parts and kits for Compaq personal computers that are mainly exported overseas.

Mitsubishi Stone Semiconductor Co., Ltd. was set up by Stone Group and the Japanese Mitsubishi Electric Corporation and Mitsui & Co. Ltd. With a joint investment totaling US$ 90.64 million, Stone holds 30 percent of the shares. Its main products are MCU, MPU, ASIC, and MEMORY.

3. Medicine and Food

Anhui Stone Pharmaceutical Co., Ltd. is a joint venture with Bangpu No. 2 Pharmaceutical Factory that was inaugurated in March 1994. Stone holds 75 percent of the shares. The second phase expansion project of vitamin C production was completed in July 1995, bringing the annual production capacity of vitamin C up to 2,000 tons.

Beijing Unistone Pharmaceutical Co., Ltd. is a joint venture with Beijing University and Medy Corporation (USA) and was inaugurated in May 1995. With a total investment amounting to US$ 7.8 million, Stone holds 51 percent of the shares. The company is mainly engaged in development and production in the field of biological technologies and medicines in China and abroad. The projected output value in 1996 will amount to RMB 60 million.

Beijing Stone Tianli Biopharmaceutical Co., Ltd. was inaugurated in October 1995 with a registered capital amounting to RMB 5 million. Stone holds 100 percent of the shares. It is mainly engaged in sales, technical consultation, and services of quality products in the field of biological technology in China and abroad. Projected sales revenue in 1996 was RMB 25 million.

Beijing Unipharm Medicine Co., Ltd., a joint venture with Beijing Municipal General Pharmaceutical Corporation, was inaugurated in December 1995. It has a total investment amounting to RMB 5 million, of which Stone holds 80 percent of the shares. Mainly engaged in the research, development, and sales of new and special-purpose medicines in China and abroad, this company projected its sales value in 1996 at RMB 40 million.

Lotte Stone Foods Co., Ltd. was inaugurated in Beijing in August 1994 as a joint venture with the Japanese Mitsui & Co. Ltd. and Lotte Co., Ltd. of the Republic of Korea. This company has a total investment amounting to US$ 20 million. Stones holds 25 percent of the shares. Its production began in October 1995. Its main products are quality cookies, children's food, candies, and soft drinks.

Beijing Bailu Office Article Co., Ltd. was inaugurated in December 1988. As a joint venture with the Japanese Monmose Heavy Industry Co., Ltd. and Changping Township General Corporation of Industrial Enterprises, Stone holds 30 percent of the shares. Its main products are high-end office furniture and office articles.

Source: www.china-stone.com.

European firms were also trying to get a share of the pie (especially Philips from Holland, which had two wholly foreign-owned units and 19 joint ventures by the end of 1995).

Word Processors. Stone's word processors were introduced in 1986 and have occupied most of the word processor market since. However, personal computers (PCs) have become strong substitutes. Recognizing that the market seemed ready for a transition, Stone has started to diversify into other businesses and become less dependent on word processors (which accounted for 6 percent of sales revenue in 1996).

The Group was involved in the development and manufacturing of sales tax electronic cash registers (ECRs) and value-added tax (VAT) invoice processors designated by the government as part of the Gold Tax project. In July 1997, it was officially announced that the Stone Sales Tax ECR would be used in an experiment in the Beijing area. Stone anticipated great revenues from the sale of ECRs and VAT invoice processors. Whereas other countries were making a transition toward PC cash registers, the development of information technology was still at an early stage in China so the ECR was perceived to be a good opportunity for years to come. A general-purpose ECR, also developed by Stone, had been launched and had ranked first in domestic sales since 1993.

The OKI series of invoice printers have maintained their market share and Stone has also launched high-speed and passbook update printers. The Group recently entered an agreement with Lexmark for the distribution of inkjet printers.

Computer Hardware. With the growth of disposable income, an emphasis on the education of a single child, and the blossoming of nongovernmental businesses (especially the financial and infrastructure sectors), the World Bank projected that China would become the world's third largest personal computer market by the year 2000. The total number of PCs was predicted to reach 2.15 million compared to only 650,000 units in 1994. As a result, many foreign computer companies set up joint ventures in China. IBM and the Great Wall Computer Group announced a joint venture to manufacture, service, and distribute PC products. AST was teaming up with Legend and Digital with Founder, another well-connected Chinese partner. Chinese partners provided not only low-cost production capabilities, but also distribution channels for the fragmented Chinese market. However, as distribution channels were becoming more standard, Chinese firms were beginning to lose their added value in this area. Some foreign companies were setting up their own representative offices in China. Compaq, a partner of Stone, set up its Beijing representative office in 1994 and, by 1997, had offices in Shanghai and Shenzhen.

The Chinese government had tried to encourage the development of domestic PC manufacturers, but could not protect them from the fierce competition of foreign firms. Only the larger local firms survived, of which Legend was the only one capable of defending its market share and even expanded sales abroad. Legend was the world's third biggest supplier of motherboards and VGA cards with 10 percent of the world market.[4] Domestically, Legend ranked fourth behind Compaq, AST, and HP, according to 1996 industry statistics. But even Legend had to review its strategy as it suffered a $68 million loss in the half-year to September 1996. The company was hit by inventory depreciation during the computer industry downturn in late 1995.

Stone quickly realized that it could not sustain under the competitive pressure of the PC industry. It adapted by entering into a joint venture with Compaq to manufacture joint brand-name (Stone-Compaq) PCs. Some said that Stone, having diversified into less competitive sectors, had been right to recognize there was little future for Chinese companies making and selling hardware. To survive, domestic companies needed to add value to foreign technology by providing Chinese solutions to end-user problems.[5]

Software Products. Stone's decision to move into software allowed it to become one of the key players in the industry. China's software industry was one of the fastest growing software markets in the world with annual sales forecasted to reach US$ 10 billion by the year 2002. The Ministry of Electronics Industry was encouraging an indigenous industry by providing low-interest loans and tax breaks, pressuring foreign companies to set up joint ventures and promoting a "buy local" policy.

Local software companies were specializing and

made sure they kept close relationships with the relevant authorities. Beijing Kelihua held 30 percent of the educational software market; the UfSoft Group was a market leader in accounting software with 40 percent of the market; Beijing Founder Electronics had sold its desktop publishing software to 80 percent of China's 3,500 newspapers, magazines, and book publishers.[6] Stone was focusing on Internet software.

Beijing Stone Rich Sight Information Technology was a joint venture formed in 1993 between the Stone Group and the Hong Kong firm Rich Sight Investment Ltd. to develop and sell software for the Chinese market. It was counting on the use of the Internet to boost its sales. Its Chinese-language software allowed users to receive Internet messages written in different codes. The software was exported across Asia and to the U.S. In China, the State Development Council, a for-profit organization, offered packages that included Hayes Modems, Microsoft's Internet Explorer, and Stone's Enable software. Stone's major software product was RichWin, a Chinese supporting environment that enabled Chinese system software to be transplanted on multiple platforms among different operating systems. The software was prebundled for brand-name microcomputers. According to Stone, sales orders for RichWin had reached approximately 3 million sets. The Group's next objective was to localize a cross-platform software system. Stone felt confident that these projects would become mainstream PC operating systems in the future.

The latest software products developed by Stone included: WarpMate, the Chinese environment of IBM OS/2 Warp; the Chinese environment of Windows NT, RichWin NT; RichWin 4.01, and the special edition of RichWin for AutoCAD, as well as the True Type Chinese compiler and the 24 True Type Chinese character. RichWin would be installed on about 85 percent of the estimated 140,000 Legend PCs to be sold in 1997. This alliance would help fight the evil of the industry: piracy.

Semiconductors. The electronics industry was identified as a pillar industry in the government's ninth Five-Year plan (1996–2000). This has led to an increase in production of electronic products which, in turn, has triggered increased demand for integrated circuits. In 1989, China used some 350–400 million integrated circuits (ICs), only 114 million of which were produced domestically. China's obsolete manufacturing facilities and its inability to utilize the technological advances developed in research laboratories induced the Chinese government to seek foreign investment help. Under government pressure, many foreign telecom equipment manufacturers transferred IC technology in order to gain access to China's booming telecom sector. Alcatel and Philips invested in separate IC plants in Shanghai. Motorola set up a wholly owned IC manufacturing plant in Tianjin. NEC invested US$ 62 million in a joint venture with Feijing's Shoudu Iron and Steel Plant (Shougang) to produce ICs. Siemens also participated through its collaboration with Jiangnan #742 Factory, once the largest IC producer in China.

For foreign manufacturers, finding local suppliers that met quality standards and just-in-time delivery expectations was not easy. Furthermore, the technology and production skills were still behind world standards. A key to succeed in this line of business was the ability to imprint ever smaller integrated circuits, or chips, in ever greater numbers on ever larger wafers of pure silicon. Chinese producers could only etch lines about one micron in width on 4–5 inch wafers compared with 0.5 to 0.35 microns on 8-inch wafers elsewhere in the world. Stone was allying with Mitsubishi to build China's largest semiconductor plant.

Stone's other areas of investments in electronics included the development in 1989 of the TISC electronic ballast for fluorescent lamps and in 1990 of the bank bill printer, which took a market share of 80 percent before 1993 and 48 percent in 1995.

2. Food and Pharmaceuticals

In order to fulfill Stone's strategic goals, the company started to diversify into different kinds of businesses. Food (confectionery) and medicine were the initial targets. By getting involved in these industries, Stone hoped to contribute to the improvement of the living standards in the country.

Food. This market was expected to grow in line with rising urban living standards. In the confectionery industry, Cadbury, Mars, and Nestlé, attracted by the number of potential customers, had set up local production bases. The influx of foreign enterprises had forced more than 60 percent of Chinese confectionery businesses to close in the last few years. But some 600 local factories remained.

As the Chinese market was highly fragmented, control of the distribution network and good relationships with wholesalers and retailers were crucial. Frequent deliveries and visits were needed to ensure fresh stock was shelved. The poor transportation network posed a major obstacle especially for food products that have limited shelf lives.

Another challenge was trademark infringement. Mars, for example, had faced infringement problems in a number of cities. It opposed the registration of products from local manufacturers, one of which had tried to sell W&Ws.

As few people consumed chocolate, this untapped demand/market was seen by many as a great opportunity for business. Import of chocolate into China had more than tripled between 1988 and 1993 (from 660 tons to 2,100 tons), with Chinese consumers favoring internationally famous brands and increasingly able to afford them.[7] Mars was a first-mover, and was now the market leader.

Stone formed a joint venture with Mitsui from Japan and Lotte from South Korea to produce chocolate cakes, quality cookies, children's food, candy and soft drinks. Although the market was expanding, Stone did not have first-mover advantages and Mars and Cadbury had a significant advantage in sales and promotion. Competition was expected to become more intense as other local and foreign manufacturers joined the race.

Pharmaceuticals. China's pharmaceutical market was estimated at US$ 10 billion in 1996 with total exports reaching US$ 3 billion. Foreign joint ventures accounted for 13 percent of total sales. The market had been steadily growing at about 15 to 20 percent in recent years. Per capita pharmaceutical consumption was low (estimated at US$ 3.6) but it was expected to grow to US$ 40 by the year 2000.

Key end-users in China were 13,917 hospitals. Pharmacies/drugstores were still limited in number and their sales represented only 15 percent of the whole pharmaceutical market. Among the top 13 categories of drugs in terms of total consumption value, anti-infectious drugs accounted for the largest portion of the pharmaceutical market in China (32 percent) and were identified as a growth sector. Vitamins accounted for only 1.2 percent of the total consumption value but accounted for the largest export value.

China's pharmaceutical industry was heavily regulated and protected, and foreign companies were restricted or forbidden to invest in several sectors such as antibiotics, vitamin C, and traditional Chinese medicine. Moreover, the industry was characterized by regional protectionism. For instance, the Ministry of Health (MOH) published lists of "essential drugs" that hospitals were encouraged to use. In Shanghai, the lists included only locally manufactured pharmaceuticals.

The pharmaceutical wholesale distribution system was very disorganized. It included more than 70,000 companies, of which 17,000 were wholesalers. The State Pharmaceutical Administration Corporation (SPAC) planned to reduce the number of pharmaceutical wholesalers to 1,500 by the year 2010, while constructing a state-managed retail network in rural areas and remote, poverty-stricken areas. Recently, large department stores had started to have pharmaceutical counters with OTC products.

In 1994, Stone formed a joint venture with Bangpu No. 2 Pharmaceutical Factory to produce vitamin C. After investments in 1995 in Beijing Unistone and Beijing Unipharm (see Exhibit 8), Stone had shown an interest in biotechnology research and development.

3. Electrical Appliances and Lighting Equipment

This market was highly fragmented and competition was very intense. Beijing Stone Matsushita Electric Works Ltd., which started production in May of 1995, was a joint venture with Matsushita and Mitsui to produce energy-saving lighting equipment, fixtures, and fittings. The joint venture produced lighting devices, accessories for electrical appliances, automatic sliding door controllers, and health devices (e.g., electronic blood pressure meters).

As in the other industries, distribution was characterized by infrastructure weaknesses, regionalized markets, and a wholesale system dominated by small, financially weak and dispersed distributors lacking a sales and service culture. The situation was gradually changing as individual entrepreneurs and other nonstate distributors had been allowed to enter the business.

CONCLUSION

Looking ahead, Mr. Shen Guojun was concerned about the following issues: What would replace word processors as the company's cash cow? To what extent should the company diversify? Which core competencies should the company build on? As the distribution channels in China became more standard and as foreign companies were getting more familiar with the channels through the establishment of regional sales offices, how could Stone sustain its competitive advantage in distribution?

One possibility was to expand further into commercial machinery production (e.g., invoice printers, ECRs). The Chinese government had announced more regulation for the compulsory use of VAT ECRs by all commercial units. Also, with its good relationships with the government, Stone could increase its participation in key government projects in taxation, post and telecommunications, commerce and industry, transport, customs, and medical services.

Another avenue would be to upgrade the quality of its electrical and electronic consumer products in order to shift from low-margin products—Compaq and AT&T computers—to higher margin products—Matsushita electrical and electronic appliances. Also providing growth possibilities were Stone's information service products (i.e., software on the Chinese platform and for integrated systems).

A few operational concerns had emerged as diversification had become more prevalent. Rapid expansion had swamped a management system that was put in place when Stone was a fledgling firm. Several tiers of middle management had been created. Middle management could potentially slow down the decision-making process and become a barrier to effective communication between management and workers. Some employees were dissatisfied with the new strategy of the company. They wanted the company to remain dedicated to research and high technology. They felt the company had diverged from its original mission that emphasized technology, innovation, and production.

In the 1980s, Stone had hoped to become China's IBM. What should be the goal now? Was Stone to be a value-added reseller and service provider for foreign companies? Or was it going to develop manufacturing skills of its own and, if so, which areas of growth should be its priority?

ENDNOTES

1. "Stone Electronic Technology Ltd.: Interim Results," *South China Morning Post*, September 29, 1997, p. 4.
2. US$ 1 = HK$ 7.74.
3. Stone's former president was forced to leave the country after giving support to the students during the Tiananmen incident in June 1989.
4. "Only One Firm Can Benefit from China's Fast Growing PC Market," *Business China*, January 8, 1996.
5. Ibid.
6. "The Race to Become China's Microsoft," *Business Week*, November 18, 1996, pp. 62–63.
7. *Multinational Companies in China: Winners and Losers*, EIU Research Report (December 1996), p. 99.

CASE 36

Sun Microsystems, Inc.

Irene Hagenbuch
Alan N. Hoffman
Bentley College

The Network is the computer's means to make all the systems work together like one big resource. Sun has always seen our customers' computing needs answered by a variety of computing resources in a heterogeneous network.

Scott G. McNealy, CEO, April 1987

COMPANY BACKGROUND

John Doerr and Klein Perkins have described Sun Microsystems, Inc., with world headquarters in Palo Alto, California, as "the last standing, fully integrated computing company adding its own value at the chip, OS and systems level."

The company's history started in 1982, when Andreas Bechtolsheim, Bill Joy, Vinod Khosla, and Scott McNealy founded Sun Microsystems, Inc. for Stanford University Network. Within a month after the introduction of the business plan, which Andreas, an electrical engineering whiz, had built for Stanford's computer network, the first Sun system, the Sun-1, a high-performance computer based on readily available, inexpensive components and UNIX was produced. After a rocky two-year start, McNealy, then vice president for manufacturing and operations, was appointed president in 1984 when Khosla left the company. Today, Sun has emerged as a global Fortune 500 leader in enterprise network computing with operations in 150 countries and over $8 billion in revenues.

The company's philosophy is to enable customers to create breakaway business strategies by using its network computing products, solutions, and services. Sun further states that in an age when information is power, it provides the technology, innovation, and partnerships that enable individuals or entire organizations to access information from anywhere to anything on any device. Thus users can better differentiate and more effectively create breakaway products and services.

Supporting and enforcing its philosophy where everything it brings to the market is predicated upon the existence of the network, where Java is on every client and every server, Sun has a vision statement. It says that its "vision is for a networked computing future driven by the needs and choices of the customer. It is a vision in which every man, woman and child has access to the collective planetary wisdom that resides on the network." Sun further explains that the Internet represents the first environment through which the company's vision can actually begin to be achieved. Sun sees its role as making the most of the opportunity by delivering open, affordable, and useful products to help as many people as possible share in the power of the network around the world.

COMPETITION

Sun's competitors in the technical and scientific markets are primarily Hewlett-Packard (HP), International Business Machines Corporation (IBM), Compaq Computer Corporation (CPQ), and Silicon Graphics, Inc. (SGI).

The information technology industry, the market for Sun's services and products, is extremely competitive. The industry is characterized by rapid, continuous change, frequent product performance improvements, short product life cycles, and price reductions. Such an environment forces Sun to rapidly and continuously develop, introduce, and deliver in quantity new systems, software, and service products. Additionally, it must offer new microprocessor technologies—giving its customers improved performance at competitive prices. The company has begun to improve, change, and implement a number of new business practices, processes, and a series of related information systems. Jim Moore from GeoPartners Research in Cambridge, Mass., compares Sun to IBM in its glory days, when customers viewed it as the repository of wisdom and competence: "Sun has suddenly become a thought leader for the whole industry."

Compared to previous years, Sun has an increasing dependence on the ability of its suppliers. Competence in designing, manufacturing, and delivering the advanced components required for timely introduction of new products is crucial to Sun's future competitiveness. The failure of any of these suppliers in delivering components on time or in sufficient quantities, or the failure of any of Sun's own designers in developing innovative products on a timely basis, could also have a serious impact on the company's operating results. To prevent any adverse affect on its net revenues and operating results, Sun frequently makes advanced payments to specific suppliers and often enters into noncancelable purchase contracts with vendors early in the design process. These commitments help secure components for the development, production, and introduction of new products. The distribution of Sun's computer systems is accomplished through the company's own systems. No customer accounted for more than 10 percent of Sun's revenues in fiscal 1997, 1996, or 1995. Sun's vision and strategy have stayed constant. With more market opportunities, an increasing number of companies are realizing the benefits of open network computing.

After Sun observed that sharing data between computers was crucial to key business tasks, McNealy worked extensively to transform Sun's product line to capitalize on networking. Today its main products can be divided into six categories: Servers and Workstations, Solaris and Solstice, SunSpectrum, WorkShop and NEO, UltraSparc and Java Processors, and Java Software (see Exhibit 1). This wide variety of products is used to implement the McNealy philosophy: "The network is the computer." Sun was refiguring its UNIX operating system for workstations, called Solaris, to run servers that coordinate work and store data on networks.

The year 1994 was marked as a big year in the computer industry. Sun faced the dramatic expansion of the Internet's World Wide Web. Millions of users came to believe that the network was indeed the computer. Since this statement had been accepted by Sun for a long time, the company had made the transition faster compared to its UNIX rivals IBM and Hewlett-Packard. This led to many customers turning to Sun for their workstations. According to Computer Intelligence, a research firm located in La Jolla, California, 26 percent of all Web servers in use in the United States were made by Sun. This is more than any other company.

By 1998, Sun was the leading provider of UNIX-based servers. Java has helped increase sales, even though the language does nothing yet to make Sun's servers better than any of its competitors'. Using Java to sell servers is a necessity, since the workstation, the computer Sun was built on, is going the way of the minicomputer. The more expensive machines made by Sun and others are being replaced by PCs incorporating cheaper Intel microprocessors. While companies are using inexpensive Windows NT servers to handle their simpler networking tasks, they still rely on UNIX for their most critical applications since Solaris servers crash a lot less than NT servers. Nonetheless, the PCs that run Microsoft's Windows NT operating system—Compaq, Dell, and others—will soon take over the market for workstations priced under $10,000.

In January 1998, however, Sun announced sweeping innovations to its award-winning power desktop line. This move, designed to capture new growth within the $19 billion market for high-end personal computers and powerful workstations, allows the company to grow market share at both the low end (less than $5,000) and high end (more than $15,000) of the workstation market. Putting its expertise in high-performance system design has enabled the company to bring advanced workstations and graphics technologies down in price. Sun's announcement of new graphics capabilities as well as the fastest workstation, the Ultra 60 multiprocessing system, ideally positioned the company to take market share from competitors like Hewlett-Packard,

1 | Consolidated Statements of Income

(In thousands, except per share amounts)	Years Ended June 30, 1998	1997	1996
Net revenues:			
Products	$8,603,259	$7,747,115	$6,392,358
Services	1,187,581	851,231	702,393
Total net revenues	9,790,840	8,598,346	7,094,751
Costs and expenses:			
Cost of sales—products	3,972,283	3,790,284	3,468,416
Cost of sales—services	721,053	530,176	452,812
Research and development	1,013,782	825,968	653,044
Selling, general and administrative	2,777,264	2,402,442	1,787,567
Purchased in-process research and development	176,384	22,958	57,900
Total costs and expenses	8,660,766	7,571,828	6,419,739
Operating income	1,130,074	1,026,518	675,012
Gain on sale of equity investment	—	62,245	—
Interest income	47,663	39,899	42,976
Interest expense	(1,571)	(7,455)	(9,114)
Income before income taxes	1,176,166	1,121,207	708,874
Provision for income taxes	413,304	358,787	232,486
Net income	$ 762,862	$ 762,420	$ 476,388
Net income per common share—basic	$ 2.04	$ 2.07	$ 1.28
Net income per common share—diluted	$ 1.93	$ 1.96	$ 1.21
Shares used in the calculation of net income per common share—basic	373,728	368,426	371,134
Shares used in the calculation of net income per common share—diluted	394,274	388,967	393,380

IBM, DEC, and Silicon Graphics at the high end of the market. Sun is pushing SGI's technology to the limits with its new price/performance levels and intends to overtake SGI's market share in the $25,000+ workstation market, which was approximately $3 billion in 1996. These new workstations allowed users to run the most popular Microsoft Windows 95 applications alongside the Solaris applications. This meant that users could run the more than 12,000 Solaris applications, which offered proven UNIX reliability/uptime, handled larger data sets, and delivered faster real-world modeling capabilities than the NT environment, in addition to PC applications such as Microsoft Office.

The new Darwin line was designed to appeal to the growing base of desktop users who were demanding more reliability and power. When Darwin systems are coupled with new accelerated graphics, it allows Sun to focus more on the needs of the rapidly growing base of digital contents creators. This desktop line sets a new low price point for workstation functionality, enabling Sun to grasp market share from Compaq and other PC vendors at the lower end of the market. Part of this move into the desktop markets was the announcement of a worldwide trade-in program designed to ensure investment protection for existing Sun customers and to attract new customers currently using other PCs and competitive workstations to the Sun platform. To specifically draw the attention of Silicon Graphics', Apple Computer's, Compaq's, and other PC vendors' customers toward the performance and speedy graphics advantages of Sun systems, Sun designed its "Jurassic-Back," "Mac-Back," and "Paq-Back" trade-in promotions.

FINANCIAL PERFORMANCE

Even though Sun's industry is fast changing and highly competitive, the company has managed to have at least 10 percent sales growth over the last several years across its product line. Its net revenue in fiscal 1998 increased to $9.7 billion, or 13 percent compared to $8.6 billion in fiscal 1997 (see Exhibit 1). Net income was flat at $762 million for fiscal 1998—the same as fiscal 1997. However, product's gross margin was 53.8 percent for fiscal 1998, compared to 51.1 percent in fiscal 1997. Research and development (R&D) expenses increased $188 million, or 22.7 percent, in fiscal 1998. Sun has one of the strongest balance sheets in the industry, with $822 million cash in the bank (see Exhibit 2). Having been the world leader in workstation sales (with 39 percent in unit sales and 35 percent in revenues, per Dataquest), the company is successfully transforming itself into an enterprise-computing firm with a focus on global network computing (see Exhibit 3). This was a necessary move as Sun's workstation sales started to slip and its server sales to gain.

Over the last 10 years, the company's revenues have grown an average of 34.1 percent annually as the demand for its open network computing products and services has risen. The revenues by geography are well balanced. Approximately 49 percent of the total revenue is generated from outside the United States. Its net income has grown 41 percent annually on average over the same time period.

CORPORATE GOVERNANCE

Scott G. McNealy

The story behind Sun's current chairman of the board, president, and chief executive officer, Scott G. McNealy, is not very typical for a Silicon Valley entrepreneur. He didn't drop out of college to realize his idea for the PC business nor did he work his way up through engineering. His background in manufacturing makes McNealy a fierce competitor who knows his business fundamentals, always keeps score, and has good moves. He is smart, complex, and fiercely ambitious. Over the many years at Sun, McNealy has become one of the industry's most respected managers. Lawrence J. Ellison, CEO of Oracle says, "There are two things I think about Scott. One is passionate leadership, and the other is his rigorous financial management. And that's uncommon to find in one person" (*Fortune*, October 13, 1997). Those talents, plus a competitive instinct and nonstop drive, have kept Sun rolling through a decade of tremendous change in the computer industry.

McNealy grew up where hard work and a fast-paced environment were part of everyday life. As a child, Scott learned a great deal about manufacturing. His curiosity in his father's work (he was vice-chairman of American Motors Corp.) led the grade-schooler to look into his dad's briefcase at night to inspect its contents. Many Saturdays, young McNealy went along to the plant and snooped around while his father caught up on paperwork. By the time he reached his teenage years, Scott was spending evenings with his father reading over memos and playing golf with industry leaders such as Lee A. Iacocca.

Graduating from Harvard University in economics, McNealy took a job for two years as a foreman at a Rockwell International Corp. plant in Ashtabula, Ohio, which made body panels for semi tractors. In 1978, he enrolled in Stanford University Graduate School of Business focusing on manufacturing at a time when finance and information technologies were the ways to the top. While many of his classmates wanted to launch a Digital Age business, McNealy signed on as a manufacturing trainee for FMC Corp. The company assigned him to a factory in Silicon Valley where it was building Bradley fighting vehicles for the U.S. Army.

McNealy's career in the computer world started in 1981 when his mentor from Harvard asked Scott for help in the troubled production department of a workstation company called Onyx Systems. After only 10 months at Onyx, a former Stanford classmate, Vinod Khosla, contacted McNealy to join him and Bechtolsheim in starting Sun. In 1982, he joined Sun to head up manufacturing and operations. Scott's manufacturing skills enabled the new company to keep up with the high demand as sales went from $9 million in 1983 to $39 million in 1984. Nonetheless, the high amount of new orders surpassed the cash available for expansion. McNealy then asked their customer Eastman Kodak Co. to invest $20 million. As a condition of the investment, Kodak insisted that McNealy take over as president. In 1984, Scott was officially named CEO of the company.

2 | Consolidated Balance Sheets

(In thousands, except share and per share amounts)	At June 30, 1998	1997
Assets		
Current assets:		
Cash and cash equivalents	$ 822,267	$ 660,170
Short-term investments	476,185	452,590
Accounts receivable, net of allowances of $235,563 in 1998 and $196,091 in 1997	1,845,765	1,666,523
Inventories	346,446	437,978
Deferred tax assets	371,841	286,720
Other current assets	285,021	224,469
Total current assets	4,147,525	3,728,450
Property, plant and equipment:		
Machinery and equipment	1,251,660	1,057,239
Furniture and fixtures	113,636	93,078
Leasehold improvements	256,233	166,745
Land and buildings	635,699	341,279
	2,257,228	1,658,341
Accumulated depreciation and amortization	(956,616)	(858,448)
	1,300,612	799,893
Other assets, net	262,925	168,931
	$5,711,062	$4,697,274
Liabilities and Stockholders' Equity		
Current liabilities:		
Short-term borrowings	$ 7,169	$ 100,930
Accounts payable	495,603	468,912
Accrued payroll-related liabilities	315,929	337,412
Accrued liabilities and other	810,562	625,600
Deferred service revenues	264,967	197,616
Income taxes payable	188,641	118,568
Note payable	40,000	—
Total current liabilities	2,122,871	1,849,038
Deferred income taxes and other obligations	74,563	106,299
Commitments and contingencies		
Stockholders' equity:		
Preferred stock, $0.001 par value, 10,000,000 shares authorized; no shares issued and outstanding	—	—
Common stock, $0.00067 par value, 950,000,000 shares authorized; issued: 430,311,441 shares in 1998 and 430,535,886 shares in 1997	288	288
Additional paid-in capital	1,345,508	1,229,797
Retained earnings	3,150,935	2,409,850
Treasury stock, at cost: 54,007,866 shares in 1998 and 60,050,380 shares in 1997	(1,003,191)	(915,426)
Currency translation adjustment and other	20,088	17,428
Total stockholders' equity	3,513,628	2,741,937
	$5,711,062	$4,697,274

3 | Sun Microsystems—Products Source (Form-10k)

Servers and Workstations: The company offers a full line of Ultra Enterprise servers to support an immense database and mission-critical business applications. With their Netra server family, Sun delivers preconfigured solutions for Intranet and Internet publishing. Their Ultra workstation series combines accelerated graphics, high-bandwidth networking and fast processing to provide outstanding performance for technical applications.

Solaris and Solstice: With Sun's installed base of more than 2 million systems, Solaris software is the leading operating environment for open client-server networks. The Solstice products consist of a highly scalable and comprehensive suite of Intranet management software, helping organizations securely access, administer and manage rapidly changing Intranet computing environments.

SunSpectrum: This newly developed portfolio of enterprise-wide support services connects Sun's customers to a highly responsive organization that supports more than half a million systems worldwide. That combination of hardware, system software and application support with premium account-level services, maximizes both system availability and customer satisfaction.

WorkShop and NEO: The WorkShop family, which includes the new Java WorkShop solution, delivers visual development tools that quickly and easily create multiplatform applications for the Internet, Intranets and enterprise networks. NEO delivers system administration tools, object-oriented development tools and transparent networking in order to reduce the cost of creating, customizing and maintaining applications.

UltraSPARC and Java Processors: Well-developed UltraSPARC microprocessors accelerate multimedia and networking applications with their innovative architecture and VIS media instruction set through powering networked systems from routers to supercomputers. The planned JavaChip microprocessor family will be optimized for Java-powered applications.

Java Software: It is the first software platform planned from start for the Internet and corporate Intranets that will run on any computer.

McNealy showed his ability as a CEO over the coming years. After the company went public in 1986, it took two years for Sun to outgrow its production capacities, which led to the company's first quarterly loss. Its troubled production facilities was reason enough for McNealy to move from Sun's executive suite to the floor of its biggest factory and revamp the company's manufacturing. In the months after production was rolling again, he showed skills nobody expected. He deliberately pruned the product line, sharpening Sun's focus to workstations built around a high-powered processor of its own design. Realizing that fixing problems on the factory floor was no job for the CEO of a company of Sun's size, McNealy reorganized the company's structure. He pushed profit-and-loss responsibility down to individual product organizations, called planets, and let them feel the troubles if things went wrong.

At Sun's headquarters, McNealy, having an image in the industry of being brash, was building a corporate culture based on his own motto: "Kick butt and have fun." Soon after that, the company became known for its aggressive marketing, featuring Network, McNealy's Greater Swiss Mountain dog, and various juvenile behavior taking place within Sun's headquarters.

This humor had an important effect on the culture. During these competitive times in the computer industry when good positions and good workers were hard to find, it helped employees live with their demanding jobs and bound the company together. Carol A. Bartz, former sales vice president of Sun, and Thomas J. Meredith, former Sun treasurer, agree that McNealy has a special gift. Using humor and a tremendous amount of energy, McNealy has the ability to raise employees enthusiastically to their feet.

Sun does not consist of McNealy alone, however. According to Ellison, Scott has complemented his leadership with very capable people. "You don't find Scott surrounded by dummies. You find Scott surrounded by real smart people, like Bill Joy and Eric Schmidt [chief technology officer] and others who do wonderful work."

JAVA—THE PROGRAMMING LANGUAGE

Java originated from a 1990 programming language, code-named Oak, that would enable all computerized devices to run simple programs distributed to them over a network. At one point, Oak was part of the effort to develop a two-way interactive cable TV system (which Sun lost out to Silicon Graphics). By the end of 1994, Oak seemed to be going nowhere. During one last presentation of Oak, McNealy recognized the potential of the programming language—to reach his ultimate goal: to harness the Internet to stop Microsoft from swallowing all of them—and became its biggest supporter. Soon after that, the language was renamed Java, a colloquial word for coffee. The fact that the name was informal and generic, compared to previous programming language names that were obscure and somewhat daunting, implied that normal people should also care about Java, whether they knew what it did or not. By May 1995, McNealy informed the public, who at that point did not know what to make of the new concept. On January 12, 1996, Sun officially released Java, its network software. With the announcement of Java, Sun entered a new era with a tremendous amount of public exposure and a heightened interest in the company.

The brand name Java refers to many things, including a programming language plus a set of components and tools. It was originally looked at as a language that would jazz up Web pages with graphic animations—dancing icons, for example. To Microsoft's dismay, Java is viewed by the public as a computing platform. Its most important part is what makes Java a self-sufficient computing system; it is the Java Virtual Machine or JVM. The JVM is a piece of software that imitates all the functions of the computing device. This allows Java to run on any machine with a JVM, insensitive to the underlying operating system (Windows, Macintosh, UNIX, etc.), and allows applications written in Java to run on all machines without being changed. The Java digital language is the first universal software that would allow all computerized devices to share programs and communicate over a network. It makes possible the rapid development of versatile programs for communicating and collaborating on the Internet.

Compared to ordinary software applications, Java applications, or "applets," are little programs that reside on the network in centralized servers. The network delivers the programs to the user's machine when needed. Because the applets are so much smaller, they require comparably less time to download. In other words, Java lets programmers write small applications that can zip across the World Wide Web. Without leaving the browser, the user will then be able to print out attractive text and charts. The user always gets the latest version of the applets. As the software is stored in only one place, corporations can keep it updated more easily. Java's designers believed that in the new environment, the program's speed would be measured by how fast a program ran on a network and not by how fast a program ran on an individual computer. In this sense, being object oriented versus speed oriented makes programs run faster or at least appear to. Java was developed to have its objects move quickly into and out of different machines and merge with other Java objects on the network, even when these objects appeared unexpectedly.

With the immense growth of the World Wide Web, Java's introduction was one of those magic moments where place and time seemed perfect. It appeared to be the language best suited for Internet computing. In addition to applying to all PCs, Java is inherently virus-proof. This is because the language was designed so that applets cannot alter data in the user's computer files or on its hard disk. Silicon Graphics and Macromedia partnered with Sun to jointly define a new set of open multimedia formats and application programming interfaces (APIs) to extend Sun's Java. The companies believe that these new API formats will enhance Java's capabilities for providing animation and interactivity, especially in the area of 3-D rendering and multimedia over the Internet or corporate networks.

With the increasing importance of the Net, McNealy once more is convinced that Java will alter the dynamics of the business. "Java opens up a whole new world for Sun," he says. It can be said that a part of the new world has already started. Java is well on its way to becoming the Internet software standard, which would make Sun the leader in Internet computing. Millions of personal computer owners already have access to Java because the software was built into the 1996 release of Netscape's Web browser. As the "intelligent network" also starts to include mobile phones, smart pagers, hand-held electronic assistants, and so on in addition to traditional computers, Java is set off to become a standard language for these far-flung devices.

Although Sun is planning to eventually donate the software language to the computer world through publicizing all the specs and letting anybody use them, Java should continue to spur profitable growth for the company. According to management, Java will increase Sun's sale of Internet servers, priced at $25,000, and start its new line of JavaStation network computers. Java will also raise the demand for Sun's software development tools and for special Sun chips, which other computer makers can incorporate into their machines to run Java faster.

McNealy's view of the future is not shared universally, however. It is very unlikely that Java will change computing so soon. The programming language still is at a fairly immature stage and its programs run significantly slower than programs written specifically for a particular computer operating system. Furthermore, there have been security issues raised by a system of distributing software on the Net.

The Java Controversy

By the first week of December 1995, many of the top names in computing, from Netscape Communications to Oracle Systems, Apple, BulletProof Corporation, Wind River Systems, Inc., Toshiba, and IBM, had endorsed Java. IBM had 2,500 programmers working to improve Java because it saw Java as the glue that could finally link its many lines of computers seamlessly. Because Java programs run on any hardware or operating system, Java could bypass and, therefore, break Microsoft's cash cow, Microsoft Office. For Java to be present on further PCs, Sun tried to persuade Microsoft to incorporate a Java interpreter into the Windows operating systems. After four months of negotiations, Sun received a fax from Microsoft in March 1996 agreeing to license Java on Sun's terms. Microsoft had changed its strategy of writing its own software for any interface or function (unless customers demanded that Microsoft adopt another) because of a software language. In its many years of business, Microsoft had rarely adopted anyone else's software or hardware standards. The company had agreed to license a product from Sun because it did not have a lot of choices.

On October 7, 1997, however, Sun Microsystems announced that it had filed a lawsuit in U.S. District Court, Northern District of California, San Jose Division, against Microsoft Corporation for breaching its contractual obligation to deliver a compatible implementation of Java technology on its products. Further, the complaint charged Microsoft with trademark infringement, false advertising, breach of contract, unfair competition, interference with prospective economic advantage, and inducing breach of contract. Sun claimed that Microsoft had deliberately violated its licensing agreement in its attempt to reduce the cross-platform compatibility made possible by the Java technology and deliver a version of the technology that worked only with Microsoft's products. Sun also charged that Microsoft illegally placed Sun's software code on its World Wide Web site. Sun asked for $35 million in damages over that one issue.

Even though there have been threats of revoking Microsoft's Java licensing agreement, Sun did not plan to cancel Microsoft's license. The company's goal was to pressure Microsoft to fulfill the obligations created in that license. Sun was seeking a court order to hinder Microsoft from improperly using the Java Compatible logo and deceiving the marketplace. The logo appeared in different locations in and on Microsoft's consumer packaging and promotional materials. Sun was further seeking to hinder Microsoft from misleading Java developers and to prevent the company from delivering anything but fully compatible Java technology implementations. Sun saw itself responsible for defending the integrity of Java. Michael Morris, Sun's VP/General

Counsel, stated, "Nowhere is the sanctity of a trademark more important than in the field of computer software. Our customers rely on the reputation and the goodwill of the trademark to make informed, efficient decisions about the technology they are using."

Any one of Java licensee's most significant contractual obligations is to pass the Java compatibility tests. These tests determine if a licensee's technology conform to the Java specifications and APIs. In Microsoft's case, the products that failed are the new Internet Explorer 4.0 browser and the company's Software Development Kit for Java (SDKJ). The new technology did not pass Sun's compatibility tests due to an improper modification of the products by Microsoft. Hence, applications written using Microsoft's development tools do not run on all machines without the necessary adjustments made to them.

The stakes are high for the two companies. McNealy is convinced that Sun can win a lawsuit against Microsoft, the most powerful software company in the world, by having a court that looks at the case, not at the companies involved. Winning the suit would enable Sun to live up to the CEO's idea behind his drive to develop Java: To free the world of the duopolistic grip of Microsoft and Intel or so-called Wintel. It would open the market for Sun and other computer companies. As Microsoft is fully aware of McNealy's concept, the strategy behind the company's allegedly illegal behavior is to encourage developers to write Java programs that are tied to Windows. This would block Sun's efforts to expand the language into a possible full-blown operating system.

Sun and its CEO are very confident that the court will see the merits of the complaint and move to a speedy resolution. Sun seems to ignore, however, that Microsoft, Intel Corp., Digital Equipment Corp., and Compaq Computer Corp. all signed an open letter on September 11, 1997, that urged Sun to turn control of Java over to the International Standards Organization (ISO). This demand would put the Java logo in the public domain. Sun seems to have missed the fact that this suit is not solely about Microsoft. It is about whether Sun can respond to the standards body. If Sun loses, its plan that the ISO would have some oversight over Java might not get accepted and Sun would have to give up control of the key components of Java and the Java brand. This, in turn, would lead to a huge future loss in revenue and a decline in any investments of many trustworthy companies like IBM, who have partnered with Sun in the development of Java. Furthermore, it would enable Microsoft to establish a Windows-only variant of Java, one that would only benefit Wintel (PCs based on Intel's microprocessor using the Windows operating system) machine users, as a competing standard that would block Sun from creating a uniform Java that can run equally well on any type of computer.

The Vendetta with Microsoft

The suit had developed into a public fight between Sun Microsystems and Microsoft, two extremely successful companies. This sniping between Sun and Microsoft is more about who controls the future of computing than the surface spat over the Java Internet programming language. Microsoft has brought its weight into play to slow Sun down further. Microsoft is using its power, market visibility, and market presence to try to reposition Java as "just another programming language".

The rivalry between the two companies has become so shrill that Aaron Goldberg, of Computer Intelligence in La Jolla, California, calls it a "urinary Olympics." After winning out over Apple, Lotus, and WordPerfect, Microsoft is convinced that it is on its way to winning the browser war as well. Netscape is still growing and finding new customers, but it may lose out to Microsoft as well. Thinking that Sun will succeed where others have failed is probably irrational.

At the same time, it may be smart to be perceived as the one company who is attacking Microsoft. Many CIOs have started to worry about the increasing costs of information technology systems and software and their dependence on Microsoft and Intel. The incredibly large sums spent on equipment and maintenance increased the CIOs' willingness to support new alternatives. In addition to the CIOs, customers have always liked to apply pressure to the market leaders in the hope of driving down prices. Consumers like the concept that no user of Java needs to buy the software in a retail store or from an electronic catalogue; it is part of the economic transaction. There is also a willingness and availability of money in the industry to help anyone who might loosen Microsoft's control over the way things will be in the future. This is why there has been

EXHIBIT 4 | Board of Directors, Corporate Officers, and Worldwide Corporate Structure: Sun Microsystems, Inc.

A. Board of Directors

Scott G. McNealy
Chairman of the Board of Directors, President, and Chief Executive Officer, Sun Microsystems, Inc.

L. John Doerr
General Partner, Kleiner Perkins Caufield & Byers

Judith L. Estrin
President, Chief Executive Officer, Precept Software, Inc.

Robert J. Fisher
Executive Vice-President and Director, Gap, Inc., President, Gap Division, Gap, Inc.

Robert L. Long
Management Consultant

M. Kenneth Oshman
Chairman, President, and Chief Executive Officer, Echelon Corporation

A. Michael Spence
Dean, Graduate School of Business, Stanford University

B. Corporate Officers

Scott G. McNealy
Chairman of the Board of Directors, President, and Chief Executive Officer, Sun Microsystems, Inc.

Kenneth M. Alvares
Vice-President, Human Resources, Sun Microsystems, Inc., and Corporate Executive Officer

Alan E. Baratz
President, JavaSoft, and Corporate Executive Officer

Lawrence W. Hambly
President, SunService Division, and Corporate Executive Officer

Michael E. Lehman
Vice-President, Chief Financial Officer, Sun Microsystems, Inc., and Corporate Executive Officer

Michael H. Morris
Vice-President, General Counsel, and Secretary, Sun Microsystems, Inc.

Alton D. Page
Vice-President, Treasurer, Sun Microsystems, Inc.

William J. Raduchel
Vice-President, Corporate Planning and Development, and Chief Information Officer, Sun Microsystems, Inc., and Corporate Executive Officer

George Reyes
Vice-President, Controller, Sun Microsystems, Inc.

Janpieter T. Scheerder
President, SunSoft, Inc., and Corporate Executive Officer

Chester J. Silvestri
President, Sun Microelectronics, and Corporate Executive Officer

Edward J. Zander
President, Sun Microsystems Computer Company, and Corporate Executive Officer

Sun Worldwide Manufacturing
2 countries

International Research & Development
8 countries

International Sales, Service, and Support
41 countries

International Distributors
Nearly 150 countries

Source: Sun Microsystems, Inc., *1998 Annual Report,* p. 47.

so much support for Java, even more than McNealy originally expected.

McNealy soon will have to decide if this almost personal vendetta to break Microsoft's power in the computer industry is in the best interest of Sun's shareholders and if it is a healthy path for Sun in the future. He could have considered cooperating with Microsoft. This would have opened Java up to the masses and could have helped Sun sell even more highly profitable servers and workstations. Stating Sun's point of view that Java does not have to make money for the company as long as it helps the company break Microsoft's business model shows McNealy's intent. Sadly enough, this might really not be in the public's best interest. McNealy is convinced "if Java catches on big, the software lock-in of the Microsoft Windows/Intel design will end. Then, computer and software companies will once again be able to differentiate their products. Indeed, they will have to." If Java does not catch on or if Sun loses the suit, no one, including McNealy, will know what Sun's future will be in the computer technology industry, especially if one considers that neither the law suit nor Java itself affects Microsoft as much as originally thought. The fact that many people like Java does not change how customers want to use the computers on their desks. They still want to calculate spreadsheets, process words, hold presentations, and manage personal information by using software that allows them to do so as conveniently as possible. It does not seem to make a difference that the new programmers will use Java to create new software. Many of the present programmers will continue using conventional languages to develop commercial software because all the new languages will end up running on Windows machines anyway, only because these are the machines the majority of the users already have.

Sun Microsystems Faces Revolt Over Java Control

Sun Microsystems is facing an industry revolt against its control of Java, the computer language which allows programs to run on any system. On November 2, 1998, 14 companies including Hewlett-Packard, Microsoft, Siemens and Rockwell announced they would start setting their own standards for creating Java programs which control devices such as cellphones and printers. The move follows several months of negotiations with Sun over industry complaints that it was being too slow at developing new software standards and was charging too much in licensing fees.

Joe Beyers, general manager of Internet Software at Hewlett-Packard, said, "We are trying to respond to customer needs but Sun has been unwilling to relinquish control of Java. If they want to go in a different direction they can, but I hope they can join us."

Sun has focused on developing Java for mainstream computer programming to the frustration of companies wishing to develop other uses. Sun has yet to start selling its own system for running Java programs on embedded processors.

Hewlett-Packard this year broke Sun's grip on Java by developing its own system for operating Java programs called Chai, which does not require a license from Sun.

*Mr. Beyers says several other companies are developing similar systems (*Financial Times, *November 3, 1998, p. 1).*

Postscript

On November 24, 1998, America Online (AOL) announced it was purchasing Netscape Communications for $4.2 billion, and entering into a multilayered strategic partnership with Sun Microsystems to develop new Internet access devices (see Exhibit 4).

REFERENCES

Alsop, Stewart, "Warning to Scott McNealy: Don't Moon the Ogre," *Fortune,* October 13, 1997.

Alsop, Stewart, "Sun's Java: What's Hype, What's Real," *Fortune,* July 7, 1997.

Bank, David, "Sun Lawsuit Is Latest Shot at Microsoft," *Wall Street Journal,* October 9, 1997.

Bank, David, "Sun Suit Says Microsoft Disrupts Java," *Wall Street Journal,* October 10, 1997.

Fitzgerald, Michael, "Sun's Threat: Microsoft Could Lose Java License," *ZDNet,* September 23, 1997.

Gomes, Lee, "Sun Microsystems 1st-Period Net, Sales Miss Expectations Due to Currency Rates," *Wall Street Journal,* October 17, 1997.

Gomes, Lee and Clark, Don, "Java Is Finding Niches But Isn't Yet Living Up To Its Early Promises," *Wall Street Journal,* August 27, 1997.

Gomes, Lee, "Profits at Sun Microsystems Increase 56%," *Wall Street Journal,* April 16, 1997.

Hamm, Steve with Hof, Robert, "Operation Sunblock: Microsoft Goes to War," *Business Week,* October 27, 1997.

Hof, Robert D. with Burrows, Peter and Rebello, Kathy, "Scott McNealy's Rising Sun," *Business Week,* January 22, 1996.

Hof, Robert D. with Verity, John, "Now, Sun Has To Keep Java Perking," *Business Week,* January 22, 1996.

Indiana Rigdon, Joan, "Sun Microsystems' Earnings Soar 41% Due to Strength at Top of Product Line," *Wall Street Journal,* January 16, 1997.

Kirkpatrick, David, "Meanwhile, Back at Headquarters . . . ," *Fortune,* October 13, 1997.

Mitchell, Russ, "Extreme Fighting, Silicon Valley Style," *U.S. News & World Report,* October 20, 1997.

Schlender, Brent, "The Adventures of Scott McNealy," *Fortune,* October 13, 1997.

Schlender, Brent, "Sun's Java: The Threat to Microsoft Is Real," *Fortune,* November 11, 1996.

Seminerio, Maria, "Java Jive: Microsoft vs. Sun Draws No Blood—Yet," *ZDNet,* September 23, 1997.

Sun Microsystems, Inc.'s home page: *www.sun.com*

"Sun Microsystems, Silicon Graphics and Macromecia Intend to Define a New Set of Open 3D and Multimedia Interfaces for Java and the Web," from Sun's home page: *www.sun.com*

Sun Microsystems, Inc.'s Annual Report 1996.

Sun Microsystems, Inc.'s Annual Report 1997.

"Wind River System's Tornado for Java Passes Sun Microsystem's Java Compatibility Tests": biz.yahoo.com/prnews/980121/ca_wind_ri+1.html. January 21, 1998.

"BulletProof Releases JdesignerPro 2.32—Advanced RAD Application Development System for Java": biz.yahoo.com/prnews/980120/ca_bulletp_1.html. January 20, 1998.

"Sun Unveils Plans to Grow Desktop Market at Expense of Compaq, H-P and SGI": *www.sun.dom/smi/Press/sunflash/9801/sunflash.980113.3.html.* January 13, 1998.

"Sun Sues Microsoft for Breach of Java Contract": *www.sun.com/smi/Press.sunflash/9710/sunflash.97107.10.html.* October 7, 1997.

"Sun Microsystems Seeks to Bar Microsoft from Unauthorized Use of 'Java Compatible' Logo": *www.java.sun.com/pr/1997/nov/sun.pr971118.html.* November 18, 1997.

CASE 37

The Merger of U.S. Bancorp and Piper Jaffray Companies

Dawn Hodges
California State University, San Marcos
Ernest E. Scarbrough
Arizona State University
John R. Montanari
California State University, San Marcos

THE MERGER

On December 15, 1997, U.S. Bancorp and Piper Jaffray issued a joint press release announcing that they had entered into an agreement and plan of merger, dated December 14, 1997. Piper Jaffray Companies will merge with and into U.S. Bancorp. The $730 million, or $37.25 a share, deal makes it the largest foray by a big commercial bank into the once-forbidden world of investment banking. The price represents over four times Piper Jaffray Companies' book value per share and a 25 percent premium over the December closing price of $29.75 per share.

The acquisition will allow U.S. Bancorp to offer investment banking and institutional and retail brokerage services through a new unit named U.S. Bancorp Piper Jaffray, Inc. This combines two powerful brand names that reflect the expanded capabilities of the new organization. (See Exhibit 1.) The deal should close in the second quarter of 1998, after all regulatory and Piper Jaffray Companies' shareholder approvals are received.

FINANCIAL SERVICES INDUSTRY

Commercial Banks

The commercial banking industry has rolled up six straight years of record profits, fed by massive consolidations and the application of new technologies. In 1997 the industry's net income hit $59.2 billion, up 13 percent from 1996, with fewer but larger institutions. According to the FDIC, 599 bank mergers took place in 1997, reducing the number of banks to 9,143 from nearly 14,000 just 10 years earlier.

Ascendancy of the Universal Commercial Bank. Industry observers predict the ascendancy of the universal commercial bank and increased competition in the commercial banking industry. On April 13, 1997, as the Bank of America–NationsBank deal was announced, Banc One chairman John B. McCoy (who once mused that in the future the industry would have just five or six major banks) announced plans to merge his $116 billion bank with the much merged $115 billion First Chicago NBD Corp. All this came just a week after insurance and brokerage giant Travelers Group announced plans to tie the knot with Citicorp, the second largest bank in the U.S.—a $76 billion marriage, not just of services but of two industry titans.

The Glass–Steagall Act

Initially, the U.S. government did not enforce a separation between commercial and investment banking. However, bank failures, which accompanied the 1929 stock market crash and subsequent loss of individuals' savings during the Great Depression, prompted Congress to enact the Glass–Steagall Act. This legislation split commercial from investment banking to protect consumers. Banks at that time had to choose between the two functions: commercial banking or investment banking. For example, Morgan Stanley was created as an investment-banking spin-off from J.P. Morgan.

In the early 1930s, the Securities and Exchange Commission (SEC) was created to enforce the new se-

1 | Pro Forma Recaps (1997)

U.S. Bancorp		Piper Jaffray Companies	
Headquartered	Minneapolis	Headquartered	Minneapolis
Chairman and CEO	John F. "Jack" Grundhofer	Chairman and CEO	Addison L. "Tad" Piper
Assets under management	$55.3 billion	Assets under management	$12.8 billion
Retail branches	1,000 in 17 states	Retail branches	89 in 19 states
Number of employees	27,566 (250 are brokers)	Number of employees	3,328 (1,235 are brokers)
Operating Income	$324.8 million	Operating income	$4.3 million

Source: Securities and Exchange Commission, Washington, D.C. Form 8-K, Commission File Number 1-6880.

curities laws. The SEC still ensures that investors have access to important information concerning public securities and regulates anyone involved in trading securities or providing investment advice.[1]

The biggest challenge affecting the industry today is the gradual collapse of the Glass-Steagall Act. The division between commercial and securities banking is tumbling downward and commercial banks are entering securities banking turf.

U.S. BANCORP

U.S. Bancorp was formed in 1997 when Minneapolis-based First Bank System bought Oregon-based U.S. Bancorp. The bank derives about one third of its earnings from corporate customers. Although it is one of the nation's most profitable commercial banks, U.S. Bancorp increasingly risks losing many of its customers to securities firms or other banks with investment-banking functions. Unless it quickly develops the ability to underwrite securities or provide merger-and-acquisitions advice, U.S. Bancorp could be a loser in the banking wars. Exhibit 2 gives a brief history of the company.

Building the Business

U.S. Bancorp looks for opportunities in existing markets and adjacent markets where economic benefits are the highest and in niche markets such as corporate trust. It pursues only those acquisitions that it believes will create shareholder value.

Amid restructuring in 1989, First Bank System hired John "Jack the Ripper" Grundhofer from Wells Fargo Bank. He slashed costs to the bone, cut out lending to large corporations, began consolidating data systems, introduced uniformity to the bank's product lines and focused acquisitions on trust businesses. In 1993 First Bank System bought Colorado National Bancshares, a Denver bank. This transaction brought it full ownership of the Rocky Mountain BankCard System, making it a leading processor of merchant-side credit card transactions. The firm bought several other banks in 1995, but the big fish, Los Angeles–based First Interstate, got away. That year the company took steps to become the U.S.'s largest corporate trust company by buying Bank of America's corporate trust business. First Bank System subsequently exited the mortgage servicing business.

In February 1996, U.S. Bancorp closed on its acquisition of FirsTier Financial, Inc., creating the second largest banking institution in Nebraska in terms of total deposits, and making that state its third largest market. U.S. Bancorp completed the integration of FirsTier within three days, quickly taking out operating expenses for the benefit of shareholders.

In its boldest move to date, First Bank System bought U.S. Bancorp (which operates in California, Idaho, Nevada, Oregon, Utah, and Washington) in 1997 for about $9 billion. This deal created a banking behemoth that retained the U.S. Bancorp name. Nineteen ninety-seven also brought the purchase of Zappco, Inc., of St. Cloud, Minn., giving U.S. Bancorp the number one market position in that area.

2 | A Very Brief History of U.S. Bancorp

1864	First National Bank of St. Paul chartered
1865	First National Bank of Minneapolis chartered
1929	First Bank Stock Corporation formed by First National Banks of St. Paul and Minneapolis; despite depression, 85 banks purchased by year-end; total assets—$122.8 million
1968	First Bank Stock Corporation changes name to First Bank System, Inc. (FBS)
1985	FBS sells 28 rural affiliate banks
1988	FBS sells portion of bond portfolio, incurs pretax loss of $500 million
1989	Jack Grundhofer brought in as chairman, president and CEO from Wells Fargo.
1996	FBS posts 1.88 percent return on assets, 21.4 percent return on common equity, 49.9 percent efficiency ratio, putting the bank among industry's top performers
1997	FBS acquires Oregon-based U.S. Bancorp, doubling in size; announces plan to acquire Piper Jaffray Companies
1998	New U.S. Bancorp is 15th largest American bank holding company, 1,000 branches in 17 states, 4,500 ATMs, 500,000 business customers, 4 million retail customers
	U.S. Bancorp acquires Zappco, Inc., of St. Cloud, Minn., giving U.S. Bancorp the No. 1 market position in that area.
Future	Proposed acquisition of Piper Jaffray Companies creates the nations 11th largest retail brokerage sales force, spanning a 19-state region, with more than $68 billion in assets under management

Brand Promise

Nineteen ninety-seven brought the introduction of a new corporate identity system that reflects the new U.S. Bancorp. One objective for the new look was to provide a "clean, clear look for a strong, progressive company." The new identity system captures U.S. Bancorp's key characteristics in "brand promise" and "brand identity" statements (see Exhibit 3).

Market Leadership

The new "brand" identity, with its implied personality and promise, symbolizes an organization that holds the number one market share in 12 markets, including Minneapolis/St. Paul, Portland/Vancouver, Boise and Salem, and ranks number two or number three in 17 additional markets, including Seattle, Denver, Omaha, Spokane and Lincoln, Nebraska.

U.S. Bancorp continues as the nation's leading issuer of VISA corporate and purchasing cards. It is also the fourth largest merchant card processor in the United States, responsible for $22 billion in credit card volume. U.S. Bancorp has the nation's eighth largest bank-owned leasing company. Its retail operation includes about 1,000 branches and 4,500 ATMs in 17 states serv-

3 | U.S. Bancorp's Characteristics

Brand Promise	Brand Identity
U.S. Bank promises to provide meaningful and relevant solutions to our customers; we simplify our customers' lives by delivering anytime, anywhere access to a comprehensive range of financial solutions.	U.S. Bancorp is a solution-oriented, progressive organization that is focused on meeting customer needs.

ing four million households. In addition, the firm manages a $31.3 billion commercial loan portfolio, serving over 50,000 businesses, and is one of the largest providers of corporate trust services in the United States.

Ultimately, U.S. Bancorp's 27,000-plus employees are the key to delivering industry-leading shareholder and customer value. The firm works hard to maximize sales from its retail clients, providing its "personal bankers" with standard sales materials and telephone scripts. "U.S. Bancorp is a top-performing company because we have top-performing individuals," says Jack Grundhofer. "Our employees are people of strong ethical standards who thrive on speed and flexibility and who are energized by a challenging environment. Our people are committed to the communities they serve and share a common commitment to create shareholder value. U.S. Bancorp employees understand that satisfying and retaining customers is the fundamental means for continued prosperity."

Tangible Community Support

U.S. Bancorp also provides considerable leadership in the area of community involvement. In 1996, the bank earned "outstanding" ratings in Minnesota and Colorado from the national agency, which oversees industry compliance with community reinvestment requirements. U.S. Bancorp annually gives approximately two percent of its pretax earnings back to its communities. Last year these contributions totaled $18 million across seventeen states. Contributions during 1998 are expected to total approximately $20 million.

Creating Shareholder Value and Meeting Customers' Needs

U.S. Bancorp offers standardized products and services supported by central operations. At the same time, it provides hands-on custom service to customers who demand it. The bank's structure reflects its sharp focus on customers. Its unique flat organizational structure, coupled with an action-oriented culture, fuels the innovation, creativity and a sense of urgency that enables it to meet the unique needs of diverse customer segments.

In 1996, U.S. Bancorp streamlined its senior management and realigned its organization into five business lines: Retail Banking, Payment Systems, Business Banking and Private Financial Services, Commercial Banking, and Corporate Trust and Institutional Financial Services. (See Exhibit 4.) Through teamwork and integrated technology, each business can quickly bring together its diverse resources to satisfy unique customer needs.

Retail Banking. U.S. Bancorp built its retail banking business on quality products, effective sales and service,

EXHIBIT 4 | U.S. Bancorp

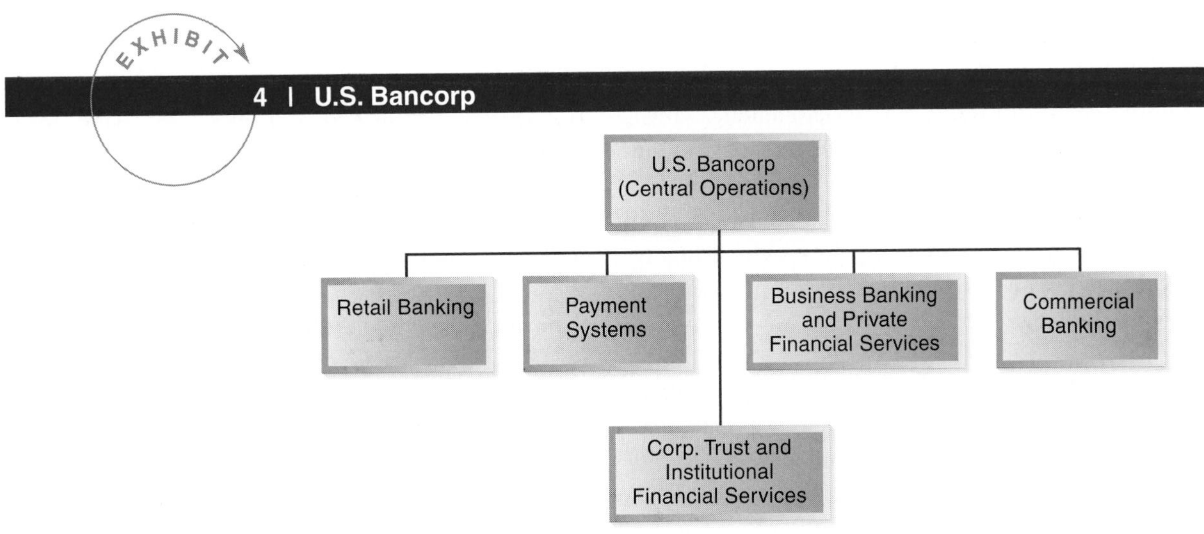

long-term relationships, and physical presence in the markets it serves. Retail banking is U.S. Bancorp's largest business. The retail banking division focuses on the broad consumer and small-business markets and serves approximately 1.9 million households and 203,400 small businesses throughout its eleven-state banking region.

Investment in new technologies has allowed U.S. Bancorp to continue to serve its customers through more convenient and efficient distribution channels. U.S. Bancorp has successfully encouraged customers to migrate to more cost-effective distribution channels such as supermarket branches, automated teller machines, and FastLine 24-hour banking. These channels offer customers the convenience of banking anytime, anywhere.

Business Banking and Private Financial Services. Business Banking and Private Financial Services, which together contribute roughly the same percentage of net income as retail banking, provide middle-market companies and ultra-affluent customers with relationship-oriented service. Many of the business owners and managers served by business banking division bankers also have needs for personal banking, personal trust, and investment services offered through the Private Financial Services division. The business banking bankers are typically among the first to identify these opportunities and are in a better position to leverage their customer relationships. Cross-selling between business and individual clients is facilitated by a joint management structure between the two services.

Commercial Banking. Commercial Banking, which provides an array of financial services to large corporate customers, is a mature and profitable business. Credit quality remains strong. Commercial Banking is successfully deepening client relationships by providing highly customized, complex financial services to increasingly demanding clients.

Corporate Trust. Scale is just one reason U.S. Bancorp is well positioned to succeed in the corporate trust niche. The bank has been investing in the infrastructure needed to absorb future acquisitions and grow existing business. The bank's continuing emphasis on automation and standardization enhances its ability to deliver the levels of accuracy, quality and timeliness that bond holders and bond issuers demand.

The strategy of maintaining local offices gives U.S. Bancorp a competitive edge in retaining and expanding its client base, particularly for municipal bonds. Through thirteen full service offices nationwide, it clearly has the size, experience and resources to compete profitably and efficiently. In addition, it is able to leverage management expertise throughout U.S. Bancorp in areas such as acquisitions and cost control.

In the corporate trust business, establishing economies of scale is necessary for competing effectively. The advantage goes to the companies with the means to invest in efficient technology and offer a breadth of high-quality products. Through recent acquisitions and internal growth, U.S. Bancorp has become one of the largest providers of corporate trust services in the industry.

In 1996 U.S. Bancorp successfully completed the integration of Bank of America's corporate trust business, doubling its corporate trust revenue and profitability. The bank continued its growth by closing on its acquisition of Comerica, Inc.'s bond indenture and paying agent business in January 1997. Having closed the acquisition, U.S. Bancorp now serves more than 10,000 clients with 33,000 bond issues in the areas of municipal, revenue, housing and corporate bond indenture trusteeships. U.S. Bancorp has built the critical mass needed to succeed in corporate trust, and will continue to grow by acquisition as other regional banks decide to exit this business.

Institutional Financial Services. The goal of Institutional Financial Services is to satisfy customers' needs, enabling U.S. Bancorp to grow non-interest income by gathering assets. U.S. Bancorp has approximately $20 billion in mutual fund assets. Total assets under management are more than $55 billion.

In 1996 institutional financial services assets under management increased 35 percent to $39.3 billion, and fee income grew 16 percent to $85.8 million. Strong long-term economic performance is fueling this division's growth and is a key reason that First American Funds, a proprietary mutual fund family of U.S. Bancorp, has enjoyed sustained performance. (See Exhibit 5.)

5 | U.S. Bancorp Businesses and Their Percentage of Third-Quarter 1997 Operating Earnings

- Retail Banking—consumer and small-business banking with an emphasis on convenience *(31 percent).*
- Payment Systems—consumer credit cards, corporate and purchasing cards, and merchant bankcard services *(12 percent).*
- Business Banking and Private Financial Services—credit and other financial services to mid-size companies, integrated services in private banking, personal trust and investment management to clients with significant assets *(22 percent).*
- Commercial Banking—credit products, treasury management and other financial services primarily to larger companies *(28 percent).*
- Corporate Trust and Institutional Financial Services—bond indenture trusteeship, payment agent and custody services to corporate and municipal debt issuers, 401(k) and other employee benefit programs, asset management, and institutional investment products *(7 percent).*

Actively Managing Capital and Delivering Strong Shareholder Results

While size is important to some aspects of the corporation, high performance is what differentiates U.S. Bancorp in the marketplace. Its strategy has been to manage capital for the benefit of shareholders now and over the long term.

Investment in Core Businesses. U.S. Bancorp invests in technology and other resources so that its core business can serve customers better, improve profitability, and increase revenues. U.S. Bancorp's Relationship Management System (RMS), launched in 1995 and expanded in 1996, generates detailed customer information that helps its people provide better service and identify the best sales opportunities. Unlike other database marketing efforts, RMS actually analyzes customer account and behavior data—and initiates action.

PIPER JAFFRAY COMPANIES

Piper Jaffray Companies, Inc., is principally engaged in general securities brokerage, corporate and public finance services, and investment management. Many of Piper Jaffray Companies' customers are the same types of midsize companies that characterize U.S. Bancorp's corporate customer base. Its largest subsidiary, Piper Jaffray, operates 89 branch offices in 17 Midwest, Mountain, Southwest and Pacific Coast states and has offices in 16 of the 17 states in which U.S. Bancorp has branches.

Although not a national powerhouse in securities banking, Piper Jaffray Companies is one of the country's largest regional brokerage firms, with more than 1,200 brokers in nineteen states and nearly $13 billion assets under management. Piper Jaffray Companies, Inc., offers investment and financial services through four complementary wholly owned subsidiaries: Piper Jaffray, Inc. (Piper Jaffray), Piper Capital Management Incorporated (Piper Capital), Piper Trust Company (Piper Trust) and Piper Jaffray Ventures, Inc. (Piper Jaffray Ventures). (See Exhibit 6.)

Piper Jaffray (Individual Investor Services). Piper Jaffray's investment executives help individuals meet their financial goals with focused planning, thoughtful advice, and an array of investment products and services. Driven by a strong growth in client assets, Piper Jaffray's Individual Investor Services group had a record revenue year in 1997. Its retail branch system, serving individual investors and small- to medium-sized businesses, had a 27 percent increase in client assets as investors increasingly saw the need to take responsibility for their financial future. Revenue of $399.1 million increased 2 percent over the prior year. This business unit contributed 59 percent of the Company's pretax income.

Piper Capital. Piper Capital has built powerful investment banking capabilities through its unwavering commitment to close customer relationships based on industry expertise, transactional experience, quality

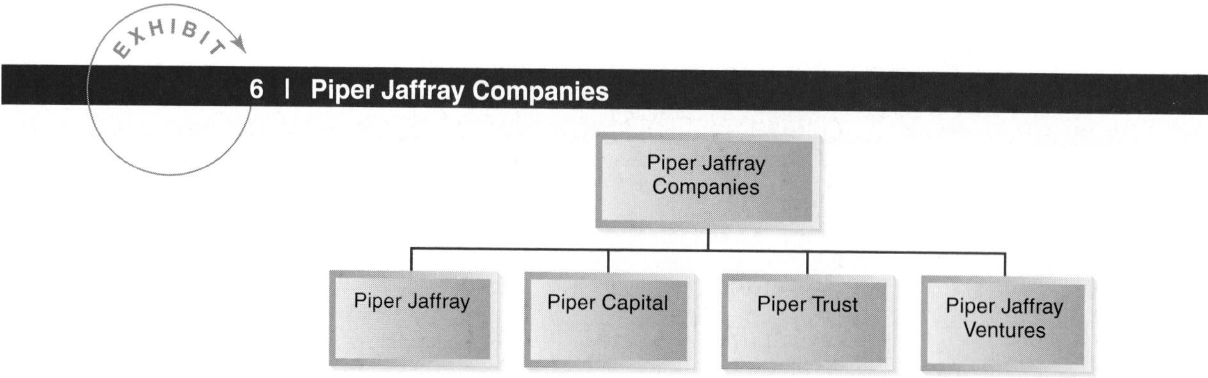

products, and outstanding performance. The Piper Capital group comprises equity research, corporate finance, mergers and acquisitions, institutional sales and trading, and corporate client services. Piper Capital's professionals offer nationally recognized capabilities in research, corporate finance, and institutional sales and trading to both issuers and investors.

Capital markets contributed 36 percent of the Company's pretax income for 1997 on revenue of $166.9 million. Strong merger and acquisition activity helped Piper Capital offset a less robust market in initial and follow-up public offerings.

Piper Trust Company (Piper Trust). Piper Trust Company is involved in three primary functions: investment banking to assist clients in issuing taxable and tax-exempt debt securities; trading of municipal government, corporate and mortgage-backed bonds; and institutional sales of these debt instruments to national and regional investors. This department employs approximately 200 people in 13 locations throughout the Midwest, Rocky Mountain, and Pacific Northwest regions.

Piper Jaffray Ventures, Inc. (Piper Jaffray Ventures). Piper Jaffray Ventures, Inc. ("PJV") organizes venture funds and invests the capital into promising emerging-growth companies in attractive market sectors. The funds' principal focus is in the areas of medical devices, and healthcare services and technology. Piper Jaffray Ventures currently manages three major funds: Piper Jaffray Healthcare Funds I and II, and Piper Jaffray Technology Fund. In addition, it manages several smaller funds that focus on investments in other specialty areas such as consumer, financial services and leveraged buyouts.

Currently, PJV's healthcare funds have approximately $80 million under management, while its technology fund as $32 million under management. In addition, other venture funds have approximately $7 million under management.

Growth Beckons as Opportunity Knocks

In the late 19th century, Minnesota's entrepreneurial soil was ready to be cultivated. As business start-ups soared, so did the need for cash. Recognizing this opportunity, former bank cashier George Bishop Lane began a commercial paper brokerage business, George B. Lane & Company, in Minneapolis in 1895.

In 1913 Harry Piper and Palmer Jaffray established a commercial paper brokerage firm, Piper, Jaffray and Company, that helped finance companies such as Northrop King (seeds), Pillsbury (flour), and Archer-Daniels-Midland (food processing). It merged with George B. Lane & Co. and created Lane, Piper & Jaffray, Inc. (LPJ) in 1917.

The firm soon moved into stock offerings, public finance, and underwriting. It gained a seat on the NYSE with the purchase of Hopwood & Co., which had been hard hit by the 1929 stock market crash. Piper Jaffray and Hopwood grew during the next forty years and went public in 1971. Three years later it changed its name to Piper Jaffray Companies.

As the economy boomed in the 1980s, Piper Jaffray

7 | Piper Jaffray Financial Highlights

(dollars in thousands, except per-share amounts)	1997	1996	% Increase
Total revenue	$601,894	$553,904	9%
Net income	$ 954	$ 7,296	—
Net income per share	$ .05	$ .04	—
Dividend per share	$ .30	$ .30	—
Shareholders' equity	$171,563	$166,825	3%
Return on average shareholders' equity	0.6%	4.5%	—
Shareholders' equity per share	$ 9.15	$ 9.17	—
Number of full-time employees	3,133	2,956	6%
Weighted average number of common and common equivalent share outstanding (in thousands)	19,727	18,377	7%
Number of shares outstanding at year end (in thousands)	18,754	18,197	3%

Companies, still under management by the Piper family, added new products and services, including asset management and mutual funds. It went through the 1987 stock crash relatively unscathed. When asked why the firm had weathered the crash of 1987 and the market's multiple aftershocks better than many in the financial service industry, observers pointed to planning, prudent investing, management by mission, and most important, people who shared the same values when the going got tough.

The firm's debacle came in 1994 when a mutual fund floundered due to a preponderance of risky derivative investments. Investors claiming they had not been informed of the risk brought class action suits against Piper Jaffray Companies. The company saw its net income plummet as it paid out over $100 million in settlements beginning in 1995; several suits were still pending in 1997.[2] Exhibit 7 displays financial highlights for 1996 and 1997.

An Environment of Interdependence

While the Piper Jaffray Companies organizational chart (Exhibit 6) once appeared in a linear schematic with separate boxes identifying functional areas, the lines and boxes have disappeared. In their place are overlapping circles (Individual Investor Services, Capital Markets, and Investment Services) that symbolize collaboration in a company that has grown dramatically in size, geographic reach, and products and services. (See Exhibit 8.)

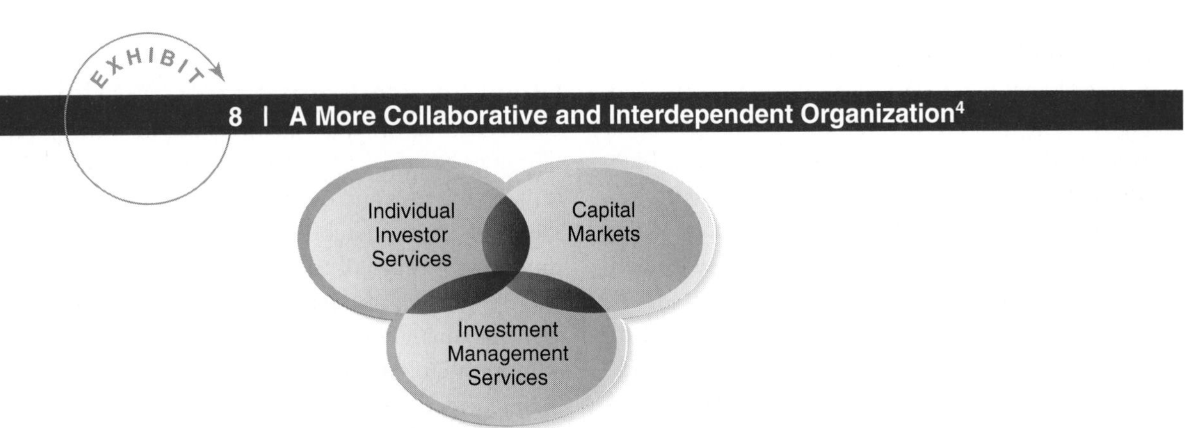

Source: Piper Jaffray Companies, "Vision 2000."

This collaboration, reflected in the interlocking circles, means that the three core business sectors within Piper Jaffray Companies share certain common markets, customers and core processes that yield a higher level of service, a significant marketplace advantage and increased operational efficiency.[3] While they all have their own strategic plans, business sectors share one clearly defined focus for the future.

Finally, Piper Jaffray Companies can tap into leadership within the Company that is broader and more diverse than ever before in its history. Entrepreneurship in the context of teamwork is emphasized and is expected to create an environment of interdependence that will benefit all of Piper Jaffray Companies' businesses.[4]

Employee Owners

Piper Jaffray Companies' employee-owners, who own 56 percent of the firm, take the challenges of ownership seriously. Employee-owners participate at many levels in strategic planning, then take responsibility for achieving the firm's goals.

Piper Jaffray Companies works hard to give employees professional development opportunities and skills, while recognizing and rewarding outstanding performance. The firm's management has taken the initiative to attract and reward the contributions of people with diverse backgrounds and ideas. To help employees lead its growth, Piper Jaffray Companies regularly brings together nearly 60 managers from across the company, giving them more opportunities to work across departments, build their leadership skills, and play a role in moving the firm forward.

Tad Piper and the Piper Jaffray Culture. As soon as he was old enough to write, Tad Piper accompanied his father to the office on Saturdays to help post customers' books. In 1963, when he was a junior in high school, Piper got his first "real" job at Piper, Jaffray & Hopwood. Like his father, Piper worked summers in the mailroom. He also worked in the cashier's "cage" and in the research department.

After earning his MBA at the Graduate School of Business at Stanford University, Piper worked in a variety of departments, including Trading, Syndicate, Sales, and Marketing. Piper advanced to senior vice president in 1980 and was named chairman of the Management Committee in 1982 and chief executive officer in 1983. Tad Piper's appointment to chief executive officer marked the third generation of Piper family leadership at the firm.

Tad Piper's office is a corner office, but not a typical one. It is simple and surprisingly small, decorated with bright Native American art and unobtrusive white furniture. One can look in from the corridor outside through glass walls. Photos of Piper's family, in a myriad of frames, line the sideboard by his desk. In many ways, his office is an appropriate symbol of a firm that prides itself on its close-knit family of bankers, down-to-earth personalities, and accessibility of even the most senior managers.

When asked about Piper Jaffray Companies' culture in a recent interview, Piper said,

> *I think our culture is quite different from New York investment banking. I think people here work just as hard or harder so it's not like "Come to the Midwest, so that you don't have to work quite as hard." But I think the environment in which we work is more supportive, both to careers and to outside activities. It's less dog-eat dog and more conducive to feeling good about the environment in which you're working so you're not competing against the people you are sitting next to.*
>
> *I think we're more understanding here, frankly, of family and personal issues. These are part of people's lives. Raising families and doing volunteer work we think are also important to a person's career and longevity here. We understand that the whole person is important.*[5]

Client Service Tradition

Guided by its mission statement (see Exhibit 9), Piper Jaffray Companies has traditionally focused on client service (internal and external) as the best way to meet the needs of its shareholders, employees and communities. In the midst of rapid change within the business, and the world around it, Piper Jaffray Companies' mission statement continues to serve its people well. The commitments of the mission statement challenge its people every day to find ways to build stronger relationships with their clients and serve them more effectively.

9 | Piper Jaffray Companies' Mission Statement

We, the people who are Piper Jaffray Companies, believe serving our clients is our basic purpose. By placing the interests of our clients first, we serve the best interests of our employees, our shareholders and our communities. We believe service is the chief contributor to our growth and profitability.

As we serve, we commit to:

- Work in partnership with our clients to understand their objectives and earn their confidence and respect;
- Provide sound advice, creative financial strategies and suitable investment to meet our clients' objectives;
- Communicate effectively and frequently with our clients;
- Cooperate with each other, promote the personal growth of each employee and preserve a high-quality work environment; and
- Contribute to the communities in which we live and work.

U.S. BANCORP PIPER JAFFRAY, INC.

The cross-town marriage pairs the nation's 15th largest commercial bank (with $70 billion in assets) with the 11th largest securities firm (as measured by the number of brokers) to form the 11th largest retail brokerage network in the U.S. This strategic partnership will help both companies grow revenues while providing clients with a broader array of creative financial solutions. (See Exhibit 10.) Sharing products, expertise and customer bases will create tremendous cross-selling opportunities and allow U.S. Bancorp Piper Jaffray, Inc., to enter the next level of competition in the marketplace.

Serving Clients with a Broader Array of Financial Products and Services

Piper Jaffray and U.S. Bancorp bring their own distinct, but complementary, strengths to U.S. Bancorp Piper Jaffray, Inc. Piper Jaffray's capabilities in equity and debt underwriting, trading, sales and research, as well as its corporate finance advisory and merger and acquisition services, will allow U.S. Bancorp to further strengthen its relations with its more than 40,000 middle-market commercial clients. Piper Jaffray customers will have access to the commercial banking products and services offered by U.S. Bancorp. Both companies will benefit

10 | Complementary Business Strengths

Value Added by Piper Jaffray

1. Corporate finance capabilities
   - Underwriting—debt & equity
   - Research
   - M&A Advisory
2. Over $12 billion of assets under management
3. Private client services/products
4. Trading expertise
5. Retail and corporate customers
   - $42.8 billion of clients funds
   - 122,000 households

Value Added by U.S. Bancorp

1. Extensive regional corporate relationships
   - 40,500 middle market customers
   - Middle market strength
   - Commercial banking products and services
2. Over $55 billion of assets under management
3. 52,000 private banking and personal trust relationships
4. Significantly greater distribution channels
   - Retail banking products & services
   - 4.0 million households
5. Technology investment

from their combined asset management experience and U.S. Bancorp's expertise in providing private banking and personal trust services.

Investing in Technology, Developing a Better Understanding of Client Needs

U.S. Bancorp has made significant investments in technology. It is successfully using technology to develop a rich database of its customers and their financial needs. Developing this kind of understanding of clients—and approaching business from a "market driven" perspective—has been a key priority of both U.S. Bancorp and Piper Jaffray Companies.

Business Model of the New Subsidiary

Tad Piper will continue his responsibilities as Chairman and CEO of U.S. Bancorp Piper Jaffray, a subsidiary of U.S. Bancorp, reporting to U.S. Bancorp President and CEO Jack Grundhofer. Andrew Duff and most other executive managers will continue in their current roles. Because U.S. Bancorp Piper Jaffray, Inc., will be a subsidiary of U.S. Bancorp, it will no longer need Piper Jaffray's external board of directors. However, in the future, an internal board may be formed. Piper Jaffray Companies' management committee will continue to lead U.S. Bancorp Piper Jaffray.

U.S. Bancorp's retail brokerage organization, fixed-income capital markets, and corporate finance group will report organizationally into Piper Jaffray Companies' existing structure, while Piper Capital Management and Piper Trust Company will report into First Asset Management First Trust. Piper Jaffray Companies' administrative functions will report to U.S. Bancorp.

Andersen Consulting has been hired to analyze the applications that support the brokerage, investment banking and investment management business. Andersen will be exploring respective applications to determine which of the applications to combine, convert or continue using. Information Systems managers from both companies will use Andersen's recommendations to develop a joint application architecture. In the meantime, business at Piper Jaffray Companies will continue as usual. Projects already in progress, like Piper PRO-File, will continue to move forward.

Stocks and Compensation. Its employees own the majority of Piper Jaffray Companies' stock directly or through company-sponsored employee stock ownership plans (ESOP). Piper Jaffray Companies' current benefits plans will continue through 1998. Shares will be voted on a pass-through basis. Employees will vote the shares that are allocated to them in the ESOP. ESOP participants who are not already vested will be vested at closing. The ESOP will be dissolved and employees will have several options for their ESOP balances, including a tax-free rollover.

ESOP. Much of the money U.S. Bancorp is paying will go to Piper Jaffray employees, who together own slightly more than 60 percent of the firm, including a 3 percent stake owned by Addison L. Piper, the firm's chairman and chief executive officer. In addition, certain employees will be eligible for a three-year package of financial incentives designed to keep them with the firm. It has been speculated that incentives could have a value of between $30 million and $70 million a year, before taxes.[6]

Piper Jaffray Companies' Employee Stock Ownership Plan (ESOP) participants who are employed by the company on the date of close will become fully vested and be eligible for a mid-year ESOP contribution. This contribution will be made shortly after close, based upon Piper Jaffray Companies' financial performance between October 1, 1997, and the date of close.

Employees may leave their account balances in the ESOP and continue to direct their investments through December 31, 1998, into the same investment options as the Piper Jaffray Companies 401(k) Plan. In early 1999, any remaining ESOP account balances will automatically be merged into the U.S. Bancorp 401(k) Capital Accumulation Plan (CAP).

Shortly after the mid-year contribution is made, employees will have a one-time option to withdraw their entire account balance in a lump-sum cash distribution. If a lump-sum cash distribution is taken, they will then have the option to either roll the funds into a self-directed IRA (to defer income taxes and avoid tax penalties) or take a cash payment.

In early 1999, a profit-sharing contribution will be made to the Piper Jaffray Companies' 401(k) Plan for the period between close and December 31, 1998. This contribution will be determined in a manner similar to past ESOP contributions. Employees will have a one-time opportunity to withdraw their profit-sharing contribution from the 401(k) plan and either take the cash or roll it into a self-directed IRA. If an employee does not choose to take a withdrawal, his or her contribution will automatically be merged into the U.S. Bancorp 401(k) CAP. Employees must be employed by U.S. Bancorp or U.S. Bancorp Piper Jaffray on December 31, 1998, to receive this year-end contribution.

In January 1999, eligible U.S. Bancorp Piper Jaffray employees will join the U.S. Bancorp retirement program.

Piper Jaffray Companies' 401(k) Plan. The Piper Jaffray Companies 401(k) plan will continue through December 31, 1998, with existing contribution matches and investment options. The plan will be merged into the U.S. Bancorp 401(k) Capital Accumulation Plan (CAP) in early 1999. Account balances will be automatically merged into the CAP. Piper Jaffray Companies employees may enroll in the U.S. Bancorp CAP beginning January 1, 1999.

Piper Jaffray Companies Stock Investment Plan. The Stock Investment Plan will be terminated and balances paid out. Eligible U.S. Bancorp Piper Jaffray employees will be able to enroll in the U.S. Bancorp Employee Stock Purchase Program (ESPP) for the July–December 1998 purchase period. To be eligible to participate in the ESPP, employees will need to have been employed by the company, in a benefits eligible position, for at least one year of continuous service as of the beginning of the purchase period. Employment tenure with Piper Jaffray Companies applies toward the one-year requirement.

Welfare Plans. Piper's medical, dental, flexible spending accounts, life insurance, accidental death and dismemberment insurance, long-term and short-term disability plans, and all other welfare plans will be transitioned into the various welfare plans U.S. Bancorp provides to its employees.

Compensation Programs. No plans have been made to change Piper Jaffray Companies' compensation programs as a result of the merger. U.S. Bancorp's compensation philosophy is to provide programs which reward employees for achieving or exceeding business objectives. In addition, different divisions of U.S. Bancorp compete in different markets and compensation must be competitive within those markets.

Joining Forces

The plans for integrating Piper Jaffray Companies into U.S. Bancorp are yet to be developed. Piper Jaffray Companies will proceed with its plans to build a new headquarters building in downtown Minneapolis and will move into that location in June 2000. Any merger plans for U.S. Bancorp banking locations with Piper Jaffray offices will be made when integration plans are developed. Both organizations will be involved in this process.

U.S. Bancorp is in a growth mode. A special retention program has been created for key Piper Jaffray Companies employees whose leadership and customer focus are critical to the success of the company going forward. Piper Jaffray Companies' senior management selected the participants and determined the size of each award under the program. While some job losses may occur, the bank is committed to creating redeployment opportunities within U.S. Bancorp. According to U.S. Bancorp policy, revenue and growth drive the decision, with cost reduction as a secondary goal. Job openings in the combined organization exceed the number of anticipated job eliminations. In cases where employees are terminated as a result of the acquisition, they will be eligible for severance.

Information about U.S. Bancorp and the acquisition will be delivered to Piper Jaffray Companies employees in a variety of ways, including meetings, publications, e-mail and inter-office mail. Piper Jaffray managers have been provided with additional materials about U.S. Bancorp and the acquisition. A feedback form included in Piper Jaffray's in-house newsletter, *Taking Stock*, can be used to forward questions directly to Tad Piper and Andrew Duff. (See Exhibit 11.) Communications will be quick and candid with all employees regarding the integration of the companies.

U.S. Bancorp Piper Jaffray, Inc., will continue to nurture meaningful community relationships, to serve as a grantmaking leader, to develop creative sponsorships, and to support employee leadership and volunteerism. These charitable contributions will continue through

11 | Letter to Employees and Feedback Form from *Taking Stock*, the Company Newsletter

Dec. 19, 1997

Dear Fellow Employees:

Since the Monday announcement of our merger with U.S. Bancorp, everyone has been working hard to maintain the high level of service our clients and coworkers expect, while at the same time trying to understand what lies ahead. As promised when we announced the merger, we want to keep you informed about the transition as quickly as the information becomes available.

We're working on how Piper Capital Management and Piper Trust will transition to U.S. Bancorp, and will share that information as decisions are made. With us on the seven-member management committee for our subsidiary are Chip Hayssen, Bruce Huber, Deb Roesler, Ross Rogers and Tom Stanberry. You'll note that the group gives us leadership continuity, which is important to us as well as to our new partner because of the experience these people can contribute to our continued success.

Our management committee has been working very closely with U.S. Bancorp this week. They've come out of those meetings feeling very positive about our new coworkers as well as the opportunities to grow our business. U.S. Bancorp clearly understands that we know our business better than anyone. They're counting on us to continue to run our business, maintaining our broker/dealer as a largely independent subsidiary.

As Jack Grundhofer and his team have made clear, in our meetings and in conversations with the media, U.S. Bancorp's motivation for this merger is to accelerate the growth plans of both companies. U.S. Bancorp is excited about our partnership because they know we have the securities industry expertise, relationships and credibility to compete effectively and grow. Jack has also pointed out that our merger creates few redundant positions or departments and we can expect few layoffs. We are continuing to hire to support our growth plans.

Some of you have been alarmed by media comments that our support functions duplicate those at U.S. Bancorp. We can be very confident that they'll continue to need our expertise in these areas. For example, we know it will take considerable time to convert to shared payroll and benefits systems, and expect that it could take until 1999 before we'll begin sharing such services. Our partners have been very clear that they're relying on us to provide the support services our business needs.

Many of you have had questions about our compensation and benefits programs. Today's employee benefits plan memo answered many questions, but please don't hesitate to call Ed Caillier, ext. 6912, if you'd like additional information or clarification. The Piper Jaffray total compensation structure remains unchanged. We also know that, with the exception of 401(k) and ESOP, other benefit programs will remain in place at least through calendar 1998.

All of us feel some anxiety in times of change. If you would like someone to talk to about such feelings or concerns, please call ext. 8808 between noon and 5 p.m. central standard time. This line is being staffed by on-site consultants with experience helping our employees through periods of transition. They will be available for telephone and one-on-one discussion, whichever is most helpful to you.

11 | Letter to Employees and Feedback Form from *Taking Stock*, the Company Newsletter *(Continued)*

Going forward, we'll keep sharing information as it's available. You can also count on us to continue to invest in our employees, to keep building our business, and to keep investing in our communities. We're really excited about our growth opportunities with U.S. Bancorp, and will enjoy helping all of you become better acquainted with our new partners.

We wish all of you a joyful holiday season and look forward to a wonderful new year.

Tad Piper — Andrew Duff

—Cut here and return to Tad & Andrew c/o Taking Stock—

What's On Your Mind? 12/19/97

What questions do you have after reading this "Taking Stock" memo? Please take a minute to jot down your thoughts and return this form to us. Please include your name.

____

____

____

____

Name: ______________________

Piper Jaffray Companies Foundation and U.S. Bancorp Piper Jaffray, Inc.

For Piper Jaffray Companies' clients, it will be business as usual. In the future, the combined company will provide a more extensive array of products, services and capabilities to meet clients' needs more effectively. Communication will be a key component of this integration and clients will be promptly notified of changes. Printed ads will run in major markets, notifying clients and communities of the change. Talking points have been provided to use with clients. (See Exhibit 12.) Tad Piper intends to send a letter to all Piper Jaffray clients announcing the merger. (See Exhibit 13.)

The Transaction[7]

U.S. Bancorp will pay about 13.5 times the last twelve months' earnings and about 11.2 times earnings on a projected 1998 earnings stream, plus synergies (modest cost and revenue gains) for its acquisition of Piper Jaffray Companies. This equates to about $65 million in net income. Piper Jaffray Companies appears to be well capitalized, with shareholders' equity equating to fifteen

12 | Merger Announcement to Customers

To Our Valued Piper Jaffray Customers
Announcing the Joining of U.S. Bancorp and Piper Jaffray Companies
December 15, 1997

U.S. Bancorp and Piper Jaffray Companies Inc. are pleased to announce an agreement for U.S. Bancorp to acquire Piper Jaffray Companies Inc. By forming this partnership, we will be able to provide our customers with increased financial solutions to better meet their needs. This acquisition is expected to be finalized in the second quarter of 1998. We will then be able to offer our customers an expanded array of financial products and services.

While we have aggressively been building our investment expertise and offerings, combining with U.S. Bancorp will make this happen even faster. The industry is changing rapidly and the walls between securities, banking and other financial services sectors are crumbling. As a result, our customers are expecting us to provide a much broader array of products, services and capabilities to address their needs. To meet this demand, we are joining forces with an established and respected banking firm that has complementary strengths and allows us to offer a broader array of financial solutions faster than trying to build those capabilities internally. And, U.S. Bancorp provides technology which will enhance our ability to serve our clients.

In addition to our many outstanding products and services, we will now be able to offer our customers the following:

- excellent asset management services delivered by First Asset management (FAM). This multi-style management group offers numerous options, including unique sector funds specializing in industries such as technology.
- access to First American Funds, a strong performing group of funds. The December 1997 issue of *Mutual Funds* magazine ranked First American Funds a five-star family. In addition, at the end of the third quarter, 11 of 32 funds earned four- or five-star ratings from Morningstar for three-year average annual return.
- additional top-performing investment products, including more mutual funds and several well-managed 401(k) programs. U.S. Bancorp has more than $55 billion in assets under management.
- expanded private banking and personal trust services.
- outstanding commercial banking products and services.

These services will complement the already strong offerings we provide, including our highly respected and experienced investment executives, our corporate finance capabilities, our established municipal underwriting services and products, our strong institutional trading capabilities, and our diverse equity and fixed income investment options.

Our customers will have easy access to these expanded investment services given the excellent geographic fit between the two organizations. Combined, we will cover 19 states stretching from the Midwest to the West Coast.

Both organizations have a long standing commitment to our communities. Our customers will be pleased to learn that our excellent tradition of contributing financially and through volunteerism will continue just as strongly as in the past.

While we begin to work behind the scenes to plan the acquisition, our customers will not notice any changes. We remain committed to providing our customers with outstanding service and the best financial solutions available. Our commitment will be further strengthened through this partnership. For now, it's business as usual.

EXHIBIT 13 | Letter to Piper Jaffray Employees Announcing the Merger

December 15, 1997

To the Employees of Piper Jaffray Companies Inc. and U.S. Bancorp:

Today we announced that U.S. Bancorp has agreed to acquire Piper Jaffray Companies Inc. We believe this new partnership between one of the nation's highest performing banks and a premiere securities firm will significantly strengthen our ability to provide customers with financial solutions.

Together, we have a tremendous opportunity to leverage our complementary strengths to benefit our customers. U.S. Bancorp has a rich array of investment products; one of the nation's largest trust companies; a deep customer base of approximately 40,000 middle market commercial relationships, 50,000 private banking and personal trust clients, and 4 million households; and significant investment capital. Piper Jaffray Companies offers expert capabilities in investment banking, trading and retail brokerage.

The purchase price is $730 million cash, or $37.25 per share. The transaction is expected to close in the second quarter of 1998.

The acquisition will create a U.S. Bancorp subsidiary, called U.S. Bancorp Piper Jaffray. Piper Jaffray Companies Chairman and CEO Addison L. "Tad" Piper will lead the new subsidiary, reporting directly to U.S. Bancorp President and CEO John F. "Jack" Grundhofer. A limited number of organizational changes designed to leverage the strengths of both organizations also will be announced.

In short, the acquisition creates a leading diversified financial services provider offering an expanded, comprehensive array of products and services to businesses, governments, institutions, and individuals. We will have the nation's 11th largest retail brokerage sales force, spanning a 19-state region that virtually mirrors the regions both companies serve today. The partnership will establish a fortified position in an increasingly competitive marketplace.

The formation of U.S. Bancorp Piper Jaffray is based on revenue enhancements that will result from building stronger capabilities to serve clients. While some job losses may occur, most likely in duplicative staff and administrative areas, we are committed to providing redeployment opportunities within U.S. Bancorp.

U.S. Bancorp's acquisition of Piper Jaffray Companies will create value for our customers, our shareholders, our employees, and our communities. We promise to keep you informed of acquisition-related developments in a timely manner through upcoming meetings and other communications. We ask for your support as we build new opportunities together. Thank you.

Sincerely,

John F. Grundhofer President and Chief Executive Officer U.S. Bancorp	Addison L. Piper Chairman and Chief Executive Officer Piper Jaffray Companies Inc.

EXHIBIT

14 | Pricing

	Acquisition Multiple	Recent Regional Securities Firm Acquisitions[c]	Publicly Traded Peers[d]
Last 12 months revenues	1.2×	1.3×	1.6×
Last 12 months net income	13.5×[a]	14.4×	18.1×
Estimated 1998 net income	11.2×[b]		16.0×
Book Value	4.2×	4.3×	3.1×

[a]Represents latest 12 months net income adjusted to a normalized operating margin (15%).
[b]Represents purchase price divided by 1998 estimated net income plus fully phased in cost savings.
[c]Alex Brown, Dillon Read, Robertson Stephens, Montgomery Securities, Oppenheimer & Co., Wheat First, Furman Seiz, Source: Company presentations.
[d]Raymond James, EVEREN, Interra, Morgan Keegan and McDonald & Co. Source: Company 10Qs. Stock prices as of 12/12/97.
Source: Securities and Exchange Commission, Washington, D.C. Form 8-K, Commission File Number 1-6880.

percent of Piper Jaffray's $1.13 billion in assets as of September 1997. This is about 4.25 times Piper Jaffray's book value, which compares to about 4.3 times book value paid for other U.S. Bancorp acquisitions—some of which were less well capitalized. (See Exhibit 14.)

In Conclusion

U.S. Bancorp Piper Jaffray, Inc., still faces many challenges as the two companies are brought together. Quite possibly this merger may set a trend in the industry and establish commercial banking in the securities banking industry. Or it could, conversely, raise a flag to the SEC and intensify scrutiny of mergers that push the limits of the Glass–Steagall Act.

ENDNOTES

1. Naficy, Mariam, *"The Fast Track."* Broadway, New York, 1997; pgs. 65–66.
2. Microsoft Investor: Research Central—Subscriber Report, Piper Jaffray.
3. Piper Jaffray Companies' "Vision 2000."
4. Piper Jaffray Companies' "Vision 2000."
5. Naficy, Mariam, *"The Fast Track."* Broadway, New York, 1997; pgs. 9–15.
6. *Wall Street Journal,* Dow Jones News; "Piper Employees Get Most of Consideration," December 17, 1997.
7. Wall Street Journal, Dow Jones News, Davis, Sally Pope; *"Goldman, Sachs & Co. Investment Research—U.S. Bancorp,"* December 17, 1997.

CASE 38

The Wall Street Journal

Print versus Interactive

Amy Hillman
University of Western Ontario

In early January 1999, Peter Kann, chief executive officer of Dow Jones & Company, pondered the future of one of the company's most valuable brands and products, *The Wall Street Journal.* A meeting with Kann's top management team had been called for the following month to discuss the future of this brand, primarily focusing on the relative positioning and performance of the print and *Interactive Journal.*

The Wall Street Journal had enjoyed an unrivaled position as the top daily business newspaper in the United States for over 109 years. The *Journal* was the largest circulation newspaper in the United States with approximately 1.8 million subscribers, reached five million worldwide readers daily, and enjoyed tremendous loyalty among readers. However, the newspaper industry was facing a future of little to no growth and mounting competition from other forms of news delivery, most recently and saliently, the Internet.

IVEY This case was prepared solely to provide material for class discussion. It is not intended to illustrate either effective or ineffective handling of a managerial situation. Certain names and other identifying information may have been disguised to protect confidentiality.

Ivey Management Services prohibits any form of reproduction, storage or transmittal without its written permission. This material is not covered under authorization from CanCopy or any reproduction rights organization. To order copies or request permission to reproduce materials, contact Ivey Publishing, Ivey Management Services, c/o Richard Ivey School of Business, The University of Western Ontario, London, Ontario, Canada, N6A 3K7; phone (519) 661-3208; fax (519) 661-3882; e-mail cases@ivey.uwo.ca.

Copyright © 1999, Ivey Management Services. One-time permission to reproduce Ivey cases granted by Ivey Management Services on November 18, 1999.

Internet news providers threatened the typical newspaper's core product and service of timely, current news reporting and delivery. The threat to *The Wall Street Journal* was felt not only from competitors on the Web, such as CNN and CBS MarketWatch who operated free sites, but from its own *Interactive Journal.* The *Interactive Journal* was introduced in 1996 and within a year became the largest paid subscription site on the Internet. But what would the rising demand for instant, Web-based news do to the company's mainstay business of the print edition? Would the *Interactive Journal* serve as a complement or a substitute for print? Given this, Peter Kann wondered how the two products should be positioned, priced and promoted in order to maximize revenue for both. The answers to these questions would fundamentally shift the industry as well as Dow Jones & Company.

DOW JONES & COMPANY

Dow Jones & Company was a global provider of business news and information. Its primary operations were in three business segments: print publishing, electronic publishing, and general-interest community newspapers.

The print publishing segment included *The Wall Street Journal, Barron's National Business and Employment Weekly, The Asian Wall Street Journal, The Wall Street Journal Europe, Far Eastern Economic Review,* and *SmartMoney Magazine.* The electronic publishing segment included *The Wall Street Journal Interactive Edition, Dow Jones Newswires, Dow Jones Interactive,* and the *Dow Jones Indexes.*

The Wall Street Journal, Print Edition

The Wall Street Journal (WSJ), Dow Jones' flagship publication, was long considered the most respected source of business and financial news in the United States. By 1999, *The Wall Street Journal* was one of the most recognized brands in the world with a subscription renewal rate of 80 percent. Its circulation rate of approximately 1.8 million subscribers remained relatively stable in the 1990s.

Over 600 reporters and editors—who also support other Dow Jones products—contributed to an outstanding record of journalistic excellence. In 1997, the company received its 19th Pulitzer Prize, an award also given to its chief executive officer in 1972. Each of the print editions of *The Wall Street Journal* drew heavily upon *The Wall Street Journal*'s worldwide news staff. *The Wall Street Journal Europe,* headquartered in Brussels, had an average circulation in 1998 of 71,000 and sold on day of publication in continental Europe, the United Kingdom, the Middle East, and North Africa. *The Asian Wall Street Journal,* headquartered in Hong Kong, had an average circulation of 62,000 in 1998 and was printed in Hong Kong, Singapore, Japan, Thailand, Malaysia, Korea and Taiwan. In addition, the company distributed special editions of *Wall Street Journal* news within 30 newspapers in 26 countries, published in 10 languages with a combined circulation of four million.

Despite its long-standing traditional front page format without full paper-width headlines, six columns, dot print photos, and the "What's News" summaries, the *Journal* innovated many new formats in the 1990s. Starting in 1993, the *Journal* expanded its business and economic trend regional coverage to select parts of the United States, including Texas, Florida, California, New England, the Northwest and the Southeast. These *Journal* editions consisted of a four-page weekly section included in papers distributed in those regions. Four-color advertising, introduced in 1995, saw increased revenue of 60 percent in 1997, contributing to overall advertising linage up 13 percent, on top of a 14 percent growth in 1996. Nineteen ninety-seven saw the addition of a daily page of international business news and in 1998, a two-page technology section. *Weekend Journal,* introduced in 1998, expanded typical content to include lifestyle issues such as personal finance, food and wine, sports, travel, and residential real estate, as well as other new editorial features appealing to new advertisers and readers.

However, these new innovations in the *Journal* served as supplements rather than substitutes to the three traditional sections of the five-day-a-week paper. Kann explains, "Visually, the Journal has a unique trademark quality. It's a uniquely recognizable page. But the main reason we haven't changed it is it's a very useful format." Section A included the front page and business and political news. Section B, "Marketplace," focused more on lifestyle and marketing issues, including regional editions, and the technology section. Finally, Section C, "Money & Investing," centered on financial news, daily stock and bond quotes and other financial information. Dow Jones also announced plans to spend US$230 million between 1999 and 2002 to expand the number of color pages and total page capacity. This investment would increase the color page capacity from eight to 24 and the total page capacity from 80 to 96.

Economics of Print Publishing

Within the relevant range (circulation and advertising within 15 percent), most print *WSJ* expenses were fixed. Variable components (including newsprint, ink, plates, production and delivery overtime) accounts for approximately 15 percent of costs. Print *WSJ* revenues came from two primary sources: sales/subscriptions and advertising. Advertising rate growth was dependent upon at least roughly preserving the circulation level. Hence, if circulation dropped 10 percent, ad revenue could fall 10 percent or more.

The paper was printed in 17 company-owned U.S. and 13 overseas plants, 12 of which were leased. Company employees (through the company's National Delivery Service, Inc. subsidiary) delivered 75 percent of U.S. subscriber copies by 6:00 A.M. daily. This system provided delivery earlier and more reliably than the postal service. Company plants were unionized, operated one shift daily, six days a week, and were important to maintaining the *Journal*'s traditional size, which was larger than typical print newspapers. This size format was believed to be more appealing to advertisers and to readers alike.

The Print Newspaper Industry

Wall Street had long found newspaper stocks appealing and therefore priced them at a premium to the rest of the

1 | Stock Performance for Dow Jones & Company

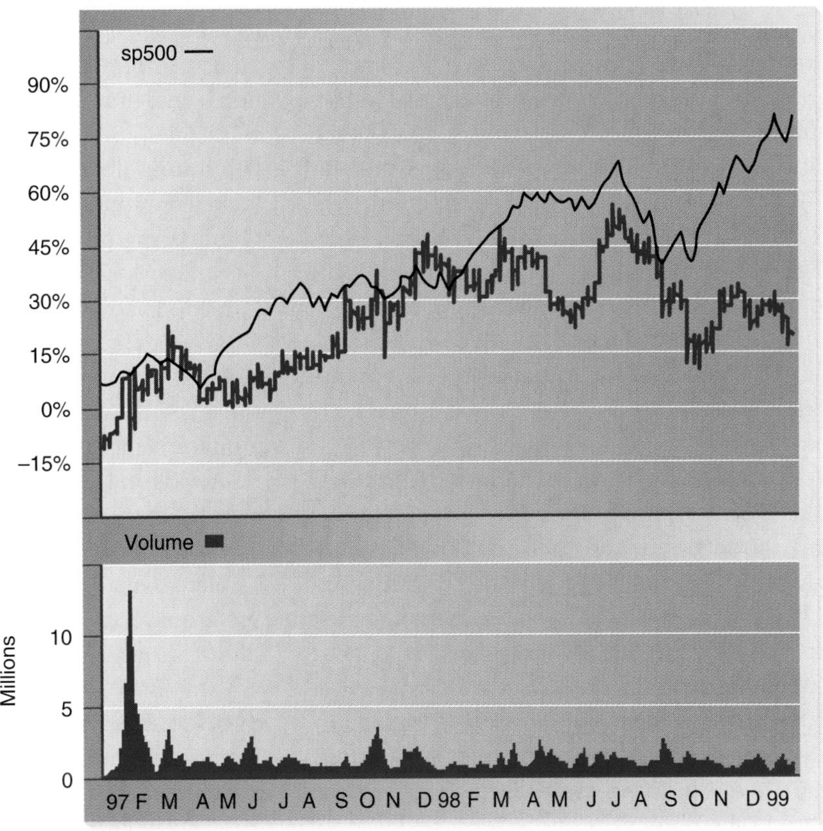

Source: Interactive Chart—dowjones.htm; October 4, 1999.

market. Exhibit 1 includes stock data for Dow Jones & Company. However, newspapers faced increasing media competition in the 1990s, making advertising sales a harder pitch. Local newspapers in general turned to supplemental advertising flyers and catalogues placed between the pages of daily and Sunday papers in order to provide more dependable cash flow. In addition, growth of classified ads was strong due to the general expansion of the economy resulting in strong real estate, automobile and job markets. Classified volume typically contributed 15 to 25 percent of total newspaper linage sales and was the industry's most profitable ad category on a per-line basis in the 1990s. However, classified ads also faced increased competition from on-line offerings. Overall, newspapers benefited from the robust economy in 1998 by encouraging more advertisers to buy more linage at increased rates. The total advertising market in the United States for print medium was US$72 billion in 1999, up from US$55 billion in 1995, and projected to exceed US$83 billion by 2001.

Despite relatively stable cash flows in the past, newspaper circulation was in a general downward trend from 1987 through late 1996, although there was some stability starting in 1997. Local distribution of newspapers, both home and newsstands, was increasingly contracted out to third parties.

The Wall Street Journal was the first national daily paper in the United States and enjoyed status as the only national daily until the advent of *USA Today* in 1985. In the late 1990s, *The New York Times* and *Los Angeles Times* also nominally entered into the nationally distributed sector of the industry. However, their entry into the nationally distributed sector did not indicate a shift towards nationally focused news; *The New York Times* and *Los Angeles Times* still concentrated on a fairly targeted geographic region in terms of subscribers and content. In addition, the business-versus-general-interest focus of *The Wall Street Journal* kept it relatively immune from direct competitors until the expansion of UK-based *Financial Times* in 1998. While the *Financial Times'* focus was primarily business news, its exposure in the U.S. market was dwarfed by that of *The Wall Street Journal,* with the circulation level of the Journal around 35 times that of the *Financial Times.*

The Wall Street Journal Interactive Journal

The Wall Street Journal Interactive Journal (http://wsj.com), introduced in April 1996, was another innovation for Dow Jones as well as for the publishing industry. While initially a free site, subscribers were first asked to pay in August of 1996. Subscribers totaled over 100,000 within the first year of launch, and reached over 266,000 subscribers by the end of 1998. While many competitors were delivering news on the Web for free, *The Wall Street Journal Interactive Edition* became the largest paid subscription site on the World Wide Web. Around one percent of the content at the web site was free access, with the remaining 99 percent accessible only to subscribers. "Our proprietary information has value, and we have the guts to charge," said Peter Kann.

U.S. News & World Report called the *Interactive Journal* "the best single financial site on the Internet." *The Interactive Journal* offered continuously updated news and market information, access to the international editions, in-depth background reports on over 20,000 companies and pay-per-view access to the Dow Jones Publication library. In addition, the *Interactive Journal* included proprietary information and coverage not found in the print editions. Within each story in the *Interactive Journal* were links to stock quotes and other information about the companies discussed.

Careers.wsj.com was a free site, launched in 1997 and linked to the *Interactive Journal,* that offered a searchable database of employment listings and content from the *National Business and Employment Weekly.*

Advertising sales were relatively stable in 1998, coming off two relatively strong years of growth. Subscription renewal rates were approximately 75 to 80 percent. Further comparison of subscribers, subscriber revenue and acquisition costs for both the print and Interactive editions is given in Exhibits 2 and 3.

Economics of Electronic Publishing

Typically for Web-based publishing, most costs were fixed or step-function fixed, except for subscriber acquisition and advertising selling expenses.

For free sites, primary revenue came from advertising, with the number of people visiting the site largely

EXHIBIT 2 | Per-Subscriber Revenue and Acquisition Costs

	Print WSJ	Electronic WSJ
1 Year Subscription Non-Print Subscriber	N/A	$59
1 Year Subscription Print Subscriber	$175	$29
Advertising Revenue Per Year Per Subscriber	$500	$40
Average Acquisition Cost New Subscriber	$160	$40
Average Renewal Cost	$5	$5
Renewal Rate	80%	75%

EXHIBIT 3 | *The Wall Street Journal* Print/Electronic Interaction

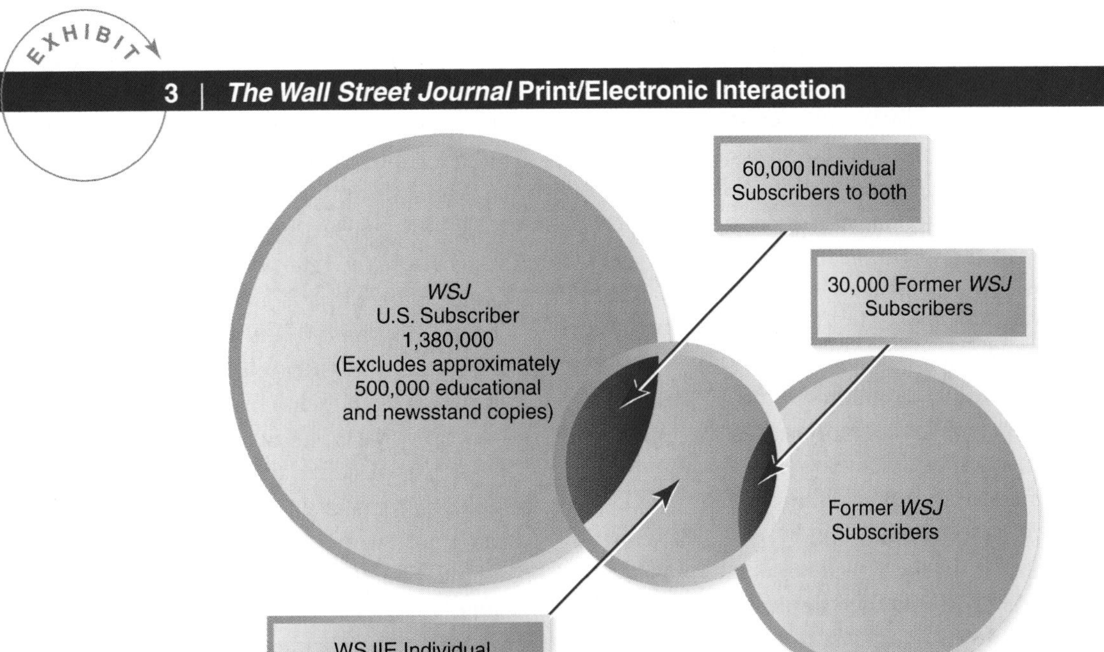

*Excludes corporate and International WSJIE subscribers.

determining the fees charged to advertisers. For subscription sites, however, revenue came from both advertising and subscriptions, similar to print publishing. A third category of revenue also became possible in electronic publishing: transaction fees. Forrester Research predicted that online revenue from subscriptions, advertising and transaction fees would grow from just over US$520 million in 1997 to US$8.5 billion within five years.

The total advertising market for Internet medium was approximately US$2 billion in 1999 and was projected to exceed US$5 billion in 2001. As a quarterly comparison, the first quarter of 1996 saw total U.S. Internet advertising spending at US$29.9 million. By the first quarter of 1998, this number had grown to US$351.3 million and second quarter of 1998 to US$423.0 million. Unlike television, radio or print advertising, an almost unlimited supply of advertising and a concurrent glut of it accompanied the advent of the Internet. As a result, advertising rates plummeted in 1998 due to the lack of target viewers. However, this trend did not apply to web sites that could offer advertisers access to more targeted demographics.

A 1998 GVU Internet survey indicated the attitudes about pay versus free sites on the Internet. Of those individuals who refused to pay for information on the Internet, 44.5 percent did so because the information was available elsewhere for free, while 32.7 percent would not pay for Internet information because they were already paying to gain access to the Internet itself. Other reasons given for the resistance to pay for site access included excessive cost and poor site quality. Similarly, a survey conducted by the BBDO advertising agency found that 60 percent of respondents replied negatively when asked if they would be willing to pay for an on-line subscription edition of their favorite print publication. Of those that answered "yes," 89 percent indicated they would not be willing to pay more than the newsstand price for an on-line version.

Unlike print publishing, editorial and news skills for a near-real time environment became necessary skills for electronic publishing. With continual news updates, reliability and quality of journalism reports became subject to increased time pressure. Accuracy, the elimination of bias, clarity and comprehensiveness in the face of a flood of information became critical for electronic publishing. In addition, new skills of technology, ease of Web site navigation, effective layout for a computer screen, etc., became necessary for Web publishing.

The Wall Street Journal Interactive Edition was expected to attain its break-even point in 1999. Forrester Research estimated the average annual operating costs of content Internet sites of US$893,000 and of transactional sites at US$2.8 million in 1998. For Income Statement information for both print and electronic products, see Exhibits 4 and 5. Companywide financial information is provided in Exhibits 6 through 8.

The electronic publishing division, which included Dow Jones Interactive, provided subscribers with a news library of over 5,000 publications, including a full-text archive of *The Wall Street Journal* and *Dow Jones Newswires* as well as roughly 1,200 non-U.S. news sources, and the 50 largest U.S. newspapers and business magazines.

The Internet/Web Publishing Market

Growth in the use of the Internet exploded in the 1990s. It was estimated that in 1998, the number of worldwide Internet users was over 147 million with over 57 million in the United States alone. The number of U.S. households joining the Internet was estimated at 760 per hour in 1999 with nearly 38 percent of households being reached by the Internet. Nearly 90 percent of Internet users gathered news and information from the Web's news, information and entertainment sites. In 1996, Pew Research Center estimated that only four percent of Americans got their news online. This number jumped to nearly 20 percent in 1999.

It was projected that by 2003, over 55 million professionals, managers and executives would be using the Internet at work. In 1999, over 17 percent of the online population preferred to receive their financial news online.

Internet penetration by age was concentrated in younger generations by the end of 1998. Fifty-nine percent of 12- to 17-year-olds used the Internet, with the

EXHIBIT 4 | Print Publishing Primarily The Wall Street Journal ($ Millions)

	1997	1998
Revenue		
Advertising	$790	$777
Circ. & Other	$353	$360
Total	$1,143	$1,137
Operating Expenses	$896	$931
Operating Income	$247	$174

EXHIBIT 5 | Electronic Products, Dow Jones Interactive, Dow Jones Newswires, The Wall Street Journal Interactive Edition ($ Millions)

	1997	1998
Revenue		
Dow Jones Newswires/Indexes	$204	$220
Interactive Publishing	$159	$172
Total	$363	$392
Operating Expenses	$302	$315
Operating Income	$61	$78

6 | Consolidated Statements of Income (Loss)

For the years ended December 31, 1998, 1997, and 1996 (in thousands except per share amounts)	1998	1997	1996
Revenues			
Advertising	$1,031,210	$1,011,864	$ 896,981
Information services	670,441	1,101,696	1,125,625
Circulation and other	456,455	458,958	458,986
Total revenues	2,158,106	2,572,518	2,481,592
Expenses			
News, operations and sevelopment	677,381	899,868	820,564
Selling, administrative and general	762,803	895,707	831,270
Newsprint	163,146	152,478	164,766
Second class postage and carrier delivery	117,649	114,442	110,256
Depreciation and amortization	142,439	250,734	217,756
Restructuring	76,115	1,001,263	
Operating expenses	1,939,533	3,314,492	2,144,612
Operating income (loss)	218,573	(714,974)	336,980
Other income (deductions)			
Investment income	12,266	3,473	4,249
Interest expense	(7,193)	(19,367)	(18,755)
Equity in losses of associated companies	(21,653)	(49,311)	(5,408)
(Loss) gain in disposition of businesses & investments	(126,085)	52,595	14,315
Other, net	(4,250)	(9,300)	(121)
Income (loss) before income taxes & minority interests	71,658	(763,884)	331,260
Income taxes	63,083	37,796	147,728
Income (loss) before minority interests	8,575	(801,680)	183,532
Minority interests in (earnings) losses of subsidiaries	(213)	(452)	6,437
Net income (loss)	$ 8,362	$ (802,132)	$ 189,969
Per share			
Net income (loss) per share:			
Basic	$ .09	$ (8.36)	$ 1.96
Diluted	.09	(8.36)	1.95
Weighted-average shares outstanding:			
Basic	95,180	95,993	96,703
Diluted	96,404	95,993	97,371
Cash dividends	$ .96	$ .96	$ .96

percentage dropping with each higher age group to 27 percent of the population aged 55 to 64, and only 14 percent of the population over age 65. In 1996 the male to female ratio of Internet use was 57 to 43 but by 1998, this ratio had changed to 51 to 49.

The *Interactive Journal* competed with a variety of business news sources on the Internet, including sites maintained by traditional print competitors such as *Business Week, Fortune, The New York Times,* and *The Financial Times.* In addition, it faced competition from non-print competitors such as CNNfn, Bloomberg, online brokerage firms, CBS MarketWatch, TheStreet.com and Yahoo and others who received their news from Reuters. Many of these competitors provided news and

7 | Financial Highlights

Income Statement Results (in thousands except per share amounts)	**1998**	**1997**	**% Increase (Decrease)**
Consolidated			
Revenues	$2,158,106	$2,572,518	(16.1)
Operating income (loss)	218,573	(741,974)	—
EBITDA[1]	437,127	510,023	(14.3)
Net income (loss)	8,362	(802,132)	—
Net income (loss) per share—diluted	.09	(8.36)	—
Excluding special items[2]			
Revenues	1,872,204	1,776,238	5.4
Operating income	327,915	335,955	(2.4)
EBITDA	418,456	454,071	(8.3)
Net income	185,039	185,707	(0.4)
Net income per share—diluted	1.92	1.92	

Financial position and cash flows (in thousands except per share amounts)	**1998**	**1997**	**% Increase (Decrease)**
Long-term debt, including current portion	$ 149,889	$ 234,124	(36.0)
Stockholders' equity	509,340	780,822	(34.8)
Capital expenditures	225,834	347,797	(35.1)
Cash from operations	306,226	459,763	(33.4)
Purchase of treasury stock, net of put premiums	291,215	—	—

Revenues and operating income (loss) by segment (in thousands except per share amounts)	**1998**	**1997**	**% Increase (Decrease)**
Revenues			
Print publishing	$1,161,939	$1,143,395	1.6
Electronic publishing[3]	393,178	363,232	8.2
Community newspapers	317,087	300,611	5.5
Segment revenues	1,872,204	1,807,238	3.6
Divested/joint ventured operations:			
Print and television operations		21,091	—
Telerate	285,902	744,189	(61.6)
Consolidated revenues	$2,158,106	$2,572,518	(16.1)
Operating income (loss)[4]			
Print publishing	$ 173,582	$ 247,191	(29.8)
Electronic publishing	56,060	61,089	(8.2)
Community newspapers	44,760	50,584	(11.5)
Corporate	(22,602)	(18,189)	(24.3)
Segment operating income	251,800	340,675	(26.1)
Divested/joint ventured operations:			
Print and televisions operations		(18,239)	—
Telerate	(33,227)	(1,064,410)	96.9
Consolidated operating income (loss)	$ 218,573	$ (741,974)	—

[1]EBITDA is computed as operating income (loss) excluding depreciation and amortization and restructuring costs.
[2]Consolidated excluding Telerate operations and loss on its sale, and other special charges/gains.
[3]1997 revenue includes $31 million of one-time index licensing fees.
[4]excluding restructuring charges, segment operating income was as follows (000s):

	1998	1997
Print publishing	$223,496	$251,903
Electronic publishing	65,921	78,138
Community newspapers	61,100	50,584
Corporate	(22,602)	(18,189)
	$327,915	$362,436

8 | Five-Year Financial Summary

(in thousands except per share amounts)	1998	1997	1996	1995	1994
Revenues					
Advertising	$1,031,210	$1,011,864	$ 896,981	$ 771,779	$ 724,990
Information services	670,441	1,101,696	1,125,625	1,092,002	976,800
Circulation and other	456,455	458,958	458,986	419,980	389,187
Total revenues	2,158,106	2,572,518	2,481,592	2,283,761	2,090,977
Expenses					
News, operations and development	677,381	899,868	820,564	748,945	642,184
Selling, administrative and general	762,803	895,707	831,270	764,161	681,244
Newsprint	163,146	152,478	164,766	157,047	107,178
Second class postage and carrier delivery	117,649	114,442	110,256	103,497	96,751
Depreciation and amortization	142,439	250,734	217,756	206,070	205,303
Restructuring	76,115	1,001,263			
Operating expenses	1,939,533	3,314,492	2,144,612	1,979,720	1,732,660
Operating income (loss)	218,573	(714,974)	336,980	304,041	358,317
Other income (deductions)					
Investment income	12,266	3,473	4,249	5,379	4,884
Interest expense	(7,193)	(19,367)	(18,755)	(18,345)	(16,858)
Equity in losses of associated companies	(21,653)	(49,311)	(5,408)	14,193	(5,434)
(Loss) gain on disposition of businesses & investments	(126,085)	52,595	14,315	13,557	3,097
Other, net	(4,250)	(9,300)	(121)	4,075	(5,981)
Income (loss) before income taxes & minority interests	71,658	(763,884)	331,260	322,900	338,025
Income taxes	63,083	37,796	147,728	139,878	157,632
Income (loss) before minority interests	8,575	(801,680)	183,532	183,022	180,393
Minority interests in (earnings) losses of subsidiaries	(213)	(452)	6,437	6,550	787
Income (loss) before cumulative effect of accounting changes	8,362	(802,132)	189,969	189,572	181,180
Cumulative effect of accounting changes					(3,007)
Net income (loss)	$ 8,362	$ (802,132)	$ 189,969	$ 189,572	$ 178,173
Per share basic					
Income (loss) before cumulative effect of accounting changes	$ .09	$ (8.36)	$ 1.96	$ 1.96	$ 1.83
Net income (loss)	.09	(8.36)	1.96	1.96	1.80
Per share diluted					
Income (loss) before cumulative effect of accounting changes	.09	(8.36)	1.95	1.94	1.82
Net income (loss)	.09	(8.36)	1.96	1.94	1.79
Weighted-average shares outstanding (000's):					
Basic	95,180	95,993	96,703	96,907	99,002
Diluted	96,404	95,993	97,371	97,675	99,662
Dividends	$ .96	$ .96	$ .96	$ .92	$ .84
Other data					
Long-term debt, including current portion, as a % of total capital	22.7%	23.1%	17.0%	13.9%	16.9%
Newsprint consumption (metric tons)	278,000	270,000	252,000	224,000	221,000
Number of full time employees at year end	8,253	12,309	11,844	11,232	10,265
Cash from operations	306,226	459,763	405,157	371,887	403,142
Capital expenditures	225,834	347,797	232,178	218,765	222,434
Cash dividends	91,662	92,116	92,969	89,131	83,360
Total assets	1,491,322	1,919,734	2,759,631	2,598,700	2,445,766
Long-term debt, including current portion	149,889	234,124	337,618	259,253	300,870
Stockholders' equity	509,340	780,822	1,643,993	1,601,751	1,481,611

information on their Web site for free (for example, CNNfn, Yahoo, Bloomberg, and The New York Times). Still others provided limited free information for non-print subscribers and free on-line access to print subscribers (e.g., *Fortune* and *Business Week*). Due to the ease of entry into Web publishing, as opposed to print publishing, competition was growing and fluid. One important difference between print competitors and purely on-line competitors had to do with branding. Companies with established brand names outside of the Internet had a cost advantage over competitors that were Internet-born (e.g., Yahoo and Amazon) due to the high costs of marketing new brands.

Print versus Interactive Customers

Since its introduction, the *Interactive Journal* was not aggressively promoted to current print subscribers of *The Wall Street Journal.* Partially, this was a result of the difference in customer profiles for the two products.

Print *WSJ* customers had a higher average age than *Interactive Journal* customers and were more likely to be retired. Print customers tended to use the Internet more at work than at home, to have a higher total value of investments, were more likely to have a home office, and were more likely to live in the eastern United States. *Interactive Journal* customers, on the other hand, were more likely to have children at home, to use the Internet at home than at work, to have a lower total value of investments, to use online brokers and other online information, and to travel internationally for business.

Simmons Market Research Bureau reported that of *WSJ* print readers, 9.3 percent had completed high school, 8.3 percent had some college education, 33.57 percent had graduated from a four-year college or university, and 30.68 percent had attended graduate school. The subscription base of *WSJ* was characterized by an average age of 52 with an average household income of US$75,000. The majority of print readers were 35 years old or older (75.7 percent), with only 24.3 percent within the 18 to 34 age group. Most print subscribers were male with a male to female ratio of 75 to 25. Nearly 74 percent of *WSJ* print subscribers read the paper every day, spending on average 50 minutes per issue. As of 1999, 40 percent of *Interactive Journal* subscribers read the edition on a daily basis and 36 percent reported using the edition a few times a week.

Current Pricing, Promotion and Positioning

Currently, the *Interactive Journal* is positioned as a supplement, not a substitute for the print edition and is priced accordingly. Non-print subscribers pay $59 per year while print subscribers pay $29 per year. The print edition is priced at $175 per year with newsstand copies for 75 cents each. The print pricing compares with other print competitors as follows: *Business Week*—US$42.95 for 51 issues; *Fortune*—US$54.55 for 26 issues; *Forbes*—US$23.97 for 17 issues; *USA Today*—US$119/year; *New York Times*—US$208/year for weekly editions only; and *Financial Times*—US$175/year,[1] although most magazine competitors did offer discount subscription rates.

The Challenge

The challenge ahead of Peter Kann was a serious one, but he was no stranger to tensions. His Pulitzer Prize was awarded for coverage of the Indian-Pakistan war. As he looked towards the next month's meeting, which would largely shape the direction of the future for *The Wall Street Journal* print and interactive, Kann wondered: Would the future mean prosperous co-existence of the two formats or a battle with but one format as the victor?

NOTES

1. This price is the effective price after taking into consideration widespread discounting.

CASE 39

Walt Disney Co.

Anthony Claro
Michelle Hill
Eric Maxwell
Russell Porter
Angela West

INTRODUCTION

At the March 3, 1997, stockholders' meeting, Michael Eisner, CEO of Walt Disney Co., made a startling acknowledgment. "People are assuming that Walt Disney Co. is going to keep growing at the same rate as it has in the past. We're having some problems with ABC, and I just wouldn't assume that."[1] This acknowledgement indicates that Disney may have reached a crossroads and that its growth may be leveling off. In 1996, the company's earnings were lower than they were the previous year, a first in the Eisner era. Some analysts say that Disney's $19 billion acquisition of Cap Cities/ABC has placed a strain on its growth potential.[2]

Even more startling than Eisner's comment was the stockholders' dissatisfaction, given that Disney's stock price had risen $19 in the six months prior to the meeting. The stockholders' dissatisfaction stemmed from several sources. First, the stockholders expressed dismay at the $100 million payout to former Disney president Michael Ovitz. They also expressed concern over Eisner's new contract, which ties his compensation to earnings per share over a target growth rate of 7.5 percent. Eisner's previous contract had tied his earnings to return on equity. Furthermore, the stockholders were unhappy with the results of the Cap Cities/ABC merger. ABC's ratings continued to lag behind other networks, and its ad revenues were falling. As a result of ABC's poor performance, Disney's net income decreased from approximately $1.4 billion in 1995 to $1.2 billion in 1996 (see Exhibits 1, 2, and 3).[3]

Eisner faces three major challenges to satisfy stockholders. First, he must formulate a growth strategy. Second, he must continue to create synergies between each of the divisions and find ways to integrate ABC. Third, Eisner must develop successors that can continue Disney traditions and growth in his absence.

MEDIA AND ENTERTAINMENT INDUSTRY: DEREGULATION, TECHNOLOGY, AND DEMAND

The large-scale consolidation of the media and entertainment industry largely has been attributable to the anticipation of regulatory changes. The recent broad changes in broadcasting regulations have caused many networks and other media organizations to position themselves for major strategic realignments. This regulatory environment influences the size of networks, which may cause media companies and others seeking to diversify to reevaluate future options. Certain regulations are now being considered that undoubtedly will change the strategic focus of firms competing in the entertainment industry.

In October 1995, the cable industry changed when Congress repealed the 1984 Communications Act. The Communications Act of 1984 was outdated and no longer addressed the realities and capabilities of current and projected communications technologies.[4] Now known as the Communications Act of 1995, the bill

This case was prepared under the direction of Robert E. Hoskisson. The case is intended to be used as the basis for class discussion rather than to illustrate either effective or ineffective handling of an administrative situation.

1 | Consolidated Statement of Income (in millions, except per share data)

Year ended September 30,	1996	1995	1994
Revenues	$18,739	$12,151	$10,090
Cost and expenses	–15,406	-9,685	-8.118
Accounting changes	–300		
Operating income	$3,033	$2,466	$1,972
Corporate activities and other	–309	–239	–279
Interest expense	–479	–178	–120
Investment and interest income	41	68	130
Acquisition-related costs	–225		
Income before income taxes	$2,061	$2,117	$1,703
Income taxes	–847	–737	–593
Net income	$1,214	$1,380	$1,110
Earnings per share	$2	$3	$2

Source: Walt Disney Co. Annual Report, 1996.

C-640

permits companies to own more than one station in a marketplace and increases the allowed viewership of a station group to 35 percent of the national audience.[5] In addition, the act opened phone service to competition, freed cable rates, allowed phone companies to carry video, and approved the use of V-chips to block out programs not suitable for children.[6] This congressional act and its implementation by the Federal Communications Commission (FCC) was intended to increase cable television competition, thus decreasing the rates for cable TV. As an industry deregulation, the bill will spur new investments in cable-TV systems and TV stations. This is critical to cable providers because they are now able to expand cable lineups and move into the telephone business, thus increasing competition.[7] At this time, many large media companies were positioning themselves for this radical change. Many "megamergers," such as the Disney/Cap Cities/ABC merger and Westinghouse's acquisition of CBS, took place at this time.

The Telecommunications Act of 1995 has also played a role in the redefinition of the communications industry. With the merger of Walt Disney and Cap Cities/ABC, the FCC had to review the applicability of the Telecommunications Act. Under the act, the current policy states that any newspaper-broadcast cross-ownership is prohibited. The FCC stated that it would make a ruling about ownership rules within the next 12 months. At present, the FCC has given Disney a temporary waiver until the matter can be reviewed further.

The four major networks, including ABC, have been experiencing competition from new sources. The recent advancement in satellite technology will increase the possible number of channel outlets to 500 in the near future. Furthermore, cable networks continue to gain market share from the four major network television stations, FOX, ABC, CBS, and NBC. In the 1970s, the big three (excluding FOX) held 91 percent of the market. That share dwindled from 61 percent in 1994 to 57 percent in 1995.[8] However, brand image is needed to compete effectively in such a diverse environment, and the networks still reach 98 percent of U.S. households.[9] Thus, the networks remain an instantaneous way to achieve a distribution channel for the mega-media players such as Disney, Time Warner, and News Corp.

The growing U.S. economy has had a profound effect on the revenue streams of the entertainment industry in general and the four major networks in particular. Optimism by analysts for the demand of major consumer products such as cars, movies, retail, and fast-food categories has led to a greater desire to advertise these products.[10] According to Larry Hoffner, head of network sales for NBC, "Network television is the single most valuable marketing tool."[11] "Upfront" sales, which are advertising time slots sold before the television sea-

EXHIBIT

2 | Consolidated Balance Sheets (in millions)

September 30,	1996	1995
Assets		
Cash and cash equivalents	$ 278	$ 1,077
Investments	454	866
Receivables	3,343	1,793
Inventories	951	824
Film and television costs	3,912	2,099
Theme parks, resorts and other property, at cost		
Attractions, buildings and equipment	11,019	8,340
Accumulated depreciation	–4,448	–3,039
	6,571	5,301
Projects in process	1,342	778
Land	118	111
	8,031	6,190
Intangible assets, net	17,978	
Other assets	2,359	1,757
	37,306	14,606
Liabilities and stockholders' equity		
Accounts payable and other accrued liabilities	6,374	2,843
Income taxes payable	582	200
Borrowing	12,342	2,984
Unearned royalty and other advances	1,179	861
Deferred income taxes	743	1,067
Stockholders' equity		
Preferred stock, $.01 par value; $.025 at September 30, 1995		
Common stock, $.01 par value; $.025 at September 30, 1995	8,576	1,226
Retained earnings	7,933	6,990
Cumulative transaction and other adjustments	39	38
	16,548	8,254
Less Treasury Stock, at cost 8 mill. shares and 51 mill. shares	462	1,603
	16,088	6,651
	37,306	14,606

Source: Walt Disney Co. Annual Report, 1996.

son begins, reached $6 billion for the first time.[12] NBC, with the popular Thursday Night "Must See TV" lineup, had the most upfront sales for 1997 with $2.1 billion, and ABC was second with $1.6 billion.[13]

While upfront sales account for 80 percent of a network's revenues, other factors determine broadcaster competitiveness. Broadcasters compete for subscribers, viewers, and listeners. Affiliates, the local stations that networks supply with creative content, and independent stations, those that lack an affiliation with the major networks, comprise the television market. Affiliates and independent stations have different cost structures. Affiliates receive payment for broadcasting network shows. The prime-time slots during the evening hours are the peak hours for showcasing network television. Because affiliates receive payment for broadcasting and the prime-time hours are filled with network television, their operating costs are low as compared to those of independents. Independents must fill prime-time slots with syndicated television because network television

3 | Consolidated Statement of Cash Flows (in millions)

Year ended September 30,	1996	1995	1994
Net income	**$1,214**	**$1,380**	**$1,110**
Change to income requiring cash outlay			
Amortization of film and television cost	2,966	1,383	1,199
Depreciation	677	470	410
Amortization of intangible assets	301		
Accounting changes	300		
Other	22	133	231
Changes in (including the impact of ABC acquisition)			
Investments in trading securities	85	1	
Receivables	-426	-122	-280
Inventories	-95	-156	-59
Other assets	-160	-288	-81
Accounts and taxes payable and accrued liabilities	-455	415	136
Unearned royalty and other advances	274	161	-141
Deferred income taxes	-78	133	283
	3,411	2,130	1,698
Cash provided by operations	4,625	3,510	2,808
Investing activities			
Acquisition of ABC, net of cash acquired	-8,432		
Film and television cost	-3,678	-1,886	-1,434
Investments in theme parks, resorts, and other property	-1,745	-896	-1,026
Purchases of marketable securities	-18	-1,033	-953
Proceeds from sales of marketable securities	409	1,460	1,494
Other		67	-968
	-13,464	-2,288	-2,887
Financing activities			
Borrowings	13,560	786	1,866
Reduction of borrowings	-4,872	-772	-1,315
Repurchases of common stock	-462	-349	-571
Dividends	-271	-180	-153
Exercise of stock options and other	85	183	76
	8,040	-332	-97
Increase (decrease) in cash and cash equivalents	-799	890	-176
Cash and cash equivalents, beginning of period	1,077	187	363
Cash and cash equivalents, end of period	278	1,077	187
Supplement disclosure of cash flow information			
Interest paid	379	123	99
Income taxes paid	689	557	320

Source: Walt Disney Co. Annual Report, 1996.

such as United Paramount Network (UPN) or Warner Brothers (WB) is limited. Independents must pay for syndicated shows, which increases their operating costs. Despite the higher costs, independents have more local advertising time to allot since national advertising occurs primarily on the network affiliates. A Standard & Poor's industry survey projects a 5.3 percent growth in television advertisement revenue compounded annually over the next five years. Radio advertising revenue is expected to increase 7.9 percent over the same time period.[14]

Both cable and direct satellite broadcasters (DSBs) receive the bulk of their revenues from subscriber fees.[15] The cable industry has a long history of providing inferior service to customers. However, despite quality issues and the maturity of the industry, the number of subscribers is expected to increase 3 percent annually over the next four years.[16] The cable industry also expects a 13.4 percent increase in advertisement in 1997 to $6.85 billion.[17] DSB subscribers mushroomed 152 percent from 1995 to 1996.[18] Standard and Poor's expects revenues to grow at an annual rate of 46.7 percent from 1996 to 2000.

COMPETITIVE ENVIRONMENT

The major shift toward consolidation of media enterprises involves the integration of content-driven companies such as Disney with distribution-driven companies such as ABC. These realignments have created powerful media conglomerates including Disney, News Corp., and Time Warner (see Exhibit 4). Media include outlets other than the four major networks, such as publishing, movies, cable, music, and retail products. Other considerations, such as diversification at Westinghouse, have driven this merger frenzy.

Disney is a primary example of a media company leveraging its core competencies from movie production to the retail outlet. Disney distributes a movie such as *Hercules* and uses its animation property rights to market toys, clothes, and other items related to the movie. Although not considered media, theme parks complement large media conglomerates by increasing brand recognition. Disney has a unique advantage in this area.

Unlike a media outlet, physical travel is required to experience a theme park. Furthermore, theme parks cater to different market segments. Parks such as Six Flags, Sea World, and Busch Gardens are more regional and can be experienced in one day. Disney World and Universal Studios are national, if not global, attractions. Visitors expect to spend up to a week at these theme parks/resorts. Theme parks allow media companies an opportunity to promote their brand image through life experiences, such as meeting Mickey Mouse at Disney World. This is becoming a more popular method of attaining brand recognition. For instance, Six Flags has an alliance with Warner Bros. to provide Looney Tunes characters to enhance the park's atmosphere.

Disney is the dominant competitor in the theme park industry. The Disneyland development gave Disney a first-mover advantage it has yet to relinquish. Its progress into other park creations keeps it ahead of its primary competitors: Universal Studios, Six Flags, and Busch Gardens. Although important, the trend toward theme parks is a less significant issue for Disney than the broader industry dynamics of creative content and finding appropriate channels of distribution, that is, broadcasting.

Time Warner

Turner Broadcasting merged with Time Warner (TW) in 1995. Ted Turner became the vice chairman of Time Warner, Inc., and Gerald Levin remained chairman and CEO. According to the Time Warner Home Page, "Time Warner journalists and artists create one new product for every half-hour of the day." Time Warner believes it creates value through "three interlocking fundamentals: creativity, libraries, and branded content combined with branded distribution."[19] Time Warner was able to increase the size of its animated library with the addition of Hanna-Barbara to its Warner Bros. line. With the acquisition of Turner Broadcasting, quality news channels such as CNN and award-winning journalists became a part of the Time Warner family. CNN complements the large publishing arm of TW, including *Time* and *Sports Illustrated* magazines. Furthermore, TW gains access to many more cable channels through brand name recognition provided by TNT, Cartoon Network, TBS, and HBO. Time Warner officials point out that "in the 1995/96 season, cable networks grew to 30% share of the total primetime viewing audience."[20]

News Corp. (FOX)

Rupert Murdoch has established a worldwide media conglomerate. In 1985, News Corp. chairman and CEO Murdoch acquired FOX. Historically a movie producer, Murdoch set out to utilize FOX as a television distribution outlet as well. FOX network was initially a lowly regarded fourth player in the network television market. Since its advent, FOX has produced such popular shows as "The Simpsons," "Married with Children," and "COPS." A high degree of "titillation television" led to ratings growth at the expense of the other three networks. By the mid 1990s, the FOX network enhanced its legitimacy with the procurement of National Football League and Major League Baseball television rights. Murdoch continued to increase the visibility of FOX and News Corp. with the acquisition of the Los Angeles Dodgers, a national cable sports network, and Pat

4 | Holdings of Disney and Competitors

Company/ Holding	Time Warner Inc.	The Walt Disney Co.
Television	WB television network; Warner Bros. Television; international Warner Bros. Programming	Walt Disney Television (International); Touchstone Television; Walt Disney Television Animation; Buena Vista Television; ABC Inc.: ABC Television Network (ABC News and ABC Sports); 10 TV Stations; Disney/ABC International Television
Cable	CNN: Headline News, CNN/SI (sports net), CNN Airport, CNNfn (The Financial Network); HBO: HBO Family Channel, HBO Animation; Cinemax; TNT; TBS Superstation; Cartoon Network; Turner Classic Movies (TCM)	ESPN; The Disney Channel; A&E Networks; A&E, The History Channel; Lifetime Television
Radio		ABC Radio Network (ABC News and ABC Sports); 26 Radio Stations: 11 AM, 15 FM; working to start Radio Disney (24-hour children's radio)
Feature Films	Warner Bros. Studios; Warner Home Video; Warner Bros. International Theaters	Walt Disney Motion Picture Groups; Walt Disney Pictures, Touchstone Pictures, Hollywood Pictures, Caravan Pictures, Miramax Films; Buena Vista Pictures Distribution; Buena Vista International, Buena Vista Home Video, Buena Vista Home Entertainment
Publications	Time Inc.: *People, Sports Illustrated, Time, Entertainment Weekly, Fortune*, specialized magazines; Time Warner Trade Publishing; Time Life Books; Warner Books; Little Brown Publishing; books; international magazines	Daily newspapers; 50 trade publications; W. magazine; Discover magazine; family magazines; books; comics
Music	Warner Music Group: Atlantic, Elektra, Warner Bros., Warner Music International, Warner/Chappell Publishing Co., 50% of Columbia House	Walt Disney Records; Hollywood Records
Retail	Warner Bros. Consumer Products; 161 Warner Bros. Studio Stores Worldwide	101 Disney Stores worldwide; clothing; toys; licensing ventures
Misc.	Book-of-the-Month Club Inc.; Warner Bros theme parks; CNN Interactive	Disney theme parks: Walt Disney World, Disneyland, Epcot Center, building Disney's Animal Kingdom and Disney's California Adventure, parks in Europe and Asia; Walt Disney Imagineering; Anaheim Sports: Anaheim Mighty Ducks NHL team; Walt Disney Theatrical Productions; Disney Online; ABC Online; Disney Interactive (CD-ROMs and online products); Disney Cruise Line
Investments/joint ventures		25% of Anaheim Angels baseball team; interests in international broadcasting companies; partnership with Ameritech to develop new cable TV networks

4 | Holdings of Disney and Competitors *(Continued)*

News Corp. Ltd. (FOX)	Viacom (Paramount)	General Electric (NBC)	Westinghouse Electric Corp. (CBS)
Fox Broadcasting Co.: 23 U.S. TV stations; Fox broadcast network; Fox News Production Inc.; 20th Century Fox Television; Twentieth Century Fox/Astral Television Distribution Ltd.; Evergreen Television Productions Inc.; Fox Children's Network Inc.	Television Signal Corp.; Riverside Broadcasting Co.; 13 TV stations; Paramount Communications Inc.; 75% of Spelling Entertainment Group, Inc.	NBC; 11 TV stations	CBS TV Network; CBS Entertainment; 14 TV Stations; CBS News/Sports
Fox Pay-Per-View services; fX Networks	MTV; Showtime; Nickelodeon/Nick at Nite; VH1; USA Networks; Comedy Central; All News Channel	Seven cable/satellite networks including CNBC and Court TV	
	12 radio stations		
	77 radio stations		
Fox Motion Pictures; 20th Century Fox Film; Columbia TriStar Films; 21st Century Fox Film; Cinemascope Products; Fox Animation Studios; Mirror Pictures; Van Ness Films; Fieldmouse Production; Fox West Pictures; San Antonio Film Features; Fox Home Video; 20th Century Fox Home Entertainment	Paramount Pictures; Viacom Productions		
HarperCollins US Inc.; Murdoch Publications; News T Magazines; News America Publications Inc.	Simon & Schuster; Macmillan Publishing USA; technical and professional books		
Fox Music; Fox Records; Fox Children's Music Inc.; Fox Film Music; Fox On Air Music; Fox Broadcast Music	Music By Video Inc.		
	Blockbuster Entertainment Corp.: home video, music		
Fox Movietone News; Fox Net; Fox Sports Productions	Discovery Zone; Paramount Parks (5 theme parks); audio/visual software; Games Productions Inc.		
		MSNBC	

Source: The Top 25 Media Groups, *Broadcasting and Cable*, July 7, 1997, 22–28.

Robertson's Family Channel. Furthermore, News Corp. is actively fostering the worldwide Direct Satellite Broadcasting (DSB) market.

Viacom (Paramount Pictures)

Viacom's largest holding is Paramount Pictures, a major motion picture studio that has existed since 1912.[21] A major portion of Viacom's assets is the Paramount movie library, which includes hits such as *The Ten Commandments, The Godfather* series, and *Forrest Gump*. But, movies are not Paramount's only business. The Paramount television studio is responsible for the "Star Trek" series. "Cheers," "I Love Lucy," and "The Honeymooners" are also a part of the Paramount TV library. Other Viacom franchises include MTV, Nickelodeon, and VH1. As a consequence, Viacom is a major participant in the music and children's television industries. Furthermore, Viacom has a large publishing arm; Simon & Schuster "is the world's largest English-language, educational, and computer book publisher."[22] In 1994, Viacom acquired Blockbuster Entertainment, a large retail outlet for movie videocassettes and music products. Thus, Viacom is a vertically integrated producer, distributor, and multimedia operator.

Westinghouse (CBS)

Westinghouse diversified its holdings with the purchase of CBS. Unlike the integration of content and distribution with the competitors described above, Westinghouse's purchase of CBS integrated two distribution companies. This purchase included local CBS television and radio stations. Industry insiders view the merger negatively. Former CBS executive Laurence Tisch was notoriously conservative. The CBS vision was considered reactive as the firm was selling its major assets, which resulted in considerable immediate earnings for CBS. Shareholders and Tisch benefited from management's actions in the short term. Westinghouse will have to revive the CBS network with an infusion of investment capital. This will be more difficult than liquidating parts of the firm to increase earnings. Despite CBS's internal problems, sporting events such as the NCAA Basketball Tournament, Master's golf tournament, and NCAA football are popular programs. In addition, television shows such as "The Price Is Right" and "The Late Show with David Letterman" are mainstays.

General Electric (NBC)

NBC is the top-rated network in the television marketplace. Its ability to continually market new situation comedies around the success of a few mainstays is one example of its competitiveness. For instance, the slogan "Must See TV" started with the network's Thursday night lineup of "Seinfeld" and "Frasier." NBC's weekend programming is filled with sports shows, such as the NFL, Major League Baseball, and the increasingly popular National Basketball Association, which have loyal viewers. General Electric, much like Westinghouse, holds NBC as a part of its diversification strategy. The financial strength of General Electric (unlike Westinghouse) increases NBC's competitiveness. NBC executives have created cable channels such as CNBC and MSNBC, which compete for the CNN-type viewer. MSNBC is unique in that it is a joint venture with software power Microsoft. This strategic alliance is designed to integrate the television medium with the information superhighway, the Internet.

HISTORY AND CURRENT BUSINESS

Walt Disney

Walter Elias Disney was born in Chicago on December 5, 1901. Walt was one of five children and came from a family that encouraged hard work and tight purse strings. As he was growing up, Walt amused himself by drawing. At the age of 14, he enrolled in the Kansas City Art Institute and began making small animated films. However, Walt never made any profits from the films because he lacked financial knowledge and business acumen.[23]

In 1923, Walt moved to California to join his brother, Roy Disney. Together they began producing animated films. Their first major hit was *Oswald the Lucky Rabbit*. However, to continue to produce these films, they had to borrow money from a New York distributor. As the character became increasingly popular, the costs to produce the films increased. Therefore, Walt asked the distributor for a raise. Instead of receiving a raise, Walt was told that he did not own the rights to Oswald, the New York distributor did. So, Walt and Roy developed the now-famous Mickey Mouse character.

To develop Mickey Mouse, Walt and Roy formed a partnership in which their mission was to provide the public with a quality product. However, their plans were often bigger than their resources and they had to take Walt Disney Productions public in 1940. Walt Disney Productions was known for taking risks and striving continuously to venture into innovative forms of entertainment. With the support of the growing Walt Disney Productions company, Walt and Roy decided to open a theme park in 1955 called Disneyland Park. This park introduced a whole new form of entertainment, the outdoor theme park. As a result, the company began to be perceived as being on the leading edge of the entertainment industry.[24]

After Walt

At the time of Walt's death in 1966, the plans for Walt Disney World in Orlando had just begun. At first, Walt's death did not affect the company; he still had a strong presence in the company and had shared his vision so well that the corporate officers were able to carry on, as Walt had once said, "after Disney." However, this growth eventually began to slow and changes could be seen within the corporation. The company was no longer taking risks on new ventures and projects and was gradually losing touch with what the public perceived as quality and innovative entertainment. The synergy between the different divisions of the Walt Disney Company had once been considered a key strength, but now it was weakening. At this time, Saul Steinberg initiated a takeover bid for the company. However, Disney's officers were able to maintain control of the company with the help of many loyal stockholders.[25]

Michael Eisner

In 1984, Michael Eisner left Paramount to become the CEO of the Walt Disney Company.[26] Eisner's original strategy was to change the company, venture into new businesses, and make acquisitions. His goal was to "continue to nurture and protect the Disney brand and to reaffirm core values such as our commitment to quality and service."[27] Eisner's first priority was to revamp Disney's film and production division and develop original and creative full-length animated films.[28] Not only did Eisner reinvent the film and production division, he also turned Disney into a premier entertainment giant with enough revenue and power to acquire Capital Cities/ABC, Inc. The majority of growth Eisner achieved came from businesses (see Exhibit 5) that did not exist

5 | Disney's Expansions Since Eisner Became CEO in 1984

- International film distribution
- Television broadcasting
- Television station ownership
- Expanded ownership of cable systems
- Radio and radio network broadcasting
- Ownership of radio stations
- Newspaper, magazine, and book publishing
- The Disney Stores
- The convention business
- Live theatrical entertainment
- Home video production
- Interactive computer programs and games
- Online computer programs
- Sites on the World Wide Web
- Ownership of professional sports teams
- Telephone company partnership
- Disney Regional Entertainment
- Disney Cruise Line

Source: Walt Disney Co. Annual Report, 1996.

prior to his tenure as the firm's CEO.[29] These businesses stemmed from acquisitions and internal ventures.

Theme Parks and Resorts

Disney's theme parks and resorts include the Walt Disney World Resort in Florida and Disneyland Park in California. The company also owns a National Hockey League team called the Might Ducks of Anaheim and has part ownership of and general management responsibility for the Anaheim Angels baseball team. Disney also receives royalties from its partially owned theme parks in Tokyo and Paris (Tokyo Disneyland and Disneyland Paris). The theme parks and resort division grew 13 percent in 1996, which brought revenues to $4.5 billion. This growth is expected to increase with the 1998 addition of another theme park at the Walt Disney World Resort in Florida, Disney's Animal Kingdom. Eisner also expects Disney to profit from the company's addition of a Wide World of Sports Complex in Orlando. This complex will be the home of the Amateur Athletes Union and the Harlem Globetrotters. It will also serve as the spring training site for the Atlanta Braves. With the help of Disney's new regional entertainment division, Disney Regional Entertainment, the company will continue to offer a diverse range of entertainment and educational experiences to children and families around the world. Disney Regional Entertainment will be in charge of operating a variety of entertainment experiences across the United States using sports concepts, interactive entertainment centers, and children's play centers. The division will run these businesses with the help of Disney's creative entertainment talents and the popularity of the Disney brand.[30]

Film

Disney's film and television division had numerous successes in 1996. It released several hit films such as *Toy Story* (Disney), *Con Air* (Touchstone Pictures), and *G.I. Jane* (Hollywood Pictures). Almost one out of four movie tickets sold each day in North America is for a Disney movie. This is not hard to believe because Disney has several different film and television companies within this division. When Eisner became CEO in 1984, his goal was to reinvent this division. In 1984 Disney released only two live-action motion pictures. However, under Eisner's leadership, in 1996 Disney increased this number to 29, which does not include the 36 films released by the Disney-owned Miramax. However, because the film market is saturated, Disney plans to reduce the number of films it releases annually. This strategy will allow Disney to focus on releasing more "high-impact, star-driven films with greater potential."[31]

Broadcasting

Disney's broadcasting division has grown significantly over the last two years. February of 1996 brought about the completion of the Disney and Capital Cities/ABC merger. Upon this merger, Disney transferred three of its units to this division: The Disney Channel, Buena Vista Television, and Disney Television International. With the Capital Cities/ABC merger, Disney gained control of several distribution channels, including ESPN, A&E Networks, and Lifetime Television. Combined, these three channels have over 90 million subscribers. ESPN is the most widely distributed cable programming network in the country. Combining Disney Television International and ABC allows Disney to form a powerful distribution operation.[32]

Consumer Products

Disney's consumer products division continues to be fueled by the popularity of the company's main characters such as Mickey Mouse, Donald Duck, Goofy, and Minnie Mouse. It also has experienced sales gains from its new animation characters such as the Little Mermaid, 101 Dalmatians, Hercules, and the Lion King. The consumer products division includes The Disney Stores, Disney Interactive, and Disney Online. Under Eisner's leadership, The Disney Stores, which promote all of the Disney characters, now have 550 units in 11 countries. Disney is also taking advantage of its merger with Capital Cities/ABC by opening an ESPN store in Southern California and a Club Disney in Thousand Oaks, California. The ESPN store will be a theme retail store offering sports merchandise with logos of various professional and college teams, sports memorabilia, and a large number of items with the ESPN logo.[33] Club Disney will offer children a virtual-reality-type play site to enjoy with their families.

Disney Interactive has increased its market share to 15 percent in the education category with its Animated Story Books. It has already released five of the best-selling children's software titles in history, such as the "Toy Story Animated Storybook" and the "Lion King Activity Center." Disney Online's goal is to increase the firm's presence on the World Wide Web via its two Web sites, Disney.com and Family.com. Disney.com acts as Disney's primary marketing and promotional Web site, while Family.com is considered a site for parents and children to visit and enjoy together.[34]

Walt Disney Imagineering

The Walt Disney Imagineering division is responsible for planning, creating, and developing all Disney resorts, theme parks, communities, and regional entertainment sites. It uses its cutting-edge creative, technical, and development abilities to update the appearance and design of all the theme parks and to create cutting-edge and creative themes for the new resorts. As a new project, the division has aided in the creation of the community outside of Walt Disney World in Florida called Celebration. This community will combine the latest telecommunication and personal computer technology with the essence of a comfortable community atmosphere. Also, this division is currently working on Disney's restoration of the New Amsterdam Theater in New York City.[35] Through the restoration of the New Amsterdam Theater, Disney hopes to lead others in an effort to recreate 42nd Street as the Main Street USA of show business.[36]

LEADERSHIP AND GOVERNANCE

In 1994, two major events occurred that changed Eisner's outlook. First, there was the accidental death of Eisner's good friend and number two man, Frank Wells. Several months later, Eisner himself had a brush with death when he suffered a heart attack and required bypass surgery. These events were complicated by shakeups at Disney. Jeffrey Katzenberg, then head of Walt Disney Studios, left Disney after Eisner refused to give him Well's job. (Wells was president of Disney.) In addition, Katzenberg took several key executives with him. However, Eisner came back from these events with a renewed focus and a new plan.[37]

Eisner appointed Richard Nanula, then CFO, as president of Walt Disney Stores and then made an unusual move by bringing in someone from outside of the entertainment industry. He recruited Steve Bollenbach from Marriott to fill the position of CFO. Bollenbach was known for his ability to finance deals, and it was Bollenbach who convinced Eisner to go ahead with the ABC acquisition.

The building block of Eisner's diversification strategy was the acquisition of Capital Cities/ABC, Inc. The Disney-ABC merger combined a content company with a distribution company. Through ABC, Disney acquired distribution capabilities in radio, television, and print. ABC owned 20 radio stations as well as network and cable television distribution channels. ABC's network television capability included eight television stations and foreign stations. ABC's cable television holdings included ESPN, A&E, and Lifetime. Finally, ABC's print distribution operations included a wide variety of magazines.

To implement Disney's diversification strategy, Eisner recruited long-time friend Michael Ovitz to serve as president of Walt Disney, Inc. Ovitz came from Creative Artists Agency, the talent agency he founded and led. Ovitz was known for his ability to recruit talent and complete business transactions. For Example, Ovitz was instrumental in the Sony/MCA merger and the MCA/Seagrams merger.[38]

Eisner also appointed Bob Iger president of ABC, Inc. At the time of the merger, Iger was six months from succeeding Tom Murphy as CEO of ABC, Inc. Iger had spent his entire career at ABC.[39]

Amid controversy, Ovitz left Disney with a $100 million settlement just over a year after he signed with Eisner. Reasons cited for Ovitz's departure included Eisner's hands-on approach to management. In addition, Bollenbach and Iger reported to Eisner rather than to Ovitz, which Ovitz claimed made it difficult to run things. Therefore, this new top-management team quickly broke apart.

Eisner has not replaced Ovitz. Instead, he has focused on building a team of number-twos (see Exhibit 6). Rather than having just one number-two person, Eisner decided to have several number-two persons for each segment of the business: Joe Roth, Walt Disney Motion Pictures; Bob Iger, ABC; Gerry Laybourne, Disney/ABC cable; Steve Bornstein, ESPN/ABC Sports; Judson Green, Walt Disney attractions; and Richard Nanula, president and CFO.[40] (Nanula was moved back

6 | Disney Management and Board of Directors

Corporate Officers
- Michael D. Eisner, Chairman and Chief Executive Officer
- Richard D. Nanula, President and Chief Financial Officer
- Sanford M. Litvack, Senior Executive Vice President and Chief of Corporate Operations

Major Subsidiaries, Divisions and Affiliates
- Robert A. Iger, President, ABC, Inc.
- Steven M. Bornstein, President and Chief Executive Officer, ESPN, Inc./President, ABC Sports
- Geraldine Laybourne, Executive Vice President, Disney/ABC Cable
- Judson C. Green, President, Walt Disney Attractions
- Joe Roth, Chairman, Walt Disney Motion Pictures

Board of Directors
- Reveta F. Bowers, Headmistress, Center for Early Education
- Roy E. Disney, Vice Chairman of the Company
- Michael D. Eisner, Chairman and CEO of the Company
- Stanley P. Gold, President and CEO, Shamrock Holdings, Inc.
- Sanford M. Litvack, Senior Executive Vice President and Chief of Corporate Operations of the Company
- Ignacio E. Lozano, Jr., Chairman, La Opinion
- George J. Mitchell, Attorney, Former U.S. Senator
- Thomas S. Murphy, Former Chairman and CEO, Capital Cities/ABC, Inc.
- Richard A. Nunis, Chairman, Walt Disney Attractions
- Leo J. Donovan, President, Georgetown University
- Sidney Poitier, Actor, Director, and Writer
- Irwin E. Russell, Attorney
- Robert A. Stern, Senior Partner, Robert A. M. Stern Architects
- E. Cardon Walker, Former Chairman and CEO of the Company
- Raymond L. Watson, Vice Chairman, The Irvine Co.
- Gary L. Wilson, Chairman, Northwest Airlines Inc. and Northwest Airlines Corp.

Source: Corporate Yellow Book, 1997.

to the position of CFO when Bollenbach left Disney for other opportunities.)

The lack of a successor at Disney is a major concern of shareholders and analysts. Eisner is noted for his ability to manage every aspect of the entertainment business. His previous experience at Paramount and ABC trained him in everything from movie production to television programming. Eisner is credited with being "one of those rare executives who is a shrewd businessman with keen creative skills."[41] Many wonder if anyone can fill his shoes. Still, Eisner refuses to appoint a successor and Disney's board of directors has been criticized for seemingly sitting idle. Some believe that Disney would benefit from having a board of directors that will stand up to Eisner's forceful dual CEO/chairman role and demand that he create a successor plan.

There are other areas of Disney's corporate governance that concern shareholders and analysts. Under Eisner's 1989 contract, his bonus was tied to the company's return on equity. Since Eisner took over, Disney has achieved average return on equity of about 20 percent a year, bringing Eisner a bonus of $9.9 million in 1994 and $14 million in 1995. Eisner's new contract abandons the return-on-equity formula. Instead, the bonus is now tied to his ability to increase earnings per share over a target growth rate of 7.5 percent. Also included in Eisner's contract is the option for 8 million Disney shares (3 million premium options and 5 million regular options) with an estimated value of anywhere from $195 to $400 million.[42] The premium options have an exercise price higher than the fair market value at the time of the grant, meaning that they become valuable only if the company's stock price rises substantially.[43]

During the annual meeting in 1997, shareholders sent a strong message about executive pay, independence of the board of directors, and the multimillion-dollar payout to former president Michael Ovitz. About 8 percent of the shareholders voted against Eisner's new contract, which will keep him at the company until 2006.[44] Approximately 12.7 percent of the company's institutional and individual investors voted to withhold their support to reelect five members of the company's board.[45] This withholding for reelection of incumbent directors represents the largest "no" vote against a major U.S. corporation since Archer-Daniels-Midland Co.'s annual meeting in October 1995.[46] When expressing disappointment about the company's payout to Ovitz, one investor suggested that Eisner personally pay for the loss.

In response to shareholders' discontent, Eisner acknowledged that Ovitz's tenure at Disney was "a mistake." Eisner said that "because he did not make it in our company, we had to give Mr. Ovitz his stock options." At another point in the meeting, Eisner brought investor Warren Buffett, who has a large stake in Disney, onstage to deliver a short speech about how happy he is with the company. "I advise you to keep your stock," Mr. Buffet said.[47]

H. Carl McCall, who controls 3.4 million Disney shares as sole trustee of New York's public pension fund, said he was voting the fund's shares against the two proposals, in part, because of the $100 million plus severance package paid to Ovitz. In addition, 24 of the 103 pension funds belonging to the Council of Institutional Investors are voting against the board reelections, the Eisner pay package, or both. The pension funds, including the California Public Employees' Retirement System and New York's Common Retirement Fund, hold at least 22 million of Disney's more than 680 million outstanding shares.[48]

McCall argues that the board has not demonstrated sufficient independence, which corresponds with criticism that is heard frequently about Disney. Twelve of the sixteen members of the Disney board have personal or professional ties to Eisner or the company. These ties include Eisner's personal lawyer, the principal of an elementary school Eisner's children attended, a Disney-commissioned architect, and three former Disney executives.[49] John Dreyer, a Disney spokesman, responds to McCall by indicating that Disney's stock performance has appreciated 2,000 percent during Eisner's 12 1/2 years, and that the market cap has risen to $53 billion from $2 billion. Dreyer maintains that the board should be measured ultimately by the performance of the company, not by some other, arbitrary standards. He argues: "I'm sure (the pensions) have what they would consider more independent boards in their holdings that are not performing well. If they really don't think the company is a good investment, they really should sell their stock."[50]

COMPETITIVE CHALLENGES

Television Disney's television holdings (ABC, ESPN, Disney Channel, Lifetime, A&E, and E!) have varied success rates. ABC currently is experiencing record low ratings and profits. However, the other channels are thriving. The critical issue is whether ABC can revive its prime-time schedule to compete against NBC and CBS. ABC's programming problems are compounded by unclear leadership. Insiders say that "Jamie's [Jamie Tarses, president, ABC programming] the figurehead. If you've got a big piece of business, you call Iger. Eisner's going to set the tone and the strategy—and he'll set the schedule."[51] The big question is who will lead ABC in its effort to regain market share.

Movie Studios Can Disney achieve its goal of producing fewer but better films than the competition? Disney must continue to compete in all markets: adults (Miramax, Hollywood Pictures, Caravan, and Touchstone), adolescents (Touchstone and Hollywood Pictures), and children (Disney and Touchstone). In addition, Disney must deal with increasing competition in animation pictures from Fox and Dreamworks SKG.

Consumer Products Consumer product success is tied to Disney's animated film success. Because of Disney's lack of hit animation films in the last year, retailers no longer see Disney products as guaranteed hits.

Theme Parks Disney faces increasing competition in the theme park segment. The challenge for Disney is to sustain the first-mover advantage by expanding the Disney experience more quickly and efficiently than competitors.

Will Michael Eisner be able to satisfy stockholders? What should his growth strategy be? Will he be able to manage the complexity that is associated with the size and maturity of Disney as a result of the ABC acquisition? Should he continue his current expansion strategy? What implications do the firm's corporate governance practices have for top management's strategy?

ENDNOTES

1. D. Turner, 1997, Disney's go-go growth days may be going, going, gone, *Los Angeles Business Journal*, March 3, 1.
2. Ibid.
3. Ibid.
4. N. M. Minow, The Communications Act, *Vital Speeches of the Day*, April 15, 1995, 389–392.
5. W. Cohen and K. Hetter, 1995, Tomorrow's media today, *U.S. News & World Report*, August 14, 47–49.
6. M. Levinson, 1995, Mickey's wake-up call, *Newsweek*, August 14, 27.
7. M. Burgi, 1995, Still bound by big brother, *Mediaweek*, May 15, 25–27.
8. Ibid.
9. Ibid.
10. E. Rathbun and D. Petrozzello, 1996, Infinity: Only the beginning?, *Broadcasting and Cable*, July 1, 7.
11. Ibid.
12. Ibid.
13. Ibid.
14. Standard & Poor's Industry Survey, "Broadcasting & Cable," June 26, 1997, 1.
15. Ibid. p. 2.
16. Ibid.
17. Ibid., p. 3.
18. Ibid., p. 7.
19. http://www.pathfinder.com
20. Ibid.
21. http://www.viacom.com
22. Ibid.
23. L. Maltin, 1995, *The Disney Films*, 3rd Edition (New York: Jessie Film Ltd.), 1–2.
24. L. Marabele (ed.), 1990, *The Walt Disney Company, International Directory of Company Histories* (Chicago: St. James Press), 2:172–174.
25. Ibid.
26. "Eisner, Michael" Microsoft® Encarta® 1996 Encyclopedia © 1993–95 Microsoft Corporation.
27. Walt Disney Co. Annual Report, 1997.
28. "Eisner, Michael" Microsoft® Encarta® 1996 Encyclopedia © 1993–95 Microsoft Corporation.
29. Walt Disney Co. Annual Report, 1997.
30. Ibid.
31. Ibid.
32. Ibid.
33. Turner, Disney's go-go growth days may be going, going, gone, 1.
34. Walt Disney Co. Annual Report, 1997.
35. Ibid.
36. F. Rose, 1996, "Can Disney tame 42nd Street?", *Fortune*, June 24, 94–98.
37. M. Meyer, 1995, How Eisner saved Disney and himself, *Newsweek*, August 14, 28.
38. E. S. Reckard, 1996, Ovitz out as Disney president, *Associated Press Online*, December 12.
39. M. Gunther and J. McGowan, 1997, Can he save ABC? Robert Iger faces the toughest challenge of a charmed career, *Fortune*, June 23, 90.
40. R. Grover, 1997, Michael Eisner defends the kingdom, *Business Week*, August 4, 73.
41. S. Coe, 1995, Disney's Michael Eisner: No Mickey Mouse CEO, *Broadcasting & Cable*, August 7, 16.
42. Turner, Disney's go-go growth days may be going, going, gone, 1.
43. B. Orwall, 1997, Disney chief's stock options exercise irks some, but street remains calm, *Wall Street Journal Interactive Edition*, http:/www.wsj.com December 5.
44. B. Orwall, 1997, Shareholders express anger over pay to Ovitz and Eisner, *Wall Street Journal Interactive Edition*, http:/www.wsj.com February 25.
45. Holders of 12.7% of Disney shares oppose 5 directors, *Dow Jones Newswires*, February 25, 1997.
46. B. Orwall, 1997, Shareholders express anger over pay to Ovitz and Eisner.
47. Ibid.
48. McCall to vote NY Pension Fund 3.4M shares against Disney board, *Dow Jones Newswires*, February 24, 1997.
49. New York State—2-: Disney says criticisms are misguided, *Dow Jones Newswires*, February 24, 1997.
50. Ibid.
51. Gunther and McGowan, 1997, Can he save ABC? Robert Iger faces the toughest challenge of a charmed career, *Fortune*, June 23, 90.

CASE 40

Western Pacific Airlines

Steve Gove
Arizona State University

I think Beauvais is onto something here.

—Airline analyst

The easiest way to become a millionaire is to start with a billion and go into the airline business.

—Investor adage

It's gone too far.

—Western Pacific Airlines stockholder commenting that he would stop flying the airline because cartoon character Bart Simpson was painted on one of the airline's Boeing 737s in an ad for Fox TV's *The Simpsons.*

In 1995, Western Pacific (WestPac) Airlines, a startup, attracted widespread interest. The attention focused not on WestPac challenging United Airlines's dominance in the Denver air travel market or WestPac's position amongst the fastest growing airlines in the nation. Rather, it was that the skin of WestPac's aircraft was painted as flying billboards. One aircraft, for Last Vegas casino chain Sam's Town, featured a 35′ scantily clad cowgirl painted on the 737's rudder (Exhibit 1). Other ads, for Colorado's Broadmoor Hotel, Thrifty Rent-A-Car, the Stardust Hotel, and the *Simpsons,* appeared in countless newspapers and several television ads. While such innovative marketing was cited as brilliant and provided WestPac with $800,000 per aircraft, would it enable WestPac to survive an industry that had seen the startup of 34 air carriers since deregulation in 1978—only two of which remained by 1996?

COLORADO AIR MARKET

The Colorado market is the seventh largest air travel market in the U.S. The population of the Denver/Colorado Springs area increased 12 percent between 1992 and 1996. The market is serviced by two primary airports: Denver and Colorado Springs. Like Wichita, St. Louis, Omaha, and Oklahoma City, Denver and Colorado Springs are roughly the geographic center of the U.S. New York, for example, is 1,623 miles away, Orlando 1,422 miles, Seattle 1,067 miles, and Chicago 911 miles. This centrality allows an airline to efficiently serve as a hub for east–west traffic.

Denver has traditionally been the center of Colorado air traffic, serving as a hub for both United and Continental Airlines. The city's former airport, Stapleton, saw passenger traffic climb from 25.2 million passengers in 1983 to 34.7 million in 1986. The FAA predicted that by 1995, yearly passenger traffic in Denver would approach 52 million. With Stapleton over capacity, the city began planning a new facility. Led by then mayoral candidate Frederico Peña, voters approved the project with a 2-to-1 margin. The new facility, Denver International Airport (DIA), was to open as early as 1990 with a budgeted cost of $1.7 billion. DIA was to be a technological marvel, covering 53 square miles, with three passenger concourses and five 12,000-foot runways designed to allow 99 planes to land every hour in any weather.

The project suffered repeated setbacks, delays, and cost overruns and opening was rescheduled for 1993. A $200 million automated baggage handling system was

Exhibit 1 | Western Pacific Airlines's LogoJets

Step 1: Design. First LogoJets are concepted; an idea is usually drawn on paper or a rough design on a computer. Next, art items are scanned into a high-end Macintosh computer with a drum scanner. Art is retouched to perfection using popular retouching software. The art is wrapped around a model using a 3-d program. Then the final is brought back to the image-editing software for the finishing touches. Then the comp is printed out using expensive dye-sublimation printers, and the design is distributed to the prospective client.

Step 2: Paint. After the design is approved, the hard part begins. From the comps, a CAD artist makes the entire jet in 3-D. Art is scanned and templates are cut using a computer. Masks are made for each color. The jet is primed and sanded very smooth. Several coats of very hard paint is added to the jet. After the jet is painted, it can weigh 2,000 more pounds!

Step 3: Fly. The jet then flies to all of our great destinations, including Colorado Springs, where Western Pacific is based.

Source: Western Pacific Airlines.

contracted for by United Airlines for their A terminal but was expanded to service all three terminals. The system was to whisk passenger luggage through 22 miles of underground tracks. High rates of system failures delayed the airport's opening by an additional 16 months. Coverage of the baggage handling system reached the national news with video of luggage shredded by the system, the source of jokes for late night television hosts. A baggage handler described the carnage as "very dramatic."

DIA finally opened on February 28, 1995. The airport was to have 120 gates on opening day and 206 by 2020. Instead it opened with 90 gates. Stapleton had 111 gates.

The much maligned baggage handling system proved to be one problem, but the opening revealed additional snafus. Contrary to what planners had envisioned, the airport lacked sufficient parking, because passengers elected to drive to the airport rather than take alternative transportation. This was due in part to one-way taxi fares near $40 for the 24-mile trip from downtown Denver. An additional 2,400 outdoor spaces were added, followed by 3,000 spaces in the employee parking area for use during peak times—an area several miles from the terminal and accessible only by shuttle bus. Underground shuttles carried passengers between the parking, main and passenger terminals. The shuttles, however, could not handle the volume of travelers during peak periods.

DIA's operations, touted as all weather, suffered as an October blizzard backed traffic up on the ice-covered airport approach road, Peña Boulevard; an airport van drove onto a runway, causing an arriving aircraft to abort a landing; ice caused an aircraft to skid off a runway; and melting snow leaked into the air traffic control tower. The airport's state-of-the-art radar system failed 75 percent of the time during a six-month period in 1995. The aircraft takeoff and landing approaches raised the ire of local residents, who had been assured of minimal airport impact on their residences, resulting in organized protests. A local TV station reported that mice were found living in the plants in the main concourse near food concessions.

DIA TRAFFIC & CARRIERS

Wary passengers avoided DIA, and Denver-based passenger traffic declined. In 1994, traffic at Stapleton totaled 33.1 million passengers. In 1995, DIA's traffic totaled 31.1 million (Exhibit 2). In addition to the airport's delayed opening and operating problems, other

EXHIBIT 2 | DIA and CSA Passenger Traffic 1983–1997

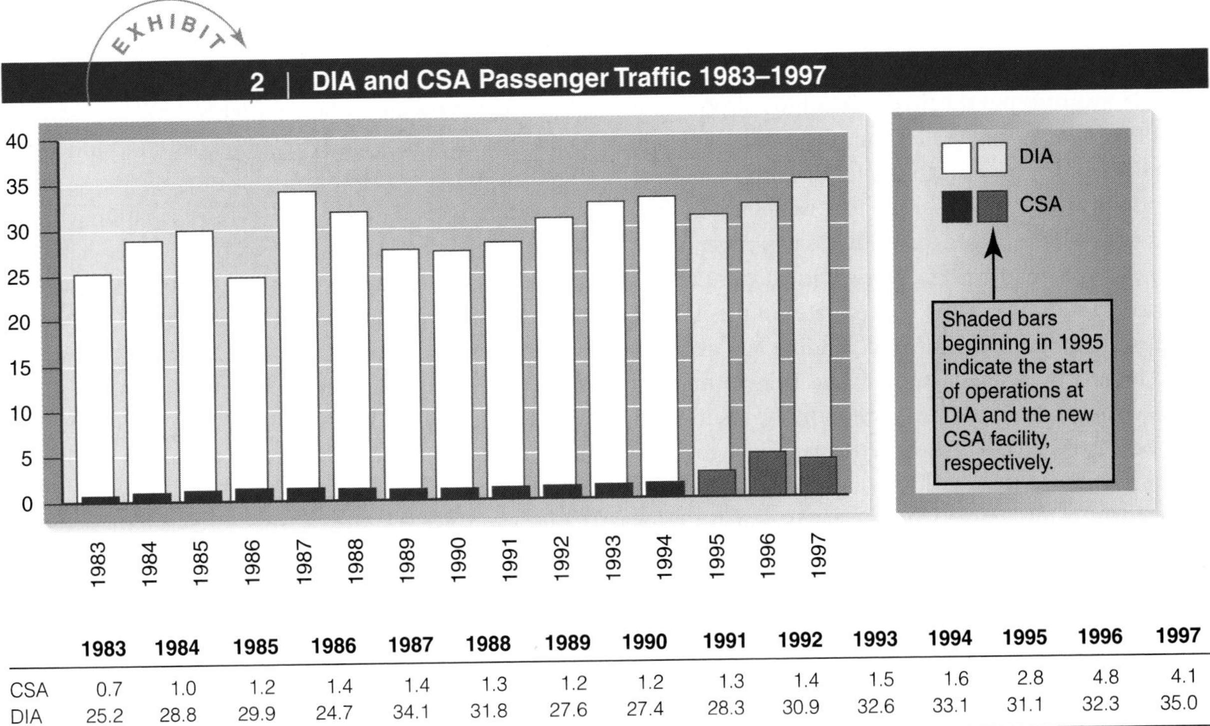

	1983	1984	1985	1986	1987	1988	1989	1990	1991	1992	1993	1994	1995	1996	1997
CSA	0.7	1.0	1.2	1.4	1.4	1.3	1.2	1.2	1.3	1.4	1.5	1.6	2.8	4.8	4.1
DIA	25.2	28.8	29.9	24.7	34.1	31.8	27.6	27.4	28.3	30.9	32.6	33.1	31.1	32.3	35.0

factors contributed to the decline in passenger traffic. DIA was to serve as a hub for two carriers: United and Continental Airlines. United, with revenues of $16.3 billion in 1996, was the nation's largest passenger carrier, with 20.6 percent of the U.S. market, followed by American (18.5 percent), Delta (16.6 percent), Northwest (12.1 percent), Continental (7.4 percent), U.S. Airways (6.9 percent), TWA (4.8 percent), Southwest (4.8 percent), America West (2.7 percent), and Alaska (1.7 percent). The Denver market is an important one for United. A battle between the United Shuttle and Southwest in California in 1994 and 1995 was seen as a draw. Southwest remained the dominant provider of air service between smaller markets, including Oakland–Seattle, Oakland–Ontario, and Sacramento–San Diego, while the United Shuttle was dominant in traffic between large markets such as San Francisco–Los Angeles, San Francisco–San Diego, and San Francisco–Phoenix. Industry analysts expected United to vigorously defend its market position in Denver.

In 1994, prior to DIA's opening, Continental Airlines greatly reduced its operations in the western U.S., eliminating its Denver hub by cutting daily jet departures from 165 in 1993 to 86 in July 1994, 59 in September 1994, and 19 as of March 1995. Continental also terminated all commuter air service, operated as Continental Express, in Denver in May 1994. Continental Express had flown as many as 110 daily departures from Denver, servicing a number of towns and ski resorts in the west. Continental's withdrawal from the market left United carrying two thirds of all passengers, a near monopoly but not a unique situation. In 1996, half of all metropolitan centers had a single airline carrying more than 50 percent of passengers. In 20 percent of those markets, the dominant carrier had a market share of 70 percent or more.

U.S. Airways and American were also in Denver, albeit with a small presence. MarkAir, Frontier, and Vanguard airlines also serviced DIA, but provided little competition to United's 300 daily flights. MarkAir filed for Chapter 11 in early 1995 and had half of its planes repossessed. Vanguard offered low-fare, nonstop service to Salt Lake City, Kansas City, and Dallas. Frontier, which started in Denver in 1994 as a low-fare carrier, flew to Tucson, Albuquerque and El Paso at the end of 1995, losing $8 million. At the end of 1996, 15 of DIA's 90 gates were still not in use.

Cost overruns put the final price of the airport near $5 billion—more than $3 billion over what voters approved. Costs for travelers to pay for the airport, paid in the form of arrival and departure fees, were initially projected to be $7 per passenger. With less passenger traffic and costs more than expected, arrival and departure fees climbed to $18, one of the highest rates in the nation. Southwest Airlines cited the high landing fees as a primary reason for its avoidance of the Denver market. These costs, and United's near monopoly, resulted in fares being among the highest in the nation. High fares, reluctance to use DIA, and the distance to the airport from downtown Denver left passengers searching for alternatives.

COLORADO SPRINGS AIRPORT & WESTPAC

Seventy-five miles south of Denver is the city of Colorado Springs and the Colorado Springs Airport (CSA). CSA, a dual-use airport shared with the U.S. Air Force, has three runways, including the longest commercial runway in the continental U.S. (13,500 feet). Like Denver, CSA experienced rapid growth through the 1980s and early 1990s. Approximately half a million passengers used the facility in 1982. By 1990, traffic had increased to 1.2 million passengers in a facility designed to handle 900,000 through six gates. A new facility was planned. In 1994, a new terminal with the capacity for handling 2.4 million passengers per year opened. Volume swelled to almost 1.6 million passengers. Despite the growth, with just 500,000 residents, CSA was assessed by many analysts as being too small to support an airline.

WestPac, chartered in 1994 as Commercial Air, was founded by Ed Beauvais, who started America West Airlines in 1981. WestPac used a business plan similar to that of Southwest Airlines: a low-fare, no-frills airline flying a single type of aircraft (Boeing 737) to high-density, high-volume markets. Like Southwest, WestPac would not be part of the national airline reservation system—passengers looking to fly WestPac would call the airline directly. Like Southwest, WestPac would be 100 percent ticketless, using only electronic ticket reservation numbers with no printed tickets provided.

Unlike Southwest, WestPac would not use a point-to-point flight program, wherein flights travel between city pairs, but instead opted for a hub-and-spoke model centered around its secret weapon—Colorado Springs. Colorado Springs was touted as a low-cost location without a low-fare carrier in a location capable of servicing the high-fare Denver market. Under the hub-and-spoke system, passengers would be gathered from surrounding spoke cities and connect at the CSA central hub, where they would transfer to subsequent legs of their flight. WestPac hoped to attract as many as 30 percent of their passengers from Denver itself, with the remaining 70 percent coming from Denver's southernmost suburbs, Colorado Springs, Pueblo, and as far south as Castle Rock.

WestPac planned to achieve low-cost status by taking a simplified approach to operations by (1) using a single type of aircraft, (2) achieving high aircraft utilization along with Colorado Springs's central geographic location, (3) using inexpensive airport facilities and servicing secondary airports when possible, (4) using both full- and part-time personnel, (5) focusing on medium-haul routes and fast aircraft turnaround, and (6) maintaining competitive wage rates. By focusing on a medium-haul route structure, as opposed to a short-haul approach such as that used by Southwest and ValuJet, WestPac would have fewer takeoffs and landings and more available revenue passenger miles per aircraft. Southwest, for example, averaged 410 miles per flight and ValuJet 507 miles in 1995. WestPac would average about 875 on its initial routes.

Startup financing was provided by Oklahoma billionaire Edward Gaylord, owner of the posh Broadmoor Hotel in Colorado Springs, and oil heiress Margaret Hunt Hill. Each provided $5.5 million for startup money and helped raise an additional $17 million from private investors.

WestPac's logo jets quickly gained media attention as their three 737s began flight operations on April 28, 1995, with daily nonstop service from Colorado Springs to Los Angeles, Las Vegas, Phoenix, Kansas City, and Oklahoma City. Future expansion called for service to San Francisco, Seattle, Portland, San Jose, Orange County, San Diego, Dallas, Fort Worth, Houston, Wichita, St.

Louis, Omaha, Minneapolis, Dayton, and New York. Most of the locations were serviced with one flight per day. The airline expected to add two aircraft by summer.

WestPac focused on the price-conscious traveler, both leisure and business, by offering advance-purchase, discounted fares; low-price unrestricted "walk-up" fares (fares for travelers with no advance booking); and additional discounts for off-peak travel times. No minimum stay, such as a Saturday night, was required. Starting fares were $49 one way between most destinations, with regular fares far lower than United Airlines's fares. For example, for a Colorado Springs to Los Angeles flight, WestPac charged $69 one way off-peak with 21 days advance notice ($138 RT), and $129 unrestricted, walk-up one-day fares ($258 RT). United's best fare was $258 with a two-week advance booking. WestPac hoped to appeal to both the leisure traveler who wanted a low fare and could book well in advance and the business traveler who sought low fares but needed the flexibility to book flights with little notice.

By the end of June 1995, WestPac was CSA's leading carrier. In July, United retaliated by reducing fares to 16 cities, including all 13 cities serviced by WestPac and three scheduled for WestPac expansion. The fares were base fares, not sale prices, but available for only a limited number of seats on specific flights. The base fares applied to flights that departed DIA at approximately the same time as WestPac flights departed Colorado Springs to the same cities. WestPac, for example, operated two nonstops to San Francisco, whereas United had 16 daily nonstops from 6:30 A.M. until 9:15 P.M. Only the base fares on two of United's daily flights (i.e., those near WestPac's 7:40 A.M. and 8:55 P.M. flights) were reduced.

By September, WestPac had grown to 800 employees, was servicing 13 cities using eight aircraft, and was expecting to add another eight aircraft within one year (Exhibit 3). Their load factor, a measure of available seats filled, was near .75. The average for major airlines was .67. In its first year of operation, WestPac became the tenth largest regional/specialty airline and perhaps the fastest growing airline in the nation. Demand was so great that Airport Express, an airport shuttle service in Denver, began offering ground shuttle service between the south metro Denver area and CSA. Service began with vans and soon expanded to full-size buses. Despite the growth, Beauvais commented that the airline wasn't interested in becoming the largest; rather it was interested in serving its niche in Colorado. The airline had a net income of $371,600 in the third quarter on revenues of $23.3 million.

WestPac's rapid growth was not without problems. September projections estimated the number of passengers at CSA at or above the facility's 2.4 million capacity—an almost 60 percent increase in one year. WestPac, using gates at both ends of the concourse, was running out of both gates and terminal space and estimated it would need a concourse of its own within the year. Such a facility, along with required parking, would cost an estimated $50 million and require two years to complete. WestPac and other CSA airlines asked the airport to purchase more jet bridges and construct three more gates to supplement the facility's existing gates. To aid WestPac's expansion, the City of Colorado Springs loaned WestPac $1 million for 15 years at 8 percent interest for the construction of a hanger at CSA, with an option for the company to purchase the hanger. The city also approved the sale of $9 million in tax-exempt bonds to finance the construction of five gates and a commuter air pad. The facilities were designed as a temporary measure to allow for WestPac's continued growth until a second concourse could be built. Other carriers at the Colorado Springs airport had refused to participate in earlier financing proposals that would have had them, in part, funding the space needed for WestPac's expansion. Under the approved funding, WestPac would be solely responsible for repaying the bonds.

Airport facilities were not the only sticking point. WestPac's private computerized reservation system suffered from demand-related shutdowns that resulted in an inability to book reservations for as long as four hours one day and intermittent ability on others. WestPac offered shares of the company to the public in an initial public offering (IPO) on December 10, 1995. The IPO raised $60 million; a portion of the proceeds were used to expand the computerized reservation system. The company's shares began trading at $19, rose to $22.75, closed at the end of the first day at $22, and ended the week at $19.

Several analysts commented that the IPO's timing was ideal. Airline stocks are highly volatile and cyclical, but conditions at the time of the IPO were favorable.

Exhibit 3 | WestPac Flight Service History

Date	Total # of Aircraft at Month's End	# of Daily Round Trips	Service Charged
April 1995	2	6	Began service to Los Angeles, Kansas City, Phoenix, Las Vegas (2), Oklahoma City
May 1995	3	9	Began service to San Francisco and added a flight to Kansas City and Los Angeles
June 1995	5	14	Began service to Chicago-Midway, Dallas/Ft. Worth (2), and Seattle and added a flight to San Francisco
July 1995	5	14	Added one flight to Phoenix and reduced one flight from Kansas City
August 1995	8	19	Initiated service to Houston, San Diego, Indianapolis, and Wichita and added a flight to Chicago-Midway
October 1995	10	20	Added flight to Oklahoma City
November 1995	12	24	Initiated service to Newark and Tulsa and added one flight to Los Angeles
December 1995	12	26	Initiated service to Washington-Dulles and added a flight to Seattle
January 1996	12	26	Initiated service to Atlanta and reduced one round trip to Dallas
February 1996	12	28	Initiated service to Nashville, San Jose, and San Antonio and withdrew from Wichita
March 1996	13	28	Added a round trip to Phoenix and Las Vegas and reduced one trip per day to both Seattle and San Francisco
May 1996	14	30	Started one round trip to Portland and added one round trip to Newark
June 1996	16[1]	33	Added a trip to San Antonio, San Diego, and San Francisco
July 1996	17	35	Added a trip to Atlanta and Seattle
September 1996	15	31	Started one round trip to Orlando and Ontario (CA); reduced one trip per day to each of Newark, Atlanta, Oklahoma City, San Antonio, Seattle, and San Francisco
December 1996	15	31	Initiated service to Miami and withdrew service from San Jose
February 1997	15	38	Added service to all cities except Houston, Miami, and Seattle and withdrew service from Ontario (CA), San Antonio, Nashville, and Las Vegas
April 1997	15	37	Withdrew service from Miami
February 1997	15	37	Added service to all cities except Houston, Miami, and Seattle and withdrew service from Ontario (CA), San Antonio, Nashville, and Las Vegas
April 1997	15	33	Withdrew service from Miami
May 1997	16	33	
June 1997	18	40	Moved the bulk of operations from Colorado Springs to Denver International Airport
July 1997	19	40	

Source: Western Pacific Airlines SEC filings.

[1]Western Pacific leased two Boeing 727-200 aircraft on a short-term basis for the seasonal period covering mid-June through early September 1996.

UAL, the parent of United, and Northwest saw their stock price double between March and December 1995, while Continental's stock increased fourfold. The gains were driven by factors favoring airline profitability: a strong economy; airlines maintaining, instead of expanding, capacity, low fuel costs; fare increases and high load factors. Historically, as load factors increased, airlines would purchase additional aircraft, which often took two years from order day to delivery. Fares would drop as the additional capacity came on-line, resulting in fare wars to fill empty seats and declining profits. At the end of 1995, this was not the case. Most carriers were ordering new aircraft to replace older aircraft; only a handful were increasing capacity. Slow aircraft sales were expected to result in aircraft manufacturers offering discounts to entice purchases. Despite the favorable market, the performance of airline stocks had been less than stellar: the S&P airline stock index had an annual 2.5 percent return since 1988, whereas the S&P 500 earned more than 15 percent.

At the end of December, WestPac had a fleet of 15 737s, with plans to add six during 1996, and reported a fourth-quarter net loss of $3 million on revenues of $24.9 million. Analysts attributed the poor financial performance to a lack of sufficient size to operate an efficient hub. With one to two flights per day to destinations, efficiencies could not be gained at spoke cities, resulting in poor performance. Analysts recommended additional growth to achieve profitability.

In early 1996 there were indications that WestPac's low-fare pricing was impacting the market. Fares on some of United's flights from Colorado Springs were one fifth that of those from Denver. For example, United's Denver to Nashville flight cost slightly less than $1,000, whereas its Colorado Springs to Nashville flight, with a stop in Denver, was $150—a fare that matched WestPac's fare. Passengers began traveling to Colorado Springs for the departing flight, but would exit the aircraft in Denver on their return. While United did not like the practice, there was little it could do about it. In March, United replaced the 138-passenger 737s used to shuttle passengers between CSA and DIA with 259-seat DC-10s.

In May 1996, ValuJet's flight 592 crashed in the Florida Everglades, killing all onboard. Started in 1993, ValuJet, like WestPac, provided low-fare, no-frills service, based out of Atlanta. Prior to the accident, ValuJet utilized 24 older DC-9 aircraft to provide 144 flights per day to 31 cities. The accident sent shockwaves through the airline industry, hitting low-fare and small carriers the hardest. Passengers rethought their decision to save money by flying low-fare airlines and instead sought the reputation for safety provided by major carriers. WestPac reported a third-quarter 1996 loss of $910,300 on revenues of $45.5 million, attributing the loss to high fuel costs and consumer hesitancy toward low-fare airlines following the ValuJet crash.

In November, WestPac expanded into the rental car business by purchasing the rights to the Colorado Springs Thrifty Rent-A-Car franchise. Thrifty had been an early advertiser in WestPac's logo-jet program. In late 1996, WestPac entered into an interline agreement with Trans World Airlines (TWA) that enabled passengers to fly to TWA-serviced destinations using both WestPac and TWA flights. Additional agreements were expected in 1997.

At the end of 1996, WestPac operated 15 aircraft and provided 37 daily round trips between Colorado Springs and 17 cities (Exhibit 4). WestPac losses for the fourth quarter of 1996 totaled $20.9 million on revenues of $37.2 million. The stock rose $1.31 to $6.94 on the news.

WESTPAC AND THE REGIONAL MARKET—MAX

The U.S. Department of Transportation (DOT) categorizes air carriers based on revenues: revenues of "majors" exceed $1 billion, "nationals" have revenues of $100 million to $1 billion, and "regionals" have revenues less than $100 million. Regionals may be commuter airlines that focus on specific geographic markets, or carriers that provide service to the entire U.S., but have revenues less than the $100 million necessary for "national" status. Major U.S. airlines carried a total of 512 million passengers in 1996, up 5.6 percent from 485 million in 1995, 479 in 1994, 449 in 1993, and 446 in 1992. Revenue passenger miles for major carriers also increased in 1996 to 539 billion, up 6.7 percent from 1995's 505 billion.

Boeing dominates the U.S. aircraft market, with McDonnell Douglas, Airbus and several other manufactur-

4 | Western Pacific Airlines's National Service Schedule (12/31/1996)

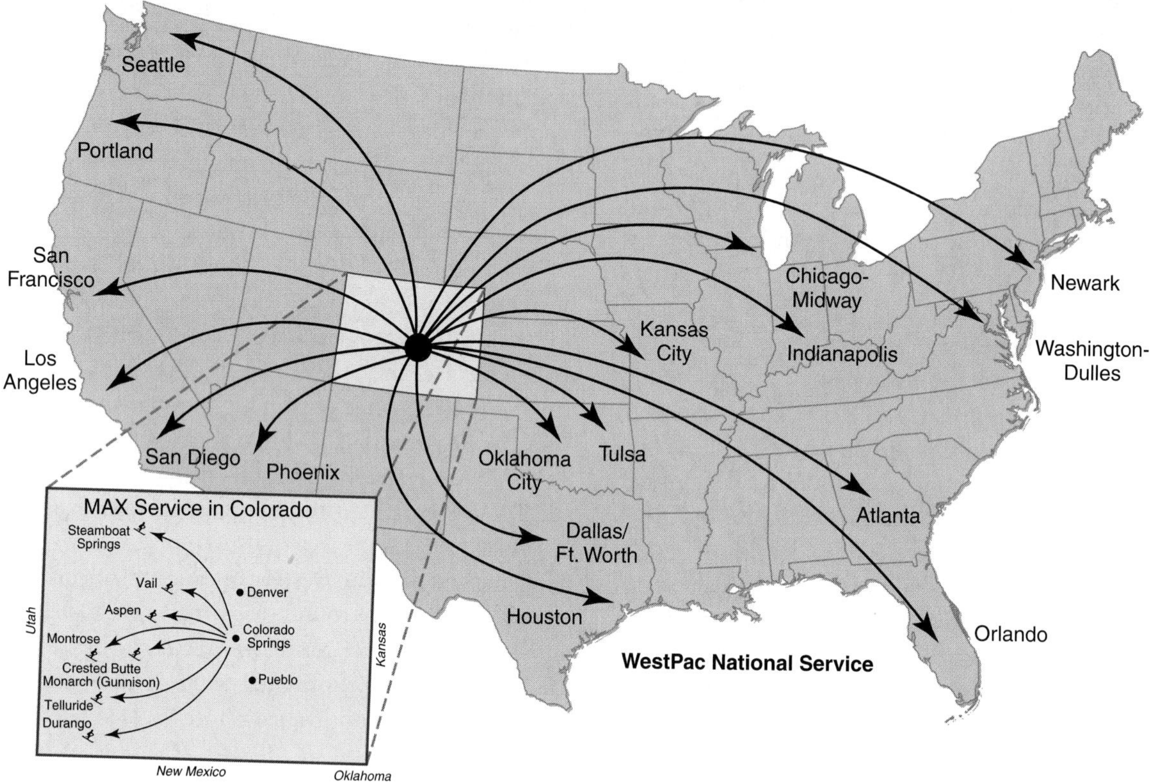

ers holding smaller market positions. Of the 4,609 aircraft in the fleets of major U.S. carriers in 1996, 1,023 (22 percent) were Boeing 737s.

Following industry deregulation in 1978, the number of regional carriers peaked at 246 in 1981 as regionals clamored to take up service gaps as major carriers abandoned unprofitable service to small cities. The number of regional carriers declined steadily through 1992. There were 130 regional carriers in the U.S. in 1993. In 1996, the top 50 regional carriers operated 2,172 planes, serviced 806 airports across the U.S., and carried a total of 32 million passengers 13.6 billion passenger miles, up from 10.6 billion in 1993. The top 50 regionals account for 97 percent of the available revenue-passenger miles on regional flights. In 1997 there were 16 manufacturers of regional aircraft, with 36 models approved for general U.S. use. Small jets, which traditionally rely on turbo prop aircraft, declined in cost, resulting in their increased use by the regionals.

Revenue-passenger miles of regional airlines are expected to grow at an annual rate of 9 percent until 2005, with miles on major airlines and international carriers expected to grow 3.7 percent and 6.5 percent, respectively. Growth of regionals is attributed to a growing trend for major and national carriers to move away from short-haul flights and use affiliated or subsidiary commuter operations. These arrangements, used by United with United Express, Continental with Continental Lite and Express, and American with American Eagle, for example, increase the perceived quality of the commuter service with passengers and provide seamless service under one carrier name.

WestPac formulated the creation of a subsidiary regional commuter airline in early 1996. Its plan called for

Mountain Air Express (MAX) to shuttle passengers from CSA to ski resorts in the outlying areas of Colorado. MAX would continue WestPac's cost strategy by offering commuter air service to the resort destinations at one third off existing prices.

Continental had been a leading provider of commuter service prior to its departure from the market. In 1995, United carried nearly half of the ski-area passengers through its regional affiliates Mesa Air and Air Wisconsin from DIA into Gunnison/Crested Butte resorts, but available seats had still not returned to the level prior to Continental's exit. Hurt by the lack of air transportation, restaurants, shops, hotels and ski resorts in several resort communities formed alliances to bolster the number of available seats, offering subsidies and guarantees to carriers. Subsidies paid a set figure for each available seat to a specific destination (reducing the cost to the traveler), whereas guarantees paid airlines cost and profit on unfilled seats (reducing the risk to carriers who offered service). The Steamboat Springs Chamber of Commerce, for example, planned to raise $150,000 to fund airline subsidies in 1996. The increased available seats resulting from the program were expected to draw an estimated 24,000 additional visitors to Steamboat and the surrounding community. Purgatory Resort had a similar program with American Air-

EXHIBIT 5 | Colorado Ski Areas and Associated Airport Facilities

	Aspen	Vail/Beaver Creek	Steamboat	Purgatory	Crested Butte & Monarch	Telluride
Airport	Aspen-Pitkin County Airport	Eagle County	Yampa Valley Regional (Hayden)	Durango-La Plata County Airport	Gunnison County Airport	Telluride (T) & Montrose Airport (M)
Airport Elevation	7,815′	6,532′	6,601′	6,683′	7,671′	9,075′ (T) 5,758′ (M)
Runways	1	1	1	1	1	1 (T) 2 (M)
Runway Length	7,004′	8,000′	6,601′	9,201′	9,402′	6,870′ (T) 8,497′ (M) 10,000′ (M)
Airlines	Aspen Mountain Air (Lone Star Airlines), United Express/Air Wisconsin, Western Pacific (MAX)	American, United, Delta, Northwest, Western Pacific (MAX)	American, Continental, Northwest, TWA, United, United Express, Western Pacific (MAX)	Air 21, America West Express, American, Reno Air, United Express, Western Pacific (MAX)	American, Delta, United Express, Western Pacific (MAX)	America West Express, Continental, United, United Express, Western Pacific (MAX)
Available Seats for '96/'97 Ski Season	220,000	286,500	155,600	100,000	80,000	80,400
% Increase in Avail. Seats over Prior Yr.	10%	74%	35%	54%	9%	46%
Revenue Guarantees & Subsidies	None	Some revenue guarantees	Some revenue guarantees & some subsidies	Some revenue guarantees	None	Some revenue guarantees

Source: Denver Post, "Ski resort skies friendlier," October 13, 1996, 1, C, 2.

lines for 160-passenger jet service from Dallas and was expanding the program to include Reno Air with jet service from Los Angeles via Albuquerque.

Several additional carriers were considering introducing direct flights to resort locations from Los Angeles, St. Louis, Newark, Chicago, Atlanta, and Houston. These carriers would service the mountain regions' larger airport facilities, such as Montrose and Durango for Telluride and Purgatory, respectively. However, not all ski areas could be serviced by large jet aircraft, as many were smaller airports designated by the FAA as "special-category" facilities due to their altitude, mountainous locations, and short runway lengths (Exhibit 5). Such facilities required special certification for both pilots and airlines. Maverick Airways, owned by former Continental Express employees, planned to provide such service by late fall 1996. Maverick planned to fly 48-seat deHavilland Dash 7 aircraft between DIA and Grand Junction and Steamboat Springs.

MAX's planned benefit to WestPac would be twofold. First, it would benefit directly from serving the Colorado ski market through profits generated by the carrier. Second, the commuter airline would allow WestPac to sell ski packages to consumers in cities it presently serviced. MAX would then provide a seamless connection for passengers from their city to their ski resort destination. WestPac could also offer all-inclusive discount ski vacation travel packages (airfare, lift tickets, and lodging) in conjunction with the resorts.

WestPac decided to proceed with MAX and scheduled operations to begin on December 4, 1996, using four, 32-seat Dornier 328 turboprop aircraft. Eight additional aircraft were expected to be brought on-line over the following four years. Twenty-five daily roundtrips were planned to destinations including Durango, Gunnison, Aspen, Montrose, Vail (Eagle County and Hayden Airports), and near Steamboat Springs (Exhibit 4 Inset). WestPac financed the $9 million project by attracting private investors and using internal funds, retaining a 57 percent ownership position.

Prior to commencing operations, WestPac and MAX would need to complete the certification process, which was expected to take several months. To ensure passenger bookings during the busy holiday season, MAX began selling tickets under WestPac's certification—a practice that the Department of Transportation investigated for legality. If certification was not completed, WestPac would be responsible for refunding tickets or providing transportation.

By late November, MAX had passenger bookings of approximately 100 passengers per day but no certification. To cover obligations, WestPac offered refunds and two daily 737 connections into Grand Junction and Montrose airports. Shuttle busses then transferred passengers to the outlying ski resorts near airports that were scheduled to be serviced by MAX but could not accommodate the larger jet aircraft. MAX commenced operations on December 15, 1996, and transported 242 passengers over two weeks in December (Exhibit 6).

CHANGES AT THE TOP

As the founder of America West Airlines in 1981, Ed Beauvais was the architect of the business plan that grew the company from a startup to a major carrier serving near 17 million passengers a year and earning revenues near $1.4 billion in just 10 years. Under Beauvais's reign, America West sought to aggressively compete against Southwest in the short-haul market. Despite Beauvais's 35 years of industry experience, the strategy proved unsuccessful.

America West changed strategy and borrowed heavily to amass a 100-plus fleet of aircraft to expand into additional cities and longer flights. The airline added international service to such cities as Tokyo, but the routes were largely unprofitable. An industrywide recession in 1990, fueled by high fuel prices and reduced air travel during the Persian Gulf War, forced America West into Chapter 11. As part of the approval of the airline's reorganization plan with creditors, Beauvais left the company in 1991. America West's operating losses totaled $32 million in 1990, $105 million in 1991, and $75 million in 1992. Net losses totaled $431 million for the period.

A reflective Beauvais commented that he had learned a great deal from his experiences at America West, emphasizing the need for sufficient startup capital and the selection of the right aircraft as being critical for success in the industry. He also called the right location one of the most fundamental factors for success, a resource he believed WestPac had with its Colorado Springs location. Industry analysts were largely in agree-

6 | WestPac and MAX Monthly Passengers (Commencement of Operations to June 30, 1997)

WestPac						WestPac–MAX			
1995		1996		1997		1996		1997	
Jan	—	Jan	160,668	Jan	111,116	Jan	—	Jan	4,600
Feb	—	Feb	119,546	Feb	101,132	Feb	—	Feb	9,248
Mar	—	Mar	164,246	Mar	146,568	Mar	—	Mar	10,756
Apr	2,748	Apr	102,414	Apr	141,356	Apr	—	Apr	8,760
May	39,594	May	137,354	May	153,450	May	—	May	4,714
Jun	69,834	Jun	141,928	Jun	153,946	Jun	—	Jun	4,964
Jul	84,436	Jul	179,534			Jul	—		
Aug	117,082	Aug	174,062			Aug	—		
Sep	91,600	Sep	133,794			Sep	—		
Oct	110,148	Oct	136,854			Oct	—		
Nov	113,276	Nov	146,112			Nov	—		
Dec	129,522	Dec	155,030			Dec	242		
Total	748,240	Total	1,731,542	YTD	807,568	Total	242	YTD	43,042

ment about the choice of location. An airline analyst, one of Beauvais's harshest critics during his reign at America West, commented that he thought Beauvais was onto something with the selection of CSA.

Despite fast growth, mounting losses in 1996 forced WestPac's investors to reassess the firm's top management. In November, Beauvais resigned as President and CEO of Western Pacific. Beauvais cited the demands of daily airline management along with the startup and expansion of Mountain Air Express as spreading him too thin. He remained the airline's Chairman, intending to concentrate his efforts on expanding CSA's facilities, obtaining additional aircraft for WestPac's fleet, and working to expand MAX.

Robert Peiser was elected as the firm's new President and CEO. Peiser was Executive Vice President of Finance and Chief Financial Officer for TWA from August 1994 through August 1996, following the carrier's emergence from Chapter 11, and a consultant specializing in turnarounds. He was widely heralded as a driving force behind TWA's successful restructuring. He left TWA citing ongoing differences in how the airline should proceed. Immediately prior to joining WestPac, Peiser was the vice chairman of Fox-Meyer Drug Co., a distributor of health-care products and pharmaceuticals that was in the process of being acquired.

Peiser was seen in the industry primarily as a turnaround specialist—a short-timer who fixes a company and then moves on. He commented that WestPac had much growth potential. The announcement of Peiser's appointment sent WestPac's stock up from $8.50 to $10.00 per share (up 17.65 percent). Peiser brought in Mark Coleman as Senior Vice President of Marketing and George Leonard as Vice President of Finance and Chief Financial Officer. Peiser and Leonard also joined WestPac's Board of Directors (Exhibit 7).

STRATEGIC AND TACTICAL CHANGE

Within a week of Peiser's appointment as President and CEO, WestPac signaled that significant changes were forthcoming to make the airline profitable. First, the route structure was reorganized to better attract business travelers. In December 1996, for example, WestPac offered three daily round trips to Los Angeles, Las Vegas and Phoenix, two daily round trips to Chicago and San Francisco, and one daily round trip between 17 other cities serviced. United was operating as many as 17 daily

7 | Western Pacific Airlines's Top Management (1997)

Edward R. Beauvais (60). Mr. Beauvais founded the Company in 1994 and is Chairman of the Board and a Director. From 1994 until November 1996, Mr. Beauvais was President, Chief Executive Officer and Chairman of the Company's Board of Directors. Prior to founding the Company, Mr. Beauvais served as General Manager of Aviation Consulting Group from 1992 through 1994. From 1981 through 1992, Mr. Beauvais was Chairman and Chief Executive Officer of America West Airlines ("America West"). America West filed for Chapter 11 protection in June 1991, and Mr. Beauvais resigned as Chairman of America West on July 31, 1992. America West emerged from Chapter 11 in August 1994.

Ivan Irwin, Jr. (63). Mr. Irwin was elected to the Board of Directors of the Company in 1995. Since 1994, Mr. Irwin has been Vice President of Hunt Petroleum of Texas, Inc. ("HPTI"), a significant stockholder of the Company, and Vice Chairman and Executive Vice President of Hunt Petroleum Corporation, the parent company of HPTI and a corporation primarily engaged in oil and gas exploration and production. Prior to assuming his position with HPTI, Mr. Irwin was engaged for over 30 years in the private practice of law in Dallas, Texas, including from February 1990 through June 1994, when he was a partner in the Dallas, Texas, office of the law firm of Vinson & Elkins, L.L.P.

Glenn M. Stinchcomb (69). Mr. Stinchcomb was elected in 1995. From October 1991 until his retirement in 1996, Mr. Stinchcomb was a director of The Oklahoma Publishing Company ("OPUBCO"), a publishing company. He was Vice President and Treasurer of OPUBCO from October 1991 to July 1995. Mr. Stinchcomb also serves as a director of Gaylord Entertainment Company ("GEC"), a diversified entertainment and communications company. He was Chief Financial Officer and Treasurer of GEC from 1974 to 1991, and he was Vice President of GEC from 1986 to 1991. Edward L. Gaylord, a significant stockholder of the Company, is an affiliate of GEC.

James R. Wikert (48). Mr. Wikert was elected in 1995. Since 1993, Mr. Wikert has been Chief Executive Officer of Express One International, Inc. ("Express One"), a cargo and charter airline, and is the controlling stockholder of Aircorp, Inc., an enterprise engaged in the ownership, lease and/or sale of commercial and general aviation aircraft. From 1987 to 1993, Mr. Wikert was the President of Express One. Mr. Wikert is the son-in-law of a controlling shareholder of HPTI, a significant stockholder of the Company.

Robert A. Peiser (49). Mr. Peiser was elected in November 1996, when he joined the Company as President and Chief Executive Officer. Prior to joining the Company, Mr. Peiser served as Vice Chairman and Chief Executive Officer of FoxMeyer Drug Company from August 1996 through November 1996. In addition, Mr. Peiser was Executive Vice President–Finance and Chief Financial Officer of Trans World Airlines, Inc. ("TWA") from August 1994 through August 1996, following TWA's emergence from Chapter 11 bankruptcy. Prior to his employment with TWA, Mr. Peiser was a consultant with BBK, Ltd., a turnaround consulting firm based in Southfield, Michigan, from November 1992 through July 1994. Prior to his employment with BBK, Ltd., Mr. Peiser was the President and Chief Executive Officer of Orange-co, Inc., a citrus processing company based in Bartow, Florida.

Clayton I. Bennett (37). Mr. Bennett was elected in 1995. Since April 1992, he has been the Real Estate and Investment Manager for The Oklahoma Publishing Company, a publishing company. Mr. Bennett is the son-in-law of Edward L. Gaylord, a significant stockholder of the Company.

George E. Leonard (56). Mr. Leonard was elected in November 1996, when he joined the Company as Vice President–Finance and Chief Financial Officer. Prior to joining the Company, Mr. Leonard was President and Chief Executive Officer of GEL Management, Inc., a company engaged in real estate and financial management and consulting services, for two separate periods, from July 1996 through October 1996 and from December 1991 through December 1995. From January 1996 through July 1996, Mr. Leonard was Chairman and Chief Executive Officer of Consumer Guaranty Corporation, an asset restructuring company.

Source: Western Pacific Airlines SEC filings.

round-trip flights to cities from Denver. WestPac saw the minimum necessary number of flights per day as 6 for popular routes such as Denver to Los Angeles. Six daily flights provided an average of 1.5 hours between flights.

The increased number of daily flights to core cities was accomplished by reducing or eliminating flights to other markets. The number of daily flights to nine cities were increased, while service to four was dropped. One city dropped, Las Vegas, was one of WestPac's most popular routes. Peiser cited fierce competition for Las Vegas traffic that resulted in the route being unprofitable. WestPac also began "wrapping" flights to several cities. Instead of servicing both Tulsa and Oklahoma City with direct flights from Colorado Springs, a Tulsa to Oklahoma City to Colorado Springs route was used. Together, these changes would allow the airline's 16 aircraft to fly an additional 28 hours per day. Hub airlines typically attract one half of their passengers from the local market, while traffic originating at the airlines spokes and connecting through the hub makes up the remainder. WestPac's daily service did not facilitate such connections, and connecting traffic was 8.7 percent of all passengers. Following the restructuring, connecting traffic increased to 32.5 percent.

In January, passenger traffic for CSA and WestPac declined over the January 1996 levels. WestPac, with 36 percent of the CSA market (Exhibit 8), attributed the decline to an increased reluctance for travelers, particularly business travelers, to drive to Colorado Springs. Smoothing operations at DIA, as well as the fact that United was meeting WestPac fares, were impacting WestPac. Increased competition at CSA was also hurting WestPac as competing airlines met WestPac's fares and captured more travelers. United's January traffic at CSA grew by 5 percent between 1996 and 1997, Continental's by 29 percent, and Northwest's by 62 percent.

DIA Service. In 1996, Frontier Airlines was emerging as a low-fare competitor with United at DIA. Frontier began operations at DIA, attempting to capitalize on the void left by Continental's departure by serving as a regional partner for United. United, however, declined the arrangement and Frontier changed its strategy, attempting to create its own hub at DIA by servicing local and connecting passengers. Frontier, with a limited number of flights, found it difficult to attract connecting passengers and began direct selling to Denver area businesses. Companies would purchase blocks of discounted tickets to locations that Frontier serviced—allowing business customers to fly on short notice for $190 to $250 rather than on United's short-notice fares of up to $600. By the end of 1996, Frontier was carrying 272,000 passengers a year to 13 cities, using a fleet of 10 leased Boeing 737s. Four additional aircraft were due to be added to Frontier's fleet within the year. Frontier hoped to expand its fleet more rapidly, but found the demand for used Boeing 737 aircraft had increased significantly in 1996 and supplies were limited.

Frontier was experiencing severe competition from United and reported a net loss of $9.7 million on 1996 revenues of $83.4 million. At the end of 1996, the company was in the process of filing a complaint with the U.S. Department of Justice alleging that United had engaged in predatory, anticompetitive and monopolistic practices at DIA, including "capacity dumping" in markets served by competitors, United's pricing practices, "exclusive dealing" with corporate customers and commuter carriers, and other tactics United allegedly used to drive competitors from its markets.

At the end of December, WestPac's Peiser announced that it would begin offering service from DIA. Peiser cited WestPac's inability to turn a profit solely from its Colorado Springs hub as driving the move. Denver's larger population base, growth in passenger traffic at DIA, and 10 empty gates at DIA made the move attractive. Peiser commented that the airline was trying to develop a way to leverage its position at CSA and enter DIA. One option was to create a "dual-hub" approach to operations by using both locations. Airline analysts were split on the move, with some focusing on WestPac's failure to turn a profit from CSA and trying to attract Denver area passengers to Colorado Springs, while others noted it would be suicidal to go head-to-head with United at DIA, citing Frontier's presence as an existing low-fare carrier and Frontier's difficulties.

In April, WestPac announced its plan to lease five gates in DIA's A terminal and add four more 737s (or one third more aircraft) upon commencing DIA operations at the end of June. To help fund the move, WestPac lobbied the Colorado legislature to approve a bill allowing fuel tax revenues to be returned to Colorado

Exhibit 8 | Colorado Springs Passenger Traffic by Carrier (1994–1997)

	Major & National Carriers										Regional Carriers			
Year	America West	American	Continental	Delta	Morris	Northwest	Reno Air	TWA	WestPac	United	Mesa	Skywest	WestPac-MAX	Total
1994	193,938	173,290	95,772	250,078	118,900	—	11,832	110,938	—	608,966	12,372	—	—	1,582,090
1995	288,484	277,052	60,696	384,358	—	77,328	108,876	138,300	758,240	711,208	15,256	1,776	—	2,831,886
1996	306,976	492,570	337,372	433,344	—	205,750	210,538	147,854	1,731,542	912,220	31,536	20,370	242	4,831,324
1997	277,112	453,830	319,260	481,996	—	189,952	197,886	144,220	1,021,918	857,058	43,324	26,668	88,608	4,098,380

airports and used for economic development. The funds, collected beginning in 1991, were to be used to pay United $115 million if the carrier were to build a $1 billion aircraft maintenance facility at DIA. United elected to build the facility in Indianapolis, and the funds remained untouched in state coffers. If passed, the bill would allow DIA to provide up to $10 million in loans to help WestPac fund the cost of moving a portion of its flight operations to the airport. Supporters of the bill cited the benefits to the traveling public of increased competition with United. United was bitterly opposed to such an arrangement, but found fighting the bill difficult given the decreased fares that had resulted from competition.

WestPac began operations at DIA as the second largest carrier, with 45 daily departures to 17 cities and fares comparable with those WestPac offered from CSA. CSA remained a WestPac hub, with 11 daily departures to destinations outside of Colorado and 12 to DIA, down from the 35 daily departures in 1996. WestPac's headquarters remained in Colorado Springs, along with 1,000 employees involved in maintenance and reservations. The carrier added 200 employees in Denver.

MAX. Shortly after arriving at WestPac, Peiser expressed concern over the amount of management time spent on MAX. Citing what he saw as a conflict between the skills required to run national and commuter airlines and the advantages of a relationship with a commuter service, Peiser stated that MAX's future as part of WestPac would be reexamined.

In April, MAX's future was known—the carrier's route was reorganized and expanded to include non-ski area destinations, including Grand Junction and Fort Collins; Colorado, Casper and Cheyenne, Wyoming; and Sante Fe, New Mexico. MAX would also supplement WestPac's jet service, flying daily between CSA and Tulsa, Oklahoma City, and Kansas City. In June, MAX, too, moved to DIA, providing 24 daily departures, and MAX's CSA operations reduced to one daily departure.

Bookings & Flight Services. Most airlines generate 60–80 percent of revenues through travel agents. WestPac, in 1996, generated only 36 percent. In early 1997, WestPac allowed travel agents "view only" access to WestPac's system—they were able to check flight schedules, but had to call WestPac's reservation center directly to book flights. Adding "view only" access resulted in call traffic increasing from an average of 20,000 calls per day to in excess of 150,000. Volume again overwhelmed WestPac's reservation system. WestPac determined that the most advantageous solution would be to join the SABRE multihost reservation system and allow travel agents booking capability. This commenced in March 1997. To spur demand, WestPac offered travel agents a 10 percent commission for bookings, as opposed to the standard maximum of $50.

At WestPac's annual stockholder meeting, WestPac announced a number of additional changes and considerations. The airline revised the logo-jet program. Instead of 80 percent of the aircraft being available for advertising, approximately 20 percent would be available. Adding premium first-class seating was also under consideration, as was a switch from a "one fare" price structure to a yield management system. Under a yield management system, airlines offer multiple fares on flights—trying to match what a prospective passenger will pay with the number of seats offered at a specific price. WestPac would limit the number of seats offered at ultra-low prices in an attempt to boost revenues while maximizing load factors. The airline also introduced its "high five" frequent flyer program wherein passengers who signed up would receive a "high five" from the ticket agent and one free one-way flight after five paid one-way segments. Upon commencing operations at DIA, WestPac began offering meals on long-haul flights to the east coast and selected west coast flights. All of these programs were being considered as ways of competing with United at DIA.

MERGER POSSIBILITIES

For the first quarter ended March 31, 1997, WestPac reported a net loss of $18 million on revenues of $35.8 million. This was followed by a reported second quarter loss of an additional $18.5 million on $44 million in revenues. The company had $6.5 million in cash and equivalents and current liabilities totaling $73.5 million.

Frontier, with 4 percent of DIA's traffic, reported a loss of $12.2 million for its fiscal year ending March 31,

1997. The stock of both WestPac and Frontier were near 52-week lows. Analysts suggested that DIA could support only one low-fare carrier.

Rumors of a merger between WestPac and Frontier began to circulate. A merger would result in a company with a fleet of 34 Boeing 737s on August 1 and the potential to add an additional four in December. Such an airline could support 101 daily DIA departures immediately and 111 in December—less than Continental's peak volume of 165. Analysts were wary of both companies' cash-poor position and United's reputation for aggressively defending its market position.

NAME INDEX

A

B

C

COMPANY INDEX

U

V

W

X

Y

Z

SUBJECT INDEX

H

I

J

K

L

M

N

O

P

Q

R

PHOTO CREDITS

pp. 1, 3: © Cindy Charles/PhotoEdit; **p. 14:** © John Neubauer/PhotoEdit; **p. 29:** © AP/Wide World Photos; **p. 34:** © Bruce Ayers/Tony Stone Images; **pp. 1, 47:** © Robert Maass/Corbis; **p. 55:** © eToys; **p. 62:** © Charles Gupton/Tony Stone Images; **p. 71:** © Mark Richards/PhotoEdit; **p. 75:** © Michael Newman/PhotoEdit; **pp. 1, 93:** © Erica Lanser/Tony Stone Images; **p. 100:** © Harry Cabluck/AP/Wide World Photos; **p. 109:** © Charles Gupton/Tony Stone Images; **p. 127:** © Alan Klehr/Tony Stone Images; **pp. 139, 141:** © Bernard Boutrit/Woodfin Camp/PictureQuest; **p. 151:** © Howard Grey/Tony Stone Images; **p. 160:** © Dean Siracusa/FPG International; **p. 171:** © Big Dog Motorcycles; **p. 192:** © Fred Jewel/AP/Wide World Photos; **pp. 139, 185:** © Davis Barber/PhotoEdit; **p. 220:** © Paul Sakuma/AP/Wide World Photos; **pp. 139, 229:** © AP/Wide World Photos; **p. 241:** © Michael Kupferschmidt/AP/Wide World Photos; **p. 247:** © Tim Ribar/Stock South/PictureQuest; **p. 257:** Stuart Ramson/AP/Wide World Photos; **pp. 139, 273:** © Martyn Hayhow/AP/Wide World Photos; **p. 279:** © Alastair Grant/AP/Wide World Photos; **p. 294:** © Paul A. Sauders/Corbis; **p. 302:** © AFP/Corbis; **pp. 139, 313:** © Ilkka Uimonen/Corbis/Sygma; **p. 319:** © Greg Baker/AP/Wide World Photos; **p. 334:** © AP/Wide World Photos; **p. 347:** © Thomas S. England/Stock South/PictureQuest; **pp. 139, 359:** © Corbis; **p. 369:** © Donna McWilliam/AP/Wide World Photos; **p. 380:** © Kim Kraichely; **p. 390:** © Paul Kuehnel/York Daily Record/AP/Wide World Photos; **pp. 399, 401:** © Marty Lederhandler/AP/Wide World Photos; **p. 403:** © Tim Brown/Tony Stone Images; **p. 423:** © Garth Vaughan/AP/Wide World Photos; **p. 430:** © AFP Worldwide; **pp. 399, 441:** © Paul Sakma/AP/Wide World Photos; **p. 452:** © AFP; **p. 462:** © Marty Lederhandler/AP/Wide World Photos; **p. 477:** © Tom Brooks/AP/Wide World Photos; **pp. 399, 485:** © AFP/Corbis; **p. 492:** © Marty Lederhandler/AP/Wide World Photos; **p. 502:** © Richard Drew/AP/Wide World Photos; **p. 506:** © AFP/Corbis; **pp. 399, 521:** © Thomas Kienzle/AP/Wide World Photos; **p. 525:** © Bob Schatz/Tony Stone Images; **p. 535:** © Frank Herholdt/Tony Stone Images.